3950

D0847516

An
Indonesian-English
Dictionary

THIRD EDITION

An
Indonesian-English
Dictionary

THIRD EDITION

BY John M. Echols

AND Hassan Shadily

Revised and edited by
John U. Wolff and James T. Collins,
in cooperation with
Hassan Shadily

Cornell University Press

Ithaca and London

First edition 1961.

Second edition 1963.

Third edition first published 1989
by Cornell University Press.

Library of Congress Cataloging-in-Publication Data

Echols, John M.
    An Indonesian-English dictionary / by John M. Echols and Hassan
Shadily. — 3rd ed. / revised and edited by John U. Wolff and
James T. Collins in cooperation with Hassan Shadily.
        p. cm.
    ISBN 0-8014-2127-6 (alk. paper)
    1. Indonesian language—Dictionaries—English. I. Shadily.
Hassan. II. Wolff, John U. III. Collins, James T. IV. Title.
    PL5076.E25 1989
499'.221321—dc19 88-21668

Printed in the United States of America

*The paper in this book is acid-free and meets the guidelines for
permanence and durability of the Committee on Production Guidelines
for Book Longevity of the Council on Library Resources.*

Contents

Editors' Preface
to the Third Edition

This work is a much-revised and much-expanded third edition of John M. Echols' and Hassan Shadily's *Indonesian-English Dictionary,* the second edition of which was published in 1963 by Cornell University Press. The present editors came to the project at the end of 1983, a year and a half after John Echols' death in 1982. At the time, a first draft of a substantial revision of the first half of the dictionary (letters A–L) was complete. This material had been prepared by John Echols and Hassan Shadily on the basis of voluminous files of citations which they had collected since publication of the second edition. We received this draft and the original file of citations, including the citations for letters M–Z, and began work in January 1984. On the basis of these materials and of a large amount of additional material provided by Professor Rufus Hendon of Yale University plus our own primary sources, a new draft was prepared for the entire dictionary over the next eighteen months. Not only were letters M–Z redone, but also the draft of the first half which had been completed before John Echols' death was extensively revised. The draft that resulted was sent to Hassan Shadily, who made many emendations.

From the middle of 1985 through 1986 the draft was corrected, emended, and augmented by both of us. We particularly profited from the summer of 1985, in which James Collins was in residence in Malang, East Java, and worked nearly full-time on the dictionary, and from the summer of 1986, when John Wolff had the same opportunity. The final draft was completed in January 1987 and was submitted to Cornell University Press after revision by Hassan Shadily. The manuscript was edited and considerably revised again in 1987–1988. The third edition contains somewhat in excess of 31,000 entries and is roughly 100 percent longer than the second. Nearly every entry of the second edition has been substantially reworked.

The revision of this dictionary could not have been completed without massive input from Indonesians and other users of the early editions. Besides Hassan Shadily, who has been coauthor of the dictionary from its earliest inception thirty years ago, a vast number of persons have been involved. Nearly every Indonesian resident at Cornell in the period 1984–1986 was consulted at some point, as were many staff members at the advanced Indonesian Summer Program at Malang Teacher Training College (IKIP Malang), in Malang, East Java. It would be impossible to name all of them. Three put in more than five hundred hours, however, and they should receive special acknowledgment: they are Dr. Dede Oetomo, of Pasuruan; Budi Susanto, S. J., of Yogyakarta and also a long-time resident of Jakarta; and Tien Hartoto of Yogyakarta. Considerable work was done in the early stages of the preparation for letters N, O, S, and T by Dr. K. A. Adelaar of the Rijksuniversiteit te Leiden, the Netherlands. Two Cornell students, Alissa Stern and Sarah Maxim, spent hundreds of hours proofreading and correcting the manuscript. Professor Rufus Hendon of Yale University prepared a complete concordance of twenty novels and generously made it available to us. This concordance was the source of innumerable citations and additional material for the entries. The material was edited on the IBM main frame computer of Cornell University with the software "Lexware" developed by Professor Robert Hsu of the University of Hawaii. We owe a debt of gratitude to Professor Hsu for making the program available and helping us to use it. The costs of the revision were partly underwritten by a grant from the U.S. Department of Education and partly by Cornell University. However, contents do not necessarily represent the policy of the Department of Education, and you should not assume endorsement by the Federal Government.

JOHN U. WOLFF
JAMES T. COLLINS

Ithaca, New York
Honolulu

Preface to the First Edition

An Indonesian-English Dictionary is intended to be a practical, comprehensive dictionary of modern Indonesian with English equivalents for the use of those who wish to read contemporary Indonesian materials. A large number of technical terms have been included, but no attempt has been made to be exhaustive. This dictionary should also be useful to Indonesians who wish to learn the English equivalent of an Indonesian utterance. It departs from the usual bilingual dictionary in one respect: it provides illustrative phrases and sentences, whereas the usual bilingual dictionary is an index of word equivalents. We hope that the inclusion of illustrations for a large number of the entries and subentries may provide the English-speaking student with examples of usage in context, thereby giving some indication of the range of meaning of the items.

A further word should be said about the illustrative phrases and utterances. Any attempt to present illustrative material involves problems of usage, of what is standard and what is substandard. Present-day Indonesian is fairly fluid, and this dictionary makes no attempt to be prescriptive (this is the prerogative of Indonesians); it merely presents the words and idioms found in print and in the speech of educated Indonesians.

Indonesian, the Malay-based national language of Indonesia, is undergoing rapid development, and its effort to become a vehicle adequate in all spheres of knowledge has placed tremendous pressure on its users to supply the necessary terms. The Komisi Istilah has done great service over the past few years in deciding on such new terms and in affirming those already existing.

Since the primary aim of this dictionary is practical utility, no attempt has been made to give etymologies. A number of Western words which would be obvious to the user have been omitted. Some obsolete and obsolescent words as well as dialectal words have been included, but there has been no intention to cover this area completely.

During the work on this project seven Indonesians assisted at various times and on certain, not all, sections of the dictionary. They were all well-educated men and women but in no sense specialists in the Indonesian language. Virtually all were from places outside Jakarta but had lived for varying periods in the capital. In education and background they represented Madura, central Java, west Java, Jakarta, and the Minangkabau and Batak areas. We checked many entries and illustrative examples with Indonesians other than those assisting us on the project, and to these, as well as to the many others who, knowingly and unknowingly, contributed to whatever merits the book may possess, deep appreciation is extended.

Thanks are expressed to Hilman Adil, Samiati Alisjahbana, Harsja Bachtiar, Idrus Nazir Djajadiningrat, Kismadi, Julia Shadily, and Odjahan Siahaan for their assistance at various stages in the dictionary's growth. Without their help publication would have been delayed much longer.

A word of appreciation should also go to the Program on Oriental Languages of the American Council of Learned Societies and to the Southeast Asia Program at Cornell University for finanacial aid and moral support.

Last, but by no means least, we owe a great debt of gratitude to Mrs. Nancy D. Echols and to Mrs. Tazu Warner, secretary in the Department of Far Eastern Studies, for typing two complete drafts of this book. Without their unstinted assistance this volume would never have reached publication.

We are aware of the limitations of this dictionary in spite of our efforts to make it as comprehensive as the resources available to us permitted. We would, therefore, be most grateful if users would supply us with any corrections or comments that might make a later edition more useful and accurate. Although assistance was received from many sources, we assume full responsibility for all deficiencies and for the arbitrary decisions necessary when the contributors could not reach an agreement.

JOHN M. ECHOLS
HASSAN SHADILY

Ithaca, New York, and Jakarta, Indonesia
March 1960

Preface to the Second Edition

The opportunity to prepare a revised edition of this dictionary presented itself far earlier than we would ever have expected. Although we are grateful for the opportunity, it has come at a period when, for various reasons, we could not devote full time to the task.

We have received much assistance from a number of scholars and interested friends, among whom we wish to mention Professors Denzel Carr and Rufus Hendon, Dr. Anthony Johns, Messrs. Valentine Ostrovsky and A. Ed. Schmidgall-Tellings, Drs. Soebardi, Mr. Renaldi Tedjasukmana, Professors A. Teeuw and Gerald Williams, and Sir Richard O. Winstedt, to all of whom we are indebted for their constructive, often detailed criticisms and suggestions for improvement. Any number of other individuals provided assistance here and there, and we are grateful for their interest and help.

In contrast to our practice in the first edition we have, at the insistence of many users, included a rather substantial number of the Western loanwords that are to be found in the Indonesian language of 1962.

We are grateful to the Program on Oriental Languages of the American Council of Learned Societies and to the Southeast Asia Program of Cornell University for financial assistance and support. Mrs. Nancy D. Echols assisted in the preparation of the manuscript and to her we express our heartfelt thanks.

Since the response to our earlier request for comments was excellent, we extend the invitation once again in the hope that each succeeding edition (by us or by others) will be a distinct improvement over the previous one.

JOHN M. ECHOLS
HASSAN SHADILY

Ithaca, New York, and Jakarta, Indonesia
May 1962

Introduction

Indonesian (Bahasa Indonesia) is the offical language of the Republic of Indonesia and is spoken as a first or second language by a majority of the population throughout the republic. Closely related dialects of this language are spoken in Malaysia, called there Bahasa Malaysia, and in Brunei. This dictionary lists forms that are used in Indonesia. Forms that are not used in Indonesia or meanings or words found only in Malaysia are excluded from this work. Because Indonesian is the official language of the Republic of Indonesia it is used for official and most public purposes: schools, mass media, books, literature, public services, governmental actions, and the like. It is the native language in Jakarta and in many regions of the country, but the majority of the population of Indonesia speaks a regional language as the home language. Indonesian is widely known and used in everyday life, however.

Coverage

This dictionary is meant primarily as a tool for English speakers who need to know Indonesian and who deal with Indonesian writings. The aim thus has been to give comprehensive coverage to forms a foreigner might run across in Indonesian readings, from this era or from the past, but excluding classical Malay literature. Much of the Indonesian written production (literary and otherwise) nowadays contains slangy, colloquial, and regional forms, and we have not excluded such forms. On the other hand, we have confined the listing of dialectal forms only to those likely to be widely known. Similarly, occasionally forms with nonstandard morphology are listed when the form cited is in common use. For example, *kerjain* "give a beating" is a Jakarta form which is widely known, and its meaning differs idiomatically from the standard form *mengerjakan*. The dictionary should also be useful to Indonesians who wish to learn English equivalents of Indonesian words, but it has not been developed primarily for that purpose, because many English words can be defined only by a sequence of Indonesian words.

Phonology and Transcription

Indonesian orthography normally allows for unequivocal interpretation of the pronunciation. Exceptions to this are marked in this work by a phonemic transcription given in slashes next to the main entry. Indonesian exists in many regional and dialectal varieties. Consequently, the number of vowels varies by dialect. Most speakers use six or eight vowels, but some dialects have as few as three vowels and some as many as ten. For our transcriptions in this work we will use six vowels as shown in Table 1.

Table 1. Vowels

	Front *unrounded*	Central *unrounded*	Back *rounded*
High	i		u
Mid	é	e	o
Low		a	

This spelling conforms to the standard spelling of Indonesian except that, in that orthography, the mid-central vowel [ə] is not differentiated from the mid-front vowel [e]; both are spelled *e*. In this dictionary, however, they are distinguished as *é* and *e,* respectively.

The diphthongs are as follows: /éy/ /oy/, and /ow/. These are spelled *ai* (occasionally *ei*), *oi,* and *au* respectively. In addition, when the suffix *-i* is added to a root ending in *a,* a vowel sequence, /ai/ also occurs; for example, *mula + i* "begin" is pronounced with three syllables /mulá-i/, with stress falling on the penultimate vowel (the *á*), as is usually the case in Indonesian. This vowel sequence also occurs as the usual pronunciation of the orthographic sequence: *ahi;* for example, *jahit* "sew" is pronounced /já-it/. Similar is the vowel sequence [au], which usually occurs in words spelled with *ahu;* for example *tahu* "know" is pronounced /tá-u/. Exceptions to these rules are noted in the text of this dictionary.

In Indonesian spelling, like vowels written together are normally pronounced with an intervening glottal stop. So *taat* "loyal" is pronounced /taʔat/. Exceptions to this spelling convention are noted in the text, for example, *boom* /bom/ "boom (post)." Sequences of unlike vowels beginning with a high vowel and ending with a low vowel (*ia, ua*) are pronounced with an intervening glide: *liar* "wild" is /liyar/; *luas* "spacious" /luwas/. As noted earlier, stress is usually penultimate. A regular exception to this rule occurs when the penultimate syllable contains /ə/ spelled *e;* in this case stress falls on the last syllable. So *taman* "park" is pronounced /táman/, but *teman* "friend" is /təmán/. Only exceptions to this rule are noted in this dictionary. For example, *anngár* "fencing" is provided with a pronunciation guide /anggár/.

The consonants are shown in Table 2.

Table 2. Consonants

	labial	apico-dental	palatal	dorso-velar	glottal
voiceless stop	p	t	c	k	ʔ
voiced stop	b	d	j	g	
spirant	f	s	sy	kh	h
nasal	m	n	ny	ng	
liquids	w	r, l	y		

Orthographic *r* is a tongue-tip trill in most dialects, but in some it is a voiced velar spirant. The palatals except for *y* do not come at the end of words. Orthographic *h* is pronounced initially, finally, and between like vowels, but between unlike vowels it is not pronounced (for example, *lihat* "see" is normally pronounced /liyat/). Orthographic *k* is normally replaced by a glottal stop at the end of a word, and in some dialects *k* is replaced by a glottal stop at the end of a root (even in suffixed forms). For example; *kontrak* "contract" is pronounced /kontraʔ/; *kontrakan* "something leased" is pronounced /kontraʔan/ or /kontrakan/.

Acronyms consisting of the first letters of a series of words are written with capitals. They are pronounced as a single word if they consist of canonical syllables. A canonical syllable consists of (C)V(C), where C is a consonant and V is a vowel. (Parentheses indicate optional elements.) Also CRV(C) is a canonical syllable where R stands for *r, l, y,* or *w.* Thus ABRI "Indonesian Armed Forces" (from Angkatan Bersenjata Républik Indonésia) is pronounced /abri/ because it consists of two cannonical syllables (*ab* and *ri*). Acronyms that consist of capitals that do not form canonical syllables are pronounced by the names of the first letters. Thus LTH "name of a company" is pronounced /éltéha/. Acronyms consisting of parts of words are written with capitals and small letters and pronounced as written: *Puskesmas* "public health clinic" (from Pusat Keséhatan Masyarakat) is pronounced /puskésmas/. Abbreviations that occur only in writing and are not pronounced are marked in this work by a period. For example, *spt.,* the abbreviation for *seperti,* is always read /seperti—that is, [səpərti]. An explanation is supplied for all acronyms and abbreviations. Any exceptions to these rules of pronunciation are indicated by a transcription in slashes placed next to the headword.

Table 3. Indonesian sounds

Symbol	Description of sound	Indonesian spelling	Examples
Vowels			
/i/	Approximately like *ee* in *see,* but shorter. Like *i* in *pit* in closed syllable [i]	i	itu /itu/ "that" pagi /pagi/ "morning" inti /inti/ "nucleus"
/é/	Like *e* in *pet¹* [ɛ] or like *a* in *make* but shorter [e]	e	bésok /bésoʔ/ "tomorrow" [besoʔ] or [bɛsoʔ]

Table 3—continued

Symbol	Description of sound	Indonesian spelling	Examples
/a/	Like *a* in *father* but much shorter	a	apa /apa/ "what" tanda /tanda/ "sign"
/e/	Approximately like *a* of *sofa* [ə]	e	ke /ke/ "to" empat /empat/ "four"
/o/	Like *o* in *coat* but shorter [o] or like the *aw* but shorter [ɔ]	o	poto /poto/ "photo" [poto] kopi /kopi/ "coffee" [kɔpi]
/u/	Approximately like the *oo* in *food* [u]. In closed syllables like the *oo* of *book* [U]	u	susu /susu/ "milk" minum /minum/ "to drink" tuan /tuan/ "sir"

Diphthongs

/éy/	Similar to the *ay* in *pay*	ai	pandai /pandéy/ "clever" lantai /lantéy/ "floor"
/ow/	Roughly equivalent to *ow* in *mow*	au	tembakau /tembakow/ "tobacco" kalau /kalow/ "if"
/oy/	Similar to *oy* in English *boy*	oi	asoi /asoy/ "beautiful!"

Vowel sequences

/ai/	Similar to the *i* of *bike*	ahi	jahit /jait/ "sew"
/au/	Similar to *ou* in *house*	ahu	tahu /tau/ "know"

Consonants

/b/	Similar to *b* in *rub*. In final position *p*	b	batu /batu/ "stone" habis /habis/ "finished" sebab /sebap/ "because"
/p/	Similar to *p* in *lip* but without puff of air	p	pukul /pukul/ "to strike" asap /asap/ "smoke"
/d/	Similar to *d* in *red*. In final position *t*	d	duduk /duduʔ/ "to sit" jihad /jihat/ "holy war"
/t/	Similar to *t* in *let* but without puff of air	t	tujuh /tujuh/ "seven" mulut /mulut/ "mouth"
/g/	Similar to *g* in *dog*. In final position *k*	g	gaji /gaji/ "wage" tiga /tiga/ "three" bedug /bəduk/ "drum"
/k/	Similar to *k* in *like* but without puff of air	k	kabar /kabar/ "news" makan /makan/ "to eat"
/j/	Similar to *j* but without the "*zh*" sound	j	jalan /jalan/ "road" meja /méja/ "table"
/c/	Similar to *ch* in *church* but without the "*sh*" sound	c	cari /cari/ "to seek" cuci /cuci/ "to wash"
/m/	Similar to *m* in *main*	m	minta /minta/ "to want" malam /malam/ "evening"
/n/	Similar to *n* in *noon*	n	nama /nama/ "name" dan /dan/ "and"
/ny/	Similar to *ny* in *canyon*	ny	nyanyi /nyanyi/ "to sing" tanya /tanya/ "to ask"

Table 3—continued

Symbol	Description of sound	Indonesian spelling	Examples
/f/	Similar to *f* in *fan*	f	fihak /fihaʔ/ "side"
			safar /safar/ "2d month of Moslem year"
		v	vak /fak/ "subject"
/s/	Similar to *s* in *send*	s	sumur /sumur/ "well"
			masa /masa/ "time"
			malas /malas/ "lazy"
/sy/	Similar to *sh* in *shoot*	sy	syukur /syukur/ "thanks"
			tamasya /tamasya/ "scene"
/z/	Similar to *z* in *zeal*	z	zat /zat/ "substance"
			azas /azas/ "principle"
/ng/	Similar to *ng* in *singer*	ng	dengan /dengan/ "with"
			ngeri /ngeri/ "to shudder"
			uang /uang/ "money"
/l/	Approximates *l* in *leave*. Tongue more advanced than English *l* in *hill*	l	lima /lima/ "five"
			boléh /boléh/ "may"
			dalil /dalil/ "proof"
/r/	Similar to *r* in British *very* or *tt* in *butter*. Not American *r* in *rule*. Sometimes trilled strongly	r	roda /roda/ "wheel"
			kiri /kiri/ "left"
			acar /acar/ "pickles"
/w/	Ranges between *v* in *vane* and *w* in *wane*	w	wasit /wasit/ "referee"
			lawan /lawan/ "opponent"
/y/	Similar to *y* in *you*	y	yang /yang/ "the one that"
			saya /saya/ "I"
/h/	Similar to *h* in *hope*. Occurs at end of words in Indonesian	h	hal /hal/ "thing"
			Tuhan /tuhan/ "God"
			sudah /sudah/ "already"
/kh/	Voiceless velar spirant similar to the sound made by a mild clearing of the throat. Often pronounced /h/ or /k/	kh	akhir /akhir/ "end"
/ʔ/	Produced by holding one's breath for a fraction of a second and then suddenly releasing it: the glottal stop	k *or* '	baik /baiʔ/ "fine"
			tunjukkan /tunjuʔkan/ "point"
			ra'yat or rakyat /raʔyat/ "people"

[1]Many dialects do not make a contrast between [e] and [ɛ] or [o] and [ɔ], and we represent the first two as *e* and the second two as *o* respectively.

Conventions

The order of the entries is strictly alphabetical, without regard to capitalization, spaces, periods, or hyphens. Within the entry, unaffixed forms with their meanings are followed by affixed forms. Verbal affixations precede nominal affixations. To list the order of the most commonly occurring affixes: root alone, doubling, *se-*, *ber-*, *ber-an*, *me-* (and its variants *mem-*, *men-*, *meng-*, etc.), *me-i*, *me-kan*, *memper-*,

memper-kan, ter-, ke-an, -an, doubling plus *-an, pe-* (*pem-, pen-, peng-,* etc.), *pe-an, per-an.* The exception to this rule is the treatment of the affixed form of phrases: affixed forms of phrases are written immediately next to the phrase to which they are affixed. Affixes are listed in bold face. Idioms are entered under the first word of the phrase; for example, *haru biru* "go on a rampage" is listed under *haru* and not under *biru.*

Cross-reference is made from spelling variants to the spelling most commonly found in publications or endorsed by the Language Center of Indonesia. Synonyms that cannot be connected phonologically are considered separate words and given separate definitions. Cross-reference is also made to forms that occur only in phrases as the second or later element. Thus *biru₂* refers back to *haru,* as it occurs only in the phrase *haru biru.* Cross-references are indicated in capital letters.

In Indonesian, kinship and other titles are often used as terms of address, but invariably these address terms are shortened. So, for example, *bapak* is usually *pak.* In this dictionary these short address terms are defined under the full entry: *pak* refers back to *bapak.*

Homonyms given under different headings are distinguished by subscript numbers. Different meanings of the same root are given under the same heading distinguished by number.

Style and Register Indications

This dictionary does not provide etymologies. Rather, as frequently as possible, information has been provided about stylistic usage. Forms that have a clear stylistic flavor or are used in certain domains or activities are so indicated. Stylistic and register indications appear in italics and parentheses preceding the definition. These stylistic indications are of three kinds: first are register indications of the domain in which the term is used. Second is the ethnic group with which a certain usage is associated; for instance, (*Jv*) indicates that the usage is assocated with Javanese speakers. This does not necessarily mean that the form is of Javanese origin (although it most often will be). Thus, *orang,* "because" is marked as (*Jv*) because the usage is closely associated with Javanese speakers, even though the word *orang* is not of Javanese etymology. Finally, we indicate words that are slang, literary, colloquial, vulgar, or derogatory. We have based these designations on the connotations conveyed to us by our informants, but in many cases the judgment is subjective: the demarcation between "slang" and "colloquial" is not always sharp. Furthermore, because much of the colloquial speech and slang comes from regional sources (especially from the Jakarta dialect), it is sometimes difficult to know whether to assign a form to Jakarta (*Jkt*) or to slang (*Sl.*) or to colloquial (*Coll.*).

Number and Gender

Indonesian normally does not distinguish number and gender. We translate as masculine or feminine, singular or plural, as the context dictates without implying thereby that the Indonesian has a number or gender meaning. For a few items of Arabic origin there is a specifically plural or a specifically feminine form. These are marked as such. Thus *almarhumah* "the late, deceased" is feminine and refers only to females. The unmarked form *almarhum* may refer to males or females. Similarly, *hadirin* "present, attending" is plural. The unmarked form *hadir* may refer to a single person or to several persons.

Abbreviations and Signs

Words that appear frequently in the Indonesian or English texts are abbreviated. Most style and register indications are also abbreviated. The following list gives our abbreviations.

Acad.	Academics	*Geog.*	Geography	sbg	sebagai
Amb	Ambonese	*Geol.*	Geology	sblm	sebeum
Anat.	Anatomy	gvt.	government	*Sd*	Sundanese
Astr.	Astronomy	hrs	harus	sdh	sudah
Auto.	Automotive	*Isl.*	Islam	sdr	saudara
Av.	Aviation	*Jkt*	Jakarta	seorg	seorang
bhw	bahwa	*Jv*	Javanese	*Sl.*	slang
Bib.	Bible	k.o.	kind of, kinds of	s.o.	someone
Biol.	Biology	kpd	kepada	spt	seperti
blm	belum	*Leg.*	legal	spy	supaya
Bp	Bapak	*Ling.*	Linguistics	ssdh	sesudah
Bri.	Bridge	*Lit.*	Literary	s.t.	something
Ch	Chinese	*M*	Minangkabau	stl	setelah
Che.	Chess	*Math.*	Mathematics	s.w.	somewhere
Chem.	Chemistry	*Med.*	Medicine	tdk	tidak
Coll.	Colloquial	*Mil.*	Military	*Tech.*	Technical
Crd.	Cards	Muh.	Muhammad	*Tel.*	Telephone or
dgn	dengan	msk	masuk		Telegraph
dlm	dalam	N.	North	tgl	tanggal
dpt	dapat	*Naut.*	Nautical	thd	terhadap
dr	dari	o.	one	*Thea.*	Theater
drp	daripada	org	orang	tlh	telah
Derog.	Derogatory	o.s.	oneself	ttg	tentang
E.	East, Eastern	pd	pada	utk	untuk
Econ.	Economics	*Phys.*	Physics	us.	usually
Elec.	Electronics,	*Pl.*	Plural	*Vulg.*	Vulgar
	Electricity	*Pol.*	Politics	W.	West
e.o.	each other	*Rel.*	Religion	yg	yang
esp.	especially	*R.R.*	Railroad	*Zod.*	Zodiac
Fin.	Finance	S.	South		

- Represents the root listed as the headword.
~ Represents the affixed form listed immediately preceding.
² A supercripted 2 indicates doubling.

A

a₁ /a/ a, the first letter of the alphabet.
a₂ well (contrastive particle). *- ndak, kalau gitu* Oh no, not if it is that way. *- tapi yg curi siapa, kan kita tahu* Well, but then we know who stole it, don't we?
a₃ at (the rate of). *- Rp750 sebungkus* at the rate of 750 rupiah for each package.
a₄, aa /a/ um (hesitation marker).
AA [*Asia Afrika*] Asia-Africa.
AAL [*Akadémi Angkatan Laut*] Naval Academy.
aam see AM.
aau /a:u/ **1** ouch! (exclamation of pain). **2** what! (exclamation of surprise).
AAU [*Akadémi Angkatan Udara*] Air Force Academy.
AB₁ [*Anggaran Belanja*] budget.
AB₂ [*Angkatan Bersenjata*] armed forces.
aba₁ -² order, command (in calisthenics, drill practice, etc.). *Ia memberi ~ utk berbaris* He gave the command to line up. **meng-kan** give orders (for drill, etc.). **peng-** drill leader. *~ genderang* drum major.
aba₂ father. *naik haji dgn -* go on a pilgrimage with father.
abab exhaled breath. **meng-i** blow on s.t.
abad 1 century. *pd - ini* in this century. **2** age, era. *- atom* atomic age. *- mesin* machine age. *- pertengahan* Middle Ages. **ber-²** for centuries. **meng-** last for centuries. *perselisihan yg ~* age-old conflict.
abadi eternal, lasting, enduring. **memper-, meng-kan 1** immortalize, record for posterity. *Tugu itu ~ jasanya* The monument immortalizes his services. **2** perpetuate. **ke-an 1** durability, permanence. **2** eternity, perpetuity. **peng-an** perpetuation.
abah₁ direction. **meng-** head for.
abah₂ see ABA₁.
abah-abah harness. *- tenun* weaving loom.
abai neglectful. **meng-kan 1** ignore, disregard. *Pegawai itu ~ perintah majikannya* The employee ignored his boss's order. **2** underestimate, minimize. **3** make light of, belittle. **ter-(kan)** slighted, ignored. **peng- 1** careless or neglectful person. **2** nonchalant or indifferent person. **peng-an 1** carelessness, indifference. **2** neglect. **3** disobedience.
abang₁ (*Jkt and some other regions*) **1** elder brother.

2 form of address for older working-class males with whom o. is not acquainted. *- bécak* pedicab driver. **3** form of address to o.'s husband or boyfriend, us. as *bang*.
abang₂ (*in some regions only*) red. *- tua* maroon.
abangan (*Jv*) o. who does not adhere strictly to the precepts of o.'s nominal religion.
abar (*R.R.*) brake. *- daya* power brake. **meng-1** brake. **2** impede, hinder. **3** remove. **4** lessen. *~ keadaan bahaya perang* lessen the danger of war. *Obat baru itu ~ keadaan payah pasién itu* The new medicine lessened the suffering of the patient. **-an** inhibition. **peng-an, per-an** braking.
abat see ABAD.
abau k.o. tortoise.
abbas abbot.
ABC /abécé, abésé/ the ABC's.
abd see ABDI.
abdas (*Isl.*) ablution before prayer. **ber-** make o.'s ablutions before prayer.
abdéi abbey.
abdi 1 servant. *- negara* servant of the state. *- dlm/ dalem* high-ranking court servant in Central Java. **2** slave. **- meng-** patron-client relationship. **meng-** serve. *~ tanahair* serve the fatherland. **meng-kan** subjugate, make subservient. *~ diri kpd partainya* devote o.s. entirely to the Party. **memper-** make subservient. *hubungan ~* patron-client relationship. **peng-** official. *~ masyarakat* public servant. **peng-an 1** service. *~ masyarakat* public service. **2** subservience, submission. **3** servitude. **4** devotion, dedication.
abdidalemisme sycophancy.
abdikasi abdication.
abdis abbess.
abdu see ABDI.
abécé [*ABC*] alphabet, ABC's.
abelur see HABLUR.
abén meng-, meng-kan cremate. **peng-an** cremation.
aberasi aberration.
aberikos see ABRIKOS.
abét 1 appearance. **2** behavior. **meng-** *bisa ~* know how to behave, act.
abib (*in families of Arabic descent*) grandfather.
abid₁ pious, devout.
abid₂ see ABADI.

1

abidin, abidun (*Isl.*) the faithful.
Abil see HABIL.
abis see HABIS.
abiturién o. who went as far as high school. *mahasiswa* - o. who went as far as the university level.
abjad alphabet. *menurut* - alphabetical. **mengkan** alphabetize. **peng-an** alphabetization.
abjadiah alphabetical.
ablak /ablak/ (*Jkt*) **ng-** open wide.
ablatif (*Ling.*) ablative.
ablur see HABLUR.
ABN [*Anggaran Belanja Negara*] national budget.
abnormal abnormal. **ke-an** abnormality.
abnormalitas abnormality.
abnus (*Lit.*) ebony.
abolisi abolition. **meng-(kan)** abolish.
abon shredded meat that has been boiled and fried. **meng-** make this dish.
aboné subscriber.
abonemén subscription (to a magazine, etc.). **ber-** subscribe. *Ia ~ bioskop* He bought a monthly book of movie tickets. **meng-kan** subscribe for s.o.
aborsi, abortus abortion. **meng-** abort (a fetus).
abrak mica.
abreg₁ **se-²** very much.
abreg₂ SEE AMBREG.
ABRI /abri/ [*Angkatan Bersenjata Républik Indonésia*] Indonesian Armed Forces.
abrikos apricot.
abrit-abritan see APRIT-APRITAN.
abruk (*Jkt*) **ng-in** slam or set s.t. down with a crash. *Langsung saja meréka nyelonong ke bangku paling depan dan ~ pantat di sana* They went directly to the first row and threw their behinds onto the benches there.
ABS [*Asal Bp Senang*] as long as the boss is happy.
absah valid, legal, legitimate. **meng-kan 1** endorse, approve. **2** legalize. **ke-an** validity, legality. **peng-an 1** endorsement, approval. **2** legalization.
absén absent. **meng-** call roll. **-an** roll. *daftar ~* attendance roll. **peng-an** taking of the roll.
absénsi take attendance. *daftar* - attendance sheet.
absés abscess.
absis (*Math.*) abscissa.
absolusi (*Rel.*) absolution (of sins).
absolut absolute. *kekuasaan* - absolute power. **meng-kan** make s.t. absolute. **-²an** in an absolute way. **peng-an** making s.t. absolute.
absolutisme absolutism.
absorpsi (*Ling., Phys.*) absorption. **meng-** absorb.
abstén abstain.
abstrak 1 abstract, summary, precis. **2** abstract, theoretical. **meng-kan** shorten.
abstraksi abstraction. **meng-kan** make abstract.
absur, absurd absurd. **ke-an** absurdity.
absurditas absurdity.
abu 1 dust. - *kayu* sawdust. **2** ashes. - *bara* cinders. - *blarak* (*Jv*) cleansing powder (of coconut frond). - *gosok* scouring sand. **-²** gray. **ber-** dusty.

meng- 1 turn to dust. **2** resemble dust. **meng-i** put dust in. *~ mata* deceive. *~ mata majikannya* deceive o.'s boss. **meng-kan, memper-kan** cremate. **ke-²an** grayish. **peng-an** *mata* camouflage. **per-an 1** urn for ashes of cremated person. **2** crematorium.
abuh 1 swollen. **2** swelling.
abuk fine powder. - *cat putih* white lead powder. - *gergaji* sawdust.
abur meng- squander, waste.
abus 1 smallest portion. **2** of no value, worthless.
abyad white, transparent, translucent.
AC /asé/ [*air conditioning*] air conditioning.
acak 1 disordered. **2** random. *sampel* - random sample. *secara* - at random. **meng-² 1** mess up, put in disorder. *Ia ~ rambutnya* She ran her hands through her hair. **2** disturb, upset, confuse. *Meréka diserbu dan di-² oléh segerombolan pengemis* They were attacked and set into confusion by a gang of beggars. **-²an** in disorder, chaos. **peng-an 1** randomization. **2** messing up, beating.
acak-acak in a hurry, hastily. *Mengapa ~ pulang? Hari baru pukul tujuh* Why hurry home? It is only seven.
acan (*Sd*) miniscule in amount. *tak* - not a bit.
acang-acang 1 confidential agent. **2** shop steward. **3** master of ceremonies.
acap 1 be under water. *Seluruh kota - karena banjir* The entire city was flooded by the rising water. **2** be stuck in s.t. deeply. *Roda mobil itu - di lumpur* The car's wheel was stuck in the mud. **meng-i 1** flood, inundate s.t. **2** soak. *Ibu ~ cucian dlm air sabun* Mother soaked the laundry in soapy water.
acapkali repeatedly, frequently.
acar pickles, salad made with raw vegetables mixed with spices and a souring agent. - *kobis* sauerkraut.
acara 1 agenda. *Apakah - rapat nanti malam?* What is on the agenda for tonight's meeting? - *basah(an)* initiation (with water). - *bébas 1* unscheduled activity or program. **2** dancing (following more formal activities). - *kebaktian* church service. - *padat* full schedule. - *penglepasan* saying farewell (at airport, funeral). - *perdana/pokok* principal item on the agenda. **2** program. - *TV* TV program. - *kerja komputer* computer program. **3** judicial procedure. - *pidana* criminal procedure. **4** jurisdiction. **ber- 1** sit, be in session (of court, etc.). **2** be on the agenda. *Pembicaraan itu akan ~ tiga soal* The discussion will have three items on the agenda. **3** be in litigation. **meng-** hand down (a court sentence). *Hakim ~ hukuman penjara lima tahun* The judge imposed a sentence of five years. **meng-i** begin the conversation. **meng-kan 1** place on the agenda. *PBB ~ soal itu sbg acara pertama* The UN placed that problem first on the agenda. **2** bring up with (a judge, etc.). **peng- 1** lawyer, attorney. **2** master of ceremonies. **kepeng-an** matters dealing with lawyers. *kode étik ~* a code of ethics for matters dealing with lawyers.
acc see ASÉSÉ.

acé see AC.

aceuk /acek/ (*Sd*) elder sister.

aci₁ 1 agreed, settled. **2** valid. *tak* - incorrect, not according to the agreement.

aci₂ (*Sumatra*) pith, starchy core. - *sagu* sago palm pith.

aci₃ see ACIK.

aci-aci example. **-nya** supposing, assuming. ~ *ia benar, pasti saja ia datang sendiri kemari* Assuming that he was right, he'd have surely come here himself. **meng-kan 1** assume, suppose. **2** imagine. **-an 1** supposition. **2** imagination.

acik (*Ch, Sumatra*) elder sister.

acir (*Coll.*) **ng- 1** in disarray. **2** helter-skelter.

aco ng- see KACAU.

acrit (*Coll.*) **ng-** come out in rush.

acu₁ ber-an having reference. **meng- 1** point. *Ia ~ bedilnya utk menémbak kijang* He aimed his gun to fire at a deer. **2** refer. *Ia ~ kpd ceramahnya* He referred to his lecture. **meng-kan 1** point at with s.t. *Iu ~ tombuknya kpd saya* IIc pointed his spear at me. **2** threaten (with a weapon). **3** refer. *Perkara tersebut tdk akan di-kan ke pengadilan* The aforementioned case will not be referred to court. **-an 1** hint. **2** reference. *karya ~* reference work. ~ *silang* cross reference. *makna ~* referential meaning.

acu₂ se- from the same mold. *bagaikan ~* a perfect fit. *Ia ~ dgn ayahnya* He looks like his father. **meng-** shape, mold, cut (cookies). **-an 1** mold. ~ *kué* cookie or cake mold. ~ *sepatu* shoe last. **2** matrix.

acu₃ ready. *Ia sdh - utk berangkat* He is ready to leave. **meng- 1** ponder a way to achieve a purpose. **2** strike a threatening pose (with gun, knife). **meng-²** plan, contrive. *Kami ~ utk pergi ke Miami* We have planned to go to Miami. **meng-kan** advocate, suggest, propose. *Ia ~ pemberantasan buta huruf* He proposed a literacy campaign.

acuh 1 care. *Ia - sekali pd tanamannya* He gives his plants a great deal of care. - *tak* - be indifferent, unconcerned, nonchalant. *Ia - tak - waktu saya . . .* He acted unconcerned when I . . . **2** not care. - *aja* Who gives a damn? Who cares? Big deal! **meng-kan** heed, care about, be concerned about. *Murid itu ~ benar segala perkataan gurunya* The pupil was very attentive to all the teacher's words. **-an** (*Jkt*) not care. *Lu ~ amé gué* You do not give a damn about me.

acum meng- to incite, instigate, provoke.

acung meng- point upward. **meng-i** point out, draw attention to. *Dlm soal baca-membaca puisi kita patut ~ Réndra dgn kedua buah jempol* When it comes to poetry reading, Rendra should be roundly applauded (lit., approved by raising both thumbs upward). **meng-kan 1** hold up (the hand to greet or answer). *Ia ~ tangannya utk menjawab pertanyaan itu* He held up his hand to answer the question. **2** point s.t. *Senapan di-kan ke bawah* The rifle was pointed downward. **ter-** pointed outward. *Tangannya ~ menunjuk ke tepi pantai* His hand shot forward pointing toward the shore. **-an 1** raising upward, lifting up. ~ *tangan* hand raising. ~ *jempol* pointing thumb upward (to indicate approval, agreement, good quality). **2** s.t. pointed forward or outward. *Mulut gua sdh penuh tersumbat oléh ~ senjata* The mouth of the cave was jammed full of rifle barrels pointing inward.

AD₁ [*Angkatan Darat*] army ground forces.

AD₂ [*Anggaran Dasar*] statutes.

ada 1 there is, are. - *anjing di sini* There is a dog here. *Dia sdh -?* Is he here already? - *kalanya* sometimes. - *tdknya déwan itu* the existence or nonexistence of the council. **2** (*Coll.*) be, be present. *Saya - di New York* I am in New York. **3** have, own. *Dia - mobil baru* He has a new car. *Ia sdh - umur* He is well along in years. **4** did (do so-and-so). *Saya - melihat film itu* I did see that film. **-kah** Is it the case that . . . *-kah anda mendengar kabar itu?* Did you happen to hear the news? **-lah 1** am, is, are. *Berdoa ~ usahanya yg terakhir* Prayer was his final recourse. *Jkt ~ ibukota Républik Indonésia* Jkt is the capital of the Republic of Indonesia. *Tuduhan itu ~ tdk benar* That accusation is not true. **2** (*Lit.*) Once upon a time there was . . . ~ *seorg raja* Once upon a time there was a king. **-pun** now, it so happens. ~ *begini agaknya* Well, it is s.t. like this. **-nya 1** presence. **2** existence. **3** situation. *Demikian ~* Such is the situation. **se-(²)nya** whatever there is, as o. finds it. *Apa anda mau makan ~?* Would you like to take potluck with us? **-² *saja** There is always s.t.; you always have s.t. to say or do (when you should not). **ber- 1** be (in a place). *Ia ~ di Chicago* He is in Chicago. **2** well-off, well-to-do. *Ia anak seorg ~* He is from a well-to-do family. **ber-²** have a hidden motive. *Tentu ia ~ memberikan uangnya begitu saja* He must certainly have a hidden motive to give his money away just like that. **keber-an** existence. **meng-²** invent, fabricate, concoct (stories). **meng-kan 1** organize, arrange. **2** give, hold, deliver (a lecture). **3** create, make. **4** launch. *Ia ~ bantahan* He launched a protest. **5** cause, bring about (a catastrophe, etc.). **6** establish (boundaries), bring about, effect (a consolidation). ~ *perbaikan* introduce improvements. **meng-²kan** say what is not true or does not exist. **ke-an** situation, condition. *Bagaimana ~mu?* How are things with you? ~ *negeri itu kurang baik* The state of the country is not good. *dlm ~ demikian* under such circumstances. ~ *badan* bodily constitution. ~ *bahaya/darurat* state of emergency. ~ *hawa* weather situation, weather conditions. ~ *keras* (*Phys.*) solid state. ~ *mendesak* emergency situation. ~ *perang* state of war. ~ *perkawinan* marital status. **peng-an 1** stock. **2** supplying, provisioning. **3** provisions. **4** procurement.

adab 1 courtesy. **2** culture. **3** knowing proper behavior. *Anak itu kurang betul -nya thd org tuanya* That child does not behave the way he should toward his parents. **ber- 1** cultured, civilized. *Bangsa itu ~ betul* That nation is very civilized. **2** polite. **keber-an** being civilized, polite. **meng-i**

respect, esteem. **memper-kan** civilize. **ke-an** politeness, refinement. **per-an** culture, civilization.
adakalanya see ADA.
adalat justice, righteousness.
Adam 1 proper name. **2** (*Isl.*) the prophet Adam. *anak* - humanity. *cucu* - men.
adan see AZAN.
Adan Eden.
adang meng- 1 intercept, block, ambush. **2** block. *Pohon ~ di jalan* A tree is blocking the road. **3** flag down. *Ia mengacungkan telunjuk ~ opelét* He raised his index finger to flag down a small bus. **4** wait for (a parade to go by, etc.). **meng-(²)i** hold up, waylay, intercept, mooch. *Kerjanya ~ rokok* His habit was to mooch cigarettes. **peng-** robber, highwayman, hold-up man. **peng-an** ambush.
adanya see ADA.
adap see HADAP.
adaptasi adaptation. **ber-** adapt, assimilate. *Orang luar itu sdh ~ dgn teman-temannya* The outsider has adapted well to his friends. **meng-** adapt.
adapun see ADA.
adas dill, fennel. - *manis* anise. - *pedas* fennel. - *pulosari* k.o. anise used in medicines.
adat₁ 1 custom, tradition. - *istiadat* (*Pl.*) customs and traditions. - *lembaga* old customs and traditions. - *resam* customs and traditions. **2** customary law. **3** manners, proper behavior. *Anak itu ndak tahu* - That child does not know how to behave! - *bahasa* good form. *kurang* - rude, impolite, ill-mannered. *Kalau menemui tamu tdk memakai jas dinamai kurang* - Receiving guests without a jacket is considered impolite. *(pd) -nya* usually. **ber- 1** customary, traditional, follows traditions. **2** well-mannered. **meng-kan** institute as a custom. **ter-** already customary. *Tlh menjadi adat yg ~ bhw . . .* It has become the custom that . . .
adat₂ ng- 1 make a fuss, cry and be naughty. **2** not run properly (of a car).
adati traditional.
a de charge /a decart/ see SAKSI.
adegan, adekan 1 scene (in a play). - *ranjang* sex scene. **2** (*Isl.*) movement.
adem 1 cool, calm. **2** cold. **3** tasteless, flat. - *ayem* cool and calm. **meng-** cool o.s. off. **ke-an** felicity, peacefulness. ~ *hidup* comfort or peacefulness in life. **peng-** apparatus for cooling. *Pinjam kipasnya dong, utk ~* Come on, lend me your fan to cool myself off.
adem pause (*Sport*) breathing spell.
adhési 1 adhesion. **2** devotion, attachment.
adhyaksa (*Leg.*) a rank for prosecutors.
adi 1 superior. - *daya* superpower. - *kawasi* force majeure. - *kodrati/kudrati* the supreme power of God. - *kuasa* superpower. - *marga* super or main highway. **2** splendid, highly valued. - *busana* haute couture.
adib respectful.
adicita ideology.

adidaya see ADI.
adiguna (*Jv*) rely too much on o.'s own abilities.
adik 1 younger brother or sister or younger cousin. - *kakak* brother and sister. - *kandung* full younger sibling (same mother and father). - *tiri* younger stepsister or stepbrother. **2** form of address to younger brother or sister and younger people in extended family (esp. first cousins). **3** form of address from husband to wife, boyfriend to girlfriend. **4** form of address for service persons of either sex (waiter, etc.) younger than the speaker. **- ber- 1** be e.o.'s siblings. **2** family, familial. **ber-** have younger siblings. ~ *berkakak* be brother and sister, be siblings. *kakak ~* be siblings. *Ada kejanggalan kakak ~ menjadi suami isteri* There is s.t. amiss if a brother and sister become husband and wife. **memper-** regard as younger sibling.
adikara dictatorial. **ke-an** dictatorialness.
adikodrat, adikodrati (*Rel.*) the supernatural, the supreme power of God.
adikuasa see ADI.
adil 1 just, fair, equitable. **2** legal. **meng-i 1** hear, try (a case). *Siapa yg ~ perkara itu?* Who is presiding over that case? **2** administer justice. **3** bring to justice. **ke-an 1** justice, justness. ~ *sosial* social justice. **2** judicature. **peng-an 1** the court. ~ *agama* religious court. ~ *bala tentara* military tribunal. ~ *negeri* court of first instance. ~ *tentara* court-martial. ~ *tinggi* appellate court. **2** trial, session. **3** courthouse. **4** jurisdiction. **per-an** judicature. ~ *terakhir* the last judgment.
adinda 1 respectful form of address and reference to younger sibling or to a younger person of either sex, esp. used in letters. **2** form of address to wife or female lover (more affectionate than *adik*).
ad interim acting, temporarily in a position.
adipati title for *bupati* (colonial era).
adiratna pekaca (*Lit.*) **1** lotus jewel, the sublime jewel. **2** young woman.
adiwarna resplendent, excellent.
adm. [*administrasi*] administration.
administrasi administration. - *kegeréjaan* ecclesiastical administration. - *negara* public administration. - *niaga* business administration. **meng-kan** administer.
administratif, administratip administrative.
administratir, administrator manager of an estate.
administratur administration.
administrir meng- administer, manage.
admiral admiral.
adolénsi tax clemency.
adon meng- knead. **-an** batter, dough. ~ *asam* leaven.
adperténsi advertisement.
adpis see ADVIS.
adpisir adviser.
adpokat see ADVOKAT₂.
adreng (*Jv*) eager.
adrés address (of letter). **meng-kan** address (a letter).

ADRI [*Angkatan Darat Républik Indonésia*] the Indonesian Army (revolutionary era).
adu₁ compete. - *ayu* beauty contest. - *cepat* race. - *domba* opposing o. side or team against the other. **memper-dombakan, meng-dombakan** play o. against another. - *gelut(an)* wrestling match. - *jotos* boxing match, brawl. - *kata* verbal dispute. - *kekuatan* power struggle. - *tenaga* trial of strength. *saling - hidung* rub noses (affectionately). **ber- 1** collide. *Mobil ~ dgn gerobak* A car collided with a cart. *~ muka* collide head-on. *Kakinya ~ dgn kursi* His foot banged against the chair. *~ gelas* clink glasses (in a toast). **2** compete. *Harvard ~ dgn Princeton* Harvard competes with Princeton. *~ lengan* compete in strength. *~ layang-layang* compete with kites. *~ tuah* take a chance. *~ untung* seek o.'s fortune, try o.'s luck. **meng- 1** pit. *Hakim ~ dua saksi itu utk mengetahui siapa yg benar* The judge pitted the two witnesses against e.o. to find out who was right. *~ kekuatannya* pit o.'s strength. *Ia ~ Sanip lawan Buyung* She pitted Sanip against Buyung. **2** bump, hit (o.'s head). **3** contest. *Dua pujangga itu ~ kepandaiannya* The two scholars are contesting their skills. *~ layang-layang* compete in kite fighting. **per-an** contest, clash. *deringan ~ cangkir* the sound of clinking cups.
adu₂ meng- 1 complain about. **2** sue, bring legal action. **3** inform, squeal, tell on, report. *Ia ~ di kantor guru besar* He squealed in the principal's office. **meng-kan** complain about. *Saya -kan pd Ibu* I will tell Mother on you. **peng-** informer. **peng-an 1** accusation, complaint. **2** denunciation, information (against). **3** indictment.
adu₃ sleep (of royalty). **per-an** royal bed.
aduh 1 ouch! ow! (expression of pain). **2** oh my! (expression of disappointed surprise). **meng-1** lament. **2** moan, groan. *Anak yg sakit itu kadang-kadang ~* The sick child sometimes uttered a groan. **ter-²** repeatedly moaning. *Si wanita menang, kedua pria yg kalah ~* The woman won, with a lot of complaining from the two men who lost. **peng-** chronic complainer, grouch.
aduhai (*Lit.*) **1** how beautiful! how sad! etc. **2** incredible, staggering. *dgn harga yg ~* at an unbelievable price.
aduk - *semén* mixture of cement and sand. **meng-1** stir (tea, etc.). **2** beat (batter, etc.). **3** mix. *~ téh Cina dgn téh Jawa* mix Ch and Jv tea. **4** scramble (eggs). **5** interfere in, meddle in (the affairs of others). **6** stir up, confuse, annoy. **meng-²** stir up (coffee, etc.). **-an 1** the mix, mixture. *~ semén* mortar. **2** mixer, beater. *~ telur* (*Jv*) eggbeater. **-²an** continuous mixing. **peng-** stirring spoon or rod. *~ telur* eggbeater. **peng-an** mixing, stirring (of). *~ lautan* churning of the ocean. *~ beton* concrete mixer.
adun₁ dress, finery. **ber-** dress up.
adun₂ see ADON.
Advén, Advént Seventh Day Adventist religious sect or adherent thereof.
advérbia adverb.

advérbial adverbial.
adverténsi see ADPERTÉNSI.
advis advice.
advokat₁ lawyer.
advokat₂ avocado.
adzan see AZAN.
aérodinamika aerodynamics.
aéronotika aeronautics.
af break off, break up. *Hubungan Joni dan Dini sdh - Joni* and Dini have broken up. **meng-(kan)** break s.t. up. *Ya, saya kira sebaiknya di- saja* Yes, I suppose it is better to break it up.
afal₁ /af'al/ (*Isl.*) works, deeds.
afal₂ waste portions of butchered animals. **2** reject products of a factory.
afal₃ see HAFAL.
afasi aphasia.
afdal 1 good, fine, nice. *Spy - berapat nanti, mari kita makan dulu* Let's eat first so that the meeting goes well. **2** (*Isl.*) ritually pure. *Jangan sembahyang kalau tdk -* Do not pray if you are not ritually pure.
afdéling section, department (colonial era). *mandor di - B* the foreman in B section.
afdlal, afdol see AFDAL.
afdruk print, copy.
affiliasi see AFILIASI.
afiat 1 healthy. **2** good health. **meng-kan** make healthy. **ke-an** fitness, healthiness.
afiks (*Ling.*) affix.
afiksasi affixation.
afiliasi affiliation.
afinitas affinity.
afirmasi affirmation. **meng-kan** affirm. *tempat org bisa ~ dirinya* where a person can affirm himself.
afiun see APIUN.
afkir see APKIR.
aflos, aflus see APLOS.
afrikat (*Ling.*) affricate.
afrit evil spirit.
afwah blessing.
agah ber-²an stare at e.o. (esp. in a fight, to start a fight). **meng- 1** stare fixedly forward (esp. in certain sports). **2** stare at (to start a fight). *~ kera* rile up a monkey by facial expressions. **3** put o.'s face forward. *~ bayi* put o.'s face near a baby to amuse it.
agak 1 rather, somewhat. *Ia - besar utk umurnya* He is rather large for his age. - *mudik* not far upstream. **2** approximately, about. - *dua bulan lamanya* for about two months. - *agih* **meng-agihkan 1** explain, state clearly. **2** be critical of. **-nya** it seems, probably. *~ ia tiada mengerti* It seems he did not understand. *Apa ~ maksudmu?* I wonder what you mean. **-² 1** guess, vague idea, fantasy. **2** careful. *~ berjalan malam* Be careful about walking in the evening. **ber-(²)** intend. *Ia ~ pergi ke Indonesia* She intends to go to Indonesia. **meng-(²) 1** suspect, guess correctly. *Ia ~ bhw tdk ada org di rumah* He guessed correctly that no o. was home. **2** consider, ponder. *Aku mencobakan baju cina dan ~ di depan cermin* I tried

on the Ch blouse and considered it in front of the mirror. **meng-kan** determine carefully. **meng-²kan** guess, figure. *tdk secepat spt ku-²kan* not as quickly as I had imagined. **ter-** long for, truly wish to meet. **peng-** 1 estimate. 2 guess, conjecture.

agam 1 virile, manly. 2 sturdy, hefty.

agama religion. **ber-** 1 have a religion. *Ia ~ Islam* He is a Muslim. 2 be religious. *~ pd uang* worship money, serve Mammon. **ke-an** religious, religiousness. *Ibu ajari aku ~, kesaléhan . . .* Mother taught me religiousness, piety . . . *Ia berdoa penuh ~* He prayed with great piety. **-²an** false religion.

agamawan religious person, religionist.

agamawi religious.

agamis religious. *nada -* religious quality or tone.

agan ber- intend, plan. **ber-²** tease, annoy. *~ mati* die suddenly, commit suicide. **meng-i** tease, annoy.

agar in order that, in order to. *Saya selalu berlatih - menang* I always practice in order to win. *- spy* in order that.

agar-agar 1 k.o. seaweed. 2 gelatin made of seaweed.

agas sandfly, gnat.

agén 1 agency, branch. *- suratkabar* local newspaper distributor. *- pembukuan/penjual karcis* booking agent. 2 agent. *- ganda* double agent. *- polisi* policeman. *- tunggal* sole agent. **meng-i** 1 distribute. 2 handle, manage. *perusahaan pelayaran yg ~ perusahaan pelayaran samudera nasional* shipping firm that handles the national oceangoing shipping lines. **per-an, ke-an** agency.

agénda agenda.

agéndaris secretary or clerk who draws up the agenda.

agendir meng- enter on an agenda.

agih meng-(kan) distribute evenly, apportion.

agitasi agitation. **ber-, meng-** agitate for.

agogo 1 Western dance 2 rock and roll.

agraria agrarian affairs. **ke-an** agrarian matters. *di bidang ~* in the agrarian sector.

agrégat 1 electric generator. 2 aggregate.

agrési aggression. **meng-** be aggressive. **ke-an** aggressiveness.

agrésif, agrésip aggressive.

agrésor aggressor.

agréssif see AGRÉSIF.

agri-bisnis agribusiness.

agri-industri agri-industry.

agronomi agronomy.

aguk locket.

agul meng-(²)kan 1 boast of. 2 make a show of, display, show off.

agung 1 exalted, high, noble. *Mahkamah -* Supreme Court. 2 impressive. *- benar kelihatannya pembesar itu* That prominent person looks very impressive. **meng-kan** 1 glorify, exalt, elevate. 2 praise. *~ diri* 1 boast. 2 be proud. **meng-²kan** indulge in glorification. **ke-an** 1 grandeur, majesty. *~ Sultan Yogyakarta dlm memberikan istanan-*

ya utk gedung sekolah tinggi tak akan dilupakan The noble gesture of the Sultan of Yogya in giving his palace for a university building will not be forgotten. 2 greatness, mastery. **peng-an** 1 exalting (of). 2 glorification. *~ diri* self-glorification.

Agustus August. *perayaan (17) -an* Independence Day celebrations.

ah₁ 1 ah! alas! 2 yechh! (exclamation of disgust). *-, kotornya kamarnya* Ugh, is this room filthy! 3 intensifying negative particle. *Ndak -!* No, of course not!

ah₂ see A₁.

aha aha!

ahad one. **meng-kan** unite in marriage.

Ahad Sunday. *- Palem* Palm Sunday.

ahadiat unity.

ahala dynasty. *- Tang* Tang dynasty.

ahdiat see AHADIAT.

ah ih éh exclamation of indecision.

ahir see AKHIR.

ahlak see AKHLAK.

ahli₁ 1 expert,. specialist. *- agama* theologian. *- alam* natural scientist. *- bahasa* linguist. *- bangsa* ethnologist. *- bangun* builder, building contractor. *- bangun-bangunan* architect. *- bedah* surgeon. *- bina wicara* speech therapist. *- busana* expert tailor. *- ceritera* storyteller. *- firasat* physiognomist. *- gaib* spiritualist. *- hayat* biologist. *- hukum* lawyer. *- kandungan* obstetrician. *- kecantikan* beautician, beauty specialist. *- keuangan* monetary expert, financial expert. *- klenik* 1 soothsayer, practitioner of black magic. 2 expert on mysticism. *- negara* statesman. *- nujum* astrologer. *- patung* sculptor. *- pembukuan* certified public accountant. *- pengetahuan* scholar, scientist. *- penggunaan tanah* soil scientist, pedologist. *- peramal* seer. *- periksa* inspector. *- pidato* orator, speaker. *- pijat* masseur. *- plastik* plastic surgeon. *- ragam* composer. *- rajah* tattooer, tattoo artist. *- rencana* planner. *- rias* makeup artist. *- sastra* 1 man or woman of letters. 2 literary scholar. *- siasat* tactician. *- sihir* magician, wizard. *- sunah/sunat* observer of the traditional law. *- tafsir* commentator, annotator. *- tarikh* 1 chronicler. 2 genealogist. *- téhnik* technician. *- tenung* fortune teller. *- varuna* hydrologist. 2 virtuoso. 3 skilled, highly competent, professional. **mengkan** *dirinya* specialize, become a specialist or expert. *Ia tlh ~ dirinya dlm pelayaran* He has become a specialist in navigation. **ke-an** expertise, skill, competence, know-how.

ahli₂ 1 members. 2 relatives. *- karib* close relatives. *- nikah* in-laws. *- pamili* family members. *- rumah* household. *- waris* heirs.

ahlubait (*Isl.*) owner of the house, host.

ahlukubur (*Isl.*) the deceased.

ahlulsuluk (*Pl.*) mystics.

ahmak 1 a fool. 2 foolish. 3 stupid.

AI [*ad interim*] acting, temporary.

ai₁ (*Jkt, Ch*) I.

ai₂ see AIH.

aib 1 shame, disgrace, scandal. **2** error, mistake. **meng-kan 1** humiliate, bring disgrace on. **2** blame, reprimand. **ke-an 1** humiliation, disgrace. **2** shame.

aidil fitri see IDUL FITRI.

aih exclamation of surprise.

ai lap yu (*Sl.*) a profession of love.

ainul yakin with the complete conviction of o. who has witnessed. *Dia bilang begitu dgn -* He said it with conviction.

air 1 water, liquid. *- abu* lye. *- aki* distilled battery water. *- alas* brackish water. *- alur* (*Naut.*) wake. *- api* hydrochloric acid. *- artésis* artesian well water. *- asam* brackish water. *- asin* brine. *- asli* pure water. *- bakat* swirling water, whirlpool. *- balik* receding tide. *- baling-baling* wake (of a ship). *- basuh tangan* 1 water to wash o.'s hands. 2 easy to obtain, in abundance. *- batu/beku* ice. *- belanda* soda water. *- bena* rising tide. *- besar* 1 flood. 2 feces. *- bor* water pumped from ground. *- buangan* sewage. *- comberan* sewage. *- dadih* k.o. watery yoghurt. *- daging* stock. *- galian* ground water. *- hidung* nasal mucus, snot. *- hidup* running water. *- kaku* hard water. *- kaldu* broth. *- kali* river water. *- kapur* whitewash. *- kelapa* coconut milk. *- kelonyo* eau de cologne. *- kemih/kencing* urine. *- keras* (hydrochloric) acid. *- ketuban* amniotic fluid. *- kirawa* floodwater from a mountain stream. *- kumur/kusur* mouthwash. *- lebah* honey. *- léding* running water. *- lendir* phlegm. *- limbah* waste water, sewage. *- lisol* creosol-based disinfectant. *- lunak* soft water. *- madu* honey. *- mani* sperm. *- mas* 1 fluid for gilding. 2 gold thread. *- masin* salt water. *- mata* tears. *- mati* 1 bay, inlet. 2 stagnant water. *- mawar* rose water or perfume. *- (me)lata* 1 waterfall. 2 mountain stream. *- (me)mancur* 1 fountain. 2 small waterfall. *- mentah* unboiled water. *- muka* 1 facial expression, countenance. 2 surface of water. *- mukabumi* surface (of earth). *- murni* pure water. *- pasang* high tide. *- payau* brackish water. *- pembersih* lotion. *- pendingin* cooling water. *- pérak* silver zinc. *- perbani* neap tide. *- permukaan* surface water. *- peres* fruit juice. *- putih* plain water. *- raja* aqua regia. *- raksa* quicksilver. *- rebusan* decoction. *- rendah* low tide. *- ruang* bilge water. *- sabun* soapsuds. *- sadah* hard water. *- saluran* tap water. *- sebak* flooding. *- seléra* saliva. *- sembahyang* water for ritual ablution. *- sembilan* water for bathing of corpse. *- seni* urine. *- serani* water for baptism. *- sinau* urine. *- soda* soda water. *- suci* holy water. *- suling* distilled water. *- sumber* spring or well water. *- sumur* well water. *- sungai* river water. *- surut* low tide. *- susu (ibu)* mother's milk. *- tadahan* stored rainwater. *- tanah* ground water. *- tapai* excess water from fermenting rice or cassava cakes. *- tawar* 1 fresh water. 2 unboiled water. *- tepung tawar* magic potion. *- terjun* waterfall, cataract. *- tétés* molasses. *- timah* tin coating. *- tuban* amniotic fluid. *- ukup* perfumed holy water. *- wangi* perfume. *- (w)udu* water for ritual ablution. *- zamzam* water

from the well at Mecca. **2** juice. *- jeruk* orange juice. **ber- 1** have water. *Sungai ini tak ~* This river has no water. **2** juicy (of fruit). **3** aqueous. **meng- 1** turn into water. *És itu ~* The ice has become water. **2** like water. **meng-i 1** irrigate (rice field). **2** dilute with water. *~ madu* dilute honey with water. **3** give to drink. **ke-an** flooded, inundated. *Rumahnya ~* His house was flooded. **per-an 1** waters. *~ wilayah* territorial waters. *~ dlm* inland waters. **2** waterworks. **peng-an** irrigation, watering.

ais -an carrying cloth. **meng-** carry on the back.

Aisyiah reformist Muslim organization for women.

aja (*Coll.*) see SAJA.

ajab₁ surprised, astonished.

ajab₂ see AZAB.

ajag see AJAK₂.

ajaib 1 miraculous. *cermin -* magic mirror. **2** astonishing, remarkable. **meng-kan** amazing, miraculous. **ke-an 1** miracle. **2** mystery, wonder. *~ alam* freak of nature. **3** remarkableness.

ajak₁ *- serta* **meng-sertakan** invite along. **meng- 1** invite, ask. *Ia ~ saya pergi dgn dia* He invited me to go with him. **2** urge. *Ia ~ org-org bekerja keras* He urged the people to work hard. **3** challenge, invite. *Ia rupa-rupanya ~ berkelahi* It seems he challenged s.o. to a fight. **-an 1** invitation. **2** challenge. **3** stimulus. **peng-** inducement.

ajak₂ (*Jv*) wild dog.

ajak₃ (*M*) similar to, as.

ajal predestined hour of death, end. *Tak ada dokter yg dpt menolong karena tlh sampai -nya* No doctor can be of any further help because his hour has arrived. *- samar* unexplained (sudden) death.

Ajam (*Lit.*) Iran, Persia.

ajan see AZAN.

ajang 1 site. *- industri* industrial estate. **2** arena. *- persaingan* competitive arena.

ajar₁ (*Coll.*) study. *kurang -* (*Derog.*) crude, extremely rude. **bel- 1** study. *Saya ~ pd Pak Ali* I study under Mr. Ali. **2** learn. *~ (me)nyopir* learn to drive. *~ kenal* make o.'s acquaintance. *Saya ingin ~ kenal anda* I would like to introduce myself. **meng- 1** teach (a subject). *Saya ~ bahasa Indonésia* I teach Indonesian. **2** teach s.o. *Saya di- oléh Bu Pomo* Mrs. Pomo teaches me. **3** give s.o. a lesson he will not forget. *Pengkhianat di-oléh kawan-kawannya* The traitor was given a lesson by his comrades. **4** train, coach. **meng-i 1** teach s.o. **2** train, coach. *Ia ~ anak-anak berbaris* He trains the children to do close order drill. **meng-kan 1** teach s.t. *Bahasa Jepang tdk di-kan di SMA* Japanese is not taught in high school. **2** lecture, rebuke. **-an 1** teaching(s). *tahun ~* school year. **2** theory. **3** doctrine, tenet. **4** lesson, punishment. **peng-** instructor, teacher. **peng-an 1** instruction. **2** doctrine. **3** teaching (of). **4** warning, reminder, admonition. **pel-** secondary school student. **mempel-i 1** study carefully, diligently, in depth. **2** study, scrutinize (proposal). **mempel-kan 1** teach, offer as instruction. *Dipel-kan mata kuliah dasar* A basic college course was taught. **2** teach thoroughly. *Semuanya sdh dipel-kan sblm aku dikirim ke sini* All of that had been drilled into me before I was sent here. **terpel- 1** educated, learned. *Ia termasuk golongan ~* He belongs to the educated class. **2** intellectual. **pel-an 1** lesson, course. *mengikuti ~* attend classes. *~ kilat* cram course. **2** training. **berpel-an 1** obtain an education. **2** educated.

ajar₂ hermit.

ajat see HAJAT. (*Jkt*)

ajé see SAJA.

ajeg, ajek steady, stable, constant. **ke-an** regularity, constancy.

ajéktif, ajéktiva adjective.

ajeng see JENG.

ajengan (*Jv*) community leader, s.o. to emulate. *Tiada seorg pun, dukun, -, kiai, ahli gaib.* There was no o., no shaman, no big shot, no religious teacher, not even a spiritualist.

aji₁ spell, charm, magical formula. *- candrabirawa* power to conjure up an ogre which upon death doubles itself ad infinitum. *- gila* 1 out of o.'s mind. **2** exclamation of surprise. *- gineng* (*Jv*) science of sexual knowledge. *- pancasona* ability to live again.

aji₂ 1 (*Lit.*) king, ruler. *- Saka* an ancient Jv ruler. **2** o. who is a champion at doing s.t. *- mumpung* opportunistic. *Saat ini banyak pejabat yg bersikap - mumpung* Right now there are plenty of officials willing to take what they can while they can.

ajidan see AJUDAN.

ajimat see AZIMAT₁.

ajinomoto any k.o. taste enhancer, monosodium glutamate.

ajir stake, marker.

ajojing k.o. rock-style dancing. **ber-** dance this dance.

ajrih respect and fear.

aju meng- 1 institute. *~ gugatan* institute a suit. **2** put, ask (a question). **3** file, submit, make (application). **meng-kan 1** file, submit (a protest). **2** file, submit. *Sebuah topi di-kan sbg bukti* A hat was submitted as proof. **3** send, submit, present. *Lamaran hrs di-kan kpdnya* Applications must be sent to him. **4** set forward, propose, put a motion. **5** indict, remand. *Ia di-kan ke pengadilan* He was remanded to court. **6** lodge, enter (a complaint). **peng-an** submission, offer, tender. *~ pernyataan tertulis* submission of a written statement.

ajubillah see AUDUBILLAHI.

ajudan 1 adjutant. **2** (*Navy*) chief petty officer. *- jénderal* (*Mil.*) adjutant general.

ajuk₁ meng- 1 observe, estimate. *Inilah waktu yg baik utk ~ hatinya* This is a good time to observe her character. **2** test, put to the test, sound out. *Curigaku timbul, mungkin ia mau ~* My suspicion increased, he was probably testing me. **ter-** measurable, estimated. *matamu yg tak ~* your unfathomable eyes. **ke-an** deeply fathomed. **-an 1** sounding. **2** guess, assumption.

ajuk₂ mimic, imitate, parrot, mock. *Murid yg nakal itu - gurunya* The naughty pupil mimicked his teacher. **-²an** mimicry.

ajun₁ purpose. **meng-** intend to, plan to. *Ayah ~ berangkat hari ini* Dad plans to leave today.

ajun₂, ajung adjunct.

Ak. [*akuntan*] accountant (used in academic degrees).

Akabri [*Akadémi Angkatan Bersenjata*] Armed Forces Academy.

akad contract, agreement, covenant. *- bawah tangan* private agreement. *- jual beli* sales contract. *- nikah* 1 marriage contract. 2 marriage ceremony performed by the groom in the presence of the *imam*. **ber-** settle an agreement or contract. **meng-kan** enter into an agreement, fix contractually.

akadémi academy. *- militér* military academy. *- ilmu pelayaran* merchant marine academy.

akadémik academic.

akadémikus an academic.

akadémis academic.

akaid dogma. *ilmu -* dogmatic theology.

akal 1 mind, intellect, reason. *Ia tajam sekali -nya* She has a very keen mind. *msk (di) -* reasonable, makes sense. *- budi* 1 reason, intelligence, common sense. 2 ingenuity. *- cerdik* sudden inspiration. *- fikiran* genius. *- melintas* sudden thought, inspiration. *- péndék* 1 narrow-minded. 2 short-sighted. 3 stupid. *- waras* common sense. **2** intelligence. **3** way, tactics. *Ia mencari - utk menangkap pencuri itu* He is seeking a way to nab the thief. *Apa - kita?* What is our recourse? **4** advice, instruction. *Ia minta - kpd seorg kawan* He requested advice from a friend. **5** deceit, trickiness, cunning. *- bulus* cunning mind, sly trick. *- busuk* dirty trick. *- geladak* vile trick. *- kancil/ keling* 1 ruse, artifice, prank. 2 shrewd, clever. *- laba-laba* trickster. *-(nya) panjang* crafty. *- palsu* frame-up. *- ubi* clever trick, stratagem. **-²** pretended, feigned. **se-², se-** *budi* with all o.'s might, strength. **ber- 1** be intelligent or smart. *Ia seorg ~* She is a smart person. **2** keep o.'s head, be calm. *Kita hrs ~* We must keep our heads. **meng-i 1** seek a way. **2** deceive, double-cross. **meng-kan** endeavor, seek a way, work s.t. out. *Bagaimana ~ spy dia bisa datang ke sini?* How can we work it out so he can come here? **-an** fabrication, invention. **-²an** machination(s).

akali intelligent. *secara -* intelligently.

akan₁ will, about to (particle marking future events). *Nasi ini - dimakan nanti* The rice will be eaten later. **-²** equally true. **se-²** as if, as though. *Ia terus bekerja ~ tak mendengar temannya* He kept on working as though he did not hear his friend. **meng-** aim, strive for. **meng-kan** suppose. **ke-an** the future, futurity. **-an** horizon.

akan₂ 1 about, regarding. *Ia lupa - janjinya* She forgot about her promise. *- utangmu itu* regarding your debt. *Saya tdk percaya - dia* I have no confidence in him. *Ia bangga - anaknya* She is proud of her son. **2** for, with purpose of. *- ganti* in lieu of. *- mendapat kepercayaannya tdk mudah* To gain his confidence is not easy. *kemampuan - membayar* the ability to pay. **3** as for. *- halnya program itu tdk perlu dipersoalkan* As for the program, there is no need to discuss it. *- tetapi* but, however; yet, still. *Walaupun dia lapar sekali, - tetapi dia tak mau makan* Although he was starved, he still would not eat.

akang (*Sd, Jkt*) term of address or reference for elder brother.

akar 1 root. *- pohon waringin* the root of the banyan tree. *- kata "menerima" ialah "terima"* The root of the word "*menerima*" is "*terima*." *- apung* floating roots. *- bahar* k.o. talisman (black coral from which a bracelet is made). *- beluru* St. Thomas's bean. *- bergantung* aerial root. *- bulu* radical root (of hair). *- cina* k.o. shrub. *- gigi* root of tooth. *- jangkar* aerial roots. *- jitah* k.o. liana. *- lembaga* root that issues from a seed. *- melata* **1** creeping root. **2** constantly on the increase (debts). *- melibat* clinging root. *- melilit* wraparound root. *- napas* air roots (erect branches of mangrove roots above water surface). *- parsi* asparagus. *- rambut* hair follicle. *- serabut* adventitious root. *- tombak/tunggang* large straight root. *- tunjang/umbi* above-ground root, tuber. *- wangi* k.o. fragrant grass. **2** root, source. *Uang adalah - segala kejahatan* Money is the root of all evil. *- bilangan* (*Math.*) root. *- pangkat (dua)* square root. *Lima adalah - pangkat dr dua puluh lima* five is the square root of 25. *- pangkat tiga* cube root. *-²nya* source, origin (of s.t.). *sampai ke ~* drastic, thorough, far-reaching. **ber- 1** have roots in. *Adat ini ~ kpd kepercayaan kuno* This custom is rooted in an old-fashioned belief. **2** take root. *Bibit ini mulai ~* The seed is beginning to take root. **meng-** take root. *Datangnya zaman emas sangat ~ pd falsafah hidup meréka* The arrival of a golden age became deeply rooted in their philosophy of life. **meng-kan** calculate the square root. **-²an 1** several k.o. roots. *Obat ini terdiri dr ~* This potion is made of many k.o. roots. **2** s.t. like a root.

akas₁ clever, handy, skillful. **ke-an** skill.

akas₂ 1 upside down. **2** the opposite.

akasa see ANGKASA.

akasia acacia.

akat see AKAD.

akaunting see AKONTING.

akbar 1 exalted, great. *mesjid -* a great mosque. **2** big. *konperénsi -* large conference. **ke-an** exaltation, elevation, glorification.

akékah ritual shaving of baby's head for first time (us. on the seventh day after birth).

akh see AH₁.

akhbar newspaper, the press.

akhir end, finish. *pd - minggu ini* at the end of this week. **-nya** final, last. *-² ini* recently, of late. **ber-1** end. *Pertemuan itu ~ jam dua* The meeting

ended at two o'clock. *Beliau ~ di Sidratil* He ended up at Sidratil. *~lah cerita* There ends the story. **2** become extinct. **keber-an** finality. **ber-kan** end in. *Peristiwa itu ~ pembunuhan yg kejam* The incident ended in a cruel murder. **meng-i** end, close. *Ia ~ pidatonya dgn ucapan terima kasih* He concluded his speech with an expression of thanks. *~ hidup* **1** conclude a life. **2** kill (euphemism). **meng-kan 1** place last. *Adiknya di-kan* His younger brother was placed last. **2** set back (a timepiece). **ter- 1** latest. *Ini kabar ~ malam ini* This is the latest news this evening. **2** last. *pd halaman-halaman ~* in the last pages. **3** ultimate. *tujuan ~ agama* religion's ultimate purpose. **-an** (*Ling.*) suffix. **peng-an** ending, concluding.

akhirat the hereafter, the beyond. *Aku menganggapmu sdr kandung di dunia dan -* I consider you a brother in this world and the next. *dunia -* **1** eternity. **2** for eternity. **ke-an** concerning the hereafter. *soal-soal ~* matters of the hereafter.

akhirulkalam in conclusion. *- saya uraikan bhw . . .* In conclusion I wish to explain that . . .

akhlak character, morals. *krisis -* moral crisis. **ber-** have a certain character. *~ tinggi* be of good character. **ke-an** morality. *nilai ~* moral values.

akhlas see IKHLAS.

akhli see AHLI₁,₂.

aki₁ storage battery.

aki₂ (*in some regions only*) grandfather.

akiau (*Jkt, Ch*) young Ch man.

akibat result, consequence. *- sampingan* side effect. *- jauh* far-reaching consequences. **-nya** finally, as a consequence. **ber-** have consequences. *~ besar* have far-reaching consequences. **meng-kan** result in s.t., cause. *Tindakan itu ~ amarah ayahnya* That action resulted in his father's anger.

akidah belief, faith.

akik carnelian, agate.

akilbalig, akilbaligh 1 of age, grown up (from age 15 on). **2** legally responsible.

akir see AKHIR.

akisir battery acid.

akkord see AKORD.

aklamasi acclamation.

aklimatisasi acclimatization.

akmal (*Rel.*) utterly perfect (of God).

Akmil [*Akadémi Militér*] Military (Army) Academy.

akomodasi accommodations. **meng-kan** accommodate, lodge, house.

akompanimén accompaniment.

a kontan cash only, no credit given.

akonting accounting.

akor see AKUR.

akord harmonic chords.

akordéon, akordion accordion.

Akpol [*Académi Kepolisian*] Police Academy.

akrab intimate, chummy. **ber-an** be chummy with, be close to. *Sejak kecil ia ~ dgn buku* He has been close to books since childhood. **meng-kan** bring close, strengthen (friendships, etc.). **ke-an 1** intimacy, familiarity. **2** solidarity.

Akrab (*Zod.*) Scorpio.
akréditasi accreditation.
akronim acronym.
aksara 1 letter of the alphabet, Ch character. - *murda* a large letter in Jv script. - *rerekan* a letter used to indicate a foreign sound in Jv script. 2 script. - *hieroglif* hieroglyphic script. - *rencong* a script used for the Kerinci language.
aksarawan o. who is literate.
aksef [*aksi sefihak*] unilateral action.
akselérasi acceleration. **meng-kan** accelerate.
aksén accent.
akséntuasi 1 (*Ling.*) accentuating. 2 accent, stress. 3 emphasis, stress. **meng-kan** accentuate, stress. ~ *rasa daérahisme dan sukuisme* stress the feeling of regionalism and ethnicism.
aksép an IOU, promissory note.
akséptabel acceptable.
akséptor acceptor, esp. o. who has agreed to practice birth control.
aksésori, akséssori accessory.
aksi 1 action. - *lamban* slowdown, job action. - *politik* political campaign. 2 lawsuit. 3 boasting, bragging. 4 pretense, airs. 5 handsome, attractive (of apparel, behavior, etc.). **ber-** 1 be in action. *Polisi ~ memberantas pengacau* The police are in action against the troublemakers. 2 show off, flaunt. *Si Amat sedang ~ memakai kacamata hitamnya* Amat is showing off with his sunglasses. **-²an** put on airs to get attention.
aksioma axiom. **meng-kan** make axiomatic.
aksiomatis axiomatic.
akta 1 official document. - *buru* hunting license. - *guru* teacher's certificate. - *lahir/kelahiran* birth certificate. - *lima* education courses required by law for tertiary-level teachers. - *kematian* death certificate. - *notaris* notarial document. - *pernikahan* marriage license or certificate. 2 diploma, certificate.
akte see AKTA.
aktentas briefcase. *pengusaha* - phony businessman.
aktif 1 active, energetic. 2 (*Ling.*) active (verb, etc.). 3 functioning. 4 favorable. *neraca pembayaran* - favorable trade balance. **meng-kan** activate. **ke-an** being active. **peng-an** activation.
akting 1 o. temporarily in charge. - *kepala jawatan* acting office director. 2 o. who assumes responsibility. *Dia menjadi - kepala rumah tangga selaku putra sulung* As the oldest son, he took over as the head of the household.
aktip see AKTIF.
aktir see AKTOR.
aktiva (*Fin.*) assets.
aktivis activist.
aktivitas, aktivitét activity. **meng-kan** activate.
aktor actor.
aktris actress.
aktual see AKTUIL.
aktualisasi actualization. **meng-kan** bring up to date, actualize.
aktualisir meng- actualize, bring up to date.
aktualitas timeliness, topicality.

aktuil recent, topical, current. **ke-an** topicality.
aku₁ I (familiar, intimate). - *katakan kpdmu* I told you. -*ku yg kedua* my alter ego. *sang* - ego. **ber-** use *aku*, be familiar when talking to another. **ber-²an** use *aku* when addressing e.o. **meng-** 1 confess, admit. *Ia ~ salah* He admitted he was wrong. ~ *dosa* (*Rel.*) confess o.'s sins. 2 guarantee, promise. *Ia ~ membayar hutangnya* He promised to pay his debt. 3 claim to be. *Ia ~ ahli hukum* He claims to be a legal expert. 4 consider as o.'s own. *Jangan ~ jasa org lain* Do not consider another's merits as your own. 5 always talk about o.s., boast about o.s. **meng-i** 1 acknowledge, admit. *Ia ~ bhw kelambatan itu disebabkan oléhnya* He admitted that he was the cause of the delay. ~ *kekalahan* concede defeat. 2 confess, admit. 3 recognize, acknowledge. *Negara itu ~ negara kami* That country recognized our country. *di-i sétan* possessed by the devil. **meng-kan** cause s.o. to confess or acknowledge. *Kartini ~ dirinya adik Rusli* Kartini admitted to being Rusli's younger sister. **ke-an** egoism. **-an** 1 confession, admission. 2 genie, spirit. **peng-** o. who confesses. ~ *iman* believer (of Christian or Isl. creed). **peng-an** 1 confession (of faith). 2 acknowledgment. 3 avowal. 4 admission (of guilt). ~ *dosa* (*Rel.*) confession. *kamar ~ dosa* (*Rel.*) confessional.
aku₂ see AKI₁.
akuaduk aqueduct.
akuarél aquarelle.
akuarium aquarium.
akuisme egocentricity, self-centeredness.
akulturasi acculturation.
akumulasi accumulation. **meng-(kan)** accumulate.
akumulatif accumulative. **meng-kan** make s.t. accumulative. *Hukumannya di-kan menjadi lima puluh enam tahun penjara* His sentence was made cumulative, totaling 56 years in prison.
akuntan accountant. - *Negara* department in charge of auditing the books of all gvt. offices.
akuntansi accountancy.
akunting see AKONTING.
akupungtur, akupunktur acupuncture.
akur agree to do, go along with. *Ia - utk pergi dgn saya* He agreed to go with me. -, *pak* Agreed, sir. *Laporanku - dgn laporannya* My report agrees with his report. **meng-i** agree with. **meng-kan** 1 reconcile. *Agén itu ~ dua org itu* The policeman reconciled the two persons. 2 check. *Ia ~ turunan itu dgn yg asli* He checked the copy against the original. 3 harmonize (colors, etc.). **ke-an** 1 conformity. 2 harmony. **-an** mutually agree. *sehingga polisi dan wartawan sdh ~ utk tenang* until the police and reporters mutually agreed to quiet down. *Tersangkut dua buah negara yg selama ini ~ saja* Inadvertently involved are two countries which have always been in mutual agreement. **peng-an** harmonization.
akurat accurate, precise, exact.
akustik, akustika acoustics.
akustis acoustic.

akut acute, critical (crisis, illness, etc.). **ke-an** acuteness, severity.

akwal (*Lit.*) words, speech. *afal dan* - in word and deed.

a.l. [*antara lain*] among others.

ala₁ in the style (of). - *barat* in the Western style. - *kadarnya* what is available, what is possible under the circumstances. *Gajinya cukup utk hidup - kadarnya* He received just enough money to make ends meet. *Minumlah - kadarnya* Have a drink. This is all we have.

ala₂, alaah /ala:h/ exclamation of exasperation. - *kamu itu* Oh you! -*, jangan begitu keras kepala!* Come on, don't be so stubborn!

alah₁ defeated, beaten, conquered. **ber-an** end in a draw. - **meng-i** give in to e.o., adjust to e.o. **meng-** concede, admit, yield, give in. *Saya ~ karena saya merasa kasihan kpdnya* I gave in because I felt sorry for him. **meng-i** conquer, overcome. *Takdir ~ segala* Destiny overpowers everything. **meng-kan 1** defeat, beat. *Perkumpulan kami ~ meréka* Our team defeated them. **2** exceed. *tdk ~* invincible. **ke-an** defeat, loss. *~ bisa karena biasa* Practice makes perfect. **-an** loss (in gambling, etc.). **per-an 1** conquest, pillaging, plundering. **2** booty, loss (in war, etc.). **peng-an 1** defeat inflicted on s.o. **2** concession, admission.

alah₂ see ALA₂.

alaihissalam (*Isl.*) Upon him be peace (used after mention of o. of the prophets other than Muh.).

alaikum salam (*Isl.*) Peace be unto you (said as a response to *assalam alaikum*).

alal bihalal see HALAL BIHALAL.

alam₁ 1 world, realm. - *arwah* world of spirits. - *baha* eternity. *barzakh* period between death and judgment. - *cita* idealism. - *dunia* the world. - *fana* perishable world. - *héwan(ah)* fauna, animal kingdom. - *khayal* fantasy world. - *klenik* world of secrets or mysticism. - *malakut* world of spirits. - *nabatah* plant kingdom. - *nasut* mankind. - *pikiran* view, philosophy, world of ideas, way of thinking. - *tumbuh-tumbuhan* plant kingdom. **2** nature, natural. *karét* - natural rubber. - *sekeliling/sekitar* environment, surroundings. - *semésta* the universe. - *terbuka* open-air. *réstoran - terbuka* open-air restaurant. **se-** of the same geographic or environmental type. *Irian ~ dgn Australia* New Guinea has the same type of environment as Australia. **ber-** *~ lapang* easygoing, not quick to take umbrage. **ke-an** quality, nature, character.

alam₂ (*Isl.*) be more knowledgeable. *wallahu -* only God knows. *Apakah dia datang atau tdk, wallahu -* Whether he came or not, only God knows. **meng-i** experience. **peng-an** experience. **ber-peng-an** have experience, be experienced.

alam₃, alamat₁ banner, standard.

alamat₂ 1 address. *Coba tulis -nya di sini* Please write the address here. - *kawat* cable address. - *pengirim* sender's address. **2** omen, sign, indication. *Itu - bhw ia sakit* That is the sign that she is sick. **3** target. **4** title (of a book). **si-** the ad-

dressee. **ber- 1** have an address. *Surat itu tdk ~* That letter has no address. **2** indicate. *Angin teduh biasanya ~ datangnya angin tofan* A calm wind us. indicates the coming of a hurricane. **3** be titled (of a book). **meng-i** put address on. **meng-kan 1** address s.t. *Ia ~ surat undangan itu kpd saya* She addressed the invitation to me. **2** indicate, foretell. *Angin sejuk ~ hujan* A cool wind indicates rain.

alami, alamiah natural, concerned with nature. *Apakah nafsu ini dorongan -* Is this passion a natural drive?

alan-alan comedian, jokester. - *istana/raya* court jester.

alang₁ middle, medium. *anak -* the third child. *tdk - much*, not a little. - *kepalang* insufficient, inadequate,. *Hanya sedikit itu? - kepalang!* Only that little bit? Not worth bothering with! **-kah** how! *~ énaknya!* How tasty! **-²(an)** indifferent, neither here nor there, halfhearted(ly).

alang₂ 1 crosswise, diagonal. **2** crossbeam, bar. **-²** partitions (of room). *~ rumah* partitioning in a house. **meng-** lie athwart or across. *Pohon ~ di jalan* A tree lies across the road. **meng-kan** place s.t. athwart.

alang₃ see HALANG₁.

alang-alang tall, coarse grass.

alap₁ -²1 hawk. **2** thief. **meng- 1** pick (fruit). **2** abduct. **peng-** abductor. **peng-an** abduction.

alap₂ nice, attractive, handsome. - *santun* handsome, dignified.

alaram, alarem alarm, danger signal.

alas₁ 1 base, foundation. - *rumah* house foundation. **2** layer, lining, covering. - *baju* jacket lining. - *cangkir/cawan* saucer. - *kaki* footwear. - *kata* introduction. - *kubur* o. who takes the blame for another's deed. - *léhér* collar. - *méja* **1** tablecloth. **2** desk pad. - *perut* **1** breakfast. **2** light snack. - *pijak* s.t. to step on (when reaching for s.t. high up). - *tilam* mattress cover. **ber-(kan) 1** be placed on as a base or covering of s.t. *tidur di ubin ~ tikar* sleeping on mats on a tile floor. **2** be based on. *Tuduhan korupsi ~ bukti-bukti yg sah* The accusation of corruption is based on valid evidence. **ber-an** have a base or foundation. *Uraiannya tdk ~* His explanation is without foundation. **meng-(i) 1** cover. *Ibu ~ méja dgn taplak baru* Mother covered the table with a new cloth. **2** lay a base or foundation for. **meng-kan 1** put s.t. down as a base (cloth, rug, etc.). **2** base (o.'s complaint, accusation). **-an 1** reason, excuse, alibi. *Apa ~nya dia tdk datang?* What was his reason for not coming? **2** layer, basis, foundation. **3** evidence, grounds, proof. **peng-** base.

alas₂ (*Jv*) forest. *sétan -* (*Derog.*) s.o.b.

alat₁ 1 instrument, tool, device, equipment. - *penghitung* computer. - *bantu* medium. - *bantuan* accessories. - *bicara* **1** microphone or telephone receiver. **2** (*Ling.*) speech organ. - *bunyian* musical instrument. - *gempa* seismograph. - *gések* string instrument. - *kearsipan* filing equipment. - *kebesaran* insignia of state. - *kelengkapan* paraphernalia. - *kerajaan* insignia of royalty. - *larutan* solvent. - *pemecah belah* instrument of divisiveness. - *pacu jantung* heart pacemaker. - *pemercik* nozzle. - *pemersatu* unifying instrument. - *pemutar lampu* light switch. - *pencatat waktu* stopwatch. - *pendarat* landing gear. - *pendengar* hearing aid. - *(pen)dérék* 1 touring equipment. 2 crane. - *penduga* water gauge. - *pengaman* safety device. - *pengampelas* scouring pad. - *penggerak* motive power. - *penghindar* deterrent. - *penghisap(an)* pumping tool. - *penguap* vaporizer. - *penguat* brace. - *penolak* (*Elec.*) insulator. - *penyedot debu* vacuum cleaner. - *penyejuk* air conditioner. - *penyemprot gemuk* grease gun. - *penyorot* projector. - *peraga(an)* audiovisual aid. - *peredam goncangan* shock absorber. - *rias* make-up equipment. - *rumah (tangga)* household furnishings. - *sinar tembus* fluoroscope. - *solék* makeup. - *tambahan* attachment. - *tetap* permanent fixture. - *tulis* stationery supplies. 2 organization. - *negara* instrument of the state. - *negara penegak hukum* law enforcement agency. 3 (*Fin.*) asset. - *likuida* liquid assets. - *penukar/pertukaran/ petukar* medium of exchange. 4 bodily organ. - *indria* the five senses. - *kandungan* womb. - *kelamin* sex organ. - *napas* respiratory organs. - *pencernaan* digestive organs. - *pencium* nose. - *penglihat* 1 eye. 2 optical equipment. - *peraba* tentacle. - *perasa* o. of the five senses. - *pernapasan* respiratory tract. - *tubuh* (*Anat.*) organ. - *ucap* organ of speech. - *vital* genitals. **-²** (*Fin.*) assets. ~ *pembayaran luar negeri* foreign exchange. **meng-i** equip s.o. with. *Ia ~ anaknya dgn pisau* He supplied his children with knives. **meng-kan, memper-** manipulate, treat or use as an instrument. **per-an** 1 instrumentation. 2 equipment, tools. ~ *analisa* analytical tools. ~ *kantor* office equipment or supplies. ~ *kesatriaan* (*Mil.*) military post equipment. ~ *olahraga* sporting goods. **- per-an** all k.o. equipment.

alat₂ 1 guest. 2 feast, party. - *lauk* (*Sumatra*) feast for wife's family held 8 days after wedding. **ber-** celebrate at a feast. **memper-kan** 1 marry off. 2 arrange a traditional feast. **per-an** feast, celebration. *Persiapan-persiapan utk ~ dilanjutkan* Preparations for the feast were continued.

album album. - *sisipan* philatelic stockbook.

alé (*Amb*) you (respectful).

alégori allegory.

alégoris allegorical.

alégro allegro.

aléksander topaz.

alem spoiled, pampered. **(me)ng-** excessively praise s.o. **-an** pampered, spoiled.

alérgi allergy, allergic.

alesduk scarf.

alfabét alphabet.

alfabétis alphabetical.

alfatihah (*Isl.*) first chapter of Koran recited every prayer time and before praying for dead (esp. at burial), etc.

algoritme algorithm.

algojo 1 executioner, hangman. 2 bully. 3 butcher, murderer.

alhamdu (*Isl.*) 1 first word of the *alfatihah*. 2 the *alfatihah*.

alhamdulillah (*Isl.*) Praise be to God (us. said in thanksgiving). *Pisau itu disambitkannya ke pintu belakang yg - tak ada kacanya* He hurled the knife at the back door, which, thank God, had no glass. *Wah, anak isteri saya bisa hidup ini, -* Why! My wife and children can now survive, praise the Lord!

alhasil 1 eventually, in the end. - *ia pergi juga* He eventually went away. 2 consequently, in sum, the result. *-, kami tak jadi pergi* The result was we did not go after all.

ali-ali man's ring. **meng-** sling, hurl (with a slingshot). **peng-** 1 slingshot. 2 catapult, sling.

aliansi alliance. **ber-** be allied.

alias 1 i.e., namely, in other words. *terpaksa luntang-lantung - menganggur* forced to loaf around, in other words be unemployed. 2 alias, otherwise called. *Ali - Samin* Ali alias Samin.

Ali Baba (*Derog.*) 1 joint Indonesian-Chinese business. 2 frontman in enterprise secretly financed by a non-Indonesian.

alibi alibi.

alif first letter of the Arabic alphabet. *berdiri tegak spt -* stand straight as a ramrod (the letter alif is written as a vertical line). - *bata* alphabet. *mulai dr - bata* start from beginning, from scratch. *tdk tahu di -* illiterate.

alih shift, change position. - *kécék* change the subject. - *kode* (*Ling.*) codeswitching. - *téknologi* transfer of technology. **-²** 1 instead of. ~ *engkau menyokong tenaga bapakmu bahkan kini engkau membinasakan daku* Instead of supporting your father's efforts, now you are even ruining me! 2 on the contrary. *Dikatakan sdh kawin, ~ masih bujang* He was supposed to be married, but in fact he was still single. **ber-** 1 change. *Zaman ~* Times change. ~ *fikiran* change o.'s mind. ~ *cakap* change the subject. ~ *haluan* change o.'s approach or direction. ~ *laku* change behavior. ~ *nama* change name. ~ *agama* change religious affiliation. ~ *perhatian* switch interests. 2 shift, move. ~ *rumah* move from o. house to another. *Ibu-ibu ~ ke Rinso* Women are turning to Rinso soap. **meng-** change, replace s.t. with s.t. else. ~ *langkah* change jobs. **meng-(kan)** shift, move s.t. *Jawatan Pengairan ~ jalan sungai* The Irrigation Department shifted the river's course. ~ *barang-barang* move goods from o. place to another. **ter-** inadvertently shifted. *Matanya ~ kpd Pak Ayub* His gaze shifted toward Mr. Ayub. **peng-an** transfer of s.t. ~ *hak guna tanah* the transferring of the rights for land use. **per-an** transfer, shift, change. ~ *pemerintahan* transfer of gvt. ~ *zaman* change of the times.

alihbahasa, alihbasa translation. **meng-kan** translate. **peng-an** *buku* book translating.

alik see ULANG.

alim 1 learned. 2 pious, religious, devout. - *ulama* (*Isl.*) religious scholar. **ke-an** 1 piety. 2 religious knowledge.

alimentasi alimony.

aliminium see ALUMINIUM.

alinéa paragraph.

aling₁ -² shelter, protective cover. *tanpa tédéng ~* straightforward, honest. **ber-²** be in the shelter of s.t. *~ pagar yg agak tinggi* hiding behind the rather high fence. **meng-i** shelter, cover s.t. or s.o. **meng-kan** hide. *Ia ~ bukunya dr mata saya* He hid the book from my eyes. **-an** shelter, cover, concealment.

aling₂ mechanical bearing.

alir₁ ber-an have an ideology. *Perkumpulan itu ~ radikal* That organization has a radical leaning. **meng-** 1 flow. *Sungai ~ di belakang rumah* The river flows behind the house. 2 pour, stream, flow (of money, people). *Ribuan org ~ ke tanah lapang* Thousands of people poured into the square. 3 stream down. *Air matanya ~* His tears streamed down. **meng-i** flow through. *Sungai Donau ~ Austria* The Danube River flows through Austria. *Semua rumah akan di-i listrik dua ratus dua puluh volt* All houses will be supplied with 220-volt electricity. *Setétés-setétés air mata ~ pipinya* Tears flowed down her cheeks, drop by drop. **meng-kan** 1 channel. *Pak tani ~ air itu ke sawahnya* The farmer channels the water into his rice field. 2 siphon. *Ia ~ cuka dr botol* She siphoned vinegar from a bottle. 3 shed (tears). *Yg bisa kulakukan hanyalah ~ air mata* All I can do is cry. 4 aim, point. **-an** 1 current. *~ air* stream flow. *~ darah* blood circulation. *~ listrik* electric current. 2 current, trend, ideology. 3 political grouping, religious sect. *~ kebatinan* (*Jv*) spiritualism, mysticism. 4 school of learning, scholarly tradition. *~ Praha* the Prague school. 5 pipeline. 6 conduit, wiring. **peng-an** 1 flow (of money). 2 trend, drift.

alir₂ smooth.

alir₃ a line with live bait (to catch crocodiles). **meng-** catch crocodiles (with a baited line).

alis eyebrow. *-nya melengkung* Her eyebrows curve.

alit see TALI.

aliterasi alliteration.

aliyah (*Isl.*) senior high school.

aljabar algebra.

Aljasair, Aljazair Algeria.

Aljir Algiers.

alkali (*Chem.*) alkali.

alkisah, alkissah 1 the story. 2 once upon a time. *- sang naga yg sedang mengantuk . . .* As the story goes, the sleepy dragon . . .

Alkitab the Bible.

alkitabiah biblical.

alkohol alcohol.

alku (*Coll.*) pimp, procurer.

Alkuran see AL-QUR'AN.

Alkus (*Zod.*) Sagittarius.

Allah God. *Demi - jangan! Dia tak berdosa* For God's sake, don't do it! He is not guilty! *- (wa) ta'ala* (*Isl.*) God the Most High. *-u Akbar* (*Isl.*) God is Great (beginning of the muezzin's call to prayer and an exhortatory shout on the battlefield). *-u subhanahu wa ta'ala* (*Isl.*) God who is

praised and most high (esp. in sermons). *Kita senantiasa memohonkan ampun kpd -u subhanahu wata'ala* We always beg mercy from Almighty God.

Allahumma (*Isl.*) O God (in prayers and Koranic recitations).

allamah (*Lit.*) very learned.

all in /olin, ol'in/ (*Coll.*) everything included, complete. *Séwa kamar ini sdh - termasuk céwéknya* The room rental includes everything, even the girl.

all round /olron/ (*Coll.*) diverse capabilities, versatile. *Dia - orgnya, segala pekerjaan kantor bisa dikerjakannya* He is versatile, he can perform every office task.

alm. [*almarhum*] the late, the deceased.

almahdi (*Isl.*) the Messiah (of the Last Judgment).

Almaktub (*Rel.*) the Holy Book.

almalun /almal'un/ (*Lit.*) the damned.

almanak 1 almanac. 2 calendar.

almarhum 1 the late, the deceased o. *Dr. Sutomo* the late Dr. Sutomo. *Kalau anda merasa teraniaya oléh - . . .* If you think you were maltreated by the deceased . . . 2 pass away. *Ali yg tlh -* Ali who passed away. **meng-kan** (*Sl.*) kill.

almarhumah the late, the deceased (of women). *- Aminah* the late Aminah.

almari see LEMARI.

al-Masih the Messiah. *kenaikan Isa -* Ascension Thursday.

alofon (*Ling.*) allophone.

alokasi allocation. **meng-kan** allocate. **peng-an** allocating of.

alokir meng- allocate.

alomorf (*Ling.*) allomorph.

alon-alon₁ (*Jv*) slow, slowly. *- asal kelakon* slow but sure.

alon-alon₂ see ALUN-ALUN.

alot 1 tough (of meat). 2 difficult.

alpa neglectful, inattentive. *Ia - akan kewajibannya* He is neglectful of his responsibilities. **meng-kan** neglect. **ter-** be forgotten, be ignored. **ke-an** 1 shortcoming, omission. *Harap dimaafkan segala ~ saya* Please forgive all my shortcomings. 2 neglect.

alpabét see ALFABÉT.

alpaka k.o. alloy.

alpukat see ADVOKAT₂.

Al-Qur'an the Koran.

ALRI [*Angkatan Laut Republik Indonésia*] Indonesian Navy.

altar altar.

alternasi alternation.

alternatif alternative. *Aku dihadapkan pd sebuah -* I was faced with an alternative.

alto alto.

altruis altruist.

altruisme altruism.

altruistis altruistic.

Altur (*Zod.*) Taurus.

alu rice pestle.

alum faded, wilted, withered. **meng-** fade, wither, wilt.

aluminium aluminum.

alumni alumnus, alumna.

alun wave, swell. **ber-(²) 1** heave, roll, pitch, billow up. *laut* ~ the pitching sea. *Tanaman padi* ~ *ditiup angin* The rice plants billowed as the wind blew over them. **2** be in steady movement. *selama darahku* ~ as long as my blood flows. **meng- 1** pitch, heave. *Lautan Teduh* ~ The Pacific Ocean is heaving. **2** be in steady, rhythmic movement. *Musik wals kedengaran* ~ *lambat* Waltz music was heard playing in a slow rhythm. *Irama napasnya* ~ *naik turun dgn rata* The rhythm of his breath moved steadily up and down. **meng-kan** put s.t. in steady motion. ~ *azan* recite the call to prayer. **-an 1** wave (in hair). **2** strains (music). *Tiba-tiba msk ke kamarnya* ~ *lagu dr radio di bawah* Suddenly there entered her room the strains of a song from a radio downstairs. *dlm* ~ *impian* in the rhythm of o.'s dreams.

alun-alun town square. - *yg tadinya sangat lapang itu kini tlh penuh* The village square, vast and empty just a while ago, is now filled.

alur₁ 1 gully, channel. - *pelayaran* ship's channel. **2** plot (of a story). *Skenario memberi - cerita yg kuat* The screenplay provides a forceful plot. **3** slot, groove. **4** space. - *jaman* space of time. **ber-** grooved. **meng-** groove, flute. **meng-²** be so thin the bones stick out. *Dadanya* ~ He was so thin his ribs protruded. **-an 1** channel. ~ *air* water trench. **2** context. *menurut* ~ *adat* fitting, proper. *Peristiwa-peristiwa berlangsung di tengah* ~ *jaman* Events occur in the context of an era.

alur₂ ber- hold a discussion. *Meréka* ~ *sblm mengambil keputusan* They held a discussion before making a decision.

alus see HALUS.

aluwung (*Jv*) preferable.

alvéolar alveolar.

am 1 general, ordinary, common. **2** universal. *geréja yg* - universal church. - *khasnya* whether in general or in detail, the long and short of it. **meng-kan** announce, proclaim.

ama₁ see HAMA.

ama₂ (*Jkt*) see SAMA₂.

amah (*in some regions only*) female Ch servant.

amal 1 deed, work. *banyak - sedikit bicara* much work little talk. **2** good deed, charity. - *baik* good deed, good works. - *bakti* dedication, service. **meng-baktikan** put to charitable use. *Ia meng-baktikan kemampuannya sbg ibu lurah* She put her abilities as the wife of the village head to work for the good of the public. - *jariah/jariat* charity. - *kebajikan* good deed. - *saléh* pious deed. - *wiyata* endowment. **ber- 1** charitable, generous. **2** pray silently. **meng-kan 1** put into practice, apply. *Ia* ~ *ilmunya utk masyarakat* He puts his knowledge to use for society. **2** do s.t. regularly. *Sdh lima belas tahun ia* ~ *membeli loteré ini* She has been buying lottery tickets regularly for 15 years. **3** carry out with devotion. *Ia* ~ *niatnya* She carried out her intention with devotion. ~ *Pan-*

casila practice the tenets of *Pancasila.* **-an 1** good deed, good works. **2** regular practice. *-nya yg sdh belasan tahun tadi tak satu yg kena* Of his steady practices for the last 10 or 20 years, not o. of them worked out. **peng-an 1** doing of good deeds. **2** sincerity in doing s.t. **3** implementing of.

amaliah charitable.

aman 1 peaceful, calm. - *sejahtera* peaceful and tranquil. **2** safe, secure. *Saya merasa - di kota ini* I feel safe in this town. **meng-kan 1** pacify, render safe. *Polisi Negara tlh* ~ *daérah ini* The State Police have pacified this area. **2** place in protective custody, hold in custody. *Polisi tlh* ~ *pencopét itu dr amarah rakyat* The police took the pickpocket into custody to protect him from public anger. **3** hand over for safekeeping. *Kakak saya* ~ *harta bendanya dr kobaran api* My sister tried to save her goods from the spreading flames. **4** reassure. **5** prosecute. **ke-an 1** safety, security. *Paman giat sekali menyusun barisan* ~ *kampung* Uncle was very active setting up village security ranks. **2** peacefulness, tranquillity. **peng- 1** safeguard. **2** pacifier, peacemaker, conciliator. **peng-an 1** (*Mil.*) pacification. **2** efforts to achieve security. ~ *kunjungan beliau diserahkan kpd Garnisun Ibukota* The security precautions during the notable's visit were entrusted to the capital garrison.

amanah, amanat 1 trusteeship, mandate. **2** instruction, mandate, commission. **3** (*Mil.*) order of the day. **4** speech, message. - *présidén* the president's message. - *Penderitaan Rakyat* Message of the People's Suffering (slogan of the Sukarno era). **ber-** instruct, issue an order. *Bung Karno* ~ *agar rakyat meningkatkan kewaspadaannya* Sukarno ordered the citizens to increase their vigilance. **meng-i** deliver a speech, give advice. *Jénderal itu* ~ *anak buahnya spy bertahan hingga titik darah terakhir* The general ordered his men to resist to the last drop of their blood. **meng-kan 1** entrust, commit. *Jawatan banyak dikan pd kaum munafik* Many positions were entrusted to the hypocrites. **2** instruct, order. *Opsir itu* ~ *budi pekerti yg baik* The officer ordered good conduct. **3** dedicate, set aside. *Ayahnya* ~ *kekayaannya kpd yayasan* His father donated his fortune to a foundation.

amandel 1 almond. **2** tonsil.

amandemén amendment.

amandir meng- amend.

amang meng-(²)kan threaten by brandishing. *Ia* ~ *tinjunya ke istana Péron* He shook his clenched fist at Peron's palace.

amar (*Lit.*) injunction, command (esp. of God). **meng-kan** (*Lit.*) order, enjoin. **-an** order, charge, injunction.

amarah (*Lit.*) anger. *penuh - dan dendam* full of anger and vengeance.

amat₁ very, exceedingly. *Kau - membencinya sejak itu?* Did you hate him very much after that time? - *penting* very important. - *rahasia* top secret.

memper-(kan) intensify, heighten. *Polisi ~ penjagaan* The police intensified the patrol. **ter-** very. *~ sangat* extremely. **ter-²** awful, very. *sakit kepala ~ sangat* an awful headache.

amat₂ meng-(²)i 1 watch closely, keep track of. *Ia ~ tingkah laku org itu* He watched that man's behavior closely. **2** inspect. *Ia ~ lukisan itu* He examined the painting. **3** monitor, guard. *Ia ~ gedung ini* He is guarding this building. **peng-** observer. *~ lingkungan* environmentalist. **peng-an 1** supervision. **2** monitoring, tracking. **3** observation. *Laporan ini berdasarkan atas ~ thd tiga puluh KK* This report is based on the observation of 30 heads of household. **peng-(²)an** surveillance. **per-an** (*Meteorology*) radiosonde.

amatir amateur. **ke-an** amateur standing. **-an** amateur contest.

ambah trade, handicraft.

ambah-ambah plague, pest.

ambai scoop net. *sampan -* fishing boat equipped with a scoop net (rather than a drag net). **meng-** fish with a scoop net or basket.

ambai-ambai k.o. sea crab.

ambal₁ carpet.

ambal₂ ber-²an in procession. **-an 1** procession. **2** troops.

ambang₁ 1 threshold, sill. *- jendéla* windowsill. *- pintu* doorstep. *- sungai* bar, shoal, bank. *di - pintu* near at hand, imminent. **2** railroad tie.

ambang₂ meng-(²) float. *kurs ~* (*Fin.*) floating rate. **meng-kan** float s.t. *~ rupiah* float the rupiah. **peng-an** floating (of currency).

ambar₁ 1 ambergris. **2** amber. *- bunga* styrax. *- kuning* amber.

ambar₂ see HAMBAR.

ambasadir, ambasador, ambasadur ambassador.

ambeg-parama-arta (*Jv*) first things first. *negara yg - a* nation that gives top priority to what is essential (the economy). **meng-kan** give priority to. *Kita hrs ~ soal yg lebih besar* We must give priority to bigger problems.

ambéien /ambéin/ hemorrhoids, piles.

ambek /ambek/ pout, be unwilling to move, work, or take part. **(me)ng-** sulk, mope. **-an** tending to sulk.

ambekan breath, breathe. *Ia makan terlalu banyak hampir tak bisa ~* He ate so much he could hardly breathe.

ambelas see AMBLAS.

ambeles see AMBLES.

ambén₁ sash worn with woman's sarong.

ambén₂ wooden or bamboo platform for sleeping.

amberol see AMBROL.

amberuk see AMBRUK.

ambet 1 diaper. **2** swaddling clothes. **3** bindings, bandage.

ambia the prophets (plural of *nabi*). *Kita semua sebaiknya meneladani para -* We should all follow the example of the prophets.

ambigu ambiguous.

ambiguitas ambiguity.

ambik (*Coll., M*) see AMBIL.

ambil take. *- alih* take over. **meng-** *alih* take over. **peng-alihan** expropriation. *- ancang-ancang* square off (for a fight, etc.). *- angin* get a breath of fresh air. *- bagian* participate, take part in. *- berat* take seriously, care about. *- buruk* take offense. *- contoh* take as a model. *Ia - contoh ayahnya* He took his father as a model. *- di/ke hati* take offense. *- haluan* determine direction, aim, direct. *- foto* take a photograph. *- gampang* take lightly. *- gusar* take offense. *- hati* **1** play up to, get on good side of. *Ia datang pagi-pagi ke kantor utk - hati majikannya* He came to the office early in order to curry favor with his boss. **2** be offended. *Aku bicara begitu lantas dia - hati* I just talked like that and right away she was offended. *- hawa* take an airing, go for an airing. *- ibarat* take as an example. *- ingatan* take notice of. *- jalan* take a road or direction. *- kesempatan* take the opportunity. *- kesimpulan* conclude, deduce. *- keputusan* make a decision. *- kias* draw a moral. *- langkah* take steps. *- langkah seribu* flee, scamper, take to o.'s heels. *- marah* be offended at. *Jangan - marah perbuatan saya* Do not be angry at what I did. *- menantu* make s.o. an in-law. *- muatan* take on cargo. *- muka* butter up, flatter, wheedle. *Murid itu suka - muka pd gurunya* The pupil likes to butter up his teacher. *- oper* take over. *- peduli* care, heed. *- perhatian* pay attention to. *- pusing* worry over, be concerned about. *Dia tdk - pusing thd itu semua* He did not concern himself with all that. *- rantang* **1** supply food in multiple unit containers. **2** get meals in containers delivered on a regular basis. *- ringkas/simpan/singkat* put briefly. *Di- ringkas, ceriteranya begini* To put it briefly, his story was like this. *- sumpah* administer an oath. *- tahu* be concerned. *- tanah* **1** plunder (an area). **2** (*Isl.*) commemoration of Hassan and Hussein, Muh.'s grandsons. *- tempat* occupy space; take a seat. *- tindakan* take action. *- ujian* take a test. *- untung karena keadaan* take advantage of the situation. *- upah* **1** work for wages. **2** accept a bribe. *- waktu* take up time. **ber-²an** give and take. **- meng- 1** take away e.o.'s property. **2** give and take. **meng- 1** take. *Siapa yg ~ buku saya?* Who took my book? **2** get, fetch. *-lah payung itu!* Go get the umbrella! *-lah sendiri ke Bandung!* Go get it in Bandung yourself! **3** subtract. *Seratus di- dua puluh menjadi delapan puluh* 100 minus 20 is 80. **4** adopt (a child, a policy). *~ alih(kan)* **1** expropriate. **2** take over, shift authority. **meng-i** keep taking. *Ia ~ kué hingga habis* She kept taking the cookies until they were all gone. **meng-kan** get or fetch for s.o. *Ia ~ isterinya uang* He got his wife some money. **-an** the take, the receipts. *Tdk banyak ~nya bulan ini* His take was not much this month. **peng-** taker. *~ inisiatif* initiator, o. who takes the initiative. *~ keputusan* decision maker. **peng-an 1** removal, withdrawal. **2** interpretation, understanding. *~ bagian* participation. *~ contoh* sampling. *~ keputusan* decision making. *~ jarak* establishing the proper distance. ~ *oper* taking over of. ~ *suara* election. ~ *sumpah* 1 administering of an oath. 2 taking of an oath.

ambin₁ strap, sling. **ber-** *lutut* squat while the knees are tied with a strap. **meng-** carry on o.'s back or side in a sling. *Di Jawa Tengah biasanya org perempuan ~ bakulnya* In Central Java the women us. carry their baskets in a sling. **-an** 1 knapsack, pack. 2 load carried on the back.

ambin₂ see AMBÉN₂.

ambing udder.

ambisi ambition. *tanpa ada - utk naik pangkat* with no ambition to rise in rank. **ber-** ambitious.

ambisius ambitious.

ambivalén ambivalent.

ambivalénsi ambivalence.

amblas disappear, vanish. *Rumahnya - kebakaran* Her house vanished in smoke. *Révolusi akan - dlm padang pasirnya* The revolution will vanish in the desert sands. *- déh saya* I am ruined.

ambleg, amblek give way, collapse (of a bridge, etc.).

ambles mire, bog down, sink in mud. *Mobilnya - di tengah paya* His car bogged down in the middle of the swamp. **-an** (*Geol.*) subsidence.

amboi hey! (exclamation of surprise or sympathy).

ambok ng- arrogant, haughty.

ambreg untidy, messy.

ambreng -²an strong-smelling. **ng-** have a pervasive odor.

ambrin (*Coll.*) sweetheart.

ambring-ambringan indescribable, unheard of.

ambrol 1 collapse (esp. of flat surfaces), sag. *- lantainya* The floor gave way. 2 be destroyed. *- keséhatannya* His health is declining. *Perusahaannya -* His firm is near bankruptcy.

ambruk collapse (houses, buildings), fall down. **ke-an** collapse. *~ kekaisaran Austria* the collapse of the Austrian empire.

ambu-ambu k.o. fish, the bonito.

ambul meng- 1 bounce, rebound, ricochet. *Bolanya tdk ~* The ball does not bounce. 2 bob up and down. **meng-kan** bounce (a ball).

ambulan, ambulans ambulance.

ambung bounce, soar. *kehilangan daya -* loss of ability to bounce. **meng-(kan)** toss up, throw upward (baby, ball, etc.). *Si Ali ~ bola utk adiknya* Ali tossed the ball for his little brother. **meng-²(kan)** 1 lift up, raise, hoist. 2 toss about (by waves). *Perahu itu di-²kan oléh ombak* The boat was tossed up and down by the waves. *~ diri* be conceited, arrogant, put on airs. **ter-²** floating about, bobbing up and down (in the water).

ambyar (*Jv*) splatter, fall apart. *Rencana yg sdh diatur baik-baik itu - karena pelaksanaannya tdk becus* The well-arranged plan fell apart because its implementation was incompetent.

ambyuk (*Jv*) 1 swarm, gather in large numbers. *Pd waktu itu, wah, banyak keluarga saya dr Kangean - ke mari mengungsi* At that time an awful lot of my relatives fleeing Kangean gathered here. 2 fall down (of a tree).

AMD [*ABRI Masuk Désa*] policy of military personnel participating in village development projects.

amé (*Jkt*) see SAMA₁,₂.

amén statement uttered when begging. **ng-** 1 beg while singing playing musical instruments or reciting prayers. 2 be persistent (like a singing beggar). **peng-** singing beggar. *rombongan ~* traveling troupe of beggars.

amendemén see AMANDEMÉN.

amendir see AMANDIR.

Amérika 1 N. or S. America. 2 America, American. *- Serikat* the United States of America. **ke-an** 1 American-ness. 2 Americanized.

Amérikanisasi Americanization.

Amérikanisme Americanism.

amfibi amphibian (vehicle, animal). *tank -* amphibious tank.

amil (*Isl.*) mosque official who collects the tithe.

amin amen. **ber-, meng-** 1 say amen. *menengadahkan tangannya sambil ~* holding palms upward, saying "Amen". 2 concur. **meng-i, meng-kan** 1 conclude a prayer with "Amen." *Org ~ doa yg dibacakan oléh imam* People said amen to the prayer recited by the imam. 2 approve of, concur. *Semua org ~ usulnya* All approved of his proposal.

amir (*Lit.*) commander, leader (of gvt.).

amirulmukminin (*Isl.*) caliph.

amis putrid taste or odor of fish. *Tanganmu - baunya bekas memegang ikan* Your hands smell putrid after handling fish.

amit-amit God forbid! *Laki-laki spt itu? -! Nggak usah, ya?* A man like that? God forbid! Forget him.

ammaba'dah, ammaba'dahu and furthermore (used in formal correspondence and speeches).

ammi illiterate.

AMN [*Akadémi Militér Nasional*] National Military Academy.

amnésti amnesty.

amoh (*Jv*) in rags.

amoi (*in some regions only*) form of address and reference to Ch girl. *- itu melirik pdku* The Chinese girl glanced in my direction.

amok see AMUK.

amonia, amoniak ammonia.

amor (*Lit.*) love. *dewi -* goddess of love.

amoralitas amorality.

amorf (*Biol.*) amorphous.

amortisasi (*Econ.*) amortization.

amour see AMOR.

amoy see AMOI.

ampai₁ slim, slender.

ampai₂ ber- *bertinju* to come to blows.

ampai₃ meng- 1 hang on, over. *Ada ular mati ~ di pagar* There is a dead snake hanging on the fence. 2 hang out s.t. to dry (e.g. tobacco). 3 hit, strike. **meng-kan** hang out in the air (to dry). **-an** 1 rack, clothes rack. 2 clothesline.

ampai-ampai jellyfish.
ampang₁ insipid, tasteless.
ampang₂ see ÉMPANG.
ampas waste, dregs. - *buangan* waste material. - *kopi* coffee grounds. - *minyak* oil waste. - *tebu* cane pulp.
ampat (*Jkt*) see EMPAT.
ampé see SAMPAI₁.
ampek 1 have difficulty breathing. **2** asthma.
ampela chicken gizzard.
ampelas see AMPLAS₁,₂.
ampelop see AMPLOP.
ampér₁ (*Madura*) porch, veranda.
ampér₂ 1 (*Elec.*) ampere. **2** electric meter. **ng-** (*Coll.*) show reaction.
Ampera [*Amanat Penderitaan Rakyat*] Message of the People's Suffering (Sukarno-era slogan).
ampera, ampéra inexpensive. *bioskop* - movie theater with cheap ticket prices. *harga* - cheap price.
amphibi, ampibi (*Coll.*) see AMFIBI.
ampir see HAMPIR.
ampiran (*Jv*) stopping-off place.
ampitasi see AMPUTASI.
ampitéater amphitheater.
ampitir meng- amputate.
amplas₁ fig tree.
amplas₂ sandpaper. **meng-(i) 1** scour. **2** sandpaper.
amplasemén see ÉMPLASEMÉN.
ampli, amplifayer amplifier.
amplop envelope. *menerima - tebal* accept a bribe. *wartawan* - a paid-off (bribed) journalist. **ber-** within an envelope.
ampo k.o. red medicinal clay for stomach upsets.
amprok meet, run into. **-an** run into. *Makanya perkémahan itu beberapa kali ~ dgn turis-turis bulé* So, several times the campers ran into European tourists.
ampu₁ meng- support, prop up. *Rumah tua itu di-* The old house was propped up. **meng-kan** rule, reign over (a country). **peng-** support, means of support. **peng-an** guardianship.
ampu₂ see EMPU.
ampuh₁ 1 endowed with magical power. **2** potent, effective (of medicine). **ke-an 1** magical power. **2** potency. *membuktikan ~ meréka léwat rekaman-rekaman di Musica Studio* prove their effectiveness through recordings at Musica Studio. *~ dlm menurunkan kadar kolésterol dlm darah* effectiveness in lowering the cholesterol level in the blood.
ampuh₂ flood, overflow, inundation. **meng-(kan)** flood, inundate. **ke-an** flooded, inundated.
ampul₁ (*Med.*) ampul.
ampul₂ meng- swell, expand.
ampun 1 pardon, forgiveness. *Ia minta - kpd ayahnya* He asked his father's forgiveness. *Minta -!* For mercy's sake! *Baunya minta -!* Good Lord! What a smell! **2** mercy. *-, Pak* Have mercy, sir! **meng-i 1** forgive s.o. *Moga-moga Tuhan ~ku* May God forgive me. **2** pardon, commute (a sentence). **meng-kan 1** forgive s.t. *-kanlah dosaku*

Please forgive my sin. **2** condone. **ter-kan** forgiven, forgivable. *dosa dan kesalahan yg tak ~ an* unforgivable sin and trespass. **ke-an** forgiveness, pardon. *~ dosa* absolution. **-an 1** forgiveness. **2** amnesty. **peng-** forgiver. **peng-an 1** amnesty. *~ pajak* tax clemency. **2** mercy.
amput (*Jv, Vulg.*) **meng-** have sexual intercourse. *Di-* Screw you! **-an 1** female genitalia. **2** mistress.
amputasi amputation. **meng-** amputate.
amputir see AMPITIR.
amra k.o. mango.
amril 1 sandpaper. **2** emery board or paper. **meng-** sand, file.
AMS [*Algemene Middelbare School*] k.o. upper secondary school (colonial era). *tamatan -* graduate of such a secondary school.
amsal 1 proverb. **2** parable. **3** (*Bib.*) Proverbs.
amsiong (*Ch*) internal injury.
amtenar gvt. official.
amtenarisme officialism, bureaucratism.
amuba amoeba.
amubawi amoebic.
amuk ber-, meng- 1 go berserk, run amuck. **2** rage violently. *di- lindu* suffered the violence of an earthquake. *Pikiranku di- kehabisan bénsin* My thoughts turned inside out because we had run out of gas. *Aku ~ memukul siapa saja yg mendekat* I went wild, striking at whoever came near. **meng-kan** (*Lit.*) incite to violence. *Ia ~ anak buahnya* He incited his men to violence. **-an 1** fight. *berkelahi ~* have a knock-down, drag-out fight. **2** uncontrolled raging. *~ angin topan* the raging of the typhoon winds. *~ kerinduannya* his violently passionate yearnings. **peng-** o. who runs amuck. **peng-an** running amuck, fury, raging. **per-an** fury, conflict. *Hébatlah ~ pikiran dgn perasaan* The conflict between thought and reason was violent.
amunisi ammunition.
ana (*Jkt, used by those of Arab descent or educated in Isl. schools*) I.
anafora anaphora.
anaforis anaphoric.
anak 1 child. - *Adam* **1** human being. **2** a man. - *agung* Balinese title of nobility. - *akut-akutan* informally adopted child. - *alamiah* natural (illegitimate) child. - *angkat* adopted child. - *angon* young cowherd. - *asuh(an)* **1** disciple, protegé. **2** foster child. - *badung* scamp, rascal. - *balim/ balita* child (under age 5). - *bangsawan* **1** member of nobility. **2** actor in a folk play. - *bawang* **1** young child whom the older children allow to play along but who doesn't count. **2** insignificant person, figurehead. *Ia menjadi - bawang di keluarga itu* He does not count in that family. - *bini* wife and child(ren). - *bungsu* youngest child. - *corot* child born to elderly parents. - *cucu* **1** children and grandchildren. **2** descendants. - *dapat* foundling. - *dara* **1** virgin. **2** unmarried girl. **3** bride. - *dara sunti* girl approaching puberty. - *dayung* oarsman, rower. - *didik* pupil, protegé. - *gadis* **1** virgin. **2** unmarried girl. - *gahara* legiti-

mate son of king. - *gedongan* offspring of the wealthy. - *gelap* illegitimate child. - *gunung* 1 boor, lout. 2 knoll. 3 torrent. - *halal* legitimate child. - *haram* illegitimate child. - *hilang* prodigal child. - *hitam* 8th child. - *ingusan* child still wet behind ears. - *jadah* illegitimate child. - *kandung* o.'s own flesh and blood. *Saya bukan* - *kemarin* I was not born yesterday. - *kembar* twins. - *kembar tiga* triplets. - *kemenakan* nephew, niece. - *kencing/kolong* bastard, illegitimate child. - *kolong* army child (born on the post). - *kompéni* 1 colonial soldier. 2 offspring of colonial soldier. - *kos(t)* boarder. - *kota* urban child. - *kualon* stepchild. - *kukut* foster child. - *laki-laki* 1 son. 2 boy. - *mantu/menantu* son or daughter-in-law. - *manusia* son of man. - *mas* 1 favorite child. 2 child taken in by another family. **meng-(e)maskan** treat as favorite. *sampai berapa jauh industri itu akan ~ produksi dlm negeri* how far that industry will favor domestic production. **peng-masan** favoring, treating as a favorite. ~ *golongan agama* favoring of the religious faction. - *mérah* newborn baby. - *muda* youth. - *murid* pupil, schoolchild. - *obat* 1 a patient. 2 child raised largely on medicine. - *ontang-anting* (*Jv*) only child. - *orok* newborn baby. - *pacu* jockey. - *pandak* 5th child. - *pénak* descendant. - *perawan* virgin, unmarried girl. - *piara* foster child. - *piatu* 1 orphan. 2 motherless child. - *pinak* descendant. - *pungut* foster or adopted child. - *putih* 7th child. - *rakyat* son of the common people. - *saudara* 1 cousin. 2 nephew or niece. - *sekolah* pupil, schoolchild. - *semang* s.o. who is taken into the family. **meng-semang** take an outsider into the family or clan. - *sétan* 1 Dammit! 2 s.o.b. - *subang* bastard, illegitimate child. - *suku* tribe. - *susuan* unweaned child. - *tanggung* adolescent, teenager. - *teruna* youth. - *tiri* stepchild. **memper-tirikan, meng-tirikan** treat like a stepchild. *Pemerintah selalu meng-tirikan daérah itu* The gvt. always treats that region like a stepchild. - *yatim* 1 orphan. 2 fatherless child. - *zadah/zina* illegitimate child, bastard. 2 offspring. - *anjing* puppy. 3 native of. *Ia - Malang* He is a native of Malang. 4 member of a group. - *buah* 1 member. - *buah pasukan Siliwangi tak pernah kenal payah* The members of the Siliwangi Division never knew fatigue. 2 crew member. 3 loyal subject, follower. 4 charge, ward. *keselamatan - buahnya* the safety of his charges. 5 younger relative. **meng-buahi** man, staff (a ship). - *kapal* 1 sailor. 2 crew member. - *komidi* member of stage cast. - *negeri* subject (of a state), national. - *perahu* sailor, member of crew. - *tonil* (*Thea.*) member of the stage cast. - *wayang* (*Thea.*) member of the cast. 5 dependent, sub, smaller variant, accessory of. - *air* brook, rivulet. - *arus* (*Elec.*) secondary current. - *baju* undershirt. - *batu giling* (*M*) stone for grinding. - *batu tulis* slate pencil. - *bedil* bullet. - *bendungan* cofferdam. - *benua* subcontinent. - *bukit* hill, hillock. - *busur* arrow. - *cabang* subbranch. - *catur* chessman. - *dacing* weights of scale. - *duit* (*Fin.*) interest. - *genta* clapper, tongue (bell). - *ginjal* (*Anat.*) adrenal. - *gobék* pestle used to pound betel preparation. - *janjang/jenjang* rung of ladder. - *jari* finger. - *jentera* wheel spoke. - *judul* subtitle, subheading. - *kalimat* subordinate clause. - *kunci* key. - *kursi* rung of a chair. - *laut* arm of the sea. - *lidah* (*Anat.*) uvula. - *limpa* (*Anat.*) spleen. - *loncéng* clapper, tongue (bell). - *lumpang* pestle. - *mata* pupil of the eye. - *méja* table or desk drawer. - *neraca* weights of scale. - *panah* arrow. - *panji* banner, pennant, streamer. - *pélor* bullet. - *perusahaan* affiliated firm, affiliate. - *rambut* 1 a hair, small hairs. 2 lock of hair. 3 ringlets at the temples. - *roda* wheel spoke. - *saku* small pocket, watch-pocket. - *séwa* **meng-séwakan** sublet. - *sungai* tributary. **meng-** *sungai* 1 be a tributary. 2 flow a great deal (of blood, tears, sweat). - *tangan* finger. - *tari* dancer. - *tangga* 1 ladder rung. 2 (stair) step. - *tekak* (*Anat.*) uvula. - *telinga* (*Anat.*) tympanum. - *timbangan* weights of scale. - *torak* bobbin. - *uang* (*Fin.*) interest. 6 term of address to a child (most often as *nak*). **-²** 1 children. 2 of a child's age. *Dia bukan ~ lagi* She is no longer a little child. **ber-** 1 have children. *Ia ~ tiga* She has three children. 2 bear, give birth to (us. of animals). *Kuda itu ~* The mare foaled. 3 breed. *Kapitalisme itu ~ impérialisme* Capitalism breeds imperialism. 4 together with the children, with o.'s wife and children. *Pak Amat tiga ~ berkeliling negeri* Mr. Amat together with his wife and child (with two children) toured the country. 5 (*Fin.*) get or obtain interest. **memper-kan** 1 bear, give birth to. *Ia ~ seorg laki-laki* She bore a son. 2 treat as o.'s own child. *Ia ~ saya di rumahnya* He treated me like his own son. ~ *uangnya* earn interest on his money. **memper-²kan** treat like a little child. *Guru itu ~ murid-muridnya* The teacher treats his pupils like little children. **ke-²an** childish, childlike. **-an** 1 (*Fin.*) interest. 2 doll. 3 shoots, young plants, saplings. ~ *pinus* pine saplings. *Pemupukan di persemaian akan menghasilkan ~ yg séhat* Fertilizing the nursery beds will result in healthy young plants. **per-an** 1 of mixed ethnic origins (Eurasian or Ch with some Indonesian ancestry). 2 uterus, womb. 3 hybrid (of cattle).

anakanda (*Lit.*) 1 child, son (respectful, used mostly in letters with the meaning I or you). 2 familiar form of address to young people. - *hendak kemana?* Where are you going, child?

anakronisme anachronism.

analis analyst, analyzer.

analisa analysis, examination. **meng-** analyze. **peng-** analyst. **peng-an** analyzing, examining.

analisawan analyst.

analisir meng- analyze.

analisis analysis. - *véktor* vector analysis.

analitik analytic.

analitikus analyst.

analitis analytical.

analog analog.

analogi analogy.

anam see ENAM.

ananda see ANAKANDA.

anarkhis 1 anarchic. **2** anarchist.
anarki anarchy.
anarkis see ANARKHIS.
anarkisme anarchism.
anasir element. *Pegawai-pegawai tlh dimasuki -²
jahat* Bad elements have infiltrated the ranks of
the employees.
anatomi anatomy.
a.n.b. [*atas nama beliau*] in his name.
anbia see AMBIA.
ancai disabled (of a ship). **meng-kan** wreck,
damage.
ancak 1 bamboo stand or container for offerings
to spirits. **2** rack, shelf.
ancak-ancak indifferent, casual, nonchalant.
ancam say s.t. threatening. *"Awas kalau tdk dibayar," -nya* "Watch out if it is not paid!" he
threatened. **- meng-** threaten e.o. **meng-** threat-
en. *Ia ~ akan memanggil polisi* She threatened to
call the police. *Bahaya kelaparan ~* Famine
threatens. *Ia di- dgn denda* He is liable to a fine.
meng-kan 1 threaten with s.t. *Kaum buruh ~
pemogokan* The workers threatened a strike.
2 threatening. **ter-** threatened, in danger. *Binatang itu ~ kepunahan* That animal is threatened
with extinction. **-an** threat. **peng-an** posing a
threat. *~ bahaya* threat of danger.
ancang -² (*Jv*) **1** the distance o. runs before taking
a leap. **2** preparations (often directional). *Si pilot
sedang mengambil ~ utk pendaratan* The pilot was
making preparations for the landing. **3** (*Ling.*)
onset. **meng-² 1** make preparations. *Ia ~ perjalanannya ke luar negeri* He is making preparations for his trip abroad. **2** take a run. *Ia ~ sblm
melompat* He took a run before he jumped. **-an**
approach (to a problem, etc.).
ancar-ancar, ancer-ancer 1 estimate. **2** target
date, time, or amount. **meng-kan** estimate at,
target. *~ pelaksanaan* scheduling.
ancoa (*Ch*) How's it going?
ancuk (*Jv, Vulg.*) **meng-** copulate. **Di-** Dammit!
Fuck you!
anda you (common in newspapers and journals,
and sometimes used in speech as a neutral
form). *- sekalian* ladies and gentlemen, all of
you.
andai if. *-kata* supposing, if we say. **peng-kataan**
assumption. **-pun** supposing that. **-²** supposition. **se-(nya), -nya** supposing or suppose that.
ber- suppose. **ber-²** suppose that s.t. might happen, talk hypothetically. *Meréka ~ menang dlm
pemilihan* They were hypothesizing they would
win the election. **meng-kan** suppose, assume.
-kanlah seorg hakim yg . . . Assume a judge who
. . . **peng-an** supposition, assumption. *kalimat ~*
(*Ling.*) conditional sentence. **per-an** assumption.
andak meng-kan 1 (*Naut.*) reef, take in (a sail).
2 limit, restrict, decrease. *Ia ~ jam bicaranya menjadi dua jam* He is reducing his office hours to
two hours.
andal meng-kan 1 rely on. *Negara OPÉC ~ pendapatan dr minyak* The OPEC countries rely on

oil income. **2** trade on. *Ia ~ kepandaiannya* He
traded on his knowledge. **-an 1** mainstay. *~ yg
kokoh* firm mainstay. *penuh ~* very reliable. *musikus ~* top musician. **2** security, pledge. **3** chief
seat (at national or territorial level).
Andalas (*Lit.*) Sumatra.
andam₁ ber- 1 trim o.'s hair or beard neatly.
2 have a hairstyle that requires care. **meng-** trim
s.t. neatly.
andam₂ lock up. *- karam* irretrievably lost. *Rumahnya - karam dimakan api* His house was totally
destroyed by fire. **meng- 1** tie, fasten. **2** lock up,
incarcerate. **-an** incarcerated. *anak ~* daughter
kept in seclusion.
andam₃ (*M*) grave.
andang torch.
andang-andang₁ (*Jkt*) mole, birthmark.
andang-andang₂ (*Naut.*) yardarm.
andap (*Jv*) able to be humble.
andapita k.o. cake.
andar₁ meng-kan explain in great detail, give a
long-winded account. **-an** protracted account,
explanation.
andar₂ see MATI.
andé see HANDAI, ANDAI.
andel see ANDAL.
andél see ANDIL.
andeng-andeng see ANDANG-ANDANG₁,₂.
andépi see ANDÉWI.
anderak elephant pit.
anderok slip, petticoat. *hanya dibungkus oléh sehelai kutang dan selembar -* covered only with a
camisole and a slip.
andéwi endive.
andi title of nobility in S. Sulawesi.
andil 1 (*Fin.*) share. *Harta itu diperdagangkan dgn
memasukkan - pd beberapa CV* The property was
put on the market by putting shares into some
companies. **2** contribution. *seniman yg tlh memberikan -nya dlm kesenian Indonésia* an artist who
has made his contribution to Indonesian art. *-
Indira menarik minat modal asing tampak besar* Indira's share in attracting the interest of foreign
investors seems substantial.
andon see ANDUN.
andong four-wheeled carriage drawn by two
horses common in Central Java.
anduk₁ meng-(kan) 1 hold up high in a strap.
2 hold. **-an 1** support, prop. **2** sling. **peng-** (*kayu*)
splint.
anduk₂ see HANDUK.
andun go to. *- perang* wage war. **-an** outsider.
pemain ~ not a local player.
andung (*M*) grandmother.
ané (*Jkt*) see ANA.
anéh strange, queer, peculiar. *- benar kejadian itu!*
What a strange thing that event was! *- bin ajaib, -
bin -* very strange. **-nya** the strange thing is.
meng-kan 1 make o. consider s.t. strange. **2** be
surprising. *Sungguh ~ mengapa dia tdk datang* It
is really strange that he has not come. **ke-an
1** oddity, peculiarity. **2** idiosyncrasy. **-²an** oddity.
anéka various, diverse, all sorts of. *- guna* ver-

satile. - *muka* multifaceted. - *ragam* varied. **keragaman** variety, diversity. - *warna* varicolored, multicolored. **ber-** *warna* variegated. **ke-warnaan** variety, miscellany, assortment. - *warta* diverse notes. **ber-** mixed, all kinds. *Dadanya tlh dipadati perasaan* ~ His heart was filled with all k.o. emotions. **meng-kan** vary, make diverse. ~ *sumber énergi* diversify sources of energy. **ke-an** variety. ~ *lingkungan budaya dan étnis masyarakat Sumut* the diversity of the cultural and ethnic setting of N. Sumatra. *faktor* ~ *étnis* the factor of ethnic diversity.

anékdot, anékdote anecdote.

anéksasi annexation. **meng-** annex, appropriate, take possession of.

anem see ENAM.

anémer building contractor.

anémi anemia. - *besi* iron deficiency.

anestési anesthesia.

anestésiologi anesthesiology.

anfal (*Coll.*) **1** attack. **2** heart attack.

ang (*M*) you (when addressing males).

angah see ENGA₂.

angan 1 thought, notion, idea. *Mémang - saya utk berjumpa dgn kamu* It has certainly been my intention to meet you. **2** chimera, illusion. **-²** **1** thought, notion, idea. **2** fantasy, illusion, daydreaming. ~ *hati* heart's desire. **ber-²** **1** dream, fantasize. *Ia* ~ *pergi ke Éropah* He is dreaming of going to Europe. *Ia tak bekerja,* ~ He does not work, he just daydreams. **2** aim, have ideals. *Ia* ~ *terlalu tinggi* His aims are too high. **meng-²(kan) 1** recall, ponder, contemplate. *Dia* ~ *waktu masih muda* He recalled his youth. **2** imagine, fantasize. *Dia* ~ *menjadi ratu kecantikan* She fantasizes about becoming a beauty queen. *Ia* ~ *naik haji* He dreams of making the hajj. **ter-²** thought, intended. ~ *oléhnya utk melihat-lihat kota Roma* He had planned to sightsee in Rome. **-an** idea, notion. *tdk msk* ~ implausible. *dimabuk* ~ intoxicated by o.'s reveries.

angcui k.o. red Ch liquor.

angél (*Jv*) **1** difficult. **2** strange, unusual.

anget see HANGAT.

angga tine, branch of antler. **ber-** be tined.

anggak conceited, arrogant, haughty.

anggal 1 light, insignificant. *Serangan malarianya tlh* - His malaria attacks have become light. **2** slack, light. *Musim panas adalah masa yg - di percétakan* Summer is a slack season at the printing shop. **3** lightly loaded (of a ship). **meng-i, meng-kan** lighten.

anggap₁ ber-an be of the opinion. **meng-** regard as, consider, deem. *Aku* ~ *kau sbg adikku* I consider you my brother. *Meréka* ~ *itu salah* They deem it wrong. ~ *énténg* take lightly. ~ *sepi* slight, ignore. *Duta besar itu* ~ *sepi konsul Aljasair* The ambassador snubbed the Algerian consul. **-an 1** opinion, belief. ~ *umum* public opinion. **2** judgment. **3** suspicion, hunch, impression.

anggap₂ meng- (*Lit.*) nod the head to invite another to join in dancing or drinking. **-an** such an invitation (by a nod) to dance or drink.

anggar₁ meng- estimate, calculate, compute. ~ *belanja* make a budget estimate. **peng-belanjaan** budgeting. **meng-kan** draw up a budget, budget out. *di-kan atau diambil dr dana taktis* budgeted or drawn from the operating funds. **-an** estimate, calculation, consideration. *tahun* ~ the fiscal year. ~ *belanja* budget. **peng-an** budgeting. ~ *berimbang* balanced budget. ~ *dasar* statutes. ~ *induk* amplified or master budget. ~ *negara* national budget. ~ *rumah tangga* rules of association, bylaws. ~ *surplus* surplus in the budget. ~ *tambahan* supplemental budget.

anggar₂ /anggár/ (*Sport*) fencing. **ber-** fence. ~ *lidah* debate, argue. ~ *péna* carry on polemics in newspaper. ~ *pikiran* debate, exchange views.

anggar₃ 1 (*Av.*) hangar. **2** shed, warehouse (at harbor). **3** quay. **-an** *burung* perch in bird cage.

anggauta see ANGGOTA.

angger fixed (of prices).

anggerék, anggerik see ANGGRÉK.

anggit meng- 1 lace, thread, string (shoes, etc.). **2** fasten or secure with rattan (for thatching). **3** compose, draft. *Siapa yg* ~ *musik itu?* Who composed that music? **-an 1** draft. **2** composition (music or written).

angglap (*Coll.*) **ng- 1** embezzle (money). **2** steal (goods). **3** default, welsh (on debts).

anggota 1 member. *Ia menjadi - pengurus* He became a member of the board. - *kehormatan* honorary member. - *peserta* partner (in business). - *tersiar* member-at-large. **2** member, limb. *Ia merasa lemah pd -nya* He felt weak in his limbs. **3** part, component. *Keréta api itu terdiri dr lima* - That train consists of 5 parts. **ber-** have as member. **ber-kan** be composed of, have as members. **ke-an** membership.

anggrék orchid. **peng-an** orchid growing. **per-an** orchid matters, orchidology.

anggrékwan orchid grower or enthusiast.

angguk nodding of head (to indicate agreement or due to dozing). - *dan géléng mobil* pitching and swaying of car. *si* - yes-man. **ber-** nod. **meng-** nod (in agreement). *Ia* ~ *menyatakan setuju* He nodded, confirming agreement. **meng-²** keep nodding. **meng-i** assent to. *Bila seseorang punya léhér longgar, ia dpt* ~ *segala omongannya* Only a person with no backbone could agree with all his blathering. **meng-kan 1** nod (the head). **2** agree to. *perjanjian yg penuh di-kan bupati* a contract to which the regional leader gave his full agreement. **ter-² 1** uncontrollably nod. **2** toss and pitch (of a boat). **-an 1** a nod. **2** pitching (of boat or ships).

anggul ber-, meng- raise the head, tip upward. **ter-²** pitch, bob up and down (of a boat).

anggun 1 neat, handsome, elegant (of building or appearance). - *kelihatannya dgn pakaian baru itu* He looks elegant in the new suit. **2** affected, pretentious. **3** haughty. - *halus* refined. **kehalusan** refinement. **ke-an 1** elegance. **2** affectation. **3** haughtiness, aloofness.

anggung meng- lift, raise.

anggur₁ (me)ng- 1 be unemployed, be idle. *Ia* ~

bulan ini He is out of work this month. **2** lie idle. *Jangan biarkan uang anda* ~ Do not let your money lie idle. **peng-** unemployed person. **peng-an** unemployment, joblessness. ~ *tersembunyi/terselubung* disguised unemployment.

anggur₂ slip, cutting (of plants). **meng- 1** prepare cutting for planting. **2** transplant, plant with a slip.

anggur₃ 1 grape. - *kering* currant, raisin. **2** wine. - *beranak/bersalin* postparturition tonic. - *obat* medicinal wine.

anggut meng- 1 nod due to drowsiness. **2** move erratically, pitch (of a ship). -²**an** keep nodding, pitching.

anghun (*Ch*) k.o. tobacco.

angin 1 wind. - *baik* fine opportunity. *dpt* - get the opportunity. - *beralih* shifting wind. - *bohorok* a strong seasonal wind on Sumatra's E. coast. *buang* - fart, break wind. - *buritan* tail wind. - *buruk* flatulence that causes stomachache. - *busuk* fart. - *darat* (*Naut.*) landward wind. - *desir* breeze. - *dingin semilir* soft cool breeze, zephyr. - *duduk* (*Med.*) k.o. of persistent cold. - *ékor duyung* wind that comes from various directions. - *gila* variable wind. - *gunung* (*Naut.*) landward breeze. - *haluan* head wind. - *kencang* stiff breeze, strong wind. - *langkisau* whirlwind. - *laut* **1** sea breeze. **2** (*Naut.*) seaward breeze. - *lesus* (*Jv*) whirlwind gale. - *mati* calm, dead calm, doldrums. - *paksa* good sailing wind. - *pancaroba* shifting wind (characteristic of transition between monsoons). - *pasat* trade wind. - *puting beliung/puyuh* tornado, cyclone, hurricane. - *ribut* typhoon. - *sakal* head wind. - *salah* unfavorable wind. - *selembubu* whirlwind. - *sendalu* moderate wind. - *sepoi/sepoi-sepoi* light or soft breeze, zephyr. - *silir semilir/siliran* zephyr. - *sipu-sipu* zephyr. - *sorong buritan* tail wind. - *sulit* hard times. - *tegang kelat* a strong wind. - *timba ruang* strong side wind (causing o. to bail a lot of water). - *topan* cyclone, hurricane, typhoon. - *turutan* tail wind. **2** air. **3** rumor. **ber- 1** windy (day). **2** have wind circulating. *Bilik ini hampir tdk* ~ There is almost no air circulating in this room. **ber-²** get some fresh air. *Marilah kita duduk di serambi* ~ Let us sit on the porch and enjoy the breeze. **meng- 1** become wind, disappear. **2** blow (of wind). **meng-i** air. *Pagi-pagi meréka* ~ *kamar* In the morning they air the rooms. **meng-(²)kan 1** air, aerate, expose to the air. *Kami* ~ *cucian spy lekas kering* We exposed the laundry to the air so it would dry quickly. **2** hint at, allude to, throw out a feeler. *Ia* ~ *keuntungan dr perusahaan bersama* He alluded to the advantages of a joint enterprise. **memper-kan** air, aerate. *Biji-biji yg bersih diper-²kan* The clean seeds were aired. *Ruangan hrs diper-kan* The room must be aired out. **ter-** perceptible, noticeable. **ter-²** spread (of news, rumors etc.). *Berita* ~ *bhw ia akan dipindahkan ke Tokyo* The news spread that he would be moved to Tokyo. -²**an** blow hot and cold, fickle, be capricious. *penyakit* ~ capriciousness. *bekerja* ~ work in spurts.

peng-(²)an aeration, airing. **per-an 1** ventilation. ~ *silang* cross ventilation. **2** balcony.

angina tonsillitis.

angit odor of burnt rice or bread.

angka 1 figure, numeral, digit. - *Arab* Arabic numeral. - *bulat* round number. - *dua* superscript 2. - *penunjuk* number on a dial. - *produksi* production figures. - *rumawi* Roman numeral. - *urut(an)* ordinal. **2** rate. - *kelahiran* birth rate. - *kematian bayi* infant mortality rate. - *selamat* survival rate. **3** mark, grade. - *saya utk sejarah baik* I got a good grade in history. - *jatuh* failing grade. *menang* - **1** win because of better grades. **2** (*Sport*) win on points. - *pandai* school grades. - *tipis* narrow margin. -² **1** number. **2** statistics, figures. ~ *bersusun* compound numbers. **meng-kan 1** mark, grade (exams, etc.). **2** mark, number. *Ia sedang* ~ *peti-peti yg akan dikirim* She is marking the boxes to be sent. **memper-kan** treat as numbers. **peng-an** numbering, marking. **per-an** statistics.

angkar see ANGKER₁.

angkara (*Lit.*) **1** greedy (for power, wealth, position). **2** egotistical, self-centered. **3** brutal violence, savagery. - *murka* greedy, self-centered, willing to use any wicked means to achieve o.'s ends. **ke-murkaan** ruthlessness, evilness. **ke-an 1** greed, covetousness. **2** ruthlessness.

angkasa 1 sky. **2** heaven, firmament. **3** atmosphere. - *luar* outer space. **meng- 1** be airborne. **2** soar, take off. **3** come to the fore. **meng-kan** develop to the fullest. ~ *segala daya kréasinya* develop all o.'s creativity to the fullest.

angkasawan 1 spaceman, astronaut. **2** broadcaster, announcer.

angkasawati 1 spacewoman, female astronaut. **2** female broadcaster, announcer.

angkat 1 lift, raise. - *barang, tuan?* Take your bag, sir? - *besi* weightlifting. - *bis* collect letters (from the corner mailbox). *jam* - *bis* letter collection time. - *gelas* raise a toast. - *jangkar* weigh anchor. - *kaki* flee, take to o.'s heels. *Pencuri itu* - *kaki waktu polisi datang* The thief fled when the police arrived. - *koper* clear out, leave. - *rumput* weed. - *senjata!* (*Mil.*) Present arms! - *suara* speak louder, raise o.'s voice. *Para pendengar meminta spy yg berbicara* - *suara* The listeners asked the speaker to talk louder. - *tangan* **1** put up hands in surrender. **2** raise o.'s hand in classroom. **2** take away, remove (esp. in petty commerce). *Baiklah,* - OK, take it away, it is yours. **3** (*in set phrases*) begin to do s.t. - *bicara/suara* begin to speak. *Siapa yg pertama* - *bicara* Who began to speak first? **ber-** leave, depart, set out. *Tadi pagi ia* ~ *ke New York* He left this morning for New York. ~ *déwasa* begin to grow up (of a child). **ber-nya** departure, leaving. **member-kan** dispatch, send. *Kepala stasiun* ~ *keréta api itu* The stationmaster dispatched the train. *Pesuruh itu diber-kan segera* The messenger was dispatched immediately. **keber-an** departure. **pember-an** sending off, dispatch. ~ *haji* the arranging of the departures of persons making the hajj. *ruang* ~

departure lounge. **meng- 1** lift (up), raise. *Ia ~ batu itu* He lifted that stone. *~ alis* knit o.'s brows, scowl. *~ bahu* shrug o.'s shoulders. *~ beban* lift weights. *~ diri* be arrogant or haughty. *~ kening* knit o.'s brows. *~ langkah seribu* flee, run, take to o.'s heels. *~ makanan* 1 serve food. 2 clear the table. *Ssdh tamu-tamu selesai, makanan di-* After the guests had finished, the table was cleared. *~ pantat* clear out fast. *~ pundak* shrug o.'s shoulders. *~ sembah* lift folded hands as a sign of obeisance. *~ tepuk* applaud. *~ topi* pay o.'s respects. **2** appoint, designate. *Ia di- menjadi kepala daérah* He was appointed regional head. *~ sumpah* 1 take an oath. *memberi keterangan dgn ~ sumpah* 1 give information under oath. 2 swear in. *Présidén ~ sumpah duta besar baru itu* The president administered the oath to the new ambassador. **3** promote. *Jurutulis itu di- menjadi sekretaris* The clerk was promoted to secretary. **4** remove, take away. *Perampok itu ~ segala barang kami* The bandit took everything of ours. **5** take up. *Tak lama lagi murid-murid itu ~ nyanyiannya* Before long the pupils began to sing. *~ senjata* take up arms. **6** adopt (a child), adapt (written material). **7** nab, pick up. *Ia di- polisi* He was nabbed by the police. **meng-²** praise. **meng-i** remove (many things). *Dgn truk dan bécak tetangga-tetangga itu ~ barang-barangnya* With a truck and a pedicab, the neighbors removed his goods. **meng-kan 1** lift up, raise. **2** roll up (o.'s sleeves). **ter- 1** able to be picked up. *Kotoran ini tak akan ~ lagi* There is more trash than they will be able to pick up. **2** unintentionally lifted up. *Atapnya ~ angin* Its roof was lifted by the wind. **-an 1** lift (of a certain weight). *Ia keluar sbg juara dgn ~ seratus kg* He came out the winner in the 100-kilogram lift. *~ gelas* a toast. **2** branch of armed forces. *~ bersenjata* armed forces. *~ Bhumiyam* Marine Corps. *~ Darat* 1 army. 2 infantry. *~ kelima* fifth force, i.e. of peasants and workers (communist slogan of 1960's). *~ kerja* work force. *~ Kepolisian* national police. *~ Laut* navy. *~ Perang* armed forces. *~ Udara* air force. **3** generation, age group, class. *~ '45* generation of '45. *~ '61* class of '61. *Meréka se~ di Fakultas Kedokteran* They were in the same class in medical school. *~ muda* the younger generation. *~ negara* appointed gvt. office. *~ tenaga (kerja)* work force. *~ tua* the older generation. **-²an** play around at lifting. *Meréka hanya melakukan sekedar ~ saja* They were only fooling around at lifting weights. **peng- 1** support. **2** instrument for lifting. **3** lifter, o. who lifts. **peng-an 1** appointment. **2** adoption (of child). **3** elevation. *~ sbg org kudus* her elevation to sainthood. *~ sumpah* taking of an oath. **per-** sets of equipment. *~ SLI/SPLI (Tel.)* international direct-dial phoning equipment. *~ keras (Tech.)* computer hardware. *~ lunak (Tech.)* software. **per-an 1** equipment. *~ adat* accoutrements required by custom (often traditional clothing). *~ nikah* wedding attire and paraphernalia. **2** forces. *Rakyat Ranteballa dgn segala ~nya menyerbu désa*

Ulusalu The people of Ranteballa with all their forces attacked the village of Ulusalu. **seper-(an)** set. *pakaian ~ lengkap dgn perhiasannya* a suit of clothes complete with accessories. *~ gamelan* a set of gamelan instruments.

angkél pocket money given to a military recruit.

angker₁ 1 eerie (esp. of haunted places). *Suasana Lapangan Ancol juga tdk se-* Lapangan *Rawamangun* The atmosphere of the Ancol field is not as eerie as the Rawamangun field. **2** (*Coll.*) terrible. *Celananya terbelah di tempat yg paling -* His trousers split in the most embarrassing place. **ke-an 1** eeriness, fearsomeness. *~ pantai ini sdh terbukti. Sdh berapa saja turis yg ditelan ombak* The eerie quality of this beach has already been proven. How many tourists have been towed under by the waves? **2** awesomeness.

angker₂ 1 anchor. **2** motor armature. *- dinamo* dynamo armature.

angkét 1 inquiry, poll. **2** questionnaire.

angkin (*Ch*) cloth waistband, sash worn by women.

angkit meng- remove hot pans or coals from the fire.

angklung musical instrument consisting of suspended bamboo tubes which sound when shaken.

angkong k.o. gambling game with three cards.

angkong-angkong sit idly, do no work.

Angkota see ANGKUTA.

angkringan (*Jv*) long carrying pole with hampers on either end.

angku see ENGKU.

angkuh₁ arrogant, conceited. *suaranya yg - dan sombong* His conceited and proud voice. **ke-an 1** arrogance, conceit. **2** vanity.

angkuh₂ form, appearance.

angkup tweezers. **-²** 1 valve. 2 tweezers. **meng-** hold with tweezers. **ter-²** opened and closed continuously.

angkut meng- 1 carry, transport. *Motor gerobak ~ barang ke pelabuhan* The truck transports the goods to the harbor. **2** carry away. *Air sungai itu ~ kotoran* The river carries away the refuse. **3** contain. *Bengkak ~ darah* The swelling contains blood. **meng-i** pick up, collect. *Sampah di-i setiap hari* The garbage is picked up daily. **-an 1** transport, transportation. *~ kota* urban transportation. *~ pedésaan* rural transportation. **2** shipment, load. *~ pos* mail pickup. **peng-1** transport, carrier. *pesawat ~* transport plane. **2** transporter, truck, van. *~ barang* longshoreman, dockhand. **peng-an** transportation, transport. *~ antar pulau* interisland transportation.

Angkuta [*Angkutan Kota*] gvt.-organized small vehicle transportation systems in small urban centers.

angkut-angkut k.o. wasp.

anglap see ANGGLAP.

angler 1 pleasant. **2** smooth. **3** quiet, tranquil. **-²an** calm, content.

anglisisme anglicism.

anglo brazier.

anglong₁ terrace.

anglong₂ speak in a confused manner.

angon -² *kerbau* water buffalo pasture. **meng-** (*Jv*) graze cattle. *Anak itu~ sapinya di hutan* The boy grazes his herd in the forest. **-an** livestock. **peng-an** pasture.

angop (*Jv*) a yawn. **meng-** to yawn.

angot 1 have a relapse, become angry or ill again. **2** be delirious.

angpau (*Ch*) gift of money in a red envelope (esp. at Ch weddings, New Year).

angsa goose.

angsana k.o. tree.

angsio (*Ch*) red-braised cooking.

angsu (*Jv*) draw water. - *kawruh* seek out learning. **(me)ng- 1** draw water. **2** absorb, draw upon. **3** gain knowledge. *Dpt di- sebesar-besarnya segala unsur* As much as possible o. can draw upon and assimilate all elements of learning.

angsur ber-(²) 1 little by little. *Ssdh menerima suntikan itu keséhatannya ~ baik* After the inoculation his health gradually improved. *Kesedihan hatinya ~ hilang* His sadness gradually disappeared. **2** move forward a little. **3** in installments. *Boléhkah saya membayar ~?* May I pay in installments? **meng- 1** do gradually. **2** pay in installments. **3** move. *Siapa yg ~ gambar ini?* Who moved this picture? **meng-i** pay for s.t. in installments. **meng-kan 1** order s.o. to move. *Ketua rapat ~ para hadirin ke muka* The chairman of the meeting ordered those present to move forward. **2** pay s.t. in installments. **3** move forward. *Leila ~ amplop itu* Leila held out the envelope. **-an** installment payment. **peng-an 1** process of paying installments. **2** process of moving gradually.

angus see HANGUS.

angut meng- 1 nap, doze. **2** fritter o.'s time away. **peng-** indolent person.

ani wooden device of loom where warp fits. **meng-** arrange warp of loom. **-an** warp. **peng-** spool rack.

ani-ani small palm-held reaping knife for cutting rice stalks.

aniaya 1 ill treatment. **2** tyranny, oppression. **3** injustice. **meng-(i) 1** maltreat, torture, beat viciously. *Ia menyadari bagaimana ia tlh ~ seorg gadis remaja* He realized to what extent he had battered an adolescent girl. **2** tyrannize, persecute. **ter-** molested, mistreated. **peng-** tyrant, maltreater. **peng-an 1** mistreatment, cruel treatment. **2** oppression, tyrannical treatment. **3** battering.

Aniem, Anim /anim/ [*Algemene Nederlandsch Indisch Electriciteit Maatschappij*] electricity (company) (esp. of colonial era).

animis animist.

animisme animism.

animo 1 zest, energy, gusto. **2** interest. - *masyarakat thd produk kita cukup besar* Public interest in our product is quite substantial.

aning-aning k.o. large wasp or bee.

anion (*Chem.*) negatively charged ion.

anis anise, anisette.

anja-anja ber-, ter- spoiled, pampered.

anjak thrust, push, shove. *bidang -* (*Geol.*) thrust plane. **ber- 1** move, get up. *Rekan itu ~ msk ke dlm* That associate moved inside. *Setapakpun ia tak mau ~* He will not budge a step. **2** shift, move. *Ia ~ ke DEPPEN* She moved to the Ministry of Information. *Ia ~ tua dan kekuatannya berkurang* He is getting old and his strength is diminishing. *Kemudian ia ~ ke soal-soal lain* Afterward she moved on to other matters. **meng-** transplant, reset (plants). **meng-kan** *langkah* take steps. **per-an** transfer, removal.

anjal meng- 1 bounce, rebound. **2** elastic, springy, resilient.

anjang-anjang₁ k.o. sea fish, the gurnard.

anjang-anjang₂ small trellis of split bamboo, lattice.

anjangkarya field trip, study tour. **ber-** make a field trip. *~ ke Taj Mahal* make a field trip to the Taj Mahal.

anjangsana a visit of a high official to the field for inspection or to another country. **ber-** tour an area.

anjar anchor.

anjiman (*Lit.*) merchant ship of the British E. Indian Company.

anjing 1 dog. - *gila* mad dog. - *air* otter. - *geladak* cur, mongrel. - *gembala* 1 sheep dog. 2 a powerless supervisor. - *hutan* jackal. - *kampung* mongrel, cur. - *laut* seal. - *ras* purebred dog. - *tanah* k.o. insect, mole cricket. - *trah* purebred dog. **2** (*Derog.*) despicable fellow. - *NICA* a cur working for the Dutch. **per-an** canine affairs.

anjing-anjing k.o. tree.

anjir k.o. tree.

anjlog 1 descend rapidly, plummet. *Harga-harga -* Prices plunged. *-nya kadar minyak* the sharp decline in the level of oil. *-nya keuntungan* the steep decline in profit. **2** shift rapidly. *Gerbong - keluar rél* The boxcar jumped the rails.

anju attempt, running start.

anjung 1 extension, annex (often an enclosed veranda). **2** ship's bridge. **3** (*R.R.*) platform (of coach). **-², -an 1** ship's bridge. **2** extension, annex, pavilion, airport platform. **meng-** jut out, protrude. **meng-(kan) 1** hold up, lift. *Ia ~ bayinya* She held her baby up. **2** praise to the skies. *~ diri* boast, brag. **-²an 1** fulsome praise. **2** raised platform at the ship's stern. **3** pavilion (at a fair). **peng-an** praising.

anjur₁ meng- 1 stick out, jut out, protrude. *Potlotnya ~ dr kantongnya* His pencil is sticking out of his pocket. **2** move on or toward. *Org-org désa tlh ~ ke pasar* The villagers moved on to the market. **meng-i 1** lead, head (a parade). **2** pioneer, take the initiative. **meng-kan 1** suggest, propose, recommend. *Penanaman jagung tdk di-kan* Planting of corn is not recommended. *Ia ~ spy saya lebih baik pulang saja* He suggested that I had better just go home. **2** extend, project, thrust s.t. out. *Penumpang-penumpang tdk boléh ~ badannya ke luar jendéla* Passengers may not lean out the window. **3** hand over, pass. *Teman saya* ~ *koper ke dlm keréta* My friend passed the suitcase into the coach. **-an 1** proposal, suggestion. **2** recommendation, advice. **peng- 1** proponent, advocate. **2** promoter, propagandist. ~ *mula* pioneer, initiator.

anjur₂ ber-, meng- withdraw. ~ *diri* retreat, withdrawal. ~ *surut* order a withdrawal, retreat.

Anm. [*Anumerta*] posthumous.

annémer see ANÉMER.

annuitét see ANUITÉT.

ano see ANU.

anoa, anoang (*Sulawesi*) dwarf buffalo.

anoda anode.

anom (*Jv*) young.

anomali anomaly.

anomi anomie.

anonim anonymous.

anonimitas, anonimitét anonymity.

anonser announcer.

anotasi annotation. **ber-** annotated.

ansambel ensemble.

ansar, ansor (*Isl.*) Muh.'s followers in Medina when he departed Mecca.

ansur see ANGSUR.

Ant. [*Antara*] Indonesian News Agency.

anta see ANTAH₂.

antagonis antagonist.

antagonisme antagonism.

antagonistis antagonistic.

antah₁ rice chaff, bran. - *lemukut* s.o. or s.t. worthless to society.

antah₂ - ber- fabled, imaginary. *negeri* ~ never-never land. *républik* ~ the republic that never was.

antah₃ see ENTAH.

antakusuma see BAJU.

antam see HANTAM.

antamér, antamir meng- undertake, tackle.

antan rice pestle. - *patah lesung hilang* o. misfortune on top of another.

antap₁ calm, quiet. **meng-kan 1** calm, soothe, appease. **2** calm s.o. down.

antap₂ see ANTEP.

antar₁ accompany. **- meng- 1** send to e.o. **2** deliver (packages, letters). **meng- 1** deliver, bring s.t. *Korannya di- terlambat* His paper was delivered late. **2** carry, transmit. *Air dpt* ~ *arus listerik* Water can transmit electric current. **meng-i** bring or send to s.o. *Selama ditawan ahli rumahnya* ~ *makanan* During his internment his family kept sending food. **meng-(kan) 1** accompany, bring s.o. to a destination. *Paman* ~ *tamu-tamunya ke pintu* Uncle accompanied his guests to the door. *Ibu tiap hari* ~ *anak-anak ke sekolah* Mother brings the children to school every day. **2** see off. *Aku* ~ *isteriku ke lapangan terbang* I saw my wife off at the airport. **3** introduce. *Ketua itu* ~ *pembicara itu* The chairperson introduced the speaker. **-an 1** (*Elec.*) conductor. **2** an order, thing ordered. ~ *kawin* dowry. **3** s.t. delivered. ~ *pos* postal delivery. **peng- 1** companion, escort. **2** o. who de-

livers. ~ *koran* newspaper boy or girl. ~ *pos/surat* postman. **3** porter. **4** bellboy. **5** (*Elec.*) conductor. **6** introduction. ~ *ékonomi* introduction to economics. ~ *kalam/kata* preface, foreword. ~ *khayal* prologue.

antar₂ inter- (used in compounds). - *agama* interreligious, interdenominational. - *angkatan* between forces. - *bagian* interdivisional, intersectional, interdepartmental. - *bangsa* international, interracial. - *benua* intercontinental. - *bintang* interstellar. - *budaya* intercultural, crosscultural. - *cabang* between branch offices. - *daérah* interregional. - *Departemén* interdepartmental. - *diri* interpersonal. - *disiplin* interdisciplinary (studies). - *golongan* intergroup. - *ilmu pengetahuan* interdisciplinary. - *jawatan* interdepartmental, interoffice (memo). - *kota* interurban. - *negara* international. **meng-negara-kan** move s.t. among countries (esp. shipping in S.E. Asia). - *negara bagian* interstate. - *planit* interplanetary. - *pribadi* interpersonal. - *pulau* interisland, interinsular. **meng-pulaukan** move s.t. among islands. *Ijin yg ada ialah utk meng-pulaukan seratus lima puluh ton kopra* The existing permit is for interisland transport of 150 tons of copra. - *ras* interracial. - *ruang* outer space. - *suku* intertribal. - *umat beragama* ecumenical. - *waktu* interim, meanwhile.

antara 1 between. *jarak* - *Ithaca dan Syracuse* the distance between Ithaca and Syracuse. - *kita dgn kita saja* just between us. *Ali yg terpandai* - *teman-temannya* Ali is the brightest among his friends. *dgn* - through the agency of. *di* - between, among. - *lain* among others. - *sebentar* intermittently. **2** in, about (of time). - *lima hari pesanan-nya akan selesai* The order will be ready in about 5 days. - *itu* **1** thereafter. *Pencuri keluar tak lama - itu* The thief came out not long thereafter. **2** at that moment. *Pd - itu juga ia merasa salah* At that moment he felt guilty. **3** not far from. *Kapal berlabuh* - *Semarang* The ship anchored not far from Semarang. **4** in the meanwhile. **-nya 1** among (them). *Banyak yg hadir* ~ *Sutomo dan Hassan* There were many attending, among them Sutomo and Hassan. *di* ~ among others. **2** distance, gap. *Berapa méter* ~ *dr rumah ke sungai?* How many meters distance is it from the house to the river? **se-** all around, entirely. *melingkari* ~ *rongga hati si gadis* completely encircle the deepest feelings of the girl's heart. **ber-(²) 1** at intervals. *Meriam berdentum* ~ *tiga puluh detik* The cannons boomed at 30-second intervals. ~ *sehari* alternate days. **2** be at a distance. *Stlh* ~ *agak jauh . . .* After being at some distance from him . . . **3** have an intermediary. *Tamu-tamu hrs* ~ The guests must have an intermediary. **meng-i 1** come or be between. *Selat Sunda* ~ *Pulau Sumatera dan Pulau Jawa* The Sunda Straits divide Sumatra and Java. **2** intercede, mediate. *Negara-negara ASEAN mencoba* ~ *Viétnam dan Kampucéa* The ASEAN countries attempted to mediate between Vietnam and Kampuchea.

per-, peng- 1 intermediary, mediator, go-between. 2 agent. *tanpa* ~ no agents. 3 agency, expediter. ~ *pertanggungan* insurance agency. **peng-an** intercession, mediation. **per-an** 1 intercession, mediation. 2 middleman, intermediary (individual or a body). *dgn* ~ via, by means of. *Pengumuman itu diberikan dgn* ~ *TV* The announcement was made via TV. *tdk dgn* ~ indirectly, in a roundabout way. 3 intervention. 4 relationship. ~ *dgn majikannya rupanya kurang baik* The relationship with his employer apparently was not good.

Antara Indonesian News Agency.

antarabangsa SCC ANTARBANGSA.

antar-antar 1 rotor. 2 piston rod.

antarbangsa international.

antari see BAJU.

antariksa 1 (outer) space, interplanetary space. 2 planetary atmosphere. *perjalanan* - space travel.

antariksawan astronaut, cosmonaut.

antariksawati female astronaut or cosmonaut.

antartika antarctic.

antarvokal (*Ling.*) intervocalic.

anteb see ANTEP.

antédatéring retroactive dating.

antédatir meng- date s.t. retroactively.

anték (*Coll.*) henchman, lackey. **ng-** be a lackey.

antelas see KAIN.

antem see HANTAM.

antén, anténa, anténe antenna, aerial. - *kamar* rabbit ear antenna.

anteng (*Jv*) 1 calm, quiet. *Ia* ~ *saja sekalipun isterinya marah-marah* He remained calm even though his wife was furious. 2 being quiet and sticking to o.'s work. *Ia - bekerja dr jam delapan hingga jam lima soré* He worked quietly without stopping from 8 to 5 o'clock. **ke-an** imperturbability, calm. *Kukira* ~*nya benar-benarlah sifat aslinya* I think his imperturbability was part of his true character.

antep (*Jv*) heavy, solid, massive. **meng-** 1 trust, believe in. *Segala org* ~ *perkataannya* Everyone believed in him. 2 be faithful to. *Pegawai itu sangat* ~ *majikannya* The employee was very faithful to his employer. 3 let, permit. ~ *org-org mengéjéknya* let people make fun of him.

anter see ANTAR₁.

anteré, anteri see ANTRÉ.

antéro whole, all, total, entire. **se-** the whole, the entire. *dijual di* ~ *dunia* sold all over the world. **se-nya** everything, entirely.

antéséden antecedent.

anti- 1 be opposed to. *termasuk Irwan yg paling - pésta* including Irwan who is very much opposed to parties. 2 anti-, resistant to. - *biotika* antibiotic. - *gemuk* nonfattening. - *histamin* antihistamine. - *karat* stainless (steel), rustproof. - *pelor/peluru* invulnerable to bullets. - *perang* antiwar. - *silau* nonglare (of headlights). - *slip* nonskid (of tires). - *toksin* antitoxin.

antih meng- spin. **peng-an** spinning mill.

antik₁ 1 antique. 2 ornate, highly embellished (furnishings, etc.). 3 eccentric.

antik₂ 1 lively. 2 cute (esp. of children).

antiklin (*Geol.*) anticline.

antilop antelope.

antimon, antimonium antimony.

anting - *neraca* weight for a small and sensitive scales. -² 1 pendant, earring. 2 pendulum of clock. **meng-** 1 dangle, sway. 2 swing. *Kera* ~ *di ranting pohon* A monkey is swinging on the tree branch.

anting-anting drongo bird.

antipati antipathy.

antipoda, antipode 1 antipodes. 2 wholly opposite (of individuals).

antisemit anti-Semite.

antiséptis antiseptic.

antisipasi anticipation. **meng-** anticipate.

antisipir meng- anticipate.

antitésa, antitése, antitésis antithesis.

antologi anthology.

antonim antonym.

antonimi antonymy.

antrasit anthracite.

antré, antri stand in line, queue up. - *beras* line up for rice. - *bénsin* queue up for gasoline. **-an** a queue. -²**an** queuing up.

antropolog anthropologist.

antropologi anthropology.

antuk₁ ber- come in contact with, touch. **ber-²an, bersi-an** collide with, hit against e.o. *Giginya* ~ His teeth were chattering. - **meng-** collide against e.o. **meng-kan** bump or strike s.t. against. *Susi* ~ *kepalanya ke batu karena mabuknya* In her drunkenness, Susi knocked her head against a stone. **ter-** accidentally bump into. *Kakinya* ~ *dgn batu* His foot bumped against a rock.

antuk₂ see KANTUK.

antul meng- bounce, rebound (of a ball).

antun see ORANG₁.

antung-antung hanging holder for earthen jugs.

antup sting. **meng-** sting.

antusias enthusiastic.

antusiasme enthusiasm.

anu 1 whatchumacallit, what's-his-name (hesitation form). *Ia mendapat surat dr si* - He received a letter from s.o. or other. -*nya* his or her genitals. 2 (*Math.*) unknown quantity. 3 say, by the way. *Menurut* - *katanya* Scuttlebutt has it . . .

anuang see ANOA.

anugerah 1 (*Rel.*) a gift from God. 2 gift from a person of higher status to o. of lower status. *Majikan kami memberi* - *kpd segala pekerjanya* Our boss gave gifts to all his workers. **meng-i** bestow on s.o. *Meréka di-i seorg puteri* They were granted a daughter. **meng-kan** bestow, confer (a degree), present a gift to s.o. *Tuhan memberi hayat serta* ~ *maut* God gives life and bestows death. **peng-an** bestowal, conferral, presentation.

anuitét annuity.

anulir meng- annul, cancel.

anum see ANOM.

anumerta posthumous. *jénderal* - posthumously promoted to general.

anut attentive, meek, pliant. *Anak itu - sekali kpd naséhat-naséhat org tuanya* That child is very attentive to his parents' advice. **meng-(i) 1** follow, submit to. *Ia ~ naséhat gurunya* She followed her teacher's advice. **2** practice, profess (a religion). *Ia ~ agama Kristen* He professes Christianity. **-an 1** adherence. **2** conviction, belief. **3** fad. *~ anak muda* a youth fad. **peng- 1** follower, adherent. **2** o. who goes along with others without sticking up for o.'s own ideas. *Ia seorg ~. Ia tak pernah membantah* He just goes along. He never argues. *~ garis keras* hardliner. *~ grubyuk* o. who follows blindly. **peng-an** taking up (a religion, political philosophy, etc.). *~ agama* professing religion.

anyal 1 peevish, petulant. **2** resentful, annoyed.

anyam meng- plait. *~ rambut* braid hair. *~ tikar* plait a mat. **-an 1** cane work, plaited mats. **2** plait, tress, braid. *~ rambut* braided hair, tresses. **-²an** plaited materials. **peng-an** plaiting.

anyang k.o. salad of raw meat and shellfish or raw fruit with spices.

anyar (*Jv, Madura*) new.

anyelir carnation.

anyep (*Jv*) **1** bland not salty. **2** clammy, damp. *Keringatnya mulai -* His sweat was becoming clammy.

anyes (*Jv*) cold and damp.

anyih, anyik see ONYAH-ANYIH.

anyir rancid, rank, smelling of fish oil.

AP [*Angkatan Perang*] Armed Forces.

apa 1 what, which. *- ini?, Ini -?* What is this? *Bunga - ini?* What flower is this? *-, ya?* What could it be, I wonder? *- akal?* What will we do? *- boléh buat?* What can o. do? *- juga* anything. *- juga baik* Anything will do. *- kabar?* What is the news? (How are you?) *- lagi?* **1** what else? **2** what in the world? *Mau - lagi ini?* What the heck do you want? *- lacur!* What can o. do? It is useless. *-mu yg kena?* Where were you hit? *- nian* whatever. *- pula?* what else? *- saja* **1** everything. *~ saja disumbangkan kpd korban banjir itu* Everything was contributed to the flood victims. **2** what all. *- saja yg dibicarakan tadi?* What all was discussed just now? *- sajalah* Anything will do! *- siapa* what and who. **meng-siapakan** write up, feature (in a journal, etc.). *Dr. Sardjito di-siapakan dlm Minggu Pagi* Dr. Sardjito's biography is featured in Minggu Pagi. *Tdk - It* does not matter. *Saya tdk - I* do not mind. *Tdk jadi -* It does not matter. **2** a question marker. *- anda sdh makan?* Have you eaten? *Ditanyakan - ia pernah pergi ke Bali* He was asked whether he'd ever gone to Bali. **-kah** whether. **3** or. *Bisa tinggal di sini - tdk?* Can we stay here or not? **4** eh (hesitation marker, filler word). *Dia sekarang mempelajari, -, mawas* Now he is studying, uh, orangutans. **-²** anything. *Kalau sampai di sana jangan katakan ~* When you get there don't say anything. *Tdk ~* It is nothing, it does not matter. **-nya** s.t. *Ada ~* S.t. is going on.

-nyapun whichever o. *merusak stratégi pembangunan pemerintah atau ~* to harm the gvt.'s development strategy or whatever. **-²nya** s.t. (behind it). *Ia terlampau baik pd saya hari ini. Tentu ada ~* She is too nice to me today. There must be s.t. behind it. **-pun 1** no matter what. *~ yg terjadi* no matter what happens. **2** of any kind. *Ia tak memerlukan senjata ~* He did not need a weapon of any kind. **ber- 1** do what. *Sedang ~ dia? Berkaca?* What is he doing? Sprucing up in the mirror? **2** see BERAPA. **meng- 1** why. *~ ia menangis?* Why is she crying? *Tdk ~* No matter, it does not matter. **2** do what. *Ibu ~ di kebun?* What is mother doing in the garden? **meng-(²)i** do s.t. to. *Kau-i anak itu?* What are you doing to that child? **meng-kan** do what to. *Mau di-kan tomat ini?* What are you going to do with these tomatoes? *Anak ini kau-kan kok menangis?* What did you do to this child? Why is he crying? **dimeng-kan** be treated in what way. *Mesti ~ barang ini?* What must we do with this thing? **ng-in** (*Jkt*) **1** do what. *~ dia* What did he do? **2** why? *~ gué mesti ke sana?* Why do I have to go there? **meng-²kan** do s.t. (harmful). *yg tak di-²kannya* those to whom he did nothing. **-an** what k.o. *Lelaki ~* What k.o. man is he? **-²an** What is going on here? *~ ini? Saya disuruh datang ke rumahnya tapi waktu saya sampai di sana dia pergi* What is going on? I was told to come to his house, but when I got there he had left. *~ kawin sama org begitu* What are you thinking of, getting married to s.o. like that?

apabila (*Lit.*) when (esp. in indirect questions). *Katakan kpd saya - ia datang* Tell me when he comes.

apak musty, moldy, sweaty. *Bajunya -* His clothes smelled musty. **ke-an** mustiness.

apakala (*Lit.*) when (esp. in temporal clauses,). *- ia merayakan hari ulang tahun . . .* When he celebrates a birthday . . . . *- kedinginan, pakailah jas* When you feel chilled, put on a jacket.

apal see HAFAL.

apalagi 1 above all, especially. *Semua gembira waktu adik datang - ibu* All were happy when the little brother came, esp. Mother. **2** even less, let alone. *Saya tdk percaya, - dia* I did not believe it (and) even less did she. *Kelakuannya tak dpt saya benarkan, - béla* I could not approve of his behavior, much less defend it. **3** moreover, besides.

apalah 1 please. *Sudi - kiranya* Would you be kind enough to . . . ? **2** What does it amount to? (Nothing!)

apam k.o. rice flour cake. *pipi spt -* full and firm cheeks. **meng-** make or make s.t. into *apam*.

aparat 1 apparatus, appliance, instrument. *- dengung(an)* buzzer. **2** institution, agency. *Hampir seluruh - pemerintah dikuasai badan dagang asing* Almost all gvt. agencies are controlled by foreign commercial interests.

aparatur apparatus. *- negara* state apparatus.

apartéid see APARTHÉID.

apartemén apartment.
apartheid apartheid.
apas₁ elegant.
apas₂ (*Coll.*) be unlucky, be jinxed. *Saya - melulu hari ini. Tadi pagi nubruk bajaj, sekarang ban kempés* I have had bad luck all day today. This morning I ran into a pedicab, and now I have a flat tire. *celana -* unlucky trousers.
apati apathy.
apatis apathetic. **ke-an** apathy.
apatisme apathy. *- yg demikian sangat membahayakan* Apathy like that is very dangerous.
APBN [*Anggaran Pendapatan dan Belanja Negara*] national budget.
apdéling see AFDÉLING.
APDN [*Akadémi Pemerintahan Dalam Negeri*] Civil Service Academy.
apdol see AFDAL.
apé-apé k.o. cake made from wheat flour.
apek see APAK.
apel apple.
apél 1 (*Leg.*) appeal. *naik -* lodge an appeal. **2** roll call. *- nama* roll call. *- kesiapan* call for preparedness. *- siaga* call for readiness. **3** rally, assembly. *- besar* large assembly to hear an address. **4** (*Sl.*) go to see s.o. when o.'s presence is expected. *- di rumah pacar* put in o.'s appearance at o.'s girlfriend's house. **meng- 1** appeal, enter an appeal. *Ia ~ ke Pengadilan Tinggi* He appealed to the High Court. **2** take roll.
apem see APAM.
apermut see HAVERMUT.
apersépsi apperception.
apes see APAS₂.
aphasi see AFASI.
api 1 fire. *- masih menyala* The fire is still going. *bagaikan - dlm sekam* like a snake in the grass (unknown threat). *- lancip* **1** blowpipe flame. **2** pilot light on gas stove. *- luka* erysipelas. *- mengangah* coal fire. *- mercun* sparks from fireworks. *- pencucian/penyucian* (*Rel.*) purgatory. *- unggun* campfire, bonfire. **2** flame, blaze. **3** spirit. *- Islam* spirit of Isl. *-² ***1** match. **2** firefly. **ber- 1** have fire. *Gunung Bromo yg katanya sdh tdk ~ itu ternyata bekerja lagi* Mt. Bromo, which is supposed to be extinct, turns out to be active again. **2** be on fire. *Puing-puing désa itu masih ~ ketika kami tiba* The ruins of the village were still aflame when we arrived. **3** fiery, fervent. *Diucapkannya pidato itu dgn ~* He orated with great vigor. **4** very angry, livid. **ber-² 1** furious, raging. **2** glitter, shine, sparkle (of eyes). **meng- 1** fan (a fire). **2** rouse (passions, spirit). **3** incite, stir up (trouble). **4** warm up. *Ia ~ kakaknya spy membeli mobil baru* She warmed her brother up to the idea of buying a new car. **per-an 1** fireplace, brazier. **2** ignition. **3** oven, range. **4** furnace.
apik 1 neat and nice, trim. *- benar rumahmu* Your house is neat and nice. **2** attractive, chic. **mengkan** tidy up. **ke-an** neatness, tidiness.
apikal apical.

apit hemmed in, wedged in. *- kayu* wooden wedge. **ber- 1** be wedged in, be hemmed in. *Ia duduk ~ timbunan beras* He sat between piles of rice. *gunung ~* a mountain located between two other mountains. **2** be close to e.o. *Anak-anak itu duduk ~* The children sat close to e.o. **3** jammed, wedged, stuck. **meng- 1** flank. *Dua penjaga ~ penjahat itu* Two guards flank the criminal. **2** press between s.t., clamp. *Ia ~ tebu spy keluar airnya* He pressed the sugarcane to get the juice. *~ minyak* press oil. **3** hold by pressing between. *Ia ~ payung itu dgn lututnya* He held the umbrella between his knees. **4** staple (paper together). **5** enclose on either side. *Tanda kurung ~ angka yg memerinci keterangan* The parentheses enclose a number which details an explanation. *Dua pohon kelapa ~ rumah itu* Two coconut trees framed the house. **memper-kan** move close together. *Supir ~ penumpang-penumpang spy yg lain bisa duduk juga* The driver moved the passengers close together so others could also sit down. **ter-** hemmed or wedged in, surrounded. *Pencuri itu ~ di antara org-org kampung* The thief was surrounded by villagers. **-an 1** clamp. **2** (*Elec.*) terminal. **3** press, extractor (sugarcane, petroleum). **4** intercalation, interpolation. **peng-1** clamp. **2** paperclip. **3** flanker. **4** maid of honor or best man at wedding.
apiun raw opium.
apkir 1 cast off. **2** rejected (for the army). **-an 1** rejected, discarded. *barang ~* rejected goods. **2** castoff. **meng- 1** reject (because of poor quality). *Dokter ~nya msk tentara* The doctor rejected him for enlistment in the army. *Di- pasangannya* She rejected her lover. **2** condemn (a building). **3** prohibit, ban. **peng-an** condemnation (of house, building etc.).
aplikasi application. **meng-kan** apply, put to use, administer.
aplos 1 relieve, take turns. *Nanti saya - kalau sdr mulai merasa capé* I will take over if you begin to feel tired. *Meréka baru - di pos* They just changed guards at the post. **2** redeem. **meng-** relieve. *Penjaga baru ~ yg lama* New guards relieved the old ones. **-an** turn, shift, swing. *Kita kan teman, ya kerja ~* After all we are friends. Let us take turns working.
aplus₁ applause. **meng-** applaud.
aplus₂ see APLOS.
apokat see ADVOKAT₂.
apolitik apolitical.
apollo kronco rides at an amusement park.
apopléksi apoplexy.
aposisi apposition.
apostolik apostolic.
apostrof, apostrofe apostrophe.
apoték pharmacy, dispensary.
apotéker pharmacist.
apotik see APOTÉK.
appél see APÉL.
Apr. [*April*] April.

APR [*Amanat Penderitaan Rakyat*] Message of the People's Suffering (Sukarno-era slogan).
APRA [*Angkatan Perang Ratu Adil*] Army of the Just King, a right-wing terrorist group in W. Java (about 1950).
aprésiasi appreciation. - *sastra* appreciation of literature. **meng-** appreciate, relish, enjoy.
APRI [*Angkatan Perang Républik Indonésia*] Indonesian Armed Forces.
April April. - *mop* April Fool's Day joke.
APRIS [*Angkatan Perang Républik Indonésia Serikat*] Army of the United States of Indonesia.
aprit-apritan run pell-mell, run feverishly.
apuh wrung dry, squeezed out.
apukat see ADVOKAT₂.
apung float, buoyed up. -² 1 floating object. 2 life buoy, float. **meng-** 1 float. *Kayu-kayu ~ ke laut* Pieces of wood are floating to the sea. 2 float upward, soar. **meng-i** hover about, float about. *Warna kelabu ~ udara peladangan* A gray mist hovered over the fields. **meng-kan** set or keep afloat (of a canoe, toy boat, etc.). **ter-** floating or drifting about, afloat, adrift. **-an** (*Geol.*) drift. ~ *benua* continental drift. **peng-** 1 buoy. 2 float, raft. **peng-an** floating (of a boat, etc.).
apuran gutter, drain, drainage ditch.
apus₁ (*Jv*) deceive, trick. **ng-i** deceive s.o., hoodwink s.o. *Dia mau ~ saya* He wants to trick me.
apus₂ see HAPUS.
aqidah see AKIDAH.
aqil-balig see AKILBALIG.
ara 1 tropical fig tree (several species). *menanti - tdk bergetah* waiting for s.t. impossible or unlikely. *hutang kayu -* a debt unlikely to be paid. 2 plants similar to *ara.*
Arafah (*Isl.*) a desert valley near Mecca which has an important role in hajj ceremonies.
arah₁ 1 direction, course. *Yg dinamai kiblat ialah - ke Mékah* The word *kiblat* means the direction toward Mecca. - *gejala* trend. (*menurut*) - *jarum jam* clockwise. - *melintang* (*Naut.*) athwart. - *penggunaan* the direction of consumption. - *penglihatan* line of vision. - *perkembangan* (*Ling.*) drift. *pd - serat* with the grain. 2 aim, direction, purpose. *Ke mana -nya pembicaraan itu?* Where is the discussion headed? -² resemble. *Rupanya ~ bapaknya* He looks like his father. **se-** in the same direction, having the same aim. **menye-kan** direct or point in the same direction. **ber-** have an aim or purpose. **meng-** 1 aim, direct. *Ia ~ langkahnya ke jurusan itu* She pointed her steps in that direction 2 aim at. *Ia ~ bola itu, tapi tak kena* He aimed at that ball, but missed. 3 manage, direct, administer. 4 head for. **meng-²** 1 resemble, favor. *Tingkah lakunya ~ pemain tonil* His behavior resembles that of an actor. 2 note, observe (in order to identify). **meng-i** give directions to. **meng-²i** 1 give (many) directions to s.o. *Dia hanya ~ kalian agar tdk sesat* He was only giving you directions so you would not get lost. 2 resemble. *Tingkah lakunya ~ pemain tonil* His behavior resembles that of an actor. **meng-kan**

1 direct, aim, point. *Pemburu itu ~ bedilnya ke kijang itu* The hunter aimed his gun at that deer. 2 make efforts in a certain direction. 3 give directions or instructions, direct. *utk mengerahkan dan ~ dana tersebut* to assemble and administer those funds. **meng-²kan** 1 repeatedly direct. *Polisi sibuk ~ arus lalu lintas* The police were busy directing the flow of traffic. 2 intend, mean. *Mémang ia ~ spy ia datang di rumahnya* He surely meant that he would come to her house. **ter-** aimed, directed, guided. **keter-an** 1 directedness. 2 state of having guidance. **-an** directive. ~ *riset* a directive to carry out certain research. **peng-** 1 (*Thea.*) manager, director. ~ *acara* director of T.V. programs. ~ *laku* stage director. 2 o. who sets the direction. *Almarhum Idrus dikenal sbg ~ satiris angkatan '45* The late Idrus was known as the man who set the satirical direction of the generation of 1945. **peng-an** 1 briefing. 2 direction, instruction, guidelines. *rapat ~* 1 meeting to give guidelines or directions. 2 meeting of the steering committee. *himpunan amanat, ~ dan laporan* collection of addresses, directives, and reports. ~ *pembangunan kebudayaan* guidelines for cultural development. ~ *dan pengerahan segala fasilitas* focusing and summoning up all services. *pidato ~* a speech laying down guidelines.
arah₂ see ARA.
arak₁ 1 rice wine, arrack. 2 liquor (esp. brandy, gin). - *cap tikus* k.o. alcoholic beverage made of distilled palm sap. - *obat* medicinal drink. **peng-an** arrack distillery.
arak₂ **ber-(an)** go in a procession. *Anak-anak sekolah ~ menuju istana Présidén* The schoolchildren went in procession to the presidential palace. **-²an** procession, review. ~ *obor* torchlight parade. **meng-** accompany in a procession. *Banyak org di désa ~ calon haji itu* The villagers formed a procession, accompanying people who were about to make the pilgrimage. *Meréka itu ~ di sekeliling madrasah* They paraded around the mosque school. *Plakat demikian itu di- oléh ribuan org* Such posters were paraded around by thousands of people. **peng-** o. who participates in a procession, parader. *awan ~ angin* cloud that precedes wind. **peng-an, per-an** procession.
arakian (*Lit.*) moreover, the next thing in the story. - *sang raja pun jatuh hati melihat budak yg rupawan itu* Moreover, the king fell in love when he saw the comely slave.
aral hindrance, obstacle. *Kalau tak ada, - saya akan datang bésok* If nothing gets in the way, I will come tomorrow. *Saya sdh siap utk pergi tapi lalu ada -* I was prepared to go, but then s.t. happened. *berasa -* feel less than good about s.t. *Kalau tdk ada - melintang . . .* If there are no obstacles ahead . . .
aram-temaram twilight.
arang charcoal. - *batok* charcoal from coconut shell. - *besi* 1 coke, slag. 2 cinders. - *di muka* shame, insult, affront. *Dia membunuh diri utk*

menghilangkan - di muka He committed suicide to remove his shame. - *kayu* charcoal. - *kokas* coke. - *pagu/para* soot. **meng-** become charcoal. **mengkan** make into charcoal. **peng-an 1** charcoal making. **2** carbonization. **per-an 1** place for charcoal making. **2** matters pertaining to charcoal making or carbonization.

arangesemén see ARANSEMÉN.

arangsir see ARANSÉR.

aransemén arrangement.

aransér, aransir 1 arrange. **2** arranger. **meng-** write the arrangement for. *Idris Sardi ~ lagu itu* Idris Sardi wrote the arrangement for that song.

Ararat (*Rel.*) Ararat, the mountain where Noah's ark rested.

ararut arrowroot.

aras₁ border, limit. **meng- 1** reach a limit. *Celananya ~ lutut* His trousers came up to his knees. **2** (*Che.*) checkmate. *Raja di-* The king was checkmated. **meng-i** define, delimit. *Utk ~ masalah tersebut* To delimit that problem. **-²an** feel too lazy to do s.t.

aras₂, arasy (*Rel.*) the throne of God. *Tampak segala org mati berdiri di hadapan -* There were seen all the dead standing before the throne of God.

arbaa see RABU.

arbab see REBAB.

arbéi strawberry.

arbitrase arbitration.

arca statue, image. **meng-kan** cast into a statue, make a likeness. *Di-kan menurut déwa yg dipujanya* A statue was made according to the image of the god he worshiped.

arde (*Elec.*) ground.

are 100 square meters.

aréal acreage.

arék (*Jv*) child. - *Suroboyo* (*Coll.*) s.o. from Surabaya.

arén sugar palm.

aréna arena.

arés (*Leg.*) arrest.

aréstasi detention, capture.

argométer fare-meter (e.g. in taxis).

argumén argument, case, plea, reason.

arguméntasi argumentation.

arhéologi see ARKÉOLOGI.

ari₁ see ARI-ARI.

ari₂ see ULAR.

ari₃ see KULIT.

ari₄ see HARI.

aria₁ 1 title of nobility. **2** the Aryan race.

aria₂ aria.

ari-ari 1 abdomen. **2** placenta. *tali -* umbilical cord.

arif 1 learned. **2** wise, clever, skillful. *Ibu menyambut dgn pandangan -* Mother responded with a knowing glance. **3** capable. **meng-i** understand, see. **meng-kan** realize, understand. **ke-an 1** learning, wisdom. **2** ability.

arifin (*Lit.*) intelligent person.

arih meng-(kan) hold out, extend. *Ibunya ~ ta-* ngan kpdnya utk memeluknya Her mother held out her hands to embrace her.

arik insomnia.

aring₁ 1 trap, snarl. **2** lasso.

aring₂ odor of urine.

ario see ARIA₁.

arip see ARIF.

aris 1 hem. **2** edge, border (of sail, etc.).

arisan regular social gathering whose members contribute to and take turns at winning an aggregate sum of money. - *call/télepon* an activity of this sort where the exchange of money is carried out by telephone and the social gathering is dispensed with. - *drop* a system where members of a group can purchase s.t. o. at a time in turn with each member putting in a set amount at stated intervals. - *piao* such a gathering in which a member can get a turn first by agreeing to contribute more than the others.

aristokrasi aristocracy.

aristokrat aristocrat.

arit 1 sickle. **2** knife for tapping rubber trees. **3** grass knife. **meng-** cut grass.

arivé established, attained a position.

Arjuna 1 the chief hero of the Mahabharata, known for his martial and sexual prowess. **2** playboy, womanizer. *Meréka tak perlu lelaki -* They do not need any playboys. **3** handsome man. *Dirman, - alim yg perkasa itu* Dirman, that handsome, pious, and well-built man.

arkais archaic.

arkaisme archaism.

arkéolog archaeologist.

arkéologi archaeology.

arkéologis archaeological.

arkian see ARAKIAN.

arkip see ARSIP.

arktika see ARTIKA.

arloji timepiece, watch. - *kantung/saku* pocket watch. - *tangan* wristwatch.

armada fleet. - *niaga* merchant (marine) fleet. - *tempur* combat fleet.

arnab rabbit, hare.

arnal hairpin, stickpin for the hair.

aroma aroma.

aromatik aromatic.

aromatis aromatic.

aron half-cooked rice.

arona sun.

arpus resin, rosin for violin bows.

arrahman (*Isl.*) the Merciful (i.e. God, esp. in prayers or sermons). - *arrohim* the Merciful and the Benevolent O. (in prayers and sermons).

arransir see ARANSÉR.

arrivé see ARIVÉ.

arrohim (*Isl.*) the Benevolent O. (i.e. God, esp. in sermons).

arsén, arsénikum arsenic.

arsip 1 archives. **2** files. - *negara* state or national archives. **ke-an 1** archival matters. **2** records. **peng-an** filing, system for keeping archives. *Di kantor kami cara ~ sedang diubah* At our office

the method for keeping records is being changed.
arsiparis 1 archivist. **2** file clerk.
arsir shade in (a drawing). **-an** hatching (in sketching), shaded-in area.
arsiték architect.
arsitéktur architecture. *- landskap* landscape architecture.
arsitékturil architectural.
arso (*Jv*) **ng-** in front of an exalted person.
ART [*Anggaran Rumah Tangga*] rules of association.
arta see HARTA.
artawan see HARTAWAN.
artésis artesian.
arti 1 meaning. *Apa -nya?* What is the meaning? **2** sense. *dlm - sempit* in the narrow sense. **3** significance, importance. *Seratus dolar tak ada -nya bagi seorg kaya spt dia* 100 dollars means nothing to a rich man like him. *- dua* ambiguity. *- kiasan* figurative sense. **-nya** that is, meaning. **se-** of the same opinion or meaning. *~ dgn* synonymous with. **ber- 1** mean. *Pemadaman listrik ini ~ kita terlambat memenuhi kuota* This blackout means we will be late in meeting the quota. *kata ini ~ apa?* What does this word mean? **2** be significant, meaningful. *Ia memberi uraian yg ~* He gave a significant explanation. *secara ~* significantly. **3** valuable, useful. **keber-an** significance. **ng-** (*Jkt, Sd*) understand, comprehend. **meng-kan 1** interpret, construe. *istilah kimia yg ku-kan ke istilah umum* a chemical term to which I gave a meaning which is the same as the general term. **2** bear a meaning for, lead o. to understand. *Kalimat-kalimat lagu itu ~ Hafid bhw . . .* The lyrics of that song led Hafid to understand that . . . **-an 1** meaning. *dlm ~ lambat* in the sense of slow. **2** idea, concept. **3** interpretation. **peng-an 1** understanding. **2** meaning, sense.
artifisial, artifisiil artificial.
artika arctic.
artikel 1 article, clause. *- karét* clause subject to various interpretations. **2** article, column. **3** (*Ling.*) article. *- tentu* definite article.
artikulasi articulation. **meng-kan** articulate. *~ pendapat* express or articulate an opinion.
artikulator (*Ling.*) articulator.
artileri 1 artillery, ordnance. **2** artillery, gunners.
artis artist.
artistik artistic. **ke-an** artistic.
arts (*Coll.*) physician.
Aru Buginese title.
aruan see HARUAN.
aruh see PENGARUH.
arum dalu k.o. night-blooming flower.
arum manis cotton candy.
arun meng- stir, mix in.
arung meng- wade across, cross. *Mari kita ~ sungai itu* Let us wade across that river. *Kapal baru itu ~ segara* The new ship crossed the ocean. **meng-i 1** cross s.t. *Meréka ~ padang pasir itu selama empat puluh hari* They crossed the desert

for 40 days. **2** sail through s.t. *~ Atlantik* sail through the Atlantic. *~ samudera hidup* go through the experience of life. **3** ford, wade across. **4** wade through, plod through (o.'s studies, work). **-(²)an 1** crossing, ford. **2** (*Naut.*) shipping corridor. **peng-an** action of crossing.
arus₁ 1 current. *Di antara Bali dan Jawa ada - kuat* There is a strong current between Bali and Java. *- air* stream flow. *- balik* feedback. *- balik belakang* undertow. *- bawah* undercurrent. *- bolak-balik* alternating current. *- hayati* vital fluid. *- laut* marine current. *- lemah* (*Elec.*) low-tension current. *- listrik* electric current. *- olak* (*Elec.*) eddy current. *- olak(an)* rollers, rolling waves. *- pasang* tidal current. *- penukar* alternating current. *- pokok* thrust. *- pusar* (*Elec.*) eddy current. *- searah* direct current. *- Teluk* Gulf Stream. **2** flow. *- barang* commodity flow, flow of goods. *- dana* cash flow. *- kas* cash flow. *- pembeli* (*Econ.*) buying surge.
arus₂ see HARUS.
arwah soul, departed spirit. **meng-kan** hold a memorial service in honor of the deceased.
Arya see ARIA₁.
aryaduta (*Lit.*) ambassador.
as₁ 1 axle. **2** axis.
as₂ (*Crd.*) ace.
as. [*alaihissalam*] Peace be with him (uttered after mention of minor prophet).
AS [*Amérika Serikat*] the USA.
asa hope. *- sia-sia* vain hope. **-²an** ever hoping.
asabat 1 nerve. **2** sinew, muscle.
Asad (*Zod.*) Leo.
Asada Buddhist holiday commemorating Sidharta's first sermon after being enlightened.
asah grind down (teeth or gem). *- bulat* a style of tooth filing. *- papan* a style of tooth filing. **ber-** filed, sharpened, polished, burnished. **meng- 1** sharpen. *Ia ~ pisau* He sharpened the knife. **2** file (teeth). **3** polish, shine, burnish (a gem). *~ intan* cut a diamond. **4** grind, whet, hone. **5** plane (a board). *Ia pandai sekali ~ hati org* He is very clever at persuading people. **-an 1** shavings. *~ kayu* wood shavings. **2** dust. **peng-1** sharpener. **2** grinder. **3** whetstone. *~ pénsil* pencil sharpener. *~ otak* brain teaser, brain twister. **peng-an 1** honing. **2** sharpening, grinding, scraping. *~ gigi* tooth filing. *Ia mendapat luka berat dr ~ batu di jalan raya* He got a serious wound from scraping against the stones on the highway.
asah asih asuh (*Jv*) a teacher's slogan: teach, love, care for.
asai mouldered, mildewed. *Di negeri panas banyak macam kayu lekas -* In tropical countries many k.o. wood quickly rot.
asak ber- 1 move, budge. *Sekalipun org lainnya mengungsi, org tua itu tdk ~* Although other people were evacuating, the old man would not budge. **2** cram, jam. **ber-²** cram, jam. **ber-²an** be jammed into. *Di akhir minggu penumpang ~ di trém* On weekends passengers crowd into street-

cars. **meng-** 1 cram, jam. *Ia ~ peti dgn beras* She crammed the box with rice. 2 urge, press, insist. *Ia ~ pamannya spy menjual saham karétnya* He insisted that his uncle sell his rubber stock. 3 move, shift. *Ia ~ pohon itu ke tempat yg lebih subur* He moved the tree to a more fertile place. 4 replace, supplant. 5 push onward. **meng-i** 1 cram, jam s.t. with. 2 urge, insist, press. **ter-** 1 be crammed, be crowded. 2 be moved, shifted. *Ia ~ ke tempat yg lain* He was moved to another place. 3 urged, pressed.

asal₁ 1 origin, source. *Di mana - sungai itu?* What is the source of this river? 2 beginning, cause. - *jasad* organic. - *kata* (*Ling.*) base, stem. - *muasal* beginnings (of an idea, etc.). - *mula* origin, very beginning. - *mula sejarah* dawn of history. - *usul* 1 pedigree, descent, origin. 2 history, origin. *Itulah - usul sengketa meréka itu* That was the origin of their quarrel. *Bagaimana - usul penyakit itu?* What is the history (etiology) of that disease. **sc-** related. *~ sepangkal* of the same family background and origins. **-nya** originally, initially. - **ber-** be of good family, wellborn. **ber-** 1 come from. *Dr mana dia ~?* Where does he hail from? *Barang-barang ini ~ dr Jepang* These goods come from Japan. 2 be from a good family. 3 be descended (from). **meng-kan** trace origin (back) to. *Ahli sejarah ~ kesenian Borobudur* A historian traces the origin of the art of Borobudur. *~ pd* (*Math.*) reduce s.t.

asal₂ 1 provided that, as long as. - *kau mau menunggu saja* as long as you want to wait for me. *Cukup - ada tikar buat alas* Provided there is a mat to lie on, that will be enough. - *bapak senang* as long as the boss is happy (an attitude of chronic sycophancy). 2 do s.t. for no good reason other than just to do it. *Aku sesungguhnya cuma - bicara* Actually, I said it just for the sake of having s.t. to say. 3 just be able to do the most important, basic thing and no more. *Tata lampunya - bisa nyalapadam* You could turn the stage lighting on and off, but that was about it. *Tata pengeras suara - bisa terdengar* You could hear with the sound system, but that was just about it. - *saja* perfunctory. *mencuci mukanya - saja* give o.'s face a perfunctory washing. **se-nya** perfunctorily. *Dia menyusun laporan itu ~ saja* He put the report together any old way. **-²an** done in any old way, perfunctorily. **-kan** provided that. *Ia boléh ke bioskop, ~ ada uang* He is allowed to go to the movies, provided he has the money. *biar lambat, ~ selamat* slow but sure.

asali 1 original, primary. 2 ancient. 3 of good family, wellborn.

asaliah see ASALI.

asam 1 sour. *Air jeruknya - lho* Hey! The lemonade is sour. *Mukanya -* He has a sour look. *tersenyum -* smile in a forced way. - *kandi* k.o. sour condiment made from a fruit. *Kurang -!* 1 How rude! (a euphemism for *kurang ajar*). 2 Darn it! 2 acid. - *air* uric acid. - *arang* carbon dioxide. - *arsénat* arsenic. - *belérang* sulphuric acid. - *borat*

boric acid. - *cuka* acetic acid. - *foli* folic acid. - *fosfor* phosphoric acid. - *garam* 1 hydrochloric acid. 2 flavoring (esp. tamarind and salt). 3 ups and downs. *Ibu ini sdh banyak makan - garam hidup ini* This woman has already experienced the vagaries of life. - *jeruk* citric acid. - *karbol* carbolic acid. - *klorat* chloric acid. - *klorida* hydrochloric acid. - *laktat/susu* lactic acid. - *lambung* gastric juice. - *limau* citric acid. - *nit(e)rat* nitric acid. - *nitrit* nitrous acid. - *salisilat* salicylic acid. - *samak* tannic acid. - *semut* formic acid. - *sendawa* nitric acid. - *sulfat* sulphuric acid. - *sulfida* sulphide acid. 3 k.o. tree, tamarind. - *caluk* k.o. tamarind with tiny leaves. - *jawa* tamarind. **meng-** 1 clean s.t. with acid. 2 turn into acid. **meng-i** 1 add acid. 2 put tamarind into o.'s cooking. **meng-kan** pickle, preserve. **ke-an** acidity. **ke-²an** sour(ish), acidic. **-an** 1 pickle. 2 acid. 3 acidity. **-²an** 1 pickled dish(es). 2 all sorts of acids.

asap 1 smoke. - *air* vapor. - *dapur* livelihood. *Mempertahankan pendapat pribadi berarti mengancam - dapur* Defending o.'s personal opinions means threatening o.'s livelihood. 2 fumes. - *kendaraan bermotor* exhaust fumes. - *kemenyan* incense fumes. **meng-kemenyani** praise. *suka meng-kemenyani mertuanya* like to praise o.'s in-laws. - *ratus* incense fumes. - *tangis* tear gas. 3 smoked. *bandeng -* smoked milk fish. **ber-** 1 smoke, issue smoke or vapor. *segelas kopi yg masih ~* a piping hot glass of coffee. 2 dim, misty. **meng-** 1 become, turn into, smoke. 2 smoke, cure (food). 3 fumigate. 4 scent, perfume (clothes). **meng-i** 1 smoke, cure (food). 2 fumigate. 3 scent, perfume (clothes). **peng-an** 1 fumigation. 2 curing. *rumah ~ karét* place to cure rubber. **per-an** 1 incense burner. 2 fumigator, fumigating agent.

asar 1 (*Isl.*) afternoon prayer (about four p.m.). *salat -* the afternoon prayer. 2 period between three and four p.m. - *rendah* about 5 p.m. - *tinggi* about three p.m.

asas 1 basis, principle. 2 foundation, base. *Pd -nya ia salah* Fundamentally he is wrong. - *rumah itu dibuat dr beton* The foundation of that house is made of concrete. **ber-(kan)** 1 be based on. *Negara Pakistan ~ keislaman* Pakistan is based on Isl. principles. 2 have principles. *Perkumpulan ini ~ sosial* This association is based on social principles. **meng-kan** 1 found, base. *Ia ~ pelajarannya pd cita-cita Islam* He founded his teachings on Isl. ideals. 2 found, establish. **peng-** founder.

asasi fundamental, basic. *hak -* basic right.

asbak ashtray.

asbés asbestos.

asbun [*asal bunyi*] speak without forethought. *Jangan - saja ah, dipikir dulu baru bicara* Don't just blurt out whatever comes to you. Think before you speak.

asbut [*asap kabut*] smog.

asé₁ k.o. curry soup with meat.

asé₂ [*air conditioner*] air conditioner.
ASEAN [*Association of S.E. Asian Nations*] ASEAN.
aseli see ASLI.
asem see ASAM.
asémbling assembling, assembled. *Ini mobil - Indonésia* This is a car assembled in Indonesia. **meng-** assemble.
asémblir meng- assemble.
asep see ASAP.
asép see AKSÉP.
asesanti (*Jv*) utter a slogan.
asésé approved, agreed. **meng-kan** approve.
asésori accessories.
asétilén acetylene.
asfal see ASPAL₁.
ashadu see ASYHADU ANLA ILA HA ILLALLAH.
ASI [*Air Susu Ibu*] mother's milk. *Sebaiknya bayi diberi - saja* The best thing would be for the baby to be given mother's milk.
asi₁ care, attention. **meng-** pay attention to. *Anak itu sama sekali tdk ~ perkataan ayahnya* The child paid no attention whatsoever to what his father said.
asi₂ disobedient.
Asia Asia. - *Kecil* Asia Minor. - *Tenggara* S.E. Asia. **ke-an** Asian-ness, possessing an Asian quality, Asia-like. *suasana ~* an Asian atmosphere.
asih₁ see ASAH ASIH ASUH.
asih₂ see MAHAASIH.
asik see ASYIK.
asimétri asymmetry.
asimétris asymmetric.
asimilasi assimilation. **ber-** assimilate.
asimot see AZIMUT.
asimptot (*Math.*) asymptote.
asimut see AZIMUT.
asin 1 salty. *Supnya terlalu -* The soup is too salty. **2** salty, briny. - *garam* worries, problems. **meng-i, meng-kan 1** salt. *Ia ~ ikan* She salted the fish. **2** pickle s.t. **-an** salted vegetables. **peng-an** pickling, salting.
asing 1 strange, foreign, alien. *Saya merasa - di sini* I feel strange here. *Kejadian spt itu - di sana* Events like that are unusual there. *tak - sbg* far from unknown as. **2** odd. *Agak - macam pakaian org itu* That man is wearing rather odd clothing. **3** remote, isolate. *Rumah itu - tempatnya* That house is isolated. **4** different. **ber- 1** isolate o.s. *Anak itu selalu ~ seorg diri* That child is always off by himself. **2** become different. **ber-²an** different o. from another. **meng-kan 1** isolate, separate. *Pemerintah ~ org sakit lépra ke pulau kecil* The gvt. isolated the lepers on a small island. **2** exile, banish. **3** segregate, separate out. **4** intern, jail. **5** alienate. *Anak-anak golongan atas sering di-kan dr masyarakat meréka sendiri* Upper-class children are frequently alienated from their own society. **memper-kan** isolate, quarantine. **ter- 1** secluded, separated, isolated. *Org itu tinggal ~ di atas gunung* That man lives isolated

up on a mountain. **2** exotic, very foreign. **keter-an 1** isolation. **2** exclusion, alienation. **ke-an 1** difference, deviation. **2** strangeness. **per-an 1** exile, banishment. **2** isolation. *~ suatu badi* isolation of a virus. **3** internment (camp). **4** alienation, estrangement.
asistén 1 assistant. - *ahli* skilled assistant. - *wedana* subdistrict head or chief. **2** assistant in a university. - *luar biasa* part-time assistant. **ke-an** assistantship. **-an** subdistrict.
asitilén see ASÉTILÉN.
askar see LASKAR.
asli 1 original. *Inilah surat keterangan -* This is the original certificate. **2** genuine, authentic. *Ini laporan - ttg keadaannya* This is an authentic report of the situation. **3** indigenous, native, autochthonous. **4** aboriginal, primitive. **5** innate, inborn. **ke-an 1** authenticity, genuineness. **2** originality.
asma₁ name (esp. of God). *dgn - Tuhan* in the name of God.
asma₂ asthma.
asmara romantic love. - *berahi* erotic love. **meng-i** love s.o. *Ia ~ dan menyatakan rasa berahi pd Tante* He loved my aunt and expressed his passion to her.
asmaragama (*Jv*) the art of sexual relations.
Asnowo [*Asli Cino Jowo*] (*Derog.*) Javanese Chinese.
aso (*Coll.*) **meng-** rest, take a break. **peng-an** resthouse, spot for resting.
asoi, asoii 1 passionate, hot. **2** wonderful, super. *tdk cuma cakep, tapi cantik, manis, pokoknya - déh!* not just cute but beautiful, attractive, hey, I mean fantastic! **3** be absorbed in s.t. *Anda jangan kéki kalau lagi - baca, tiba-tiba terdengar suara keras* Don't be startled if you suddenly hear a loud noise while you are absorbed in your reading.
asonansi assonance.
asor (*Jv*) lowly. **ke-an 1** lowliness. **2** defeated.
asosiasi association. **ber-** associate. **meng-kan** associate s.t. **peng-an** the act of associating (with s.o.).
asoymasoy see ASOI.
aspal₁ asphalt. **meng-** asphalt a road. **-an** pavement. **peng-an** asphalting (of a road).
aspal₂ [*asli palsu*] (*Humorous*) s.t. that looks original but is falsified. *diploma - a* falsified diploma.
asparaga k.o. vine used in floral arrangements.
aspék aspect.
aspéktual aspectual.
aspérges, aspérjis asparagus.
aspiran aspirant, candidate. - *kontrelir* junior district officer on probation.
aspirasi aspiration.
aspirat (*Ling.*) aspirate.
asprak (*Coll.*) appointment.
Aspri [*Asistén Pribadi*] personal assistant.
Asrafil see ISRAFIL.
asrakal a ceremonial meal.
asrama 1 dormitory, hostel, residence hall. - *cam-*

puran coed dorm. **2** barracks. - *tuna tertib* (*Mil.*) (detention) stockades. **per-an** billeting. ~ *prajurit* billeting of soldiers.

asri 1 beautiful. **2** harmoniously chic. **ke-an** beauty. ~ *pepohonan* the beauty of landscaping.

assalam alaikum (*Isl.*) Peace be unto you (a greeting). - *warahmatullohi wabarakatuh* (*Isl.*) Peace be to you and Allah's mercy and blessing as well.

assémbling see ASÉMBLING.

assét (economic) assets.

assoi see ASOI.

assumsi see ASUMSI.

assyooi see ASOI.

astaga Heaven forbid, For heaven's sake. **ber-** say *astaga.*

astaganaga (*Sl.*) gee whiz!

astagfirullah, astagh firullah, astagh firullahal'azim (*Isl.*) May God forgive me! (uttered when o. is shocked by immoral behavior).

astaka see BALAI₁.

astakona 1 octagon. **2** polygon. **ber-** octagonal.

astana see ISTANA.

Asteng [*Asia Tenggara*] S.E. Asia.

aster see BUNGA.

astma see ASMA₂.

astrolog astrologer.

astrologi astrology.

astronaut astronaut.

astronautika astronautics.

astronomi astronomy.

astronomis astronomical, celestial.

astronot see ASTRONAUT.

astronotik see ASTRONAUTIKA.

asu (*Jv*) dog! bastard!

ASU [*Ali-Surachman*] (*Derog.*) 1960s leftist faction of the *PNI*.

asuh meng- 1 care for, take care of, rear, bring up (a child). **2** educate, bring up. **3** train, prepare. *Opsir itu hrs* ~ *tentara-tentaranya* The officer must train his soldiers. **4** maintain, lend support to. **-an 1** upbringing, rearing. *salah* ~ poor upbringing. **2** education. **3** leadership, direction. **4** sponsorship. **peng- 1** nurse, nursemaid. ~ *anak* o. who takes care of a child. **2** guardian, caretaker. **peng-an** care. *dlm* ~ in the care of the orphan's court.

asumsi assumption.

asung (*M*) incite, stir up. **meng-** stir up. *Dia* ~ *Ali memukul Hadi* He incited Ali to hit Hadi. **-an** incitement.

asuransi 1 insurance. - *bendasraya* property insurance. - *ganti kerugian* insurance for damages. - *jiwa(sraya)* life insurance. - *kebakaran* fire insurance. - *laut* marine insurance. **2** insurance payment or installment. **3** insurance payment received. **meng-kan** insure s.t. **per-an** insurance system.

asusila immoral.

asut see HASUT.

aswo [*asli Jowo*] authentic Javanese.

asyar see ASAR.

asyhadu an la ila ha illallah (*Isl.*) **1** the first part of the confession of the faith. - *waasyhadu anna Muhammadar rasulullah* I witness there is no God but Allah and Muh. is His prophet (uttering this is o. prerequisite to becoming Muslim). **2** I testify there is no God but Allah (an exclamation of astonishment upon hearing or seeing s.t. forbidden by religion).

asyik 1 passionate. *Ia* - *mencintai kekasihnya* He passionately loves his sweetheart. *Ia* - *akan perangko* He is passionate about stamps. **2** be infatuated. *Ia* - *kpd gadis itu* He is infatuated with that girl. **3** busy, occupied. *Ia sedang* - *makan siang* She is occupied with eating lunch. **4** absorbed, eager. *Ia* - *belajar bahasa Indonésia* He is absorbed in studying Indonesian. *Wah,* - *nak, naik sepéda waktu itu* Why, son, it was exciting riding a bike in those days! - *berahi* infatuated. *Ia* - *berahi akan perempuan itu* He is infatuated with that woman. - *dan masyuk* deeply in love with e.o. **meng-i** eat up, devour (movie magazines, etc.). **meng-kan 1** preoccupy, engross, absorb. **2** fascinate. **3** fascinating, attractive. *bacaan yg* ~ absorbing reading. **4** making s.o. ardent or amorous, infatuating. **ke-an** preoccupation, obsession. **ke-²an 1** deeply absorbed. **2** infatuated, enamored, smitten.

asyoi see ASOI.

Asyura (*Isl.*) 10th day of Muharram, which commemorates Muh.'s grandsons Hassan and Hussein, Day of Atonement.

AT [*Asia Tenggara*] S.E. Asia.

atak k.o. three-wheeled vehicle similar to the *bémo.*

Atal [*Atasé Angkatan Laut*] naval attaché.

atap 1 thatched roof of palm leaves. **2** roof. - *séng* corrugated metal roof. - *kaca* skylights. - *langit* in the open air, al fresco. **ber-** have a roof, roofed. **ber-kan** covered with. **meng-(i)** *Ia* ~ *rumahnya dgn ijuk* He put an arenga palm fiber roof on his house. **peng-an** roofing (of a house).

atar k.o. perfume.

atas 1 on, upon, on top of. *Dr* - *bukit itu saya lihat laut* From the top of that hill I see the sea. *Yg tersebut di* - *tdk benar* That mentioned above is incorrect. *Di* - *méja ada buku* A book is on the table. *mohon kpd yg di* - request to the superiors. *Lampu bergantung di* - *méja* A lamp hangs over the table. *Pesawat itu terbang di* - *Bangkok* A plane flew over Bangkok. *binasa di* - *ditindas* annihilation over oppression. - *angin* windward. - *sungai* upriver. **2** upper. *Pintu itu rusak di bagian* - The upper section of the door is damaged. *Sebelah* - *méja itu dicat kuning* The upper surface of the table is painted yellow. **3** above, upstairs. *Ia mendapat peringatan dr* - *bhw pekerjaannya tdk béres* He received a warning from above that his work was not in order. *Jl. Braga 132 (-)* 132 Braga Street (2d floor). **4** over (an amount), in addition. *anak tiga tahun ke* - children three years and older. *dr ini ke* - from now on. *Tambah tiga puluh di* - *yg sdh*

diterima Add 30 in addition to what had been received. **5** for, because of. - *kebaikanmu itu saya ucapkan terima kasih* I thank you for your kindness. - *usaha teman saya* thanks to the effort of my friend. **6** in(to). *Buku itu terbagi - tiga bagian* The book is divided into three parts. **7** at, upon. *Saya datang di sini - undangan ayahmu* I came here at your father's invitation. - *dasar* on the basis of. - *dasar bagi dua* on the basis of a 50-50 split. -*mu* you should, it is obligatory for you. - *nama* in the name of. - *nama perkumpulannya* in behalf of his organization. - *nama umat Islam* in the name of the Isl. community. **meng-namai** put in the name of. *gambar yg di-namai Hendro* the painting Hendro claimed as his. **meng-namakan, member-namakan** act on behalf of, do in the name of. *Ia meng-namakannya tanpa izin* He did it in the name of s.o. without receiving his permission. - *perintah* done by order of . . . - **meng-** go up and up. - **meng-, ber-²an** excel o. another. - **meng-i** contend. **meng-** **1** rise, go upward. *Debu ~ karena tiupan angin* The dust rose because of the wind. *Harga makanan makin lama makin ~* The price of food rises more and more. **2** aspire, rise. *Cita-citanya selalu ~* Her ideals are always rising. **3** appeal. *Ia ~ kpd kepala sekolah* She appealed to the school principal. **meng-i 1** top, surpass, exceed. *Pak Tomo kaya, tapi Pak Darmo masih ~nya* Tomo is wealthy, but Darmo still surpasses him. **2** overcome, master, surmount. *Ia dpt ~ kesukarannya* She was able to overcome her difficulty. *tak dpt di-i* insurmountable. **meng-kan 1** lift up, hike up. *Ibu ~ ampaian* Mother raised the clothesline. **2** place higher, favor. *Ia selalu ~ bangsanya* She is always favoring her own people. **menge-kan 1** raise. *Persoalannya tlh dike-kan* The matter has been raised. **2** hike up. *Kain itu dike-kan* The sarong was hiked up. *Yg* **Diper-**God. *memohon kpd yg ~, spy* . . . beseech Him on High to . . . **ter-** uppermost, highest. *tempat ~* uppermost place. **ter-i** can be overcome. *Segala kesukaran di bidang industri akan segara ~* All difficulties in the industrial sector will be overcome right away. **-an** higher, superior. *Golongan ~ pun hidupnya sangat sederhana* Even the upper class live very simply. *org ~* superiors, upper class. *pendidikan ~* higher education.
atasé attaché. - *angkatan laut* naval attaché. - *kebudayaan* cultural attaché. - *militér* military attaché. - *perdagangan* commercial attaché.
atau or. *Pergilah main ténis - badminton* Go out and play tennis or badminton. *-pun* or. **-kah 1** or (in questions). **2** whether. *~ kau mau hidup ~ ingin mati terserah kau sendiri!* Whether you want to live or want to die is entirely up to you!
atawa (*Coll.*) see ATAU.
atéis atheist. **ke-an** atheism.
atéisme atheism.
aténsi attention.
Athan [*Atasé Pertahanan*] defense attaché.
ati see HATI.
atlas atlas.

atlét athlete.
atlétik athletics.
atlit see ATLÉT.
atma (*Lit.*) **1** breath (yoga exercises). **2** soul.
Atmil [*Atasé Militér*] military attaché.
atmosféra, atmosfir atmosphere.
atol (*Geog.*) atoll.
atom atom.
atomisasi atomization.
atop burp, belch.
atos hard. - *benar bola ini* This ball is very hard.
atraksi attraction.
atrét (*Coll.*) back up, go in reverse.
atribut attribute. - *plonco* all k.o. paraphernalia worn by university freshmen during hazing.
atributif (*Ling.*) attributive.
atsiri volatile. **ke-an** volatility.
Atu, Atud [*Atasé Udara*] air attaché.
atuh (*Sd*) oh, hey. - *jang* Hey, sonny!
atung see KATUNG.
atur₁ arrange. - *tepat* arrange precisely. **meng-tepatkan** adjust, regulate. **peng-tepatan** adjustment. **ber-** be arranged, be in order. *Segala ~ baik-baik* All has been carefully arranged. **ber-an** uniform. *bangunan-bangunan yg tak ~* buildings that are not uniform. **meng- 1** put in order, straighten up. *Saya akan ~ dapur dulu* I will get the kitchen in order first. **2** regulate, organize. *Agén polisi itu ~ lalu lintas* The policeman regulated the traffic. **3** arrange, settle. *Saya akan ~ urusan saya* I am going to settle my own affairs. **4** string, thread. *Gadis itu ~ mutiara dijadikan kalung* The girl strung the pearls into a necklace. *~ sikap* come to o.'s attention. **meng-kan** put in order for s.o. **ter- 1** in order, regulated nicely. *Keamanan tlh ~ kembali* Security has been restored. *Meréka berjéjér dgn ~* They stood side by side in orderly fashion. **2** regular, arranged. *Pengajaran diberikan dgn waktu yg ~* Teaching is done at regular periods. **keter-an** orderliness, regularity. **-an 1** arrangement, set-up. *Gedung ini baik benar ~nya* This building has quite a nice arrangement. *~ tertib* rules of proper conduct. **2** regulation, rule. **3** directions, instructions. *~ pakai* directions for use. **4** manner, behavior. *Rupanya ia tak tahu ~* He does not seem to have any manners. **5** routine (of a household). **-annya 1** according to the regulations. *~ tiap kelahiran hrs didaftarkan* According to the regulations, every birth must be registered. **2** in fact, as a matter of fact. *~ ia hrs sdh di sini sblm saya datang* Actually she should have been here before I came. **peng- 1** (*Tech.*) regulator, governor. *~ peledak* detonator. **2** controller, technician. *~ lalu lintas* traffic cop. *~ muda* a rank in the civil service. *~ rawat gigi* dental hygienist. **3** arranger. *Siapa ~ pésta itu?* Who arranged that festival? *~ perjalanan* tour operator. **peng-an** arrangement, control. *~ hawa* air conditioning. *~ kembali* rearranging, rescheduling. *~ huruf* typesetting. *~ langkah* coordination of steps. **per-an 1** regulation. *~ menteri* ministerial regulation. *~ pem-*

bangunan building code. ~ *permainan* rules of the game. ~ *présidén* presidential regulation. ~ *rumah tangga* bylaws. ~ *tingkah laku* rules of behavior. **2** system of organization. ~ *gaji* salary scale. ~ *dua kamar* bicameral system.

atur₂ (*Jv*) **meng-kan 1** offer, give (used on solemn occasions or to s.o. of higher authority). *Bersama ini kami -kan dgn hormat kpd Tuan* We herewith respectfully offer you . . . **2** say, express to a person of high status. ~ *bélasungkawa* express sympathy or condolences. ~ *selamat* congratulate.

au exclamation of pain or amazement.

AU [*Angkatan Udara*] air force.

aubade solemn evening ceremony of taking down the flag. *Semua murid berlatih - di tanah lapang sépak bola* All the students practice the evening flag ceremony on the soccer field.

audiénsi audience (with royalty, etc.). **ber-** have an audience.

audio-visuil audiovisual.

audisi audition.

audit audit. **meng-** conduct an audit.

audubillahi, audzubillahi (*Isl.*) I take refuge in God, may God protect me (uttered when o. is shocked by immoral or impious behavior).

auk meng-(²) 1 bark (of a dog). **2** caw, cackle.

aula hall, auditorium.

aulia (*Isl.*) saints, pious personages.

aum 1 roar (of lion or tiger). **2** raging (of storm). **meng- 1** roar, bellow. **2** buzz. **meng-²kan** boast, tout, make widely known. **-an** roaring, buzzing. ~ *singa* the roaring of the lion.

aung see RAUNG.

aur₁ k.o. thin bamboo. - *cina* k.o. thin bamboo used in making fences. - *duri* thorny bamboo. - *gading* yellow bamboo. - *temiang* k.o. thin bamboo.

aur₂ see AWUR₁.

aurat 1 (*Isl.*) part of the body which may not be visible while performing a ritual. **2** genitals.

AURI [*Angkatan Udara Républik Indonésia*] Indonesian Air Force.

auriol /oriol/ halo.

aus 1 worn-out, threadbare. - *tanah* erosion. **2** worn down (of a knife, etc.). **meng-i 1** wear s.t. out. **2** wear s.t. away, erode s.t. **meng-kan** cause s.t. to wear out. **ke-an 1** wearing out. **2** weathering.

Australi, Australia Australia.

aut (*Sport*) out.

autarki economic self-sufficiency.

auténtik see OTÉNTIK.

auto see OTO₁.

autobiografi autobiography.

automatis see OTOMATIS.

autonomi see OTONOMI.

autopéd see OTOPÉT.

autopsi autopsy. **meng-** perform an autopsy.

autorisasi see OTORISASI.

Avgas [*aviation gasoline*]

aviasi aviation.

Avigas see AVGAS.

avontir see AVONTUR.

avontirir adventurer.

avontur adventure.

avonturir see AVONTIRIR.

avonturisme adventurism.

Avtur [*Aviation Turbo Fuel*] airplane fuel.

awa- negating prefix used in formal neologisms. *-suara* devoice.

awahama meng-kan disinfect, sterilize. **peng-an** sterilization.

awahidrat peng-an dehydration.

awahutan meng-kan deforest. **peng-an** deforestation.

awak 1 body, self. *Asap kelihatan dr - kapal itu* Smoke was coming from the body of the ship. *Saya merasa tdk énak -* I do not feel well. *Mengapa -ku hrs sakit di sini?* Why must I be sick here? **2** crewman, crewwoman. - *kabin* cabin boy. - *kapal* member of ship's crew. - *pesawat* flight crewman or crewwoman. **3** I, my. - *tak dpt pergi* I cannot go. - *sama -* just between ourselves. *Janganlah malu; kita hanya - sama -* Don't be shy; we are among friends. **4** (*Sumatra*) Minangkabau. *Ia org -* He is Minangkabau. **5** you, your. **member-, meng-i** man (a ship, etc.). **meng-kan** house in barracks or dormitory, billet. **peng-an 1** figure, shape, silhouette. **2** crew. **per-an 1** figure, shape. *gadis cantik dgn ~nya yg ramping itu* the pretty girl with the slender figure. **2** build, physique. **berper-an** have a certain build. ~ *gagah* have a handsome build.

awal 1 beginning. - *tahun ini* the beginning of this year. **2** beginning, initial. *Hujan - tlh jatuh* The first rain has fallen. **3** first, early. *Lebih baik datang - drp akhir* It is better to come first than last. *yg datang paling -* those who come earliest. **ber-an** prefixed. **meng-(i) 1** head, be first. ~ *pawai raksasa* head a gigantic parade. *Ia ~ teman-temannya memberi sumbangan* He was first of his friends to give a contribution. **2** precede. *Dialog itu di-i dgn musik* The dialogue was preceded by music. **-an** (*Ling.*) prefix. **peng-** pioneer, the first. *Alif ~ huruf alfabét Arab* Alif is the first letter of the Arabic alphabet.

awam 1 common, general. **2** lay, nonexpert. **meng-(kan) 1** promulgate, announce (a decree, etc.). **2** propose. **3** advocate. **ke-an** generalness, commonness. **peng-** advocate, promoter.

awan 1 cloud. - *berarak* moving clouds. - *gemawan/kemawan* cumulus. - *guntur* cumulonimbus, thunderhead. - *hitam* dark cloud. **2** cloudlike decoration. **ber-** cloudy, overcast. **meng-** climb into the sky. *Pesawat ~ ke udara itu* The plane climbed into the sky.

awangan impromptu, extemporaneous.

awang-awang 1 atmosphere. **2** up in the air, uncertain, far off. *Persetujuan masih di -* An agreement is still far off. **3** dizzy. **meng- 1** go up into the air. **2** indulge in fancies. **meng-kan** brandish, wave (a sword) (as if slashing the air).

awas 1 careful, watch out. *-, keréta api sdh datang* Be careful, the train is coming. *- pencopét* Beware of pickpockets! - *kalau kamu tdk mau bayar utang-mu* Do not pay your debt and see what happens. - *waspada* be careful, be alert. **2** sharp-sighted, far-sighted. *Matanya masih* - His eyes are still sharp. *Ia terkenal sbg ahli nujum yg* - He is known as a far-seeing astrologer. **3** (*Sport*) get set! **ber(²)- 1** be careful. *Kita hrs ~ jika berbicara dgn penipu itu* We must be careful when we talk with that fraud. **2** control, check. **meng-i 1** supervise, control, administer. *Siapa yg ~ pekerjaan ini?* Who is supervising this work? **2** supervise, oversee, look after. *Ia ~ anak itu* She looked after the child. **meng-kan** observe, note. **peng- 1** supervisor, superintendent, overseer. *~ lalu lintas udara* air traffic controller. **2** keeper, caretaker. **peng-an 1** supervision, care, oversight. **2** control, checking. **3** surveillance. *~ senjata* arms control. **kepeng-an** monitoring.

awé, awé-awé (*Jv*) wave (hand). - *salam* wave in greeting. **meng-** wave. **meng-kan** wave s.t.

awét, awit durable, lasting. *Sepatu ini - sekali* These shoes are very durable. - *muda* staying young. *Ia - muda karena hidupnya selalu senang* He stayed young because he always led a happy life. **meng-(kan)** can, preserve (fruits, etc.), stuff (animals). **ke-an 1** life, duration (of appliances). **2** preservation. **-an** s.t. preserved. *dua kera Mentawai ~ yg dihadiahkan kpd Présidén itu* two stuffed Mentawai monkeys which were given to the president. **peng-** preservative. **peng-an** preserving, conservation. *~ tanah* soil conservation.

awloh see ALLAH.

awur₁ meng- scatter, sow. **meng-i** scatter, sow (a field). *Gadis itu ~ bunga di makam* The girl spread flowers on the grave. **meng-kan** spread, scatter, sow s.t.

awur₂ (me)ng- do s.t. at random, blindly. **ke-an** recklessness. **-²an 1** randomly. **2** scattered at random.

awut (me)ng- do s.t. blindly, carelessly. **-²an 1** tangled (of rope, thread, etc.). **2** tousled (of hair). **3** chaotic, haphazard. *rumah ~* chaotic household. *Kerjanya ~* His work is haphazard.

AX part of a license plate number given to vehicles not paying import duties. *Mobil bapaknya masih - sdh dipamér-pamérkannya* His father's car still has an AX plate but he is already showing it off.

ay. [*ayat*] verse (of the Koran, Bible), article (of a law, etc.).

ayah father, as a term of address, us. *yah*. - *bunda* parents. - *tiri* stepfather. *se- seibu* having the same mother and father. **ber-(kan)** have a father. *Énak dia ~ jénderal!* How lucky he is to have a general for a father! **meng-i** father (a child). **ke-an 1** fatherhood. **2** parental.

ayahanda father (used in letters).

ayak sieve, sifter. **meng-** sift (flour, etc.). **-an, peng- 1** sieve, sifter. **2** o. who wobbles or waddles.

ayak-ayak k.o. insect with long legs us. found on top of water.

ayal 1 slow. **2** doubtful. *Saya tdk - sedikitpun akan kemenangan* I was not the least bit doubtful about the victory. *Tak - lagi bekas sénator itu yg dituduh* Indubitably the ex-senator was the o. accused. **(ber)-²an** delay, tarry, linger. *Ia masih juga ~ di pintu itu* He was still lingering by the door.

ayam chicken. - *aduan* fighting cock. - *alas* jungle fowl. - *belanda* turkey. - *beroga* jungle fowl. - *biang* laying hen. - *bibit* fledgling. - *bugil* featherless chicken. - *daging* broiler. - *dara* pullet. - *jago* cock, rooster. - *jalak* speckled cock. - *kampung* free-range chicken. - *katik* short-legged Bantam chicken. - *ke(m)biri* capon. - *mutiara* guinea fowl. - *negeri* domestic poultry. - *pedaging* broiler. - *(pe)laga* fighting fowl. - *penelur/(pe)telur* laying pullet. - *potongan* chicken raised for food. - *pungguk* tailless chicken. - *ras* purebred chicken. - *sabungan* fighting cock. - *sayur* potpourri. - *trah* purebred chicken. **-²** waterfowl. **-²an 1** weather vane. **2** bird resembling a chicken. **3** toy chicken.

ayan₁ epilepsy. **-an 1** prone to epilepsy, epileptic. **2** have an epileptic fit.

ayan₂ 1 tin. **2** tin can.

ayaran *tukang* - pickpocket.

ayat 1 (*Rel.*) verse. *menghafal - Al Qur'an* memorizing verses of the Koran. *Markus lima - enam (Markus 5:6)* Mark 5:6. - *kursi* verses in Koran that explain the powers of God. **2** (*Leg.*) article, subsection. **3** clause. **4** paragraph.

ayé (*Jkt*) I.

ayem (*Jv*) calm, assured. - *tentrem* contented, quiet.

ayeng -²an 1 go here and there. **2** go around in circles, accomplishing little or nothing.

ayér see AIR.

ayo, ayoh, ayok 1 come on! -, *pulang* Come on, let's go home. *-lah* well then, come on then. - *duluan!* Go ahead (before the others)! *Kenapa salah semua? -!* Why is everything wrong? Come on, tell me! **2** goodbye. - *déh!* See you! So long!

ayom protected, sheltered. **meng-i** protect, shelter, guard. **peng-** protector. **peng-an** protection, care, guardianship.

ayu pretty, beautiful. **ke-an** beauty.

Ayub 1 (*Isl.*) o. of the prophets. **2** (*Bib.*) Job.

ayubagya meng- celebrate. *~ HUT* celebrate a birthday.

ayuh see AYO.

ayuhai (*Lit.*) an exclamation.

ayun - *ambung* swing, sway. **meng-ambungkan** sway, rock s.t. *gondola yg di-ambungkan oléh angin* a gondola rocked by the wind. **ber-** sway, swing, oscillate. *~ tambang* (*Mil.*) cross by swinging on a taut rope. *~ kaki* swing o.'s feet in a relaxed way. *~ temayun* go down, set (of the sun). *air ~ temayun* waterfall. **meng- 1** rock (child, cradle). **2** swing, wield. *Suwondo berdiri ~ kata diatas podium* Suwondo stood at the podium wielding his words. *~ cangkul pertama* break ground, wield the first spadeful of earth (for a building, etc.). *~ kaki* move away. *Ia pergi ~ kaki asal meninggalkan pasar* He shuffled away. All he wanted to do was get out of the market. ~ *kepal* shake o.'s fist. **meng-kan 1** swing s.t. at. *Hardjo ~ tinjunya ke perut Dadang* Hardjo swung his fist at Dadang's belly. **2** hurl s.t. by slinging it. **ter-** swung. *Tangan yg memegang pisau ~ keras* The hand holding the knife swung out. **ter-²** sway (as though drunk), reel, pitch. *Perahu kami mulai ~* Our boat began to pitch. **-an 1** (baby) cradle. **2** swing. **3** pendulum. **4** sling (shot). **5** swaying, oscillation, wielded by swaying. *~ cangkul pertama* breaking of ground. *~ pohon-pohon oléh bayu* the swaying of the trees by the storm. *~ rém* brake handle. *~ tangan* oscillating gesture of the hand. **peng-** pendulum. **peng-an** action of swinging. *~ cangkul pertama* ground breaking (ceremony). **peng-kan** sling to hurl s.t. away.

ayunda (*Jv*) elder sister (respectful), esp. in letters.

ayut (*Vulg.*) **meng-** fornicate.

azab torment, punishment. *- sengsara* misery, distress, suffering. **meng-** torment, persecute, harass.

azal₁ endless past, eternity without beginning.

azal₂ see AJAL.

azali see ASALI.

azam₁ highly respected. *Nama Allah adalah nama -* God's name is highly respected.

azam₂ intention. **ber-** have a firm intention, be resolute. **meng-kan** intend, propose. *Ia ~ akan berangkat bésok* She intends to leave tomorrow.

azamat see AZMAT.

azan (*Isl.*) call to prayer. **meng-i** (*Isl.*) recite the call to prayer at s.o. *~ bayi* (*Isl.*) recite call to prayer over newborn male child. *~ mayat* (*Isl.*) recite call to prayer over deceased in funeral rites.

azas see ASAS.

azasi see ASASI.

azimat₁ 1 amulet, charm, talisman. *Panca - Révolusi Indonésia* Five Talismans of the Indonesian Revolution (Sukarno-era slogan). **2** mascot.

azimat₂ see AZMAT.

azimut (*Astr.*) azimuth.

aziz 1 enormous, great. *Kota itu memperlihatkan perhatian yg - thd rombongan tari Bali* The city showed enormous interest in the Balinese dance group. **2** awe-inspiring. *Sorak penonton itu - The applause of the spectators was extraordinary.*

azmat extraordinary, fantastic.

azza wa jalla (*Isl.*) to whom belongs glory and majesty (in reference to God).

B

b /bé/ b, the 2d letter of the alphabet.

ba₁ name of the 2d letter of the Arabic alphabet.

ba₂ *tanpa bilang - dan bu* without uttering a sound, without warning.

ba' see BAK₁.

baal without feeling, asleep (of foot, leg).

bab 1 chapter (of book). **2** matter, subject, topic. **3** gate, door.

baba₁ 1 father (form of address). **2** older man. *- Markus* old man Markus.

baba₂ (*Lit.*) see BABAH, ALI BABA.

babad history, chronicle. *- Tanah Jawa* Chronicle of Java.

babah 1 elderly Indonesian-born Ch man. **2** title for elderly Ch (as a term of address, us. *bah*). *- Liong* Mr. Liong.

babak₁ 1 stage, phase. *- baru dlm sejarah perkapalan* a new chapter in the history of shipping. *Perang itu sdh mencapai - terakhir* The war has reached the final stage. **2** (*Sport*) round, heat, period. *- penyisihan* elimination round. **3** (*Thea.*) act. **4** stanza. **-an** (*Sport*) round, set. *di ~ kedua* in the 2d set. **pem-an** dividing into phases. *~ waktu* periodization.

babak₂ *- belur/bundas* black and blue (from a beating or accident), skinned and bruised.

babakan bark (of tree).

baban see BEBAN.

babang gaping (of mouth, wound, abyss).

babar **mem-** spread, unfurl. *Layar ~ ditiup angin* The sail unfurled in the wind. **mem-kan 1** spread, unfurl. *Tak lama lagi perahu itu ~ layar-nya* Before long the boat unfurled its sails. **2** lay out, set out. *Penjual itu - barang-barang dagangannya di pinggir jalan* The vendor laid out his merchandise at the roadside. **3** explain, set forth. *Penaséhat itu ~ pendapatnya ttg rencana baru itu* The adviser explained his view of the new plan. **4** extend, spread. *Raja itu ~ kekuasaannya* The king extended his sway. **ter- 1** be driven off course, drift off course. *Karena udara buruk, penerbangan ke Ambon ~ ke Masohi* Because of bad weather the plane for Ambon had to land in Masohi. **2** carried away, swept away, washed out (in a flood, etc.). **3** go by mistake. *Karena disangka hotél, banyak org ~ ke rumah itu menanyakan kamar penginapan* Because they thought it was a hotel, many people mistakenly went to that house to seek a room. **pem-an 1** spread, development. **2** account, statement. **3** exposé.

babar pisan (*Jv*) completely.

babat₁ **mem-** clear away, cut through (jungle,

grass, etc.). ~ *rumput* mow the grass. ~ *bécak* ban (clear away) pedicabs (from an area). *Seorang bék kesebelasan* ~ *dgn taktik sapu bersih* A backfield player of the team cut through with his clean-sweep tactics. **pem-an** clearing away. ~ *hutan* clearing of a forest. ~ *dan pemupukan tiap empat puluh hari* weeding and fertilizing every 40 days.

babat₂ mem-kan give a blow, strike with s.t. **-an** a lateral blow, swipe (of a sword).

babat₃ tripe of ruminants and pigs. *soto* - tripe soup.

babat₄ group. *Dlm pergaulan masyarakat org mencari sama -nya* In social intercourse o. looks for o.'s own kind. **se-** of the same kind or type.

babat₅ see BEBAT.

babé (*Jkt*) **1** boss. *penyakit* - corruption. **2** see BABA₁.

babi 1 pig, hog, pork. - *alu* tapir. - *asap* smoked pork, bacon, ham. - *buta* **mem-** *buta* **1** storm, rage. **2** act blindly, at random. - *duyung* manatee, sea-cow, dugong. - *guling* roast (whole) pig. - *hong* (*Ch*) pork braised in a red sauce. - *hutan/jalang* wild boar. **mem-** *jalang* **1** act wildly. **2** fornicate. - *kécap* pork stewed in soy sauce and other spices. - *laut* sea urchin. - *nangui* bearded pig. - *putih* wild boar (of Kalimantan). - *rusa* deer-hog (of Sulawesi and nearby islands). - *tanah* k.o. anteater. **2** swine (term of abuse). - *lu!* You swine! **3** (*Crd.*) a card suit in *ceki*. **-²an** toy pig.

babil quarrelsome. **ber-** squabble, quarrel. **per-an** squabble, row, quarrel, ruckus.

Babil Babel.

Babinsa [*Bintara Pembina Désa*] noncommissioned law enforcement officer posted in villages and wards and affiliated with the civilian administration.

babit mem-kan involve, implicate s.o. *Ia* ~ *saya dlm pertikaiannya* She involved me in her argument. **ter-** involved, implicated.

babon 1 (*Jv*) (laying) hen. **2** original (text), master copy. - *naskah* original manuscript.

babtis see BAPTIS.

babu (*Derog.*) female domestic servant. - *anak* children's maid, nursemaid. - *cuci* laundress. - *dlm* chambermaid. - *masak* female cook. - *nyai* a woman who is both servant and concubine of a European or a Ch. - *susu/téték* wet nurse. **mem-** work as maid. **mem-kan** place s.o. as maid. **memper-** treat s.o. as maid.

babut rug, carpet. **mem-i** carpet (a room).

baca mem- 1 read. *Ia suka* ~ *buku* She likes to read books. ~ *batin* read to o.s. ~ *batin org* read s.o.'s mind. ~ *dlm hati* read to o.s. ~ *nyaring* read aloud. **2** recite or chant (holy text, prayer, magic formula, etc.). ~ *doa* say a prayer. **mem-²** read repeatedly or rapidly. **mem-i 1** read over and over, read thoroughly. **2** pronounce, recite. **mem-kan 1** read aloud, read for s.o. *Ia* ~ *suratkabar kpd ayahnya* She read the paper to her father. **2** recite (prayer, scripture verse, etc.) aloud. **ter-** be read. *tak* ~ illegible. **-an 1** read-

ing, literature. **2** reading material. ~ *cabul* pornography. **3** style of (Koranic) recitation. **4** incantation. ~ *Bismillah* the incantation involving the name of Allah. **pem-** reader. **pem-an 1** reading aloud (esp. in formal circumstances). ~*nya kurang jelas* His reading is not very clear. **2** lecture.

bacak 1 moistened, wet. **2** soft from moisture, water-soaked. - *tinta* inkblot.

bacam mem- impregnate. **pem-an** impregnation.

bacang₁ (*Ch*) preparation of glutinous rice wrapped in bamboo leaves, shaped into a diamond, filled with meat, and steamed.

bacang₂ see EMBACANG.

bacar garrulous, talkative. - *mulut* loves to talk, runs off at the mouth.

baccalauréat see BAKALORÉAT.

bacek see BACAK.

bacem steeped prior to cooking. **mem-** steep, soak (bean curd, etc.).

bacet see MACAT.

baciluk see MAIN.

bacin 1 odor of s.t. rotten or spoiled. **2** rotten-smelling.

back see BÉK₁.

backing see BÉKING.

backingisme see BÉKINGISME.

bacok a jab (with sharp instrument). **mem- 1** hit with a sharp edge. *Ia* ~ *lengan pacarnya dgn badik* She gashed her boyfriend's arm with a dagger. **2** chop up, cut up, cleave. **mem-kan** cut with s.t. *Ia* ~ *pisaunya ke dada lawannya* He slashed his enemy's chest open with his knife. **ke-** accidentally wounded with a knife. **-an** gash. **pem-** o. who cuts others with a knife. **pem-an 1** (act of) gashing, knifing. **2** scuffle or brawl involving a knifing.

bacot 1 snout. **2** (*Derog.*) mouth. **ber-, mem-** (*Vulg.*) open o.'s trap.

bacul 1 spiritless. **2** lacking spunk, cowardly.

bada₁ (*Lit.*) *tak* **ter-²** beyond words, inexpressible. *amarah yg tak* ~ indescribable wrath.

bada₂ see BAKDA.

badai₁ 1 sudden storm. - *salju* blizzard. - *pasir* sand storm. **2** hurricane, typhoon, gale. **ber-** accompanied by a gale. *hujan* ~ rain accompanied by a gale. **mem- 1** become a strong storm. **2** rage, storm about. *Ia* ~ *di kantor, sebab pegawai-pegawai datangnya terlambat* He was in a rage because the employees came late.

badai₂ ter- be stretched out. *Ia* ~ *di dipan* He was stretched out on the sofa.

badak 1 rhinoceros. - *babi* tapir. - *kerbau* Sumatran (two-horned) rhinoceros. - *sumbu* Sundanese (one-horned) rhinoceros. - *tampung* tapir. - *tenggiling* one-horned rhinoceros. **2** o. oblivious to implied or overt criticism, a thick-skinned person. *Dasar (kulit)* -, *tak tahu malu* He is so thick-skinned he does not know shame. *pekak* - stone deaf.

badal representative, substitute, assistant. *Pak Af-*

lus menjadi - rombongannya Aflus became the representative of his group.

badam almond. *- hijau* pistachio.

badan 1 body. *Saya merasa sakit di seluruh -* I feel sick all over. *- bentuk puting (Anat.)* ventricle. *- mobil (Auto.)* panel body. *- perahu (Naut.)* ship's hull. **2** torso. *- bulat* stripped to the waist. **3** body, group, agency. *- kontak* liaison group. *- pekerja* working committee. *- pelaksana* executive body. *- penerangan* clearing house. *- perantara(an)* liaison bond. *- perwakilan* representative body, parliament. *- pusat* central committee. *- usaha* 1 committee. **2** executive branch. **4** corporation. *- hukum* corporate body. **ber-** have a body. *~ kecil* having a small physique. *~ séhat* physically healthy. *~ dua* be pregnant (polite usage). **member-i** organize into a group. *~ perkumpulan* incorporate a group.

badang large sieve, winnower.

badani, badaniah physical, bodily. **ke-an** physical matters. *pengalaman ~nya* his physical experience.

badar₁ 1 k.o. fish. **2** term for side dishes of meat or fish.

badar₂ full moon.

badar₃ k.o. crystal.

Badawi Bedouin.

badég, badék₁ an intoxicant beverage made from fermented cassava, rice, etc. **mem-kan** ferment s.t.

badék₂ (*Jv*) a guess. **mem-** guess, divine. **-an** guess, estimate. *~ saya ternyata benar* It turned out that my guess was right. **-²an** puzzle.

badge badge.

badi 1 evil influence (emanating supernaturally from a dead creature). **2** virus.

badik k.o. small dagger.

badkuip /batkép, bétkap/ bathtub.

badminton badminton.

badog (*Jv, Derog.*) eat gluttonously. **m-, nge-** eat like a dog. **-an** food.

Badui₁ ethnic group in W. Java.

Badui₂ see BADAWI.

baduk /baduk/ (*Jv*) low wall near gate or doorway where o. can sit.

badung (*Jkt*) **1** naughty but witty (of children). **2** naughty, delinquent.

badut clown. **mem-** act like a clown. **mem-i** *diri* pretend to o.s. **ke-an 1** clowning, buffoonery. **2** ridicule. **3** absurdity, ridiculousness. **-an** laughing stock, butt (of jokes). *Kawin lari akan dibikinnya sbg komédi, tapi bukan ~* He is treating elopement as a comedy, but it is no joke. **-²an be** a smart aleck. **pem-an** clowning, buffoonery.

baduta [*bawah dua tahun*] (children) under two.

bagadang see BEGADANG.

bagai 1 like, as if (often used to introduce idioms and proverbs). *- ayam bertelur di padi* be in clover (lit., a hen nesting in the rice). *Penerangan di kamar ini terang - siang* The illumination in this room is bright like daylight. *Wanita itu menundukkan kepalanya - menanti* The woman bowed her head as if she were waiting. *Hujan - dicurahkan* It was raining as if it was being poured out in buckets. **2** (*Lit.*) equivalent, peer. *Gunung itu indah sekali. Tak ada -nya* That mountain is very pretty. It has no peer. **3** (*Lit.*) kind, type. **se-** as, like. *~ saya katakan tadi . . .* As I was saying just now . . . *Ia memimpin pasukan itu ~ kaptén* He led his troops as captain. *Ia dipilih ~ pemimpin* She was chosen as leader. *dan ~nya* and so forth, and so on, etc. *~ pula/lagi* as moreover. **ber-** various, all sorts of. *~ bahasa terdapat di negeri itu* All sorts of languages are found in that country. *~ ragam* all kinds. **keber-ragaman** diversity, assortment. **ber-²** various. **mem(per)-(²)kan** ridicule. **-kan 1** as if, like. *Ia tak melihat kpd saya, ~ tak mendengar panggilan saya* He did not look at me, as if he had not heard me call. **2** similar to. *Ia ~ burung di sangkar emas* She is like a bird in a gilded cage.

bagaimana 1 how. *- (kabarnya)?* How are things? *- dia sekarang?* How's she now? **2** how about it? *- kalau saya . . .* How about it if I . . . *- nanti* What is going to happen? *Tunggu - nanti* Wait and see what happens. *-(pun) juga* however it may be, in any case. *kondisi jalan dan cuaca yg - juga* regardless of road and weather conditions. *- pun juga tdk* under no condition. *yg - pun* whatever. **-²nya** the ins and outs of s.t. *Saya tdk tahu ~* I do not know the details of it. **se-** in the same manner as. *Kerjakanlah ~ tlh saya uraikan tadi* Do as I just explained. **di-kan** be done to, be done with. *Mau ~ daging ini, digoréng ataukah direbus?* How are we to do this meat, fry it or boil it?

bagak dauntless, confident. **ke-an** poise, self-confidence, self-assurance.

bagal mule.

bagan₁ 1 draft, blueprint, design. **2** skeleton, frame. *Lihatlah - rumah terbakar itu* Look at the skeleton of that burned-out home. **3** program, schedule. *- latihan* training program or schedule. *- pengajaran* study plan. *Kami membuat - perjalanan ke Éropah* We have worked out an itinerary for the trip to Europe. **4** chart, diagram. *- susunan organisasi* organization chart. **mem-** design. *~ di papan* draw the design on the blackboard. **pem-** designer.

bagan₂ k.o. fishing platform. **-²** fish trap.

bagap see BEGAP.

bagar k.o. curry. *- kambing* k.o. goat curry.

bagas 1 robust, sturdy (body). **2** strong (wind).

bagasi 1 baggage, luggage. *- tercatat* checked baggage. *- cuma-cuma* free baggage allowance. *- lebih* excess baggage. **2** luggage rack. **3** (*Auto.*) trunk. **4** (*R.R.*) baggage car. **mem-kan** check baggage.

bagéa (*Amb*) a brittle cake made of sago flour and coconut or *kenari* nut.

bagéro see BAKÉRO.

bagi 1 for. *Kursi itu - ibu saya* That chair is for my mother. **2** divide. *- dua* divided in two. *atas dasar - dua* on a 50-50 basis. *- hasil* sharecropping, profit sharing. *- rata* equally (shared or divided).

mem-ratakan divide equally. *Bagaimana manfaat tersebut akan di-ratakan?* How will that benefit be equally divided? **ber-** split up, divisible, shared out. *Kasih sayang tak pernah* ~ Loving affection is never divisible. **mem- 1** divide. *Ia* ~ *tiga puluh dgn lima* She divided 30 by five. ~ *dua* bisect. ~ *ékor* do long division. ~ *lagi* subdivide. ~ *tiga* trisect. **2** share, distribute. ~ *makanan kpd penduduk* distribute food to the inhabitants. ~ *kartu* deal cards. **mem-²** divide into separate parts. **mem-(²)kan 1** share, distribute. *Ia* ~ *bukunya kpd teman-temannya* He distributed his books among his friends. *Laut biru itu seolah-olah* ~ *keluasannya pd hatiku* The blue sea seemed to share its breadth with me. **2** allot, allocate. **ter- 1** divisible. *tak* ~ indivisible. **2** divided, split up. *Di kampung kami penduduk mulai* ~ In our village the people are beginning to form sides. **ke-an** be allotted (a place, a share). *Aku cuma* ~ *sayapnya saja!* I only got a chicken wing! **-an 1** part, share. *Berapa* ~ *saya dlm keuntungan ini?* How much is my share of the profit? ~ *mutlak* undivided share. **2** part, participation. *mengambil* ~ *dlm* take part in. ~ *hasil* production sharing. **3** section, division. ~ *kalimat* 1 phrase. **2** sentence constituent. ~ *waktu* period of time. ~ *administrasi* administrative section. ~ *anak* pediatrics section, children's section. ~ *bahan* component. ~ *bawah* underside. ~ *belakang* 1 rear (of building, etc.). **2** posterior. ~ *jenang* purser's department. ~ *kedua dr abad ke-18* the latter half of the 18th century. ~ *perlengkapan* maintenance department. **4** lot, fate, fortune. **se-an** a part, some. *Penduduk kota itu* ~ *miskin* Part of the population is poor. ~ *besar* a large part, the majority. ~ *karena* partly because. ~ ~ little by little, bit by bit. **pem- 1** divider (person or thing). ~ *hasil* sharecropper. **2** (*Math.*) divisor. ~ *persekutuan bersama terbesar* largest common denominator. **3** (*Tech.*) distributor. *Débit air yg keluar dr* ~ *utama itu 7.5 meter kubik per detik* The water debit coming out from the main distributor is 7.5 cubic meters per second. ~ *arus* (*Auto.*) distributor. **4** (*Crd.*) dealer. **pem-an 1** distribution. ~ *rezeki* distribution of wealth, jobs. **2** (*Math.*) division. ~ *koték* long division. **3** allotment, division. *Kita hrs mengadakan* ~ *waktu yg baik* We must arrange a good division of time. **4** sharing, share. ~ *tugas* division of labor. ~ *wewenang* delegation of authority. **per-an** quotient.

bagia see BAHAGIA.

bagimana see BAGAIMANA.

baginda 1 His Majesty (for royalty). **2** (*Isl.*) a respectful term of reference for Muh. **3** (*M*) title of nobility.

bagong₁ 1 pot-bellied, portly. **2** cumbersome, ponderous. **3** name of a pot-bellied clown in a *wayang* performance.

bagong₂ (*Sd, Jkt*) **1** wild boar. **2** willing sexual partner.

bagor k.o. coarse plaitwork of palm leaves.

baguk see BEGUK.

bagur hulking, ponderous, massive.

bagus 1 fine, good. - *benar kalau ia dpt datang* It will be nice if he can come. *Cuacanya* - The weather is fine. **2** good, exemplary. - *kelakuannya* His conduct is exemplary. **mem-i** improve. ~ *diri* dress up. **mem-kan** embellish, beautify. **mem-²kan** flatter, play up to. **memper- 1** embellish, beautify. *Ia* ~ *rumahnya* She improved the appearance of her house. **2** touch up (a photograph). **ke-an 1** exaggerated praise. **2** beauty, splendor. **-an** (*Coll.*) better.

Bagus title of Jv and Balinese nobility.

bah₁ inundation, flooding. - *betina* subsidence (of river). - *jantan* rise (of river). **mem-** overflow, flood. *Air* ~ *sedikit* The water overflowed a little.

bah₂ exclamation of disgust or denigration. -*! Siapa mau kawin sama dia?* Ha! Who would want to marry him? -*! Tak tahu malu* Humph! Have you no sense of shame?

bah₃ see BABAH.

bahadur 1 knight, hero. **2** bold, courageous.

bahaduri heroic, chivalrous, knightly.

bahagi see BAGI.

bahagia happy. *kabar* - good news. **ber-** be happy. *Ia sangat* ~ *mendapat rumah di Jkt* He was very happy to find a house in Jkt. **mem-kan** make happy, bring happiness. *Surat itu* ~ *ibunya* That letter made his mother happy. **ke-an** happiness, well-being, bliss.

bahagian see BAGI.

bahagiawan blessed o.

bahak₁ burst of laughter. *tawa -² pd adegan yg lucu* fits of roaring laughter at the funny parts. **ber-** uproariously (laugh). *Ucin tertawa* ~ Ucin laughed uproariously. **ter-(²)** roar with laughter.

bahak₂ white-bellied sea eagle.

bahala see BALA₂.

baham (*Anat.*) molar. **mem-** chew with mouth closed.

bahan 1 matter, substance, material, cloth. - *yg mudah terbakar* inflammable material. - *anti-beku* antifreeze. - *bakar* fuel. - *buangan* waste matter. - *buatan* artifact. - *galian* extractive, mineral, ore. - *gizi* nutrient. - *hidup* provisions. - *keras* caustic agent. - *keterangan* data. - *lekat* adhesive. - *letupan/letusan* explosive(s). - *lumas* lubricant. -*(pe)ledak/peletus* explosives, blasting material. - *masukan* input. - *mentah* raw material. - *pangan* foodstuff. - *pelicin* 1 lubricant. **2** bribe. - *pembantu* auxiliary material. - *penambah* additional material. - *pendidik/pengajaran* teaching or instructional material. - *pengepak* packing material. - *penolong* auxiliary material. - *perekat* adhesive. - *pokok* staple supplies. - *ramuan* 1 spices. **2** perfume extracted from herbs. - *ujian* examination paper. **2** material for producing s.t. - *penyamak* tannin. - *pencegah ketularan* disinfectant, germicide. - *baku* raw material from which s.t. is produced. - *bangunan* construction, building material. - *pembersih* cleanser, cleaning material. - *pembersih air* chlorine. - *pencegat* prophylactic. - *(peng)gigit* corrosive material. - *peng-(k)urus* thinner, thinning agent. - *perumahan* building material. - *warna* coloring matter, pigment. **3** object (of criticism, etc.). - *pembicaraan* material of discussion. - *sengkéta* s.t. to quarrel over. - *adukan pasangan* mortar.

bahana 1 loud noise, din. **2** echo. **ber-, mem-1** sound. **2** echo, reverberate.

bahar₁ large body of water (such as river, sea, large lake).

bahar₂ a measure of weight (about 400 lb.).

bahar₃ see AKAR.

bahara see BARA BAHARA.

bahari₁ 1 antique, ancient. *Itu kepercayaan* - That is an ancient belief. **2** charming.

bahari₂ maritime, nautical. **ke-an** nautical matters. *sejarah* ~ maritime history.

bahariwan, bahariawan seaman. **ke-an** seaman matters. *bidang* ~ nautical studies.

bahariwati, bahariawati female sailor.

baharu see BARU₁.

bahas 1 research, investigation, study. **2** criticism. **ber-** confer. *Meréka* ~ *ttg peraturan baru itu* They conferred about the new regulation. **mem-1** discuss. **2** criticize. *Kaum kiri* ~ *politik pemerintah* The leftists criticized gvt. policy. **3** investigate, examine. *Polisi* ~ *kecelakaan itu* Police investigated the accident. *Laporan ini* ~ *masalah korupsi* The report examines the issue of corruption. **ter-** be discussed, studied. *Pd hari pertama konperénsi tdk semua makalah* ~ On the first day of the conference not all of the articles were discussed. **-an 1** criticism. **2** discussion. **pem-** discussant, panelist. **pem-an 1** discussion. **2** criticism. **3** study. **per-an** discussion, debate.

bahasa₁ 1 language. - *Indonésia* Indonesian language. **mem-Indonésiakan** put into Indonesian. - *antarwarga* lingua franca. - *baku* standard language. - *beradat* polite language. - *berton* (*Ling.*) tone language. - *campuran* mixed language. - *daérah* regional language, vernacular. - *dlm* language used at royal courts. - *gelap* jargon, cant. - *golongan* jargon, argot, slang. - *gunung* rural language. - *ibu* mother tongue. - *induk* (*Ling.*) parent language. - *kacauan* mixed language. - *kacok(²)an* colloquial Malay. - *Kawi* old Javanese. - *kebangsaan* national language. - *kerabat* (*Ling.*) cognate language. - *kesat* abusive language. - *kuno* 1 old-fashioned language. 2 (*Ling.*) archaism. - *lisan* spoken language. - *manusia* natural language. - *nada* (*Ling.*) tone language. - *pantang* taboo language. - *pasar/pasaran* 1 trade language. 2 simplified form of a language used as lingua franca. - *pengantar/perantara(an)* medium of instruction. - *pinggiran* peripheral language. - *prokém* (*Jkt*) argot used by criminals and street kids. - *purba* (*Ling.*) proto-language. - *sehari-hari* colloquial language. - *Tarzan* (*Sl.*) sign language. - *tulis(an)* written language. - *turunan* (*Ling.*) daughter language. **2** speech. - *sulung* (*Ling.*) infant speech. **3** good manners. *Anak itu tak tahu* - That kid has no manners. **ber- 1** speak (such and such a language). *Ia* ~ *Arab* She speaks Arabic. **2** well spoken, well mannered. *Ia seorg yg* ~ He is well mannered. **ber-² 1** shy, extremely polite. **mem-kan, memper-kan 1** express. *Ia tak dpt* ~ *apa yg disaksikannya itu* He could not put into words what he had just witnessed. **2** call, address. *Ia* ~ *anak pd saya* He called me son. **3** show respect, invite. *Ia* ~ *tamunya utk duduk di muka sekali* He showed his guest respect by having him sit in the front row. **ke-an 1** language. *kebijaksanaan* ~ language policy. **2** linguistic. *masalah* ~ linguistic problem. **per-(an) 1** proverb. **2** good manners, politeness.

bahasa₂ that. *Ia mengatakan* - *ia tak datang* He said that he was not coming. **-nya** (*Lit.*) that, namely, the following.

bahasa₃ a little, slightly. *Bajunya basah* - *terkena hujan* His suit was slightly wet from the rain.

bahasawan linguist.

bahasi see BAGASI.

bahath see BAHAS.

bahawa see BAHWA.

bahawasa see BAHASA₂.

bahaya danger, peril, jeopardy. - *kebakaran* danger of fire. - *kelaparan* danger of starvation. - *latén komunis* latent danger posed by the communists. - *maut* mortal danger. - *rugi* risk of financial loss. *Org hrs berani menanggung* - *rugi* O. must run risks. **ber- 1** dangerous, hazardous, risky. *Jalan ini* ~ This road is dangerous. **2** (*Crd.*) vulnerable. **mem-kan 1** endanger, imperil, threaten. *Serangan musuh* ~ *pembélaan kita* The enemy's attack endangered our defense. *Ia* ~ *keselamatannya sendiri* He risked his own safety. **2** dangerous, perilous.

bahela see BAHEULA.

bahénol nicely shaped, sexy, voluptuous.

baheula /bahela/ **1** old-fashioned, antiquated. **2** ancient. *peninggalan jaman yg* - relics of an ancient period.

bahkan 1 in fact, even. *Berpuluh-puluh,* - *beratus-ratus tahun . . .* For decades, in fact even for centuries . . . **2** moreover, on top of that. *Ia mengetahui,* - *ia sendiri yg mengatakan itu* He knew, moreover, it was he himself who said that. **3** on the contrary, in fact. *Ia tdk miskin;* - *yg terkaya di kota itu* She is not poor; in fact, she is the wealthiest person in town. **4** indeed. -, *tuan, mémang benar apa yg tuan bilang itu* Indeed, sir, what you said is certainly true.

bahna (*Jkt, Sd*) on account of. *"Keluarkan gua dr tempat ini!" teriak Arjuna* - *marahnya* "Get me out of this place!" Arjuna shouted because of his anger.

bahri see BAHARI₂.

bahtera 1 (*Bib.*) ark. **2** boat, ship. - *rumah tangga* marriage.

bahu₁ shoulder. - *jalan* shoulder of the road. - **mem- 1** shoulder to shoulder. *Meréka berdiri* ~

They stood shoulder to shoulder. **2** support e.o. **mem-** **1** shoulder, support with the shoulder. *Ia ~ tiang* He supported the pole with his shoulder. **2** carry on the shoulder. *Ia ~ keranjang yg berat itu* She carried the heavy basket on her shoulder.

bahu₂ (*Jv*) hamlet headman.

bahu₃ see BAKHU.

bahu₄ see BAU₂.

bahubahasa (*Ling.*) multilingualism.

bahureksa see BAUREKSA.

bahwa that. *Ia mengatakan - harga daging naik* She said that the price of meat was going up.

bahwasanya (*Lit.*) **1** that. **2** truly, indeed.

baiat /bai'at/ (*Isl.*) oath. **mem-** take o.'s oath. **pem-an** oath taking.

baid /ba'it/ distant (of relatives).

baiduri opal (and other semiprecious stones).

baik 1 good, fine, kind. *Ia org -* He is a good person. *Saya tdk bisa melihat dgn -* I cannot see well. *- kita tunggu* It would be good for us to wait. *Guru - sekali kpd saya* The teacher was very kind to me. *dgn -* **1** well. *Kedatangan kami diterima dgn -* Our arrival was well received. **2** carefully. *- bahasa* polite, kind, amiable. *- hati* kind-hearted. *- rasi* born under lucky stars. **2** healthy. *Apa dia sdh - lagi dr penyakitnya?* Has he recovered from his illness? **3** yes, all right. *- tuan, saya mau pergi* All right, sir, I will go. *-lah* OK. *- . . . -* (*Lit.*) both . . . and. *- dia - saya suka makanan yg énak* Both she and I like good food. *- buruknya* good and bad aspects of s.t. *- . . .atau* either . . . or. *- dékan atau réktor tdk tahu-menahu ttg rencana penataran itu* Neither the dean nor the president knew anything about the plans for a program to upgrade employees. *- . . . .maupun* both . . . and. *- ini maupun itu tak diterimanya* She accepted neither this nor that. **-² 1** well, carefully. *Bungkus barang-barang itu ~* Wrap those things well. *~ lho!* Do be careful! **2** in good condition. *Tentara yg bertugas ~ semuanya* The soldiers who were on duty all came out all right. *Kuharap kau ~ saja* I hope you are fine. **3** good, respectable. *pergaulan org ~* the society of respectable people. **se-1** as good as. *Mobil ini tdk ~ mobil itu* This car is not as good as that car. **2** as soon as. *Seluruh negeri berduka ~ diterimanya kabar* The entire country was in mourning as soon as it received the news. **se-nya** better, best, preferable. *~ kita pergi lebih dulu* It is best for us to go first. **se-²** however good. *~ org, tak ada yg melebihi ayahnya* No o., however good, can surpass her father. **se-²nya** as well or good as possible. **ber-** **1** be on good terms. **2** be kind. **ber-² 1** make peace. **2** be on good terms. **ber-an** be on good terms with e.o. **mem-** improve, become better. *Kapan harga kayu akan ~?* When will timber prices improve? *Keadaan ~* The situation is improving. *Ia mulai ~ dr sakitnya* She is beginning to get better after her sickness. **mem-i 1** improve s.t. **2** repair. **3** treat nicely. **mem-kan 1** improve s.t. *Di-kannya duduknya* He rearranged himself in his seating. **2** treat well, do well by s.o. **memper-i 1** repair

(road, etc.). **2** correct (mistake, etc.). **3** improve s.t., reform. **4** improve upon, break (record). **ter-** best. **ter-i** reparable. *tdk ~* irreparable, beyond repair. **ke-an 1** goodness, good quality. **2** kindness, goodness. *~ hati* goodness of o.'s heart. **3** advantage, benefit, interest. *Aku melakukan ini utk ~ sendiri* I am doing this for my own benefit. *demi ~ keluarga* in the interest of the family. **4** good deed, meritorious action. *Bu Lurah disegani karena ~nya* The district chief's wife is respected because of her good deeds. **-an** (*Coll.*) **1** better (than). **2** improve. *Dia mulai ~* She is on the mend. **-²an** be amicable to e.o. *AS ingin ~ dgn US* The US wants to be on good terms with the Soviet Union. **pem-an** construction. **per-an 1** repair. *~ jalan* road repairs. **2** improvement, betterment. *Adakah ~?* Is there any improvement? *~ sosial* social rehabilitation. **3** upgrading.

baikut (*Ch*) spare ribs.

bait₁ abode, house (often used in names of mosques). *- Allah* **1** (*Bib.*) the temple in Jerusalem. **2** (*Isl.*) the holy mosque in Mecca.

bait₂ 1 distich, couplet. **2** (*Isl.*) verse. **ber-²** by the verse, lots and lots of verses.

baitullah the holy mosque in Mecca.

Baitul Makdis see BAITUL MUKADDIS.

baitulmal (*Lit.*) treasury.

Baitul Mukaddis (*Isl.*) the holy city of Jerusalem.

baja₁ 1 steel. *Ia berkemauan -* He has an iron will. *- keras manggan* manganese. *- krom* chrome steel. *- lembik* ingot steel. *- putih/tahan korosi/tahan karat* stainless steel. **2** armor. **ber-** armored, armorplated. **mem- 1** become steel. *Karena panas api yg keras itu besi mudah ~* Because of the intense heat the iron easily turns into steel. **2** become hard, become strong. *Kepercayaan rakyat tlh ~ thd pemimpin itu* The people's confidence in that leader has strengthened. **mem-kan** steel, harden, strengthen (o.'s spirit). *Partai adalah kekuatan perkasa yg ~nya* The party was a mighty force that made him into a man of steel. **ke-an 1** hardness, toughness. **2** resistance. **pem-an 1** obdurancy, doggedness, obstinancy. **2** hardening, steeling.

baja₂ fertilizer, manure. *- kandang* dung. **mem-i** fertilize.

baja₃ (*Jv*) **1** mixture of oil and burnt coconut shell for blackening teeth. **2** dentifrice. **mem-i** blacken (teeth).

bajag k.o. sweet and fried chili-spiced condiment.

bajaj /bajai, bajéi/ two-passenger pedicab with motor scooter engine.

bajak₁ plow. **mem- 1** plow (field). **2** make furrows in the water (as in wake of boat). **-an** plowing. *bekas ~* traces of plowing. **pem-an** plowing.

bajak₂ bandit. *- laut* pirate. **mem- 1** carry on piracy, plunder. **2** hijack. **3** illegally reproduce tapes, books, etc., pirate. **-an 1** loot, plunder, s.t. pirated. *Kasét ~* pirated cassette. **2** illegal profit. **pem- 1** pirate. **2** hijacker. *~ udara* skyjacker. **pem-an 1** hijacking. **2** plundering, pirating (of

books, cassettes, etc.). ~ *lagu ciptaannya membuatnya gusar* It made her angry that they pirated her composition.
bajan 1 basin. **2** see WAJAN.
Bajau Samal-speaking sea nomads off the coasts of E. Kalimantan, Sulawesi, and elsewhere in E. Indonesia.
baji 1 wedge. **2** peg. **mem-1** split s.t. with a wedge. **2** hold together with a peg.
bajigur k.o. hot drink made of coconut milk and spices.
bajik good, wholesome, virtuous (life). *uang* - bonus for special services to an organization. **ke-an** good deeds, benevolent service. *Ia banyak berbuat ~ di masyarakat* He has rendered considerable service to society.
bajing squirrel. **-an 1** scoundrel, gangster. **2** thief.
baju 1 jacket, blouse, shirt. - *antakusuma* magical cloak that enables its wearer to fly. - *antari* long inner vest worn by pilgrims to Mecca. - *bébé* woman's Western-style dress. - *belah dada* jacket opening in the middle. - *besi* armor, coat of mail. - *béskét* waistcoat, vest. - *blus* blouse. - *bodo* woman's sleeveless tunic of S. Sulawesi. - *buntung* short-sleeved woman's jacket. - *cina* pajamas. - *dlm* undershirt. - *dingin* winter clothes. - *hangat* thick and warm clothing. - *hijau/ijo (Derog.)* soldier. - *hujan* raincoat. - *jas* coat. - *jubah* **1** tunic, mantle, flowing robe (Arab, judge). **2** *(Rel.)* habit. - *kelepak* open-fronted shirt or blouse. - *kembang* flowered shirt, sports shirt. - *kurung (Sumatra)* woman's long tunic. - *las* welder's outfit. - *lasak* everyday dress or work clothes. - *loréng (Mil.)* camouflage uniform. - *mandi* swimsuit. - *maskat* vest. - *monyét* **1** overalls. **2** child's o.-piece playsuit. - *pelampung* life jacket. - *pengantin* **1** bridal gown. **2** regional costumes for bride and groom. - *perang* battle attire. - *rompi* vest, sleeveless sweater. - *safari* short-sleeved four-pocket shirt (us. worn by civil servants). - *sika* close-fitting blouse. - *sirap* coat of mail. - *teluk belanga* collarless man's blouse or jacket. - *terusan* full-length dress. - *tidur* nightshirt, nightgown, pajamas. - *zirah* coat of mail. **2** clothing, apparel. **ber-** wear clothing, shirt, jacket, etc. ~ *hijau (Derog.)* be a soldier. ~ *putih* be a civilian. *tak* ~ naked. **ber-kan** dressed as. *singa ~ domba* wolf in sheep's clothing. **mem-i** put a jacket on s.o., dress (a doll, etc.).
bajul *(Jv)* **1** crocodile. **2** scoundrel, rascal. - *buntung* womanizer, molester of women. **3** pickpocket. **mem-1** womanize, chase women. **2** show off in order to attract a woman's attention.
bak₁ *(Lit.)* like, as. - *buku-buku tiga puluhan* as in books of the 1930s.
bak₂ /bak/ **1** basin, vessel. - *potrét* photo-developing tank. **2** large container. - *cuci* **1** sink. **2** laundry tub. - *kamar mandi* an open tank for splash baths. - *karter* crankcase. - *makan(an)* feeding trough. - *mesin* crankcase. - *pasir* sandbox. - *persnéling* transmission, gear box. - *sampah* trash

bin, trash can. - *siram* flushing tank of toilet. - *tinja* septic tank.
bak₃ Ch ink.
bak₄ sound of a thud.
baka₁ eternal, everlasting. *alam* - eternity, the hereafter. *persahabatan yg* - lasting friendship. *negeri yg* - world without end, world hereafter. **mem-kan** immortalize. **ke-an 1** eternity. **2** durability, perdurability.
baka₂ **1** family, descent, line. **2** genetic origins. *Puteri itu membuang - utk menikah dgn org biasa* The princess renounced her heritage to marry a commoner.
bakal 1 future, prospective. *Ia - présidén* He is the future president. - *baju (Jv)* material for clothing. - *buah (Biol.)* ovule. - *guru* student teacher, prospective teacher. - *isteri* fiancée. - *manusia* fetus. - *menantu* future son or daughter-in-law. - *pelanting (R.R.)* rolling stock. **2** in the making. *Ia - musikus* She is a musician in the making. **3** shall, will. *Dia - bertemu dgn ahli-ahli bahasa di sana* He will meet linguists there. *Pertemuan itu - diawali oléh suatu proséminar* The meeting will be preceded by a proseminar. **-an** shall, will. *Kami ~ punya perusahaan pompa bénsin* We will own a filling station (business). *Mesjid ini ~ menjadi mesjid yg termegah di Asia* The mosque is to become the most glorious mosque in Asia.
bakaloréat baccalaureate.
bakantan see BEKANTAN.
bakap k.o. fish, murral.
bakar 1 burn, set on fire. *bahan* - fuel. *kayu* - firewood. *motor* - combustion engine. **2** roasted. - *ikan* roasted fish. **mem-1** burn, set on fire. ~ *diri* immolate, set o.s. on fire. ~ *habis* incinerate. ~ *hati* **1** anger, mortify. **2** arouse passions, inflame. *Ia ~ hati tetangganya* He made his neighbor mad. ~ *jenazah* cremate. ~ *rokok* light a cigarette. ~ *téwas* burn s.o. to death. **2** inflame (emotions). *Kurasa darahku naik ~* I felt my blood boiling up. ~ *angan-angan* arouse desire. **3** bake, roast. ~ *arang* make charcoal. ~ *bata* make bricks. **mem-i** burn up. *Ia sibuk ~ surat-suratnya* She is busy burning up her letters. **mem-kan** burn s.t. for s.o. **ter-1** on fire. *Rumahnya ~* His house is on fire. ~ *hati* angry, furious. **2** burned down (of a building). ~ *melepuh kedua* second-degree burn. **ke-an** fire, conflagration. ~ *jénggot* be frantic, beside o.s., distraught. ~ *tambang* firedamp. **-an** grill. ~ *roti* toast. **pem-1** burner. ~ *bunsén* Bunsen burner. ~ *hémat* (gas) pilot light. **2** arsonist, firebug. **3** agitator, fomenter. **pem-an 1** burning, incineration. ~ *mayat* cremation. **2** ignition, lighting (of fire). ~ *hutan* slash and burn. **3** place for burning. ~ *kapur* lime kiln. **4** roasting. ~ *kopi* roasting of coffee.
bakarat baccarat.
bakat 1 trace, trail. *Ada - kaki harimau di halaman* There are footprints of a tiger in the yard. **2** sign, omen. *Méga mendung adalah - hujan* Cloudiness is a sign of rain. - *penyakit* symptom.

3 crest, head. - *ombak* crest of waves. **4** talent, aptitude, propensity. *Ia menunjukkan - menggambar* She shows a talent for drawing. *Sdh - dia gemuk* He has a tendency to put on weight. - *alam* genius. - *seni* artistic. **ber-** 1 scarred, marked. *Mukanya ~ cacar* His face is pockmarked. **2** talented, gifted. *pemuda yg ~ a* talented youth. **mem-** 1 indicate. **2** impending, imminent. *Sunyi senyap di laut ~ datangnya angin ribut* Calm at sea announces the arrival of a storm.

bakau k.o. mangrove tree.

bak bak kur 1 sounds of birds and chickens. **2** k.o. children's game.

bakcang see BACANG₁.

bakda 1 after. *Kami berangkat - makan malam* We left after supper. - *magrib* after the sunset prayer. **2** (*Jv*) the celebration at the end of the fasting month.

bakelit Bakelite (plastic).

bakéro (*Japanese*) idiot, imbecile.

bakhil stingy, miserly. *Si - The Miser.* **ke-an** avarice.

bakhsyis see BAKSIS.

bakhu (*Ch*) thin strips of spiced, fried pork.

baki₁ small tray. **ber-²** by the tray, trays and trays of.

baki₂ remainder, residue, balance. **mem-kan** set aside, reserve. *coklat yg di-kan utk anak-anak itu* chocolate that was set aside for the children.

bakiak wooden clog.

bakik betel vine (leaves are chewed with areca and other ingredients).

bakikuk, bakiluk see MAIN.

Bakin [*Badan Koordinasi Inteligéns Negara*] State Intelligence Coordinating Agency.

bakmi Ch noodles (flavored with meat). - *basah* semicooked noodles. - *goréng* sautéed noodles. - *pangsit* Ch noodle soup with wonton.

bako₁ the relation on the paternal side. *Karena banyak teman yg baik-baik ia merasa di rumah induk -* Thanks to his many good friends he felt quite at home (lit., as if in his father's relatives' house). *cari* - seek a son-in-law.

bako₂ see BAKAU.

bako₃ see BAKU₂.

bakpao steamed bun stuffed with meat or other ingredients. *Pipinya kayak -* She has rounded cheeks.

bakpuder baking powder.

baksi mizzen sail. **mem-** set the mizzen sail.

baksil /baksil/ bacillus.

baksis tip, gratuity, bribe.

bakso 1 Ch meatballs. **2** soup with meatballs, sliced cabbage and bean threads. **nge-** (*Coll.*) eat such a soup.

baktau (*Ch*) madam (of a brothel), procuress.

baktéri /baktéri/ bacteria. - *bundar* coccus.

baktériologi bacteriology.

bakti 1 homage, devotion. **2** service. *Meréka msk tentara utk berbuat - pd negara* They entered the military to perform a service to their country.

3 faith, loyalty. *Ia melupakan - kpd negaranya* She forgot her loyalty to her country. **4** filial piety. **5** staunch, loyal, faithful, devoted. *seorg isteri yg amat - thd suaminya* a wife who is devoted to her husband. **ber-** 1 be loyal, serve devotedly. **2** perform a (public) service. **mem-kan** dedicate, devote. *Ia ~ tenaganya kpd tanah air* He dedicated his energies to his country. *~ hidupnya kpd . . .* devote o.'s life to . . . **ke-an** 1 loyalty, dedication. **2** religious service. **pem-an** 1 devotion, dedication (to a cause). *~ kpd tanah air* devotion to o.'s country. **2** loyalty, faithfulness. **3** service, aid, assistance.

baku₁ 1 standard. *karya -* standard work. **2** full-fledged (teacher, etc.). **3** basic. *bahan -* basic commodity. *harga -* basic price. - *emas* gold standard. **mem-kan** standardize (the language). **ke-an** standardness. *masalah ~* standardization problem. **pem-an** standardization.

baku₂ (*Coll.*) mutual, reciprocal. - *bunuh* fight to the death. - *débat* debate e.o. - *ganti* interchangeable. - *hadap* facing e.o. - *hantam* 1 hit e.o. 2 scuffle, fistfight. - *témbak* shoot e.o. - *tubruk* 1 crash into e.o. 2 collision. - *tuduh* mutually accuse.

bakul₁ .basket. - *beramin* bamboo storage basket (us. hung on wall). - *berombong* round basket with lid. - *bilah* finely woven basket. - *kerau* bamboo basket. - *nasi* a large container for rice.

bakul₂ (*Coll.*) small tradeswoman.

bakung 1 wild lily. **2** k.o. onion.

bakup red and swollen (of the eyes).

bakwan 1 corn fritter (sometimes with shrimp). **2** soup with Ch meatballs.

bakyu see MBAK.

bal₁ 1 ball. **2** balloon. - *békel* ball for playing jacks.

bal₂ bale. **ber-²** by the bale.

bala₁ troops, army. - *bantuan* reinforcements. - *Keselamatan* Salvation Army.

bala₂ disaster, catastrophe. - *bencana* distress, emergency. - *dosa dr Tuhan* just deserts from God.

balah **ber-** argue, quarrel. **mem-** oppose, argue against. *Semua anggota ~ anjuran itu* All members opposed the proposal. **pem-an** disputation, arguing. **per-an** dispute, argument.

balai₁ 1 public hall or building. - *adat* ceremonial hall. - *angin/peranginan* summer house, gazebo. - *apit (tengah)* waiting or reception room. - *astaka* royal viewing platform. - *bayu* pavilion. - *bendul* royal reception hall. - *benih* greenhouse. - *bersalin* lying-in hospital. - *budaya* cultural center. - *derma* almshouse, poorhouse. - *désa* village meeting hall. - *istirahat* rest house. - *kambang* artificial island (in a garden pond). - *lélang* auction hall. - *keséhatan* medical clinic, polyclinic. - *kota* town hall, municipal building. - *penghadapan* reception hall. - *pengobatan* medical clinic. - *perguruan tinggi* university building. - *pertemuan* meeting hall. - *prajurit* army clubhouse. - *senirupa* art gallery. - *sidang* convention hall. - *wartawan* press club. **2** office or bureau, association. - *dagang* chamber of commerce. - *harta pening-*

galan probate court. - *penerangan* information office. - *perancang tatabumi* land utilization bureau. - *Pustaka* Gvt. Printing and Publishing House (formerly Bureau for Popular Literature). 3 house (of parliament). - *rendah* House of Commons, House of Representatives, Lower Chamber. - *tinggi* House of Lords, Senate, Upper Chamber.

balai₂ see BURUNG.

balai-balai wooden or bamboo couch or sleeping platform.

balairung 1 royal audience hall. **2** market shed or stall.

balam₁ turtledove, banded ground dove.

balam₂ ber-, mem- be barely visible. *Karena kabut itu penglihatan sangat* ~ Because of the fog, visibility was extremely poor.

balang₁ long-necked bottle.

balang₂ see HULUBALANG.

balang₃ see BELANG.

balans₁ (*Coll.*) weighing scales.

balans₂ bank balance.

balansir mem- balance (wheels, scales, etc.).

balantara see BELANTARA.

balap race, racing. - *sepéda* bicycle race. **ber-** compete. **mem- 1** race, compete. **2** speed, hurry along. **mem-kan** race (a vehicle), run s.t. at high speed. **-an 1** race. ~ *mobil* car racing. **2** race track. **pem-** racer.

balapecah (*Jv*) crockery.

balar 1 albino. **2** with white spots (of cattle).

balas reply, response. - *bicara* retort, rejoinder. - *budi* gratitude. - *bunyi* echo. - *dendam* revenge. - *hadiah* thank-you gift. - *jasa* **1** recompense. **2** fringe benefits. - *kata* reply, response. - *pati* retribution of honor. - **ber-** mutual response. *kebaikan* ~ mutual kindness. **ber- 1** have a response. *Kebaikannya tak* ~ Her kindness had no response. **2** reverberate, echo, respond. *Dlm sumur itu suara* ~ *riuh* A sound reverberated loudly in the well. **ber-an** exchange replies, gunfire, etc. **ber-²an** correspond with e.o. - **mem-** reply to e.o. *Sdh dua tahun meréka* ~ *berkiriman surat* They have been corresponding for two years. *atas dasar* ~ on a quid-pro-quo basis. **mem- 1** answer, reply. ~ *surat Tuan tertanggal tiga Maret* . . . In reply to your letter of March 3d . . . *Ia blm* ~ *surat saya* She has not answered my letter yet. ~ *guna* render service, be useful. ~ *jawab* reply, respond. ~ *salam* greet, extend greetings. **2** repay, reward. *Ia* ~ *kebaikan temannya* He repaid his friend's kindness. ~ *budi* reciprocate s.o.'s kindness. ~ *jasa* repay a service. **3** avenge, take revenge, punish. *Ia tlh disakiti oléh org itu dan hendak* ~ She was hurt by that person and wants revenge. ~ *dendam* take revenge, avenge. **mem-i 1** reply to. ~ *suratnya* reply to his letter. *Aku* ~ *itu semua dgn senyuman* I responded to it all with a smile. **2** reward, requite. **mem-kan** avenge. *Dendamnya bisa betul-betul di-kan* He can really avenge himself. **ter-** requited, responded to. *Cinta Fran ini tdk* ~ Fran's love is unrequited. **-an**

1 answer, reply. **2** response. **3** revenge. **4** reprisal, retaliation. ~ *Tuhan* divine judgment. **pem- 1** avenger. **2** responder, replier. *Siapakah* ~ *surat itu?* Who replied to that letter? **3** response, reply. **pem-an 1** reply, replying, response, responding. *serangan* ~ counterattack. **2** recompense. **3** revenge, retribution, retaliation, reprisal.

balatentara troops.

balau confused, in disorder. **ber-** mix, mingle. **ke-an** disorder, confusion, chaos.

balé-balé see BALAI-BALAI.

baléla rebellion. **mem-** rebel, resist authority.

bales see BALAS.

balét ballet.

balgam, balgham mucus, phlegm.

bali₁ placenta.

bali₂ culinary style characterized by large quantities of chili, tamarind, and other spices.

balian 1 shaman, traditional medicine practitioner. **2** transvestite medium among the Ngaju Dayak.

balig, baligh /balikh/ be of age, attain o.'s majority, mature. **ke-an 1** adulthood. **2** puberty.

baliho billboard (esp. for movies).

balik 1 return. *Ia blm* - *dr Éropah* He has not returned from Europe yet. - *hari* return the same day. - *kucing* turn back in cowardly fashion. - *sadar* return to consciousness, revive. *tdk dpt* - irreversible. **2** the reverse side, behind. *di* - *pintu* behind the door. *Ia berdiri di* - *méja* She was standing behind the table. *di* - *jas hujan* under the raincoat. - *belah* upside down. - *belakang* behind (the back). - *bokong* inside out, back to front. *di* - *awan* walking on air, being in a cloud. - *mata* **1** pretend not to know, close o.'s eyes to. **2** plot, scheme. - *pembelakangan* behind (the back). **3** the reverse, the contrary. *Ia bertindak* - *hukum* He acted against the law. - *adab* rude, discourteous. - *gagang* defect, go over to the enemy. - *jung* (do a) somersault. -*! Kanan!* (*Mil.*) Right face! - *nama* transfer the title of ownership. **mem-namakan** transfer ownership (of motor vehicles). **4** again. - *sakit* (have a) relapse. *Stlh tiga hari sepi, maka pasar itu* - *ramai* After three quiet days, the market is busy again. *di* - *itu* besides, moreover. - *kerak/rujuk* remarry o.'s divorced wife. **se-** the opposite. *di* ~ *dinding* on the other side of the wall. **se-nya** on the contrary, just the opposite, the other way. *Lihat* ~ See the other side (of the page). **ber- 1** turn over or upside down. *Anjing laut itu* ~ *hingga kelihatan perutnya* The seal flipped over, and we saw its belly. **2** change, take a different course. *Perkataanya* ~ His words took a different course. **3** turn around. *Ia* ~ *melihat isterinya* He turned around to look at his wife. **4** turn back. *Kedengkian itu akan* ~ *kpd dirinya sendiri* That cruelty will turn back on him. **5** reflect. *Sinar matahari yg* ~ *dr kaca itu sangat kuat* That glass strongly reflected the rays of the sun. **6** return. **7** retrograde. ~ *arah* **1** change direction. **2** make a

U-turn. ~ *bertanya* reply to a question with a question. ~ *haluan* 1 change direction. 2 (*Naut.*) tack. ~ *hati* have a change of heart. ~ *muka* 1 turn around. 2 deflect. ~ *pikiran* change o.'s mind. ~ *pulang* 1 return. 2 return to consciousness. **ber-²** keep turning, keep returning. **ber-an** be the opposite. *Semuanya ~ dgn dulu* Everything is the opposite of the way it used to be. **mem-** 1 turn around. *Ia ~ menghadap ke arah saya* She turned and faced in my direction. 2 turn s.t. over. ~ *ikan itu spy lekas masak* Turn the fish over so it will cook quickly. 3 ricochet. *Ia luka kena peluru yg ~ dr tiang besi* He was wounded by a bullet which ricocheted from an iron pole. 4 turn over, capsize. 5 reverse, change. *Ia ~ perintah majikannya* He reversed his boss's order. ~ *belakang* turn o.'s back. ~ *ke kiri* turn to the left. ~ *rambut* ruffle or muss up the hair. **mem-²** 1 turn over and over. ~ *kotak itu sblm membelinya* She turned the box over and over before buying it. 2 turn repeatedly (pages). **mem-i** 1 return to. *Ia ~ isterinya* He returned to his wife. 2 repeat. ~ *permintaan* repeat a request. 3 go back on (a promise). **mem-kan** 1 turn s.t. *Ia ~ méja tulisnya menghadap pintu* He turned his desk so it would face the door. ~ *tanah* turn over the soil. ~ *haluan* change course. ~ *muka* 1 turn or avert o.'s face. 2 make an about-face. ~ *hujan ke langit pula* demand the impossible (lit., return the rain to the skies). 2 place upside down. 3 return. ~ *serangan musuh* return the enemy's attack. ~ *penghinaan* return an insult. 4 misrepresent. *Ia selalu ~ perkataannya* He is always distorting her words. ~ *punggung ke* turn o.'s back on. 5 reverse (the course of history). **mem-²kan** keep turning (pages). **ter-** 1 be upside down. *Bis yg jatuh di jurang itu ~* The bus that fell into the ravine was upside down. 2 reverse, the other way around. *Buku ini ~* According to this book it is just the other way around. 3 inside out. *Piyamanya ~* His pajamas were inside out. 4 capsized, upside down (of a boat, etc.). 5 backwards. ~ *akal* out of o.'s mind, crazy. ~ *lidah* change the subject. ~ *mata* have waited too long. **ter-²** 1 heave (of the stomach). 2 rolled back. *Matanya ~* His eyes were rolled back. **menter-²kan** roll (o.'s eyes) back. **ke-** (*Coll.*) upside down. **ke-an** be the contrary, the opposite. **ber-ke-an** be the opposite, be the contrary. **pem-** (*Elec.*) commutator. **pem-an** 1 reversal. 2 inversion. 3 sudden change of fortune, reversal.

baling -² 1 propeller. ~ *angin* fan. 2 ship's screw. 3 weathercock. 4 toy windmill. *hati bagai ~ di atas bukit* vacillating, indecisive (lit., heart like a windmill on a hill). **ber-** turn, revolve (like a propeller). **-an** revolution, turn (of a propeller).

balir see BALIG.

balistik 1 ballistic. 2 ballistics.

Balita [*Bawah Lima Tahun*] *anak ~* children under five.

Balkanisasi Balkanization.

balkon 1 balcony. 2 (*R.R.*) platform.

ballada, ballade ballad.

ballpoint /bolpoin/ ballpoint pen.

balmaski masquerade ball.

balok 1 beam (of wood). - *és* block of ice. - *induk* main beam. - *lintang/silang* cross beam. 2 crossbar, joint, girder. - *rél* (*R.R.*) tie. 3 bar (as in military insignia, line drawn, etc.). - *not* music bar. **-an** s.t. produced in bars. ~ *timah* tin ingot.

balolo [*barisan lonte lanang*] line-up of male prostitutes. (Sl)

balon₁ balloon. - *gelembung* - o. who is empty like a bubble (but pretentious). - *kabel* captive baloon. - *lampu listrik* lightbulb. - *sabun* soap bubble. **-an** 1 made of balloons. 2 similar to balloons. **-²an** 1 soap bubbles. 2 trial balloon.

balon₂ (*Jv*) prostitute.

balong 1 pond, pool. 2 fishpond. 3 puddle, mud hole.

balsa balsa.

balsam, balsem balsam, ointment. **mem-** apply balsam. ~ *tubuh* embalm. **pem-an** embalming.

balu widow.

baluarti fortress, bastion.

baluhan 1 wooden frame for seat on elephant. 2 wooden frame for drum.

balui (*Sport*) draw, tie.

balun₁ **mem-** beat (with a stick). *Ia ~ kentongan itu dgn kerasnya* He beat the drum loudly.

balun₂ **mem-** fold, roll up. *Ia ~ lengan bajunya utk bekerja* He rolled up his sleeves for work.

balung₁ 1 cockscomb. 2 cockscomb plants.

balung₂ bone. - *sumsum* bone marrow. *Dia seorg romantikus sampai ke - sumsum* He is a romantic to his very marrow. **mem-** *sumsum* deep-seated, deep-rooted.

balung₃ k.o. snakelike fish that swims near water surface.

balur₁ 1 jerky, dried meat. 2 thick skin around neck (of certain animals). **mem-kan** spread, smear, coat. ~ *minyak babi pd badannya* spread lard on o.'s body.

balur₂ see HABLUR.

balut₁ bandage, dressing, wrapping. - *kepala* headband. - *luka* bandage. - *rokok* cigarette paper. **ber-** 1 wrapped. *Tubuh gadis itu hanya ~ kain sarung* The girl's body was covered only with a sarong. 2 bandaged. - **mem-** first aid. **mem-** 1 dress, bandage. 2 wrap. *Ia ~ bukunya dgn kain hijau* He wrapped his book in green cloth. 3 envelop, mold (the body). *Bulan sabit di- awan hitam sebentar* For a moment the crescent moon was enveloped by dark clouds. ~ *ke arah* ogle at. **mem-i** 1 wrap. *Kakinya hanya di-i kulit* His leg was just skin and bones. 2 dress (a wound). **mem-kan** 1 put s.t. on as a bandage, wrap s.t. around. *Angin ~ rok rapat-rapat ke paha dan betisnya* The wind wrapped the skirt tightly around her thighs and calves. 2 wrap for s.o. **-an** 1 bandage, dressing. 2 packing, wrapping, envelopment. *Dia merasa bhw dirinya sedang berada dlm ~ kekotoran* He felt that he was entangled in filth. **3** parcel, package. **pem-** 1 bandage, dressing. ~ *tekan/ténsi* tourniquet. **2** wrapping. ~ *wanita* sanitary napkin. **pem-an** 1 bandaging, dressing (of a wound). **2** covering, upholstering (of a chair, etc.).

balut₂ red and swollen (of eyes).

bam₁ cross beam to hold rudder.

bam₂ sound of a drum.

bam₃ (*Coll.*) gun.

bambang₁ vast, extensive. *tanah* - vast area. **bersean** 1 extended, spread out (of area). **2** act big. **ter-** 1 extend. *Lapangan yg luas ~ di antara dua gunung itu* A vast plain extends between the two mountains. **2** be displayed. *Panji-panji memuat semboyan-semboyan ~ di sepanjang jalan* Banners were displayed along the road.

bambang₂ *se-* elope. **mem-** elope, run off with a willing girl.

bambu bamboo. - *ampel/apus/ater/betung/bunar/duri/gombong/hitam/kuning/pagar/perling/talang/tamiang* names of various k.o. bamboo. - *runcing* bamboo spear. **mem-runcingkan** run through with a bamboo spear.

bambung, bambungan (*Jv*) squatter, street people.

bami see BAKMI.

bamper see BUMPER.

ban₁ 1 tire. - *angin* pneumatic tire. - *dlm* inner tube. - *hidup* tire with inflatable inner tube. - *luar* tire casing. - *mati* solid tire with no inner tube. - *pinggiran putih* whitewall tire. - *renang* swimming tube. - *serap/sérep* spare tire. - *tanpa - dlm* tubeless tire. - *udara* pneumatic tire. **2** ribbon, band. *Ia memakai - hitam* He wore a black sash or arm band. - *bahu* shoulder plate. **3** sash, belt. - *opsir* officer's sash. - *bergerak/berjalan* conveyor belt, assembly line. - *jalan* conveyer belt. - *kipas* fan belt. - *pengangkut* conveyor belt. - *transpor* conveyor belt. **4** tire tread. - *baja berigi* caterpillar tread. - *ulat* caterpillar tread. **ber-** 1 have a certain k.o. tire. **2** wear a band, sash, etc.

ban₂ 1 (tennis, badminton) court. **2** train track. **3** (race) track.

ban₃ see BAND₂.

banal banal, trite.

banat mem- whip, thrash, defeat.

bancakan 1 (*Jv*) k.o. ritual feast. **2** victim of mob attack. *Maling itu dijadikan - oléh org kampung* That thief was battered pitilessly by the villagers.

bancang tether (an animal).

bancar (*Jv*) flow copiously. **men-kan** make s.t. flow copiously.

bancét k.o. small frog.

banci₁ 1 effeminate or transvestite homosexual. - *lu!* You queer! **2** hermaphrodite. **3** effeminate. **4** powerless. *partai politik* - powerless political parties. **mem-kan** render powerless. **ke-an** effeminacy. *dgn gaya lawak ~* with an effeminate style of clowning.

banci₂ Ch or Hindu census.

banci₃ k.o. large ax.

bancuh mixed up, confused. *Tempat duduk ini* - These seats are mixed up. **mem-i** mix s.t. with. *kalau dpt di-i apiun* if it can be mixed with (raw) opium. **mem-kan** mix, blend. ~ *kartu* shuffle cards. **-an** mixture, blend.

bancut protruding (of eyes).

band₁ /bén/ band.

band₂ /ban/ radio band. *transistor tiga* - three-band transistor radio.

band₃ see BAN₁.

bandal see BANDEL.

bandang large. *banjir* - flash flood.

bandar₁ harbor, port. - *udara* airport. **ber-** have a certain k.o. port. **per-an** system of docks. - *duane* customs office.

bandar₂ 1 water course, channel, duct. **2** ditch, drain. - *sampah* sewage ditch. **mem-kan** irrigate, flood water. *bagai ~ air ke bukit* perform a Sisyphean task. **ter-** irrigated. **-an** channel, draining.

bandar₃ 1 croupier. **2** o. who directs or finances illegal or underhand activities. *Nénéknya menjadi - di gelanggang perjudian* His grandmother became an illegal operator in gambling activities. **mem-** 1 trade. *Ia ~ sbg penghidupannya* He trades for a living. *modal ~ kain* capital to trade in dry goods. **2** serve as a croupier. **mem-i** be a croupier.

bandara [*bandar udara*] airport.

bandel 1 obstinate, stubborn, recalcitrant. **2** undisciplined, disobedient (of children). **mem-** be naughty. **ke-an** obstinacy, insistence on being naughty. **pem-** recalcitrant or stubbornly undisciplined person. *Rendra bukan lagi ~ thd kehalusan istana* Rendra is no longer in rebellion against the refinement of the court. **pem-an** acting undisciplined and naughty.

bandela bale. - *kapas* bale of cotton.

bandeng k.o. fish, milkfish.

banderék₁ k.o. ginger drink served hot.

banderék₂ master key, any device used to pick a lock. **mem-** 1 pick a lock. **2** modify engines or machinery. ~ *motor* modify a motor to change the k.o. fuel used.

bandering slingshot. **mem-** use a slingshot.

banderol 1 strip of paper verifying payment of tax on package of cigarettes, revenue stamp. **2** official price, controlled price.

bandés₁ [*bantuan désa*] village assistance program.

bandés₂ [*pembangunan désa*] rural development (body).

bandikut bandicoot.

banding 1 equivalent, equal. *Ia pandai sekali; tak ada -nya* He is very clever; he has no equal. - *berganda* constantly. *satu - satu* ratio of o. to o. **2** consideration, appeal. *Ia ingin minta - lagi kpd hakim yg lebih tinggi* He wanted to appeal to a judge at a higher court level. **se-** 1 comparable (value, type, etc.). **2** proportional. *Kekuatannya ~ dgn bentuk badannya* His strength is proportional to his body. **ber-** proportionate, in proportion to. *Gajinya ~ dgn kecakapannya* His salary is in proportion to his ability. *~ balik* inversely proportional. *~ sbg* in the ratio of. *~ sbg lima tujuh* in the ratio of five to seven. **ber-an** 1 match, be congruent, in harmony. *Warna rambutnya ~ dgn warna pakaiannya* Her hair matches the color or her dress. 2 in accordance. *Itu tdk ~ dgn kejadian yg sebenarnya* That is not in accordance with the facts. **- mem-** compare with e.o. **mem-** 1 (*Leg.*) appeal. *Ia ~ perkaranya ke Mahkamah Agung* He appealed his case to the Supreme Court. 2 compare. **mem-i** 1 balance, counterbalance. 2 equal, match. *Tdk mudah ~ rékor Rudy Hartono* It will not be easy to match Rudy Hartono's record. **mem(per)-kan** compare s.t. **ter-kan** comparable. *tiada ~* incomparable, beyond compare. **-an** 1 comparison. *Tak ada ~nya* There is no comparison. *~ tetap* constant proportion. 2 (*Leg.*) appeal. 3 criticism. **pem-** 1 standard of comparison. *Universitas Airlangga jadi ~ banyak universitas di Jawa Timur* Airlangga University has become a standard for many universities in E. Java. 2 discussant. **pem-an** process of comparing. *Dgn adanya ~, kita bisa menilai* We are in a position to make evaluations because of the existence of a procedure for making comparisons. **per-an** 1 comparison. *ilmu bahasa ~* comparative linguistics. 2 proportion, ratio, scale. *~ kelamin* sex ratio. *~ kekuatan* balance of power. *~ nilai* rate of exchange, rate of equation. 3 example. 4 (*Leg.*) appeal.

bandit 1 gangster, bandit. *- picisan* small-fry hoodlum. 2 scoundrel, villain. **mem-** commit a heinous crime. **ke-an** banditry, gangsterism.

banditisme 1 banditry, highway robbery. 2 mentality characterized by thoughtless commercial exploitation of the public.

bando k.o. large headscarf, us. silk. *Gadis itu memakai - melingkari rambutnya* The girl wore a scarf around her hair.

bandong see BENDUNG.

bandos a sweet tidbit made of cassava.

bandosa see BENDOSA.

bandot 1 billy goat. 2 lascivious old man. 3 womanizer, ladies' man.

bandrék see BANDERÉK₁. → **bandrék** see BANDERÉK$_1$.

bandrol see BANDEROL.

bandul 1 pendulum. *- loncéng* clapper (of a bell). 2 hanger. **mem-** 1 swing. *Tentara payung ~ di langit* The paratroopers were swinging in the air. 2 hang. *Ada sarang ~ di ranting pohon itu* A nest is hanging on that tree branch. **mem-i** counterbalance, offset. **-an** 1 pendulum. 2 hanger. *~ pemberat* hanger to increase weight. 3 swing. 4 (*Coll.*) testicles.

bandung pair, set, duo. **se-** 1 twin. *Ia ~ dgn sdrnya* She is o. of twins. 2 pair, set. *~ permata dimuat di cincin mas* A pair of jewels was mounted in a gold ring.

bandut cord, string, twine. **mem-** 1 tie together, join together. 2 patch up. **pem-** 1 strap, band. 2 string, twine, cord.

bang₁ sound of a bang.

bang₂ 1 muezzin's call to prayer. 2 call others to prayer. *Tadi ia sdh -* A moment ago he recited the call to prayer.

bang₃ see BANK.

bang₄ see ABANG₁.

bangai ter- 1 neglected. *Rumahnya ~* Her house was neglected. 2 given up, abandoned. *Pekerjaannya ~ karena kekurangan ongkos* His work was given up because of lack of funds.

bangar see BANGER.

bangat₁ fast, quick, soon. **ber-** hasten. **mem-kan** quicken, speed s.t. up.

bangat₂ see BANGET.

bangau white egret, tufted heron. *- air* blue heron. *Setinggi-tinggi terbang - surutnya ke kubangan juga* No matter how high the heron flies, he always returns to his nest, i.e. o. cannot escape o.'s background or origins.

bangbong sound of an empty barrel when struck.

bangdés [*pembangunan desa*] rural development.

banger stinking, rotten (odor).

banget (*Jv*) very, excessively. *besar -* very big. *Akur -!* I heartily agree! **ke-an** excessively, terribly, overly.

bangga rightfully proud. *Ia - akan anaknya* She is proud of her child. **ber-, mem-(²)** be proud. **mem-(²)kan** 1 make s.o. proud. *Anak itu ~ ayahnya* The child made his father proud. 2 be proud of. *Ia dpt ~ kudanya* She can be proud of her horse. **ke-an** s.t. o. is (rightly) proud of. *Istana itu pernah menjadi ~ seluruh Palopo* That palace was once the pride of all Palopo.

bangir (*Jv*) pointed (of nose).

bangka tough and stiff (of rug, etc.).

Bangkahulu see BENGKULU.

bangkai 1 carcass, carrion. 2 (*Derog.*) corpse. *Ia menjemur - ke atas bukit* He laid his corpse on the hilltop, i.e. he was exposed to shame. 3 (*Av.*) fuselage (of a crashed plane). *- kapal* remains of sunken or beached ship. *- mobil* wrecked car. **mem-** become a carcass, deteriorate. *tempat bisbis ~* where old buses rot away.

bangkang mem- rebel, resist, oppose. *Ia tdk ~ thd pemerintah* He did not rebel against the gvt. **mem-i** rebel against, resist s.t. *Ia sengaja ~ ajaran-ajaran agama* He purposely rebelled against the doctrines of religion. **pem-** 1 rebel, resister, dissident. 2 intractable person, insubordinate person. **pem-an** 1 insubordination, disobedience, rebelliousness. *~ sipil* civil disobedience. 2 protest.

bangkar 1 tough and stiff, coarse. 2 rigid. 3 rigor mortis, rigidity. 4 rough to the touch. **mem-** 1 become tough and stiff. 2 become rigid.

bangkerut see BANGKRUT.

bangkés see BANGKIS.

bangkét₁ banquet.

bangkét₂ k.o. fancy cookie.

bangking see BUNGKANG.

bangkir see BONGKAR.

bangkis sneeze. **ber-(²)** sneeze.

bangkit 1 get up from seated or prone position. *Ia - dr duduk* He got up from a sitting position. **2** come up. *- perasaan benci thd gurunya* A feeling of strong dislike for his teacher arose. *Angin -* The wind came up. *Penyakit sampar sdh - lagi di daérah saya* The plague has reappeared in my area. *Matahari -* The sun rose. **3** be revived, resuscitated. *Stl sebentar pingsan ia -* After losing consciousness for a moment, he revived. *Disangka mati lemas, tahu-tahu - juga dia* Everyone thought he had drowned but he came to after all. **ber- 1** rise, get up. **2** break out (of epidemic, etc.). **mem- 1** arouse, inspire, instigate. *Ia ~ ketakutan di kalangan siswa* He inspired fear among the pupils. **2** rise up, come alive. *Seléra ~* His appetite picked up. **mem-kan 1** raise, resurrect. **2** arouse, provoke, awaken. *Anjuran itu ~ perasaan bersatu* That proposal aroused a feeling of unity. *~ gairah* arouse desire. **3** generate (energy). *Mesin baru itu ~ tenaga listrik utk seluruh kota* The new generator produces electricity for the whole city. **mem-²kan** dig up. *Apa guna ~ hal yg tlh liwat?* Why dig up the past? **ke-an 1** resurgence, rise. *~ negeri-negeri Asia* resurgence of many Asian countries. *Hari ~ Nasional* Day of National Resurgence, May 20, commemorating the early nationalist movement. **2** resurrection, awakening. *~ kembali* renaissance, revival. **-an 1** s.t. that has been resurrected from the past. **2** attack (of flu, etc.). **3** production, generation (of energy). **pem- 1** generator. *~ tenaga listerik* electric power station, electric generator. *~ tenaga nuklir* nuclear power plant. **2** instigator, initiator, motivating force. *~ seléra* appetizer. **pem-an** generation (of energy).

bangkong k.o. large frog.

bangkot, bangkotan (*Jv*) **1** old, advanced in age. **2** old and cantankerous.

bangkrut bankrupt. **mem-kan** cause s.o. or s.t. to become bankrupt. **ke-an** bankruptcy, default.

bangku bench, seat. *- geréja* pew. *- kaki* footstool. *kawan se-* classmate (seated on same school bench). *- komuni* (*Rel.*) communion rail.

bangkuang, bangkuwang k.o. juicy tuber.

banglas vast, extensive (of a view).

banglé see BENGLÉ.

banglo see BUNGALO.

bango see BANGAU.

bangor naughty, annoying.

bangsa 1 nation, people, race. *- bahari* seafaring people. *Ia - Indonésia* She is Indonesian. *- banténg* fighting, struggling nation. *bunga -* fallen soldier. *- cacing* an inferior or meek people. *- kintel* an inferior or insignificant people. *- négro* black race, the blacks. *- témpé* 1 an inferior class of people. **2** weak nation. *- terbelakang* 1 a backward people. **2** underdeveloped nation. *- tutul* fighting (struggling) nation. *- yg sedang berkembang/membangun* developing nation. **2** family, breed, category, sex. (*Biol.*) order. *Héwan yg menggigit itu - kucing* The animal that bit was a feline. *- déwék* compatriots. *- kerdil* 1 pygmy.

2 defeatist. **3** (*Derog.*) Japanese. *- raja* royal family. **3** class, group, type. *Ia bukan dr - yg tinggi di masyarakatnya* He was not from an eminent social class. *pesawat terbang - pelémpar* bomber-type plane. **se- 1** of o. nationality. *Meréka adalah ~ dan setanah air* They are fellow nationals. **2** a type of, a species of. *Padi adalah ~ rumput* The rice plant is a k.o. grass. **ber- 1** have a nation. *Kami putera dan puteri Indonésia mengakui ~ satu, ~ Indonésia* We sons and daughters of Indonesia acknowledge that we are o. nation. **2** be of noble birth. **3** be related to. *Ia ~ kpd isterinya* She is related to his wife. **ke-an 1** nationality. **2** nationalism, nationalist. *pergerakan ~* nationalist movement. **3** national. *lagu ~* national anthem. **berke-an** have the nationality. *seorg ahli ilmu bahasa ~ Jerman* a linguist of German nationality.

bangsai 1 rotten. *Kayunya -* The wood is rotten. **2** fragile, brittle. **3** thin, frail.

bangsal 1 shed, warehouse (of wood). *- lokomotip* roundhouse. *- pengeringan* drying shed. **2** public building. *- pertemuan* meeting hall. *- olahraga* gymnasium. **3** market stalls. **4** ward (in hospital). **5** emergency housing, lean-to.

bangsat 1 (*Derog.*) scoundrel, rascal. *- kau!* You s.o.b.! **2** (*Jkt*) poor person, pauper. **3** bedbug. **ke-an** hooliganism, rowdyism, ruffianism.

bangsawan₁ 1 noble, of nobility. **2** nobility. **3** o. who is not punctual, comes late to work. **ke-an** nobility, aristocracy.

bangsawan₂ k.o. drama, often with singing based on European or Arabian themes.

bangsawati noblewoman.

bangsi k.o. bamboo lute.

bangun 1 wake up. *Ia -, tdk dpt tidur* He woke up, he could not sleep. *- siang* sleep in, sleep late. *- tidur* arise from sleep. **2** get up. *Ia duduk dan - lagi* She sat down and got up again. **3** rise (of dough). **4** structure, form. *Indah sekali - rumah itu* The structure of the house is very beautiful. *- mukanya spt org barat* His face is the shape of a Westerner's. *- bawah* foundation. **5** model, type. *Mobil ini - 1958* This is a 1958 model car. **se-** uniform, unvarying. *~ dgn* same as. **ber-** get up, rise. **ber-an** have a certain k.o. building or construction. *Di jalan ini banyak rumah yg ~ modél Belanda* This street has lots of houses constructed in the Dutch style. **mem- 1** build, construct, pay. *Kejahatan tdk ~* Crime does not pay. **2** develop. *~ industri nasional* develop a national industry. *kecaman ~* constructive criticism. *negara yg sedang ~* developing nations. **3** rise. *Asap ke langit* Smoke rose to the sky. **mem-i** (*Jv, Coll.*) repeatedly build. *Buat apa sih pemerintah ~ pertokoan terus* What is the point of the gvt.'s continually building shopping complexes? **2** awaken, wake up s.o. *Dia lupa ~ saya kemarén* He forgot to wake me up yesterday. **mem-kan 1** wake s.o. up. **2** build, erect, construct. *~ rumah yg roboh itu* rebuild the collapsed house. **3** build up (a country). **4** shape, fashion. *Ia ~ anak-*

anakan dr tanah liat She fashioned a doll from clay. **5** constitute, make up. *Sél-sél dan jaringan-jaringan ~ makhluk hidup* Cells and tissues make up a living creature. **6** arouse, excite. *~ semangat* arouse enthusiasm. **ter-** **1** awaken (suddenly). *Ia ~ pd tengah malam* He was awakened in the middle of the night. **2** become aware, come to o.'s senses. *Stlh berlumuran dgn dosa, ia tersadar dan ~* After wallowing in his sins, he woke up and came to his senses. **3** be constructed, created. **ke-an** **1** awakening. *~ bangsa-bangsa jajahan* the awakening of the colonial peoples. **2** insurrection, uprising. **3** renaissance, resurgence, revival. *~ rohani* spiritual revival. **-an** **1** building, structure. **2** construction. *~ liar* illegal construction, squatters' buildings. **3** installation. *~ militér* military installation. **4** scaffolding. **5** building (of character). *~ air* waterworks. *~ jembatan air* aqueduct. *~ atas* superstructure. **-²an** **1** buildings, structures, edifices. **2** mock-up model. **3** scaffolding. **pem-** builder, constructor. **pem-an** **1** (re)construction. **2** development. *rencana ~* development plan. *~ diri* self-development. **3** foundation, establishment.

bangus (*Jv*) snout.

bani (*Rel.*) children of, descendants of. *- Adam* descendants of Adam.

baning k.o. tortoise.

banir buttress root.

banjang (*Jv*) fishing platform.

banjar₁ **1** line, row, series. *- pulau* series of islands. **2** train of events. **se-** of the same row, line, series. **ber-(²), ber-an** form a line, line up. *Murid-murid ~ menurut kelas masing-masing* The students formed rows according to their respective classes. **mem-kan** line up, arrange in rows. **-an** line, row, file. *~ bukit* range of hills.

banjar₂ (*Bali*) hamlet association, neighborhood organization.

banji lattice work (as in wall decorations), motif in form of a swastika.

banjir **1** flood, deluge. *Ada - besar ssdh hujan itu* There was a big flood after that rain. **2** flood, overflow. *Sungai -* The river overflowed. *- bandang* flash flood. **mem-** **1** in floods, in a large quantity. **2** rush en masse. *Laki-laki yg banyak itu ~ ke tempat pencuri itu jatuh* That mob of men surged toward where the thief fell. **mem-i** **1** flood, inundate (an area). **2** flood, swamp, overwhelm. *Barang-barang ini ~ pasar Jkt* These goods are flooding Jkt's markets. *Nénék ~nya dgn pertanyaan* Grandmother swamped him with questions. **ke-an** **1** flooded, inundated. *Negeri Belanda ~ air laut* Holland was inundated by the seawater. **2** overwhelmed. *Keluarga yg melarat itu ~ beras dan barang-barang kaléngan* The poor families were overwhelmed with rice and canned goods. **pem-an** flooding, inundating, deluging (of the market).

banjur sprinkle, pour. **mem-i** sprinkle, pour on s.t. **mem-kan** sprinkle s.t. on.

bank /bang/ bank, financial body. *- 46 o. of the*

national savings banks. *- beroda/keliling* bank on wheels, mobile bank. *- dagang* commercial bank. *- devisa* foreign exchange bank. *- hipoték* mortgage bank. *- pasar* bank specializing in small, low-interest loans to petty traders. *- séntral* currency-issuing bank. *- sirkulasi* bank of issue. *- tabungan* savings bank. **per-an** banking.

bankét see BANGKÉT₂.

bankir **1** banker. **2** moneylender.

Banpol [*Pembantu Polisi*] auxiliary police.

Banprés [*Bantuan Présidén*] special presidential aid.

bansai (*Japanese*) long live!

bantah say in disagreement. *"Tapi wanita itu!" -nya* "But that woman!" he objected. *- bentoh* quarrel, squabble. **ber-** **1** remonstrate. **2** quarrel, argue, dispute. *Tetangga kami ~ sepanjang hari* Our neighbors quarrel all day long. **ber-(²)an** quarrel with e.o. *Itu amat ~ dgn prinsipku* That is very much in conflict with my principles. *- mem-* dispute with e.o. **mem-** be opposed, be disputatious. *Dilarang ~ dan menentang* It is forbidden to be contentious and rebellious. **mem-i** **1** argue with, contest, refute, deny. *Ia ~ kebenaran kabar itu* He contested the accuracy of that report. *Kabar ini ~ kabar tadi pagi* This news report contradicts this morning's. **2** oppose, protest. *Kau ~ setiap kata suamimu* You protest your husband's every word. **mem(per)-kan** **1** dispute, argue over. **2** debate, discuss (heatedly). *Meréka ~ soal politik* They debated political matters. **ter-kan** subject to complaint. *Cepat ~ hal itu, kan?* That matter was quickly the object of protest, wasn't it? *tak ~* irrefutable, incontrovertible. **-an** **1** protest, objection. **2** contradiction. **3** back talk. **4** protestation. **pem-** disputant. **pem-an** rebuttal. **per-an** **1** quarrel, dispute, argument. **2** conflict.

bantai **1** butcher. **2** beat up severely. **mem-** **1** slaughter, butcher. **2** finish up. **ter-** butchered. **-an** **1** butcher's block. **2** slaughterer. *lembu ~* beef cattle. **pem-** butcher. **pem-an** **1** abattoir. **2** butchering, slaughtering. *~ org-org désa ini sdh dilupakan org* People have forgotten the butchering of these villagers.

bantal pillow, cushion. *- angin* air cushion. *- guling* bolster, Dutch wife. *- kembung* round pillow. *- listrik* (*Chem.*) heated stand (for beakers, etc.). *- mampung* a light cushion. *- peluk* bolster, Dutch wife. *- peniti* pincushion. *- pipih* flat pillow. *- sandar* back of seat, pillow for propping s.o. up. *- téko* tea cozy. *- tikar* belongings. **ber-** **1** sleep with s.o. or share s.o.'s bed. **2** use as a pillow. *Ia tidur ~ gulungan koran* He slept using rolled-up newspapers for a pillow. **ber-kan** use as a pillow. *~ paha ibu* with her head resting on her mother's thigh. *~ kedua belah tangan* pillowed on both his hands. **mem-i** **1** provide with a pillow. **2** pillow, support with s.t. *~ kepala anaknya pd* pillow her child's head on. **mem-kan, memper-(kan)** use as a pillow, cushion. *Ia merebahkan badannya dan ~ lengannya* He threw himself down and used his arm as a pillow. **-an 1** (pin) cushion. **2** underpinning. ~ *rél (R.R.)* tie. **3** bolster, cushion, pillow. ~ *gulung/peluru/poros* ball bearing. ~ *stémpel* stamp pad. ~ *udara* air cushion.

bantam (*Sport*) bantam weight.

bantang see BUNTUNG.

bantar (*Med.*) present (illness).

bantaran (*Geog.*) flood plain.

bantat not well done, partially cooked (of bread, etc.).

banténg the wild ox of Java. *bagai - ketaton* with great bravery or fierceness (like a wounded ox). *Pasukan kami bertempur bagai - ketaton* Our troops fought fiercely. *massa -* supporters of the Nationalist party (whose election symbol was the wild bull).

banter 1 fast, quick, speedy. *paling -* at most, at the worst. *Paling - ia akan meléwati seratus mil dgn ban yg sdh tua itu* At most he will cover 100 miles with that old tire. **2** loud, projects or carries well (of voice).

banteras see BERANTAS.

banting throw down forcefully. *- stir* change directions sharply. **mem-** *stir* **1** veer sharply. *Ia ~ stir ke kanan ketika melihat anak lari memotong jalan* He turned the wheel sharply to the right when he saw the child running across the street. **2** change directions (in o.'s politics, opinion, attitudes). **mem-stirkan** turn s.t. sharply. **pem-an** *stir* sharp change of political direction away from the W. (proposed by Sukarno). **ber-an** swirl around (of a stream against rocks). **mem-1** throw, fling. *Ia ~ gadis itu ke tanah* He threw the girl to the ground. *Jangan di-!* Handle with care! **2** strike (downward) violently. *Ibunya ~ cuciannya pd batu* His mother beat the laundry on a stone. ~ *harga* slash prices. ~ *kaki* stamp the foot. ~ *otak* rack o.'s brains. ~ *pintu* slam a door. ~ *tulang* do all in o.'s power, make every effort, do o.'s utmost, exert o.s. to the fullest, apply o.s. fully. *Meréka ~ tulang utk menyekolahkan anaknya* They did everything in their power to send their children to school. **mem-²1** rattle, shake. *Mobil truk itu ~ di jalan* The truck rattled along the road. **2** keep tossing up and down. *Karena ombak besar kapal ~* Because of the big waves the boat kept tossing. **mem-kan 1** slam. *Pintu ku-kan sekuat tenaga* I slammed the door as hard as I could. **2** smash, throw down. *Ia lari ke pojok kamar dan ~ diri* She ran to the corner of the room and threw herself down. *Ombak bergulung hampir ~ tubuhnya ke dasar laut* The crashing waves almost slammed his body to the bottom of the sea. ~ *kaki* stomp. **ter-** struck, knocked to the ground. **ter-²** beaten, thrashed (as by waves). *Truk itu ~ di jalan yg berlubang-lubang itu* The truck was tossed around on a pot-holed road. **ke-** (*Coll.*) accidentally thrown down forcefully. **-an 1** beating. ~ *rantai di ubin* the rattling of chains on the floor-tiles. **2** steep reduction (in price). **3** (sudden) shock or swaying. **pem-an 1** drastic reduction (of prices). **2** blow, shock. ~

harga sharp reduction of prices. ~ *tenaga/tulang* exertion of energy.

bantu 1 assist. *Tetangga sebelah turut - memegangkan dia* The next-door neighbors also helped to hold him down. **2** auxiliary. *kata kerja -* auxiliary verb. **ber-an** receive aid. *sekolah ~* a school with gvt. subsidy. **mem- 1** help, aid, assist. *Saya selalu ~ di rumah* I always help around the house. **2** support, back up. *Kita hrs ~ pemerintah* We must support the gvt. **mem(per)-kan 1** put at the service of, assign. *Pemerintah ~ seorg ahli ékonomi kpd panitia itu* The gvt. placed an economist at the service of the committee. **2** assign, detail. *Létkol itu diper-kan kpd staf* The lieutenant-colonel was detailed to the staff. **-an** aid, help, assistance. ~ *luar negeri* foreign aid. ~ *hukum* legal assistance. ~ *krédit* loan assistance. ~ *moral/moril* moral support. ~ *peradilan* legal assistance. ~ *téknis* technical assistance. *- tembakan* (*Mil.*) fire support. ~ *uang* financial support. ~ *udara* (*Mil.*) air support. **pem- 1** helper, assistant. ~ *utama* chief aide. ~ *bupati* assistant to the bupati. ~ *dékan* deputy dean. ~ *gubernur* assistant to the governor. ~ *létnan* (*Mil.*) warrant officer, 2d lieutenant, ensign. ~ *menteri* assistant to the minister. ~ *réktor* deputy president (university). ~ *tindak pidana* criminal accomplice. ~ *tukang cétak* printer's devil. **2** (domestic) servant. ~ *rumah tangga* domestic help. **3** (*Leg.*) accessory, accomplice. **4** stringer (in journalism). **pem-an** provision of assistance. **per-an** assignment, task.

bantun mem- 1 weed (yard). **2** extract, pull out (a tooth, etc.). **mem-i 1** extract o. by o. **2** weed thoroughly.

bantut blocked, aborted. **mem-** hinder, prevent. *Sénsur yg keras itu ~ perkembangan persuratkabaran* The severe censorship hindered the development of the newspaper industry. **mem-i** clog s.t. *Kotoran itu ~ got* Dirt clogged up the ditch. **ter- 1** stunted, thwarted (in growth). **2** stopped up, clogged up. **3** futile.

banyak₁ 1 many, much. *Bukunya -* He has many books. *- mobil di sini* There are many cars here. *Terima kasih -/ - terima kasih* Thanks very much. *- kali* frequently, often. *- mulut* loquacious, talkative. *- pikiran* much thought, worry, or concern. *- sedikitnya* 1 amount, extent. *- sedikitnya kerusakan* extent of the damage. **2** more or less. **2** have a lot of s.t. *Ia - anak* He has a lot of children. **3** excessively. *Ia - menangis* He cries a lot. **4** in great quantities. *Ia - membeli buku* She bought many books. **-nya 1** amount, quantity. ~ *beras terbatas* The quantity of rice is limited. *menurut ~* quantitatively. **2** number. ~ *org di toko itu dua puluh* The number of people in the shop was 20. **-² very** much, do s.t. much or often. **se-** as many as, as much as, amounting to. ~ *itu kantor-kantor yg kumasuki, inilah yg paling cocok* Of all the offices I have entered, this is the o. most suitable. *Uangnya ~ itu* His money amounted to that much. **se-²nya** as much or many as possible. **ber-²** in great numbers. *Org kota ~ pergi ke désa mencari* *makanan* City people went to the village in great numbers in search of food. *makan buah-buahan* ~ eat great quantities of fruit. **mem-** increase. *Prajurit kian* ~ The number of soldiers swelled all the more. **mem(per)-(i)** increase, raise (wages, etc.). *Kita hrs* ~ *pengiriman mahasiswa ke luar negeri* We have to increase the number of students sent abroad. *diper-* *terima kasih* many thanks. **mem(per)-kan 1** (*Math.*) multiply. **2** increase, augment. **3** reproduce, duplicate. **ter-1** the greatest number. *bagian* ~ *penduduk kota itu* the greater part of the city's inhabitants. **2** majority. *dgn suara* ~ by a majority vote. *rakyat* ~ common folk. **3** more. ~ *di sini drp di sana* There are more here than there. **ke-an 1** majority, the greater part. ~ *org di negeri Amérika mempunyai mobil* The majority of Americans own cars. **2** too much. ~ *tidur tdk baik* Too much sleep is not good. **3** ordinary. *Ia berasal dr keluarga org* ~ *saja* He is from just an ordinary family. *org* ~ the man in the street. **-an** perhaps, possibly. **per-an 1** (*Math.*) multiplication. **2** increase.

banyak₂ (*Jv*) goose.

banyo banjo.

banyol 1 joke, jest, gag. **2** clown, jokester, wag. **3** rascal, scamp. **mem- 1** tell jokes. **2** play the clown, buffoon. **3** joke. **nge-** clown around. **-an** joker, jester, wag. ~ *Aprilan* April Fool's Day prank.

banyu bening (*Jv*) a high degree of spiritual enlightenment and peace. *nyecép* - absorb spiritual knowledge.

banzai see BANSAI.

bapa, bapak 1 father. - *angkat* foster father. - *ayam* unworthy father. - *badari* exploiter, o. who exploits his subordinates. - *besar* big shot, important personage. - *cilik/kecil* uncle (younger brother of father or mother). - *gedé* (*Jv*) uncle (father's eldest brother). - *guru* the teacher. - *kami!* (*Amb*) Good Lord! - *kualon* stepfather. - *mertua* father-in-law. - *muda* uncle (younger brother of father or mother). - *permandian* godfather. - *serani* (*Amb*) godfather. - *tiri* stepfather. - *tua* uncle (older brother of father or mother). **2** form of address to an older man, esp. as *pak*. *Mau ke mana, -?* Where to, Sir? **3** part of a respectful title, esp. as *pak*. - *Komandan Pasukan* commander of the forces. - *aljabar* algebra instructor. - *tani* peasant. **4** founder of a cause, movement. *Sukarno terkenal sbg - kemerdékaan* Sukarno is famous as the father of independence. **5** spiritual father. - *pengakuan* (*Rel.*) father confessor. - *suci* (*Rel.*) Holy Father, Pope. **-²1** fathers. **2** you gentlemen. **3** of an age to be a father. *O masih muda! Saya kira sdh* ~ Oh, you are still young! I thought you would be much older. **se-** having the same father but different mother. *Ia* ~ *dgn aku* He has the same father as me. ~ *seibu* children of the same parents. **ber- 1** have a father. *Ia tak* ~ *lagi* He no longer has a father. **2** call father. *Ia* ~ *kpd pamannya* She called her uncle father. **ke-an 1** fatherly, paternal. *sikap* ~

majikan the boss's fatherly attitude. **2** paternalistic. **per-an** fatherhood.

bapakisme /bapa'ism/ paternalism.

bapanda respectful form of address to o.'s father (esp. in letters).

bapao see BAKPAO.

Baperki [*Badan Permusyawaratan Kewarganegaraan Indonésia*] political movement of the 1950s and 1960s to integrate ethnic Ch into Indonesian society.

bapét 1 penniless, broke. **2** bad, wicked, rude.

baplang large and thick (of a moustache).

Bapparda [*Badan Pembangunan Pariwisata Daérah*] Regional Tourism Development Board.

Bappeda [*Badan Pembangunan Daérah*] Agency for Regional Development.

Bappenas [*Badan Perancang Pembangunan Nasional*] National Planning Board.

baptis 1 (*Rel.*) baptism. **2** the Baptist sect or adherent thereof. **mem-(kan) 1** baptize. *Seolah-olah aku di-kan msk ke dunia baru* It was as if I had been baptized and entered a new world. **2** convert (to Christianity). **-an** baptism. **pem-** baptist. **pem-an 1** baptizing. **2** christening.

Bapus [*Badan Penerangan Uni Soviét*] Information Agency of the Soviet Union (common in cities until mid-1960s).

baqa see BAKA₁.

bar bar, cocktail lounge.

bara 1 ember, live coal. - *api* ember. - *halus* coal dust. **2** heat, warmth. **3** fire, fervor. **mem- 1** be aglow, smoulder. **2** blaze, burn. *berkat semangatnya yg* ~ thanks to his glowing enthusiasm. **mem-kan 1** set ablaze. **2** illuminate. **3** inflame, excite. **pem-an** the burning of s.t. **per-an** brazier, hearth, furnace.

bara bahara ballast.

baragajul see BERGAJUL.

barah boil, abscess. **mem-** fester, become abscessed.

barak 1 barracks. **2** quarantine quarters. **mem-** quarantine, segregate. *Karena penyakit yg menular itu ia di-* Because of his contagious disease he was quarantined.

barakah blessed. **ke-an** bliss, blessedness.

baran swampy forest.

barang₁ 1 goods, commodity. - *andalan* security guarantee. - *angkutan* freight goods. - *bergerak* moveables, chattels. - *curah* bulk goods. - *gelap* contraband goods. - *hantaran* goods to be delivered. - *impor* imported article. - *jadi* finished products. - *kerajinan* handcrafted article. - *kumango* sundries, toiletries. - *légoan* articles bought in quantity. - *lepas* bulk articles. - *loakan* secondhand goods. - *lux/méwah* luxury item. - *makanan* foodstuffs. - *mindringan* goods sold on an installment plan of daily payments. - *modal* inventory, stock. - *tanggungan* security, warranty. - *tangkapan* confiscated goods. - *tenun* textiles. **2** article, object. - *batil* prohibited objects. - *bukti* (*Leg.*) material evidence. - *cair* liquid. - *cétakan* printed matter. - *ékstraktif* extractive. - *galian* mineral. - *kemas* object of value. - *keras* pistol. - *mati* inanimate object. - *pecah* s.t fragile. - *pecahan* table service, china. - *purbakala* antiquities. - *pusaka* heirloom. - *rampokan* loot, booty. - *rombéngan* rummage, trash. - *sekali pakai* article used once then disposed of. - *seni* art object. *sdh - tentu* for certain, positively, positive fact. *Bhw ia seorg kaya, itu sdh - tentu* That he is a wealthy man is a fact. - *tak bergerak* immovables. - *tambang* minerals. - *tanah* earthenware, pottery. - *tetap* real estate. - *tiruan* 1 reproduction. 2 imitation. *Awas - tiruan* Beware of imitations. - *tontonan* s.t. to be gawked at. - *tuangan* cast-iron article. 3 (*Coll.*) s.t. whose direct mention should be avoided (i.e. marijuana, genitals, etc.). *-nya kelihatan!* You could see his whatsis (genitals)! 4 baggage, luggage. -² 1 belongings. 2 goods, commodities. ~ *amanat*, ~ *bersyarat konsinyasi* goods on consignment. 3 matter. *Berhutang adalah ~ yg biasa bagi org itu* Accumulating debts is a common matter for that person.

barang₂ any. - *apa* anything, whatever. - *apa yg diceriterakannya selalu benar* Whatever she said was true. - *bila* whenever. - *bila ia ingin pergi selalu jatuh hujan* Whenever he wanted to go it always rained. - *di mana* wherever, anywhere. - *di mana kita pergi* Wherever we go. - *kala* whenever. - *kala ia berkata, semua turut* Whenever he speaks, everyone listens. - *ke mana* to wherever. - *org* anyone. - *org pergi ke sana mesti dirampok* Anyone who went there was sure to be robbed. - *sesuatu* anything, everything. - *sesuatu yg dibawanya mesti diperiksa oléh polisi* Everything he brought had to be inspected by the police. - *siapa* anyone, whoever. *siapa mau msk ke paberik itu mesti membawa keterangan* Anyone who wishes to enter that factory must have an ID. **se-(an), sem-(an)** any old, just any. *Bukan ~ org diundang pd pertemuan itu* Not just anyone was invited to that meeting. ~ *waktu* at any time. **se-²** nothing, a trifle. *Mintanya bukan ~* It is not a trifle he is requesting.

barang₃ more or less, approximately. *Pergi beli jeruk dulu - lima biji* First go and buy some oranges, say about five. *Ia boléh menunggu di sana - setahun* He can wait there for more or less a year. *Meréka masih punya waktu - sejam menunggu* They may have another hour or so to wait. - . . . *.pun* not even . . . *Ia tak pernah - satu malam pun di sini* He has never been here, not even for a single night. - *sedikit* a little. - *sekali* one time.

barangan see BERANGAN₁.

barang-barang may it happen that, would that. ~ *luluslah ia dlm ujiannya itu* May she pass her exam.

barangkali perhaps, maybe. *Org tak menyukainya* Maybe people did not like him.

baras leprosy.

barat 1 west. - *daya* S.W. - *laut* N.W. 2 western, occidental. **mem-** go west(ward). **mem-kan** Westernize. **ke-²an** be like a Westerner. *Wajahnya mirip org Arab dan sedikit ~* His face was s.t.

like an Arab's and a bit like a Westerner's. **peman** Westernization.

barau-barau k.o. bird, the yellow-crowned bulbul.

barbar barbarian.

barbarisme barbarism.

barbir barber (in expensive hotels, posh salons).

barbur 1 splash, spill. *Org mandi - di air* People were bathing and splashing noisily in the water. 2 waste. *Ia - dgn uangnya* He is wasting his money.

barél barrel, a measurement for petroleum.

bareng (*Jv*) with, together with. *Ia pergi - ibunya* She went with her mother. -² together. *Meréka teriak ~* They screamed together. **ber-** 1 together. *Mari kita ~* Let us go together. 2 at the same time. *Ia dilahirkan ~ dgn kematian ayahnya* He was born at the time of his father's death. **ber-an** 1 together with, accompanied by. 2 at the same time. ~ *dgn diterimanya kabar itu, mobilnya ketabrak* At the same time he got that news, his car was in a collision. 3 coincide. **mem-i** 1 accompany. *ledakan membahana di-i réntétan tembakan* an echoing explosion accompanied by rapid fire. 2 be close to, be proximate to. *Suamiku ~ perawat di méja réstoran* My husband sat with a nurse at a restaurant table. **mem-kan** synchronize. **se-an** o. who accompanies. *Dia teman ~ saya waktu ke Jkt* He went with me when I went to Jkt. **pem-an** synchronization.

bares -²an honest, straightforward.

barét₁ beret. - *mérah* nickname for army commandos.

barét₂ 1 laceration, scratch, abrasion. 2 lacerated, scratched. **ter-** scratched.

bari see BAHARI₂.

bari-bari fruitfly.

barik-barik 1 grain (in wood). 2 vein (in marble). 3 spotted, speckled (of eggshell). **ber-** veined, grained.

barikade barricade. **mem-** obstruct with barricades. *Seluruh kota di- bersiap-siap menghadapi serangan musuh* The whole city was barricaded in preparation for the enemy attack.

baring₁ lie down. *Aku - agak jauh drnya* I lay down a bit of a distance from him. *Ia bangkit dr -nya* She got up from her prone position. **ber-** 1 lie down. *Ia ~ di bawah pohon* He is lying under a tree. 2 be stretched out (in a lounge chair). 3 be in bed (in hospital). **ber-²** relax, loll about in a lying position. *Sambil ~ kami bercerita terus* As we lounged, we continued to talk. **ber-an** be lying alongside e.o. **mem-i** lie on s.t. **mem-kan** put to bed, place on a bed. *Wanita itu ~ anaknya di tempat tidur* That woman put her child on the bed. *Jenazah di-kan* The body was laid out. ~ *diri* stretch out (on a bed). **ter-** lie, be stretched out. *Org tua itu ~ di tanah* The old man lay stretched out on the ground. **-an** rest, nap. *Aku cuma mau ~* I just want to lie down and rest a bit. **pem-an** bed, couch.

baring₂ **mem-** take a bearing. **-an** (*Naut.*) bearing.

baris₁ 1 row. *Tempat saya di - pertama* My place was in the first row. **2** line. *Mulailah dgn - baru spy mudah membacanya* Begin a new line so it will be easy to read. *- kembar* hyphen, dash. *- kepala* running title. **3** line, queue. **4** ranks. **5** slide rule. **6** (*Mil.*) drill. **7** verse. **ber- 1** form a line (of trees, etc.). **2** march. *Meréka ~ ke rumah jénderal* They marched to the general's house. **3** line up, form a queue. *~ membeli karcis* form a queue to buy tickets. **4** (*Mil.*) to drill. *Meréka ~ di lapangan* They were drilling on the field. *~ keluar* exit in line. **ber-² line** up, be in line. **mem-** form a line, line up. *Pengungsi-pengungsi ~ di muka Kantor Palang Mérah* the refugees lined up in front of the Red Cross Office. **mem-kan 1** line s.t. up. *Wasit itu ~ kesebalasan-kesebalasan* The referee lined up the soccer teams. **2** arrange in rows, series. *Di-kannya daun-daun yg tlh dilajur di lantai* He straightened the leaves in rows on the floor. **3** (*Mil.*) drill a group. *Opsir itu ~ pasukan* The officer drillled his troops. **-an 1** ranks. *dlm ~* in the ranks. *~ belakang* **1** rear echelon. **2** rear guard. **3** (*Sport*) backs (soccer). *~ depan* front line. *~ kehormatan* honor guard. *~ musik* marching band. *~ pemadam api/kebakaran* fireman, firefighter. *~ pengawal* escort platoon. **2** front. *~ Nasional* National Front. **3** row, organized arrangement. *~ pohon karét* row of rubber trees. *~ buku* row of books. *~ truk* fleet of trucks. *~ tiang* colonnade.

baris₂ (*Bali*) k.o. male dance.

barit messenger who delivers letters.

bariton baritone.

barjah see BARZAKH.

barkas k.o. small steamship.

barokah see BARAKAH.

barométer barometer.

baron baron.

barong₁ national dress of Filipino men.

barong₂ (*Bali*) k.o. dance with mask.

barongan (*Jv*) folk entertainment featuring performer dressed as monster.

barongsai lion dance us. performed on Ch New Year.

baros₁ (*Jv, Sd*) k.o. tropical magnolia.

baros₂ see BERUAS.

barter barter. **mem-** barter, exchange.

baru₁ 1 new, recent. *Ia masih - di sini* He is still new here. **2** modern. *kesusasteraan -* modern literature. **3** fresh. *daging -* fresh meat. **4** just, only so much up to now. *Uangnya - lima ribu* He has just got 5,000 (rupiah). **5** only now, just at a certain time. *- saja datang* just arrived. *Ia - kemarin datang di sini* He just arrived here yesterday. *- terima* just received. **6** not until, only then. *Ssdh kata itu ditulis - ia mengerti maksudnya* Not until the word was written down did he understand its meaning. *Petang hari -lah ia pulang* She did not return until the evening. *Kalau ada anggota parlemén yg mengantarkan - boléh* You may do it only if you are accompanied by a member of parliament. **7** be in the process of. *Ia - makan* He is eating. *Saya - mau pergi ketika kau msk* I was just about to leave when you came in. *-²* recent, just a minute ago. *~ ini* quite recently, of late. **mem-(per)-i 1** renew. *~ kontrak* renew a contract. **2** modernize, renovate, remodel. *~ pendapatnya ssdh datang dr Éropa* He brought his views up to date after his return from Europe. **3** refurbish, recast. **4** regenerate. **5** reform. *Penjahat itu ~ kehidupannya stl bébas dr penjara* The criminal reformed his life after his release from jail. **mem-kan** make over, make new. *~ sistém kerja* renovate the system of employment. **ter-** newest, latest (style, etc.). *plat ~ dr luar négeri* the latest foreign record. **ke-an 1** newness, inexperience. *Karena ~nya ia tak tahu apa yg dikerjakan lebih dulu* Because he was new he did not know what to do first. **2** novelty, innovation. **pem- 1** renewer, reformer. **2** innovator. **pem-an, per-an 1** renewal. *~ nomer mobil hrs dilakukan sblm tgl 31 Januari* Renewal of auto licenses must take place before January 31. **2** renovation. **3** reform. *~ masyarakat* social reform. **4** modernization. **5** innovation. **6** regeneration.

baru₂ k.o. tree of seashore with large yellow flowers, beach hibiscus.

baruh lowlands.

Baruna Hindu god of the sea.

barung-barung 1 watchman's hut (in field or orchard). **2** stall, booth, stand. **3** hut, hovel.

barus see KAPUR.

barusan₁ (*Coll.*) just, just now. *- saja suami saya berangkat* My husband just left. *- ini* recently, of late.

barut₁ 1 bandage, dressing. **2** diaper. *- gantung/keréta* swaddling cloth. *- panjang* pregnancy girdle. **mem- 1** dress, bandage (a wound, etc.). **2** swathe, bind up (a baby). **pem-** bandage, dressing. **pem-an** bandaging, dressing (of wounds).

barut₂ mem- 1 scrub, clean, polish, wipe (floors, etc.). **2** grease (a pan).

barut₃ mem- scratch deeply. **ter-** be scratched.

barzakh (*Isl.*) the place and time between death and the Last Judgment.

barzanji (*Isl.*) chant recounting Muh.'s life, us. recited on 10th of *Muharram*.

bas₁ boss, foreman, overseer.

bas₂ 1 bass (voice). **2** double bass. **3** bass guitar.

bas₃ (*Chem.*) base.

basa₁ (*Chem.*) alkali. *- cair* (*Chem.*) liquid base. *asam dan -* acids and bases. **mem-kan** alkalize. **ke-an** alkalinity.

basa₂ see BAHASA₁.

basa-basi 1 good manners, courtesy, politeness. **2** conventional phrase of greeting, etc., conventionality. *Jumpailah beliau sekedar -, siapa tahu ada gunanya* Meet him just for the sake of courtesy, who knows it might be of some use. **ber-** be courteous.

basah 1 wet, soaked. *Tangannya - His hands are wet. - diri* be wringing wet after fever breaks. *- kuyup/lecap/léncong* soaking wet, wringing wet.

mem-kuyupi soak, inundate. **2** damp, moist. *Hawanya* - The weather is damp. *kué* - soft sweetmeat or cake (us. steamed or boiled). **3** fresh (not dried). *ikan* - fresh fish. **4** remunerative. *pekerjaan yg* - well-paying job. **ber-²** be soaking wet, wet through and through. **mem-** be(come) moist. *Matanya* ~ Her eyes became moist. **mem-i 1** wet, dampen, moisten. *Ia* ~ *handuknya* She dampened her towel. ~ *kerongkongan* wet o.'s whistle. ~ *diri* be wringing wet after fever breaks. **2** freshen. *Sesuatu yg samar* ~ *ingatanku pelan-pelan* S.t. obscure was slowly refreshing my memory. **mem-kan** moisten, dampen, (make) wet. *Air hujan* ~ *ladang yg kering itu* Rain water made the dry field wet. **ke-an 1** get soaked. **2** wetness, dampness. ~ *udara* humidity. **-an 1** s.t. to work in. *pakaian* ~ work clothes. **2** cloth wrapped around the body while bathing. *mandi tanpa* ~ bathe in the nude. **3** humidity. **pem-an 1** moistening, dampening. ~ *tanah pertanian* soaking of farmland. **2** (bed)wetting.

basal₁ 1 dropsy. - *api* erysipelas. **2** scab, scar.
basal₂ basalt.
basi₁ 1 spoiled, stale. *Nasinya sdh* - The rice is spoiled. **2** stale, out-of-date, not topical. *Kabar itu sdh* - The news is stale. *peraturan yg sdh* - outdated, ineffective regulations. **mem-kan** let spoil, let go to waste.
basi₂ 1 commission, fee. **2** overtime or extra pay. **3** reduction (in price), discount. **mem-** take a commission, give a discount.
basi₃ 1 bowl, dish. **2** serving dish. - *sup* soup tureen.
basi₄ see BASA-BASI.
basil bacillus, germ.
basis 1 basis, principle. **2** (*Mil.*) base. **ber-kan** have as a base. **pem-an** efforts to establish a base. ~*nya atas faktor-faktor yg kurang mendalam* basing o.s. on factors which are not substantial.
basit 1 all-embracing (of God). **2** (*Math.*) indivisible.
baskara sun (used in mottoes).
baskét (*Sport*) basketball.
baskom washbasin.
basmi mem- 1 exterminate (rodents, etc.). **2** eradicate, root out, eliminate (crime, etc.). *Polisi* ~ *pelacuran* The police wiped out prostitution. ~ *ketombé* get rid of dandruff. **3** burn off, clear by burning. *Meréka* ~ *hutan utk dijadikan ladang* They burned off the jungle in order to turn it into a field for cultivation. **ter-** eliminated, obliterated. *Komunis tdk akan* ~ *oléh kekuatan mana pun* Communism will not be eliminated by any force, no matter what. **pem-** eradicator, exterminator. **pem-an 1** eradication, extermination (of malaria, rodents, etc.). ~ *serangga* insect eradication. **2** removal, demolition (of slums).
baso see BAKSO.
basoka see BAZOKA.
bassdrum /bas dram/ bass drum.
bastar bastard. **mem-** interbreed. **-an** mixed descent. *anjing* ~ mutt, mongrel. **pem-an 1** cross-

breeding. *seléksi* ~ *berganda* multiple cross-breeding. **2** bastardization.
basuh washing. **mem- 1** wash (hands, clothes, dishes). **2** rinse. **pem- 1** cleansing material. *air* ~ *tangan* water for washing hands. ~ *balai (méja)* legal costs. ~ *dosa* pardoner of sins. ~ *mulut* dessert. ~ *tangan* gratuity, reward, recompense. **2** washer, washing machine. **3** o. who washes dishes. **pem-an** washing.
basuki (*Jv*) prosper, flourish.
basung₁ two dozen.
basung₂ mem- kick (a ball) high. **-an** high kick (of ball).
basung₃ corklike root.
bata concrete brick. *batu* - brick. - *emas* gold ingot or bar. - *garam* salt brick. - *genting* cinder block. - *jemuran* adobe.
bata-bata mem- ambivalent, unsettled, wavering. *Pikirannya dgn senulirinya* ~ His thoughts wavered involuntarily. **ter-, ke- 1** in bursts, haltingly (of speech). "*Jaya . . . Jaya di mana . . . nah?*" *tanyanya* ~ "Jaya, where is . . . Jaya . . . , son?" she asked haltingly. **2** hesitant, vacillating. *Meréka* ~ *menceritakan keadaan yg sesungguhnya* They were reluctant to tell the true story.
batak 1 hobo, vagabond. **2** soldier of fortune, adventurer. **mem- 1** rob, plunder, pillage. **2** wander, roam. **pem- 1** plunderer, pillager, robber. **2** soldier of fortune, adventurer.
Batak Batak (a people of N. Sumatra).
batako k.o. concrete brick (manufactured in a modern factory, not in a cottage industry).
batal 1 canceled, null and void. *Perjalanannya* - Her trip was canceled. **2** in vain. **3** invalid, invalidate. *Puasanya - stl ia minum* His fasting became invalid after he drank. **4** cancel out, omit. *Dia beli rokok tapi - beli buku* He bought cigarettes but changed his plan to buy books. **mem-kan 1** cancel, abrogate. *Ia* ~ *penerbangannya* He canceled his flight. ~ *cék* stop payment on a check. **2** revoke, rescind. *Ijazah sopirnya di-kan* His driver's license was revoked. **3** quash, nullify. **4** renounce, withdraw. *Meréka* ~ *tuduhan itu* They withdrew the charge. ~ *diri* forgo, give up the idea of. **ke-an** nullification. ~ *pertemuan itu berpangkal pd ketidaksepakatan* The failure to hold the meeting originated from disagreement. **pem-an 1** cancellation, abrogation. **2** annulment, renunciation. **3** abolition. **4** disqualification.
batalion, batalyon battalion.
batang 1 stem, stalk, blade (grass). - *padi* rice stalk. **2** stick, pole, shaft. - *air* tributary. - *arang* carbon. - *dacing* arm of a weigh-beam. - *dayung* oar handle. - *éngkol* connecting rod. - *hambatan* barrier. - *hari* **1** noon. **2** mainstream (of river). - *hidung* bridge of nose, tip of nose. - *kaki* leg. - *kalam* writing pen. - *kali* river. - *léhér* nape of the neck. - *lengan* arm. - *nadi* aorta. - *palong* cross beam. - *penggerak* rod, lever. - *pengungkit* crowbar. - *pengukur* rule(r), yardstick. - *sepéda* bicycle frame. - *tenggorok* trachea. - *terak* connecting

rod. - *tubuh* 1 torso, trunk. 2 body (of constitution excluding preamble and amendments). - *zakar* penis. 3 trunk. - *pohon* tree trunk. 4 classifier for oblong, cylindrical objects. *Tiga - coklat* three chocolate bars. *dua - potlot* two pencils. 5 (*Jv*) stem, handle. - *payung* umbrella handle. 6 corpse. -² (*Coll.*) go stag. se- a single (stick, bar, etc.). ~ *rokok* a single cigarette. ~ *besi* a bar of iron. ~ *kara* all alone in the world. ber- have a certain k.o. stem. ber-² by the bar, lots and lots of bars. mem- erect, become stiff. *Zakarnya* ~ He had an erection. -an 1 boom (in estuary or harbor). 2 barrier. 3 cross beam. 4 bar. ~ *emas* gold bar. 5 (sold) by the bar. 6 trunk. *Semuanya berlindung di balik* ~ *pohon* Everyone hid behind a tree trunk.

batara god, male deity. - *Kala* (*Jv*) divine ogre said to cause eclipses by swallowing the sun.

batari goddess, female deity.

batas 1 limit. - *kecepatan* speed limit. - *akhir* 1 extreme limit. 2 death, the end (of life). - *salju* snow line. - *tinggi* (*Av.*) ceiling. - *umur* age limit. - *waktu* deadline, time limit. *sampai pd - kesanggupannya* to reach the end of o.'s rope. 2 border, confine, boundary, limits. - *kota* city limits. *Pagar ini - halaman saya* This fence is the boundary of my yard. - *kesabaranku hilang* The limits of my patience were exceeded. *dlm - kesusilaan* within the bounds of decency. - *kata* (*Ling.*) word boundary. - *luar* outer limits. se- to the point or limit of. *Celananya digulung* ~ *lutut* His trousers were rolled up to his knees. ber- have a boundary. *tak* ~ boundless, limitless. ber-an border on, be adjacent to, be contiguous with, adjoining. *Negeri Birma* ~ *dgn Muangthai* Burma borders on Thailand. ber-kan have as a border. mem-i 1 form the boundary or border of. 2 limit, restrict. *Ia* ~ *perbelanjaannya* He limited his expenses. *Kita mesti* ~ *diri pd . . .* We must limit ourselves to . . . ~ *kelahiran* control the birthrate. 3 curb, curtail. mem(per)-kan limit, restrict. *Fokus studinya di-kan pd segi hukum* The focus of his study was limited to legal aspects. ter- limited, restricted. *Penjualan karcis itu sangat* ~ The sale of tickets was very restricted. *tak* ~ unlimited. keter-an limitedness, limits. -an 1 border, boundary. 2 limitation, restriction. 3 circumscription, definition, demarcation. *Apalah* ~ *anak pungut dan anak kandung?* So what is the difference between an adopted child and o.'s own flesh and blood? pem- 1 divider, circuit breaker. *Gordin digunakan sbg* ~ *ruang* A curtain was used as a space divider. *Inilah mélodi yg dominan, yg setiap kali terdengar kembali sbg* ~ *adegan* This is the dominant melody, repeated as a divider of the movements. 2 restraint (of trade). *faktor* ~ limiting factor. pem-an 1 restriction. 2 delimitation. 3 curtailment. ~ *kelahiran* birth control. ~ *diri* self-control. per-an border, division. ~ *és* (*Geol.*) ice line.

batau see BAKTAU.

baterai, bateré 1 dry-cell battery. 2 (*Mil.*) battery.

bathal see BATAL.

bathcup see BADKUIP.

bathil see BATIL₂.

bathin see BATIN.

bati (*Jv*) gain, profit. *Berapa -nya menjual kain itu?* How much profit do you make selling that material?

batih 1 o.'s household. 2 (nuclear) family.

batik₁ 1 batik. - *cap/cétak* printed batik. - *sandang* batik to wear, batik material for dresses. - *tulis* handmade batik. 2 batik work. mem- do batik work. mem-i apply a batik pattern on s.t. ~ *bagian-bagian yg tertentu* apply batik patterns on certain parts. mem-kan transform into batik. *Maka para pelukis pun makin rajin* ~ *keseniannya* Thus the painters too have produced more and more art in the medium of batik. pem- worker in batik. pem-an 1 batik work. 2 batik workshop.

batik₂ see BETIK₁.

batil₁ 1 copper bowl. 2 plate. 3 tray.

batil₂ 1 invalid, null and void. 2 false, wrong. *Korupsi adalah tindakan -* Corruption is an evil deed. 3 evil, bad. ke-an evil.

batin 1 inner, internal, spiritual. *Maaf lahir -* (*Isl.*) Forgive my sins, both those of the world and those within in me (a formula of greeting at the Isl. New Year). 2 mind, heart. *Dlm - ia mencurigai kawannya itu* In his heart he suspected his friend. *kekuatan -* moral force. *pertolongan -* moral support. *tekanan -* psychological strain or stress. 3 arcane, esoteric. ber- mull over. mem- say to o.s. *Saya menoléh kpdnnya dan dlm hati* ~*: anak-anak kok diadili* I looked at him and said to myself: why should a child be brought before the court? mem-kan keep to o.s., keep secret. ke-an 1 mysticism, spiritualism. 2 related to o.'s inner self. 3 spirit. pem-an interior meditations. *léwat cakapan,* ~ *tindak dan sikap* through discussion, meditation, acts and attitude.

batiniah spiritual, internal, moral.

batis batiste, cambric.

batkép see BADKUIP.

batok 1 coconut shell. - *kepala* skull. 2 dry measure, about a liter.

batu 1 stone. - *air* pebble. - *akik* k.o. gemstone. - *alam* natural stone. - *anggur* tartar. - *anting* pendulum (of clock). - *apung* pumice. - *arang* coal. - *aspal* stone with asphalt. - *badar* crystal. - *bara* coal. - *bara kilap* anthracite. - *bara kusam* cannel coal. - *bara pijar* live coals. - *beku* (*Geol.*) igneous rock. - *berani* magnet. - *bersurat/bertulis* epigraph, inscribed stone. - *besi* granite. - *bintang* meteorite. - *bulan* birthstone. - *cadas* rubble. - *canai* whetstone. - *catur* chessman. - *dacing* weights. - *dapur* hearthstone. - *darah* hematite. - *dasar* 1 foundation stone. 2 (*Geol.*) bedrock. - *duga* sounding lead. - *empedu* gallstone. - *endapan* sedimentary rock. - *gamping* limestone. - *geliga/guliga* bezoar. - *genténg* roof tiles. - *gerinda/gurinda* sandstone, whetstone. - *giling* millstone. - *ginjal* kidney stone. - *giok* jade. - *hampar* flagstone. - *hidup* magic stone. - *hitam* black hornblende. - *jemala* skull, cranium. - *kaca* obsidian. - *kail* sinker (for fishing line). - *kali* river stone or pebble. **mem-** *kali* refuse to talk. - *kambang* pumice. - *kapur* limestone. - *kawi* manganese. - *kecubung/kecumbung* amethyst. - *kencing* kidney stone. - *kepala* skull. - *kétel* tartar. - *kisaran* milkstone. - *kolar* pebble. - *kubur(an)* tombstone, headstone. - *kulansing* granite. - *lada* gravel. - *ladung* sinker (for fishing line). - *loncatan* 1 stepping stone. 2 beachhead. - *lumpur* mudbrick. - *lumut* jade. - *méjan* headstone, tombstone. - *mérah* brick. - *minyak* whetstone. - *mulia* precious stone. - *nikmat* magic stone. - *nilam* sapphire. - *nobatan* stone inscription to commemorate a coronation. - *panas* slag, hot cinders (from volcano). - *paras* sandstone. - *pasir* sandstone. - *pateri* soldering iron. - *pecahan* highway crushed stone. - *pelinggam* marble. - *penarik* yellow amber. - *penarung* 1 stumbling block. 2 obstacle. - *pertama* cornerstone. - *pijak* stepping stone. - *sabak* slate. - *sabun* soapstone. - *sendi* 1 cornerstone. 2 foundation. - *siam muda* carbuncle. - *sontokan* stumbling block. - *sudut* cornerstone. - *tahu* gypsum. - *tanduk* hornfels. - *témbok* brick. - *timbang(an)* weights. - *timbul* pumice. - *tulis* slate (for writing). - *tumpuan* base of operation. - *ujian* 1 touchstone. 2 criterion. 3 test case. - *ukuran* benchmark. 2 milestone, milepost. - *pal* milestone, pile post. - *sempadan* boundary marker. - *tapal* boundary stone. 3 artificial diamond. - *belanda* imitation diamond. 4 (*Coll.*) flint (of lighter), battery. - *api* 1 flint. 2 firebrand, instigator. - *gerétan* flint. 5 classifier for teeth. *gigi empat* - four teeth. **ber-** stony, rocky. ~ *hati* hardhearted, insensitive, callous. **ber-(²)** covered with rocks. **mem-** 1 petrify, fossilize. 2 harden. *Hatinya* ~ Her heart hardened. *Kuéhnya* ~ The cookies became hard as a rock. 3 remain silent. *Dia* ~ *sampai terpaksa saya menilpon polisi* He refused to talk so I was forced to call the police. *Yg dibujuk sendiri* ~ *dan keras menolak* Even the o. who had been coaxed into agreeing clammed up and firmly refused. **mem-i** 1 pave, asphalt (a road, etc.). 2 stone, throw stones at. 3 arrange stones, lay bricks. *Ia* ~ *rumah* He built a brick house. **-an** (*Geol.*) rock, boulder. ~ *beku* igneous rock. ~ *endapan* sedimentary rock. ~ *léléhan* volcanic rock. **-²an** 1 rocklike. 2 pebbles. 3 boulders. **pem-an** fossilization. **pe(r)-an** rocky place.

batuk 1 a cough. *Ia sakit* - She is suffering from a cough. - *darah* spitting (up) of blood. - *kejang* whooping cough. - *kering* 1 any cough with little or no phlegm. 2 tuberculosis. - *lelah* asthma. - *rejan/sisik* whooping cough. 2 to cough. -² *kambing* 1 nervous cough. 2 coughing spell. - *kecil* clear o.'s throat. **ber-** cough. **mem-kan** cough or spit up (blood). **ter-²** 1 have a coughing spell. 2 sputtering or coughing of an engine.

batur₁ shelf. - *benua* continental platform, shelf.

batur₂ (*Jv*) servant.

bau₁ 1 scent, smell, aroma, odor. - *harum* fragrant smell. *masih* - *kencur* still young. 2 unpleasant odor, stench, stink. 3 fumes. 4 (*Coll.*) give off an odor. *Kamarmu* - *benar!* Your room reeks! 5 suggest an element of. *oléh-oléh yg* - *Jkt* a present which has s.t. of Jkt in it. **se-** 1 be of the same odor. 2 be in harmony with. **ber-** 1 smell, give off an odor, be odorous. *Masakannya* ~ *énak sekali* Her cooking smelled delicious. ~ *bir* the smell of beer. 2 suggest an element of. *Ajarannya* ~ *fanatisme ala Khomeini* His teachings reek of Khomeini-like fanaticism. ~ *dua* suggest duplicity. **mem-** smell a rat, suspect s.t. wrong. *Saya* ~ *adanya kecurangan* I smell s.t. rotten in Denmark. **mem-i, mem-ni** 1 smell s.t., sniff s.t. *Anak gadis itu* -- *bunga mawar* The young girl sniffed the rose. 2 be on the track of, track down. *Polisi* ~ *pembunuh* The police are on the track of the murderer. **ter-** 1 smelled, sniffed. ~ *oléhnya asap kebakaran* He smelled smoke from the fire. 2 known, detected. *rahasia* ~ a secret was detected. **-²an** 1 odors, scents. 2 perfume, fragrance. **pem-** 1 (sense of) smell. 2 o. who tests by sniffing.

bau₂ surface measurement, 7096.5 square meters.

baud see BAUT.

bauk 1 down between chin and neck. 2 feathers beneath jaw or beak. 3 (*Coll.*) beard, sideburns. **ber-** bearded.

bauksit bauxite.

baulu see BOLU.

baung k.o. freshwater catfish.

baur mixed. **ber-(an)** 1 be mixed. *tepung* ~ *dgn gula* flour mixed with sugar. 2 mix, associate. *Ia suka* ~ *dgn org* She likes to socialize with people. 3 live together. **mem-** 1 diffuse. *warna* ~ *the* colors diffused. *Sejenak bapak menatap asap-asap* ~ Just a quick look from you and the smoke diffuses. 2 assimilate. *Kami sdh lama* ~ *dgn masyarakat lain, menghadiri upacara, bergotong-royong, dll.* For a long time now we have been assimilating with other social groups, attending ceremonies, undertaking communal work together, etc. **mem-i** blend into, mingle with. *WNI dihimbau agar* ~ *masyarakat sekitar* Naturalized citizens have been urged to mix with the community around them. **mem-kan** 1 mix s.t. *Ia* ~ *gula dgn terigu* She mixed sugar with wheat flour. 2 mix, incorporate. **mem-²kan** mix up. *Feisal* ~ *rambut anaknya* Feisal messed up his son's hair. **mem-per-kan** unite, join s.o. together. **ke-an** mixture, mix-up. ~ *antara dosa agama dan dosa kemanusiaan* confusion between religious and human sin. **-an** mixture. **pem-an** 1 mixing, blending. *Di sekolah itu ada* ~ *laki dan wanita* At that school the boys and girls are integrated. 2 association, social intercourse. ~*nya dgn pencuri itu menjadikan ia pencuri juga* His association with the thief made him a thief too. 3 assimilation (of a group). **per-an** diffusion, mixture. ~ *warna menciptakan warna baru* A mixture of colors creates a new color.

baureksa (*Jv*) ghost or spirit inhabiting (and

guarding) a certain place. **mem-** settle in and guard over (of tutelary spirits).

bausastra (*Jv*) dictionary.

bausuku unpaid laborer.

baut 1 bolt. - *jangkar* anchor bolt. **2** bully, strong-arm man, bouncer. **mem-** bolt. *Kayu di- pd bangunan* Wood was bolted to the structure. **pem-an** bolting.

bavian baboon.

bawa bring, bring along. **ber-an** match. *Celananya ~ dgn jasnya* His trousers and coat match. **mem- 1** carry (bag, suitcase, etc.). *Saya mau ~ koper ini* I want to carry this suitcase. *~ mobil* drive a car. *~ mulut* come for the purpose of chatting and eating. *~ perut* come seeking food. *~ senjata api* bear arms. **2** bring, take along. *Saya tdk ~ uang waktu pergi ke toko* I did not take any money when I went to the store. *Anaknya di- ke dokter* He took his child to the doctor. *Ia ~ anjingnya ke sekolah* She took her dog along to school. *~ adat* well mannered. *~ agama* be religious. *~ ajalnya* cause o.'s death. *~ alamat* betoken, indicate, denote. *~ aturan sendiri* do as o. likes. *~ bekas* leave traces. *~ bendéra mérah/bulan* (*Sl.*) menstruate. *~ cemar* cause to besmirch o.'s name. *~ diri* **1** get along (with others). **2** attitude. **3** betake o.s. *Ia ~ dirinya ke London* He went to London. *dpt di-* portable. *~ duduk* invite to sit. *~ iman* embrace the faith. *~ jalan* show the way, guide. *~ kakinya* go anywhere. *~ kabur* **1** flee. **2** take away, abscond with. *di- ke sungai* circumcised. *~ lagu* sing a song. *~ lari* run away with. *Anaknya di- lari* S.o. ran off with his child. *~ nasib* try o.'s luck, seek a livelihood. *~ nyawa* seek to save o.s. *~ salah* misunderstand. *~ serta* accompany. *~ singgah* invite to stop in. *~ suara* make a speech. *~ tempurung* beg. **3** bring, transport. *Truk itu ~ barang-barang dr pelabuhan ke kota* The truck brought the goods from the harbor to the city. **4** bring about, cause. *Siaran itu ~ akibat kebingungan di antara pendengar-pendengar* That broadcast caused confusion among its listeners. *Mulut yg usil ~ fitnah* Talkativeness leads to slander. *~ gelak* cause laughter. *~ kacau* cause confusion. *~ kenangan* evoke memories. *~ mati* **1** cause death. **2** take along when o. dies. *Ia ~ mati rahasia itu* He carried the secret to the grave. *~ untung* **1** bring good fortune. **2** seek o.'s livelihood or luck. **5** involve (in a matter). *di- arus* swept away by the current. **mem-²** involve, mention. *Jangan ~ nama saya dlm soal itu* Do not mention my name in connection with that matter. **mem-kan 1** bring s.t. for s.o. *Ayah ~ air minum utk adikku* Dad brought some water for my younger brother. *Ia ~ kita obat mujarab* He brought us some effective medicine. **2** present (a song, violin solo, working paper, etc.), perform. **3** portray, present. *~ peranan* play the role. *~ diri* comport, conduct o.s. **4** recite (a poem). **ter-1** brought, taken along (accidentally). *Kunci rumahnya ~ ke kantor* His house key was accidentally taken to the office. **2** involved. *Ia ~ dlm*

perkara itu He was involved in that matter. **3** because of, influenced by. *~ tabiat ibunya yg ramah-tamah, tabiatnya pun menjadi baik* Because of his mother's friendly nature, he too became a man of good character. **ter-²** carried over, persisting for some time. *Sifat kekanak-kanakannya masih saja ~* His childish attitude still persisted. **-an 1** load. **2** gift, item brought back home. *Barang ini ~ saya dr Hong Kong* This item I brought back from Hong Kong. **3** nature, temperament, disposition. *Sdh ~nya dr kecil* His temperament was like that since he was a child. **4** congenital, innate. *kelainan ~* congenital defect. *gagasan ~* innate ideas. **5** result, consequence. **pem- 1** porter, bearer. *~ surat ini bernama Amat* The bearer of this letter is named Amat. *~ acara* master of ceremonies. *~ barang* deliveryman. *~ berita/kabar* correspondent, reporter, newsman. *~ peti jenazah* pallbearer. *~ suara* spokesman. **2** means of obtaining, cause. *Anjing itu ~ tuah* That dog brings good luck. *Kesunyian ~ kedamaian hati* Silence is a means to inner peace. **sepem-** as far as o. can carry. *~ kakiku* as far away as my feet could carry me. **pem-an 1** nature, character, temperament. **2** talent, gift. **3** transporting, delivery. *~ bahan makanan dikerjakan dgn hélikopter* The delivery of food was made by helicopter. **4** result, consequence. **berpem-an 1** have talent, have a gift for. *Ia ~ menggambar* She has a talent for drawing. **2** have a disposition (for).

bawab (*Lit.*) gatekeeper.

bawah under, beneath. - *angin* leeward, windward. - *baku* substandard. - *kulit* subcutaneous. - *laut* submarine, undersea, underwater. - *sadar* subconscious. - *tanah* **1** subterranean, underground. **2** underground, clandestine, covert. - *tangan* underhanded, furtive, deceitful. *di -* **1** under, beneath. *Buku itu ada di - méja* The book is under the table. *Semua berada di - nilai* Everything was substandard. *di - pimpinannya* under his leadership. *di - garis kemiskinan* under or below the poverty level. *di - harga* below the fixed price. *di - langit* on the earth, in the world. *di - tangan* behind the scenes, sub rosa. *di - umur* underage. **2** on the floor, below. *Ia duduk di -* She is sitting on the floor. **3** as follows. *Ucapannya tertulis sbg di - ini* The pronunciation is written as follows. *ke -* **1** downward, to place under. *Ia turun dr atas ke - gunung* He descended from the mountain. *Anjing itu lari ke - méja* The dog ran under the table. **2** and under. *umur tujuh belas tahun ke - 17* (years old) and under. **mem-i 1** be under or beneath. *Pesawat pengebom itu terbang ~ méga* The bomber flew beneath the clouds. **2** supervise, have under. *Ia ~ sepuluh mahasiswa* She supervises 10 students. *Dépkés ~ yayasan itu* The Ministry of Health supervises that foundation. **mem-kan** be in charge of, supervise. *Gubernur itu ~ daérah yg luas* The governor is in charge of a vast area. *Mandor itu ~ tiga puluh org pekerja* That foreman supervises 30 workers. **ter-** lowest. *Sepatu saya ada di rak ~* My shoes are on the lowest shelf. **-an 1** subordinate, underling. *rekan-rekan ~nya* his subordinates. **2** (*Mil.*) enlisted man or woman.

bawak see BAWA.

bawal k.o. fish, pomfret.

bawang onion. *- acar* pickled onion. *- Benggala* large onion. *- Bombay* large yellow onion. *- cina* white spring onion. *- daun/hijau* scallion. *- kucai* leek. *- mérah* red onion. *- perai* leek. *- putih* garlic.

bawasir hemorrhoids.

bawél (*Coll.*) fault finding, carping. **ke-an** quibbling, carping.

bawon (*Jv*) share of rice harvest received for o.'s service during harvesting.

baya old. *Seorang wanita - bersujud syukur* An old woman bowed in thanksgiving to God. *separuh/setengah -* middle-aged. **se-** of the same age, a contemporary. *Ia ~ dgn guru saya* She is the same age as my teacher. *~ dan sejuman* be a contemporary of.

bayak fat, corpulent. **ke-an 1** overly fat, quite obese. **2** very stout. **3** plumpness, stoutness, obesity.

bayam amaranth used as a vegetable. *- (ber)duri* k.o. vegetable, the roots of which are medicinal. *- putih* k.o. amaranth.

bayan₁ k.o. parrot, long-tailed parakeet.

bayan₂ clear, distinct. **mem-kan** explain, expound, elucidate.

bayan₃ see KEBAYAN₁.

bayang 1 shadow, shade. *- gelap* dark shadow. **2** image, reflection. **3** imagination. *- kias* **mem-kiaskan** imply. *Baru ku- kiaskan pd adik* I just explained (it) indirectly to my brother. *-² sepanjang badan* in accordance with expectations. *-² tdk sepanjang badan* do s.t. beyond o.'s abilities. **ber-** be reflected. *Pohon itu ~ di air* That tree was reflected in the water. **ber-²** hover, be in o.'s thoughts. *Selama ia sakit ayahnya selalu ~ di dlm fikirannya* During his illness his father was always in his thoughts. **mem- 1** cloud over, darken. **2** be reflected. **3** appear (on o.'s face). **mem-i 1** shade. *Pohon itu ~ rumahnya* The tree shades his house. **2** shadow, follow closely. *Kapal terbang kami di-i oléh kapal terbang asing* Our plane was shadowed by a foreign plane. *Ia selalu ~ Amat ke mana pun Amat pergi* She shadowed Amat wherever he went. **3** hover about ominously. *Bahaya narkotika tetap ~ anak-anak kita* The peril of drugs constantly hangs over our children. *Masa lalu waktu kecil itu selalu ~ku* The shadow of my childhood always haunts me. **mem-²i** keep watch over, keep an eye on. **mem-kan 1** reflect an image. **2** show s.t., describe. *Pak lurah ~ betapa sulitnya keadaan di desa itu* The village leader described how difficult the situation in that village was. **3** reflect on, imagine. *-kan saja!* Just imagine! *Sedih aku ~ kenangan di tempat ini dulu* Sadly I reflect on the memories of this place in the past. **mem-²kan** try to imagine, imagine. *Dapatkah kamu ~ betapa girang ibumu nanti?* Can you imagine how happy your mother will be? **ter- 1** be

visible. **2** be imagined. *bahaya ~* imaginable danger, clouds on the horizon. **ter-²** appear. **ter-kan** *tak ~* unimaginable. **-an 1** shadow. **2** imagination. **3** estimation. **4** (*Thea.*) understudy. **5** image, phantom. *~ khayal* phantasmagoria. **-²an 1** estimate. **2** shadows. *~ merangkak dr sudut ke sudut* Shadows crept from corner to corner. **pem-an** act of shadowing or keeping close watch over.

bayangkara (*Lit.*) policeman.

bayangkari (*Lit.*) **1** policewoman. **2** policemen's wives' association.

bayar mem- 1 pay. *Ia ~ lima rupiah* She paid five rupiah. *Saya mau ~ di muka* I want to pay in advance. **2** pay for. *~ kejahatan* pay for, expiate, a crime. *~ (di) belakang* pay later or afterwards. *~ kaul/niat* fulfill a promise. *~ utak* repay, redeem, pay off. **3** pay s.o. *Saya blm di-* I have not been paid yet. **mem-i** pay for. **mem-kan** pay out, expend, disburse. *Ayah saya ~ separuh gajinya* My father paid out half of his salary. *~ nyawanya* pay with o.'s life. **ter-** paid. *tak ~* unpayable. *Hutangnya begitu besar sehingga tak ~* His debts accumulated and became unpayable. **ter-kan** accidentally paid for. **-an 1** payment. *Berapa ~ menjaga anak satu jam?* How much is babysitting per hour? *~ msk* entrance, admission fee. *Paméran foto umum tanpa dipungut ~* Public photo exhibition. Admission free. **2** for pay. *kendaraan ~* a rented vehicle. *Semua ~* All are salaried or paid. **pem-** payer. **pem-an** payment. *~ (di) muka* advance payment. *~ kembali* refund.

bayas k.o. palm tree.

bayat 1 (*Acad.*) freshman. **2** homage. **mem- 1** initiate. **2** honor, respect. **pem-an** hazing.

bayem see BAYAM.

bayi baby, infant. *- mérah* newborn baby. *- terlantar* foundling. **ke-²an** babyish.

bayonét bayonet. **ber-** be provided with a bayonet. **mem-** bayonet s.t. or s.o.

bayu₁ (*Lit.*) **1** wind, breeze. **2** Hindu god of wind.

bayu₂ 1 s.t. that has turned, i.e. fermented. **2** stale (of food), tasting of leftovers. **ke-an 1** fermented. **2** stale. **-an** leftovers, stale food.

bayu₃ (*Lit.*) slave, servant.

bayuh wife's right of access to her polygynous husband.

bayung see LEMBAYUNG.

bayur k.o. tree.

bazar charity fair, church bazaar.

bazir see MUBASIR.

bazoka, bazooka bazooka.

BB₁ [*Binnenlands Bestuur, Binnenlandsch Bestuur*] Civil Service during the colonial period.

BB₂ [*Bau Badan*] body odor.

BBD [*Bank Bumi Daya*] state-controlled bank.

BBM [*Bahan Bakar Minyak*] refined fuel oil.

BBN [*Béa Balik Nama*] fee for conversion of vehicle ownership.

BD [*Barat Daya*] S.W.

bé see BABÉ.

béa 1 excise, tax, duty, toll. *- Balik Nama* fee for

conversion of vehicle ownership. - *dan Cukai* Customs Office. - *keluar* 1 export duty. 2 exit fee. - *msk* import duty. - *meterai* tax or revenue stamp, duty. - *pemasukan* import duty. - *tetap* fixed duty or tax. - *warisan* inheritance tax. - *légalisasi* notary public fees, fees for official documents. - *pos* postal rate, postage. 2 cost, expense. - *angkut* fare, charge. - *labuh* anchorage or harbor fee. **mem-** tax. *Pemerintah ~ segala barang méwah* The gvt. is taxing all luxury goods.

béasiswa scholarship, fellowship. **mem-i** grant a scholarship to s.o. **ke-an** matters regarding fellowships.

béaya see BIAYA.

bebal 1 stupid, imbecilic, slow. 2 silly, foolish, asinine. **ke-an** imbecility, stupidity, stupidness.

beban 1 load (in vehicles or on back or shoulders). - *maksimum* peak load, maximum capacity. - *komunikasi* communication load. 2 burden, responsibility. 3 (*Elec.*) load, charge. **mem-** burdening. *masa datang yg ~ a* future full of burdens. **mem-i** 1 load on s.t. *Ia ~ mobilnya dgn beras* He loaded his car with rice. *~ lebih* overload. 2 burden, be a burden to s.o. 3 burden, weigh down, oppress. *Ia ~ rakyat dgn bermacam-macam pajak* He burdened the people with various taxes. *Ia tlh begitu di-i perasaan takutnya* He was so very oppressed by a feeling of fear. **mem-kan** 1 burden with s.t., load s.t. on. *Ayah ~ kewajiban yg berat kpd kami* Father placed a heavy responsibility upon us. *Apa saja yg di-kan pdku akan kupikul* Whatever duty is thrust on me, I shall do. 2 impose financial responsibilities, charge s.t. to. *Segala biaya akan di-kan kpd bank itu* All expenses will be borne by the bank. **pem-an** 1 load, burden. *~ sebagian* partial load. 2 loading (of).

bebandos see BANDOS.

bebang 1 stillborn. 2 asphyxia. **mem-, mem-kan** strangulate, asphyxiate. **ke-an** strangled in the course of birth.

bebar ber-an scattered, spread about. *Bukunya ~ di mana-mana* His books were scattered all about. **ter-** spread, scattered.

bébas 1 free, unhampered, unimpeded. *Ia membuka pintu dgn tangan yg masih - itu* She opened the door with her o. free hand. *daérah - bécak* area in which pedicabs are prohibited. *terjun -* free fall. - *bocor* leak-proof. - *buta huruf* free of illiteracy. - *cacing* worm-free, dewormed. - *ongkos kirim* no postage required. - *tugas* relieved of duty. **mem-tugaskan** relieve from duty. *Empat org perwira AURI tlh di-tugaskan* Four Air Force officers have been relieved of duty. **pem-tugasan** relief from duty. 2 free(d), be free. *Negeri itu sdh - dr penjajahan* That country is free from colonialism. *Sbg anggota korps diplomatik ia - dr pajak penjualan apa pun* As a member of the diplomatic corps he is exempted from any sales tax. *politik -* independent policy. *pelabuhan -* free port. 3 released, acquitted. *Ssdh ditahan tiga minggu ia - kembali* After being detained for three weeks he was released. **mem-kan** 1 set free, release (a prisoner, etc.), liberate. *Di-kannya sepasang merpati* A pair of doves was set free. *-kanlah kami dr kejahatan* Deliver us from evil. 2 exonerate, absolve. 3 exempt, dispense from. *Pemerintahan tlh ~ bahan makanan dr béa* The gvt. has exempted all foodstuffs from duty. 4 allow, let o. be free to (do s.t.). *Ku-kan kau bergaul dgn anakku* I allow you to associate with my son. **ter-** be freed. *Penduduk désa itu tlh ~ dr wabah muntah bérak* The inhabitants of the village were freed from a cholera epidemic. **ke-an** freedom, liberty. *~ (ber)bicara* freedom of speech. *~ mimbar* academic freedom. *~ pribadi* personal freedom. **-²an** 1 permissive. 2 licentious. **pem-** liberator, emancipator, deliverer, savior. *~ dunia* (*Rel.*) savior of the world. **pem-an** 1 liberation, deliverance, emancipation. 2 dispensation, exemption. *~ pajak* tax exemption. 3 acquittal.

bebat bandage, dressing. **mem-(i)** bandage, dress (a wound). **mem-kan** use s.t. to bandage (a wound). *Ia ~ selendang pd lukanya* He used a scarf to bandage his wound. **-an** bandage, dressing. **pem-** bandager, dresser. **pem-an** bandaging, wrapping, dressing (of a wound).

bébé see BÉBI.

bébék₁ duck. **mem-** 1 quack. 2 imitate, parrot. 3 follow unthinkingly. **pem-** 1 imitator, parrot. 2 o. who follows along without thinking.

bébék₂ bleat. **mem-** bleat (of goat).

bébék₃ k.o. motorcycle of less than 100 cc.

bébékisme a mental outlook characterized by unthinking loyalty to a leader or society.

bebel see BEBAL.

bebenah see BENAH₁.

bébér - *bentang* **meng-bentangkan** disclose in detail, unfold fully. **mem-** 1 spread, unfold, display. 2 open up (a map). 3 unfurl. 4 reveal, disclose (a secret). **mem-kan** 1 unfold, unroll. *Pedagang itu ~ kain batiknya* The merchant unfolded and laid out her batik cloth. 2 explain, unfold. *~ rencana* explain a plan. 3 open up (a map, etc.). 4 reveal, disclose (a secret). *Ia ~ keinginannya* He disclosed his desires. **-an** 1 s.t. unrolled or displayed. 2 explanation, analysis. **pem-an** 1 explaining, narrating. 2 presenting an exposé.

beberapa some, several. - *buku* several books. - *lama* for some time.

bebesaran see BESARAN.

bebet (*Jv*) wraparound indicating rank, worn by males.

bébét (*Jv*) ancestor. -, *bebet, bobot, bibit* lineage, rank, wealth, and origins: criteria for ranking prospective son-in-law.

bébi infant. *pakaian -* baby clothes.

bebingka see BINGKA.

béblat supplement, esp. to colonial-period legal gazette.

bebotoh see BOTOH₂.

bebotok 1 fried chicken leg or thigh. 2 large chunk of cooked chicken.

bebuka (*Jv*) foreword.
bebuyutan senile.
béca see BÉCAK₂.
bécak₁ spot, dot. **ber-²** spotted, dotted. *Citanya ~* The material has a polka-dot design. **mem-i** pock(mark).
bécak₂ 1 pedicab, tricycle. *- komplit* pedicab plus prostitute. 2 DC-3 plane. **ber-** ride a pedicab. **ber-²an** go here and there in a pedicab. **(me)m-** 1 work as pedicab driver. 2 ride a pedicab.
bécak₃, bécék muddy. **mem-kan** cause s.t. to be muddy, dirty.
becok noisy, loud (of talking).
becus capable. *tdk -* incapable, incompetent. *tdk - kerja* unable to work.
béda 1 difference. *- tinggi kedua org itu delapan sénti* The difference in height between those two men is eight cm. *- dgn* in contrast to. *- dgn pasién lain . . .* in contrast to other patients . . . 2 remainder, balance. *- halus* nuance, shade, fine distinction. **ber-** 1 be different, differ, diverge. *Usianya tdk ~ jauh dr aku* He is not very different in age from me. *~ dgn yg lain* different from the others. 2 have a difference (of). *Hanya ~ tiga tahun* There is a difference of only three years. *~ pendapat* have a different opinion. **ber-², ber-an** be different (from e.o.). *Uraiannya ~ tapi maksudnya sama* The explanations differ, but the intent is the same. **keber-an** difference. *~ pendapat* difference of opinion. **mem-²kan** differentiate between. *Kamu terlalu ~ Ami dan Arti* You treat Ami and Arti too differently. **mem(per)-kan** 1 discriminate, treat differently. *Ia ~ anak angkat dan anak kandungannnya* She treats her stepson differently from her own son. 2 distinguish, tell apart. *Ia tak dpt ~ yg mana kudanya* She could not tell which horse was hers. **ter-kan** distinguishable. **pem-** distinguishing factor. *ciri ~* (*Ling.*) distinctive feature. **pem-an** 1 distinction, differentiation. *Di tentara hrs diadakan ~ antara prajurit dan opsir* In the army there must be a distinction between enlisted personnel and officers. 2 discrimination. *~ ras* racial discrimination. 3 classification, division. **per-an** 1 difference. *~ paham* difference of opinion. *~ umur* age difference. 2 distinction. *~ warna* color distinction.
bedah surgical operation. *- mayat* autopsy. *- pintas* by-pass (heart) surgery. *- rongga dada* thoracic surgery. **mem-** operate (surgically). **-an** surgical incision. *~nya panjang sekali* The incision was very long. *menjalani ~* undergo surgery. *~ kecil* minor surgery. *~ plastik* 1 plastic surgery. 2 dissection. **pem-** instrument for performing surgery. **pem-an** surgical operation.
bedak face powder, talcum powder. *- dingin* cooling facial powder applied before going to sleep. **ber-** 1 powder o.s. *Segala gadis asyik ~ dan bergincu* All the girls are busy putting on makeup and lipstick. 2 powdered. *Mukanya ~ putih* Her face is white with powder. **mem-i** 1 put powder on s.t. *Dipakaikannya baju pd Irwan dan di-inya* He

put a shirt on Irwan and applied powder to him. 2 make superficial improvements to s.t. *Alah! Gedung ini hanya di-i saja, sebulan lagi sdh bobrok lagi* My! They're just patching this building up; in another month it will fall apart again. **mem-kan** apply s.t. in a powder form.
bedal₁ **mem-** whip, thrash s.o.
bedal₂ run wild, bolt (of a horse).
Bedawi see BADAWI.
bedaya /bedaya, bedoyo/ k.o. sacral Central Jv court dance.
bedebah ill-omened (used in terms of abuse). *si -* the scoundrel. *si - itu mencurinya dr saya* The scoundrels stole it from me. **mem-(²)kan** accuse s.o. of being a rascal.
bedegap sound of a strong blow.
bedegong 1 obstinate, stubborn, headstrong. 2 opinionated, conceited.
bedék see BADÉK₂.
bédék see BIDIK.
bedél (*Coll.*) surgical operation. **mem-** 1 operate on. *Ia tlh di-* He is been operated on. 2 lance. *Bisul itu di-* The boil was lanced. **-an** incision, scar. **pem-an** operation.
bédéng₁ shed, barracks.
bédéng₂ 1 dike embankment of a paddy field. 2 ditch. 3 flowerbed, seedbed. *- cengkéh* clove tree nursery. **-an** 1 embankment. 2 vegetable bed.
bedil gun, rifle. *- angin* air rifle. *- bambu/buluh* 1 toy gun. 2 empty bluff, boasting, bragging. *- bedal* various firearms. *- locok* k.o. musket, blunderbuss. *- mesin* machine gun. **ber-** armed. **mem-** 1 fire, shoot. 2 use a rifle, have a rifle. **mem-i** shoot at. *Ia ` macan* He fired at a tiger. **-an** 1 shooting match. 2 toy gun, wooden training gun. **-²an** play gun, play guns. **sepem-** within gunshot.
bedol *- désa* immigration of an entire village. **mem-** uproot. **-an** drop-out (from school).
bedudak (*Jv*) viper.
bedug, beduk large drum suspended horizontally at mosque to summon to prayer. *Sebentar lagi - subuh berbunyi* In a moment the drum call to dawn prayer will sound.
bedukang k.o. freshwater catfish.
bedung **mem-** swathe, put on a diaper. **-an** swathing, swaddling.
bééng (*Sl.*) very, extremely. *Kerén -!* You really look like a dandy!
béga₁ **ber-, mem-** circle around (of a bird). **mem-i** circle around s.t. *Burung elang ~ lapangan tempat mangsanya* The hawk circled around the field where his prey was.
béga₂ **mem-** aim, take aim.
begadang (*Coll.*) stay up and talk all night.
begadrung gathering, meeting, assembly.
bégal robber. **mem-** 1 rob. 2 hijack, holdup. **pem-** 1 robber. 2 hijacker. **pem-an** 1 robbery. 2 hijacking. 3 misappropriation.
begap sturdy, stout, stocky.
begar confirmed, inveterate. *pemabuk yg -* con-

firmed drunkard. *penjahat yg* - hardened criminal.

bégar, béger ber-, mem- circle around, pivot. *Kau hanya tahu ~ di sekitar dapur* All you know is hanging around the kitchen. **mem-i** circle around s.t. **per-an** merry-go-round, carousel.

begasi see BAGASI.

begawan title for Hindu priest or ascetic (in shadow plays, etc.).

begini 1 thus, like this. *- ceriteranya* The story goes like this. *- besarnya* It is this large. **2** well, so (often used to start a conversation). *-, pak . . .* Well, sir . . . *-lah* **1** It is like this. **2** Let us do it like this. **-²** just like this. *~ aja kerjanya* This is all we do. **se-** as . . . as this. *~ banyaknya* as much as this. **mem-kan** treat in such a way, handle like this. *Gurunya ~ dia* His teacher treated him like this. **-an** *(Coll.)* **1** s.t. like this. *Utk apa kau beli yg ~* What did you buy stuff like this for? **2** terrific (said simultaneously with upward gesture of thumb).

begitu 1 like that. *Jangan - kalau membutuhkan pertolongan* Do not be like that if you need help. **2** so, very. *Rumahnya - besar* Her house is so large. *Adiknya tdk - pandai* His younger brother is not so clever. **3** how very. *- bagus rumahnya!* How beautiful his house is! **4** just at the moment. *- berbunyi lonceng, meréka terjun* Just as the bell sounded, they dove. *- juga* even so. *- mahal* very expensive. *- rupa sehingga . . .* in such a way that . . . *- saja* just like that. *Bagaimana kita membuangnya - saja?* How can we throw him out just like that? *~ keadaannya ssdh ditinggal oléh isterinya* Such was his situation after his wife left him. *~ kira-kira* That is about the way it is. **-pun 1** likewise, and so, also. *Ia kaya ~ pamannya* He is rich and so is his uncle. **2** in spite of. *~ ia pergi juga ke rumahnya* In spite of it, he went to his house anyway. **-² 1** like all that, after all that. *~, saya blm tahu apa saya dpt pergi* After doing all that, I still do not know if I can go. **2** just so-so, nothing special. *Makalahnya ~ saja* His seminar paper was just so-so. **se-** like that. *~ banyaknya* as many as that. *~ jauh* to the extent that, to that extent. **mem-kan 1** treat s.o. like that. *Saya tdk mau di-kan* I do not want to be treated like that. *Pintunya di-kan kok masih ndak mau nutup sih!* After doing all that to the door it still does not want to shut! **2** compel s.o. to have sex. *Ia di-kan oléh pamannya* She was raped by her uncle. **-an** *(Coll.)* **1** s.t. like that. **2** have sex.

bégo, bégok stupid, imbecilic, idiotic.

begondal see BEGUNDAL.

bégonia begonia.

begroting /behroting/ *(Coll.)* budget.

beguk 1 goiter. **2** mandible, lower jaw.

begundal hoodlum.

béha see BH.

behandel *(Coll.)* **mem- 1** take care of, treat (patient, wound, etc.). **2** manage, handle. **-an** treatment.

behaviorisme behaviorism.

bejana 1 container, vessel, receptacle. *- pasir* sandbox. *- sorong (Med.)* bedpan. *- susu* milk can, milk jug. **2** vase.

bejat 1 damaged, spoiled (esp. of baskets, bags, etc. with split seams). *mobil -* jalopy. **2** depraved, wanton. **mem-i, mem-kan** damage, harm. **ke-an** turpitude, depravity, debauchery. **pem-an** damaging, harming. *~ moral* damaging to morals, immoral.

bejo *(Jv)* lucky.

bék₁ /bék/ *(Sport)* backfield player.

bék₂ *(Coll.)* head of a village.

béka ber-(²) chat, discuss. *Stlh lama ~, meréka minta diri pulang* After chatting for some time, they took their leave.

bekak ber- be cruel.

bekakak *(Sd)* whole baked chicken, esp. in weddings when bridal couple pulls it apart.

bekakas see PERKAKAS.

bekal stock, supplies, provisions. *org yg cukup -nya* a person of sufficient means. *- hidup* a foothold in life (skills, wisdom, etc. necessary to be successful). **ber-** have a supply. *Ia ~ nasi dlm perjalanan itu* He had a supply of rice along on the trip. **ber-kan** supplied with. *~ keinginan* supplied with a desire. *~ téhnik dan patokan* provided with a technique and a standard. **mem-kan** supply, provide s.t. *~ kebutuhan pokok* provide the basic needs. **mem(per)-i** supply s.o. *Setiap org di-i dgn sebuah granat* Each man was supplied with a grenade. **pem-an** supply(ing), provisioning. **per-an 1** supplies, provision. *~ modal* the amount of capital provided. **2** talents, necessary skills. *Kita dilahirkan dgn ~ yg sama* We are born with the same aptitudes.

bekam₁ bruise. **mem-** pinch, nip.

bekam₂ mem- 1 bleed s.o. **2** seize (prey). **pem-an** bloodletting, bleed.

bekantan proboscis monkey (of Kalimantan).

bekas₁ 1 print, trace. *- jari* fingerprint. *- kaki* footprint. *- luka* scar. **2** former (site, wife, etc.). *Ia menjenguk - tangsi* She looked at the old site of the barracks. *- kawah* extinct crater. **3** ex-, former. *Ia - guru* He is an ex-teacher. *Dia - pacar saya* She is my ex-girlfriend. **4** used, secondhand. *piring - saya* the plate I used. *buku -* secondhand book. *- tubuh/baju -* secondhand clothes. **ber-, mem- 1** have a print, leave a trace. *Tangannya tdk ~* His hand left no print. *kenangan yg ~* memories which leave an imprint. **2** have results. *Usahanya tiada ~* Her efforts were fruitless. **mem-i** leave a print on s.t. *Wajahnya masih di-i airmata* Her face was still traced with tears. **mem-kan** leave behind. *Pengajarannya ~ perasaan bersatu yg kuat* His teachings left behind a strong feeling of unity. **-an** secondhand. *piano ~* secondhand piano. **-²an** remainder, residue.

bekas₂ receptacle, container. *- sirih* betel nut holder. *- tinta* inkwell.

bekatul 1 bran. **2** rice siftings.

bekécot see BEKICOT.

bekék see BERKIK.
bekél game of jacks.
békel$_1$ see PERBEKEL.
békel$_2$ see BEKÉL.
bekén (*Coll.*) well known, familiar. *Namanya cukup* - Her name is quite well known. **mem-kan** cause s.o. to be well known. **ke-an 1** fame. **2** notoriety.
béker$_1$ alarm clock.
béker$_2$ **1** trophy. **2** cup, beaker.
bekicot k.o. edible snail, similar to escargot.
bekil k.o. fish, snapper.
béking backing, support. *Ia mendapat - dr Présidén* He got the president's backing. **mem-(i)** support. *Ia ~ adiknya* He supported his brother. **-an** collusion. **-²an** do business on a system depending on patronage.
békingisme practice of seeking and relying on support from influential figures in (often) questionable projects.
bekisar cross between domestic chicken and jungle fowl.
bekléding upholstery or covering of car interior, chair, wall.
békles backless gown.
beklit mem- upholster s.t. **mem-kan** have s.t. upholstered. **-an** upholster. **pem-an** upholstering s.t.
békot see BOIKOT.
beku 1 frozen. *Airnya* - The water's frozen. *Uangnya di bank* - His bank account is frozen. *- kering* freeze-dried. **mem-** *kering* freeze dry. **2** congealed, coagulated. *darah* - congealed blood. **3** rigid, inflexible, unbending. *Pikirannya* - He is rigid in his thinking. **mem- 1** freeze over. *Sungai itu ~ semalam* The river froze over last night. **2** clot, coagulate. *Darah ~* The blood clotted. **3** congeal, solidify. *Agar-agar ~* The gelatin congealed. **4** become immobile, become inoperable. *Mulutku ~* I was speechless. **mem-kan 1** freeze. *Hawa dingin ~ air* Cold weather froze the water. *Pemerintah ~ segala pembayaran* The gvt. froze all payments. **2** put on ice. *~ rencana* put a plan on ice. **ke-an** rigidity, congealment. **-an** clot. **pem-an 1** freezing. *~ keuangan* freezing of accounts. **2** congealing, coagulating.
bekuk$_1$ **mem-** bend in two, fold. *Ia ~ kawat itu* He bent the wire in two.
bekuk$_2$ **mem- 1** capture, arrest. *Polisi ~ penjudi itu* The police arrested the gambler. **2** swindle, trick, fool. *Toko itu ~ pembeli-pembeli* That shop swindled the customers. **ter-** caught, captured. **pem-** catcher, capturer. **pem-an** capture, arrest.
bekuku, bekukung k.o. fish, sea bream.
bel- see also entries with **bl-**.
bél bell. *- pengaman* alarm buzzer. **mem-, menge- 1** ring a bell. *- saja kalau Tuan memerlukan sesuatu* Just ring the bell if you need anything, sir. **2** telephone s.o.
bela care for, nurture. **mem- 1** look after, provide material support. *Ia ~ ibunya* He is providing for his mother. **2** help, assist s.o. **-an** protection.

dlm bimbingan dan ~ org under the direction and protection of others. **pem-** protector. **pem-an 1** act of caring for s.o. **2** protection.
béla$_1$ say in defense. *"Bukan dia!"* - *ibunya* "Not him!" his mother said in defense. **mem-** defend. *~ tanah air* defend the fatherland. **pem- 1** defender. **2** defense lawyer. **pem-an 1** defense. **2** (*Leg.*) plea, advocacy. *~ diri* self-defense.
béla$_2$ **1** sacrifice, suicide, suttee, self-immolation. **2** sacrificial victim. **mem- 1** sacrifice o.s. in death, commit suicide, join (another) in death. **2** avenge.
belacan shrimp or fish paste condiment.
belaco, belacu unbleached cotton, gray shirting.
beladau k.o. bolo knife.
belado (*M*) a dish with red pepper sauce. *ikan -* fish prepared in this way.
belagu put on, act affected.
belah 1 crack, gap, crevice. *Ada - di témbok itu* There is a crack in the wall. **2** half, cut in half. *- dua* split, divided in two. *Ia menangkul kepala bangsat itu sampai -* He split the scoundrel's head in two with a hoe. *- hancur* fall out into pieces. **mem-hancurkan** rip apart, destroy. *Ledakan mem-hancurkan kesunyian malam itu* Explosions destroyed the stillness of the night. *- ketupat* rhombus. *spt pinang - dua* identical, like two peas in a pod. **3** side. *- bumi* hemisphere. *kedua - tangan* both hands. *kedua - pihak* both sides (of an issue). *- paru* lobe of lung. **se- 1** one half. *Sandal saya hilang ~ O.* of my sandals has disappeared. **2** beside. *kamar ~* the room next door. *di ~* beside, on the side of. *Di ~ rumah itu ada pohon apel* There is an apple tree beside the house. **3** in the direction of. *~ utara* toward the N. *~ kiri* on the left-hand side. *~ sini* on this side. *~ matahari mati* the W. **berse-(²)an** contiguous, side by side, neighboring. **se- menye- 1** side by side, contiguous. *Rumah saya ~ dgn rumah kawan saya* My house is beside that of my friend. *Meréka duduk ~* They are sitting side by side. **2** on both sides. *~ jalan itu terdapat pohon-pohon* There are trees on both sides of the street. **menye-i** be on the side of s.t. or s.o. *Mobil saya ~ mobilnya* My car was neck to neck with his. **menye-kan 1** shunt aside, shunt to the side. **2** put, place beside. **3** separate, split up (fights). **ber-** be split in two. *Hatinya sdh ~* His heart was unable to choose. *~ bagi* split and divide (inheritance, etc.). **mem-1** split. *~ rotan* split rattan. **2** cleave, cut through. *Perahu nelayan ~ permukaan air* The fisherman's boat cleaved the water's surface. *~ dua* bisect. **3** rip apart. *Granat ~ bumi* The grenade fissured the earth. **4** cut across. *Sungai Cerucuk ~ kota Tanjungpandan* The Cerucuk River cuts across Tanjungpandan town. **5** take a short-cut across. *Meréka berjalan ~ di padang rumput* They took a short-cut across the grassy field. **ter-** split, rent, cracked. *Tanah ~ karena gempa bumi* The ground was rent by an earthquake. *Celananya ~ di tempat yg paling angker* His pants split at the most dangerous place. **keter-**

an halfheartedness, irresoluteness, shilly-shallying. **-an 1** split, crack, cut. ~ *di témbok* crack in the wall. ~*jahitan* seam. **2** (*Geol.*) fissure. **3** splinter, fragment. ~ *gelas* glass fragments. **4** slice, cut. ~ *buah semangka* slice of watermelon. **5** half. *di bagian* ~ *utara* in the northern half. ~ *bumi* hemisphere. ~ *diri/jiwa* **1** better half, helpmate. **2** sweetheart. **pem-an** fission. ~ *inti* nuclear fission. ~ *bibit* seed casing separation.

belahak mem- clear o.'s throat, expectorate.

belai mem- 1 caress, stroke. *Ia nampaknya sangat mesra* ~ *kepala Rukini* She seemed very intimate caressing Rukini's head. **2** flatter. **mem-²** repeatedly caress. *Ia* ~ *rambutnya* He kept stroking her hair. **mem-kan** use s.t. to caress with. **-an 1** caress, pat. **2** flattery.

belajar see AJAR₁.

belak 1 black spot (on wood). **2** white spot (on skin). **ber-** spotted, dotted.

belaka 1 entirely, completely. *Janjinya palsu* - His promise was wholly false. *Gelang itu terbuat dr pérak* - The bracelet was made entirely of silver. **2** quite, very. *Mempelai itu masih muda* - The bride was still quite young. **3** only, merely. *Ia - yg datang* He was the only o. who came.

belakang 1 back, backside. *Saya gatal di* - My back itches. **2** behind, back of. - *rumah* behind the house. *Musuhnya datang dr* - The enemy approached from the rear. **3** later. *Ambillah barang-barang itu dulu; bayarannya urusan* - Take the goods now; payment can be arranged later. - *hari* future, in days to come. *Ia menyimpan uang utk* - *hari* He has saved money for the future. - *tangan* back of the hand. *di* - **1** behind. *Ia berdiri di* - *pintu* He is standing behind the door. **2** after. *Di* - *pidatonya ada nyanyian lagu kebangsaan* After the speech the national anthem is sung. **3** later. *Bangsa Indonésia yg di* - *akan mengalami kemajuan* Generations of Indonesians to come will experience progress. **4** on the back of, the reverse side. *Ia luka di* - *tangannya* He hurt the back of his hand. *ke* - **1** to the rear. *Ia pindah ke* - He moved to the rear. **2** behind. *Ia pergi ke* - *rumah* He went behind the house. **3** to the toilet. *Saya perlu ke* - I need to go to the bathroom. *Permisi ke* - *sebentar* Excuse me while I go to the restroom. **mengekan 1** move s.t. back. *Ia* ~ *layar putih itu spy gambarnya lebih jelas* He moved the screen back so that the picture would be clearer. **2** turn back, move back. *Ia* ~ *arlojinya* He turned his watch back. **3** neglect, ignore. *Tak lama lagi ia* ~ *ibadatnya* Before long he was neglecting his religious duties. **terke- 1** be left behind, put in the background. *Kalau berjalan kaki ia selalu* ~ When he was walking, he was always left behind. *Ia merasa* ~ He felt he had been pushed into the background. **2** neglected. *Pelajarannya* ~ Her studies were neglected. *negeri* ~ underdeveloped country. **ber-²an** back to back. *duduk* ~ sit back to back. **- mem-i** back to back. **mem-** turn o.'s back. **mem-i 1** turn o.'s back on, give s.o. the cold shoulder. *Ia* ~ *anaknya* He turned his back on

his child. **2** have o.'s back to. *Ia duduk* ~ *papan tulis* She sat with her back to the blackboard. **mem-kan 1** postpone, put off, delay. *Meréka* ~ *rapat itu* They postponed the meeting. **2** neglect, ignore. *Ia* ~ *hal keduniaan* He has neglected worldly matters. **3** pass over (for promotion). **ter- 1** last. *Ia duduk di tempat yg* ~ He sat in the last seat. **2** latest. *kabar yg* ~ the latest news. **3** retarded, backward. **keter-an** backwardness, underdevelopment, retardation. **-an 1** later. *Saya pergi* ~ *saja* I will just go later. **2** eventually. *Mula-mula tdk ada harapan* ~ *ikhtiarnya berhasil* Initially there was no hope, but eventually his effort was successful. **3** later on. ~ *ia mengaku bhw ia salah* Later on he admitted he was wrong. *Aku msk* ~ I entered later on. ~ *ini* recently, lately, of late, recent times. ~ *ini ia menyurat kpd saya* Recently he has been writing to me. *yg* ~ *ini* the latter. *Dia lebih besar drp yg* ~ *ini* He is larger than the latter.

belalai 1 trunk, snout. **2** proboscis. **3** tentacle, feeler.

belalak mem- stare, open wide. *Ia* ~ *matanya* She stared wide-eyed. ~ *kpd* stare at. **mem-i** outstare, stare down. **mem-kan 1** open (eyes) wide to stare. *Ia* ~ *matanya* He opened his eyes wide. **2** look at s.o. with big eyes. **ter- 1** wide-open (eyes). **2** surprised. **-an** wide-eyed stare.

belalang₁ locust, grasshopper. - *centadu/kacung/sentadu* praying mantis. - *kerit-kerit* cricket.

belalang₂ mem- stare. *Ia* ~. *Tampaknya ia marah* He was staring. He seemed angry. **mem-i** stare at. *Ia* ~ *aku kembali* He stared right back at me.

belam see BALAM₁.

belan bolt. **mem-** fasten with crossbar.

belanak k.o. fish, gray mullet.

Belanda 1 Dutch. *Negeri* - The Netherlands. - *hitam* **1** Indonesian with Dutch citizenship. **2** (*Derog.*) Indonesian who feels and acts like a Dutchman. - *Indo* Dutch Eurasian. - *kertas* (*Derog.*) Indonesian with Dutch citizenship. - *témpé* (*Derog.*) Dutch Eurasian. - *totok* **1** full-blooded Dutchman. **2** (*Coll.*) any Caucasian. **mem-kan 1** put into Dutch. *Ia* ~ *kitab al-Qur'an* He translated the Koran into Dutch. **2** treat as Dutch. *Pemerintah itu* ~ *meréka yg memintanya* The gvt. conferred European status upon those who requested it. **ke-(²)an** Dutch-minded, act Dutch.

belandang (*Jv*) **mem-** run fast.

Belandanisasi Hollandization.

belandong see BLANDONG.

belang 1 spot, band, stripe. *Harimau menunjukkan -nya* A tiger shows its stripes. **2** skin blemish. **3** blemished, spotted. - *cecak* spotted mark. **ber-(²)** striped. **mem-i** create spots on s.t.

belanga earthen cooking pot.

belangkas₁ horseshoe crab.

belangkas₂ k.o. small bolo knife.

belangkin 1 asphalt. **2** black shoe polish.

belanja 1 expense, expenditure. *Berapa - sehari-hari?* How much are the daily expenses? **2** cost, expense. - *dapur* kitchen expenses. - *mati* fixed expense or wage. - *negeri* gvt. expense. - *pasar* money for marketing. - *rokok* cigarette allowance. **3** go shopping. **ber- 1** shop, go shopping. *Banyak org ~ di toko itu* Many people shop at that store. **2** buy, purchase. **mem-i 1** finance, defray expenses of. *Pemerintah ~ perjalanannya* The gvt. financed his trip. **2** bear the expense of. *Kau lebih suka ~ anjingmu drp anakmu!* You'd rather support your dog than your child! **mem-kan** spend s.t. *Semua uangnya di-kan utk pakaian* He spent all his money on clothes. **-an** items purchased. *bakul ~* marketing basket. *pusat ~* shopping center. **pem-** shopper. **pem-an** financing. **per-an 1** expenses, (national) budget. **2** financing. **3** shopping. *pusat ~* shopping center.

belantan club, cudgel, nightstick.

belantara forest, jungle. *hutan -* thick forest.

belantik₁ k.o. spear used in hunting.

belantik₂ see BLANTIK₁.

belantik₃ see BINTANG.

belarak see BLARAK.

belas₁ mercy, pity. *- kasihan* pity, have pity. **ber-** *kasihan* have pity. **mem-kasihani** pity, be sorry for, commiserate with. **ber-²an** be compassionate toward e.o. *Kedua keluarga itu ~ dlm hubungan sehari-hari* The two families maintained a compassionate relationship on a day-to-day basis.

belas₂ teens, tens (used in numbers from 11 through 19). *dua-* twelve. *se-* eleven. **-an 1** between 10 and 20. *Ia pingsan selama lima ~ jam* She was unconscious for some 15 hours. *utk ~ tahun* for decades. *Pimpinan perusahaan hanya ~ org* The management of that company consists only of some 10 or 20 men. **2** characterized by being in the teens. *~ tahun* teenaged. *gadis tujuh ~ tahun* a girl of about 17. **3** celebration marking an anniversary in age or date of the teens. *Perayaan tujuh ~ kali ini lebih meriah* This time the 17th of August celebration was more lively.

belasah mem- whip s.o.

belastar see BLASTER.

belasteng, belasting (*Coll.*) **1** tax. **2** duty, tariff.

bélasungkawa condolences. *menyampaikan -* express condolences.

belasut growl, snarl. **mem-** growl, snarl. *Anjingnya ~ pd org gémbél itu* The dog snarled at the tramp. **mem-i** snarl at. *Ia marah sekali dan ~ saya* He was angry and snarled at me. **-an** a snarl, growl.

belat 1 bamboo screen. **2** fish trap of plaited bamboo. **3** splint. **mem- 1** catch fish with a plaited trap. **2** put in splints. *Dokter ~ lengan yg patah itu* The doctor put the broken arm in splints.

belat-belit devious, surreptitious. *Mulutnya ~ O.* cannot trust his words.

belati k.o. broad-bladed knife.

belatik, belatuk woodpecker.

belatung maggot.

belau₁ (ber)-²an flicker, glitter, shine.

belau₂ see BLAU.

beldu see BELUDRU.

belebas 1 lathe. **2** ruler, yardstick.

beledang sea eel.

beledu see BELUDRU.

belegar booming noise of explosion.

beleguk bubbling sound of water.

beléh see SEMBELIH.

beléid /beléyt/ policy. *- pendidikan menteri* the cabinet minister's education policy. *- ékspor* export policies.

belék₁ mem- operate on, cut open. **-an** incision.

belék₂ see BLÉK.

bélék₁ 1 conjunctivitis. **2** inflamed. *Matanya -* His eye was inflamed.

bélék₂ mem- peer at, watch.

belekok see BLEKOK.

belél bell-bottom style trousers, wide at the cuff. *celana jeans -* bell-bottom jeans.

beléncong see BLÉNCONG.

belendung (*Jv*) **mem-** be sticking out (of stomach).

béléng ber- turn around. **mem-²** turn s.t. around. *Ia ~ kepalanya* He turned his head around.

beléngéh mem-kan *bibir* distort o.'s lips, grimace.

belenggu handcuff, fetter, shackle of wood or iron. *Lepaskan dirimu dr - Sétan* Free yourself from the shackles of Satan. **mem-** handcuff, shackle, manacle. *Kita ~ diri dgn adat kuno* We shackle ourselves with old-fashioned traditions. *Tangannya di-* He was handcuffed. **mem-kan** use s.t. to shackle s.o. **ter-** in fetters, repressed. **pem-an** handcuffing, shackling.

beléngkét mem- stick, cling, adhere. **mem-kan** paste s.t. up, to stick s.t. on. *Ia ~ pengumuman itu di papan pengumuman* She pasted the announcement on the bulletin board.

beléngkik turn. **mem-** curve, turn. *Sungai ini ~ ke kanan* This river bends to the right. **-an** curve, bend, turn.

beléngkong curve, arch.

beléngsét ectropion, with the lower eyelid turned inside out.

belenong sound of a bell.

belér m-i (*Jv*) cut into s.t. **ke-** (*Coll.*) accidentally cut o.s. with a sharp object.

belérang sulphur. *- bang* arsenic (for rat poison). **mem- 1** treat with sulphur. **2** fumigate.

belérong market stall.

belesek see BLESEK.

belet (*Jv*) **ke-** have the need, have compelling urge (esp. to urinate or defecate). *~ ke belakang* an urge to go to the toilet. *Rupanya, rasa ~ utk modernisasi tak dpt diélakkan* Apparently there is no way to avoid the compelling urge to modernize.

belét 1 appointment to a job. **2** permission to appear before a higher-up. *Ia minta - utk menghadap Gubernur* He asked for an appointment to see the governor.

beletak-belenong clang-clang (of streetcar bell).

Bélgia Belgium.

beli buy. *Bp bisa - sawah* Father can buy a paddy field. **ber-²an 1** buy for e.o. **2** shop, go shopping.

mem- 1 buy, purchase. *Saya sdh ~ mobil* I have bought a car. *~ murah bisa berarti terbeli mahal* A cheap buy may turn out expensive. 2 buy, obtain (with). *~ dgn pengorbanan* obtain through sacrifice. *dpt di-* 1 obtainable, can be purchased. 2 bribable. **mem-kan** 1 buy for. *Ia ~ ayahnya sebuah kursi* He bought his father a chair. *Aku bisa ~ Bp seékor kerbau* I can buy a water buffalo for you. 2 use s.t. to buy, spend s.t. on. *Uang ini bisa di-kan méja* You can use this money to buy a table. **ter-** 1 affordable. *Mobil itu ~ oléh awam* That car is affordable for the masses. 2 bought, bribed. 3 (*Lit.*) manage to buy s.t. *Wan Saleh ~ dgn murah* Wan Saleh managed to buy things cheap. 4 happen to buy. **-an** s.t. purchased. *Apa ~nya di New York?* What did you buy in New York? **-²an** purchases of all kinds. **pem-** 1 buyer, purchaser. 2 s.t. sufficient for a purchase. *Aku tak punya uang ~ nasi* I do not have the money to buy rice. **pem-an** 1 purchasing, buying. *~ balik* counterpurchase. 2 procurement.

belia 1 youth. 2 young. *usia - a* young age. *masih muda -* still very young.

beliak mem-, ter- wide open and staring (of eyes). **mem-kan** open eyes wide.

belian see BERLIAN.

beliau (*respectful form of reference*) he, she. *- mendapat gelar doktor kehormatan* He received an honorary Ph.D.

belibis k.o. wild duck, the teal.

belida k.o. fish.

beligo wax gourd.

belik see BLÉK.

belikat scapula, shoulder bone.

beliku bend, curve (in road etc.).

belimbing 1 ridged longitudinally. 2 star fruit, carambola. *- sayur* k.o. carambola used in vegetable soup. *- wuluh* small, sour carambola for cooking. **mem-** ridged like bars in a row, corrugated. *Sebuah tangan yg ~ tiba-tiba datang menjemba léhér baju* A gnarled hand suddenly came fumbling at the shirt collar. **-an** s.t. shaped like carambola. *alat judi yg berupa ~ bermata* gambling device shaped like carambola with markings (roulette wheel).

belincung pickax.

beling 1 porcelain. *piring -* porcelain plate. 2 shards (of glass, platter, etc.).

belingkang ter- sprawled. *Ia jatuh ~* He fell sprawling.

belinjo₁ bullet (of gun, rifle).

belinjo₂ see MELINJO₁.

belintang ber-(an), ter- lie across, be athwart. *Bis yg terbalik ~ di jalan* The overturned bus lay across the road. **mem-** cross s.t. *Ia ~ di Sungai Malili* He crossed the Malili River. **mem-kan** place across, place athwart.

belit 1 coil. 2 curve, bend. **ber-** wind, twist in and out. **ber-²** 1 wind, twist in and out. *Sungai itu ~ di pegunungan* The river winds through the mountains. 2 complicated, intricate. *Soal ini ~* This matter is complicated. 3 involved, has ramifications. *Soal ini ~ dgn pembunuhan janda itu* This matter is involved with the widow's murder. **- mem-** intertwined, interwoven, interlaced. **mem-** 1 wind around s.t. *Kami melihat anak rusa di- ular kemarin* Yesterday we saw a snake coiling around a fawn. 2 bind, wrap together. 3 involve s.o. *Kau sdh di- ulah si Jamal* You've already been trapped in Jamal's tricks. **mem-²** move in serpentine fashion, wind. *Jalan ini ~ di gunung* The road makes serpentine turns in the mountains. **mem-i** wind, wrap around s.t. *Roda itu di-i dgn rantai besi* The wheels were fitted with chains. **mem-kan** wind s.t. *Kalau ku-kan demikian rupa ...* If I wind it like that ... **ter-** 1 involved, wound about. 2 twisted. *Kakinya ~* She twisted her foot. **-an** 1 kink, coil, twist. 2 twist. *~ nasib* twist of fate. *menceritakan ~ penderitaan yg menimpa seorg gadis cilik* relates the ins and outs of the suffering which struck a young girl. 3 association. *Kenangannya mempunyai ~ yg tak menyedapkan* His reminiscences have unpleasant associations.

Belitung Billiton, an island S. of the Riau archipelago.

beliung 1 carpenter's adze. 2 pickax.

beliut bent and crooked.

belodok 1 k.o. fish, goby. 2 protruding (of eyes), similar to goby eyes.

belok₁ 1 muddy. 2 mud. 3 clayey soil.

belok₂ 1 pulley. 2 stocks, fetters. **mem-** fetter, place in stocks. **pem-an** prison, jail.

belok₃ see BLOK₁,₂.

bélok curve, bend, sharp turn. **-²** (*Naut.*) tack. **ber-** turn. *Mobil itu ~ ke kanan* The car turned to the right. **ber-²** 1 have curves. *Jalan itu ~* That road has many curves. 2 zigzag. **mem-** turn, veer, bear. *Lalu ~lah ia ke kiri* Then he veered to the left. **mem-i** turn at a place. *Sekali ~ tikungan, Agus mendengar siréne* As soon as he turned the corner, Agus heard a siren. **mem-kan** 1 turn s.t. *Ia ~ mobilnya ke kanan* She turned her car to the right. 2 divert, distract. *Ia ~ perhatian para pendengar* He diverted the attention of the listeners. *~ percakapan* change the conversation. 3 distort. *Katanya Deng dkk. ~ ajaran Mao* He says that Deng and his colleagues are twisting Mao's doctrines. **-an** curve, bend, sharp turn. *~ empat puluh empat* a road with 44 hairpin curves (leading to Lake Maninjau). **pem-an** 1 turning, shift (in policy, etc.). 2 distortion. *Apakah arti ~ ini?* What does this shift mean? **per-an** shift, change. *~ jiwa* psychological change.

belon (*Jkt*) see BELUM.

belongkang barge, river freighter.

belongsong wrapper.

belontok k.o. fish, large goby.

belorok see BLOROK.

belorong see BLORONG.

bélot 1 turncoat, renegade, traitor. 2 be a turncoat. 3 (*Rel.*) apostate. **ber-, mem-** 1 be a turncoat, desert to the enemy. 2 (*Rel.*) be an apostate. **pem-** deserter, turncoat. **pem-an** desertion.

belu-belai chatter, gossip.

belubur storage place for rice.

beludak₁ outburst (of laughter, applause). **mem-1** explode, burst out. *terbukti dr ~nya penonton* proved by the outburst of the audience. **2** rage, boil up. *Kebanggaan ~ memenuhi rongga tubuhku* Pride rose up and filled my breast.

beludak₂ viper.

beludar k.o. round rice cake.

beludru velvet, velveteen.

beluk₁ k.o. insect, stalk borer.

beluk₂ see SELUK₁.

belukar 1 thicket, underbrush. **2** shrub. **mem-** become scrub, go to weeds. *pohon dan rumput yg sdh ~ trees* and grass which became a thicket. **mem-i** overgrow, cover up. *Rambut ~ mukanya* His face was covered by a thicket of hair.

beluku see WALUKU.

belulang 1 tough, dry. **2** callus (on foot or hand). **3** rawhide. **4** (*Lit.*) bones. *atas - rakyat yg melarat* on the very bones of the suffering citizens. **ber-, mem-** calloused. *~ di karét* formed lumps like calluses on the rubber sheet.

beluluk young coconut.

belum 1 not yet. *Sdh jam empat, ia - datang* It is four o'clock and he has not come yet. *- coba tapi sdh dikatakan gagal* You have not tried yet, but you are already saying you have failed. *- juga/ lagi/saja* still not yet. *Saya - lagi berbuat salah* I still have not done anything wrong. *- lama ini* just recently, not so long ago. *Saya melihat di toko - lama ini* I saw him at the store a little while ago. *- pernah* never have up to now. *Saya - pernah melihat buku sebesar itu* I have never seen a book as large as that. **2** not (yet) including. *Biasanya Rp2.000, - supirnya* It us. costs 2,000 rupiah, not counting the (cost of the) driver. *- lagi* **1** not to mention. *Yg dua ribu itu sdh cukup mahal - lagi tambahan ongkos utk transpor* 2,000 rupiah is expensive enough, not to mention the extra transportation costs. **2** still not yet. *Ini sdh jam delapan dan dia - lagi makan* Here it is already eight and she still has not eaten. *- pula* exclusive of, not including. *Ia banyak memiliki tanah - pula yg di luar negeri* He owned a lot of land not including his property abroad. **-²** nothing has happened yet. *~ kok sdh menangis* I have not done anything yet and you are already crying. **se-** before, prior to. *~ perang* before the war. *~ pergi, makanlah dulu* Eat first before you go. *~ waktu/waktunya* prematurely. **se-nya** previously, formerly. **ke-adaan** temporary unavailability. *~ persediaan utk jamuan itu amat membingungkannya* The temporary shortage of supplies for the reception thoroughly confused him. **ke-déwasaan** immaturity.

belun (*Jv*) see BELUM.

belungkang 1 butt end of palm leaf stalk. **2** young coconut halved.

belungkur k.o. fish, Queensland smelt.

belunjur see UNJUR.

beluntas k.o. gardenia with edible leaves used for hedges.

belur welt up (of skin). **ber-(²)** harden into welts, raise up welts. *Ia mendera aku sampai pantatku ~ mérah kebiru-biruan* He whipped me until my buttocks welted and became severely bruised.

beluru see AKAR.

belus₁ loose-fitting (of ring, clothing).

belus₂ blouse.

belut eel.

bembam mem- roast in hot ashes.

bemban₁ k.o. shrub the leaves of which can be plaited.

bemban₂ k.o. staked fish trap.

bembem thick and swollen. *Bentuk kakinya bagus, tdk -* The shape of her foot was beautiful, not swollen.

bémo [*bécak bermotor*] k.o. small motorized vehicle used for public transportation. **mem- 1** go with this vehicle. **2** work as a driver of this vehicle.

bémper see BUMPER.

bén see BAND₁.

béna 1 particularly, very. *Ia tak - besarnya* He is not very big. **2** care, attention. *Anjing ini tak dpt - dr pemiliknya* This dog received no attention from its owner. *- tak -* be indifferent. **mem-kan** like, care about. *Ia tak begitu ~ pekerjaannya* He does not care so much for his job.

benah₁ be(r)-(²) straighten up, tidy up, clean up. *~ diri* straighten up o.s. *Sementara ia masih saja ~ di wisma* For the time being he is still readying things at the villa. *Saya ~ utk segera tidur* I got ready for bed right away. **mem-i** fix, get ready, straighten out. *~ diri* fix o.s. up, straighten o.'s clothes. *~ kehidupan negara yg kacau* straighten up the chaotic state of the nation. *~ rambutnya* straighten o.'s hair. **mem-kan** put in order. *Ia ~ nasi goréng di méja makan* She set out the fried rice on the table. **ter-i** can be straightened out. **pem-an** repairing, mending. *~ kota* city beautification. *~ kehidupan politik* mending of political life.

benah₂ k.o. small insect harmful to rice.

benak₁ 1 marrow. *- gigi* soft interior of the tooth, pulp. **2** brain, mind. *Mat Coléng akan menembak -nya* Mat Coleng was about to shoot his brains out. *Camkan peringatan ini di -mu* Keep this reminder in mind. **ber-** have brains.

benak₂ 1 hard of hearing. **2** stupid, dull-witted.

benalu 1 arboreal parasitic plant, epiphyte. **2** parasite. **3** sponger, freeloader. **mem-** be a parasite. **mem-i** mooch off s.o. **pem-an** sponging, mooching.

benam ber-, mem- sink out of sight, hide. *Di mana kau ~?* Where have you been hiding? *~ diri* be deep in, hide behind (a newspaper, etc.). **mem-** envelop. *Sebuah gelombang ~ kami* A wave enveloped us. *Ia menelungkup ~ aku dlm dekapannya* He stretched out to envelop me in his embrace. **mem-kan 1** drown, immerse. *~ diri di balik koran* bury o.s. behind a newspaper. **2** suppress. *Ayahnya ~ tuduhan anaknya* The father suppressed his son's accusation. **3** sink (a knife in s.o.). **4** sink, scuttle (a ship). **5** incarcerate, jail. **ter-**

1 disappear, go down. *Matahari ~ di barat* The sun sets in the W. 2 be buried. *Rumah itu ~ di bawah salju* The house was buried in snow. *Ia ~ dlm hutang* He is buried in debts. **-an** what has been produced by immersing s.t. *~ air merang dipakai keramas* The water in which the rice stems were immersed can be used to rinse the hair.

benang thread, yarn. *- arang* carpenter's charcoal line. *mendirikan - basah* make a wet thread stand erect, i.e. do the impossible. *- bol* wrapping string (us. on spool). *- gelasan* string onto which ground glass has been stuck for kite fighting. *- ikat* twine. *- lungsing* warp. *- pakan* woof. *- raja* rainbow. *- sayét* knitting wool. *- salib* cross wire. *- sari/serbuk* stamen. *- sela* thread with several strands. **se-** a little bit. *Ia tetap blm luka ~ pun* Not a single hair was harmed. **ber-** have a certain type of thread. **ber-²** fibrous. **mem-** 1 stringy, fibrous. 2 be interminable. *Ceriteranya ~* His story stretches on and on.

benar 1 correct, right. *Taksiran itu -* That estimate is correct. 2 right, honest, true. *Ia berpegang pd pedoman yg -* She sticks to the right course. 3 just, honest. *Ia terkenal sbg hakim yg -* He is known as a just judge. 4 true, not false. *keadaan yg - the* true situation. 5 sincere, true. *Ia menjalankan kewajiban dgn hati yg -* She performed her duty with sincerity. 6 valid. *Surat perjanjian itu tdk -* That contract is not valid. 7 truthful. *Berkatalah yg -* Tell the truth. 8 very, quite, really. *Film itu bagus -* That film was very good. *Yg - saja dong!* You cannot be serious! **-²** 1 real, actual. 2 seriously. *Pelajari keadaan itu ~* Study the situation seriously. **se-** so true as. *Blm ada pernyataan ~ itu* No statement has yet been made as true as that. **se-nya** 1 in fact, as a matter of fact, actually. *Katanya ia kaya tapi ~ tdk* He says he is rich but actually he's not. *Keadaan yg ~ ialah spt ini* The true situation is like this. 2 proper, fitting. *Sdh ~ kalau ia menyokong ibunya* It was proper that he should support his mother. **ber-(²)** 1 be sincere. *Ia ~ ketika menceritakan kesedihannya itu* He was sincere when he talked about his miseries. 2 state frankly, admit candidly. **mem-(²)** adjust, put in the proper position. *~ taplak méja* straighten the tablecloth. *Tangannya ~ kain kepalanya* His hands straightened his headdress. **mem-i** 1 advise. 2 persuade, induce. **mem-²i** 1 take seriously. 2 do seriously. **mem-kan** 1 correct (a mistake). 2 straighten, arrange, fix (o.'s hair). 3 confirm, substantiate, verify (a report). 4 justify, condone (an act). 5 approve of. *Ia ~ perkawinan itu* She approved of the marriage. 6 permit, allow. *Polisi tdk ~ mobil berjalan malam* The police do not permit cars to run at night. 7 acknowledge (receipt). **ke-an** 1 correctness, rightness. 2 truth. 3 righteousness, justness. 4 honesty. 5 fidelity. *~ piring hitam* fidelity of the recording. 6 proof, acknowledgment. *Inilah ~ yg menyatakan bhw ia berhak pd tanah itu* This is the proof that he is entitled to the land. 7 by chance, by accident, coincidentally. *~ saya akan pergi ke*

Cirebon By chance I am going to Cirebon too. **-an** (*Coll.*) do s.t. properly. *~ aja dong!* Come on, do it right! **pem-** justifier, corrector. *alasan ~* justifiable cause. **pem-an** 1 correction. 2 justification. 3 confirmation, acknowledgment. 4 approval.

benatu see PENATU.

bencah muddy (of ground after storm). **ber-(²)** swampy, marshy.

bencana disaster, calamity, debacle, havoc. *Kau dipelihara di situ akan menjadi - saya nanti* Your being cared for there will become a personal calamity for me later. *- alam* natural disaster, catastrophe. *- jiwa* trauma, mental shock. **mem-i** 1 disturb, cause trouble. 2 deceive, swindle. **mem-kan** 1 endanger, imperil, jeopardize. 2 disturb, annoy, irk.

bencarung k.o. bird, oriole.

bencat stunted in growth, dwarfed.

benci hate, dislike, aversion. *Ia - akan org itu* He hates that person. **ber-an, - mem-** hate e.o. **mem-** hate, dislike, detest. *Ia ~ org itu* She hates that person. **mem-kan** 1 hate, dislike. 2 odious, abominable. **ke-an** 1 hate, hatred. 2 dislike, aversion. 3 loathing, abomination. 4 hostility. **pem-** hater.

bencirit see CERÉT.

béncong (*Sl.*) female impersonator, transvestite.

benda thing, article, inanimate object. *- angkasa* celestial body or object. *- asing* foreign body, matter, or object. *- buang* excrement, manure. *- duniawi* worldly things. *- cair* fluid matter. *- hidup* living matter. *- letupan* explosive material. *- mati* immovable, nonliving object. *- padat* (*Phys.*) solid matter. *- tetap* stationary object, immovable. *- tuang* casting from mold. **ber-** wealthy, rich. **mem-kan** make into money. **ke-an** 1 matter. 2 material, physical, substantive. 3 material wealth. **pem-an** objectification. **per-an** 1 stock, supply. 2 matters concerning goods.

bendahara 1 treasurer, esp. of clubs, organizations, etc. 2 (*Lit.*) grand vizier. 3 (*Che.*) queen. **per-an** 1 treasury. *~ negara* state treasury. 2 wealth, riches. 3 repertory. *~ bacaan* repertory of reading materials. *~ kata* vocabulary.

bendaharawan 1 treasurer, esp. gvt. officials. 2 (*Acad.*) bursar. 3 office accountant.

bendahari (*Lit.*) treasurer.

bendalu see BENALU.

bendar irrigation canal in rice field.

bendasraya see ASURANSI.

bendawi, bendawiah material, substantive. *pemujaan -* worship of material objects.

bendé small bronze or copper gong.

béndék, béndéks (*Auto*) starter drive pinion.

bendel, béndel see BUNDEL₁.

bendéra flag, colors. *- kebangsaan* national flag. *- mérah putih* Indonesian flag. *- salah* (*Sport.*) penalty flag. **ber-** fly a flag. *~ asing* fly a foreign flag. **mem-i** decorate with flags.

benderang bright, brilliant. **mem-i** make s.t. bright or brilliant.

benderung empty space between two buildings.

béndi two-wheeled carriage.
bendo large-bladed knife for cutting wood.
bendoro (*Jv*) a title of nobility.
bendosa (*Jv*) catafalque.
bendul₁ cross beam. - *jendéla* windowsill. - *pintu* threshold beam.
bendul₂ (*Coll.*) swollen.
bendung 1 dike. 2 dam. - *peti* cofferdam. **mem-** 1 dam up. 2 dam, stem, check. *Meréka ~ serangan musuh* They stemmed the enemy attack. 3 repress. *Ia tak dpt ~ tangisnya* He could not check his tears. **mem-i** dam up. **ter-** 1 dammed (up). 2 held back. *tdk ~ irresistible.* **-an** 1 dike. 2 dam, weir. *~ batu* rockfill dam. *~ gelombang* breakwater. **pem-** 1 o. who checks or stems s.t. 2 s.t. that dams up or stems s.t. *Perbukitan di sebelah timur menjadi ~ bagi hujan yg datang* The range of hills to the E. was a barrier to rain sweeping in. **pem-an** 1 damming up. 2 im pounding. 3 stemming, checking.
bené (*Jkt*) see BENAH₁.
bener see BENAR.
benerang see BENDERANG.
bengah 1 pedantic. 2 proud, conceited, arrogant, haughty. **ke-an** pedantry.
bengal 1 momentarily deaf (as from a blow), stunned. *Ia ~ karena kepalanya terpukul ke pintu* He was stunned from hitting his head on the door. 2 stubborn, obstinate. *Anak - itu tdk pernah lagi pulang ke rumah* That naughty child never goes home when he is supposed to any more. 3 forward, impertinent, rude. **ke-an** stubbornness, impertinence.
bengalo see BUNGALO.
bengang₁ ringing in the ears. **ber-** ring in the ears.
bengang₂ wide open. **mem-** open wide. **ter-** 1 wide open. *Mulutnya ~* His mouth was wide open. 2 flabbergasted. *Ia ~ melihat suaminya datang* She was flabbergasted to see her husband coming.
bengap 1 slight deafness (from a cold or from descent of a plane). 2 have difficulty speaking, incoherent (from embarrassment, shyness, or hesitation).
bengawan (*Jv*) river. - *Solo* Solo River.
bengék₁ 1 asthma. 2 asthmatic.
bengék₂ teat, nipple.
benggal-benggil bump, bruise.
benggalo₁ k.o. cassava.
benggalo₂ see BUNGALO.
benggang have space between. **mem-** make space between.
benggil ber- have bumps, be bumpy (of road).
benggol bump, bruise.
bénggol₁ leader of gang. **mem-i** make into gang leader, put into authority. *jéndral-jéndral kanan yg ~nya dgn dukungan CIA* rightist generals who put him into power with CIA support.
bénggol₂, bénggolan coin worth two and a half cents in colonial period.
bengik see BENGÉK₁.
bengis 1 cruel, strict, harsh. *Guru itu sangat -* The

teacher was very strict. *Anak itu - kpd adiknya* The boy was harsh to his younger brother. *Perkataannya -* His words were harsh. *- bertimpal -, kejam berbalas kejam* an eye for an eye, a tooth for a tooth. 2 angry, snappish. 3 penetrating, pungent. **mem-(i)** 1 be angry with. *Ia ~ adiknya* He was angry with his younger brother. 2 be cruel to. *Penjaga itu ~ tawanan* The guard was cruel to the prisoner. **mem-kan** cause s.o. to be angry, incite to cruelty. **ke-an** 1 cruelty. 2 severity, harshness.
bengkak 1 swollen, puffy. *Kakinya -* Her foot is swollen. 2 swelling, tumor. 3 abscess. - *léhér* cervical abscess. - *bengkil* lump, bump, bruise. **mem-** 1 swell, puff up. 2 increase, expand. *Angka kematian ~ menjadi seribu org* The casualty figure reached 1,000. **mem-kan** cause s.t. to swell up. **-an** lump, swelling. **pem-an** 1 swelling (of abdomen, etc.). 2 expansion, incrcasc. *- aréal tebu di beberapa tempat di Jawa* expansion of sugarcane acreage in some places in Java.
bengkal ke-an choke, swallow the wrong way. *Ia ~ air* She choked on the water. *Anak itu ~ jarum* The child accidentally swallowed a needle.
bengkalai mem-kan neglect, leave unattended or unfinished. *Ia ~ pekerjaannya* He left his work unfinished. *~ RUU* sabotage (by leaving unfinished) a proposed law. **ter-** 1 left in an unfinished state. 2 neglected. **keter-an** state of having been left incomplete.
bengkal-bengkil bruise, lump.
bengkang 1 crooked, curved. 2 curve. - *bengkok* zigzagging. - *bengkung* curved. *Jalan ini - bengkung* This road is curvy.
béngkap see BINGKAP.
bengkar mem- 1 expand. *Jagung ini ~ kalau digoréng* This corn expands when fried. 2 be in bloom. *Bunga mawar ~* The rose was in bloom.
bengkarak 1 skeleton. 2 bones. 3 carcass.
bengkarung k.o. smooth-scaled lizard.
bengkawan 1 lath around which palm thatch is made. 2 numeral classifier for thatch. *sepuluh - atap* 10 pieces of thatch.
bengkawang k.o. fern.
bengkayang gorged, stuffed (from overeating).
béngkél 1 workshop. - *lukis* artist's studio. - *téater* theater workshop. 2 machine shop. - *canai* rolling mill. - *las* welding shop. 3 repair shop, garage. - *mobil* auto repair shop. **mem-** operate a workshop. **mem-kan** send s.t. (car, etc.) out for repairs. *perunggu yg sdh di-kan* bronze already sent out for repair. **per-an** 1 repair shop. 2 workshop affairs.
bengkelai (*Coll.*) have a fight.
béngkéng irritable, irascible, touchy, testy. **mem-i** 1 anger. 2 nag, tease, bully.
bengkok land for use of village employees in place of salary.
béngkok 1 crooked, bent, warped. *Tiang itu -* That pole is bent. 2 crooked, dishonest, sly. *Maksudnya -* His intention is unscrupulous. *mengambil jalan -* do s.t. immoral. **mem-** 1 turn, make a turn. 2 bend. *Tongkatnya ~* The cane bent.

mem-kan 1 cause s.t. to bend. *Ia ~ badannya* She bent over. **2** warp, distort. **3** clamp, clinch (a nail). **pem-an** bending.
béngkol bent, curved.
béngkong₁ crooked, bent.
béngkong₂ a professional circumciser.
bengkos mem- gasping. *Nafasnya ~* He was gasping for breath.
bengkuang see BANGKUANG.
bengkudu small tree the root of which produces dyes, morinda.
Bengkulu Bencoolen (town and province in S.W. Sumatra).
bengkunang k.o. mousedeer.
bengkung₁ 1 long waist sash used by women wearing sarongs. **2** abdominal sash worn after giving birth.
bengkung₂ bent, crooked. **mem-kan** bend s.t.
benglé plant used in medicines.
bengok goiter.
bengong 1 dazed, stupefied. **2** crestfallen. **3** expressionless, vacant, blank. **mem-** act dazed, become stunned. **mem-kan** stun s.o. **ter-²** completely dazed.
béngot slanting, sloping.
bengu stale (of air).
benguk 1 angry, surly. **2** sulking. **3** downhearted. **mem-** be angry. *Ia kelihatannya ~ saja* He just looks angry.
bengul red and swollen (of eyes after crying).
benian 1 strongbox. **2** jewelry box.
benih 1 seed. **2** germ. *- penyakit cacar* smallpox germ. **3** semen. **4** origin, descent. *Ia adalah - raja-raja* He is a descendant of kings. **5** cause, origin. *Itu - perselisihannya* That was the cause of the conflict. **mem-** be at the root. *Kesedihan ialah naluri kodrati manusia yg ~* Sadness is a deep-seated natural human instinct. **mem-kan 1** germinate s.t. **2** conceive (of women). **pem-an 1** germination. *- buatan* artificial insemination. **2** seedbed. **per-an** (*Biol.*) culture medium.
bening clear, transparent. *Motor itu -* The engine is running like a top. *dgn suara yg - jelas* a crystal-clear voice. *wajah -* shining or radiant countenance. *-² air mata* teardrops. **mem-kan 1** purify (water). **2** clear, make s.t. clear. **ke-an** clearness, clarity (of water, etc.). *Maksudku lahir dr ~ pikiran* My intentions spring from a clarity of thought. **pem-an** purification. *~ air* water purification.
bénjal-bénjol bumpy and rocky (of road, path), lumpy (mattress).
bénjol 1 lump, bump, protruding tumor. **2** bruised, swollen. **ber-²** covered with bumps or bruises. **-an 1** bruise. **2** lump, swelling. **3** bump (in the road).
benjut having a large lump or bump from being struck. **-²** have lumps all over.
bénsin gasoline. *- campur(an)* mixed gasoline. *- murni* pure gasoline. *- serap* reserve gasoline (in a vehicle).
bénsol high-octane gasoline for planes.

benta sore, boil (on upper lip).
bentak say in a harsh manner. *"Kurang ajar, kau!" -nya* "You are a rude s.o.b.!" he snapped. **mem-1** snap at, bawl out. *Ia ~ org tua itu* He snapped at the old man. **2** bark out (orders). **mem-i** shout at s.o. harshly. *Ia takut di-i sépnya* He was afraid his boss would shout at him. **-an** bark, bellow, growl.
bentan relapse. *Jagalah spy sembuh sama sekali, jangan sampai -* Be sure to recover completely lest you have a relapse.
bentang - *alam* landscape. **mem- 1** spread out, extend. *Daérah ini ~ ke pantai ini* This area extends to the shore. *Cahaya timur ~* The dawn breaks. **2** reach. *jembatan ~* extending bridge. **mem-i 1** spread over s.t. *Siaran TVRI sdh ~ seluruh negara* Indonesian Television broadcasts now cover the whole country. **2** fit out (with a rug). **mem-kan 1** spread s.t. out, extend. *Ia ~ babut* He spread out a rug. **2** explain. *Ia ~ pendapatnya* She explained her opinion. *~ segala maksudnya* place all o.'s cards on the table. **ter-1** be spread out. *Peta Asia ~ di méja* A map of Asia was spread out on the table. **2** extend outward (of sail, etc.). **-an 1** expanse. *~ langit* the firmament. **2** s.t. extended. **3** disquisition, exposition. **pem-an 1** unfurling (of flag), unrolling (of rug). **2** exposition, setting forth. **per-an** extension (of a building, etc.). *skala ~* extension scale.
bentangur k.o. tree growing on seashore.
bentar₁ see SEBENTAR. **-an** (*Jkt*) momentary.
bentar₂ see CANDI.
béntar mem- be running around. *Ia membawa kudanya ~ di lapangan itu* He ran his horse around the field. **mem-i** run around s.t. *~ lapangan* run around a field.
bentara herald.
bentaran (*Jkt*) see SEBENTAR.
bénténg ber- wrestle with the legs intertwined.
bénténg 1 fortress, bastion, rampart. **2** fortification, entrenchment. **3** (*Che.*) rook, castle. **ber-** be fortified. **mem-i 1** fortify. **2** function as a fort for. *Jembatan beton itu ~ kota* That concrete bridge serves as a fort for the city. **per-an** fortification. *~ Maginot* Maginot line.
bénter ber-(²) 1 turn, revolve. *Dunia ~* The earth revolves. **2** turn off, detour. *Ia mengambil jalan ~* He took a detour. **mem-i** circle. *Harimau itu ~ mangsanya* The tiger circles its prey. **memper-kan** take (a horse) around in a circle. **per-an** arena for parading a horse.
bentét cracked open, burst open.
bentil nipple, teat. *- susu* 1 teat, nipple. **2** udder.
bentoh see BANTAH.
bentok ke- hit against, bump against. *Lengannya ~ témbok* His arm hit the wall.
béntol small bump (like a mosquito bite).
bentong large splotch. **ber-²**, **ber-an** having splotches. **mem-i** make large splotches on s.t.
bentrok quarrel, clash. **ber-** quarrel, clash. **ber-an** quarrel with e.o. **mem-kan** bring into conflict. *Ia*

~ *ayahnya dgn gurunya* She brought her father into conflict with her teacher. **-an** quarrel, clash, run-in. ~ *senjata* cross fire. **pem-an** struggle, contention. **per-an 1** conflict, dispute, clash. **2** collision, crash.

bentuk 1 shape, form, type. *Saya suka - rumah itu* I like the shape of the house. *- kembar* (*Ling.*) doublet. *- seasal* (*Ling.*) cognate form. *- semi* block style. *- tasrif* (*Ling.*) conjugated form. *- tegun* (*Ling.*) hesitation form. **2** bend, curve. **3** classifier used for round or curved objects. *se- cincin* a ring. **ber- 1** have the shape of. ~ *léhér angsa* goose-necked. ~ *manis* have a pleasant shape, good figure. **2** have the form of. *Negara kami ~ républik* Our country has the form of a republic. **mem- 1** form, compose. *Dapatkah kamu ~ kata dr tiga huruf ini?* Can you form a word from these three letters? *Perdana Menteri itu ~ kabinét* The prime minister formed a cabinet. ~ *panitia* establish a committee. **2** fashion, mold, transform. *cétakan utk ~ modél* a mold to make a model. **3** curve, bend. *Élok sekali dahan itu ~!* How nicely that branch curves! **ter-** formed, shaped, molded, fashioned. **-an 1** form, shape. **2** s.t. shaped or formed. *kabinét ~ kaum kiri* cabinet formed of the leftists. **3** derivative. **pem-1** framer, shaper, maker. **2** (*Pol.*) o. delegated to form a gvt. cabinet. **pem-an** formation, establishment.

bentul k.o. large aroid.

bentur ber- collide. *Dokar dan mobil ~* A horsecart and a car collided. **ber-an** collide repeatedly by accident. **mem- 1** bend, bow. *Pohon itu ~ karena angin yg keras* That tree bent from the strong wind. **2** collide, crash, come in contact with. *Biduk itu ~ karang* The boat ran aground on the coral. *gelas ~ marmar* glass flush with marble in building. **mem-kan** make s.t. ram into or collide. *Kesenian tdk boléh di-kan dgn kritéria-kritéria moral* You cannot force art to confront moral criteria. **ke-, ter- 1** collide with. **2** failed, blocked. *Rencananya selalu ~ pd masalah keuangan* His plans always stumbled on money problems. **-an** impact. **pem-an** clash. ~ *nilai-nilai* clash of values. **per-an 1** clash. ~ *kepentingan* clash of interests. **2** difference, clash. ~ *pendapat* differences of opinion.

bentus (*Jv*) see BENTUR.

benua 1 continent. **2** (*Lit.*) country.

benum mem- (*Lit.*) appoint. *Suaminya di- Belanda menjadi anjing NICA* The Dutch appointed her husband to the ranks of the NICA dogs. **-an 1** (*Lit.*) appointment, nomination. **2** (*Rel.*) ordination, installation. **pem-an** act of appointing.

benur shrimp fry.

benyai 1 soft, mushy. **2** weak, impotent.

benyawak see BIAWAK.

bényék soft, mushy (of fruit, cereal, mud).

bényot awry, askew, skewed.

béo myna bird. **mem-** parrot, imitate. **pem-** o. who likes to imitate. **pem-an** parroting, imitating.

béol /bé?ol/ (*Sd*) defecate.

ber- see also entries with **br-**.

bera₁ 1 dark red. **2** red and swollen. **mem-** become dark red. *Mukanya ~ karena malu* Her face reddened from embarrassment.

bera₂ mem-kan leave (paddy) fallow temporarily. *Tanah sawahnya di-kan dlm musim kemarau* His rice field lay fallow in the dry season. ~ *musiman* seasonally fallow.

berabé 1 nuisance, annoying. *- kalau mesinnya rusak* It is a nuisance when the engine breaks down. *Wah, itu kan -* Oh, it is too much trouble, isn't it? **2** bad luck. *Keadaannya - sdh* Now things are really unfortunate. **3** (*Coll.*) Darn! (exclamation of exasperation). *-! Kita ketinggalan kapal* Darn! We missed the boat.

berahi 1 sexual desire. *masa* period of heat, rut. **2** passion, lust. **3** passionate, lustful. **mem-kan** stimulate s.o.'s sexual desires, titillate. *Penari itu ~ penontonnya* The dancer enticed her audience. **ke-an** passion, lust.

berahmana see BRAHMANA.

berai ber- be spread, dispersed. **mem-²kan 1** spread, scatter (news, the enemy). **2** disperse.

berak mired (in mud, quicksand).

bérak 1 feces, excrement. *- air* diarrhea. **2** defecate. **-²** diarrhea. **ber-, mem-** defecate. **mem-i 1** defecate on s.t. **2** disgrace, dishonor. *Ia ~ nama keluarganya* He dishonored his family's name. **ter-²** (*Vulg.*) defecate in o.'s pants (e.g., out of fright).

berak-berok (*Jv*) scream and shriek.

beraksa mythical winged creature, Pegasus.

beram intoxicating beverage made of fermented rice or tapioca.

berambang see BRAMBANG.

beranda 1 veranda, porch. **2** (*R.R.*) station platform. **3** (*Naut.*) quarterdeck.

berandal see BRANDAL.

berandang 1 conspicuous, clearly visible. **2** striking, noticeable.

bérang 1 angry, furious, irate. **2** anger. *Mukanya mérah menahan -* His face reddened as he held back his anger. **mem-** become angry, furious. **mem-i** be(come) angry at s.o. *Ia ~ suaminya* She was angry with her husband. **ke-an** anger, fury, wrath. **pem- 1** hothead. **2** hotheaded, bad-tempered.

berangan₁ arsenic.

berangan₂ k.o. tropical chestnut and other related trees.

berangas barnacle.

berangasan hot-tempered, hotheaded.

berang-berang, berang-berangan otter.

berangsang mem- be very angry. **mem-kan 1** make angry. *Éjékannya ~ temannya* His ridicule made his friend angry. **2** instigate, incite, foment. **-an** instigation. **pem-** hothead.

berangus see BRANGUS.

berani audacious, brave, bold, courageous, dauntless. *Ia - mengatakan itu kpd ayahnya* He dared say it to his father. *Ambé - berjalan sendi-*

rian? Are you brave enough to go by yourself, Ambe? - *candang* 1 reckless, foolhardy. 2 bold, courageous. - *lalat* pretend to be brave. - *mati* have contempt for death. *pasukan - mati* suicide squad. - *sumpah* dare to swear. - *sumpah saya tdk mencuri arloji itu* I swear I did not steal the watch. - *udang* be frightened, scared. **mem-kan** encourage, foster. *Ia ~ anaknya pergi sendirian* She encouraged her son to go alone. *~ diri* summon or muster up the courage. **ke-an** bravery, courage, boldness, pluck. **-²an** act brave. *Jangan dia dibiarkan ~!* Do not let him put on his brave act! **pem-** 1 courageous person. 2 daredevil.

berantak mem-kan put s.t. into disorder. **ke-an** disorder. **-an** 1 in a mess, in disarray. *Pekerjaannya ~* His work is in a mess. 2 fall to pieces, be dilapidated (of a car etc.). *Gedung dan geréja hancur ~* Buildings and churches were smashed to smithereens.

berantas mem- 1 fight (against), combat. *~ penyakit gigi* combat tooth decay. 2 wipe out, remove (corruption, smallpox, inflation). **ter-** eliminated, wiped out. **pem-** 1 s.o. or s.t. which abolishes. *uang ~ kemiskinan* money to wipe out poverty. 2 exterminator (of malaria, etc.). **pem-an** efforts to eliminate. *~ buta huruf* the elimination of illiteracy. *~ hama* pest control, battle against pests.

berapa 1 how much, how many. *- harga buku ini?* How much does this book cost? *- duit* How much? What is the price? *-pun juga* no matter how much. *- org datang ke rumahmu?* How many people came to your house? 2 how (big, little, etc.). *- kecil rumah itu?* How small is your house? *- lama sdr tinggal di sini?* How long have you lived here? *- jauh rumahmu dr sini?* How far is your house from here? *tdk - lama* after a little while, in a short time. *- lama pun* no matter how long. *- lama pun dicari uangnya tak ketemu juga* No matter how long he searched for the money it still could not be found. *- saja* any amount whatever. **se-** 1 as much as. *~ dpt saya* as much as I can. 2 so and so many. *tdk ~* not so much. *Bédanya tdk -* There is not so much difference. **be-** several, some, a few. *~ buku* several books. *Ia berdiri di sana ~ menit lamanya* He stood there for a few minutes. *~ waktu yg lalu* some time ago. **ke-** 1 the how-manyeth, which (in numerical series). *Entah malam ~?* Who knows which night (of series of nights). 2 the umpteenth. *Yg ~ kali ia menaséhatiku* For the umpteenth time he gave me advice.

beras hulled rice. *- belanda* pearl barley. *- bertih* parched rice. *- cerah* white rice (cleaned). *- giling* milled rice. *- kencur* medicinal beverage of rice and herbs. *- kepala* finest quality rice. *- ketan* glutinous rice. *- kuning* tumeric-stained (raw) rice scattered or offered at ceremonies (funerals, weddings, etc.). *- menir* rice bits (used for cakes, porridge). *- perelek* rice that falls out of sack while being transported. *- petas* various k.o. rice. *- pulut* glutinous rice. *- recak-recak* cracked rice. *-*

sosoh rice husked with mortar and pestle. *- tumbuk* stamped rice.

beras-beras k.o. fish, drumfish.

berat 1 heavy. *Ranselku terasa - sekali* My backpack was quite heavy. *Tugas yg dipikulnya -* The task he had undertaken was heavy. *Tugas yg - a* heavy task. *alat-alat -* heavy-duty equipment. *- bibir* taciturn, a silent type. *- ékor* lazy, shiftless, indolent. *- hati* 1 suspect. *Ia - hati kpd org itu* She suspected that person. 2 heavyhearted, sad of heart. **ber-** *hati* feel sorry or sad. *- kaki* lazy. *- pd/kpd* favor. *- kepala* dull (-witted), mentally slow. *- (ke) puncak* topheavy. *- lidah/mulut* taciturn. *- otak* troubled, worried. *- sebelah* biased, partisan, one-sided, partial. **ke-sebelahan** partiality. *- siku* shiftless, lazy. *- sama dipikul ringan sama dijinjing* sharing good and bad. *tersenyum -* force a smile. 2 serious, severe. *Ia dihukum -* She was severely punished. 3 hard, difficult. *Pelajaran ini sangat -* This lesson is extremely difficult. *Apakah saya mesti menjaga di muka rumah sepanjang malam? - ni!* Do I have to guard the house all night long? That is quite a job! 4 close, oppressive, sultry. *Hawa -* The weather is close. 5 weight. *Berapa - barang itu?* What is the weight of this item? *Mobil itu -nya satu ton* That car weighs o. ton. *- bersih* net weight. *- dibongkarkan* weight (of item) delivered. *- dimuatkan* weight (of item) shipped. *- imbangan* counterbalance, counterweight. *- jenis* (*Phys.*) specific gravity. *- khusus* specific weight. *- kotor* gross weight. 6 strong (of drink, cigarettes, etc.). *- minuman -* strong (distilled) alcoholic beverage. **-²** extremely difficult, strained. *Nafas - menindih perasaannya* His heavy breathing exacerbated his feelings. **mem-** become heavy. *Kepalanya mulai ~* His head began to get heavy. *~ dadanya* She feels sick at heart. *Matahari mulai ~ condongnya* The sun began to set. **mem-i** 1 weigh down (of ballast, etc.). *sepatu yg di-i dgn lumpur* shoes weighed down with mud. 2 weigh on. *Apakah yg ~ fikiranmu?* What is weighing on your mind? *~ belanja dapur org lain* be a burden on s.o. else's household budget. 3 saddle, burden. *~ dgn hipoték* saddle with a mortgage. **mem-kan** 1 make things difficult for, worsen. *Kelelahan bisa ~ penyakit Aki* Exhaustion can worsen Grandfather's illness. *Harga patokan karét tak ~ éksportir karét* The standard price of rubber is not objectionable to rubber exporters. 2 load with ballast. 3 strengthen, stiffen. *Ia ~ tuduhanya dgn bukti-bukti nyata* She strengthened her accusation with factual proof. 4 stress, emphasize. *Meréka ~ pertahanan negeri dlm pembicaraan perbelanjaan itu* They stressed national defense in the budget discussion. 5 (*Leg.*) incriminate, implicate. *kesaksian yg ~ kawan sendiri* testimony which implicates her own comrade. *~ diri* implicate o.s. **memper-** make heavier. *~ hukuman* make the punishment heavier. *~ payah jantung* to burden the heart's effort still more. **ke-an** 1 objection. 2 raise objections, be unwilling. *Ia ~ menjalankan perintah itu* She objected to carrying out

that order. **3** drawback. **4** (*Coll.*) too heavy, overloaded. *Motor gerobak itu rupanya ~* That truck appears to be overloaded. **berke-an** have objections. **pem-** ballast. **pem-an** weighing down.
bercak pockmarked, spotted. *- bawaan* birthmark. *-² darah* red spots on the skin. *-² di jalan* holes in the road.
bercik see PERCIK.
bercokok see BICOKOK.
berdikari [*berdiri di atas kaki sendiri*] stand on o.'s own feet, be self-reliant.
berdus obese, corpulent, potbellied.
berebet see BREBET.
bérék-bérék k.o. bird. *- besar* blue weaving thrush.
berem see BERAM.
béreman edge, verge (of road).
beremban 1 cross beam. **2** dam.
berenga maggot.
béréng-béréng flat knobless gong.
beréngos see BRÉNGOS.
berengut mem- surly, sullen.
berentang mem- be stretched, taut. **mem-kan** make s.t. taut.
berenti see HENTI.
beréo, beréok (*Jkt*) see BRÉWOK.
bérés 1 in order, well done. *Pikirannya kurang -* His thoughts are befuddled. *Semua pekerjaannya ditanggung -* All her work is certain to be well done. **2** finished, settled. *Perkara itu sdh -* The matter is settled. *Tahu - !* Do not worry about anything. Everything will be fine. *hidup hanya tahu -* lead a life in which everything is done for o.'s own benefit. **mem-i 1** put in order. *Aku dan bibi bisa ~ semuanya* My aunt and I can handle everything well. **2** take good care of. *Ia asyik ~ tanaman* He was busily taking good care of the plants. **mem-kan 1** clear up, settle (a matter, disturbance). **2** put in order, straighten up. *Ia ~ pekerjaan yg kacau-balau itu* She put the chaotic work in order. *~ tempat tidur* make the bed. **3** finish off s.o. **ke-an** order, neatness, tidiness. **pem-an** settlement, resolution (of conflict, problem, etc.).
berésok see ÉSOK.
bérét demanding, exacting.
berét (*Jv*) see BARÉT₂.
beréwok see BRÉWOK.
bergajul scoundrel. **-an** act like a scoundrel. **ke-an** matters pertaining to scoundrels.
bergedél k.o. spherical croquette (of meat and mashed potato).
berguk dress covering entire body except eyes and hands sometimes worn by Muslim women.
berhala idol, image. **mem-kan** worship, idolize. **ke-an** idolatry. *~ atau kepercayaan kpd tuhan serba berhala* idolatry or belief in all k.o. idolatrous gods. **pem-an** idolization, idolatry.
beri - mem- give and take. **mem- 1** give, bestow. *Ia ~ hadiah* He gave a gift. *~ kesempatan* give a chance. *~ alamat* **1** signal. **2** drop a hint. *~ angin* give an opportunity. *Pemerintah ~ angin kpd*

beberapa perusahaan konstruksi The gvt. offered an opportunity to some construction firms. *~ celaan* criticize, find fault. *Ia ~ celaan kpd teman-temannya* She found fault with her friends. *~ betis hendak paha* give s.o. an inch and he will take a mile. *~ gelar* award a degree, bestow a title. *~ hati* **1** make happy, cheer up. **2** encourage. *Ia ~ hati kpd saya utk menerima tugas itu* He encouraged me to accept the task. **3** give in to s.o.'s whims. *Bapanya selalu ~ hati kpd anaknya* Her father is always giving in to her whims. *~ hormat* **1** extend regrets. *Ia ~ hormat kpd kawannya* He extended his regards to his friend. **2** (*Mil.*) salute. *~ ingat* remind s.o. of s.t. *~ isyarat* **1** signal. **2** drop a hint. *~ leta* show contempt for. *~ malu* cause s.o. shame. *~ pinjaman* lend. *~ rezeki* **1** give a living. **2** bring luck. *~ salam/selamat* **1** greet say hello, extend greetings,. *Ia ~ salam kpd temannya* He extended greetings to his friend. **2** salute. *~ semangat* inspire, cheer up. *~ suara* vote. *~ tanda* signal (with the hands). *~ telinga* listen, lend an ear. *~ tempat* make room. **2** offer, put up. *~ perlawanan yg sengit* put up stiff resistance. **3** (*Coll.*) let. **4** put on, apply s.t. *Ia ~ warna hijau kpd dinding kamar duduk itu* He painted the living room green. **5** (*Coll.*) hit, strike. **6** add (in recipes). **mem-kan 1** give, hand over. *Ia ~ uangnya kpd adiknya* He handed over his money to his younger brother. **2** extend, confer. *~ perlawanan* put up resistance. *~ suara* vote, participate in election. **pem-** giver, donor, bestower. *~ sedekah* alms-giver. **pem-an 1** gift, present. **2** conferral, awarding, bestowal (of degree). **3** distribution, act of distributing. **4** issue. *tempat -* place of issue. *- kuasa* delegation of authority. **5** giving, extending. *~ krédit* extension of credit. *~ izin* licensing. *~ tahu* (*Coll.*) announcement.
beriang k.o. monitor lizard.
béri-béri beri-beri.
beringas 1 hot-tempered, wild. *mata -* wild eyes. **2** furious. **ke-an** wildness, savagery.
bering-bering large cymbal with center boss.
beringin banyan tree.
beringis, beringisan grin.
beripat traditional game in Billiton in which players strike e.o. with rattan rods.
berisik 1 noisy, tumultuous. **2** uproar, noise. **ke-an** noise, din.
berita 1 news (report). **2** announcement, report. *- acara* official report, minutes, record. *- bulanan* monthly report. *- dlm negeri* home news. *- dengkul* secondhand news. *- kilat* bulletin. *- pelaut* notices to mariners. *- rapat* minutes (of meeting). *- sepekan* weekly news. **be(r)-** have news. **mem-kan** report about s.t. *Ia ~ bhw ayahnya tlh sampai dgn selamat* He reported that his father had arrived safely. **ter-** reportedly. **pem-** reporter, news correspondent. **pem-an 1** news release, announcement, report. **2** communication. **3** notification.
beritahu mem- 1 inform s.o. *Aku segera ~ Simun* I

quickly informed Simun. **2** report, tell about. *Ia tdk ~ ke mana perginya* He did not say where he was going. **mem-kan 1** inform about. *Ia sengaja ~ kode kpd musuh* He purposely revealed the code to the enemy. **2** announce. *Akhirnya guru ~ siapa-siapa yg naik kelas* Finally the teacher announced who was promoted to the next grade. **ter-** reportedly, it was told that. **pem-an** announcement, notification. *~ pengiriman* notice of shipment. *tanpa ~ terlebih dulu* without prior notice.

berjuis see BORJUIS.

berkah see BERKAT.

berkas 1 bundle, sheaf. *se- kayu bakar* a bundle of firewood. *- cahaya* shaft of light. *- isoglos (Ling.)* isogloss bundle. **2** dossier. **mem- 1** bind, put in bundles. **2** place together in a file. **3** concentrate into a single force. *Lampu kota ~ cahaya di aspal* The street lights projected a beam of light onto the pavement. **mem-kan** put s.t. together in a dossier. **-an** bundle.

berkat 1 blessing, favor. *Ia meminta - org tuanya* She asked for her parents' blessing. **2** thanks to, owing to, due to. *- doa ibuku* thanks to my mother's prayers. *- usahanya* owing to his efforts. **3** profitable, doing well (of an enterprise). **4** small amount of food taken home after ceremonial meal. **mem-i 1** bless, give o.'s blessing. *Pengairan ini ~ penduduk désa ini dgn kehidupan yg baik* This irrigation system has blessed the villagers with a good life. **2** endow, bless with. *Tuhan tlh banyak ~mu* God has blessed you with many things. **te(r)-i** blessed. *Engkau hrs merasa ~* You should feel blessed. *Perawan Maria yg ~ (Rel.)* Blessed Virgin Mary. **ke-an** blessing. **-an** food taken home from ceremonial meal. **pem-an** bestowal of blessing.

berkik k.o. bird, pintail snipe.

berkil k.o. fish, the perch.

bérko bicycle lamp.

berlian polished diamond. *intan -* all sorts of diamonds, gems of all sorts.

bernas 1 filled out. *Lihatlah buah apel yg - rupanya* Look at the filled out apple. *Tanamannya - sekali rupanya* His plants look very promising. **2** full (of breasts). **3** pithy, terse, spirited. *Ia mengadakan pidato yg -* He delivered a spirited speech. **mem-kan** give shape to, fill out. *Ia ~ idé tersebut* He made a reality out of the idea.

bernga see BERENGA.

bero see BERA₂.

beroerte see BERURTE.

berok see BURUT.

berondong see BRONDONG.

berongsang see BERANGSANG.

berongsong 1 muzzle (for dogs). **2** muzzle, gag. **mem-** muzzle, gag.

beronok k.o. sea slug.

berontak 1 struggle, wriggle. *Ia - sekuat-kuatnya mau lepaskan diri* He struggled with all his might to get out (of the hold). **2** revolt, rebel. *Hatinya -* His heart rebelled. **mem- 1** break loose. *Ia ~ dan*

membanting gadis itu ke tanah He broke loose and slammed the girl to the ground. **2** rebel, revolt. **mem-i 1** rebel against. **2** resist. *Keletihan hrs dilawan dan di-i dgn berbagai cara* Weariness must be opposed and resisted in various ways. **pem-** rebel, insurrectionist, mutineer. **pem-an** rebellion, revolt, uprising, mutiny.

beronyong k.o. basket.

beroti slat.

bersih 1 clean, neat. *Piring-piring ini -* These plates are clean. *- suci* 1 unblemished. 2 innocent. **mem-sucikan** purify. **2** innocent. *Ia - dlm hal itu* He was innocent in that matter. **3** pure, unadulterated. *di désa itu masih terdapat adat-istiadat yg -* in that village genuine customs and traditions still exist. **4** net. *penghasilan -* net income. **mem-kan 1** clean up. *Ia ~ tangannya* He washed his hands. *Ia ~ kamarnya* She cleaned up her room. *~ hidung* blow or pick o.'s nose. **2** purify. *Air itu di-kan dan diolah di Pejompongan* The water was purified and processed at Pejompongan. *Sblm kau berani mencintai dia, -kan dulu hati nuranimu* Before you dare to love him, first purify your heart. **ke-an 1** cleanliness, tidiness, neatness. **2** purity. *~ hati* purity of heart. **pem-1** janitor, custodian. **2** cleaner, cleanser. *~ lantai* floor cleanser. **pem-an 1** cleaning, cleansing. *~ rumah* housecleaning. **2** purification (of soul, water). **3** (Pol.) purge. **4** (Mil.) mopping-up. *gerakan ~* mopping-up operation. **5** catharsis. **6** raid, round-up.

bersil mem- protrude.

bersin sneeze.

bersit se- 1 a burst of. **2** a little of. *Tdk ~ pun pikiran mendekati kebenaran!* Thoughts do not come close to reality, not even a little! **mem-1** burst out, gush forth. *Ssdh lama menggali, akhirnya ~ air kehitam-hitaman* After we dug for a long time, at last blackish water gushed forth. **2** protrude, stick out. *~ hidungnya* His nose sticks out. **3** be prominent. *Keseganan ~ dlm hatinya* Reluctance dominated his feelings. **mem-kan 1** whip out. *Ia ~ pistolnya* He whipped out his pistol. **2** exude (odor). *Dagangan kita yg ~ bau asing* It is our merchandise which puts out a strange smell. **ter-** unexpectedly or involuntarily gush forth. *~ rasa dongkol di dadanya* Spiteful feelings welled up in his heart.

bersut mem- 1 hiss, spit at (of dogs, cats). **2** glare at, glower at.

bertam₁ k.o. palm.

bertam₂ k.o. bird, Malayan black wood partridge.

bertih roasted rice kernel.

beruang₁ Malayan bear. **-²an** teddy bear.

beruang₂ see UANG.

beruas k.o. wild mangosteen.

berudu tadpole.

berujul small plowshare.

beruk short-tailed macaque (often trained to pick coconuts). *- mentawai* k.o. macaque.

berumbung tubular, cylindrical.

berungut mem- grumble, gripe. **mem-i** grumble about, have a gripe against. *Ia ~ kakaknya* She had a gripe against her older brother.

beruntusan pimple, rash (prickly heat, etc.).

berurte suffer a stroke.

berus brush. **mem-** brush, groom.

berzanji see BARZANJI.

bés see BIS₄.

bésan 1 relationship between parents whose children are married to e.o. *Amin dan saya adalah -* Amin is related to me as the father of my son-in-law. **2** title used between people in this relationship. **ber-, -an** be related as parents-in-law. **per-an** the relationship between parents-in-law.

besar 1 big, large, huge. *Herman bertubuh -* Herman is a big man. *- cakap* **1** garrulous, talkative. **2** arrogant. *- gabuk* large but weak. *- hati* **1** proud. **2** happy, pleased, elated. *Ia - hati mendengar anaknya lulus ujiannya* He was proud to hear that his son had passed the examination. **ber-** *hati* receive s.t. with joy or pride. *- kecilnya* size. *- kepala* **1** stubborn, obstinate. **2** conceited, vain, stuck-up. *- lambung* greedy, voracious, gluttonous. *- lengan* powerful, influential. *- meriah* grandiose, lofty, pretentious. *- mulut* **1** proud, arrogant. **2** insolent. *- perkataan* conceited, boastful. *- terak* quite large. **2** great, momentous, important. *penemuan* - important discovery. **3** adult, grown. **4** (*Coll.*) grow up. **se- 1** as big as. **2** in the amount of. *cék ~ Rp10.000* a check in the amount of 10,000 rupiah. **se-²nya** as great as possible. *minta maaf ~* deeply apologize. **ber-²** increase. **mem- 1** expand, become big. *Balon itu ~* The balloon expanded. *kesenjangan yg senantiasa ~* ever-widening gap. **2** grow up. *Cepat sekali anakmu ~* Your kid is really growing up fast. **3** increase. *Ketakutannya ~* Her fear increased. **mem-kan 1** enlarge, increase. *Ia ~ lampu* She turned the light on brighter. *~ modal* increase the capital. **2** raise, bring up, rear. *Ia dikan di Malang* He was raised in Malang. **3** magnify, increase. **4** revere, esteem, hold dear. *Ia ~ sejarah negerinya* He speaks with great reverence about his country's history. **5** make great. *Kemenangannya ~ negerinya* His victories made his country great. *~ diri* boast, brag. *~ hati* **1** encourage. **2** please. **3** encouraging. *Situasi ékonomi itu ~ hati* The economic situation is encouraging. **6** extend, expand. *Kawan saya ~ perusahaannya* My friend expanded his business. *Raja itu ~ pengaruhnya* The king extended his influence. **mem-²kan** exaggerate, magnify out of proportion, overstate s.t. **memper- 1** increase. *Bapa tekun bersujud dan ~ amalnya* Father prayed with regularity and increased his charitable acts. *~ lampu minyak* increase the lighting power of the lamp, raise the wick. **2** maximize, enlarge. **ter-** largest, biggest. **ke-an 1** (*Coll.*) too big, oversized. *Sepatu itu ~* Those shoes are far too big. **2** amount, volume. *~ biaya itu tdk disetujui oléh rapat* The meeting did not agree upon the amount of the cost. **3** greatness, grandeur,

might. *~ kerajaan Roma* the grandeur of the Roman empire. *~ alam* nature's grandeur. **4** pomp, ceremony. **-an** bigger. **-²an** on a large scale. *merayakan secara ~* celebrate on a large scale. *operasi ~* large-scale operation. **pem- 1** an official, authority, functionary. **2** high-ranking official, prominent person, big shot. **pem-an 1** expansion, increase. **2** enlargement. *~ hati* **1** encouragement. **2** shot in the arm, incentive, spurt. **3** enlargement (of photos, glands etc.). **per-an** enlargement, magnification.

Besar (*Jv*) 12th month of the Muslim calendar.

besaran mulberry.

bések k.o. covered square basket of plaited bamboo.

besel bribe.

besengék k.o. side dish of chicken.

besér tend to urinate frequently.

beséro see SÉRO₁.

beset₁ scraped (of skin). **mem-** skin, flay, scuff.

beset₂ occupied, taken. *Apakah kursi ini -?* Is this chair taken? **mem-** occupy, take over. **ter-** occupied. *Sementara ia pulang ke kampung tempatnya ~ adiknya* While he was visiting in his village his place was taken by his brother.

besi iron. *- baja* steel. *- belérang* ferrous sulfide. *- berani* magnet. *- berombak* corrugated iron. *- beton* iron rods for reinforced concrete. *- buruk* scrap iron. *- cor* cast iron. *- galbani* galvanized iron. *- gubal* pig iron. *- kuda* horseshoe. *- kuning* k.o. metal said to have magical power, often used in forging weapons. *- lantai* sheet iron. *- lantak(an)* iron bar. *- lémpéng* sheet iron. *- lunak* nonmagnetic iron. *- papan* iron plate. *- putih* tin plate. *- sudur séng* zinc-plated iron. *- sadur timah* tin-plated iron. *- sembrani* magnet. *- sponse* sponge iron. *- tempa* wrought iron. *- tua* scrap iron. *mem- tuakan* turn into scrap iron. *- tuang* cast iron. **mem-** like iron, very strong.

besit see BERSIT.

béskat, béskét vest.

beskit cookie.

beslah seizure, confiscation. **mem-** seize, confiscate. *Karena tdk bisa membayar hutang, mobilnya di-* Because he could not pay, his car was confiscated. **-an** booty, confiscated goods. **pem-an** seizure, confiscation.

beslit 1 gvt. decree. *- kenaikan gaji* decree for pay raise. **2** letter of appointment. *- (peng)angkatan* official letter of appointment.

bésmén (*Coll.*) best man (at wedding).

bésok 1 tomorrow. *- lusa* **1** day after tomorrow. **2** some time in the future. *- malam* tomorrow night. *- paginya* the next morning. *- soré* tomorrow afternoon. **2** later on, in the future. *Anak ini - akan menjadi org yg terpelajar* This child will become a scholar later on. **3** (*Coll.*) later. *Ia akan pergi - bulan Juni* She will go later in June. **4** coming. *Beliau akan dilantik tgl 22 Januari -* He will be installed this coming January 22. **-²** the future. **-nya** the next day.

besot scraped, scratched (of foot).

bestari 1 expert, skilled. **2** bright, clever.

besték₁ specifications, plan (of construction). *menyalahi* - not according to the specifications.

besték₂ see BESTIK.

bestél 1 order s.t. *Apakah Tuan sdh -?* Have you ordered? **2** an order. **mem-** order s.t. **-an 1** an order, s.t. ordered. *~nya sdh datang* The order has arrived. **2** package, bundle, parcel. **pem-an** act of ordering s.t. *~ melalui pos* mail order.

bestik beefsteak.

bestir 1 administration. **2** gvt. **3** board of directors.

bestral radiation (for medical treatment). **pem-an** treatment by radiation.

besuk /besuk/ visit (to patient in hospital). *Kita - Ibu di rumah sakit* We visited Mother at the hospital. *Jam - jam berapa?* What are the visiting hours? **mem-** pay visit to patient.

bésuk see BÉSOK.

besut₁ mem- flow, gush (of blood). **mem-kan** spray, spout, gush (blood).

besut₂ mem- 1 remove rust from metal. **2** improve, refine.

besutan (*Jv*) k.o. comedy show.

bet sound of a sheet (of s.t. being flapped, snatched, etc.).

bét₁ bat (in ping-pong).

bét₂ badge.

béta 1 I (polite form in classical texts). **2** I (used by Malay royalty). **3** (*Amb*) I. **mem-** refer to o.s. as *béta* (as a king would).

betah 1 stand, endure. *Ia - menahan perasaan sakit* She can stand pain. **2** like, feel at home. *Saya baru - tinggal di sini ssdh enam bulan* I only began to like it here after six months. **mem-i** like (a place), feel at ease in (a place). *tempat yg di-i oléh masyarakat* a place in which the community felt at ease. **mem-(²)kan** put at ease, make o. feel at home. *suasana yg ~ an* atmosphere that makes o. feel at home. **ke-an** adjustment. *~ pd hidup* adjustment to life.

betahak see TAHAK.

betak-betak in shreds, in tatters.

betapa 1 how very. *- girangnya org itu menjumpai anaknya lagi* How happy he was to see his child again. **2** as. *Kerjakanlah ini - biasa* Do this as usual. *- lagi/pula* the more so, even more, let, alone. *Ia kaya - lagi ayahnya* He is rich and his father even more so. *Ia tak berani berjalan sendirian, - lagi isterinya* He himself did not dare go alone, much less his wife. *- pun* however.

betara see BATARA.

betas 1 torn, ripped (of jacket, hem). **2** cracked (of egg). **mem- 1** rip, tear. **2** crack.

Betawi 1 Batavia (now Jkt). **2** name of ethnic group indigenous to Jkt. **pem-an** Jakartanization.

bétel chisel.

bétét (*Jv*) k.o. parrot, long-tailed parakeet.

betik₁ ter- 1 be announced. *Kabar ~ bhw buruh akan mogok* It was announced that the workers would strike. **2** leaked out, came to light (of secret).

betik₂ (*in some regions only*) papaya.

betik-betik 1 pimple. **2** rash, prickly heat. **ber-** spotted. *Kulitnya ~* Her skin is spotted.

betina 1 female (of animals). *jantan -nya* its sex. **2** (*Derog.*) woman.

beting shoal, reef, sandbank. **mem- 1** like a shoal. **2** constitute a shoal. **ter-** run aground on a shoal.

betis calf (of leg). *Diberi -, hendak paha* Give him the calf and he wants the whole leg, i.e. give him an inch and he takes a mile. *pagar -* encirclement by people. *Pencuri itu tak bisa lari ketika dikepung pagar -* The thief could not escape when he was encircled by the village people.

betok₁ k.o. fish, climbing perch. *- laut* damsel fish.

betok₂ burned by acid.

beton concrete. *- bertulang* reinforced concrete. *- molen* cement mixer. *- pratekan* prestressed concrete. **mem-** enclose in concrete, build with concrete. *Meréka ~ rumahnya* They rebuilt their house with concrete.

betonisasi program of changing (paths, walls, etc.) to concrete.

betot snatch, pull off. **mem-** remove forcibly, extract. *Pakaian ini banyak ~ mata kaum remaja* This clothing is catching the eye of the teenage crowd. **ke-, ter-** accidentally snatched.

betul 1 right, correct. *Ini alamat yg -* This is the right address. *- salah* appropriateness, correctness. **2** true. *ceritera yg -* true story. *- hati* honest, straight, square, on the level. *Yg - aja dong* Be truthful, huh! **3** exact, right. *Méja ini - ditengah-tengah kamar itu* This table is right in the middle of the room. *Ya -* Yes, exactly. **4** very, really. *Rumahnya besar -* Her house is very big. **-²** truly, sincerely. *Ia percaya ~ kpd org itu* He sincerely trusted that person. **se-nya** actually, in fact, as a matter of fact. *~ saya sdh capé* As a matter of fact I am tired. **ber-an** coincide. *Perkawinannya ~ dgn akhir ujiannya* Her wedding coincided with the end of her exams. **mem-** straighten o.s. out, correct o.'s behavior. *Ia ~ dr kehidupannya yg tdk becus* He straightened up and ceased leading a useless life. **mem-i 1** repair. **2** correct (by repeated efforts). *Ia ~ harapan anaknya* She worked hard to straighten out her child's aspirations. **mem-kan 1** repair, fix (bicycle, etc.). **2** rectify, correct (a mistake). **3** straighten (a tie). **4** revise. **ke-an 1** by chance, coincidentally. *Ia ~ mau pergi juga sehingga kami dpt pergi bersama-sama* Just by chance he was going too so we could go together. **2** happen to, chance to, it so happens. *Saya ~ tahu ttg soal itu* I happen to know about that matter. **3** just right. *~ sekali kamu datang* You came at just the right time. **berke-an** coincide. **-an 1** (*Coll.*) precisely. *Kecelakaan terjadi ~ di prapatan* The accident occurred precisely at the crossing. *yg terletak ~ di tanjakan Nagrek* lying right at Nagrek slope. **2** actually. *Awas, nanti terjadi ~* Watch out or it might really happen. **-²an** real. *main ~* playing for real. *~ ini!* It is for real! *rusak ~* really damaged. **pem-an 1** repair.

2 improvement. **3** correction, rectification. **4** revision.

betung k.o. large bamboo. *membelah* - be one-sided (lit., split a bamboo). *Dlm urusan itu ia membelah* - In that matter he was biased.

bewés see NOMER.

béwok see BRÉWOK.

bewust /bewis/ (*Coll.*) conscious. **ke-an** consciousness.

béza see BÉDA.

bezuk see BESUK.

BF [*blue film*] pornographic movie.

BFO [*Bijeenkomst voor Federaal Overleg*] Conference on Federal Deliberations (Dutch-sponsored committee that helped arrange federal gvt. in Indonesia before 1950, often called Federal Consultative Assembly).

bg. [*bagian*] part, section.

Bg. [*Baginda*] (*M*) title of nobility.

bh. [*buah*] a numeral classifier. *dua belas* - *kapal* 12 ships.

BH /béha/ [*bustehouder*] bra.

bhakti see BAKTI.

bhayangkara see BAYANGKARA.

bhg. [*bahagian*] part, section.

bhinnéka (*Lit.*) diversity. - *Tunggal Ika* Unity in Diversity (Indonesia's national slogan). **mem-kan** diversify. **ke-an** diversity.

bhs. [*bahasa*] language.

bhw. [*bahwa*] that.

b.i., B.I. [*bulan ini*] this month, instant. *sepuluh* - the 10th instant.

bi see BIBI.

BI₁ [*Bahasa Indonésia*] Indonesian language.

BI₂ [*Bank Indonésia*] Bank of Indonésia.

bia see BÉA.

biadab (*Derog.*) **1** ill-mannered, impolite, uncouth. **2** uncivilized, barbaric, savage. *suku bangsa yg* - savage tribe. **3** uneducated, uncultured. **ke-an 1** impertinence, rudeness, insolence. **2** brutishness.

biadi thread worm, pin worm.

biak₁ fertile, prolific, fruitful. - *dara* parthenogenesis. **ber- 1** multiply, flourish. *Pemberantasan buta huruf* ~ Efforts to eliminate illiteracy are flourishing. *Kumisnya* ~ *dgn cepat* His mustache grew rapidly. **2** breed. *Ikan* ~ *subur di sawah ini* Fish breed rapidly in this wet rice field. **mem-**flourish, multiply. *Kupu-kupu malam sdh* ~ *sejak dua-tiga tahun ini* Prostitutes have multiplied in the past two or three years. **mem-kan** cultivate, breed, rear. *Ia* ~ *ikan tambak* He breeds freshwater fish. **-an** s.t. cultivated. *ikan* ~ cultivated fish. ~ *murni* (*Biol.*) pure culture. **pem-an** breeding, rearing, cultivation. ~ *ternak* cattle breeding.

biak₂ wet, damp. **mem-i** wet, dampen.

biak₃ cud. *mamah* - chew the cud.

biang 1 mother (of animals), parent species (of plants). - *ayam* purebred chicken. - *keladi* 1 taro (main root stock). **2** ringleader, mastermind. **mem-keladikan** mastermind in political party.

2 origin, source. - *penghidupan* source or livelihood. - *selisih* source of disagreement. **mem-selisihkan** confuse. *Jangan* ~ *penafsiran* Do not confuse the interpretation. **3** essence. - *cuka* essence of vinegar. - *roti* leaven. - *besi* iron ore. - *jari* thumb. - *keringat* prickly heat. - *kérok* culprit.

biang-biang saltwater herring.

bianglala rainbow.

biar 1 let, permit. - *saya pergi sekarang* Let me go now. - *dia menangis; itu tdk apa* Let him cry; it does not matter. - *mati drp kalah* better dead than defeated. - *lambat asal selamat* slow but sure. - *dahulu* leave it as it is. - *saya urus* leave it to me. - *putih tulang jangan putih mata* better death than disgrace. **2** so that. *Beri makan banyak* - *lekas besar* Give him a lot of food so that he will grow fast. *Lepaskan talinya* - *dia lari* Let go of the rope so she can run. **3** (al)though. - *kecil ia berani* Although she is small she is brave. *bagaimanapun* be that as it may. - *begitu* 1 nonetheless, yet. **2** nevertheless. **-lah** this will do, all right. **-pun** although. ~ *menyembah-nyembah dia tak akan diterima* even if he gets down on his knees and begs, he will never get in. ~ *demikian* be that as it may. **mem-kan 1** let, permit, allow. *Ia* ~ *anjingnya tidur* She let her dog sleep. **-kan!** (*Coll.*) Who cares! So what! ~*! Aku mau meludahinya* Who cares! I want to spit on him. **2** neglect, let go. *Ia* ~ *segala kewajibannya* He neglected all his responsibilities. **3** leave s.o. alone. **4** connive. *Ia* ~ *org mencuri garam pemerintah* He connived with people in stealing gvt. salt. **-in** (*Coll.*) forget it, let it be!

biara 1 monastery, abbey, friary. **2** convent, nunnery. - *induk* cloister. **mem-** become a member of a cloistered community. *panggilan* ~ vocation to enter convent or monastery.

biarawan monk.

biarawati nun, religious sister.

biar-biar k.o. small intestinal worm.

bias 1 ray. *se- sinar lampu* a ray of lamplight. **2** refraction. **ber-** reflect, deflect. **mem-** drift off, deviate. **mem-kan** refract, deflect. *pagi* ~ *teriknya* The morning sun poured out its heat. **-an** refraction, reflection. **pem-an** refraction.

biasa 1 usual, customary. *Ia makan spt* - He ate as usual. *yg* - the usual. **2** used to, accustomed to. *Ia* - *pergi ke sana* She is accustomed to going there. **3** ordinary, commonplace, common. *Di sini tinggal banyak org* - Many ordinary people live here. *Itu* - *saja* It is nothing. **-nya** usually, customarily. **se-²nya** as ordinary as possible. **mem-kan 1** make s.o. accustomed. ~ *diri kpd* adjust o.s. to. **2** make s.t. usual. **mem-²kan** cause to be natural. *Meréka* ~ *sikapnya* They tried to make her behavior seem natural. **ter- 1** habitual. **2** have become accustomed. *Kita* ~ *dgn cuaca buruk dlm bulan ini* We have become accustomed to bad weather this month. **ke-an 1** usage. **2** habit, custom. ~ *dagang* commercial practices. ~ *sehari-hari* daily routine. *menurut* ~ conventional. **pem-an** making people accustomed.

biawak monitor lizard.

biawas k.o. guava.

biaya expense, fee, cost. - *administrasi* administrative fee. - *éksploitasi* operating costs. - *fiskal* departure tax. - *hidup/penghidupan* cost of living. - *kebatalan* opportunity costs. - *pelabuhan* dockage, harbor fees. - *penundaan* towage fees. - *perang* war expenditures. - *perjalanan* travel expenses. - *sampan* lighterage. **mem-i** finance, fund. *Berat sekali utk ~ anaknya bersekolah* It is very hard to finance his child's schooling. **mem-kan** spend, pay out, disburse. *Ia ~ segala simpanannya utk menyekolahkan anaknya* He spent all his savings to send his son to school. **pem-** financier. **pem-an** funding, financing.

Bibel Bible.

bibi, bibik 1 aunt. **2** form of address to older woman (often as *bi*).

bibir 1 lip. *Tutup -mu* (*Vulg.*) Shut your mouth! *Hanya di - saja ia berjanji akan menolong* He was just talking when he promised to help. *-nya spt delima merekah* full, well-shaped lips. - *sumbing* harelip. **2** genital labia. **3** edge. - *hutan* edge of forest. - *mangkok* edge of cup. - *mata* edge of eyelid. *Kecelakaan itu terjadi di - mata saya* That accident took place right in front of my very eyes. - *sumur* edge of well. - *tangan* side of hand. **pem-an** (*Ling.*) palatization.

bibit₁ 1 seed, germ. **2** seedling. **3** germ, bacteria. **4** cause, origin. **5** prospective, future. *Ia - guru* She is a prospective teacher. **6** fledgling, neophyte, novice. **ber-** have a certain k.o. seed or germ. **mem-** create a certain type of seedling. **mem-kan 1** (trans)plant seedlings. **2** yield. *Waktu yg panjang itu tlh ~ sesuatu yg baru* That long stretch of time yielded s.t. new. **pem-an 1** cultivation of seedlings. **2** talent scouting (for new singers, etc.).

bibit₂ see BIMBIT.

bibliograf bibliographer.

bibliografi bibliography.

bibliografis bibliographic.

bicara 1 speak. *Ia - bahasa Perancis* She speaks French. *sedikit - banyak kerja* saying little but doing much. *memotong -* interrupt another's conversation. *(Sedang) -* (*Tel.*) The line is busy. *tanpa - apapun* without saying a thing. - *soal* talk about. *Kita - soal jilbab* Let us take the case of the headcovering. **2** stated opinion, comment. *Apa -mu ttg keadaan itu?* What is your opinion about that situation? **3** (*Leg.*) matter, case, cause. **4** meaningful. **ber- 1** speak. *Ia ~ bahasa Inggeris* She speaks English. *Ia ~ dgn ayahnya* He is talking with his father. *Ia ~ ttg perbelanjaan negara dgn présidén* He discussed the gvt. budget with the president. *kebébasan ~* freedom of speech. **2** meaningful. *Cara hidupnya sekarang tlh ~ ttg keberhasilan kariérnya* His life-style says a lot about his successful career. **mem-kan, memperkan** discuss, talk about s.t. or s.o. *Énak saja kamu ~ anak org!* Aren't you having a good time gossiping about other people's kids! *Dlm rapat itu*

meréka ~ pembélaan negeri In that meeting they discussed national defense. **pem- 1** speaker. **2** adviser, spokesman. **3** lawyer, attorney. **4** discussant. **pem-an 1** discussion, deliberation. **2** conversation.

bicokok 1 small crocodile. **2** (*Jkt*) accomplice, partner in crime. **3** (*Jkt*) rogue, rascal.

bicu, bicu-bicu jack for raising weights.

bid (*Fin.*) bid.

bidaah see BIDAH.

bidadara male sprite.

bidadari 1 fairy. **2** beautiful woman.

bidah /bid'ah/ **1** (*Isl.*) heresy. **2** (*Coll.*) lie, falsehood.

bidai 1 bamboo or rattan screen. **2** basket work. **3** splint. **4** (*Sport*) base (as in baseball). **ber-²** be black and blue (from beating or accident). **mem-** place in splints. *Meréka ~ lengan yg patah itu* They put the broken arm in splints.

bidak (*Che.*) pawn.

bidal₁ proverb, maxim.

bidal₂ thimble.

bidan midwife. **ber-** have a midwife. **mem-i** serve as midwife for s.o. *Siapakah yg ~ isterimu?* Who served as midwife for your wife? **ke-an** midwifery, midwife service.

bidang 1 area, field, sector. - *lingkup* scope. - *percobaan* experimental stretch (of road, etc.). - *penelitian* research area. - *pendidikan* field of education. **2** plane, level, surface. - *alas* base. - *batas* plane to level s.t. - *penyejukan* cooling surface. - *rata* (*Math.*) even level. **3** broad, wide. *Bahunya -* His shoulders are broad. **4** classifier for things broad and flat, e.g. sails, land, mats. *se- tanah* a tract of land. **mem-i** be expert in a certain field. **mem-kan 1** classify, categorize, specify. **2** enlarge, expand. *~ perindustrian* **1** expand industry. **2** specialize industry. *~ tugas meratakan jalan* set up a special division in charge of upgrading the roads. *~ dada* **1** puff up chest. **2** stretch. *~ bahunya* square o.'s shoulders. **-an** stretch, sector, plot. **pem-an 1** tenter, stretcher for cloth. **2** classification. *~ ilmu agama Islam* classification of Isl. theology.

bidara jujube or date tree.

bidari (*Sport*) base (as in baseball).

bidas mem- 1 penetrate, pierce (of attack). *Barisannya ~ jauh di daérah musuh* His troops penetrated far into enemy territory. **2** spring back, fly back (when released) (of trap, bedsprings, etc.). **3** fly from, shoot away. *Batu ~ dr pelanting* The rock flew from the slingshot. **4** attack verbally. *"Apa mau lapar?" ~ ibunya* "What? Do you want to go hungry?" his mother countered. **mem-kan** release s.t. with a springing force. *menyentik dgn belakang ujung jari yg di-kan dgn jempol* snap at with the exterior of the fingertip released from thumb (pressure). *~ tombak* release a spear. **-an 1** reaction. **2** attack. **3** spring movement. **pem-** release device. *~ tombak* javelin releaser with a spring. **pem-an** release, relieving.

bidder (*Fin.*) bidder.

bidding (*Fin.*) bidding.
bidik aim. **mem-** 1 peer, look. *Ia ~ dlm gelap gulita* He peered into the darkness. 2 take aim, draw bead on (by closing o. eye). 3 engage in sharpshooting. *Pemuda-pemuda désa berbaris dan ~* Village youths drilled and fired at targets. **mem-kan** aim. *~ brénnya* aim o.'s machine gun. *~ kamera* aim camera, snap picture. **-an** 1 aim. *Kecepatan keréta api memelesétkan ~nya* The speed of the train ruined his aim. 2 selection, choice. *hasil ~* result of careful selection. **pem-** 1 sight (on gun). 2 o. who aims. *Kalau ~ mengejar angka sepuluh pd témbakannya . . .* If the sharpshooter is going after a score of 10 in his shooting . . . **pem-an** aiming. *~ yg cermat* precise aiming.
bidston, bidstond (*Rel.*) prayer group.
biduan male vocalist, crooner.
biduanda (*Lit.*) palace servant.
biduanita female vocalist.
biduk river craft for cargo or fishing. **ber-** 1 use river craft. 2 go by river craft. 3 go boating.
bidur slab of tin weighing about 2.75 lb.
biduren (*Jv*) suffer from rash (due to cold weather, allergy, etc.).
biduri see BAIDURI.
bier see BIR.
bigami bigamy.
bihara see BIARA.
bihun see MIHUN.
bihus see BIUS.
bijak 1 able, smart, experienced, wise. 2 witty, articulate. **ke-an** 1 wisdom. 2 policy.
bijaksana 1 wise, astute, farsighted. *tindakan yg -* a wise measure. 2 prudent, tactful, discreet. **ber-** be wise. **ke-an** 1 wisdom, prudence. 2 policy. *~ Nopémber 20* rapid devaluation policy promulgated November 20. 3 discretion. *ruang ~* room for discretion.
bijan sesame.
biji 1 seed, kernel. *- jeruk* orange seed. *- padi* unhusked rice. *- polongan* bean seed. 2 stone, pit. *- pala* nutmeg. 3 classifier for small round objects. *tiga - bola* three balls. *- mata* 1 eyeball. 2 darling, sweetheart, apple of o.'s eye. *- sabak* **ber-** *sabak* cry, weep. 4 grade, mark. *Ia mendapat - yg baik di kelasnya* She got good grades in class. 5 (*Sport*) point. *Regu kita mendahului lawan dgn sepuluh -* Our team came out ahead by 10 points. *- kemenangan* (*Sport*) set point. 6 (*Coll.*) testicles. *- kemaluan/pelér* testicle. **mem-** (give a) grade. *Guru itu tak pernah ~ banyak* That teacher never gives very high grades. **-an** digit. **-²an** cereals, various k.o. seeds. **pem-an** 1 grading, giving marks. 2 taking care of seeds, seeding (developing seeds). *peranan ~ dlm kehutanan* role of seeding in forestry.
bijih ore. *- besi* iron ore, hematite.
bik see BIBI.
bika, bikang k.o. rice-flour cake. *- Ambon* k.o. yellow-colored rice flour cake often with bits of jackfruit. **pem-an** cookie pan or mold.
bikel see BEKÉL.

bikin (*Coll.*) make, cause. *- besar* enlarge. *Ia - besar rumahnya* He enlarged his house. *- kejutan* cause a shock. *- malu* shame, embarrass. *- takut* frighten, scare. **-²** pretend, make up. **mem-** 1 make, build. 2 fix, repair. 3 cast a spell. *Kasihan! Anak itu di- org* It is too bad! S.o has put a spell on that kid. **mem-²** fabricate. *pertunjukan yg di-²* a fabricated performance. **mem-kan** make on behalf of s.o. **ter-** made from. **-an** 1 product. *~ Belanda* Dutch product, made in Holland. *~ tahun berapa mobil ini?* What year car is this? 2 fib, lie. *Itu hanya ~ saja, tdk mungkin benar* That is just a fib, it cannot be true. **pem-** maker, builder. *~ uang palsu* counterfeiter. **pem-an** manufacture, construction.
bikini bikini, bikini-style.
biksu /biksu/ Buddhist monk. **ke-an** Buddhist monkhood.
biksuni /biksuni/ Buddhist nun.
biku₁ lace edging. **ber-²** 1 notched, toothed. 2 curve, zigzag.
biku₂ see BIKSU.
bikulturalisme biculturalism.
bikuni see BIKSUNI.
bila 1 when. *- kamu akan pergi?* When will you be going? 2 when, if. *Bawalah buku ini - sdr pergi* Take this book when you go. *Selesaikanlah sekarang - mungkin* Finish it now if possible. *- perlu* if needed or necessary. *-(²) saja* any time. *Datanglah di rumah - saja* Come and see me any time.
bilabial bilabial.
bilah 1 lath. 2 wood chip. 3 knife blade. *- bambu* bamboo blade traditionally used to sever the umbilical cord. 4 classifier for long, narrow objects. *tiga - pisau* three knives. *se- cemeti* a whip. *se- pengaduk* o. blade of a mixer.
bilai 1 hem, border, edge. 2 addition. **mem-** 1 lengthen. *Ia ~ pipa celananya* He lengthened his trouser leg. 2 fill teeth. *Dokter giginya ~ gigi dgn emas* His dentist put in a gold filling. 3 add. *Ia bekerja malam juga utk ~ penghasilannya* He worked at night to supplement his income.
bilal (*Isl.*) muezzin.
bilamana (*Lit.*) when. *Saya pergi - saya selesai* I will go when I am ready. *- juga* any time.
bilang₁ every. *- hari* every day. *- waktu* each or every time. **ber-** some, a few, several. *Ia akan pergi ~ hari* She will be away for several days. *~ kali* several times. **mem-** 1 count. *Ia ~ uangnya* She counted her money. *~ dr satu hingga seratus* count from o. to 100. 2 take into account, consider. *Ia hanya ~ pembesar-pembesar saja* He paid attention only to the big shots. **ter-** 1 be calculated. *Banyaknya kursi ini ~ seratus buah* The number of these chairs was calculated at 100. *Tak ~ banyaknya org di lapangan itu* There were incalculable numbers of people on the square. 2 be regarded as, reckoned as. *Ia ~ org kaya* She is regarded as a wealthy woman. **ke-an** (*Coll.*) prominent, well-known. **-an** 1 amount, sum. *dlm ~ yg besar* in large numbers. 2 (*Math.*) numeral, number. *~ satu seribu* the numbers o. to 1,000.

~ *asli* integers including zero. ~ *bulat* round number. ~ *cacah* integers. ~ *ganjil* odd number. ~ *genap* even number. ~ *khayal* imaginary number. ~ *pecahan* fraction. ~ *persepuluhan* decimal. ~ *pokok* cardinal number. ~ *prima* prime numbers. ~ *tingkat* ordinal number. ~ *urut(an)* ordinal. ~ *utuh* round numbers. **3** area, district, territory. *Ini termasuk ~ kecamatan Obi* This is included in the area of the Obi district. **4** calculation. **5** fate. *Kalau masih bukan ~nya org tak mudah mati* If o.'s number has not come up yet, it is not easy to die. **6** group, sphere. *Ia msk ~ org terpelajar* She belongs to the educated group. **pem-** **1** (*Math.*) numerator. **2** counter, reckoner, teller. **3** quantifier. **pem-an** counting.

bilang₂ (*Coll.*) say. *Apa dia -?* What did she say? *Aku kan sdh* - Haven't I told you? **mem-i** say to s.o., us. scolding. **mem-kan** say, tell. *Ia ~ apa?* What did she say? *Ia tdk ~ nama saya* He did not mention my name. *Di negeri itu boléh di-(kan) tak ada pengemis* In that country o. may say there are no beggars.

bilas mem- rinse, wash off. **mem-i** wash off s.t. *Ibu ~ kain* Mother rinsed off the cloth. *Corong di-i dlm dan luarnya dgn air* The funnel was washed inside and out with water. **-an** flushing, rinse. **pem-an** **1** rinsing, flushing, washing off. **2** ablution.

bilik **1** room, chamber. - *gerbong* (*R.R.*) compartment. - *jantung* (*Anat.*) ventricle. - *markonis* telegraphist's cabin. - *suara* voting booth or room. **2** woven bamboo room divider, plaited screen. **ber-** have a room.

bilingual bilingual.

bilingualisme bilingualism.

bilion bouillon.

bilis bloodshot and burning (of the eyes).

biludak see BELUDAK₂.

bilur welt, wound caused by whip. **ber-²** be hurt by lashing.

bilyar billiards.

bilyét ticket.

bilyun trillion.

Bima Bhima, hero of the Mahabharata.

Bimas [*Bimbingan Masal*] package-deal credit plan offered by gvt. **mem-kan** extend such gvt. credit. *Ssdh di-kan, semua hutangnya dpt dilunasi* After being given gvt. assistance, he could pay all his debts. **pem-an** procedure of extending gvt. credit. *Sebab petani dlm ~ dibébaskan dr pembayaran krédit* . . . Because a farmer included in the credit assistance program is exempted from paying credit charges . . .

bimasakti Milky Way.

bimbang **1** worried, anxious. *Ia - memikirkan ayahnya yg sakit* He was worried about his sick father. **2** hesitate, be dubious about, vacillate. *Ia - akan pergi atau tdk* She hesitated about whether to go or not. - *hati* doubtful. **mem-kan** cause hesitation, make o. restless. *Kabar itu ~ hatinya utk pergi atau tdk* The news caused her to hesitate about whether to go or not. **ke-an 1** vacillation,

doubt, hesitation. **2** worry, anxiety. **3** in doubt. **pem-** worrywart.

bimbing ber- find guidance. *Ia ~ pd Kitab Injil* She found guidance in the New Testament. **ber-², ber-an 1** hold hands, go hand in hand. **2** cooperate, help e.o. **mem- 1** lead by hand. **2** lead, guide. *Présidén ~ rakyat* The president leads the people. **3** conduct, lead. *Ketua itu ~ rapat* The chairperson conducted the meeting. ~ *keluar* show s.o. to gate or exit. **4** introduce. *Mata pelajaran baru di- oléh guru* The teacher introduced a new course. **-an** leadership, guidance. ~ *Massal* gvt.-sponsored program to provide credit. ~ *dan penyuluhan* guidance and counseling. **pem- 1** guide, counselor. ~ *pembaca* reader's guide. **2** leader. **3** (*Acad.*) adviser. **pem-an** leading, guiding, leadership.

bimbit mem- 1 carry by hand. *Ia ~ tas* He was carrying a briefcase. **2** lead by hand. **-an 1** leadership. **2** foreword, preface.

bin 1 (*Isl.*) son of. *Ali - Amar* Ali, son of Amar. **2** (*Coll.*) and furthermore (when between words of similar meaning). *anéh - ajaib* very strange and mysterious. *marah - dongkol* mad and angry.

bina building, construction. - *raga* body building. **mem- 1** build, found, construct. *Ia ~ negara* He founded a state. **2** develop, cultivate. **ter-** cultivated. *kepahlawanan yg ~* carefully nurtured heroism. **pem- 1** builder, cultivator. **2** elder members (of organization). **3** Boy Scout rank similar to Explorer. **4** (*Sport*) coach (esp. training coach). **5** highest rank in civil service. **pem-an 1** founding, establishment. **2** creation, construction. ~ *kembali* reconstruction, restoration. ~ *méntal* character building.

Bina Graha president's executive office.

binal 1 rebellious (of child), uncontrollable. **2** disobedient, obstinate. **3** wild, untamed. **ke-an 1** disobedience. **2** wild behavior. ~ *Tante Monica* Aunt Monica's craziness.

Bina Marga directorate general of highway construction and maintenance.

binang poinsettia.

binar bright. *cahaya yg -* bright light. **ber-²** be very bright. *Penglihatannya ~* He was temporarily blinded; he saw stars. **mem-** radiate. *Eksisténsi individunya ~* O.'s personal existence shines out. *Fajar harapan ~ dgn cemerlang* Rays of hope shine brightly.

binaraga body building.

binaragawan body builder.

binaragawati woman body builder.

binasa destroyed, wiped out. *Kota itu - karena bom atom* That city was wiped out by an atom bomb. *hancur -* utterly smashed to pieces. **mem-kan 1** destroy, annihilate. **2** exterminate. **ke-an** death, demise. **pem-** destroyer, annihilator, eradicator. **pem-an 1** total destruction. **2** extermination, annihilation.

binatang animal. - *berkantung/beruncang* marsupial. - *buas* wild animal. - *hantu barat* tarsier. - *kerat/mengerat/pengerat* rodent. - *melata* reptile. -

lunak mollusc. - *menyusui* mammal. - *perusak* destructive animal, pest (rodents, etc.). - *piaraan* domesticated animal. - *rumah* house pet. - *timangan* pet. **mem-kan** degrade, debase. **ke-an** bestiality, brutality.

binatu laundryman.

bincacak small, spritelike evil spirit.

bincang ber-(²) discuss, deliberate. *Meréka ~ hingga jauh malam* They had a discussion until far into the night. **mem(per)-kan** discuss, talk about s.t. *Ia ~ soal keamanan* He discussed the problem of security. **per-an 1** discussion, deliberation. **2** conference.

bincul lump, bump, bruise. **mem-** bruise.

bindeng (*Jv*) nasal (of speech). *Suaranya -* He has a nasal twang.

bindu lathe. **mem-** use or work a lathe.

binéka see BHINNÉKA.

binen see BINNEN.

binér binary.

bingar see HINGAR.

bingas quick-tempered, short-tempered, irascible.

bingit 1 ill at ease, uncomfortable. **2** jealous, envious.

bingka hemispherical-shaped cake of leavened rice flour.

bingkah bit, lump, fragment, chunk. **ber-²** in bits, in fragments. **mem-** smash to bits, break into chunks. **-an** lump, chunk.

bingkai 1 brim, rim, fringe, edge. **2** frame. - *gambar* picture frame. - *hiasan* trim. *rumah putih dgn - hiasan hitam* white house with black trim. - *mata* rim of eye. - *pintu* doorframe. - *roda* rim of wheel. **ber-kan** framed with. *lukisan ~ bambu* picture framed in bamboo. **mem-(kan)** frame, border (picture). **-an** frame.

bingkap legging, puttee.

bingkas 1 resilient, elastic. **2** elasticity. **ber-** bounce, rebound. **mem- 1** bounce, rebound. *Bola ténis ~* the tennis ball bounced. **2** jump up. *Ia ~ dr tempat duduknya* He jumped up from his seat.

bingkil see BÉNGKÉL.

bingkis mem-kan send gift. **-an 1** gift, present. **2** souvenir. **3** parcel, package.

bingung 1 confused, bewildered, flustered. **2** disoriented, unsure of direction. **3** panicky. **4** perplexed. **mem-kan 1** confuse, bewilder, fluster. *Peraturan ini ~ rakyat* This regulation confuses the people. **2** perplexing, disconcerting. **ke-an 1** suffering from disorientation. **2** confusion, bewilderment. **3** panic. **4** perplexity.

bini (*Derog.*) wife. *mencari -* (*Coll.*) chase after girls. - *aji* concubine. - *gahara* legal wife. - *muda* **1** additional (2d, 3d, etc.) wife. **2** mistress. - *simpanan* mistress. - *tua* first wife. - *yg terang* legal wife. **ber-** have a wife. *Ia ~ org asing* He has a foreign wife. *Ia ~ dua* He has two wives. **ber-kan** take as wife, marry with (a woman). **memperkan 1** make s.o. o.'s wife. **2** marry off (o.'s male relative). *Ia ~ anaknya yg sulung* He married off

his eldest son. **-²an** (*Coll.*) **1** keep taking wives, womanize. **2** mistress, paramour. *Ia bukan -nya, ~ saja* She is not his wife, but just s.o. he is playing around with.

binkap see BINGKAP.

binneka see BHINNÉKA.

binnen (*Coll.*) elite, established.

binomium binomial.

bint see BINTI.

bintak stain.

bintang 1 star. - *babi* Vesper, evening star. - *Belantik* Orion. - *beralih* meteor, shooting star. - *berasap/berbuntut* comet. - *berédar* planets. - *berékor/berkoték* comet. - *biduk* Big Bear. - *bulan* crescent moon and a star, symbol of Isl. - *corat-corat* meteor, falling star. - *gugut* falling star. - *Jadi* Capricorn. - *johar* Venus. - *jung* Big Bear. - *Kala* Scorpius. - *Kartika/Ke(r)tika* Pleiades. - *kejora* Venus. - *(ke)mintang di langit* starry host, stars in firmament. - *kukus* comet. - *laut* starfish. - *Marikh* Mars. - *Mayang* Virgo. - *Musytari* Jupiter. - *Pari* Southern Cross. - *penganjur/pengarak siang* morning star. - *sapu* comet. - *siang* morning star. - *sayarah/siarah* planet. - *Timur* Venus. - *Tohok* Southern Cross. - *Tujuh* Pleiades. - *Utara* N. Star. - *Waluku* Orion. - *Waruna* Neptune. - *Zahal* Saturn. - *Zuhara* Venus. **2** star, fate, luck. *-nya naik* His star is rising. **3** s.o. with notable qualities. - *kelas* top pupil in class. - *layar putih* film star. - *pelajar* best student at final exam. - *pendukung* supporting star or cast. - *sandiwara* stage star. **4** medal, decoration. - *jasa* service medal, medal for meritorious service. - *kehormatan* military or civilian decoration. **se-** born under same star. *Saya ~ dgn dia* I have the same zodiac sign as he has. **ber- 1** starry. *malam ~* starry night. **2** be lucky. *Hidupnya tak ~* He is unlucky. *~ gelap* have bad luck. *~ terang* have good luck. *Ia ~ terang selama ada di negeri asing* He had good luck while abroad. **ber-² 1** starry. *langit terang yg ~* clear sky with many stars. **2** starry-eyed. **3** see the stars. *Stlh terlempar ke méja, pandangannya ~* After being slammed to the table, he saw stars. **4** shine through, glitter (esp. from holes in the roof). **mem-i** star in (movie, etc.). *Langit Malam di-i oléh Usman* Usman stars in the film *Evening Sky.* **-an 1** constellation. **2** artificial star. **per-an 1** astronomy. **2** astrology. **3** horoscope.

bintangur see BENTANGUR.

bintara soldier in lowest grades. - *pelatih* noncom, training officer. - *tinggi* (*Mil.*) senior noncommissioned officer, petty officer.

binténg jahé chewy confection of sticky rice flour, ginger, and sugar.

binti (*Isl.*) daughter of. *Salimah - Saléh* Salimah daughter of Saleh.

binti-binti daughters.

bintik spot, stain. - *hitam* blackhead. - *tinta* ink-spot. **ber-² 1** having small spots. **2** bead (of sweat). *Peluh ~ di dahinya* Sweat beaded on his forehead.

bintil 1 small pimple, pustula. **2** nodule.

bintit sty in eye.
bintul slight bump, e.g. from insect bite.
bintur k.o. trap for crabs.
binturung bear cat.
bio (*Ch*) Confucian temple.
biografi biography.
biokimia biochemistry.
biokimiawan biochemist.
biokimiawi biochemical.
biola violin.
biologi biology. - *laut(an)* marine biology.
biologik, biologis biological.
biologiwan biologist.
biopsi biopsy. - *ginjal* renal biopsy.
bioritme biorhythm.
bioskop movie theater, cinema. **per-an** 1 cinematic matters. *masalah* ~ problems pertaining to movie theaters. 2 movie theater management.
bipang k.o. sugared, puffed-rice cake.
bipolar bipolar.
bipolarisasi bipolarization.
bipolér see BIPOLAR.
bir beer. - *hitam* stout. - *kaléng(an)* beer in cans. - *tong(an)* draft beer.
birah 1 k.o. large aroid with edible tuber and sap that causes itching. 2 lascivious, salacious. **ke-an** lasciviousness.
birahi see BERAHI.
birai 1 low wall, balustrade. 2 banister, railing. 3 curb, edge, border.
biras 1 relationship between two men marrying sisters or between two women marrying brothers. 2 coreferent title between two persons in such situations.
birat scar or scab around mouth.
biri-biri₁ sheep.
biri-biri₂ see BÉRI-BÉRI.
birih see BIRAI.
biring₁ k.o. extremely itchy skin disease. - *paluh* prickly heat.
biring₂ yellowish red.
birit buttocks, bottom, rear. **ter-²** 1 helter-skelter, hurriedly (scramble). *Kami* ~ *menuruni jurang dlm itu* We scrambled down the steep ravine. *lari* ~ run head over heels, hurry. 2 suffer from slight diarrhea.
biro office, bureau. - *iklan* advertising bureau. - *perjalanan/wisata* travel bureau.
birokrasi bureaucracy.
birokrat bureaucrat.
birokratis bureaucratic.
birokratisasi bureaucratization.
birokratisme bureaucratism.
birput cesspool.
birsam pleurisy.
biru₁ 1 blue. - *cuci* bluing. - *langit* sky blue. - *laut* aquamarine, navy blue. - *legam* black and blue. - *muda* light blue. - *sembam* bruise. - *telar asin* aquamarine. - *tua* dark blue. *mata yg* - 1 blue eyes. 2 a black eye. 2 above average (grades), C or better. **mem-** turn blue. *Bibirnya* ~ *karena*

dingin Her lips turned blue from the cold. **mem-kan** color s.t. blue (by painting, dyeing, etc.). **ke-²an** bluish.
biru₂ fold, hem, pleat. **ber-** pleated.
biruang see BERUANG₁.
bis₁ bus. - *antarkota* intercity bus. - *kilat* express bus. - *kota* city bus. - *luar kota* intercity bus. - *malam* express night bus. **nge-** (*Jv*) go by bus. **mem-kan** (*Coll.*) send by bus. *Ia* ~ *barang-barang* She sent the packages by bus.
bis₂ box. 2 post office box, mailbox. - *surat* letter box, mailbox.
bis₃ 1 twice. 2 encore. 3 (*Leg.*) supplement, annex, codicil.
bis₄ 1 tube, duct. 2 pipe.
bis₅ 1 covering for ornamentation or protection. 2 piping, thin strip sewn on cloth, trimming. - *ban* wide strip of cloth sewn as trim. *Ia memakai jubah hitam dgn - biru* He wore a black robe with blue trim. 3 (*Elec.*) bushing.
bisa₁ be able, can, could. *Ia tdk - datang* She cannot come. - *jadi* possible, likely. *tdk - jadi* impossible, out of the question. **-²** possible, quite likely. ~ *lu dikeluarin* You are liable to get fired, buddy! **-²nya** just manage to do. *Dr mana dpt uang* ~ *beli tustél?* Where did he get money so he could manage to buy a camera? **se-nya** where possible. *Pd tiap sajak* ~ *disebutkan sumber* Wherever possible the source of every poem is given. **se-²nya** 1 as much as possible. 2 to the fullest extent. *Meskipun cedera,* ~ *ia membaca doa* Although he was injured, he recited a prayer as best he could. **ke-an** ability, capacity.
bisa₂ 1 poison. 2 poisonous. *ikan* - poisonous fish. **ber-** poisonous, venomous (of injected poison). **ke-an** 1 virulence, toxicity. 2 poisoned. *Kambing itu mati* ~ The goat died from poisoning.
bisép (*Anat.*) biceps.
bisik 1 whisper. 2 say in whisper. **ber-(²)** 1 whisper. *Ia* ~ *kpd temannya* She whispered to her friend. 2 speak confidentially. *Meréka* ~ *utk membékot majikannya* They spoke in secret in order to exclude their boss. **ber-an** whisper to e.o. *Dua org tentara msk saling* ~ Two soldiers came whispering to e.o. **mem-i** 1 whisper to s.o. *Ia* ~ *kawannya spy pergi* He whispered to his friend to go. 2 whisper at. 3 (*Thea.*) prompt. **mem-kan** 1 whisper. ~ *perintah* whisper an order. 2 suggest, imply. *Kejadian itu* ~ *rencana yg tetap kpdnya* That incident suggested a definite plan to him. *Ada yg* ~ *bhw saya hrs tinggal di sini* S.t. tells me I should stay here. **-an** 1 whisper. 2 whispering. ~ *hati* 1 conscience. 2 outpouring of o.'s heart. **pem-** (*Thea.*) prompter.
bising 1 noise, uproar, hullabaloo. 2 noisy. 3 buzzing (in ear). *Pilek ini membikin telinga kita* - This cold has made my ears ring. **ber-** 1 make noise. 2 be dazed. **mem-kan** 1 cause s.o. to suffer from noise, deafen. *Suara TV* ~ *tetangga di sebelah* The noise from the TV was too loud for the next-door neighbor. 2 cause ringing in ears.

Bunyi itu ~ *telinga* The noise rang in his ear. **ke-an 1** noise, uproar. **2** suffer from buzzing in ears.
biskit see BISKUIT.
biskop bishop.
biskuit /biskwit/ **1** cracker. **2** Dutch rusk.
bislah see BESLAH.
bislit see BESLIT.
bismillah (*Isl.*) in the name of God (recited at beginning of each *surah*). *baca* - say grace before meal, utter prayer before undertaking task.
bismut bismuth.
bisnis business.
bisték, bistik rump steak, roast beef, beefsteak.
bisu 1 dumb, mute. - *batu* **ke-batuan** totally mute. - *tuli* deaf and dumb. *si* - deaf-mute. **2** quiet, noiseless. *kepekatan malam yg* - the unspeaking depth of the night. *Sampan melaju dgn* - The dugout glided on noiselessly. *Ia mengangguk* - He nodded without saying anything. *film* - silent movie. - *(seribu) bahasa* not say a thing. *Jawabannya* - *seribu bahasa* She refused to answer a word. **bersi-, ber-an** not speaking to e.o. *Dgn* ~ *kedua anak itu saling bersuratan* Though not speaking to e.o., the two children were exchanging letters. **mem-** keep quiet, say nothing. ~ *seribu bahasa* refuse to say a word. *Dia ditanya tapi* ~ *seribu bahasa* They asked him, but he kept totally silent. **mem-kan** eliminate (noise), effect quietness. ~ *kesusastraan* kill literature. **ke-an 1** muteness. **2** silence. *memecahkan* ~ break the silence.
bisul 1 boil, abscess, ulcer. - *benata* small abscess on upper lip. - *jerawat* pimple on face. - *lada* small boil. - *perut* gastric or stomach ulcer. - *sabut* carbuncle. **2** tumor. **mem-** ulcerate, develop boils. **-an** suffer from ulcers or boils.
bit beet.
biting coconut leaf rib splinters sharpened to point, for pinning packets wrapped in leaves. - *keju* cheese on skewer.
biuku k.o. freshwater turtle.
bius drugs. **mem- 1** make unconscious by using drugs. *Ia di- tak ingat pula* He was drugged and could no longer remember. **2** anesthetize. **mem-i, mem-kan 1** drug s.o. **2** captivate, attract. *Naséhat itu* ~ *hatinya* That advice captured his attention. **ter- 1** drugged. **2** intoxicated, exhilarated. *Jangan* ~ *dgn tarian ngak ngik ngok itu* Do not get high on those gyrating rock and roll dances. **keter-an** state of being under influence of drugs. **ke-(an)** be unconscious (due to drugs). **pem-** anesthetist. **pem-an** anesthetization. ~ *umum* general anesthetization.
bivak bivouac.
biyaya see BIAYA.
biyuh (*Jv*) oh no! (an exclamation of astonishment, pity).
biyung (*Jv*) **1** mother. **2** Mama! (exclamation of pain or emotional duress). *"Aduh! -!" tangisnya menggaung* "Ow! Mama!" he cried loudly.
BKPM [*Badan Koordinasi Penanaman Modal*] Co-ordinative Agency for Investments.

BKR [*Badan Keamanan Rakyat*] People's Security Body (forerunner of Indonesian national army).
bl- see also entries with **bel-**.
BL [*Barat Laut*] N.W.
bl., bln. [*bulan*] month.
B/L [*bill of lading*]
blacksweet /blékswit/ (*Coll.*) dark and attractive.
blaf (*Coll.*) bluff.
blak-blakan outspoken, blunt. *Ia tdk* ~ *mengatakan begitu* She did not come right out and say so.
blam sound of explosion.
blanco see BLANGKO.
Blandis pro-Dutch (esp. during revolutionary period).
blandong lumberjack. **-an 1** timber. **2** lumber-jacking.
blang sound of explosion. --*bleng* sound of repeated explosions.
blanggur (*Jv*) large firecrackers, esp. to mark end of each fasting day during Ramadan.
blangko 1 form to be filled in. - *pos wésél* postal money order blank. **2** abstention in voting. **3** blank (of paper).
blangkon (*Jv*) male batik headdress.
blangwér, blangwir (*Coll.*) fire engine. *Kuur, pi, pi alamat* - *mau datang* The whining sirens and clanging bells meant the fire engine was on its way.
blanko see BLANGKO.
blantik₁ (*Jv*) broker, middleman in livestock.
blantik₂ see BELANTIK₁.
blantika world, arena. *dlm* - *rekaman* in the world of recordings. *dlm* - *nyanyi internasional* in the international arena of song. *Indriasari muncul di* - *musik pop blm lama* Indriasari has not been in the music scene very long.
blarak dried coconut leaf.
blasak mem- make o.'s way through scrub or forest.
blaster mem- crossbreed. **-an 1** crossbred (of animals). **2** (*Derog.*) of mixed blood, mulatto.
blau (*Coll.*) **1** blue. **2** laundry bluing. **ke-an** bluish.
Bld. [*Belanda*] **1** Dutch. **2** Holland.
blecas-blecos (*Coll.*) speak without thinking, talk off top of o.'s head. *Kamu omong* - *tanpa didasari pengetahuan* When you talk you say any old thing without any factual basis. *omongan* - gossip.
bledak-bleduk sound of objects randomly striking e.o. repeatedly. *Barang-barang di bak truk bergoyang* - The goods in the back of the truck shook with a rattling noise.
bledék thunder.
bléjét mem-i 1 strip s.o. (of possessions). *Bu Samirah di-i kalungnya oléh dua gali* Two gangsters ripped off Bu Samirah's necklace. **2** strip (of pretensions), expose (a criminal). *Penguasa AS sdh di-i dan dikorék habis-habis oléh pérs* The US gvt. was exposed and strongly criticized by the press.

blék tin can.
blekék see MBLEKÉK.
blekok k.o. heron.
bléncong (*Jv*) oil lamp used in *wayang* performance.
blendok see SAKIT.
bleng₁ sound of explosion.
bleng₂ (*Jv*) natural brine.
blépotan (*Coll.*) 1 be smeared all over with s.t. 2 be messy.
blesek (me)m- pushed in, be sunk in. *Hidungnya ~* He has a flat nose. *Tubuhnya ~ ke dlm rawa-rawa* His body sunk into the swamp. mem-i cram into. *Bis penghabisan itu di-i dgn karyawan* The last bus was jammed with workers. mem-kan cram s.t. into a hole, shove s.t. into. *Kura-kura ~ kepalanya* The turtle pulled its head into its shell. ke- fallen into a hole, sunk in mud.
blétok mud, muddy.
bléwa, bléwah k.o. melon.
bléyer (me)m- (*Coll.*) race (engine), rev up.
blinger ke- (*Coll.*) very wrong, led astray.
blingsatan 1 wriggle (because of excessive heat). 2 feel awkward, be ill at ease.
blobor m- blot, smear while writing (of ink, water colors, paper). *Tintanya ~* This ink causes the paper to blot.
blok₁ 1 bolt, roll. - *cita* bolt of cloth. - *silinder* (*Auto.*) cylinder block. 2 block, street block. - *rumah* block of houses. 3 bloc, alliance. - *Timur* Eastern bloc. nge- (*Coll.*) favor o. bloc. *Malaysia sedang ~ ke Barat* Malaysia is siding with the W. now.
blok₂ mem- (*Coll.*) obstruct.
blokade blockade. mem- to blockade.
blokir mem- 1 blockade. 2 obstruct. 3 (*Fin.*) freeze (account), stop (check). pem-an blockading.
bloknot note pad.
blong 1 free from tension, relieved. 2 not properly tensile, not holding or catching (of mechanical parts). *Rémnya - dan dia tdk bisa berhenti lagi* Her brakes gave way and she was no longer able to stop.
bloon 1 stupid, idiotic, dumb. 2 wacky, crazy, loony.
blorok motley (of chickens).
blorong (*Jv*) 1 black and white striped. 2 k.o. viper. - *imperialisme Amerika* American imperialistic viper.
blouse /bluse, blus/ see BLUS.
bludag see BELUDAK₁.
bludas-bludus (*Jv*) go in and out (without permission).
bludrék hypertension.
blujin denim trousers, blue jeans.
bluk thump! (sound of heavy object falling on soft surface).
blumkol cauliflower.
blus woman's blouse.
blusuk (*Jv*) mem- go through place in which passage is difficult (crowds, scrubs, narrow alleys,

etc.). *Ia suka ngeluyur atau ~ ke tempat-tempat keramaian umum* He likes to wander about squeezing into busy public places.
bluwok k.o. bird.
B'masin city of Banjarmasin.
Bn. [*batalyon*] battalion.
BNI [*Bank Negara Indonésia, 1946*] the 1946 National Bank of Indonesia (a national bank).
boat /bo'at/ (*Sl.*) drugs.
bob bouffant. *Rambutnya dipotong -* Her hair is done in a bouffant style.
boba (*Amb*) ulcerations caused by frambesia.
bobo, bobok₁ sleep (of young children or in children's speech). mem-kan put to sleep.
bobok₂ (*Jv*) mem- 1 pierce, break open. 2 forge a way through. -an 1 hole, aperture. 2 site of break-in.
bobok₃ (*Jv*) k.o. soothing powder.
bobol give way, collapse. *Dam yg baru dibangun itu -* The newly constructed dam gave way. mem- break into. *Tukang itu ~ témbok* The workman broke an opening into the wall. *Rumahnya ludes di- pencuri* Thieves broke into the house and stole everything. mem-i tear down several things. *Buldozer sibuk ~ pagar-pagar liar* The bulldozer is busy tearing down illegal fences. mem-kan 1 pierce, penetrate, breach. *~ tanggul Ciserut sepanjang empat méter* breach the dike at Ciserut for four meters. 2 (*Sport*) penetrate, pierce (opponent's goal). *~ gawang regu lawan* make a score against rival team. 3 ruin, destroy. *~ apartemén luks* ruin a luxury apartment. ke-an 1 pierced, penetrated. 2 penetration. *~ jala* (*Sport*) penetration of the net. 3 caught unawares, hit (by theft). *Dlm waktu dua minggu Bank Umum Nasional ~ Rp64.000.000* In two weeks' time Bank Umum Nasional was hit with 64 million rupiah's worth of bad checks. -an pierced hole. *~ tanggul* a pierced dike. pem-an 1 piercing. 2 making a score.
bobos breach, crack, tear. *Témboknya -* There is a crack in the wall. mem- pierce, penetrate. *Peluru itu ~ témbok* The bullet pierced the wall.
bobot 1 heavy. *Berapa -nya?* How heavy is it? 2 weight, heaviness. - *atom* atomic weight. - *mati* dead weight. - *setara* balanced weight. 3 integrity, quality (of literature, persons, etc.). memberikan - *perhatian* center o.'s attention. -, *bibit, bébét* (*Jv*) quality, origin, and rank: qualities for ranking a prospective son-in-law. ber- have weight. *Pidatonya ~* Her speech carried weight. *seniman ~* an artist who has s.t. to say in his field. mem-i add weight to s.t.
bobrok 1 dilapidated, shoddy, ramshackle. *Rumahnya -* His house is dilapidated. 2 rotten, degenerate. *Masyarakatnya -* The society had degenerated. - *akhlaknya* immoral. mem-kan collapse, topple, bring down. ke-an 1 collapse. 2 evil, badness.
bocah kid (of prepuberty age). *Ia masih -* He is still a child. ke-²an childish.
bocél chipped. mem-kan chip s.t. -an chip, nick.

bocong jug.
bocor 1 leak. *Ia menambal -* He plugged the leak. **2** leak, be leaky. *Atapnya -* The roof leaks. *Rahasianya -* The secret leaked out. *- mulut* garrulous, talkative, run off at the mouth. **3** (*Coll.*) urinate (frequently). **4** (*Coll.*) suffer from diarrhea. **5** (*Coll.*) bleed. **mem-kan 1** divulge, leak (secret). **2** cause leak, puncture (tire, etc.). **ke-an 1** damaged by leakage. *Kamarnya basah karena ~* The room is wet from leaking. **2** leakage, divulgence. *~ rahasia itu merugikan pemerintah* Leaking the secret hurt the gvt. **3** puncture. **-an 1** leak. **2** leakage. *air ~* leaking water. **pem-** o. who reveals secrets. **pem-an 1** leaking. **2** divulging (secrets, etc.).
bodo₁ see BAJU.
bodo₂, bodoh stupid, dumb, dull-witted. **se-** *amat* I do not give a darn. **ber-², ber-** *diri* pretend to be stupid, feign stupidity. **mem-** act stupid. **mem-i** fool, take in. *Ternyata rakyat tdk bisa di-i* It turned out that the people could not be fooled. **mem-kan 1** keep ignorant. *Pemerintah itu mencoba ~ jajahannya* That gvt. attempted to keep its colony in ignorance. **2** dupe, take s.o. in, make a fool of. *Saya sama sekali di-kan* I was completely taken in. **3** consider a fool, consider ignorant. **mem-per-** keep s.o. ignorant. **ke-an 1** stupidity, idiocy, folly. **2** ignorance. **3** mistake, error. **-²an** pretend to be stupid. **pem-an** duping, tricking, fooling. *~ rakyat besar-besaran* large-scale deception of the people.
bodok initial stages of leprosy.
bodol₁ windfall.
bodol₂ (*Jkt, Jv*) torn or with holes. *celana -* old and ragged pants. *karung -* basket full of holes.
bodong protruding, bulging (of navel).
bodréks k.o. patent medicine for colds.
bof swollen thyroid glands.
bogél see BUGIL.
bogem *- mentah* blow with the fist.
bogénvil see BUGÉNFIL.
bogi₁ bogey (in golf).
bogi₂ see KERÉTA₁.
bogot see HITAM.
boh curve, arch (as in pipes, etc.). **nge-** (*Coll.*) make a sharp turn. **-²an** (*Coll.*) turning, way of making a turn.
bohong 1 lie, falsehood. *-! Kau hanya malas* Lies! You are only lazy. *kabar -* false news. **2** lie, prevaricate. *Kau -! Kau betul-betul mengkhianati kami* You are lying! You are really betraying us. **ber-, mem-** lie, tell a lie. **mem-i** lie to s.o., deceive s.o. *Ia ~ saya* She lied to me. *~ janji* break a promise. **mem-kan 1** lie about s.t. **2** deny. *~ segala tuduhan* deny all accusations. **ke-an 1** lie, falsehood, untruth. **2** lying. **-²an** fake, false. **pem-** liar. **pem-an** lying.
bohorok a seasonally strong wind in E. Sumatra.
boikot boycott. **mem- 1** boycott. **2** ostracize (playmate, etc.). *Kami sepakat ~ Nono* We all agreed not to speak to Nono. **-an** s.t. boycotted. **pem-an** boycotting.

bojo (*Jv*) spouse.
bok₁ /bok/ playpen.
bok₂ see MBOK₁,₂.
boké₁ see BUKÉT.
boké₂, bokék (*Sl.*) broke, destitute. *Gué lagi - nih. Pinjamin Rp500 dong* I am broke right now. Lend me 500 rupiah, will you?
bokét see BUKÉT.
bokong 1 buttocks. **2** hindpart first, the wrong way around. **3** back. *memikul beban di -* carry a load low on the back. **mem- 1** attack from the rear. **2** secretly, on the sly. **mem-i** turn the buttocks to. *~ adiknya* She stuck out her butt at her younger sister. **pem-an** treacherous attack.
bokor 1 copper or silver bowl with wide rim. **2** (*Sport*) loving cup, trophy.
boks₁ box on a newspaper or magazine page.
boks₂ see BOK₁.
buksen (*Coll.*) boxing.
bokser (*Coll.*) boxer.
boksit bauxite.
bol₁ (*Jv*) anus.
bol₂ (*Coll.*) testicles.
bol₃ see BENANG.
bol₄ see JAMBU.
bola 1 ball. *- bopéng* golf ball. *- bulu tangkis* shuttlecock. *- huruf* typewriter ball. *- kaki* soccer. *- kasti* game of catch. *- keranjang* basketball. *- sépak* soccer ball. *- sodok* billiards. *- tampél* tennis ball. *- tangan* handball. *- tojok* billiards. *- tongkat* field hockey. **2** globe. *- bumi* terrestrial globe. **3** spherical object. *- lampu* 1 lightbulb. 2 lamp globe. *lampu - kilat* flashbulb. *- lampu pijar* lightbulb. *- langit* fireball, meteorite. *- mata* eyeball. *- sépok* bladder. *- turut bunyi* resonator.
bolak-balik 1 to and fro, back and forth. *Bis ini pergi - ke Semarang* This bus goes to Semarang and back. *Berapa harga karcis - ke Cirebon?* How much is the round-trip ticket to Cirebon? *Malam itu ia habisi dgn berbaring -* He spent the whole night tossing and turning. *fotokopi -* back-to-back photocopy. **2** frequently, again and again. *Ia - pergi ke kantor imigrasi* He keeps going back and forth to the immigration office. **3** contradictory. *Omongnya -* Her conversation was contradictory. **mem- 1** turn s.t. again and again. *Titi ~ surat ibunya* Titi turned her mother's letter over and over. **2** turn over and over. *Sampai jauh malam ia ~ di tempat tidur* Till late at night he tossed and turned in his bed. **mem-(kan) 1** turn s.t. again and again for s.o. **2** twist, distort. *Ia pandai ~ perkataannya* He was clever at twisting her words. **pem-an** repeated turning back and forth. *~ kompas* erratic spinning of compass.
bolang-baling₁ 1 propeller. **2** weathervane, whirligig. **ber-** be provided with propeller or weathervane.
bolang-baling₂ k.o. fried sweet roll.
bolbal [*bolak-balik*] back and forth. *pesawat -* space shuttle vehicle.
boléh 1 be permitted, may. *Meréka - berumah di sini* They are permitted to live here. *Mana -?*

How is it possible? How could it be? **2** (*Lit.*) be able, can. *Apa - buat?* What can o. do? *Seberapa - pekerjaan ini hrs diselesaikan bésok* Insofar as possible, this job must be completed tomorrow. *- jadi* probable, probably. *ke- jadian* probability. *Tak - jadi* It cannot be. *- juga* **1** fair, not bad. *- juga pekerjaannya itu* His work is not too bad. **2** maybe, likely. *- juga ia ikut ayahnya* It is not unlikely that he went with his father. *tak - tdk* have to, unable to avoid. *Ia tak - tdk hrs pergi* She cannot avoid having to go. **-lah** all right. *~ kalau begitu* very well then. **se-²nya** to the extent possible, as much as possible. **mem(per)-kan** permit, allow. *Tdk diper-kan msk* It is forbidden to enter. **ke-an** ability, skill, cleverness. **berke-an** able, skillful, clever.

boling bowling. **pe-** bowler, o. who bowls.

bolong 1 perforated, pierced. *- melompong* completely empty. *uang -* coin with hole in the center, esp. five-cent piece of colonial era. **2** precisely. *Ia tiba pd tengah hari -* She arrived precisely at noon. *siang/tengah hari -* broad daylight. **ber-²** pierced, perforated. **mem-i** put a hole in s.t. **ke-an** perforation. **-an** place where handle of shadow puppet is affixed.

bolos₁ 1 penetrated, with a hole. *kertas itu -* the paper has a hole in it. **2** (*Coll.*) truant. **mem-1** desert, go AWOL. **2** play hooky, cut class. **3** escape from captivity. **pem- 1** truant, absentee. **2** deserter. **pem-an** absenteeism. *Produksi berkurang karena ~* Production goes down due to absenteeism.

bolos₂ see BULUS₂.

bolot mem- wrap up.

bolpén, bolpoin ballpoint pen.

bolsak see BULSAK.

Bolsyéwik Bolshevik.

bolu k.o. spongecake.

bom₁ 1 bomb. *- atom* atomic bomb. *- (pem)bakar* incendiary bomb. *- brisan* high explosive bomb. *- kambang* sea mine. *- laut* depth charge. *- peledak* high explosive bomb. *- tarik* land mine. *- waktu* time bomb. *- zar(r)ah* atom bomb. *- zat air* hydrogen bomb. **2** (*Coll.*) fart. **nge-** (*Coll.*) pass gas, fart. **mem-(i), menge-(i)** bomb. *Musuh ~ kota* The enemy bombed the city. **pem-** bomber. *~ tempur* fighter bomber. **pem-an** bombing.

bom₂ 1 boom (at a barrier), gate, bar. **2** customs. **3** wagon tongue. **4** (*Naut.*) boom.

bombardemén bombardment, bombing.

bombardir mem- 1 bombard, shell, bomb. **2** appoint without regard for qualifications. *Ia ~ adiknya menjadi menteri pertahanan* He appointed his younger brother minister of defense. **3** shower, bombard. *Ia ~ kawannya dgn pertanyaan* He bombarded his friend with questions.

bombasme bombast.

bombastis bombastic.

bombon bonbon.

bomo, bomoh medicine man, native practitioner, shaman.

bon₁ 1 check, bill. *Minta -, ya!* The check, please.

2 voucher for payment, IOU. **(me)nge- 1** put on a (monthly) account, pay with an IOU, buy s.t. and pay later. *~ dulu, ya, tgl tua nih* Put it on my account, okay, it is the end of the month now. *Buruh Filipina diperboléhkan ~, tetapi buruh kita jangan harap bisa begitu* Filipino workers are permitted to charge, but our workers cannot even hope to be able to do so. **2** borrow (prisoners), temporarily shift custody of detainees (to put them to work). *~ tahanan yg biasa dilakukan oléh polisi* the lending out of prisoners for work details which the police like to engage in.

bon₂ alliance, league.

bonafide /bonafit/ bona fide, without fraud.

bonafiditas reliability, genuineness.

bonang gamelan instrument consisting of row of tuned inverted bronze bowls.

bonbon candy. *- karét* chewing gum.

boncéng get a ride on a two-wheeled vehicle. **ber-an** ride along with s.o. on a two-wheeled vehicle. **mem- 1** get a ride on a two-wheeled vehicle. *Boléhkah saya ~ pulang* May I get a lift home? **2** sponge on. *Ia ~ ayahnya* He sponges on his father. **3** share in another's fame, bask in another's limelight. **4** get a free ride (on train, bus, etc.). **mem-i** get a free ride with s.o. *PKI ~ legalitas* The Communist Party developed under the aegis of legality. *Perjuangan kami tlh di-i oléh kaum munafik* Hypocrites have gotten a free ride from our struggle. **mem-kan** give s.o. a ride. **ter-** ride along, be a rider with s.o. **-an 1** ride double. **2** s.t. carried on the back of bicycles and motorcycles. **3** bicycle rack. **pem-** sponger, freeloader, o. who bums a ride. *~ gelap* illegal passenger. **pem-an** obtaining a ride.

boncol see BONJOL.

bondo (*Jv*) goods, capital.

bondong group, throng, crowd. **-an** throng, crowd. *~ org* throng of people. **ber-(²), ber-an** in throngs, in great numbers. *Buruh berdatangan ~ memprotés potongan gaji* The laborers arrived in great numbers to protest the cut in pay.

bondot bundle, bunch. **mem-** bundle, tie up.

bonéka 1 doll. *- pajangan* mannequin. **2** puppet, marionette. *- jari* finger puppet. **3** figurehead, front. *pemerintah -* puppet gvt. **mem(per)-kan** use as a puppet. *Negara itu ~ pemimpin bekas jajahannya* That country made puppets of the leaders of its former colonies. **-²an** stooge, puppet.

bonét (*Leg., Acad.*) cap, mortarboard.

bong₁ Ch grave.

bong₂ bang!

bong₃ professional circumciser.

bongak 1 proud, arrogant. **2** stupid. **mem-** boast.

bonggol₁ 1 hump. **2** outgrowth. **3** knot on tree. *- jagung* corn cob.

bonggol₂ mem- strike over and over, hit repeatedly.

bongkah numeral classifier for lumps, chunks, etc. *se- batu* a slab of stone. *se- daging* a hunk of meat. *se- mas* a gold nugget. *se- uang* a wad of money. **mem-** dig up into clumps. **-an** hunk, chunk, nugget.

bongkak 1 proud. **2** insolent, arrogant.

bongkar take apart. *- muat* loading and unloading. *- pasang (Auto.)* overhaul. **mem- 1** force open, dig up. *Ia ~ pintu* He forced the door open. **2** break in. **3** demolish, wreck (building). **4** disclose, uncover, expose (plot, secret). *~ kejahatan* expose evils. **5** unload, discharge (ship). **6** open up, uncrate, unpack. **7** dismantle, disassemble, take apart (engine). *~ pasang* overhaul (engine). *~ sauh* weigh anchor. **mem-i** take apart. **ter-** disclosed, bared, uncovered. *Komplotan itu ~* The plot was uncovered. **ke-an** get broken into. *Rumah kami ~ tadi malam* S.o. broke into our house last night. **-an** unloaded goods. **pem- 1** o. who breaks open (doors, houses, etc.), house burglar. **2** demolisher, wrecker. **3** o. who discloses s.t. **pem-an 1** disclosure, expose. **2** demolition, removal. *~ bangunan* clearance of buildings.

bongkar-bangkir scattered, spread about. **mem-** spread, scatter about (often in anger).

bongkok see BUNGKUK.

bongkol 1 knob. **2** hump. **3** head (of lettuce). **ber-** having a hump. *lembu yg ~* (Brahman) cattle characterized by fatty deposits above withers.

bongkong stupid.

bongkot 1 tree trunk. **2** tree stump. **3** base of plant stem, etc. *- kol* cabbage stalk. *- sapu lidi* base of broom (handle). **-an** with a stump. *bambu ~* bamboo with stump.

bongkrék (*Jv*) inedible (of misshapen, diseased tubers or fruits). *tempé -* fermented cake made from peanuts after the oil has been pressed out; this foodstuff is often poisonous.

bonglai see BENGLÉ.

bongméh mem- 1 feel o.'s pulse. **2** note, observe.

bongok short and fat.

bongpai (*Ch*) tombstone.

bongsang small fruit basket.

bongsor 1 oversized, overweight. **2** big, tall.

bonjol 1 lump. **2** projection. **3** protrude.

bonjor fortification.

bontak chubby, bulging (of cheeks, etc.).

bontot₁ (*Jv*) rice wrapped in leaves to eat away from home. **mem-** bring food on trip. **-an 1** s.t. wrapped (in cloth, etc.) for carrying, (cloth) bundle. **2** food for journey.

bontot₂ (*Jv*) youngest (child).

bonyok, bonyor 1 flabby (of flesh). **2** soft, mushy (of fruit). *- hancur* really beat up, finished. **3** tainted, rank (of meat, fish).

boom /bom/ see BOM₂.

booking /buking/ see BUKING.

boong see BOHONG.

boorwater /borwater/ see BORWATER.

bop see BOB.

bopéng 1 pockmarked. **2** full of pot-holes (of roads). **mem-kan** create pockmarks. **ke-an** covered with pockmarks.

boper buffer.

bopét see BUFÉT.

boplo construction unit or group.

bopong mem- hold s.o. up against o.'s chest. **-an** sling to hold a baby against o.'s chest. **pem-** supporter. *~ yg bergairah* enthusiastic supporters.

bor drill, brace and bit. *- bit* auger. *- kecil* gimlet. *- listrik* electric drill. **mem-, menge-** drill, bore. **-(²)an** drilled (of water, well, etc.). **penge-** driller. **pem-an, penge-an** drilling. *anjungan ~* drilling platform.

borak (*Isl.*) winged steed that carried Muh. to heaven.

boraks borax.

boraq see BORAK.

bordél see BORDIL₁.

bordés balustrade.

bordil₁ bordello, brothel.

bordil₂, bordir embroidery. **mem-** embroider. **mem-kan** embroider s.t. *Ia ~ tanda silang ke bajunya* He embroidered a cross on his shirt. *Sutera kuning di-kan di roknya* Her dress was embroidered with yellow silk. **-an** embroidered object, embroidery.

bordu (*Naut.*) gunwale.

boreg, boreh 1 guarantee, security, warranty, collateral. **2** guarantor. **mem-kan** make s.t. collateral. *Kalau pinjam uang dr Tuan Abdullah mesti ~ emas* If o. borrows money from Abdullah, he must use gold as collateral.

boréh medicinal powder mixed with water used as ointment or liniment. **mem-i** rub an ointment on s.o. or s.t. **meng-kan** rub s.t. as a liniment on.

borék see BURIK.

borg see BOREG.

borgol handcuffs. **mem-** handcuff. **pem-an** handcuffing.

borhan proof.

borjuasi bourgeoisie.

borjuis bourgeois. **-²an** similar to or related to bourgeoisie. *soal ~* bourgeois issue.

boro-boro (*Jkt*) do not expect even that much (s.t. less is even unlikely). *- dia datang, nulis surat ajé nggak sempat* Don't even think about his coming, he doesn't even have time to write.

borok 1 ulcer, boil, sore. **2** ulcerous, mangy, itchy. **3** bad, rotten. *Ia - hatinya* He is very bad. *- kejahatan* the ulcer of crime. **ber-, mem-** fester, be ulcerous. *Luka yg tak dirawat bisa ~* Untreated wounds can fester. **pem-an** festering.

borong the entire stock. **mem- 1** buy up the entire stock, take all of s.t. *Rudi Hartono ~ beberapa piala kejuaraan dunia* Rudy Hartono took several world championship cups. **2** do an entire job. *Perusahaan itu ~ segala pembangunan* The firm contracted to do the entire construction job. **3** hold various positions. *Berapa jabatan aja yg di-nya?* How many jobs has he commandeered for himself? **mem-kan 1** sell wholesale. *Ia ~ barang-barangnya kpd pembeli itu* He sold the goods wholesale to the buyer. **2** give the entire contract. *Ia ~ pembangunan rumahnya kpdnya* He gave the entire contract for construction of his house to him. **-an 1** total sale. **2** work contracted for. *pekerjaan* ~ contract work. *penerbangan* ~ *Denpasar-Manila* charter flight from Denpasar to Manila. **pem- 1** contractor. ~ *bangun-bangunan* building contractor. **2** (wholesale) supplier, purveyor. **pem-an 1** wholesale buying or selling. **2** contracting, chartering.

boros 1 wasteful, extravagant. *Ia sangat - tak bisa menyimpan uang* He was very wasteful and could not save any money. **2** lavish. **mem-** be wasteful. **mem-kan** waste, squander. *Mandi semacam itu sangat* ~ *air* Bathing like that really wastes water. **ke-an** wastefulness. **pem- 1** squanderer, wastrel. **2** big spender. **pem-an 1** wasting, squandering. **2** extravagance, lavishness.

bortel, bortol see WORTEL.

boru Batak kinship term, daughter of a clan. - *Ginting* daughter of the Ginting clan.

borwater boracic solution.

bos₁ bunch, bundle. *satu - kayu bakar* o. bundle of firewood. *satu - rokok* a carton containing 10 packs of cigarettes.

bos₂ (*Auto.*) bushing.

bos₃ (*Sl.*) boss.

bosan 1 bored. *Lama-lama kami - juga menunggu* After a while we were bored waiting. **2** tired of, fed up. - *hidup* weary of life. *Ia - mendengar perkataan itu* She was fed up with those words. *tak -²* never flagging, never tiring. *Ibunya tak -² menghibur Munah* His mother never flagged in her efforts to divert Munah. **mem-kan 1** bore, leave cold. **2** boring, humdrum, tedious. *kata-kata* ~ hackneyed phrases. **ke-an** boredom, ennui. **pem-** o. who becomes bored easily.

bosen (*Coll.*) see BOSAN.

bosman₁ boatswain.

bosman₂ Bushmen (of Africa).

bosor pierced, full of holes. - *makan* greedy, ravenous.

bot₁ motorized boat (us. with outboard motor).

bot₂ boot.

botak bald (headed). **mem-** become bald. **mem-i 1** shave off all hair, shave s.o. bald. *Kepala kamp menyuruh meréka* ~ *tawanan* The leader of the camp ordered them to shave the heads of the detained persons. **2** strip completely bare. *Pengambilan kayu bakar* ~ *hutan* The taking of firewood stripped the forest bare.

botani botany.

botanikus botanist.

botik see BUTIK.

boto, botoh₁ shapely, nice, comely. *jago -* handsome champion.

botoh₂ croupier, gambling chief (cockfighting, etc.).

botok dish made of coconut and meat, fish, etc. wrapped in banana leaf and steamed. - *tahu* bean curd cooked in such a way.

botol 1 bottle. - *hampa udara* vacuum bottle. - *susu* baby bottle. - *takaran* graduated flask. **2** bottled (in set expressions). *téh -* tea in bottles (or cartons). **ber-²** bottled. *Dia mentraktir bir* ~ He picked up the tab for the beer, bottle after bottle. **mem-kan** bottle s.t. **pem-an** bottling.

bougie see BUSI.

boven see NAAR BOVEN.

boyak see BAYAK.

boyas potbellied, fat, obese.

boyok small of back.

boyong a move from o. place to another. - *pulang* return home. **ber- 1** move, shift, change, remove. *Ia sdh* ~ *ke tempat yg baru* She has already moved to a new place. **2** emigrate, settle. **(me)m-1** move, shift. ~ *modalnya ke Jkt* move o.'s funds to Jkt. **2** capture, take away s.t. *Ia dpt* ~ *empat buah medali* He captured four medals. **mem-kan** move s.t. *Ia* ~ *pendiriannya melalui ucapan-ucapannya yg tepat* He shifts his position under the cover of pat phrases. **-an** moving, removal. *Apakah engkau sdh* ~? Have you already moved? **pem-an 1** emigration, settlement, colonization. **2** removal, shifting. ~ *benda-benda kebudayaan* removal or shifting of cultural objects.

BP [*Balai Pustaka*] Gvt. Printing and Publishing House.

BPKB [*Buku Pémilik Kendaraan Bermotor*] certificate of ownership of motor vehicles.

BPS [*Biro Pusat Statistik*] Central Bureau of Statistics.

br- see also entries with **ber-**.

brahmana Brahmin.

brahmani Brahmin (woman).

brai bell bottom, flared (of trousers).

brambang shallot.

brandal 1 rascal, scoundrel. **2** gangster, bandit. **mem- 1** be a gangster or bandit. **2** commit an act of banditry, commit rascally act. **ke-an** rascally, villainy, wantonness. **-an** madcap, hothead. *rencana* ~ madcap scheme.

brangus muzzle (of dogs). **mem-** censor, muzzle. *Pemerintah Afrika Selatan selalu* ~ *pers yg antiapartheid* The gvt. of S. Africa always censors the antiapartheid press. **pem-an** censorship.

brankar hospital cart, stretcher.

brankas safe, strongbox.

brantam see HANTAM.

branwir see BLANGWÉR.

bratawali 1 k.o. vine the leaves of which are used in bitter medicinal concoctions. **2** a concoction containing such leaves, often used in university initiations.

bray see BRAI.

brayat nuclear family.

brebet (me)m- make sound of static. **mem-kan** cause s.t. to emit static.

brédel see BRÉIDEL.

breg sound of s.t. heavy falling.

bréidel bridle. **mem- 1** check, curb. **2** muzzle (critics), close down (press). ~ *koran itu* shut down that newspaper. **pem-an** muzzling.

brem (*Bali*) see BERAM.

brén k.o. light machine gun.

bréndi brandy.
breng-brengan pungent, excessive (of fragrance).
bréngos (*Jv*) moustache. **-an** mustachioed.
bréngsék /bréngsék/ **1** useless, in bad condition, no good. *réklame yg* - a lousy advertisement. *sopir yg* - a no good driver. **2** Hell! It is all messed up! (exclamation of disapproval). **ke-an** lousiness. ~ *administrasi* breakdown in administration. ~ *suatu rejim yg berkuasa* lousiness of a regime in power.
bret sound of a sheet (of s.t.) snatched away.
brétél suspenders.
brévét certification, license, flying certificate.
brevir (*Rel.*) breviary.
bréwok (*Jv*) whiskers, sideburns. **-an** (*Coll.*) be-whiskered, bearded.
BRI [*Bank Rakyat Indonésia*] People's Bank of Indonesia (state-controlled bank).
bridge /brits/ bridge, the card game.
briefing /brifing/ short oral summary of a project or organization. **mem-** deliver a short summary.
brigade brigade.
brigadir jénderal brigadier general.
brigjén [*brigadir jénderal*] brigadier general.
brikdan, brikdans breakdance.
brikét briquet.
bril (*Coll.*) eyeglasses.
brilyan₁ brilliant, highly intelligent.
brilyan₂ brilliant (cut of diamond).
brintik curly (hair).
brisik see RISIK₂.
Britania Raya Great Britain.
brocél (*Jv*) having a rough surface, uneven and not smooth.
broche see BROS₁.
brojol m-, mem- (*Jv*) come out (from within o.'s body) unexpectedly. *Mau ke RS bersalin, éh bayinya* ~! We were on the way to the maternity hospital, and all of a sudden the baby came! *Anak itu tak tahan, ya*, ~ *di celana* That kid could not hold it, so he did it in his pants.
brok sound of s.t. heavy falling. **nge-i** (*Jv*) defecate on s.t. (us. of babies).
brokat brocade.
bromfits see BROMPIT.
bromida bromide.
bromocorah repeat offender.
brompit moped, motor bicycle.
brondol featherless, hairless.
brondong fusillade. *jagung* - popcorn. **mem-1** fire a volley. *Kalau Belanda dengar, di-nya kamu!* If the Dutch hear you, they will shower you with bullets. **2** shell, bombard. *Meréka ~nya dgn pertanyaan-pertanyaan* They bombarded her with questions. **-an** barrage, volley of gunfire, spray of bullets. **pem-an** bombardment.
brongkol (*Jv*) lump under skin.
bronhitis bronchitis.
bronjong concertina (barbed) wire. *memasang - kawat* unroll the concertina wire.

bronsitis bronchitis.
bros₁ brooch.
bros₂ crisp, brittle.
brosur brochure. **mem-kan** put in form of a brochure.
bruder religious brother, friar. **-an 1** friary, abbey. **2** place (esp. school) operated by religious brothers.
brujul (*Jv*) *sapi* - oxen for plowing. **mem-** plow. **-an** plowing.
bruk sound of many hard things falling together.
brul sound of rapid movement of many. *Begitu bendera dikebut, -, seluruh rombongan melangkah aducepat* As soon as the flag was waved, with a thunderous noise, the whole group raced forward.
brur brother, a reference and address term, esp. in Protestant circles.
brutal 1 very violent, brutal. *film yg* - graphically violent film. **2** impudent, insolent. **ke-an** brutality.
bruto gross. *berat* - gross weight. *pendapatan* - gross income.
brutu fleshy part of fowl's tail.
BS₁ [*Burgerlijke Stand*] (office of) civil registration. *kawin* - civil marriage.
BS₂ [*Bayar Sendiri*] (*Sl.*) pay o.'s own way, Dutch treat.
bt. [*binti*] daughter of (in Isl. names).
BTN [*Bank Tabungan Negara*] National Savings Bank (state-controlled bank).
bto. [*bruto*] gross.
bu₁ (*Amb*) brother (term of address to men somewhat older than o.s.).
bu₂ see IBU.
bu₃ see BA₂.
buah 1 fruit. - *méntéga* avocado. - *punti* k.o. large, sweet banana. - *sulung* beginning, first fruits. - *tempayan* pitcher plant. - *terlarang* forbidden fruits (us. sex). **2** s.t. shaped like a fruit. - *baju* button. - *betis* calf of leg. - *catur* (*Che.*) chessman. - *dacing* weights. - *dada* breast, bosom. - *dam* checker (game). - *geli(-geli)/ginjal* kidneys. - *kandungan* fetus. - *kerinjal* kidney. - *khuldi/kuldi* apple of Garden of Eden. - *lengan* biceps. - *pantat* cheek (of buttocks). - *pelir* testicles. - *pinggang/ punggung* kidney. - *zakar* testicles. **3** result. *Usahanya tak ada -nya* His efforts are fruitless. - *perundingan* result of the discussion. - *kalam* essay, writing. - *karya* literary work. - *keringat* result of o.'s efforts. - *péna* essay, writing. **4** focus, topic. - *bibir/bicara/cakap* subject or topic of conversation. - *hati* **1** heart. **2** sweetheart. - *mimpi* dream. - *mulut* subject or topic of conversation. - *pelajaran* **1** subject of study. **2** result of study. - *pikiran* opinion. **5** a classifier of large objects. *serumah o.* house. *tiga - negeri* three countries. **ber-1** bear fruit, yield a harvest. **2** have results. *Usahanya* ~ Her efforts bore fruit. **ber-kan** yield s.t., result in s.t. *téori* ~ *kerja* a theory resulting in action. **mem-i** impregnate, fertilize. *Spérma* ~

ovum pd saat senggama Sperm fertilizes the ovum at the moment of sexual union. **mem-kan 1** bear (fruit, child, etc.). ~ *keturunan* bear a descendent. **2** produce, yield, result in. *Harapan tdk selamanya ~ kenyataan* Hope does not always yield realities. **-²(an)** fruit of all kinds. ~ *campur* mixed fruit. **pem-an** conception, fertilization.

buai₁ swing. **ber-(²)** swing. *Anak itu ~ di udara* The child was swinging in the air. **mem-(kan) 1** swing s.t., rock s.t. *Ia ~ anaknya* She rocked the child in her arms. *org yg ingin ~ diri dlm kenang-kenangan nostalgis* s.o. who wants to lose himself (lit., swing himself back and forth) in nostalgic memories. **2** cause s.t. to fluctuate. **-an** swing, cradle, hammock.

buai₂ mem- stroke (hair, cat, etc.). **ter-** in a state of oblivion because of bliss. *Gadis itu ~ oléh rayuan pacarnya* The girl was lulled into security by her lover's sweet talk.

bual 1 bubbling over (of liquid). - *sumber* bubbling of the spring. **2** boasting, big talk, bragging. *Saya benci mendengar - org itu* I am sick and tired of hearing that man's big talk. **ber-(²), mem-(²) 1** bubble up, fizz, foam (of liquid). **2** brag, boast, talk big. *Ia ~ kpd teman-teman* He boasted to our friends. **mem-kan 1** spout, expel (a liquid). *Sumber itu ~ air panas* The well spouted forth hot water. **2** brag about s.t. *Ia ~ ceritera yg tdk-tdk* She spouted forth nonsense. **pem-** loudmouth, braggart.

buana (*Lit.*) earth, universe.

buang throw (away). - *angin* break wind. **mem-1** throw, cast. *Ia ~ bola kpd saya* He threw a ball to me. ~ *aksi* pose, posture, strike an attitude. ~ *arang (di muka)* cause shame, humiliate. ~ *belakang* 1 run, flee. 2 unwilling to know. ~ *dadu* play at dice. ~ *jangkar* cast anchor. ~ *lambai* wave. ~ *langkah* 1 flee, escape. 2 execute a step back in fencing, martial arts, etc. ~ *mata* throw a glance, look around. ~ *muka* 1 avert o.'s eyes. 2 dislike, have no use for. ~ *peluru* (*Sport*) put the shot. ~ *sauh* cast anchor. ~ *sipat* do s.o. bodily harm. ~ *tangan* move hand to deliver blow (in martial arts, etc.). ~ *undi(an)* 1 play at dice. 2 draw lots. **2** throw away, cast off, discard. *Ia ~ pakaian yg tlh sobék* He threw away his torn clothes. ~ *air besar* defecate. ~ *air kecil* urinate. ~ *ancak* make an offering (of food) to spirits. ~ *angin* pass gas, break wind. ~ *bini* divorce o.'s wife. ~ *diri* 1 commit suicide. 2 isolate o.s., go into seclusion. ~ *hajat besar* defecate. ~ *hajat kecil* urinate. ~ *hamil* have an abortion, abort. ~ *ingus* blow o.'s nose. ~ *lelah/letih* take a break, rest. ~ *malu* 1 cause shame, humiliate. 2 take revenge. ~ *nama* disgrace s.o.'s name. ~ *nafas* exhale strongly (in swimming, etc.). ~ *nyawa* 1 throw o.'s life away. 2 die. 3 court death. ~ *pandang* look or glance around. ~ *penat* take a break, rest. ~ *seluruh adat* leave tradition behind. ~ *sepanjang adat* expelled and ostracized by the community. ~ *sial* break an unlucky streak (often by undergoing ceremonies, hair cutting, etc.). ~ *sikap/tingkah* 1 remove,

get rid of an attitude. **2** act, walk, or talk in an affected manner. **3** exile, banish. *Pemerintah ~ org hukuman* The gvt. exiled the convicts. **4** waste (time, energy, money). ~ *mulut* speak insincerely. ~ *obat* fire or shoot wildly. ~ *pukulan* parry a blow. ~ *témbakan* fire or shoot wildly. ~ *témpo/waktu* waste time. **mem-kan 1** throw, toss, cast. **2** discard s.t. on s.o.'s behalf. **ter- 1** expelled. **2** in vain. **ter-²** neglected. **-an 1** s.t. cast off, discarded object. **2** exile, outcast. **pem-** thrower, hurler. ~ *bom* bomber. **pem-an 1** exile, banishment. **2** elimination, removal. ~ *sampah* garbage disposal. ~ *air* 1 run off, drainage. 2 spillway. **3** renunciation (of o.'s rights), renouncement.

buani (*Lit.*) universal.

buar extravagant, wasteful. **pem-** spendthrift, lavish spender.

buas 1 wild (of animals, natural phenomena). **2** cruel-hearted, ruthless. **mem-** be cruel. **mem-kan** make wild, excite. *Manusia tak akan jadi begitu kalau tak ada yg ~* Man does not get like that if there is no o. exciting him. **ke-an** cruelty, savagery, ferocity. **pem-an** activation, excitement.

buat 1 do, make. **2** for. - *apa?* For what? - *saya* for me. - *sementara* for the time being. **3** in order to. *Ia pergi - belajar* She went in order to study. **ber-** do, act. *Ia tak ~ apa-apa* He does not do anything. ~ *jahat* do wrong. ~ *olah* be tricky, make difficulties. ~ *sérong* cheat (in love relationship). **mem- 1** make. ~ *salah* make a mistake. ~ *perkara* take legal action, sue. ~ *rencana* draw up a plan. **2** do. *Akan ~ apa kalau sdh begini?* What are we going to do if it is like this? ~ *logika* draw a logical inference. **3** cause. *Ia ~ anaknya takut* He frightened his child. **mem-²** feign, pretend. *basa-basi yg di-² saja* polite conversation that was merely feigned. **memper- 1** make, build. **2** do, perform. **3** make into. **ter-** made. *rumah yg ~ dr bambu* house made of bamboo. **-an 1** make, brand. ~ *luar negeri* foreign make. ~ *mana jam itu?* Where is the clock made? **2** product. ~*nya baik* It is a good product. **3** artificial, false. *gigi ~* false teeth. *mata ~* artificial eye. *pemijahan ~* induced spawning. *perkawinan ~* artificial insemination. *pupuk ~* commercial fertilizer. **4** pretense, sham. **-²an** artificial, false. *kesopanan ~* artificial courtesy. **pem-** maker, producer. ~ *jalan* road builder. ~ *undang-undang* legislator, framer of laws. **pem-an** production, manufacture. ~ *jalan* road construction. **per-an 1** deed, act. ~ *Rasul-rasul* (*Bib.*) Acts of the Apostles. **2** action. **3** performance. **4** conduct, behavior. ~ *melanggar hukum* illegal act.

buaya 1 crocodile, alligator. **2** villain, scoundrel, bounder. - *darat* 1 thief, scoundrel. 2 woman chaser. - *pasar* pickpocket. - *tangsi* bullying soldier's son. - *uang* usurer. **mem- 1** creep on the belly. **2** chase women, be a Don Juan. **mem-i 1** cheat, deceive. **2** scare, bully.

bubar 1 disperse, scatter. *Org banyak itu - karena kedatangan tentara* The crowd dispersed upon the arrival of the army. *Rapat itu - jam tujuh* The meeting broke up at seven. **2** (*Mil.*) Fall out! Dismissed! **mem-kan 1** disperse s.t., break up. *Polisi ~ org-org yg berkumpul di muka kantor itu* The police broke up those gathered in front of the office. *Hadirin yg lebih lima ratus org itu ~ diri* The more than 500 present dispersed. **2** dissolve, liquidate. *~ perséroan* dissolve a partnership. **3** close down (a factory). **-an** dispersal. *sampai ~ skor 3-0 utk Semarang* At the end (of the game) the score was 3-0 in favor of Semarang. **pem-an 1** dispersal, breaking up. *~ tentara sukaréla* disbandment of the volunteer army. **2** dissolution (of firm, association, cabinet, etc.). **3** abrogation (of treaty, agreement).

bubrah (*Jv*) fall apart, scatter all over.

bubras (*Jv*) scraped off (of skin). *Saya jatuh dan siku saya -* I fell and scraped my elbow.

bubu a plaited rattan fish trap. **mem-** make o.'s living by catching fish with such a trap.

bubuh mem- put or place on. *~ garam* add salt to. *~ harga* set a price. *~ tanda tangan* sign, affix a signature. **mem-i 1** add to s.t., affix to s.t. *~ garam sedikit sopnya* add a little salt to the soup. *~ kode* program (in computer). **2** apply s.t. to. *~ cat* daub, paint on. **mem-kan** add, append, attach, affix. *~ titik pd kalimat itu* add a period to a sentence. **ter-i** get placed onto. *Surat-surat yg sdh ~ tanda tangan disendirikan* Put the letters that already have a signature attached off to o. side. **-an** addition. **pem-an** placing. *~ tanda lalu lintas* placing of traffic signs. *~ kode* programming (of computers).

bubuk₁ 1 powder. *- beras* rice powder. *- besi* iron dust. *- kayu* sawdust. *hopi coffee powder. - roti* breadcrumbs. *- sabun* soap powder. *- tulang* bonemeal. **2** s.t. which has been pulverized. *kopi -* powdered coffee. *merica -* ground pepper. **mem- 1** become or turn into dust. **2** grind, pulverize. **-an** s.t. ground up. *~ kaca/glas* ground glass. **pem-an** pulverization.

bubuk₂ k.o. insect, woodborer.

bubul₁ 1 sore on palm or sole. **2** corns on hooves of animals. **-an** suffer from such sores.

bubul₂ mem- repair, fix (net, etc.).

bubul₃ mem- soar, rise skyward (of fire, swarm of insects). **mem-kan** cause to rise upward. *~ perasaan yg anéh* enkindle a strange feeling.

bubun-bubun (*M*) fontanel.

bubung 1 top, ridge. **2** ridgepole. **mem-** rise, go upward. *Pesawat terbang ~* The plane rose. *Harga kopi ~* The price of coffee rose. *~ tinggi* soar, skyrocket (of prices). **mem(per)-kan** raise, increase (prices). **-an 1** ridge (of house). **2** ridgepole. **3** cam.

bubur porridge, gruel, mush. *Nasi sdh jadi -* The rice has turned into porridge, i.e. there is no use crying over spilt milk. *- kacang ijo* porridge of mung beans. *- kayu* wood pulp. *- ketan* porridge of glutinous rice. *- mérah* ceremonial rice porridge with palm sugar. *- sumsum* porridge of rice powder. **mem- 1** make porridge. **2** become mush.

bubus mem- swarm out. *Semut ~ dr lobang* Ants swarmed out of the hole. **-an** culvert.

bubut₁ *mesin -* lathe. **mem-** operate a lathe. **-an** lathe. **pem- 1** lathe worker, turner. **2** lathe.

bubut₂ mem- 1 pull up, pluck (grass, hair, etc.). **2** extract (a tooth). **mem-i** pluck hair, fur, etc. from s.t. *~ ayam* pluck a chicken.

bubut₃ (*Naut.*) stay, brace. **-an** guy, stay.

bubut₄ k.o. bird, coucal.

bucu angle, corner.

Buda see BUDHA.

budak 1 servant, slave. *- belian* bondslave. *- gembala* herdsman, shepherd. **2** (*Lit.*) youngster. **mem-** become a slave. **memper-, mem-kan 1** treat as slave. *Raja itu ~ rakyatnya* The king treated his subjects as slaves. **2** enslave. **pem-an** enslaving. **per-an** slavery, bondage, servitude.

budanco rank in defense units during Japanese occupation.

budaya 1 culture. *org yg -nya tdk begitu tinggi* person who is not very refined. *antropologi -* cultural anthropology. **2** practice. *- semacam ini jangan diteruskan* A practice like this should not be continued. *- télepon* practice of directing editors to remove sensitive news items. **ber- 1** cultured, civilized. **2** have a certain culture. **mem-** be entrenched, be part and parcel (of a society). *Korupsi blm ~ dlm negeri itu* Corruption has not yet become entrenched in that country. *Tradisi ini sdh ~ di Indonésia* This tradition has become part and parcel of life in Indonesia. **mem-kan 1** cultivate, develop (art, music, etc.). **2** civilize, bring into mainstream of civilization. *~ suku asli* bring the aborigines into the mainstream of civilization. **ke-an** culture, civilization. **pem an 1** cultivation. *~ kritik yg berarti* cultivation of meaningful criticism. **2** civilizing.

budayawan cultural observer, o. who writes about art, drama, etc.

budayawi cultural.

budeg (*Jv*) **1** deaf. **2** anonymous. *surat -* anonymous letter.

budel (*Coll.*) inheritance.

budeng (*Jv*) k.o. ape, black gibbon.

budgét see BUJÉT.

budgetér see BUJETÉR.

Budha Buddha.

Budhis Buddhist.

Budhisme Buddhism.

budi 1 mind, reason, right thinking. *- bakti* total submission or sacrifice. *- bicara* common sense, intelligence. *- manusia* human intelligence. **2** character. *Ia baik -* She is of good character. *- bahasa* good manners, nice behavior. **ber-** *bahasa* suave, polite. *- luhur* noble character. *- pekerti* **1** character. **2** conduct of life. **3** morals. **3** sensibleness, reasonableness, level-headedness. **4** trick, cunning. *main -* cheat. *Ia mencari -* He sought a scheme (which would help him). **se-akal** with heart and soul, by all possible means. *Ia mengerjakan tugasnya ~ akal, tapi tak ada hasil juga* He performed his task to his utmost, but still failed. **ber- 1** be of good character. **2** wise. **3** well behaved, nice. **memper-kan** trick, fool, deceive.

budidaya cultivation. *peningkatan produksi - ubi* increase in the production in tuber cultivation. *- kopi* coffee cultivation. **mem-kan** cultivate. *tanaman hias yg di-kan penduduk kota* decorative plants that city dwellers cultivate. **pem-an** cultivation. *~ jenis bambu* cultivation of species of bamboo.

budiman wise, prudent, sensible. *pembaca -* esteemed reader.

buduk₁ mangy (of dogs).

buduk₂ see BODOK.

budur ter- prominent, protruding (of eyes).

bufé, bufét, buffét 1 buffet, side table, counter, bar. **2** food and drink stand, lunch counter, refreshment bar.

bugar see SEGAR, SÉHAT.

bugénfil k.o. flowering ornamental shrub, bougainvillea.

bugil completely naked. *mata -* the naked eye. **mem-i, mem-kan** undress s.o. completely. **ke-an** nakedness.

buh sound of blowing (candle, etc.).

buhuk goiter.

buhul₁ knot (of rope or string). *- mati* hard knot. **mem- 1** tie, make a knot. **2** conclude (an agreement). **mem-kan** make into a knot. *Pita di-kannya spt dasi kupu-kupu* He tied a ribbon like a bow tie. **-an** knot.

buhul₂ appear slightly or partly from beneath or inside.

bui₁ jail. **mem-** jail, lock up. **pem-an** jailing, incarceration.

bui₂ buoy.

buih foam, froth. *- sabun* soapsuds. **ber-(²), mem-(²)** foam up. *Mulutnya ~* He foamed at the mouth. **mem-kan** cause to foam. **pem-an** act of causing s.t. to foam.

Buitenzorg /bétensorekh, boitensorekh/ Bogor in the colonial period.

bujah protruding, prominent.

bujang 1 single, unmarried. **2** bachelor. **3** male servant. **mem- 1** be single. *Ia hidup ~* He leads a bachelor's life. **2** work as servant. *Ia ~ pd keluarga* He works as a servant for a family. **-an** unmarried (person). **pem-** o. who stays unmarried (beyond the usual age). **pem-an** maintaining o.'s bachelorhood.

bujangga 1 sage, scholar, learned or wise person. **2** poet, man of letters. **ke-an** literary, poetic. *dunia ~* literary world.

bujét budget.

bujetér budgetary.

bujuk coaxing, persuasion. *- rayu* gentle persuasion, enticement. **mem- 1** persuade s.o. **2** trick, cheat s.o. **mem-i 1** repeatedly persuade s.o. **2** repeatedly trick s.o. **mem-kan** persuade s.o. on behalf of another. **ter-** talked into, tricked into. **-an** blandishment, enticement, cajolery. **pem-1** flatterer. **2** cajoler, coaxer. *~ hati* s.o. or s.t. used to cajole (esp. children). **pem-an 1** persuasion. *~ agama* religious persuasion. **2** wooing,

soliciting. *~ konsumén oléh produsén* wooing of consumer by producer.

bujur 1 lengthwise, longitudinal. *- panjang* oblong. *- sangkar* **1** rectangle. **2** square. *lima méter - sangkar* five square meters. *- sirih/telur* oval-shaped. **2** longitude. *- barat* W. longitude. **3** a numerical classifier for long objects. *tiga - bom dinamit* three sticks of dynamite. **mem- 1** stretch out. *Ia tidur ~ di tanah* He slept stretched out on the ground. **2** lie alongside. *Pohon yg jatuh itu ~ rumah* The fallen tree is alongside the house. **3** stretch, run. *Pegunungan ~ Timur-Barat* The mountain range lies E. to W. **4** horizontal. **mem-i** travel the length of s.t. **mem-kan** lay out lengthwise, die. **ter-** stretched out. **-an** length. *di ~ Jalan Pemuda* alongside Jalan Pemuda. *~ pipa* pipeline.

buk₁ /buk/ sound of thud.

buk₂ /buk/ **mem-** book (up). *Hostés yg cantik itu selalu di-* That pretty bar girl is always booked up.

buk₃ cement bench us. placed in front of gate to yard of home.

buk₄ (*Jv*) see IBU.

buka 1 open. *Toko ini - jam tujuh* This shop opens at seven. *- jalan* give way, open a path. **2** breaking of fast, food consumed at breaking of fast. *Jam berapa - hari ini?* What time does the fast end today? **ber- 1** remove, take off s.t. of o.'s own. *~ baju* remove o.'s shirt. **2** break the fast. **mem-1** open. *Ia ~ pintu* She opened the door. *Ayahnya ~ toko* His father opened a shop. *~ mulut* talk, speak. *~ paha* spread apart the thighs (for sexual activity). **2** clear, reclaim (land). **3** remove, take off (glasses, shoes, etc.). *Mur itu di-* The nut was removed. **4** disclose, expose, betray, divulge, reveal (secret). *~ bungkusan* unwrap or open package. *~ faal* study diviner's signs. *~ kedok* uncover o.'s real intention. *~ nujum* consult the stars. *~ warna* show o.'s true colors. **5** begin, start. *Isterinya ~ bicara* His wife began to speak. *~ prakték* open a medical practice. *~ rapat* open a meeting. *~ serangan* launch an attack. **6** unfurl (sails), unfasten (rope, safety pin). *~ pisau* unfold a (pocket) knife. *~ puasa* break the fast. **mem-² 1** leaf through (a magazine). **2** rummage through (a drawer). **mem-i 1** open repeatedly. **2** open for s.o. *Jangan di-i pintu org gila itu* Do not open the door for that madman. **mem-kan 1** open. **2** open for s.o. **3** divulge, disclose, reveal. *~ perasaan* bare or disclose o.'s true feelings. **ter- 1** opened. *Pintunya ~* The door is open. The door came open. *dgn tangan ~* open handed. **2** in the open. *rapat ~* open or public meeting. **3** open, outgoing, extroverted. **4** available. *Kesempatan bersekolah ~ bagi semua anak* The chance to attend school is open to all children. **keter-an** openness. *~ hati* openness of mind. **-an 1** (*Coll.*) opener. *~ botol* bottle opener. *~ kaléng* can opener. **2** opening, aperture. **3** cutaway drawing. **-²an** run around naked. *Aktris itu tdk bersedia main ~* That actress is not willing to play roles in which she runs around naked. **pem-** opener. ~ *akal* broadener of the mind. ~ *jalan* trail-blazer, pioneer. ~ *kata* preface, introduction. **pem-an 1** opening. *Apa nama lagu ~?* What is the name of the opening song? *Banyak terima kasih atas kata* ~ Many thanks for the words of introduction. ~ *tanah* clearing of land. **2** preamble, preface. **per-an** food served at breaking of fast.

bukan 1 not, no (negates nouns, pronouns or nominal phrases). *Dia - org Inggeris; dia org América* He is not an Englishman; he is an American. *- itu yg saya katakan* That is not what I said. *- Amat dan - Dul yg datang. Si Dadap yg datang* Neither Amat nor Dul came. It was Dadap who came. **2** it is not the case that. *Saya - belajar, tetapi membaca-baca saja* I am not studying, but just reading. *Ia - tdk mau, akan tetapi ia berhalangan* It is not that he does not want to, but that he cannot. *- (alang) kepalang/buatan/main/* very extraordinary. *- main indahnya* It is extraordinarily beautiful. *Saya malu - buatan* I was terribly ashamed. **3** isn't it?, aren't you?, etc., often as *kan. Ini bukumu, -?* This is your book, isn't it? *Kita ke pasar, -?* We were going to the market, right? *-kah* is it not the case that? *-kah org yg pakai topi itu pamanmu?* Isn't the man with the hat your uncle? *-tah* (*Lit.*) is it not? ~ *Adinda yg meminta dahulu?* Wasn't it you who first requested it? *yg -²* nonsense, impossibility. *Ia mengharapkan hal yg* ~ He expected the impossible. **-nya** it is not the case that. *Ia ~ malas melainkan bodoh* He is not lazy, but stupid. **mem-kan** deny, disclaim, disavow.

bukat dirty, muddy. *- likat* very turbid.

bukau see BUKIT.

bukét bouquet.

buking booking, previously arranged reservation. **mem- 1** program, schedule. **2** book (ticket, etc.), reserve (room, etc.). *Kamar lantai tiga semua sdh di-* All the 3d floor rooms have been booked. **mem-kan** reserve a space, etc. for s.o. *Meréka di-kan tempat utk malam nanti* Reserve them a seat for tonight. **ter-** booked. **-an** s.o. who is booked. **pem-an** act of booking s.o. or s.t.

bukit hill, mountain. *- bukau* wilderness, wildwood. *- pasir* (sand)dune. **ber-²** hilly, mountainous. **mem- 1** form a hill or heap. *Buah kelapanya* ~ The coconuts piled up. **2** resemble a hill. **pe(r)-an** range of hills.

bukti proof, evidence. *- dpt diasuransikan* evidence of insurability. *- diri* ID card. *- garansi* warranty, guarantee. *- nyatadiri* ID card. *- pelanggaran (tilang)* traffic ticket. *- saksi* **1** evidence. **2** testimony. **mem-kan** prove, demonstrate, establish, show. **ter-(kan)** proven. **pem-an** authentication.

buku₁ book. *- acara* program, agenda. *- agenda* datebook, diary. *- alamat* directory, address book. *- bajakan* pirated book. *- besar* **1** ledger. **2** guest register. *- catatan* notebook. *- dagang* commercial, business, or trade directory. *- geréja*

prayer book. *- harian* diary, journal. *- hitam* **1** black book. **2** blacklist. **mem-hitamkan** blacklist, blackball. *- kas* ledger. *- kir* paper listing automobile parts and their condition for automobile inspection. *- nilai* teacher's grade book. *- panduan/pedoman/pegangan* guidebook, handbook, manual. *- pelajaran* textbook. *- pemutaran* scenario. *- pengumpulan* compilation. *- penuntun* manual, handbook. *- petunjuk* directory. *- petunjuk dagang* trade or commercial directory. *- (petunjuk) télépon* telephone book, directory. *- pintar* reference book. *- pokét* pocketbook, paperback. *- putih* white paper (of gvt.). *- rapor* report card or book. *- saku* pocket book. *- sebaran* pamphlet, brochure. *- simpanan* savings book. *- suci* book carried by freshmen (during hazing period) which requires signatures of older students. *- tamu* guest book. **mem-kan 1** (*Fin.*) enter in a book. **2** put into book form. ~ *kisah nyata* make a book out of a real event. **pem-an 1** (*Fin.*) entry, bookkeeping. ~ *berpasangan* double-entry bookkeeping. **2** booking. ~ *muatan* cargo booking. **per-an** book matters.

buku₂ 1 knuckle, joint. *- jari* knuckle. *- kaki/lali* ankle. *- léhér* cervical vertebra. **2** knot. *- benang* bobbin. **3** grain, pellet, lump (of salt, sand, etc.). *garam dua* - two lumps of salt. *tanah se-* o. lump of earth. *- sabun* cake of soap. **ber-** jointed, have joints. **mem-² 1** form knots or joints. **2** be pent up (of emotions). **per-an 1** (*Anat.*) joint. ~ *kaki* joint of foot. **2** foundation, cornerstone.

bukung 1 tailless. **2** (*Coll.*) woman's short hairstyle.

bukur grain, granule.

bukut mem- 1 cover up, keep secret. **2** cover. **pem- 1** covering, cover, lid. **2** wrapping, wrapper.

bul see BOL₁.

bulai 1 albino. **2** (*Derog.*) white person, Caucasian.

bulak lonely place in a road. *Di - itu sering terjadi penjambrétan* In that lonely area there are lots of purse snatchers.

bulak-balik see BOLAK-BALIK.

bulan 1 month. *- apit* 11th month of Muslim year. *- arwah* 8th month of Muslim year. *- haji* 12th month of Muslim year. *- puasa* 9th month of Muslim year. *- setor* month of deposit. *- suci* (*Isl.*) fasting month. *- tabut* first 10 days of month of Muharram. **2** moon. *- bintang* crescent moon and star, the symbol of Isl. *- gelap* dark of moon. *- kesiangan* pallid moon in daylight. *spt - kesiangan* very pale. *- madu* honeymoon. *- mati* dark of moon. *- muda* **1** first phase new moon. **2** first days of month. *- perbani* crescent (moon). *- purnama* full moon. *- sabit* crescent (moon). *- susut* waning moon. *- tiga persegi* 12th day of month. *- timbul* waxing moon, new moon. *- tua* **1** last phases of moon. **2** last days of month (when o.'s salary is exhausted). **ber-(²)** for several months. **mem- 1** become like a moon. *Wajahnya berseri* ~ His face lit up like the moon. **2** land on moon.

Pesawat Apollo sdh ~ The Apollo space vehicle has landed on the moon. **mem-kan** send to the moon. **-an** monthly. *majalah* ~ a monthly journal. *kotoran* ~ menses. **-²an** target, goal.

bulang 1 wrapper, headdress, wraparound. **2** tape, ribbon, etc. for fastening spur to fighting cock's foot. **-²** s.t. wrapped around or placed on head. **ber- 1** wear headdress or turban. **2** wind, wrap. *Ia* ~ *kain putih pd pinggangnya* She wrapped a white cloth around her waist. **3** wear a spur. **mem- 1** wear, wrap around. **2** tie on. **3** attach cock's spur.

bulang-baling see BOLANG-BALING₂.

bular cataract of eye.

bulat 1 circle, spherical, round. - *bujur* elliptical, oval. - *buluh* cylindrical. - *cekung* concave. - *cembung* convex. - *gépéng* round and flat. - *lipir* round and flat. - *panjang* cylindrical, oblong. - *pipih* round and flat (as a coin). - *telor* oval-shaped. - *torak* 1 cylinder. 2 cylindrical. **2** complete, overall. - *hati* 1 resolute, determined. 2 frank, sincere. *rencana* - 1 overall plan. 2 globular. **3** unanimous. *pendapat* - unanimous opinion. - *kata* 1 agreement. 2 resolution, determination. 3 conclusion, decision. *dgn suara* - unanimously. **-²** 1 round object. 2 flatly, totally, completely. **se-²nya** completely. **mem- 1** become round, spherical. **2** be unanimous. **mem-i 1** draw circle around s.t. **2** (*M*) take all. **mem-kan 1** round off. *Ia* ~ *bilangan* He rounded off the figures. **2** complete s.t., perfect s.t. ~ *hati* 1 concentrate. *Ia* ~ *hati dlm pelajarannya* She concentrated on her studies. 2 make a decision. *Ia* ~ *hati utk mengalahkan musuhnya* He resolved to defeat his opponent. ~ *ingatan* concentrate. ~ *mufakat* arrive at, reach agreement. ~ *niat* make up o.'s mind. ~ *pikiran* concentrate. ~ *suara* come to agreement. ~ *tékad* make a definite decision. ~ *tinju* clench the fist. **ke-an 1** roundness. ~ *bumi* roundness of the earth. **2** resoluteness, determination. ~ *tékad* resoluteness, firm determination, resolve. **3** unanimity. ~ *hati* agreement, single-mindedness. **-an 1** circle, sphere. *setengah* ~ *selatan* southern hemisphere. **2** rotundity, roundness. **pem-an 1** rounding off. ~ *bilangan* rounding off of figures. **2** integration, completing. ~ *fikiran* decision. ~ *suara* agreement.

bulbul k.o. bird, tropical nightingale.

buldog bulldog.

buldoser, buldozer bulldozer.

bulé, bulék see BULAI.

buletin bulletin.

bulgur grain product made of the nutritious portions of wheat, bulgur.

bulian k.o. ironwood tree.

buli-buli gourd for storing liquids.

bulir 1 ear (of corn). **2** counter for long, cone-shaped objects, esp. grains. *se- padi* a grain of rice. *se- air mata* a tear.

bulkpos bulkpost.

bulldozer see BULDOSER.

bulsak 1 upholstery. **2** mattress.

bulu 1 body hair. - *kuduk* hair on nape of neck. *membuat - kuduk berdiri* make hair stand on end. - *suak* hair at nape of neck. - *roma* fine body hair, down on face. - *tengkuk* 1 hair at nape of neck. 2 mane. **2** fur. - *babi* sea porcupine or urchin. - *kaca* glass wool. **3** feather. - *ayam* 1 chicken feather, quill. 2 feather duster. - *balik* fowl's feathers ruffled. - *kalong* 1 down. 2 anal hair. - *tangkis* badminton. **per-tangkisan** matters pertaining to badminton. **-²** feather duster. **ber-** have body hair, fur, feathers. ~ *hati* angry. ~ *kapas* fluffy. ~ *mata melihat* hate the sight of. **mem-²** dust, wipe off. **mem-i** remove body hair, fur, feathers.

buluh bamboo. - *perindu* mythical k.o. bamboo used to make flutes that produce melodies irresistible to women. *bagai - perindu* very melodious (of voice). **pem-** (*Anat.*) artery, corporal passages. ~ *balik* vein. ~ *darah* blood vessel. ~ *Estachio* Eustachian tube. ~ *karét* rubber hose. ~ *kencing* urethra. ~ *kerongkongan* trachea, windpipe. ~ *makanan* alimentary canal. ~ *nadi* artery. ~ *napas* respiratory tract. ~ *rambut* small artery.

buluk, bulukan 1 moldy, mildewed. **2** stale (of cigarette smoke).

bulur starving, overpowering hunger. **ke-(an)** overcome by hunger.

bulus₁ 1 totally bald, smooth (of head). **2** childless. **3** robbed, fleeced, wiped out.

bulus₂ be struck (by blow).

bulus₃ small freshwater or land turtle.

bulus₄ pierce, penetrate.

bulus-bulus k.o. fish.

bulutangkis badminton.

bulyon₁ bouillon (for broth).

bulyon₂ bullion.

bum see BOM₂.

bumban wreath, garland.

bumbu cooking spices, flavor. - *karé* curry powder. **mem-i 1** season s.t., add spice to s.t. *Ia* ~ *daging utk gulai* She seasoned the meat for the stew. **2** add flavor to s.t., add color to s.t. (speech, conversation, etc.). ~ *hidup* spice up o.'s life. *Ia* ~ *pidatonya dgn lelucon* He spiced his talk with jokes. **-²an** various k.o. spices.

bumbun₁ 1 shady, shaded. **2** shelter for hunters.

bumbun₂ 1 heap, pile. - *beras* rice pile. **2** heaped up. *Piringnya - dgn nasi* His plate was piled high with rice. **mem-** pile, store, hoard. ~ *bahan makanan utk musim dingin* store up food for food supplies for winter. *satu sendok kopi* ~ o. heaping spoonful of coffee.

bumbung₁ bamboo cylinder used as container. **2** tubing. - *pengembun* tubing for condensation.

bumbung₂ see BUBUNG.

bumel local train.

bumerang boomerang.

bumi 1 earth. *bagai - dan langit* different as night and day (lit., like the earth and heaven). **2** (*Lit.*) soil. - *Indonésia* Indonesian soil. - *hangus* scorched earth. **mem-hanguskan** subject to scorched-earth policy, reduce to rubble. **pem-hangusan** total destruction. - *rata* leveled to the ground. **mem-ratakan** level an area to the ground (in war). **mem-** return to earth. *Ia bisa ~ kembali utk disérvis* It can return to earth to be serviced (of space shuttle). **mem-kan** cause s.t. to return to earth. **menge-kan** bury, inter. **penge-an** burial, interment.

bumiawi earthly, terrestrial. *benda* - terrestrial object.

bumiputera native (of country). **ke-an** native-ness, indigenousness.

BUMN [*Badan Usaha Milik Negara*] state-owned corporation.

bumper /bumper, bimper/ (*Auto.*) bumper.

bumpet clogged up (gutters, thoughts, etc.).

bun₁ small brass box.

bun₂ see EMBUN.

bunar see BAMBU.

buncah (*M*) disturbed, upset. *Pikirannya* - She is upset. **mem-(kan)** upset, disturb. **ke-an** frustration, trouble.

buncéng see BONCÉNG.

bunci capital for small-scale business.

buncis stringbean. - *mérah* kidney bean.

buncit₁ 1 distended, bloated, puffed up. 2 pregnant. **mem-kan** distend, expand, puff out (abdomen).

buncit₂ recent, last. **-an** latest. *nomor ~* latest issue.

bunda mother, respectful term of reference and address. - *Kudus* (*Rel.*) Holy Mother. - *Maria* (*Rel.*) Mother Mary.

bundar₁ round, circular, spherical. *Mukanya* - Her face is round. *bunyi* - (*Ling.*) rounded vowel. *Méja* - Round Table. - *gemuk* plump. - *telur* oval. **mem-** 1 be rounded. 2 form a circle. **mem-kan** make s.t. round. **-an** 1 circle. 2 traffic circle. *~ semanggi* highway cloverleaf. 3 hoop, disk, etc. **pem-an** rounding. *~ bibir* (*Ling.*) labialization, lip-rounding. *~ ujung* rounding of an edge.

bundar₂ clothesbrush.

bundas all bruised up.

bundel₁ 1 bundle, sheaf, wad. 2 collection. *~ puisi* poetry collection. 3 bound volume of journal. **mem-(kan)** 1 bundle s.t., place in bundles, file. 2 bind (papers, journal issues). 3 collect, assemble, gather (poetry, etc.). **-an** bundle. **pem-an** placing of items in bundles.

bundel₂ knot. **mem-** become knotted (of string, thread, etc.). **mem-i** tie knot on s.t. **-an** knot.

bunder see BUNDAR₁.

bung₁ 1 fellow, buddy. *Ayo pulang, -!* Let us go home, fellow! 2 brother (affectionate title for some popular leaders). - *Hatta* Brother Hatta.

bung₂ sound of a drumbeat.

bung₃ see REBUNG.

bunga 1 flower, blossom. - *bangkai* various k.o. parasitic plants, rafflesia. - *bibir* flattery, sweet words. - *karang* sponge. - *keras* artificial flower. - *laut* coral. - *lawang* aniseed. - *mas* artificial flower

of gold. - *matahari* sunflower. - *pala* mace (spice). - *rampai* 1 bouquet, bunch of various k.o. flowers. 2 anthology. - *raya* 1 hibiscus. 2 prostitute. - *sakura* 1 cherry blossom. 2 k.o. tree with pink blossoms. 3 heroine. - *sepatu* hibiscus. - *tanjung* fragrant flowers of k.o. shade tree. - *teluki* k.o. hibiscus. - *wijayakusuma* k.o. flower. 2 the best part, cream. *Pemuda - bangsa* Youth are the flower of a nation. - *angin* zephyr. - *désa* village belle, toast of village. - *latar* prostitute, streetwalker. - *tanah* humus. 3 floral design, s.t. flowerlike. - *api* 1 fireworks. 2 spark. - *badan* reddish skin (skin disease). - *barah* rash of small white spots after initial symptom of yaws, leprosy, etc. - *és* frost. - *kol* cauliflower. - *kuku* halfmoon at base of fingernail. - *kusta* leprosy markings. - *lalat* larva of fly. - *pan(a)u* pale blotches on skin (caused by dermal fungus). - *pasir* very fine-grained sand. - *puru* white spots on skin. - *tahi* dirty, offensive words. 4 (*Fin.*) interest. - *majemuk* compound interest. - *modal* interest on capital. 5 tire tread. 6 (*Crd.*) suit. **ber-** 1 be in bloom, flower. *Pohonnya ~* The tree is in bloom. 2 (*Fin.*) bear interest, interest bearing. 3 yield s.t. useful. *Anjurannya ~* Her suggestion is bearing fruit. **ber-²** patterned (of cloth). **mem-** 1 become like a flower. 2 earn interest. **mem-i** 1 decorate with flowers. 2 place a wreath. 3 pay interest. 4 embellish, enhance (a speech) with. *Biasanya kelahiran di-i berbagai sambutan* Usually the occasion of a birth is embellished with all k.o. welcoming events. **mem(per)-kan** lend at interest. **-²an** 1 flowers. 2 artificial flowers. 3 floral decoration. **pem-** money lender. **pem-an** 1 flowering, blossoming, blooming. 2 acquiring interest. *Isterinya menjalankan ~ uang* His wife operated a money lending enterprise. **per-an** budding, blossoming.

bungalo lodge, country retreat.

bungkah see BONGKAH.

bungkal 1 lump, piece, chunk. 2 leaden weight, sinker. 3 measure of weight for gold. **ber-²** in chunks. **mem-** dig up (land) into chunks. *Tanah itu di- dgn bajak* That land had just been turned into chunks by a plow. **-an** piece. *~ mas* lump of gold.

bungkam 1 quiet, silent. 2 speechless, struck dumb. - *(dlm) seribu basa* completely quiet, silent. 3 not go off, not explode (of firecracker, etc.). **mem-** 1 remain silent. 2 gag, silence. **mem-kan** gag, stifle, silence. *~ segala kebébasan kréatif* stifle all creative freedom. **ke-an** silence, stillness. **pem-** 1 magic formula for keeping s.o. silent. 2 silencer, gag, muzzle. **pem-an** gagging, silencing, stifling. *~ suara yg bernada protés* the stifling of protesting voices.

bungkang laid out like a corpse. --*bangking* lying stretched out.

bungkem see BUNGKAM.

bungkil residue of copra after extracting oil. - *kedelai* soybean meal.

bungkuk crooked, bent (over), humped. *Badan-*

nya - He is hunchbacked. **mem-** stoop or bend over. ~ *kpd* bow to. *Ia* ~ *di hadapan tentara Jepang* He bowed before the Japanese soldier. **mem-²** 1 bow respectfully. 2 lower or demean o.s. 3 bend (the back). **mem-i** stoop in direction of s.t. *Pelan-pelan ia* ~ *kaléng itu mengambil air wudhu* Slowly he stooped toward the tin can to perform the ritual ablution. **mem-kan** bend (the back). **ter-²** bent (from age, etc.). **-²an** 1 repeatedly bowing or bending. *Tak usah* ~ There is no need to keep bowing. 2 engage in foolish bowing. **pem-an** bending, stooping, bowing. *akibat* ~ as a result of stooping.

bungkul₁ cauliflower.

bungkul₂ see BONGKOL.

bungkus 1 parcel, pack. --*bingkis* all k.o. of packages. *se- rokok* a pack of cigarettes. 2 wrapper, wrap. - *rokok* cigarette wrapper. - *ulang* rewrapping. **ber-** wrapped up. **mem-** 1 wrap up (book, etc.). 2 conceal, keep secret, cover up. *Serbuk ini di- dgn kertas halus* This powder is wrapped in fine paper. **mem-i** 1 wrap up, envelop. *Kemelaratanlah yg* ~ *hidup bersama adiknya* It was misery that surrounded his life with his brother. 2 repeatedly wrap s.t., wrap many things. **-an** parcel, package. **pem-** 1 wrapping, wrapping paper. ~ *mayat* shroud. 2 wrapper, packer. **pem-an** packing, packaging.

bunglai see BENGLÉ.

bunglon₁ 1 chameleon. 2 vacillator. 3 opportunist. **mem-** shilly-shally, vacillate. *Dlm rapat itu ia kelihatan selalu* ~ In the meeting he seemed to vacillate.

bunglon₂ tube, valve housing.

bungsu 1 youngest offspring. *si -* youngest son or daughter in family. 2 the last in series. *hujan -* last rain of season. *isteri - o.*'s most recent wife.

bungur k.o. timber tree.

buni₁ k.o. tree bearing small sour fruits.

buni₂ see BUNYI.

bunian race of invisible people of forest, thought to kidnap humans.

bunker /bungker/ bunker.

buntak (*M*) short and stout, out of proportion. **ke-an** compactness.

buntal swollen, bloated. **-an** 1 s.t. swollen. 2 bundle. *Dia melihat* ~ *si tukang perahu* He saw the boatman's bundle.

buntang 1 staring (of choking or dying person). 2 stiff (of carcass). **ber-, mem-, ter-** 1 stretched out stiffly (of corpse). 2 rise, emerge (to surface). 3 wide open (eyes). **mem-kan** 1 stretch, strain. 2 raise, pull up.

buntar see BUNDAR₁.

buntat₁ gallstone. - *hendak jadi gemala* He has absurd pretensions.

buntat₂ blocked, clogged, stopped up.

buntel₁ (*Jv*) 1 wrapping. 2 dish of spices wrapped in taro leaves. **mem-** wrap, bundle. **-an** s.t. wrapped (in cloth, leaves, etc.). **pem-an** coating (on teeth), plaque.

buntel₂ knapsack. **mem-** wrap up. **-an** 1 s.t. wrapped. 2 knapsack.

buntet 1 clogged. 2 stifled (of thoughts).

buntil₁ dish of roasted taro leaves wrapped around spices.

buntil₂ knapsack, clothes bag.

bunting 1 pregnant (of animals). *Anjing itu -* That bitch is pregnant. 2 full, filled out (of paddy, etc.). *Dikiranya péstol itu tak -* She did not think the pistol was loaded. 3 (*Derog.*) pregnant (of women). - *bantang/besar* advanced pregnancy. - *gelap* secretly pregnant. - *jolong* first pregnancy. - *kecil* early stage of pregnancy. - *sarat/tua* advanced pregnancy. **mem-** fill up, become full. ~ *padi* have the shape of a fully formed rice grain. *Betisnya* ~ *padi* Her calves are beautifully formed. **mem-i, mem-kan** 1 impregnate (of animals). 2 (*Derog.*) knock up (a woman). **-an** gestation (of animals). **pem-an** insemination, impregnation (of animals).

buntu 1 blocked, stopped (up), dead end. 2 deadlocked. 3 stumped, stymied. - *akal* be at a loss, be at o.'s wits' end. **mem-kan** 1 block (alley, road, etc.). 2 cause impasse, block. **ter-** clogged up. **ke-an** deadlock, impasse, blind alley. ~ *pikiran* out of ideas.

buntung 1 lopped off or amputated (arm, leg, tail etc.). 2 bad luck, misfortune. *Kami sedang -* We are having bad luck. *Ingin untung malah -* We wish for good luck but instead get bad luck. **mem-kan** amputate, lop off.

buntut 1 tail. *sup - oxtail* soup. *Ia selalu menjadi - sdrnya* He is always trailing after his brother. - *kuda* ponytail (hairdo). 2 rear end, latter part. *Mereka semua mau jadi kepala, tdk mau jadi -* They all want to be at the head and not at the rear. *pd - bulan ini* (*Coll.*) at the end of this month. - *kapal* ship's stern. - *perarakan* tail end of procession. 3 aftermath, consequence. *Kejadian itu pasti ada -nya* There will be an aftermath to that incident. 4 k.o. gambling based on last three digits of lottery. *lotré -* lottery based on this type of gambling. **ber-** 1 have a tail. 2 have consequences. *Konflik itu* ~ That conflict has consequences. **ber-²** in succession. *Meréka datang* ~ They came o. after the other. **mem-** imitate s.o., follow what s.o. is doing. **mem-i** 1 follow, trail, shadow. *Ia selalu* ~ *ayahnya* He is always following after his father. 2 follow at rear. *Mari kita* ~ *arak-arakan ini* Let us follow at the rear of this procession. **-an** plow handle. **pem-** follower.

bunuh **ber-(²)an, -** **mem-** kill e.o. **mem-** 1 kill. *Anjing itu hrs di-* That dog had to be destroyed. ~ *diri* commit suicide, take o.'s life. 2 put out, extinguish, quench, douse (fire, lamp). 3 remove, cross out, cancel. *Ia* ~ *kalimat* She crossed out a sentence. 4 plug (leak, hole). **mem-i** kill many victims. *Badak sdh banyak di-i* Rhinoceroses have been slaughtered in great numbers. **ter-** accidentally killed. **pem-** killer. ~ *bayaran* hired assassin or killer. **pem-an** killing, slaying.

bunut k.o. small tree.

bunyi 1 sound, noise. - *janggal* dissonance. - *kerap* a creaking sound. - *memanjang* dial tone. - *menggelegar* sonic boom. - *suara cina karam* very loud or noisy. **2** (*Ling.*) sound. - *alir* liquid. - *desis* sibilant. - *geletar/getar* trill. - *gésér* spirant, fricative. - *hidup* vowel. - *kembar* diphthong. - *letupan* stop, plosive. - *pepet* shwa, the mid-central vowel. - *sampingan* lateral. - *sengau* nasal. - *sentuhan* flap, tap. - *serangkap* diphthong. **3** contents. *Bagaimana - surat itu?* How does the letter read? -*nya begitu* It sounds like this. It goes as follows. **se-1** of the same sound. **2** true copy of document, letter etc. **ber- 1** make a noise. *Suaranya ~ keras* His voice sounds loud. *Bomnya tdk ~* The bomb did not go off. **2** sound. *Surat itu ~ begini* Her letter goes as follows. **mem-kan 1** cause s.t. to make a noise. *Siapa yg ~ bél?* Who rang the bell? *~ suling* play the flute. *~ lidah* click (the tongue). *~ mercon* set off, fire (firecrackers). **2** sound, pronounce (words, etc.). **3** read aloud (letter, etc.). -²**an 1** music. **2** musical instruments. **pem-an** (*Ling.*) phonation.

bupati regent, gvt. officer in charge of a regency.

bupét see BUFÉ.

bur sound of splashing.

bura spittle, spit. **mem- 1** spit, spew out. *Api ~ dr jendéla* Fire spewed forth from a window. **2** spit out s.t. *Ular itu ~ bisa* The snake spit poison. **3** fly apart, go to pieces (of o.'s mind). **mem-kan** spray, spout, spew forth (water, fire, etc.).

burai ber-, mem-, ter- hang out in strands (of hair, etc.), spill out in streams (rice, cement, etc.). *Beras ~ dr kantung yg terkoyak* Rice spilled out in a continuous stream from the rip in the bag.

burak see BORAK.

buraksa see BERAKSA.

buram₁ 1 blueprint, design, plan. **2** sketch, draft, outline. - *naskah* manuscript copy. **3** unregistered.

buram₂ 1 not clear, dull. **2** dark, be clouded (of face). **mem-kan** darken, becloud s.t. **ke-an 1** vagueness. **2** unclearness (of light). *~ lampu* haziness of the lamp.

buraq see BORAK.

buras₁ chitchat, small talk. -² chat, talk. **mem-1** discuss, talk about. **2** coax, soothe by making small talk. **mem-kan** talk about s.t. **pem-** chatterer, chatterbox.

buras₂ k.o. rice cake made with coconut cream wrapped in banana leaves.

buras₃ erased, wiped out, eradicated. *Duit gua udah - nih* My money is all gone!

burat see BORÉH.

bureng hazy, unclear, dim (of glasses, etc.). **pem-an** efforts to obscure, obfuscation.

bures see BURAS₁,₂,₃.

burik 1 dotted, speckled (of feathers, skin). **2** pockmarked.

burit posterior, rear, behind. **se-** sodomy. *main ~*

commit sodomy. **berse-** commit sodomy. **menye-** sodomize. **mem-** commit sodomy. -**an** ship's stern. *angin ~* wind from behind.

burjasmani (*Tech.*) elliptical.

burjuasi see BORJUASI.

burjuis see BORJUIS.

burjul'hamal (*Zod.*) Aries.

burju'ssunbulat (*Zod.*) Virgo.

burkuk see BERGUK.

buro see BIRO.

burokrasi see BIROKRASI.

buron, buronan fugitive from justice, s.o. wanted.

bursa stock exchange. - *éfék* stock exchange. **mem-kan** place on the stock exchange.

bursuasi see BORJUASI.

buru -², **ter-**(²), **ke-**(²) hurried, in a rush. *Ia ~ pulang* He was in a great hurry to get home. **ber-** go hunting. *binatang ~* predator. **mem- 1** chase after. *Ia segera ~ kami* She immediately chased after us. **2** pursue (wealth, position). **mem-i** hunt, pursue (animals). **mem-²kan** cause s.o. to hurry up. -**an 1** prey. **2** fugitive from justice, hunted person. **pem-** hunter. - *sergap* (*Av.*) fighter interceptor. **per-an 1** the hunt. **2** prey, game. *~ besar* big game. **3** persecution.

buruh worker, laborer. - *borongan* piece worker. - *cuci* washerwoman. - *kasar* manual laborer, unskilled worker. - *lepas* temporary laborer. - *musiman* seasonal worker. - *pelabuhan* dockworker, longshoreman. - *rendahan* lower-paid workers. - *tani* farmhand. **mem-** work as laborer. *Ia ~ pd pabrik* He worked as a laborer at a factory. -**an** wages as a laborer. *org ~ o.* who receives wages. **per-an** labor, matters concerning workers. *Departemén ~* Ministry of Labor.

buruk 1 old, worn out, dilapidated. **2** decayed (of teeth), rotten (of wood, etc.). **3** bad, foul, nasty. *cuaca -* foul weather. *Ia berbuat -* He does bad things. *Ia mempunyai nama -* He has a bad reputation. - *ambil* unjust, unfair. - *gizi* malnutrition. - *hati* bad. - *laku* bad behavior. - *mulut* coarse, crude (in speech). - *perut* gorge, eat a lot. - *sangka* misunderstand. - *siku* mean, speak only ill of people. **se-²nya** at the worst. **mem-** worsen, deteriorate. *Cuaca ~* The weather worsened. **memper-, mem-kan** aggravate, make worse, worsen. *Tindakan itu ~ hubungan kedua negeri itu* That action aggravated the relationship between the two countries. **mem-²kan** defame, vilify. *Budi ~ Udin pd tetangganya* Budi defamed Udin when talking to his neighbor. **ke-an 1** bad aspect, badness. *~ urbanisasi* bad features of urbanization. **2** evil, badness, wickedness. **pem-an** deterioration, decay, decomposition.

burung 1 bird. - *angin ribut* albatross. - *babi* adjutant crane, stork. - *badak* hornbill. - *balai* shrike. - *berkik* snipe. - *buaya* stork-billed kingfisher. - *dara* pigeon. - *déwata* bird of paradise. - *geréja* sparrow. - *hantu* owl. - *hong* (*Ch*) phoenix. - *kékék/kékék* k.o. kingfisher. - *manintin* (*besar*) k.o. bird. -

manyar weaverbird. - *nasar* vulture. - *nilam* golden oriole. - *pingai* s.t. miraculous (lit., white crow). - *putar* island turtledove. - *suangi* owl. - *udang* kingfisher. - *unta* ostrich. - *wilis* k.o. emerald-colored bird. **2** (*Coll.*) penis. **-²(an) 1** imitation bird. **2** clay pigeon.

burut hernia.

burwater see BORWATER.

bus see BIS$_{1,2}$.

busa₁ 1 foam, lather. - *sabun* soapsuds, (soap) lather. - *budaya* cultural froth. **2** scum, suds. **ber-** be full of foam. **mem-** become foam.

busa₂ mem- 1 gasp, pant. **2** blow. *Ia ~ debu di méja* She blew the dust on the table. **mem-kan 1** blow up (balloon, etc.). **2** blow out, spray (water, etc.). **pem-** (glass) blower. ~ *api* bellows.

busana clothing, esp. in fashion circles. *dunia* - haute couture. - *malam* evening fashion. **mem-kan** cause s.o. to wear clothing.

busar see BUSUR₁.

busét Hell! (exclamation of disapproval). -*! Apa betul dia buat gitu?* Hell! Did he really do s.t. like that? - *mobilnya mogok lagi* Damn, the car is stalled again.

busi sparkplug.

buster (*Auto.*) booster.

busuk 1 putrid, rotten, spoiled, decomposed, putrefied. *Dr mana datang bau - itu?* Where is that putrid odor coming from? **2** low, depraved, corrupt, vile. *Hatinya* - He is depraved. - *hati* evil-minded. **-²** *embacang* appear to be stupid, but actually be quite clever. **mem- 1** rot, decay, putrefy. *Mayat itu mulai ~* The corpse began to decompose. **2** become infected, fester. *Lukanya ~* Her wound was festering. **mem-kan 1** cause to rot. **2** slander, denigrate, defame. **ke-an 1** rottenness, putridness, decomposition. **2** badness, wickedness, evil. **pem-an 1** decaying. **2** putrefaction, disintegration, spoiling, spoilage (of fish, etc.). **per-an** decayed state. ~ *gigi* tooth decay, caries.

busung₁ 1 bloated, distended. - *dada* proud, conceited. - *muka* puffed-up face. **2** (*Med.*) edema. - *air* dropsy. - *darah* edema caused by failure to menstruate. - *kelaparan/lapar* bloating due to starvation. - *kencing* edema caused by bladder disease. **3** bulging, packed, stuffed (of pocket, chest, breast). **mem-** be distended, bloated, puff up. *Perutnya ~* His belly is distended. *Dadanya ~* She feels proud. **mem-kan 1** pump up, inflate (a tire). **2** puff up (o.'s chest). -*kan dadamu* Throw out your chest.

busung₂ 1 elevated land. **2** sandbank, shoal. **mem-** form sandbank.

busur₁ 1 archer's bow. **2** arch, arc. - *cahaya* arc of light, electric arc. - *derajat* protractor. **mem-1** shoot with bow and arrow. **2** be curved. *Alisnya ~* Her eyebrows are curved.

busur₂ cotton gin. **mem-** gin (cotton).

busut 1 small mound. **2** anthill, termite nest (in the ground). - *betina* large rounded anthill. - *jantan* small pointed anthill.

busyét see BUSÉT.

buta 1 blind, sightless, unseeing. - *ayam* 1 near-sighted. 2 twilight blindness. - *belakang* blind stare. - *cémér* incurably blind, optic atrophy. - *hati* heartless, unfeeling. - *larang* poor, weak eyesight. - *malam* night blindness. - *picak* blind through loss of eye. - *siang* day blindness. - *warna* color-blind. **2** blank. *dinding* - blank wall. **3** forgetful. **4** unknowledgeable. *Saya samasekali - dgn alat-alat listrik* I do not know a thing about electrical appliances. - *hukum* ignorant of the law. - *huruf* illiterate, illiteracy. **ke-hurufan** illiteracy. - *pendengaran* 1 deaf. 2 refuse to listen to. - *perasaan* insensible. - *perut* 1 inability to distinguish o. taste from another. 2 eat food by mistake or pretended mistake. - *politik* ignorant of politics. - *tuli* 1 blind and deaf. 2 be completely ignorant of s.t. **mem-** *tuli* be reckless or rash. **mem-tulikan** keep s.o. completely in the dark. - *warta* without news of current events. **-²** blindly, instinctively. **mem- 1** become blind. **2** pretend to be blind. **3** do as o. pleases. **mem-kan** blind, strike or make blind. **ke-an 1** blindness, sightlessness. **2** darkness.

butak₁ see BOTAK.

butak₂ see BUTEK.

butas [*Buton Asphalt*] popular k.o. asphalt.

but-but see EMBUT.

butek 1 turbid, thick, muddy. **2** (*Coll.*) troubled.

butik /butik/ boutique.

butir 1 grain, granule, pellet. - *padi* grain of rice. - *obat tidur* sleeping pill. - *sabun* soapflake. **2** numeral classifier for round objects. *tiga - telur* three eggs. *empat - mangga* four mangoes. **3** small object. **4** item (in a list). *Lihat pemberitahuan kami - dua* See our announcement item two. **-²** details, items. *Dgn perkakas itu org dpt melihat ~nya pd bagian bulan* With that instrument o. can see small objects on a section of the moon. **se-** a, one (thing the size of a grain). ~ *harapan* a sliver of hope. **mem-** granulate, become grains. **-an** a small object (granule, trickle, etc.). **-²an 1** grains. ~ *beras* grains of rice. **2** grains, cereals.

BUTSI [*Badan Urusan Tenaga Sukaréla Indonésia*] coordinating body for volunteers, foreign and domestic, in Indonesia.

butsir mem- model objects from clay or wax.

butuh₁ need, necessity. *Pemerintah - dia, makanya tdk dipecat* The gvt. needed him so he was not fired. **mem-kan** need, require. **ke-an** need, necessity. *memenuhi ~ pokok* fulfill the basic requirements. ~ *zat asam* oxygen requirement.

butuh₂ (*Coll.*) penis.

butut worn out.

buwés see RÉBEWÉS.

buya (*Isl.*) title for respected religious experts and leaders. - *Muh. Yunus* Leader Muh. Yunus. - *Hamka* Leader Hamka.

buyar 1 run (like ink on blotting paper), spread. **2** scattered, dispersed, blown about. *awan* - scattered clouds. **3** scatterbrained, unable to concentrate. **mem-kan 1** scatter, disperse. **2** interrupt.

Apa yg kaufikirkan? tanya Rima ~ *kenanganku* "What are you thinking of?" asked Rima, scattering my recollections. *kesempatan angin utk* ~ *gumpalan awan* a chance for the wind to disperse the clouds.

buyung₁ narrow-necked, big-bellied earthenware or metal jar.

buyung₂ form of address to young boy.

buyur see GUYUR.

buyut 1 term of reference for great-grandparent or great-grandchild. *Org itu sdh - kok masih naik sepéda* That man is old enough to be my great-grandfather, what is he doing riding a bicycle! **2** (*Jv*) ancestral and sacred (of places, such as cemeteries). **be-an** longstanding (of enemies). **ke-an** principal. *naluri* ~ principal instinct. **-an** senile.

byar (*Jv*) on (of lights). *- pet* on and off (of lights). *Kalau musim hujan, listrik di Jkt masih - pet* During the rainy season the lights in Jkt go on and off frequently.

byur (*Jv*) splashing noise when s.t. falls or is thrown into water.

C

c /cé, sé/ c, the 3d letter of the alphabet.

C. [*Celsius*]

ca (*Ch*) stir-fried dish. **menge-** stir-fry with soy sauce.

cabai red pepper, chili. *- jawa* long pepper. *- mérah* ordinary chili. *- rawit* a small, very pungent k.o. chili. *mendapat - rawit* get a dressing down. *kecil-kecil - rawit* small but courageous. **ke-an** feel hot about the lips from chilis. *spt org* ~ jittery, jumpy.

cabak k.o. night bird.

cabang 1 branch, bough, prong. *- atas* upper echelon, top-level group. *- dua* bifurcation. *- pegunungan* mountain spur. **2** branch (office, department, academic field, etc.). **3** fork (in the road, river). **4** chapter, affiliate (of club, association, etc.). **ber- 1** have branches (of trees, firms, etc.). *Ia akan tumbuh berdandan dan* ~ It will sprout up and grow replete with boughs and branches. **2** branch off, split, bifurcate. *Di situ jalan itu* ~ The road branches off there. *Fikirannya* ~ His thoughts are divided. **ber-²** have many branches or subdivisions. **men-kan** set up a branch or affiliate. **memper-kan** bifurcate, make into a branch. **pen-an** grafting. **per-an** branching, forking, bifurcation.

cabar *- hati* **1** cowardly, fear-stricken, timorous. **2** discouraged, dejected, downhearted. **3** careless, unheeding. **men-kan** *hati* **1** discourage, dishearten s.o. **2** frighten. **ke-an** discouragement, dejection, downheartedness.

cabé see CABAI.

cabik 1 torn, ripped, snagged. **2** strip, piece. *sekertas* a piece of paper. *se- sandang* a bit of clothing. **-² 1** torn, ripped, snagged. ~ *arang* tenuous (of nearly broken relationships). **2** a piece of paper. **men-²** repeatedly tear at, shred. *Mau ia rasanya* ~ *daging pengkhianat itu* He felt like ripping apart the traitor's flesh. *Kota ini hancur lumat di-² oléh api revolusi* This city was destroyed by the flames of the revolution. **men-(kan) 1** rip s.t. ~ *baju dadanya* embarrass or humiliate o.'s family. **2** lacerate. **ter-** be torn, get ripped. **ter-²** shredded, torn to pieces. *Jangan biarkan kehormatanmu* ~ Do not let your honor be torn to shreds. **-an** tear, snag, rip. **pen-an** laceration.

cabir long rip or tear. **ber-an** in tatters, in shreds.

cabo (*Ch*) prostitute, whore. **ny-** (*Vulg.*) engage in promiscuous sex (esp. of woman).

cabuh in an uproar.

cabuk₁ 1 carbuncle. **2** foul-smelling ulceration.

cabuk₂ k.o. fish, wolf herring.

cabuk₃ see CAMBUK.

cabul₁ 1 indecent, obscene. **2** pornographic. *bacaan -* pornographic reading material. **ber- 1** have illicit sexual relations. *Ia* ~ *dgn perempuan itu* He had illicit sex with that woman. **2** rage, spread (epidemics). *Penyakit koléra sedang* ~ *di sana* Cholera is raging there. **men-i 1** rape. *Bangsat itu* ~ *anak gadis pungutnya* That s.o.b. raped his foster daughter. **2** violate, transgress (sovereignty, etc.). *Uni Sovyét* ~ *wilayah Afghanistan* The Soviet Union violated the territory of Afghanistan. **ter-i** get raped or violated. **ke-an** lewdness, salaciousness, obscenity. **pen-an** violation, outrage. **per-an** indecent activities (adultery, exhibitionism, etc.).

cabul₂ see CÉBOL.

cabur ke-an disturbance, commotion, tumult.

cabut 1 yank out, withdraw. *beroda atau bertiang -* equipped with removable wheels or poles. *- bulu* hair tweezers, plucker. *- malu* save face. *- kartu* draw a card. *- untung* extract a profit. **2** (*Coll.*) take off, leave. *Mari kita -!* Let us go! *- lari* flee, scram. **ber- 1** drawn, unsheathed. **2** (*Crd.*) blackjack, the game of 21. **(ber)-²an** mutually yank out. *Kedua monyét itu* ~ *bulu* The two monkeys were tearing out e.o.'s fur. **men- 1** draw, pull (a pistol, gun, card, lots). *Irwan* ~ *pisau yg disimpannya di dlm botnya* Irwan pulled out the knife he kept in his boot. **2** pull out, extract (a tooth). **3** revoke, rescind, abrogate (regulation, law). ~ *jiwa/nyawa* take away a life. *Tuhan* ~ *nyawanya* God took her life. ~ *kata* withdraw a statement. ~ *paspor* revoke a passport. **4** unsheathe (sword, pistol, knife). **5** excerpt (a paragraph, etc.). **men-i** pluck, pull repeatedly. *Hamida sibuk* ~ *rerumputan yg tumbuh di punggung pusara itu* Hamida was busy yanking out weeds growing on the grave mound. **men-kan 1** have s.o. pull out, extract. *Saya mau ke dokter gigi* ~ *geraham bungsu saya* I am going to the dentist to get my wisdom tooth extracted. **2** pull, draw, extract for s.o. **ter-** yanked out, forcibly removed. **-an** an object that is extracted, etc. **pen- 1** s.t. or s.o. that withdraws or removes s.t. ~ *bulu* hair plucker. **2** rescinder. ~ *nyawa* o. who takes a life. **pen-an 1** revocation, cancellation, annulment. ~ *nama itu akan lebih sukar* The withdrawal of that name will be more difficult. ~ *hak milik* revocation of title. **2** retraction (of a statement). **3** extraction (of tooth, etc.).

cacad see CACAT.

cacadan (*Jv*) whiffletree, pole to connect the yoke to the plow.

cacah₁ number, amount. - *jiwa* census. **-an** digital. *komputer* ~ digital computer. **pen-** census taker. **pen-an** census taking.

cacah₂ cut up. *daging* - minced meat. **men-1** chop s.t. into fine bits, mince (meat, etc.). **2** chop up food for animals. **pen-** s.o. or s.t. that chops.

cacak₁ vertical, upright, perpendicular. **men-1** be upright, stand upright. **2** stand s.t. upright, stick into (the ground). **men-kan** erect (a statue, etc.).

cacak₂ 1 pinch. **2** steal, swipe.

cacak₃ (*Jv*) **1** elder brother. **2** form of address to elder man. **3** comrade, buddy (esp. to pedicab drivers in Surabaya, as *cak*). -, *berapa ke Tunjungan?* Hey buddy, how much is it to Tunjungan?

cacap₁ hair remedy (to ensure growth). **men-** treat hair with such a remedy.

cacap₂ men-i flood, inundate.

cacar 1 pustular skin eruption. **2** smallpox. - *air/bagus/cair/jeluntung/jeluntur/monyét* chicken pox. - *sapi* cowpox. - *ulang* revaccination, booster shot. - *unggas air* pox that affects fowl. **ber-** vaccinated. **men-** vaccinate. **pen-an** vaccination, vaccinating.

cacat 1 physical defect, deformity. - *badan* physical defect or handicap. - *cedera/cela* various defects. - *lihat* impaired eyesight. - *logat/wicara* speech defect. **2** flawed. *Mobilnya* - His car has its defects. *Namanya sdh* - He has become disreputable. **ber- 1** disabled, handicapped, infirm. **2** have a defect. **men-** criticize, find fault with. **men-i** damage, injure, impair. *Dilarang* ~ *héwan* It is forbidden to harm the animals. ~ *nama ayahnya* damage the name of o.'s father. ~ *undang-undang* break the law. **men-kan** cause damage. *Janganlah* ~ *kakimu dgn memakai sepatu*

sempit Do not harm your feet by wearing narrow shoes. **ter-** flawed, defective. **ke-an** disablement. **-an** criticism. **pen-** faultfinder, critic, caviler. **pen-an** deformation, disfigurement, malformation.

cacau fickle, inconstant, capricious, changeable. **men- 1** rave, be delirious. **2** be fickle, capricious. **3** be nervous.

caci abuse verbally. - *maki* curses and obscenities. **men-** *maki* taunt with vile language, heap on curses. **-makian** vile language used to insult s.o. **ber-²an** scold e.o. with strong language. **men-1** scorn, jeer at, ridicule. **2** curse out, swear at. **-an** scornful, vile remarks.

cacing worm, maggot. - *gelang/gerumit* tapeworm, roundworm. - *gila* **1** worm that turns when touched, earthworm. **2** (*Derog.*) woman who fails to stay home. - *gulung/kalung* earthworm. *Selagi menunggu kabar ia spt* - *kepanasan* He wriggled like a worm in the sun waiting for the news. - *kerawit* pinworm. - *kermi* **1** worm. **2** maggot. - *menjadi naga* from a humble beginning to power. - *perut/pipih/pita* tapeworm. - *tambang* hookworm. **ber-** have worms in it. **-an** suffer from intestinal worms.

cadang *suku* - spare parts. **ber-** ready, prepared. **men-kan 1** reserve, set aside. ~ *tempat duduk utk tamu* reserve seats for guests. ~ *uang utk hari tua* lay aside money for o.'s old age. **2** plan s.t. ~ *proyék baru* plan a new project. **3** propose, suggest, put forward for nomination. ~ *seorg utk diréktur* nominate s.o. for director. **-an 1** reserve, back up, spare. ~ *emas* gold reserves. *uang* ~ reserve funds. *pasukan* ~ reserve troops. **2** a proposal. ~ *perdamaian* peace proposal. **3** plan, long-range project. ~ *sepuluh tahun* 10-year plan. **4** a vote. ~ *tdk percaya* a vote of no confidence. **pen-** proposer or mover (of a motion). **pen-an 1** act of setting s.t. in reserve. **2** nomination. **per-an** reserves, preserves. ~ *hutan* forest preserves.

cadar veil (worn by Isl. women, bride, etc.). *Ia bercerita membukakan - hatinya* She talked and told everything honestly (lit., removed the veil from her heart).

cadas (*Geol.*) **1** sedimentary rock formation (such as sandstone or tuff). **2** rocky ground or area.

cadél (*Jkt*) see CEDAL.

cadik₁ (*Naut.*) **1** leeboard. **2** outrigger. **ber-** be fitted with outriggers. *perahu* ~ boat with outriggers.

cadik₂ (*Coll.*) **ny-** addicted.

cadik₃ see CERDIK.

cadok nearsighted, myopic.

cadong share, portion. **men-kan** divide s.t. up to be shared. **pen-** o. who gets a share.

caela expression of exasperation.

caem /ca'em/ (*Sl.*) cute.

cafétaria /kafétaria/ canteen, small restaurant (not necessarily self-service) attached to school or office.

cagak₁ 1 a forking branch. **2** crossing. *jalan* ~

crossroad. **ber-** forked, branched. *jalan* ~ forked road.

cagak₂ (*Jv*) pole, post used for support. - *hidup* 1 source of subsistence. 2 life annuity. *Tanah ini bisa saya jadikan - hidup saya* I can make this land into a source of my livelihood. - *potrét* camera tripod. - *télpon* telephone pole. **ber-** supported. *Témbok ini* ~ *besi* This wall is supported by iron props. **men-** 1 support, prop up, brace. ~ *témbok spy tdk rubuh* prop up a wall so it will not collapse. 2 stand upright. **men-kan** 1 implant, stick (in the ground). 2 place on a post. **ter-** 1 implanted, standing (up). 2 sticking out, conspicuous. 3 supported on a stand. *Kamera ini tdk akan bergerak karena* ~ This camera will not move because it is on a stand. 4 be straight and motionless. *Lama juga aku* ~ *di tepi jalan* For a long time I stood motionless on the side of the road.

cagar 1 security, guarantee, pledge. - *alam* nature preserve. 2 advance payment. **men-kan** offer as security. **-an** security, guarantee.

cagu, caguh whitlow.

cagut men- peck, bite.

cah₁ hah! (exclamation of disagreement).

cah₂ see BOCAH.

cahar loose (of feces). **pen-** laxative.

cahari see CARI.

cahaya 1 radiance, brilliance, glow. - *muka* 1 shining (of countenance). 2 complexion. 2 light. - *baur* diffused light. *pd* - *pertimbangan* in the light of a consideration. 3 ray. - *kilat* flash of lightning. - *matahari* sunlight. - *silau* glare. - *hati* sweetheart. - *majemuk* (*Phys.*) light that consists of component parts. - *mata* 1 a sparkling (of eyes). 2 sweetheart, beloved. **ber-(²)** 1 luminous. *cat* ~ luminous paint. 2 shine, gleam, radiate. **ber-kan** (*Lit.*) reflect light of a certain kind. *malam yg* ~ *bintang* a night lit by the stars. **men-i** 1 illuminate. *Jalan ini gemilang di-i lampu terang* This street is brilliant, illuminated with bright lights. 2 pour rays on, shed light on. *Bila matahari tdk lagi* ~ *pohon-pohon nyiur . . .* When the sun no longer pours its rays on the coconut palms . . . 3 expose (in photography). **men-kan** radiate, beam s.t., send out (light rays). **pen-an** 1 illumination, lighting. 2 exposure (in photography).

cailah /ca'ilah/ Lord! (exclamation of surprise).

caing-caing in shreds, in tatters. **men-** rip up, tear to shreds.

cair 1 liquid, fluid. 2 thin, weak, diluted. *susu* - diluted milk. *Hubunganku dgn isteriku sdh* - My relationship with my wife has become very tenuous. **men-** 1 liquefy, melt. *Ésnya* ~ The ice melted. 2 diffuse in liquid, become part of larger whole. *Kalau basah, gula itu* ~ *nanti* If it gets wet, the sugar will dissolve. *Utk keperluan ini pejabat perlu* ~ *dgn rakyat* For this reason officials should integrate themselves within society. 3 weaken, become watery. *Perang dingin kini* ~ *menjadi gugatan-gugatan yg pedas* The cold war has now weakened into sharp recriminations.

men-kan 1 liquefy s.t. *Matahari* ~ *salju di puncak gunung* The sun melted the snow on the mountain peak. 2 water down, dilute. 3 smooth the way, thaw out. *Ketidaknikmatan org thd sastra perlu kita -kan* We need to remedy people's lack of interest in literature. 4 (*Fin.*) release. ~ *cék* clear a check. ~ *uang* free an account or money supply. *Di-kan krédit koperasi utk sapi perah impor* Clearance was given for the cooperative to import milch cows. **memper-** cause s.t. to become liquid. *Hujan masih* ~ *debu kampung-kampung Jkt* Rain was still turning the dust of Jkt's neighborhoods into mud. **ter-** 1 suddenly become liquid. 2 (*Fin.*) released. **ke-an** (*Fin.*) liquidity. **-an** liquid. ~ *keras* corrosive liquid. ~ *malam* liquid wax. **pen-** solvent. **pen-an** 1 liquefaction. ~ *gas alam* liquification of natural gas. 2 smoothing out. ~ *hubungan* normalization of relations.

cais reins.

caisim k.o. Ch vegetable, mustard greens.

cak₁ smack (of the lips). **ber-²** repeatedly make a clicking sound (as in the Balinese *kecak* dance).

cak₂ - *padang* sparrow.

cak₃ see CACAK₃.

cakah at an obtuse angle.

cakalang (*E. Indonesia*) k.o. tuna, skipjack.

cakal-bakal (*Jv*) founder of a village, pioneer.

cakalélé war dance in the Moluccas and Minahasa.

cakap₁ 1 able, capable. *Ia - menjalankan tugasnya* She was able to perform her task. 2 adroit, clever, skillful. *pemanjat - dan berani* a brave and skilled climber. 3 good-looking. *Ia - sekali rupanya* He looked very handsome. *gadis cantik -* a very attractive girl. **ber-** be able, be capable. *Ia* ~ *mangalahkan musuhnya* He was able to defeat his enemy. **memper-(kan)** enable, empower. **ter-** most qualified, highly capable. **ke-an** skill, ability. *Aku tlh membuktikan* ~*ku bekerja* I have proven my ability to work.

cakap₂ words, statement. - *Inggris* speak English. *Kuputuskan - ayah* I interrupted father's statement. *banyak -* much talk. - *angin* chatter, empty talk. - *olah-alih/pancaroba* inconsequential chatter. -² chatter, prattle. *Kemudian saya mendengar* ~ *meréka* Then I heard their prattle. **ber-** speak, talk. *Tlh sepuluh hari ia tak* ~ *dgn bininya* It has been 10 days since he talked to his wife. - *perut* ventriloquize. **ber-²** 1 be engaged in conversation. *Komandan* ~ *dgn Patiwiri di atas rumah* In the house the commandant was conversing with Patiwiri. 2 chat, chatter. **men-kan** discuss s.t. *Katakanlah apa yg ingin kau-kan* Tell me what you want to talk about. **memper-kan** 1 discuss, talk about. ~ *soal politik* discuss political matters. 2 speak. *Ia pandai* ~ *bahasa itu* He was good at speaking that language. **per-an** 1 conversation, dialogue. *bahasa* ~ conversational language. 2 discussion.

cakar 1 claw, talon (of birds). - *besi* iron pincers. 2 paw. 3 scratch. - *ayam* scrawl, poor handwriting. - *balar* scratches everywhere, scratches all over. **4** rasp, file. **bersi-** claw at e.o. **(ber)-²an** **1** scratch e.o. with claws. **2** fight, quarrel. **3** engage in polemics. **men- 1** claw, scratch. *Mukanya cacat di- oléh seékor kucing* His face was disfigured because it had been scratched by a cat. **2** scratch, scrape (of chickens in search of food). ~ *langit* be a skyscraper. **men-kan** scratch, scrape after s.t. (for s.o.). **ter-** get clawed. **-an 1** scratches. **2** clawing. **-²an** have a violent argument with s.o. *Christine malahan sampai berkelahi ~ dgn anak-anak lain* Christine even got to the point of fighting and arguing violently with the other children. **pen-** scraper, rasp. ~ *awan/langit* skyscraper.

cakatan see CEKATAN.

cakau see CEKAU.

cakep see CAKAP₁.

cakera see CAKRA.

cakeram see CAKRAM.

cakil 1 noble shadow-play character with protruding lower jaw. **2** prognathous. **ny-** having a lower jaw protruding.

caklat see CIAKLAT.

cakra Vishnu's mythical weapon.

cakrabirawa presidential palace guards in Sukarno era.

cakrak (*Jv*) well-formed body, good-looking (of humans, animals).

cakram 1 disk. - *optik* optical disk. - *angka/nomor/putar* (*Tel.*) dial. - *rantai* bracketwheel. **2** (*Sport*) discus.

cakrawala 1 firmament, heavens, sky. **2** rotation of heavenly bodies.

cakrawati rule, sway.

cakruk (*Jv*) small market. **ke-an** rule, sway.

cakué see CAKWÉ.

cakup₁ men- 1 catch with the mouth, snap at. **2** arrest, round up (prostitutes, illegal vendors, tramps). *Suaminya di- menjadi tentera anjing Belanda* Her husband was arrested and forced to become a Dutch mercenary. **3** embrace, entail, include. *bahan bacaan yg di- oléh kumpulan ini* reading material that is included in this compilation. *Ajaran-ajarannya ~ segala segi hidup manusia* His teachings encompass all aspects of human life. **men-²** open and close mouth repeatedly. **men-i** embrace, include. *Apa saja yg di-i oléh JAL Executive Service?* What all is included in JAL's Executive Service? **ter- 1** rounded up. *Seorg bandit ~ dlm tangkapan* A bandit was caught in a trap. **2** caught up in, embroiled in. *Ia merasa ~ pula dlm masalahnya* He felt entangled in her problem as well. **3** covered, protected. *Saya sdh ~ oléh asuransi* I am already covered by insurance. **-an 1** scope. ~ *tugas* term of reference. **2** low quality because of being acquired at random, as in a police raid. **pen-** k.o. snapping trap. **pen-an** coverage. ~ *data* coverage of data.

cakup₂ (*Jv*) scoop, ladle out. **se-** a ladleful. **men-** serve up a ladleful.

cakwé (*Ch*) k.o. fried cake, fritter of twisted dough.

cala see COLA-CALA.

calabikang k.o. multicolored cake made from rice.

calak₁ superimposed (of o. color on another).

calak₂ (*M*) sharp-tongued, glib. -² *ganti asah* stopgap, makeshift, do s.t. halfheartedly. **men-** sharpen.

calak₃ (*Jv*) o. who performs traditional circumcision.

calang 1 bare, almost leafless. **2** unadorned (of furniture, etc.).

calar laceration, scratch (on skin). - *balar* a number of scratches. **ber-** be lacerated or scratched.

calincing k.o. weed.

caling₁ tusk, canine tooth.

caling₂ see COLANG-CALING.

calipso see CALYPSO.

calit smear, stain, spot. **ber-** stained, spotted, smeared. **men-kan** stain s.t., make a stain. ~ *tinta pd lengan* smear ink on the arm.

calo 1 passenger recruiter for public vehicles. **2** ticket scalper.

caloisme a mentality and system characterized by using the power of o.'s position for personal gain (i.e., by farming out projects, etc.).

calon 1 candidate, aspirant. **2** applicant. **3** recruit. - *biarawan/biarawati* (*Rel.*) novitiate. - *guru* student teacher. - *ibu* mother-to-be. - *isteri* **1** prospective wife. **2** bride. - *opsir* cadet. - *penerbang* fledgling pilot. - *penulis* would-be writer. - *perwira* officer candidate, cadet. - *présidén* presidential candidate. - *suami* **1** prospective husband. **2** groom. **men-kan** nominate, run s.o. for office. ~ *diri* run for office. **pen-an** nomination, designation.

caluk see ASAM.

calung₁ 1 bamboo water scoop. **2** cup for latex.

calung₂ k.o. bamboo xylophone.

calypso /kalipso/ **1** k.o. Latin American dance. **2** pomaded, brushed-back hair style (1950s).

cam₁ interest, attention (us. only in negative constructions). *tak berapa -* **1** pay little attention. **2** understand little. *kurang -* pay little attention. *Ia tak berapa - akan usul itu* He was not much interested in the proposal. **men-** bear in mind. **men-kan 1** note, observe carefully. *Ia ~ naséhat ayahnya* He paid close attention to his father's advice. **2** criticize. ~ *tindakan pemerintah* criticize the gvt.'s action. ~ *pd* remind. *Ia ~ pd temannya spy bekerja keras* She reminded her friend to work hard. **3** review, implant (in the mind).

cam₂ see KECAM.

cama₁ have a large appetite.

cama₂ [*calon mahasiswa*] freshman, new university student (during hazing). - *cami* freshmen boys and girls.

camar seagull, tern.

camat subdistrict head. **ke-an** subdistrict.

cambah see KECAMBAH.

cambang whiskers, sideburns. - *bauk* full beard. **ber-** bearded, whiskered.

cambuk whip, cat-o'-nine-tails. - *pemacu* stimulus, s.t. to spur the process. - *petir* thunderclap. **men- 1** lash, (strike with a) whip. **2** exhort, spur. *hari* *depan yg selalu ~nya utk rajin belajar* a future which ever spurred him to study hard. **men-i** whip repeatedly, lash s.o. or s.t. *Ia ~ suaminya* She lashed her husband. **men-kan** whip, apply the whip. **-an 1** lash, stroke (of whip). **2** exhortation.

cambul see CEMBUL.

cambung large bowl, tureen (for rice, fruit, etc.).

camca (*Sumatra*) tea or soup spoon.

cami [*calon mahasiswi*] female freshman (during hazing).

camik meny- eat a little. **ny-an** snacks.

camilan (*Jv*) snacks.

campa coarse, not ground finely (of tea leaves or coffee).

campah flat, insipid, tasteless.

campak₁ a throw, toss. *- buang* k.o. simple wooden javelin. **men-** throw carelessly, toss (money to beggars, etc.). **men-kan 1** throw, toss. *~ jala* throw a net. *Temannya ~ jambu sebuah kpdnya* His friend tossed a guava to him. **2** toss out, dispose of. *Stlh bertemu, dia ~ aku* After we met, he threw me out. *Ia ~ segala tugas itu* He abandoned all his duties. **ter-** be thrown out, regarded as useless.

campak₂ measles.

campak₃ k.o. folk dance from Beliton.

campin 1 skillful, handy. **2** clever, adept.

camping in rags, in tatters. **ber-(²)** be in rags, be in tatters.

campung lopped off, clipped. **men-(i)** chop off, lop off.

campur 1 mixed, mingled, blended. *- aduk* 1 mixed, hodge-podge. 2 upset, confused. **men-adukkan** mix up, confuse. **pen-adukkan** mixing up, confusion. *- baur/gaul* 1 mixed up. 2 associated with. **ber-** *baur/gaul* associate with, have contact with. **men-baurkan** mix up. *men-baurkan pernyataan* mix up statements. **pen-bauran** mixing up. *- kode* (*Ling.*) code switching. **2** get involved. *Kami tdk perlu -* We do not need to get mixed up in it. *turut/ikut -* involve o.s. *- bicara/mulut* break or enter into conversation. *- tangan* 1 interfere in, invade the rights of another. **2** intervene. **ber-** *tangan* be involved with. **ber-1** mixed with. *susu ~ air* milk mixed with water. *bingung ~ haru* confusion mixed with deep emotion. *~ darah* of mixed blood. *Ia ~ darah dgn bangsa Swédia* She has some Swedish blood. **2** mix. *Minyak tdk ~ dgn air* Oil and water do not mix. *Org itu tdk mau ~ dgn tetangganya* That person does not want to mix with his neighbors. **ber-kan** mixed with. *Wah, gula ini sdh ~ garam* Hey, this sugar is mixed with salt. **men-** mix together, blend. *~ air dgn minyak* mix oil and water. **men-i 1** mix into. *Darahnya mengalir ~ air dr sungai* His blood flowed mixing with the river water. **2** participate, join in. *Ia mémang tdk pernah ~ apa-apa* Of course he never joined in anything. *~ perdébatan* participate in the debating. **3** adulterate, mix s.t. into s.t. *Ia ~ susunya dgn air* He adulterated the milk with water. **men-kan** mix s.t. into, blend s.t. in. *Aku ~ warna hijau pd*

yg putih I mixed a green color into the white. **ter-i** get s.t. mixed into it. **ke-an** (*Jv*) get s.t. mixed into it. **-an 1** intervention. **2** alloy, mixture. **3** intercourse, association. **4** medley. **5** interference, meddling. **pen- 1** s.o. or s.t. which mixes into. *tawas ~ getah* alum, the substance that mixes with sap. **2** blender, mixer. **per-an 1** interference, meddling. *~ tangan* interference, meddling. **2** social intercourse. **3** mixing, blending. **4** promiscuity.

camuk stab. **men-** stab, strike.

canai grind down. *batu -* a round grinding stone. **men- 1** sharpen, polish (on grindstone). **2** make even (with ruler). **3** smooth (the way). **-an 1** s.t. polished or sharpened. **2** manner of sharpening. **3** baptism of fire.

canang crier's cymbal. **ber- 1** use a cymbal. **2** state a message. *Senyumnya terus ~ di wajah hitamnya* His smile continued to express a message on his dark face. **men-kan 1** proclaim (by beating on drum, etc.). **2** announce with ceremony. *~ perang thd kemiskinan* declare war on poverty. **3** propagandize, tout. **ter-** proclaimed. **ter-kan** be proclaimed. **-an 1** summons. **2** description, message. **pen-** crier. **pen-an** issuing (a formal statement), proclamation.

cancang₁ ter- be standing on end.

cancang₂ men-, ny- 1 tie up. *Pakaian Listi di- di ujungnya* Listi's clothes were knotted at the ends. **2** put on a leash. **men-kan** tie to s.t. else, tether. **ter-** be tied.

cancut (*Jv*) loincloth. **ber-** wear a loincloth. *~ tali wondo* roll up o.'s sleeves and get (down) to work.

canda (*Jv*) **1** joke (esp. of teasing nature). *gelak ~* jokes and laughs. **2** caprice. **ber- 1** joke, act playfully, tease. *Biasanya org berpacaran ~* Usually lovers behave playfully. **2** be capricious.

candak *sistim - kulak* system of gvt. credit for small investors. **ke-** (*Jv*) **1** can be handled or picked up. **2** caught, seized.

candi ancient Hindu or Buddhist temple or shrine. *- bentar* (*Bali*) split gate to a Balinese temple. **men-kan, memper-kan** enshrine. *Ia dikan di Tumapél* Upon his death a temple was built for him at Tumapel. **per-an 1** enshrinement. **2** monument matters.

candit (*Naut.*) fluke (of anchor).

candra₁ (*Lit.*) moon. *- sangkala* chronogram based on lunar calculations.

candra₂ men- give s.t. a symbol or label. *Kita tlh menginjak jaman baru yg dpt di- sbg jaman Palapa* We are entering a new era which can be given the title of the Space Age.

candrabirawa see AJI₁.

candradimuka 1 (*Lit.*) a legendary crater from which infants immediately emerge as adults. **2** (*Mil.*) officer candidate training.

candrasangkala see CANDRA₁.

candu 1 opium (ready for use). **2** s.t. hallucinogenic or intoxicating, like a drug. *Cinta pd tanah air adalah - yg paling nikmat* Love of the fatherland gives the greatest high. **men-1** smoke opium. **2** be addicted to. *Ia tlh ~ minum* *kopi* She has become addicted to coffee. **men-i** become devotee of. *Lagu ini di-i anak muda* This song is madly popular among youth. **men-kan** habit forming, addictive. **ke-an** addicted. *Kamu sdh ~ cara roman yg dilihat di film* You are addicted to the romantic ways you have seen in the movies. **pe(n)- 1** opium addict. ~ *morfin* morphine addict. **2** fan, devotee. ~ *bir* beer lover. ~ *bioskop* movie fan.

candung meat cleaver.

cangah ter- be opened wide, agape. *Ia ~ melihat mayat adiknya* He was stunned to see his little sister's corpse.

cangak₁ men- raise the head in order to see.

cangak₂ k.o. heronlike bird.

cangap 1 notch on end of a pole. **2** forked branch. **men-** force (the mouth of animals) open.

cang cing cong (*Derog.*) speak a Ch dialect.

canggah₁ two-pronged pole or branch. **ber- 1** use a forked pole. **2** two-pronged, forked.

canggah₂ (*Jv*) **1** great-great-grandchild. **2** great-great-grandparent.

canggai₁ long, decorative fingernail.

canggai₂ peanuts fried with a confectionery shell.

canggi, canggih sophisticated. *gadis yg -* a sophisticated girl. *téknologi -* sophisticated technology.

canggung₁ 1 clumsy, awkward. *Ia - benar naik sepéda* He is really clumsy on a bicycle. *Ia merasa - mengendarai mobil di kota yg ramai itu* He felt uneasy driving in that busy city. **2** gauche, ill at ease, bashful. *Ia merasa - bercakap-cakap dgn gurunya* She feels ill at ease when she talks with her teacher. *Agak - kurasa pidato-pidatoan* I feel rather uneasy giving speeches. **3** ill-mannered, curt. *Perkataannya kasar dan -* His words were coarse and ill-mannered. **4** insufficient, inadequate. *kepandaian yg -* insufficient ability. *penghasilan yg -* inadequate income. **men-kan** cause awkwardness. *Sikap org tuanya ~* His parents' attitude created difficulties. **ke-an 1** clumsiness, awkwardness. **2** (physical) handicap.

canggung₂ half-submerged tree trunk.

cangkang eggshell.

cangkat (*in some regions only*) low hill.

cangkél stuck fast. **men-kan 1** hook (up). **2** attach (a condition).

cangkih-mangkih stick out in all directions.

cangking men- carry by the hand while walking. **meng-kan** carry on behalf of s.o. **-an** s.t. carried in the hand. *bagasi ~* hand baggage.

cangkir₁ cup, small mug. *se- kopi* a cup of coffee. *- piring* china(ware). *- tinta* inkwell.

cangkir₂ spur (of a fowl, bird).

cangklék mem- carry on the hips.

cangklong k.o. pipe with curved stem. **-an** s.t. similar to a long pipe. *tas ~* a carrying bag with a strap.

cangkok see CANGKUK₁.

cangkrang 1 leafless branch. **2** cover of a battery lamp. **3** (*Auto.*) chassis.

cangkriman riddle, conundrum.

cangkring k.o. tree.

cangkruk sit around doing nothing.

cangkuk₁ 1 shoot, cutting. **2** graft, transplant. *- sumsum tulang* bone marrow transplant. **3** false, imitation. **men-kan** transplant, graft. **ke-an** transplantation. **-an 1** a transplant, a graft. **2** false, imitation. *pemimpin ~* false leader. **pen-an** transplanting. *~ jantung* heart transplant.

cangkuk₂ 1 elephant goad, gaff. **2** hook. *- pangkal* butt hook. *- tanjul* choker hook. **ber-** use a goad, have a hook. **men-** hook, catch (by using a pole with hook).

cangkuk₃ k.o. tree whose dried flowers provide a medicine.

cangkuk₄ preserved or pickled fish.

cangkul mattock, hoelike tool. *- burung* pickax. **men-, meny-** be engaged in hoeing, prepare (ground) for cultivation. **men-i** hoe at s.t., break up s.t. with a hoe. *Berhari-hari para petani ~ sawah mencari antik* For days and days the farmers dug up the paddy fields looking for antique ceramics. **pen-** o. who hoes. **pen-an, peny-an** hoeing. *upacara ~* ground-breaking ceremony.

cangkum men- embrace, hug, clasp.

cangkung squat. **ber-, men-** squat, hunker.

cangkup men- eat by tossing food into the mouth with the hand.

canguk men- sit with head bowed down.

cangut men- protrude, stick out (as of the hilt of a dagger from the sheath).

cantas (*Jv*) sharp-tongued.

cantél ny- (*Coll.*) be hooked on s.t. **men-i** put a hook on. **men-kan** put s.t. on a hook. **ke-** (*Coll.*) hooked on. *Sialan, bajuku ~ kawat berduri!* Darn! My shirt snagged on barbed wire! **-an 1** hook, clasp. **2** clip.

cantengan whitlow.

cantik 1 pretty, beautiful (in appearance). *- molék* very attractive. *- rupanya* have a pretty appearance. **2** (*Sport*) well executed (smash, goal, etc.). **ber-²** be dressed up, dress up. **memper-** make pretty, beautify. *~ wajahnya* fix up her face. **ke-an 1** beauty, pulchritude. *salon ~* beauty parlor. **2** charm, sweetness, attractiveness.

canting 1 small dipper used to apply wax in batik process. *- cap* instrument for printing on cloth. **2** bamboo water scoop.

cantol hook. **men-** get hooked, attached to. **men-i** attach to, hook on to. *Talinya ~ kawat listrik* The string hooked onto an electric wire. **ke-** (*Coll.*) caught, snagged. *Jangan ~, bung!* Don't get hooked (by a girl), man!

cantrik pupil, disciple (of Buddhist or Hindu guru).

cantum graft. *- hijau* green budding. *- jemala* crown grafting. *- sanding* approach grafting. **ber-** joined together. **men- 1** fuse, close, bring together. **2** pin. **men-i** add on to. *Pengarang ~ buku ini dgn tanda tangannya* The author added his signature to his book. **men-kan 1** include. *Harian ~ kabar baik* The daily carried good news. ~ *nama* sign up. **2** stitch (up). ~ *lubang di* *pakaian* stitch up a hole in a garment. **3** attach, stick. *Gambaran itu saya -kan di dinding itu* I stuck the poster on the wall. **4** pin on (a medal), stick (a knife in s.o.'s back). **ter- 1** included, added to. *Nomormu ~ di papan lulus* Your number was included on the passing list posted on the bulletin board. **2** inserted, attached. **-an** s.t. added, attached. *O, itu hanya nama ~ saja. Sebenarnya dia tdk ada di sini.* Oh, that name is just on the list for official purposes. Actually, he does not work here. **pen-an** inclusion, incorporation.

cao₁ (*Ch*) run.

cao₂ see CINCAU.

caos see SAUS.

cap₁ 1 stamp, seal. *surat - Semarang* a letter postmarked Semarang. *- pemerintah* gvt. seal. *- air* watermark. *- batu* lithography. *- jari* fingerprint. *- jempol* thumbprint. *- lak* wax seal. *- mohor* **1** gvt. seal. **2** (*Lit.*) seal on coins. *- pos* postmark. **2** trademark, brand name. *pistol - kuda* pistol with a horse label. *dagang* trademark. **3** printed. *huruf - printed* letter. **4** quality, feature. **5** Ch seal. **men-, menge- 1** stamp, place a seal on, brand (a steer). **2** brand, stigmatize. *Kawan-kawan sekantor ~ aku santri yg kolot* My office mates labeled me an old-fashioned religious believer. **men-i 1** affix seal or label to s.t. *Kerja tukang pos bukan cuma ~ surat* A postal clerk's work is not merely stamping letters. **2** label s.o. as. **men-kan 1** have s.t. stamped. **2** stamp for s.o. **-²an 1** made with a stamp. *batik ~* printed batik. **2** not genuine, bearing a fake seal. **penge-an, pen-an** labeling. **~ sosial** social labeling.

cap₂ sound of sharp instrument perforating a target. *-! Pisaunya tertancap tepat di tengah-tengah lingkaran* Wham! His knife stuck right in the center of the bull's-eye.

cap₃ (*Ch*) ten. *- go* fifteen. *- go céng* 15,000. *- tiau* 10,000,000.

capa₁ [*calon perwira*] senior military cadet's rank.

capa₂ k.o. wild camphor plant.

capa₃ game of heads or tails.

capai₁ men- 1 reach out for and touch. *Ia ~ kotak peluru di ujung méja* He reached for the ammunition box on the edge of the table. **2** reach, attain. *Haji Anwar tlh ~ usia tujuh puluh tahun* Haji Anwar has reached the age of 70. *Dicobanya ~ Makassar berjalan kaki* He tried to reach Makassar on foot. **3** achieve, attain. *~ maksud* achieve a purpose. *~ gelar doktor* obtain a doctorate. **ter-** reached, achieved. *bisa ~ oléh kantong org biasa* within reach of the average man's wallet. **sepen-** as far as o. can reach. **pen-an** achievement, achieving.

capai₂ tired, exhausted, weary. *- lelah* thoroughly exhausted. **ber-²** exhausted. **ke-an 1** weariness, fatigue. **2** fatigued, worn out. *Karena ~ tertidur jugalah Ny. Iskandar* Out of exhaustion Mrs. Iskandar fell asleep after all.

capak₁ men-, memper- 1 slight, ignore. **2** take lightly, show disdain for. **ter- 1** humiliated. **2** ignored, left alone.

capak₂ men-, men-² smack o.'s lips (while eating).

capak₃ ter- sit straddling s.t.

capal k.o. sandal.

capang wide-spreading (of ears, nostrils, mustache, horns).

capcai (*Ch*) **1** stir-fried vegetables. **2** hodgepodge, mishmash. *musik -* music of mixed styles. *Pendidikannya pendidikan -. Segala macam sekolah pernah dimasukinya* His education was a hodgepodge. He is been enrolled in every k.o. school.

capeg /capek/ [*calon pegawai*] candidate for civil service.

capék see CAPAI₂.

capelok see CAPLOK.

capéo (*Amb*) hat.

capgomé, capgomék celebration of 15th day of the first Ch month.

capik lame, paralyzed.

capil k.o. broad sun hat made of palm or pandanus leaves.

caping head covering of woven bamboo of broad conical shape.

capit tweezers. **men-** snap at, bite (of crabs).

capita sélecta /kapita sélékta/ anthology of selected topics.

capjai see CAPCAI.

capjiki Ch card game with 12 cards or dice.

caplak 1 dog flea. **2** skin blemish.

caplok snatch and swallow. **men- 1** snatch (a purse). **2** swallow, gulp down. **3** seize, annex (a country). *Musuh sdh mengepung kota ini dan tinggal ~nya* The city is surrounded and all but seized. **4** carry, win, capture. *Politikus itu ~ distrik ini* The politician carried this district. **ter- 1** swallowed (up). **2** annexed. **pen-an** annexation.

capuk pockmarked.

capung dragonfly.

cara 1 manner, mien. *Ayahku senang melihat - Fiansyah bekerja* My father was pleased to see the way Fiansyah worked. *dgn - yg tenang* in a calm way. *bercakap - Cina* **1** talk in the Ch way. **2** speak Chinese. *- artikulasi* (*Ling.*) manner of articulation. **2** style, fashion, tradition. *- Barat* Western style. *- menulis* writing style. *menulis - Arab* write in Arabic script. **3** method. *- lepas* free-range method (for poultry). *- mengajar* method of teaching. *- beristirahat* at ease, parade rest. *- berpikir* way of thinking, world view. *- bersiap* at attention. *- hidup* way of life. *- kerja* procedure. *- pemeristiwaan* case method. *- pendekatan* approach. *- pengerjaan* method of operating. *- terakhir* last resort. **se- 1** in a ... manner. *~ anumerta* posthumously. *~ sepihak* unilaterally. *~ tdk merata* unequally, unevenly. **2** on a ... scale. *~ besar-besaran* on a large scale. **3** as (if). *Ia diperlakukan ~ tuan besar* He was treated like a big shot. *diterima ~ tamu* be received as a guest. **4** according to, in accordance with. *merayakan ~ adat lama* celebrate according to long-standing customs.

carah ber- in small lots. **men- 1** cut into small bits. **2** sell piecemeal. **men-kan** sell by the piece.

carak₁ men- swallow in a gulp (such as sucking a raw egg, pouring water down o.'s throat, etc.).
carak₂ men- begin to be visible (e.g., rising sun).
caraka 1 envoy, emissary. - *negara* foreign service officer. **2** (*Lit.*) messenger.
carang tendril.
cari look for. - *angin* take a break. - *bola* (*Sport*) go for a serve. - *gampang* easygoing. **ber-²an 1** look for e.o. **2** play hide-and-seek. **men-** seek, hunt for, look for. *Ia ~ salah* She is looking for mistakes. *di-segera* wanted immediately. *~ akal* endeavor, strive. *~ béla* kill s.o. in order that his spirit will accompany the spirit of another dead person, suttee. *~ fasal* provide an excuse for. *~ hitungan* solve an arithmetic problem. *~ kelebihan* better o.s. *~ kesalahan* endeavor to know others' faults. *~ kutu* investigate, look into. *~ makan* make a living. *~ muka* 1 ask a favor. 2 seek praise. *~ nafkah* seek a living. *~ nama* seek fame, make a name for o.s. - *nasi* earn o.'s living. *~ penyakit* look for trouble. *~ rezeki* seek a living. *~ risik* make (secret) inquiries. *~ selisih* seek an excuse to fight, look for a fight. *~ tahu* desire to find out. *~ uang* try to obtain money. *~ umbut dlm batu* be in a hopeless situation. *~ untung* try to obtain a profit. **men-² 1** look for thoroughly, repeatedly search for. *Tangannya ~ di antara amplop* His hands rifled the envelopes. **2** pretend to look for, fabricate. *alasan yg di-²* a trumped-up charge. *~ muka* make a scene. **men-kan 1** look for or seek s.t. for s.o. *Ia ~ adiknya bunga mérah* He looked for a red flower for his little brother. **2** seek (a solution, etc.). **pen-** s.o. or s.t. that searches for s.t., seeker. *~ arah* direction finder. *~ kerja* s.o. looking for a job. *~ mutiara* pearl diver. *~ nafkah* breadwinner. **pen-an 1** livelihood. *Nelayan-nelayan kematian ~* The fishermen have lost their livelihood. **2** income. *Tdk layak aku makan ~mu* It is not right for me to live off your earnings. **3** quest. *~ pelikan* (*Geol.*) prospecting. **se(pen)-an** common property (of husband and wife).
carik₁ 1 torn, ripped (of paper, cloth). **2** classifier for paper. *se- kertas* a piece of paper. **3** (ticket) stub, remnant, scrap. *se- kain beludru* a scrap of velvet. **ber-²** in strips, tears, rags. **men-** tear, rip to pieces. **-an** a scrap torn off. *~ kertas* a scrap of paper.
carik₂ chief clerk of a village.
caring lie in the sun.
carok (*Madura*) duel to defend o.'s honor.
carter charter. **men-** charter (vehicle etc.). **-an** chartered. *pesawat terbang ~* chartered plane. **pen-** o. who charters a vehicle.
caruk₁ men- 1 notch, indent. **2** tap (for rubber).
caruk₂ ravenous, gluttonous. **men-** be gluttonous.
carut obscene, filthy (of speech). --*marut* abusive speech, obscene language. **ber-, men- 1** use foul language, utter obscenities. **2** curse s.o. with foul language. **memper-i** revile, berate, abuse (verbally) using foul language. **ke-an** obscenity. **pen-** foul-mouthed person.

cas 1 (*Elec.*) charge. **2** (*Sumatra*) charge (a battery). **3** (*Sl.*) eat. **men-(kan)** (*Sumatra*) charge (a battery).
casanova /kasanofa/ womanizer.
cas-cis-cus, cas-cus (*Coll.*) chatter, prattle. **ber-** (*Derog.*) speak a European language.
casis (*Auto.*) chassis.
cassette see KASÉT.
cat₁ 1 paint. - *air* water color. - *alis* eyebrow pencil. - *dasar* primer, undercoat. - *duko* spray paint. - *luar* outer coat (of paint). - *minyak* oil paint. **2** tint, tinge. - *rambut* hair tint. - *batik* coloring material for coloring batik. - *bibir* lipstick. - *kuku* nail polish. **ber-** painted. *rumah yg ~ mérah* red-painted house. **men-, menge-** paint or color s.t. **penge-an, pen-an** painting, paint job.
cat₂ Charge! (exclamation when attacking).
catak horsefly.
catat, catet record, note. - *pinggir* **men-pinggiri** comment on. **ber-an** annotated. **men- 1** make a note of, record. *Radio kemarén ~ harga yg agak merosot* Yesterday the radio noted a slight decline in prices. *~ pemasukan barang* make a note of incoming goods. **2** register, chalk up. *~ waktu tiga menit tiga puluh satu detik* Chalk up a time of three minutes 31 seconds. **men-i** note down. *Pak Pono ~nya pd notés kecil* Pak Pono entered it in his little notebook. **men-kan** note s.t. down. *~ diri* register, sign up. *~ dirimu sbg sukarélawan* sign up as a volunteer. **ter- 1** noted down, recorded. *~ dlm sejarah* recorded in history. **2** registered. *surat ~* registered letter. **menter-kan** register (a letter). **-an 1** note, documentation. *~ bawah/di kaki halaman/kaki* footnote. *~ harga* price notation. *~ harta benda* inventory. *~ jiwa* census. *~ kesimpulan* summary remarks. *~ pinggir* 1 marginal notes. 2 commentary. *~ sipil* vital statistics. *~ tambahan* postscript. *dgn ~* 1 with the endorsement of. 2 with the annotation. *menurut ~ terakhir* at last count. **2** records. *~ hidupnya* the records of his life. *buku ~* journal, record book. **pen-** registrar, recorder. *~ biji* (*Sport*) scorer. *~ télegram* clerks who register telegrams. *~ waktu* timekeeper. **pen-an 1** registration. *~ jiwa* census. **2** (price) quotation. *~ data* data recording.
catok, catokan vise, clamp.
catu share, portion, ration. - *beras* rice ration. **men- 1** ration, limit amount (i.e. of gasoline per day), allot. **2** distribute, dole out (bit by bit). **men-kan** dole out, ration. *Pemerintah memutuskan ~ beras karena tdk cukup* The gvt. decided to dole out rice because the supply was insufficient. **-an** share, portion, ration. **pen-an 1** rationing, doling. **2** allocation.
catuk₁ 1 peck at, nibble (of fowl). **2** rap, tap on. **3** hit, harm with the edge of a weapon. **4** cut into (a coconut). **5** a hammer.
catuk₂ 1 a spoonful. **2** contents of half a coconut shell.
catuk₃ ter- sit with head bowed.
catur₁ chess. **ber- 1** play chess. **2** checkered. **-an** checkered embroidery. **pe(n)-** o. who plays chess. **per-an 1** chessboard. **2** constellation, set-

up (political, economic, etc.). ~ *internasional* international constellation, geopolitics.

catur₂ four (only in slogans, titles). - *tunggal* a four-part board of authority: governor, military commander, police chief, and public prosecutor (a political concept of the 1960s). - *warga* the ideal (planned) family of four. - *wangsa* four-caste system. - *wulan* quarterly.

catur₃ (*Jv*) talk. **-an** topic of conversation.

caturangga chessboard.

caturisme political chess.

catus see CETUS.

catut 1 tweezers, forceps. **2** tongs, pincers. - *kawat* wire clipper. **3** black marketer, scalper, corrupter. **men-, meny- 1** extract, pull (a tooth, nail, etc.). **2** operate on the black market, be a scalper. **3** swindle, cheat, misuse o.'s position for gain. **men-kan 1** sell on the black market. **2** scalp. **-an** income from black marketing, scalping, abuse of authority, etc. ~ *darah* commercialization of blood (for transfusions). **pen- 1** black marketer. **2** profiteer, scalper. **pen-an** profiteering. **per-an** black marketing.

catutisme mental attitude characterized by efforts to make a profit from o.'s official position.

caul see KAIN.

caung sunken (face). *Mukanya - karena kurang makan* His face was sunken from lack of food.

cawak₁ leash.

cawak₂ dent. - *pipi* dimple. **ber-** have a dimple.

cawan cup (without handle). - *kaléng* tin cup or bowl. - *lebur* crucible. - *pétri* petri dish. - *pinggan* porcelain.

cawang₁ check mark. **men-i** mark s.t. with a check. **ter-** given a check mark.

cawang₂ see CABANG.

cawat loincloth, G-string. **ber-** wear a loincloth. ~ *ékor* **1** with its tail between its legs (of a dog). **2** be very scared.

cawé-cawé (*Coll., Jv*) pry into, be a busybody.

cawik handful. *se- beras* a handful of rice. **men-** take up liquids or grains of s.t. in cupped hands.

cawis men-kan prepare. **-an** stock, materials that have been prepared. ~ *enam botol* six bottles in stock.

caya see CAHAYA.

cb. [*cabang*] branch (of a firm, etc.).

CB /sibi/ [*Citizens' Band*] citizens' band radio.

cc /cécé/ cubic centimeter.

CC /cécé, sésé/ [*Comité Céntral*] Central Committee of Communist party.

cd /cédé/ see KERTAS.

CD /sidi, cédé, sédé/ [*Corps Diplomatik*] license plates and cars used by diplomats.

cebak men- dig, mine. **-an 1** mineral deposit. ~ *bijih* ore deposit. **2** mine.

ceban (*Jkt, Ch*) 10,000, in commercial transactions.

cebar-cebur sound of splashing. - *terdengar org mandi di kali* Splash! We could hear people bathing in the river.

cebik men- extend lower lip as sign of derision.

cebir₁ piece. *se- kertas* a scrap of paper.

cebir₂ see CEBIK, CIBIR.

cebis see CEBIR₁.

ceblék men- slap lightly. **-an** a light slap.

cébok wash the genitals or anus with water after defecating or urinating. **men-** wash o.s. after urinating or defecating. **men-(i)** cleanse s.o. after defecating. *Ia ~ adiknya* He cleaned up his little brother (after he had defecated). **-an** a small trough for storing water used for cleaning o.s., o.'s feet, etc.

cébol dwarf. *si - merindukan bulan* seek the impossible (lit., the dwarf is longing for the moon).

cébong tadpole.

cebur men- 1 splash. **2** jump, plunge. **3** splash down (of astronaut). **men-i** become involved in s.t. not o.'s business. *Tdk boléh anak kecil ~ urusan org déwasa* Children aren't supposed to mix into adults' business. *Pujangga Baru tdk juga di-i Achdiat* Achdiat did not get involved in the *Pujangga Baru* movement, either. **men-kan** plunge s.t. into. ~ *diri* plunge, throw o.s. into. *Ia ~ diri ke dlm kancah politik* He threw himself into the political arena. **ter- 1** fallen, plunged. **2** entered. **ter-i** get dirt in it (of water). *Sumurnya -- kotoran* The well got polluted with dirt. **pen-an** splashdown (of astronaut).

cecah se- 1 a moment, awhile. ~ *mata* in a wink. **2** a little, a touch of, dash of. ~ *gula* a dash of sugar. *Pikirannya tak ~ pun memperhatikan apa yg ditatapnya* Not even a little did his thoughts focus on what he was staring at. **ber-** a little bit. **men-1** touch lightly, hit slightly. ~ *bahu* touching the shoulders (of hair). ~ *bumi* tread the earth (a ceremony of infancy). *sejak ~ bumi* from childhood. **2** pinch (of salt, etc.). **men-kan 1** dip. *Dia ~ telapak tangannya ke permukaan air* She dipped the palm of her hand into the water's surface. **2** cause to touch lightly. ~ *bibirku ke bibirnya* touch my lips to his. **ter-** touch slightly, brush against.

cecak₁ dot, spot, fleck.

cecak₂ men- 1 pinch, tweak, nip. **2** pick (pocket). **pen-** pickpocket.

cecak₃ see CICAK.

cecap men- taste, savor.

cecar men- bully, pester, cross-examine.

cécé₁ cubic centimeter, esp. in engine measurements.

cécé₂ see CICIT₁,₂.

cécél chipped.

cecéng (*Jkt, Ch*) 1,000, in commercial transactions.

cécér spilled, scattered (in small quantities). **(ber)-an** spilled and scattered (on the ground). **men-kan 1** spill, scatter about. **2** sow, scatter (seed). **ter- 1** scattered about, spilled out. **2** lost, lose o.'s way. *Benarlah ini adikku yg pernah ~ di ladang* Yes, it is indeed my little sister who had long ago gotten lost in the fields. **3** get lost from the mainstream, get left behind in progress made by a majority. *Dlm hubungan ini Yassin mungkin tlh ~ dr perbauran* In this respect Yassin probably lagged behind in assimilating. **ter-i** get s.t. scattered over it. **keter-an** backwardness, lagging behind. **ke-** scattered about, leaked out. *berita-berita kepolisiannya yg* ~ police news which leaked out. **ke-an 1** scattered, spilled about. *Kalau kebetulan* ~ *di jalan tak jadi apa* If it happens to get spilled on the way, that is all right. **2** stolen, pilfered. *Ia ingin agar barang sumbangan itu cepat sampai di tempat tujuan tanpa* ~ *sepotong pun* He wanted the contribution to reach its destination quickly without losing even a little to pilferage. **berke-an** scattered, spilled.

cecincin annular.

cécok see CÉKCOK.

cecuit low hissing or hushing sound. **-an** a low whistle or hiss.

cecunguk 1 (*Sd*) cockroach. **2** (*Coll.*) shady character, spy. - *dan mata-mata* shady characters and spies. **3** secret police.

cecuping auriculate.

cecurut shrew.

cedal *berlidah* - (*Jv*) suffer from speech defect characterized by pronunciation of /r/ as a tap or as /l/.

cedera₁ disagreement, conflict, bickering. **ber-** quarrel, bicker. **per-an, ke-an** conflict, quarrel, feud.

cedera₂ 1 be flawed, defective. *Hubungan kami sdh* - Our relationship is tainted. **2** injury. *-nya parah* His injuries are severe. - *janji* break a promise. **ber-** have a defect, be flawed. **men-i** do irreparable damage. *Bom musuh* ~ *banyak penduduk* The enemy's bombs did irreparable damage to many residents. **men-kan** injure. **ter-** hurt, damaged.

cedera₃ 1 traitorous, faithless, untrustworthy. **2** murder through treachery. **men-(kan) 1** betray. **2** kill by stealth or through trickery. **ke-an 1** treachery, perfidy. **2** faithlessness, infidelity, disloyalty. **pen-an** act of betraying.

cedera₄ see CANDRA₁,₂.

ceding small, scrubby, undersized (of plants, fruits, etc.).

cédok (*Jkt*) dipper. **men- 1** scoop up (of sand, etc.). **2** dip up, ladle out (liquids). **men-kan** use s.t. to scoop with. *Ku-kan senduk ke dlm kancah* I dipped the spoon into the cauldron. **pen-** ladle, scoop, dipper.

cédong see CÉDOK.

ceduk shrunken (of cheeks), sunken (of eyes).

cedut-cedut slight twitching feeling, low-level pain in an infection.

cegah say s.t. by way of prohibition. *"Sekarang sdh tengah malam,"* - *isterinya* "It is the middle of the night now," said his wife, keeping him from going out. **men- 1** restrain, prevent, prohibit. *Ia* ~ *anaknya bermain-main di jalan* He prohibited his child from playing in the street. ~ *bahaya api* prevent the danger of fire. ~ *makan banyak* restrain from eating a great deal. **2** combat, guard against. ~ *karat* prevent rust. *utk* ~ *spy pakaian anda jangan kena tinta* in order to guard against getting ink on your clothes. **-an** prohibition,

prevention. **pen-** preventative. ~ *karat* rust preventative. ~ *kehamilan/penghamilan* contraceptive. **pen-an 1** prevention. ~ *kebakaran* fire prevention. **2** combating, the fight (against).

cégak, cegak strong and active, vigorous, robust.

cegat men- 1 hail (taxi), flag down. *Di sini saja kalau* ~ *bus yg ke Tanjung Pérak* Right here is where you stop buses to Tanjung Pérak. **2** waylay, hold up. *Tentara kita siap* ~ *musuh* Our forces are prepared to intercept the enemy. *Keréta api di- perampok* The train was waylaid by bandits. **men-i** repeatedly stop s.t. or s.o. *Kerjanya* ~ *pedagang pasar saja* Their job is just to detain merchants en route to market. **-an 1** interception. *prakték* ~ the practice of setting up checkpoints to extort money from commercial vehicles with code violations. **2** checkpoint (army, police, officials, etc.). **3** (*Sport*) sliding tackle. **pen-** s.o. who stops people on the road. **pen-an** act of stopping people.

ceguk gulp. **-an** (*Coll.*) hiccup.

cék₁ /cék/ (*Fin.*) check. - *kosong* bad check. - *mundur* postdated check. - *perjalanan/turis* traveler's check. - *pos* postal money order. - *selang* nonnegotiable check for account only.

cék₂ /cék/ examine, check out. **men(ge)-** check. *Aku kembali* ~ *barang itu* I returned and examined the goods. **penge-an** verification.

cék₃ see ENCIK.

cekah split open. **ber-** be split open. **men-** split (fruit, etc.) open.

cekak₁ se- a pinch, what can be seized between finger and thumb. **ber-** ~ *pinggang* with arms akimbo. **men-** seize between finger and thumb.

cekak₂ 1 short. **2** insufficient, inadequate. **3** too narrow, tight (of clothes). **4** rude, coarse (behavior).

cekak₃ fight. **ber-** fight.

cekakak - *cekikik* sound of laughter, giggles. **-an** loud (of laughter).

cekal stalwart, gallant. **men- 1** hold firmly, grasp tightly, seize. *Seorg mencoba* ~ *kaki lawannya yg menyépak* S.o. tried to grasp the legs of his kicking opponent. ~ *corong mikrofon* seize the microphone. **2** arrest, capture. **-an** s.t. to grasp.

cekalang see CAKALANG.

cekam₁ dibble. **men-** dibble, plant with a dibble.

cekam₂ see CENGKAM.

cekap₁ fight.

cekap₂ see CAKAP₁.

cekatan adroit, deft, adept. **ke-** adroitness, dexterity.

cekau men- grasp, seize. *Burung elang* ~ *anak ayam itu* A hawk snatched that chick. **-an** grasp, grip, hold.

cék cék cék sound of pieces of metal striking e.o.

cékcok quarrel, squabble, bicker, fall out. **ber-** bicker, squabble, fall out. **ber-an** squabble with e.o., fall out. **memper-kan** bicker about s.t., dispute about s.t. **per-an** quarrel.

cekék see CEKIK.

cékél stingy, miserly.

cékér 1 foot (esp. of birds). **2** claw.

cekeram see CENGKERAM.

ceki k.o. Ch card game. *daun* - the small cards used in this game.

cekibar flying lizard.

cekik ber- *merih* quarrel. **men-** strangle, choke, throttle. *Harganya* ~ Its price was murderous. ~ *napas* asphyxiate, stifle, suffocate. **men-i** repeatedly smother, choke. *Ia* ~ *bayi-bayi itu karena dikiranya meréka kemasukan sétan* He choked the babies because he thought they were possessed by the devil. **men-kan 1** strangle. **2** strangle by means of s.t. *Tangannya di-kan pd léhér Mulyadi* His hands were wrapped around Mulyadi's throat. **memper-kan** squabble, quarrel, dispute over. **ter- 1** strangled. *Ia mati* ~ She died from strangulation. **2** abruptly and completely halted. *Percakapan meréka* ~ *oléh ketakutan* Their conversation was cut off because of their fear. **-an** strangulation. *tertawa* ~ laugh till o. is out of breath. **pen-** strangler. **pen-an** strangling, throttling.

cekikik sound of a giggle. **-an** chuckle, giggle. *Tahu-tahu meréka dengar org* ~ All of a sudden they heard chuckling. *Kali ini penonton masih banyak yg* ~ This time many spectators were still chuckling.

ceking 1 thin, slender, wasted. *Potongannya sempit di paha dan - di betis* She was built with thin legs and calves. **2** frugal, economical. **ke-an 1** thinness. **2** suffer from thinness.

céking examination, checking.

cekit -² small pricking pain. **men-** nibble at, peck at.

ceklék see CEKLIK.

cekli small and attractive (of house and furnishings).

ceklik 1 sound of clicking. **2** (*Ling.*). click. **men-** switch on the light. **men-kan** close with clicking noise, shut (of locks). **-an 1** click, clicking sound. **2** light switch.

Céko Czech.

cekok medicine forcibly given. **men-i 1** force s.o. or s.t. to take medicine. **2** indoctrinate. **men-kan** ram s.t. down, force s.t. down. *bantuan yg di-kan di dlm mulut kita* aid that is rammed down our throats. **-an** s.t. force-fed (medicine, etc.).

Cékoslowakia Czechoslovakia.

cekot-cekot throbbing pain in head.

ceku men- prick, dent (with fingernail).

cekuh men- search (in o.'s pocket). *penonton-penonton yg di- kantongnya* spectators whose pockets were picked.

cekuk₁ niche, depression in surface. **-an 1** notch (in coconut trunk for a foothold). **2** thumb index (of a dictionary).

cekuk₂ see CEKOK.

cekukrak-cekukruk 1 in bad health (of chickens). **2** listless, not feeling up to doing anything.

cekung 1 sunken (of cheeks). *mata* - hollow eyes. **2** concave. - *batu bara* coal basin. **men-** sink inward. *Pusaran cinta senantiasa* ~ *dlm-dlm* The vortex of love always spins deeply inward. **men-**

kan form a concavity, make s.t. concave. ~ *tangan* cup o.'s hands. **ke-an** concaveness. **-an 1** cavity. **2** basin. ~ *Atlantik Utara* N. Atlantic Basin. **3** (*Coll.*) be sunken. *kakék yg pipinya* ~ a grandfather with sunken cheeks.

cekup₁ men- seize with closed hand (a fly, etc.).

cekup₂ see CEKUT.

cekur k.o. small cultivated plant of ginger family used as medicine.

cekut men- pick up with fingertips.

cél /sél/ battery cell.

cela₁ 1 defect, flaw, blemish. **2** shortcoming, failing. **3** disgrace, shame. **ber-** have shortcomings, have defects. *tdk* ~ flawless. **men- 1** disapprove of, condemn. ~ *politik pemerintah* disapprove of gvt. policy. **2** criticize, find fault, deprecate. *Anak buah tdk boléh* ~*nya* His followers were not allowed to criticize him. **men-kan** chide s.o. on behalf of s.o. else. **ter- 1** disabled, deformed. **2** disgraceful, shamefully bad. *tindakan yg* ~ a disgraceful deed. **ke-an 1** shortcoming, fault, defect. **2** disgrace, shame. **berke-an 1** have shortcomings, have defects. **2** suffer ignominy. **-an 1** reproach, denunciation, censure. **2** shortcoming. **pen-** critic, faultfinder, detractor. **pen-an** faultfinding, scolding, upbraiding.

cela₂ see CELAH.

celad see CEDAL.

celadi woodpecker.

celaga (*Naut.*) helm, tiller (of boat).

celah gap, space, fissure, rift, slot. - *gigi* gap between teeth. - *glétser* (*Geol.*) crevasse. - *gunung* mountain pass. - *jari* space between fingers. - *kening* furrow in brow. - *paha* groin. - *suara* (*Anat.*) glottis.

celak k.o. cosmetic used to blacken eyelid. **ber-** made-up with such a cosmetic. **men-(i)** apply blackening to eyelids.

célak ber-, men-, ter- sparkle, shine, glisten, gleam.

celaka 1 misfortune. *Kematiannya - besar bagi org tuanya* Her death was a severe blow to her parents. **2** bad luck, unlucky. **3** dammit!, darn it! - *benar, dompétku ketinggalan di rumah* Darn it, I left my wallet at home. - *aku!* I am out of luck! - *dua/ tiga belas* very bad luck. *si* - scoundrel. **men-kan** bring misfortune on, ruin. *Aku sekarang menyesal tlh* ~ *kesatuannya* I now regret having brought about the downfall of his team. **ke-an 1** accident, mishap. **2** bad luck.

celam-celum 1 go in and out of a house. **2** unsure, uncertain.

celampak men-(kan) fling, hurl, throw away.

celana trousers, pants. - *(be)renang* swim trunks. - *buntung* cut-offs. - *(cut)bray* bell bottoms. - *dlm* underpants, panties. - *jengki* dungarees. - *katok* short pants, shorts. - *kolor* shorts with a drawstring. - *mandi* swim trunks. - *monyét* children's pajamas or playsuit. - *Napoléon* blue jeans. - *péndék* shorts. - *tanggung* knickers. **ber-** wear trousers. **men-i** put trousers on s.o. or s.t.

celang men- stare (with eyes wide open).

celangak wide open (of a door, etc.). **men-kan** open (a door) wide.

celangap agape, wide open (of the mouth). **men-kan** *mulut* open the mouth wide. **-an** tending to speak in a disrespectful or impolite way.

celapak **men-i** straddle. **ter-** be astride, straddling.

celas-celas go in and out of (a house).

celat men- jump far, jump high.

celatuk ber- chat, joke, gossip.

celebuk sound of a stone hitting water, splashing sound.

celékéh 1 stain, blemish, spot. 2 dirty, soiled.

celekit ny- hurting o.'s feelings.

celemék (*Coll.*) apron.

celemot crumbs or leftovers from eating. *Di bibirnya ada - yoghurt* He had dribbles of yoghurt on his lips.

celempung k.o. zitherlike musical instrument.

céléng 1 wild boar. 2 pig. 3 (*Derog.*) jerk. **men-i** put money in a piggy bank. ~ *uang* save money, hoard money. **-an** 1 savings. 2 money box, piggy bank.

celéngkang-celéngkok 1 winding, twisting. 2 bent.

celentang lie face up. **ber-, men-** lie face up. - *menatap loténg* lie face up staring at the ceiling. **men-kan** place s.t. face up.

celep dye. **men-** dye. **-an** dyed goods.

celepik 1 sound of a small object falling. 2 tick.

celepok, celepuk₁ 1 sound of a fall, thud, plop. 2 fall with thud or plop. **ter-** fall suddenly into a sitting position. *jatuh* ~ fall flat on o.'s butt.

celepuk₂ k.o. owl.

celetuk say s.t. abruptly. *-nya "Bagaimana, Pran? Cocok, ndak?"* He burst out, "How about it, Pran? Is she for you or not?" **men-, meny-** interrupt, break in. **ter-** interrupted.

celi 1 keen, sharp-eyed. 2 careful, precise.

celik 1 open (of eyes). 2 see. - *huruf* literate. **ke-hurufan** literacy. **men-** see. **men-kan** open (the eyes). **ke-** 1 realize the truth, have o.'s eyes opened. *Penduduk Sulsel bukan sekali ini* ~ It was not the first time the people of S. Sulawesi had a rude awakening. 2 disappointed, fail to meet s.o. at his home and feel bad about it. 3 feel cheated or fooled, feel o. has been made a fool of. ~ *bulé* completely fooled.

celingak-celinguk look around in a dazed way.

celingukan look around in a dazed way.

celis men- chop up, cut in bits.

célló /sélo/ cello.

celomes 1 ail, suffer chronically. 2 fussy, hard to please, finicky.

celomok pockmarked (of face).

celopar 1 fussy, finicky. 2 talkative, garrulous.

celoréng men- 1 gash, cut. 2 mark with a stripe or slash. *Bajunya di- dgn warna mérah dan putih* His shirt had red and white stripes.

celotéh empty talk. *Org kaya banyak -* The rich are full of useless chatter. **ber-, men-** 1 make the noise of a small gecko. *Cicak ~ di dinding itu* The

geckos are chirping on the wall. 2 chat, babble. *Dia langsung saja* ~ Right off she started to babble. **men-i, men-kan** babble about s.o. or s.t.

Célsius see SÉLSIUS.

celung₁ sunken (of eyes), hollow (of cheeks).

celung₂ narrow corral for elephants, water buffalo. **men-(kan)** place in a corral.

célung red flower of *Erythrina* tree.

celung-celang jingle, tinkle.

celup men-(kan) 1 dip, immerse. *Anak kami senang ~ roti di susu* Our child likes to dip his bread in milk. *Meréka ~ kwas lalu mulai menulis* They dipped their brushes in and then started to write. 2 dye. **ter-** gotten immersed. **-an** 1 dyed article. 2 dyeing. **pen-** 1 o. who dyes. 2 the dyeing medium. **pen-an** 1 immersion. 2 dyeing.

celupak (*Jv*) oil lamp without a chimney.

celupar see CELOPAR.

celur immersion into boiling liquid. **ber-** *tangan* (*Lit.*) swear by placing the hand in boiling water or oil. **men-** 1 boil (an egg). 2 scald (a chicken to remove feathers).

celurit see CLURIT.

celurut musk shrew.

celus 1 loose fitting (of rings, clothing, etc.). 2 slip through, get through. **men-** become loose.

celutak willing to eat anything.

celutuk k.o. sandpiper or plover.

céma accuse. *tanda -* sufficient evidence to make a charge. **men-** make a charge. **ter-** the accused.

cemar 1 dirty, soiled, filthy. *perkataan yg -* filthy words. 2 besmirched, blackened (name, etc.). *-noda* **men-nodai** cast aspersions, deeply insult. *Saya tak mau men-nodai pengertian wahyu* I do not mean to insult the meaning of divine revelation. **ber-** dirty, soiled. *Ia ~ lumpur* He is covered with mud. ~ *kaki* dirty o.'s feet (be kind enough to visit the speaker's house). **men-i** 1 soil, stain, dirty (a room, etc.). 2 defile, outrage, desecrate. *Terlalu banyak turis bisa ~ budaya kita* Too many tourists can pollute our culture. **men-kan** 1 soil, make dirty. *Saya mencari org yg ~ isteri saya* I am looking for the man who defiled my wife. 2 besmirch, cast aspersions on. **ter-** befouled, besmirched, polluted. *Nama keluarga kita* ~ Our family name was dragged through the mud. **ke-an** 1 dirt, filth. 2 slander, calumny. **pen-an** 1 pollution. ~ *air* water pollution. 2 vilification. ~ *nama* libel.

cemara₁ casuarina tree.

cemara₂ long switch of hair or wig twisted into chignon.

cemas 1 worried, disturbed, apprehensive, frightened. *Negeri itu - akan serangan itu* That country is disturbed about the attack. *Ia - rupanya mendengar bunyi meriam* He seemed to be apprehensive at the sound of a cannon. 2 discouraged. *Ia - ssdh mengalami kerugian itu* He was restless after experiencing that financial loss. **ber-** be worried, on edge. **men-** become anxious. *Suara Nunuk itu tampak kian* ~ Nunuk's voice seemed to become increasingly edgy. **men-i**

worry about s.t., be alarmed at. *Ibunya pun turut ~ kehilangan pacarnya* Her mother too was alarmed at her boyfriend's disappearance. **men-kan 1** alarm, disturb. *Kabar itu ~ penduduk* The news disturbed the population. **2** worry about, fear. *Ia ~ keselamatan keluarganya* She worried about the safety of her family. **ke-an** anxiety, worry, concern, apprehension. **pen- 1** pessimist. **2** coward.

cemat pull (boat). *tali - (Naut.)* rope used to warp a boat. **men-** shift (a ship) by warping.

cemberut sullen, glum, morose.

cembul small metal box for tobacco. *serasi spt - dgn tutupnya* fit together like a tobacco box and its top, i.e., get along very well.

cembung 1 chubby (of cheeks). **2** dome-shaped. **men-** curve. **men-kan** curve s.t. **ke-an** curvature of the earth.

cembur see CEBUR.

cemburu 1 jealous. *Si Joni melihat pacarnya bercanda dgn cowok lain* John is jealous when he sees his girl joking around with another guy. **2** envious. *Ia selalu - pd org asing* She is always envious of foreigners. **ber-** be jealous of, be envious of. *Ia ~ kpd temannya* He is jealous of his friend. **men-i** be jealous of. *Nyona itu ~ tetangga baru yg muda itu* That lady is jealous of the new young neighbor. **men-kan 1** be jealous of or about. **2** rouse jealousy, stir up suspicion. **ke-an** jealousy. **-an 1** jealousy. **2** (*Coll.*) of a jealous kind. *org ~* jealous person. **pen-** person given to fits of jealousy. *suami ~* jealous husband.

cemééh /cemé'éh/ jeer, insult. **men-(kan)** ridicule.

céméh₁ 1 blind on o. side. **2** blind but with eyelids open.

céméh₂ card game.

cemekian, cemengkian k.o. croton tree (seeds used for purges and abortifacients).

cémér see CÉMÉH₁.

cemerlang 1 sparkle, shine, gleam, glisten. *cuaca yg -* glorious weather. **2** bright, gleaming, dazzling. *dua pujangga yg -* two writers who were in their glory. *Suaranya lebih -* The sound is clearer. **men-kan** brighten, dazzle. *gigi yg ~* dazzling teeth. *Salah satu di antaranya pasti akan ~ hari depan dunia* O. of them is sure to brighten the future of the world. **ke-an 1** glitter, luster, glow, radiance. **2** glory. **3** brilliance, wittiness.

cemerut see CEMBERUT.

cemeti whip. *- déwa* lightning. **men-** whip, lash.

cemil *se-* a little bit.

cemomot dirty (of face).

cemong 1 dirty, soiled. **2** scratched (face).

cemooh see CEMUH.

cempaka 1 k.o. tropical magnolia, champac. **2** frangipani (and other similar flowering shrubs).

cempakul k.o. fish with protruding eyes.

cempedak k.o. tree similar to jackfruit.

cempelung see CEMPLUNG.

cempera k.o. seashore shrub.

cemperling k.o. small bird.

cempiang rowdy, roughneck, ruffian, hoodlum.

cemping rag, piece of ripped-off cloth.

cemplak men- kick a horse to make it go, step on the starter of a motorcycle.

cemplang bland.

cemplung 1 sound of a splash. **2** plunge into water. **men-** fall or dive into water with a splash. *Dua tubuh ~ ke bawah sana* Two bodies dove with a splash. **men-kan** cause to sink into water with a splash. **-an** (*Coll.*) cesspool.

cempoa see SEMPOA.

cempolong plastic piping for sanitation, insulation, etc.

cempor k.o. wall lamp with chimney.

cempréng shrill (of voice).

cempung sound of a splash. **ber-²** splash (in water). **men-** plunge (into), splash. **men-i** jump into, plunge into. **men-kan 1** plunge s.t., immerse. *~ diri* plunge, throw o.s. (into). **2** (*Sport*). dunk. *~ bola ke jala* dunk the ball in the basket. **ter-** drowned.

cemuh 1 insult, taunt. **2** ridicule. **men-** jeer at. *Lelaki itu tertawa ~ Purnama* The man laughed, jeering at Purnama. **men-kan** ridicule, deride. *Aku bukan ~ kerinduanmu pdnya* It is not that I am ridiculing your missing her. **-an** belittling comments. **pen-** jeerer, taunter.

cemuk₁ shaft. *- tambang* mine shaft.

cemuk₂ shake (stick). **men-** hit (with stick).

cemuk₃ pod (of legumes).

cemuk₄, cemung large metal cup for drinking.

cenangau k.o. insect.

cenangga congenital defect, deformity.

cenangkas k.o. straight-edged sword.

cenayang medium, spiritualist.

cencala k.o. bird.

cencaluk k.o condiment made of fermented, raw shrimp.

cencang see CINCANG.

cencaru k.o. fish, horse mackerel.

céncong see CINGCONG.

cendala low, base, mean. **ke-an** baseness, meanness.

cendana yellow sandalwood. *Sdh gaharu - pula* You already know, why ask? (rhymes with *Sdh tahu mengapa bertanya pula*).

cendawan 1 mushroom, toadstool. **2** fungus, mildew, mold. *sbg - tumbuh dlm musim hujan* multiply quickly, appear rapidly during rainy season. **ber-** moldy. **men-** mushroom up, appear suddenly.

cendekia 1 learned, educated. **2** clever, shrewd. **ke-an 1** learnedness. **2** shrewdness. **pen-an** intellectualization. *~ Bahasa Indonésia* the intellectualization of Indonesian.

cendekiawan 1 an intellectual. **2** the educated (class). **ke-an** intellectualism.

cenderamata souvenir or memento (esp. exchanged or presented on official visits).

cenderawasih bird of paradise.

cenderung 1 inclined, lean, disposed. *Hatinya -*

kpd mobil yg hitam She was inclined to buy the black car. **2** sloping, leaning. *Tiangnya agak -* The pole leans a bit. **men-kan** tend. *~ pd keruntuhan moral* tend toward moral collapse. *~ diri* lean, duck (to avoid being hit). **ke-an 1** inclination, preference. **2** tendency, willingness. **3** trend.

céndol 1 small, doughy rice-flour droplets used in cold drinks. **2** a beverage made with such droplets.

cendong k.o. children's guessing game with pantuns.

cenéla embroidered slippers or sandals.

céng syrup, molasses.

cengal k.o. large hardwood tree yielding commercial timber.

cengam men- snap at, seize with mouth or beak (as dog, crocodile, etc.).

cengang ber- surprised, astonished, amazed. *Ia ~ melihat kemajuan téknik* He was amazed to see the technical progress. **men-i** be amazed at. *Ketua itu ~ saya* The chairman was amazed at me. **memper-kan, men(ter)-kan 1** amaze, astonish. *Kepandaiannya ~ teman-temannya* Her ability amazed her friends. **2** baffle, perplex, confound, mystify. **3** amazing, astonishing. **ter-(²)** astonished, amazed, dumbfounded. **-an** (*Coll.*) amazement.

cengap men- 1 snap at. **2** gape, pant (for breath).

cengar-cingir grin foolishly, grimace. *Ia - sambil menggaruk kepala yg tdk gatal* He smiled sheepishly while scratching his head even though it did not itch.

céngbéng (*Ch*) grave-cleaning festival.

céngcéng (*Bali*) k.o. cymbals.

céngéng 1 whine, be a crybaby, snivel. **2** tearful, sentimental, overly emotional. **ke-an 1** bathos, sentimentality, sappiness. *Manusia mémang kotak ~* Man is indeed a fount of emotionalism. *mengatasi segala ~* overcome all sentimentalities. **2** sappy, bathetic.

cengéngés (*Jv*) **men-** jeer or sneer at. **-an 1** jeering, sneering at, ridiculing. **2** smile sheepishly.

cengér very young (of infants about 1-2 months old), crying stage. *Anaknya masih - sdh mati* His baby died at less than 2 months. *cengar -* bawl, cry incessantly.

cénggér see JÉNGGÉR.

cénggéréng grated coconut or onions fried for use in cooking.

cenggérét k.o. locust.

cénggo (*Ch*) 1,500 in business transactions.

cengir wry smile, grin. **ny- 1** (*Jkt*) grimace, expression made by screwing up o.'s face. **2** smile sheepishly. **meny-kan** *senyum* grin sheepishly.

cengis 1 bad odor or taste. **2** loathsome, nauseating.

cengkah quarrel.

cengkal₁ unit of length (about 3.75 m.). *Petani kecil itu hanya memiliki se- tanah* That peasant farmer owns only a tiny piece of land.

cengkal₂ a framelike device worn to keep o.'s sarong from touching his healing circumcision wound.

cengkam grip, squeeze, hold. *lapis -* supporting layer of road between surface and bed. **men-1** seize, grasp. *Burung elang ~ mangsanya* The eagle seized its prey. *~ kekuasan dunia* seize world domination. *Rasa takut ~ hatiku* Fear gripped me. **2** ingrown (of toenail). **3** gripping, tenacious, engrossing. *~ pikiran* to engross o.'s thoughts. **men-kan** fasten (the claws in), grip (by planting fingernails in the skin). *suasana yg ~* an atmosphere which grips o. with fear. **ter-** be gripped. **-an** grip, hold, squeeze.

cengkar fallow, barren (land). **ke-an** fallowness, barrenness.

cengkaruk fried sticky rice for use in confection.

cengkat stand on o.'s heels.

cengkau₁ middleman, broker.

cengkau₂ see CEKAU.

cengké, cengkéh see CENGKIH.

cengkelong men- withdraw (money).

cengkeram grip, hold. **men- 1** hold firmly (in o.'s hands). *~ kukunya dlm* sink its claws into. **2** firmly grip. *Si suami di- perasaan dln yg dlm* The husband was gripped by deep emotional feelings. *~ pikiran* have a hold on o.'s thoughts. **meng-kan** grip with (the hands, nails, etc.). **-an** grip, hold.

cengkerama chat, talk. **ber-** (*Lit.*) chat, talk. *Pembesar lain ~ dgn duta-duta besar* The other high officials talked with the ambassadors.

cengkerawak k.o. bird, yellow-crowned bulbul.

cengkerik see JANGKRIK₁.

cengki run of luck in cards.

cengkih 1 clove. **2** (*Crd.*) club. **ber-** spiced with cloves. **per-an** matters pertaining to clove cultivation.

cengking yelping, squealing (of a dog). **ber-** yap, squeal.

cengkir half-ripe coconut.

céngkok₁ crooked, twisted, bent.

céngkok₂ leaf monkey.

céngkol twisted, bent.

cengkong deformed, misshapen.

cengkung₁ hollow, sunken (of eyes, cheeks). *--mengkung* very hollow, deeply sunken.

cengkung₂ yapping, barking, yelping. *--cengking* much yelping.

cengkung₃ ber- squat. **men-kan** cause to stoop, bend down. *Ia ~ lagi badannya lebih menyusuk di belakang babah itu* He bent his body so as to hide even better behind the Ch.

cengkur see CEKUR.

céngli (*Ch*) reasonable, logical.

céngor (*Madura*) see CINGUR.

centadu see BELALANG₁.

centang *- perenang/perentang* in total disarray, in a mess.

céntang₁ men- hit, slap.

céntang₂ men- tick off, place a check mark against.

céntél see CANTÉL.

centéng 1 guard, watchman. 2 foreman on private land. 3 hired thug, hit-man.

centerik see CANTRIK.

centét 1 stunted, runty (in growth). 2 shrunken. 3 economical.

centil coquettish. *Sinta benar-benar gadis -* Sinta is truly a coquettish girl.

céntong 1 rice ladle. 2 dipper with handle. **men-** ladle out, scoop out (rice).

centung 1 lock, tuft of hair. 2 tuft, crest (of bird).

cenung **ter-** stunned into silent pondering. *Aku ~ memandang ke arah timur* I was blankly gazing toward the E.

cep₁ silent, quiet, sudden silence. *--klakep* stunned into silence.

cep₂ see CP.

cepak smacking (of lips). **men-** *-cepok* smack o.'s lips (while eating).

cepat fast, speedy, quick. *Ia berjalan -* She walked fast. *Yg - dpt* First come first served. *Ia - pulang* He hurried home. *-nya 50 mil dlm satu jam* The speed is 50 miles an hour. *Terlalu - bisa tersesat* Haste makes waste. *- kaki* swift of foot, fleet, speedy. *- kiri* left-handed. *- lidah* rash, hasty, garrulous. *- mulut* garrulous, talkative. *- pikir* mentally agile. *- réaksi* (*Chem.*) reaction time. *- tangan* pilferer, filcher, thief. *- tepat* 1 fast and accurate. 2 quiz contest. **se-** as fast as. *~ kilat* quick as lightning. **ber-²**, **berse-**, **bersi-** 1 race, compete. 2 in a hurry, hastily. **men-** accelerate, become fast, speed up. *Mobilnya ~* The car speeded up. **men-kan, memper-kan** speed up, accelerate. *Mesin ini ~ produksi* This machine speeds up production. **ke-an** 1 speed, velocity. 2 (*Av.*) cruising speed, landing speed. *~ jelajah* cruising speed. 3 too fast. **-an** (*Jkt*) faster. *~ dong!* Speed it up, please! **pemer-an** acceleration. *~ prosés pembangunan* the acceleration of the development process. **pen-an** speeding up, hastening. **per-an** 1 acceleration. 2 speeding up. *~ pembicaraan soal itu menguntungkan bagi semuanya* Speeding up of the discussion was advantageous to all. 3 velocity.

cepék 1 (*Jkt, Ch*) 100, in commercial transactions. *- céng* 100,000. 2 k.o. motorcycle with 100 cc. gas tank. *Dua ban honda - pak guru dikempéskan* S.o. let the air out of both tires of the teacher's 100 cc. Honda.

cepékcéng see CEPÉK.

cépéng half a cent. *Tdk bayar se- pun* We did not pay a cent. **-an** cheap, not worth much. *cinta ~* cheap (false) love.

cépér shallow and rimmed (of bowl, saucer). *piring -* soup dish. *dpt piring -* get a dish for soup, i.e., be unfortunate, have small livelihood.

cepet see CEPAT.

cepiau hat (of kind worn by stationmasters).

cepit₁ **men-** sandwich between, jam. **ter-, ke-** sandwiched between.

cepit₂ see SEPIT.

ceplas-ceplos 1 speak out frankly. 2 speak uninhibitedly. *Di depan org tua anak itu - saja ngomong* Even in front of his elders that kid says what he wants.

ceplek gambling.

ceplok₁ circle-shaped. *kain -²* cloth with a large polka dot pattern. *telur -* fried egg. *- piring* k.o. flower. **men-** fry (of eggs).

ceplok₂ sound of stamping feet. *-²* repeated stamping sound. *Sdh tahu ada org tidur kok jalan ~ di dlm rumah* You know s.o. is sleeping but still you shuffle and stamp in the house.

ceplos **men-kan** blurt out. *Penonton yg menyaksikan wayang kulit itu ~ émosinya* The shadow play audience freely expressed its emotions. **ke-** blurted out s.t. **-an** uninhibited comment. *Wajahnya mérah mendengar ~ itu* He grew red in the face upon hearing that uninhibited comment.

céplukan /céplu'an/ k.o. cherry tomato that grows on bush.

ceplus **men-** press. *Beberapa cabé di-nya lebih dulu* First he pressed a few chili peppers (into his mouth).

cepol 1 come off (of a handle). 2 break off. 3 broken, damaged. **men-** strike, hit.

ceprat-ceprot sound of pounding (in a small mortar, etc.).

ceprét sound of clicking (cameras, etc.), sound of squashing (an insect). **men-** 1 squash flat. *Sengaja kau ~ kacoak itu di pintu* You purposely smashed that cockroach on the door. 2 snap a photograph. *Aku selalu ~ kalau ada peristiwa penting* I always take a photo if there is an important event. **men-i** squeeze on to s.t. *Lukanya di-i dgn jeruk nipis* They squeezed limes on his wounds.

céprét good luck. **ny-** give others a share in what o. has acquired. **ke-an** get a share from what s.o. else acquired by luck.

cepu, cepuk₁ wooden or metal box (for betel, etc.). *- bunga* (*Bio.*) anther.

cepuk₂ tube.

cepung 1 sound of a splash. 2 splash. *Tiap - air hrs dipertahankan* Every time you get splashed you have to defend yourself.

cerabut uproot. **ter-** uprooted, rootless. *kehidupan yg ~* an uprooted life. *Jangan sampai ~ dr akar* Be careful not to yank it by its roots. **keter-an** rootlessness, state of being uprooted.

ceracah sound of rain, brooks, etc. **men-** babble (brook), drum (rain). *anak air yg ~* babbling brook.

ceracap cymbal, castanets.

ceracau babble, prattle. *Masih banyak ~ lainnya yg menyangkut masalah ini* There are many other nonsensical comments related to this problem. **men-** be delirious, rave. **pen-** chatterbox, blabbermouth.

cerah 1 bright and clear. *cuaca -* clear weather. *warna -* bright color. *harapan -* auspicious (beginning). *saat-saat -* happy moments. 2 sharp (of a photo). **men-** brighten up. *Hari pun ~ dan kami* *berangkat* The day brightened and we left. **men-kan** brighten, illuminate. **ke-an 1** brightness, radiance, brilliance. **2** sharpness (of photo). **pen-** brightening agent. ~ *bibir* a substance that puts a gleam on o.'s lips. **pen-an** enlightenment.

cerai 1 divorce. *Isterinya minta - di pengadilan agama* His wife petitioned for divorce at the religious court. *Saya mau minta - dr suami saya* I want to ask for a divorce from my husband. *- tembilang* separation of a married couple through death of o.'s partner. **2** separate. *Anak ayam itu - dr induknya* The chick has separated from its mother. *- berai* dispersed, scattered, in disorder. **ber-** *berai* be scattered, become dispersed. *Pencuri itu lari ~ berai* The thieves ran in all directions. **men-beraikan** disperse, scatter (a crowd). **ter-** *berai* **1** separated, not together. *Sapu lidi jadi ~ berai* The rake made of a bundle of twigs came apart. **2** dispersed (of things that should remain together). *- susu* weaned. **ber-1** be divorced, separated (of married couple). **2** part, separate. *Di sini jalan kami ~* Our ways part here. **3** disconnected, noncontiguous. **ber-an** separated from e.o. **men-** separate, part. ~ *rambutnya* part o.'s hair. **men-kan 1** divorce (o.'s spouse). *Kau akan bosan lalu kau ~ aku* You will get bored and divorce me. **2** separate s.t. from s.t. else. **3** separate from e.o. **4** (*Ling.*) parse, analyze. **memper-kan** separate (fighters). **ter-** divorced. **pen-an 1** separation. **2** divorce, separation. **per-an 1** divorce, separation. **2** dissociation.

ceraka₁ a stand on which clothes are laid for fuming with incense.

ceraka₂ see CARAKA.

cerakin (*Lit.*) small chest with compartments for medicinal herbs.

ceramah 1 extracurricular lecture, talk, speech. **2** talkative, communicative, sociable. **ber-** give a lecture. *Ia ~ selama dua jam* She lectured for two hours. **men-i** give a lecture to s.o. *Sdh déwasa, kok di-i begini!* Here I am an adult being lectured to like this! **men-kan** lecture on. *Ia ~ perjalanannya ke Éropah* He lectured on his trip to Europe.

cerana metal container for betel-chewing paraphernalia.

cerancang ber-(an) prickly, thorny.

ceranggah ber-, men- 1 forked, branched. **2** prickly, thorny.

cerap *kurang* - uninterested, unresponsive. **men-1** note, observe. **2** show interest in. **3** sense, apprehend, respond. **men-kan** respond to. ~ *alam sekitarnya* respond to o.'s environment. **-an** response, sense, perception. ~ *salah* illusion. *citra ~* perceptive image. **pen-an 1** perception. **2** observation.

cerat 1 faucet, spigot, tap, nozzle. **2** pour through a spout. **3** drain or draw off (liquids). **men-** squirt. *Air ~ ke segala jurusan* The water squirted in all directions.

ceratuk ber-, men- sit with head bowed slightly.

cerau sound of a heavy downpour.

cerawat rocket. *- bahaya* distress flare.

cerbak not squeamish, willing to eat anything.

cerber [*ceritera bersambung*] serialized story.

cerbergam see CERGAM.

cerbersam see CERBER.

cerca 1 a censure, reprimand. **2** derision. **3** scorn, disdain. **men-(i) 1** deride. **2** censure, reprimand. *Pemerintah ~ tindakan semacam itu* The gvt. censured such an action. **3** revile, call s.o. names. **men-kan** criticize mockingly. **-an** disdain, mocking criticism. **pen-** critic, faultfinder, caviler, scold.

cercah se- a slight s.t. *Tak ~ pun yg dpt kuhadiahkan kpdnya* I could not give him a thing. ~ *cahaya kebahagiaan* a slight ray of happiness. ~ *harapan* a slight ray of hope. ~ *sentuhan* a slight touch. ~ *tangkapan* a very small catch.

cercak slightly pockmarked.

cercap men- flop about, squirm (as fish out of water).

cerdas 1 intelligent, educated. **2** shrewd, clever. *Ia - berdagang* He is shrewd in business. **3** mentally agile. *- cermat tangkas* quiz contest. **men-kan** develop o.'s mind, sharpen o.'s mind. *latihan utk ~ pikirannya* exercise to sharpen o.'s mind. *buku ~ bangsa* books develop the mentality of the nation. *Manusia hrs ~ diri* O. must develop o.'s mental capabilities. **ke-an 1** intelligence. **2** shrewdness, astuteness. ~ *berdagang* business acumen. **pen-an** development of the mind. ~ *kehidupan bangsa Indonésia* process of developing the intellectual life of the Indonesian nation.

cerdét [*ceritera détéktif*] detective story.

cerdik 1 smart, clever, bright. *- pandai/cendékia* intelligent, brainy. **2** cunning, shrewd, tricky. **ke-an 1** intelligence, cleverness, astuteness. **2** cunning, shrewdness, chicanery.

cerecak₁ slightly spotted, lightly pockmarked.

cerecak₂ see CICAK.

cerecat sound of chirping. **ber-²** cheep and chirp. *Suaranya ~ spt di pasar burung* His voice was a medley of chirps and cheeps like in a bird market.

cerécéh sound of a chirping house lizard. **ber-** make a chirping noise. *Cicak-cicak ~ sepanjang malam* The lizards clicked and chirped all night long. **men- 1** make a noise like a lizard. *Pérs déwasa ini hanya bisa ~ tanpa mungkin bersuara* Nowadays the press can only chirp like lizards without really being able to speak. **2** blather, speak nonsense.

cerécék k.o. freshwater fish.

cerecis sound of sizzling and hissing. **ber-²** make a hissing noise. *kawah minyak yg ~ suaranya* a huge pan of oil making a sizzling noise. ~ *spt air dlm kawah* sizzle and spit like water in a greased pan.

cérék 1 kettle. **2** watering can.

ceremai see CERMAI.

cerempung see CELEMPUNG.

cerenah see CERNA.

cerét diarrhea. --*berét* serious diarrhea. **men-, mén-** have diarrhea.

céret kettle.

ceréwét 1 fussy, finicky, hard to please. *org -* grumbler, carper, malcontent. **2** sharp-tongued. **men-i 1** criticize, find fault with. **2** order about. **ke-an** fussiness, faultfinding. ~ *logika* the nit-picking of logic.

cergam [*cerita bergambar*] story in comic strip form.

cergas enterprising, active, energetic. **men-kan** activate, enliven. **ke-an 1** activity. **2** verve, dash, vim, push.

céri cherry.

ceria₁ **1** pure, clean, cleaned. **2** cloudless. **3** cheerful. **men-kan** purify, cleanse. **ke-an** purity.

ceria₂ (*Lit.*) oaths and formulas read at the installation of a king.

cericip sound of chirping or chatter (of birds).

cericit sound of chicks. **men-** peep. *Anak ayam ~ di kerampang induknya* Chicks were peeping under their mother's protection.

ceriga see CURIGA.

ceringis wide grin.

ceriping see CRIPING.

cerita, ceritera story, account, narrative, tale, yarn. - *perjalanannya* account of her trip. - (*ber*)*sambung* serial, continued story, feuilleton. - *berbingkai* story within a story (such as the 1,001 nights, etc.). - *burung* gossip, rumor. - *gambar* comics, comic book. - *kriminil* detective story, murder mystery. - *panjang* novelette. *péndék* short story. - *rakyat* folktale. - *rékaan* prose fiction. - *silat* martial arts stories (often with illustration). **ber-** tell, relate, spin a yarn. *Ia ~ ttg pengalamannya di negeri Turki* He told about his experiences in Turkey. **men-i** narrate to s.o. *Ia ~ anaknya ttg perjalanannya* She told her child about her trip. **men-kan** narrate, tell, recount. *Ibu ~ lagi dongéng Joko Kendil* Mother once again told the *Joko Kendil* tale. **-an** story. **pen-** narrator, storyteller.

ceriwis talkative when o. should not talk, open o.'s big fat mouth.

cerkas see CERGAS.

cerkau men- grab at. **-an** a grab, snatch.

cerkrim [*cerita kriminal*] detective story, murder mystery.

cerlang bright, gleaming. --*cemerlang* bright, gleaming. **ber-** glisten, shine. **ke-an** beauty.

cerlih see TUPAI.

cerling men- **1** ogle. **2** look at from the corner of the eye.

cermai k.o. small red fruit often candied.

cermat **1** accurate, precise, punctilious. **2** careful, prudent, cautious, frugal. **3** neat, orderly, conscientious. *mengatur kamarnya dgn -* arrange o.'s room neatly. **men-i** pay close attention to. *~ uraian gurunya* pay close attention to the teach-

er's explanation. **men-kan 1** be accurate in. ~ *pekerjaannya* be precise in o.'s work. **2** economize on, be thrifty with. ~ *pengeluaran uang* economize on expenditures. **ke-an 1** neatness, orderliness, meticulousness. **2** accuracy. **3** frugality.

cermin **1** mirror. *melihat di -* look in the mirror. - *mata* **1** sweetheart. **2** (*M*) spectacles. - *muka* looking glass. - *wasiat* magic mirror. **2** shining example, exemplar. *Pemimpin hrs jadi - rakyat* A leader must be a shining example for the people. **ber-1** have, be provided with, mirrors. **2** look in the mirror. *Lama sekali ia ~* She looked in the mirror for a long time. **3** take as an example. *Ia selalu ~ kpd ibunya* She always takes her mother as an example. ~ *bangkai* have a guilty conscience, feel shame (lit., take a dead body as an example). *Drpd hidup ~ bangkai lebih baik mati berkalang tanah* Better dead than live in shame. ~ *dlm hatinya* reflect in o.'s heart, search o.s. **men-i 1** hold the mirror in front of s.t. *Ia ~ ibunya* She held the mirror in front of her mother. **2** look at s.t. by holding a mirror in front of it, examine carefully. *Ia ~ lukanya* He looked at his wound in the mirror. *Anak-anak sekarang ~ masyarakat di sekitarnya* Nowadays young people observe with attention the society around them. **men-kan** reflect, mirror s.t. ~ *pendapat org banyak* reflect the view of the crowd. **mempe(r)- 1** use as a mirror. **2** see, observe, note. **ter-** mirrored, reflected. *Wajah kekasihnya tetap ~ dlm hatinya* His sweetheart's face was permanently mirrored in his mind. **-an** reflection, shadow. **pen-an** reflecting, mirroring.

cerna **1** digested, absorbed, assimilated. **2** dissolved. **men-** become dissolved. **men-(kan) 1** digest, dissolve. *Obat ini ~ segala bagian makanan yg keras* This medicine dissolves all hard parts of food. ~ *rencana besar-besaran* digest a large-scale plan. **2** absorb, register, take in. ~ *segala naséhat gurunya* absorb all his teacher's advice. *Dia dpt ~ pengalaman yg lampau* He was able to absorb all his past experience. **ter- 1** digestible. **2** dissolved, absorbed. **pen-an** digestion, assimilation, absorption.

cernak [*cerita anak*] children's story.

ceroboh **1** improper, indecent, immoral. *tindakan yg -* improper act. **2** cruel, merciless. **3** untidy, careless, sloppy, messy. *Kabar ini dipilih dgn -* This news was carelessly chosen. **men- 1** act improperly, act indecently. **2** defile, soil. **men-i** perform an improper act on s.o. **ke-an 1** indecency, impropriety. **2** carelessness, sloppiness.

cerobong **1** chimney, smokestack. **2** ship's funnel.

cerocok₁ funnel, spout. **ber-** spout. *Cairan mérah muda ~ ke dlm gelas* A light-red fluid flowed into a glass.

cerocok₂ **1** palisade at sea's edge, landing stage, berthing area. **2** breakwater.

cerocos see CROCOS.

cerompong see CEROPONG.

ceronggah see CERANGGAH.

ceropong muzzle of gun, mouth of cannon.

cerpelai mongoose.

cerpén [*ceritera péndék*] short story.

cerpénis short story writer.

cerpu k.o. sandal.

cersil [*ceritera silat*] martial arts stories.

certa (*Geol.*) chert.

cerucuk see CEROCOK₁.

cerucup pointed, tapering, funnel-shaped. - *atas* gable. **ber-, men-** project, protrude, stick out (to a point). *pagar yg ~ tajam-tajam* hedge with sharp projecting point.

cerucut cone. - *és* icicle.

ceruh completely milled (rice).

ceruk 1 hole, cleft, niche. 2 cranny, nook. 3 compartment (in drawer, etc.). 4 shaft (in a mine). 5 lane, path. - *meruk* various nooks and crannies. *dr segala - rantau* from everywhere. **men-** 1 dig a hole in the earth. 2 enter a hole, niche, etc.

cerup 1 sound of sucking in water. 2 sound of a small object falling. **men-** suck, inhale.

cerurut see CELURUT.

cerut men- wind around tightly, squeeze, constrict (as of a snake). **pen-** (*Naut.*) guy wire.

cerutu cigar, cheroot.

cespleng cure instantly, provide instant relief. *Obat ini - utk sakit kepala* This medicine cures headaches instantly.

cét see CAT₁.

cét. [*cétakan*] edition or printing. - *kedua* 2d edition.

cétak mold, form, cast, matrix. - *batu* lithoprinting, lithography. - *biru* blueprint. - *coba* proofs, proof sheets. - *talam* galleyproof. - *tambahan* reprint. - *tinggi* letterpress. - *ulang(an)* reprint. **ber-** printed. **men-** 1 print (books, banknotes, etc.). *sedang di-* in press. *~ ulang* reprint. 2 cast, shape, mold. *~ kuéh* shape cookies. *~ roda* cast a wheel. 3 produce, stamp (coins, etc.). 4 achieve, produce. *~ kemenangan yg gemilang* achieve a glorious victory. *Dia adalah anak angkat almarhum dan bukan anak yg di- almarhum* He is an adopted, not natural, son of the deceased. *Angka satu itu di- oléh Nina* Nina got an A. *~ gol* (*Sport*) score, make a goal. **men-kan** print s.t. for, publish s.t. for. **ter-** 1 published. 2 unintentionally shape s.t. *Bentuk jendéla yg terbuka ~ pd tanah di sekitar rumah* A rectangle of light was cast from the open window onto the yard. **-an** 1 publication. *Buku ini ~ Pembangunan* This book is published by Pembangunan Press. 2 printing. *Karena sukar kertas ~ buku mahal* Because of the scarcity of paper, book printing is expensive. 3 edition, printing. *~ biru* blueprint. *~ percobaan* proofs, proofsheets. *~ percontohan* rush print. 4 mold, matrix. *~ kué* cookie mold. *~ roda* mold for casting wheels. **pen-** printer. **pen-an** process of printing. *~ piringan hitam* pressing of records. **per-an** printing house, press. *~ Negara* Gvt. Printing Office.

cetar-cetér sound of gunshots, fireworks.

ceték₁ 1 shallow (river, etc.). 2 superficial, shallow. *pengetahuan yg -* shallow knowledge.

ceték₂ sound of a click. **men-kan** click on (a switch).

céténg men- carry by hand.

cetér see CETAR-CETÉR.

cetét see CETÉK.

céti₁ Indians, often merchants, from Coromandel or Malabar.

céti₂ 1 moneylender (often at high rate of interest). 2 pimp, procuress.

cetiao, cetiau (*Jkt, Ch*) o. million, in commercial transaction.

cetit small pinch, impression made on skin by a rough surface. **men-** pinch, cause a small pressure mark. **ter-, ke-** pinched, having marks of pressure in it. **-an** small pressure mark or pinch mark.

cetok₁ 1 k.o. large Ch hat. 2 European style hat, pith helmet.

cetok₂ sound of a valve in an engine.

cétok (*Jv*) trowel.

cetrék sound of a switch, a clicking noise. **men-kan** turn off, turn on (a switch). **men-²kan** repeatedly operate a switch. *Anwar ~ lampunya* Anwar kept trying to switch on his light. **-an** 1 switch (of a knob, electrical switch). *~ kedua menggelapkan segala sinar* The 2d switch turned out all the lights. 2 flick of a switch.

cetus 1 sound of s.t. being struck against stone. - *api* lighter. 2 say s.t. unexpected, unrelated to previous discourse. *"Janji palsu!" -nya* "Empty promises!" he said in an outburst of emotion. **men-** 1 scratch, scrape. *~ korék api utk membuat api* strike a match to make a fire. 2 flash, burst out. *Api mercun ~ dgn tiba-tiba* The fire of the firecrackers suddenly flashed. *"Cantik juga anak ini!" ~ dr mulutku dgn tak sengaja* "What a beautiful child!" burst inadvertently from my lips. 3 find fault. *Ia suka ~ ttg tetangga* He likes to find fault with his neighbors. **men-kan** 1 ignite, light, strike (a match). *~ keluar* ignite, set off. 2 spark, kindle, initiate. *Program itu di-kan oléh walikota* The program was sparked by the mayor. *~ pemberontakan* kindle a rebellion. 3 let go with (words). *Aku ~ kata-kata yg tak pantas diucapkan kpd wanita* I let go with words unfit for the ears of a woman. **ter-** 1 enkindled, sparked. *Résolusi yg ~ dlm konperénsi non-blok tdk diterima oleh Menlu Amérika* The resolution initially proposed in the conference of nonaligned nations was not accepted by the US secretary of state. 2 said unexpectedly. *"Itu sanjaknya," ~ dr mulutku* "That is his poem," the words leapt from my lips. **-an** 1 spark, flash. 2 spontaneous outburst. *~ ketawa* burst of laughter. *menyampaikan ~ hati* express emotions springing from the heart. *Suparno menghargai ~ Ny. Nur* Suparno values Mrs. Nur's spontaneously expressed opinion. **pen-** spark, impetus, founder of an idea. - *idé* sparker of ideas. **pen-an** initiation, kindling.

ceuk see ACEUK.

cewang not clear, clouded.

céwék (*Sl.*) girl, gal.

cewir see CEBIR₁.

céwok see CÉBOK.
CGMI [*Céntral Gerakan Mahasiswa Indonésia*] left-wing student organization (pre-1965).
chrom, chroom see KHROM.
chrysant /krisan/ chrysanthemum.
chudancho /cudanco/ (*Japanese*) military rank in Indonesian auxiliary units during Japanese occupation.
chusetsu /cusétsu/ (*Japanese*) submission to the fatherland.
ci 1 $\frac{1}{10}$ of a *tahil* or $\frac{2}{15}$ of an ounce. *duit* - k.o. Ch coin with a square hole in the middle. **2** a measure of weight used in illicit drug deals.
ciak₁ cheep, sound of birds and chicks. **ber-, men-(²)** chirp. *Anak ayam* ~ The chicks were chirping. ~ *miak* cheeping and twittering. **-an** peep, cheep.
ciak₂ k.o. bird. *padi/uban* white-headed munia. - *raya* weaver finch.
ciak₃ (*Ch*) eat.
ciaka /cia'ka/ (*Ch*) barefooted.
ciaklat, cialat (*Ch*) Uh-oh! Troubles! -*! Bénsinnya mau habis ini* Now we are in trouble! The gas is almost gone.
ciami, ciamik 1 handsome, beautiful. **2** (*Ch*) of good quality.
ciap see CIAK₁.
ciar men-² bawling, squalling (of babies).
ciat en garde! (sound made when attacking in martial arts).
ciat-ciut sound of creaking or squeaking.
cibir men- curl o.'s lips. *Kulihat ia ~ setiap mendengar cerita pahlawan* I saw him sneer every time he heard a heroic story. **men-i** scorn, look down at. *Asap itu yg ~ku, aku rasa* I felt as if the very smoke were ridiculing me. **men-kan 1** cause to curl o.'s lips in scorn. *Kaptén infanteri inipun berlalu dan ~ mulutnya* Even that infantry captain passed by and sneered in derision. **2** turn up o.'s nose at, scorn, look down on. *Ia ~ temannya* He scorned his friend. *Titi ~ penjual buku itu dgn menjulurkan lidahnya* Titi ridiculed the bookseller by sticking out her tongue at him. *"Ha," Patiwiri ~, "Masihkah engkau penakut?"* "Hey," sneered Patiwiri, "Are you still a coward?" **-an** scorn, contempt, disdain.
cibuk (*Jv*) dipper.
cicak k.o. small house lizard. - *terbang* flying lizard.
cicik₁ men- **1** whistle (of water boiling). **2** flow (of sweat).
cicik₂ affectionate form of address and reference for o.'s elder sister.
cicil men- pay in installments. *Nyatanya kami tdk bisa ~ dan sepéda itu jadi korban* It turned out we could not make the payments and we had to give up the bicycle. *penyediaan rumah secara ~* making houses available on an installment basis. **-an** installment. *Berapa ~nya satu bulan?* How much is the monthly installment? **pen-an, peny-an** paying in installments.
cicip₁ men- **1** taste (during preparation of food). **2** sip at, eat (a bit). *Pengunjung baru ~ kacang*

hijau itu The visitor had just taken a taste of the bean porridge. **men-i 1** taste (repeatedly), nibble at a small quantity. *Pandito ~ madu yg melekat di tangannya* Pandito licked at the honey on his hand. **2** experience s.t. pleasant. **-an** sample for tasting. **pen-, peny-** taster.
cicip₂ sound of birds, chicks, etc. **men-** chirp, twitter, cheep.
cicir see CÉCÉR.
cicit₁ great-grandchild, great-great-grandchild.
cicit₂ sound of an animal squeaking. **men-1** squeak (of a mouse, etc.). **2** tweet (of a canary).
cidera see CEDERA₁,₂.
ciduk₁ (*Coll.*) **men-** arrest. **-an** detention.
ciduk₂ see CÉDOK.
cigak k.o. monkey.
cih exclamation of scorn, disgust, disapproval. *Kau hébat dlm soal wanita, ya? -!* So, you're hot stuff with the girls, huh? Shit!
cihui whoopee! (exclamation of delight). -, *aku pulang bésok* Hooray! I am going home tomorrow.
cik₁ get out! shoo!
cik₂ see ENCIK.
cik₃ see CI.
cik₄ see TACI, CICIK₂.
cikal (*Jv*) young coconut.
cikalan remnants (of cloth, cake, tin can, etc.).
cikal bakal see CAKAL-BAKAL.
cikar k.o. two-wheeled bullock cart.
cikrak₁ 1 waste basket. **2** dustpan.
cikrak₂ see JINGKLAK.
cikutan hiccup.
cilaka see CELAKA.
cilap ter-² flicker.
cili (*Amb*) chili.
cilik, cilikan /cili', cili'an/ (*Jv*) little, small (esp. of children). *gadis* - a little girl.
ciling see CÉLÉNG.
cilok men- **1** steal, pilfer. **2** pick pockets. **pen-1** thief. **2** pickpocket.
ciluk ba, cilup ba peekaboo (exclamation to babies).
cim see ENCIM.
cimplung food prepared by boiling with sap or juice that is being boiled down for sugar. **men-** candy s.t. in this way. **-an** s.t. candied.
Cina (*us. Derog.*) China, Chinese. - *gundul* (*Derog.*) a cheat, s.o. who takes advantage of a peasant. *spt* - *karam* noisy, boisterous. - *kuncir* (*Derog.*) pigtailed Chinese. - *mindering* itinerant Ch vendor. **men-** become Chinese. **Pe-n** Chinatown. **per-an** Chinese affairs.
cina buta the intermediate husband which a thrice-divorced Muslim woman must have before remarrying her original husband.
cinafikasi (*Derog.*) sinicization.
cinangga deformed.
cincai (*Ch*) not important, it does not matter. -*lah! Buat Bp boléh Rp20.000* No problem! For you, Sir, I can make it 20,000 rupiah.
cincang hack, chop, mince. *daging* - chopped meat, hamburger. - *air* unbreakable (relation-

ship). *memainkan - babi* play chopsticks. *- dua segeragai* kill two birds with o. stone. **ber-** be chopped into bits. **men-** chop up, cut into small pieces. *Tubuh manusia itu di- dan disusun kembali* That human corpse had been chopped to pieces and then put back together. *Tanganku ~, bahuku memikul* Crime must be punished, the punishment must fit the crime. **-an** s.t. minced, s.t. chopped up.

cincau 1 k.o. gelatin used in cool drinks. **2** drink made from this gelatin. **3** k.o. plant the leaves of which are used to produce this gelatin.

cincin 1 ring. *- pertunangan* engagement ring. *- berapit* ring with two stones. *- cap* signet ring. *- garam sebuku* ring with single stone. *- marcis* diamond-shaped ring. *- mata tiga* ring with three stones. *- stémpél* signet ring. *bagai - dgn permata* perfect match. **2** washer for bolts, faucets, etc.

cincing men- rise up (of skirt, pants). **men-kan** raise up (clothing) for s.o.

cincoang k.o. bird, blue shortwing.

cincong see CINGCONG.

cincu boat owner, ship's captain.

cindai, cindé k.o. elaborately dyed cloth.

cindil baby mouse. *- abang* (*Jv*) child.

cindur mata 1 sweetheart. **2** souvenir.

cinématografis /sinématografis/ cinematographic.

cingah see CINGANGAH.

cingam k.o. small tree found in mangrove swamps.

cingangah ter- startled, surprised.

cingbing see CÉNGBÉNG.

cingcai see CINCAI.

cingcong ado, fuss. *Jangan banyak -* Do not make a lot of fuss and bother.

cinggé (*Ch*) parade featuring floats and pantomimes.

cingkéh see CENGKIH.

cingur cartilage and meat of the nostrils and ears of cattle (often used in salads).

cinkolim [*Cina Kolonialis Impérialis*] Colonialist-Imperialist China.

cinsé see SINSÉ.

cinta 1 love, affection. *- yg dlm* profound love. *Ia berjuang karena - kpd tanah airnya* He fought out of love for his country. *- berahi* sexual love. *- kasih* loving affection. *- monyét* puppy love. *- rasa* affection. *- segi tiga* love triangle. **2** love s.o. *Aku tetap - padamu* I still love you. **3** have a great interest in. *- laut* sea-minded. *Aku muridnya yg - déklamasi dan sastra* I am his student with a passion for poetry reading and literature. **4** (*Lit.*) sorrow, regret. **ber- 1** be in love, fall in love. *Aku ingin ~ lagi* I want to be in love again. *Tak ada gunanya ~ sekarang* There is no point in being in love now. **2** be in love with e.o. *Meréka berdua tdk ~ cuma bersahabat* They were not in love with e.o., they were only good friends. **ber-(²)an 1** be in love with e.o. **2** fall in love repeatedly. *Sejak di sekolah rendah aku ~* Since grade school I have been falling in and out of love. **- men-i** be in love with e.o. **men- 1** be in love. *Kau tak berhak buat ~*

You do not have a right to be in love. **2** loving. *ibu yg ~* a loving mother. **men-i** love. *Ayah ~mu, nak* Father loves you, son. **ter-** beloved. *ibuku yg ~* my beloved mother. **ke-an 1** love, loving emotion. *Tiada sesuatu ~ dlm dirinya* There was no feeling of love in him. **2** devotion, loving commitment. *~ku thd Tanah Air masih kekal* My loving devotion to the fatherland remains constant. **3** beloved, favorite. *lagu ~nya* his favorite song. **pe-** lover. *~ alam* outdoorsman, nature lover. **pen- 1** lover. **2** devotee, aficionado. *~ alam* nature lover. *~ tanah air* patriot. **per-an 1** love. **2** romance, love affair. *~ Dirman dan Ida menjadi buah bibir* Dirman and Ida's love affair was on everybody's lips. **3** (*Lit.*) mourning.

cintrong (*Sl.*) love.

cintuh see SENTUH.

ciongsam see CONGSAM.

cip₁ sound of cheeping. **men-(²)** cheep, peep.

cip₂ (*Sport*) a chip (golf). **men-** to chip (in golf). *Ia ~ bolanya, dan bola msk dgn satu pat* He chipped the ball, and it went in with a single putt. **-an** a chip (golf).

cipan Malay tapir.

ciplak₁ (*Jv*) **ny-** chew s.t. noisily. *Dia ngomong sambil ~ kwaci* He talked as he was chewing his watermelon seeds.

ciplak₂ see JIPLAK.

ciplukan k.o. weed.

cipoa₁ (*Coll.*) cheat, deceive. **men-** cheat or trick s.o.

cipoa₂ see SEMPOA.

cipok (*Coll.*) kiss.

ciprat splash. **ber-an** spray e.o. **men-** spray, splash. **men-i 1** spray on repeatedly. **2** share a large sum of money or s.t. lucrative. **men-kan** cause to spray, shake off water so that it sprays. *~ air dr mantel* shake the water from a coat. *Ia ~ air dr muka dan tangannya* He shook the water from his face and arms. **ke-an 1** sprayed, hit with spray, be splashed. *Ada lima org yg ~ api mercun* Five people were hit with fragments of exploding firecrackers. **2** be showered, get a share. *~ sumbangan pengusaha gedé* be showered with contributions from a big entrepreneur. *Rupanya Yayub ~ juga* It looks like Yayub got a piece of the action too.

cipta 1 creative force, creative power. **2** thought, idea. **men- 1** compose. *Udin yg ~ sajak itu* Udin was the o. who wrote the poem. **2** be creative. *Aku akan belajar dan ~!* I will study and be creative! **men-kan 1** create, conceive. *~ dunia* create the world. *Engkau hrs ~ ketenteraman* You must create serenity. **2** make, produce. *Hiasan itu di-kan oléh buruh-buruh sendiri* The laborers themselves made the decorations. *~ rékor* break or set a record. **ter-** created, produced. *~nya akhlak yg tinggi* the creation of a deep morality. **-an** creation, product, composition. *Liebestraum ~ Frans Liszt* Franz Liszt's composition *Liebestraum*. **pen- 1** creator, maker. **2** author, composer. **pen-an** creating, composition. *~ lagu-lagu baru* composition of new songs.

Ciptakarya directorate of housing, planning, and urban development.
ciput₁ (*Coll., Vulg.*) female genitalia.
ciput₂ see SIPUT.
circir small bell.
ciri₁ 1 feature, characteristic. - *gaya* stylistic. - *pemusatan* centricity. 2 identifying mark, earmark. - *khas* distinctive feature. **ke-khasan** distinctiveness. 3 (*Ling.*) feature. - *melimpah* redundant feature. - *pembéda* distinctive feature. 4 have a defect, marked by not being good. *Org itu sdh - namanya di perusahaan kami* That man has gotten a bad name in our factory. **ber-** have the characteristic of. **ber-kan** be characterized by, have s.t. as an earmark. *Abad ke-18 ~ konsolidasi* The 18th century was characterized by consolidation. **memper-, men-kan** type, characterize. **ke-an** identifying characteristic. *Ia punya ~ suara yg tinggi* O. of her characteristics is her high voice.
ciri₂ (*Lit.*) words (of fidelity) read at the installation of a ruler.
cirit 1 diarrhea. - *birit* diarrhea. - *bintang* meteor. 2 sediment. - *kopi* coffee dregs or grounds. **men-** have diarrhea. **men-kan** discharge, eliminate s.t.
cis₁ exclamation of disgust, bah! -, *tak ingat pd anak-isterinya* It is disgusting how he forgets about his family.
cis₂ k.o. light rifle.
cit squeak (of mouse, baby bird).
cita₁ feeling, sentiment. - *rasa* taste, savor, flavor. **ber-** *rasa* 1 having savoir vivre, discerning. *pria ~ gentleman of taste*. -² 1 desire, hope. ~ *utama* prime desires. 2 ideal, aspiration. ~ *kehidupan* life's ideals. **ber-²** 1 desire, long for. *Ia ~ pergi ke Éropa* She longed to travel to Europe. 2 aspire. ~ *tinggi* have high aspirations. *Ia ~ utk menjadi dokter* His ideal was to become a doctor. 3 longing, yearning. 4 idea (esp. in slogans). **ber-²kan** 1 have s.t. as its ideal or goal. ~ *satu masyarakat sosialis* have a socialist society as its ideal. 2 aspire to s.t. *Dia ~ menjadi jurnalis* He wanted to become a journalist. **men-²(kan)** desire, want, wish for. *Ia mendapat segala yg di-kannya* She got everything she wanted. *Dua puluh per sén ~ menjadi pedagang* Twenty percent wished to become traders.
cita₂ see KAIN.
citra image. - *diri* self-image. *Yustejo dianggap dpt merusak - nasional* They thought Yustejo could ruin the national image. **men-kan** project an image. ~ *nilai-nilai baru* project an image of new values. **-an** imagery. **pen-an** image projection.
Citra name of the annual film festival awards.
cituk men- snatch. *di- tentara* snatched away by the army.
ciu (*Ch*) intoxicating distilled beverage. - *bumbon* (*Jv*) a spiced intoxicating beverage.
cium 1 smell. 2 kiss. **ber-(²)an, -²an** kiss e.o. **men-** 1 kiss. ~ *tangan ibunya* kiss (sniff at) his mother's hands (in respect). 2 smell, sniff. ~ *bau apak* smell a rancid stink. 3 sense, learn about. *Rencana penyerangan kita sdh di- Belanda* The Dutch

had detected our plans to attack. 4 bump against. *Sekoci itu ~ pasir* The boat bumped against the sand. *Irwan hrs ~ lantai gudang itu lagi* Once again Irwan was slammed to the warehouse floor. **men-i** 1 kiss repeatedly. *Ia ~ anaknya sblm pergi* She kissed her child repeatedly before she left. 2 sniff out (secrets, news, etc.). *Anjing pelacak ~ jejak pelarian itu* The bloodhounds caught the scent of the traces of the escaped. **men-kan** cause s.o. to kiss or sniff. **ter-** 1 kissed (accidentally). 2 learned, sniffed out. ~ *kabar padanya . . .* she came to learn . . . **-an** 1 kiss. 2 whiff, sniff. **pen-** s.t. to sniff with. *Hidung adalah alat ~* The nose is the organ of smell. **pen-an** 1 sense of smell. 2 (act of) kissing. 3 sniffing out (of news). *mempunyai ~ ttg keonaran* have a nose for scandal.
ciut₁ 1 shrunk(en), shriveled. *Hatiku jadi -* My heart shriveled up. - *hati* scared, afraid. **men-hati** become afraid. 2 narrow, tight. *Jalannya -* The road's narrow. *Hari makin -* The days get shorter and shorter. **men-, meny-** 1 become narrow, tighten. *Bahan-bahan makanan ~* Foodstuffs are becoming tight or scarce. *Kankernya terus menyempit dan ~* The tumor continues to shrink and reduces in size. 2 be narrow-minded. *karena ~nya pendapatnya* because of his narrowness of opinion. *Partai itu bertambah ~ dan mengecil* That party is becoming increasingly narrow and petty. **men-kan** 1 narrow, reduce. ~ *jumlahnya* reduce the amount. *Sistim ini ~ kesempatan bintang-bintang baru utk tampil* This system reduces the opportunity for new movie stars to emerge. ~ *keuntungan* reduce the profit. ~ *muatannya jadi seribu lima ratus ton* reduce the load to 1,500 tons. ~ *hati* shrivel up the heart. 2 reduce in size. *Toko di-kan* The store was made smaller. **memper-(kan)** narrow, tighten. ~ *halaman* narrow the yard. ~ *pasaran* narrow the market. *Dgn sendirinya langkah itu ~ pemasukan dana* By itself that measure restricted the inflow of funds. **ke-an** 1 narrowness. ~ *pikirannya yg tdk kusenangi* It is his narrow mentality that I do not like. 2 astringency, contraction. **pen-an** 1 shrinkage. 2 narrowing down, thinning out, reduction. ~ *dan merger bank-bank* the thinning out and merger of banks. ~ *parpol-parpol* reduction (in number) of political parties. 3 attrition.
ciut₂ sound of squeaking. **ber-², men-²** 1 squeak (of shoes, brakes, etc.). 2 whistle (of wind through trees). **-an** squeak, squeal, screech. *bunyi ~ jip* the screeching sound of jeep.
ck ck ck (representation of) a smacking of the tongue tip, an exclamation of astonishment and often disapproval. -, *sampai begituan!* Tsk, tsk, it has gone that far!
claim /klém/ insurance claim. **men-** make a claim.
clash /klés/ 1 Dutch attacks on Indonesian territory in 1947 and 1948. 2 (*Coll.*) conflict, disagreement.
cleguk sound of swallowing liquid.
clik men- snip. ~ *pita* cut a ribbon.
clila-clili (*Jv*) flustered, embarrassed.

clingak-clinguk (*Jv*) look bewildered.
clingus (*Jv*) bashful but coy.
clola-clolo (*Jv*) act stupid.
clupak see CELUPAK.
clurit k.o. sickle (often used as weapon).
clurut see CELURUT.
clutak (*Jv*) **1** always getting at food. **2** always getting into other's business.
cm. /séntimétér/ centimeter.
coaching /kocing/ (*Coll.*) directions given before a speech, etc. *- indoktrinasi politik* directions based on political indoctrination. **men-** give pointers, coach. *Pantas dia kedengaran lancar, sdh di-* No wonder he sounds good, he has been coached.
coan (*Ch*) gain a profit.
coang ber-(an), men- protrude, stick up. **men-kan** stick s.t. upward.
coba, cobak 1 try, make an attempt. *Jangan kau - mengajar anak itu* Do not try to teach that child. *perhitungan-perhitungan -* trial calculations. **2** try s.t. out. *-lah mobil ini dulu* Try this car first. *-lah pakaian ini dulu sblm kancingnya dipasang* Try this suit on before I sew on the buttons. **3** (*Coll.*) please (with a request to a person on equal or lower footing). *- pegang ini* Please hold this. **4** (*Coll.*) just imagine, try considering. *- bagaimana ini?* Look, what does this mean? *- lihat, pekerjaan apa ini?* Just look! What k.o. work is this? *-! Ini dia!* What do you know! Here it is! **5** (*Coll.*) just try, let us see you prove (in challenge). *-! Mana orgnya?* Come on then! Where is the man? *-! Mana peraturannya?* Let's see it! Show me those regulations! **6** (*Coll.*) if, supposing. *- ayahnya tak ada, siapa yg akan membayar hutangnya* Supposing his father were not there, who would pay his debt? **-²** **1** attempt repeatedly. *Ia ~ membuka pintu yg terkunci itu* He was attempting to open the locked door. **2** try (not in a serious way). *Rupanya ia ~ saja* Apparently he was just trying it out. **men- 1** try, attempt. *Ia ~ menipu aku* She tried to cheat me. **2** test s.t. *Ia ~ kepandaian temannya* He tested his friend's skill. *Ia ~ masakan isterinya* He tried his wife's cooking. **men-²** try repeatedly. *~ keuntungan* try o.'s luck. **men-i 1** try on. *Darmi terus ~ baju yg bergantungan di lemari* Darmi kept on trying on the dresses hanging in the armoire. **2** test, put to the test. **men-kan 1** try out, test on s.o. *Ia ~ kepandaiannya* She tried out her skill. **2** try (clothing) on s.o. *~ pakaian kpd anaknya* try a suit on o.'s child. **-an 1** test. **2** trial, ordeal. **3** (*Rel.*) temptation. **pen- 1** o. who tests s.t. *penerbang ~ test* pilot. **2** tempter. **pen-an 1** effort, attempt. **2** testing. *~ mesin baru* testing of a new engine. **3** temptation. **per-an 1** trial, affliction, ordeal. **2** experiment. *~ berlayar* trial run (of a ship). **3** specimen, trial. *nomor ~* specimen copy. **4** attempt. *~ membunuh* murder attempt. **5** tryout. **6** probation. *Ia dijatuhi hukuman ~* He was sentenced to probation.
cobak-cabik all torn up.
coban k.o. broad, coarse needle for making nets, etc.

cobar-cabir see CABIR.
cobék₁ mortar (for braying condiments).
cobék₂ see SOBÉK.
coblong small hole. **-², ber-** have holes in it. **men-** make a hole. **men-i** make a hole in s.t. **ter-i** have gotten a small hole in it. **-an** a hole made in s.t.
coblos men- 1 perforate, punch. **2** vote by punching ballot. *Penduduk taat dan tenang ~* The inhabitants obediently and calmly voted. **-an** (*Coll.*) elections. **pen-** voter. **pen-an 1** punching, perforating. **2** voting. *hari ~* voting, ballot day.
cocakrawa see CUCAK RAWA.
cocok₁ 1 agree, tally, jibe. *Uraiannya tdk - dgn kenyataan* His explanation does not agree with the facts. *-!* Agreed! OK! **2** correct, exact. *Jamnya tdk -* Her watch is not correct. **3** come true. *Ramalannya -* His prediction came true. **4** like, be agreeable. *Kalau - boléh ambil* If you like it, you may have it. **5** compatible (people, colors, etc.). **6** suitable. *yg kulit kayunya - utk . . .* the bark of which is suitable for . . . *Ssdh arloji jatuh, jalannya tdk - lagi* After I dropped my watch, it no longer kept good time. *- dgn* match. *Bunga itu - dgn warna témbok* The flowers match the color of the wall. *Tanah itu tdk - dgn tanaman tembakau* That soil is not suited for tobacco plants. *- pd* fit. *Kunci ini tdk - pd pintu itu* This key does not fit the door. **men-i** be suitable with s.t., fit in well with s.t. *Pekerjaan ini yg paling di-i oléh para pengrajinnya sendiri* This job is the o. the craftsmen themselves like the most. **men-kan 1** compare, check. *~ hasil hitungan* compare the results of the calculation. **2** adjust. *~ diri kpd iklim* adjust o.s. to the climate. **3** correct, set right, synchronize. *~ arloji* synchronize the watch. **4** fit s.t. to s.t. **ke-an 1** agreement, harmony. **2** compatibility. **pen-an** verification, checking, collation. *~ data sekundér* checking of secondary data.
cocok₂ 1 pin, needle. **2** skewer. *dua - saté* two skewers of barbecued meat. *- keluan* nose rope for cattle. *- kondai/sanggul* hairpin. **ber-** *tanam/tanah* till or work the soil. **men- 1** stick, prick. *rasa perut spt di-²* the stomach feels like it is being pricked with needles. **2** pin. **3** fasten (a nose ring). *spt kerbau di- hidung* like a water buffalo being led by the nose. **4** puncture. *Duri ~ ban* A thorn punctured a tire. *~ tanda gambar* vote (by punching out a picture, illustration, etc.). **5** string, thread (by sticking through). **men-i** pierce s.t. repeatedly. **men-kan 1** pin, fasten with a pin. **2** prick, stab, stick s.t. in. *~ jarum ke bantal* stick a needle in a cushion. **ter-** pricked, stuck, stabbed. *Kakinya ~ paku* His foot got pricked by a nail. **-an** skewer. **pen- 1** skewer. **2** electric light plug.
cocol₁ men- extend, thrust out, protrude. *Potlotnya ~ dr kantongnya* His pencil stuck out from his pocket.
cocol₂ men- 1 dip with finger. **2** eat ravenously. **men-kan** stick in, insert.
cocor men- 1 hit with o.'s fist. **2** kick (a ball) with the tip of the foot.
cocor bébék k.o. flower.

cocot 1 mouth of animals. **2** (*Vulg.*) human mouth.

codak men- hold up (of head). **men-kan** hold out (o.'s head).

codét scar (on face).

codot k.o. fruit-eating bat.

coél men- 1 touch with the tip of the finger. **2** reprimand, rebuke, admonish.

cogan 1 emblem. **2** standard, ensign. - *kata* slogan.

cogok₁ 1 be erect, vertical. **2** appear, occur. **ter-** standing straight. *Beberapa méter dr rumah Uca ~ kantor polisi séktor Banjaran* The Banjaran sector police station stood several meters from Uca's house.

cogok₂ k.o. taper lamp made from empty bottle.

cokék k.o. Ch-Jkt dance show.

cokelat see COKLAT.

cokér men- scratch around for food.

cokét men- take a small piece. *Ia ~ kué* She broke off a small piece of cake.

coklak-caklik sound of clicking.

coklat 1 brown. - *hitam* dark brown. **2** chocolate. - *susu* milk chocolate. **3** cocoa. **men-** become brown. **ke-(²)an** brownish.

cokmar (*Lit.*) club, cudgel.

cokok men- seize, catch (chicken, fish, etc.).

cokol ber- 1 settle, reside. *Ia lama ~ di Paris* She has long resided in Paris. **2** squat. **3** be in existence s.w., extant. *dr dua ratus lima belas naskah yg ~* of the 215 extant manuscripts. **men-** occupy, be headquartered. *Belanda yg ~ di Surabaya menyerang désa kami* The Dutch entrenched in Surabaya were attacking our village. **men-i** dominate s.t. *Sdh lama Lee Kwan Yew ~ pemerintahan Singapura* Lee Kwan Yew has been dominating the Singapore administration for a long time.

cokot ny- take a large bite out of s.t. **-an** large bite.

cola-cala, cola-colo talk nonsense.

colak-caling in disarray.

colak-colék touch lightly, pinch lightly.

colang-caling in disorder.

colék touch lightly with the fingertips and pinch. **se- 1** a pinch, dash (of salt, etc.). **2** dab, pat (of butter, etc.). **men- 1** take a small piece of s.t. **2** squeeze, press (a boil, etc.). **3** remove, dig out (wax from ear, thorn from foot). **4** scratch, scrape. **5** squeeze, embrace. *Tangan Erlin ~ pinggang Ratna* Erlin's hands squeezed Ratna's waist. *~ tangan* squeeze the hand. **men-kan** press s.t. out or onto. *Seorg tukang batik ~ lilin ke kain mori* A batik craftsman pressed wax onto the cotton cloth. **ke-** be accidentally touched and pinched.

coléng men- hold up, steal by force, rip off. **pen-** thief. **pen-an** theft.

colét se- a bit. *Batik-batik ini tdk disentuh ~ warna dgn kwas* These batik cloths were not touched by even a bit of brushed-on color. **men-kan** daub, smear. *Adik ~ sambal ke hidung anjing* My kid brother smeared some chili sauce on the dog's nose.

collecte /kolékte/ collection (at church).

colok₁ 1 piece of cloth dipped in oil and used as a light. **2** fuse, wick. **men-(i)** light with a torch.

colok₂ men-, meny- striking, glaring. *Bajunya ~* He is wearing a loud shirt.

colok₃ men- poke with finger, poke finger into s.t. **ke-** get s.t. poked into it. *Mata Hani ~ bola* A ball struck Hani in the eye.

colong (*Jkt, Jv*) **men-, ny-** steal. **ke-** stolen. *Wajahnya ~ bidikan kameraku* I managed to steal a snapshot of her face. **ke-an** have s.t. stolen from. *Pimpinan BRI Tanjung Pinang merasa ~* The leadership of the Tanjung Pinang branch of the Indonesian People's Bank felt that s.t. was stolen from them. **-an** booty.

culot men- spring, leap, jump (like a frog).

colt /kol/ a brand of light pick-up truck frequently rebuilt as a minibus and used as a passenger vehicle. *Mobil - yg kami tumpangi mogok* The passenger van we were riding in broke down.

comat-comot pick in a variety of ways.

combéran drainage ditch, sewer. *air -* sewage water. **pe-** sewer.

combi /kombi/ k.o. minibus.

comblang 1 matchmaker, go-between. **2** (*Sl.*) pimp, procurer.

combol see TOMBOL.

combong see KECUBUNG₁.

combor horse feed (grass, rice bran and rice husks mixed with water).

comék₁ small goatee just beneath the lower lip.

comék₂ k.o. cuttlefish.

comél₁ grumbling, nagging. *Jangan terlalu -* Don't grumble so much. **men-** grumble, grouse, nag. *Ia tak takut ~ di muka ibu tiri kami* He was not afraid to grumble right in front of our stepmother. **men-i** scold, rebuke, reprimand. *Ia ~ anaknya* She scolded her child. **-an** scolding, rebuke, reprimand. **pen-** grumbler, complainer.

comél₂ (*Lit.*) **1** dainty, exquisite. **2** winsome, pretty. - *cantik* extremely beautiful.

comité see KOMITÉ.

comot₁ grimy, dirty, filthy. *Mulutnya - dgn gula-gula* His mouth was dirty from eating candy. *momot* stained, soiled, smeared. **ber-** be dirty, grimy. *~ minyak* be smeared with oil.

comot₂ men-, ny- 1 seize, nab, grab and hold. *Tiga penjambrét kalung di- Réskrim* Three necklace snatchers were seized by the criminal investigation bureau. **2** snatch off. *Kepala udang di-* The heads of the shrimp were ripped off. **3** pick. **men-i, ny-i** snatch s.t., steal. *Ia ~ jatah léwat jalan belakang* He stole rations through his inside connections. **men-kan** steal on behalf of s.o. **-an 1** stolen goods. **2** whatever o. picks up.

compang-camping in tatters, frayed, ragged. *Pakaiannya yg - terkibar-kibar dimainkan angin* His ragged clothes flapped wildly in the wind. *Aku juga berdiri, senyum -* I got up too with a ragged smile on my face.

compéng torn on the edge.

compés chipped, jagged on the edge (chinaware, etc.).

concong men- go forward without turning around.

conderong see CENDERUNG.

condong 1 leaning, inclining to o. side. *menara Pisa yg* - Leaning Tower of Pisa. **2** inclined, sympathetic. *Ia - ke pihak kanan* He inclined toward the rightist party. **3** set. *Matahari tlh* - The sun has set. **4** off, insane. *Pikirannya* - He was slightly insane. *- ingatan* slightly crazy, a bit off (mentally). *- mondong* greatly inclined. **men-kan 1** bend s.t. **2** cause to incline. *Penawaran semacam itu mudah sekali ~ hati* An offer like that easily tempts o. **ke-an 1** leaning. **2** tendency, inclination.

Conéfo [*Conference of the New Emerging Forces*] 3d-world organization created by Sukarno.

conét upturned. **men-** turn upward (of moustache, tail, etc.).

cong menge- brew tea. **penge-an** brewing of tea.

congak men- 1 raise o.'s head, hold o.'s head high. **2** calculate in o.'s head. **3** dictate mathematics problems. **men-kan** *kepala* cock o.'s head.

congék 1 deaf. **2** inflamed (of the ear).

conggét ter-² move up and down (of tail, etc.).

conggok erect. **men-** stand or sit erect. **men-kan** erect s.t.

congkah --*cangkih* stick out at an angle, uneven, irregular. --*mangkih* in disorder or disarray.

congkak₁ proud, arrogant, snooty. - *bongkak* very arrogant. **men-** hold up the head arrogantly. **ke-an** pride, arrogance, haughtiness.

congkak₂ 1 cowrie shell. **2** k.o. board game with receptacles often played with shells as tokens.

congkar-cangkir protruding everywhere.

congkél see CUNGKIL.

congklak see CONGKAK₂.

congklang sound of galloping hooves. **men-** gallop.

congkong₁ guard house, sentry post.

congkong₂ men- squat.

congkrah (*Jv*) quarrel.

congok see CONGGOK.

congol men- stick out suddenly (through a small hole).

congor (*Jv*) snout, muzzle.

congsam k.o. sleeveless, high-collared Ch dress.

container /konténer/ container (as in shipping). **men-kan** pack in containers.

containerisasi /konténerisasi/ changing over to shipping by containers.

conténg smear, stain, blemish. --*moréng* smeared and streaked. **ber-²** be smeared. **men-(²)** smear, stain (with paint, charcoal, etc.). **men-kan** smear, stain.

contoh 1 specimen, sample. **2** model. **3** pattern, design. **4** example. **ber-kan** complete with examples. *keterangan yg tdk ~* an explanation with no examples. **men- 1** copy, imitate. *Ia coba ~ pamannya* He tried to follow his uncle's example. *pejuang yg patut di-* a model fighter. **2** copy (another's essay, homework, etc.). **men-i 1** give s.t. as an example. **2** give answers to s.o. (in a test).

men-kan show by example, set an example. *Kalau kamu ndak tahu, biar saya ~* If you do not know, let me show you. *Boediardjo ~ Muang Thai sbg negara yg* . . . Boediardjo used Thailand as an example of a country that . . . **memper-kan** exemplify, give as an example. **per-** sample. *~ acak/rambang* random sample. **pen-an** process of giving example, elucidation with examples. **per-an 1** specimen, sample. *nomor ~* trial number, sample issue. **2** model. *désa ~* model village. *proyék ~* pilot project.

contong cone-shaped container made from paper or banana leaf. *se- kacang goréng* a paper cone of fried peanuts.

cop₁ 1 electric plug or socket. **2** lightbulb socket.

cop₂ see CUP₁.

copét pickpocket. *Awas, -!* Beware of pickpockets! **men-** pick pockets. **men-i** pick s.o.'s pockets (repeatedly). *Bangsat mana yg ~ org-org yg tdk berdaya!* What scoundrel rips off helpless people! **ke-an** be a victim of pickpocketing, be pickpocketed of s.t. *Ia ~ dompétnya di keréta api* His wallet was stolen on the train. **pen-** pickpocket. **pen-an** pickpocketing, pilfering.

coplok 1 come loose, break off. *Kaki méja* - A table leg came off. **2** detached, apart. **men-** (*Coll.*) detach, take off. *Ini mesti di- dan diserahkan kpd* . . . This has to be detached and handed over to . . . **men-i** remove s.t. repeatedly or in large numbers. *Karto sudi ~ giginya* Karto was willing to pull out his teeth.

coplot see COPLOK.

copot 1 dislodged. **2** broken off, detached, loosened. *Pakunya blm* - I have not gotten the nail out yet. *Giginya* - His tooth fell out. *- ban* remove a tire from a wheel. **3** Gracious! (exclamation of surprise, somewhat effeminate). **men-, ny-1** take off, remove (shoes, etc.). **2** pull out, extract (a nail). **3** untie. **4** remove, take away. *usaha-usaha utk ~ semua kekuasaan dr raja* efforts to remove all authority from the ruler. *Dialah bangsawan pertama yg ~ gelar "andi" dr namanya* He is the first aristocrat to remove the title *andi* from his name. **men-i** take off s.t. repeatedly. **men-kan** take off s.t. on behalf of s.o. **pen-an 1** removal. **2** dismissal, firing.

cor men- 1 cast, found. **2** pour concrete. *~ fondasi* pour a cement foundation. *-²an* concrete. **pen-an** casting. **penge-an** foundry.

corak 1 design, motif, pattern. *- batik* batik design. **2** color. *-nya mérah* The color is red. **3** stripe (of flag). **4** type, form. **5** feature, characteristic, color. *Perkumpulan itu -nya nasionalis* The character of that organization is nationalistic. *Ia ramah - wataknya* He has a friendly disposition. **ber-1** have the design of. *Kain yg ~ burung dan padi* cloth with bird and rice-plant design. **2** striped, with bars. **3** have the character of. *perkumpulan yg ~ politik* an organization with a political character.

corak-carik in tatters, in shreds. **men-kan** tear to shreds.

corat-corét 1 rough (of draft, sketch). **2** first draft (of composition). **3** scrawled. **men-** make doodles or rough sketches on s.t.
corék 1 long line, scratch. **2** streak. **men- 1** underline. **2** scratch out.
coréng 1 scratch, streak. **2** smear. ~ *moréng* full of streaks and scratches. **ber-** *moréng* be filled with many dirty marks and streaks. **ber-** streaked, striped. *macan* ~ striped tiger. **men-1** cross out. **2** draw lines over, streak s.t. *Rasa malu* ~ *mukanya* His face was streaked with the shame he felt. **men-i** scratch repeatedly. **men-kan** streak or scrape s.t. on. *Ia* ~ *kapur mérah ke témbok* She scratched red chalk on the wall. **ter-** streaked. **-an 1** scratch, streak. **2** smear (of lipstick).
corét 1 scratch. **2** streak, smear. **-²** doodling, graffiti. **ber- 1** underlined. **2** streaked, smeared. **men- 1** scratch, streak, ~ *témbok dgn arang* streak the wall with charcoal. **2** rule, make lines. **3** scratch out (the wrong words). *Ia* ~ *nama Abdul dan menggantinya dgn nama lain* He crossed out Abdul's name and replaced it with another. **4** do a pen drawing. **5** not enter s.t. into the calculations. **6** remove from consideration (participants in a competition). **7** (*Coll.*) write. **men-²** scribble down, jot down. **men-i 1** streak repeatedly. *Langit di-i oléh warna yg duka* The sky was streaked with various somber colors. **2** scribble on. *Ia* ~ *bukuku ketika masih kecil* He scribbled on my books when he was still little. *Meréka* ~ *gedung-gedung itu dgn slogan révolusi* They repeatedly scratched revolutionary slogans on the building. **men-kan** scrape s.t. on s.t. else. **ter-** marked, streaked. **-an 1** scratch, line, stripe. **2** pen drawing. **3** graffiti. **pen-an** removal, eradication, scratching out.
coro 1 (*Jv*) cockroach. **2** (*Derog.*) creep, bum.
corong₁ 1 funnel (for bottles, etc.). - *utk menuang minyak* funnel for pouring oil (into container). - *dengar* hearing trumpet. - *tuang* hopper (car). **2** shaft (for ventilation), funnel (ship). - *asap* **1** chimney. **2** flue. - *hawa* ventilation duct. - *lampu* lamp chimney. **3** microphone, megaphone. - *bicara* megaphone. - *cukong* mouthpiece of a financier. - *halo-halo* bull horn. - *pembesar suara* loudspeaker. - *radio* microphone. - *télpon* receiver. **4** mine shaft. **men-kan 1** broadcast. **2** shape s.t. into a funnel. *dgn tangan di-kan pd mulutnya* with his hands cupped around his mouth.
corong₂ men- 1 shine, glare. *lampu mobil yg* ~ glaring headlights. **2** radiate. **men-kan** shine on s.t.
corot spout, nozzle (of watering can). - *pelita* the rays of a lamp. - *selang* nozzle of hose. **memper-kan, men-kan** spray, spout forth (water, etc.).
corps /koreps/ corps. - *kehakiman* (*Mil.*) judge advocate corps.
cotok beak, bill. **men-** peck at.
cowboy /koboi/ **1** cowboy. **2** rough, rowdy. **-²an** rough(ly).
cowék see COBÉK₁.

cowok (*Coll.*) young fellow, guy, boyfriend. **-an** be fond of boys.
cp /cep/ (representation of) sound made by smacking tongue and closing lips, used to calm children.
CPM [*Corps Polisi Militér*] Military Police.
cq /céki/ [*casu quo*] (*Leg.*) in this case.
crat 1 sound of s.t. squirting. **2** shit! strong exclamation of disapproval. **--crét 1** emission of feces in diarrhea. **2** go to the bathroom frequently.
crét see CRAT, CÉRÉT.
cring sound of jingling. *Peggy menekan mesin hitung,* -² *Peggy pressed the adding machine making a jingling noise.*
criping fried cassava chips.
crocos rattle on. **ny-** (*Coll.*) talk glibly and fast. *Suaminya ternyata* ~ *terus omong Rusia* It turned out her husband rattled on and on talking Russian.
crongos buck-toothed. **ny-** sticking out, growing outward. *Rambut-rambut* ~ *keluar dr lubang hidungya* Hairs were growing out of his nose.
crop-crop sound of metal pieces hitting e.o.
crossboy /krosboi/ punk, delinquent.
cruat-cruit talk in large groups all at once. *Meréka terus saja* -. *Ribut sekali* It was very noisy the way they were all talking at once.
cs [*cum suis*] and associates. *Mat Coléng* - Mat Coléng and his buddies. **di-** (*Jv*) be made an accomplice.
cuaca weather. *-nya terang ssdh angin ribut semalam* The weather was clear after last night's storm. - *bak* neither overcast nor rainy. - *buruk* foul weather.
cuai insignificant, unimportant, trivial, **men-kan 1** neglect. **2** look down on, hold in contempt. **3** ignore.
cuap (*Coll.*) talk.
cuar, cuat₁ men-, ter- 1 stick up high, project upward. *mengeluarkan air dr tiang bor yg* ~ *tinggi* extract water from a drilling rig which extends high up. **2** stretch out o.'s legs. **3** stick out, be too visible. *Tempat-tempat hiburan semakin* ~ Places for entertainment are popping up more and more.
cuat₂ men- 1 be flipped, pushed away with a springy motion. *Krikilnya* ~ *digilas ban mobil* The gravel flew off to the side when the car ran over it. **2** spring back. *Ujung bambu yg ditekuk akan* ~ If you bend the bamboo at the tip it will spring back. **3** bend outward to project in a point. *Hidungnya* ~ She has a pointed nose. **men-²** vibrate at the end with the base steady. **-an** amount of spring in s.t. ~ *besi itu kuat sekali* That piece of iron has a hefty spring to it.
cuat-cuit see CRUAT-CRUIT.
cubit pinch between forefinger and thumb. - *getil* a slight pinch. **se- 1** a pinch. **2** a bit, a little. **ber-an** pinch e.o. **men- 1** pinch. **2** (*Coll.*) swipe, steal. **men-i** pinch repeatedly. **-an** a pinch. **-²an** (*Coll.*) pinch e.o.

cublik k.o. oil lamp with chimney and reflector.

cubung see KECUBUNG₁.

cubung-cubung fly larva.

cuca magic formula (for treating wounds). men- pronounce a spell.

cucak rawa, cucak rowo k.o. bird, yellow-crowned bulbul.

cuci wash. - *asam* pickling, curing. - *darah* 1 dialysis (kidney). 2 eat certain foods thought to purify sluggish blood. - *mata* 1 window shopping. 2 girl watching. - *muka* 1 wash the face. 2 washstand, basin. - *perut* laxative. - *rambut* shampoo. men-, ny- 1 wash. ~ *rambut* shampoo the hair. 2 wash, launder, do the laundry. 3 develop (a film). men-kan 1 wash s.t. for s.o. *Ia* ~ *sehelai cita utk adiknya* She washed a piece of chintz for her younger sister. 2 have s.t. washed. *Ia* ~ *jasnya* He had his jacket washed. -an 1 laundry, wash. 2 manner of washing. pen- laundress, laundryman. ~ *mulut* dessert. ~ *rambut* shampoo. pen-an 1 washing of. 2 catharsis.

cucimaki verbal abuse.

cucu grandchild. - *Adam* humanity. ber- have grandchildren.

cucuh 1 kindle, light. 2 switch on (a light).

cucuk₁ 1 bill, beak. 2 (*Mil.*) front line.

cucuk₂ see COCOK₂.

cucunda your grandchild (respectful form, esp. in writing letters).

cucung grandchild.

cucunguk see CECUNGUK.

cucup 1 a kiss. 2 suck, slurp. men-, meny- suck in, drink through a straw.

cucur₁ a flow, trickle. - *darah* hemorrhage. ber-an flow, stream, gush. *Air matanya* ~ Tears flowed down her cheeks. men-i pour or drip on. ~ *matanya dgn tétés mata* put drops in o.'s eyes. men-kan 1 drip s.t. on. ~ *obat pd lukanya* put medicine on o.'s wound. 2 let s.t. drip or pour. ~ *air di kepalanya* let water fall on his head. ~ *air mata* shed tears, weep. ~ *darah* shed blood, cause blood to flow. ~ *keringat* perspire, sweat. -an pouring, flood. ~ *air mata* flood of tears. ~ *atap* eaves. ~ *keringat* sweat, perspiration.

cucur₂ fried cake made of rice flour and sugar.

cucur₃ k.o. bird, large frogmouth.

cucur₄ (*Naut.*) bowsprit (of ship).

cucurut see CECURUT.

cucut₁ shark. - *rongcéng* hammerhead shark.

cucut₂ men- 1 kiss. 2 suck.

cuenosit /sénosit/ (*Phys.*) coenocyte.

cuh₁ sound of expectoration.

cuh₂ huh! (exclamation of distaste, cynical disfavor, etc.).

cuik men- steam and salt (fish).

cuil 1 chunk. 2 chipped. se- a little bit. ~ *senyum* a slight smile. ~ *usaha* a bit of effort. *tanpa ada catatan* ~*pun* without any notes whatever. men- touch slightly, nudge, poke.

cuilah (*Coll.*) Lord! Gosh! (exclamation of distaste). -! *Lu kayak babé gué ajé!* Lord! You are just like my old man!

cuing-cuing men- shred meat with the fingers.

cuit₁ sound of squeaking. -, -, - *begitu bunyinya* Screech, screech, screech, that is how it sounded. ber-(²) screech, squeak. *Keréta api* ~ *tajam suaranya* The train screeched shrilly. men- make a shrill noise. *Aku kontan* ~ *dgn siul* Right away I let out a shrill whistle.

cuit₂ movement of fingers. - *gamit* nervous movement of fingers. men- poke, nudge, tap. -an nudge.

cuk₁ (*Auto.*) choke.

cuk₂ mosquito larva.

cuk₃ see CUKULÉLÉ.

cuka vinegar. - *belanda* artificial vinegar. - *jawa* vinegar made from juice of palm blossoms. - *minyak* (*Amb*) Gosh! (exclamation of surprise, euphemism for *cuki mai*). men-i put vinegar in.

cukai, cuké 1 (customs) duty, toll, tax. 2 excise duty. - *tembakau* duty on tobacco, tobacco tax. 3 tariff. men- impose a duty.

cuki₁ game of draughts. ber- play the game of draughts.

cuki₂ (*Vulg.*) have sexual intercourse. - *mai* Dammit! (strong exclamation of exasperation or contempt).

cukil see CUNGKIL.

cukin bib.

cukit 1 pick. 2 fork (for eating).

cukong 1 well-to-do financier, financial backer. 2 capitalist (engaged in illegal practices). 3 broker, wholesale distributor. men-i 1 finance, underwrite the costs. 2 treat s.o. to s.t. per-an matters regarding big financiers.

cukongisme a mode of (often illegal) cooperation between authorities and (us. Ch) financiers.

cukulélé ukulele.

cukup 1 enough, sufficient, adequate. - *utk hari ini* enough for today. *persediaan yg* - adequate supply. *Sdh - panjangnya* It is long enough. - *saja untungnya* The profit was just enough. 2 exactly, precisely. *Umurnya - enam tahun* She is exactly six years old. *Uangnya - enam ratus rupiah* He has precisely 600 rupiah. *tdk - sepuluh menit* in less than 10 minutes. - *bulannya* end of term for childbirth. 3 well-to-do, prosperous. *Ia termasuk keluarga yg* - He belongs to a well-to-do family. 4 complete. *sebuah rumah - dgn dapur dan kamar mandi* a house complete with kitchen and bathroom. 5 quite, rather. *Usahanya - terbatas* His efforts were quite limited. se-nya sufficient, adequate. *Perangkoilah kiriman-kiriman pos* ~ Please place sufficient postage on the mail. *dan garam* ~ and salt to taste. men-i 1 make up a lack, complete. *Ia* ~ *uangnya utk membayar hutangnya* He supplemented his money to pay his debts. 2 fulfill. ~ *segala syarat-syarat* fulfill all conditions. 3 be sufficient, suffice. *Gajinya tdk* ~ Her salary was not sufficient. men-kan 1 make sufficient or adequate. *Ia* ~ *uangnya dulu sblm beli karcis* He saw to it he had enough money before he bought the tickets. 2 make suffice, make do with. *Ia* ~ *gajinya utk satu bulan* She made her salary suffice for a month. **men-²kan** try to make (both) ends meet. **ter-i** fulfilled. *Isterinya blm ~ kebutuhannya* He has not succeeded in providing his wife's needs. **ke-an 1** sufficiency, adequate amount. *~ kebutuhan pangan* sufficiency of food requirements. **2** have enough to live. **berke-an** be in moderate circumstances, have an adequate amount. *Iapun tdk ~* She does not even have enough. *hidup ~* live in a moderate style. **-an** (*Coll.*) just enough, adequate. *~ saja* just average, not too much. *~ saja untungnya* The profit was not bad. **pen-an** efforts to achieve sufficiency.

cukur 1 razor, shaver. *tukang -* barber. *- batok* cut hair (as if) by using a coconut shell as guide. **2** tonsure. *- suci* (*Rel.*) holy tonsure. **ber- 1** shave. *Ia sedang ~* He is shaving. **2** shaved, have a shave. **3** get a haircut. **men- 1** shave s.o. or s.t. **2** (*Sport*) defeat, drub. *Regu kami di- gundul* Our team was scalped. **men-kan** shave with s.t. **-an 1** shavings. **2** instrument for shaving. *~ listrik* electric shaver. **pen-an** shaving, trimming down. *Terjadilah ~ gencar thd kesenian tradisionil* Thus, traditional art was extremely curtailed.

cula rhinoceros horn.

culan k.o. shrub, the flowers of which are used to perfume tea and clothes.

culas₁ 1 lazy, indolent. **2** slow, plodding, poky. **3** clumsy, awkward.

culas₂ deceitful, dishonest, not straightforward. **ke-an** deceit, fraud.

culik men- kidnap, abduct. **pen-** kidnapper, abductor. **pen-an 1** kidnapping, abduction. **2** hijacking.

cuma 1 only, merely. *Kuénya - tinggal dua* There were only two cookies left. *Saya - dua hari di sana* I was there for only two days. **2** only, but. *Saya mau ke Éropa, - tdk punya uang* I want to go to Europe, but I do not have the money. *- saja* on the condition that . . . **-²**, **per- 1** in vain, useless, ineffectual. **2** free, free of charge, gratis. *mendapat makan dan minum ~* get food and drink free. **memper-kan 1** waste (time, energy). **2** provide s.t. gratis.

cuman (*Coll.*) only. *- itu saja?* Is that all?

cumbu 1 flattery. **2** sweet talk, honeyed words. **3** joke, jest, good-natured banter. *- rayu* flirtatious flattery. **ber-** *rayu* flirt. **men-** *rayu* flatter, sweet-talk s.o. *Asyik benar cowok itu ~ rayu pacarnya* That fellow sweet-talks his girlfriend like mad. **ber-²an 1** joke flirtatiously, banter, repartee. **2** fondle e.o., be engaged in petting. **men-i 1** woo s.o. **2** fondle, pet. **-an 1** sweet words, flattery. **2** joke, jest, banter. **-²an** advances, approach. **per-an** flirtation, courtship.

cumi-cumi₁ squid.

cumi-cumi₂ 1 evildoer, criminal. **2** traitor. **3** enemy spy.

cumlaude /kumlot/ with distinction (esp. of academic achievements). *lulus -* graduate with distinction.

cumpang-camping see COMPANG-CAMPING.

cun₁ inch.

cun₂ (*child language*) kiss.

cunam pliers, pincers.

cunang-cuning time at random.

cuncum k.o. cone-shaped pastry with sweet filling.

cunda see CUCUNDA.

cundang₁ men-i, menge-kan defeat. **ke-, terke-** defeated. **pe-** o. who is defeated.

cundang₂ men- incite, instigate, foment. **pe-** troublemaker, instigator, fomenter.

cundrik k.o. small kris.

cunduk large pin for holding a chignon in place.

cung₁ (*Jv*) laddy, sonny, a term of address.

cung₂ k.o. machine gun.

cungap *- cangip* gasp for breath, be short of breath. **meng-, ter-** pant, gasp (for breath).

cungkil crowbar, lever. **men- 1** pry up or off. *Ia ~ batu besar itu dgn kayu* He pried the big rock with a piece of wood. *~ ban* remove a tire from the wheel. *~ kelapa* pry loose the meat of a coconut. **2** dig or gouge out. *Mata-mata itu di- matanya* The spy's eyes were gouged out. **3** pick. *~ giginya* pick o.'s teeth. *~ telinga* remove wax from the ear. **men-i 1** pick repeatedly. *~ giginya* keep picking o.'s teeth. **2** pry off repeatedly. **men-kan** pry off on behalf of s.o. **-an** chunks pried from s.t. (coconut, etc.). *~ kayu* woodcut. **pen-** lever. *~ ban* tire iron.

cungkup dome or cover over grave.

cunguk see CECUNGUK.

cungul see CONGOL.

cungur see JUNGUR.

Cuo Sangiin Indonesian advisory body assisting the Japanese occupation.

cup₁ smack (of kiss). **-²an** smooching, kissing.

cup₂ That is mine! (assertive exclamation).

cupai men-kan neglect, ignore.

cupak₁ a measure of volume, esp. for rice. **men-** measure by the *cupak*.

cupak₂ bowl (of an opium pipe).

cupang (*Coll.*) love-bite, hickey.

cupar₁ deride, sneer at. **men-** twist things around, confuse matters.

cupar₂ a man who is stingy and a busybody in the kitchen.

cupat, cupet 1 inadequate, short, insufficient, skimpy. **2** shortsighted. *pandangan yg -* shortsighted view. **3** petty, narrow, bigoted. **ke-an** narrow-mindedness.

cuping ear lobe. *- hidung* nostril.

cuplak see CELUPAK.

cuplik pick out a small portion. **men-(i) 1** cite, name, quote. **2** borrow. **-an** citation, quotation.

cupu, cupu-cupu 1 box for pills. **2** posthole, hole for mast.

cupul too short.

cur sound of spouting.

cura joke, jest. **ber- 1** joke, jest. **2** call s.o. names, be insulting. *tdk ~* serious, no kidding.

curah *- hujan* rainfall. *- hujan setempat* amount of rainfall at that place. *barang -* bulk goods. **men-**

fall (of rain). *Hujan terus ~ dr langit* The rain kept falling from the sky. **men-i 1** pour on. *Hujan ~ sawah* Rain poured down on the rice fields. **2** bestow upon, shower. *Anak itu di-i pemberian* The child was showered with gifts. **3** expend. *Di-i air dingin dan diaduk* Pour cold water all over it and mix. **men-kan 1** pour s.t. on. *~ air ke kepala* pour water on the head. **2** pour s.t. out, unload. **3** lavish, expend. *Ia ~ segala kekuatannya utk mengangkat batu itu* He exerted all his strength to lift that stone. *~ isi hati* speak freely. *~ perhatian* devote attention. *~ perhatian istiméwa* take special pains. **ter-(kan) 1** poured down. *Sesalannya ~ kpd kami* He showered us with his regrets. **2** focused. *Perhatian meréka ~ kpd pengejaran tawanan itu* Their attention was focused on the pursuit of that prisoner. **-an 1** precipitation (of rain, etc.). **2** outpouring, outflow. *~ air dr mulut* water spit from the mouth. **pen-an 1** outpouring. *~ rasa* outpouring of feelings. **2** bestowal. *~ pemberian* bestowal of gifts.

curai 1 loose, detached, apart. *Adakah uang -?* Do you have any loose change? *Ada yg diikat ada yg ~* There are bound o.'s and there are loose o.'s. **2** clear, evident, real. **men-kan 1** loosen s.t. **2** explain, clarify. *~ duduknya perkara* explain the position of the case. **3** separate, isolate. *~ uang kertas dr uang -* separate the banknotes from the loose cash. **-an 1** explanation. **2** separation.

curam steep, precipitous, sheer, abrupt (cliff, abyss, etc.). **men-** become steep. **ke-an** steepness, precipitousness, abruptness.

curang dishonest, fraudulent, deceitful. *main -* play foul. *suami yg -* two-timing husband. **men-i 1** deceive, defraud, cheat. **2** (*Sport*) commit a foul. **ke-an 1** deceit, fraud. **2** corruption. **3** (*Sport*) foul.

curat spout, nozzle. **men-** gush out, spew forth, spout.

curat-corét see CORAT-CORÉT.

cureng deep-socketed (of eyes). **ny-** (*Jv*) put on serious face, frown.

curi 1 steal. **2** surreptitious. **-²** surreptitiously, stealthily, on the sly. *Ia ~ menemui kekasihnya* She was meeting her sweetheart clandestinely. **men-1** steal, pilfer. **2** rob. *~ pandang(an)* steal a glance. **men-²** do on the sly. **ke-an 1** experience a theft, be stolen from. *Ia ~ kudanya* Her horse was stolen. **2** theft. **-an** stolen goods. **pen-** thief. *~ hati* stealer of hearts. **pen-an 1** robbing. *~ paksa* armed robbery. **2** looting.

curiga suspicious, distrustful. *Meréka - akan menerima temannya itu* They were suspicious about receiving that friend of his. **men-i** suspect, distrust s.o. *Semua yg di-i ditangkap* All those suspected have been caught. **men-kan** arouse suspicion. *Jangan ~ karena gerakmu* Do not give yourself away through your movements. *Sikapnya yg ganjil itu ~ temannya* His strange attitude aroused his friend's suspicion. **ke-an** suspicion, distrust.

curu-curu diarrhea or dysentery.

curuk (*Jv*) waterfall.

cus sound of fizzing or sizzling (i.e. water poured on a fire).

cutbrai, cutbray see CELANA.

cuti leave, furlough. *Ia lagi -* She is on leave. *- darat* shore leave. *- dinas* official leave. *- tahunan* annual leave. **ber-** be on leave. *Ia pergi ~* He left on furlough.

cuwil see CUIL.

CV [*Commanditaire Vennootschap*] Limited Partnership.

D

d /dé/ d, the 4th letter of the alphabet.

D. [*danau*] lake.

D-1 [*diploma satu*] o.-year diploma program.

D-2 [*diploma dua*] two-year diploma program.

D-3 [*diploma tiga*] three-year diploma program.

d.a. [*dgn alamat*] c/o., in care of.

da₁ (*Ch*) at, on, in.

da₂, daa, daag /da:, da:kh/ (*Coll.*) goodbye.

dab men- dub a film. **pen-an** dubbing.

dabing dubbing.

dabung (*Lit.*) **ber-, men-** file teeth (for aesthetic or religious reasons).

dabus see DEBUS₂.

dacin, dacing k.o. portable balanced scale. **men-** weigh items with such a scale.

dada 1 chest, thorax. *- bidang* broad-chested. *- burung/manuk* pigeon-chested. **2** bosom. *Ini -ku! Mana -mu?* This is my chest. Where is yours? (I dare you to fight.). *- lapang* passive, phlegmatic. *- lega* relieved, have burden lifted from o.'s chest. *-nya lega stl membaca surat itu* She was relieved after reading the letter. **ber-²an** fight hand to hand.

dadah₁ medicine, medicinal herb. **pe-** (*Lit.*) container for such herbs.

dadah₂ (*Coll.*) wave goodbye, bye-bye.

dadak men- sudden. *serangan yg ~* sudden attack. *Hujan turun dgn ~* It suddenly began to rain. *Makannya ~ terhenti* She suddenly stopped eating. *keperluan ~* s.t. that suddenly comes up and requires immediate attention. ~ *sontak* very suddenly. **-an** (*Jv*) all of a sudden. **pen-an** (*Mil.*) surprise attack.

dadal fall down or burst apart (as of dike or dam).

dadap flowering trees of *Erythrina* spp. *si - dan si Waru* John Doe and Joe Blow (terms used to avoid referents' real names).

dadar 1 fry a mixture spread into a pan. *kué* - k.o. pancakelike cake. **2** omelette. - *kécap* sweet soy-sauce-flavored omelette. **men-** make an omelette of. *Telurnya di- saja* Just make an omelette of the eggs.

dadih (*Lit.*) fermented water buffalo milk. - *darah* coagulated blood. - *kerang* butter. **men-kan** condense a liquid. *~ latéks* cause latex to coagulate. **pen-** fermenting agent that causes coagulation. **pen-an** process of coagulating.

dadu₁ 1 dice. - *putar* roulette. **2** cube. **ber-** shoot dice.

dadu₂ pink, light brownish-red. *pipi berwarna - pink cheeks*.

daduh, dadung₁ (*Lit.*) **ber-** sing a lullaby. **men-(kan)** sing s.o. to sleep.

dadung₂ (*Jv, Sd, Naut.*) hawser. - *kapal* moorings.

daéng (*Makassar*) **1** title of rank in S. Sulawesi. **2** respectful term of address for pedicab drivers.

daérah 1 territory, esp. the size of a province. - *bahagian* component state. - *istiméwa* special (administrative) territory (Yogyakarta). - *khusus ibukota* municipality of Jkt. - *perwalian* trust territory. - *seberang* overseas territory. - *swapraja* self-governing unit. - *swatantra* local gvt. unit. - *takluk* dependency, possession. - *tatapraja* regional administration unit. **2** area, region. - *aliran sungai* river basin. - *antar* 1 inter-regional. **2** postal zone. - *bayang-bayang hujan* an area with high rainfall frequency. - *belakang* hinterland. - *bina* target area (in agricultural development, etc.). - *hawa panas* tropical zone. - *hawa sedang* temperate zone. - *hitam* crime-infested part of town or countryside. - *kantong* enclave. - *minus* depressed area. - *mérah* a region strongly pro-Communist. - *pasang surut* tidal area. - *pedaluman* hinterland. - *penangkapan* fishing grounds. - *pengaruh* sphere of influence. - *penyangga* buffer zone. - *penerjunan* (*Mil.*) drop zone. - *plus* surplus-food-producing area. - *singgahan* staging area. - *tdk bertuan* no man's land. **3** outlying district. **se-** from the same region. *Kami asal ~* We come from the same area. **sese-** a certain local region. *Jangan gunakan ukuran ~* Do not use a standard of just a certain region. **per-an, ke-an** pertaining to a certain region. *rasa ~* a feeling of regionalism.

daérahisme provincialism.

daftar 1 list, roster. **2** (*Pol.*) slate. - *abjad* alphabetical list. - *absénsi* roster. - *darab* multiplication table. - *gaji* payroll. - *hadir* roll, roster. - *hitam* blacklist s.o. **men-hitamkan** blacklist. - *induk* master list. - *isi* table of contents. - *kali-kali(an)* multiplication table. - *kartu* card index. - *kata* glossary, wordlist. - *kelahiran* registry of births. - *kematian* mortality table. - *logaritma* logarithmic table. - *makanan* menu. - *muatan* waybill. - *pasang surut* tide table. - *penunjuk* index. - *perjalanan* schedule, timetable. - *pertanyaan* 1 questionnaire. **2** application form. - *presénsi* roster. - *pustaka* bibliography. - *sérep* waiting list. - *usaha* program, schedule. **men-** register s.o. or s.t. *Penduduk di daérah ini sdh di-* The inhabitants of this area have been registered. **men-i** make a list of many items, register a large number. *Rakyat di daérah itu di-i* They registered the people of that region. **men-kan 1** register, record s.t. **2** enroll, enlist s.o. *Saya ~ diri di kantor administrasi* I registered at the administration office. **ter-** registered, enrolled. *surat ~* a certified or registered letter. **-an** list. **pen-** registrar, recorder. **pen-an 1** process of registration. **2** registry.

daga₁ (*M*) resistance, civil unrest. **--dagi** civil disorder.

daga₂ see DAHAGA₁.

dagang₁ from outside the region. *anak/org -* a person not originally from a certain place. **ber-** (*Lit.*) travel far from home.

dagang₂ trade, commerce. - *gelap* smuggling trade. - *sapi* (*Pol.*) make a political deal (in apportioning cabinet seats, etc.), horse trade. - *transito* transit trade. **ber-** trade, deal, barter. **memper-kan, men-kan** trade in s.t. *Kami dilarang ~ pérak* We are forbidden to deal in silver. *tdk diper-kan* not in the trade, for private circulation. **-an** merchandise, wares. **pe-** trader, merchant. *~ keliling* traveling salesman. **per-an** trade, commerce. *~ sapi* (*Pol.*) horse-trading.

dagang₃ **men-** carry on shoulder. **-an** load on shoulder. **pen-** carrying pole.

dag-dig-dug sensation of rapid heartbeat (caused by fear, anxiety, etc.). *Jantungnya -* His heart was throbbing. *Kaum pejabat merasa -* The authorities were greatly concerned.

dagel **men-** joke, clown about. **-an 1** joking, clowning. **2** short humorous skit.

dagi see DAHAGI.

daging 1 meat. - *asap* smoked meat. - *awét* preserved meat. - *has* sirloin. - *mati* (*Isl.*) meat of an animal not ritually slaughtered. **2** flesh. *Salak hanya dimakan - buahnya* You only eat the flesh of salak fruits. - *buah* pulp. - *kain* unprocessed material to be woven into cloth. - *kancing* muscle. - *menémpél* calloused wart. - *mentah* 1 raw meat. **2** (*Sl.*) prostitute. - *tumbuh* wart. **ber- 1** fat, plump. **2** wealthy, well-to-do. **men- 1** become flesh or meat. **2** begin to heal and become flesh (of wound). *~ ayam* firm of flesh (of durian). **3** regain o.'s weight (after illness). **ter- 1** sliced into the flesh. **2** hurt s.o.'s feelings, cut to the quick. **ke-an** having to do with the flesh. **pen-an** bringing s.t. to realization. *~ dr nafsu-nafsu dan keinginan-keinginan* materialization of desires and wants.

dagu chin.

dah₁ see DÉH.

dah₂ see DA₂.

dah₃ see SUDAH.
dahaga₁ thirst. **ber-** thirst. **men-kan** thirst for s.t. ~ *pendidikan* thirst for an education. **ke-an** thirstiness.
dahaga₂ 1 opposition. - *dahagi* various k.o. opposition or resistance. 2 subordination. **men-** be in opposition, be insubordinate.
dahagi oppose orders.
dahak phlegm, sputum. **ber-, men-** expectorate, cough up and spit out phlegm.
daham see DEHAM.
dahan bough, branch.
dahar (*Jv*) eat (referring to respected person).
dahi forehead, brow. - *layar* wood attached to mast to strengthen sail. - *sehari bulan* well-shaped forehead.
dahlia dahlia.
dahsat, dahsyat 1 horrifying, terrifying. *Dentuman meriam* - The rumbling of the cannons was dreadful. 2 awe-inspiring, imposing. *Di New York banyak gedung yg* - There are many enormous buildings in New York. **men-** get worse, become terrifying. *Angin taufan itu makin* ~ The typhoon became more and more terrifying. **memper-, men-kan** terrify. *Pertumpahan darah itu* ~ *hati saya* The bloodshed terrified me. **ke-an** awesomeness.
dahulu (*Lit.*) previous. **- men-(i)** try to surpass e.o. **men-i** 1 precede s.t. or s.o. *Dia* ~ *waktu yg sdh ditentukan* He did it ahead of the determined time. *Suaminya* ~ *isterinya ke alam baka* The husband preceded his wife to the life everlasting. 2 pass by s.o. **men-kan** give precedence to. *Kakék mesti di-kan* We must give precedence to Grandfather. **ter-** 1 first. 2 earlier. **ke-an** 1 be the first. *Aku* ~ *mengangguk* I happened to be the first to nod. 2 preliminaries. *pemeriksaan* ~ preliminary investigation. **pen-** predecessor, pioneer, first comer. **pen-an** preface, introduction.
dahyang (*Jv*) guardian spirit.
dai /da'i/ (*Isl.*) 1 proselytizer. 2 revival mullah.
daidan (*Japanese*) battalion.
daidancho, daidanco (*Japanese*) battalion commander.
daif /da'if/ 1 weak, powerless. *Alasannya itu* - His argument is weak. *Abdi tuan yg* - Your humble servant. 2 incompetent. *Ia* - *menandatangani surat itu karena ia mabuk* He is not competent to sign that letter because he is intoxicated. **men-kan** 1 weaken s.o. 2 consider s.o. weak or incompetent. *Jangan* ~ *org miskin* Do not look down on poor persons. **ke-an** 1 weakness. ~ *alasannya* weakness of her argument. 2 contempt, scorn. 3 humbleness.
daim (*Isl.*) eternal, enduring.
daing dried fish or meat.
dajal 1 (*Isl.*) a being of the days preceding the Last Judgment who tempts humans to evil, esp. licentious activities. 2 (*Isl.*) irreligious person who tempts others to be antireligious and licentious. 3 liar, deceiver. 4 (*Coll. Christian usage*) k.o. devil.
dak₁ see TIDAK.

dak₂ /dak/ (*Coll.*) roof.
dak₃ sound of s.t. exploding.
dakap see DEKAP₁.
dakar₁ stubborn, obstinate, hardheaded.
dakar₂ see ZAKAR.
dakep see DEKAP₁.
dakhil 1 inner life. 2 intimate. *Persahabatan meréka* - *benar* They are on very intimate terms.
daki₁ grime, esp. on o.'s body. - *dunia* filthy lucre. **ber-** begrimed, filthy.
daki₂ **men-** climb (hill, mountain). *jalan* ~ an ascending road. *Matahari* ~ The sun is getting higher in the sky. **men-kan** cause to climb. *Ia* ~ *keranya ke atas pohon* He had his monkey climb a tree. **-an** slope, incline. **pen-** climber. ~ *gunung* mountain climber. **pen-an** 1 pass, defile. ~ *Khyber* Khyber Pass. 2 path or steps up which o. climbs. 3 climbing.
dakocan, dakocang 1 k.o. black inflatable doll. 2 defamatory nickname for Malaysia (1960s).
dakon game played on board with depressions to be filled with cowrie shells.
dakron Dacron.
daksa 1 skilled, able. 2 proper.
daksina (*Lit.*) 1 right side. 2 south.
daktiloskopi dactylography.
daktur see REDAKTUR.
daku (*Lit.*) me. *Tolonglah* - Help me. **men-** claim as o.'s own. *Ia suka* ~ *karangan mahasiswanya* He often claims that his students' compositions are his own.
dakwa charge, accusation, indictment. **--dakwi** mutual recriminations, esp. about land and contracts. **ber-** litigate. *Ia sedang* ~ He is engaged in litigation. **men-** 1 accuse, charge. *Ia* ~ *saya mencuri* She accused me of stealing. 2 sue. **men-i** claim, lay claim to. ~ *hak-haknya* claim o.'s rights. **men-kan, memper-kan** indict, bring to court. **ter-** defendant, the accused. **-an** accusation. **pen-** plaintiff, complainant, accuser. **pen-an** 1 indictment. 2 charge, accusation, complaint.
dakwah religious proselytizing, missionary endeavor. **me-kan** missionize, proselytize, propagate (the faith). **pen-** proselytizer, missionary.
dal (*Jv*) 5th in series of eight years.
dalal 1 go-between, intermediary. 2 agent, broker.
dalam 1 interior, inside. *Banyak tamu di* - *rumah* There are a lot of guests in the house. - *hati* to o.s., in o.'s own mind. *membaca* - *hati* read to o.s. - *negeri* 1 domestic, internal. *produksi* - *negeri* domestic production. 2 inland, interior. *Départemén* - *Negeri* Department of Internal Affairs. *di* - *rumah* inside the house. 2 in, within. - *sejam kita akan sampai di Jkt* We will reach Jkt in an hour. - *tidur* while sleeping. - *pd itu* in the meantime. - meanwhile, at that time. *Bekerjalah keras, tetapi* - *pd itu keséhatan hrs selalu dijaga* Work hard, but meanwhile always take care of your health. 3 deep. *Samudera itu sangat* - That ocean is very deep. *pengetahuan yg* - profound knowledge. 4 thoughtful, serious, deep. **-²** very deep. *Ia membungkuk* ~ She bowed deeply. **-nya** depth. ~

sungai dua puluh méter The river's depth is 20 meters. **ber-²** grow worse, worsen. *Perselisihan itu ~* The quarrel worsened. **men- 1** become deep, going deep. *Akibat aliran air yg deras saluran itu ~* Because of the rushing water, the ditch deepened. *pengetahuan yg ~* a profound knowledge. **2** sink in, penetrate (of problem, idea, etc.). *Kebudayaan Hindu sangat ~ di Indonésia* Hindu culture is very deeply rooted in Indonesia. **3** deepen, intensify (of illness, etc.). *Malam ~* The evening deepened. **men-i 1** deepen o.'s understanding, penetrate. *~ ilmu bintang* steep o.s. in astronomy. **2** obtain a deep understanding of. *Ia dpt ~ hati wanita* She can understand a woman's mind. **memper-, men-kan 1** deepen (ditch, etc.). *~ sumur* deepen a well. **2** deepen, broaden (o.'s knowledge, etc.). *Ia merasa perlu ~ ilmu silat* He feels the need to broaden his knowledge of the art of self-defense. *~ persoalan* make a problem more complicated. **ke-an** depth, profundity. **pe-an** hinterland, interior, back country. **pen-an** deepening of s.t. *~ prosés Islamisasi* intensification of the process of Islamization.

dalang 1 narrator and puppeteer of traditional shadow plays. **2** mastermind, power behind the scenes. *Siapa - komplotan itu?* Who is the mastermind behind that plot? **ber-, men-** perform a shadow play. **men-i** mastermind, manipulate. *Ia dituduh ~ pemberontakan itu* He was accused of masterminding the rebellion. **men-kan 1** manipulate the puppets (in shadow play). **2** mastermind, pull the strings. **pe-an 1** narration by a *dalang.* **2** shadow play puppetry.

dalem₁ (*Jv*) **1** residence of high official, palace of king. **2** title for person who possesses such a residence.

dalem₂ see DALAM.

dalfin dolphin.

dalih excuse, pretext. **ber- 1** seek an excuse. **2** equivocate, quibble. **ber-²an** express mutual recriminations. *Meréka ~ mengenai kerugian meréka* They blamed e.o. for their losses. **ber-kan** be evasive or equivocate about s.t. *~ ibunya sakit, ia tdk datang ke rapat* Claiming his mother was ill, he did not attend the meeting. **men-** say s.t. as an excuse. *Dia ~ menyalahkan situasi* He claimed that the situation was at fault. **men-kan** make s.t. an excuse. *Ia selalu ~ cacat tubuhnya* He always blames things on his disability.

dalil 1 (*Isl.*) argumentation. *- akali* rational argumentation. *- naqli* argumentation by reference to relevant passages of the Koran. **2** proposition, theorem. *- lancung* (false) syllogism. *- Arkhimédés* Archimedes' Theorem. **ber-** valid, well founded. *tak ~* groundless, unfounded. **men-kan 1** elucidate, set forth an opinion. *spt di-kan pemuka-pemuka* as postulated by the leaders. **2** defend an opinion. **pen-** o. who argues in favor of a certain theory. **pen-an** basing o.s. on, setting forth evidence. **per-an** proof.

dalu (*Jv, Sd, Jkt*) ripe.

Dalu (*Zod.*) Aquarius.

daluwarsa 1 overdue, expired. *Perjanjian itu sdh -* That agreement is long overdue. **2** expiration date (of food products). **ke- 1** expired, too old. *Céknya sdh ~. Tdk bisa ditunaikan lagi* The check has expired. You cannot cash it any longer. **2** expired through the statute of limitations. *waktu ~* expiration date, statute of limitations.

dam₁ 1 checkers. **2** checkered (design).

dam₂ sound of thump of drum.

dam₃ (*Ch*) greedy. *- ciak* gluttonous.

dam₄ dam.

damai peace, tranquillity. *harga -* reasonable price. **ber- 1** be peaceful, be on good terms. **2** make peace, come to an agreement. *Kedua negeri itu tlh ~* The two countries have come to terms. *Meréka ~ ttg itu* They reached an agreement on that. **memper-kan, men-kan 1** resolve peacefully. *~ kedua negeri itu* bring peace between the two countries. **2** reconcile, bring to terms. *~ pendirian meréka* reconcile their stands. **ter-kan** reconcilable. **ke-an** peacefulness, tranquillity. *~ hati* peace of mind. **pen-** peacemaker. **per-an** peace, reconciliation.

damak blowpipe dart.

daman (*Naut.*) sheet (of large sail).

damar 1 resin of certain trees collected as an article of trade. *- batu* hard resin. **2** resin torch. **3** oil lamp. **ber- 1** collect resin. **2** use resin. **men-** collect resin. **men-i 1** apply resin to s.t. (violin string, pottery surfaces, etc.). *Tukangnya ~ bagian luar belanga itu* The potter applied resin to the surface of the cooking vessel. **2** illuminate (with a torch). **pen-** resin collector. **pen-an 1** forest area with a concentration of resin bearing trees. **2** resin collecting. **3** torch or taper using resin fuel.

damast damask.

damba long, yearn. *Saya - pdnya* I miss him. **men-kan** long for, crave. *Ia ~ kedudukan yg paling tinggi* He coveted the highest position. **ke-an** longing, yearning. **-an** s.t. longed for. *bayi ~* yearned-for baby. *~ hati kami* what we have been longing for. **per-an, pen-an** desire.

damban see LAMBAN.

dambin sound of thud, plop, or thump. *--dambun* sound of a series of thuds. **ber-** (make a) thud or plop. *Batu besar jatuh ~ di tanah* A large rock fell on the ground with a thud.

dambun sound of sonorous thud. **ber-²** repeated booming. *~nya bedug mesjid* the booming of the mosque drum.

damé see DAMAI.

damén (*Jv*) rice straw.

dami see DAMAI.

damir symbol in Arabic script to indicate closed syllable.

dampak impact. *mempunyai - bagi lingkungan* has an impact on the environment. **men-** bump into, collide with. *Sepédanya ~ mobil saya* Her bicycle collided with my car.

dampar **men- 1** cast s.t. ashore. *Meréka ~ perahu meréka di suatu pulau kecil* They cast ashore on a small island. **2** break (of nerves). **men-kan**

1 wash ashore, cause to go aground. *Gulungan ombak tlh ~ perahu itu pd batu karang* The waves cast the boat up on a coral reef. **2** beach (boat etc.). **ter- 1** gone aground, cast ashore. *Kapal itu ~ pd karang itu* The ship went aground on a coral reef. *Sisa-sisa kapal itu ~ ke pantai* The wreckage of the ship was cast onto the beach. **2** dumped off at, (inadvertently) located at. *Dlm pengembaraanku di dunia ini aku ~ di pojok kota Jkt* In my travels in the world, I found myself in a corner of Jkt.

damping close, near. *keluarga yg -* a close family. *sahabat -* an intimate friend. **se-²nya** most closely related or located. **ber-(an)** contiguous, side by side. *duduk ~* sit side by side. **men-i 1** accompany. **2** flank, stand beside (esp. of o.'s spouse). **3** closely assist s.o. *Wakil présidén ~ présidén* The vice-president worked closely with the president. **men-kan** move s.t. or s.o. close. *Tukang foto ~ kedua pengantin* The photographer moved the newlyweds close together. **ke-an** closeness. *~nya kpd keluarganya mengharukan* Her closeness to her family is touching. **pen-** associate, colleague. *~ menteri* the right-hand man of the minister. *~ hidup* spouse (lifelong companion). **pen-an** assistance.

damprat abuse, scolding. **men-(i)** verbally abuse. *Siapa yg kau-/kau-i?* Who are you scolding? **men-kan** pour (o.'s anger, bitterness, etc.) out. **-an** scolding, verbal abuse.

Damsyik Damascus.

dan₁ and.

dan₂ particle requesting confirmation, right? *Dia punya minat -* She is interested, right?

dan₃ (*Sport*) ranking. *Karatéka - 4* s.o. at the fourth level of skill in karate.

dana 1 donation. **2** fund. *- bantuan* assistance funds. *- piatu perang* war orphan fund. **ber-** donate. *Ia suka ~* She likes to donate. **men-kan** donate s.t. **ke-an** matters pertaining to funds. *Yayasan itu mengadakan hari ~* The foundation organized a drive. **pen-an** funding, financing. *Porkas tdk hanya utk menyelenggarakan ~ olahraga* The *porkas* lottery is not only for the financing of sports.

danau lake.

danawa ogre.

dandan₁ grooming, personal embellishment. **ber- 1** dress up, get dressed. *Ia ~ indah* She was beautifully attired. **2** decorated, made elaborate. *Karangannya ~ kata-kata yg indah* His article was adorned with beautiful words. **men-i 1** dress s.o. *Pengantin itu di-i ibunya* Her mother dressed the bride. **2** equip. *Para kelasi ~ kapal selam itu* The sailors equipped the submarine. **3** repair. *Tukang jam ~ arloji saya* The repairman fixed my watch. **-an 1** clothing, outfit. **2** makeup, adornment. **3** equipment.

dandan₂ (*Lit.*) additional platform on a ship's deck.

dandang₁ large metal vessel for steaming rice.

dandang₂ (*Lit.*) cormorant.

dandi 1 (*Lit.*) k.o. drum. **2** (*Bib.*) k.o. lyre.

dang (*Lit.*) title for female nobility.

dangai k.o. cake.

dangau₁ loom up.

dangau₂ small temporary hut in agricultural fields.

dang dang dut, dangdut 1 beating of drums (in Indian movies). **2** popular music with strong beat reminiscent of Hindi and Arabic music. **3** dance to such music. **ber-** dance to such music. **per-an** matters pertaining to such music and dance.

dangir (*Jv*) **men-(i)** hoe before planting. **pen-1** o. who hoes. **2** hoeing equipment.

dangkal 1 shallow. **2** superficial (of knowledge, etc.). **memper-** make shallow. *Érosi ~ pelabuhan di muara itu* Erosion has made the river mouth anchorage shallow. **men-kan 1** make shallow. **2** consider superficial. *~ téori* consider a theory superficial. **ke-an** shallowness, superficiality. **-an** shoal, shallows. **pen-an 1** silting up (of river, etc.). **2** trivialization, process of making s.t. superficial. *~ sosialisme* the trivialization of socialist principles.

dangkung k.o. leprosy.

dangsa see DANSA.

danguk ber-, men-, ter- sit with chin in hands and stare.

Danramil [*Komandan Rayon Militer*] commander of the army administrative unit at the level of the *camat* .

dansa Western-style dancing. *- pergaulan* social dancing. *- dansi* various k.o. Western-style dancing. **ber-** dance (Western style). **men-kan** dance a certain k.o. dance.

dansanak (*M*) relative, kin. *- bapak/ibu* cousin. **ber-** be related.

dansi see DANSA.

danta (*Lit.*) elephant tusk, ivory.

Danu, Danuh (*Zod.*) Sagittarius.

dapat 1 can, be able. *Ia - membaca* He can read. *- mengemudi mobil* be able to drive a car. *- dibalik* reversible. *- larut* soluble. *Tak - tdk* 1 it cannot be avoided. **2** without fail. *Tak - tdk dialah yg bersalah* It cannot help but be his fault. **2** may. *-kah saya datang?* May I come? **3** get, obtain. *- kenaikan pangkat* get a promotion. *Aku harap kau - jawaban yg menyenangkan* I hope you will have a favorable reply. *- angin* get the opportunity. *- penghinaan* be humiliated. *- hati* 1 take courage. 2 be happy with, like. 3 have o.'s way. *- malu* be embarrassed. **4** be obtained. *Tikétnya sdh - blm?* Have you gotten the ticket yet or not? **5** be found, be met with. *Walaupun diperiksa seteliti-telitinya, kesalahan dlm buku masih tak - juga* Although the ledger was checked thoroughly, the mistake still could not be found. *-pun . . . takkan* even though . . . will not. *-pun demikian, takkan saya berubah pendirian saya* Even though that is the case, I will not change my stand. **se-** upon receiving. *~ surat ini* upon receipt of this letter. **se-(²)nya** as much as o. is capable of. *Kerjakanlah ~* Do what you can.

ber-an meet e.o. **men-** 1 get, receive. ~ *teguran* get a reprimand. ~ *kabar* receive news. ~ *kain kotor* menstruate. ~ *nama* become famous, acquire a name for o.s. 2 find, come across. ~ *kecelakaan* meet with an accident. ~ *rezeki* have success or luck. 3 meet, see. *Ia* ~ *dia di rumahnya* He met her at her house. **men-i** 1 find, discover. *Polisi* ~ *béngkél pemalsu uang* Police found the counterfeiter's workshop. 2 unexpectedly meet up with. *Ia* ~ *adiknya di stasiun* He met his brother at the station. ~ *kesialan* run into misfortune. **men-kan** 1 procure, obtain. *Ia* ~ *pekerjaan bagi saya* He got me a job. 2 visit, meet, go to where s.o. else is. ~ *anaknya di rumah sakit* visit o.'s child at the hospital. ~ *Tuan Ali* to Mr. Ali (in a letter). ~ *kesusahan* meet with sadness (death in family, etc.). ~ *diri* repent, realize o.'s wrongs. 3 discover, invent. *Edison* ~ *lampu listrik* Edison invented the electric light. 4 shortly before, coming up on. ~ *jam lima* shortly before five o'clock. **memper-** obtain, get. ~ *persetujuan stl lama berunding* reach an agreement after long negotiations. **ter-** be found, exist. *Kera tak* ~ *di Kanada* The monkey is not found in Canada. ~ *tiga faktor* There are three factors. **keter-an** occurrence. **ke-an** be found, be uncovered as. *Pencuri itu* ~ *oléh polisi* The thief was found by the police. *Ia* ~ *menerima suap* He was discovered to have taken bribes. **pen-** opinion, judgment. *Pd* ~ *saya* in my opinion. **sepen-** of the same opinion. **berpen-** be of a certain opinion. **pen-an** 1 income, earnings. ~ *bulanan* monthly earnings. 2 yield, output. ~ *sawah* yield of wet rice fields. ~ *ikan* catch of fish. 3 (*Math.*) product, result, solution.

daptar see DAFTAR.
dapur 1 kitchen, galley. 2 stove, kiln. - *arak* distillery, still. - *batu* brick kiln. - *kapur* lime kiln. - *leburan* blast furnace. - *matahari* solar oven. - *pemanas listrik* hot plate. - *pengering* drying kiln. - *tinggi* blast furnace. - *tukang besi* forge. 3 firebox (in furnace, locomotive). 4 (*Coll.*) place where s.t. other than food is cooked up. - *koran* place journalists write up their reports. -² ~ *bahu* (*Anat.*) thoracic cavity. **pen-an** furnace. **per-an, ke-an** culinary matters. *profési* ~ culinary profession.
dar sound of loud crash or explosion. --*dir-dor* sound of firecrackers or shooting. --*dor/dur* repeated booming (of cannon, heavy artillery).
dara₁ virgin, young girl. - *sunti* young, preadolescent girl. - *tua* spinster. **per-an** (*Med.*) virginity.
dara₂ see BURUNG.
darab (*Math.*) multiplication. **men-** multiply. **pen-** multiplier.
darah blood. - *daging* 1 blood relative, o.'s flesh and blood. 2 2d nature. *Kebiasaan itu tlh menjadi - dagingnya* That habit has become 2d nature for him. 3 o.'s mortal existence. *Marilah membéla tanah air kita dgn - daging kita* Let us defend our country with our lives. **men-** *daging* 1 be a blood relative. 2 be 2d nature, be thoroughly incul-

cated. ~ *daging sumsum* deeply rooted, ingrained. **men-dagingkan** make part and parcel of. **pen-dagingan** process of inculcation. - *dingin* phlegmatic, imperturbable. - *hidup* fresh blood. - *jernih* of noble blood. - *kental* gore. - *kotor* menstrual blood. - *lintah* thick and sticky. *Kopi itu spt - lintah saja* That coffee is too thick. - *mati* congealed blood. - *nifas* (*Med.*) 1 postnatal hemorrhage. 2 afterbirth. - *panas* hotheaded. - *putih* of noble descent, blue-blooded, well born. - *tinggi* high blood pressure. **ber-** 1 bleed. *Hidungnya* ~ His nose is bleeding. 2 be of a certain ethnic background, be of a certain tendency. *Ia* ~ *Tionghoa* She has Chi blood. ~ *dagang* have business in o.'s blood. 3 bloody, gory. *Pakaiannya itu* ~ His clothing is bloody. **men-** be like blood, become dark red. **men-i** smear s.t. with blood. **pen-an** bleeding, hemorrhaging. ~ *dlm* internal bleeding, hemorrhaging. ~ *otak* cerebral hemorrhage.
darajat see DERAJAH.
daras men- 1 (*Isl.*) recite the Koran. 2 study, investigate deeply. **pen-an** 1 study. 2 reading of the Koran.
darat 1 land, shore. - *pokok* mainland. 2 upland, hinterland. **men-** 1 land, reach the shore. *Penumpang perahu itu* ~ *di pantai* The boat passengers got off at the beach. *Pesawatnya* ~ *di lapangan udara* The plane landed on the airfield. 2 go inland. 3 (*Tel.*) sign off. **men-i** land on s.t. *Org blm pernah* ~ *pulau ini* Nobody has ever set foot on this island. **men-kan** 1 put ashore. *Kapal itu* ~ *muatannya* The ship put its cargo ashore. 2 cause s.t. to land. ~ *kapal ruang angkasa di bulan* land a spaceship on the moon. **-an** 1 mainland. 2 landing. **pen-an** 1 landing, disembarkation. ~ *darurat* emergency force landing. ~ *empuk* soft landing. 2 dock, pier.
dari 1 from. *Ia datang - Indonésia* She comes from Indonesia. *menerima surat - isteri* receive a letter from o.'s wife. - *mana* 1 from where, whence. - *mana dia datang?* Where does she come from? - *mana tahu?* How do you know? 2 Who's calling? *dibuat/terbuat - pérak* made of silver. - *hal* about, concerning. - *hal soal ini* concerning this matter. - *itu* for that reason, therefore. *Saya lapar, - itu saya mau makan* I am hungry, therefore I want to eat. 2 (*Coll.*) of. 3 out of (a series). *Sabun ini dipakai oléh sembilan - sepuluh bintang pilem* This soap is used by nine out of 10 movie stars. 4 starting at or from. - *pagi hingga malam* from morning to evening. - *tadi* for some time. 5 than. *Dia lebih besar - kamu* She is bigger than you. **se-** since. ~ *masa kecilnya ia sakit saja* He has been sickly since childhood.
daripada 1 (*Lit.*) from. *dibuat -* made of. *Méja itu dibuat* ~ *kayu* That table is made of wood. 2 than. *Ia lebih pandai* ~ *saya* He is smarter than I am. 3 better than. - *tdk ada* (So-and-so) is better than nothing.
darma (*Lit.*) 1 duty, obligation. 2 service, good deed. - *warga* civic mission.

darmabakti volunteer work, service of value to the state. **ber-** perform a volunteer service. **men-kan** give o.'s services to a cause. ~ *kepandaian pd negara* devote o.'s knowledge to the nation.

darmasiswa (*Lit.*) student scholarship, fellowship.

darmatamu (*Lit.*) leadership grant.

darmawisata 1 excursion, outing. **2** field trip. **ber-** go on an excursion.

darmawisatawan excursionist.

darsana, darsono see JAMBU.

daru-daru k.o. tree used for commercial timber.

Darulbaka (*Isl.*) The hereafter.

Darulfana (*Isl.*) present transitory world.

darun se- in unison. *"Pembohong!" meréka berteriak* ~ *"Liar!"* they shouted in unison.

darurat emergency. *Dlm keadaan - panggillah polisi* In an emergency call the police. *Negara ada dlm keadaan -* The country is in a state of emergency. *jembatan -* temporary bridge.

darus see DARAS.

Darusalam 1 Jerusalem. **2** (*Lit.*) abode of happiness.

darwis dervish, fakir.

das boom (of gun), bang (of gun).

dasa- (*Lit.*) in intervals of 10.

dasadarma the 10 duties of Indonesian Boy Scouts.

dasalomba decathlon.

dasar 1 base, foundation. *- rumah* house foundation or floor. *- laut/samudera* bottom of the sea. *- sungai* riverbed. *- tengkorak* (*Anat.*) base of the skull. **2** basis. *Itu bertentangan dgn - démokrasi* That is contrary to democratic principles. *Saling hormat-menghormati adalah - persahabatan* Mutual respect is the basis of friendship. *- bunga/perbungaan* (*Fin.*) rate of interest. *- timbal-balik* principle of reciprocity. **3** nature. *kepandaian -* natural aptitude. *Itu mémang sdh -nya* That is really the way she is. *pd -nya* basically, by its nature. *Pd -nya ia org baik* Basically he is a good person. *- mudasir* through and through by nature. *- mudasir anak tolol* He was born stupid, and that is the way he will always be. **4** (so-and-so) is like that because that is the way people of his or her type are. *Yah, - laki-laki!* Hmph! That is just like a man! *- dosén selalu mengira pintar sendiri* Just like a university professor, he always thinks he knows best. *- pelancongan* nothing but a drifter. **5** background. *- lukisan itu biru* The background of the painting is blue. *- panji* field of a banner or flag. **ber- 1** have a basis. *Pendapatnya itu sama sekali tak* ~ His view has no basis whatever. **2** have as a background. *Baju* ~ *mérah* Her blouse has a red background. **ber-kan** be based on. *Negara kita* ~ *asas démokrasi* Our country is based on the principles of democracy. **men- 1** be basic, going on the basis of. *Pendidikan vokal* ~ Vocal training starts with the basics. *sikap kritis yg* ~ a critical attitude that deals with the basics. *perbédaan yg* ~ basic difference. **2** display, spread out (goods). *Penjual itu* ~ *contoh barang-*

barang baru The salesman displayed samples of his new wares. **men-i** serve as a basis for s.t. *Gagasan itu* ~ *malam sastra* That idea provided the basis for a literary evening. ~ *gugatannya* provide a basis for his lawsuit. **men-kan** base s.t. on s.t. *Ia* ~ *dakwaanya itu atas hasil penyelidikannya* He based his accusation on the result of his investigation. **pen-** thing that stands as base. *Suatu téater remaja mendadak menjadi* ~ *konsépsi baru ttg téater* A youth theater suddenly became the basis of a new concept of theater. **pen-an** action of basing on. ~ *téologis* basing s.t. on theological grounds.

dasariah basic.

dasasila the Ten Commandments.

dasawarsa decade, decennial.

dasi necktie. *- jepitan* clip-on tie. *- jerat* garotte. *- kupu-kupu* bow tie.

daster 1 house dress, lounging gown. **2** doctor's lab coat.

dasun (*Lit.*) k.o. garlic. *Hidungnya bagai - tunggal* He has a well-shaped nose (lit., like a clove of garlic).

Daswati [*Daérah Swatantra Tingkat*] autonomous administrative region (pre-1970s). *- I* province. *- II* regency or municipality.

data data. *- taksasi* appraisal data. **men-** encode for processing (on computer). **men-kan** collect data about s.t. **pen-an 1** data collection. **2** encoding for processing.

datang 1 come. *Dia - dua bulan yg lalu* He came two months ago. *- dr* come from. *minggu -* the coming week. **2** arrive. *- bulan/haid* menstruate. *yg akan -* next, future, coming. *minggu yg akan -* next week. *dua tahun yg akan -* two years hence. *Kapan sdr -?* When did you arrive? *- bertandang* pay a visit. **-² 1** upon arrival. **2** suddenly, all of a sudden. ~ *ia menyalahkan saya* All of a sudden, he threw the blame on me. **3** keep coming, come repeatedly. *Apa kerja org itu? Ia* ~ *saja kemari* What does that fellow want? He just keeps coming here. ~*lah lagi!* Continue to keep coming by! *tak* ~ never comes. **ber-** *sembah* approach respectfully. **ber-an** arrive (o. after another). *Sdh jam sepuluh tapi tamu-tamu masih* ~ *terus* It was already 10 but the guests kept coming. **- men-i** visit e.o. **men- 1** arrive, come. *Malam* ~ Night fell. **2** upcoming. *tgl dua puluh* ~ the coming 20th of the month. **3** occur, happen. *Hal itu* ~ *pd pikiran saya* It flashed across my mind. *Akibat yg* ~ *itu menginsyafkan dia akan kesalahannya* The resulting consequence made him realize his mistake. **men-i 1** visit, pay a call. *Polisi* ~ *kantornya* Policemen visited his office. *Ia* ~ *Garut pd tahun 1936* She visited Garut in 1936. **2** come to s.t. *Kampung di-i musuh* The enemy approached the village. **men-kan 1** cause to be brought in. *Polisi* ~*nya* The police had him brought in. ~ *bala bantuan* bring up reinforcements. **2** import. **3** bring about, cause. *Kelalaiannya itu* ~ *kerugian* Her negligence caused a loss. **ke-an 1** arrival. **2** be unexpectedly visited by s.o. *Saya* ~ *tamu* I had an unexpected visitor. **3** attacked, invaded. *Kota itu ~ musuh semalam* The city was attacked last night. **pen-** outsider, stranger. *~ baru* newcomer, new arrival.

datar 1 flat, level, smooth. *Permukaan laut itu -* The sea's surface is smooth. *Wajahnya -* Her face is flat. **2** superficial. *Pengetahuannya -* His knowledge is superficial. **men-** **1** be level. *Jalan itu ~* The road is level. **2** horizontal, across. *balok ~* crossbeam. **men-kan 1** level, (make) smooth. *~ tanah yg tak rata* make uneven land level. **2** ease (feelings). *Kabar itu ~ fikirannya* The news made her feel more at ease. **ke-an** being level. *~ tanah itu memudahkan pembangunan* The smoothness of the field made development easy. **-an** plain, level land. *~ rendah* lowland. *~ tinggi* upland, plateau. *~ kontinéntal* continental shelf. **pen-an** leveling, smoothing.

Dati [*Daérah Swatantra Tingkat*] autonomous administrative region.

datu (*in some regions only*) title of headman.

datuk 1 oldest male of family clan, headman. *Apa kabar, -?* How are you, sir? **2** grandfather (in some parts of Indonesia and Malaysia). *- nénék* ancestors. **3** honorific term of reference and address (for strangers, dangerous animals). **4** k.o. title for persons in certain high positions. *- bendahara* high-ranking Malay court official, grand vizier. **5** term of address to persons in high position, us. as *tuk* or *to*.

dauk 1 gray. **2** roan.

daulat (*Lit.*) **1** good fortune. **2** expression of deference to nobility. *-, tuanku!* Hail, milord! **ber- 1** sovereign, independent. *pemerintah yg ~* sovereign gvt. **2** become predominant. *Malam merangkak dan harum cempaka manis ~* The night slowly progressed and the sweet smell of the magnolia blossoms predominated. **men-1** spontaneously elect s.o. to position of authority. **2** (*Coll.*) force. *Dia ~ saya menyanyi* He forced me to sing. **men-i** become predominant over. *Malamnya wajah yg jelita itu ~ kenanganku* That night that beautiful face dominated my reveries. **men-kan 1** put s.o. in authority by popular acclaim. *~ diri* put o.s. in authority. *Kolonél itu tlh di-kan penduduk setempat* The local people put the colonel in authority. **2** appropriate, take over illegally. *Kaum pemberontak ~ harta benda penduduk* The rebels appropriated the property of the inhabitants. **3** oust s.o. by popular agreement. **ke-an** sovereignty. **-²an** (*Coll.*) passing the buck. **pen-an** ousting, firing, dismissal.

daun 1 leaf. *- bawang* leek. *- bunga* petal. *- hidup* touch-me-not. *- kaki kuda* k.o. vine with edible leaves planted on the sides of bunds to prevent erosion. *- lindung* calyx or sepal. *- penumpu* stipulate. *- penutup* sepal or calyx. *- salam* laurellike leaf used in cooking. **2** playing card. **3** blade or other flat thing. *- baling-baling* propeller blade. *- dayung* oar blade. *- gergaji* saw blade. *- jendéla* shutter, window leaf. *- kemudi* (*Naut.*) afterpiece of rudder. *- méja* table leaf. *- neraca* scales for

weighing. *- pedang* sword blade. *- pintu* door. *- rokok* cigarette paper. *- telinga* auricle of ear. **ber-** have leaves, be leafy. **men-** be like a leaf. **-²an** foliage, leaves.

daur 1 cycle (of years). *- besar* cycle of 120 years. *- kecil* cycle of eight years. **2** rotation. *- haid* menstrual cycle. *- ulang* recycling.

da'wa see DAKWA.

da'wah see DAKWAH.

dawai fine wire. **-²** strings (for musical instruments).

dawat, dawet₁ ink. *- cina* India ink.

dawet₂ cold drink made from rice or arrowroot flour, coconut milk and palm sugar.

dawuh (*Jv*) order, command.

daya₁ **1** power, energy, capacity. *Ia sdh habis segala -nya* She is at her wit's end. *- air* water power. *- angan* inspiration, inspirational force. *- angkat* lift, lifting capacity. *- antar* (*Elec.*) conductivity. *- apung* buoyancy. *- atom* atomic power. *- baca* reading capacity. *- bahar* degree to which s.t. can burn. *- baut* **1** psychic power. **2** inner strength. *- beli* purchasing power. *- berobah* changeability. *- bertahan* stamina. *- biak* procreative capacity. *- biaya* funding capacity. *- cahaya* illuminating power. *- capai* capacity for achievement. *- cengkeram* power to grip (e.g. tire). *- cerap* applicability. *- cerna* digestibility. *- cipta* **1** creativity. **2** imagination. *- dorong* **1** motivation, incentive. **2** (rocket) thrust. *- gaib* supernatural power or force. *- gerak* **1** mobility. **2** kinetic energy. *- guna* **1** efficiency. **2** usefulness. **ber-** *guna* efficient, useful. **men-gunakan** using s.t. efficiently. **ke-gunaan** efficiency, usefulness. **pen-gunaan** making efficient use of s.t. *pen-gunaan pegawai* making efficient use of the employees. *pen-gunaan pekarangan sbg salah satu usaha pertanian* making efficient use of backyard gardens as an effort to improve agriculture. *- hantar* (*Elec.*) conductivity. *- hasil* productivity. *- hembus* windpower. *- hidup* vitality. *- hisap* absorptive capacity. *- ikat* binding capacity. *- ikhtiar* initiative, drive. *- jangkau* projection capacity (of missiles). *- jelajah* cruising range or capacity. *- juang* fight, fighting spirit. *- kebal* immunity, resistance. *- kecambah* sprouting capacity. *- kembali/kenyal* resiliency, spring. *- kerja* work capacity, efficiency. *- khayal* imagination, imaginative power. *- kritis* critical ability. *- kuda* horsepower. *- laksana* feasibility. *- laku* validity. *- larut* solubility,. *- lekat* adhesiveness. *- lenting* flexibility. *- muai* power of expansion. *- muat(an)* load capacity. *- pakai* life span (of mechanical parts). *- paksa* capacity to force. *- pegas* elasticity. *- peka* sensitivity, sensitiveness. *- pemikat* capacity to appeal. *- penalaran* reasoning power. *- penarik* power of attraction, drawing power. *- penerimaan* receptivity. *- pengangkut* carrying capacity. *- pengantar* conductivity. *- penggerak* (*Phys.*) **1** motive power. **2** motivation. *- pengisap* absorptive capacity. *- penjiwa* power of inspiration. *- penyatu* power to unify. *- peramal* predictive power. *- perang* fighting capacity. *-*

perusak power to destroy. - *pikat/pukau* charm. - *pukul* (*Mil.*) striking power. - *rambat* reproductive power. - *regang/rentang* tensile strength. - *saing* competitive ability. - *serap* absorptive power. **ke-serapan** absorptiveness, absorptivity. - *serbu* striking power. - *surut* retroactive. *Peraturan ini berlaku dgn - surut hingga 1 Januari 1987* This regulation is retroactive to January 1, 1987. - *tahan* 1 durability, stamina, endurance. 2 resistant. - *tampung* capacity, accommodation. - *tanam* planting capacity. - *tanggapan* responsiveness. - *tangkis* ability to resist. - *tarik* 1 power of attraction. 2 gravitational force. - *témbak* (*Mil.*) fire power. - *tembus* transparency. - *tempuh* stamina. - *tempur* (*Mil.*) combat power. - *tenaga* energy capacity. - *terbang* cruising range (of flight). - *timbang* judgment. - *ungkapan* expressiveness. 2 effort. *Tiada berhasil segala -nya* All his efforts were unsuccessful. *Apa -?* What is to be done? - *upaya* all k.o. efforts. **se-upaya** utmost. *Ia berusaha ~* He does his utmost. **ber-**upaya* endeavor. *Indonésia ~ upaya spy mencapai kemakmuran* Indonesia is endeavoring to achieve prosperity. **men-upayakan** endeavor. - *usaha* enterprise, initiative, drive. **ber-** forceful, energetic. *tdk ~* powerless. **men-i** provide power. *~ kampanye pemilihan dgn penyediaan dana yg besar* give steam to the election campaign by providing large sums of money.

daya₂ trick, ruse. **men-(kan), memper-(kan)** deceive, trick. *Seorang pendéta yg murtad tlh ~ para wanita* An apostate minister deluded the women. **teper-** deceived, taken in. *Saya ~ karena kata-katanya yg manis itu* I was taken in by his sweet words. **pen-an** 1 deceit, trick. 2 way out, expedient. **per-an** ruse, stratagem.

daya₃ see BARAT.

dayah 1 foster mother. 2 wet nurse.

Dayak 1 native ethnic groups of Kalimantan. 2 (*Coll.*) American Indian.

dayang (*Lit.*) lady-in-waiting.

dayu men- rumble like distant thunder.

dayung 1 oar. 2 pedal (bicycle). **ber-** 1 row. 2 pedal (bicycle). **men-** 1 row s.t. *~ antara dua karang* between the devil and the deep blue sea (lit., row between two coral reefs). 2 pedal s.t. **pen-** 1 oarsman, rower. 2 oar.

db. [*di bawah*] below, under, beneath.

DB [*drum band*] marching band.

DBB [*daérah bébas bécak*] area in which pedicabs are not allowed to operate. **men-kan** clear pedicabs out of. *Jalan ini sdh di-kan* Pedicabs are no longer allowed to operate in this street.

dbp. [*di bawah pimpinan*] under the direction of (referring to bands).

debak sound of thud, esp. blow hitting the mark. **ber-** thud (of boxer's blows, collision in sports, etc.).

debam sound of heavy object falling with resonant thud (such as coconut falling to ground). **ber-** thud. *Buku itu ~ jatuh ke lantai* That book fell to the floor with a thud.

debap sound of object hitting ground.

debar sensation of pulse beat. - *jantung* pulse. **ber-** throb, beat, pulsate. **ber-²(an)** pound, beat rapidly. *Hatinya ~ ketakutan* Her heart pounded from fear. **men-kan** make the heart beat rapidly. *~ hati umat manusia* make the hearts of men pound. *adegan-adegan yg ~ anak tanggung* scenes that excite youth. *pendaratan yg ~* a heart-pounding landing. **-an** beat, throb. *~ jantung* heartbeat. **per-an** pulsating, palpitating.

débarkasi debarkation.

debas sound of exhaling.

débat debate, discussion. - *kusir* silly talk. **ber-(²)** debate, have heated discussions. *Meréka ~ selama dua jam* They debated for two hours. **men-** contradict, take issue with. *Meréka ~ pendapat saya* They took issue with my opinion. **memper-kan** debate s.t., argue about s.t. *~ soal ékonomi negara* argue about the national economy. **pen-** debater. **per-an** 1 debate, discussion. 2 subject of debate. *Lama juga bahan-bahan ini jadi ~* For some time these materials have become the subject of debate.

débét debit. **men-kan** debit s.t. **pen-an** debiting.

debik sound of a goat bleat. **ber-** bleat.

debil mentally retarded, psychologically unstable.

debing sound of light object falling.

débirokratisasi debureaucratization.

débit rate of flow, discharge (of water).

débitur debtor.

déboasasi deforestation.

debos (*Coll.*) **nge-** boasting.

debu dust, grit. - *mérah* red haze. **ber-** dusty. **men-** be or become like dust.

debuk sound of thud. **ber-** make a thudding noise. *~ -debak* make repeated sounds of thumping and pounding.

debum sound of muffled blow (such as when striking mattress). *--debam* sound of various blows.

debung sound of resonant blow such as drum beat.

debup sound of light object falling.

debur 1 sound of splashing (object falling into water, surf, etc.). 2 pounding of heart. **ber-, men-** pound (of surf, heart, etc.). *Hatinya sekonyong-konyong ~ kencang* Her heart suddenly pounded rapidly. **-an** pounding (of surf, heart, etc.).

debus₁ sound of whistling, sound of howling wind.

debus₂ ritual display of invulnerability in W. Java.

debut sound of light popping (e.g. breaking wind).

début first appearance before the public.

decak sound of click, esp. of tongue to express astonishment, enjoyment, etc. **ber-** make such a clicking noise. *~ nikmat* express o.'s pleasure by clicking. **men-kan** click (the tongue softly).

decap sound of smacking o.'s lips. **ber-(²), men-(²)** smack o.'s lips.

decéh, decih sound of clicking with tongue and teeth to express disapproval, tsk tsk. **ber-, men-** make this sound (us. to express disapproval).

decing sound of light metallic ringing.

decit sound of chirp (of chicks, etc.). **ber-, men-** chirp, cheep.

decur sound of water spraying. **men-** spray, spout.

dedah exposed, uncovered. **men-kan** open, expose. ~ *pakaian* undress. ~ *sarong* take off o.'s sarong. **ter-** 1 wide-open (of door, etc.). 2 uncovered (of lid, o.'s chest, etc.).

dedak mixture of rice and bran, by-product of milling used as animal feed.

dedangkot see DEDENGKOT.

dedas sound of crackling of small arms.

dedau men- cry out loudly, scream.

dedaunan foliage, leaves.

dédé see DIDÉH.

dedek (*Jv, Jkt*) see DEDAK.

dédél ripped. **men-(i)** rip out (a scam, etc.).

dedemenan (*Jkt*) o.'s favorite thing or person.

dedemitan 1 ghost, apparition. 2 (*Jv*) do s.t. secretly.

dedengkot (*Coll.*) prominent figure, big shot. - *fotografi* well-known photographer.

dédés₁ 1 civet cat. 2 musk.

dédés₂ men- slice thinly.

dédikasi dedication. **men-kan** dedicate. ~ *diri utk* dedicate o.s. to.

dédolarisasi (*Fin.*) removal of dollar as standard of currency valuation.

déduksi deduction.

déduktif deductive.

dééskalasi de-escalation.

dé facto, dé fakto de facto.

défaitis (*Lit.*) defeatist.

défaitisme defeatism.

défénsif defensive.

défilé 1 (*Mil.*) review, march past. 2 file past (a coffin). **ber-** pass in review.

définisi definition. **men-kan** define. **pen-an** defining.

définitif definitive.

défisiénsi deficiency.

défisit deficit.

déflasi deflation.

défléksi deflection.

déformasi deformation.

degam sound of boom, such as thunder, cannon, etc.

degan (*Jv*) young coconut.

degap₁ sturdy, robust.

degap₂ 1 sound of nonmetallic surface being struck. 2 heartbeat. --*degup* pounding heart (due to stress, etc.). **(ber)-²(an)** 1 make repeated pounding noises. 2 pound, beat hard (of heart). *Dadaku* ~ my heart pounded. **-an** pounding, throb.

degar 1 sound of a surface being struck hard. 2 sound of breaking down a door.

degdeg, degdegan sensation of pounding (of

heart). *Dgn* ~ *aku menghampirinya* I approached him with a pounding heart.

dégen (*Sport*) foil in fencing.

dégénerasi degeneration.

degil obstinate, headstrong. **ke-an** obstinacy, stubbornness.

deging ber- persevere through thick and thin.

déglén slanting (of walls of decrepit buildings).

degradasi degradation.

degub see DEGUP.

deguk sound of gurgle. **ber-, men-** gurgle.

degum sound of boom, such as cannon being fired. **-², --*degam*** various or repeated booming noises. **ber-** make a booming noise.

degung 1 sound of gong. 2 (*Sd*) gamelan.

degup sound of gulp. - *hati* heart beat. **ber-, men-(²)** 1 make a gulping sound. *Air kendi* ~ *karena hausnya* She gulped the water noisily because of her thirst. 2 beat, pound. *Hatinya* ~ *lebih kencang* Her heart beat faster. **men-kan** exciting, cause to beat. ~ *hidup* make life exciting.

degur sound of surf. **ber-** make the sound of surf. *Ombak* ~ *di tepi pantai* The waves splashed on the beach.

déh (*Jkt*) 1 come on, please do (an urging particle). *Makan -!* Come on! Eat! *Lima ratus aja -!* Come on! Let me have it for 500! *Ayo! Pulang -* Come on. Let us go home. 2 Oh, all right, I will agree. *Baik -. Saya coba aja -* OK. I will just try. *Lima ribu? Ambil -* 5,000? OK, take it! 3 that is the way it is, I guarantee you. *Dicicipi aja. Énak -* Just take a taste. It is delicious, I guarantee you.

deham, dehem clearing of throat. **ber-, men-** cough slightly, clear throat (often to signal o.'s presence). **men-i** hint, give s.o. a signal by clearing the throat. *Kudengar seorg perempuan* ~ *aku* I heard a woman signaling to me (by clearing her throat).

déhidrasi dehydration. **men-** dehydrate.

dehoi see INDEHOI.

dék₁ /dék/ (*Naut.*) deck. *penumpang* - deck class passenger.

dék₂ /dék/ (*Coll.*) blanket.

dékadén decadent.

dékadénsi decadence.

dekah-dekah see TAWA.

dekak-dekak abacus.

dekam ber- men- 1 be in crouching position (of cat, etc.). 2 be cooped up. *Gadis itu* ~ *saja di rumahnya* That girl just stays cooped up at home. *Ia terpaksa* ~ *sembilan belas hari di rumah sakit* He was forced to spend 19 days at the hospital. 3 be incarcerated.

dekan bamboo rat.

dékan (*Acad.*) dean. - *ahli* academic dean, dean of academic affairs. - *fakultas* dean of the faculty. **men-i** be the dean of a certain faculty. ~ *FSUI* be the dean of the Faculty of Letters of the University of Indonesia.

dekap₁ with folded arms. **ber-, men-** embrace, hug. ~ *tangan/tubuh* 1 fold o.'s arms on o.'s chest. 2 not work, be idle. **ber-(²)an** embrace e.o.

berse- with arms folded. *Ia ~ tegak* He stood erect with folded arms. **men-i** embrace s.o. *Ku-i meréka dgn tangis yg tak kukuasai lagi* I embraced them, weeping uncontrollably. **men-kan** press s.t. in an embrace. *Bunda ~ mukaku ke dadanya* Mother pressed my face against her breast. **-an** hug, embrace. *mempererat ~nya* tighten o.'s embrace. **sepen-** a measure of circumference equal to the extent of an embrace.

dekap₂ near. **men- 1** be near. **2** be situated. *Pembantu membuka sekerup peti tempat ia ~ tadi* The assistant opened the screws of the box where he had just been sitting. **memper-kan** bring near, reconcile.

dekap₃ noise of a heartbeat. **ber-** beat (of heart).

dékar men- fight with a sword. **pen- 1** master of swordsmanship or martial arts. **2** champion. *~ lidah* **1** highly skilled advocate. **2** champion of a cause. *~ péna* skillful writer.

dekat 1 near, close by. *duduk - suaminya* sit next to her husband. *Rumah saya - kantor pos* My house is near the post office. *Hari Natal sdh -* Christmas is near. *Sdh - saatnya* It is almost time. **2** vicinity. *Rumahnya di - setasiun* Her home is near the station. **ber-(²) 1** be close to e.o., be next to e.o. **2** associate. *Jangan ~ dgn anak-anak yg nakal* Do not associate with naughty children. **ber-an** adjacent, contiguous. *Rumah kami ~* Our houses are next to e.o. *menurut sumbér yg ~ dgn . . .* according to sources close to . . . **ber-²an** side by side. **men- 1** draw near, approach. *Hari Natal sdh ~* Christmas is drawing near. **2** draw closer (of agreement, etc.). **men-i 1** approach s.t. or s.o. *Kami sdh ~ tujuan kami* We have come near to our goal. **2** resemble. *Lukisannya ~ org yg sebenarnya* The painting resembled the man himself. **men-kan** bring s.t. close, cause s.t. to be close by. *Ibu ~ méja ke dinding* Mother brought the table closer to the wall. *~ diri bring o.s.* closer. *~ diri kpd Hinduisme* bring o.s. closer to Hinduism. **memper-kan 1** bring things near to e.o. *Dia berusaha ~ hubungan dagang Indonésia dgn Jepang* He is endeavoring to bring Indonesia and Japan into closer trading relations. **2** reconcile s.o. **ter-i** approachable. **ke-an 1** nearness, propinquity. **2** too close. **-an** (*Coll.*) come closer. **pen-an 1** approach. *Dgn ~ baru masalahnya bisa cepat diselesaikan* With a new approach the problems can be readily resolved. **2** (*Pol.*) rapprochement, reconciliation. **per-an** approach. *~ kpd kejituan* an approach to accuracy.

dekih sound of a chuckle. **men-(²), ter-(²)** chuckle, chortle.

dekik small indentation. *- pipi* dimple.

dekil caked with dirt.

déking 1 protection, shelter, cover. *mencari - di balik sebuah rumah* seek cover behind a house. *mendapat - dr baju ijo* get protection from the military. **2** patron, protector. **3** (*Fin.*) reserve funds. **men- 1** protect, defend (a goal). *Pemerintah ~ usaha pribumi yg lemah* The gvt. is protecting native enterprises which are weak. **2** detain, cut off.

déklamasi formal stylized recitation of poetry, etc. **ber-** engage in formalized poetry recitation. **men-kan** recite literature in a formal style. **pen-an** act of declaiming.

déklamator orator (esp. of poetry).

déklarasi 1 customs declaration. **2** voucher.

deklérer (*Crd.*) declarer.

déklinasi 1 (*Astr.*) declination. **2** (*Ling.*) declension.

dékolonisasi decolonization.

Dékon [*Déklarasi Ékonomi*] Economic Declaration (enunciated by Sukarno in 1963).

dékonséntrasi deconcentration. **men-kan** deconcentrate.

dékor decor. *- gaya disko* disco-style décor.

dékorasi 1 decoration, decor. **2** (*Mil.*) medal, ribbon.

dekrét, dekrit decree, edict. **men-kan** decree s.t.

dekuk ber- work hard. **ke-an** working hard.

dekur see DEKUT.

dekus sound of hissing or snorting. *Nafasnya kedengaran spt - kuda* His breathing sounded like the snort of a horse. **ber-, men-** hiss (of cats), snort.

dekut sound of cooing. *- puyuh* the cooing of quails. **ber-, men-** coo.

delah k.o. saltwater fish.

delapan eight. *- belas* eighteen. *- puluh* eighty. **ber-** be in a group of eight. **ke- 1** all eight. *~ org* all eight persons. **2** the eighth. *org ~* the 8th person.

délégasi delegation. **men-kan** delegate s.t. *~ wewenang kpd bawahan* delegate authority to subordinates. **pen-an** delegation of authority.

delep (*Jv*) **men- 1** sink, go below surface. **2** make o.s. unobtrusive. *Karena tdk siap dia ~ terus-menerus dlm diskusi* He was not prepared for his lecture, so he saved himself by opening a discussion.

deles pure-blooded.

déligir men- delegate (power).

delik wide-open (of eyes). **men-** glare at. *Mimi ~ kpd Galih* Mimi glared at Galih. **men-i** glare at.

délik offense. *- aduan* offense that warrants complaint. *- tunggal* sole offense.

delikan /deli'an/ (*Jv*) game of hide and seek.

délikuénsi delinquency.

delima pomegranate.

délman k.o. two-wheeled buggy.

delung sunken (of eye). **men-** look sunken (of eyes).

délta delta.

delujur see JELUJUR.

déma [*déwan mahasiswa*] student council.

démagog demagogue.

démagogi demagoguery.

demah warm compress. **men-** apply a warm compress.

demam 1 fever, feverish. *Ia -* She has a fever. *- berselang* intermittent fever. *- dingin* have a clammy fever. *- puyuh* slight fever. *- selesma* influenza. *- siput* schistosomiasis. **2** (*Coll.*) fad. *Surabaya ditulari - breakdance* The breakdance fad has reached epidemic proportions in Surabaya. -² feverlike. ~ *puyuh* pretend to be ill.

deman like, be fond of. *Saya - mangga* I like mangoes.

demang 1 village headman in Java. **2** customary law expert. **3** village gvt. officer. **ke-an** customary law area.

démarkasi demarcation.

dembam see DEBAM.

dembum see DEBUM.

demek moist, still wet.

demen see DEMAN.

demés flat (of nose).

demi₁ 1 for the sake of. - *kepentingan nasional* in the national interest. - *hari depan anakku* for the sake of my son's future. - *alasan keamanan* for reasons of security. *Dibuatnya juga - tdk mengecéwakan meréka* He did it anyway only so as not to disappoint them. **2** by (in oaths). *Saya bersumpah - Allah bhw itu tdk benar* I swear by God that it is not true. - *kehormatanku* on my honor.

demi₂ 1 as soon as. - *dilihatnya rumah itu terbakar ia memanggil polisi* As soon as he saw the house was on fire, he called the police. - *pertempuran mulai . . .* As soon as the battle started . . . **2** (immediately) after, by. *gelas - gelas* glass after glass. *satu - satu* o. by o.

demikian 1 such. *Saya ingin baju yg - ini* I want a shirt such as this. *Sdh - lamanya ia tak muncul* He has not shown up in such a long time. *dlm hal yg - in* such a case. *tak - mudah* not so easy. - *rupa sehingga* in such a way that. **2** thus, such was the case. *-lah akhir cerita ini* Thus ends this story. - *pemberita kita melaporkan* Thus our correspondent reports (according to our correspondent). *dgn -* thus, so. - *juga* likewise. - *juga engkau hrs bertindak* You should act likewise. **se-** of this sort, of that sort. *Laki-laki ~ itu tak dpt dipercayai* A man like that cannot be trusted.

démilitérisasi demilitarization. **men-kan** demilitarize.

démisionér (*Pol.*) *kabinét -* outgoing cabinet which still carries out routine tasks. **men-kan 1** ask for the resignation of a cabinet. **2** strip (of authority, power). **pen-an** dissolution of cabinet, stripping of authority. ~ *yg mendadak* sudden firing (of a cabinet).

demit see DEDEMITAN.

démo₁ [*délman bermotor*] small motorized three-wheeled vehicle used for public transportation.

démo₂ see DÉMONSTRASI.

démobilisan demobilized member of armed forces.

démobilisasi demobilization. **men-kan** demobilize.

démograf demographer.

démografi demography.

démografis demographic.

démokrasi democracy. - *terpimpin* guided non-parliamentary democracy (practiced in last years of Sukarno era). **ber-** democratic. **men-kan** democratize. **pen-an** democratization.

démokrat democrat.

démokratis democratic. **men-kan** democratize.

démokratisasi democratization.

démokratisér, démokratisir men- democratize.

démonstran participant in a demonstration, protester.

démonstrasi 1 demonstration, protest. **2** demonstration (of cars, radios, etc.). **ber-** participate in a demonstration. **men-** demonstrate against. *Peraturan baru itu di- mahasiswa* The students demonstrated against that new regulation. **men-kan 1** protest s.t. **2** demonstrate (quality, etc.).

démoralisasi demoralization.

démoralisir men- demoralize. ~ *masyarakat perbankan* demoralize the banking community.

démotrasi see DÉMONSTRASI.

dempak 1 low and flat. *Atap rumah itu -* The house roof is flat. **2** stocky. *Tubuh org itu -* The man is stockily built.

dempal (*Jv*) physically strong.

dempang hollow sounding (as the fall of empty barrel). **ber-² 1** sound hollow. **2** chatter, babble, prattle.

démpél near to. **ber-an** nearby, close to e.o. *Rumahnya ~ dgn kantor polisi* His house is next to the police station. **men-** crowd together. *Meréka ~ di pangkuan ibu* They crowded together in Mother's lap.

dempét, démpét stuck together. *kembar -* Siamese twins. *Kedua pisang itu ~* The two bananas are stuck together. **ber-** stick together. **ber-²(an), - men-** be jammed together. *Rumah ~ dlm kota ini* The houses are jammed together in this town. *Lalu lintas ~ di Jln Majapahit itu* The traffic was jammed on Majapahit Street. **men-** get stuck. *Anyelir yg kering ~ di kertas lembaran album* The dried carnation stuck to the leaves of the album. **men-kan** press together. **ke-** jammed, wedged in.

dempir sound made by cymbal.

dempit see DEMPÉT.

démplon (*Jkt*) cute, pretty.

dempok, dempuk ber- bump against, collide with. **ter-** bump accidentally against. *Saya ~ méja* I bumped against a table.

dempul glazier's putty, boat caulking. **men-** apply putty or caulking.

dempung sound of s.t. falling into water.

dén see RADÉN.

dénah sketch, blueprint, ground plan. - *vokal* (*Ling.*) vowel chart.

denai trail, track (of wild game).

denak decoy (used in hunting).

Dénas [*Déwan Nasional*] national council.

dencang ber- rattle, clang.

dencing see DENTING.

déncis see SARDÉN.

denda fine. - *lima ribu rupiah* a 5,000-rupiah fine. **men-** fine, assess. **-an** fining. **pen-an** fining.

dendam 1 revenge, vengeance. *Saya ingin membalas -* I want to take revenge. **2** grudge, resentment. *menaruh -* bear a grudge. - *benci* grudge and hatred, deep resentment. - *kasemat/khasumat/kesumat* enmity, rancor. **3** yearning, longing.

- *berahi* passionate love or desire. **ber-** bear a grudge. ~ *hati* bear malice. **ber-²an** have hard feeling toward s.o. **men-(i)** resent. *Ia ~ kata-kata saya* She resented my words. **ke-an** resentment. **pen-** s.o. who bears a grudge.

dendang₁ crow (bird).

dendang₂ see DANDANG₁.

déndang chant sung while working. *dgn* - in good spirits, easily, happily. **ber-** sing happily. *Gadis-gadis memotong padi sambil* ~ The girls sang while harvesting rice. **men-** sing. ~ *pantun* recite pantuns. **men-kan** sing s.t. *Loudspeaker terus ~ "Auf Wiedersehen"* The loudspeaker continually sang out "Auf Wiedersehen".

déndéng jerked meat. - *belado* (M) jerked meat fried with red peppers. **men-** to dry meat.

denderang sound of drum or heavy steps. **-an** weary steps or drum beats.

dengan 1 with, accompanying. *Ia pergi - ayahnya* She went with her father. - *ini* herewith. - *ini saya menjawab* I herewith reply. **2** and. *Siti - Amat akan datang bésok* Siti and Amat will come tomorrow. **3** by, by means of. *datang - keréta api* come by train. *menulis - potlot* write with a pencil. **4** in. - *nama Tuhan* in the name of God. *suhu - C* temperature in Celsius. **5** by way of. - *alamat* in care of. - *jalan* 1 by means of. - *jalan menipu ia mencapai kedudukan yg tinggi* By cheating he reached a high position. 2 by way of, via. **6** in the manner of. - *begitu* thus. - *cara bagaimana* how. - *cara bagaimana ia melamar utk pekerjaan itu?* How did he go about applying for that job? - *hormat* with respectful greetings (used in correspondence). - *harga* at a cost of. - *kadarnya* in a modest fashion. - *lisan* verbally. - *sekaligus* 1 simultaneously, all together. *menyudahkan dua pekerjaan - sekaligus* complete two jobs simultaneously. *Mereka datang - sekaligus* They came all together. 2 promptly. - *sekaligus musuh menduduki kota itu* The enemy promptly occupied the city. - *sendirinya* 1 automatically, of itself. *Radio itu akan mati - sendirinya* That radio will turn off automatically. 2 obviously. *Sdh - sendirinya ia susah kalau tdk lulus* He is obviously going to have problems if he fails. - *sepatutnya* fittingly. - *sepatutnya engkau meminta maaf* It is fitting that you request an apology. - *sewajarnya* naturally. - *tiada/tdk* without. *Ia pergi - tiada izin* He went without permission. - *tdk malu-malu* 1 shamelessly. 2 with no reservation. - *tulisan* written, in writing.

dengap ber- 1 pound, beat (of heart). **2** pant, be out of breath, gasp (for breath).

dengar hear. *Saya - kamu sdh dpt rumah* I hear you have found a house. **men-** 1 hear. *Dia sdh tua dan tdk dpt* ~ *lagi* He is old and cannot hear any more. ~ *suara* hear a voice. ~ *kabar* hear the news. **2** (*Leg.*) noted (in resolutions, decrees, etc.). **men-kan** 1 listen to. *Ia ~ radio* She listens to the radio. **2** heed, pay attention to. *Kita hrs ~ perintah Tuhan* We must obey God's commandments. **memper-kan** 1 let s.t. be heard or listened to. **2** perform, present (a program, etc.). *Penyanyi itu ~ suaranya yg merdu itu* The vocalist

let people hear her beautiful voice. **ter-** heard, audible. *tak* ~ inaudible. **ke-an 1** can be heard. *Satu-satunya bunyi yg* ~ The only sound that could be heard. *Tdk énak* ~ Not nice to hear. ~ *pula si isteri bicara* The wife was also heard to speak. **2** seems, strikes o. as. *Itu ~ anéh* That sounds odd. **-²an** hear a rumor, seem to hear. *Kami ~ bhw sdr akan pergi* We heard rumors you are going to go. *Dia sering ~ suara ibunya yg sdh meninggal* He often thought he heard his dead mother's voice. **pen-** 1 listener, audience. **2** (sense of) hearing. ~ *tengah* (*Anat.*) middle ear, tympanum. **3** telephone receiver. **pen-an** 1 sense of hearing. 2 what has been heard. **se-pen-an** according to what has been heard.

denger (*Jv, Jkt*) see DENGAR.

dengih sound of rapid breathing or gasping.

denging sound of ringing (in ears). **ber-, men-** buzz, ring (in ears). *Telinga saya* ~ My ears are ringing.

dengkang sound of croaking frogs. *si* - frog. **ber-²** 1 croak (of frog). 2 laugh hard.

déngkang-déngkol crooked, bent and bowed (of hand, tree branch, etc.).

dengki envy, spite. **ber-** be full of hatred and envy. **men-** envy, be jealous of s.o. **ke-an 1** spite, spitefulness. **2** jealousy. **pen-** o. who is invidious and spiteful.

dengkik become weak from lack of food.

dengking 1 sound of dog yelping. **2** a yelp, squeal, or scream. **ber-, men-** 1 yelp, squeal. **2** scream. *suara yg ~* strident voice. **men-kan** scream out s.t. *Ia ~ kesedihannya* She screamed out her sorrow. **-an** a yelp.

dengkir men- chirp.

dengklang lame, limping. **men-kan** cripple, hobble s.o.

dengkul (*Jv, Jkt*) knee. *modal -* with only o.'s own strong back to rely on (lit., with o.'s knee as capital). *seénak - sendiri* do as o. likes. - *kopong* having too much sex (lit., having a hollow knee). *Dasar - kopong* He is like that because he has sex too much. **men-** 1 kneel. 2 knee s.o.

dengkung 1 growl (of dog). **2** sound of metal on metal. **ber-, men-** 1 make a grating metallic sound, rumble. 2 to growl (of dog).

dengkur 1 snore, snoring. **2** grunt. **3** purr. **ber-, men-** 1 snore. 2 grunt. 3 purr. **-an** snore. **pen-** snorer.

dengkus, dengu₁ whinny, snort. **ber-, men-** 1 whinny, snort. 2 sigh.

dengu see DUNGU.

denguk sound of sobbing. **ber-, men-** utter sobbing sounds.

dengung sound of droning, buzzing, purring, etc. **ber-, men-** 1 wail (of siren, foghorn, etc.), drone (of plane). 2 resound, reverberate. *Tepuk sorak ~ dlm gedung itu* The building resounded with applause. **men-kan** 1 sound (siren, gong, etc.). *Harimau ~ suaranya di hutan* The tiger's roar filled the jungle. 2 tout, propagandize. **-an** 1 wail, drone. 2 propaganda. **pen-** buzzer.

dengus 1 snort (of animals). **2** deride with a

snort. **ber-, men-** snort. *Keréta api itu datang ~ memasuki stasiun* The train came chugging into the station. **men-kan** make s.t. snort. **-an** a snort.

dengut sound of murmuring (of quail), sound of vibrating (of xylophone, gong). **ber-²** resonate, reverberate. *Bunyi burung puyuh ~ di kejauhan* The sound of a quail resonated in the distance.

denok (*Jv*) term of address to young girl, esp. as *nok.*

dénok svelte. **ke-an** svelteness.

dénotasi denotation.

dénsitas density.

dentam sound of gunfire, pounding on anvil, etc. *--dentum* repeated sound of gunfire. **ber-** 1 produce sound of gunfire, etc. 2 resound. *Beduk ~ tak putus-putusnya* The drum sounded incessantly. **ber-an** beat. *Hatiku ~* My heart was beating loudly. **men-kan** pound with s.t. *Hakim ~ palunya ke méja* The judge pounded on the table with his gavel. **-an** 1 pounding. 2 sound of gunfire, beating, etc.

dentang sound of clanging or loud explosion. *--denting* a jingle-jangle sound. **ber-** *denting* jingling and jangling. **ber-** clang, peal. **ber-an** clang repeatedly or of many things. **men-kan** peal out s.t. *~ tanda waktunya* peal the time of day.

dentar clang. **ber-** clang, peal.

denting sound of jingle or tinkle (of money, piano, keys, etc.). *- pelatuk* click of the trigger. **ber-, men-** jingle, tinkle. *Garpunya ~ ketika jatuh ke lantai* Her fork rang when it fell to the floor. *Gitarmu ~* Your guitar gives out a nice tinkling sound. **ber-²**, **ber-an** make repeated jingling sounds. *Loncéng geréja ~* The church bell pealed. **men-kan** cause a ringing, tinkling noise. *gerak dan suara yg ~ hati Buyung* a movement and voice which struck a note in Buyung's heart.

dentum sound of boom (explosion, cannon, etc.). *-nya gelombang* booming of the waves. **ber-** boom out. *Meriam-meriam itu ~ di pelabuhan* The cannons boomed in the harbor. **ber-(²)an** make repeated booming noises. **-an** booming. *~ meriam 21 kali* 21-gun salute.

dentung sound of clap of thunder. **ber-** clap (of thunder).

dentur sound of pop, small explosion, etc. **ber-, men-** crackle, pop. *Senapan-senapan itu ~* The rifles crackled.

dénudasi denudation.

denyak see ENYAK.

denyar flash. *- kilat* flash of lightning. **ber-, men-** flash. *~ kilat di kepalaku* s.t. flashed in my mind. **-an** flash, gleam.

denyit sound of shrieking and high-pitched noises. **ber-** screech. *Rémnya ~ di pojok itu* The brakes screeched at the corner. **-an** a screech, shriek.

denyut throb, beat. *- hati/jantung* heartbeat. *- nada* pulse. **ber-, men-** beat, throb (of heart, pulse). *Kepalaku ~ karena pusing kepanasan* My head is throbbing with a headache from too much sun. **-an** beat, throb. *~ jantung* heartbeat.

déodoran deodorant.

dép **men-, menge-** pigeonhole, shelve (a question). **pen-an** shelving (of question).

Dép [*Départemén*] ministry, department of gvt.

depa fathom. **men-** measure in fathoms. **men-kan** reach the length of a fathom. *~ tangan* spread out the arms sideways.

Dépag [*Départemén Agama*] Department of Religious Affairs.

depak₁ a kick. **men-** 1 kick (ball, etc.). *Mulyadi diterpelanting* Mulyadi lay sprawled on the ground after being given a kick. 2 fire, dismiss, kick out, expel s.o. *Sementara inflasi terus ~ harga-harga barang kebutuhan pokok si petani* Meanwhile inflation continues to give the prices of the peasants' basic needs an upward kick. **-an** a kick. **pen-an** 1 act of kicking. 2 firing, dismissal, expulsion.

depak₂ sound of clap, clip-clop (esp. of horses' hoofs, etc.). **ber-** make a clapping noise (of horses, etc.). **men-kan** cause a clapping or smacking noise. *~ lidah* smack o.'s lips.

dépak see DEPAK₁.

depan 1 front. *Di - rumah ada pohon* In front of the house is a tree. *Ia berjuang di garis -* He fought on the front line. 2 ahead. *Itu dia di -* That is it up ahead. 3 coming, next. *bulan -* next month. *ke -* to the front. *tampil ke -* step to the front. **ber-²** face to face. **ber-an** face e.o. *Rumahnya ~ dgn rumah saya* His house faces mine. **menge-kan** 1 put in the front. *Ia ~ méja* He placed the table forward. 2 put forward, propose. *Ketua ~ usulnya* The chairman submitted his proposal. **ter-** 1 foremost, front (seat, etc.). 2 in the lead (in contests, etc.).

depang ber- stretch out both arms sideways. **men-** 1 stretch out both arms sideways. 2 block the way with both arms. *Ia ~ jalanku sampai saya terpaksa berhenti* She blocked my way to the point that I was forced to stop. **men-kan** stretch (o.'s arms) out.

depap sound of slap (i.e. palm of o.'s hand striking table, etc.).

Déparlu [*Départemén Luar Negeri*] Department of Foreign Affairs.

déparpolisasi (*Pol.*) simplification of political party structures, decreasing of number of political parties.

départemén ministry.

Dépdagri [*Départemén Dlm Negeri*] Department of Internal Affairs.

dépendénsi 1 dependency, dependence. 2 (colonial) possession.

Déperdag [*Départemén Perdagangan*] Department of Commerce.

dépersonalisir men- depersonalize.

Dépertan [*Départemén Pertanian*] Department of Agriculture.

dépinisi see DÉFINISI.

dépisen see DÉVISA.

Dépkéh [*Départemén Kehakiman*] Department of Justice.

Dépkes [*Départemén Keséhatan*] Department of Health.

Dépkéu [*Départemén Keuangan*] Department of Finance.

Déplu [*Départemén Luar Negeri*] Department of Foreign Affairs.

Depnaker [*Départemén Tenaga Kerja*] Department of Labor.

Depnakertranskop [*Départemén Tenaga Kerja Transmigrasi dan Koperasi*] Department of Labor, Population Resettlement, and Cooperatives (until 1978).

depo see DEPOT.

dépo storehouse, warehouse.

depok men- reside. **pen-an** camp, dormitory. **pa-an** residence.

dépolitisasi depoliticization.

déponir men- delay, put on ice. *Kepala kantor ~ soal itu* The head of the office put that question in deep freeze.

déportasi deportation. **men-kan** deport.

déposan depositor.

déposito (*Fin.*) fixed deposit (us. bearing high interest). **men-kan** put o.'s money in a time certificate or fixed deposit.

depot refreshment stand. **- és** iced drinks stand.

Déppén [*Départemén Penerangan*] Department of Information.

déprési financial depression.

déprésiasi (*Fin.*) depreciation.

déprok (me)n- 1 sit on floor without folding legs. 2 (*Coll.*) sit s.w. uninvited. *~ sambil memandangi* sit down uninvited and stare at s.o.

Dépsos [*Départemén Sosial*] Department of Social Services.

dépteri diphtheria.

depus sound of sighing, exhaling air, etc.

députasi deputation, delegation. **men-kan** delegate s.o.

députi deputy.

dér sound of explosion.

dera lash (of whip), lashing. *dihukum -* sentenced to a whipping. **men-** 1 whip, lash. 2 be stingingly painful. *sakit yg kian ~* the pain that became ever more stinging. **-an** whipping.

derai₁ sound of water dripping on or beating against glass, etc. *- air mata* dripping of tears. *- angin* the swishing of the wind. **ber-(²)** 1 drip (of water). 2 make spattering sound. **men-(²)kan** make s.t. patter, drip. *~ air mata* shed tears. **-an** 1 pattering sound. *~ hujan* patter of rain. 2 flow of drops. *~ air mata* the stream of tears.

derai₂ ber-² 1 in droves. *Penonton-penonton ~ datang di pekan raya* Spectators arrived in droves at the fair. 2 continuously. *Dokter itu tertawa ~* The doctor laughed continuously.

derai₃ grain. **ber-** 1 in grains, become grains. 2 loose (of soil). **men-(²)kan** turn into particles.

derajah, derajat 1 degree. *- panas* temperature. *Panasnya dua puluh enam -* It is 26 degrees. *sudut tujuh puluh lima -* an angle of 75 degrees. *- busur* degree of a circle. 2 rank, level. *- pengetahuan* level of knowledge. 3 standard. *- penghidupan* standard of living. *- tolok* standard meridian. *-*

utama prime meridian. 4 Latinate qualifiers of university degree (e.g. *cum laude*, etc.). **se-** of the same degree or level. *Mantuku kelak hrs ~ dgn kita* My son-in-law will have to be of the same status as we are. **menye-kan** place on the same level.

derak sound of snap (such as tree branch breaking, gnashing of teeth, etc.). *--deruk* repeated cracking noises. **ber-(²)** creak, squeak (of tree branches, bedsprings, etc.). **men-²** repeatedly make squeaking noises (gnash o.'s teeth, etc.). **-an** creaking, squeaking. *suara ~ rantai sepéda* sound of squeaking of the bicycle chain.

deram sound of rumble (thunder, tiger's roar, drum roll, etc.). *--derum* sound of repeated rumbling of various tones. **ber-(²), men-** 1 rumble (of thunder, etc.). *Suara tinju ~ di daun pintu* The sound of blows resounded on the door. 2 hum deeply.

derang sound of ringing clank (chains or coins falling, of small gongs, etc.). **ber-, men-** make a resonant, often metallic sound. *- siang* 1 signal daybreak (with drums). 2 broad daylight.

derap sound of stamping on flat surface (horse's trot, marching feet, etc.), a trot, clop. *- irama* rhythmic trot. *- langkah barisan wanita dlm pawai* sound of the marching feet of the women's unit in the parade. *- sepatu* footstep. *- révolusi/pembangunan* steady forceful progress of the revolution or development. **ber-** 1 make a clopping sound. 2 trot. **men-** move at slow and regular pace. *Keréta api ~ sambil membunyikan peluit* The trains slowly moved out while letting out a whistle. **men-kan** cause to move a steady pace. *~ kuda* trot a horse. **-an** steady movement (of footsteps, etc.).

deras₁ swift (esp. of flowing liquids). *Kali itu - arusnya* The river has a fast current. *Hujannya sangat -* The rain came down hard. *lari - run* swiftly. *-nya tikaman* a torrent of stabs. **ber-** rush (of water). **men-** 1 flow rapidly. 2 energetic. *Pemuda ~ tentu majunya* Energetic youth will surely get ahead. **men-kan** increase speed of s.t. (esp. water). *Ia ~ larinya* She ran faster. **ke-an** speed, swiftness. **pen-** 1 accelerator. 2 hired worker. **pen-an** rapids, cataract.

deras₂ sound of trash or sand being stepped on.

deras₃ see DARAS.

derau sound of roaring (wind-borne rain, etc.). *- keréta api* roaring of a train. **ber-(²), men-(²)** make a roaring sound like that of wind-borne rain, etc. *~ ribut di pepohonan* a roaring sound in the shrubs.

dérék₁ /dérék/ crane, cargo boom. **men-** lift by crane or boom.

dérék₂ see DÉRÉT.

derep men- harvest rice.

dérés₁ men- tap tree to extract sap (sugar palm). **pen-** tapper.

dérés₂ men- recite the Koran.

dérési (*R.R.*) passenger car.

dérét row, line, series. *dua - tanaman* two rows of

plants. - *hitung* arithmetical progression. - *ukur* (*Math.*) geometrical progression. **se-** 1 abreast, in the same line. 2 a line of. ~ *kata-kata sederhana* a sequence of simple words. **ber-** in a row, in rows. *Meréka duduk* ~ They sat in rows. **ber-²** line up. *Org-org* ~ *sepanjang jalan* People lined up along the road. **men-i** line s.t. *Sungai itu di-i dgn pohon* The river was lined with trees. **men-kan, memper-kan** line s.o. up. *Guru itu* ~ *murid-muridnya* The teacher lined up her pupils. **-an** row, line. ~ *berbagai ilustrasi* a line of various illustrations (as in a comic strip). ~ *meriam* a battery of cannon.

deretak sound of repeated rattling. **ber-²** rattle (of machinery, teeth).

derhaka see DURHAKA.

deriji see JERUJI.

derik creaking sound. **ber-** make a creaking sound. *Di belakangnya bangku* ~ Behind him a bench creaked. **ber-²** make repeated creaking noises. *Giginya* - He grated his teeth.

deril see DRIL.

dering 1 sound of tinkling (bells, etc.). - *kunci* tinkle of the key. - *bél itu merdu* That bell has a nice ring. 2 sound of crickets chirping. **ber-, men-** 1 ring, tinkle. *Télepon* ~ The phone rang. 2 clink. *Uang récéh jatuh* ~ *di atas lantai batu* The small change fell with a clinking noise on the cement floor. 3 chirp (of crickets, etc.). **-an** tinkling, clinking noise.

deris sound of rustling (of stepping on dry grass, of cutting cloth, etc.). **ber-, men-** make a rustling sound.

derit sound of squeak (a brake, etc.).

derita suffering. **men-** suffer (illness, defeat, etc.). ~ *kemiskinan* suffer from poverty. **ter-kan** bearable (of suffering). *kesedihan hati yg hampir tak* ~ *oléhnya lagi* a sadness that she could hardly stand to bear any longer. **pen-** 1 sufferer, victim. *Ia* ~ *penyakit paru-paru* She is a victim of lung disease. ~ *cacat (tubuh)* the physically handicapped. ~ *kecelakaan* accident victim. 2 (*Ling.*) object. **pen-an** suffering, anguish.

derma alms, donation. - *korban banjir* donation for the flood victims. **ber-** give a donation. **men-kan** donate s.t. **pen-** donor. ~ *darah* blood donor. **pen-an** act of donating. ~ *darah* blood donation.

dermaga quay, pier.

dérmatalog dermatologist.

dérmatologi dermatology.

dermawan donor, philanthropist. **ke-an** philanthropy, generosity.

dermimil (*Jv*) 1 mumble. 2 talk incessantly.

derobos see TEROBOS.

dersana see JAMBU.

dersik sound of sighing or rustling (leaves in wind).

deru sound made by storm, thunder, large trucks, planes, etc. **men-** roar, howl. *angin yg* ~ howling wind.

deruji see JERUJI.

deruk sound of heavy object crashing.

derum₁ sound of muffled rumble (distant thunder, whir of engine). **ber-, men-** make a muffled rumbling sound. **-an** a rumbling sound. **pen-an** rumbling.

derum₂ men- kneel (of elephant, camel, etc.). **men-kan** cause to kneel.

derum₃ see DRUM.

derun, derung see DERUM₁.

derup-derap sound of many footsteps.

derus, derut sound of objects being rubbed or shifted.

derwis, derwisy see DARWIS.

désa village. - *keputihan* village of religious inhabitants, us. free of village tax or other obligations. - *praja* village administration. - *swadaya/swasembada* self-sufficient village. **ke-an** villagelike, pertaining to villages. **pe-an, per-an** rural. *sosiologi* ~ rural sociology. *Jawatan* ~ Office of Village Affairs.

desah 1 sound of wheezing or huffing. - *keréta mulai terdengar* The puffing of the train began to be heard. --*desau* sigh of the wind. 2 swishing (of leaves, etc.). - *ban pd aspal basah* the swishing sound of wheels on wet pavement. 3 sigh. **ber-, men-** 1 wheeze, huff. *Ia mengangkat wajahnya dan* ~, "*Terima kasih*" He lifted his face and wheezed, "Thank you." 2 sigh (of wind, etc.). *Bunyi air terjun* ~ *jauh dr gunung* The muffled whisper of a waterfall came from the distant mountains. **ber-an** make repeated huffing or swishing sound.

desak₁ sound of crumpling paper. **ber-, men-** make the sound of paper being crumpled.

desak₂ ber-(²) crowd, jostle. **ber-(²)an** crowd e.o. aside. **men-** 1 push, shove. *Ia* ~ *saya ke dinding* He pushed me to the wall. 2 urge, insist. *Ibu* ~ *dia spy kawin* Mother urged him to get married. *Waktu sdh* ~ Time is pressing. *soal* ~ an urgent matter. **kemen-an** urgency. **men-i** press in on, make crowded. *Pengunjung sandiwara* ~ *pintu msk* The audience of the play crowded the entrance. *Perasaan sedih* ~ *dadanya* A sad feeling filled her breast. **men-kan** 1 press s.t. against. *Isterinya* ~ *tubuhnya ke tubuh suami* The wife pushed her body against her husband's. 2 force s.t. on s.o. *Surat itu di-kannya ke dlm tanganku* She pushed the letter into my hand. **-an** 1 push, shove. 2 pressure, request. **-²an** shuffle. **pe-** o. who presses. *golongan* ~ pressure group, lobby. **pen-an** act of ousting.

désapraja see DÉSA.

desar sound of sizzling or hissing. **ber-, men-** 1 sizzle, hiss. 2 lisp.

desas-desus 1 sound of hissing or whispering. 2 rumor. **men-kan** spread rumors about s.t. *Di-kan bhw dia akan dipindah* It was rumored that he would be transferred.

desau sound of soft rustling. - *kipas angin* the humming of the fan. - *angin pd cemara* the rustle of the wind through the casuarina trees. **ber-, men-** make a rustling or swishing. *Airnya* ~

lemah The water was making a soft rushing sound. **-an** rustling.

déségregasi desegregation.

Désémber December.

déséntralisasi decentralization. **men-kan** decentralize.

déséntralisir men- decentralize.

désérsi desertion.

désértir deserter, defector.

desik sound of light snapping (branch breaking, etc.). **ber-, men-** rustle.

désimal 1 decimal. **2** decimal fraction.

désiméter 10 centimeters.

désinféksi disinfection.

désinféktan disinfectant.

desing sound of whizzing (wind blowing, shot fired, etc.). **ber-, men- 1** make whizzing sound. **2** buzz (in ear). **ber-an** make repeated whistling sounds. *Peluru* ~ Bullets whistled about. **-an** whizz. ~ *ban yg berjalan di atas aspal yg licin* the whirring sound of the tires on the slippery pavement.

désintegrasi disintegration.

desir sound of hissing, rustling, or slurping. - *sarung* rustle of a sarong. - *penghapus kaca* the swish of the windshield wiper. **ber-, men-1** make a hissing or swishing sound. *Gelombang* ~ The waves made a hissing sound. **2** make a chirping sound. *Hatiku* ~ *melihat senyumnya* My heart sang to see her smile. **-an** hiss. ~ *daun rumbia yg ditiup angin* the swishing of the sago palm fronds blown by the wind.

desis, desit sound of hissing or sizzling. **ber-, men-** hiss, sizzle. *Api sigarétnya* ~ *padam* The cigarette went out with a hissing sound. *Ani* ~ *tajam* Ani hissed sharply. *Peluru-peluru* ~ Bullets hissed by. **men-kan** express s.t. with a hiss.

déskripsi description. **men-kan** describe. **pen-an** act of describing.

déskriptif descriptive.

déspot despot.

déspotisme despotism.

déstar Jv head cloth, k.o. turban. **ber-** wear this k.o. head gear.

déstilasi see DISTILASI.

déstruksi destruction. **men-** destroy.

déstruktif destructive.

desuk see DESAK₁.

desur sound of forceful rustling. **ber-** make a forceful rustling sound. *Kedengaran bunyi* ~ *sekuat-kuatnya* They heard a loud rustling noise.

desus sound of light whispering. **ber-², men-²** whisper. **men-kan** spread s.t. as gossip.

desut sound of forceful blowing. **men-** make a blowing sound.

détail see DETÉL.

détailer medical sales representative.

detak sound of tapping. - *hati/jantung* heartbeat. - *loncéng jam dinding* ticking of the clock on the wall. - *pintu mengunci* the click of a door being locked. **ber-, men- 1** make a tapping sound. ~ *tiang roboh* The pole fell with a bang. *langkah kuda yg* ~ the steps of the horse which made a

clip-clop sound. **2** beat (of heart). **ber-an** make repeated tapping sound. **men-kan** cause s.t. to make a tapping sound. ~ *lidah* clack (the tongue). **-an** tapping sound. *di antara* ~ *tongkat dan langkah sepatu* between the tapping sound of a cane and footsteps.

detar sound of sizzling or whirring (roasting corn, wheels turning, etc.). **ber-, men-** sizzle. *Di sini berderak, di sana* ~ There was a crackling sound here, a sizzling sound there.

detas sound of light crackling explosion (eggshell breaking, etc.). **ber-an** give off a popping sound (wet leaves burning, etc.).

détasemén (*Mil.*) detachment.

détaséring temporary deployment to another place of work.

détasir men- (*Mil.*) detail, detach to another unit.

détdot sound of tooting. **ber-(²)** sound the horn. *Mobil* ~ Cars were honking their horns.

détéksi detection, discovery. - *gas* detection of gas. **men-** detect (radiation, etc.).

détéktif, détéktip detective.

détéktor detector.

detél detail. **men-** going into detail.

déterjén detergent.

déterminan determinant.

déterminasi determination, decision. **men-kan** determine, decide.

déterminisme determinism.

detik 1 sound of ticking (of clock). - *jantung* heartbeat. **2** second (unit of time), moment. *sampai pd - terakhir* up to the very last moment. **se-** a moment, momentary.

detil see DETÉL.

deting sound of light twanging (i.e. of plucked guitar string, etc.).

détonator detonator.

detup, detus sound of light explosion (gun firing, firecracker, etc.). **ber-, ber-an 1** explode. **2** make throbbing sound. *Dgn hati* ~ *ia memasuki rumah* She entered with her heart throbbing.

dévaluasi (*Fin.*) devaluation. **men-(kan)** devaluate.

dévaluir (*Fin.*) **men-** devaluate.

déviasi deviation.

dévisa, dévisen, dévizen (*Fin.*) foreign exchange.

déwa god, idol. *-dewi* gods and goddesses, various divinities. **men-(²)kan, memper-(kan) 1** deify. *Suku Indian itu* ~ *semangat jagung* That Indian tribe deified the corn spirit. *Aku terlalu tua utk* ~ *kecantikan* I am too old to deify beauty. **2** idolize s.o. *Ia* ~ *isterinya* He idolizes his wife. **ke-an** divine powers. **pen- 1** idolater. **2** admirer. ~ *pikiran Marx* o. who idolizes the ideas of Marx. **pen-an, per-an 1** deification. **2** idolization.

déwan 1 council. - *Keamanan* Security Council. **2** board. - *niaga* board of trade. - *geréja* synod. - *Geréja-geréja di Indonésia* Indonesian Council of Churches. - *juri* judges in a competition. - *komisaris* board of directors. - *Mahasiswa* Student Representative Council. - *menteri* cabinet. - *penaséhat* advisory council. - *pengawas* 1 supervisory council. 2 inspectorate. - *pengawas keuangan* financial audit board. - *penguji* board of examiners. - *pengurus* board of management. - *penyantun* board of trustees. - *perancang* planning board. - *Pertimbangan Agung* Supreme Advisory Council. - *Perwakilan Rakyat* Indonesian legislative assembly. - *Perwakilan Rakyat Daérah* Assembly at provincial, regency, or municipal level. - *pimpinan* board of directors. - *Rakyat* People's Council. - *rédaksi* editorial board.

déwangga k.o. cloth design. - *raya* firmament of heaven.

déwani 1 council member. **2** council.

déwasa 1 adult, of age. *Ia sdh* - He has come of age. *He is an adult.* **2** (*Lit.*) time. *Sdh datang -nya utk bekerja giat* The time has come to work energetically. - *dulu* formerly. - *ini* at the present time, nowadays. **men-kan** mature s.t. **pen-an 1** maturation, bringing to adulthood. **2** raising the age. ~ *usia kawin* raising of the marrying age.

déwasawan a mature person.

déwata gods.

déwé, déwék (*Jv*) o.'s own. *Ia mau énaknya* - He wants to do as he likes. *Kan juga kau bangsa* - You are o. of us, too, aren't you?

déwi 1 goddess. - *Pertiwi* earth goddess. - *Sri* goddess of rice crop (wife of Vishnu). **2** darling, beloved.

déwi-déwi (*Naut.*) davit.

Dg. [*daéng*] title in S. Sulawesi.

dg.₁ [*désigram*] decigram.

dg.₂, dgn. [*dengan*] with.

dh.₁ [*dahulu*] formerly.

dh.₂ [*dgn hormat*] with respectful salutations (in correspondence).

dhalim see LALIM.

dharma₁ term used in names of associations. - *Partiwi* Association of Military Wives. - *Tirta* an association of peasant water users in Central Java. - *Wanita* Association of Retired Civil Servants and the Wives of Civil Servants.

dharma₂ see DARMA.

dhat see ZAT.

dholim see LALIM.

di 1 in, at, on, upon (general locative preposition). - *dapur* in the kitchen. - *Jawa* on Java. - *rumah* at home. **2** (*Coll.*) at, on (temporal preposition). - *hari kemudian* later on. - *hari Kemis* on Thursday.

di- 3d person passive verbal prefix.

dia 1 he, she. - *lagi makan* She is eating. *si* - that certain s.o. (often a lover). **2** (*Coll.*) it. *itu* - 1 That is it. 2 Precisely! *Mana pasarnya? Itu - di depan* Where is the market? There it is, ahead. - *org* they. **-nya** he, she (as opposed to another). *Yg penting* ~ *dulu baru isterinya* What is important is that he himself get taken care of first and his wife only afterwards. **men-kan** treat s.o. with less respect than proper by referring to him as *dia. Jangan -kan Présidén tetapi pakailah beliau* Do not use *dia* to refer to the president. You must use *beliau*.

diabét diabetes.

diafan diaphanous.

diafragma, diafrakma (*Anat.*) diaphragm.

diagnosa, diagnose diagnosis. **men-** diagnose. **pen-an** act of diagnosing.

diagnostik diagnostic.

diakon (*Rel.*) deacon.

diakritis diacritical.

dialék (*Ling.*) dialect.

dialéktik, dialéktika dialectic. **men-kan 1** use dialectics in analyzing s.t. **2** cause a confrontation.

dialéktis dialectical.

dialog, dialoog /dialok/ dialogue. **ber-** hold a dialogue.

diam₁ 1 silent, quiet. *Ia - saja, tdk berkata apa-apa* She was silent and said nothing. *Keadaan di kampung itu - saja* It was completely quiet in the village. -*!* Quiet! - *dlm seribu bahasa* absolutely quiet. **2** motionless. *Bola itu tdk bergerak; tinggal - saja* The ball did not move; it just remained motionless. **3** idle. *Ia tak pernah -, selalu ada yg dikerjakannya* He was never idle but was always busy doing s.t. **-²** quietly, secretly. *Meréka kawin dgn* ~ *saja* They were married secretly. ~ *ubi* still waters run deep. *pengakuan secara* ~ implicit admission. **ber-** be silent, say nothing. ~ *diri* be silent. **ber-** (²)**an** refuse to speak to e.o. **men-** be silent. **men-i** keep silent toward, not speak to s.o. **men-kan, memper-kan 1** keep quiet about s.t. (scandal, etc.). *Mula-mula maksud kami hendak* ~ *hal itu* Initially it was our intention to keep the matter quiet. **2** ignore, disregard. **3** keep s.o. or s.t. silent. *Anjingnya di-kan biar tdk menggonggong lagi* He silenced his dog to stop it from barking. **4** keep s.t. motionless. **ter-** 1 fall silent or motionless. *Ia* ~ *mendengar berita itu* She fell silent upon hearing that news. **2** quietest. **pen-** s.o. taciturn. *Ia adalah kepala pasukan yg* ~ He is a closemouthed troop commander. **kepen-an** taciturnity.

diam₂ ber- reside. *Meréka* ~ *di kota* They live in town. **men-i, menge-i 1** reside at. **2** inhabit (an island, etc.). **ke-an** residence.

diaméter diameter.

diamétrikal, diamétris diametrical.

dian taper or oil lamp. **men-i** illuminate s.t. with taper or oil lamp.

diang₁ ber- warm o.s. near the fire (esp. after childbirth). **men-kan 1** warm, heat. *Ia* ~ *badan di api unggun* He warmed himself up at the open fire. **2** roast. **pen-an 1** hearth, fireplace. **2** temporary hearth constructed to warm a mother soon after childbirth.

diang₂ see MENDIANG.

diaré diarrhea.

diaspor diaspora.

diat (*Isl.*) fine imposed for failure in o.'s religious responsibilities. **men-kan** pay such a fine.

didaktik, didaktis didactic.

didéh (*Jv*) coagulated chicken or beef blood as food.

didih men- 1 boil. *Air itu sdh* ~ The water's boiling. **2** boil, rage. *Darahnya* ~ His blood was boiling. **men-kan** boil s.t.

didik *anak* - pupil. **men-** 1 educate. *sifat* ~ educational quality. 2 bring up, raise (children). **men-kan** teach or practice s.t. **ter-** educated. *kaum* ~ intelligentsia. **keter-an** state of being educated. **-an** 1 education, upbringing. 2 pupil, product of a certain teacher, alumnus. *Ia* ~ *Bandung* He was educated in Bandung. **pen-** educator. **pen-an** education. ~ *kejuruan* vocational education. ~ *masyarakat* continuing education, adult education. **berpen-an** have an education, be educated.

didis$_1$ men- slice thinly.

didis$_2$ (*Jv*) **men-** removes nits and lice from o.'s hair.

dido, didong$_1$ (*Sl.*) 1 Frenchman. 2 European. *Belanda* - full-blooded Dutch.

didong$_2$ stubborn, obstinate.

didong$_3$ k.o. dance in Aceh.

diesel 1 (*Coll.*) diesel motor, electric generator. 2 diesel fuel. **men-kan** change (bus engines, etc.) to diesel fuel.

diés natalis anniversary (of educational institutions, universities, college departments, etc.).

diét diet. **ber-** diet.

diferénsial (*Math*) differential.

diferénsiasi differentiation. **men-kan** differentiate.

difinisi see DÉFINISI.

difraksi diffraction.

diftéri diphtheria.

diftong diphthong.

difusi diffusion.

digdaya (*Jv*) invulnerable.

digital digital. *jam tangan* - digital wrist watch.

digjaya see DIGDAYA.

Digul Boven Digul, place of political exile in Irian Jaya during Dutch period. **men-kan** send s.o. into exile at Boven Digul. **pen-an** exiling at Boven Digul.

Digulis *org* - o. who was exiled at Boven Digul.

diit see DIÉT.

dik see ADIK.

dikau (*Lit.*) you.

dikhotomi see DIKOTOMI.

dikir (*Isl.*) repeatedly chant part of the confession of faith, often in unison, as a form of worship. **ber-** engage in such a form of worship. **men-kan** chant s.t. in praise of God. **pen-** chanter of phrases in praise of God.

dikit little, small. *Cepatan* - Make it a bit faster. - *demi sedikit* bit by bit. **se-** see SEDIKIT. **se-^{2}nya** at (the very) least. *Engkau hrs belajar* ~ *sejam sehari* You must study at least an hour a day. **sese-^{2}nya** as little as possible. **ber-^{2}** 1 little by little, bit by bit. ~ *menjadi bukit* Acorns become oaks. 2 be thrifty. *Asal* ~ *saja cukuplah gajimu itu* Provided you are thrifty, your wages are sufficient.

diklat [*pendidikan dan latihan*] training and education program for gvt. and military personnel.

diko see DUKO.

dikotomi dichotomy.

dikrit see DEKRÉT.

diktat written summary of lectures, often used as a university textbook.

diktator dictator. **men-i** rule over (with iron hand). ~ *wilayahnya* rule over o.'s region with iron hand. **-^{2}an** 1 act like a dictator, be domineering. *Jgn main* ~ Do not act like a dictator. 2 false dictator. **ke-an** 1 dictatorship. 2 dictatorialness.

diktatoris dictatorial.

diktatur dictatorial gvt.

dikté dictation. **men-** 1 dictate to s.o. *Caranya mengajar* ~ *saja; ndak pernah menerangkan* The way she teaches is just to read off her notes; she never explains anything. 2 command s.o. *Dia* ~ *saya, sialan!* He lords it over me, dammit! **men-kan** 1 dictate s.t. *"Dgn hormat," beginilah akan dikannya* "Greetings" that is what he will dictate. 2 dictate, determine. *Pemesan* ~ *tawaran* The buyer dictates the price offered. **-an** dictation.

diktum decision of a high authority.

dilak men- roll o.'s eyes.

dilalah (*Jv*) by God's will, by chance. *Saya sedang lapar, eh kok - ada yg bawa kué* I was hungry, when can you believe it, by chance s.o. brought some cake.

diléma dilemma.

dilétan dilettante.

dilétantisme dilettantism.

dim$_1$ a linear measurement, decimeter.

dim$_2$ (*Auto.*) bright headlights. **(me)nge-** dim the headlights. *Ia* ~ *lampunya spy tdk menyilaukan mobil yg berpapasan dgnnya* He dimmed his lights so they would not blind the oncoming car.

dimas (*Jv*) term of address for younger brother.

diménsi dimension.

dimésionir see DÉMISIONÉR.

dimpit see DEMPÉT.

dina of low esteem, ignoble.

dinamik dynamic. **ke-an** dynamism.

dinamika dynamics. - *kelompok* group dynamics.

dinamis dynamic. **men-kan** dynamicize s.t. **pen-** dynamist.

dinamisasi dynamicization. **men-kan** dynamicize.

dinamisator dynamist.

dinamisir men- make dynamic. ~ *pelaksanaan tugasnya* render dynamic the implementation of his task. **pen-** o. who makes s.t. dynamic. *penggerak dan* ~ *pembangunan* the prime mover and dynamicist of development.

dinamisme dynamism.

dinamit dynamite.

dinamo dynamo.

dinar 1 various k.o. gold coins, now used as jewelry. 2 unit of money in Middle East.

dinas 1 official (gvt.). *mobil* - an office car. *surat* - an official letter. *utk* - for official use. 2 agency, department. - *kehutanan* forest service. - *pemerintah* gvt. department. - *kepanduan* (*Naut.*) pilot service. - *(jaga) malam* night duty. - *pendahulu* office that serves pioneer transmigrants. - *penyelidik* intelligence service. - *selip* towing service. - *tata kota dan daérah* office of city and regional planning. - *tentara* military service. - *traksi* traction, haulage service. 3 gvt. service, official duty.

- *saya sdh sepuluh tahun* I have served 10 years. *Ia sedang -* He is on duty. **4** church service. **ber-** serve in a certain office. *yg baru ~ kurang setahun* those who have had less than a year of service. **men-kan** put s.o. into service. **ke-an** service. *~ umum* public service.

dinasti dynasty. *- ékonomi* large firms that control the economy. *- lama* long established firm or family with vested interest.

dinda see ADINDA.

dinding 1 interior wall, partition. *- antara* partition. *- hias* paneling. *- jantung (Anat.)* cardiac partitions. *- pisah* partition. **2** buttress. *- penupang/tupang* retaining wall. **ber-** have a wall or partition. **ber-kan** walled with s.t. *~ tebing-tebing curam* walled in by steep embankments. **men-1** constitute a wall. **2** wall in, shut off, block. **men-i 1** wall s.t. in. *~ kebun* wall off a garden. **2** block, shut off (a blow, imports, etc.). **men-kan** use as a wall. *~ tangan* use o.'s hands to block s.t. **ter-** walled in, partitioned off. **pen- 1** partition, screen, shield. **2** cover. **3** hindrance, restraint. **pen-an 1** act of walling in, partitioning off. **2** brickwork.

dines see DINAS.

ding *(Coll.)* particle that contradicts o.'s own statement. *Tadi Anna ke sini, ndak, -, kemarin* A few minutes ago Anna came by, no, I guess it was yesterday.

dingdong arcade games, esp. pinball and video.

dingin cold. *- hari ini* It is cold today. *Ia diterima dgn -* She was received coolly. *- hati* indifferent, with a certain detachment. *- kepala* cool (headed). *- tangan* have a green thumb. *- tertulang* very cold, chilled to the bone. *-² * when it is cold. *Merokok, pak, énak ~* It sure is nice to smoke when it is cold. **ber-²** enjoy the coolness. **men-** become cold. *Malam mulai ~* The evening is getting cold. **men-i** cool s.t. off. *Ia ~ kakinya dgn és* He cooled his feet off with some ice. **men-kan 1** refrigerate, chill s.t. (a drink, etc.). **2** cool down (an engine, etc.). **3** calm down (s.o.'s anger, etc.). **ke-an 1** coldness. *~ malam* the coldness of the night. **2** be very cold. *Ia menggigit ~* He trembled with cold. **3** too cold. *Ini ~. Panasin dikit* This is too cold. Heat it up a bit. **pen-1** cooler. *~ air minum* watercooler. *sistim ~* cooling system. **2** o. who soothes away problems, peacemaker. **pen-an** refrigeration, cooling off. *masa ~* a cooling-off period.

dingkik men- watch, spy on.

dingklik stool, seat with no back.

dini early. *lahir -* born prematurely. *diagnosa -* early diagnosis. *- hari* early dawn. **se-²(nya), se-** *mungkin* as early as possible.

diniyah religious (in school names). *Sekolah - Puteri* Girls' Religious School.

dioksid, dioksida dioxide.

diorama diorama.

diosis diocese.

DIP [*Daftar Isian Proyék*] budget proposal for a project.

dipan divan, sofa.

dipati see ADIPATI.

dipisi see DIVISI.

diploma diploma, certificate.

diplomasi diplomacy. **ber-** be diplomatic, engage in diplomacy. *Kita hrs ~ dgn ibu spy masih bisa nonton* We have to engage in some diplomacy with Mother so we can still go to the movies. **men-kan** negotiate s.t.

diplomat diplomat.

diplomatik, diplomatis diplomatic.

diréksi management, administration.

diréktif, diréktip directive.

diréktorat 1 directorate. *- jénderal* directorate general. **2** department, division. *- géologi* geological division. *- inténdans (Mil.)* quartermaster or supply corps.

diréktori directory.

diréktris, diréktrise 1 directress, headmistress. **2** Catholic mother superior.

diréktur director, headmaster. *- jénderal* director general. *- pelaksana/utama* managing director.

dirgahayu long live! long life.

dirgantara sky, upper atmosphere. **ke-an** aerospace affairs.

diri₁ self. *Ia membunuh -* She killed herself. *Jagalah -mu* Take care of yourself. *- sendiri* (by) o.s. *Jika tdk hati-hati -mu sendiri akan rugi* If you do not watch out, you yourself will be the loser. *menganggap - tinggi* consider o.s. superior.

diri₂ ber- 1 stand. *Ia ~ di pintu* She is standing at the door. *~ azamat* stand in a respectful position. *~ di atas kaki sendiri* stand on o.'s own two feet, be self-reliant. *~ sendiri* 1 be on o.'s own. *Sejak saya déwasa saya ~ sendiri* Since I have grown up I have been on my own. **2** independent. *Negara kita sekarang ~ sendiri* Our country is now independent. *~ tegak* 1 stand erect. **2** *(Mil.)* stand at attention. *~ urut* stand in line. **2** exist. *Negara kita tlh ~ beratus-ratus tahun* Our country has existed for hundreds of years. *Gedung itu masih ~* That building still stands. *atas/dr* consist of. **member-kan** cause s.o. or s.t. to stand again. **men-kan 1** cause to stand up. *~ bulu roma* make o.'s hair stand on end. **2** build erect (building, etc.). *~ kémah* pitch a tent. **3** found, establish (business, cooperative, etc.). **ter-1** suddenly stand up. **2** consist. *Usulan itu ~ atas dua bagian* That proposal consists of two parts. *~ atas/dr* consist of. **ke-an** the way o. is, personality, individuality. *~nya sangat kuat. Sukar bekerjasama dgn dia* He is very much an individual. It is hard to work with him. **pen-** founder, organizer. **sepen-** the height of a person. **pen-an 1** building, founding. *~ tugu* erection of a monument. *~ negara kita* founding of our country. **2** stand(point), convictions. **3** *(Mil.)* installation. *Tugas dr ~ darat ialah membekali kesatuan-kesatuan operasionil* The task of a land installation is to supply the operational units. **berpen-an** have a stand, be of the opinion.

dirigén musical director, conductor.

dirigir men- direct (an orchestra).

diris men- water (plants).

Dirjén [*Diréktor Jénderal*] director general.
dirus men- flush with water. ~ *kakus* clean a latrine by flushing it with a lot of water. **men-kan** pour s.t. on or over.
Dirut [*Diréktor Utama*] managing director. **ke-an** adulthood, maturity.
dis.₁ [*dinas*] service, agency.
dis.₂ [*diskualifikasi*] disqualification.
disain design, pattern. - *riset* outline of research. **ber-** have a certain pattern. **men-** design. **pen-** designer. **pen-an** designing.
disainer fashion designer.
disél see DIESEL.
disémbarkasi disembarkation.
disén see DISAIN.
disénteri, diséntri dysentery. - *amubawi* amoebic dysentery.
disérsi see DÉSÉRSI.
disértasi dissertation.
disértir see DÉSÉRTIR.
disharmoni disharmony.
disidén dissident.
disintégrasi organizational disintegration (of parties, cabinets, etc.).
disipasi dissipation.
disipel disciple.
disiplin discipline. **ber-** disciplined. **men-(kan)** discipline, punish (children, etc.). **ke-an** discipline, training. **pen-an** disciplining.
disiplinér disciplinary.
disjoki (*Coll.*) disc jockey.
diskét floppy disc. **men-kan** store on a disc.
disko discotheque. **ber-** dance to disco music. **-²an** lead the disco life-style.
diskontinuitas discontinuity.
diskonto (*Fin.*) discount. **meng-kan** discount. *wé-sél yg di-kan* discount draft.
diskoték, diskotik 1 discotheque. 2 collection of phonograph records. 3 producer of music cassettes.
diskrédit discredit. **men-kan** discredit. ~ *poténsi Kristen* discredit Christian potential. *manusia yg di-kan* a human being who is discredited. **pen-an** discrediting.
diskrépansi discrepancy.
diskridit see DISKRÉDIT.
diskriminasi discrimination. **men-(kan)** discriminate against. ~ *org asing* discriminate against foreigners.
diskriminatif discriminatory.
diskualifikasi disqualification. **men-(kan)** disqualify.
diskualifisir men- disqualify.
diskusi discussion. **ber-** engage in discussion and conversation. **men-kan** discuss s.t. *Masih banyak yg hrs kita -kan* We still have lots to discuss. **pen-an** discussing.
dislokasi 1 (*Med.*) dislocation. 2 disturbance.
disonan dissonant.
disonansi dissonance.
disorganisasi disorganization.
disparitas disparity.

dispénsasi 1 (*Rel.*) dispensation. 2 exemption (from tax, official responsibility, etc.). *Saya diberi - utk tdk mengikuti ceramah itu* I was given permission not to attend that talk.
dispérsi men-kan disperse.
disposisi authorizing signature.
disproporsi disproportion.
disproporsional disproportionate.
distilasi distillation. **men-** distill.
distilat distillate.
distilir men- distill.
distorsi distortion. **men-kan** distort. **pen-an** distorting.
distribusi distribution. **men-kan** distribute, allocate s.t. **pen-an** distributing.
distrik administrative district.
ditéksi see DÉTÉKSI.
ditéktif see DÉTÉKTIF.
ditél see DETÉL.
diter. [*diterjemahkan*] translated.
Ditjén [*Direktorat Jéndral*] Directorate General.
dito ditto.
Div. [*divisi*] division.
divan see DIPAN.
divérsifikasi diversification. **men-kan** diversify.
dividé et impéra divide and rule.
dividén dividend.
divisi 1 (*Mil.*) division. 2 (*Bio.*) phylum. **ber-²** be myriad in number. *Kami menghadapi tikus yg ~ itu* We faced rats that came like an army.
DIY [*Daérah Istiméwa Yogyakarta*] Special District of Yogyakarta.
DK [*daya kuda*] horsepower.
DKI (Jaya) [*Daérah Khusus Ibukota*] Special Capital District (of Jkt).
dkk. [*dgn kawan-kawan*] et al.
dl. [*dalam*] in.
dléwéran (*Jv*) ooze and trickle down slowly. *Pe-luhnya -* Her sweat flowed.
dll. [*dan lain-lain*] and others, etc.
dlm. [*dalam*] in.
dls., dlsb. [*dan lain sebagainya*] and so forth.
DN [(*Départemén*) *Dlm Negeri*] (Department) of Internal Affairs.
dng. [*dengan*] with, by means of.
doa /do'a, doa/ prayer. - *kunut* (*Isl.*) prayer said at a certain point, e.g. early morning, the 17th night of the fast, etc. - *pendinding* prayer to save o.s. from danger or calamity. - *réstu* blessing (esp. from o.'s elders). - *selamat* blessing, grace. - *sya-faat* the Catholic creed. **ber-, men-** pray, say prayers. **men-i** say a prayer on behalf of s.o. *Ssdh di-i, meréka berangkat* After having prayers said for them, they departed. **men-kan** pray for s.t. (to happen). *Ibulah yg selalu saya -kan* I always pray for Mother.
doane see DUANE.
doang, doangan (*Jkt*) only, no more than. *Itu membuang duit -* That is nothing but throwing money away.
dobel 1 double. *Kenapa saya di suruh bayar -?* Why must I pay twice? - *gardan* four-wheel drive.

2 (*Sport*) doubles. - *campuran* mixed doubles. - *pria/putri* men's and women's doubles. **men-** (*Crd.*) double. **men-kan** double, duplicate. **-an** s.o.'s double, counterpart.

dobelop double-barreled rifle.

dobi (*Lit.*) laundryman. **ber-, men-** go to a laundryman. **men-kan** send s.t. out to be washed.

dobis caps (for toy guns).

doblé gold-plated.

dobol₁ perforated, torn. *Karung itu -* The sack has a hole in it. *- mulutmu!* (*Vulg.*) You are talking irresponsibly! **men-kan** pierce, puncture. *Ia siap akan - kartu pemilihan itu* He was ready to pierce the election card.

dobol₂ see DOBEL.

dobrak smashed, broken open (of door, gate, fence, etc.). **men-** **1** batter down, break in. *Meréka ~ pintu itu* They battered the door down. *~ kemacetan* break (through) bottleneck. **2** (*Mil.*) penetrate (defenses). **-an** breakthrough. *~ Bannister atas waktu empat menit* Bannister's breakthrough of the four-minute (mile). **pen-** **1** batterer. **2** wrecker, demolisher. **3** k.o. crowbar to remove nails, boards, etc. **pen-an** **1** battering. *~ rumah* housebreaking, burglarizing. **2** break through.

dodét (*Sl.*) **men-** rip open the belly.

dodok₁ (*Jv*) squat, kneel sitting on the hams.

dodok₂ /dodok/ **men-** smooth out a metal sheet by hammering.

dodol k.o. taffy made of sticky rice, coconut milk, and palm sugar (often with durian).

dodor ke-an loose and ill-fitting (of clothing). *Pakaiannya ~* His clothes were too big for him.

dodos men- plane s.t. *~ papan perahu* plane boat planks. **men-i** **1** dig s.t. up. *Umbi-umbi tlh habis di-i* She dug up all the tubers. **2** (*Coll.*) steal little by little.

dodot (*Jv*) k.o. batik wraparound worn by courtiers and bridegrooms.

dogdog **1** sound of repeated knocking (at door, etc.). **2** make such a sound. **3** (*Sd*) small drum.

dogér (*Sd*) k.o. folk dance performed by women. **men-** dance this dance.

dogma dogma.

dogmatika (*Rel.*) dogmatics.

dogmatis dogmatic. **ke-an** dogmatism.

dogol **1** without horns (of horned animals). **2** without combs (of fowl). **3** stupid. **ke-an** stupidity.

doha (*Isl.*) nonobligatory prayertime around 10 a.m.

doi /do'i/ (*Sl.*) he or she (of o.'s lover).

dok₁ /dok/ (*Navy*) dock. *- apung* floating dock. *- darat/galian* drydock. **menge-, men-kan** dock (a ship). **penge-an** docking.

dok₂ /dok/ see DOKTER.

dokar horse-drawn buggy. **ber-** ride a buggy.

doking docking (of ship, etc.).

doklonyo (*Coll.*) cologne.

dokoh₁ pendant for a necklace.

dokoh₂ see DUKUH.

dokok-dokok see KUÉ.

dokter doctor, physician, esp. *dok* as a term of address. *- ahli* medical specialist. *- anak* pediatrician. *- gigi* dentist. *- héwan* veterinarian. *- jaga* doctor on call. *- Jawa* prewar Indonesian doctor educated in Java. *- jiwa* psychiatrist. *- kandungan* obstetrician. *- mata* ophthalmologist. *- umum* general practitioner. **ber-** be provided with a doctor. **men-i** provide medical treatment for s.o. *Dr. Bhé yg ~ Ayah dulu* It was Dr. Bhe who treated Father at that time. **men-kan** bring s.o. to the doctor's. **ke-an** medical. *fakultas ~* school of medicine. *~ gigi* dentistry. *~ pencegahan* preventive medicine.

doktor holder of doctorate. *- ékonomi* PhD in economics. *- kehormatan* honorary PhD.

doktoral doctoral studies. *ujian -* doctoral examination.

doktoranda **1** female holder of postgraduate degree in humanities below doctoral rank. **2** female college graduate (post-1980).

doktorandus **1** s.o. with postgraduate degree in humanities below doctoral rank (pre-1980). **2** academic degree in humanities equivalent to baccalaureate (post-1980).

doktrin doctrine. **ber-** have a doctrine. **men-** indoctrinate.

doktrinér doctrinaire.

doku (*Sl.*) money.

dokumén document. **pen-an** documentation.

dokuméntalis documentalist.

dokuméntasi documentation. **men-** document. **men-kan** document. **pen-an** system of documentation, documenting.

dol **1** damaged or worn because of overuse. **2** (*Coll.*) crazy, mad.

dolak-dalik constantly changing, vacillating.

dolan (*Jv*) **1** make a visit for pleasure. *Ia - ke rumah temannya* He went out to his friend's home. **2** play. *Temannya diajak -* He invited his friend to play with him. **-an** play.

dolar **1** dollar, esp. the US currency. *- Malaysia* the Malaysian *ringgit*. **2** (*Coll.*) any gold coin. *- Meksiko* Mexican gold pesos. **3** k.o. round, sweet wafer. **men-kan** convert s.t. to US dollars.

dolarsén (*Coll.*) cent of US currency.

dolfin dolphin.

dolim see LALIM.

dollar see DOLAR.

dolle Mina radical feminist.

dolog [*dépot logistik*] warehouse for foodstuff.

dolok (*Batak*) mountain.

dom (*Coll.*) compass.

domba **1** sheep. *- Allah* (*Rel.*) Lamb of God. **2** (*Rel.*) the congregation.

domblong (*Jv*) open-mouthed due to surprise.

dombrong ke-an baggy, fitting too loose (of clothes).

doméin domain (of authority).

doméstik domestic.

domina term of reference for female Protestant minister.

dominan dominant.
dominasi domination. **men-** dominate.
dominé term of reference for Protestant minister.
dominir men- dominate.
domino dominoes.
domisili (*Leg.*) domicile. **ber-** be domiciled.
dompak₁ ber- 1 leap, jump (in fighting). **2** prance (of horses). **men-** leap up, rear (of horses).
dompak₂ densely packed (of houses, etc.).
dompét 1 wallet. - *kempés/tipis* short of money, broke. **2** relief fund (often organized by a publication). - *Galunggung* relief fund for victims of the Galunggung eruption. - *banjir* flood relief funds.
domplang see-saw. **-an** *sepur* railroad crossing gate.
dompléng men- join, double up. *Kami mencoba ~ kendaraan* We will try to double up in the vehicle. *Boléh ~ satu org?* May I hitch a ride? *~ dgn réklame* get use out of another's advertisement. **men-i** join on to s.t., double up with. **pen-** non-paying passenger. **-an** doubling up, hitching a ride.
dompol bunch. *se- anggur* a bunch of grapes.
donasi donation.
donat doughnut.
donatir, donatur donor, benefactor.
Donau Danube River.
doncang men- jump, leap.
dondang cradle. **ber-** rock back and forth. **men-(kan)** rock (a baby). **-an** cradle.
donder (*Coll.*) scolding. *Ia kena - pacarnya* He really got chewed out by his girlfriend. **men-** severely scold s.o. **-an** scolding.
dong₁ (*Coll.*) particle asserting that interlocutor should already know or do what o. is asserting. *Kamu turut pergi? Ya -!* You going along? Of course! *Sama siapa? Sama dia -. Sama siapa lagi?* Who with? With him, of course. Who else? *Jangan begitu -!* Don't do it that way, dummy! *Kasi sedikit -!* Give me a bit (you know you should).
dong₂ (*E. Indonesia*) they.
dongak men-, ter- 1 pointed upward (of head, rifle muzzle, etc.). **2** gaze up(ward). *Aku ~ I* raised my head. I looked up. **men-kan** cock o.'s head. *Bunga-bunga ~ kembali kepalanya* The flowers lifted their heads again.
dongéng 1 fairy tale, legend. - *perumpamaan* fable. - *rakyat* folktale. - *sasakala* legend. **2** nonsense. - *saja!* That is just nonsense! **men- 1** tell a tale. **2** tell a falsehood. **men-i** tell tales to. *Ia suka ~ aku* She likes to tell me tales. **men-kan** narrate (stories, etc.). **-an 1** myth. **2** false story. **pen-1** storyteller, narrator. **2** o. who tends to tell tall tales.
dongkak leap up.
dongkél lever, jack. **men- 1** lift up, pry loose. *Jendélanya di- pencuri* A thief pried the window open. **2** remove by force, oust s.o. *Apa sebab pangkalan militér asing hrs di- habis?* Why must foreign military bases be done away with? **3** re-

veal (secrets). **-an, pen-** lever. *~ utama* prime mover. **pen-an** removing by force. *Empat perwira ditahan karena merencanakan ~ thd pimpinannya* Some officers were detained because they planned a forcible removal of the leadership. *aksi/gerakan ~* action or movement for forcible removal.
dongkol₁ 1 resentful, acrimonious. **2** irked, vexed. *Saya - menantikan dia sekian lamanya* I was irked waiting for him so long. **men-** be resentful. **men-kan** irksome, aggravating. *~ hati saya apa yg dikatakannya* It really irks me what he said. **ke-an** anger.
dongkol₂ ex-, former. *Dia sekarang jadi lurah -* He now is the former village head.
dongkrak (*Auto.*) jack. **men- 1** jack up (car, etc.). **2** assist s.o. in achieving his purpose. **3** praise, esp. in sycophantic manner.
dongkrok (*Jv*) **n-** remain motionless. *Karena keseléo kaki, dia ~ saja* He just remained still because he sprained his foot.
dongok 1 ponderous, hulking. **2** stupid.
dongong men- stare open-mouthed.
Don Juan see DON YUAN.
donor donor. - *darah* blood donor.
Don Yuan womanizer. **ke-an** womanizing.
doorslag see DORSLAG.
dop₁ 1 hubcap. **2** caps (for toy guns).
dop₂ (*Coll.*) baptism. **menge-** baptize.
dop₃ lightbulb.
dopércis, dopérten (*Coll.*) canned sweet peas.
dopis see DUMPIS.
dor sound of gunshot. **-²an** gunfire. **men-(kan) 1** make a sound like the crack of a rifle. **2** (*Sl.*) shoot. *Tukang catut di-* They shot the black marketer.
doraka see DURHAKA.
dorang₁ k.o. fish.
dorang₂ (*E. Indonesia*) they.
doréng (*Coll.*) striped.
Dorna see DURNA.
dorong men- 1 push. *Meréka ~ mobil itu* They pushed the car. *Ia ~ ke depan* She pushed forward. **2** motivate, provide the impetus. *Kejadian itu yg ~nya utk msk fakultas hukum* It was that event which motivated him to enter law school. **3** urge. *Ibu ~ Ida spy menerima pekerjaan itu* Mother urged Ida to accept that job. **ter-** pushed, shoved. *Ia ~ ke dinding* He was pushed to the wall. *~ waktu* pressed for time. **-an 1** pushing. *Karena ~ kami mobil itu berjalan* Because of our pushing the car started. **2** urging, stimulus. *atas ~ ibunya* at her mother's urging. *~ hati* impulse. **3** impetus, motivation. *~ batu* motive, motivation. *~ kehendak* willpower. **pen-1** promoter, organizer. *~ pergerakan perburuhan* organizer of the labor movement. **2** impetus, incentive. **pen-an** instigation, stimulus.
dorslag, dorslah onionskin paper.
dortrap k.o. bicycle with pedal brakes.
dos 1 small box. - *obat* pillbox. **2** carton, case.
dosa sin. - *asal* (*Rel.*) original sin. **ber-** commit a

sin, be sinful. *Dia tdk ~!* She is innocent! **ke-an** sinfulness. **pen-** sinner.
dosén university-level instructor. *- terbang* university professor engaged by more than o. institution and flying between them. **ke-an** having to do with lecturers.
dosin see LUSIN.
dosir dossier.
dosis (*Med.*) dose. **men-kan** determine the dosage.
dot₁ 1 nipple. 2 pacifier. **men-** suckle, esp. pacifiers.
dot₂ sound of a car horn.
dowér (*Jv*) having a drooping lower lip.
doyan (*Jkt*) be fond of. *Saya tdk - mangga* I do not care for mangoes. **men-i** be fond of s.t. **ke-an** fondness for s.t. to eat.
doyong inclined, not straight. *menara - Pisa* the Leaning Tower of Pisa. **men-** 1 inclined, tilting. *Rumah itu ~* That house leans. 2 make s.t. inclined. **-an** inclination.
dozer bulldozer.
d/p [*dgn perantaraan*] via s.o.
DPC [*Déwan Pimpinan Cabang*] leadership of political party at local level.
DPD [*Déwan Pimpinan Daérah*] leadership of political party at regional level.
DPP₁ [*Déwan Pimpinan Pusat*] leadership of political party at national level.
DPP₂ [*dada, pinggang, pinggul*] chest, waist, hip measurements.
DPP₃ [*dana pembinaan pendidikan*] k.o. gvt. subsidy to state universities to supplement tuition fees.
DPR [*Déwan Perwakilan Rakyat*] Indonesian legislative assembly.
DPRD [*Déwan Perwakilan Rakyat Daérah*] Assembly at provincial, regional, or municipal level.
DPRGR [*Déwan Perwakilan Rakyat Gotong Royong*] The Indonesian Parliament (1959-1973).
dpt. [*dapat*] can, be able.
DPT [*diphteri, pertussis, tetanus*] diphtheria, whooping cough, tetanus vaccine.
dr- see also entries with **der-**.
dr.₁ [*dari*] from.
dr.₂, Dr.₁ [*dokter*] doctor (of medicine).
Dr.₂ [*doktor*] doctor (of philosophy).
Dra. [*doktoranda*] title of woman holding postgraduate degree in humanities below doctoral rank.
draf draft (of plan, etc.).
dragon manual water pump.
draimolen carousel.
drainase drainage.
dram see DRUM.
drama drama. **men-kan** dramatize. **pen-an, per-an** dramatization.
dramatari dance drama.
dramatis dramatic. **men-kan** dramatize, make into a play.
dramatisasi men-kan dramatize, make into a play.

dramatisir men- dramatize, make into a play.
dramaturg dramatist.
dramaturgi dramaturgy.
dramawan stage actor, performer.
drambén see DRUMBAND.
drastis drastic.
drat 1 wire thread. 2 thread of a screw. **men-** thread (a screw).
dréi k.o. drill.
drél sound of staccato crackling (gun salvo, etc.). **men-** spray with bullets. **pen-an** spraying with bullets.
dréssoar /dréswar/ sideboard, buffet.
drg. [*dokter gigi*] dentist.
drh. [*dokter héwan*] veterinarian.
dribbel, dribel men- (*Sport*) dribble.
dril k.o. cloth.
drive /drayp/ (*Sport*) drive in golf.
drodok /drodok/ (*Coll.*) dry dock.
dromedaris dromedary.
drop₁ men-, menge- 1 provide aid outside of ordinary budget. *Pemerintah ~ makanan utk korban banjir* The gvt. came up with food for the flood victims. 2 deliver, drop off, unload. *Dia ~ barang itu di depan rumah saya* He delivered the goods in front of my house. **pen-an, penge-an** dropping (of supplies, etc.).
drop₂ mints, cough-drops.
droping, dropping allocation, us. from outside ordinary channels (direct order of president, etc.).
Drs. [*Dokterandus*] title of o. holding graduate degree in humanities below doctoral rank.
drum 1 drum. 2 oil drum, canister for chemicals. *- sampah* rubbish container.
drumband /drambén/ marching band.
ds. [*dominé*] Protestant clergyman.
dsb. [*dan sebagainya*] etc.
dsl. [*dan selanjutnya*] and so forth.
dst., dstnya. [*dan seterusnya*] and so on.
Dt. [*Datuk*] title in Malaysia and certain parts of Indonesia.
DT see DASWATI.
dtk. [*detik*] second moment.
dto. [*ditandatangani oléh*] signed by.
dua two. *- belas* 12. *- bulanan* bimonthly. *- hati* be hesitant. **men-hatikan** arouse hesitation. *- jurusan* two-way (ticket, etc.). *- kali* two times, twice. **men-kalikan** double s.t. *- mingguan* biweekly, semimonthly. *- puluh* 20. *- sama* (*Sport*) two-all. *- sejoli* couple (of lovers). *- spasi* double-space. *Tak ada -nya* incomparable, without peer. *dlm - tengah tiga* dishonest, deceitful. *sdh - kepalanya* intoxicated. *-(²)nya, ke-²(nya)* both of them. **ber-** both, the two. *Meréka ~ pergi* Both of them went. *antara kita ~* just between the two of us. **(ber)-²** 1 two by two. 2 both. **ber-(²)an** be or do s.t. as two together. *Mariam dan Stewart tdk sering terlihat ~* Mariam and Stewart were infrequently seen together. **men-** become two. *Tongkat patah ~* The cane broke in two. *Hatinya ~* He is of two minds. **kemen-an** indecisiveness. **men-i** take a

2d wife (i.e. cause o.'s wife to be o. of two wives), give o.'s wife a rival. *Ia tdk hendak ~ isterinya* He does not want to take another wife (and make his wife share her rights with another). **men-kan** double, duplicate. *~ Allah* duplicate God, i.e. have another deity besides God. *~ hati* cause hesitation. **memper-(kan)** halve, divide into halves. **menye-kan, menye-i** let s.o. care for the livestock or till the rice field and divide the profit. **ke-** 1 second. *Itu buku yg ~* That is the 2d book. 2 two, both. *Itu ~ bukunya* Those are the two books. *~ belah* both. *~ belah pihak* both sides. **-an** be a pair, esp. of married or courting couples. *~ waé* (*Jv*) just the two of them. **seper-** half. *~ umur* middle-aged. **pen-an** sharecropping on a 50-50 basis. **per-an** 1 50-50 sharecropping. 2 (*Math.*) over two. *tiga ~* three over two (that is, three halves).

duai see IPAR.

duaja banner, ensign.

dualis (*Ling.*) dual.

dualisme dualism.

duane customs.

dub see DAB.

dubang (*Jv*) saliva reddened by betel chewing.

Dubes [*Duta Besar*] ambassador. **men-kan** appoint s.o. ambassador.

dubilah (*Isl., Coll.*) God forbid!

dubun hyena.

dubur anus.

duda widower. *- kembang* childless widower. **men-** be a widower.

dudu men- follow s.o., continue on (without looking back).

duduk 1 sit. *Ia - di korsi* He sat in a chair. *- berjuntai* sit with legs dangling. *- berkokol* sit hunched over. *- bersanding* 1 sit side by side, esp. of a bridal pair. 2 get married. *- bersila* sit cross-legged. *- bersimpuh* sit with o.'s legs folded to o. side and back (a posture for women). *- bertinggung* squat. *- perut* pregnant. *- simpuh* sit with o.'s legs folded to o. side and back (a posture for women). 2 state, situation. *Bagaimana - perkara itu?* What is the state of the case? *-nya kota di sebelah selatan* The city is situated in the south. 3 live, dwell, reside. *- dgn* be engaged or married to. 4 settle, go to the bottom (of dregs). **ber-** be seated. *~ dgn* wedded to. **menge-i, men-i** 1 sit on. 2 occupy a territory. **men-kan** 1 seat s.o. *Dikannya aku di kursi* He seated me in a chair. 2 marry off, betroth. 3 put a matter in perspective. **ter-** 1 fall to seated position. 2 sedimented, settled. *Bubuk kopi tlh ~* The coffee grinds have settled. **ke-an** 1 situation, state. *~ perkara itu sdh jelas* The state of affairs regarding that case is clear. *~ perkawinan* marital status. 2 position. *~ negara itu sangat penting* The position of that country is very important. *~nya dlm pemerintahan* his position in the administration. *~ penyangga* buffer position. 3 status. **seke-an** of the same status. **berke-an** 1 be located. *Kedutaan Inggeris ~ di Jl. Imam Bonjol* The British embassy is located on Imam Bonjol Street. 2 hold the position. *Ia ~ redaktur surat kabar* He is editor of a newspaper. **berseke-an** (*Lit.*) cohabit, live as man and wife. **pen-** inhabitant. *Jumlah ~nya tdk besar* The population is not large. **pen-an** 1 inhabiting. 2 occupation. *~ Jérman* German occupation. 3 bottom, backside. **kepen-an** demography. *soal-soal ~* population affairs.

dudut₁ (*Jv*) **men-** pull, tug at. *Lidahnya akan di- dr kerongkongan* They will pull his tongue from his throat.

dudut₂ (*child language*) penis.

duél 1 duel. 2 (*Coll.*) traffic collision.

duét duet. **ber-** perform a duet.

duga guess, estimate. **-(²)nya** apparently, seemingly. **bersi-** sink out of sight. *Kaum pelarian ~ cepat-cepat msk got* The refugees sank out of sight by jumping into the drainage ditches. **men-** 1 (*Naut.*) take depth bearings. *Ia ~ dlmnya laut* He took soundings of the sea's depth. 2 understand, fathom. *Saya tdk dpt ~ hatinya* I cannot fathom his mind. 3 presume, expect. *Meréka ~ saya akan datang hari ini* They expected that I would come today. **men-²** repeatedly estimate. *secara ~* presumably, likely. **men-kan** guess at s.t. **ter-** presumed, assured. *tdk ~* 1 unfathomable. 2 unexpected. **-an** 1 guess, hunch. 2 assumption. *di luar ~* beyond expectations. **pen-** gauge, depth finder. **pen-an** fathoming, sounding. *~ kompas* compass bearing.

dugal (*Jv*) naughty.

dugang men- restrain s.t. with a rope so that it will not fall.

dugdén (*Jv*) invulnerable.

dugdér (*Jv*) week-long festival before fasting month.

dugong dugong.

duh see ADUH.

duhai see ADUHAI.

duilah, duillah (*Coll.*) My gosh! (exclamation of surprise or astonishment). *-! Rumahnya gedé banget* Gosh! Her home is really big.

duit money. *Berapa - harganya ini?* How much does this cost? **ber-** well-to-do, wealthy. **men-kan** sell o.'s property. **-an** concerning money. *mata ~* loving money (lit., eye for money).

duk /duk/ kerchief.

duka grief, sorrow. *- nestapa* 1 grief, sorrow. 2 wretched, miserable. **ber-** (*hati*) be sorrowful. **men-kan** distress, distressing. *Kamu ~ org tuamu saja* You just distress your parents. **ke-an** sorrow, misery. *tujuh ~ Santa Perawan Maria* (*Rel.*) seven sorrows of the Holy Virgin Mary.

dukacarita, dukacerita tragedy, story with sad theme.

dukacita profound sorrow. *Terimalah - kami* Please accept our sympathy. *- atas kehilangan anaknya* grief over loss of o.'s child. **ber-** grieve, mourn. *Ia ~ karena anaknya meninggal* She grieved because her child died. *Seluruh negara ~ ketika raja wafat* The entire country went into mourning when the king passed away. *ayah yg ~*

a grief-stricken father. **men-kan 1** mourn, grieve over. **2** cause sorrow or displeasure.

dukana taking pleasure in sex, lascivious.

duko spray paint (for cars, etc.). **men-** apply spray paint to s.t.

duku lanseh tree or its fruit.

dukuh hamlet. **se-** the whole hamlet. **pe-an 1** cluster of hamlets. **2** pertaining to the hamlet.

dukun indigenous medical practitioner, shaman. *- bayi/beranak* midwife. *- buntut* fortune teller for a lottery. *- klenik* shaman who goes into a trance. *- paés* (*Jv*) o. who makes up a bride. *- paraji* (*Sd*) traditional midwife. *- tiban* shaman who received his power through s.t. which suddenly befell him. **ber- 1** receive treatment from a shaman. **2** serve as a shaman. **men-i** minister to s.o. as a shaman. **men-kan** take s.o. to a shaman to get his problem cured. **ke-an** having to do with shamanism. *dunia ~* the world of shamans. **pe-an, per-an** native healing, shamanism. *praktek ~* practice of native healing.

dukung ber- be carried on the back or hip like a child. **men- 1** carry as o. would carry a child, on the back or straddling the hip (with support of the arm). *Anak itu di- di punggung ibunya* The mother carried the child pickaback. **2** support, espouse (a cause). **-an** support, endorsement (esp. in politics). **pen-** supporter, proponent. **pen-an** supporting, endorsing (a cause, etc.).

dulang₁ food tray. *- alas* coaster. *- pelanda* pan for mining gold. **men-** pan for gold. **pen-** prospector. *~ mas* gold prospector. **pen-an** panning (for gold).

dulang₂ printer's galley. **pen-an** setting up and printing a galley.

dulang₃ men- feed (a child).

duli (*Lit.*) **1** dust. **2** expression in royal titles. *- baginda* Your majesty (i.e. in the dust of your highness). **ber-** be dusty.

dulu 1 formerly, previously. *- ia tinggal di sini* He formerly lived here. *Pd zaman - blm ada mobil* In former times there were no cars. *Isterinya yg - sdh dicerainya* He has divorced the wife he had formerly. *- kala* long ago. **2** first (before doing s.t. else). *Makanlah - sblm pergi* Eat first before you go. **3** before, prior. *- drp surat ini kami tlh mengirim surat yg lain* Prior to this letter we sent you another o. *lebih -*, first, before others. *Saya pergi lebih -*. *Kalian nanti saja menyusul* I will go beforehand. You all follow later. **4** for the time being. *Duduklah -, Tuan* Sit down for now, Sir. *Tunggulah -!* Wait a moment! **-² 1** previous, former. **2** earlier. **-nya** formerly. **ber-²an, -** **men-i** race o. another. **men-i** be ahead of, precede. **men-kan** give precedence or priority to. **ke-an** be preceded by. *Saya tlh ~ org lain* S.o. else got there first. **-an** (*Coll.*) first before others.

dulur (*Jv*) kin, family.

dum-dum sound of drum or cannon.

dumel (*Jv*) nag, complain.

dumpis caps (for toy guns, etc.).

dung sound of drum.

dungak see DONGAK.

dungu 1 dull-witted, mentally slow. **2** gullible. **men-kan** render dull-witted. **ke-an** stupidity.

dunia 1 world. *- akhirat* the hereafter. *- barat* the Western world. *- gaib* world of magic or mystery. *- Ketiga* the Third World. *- luar* outside world. *- olahraga* sports world. *- merdéka* the free world. *- perdagangan* world of commerce. *- rohani* spiritual world. **2** (*Bio.*) kingdom. **se-** the whole world. *fédérasi mahasiswa ~* international student federation. **ber- 1** live in the world. **2** compete for worldly goods and pleasures. **men-** being of the world, secular. *bagi kebudayaan kita yg ~ ini* for this secular culture of ours. **men-kan** secularize, make profane. **ke-an 1** affairs of mortal life. **2** worldly, profane. **pen-an** secularization, worldliness.

duniawi worldly, secular. *kekayaan -* earthly riches. **men-kan** secularize. **ke-an 1** worldly, secular. **2** transient, impermanent. **pen-an** secularization.

duniawiah worldly, profane.

dunsanak (*M*) relatives.

dup see DOP₂.

dupa incense. **men-i** burn incense for. **pe-an, per-an** censer.

dupak see DEPAK₁.

duplik (*Leg.*) rejoinder, rebuttal.

duplikasi duplication (of effort, etc.).

duplikat, duplo duplicate, carbon copy.

dur sound of explosion.

durén (*Jv*) see DURIAN.

Durga Hindu goddess of destruction.

durhaka rebellious, insubordinate. *isteri -* faithless wife. **ber- 1** rebel. **2** commit an act of insubordination. **men-** be rebellious. *~ sumpah sendiri* break o.'s vow. **men-i** rebel against. *~ révolusi* betray the revolution. **ke-an** rebelliousness. **pen- 1** traitor. **2** rebel, insurgent. **pen-an 1** treachery. **2** rebellion, insurgency.

duri 1 thorn, burr, spine. **2** fish bone. **ber-** thorny, prickly. **ber-² 1** very thorny, prickly. **2** with many difficulties. **men-** sharp, stinging (remarks, etc.). *~ hati* be annoyed.

durian durian fruit and tree. (*dpt*) *- runtuh* (have) a windfall or an unexpected piece of luck.

durja see MURAM.

durjana (*Lit.*) evil, wicked. **ke-an** evil, crime.

Durna 1 (*Jv*) name of character in the *wayang*, adviser first to o. side and later the other. **2** intrigue-ridden adviser. **men-i** incite, foment.

dursila (*Jv*) unethical.

dus₁ shower (bath).

dus₂ (*Coll.*) so, consequently. *-, kamu yg bersalah* So, you are the o. at fault.

dus₃ see DOS.

dusel (*Jv*) **n-, men-** snuggle up close.

dusi men- continue to feel drowsy after nap.

dusin men- 1 be awake. *Ia sebentar ~ lalu tertidur lagi* He was awake for a moment then fell back asleep. **2** be conscious of, realize. *Ia tdk ~ maksudnya* She was not aware of his intentions.

dusta 1 lie, falsehood. **2** tell a lie. **ber-, men-** tell a lie. **men-i** lie to s.o. *Ia ~ saya* He lied to me. **men-kan** deny, denounce as a lie. *Ia ~ segala desas-desus itu* She denounced as a lie all the rumors. **ke-an** prevarication. **pen-** liar. **pen-an** lying.

dusun 1 (*Lit.*) orchard. **2** village far from urban areas. **pe-an** cluster of villages.

dut (*Coll.*) dead.

duta ambassador. *- besar luar biasa dan berkuasa penuh* ambassador plenipotentiary and envoy extraordinary. *- istiméwa* special envoy. *- keliling/ pengembara* ambassador-at-large, roving ambassador. *- pribadi* personal envoy (of president, etc.). *- besar* ambassador. **men-besarkan** appoint s.o. as ambassador. **ke-an** embassy. **pe-/pen-** envoy, emissary. **per-an** delegation, mission.

dutawati ambassadress.

duyun ber-² in throngs. *Meréka datang ~ hendak melihat filem itu* They came flocking in to see the movie.

duyung see DUGONG.

dwi- two (formal and only in certain constructions).

dwiarti ambiguous. **ke-an** ambiguity.

dwibahasa bilingual. **ber-** be bilingual. **ke-an** bilingualism.

dwibahasawan a bilingual.

dwidasawarsa 20th anniversary.

dwifungsi dual function, esp. of the military, referring to its soldierly and political roles. **ber-** have a dual function. **ke-an** dual functionalism. **pen-an** having a dual function.

dwiguna dual-purpose.

dwihuruf (*Ling.*) digraph.

dwikewarganegaraan dual citizenship.

dwikora [*dwikomando rakyat*] The people's two mandates: crush Malaysia and defend the revolution (slogan of Sukarno era).

dwimakna ambiguous. **ke-an** ambiguity.

dwipekanan biweekly.

dwisuku (*Ling.*) disyllabic.

dwitunggal duumvirate, two working as o. *Bung Karno dan Bung Hatta merupakan - dlm memproklamasikan kemerdékaan* Sukarno and Hatta as a duumvirate declared Indonesia's independence.

dwiwarna the Indonesian flag, the Red and White.

dwiwulanan bimonthly.

dynamo see DINAMO.

dyséntri see DISÉNTRI.

dz see also entries with **d-, l-,** or **z-.**

E

e uh, hesitation particle. *Kami - aku sesungguhnya cuma asal bicara* We, eh, I was just talking for the sake of saying s.t.

é₁ /é/ e, the 5th letter of the alphabet.

é₂ Ha! emphatic particle. *-, mati lu!* Ha, serves you right! (e.g. in killing an insect). *-,-, sabar dong!* Now, now, please be patient.

é₃ Hey! interjection to attract attention or to express astonishment. *Darah! -, siapa membunuh Kasan?* Blood! Hey! Who killed Kasan? *-, kau tdk pakai cat bibir?* Hey, don't you use lipstick?

ébam porcelain pot with lid.

éban see HÉBAN.

ebang see BANG₂.

ébék awning.

ébéng see IBING.

ébi dried shrimps.

éboh see HÉBOH.

ebom see BOM₁.

ébonit ebonite.

ebor see BOR.

ébro two- or four-wheeled carriage.

Ec. [*ékonomi*] economics (used in academic degrees).

écé meng- make a fool of, kid, make fun of. **-an** kidding, fooling.

écék apparently, outwardly. **-²** not be serious, just appear as.

écék-écék k.o. legume.

ecéng, écéng k.o. water plant with red leaves and edible flowers. *- gondok* k.o. water hyacinth.

écér meng-(kan) sell retail. *Harian yg di-kan laku keras* The newspapers sold in retail were selling fast. **-an** retail, price of a single item. *harga ~* retail price. *Majalah Témpo kalau ~ harganya sdh dua ribu Tempo* magazine already costs 2,000 rupiah per copy. **peng-** retailer.

éco (*Jv*) tasty, delicious.

édah see IDAH₁.

édan 1 wild, frantic. **2** (*Coll.*) insane, mad, crazy. **ke-an** craziness, foolishness.

édap see IDAP.

édar ber- 1 turn, revolve. *Bumi ~* The earth revolves. **2** circle (of flying plane). **3** circulate (of money, etc.). **meng-i 1** revolve around s.t. *Bumi ~ matahari* The earth revolves around the sun. **2** circle around, encircle. *dr semua jalan yg ~ Bengkulu* from all roads that go around Bengkulu. *Matanya ~ setiap org* His gaze fell on everyone around him. **3** explore, roam (the seas, etc.). **meng-kan, memper-kan 1** circulate (a letter, etc.). **2** circulate, issue (money). **3** pass around.

Di-kan org bekas kaléng sardéncis S.o passed around an old sardine can. **-an 1** s.t. circulated. *surat* ~ a circular. ~ *pérs* press release. **2** orbit, cycle. **peng-** circulator, dealer. ~ *cék kosong* passer of bad checks. ~ *morfin* dealer in morphine. **peng-an** act of circulation. ~ *uang palsu dpt dihukum* You can go to jail for circulating counterfeit money. **per-an 1** rotation, revolution (of wheel). ~ *dunia* the ways of the world, life's ups and downs. ~ *zaman* changing of the times. **2** orbit. **3** circulation. ~ *darah* circulation of blood. ~ *udara* ventilation, circulation of air.

édisi edition (of book, etc.). - *istiméwa* special issue (of newspaper or magazine). **meng-kan** issue, publish (book, etc.).

édit meng- edit (manuscript, etc.). **peng-** editor. **peng-an** editing.

éditor, éditur editor (of manuscript, etc.).

édukasi education.

édukatif, édukatip educative, instructive.

é é é Say! interjection of amazement or of being amusingly offended. - *benar! Di tempat tidur tampaklah tubuh seorg manusia* My God, it is true! I saw a human body on the bed. - *ini beli sendiri, bukan punya kantor!* Hey wait a minute, I bought this myself, it does not belong to the office!

é-é (*child language*) doo-doo, feces.

eem-eem (*child language*) yummy, tasty.

éfék₁ /éfék/ effect. - *sampingan* side-effect.

éfék₂, éfékten /éfék, éfékten/ (*Fin.*) share, stock.

éféktif, éféktip effective. **meng-kan** cause s.t. to be effective. ~ *pelaksanaan tugas-tugas* make the implementation of tasks effective. **ke-an** effectiveness. **peng-an** effort to make s.t. effective. ~ *peraturan itu mendatangkan kelancaran perdagangan* The effective enforcement of the regulations has yielded a smooth flow of trade.

éféktivitas effectiveness.

éffékten see ÉFÉK₂.

éfisién efficient. **meng-kan** render efficient. **ke-an** efficiency. **peng-an** efforts to make s.t. efficient.

éfisiénsi efficiency. **peng-an** efforts to make s.t. efficient.

egah glorious. **meng-kan** *diri* glorify o.s., boast.

égah meng- shuffle, stagger.

égois egoist, egoistic. **ke-an** egoism.

égoisme egoism.

égoistis egoistic.

égol meng- 1 pry up, lift with a lever in a jerky motion. **2** sway o.'s hips. **meng-i 1** pry (several things). **2** move s.t. with a jerk. *Penari itu* ~ *pasangannya utk menarik perhatiannya* The dancer jerked her partner to draw his attention. **ter-²** jerkily, in jerks. *Mesin giling sedang* ~ *maju mundur meratakan sebuah pelataran* The roller was jerkily moving back and forth to level a yard.

égos meng- 1 evade. *Dia tdk bisa* ~, *jadi kena* He could not get out of the way so he was hit. **2** evade, get around s.t., get out of the way of s.t. *Dia* ~ *sénsor itu* He got around the censor. **meng-i** evade, get around s.t. **meng-kan** move s.t. to

get it out of the way. *Ia* ~ *mobilnya utk menghindari tabrakan* He swerved his car abruptly to avoid an accident. *Ia* ~ *pembicaraanya* He avoided what they were speaking about by changing the topic.

égoséntris egocentric.

égoséntrisme egocentricity.

égrang stilts. *main/berjalan dgn* - walk on stilts.

egung see GONG₁.

eh ugh, interjection expressing disgust.

éh see É₂.

ehm₁ whatsit (particle used to avoid saying actual word). *Dia sdh punya . . . -* She has already got a . . . ehem (boyfriend).

ehm₂ (*Coll.*) uh-huh, yes.

éi see É₂.

éit exclamation used when trying to avoid physical or verbal attack.

éja meng- spell. *Susah benar* ~ *namanya* It sure is difficult to spell his name. **meng-kan** spell out to s.o. **-an** spelling, orthography. ~ *Yg Disempurnakan* official Indonesian and Malaysian spelling system adopted in 1972. **peng-an** spelling.

éjakulasi ejaculation of semen.

ejan meng- strain abdominal muscles when defecating.

éjawantah visible, manifest. **(me)ng-** materialize, become visible. **meng-kan** manifest, materialize. *Déwa itu* ~ *diri sbg seékor burung* The deity manifested itself as a bird. ~ *suara hati nurani* manifest o.'s deepest feelings. **ter-** manifested. **peng-an** manifestation, embodiment, materialization.

éjék mock, ridicule, make fun of. **meng-** mock, ridicule, deride. ~ *org* mock s.o. **meng-kan** mock on account of s.t. ~ *celananya yg pakai rénda* make fun of the pants with lace on them. **-an 1** mockery, derision, ridicule. *Terasa nada* ~ *di dlmnya* He felt the tone of mockery in it. **2** object of ridicule, butt of joke. *Kalau ada org yg tahu, pastilah kau akan jadi* ~ If s.o. finds out, you will be a laughing-stock for sure.

ék₁ meng- /meng'ék/ calibrate.

ék₂ oak.

éka one, single (in formal compounds and slogans).

ékabahasa (*Ling.*) monolingual.

ékabahasawan, ékabasawan (*Lit.*) monolingual person.

ékamarga one-way (traffic, road).

ékamatra unidimensional.

Ékaprasetia Pancakarsa title of 1978 speech by Suharto, in which he gave his interpretation of the *Pancasila*.

ékaristi (*Rel.*) Eucharist.

ékasila condensation of the *Pancasila* into o. principle (1960s).

ékasuku (*Ling.*) monosyllabic.

ékawarna monochromatic.

ékawarsa o. year.

ékéh-ékéh ter- panting, out of breath.

ékivalén see ÉKUIVALÉN.

ékivalénsi see ÉKUIVALÉNSI.

éko echo.

ékologi ecology.

ékologis ecological.

ékonom economist.

ékonométri econometrics.

ékonomi 1 economics. - *pertanian* agricultural economics. *(jurusan)* - *perusahaan* (department of) business economics. **2** economy. - *berancangan/berencana* planned economy. - *terpimpin* guided economy. **3** household management. **ke-an** economy, economic matters. **per-an 1** economic matters. **2** economy.

ékonomis economical. **ber-** economize. **meng-kan** make s.t. economical. ~ *pelabuhan* make the port economical. **ke-an** economy, frugality, thriftiness.

ékor 1 tail (of animals). - *ayam* chicken's tail. - *anjing* tail of dog. - *tupai* k.o. grass. - *kuda* 1 horse's tail. 2 frayed piece of cloth. 3 ponytail (hair). - *tikus* small round file. **2** classifier used for animals. *tiga - kuda* three horses. *Aku blm bertemu dgn burung bangau se-pun* I have not seen even a single heron. **3** tail (end) (of kite, parade, train, etc.). - *lipas* hair at nape of neck. - *mata* outer corner of eye. - *pipi* lower part of cheek. - *pulau* downstream end of island. **4** follower, adherent, hanger-on. **5** bad consequence, aftermath. *Inilah mestinya - satu politik yg lepas dr cita-cita yg usul* This has to be the result of a policy that has lost sight of its original ideals. **6** the last digits in a lottery number. **ber-** have a tail, tailed. ~ *panjang* have many unpleasant or complicated consequences. *Hal tadi pagi itu akan ~ panjang* The matter that came up this morning is going to have some rather unpleasant consequences. **ber-²** o. behind the other, in single file. **meng- 1** dangle like a tail. **2** tail, trail, follow. *Bisnya ~ di buritnya* The bus brought up the rear. **meng-²** follow without much thought or purpose. **meng-i** follow, walk behind, tail. **peng-** follower, hanger-on.

ékosistém ecosystem.

éks₁ 1 *(Leg.)* (cited) from. - *Pasal 281 KUHP* from Section 281, Code of Criminal Law. **2** imported from. *barang - Jepang* goods imported from Japan.

éks₂, éks- ex-, former. *Ah, dia kan sdh -!* Come on, she is a has-been, isn't she?

éks. [*éksemplar*] copy, issue, number.

éksak, éksakta exact sciences (mathematics and physics).

éksamen *(Acad.)* examination. **meng-** examine.

éksaminator *(Acad.)* o. who administers an examination.

éksekusi 1 execution, carrying out. **2** execution, putting to death.

éksekutif executive.

éksém, ékséma eczema.

éksemplar copy (of book), issue (of periodical).

ékséntrik eccentric. **ke-an** eccentricity.

éksépsi *(Leg.)* demurrer, exception.

éksés excess.

ékshibisi, éksibisi exhibition. *pertandingan* - exhibitionary matches (sports).

éksim see ÉKSÉM.

éksisténsi existence.

éksisténsialisme existentialism.

éksit exit permit from the immigration office. **meng-kan** expel, dismiss. *Pd masa jayanya LEKRA Yassin di-kan dr UI* At the height of *LEKRA*'s influence Yassin was dismissed from the University of Indonesia.

ékskavasi excavation.

éksklusif 1 exclusive, select. **2** excluded, without. **meng-** exclude o.s. **meng-kan** make s.t. exclusive. **ke-an** exclusivity, exclusiveness.

éksklusivisme exclusivism.

ékskursi excursion. **ber-** go on an excursion.

éksodus exodus, mass migration out of a place.

éksogami exogamy.

éksogén exogenous.

éksotik, éksotis exotic.

ékspansi expansion (of territory, gas, etc.). **ber-** carry out an expansion (of territory).

ékspansif expansive.

ékspansionis 1 expansionist. **2** expansionistic.

ékspédisi₁ 1 shipping, forwarding. *Kirim surat ini dgn* - Send this letter by a private mail carrier. **2** mail room (of large institution). **meng-kan 1** send s.t. by private dispatch. **2** expedite. **peng-an** forwarding, shipping.

ékspédisi₂ 1 expedition, jaunt, campaign. **2** *(Mil.)* dispatching of troops.

ékspéditur shipping agent.

ékspérimén experiment. **ber-** experiment with s.t.

ékspériméntal experimental.

ékspériméntasi experimentation.

ékspériméntil see ÉKSPERIMÉNTAL.

éksplisit explicit. **meng-kan** make s.t. explicit.

éksploatasi see ÉKSPLOITASI.

éksploatir see ÉKSPLOITIR.

éksploitasi 1 development, working. **2** exploitation, use, operation. **meng-(kan) 1** use, work, operate for profit. *Aku mau ~ trayék Jkt-Bandung* I would like to work the Jkt-Bandung route. **2** exploit (people). *Ah, si Jalal, kerjanya hanya ~ anak buahnya* Oh, that Jalal, he only exploits his staff. **peng-an 1** using, working s.t. **2** exploiting.

éksploitir meng- 1 work, use. **2** exploit.

éksplorasi exploration. **meng-** explore.

éksplosi explosion.

éksplosif explosive.

éksplotasi see ÉKSPLOITASI.

ékspo see ÉKSPOSISI.

éksponén 1 *(Math.)* exponent. **2** exponent (of idea, theory, etc.). - *daérah* regional activists of an organization.

ékspor export. **meng-** export. **peng-** exporter. **peng-an** exportation, exporting.

éksportir exporter.

ékspos meng- expose, reveal, uncover. *Dgn pengumuman itu ia ~ kejahatannya sendiri* By that announcement he revealed his own crime.

éksposé exposé.

éksposisi 1 exposition, fair. 2 exposition, explanation.

éksprés 1 express, fast (public transport). 2 special delivery.

éksprési 1 expressiveness. *kekuatan - di wajah perempuan Bali* the expressive power in the faces of Balinese women. 2 expression. *- keinginan* expression of will. **meng-kan** express. *~ suatu perasaan* express a feeling. **peng-an** the expression of s.t. *dlm ~ iman kepercayaannya akan Tuhan* in his expression of faith in God.

éksprésif expressive. **ke-an** expressiveness.

éksprésionis expressionist (art).

éksprésionisme expressionism (art).

éksprésionistis expressionistic (art).

ékstase ecstasy.

éksténsif extensive.

ékstérn 1 external. 2 not a resident. *mahasiswa -* a day or commuting student.

ékstra₁ 1 extra, more. *Kalau hasil pekerjaannya baik, nanti kami beri -* If he works well, we will give him s.t. extra. 2 extraordinary, in a special way. *Selalu berdandan - kalau ke dokter* He always dressed up, esp. well when he went to the doctor. 3 previews or shorts shown in addition to the main film.

ékstra₂ outside of a certain institution. *kegiatan -* activities not within (the institution).

ékstradisi extradition. **meng-(kan)** extradite.

ékstrak extract. **meng-** extract s.t.

ékstrakurikulér extracurricular.

ékstrané (*Acad.*) outside participant in an examination.

ékstraparleméntér extraparliamentary.

ékstrapolasi extrapolation. **meng-(kan)** extrapolate.

ékstrauniversitér outside of the university.

ékstrém extreme. *dlm bentuk -nya* in its most extreme form. **meng-kan** make extreme, carry or put to the extreme. **ke-an** extremism.

ékstrémis extremist.

ékstrémisme extremism.

ékstrémitas extremity.

ékstrim see ÉKSTRÉM.

ékstrovért extrovert.

Ekuin [*Ekonomi, Keuangan dan Industri*] economy, finance, and industry.

ékuivalén equivalent.

ékuivalénsi equivalency.

ékuménis ecumenical.

ékwivalén see ÉKUIVALÉN.

ékwivalénsi see ÉKUIVALÉNSI.

éla unit of linear measure, 91.4 cm. or about o. yard.

élaborasi elaboration. **meng-(kan)** elaborate.

élah 1 trick. 2 pretext, excuse. **-an** 1 trick. 2 pretext, excuse.

élak said in evasion. *Nggak tahu, -nya* I do not know, she said evasively. **meng-** 1 get out of the way, move to evade. *Susy ~ ketika Herman hendak mencekal lengannya* Susy dodged when Herman tried to grab her arm. *~ dr para wartawan* avoid the journalists. 2 avoid doing s.t. *Tuti selalu ~ berbicara dgnnya* Tuti always avoids speaking with him. **meng-²** evasive (reply). **meng-i** avoid s.t., dodge s.t. *tantangan serius yg sulit di-i* a serious challenge that is difficult to dodge. **meng-kan** 1 dodge (blow, tax, etc.). *~ serangan* evade an attack. *Wajahnya ~ tatapan mataku* His face avoided my eyes. 2 shunt to the side, deflect. *Ia ~ tangan Mantri* She pushed Mantri's hand aside. 3 shirk (o.'s duty). *~ tanggungjawab perbuatannya* shirk the responsibilities of o.'s actions. **ter-kan** avoided, avoidable. **peng-** dodger, avoider. *~ pajak* tax dodger. **peng-an** 1 avoidance, evasion. 2 deflection.

elang hawk, eagle or any large bird of prey.

élastik, élastis elastic.

élastisitas, élastisitét elasticity.

élégi elegy.

éléktrifikasi electrification. **meng-(kan)** electrify.

éléktris (*Coll.*) electrical. **meng-kan** electrify.

éléktrisir meng- electrify.

éléktro 1 concerning electrical matters. *insinyur -* electrical engineer. *téknik -* electrical engineering. 2 electrical engineering.

éléktroda, éléktrode (*Phys.*) electrode.

éléktrodinamika electrodynamics.

éléktrolisa electrolysis.

éléktrolit electrolyte.

éléktrolitis electrolytic.

éléktromagnit electromagnet.

éléktron electron.

éléktronik 1 electronic. 2 electronics.

éléktronika electronics.

éléktronis see ÉLÉKTRONIK.

éléktrotéknik electrical engineering.

elemén 1 element. *Partai itu dikuasai -² radikal* That party is under the control of radical elements. 2 (*Chem.*) element. *- kering* dry cell.

eleméntér elementary.

éléng rock (of boat).

éliminasi meng-kan eliminate.

éliminir eliminate.

éling (*Jv*) remember (esp. in spiritualism). *Org hrs selalu - sama Tuhan* O. must always remember God.

élips ellipse.

élipsis (*Ling.*) ellipsis.

élipsoide ellipsoid.

élit, élite elite. *golongan/kaum -* the elite.

élitis elitist.

élitisme elitism.

élo see ÉLA.

élok 1 beautiful, lovely. 2 good. *- laku* well-behaved. **meng-kan, memper-** beautify. **ke-an** beauty, loveliness.

elon see KELON.

élon (*Jv*) **meng-i** side with, espouse the cause of, defend.

élpiji [*liquid propane gas*] liquid propane gas.

ELS [*Europese Lagere School*] k.o. elementary school of colonial period with instruction in Dutch for Europeans and the indigenous elite.

éltor (*Med.*) eltor, k.o. cholera.

elu see LU.

elu-elu₁ meng- come in waves (of sound), reverberate. *Suara lembut-halus ~ di telinga saya* Her soft voice reverberated in my ears.
elu-elu₂ acclaim, give applause. **meng-** applaud. **meng-kan 1** welcome, meet (guests, etc.). **2** stick o.'s head out. **-an** welcome given, acclamation. **peng-an** welcoming of guests.
eluk see LUK.
elus meng- stroke. *~ dada* feel sad and helpless. **meng-² 1** caress, stroke. *~ rambutnya* stroke her hair. **2** coax. **meng-i** make a stroking motion on s.t. *Kabut terasa ~ muka* We could feel the mist stroking our faces. **meng-kan** stroke with s.t. *~ tangan ke rambut* stroke o.'s hair with o.'s hand. **-an 1** a caress. **2** flattery.
ém see M₁.
émail enamel. **meng-** to enamel.
emak see MAK.
emam (*child language*) eat.
emang (*Sd*) term of address and reference for o.'s uncle.
émang see MÉMANG.
émansipasi emancipation.
emas gold. *menilai mana yg - mana yg loyang* distinguish good from bad. *- batang* gold ingot. *- belanda* 18-karat gold. *- hijau* timber. *- hitam* petroleum, oil. *- juita* sweetheart. *- kawin* bride price. *- ker(a)jang/kerancang* **1** tinsel. **2** tinfoil. *- kertas* gold leaf. *- kodok* platinum. *- lantak(an)* gold ingot. *- liplap* imitation gold. *- muda* 18-karat gold. *- pasir* gold dust. *- perada* gold leaf. *- putih* platinum. *- tua* gold of high alloy. *- urai* **1** particles of gold. **2** gold dust. **ber- 1** have gold, wear gold. **2** be well-to-do. **meng-** resemble gold, become golden. *Padinya ~* The rice turned golden. **meng-i 1** gild. **2** bribe. **ke-an 1** golden. *Jaman ~* Golden Age. **2** gilded. **per-an** gilding.
emat₁ (*Che.*) checkmate. **meng-** checkmate.
emat₂ see MAT₂.
embacang k.o. mango.
embah (*Jv*) **1** term of address and reference for o.'s grandparent. **2** term of address and reference for old person, teacher, or mystic.
embalau shellac.
emban₁ 1 breastband, waistband, sash. **2** belly band (for horses). **meng-** carry in a sash slung over the shoulder.
emban₂ meng- 1 carry out, execute, perform. *~ tugas* carry out a task. **2** support. **meng-i** assign to carry out. *Dia cakap utk di-i tugas itu* She is capable of performing that task. **meng-kan 1** carry out, execute for s.o. **2** give s.t. as a task. *Tugas penting di-kan kpdnya* An important task was entrusted to her. **peng-** guardian, caretaker of culture. *sbg ~ kebudayaan* as o. who has the task of carrying out the duties of the culture. **peng-an** carrying out, execution.
emban₃ nursemaid.
embara meng- roam, rove, wander. **meng-i** wander over, roam in. *Ia ~ Éropa* He roamed over Europe. **peng- 1** wanderer. **2** nomad. **peng-an 1** wandering, roaming, roving. **2** place of wandering. **3** adventure.

embarau 1 palisade, wood or stone embankment. **2** piling (of pier, etc.).
émbargo embargo.
émbarkasi embarkation.
embat meng- lash s.o. down with strip of bamboo, rope, etc.
embék see EMBIK.
embel (*Jkt*) swamp covered with plant growth.
émbél meng-i cause to fray or unravel.
émbél-émbél 1 details. *Pokok-pokoknya dulu. -nya nanti saja* First let us talk about the main points. We can do the details later. **2** insignificant addition, supplement. *Nasution pun jadi - saja tanpa kekuasaan* Nasution became a fancy appendage in the gvt. with no power. **3** side issue of little importance. *Yg dibicarakan tadi hanya - saja, tdk pokok* What they talked about was a side issue of little importance, not the main thing. **meng-i** add a detail. *Dia ~ persoalan itu dgn memasukkan hal-hal kecil* She unnecessarily added to the problem by introducing numerous details. **-an** small or insignificant detail.
émbér pail, bucket.
embi (*Jkt, Sd*) term of address for o.'s aunt.
embik 1 a bleat. **2** sheep, goat. **meng-** bleat. **-an** a bleat.
embok see MBOK₂.
émbol meng- swell, puff up.
émbrat see ÉMRAT.
émbrio (*Biol.*) embryo, fetus.
émbriologi (*Biol.*) embryology.
embun 1 dew. *- asap* fog. *- betina* a fine dew. *- jantan* dew with large drops. *- kering* about seven a.m. *- pagi* early morning dew. *- rintik* small dew drop. *- di ujung rumput* transitory, evanescent. **2** condensed vapor. **3** haze. **ber- 1** dewy. **2** spend the night in the open. **meng- 1** resemble dew. **2** turn into dew, condense. **meng-i** drip on. *Mukanya di-i air mata* Her face was wet with tears. **meng-kan, memper-kan** expose to dew, make s.t. or s.o. stay out overnight. **-an** moisture, condensate. **peng-an** condensation.
embus₁ aspirate. *p - (Ling.)* aspirated "p." **ber-, meng- 1** exhale, breathe. **2** blow (wind). *Angin ~ kencang* The wind blew hard. **meng-kan 1** blow (smoke, etc.) off. *~ uap* blow off steam. **2** exhale. *~ napas penghabisan* breathe o.'s last. **-an 1** bellows. **2** blowing, blast (of wind). *~ napas* a sigh. **3** (*Ling.*) aspiration. **4** suggestion. **peng-an** exhalation.
embus₂ scoot! go away! **meng-** flee, take to flight, take to o.'s heels.
embut meng-², ter-² move up and down (i.e. of the chest of sleeping person).
émigran emigrant.
émigrasi emigration. **ber-** emigrate. **meng-kan** make s.o. emigrate.
emik (*child language*) drink.
émirat emirate.
emis see KEMIS₁.
émisi 1 issue (of banknote, security, stock, etc.). **2** emission (of semen, light, etc.).
émiter o. who issues a security or banknote.

emoh (*Jv*) be unwilling. *Negeri itu - ikut SEATO* That country was unwilling to join SEATO. *Aku - hidup dlm kesusahan* I am unwilling to live in poverty. **meng-i** not want s.t. or s.o. *Rendra di-i oléh wong Yogya* Rendra was rejected by Yogyakartans.

émolumén emolument, perquisite.

emong meng- 1 care for, look after. 2 direct an enterprise. **-an** s.t. taken care of.

émosi 1 emotion. 2 emotional. *Kataku bergairah dan -* My words were passionate and emotional. 3 be emotional. *Dia - maka itu dia bilang begitu* He was seized by emotion. That is why he talked like that. **ber-** emotional, have emotional feelings.

émosional, émosionil emotional.

empal (*Jv*) spiced and fried chunks of beef.

empang, émpang 1 (fish)pond. 2 embankment. 3 dam. - *KA* railroad crossing barrier. **meng-** 1 dam (up), block (stream). 2 lie athwart (road, etc.). 3 block (import of drugs, s.o.'s way, etc.). *Dgn dadanya yg besar tegap ia ~ jalan* With his broad sturdy chest he blocked the way. **ter-** blocked, barred. *Tiada ~ peluru oléh lalang* Grass does not stop a bullet, i.e. a powerless person cannot block the will of higher-ups. **-an** 1 fishpond. 2 dam. 3 barrier. *~ jalan* road barricade. **peng-** dam. *~ air* sluice. **peng-an** damming up, blocking.

empap ber- gamble by tossing a coin. **meng-** strike with heavy or flat object (oar, palm of hand, etc.). **meng-kan** 1 strike s.t. flat onto s.t. 2 throw down hard.

émpar meng- drift off, be off course (of ship, etc.).

empas meng- be tossed, dashed against, throw o.s. down. *Ombak ~ ke batu* The waves dashed against the rocks. **meng-kan** 1 throw, dash, hurl s.t. against. *Ombak ~ perahu itu ke pantai* The wave hurled the ship onto the beach. 2 slam (door, etc.). **ter-** tossed, flung, hurled. **-an** violent crashing (waves, wind). *~ gelombang* breaker.

empat four. - *penjuru alam* the four points of the compass. - *belas* 14. - *likur* (*Jv*) 24. - *puluh* 40. **meng-** *puluh hari* hold a religious meal 40 days after s.o.'s death. - *dasawarsa* 40 years, 40th anniversary. - *mata* face to face, privately. *Kedua menteri itu berunding - mata* The two ministers met privately. - *(per)segi* quadrangle. - *persegi panjang* rectangle. - *satu* card game similar to black jack. - *suara* in four-part harmony. **ber-** be four. *Kami ~ pergi* The four of us went. **ber-²** four by four. *Prajurit-prajurit berbaris ~* The soldiers lined up in rows of four. **memper-** divide into four parts. **ke-** 1 fourth. *Org ~ datang* The 4th person came. 2 (all) four. *~ org itu datang* All four persons came. **ke-²** all four. **per-** quarter, one-fourth. *se~ jam* a quarter of an hour. *tiga ~* three quarters. **per-an** 1 crossroad, intersection. 2 a fourth.

empedal gizzards.

empedu gall, bile. *Susu dibalas -* Repay milk with bile, i.e. bite the hand that feeds you.

empé-empé see EMPÉK-EMPÉK.

empék 1 (*Ch*) term of address and reference for o.'s parent's older brother or brother-in-law. 2 (*Coll.*) term of address for old Ch man.

empék-empék k.o. fishcake (S. Sumatran specialty).

empelas see AMPLAS₁,₂.

émpelop see AMPLOP.

empénak meng- 1 spoil, coddle, pamper. 2 (friendly) persuasion, praise, flattery.

empéng see EMPING.

émpér, émpéran 1 veranda, porch. 2 overhang, awning.

empet (*Jkt*) annoyed, angry.

empét-empét paper trumpet, balloon with a whistle.

empéyék cracker made of dried fish or other viand fried with rice flour.

empik (*Jv*) eager, want to.

emping 1 chips made of pounded new rice toasted and served with palm sugar. 2 fried chips made of *Gnetum gnemon* fruit. **meng-, memper-** make such chips.

émpiris empirical.

émpirisisme, émpirisme empiricism.

émplasemén 1 (*Mil.*) emplacement. 2 (*R.R.*) railway yard. - *langsir* siding.

emplék 1 (*Jv*) sheet, layer. 2 (*Coll.*) classifier for sheet of mosquito coils.

émplék (*Jv*) roof eaves.

émpoh rise, overflow (of water). **meng-i** inundate, flood. **ke-an** flooded, inundated, submerged. **peng-an** flooding, submersion (of field).

empok (*Jkt*) 1 term of address and reference for o.'s older sister. 2 term of address to lower class women.

empon-empon (*Jv*) spices.

empos, émpos meng- 1 breathe, blow on. 2 expose fruit to smoke to speed up ripening process. **-an** fruit ripened by smoking process.

empu 1 (*Lit.*) master craftsman. - *keris* master kris-maker. 2 armorer. 3 master. - *jari* thumb. - *kaki* big toe. **meng-kan** acknowledge s.o.'s mastership. *Beliau di-kan sbg kritikus sastra Indonésia* He was acknowledged as the master critic of Indonesian literature. **ke-an** 1 craftsmanship. 2 quality of being a master craftsman.

empuk 1 soft (mattress, etc.). *Kedudukannya -* She has a soft job. 2 tender, well-done (of food). 3 easy to defeat or cheat. *Janda itu jadi sasaran -* The divorcee is easy prey. 4 well-worn (of cloth). 5 soft and pleasant (of voice, sounds). **meng-kan** soften s.t. **peng-** 1 softener. *~ daging* meat tenderizer. 2 padding, stuffing (in chair, etc.). **peng-an** softening.

empul meng- bob up and down (of boat, etc.).

empulur pith or soft core of palm tree.

empunya owner. *si-/yg -* the owner. *yg - rumah* the landlord. *si - toko* the owner of the shop. *si - cerita* the storyteller.

émrat (*Jkt*) large watering can.

émulsi emulsion. **meng-** emulsify.

emut ng- have in o.'s mouth, suck.

én (*Coll.*) and.

énak 1 nice, tasty, delicious. *Alangkah -nya buah apel itu!* How delicious this apple tastes! **2** nice, pleasant. *nyanyian yg -* a nice song. *-nya pindah ke kota!* How nice to move to the city! *Kalau mau -, diam ajé!* If you want to have it easy, just do not say anything. *- saja sendiri* do whatever o. likes (regardless of others). *- saja lupa, ya?* You just forget if you do not feel like remembering, right? **3** well. *Perasaan saya tak -* 1 I do not feel well. 2 I feel ill at ease, I am worried. *- kepénak* (*Jv*) comfortable. *-²* absorbed in s.t. *sedang ~ bekerja* while she was absorbed in her work. **-nya** the easy way to do it. *~ diangkat dr bawah* The easiest way is to lift it from the bottom. **se-** as delicious. *~ udelnya* (*Jv*) as o. pleases regardless of others (as o.'s belly-button dictates). **se-(²)nya** as o. wishes, as o. likes. *Meréka itu ~ saja jalannya* They drive however they please without following traffic regulations. **ber-²** enjoy. **meng-kan** reassure, put at ease. *berita yg ~ (hati)* reassuring news. **meng-²kan** make o.'s mouth water. **memper-** make more pleasant, more comfortable. *Ia ~ letak duduknya* She made herself more comfortable in her chair. **ter-** most pleasant. **ke-an 1** pleasantness. **2** have too much fun or pleasure (doing s.t.). *Kita ~ ngobrol jadi lupa waktu* We have been so engrossed in our conversation we forgot the time. **-an** (*Coll.*) preferably, more pleasant, more comfortable. *Kalau begitu, ~ aku tinggal di rumah sakit* In that case, it would be more comfortable to stay in the hospital. *Anak-anak muda mémang ~* Young people really do have it easier. **-²an 1** (*Coll.*) relax, take it easy. *Pantas saya jadi malas-malasan dan ~* No wonder I became lazy and took it easy. **2** (*Lit.*) various k.o. delectable foods. **p-, kep-** (*Jv*) *hidup p- dan kep-* live in luxury.

enam six. *- belas* 16. *- likur* (*Jv*) 26. *- puluh* 60. **ber-** be six, in sixes. *Mari kita pergi ~!* Let the six of us go! *saya ~* me and my five friends. **ke- 1** sixth. *hari ~* the 6th day. **2** all six. *~ hari itu* all six days.

enap₁ ponder, consider deeply, give a great deal of thought to.

enap₂ see ENDAP₁.

enau sugar palm.

encék₁ (*Jv*) stand on s.t.

encék₂ see ENCIK.

encéng see ECÉNG.

encér see INCAR.

éncér 1 liquid, not so thick that it fails to flow. *Getahnya masih - hingga sukar mengental* The sap is still watery so that it does not thicken easily. **2** weak, thin. *Kopi itu -* The coffee is weak. **3** smart, quick (of the mind). *Otaknya -* She is intelligent. **meng-kan** dilute, thin s.t. *~ susu* dilute milk. **memper-** make s.t. more dilute. **-an** diluteness. **-an** liquid, solution, fluid that results from dilution. **peng-** thinning agent, thinner. **peng-an** dilution, thinning.

encik 1 (*Ch*) term of address and reference for father's younger brother. **2** (*Ch*) term of address for a man of o.'s father's generation. **3** (*Lit.*) term of address for a woman teacher. **-²** full-blooded Chinese.

encim 1 (*Ch*) term of address for father's younger brother's wife. **2** (*Ch*) term of address or reference for woman of o.'s mother's generation. **3** wife of the store owner.

encit (*Ch*) cloth, fabric.

éncok 1 rheumatic, stiff. **2** rheumatism. **3** gout.

éncot see INCUT₂.

endak₁ see NDAK₁.

endak₂ see HENDAK.

endal meng- 1 stuff, cram (into bag, etc.). **2** elastic, resilient, springy.

endap₁ *- tuang* **meng-tuangkan** pour out excess liquid after solid has settled at bottom (of container, etc.). **-²** sediment, deposit. *~ darah* blood precipitate. **meng- 1** settle, precipitate. **2** be present, be there (but not put to any use). *barang yg ~ di gudang* goods stored without any purpose in a warehouse. *kemanisan yg ~ pd air tapé* the sweetness that is present in water from fermented cassava. **meng-i** settle at. *Lumpur ~ lembah stl habis banjir* Mud settled in the valley when the flood was over. **meng-kan** let s.t. settle. **-an, -²an** sediment, deposit. *~ darah* blood precipitate. **peng-an** process of sedimentation. *bak ~* sedimentation vessel.

endap₂ meng-(²), ber-(²) move stealthily, move in crouching position. *Aku lihat dia ~ dan menyuruk di antara rumput* I saw him crouching and hiding himself in the tall grass. **meng-kan 1** bend s.t. down. *Ia ~ badannya menhindari hujan batu itu* He bent his body in a crouching position to avoid the hail of stones. **2** conceal s.t.

endap₃ see TANAH.

endasan chopping board.

éndémi endemic disease.

éndémis endemic. *Penyakit itu sdh menjadi -* The disease has become endemic.

enderia see INDERIA.

endon (*Jv*) **(me)ng-** stay for a considerable length of time. **-an** o. who stays for some time.

éndong (*Sd*) see ENDON.

éndosemén endorsement (of checks).

éndosir meng- endorse (checks).

éndrin brand of pesticide. **meng-** kill with Endrine.

enduk see GENDUK.

endus meng- 1 get wind of, smell, whiff. *~ bau daging, harimau itu beringas* When it smelled the meat, the tiger went wild. **2** get wind of, find out, discover. *Rupanya petugas-petugas Opstib ~ kunci mistéri itu* Apparently the officials of the anticorruption brigade discovered the key to that mystery. **-an** whiff. *mendapat ~* get wind of, find out.

endut -²an throb, beat, pound.

enek nauseated, feel sick.

énérgi, énérji energy. *~ surya* solar energy.

énerjétik, énerjik energetic.

énérsi see ÉNÉRGI.

enes (*Jv*) **meng-** languish from sadness. **meng-kan** make s.o. languish.

enga₁, engah₁ (*Jkt*) be aware, be conscious.

enga₂, engah₂ ter- 1 excited, nervous, upset. 2 gasping for breath. *Anak itu ~ ketakutan* The child was gasping for breath out of fear. **(meng)-², ter-²** 1 panting, puffing. *Kulihat badannya gemetar, dadanya ~* I saw his body tremble and his chest heave with panting. 2 in a hurry. **-an** panting, puffing. *dlm ~ napasnya* in her panting for breath.

engak 1 drowsy, sleepy. 2 (*Med.*) comatose. 3 dazed.

engap 1 panting, puffing. 2 tight in the chest, breathe with difficulty.

engas stink, stench, foul odor.

enggak see NGGAK.

enggan reluctant, averse, unwilling. *Ia - memberi penjelasan* He did not want to give an explanation. *Aku mempunyai rasa - pdnya* I have a feeling of disgust toward him. **-²** 1 somewhat reluctant. 2 hesitate, waver. **meng-i** 1 dislike s.t. or s.o. 2 reject. *gadis yg di-inya* the girl he rejected. **meng-kan** 1 dislike, have no use for. 2 not permit, not allow. **ke-an** 1 aversion, dislike. 2 unwillingness.

enggang hornbill.

énggét (*Jkt*) **meng-** hook (fruit, etc.).

enggil ber- toothed, serrated, notched.

énggokan (*Jkt, Jv*) curve (in road, etc.).

engkah₁ wood glue.

engkah₂ 1 half ripe, partially ripe. 2 partially cooked.

engkak (*Jv*) k.o. crow.

éngkang meng- walk with legs wide apart.

éngkar see INGKAR.

engkau 1 you, familiar pronoun for 2d person singular, often abbreviated as *kau*. *Apa - sdh dengar ttg kabar itu?* Have you heard the news? 2 (*Coll.*) your. 3 (*Rel.*) Thou, Thee. **ber-** use *engkau*, be on familiar terms with s.o.

éngkel single, not manifold. *Kaca mata -* eyeglasses that are not bifocals. *kain -* cloth of single width (rather than double width).

éngkél keep arguing. **ng-** keep arguing.

engkim (*Ch*) term of address and reference for mother's younger brother's wife.

engko see ENGKAU.

éngko partner, business associate. **ber-** be in partnership, operate jointly. **-an** be partners in business.

engkoh (*Ch*) term of address and reference for elder brother or male of age similar to o.'s elder brother.

éngkol 1 crank (of machine). 2 wrench. **meng-** 1 crank (motor, etc.). 2 loosen or tighten nut and bolt with wrench.

engkong (*Ch, Jkt*) term of address and reference for grandfather.

engku 1 (*Ch*) term of address and reference for mother's younger brother. 2 (*Lit.*) term of address and reference for highly respected individuals of both sexes. *- muda* 1 form of address to newlywed son-in-law. 2 form of address to young gentleman.

engkuk₁ k.o. bird similar to barbet.

engkuk₂ meng-(²) bend or push s.o. down.

éngsél 1 hinge. 2 (*R.R.*) switch.

engso (*Ch*) 1 term of address and reference for older brother's wife. 2 respectful term of address for woman old enough to be married but not of a generation older than the speaker.

enjak see INJAK.

enjal₁ meng- stuff, cram.

enjal₂ see ANJAL.

énjima see ÉNSIM.

enjot, enjut meng- 1 push or pull with a jerk. 2 pedal (a bicycle, etc.).

énsiklik (*Rel.*) encyclical.

énsiklopédi encyclopedia.

énsim, énsima enzyme.

énsopor (*Coll.*) et cetera.

entah who knows, I do not know. *- berapa banyaknya tamu yg datang itu* Heaven knows how many guests came. *- bagaimana* somehow. *- bagaimana dia ditemukan tertidur di atas atap dangau* Somehow he was found sleeping on the roof of a hut. *- . . . - . . .* whether . . . or . . . *- betul - salah, saya tdk tahu* Whether it is true or false, I do not know. **-²** 1 not know. *~ kalau dia sdh punya pacar* I do not know if she already has a boyfriend. 2 maybe, possibly (but o. hopes not). *~ dia datang* O. hopes he will not come (but who knows). **- ber-** fabled, imaginary. *negeri ~* never-never land. *république ~* the republic that never was. **-kan** 1 (*Lit.*) do not know. 2 or perhaps . . . , I do not know. *air yg jernih, dangkal ~ dlm* clear water which was shallow or perhaps it was deep, I do not know.

entah-berentah see ENTAH.

entak men- 1 stamp on with force. 2 thrust, stab. 3 pound, throb as if being stamped on. **meng-kan** pound or stamp with s.t. *Dgn jéngkél di-kan kakinya ke tanah* He stamped his foot on the ground in irritation. **ter-** be thrown down. *Beberapa saat aku ~ diam di tanah* For a short while I lay sprawled on the ground. **-an** stamping, pounding. **peng-** pounder, pestle.

entar (*Jkt*) later. *- pacarnya marah* Her boyfriend will be mad in a while. *- malam* tonight.

entas meng- take or pull s.t. out. *Ia ~ krupuk dr penggoréngan* She took the chips out of the frying pan. *~ jemuran* take in the laundry. **meng-kan** raise a child to adulthood so that it becomes s.t. *Org tua saya berhasil ~ semua anaknya* My parents have managed to raise all of their children successfully.

énté (*Jkt and among Arabs*) you.

énten meng- graft, implant.

énténg 1 light (in weight). 2 light (feelings, etc.). *- sekali perasaannya tiba-tiba* She suddenly felt very relieved. 3 easy, inconsequential. *cerita -* light story (easy to read). *dianggap -* considered unimportant. 4 mild (of cigarettes, etc.). **meng-kan**

1 lighten, ease. 2 alleviate, mitigate. 3 take for granted. **-an** lighter, easier.

énternit see ÉTERNIT.

entimun see MENTIMUN.

entit (*Jv*) **ng-** steal (small and trivial objects).

éntog (*Jv*) Manila duck.

éntomolog entomologist.

éntomologi entomology.

entomologis entomological.

éntot (*Vulg.*) **(me)ng-** fuck, screw.

éntri entry (in dictionary, etc.).

entrog meng-(²) shake.

enyah go away, get out. *-lah kau dr sini!* Go away from here! Beat it! **meng-kan** chase away, evict. **peng-an 1** fleeing. 2 expulsion. 3 abolition.

enyak meng- tread on, step on, press, stamp. ~ *tanah* stamp down the soil. **meng-kan** *diri* fall back down. ~ *diri di kursi* drop into chair. **te(pe)r-** fall back with thud (in a chair etc.).

enyék (*Jv*) answer in a mocking way. **(me)ng-** mock, put s.o. down, look down on, belittle.

énzim, énzima see ÉNSIM.

epak see PAK₁.

épék (*Coll.*) belt.

épidémi epidemic.

épidémiologi epidemiology.

épigrafi epigraphy.

épik epic.

épilépsi epilepsy.

épiséntrum epicenter.

épisode episode.

épistemologi epistemology.

épok k.o. plaited bag to hold ingredients for betel chewing.

épolét epaulette.

épos epic.

éra era.

erak screeching sound. **meng-** make a screeching sound. *kursi yg* ~ *di lantai* a chair that made a screeching sound on the floor.

érak ber-, meng- 1 unwind, uncoil (of rope, snake, etc.). 2 separate, part. **meng-(kan) 1** unwind, untie, uncoil s.t. 2 separate, part s.t.

eram meng- 1 hatch, brood. 2 crouch on all fours (as of water buffalo in pond, tiger set to pounce on prey, etc.). 3 brood. *Gadis itu* ~ *terus di dlm rumah* The girl stayed in the house brooding. **meng-i** brood s.t., sit on (eggs). ~ *telur org* l take care of s.o. else's affairs without getting the benefits of it. 2 (*M*) have intercourse with a pregnant woman. **meng-kan** hatch eggs. **peng-** incubator. **peng-an** hatching.

erang groaning, moaning from pain. **meng-** groan, moan. **-an** a groan.

érang black, dark blue.

érang-érot zigzag, askew, awry.

erat 1 tight, firm. *Pintunya tertutup -* The door was firmly closed. 2 firm (of promise, etc.). 3 close (of relationship). *- hubungannya dgn ibunya* She had a close relationship with her mother. **se-²nya** as tightly as possible. **meng-kan, memper-(kan) 1** tighten (belt, embrace, etc.). 2 firm

up, strengthen (friendship, etc.). **ke-an** closeness. ~ *hubungan dgn adiknya* closeness of the relationship with her brother.

ércis peas.

eréng see RÉNG.

éréng leaning, sloping. *- géndéng* improper or indecent matters. *Sindir-menyindir tak putus-putus, - géndéng jangan disebut* The hurling of insults at e.o. went on an on, not to mention other shocking behavior. **meng-** slope, lean, slant.

érét meng- 1 drag, pull. 2 snare, lure, take in s.o. **-an** sleigh, sledge. ~ *sungai* barge pulled along guide rope used as ferry across river. **peng- 1** puller, dragger. 2 (*Jkt*) o. who is clever at winning another's favor for personal gain. **peng-an** baggage cart.

erik meng- scream, shout, trumpet (of elephant).

ering k.o. bird of prey.

érloji see ARLOJI.

érobik 1 aerobic. 2 exercise.

érong *lubang -* (*Naut.*) scupperhole. **-²** (*Naut.*) scupperhole.

Éropa, Éropah Europe, European.

Éropanisasi Europeanization.

érosi erosion.

érot₁ distorted, wry (of face). *- bényot/bérot* askew, awry. **meng-kan 1** distort, twist (face in pain, etc.). 2 make s.t. askew.

érot₂ ber- in a row, following exactly in e.o.'s traces. *Yusiwo pun latah, ngikut* ~ *di pantat Nina* Yusiwo started acting crazy, following Nina's buttocks and imitating her. *Org beriringan* ~ People were going in duck formation. **ber-an** go in single file in a large group.

érotik 1 eroticism. 2 erotic.

érotis erotic.

érpah land leased on a long-term basis.

érpékad see RPKAD.

érté see RT.

erti (me)ng- 1 understand. *Ia* ~ *maksud surat itu* She understands the meaning of that letter. 2 (*Jv*) know. **dimeng-** be understood. *Apakah soal itu dpt dimeng-?* Could the problem be understood? **meng-kan 1** explain, cause to understand. *Saya* ~ *maksud surat itu kpd Ibu* I explained the purpose of that letter to Mother. 2 understand, explain to o.s. *Isterinya merenung-renung sia-sia* ~ *tingkah lakunya* His wife pondered, in vain trying to explain his behavior to herself. **peng-an 1** understanding, way s.o. understands s.t. *penuh* ~ *serta kasihan* full of understanding and compassion. ~ *saya ttg Islam* my understanding of Isl. ~ *umum* generalization. 2 explanation, interpretation. *Ia insaf berkat* ~ *yg diberikan oléh Komandan* He came to his senses thanks to the Commander's explanation.

eru the Australian pine (*Casuarina sp.*).

érwé see RW₂.

és 1 ice. *- balok/batang* block of ice. *- batu* ice cube. *- gepukan* (*Jv*) crushed ice. *- kas* icebox. *- longsor* avalanche. *- perongkol* ice cube. *- serut* shaved ice. 2 confection or drink with ice. *- blok* cube-shaped flavored ice. - *campur* iced mixed with fruits and syrup. - *gandul* a ball of crushed ice soaked with syrup. - *ganéfo* flavored ice in a plastic bag. - *jus* blended fruit juice and crushed ice. - *kombor serut* ice shavings with sweeteners and milk or coconut milk plus s.t. else. - *krim* ice cream. - *lilin/loli/mambo/roli* popsicle. - *syanghai* iced fruit cocktail. - *tébak* shaved ice made with a spinning shaving machine. - *téh* ice tea. - *télér* iced fruit-cocktail with topping of condensed milk. **meng-** 1 become ice, freeze. 2 freeze s.t. *Buah pepaya énak di-* Papaya is delicious frozen. **peng-an** freezing s.t.

esa, ésa (*Lit.*) single, one. *Tuhan yg -* the o. and only God. *Yg -* God. - *hilang, dua terbilang* For each o. lost, two new o.'s will take his place. **meng-kan** *Tuhan* acknowledge the oneness of God. **ke-an** oneness, unity. **-²an** 1 alone. 2 lonely.

esah see SAH₁.

esak *sakit -* be short of breath. **meng-** sob. **ter-(²)** sobbing.

esang see KESANG.

ésdé see SD.

éséi essay.

éséis essayist.

ések see DEMAM.

éselon 1 echelon. - *atas* the top echelon. 2 (*Mil.*) echelon, battle-array.

éséma see SMA.

ésémbling see ASÉMBLING.

ésémpé see SMP.

éséns essence, odor, scent.

ésénsi essence, quintessence, gist.

ésénsiil essential.

ésér see SR.

ését see EZ.

ésha see SH.

éskadron squadron.

éskalasi escalation.

éskas icebox, refrigerator.

éskatologi eschatology.

éskatologis eschatological.

Éslandia Iceland.

ésok tomorrow, the next day. *pelajaran -* the next days lesson. - *hari* tomorrow. *hari -* the future. - *lusa* day after tomorrow. - *pagi, pagi -* tomorrow morning. **-nya** the next morning. **ber-** tomorrow. *Kalau tdk sekarang ~* If not today, tomorrow. *~ hari* in the future. **meng-kan** postpone s.t. a day. **ke-an** (*harinya, paginya, sorénya* etc.) the following (day, morning, evening, etc.). **ke-annya** the following day.

ésot see INGSUT.

éspos see ÉKSPOS.

ésprés see ÉKSPRÉS.

esrar see TANDA.

éstafét, éstapét (*Sport*) relay race. **meng-kan** pass s.t. rapidly from o. person to another. *Modal itu akan saya -kan* I will distribute the capital in rapid consecutive installments.

éstétika aesthetics.

éstétis aesthetic.

ét see ÉIT.

étalage, étalase shop window.

étatisme statism.

éték₁ ng- crave.

éték₂ (*M*) term of address for mother's younger sister.

éter 1 ether, upper air. 2 (*Med.*) ether.

éternit plasterboard.

éthika, étik, étika ethics.

étikét₁ label (on bottle, etc.). - *harga* price tag. **ber-** be labeled.

étikét₂ etiquette.

étimologi etymology. **meng-kan** etymologize.

étiologi etiology.

étis ethical.

étnis ethnic.

étnisitas ethnicity.

étnografi ethnography.

étnolinguistik ethnolinguistics.

étnologi ethnology.

étnologis ethnological.

étos ethos, ethics. - *kerja* work ethic.

étsa etch. **meng-** etch.

évakuasi evacuation. **ber-** evacuate. **meng-** evacuate s.t. or s.o.

évaluasi evaluation. **meng-** evaluate.

évaluir meng- evaluate facts, etc.

évangelis 1 evangelist. 2 evangelical.

évangelisasi evangelization.

évolusi evolution. **ber-** evolve.

éwa (*Jv*) averse, unwilling.

éwé (*Vulg.*) **meng-, ng-** copulate, have sexual intercourse.

ex- see also entries with **eks-**.

éyang (*Jv*) term of address and reference for grandparent. - *putri* grandmother. - *kakung* grandfather.

EYD. [*Éjaan Yg Disempurnakan*] official Indonesian and Malaysian spelling system since 1972.

éyél obstinate in argument. **ng-** be obstinate in argument. **-an** sticking to o.'s own view in an argument.

EZ, ez, é-zét, ézét [*Economische Zaken*] Ministry of Economic Affairs (in colonial period). *harga -* price determined by (colonial) Ministry of Economic Affairs.

F

f /éf/ f, the 6th letter of the alphabet.

FA [*firma*] firm.

faal₁ 1 deed, work. - *tobat/iman* (*Isl.*) prayer reaffirming faith. 2 (*Med.*) function, action (of body, organs, etc.). - *jantung* functions of the heart.

faal₂ sign, omen. *membuka* - study signs, view horoscope. **memf-kan** prophesy.

faali physiological.

fabel fable.

fabrik see PABRIK.

fabrikan maker, manufacturer. - *roti, biskit dan mi* maker of bread, cookies, and noodles.

fabrikasi manufacture, product.

fadihat disgrace, shame, ignominy. **memf-kan** disgrace, humiliate.

fadil prominent, eminent, famous.

fadilat, fadzilat excellence, prominence.

faédah use, benefit, profit. *Kedatangannya ke mari ada -nya juga* There is an advantage in his coming here anyway. *bagi* - in the interest of. **ber-** useful, advantageous. ~ *utk rambut* good for the hair. **memf-kan** make use of. **ke-an** utility, usefulness.

faham see PAHAM.

failasuf see FILSUF.

failit see FAYIT.

fait accompli /fétakompli/ fait accompli.

fajar dawn. - *kizib* dawn before sunrise. - *menyingsing/merekah* daybreak, crack of dawn. - *sidik/siddik* true dawn. - *sumirat* first crack of dawn. **ber-** dawn.

fakih (*Isl.*) expert in canon law.

fakir 1 poor, destitute, indigent. - *miskin* the poor and needy, the indigent. 2 Muslim or Hindu religious mendicant. **ke-an** poverty, destitution.

fakta fact. **mem-kan** 1 make factual. 2 prove with facts.

faktor /faktor/ 1 factor, element. - *keadaan* environmental factor. 2 (*Math.*) factor.

faktual, faktuil factual.

faktur /faktur/ invoice.

fakultas school of a university, faculty. - *hukum* faculty of law. - *keguruan* School of Teacher Training. - *téhnik* school of engineering.

fakultatif, fakultatip optional.

fakultét see FAKULTAS.

falak 1 celestial sphere. *ilmu* - (*Isl.*) astronomy, esp. to calculate the proper dates for ritual. 2 (outer) space.

falsafah, falsafat 1 philosophy, philosophical system. - *Tagore* Tagore's philosophy or philosophical ideas. 2 philosophical base, ideology, idea. **ber-** philosophize.

falsafi philosophical.

fam family name (esp. in E. Indonesia).

famili 1 relative. 2 family. **ber-** 1 have a family. 2 be related. *Hassan ~ dgn isteriku* Hassan is related to my wife. **ber-kan** have in o.'s family. *Tdk pantas kami org kaya ~ org miskin* It is not right that we who are rich should be in the same family as poor people. **ke-an** the state of being familylike in nature. *pendekatan-pendekatan ~* familylike approaches. **per-an** family affairs.

familial familylike.

familiér 1 accustomed, used to doing. 2 intimate. 3 have an intimate or homelike atmosphere. *Tinggal di asrama énak. Ibu asramanya* - It is nice to stay in the dorms. The house-mother is very motherly.

fana 1 transitory, fleeting. *dunia yg* - this world. 2 perishable. **ke-an** transitoriness, impermanence, fleetingness.

fanatik adhering strictly to a religion. **ke-an** strongly adhering to a religion.

fanatisme fanaticism.

fani perishable.

fantasi 1 fantasy, illusion, fancy. 2 imagination. 3 fancy. *saputangan* - a fancy handkerchief. **ber-** fantasize, give rein to o.'s imagination. **memf-kan** imagine or envision s.t.

fantastis fantastic.

faraid, faraidz /fara'id, fara'idz/ (*Isl.*) law of inheritance.

faraj see FARJI.

fardhu, fardu 1 obligatory. 2 (*Isl.*) religious obligation. - (*l*)'*ain* individual obligation of a Muslim. - *kifaya* communal obligations of a Muslim. - *puasa* obligation to fast during the prescribed month. **memf-kan** oblige (in religious sense).

faring (*Anat.*) pharynx.

farji vulva.

farmakologi pharmacology.

farmakopé pharmacopoeia.

farmasi pharmacy, drugstore. **ke-an** pharmaceutical affairs.

fasal see PASAL.

fase phase.

fasét facet.

fasid imperfect. **memf-kan** render imperfect. *Pengadilan agama ~ perkawinannya* The religious court annulled their marriage.

fasih 1 fluent. *Ia - berbahasa Indonésia* She is fluent in Indonesian. 2 eloquent, quick-witted. 3 glib. -

lidahnya He has a ready tongue. **ke-an** fluency, articulateness.
fasihat eloquence.
fasik godless, atheistic.
fasilita, fasilitas facilities or conveniences put at o.'s service.
fasis fascist. **-²an 1** fake fascist. **2** act fascistically.
fasisme fascism.
fatal fatal. *Kejadian itu - baginya* This was fatal to her. **ke-an** fatalism.
fatalis fatalist.
fatalisme fatalism.
fatihah see ALFATIHAH.
fatsal see PASAL.
fatwa 1 (*Isl.*) a binding ruling in religious matters. **2** instructions, guidance of an older person. *Présidén memberi - kpd tentara yg akan berangkat ke médan perang* The president gave instructions to the troops which would be leaving for the field of battle. **ber-** give instructions, advice on religious matters. **memf-kan** advise, give instructions, instruct. *Tepatlah apa yg di-kan oléh Nabi junjungan kita* What the Prophet has instructed is precise.
favorit favorite.
fayit bankrupt.
FE [*Fakultas Ekonomi*] School of Economics.
Féb [*Fébruari*] February.
Fébruari February.
féderal federal.
féderalis federalist.
féderalisme federalism.
féderalistis federalistic.
féderasi federation.
félbét cot.
féminin feminine.
féminisme feminism.
fenér see FINEER.
fénomén, fénoména, fénomin phenomenon.
féntilasi see VÉNTILASI.
féodal feudal. **ke-an** feudalism.
féodalisme feudalism.
féodalistis feudalistic.
féri ferry.
férméntasi fermentation. **memf-kan** ferment s.t.
fértilitas fertility.
féstival festival. **memf-kan** celebrate with a festival.
fétsin see VÉTSIN.
FH [*Fakultas Hukum*] School of Law.
FHIPK, FHPK [*Fakultas Hukum dan (Ilmu) Pengetahuan Kemasyarakatan*] School of Law and Social Sciences.
fiasko fiasco.
figur 1 figure, shape. **2** figure, personage (in a story).
figura see PIGURA.
figuran supernumerary (actor or actress), extras (in a movie).
fihak see PIHAK.
fiil 1 behavior, deeds. **2** (*Lit.*) verb.
fikh see FIQH.

fikir see PIKIR.
fiksi fiction.
fiktif fictitious. **ke-an** fictitiousness.
filamén filament.
filantrop philanthropist.
filantropi philanthropy.
filantropis philanthropical.
filatéli philately.
filatélis philatelist.
filem see FILM.
filial branch (of a firm, etc.).
filing (*Coll.*) **1** feeling, intuition. *Saya ada - hari ini kamu akan datang* I had the feeling that you'd come today. **2** lottery hunch.
Filipin, Filipina, Filipinas the Philippines.
film 1 film for camera. **2** film, movie. *- berita* newsreel. *- bicara* talkie. *- biru* pornographic movie. *- bisu* silent film. **memf-kan** film, make a film of. *~ perahu di pelabuhan Padang* film boats in the harbor of Padang. *~ Siti Nurbaya* film (the novel) *Siti Nurbaya.* **per-an** the movie industry.
filolog philologist.
filologi philology.
filologis philological.
filosofi philosophy.
filosofis philosophical.
filsafah, filsafat 1 philosophy, ideology. *- Pancasila* the ideology of *Pancasila.* **2** philosophical system. *ilmu -* philosophy. *- ilmu pengetahuan* philosophy of science. **3** (*Coll.*) mysticism. **ber-** philosophize, speculate. **memf-kan** philosophize about s.t. *~ Pancasila* philosophize about the *Pancasila.* **ke-an** pertaining to philosophical matters. *dlm perspéktif kesejarahan dan ~* in a historical and philosophical perspective. **ke-²an** pseudo-philosophical.
filsafati philosophical.
filsuf philosopher.
filum (*Biol.*) phylum.
filusuf see FILSUF.
final (*Sport*) finals. **memf-kan** make final, finalize.
finalis finalist.
finansial, finansiil financial.
finansir financier. **memf-** finance, fund, back (enterprise, etc.).
fineer, finir /finér/ veneer.
Finlandia Finland.
FIPA, FIPPA [*Fakultas Ilmu Pasti dan (Pengetahuan) Alam*] School of Mathematics and Physical Sciences.
FIPIA [*Fakultas Ilmu Pasti dan Ilmu Alam*] School of Mathematics and Physics.
fiqh, fiqih /fik, fikih/ (*Isl.*) study of laws pertaining to ritual obligations.
firaon /fira'on/ see FIRAUN.
firasat 1 reading of s.o.'s character (by palmistry, physiognomy, etc.). **2** ability to prophesy the future. **3** presentiment, hunch, foreboding. *Nalurinya sendiri mencengkap ~ yg tdk baik* His own instincts gave him a foreboding of s.t. bad.
firaun /fira'un/ **1** pharaoh. **2** tyrant.
firdaus paradise.

firdausi heavenly, paradisiacal.
firma firm, company, enterprise.
firman saying, decree (divine or royal). - *Allah* Commandment of God. **ber-** decree, speak. *Tuhan ~ kpd Yeremia* the Lord said to Jeremiah. **memf-kan** decree, proclaim s.t.
firus k.o. gemstone, turquoise.
FIS [*Fakultas Ilmu Sosial*] School of Social Sciences.
fisik physical.
fisika physics. - *inti* nuclear physics. - *perbintangan* astrophysics. - *terapan* applied physics.
fisiografi physiography.
fisiografis physiographic.
fisiologi physiology.
fisiotérapi physiotherapy.
FISIP [*Fakultas Ilmu Sosial dan Ilmu Politik*] School of Social and Political Sciences.
fisipén (*Sport*) kingpin.
fiskal 1 fiscal. *tahun* - fiscal year. **2** (*Mil.*) judge advocate. **3** departure tax. *surat* - document showing that the exit tax was paid, exit-tax receipt.
fissi (*Phys.*) fission.
fiting see FITTING.
fitnah slander, calumny. **memf-** slander, calumniate, libel. ~ *perusahaan saingan* slander a competing firm. **pem-** detractor, slanderer. **pem-an** libeling, slandering, defamation.
fitrah₁ (*Isl.*) tithe in rice or cash paid at end of fasting month. **ber-** tithe, purify (by paying the tithe). **memf-kan** give away as a tithe.
fitrah₂, fitrat natural tendency, disposition, character.
fitri pure, natural. *secara* - in a pure way. *dasar* - true principle, foundation or base.
fitting light socket, fixture. - *imbo* light socket or wall plug built into wall or ceiling.
FK [*Fakultas Kedokteran, Fakultas Keguruan*] School of Medicine, School of Teacher Training.
FKG [*Fakultas Kedokteran Gigi*] School of Dentistry.
FKH [*Fakultas Kedokteran Héwan*] School of Veterinary Medicine.
FKIP /éfkip/ [*Fakultas Keguruan dan Ilmu Pendidikan*] Normal School.
flai (*Sl.*) euphoric and disoriented due to drugs or intoxicating beverages. **-²** get high (us. in a group).
flamboyan poinciana tree.
flanél flannel.
flat /flét/ apartment.
fléksibel flexible.
fléksibilitas flexibility.
flés see PLÉS.
flét see FLAT.
flipper (*Coll.*) dolphin.
florét (*Sport*) foil.
floridasi fluoridation.
flu influenza, a cold.
fluktuasi fluctuation. **ber-** fluctuate.
fluor fluoride.

fluoroskop fluoroscope.
fly see FLAI.
fly-over /flai ofer/ traffic overpass.
fobi see PHOBI.
fohte, fokhte (*Coll.*) humid.
foklor folklore.
fokus 1 focus (of lens). **2** focus (of attention). **ber-kan** focus on. **memf-kan** focus s.t. *Kami hendak ~ kajian ini pd anak-anak kecil* We would like to focus this study on small children. **pemf-an** focusing.
folio foolscap-size paper. *Naskah diketik - spasi renggang* The document was typed double-spaced on foolscap-size paper.
fondamén foundation.
fondasi foundation.
fonds /fon, fons/ (*Fin.*) fund.
foném (*Ling.*) phoneme.
fonémik (*Ling.*) phonemics.
fonémis (*Ling.*) phonemic.
fonétik (*Ling.*) phonetics.
fonétis (*Ling.*) phonetic.
fonologi (*Ling.*) phonology.
fonologis (*Ling.*) phonological.
forklif /foklif, poklip/ forklift.
formal formal. **mem-kan** formalize. **ke-an** formality. **-²an** do in a formal way, be formal. *Ah, jangan ~, kan hanya antara teman!* Oh, don't be formal, aren't we among friends!
formalisir memf- formalize.
formalitas formality.
formasi 1 formation. **2** (*Mil.*) formation. **3** position, a line item in the official budget for a certain employee. - *dlm Départemén Dalam Negeri sdh penuh* There are no vacant positions in the Department of Internal Affairs. *Dia berada dlm - tinggi di departemén itu* He is in a high position in that department.
format format, form.
formatir, formatur (*Pol.*) person or committee appointed by an assembly to form the executive leadership, cabinet, etc.
formika Formica.
formil see FORMAL.
formulasi formulation. **memf-kan** formulate.
formule formula.
formulir form, declaration, blank. - *lamaran* application form. - *pertanyaan* questionnaire. **memf-kan** put in a form.
forsir memf- force, compel. ~ *suaranya* force o.'s voice out of its range.
forum forum, open discussion.
fosfat phosphate.
fosfor phosphorus.
fosil fossil.
foto photograph, picture. - *Rontgén* x-ray. - *tustél* camera. - *udara* aerial photo. **mem-** take a picture.
fotograf, fotografer photographer.
fotografi photography.
fotokopi 1 photocopy. **2** (*Coll.*) print of a video cassette. **memf-(kan)** make a photocopy of s.t.
fotosintésa, fotosintésis (*Biol.*) photosynthesis.

foya, foya-foya (ber)- be extravagant with money, throw money around.

FPS [*Fakultas Pasca Sarjana*] Graduate School.

Fr. [*frater*] (*Rel.*) brother, friar.

fragmén, fragménta fragment.

fragméntaris fragmentary.

fraksi faction (in parliament), section (of political party).

framboesia frambesia, yaws.

frambos raspberry.

frambosen raspberry flavored syrup.

frambus see FRAMBOS

frambusia see FRAMBOESIA

franco, frangko /frangko/ surcharge paid to an expediter for shipments sent to a certain place. *dikirim - Semarang* sent to Semarang with shipping charges paid.

frasa, frase (*Ling.*) phrase.

frater (*Rel.*) friar, brother. *sekolah -* school taught by Catholic brothers. **-an** friary, abbey, priory.

fraude fraud, swindle.

frégat frigate.

frékuénsi, frékwénsi frequency.

frigiditas sexual frigidity.

frikatif (*Ling.*) fricative.

friksi friction.

friser (*Coll.*) freezer, freezer compartment.

frobel (*Coll.*) kindergarten.

front /fron/ **1** (*Pol.*) front, cadre. **2** (*Mil.*) front (line). *di - terdepan* on the front lines.

frontal frontal, head-on. *konfrontasi -* head-on confrontation.

fronton jai alai arena.

fruktosa fructose.

frustrasi 1 frustration. **2** frustrated. **ber-** be frustrated. **ke-an** frustration.

FS [*Fakultas Sastra*] School of Literature.

fuad (*Lit.*) heart. *- (al) zakiah* a pure heart.

fufu meat of copra dried by heat.

fulan see POLAN.

fuli mace, the whorled interior skin or membrane of nutmeg.

fulus 1 filthy lucre. **2** (*Coll.*) money.

fumigasi fumigation. **mem-** fumigate.

fundaméntal, fundeméntil fundamental.

fungisida fungicide.

fungsi 1 function, office, job. **2** function, purpose. *- sosial* social function, societal function, public service role. **ber-** *sbg* function as. **memf-kan** make s.t. function, put s.t. into function.

fungsional see FUNGSIONIL.

fungsionalisasi functionalization. **memf-kan** functionalize, render functional.

fungsionalisme functionalism.

fungsionaris, fungsionér functionary, official.

fungsionil functional.

Funisia Phoenicia.

fuqoro wal masakin (*Isl.*) the poor and the needy.

furak difference, dissimilarity.

furuj (*Lit.*) star.

furuk teaching of ethics based on principles of religion.

fusi 1 (*Phys.*) fusion. **2** (*Pol.*) fusion, coalition. **ber-** fuse, coalesce. **memf-kan** merge s.t. **per-an** coalescence, state of having merged.

futbal soccer.

futur (*Ling.*) future.

futurolog futurologist.

futurologi futurology.

futurologis futurological.

fuyonghai (*Ch*) foo young, an omelette with meat and vegetables served with sweet and sour sauce.

G

g /gé/ g, the 7th letter of the alphabet.

G.₁ [*gunung*] mt., mount.

G.₂ [*gerakan*] movement.

G30S [*Gérakan 30 Séptémber*] September 30th Movement, the 1965 attempt to seize control of the gvt.

gaang mole cricket.

gabag German measles. **-en** (*Coll.*) have German measles.

gaba-gaba (*Amb*) **1** garlands and other decorations made of palm fronds. **2** bamboo gate decorated with garlands of fronds, etc. **3** roof of sago palm fronds. **4** dried sago palm stems, esp. as building material. **meng-i** decorate with garlands of leaves, etc.

gabah unhulled paddy separated from the stalks. **meng-kan** leave as unhulled rice. **peng-** huller. *mesin ~* huller.

gabai see GAPAI.

gabak₁ cloudy, overcast. **meng-** gloomy, dark. *Cuaca ~* Dark clouds are closing in.

gabak₂ see GABAG.

gabardine gabardine.

gabas₁ in a hurry, hurriedly. **meng-** hurry s.t. up. **ter-** in a hurry.

gabas₂ rough, coarse, not tidy.

gabir clumsy, awkward, maladroit.

gableg, gablek (*Jv*) be capable of doing s.t. *Anak umur sepuluh tahun masak mompa sepéda saja nggak - You are 10 years old. How is it possible you do*

not even know how to pump up a tire? *Habis org itu -nya cuman kawin-kawin melulu* All that man can do is take up with o. woman after another.
gabruk sound of banging. **meng-** strike with a bang.
gabug, gabuk 1 empty (of rice, kernels, etc.). **2** sterile. **3** childless.
gabung 1 bundle, sheaf. *se- bunga* a bunch of flowers. **2** cluster. **ber- 1** gather together, collected together. *Org-org tlh ~ di balai kota* People have gathered at the community hall. **2** merge, fuse. *Kedua pergerakan buruh itu ~ menjadi satu* The two labor movements have merged into o. **meng- 1** place in bundles or sheaves (of paddy, wood, etc.). **2** join together with. **meng-kan 1** bundle, bale. **2** fuse, unite, join s.t. to s.t. else. *Pemerintah ~ semua partai politik* The gvt. united all the political parties. *~ diri* join. *Ia ~ diri pd perkumpulan itu* He joined the club. **ter-** fused, united, joined together. **-an** federation, merger, consolidation (of several firms, etc.). *~ partai-partai oposisi menyerang pemerintah* A combination of opposition parties attacked the gvt. *armada ~* combined fleet. **peng-an** fusion, merging, annexation. **per-an** federation, grouping of things merged. *~ buruh se-Indonésia* The Indonesian Federation of Labor.
gabus₁ 1 k.o. tree, the soft wood of which is used as cork, scraper, etc. *- kaki* floor mat. **2** cork. *topi - pith-*helmet (lined with cork). *- botol* cork of bottle. **meng-** polish with cork. **peng-** abrasive, polisher.
gabus₂ k.o. widely eaten freshwater fish, snakehead.
gacok, gacuk the marble, card, etc. which o. picks as the means of winning in children's game of marbles, cards, etc., where the object is to accumulate marbles, etc. **-an** /gaco'an/ **1** preferred marble, card, etc. **2** (*Coll.*) boyfriend, girlfriend.
gada club, bludgeon, cudgel. **meng-** bludgeon, club. **peng-** truncheon.
gada-gada ship's weathervane.
gadai 1 pawning. **2** security. *memberikan jamnya sbg - atas pinjaman* give o.'s watch as security for o.'s loan. *- gelap* illegal pawn. **ber-** borrow money by pawning s.t. **meng-** take in pawn. *Ia ~ sawah org itu* He took the man's wet rice fields as security. **meng-kan** pawn s.t. *Ia tlh ~ sawahnya* He has mortgaged his rice field. **ter-** pawned. **-an** pledge, security. **peng-** pawner. **pe-an** pawnshop. *jawatan ~ pawnshop* service. **peng-an** pawning.
gadang₁ large, big. *rumah - (M)* large sprawling house, esp. the matrilineal clan house. **meng-** be arrogant, swagger.
gadang₂ large sieve.
gadang₃ ber- see BEGADANG.
gadang-gadang meng- hope for s.t. *Orangtuanya ~nya utk menjadi dokter* His parents fervently hope he will become a doctor.
gadar see KADAR₁.
gadas bowling pin.

gadén see SURAT.
gading 1 elephant tusk. **2** ivory. *Tak ada - yg tak retak* Nothing is perfect (lit., there is no ivory which is not cracked). **3** ivory color. **ber- 1** be of ivory. **2** use ivory. **meng- 1** resemble ivory. **2** puncture or stab with a tusk.
gading-gading 1 joist, truss. **2** ribs of ship.
gadis 1 girl. *- bar* barmaid. **2** maiden, virgin. *tdk ber-* no longer a virgin. **meng-** remain single, stay unmarried (of women). **meng-i** have sexual relations with a virgin. **ke-an 1** virginity. **2** chastity, continence. **ke-²an** behave like a girl, girlish. *Janda itu tingkah lakunya ~ saja* The divorcée acted just like a young girl.
gado meng- eat side dishes without rice. **-² 1** k.o. salad eaten with peanut sauce. **2** s.t. consisting of various elements. *lagu ~* potpourri. *bersifat ~* heterogeneous.
gaduh₁ 1 noisy. *Jangan -, saya mau tidur* Don't be noisy, I want to sleep. **2** boisterous, rowdy. **3** tumult. **ber- 1** make a row. **2** quarrel, fight. *Kedua org itu ~* The two people quarreled. **3** be confused, mixed up. **meng-** disturb s.o. **meng-kan 1** disturb, upset, stir s.o. up. *~ keamanan* disturb the peace. *Hal itu ~ hati saya* That matter distresses me. **2** be in commotion over. **ke-an 1** commotion, tumult. **2** brawl, rumpus. **per-an** commotion, tumult.
gaduh₂ meng- farm s.o.'s land or raise s.o.'s animals for a share in the product. *Penduduk désa diberi kesempatan ~ sapi bantuan pemerintah* The villagers were given the opportunity to raise the gvt. cows for a share in the produce. **meng-kan** rent out o.'s land or o.'s animals for a share. *Pemerintah ~ seratus ékor sapi pd penduduk désa* The gvt. gave 100 cows to the villagers to raise for a share. **-an** s.t. lent out under this system.
gaduk arrogant, conceited.
gadung k.o. creeping edible tuber which is toxic if not cooked properly.
gadungan fake, bogus, imitation. *patriot -* bogus patriot. *intan -* fake diamond.
gaé, gaék (*Coll.*) old. *org -* an old man.
gaét hook, snare. **meng- 1** snatch, hook. **2** rake in. *~ ratusan dolar* rake in hundreds of dollars. **3** tickle with fingers to catch s.o.'s attention. **meng-i** hook, grab several things. **ter- 1** get hooked. **2** get caught up in s.t. bad. *~ oléh rayuan laki-laki* get caught by a man's flattery. **-an** a hook, catch.
gaga see GOGO₁.
gagah 1 strong. *Ia masih - meskipun sdh tua* He is still strong although he is old. **2** brawny, muscular. **3** handsome, dashing. *Sangat - kelihatannya dlm uniformnya* He looked very dashing in his uniform. **4** heroic, brave, dauntless. *- berani/ perkasa/perwira* courageous, brave, bold. **ber-1** have strength, influence. *yg dulu ~ dlm grup itu* who formerly had influence in the group. **2** act with firmness. **ber-²an 1** test e.o.'s strength. **2** brag or boast to e.o. **meng-** act with firmness. *Ia ~ thd kaum pemberontak* He acted with firm-

ness against the rebels. **meng-i 1** subjugate, overpower, take by force. **2** rape, molest sexually. **3** consider great and heroic. ~ *kehidupan kesenian tradisi kita* Take pride in our traditional artistic life. *Ia ~ Muh. Ali sbg jagonya yg tdk terkalahkan* He took pride in Muh. Ali as the undefeatable champion. **meng-kan 1** consider strong and heroic. *yg di-kan sbg tugu-iman yg tak tergoncangkan* which was considered an unshakeable monument of faith. **2** make s.t. strong and heroic or handsome. **meng-²kan** make s.t. falsely heroic. *Lafal "p" yg di-²kan jadi "f"* The pronunciation of "p" was fancied up by making it an "f." **ke-an 1** courage, valor. **2** strength, firmness. **3** handsomeness. **4** conceitedness. **-²an** for show, showing off. *"Api Islam" lahir bukan utk ~, tapi utk disebarluaskan* The *Spirit of Islam* was founded not for show but to have a broad effect. **peng-an 1** rape. **2** suppression of o.'s rights.

gagai meng- climb a tree by embracing the trunk.

gagak raven, crow.

gagal fail. *Segala usahanya -* All her efforts failed. *- (ujian)* fail an exam, flunk. **meng-kan** foil, cause to fail, defeat. *-kan regu meréka* Defeat their team. **ke-an** failure, abortive attempt.

gagang 1 handle. *- péna* penholder. *- pintu* doorhandle. *- pisau* handle of a knife. *- senapan* rifle butt. *- télpon* telephone receiver. **2** stem, stalk, spadix. *- bunga* flower stem, peduncle. **ber-** have a handle, stem.

gagap₁ stammer, stutter. **ber-(²), meng-(²) 1** stammer, stutter. **2** in a hurry, hurriedly. **ter-²** stammer from being upset. **ke-an** stammer. **peng-an** stuttering.

gagap₂ meng- feel, grope. **meng-i** feel for, grope for. *Ia ~ kantong bajunya* He groped in his shirt pocket.

gagas meng- have an idea. **-an 1** idea. **2** concept. **peng-** designer, o. who thought up s.t. **peng-an** thinking out of s.t.

gagau₁ meng- grope. *Ia ~ dlm gelap* She groped in the dark. **ter-²** walk gropingly.

gagau₂ ber-²an scream uncontrollably. **ter-** suddenly scream out.

gagu 1 mute, dumb. **2** empty-minded, void of ideas. **ke-an** muteness. *~ inteléktuil* void of ideas.

gaguk see GAGAP₁.

gahar meng- scrub, scour.

gahara (*Lit.*) of royal descent.

gahari moderate.

gaharu k.o. tree, eaglewood, the rotted xylem of which yields fragrant resinous material. *sdh - cendana pula* ask for the sake of asking (a rhyme with *sdh tahu tanya pula* You already know, so why ask?)

gaib /ga'ib/ **1** mysterious. *Kejadian - itu sangat menakutkan* The mysterious incident was very frightening. **2** invisible, hidden, inscrutable (meaning, etc.). *sebuah tangan -* an invisible hand. **3** disappear, vanish (of gods, etc.). **4** belonging to the invisible (divine or supernatural)

sphere. **5** in absence. **meng-kan** make invisible. *~ diri* make o.s. invisible. **ke-an 1** mystery. **2** mysteriousness. **-²an** mysterious happenings.

gaing (*Naut.*) sheer.

gairah, gairat passion, strong desire. **ber- 1** passionate. **2** very enthusiastic. **meng-i** arouse a desire or passion in. **meng-kan 1** stir, arouse, stimulate. *Perempuan itu ~ nafsunya* The woman stirred his desire. *mata yg ~ alluring* eyes. **2** enrapture, delight. *Musik itu ~ hati* That music delights the heart. **3** stimulate, encourage (exports, etc.). **ke-an 1** passion, fervor. *~ séks* sexual desire, lust. **2** enthusiasm. *~ kerja* enthusiasm for work. *belajar bahasa Inggeris* enthusiasm for studying English. **peng-an** stimulate, encouragement.

gait meng- 1 pull, hook, pluck (fruit, etc. with a pole). **2** wheedle (money, etc. from s.o.). **3** swipe, steal, purloin. **meng-kan** pluck, wheedle, swipe on behalf of s.o. **-an, peng- 1** hook, snare. **2** method for catching s.o. *Ketagihannya akan candu menjadi ~ bagi polisi* His addiction to opium became a way for the police to snare him.

gajah 1 elephant. *- kuning* bulldozer. *- lalang* tame elephant. *- Mada* 1 the Prime Minister of Majapahit. 2 name of a university in Yogyakarta. *- menyusu* shed connected to house. *- mina* whale. *- oling* k.o. batik pattern. **2** (*Che.*) bishop. **ber-1** provided with an elephant. **2** ride an elephant. **meng-** be like an elephant. **-²an** toy elephant, to play elephant.

gaji wage, salary. *- bermula* beginning wage or salary. *- bersih* net wages. *- borongan* piece rate. *- bulanan* monthly pay. *- buta* pay without working. *- kotor* gross wages. *- pokok* base pay. **ber-** have a certain wage. **meng- 1** hire, employ. *Ia ~ lima org pekerja* He employs five workmen. **2** pay a salary or wage. **ter-** salaried. *pegawai ~ salaried* employee. **-an 1** payday. **2** wage laborer. **peng-an** payment of wages.

gajih (*Jv*) fatty portions of meat. **ber-** fatty.

gajul scoundrel, rascal. **ber- 1** hang around engaging in petty criminal activities. **2** act like a scoundrel. *anak ~ juvenile* delinquent. **ber-an** act criminally. *anak-anak muda ~ kids* engaged in petty criminal activities. **per-an** criminal actions.

gajus cashew.

gak see NGGAK.

gakang /ga'ang/ see GAANG.

gala₁ 1 resin, pitch. *- lembut* tar. **2** caulking. **3** a resin-collecting bee. **-²** putty.

gala₂ gala. *- yudha* (*Mil.*) field test. **meng-prémiérkan** show a film at a gala premiere.

gala₃ *main - asin* k.o. children's game.

gala₄ see SEGALA.

galagasi (*Jkt*) k.o. poisonous spider.

galah₁ 1 punting pole. **2** spear. **ber-** use a punting pole, punt. **meng-, men-i 1** get s.t. with a pole. *Ia ~ buah* He got fruit from the tree with a pole. **2** push with a pole. *Ia ~ perahunya ke pantai* He punted his boat to shore. **meng-kan** push with a pole. **peng-** piece of wood or bamboo used as a pole. **sepeng-(an)** a pole's length. *sepeng- hari* half a day's length (from 6 to 12 or from 12 to 6), the times the sun casts a shadow of a pole's length.

galah₂ see GALA₃.

galak 1 fierce, vicious. *anjing -* a vicious dog. **2** sharp and mean. *Matanya sangat -* His eyes blazed. **3** impudent, forward. **ber-** act fierce. **meng- 1** become fierce. **2** rage. *Api kebakaran itu ~* The flames raged. **meng-kan, memper- 1** incite, stir up. *Ia ~ org-org agar memberontak* He incited the people to revolt. **2** encourage, encouraging, activate. **ke-an 1** fierceness, ferocity. **2** gruffness. **3** audacity, impudence. **peng-an** encouragement.

galaksi galaxy.

galang girder, supporting beam. *- atap* girders that support the roof. *- kepala* head support, headrest. *- perahu* (*Naut.*) slip, dry dock. **ber-1** use a girder, have a girder as support. **2** (*Naut.*) be on the ways. **meng- 1** lie athwart, block. *Ada pohon tumbang ~ di jalan* A fallen tree is lying across the road. **2** support (o.'s head, roof, etc.). **3** (*Naut.*) place on the ways. **4** give s.t. a firm footing, lay a base for. *~lah kerjasama!* Let us put cooperation on a firm footing! *~ persatuan* Build unity. **meng-i** support, give s.t. a firm footing. **meng-kan 1** use as a support. **2** rest s.t. on. *Ia ~ atap itu pd tiang-tiang baja* He rested the roof on steel posts. **3** (*Naut.*) place in dry dock. **ter-1** supported, placed on the ways. **2** blocked, hindered. **-an 1** (*Naut.*) slip, dry dock. **2** shipyard. *~ kapal* dockyard. *~ sérét* slip(way). **3** beams around the edge of s.t., bunds around a rice field, etc. **peng- 1** o. who provides leadership. **2** a Boy or Girl Scout on the 2d level (age 12-15). **pe-an** dock.

galant gallant.

galantin galantine, k.o. meatloaf.

galar 1 k.o. mat made of bamboo pounded flat. **2** board, two-by-four.

galas 1 carrying pole. **2** goods carried on a shoulder pole. **meng- 1** carry with a shoulder pole. **2** peddle merchandise (carried in containers suspended from carrying poles). **peng-** peddler, hawker. **peng-an 1** peddling, hawking. **2** sales area for peddlers.

galat see RALAT.

galau hubbub, confusion. **ber-(an)** be in a hubbub, in the midst of confusion. **meng-** become confused. **meng-kan 1** make confused. **2** be confused about. **ke(-an)** confusion, hubbub, uproar.

galbani meng- galvanize.

galengan (*Jv*) small dike in rice field.

galenika k.o. patent medicine.

galgal hurried and rude (in activity, behavior, etc.).

gali₁ meng- 1 dig (hole, well, mine, grave). *~ emas* mine for gold. **2** dig up (potatoes, etc.), excavate, unearth, exhume. **3** delve. *Polisi ~ ke dlm*

masa hidupnya yg lalu The police delved into her past. **4** unearth, discover. *Pancasila yg di- oléh Bung Karno* the principles of *Pancasila* which Sukarno had discovered. **-an 1** the result of digging. *barang ~* excavated object. **2** entrenchment. **-²an 1** plants dug up (e.g. tubers). **2** various mined products. **peng- 1** digger, excavator. **2** shovel, scoop, spade. **peng-an 1** quarrying. **2** excavating, digging. *~ kenangan* digging up old memories.

gali₂ [*gabungan anak liar*] (*Sl.*) **1** gang of street toughs. **2** racketeers.

galib normal. *pd -nya* normally, customarily, generally. *sdh -* the customary thing, the normal. **meng-kan** accustom, habituate. *pakaian yg dikan bangsa lain* clothing which other nations use customarily. **ke-an** customs, normal behavior.

galing see IKAL.

galing-galing k.o. wild climbing vine.

galir 1 loose (of screws, key, ring, etc.). **2** fluent, glib, articulate. **3** agile, nimble, spry.

galon gallon. **ber-²** by the gallon.

Galungan Balinese celebration, lasting 10 days and occurring once every 210 days according to the *wuku* calendar.

galur 1 furrow, groove. **2** channel. **ber-²** furrowed, grooved. **meng-** trace the course of s.t. *~ sejarah kerajaan kuno* trace back the history of an ancient kingdom. **meng-kan** regain or clarify the origin of s.t. **-an** probing back into s.t.

galvanisasi meng-kan galvanize.

Gama [*Gajah Mada*] Gajah Mada University in Yogyakarta.

gamak meng-(²) 1 take s.t. in hand to feel size or estimate its weight. **2** estimate, make a guess. **3** put o.'s hand threateningly on the hilt of a dagger. *tdk* **ter- 1** incalculable, invaluable. **2** undaunted.

gamal [*ganyang mati alang-alang*] k.o. tree that exterminates elephant grass.

gamalisasi planting of *gamal* trees to eliminate elephant grass.

gamam see GAMANG.

gaman weapon. **ber-** armed.

gamang 1 nervous, afraid. **2** feel dizzy from heights. **meng-** be nervous. *Suaranya ~* Her voice sounded nervous. **meng-kan** dizzying (heights), making nervous. **ke-an** dizziness, vertigo. **peng-** o. who tends to be nervous or afraid of heights.

gamat sea cucumber, sea slug.

Gamawan male student at Gajah Mada University, Yogyakarta.

Gamawati female student at Gajah Mada University, Yogyakarta.

gamb. [*gambar*] illustration, picture.

gambang traditional instrument similar to xylophone. *- keromong* **1** small popular Chinese-Indonesian orchestra. **2** Jkt gamelan.

gambangan yoke. *- rél* (*R.R.*) railroad ties.

gambar 1 picture, drawing. *- angan-angan* imaginary picture. *- cermin* image, reflection. *- corét* pencil drawing, sketch. - *éjékan* caricature. - *hidup* motion picture, movie. - *kaca* slides used in movie theaters for projecting advertisements. - *kulit* dust jacket. **meng-kuliti** provide (book) with illustrated dust jacket. - *mati* portrait, still. - *muka* frontispiece. - *renik* microphoto. - *sénter* (lantern) slide. - *sindiran* 1 caricature. 2 political cartoon. - *sorot* 1 movie. 2 slide. - *témpél* illustrated poster. - *timbul* bas-relief. 2 sketch. - *bagan* 1 sketch, draft. 2 blueprint. - *bumi* map. - *cétak-biru* blueprint. - *denah* outline map, sketch. - *situasi* location map. **ber-** 1 illustrated (magazine, etc.). 2 have o.'s picture taken or painted. **meng-** draw, make a picture of. *Ia punului binatang* He is skilled at drawing animals. **meng-i** draw a picture on or in, illustrate (magazine, etc.). ~ *grafik* plot a graph. **meng-kan** 1 explain s.t. by drawing it. 2 depict, describe. *cerita yg ~ kesusahan hidup* a story that depicts the difficulties of life. **ter-** pictured, depicted. *Rupa ibunya bagai ~ dlm pikirannya* It was as if his mother's face was etched into his mind. **ter-kan** describable. *tdk ~* indescribable, beyond description. **-an** 1 illustration, picture of s.t. 2 image. **-²an** pictures to play with (e.g. baseball cards). **peng-** draftsman. **peng-an** 1 drafting. 2 description, depiction.

gambas k.o. squash.

gambir 1 gambier, ingredient used in betel chewing, tanning, and dyeing. 2 the climbing plant that produces gambier.

gamblang (*Jv*) 1 clear, understandable. 2 explicit, mincing no words. *Dia bilang secara - dia nggak senang* He said without mincing words that he did not like it. **meng-kan** make s.t. clear and explicit. **ke-an** explicitness, clarity.

gamblok ng- 1 be attached to, hold on to. 2 join.

gambuh (*Jv*) 1 a male dancer. 2 k.o. dance. **ber-** perform such a dance.

gambus 1 k.o. six-stringed, plucked instrument of Arabic origin, us. accompanied by a drum. 2 band with such an instrument or a harmonium and with other instruments playing Arabian songs. **meng-** perform with such a band. **meng-kan** put a song into the style played by such a band. **-an** musical band of this sort.

gambut 1 peat moss. 2 turf.

gambyong (*Jv*) k.o. woman's dance. **ng-** perform this dance.

game /gim/ 1 expression signalling end of a game. 2 (*Sl.*) dead.

gamelan gamelan orchestra.

gamik see GAMIT.

gamis k.o. Arab-style shirt.

gamit ber-(an) 1 nudge, tap s.o. on the shoulder, arm. 2 attract s.o.'s attention. *Meréka ~ saling memberi kedip mata* They gave e.o. a sign by exchanging winks. **meng-** 1 nudge, tap s.o. to attract attention. *Kelembutan suara itu ~ mataku mencari wajahnya* The softness of the voice led my eyes to look for her face. *Di-nya bahuku* He tapped me on the shoulder. 2 pluck, pick, strum

(guitar, etc.). **meng-(²)kan** tap o.'s fingers. **ter-** be flicked with the fingers to attract attention. **-(²)an** 1 nudging, tapping to draw attention. 2 s.t. people nudge e.o. about to ridicule.

gampang easy. **meng-kan** 1 facilitate, smooth (the way). *Perjalanan secara modern ~ perhubungan antara semua negara* Modern travel facilitates communication among all nations. 2 take lightly, consider s.t. easy which is hard. *Jangan ~ pekerjaanmu itu* Do not take your work lightly. **memper-** alleviate, make easy, ease. *Alat ini akan ~ pekerjaanmu* This tool will make your job easier. **ke-an** easiness, ease. **-an** easier. **-²an** easygoing, taking things easy.

gampar meng-i strike, slap. **-an** 1 slap, stroke. 2 wooden clog, flapping slipper.

gamping limestone.

gamuh k.o. water jar.

gan see JURAGAN.

gana-gini see GONO-GINI.

ganang see GUNUNG.

ganas 1 savage, ferocious, vicious. *Dgn - musuhnya dibunuhnya* He ferociously killed his enemies. *Buaya binatang -* The crocodile is a savage animal. 2 malignant (tumor). **meng-** 1 rage, rampage, storm. *Perang ~ di seluruh dunia* War raged over the whole world. 2 be ferocious, be vicious. **meng-i** attack viciously. *Topan ~ daérah kami* Our area was attacked by a fierce storm. **ke-an** ferocity, viciousness. **peng-** terrorist, o. who acts viciously.

gancang quick, spry, alert.

gancaran (*Jv*) prose.

ganco, gancu 1 pole with a hook (e.g. to pluck fruit from trees). 2 boat hook. 3 pickax. **meng-** remove with a *ganco*.

ganda₁ -fold. *tujuh -* sevenfold. *Uang saya dua kali - uangmu* I have twice as much money as you. - *putera/puteri* (*Sport*) boys and girls doubles. **ber-** doubled. **ber-²**, - **ber-** double, become several times over. **memper-kan, meng-kan** make s.t. become two- or more-fold. *Meréka ~ hasil tanaman mereka* They doubled their crops. **member-²kan** multiply, become several times over. **peng-an** 1 multiple, doubling. 2 reduplication. 3 (*Tel.*) multiplexing. **per-an** 1 multiplication, becoming several-fold. ~ *sepuluh* tenfold increase. 2 reduplication.

ganda₂ 1 opponent of unequal strength. 2 (*Sport*) handicap.

gandal -an, peng- obstacle, hindrance.

gandapita k.o. cake.

gandapura k.o. tree whose fragrant leaves are used for medicinal purposes and whose seeds smell like musk.

gandar₁ 1 lever, arm of scales. 2 axle of wheel. 3 carrying pole. **ber-** having an axle. ~ *dua* biaxial. **meng-** carry on shoulders with pole. **-an** load carried on shoulders with pole.

gandar₂ drive a vehicle. **-an** motorcade.

gandaria, gandariah k.o. tree bearing edible fruit, used for medicinal purposes.

gandarukam k.o. tree that provides resin used for caulking, soap, etc.

gandarusa various k.o. small trees the leaves of which are used for medicinal purposes.

gandaruwa see GENDRUWO.

gandasuli k.o. medicinal herb.

gandel clapper (bell).

gandén see GANDIN.

gandéng ber- 1 side by side, arm in arm. *Kedua pengantin baru itu ~ memasuki hidup baru* The newlyweds entered their new life side by side. *Meréka berjalan ~* They walked arm in arm. **2** coupled. *Kedua gerbong keréta api itu tlh ~* The two railway coaches were coupled. **ber-an 1** side by side, arm in arm. *~ tangan* 1 hand in hand. **2** lock arms. **2** coupled. **3** related to. *Persengkétaan ini ~ dgn pemberontakan itu* This dispute is related to the rebellion. **meng- 1** pull, tow. **2** hold (hands). *Dia ~ adiknya menyeberang jalan* He took his little brother by the hand to cross the street. **meng-i** accompany, go hand in hand with. **meng-kan 1** link, hook together, join. *Nasionalisme ~ rakyat Indonésia* Nationalism links the peoples of Indonesia. *Dua tempat tidur hrs dikan utk menempatkan tiga org penderita* Two beds had to be joined in order to accommodate three patients. **2** (*R.R.*) couple. **ter-** coupled, hooked together. **-an 1** connection, link(ing). *~ antara kedua kawat itu kurang kuat* The connection between the two cables is not strong enough. **2** truck trailer, sidecar. *grobak ~* truck with trailer. **3** appendix to a document. **4** go side by side, arm in arm. **peng-an** act of coupling. **per-an** parallelism.

ganderuwo see GENDRUWO.

gandes (*Jv*) graceful, charming, elegant.

gandik 1 golden ornament worn on forehead by bride. **2** ornament on top of a kris. **3** milling stone.

gandin large mallet.

ganding see GANDÉNG.

gandol see GANDUL.

gandos k.o. cookie made of rice flour and coconut.

gandrung 1 infatuated, in love, crazy about. *Ia - pd gadis itu* He was enamored of that girl. **2** devoted to a cause. **meng-** be crazy about, be crazily in love with. *Tentu saja aku tdk akan campur kalau perempuan yg di-nya bukan kau* I certainly will not interfere if you are not the woman he is crazy about. **meng-i** enamored of, infatuated with. *Gadis-gadis itu selalu ~ puisi yg terbit di majalah itu* Those girls are always crazy about the poetry which appears in that magazine. *Ia ~ laki-laki itu* She is enamored of that man. *mode yg ada saatnya di-i* a fashion that people are crazy about at a certain time. **meng-kan** be keen on having, be crazy over. *alat-alat pengangkutan yg di-kan pula di désa-désa* vehicle for transporting goods which people in the rural areas are crazy to have as well. **ke-an** love, infatuation, craze for.

gandu k.o. flat black seed used as a marble.

ganduh ber-, meng- barter, exchange by providing s.t. extra in the exchange. **meng-(²)kan** barter or exchange s.t. by providing s.t. extra.

gandul ber-an hang down (of several things). *Monyét ~ di pohon* The monkeys were hanging in the trees. **ber-, meng-** hang, suspend (of holster, etc.). **meng-i** hang on (of several things). **meng-kan** hang, suspend s.t. *Ia ~ lampu itu pd paku* He hung the lamp on a nail. **-an 1** hanger. **2** s.t. hanging on s.t.

gandum 1 wheat. **2** wheat flour.

gandung outrigger. **ber-** use an outrigger. **meng-** load cargo to carry on outrigger. **peng-** outrigger.

gandungan see GADUNGAN.

Ganésa Ganesha, Hindu elephant god.

gang₁ 1 alley, narrow street. *- buntu* dead-end alley. *- mobil* driveway. **2** corridor, passageway.

gang₂ gang (of thieves, etc.).

ganggang₁ algae, seaweed.

ganggang₂ space between two objects. **ber-1** have a space or gap between. **2** be divorced. **meng- 1** to crack or split (board). **2** be open a crack (of window or door). **meng-kan** crack (a door, window) open.

ganggang₃ ber- 1 warm o.s. by a fire. **2** warm things on a fire. **meng-** warm s.t. by laying it over the fire. **-an** warmth, warming. *~ panas matahari* the warmth of the sun's rays.

ganggu meng- 1 disturb. *Perampok itu ~ ketertiban* The robber disturbed the peace. **2** disturb, intrude on, interfere with. *Jangan di-, dia lagi bekerja* Do not disturb him, he is working. *Tak ada sesuatu pun juga yg dpt ~ pekerjaannya* There was nothing that could interrupt his work. **3** annoy, molest. *Ia ~ gadis yg berjalan sendirian* He molested girls who were walking alone. *~ gugat* take issue with a law, regulation, or decision issued by s.o. in authority. **ter- 1** disturbed. *Saya harap Bp tdk ~ oléh keributan di sini* I hope you will not be disturbed by the noise here. *Pidatonya ~ oléh éjékan hadirin* Her speech was interrupted by jeers from the audience. **2** hampered, obstructed. *Pekerjaannya ~ oléh kekurangan tenaga* His work was hampered by lack of manpower. *Ia ~ keséhatannya* He fell ill (His health was disturbed). *tdk ~* imperturbable. **-an 1** interference, hindrance. *~ listrik* disruption of electrical service. *~ perut* stomach upset. **2** nuisance, bother, annoyance. **3** attack, assault. **peng- 1** intruder. **2** disturber (of the peace). *~ gugat* o. who refuses to accept the decision handed down by an authority. **peng-an 1** teasing, annoying. **2** creating an intrusion, interfering.

ganggut meng- pull, tug.

gangsa₁ brass.

gangsa₂ k.o. meat dish. **meng-** fry with little oil.

gangsa₃ see ANGSA.

gangsal see GASAL.

gangsang see GASANG.

gangsar see GANGSIR.

gangsing see GASING.

gangsir (*Jv*) mole cricket. **meng-** undermine, dig a tunnel, furrow. *Pencuri ~ utk memasuki rumah* The thief dug a tunnel in order to get into the house. **peng-** s.t. that burrows. *binatang ~ a* burrowing animal.

ganja 1 hemp plant. **2** hashish, marijuana. **peng-** drug addict.

ganjak ber- budge, move a bit. **meng-(kan)** move, shift s.t. slightly. *tdk* **ter- 1** immovable, stationary. **2** unflinching.

ganjal 1 a wedge. **2** a prop, support. - *kaki* footrest. **meng-(i) 1** wedge in, wedge tight. *Pintunya di-(i)* The door has been wedged closed. **2** prop up, shore up, support. *Ia ~ méja yg goyang itu* He propped up the wobbly table. **ter-** tight, firmly wedged. **-an 1** a wedge. *~ hati* problems, thing that weigh on o.'s mind. **2** prop, support. *~ perut* s.t. to fill o. up when o. cannot get proper food. **peng-** used as a prop or support. *~ perut* food. **peng-an** wedging, propping.

ganjar reward. **meng-** reward, compensate. *Raja ~ abdinya yg setia* The king rewarded his faithful servant. *Pencuri itu di- tiga tahun penjara oléh hakim* The judge rewarded the thief with three years in jail. **meng-kan** give s.t. as a reward. **ter- 1** rewarded. **2** be blessed with. *Kita ~ keséhatan yg baik* We have been blessed with good health. **-an 1** reward. **2** just deserts, punishment, retribution. **peng-an** rewarding.

ganjat 1 have a cramp (in muscles, etc.). **2** tangled (of thread, etc.). **ter-** get a cramp. *Kakinya ~* He got a cramp in his legs.

ganjel see GANJAL.

ganjen (*Coll.*) coquettish.

ganjil 1 uneven, odd (of numbers). **2** queer, odd, abnormal. **meng-kan 1** make (a number) odd or uneven. **2** arouse a strange or mysterious feeling. **ke-an** strangeness, peculiar nature. *~ kelakuannya itu menakutkan* The strangeness of his behavior is frightening.

ganjur₁ k.o. lance or pike. **meng-i** spear s.t.

ganjur₂ k.o. rice borer.

ganjur₃ ber- withdraw, pull back. **ber-²** *surut* be in doubt, keep pulling back. **meng-** pull s.t. back, postpone. *~ diri* withdraw, pull back. *~ hari keberangkatan* postpone the day of departure.

gantang measure of rice equivalent to 3.125 kg, around o. quart. *se- beras* a quart of rice. **meng-** measure by this unit. *~ asap* build castles in the air, seek the impossible (lit., measure out quarts of smoke).

gantar stake, post.

gantél₁ (*Jv*) **meng-i** hang from. *Kupingnya di-i anting-anting* Earrings hung from her ears. **méng-kan** (*Jv, Jkt*) hang s.t. so that it dangles.

gantél₂ stick.

ganteng handsome, dashing. **ng-, meng-** acting with the knowledge o. is handsome.

ganténg coagulated, congealed.

gantét (*Jv, Jkt*) stick.

ganthol see GANTOL.

ganti 1 substitute, replacement. *memakai minyak sbg - mentéga* use oil as substitute for butter. *Inilah - gelas yg pecah itu* This is a replacement for the broken glass. **2** change (name, clothes, etc.). - *kerugian perang* war reparations. - *rugi* **1** compensation, indemnity. **2** redress. - *skéna* scene change. - *tikar* marriage with sister of o.'s deceased wife. **3** over (of radio operators). - **ber-** take turns, by turns. *tidur ~* take turns sleeping. *Matanya ~ dr lukisan itu ke wajahku* He looked at the picture and then at my face by turns. **ber-** change (name, clothes, etc.). *~ haluan* change course. *~ keréta api* change trains. *~ bulu* **1** shed feathers, molt. **2** change o.'s attitude. *~ keméja* change shirts. **ber-² 1** take turns, by turns. *~ meréka menjaga rumah itu* They took turns guarding the house. **2** keep on changing. *Pimpinan negara itu ~ saja* The country's leadership just keeps changing. **ber-an** by turns. *Meréka ~ menjabat tangan Irwan* They shook hands with Irwan by turns. **meng-** replace, substitute for, make up for. *~ gelas yg pecah itu* replace the broken glass. *~ ban* change a tire. *~ mentéga dgn minyak* replace butter with oil. *Saya hrs ~ kerugiannya* I have to make up her losses. *~ pengawal* relieve the guard. *~ persnéling* (*Auto.*) shift gears. *~ tanaman* rotate crops. **meng-kan** continue as a replacement, be given as a substitute. *Siapa yg ~ réktor yg lama?* Who will take over for the old rector? *Minyak yg di-kan utk mentéga* It was oil they used to substitute for butter. **memper-²kan** keep changing s.t. **ter-kan** replaceable. *tdk ~* irreplaceable. **peng- 1** replacement, substitute. **2** the o. who replaces or succeeds. *~ raja* the king's successor. **peng-an 1** change, substitution, replacement. *~ alamat* change of address. *~ pemerintahan* change of gvt. **2** giving or compensation. **per-an** change. *~ nada suara* modulation. *~ pegawai* employee turnover.

gantol (*Jv*) **meng-** catch with a large hook. **-an** good-sized hook to seize with.

gantolé hang glider.

gantung - diri hang o.s. **ber- 1** hang. *Lukisan itu ~ pd dinding* The painting hangs on the wall. **2** depend. *Itu ~ sama sekali pd keadaan* That depends entirely on the situation. *Itu ~ pdmu sendiri* It is up to you. *~ di ujung rambut* hang by a thread. **ber-an** be hanging (of several things). *saling ~* be interdependent. **meng- 1** hang (a person). *~ diri* hang o.s. **2** hang up (clothes). **3** adjourn, suspend (a legal case). **4** be suspended. *asap rokok yg ~ di udara* the cigarette smoke that was suspended in the air. **meng-i 1** hanging (several persons or things). **2** hang s.t. onto. *Ia ~ dinding dgn lukisan-lukisan* She decorated the wall with paintings. **3** be hanging on to. *Pergaulan kami yg kian rapat membuat ia ~ aku* The more intimate our relationship the tighter she hung on to me. **memper-i** depend on s.o. **meng-kan 1** hang s.t. *Ia ~ bajunya di paku di témbok* He hung his shirt on a nail in the wall. **2** make s.t. dependent. *Saya ~ nasib saya pdmu* I entrust my fate to you. *Ia ~*

keputusannya pd hasil rapat itu He made his decision dependent on the results of the meeting. ~ *bahan bakunya dr luar negeri* depend on their basic materials from abroad. **3** suspend, adjourn (a legal case). **memper-kan** make dependent. *Sikap itu diper-kan kpd situasi aktuil* The attitude depends on the current situation. **ter-** **1** suspended, be hanging on. *Lampu itu ~ pd langit-langit* The lamp was suspended from the ceiling. **2** dependent. *Nasib saya ~ pdmu* My fate is in your hands. *Suratkabar ~ dr pembayaran langganan utk hidup* A newspaper is dependent upon payment from its subscribers for its survival. **keter-an** dependence. **-an 1** hanger, hook. **2** gallows. **3** s.t. o. depends on, bulwark, refuge. **peng-** s.t. to hang s.t. else from. **peng-an** action of hanging (a criminal).

ganyah meng- 1 polish (with sandpaper, etc.). **2** rub or massage vigorously, scrub. **3** strike hard (with a fist).

ganyang meng- 1 eat raw, devour. *Capai berdiskusi meréka ~ pisang di méja* After their tiring discussion, they attacked the bananas on the table. **2** smash, crush. *~ féodalisme!* Crush feudalism! *Sasak rambut isterinya nyaris di-nya* He nearly ruined his wife's bouffant hairdo. **3** eliminate, wipe out. *di- dgn Diditox!* Get rid of it with Diditox! **ter- 1** devoured. **2** smashed, eliminated. **-an** blow delivered. *~ mahasiswa akhirnya menggulingkan présidén* The students delivered a blow which in the end toppled the president. **peng-** destroyer, demolisher, annihilator. **peng-an** crushing, destroying of.

ganyar hard (of uncooked tubers).

ganyong (*Jv, Sd*) k.o. edible tuber.

ganyut see GANYAR.

gaok (*Jv*) **1** k.o. bird, crow. **2** cawing sound. **meng-** caw. **-an** sound of crowing.

gap 1 sound of slapping on a table. **2** sound of heartbeat.

gapa, gapah₁ skillful, adroit, agile.

gapah₂ see GOPOH.

gapai ber-an, meng-(²) 1 reach for, extend the hand for, grasp after. *Ia ~ hendak bergantung pd dahan* He reached out to hang onto a branch. **2** wave (o.'s hand) to. **3** achieve, attain. *~ gelar kesarjanaan* attain a master's degree. **meng-(²)kan** extend (o.'s hand). **peng-an** waving of hand.

gapak see GAPA.

gapik see GOPOH.

gapil - *mulut* quick to protest, criticize. - *tangan* **1** pilferer, shoplifter. **2** o. who interferes. **meng-** interfere in.

gapit pincers, tweezers, clamp. **meng-** pick up, hold, with tweezers.

gaplé dominoes.

gaplék dried cassava.

gaplok (*Jv*) **meng-** slap s.o. on the back. **meng-i** slap on the back several times. **-an** a slap on the back.

GAPMNI [*Gabungan Pengusaha Makanan-Minuman*] Association of Food and Drink Producers.

gapu meng- reach, extend to.

gapura gate, gateway, portal.

gara-gara 1 (*Jv*) scene in traditional *wayang* depicting turbulence and war. **2** turbulence, commotion (in war or of nature). *Rupanya kau cari ~* Apparently you are looking for trouble. **3** natural phenomenon (earthquake, typhoon, etc.) regarded as an omen (us. bad). **4** just because (of). *~ bertengkar dgn atasannya dia dikeluarkan* He was fired just because he quarreled with his boss. *~ perempuan* all on account of a woman. **ber-** make a fuss.

garage /garase/ see GARASI.

garah₁ frighten away, chase away (birds, etc.). **peng-** rope with noisemakers attached stretched across rice field, which when shaken frightens birds away.

garah₂ -² joking, jesting. **ber-(²)** joke, jest.

garam 1 salt. - *bata(an)* block or brick salt. - *batu/darat* rock salt. - *hancur(an)* table salt. - *di laut asam di gunung bertemu di belanga* married couple with quite different origins (lit., the salt of the sea and the acid of the uplands meet in the pot). *membuang - ke laut* carry coals to Newcastle (lit., throw salt in the sea). **2** a mineral salt. - *inggeris* Epsom salts. - *kapur* calcium. - *mesiu* saltpeter. - *niterat* sodium nitrate. - *sian* cyanide. **3** experience, effectiveness (in idioms). *banyak makan - di hidupnya* having had plenty of experience in life. *KB kurang - bila tdk disertai dgn pendidikan séks* Family planning is ineffective if it is not coupled with sex education. **ber- 1** salted. **2** be like salt. **3** be effective. *leluconmu itu kurang ~* Your jokes do not hit the mark. **meng- 1** become salty. **2** make or produce salt. **3** lick at salt (of animals). **meng-i 1** salt s.t. **2** make worse. *~ keadaan* worsen the situation. **meng-kan** turn s.t. into salt. **-²an** various salts. **pe(ng)-an 1** work with salt. **2** salt-making location.

garan (*Jv*) handle. - *pisau* knife handle.

garandir meng- guarantee.

garang₁ 1 fierce, cruel, ferocious. **2** vivid (of colors). **3** very strong. - *bekerja* work very hard. **4** angry. **meng-** rage, storm. **ke-an** fierceness, ferocity.

garang₂ (*Jv*) **meng- 1** roast s.t. **2** dry s.t.

garangan mongoose.

garansi guarantee, warrant. **ber-** having a guarantee. *membeli jam ~* buy a watch with a guarantee.

garap meng- work on. *~ tanah* work the land. **meng-kan** work on on behalf of s.o. **-an** s.t. produced. **peng-** o. who works on s.t. **peng-an** the process of making. *~ filem* the making of the film.

garas₁ shin.

garas₂ meng- eat, gobble up. *Ku- kapitalisme!* I will gobble up capitalism!

garasi garage.

garau hoarse.

garba, garbha (*Biol.*) embryo.

garbis (*Jv*) k.o. round, yellow and black melon.

garda guard. - *depan* avant-garde, vanguard.

gardan (*Auto.*) differential gear.
gardén, gardin see GORDÉN.
gardu 1 guardhouse, sentry post, ticket booth (on toll road). - *penilikan bintang* astronomical observatory. **2** bus shelter. **3** (*Mil.*) depot, dump, magazine. **4** (*Tech.*) relay station. - *listrik* electrical relay station. - *télpon* telephone relay station.
Garebeg (*Jv*) o. of the three major Muslim religious festivals. - *Besar/Haji* day of sacrifice, celebration on 10th of *Zulhijah*. - *Maulud* festival commemorating Muh.'s birth. - *Puasa* festival at end of Muslim fasting month.
garéng (*Jv*) k.o. cicada that appears at end of rainy season.
Garéng son of Semar in Jv shadow play.
gari handcuffs. **meng-** handcuff, shackle, manacle.
garib strange, peculiar, exotic.
garing 1 dry and crispy, crunchy. **2** cool (of a relationship). *Hubungan keduanya boléh dikatakan* - The relationship between them can be said to be tenuous. **meng-kan** make s.t. crisp and dry. **ke-an** crispness, crunchiness.
garis 1 line. - *akhir* (*Sport*) finish line. - *alas* base line. - *arah* alignment. - *arsiran* hatching line (in a drawing). - *bagi* (*Math.*) bisecting line. - *balik* tropic. - *balik sartan/selatan* Tropic of Capricorn. - *balik utara* Tropic of Cancer. - *batas* 1 line of demarcation. **2** (*Sport*) finish line. **3** frontier, border. **4** (*Sport*) boundaries, bounds. - *bawah* underlining. **men-bawahi 1** underline, underscore (word, sentence, etc.). **2** emphasize. **peng-bawahan 1** underlining, underscoring. **2** emphasizing - *belakang* 1 rear guard, 2 home front. **3** base line. - *berat* (*Math.*) median. - *besar* broad outline. - *biku-biku* zigzag. - *bukur/busur* (*Geog.*) meridian. - *dasar* base line. - *démarkasi* line of demarcation. - *depan* front line. - *grafik* curve (on a graph, etc.). - *haluan* line of action. - *kaki* base line. - *khattulistiwa* equator. - *kodrat* fate. - *(me)lintang* (*Geog.*) latitude. - *pemisah* dividing line. - *penyekat* slant line. - *perhatian* underlining, underscoring. - *pilih* slant line. - *potongan* (*Math.*) secant. - *samping* line at side of paper to indicate margin. - *sekat* slant line. - *sempadan* alignment. - *silang* intersecting line. - *singgung* (*Math.*) tangent. - *sipat* alignment. - *sudut-menyudut* diagonal. - *tgl* (*Geog.*) date line. - *tegak* perpendicular. - *tengah* diameter. - *tepi* margin-setting line on paper. - *tinggi* (*Math.*) 1 perpendicular. 2 contour line. - *tinggian* high-water mark. - *titik* dotted line. - *tolak* starting line. **2** dash, stroke. - *balok* bar of music. **3** contour. - *édar* orbit. - *segi tiga* triangle. **ber-** lined (of paper). **ber-²** decorated with lines. **meng-1** scratch. **2** draw lines, rule (a page). **3** be a thin line. *jalanan kecil yg* ~ *di lembah itu* the narrow path that was like a line in the valley. **meng-i** draw a line on. **meng-kan 1** underline, underscore s.t. *Keputusan-keputusan ini* ~ *peranan organisasi itu* These decisions underscore the role of that organization. **2** trace the lines of. **3** outline. *Haluan negara sdh di-kan* The direction of the

state has been outlined. **ter-** be scratched into s.t. **-an 1** ruler. **2** line etched or drawn. **peng-ruler.** ~ *beléid (kebijaksanaan) téknis* rule of technical policy. **pe-an** indication by lines. ~ *batas tanah* boundary markings. **peng-an 1** drawing lines. ~ *silang* cross-hatching. **2** line, policies set. ~ *dr Purék* the rules set forth by Purek. ~ *tata guna tanah* policy regarding land use.
garisah instinct.
garit₁ scratch. **meng-** scratch. **ber-** be scratched. *tak* ~ unscathed.
garit₂ meng- move. **meng-kan** move s.t. ~ *tangan* move o.'s hand.
garnéren, garnéring /harnéren, harnéring/ (*Coll.*) cake icing or decoration.
garnisun (*Mil.*) garrison.
garong robber. **meng- 1** rob, commit a robbery. **2** plunder, loot, pillage. **ke-an** be robbed from. **peng- 1** robber. **2** plunderer, pillager, looter. **peng-an 1** robbery, banditry. **2** looting, pillaging.
garpu fork. - *(pe)nala* tuning fork. - *tanah* 1 harrow. 2 pitchfork. **ber-** use a fork. **meng-** pick up with a fork.
garu₁ harrow. **meng-** harrow. **peng-** a harrow.
garu₂ see GAHARU.
garuda 1 mythical bird, mounted by god Vishnu. **2** bird in official seal of Republic of Indonesia. **meng-i** give wings to. ~ *Indonésia* give wings to Indonesia.
garuk round up. *Para tuna susila kena - tadi malam* They had a round up of the prostitutes last night. **ber-(²), -²** scratch. *Monyét itu* ~ The monkey is scratching. **meng- 1** scratch (head, arm, etc.), curry (horse), scrape (pan, etc.), rake. **2** round up people (in a raid). **3** rob, clean out. *Hartanya di- habis oléh garong* She was cleaned out by the robbers. **meng-²** keep scratching. ~ *kepala* scratch the head because o. is at a loss for what to do. **meng-i** scratch repeatedly. **meng-kan** scratch or scrape with, harrow. *Ia* ~ *besi itu pd tanah* He used that iron rod to scrape the earth. **-an 1** scratch(es). **2** scratching. **peng-** rake, curry, comb, scraper. **peng-an** scraping, scratching.
garung₁ meng- 1 growl, roar. **2** cry or weep loudly.
garung₂ see GARONG.
garut meng- abrade, chafe.
garwa, garwo (*Honorific, Jv*) spouse. - *ampil* concubine, mistress.
gas 1 gas. - *air mata* tear gas. - *alam* natural gas. - *buang* exhaust (from car, etc.). - *bumi* natural gas. - *cair* liquid gas. - *karbit* acetylene. *lampu* - gas lamp. - *letus* explosive gas. - *rawa* methane gas. **2** vapor from gasoline. *menancap* - step on the gas. **ber-** be filled with gas. **meng- 1** evaporate. *Alkohol itu mudah* ~ Alcohol evaporates easily. **2** accelerate, give gas to. **meng-i** (*Coll.*) step on the gas, give the gas to.
gasak 1 fight. **2** hit. **ber-** fight, hit e.o. *Kedua anak itu* ~ The two boys fought. **meng- 1** rub hard. **2** attack, assault (by hitting or kicking). **3** take by

force. **4** pilfer, steal. **5** thrash. *Tiba di final, Indonesia kembali di- satu-tiga oléh Tin Aung* Reaching the finals, Indonesia was again thrashed 1-3 by Tin Aung. **6** devour. *Di-nya semua suguhan sampai tak tersisa* She went at the refreshments until there were none left. **-an** blow, drubbing, hitting e.o. **peng-an** hitting, breaking. *~ pintu terjadi lagi oléh perampok* Robbers again broke down the doors.

gasal (*Math.*) uneven, odd (of a number).

gasang lustful, lecherous, lascivious.

gasing a top. **ber-** spin a top. **-an** a spin of a top.

gaskét gasket.

gasolin gasoline.

gasung sandbar.

gatal 1 itch. *Kaki saya -* My foot itches. *- gusi* mouth-watering. *- hati* itchy. *- mulut* talkative, garrulous. **2** eager for s.t. (money, etc., but esp. sex). *Mau jadi janda -, jadilah!* OK if you want to be a lecherous divorcée, be o.! *- tangan saya hendak memukul dia* My hand itches to hit him. **meng-kan 1** cause to itch. *Awas, daun itu ~* Watch out, those leaves will make you itch. **2** irritating. *Sikapnya sungguh ~* Her attitude was really irritating. **ke-an 1** itchiness. **2** irritation. **-an** prone to have strong desires.

gatot (*Jv*) sliced dried cassava boiled with coconut milk.

gatra phrase (in a sentence or in music).

gatuk (*Jv*) match, meet, coincide. *-nya derap-irama* being together in their rhythm. **-an** being matched, being close in harmony.

Gatutkaca son of Bima, o. of the Pendawa brothers in the Jv *wayang* .

gaul ber- associate. *Ia hanya ~ dgn org-org terkemuka saja* He only associates with prominent persons. *~ intim dgn* have an intimate relationship with. **meng-** mix, stir (food). **meng-i 1** have intercourse with. *Toh meréka itu yg hrs ku-i dlm hidupku yg akan datang* However, those are the people I will have to have social relations with in my future life. **2** have sexual intercourse with. **memper-i** associate with, go around with. *Segala lapisan masyarakat diper-inya* He has moved in all strata of society. **memper-kan** make s.t. blend. **per-an 1** association, social intercourse. **2** society. *~ hidup* social intercourse. **3** sexual intercourse. *~ bébas* free sex, promiscuity.

gaun gown, W.dress. *- rumah* housecoat, dressing gown. *- tidur* nightgown. **ber-** have, wear a gown.

gaung₁ echo, reverberation. **ber-, meng-** echo, reverberate.

gaung₂ hole, ravine. **meng-** dig, excavate.

gawai see GAWÉ.

gawal mistake, error. *Sepandai-pandai tupai melompat, sekali - juga* No matter how well a squirrel jumps, o. day he will miss.

gawang 1 gate. **2** (*Sport*) goal posts. **3** (*Sport*) hurdles. **-²an** (*Sport*) wicket.

gawar warning sign (us. by means of ropes).

gawat 1 critical, serious, grave. **2** dangerous, risky. **3** bad, terrible. *- temanmu itu! Masa isteri*

org dibawa-bawa seénak udelnya Your friend is awful. Imagine, going wherever he wants with s.o. else's wife. **meng-** be critical, be grave. **meng-kan 1** endanger, render critical. *~ kehidupan surat kabar berbahasa daérah* endanger the life of regional language newspapers. **2** dangerous, precarious, critical. **ke-an 1** criticalness. **2** danger, gravity. *Menghentikan ~ di wajah anda* Stop looking so grave.

gawé (*Jkt, Jv*) work. *nyari -* look for work. *punya -* hold a celebration or feast.

gawir (*Sd*) escarpment.

gaya 1 energy, force. *- air* waterpower. *- apung* buoyant force, buoyancy. *- basa* (*Chem.*) basicity. *- berat* gravity. *- bobot* gravity. *- dorong* thrust, propulsion. *- dukung* supporting or carrying capacity. *- gabung* affinity. *- gerak* motive power. *- hidrolik* hydraulic force, hydraulic power. *- lentur* flexibility. *- pegas* resilience, elasticity. *- pusingan* centrifugal force. *- putaran* torque. *- rentang* tensile strength. *- semu* inertia. *- séntrifugal* centrifugal force. *- séntripetal* centripetal force. *- séx* sex appeal. *- tahan* resistance. *- tarik/tegang* tensile strength. *- uap* steam power. **2** style, form, manner. *- yg élok* a graceful manner. *- aku* the style of writing using *aku* for the first person. *- bahasa* literary style. *- baru* new style. **meng-barukan** bring a new style to s.t. *~ pengurusnya* bring a new style to the board, change the board into personalities representing a new style. *OPS Écéran Jkt yg di-barukan* The organization of retailers in Jkt which was set in a new style. *- bébas* (*Sport*) free style, catch as catch can. *- berganti* (*Sport*) relay race. *- berkecambah* way s.t. sprouts. *- dada katak* (*Sport*) breast stroke. *- kupu-kupu* (*Sport*) butterfly stroke. *- laku* behavior. *- punggung* (*Sport*) back stroke. *- tulis* (writing) style. **3** musical note, melody. **-²nya** affectedly, seemingly. **ber- 1** strong, energetic, powerful. **2** stylish. *gedung yg ~ baru* new-style building. **3** be in a certain style. *~ Perancis* be in a French style. **meng- 1** inspire, encourage. *Ia ~ rakyatnya spy berontak* He inspired his people to revolt. **2** put on airs, be affected or pretentious in manner. **meng-kan** lend beauty, strength to. *Dékor di-kan dgn warna-warni* The decor was given beauty by the various colors.

gayal 1 elastic. **2** tough of meat.

gayam k.o. semicultivated *Inocarpus* tree with pulpy fruits eaten cooked.

gayang staggering, reeling (from dizziness, drunkenness, etc.).

gayang-gayang a rack.

gayem (*Jv*) **meng-(i)** chew the cud.

gayeng (*Jv*) **1** pleasant, warm, cordial (attitude). **2** cheerful, interesting (conversation). **ke-an** cordiality, warmth, pleasantness.

gayuh₁ hang low (of fruit on tree or bush).

gayuh₂ aspiration, ideal, objective. **meng-** achieve.

gayung₁ water dipper, scoop. **ber-** use as a water dipper.

gayung₂ attack (with sword or blow). **ber-** (*Sport*)

engage in boxing or fencing. **meng-** 1 strike, slash. 2 cast an evil spell on. 3 stab. 4 do footwork (in *silat* or other self-defense art).

gayut ber- hang, swing. *Anak itu ~ di léhér ibunya* The child is hanging from its mother's neck. **ber-an** swing (of several things or people). *Meréka suka ~ dr pohon ke pohon* They like to swing from tree to tree. **meng-** be hanging. *Buah dadanya ~* Her breasts sagged. **meng-i** 1 hang on to. *Kita adalah putera-putera yg di-i harapan* We are young people upon whom hope hangs. 2 be present in a place. *Di-i oléh sebanyak tiga puluh juta anggota* attended by 30 million members. *Ada semacam rasa rindu yg ~ hatiku* A k.o. nostalgia engulfed me.

gb. [*gambar*] illustration.

GBHN [*Garis-garis Besar Haluan Negara*] (*Pol.*) Broad Outlines of the Nation's Direction.

gbr. see GB.

gebah meng- chase away, chase out.

gebang (*Jv*) tall thornless jungle palm with large leaves.

gebar see KAIN.

geber₁ meng- vibrate (of an engine).

geber₂ meng- give too much of s.t.

gébér (*Jv*) wattle on birds.

gebes meng-kan move s.t. *Ia ~ tangannya* He waved his hand.

gébés (*Jv*) 1 shake o.'s head in disagreement. 2 be unwilling.

geblak (*Jv*) **ng-** fall backward.

geblas (*Jv*) **meng-** go away hurriedly. *Ia ~ léwat pintu belakang* He left hurriedly through the back door.

geblek see GOBLOK.

geblok (*Jv*) 1 bolt of cloth. *dua - kain katun* two rolls of cotton cloth. 2 wad of money.

gebok bolt of cloth.

gébok meng- hit with a ball or s.t. thrown.

gebos₁ meng- scold, snap at, snarl at.

gebos₂ (*Jv*) **meng-** suddenly let off smoke.

gebrak sound of a door slamming, board crashing to floor, etc. **ber-(an)** pound e.o. (of boxers, etc.). **meng-** 1 thump, pound on (a table, etc.). 2 crash. *Mobilnya di- oléh bintara AL* Her car was hit by a Navy non-com. 3 hit. *Beberapa sastrawan ~ balas* Several literary persons hit back. 4 instigate, urge, move. *Ia berhasil ~ anak buahnya utk menggali* He succeeded in urging the crew to dig. 5 shake off. *~ kelesuan pikiran* shake off tiredness from thinking. **-an** 1 (karate) blow, chop. 2 blow, slap (on table, etc.), beat (of music). *menyaksikan ~ musik Arék-Arék Surabaya ini* to experience the Surabaya boys' beat.

gebrés (*Jv*) sneeze.

gebu meng-(²) 1 flare up (of fire, revolt). 2 rage. *Biarkan topan ~!* Let the storm rage! 3 be tense and excited with enthusiasm, worked up for action.

gebuk meng- beat (a drum). **meng-i** pummel, beat up. **meng-kan** beat with s.t. *Tasnya di-kan-nya pd org yg menjahilinya* With her purse, she pummeled the man who was molesting her. **-an**

beating, pummeling. **-²an** beating e.o. **peng-** drum.

gebyah (*Jv*) **meng-** *uyah* consider all to be the same, make no distinction. *Jangan ~ uyah karena tdk semua org spt dia* Do not think everybody is the same because not everybody is like him.

gebyak (*Jv*) **meng-** perform, stage. **-an** performance. *Jangan mengadakan ~ pd sekitar hari-hari ulangan* Do not organize performances during examination times.

gebyar (*Jv*) sparkle, shine, glitter. *Ia tdk kalah dgn - Nixon* Nixon did not outshine him.

gebyur (*Jv*) **meng-** splash a large amount of water on s.o. or s.t. **meng-kan** pour s.t. out with a splash. **-an** water splashed out. *kena ~ bekas air cucian* get the water from the laundry splashed on o.

gecak see GECEK.

gecar trembling, fright. **meng-** shudder, tremble (from fear).

gecek (*Jv*) **meng-** 1 crush, smash (i.e. food to soften it, etc.). 2 catch, seize, grasp.

gedabah triangle-shaped gold hair ornament.

gedang₁ large, big. **meng-kan** enlarge, increase, expand.

gedang₂ (*Sd*) papaya.

gedé (*Coll.*) big, large. **meng-kan** enlarge. **ke-an** too big. **peng-** (*Sl.*) big shot.

gedebak --*gedebuk*/*gedebur* 1 sound of s.t. heavy having fallen. 2 sound of footsteps on a floor. **ber-(-*gedebuk*)** make heavy steps. *Langkahnya ~ -gedebuk* His steps were heavy-sounding. **ber-an** sound heavily (of many things). *Kembali gedung itu ~* Again there were heavy pounding noises in the building. **meng-kan** stamp s.t. down hard. *Ia ~ kakinya karena marah* He stamped his foot in anger.

gedebar-gedebur sound of beating or throbbing, beat or throb. *- jantungnya* the pounding of her heart, her heart pounded.

gedeblak-gedebluk sound of wrestling and fighting.

gedebok₁ (*Jv*) trunk of a banana plant, esp. as a place to arrange *wayang* puppets.

gedebok₂ see GEDEBUK.

gedebrak-gedebruk loud sound of s.t. heavy falling, very loud stamping of the feet.

gedebuk sound of heavy footsteps. **ber-** with a thud. **(ber)-an** make a pounding or thudding noise. *suara sepatu ~ menjejak tanah* thudding sound of shoes hitting the ground.

gedebum see GEDEBUK.

gedebung square of cloth formed into a pouch often for betel leaves and tobacco.

gedebur see GEDEBAR-GEDEBUR.

gedék panel of woven or plaited bamboo (for house walls, etc.). *rumah -* a house with walls of this material.

gedempak tambourine.

gedempol fat, obese. *gemuk -* fat and pudgy.

gédéng (*Jv*) sheaf (of rice).

gedobros (*Jv*) **ng-** talk nonsense.

gedok meng- weave. *~ benang hingga berbentuk*

sarung weave thread into the form of a sarong. **-an** primitive handloom.

gedombrongan (*Coll.*) too large (of clothes).

gedoncak ber- beat (of heart).

gedong fancy house, mansion. **-an** having or living in a large, stone house. *anak* ~ children from well-to-do classes (living in expensive houses).

gedor meng- 1 pound on. *Bp* ~ *pintu* Father pounded on the door. 2 break in to plunder. **meng-i** pound on (repeatedly or several things). **meng-kan** slam (a door, etc.). **-an** loot, plunder. **peng-** burglar, looter. **peng-an** 1 looting, plundering. 2 burglary.

gedruk (*Jv*) **meng-** stamp. **meng-kan** stamp (feet). **-an** stamping (of feet).

gedubrak /gedubrak/ (*Jv*) **meng-** make a sudden popping or crashing noise.

gedubrang see GEDUBRAK.

gedumbreng sound of jangling or clanking (e.g. of cans banging against e.o.). **-an** keep making this sound.

gedumel see KEDUMEL.

gedung building (us. of brick or concrete), edifice. *- acara* law court. *- arca* museum. *- bertingkat* multistoried building. *- bicara* meeting hall. *- bioskop* movie house, movie theater. *- flat* apartment building. *- induk* main building. *- instansi* 1 public building. 2 building owned by a firm. *- pemerintah* public building. *- Putih* US White House.

geduyut ber- droop, bend (from heavy branches, etc.).

gegabah rash, reckless, hasty. *tindakan -* reckless deeds.

gegak see GEGAP₁.

gegaman hand weapon.

gegaokan (*Jv*) caw.

gegap₁ *- gempita* uproarious, noisy, clamorous. **ke- gempitaan** clamor, uproar, tumult. **meng-gempita(kan)** make uproarious. ~ *seluruh rakyat* bring the crowd to a roar. **meng-** make a huge noise. **meng-kan** ear-shattering, ear-splitting.

gegap₂ ter-² haltingly, falteringly (in speaking).

gegar shaking, swaying. *- budaya* culture conflict. *- otak* brain concussion. **ber-, meng-** 1 shake. *Suaranya* ~ Her voice shook. 2 rumble (of cannon, thunder). **ber-an** tremble, shake, rumble (plurally). ~ *org bersorak pula* The people once again let out a thunderous cheer. *Hujan melampias* ~ *jatuh* The rain roared as it rushed down. **ber-²an** thunder. *dlm sorak riuh yg* ~ with wild applause which thundered out. **meng-²** rumble and thunder. *Guntur* ~ Thunder kept rumbling. **meng-kan** shake. *Gempa* ~ *bumi* An earthquake shook the earth. ~ *dan menjungkir-balik-kan keseimbangan* shake and upset the balance.

gegares stuff, gorge o.s. *Kerjanya - melulu* All he does is stuff himself.

gegas lots of movement and activity. *persimpangan yg penuh* - a busy intersection. **ber-(²),** **ter-(²)** hurry up, be in a hurry. *Meréka* ~ *ke sekolah* They hurried to school. *~lah!* Hurry (up)!

Dgn ~ *meréka berpakaian* They got dressed in a hurry. **ber-an** hurry. **meng-(kan)** hurry or speed s.t. up.

gegat₁ k.o. insect, silverfish.

gegat₂ see KEGAT.

gegau ter- startled, wake up with a start.

gégép pliers, tweezers.

gégér 1 commotion, tumult. *- guntur* sound of thunder. *- otak* brain concussion. 2 be in a tumult. *Seluruh dunia -* The whole world is in a tumult. **(ber)-an** make a commotion (in large numbers). **meng-kan** stir, cause a commotion. *Dunia penerbangan di-kan dgn berhasilnya sputnik* The world of aviation was thrown into a tumult by the success of Sputnik. *Insyallah itu akan* ~ *kubu-kubu impérialisme* God willing, that will shake the ramparts of imperialism. *tahun-tahun yg* ~ years of turbulence. **ke-an** commotion, clamor, tumult.

gegetuk see GETUK₁.

gegetun surprised, dumbfounded.

geguyon joke, make a joke.

gejala 1 symptom, indication. *memperlihatkan -²* *penyiaran radioaktip* show symptoms of radioactivity. *- hamil* sign of pregnancy. 2 tendency. *bertindak menentang -²* *yg jahat dlm golongan* act to counter the evil tendencies in the group. **ber-** have symptoms. **meng-** 1 become, have the symptom of. 2 be indicated, conspicuous. *Rupanya konstruksi "yg" plus kata benda mulai* ~ *di dlm pemakaian BI* It seems that the construction *yg* plus noun is beginning to become conspicuous in Indonesian usage. **peng-an** process of becoming conspicuous.

gejolak 1 flaming, fire. 2 fluctuation (in prices). **ber-** 1 flare up (of fire, temper, etc.). *Apinya* ~ *tinggi* The fire blazed with high flames. 2 fluctuate (of prices).

gejos sound of sizzling (when water is poured over hot coals, etc.). **meng-** sizzle (when hot object comes into contact with cold water). **meng-kan** pour s.t. hot in water. *Puntung rokok di-kannya ke dlm sisa minumannya* He snuffed out his cigarette in the remains of his drink.

gejug (*Jv*) **meng-** kick in fighting (in martial arts, dance). **meng-kan** kick (the feet) outward. **-an** kick, blow with the feet.

gejuju meng- build up, pile up (of clouds).

gclabak see GELÉTAK.

gelabur meng- plunge into water.

geladah see GELÉDAH.

geladak₁ (*Naut.*) deck. *- belakang* afterdeck. *- muka* foredeck.

geladak₂ 1 mongrel dog. 2 criminal.

geladi rehearsal. *- resik* dress rehearsal.

geladir 1 mucus, phlegm. 2 slime.

gelagah wild sugarcane.

gelagak see GELEGAK.

gelagapan 1 stutter, stammer. 2 confused, flustered, upset. 3 losing direction. 4 make gasping noises when drowning.

gelagar ber-an thunder (of cannons).

gelagat 1 sign, indication. *Méga adalah - hujan*

Clouds indicate rain. **2** symptom. **3** attitude. *Dr -nya saya lihat dia lagi susah* From his attitude I noticed that he was sad. **4** habits. *Meréka mempelajari - musuh sblm menyerang* They studied the habits of the enemy before attacking.

gelagepan see GELAGAPAN.

gelak 1 laughter. **2** laugh, chortle. *- gejolak* loud laughter. *- manis* smile. *- nabi* derisive smile. *- senyum* smile. *- sétan* booming laughter. *- sumbing* sickly laugh. *- tawa* hearty laugh(ter). **ber-², ter-²** chuckle, chortle.

gelakak hearty laugh.

gelam k.o. Melaleuca tree and its bark which is used for caulking.

gelama₁ k.o. sea fish.

gelama₂ mucus, phlegm.

gelamai sweet made of pounded sticky rice, coconut, and sugar. **meng-** prepare this sweet.

gelambir wattle of fowl, jowls, or other wattlelike skinfold in animals. **ber-** have wattles, jowls. **ber-(an), meng-** hang down like jowls. *Buah dada nénék itu sdh ~* The breasts of the old woman hang down.

gelandang (*Sport*) halfback. *- tengah* center halfback. **ber-an** loaf about, loaf around, wander aimlessly. **meng- 1** take in, arrest for vagrancy. **2** be a vagrant. *dlm dunia jambrét dan ~* in the world of (purse) snatching and vagrancy. *~lah ke-35 anggota rombongan kami di lantai gerbong* The 35 members of our group were just lying around on the floor of the freight car. **-an** vagrant, homeless drifter. **per-an** vagrancy.

gelang bracelet. *- jam* watchband. *- kaki* anklet, ankle bracelet. *- karét* rubber band. *- keroncong* a series of brackets or bangles. *- kunci* key ring. *- penutup* washer (plumbing). *- panggul* pelvic region. *- rantai* link (in a chain). *- raya* spindle worm. *- silinder* piston ring. *- tanah* earthworm. **-²** tapeworm. **ber-** wear a bracelet. **-an 1** hoop. **2** bracelet. **per-an** circle. *~ kaki* (*Anat.*) tarsus. *~ tangan* wrist.

gélang purslane.

gelanggang 1 a circular area in which an event takes place: arena, forum, pit, ring. *- bergumul* wrestling ring. *- buku* book fair. *- dagang* trade fair. *- perang/perjuangan* battlefield, battle arena. *- remaja* youth center. *- tinju* boxing ring. **2** a round area which forms the background for s.t. *- matahari* halo around the sun. *- susu* (*Anat.*) areola. **ber- 1** be a circular area for a public event. *~ di mata org banyak* perfectly clear, obvious. **2** have a halo around it. **meng-** arrange a circular area.

gelangsar meng- slide, slip up.

gelantang meng- bleach, dry in the sun.

gelanting, gelantung ber- hang down, dangle, steady o.s. by holding onto s.t. above. *Anting-antingnya - dgn manisnya* Her earrings dangled attractively. **ber-an** hang down (of many persons or things). *Org di bis ~ di besi-besi pegangan* The people in the bus were hanging onto the overhead bars. **meng-** dangle, swing (on gallows, etc.). *Meskipun jatuh dia masih sempat ~ pd akar*

tanaman He fell, but he was able to hang on to the root of a plant. **ter-** be hanging from.

gelantur meng- flow forth, come forth. *pendapat sepihak yg ~ bila membaca koméntar* a personal opinion which is expressed upon reading the commentary.

gelap 1 dark. *- bulan* dark of the moon. *- buta/ gelita/gerelap/gulita/katup* pitch-dark. *- mata/pikiran* **1** go berserk, run amuck. **2** desperation, mental derangement. **2** unclear, obscure. *Hal itu masih - bagi saya* That matter is still not clear to me. **3** secret, illicit, clandestine (organization). *hubungan -* secret liaison. *garam -* bootleg salt. *mata-mata -* secret police. *bapak -* unwed father. **ber-² 1** sit in the dark. **2** be less than frank, less than candid. **meng- 1** turn dark. **2** disappear in the dark. **3** run amuck, act crazy. **meng-i** darken. **meng-kan 1** darken, obscure. **2** embezzle. **3** tamper with legal papers. **ke-an 1** darkness, obscurity. **2** overtaken by darkness. **3** become raving mad. **-an** darkness. **-²an** in a secret, illegal manner. *secara ~ meréka menanam ganja* They planted marijuana clandestinely. **ke-²an 1** fairly dark. *kamar yg ~* a rather dark room. **2** become furious. **peng-** embezzler. **peng-an 1** blackout (as a precaution). **2** darkening. **3** embezzling. **4** tampering with legal papers, cover-up.

gelapai meng- fight feebly (of cocks).

gelar₁ 1 title. **2** academic title, degree. *Saya ingin meraih - doktor* I want to get a doctor's degree. *- bangsawan* title of nobility. **3** alias. *Aman - si Kucing* Aman alias "The Cat." **ber- 1** have a title. *Ia ~ doktor* She has the title of doctor. **2** titled, noble. **meng-(i) 1** to name. *Ia ~ anaknya Budiman* He named his child Budiman. **2** give a title to. *Menurut adat Acéh ulama di-i Teungku* According to Achehnese custom a religious scholar is called *Teungku*. *UI sdh ~ tujuh org menjadi Doktor Ilmu Sastra* The University of Indonesia has given seven Doctorates in Letters. **memper-kan** stage, present (a play, etc.). *Nomor-nomor diperkan oléh . . .* The numbers were presented by . . . **-²an** designation, a so-called title. *~ Agung hanya mode saja* People use the title *Agung* with no real meaning. It is merely a matter of fashion. **pe-an, per-an** presentation, staging, performance. **peng-an** bestowal of degree or title. *pidato ~ pertama* the first speech upon the bestowal of degrees.

gelar₂ meng- spread out. *~ tikar* **1** roll out a carpet. **2** set up shop. **ter-** spread out. **-an** carpet, mat to sit on.

gelas glass (for drinking). *- baterai* (*Chem.*) battery jar. *- kimia* (*Chem.*) beaker. *- takar/ukur* calibrated beaker. **ber-²an** kite fighting (with ground glass on string). **meng-** coat kite string with ground glass. **-an** coating of ground glass or glass shards. *~ mati* **1** hard glass. **2** glass shards which have been affixed s.w.

gelatak₁ meng- tickle.

gelatak₂ meng-i hunt or search through (pockets, drawers, etc.).

gelatik k.o. bird that eats rice crops, Java finch.

gelayangan meander, roam, ramble.

gelayaran stagger.

gelayut see GAYUT.

gelebap sound of an object falling, plop.

gelebar ber-, ter- flap (of sail, shirt, tail, etc.). **meng-** plop o.s. down.

geleber, geleberan hang loosely, hang in folds (of skin, clothing).

gelebuk sound of an object falling.

gelebur meng- plunge, jump into (a fire, etc.).

gelebyar ber- fly around. **ber-an** fly all over (of many things). *Kertas ~ ditiup angin* The wind blew paper all over the place. **meng-** fly about (of a bird).

gelécék, gelecik meng- skid, slip, slide.

geledah meng- search (a building), frisk (a person), ransack. *- diri* self-searching. **meng-i** ransack repeatedly or many things. **peng-** raider. **peng-an 1** raid. **2** ransacking.

geledang meng- extend the arms (as if to ward or hold off s.t. or s.o.).

geledék thunder, lightning. **meng-** thunder, rumble. *Guruh ~ di kejauhan* Thunder rumbled in the distance. *Suaranya ~ mengucapkan pidatonya* His voice thundered as he delivered his speech. **meng-i** thunder at. *Ia di-i oléh Ayah ketika pulang tengah malam* Father thundered at her when she returned home at midnight.

geleding meng- twist, warp (of wood, etc.).

geledur have folds (of fat around the abdomen).

gelegak ber-, meng- 1 bubble, effervesce, fizz, seethe. *Air laut ~* The sea seethed. *Dunia masih ~ dgn perang* The world is still seething with war. *Bubur panas itu ~ di atas tungku* The hot porridge bubbled on the stove. **2** wheeze. *suara ~* wheezing sound. **meng-kan** bring to a boil, make s.t. seethe or wheeze.

gelegapan see GELAGAPAN.

gelegar₁ (floor) beam, girder, joint.

gelegar₂ thundering, rumbling, sound of cannon. *- buluh* boastful. **meng-** thunder, rumble. *Protés-protés ~ di AS* Protests thundered throughout the US. *Letusan senjata api ~ di hutan* The sound of gunfire rumbled in the forest. *Guruh kembali ~* Thunder rumbled again. **meng-kan 1** announce in a thunderous way. *~ segala pembantingan tulang* making known noisily the great efforts they were making. **2** make s.t. thunder. *lédakan yg ~ bumi* an explosion that made the earth thunder.

gelegata itchy rash, prickly heat.

gélék₁ meng- 1 roll over. *Kuda ~ di rumput* The horse rolled over in the grass. **2** roll. *Ia ~ lilin di antara telapak tangannya* She rolled a piece of wax between the palms of her hands. **3** run over, crush as in mortar. *Mobil grobak ~ anjing* A truck ran over a dog. **4** dodge, get out of the way. **meng-kan** avoid, evade s.t. *~ diri* get out of the way. **ter-** run over, crushed, knocked down (by car, train, etc.).

gélék₂ (*Sl.*) marijuana.

gelekak meng- peel (of paint, scabs, etc.).

gelekek meng- giggle, snicker.

gelemat (*Naut.*) forecastle.

gelémbéran wattle of fowl.

gelembung 1 bubble. *- air* water bubble. *- sabun* soap bubble. *- udara* air bubble. **2** (*Anat.*) vesicle. *- paru* alveolus (of lung). **3** swollen. *Perutnya -* His stomach is distended. **ber-, meng-** be inflated. *Bola itu ~* The ball is inflated. **ber-²** bubble, fizz. **meng-kan 1** inflate s.t. **2** distend (the abdomen, etc.). **-an** bubble. **-²an** bubbles of various kinds. *main ~* blow bubbles.

gelembur ripple. **meng-** be wrinkled. *Kulitnya ~* His skin is wrinkled. **meng-kan** wrinkle (the skin, etc.).

gelémpang see GELIMPAH.

gelémprang ber- high-pitched, piercing (of sound).

geléndong s.t. to wind s.t. around: bobbin, spool, coil, reel. *- kabel* cable drum. **meng-** wind s.t. around a spool, reel, etc.

geléndot meng- pull to attract attention. *~ di bahu ibunya* pull on his mother's shoulder (to get her attention). **meng-i** pull on s.t. to get o.'s attention.

géléng move from side to side (of o.'s head). **ber-, meng-** shake (of the head). **(ber-)², meng-²** keep shaking back and forth (of the head). **meng-kan** *kepala* shake o.'s head. **meng-²kan** shake (the head) back and forth. **-an** a shake of the head.

gelénggang see GELINGGANG.

gelentang ber- roll over. *Ia ~ di tikar mendekati saya* He rolled over on the mat closer to me.

gelentar see GELETAR.

gelenyar meng- tingle. *Kaki saya -* My foot tingles.

gelepak sag, collapse (of bridge, etc.).

gelepar fluttering. **meng-(²), ber-(²)** flutter, twitch, flap (as of wings, of dying fowl), flounder, squirm (of fish in net). **meng-kan** make s.t. flutter, flap. *Aduh! Ular! Dan aku ~ kaki* Heavens, a snake! And I shook my foot violently. **-an** flutter(ing).

gelepék meng- hang loosely, hang limply (of flag, etc.).

gelepok, gelepot muddy, muddied.

gelepung sound of heavy object hitting water.

gelepur flapping, fluttering (of dying or fighting fowl). **meng-** flounder, flutter.

gélér see GILIR.

geléser meng- 1 begin to turn, begin movement. **2** flutter, move agitatedly.

geléta long-necked jug.

gelétak flounder, flutter. **--geletik** floundering, fluttering. **ber-an** be sprawled, scattered, strewn about. *Kami ~ hendak tidur* We were sprawled in sleep. *buku-buku yg ~* scattered books. **meng-** sprawl. *Ia ~ di lantai* He sprawled on the floor. **meng-kan 1** put down in a sprawling position. **2** scatter s.t. about. **ter-** sprawled, laid out. *Korban ledakan itu ~ di tanah* The victims of the explosion lay sprawled on the ground.

geletar ber-, meng- 1 shiver, tremble. *Bumi ~* The earth trembled. 2 beat (of o.'s heart). **ber-an** shiver (plural). **meng-i** make s.t. shiver. *Hawa dingin ~ tubuhnya* The cool weather made his body shiver. **meng-kan** move s.t. rapidly in trembling way.

geletik meng- 1 move agitatedly, twitch, squirm. 2 make tick-tock sound (of watch or clock). 3 throb, beat (of o.'s heart).

geleting meng- tinkle (as of ice in a glass).

geletis meng- twitch, squirm.

geletuk chattering (of teeth). *Terdengar - giginya karena kedinginan* You could hear his teeth chattering from cold. **ber-an** chatter strongly (of teeth). **meng-** chatter (of teeth).

geli₁ 1 amused, tickled. *Saya ~ melihat org itu* I was amused watching that person. *- hati* feel like laughing. *- pahit* feeling amused and bitter at the same time. *- sendiri* laugh up o.'s sleeves. 2 ticklish. *Jangan pegang saya. Saya - Do not* touch me. I am ticklish. 3 set o.'s teeth on edge, give o. the creeps. *- geman* 1 irritating, get on o.'s nerves. 2 horrifying, horrible. **meng-kan** 1 encourage. 2 ridiculous, absurd. *Topi ~ absurd* hat. 3 tickle s.o. **ke-an** 1 amused, tickled. 2 feeling of amusement. *~ hati* amusement. **peng-** s.t. to make o. amused. *~ hati* joke, jest.

geli₂ see BUAH.

geliang, geliang-geliut writhe, wriggle. **ber-** wriggle, squirm.

geliat *--geliut* writhe, wriggle. **ber-an** squirm about (plural). **meng-** 1 twist. 2 stretch after sleeping. **meng-kan** stretch (the body) after sleeping. **ter-** twisted. *Kakinya* She twisted her ankle.

gelibir see GELIMBIR.

gelicik meng-kan avoid, evade. **ter-** skid, slip.

geliga see GULIGA.

geligi see GIGI.

geligir *- hidung* bridge of nose.

geligis meng- 1 tremble, quiver, shudder, shake. 2 chatter (of teeth).

geligit meng- bite repeatedly.

gelimang *dlm - lumpur* smeared by mud. **ber-** be soiled, smeared, covered with s.t. wet. **ber-an** smeared (plural). **meng-** be smeared over s.t. *Kakinya basah oléh darah yg ~ di tanah* His feet got wet from the pool of blood on the ground. **meng-i** cover s.t. with, smear s.t. with. **-an** shallow pools of liquid, mud, etc.

gelimbir hang loosely, hang in folds. **meng-** dangle, be pendulous. **-an** sagging. *pipi ~* sagging jowls (as in old people).

gelimpah, gelimpang ber-an be sprawled face up all over. *Korban pengeboman itu ~ di mana-mana* The victims of the bombardment lay sprawled everywhere. **meng-** lie sprawled face up. *Anak-anak kecil ~ tak bernyawa di pinggir jalan* Small children lay sprawled, lifeless, at the edge of the road. *tidur ~* sleep sprawled over e.o. **meng-kan** put (the body) in a sprawled and face-up position. **ter-** sprawl, lie sprawled.

gelinang meng- form in the corners of the eyes (of tears).

gelincir meng- slip, skid. *Mobil itu ~ di atas jalan yg basah* The car skidded on the wet road. **meng-kan** 1 cause s.t. to slip or skid. 2 sidetrack, derail s.t. or s.o. **ter-** 1 slip, skid. *Ia ~ di jalan yg licin itu* She slipped on the slick road. 2 (*Sport*) lose, be defeated. 3 make a slip (of the tongue). *Ia ~ lidah dan membuka rahasianya* He made a slip of the tongue and disclosed his secret. *Pengarang tdk ~; ia hanya terpelését sedikit* The writer did not slip; he merely was a bit off the mark.

gelincuh ter- stumble.

gelinding wheel. **ber-, meng-** 1 roll (of ball, etc.). 2 revolve. 3 (*Sl.*) get moving. *Lekas ~ lu. Pergi sblm aku sérét kau ke kantor polisi* Get moving before I drag you to the police station. **ber-an** roll (plural). **meng-kan** roll s.t. *~ ban mobil di antara tiang-tiang* roll a tire between posts. **-an** caster.

gelinggam 1 red lead. 2 red dye, red paint.

gelinggaman shudder, get the creeps.

gelinggang k.o. shrub, used to treat ringworm.

gelingsir ber-, meng- 1 slide or slip down while revolving. *Batu itu ~ dr léréng gunung* The rock slid from the mountain slope. 2 descend, go down (of the sun). 3 shift or move downward or forward. **meng-kan** cause s.t. to slip down (esp. with application of lubricant).

gelinjang meng- 1 jump up and down. *Ia hanya ~ saja waktu api menjilati seluruh kulitnya* He simply jumped up and down as the flames licked at his skin. 2 wriggle with pleasure. *céwék yg ~ di tempat tidur* the girl that writhed in pleasure in the bed. **ter-** jump up and down in response to s.t. that happened. *Aku ~ mendengar itu* I jumped up and down when I heard that.

gelintang ter- sprawled.

gelintin ber- 1 sticky. 2 thick, concentrated.

gelinting meng- 1 roll (cigarette, etc.). 2 writhe, squirm. *Dia ~ di lantai* He writhed (in pain) on the floor. **-an** s.t. rolled (cigarettes, etc.). **peng-** roller (of cigarettes). *~ rokok dan pengécér sandal plastik* roller of cigarettes and seller of plastic sandals.

gelintir 1 pellet. 2 counter used with small pelletlike objects. *Saya mempunyai tiga - intan* I have three diamonds. 3 counter used with persons. *beberapa - guru* several teachers. *se- penyair* o. poet. *hanya se- masyarakat* only a small segment of society. 4 a general all-purpose counter. *se-mata kuliah* a subject of instruction. **meng-** roll into a pellet. **meng-i** roll into little pellets.

gelis (*Sd*) lovely, pretty.

gelisah 1 nervous, on edge, restless. *Semalam tidurnya - saja* He had a restless sleep last night. 2 worried, concerned. *Ia - ketika anaknya tdk lekas pulang* He was worried when his son did not come home right away. **ber-** worry. *Ia duduk saja dan ~* She just sat and worried. **meng-i** disturb, bother. **meng-kan** 1 worry about. *Ia ~ anaknya yg pergi berperang itu* She worried about her son who went to war. 2 perturb, upset. *Surat itu ~*

ibunya That letter upset her mother. **peng-**alarmist, scaremonger. **ke-an 1** nervousness, restlessness. ~ *sosial* social unrest. **2** concern, worry, anxiety.

gelisir meng- slide s.t. a short distance.

gelita see GULITA.

gelitar meng- struggle, move about to free o.s.

gelitik 1 tickle, tickling. **2** stimulus, incitement, inducement. **meng- 1** tickle. **2** prod, encourage, incite. *berusaha* ~ *penonton tivi* endeavor to excite the interest of the TV audience. **3** beat of o.'s heart. **meng-i** tickle. **-an** tickling, tickle. *melindungi perutnya dr* ~ *ibunya* protect her stomach from her mother's tickling. *tudingan yg disertai dgn* ~ accusation accompanied by jesting. **peng-**stimulus.

geliut ber- writhe, squirm. ~ *kesakitan* writhe in pain.

gelo (*Jv*) be disappointed and therefore be hurt and angry.

gélo, gélok 1 out of o.'s mind, crazy. **2** unmannered, foolish.

gelobok meng- make a sound like a bottle being filled with water.

gelocak see GELOJAK.

gelodar₁ meng- squirm, writhe.

gelodar₂ turbid from mud.

gelogok₁ swig (of whiskey), gulp (of water). **meng- 1** gulp down. *Ia* ~ *air kopinya* He gulped his coffee down. **2** seethe, boil. **3** spill a large quantity.

gelogok₂ a threat. *salah* - do s.t. without haste.

gelohok ter- opened wide.

gelojak ber-, ter- slap, wash against (of waves against side of boat).

gelojoh 1 gluttonous. **2** greedy. - *laki* eager to catch a man. **meng-** be gluttonous.

gelokak see GELOPAK.

gelomang see GELUMANG.

gelombang 1 a long unbroken wave or swell. - *bunga lepang* foam-crested wave. - *getaran* shock wave. - *mangkuk* whirlpool, eddy. - *péndék* short wave. - *samudera* ocean waves. - *radio* radio waves. *Musuh menyerang dlm beberapa* - The enemy attacked in several waves. **2** phase, facet. **ber- 1** wave, surge. *Pertempuran* ~ *kian kemari* The battle surged back and forth. **2** fluctuate. *Harga-harga* ~ *naik turun* Prices fluctuate. **3** wavy, bumpy (of roads, etc.), corrugated. *Rambutnya* ~ She has wavy hair. **ber-an** wavy. ~ *ringan* rolling (of water). **meng-** wave, surge. *Huru-hara rasial* ~ *di* . . . Racial unrest is surging in . . . **peng-an** causing s.t. to surge.

gelompar meng- leap or jump up.

gelondang (ber)-an make a resounding sound (e.g. an empty can).

gelondong roll, bunch. *se- tembakau* a roll of tobacco.

gelonéng small gong.

gelonggong ber- eat through, nibble at.

gelongsor see GELOSOR.

gelonjak jumping up and down. **ber- 1** jump up and down. **2** go around. **ber-an** jumping

around. *Anak* ~ *di kamar mandi* The children were jumping around in the bathroom. **meng-**arise. *Perasaan tak senang* ~ *selagi meraba kain itu* O. gets an unpleasant sensation on touching that cloth.

gelontor meng- 1 spray with water in order to remove s.t. **2** drink a great deal. **peng-an** spraying of water to clean.

gelopak meng- peel off (of bark, paint, etc.).

gelora₁ 1 seething, tempestuousness, turbulence. - *laut* seething of the sea. **2** enthusiasm, violent passion. - *hati* impulse, passion. - *semangat* joy, happiness. **ber-, meng- 1** rage, seethe (of sea). **2** impassioned (of speech), full of spirit. **meng-kan** stir up, whip up, incite. ~ *semangat pengabdian perjuangan bangsa* whip up the spirit of service to the nation's struggle. **peng-an** stirring, whipping up.

gelora₂ [*gelanggang olahraga*] Sport Stadium.

gelosang meng- hurry up, speed s.o. up.

gelosok meng- rub hard, scrub vigorously.

gelosor ber- slip. *Kakinya* ~ *spt di atas és* Her feet slipped as though she were on ice. **meng-** slide down. *Mantelnya* ~ *dr bahunya* Her coat slid from her shoulders. **ter-** slip down, slide down.

gelotak meng- split a coconut shell.

gelotrak rattle. **meng-** rattle (of chains).

geluduk deep, far-off thunder. **ber-** thunder, rumble. **-an** characterized by thunder. *Dgn cuaca* ~ *begini saya tdk jadi pergi* In this thunder I decided not to go.

geluga red lead.

gelugur k.o. forest tree with yellow edible fruits similar to mangosteen but sour.

gelugut meng- shiver from cold, chatter (of teeth).

geluh loam.

geluk coconut shell.

gelulur meng- 1 slide down, fall. **2** slip down (of trousers).

gelumang muddied, wet with s.t. dirty. **ber-** be muddied. *Kumisnya* ~ *dgn darah dan abu* His mustache was besmeared with blood and ashes. **meng-i** spread on, smear with.

gelumbang see GELOMBANG.

geluncur see GELINCIR.

gelundung₁ ber-an roll downward (of several things). **meng-** roll downward or along (of large objects). **meng-kan** make s.t. heavy roll.

gelundung₂ see GELONDONG.

gelung 1 coil (of rope, etc.), bun of hair. **2** curve, turn. **ber- 1** coil (of a rope, snake), curl, become twisted. *Kertas yg sedang terbakar* ~ Burning paper curls. **2** wear o.'s hair in a coil. **ber-²** rolled up in coils. *pikiran* ~ confused thoughts. **meng-** coil s.t., tie o.'s hair into a knot. **meng-i** make s.o.'s hair into a coil. *Ia* ~ *ibunya* She tied her mother's hair into a bun. **meng-kan** make s.t. into a coil. *Ia sering* ~ *kakinya selagi membaca* She often curls up her feet under her while she reads. **ter-1** curled up, coiled up. **2** knotted, in a knot. **-an 1** coil (of rope, etc.). **2** curve (in road).

gelungsur see GELOSOR.

geluntung (ber)-an laze around in bed.
geluntur meng- glide, slide, ride smoothly along. **peng-an** riding smoothly along.
gelup fall out, drop out (of teeth).
gelupur see GELEPUR.
gelusak meng- trouble, throw (thoughts, etc.) into turmoil. *Ada sesuatu yg ~ dlm dadanya* There was s.t. that was causing a turmoil in his breast.
gelut ber- 1 wrestle. 2 romp, play in rough-and-tumble fashion. 3 quarrel. **ber-²an** roughhouse. **meng-** 1 seize or embrace in o.'s arms. 2 come over o. (of feelings). *Aku di- kekecéwaan* I was overcome by disappointment. **meng-i** 1 embrace. *~ tubuh* embrace the body. 2 wrestle with. *~ ilmu pengetahuan* wrestle with science. *~ dunia sépak bola* be deeply involved in the world of soccer. *~ ilmu ini secara mendalam* wrestle with this knowledge profoundly. 3 seize, embrace. *Kesunyian ~ diriku* Loneliness seized me. **per-an** 1 wrestling. 2 wrestling match.
gelutuk see GELETUK.
geluyur see KELUYUR.
gema echo, reverberate. **ber-, meng-** echo, reverberate. *Suara guruh itu ~ di dlm lembah* The sound of thunder reverberated in the valley. *Panggilan pemimpin negara ~ ke seluruh penjuru negara* The call of the nation's leader reverberated in every corner of the country. **meng-i** fill with reverberations. *Musik ~ ruangan besar itu* Music filled the hall with reverberations. **meng-kan** (cause to) echo, reflect. *Ia ~ jeritan hati rakyatnya ke seluruh dunia* She made the intense suffering of her people reverberate throughout the world.
gemaca plaited bamboo for walls and ceiling.
gemah ripah (*Jv*) very prosperous. *- loh jinawi* very prosperous and very fertile (description of a place in traditional *wayang* tales).
gemak₁ meng-(²) handle, finger.
gemak₂ k.o. wild quail.
gemal bunch (of twigs, paddy), sheaf. *se-* a handful, a bunch. **ber-²** in bunches. **meng-** 1 put together in sheaf or bunch. 2 hold, grasp.
gemala magic stone, probably bezoar.
geman afraid, frightened. *Ia - melihat gunting ahli bedah itu* She was frightened upon seeing the surgeon's scissors. **meng-i** be afraid of. **peng-** coward.
gemang₁ thick, cylinder-shaped (log, etc.).
gemang₂ see GAMANG, GEMAN.
gémang k.o. fish.
gemap ter- astounded, dumbfounded.
gemar be fond of, delight in. *Ia - minum téh* He is fond of drinking tea. *- akan gambar hidup* fond of movies. **ber-** enjoy o.s., have a good time. *Meréka ~ di pantai* They enjoyed themselves at the beach. **meng-i** be fond of, delight in, like very much. *~ buah-buahan* be fond of fruit. **meng-kan** make happy, give pleasure to. *Ia selalu mencoba ~ org tuanya* She always tries to please her parents. **ke-an** 1 o.'s hobby, what o. is fond of, amusement. *~nya berburu* His hobby is hunting. 2 fondness, passion. **peng-** devotee, lover, fan.

Ia ~ makanan énak She is a lover of good food. *~ sépak bola* devotee of soccer. *~ perangko* stamp collector, philatelist.
gemas 1 annoyed, put out, irritated. 2 passionate, with heat. *Saya pelototkan mata saya, spt harimau* - I rolled my eyes like an angry tiger. 3 be moved emotionally to do s.t. physical from anger, love, etc. *- aku melihat anak ini* That child is so cute I could eat it up. **meng-kan** annoy, put s.o. out. **ke-an** 1 anger, spite, annoyance. 2 passion. *~ révolusionér* revolutionary passion.
gemawan clouds moving rapidly by in sky.
gembala 1 shepherd, herdsman. *- pintu* gatekeeper. *gajah seékur - dua two lovers* of o. girl (lit., o. elephant, two keepers). 2 (*Rel.*) shepherd (of the flock). *Tuhan adalah - saya* The Lord is my shepherd. **meng-(i)** tend, look after. *budak-budak yg ~ kami* servants who look after us. **meng-kan** herd, tend. *~ sapinya* tend his cows. *Tuhan ~ umatnya* God shepherds his flock. **ke-an** leadership, being a herder. **peng-** o. who herds. **peng-an** shepherding, herding, tending.
gembang pudgy.
gembar-gembor ranting. *tanpa -* without fanfare. **ber-** rant, shout, cry out. **meng-kan** propagandize, tout, shout about. *Ia ~ keberhasilan usahanya* He bragged about the success of his efforts.
gémbél see JÉMBÉL.
gembéréng see GEMBRÉNG.
gembili see KEMBILI.
gembira 1 glad, happy. *Ia - melihat saya* He was glad to see me. 2 cheerful, gay. *Ia selalu -* She is always cheerful. *- ria* be happy and gay. **ber-** rejoice, be cheerful, be full of spirit. *Marilah kita ~* Let us be cheerful! **meng-i** cheer s.o. up. **meng-kan** 1 cheer up, make happy, gladden. *Uang itu ~ ibunya yg miskin itu* The money made his poor mother happy. 2 enliven (a party, etc.). 3 rejoice over s.t. **ke-an** 1 happiness, gladness. 2 cheerfulness. **peng-** cheerful type. *Antonino tampaknya lebih ~ dr rekannya* Antonino appeared to be more cheerful than his friend. *perangai ~* cheerful disposition.
gembleng ber-, ter- united, welded into o. **meng-** unite. **peng-an** unification.
gembléng meng- 1 forge. 2 harden (the spirit). 3 train, indoctrinate. **-an** 1 discipline, training, indoctrination. *~ semangat* spiritual or ideological indoctrination. 2 the product of s.o.'s training. *Anak ini ~ Pak Umar* This child has been trained by Mr. Umar. **peng-** trainer, forger, uniter (of people). **peng-an** hardening discipline. *~ watak* character building.
gemblok meng-i cling to. *Mak Likin yg sering aku -i* It was Aunt Likin whom I often clung to.
gembok padlock. **ber-** be locked or provided with a padlock. **meng-** to padlock. **ter-** padlocked.
gembol meng- carry (in bag, pocket, piece of cloth). **-an** s.t. carried (in bag, etc.).
gembong, gémbong leader, brains, prominent figure. *- rakyat yg tertindas itu* champion of the oppressed. *- gerombolan* leader of a gang. *- politik* politico. **meng-i** be the brains of, be the ring-

leader of. *Yg ~ Barat ialah impérialis AS* The W. is led by the US, the ringleader of the imperialists.
gembor₁ see GEMBAR-GEMBOR. **meng-kan 1** bruit about, noise about. *yg sdh di-kan di koran-koran* which was bruited about by the papers. **2** ballyhoo, plug, pour out. *~ slogan ékonomi* ballyhoo economic slogans. **-²an** ballyhooing.
gembor₂ watering can.
gembos deflated. **meng-kan** deflate a tire.
gembréng k.o. flat knobless gong.
gembrot (*Jv*) big-bellied, paunchy. *Dulu waktu muda ia langsing, sekarang sdh -* When he was young, he was thin. Now he is fat. **ke-an** paunchiness.
gembul₁ always hungry, never satisfied. *Dasar - makannya lima piring* He is a big eater and finished off five helpings.
gembul₂ full, fat. *Wajahnya -* He had a fat face. **ke-an** distention (of stomach).
gembung 1 swollen, distended, puffed (of stomach, cheek, etc.). **2** stuffed, filled. **ber-** be swollen. *~ dada* be proud, be puffed with pride. **meng-** fill up, swell up (of balloon, etc.). *Tentu kas penyelenggara bakal ~* Certainly the executive coffer will swell. **meng-kan 1** swell s.t. up, inflate. **2** puff up o.'s cheeks. **-an** swelling.
gembur 1 loose (of soil). **2** crumbly (of bread). **meng-** become loose (of soil). **meng-kan** loosen (soil, etc.).
gemelai see GEMULAI.
gemelegar see GELEGAR₂.
gemelentam sound of booming cannon fire.
gemeletak shiver, chatter (of teeth).
gemeletap sound of tapping (of fingers on table or glass pane, etc.).
gemeletuk see GELETUK.
gemelugut 1 shake, shiver (from cold). **2** shudder.
gementar see GEMETAR.
gemercak splatter, splashing. **ber-** splatter, splash (of water, etc.).
gemercik see GEMERICIK.
gemercing see GEMERINCING.
gemerencang sound of clanging. **ber-** clang (of swords, etc.).
gemerencik sound of splattering.
gemerencing see GEMERINCING.
gemerencung see GEMERENCANG.
gemeresik 1 sound of rustling (of leaves). **2** sound of paper being crumpled. **ber-** rustle. *Daun-daun itu ~ ditiup angin* The leaves rustled in the wind.
gemeretak sound of chattering teeth.
gemeretuk, gemeretup sound of rattling or clanging.
gemericik, gemerincik sound of water flowing in a small stream.
gemerincing sound of clinking or tinkling (e.g. glass breaking, jingling money, etc.). **ber-** tinkle (of bells). **-an** tinkling, clinking. *~ piring* clatter of dishes. *~ rantai* the clinking of chains.
gemerlap shining, gleaming, sparkling brightly.

ber-an be gleaming, sparkling (plural). **ke-an** luxury, shining quality. **-an** of a sparkling quality. *batu ~* sparkling stone. *mérah ~* shining red. *perabot rumah yg ~* shining household utensils.
gemerocok see GEMERCAK.
gemertak, gemertakan sound of a crack or rattle. *- api* crackle of fire.
gemertuk, gemertup see GELETUK.
gemerusuk rustle. *Daun ribut - dikacau angin* The leaves rustled in the wind.
gemerutuk see GELETUK.
gemes see GEMAS.
gemetar tremble. *Ia - ketakutan* She trembled with fear. **ber-an** tremble. *Tangannya ~* His hand trembled. **meng-kan** make s.t. tremble. **-an** trembling, tremor.
gemi see IKAN.
gemik meng- signal with the finger.
gemilang brilliant, shining, bright. *bintang-bintang yg -* brilliant stars. *kemenangan yg -* brilliant victory. *masa depan -* brilliant future. **ke-an** brilliance.
gemilap see GEMERLAP, GILAP. **ke-an** glitter.
géminasi (*Ling.*) gemination.
geming ber- keep quiet, be motionless.
gemintang full of stars. *langit yg-* the sky full of stars.
geminte /kheminte/ (*Coll.*) municipality.
gempa *- bumi* earthquake. *- gelora* **meng-gelora-kan** shake turbulently. *Kemenangan luar biasa itu ~ dunia olahraga* The unusual victory shook the world of sports. *- kiamat* the final earthquake at doomsday. **ber-** shake, quake (of the earth). **meng-kan** shake, jolt. *Kejadian itu ~ seluruh dunia* That incident jolted the whole world. **ke-an** subject to earthquakes. *wilayah ~* seismic zone.
gempal₁ sturdy, plump (of build). **ke-an** sturdiness. *~ tubuhnya amat mengesan* His physical fitness was impressive.
gempal₂ see GUMPAL.
gempar uproar, commotion. **meng-kan** cause a stir, cause a commotion, stir up. *yg ~ dunia* earth-shaking. *kabar yg ~* sensational news. **ke-an** tumult, stir.
gempel adhere, fuse. *Séménnya jelék sdh -* The cement is no good. It is sticking together.
gempét, gempit meng- push into a corner.
gempil (*Jv*) chipped, damaged. **-an** chip, splinter, sliver.
gempita loud. **meng-** be noisy, loud. *keplokan yg ~* loud applause.
gempul-gempul panting, out of breath.
gempur - meng- attack o. another, attack by turn. **meng- 1** attack and destroy. *Kita ~ bénténg itu* We attacked and destroyed that fortress. **2** demolish (an argument, idea, etc.). *Partai opposisi ~ tindakan pemerintah* The opposition party ripped into the measures taken by the gvt. *Jaksa ~ alasan terdakwa* The prosecutor tore the defendant's argument to pieces. **3** demolish. *Meréka ~ gedung tua itu* They tore down the old building.

-an attack, assault, charge, onslaught. **-²an** feign an attack. **peng-** attacker, aggressor. **peng-an** destruction, crushing.

gemuk 1 fat, corpulent, obese. *- lembék* flabby. **2** fat, grease. *Minyak itu dibuat dr - tanaman* That oil is made from vegetable fats. *- talek* tallow. **3** rich (of soil). **4** fertilizer. **meng-** become fat. **meng-i** grease, lubricate. *Ayah ~ mobilnya* Father greased the car. **meng-kan 1** fatten up. *Ia ~ diri* He is putting on weight. **2** fattening (food). **3** fertilize. **peng-an 1** fattening up. **2** greasing, lubricating. **ke-an** too fat, overweight.

gemulai 1 supple, pliant. *Gerak-geriknya -* Her movements were supple. **2** swaying (of leaves in wind, etc.). **meng-kan** cause s.t. to sway.

gemulung rolling (of waves). **ber-** roll gently (of people, waves, etc.).

gemuruh 1 thundering, cannonading. **2** clamorous, tumultuous. **ber-, meng-** thunder. *Panggilan présidén ~ di seluruh negara* The president's appeal thundered throughout the entire nation. **meng-kan** do s.t. in a thunderous way. **ke-an** thundering quality.

géna gene.

genah (*Jv*) **1** proper. *Kelakuannya tdk -* His behavior was improper. **2** straightened out, settled. *Perkara itu sekarang sdh -* That case is now settled. **se-nya** properly. **meng-kan** straighten out (a problem, error, etc.).

genang ber-, meng-, ter- filling a place and not flowing (water). *Air matanya ~* His tears welled up in his eyes. *Peluh ~ di dahinya* Sweat bathed his brow. *Air ~ di rawa-rawa* Water stagnated in the swamps. **meng-i** inundate, whelm s.t. *~ sawah* flood a rice field. *Matanya di-i air mata* Her eyes were flooded with tears. **-an** puddle, flooded area (caused by water backup, etc.). *Gangnya bécék karena ~ air selokan yg meluap* The lane was muddy because of the backup of water from the overflowing gutters. **peng-an** overflowing, flooding. *dgn pembajakan dan ~ di sekitar tanaman* by turning up the soil and flooding the area around the plants.

genap 1 exactly enough, whole. *Uangnya - seribu rupiah* She has exactly 1,000 rupiah. *Pikirannya -* He is (quite) sane. *- bulannya* end of pregnancy period. *Umurnya mencapai - enam puluh tahun* He has reached the exact age of 60. **2** even (numbers). **se-** all, entire. *~ usahanya gagal* All his attempts failed. *~ warga negara* all citizens. *~ tubuhnya gemetar* Her entire body trembled. **meng-i 1** fulfill (a promise). **2** make complete, complement. *Bergabungnya Amin ke klub kami ~ kekuatan kami* Amin's joining our (ball) club rounds out our strength. **meng-kan 1** bring s.t. to completion, complete s.t. *~ pekerjaan itu* complete the job. *Hari berganti hari dan sebulan demi sebulan ~ setahun* Days go by and o. month after the other to complete a year. **2** make (a number, etc.) even. *~ bilangan itu* make the number even. **ke-an 1** completeness. **2** evenness (of numbers). **peng-** complement, supplement.

Undang-undang ini membutuhkan ~ This law needs a supplement. **peng-an** fulfilling, fulfillment. *~ janji Allah* fulfillment of God's promise.

gencar unceasing, incessant, unbroken. *hujan yg -* ceaseless rain. *Témbakan-témbakan makin -* The shooting became incessant. **-²nya** incessantly. **meng-** become incessant or rapid. **meng-kan** accelerate (the pace, etc.). *~ serangan* speed up the pace of the attack. **memper-** make s.t. uninterrupted, accelerate. *Tuduhan itu makin diper- stl pérs tahu bhw . . .* The accusation was made incessantly after the press knew that . . . **ke-an 1** too fast, too often. **2** rapidity.

gencat 1 stopped, suspended. *Pemeriksaan - karena kekurangan bukti* The investigation was suspended for lack of evidence. **2** stunted (in growth). **meng-** cease, stop. *~ senjata* cease firing. **ter- 1** halted, stopped. **2** oppressed. **-an** cessation. *~ senjata* armistice, truce.

gencér see GENCAR.

gencét meng- 1 (*Jkt*) squeeze, press. *Ia ~ tanganku* She squeezed my hand. **2** urge, press. *Saya dirakyat utk jadi lurah* I was pressed by the people to become the village headman. **3** (*Jkt*) crush. *Ia ~ kepala ular dgn batu* He crushed the snake's head with a rock. **4** suppress, crush. *Mengapa mahasiswa di-?* Why were the students suppressed? **ter-** pressed, squeezed. *Saya ~ sedikit* I am in somewhat of a bind. **-an 1** physical or psychological pressure. **2** suppression.

géncét (*Jkt*) grown together (of fingers, bananas, etc.).

gendak (*Jkt, Jv*) mistress, concubine. **ber-** have a mistress. **ber-kan** have a certain person as a mistress. **meng-i** establish a concubinal relationship with s.o. **per-an** concubinage.

gendala hindrance, obstacle. **meng-kan** obstruct, hinder, hamper. **ter-** obstructed. *Jalan itu ~ oléh pohon yg tumbang* The street was obstructed by a tree that had fallen down.

gendang₁ 1 k.o. drum. *- hati* inner voice. *- raya* large drum. *- pendengar/telinga* (*Anat.*) eardrum. **2** mosque drum. **-²** (*Anat.*) membrane (of the ear). **ber-** play the drum. *~ paha* gloat over another's misfortune (lit., slap o.'s thigh). *~ tangan* clap hands, applaud. **meng-i 1** play down accompaniment to s.t. **2** agree with. *Terdengar Onih ~* Onih was heard agreeing.

gendang₂ a roll (of paper).

gendeng (*Jv*) dumb, stupid.

géndéng (*M*) oblique, inclined. **meng-kan** cause s.t. to be slanted, incline s.t. **ter-** placed at an angle.

gendér k.o. metallophone with keys suspended on thongs or cords over sounding tubes, a gamelan instrument.

genderang k.o. large drum. *- suling* drum and flute.

genderuwo see GENDRUWO.

gendi see KENDI.

gending (*Jv*) musical composition for gamelan.

gendir see GENDÉR.

géndong **meng-** carry (esp. children) on the small of the back or the hip, supported by the waist and o. arm, often with the help of a cloth sling, carry (a child) astraddle. *Nina di- pd pinggang kiri ibunya* Nina's mother was carrying her hitched on her left side. *Tangannya masih ~ mayat anak itu* Her hand still supported the child's corpse slung on the side of her waist. **meng-kan 1** hang (the hands) in a sling. **2** carry for s.o. **-an 1** carrying cloth. *ayam sabung dlm ~nya* a fighting cock in his carrying cloth. **2** s.t. carried on back or waist (often in such a sling). **peng-** o. who carries s.t. on the back or waist.

gendruwo (*Jv*) malevolent (male) spirit.

genduk (*Jv*) **1** girl. **2** term of address for girls, esp. as *nduk* for little girls or for waitress or maid.

gendut **1** corpulent, potbellied. *perempuan kaya dan -* a rich and corpulent woman. **2** (*Coll.*) pregnant. **3** (*Coll.*) very profitable. **meng-kan** fatten s.t. *Bir ~ perut* Beer causes a potbelly. *~ kantong* line o.'s pockets. **ke-an 1** corpulence. **2** too fat.

généalogi genealogy.

généalogis genealogical.

généralisasi generalization. **meng-kan** generalize.

généralisir **meng-** generalize.

génerasi generation. *- penerus* the generation responsible for continuing (the national aspiration), i.e. the 2d generation after the revolution.

géneratif (*Ling.*) generative.

génerator generator.

génétika genetics.

genggam handful. *beras beberapa -* several handfuls of rice. *- tangan* stingy, tightfisted. *- bara terasa panas dilepaskan* A difficult task is evaded. **ber-²** in handfuls, by the handful. **meng-** clutch, hold in o.'s grasp. *Ia ~ uang itu erat-erat* She held the money tightly in her fist. *Ia ~ kekuasaan yg tertinggi dlm negara* He holds the highest authority of the state in his hands. *~ rahasia* keep a secret. *~ tangan* clench the fist. **meng-kan** hold tightly in o.'s grasp. **ter-** grasped, clasped. *Di tangannya ~ sepucuk sténgun* Clutched in his hands was a machine gun. **-an 1** s.t. held in the hand, a handful. **2** grasp, grip, clutch. *Ia jatuh dlm ~ seorg peminjam uang* He fell into the clutches of a moneylender.

genggang₁ **1** ajar, slightly open. **2** fissure, split. **ber-, ter-** be ajar (of a door, etc.).

genggang₂ gingham.

génggong₁ **1** bamboo jew's harp. **2** harmonica.

génggong₂ (small) house surrounded by water.

géngsi₁ (*Lit.*) collateral relative.

géngsi₂ **1** prestige. *Saya tdk mau terima upah sekecil tu, - dong!* I cannot accept such a small fee, think of my prestige! **2** (*Sl.*) put on airs. *Jangan -, dong!* Stop putting on airs! **ber-** prestigious.

géngsot k.o. dance. **ng-** dance such a dance.

génial genial.

génialitas geniality.

genit flirtatious, vain. **meng-kan** cause s.o. to be flirtatious. **ke-an** coquettishness.

génitif, génitip (*Ling.*) genitive.

génjah early-ripening (of certain rice or fruit varieties).

génjang **1** askew. **2** (*Math.*) rhomboid, parallelogram. *- génjot* **1** zigzag. **2** awry, askew.

génjér k.o. edible riverine plant.

génjér-génjér song associated with Indonesian Communist party.

genjik (*Vulg.*) an imprecation: you pig!

génjot **meng- 1** operate a pedal or treadle. *~ bécak* pedal a pedicab. **2** do s.t. all at once, push s.t. to the limits. *Seorg atlit di- pd saat-saat latihan terakhir* An athlete is pushed to his limits during the last phases of his training. *Ia di- dgn denda yg besar* She was hit with a big fine. **3** (*Mil.*) attack (en masse). **meng-kan** pedal s.t. on behalf of another. *Ali ~ bécak temannya selama dia sakit* Ali pedaled his friend's pedicab while he was was ill.

génjot see GÉNJANG.

genjur stiff (of hair).

génsi see GÉNGSI₂.

genta bell (in churches, worn by cattle, etc.). *- tangan* handbell. *- suara* forceful echo, peal of the voice. **ber-** ring out. *Loncéng geréja ~ beberapa kali* The church bell rang a couple of times.

gentar **1** vibrate (of plucked string), quiver. **2** tremble (with fear), fear. *Saya tdk - menghadapinya* I am not afraid to confront her. **ber-, meng-** vibrate, quiver, tremble. *Ia ~ ketakutan* She was trembling with fear. **meng-i** frighten s.o. **meng-kan 1** pluck (guitar, etc.). **2** shake, cause to tremble. *Tenaga atom ~ seluruh manusia* Atomic energy has severely shaken all human beings. **memper-** frighten. **-an** vibration, tremor. **ke-an 1** vibration. **2** fear, nervousness. **peng- 1** coward. **2** instrument for plucking a guitar. **peng-an 1** terrorism. **2** vibrating.

gentas **1** pinched off (with thumbnail), broken off (of stem of flower). **2** finished. *Masa peralihan blm -* The transitional period is not over yet. **meng-** pinch off, break off (of flower stalk).

gentat (*Lit.*) dented.

gentayangan (*Jkt*) roam about, wandering. *Pemuda-pemuda désa - di kota* Village youth were roaming all over the city. **ber-** roam.

géntél pill, pellet. **meng-i** roll s.t. into a pellet.

genténg roof-tile. *- berombak* corrugated tile. *- kodok* k.o. thick tile. **meng-** put roof-tiles on a house. **per-an** imbrication, overlapping.

gentik see GETIK.

genting₁ (*Lit.*) **1** narrow, thin, slender in the middle. *bagian - dr jam pasir* the waist of an hourglass. *- tanah* (*Geog.*) isthmus. **2** frayed, worn thin. *Ada beberapa bagian - pd tali itu* There are several frayed spots on that rope. **3** critical, tense. *Keadaannya sangat -* The situation is quite critical. **meng-** become critical. *Keadaan makin ~* The situation became more and more critical. **meng-kan** render s.t. critical, endanger s.t. *Tindakannya yg tak bijaksana itu ~ keadaan* His unwise measure made the situation critical. **ke-an** crisis, critical junction. *~ keadaan daérah ini* the critical situation of this region. **pe-an** (*Geog.*) isthmus. **peng-an** causing s.t. to be critical.

genting₂ see GENTÉNG.

gentong large earthenware bowl for water.

gentus (*Jkt*) surly, offensive (of speech, words).

gényot awry, askew.

géodési geodesy.

géofisik geophysical.

géofisika geophysics.

géofisikawan geophysicist.

géografi geography.

géografis geographical.

géokimia geochemistry.

géol (*Sd*) **ber-, meng-** sway, swing. *Jalannya* ~ She walks with her hips swaying.

géologi geology. - *ékonomi* economic geology. - *téknik* engineering geology.

géologis geological.

géologiwan geologist.

géométri, géométrika geometry.

géométris geometrical.

géopolitik geopolitics.

géopolitis geopolitical.

géotérmis geothermic.

gepak, gépak₁ see KEPAK₁.

gépak₂ (*Jkt*) kick.

gepar see GELEPAR.

gépéng flat and rather thin, us. of s.t. not flat (a cake that fails to rise, a malformed head, a plate rather than a soup bowl, etc.). **meng-kan** flatten s.t.

geplak₁ (*Jv, Jkt*) k.o. sweet cake.

geplak₂ meng- strike with the back of the hand.

gepok bundle, sheaf. **se-** a sheaf or bundle, a numeral marker. ~ *uang* a wad of money. **ber-²** have several bundles, in bundles or wads. **-an** bundle, sheaf, wad.

geprak meng- hit with banging sound (us. the head).

gepuk₁ (*M*) fat, obese.

gepuk₂ meng- 1 beat, pound. **2** crack (with hammer). ~ *és* crush ice.

ger- see also entries with **gr-.**

gera meng- frighten, threaten (by startling actions). **peng-** s.o. or s.t. who frightens or startles. ~ *burung* scarecrow.

gerabah earthenware vessels.

gerabak meng- trickle, flow (of tears). **meng-kan** cause to flow.

gerabak-gerubuk 1 sound of repeated, various thumping noises (of heavy footsteps, falling chairs, furniture being moved). **2** do s.t. hurriedly or without care or regard for others.

gerabang 1 large rip. **2** gaping hole (in wall).

geradakan 1 uneven, coarse (surface, etc.). *permukaan* - pockmarked surface. **2** rough (action, handling, etc.).

geragai k.o. hook for catching crocodiles.

geragap meng- be nervous and uncontrolled (of speech). **-an** have difficulty speaking (from nervousness, fear, etc.).

geragas (*Jv*) **ng-** gluttonous.

geragau₁ meng- claw at.

geragau₂ see UDANG.

geragot meng- damage s.t. slightly by nibbling or gnawing at it. **meng-i** damage several things or s.t. over a period of time by gnawing or nibbling at it.

gerah₁ 1 stiflingly hot, sultry. **2** (*Coll.*) sick. **ke-an 1** suffer from sultry weather. **2** mugginess. **-an** difficulty. ~ *mengimpor barang* difficulty of importing goods.

gerah₂ see GERUH₁.

geraham molar. - *bungsu* wisdom tooth.

gerai₁ meng- dig, excavate.

gerai₂ (*Lit.*) small stand or platform.

gerai₃ meng-, ter- be loose (of hair). ~*lah rambut Nari sampai ke bahu* Nari's hair hung down to the shoulder. **meng-(²)kan** loosen o.'s hair. *Aku* ~ *rambutku dgn tanganku* I loosened my hair with my hand.

gerak 1 movement. *Tarian itu mempunyai - yg indah* That dance has beautiful movements. - *badan* physical exercise, calisthenics. - *bangkitnya* upward movement. - *batin* impulse, intuition. - *gerik* **1** movements. **2** gestures. **3** steps. **meng-gerikkan** move s.t. repeatedly. - *hati* impulse, intuition. *mengikuti - hatinya* follow o.'s impulse. - *jalan* **1** race walking. **2** hike, long walk, march. - *jalan beranting* relay march. - *kaki* footwork. - *langkah* manipulations, steps. - *lintas alam* cross-country march. - *putar* rotary motion. - *surut* ebb tide. - *tangan* gesture. - *tipu* (*Sport*) trick move. - *torak* piston stroke. **2** twitch, jerk (of eyelid, shoulder, etc., often regarded as an omen). **ber-1** move, be in motion. *Keréta api itu* ~ The train moved. *tanpa bicara ataupun* ~ without talking or even moving. ~ *maju* (*Mil.*) advance. **2** be active. *Ia* ~ *dlm lingkungan politik* She is active in political circles. *tdk* **ber-²** not make any motions at all. *Badannya tdk* ~ *lagi stl ia jatuh* His body showed no sign of life after he fell. **meng-kan 1** move s.t., set s.t. in motion. *Ia* ~ *badannya* He moved his body. *Ia* ~ *mesin itu* He started the engine. *Keréta api itu di-kan turbin* That train is turbine-propelled. **2** motivate, activate. *Ia* ~ *koperasi yg sdh hampir mati itu* She activated the cooperative which had nearly died. **ter-** moved. *Hati saya* ~ *melihat penderitaannya* My heart was moved at seeing his suffering. *Dgn tdk sengaja buku itu* ~ *oléhnya* He accidentally moved the book. **ter-kan** movable. **-an** movement. ~ *politik* political movement. ~ *hati* presentiment. ~ *maju* (*Mil.*) advance. ~ *Séptémber 30* movement of September 30th, the 1965 attempt to seize control of the gvt. **peng-** moving spirit, activator. **peng-an** activation. ~ *kekuatan rakyat* the activation of the strength of the people. **per-an 1** movement. ~ *politik* political movement. **2** cause, crusade.

geram₁ 1 infuriated. **2** (*Lit.*) passionate. **meng-** be furious. **meng-kan** infuriate, stir up passion. *Kejadian itu sungguh* ~ *hati* That event was truly infuriating. **ke-an** furious anger.

geram₂ sound of growl. **meng-** growl.

geramang k.o. long-legged ant.

gerami see GURAMI.

geranat see GRANAT.

gerang tooth blackener. **meng-** blacken the teeth.

gerangan can it be?, an expression of wondering or doubt. *Siapa - yg datang terlambat semalam itu?* Who might it be that came late last night? *Benarkah - hal itu terjadi?* Did it really happen?

geranggang (*Jv*) bamboo spear.

gerantam sound of cannon, explosion, etc.

gerantang 1 tumult, din, racket. 2 snarl, growl. - *keling* empty bluff. **meng-** 1 snarl at s.o. 2 intimidate (with o.'s speech).

geranyam₁ meng- have a tingling sensation (from striking o.'s funny bone, etc.).

geranyam₂ (*M*) **meng-** come up in waves (e.g. heat off a tin roof).

gerapai meng- grope.

gerasakan rough (of a surface).

gerat meng-kan gnash. ~ *gigi* gnash the teeth.

geratak (*Jkt*) **meng-** search, look for (everywhere).

geratih (*M*) canter.

gerayang₁ meng- 1 crawl (of insects, snakes, etc.). 2 scratch (the head).

gerayang₂ (*Jkt*) **meng-** grope, esp. probe stealthily (in order to steal). **meng-i** touch. ~ *tuts piano* touch the piano keys. **-an** a touch, a grope.

gerbak meng- pervade (of odors).

gerbang₁ disheveled (of hair). **--gersul** tangled, tousled (of hair). **meng-kan** 1 let down o.'s hair, undo o.'s hairdo. ~ *rambut* let o.'s hair down. 2 spread out. *Burung itu* ~ *sayapnya* The bird spread its wings.

gerbang₂ gate, esp. ceremonial arches.

Gerbangkertasusila [*Gersik-Jombang-Kertosono-Surabaya-Sidoarjo-Lamongan*] metropolitan Surabaya area.

gerbas-gerbus sound of rustling.

gerbong railway coach. - *barang* freight car. - *réstorasi* dining car.

gercik see GEMERICIK.

gerdak sound of s.t. hard falling suddenly.

gerdam sound of loud slamming. **meng-** fall with loud noise (as of heavy object hitting floor).

gerdum sound of loud thud.

gerebak, gerebeg, gerebek meng- 1 come up (in large number) on s.o. unawares. 2 raid s.t. *Polisi* ~ *tempat perjudian itu* The police raided the gambling den. 3 (*Jkt*) gang up on s.o. **-an** raid, sudden attack. **peng-an** raiding.

gerecak sound of fizzing. **meng-²** fizz, seethe.

gerecok meng- annoy, bother, nag. **meng-i** nag at s.o. **peng-** a nuisance, a nagger.

geréformeerd, geréformir reformed (church), Calvinist Protestant sect.

geregetan tense from restraining pent-up emotions. *Ia* ~ *melihat kamar temannya yg berantakan itu dan ingin merapihkannya* She could hardly restrain herself when she saw her friend's room in disorder and wanted to clean it up.

geréh (*Jv*) dried salted fish of any kind except anchovy.

geréja 1 church. - *Injili* Church of the Gospel. - *ayam* 1 a Protestant church (i.e. church with weathervane). 2 the English church in Jkt. 2 (*Coll.*) church services. **ke-an** ecclesiastical, concerning the church. *kebaktian* ~ church service.

geréjani ecclesiastical.

geréjawan churchman, an ecclesiastical.

geréjawi ecclesiastical.

gérék drill. - *kayu* auger, gimlet. - *kotrék* ratchet drill. **ber-²** perforated. **meng-** 1 drill (a hole), perforate. 2 bore (of a rodent). **meng-kan** drill or bore s.t. for s.o. **peng-** drill, auger. ~ *kecil* gimlet. ~ *polong* pod auger.

gerelap see GELAP.

geremeng vibration. *-nya tertinggal beberapa saat* Its vibration lingered for a while.

geréndel (*M*) see GRÉNDEL.

geréndéng meng- strike a threatening posture (e.g. bull about to attack).

gerentang see GERANTAM.

gerenyam see GERANYAM.

gerenyau impertinent, saucy.

gerényéng, gerénying 1 display the teeth (of dog, monkey, etc.). 2 grin broadly. **ter-²** grin broadly.

gerényét, gerényit 1 muscle spasm, twitching (of muscles). 2 sound of squeaking. **ber-, meng-** 1 have a muscle spasm. 2 wince. 3 make a squeaking noise.

gerényot, gerényut 1 with the corners of the mouth pulled up or down. 2 sneering, grimacing. **meng-kan** *bibir* curl the lips.

gerépés₁ meng- fidget, fiddle (with o.'s fingers).

gerépés₂ ber- uneven, rough (of a surface, etc.).

geréséh-péséh see KARÉSÉH-PÉSÉH.

gerésék sound of rustling. **meng-** rustle (of leaves, etc.).

gerét meng- 1 scratch, scrape. 2 screech, squeak. *Éngsélnya* ~ *lantaran lama tak kenal minyak* The hinge squeaked because it had not been greased for a long time. **meng-kan** scratch with s.t. *Ia* ~ *intan itu pd kaca* She scratched the diamond across the mirror. **-an** matches, lighter.

gérét meng- drag along, tow. **-an** a pull. *Mobil itu tdk bisa digerakkan hanya dgn* ~ *dua org* That car cannot be budged if only two people pull it.

geretak, geretek meng- 1 crackle. *Api rokok kréték* ~ The lit end of the clove cigarette crackled. 2 gnash o.'s teeth. **meng-kan** gnash o.'s teeth. *Ayah* ~ *giginya* Father gnashed his teeth.

gerétang (*M*) **meng-** adopt a fighting posture.

gergaji saw. - *bolak-balik* crosscut saw. - *bundar* buzzsaw. - *piring* circular saw. - *pita* band saw. - *tarik* crosscut saw. - *vertikal* jigsaw. **meng-** 1 saw. 2 (*Naut.*) tack. **-an** s.t. sawed. *kayu* ~ sawdust. **peng-** sawyer. ~ *kayu* sawyer of wood. **peng-an** sawing. ~ *kayu* 1 sawmill. 2 sawmilling.

gergajul (*Jkt*) scoundrel, blackguard.

gergasi giant.

ger-ger 1 sound of boisterous laughter. 2 sound of snoring. **-an** laugh boisterously.

gerham see GERAHAM.
gerhana₁ eclipse. - *bulan* lunar eclipse. - *mutlak* total eclipse.
gerhana₂ in difficulty.
geriap meng- become small (of drooping eyelids, fading lamps).
gériatri, gériatria geriatrics.
gériatrik geriatric.
gericau sound of repetitive twittering or chattering (e.g. birds, geese, monkeys, etc.). **meng-** twitter, chatter.
geridik meng-kan (*bulu roma*) make the hair stand on end.
geridip meng- blink.
gerigi serration, a series of notches. **ber-** 1 serrated, toothed (saw, etc.). **2** jagged (edge).
gerigik k.o. bamboo water-scoop, with a handle.
gerigis ber- serrated, cogged (file, etc.).
gerigit meng- gnaw at.
gerik see GERAK.
gerilya guerrilla. **ber-** wage guerrilla warfare. **meng-i** attack s.t. with guerrillas.
gerilyawan male guerrilla fighter.
gerilyawati female guerrilla fighter.
gerim k.o.coarse flannel.
gerimis drizzle. **ber-, meng-** drizzle. *Air mataku ~* My tears trickled.
gerincing sound of tinkling. **meng-kan** jingle s.t. (keys, etc.).
gerinda grindstone, emery wheel. **meng-** hone s.t.
gerindin (*M*) suffer from shivers (esp. a horse disease).
gerinding₁ k.o. jew's harp.
gerinding₂ ber-, meng- get goose bumps from fear, stand on end (of body hair from fear). *Bulu romaku ~* I got goose bumps (lit., my body hair stood on end).
gering 1 (*Jv, Jkt*) ill, esp. of animals. **2** (*Lit.*) ill (of royalty). **peng-** 1 sickly. **2** potion to cause illness.
geringsing₁ k.o. batik pattern.
geringsing₂ see GERISING.
gerinjal see GINJAL.
gerinjam₁ whetstone for filing teeth.
gerinjam₂ ear scoop (for clearing outer earduct). **meng-** clean with an ear scoop.
gerinting k.o. grass.
gerinyau meng- feel itchy.
gerinyit see GERÉNYOT.
gerip slate pencil.
geripir (*Coll.*) court clerk.
gerisik sound of rustling. **meng-** rustle.
gerising distort o.'s face (from pain).
gerit₁ sound of scratch (e.g. chalk across blackboard). **ber-, meng-** screech (from scraping), squeak (of chair on floor). *Gerip itu ~ di atas batu tulis* The slate pencil screeched over the slate.
gerit₂ meng- nibble, gnaw.
gerita see GURITA₁.
gerit-gerit k.o. vine yielding k.o. latex.
gerlap see KERLAP₁.
gerlip see KERLIP₁.

germo 1 pimp, procurer, panderer. **2** brothel keeper. **per-an** matters pertaining to pandering. **peng-an** pimping.
germut meng-i crowd, swarm around.
geroak have a large, gaping tear, esp. in clothing.
gerobak 1 cart, wagon. - *lembu* oxcart, bullock cart. - *gandéngan* trailer truck. - *roda* wheelbarrow. - *sorong* handcart, pushcart. - *tambahan* trailer. **2** (*R.R.*) car. - *batu bara* coal car or hopper. - *héwan* cattle car. - *ungkit* coal car that tips to spill out contents. **ber-** in carloads. *Pelurunya ~* There were carloads of ammunition.
gerobok₁ 1 (*Jkt*) k.o. bamboo cupboard for food storage. **2** (*Lit.*) large clothes wardrobe.
gerobok₂ meng- bubble, gurgle.
gerocok sound of falling water. **ber-an** foam (of fountain). *air ~* foaming water.
gerodak sound of clattering (stone rolling on floor, stamping of feet, etc.). **meng-** 1 rumble, clatter about. **2** break into, enter, burst into (house).
gero-gero (*Jv*) wail.
gerogi 1 somewhat afraid. *Ia - stl dimarain bosnya* He was afraid after his boss scolded him. **2** embarrassed. *Suaminya - stl diketahui bhw ia menipu isterinya* The husband was embarrassed when it became known that he was cheating on his wife. **3** dazed, dizzy. *Ia - stl minum obat keras itu* He became dizzy after drinking that strong medicine.
gerogoh meng-(i) grab at, grope.
gerogol (*Lit.*) palisade.
gerogot meng-i 1 (*Jkt*) gnaw on (of rats, etc.), chew at. *Ia ~ jagung bakar* He was gnawing at roasted corn on the cob. **2** undermine (a plan or duty). *~ kekuasaan pemerintah* undermine gvt. authority. **3** embezzle, steal little by little. *Ia mendapat dua tahun penjara karena ~ uang bank sekitar Rp300.000* He was sentenced to two years in prison because bit by bit he embezzled about 300,000 rupiah from a bank. **-an 1** gnawing. *Dos itu rusak akibat ~ tikus* The box was ruined by the gnawing of the mice. **2** embezzlement, despoilment. *luput dr ~ penguasa* managed to escape despoilment by the authorities. **3** erosion. *~ air pd tepian sungai* water erosion of riverbank. **peng-an** embezzling, plundering. *~ uang negara* embezzlement of state funds.
gerohok hollow, empty. **ber-** 1 be hollow (of tree). **2** have a cavity (of tooth).
gerombol ber-, meng- assemble, collect. *Penduduk desa itu ~ di depan rumah lurah* The villagers gathered in front of the headman's house. **-an 1** group, bunch, cluster. *~ rumah* a cluster of houses. **2** gang, band (of thieves, etc.). *Perkebunan itu semalam diserang oléh ~* The plantation was attacked by a gang of bandits last night. *~ bersenjata* armed band.
gerong 1 (*Jkt*) hole or cavity in the earth. **2** (*Jv*) sunken (of eyes).
geronggang₁ k.o. tree yielding house timber.
geronggang₂, geronggong 1 cavity (in tree, etc.),

large hole. **2** be hollow. **ber-** have a large hole in it. *Témbok itu ~ terkena ledakan mortir* When the artillery shell exploded, the wall got a huge hole in it. **meng-** go through s.t. making a huge hole in it. *Trowongan ~ ke dlm bukit* The tunnel made a huge hole in the mountain. **meng-i** make a large hole in s.t. **ter-** get a hole in it.

gerontang sound of erratic chattering or clattering (falling cans, etc.). *- keling* empty threat, bluff. **meng- 1** make such a noise. **2** threaten with loud noises.

gérontologi, gérontologia gerontology.

geronyot 1 throb with pain. **2** twitch.

geropés see GERUPIS.

geropyak (*Jv*) sound of a crash. **ber-** thump, thud (of tree falling, etc.).

geropyok meng- (*Jv*) **1** stage a raid, give chase. *Seluruh kampung ~ si pembunuh* The whole village joined in chasing the killer. **2** round up. **-an** raid. **peng-an** rounding up (of criminals, etc.).

geros₁ (*Jkt*) **meng-** snore.

geros₂ see GROS₁.

gerosok₁ sound of rustling (e.g. dry leaves when walked over). **ber-, meng-²** make such a rustling sound. **-an** seething, roaring. *~ arus* the seething sound of the waves.

gerosok₂ meng-² wade.

gerowot see GEROGOT.

gerpol [*gerilya politik*] political guerrilla.

gerr sound of laughter, snoring, purring of a cat.

gersah, gersak sound of crackling (e.g. dried twigs, leaves, etc.). **meng-kan** make s.t. rustle.

gersang 1 dry, barren (of hair, land, etc.). **2** coarse (of hair). **meng-** be dry and barren. **ke-an** dryness, barrenness.

gersik k.o. coarse sand.

gertak 1 snarl, snapping. **2** threaten. *Itu hanya - kosong saja* That is just an empty bluff. *- gerantang/kosong/sambal* empty threat. **meng-(i) 1** snap at. **2** threaten s.o. *Hanya di- sdh menyerah* All you have to do is snarl at them and they surrender. **3** spur (a horse). **4** gnash (teeth). **meng-kan 1** intimidate. **2** spur (a horse). **3** gnash o.'s teeth. **-an 1** snarling, snapping. **2** threat, intimidation. *Dia makin liar, kadang-kadang dgn ~ mau memukuli adiknya* He became wilder and wilder, sometimes threatening to beat his brother. **3** spurring (of a horse). **peng- 1** s.o. who snarls. **2** intimidator, threatening person.

gertap sound of repeated tapping.

gertik meng- make a grating noise. *Ada yg ~ pd kaca jendéla* S.t. is grating against the window pane.

geru (*Lit.*) **meng-** roar (of tiger, etc.).

gerubuk see GERABAK.

gerudug (*Jv*) **meng-** attack en masse.

gerugul see GEROGOL.

gerugut grooved, corrugated.

geruh₁ misfortune, bad luck. *--gerah* all sorts of misfortune. **ke-an** misfortune, bad luck.

geruh₂ meng- 1 snore. **2** roar (of animals).

geruit see KERUIT.

geruk sound of objects scraping across hard surface. *--gerak* sound of various objects clattering across floor, etc. **meng-²** make screeching or scraping sound when dragged.

gerumbul density. **meng-** be gathered in a place. *org yg ~ di depan lokét* the people crowding around the ticket window. *Semak-semak ~ menghalangi pandangan* The clumps of bushes impede the view.

gerumit meng- perform fine, meticulous work.

gerumpung mutilated, deformed (nose).

gerumuk meng- sit hunched up.

gerumus meng- murmur (of voices).

gerumut meng- swarm. *semut yg ~ di gelas* ants swarming over the glass. **meng-i 1** swarm over s.t. (of ants, etc.). **2** crowd (the thoughts). *Pikiranku di-i oléh persoalan perkawinanku* The problems about my wedding crowded my thoughts.

gerun overwhelming fear (on seeing a serious car accident, etc.). **meng-kan** cause fear or panic.

gerundang (*M*) tadpole.

gerundel meng- complain, pout.

gerung sound of roaring. *antara - dan gemuruh mesin* amidst the roaring and rumbling of the engines. **meng- 1** make a roaring noise (elephant, engine, etc.). *Mobilnya ~ spt kekurangan oli* Her car sputtered as if it was running out of oil. **2** cry loudly. *Dia ~ melihat suaminya yg pucat dgn darah meléléh* She shrieked when she saw her husband all pale and covered with dripping blood. **meng-²** cry loudly. *nangis ~* wail loudly. **ter-** burst out in wailing.

gerunggung k.o. tree.

gerunjal meng- 1 jolt. **2** appear suddenly. **3** cause jolts.

gerup the portion of the loom in which the comb is fixed.

gerupis meng- tinker at, putter at (o.'s work). **ter-** (*M*) trip and fall, stumble.

gerus shell used to polish cloth. **meng- 1** polish s.t. with a shell until it shines. **2** crush, grind. *Air hujan ~ aspal* The rain ground at the asphalt. *~ pinggir laut* erode the sea's edge. **3** bray (in a mortar). **ter-** scraped, rubbed down. *-nya pantai* scouring action on the beach. **-an 1** scraping, rubbing. *~ air laut* scouring (effect) of sea water. **2** s.t. scraped. **peng-** scraper, s.t. for rubbing or grinding. *alat ~ bumbu dan sambal* a tool for rasping spices and condiments. **peng-an** process of scraping down.

gerut 1 sound of scratching. **2** scraping, scratching. **-an 1** scratch. **2** claw.

gerutu₁ rough, coarse (of texture).

gerutu₂ say s.t. in complaint. *"Terkutuk!" - Irwan sambil berbisik* "Dammit!" Irwan grumbled in a whisper. **meng-** grumble, complain. *Semua ~ kekurangan air* All complained about the shortage of water. **meng-i** grumble about. *Kenapa ada org yg ~nya?* Why were there people grumbling about him? **-an** complaint, gripe. *~ tetap sama saja: air mahal* The complaints were always the same: the water was expensive. **peng-** grumbler.

gerutup, gerutus sound of rattling explosion (of machine gun, firecrackers, etc.).

geruyak meng- shake, make s.t. turbulent. ~ *imannya* shook the foundations of his faith.

gesa ber-, (ber)-² in a hurry, in haste. ~ *ia msk kamarnya* She hurried into her room. **meng-(²)** hurry s.o. up, rush s.o. **meng-²kan, memper-** hurry s.t. up. **ter-²** in a hurry, in haste. *pernyataan yg* ~ hasty statement. **keter-an** hastiness.

gésék ber- rub, scrape. **ber-an** rub against e.o. **meng-** rub. *Sandalnya* ~ *lantai* His sandals dragged across the floor. ~ *biola* play the violin. **meng-i** rub s.t. ~ *rebabnya* bow o.'s *rebab*. **meng-²kan** rub s.t. against. **memper-²kan** rub things together. **-an 1** rubbing, friction. ~ *biola* the bowing of a violin. **2** stringed instrument. **peng-** s.t. that rubs. ~ *biola* violin bow. **per-an** friction.

gésél, gésér (*Ling.*) fricative. **ber- 1** shift, move. *Kursi* ~ *dr tempatnya* The chair shifted from its position. *Pemimpin itu sedang* ~ *ke kiri* That leader is shifting to the left. **2** rub. *Lengannya* ~ *pd témbok* His arm rubbed against the wall. **ber-an** rub against e.o. *Gigi* ~ The teeth ground against e.o. **meng- 1** rub against. **2** shift, move s.t. a bit. *Ia* ~ *kursinya* She moved her chair a bit. **3** replace, push to o. side. *Mungkinkah softball mampu* ~ *bola baskét di perguruan tinggi?* Can softball possibly replace basketball at colleges? **meng-kan 1** rub against. **2** shift or move s.t. ~ *sebuah kursi* draw up a chair. **ter- 1** shifted, moved. **2** removed (from a position). **ter-² 1** *Sandalnya* ~ *menyayat* Her sandals rubbed blisters into her foot. **-an 1** s.t. rubbed. **2** (*Ling.*) fricative. **-²an** (*Coll.*) act of shoving e.o. **peng-an 1** shifting, moving. **2** rubbing. **per-an 1** shift, transfer. ~ *kabinét* cabinet reshuffle. **2** (*Geol.*) displacement. **3** friction. *Ia selalu ada* ~ *dgn ayahnya* There was constant friction between her and her father.

gesit 1 nimble, adroit, agile. *Dgn - diélakkannya pukulan lawannya* He nimbly parried his opponent's blow. **2** skillful. *Aku sdh - benar dlm hal menggait ikan* I am really skillful in snagging fish. **ke-an** nimbleness, agility.

géspér clasp, buckle. **meng-kan** buckle (belt, etc.).

Gestapu [*Gerakan Séptémber Tiga Puluh*] September 30th Movement, the 1965 attempt to seize control of the gvt.

getah 1 sap, latex, resin. *- arab* gum arabic. *- asap* smoked sheet of rubber. *- burung* birdlime. *- karét* rubber sap. *- perca* gutta-percha. **2** (*Biol.*) gland secretion. *- bening* lymph. *- lambung* gastric juice. *- lendir* mucus. *- perut* gastric juice. *- tubuh* bodily secretion. **ber- 1** have or exude sap. ~ *bibirnya* cajole, persuade. **2** sticky (of fruit, sweat, etc.). **meng- 1** tap (a tree), collect sap. *pergi* ~ *ke hutan* go to the jungle to collect sap. ~ *bawang* use sharp words (lit., collect juice from garlic). **2** catch birds with birdlime.

getak-getuk sound of knocking or pounding (e.g. butcher's cleaver on cutting block).

getang cover of thin material (paper, cloth, skin) tightly drawn over an opening. **meng-** draw s.t. taut to cover s.t.

getap₁ broken. **meng-** grate, crunch. ~ *geraham* gnash o.'s teeth.

getap₂, getapan 1 quick-tempered. **2** easily shocked.

getar 1 tremble. **2** (*Ling.*) trill. **se-** just a light movement, a small tremble. ~ *senyum* a momentary smile. **ber-, meng- 1** shake, tremble. *Ia* ~ *ketakutan* She trembled with fear. **2** vibrate, quiver. *dgn suara* ~ with a quivering voice. **meng-i** cause s.t. to quiver repeatedly. **meng-kan** cause s.t. to quiver. *Sentuhan tangan itu* ~ *seluruh badannya* The touch of that hand caused his whole body to quiver. ~ (*hati*) heart-moving. **ter-** be made to tremble, trembled. ~ *hati Ny. Martini* Mrs. Martini's heart quivered (at the events). **-an 1** vibration, quiver, shiver. **2** (*Ling.*) trill. **3** (*Med.*) pulsation. **4** frequency. *Radio pemancar bekerja pd* ~ *20084* The station operates on a frequency of 20084. **peng-** s.o. or s.t. causing vibrations or quivering.

getas₁ 1 brittle (of wood, etc.). **2** easily heart-broken, oversensitive.

getas₂ (*Jkt*) clear, distinct (change, etc.).

gétték₁ (*Jkt*) small raft.

gétték₂ see GITIK.

getik meng- 1 tap lightly, flick (with finger). **2** nip between o.'s fingers. **-an** a pinch, a nip.

getil se- a pinch of s.t. ~ *garam* a pinch of salt. **meng-** pinch, hold between two fingers.

getir₁ bitter. *Ia tertawa -* He laughed bitterly. *kepahitan yg -* very bitter. **meng-kan** make bitter, embitter. *Kelakuan anaknya* ~ *kehidupannya* Her child's behavior embittered her life. **ke-an** bitterness. ~ *hidup* the bitterness of life.

getir₂ see GETIL.

getis 1 brittle. **2** frail (of health).

getok sound of pounding. **ber-** make a pounding sound. **meng- 1** hit, strike. **2** knock on (with a hammer, gavel, knuckles, etc.). **-an** stick to hit with. ~ *golf* golf club. ~ *hoki* hockey stick.

getol diligent, industrious, hardworking. **ke-an** industry, industriousness, diligence.

getrok sound of flailing (e.g. palm fronds). **meng-** strike repeatedly (to remove contents of can, jar, etc.).

getu meng- crush with fingernail.

getuk₁ (*Jv*) k.o. sweet steamed loaf of pounded cassava. *- lindri* multicolored confection of steamed cassava.

getuk₂ see GETOK.

getun ke-an surprise, astonishment.

geulis /gelis/ see GELIS.

géwang₁ mother-of-pearl.

géwang₂ see GIWANG.

géyong (*Jkt*) large-buttocked.

géyong-géyong (*Jv*) dangle.

gh- see also entries with g-.

ghaib see SEMBAHYANG, GAIB.

gi (*Coll.*) see PERGI.

GIA [*Garuda Indonesian Airways*] the Indonesian national airline.

giam k.o. hardwood tree.

giat energetic, active. *Ia bekerja dgn -* He worked energetically. *dgn - memerangi kejahatan* wage war on crime forcefully. **ber-** engage in s.t. energetically. *Ia ~ memajukan kebudayaan nasional* He was active in promoting national culture. *Gerombolan itu ~ lagi dlm daérah ini* That gang is active in this area again. **meng-** become active. *Meréka makin ~* They are more and more active. **mengkan, memper-(kan) 1** activate. *Dianjurkan ~ produksi, malah produksi turun!* He proposed that we step up production, but it has gone down all the more! **2** encourage. *Pertunjukan-pertunjukan spt ini hrs di-kan selalu!* Performances like these should always be encouraged! **ke-an 1** energy, ardor. **2** activity. *Tentara selalu memegang pimpinan segala ~* The army always holds authority over all activities. **peng-** activator, motivating force. **peng-an** activation.

gibas₁ see KIBAS₁.

gibas₂ see KAMBING.

gidig, gidik ber- shudder, shiver (e.g. due to gruesome situation). **meng-(²)** cause s.o. to shudder with fear.

gigau see IGAU.

gigi 1 tooth. *- asu* eyetooth, upper canine tooth. *- benar* permanent tooth. *- bungsu* wisdom teeth. *- geligi* denture. *- manis/pengiris* incisor. *- sejati* permanent teeth. *- seri* incisor. *- sulung* baby teeth. *- susu* milk teeth. *- taring* 1 canine teeth. 2 fang. *- tikus* small, evenly spaced teeth. *- tiruan* false teeth, dentures. **2** toothlike object. *- garpu* tine (of a fork). **3** cog, gear. *- jentera* sprocket. *- persnéling* transmission gears. **4** edge or extremity. *- air* the line where the water and the sky meet at the horizon. *- hutan* edge of forest. *- laut* 1 sea's edge. 2 horizon. **-² 1** tread (of tires). **2** perforation (on stamps). **ber-** have teeth. *tdk ~* 1 toothless. 2 ineffective, powerless. **per-an** dentition, dentistry.

gigih₁ persevering. *jagoan yg paling - dan berani* the most persevering and courageous champion. **ber-** persevere. **ke-an** persistence, perseverance. *kepahlawanan dan ~ putera-putera Indonésia* the heroism and perseverance of Indonesia's sons.

gigih₂ half-cooked rice.

gigih₃ see GIGIL.

gigil, gigir meng- shiver, tremble. *Ia ~ kedinginan* He shivered from cold. **meng-kan** make s.o shiver. *Udaranya ~ seluruh pribadiku* The air makes my whole body tremble.

gigir gunung (*Jv*) mountain ridge, range of hills.

gigis (*Jv*) see KIKIS.

gigit bite s.t. *- jari* feel disappointed or left out (i.e. bite at o.'s fingers). **se-** a bite. *daging ~* a bite of meat. **ber-²** bite e.o. **meng-** 1 bite s.t. *Mengapa aku hrs takut? Kau tdk akan ~ku* Why should I be afraid? You are not going to bite me. *di- nyamuk* bitten by a mosquito. **2** scathing (critique, etc.). *teguran yg ~* a biting reproach. **meng-i** keep biting, bite all over. *Nyamuk berkeliaran ~ tubuh meréka* Swarms of mosquitos bit them all over their bodies. **ter-, ke-** bitten. *Lidah saya ~* I accidentally bit my tongue. **-an** a bite. *~ nyamuk* mosquito bite.

gila₁ 1 insane, crazy. *- anjing* rabies. *- babi* epilepsy. *- bahasa* slightly mad, eccentric. *- renang* somewhat off mentally. *- tujuan* at a loss where to turn. **2** obsessed, infatuated. *Saya - pdmu* I am crazy about you. *- harta* money-mad. *- wanita* woman-crazy. *- asmara* madly in love. *- asyik* fall in love. *- bayang-bayang* a desire for the impossible. *- gadis* girl-crazy. **-²** somewhat crazy. **ber-²** 1 act in a crazy manner. *~ dia mengeluarkan uangnya* He spent his money madly. 2 go crazy over, become engrossed in. **ber-²an** fool around. *Jangan ~ dgn pegawai perempuan saya* Do not fool around with my female employees. **meng-** 1 drive s.o. mad. *Musik di dlm rumah ~* The music in the house was maddening. 2 reach a mad state or frenzy. **meng-i** be very fond of, be crazy about. *~ asinan* have an insane desire for pickles. *Ia ~ gadis itu* He is madly in love with that girl. **meng-kan** 1 drive s.o. insane. *nyanyian-nyanyian yg membosankan dan ~ telinga* boring songs that drive o. crazy. 2 treat s.o. as insane. **ter-²** be mad about, be infatuated. *Dia ~ pd seorg lonté* He is mad about a prostitute. **ke-an 1** madness, insanity. **2** folly, stupidity. **3** mania, passion, obsession. *~nya akan wanita* his passion for women. **ke-²an 1** rather insane. **2** appear crazy. **-²an 1** foolhardy, foolish. **2** frantic, like mad. *berbuat ~* act crazily. **3** excessive, beyond reason. *Bunganya ~* The interest is crazily high.

gila₂ meng-i, meng-kan (*M*) look after, take care for s.o.

gilang-cemerlang glittering and bright.

gilang-gemilang bright and brilliant. *dgn hasil -* with brilliant results. *zaman -* a glorious age.

gilap - gemilap brilliantly shining. **meng-** lustrous, shining (of s.t. polished). **meng-(kan)** cause s.t. to shine.

gilas meng- 1 crush, pulverize. 2 run over. *Mobil sedan itu ~ anjingku* That sedan ran over my dog. 3 overrun, cross over. *Garis tsb tdk boléh di- oléh roda-roda kendaraan* The vehicle's wheels may not cross the aforementioned line. *~ cucian* scrub or rub laundry. **meng-kan** run over. **ter-** 1 be run over. *Ia mati ~ mobil* She was killed when a car ran over her. 2 crushed, pulverized. *~ roda ékonomi* ground down by the wheels of the economy. **-an 1** s.t. run over or crushed. 2 instrument for crushing. **peng-** crusher, pulverizer. *batu ~ lombok* a stone to crush pepper. *~ és* ice crusher. *~ jalan uap* steam roller.

giles see GILAS.

gili (*M*) **meng-(²)** 1 tickle. 2 incite, egg on, needle.

gili-gili 1 bund, earthen dike. 2 sidewalk.

gilik₁ meng- roll over s.t. to crush it. *Mesin itu ~ batang besi menjadi lembaran-lembaran* The machine rolled the iron bars into sheets.

gilik₂ see GILI.

giling -² steam roller. **meng-** 1 roll (cigarette,

steel). **2** mill, grind (wheat, coffee, pepper, etc.). ~ *padi* mill rice. **3** flatten (s.t. with a roller). ~ *tebu* press sugarcane. **meng-kan** mill or grind for s.o. else. *Ia tolong ~ beras* He was kind enough to mill the rice for me. **ter-** milled. **-an 1** mill. ~ *beras* rice mill. **2** s.t. milled, result of milling. ~*mu kurang halus* What you ground is not fine enough. **peng-** s.t. to crush or grind, grinder. ~ *beton* cement mixer. ~ *jalan* steam roller. **peng-an 1** action of milling. **2** mill.

gilir ber- 1 alternate, pass through cycles. *Musim hujan ~ dgn musim kering* The rainy season alternates with the dry season. **2** take turns. *Meréka ~ menjaga rumah itu* They take turns guarding the house. *kerja ~* work in shifts. ~ *ganti* take turns. **ber-², ber-an** take turns. *Meréka mentraktirnya secara ~* They took turns in treating her. **memper-kan, meng-kan** rotate a position. *Ketua dan sékrétaris fakultas itu di-kan* The office of chairman and secretary of the faculty are occupied in rotation. **ke-an** in turn, get o.'s turn. **-an 1** turn, shift. **2** serve (in tennis). **peng-an** rotating s.t. ~ *selang sepuluh hari* rotating every 10 days. **per-an** rotation (of crops, positions).

gim₁ gold thread.

gim₂ 1 the gymnasium of colonial period offering Latin and Greek courses. **2** attend such a school.

gim₃ see GAME. (*Coll.*)

gimana (*Coll.*) see BAGAIMANA.

gimnastik gymnastics.

gimpal locket, pendant.

gin gin.

ginang-ginang sticky rice sweetmeat.

gincu lipstick. - *bibir* lipstick. - *pipi* rouge. **ber-** put on makeup, esp. lipstick.

ginékolog gynecologist.

ginékologi gynecology.

gingsir see GELINGSIR.

gini (*Coll.*) see BEGINI. **se-** this much.

ginjal, ginjel kidney.

giok (*Ch*) jade.

gips 1 gypsum. **2** plaster cast (on sprain or fracture). **meng-** put s.t. in a cast. *Kakinya hrs di-* His foot had to be put in a cast.

gir gear wheel, cogwheel (of car, bicycle, etc.).

girang glad, happy. *Ia - mendapat uang itu* She was glad to get the money. *Ia bernyanyi dgn -* He sang merrily. **ber- 1** be happy. ~ *hati* elated. **2** be cheerful. **meng-kan** cheer s.o. up, gladden. *berita yg ~* cheering news. **ke-an 1** gladness, happiness. **2** be gleeful. *Limah menangis ~* Limah wept with joy. *Dia ~ ; suaminya pulang dr luar negeri* She was overcome with joy; her husband had returned from abroad. **ke-²an** overjoyed. **peng-** cheerful person.

giras k.o. coarse linen.

girik 1 ID card. **2** chit, voucher. **3** title of land ownership (containing land measurements). **4** schedule of rounds by guards.

girik-girik areca nut crusher.

giring₁ meng- 1 herd, drive (livestock). ~ *bola* (*Sport*) drive the ball toward the goal. **2** escort a criminal (to prison, court, etc.). *Mulyadi di- msk*

ruangan pemeriksaan Mulyadi was brought into the interrogation room. **meng-kan** herd on behalf of s.o. **-an** procession. **peng-an 1** driving, herding. ~ *wanita-wanita gelandangan* rounding up of homeless women. **2** escorting a criminal s.w.

giring₂ see TEMU₁.

giring-giring₁ bell (on bicycle, clothing, etc.).

giring-giring₂ plants used for fertilizer.

giris (*Jv*) feel fear and horror. **meng-kan** make o. feel horror and fear. *ulat yg ~* a horrid worm.

giro (*Fin.*) **1** clearing, clearing account. **2** credit transfer. **3** check for deposit only. **peng-an** transfer of funds through a credit transfer.

giro pos 1 postal money transfer. **2** postal clearing.

giroskop gyroscope.

gisar₁ see KISAR.

gisar₂ see GÉSÉL.

gisik (*Jv*) beach.

gisil see GÉSÉL.

gita (*Jv*) hymn, song.

gitar guitar. **ber-** play the guitar.

gitaris guitarist.

gites (*Jv*) **meng-** crush lice between tips of o.'s fingernails.

gitik (*Vulg., Sl.*) **meng-** have sex with a woman.

gitu (*Coll.*) see BEGITU. **-²** so-so, all the same. *Keadaanya ~* His condition is always so-so, never changes. *Saya nggak apa-apa. ~ aja* I am not doing anything. Just the same old thing. **se-** that much. **di-kan** be treated like that (badly). *Saya kok di-kan?* Why do they treat me like that? **-an** that sort of (bad, dirty) thing. *Saya nggak mau barang ~* I do not want that k.o. junk. *filem ~* that k.o. (dirty) movie. **-²an** in that sort of (bad) way. *Jangan ~ dong!* Don't do it like that!

giuk (*Naut.*) guy.

giur meng-kan 1 arouse sexual excitement. *Kecantikannya ~* Her beauty is enchanting. **2** arouse interest, tempt. *Kita di-kan léwat TV utk membeli* Through TV we are enticed to buy. **ter-1** aroused (sexually). **2** tempted. **peng-** s.t. or s.o. arousing. *buku ~* enticing book.

giwang ear stud.

gizi nutrient. **ber-** nutritious, nourishing.

gk [*gaya kuda*] horsepower.

gl- see also entries with gel-.

gl. [*gelar*] title.

gladi rehearsal. - *bersih/resik* dress rehearsal. - *kotor* rehearsal. - *tangguh* survival exercise.

gladiol, gladiole gladiolus.

glasiasi (*Geol.*) glaciation.

glasir see GLAZUR.

glaukoma glaucoma.

glazur 1 glazing (of tile, etc.). **2** tooth enamel. **3** cake frosting.

glek-glek-glek sound of gulping down liquids.

glendem, glenggem₁ sound of s.t. heavy rolling slowly (wheels of train, etc.).

glenggem₂ (*Jv*) **ng-** eat s.t. or put s.t. in o.'s pocket quietly without letting anyone know to avoid sharing it.

glétser glacier.
glikosa see GLUKOSA.
gliserin glycerine.
global 1 global, overall. *keadaan* - overall situation. **2** broad, all-encompassing. *secara* - roughly, broadly.
glondongan (*Coll.*) unprocessed timber.
glos (*Ling.*) gloss.
glosarium (*Ling.*) glossary.
glotal (*Ling.*) glottal.
glotalisasi (*Ling.*) glottalization.
glotis (*Ling., Anat.*) glottis.
glotokronologi (*Ling.*) glottochronology.
glugut (*Jv*) fine hairs of the bamboo.
glukosa glucose.
go₁ (*Ch*) five. - *ban* 50,000. - *cap* 50. - *céng* 5,000. - *pék* 500. - *tiau* five million.
go₂, GO gonorrhea.
goa see GUA₁.
goal see GOL.
gobah see KUBAH.
goban see GO₁.
gobang k.o. colonial era coin (valued at two-and-a-half cents) with hole in middle.
gobar somber. - *hati* sad.
gobék metallic cylinder with plunger to mince betel chew, esp. for toothless elders. **meng-** pound areca nut with such a device.
gobernor see GUBERNUR.
gobét meng- cut very thin, grate.
goblék /goblék/ **1** finished, done. *Biarlah, asal - saja* Never mind, so long as it gets done. **2** done as o. pleases. *ngomong asal - aja* talk uninhibitedly.
goblok stupid. **ke-an** stupidity, folly.
gocan (*Jkt*) toss and turn (in o.'s sleep).
gocap see GO₁.
gocek meng- (*Sport*) maneuver with the foot. *Dia pintar* ~ His footwork is excellent.
gocéng see GO₁.
gocét see GOCEK.
gocoh ber- fight, pummel. **ber-(²)an** pummel e.o. **meng-** pummel severely. **meng-kan** punch s.o. with s.t. (e.g. fist).
goda meng- 1 tempt. *Ia menggunakan uangnya utk* ~ *seorg wanita cantik* He used his money to tempt a beautiful woman. **2** plague, tease, torment. *Kecurigaan* ~ *hatinya* Suspicion plagued his mind. *Angin dan badai* ~ *perjalanannya* Wind and storm plagued her journey. **meng-i** tempt or disturb repeatedly. **ter-** tempted, seduced. ~ *oléh harta yg berkilauan* tempted by glittering wealth. **-an** temptation. **peng-an** tempting.
godam sledgehammer. **meng-** strike, pound (of fist, club, etc.). ~*lah kepalan Anwar di atas méja* Anwar pounded his fist on the table. **peng-** mace, club.
godék side whiskers, sideburns. **ber-** growing side burns. *Mukanya* ~ He is growing side burns.
godog, godok /godok/ s.t. boiled. *mi* - boiled noodles. *telur* - boiled egg. **meng- 1** cook by boiling (e.g. poach egg, boil stew, etc.). **2** train inten-

sively. **3** discuss, debate, think over deeply. *Gagasan itu sdh lama di- oléh panitia* The idea had long been thought about by the committee. **-an 1** boiled food. **2** s.o. who underwent training. **peng-an** intensive training. ~ *dgn komputer* intensive training with a computer. *tempat* ~ *tokoh-tokoh sipil Viétnam* a place for the training of Vietnamese civilian leaders.
godot meng- slice, saw thinly.
goék sound of clearing the throat. **ber-** clear o.'s throat.
go-go see SISTÉM.
gogo₁ nonirrigated rice field.
gogo₂ go-go dance.
gogoh meng- shiver.
gogok (*Jv*) **meng- 1** drink straight from a pitcher or bucket. **2** guzzle, swill.
gogos see GUGUS.
gohok (*Jkt*) k.o. plant bearing sour purple fruit.
gohong (*M*) hole, cave.
gojlog, gojlok meng- 1 shake up (from accident, etc.). *Bémo remuk di- bis umum* The minivan was totally damaged in a collision with a bus. **2** haze (new students, etc.). *Para sarjana baru dr FT sedang di- habis-habisan* The new graduates of the Engineering School underwent a thorough hazing. **ke-²** (*Jkt*) shaken up, jolted (by rough road, etc.). **-an, peng-an** hazing. *Akan diskors mahasiswa-mahasiswa yg melakukan* ~ Those students who engage in hazing will be suspended.
gokart go-cart.
gol 1 goal, score, point. **2** achieve a goal. *Ujiannya blm* - She has not yet passed her exam. **3** (*Sport*) goal, goal post. - *balasan* (*Sport*) equalizer. **meng-kan 1** achieve, push through until accepted. *Saya berhasil* ~ *anggaran belanja utk proyék itu* I succeeded in pushing the budget for the project through. **2** (*Sport*) make a goal. ~ *bola* score a goal (with the ball).
gol. [*golongan*] group.
golak - *gejolak* flare-up, outburst. **ber- 1** boil (of water). **2** seethe, churn,. *Laut* ~ The sea churned. *Pemberontakan* ~ *di seluruh negara* Rebellion seethed all over the country. **meng-** brew, boil. **-an 1** seething. **2** violent move, stir. **per-an** turbulence, upheaval. ~ *dlm batinnya* the turbulence in her mind.
golak-galik 1 up and down. **2** to and fro.
golbi fly (of trousers).
golék₁ -² lie around, lounge around. **ber- 1** roll. *Batang kayu itu* ~ The tree trunk rolled over. **2** lie down. **ber-² 1** roll repeatedly. **2** lounge about. **(ber)-an** lying down relaxing, lounging about. *Kita sedang* ~ *di lantai* We were lying around, relaxing on the floor. **meng- 1** roll s.t. over, make s.t. sprawl. **2** lay s.t. down. **meng-kan** roll s.t. over, make s.t. sprawl. ~ *badan* lie down. **ter-** rolled over, sprawled. *Menara* ~ *oléh angin badai* The tower toppled over from a storm. *Ia* ~ *ketubruk mobil* He went spinning after being hit by a car. *Ia* ~ *di atas tempat tidurnya* He was sprawled on his bed.

golék₂ (*Coll.*) k.o. wooden rod-puppet used in a genre of *wayang. wayang* - that genre of *wayang* that treats epic themes in puppet, not shadow, theater. **-an** (*Jv*) doll, puppet.

golér lie down. **ber- 1** turn or roll over. **2** lie down. **meng-kan** roll s.t. over. **ter-** thrown down, lie down collapsed.

golf /golef/ golf. **pe-** golfer.

Golkar [*Golongan Karya*] (*Pol.*) the Group of Functionaries, a political party established by gvt. for technocrats and civil servants.

Golkarisasi (*Pol.*) process or movement to enlist support and secure victory for *Golkar.*

golok machete (often somewhat short). **meng-** slash with such a weapon.

golong meng-kan classify, group. ~ *org-org menurut pekerjaan meréka* classify people according to their professions. **ter- 1** classified. **2** belong to. *Ia ~ kaum ningrat* She belongs to the aristocratic class. **-an 1** group. ~ *desakan* pressure group. ~ *(ter)kecil* the minority (group). ~ *darah* blood type. ~ *gaji* wage scale. ~ *karya* (*Pol.*) gvt. party comprising technocrats, bureaucrats, and military. ~ *umur* age group. **2** class, category. *Ia termasuk ~ masyarakat yg tertinggi* He belongs to the highest social class. ~ *atasan* elite, upper class. ~ *ménak* the feudal class. **peng-an** grouping, classifying. **per-an** classification. ~ *menurut umur* classification according to age.

golonganisme mentality characterized by divisiveness and group-orientation.

gombak 1 forelock. **2** tuft, crest. - *keméja* shirt ruffles (e.g. on a tuxedo shirt).

gombal empty, false. *rayuan* - false flattery. **ber-1** old and torn, worn out. **2** poorly made. *cinta* - cheap love.

gombang₁ glazed earthenware jar.

gombang₂ (*M*) handsome, good-looking.

gombéng meng- enlarge (a hole), interspace s.t.

gombinis see KOMUNIS.

gombol bunch (of keys, etc.).

gombrong (*Jkt*) loose-fitting (of clothing). **ke-an** too large, too loose. *Bajunya ~* His shirt is too large.

gombyok (*Jv*) tassel, fringe.

gombyor baggy (of k.o. pants).

gomok see GEMUK.

gompal (*Jkt*) torn down, broken.

gompyok₁ 1 thick (of hair, leaves). **2** betasseled.

gompyok₂ (*Jv*) bunch (of vegetables, etc.).

gonada (*Biol.*) gonad.

goncang 1 shake. *cinta yg tak kan* - unshakable love. - *gancing* repeated shaking and swaying. **2** shaky, swaying. **3** unstable, changeable. **ber-1** shake, move violently. *Seluruh badanku ~* My whole body was shaking. **2** be unstable, fluctuate. *Keyakinanku jadi ~ oléh keterangan itu* My conviction was shaken by that information. **meng- 1** shake s.t. *Meréka mesti di- dan dihajar* They should be roughed up and beaten. **2** agitate, cause s.t. to be unstable. **meng-kan 1** shake s.o. or s.t. *Sedu-sedan ~ seluruh badannya* His

sobbing made his whole body shake. **2** jar, jolt. **3** make s.t. fluctuate, render unstable. ~ *iman* shake o.'s faith. **ter-** shaken. - *otak* brain concussion. **ter-(²)** moved rapidly. *Dadanya ~ spt ditumbuk* His chest heaved as if it had received a blow. **ter-kan** shakable. **ke-an 1** jolt, jarring. **2** shock. ~ *batin* mental shock. ~ *politik* political turmoil. **-an 1** a shake, a jolt. ~ *dan hempasan kapal terbang begitu keras* The bumpiness and the tossing of the plane were rather strong. **2** shock. *Ia mengalami ~ dlm pertempuran yg mengerikan itu* He received a shock in that horrible battle. **per-an 1** shaking. **2** shock, commotion.

goncéng see BONCÉNG.

gondang (*Jv*) **1** snail, slug. **2** name for various k.o. mollusks.

gondok₁ goiter. - *laki* Adam's apple. - *nadi* (*Med.*) aneurysm.

gondok₂ (*Jv*) angry in a suppressed way. *Ia - karena ia tdk mendapat uang dr bapaknya* Although he did not show it, he was angry because he did not get any money from his father. **-an** easily irritated.

gondol₁ meng- 1 (*Jv*) carry in mouth (of dog, etc.). **2** walk away with or win (a championship). *Anaknya ~ kejuaraan mahasiswa* Her child won the student championship. ~ *ijazah* get o.'s diploma. **3** (*Coll.*) steal or swipe. *Orgnya ~ emas dr bank* That person stole gold from the bank. **ter-1** attained (of prize, diploma, etc.). **2** stolen. **peng-** winner, champion (of tournament, etc.).

gondol₂ see GUNDUL.

gondong goiter. **-an** s.t. similar to goiter. *sakit ~* mumps.

gondorukem see GANDARUKAM.

gondoruwo see GENDRUWO.

gondrong long-haired, esp. of men. **meng-kan** allow (hair) to grow long. **ke-an** excessive length (of hair). *Dgn ~ rambutnya menjurai ke bahu* With its excessive length, his hair reached his shoulders.

gong₁ gong. **meng-kan** second a motion, idea, etc. *Ia ~ laporan itu* He seconded the report.

gong₂ sound of barking.

gonggong₁ sound of barking. **ber-, meng- 1** bark (of dog). **2** (*Coll.*) scold. **meng-i 1** bark at s.t. or s.o. *Anjing ~ pencuri* A dog barked at the thief. **2** (*Coll.*) scold s.o. severely. **-an** a bark, barking.

gonggong₂ (*Lit.*) **meng-** carry in mouth (of animals).

gongli (*Sd*) [*bagong lieur*] willing sexual partner.

gongséng meng- fry s.t. without oil. ~ *kelapa* fry grated coconut.

goni 1 jute. **2** gunny-sack.

goniométri goniometry.

gonjong (*Lit.*) steep and pointed, pitched (of roof, etc.).

gono-gini property acquired jointly, esp. during marriage, and which is divided equally in event of divorce.

gonoréa, gonori gonorrhea.

gonta-ganti 1 mutually, reciprocally. **2** take turns,

changing repeatedly. **ber-** alternate. ~ *kalah menang dgn Pomo* alternate with Pomo in winning. **peng-an** constant changing.
gontai slow. **ber-(an)** move slowly and leisurely. **memper-** slow s.t. down. **meng-kan** move s.t. slowly. **ter-²** slowly. **ke-an** slowness of movement.
gontok -an 1 quarrel. **2** engage in a conflict, fistfight, etc. **-²an** hit with the fists in anger.
gonyak meng-kan (*Lit.*) ridicule, deride.
gonyok meng- wipe, scour, make clean. **-an 1** wiping, cleaning. **2** scourge, wiping out. *selamat dr* ~ *wereng* free from the scourge of the rice weevil infestation.
gopék see GO₁.
gopoh quick. **-²** in a hurry, hurriedly. ~ *mamang/gapik* hurriedly, in a hurry. **ter-(²)** hurry, hurriedly, hastily. *Karena sakit ibunya datang* ~ Because she was ill her mother came in a hurry. **ke-an** haste, hurry.
gordén, gordin curtain. - *gulung* windowshade, blinds.
gordon see KORDON.
gorék - *api* matches. **meng-** scratch. **meng-²** repeatedly scratch. *hati* ~ itching to do s.t. **meng-kan** cause a scratch, scrape s.t. **peng-an** scratching, scraping.
goréng s.t. fried, fried food. - *ikan* fried fish. - *kacang* peanuts (fried in a wok). **meng-** fry. **meng-²** repeatedly fry, stir-fry. ~ *bola* (*Sport*) move the ball down the field. **meng-kan** fry on behalf of. **-an** s.t. fried. **-²an** various fried foods. **peng-** frier. *panci* ~ frying pan. **peng-an 1** wok. **2** process of preparing food in a wok or skillet. ~ *kopi* roasting and stirring coffee beans in greaseless wok at low temperature.
gorés 1 scratch. *Lututnya penuh* - His knee was full of scratches. **2** etch lines into s.t. **-²** *di wajahnya* the lines etched on his face. - *api* matches. **ber-(²) 1** lined, have lines. **2** be scratched. *Lengannya* ~ Her arm was scratched. **meng- 1** scratch, notch. ~ *hati* offend, give offense. **2** write or draw s.t. roughly. *Ia* ~ *angka di atas kertas* He scratched numbers on the paper. *Kesan ini di- dgn kuat di angannya* This impression was etched in his memory. **meng-i** scar s.t., scratch lines into s.t. **meng-kan 1** scratch with s.t. **2** write or draw with s.t. *Ia* ~ *péna pd kertas* She scratched the pen over the paper. **ter-, ke-** be scratched. ~*lah dlm kalbu saya* It was etched on my heart. *Mobilnya* ~ Her car was scratched up. **-an** scratch. ~ *péna* pen sketch. **peng-** s.t. to scratch or draw with. **peng-an** scratching. **per-an** striation.
gorét see GORÉS.
gori (*Jv*) unripe jackfruit.
gorila gorilla.
gorok cut (a throat). - *léhér* cut-throat. *persaingan - léhér* cut-throat competition. **meng- 1** cut or slit (a throat). *Bila mengingat tajamnya belati yg siap* ~*ku . . .* When I think of the sharp knife that was going to slit my throat . . . **2** (*Coll.*) charge cut-throat prices. **peng-an** slaughtering.

gorong-gorong water-channel.
gosip gossip. **meng-kan** gossip about s.t. **memper-** gossip, chat. *Jangan diper- sama dia* Do not gossip about it to her. **-²an** spreading by word of mouth. *Saya tdk keberatan* ~ *yg sifatnya membangun* I have no objection to constructive gossiping.
gosok - *gigi* (*Coll.*) toothbrush. **ber- 1** rub. **2** have a shine (of furniture, shoes, etc.). **ber-an** rub against e.o. **meng- 1** rub. ~ *mata* rub o.'s eyes. ~ *biola* play the violin. **2** incite, instigate. **3** shine or polish s.t. ~ *gigi* brush the teeth. **4** iron (clothing). **meng-² 1** repeatedly rub. **2** incite. **3** rub the wrong way. **meng-i** rub s.t. repeatedly. *Ia* ~ *kacamatanya dgn secarik kain beludru* He rubbed his glasses with a piece of velvet. **meng-kan** rub s.t. on to s.t. *Sabun itu di-kannya pd mukanya* He rubbed the soap on to his face. **memper-kan** make things rub against e.o. **-an 1** rubbing. **2** polishing. **3** instigation. **-²an** incitement, instigation. **peng- 1** abrasive, polisher. **2** s.o. who polishes. ~ *sepatu* o. who polishes shoes. **3** instigator, inciter, provoker. **peng-an 1** rubbing, polishing. **2** incitement.
gosong₁ sandbar.
gosong₂ (*Jv*) burnt, scorched, singed. **meng-kan** scorch or singe s.t.
gossip see GOSIP.
got gutter, drain.
gotés meng- pluck, pick, gather.
gotiau see GO₁.
gotong meng- carry s.t. so heavy two or more people must cooperate. *Di-nya Iswadi ke rumah sakit* They carried Iswadi to the hospital. **-an** heavy burden, shared load.
gotong-royong community self-help, mutual cooperation. **ber-** cooperate, share work. **meng-kan** cooperate in. *Proyék-proyék Inprés di-kan* Projects funded, esp. from Jkt were carried out with the addition of local resources. **ke-an** cooperativeness.
gotri (*Jv*) pellet, buckshot.
gotrok (*Jv*) k.o. narrow-gauge railway (used for transporting sugar).
goyah loose, wobbly (of teeth, chair legs, etc.). *Kedudukannya* - His position is shaky. - *hati* uncertain. **meng-kan 1** make s.t. wobble or shake. **2** make s.t. uncertain. *Sengkéta itu* ~ *kedudukannya* The legal case made her position uncertain. **ter-** shakable. *iman yg tdk* ~ unshakable faith. **ke-an** shakiness.
goyak meng- (*M*) shake or rock s.t.
goyang shaky, wobbly, unsteady. *Langkah-langkahnya* - His steps were unsteady. *Harga-harga barang masih* - The prices of goods are still unsteady. - *kaki* take it easy, live in a leisurely fashion. **ber-** *kaki* take it easy, live in a leisurely fashion. *Banyak org sibuk, tetapi ia* ~ *kaki saja* Many people were busy, but he merely took it easy. - *lidah* gossip, wag the tongue. **ber- 1** rock, wobble. ~ *kepala* shake the head. **2** sway, swing (of branches, foot, etc.). *Pohon* ~ *ditiup angin* Trees

swayed in the wind. **3** fluctuate. *Harga karét ~* The price of rubber fluctuates. **meng- 1** shake, rock, jolt s.t. **2** make s.t. unstable, cause s.t. to fluctuate. *~ pemerintah* destabilize a gvt. **meng-kan** cause s.t. shake. *Madé ~ badanku* Madé shook my body. **ter- 1** shaken. **2** rocked, swayed. **ter-²** shake repeatedly. *Tubuhnya ~ karena menangis* Her body heaved from weeping. **ke-an** unsteadiness. **-an 1** oscillation, staggering. *~ pinggul* swinging of the hips. **2** fluctuation. **peng-pantat** (*Sl.*) swayer of hips.

goyor see GUYUR.

gr- see also entries with **ger-**.

GR [*Gotong Royong*] mutual aid.

grad degree. *seribu - Celsius* 100 degrees Centigrade.

gradag (*Jv*) sound of dragging or moving over a rough surface. **-an** clatter, tumult.

gradah, gradak see GELÉDAH.

gradasi gradation.

graduil gradual.

graf (*Ling.*) graph, letter (of a writing system).

grafik, grafika on a graph. *- jantung* (*Med.*) cardiogram.

grafis graphic.

grafit graphite.

gragal bits of plaster, cement, rocks left over from construction.

gram gram.

gramang see GERAMANG.

gramatika (*Ling.*) grammar. *- géneratif* generative grammar. *- semésta* universal grammar.

gramatikal (*Ling.*) grammatical.

gramopon phonograph.

granat grenade. *- bénsin* Molotov cocktail. **meng-** throw a grenade at, attack with a grenade. **peng-an** grenade attack.

granit granite.

grapik see GRAFIK.

grasi clemency granted by head of state.

gratifikasi 1 bonus (for workers). **2** dividend (for shareholders).

gratis free, gratis. **meng-kan** give away for free. **-an** s.t. for free. *pertunjukan ~* a free show.

gravir engraving (in trophies, etc.).

gravitasi (*Phys.*) gravity.

grebeg, grebek see GAREBEG.

gregatan see GEREGETAN.

grégél (*Jv*) **ng-i** nervous to the point of quivering (and losing grip of s.t.).

greges (*Jv*) feverish. **ng-** suffer or tremble from a fever.

greget see GEREGETAN.

gréhon greyhound.

gremet (*Jv*) **meng-** advance very slowly. **meng-i** crawl on s.t. *Semut ~ gulanya* Ants were crawling over the sugar.

gréndel latch, door bolt. **meng-** secure a latch. **peng-an** latching.

grengseng (*Jv*) feeling of excitement or anticipation. **ng-** feverish.

grépé see GERAPAI.

grés (*Sl.*) brand new (car, etc.). *karyanya yg paling -* her latest work.

grifir, gripir see GERIPIR.

grimis see GERIMIS.

grobak see GEROBAK.

grodok sound of dragging or bumping (i.e. metal banging against metal, etc.).

grogi see GEROGI.

grogol see GEROGOL.

grogot see GEROGOT.

grojok meng- gush forth. **meng-i** gush forth over s.t. *~ kakus* flush the toilet. **-an** flushing.

grombolan see GEROMBOL.

gros₁ gross, unit of measure.

gros₂ (*Amb*) large.

grosir wholesaler, distributor.

growak having a hole or flaw. *perempuan dgn tampang yg tdk -* a woman with a flawless appearance.

grumbul see GEROMBOL.

grundel see GERUNDEL.

grup group.

gua₁ cave, grotto. *- garba* (*Lit.*) womb.

gua₂ (*Jkt, Ch, Coll.*) I, familiar first person pronoun.

gual-gail loose, wobbly (of teeth).

guam thrush (children's disease).

Gub. [*gubernur*] governor.

gubah₁ meng- 1 arrange (flowers, music). **2** compose (stories, melodies, etc.). **-an 1** arrangement or composition (of music, flowers). **2** literary work. **peng- 1** arranger. **2** composer. **3** author. *~ sandiwara* playwright. **peng-an** arranging. *cara dan corak ~ sang kawi* the manner and style of arranging of the poet.

gubah₂ see KUBAH.

gubal₁ clump, pile (of stone, soil etc.).

gubal₂ cambium, soft wood between bark and xylem.

gubang₁ notch in tree for foothold when climbing.

gubang₂ ber- roll over to clean itself (of animals).

gubang₃ see GOBANG.

gubel meng- coax, urge.

gubernemén 1 gvt. (colonial period). **2** residence of the governor.

gubernur governor. *- jénderal* governor-general. **(ke)-an** colonial governor's residence or office.

gubit (*M*) **meng-** beckon to.

gubris meng- heed, pay attention to (a request, etc.). *permintaan yg tdk di-* an unheeded request. *Tanpa di- org saya sdh lenyap ke dlm kamar tidur* Without being noticed I disappeared into the bedroom. **-an** attention.

gubuk /gubuk/ **1** hut, shack. **2** shelter in rice field.

guci porcelain or earthenware jug. *- wasiat* secret.

gudang 1 warehouse, storehouse. *- gandum* granary. *- persediaan* stock room. **2** storeroom, pantry. **ber-² 1** with several warehouses. **2** by the warehouse. **meng-kan** store, place in a storeroom. **peng-an** storing, storage. *fasilitas ~* storage facilities. **per-an** warehousing.

gudangan (*Jv*) steamed mixed vegetables with grated coconut and chili peppers.

gudeg (*Jv*) young jackfruit cooked in coconut milk with spices.

gudél₁ water buffalo calf.

gudél₂ plaque (on o.'s teeth).

gudik₁ scabies. **-an** mangy.

gudik₂ ter-² flop about (of dog's tail, fish on land, etc.).

gué see GUA₂.

gugah₁ meng- 1 waken, arouse. 2 move (s.o.'s heart, conscience). *Jerit kawan-kawan ~ semangat kami* The screams of our friends gave us inspiration. **ter-** awakened, aroused. *~lah suatu pertanyaan* A question cropped up. *Hatinya ~ utk membantu* Her heart was moved to extend help. **-an** the moving of s.t. **peng-** arouser, awakener. **peng-an** arousing, awakening.

gugah₂ meng-(kan) grouse, complain, grumble.

gugat₁ a shock, jerk, jolt. **meng-** shake, rock s.t.

gugat₂ meng- 1 accuse, charge. *Pengadilan ~ dia dgn pembunuhan* The court charged him with the murder. 2 criticize, judge. 3 claim, demand. *Ia ~ hak-haknya* She claimed her rights. *Meréka ~ pembubaran kabinét* They demanded the dismissal of the cabinet. **ter-** 1 accused. 2 criticized. *Ia boléh hidup sesuka hati, tak ~ oléh siapa pun* She can live as she pleases without being criticized by anyone. **-an** 1 accusation. 2 (*Leg.*) suit. 3 claim. 4 criticism. **peng-** plaintiff, litigant. **peng-an** 1 accusing (of s.o.). 2 claiming. 3 criticism.

gugu (*Jv*) **meng-** listen to and obey s.o. *Ia di- oléh anak-anaknya sendiri* Her own children listened to her. **ter-** trusted, relied on.

guguh₁ meng- 1 beat (a drum). 2 knock on (a door).

guguh₂ (*Jkt*) very old.

guguk₁ hillock, knoll.

guguk₂ meng-, ter- cry with gasping, boo-hoo sounds. *nangis ~* crying softly.

gugup panicky, nervous, jittery. **meng-kan** make s.o. panicky. *Ia selalu ~ku* He always makes me nervous. **ke-an** nervousness, jumpiness. **peng-** a nervous person.

gugur 1 fall (of leaves, hair, etc.). 2 fall prematurely (of fruit, fetus, etc.). *Ia - dlm pertempuran* He fell in action. *- kandung* miscarriage. *- talak* divorced by the husband. *- tempur* killed in action. *- hati* enchanted, enthralled. **ber-an** fall (of several things). *Butir-butir air ~ di atas kepalaku* Drops of water fell on my head. *Rambutnya ~* His hair fell out all over. **meng-i** cover s.t. by sprinkling or dropping s.t. over it. *Mayat itu di-i tanah* The corpse was covered with earth. **meng-kan** 1 cause s.t. to fall out prematurely. *~ kandungan* 1 abort. 2 cause a miscarriage. 2 topple, bring down. *~ takhta* dethrone. **ke-an** 1 have a miscarriage. *Perempuan itu ~* The woman had a miscarriage. 2 loss (of hair, etc.) by falling out. *~ rambut* hair loss. **-an** s.t. fallen. *~ nuklir* nuclear fallout. **peng-an** 1 abortion. 2 discharging (of athletes, students, etc.).

gugus group, cluster. *- kata* row of words. *- konsonan* (*Ling.*) consonant cluster. *- tugas* (*Mil.*) task force. *- vokal* (*Ling.*) vowel cluster. **se-** a cluster, a group. *~ pisang* a bunch of bananas. *~ bintang* a cluster of stars. **ber-²**, **meng-** in bunches or groups. **-an** group, cluster. *~ pulau* group of islands.

guha see GUA₁.

guik meng-² squeal (of pig).

guit meng- 1 touch with the feet. 2 infringe on.

gul see GOL.

gula sugar. *- di dlm mulut* an easy job. *Ada - ada semut* People go where s.t. is to be had (lit., where there is sugar there are ants). *- arén* sugar derived from sap of arenga palm. *- batu* 1 lump sugar. 2 rock candy. *- enau* sugar derived from arenga palm. *- halus* refined or granulated sugar. *- hias* confectionery sugar. *- hitam* caramel. *- jawa* palm sugar. *- kacang* k.o. peanut brittle. *- kelapa* coconut palm sugar. *- kembang* lump sugar. *- kinca* molasses. *- mangkok* unrefined cane sugar made in bowl shape. *- mérah* 1 brown sugar. 2 palm sugar. *- nyiur* coconut palm sugar. *- pasir* granulated or refined sugar. *- rawak* sugar syrup. *- sakar* caramel. *- tétés* molasses. *- tebu* cane sugar. *-² 1* sweets, candy. 2 mistress. **ber-** contain sugar, sugared. **meng-** flatter, butter up. **meng-i** sugar s.t., sweeten s.t. **per-an** sugar industry.

gulai k.o. curry. **meng-** prepare a curry. **meng-kan** 1 cook s.t. as a curry. 2 prepare a curry for others.

gulali 1 taffy. 2 k.o. syrupy sweet.

gulana see GUNDAH.

gulat ber- wrestle e.o. *Dua org itu ~* The two people wrestled e.o. **meng-i** wrestle with s.o. or s.t. *Dgn senang hati aku ~ pekerjaan ini* Happily I tackled this job. **ter-** entangled, enmeshed, caught up in. *Ia selalu ~ pd persoalan diri sendiri* He is always enmeshed in his own problems. **pe(ng)-** wrestler. **per-an** 1 wrestling. 2 struggle, encounter, contact.

gulden guilder (monetary unit in colonial times or the current Dutch unit).

gulé see GULAI.

gulet₁ see GULAT.

gulet₂ see GELUT.

guli marbles.

guliga bezoar, esp. when used as amulet.

guling *- gentang/gelantang* roll over and over. **ber-** 1 roll. *~ (diri) di lantai* roll on the floor. 2 sleep with a bolster. **ber-an** roll, wallow (of several things). **meng-** roll. **meng-kan** 1 roll s.t. *Ia ~ tubuhnya di lantai* He rolled his body over the floor. 2 topple, overthrow. *Révolusi ~ kekuasaan penjajahan Belanda* The revolution overthrew Dutch colonial power. 3 (*Sport*) defeat. *Bandung ~ regu Solo dgn tiga-satu* Bandung downed Solo 3-1. **ter-** 1 rolled. *Batu itu ~ dr tempatnya* The stone was rolled from its place. *Truknya ~ ke sawah* The truck rolled over into a rice field. 2 overthrown. **peng-** overthrower, deposer.

peng-an overthrow. **per-an** revolution on a vertical axis. *sekian ~ per detik* so-and-so many revolutions per second.

gulir ber- move, roll on, go. *Waktu ~ dgn cepat* Time goes fast. **meng-** roll. *Bola ~ riang menyusup jala dgn manis* The ball rolled nicely into the hoop. **meng-kan** make s.t. roll.

gulita dark. *malam -* a dark night.

gulma weeds.

gulu banyak (*Auto.*) curved part of exhaust pipe.

gulung 1 roll. *Saya membeli kertas beberapa -* I bought several rolls of paper. *- ombak* wave. *--gemulung* in numerous rolls. **2** coil (of rope). **ber- 1** roll (of waves). *~ (dgn) utang* with many debts. **2** be rolled up (of sleeves, etc.). **3** coiled (of rope, etc.). **ber-² 1** by the roll, several rolls. **2** keep rolling in (of waves). *ombak yg ~ ke pantai* waves rolling up on the beach. **meng- 1** come in rolls or waves. *Ombak ~ di jalan* Waves rolled up over the road. **2** roll s.t. *~ benang* wind thread. *~ rokok* roll a cigarette. *~ lengan baju* **1** roll up o.'s sleeves ready to go to work. **2** roll up o.'s sleeves. *~ tikar* **1** roll up a mat. **2** go out of business. **3** (*Sport*) defeat. **meng-kan 1** wind or roll up for s.o. **2** (*Naut.*) furl or reef (a sail). **ter- 1** rolled, wound, reeled. **2** (*Sport*) defeated. **-an** s.t. which is wound or rolled up (e.g. spool, bolt, coil). **se-an** a spool, bolt, etc. of s.t. *~ kertas koran* a rolled newspaper. *~ kasur* a mattress. **peng-** roller. *~ rambut* hair roller. **peng-an 1** rolling up of s.t. *~ rokok* making (rolling) of cigarettes. **2** bringing s.t. to defeat or to complete end. *~ komplotan pencuri* the eradication of a gang of thieves.

gulut ber-(²), ter-(²) in a hurry, hastily, in haste. **meng-** hurry s.t. up, accelerate.

gum sound of boom (cannon, etc.).

gumal 1 wrinkled, creased (of cloth). **2** rumpled, crumpled (of paper). **meng-kan 1** wrinkle s.t. **2** rumple or crumple s.t.

gumala see GEMALA.

gumalai see GEMULAI.

gumam ber- 1 mumble. **2** suppress (laugh or smile). **meng- 1** mutter. *"Ny. Iskandar," ~ dokter membaca nama di kartu pasién* "Mrs. Iskandar," the doctor murmured while he read the name on the patient's card. **2** suppress (o.'s laughter, o.'s words). **meng-kan** mutter s.t. *tanpa dengar apa yg di-kan* without hearing what was murmured. **-an** a murmur. *Meréka menjawab dgn ~ yg tdk jelas terdengar Agus* They answered with a murmur which Agus could not hear clearly.

gumpal 1 clod, clump (of earth, clay, clouds, etc.). *- darah* blood clot. *- emas* gold nugget. *- lemak* glob of fat. **2** wad, ball. *se- katun* a wad of cotton. **ber-** in clumps, wads etc. *darah yg ~* clots of blood. **ber-²(an), ber-an** in many clumps. **meng- 1** lump up, clot. *Ia sdh berusaha menahan segala yg ~ di dlm hati* She tried to retain all that was welling in her heart. **2** cause s.t. to congeal or clot. *~ latéks* coagulate latex. **3** cause s.t. to be in clumps (soil, etc.). **meng-kan 1** make s.t. into a

lump. **2** make s.t. coagulate. **-an 1** clod, clump. **2** lump, agglomerate. *~ asap* cloud of smoke. **peng-an 1** clotting. *~ darah* blood clotting. **2** (*Ling.*) agglutination. **3** (*Phys.*) agglomeration.

gumuk (*Jv*) knoll.

gumul ber- 1 wrestle. **2** struggle. *Org tuanya tetap ~ dgn hidup yg susah* His parents were constantly struggling with a difficult life. **meng-(i) 1** engage s.o. in wrestling. *~ adiknya* wrestle with his brother. **2** wrestle with (a problem). *Ia tetap di-i perasaan prasangka* He was constantly being made to wrestle with his prejudices. **-an** a tangle (of issues, boys wrestling, etc.). **-²an** playfully wrestle e.o. **per-an 1** wrestling. **2** struggle. *~ kecil dgn bapaknya* a little struggle with her father.

gumun (*Jv*) astonished, surprised. *Ia ~ melihat saya muncul lagi* She was surprised to see me show up again.

gun₁ (*Ch*) sleep.

gun₂ fine-toothed comb in weaving machines to separate threads.

guna 1 use, purpose. *Karét banyak -nya* Rubber has many uses. *Apa ~nya kita pergi ke sana?* What is the point of our going there? **2** for, in order to. *- kepentingan anaknya* for the sake of her child. *Saya menyurat - minta uang* I write in order to ask for money. **se-** *sekaya* property held between husband and wife; upon divorcing, it must be divided equally. **ber-** useful, beneficial. *nasihat yg ~* useful advice. *seorg yg tdk ~* a useless person. *Ia mau berbuat yg ~ bagi rakyat* He wanted to do what was good for the people. **meng-kan, memper-kan 1** use, utilize. **2** make use of, resort to. **ke-an** use, purpose. *~nya sangat kurang* Its use is minimal. **peng-** user. **peng-an** employing, using, utilizing. *~ air* the (making) use of water. **per-an** use, utilization, application.

guna-guna magic, magical formulas. **meng-(²)i** use magic on s.o., bewitch s.o.

gunapa (*Coll.*) what for?

gunawan 1 (*Lit.*) virtuous, noble. **2** useful (person).

guncang see GONCANG.

gundah depressed, dejected. *--gulana* despondent. **ber-** *gulana* heartsick, sick at heart. **ber-hati 1** depressed. **2** anxious, restless. **meng-kan** depress s.o., deeply sadden s.o. **ke-an** depression, dejection, despondency.

gundal₁ 1 notch (in wood). **2** knot (in string) as indicator in counting. **-an** s.t. notched or knotted (e.g. string).

gundal₂ see BEGUNDAL.

gundar coarse brush (for cleaning a horse, etc.). **meng-** use such a brush.

gundi see LEGUNDI.

gundik concubine, mistress. **memper-(kan), meng-i** take s.o. as o.'s mistress. **per-an** concubinage.

gundu 1 k.o. nut used as a marble. **2** marble. **ber-** play marbles.

gunduk ber-² be piled up in several heaps. **meng- 1** pile up. **2** be shaped like a heap. *Jauh di bawah* *sana tampak rumah-rumah* ~ *kecil-kecil* Far below the houses appeared like tiny mounds. **meng-²kan** pile things up in heaps. **-an** heap, pile. *se~ tanah* a pile of earth.

gundul 1 bald. *mencukur* - shave o.'s head bald. **2** bare, barren (of land). *bukit yg* - deforested hill. **3** leafless. *pohon* - leafless tree. **ber-** bald, bare, leafless. **meng- 1** become or be bald or barren. **2** (*Sport*) trounce, thrash. *PSMS* ~ *Palémbang dgn lima-nol* PSMS trounced Palembang 5-0. **3** strip s.o. of possessions, etc. *Penjudian ~nya* Gambling stripped him of everything. **4** shave off o.'s head hair. **meng-i 1** shave s.o. bald. *Mahasiswa baru di-i kepalanya* New students are shaved bald. **2** clean s.o. out (financially). **3** make barren, denude (forests, etc.). **ke-an** being denuded, baldness. **peng-an 1** shaving s.o. bald. **2** denudation (of land, etc.).

gung see GONG₁.

gunggung sum total. **meng-kan** total up. **-an** the total.

gungli see GONGLI.

guni see GONI.

gunjai tassel, tuft.

gunjing gossip. **ber-** gossip with s.o. else. **meng-gossip. meng-i** always speak badly about s.t. **meng-kan** say s.t. bad about s.o. **memper-kan** gossip with e.o. about. *Kakak saya diper-kan* They are gossiping about my sister. **-an** slanderous gossip. **peng-** a gossip. **per-an** gossiping.

guntai₁ owned by an absentee landlord. *pemilikan* - *tdk dibenarkan* Land may not be owned by an absentee landlord.

guntai₂ see GONTAI.

guntak rattling (e.g. of seeds in fruit). **ber-** rattle.

gunting 1 scissors, shears, clippers. - *kebun* pruning shears. - *kuku* nail clippers. - *mesin* hair clippers. - *pagar* hedge clippers. - *besi* iron cutter. - *karcis* ticket puncher. **2** (*Coll.*) cut, clip, trim. - *rambut* haircut. - *papan* crew-cut. **meng- 1** cut with scissors or shears. **2** (*Coll.*) deceive, swindle. **meng-i** cut s.t. with scissors. **ter-** accidentally cut. **-an 1** clipping (from newspaper, etc.). **2** cut, style of cutting (a pattern, etc.). *Baju itu bagus ~nya* That jacket has a nice cut. **peng-** s.t. used as scissors. **peng-an** cutting, snipping (of ribbon, etc.). ~ *uang* 1 (*Fin.*) physically cutting a bank note in half (the two halves then equal two notes of that denomination). **2** devaluation of the currency.

guntung 1 flat, level, smooth. **2** short. *celana* - cut-off trousers. **3** blunt, flat. **meng-** top (a tree, pole, etc.).

guntur thunder. **ber-** be accompanied by thunder. *hujan* ~ rain with thunder. **meng- 1** thunder. **2** boom out (of a sound). *Suaranya* ~ He has a thundering voice. **meng-kan** utter s.t. with a booming voice.

gunung mountain. - (*ber*)*api* volcano. - *ganang/ gemunung* various mountains, ranges of mountains. **ber-² 1** mountainous. *Daérah itu* ~ That region is mountainous. **2** in large piles like mountains. *padi yg* ~ mountains of rice. **meng-1** pile up, mount up. *Buah-buahan itu* ~ *di atas méjanya* Fruit piled up on her table. *Hutangnya* ~ His debts piled up. **2** resemble a mountain. *Perutnya* ~ Her belly resembled a mountain. **meng-kan** make into a mountain. **-an 1** (*Jv*) mountainlike figure in the *wayang* play symbolizing the universe. **2** imitation mountain. **-²an 1** imitation mountain. **2** hillock, hill. **3** heap, pile. **pe-an** mountain range.

gup sound of muted thud.

gurah ber- gargle, rinse. **meng-** rinse s.t. out (vat, o.'s mouth, bottle, etc.).

guram₁ dull, dim, hazy.

guram₂ 1 chicken flea. **2** insignificant, inconsequential.

guram₃ gums.

gurami k.o. fish, gurami.

guras see KURAS₂.

gurat 1 scratch, line. - *batu* obstinate, implacable. **2** (*Jkt, Sl.*) lines in the palm. **ber-** have a scratch or line in it. **ber-²** full of scratches or lines. **meng-(kan) 1** scratch, make lines. **2** scratch out, remove. **meng-i** sketch (the face, etc.). **-an 1** sketch, outline. **2** facial wrinkle. *Tak ada* ~ *di wajahnya* There were no lines in his face. **peng-an** inscribing, relief-making.

gurau 1 a joke. **2** say jokingly. *"Dua-duanya juga boléh," -nya* "I will take both," he said jokingly. **ber-** joke, jest. *"Kau tertarik pdnya?" tanya Mulyadi* ~ "Are you attracted to her?" Mulyadi asked jokingly. **ber-an** joke with e.o. **meng-kan, memper-kan 1** joke about s.t. **2** ridicule, make fun of. **-an** joke, prank. **per-an** joking, jesting. *Asal ada* ~ *akan dibalasnya dgn* ~ *juga* Joking is always reciprocated by joking.

gurdi drill, auger. - *kecil* gimlet. **meng-** drill, bore. **peng-an** drilling, boring.

gurem (*Jkt, Jv*) see GURAM₁,₂.

guri small earthen pot.

gurih 1 deliciously oily (and salty) but causing thirst (of fried fish, etc.). **2** delicious in general. **ke-an** too salty and crisp.

gurinda see GERINDA.

gurindam (*Lit.*) **1** aphorism in two lines. **2** rhapsodical type of free verse.

guris see GORÉS.

gurit 1 philosophical verse. **2** simple verse in rhyme. **meng-** poetize, versify, write poetry.

gurita₁ octopus.

gurita₂ baby's vest.

guru teacher. - *agama* teacher of religion. - *bantu* auxiliary teacher. - *besar* professor. - *besar luar biasa* acting professor. - *injil* preacher, evangelist. - *jaga* substitute teacher. - *kencing berdiri, murid kencing berlari* Given a bad example, pupils (followers) will do s.t. even worse. - *kepala* principal, headmaster. - *mengaji* teacher of Koranic reading. - *penolong* auxiliary teacher. - *putri* female teacher. **ber- 1** be a student of s.o. *Ia* ~ *pd Prof. Hamka* She studied with Prof. Hamka. **2** act like a teacher. **meng-** act like a teacher.

meng-i act like a teacher to s.o., be a know-it-all to s.o. *Aku jangan di-i* Do not try to give me a lecture (on how to act). **ke-an** matters pertaining to teachers. *fakultas* ~ education faculty, school of education. **per-an 1** institution, school. ~ *tinggi* tertiary educational institution. **2** school (building). **3** instruction. ~ *déwasa/masyarakat* adult education.

guruh thunder. *--gemuruh* thunder. **ber-, meng-** thunder, boom. *Meriam itu* ~ The cannon boomed. *sambutan yg* ~ a thunderous reception.

gurun wasteland, desert. - *pasir* desert. **peng-an** turning s.t. into wasteland or desert. *prosés* ~ *tanah air kita* process of turning our lands into a desert.

gurung (*Jv*) windpipe, esophagus, gullet. **-an** water channel.

gus₁ (*Jv*) respectful term of address by adults to boys or youth.

gus₂ see BAGUS.

gusah (*Jv*) **meng-** chase away. *Anjing itu di- dgn sapu* Chase the dog away with a broom.

gusar angry. - *hati* angry. **meng-i** be angry at s.o. **meng-kan** provoke s.o. to anger. **ke-an** anger, ire.

gusi gums.

Gusti 1 the Lord. *Ia mohon ampun kpd - yg Maha Agung* She begged the Lord Almighty for forgiveness. **2** Lord! exclamation of hope. *Ya -, minta ampun!* Lord almighty! That is too much! **3** aristocratic title. - *Kanjeng* His Lordship.

gusur meng- 1 haul, drag. *Air* ~ *kotoran ke dlm lobang* Water swept away the filth into a hole. **2** condemn (property for public use, etc.), re-

move (people from their land). *Lombok Selatan sdh membabat seribu Ha. sawah dan* ~ *banyak penduduk S.* Lombok has cleared away 1,000 hectares of irrigated rice fields and removed many inhabitants. **3** (*Jkt*) flatten, level to the ground (buildings). **ter-** be removed by condemnation. *Rakyatnya* ~ *ke pedalaman* The population was evicted and sent to the interior regions. **-an** an area condemned for right of way or public use. **peng-an** condemnation (of buildings, etc.). ~ *rumah-rumah liar* condemnation of illegal residences. ~ *tanah pertanian* condemnation of agricultural lands (for public use).

gutik meng- touch with tips of fingers. *tali biola* pluck the strings of a violin.

gutural guttural.

guyah see GOYAH.

guyon (*Jv*) **ber-** joking. *Jangan* ~ *kalau saya sedang memberi nasihat* Do not joke when I am giving advice. **-an** joke, object of fun.

guyub₁ (*Jv*) friendly, close, mutually helpful. **ke-an** communality. **pe-an** community organization based on ascribed status.

guyub₂ see KUYUP.

guyur ber- bathed in (sweat, etc.). **meng- 1** spray, splash. ~ *seluruh badan dgn air* splash the entire body with water. *Meréka di- hujan lebat* A heavy rain showered down on them. **2** pour (liquid) in large quantities. ~ *kakus* flush (out) the toilet. **meng-kan** pour s.t. out. **-an** splash. *perut kenyang ditambah* ~ *bir yg melimpah* a full stomach plus an excessive amount of beer.

Gwo-yeu /kwo-i/ see KUOYU.

H

h /ha/ h, the 8th letter of the alphabet.

H.₁ [*Haji*] (*Isl.*) title of o. who has made the pilgrimage to Mecca.

H.₂ [*Hijriah*] year of the Arabic calendar. *1406 -* in the year 1406 of the *Hijriah*.

ha. [*héktar*] hectare.

ha₁ huh (question marker). *Kenapa ia tak diobati, -?* Why hasn't she been treated, huh?

ha₂ 1 Humph! (exclamation of derision). *-! Dgn apa kau kawin?* Humph! And just what k.o. of money are you getting married on? **2** Aha! (exclamation of discovery). *-! Itu dia* Aha! That is it. **3** Ha! (exclamation of disbelief).

haacih, haaciu see HACIH.

haah see HA₂.

haak /hak/ see HAK₃.

habelur see HABLUR.

habib respectful term of address for ethnic Arabs who can trace their ancestry to Muh.

Habil (*Bib.*) Abel, o. of Adam's sons.

habis 1 finished, used up. *Uang saya sdh -* My money is gone (I have spent all my money). *Waktu sdh -* time is up. *- akal* at o.'s wit's end. *Persediaannya -* The supply is exhausted. *- tenaga* exhausted, worn out, spent. *- terjual* sold out. **2** completed, through, concluded. *Pendidikannya sdh -* His education is completed. *Pertunjukan sdh -* The performance is over. *- itu* afterwards, then. *Kita makan. - itu kita pergi ke bioskop* We ate, and afterwards we went to the movies. *- bulan* end of the month. *- perkara* end of the matter. *Saya tak akan memberi izin, - perkara!* I will not give my permission, and that is final! *- tahun* **1** year's end. **2** beginning of the coming year. *-*

tam(m)at It is all over! - *témpo* due date, date of expiration, deadline. **3** completely, entirely. *Rumahnya - terbakar* Her house burned down completely. **4** well, that is the way it is, what do you expect (particle proposing a reason). *Mémang saya tdk datang. - saya tdk diundang* Of course, I did not go. What did you expect? I was not invited. **-²** completely. *Diminum isinya ~* He drank it all down. *tak -²(nya)* endlessly. *Ia bicara tak ~nya* She talked on without end. **se-** after. *~ kita makan, kita pergi* After we ate, we left. **se-²nya 1** to the utmost. *mengalami hidup ini ~* experience life to the fullest. *Ia bekerja ~* She worked as hard as she could. **2** to the bitter end. **ber-** waste, spend (money, energy, time). *~ air liur* spend too much time chatting. **meng-i 1** end, finish (speech, etc.). *Ia ~ sembahyang* He finished praying. **2** finish off, wipe out. *Diktator itu ~ semua musuhnya* The dictator finished off all of his enemies. *~ nyawanya* commit suicide, take o.'s life. **3** spend (time). *~ malam* spend the night. **meng-kan 1** finish (o.'s story, job, etc.). **2** spend (time). *~ dua jam* spend two hours. **3** use (up), consume. *Setiap hari sebuah truknya yg besar bisa ~ sebanyak tujuh puluh lima liter* A big truck can use up 75 liters every day. **4** finish off. *~ nyawa/riwayat* end o.'s life. **ke-an** run out of, no more left. *Ia ~ uang* He ran out of money. *Lekas pesan! Jangan ~* Order right away! Do not wait till the supply is exhausted. *tak pernah ~* inexhaustible. *~ akal* be at the end of o.'s wits. **-²an** completely. *menyerang ~* attack vehemently. **peng-an** end, conclusion (of a story). *hari sekolah yg ~* last day of school. *ujian ~* final exam. *utk ~ kali* for the last time.

hablur crystal. - *gunung* rock crystal. **meng-** crystallize. *Cairan itu ~* The liquid crystallized. **meng-kan** crystallize s.t. **peng-an** crystallization.

Habsyi 1 Ethiopia, Abyssinia. **2** African.

hacih, hacing, haciu, hacu Atchoo! (sound of a sneeze).

had boundary, limit. *sampai - itu* up to there. **ber-** limited, have a boundary or limit. **meng-kan** limit, border, restrict. **ter-** limited.

hadang see ADANG.

hadap 1 across (the street). *di - rumah* across from the house. **2** side. *satu -* **1** one-sided, prejudiced, biased. **2** unilateral (of contract, agreement). **3** facing in a certain direction. - *timur* facing E. **ber-an 1** face, front on. *Rumah saya ~ dgn geréja* My house faces a church. **2** be faced with. *Ia ~ dgn banyak kesukaran* She is faced with many difficulties. *~ dgn saya (Leg.)* in my presence. **3** face to face. *duduk ~* sit face to face. **ber-²an** face to face. *~ utk berkelahi* square off for a fight. **meng-1** face, front, look out. *Rumahnya ~ ke laut* His house looks out on the sea. *~ surut* look to the rear. **2** make a formal appearance (before s.o.). *~ kaptén* appear before the captain. *Kamu diminta segera ~* You are requested to appear immediately. *~ ke pengadilan* appear before a court. **meng-i** face, be up against (difficulties, problems, danger, etc.). *~ ajalnya* meet o.'s end,

die. *~ ujian akhir* facing the final exam. **meng-kan 1** aim. *~ meriam itu ke arah kapal musuh* aim the cannon in the direction of enemy ships. *~ perhatian* concentrate. **2** point s.t. *~ mesjid ke Mekkah* orient a mosque toward Mecca. **3** bring face to face. *Ini akan ~ kita pd masalah pilihan* This will bring us face to face with the problem of selection. **4** present s.o. formally. *Pahlawan itu di-kan kpd présidén* The hero was presented to the president. **5** bring up, present (a matter). *Perkaranya akan di-kan ke Pengadilan Tinggi* His case is being presented before the High Court. *~ terdakwa kpd hakim* bring the accused before a judge. **memper-kan** make two things confront e.o. *~ kekuasaan dgn kekuasaan* meet force with force. **ter- 1** about, concerning. *Ia tak peduli ~ celaan itu* She was indifferent to the criticism. **2** to, toward. *cinta ~ isterinya* his love toward his wife. **-an 1** front. *gigi ~* front teeth. *pintu ~* front door. *di ~ mesjid* in front of the mosque. **2** future. *bulan ~* the month to come. **3** presence. *ke ~ (Lit.)* in the presence of, to. **peng-** *(Leg.)* party to a case. **peng-an 1** reception hall. **2** orientation. *ditentukan oléh ~ meréka thd ajaran agama* determined by how they face religious teaching. **per-an** confrontation. *menjadi ~ antara permerintah dan mahasiswa* become a confrontation between the gvt. and the students.

hadas *(Isl.)* ritual impurity. - *besar* a state of ritual uncleanness which requires bathing. - *kecil* a state of ritual uncleanness which requires ablutions.

hadat see ADAT₁.

hadiah 1 prize. - *pertama* first prize. - *penghibur/hiburan* consolation prize. **2** reward. **3** gift. - *kerja* bonus. - *Lebaran* bonus on day ending the fasting period. **ber-** with a gift. *undian ~* a drawing with a prize. **meng-i** give a gift to s.o. *Dia ~ saya pelbagai buku* He gave me various books as a present. **meng-kan** present s.t., donate. *Ia ~ jam tangan kpd anaknya* She presented her child with a wrist watch. **peng-an** giving, rewarding.

hadir be present. **meng-i** attend, be present at. **meng-kan** cause s.t. or s.o. to be present. *Bulan lagi purnama ketika ia di-kan di dunia* The moon was full when he appeared in the world. *~ diri* make o.'s appearance, present o.s. **ke-an** presence, attendance. **peng-an 1** attending. *~ génerasi muda* the presence of the young generation. **2** act of causing s.o. to be present.

hadirat 1 *(Rel.)* presence (of God). *Kami memanjatkan doa ke - Allah* We send up our prayers to the presence of God. **2** female members of the audience. *Para hadirin dan -!* Ladies and Gentlemen!

hadirin those present, audience. - *berdiri dan bertepuk tangan* The audience stood and applauded. *Para - yg terhormat!* Ladies and Gentlemen!

hadis *(Isl.)* traditional collection of stories relating words or deeds of Muh., the chief source of guidance for understanding religious questions.

hadlir see HADIR.

hadlirat see HADIRAT.

hadlirin see HADIRIN.

hadrah 1 (*Isl.*) communal gathering, us. mystical, sometimes including group chanting with tambourine accompaniment. **2** tambourine.

hadrat 1 (*Isl.*) religious gathering. **2** presence.

hafal 1 know by heart, memorize. *Ia sdh - pelajarannya* He knows his lesson by heart. **2** know s.t. very well. *Org Jkt sdh - bhw télpon sering macet* Jakartans know very well that the telephone is often out of order. **meng-(kan)** memorize, learn by heart. **-an** material to be memorized. *dgn ~* from memory.

hah see HA₂.

haha sound of laughter. *- hihi* (*Sl.*) perform in front of a group. *anak wayang yg - hihi di tempat lain* the *wayang* performers that are playing elsewhere. **meng-** laugh.

hai 1 Hey! (exclamation to call s.o.'s attention). *-, Amin, ke mana kau pergi?* Say Amin, where are you going? **2** What! (exclamation of surprise).

hai alai see HAILAI.

haid menstruation.

haik Charge! (exclamation shouted when attacking).

hailai (*Sport*) jai alai.

hairan see HÉRAN.

haisom (*Ch*) k.o. dish made of sea cucumber.

haiwan see HÉWAN.

haiyaa /haiya:/ (*Ch*) **1** Greetings! **2** exclamation of disapproval.

haj (*Isl.*) pilgrimage to Mecca.

hajah see HAJJAH.

hajar meng- beat up, thrash soundly. *Kalau hal itu terjadi lagi kau akan ku* If that happens again, I will give you a sound thrashing. **-an** beating, thrashing.

hajat 1 wish, desire. *punya -* plan to have a ritual or ceremonial feast. **2** intent, intention. *Apa -mu?* What is your intention? **3** (*Euphemism*) urination or defecation. *- besar* defecation, defecate. *- kecil/seni* urination, urinate. **ber-** intend. *Dia ~ hendak pergi ke Éropa* She intends to go to Europe. **meng-i 1** desire, wish for s.t. **2** hold a party or feast for s.o. *Paman akan ~ aku nanti* My uncle plans to hold a feast for me soon. **mengkan 1** intend s.t. **2** want, desire s.t. **3** need, require s.t.

haji (*Isl.*) **1** o. who has made the pilgrimage to Mecca. **2** title and term of address for such a pilgrim.

hajing see HACIH.

hajjah (*Isl.*) female pilgrim to Mecca.

hak₁ /ha', hak/ **1** right. *- asasi* basic rights. *Kemerdékaan adalah - tiap-tiap bangsa* Freedom is the right of every people. *mempertahankan -nya* defend o.'s rights. *- berkumpul dan berapat* right of assembly. *- bersuara* suffrage. *- cipta* **1** copyright. **2** patent rights. *- guna/usaha* concession, rights to engage in an enterprise. *- ingkar* right of refusal. *- khusus* privilege. *- lintas damai* right of peaceful passage. *- memilih* the franchise. *- milik* proprietary rights. *- penerbit* publisher's copyright. *- pengarang* copyright. *- pilih* the franchise. *- pungut* tap concession. *- tolak* right of refusal. **2** rightful authority. *- hukum* jurisdiction. **ber- 1** have the right (to). *présidén ~ menunjuk dan memecat menteri* The president has the right to appoint and dismiss cabinet members. *~ atas* have the right to s.t. *~ mendapat perhatian* deserve attention. **2** reserve the right. *Redaksi ~ menyingkat karangan di mana perlu* The editors reserve the right to shorten an article where necessary. **meng-i** have a right over s.t. *~ Indonésia merdéka* have right to (have) an independent Indonesia. **meng-kan** give the right to s.o. *UUD ~ Présidén menyatakan perang* The Constitution gives the president the right to declare war.

hak₂ /hak/ heel (of shoe). *- tinggi* high heel (shoe).

hak₃ /hak/ knit.

hakékat, hakikat 1 truth, reality. **2** essence. *pd -nya* actually, in fact.

hakiki true, real, authentic. *pd -nya* in truth, actually.

hakim judge. *- agung* justice of the supreme court. *menyerahkan perkara kpd - turn* a case over to the court. *Para -* (*Bib.*) Judges. **ber-** seek justice. **meng-i** pass judgment on, judge s.t. **ke-an** judicial affairs. *Départmén ~* Ministry of Justice. *hal-hal ~* judicial matters. **peng-an** judging, judgment.

hakjing see HACIH.

hakul yakin (*Lit.*) be truly convinced of s.t.

hal₁ 1 matter, thing. *Itulah - yg penting* That is the important thing. *memperbincangkan -* discuss a matter. *- demikian itu mengakibatkan . . .* Such a thing resulted in . . . *- apa* what. *pd-* while, even though. *Hidupnya sangat sederhana, pd- uangnya banyak* He lived very simply, though he was quite well off. *- ihwal/ahwal* **1** events, circumstances. **2** particulars. *- kewiraan/wiryaan* act of heroism or bravery. *- mana* which. *(se)suatu -* some reason (not being discussed). *Mungkin ada suatu - hingga ia tdk bisa datang* Maybe s.t. happened so he could not come. **2** case. *Demikian -nya* Such was the case. *dlm - itu* in that case. *Lain -nya* It would be a different matter. **3** concerning. *Bagaimana -nya dgn dia?* How are things with him? *pidato - gerakan pemberontakan* a speech concerning the rebellion.

hal₂ galvanized sheet iron.

hal. [*halaman*] page of book.

hala direction. **se-** o. direction. *jalan ~ o.-way* street. **kese-an** state of being of o. attitude (in ideals, emotions, etc.). **ber-** in the direction of. **meng-kan 1** direct, guide, steer. **2** aim at. *~ panah pd musuhnya* aim an arrow at o.'s enemy. **ke-an** directionality.

halai-balai 1 ignored, neglected. **2** in confusion. **meng-kan 1** neglect, disregard. **2** confuse, muddle, foul up.

halal 1 (*Isl.*) allowed, permitted. *ditanggung -* guaranteed kosher. **2** rightful, legal. *Uang ini saya peroléh dgn jalan -* I obtained this money by lawful means. **meng-kan** allow, permit, autho-

rize. *Beijing diam-diam ~ perdagangan swasta* Quietly Peking has permitted private enterprise.
halal bihalal, halal bilhalal 1 (*Isl.*) ask and give forgiveness at the end of the fasting period. **2** a gathering of social group (workers at same office, people of same ethnic origin, etc.) soon after Isl. fasting month for such a purpose.
halaman 1 yard (of a house). *- rumah* yard of house. *- rumput* lawn. *- sekolah* schoolyard. **2** premises. **3** page (of book). *- luar* outer cover (of book). *- muka* 1 front yard. 2 front page. *- nama buku* title page. *- tengah* 1 center fold of magazine. 2 courtyard.
halang₁ ber-an be hindered, handicapped. **meng-** prevent. *Ia ~ saya pergi* He prevented me from going. **meng-i 1** block s.o.'s way. **2** hamper. *Ia ~ spy saya tdk lulus ujian* He kept me from passing the exam. **meng-²i** obscure, cut off. *Pohon rimbun ~ pemandangan indah itu* A leafy tree cut off the beautiful view. **-an** hindrance, obstacle. *Apa ~nya sehingga anda tdk bisa datang?* What kept you from coming to the party? **peng-** hindrance, obstacle, stumbling block.
halang₂ see ALANG₁.
halat₁ see HÉLAH.
halat₂ see ALAT₂.
halau expel s.o. **meng-(kan) 1** chase away, drive away. *Ia ~ anjing itu dr kamarnya* She chased the dog from the room. **2** drive, herd. *Ia ~ sapinya ke pasar* He drove his cattle to market. **peng-** driver, herder, drover. **peng-an 1** driving, chase, expelling. **2** herding.
halia ginger.
halilintar 1 flash of lightning. **2** thunderbolt.
halimbubu whirlwind.
halimun mist, fog.
halintar see HALILINTAR.
halipan see LIPAN.
halkum Adam's apple.
halma Chinese checkers.
halo hello.
halsduk neck scarf.
halte stopping place for public vehicles. *- bis* bus stop.
halter dumbbell, bar bell.
haluan 1 (*Naut.*) bow, prow. **2** direction. *mengubah - change* course. *Kapal itu berlayar ke - timur* The ship sailed in an easterly direction. *Partai itu mengikuti - kiri* That party followed a leftist course. *- hidup* life's aim. **3** foremost section. *balatentara -* advance troop. *- kata* foreword, preface. **se-** of the same course. *~ sama tengah* impartial, neutral. **ber-** follow a course. *Partai itu ~ liberal* That party followed a liberal course. **meng-kan** direct or orient s.o.
halus 1 refined, cultured, sensitive. *Bahasanya -* Her language is cultured. **2** soft, delicate, smooth (of skin, cloth, etc.). *Suaranya -* She has a soft voice. **3** unseen (of spirits). *bangsa -* the invisible race. *penghuni -* tutelary spirit. **4** small. *Kacang hijaunya kok -!* The mung beans are surprisingly small! **5** finely pounded or granulated

(of flour, etc.). **meng-** become fine. **meng-i 1** treat s.o. gently. **2** improve s.t., touch up. **meng-kan, memper-** refine, touch s.t. up with. *~ kayu* finish wood. *~ kulit* make o.'s skin smooth. *~ sawah* make a rice field even. **ke-an 1** refinement, breeding. **2** gentleness. **3** daintiness, smoothness, softness (of skin, etc.). **peng-** refiner. *~ bahasa* refiner of the language. *partikel ~* (*Ling.*) politeness particle. **peng-an** refining. *~ adat* refinement of customary law. *~ bahasa* euphemism. *~ pemikiran* refinement of thought.
halusinasi hallucination.
halwa fruits preserved in sugar.
ham ham.
hama 1 plant disease, pest. *- ganjur* midge. *- penggérék* borer. *- sundep* paddy borer. *- tebu* sugarcane pest. *- tikus* infestation of mice. *- uret* harmful grub. *- wereng* plague caused by the planthopper. **2** infection. *- penyakit* germ, microbe. **3** pest, scourge. **meng-kan** contaminate. **ter-1** blighted. **2** contaminated.
Hamal (*Zod.*) Aries.
hamba 1 slave, servant. *- abdi* slaves of all kinds. *- Allah* Servant of God. *- hukum* officer of the law. *- péna* journalist. *- sahaya* slaves of all kinds. *- wét* police. **2** (*Lit.*) I, esp. when talking to s.o. of higher rank, often in formal prayers. **3** (*Lit.*) yes. *-, Tuanku* Yes, My Lord. **ber- 1** be a servant. *Ia ~ pd raja itu* He was a servant to the king. **2** have a servant. **meng-** serve. *Ia ~ pd nusa dan bangsa* He served his country and people. **meng-i 1** serve s.o. or s.t. *~ si penjajah* serve the colonial master. **2** equip s.o. with slaves. **meng-kan** treat as a servant, domineer. **memper-i** serve, wait upon, be a servant to. **memper-kan** make s.o. a slave. **ke-an** servitude. **ke-²an** humbly, in humble fashion. **peng-an** serving, slaving. **per-an** slavery, serfdom.
hambalang a great deal of violence (esp. in reference to martial art films).
hambar 1 tasteless, flat, insipid. *- rasanya masakan ini* This food lacks salt. **2** vapid, trite. *Ia tersenyum -* She smiled without expression. **meng-kan 1** render tasteless or insipid. **2** disappoint. **3** nullify, annul, cancel. *Sikap itu ~ aprésiasi yg tlh ditunjukkan kpdnya* That attitude nullified the appreciation shown him. **ke-an** vapidness, insipidness.
hambat checked, blocked. **meng- 1** hamper, impede. *Kerusakan mesin ~ perjalanannya* Engine trouble hampered his trip. *Démokrasi di- oléh penguasa-penguasa* Democracy is being inhibited by the authorities. **2** head off s.o. or s.t., obstruct. **ter-** obstructed, impeded, hampered. **-an 1** obstacle, obstruction. **2** barrier, fence, wall. **3** (*Ling.*) closure. **peng- 1** barrier, obstacle. **2** s.o. or s.t. that obstructs s.t. *faktor ~* inhibiting factor. **peng-an** obstruction.
hambung see AMBUNG.
hambur₁ ber-(an) 1 scattered about. *Uangnya ~ di lantai* Her money was spread about the floor.

lari ~ run helter-skelter. **2** flow, trickle (of tears). **meng-** **1** be dispersed or diffused. *Bau minuman keras* ~ *dr mulutnya* His breath reeked of alcohol. *Anak-anak* ~ *keluar rumah* Children poured out of the house. **2** scatter. *Truk itu meledak dan* ~ The truck exploded and was scattered all about. **3** rush, move suddenly. *Ami* ~ *ke pangkuan ibu* Ami rushed to Mother's lap. **meng-i** spread s.t. with. ~ *air mata* shed tears. **meng-(kan)** **1** scatter s.t., spread s.t. about. ~ *uang* throw away, waste money. ~ *pasir* throw sand about. **2** throw, cast (a net). ~ *kata* talk a great deal. **ter-** scattered all about. **an** s.t. scattered about. **peng-an 1** dispersal. **2** waste. ~ *inséktisida* spreading of insecticide.

hambur₂ ber-an, meng- jump. *-lah!* Beat it! Get lost! **meng-i** jump into s.t. **meng-kan** cause s.o. to leap. ~ *diri dr jendéla* throw o.s. from a window.

hamburger k.o. sandwich, served with sauces in sliced bun. *- daging* hamburger. *- kéju* cheese sandwich in round bun. *- tomat* tomato sandwich in round bun.

hambus see EMBUS₁.

hamenworst /hamemwors/ luncheon meat.

hamil pregnant, pregnancy. *- muda* early stage of pregnancy. *- pertama* first pregnancy. *- tua* advanced stage of pregnancy. **meng-i, meng-kan** impregnate, make pregnant. **ke-an** pregnancy. **peng-an 1** impregnation, insemination. **2** conception.

haminte see GEMINTE.

hamis see AMIS.

hampa 1 empty. *tangan -* empty-handed. *- udara* vacuum. *- hati* disappointed. **2** without result. **meng-kan 1** empty s.t. **2** disappoint. **ke-an 1** emptiness. **2** disappointment. **3** vacuum. **peng-an 1** emptying. **2** causing disappointment.

hampai see AMPAI₁.

hampar ber-an be spread out. **meng-** be spread out evenly. **meng-i** spread s.t. on s.t. ~ *lantai dgn tikar* spread a mat on a floor. **meng-kan 1** spread (rug, etc.). **2** explain, elucidate. **ter-** spread out evenly. **-an 1** rug, carpet. **2** spread out area. **peng-an** spread(ing). ~ *ke timur* spread to the E.

hampedal see EMPEDAL.

hampedu see EMPEDU.

hampir 1 near, close. *Hari Natal sdh -* Christmas is near. **2** almost. *Saya - terlambat* I was almost too late. *- satu abad* close to a century. *- saja* very close to s.t. bad happening. *Saya - saja mati!* I came very close to dying. *-²* very nearly. ~ *celaka!* We came quite close to disaster! **ber-an** be near to e.o. *Rumah saya* ~ *dgn sekolah saya* My house is near my school. **meng-** approach, come near. *Langkahnya* ~ His steps came closer. **meng-i** approach, come close to. *Ia* ~ *ayahnya* She approached her father. **meng-kan** bring s.t. near. ~ *gelas itu pdnya* move the glass closer to him. **ter-** nearest. **-an** vicinity, neighborhood. **peng-an** approach, coming close to s.t.

hamud acid.

hamun ber-² rail at, be abusive. **meng-i 1** abuse s.o., revile s.o. **2** curse.

hamzah letter of Arabic alphabet representing glottal stop.

hana 1 wide and uninhabited. **2** empty, deserted.

hanacaraka the Jv, Sd, or Madurese syllabary.

hancing stench, foul odor.

hancur 1 shattered, smashed. *Gelas itu - sama sekali* The glass was completely shattered. *- berantakan/binasa* thoroughly shattered, smashed to pieces. *- hati* crushed, broken-hearted. *- hatinya mendengar isterinya tlh meninggal* He was crushed upon hearing of his wife's death. *jantungnya* His heart could not take it. *- lebur/luluh* **1** smashed, shattered. **2** dissolved. **meng-lebur-kan, meng-luluhkan** shatter, smash, crush to bits. *- rembas* completely destroyed. *- remuk* **1** crushed to bits, completely shattered. **2** split asunder. **2** dissolved. *Gula itu - dlm air* The sugar was dissolved in the water. **meng-kan 1** smash, shatter (building, glass, hopes, etc.). **2** dissolve (sugar in water, etc.). **3** crush (a stone). **-an 1** debris. **2** solution. **ke-an** destruction. **peng-** destroying force or agent. **peng-an 1** smashing, crushing of. **2** annihilation, total destruction. ~ *modal* destruction of the capital. **3** dissolving of, disintegration.

handai friend, companion. *- taulan* friends. **ber-²** engage in friendly exchange, be on intimate terms with e.o.

handal see ANDAL.

handikap (*Sport*) handicap. **ber-** have a certain handicap.

handuk towel. **meng-i** wipe s.o. or s.t. with a towel. *Ia* ~ *anaknya* He wiped his child off with a towel.

hang (*Lit.*) male title. *- Tuah* a legendary figure of Malay literature.

hangar see HANGGAR₁.

hangat warm. *berita -* current news. *- hati* delighted. *keadaan -* critical situation. *pikiran -* hot under the collar. *débat -* heated argument. *air -* lukewarm water. *- kuku* lukewarm. *- pijar* white-hot, incandescent. *-²* while hot. ~ *tahi ayam* a fleeting enthusiasm. **meng-** become hot. *Suasana politik makin* ~ The political atmosphere became more and more heated. **meng-i 1** warm up (food, etc.). **2** incite. **meng-kan 1** warm up (food). **2** heat s.t. *Pertentangan kedua partai itu* ~ *suasana politik* The controversy between the two parties heated the political atmosphere. ~ *hati* warm the heart. ~ *ingatan* refresh o.'s memory. **ke-an 1** heat, warmth. *Dlm* ~ *kemarahannya ia mengumpat-umpat* In the heat of his anger he kept cursing. ~ *bibirnya* the warmth of her lips. **2** tenseness. ~ *suasana politik* the tenseness of the political atmosphere. **3** eagerness. **-an** warming up. *tempat -* warming up place. **peng-** warmer.

hanggar₁ 1 airplane hangar. **2** sports hall.

hanggar₂ see ANGGAR₂, ANGGAR₃.

hangit see ANGIT.

hangus 1 burnt, scorched. *Nasinya* - The rice is burnt. *Rumahnya* - *terbakar* The house has burned down. **2** singed. - *hati* extremely irritated. **3** (*Coll.*) completely used up (of money). *Yah, uang hasil judi, cepat* - Lord! Gambling earnings get used up fast. **meng-kan 1** roast until burnt. *Kopi hrs di-kan sblm dijadikan bubuk* Coffee must be roasted before being pulverized. **2** burn, singe, scorch. ~ *hati* anger s.o. *Jangan* ~ *hati org* Do not make him mad. **ke-an** state of being charred. *Saya membau* ~ *di dapur* I smell s.t. burning in the kitchen. ~ *hati* **1** anger. **2** longing.

hanjut meng- hit s.o., crush s.o.

Hankam [*Pertahanan dan Keamanan*] Defense and Security.

Hanra [*Pertahanan Rakyat*] lower level civilian defense units.

Hansip [*Pertahanan Sipil*] civilian defense units often given neighborhood patrol tasks.

hansop child's play- and sleepwear with short sleeves and short legs.

hantam - *kromo* do as o. likes without regard to propriety, be completely at random. - *kromo AS di Viétnam* what the US arbitrarily did in Vietnam. *kesimpulan* - *kromo* a conclusion drawn without regard to facts. - *saja* do as o. likes. **ber-1** fight, scuffle. *Mari kita* ~*!* Let us fight! **2** collide with. **3** infringe on. **meng-1** strike hard. *Ombak* ~ *kapal* The waves rammed into the ship. **2** pound, pummel. *Polisi Tokio* ~ *kepala mahasiswa* The Tokyo police bashed the students' heads. **3** attack vigorously. *di- malaria* severely attacked by malaria. **4** (*Coll.*) go at (o.'s food). *Kuénya di- saja!* Let us attack that cake! **meng-i** strike repeatedly. **meng-kan 1** strike s.t. **2** strike with s.t. *Penduduk* ~ *senjata tumpul pd tubuh pencuri* The inhabitants pounded the thief with blunt weapons. **-an** blow, smack, punch.

hantar see ANTAR₁.

hantir meng- wield, manage, handle. ~ *politik ékonomi* apply an economic policy.

hantu 1 ghost. - *bungkus/kapan/pocong* ghost in form of corpse in a shroud which feeds on the blood of babies. **2** evil spirit. *rumah* - haunted house. - *rimba* spirit of the woods, jungle spirit. **ber- 1** haunted. **2** possessed by a spirit. **meng-1** become a ghost. **2** become s.t. that haunts. *Persoalan itu sdh* ~ *bagi dia* That problem has become a persistent source of fear for him. **meng-i 1** frighten. **2** haunt, obsess. *Ketakutan* ~ *pikirannya* Fear haunted his mind.

Hanuman (*Lit.*) the white monkey, sacred hero of the Ramayana.

hanya 1 only. *Saya* - *mempunyai lima ratus rupiah* I only have 500 rupiah. - . . . .*saja* only . . . . - *tiga org saja* just three men. **2** only, however. *Saya sebenarnya mau,* - *tak boléh* I want to, only I cannot. - *dia tdk tahu bagaimana caranya* Only he did not know how. - *saja* only, on condition that. *Kamu*

boléh pergi - *saja hrs kembali jam enam* You can go on condition that you come back by six.

hanyir see ANYIR.

hanyut 1 washed away, drift. *Pohon itu* - *di sungai* The tree was washed away in the river. **2** drift, wander. *Ia* - *ke negeri asing* He drifted to foreign countries. **3** lose o.s. (in reveries, etc.). *Ia* - *dlm buaian lelaki* She has lost herself in the embraces of men. **ber-(²) 1** drift. *Ia* ~ *di sungai* He drifted in the river. **2** wander, roam. **3** drag on (of conversation). **meng-kan** sweep away (of floods, currents, critical events, etc.). *Banjir itu* ~ *banyak ternak* The flood washed away many cattle. *Peristiwa G30S* ~ *segala harapannya* The events of the 1965 coup swept away all his hopes. **-an 1** drift (of flooding water, events, etc.). **2** flowing movement. ~ *tubuh* smooth flowing body movements. **peng-an** washing away (of). ~ *tanah* soil erosion.

hao (*Ch*) filial piety.

hapak see APAK.

hapal see HAFAL.

hapermot see HAVERMUT.

hapus meng- 1 completely remove. ~ *bibirnya* be left out in the cold. ~ *dosa* wash, wipe away sins. **2** clean s.t., wipe off (blackboard). ~ *keringat* wipe away sweat. **meng-kan 1** eliminate s.t., wipe out. ~ *hutang* cancel a debt. ~ *perbudakan* abolish slavery. *Satu bom atom dpt* ~ *seluruh kota* One atomic bomb can wipe out an entire city. ~ *dahaga* quench a thirst. **2** nullify (a contract), expunge (a record). **ter-** vanished, disappeared. *Noda itu* ~ The stain vanished. **peng-** tool used to wipe s.t. clean (eraser, etc.). ~ *kaca* windshield wiper. ~ *tinta* ink eradicator. **peng-an 1** wiping out, erasing. **2** abolition. ~ *pesawat terbang* retiring of (old) planes. **3** nullification. **4** remission (of sins).

harab (*Lit.*) war.

harafiah see HARFIAH.

harakah, harakat vowel (in Arabic grammar).

harakiri (*Japanese*) suicide. **ber-** commit suicide.

haral see ARAL.

haram 1 (*Isl.*) forbidden, proscribed. *Daging babi* - *bagi org Islam* Pork is forbidden to Muslims. *Masjid Al-* The holy mosque of Mecca. *anak* - illicit child. *tanah* - (*Isl.*) Mecca (which is proscribed to unbelievers). **2** (*Coll.*) on no account, under no circumstances. - *sekali dia yg harus bayar, selalu kami yg kena* It was absolutely unthinkable that he would be the o. to pay. We would always get stuck with the bill. **3** Never! (an exclamation of strong denial). -*! Aku bukan pencuri* Never! I am no thief. **meng-kan 1** forbid, prohibit. *Selama menjalankan tugas minum minuman keras di-kan* The consumption of liquor while on duty is expressly prohibited. **2** abjure, abstain from. ~ *minum rokok* abstain from smoking (once and for all). **peng-an** act of proscribing s.t.

haramjadah, haramzadah illegitimate (child).

harangaso (*Sd*) k.o. tuber.

harap 1 hope. - *hati* heart's desire. **2** please, we hope that (part of a formal command). - *diam!* Please be quiet! - *maklum!* Please take note! -² *cemas* with fear and hope. **ber-** hope, expect. *Kami ~ engkau akan lekas sembuh* We hope you will soon be well. *Kami ~ engkau akan kembali* We expect you to come back. **ber-an** have hope. **ber-²an** always hoping. **ber-kan** have hopes for. **meng-(kan) 1** hope for s.t. *Petani-petani ~ hujan* The farmers are hoping for rain. **2** expect. *Kami ~ kehadiran présidén pd rapat kami* We expect the président to be present at our meeting. *Jangan ~ pertolongan org lain* Do not count on the help of others. **3** with the approach of. *~ Hari Natal banyak org berbelanja* As Christmas approaches, many go shopping. **ter-²** ever hoping. *Akhirnya hari yg tlh lama ~ itu datang* At last the long-waited day arrived. *~ saja* disappointed, let down. **-an 1** hope. *~ bangga* the nation's hope (the youth). *~ tipis* little hope, only a sporting chance. *Tiada ~* There is no chance. **2** expectation. *bintang ~* a movie star with good prospects. *~ hidup* life expectancy. **peng-an 1** hope. **2** placing o.'s hopes, reliance, expectation. *~ pertolongan org lain* reliance on the assistance of others.

harapiah see HARFIAH.

harasia (*Sl.*) see RAHASIA.

harbor, hardbord beaverboard, hardboard.

hardik say s.t. sharply, snarl. **meng- 1** snap at. **2** scold, dress down, rebuke. *Malah dia pernah ~ menteri* Why, he has even rebuked state ministers. **-an** rebuke, scolding, harsh words.

harfiah literal, word for word. *terjemahan* - a literal translation.

harga price, cost, value. *Berapa - jam itu?* How much does that watch cost? *dgn* - at a cost of. - *banderol* **1** price found on official seal. **2** gvt.-fixed price. - *banting(an)* bargain price. - *bébas* free market price. - *borongan* **1** wholesale price. **2** price contracted for. - *diri* self-esteem, self-respect. - *diri nasional* national dignity. - *gelap* black market price. - *gila* a ridiculous price. - *jadi* price fixed after bargaining. - *jual* sale or selling price. - *luar(an)* free market price. - *mati* fixed price. *Ini - mati, tdk boléh tawar* This is a fixed price. You are not permitted to bargain. - *melawan* competitive price, a price that undersells the competitors. - *paku/pasti* fixed price. - *patokan* **1** fixed price. **2** ceiling price. - *pokok* cost price. - *plafon* top/ceiling price. - *rincih* retail price. - *satuan* unit price. - *séwa* rental price, rent. - *uang* rate of exchange. **se- 1** be at the same price. *Kedua cincin itu ~* The two rings are the same price. **2** at the price of. *~ seribu rupiah* in the amount of 1,000 rupiah. - **meng-i** bear mutual respect. **ber- 1** have a price of, cost. *Barang ini ~ seratus ribu rupiah* This article costs 100,000 rupiah. **2** valuable. *barang ~* valuable goods (esp. gold jewelry). *tdk ~* worthless. **meng-i, meng-kan 1** value at, appraise s.t. *Kita ~ barang itu seribu rupiah* We value that article at

1,000 rupiah. **2** appreciate s.t. or s.o. *Kita sangat ~ pertolonganmu* We appreciate your help very much. **3** reward (services, etc.). **peng-an 1** appreciation, respect. *~ saya bagimu sangat besar* My respect for you is very great. **2** valuation. *~ intan itu terlalu rendah* The valuation of that diamond is too low.

hari day. - *sdh jauh malam* It is late at night (lit., the day has advanced far into night). - *Angkatan Bersenjata* Armed Forces Day (October 5). - *acara* session (of court). - *arwah* (*Rel.*) All Souls' Day. - *baik* **1** feast day. **2** lucky day. - *batal* expiration date. - *berbangkit* (*Rel.*) Resurrection Day. - *berganti hari* alternating days. - *berlukunya* date of validity. - *besar* **1** holiday. **2** holy day, feast day. - *bulan* (*Lit.*) date. - *buruk* unlucky day. - *cerah* **1** a beautiful day. **2** in broad daylight. - *depan* later on, future. *gelap* dark, gloomy day. - *hujan* **1** rainy day. **2** It is raining. - *jadi* birthday. - *jatuh* due date. - *Kebangkitan* Easter. - *kebangsaan* national day. - *Kejadian* Christmas. - *kelabu* dark, gloomy day. - *kemudian* the future. - *keramat* sacred day. - *kerja* working or business day. - *kiamat* doomsday. - *kuning* unfavorable sign. - *lahir* birthday. - *libur* **1** holiday. **2** day off. - *Mahsyar* day of judgment, resurrection day. - *naas* o.'s unlucky day. - *Pembalasan* Judgment Day. - *peringatan* anniversary. - *raya* holiday, esp. marking end of fasting month. - *raya org kudus* (*Rel.*) All Saints' Day. - *sarjana* graduation or commencement day. - *setor* day of deposit. - *sidang* (*Leg.*) court day. - *témpo* holiday. - *tua* old age. - *ulang tahun* birthday, anniversary, commemoration. - *wafat* day of death. **se-** each day, a day. *tiga kali ~* three times a day. *~ suntuk* the whole day. **se-²** every day. *Apa kerjamu ~* What is your daily work? *pakaian ~* everyday clothes. **se-²an** all day long, the entire day. *Ia bermain-main saja ~* He just plays all day long. **ber-** spend a day. *Kami ~ Minggu di Puncak* We spent Sunday at Puncak. *~ Raya* spend the fasting month holiday. **ber-(²)** day after day, for several days. **-an 1** daily. *catatan ~* daily record. *pekerja ~* worker who receives daily wages. **2** daily newspaper. *Kami berlangganan ~ Sinar Harapan* We subscribe to the *Sinar Harapan*.

haribaan lap. *di - masyarakat* in the midst of society.

harim wife, female members of the family (esp. among those of Arabic descent or educational background).

harimau tiger. - *belang* striped tiger. - *campa* fierce striped tiger. - *dahan* clouded leopard. - *gadungan/jadi-jadian* a person capable of assuming the shape of a tiger. - *kumbang* black panther. - *di belakang rumah dan serigala di depan rumah* between the devil and the deep blue sea (lit., a tiger at the back of the house and a wolf at the front). - *tutul* leopard.

haring₁ herring.

haring₂ see ARING₁,₂.

harini (*Coll.*) today.
harkah, harkat 1 level, standard. **2** rate, value. - *uang* (*Fin.*) rate of exchange. - *pengikisan* rate of loss. **3** dignity. *tak sesuai dgn - pangkatnya* not in keeping with his rank. **peng-an** rating.
harlah [*hari lahir*] anniversary, birthday.
harmoni harmony. **ke-an** harmony. **peng-an** harmonizing.
harmonik see HARMONIS.
harmonika harmonica.
harmonis 1 harmonious. **2** harmonic. **meng-kan** harmonize, reconcile. ~ *hubungan* restore harmonious relations. **ke-an** harmony.
harmonisasi harmonization.
harmonium harmonium.
harpa harp.
harpis harpist.
harpus resin used by violinists.
hart (*Crd.*) heart.
harta property, wealth. - *bawaan* dowry. - *benda* wealth, riches, property. - *bergerak* movable goods. - *bersama* common property. - *dunia* wordly possessions. - *karun* 1 hidden treasure. 2 pay dirt. - *milik* property, possessions. - *pencarian* earned (not inherited) wealth. - *(pen)dapatan* dowry. - *pusaka* inherited wealth, legacy. - *tetap* unmovable goods. - *wakaf* charitable legacy. - *warisan* legacy. **se-** ~ *semilik* joint property and wealth. **ber-** propertied, landed.
hartawan wealthy person, person of means.
haru - *biru* commotion, uproar, tumult. **mengbirukan 1** start a commotion, cause chaos. **2** upset, make a stir. **meng-** confuse. **meng-kan** touch o.'s emotions, move the heart. *Ceritanya* ~ *hati saya* His story touched me. I was moved by his story. **ter-** moved, touched, affected. **keter-an** state of being highly affected by an emotion. **ke-an** emotional. *suara* ~ *bercampur sinis* a voice at once emotional and cynical. **peng-** agitator, troublemaker, rioter. **peng-an** confusion.
haruan k.o. freshwater fish.
haru-biru see HARU.
harum 1 fragrant, aromatic. **2** fragrance, aroma. - *namanya* famous. **meng-** be fragrant. **meng-i 1** perfume, scent s.t. with. *Pahlawan kita* ~ *persada ibu Pertiwi* Our heroes perfume the gardens of the motherland. **2** put fragrance in s.t. **meng-kan** aromatize, give a scent to. *Bunga-bunga itu* ~ *udara* The flowers made the air fragrant. ~ *namanya* make o.'s name famous. **ke-an 1** fragrance. **2** fame, renown. ~*nya selalu disebut org* His fame is on everyone's lips. **-an** perfume. **-²an** various k.o. fragrances.
Harun 1 (*Bib.*) Aaron. **2** (*Isl.*) o. of the prophets.
harung see ARUNG.
harus 1 have to, must. *Saya - belajar* I have to study. *tdk -* not obligatory. *Anda tak - bayar tapi sebaiknya anda bayar* You do not have to pay, but it will be best if you do. **2** (*Isl.*) permitted by religion, neither sinful nor meritorious, e.g. eating, bathing, etc. **se-nya 1** should, ought to. *Saya akan menolong tuan, tetapi* ~ *tuan pergi ke kantor*

polisi dulu I will help you, sir, but you ought to go to the police first. **2** proper(ly). *Sdh* ~ *kita menghormati org tua* It is proper that we respect our parents. **meng-kan** compel, require. *Kursus ini di-kan* This course is required. **ke-an 1** necessity, requirement. **2** imperative, must.
has₁ filet, tenderloin.
has₂ gauze, fine screening.
hasa (*Amb*) sail along the shore.
hasad envy, spite.
hasan good, beautiful, handsome.
Hasan (*Isl.*) a grandson of Muh. martyred in religious war. Hasan's and his brother Husain's deaths are commemorated on *Asyura*.
hasiat see KHASIAT.
hasil 1 yield, crop. - *alam/bumi* agricultural produce. - *utama* staple crop. **2** product. - *bagi* (*Math.*) quotient. - *ikutan* by-product. - *kali* (*Math.*) product. - *karya* 1 work, product. 2 brainwork. - *kotor* gross output. - *mahsul* products (of a country). **3** result, outcome, output. *Apakah - perundingannya?* What is the outcome of the discussion? - *guna* effect. **ber-** *guna* useful, effective. *télékomunikasi yg cepat dan* ~ *guna* fast and effective telecommunications. **se-²nya** as successfully as possible. **ber-** succeed. *Ia* ~ *memperoléh gelar* She succeeded in getting a degree. *Usahanya tak ada yg* ~ None of his attempts were successful. **keber-an** success. **meng-kan 1** produce. *Indonésia* ~ *karét* Indonesia produces rubber. *Sawah saya* ~ *dua panén dlm setahun* My wet rice field yields two crops a year. *Rencana itu akan* ~ *buah* That plan will bear fruit. **2** deliver, produce results. **peng-** producer. *salah satu* ~ *karét yg terutama* o. of the main rubber producers. **peng-an 1** production. **2** yield. **3** income, earnings. ~ *nyata* real earnings.
hasrat 1 longing, desire. **2** propensity. - *hati* motivation. **ber- 1** desire, wish. *Ia* ~ *mengelilingi dunia* He had a desire to circle the globe. **meng-kan** wish for s.t. *Bp tlh lama* ~ *mobil baru* Dad has long wished for a new car. **ter-** wished for. **ke-an 1** wish, desire. **2** longing.
Hassan see HASAN.
hasta cubit. **meng-** measure in cubits.
hastakarya 1 handicrafts. **2** (*Sl.*) petting.
hasud see HASAD.
hasung see ASUNG.
hasut meng- incite, goad, stir up. *Ia* ~ *karyawan minyak spy mogok* He incited the oil refinery workers to strike. **-an 1** instigation, provocation, fomentation. **2** agitation (for civil rights, etc.). **peng-** agitator, provocateur. ~ *rakyat* demagogue, rabble rouser. **peng-an** instigating, provoking.
hasyiah 1 edge, border. **2** marginal annotation.
hasyis hashish.
hati 1 liver. *jantung -* 1 internal organs. 2 sweetheart. - *kisut* cirrhosis of the liver. **2** seat of emotions. -*ku jadi besar* I am much encouraged (lit., my liver has become big). *membaca dlm -* reads to o.s. *dr - ke -* from o. person to another. *Yg saya*

katakan itu adalah dr - ke - I am telling you this in all candor. *- beku* cold heart. *- bercagak* insincere (heart). *- bejar* courageous (heart), encouraged. *- buntu* afraid, uneasy. *- kecil* conscience, inner voice. *dlm - kecilku* deep down, in my heart of hearts. *- kecut* cowardly, timid. *- luluh* 1 be won over. 2 become of o. heart and mind with. *- nurani/sanubari* conscience, inner feelings. 3 (*Crd.*) heart. **-²** 1 be careful, be on o.'s guard. 2 carefully. **se-** 1 of o. mind, like-minded. 2 unanimous. **kese-an** unanimity in ideals, emotions, etc. **ber-** have a heart, show compassion. ~ *batu* without compassion, have a heart of stone. ~ *berjantung* be sensitive or compassionate. ~ *dendam* have a vengeful heart. ~ *iblis* have a rotten heart, be a bad person. ~ *mutu* be at a loss, in despair, despairing. ~ *rawan* be melancholic or depressed. ~ *tungau* be a coward, be cowardly. ~ *walang* be concerned, worried, anxious. **ber-²** be careful. **memper-kan** 1 pay attention, take note of. *Per-kanlah!* Attention, please! 2 watch, observe. **pemer-** observer (for the purpose of study, etc.). **per-an** 1 attention, notice. ~*!* ~*!* Attention, please! 2 interest. *menaruh* ~ *thd soal* show interest in a problem.

hatsil see HASIL.

hatta (*Lit.*) then, thereupon.

hatur see ATUR₂.

haus₁ 1 thirsty. *- dahaga* great thirst. 2 thirst, thirstiness. *- pengetahuan* thirst for knowledge. **meng-kan** 1 cause thirst, make thirsty. *Perjalanan itu sangat* ~ *saya* The trip made me very thirsty. 2 thirst for (knowledge, etc.). **ke-an** 1 suffer thirst, be thirsty. 2 thirst, thirstiness.

haus₂ see AUS.

havermut oatmeal.

hawa 1 air. 2 climate, weather. *-nya panas hari ini* The weather is hot today. *- daba* odor, smell. *- darat* continental climate. *- laut* marine climate. *- panas* tropical climate. *- sedang* temperate climate. **meng-** evaporate. *Minyak wangi itu* ~ The perfume evaporated.

Hawa (*Bib.*) Eve. Siti - (*Isl.*) Eve. *si -* woman, female. *kaum -* womanhood.

hawai, hawaian Hawaiian-style music.

hawa nafsu carnal desire, lust.

hawar blight. *- daun* leaf blight.

hawatir see KUATIR.

hawé see AWÉ.

hawiah (*Isl.,Lit.*) depths of hell.

hayal see KHAYAL.

hayali see KHAYALI.

hayat life. *sampai akhir -nya* to the end of her life. *selama - dikandung badan* as long as o. lives. **meng-i** 1 experience to the full, comprehend fully. ~ *pengalaman kemerdékaan* experience freedom to the fullest. *Perkembangan antropologi perlu di-i oléh sarjana-sarjana Indonésia* The development of anthropology must be experienced by Indonesian scholars. 2 inspire, vivify. *Jiwa Pancasila* ~ *kehidupannya* The spirit of *Pancasila* inspired her life. **peng-** o. who compre-

hends s.t., o. who practices s.t. **peng-an** full and total comprehension. ~ *agama* full religious experience.

hayati biological, vital. *bahan -* living matter. *sumber-sumber -* biological resources. *baik - maupun nabati* both animal and vegetable.

hayo 1 Come! (in exhortations). *-! Kaum tertindas* Come, you the oppressed! 2 Behold! There you have it! *-! Apa lagi itu?* See! What else could it be?

hayun see AYUN.

hb /habé/ k.o. pencil.

hb. [*hari bulan*] (*Lit.*) date.

HB [*Hindia Belanda*] Dutch E. Indies.

HBS [*Hoogere Burger School*] four-year secondary school for children of the elite (colonial period).

hc. [*honoris causa*] honorary. *Dr. -* honorary doctor(ate).

HCS [*Hollandsch Chineesche School*] Dutch-medium primary school for well-to-do Ch (colonial period).

hé₁ huh (interrogative particle). *Kalau dilepas, kau lari, -?* If I untie you, you will run away, huh?

hé₂ umm (hesitation particle).

hé₃ see HAI.

héban (*Lit.*) hurl, throw s.t. heavy, throw with both hands,. **meng-** hurl, throw (s.t. heavy).

hébat unusually intensive (excitement, attractiveness, intelligence, violence, etc.). *sambutan -* a tremendous reception. *Filem ini -!* This movie is great! *- benar kamu!* You are terrific! *Ada tabrakan - di Jalan Thamrin* There was a dreadful collision at Jalan Thamrin. **meng-** increase in intensity. *Keadaan itu* ~ The situation grew worse. *Suasana sedang* ~ The atmosphere is becoming hectic. **meng-kan, memper-(kan)** intensify, step up. ~ *usaha pembangunan* step up developmental efforts. *Sabun itu diper-kan dgn busa super aktif* The soap is vitalized with superactive suds. **ke-an** 1 intensity (of excitement, violence, natural phenomena, etc.). 2 (*Coll.*) flap, furor. **-²an** intensive. *Di negeri itu org kaya dipajak* ~ In that country, the rich are heavily taxed. *kampanye* ~ vigorous campaign. **peng-an** intensification. ~ *peperangan* escalation of the war.

héboh 1 commotion, uproar. 2 fuss, row, stir. 3 sensational. **meng-i, meng-kan** cause a commotion. *Karangan itu sdh* ~ *pendapat umum* That article has caused a stir in public opinion. **ke-an** fuss, ado, stir.

hédonisme hedonism.

hee (*Coll.*) uh huh, yes.

héé see HAI.

hééh see HA₂.

hééhm see EHM₁.

hégemoni, hégémoni hegemony.

héh see HÉ₁.

héi see HAI.

héiho indigenous militia during the Japanese period.

hejan see EJAN.

héjrah see HIJRAH.

hék /hék/ (*Coll.*) fence (around yard, etc.).

héktar hectare.
héktoliter hectoliter.
héla meng- drag, haul, pull (carriage, wagon, etc.). ~ *ke pantai* drag ashore. ~ *napas* take a breath. ~ *napas lega* breathe a sigh of relief. ~ *surut* pull back. ~ *kambing dgn tali* pull a goat by a rope. **ter-** dragged along. *tdk* ~ unwavering, unshakable. **-an** s.t. pulled. ~ *nafas* breath. **peng-** s.t. or s.o. that pulls, draws, or tows. *kerbau sbg tenaga* ~ the water buffalo as a draft animal. **peng-an** pulling, drawing, towing (of).
hélah (*Lit.*) **1** trick, ruse. *tipu* - chicanery. **2** excuse, pretext. **ber- 1** use a trick. **2** use as an excuse. **meng-** fool, trick s.o. **peng-an** making a pretext.
helai 1 sheet (of paper, etc.). **2** a counter for paper, cloth, leaf, etc. *sepuluh - serbét* 10 napkins. *tinggal se- sepinggang* possess only the clothes on o.'s back. **ber-** in sheets, unbound. **-an** sheet (of paper, etc.).
hélak ber- be wafted or lifted back (of long things, whips, etc.). **meng-** lift (whip, sword, tail, etc.) in back of o.
hélat₁ celebration, party. **ber-** celebrate with a party.
hélat₂ see HÉLAH.
héléng meng- turn, look. ~ *ke arah Miharti* look in Miharti's direction. **meng-kan** turn s.t. *Ia* ~ *kepalanya melihat ke kiri* He turned his head looking to the left.
héli [*hélikoptér*] helicopter.
hélicak [*hélikoptér bécak*] three-wheeled motorized pedicab.
hélikoptér helicopter.
hélipad [*hélikoptér pad*] helicopter pad.
hélium helium.
hélm /hélem/ motorcycle helmet, hard hat.
hem um (exclamation of distaste, scorn). -*! Kau tak tahu!* Humph! You do not know!
hém shirt.
hémat₁ judgment, observation. *pd - saya* in my opinion.
hémat₂ thrifty, economical, thrift. - *pangkal kaya* thrift is the basis of wealth. **ber-, meng-** be thrifty, economize. **meng-kan** be thrifty with s.t., economize on. *Engkau hrs* ~ *uangmu* You must be thrifty with your money. ~ *tenaganya* conserve o.'s energy. ~ *waktu* save time. **peng-an 1** economizing. ~ *bahan bakar* economizing on fuel. **2** retrenchment, economy.
hembalang ber- tumble head over heels. *lari* ~ run pell-mell. **meng-(kan)** hurl, esp. in martial arts films. **ter-** be hurled head over heels. *Ia jatuh* ~ He fell head over heels.
hembus see EMBUS₁.
hémong (*Sl.*) homo, male homosexual.
hempang see EMPANG.
hempas see EMPAS.
hémpét see HIMPIT.
hendak 1 wish (to do s.t.). *Saya berjanji - menjalankannya* I promise I will do it. -*lah* please, kindly. -*lah dikirim dgn segera* Please send (it)

immediately. **2** intend, be going to. *Ia - bicara dgn gurunya* She is going to talk to her teacher. **3** be about to. *Gunung berapi itu - meletus* The volcano is about to explode. **-nya** be desirable that, should. *Org yg bersangkutan* ~ *dipanggil* The relevant person should be summoned. ~ *maklum* Please (take) note. ~ *kita tunggu dahulu* Let us wait first. *Jangan* ~ *ia tersesat di jalan* Let us hope he did not lose his way. ~ *jangan sampai terjadi hal itu* It is hoped it will not happen. ~ *pun* if o. were to. ~ *pun ingin membelinya, saya tdk mampu membayarnya* Although I would like to buy it, I cannot afford it. **meng-i 1** wish for s.t. ~ *bencana* court disaster. **2** require, demand. *Soal ini* ~ *penyelidikan yg teliti* This problem requires careful investigation. **ke-** wish, desire. *Apakah* ~*mu sebetulnya?* What do you really want? ~*nya akan menjadi kaya menyesatkan dia* His desire to become rich made him go wrong. *Menipumu, itulah* ~*nya!* To cheat you, that is his intention! *atas* ~ *sendiri* on his or her own initiative. **sekehatinya** to o.'s heart's content. **berke-** have an intention. ~ *baik* have good intentions. **menge-i** (*Lit.*) want s.t., desire s.t. *tdk dike-i* wanted.
hendam-karam destroyed, wiped out. *Kota yg kena bom atom* - The city was wiped out, hit by an atom bomb.
hendap see ENDAP₁.
héndel handle (of door, etc.).
héng (*Sport*) Hands! (said when soccer ball is touched with hands).
hengah see ENGA₂.
héngkang see ÉNGKANG.
hening 1 clear. *Air telaga itu* - The water of the lake was clear. *Pikirannya* - His mind is clear. *hati yg* - a pure heart. **2** silent, quiet. **meng-kan 1** clear. ~ *pikirannya* clear o.'s thoughts. **2** silence, make quiet. *Kata-kata yg tenang itu* ~ *org* His words calmed down everyone. ~ *cipta* **1** observe a brief silence (in honor of s.o. or s.t.). **2** meditate. **ke-an 1** clarity, purity. ~ *pikiran* clarity of thought. ~ *hatinya* the purity of her heart. **2** stillness, silence, quietness.
hentak see ENTAK.
hentam meng-kan stamp (the foot). **-an 1** foot stamping. **2** big explosion.
henti stopping, stoppage. *Lalu lintas ibukota tak kenal* - The traffic in the capital has not let up. *tak* -²**nya** ceaseless, incessant. **ber- 1** stop. *Mobil itu* ~ The car stopped. *Jangan* ~ Do not stop. **2** end, cease. *Perang itu* ~ The war ended. **ber-²** repeatedly stop. *tak* ~*(nya)* incessantly. **member-kan 1** stop (a vehicle). **2** dismiss s.o. from his job. **pember-an 1** discharge, dismissal. **2** stoppage. ~ *buruh* work stoppage. **keber-an** cessation, stopping. **meng-kan, memper-kan 1** stop, halt (car, production, etc.). ~ *kemajuan tentara musuh* halt advance of the enemy army. **2** end, put an end to s.t. **3** fire, dismiss. **4** (*Av.*) feather (a motor). **ter- 1** stopped, halted. *ékonomi yg* ~ stagnant economy. **2** broken off. **keter-an** impasse. **-an** (*Ling.*) stop. ~ *tunggal* simple stop. **peng-an**

bring to a halt, ceasing. **per-an 1** cessation, discontinuance, closing down (of factory, program, etc.). **2** stopping place (of bus, etc.).

henyak see ENYAK.

héos meng- blow with a bursting sound (of steam, etc.).

hépatitis hepatitis.

hér 1 retake (an exam). *Ia hrs - utk naik kelas* She had to take her exam over in order to be promoted. **2** makeup exam.

héran 1 surprised, amazed. *Ia - melihat saya* She was surprised to see me. *Tdk -* It is not surprising. **2** astonishment *-ku tak kusembunyikan* I did not hide my surprise. *- bin ajaib* very strange. **ber-²** act surprised. **meng-kan 1** cause amazement, be astonishing. *Pertunjukannya sangat ~ aku* His show really amazed me. *Peristiwa itu tak ~* That event was not surprising. **2** be surprised at s.t. *Ada hal yg di-kan tetangga kami* There was s.t. our neighbor was surprised at. **ter-²** greatly amazed, astonished. *Pencari berita ~ melihat anak kecil ngomong ttg politik* The reporters were greatly amazed seeing a small boy talking about politics. **ke-an 1** wonder, miracle. **2** be amazed. *Ia melihat ~* He looked on in amazement. **ke-²an** greatly surprised.

hérba herb.

hérbisida herbicide.

hérder German shepherd dog.

hérdislokasi re-dislocation (of shoulder, etc.).

héréng see ÉRÉNG.

herik see ERIK.

héring k.o. fish, herring.

héro 1 popular sports figure. **2** s.o. of considerate prowess. *- ranjang* terrific lover.

héroik heroic.

héroin heroin.

héroisme heroism.

hérot see ÉROT₁.

hert, herrt sound of s.t. being ripped.

hétero heterosexual.

héterogén heterogeneous. **ke-an** heterogeneity.

héteroséks heterosexual.

heuristis heuristic.

héwan 1 domesticated animal. *- piara(an)* **1** domestic animal. **2** pet. **2** animal (as a class). *- bantai* **1** beef cattle. **2** livestock for food. *- kunyah* ruminant. *- menyusui* mammal. *- penarik* draft animal. *- pengerat* rodent. *- bertulang belakang* vertebrate. **ke-an** pertaining to animals. *fakultas ~* department of veterinary science.

héwani, héwaniah of an animal. *nafsu - bestial* desires. *protéina - animal protein.

hey see HAI.

hi Ha! (exclamation uttered when teasing s.o.).

hianat see KHIANAT.

hiansay (*Ch*) son-in-law.

hias ber- 1 be decorated, adorned. **2** dress o.s., groom o.s. *Mengapa engkau ~* Why are you dressed up? *Aku lagi ~* I am still primping. *~ diri* dress up. **ber-kan** decorated with. *Ia ~ kalung emas* She was adorned with a gold necklace.

meng-(i) 1 decorate, adorn s.o. or s.t. **2** garnish, embellish (food, language, etc.). **3** illustrate (a magazine). **-an 1** decoration. *~ dinding* wall decoration. *~ janur* decoration made of young palm leaves. **2** illustration. **peng-** decorator, illustrator. *alat ~* cosmetic devices. *daun-daun ~* leaves for decoration. **peng-an 1** decorating. **2** embellishment, ornamentation. **per-an 1** jewelry (esp. gold). **2** decoration (in building, etc.).

hiatus hiatus.

hiba see IBA.

hibah bequest, grant (from foundation, etc.). *- wasiat* legacy, bequest. **meng-kan 1** give grant, award. **2** donate, bequeath. **-an** bequest. **peng-an** making a bequest.

hibernasi hibernation.

hibrida hybrid.

hibuk see SIBUK.

hibur ber- entertain o.s. **meng- 1** comfort, cheer up, divert. *~ anak yg menangis itu* comfort the crying child. **2** entertain. *Para penari ~ tetamu* The dancers entertained the guests. **meng-kan** cheer s.o. up. **ter-** consoled, comforted. *tiada ~* inconsolable, disconsolate. **-an 1** consolation, solace, comfort. **2** entertainment. **peng- 1** comforter, consoler. **2** s.t. diverting. *~ hati* diversion, entertainment. *hadiah ~* consolation prize. **peng-an** act of entertainment. *Malam ini diadakan ~ anak yatim* This evening they will put on a show by the orphans.

hidam see IDAM.

hidang meng-i serve with. *Tamu itu hanya di-i téh* The guest was only served tea. **meng-kan 1** serve (food, drink). **2** present (entertainment, etc.). **ter-** be served. *Di hadapan méreka di atas méja ~ pelbagai macam énak-énakan* On the table were several varieties of goodies set out before them. **-an 1** serving. *se~* a plateful. **2** presentation. *~ lagu* song performance. *~ sandiwara* stage performance. **peng-** server. **peng-an 1** the serving of. **2** presentation.

hidap see IDAP.

hidayah, hidayat (God's) guidance.

hidmat see KHIDMAT.

hidrat (*Chem.*) hydrate. *- arang* carbohydrate.

hidrogén hydrogen.

hidrolik hydraulic.

hidrolisis hydrolysis.

hidrolistrik hydroelectric.

hidrologi hydrology.

hidrologis hydrological.

hidu meng- sniff in, inhale.

hidung nose. *- belang* womanizer, philanderer. *- cérét* spout of a kettle. *- mancung* sharp, fine-shaped nose. *- péok* pug nose. **meng- 1** nasal. **2** acquiescent, submissive, passive, compliant. **ke-²an** nasal.

hidup 1 be alive, live. *Hanya ibunya yg masih -* Only her mother is still alive. *Api masih -* The fire is still burning. *siaran - live broadcast. ular - live snake. *Pabrik gula terus - The sugar factory continued to operate. *Apakah perkumpulan sépak bola itu masih -* Does that soccer club still exist? *- dlm batas kemampuannya* live within o.'s means. *- seranjang mati seliang* together in life and in death. *se- semati* in life and death. **2** life. *Cerita -nya menarik* The story of her life is interesting. *- bahagia* the good life. *- berbaur* lead a married life. *- berdampingan* coexistence. *- kelamin* sex life. **3** fresh. *sayur -* fresh vegetables. *cerita yg -* a vivid story. **4** (*Coll.*) run, go, esp. of machines. *Jam ini tdk -* This clock is not running. *Selama siang hari lampu ini tetap -* During the daytime this light continues to burn. *Di zaman perang jalan ini - kembali* During the war this road was again in use. *Mesin itu tdk mau -* The engine will not start. *Mesin mobilnya masih -* Her engine is still running. **5** long live! **6** (*Ling.*) prevocalic (of consonants). **-²(an)** alive. *Ia ditangkap ~* He was captured alive. *menguburkan ~* bury alive. *membakar ~* burn alive. **meng-i** support, provide sustenance for. *Ia hrs ~ delapan org anak* She has to support eight children. *Tanah itu dpt ~ kita* That land can sustain us. *LAPAN hrs ~ industri swasta* The National Aeronautics and Space Agency must sustain private industry. *~ diri* sustain o.s. **meng-kan 1** revive, bring to life. **2** turn on (radio, TV, light, etc.), start (engine). **3** light (stove, lamp, etc.). **4** rekindle (interest, political party, etc.). **memper-** invigorate, stimulate, enliven subsistence. *~ kembali* revival. **ke-an 1** life. **2** existence. **peng-an 1** o.'s way of living. *~nya lumayan sekarang* His life-style is rather good now. **2** livelihood.

hierarki see HIRARKI.

higiéne hygiene. *~ perusahaan* industrial hygiene.

higiénis hygienic.

hih Ugh! (exclamation of distaste, disgust). *-! Anak haram, kau berdusta* Dammit! Bastard, you're lying!

hihi sound of twittering and giggling.

hii, hiih (*Ch*) Oh! (exclamation of terror).

hijau 1 green, verdant. *- daun* chlorophyll. *- gadung/kemuda-mudaan* light green. *- lumut* moss green. *- tentara* army green. **2** inexperienced. *Ia masih -* He is still green. **meng-** be or turn green. *Sawahnya sedang ~* His rice fields were in the green stage. **meng-kan 1** make s.t. green. **2** plant (us. on barren land). *Meréka akan ~ 365 ha. tanah tandus* They will plant on 365 hectares of barren land. **3** reforest, replant. **ke-an 1** greenness, verdancy. **2** verdure. **ke-²an** greenish. **-²an** greenery. **peng-an 1** greening of s.t. **2** planting, us. on implanted land. **3** reforesting, reforestation.

hijrah (*Isl.*) flight of Muh. from Mecca to Medina. **ber-** evacuate. *Tentara kita ~ dr daérah itu* Our army evacuated that region. **meng-kan 1** cause s.o. to move to another place. **2** (*Mil.*) evacuate s.o. **peng-an** evacuation (of troops).

hijriah of the Isl. calendar.

hikayat 1 tale, story, romance. **2** history, account. **ber-** narrate, tell stories. *Kita gemar mendengarkan nénék ~* We enjoy listening to grandmother tell stories. **meng-kan** narrate stories.

hikmah, hikmat 1 wisdom, philosophy. *Jangan terlalu sedih. Ambillah - kejadian ini* Do not be too sad. Take what happened as a lesson. *- Illahi* Divine Wisdom. **2** magical power. **3** power in general. **ber- 1** possess wisdom. **2** possess magical power. **meng-i 1** cast a spell over s.o. **2** enchant, bewitch s.o. *Kecantikannya ~nya* Her beauty enchanted him.

hikwan (*Ch*) fish balls.

hilang 1 be lost, vanish. *Segala miliknya - selama peperangan* All his property was lost during the war. *Kapal itu - di laut* The ship vanished at sea. *Perasaan sakitnya -* The sick feeling went away. *- akal* lose o.'s senses, be rattled. *- ingatan* unconscious, fainted. *- terkikis* **1** carried away. **2** lost, vanished, evaporated. *- lenyap* completely vanish, disappear without a trace. **meng-lenyapkan** cause to disappear. *- muka* lose face. *- pencaharian* lose o.'s livelihood. *- pikiran* unconscious, fainted. *- seri* **1** (*Chem.*) volatile. **2** melt into thin air. *- tempur* missing in action. **2** pass away, die. *Ibunya tlh -* His mother has vanished. *- arwah* faint, unconscious. *- nyawa* be dead. *- semangat* discouraged. **meng-** disappear. *Pencopét itu ~ di tengah org ramai* The pickpocket disappeared in the crowd. **meng-kan 1** cause s.t. to be lost, make disappear. *Tukang sulap itu ~ saputangan* The magician made a handkerchief disappear. *~ diri* disappear. *~ haus* quench a thirst. *~ lapar* still o.'s hunger. *~ sakit* deaden the pain. **2** omit, leave out, delete. *Ketika ia membaca buku itu, ia ~ beberapa fasal* When she read the book, she omitted several sections. *-kan pernyataan itu dr laporan* Strike that statement from the record. **ke-an 1** suffer from a loss. *Indonésia tlh ~ seorg putra besar* Indonesia has lost a great son. *Bp ~ kerja* Dad lost his job. *Aku akan ~ kau, jika kau pergi* I will miss you if you go. **2** loss. *~ akal* lose o.'s head, be desperate. *~ darah* loss of blood. *~ muka* lose face. **peng-** remover. *~ cat kuku* nail polish remover. **peng-an 1** removal. **2** eradication, elimination.

hilap see KHILAF.

hilat see HÉLAH.

hilir lower course, downstream. *Kayu hanyut ke -* Wood floated downstream. *- mudik* up and down, back and forth. *berjalan - mudik dlm kamar* walk up and down in a room. *tak tentu - mudiknya* making no sense. *Ceritanya tak tentu - mudiknya* I could not make head or tail of her story. **meng-mudikkan** steer, lead by the nose. *Ny. Abadi ~mudikkan suaminya* Mr. Abadi does whatever his wife says. **se-** *semudik* be of the same view. **ber-an** stream down. *Keringatnya ~* The perspiration streamed down. *Mukanya ~ darah* Blood streamed down his face. **meng-** go downstream. *mendayung ~* row downstream. **meng-i** travel s.t. downstream. **meng-kan 1** let go downstream, set adrift in a downstream direction. ~ *perahunya* let o.'s boat drift away. **2** steer s.t. ~ *débat* steer the debate. **ke-an** have s.t. genetically inherited. *Apakah dia ~ darah bangsawan di badannya?* Does he have noble blood in his veins? **-an 1** downstream course of a river. **2** (*Med.*) fistula.

himar zebra.

himbau see IMBAU.

himmah, himmat see HÉMAT$_{1,2}$.

himne a solemn song, often the anthem of an organization.

himpit ber- 1 be very close together. ~ *kaki* crosslegged. **2** (*Math.*) coincide. **ber-²** pressed together. **ber-an** very close to e.o., pressing close on e.o. **meng-** squeeze, press. ~ *kertas dgn batu* hold papers down with a stone (as paperweight). *Dlm kecelakaan itu ia di- mobilnya* In the accident he was pinned under his car. **meng-kan 1** squeeze against. **2** lap over (of seams). **memper-(²)kan** bring s.t. together, wedge together. **ter- 1** weighed down. **2** wedged in. **3** be in a tight spot, be in a jam. **-an** press, crush. **peng-an** pressing, squeezing.

himpun ber- assemble, gather. **ber-²** collect together. *Harga ~* The costs pyramided. **meng-kan 1** assemble, gather (o.'s friends, etc.). **2** collect. ~ *tulisan-tulisan penyair* collect the writings of a poet. **3** accumulate (wealth, etc.). **ter-** collected, assembled. **-an 1** association, club. **2** collection, compilation. ~ *syair* collection of poems. **peng- 1** gatherer, collector. ~ *listrik* storage battery. **2** compiler. **peng-an** accumulation, collection. **per-an 1** association, organization. ~ *mahasiswa* student federation. **2** gathering place, place of assembly.

hina contemptible. *Itu perbuatan yg -* That is a contemptible thing to do. *gubuk -* a humble hut (in self-deprecating reference to o.'s home). *- dina/lata/papa* **1** very humble, lowly. **2** abject (poverty, etc.). **meng- 1** humiliate, insult. *Itu ~ dong!* Hey, that is insulting! **2** affront, offend s.o. ~ *diri* abase or degrade o.s. **meng-kan** insult on behalf of s.o. **ter-** degraded, insulted. **ke-an 1** humbleness, humility. **2** humiliation. **3** baseness, meanness, opprobrium. **-an 1** insult, indignity, affront. **2** taunt, gibe. **peng-an** degradation, causing humiliation.

hinai see INAI.

hindar meng- 1 pull to o. side. *Mobil itu ~ memberi jalan kpd mobil yg lain* The car pulled to the side to make way for the other car. **2** avoid (a blow, etc.). *Ia ~ ketika saya memukulnya* She dodged when I tried to hit her. *Sulit sekali menemuinya sebab ia selalu ~* It is really hard to meet her because she always avoids visitors. **meng-i** avoid s.t. *Saya selalu mencoba - kesukaran* I have always tried to avoid difficulties. ~ *pajak* evade taxes. **meng-kan** put s.t out of the way so that it can be avoided. *Ia ~ pukulan saya* He deflected

my blow. ~ *rasa curiga* remove suspicion. **terspared**. *Ia ~ dr bahaya* She escaped from danger. **ter-kan** can be avoided. **peng-** evader. ~ *pajak* tax evader. **peng-an 1** avoidance, prevention. **2** evasion (of taxes, etc.).

Hindia (*Lit.*) Indies. *- Belanda* Netherlands E. Indies. *Lautan -* Indian Ocean.

hindu see INDUK.

Hindu 1 Hindu. *- Dharma* Balinese Hinduism. **2** (*Amb*) pagan. **meng-kan** hinduize.

hinduisasi hinduization.

hingar noisy. *--bingar* tumultuous. **ke-bingaran** boisterousness. **meng-** become noisy. **meng-i** annoy s.o. by being boisterous.

hingga until, up to. *Ia makan - kenyang* He ate until he had enough. *- kini/sekarang* up till now, until now. *dr perut - ke kepala* from the belly up to the head. **se- 1** until. *Ia makan ~ ia merasa puas* She ate until she felt satisfied. **2** with the result that. *begitu . . . ~ so . . . that. Ia begitu sakit ~ ia hrs msk rumah sakit* He was so sick that he had to go to the hospital. **ber-** limited, finite. *Keajaiban alam tdk ~* Nature's wonders are boundless. **memper-kan, meng-kan** set a limit, limit, determine. **ter-** limited. *terima kasih saya yg tiada ~* my unbounded thanks. *tdk ~* infinite. **per-an** limit, boundary.

hinggap 1 perch, alight. *Burung itu - di atas dahan* The bird perched on the limb. **2** attack (of disease, infection, etc.). *Penyakit itu - pd meréka* The disease struck them. **meng-** alight (on s.t.). **meng-i 1** alight, perch on. *Burung itu ~ dahan* The bird alighted on a branch. *Stoplés itu di-i lalat* A fly alighted on the stoppered jar. **2** descend (up)on. *Demam industrialisasi ~ negara-negara berkembang* The frenzy of industrialization is descending on the developing nations. **3** get attacked by. *Ia di-i penyakit* She got an illness. **meng-kan 1** cause to perch. *Ia ~ burung di ranting* He let the bird perch on a branch. **2** set in place. *Kejadian itu hrs di-kan dlm proporsi yg sebenarnya* The event must be put in its true proportion.

hintai see INTAI.

hio (*Ch*) joss stick.

hiolo (*Ch*) incense burner.

hioswa see HIO.

hiperbole hyperbole.

hiperbolis hyperbolic.

hiperbolisme hyperbolism.

hiperténsi hypertension.

hipis 1 young Western traveler on a low budget. **2** a style of Western-influenced grooming characterized by unkempt hair and clothing. *celana -* frayed pants.

HIPMI [*Himpunan Pengusaha Muda Indonésia*] Indonesian Association of Young Businessmen.

hipnotis hypnotic. **meng-** hypnotize.

hipnotisir meng- hypnotize.

hipnotisme hypnotism.

hipokrasi hypocrisy.

hipokrit hypocrite.
hipoték mortgage. **meng-kan** mortgage (o.'s house, etc.).
hipotenusa (*Math.*) hypotenuse.
hipotésa, hipotésis hypothesis.
hipuk see IPUK.
hirap disappear, vanish. **meng- 1** disappear, vanish. **2** hide.
hirarki hierarchy.
hirarkis hierarchical.
hirau meng-kan heed, note, pay attention to. *Ia tdk ~ kata-kata bapaknya* She ignored her father's words.
hiris see IRIS.
hiru-biru see HARU-BIRU.
hiru-hara see HURU-HARA.
hiruk -*pikuk/piruk* tumult, hullabaloo, hurly-burly (of the crowd). **ke-pirukan** racket, noise, din. **meng-kan 1** make a fuss over s.t. **2** cause a commotion, disturb. **peng-** o. who causes a disturbance.
hirup meng- 1 draw on, inhale (cigarette, etc.). **2** slurp (up), sip at. ~ *kopi* sip at coffee. **3** sniff in. ~ *udara segar* suck in fresh air. **4** (*Ling.*) implosive. **-an** whiff, sniff. ~ *kopi* a whiff of coffee. **peng-an** inhalation.
his₁ 1 Shame! (explanation of scorn). **2** Shhh!
his₂ (*Coll.*) yeast.
HIS [*Hollandsch Inlandsche School*] Dutch medium primary school for the indigenous elite (colonial period).
hisab computation, calculation, reckoning. **meng-** (*Astr.*) calculate, compute. **ter-** counted. **peng-an** computing, calculating of.
hisak see ISAK.
hisap see ISAP.
hisit (*Ch*) shark fin (for soup).
histéri hysteria.
histeris hysterical.
histologi (*Med.*) histology.
histologik (*Med.*) histological.
historikus historian.
historiografi historiography.
historis historic, historical.
historisitas historicity.
hit extremely popular. *Lagu ini lagi jadi - bulan ini* This song is still very popular this month.
hitam 1 black. - *arang* carbon black. - *bogot* hideously black. - *di atas putih* in black and white, in writing. - *hangus* carbon black. - *jengat/kumbang/ legam/lotong* pitch or jet black. - *mata* iris (of eye). - *pekat* pitch black. - *putihnya* decisiveness, certainty. - *seram* black or dark and frightening (look). - *tedas* pitch black. **2** dark, swarthy. - *manis* dark and attractive (complexion). **meng-** become black. *Malam* ~ The night deepened. **meng-i** blacken (hair, teeth). *Asap* ~ *angkasa* Smoke blackened the sky. **meng-kan 1** blacken (hair, teeth). **2** blacken, denigrate, sully (a reputation). **ke-an 1** blackness. ~ *rambut* the blackness of hair. **2** very black. *rambut* ~ very black hair. **ke-²an** blackish. **peng-** blackener, blacking

agent. ~ *alis* eyebrow pencil. **peng-an** blackening. ~ *gigi* tooth blackening.
hitung (*Coll.*) arithmetic. **ber- 1** count. *Anak itu dpt ~ sampai sepuluh* That child can count to 10. ~ *kepala* mental arithmetic. **2** confer, discuss. **meng- 1** count, do sums. *boléh di- dgn jari* can be counted on the fingers of a hand. ~ *uang* count the money. **2** calculate. ~ *dgn dolar* calculate in dollars. *Gaji saya di- dr bulan April* My salary is calculated from April. **3** count in, reckon. *Ménténg di- sbg daérah méwah* Menteng is considered a wealthy neighborhood. **meng-i** count repeatedly. **meng-kan** count for s.o. **memper-kan 1** calculate, estimate. ~ *banyaknya tamu yg akan datang* calculate the number of guests coming. **2** calculate on, take into consideration (when calculating). *Ia lupa* ~ *kemungkinan pergantian politik perdagangan pemerintah* He forgot to take into consideration the possibility of a change in the gvt. trade policy. **3** count on. *Ia tak dpt diper-kan* She cannot be counted on. **4** cover. ~ *hutangnya dgn uang yg dijanjikan oléh ayahnya* cover his debt with money promised by his father. **ter- 1** counted, calculated. *tak* ~ innumerable, countless, numberless. **2** counted, included. *Dlm bilangan itu blm* ~ *meréka yg datang terlambat* Those who came late were not included in that number. **-an 1** count. *Apakah ~mu benar?* Is your count correct? ~ *angka-angka* numerical count. ~ *dagang* commercial or business arithmetic. **2** (*Sport*) count (boxing, wrestling, etc.). **peng- 1** bank teller. **2** counter, checker. ~ *cepat* speedometer. ~ *detik* stopwatch. **peng-an** counting, enumeration. **per-an 1** calculation, computation. ~ *laba rugi* balance sheet. **2** accounting. **3** consideration. *Itu sdh msk ~ saya* I have already taken that into consideration.
hiu shark. - *gergaji* k.o. sawfish. *keméjan* k.o. shark. - *kepala martil* hammerhead shark. - *pari* beaked ray. - *pedang/todak* k.o. sawfish.
hiung meng- whistle.
hiur see IUR.
hiwan see HIKWAN.
HKBP [*Huria Kristen Batak Protéstan*] The Batak Protestant Church.
hla see LHA.
hlm. [*halaman*] page (of book).
hlo see LHO.
HMI [*Himpunan Mahasiswa Islam*] Muslim Students' Association.
ho oh! -*! Seharusnya kupalu kepalamu!* Oh! I should knock you on the head!
HO, ho. [*hongeroedeem*] malnutrition.
Hoakiau, Hoakiauw overseas Chinese.
hobat see OBAT.
hobi 1 hobby, s.t. o. likes. **2** like s.t. *Dia - main bola* He likes to play soccer.
hodeng comportment, the way o. carries o.s.
hofméster chief musician of a palace (colonial period).
ho ho sound of laughter.
hoi Hey! (esp. when calling s.o. from afar).

hojat see HUJAT.

hokah hookah.

hoki (*Ch*) good luck. *Rumah itu sdh - bagi saya* This house brings me luck. *Kami sedang -* We're in luck.

hokki field hockey. *- és* hockey.

hol (*Isl.*) annual, ritual feast to commemorate the dead.

Holan, Hollan (*Coll.*) Netherlands.

holopis (kuntul baris) Yo-heave-ho (exclamation to summon up strength when lifting things). **ber-** work together.

homo male homosexual. **ber-** (²) engage in (male) homosexual activities.

homogén homogeneous. **ke-an** homogeneity.

homonim homonym. **ke-an** homonymy.

homonimi homonymy.

homoséksual, homoséksuil, homoséks see HOMO.

homoséksualitas homosexuality.

honar see ONAR.

honda (*Coll.*) motorcycle.

hong₁ (*Sport*) home base.

hong₂ earthen pipe for drainage.

hong₃ see BURUNG.

Hongaria Hungary.

hongeroedeem, hongerudim malnutrition, undernourishment.

honggi see HONGI.

honghouw (*Ch*) empress.

hongi punitive 17th-century expeditions by Dutch in the Moluccas to extirpate spice trees.

hongsi (*Ch*) rheumatism.

honor, honorarium 1 honorarium, stipend. 2 payment for services. **meng-** give a honorarium. *Pengarang itu di- Rp10.000* The author was given a 10,000 rupiah honorarium.

honorér 1 honorary. *anggota -* honorary member. 2 not officially confirmed (in o.'s job) and so paid by stipends not salary. *pegawai -* employee paid by honorarium.

honorifik honorific.

hooi see HOI.

hop₁ (*Coll.*) head, chief. *- jawatan* department or division chief. *- agén* police sergeant. *- biro* police headquarters. *- kantor* head office. *- komisaris polisi* chief police commissioner.

hop₂ Stop! Whoah! (exclamation only). *-! tunggu dulu!* Stop, just a minute!

hopbiro (*Coll.*) central (gvt.) office.

hopéng, hoping (*Ch*) close friend.

hopyes hard coffee-flavored caramel.

horas Greetings! Long live! (Batak greeting).

hordén, hordéng curtains, drapery.

horé Hurrah! Hurray!

horison horizon.

horisontal horizontal.

hormat 1 honor, respect, esteem. *Sampaikanlah - saya pd bapakmu* Please give your father my regards. *memberi - kpd* pay homage to. *- dan salam (dari)* with the compliments (of). 2 respectful. *Sikapnya selalu ramah dan -* His attitude is always

friendly and respectful. *Dgn -* Dear Sir (in letters). *- saya* Respectfully yours. **ber-** 1 pay respect. 2 respected (person). **ber-²an, - meng-i** 1 show mutual respect. 2 salute e.o. **meng-** (*Mil.*) salute. **meng-i** honor, respect, revere. *~ org tuamu* Honor your parents. *~ undang-undang negara* respect a country's laws. **ter-** esteemed, respected, honored. *warganegara yg ~ a* respected citizen. *Yg ~ . . .* Dear . . . (in letters). *Sdr-sdr yg ~!* Ladies and Gentlemen! *Tuan-Tuan yg ~* Dear Sirs. **ke-an** 1 honor. *Itu suatu ~ bagi kami* That is an honor for us. *pengawal ~* honor guard. *merusak ~ wanita* damage a woman's honor, rape a woman. *~ diri* self-esteem, self-respect. 2 honorary. *anggota ~* honorary member. *nama ~* epithet. *visa ~* courtesy visa. **peng-an** giving honor, respecting. *mengibarkan bendéra sbg ~ kedatangan présidén* fly flags in honor of the president's arrival.

hormon hormone.

horn /horen/ ice-cream cone.

horoskop horoscope.

hortikultura horticulture.

hortikulturis horticulturist.

hoskut housecoat, dressing gown.

hospés (*Biol.*) viral or bacterial host. *- intermédiér* intermediate host.

hospital hospital. **meng-kan** hospitalize.

hospitalisasi hospitalization.

hostés 1 taxi dancer, bar waitress. 2 prostitute.

hosti (*Rel.*) host, consecrated wafer. *- Suci* Holy Eucharist.

hot (*Coll.*) 1 sexy. *celana -* hot pants. 2 sexually aroused. *Aku rasa -* I feel horny. 3 very popular. *lagu -* hot song.

hotdog /hotdok/ sandwich in hot dog bun.

hotél hotel. *- kelas kambing* fleabag hotel. *- megah* luxury hotel. *- perdéo/prodéo* (*Coll.*) jail, prison. **meng-prodéoan** jail, imprison, confine, incarcerate. **meng-kan** put s.o. in a hotel. **per-an** hotel affairs, hotel management. *sekolah ~* hotel school.

houder /hoder/ cartridge pouch or box on soldier's belt.

hower k.o. artillery piece.

hoyak see OYAK₂.

hoyong see HUYUNG.

HPH [*Hak Pengusahaan Hutan*] logging concession.

hr. [*harian*] daily newspaper.

Hr. [*honor*] stipend, honorarium.

hrs. [*harus*] must.

huap see SUAP.

hubaya-hubaya make sure that . . ., above all, by all means. *Kalau ingin berhasil - engkau bekerja teliti* If you want to succeed, by all means work accurately. *Kami harap - hal itu tdk terjadi* We surely hope that it will not happen.

hubung ber- connected, related. *Kedua kejadian itu ~ satu sama lain* The two incidents are related. *~ dgn* 1 due to, owing to, seeing that. *Keberangkatan kami diundur ~ dgn keadaan udara* *yg buruk* Our departure was postponed owing to bad weather. **2** with regard to, in connection with. *~ dgn pentingnya hal itu, kita hrs bertindak cepat* With regard to the importance of that matter we have to act quickly. **ber-an 1** related to s.t. **2** get in touch, be in contact. *Saya hrs ~ dulu dgn pemerintah saya* I must first get in touch with my gvt. *Selama perjalanan itu ia selalu ~ dgn saya* During that trip he was always in contact with me. **meng-i 1** contact, get in touch with. *-ilah kantor kami* Please contact our office. **2** get ahold of. *Ia ~ alamat itu* He got ahold of the address. **meng-kan 1** connect, join. *Keréta api ini ~ kedua kota itu* This train connects those two cities. **2** put s.o. in contact with s.o. *Nanti saya -kan Bp dgn diréktur saya* Wait, I will put you in contact with my director. *~ diri* merge, ally (o.s.). **-an 1** connection, relationship. *Antara kedua kejadian itu ada ~nya* There is a connection between the two incidents. *dlm ~ ini* in this connection. *~ keluarga* family relationship. *~ antaragama* interreligious relationship. *~ diplomatik* diplomatic relations. *~ jajar (Elec.)* parallel connections in wiring. *~ masyarakat* public relations. *~ nyawa* sweetheart. *~ péndék/singkat (Elec.)* short circuit. *(Tel.) ~ télpon langsung* hot line. *~ tertutup/terbatas (Elec.)* closed circuit. *~ timbal balik* interaction. **2** contact. *Itulah ~ saya yg terakhir dgn dia* That was my last contact with him. **3** context. *dipandang dlm ~ zamannya . . .* viewed in the context of its time . . . *~ kalimat (Ling.)* sentential context. **4** coupling (in poetry). **se-an** *dgn* in connection with. **peng-** s.o. or s.t. which connects. *perwira ~* liaison officer. *~ télpon* telephone operator. *saluran ~* connecting channel. **peng-an** connecting, relating. **per-an 1** communications (radio, highway, etc.). **2** liaison. **3** relationship. *~ perdagangan* trade relations.

huduh see ODOH.

huh Ha! (exclamation of derision, scorn, etc.). *Hidup méwah, -!* You call that living luxuriously!

hujah proof, evidence. **ber-** argue, adduce arguments.

hujan rain. *- batu/beku* hail. *- buntut* steady drizzle. *- deras* downpour. *- batu di negeri sendiri, drp - emas di negeri org* There's no place like home (lit., better a shower of stones at home than a shower of gold abroad). *- és* hail, sleet. *- gerimis* drizzle. *- kerikil* hail. *- lebat* downpour, cloudburst. *- panas* rain while sun is shining. **meng-panaskan** soak s.o. with rain and sweat. *- peluru* hail of bullets. *- renyai-renyai/renik-renik/rintik-rintik* drizzle, drizzling. *musim -* rainy season. **ber-** rainy. *senja ~ a* rainy dusk. **ber-²** go about in the rain. **meng-** become like rain (of arrows, etc.). **meng-i 1** rain on s.o. or s.t. **2** shower s.o. with s.t. *Meréka ~ saya dng pemberian* They showered me with gifts. **meng-kan 1** shower s.t. on s.o. **2** let s.t. get rained on. **memper-kan** let s.t. get rained on, expose to weather. *~ garamnya* neglect o.s. or o.'s family. **ke-an** get caught in rain. **peng-** rainy. *musim ~* times when there is a great deal of rain.

hujat blasphemy. **meng-** blasphemy. **peng-an** act of blasphemy.

hujung see UJUNG.

huk₁ /huk/ (*Sport*) hook. *- kanan* right hook. *Bolanya -* His (golf)ball hooked.

huk₂ (*Coll.*) **1** corner (of room). **2** intersection.

huk-huk 1 sound of coughing. **2** coughing. *Ia - saja sehabis makan buah* She did nothing but cough after eating the fruit.

hukum 1 law. *- acara* law of procedure. *- acara pidana* law of criminal procedure. *- adat* a traditional law. *- alam* **1** law of nature, natural law. **2** law of the jungle. *- bunyi (Ling.)* sound law. *- dagang* commercial law. *- keuangan* monetary law. *- lingkungan* environmental law. *- maddi* material law. *- niaga* business or commercial law. *- pembuktian* law of evidence. *- perdata* civil law. *- perikatan* contract law. *- perselisihan* law of conflict. *- pidana* criminal law. *- resam* traditional law. *- rimba* mob rule, law of the jungle. *- syarak* Isl. canon law. *- tantra* public law. *- tatanegara* constitutional law. *- tuntutan* law of procedure. *- warganegara* citizenship law. *- waris* inheritance law. *- yg sepuluh (Rel.)* the Ten Commandments. **2** verdict. *- bunuh/mati* death verdict. *- gantung* sentence to hang (till death). *- pasung* sentence to stocks. *- penjara* imprisonment. *- taklik* suspended sentence. **ber-** have rules, follow laws. **meng- 1** punish s.o. *tindakan ~* punitive action. **2** judge, criticize. *Org terlalu mudah ~* People judge too easily. **3** sentence to. *Dia di- lima tahun* He was sentenced to five years. *~ denda* fine s.o. **ter- 1** sentenced. **2** punished. **-an 1** punishment. *~ badan* corporal punishment. *~ bersyarat* suspended sentence. *~ gantung* a sentence to hang. *~ kawalan* sentence of restricted freedom of movement. *~ kerja* punishment by hard labor. *~ kurungan/penjara/tutupan* imprisonment. *~ mati* death sentence. *~ picis* archaic form of public execution in which passersby were required to cut the body of the condemned. **2** o. who has had a sentence passed on him. *org ~* prisoner. **ke-an** legal, juridical. *syarat-syarat ~* legal conditions.

hulam see ULAM.

huler rice huller.

hulu₁ 1 upper course (of river). *- sungai* upper reaches of river, headwaters. **2** beginning of s.t. (in set phrases). *- dinihari* around four a.m. *- malang* the beginning of all misery. **ber-(kan)** have its upper reach at. **meng-** go upstream, go to the headquarters. **-(²)an** upriver region. **peng-** see PENGHULU. **pe(r)-an** interior. *di ~ Kalimantan* in the interior of Borneo.

hulu₂ 1 upper end (of a pole). **2** hilt. *- keris* hilt of a kris. **3** top of head, head (in certain phrases only). *- kepala* crown of head. *beradu -* meet head on. **ber-kan** have a handle, be adorned with a hilt. **meng-kan** (*Lit.*) serve as leader of. *Ia ~ seisi rumah dlm pembacaan do'a* He led the whole family in the reciting of prayers.

hulubalang 1 commander, war chief. **2** district chief (in Aceh). **meng-i** command s.o.

hulur see ULUR₁.

huma 1 field for dry rice cultivation. **2** newly cleared land for agriculture. **ber- 1** grow rice on dry field. **2** clear land for cultivation. **per-an 1** dry rice cultivation. **2** clearing (of field). ~ *berpindah-pindah* shifting cultivation.

humaniora the humanities.

humanisme humanism.

Humas [*Hubungan Masyarakat*] public relations.

humbalang see HEMBALANG.

humor joke. *cerita* - funny story.

humoris humorist.

humoristis humorous.

hun (*Ch*) unit of measure for weight (¹⁄₁₀ *tael*) or length (¹⁄₁₂ inch).

huncué (*Ch*) tobacco pipe.

huni ber- occupied. *rumah yg* ~ an occupied house. **meng-** occupy, dwell or reside in. *Hanya hantu-hantu saja yg* ~ *rumah itu* Only ghosts dwell in that house. **meng-kan** cause s.o. to settle. **pe(ng)-** 1 occupant, inhabitant, dweller. **2** denizen, inmate. **3** guardian spirit. *Rumah itu ada* ~*nya* 1 The house is occupied. 2 There is a ghost in that house. **peng-an** occupancy. **ke-peng-an** occupancy, occupation.

hunjam meng- 1 pierce s.t. so it is fixed. ~ *tusu-kan ke tubuhnya* thrust a stab at his body. **2** penetrate. *Naséhat itu* ~ *ke dlm hatinya* The advice penetrated her mind. **3** (*Av.*) dive. **meng-kan 1** thrust in, insert (by stabbing). *Ia* ~ *pisaunya ke perut lawannya* He planted his knife in his opponent's belly. **2** shower on. *Ia* ~ *pukulan-pukulan smash pd lawannya* He battered his opponent with smashes. **ter-** stuck, inserted. *Tiangnya* ~ *di dlm tanah* The stick was stuck into the ground. **peng-** ~ *tenggala* plowshare.

hunjuk see UNJUK.

hunkwé k.o. gelatin made from mung bean flour.

hunus meng- unsheathe, draw (sword). **ter-** unsheathed (sword, dagger).

hunyi see HUNI.

hup hup exclamation to encourage o. to jump.

hura Hooray! (exclamation of pleasure, delight). **ber-** shout hurrah.

hura-hura (*Sl.*) not to be taken seriously.

huria (*Sumatra*) district.

huruf letter, characters. - *buta* vowelless Arabic script. - *balok* block letters. - *besar* capital letters. - *bunyi* vowel. - *cétak* printed characters. - *emas* gold lettering. - *gajah* capital letters. - *gundul* vowelless Arabic script. - *harakah/hidup* vowel. - *jawi* Arabic script for Indonesian and Malay. - *kanji* Ch characters in Japanese. - *kecil* lower case letter. - *latin* roman script. - *lepas* printed-style letters. - *majemuk* digraph. - *mati* consonant. - *miring* italics, cursive script. - *rangkap* digraph. - *saksi* vowel mark in Arabic script. - *sambung* cursive script letters. - *tebal* boldface type. - *timbul* raised embossed letter. - *tulis* cursive writing. *menurut* - word for word, literal. **ber-** use letter characters.

hurufuah see HARFIAH.

huru-hara 1 disturbance. - *rasial* racial disturbance. **2** hurly-burly. **3** riot. *pasukan* - riot police. **ber-** (run) riot. **meng-kan** excite to violence, bring about confusion.

hurung see URUNG.

hurup see HURUF.

hus hush! be quiet! **meng-²kan** hush s.t. up.

husap see USAP.

husaren sla k.o. vegetable and fruit salad with mayonnaise and sometimes bits of cold meats.

husé Hurrah!

Hussain (*Isl.*) grandson of Muh. martyred in religious war. Hussain's and his brother Hassan's deaths are commemorated on *Asyura*.

hustis see HOSTÉS.

husuk see KHUSYU.

husus see KHUSUS.

husy see HUS.

Hut (*Zod.*) Pisces.

HUT [*hari ulang tahun*] anniversary, birthday.

hutan woods, forest. - *belantara/belukar* 1 dense forest, jungle. 2 wilderness. - *larangan* forest preserve. - *lepas* extensive jungle, jungle expanse. - *lindung* protected forest. - *payau* tidal forest. - *perawan* virgin forest. - *rimba* extensive jungle, jungle expanse. - *suaka* forest preserve, national park. - *tropika basah/humida* tropical rain forest. - *tutupan* forest preserve. - *wisata* national park. **meng-** be a forest. **meng-i** forest s.t, cause a forest to grow. **meng-kan 1** reforest, turn s.t. into a forest. **2** abandon to the jungle. **ke-an** forestry, silviculture. *Jawatan* ~ Bureau of Forestry. **peng-an** forestation. **per-an 1** forestry affairs. **2** forestry service.

hutang debt, obligation. - *negara* national debt. - *budi* debt of honor. **ber-** *budi* 1 be deeply indebted. **2** credit. **ber-** owe. *Ia* ~ *seratus ribu rupiah* She owes 100,000 rupiah. ~ *nyawa* owe o.'s life. ~ *piutang* debit and credit. ~ *tiap helai bulu* up to o.'s ears in debt. **meng-i** lend. *Ia* ~ *temannya lima ratus rupiah* He lent his friend 500 rupiah. **2** put s.o. in o.'s debt. *Dia* ~ *saya* He put me in his debt. **meng-kan** lend s.t. **memper-kan 1** lend s.t. to s.o. **2** borrow. **ter-** owed. **-an** having a debt. **peng-** debtor.

huyung meng-kan cause o. to stagger. **ter-²** stagger, falter. *Ia berjalan* ~ *keluar dr kamar* He staggered out of the room.

HVS [*houtvrij schrijfpapier*] bond paper of 60-100 gram thickness (lit., bondpaper free of wood).

hwa-hwé (*Ch*) popular game of numbers for gambling.

hwéé (*Ch*) association.

hyang title of autochthonous or Hindu deity. - *Wisnu* Vishnu.

hydrolistrik see HIDROLISTRIK.

hygiéne see HIGIÉNE.

hygiénis see HIGIÉNIS.

hyperténsi see HIPERTÉNSI.

hypnotisir see HIPNOTISIR.

I

i /i/ i, the 9th letter of the alphabet.

ia₁ (*Lit.*) he, she, it.

ia₂ yes. *-lah* yes, indeed. **se-** unanimous. *Meréka ~ membeli gedung itu* They were unanimous in their decision to buy that building. *~ sekata* unanimous. *Meréka ~ sekata utk menutup pertemuan* They were unanimous about adjourning the meeting. **ber-** say yes. *~ berbukan* consult, negotiate. *Meréka ~ berbukan dlm perembukan menjualbeli tanah* They negotiated in their discussion about buying and selling land. **ber-²** 1 agree repeatedly, always answer in the affirmative. *Ia ~ saja* He says yes to everything. 2 discuss, deliberate. **meng-kan** agree to s.t., answer s.t. in the affirmative. *Aku hanya mengangguk ~* I just nodded in agreement. **peng-** yes-man. **peng-an** comparison.

IAIN [*Institut Agama Islam Negeri*] Gvt. Institute for Isl. Studies.

ialah is, are (in formal statements of equivalence). *Bahasa Indonésia - bahasa nasional* Indonesian is the national language.

iau see NGIAU.

IB [*Irian Barat*] Irian Jaya (Indonesian New Guinea).

iba 1 pity, compassion. 2 moved, touched, compassionate. **ber-(²)** ask for compassion. *~ meminta* ask beseechingly. **meng-²** moved to compassion. **meng-i** pity s.o. **meng-kan** 1 cause s.o. to feel compassion. 2 feel compassion for. **ter-²** melancholic, sad. *Lagu Wilhélmus mendenging lemah berirama tenang ~* The Dutch anthem tinkled softly with a slow and melancholy rhythm. **ke-an** emotion, compassion. **peng-** tending to be compassionate.

ibadah, ibadat 1 act of devotion. 2 religious service. *rumah* - house of worship. *- suci* divine service. **ber-** 1 devout, pious. *org yg ~* a devout person. 2 worship, perform a religious service. *~ solat* (*Isl.*) observing the required prayers five times a day. **per-an** observance of religious duties.

ibah see HIBAH.

ibarat 1 like. *Tuti - kembang* Tuti is like a flower. 2 simile, metaphor. *Apa yg terkandung dlm kata-kata - itu?* What is contained in those metaphorical words? **ber-** contain a simile, be figurative. **meng-kan** 1 follow s.o.'s example. 2 compare s.t., say s.t. is like. *Dunia ini di-kan lembah kesusahan* This world is like a vale of sorrow. 3 utter a comparison. 4 treat like s.t. *Saya di-kannya kuda saja* He treated me just like a work horse.

ibing (*Sd*) **meng-** dance a traditional dance with a woman who is a professional entertainer. **peng-** female entertainer who dances with men in the audience. *~ ronggéng* female dancer.

iblis devil, Satan.

ibni, ibnu see BIN.

Ibrani (*Lit.*) Hebrew.

ibrit see NGIBRIT.

ibtida (*Lit.*) beginning.

ibtidaiyah (*Isl.*) primary school.

ibu 1 mother. *- angkat* foster mother. *- bapak* parents. **ke-bapakan** parental. *- kandung* natural mother. *- negara* first lady (president's wife). *- pertiwi/pratiwi* fatherland. *- suri* queen mother. *- tiri* stepmother. 2 form of address to older woman or o. in higher position, i.e. teacher, employer, etc., esp. as *bu. - guru* form of address to female teacher. *- kos* woman operating a boarding house. 3 lady, woman of high standing. *Ada seorg - yg mau menemui Bp* A lady has come to see you. *- rumah tangga* housewife. 4 most important or main part of s.t. *- akar* main root, taproot. *- jari* thumb. *- kaki* big toe. *- kota* capital city. *- kunci* lock, padlock. *- mata angin* cardinal points of the compass. *- negeri* capital. *- panah* bow (weapon). *- pasir* pebble. *- sungai* principal river. *- tangan* thumb. *- tangga* banister. *- tentara* main body of the army. **-²** 1 mothers. 2 Ladies (term of address). 3 of an age to be a mother. *O! Saya kira sdh ~* Oh! You're much younger than I thought you would be (lit., you are already of an age to be a mother)! **se-** having the same mother. *sdr ~* a sibling by virtue of having the same mother. **ber-** 1 have a mother. 2 call s.o. *ibu. Saya ~ kpd isteri kawan saya* I call my friend's wife *ibu.* **ber-kan** have a certain person as a mother. *~ seorg yg sangat miskin* have a very poor person as a mother. **meng-** call s.o. *ibu.* **ke-an** maternal, motherly. *kasih ~* motherly love. **ke-²an** feminine, motherly. **per-an** matriarchal. *masyarakat ~* matriarchal society.

ibuk see SIBUK.

ibul k.o. large thornless palm that yields poisonous fruit.

ibunda (*Lit.*) mother (used in letters).

ibus k.o. palm whose leaves are used for plaiting mats, etc.

icak-colé defaulter on payments.

icak-icak 1 pretend, act as if. 2 fake, spurious. **ber-** pretend, simulate. *Ia ~ pincang* He pretends to walk with a limp. **-an** false, pretended.

icip -² food sample. **meng-(i)** taste, try. *Meréka ~ makanan ini dulu* They had a taste of this food.

id (*Isl.*) holiday (in the names of certain celebrations).
ida (*Bali*) title of nobility.
idah₁ gift to establish ties of love between men and women, love token. **meng-** court by giving presents. **meng-kan** offer a gift as an introduction to courtship.
idah₂ see IDDAH.
idam 1 craving. **2** craving of pregnant woman for special foods. **3** desire, aspiration. **meng-1** crave, long or yearn for. **2** crave specific foods in the early stages of pregnancy. **meng-(²)kan** desire ardently, crave greatly. *sampai tercapai apa yg kita -kan* until we have achieved what we yearn for. **-an 1** what o. craves for, longs after. ~ *keibuan* maternal longing. **2** what o. aspires to. ~ *seluruh negara* the aspiration of the whole nation. **-²an** aspirations, ideal. *~nya tercapai* She achieved her aspirations.
idang see HIDANG.
idap meng-1 ail, be ill over a long period. *Kota itu masih ~ utang besar* That city suffers from a large debt. **2** contract (a disease). ~ *kanker* contract cancer. **meng-kan** suffer (a disease) over a long period. *Beratlah penyakit yg di-kannya* He has been suffering from a serious illness. **-an 1** persistent illness, disease. **2** sickly.
idayat see HIDAYAH.
iddah (*Isl.*) 100-day waiting period before a widow or divorced woman may remarry.
idé idea.
idéal ideal. **meng-kan** idealize.
idéalis idealist.
idéalisasi idealization. **meng-kan** idealize. ~ *tradisi asli* idealize native traditions.
idéalisir meng- idealize.
idéalisme idealism.
idéalistis idealistic.
idem idem, same as what went before.
idéntifikasi identification. **meng-kan** identify. **peng-an** identifying of.
idéntifisir meng- identify. ~ *beberapa tuntutan* identify several demands.
idéntik identical. **meng-kan 1** make identical. **2** consider identical.
idéntitas 1 identity. **2** identification.
idéologi ideology. **ber-kan** have a certain ideology. ~ *Pancasila* have the *Pancasila* as the ideology. **meng-kan** make s.t. the ideology. ~ *Islam* make Isl. the ideology.
idéologis ideological.
idep eyelash.
idep-idep better to do (so-and-so) than ... *Drp dibuang - diberikan org* Instead of throwing it away, it would be better to give it to s.o.
IDI [*Ikatan Dokter Indonésia*] Indonesian Physicians Association.
idih, idii ugh!, exclamation expressing distaste.
idil see IDUL.
idin see IZIN.
idiom idiom.
idiomatis idiomatic.

idola popular idol. - *remaja masa kini* the idol of today's teenagers.
idul (*Isl.*) - *Adha/Korban* feast of the sacrifice, the day that commemorates the sacrifice of Ismail by Ibrahim, a holy day associated with the pilgrimage to Mecca. - *Fitri* feast celebrating the end of fasting period.
idung see HIDUNG.
idup see HIDUP.
idzin see IZIN.
ied see ID.
ifaf, iffah (*Isl.*) sexual abstinence.
ifitah (*Isl.*) opening prayer.
ifrit evil spirit.
iftar (*Isl.*) ending of fast.
iga (*Jv*) rib. - *péndék* (*Anat.*) floating rib. - *selungkang* (*Anat.*) false rib.
igal meng-1 strut, show off. **2** display its feathers. **3** dance in a strutting way. **meng-kan** make s.t. dance. *Pantatnya di-kan, sangat tak pantas* It is very improper the way she wiggles her rear end. **-²an** dancing.
igama see AGAMA.
igau meng-1 talk in o.'s sleep. **2** be delirious, rave. **meng-kan** talk about s.t. while sleeping or delirious. **ter-** be talked about in a dream. *Kehilangan temannya selalu ~ oléhnya* He always talks in his sleep about the death of his friend. **-an 1** what is said in o.'s sleep or ravings. **2** delirium. **3** nonsense. **-²an** feel half asleep, still not fully awake. ~ *mimpi* nightmare.
igel see IGAL.
I'gris. [*Inggeris*] England, English.
ih ugh, exclamation showing disgust.
ihlas see IKHLAS.
ihram (*Isl.*) consecration for use in the pilgrimage to Mecca. *pakaian* - special clothing worn during pilgrimage to Mecca.
ihsan 1 good deeds. **2** charity.
ihtiar see IKHTIAR.
ihtilam nocturnal emission.
ihtimal meng-kan 1 order s.o. to do. **2** assign a task to.
ihwal see HAL₁.
ii see HII.
ijab 1 final offer. **2** agreement, consent. - *kabul/nikah* consent given by the bride's family at wedding ceremony. **3** answer to prayer. **meng-kan 1** offer, tender a bid. **2** perform a wedding ceremony. **3** answer a prayer, give consent.
ijabah, ijabat approval.
ijajah see IJASAH.
ijajil devil.
ijasah, ijazah 1 diploma. - *SMA* high school diploma. **2** certificate to practice a profession. - *guru* teacher's certificate. **ber-** licensed, certified. *bidan* ~ certified midwife. *penerbang* ~ licensed pilot.
ijén, ijin see IZIN.
ijma, ijmak 1 (*Isl.*) consensus of opinion among scholars. **2** unanimous agreement or approval.
ijmal resumé, summary.

ijo₁ meng- 1 buy rice from a farmer by paying for it long before the harvest. 2 give a scholarship to o. who promises to work for the donor after graduation. **meng-kan** sell o.'s rice long before the harvest. **-an** rice contracted for long before the harvest. **peng-an** practice of buying and selling rice long before the harvest.

ijo₂ see HIJAU.

ijon see IJO₁.

ijtihad 1 individual interpretation and judgment. *pd -nya* in his judgment. 2 personal examination of s.t. 3 diligence, effort. **ber-** interpret according to o.'s opinion.

ijtima astral conjunction.

ijuk₁ palm fiber from the sugar palm. **meng-** bristly (of mustache).

ijuk₂ ter- embarrassed, abashed, ashamed.

ik (*Coll.*) I.

ika see ÉKA.

ikal 1 curl, lock. - *galing* ringlet. - *tembaga* copper shavings. 2 curly, wavy. - *mayang* curly hair. **meng-** curl (the hair, etc.). **meng-kan** curl the hair for s.o. **ke-an** curliness. **-an** string, thread, etc. rolled up in a ball. ~ *benang* a ball of thread.

ikamat (*Isl.*) final call to prayer.

ikan 1 fish. - *asin* salted fish. - *babi* k.o. fish of the coral reef. - *balur* small, flat, round dried fish. - *basah* fresh fish. - *buntal* puffer fish. - *cuik* steamed, salted fish. - *darat* freshwater fish. - *duri* catfish, stonefish. - *garing* freshwater fish. - *gemi* sucker (fish), remora. - *gerut-gerut* grunter. - *glodok* mudskipper. - *hiu* shark. - *jolong-jolong/ julung-julung* garfish. - *juara* river catfish. - *kakap* 1 k.o. big fish. 2 big-shot, s.o. important. - *kakatua* parrot fish. - *layang* flying fish. - *lélé* freshwater catfish. - *lemuru* sardine. - *lidah* sole. - *limbat* catfish. - *lindung* eel. - *lodan* whale. - *lomba-lomba/lumba-lumba* dolphin. - *mangsi* cuttlefish. - *mas* goldfish, carp. - *mua* eel. - *mujair* k.o. freshwater fish often raised for food. - *nun* whale. - *oték* k.o. catfish. - *paus* whale. - *pépés* fish spiced and roasted in a banana leaf. - *raya* whale. - *salam/salem* salmon. - *sebelah* flatfish. - *senjolong/ senjulong* k.o. garfish. - *tambera* k.o. fish. - *teri* 1 small fish (esp. small anchovies). 2 (*Coll.*) small fry, s.o. unimportant. 2 meat. - *ayam* chicken meat. - *sapi* beef. **-²** (*Naut*) float for measuring a ship's speed. **peng-** 1 fisherman. 2 fond of fish. **per-an** 1 fishery. 2 fishery affairs. *Jawatan* ~ Department of Fisheries.

ikat 1 string, cord to tie. - *cincin* band of a ring. - *duduk/kursi/pinggang keselamatan* seat belt. - *satu* **meng-satukan** tie together. - *erat/teguh* **meng-eratkan, meng-teguhkan** tie s.t. up tight. 2 bunch, bundle, sheaf. *wortel dua* - two bunches of carrots. 3 band. - *kepala* headband. - *léhér* scarf. - *pinggang* belt. 4 method of tie-dying material being woven. **se-** a bundle, tied-up bunch, sheaf. ~ *kayu bakar* a bundle of firewood. **ber-** bound, tied. *Kacangnya sdh tersedia dan* ~ *seluruhnya* The string beans were ready and all bundled. ~ *mas* gilded. **ber-kan** use s.t. as a

band. ~ *kain putih* use a white piece of cloth as a headband. **meng-** 1 tie, fasten, tie up (in a bundle). *Tangannya di-* His hands were tied. 2 bind. *yg* ~ *penduduk* which binds the inhabitants together. *perjanjian yg* ~ a binding agreement. *cerita yg* ~ *hati* an interesting story. 3 compose (a poem, a sentence). 4 mount (gem or jewel). **meng-i** tie a number of things into a bundle. **meng-kan** fasten or secure s.t. to s.t. else. ~ *spalk pd lengan kiri* tie a splint on the left arm. **ter-** 1 bound, fastened. *Kakinya* ~ His feet were tied together. 2 attached, bound (not free). ~ *secara hukum* legally bound. ~ *pd tradisi* bound to tradition. **keter-an** being bound. **ke-an** commitment, being tied to certain obligations. **-an** 1 s.t. bound. ~ *sayur* a bundle of vegetables. 2 union society, league. ~ *Penerbit Indonesia* Indonesian Publishers' Association. 3 bond, tie, knot. *Kurang teguh* ~*nya* The knot is not tight enough. *Tangannya menjadi mérah bekas* ~ His wrists were red where he had been tied. 4 tie that binds. ~ *kawin* marriage tie. ~ *ke daérah pedésaan* ties to the rural area. ~ *dinas* contract to serve with the gvt. upon graduation. *tanpa* ~ *apa-apa* without any strings whatever. 5 (*Chem.*) bond. **se-an** belonging to the same organization. **peng-** binding agent, fastener. ~ *gigi* orthodontic braces. **peng-an** 1 binding, tying (of). 2 connection, relationship. 3 association, federation.

ikel see IKAL.

iket see IKAT.

ikhlas sincere, with all o.'s heart and soul. *Direbahkannya badannya dgn - pd rél-rél keréta api itu* Earnestly desiring death, he hurled his body on to the railroad tracks. **meng-kan** 1 accept s.t. with all o.'s heart and soul. *Ia* ~ *hidup demikian* He accepted his life wholeheartedly. 2 give s.t. with devotion, sacrifice s.t. for a cause. *Monyét itu di-kan utk kepentingan penelitian* Those monkeys were sacrificed for the good of science. **ke-an** sincerity, wholeheartedness. *penderitaan yg diterima dgn seluruh* ~ the suffering which he accepted with his whole heart.

ikhtiar 1 initiative. 2 free choice, decision. *Pulang - kpd engkau* It is up to you. 3 course, means of action. *Ia tdk mengindahkan -ku* She did not appreciate my efforts. **ber-** endeavor, seek the means to. ~ *sebaik-baiknya* do o.'s utmost. **meng-kan** 1 make an effort to. *Saya akan* ~ *pemasukan pengertian ini dlm rencana undang-undang* I will endeavor to have this concept included in the bill. 2 arrange for. ~ *tandu* arrange for a stretcher. 3 make a suggestion. **peng-an** making of an effort.

ikhtiari optional.

ikhtilaf 1 difference, divergence, discrepancy. 2 deviation.

ikhtirafan recognition.

ikhtisar 1 summary, recapitulation. - *Parlemén* Parliamentary Record. 2 synopsis, abstract, outline. - *warta berita* news in brief. **meng-kan** summarize, recapitulate, condense. **peng-an** abstracting.

ikhtisariah succinct, brief. *gambaran* - overview.

ikhwal see HAL₁.

ikhwan 1 brother, comrade. **2** fraternal, brotherly. **se-** compatriot, fraternal.

IKIP [*Institut Keguruan Ilmu Pendidikan*] Teachers' Training College.

ikke (*Coll.*) I, me, my. - *yg akan bayar* I will pay.

iklan advertisement. - *mini* classified ad. - *udara* skywriting. **meng-kan** advertise. **ke-²an** in the style of advertisement. **peng-** advertiser. **peng-an** advertising of s.t. **per-an** the advertising business.

iklanisasi commercialization of publications. **per-an** advertising.

iklas see IKHLAS.

iklim 1 climate. - *panas* tropical zone. - *sedang* temperate zone. **2** climate (political, etc.). **meng-i 1** climatize. **2** influence, set the tone for. *Korupsi ~ masa ini* Corruption sets the tone for this era. **ke-an** climatological. **peng-an 1** climatization. **2** characterizing of s.t.

iklimatisasi acclimatization.

ikonis iconic.

ikonografi iconography.

ikrab see AKRAB.

ikrar promise, pledge, declaration of intent. - *Lautan Teduh* the Pacific Charter. **ber-** make a promise or pledge. ~ *sumpah* take an oath. **meng-kan** pledge, promise s.t.

iktibar see ITIBAR.

iktidal (*Isl.*) proper standing posture when performing prayer ritual.

iktikad see ITIKAD.

iktikal religious retreat. **ber-** go on a retreat.

iktisab legal profit.

iktisad (*Lit.*) economy, economic matters.

ikut 1 follow, go along. *Saya - ke Jkt* I will be going along to Jkt. - *serta* accompany, go along. *Dlm rombongan présidén - serta . . .* In the president's party were included . . . **meng-sertakan** include s.o. in the company, allow s.o. to join in. **peng-sertaan** inclusion in, participation. **2** participate, join (in), also do. *Boléhkah saya - main ténnis?* May I join your tennis game? *Kami - berduka cita* Please accept our condolences. *Dia pun - terlibat dlm perkara itu* He was also involved in that affair as well. - *baris* take part in a march or parade. - *bersuara* have a voice or say (in a matter). - *campur* intervene. **3** stay with s.o. in his or her house. *Saya - paman saya di Malang* I stay with my uncle in Malang. **4** be a follower or servant of s.o. *Saya lima tahun - org Cina* I stayed with a Ch family as their servant for five years. **-²** **1** be a hanger on. **2** pry into things none of o.'s business, meddle. **ber- 1** accompanying, together with. ~ *uang itu saya mengirim tanda penerimaan* Along with money I am sending a receipt. *Kapal ~ penumpangnya binasa dlm badai* The ship with its passengers was lost in the storm. **2** as follows, following. *Kabar itu sbg ~*

The news is as follows. *pd halaman yg ~* on the following page. *Siapa yg ~?* Who is next? **ber-²** successively, consecutively. ~ *kelinci keluar dr lobang* O. after another the rabbits came out of the hole. **meng- 1** follow, obey. *Ia tak pernah ~ perintah saya* She never obeys my command. **2** act like, follow after. *Ia ~ kelakuan ibunya* She behaves like her mother. **meng-i 1** follow, accompany. *Saya ~ anak saya* I accompanied my son. **2** take, follow a course. *Ia ~ beberapa kuliah ttg fisika* He attended several lectures on physics. **3** follow a trail. **4** obey. ~ *perintah ayah* follow father's instructions. **5** keep up with (news, etc.). **6** be part of the audience of s.t. - *upacara* participate in a ceremony. **meng-kan 1** include, send or give along with s.t. else. *Pd suratnya ia ~ sekadar ttg riwayat hidupnya* She added a biographical sketch to her letter. *Ia ~ puteranya dgn bis pagi* She put her son on the early bus. *Apa perabot rumah ini juga di-kan?* Are you including the furniture (in the rental)? **2** follow s.t. with eyes. **ter- 1** included. **2** be influenced to go along. **ter-²** eagerly follow (a fad, etc.). **ke-an** participation. ~ *masyarakat yg aktif* active participation of society. **-an** s.t. to be followed or imitated. **-²an** always a follower, going along with whatever happens to be the prevailing view, fashion, etc. **peng- 1** follower, adherent. ~ *buta* blind follower. **2** participant.

ilah a god. *Org primitif masih menyembah banyak -* Primitive people still worship many gods. *tak ber-* atheistic, godless. **meng-kan** deify. **ke-an** divinity, godliness.

ilahi (*Isl.*) God (in set expression). *Kodrat -* God's Will. *ya -* O God!, exclamation of surprise or distress. **ke-an** godliness.

ilahiat godliness, divineness.

ilai meng-(²) 1 neigh. **2** laugh uproariously.

ilalang see ALANG-ALANG.

ilam-ilam hazy, vague, barely visible.

ilang see HILANG.

ilanun see LANUN.

ilar see ILER.

ilas meng- squash, crush, or mash underfoot.

ilas-ilas k.o. small tuber.

ilat physically handicapped, physical defect.

ilat-ilat k.o. sole or flounder.

iler slobber, spittle. **meng-** slobber, drool. **meng-kan** cause s.o. to drool. **-an** drool.

iles see ILAS.

iles-iles see ILAS-ILAS.

ilham 1 divine inspiration. **2** inspiration, brainstorm. **meng-** receive or try to find inspiration. **meng-i** inspire, give inspiration. *sajak-sajak yg di-i agama* poems inspired by religion. **meng-kan** inspire with s.t. ~ *kesedihan* inspire sadness. **peng-** inspirer.

ilir see HILIR.

illustratif illustrative.

ilmiah scientific. **meng-kan** cause s.t. to be scientific. ~ *Pancasila* give the *Pancasila* a scientific foundation. **ke-an** scientificness.

ilmiawan scientist, scholar.
ilmiyah, ilmiyawan see ILMIAH, ILMIAWAN.
ilmiyawan see ILMIAWAN.
ilmu 1 knowledge. - *padi* the ability to be well educated but humble (lit., be like rice which bends more, the fuller the ear). **2** science, branch of science. - *adab* ethics. - *agama* theology. - *akaid* dogmatics. - *akhirat* eschatology. - *alam* physics. - *alat* study of Arabic and related subjects. - *bahari* seamanship. - *bahas* dialectics. - *bahasa* linguistics. - *bantu* auxiliary sciences. - *bayan* exegesis. - *bedah* surgery. - *bumi* geography. - *fakih (Isl.)* canon law. - *falak* 1 cosmography. **2** astronomy. - *faraid (Isl.)* law of inheritance. - *firasat* science of physiognomy. - *gaya* mechanics. - *hisab/hitung* arithmetic. - *hukum* jurisprudence, legal science. - *jiwa* psychology. - *maani* rhetoric. - *mantik* logic. - *pasti* mathematics. - *pengetahuan* knowledge, science. - *pesawat* mechanics. - *surahi (Isl.)* knowledge of the Koran. - *ukur* geometry. - *urai* anatomy. **3** esoteric knowledge. - *alik* mysticism. - *batin* mysticism, spiritualism. - *gaib* magic. - *gayung* incantation for harming or killing s.o. from afar. - *hitam* occult sciences. - *kebatinan* mysticism, spiritualism. - *klenik* occult science, teaching of black magic. - *perapuh* magic that destroys the enemy's weapon. - *sihir* occultism, shamanism. - *sufi/suluk/sunyata (Isl.)* mysticism. - *tarékat/tasawuf (Isl.)* mysticism. **ber-** learned, erudite, scholarly. **meng-kan** study, practice as science. **ke-an** scientific, scholarly. **ke-²an** pseudo-scientific.
ilmuwan see ILMIAWAN.
ilusi illusion. **ber-** have illusions.
ilustrasi illustration.
image see IMAJ.
imaginatif imaginative.
imaj /iméj/ image.
imajinasi imagination. **meng-kan** imagine, picture for o.s. *Ia ~ masyarakat yg adil dan makmur* He pictured a society that was just and prosperous.
imajinatif see IMAGINATIF.
imajinér imaginary. *angka bilangan* - imaginary number.
imak meng-²i mock, parrot s.o.
imam 1 (Isl.) leader of communal prayer. **2** title of chief of an Isl. state. - *agung* 1 title of principal mosque leader. **2** great Muslim leader. **3** Catholic priest. - *mahdi* messiah. - *tentara* army chaplain. **meng-i** lead prayer services at mosque. **ke-an** Catholic priesthood. **peng-an** leading prayer services.
imamat 1 leadership. **2** priesthood.
iman 1 faith, belief, creed. *-nya teguh* She is strong in her faith. *kurang* - weak, easily enticed. *membawa* - provide religious guidance. **2** confidence, belief in s.t. **ber-** faithful, believing. *yg ~ the* faithful. **meng-i, meng-kan** believe in, have faith in. **peng-** believer, zealot.
imanén immanent.
imani, imaniah religious, pious.

imbak meng-(²) imagine, dream of.
imbal 1 lopsided, askew, awry. **2** unbalanced, off balance, o.-sided. **meng-** slanting, unbalanced, unequal. *Rumahnya ~* The house was leaning. *Jumlahnya ~* The amount was unequal. **meng-i** repay for s.t. good. *Ia ~ jasa Tomo dgn seribu rupiah* He gave Tomo 1,000 rupiah as recompense for his services. **-an** repayment for s.t. good. *penuntutan ~ jasa yg berlebih-lebihan* demand for repayment of services that is excessive.
imbang 1 balance. **2** match, equal. **se-** 1 balanced. *pendidikan yg ~* a balanced education. **2** equal, balanced out. *Kekuatan meréka ~* They are equally strong. **memperse-kan, mense-kan, menye-kan** equalize, balance out. *~ jumlah uang berédar dan jumlah barang* adjust the amount of money in circulation to the quantity of goods available. **kese-an** balance, equilibrium. *Kedua lengannya diayun-ayunkan utk mempertahankan ~nya* He waved his arms around to retain his balance. **ber-** 1 balanced. *anggaran yg ~* a balanced budget. **2** matched. *pernikahan yg ~* a well-matched marriage. **3** comparable. *kota-kota yg ~ besarnya* cities comparable in size. **ber-an** balanced out. *Kekuatan AS ~ dgn kekuatan US* The strength of the US is balanced with that of the USSR. **meng-i** equal. *Negara itu bekerja keras utk ~ kekuatan musuhnya* That country worked hard to keep its strength equal to that of the enemy. *saling ~* balance e.o. out. **meng-kan, memper-(kan)** balance, keep in balance. *Kamu hrs ~ perbelanjaan rumah tangga dgn gaji bulanan* You must keep your household expenses in balance with your monthly salary. **-an 1** match, s.t. equal in weight. *Partai Liberal menjadi ~ bagi partai yg sedang berkuasa* The Liberal party is a counterweight for the party in power. **2** balance. **-²an** approximately equal. *Kekuatan meréka ~* Their strength is approximately the same. **peng-, per-** counterpart, opposite number. **peng-an** equalization, balancing out. **per-an** 1 balance. *Pendapatan turun sehingga ~ bujét itu terganggu* The income dropped and the balance of the budget was effected aversely. **2** proportion, ratio.
imbas 1 air current. **2** (*Phys.*) electrical current. **se-** at first glance, superficially. *~ lalu* at first glance. **meng-** 1 blow. *Angin sepoi ~ di gang itu* A breeze was blowing in the passageway. **2** (*Tech.*) induce (air flow or electrical current). **meng-i** blow on, pass an electric current through. **-an** air or electrical current.
imbau meng- appeal. **meng-kan** call out or appeal for. *~ spy karya terjemahan banyak diterbitkan* issue an appeal for translations to be published in large numbers. **-an** appeal.
imbo built in. *Sakelar dan stop kontak rumah ini memakai yg -* The electrical switches and outlets in this house are built in.
imbuh 1 supplement. **2** extra, small addition given in the bargain to please a customer. **meng-** give s.t. extra. *Ayah ~ uang sakuku seribu rupiah*

Dad added 1,000 rupiah for my pocket money. **meng-i** provide a supplement to. **-an 1** s.t. extra given. *Mana ~ saya?* Aren't you going to give me an extra o. (since I already bought so many)? **2** (*Ling.*) affix. **peng-an** (*Ling.*) affixation.

iméj see IMAJ.

imigran immigrant. *- gelap* illegal immigrant.

imigrasi 1 immigration. **2** Bureau of Immigration. **meng-kan** bring to the Immigration Bureau. *Berkas ini di-kan* This dossier should be brought to the Bureau of Immigration. **ke-an** matters pertaining to immigration. *Akadémi ~ academy* for training members of the Bureau of Immigration.

iming meng-(²) tantalize, entice. **meng-kan** use s.t. to entice. **-an** s.t. that tantalizes.

imitasi imitation.

IMKA [*Ikatan Maséhi Kepemudaan Am*] YMCA.

imla, imlah, imlak dictation. **ber-** do dictating. **meng-kan** dictate s.t. **peng-an** dictating.

imlék 1 Ch calendar. **2** Ch New Year. *tahun baru -* Ch New Year.

imobilitas immobility.

imoral, imoril immoral.

impak /impék/ impact.

impas₁ impasse, deadlock.

impas₂ 1 paid off (of debt). *Ini uangnya. Sekarang kita sdh -* Here's the money. Now we're square. **2** square, equal. *Skornya -* The score is equal. *titik - break-even point.* **meng-** pay off (a debt).

impék see IMPAK.

impératif imperative.

impérialis imperialist.

impérialisme imperialism.

impérialistis imperialistic.

impérium empire.

impersonalitas impersonality, impersonal character.

impi meng- dream, hope. **meng-kan** dream of. *Benda itu lama ku-kan* I had been dreaming of possessing that thing for some time. **-an** dream, vision, wish. *perempuan ~ku* the woman of my dreams. *~ jebol* broken dream.

impit see HIMPIT.

implemén implement, tool.

impleméntasi implementation.

implikasi implication. **meng-kan 1** implicate. **2** imply.

implisir meng- 1 implicate. **2** imply. *~ suatu tantangan* imply a challenge. **ter-** implied. *téma ~* implied theme.

implisit implicit.

impor import. **meng-** import, bring in. **-an** an import, s.t. imported. **peng-** importer. **peng-an 1** import business. **2** importation.

importir importer.

impotén impotent.

impoténsi impotence. *- kelamin* sexual impotency.

impréalisme see IMPÉRIALISME.

imprégnasi impregnation.

imprésaris impresario.

imprési impression.

imprésif impressive.

imprésionis Impressionist.

imprialis see IMPÉRIALIS.

improvisasi improvisation. **ber-** improvise.

improvisator improviser.

improvisir meng- improvise.

impuls impulse.

impulsif impulsive.

impun see HIMPUN.

imsak (*Isl.*) predawn, time that the fast must begin.

imsakiah (*Isl.*) fasting calendar.

imun (*Med.*) immune.

imunisasi (*Med.*) immunization.

imunitas (*Med.*) immunity.

imunologi (*Med.*) immunology.

in abséntia /in absénsia/ in absentia.

inai 1 henna. **2** red nail polish. **ber-** have o.'s nails stained with henna (in preparation for marriage ceremony). *malam ~* (*Sumatra*) wedding night. *~ curi* hold prenuptial wedding party for the bride where her nails are stained, supposedly on the sly. **meng-** apply henna to the fingernails.

inang 1 wet nurse, nursemaid. **2** (*M*) female trader. **-² 1** mistress. **2** (*N. Sumatra*) female peddler of smuggled goods.

inap meng- spend the night, stay overnight. **meng-kan** put s.o. up overnight. **peng-an 1** lodging for the night. **2** inn.

inas carbuncle on nape of neck.

inaugurasi inauguration.

inayah, inayat help, aid, assistance.

incang meng- 1 aim at. *Dia ~ anak petani kaya itu* He is setting his sights on that rich farmer's daughter. **2** peek. *Ada anak yg ~ dia mandi* There was a child peeking at her while she bathed.

incang-incut 1 zigzag. **2** askew, not of equal length (of things that are supposed to be equal, e.g. chair legs).

incar drill, borer. **meng- 1** aim (gun, pistol, etc.). **2** have o.'s eye on s.o. or s.t., set o.'s sights on s.o. *~ gadis itu* have an eye on that girl. **-an 1** aim (of gun, etc.). **2** target, thing aimed at. *~ polisi* s.o. sought by the police.

incek tread on s.t.

incék see ENCIK.

inci inch.

incir see INCAR.

incit be off! go away! **meng-kan** shoo, chase s.o. away.

incrit-incrit dole out.

incut₁ lame, crippled. **ter-²** be crippled.

incut₂ see INCANG-INCUT.

indah₁ *tak - akan* be indifferent to. **meng-kan** heed, pay attention to. *~ petunjuk-petunjuk* heed the instructions. **peng-an** attention, heed. *Tak ada ~ pd peraturan sama sekali* There is no regard for the regulations whatsoever. **per-an** appreciation, interest.

indah₂ 1 beautiful, attractive, handsome. *- permai* very beautiful. **2** precious, valuable. **memper-**

1 beautify. 2 embellish. **ke-an** beauty. **peng-an** 1 beautification. 2 embellishment.

indang meng- winnow (rice).

indap see ENDAP$_{1,2}$.

indar see HINDAR.

indarus (*Sport*) cock that has been defeated and forfeited to the winner.

indayang coconut palm frond.

indehoi, indehoy have sex or pet heavily. **ber-** engage in sexual activity. **-an** be on a heavy date, be making out with e.o.

indék see INDÉKS.

indekos rent room and board. *Saya - pd Pak Ali* I room at Mr. Ali's. **meng-i** rent a room at. **meng-kan** have s.o. rent a room s.w.

indéks 1 index. 2 (*Econ.*) price increase. *- biaya* offical cost. *- hidup* price index. **meng-** index s.t. **peng-** indexer.

indéksasi (*Econ.*) indexing. *- gaji* wage indexing.

indén$_1$ pivot.

indén$_2$ partially prepaid. *pesanan - partially* prepaid order. **meng-** order s.t. by making a down payment.

indéntifikasi see IDÉNTIFIKASI.

indéntitas see IDÉNTITAS.

indéntor 1 o. who orders s.t. prepaid. 2 depositor.

independén, indépéndén, indépénden independent.

indera$_1$ 1 the god Indra. 2 the gods. **ke-an** (*Lit.*) the heavens, abode of the gods.

indera$_2$ o. of the five senses. *- mata* sense of sight. *- warta* nose for news. **peng-an** sensation, sensory perception. *~ jarak jauh* (*Tech.*) remote sensing (as a discernment of geographic facts from the outer atmosphere, etc.). *~ waktu* sense of time.

inderaloka (*Lit.*) the abode of the gods.

inderia o. of the five senses. **peng-an** sensation.

indéx see INDÉKS.

Indian American Indian.

indik meng- approach crawling or bent over.

indikasi 1 indication. 2 suspicion that s.o. is a communist. **meng-kan** indicate s.t.

indikator indicator. *- ékonomi* economic indicator.

inding meng- 1 listen attentively for s.t. 2 be on the lookout for, lie in wait for.

individu an individual. **ke-an** individuality.

individual individual.

individualisasi individualization.

individualisir meng- individualize.

individualisme individualism.

individualistis individualistic.

individualitas individuality.

individuil see INDIVIDUAL.

Indo a Eurasian. *- Belanda* o. who is of Dutch and Indonesian parentage. *- Tionghoa/Cina* o. who is from Ch and European parentage.

indoktrinasi indoctrination. **meng-kan** indoctrinate.

indoktrinator indoctrinator.

indoktrinir meng- indoctrinate.

Indologi Indonesian Studies.

Indonésia 1 Indonesia, Indonesian. *- 1* presidential limousine. *- 2* vice-presidential limousine. 2 Indonesian language. *Bagaimana -nya?* What is it in Indonesian? **meng-kan** 1 Indonesianize. 2 put into Indonesian. **ke-an** 1 Indonesian. *cara hidup ~* Indonesian way of life. 2 Indonesianized. *Org Arab itu tlh ~* That Arab has become Indonesianized. **peng-an** Indonesianization.

Indonésianisasi Indonesianization.

Indonésianisme Indonesianism.

Indra see INDERA$_1$.

indrawi sensory. *kenikmatan -* sensual enjoyment.

indria see INDERIA.

induk 1 mother (us. only for animals). *- ayam* mother hen. *- babi* sow. *- bako* the paternal relatives. *- semang* 1 adoptive mother. 2 female employer. 3 landlady. 2 chief, main, prime. *- penyalur* chief distributor. *perusahaan -* home or parent firm. *- pasukan* (*Mil.*) 1 home army. 2 main body of troops. *- pipa* main pipe. *- rumah* main building. *- taman ternak* cattle breeding center. *- tentara* (*Mil.*) main body of an army. *- utang* principal debt. 3 s.t. that can be regarded as a mother, thing from which s.t. else descends, the essence of a substance from which a large amount develops. *- bangsa* stock, race. *- cuka* essence of vinegar. *- jari* thumb. *- kaki* big toe. *- kalimat* (*Ling.*) main clause. *- karangan* editorial. *- karbol* concentrated carbolic acid. *- keluarga* (*Biol.*) superfamily. *- keréta api* (*RR.*) locomotive. *- madu* honeycomb. *- roti* leaven. **ber-, meng-** 1 have its main office. *Bank ini ~ di Jkt* This bank has its main office in Jkt. 2 have as its mother. *Anjing itu ~ anjing boksér* That dog is an offspring of a boxer. **per-an** brood, family. **seper-an** of the same litter or brood.

induksi induction. **meng-kan** induce. *~ perobahan-perobahan di masa yg akan datang* induce changes in the future. *Itu dpt di-kan dr . . .* That can be induced from . . .

induktif inductive.

indulgénsi indulgence.

indung 1 mother (of animals). 2 the thing from which s.t. else springs. *- madu* honeycomb. *- mutiara* mother-of-pearl. *- telur* (*Biol.*) ovary.

indusemén inducement.

industri industry. *- kecil* small-scale industry. *- perbukuan* book industry. *- rumah* home industry. **meng-kan** industrialize. **per-an** industry, industrial affairs.

industrialis industrialist. *- besar* captain of industry.

industrialisasi industrialization. **meng-** industrialize.

industrialisir meng- industrialize.

industriawan industrialist.

industriil industrial.

industriwan see INDUSTRIAWAN.

inéfisiénsi inefficiency.

inep see INAP.

inérsi, inértia /inérsia/ inertia.
infanteri infantry.
infark, infarkt (*Med.*) infarct.
inféksi infection.
infertil (*Med.*) infertile.
infiks (*Ling.*) infix.
infiltran infiltrator.
infiltrasi infiltration. ber- infiltrate, carry out infiltration. meng- infiltrate s.t.
infiltrir meng- infiltrate s.t.
infinitif (*Ling.*) infinitive.
inflasi (*Econ.*) inflation. ke-an suffer from inflation.
inflatoir (*Econ.*) /inflatwar/ inflationary.
infléksi (*Ling.*) inflection.
influénsa influenza.
info see INFORMASI.
informan informant, source.
informasi information. meng- inform s.o.
informatif informative.
informil informal. ke-an informality.
infrastruktur infrastructure.
infus (*Med.*) meng- give an infusion or intravenous feeding. *Pasién itu di- makanan cair* The patient was given an intravenous feeding. peng-an intravenous feeding.
infusi infusion.
inga ter-² 1 dazed, lost in thought. 2 surprised.
ingar see HINGAR.
ingat 1 remember, recall. *Saya tak - akan tuan* I do not remember you. *-lah pd saya* Keep me in mind, Think of me. *- akan diri* 1 be conscious. *Ia tak - akan diri selama dua hari* He was unconscious for two days. 2 be in control of o.s. *Tak - akan dirinya lagi* She completely lost control of herself. 2 attentive, careful. *Ia kurang -* He is not attentive. 3 plan, intend. *Ia - akan pergi ke pasar* He plans to go to the market. *tak -* unconscious. *-²* be careful or attentive. *~ sedikit dgn mulutmu!* Be careful what you say! se- as far as s.o. remembers. *~ saya* as far as I remember. ber-² be careful. *-* meng-i be considerate or mindful of e.o. meng- 1 remember, recall, recollect. 2 think of, keep in mind. *Ia maunya berhenti, tapi ~ pensiunnya ia diam saja* She wanted to quit, but upon thinking about the pension she had coming to her, she just kept quiet. 3 considering, in the light of. *~ hal-hal yg dikatakan kemarin ...* In view of the matters discussed yesterday ... *~ keadaan finansiil* in view of the financial condition. meng-² 1 keep in mind. *Ia hrs ~ bhw anak kecil itu adik ayahnya* She has to keep in mind that this small child is her father's younger brother. 2 keep thinking about s.t. meng-i 1 be mindful of, not fail to forget. *-ilah ajaran gurumu* Remember what your teacher taught you! 2 remind, warn. *Guru ~ anak-anak jangan berenang jauh-jauh* The teacher cautioned the children against swimming too far out. 3 advise. *Temannya ~ dia ttg jalan yg hendak ditempuhnya* Her friend advised her about the course she planned to take. meng-kan 1 remind, make o. think

about s.t. *Hal ini ~ Mutia pd masa kanak-kanaknya* This incident reminded Mutia of her childhood. 2 think of, keep s.t. in mind. *Tapi satu hal yg senantiasa hrs meréka -kan ...* But o. thing they must always bear in mind ... 3 warn, admonish. *Ku -kan kau spy jangan ...* I warn you not to ... 4 record. *Yg dilihat itu ia -kan dlm buku catatan* He recorded his observations in a notebook. memper-i 1 commemorate, celebrate (an occasion). 2 note down, record s.t. memper-kan warn, admonish, caution. ter- 1 enter o.'s mind, occur to o. *~ pd saya* It occurred to me. 2 be reminded. *Ia ~ akan anaknya yg gugur* He was reminded of his son who died in the war. ter-² be constantly reminded. -an 1 memory, remembrance. *sepanjang ~ saya* as far as I can recall. 2 thought, idea, notion, purpose. *~ku berpusat ke satu arah* My thoughts were concentrated on o. thing. *berubah ~* somewhat crazy. -²an 1 souvenir, keepsake. 2 recall vaguely. peng- 1 o. who has a retentive memory. 2 reminder. per-an 1 remembrance, memory. *sbg ~ kpd* in memory of. *~ Hari Kemerdékaan* Independence Day celebration. *tugu ~* monument. 2 warning, admonition. *surat ~* letter of warning.
ingau see IGAU.
inggang-inggung stagger, totter.
Inggeris England, English. *Ia berbicara bahasa -* She speaks English. *Negeri -* England. *- Raya* Great Britain. ke-²an Anglicized.
inggih (*Jv*) yes (to s.o. of higher position).
Inggris see INGGERIS.
inggu₁ asafetida.
inggu₂ k.o. coral fish.
inggung see INGGANG-INGGUNG.
ingin wish, desire. *Saya - pergi* I want to go. *Betapa -nya!* How he wished it! *- damai* peace-loving. *- tahu* curious. ke-tahuan curiosity. meng-i, meng-kan, memper-i desire s.t. *Ia tdk tahu apa yg di-kannya sebenarnya* He did not know what he actually wanted. ke-an wish, longing, desire. *~ tahu* curiosity. berke-an have a desire. per-an desire, longing.
ingkar 1 reluctant. 2 refuse, fail to keep o.'s word. *- akan* deny (a fact). 3 (*Ling.*) negative. *- ganda* double negative. meng-i, meng-kan 1 disavow, go back on. *~ janji* break a promise. *~ sumpahnya* go back on his oath. 2 deny (a fact). *~ kenyataannya* deny the evidence. *Saya tdk dpt ~ kata hati* I cannot disavow my conscience. *~ hubungan darah* deny that there is a blood relationship. ke-an 1 denial, disavowal. 2 refusal. peng-an 1 negation. 2 denial. *~ kehidupan yg layak* denial of a reasonable way of life.
ingkel meng-(²) 1 tease, pester. 2 oppress, maltreat, torture.
ingko see ÉNGKO.
ingsut ber- shift, move slowly. *Sebuah keréta api ~ meninggalkan setasiun* A train started to move slowly out of the station. ber-an move slowly (of several things). meng- 1 move slowly. 2 move s.t. slightly. *Tangan kanannya ~ lengan kebayanya* She

pushed the sleeve of her blouse up a bit with her right hand. **meng-kan** move s.t. slightly, shift s.t. ~ *duduknya ke dekat dinding* shifted his sitting position nearer to the wall. **ter-kan** can be budged.

ingus nasal mucus, snot. *Ketika -nya menjulur-julur* . . . When she was young (lit., when her mucus was hanging down) . . . **ber-** have a runny nose. **-an** 1 runny-nosed. 2 inexperienced. *gadis* ~ inexperienced girl. *masih* ~ still wet behind the ears.

inhalasi inhalation.

inhérén inherent.

inhibisi inhibition.

ini 1 this, these. *buku* - this book. - *buku* This is a book. - *pula lagi!* This thing again! *yg* - this o. (as opposed to others). - *dia!* 1 That is it! 2 That is the way, that is good! 3 Here he is! - *itu* such and such, this and that. *mempercakapkan* - *itu* talk about this and that. 2 now. - *sdh jam lima* It is already five o'clock now. 3 this (coming period of time). *dlm tiga hari* - In the next three days. *malam* - tonight. *sekarang* - nowadays. 4 here (in introductions). - *ada Pak Makso* Here is Pak Makso. 5 hesitation word when o. does not wish to plunge directly into s.t. -, *Bu, saya mau* . . . Umm, I would like to . . .

inisial 1 initial. 2 initials.

inisiasi initiation. **meng-kan** initiate.

inisiatif initiative. **ber-** 1 take the initiative. 2 have initiative.

inisiator o. who initiates s.t.

injak -² 1 pedal (esp. for gas in cars). ~ *rém* brake pedal. 2 stirrup. 3 running board. **meng-** 1 tread or step on. *Kakinya di- org* S.o. stepped on her foot. *Dilarang* ~ *rumput* Keep off the grass. ~ *beling* step on broken glass. ~ *dua perahu* vacillate, be unable to make up o.'s mind. 2 enter a certain age or status. *Ia* ~ *tahun kesepuluh* He entered his 10th year (of age, service, etc.). **meng-²** 1 disobey, disregard, ignore (a law, regulation, etc.). 2 be disrespectful of, hold a low opinion of. **meng-kan** *kaki* set foot on. **ter-** stepped or trampled on. **ter-²** 1 trampled upon. 2 ignored, disregarded. **-(²)an** pedal, stirrup, running board. **peng-** o. who is entering a certain status or stage. ~ *umur tua* o. who is entering old age. **peng-an** treading, trampling. ~ *hak-hak manusia* a trampling on human rights.

injap having spikes turned inward (of fish traps that permit entrance, but make egress impossible). **meng-** have inward-turned spikes.

injéksi (*Med.*) injection. **meng-** inject, give an injection. **peng-an** injecting.

Injil 1 (*Bib.*) Gospel. - *Al-Kudus* Holy Gospel. 2 (*Bib.*) New Testament. 3 (*Isl.*) the sacred book revealed to the prophet Jesus. **peng-** evangelist, preacher.

injili, injiliah evangelical.

injin (*Coll.*) engine.

inkarnasi incarnation. **meng-kan** incarnate.

inkaso payment, collection, cashing of a check.

meng-kan present a check to the issuing bank for payment.

inklaring banking clearance.

inklinasi inclination.

inklusif inclusive.

inkompatibilitas incompatibility.

inkonsekwénsi inconsistency.

inkonstitusional, inkonstitusionil unconstitutional.

inkonvénsional, inkonvinsionil unconventional.

inkorporasi incorporation. **meng-kan** incorporate.

inkubasi incubation.

inkubator incubator.

inkuisisi inquisition.

inlander indigene (during colonial times, often *Derog.*).

Inmas [*inténsifikasi massal*] program of agricultural intensification on a massive scale.

inna lillahi wa inna ilaihi raji'un (*Isl.*) We are truly Allah's and to Him we return (in obituaries and eulogies).

inokulasi inoculation.

inovasi innovation.

inovatif innovative.

inpéntaris see INVÉNTARIS.

inplénsa, inplinsa see INFLUÉNSA.

inporman see INFORMAN.

Inprés [*Instruksi Présidén*] Presidential Directive. *sekolah* - a school built with funds specially allocated by a particular presidential directive. **meng-kan** issue an executive order.

inréyen meng- break in a motor or motorized vehicle. *Kalau membeli spéda motor baru mesinnya hrs di- dulu kurang lebih 1.500 km* If you buy a new motorcycle you have to break the motor in for around 1,500 km.

insaf - *akan* realize, understand. **meng-i** realize, be aware of. **meng-kan** 1 make s.o. aware or realize. *Bisakah kau* ~ *suamiku?* Can you make my husband aware of it? 2 be aware of s.t. *Dia* ~ *kesalahannya* He is aware of his mistakes. **ter-i** can be realized. *Salahku tak* ~ *lagi oléhku* It was no longer possible for me to be aware of my mistake. **ter-kan** can be made to realize. **ke-an** awareness, realization.

insan man, human being. **ke-an** being a person, o.'s humanity.

insang fish gills.

insani, insaniah human. *hubungan* - human relations. *tubuh* - human body.

inséktisida insecticide.

inséminasi insemination. - *tiruan* artificial insemination.

inséntif incentive.

insérsi insertion.

inseting see INSTING.

insidén incident.

insidénsi incidence. *angka* - rate of incidence.

insidéntil incidental.

insinuasi insinuation. **meng-kan** insinuate.

insinye badge, identifying button.
insinyur engineer. - *éléktro* electrical engineer. - *mesin* mechanical engineer. - *tambang* mining engineer. **ke-an** engineering.
insisi incision.
inskripsi inscription.
insolvénsi insolvency.
inspéksi 1 inspectorate. 2 inspection. **meng-** inspect.
inspéktorat inspectorate.
inspéktur inspector.
inspirasi inspiration. **meng-kan** inspire. **ter-** inspired.
Instalasl 1 installation (of the new chairman, etc.). 2 installation. - *pemanas pusat* central heating installation.
instalatur installer, fitter, electrician.
instansi 1 (*Leg.*) level of a court's jurisdiction, instance. 2 institute, agency. - *pemerintahan sipil* civil administration authority.
insting, instink instinct.
institusionalisasi institutionalization.
institusionil institutional.
institut institute.
instruksi 1 instruction, directive. 2 briefing. **meng-kan** instruct.
instruktur instructor.
instrumén instrument.
instruméntal instrumental.
instruméntasi instrumentation.
insubordinasi insubordination.
insya Allah (*Isl.*) God willing. *"Sekali-sekali main-main di rumah!" "Ya tentu. Sekali waktu -"* "Come over to the house once in a while." "Surely. I will some time, God willing."
insyaf see INSAF.
intai meng- 1 spy on, watch surreptitiously. 2 lurk, lie in wait. **-an** place from which o. can spy. **peng-** (*Mil.*) look out, observer, scout. **peng-an** 1 observation, reconnaissance. 2 espionage.
intan diamond. - *berlian/permata* jewelry. - *mentah* diamond in the rough.
integral, intégral integral.
integrasi, intégrasi integration. **meng-kan** integrate. **peng-an** integrating.
integratif, intégratif integrative.
integrir meng- integrate.
integritas, intégritas integrity.
intél 1 intelligence (service). 2 intelligence agent, informer. 3 agent provocateur.
intelék intellect.
inteléktual intellectual.
inteléktualisme intellectualism.
inteléktuil intellectual.
inteligénsi, inteligénsia intelligence. *-nya kuka-gumi* I am amazed at his intelligence.
intelijén, intelijéns 1 intelligence, intelligent. 2 intelligence service.
inténdan, inténdans (*Mil.*) quartermaster.
inténs intense.
inténsi intention.
inténsif intensive. **meng-kan** intensify.

inténsifikasi intensification. **meng-kan** intensify, step up. ~ *pemungutan-pemungutan pembayaran* step up collection of payments.
inténsitas, inténsitét intensity.
interaksi interaction. **ber-** interact.
interdépendénsi interdependence.
intéren see INTÉRN.
interés interest in s.t.
interésan interesting.
interferénsi interference.
interim interim.
interinsulér interinsular.
intériur interior.
interjéksi interjection.
interkom intercom.
interlokal (*Tel.*) long distance call, make a long distance call. - *kilat* express call. **meng-** make a long distance call.
interméso, intérméso intermezzo.
intérn 1 internal, domestic. *urusan* - internal matter. 2 within the local school and not at national level (e.g. of examinations).
internasional international. **meng-kan** make s.t. up to international standards. **ke-an** on an international scale.
internasionalisasi internationalization. **meng-kan** internationalize.
internasionalisme internationalism.
internat dormitory, esp. in the colonial period.
internir meng- intern, imprison. **-an** 1 internee. 2 internment camp. **peng-an** internment.
internis, intérnis (*Med.*) internist.
internit see ÉTERNIT.
interogasi, intérogasi interrogation. **meng-** interrogate.
interogatif, intérogatif 1 interrogative. 2 questioning. *pandangan* - a questioning look.
interpélan (*Leg.*) questioner.
interpélasi (*Leg.*) interpellation.
interpiu see INTERVIU.
interpolasi interpolation. **meng-kan** interpolate.
interpretasi, interprétasi interpretation. **meng-kan** interpret, construe.
intertip Intertype.
interupsi interruption. **meng-** interrupt.
intervénsi intervention.
interviu interview. **meng-** interview.
inti 1 kernel, nucleus. - *atom* (*Phys.*) nucleus of an atom. - *bumi* (*Phys.*) earth's core. - *suku kata* (*Ling.*) syllabic nucleus. 2 gist, core. *kurikulum* - core curriculum. - *persoalannya* gist or heart of the matter. - *hidup* the meaning of life. 3 filling, contents (of pie, etc.). - *pati/sari* 1 (quint)essence. 2 digest, abstract. **meng-sarikan** make an abstract of. **ber-kan** contain, have as a core. *agama yg* ~ *ketuhanan* a religion that has the existence of God as its nucleus. **-an** core. *sistim* ~ core system.
intikad (*Lit.*) criticism.
intil meng- follow on s.o.'s heels.
intim intimate, close (friend, etc.). **meng-kan** make s.t. intimate.

intimidasi intimidation. **meng-** intimidate.
intip meng-(i) spy on, peep at. **-an 1** s.t. spied on.
2 surveillance. **peng-an** spying, surveillance.
intisari see INTI.
intoléran intolerant.
intonasi intonation.
intra see INTRA-UNIVERSITÉR.
intransitif (*Ling.*) intransitive.
intra-universitér intrauniversity.
intrik intrigue, conspiracy, plot. **meng-** engage in
  intrigue.
intrikatif full of intrigues.
introduksi introduction.
introdusir meng- introduce.
introspéksi introspection.
introvérsi introversion.
intrusi intrusion.
intuisi intuition.
intuitif intuitive.
invalid, invalide invalid, o. who is sickly.
invasi invasion.
invéntaris inventory, list of stock in a store. **peng-
  an** inventorying.
invéntarisasi stock taking. **meng-(kan)** inventory, take stock.
invéntarisir meng- to inventory.
invérsi inversion.
invéstasi (*Fin.*) investment. **meng-(kan)** invest.
invéstigasi investigation.
invéstor investor.
invitasi 1 invitation. **2** (*Sport*) invitational (tennis,
  golf, etc.).
inyéksi see INJÉKSI.
ionis (*Chem.*) ionic.
ionisasi (*Chem.*) ionization.
ionosfér, ionosfir (*Phys.*) ionosphere.
IPA [*Ilmu Pasti/Alam*] mathematical and natural
  sciences.
ipar brother, sister, or cousin-in-law. - *lamai/duai*
  cousin of o.'s spouse. **ber-** be a brother or sister-
  in-law of. **ber-an** be brothers or sisters-in-law
  with e.o. **per-an, ke-an** relationship through
  marriage.
IPB [*Institut Pertanian Bogor*] Bogor Institute of
  Agriculture.
Ipéda [*Iuran Pembangunan Daérah*] land or crop
  tax for regional development.
ipil-ipil k.o. tree, *lamtoro*, a rapidly growing
  leguminosa planted as a shade tree for coffee
  plants and for firewood and animal fodder.
iprit₁ meng- run away out of fear.
iprit₂ (*Sd*) **ng-** marry a beautiful woman who is in
  reality a supernatural snake that can make her
  husband rich.
IPS [*Ilmu Pengetahuan Sosial*] social studies.
ipuh 1 k.o. tree, the sap of which is used as poison
  for weapon tips. **2** the poison from this tree.
  3 vicious (of person). **ber-** having this poison
  applied to it.
ipuk meng- grow, cultivate. **-an** seedling. **peng-
  an** seedbed.
Ir. [*Insinyur*] title of o. who has received an engineering degree.

ira 1 section (of lemon, orange, durian). **2** sinew
  (in meat). **3** grain (in wood).
iradah, iradat (*Isl.*) will of God.
iram change color, turn pale.
irama rhythm, cadence. **se-** in rhythm with.
  *Dadanya turun naik ~ dgn jantung yg berdebar-
  debar* His chest heaved in rhythm with his wildly
  beating heart. **ber-** rhythmical, having rhythm.
  meng-kan provide a rhythm to.
iras se- similar. **meng-** resemble.
irasional, irasionil irrational.
irat meng- split into thin strips. **-an** thin strip (of
  bamboo, etc.).
Irbar [*Irian Barat*] Indonesian (W.) New Guinea.
Iréda [*Iuran Réhabilitasi Daérah*] a tax on commercial properties for regional rehabilitation.
irélevan irrelevant.
iri jealous of s.o.'s attainments or status, full of
  envious resentment. - *hati* envious, jealous. **ber-
  hati** be jealous. *Ia ~ kpd harta benda saya* He is
  jealous of my wealth. **meng-hatikan** be jealous
  of. **meng-kan** be jealous of. **ke-an** jealousy.
  peng- o. who easily becomes jealous.
Irian New Guinea. - *Barat/Jaya* Indonesian New
  Guinea. - *Timur* Papua New Guinea.
irid see IRIT₁.
irigasi irrigation. **meng-kan** irrigate.
irik meng- thresh by stamping with the feet. **ter-
  get** sifted out. *Hanya butir-butir pasir halus yg jatuh ~* Only the finest grains of sand fell through
  the sieve. **peng-** a flail.
iring se- 1 in a row. **2** of o. mind, unanimous.
  3 together or along with. *~ dgn irama la ilaha
  illalla* together with the rhythm of the chant,
  "There is no God but God." *kawan ~* companion, mate, comrade. **ber-** successive, consecutive. *Ramai-ramai meréka secara ~ teratur meléwati
  jalan-jalan raya* Large groups passed through
  the main streets successively. *hujan keras ~ badai*
  a heavy rain accompanied by high winds. **ber-
  ²(an)** o. after the other, in a procession, in single
  file. **meng-** accompany, escort, go along. *Akupun
  ~ dr belakang* I too went along following behind.
  meng-(i) 1 together with. *Di- dgn muka-muka yg
  kurang sedap kutinggalkan rumah itu* They gave
  me unpleasant looks as I left the house (lit., I left
  the house accompanied by unpleasant faces).
  seorg ibu di-i anak kecil a mother accompanied by
  a small child. **2** join in, accompany. *Saya ~ meréka berjogét* I joined them in their dance. **meng-
  kan 1** escort. *~ jenazah ke kuburan* escort the
  corpse to the grave. **2** have s.o. follow. *Ia ~
  anaknya utk menunjukkan jalan* She had her son
  go with her to show her the way. **ter-** accompanied. *~ salam kami* with our compliments. **-an
  1** follower. **2** accompaniment. *~ piano* piano
  accompaniment. *~ tertawanya* accompanied by
  his laughter. **3** procession accompanying s.t.
  -²an procession. *~ semut di lantai* the procession
  of ants on the floor. **peng- 1** follower, escort,
  retinue. **2** accompanist (on piano, etc.). **peng-an**
  escorting.
iris slice very thin. **se-** a slice. **meng-** slice s.t. ~

bawang slice onions. *pepatah yg sbg sembilu ~ hatiku* a saying that sliced into my heart like a razor-sharp blade of bamboo. **meng-kan** slice s.t. for. **-an** slice, section. **peng-an** act of slicing.

irit₁ economical, frugal. **meng-, meng-kan** economize on, save. *~ bénsin* economize on gas. *~ air* save water. **peng-an** economizing.

irit₂ see ÉRÉT.

iritasi irritation.

Irja [*Irian Jaya*] Indonesian New Guinea.

ironi irony.

ironis ironic.

irup see HIRUP.

irus 1 ladle made of a coconut shell. **2** ladle.

isa₁ see SEMBAHYANG.

isa₂ (*Coll.*) see BISA₁.

Isa (*Isl.*) Jesus.

isak sob. *- tangis* crying and sobbing. **ber-, meng-, ter-** sob. *Gadis itu menangis, mengusap air mata dan ~* The girl cried, wiped her tears, and let out a sob. **-an** sob. *~ itu reda* Her sobbing let up.

isang see INSANG.

isap **meng- 1** suck. *~ benak* think hard. *~ darah* demand excessive interest on a loan. *~ nafas* inhale. **2** smoke. *~ pipa* smoke a pipe. **3** absorb (liquid). **-an** s.t. inhaled or sucked. *~ jempol* lie, useless rumor. **peng- 1** s.t. that sucks. *~ debu* vacuum cleaner. *~ pasir* suction pump for sand. **2** extortionist. *~ dan penindas féodal* feudal extortionists and bloodsuckers. *~ darah* usurer, bloodsucker. **3** o. who smokes. *~ ganja* smoker of marijuana. *~ serutu* cigar smoker. **peng-an 1** exploitation, gouging. **2** smoking. *~ ganja* smoking of marijuana.

isarah, isarat see ISYARAT.

isbat 1 confirmation, ratification. **2** positive. *langkah yg* - a positive step. *aliran listrik -* (*Elec.*) positive electrical current. **meng-kan** confirm, ratify.

iseng do s.t. for fun, do s.t. without any serious purpose. *pertanyaan-pertanyaan -* questions just asked without really caring about the answer. **-²** **1** do s.t. just to amuse o.s. *Aku berjalan ~* I walked around, just to kill time. *Lalu ~ kuberitahu dia bhw aku punya tivi* Then just for fun I told her I had a TV. **2** casually, leisurely. **-an, ke-an** s.t. o. does just for fun. *Masih ada saja ~ lain di samping menanyakan harga buah apel* Of course there are other things o. can do to kill time besides asking how much an apple costs (without really wanting to know).

isi 1 contents. *- lemari itu* the contents of the wardrobe. *- senapan* charge in a rifle. *- perut* **1** intestines, bowel. **2** thoughts. *- sesak* **meng-sesakkan** fill s.t. chock-full. **2** volume, capacity, content (of barrel, jar, etc.). **3** substance. *Surat ini tdk ada -nya* This letter does not say anything. *hidup tanpa -* a life with no substance. *- kawin* bride-price. **4** the people who live in a certain place. *- negeri* inhabitants of a country. *- rumah* the entire household. **se-** the entire population of, the entire contents of. *~ kampung* all of the people in the village. *~ rumah* everyone in the house. **ber- 1** have contents. *timba yg ~ air* a pail

with water in it. *senapan yg ~* a loaded gun. **2** have substance. *pidato yg ~* a speech with substance. **ber-kan** contain a certain thing. *dua cangkir ~ kopi panas* two cups full of hot coffee. **-meng-** fill up for e.o. **meng-** fill up. *~ téng bénsin* fill up a gas tank. *~ malam itu* take up the evening. *~ aki* charge a battery. *~ bahan bakar* take on fuel. *~ latar belakang* fill in the background. *~ waktu* pass the time. **meng-kan 1** fill on behalf of s.o. *Isterinya menolong ~ kwitansinya* His wife helped him by filling in the receipt for him. **2** put s.t. in as contents. *Minyak yg di-kan ke dlm botol* Oil that is to be filled into a bottle. **ter-** filled. *Lowongan tlh ~* The vacancy has been filled. **-an** filler, s.t. to be filled in. **peng- 1** filler. **2** fill-in. *~ halaman* filler on a page. *~ pojok* columnist. *~ waktu* pastime, timekiller. **peng-an** filling up. *~ suara* addition of sound (to a silent movie).

isim 1 (*Isl.*) o. of God's names or attributes. **2** (*Ling., in old or Arab-style grammars*) nominal. *- al'ain* concrete noun. *- alam* proper name. *- al'adad* numeral. *- al fŭl* verbal noun.

isin (*Jv*) shy, embarrassed, ashamed.

isit gums. *Bukan sakit gigi, tapi -nya yg sakit* She did not have a toothache; she had sore gums.

islah settlement of a dispute.

Islam Islam. *- putih* practicing Muslim. **meng-kan 1** Islamize, convert to Islam. **2** circumcise. **ke-an** Islamic. **peng-an** Islamization.

Islamisasi Islamization.

ism see ISIM.

isme -ism. *pelbagai -* various -isms.

Isnin see SENÉN.

isolasi₁ cellophane tape. *- ban* friction tape.

isolasi₂ isolation. **meng-kan** isolate.

isolasionisme isolationism.

isolemén isolation.

isolir **meng-kan 1** isolate. **2** (*Elec.*) insulate.

isomorfis isomorphic.

isotop (*Chem.*) isotope.

Israfil (*Isl.*) angel of great size who will blow the trumpet on the Last Day.

Israk, Isrok (*Isl.*) Muh.'s miraculous flight from Mecca to Jerusalem.

issue see ISU.

istal horse barn, stable.

istana palace, castle. *- présidén* the president's residence. **ber-** dwell in a palace.

istanggi see SETANGGI.

isteri see ISTRI.

istiadat custom, tradition. **meng-kan** institute s.t. as a custom.

istibra (*Isl.*) period of sexual abstinence for a woman after divorce or widowhood so that there may be no question of the paternity of a baby she might be carrying.

istigfar utter *astaghfirullah* to ask God's forgiveness thereby. **ber-** utter this formula.

istilah technical term. *Komisi -* Terminology Commission. **meng-i, meng-kan** give a term or name to s.t. **per-an** terminology.

istimal utilization.

istiméwa 1 special, extraordinary, different from others. *sidang - * special session. *daérah - Yogya* the special district of Yogyakarta. *- lagi/pula* esp., more so. **2** special, better than normal. *makan yg - * special food. **meng-kan** regard or treat as special. *Segala sesuatu mesti kakék didahulukan, di-kan* In everything Grandfather has to be given priority, to be treated as special. **ter- 1** special, extraordinary. **2** most specially, in particular. **ke-an 1** peculiarity, peculiar feature. **2** special treatment, s.t. better than the normal. *Ny. Iskandar berterima kasih atas ~ yg diberikan oléh dokter* Mrs. Iskandar expressed her thanks for the special treatment that the doctor had given her.

istinja (*Isl.*) cleansing after defecation and urination or before ritual ablution.

istiqlal liberty, freedom, independence.

istirahat 1 rest. *- sakit* sick leave. **2** pause, break, intermission, recess. **ber-** rest, take a break. **meng-kan** give s.o. a rest or pause. *~ badan* lay s.o. to rest, bury. **peng-an 1** giving s.o. a rest. **2** putting s.o. into retirement. **per-an** place provided for employees or members of a given group to spend their vacation.

istri wife, married woman. *- bungsu/muda* 2nd (or most recently wed) wife, esp. in polygamous family. *- piaraan* mistress, concubine. *- sulung/tua* the first wife (in polygamous family). **ber-** have a wife, be married (of a man). **ber-kan** have or take a certain person as a wife. *~ seorg wanita Indo* have a Eurasian woman as a wife. **memper-kan** take s.o. as wife. *Ia ~ seorg janda* He took a divorcée to wife. **-²an** mistress.

isu 1 issue, problem. **2** rumors. **meng-kan 1** make an issue of. *Meréka ~ soal pembelian tanah itu* They made an issue over the purchase of that land. **2** gossip about s.t. *Dia di-kan dgn Pram* The gossip is that she is going with Pram.

isya see SEMBAHYANG.

isyarat sign, signal. *- bahaya* danger or "help" signal. **meng-kan** beckon, signal.

isytihar proclamation. **meng-kan** proclaim. *~ kemerdékaan* proclaim independence.

isyu see ISU.

itam SCC HITAM.

ITB [*Institut Téknologi Bandung*] Bandung Institute of Technology.

itibar /itibar, i'tibar/ (*Isl.*) moral lesson, example, comparison. *Sbg - kita perhatikan sikapnya yg ramah thd seorg pengemis* We can take for our example the generous attitude he showed toward a beggar.

itidal /itidal, i'tidal/ (*Isl.*) symmetry, equilibrium.

itik₁ duck. *- air/laut* k.o. wild duck. *- Manila/serati* k.o. large duck.

itik₂ meng- *air liur* make s.o. drool for s.t., stimulate a desire to eat s.t.

itikad /itikad, i'tikad/ **1** conviction. **2** determination, will. *dgn - baik* with good intentions. **ber-** have conviction, faith. **meng-kan** convince s.o.

itil (*Vulg.*) clitoris.

itlak acceptance of a theory without examination. **meng-kan** generalize.

ittifak (*Isl.*) agreement, compromise. *Tercapailah suatu - yg mengakhiri perselisihan itu* An agreement was reached whereby they could end the conflict.

itu 1 that, those. *topi - * that hat. *- topi* That is a hat. *- dia* 1 That is it! That is right! 2 There he is! *- juga* just exactly that. *Pd hari - juga* On that very day. *-lah* what did I tell you, that is just it. *-lah! Beberapa kali saya katakan kpdmu jangan berbuat demikian* Now look! I told you several times not to do that. **2** the. *Perjanjian - ditandatangani semalam* The treaty was signed last night. **3** there. *- kakak saya. - di sana* There, that is my sister. There, over there. **4** hesitation word when o. cannot find the right word. *Kita cari -, anu, lobang yg bisa dimasuki, ya kan?* We should look for a, you know, umm, a hole we can crawl into, don't you think? **5** clause marker: when, if, in the particular case that, at the particular time that. *Jadi org -, jangan kasar* If you want to grow up to be a good person, do not act rough. *Saya pas kembali dr Magelang - capai bukan main* When I have just gotten back from Magelang I am terribly tired. **-²** those very same things, that and nothing else. *hari ~* those very selfsame days. *Pembicaraannya selalu ~ saja* She always says the same old things.

itung see HITUNG.

iur ber- contribute. *Mari kita bersama-sama ~ dharma* Let us contribute our services together. **-an 1** contribution. **2** subscription, levy. **3** premium (insurance, etc.). **4** dues. **peng-** o. who contributes.

iya see IA₂, YA₁.

iyal dependants.

iyuran see IUR.

izin 1 permission. **2** permit, license, franchise (to operate bus line, etc.). *- kembali* reentry permit. *- keluar* 1 exit permit. 2 clearance. *- leluasa* freedom of action. **se-** with the permission of. *Ini diadakan ~ lurah* This is being done with the village chief's permission. **meng-kan 1** permit, allow. *batas-batas yg di-kan* permissible limits. **2** license s.o. or s.t. **per-an, ke-an 1** permission. **2** licensing.

J

j /jé, yé/ j, the 10th letter of the alphabet.
j-₁ [*jam*] o'clock.
j-₂ [*jilid*] volume.
ja see SAJA.
jab /jép/ (*Sport*) jab (in boxing).
jabal₁ mountain. **men-** loom large (of mountain, etc.).
jabal₂ men- **1** rob, mug. **2** steal from s.o. **ke-** get robbed. **-(²)an** robber band or gang. **pen-an** robbery, mugging.
jabang bayi (*Jv*) **1** newborn baby. **2** exclamation of great surprise.
Jabar [*Jawa Barat*] W. Java.
jabar₁ (*Isl., in fixed phrases only*) almighty.
jabar₂ men-kan **1** spell out, clarify. *GBHN ~ Pancasila* The outline presented in the national laws spells out how *Pancasila* is to be practiced. *Ruang lingkup dr permasalahannya tlh di-kan dlm mémorandum* The dimensions of the problem have been spelled out by the memorandum. **2** (*Math.*) reduce a fraction, convert. **3** announce widely, popularize. *~ hidup sederhana* popularize a simple way of life. **pen-an 1** spelling out. *GBHN merupakan ~ dr UUD '45* The outline presented in the national laws are what the 1945 Constitution spells out. **2** (*Math.*) reduction, conversion.
jabat - *tangan* handshake. **ber-(an)** *tangan* shake hands. **se-** colleague from the same office. **se-an** working in the same office. **men- 1** take hold of, grasp. **2** occupy an office. *Beliau ~ walikota Bandung* He is the mayor of Bandung. **men-kan** extend the hand to give a handshake. **-an 1** function, duty. *~nya melayani tamu luar negeri* His function is to take care of foreign visitors. **2** position, post. *~nya sdh tinggi* She occupies a high position. *~ kepercayaan* position of trust. *~ jaksa agung* office of attorney general. *tunjangan ~* an addition to o.'s salary for holding a high post. *~ penting* key position. *~ sampingan* secondary post or occupation. *~ utama* main occupation. **3** shake of a hand. *~ tangan* handshake. **pe-** functionary, official. *~ tinggi* senior official, high functionary. **pen-** functionary, official. *~ negeri* **1** gvt. official, office holder. **2** holder of temporary post. *~ présidén* acting president. **pen-an** office, service. *~ hidrografi* hydrographic service.
jabel see JABAL₂.
jabir-jabir ber- slovenly, sloppy (of clothes).
Jabotabék [*Jkt Bogor Tangerang Bekasi*] the megalopolis of Jkt and its satellite cities.
jabung resin.
jabur see ZABUR.

jaburan 1 snacks, sweet tidbits. **2** (*Isl., Jv*) light repast for congregation after evening prayers during fasting month.
jada see JUADAH.
jadah *anak* - illegitimate child. **men-kan** *anak* father an illegitimate child.
jadajat (*Zod.*) Capricorn.
jadam k.o. strong laxative.
jadi 1 become, get. *- pemandian* turn into a bathing place. *- kering* get dry. *-lah terang* Let there be light. *Maka -lah manusia itu* And man was born. *- org* grow up to be s.o., grow up to be successful in life. *- umum* (*Fin.*) go public. **2** so, therefore, thus, hence. *-, kalau begitu, saya pulang saja* So, if that is the case, I might as well go home. *-, semuanya berjumlah seribu rupiah* Let us see, the total amounts to 1,000 rupiah. **3** end up doing s.t. *Saya - lihat film* I did get to the movies. *Saya tdk - pergi* I ended up not going. **4** work (out), become effective, come off. *Suntikan itu -* The inoculation took. *Kalau tdk ada pulpén, potlotpun -* If there is no fountain pen, a pencil will do. *Ujian tak -* No exam will be held. **5** finished, accomplished. *Pekerjaan itu sdh -* That job is accomplished. **6** be, serve or work as. *Ia - dokter di rumah sakit* She is a doctor at a hospital. *- landas* serve as a scapegoat. **-nya 1** outcome. *Begitulah ~ kalau tdk hati-hati!* That is what happens if you are not careful! *Saya tdk tahu apa ~ anak itu kelak* I do not know what will become of that child. **2** consequently. *~, bagaimana?* So, what happened? *Bagaimana ~ ?* How did it end? **se-nya** as it turns out. *Kita makan saja kuénya ~* We will just eat the cake however it turns out. **se-²nya** as much or hard as possible. *bekerja ~* work as hard as possible. *menjawab ~* answer as harshly as possible. **men- 1** become. *Ia ingin ~ serdadu* He wants to become a soldier. *~ pengantin* marry (lit., become a bride or bridegroom). *Sedikit-sedikit ~ bukit* A bit (of dirt) at a time eventually becomes a mountain. *makin tua makin ~* the older o. gets the worse the sickness becomes (us. said of man-woman relations). **2** be. *Nénék moyangnya ~ raja* Her ancestors were kings. *Usia tdk ~ soal* Age is no problem. **3** as, be. *Ia dipilih ~ lurah* He was chosen to be village chief. *Kota itu dibagi ~ tiga bagian* The city is divided into three sections. **4** boil down to. *Soal itu ~ demikian* The problem boils down to this. **5** succeed, win out, go through with. *Sekali ini rencananya ~* This time her plan succeeded. **men-²** increase, worsen (of illness, vices, etc.). *Hutangnya ~* His debt increased. *Penyakitnya ~* She got sicker and

sicker. **men-kan 1** make into s.t. *Ia ~ saya wakilnya* He made me his deputy. *Présidén ~ dia perdana menteri* The president made him prime minister. **2** conclude, bring into being. *Saya ~ kontrak* I signed the contract. **3** create, make. *Tuhan ~ bumi ini* God created the world. **4** cause, bring about, bring to pass. *Kemalasannya ~ kemarahan bapaknya* His laziness brought on his father's anger. **men-²kan** worsen, make s.t. become worse. *Tindakannya ~ kebencian rakyat pdnya* His action made the people hate him even more. **ter-1** happen, occur, take place. *Itu juga pernah ~ di sini* That also has happened here. *Apa yg ~ dgn buku yg baru itu?* What has become of the new book? **2** consist. **ke-an 1** (*Bib.*) creation, Genesis. *~ bumi ini* creation of the world. **2** incident, event, occurrence. *~ alam* natural phenomenon. **3** affair, party, get-together. **4** case. **-an** invented, made up, derived. *harimau ~* a human who changes his shape to a tiger's. *kata-kata ~* derived words. **-²an 1** an animal with supernatural powers which is owned by s.o. and visible only to its owner. **2** imitation. *Bunga ~ itu dibuat dr kertas* Those imitation flowers are made of paper. **pen-** developer, doer. **pen-an 1** outbreak (of disease, epidemic, etc.). **2** development, creating (of).

Jadi see BINTANG.

jadwal 1 schedule. **2** table, list. *- logaritma* logarithmic tables. *- KA* railroad timetable. *- perjalanan* itinerary. *- imsakiah* (*Isl.*) table showing the time when fasting begins during the fasting month. *- waktu* timetable. **men-** schedule, line up. *Dosénnya sdh ~ pertemuannya dgn para mahasiswa* The lecturer set up his meeting times with the students. **men-kan 1** plan s.t. on schedule. *Ia ~ waktunya* He made a schedule of his time. **2** schedule s.t. to happen. *Penandatanganan resminya di-kan tgl satu* The official signing is scheduled for the first. **pen-an** scheduling.

jaga 1 wake up. *Ia - dr tidurnya* He woke up from his sleep. **2** guard, watchman. *- anak* baby sitter. *- malam* night watch. *- mobil* o. who is assigned to watch a parked car. **3** be on duty (of physician, pharmacist, etc.). *dokter -* the doctor on duty. **4** preserve. *- kebersihan* Do not litter (Maintain cleanliness). **5** be on the lookout for. *- tgl mainnya* Watch for coming attractions (movies). **-² 1** be on the safe side. *Dia membawa sedikit duit utk ~* He brought a little money along to be on the safe side. **2** be on the lookout, on o.'s guard. **ber-1** stay awake (to watch over a sick person, etc.). **2** stand guard. **3** be on o.'s guard. **ber-² 1** stay awake all night long (at a wedding, etc.). **2** be on o.'s guard, be careful. *~ sedikit membawa piring itu* Be careful carrying those plates. **men- 1** watch over, keep an eye on. *Siti ~ adiknya* Siti looked after her baby brother. *~ dirimu baik-baik* Take good care of yourself. **2** guard against (a danger). *utk ~ hal yg tdk diinginkan* to guard against s.t. that is not desired. **3** guard. *~ jalan ke gua* guard the way to the cave. **4** keep, maintain,

preserve. *~ kebersihan nama Indonésia* Keep Indonesia's name pure. *~ ketertiban* keep order. *~ nama* maintain o.'s prestige. **5** be on the lookout. **men-i** watch over. **men-kan 1** wake s.o. up. *Si suami di-kan dr tidur* The husband was awakened from his sleep. **2** guard for s.o. *Coba -kan anak saya sebentar* Watch my child for me, would you? **ter- 1** be awakened. **2** guarded. *Penjara itu tak ~* That jail is not guarded. **3** looked after, watched over. **ke-²an** sleepless, wakeful. **-an 1** surveillance. **2** thing guarded. **pen-** guard, o. who takes care of. *~ anak* babysitter. *~ dada* (*Sport*) chest protector. *~ garis* (*Sport*) linesman. *~ gawang* (*Sport*) goalie, goalkeeper. *~ lift* elevator operator. *~ pintu* doorman, doorkeeper. *~ pompa bénsin* gas station attendant. *~ télpon* telephone operator. *~ tempat duduk* usher. **pen-an 1** guarding, security. **2** surveillance. *~ udara* aerial surveillance. **3** guardpost. *~ polisi* police station.

jagabaya (*Jv*) village constable.

jagad see JAGAT.

jagal₁ small-scale trader. **ber-** trade in retail goods, hawk wares. **-an** small wares.

jagal₂ butcher, slaughterer. **men- 1** butcher, slaughter. *Tentara ~ musuhnya* The army slaughtered the enemy. **2** be a butcher. **pen-** butcher, slaughterer. **pe-an** abattoir, slaughterhouse. **pen-an 1** slaughtering, butchering. **2** murder. **3** abattoir.

jagang₁ support, prop, stand, pole (used for support). *- sepéda* bicycle stand.

jagang₂ moat.

jagat world. *- buana* the universe, cosmos. *- besar* macrocosm. *- kecil* microcosm. *- raya/semesta* universe. **se-** universal, world-wide. *féderasi buruh ~* international labor federation. *lomba ratu kecantikan ~* the Miss Universe beauty contest.

jago 1 cock, rooster. **2** gamecock. *Tingkahnya spt dia sendirilah yg paling -* He behaves as if he were cock of the walk. **3** champion, athlete. *Dialah yg menjadi - dlm kelasnya* He is the o. who is tops in in his class. *- nonton* inveterate movie-goer. *- (be)renang* swimming champ. *- bola* soccer player. *- gelut* 1 brawler. 2 wrestler. *- gulat* wrestler. *- jotos* boxer. *- kepuk* soccer player. *- kepruk* brawler, troublemaker. *- mérah* fire. *- tinju* boxer. **4** (*Pol.*) candidate. **5** charismatic leader of a group. *- tua* grand old man. **men-i 1** champion, root for. *Pihak mana yg kau-i?* Which side are you rooting for? **2** lead, be at the head of. *Indonésia ~ Swédia enam-tiga* Indonesia leads (over) Sweden 6-3. **men-kan 1** sponsor, back, champion. *Negara itu ~ démokrasi* That country champions democracy. **2** make into a candidate. **ke-an** prowess, mastery. **-an 1** gamecock. **2** champion, leader. **-²an** do s.t. recklessly, as if o. were a champion at it when o. is actually not. *Ia selalu ~ naik motornya* He must think he is a professional racer the way he drives his motorcycle.

Jagorawi [*Jkt Bogor Ciawi*] expressway between Jkt and Ciawi via Bogor.

jagung₁ corn, maize. *- bakar* roasted corn. *-*

beleduk/brondong/meletus popcorn. - *pipilan* dry-shelled corn. **men-** sprout (of rice, acne, etc.). *Gigi anak saya* ~ My child's teeth are making their appearance.
Jagung₂ [*Jaksa Agung*] attorney general.
jagur robust, sturdy, big for o.'s age. *Ki -, si -, pen-* name of the sacred cannon in Jkt.
jahan k.o. catfish.
jahanam 1 (*Rel.*) hell. **2** (*Vulg.*) a strong oath. *-! Pergilah!* Damn you! Get out of here! **men-i, men-kan 1** ruin, destroy. **2** curse, swear at. **ke-an** accursed experience.
jahat had, wicked, evil. **ber- 1** sin, do wrong. **2** defame, malign s.o. **3** seduce (a female). **men-i 1** do bad things to s.o. or s.t. *Pemuda-pemuda ~ mobil-mobil yg diparkir di depan* Some youths damaged the cars parked out front. **2** tease. *Dia suka ~ adiknya kalau ibunya sedang pergi* He is fond of teasing his little sister when his mother has gone out. **men-kan 1** make s.t. look bad. *Ia ~ nama org tuanya* He gave his parents a bad name. **2** consider s.o. evil. **ke-an 1** evil, wickedness. **2** felony, misdeed, crime. *~ anak* juvenile delinquency. *~ dlm jabatan* malfeasance in office. *~ kesusilaan* moral offense. *~ moril* moral turpitude. **pen-** criminal, crook, felon. *~ perang* war criminal.
jahé ginger. *- telur* a dish of ginger syrup and raw eggs.
jahid see ZAHID.
jahil₁ 1 stupid, ignorant, unenlightened. **2** (*Isl.*) ignorance of religion's teachings. **3** cruel. **4** rascal, scamp. **ke-an** ignorance.
jahil₂ see JAIL.
Jahiliah (*Isl.*) age of pagan ignorance preceeding the Isl. era.
jahit sewing. **ber-** seam, having stitches in it. *BH yg tdk ~* A bra with no stitches. **- men- 1** sewing, tailoring. **2** needlework. **men- 1** sew, stitch. **2** tailor. **men-i** sew. *Pakaian itu di-inya dgn benang emas* She sewed the clothing with golden thread. **men-kan 1** sew for s.o. **2** sew (cloth) into s.t. *Baju ini di-kan pd Pak Amat* Have this shirt sewn at Pak Amat's. **-an 1** sewn item, sewing to be done. *Apakah ada ~ yg hrs dikerjakan hari ini?* Is there any sewing that has to be done today? **2** seam, stitch, suture. *~ bersilang* cross-stitch. **pen-** tailor, seamstress. **pen-an** sewing.
jail /ja'il/ mischievous, sneaky. **men-i** mistreat, pick on s.o.
jailangkung device used in a seance: a straw man into which the spirit of a departed person not personally familiar to the audience has entered; this is fitted with s.t. to write responses to questions. *- jailangsék* formula used in calling out this device.
jaitun see ZAIT.
jaiz (*Isl.*) allowed but not required.
jaja ber-, men- hawk, peddle, vend. *Ia ~ berkeliling kota* He went around town peddling. **men-kan** peddle, hawk s.t. **-an** merchandise that is peddled. **pen-** hawker, peddler.
jajag see JAJAK.

jajah men- 1 colonize, take over (a country). **2** traverse, tour. *~ seluruh dunia* traverse the whole world. **men-i** traverse, tour. **ter-** colonized. **-an 1** colony, subjugated territory. *~ seberang lautan* overseas territory. **2** (*Lit.*) district. **pen-** colonizer. **pen-an 1** colonial domination. **2** colonization.
jajak men-i 1 probe, sound out. *Misi ini ~ kemungkinan invéstasi di . . .* This mission is sounding out the possibility of investment in . . . **2** (*Naut.*) fathom, take soundings, plumb. **ter-i** probed, sounded out. *Kemungkinan pembangunan PLTN blm ~* The development of nuclear-powered electric plants has not been investigated. **pen-** s.t. which probes, sounds out. *~ perdamaian* peace-feeler. **pen-an** sounding out, plumbing. **per-an 1** measuring. **2** investigation.
jajal men- try, test.
jajan 1 a sweet, snack. **2** eat snacks. **3** (*Humorous*) patronize a prostitute (of married men). **ber-** eat snacks. **-²an** various k.o. snacks.
jajar₁ row, line. **se- 1** parallel. *Dua jalan ini ~* These two roads are parallel. **2** in a row. **3** equal at the same level. *Kedua papan itu ~* The two boards are level with each other. **mense-i** equal, parallel s.t. **mense-kan 1** make s.t. parallel. **2** equate, place on a par. *Peraturan baru ~ pangkat komisaris polisi dgn pangkat létnan kolonél* The new regulations equate the rank of police commissioner with that of lieutenant colonel. **kese-an** parallelism. **perse-an, pese-an** parallelization. **ber-** in a row or line. *duduk ~* sit in row. **ber-an 1** side by side. **2** in rows. **men-i** come to the side of. **men-kan 1** place in a row, align. **2** make parallel. *~ dua papan* lay two planks parallel. **ter-** placed in rows. *Buku-buku ~ rapi dlm almari* The books were neatly arranged in the cabinet. **-an 1** row, line. **2** series. **3** array. *~ génjang* (*Math.*) parallelogram. **pen-an** alignment, juxtaposition, making parallel.
jajar₂ men- plow. **men-kan** pull, drag s.t. **-an** furrow.
jajat imitation. **men-** imitate.
jaka bachelor. *- tingting* (*Jv*) young man who has never had sex. **per-** bachelor. **keper-an** bachelorhood.
jakal jackal.
jakar see ZAKAR.
jakas k.o. pandanus tree.
jakat see ZAKAT.
Jakbar [*Jkt Barat*] W. Jkt.
jakét jacket, sport coat.
jakpot jackpot.
Jakpus [*Jkt Pusat*] Central Jkt.
jaksa (*Leg.*) public prosecutor, district attorney. *- agung* attorney general. *- panitera* prosecutor at the court of first instance. *- penuntut* prosecuting attorney. *- tinggi* chief public prosecutor. *- umum* public prosecutor. **ke-an 1** office of the counsel for the prosecution. **2** attorney (general). **3** judiciary. *~ tentara* military tribunal.
Jaksel [*Jkt Selatan*] S. Jkt.
Jaktim [*Jkt Timur*] E. Jkt.

jakum, jakun Adam's apple.
Jakut [*Jkt Utara*] N. Jkt.
jala net, esp. a hand-held casting net. - *kawat* wire netting. - *kerap* small-mesh casting net. - *sérét* dragnet. **-²** a small net. ~ *rambut* hairnet. **men-**fish with a casting net. **pen-** fisherman who uses a casting net.
jalad frost, cold air.
jalak various k.o. starlings and mynas. - *hitam* the common myna. - *kaleng* the jungle myna. - *putih* k.o. white starling with black wings. - *suren* k.o. white-breasted starling.
jalal (*Rel., in fixed phrases only*) most holy, supreme. *Allah yg* - God Almighty, the Supreme God.
jalan 1 road, path, street. - *Maluku* Moluccas St. - *aspal* paved road. - *bébas hambatan* freeway. - *bentar* bypass. - *besar* highway, main road. - *buntu* 1 dead end, blind alley. 2 deadlock, impasse, stalemate. - *butulan* access road. - *cukai* toll road. - *dagang* trade road. - *mati* dead end. - *niaga* trade route. - *pelayaran* shipping lane. - *péndék* short cut. - *pintas(an)* short cut. - *protokol* main road of an area (over which official visitors enter). - *raya* highway. - *raya lintas* cepat thruway, expressway, turnpike. - *samping* access road. - *serap/setapak* footpath. - *simpang* side road. - *singkat* short cut. - *tambak* roadway, embankment, causeway. - *tembus* thoroughfare. - *tikus* tiny path. - *tol* toll road. - *utama* main highway. **2** course s.t. follows. - *air* waterway. - *angin* exhaust pipe. - *darah* blood stream. - *napas* respiratory tract, trachea. - *peluru* bullet trajectory. - *perkencingan* urinary tract. - *pikiran* train of thought. **3** way, manner. *dgn* - by means of. *Bagaimana -nya membuat bom atom?* What is the process for making an atomic bomb? *léwat - belakang* underhanded, through the back door. - *serang* cunning ways. *Itu tdk pd -nya* That is not proper. **4** course. *-nya pemeriksaan lambat* The course of the investigation is slow. **5** be going on, be approaching. *Ia sdh - sepuluh tahun* He is going on 10. **6** lineal family relation. *Menurut - bapak, saya berasal dr Sumatra* On my father's side, I come from Sumatra. **7** pass, go. *Minta -, tuan* May I get by, sir? **-²** (go for a) stroll. *Mari ~* Let us take a walk. **se- 1** parallel. *Garis-garis itu ~* Those lines are parallel. **2** be in accordance, in compliance. *Kelakuannya tdk ~ dgn kedudukannya* His behavior is not in accordance with his position. ~ *dgn permintaannya* in compliance with her request. ~ *jadi* of the same mother. **menye-kan** make s.o. be in compliance or accordance. ~ *program dgn anggaran yg tersedia* Make the program comply with the budget available. **kese-an** being of o. mind. *Ia dan saya ~ tafsir dlm persoalan itu* He and I are of the same mind in the way we interpret that problem. **ber- 1** walk. *Jangan ~ di tengah-tengah* Do not walk in the middle of the road. ~ *béngkok* follow the crooked path. ~ *dahulu* 1 precede s.o. 2 predecease. ~ *darat* go overland. ~ *dr pintu bela-*

kang be dishonest. ~ *di atas rél* stick to the business at hand. ~ *émpar* walk with the toes turned outward. ~ *kaki* go on foot. ~ *lurus* follow the straight and narrow path. **2** run (of an engine). *Tutuplah penutup radiator sambil mesin ~* Close the radiator cap while the engine is running. ~ *stasionér* idle (of motor, etc.). **3** run, go, work. *Pekerjaannya ~ dgn lancar* Her work is going smoothly. *perusahaan yg ~* a going concern. **4** be going on a certain age. *Ia sdh ~ sepuluh tahun* He is going on 10. **ber-² 1** take a stroll. **2** take a pleasure trip. **men-i 1** walk on. **2** undergo, endure (an operation, military training, punishment, etc.). **3** go through a period of o.'s life or certain exiences. ~ *hidup baru* enter on a new life. **4** travel through s.w. **men-kan 1** drive (car, etc.), operate (machine). **2** start, put into operation (a car, etc.), make s.t. go. *Ia ~ kudanya kencang* She made her horse go fast. ~ *uang* lend out money at interest. **3** carry out, perform (o.'s duty), put into effect. *Di-kannya peraturan baru itu* He put that new regulation into effect. **4** serve (prison sentence). **-an 1** pathway. **2** road, track. ~ *msk* driveway. **pe-** walker. ~ *kaki* pedestrian. **per-an 1** trip, journey, tour. ~ *dinas/jabatan* official travel. ~ *tunggal* o.-way trip. ~ *perdana* maiden voyage. **2** course. ~ *bintang* course of a star. ~ *darah* circulation of the blood. ~ *napas* respiratory tract.
jalang wild, untamed, undomesticated (of animals). *perempuan* - prostitute. **men-, ny-** be or become wild. **ke-an** wildness.
jalangkung see JAILANGKUNG.
jalar creeping (vines). *ubi* - sweet potatoes. **ber-**spread over. *Garis pendiriannya ~ di seluruh bukunya* His principle runs through his entire book. **ber-an, ber-² 1** crawl, creep (of snakes, etc.). **2** spread, creep (of plants). **men- 1** creep, crawl (of snakes, plants). *Tanaman itu ~ di pagar* That plant climbed on the fence. **2** spread (of fire, disease, etc.). *Penyakit ~ ke mana-mana* The disease spread everywhere. **men-i 1** crawl all over. *di-i semut* have ants crawling all over it. **2** spread over. *Rasa panas ~ wajahku* A hot flash spread over my face. **men-kan** cause s.t. to spread, spread s.t. ~ *minyak di jalan raya* spread oil on the highway. **ter-** spread out. *jatuh ~* fall flat on o.'s face. **-an 1** climbing pole. **pen-an 1** climbing, creeping. **2** pole or stake for climbing plants.
jali see TAJALI.
jali-jali 1 k.o. grass which produces hard edible seeds: Job's tears. **2** name of popular song of old Batavia.
jalil (*Isl., in fixed phrases only*) sublime, exalted.
jalin - *anyam* **men-anyamkan** weave and braid together. *Kita bisa men-anyamkan tujuan hidup kita* We can weave a life for ourselves together. - **ber-**intertwined. **ber-** tied together. *Papan-papan itu ~* The boards are tied together. **ber-²** complicated, intricate, involved. *Perkara itu sungguh ~* That is quite an intricate case. **ber-kan 1** involved in. **2** interlaced, intertwined. **men-**

1 weave, plait together (into a rattan blind, wickerwork, etc.). **2** make s.t. be closer or more intense. ~ *kerjasama di bidang perikanan* work out a closer cooperative program in the fishery industry. **3** compose (stories, etc.). **men-kan, member-kan** include, interweave s.t., weave s.t. in. *Kita bisa ~ agama di dlm kehidupan kita* We can make religion an integral part of our life. **ter-1** tied in. ~ *rapat dgn* closely tied in with. **2** involved. **keter-an** involvement, entanglement. **-an 1** s.t. braided, wickerwork. **2** combination. **pen-** thread, rope, or rattan for weaving or braiding.

jalma (*Jv*) creature.

jalu cock's spur. **ber-** have a spur. **men-** use the spur on.

jalur 1 strip, stripe. **2** traffic lane. - *hélm* street on which motorcycle drivers must wear helmets. - *hijau* median (on highway), green belt. - *jalan* traffic lane, line of traffic. - *jalan matahari* sun's course. - *lambat* slow lane. - *pemisah* median (on highway). *penahan angin* windbreak. - *sébra/zébra* pedestrian crossing. **3** (*R.R.*) track. - *dua belas* track 12. **4** space between two rows of plants, column between two lines. - *gempa* earthquake belt. - *hias* louvre. - *suara* sound track. - *tambahan* contiguous zone. **ber-(²) 1** striped, have stripes. **2** be in columns or rows spaced evenly apart (of plants). **men-i** provide with streaks, streak o.'s hair. **-an** wake of a ship.

jalus see JELUS.

jalusi jalousie, venetian blinds.

Jalut (*Bib.*) Goliath.

jam 1 hour. *dua* - two hours. **2** o'clock. - *berapa?* - *dua* What time is it? It is two o'clock. **3** time for doing s.t. - *besuk* visiting hours in hospital. - *bicara* visiting hours for a doctor. - *karét* not on time (lit., rubber time). - *kerja* working hours. - *kuliah* class hours. - *main* (*Thea.*) curtain time. - *makan* meal time. - *malam* curfew. *Karena kekacauan sdh memuncak,* - *malam diberlakukan dr jam enam soré sampai jam lima pagi* Because the disorders have reached a peak, curfew has been put into effect from six p.m. to five a.m. **4** watch, clock. - *békér* alarm clock. - *gadang* a well-known clock in Bukittinggi located directly on the equator. - *pasir* hourglass. - *saku* pocket watch. - *salon* grandfather clock. - *tangan* wristwatch. - *wékér* alarm clock. **ber-²** for hours, hours on end. ~ *ibu menantikan kedatangan Bp* For hours Mother waited for Father's arrival. **men-i** time s.t. or s.o. **-²an** on an hourly basis.

jamaah see JEMAAH.

Jamaah (*Isl.*) name of a fundamentalist sect.

jamadah inanimate.

jamah men-(i) 1 touch, feel, handle s.t. or s.o. **2** sleep with, have sexual relations with. **3** attack. *Jangan ~ wilayah ini* Do not attack this area. **ter-** toucheable. *tak* ~ never touched, cannot be touched. **-an** s.t. touched. ~ *manusia* touched by human hand. **pen-an** touching, feeling, handling of s.t.

jamak₁ plural. **men-kan** pluralize. **ke-an** pluralization. **pen-an** pluralizing.

jamak₂ ordinary, customary. *Hal itu bukanlah suatu perkara yg* - That is not an ordinary case. **se-nya** normally. ~ *org tua dihormati anak-anaknya* Children should normally respect their parents. **men-kan** make or consider s.t. customary. *Anak-anak muda yg* ~ *pemakaian bahasa Indonésia di daérah ini* It is the young people who are making the use of Indonesian a normal thing in this area.

jamal (*Isl., in fixed phrases only*) beauty.

jaman period, epoch. - *Belanda* the Dutch times. - *édan/gégér* time of turmoil. *sdh dimakan* - old, archaic. - *malaise/meléset* the Great Depression. - *Madya/Pertengahan* Middle Ages. - *sekarang* nowadays. *bukan -nya lagi* no longer in style. **se-cocval. men-** be up-to-date.

jamang₁ diadem.

jamang₂ moment. **se-** a moment.

jambak₁ 1 bunch (of flowers, onions, keys, etc.). *org se-* o.'s family, ancestors. **2** tuft (of hair), plume (on horses). **ber-²an** pull e.o.'s hair out. **men-** pull, tear out hair, seize by the forelock. **-an** hair that has been pulled out.

jambak₂ k.o. fruit, jambu or rose-apple.

jambal k.o. fish.

jamban privy, toilet, latrine. - *kencing* a privy for urinating only.

jambang₁ 1 vase, pot. **2** large earthen cooking pot. **-an 1** vase, pot. **2** toilet stool.

jambang₂ see CAMBANG.

jambar₁ shelter, temporary shed or hut.

jambar₂ serving, portion. *makan se-* eat o. serving.

jambatan see JEMBATAN.

jambé, jambi (*Lit.*) areca nut.

jambian k.o. fish.

jamblang k.o. sweet-sour and astringent fruit, dark purple about the size of an olive.

jamboré jamboree.

jambrét o. who snatches purses, jewelry, etc. **men-** snatch, seize (purse, etc.). **ter-** snatched. **-an 1** loot gotten by snatching. **2** plagiarism. **pen-** snatcher. ~ *dompét* purse snatcher. **pen-an** snatching.

jambrut see JAMRUD.

jambu k.o. fruit, the rose-apple. - *air* k.o. tree with edible fruit. - *bol/dersana/darsono* variety of rose-apple. - *biji/keletuk/klutuk/lambo* guava. - *médé/medék/ménté* cashew fruit.

jambu-jambu tuft, tassel.

jambul 1 tuft, plume (on horse). **2** crest (on bird). **3** front wave (in hair), tuft of hair. **-²** cowlick. **ber-** have a tuft. **men-** develop a crest. *Stlh diberi hair-spray rambutnya* ~ She arranged her hair into a crest with hair spray.

jamhur (*Lit.*) o. well-versed in religion.

jami (*Isl.*) mesjid - principal mosque.

jamiah, jamiat 1 gathering. **2** association.

jamik see JAMI.

jamin 1 guarantor. **2** guarantee, security. **ber-kan**

have as collateral. *Pinjaman itu* ~ *rumahnya* The collateral for the loan is his house. **men-** guarantee. *Saya* ~ *jam ini tahan air* I guarantee that this watch is waterproof. **ter-** guaranteeed. ~ *dr* free from. **keter-an** security, assuredness. ~ *kerja* job security. **-an 1** guarantee. ~ *hak* patent. ~ *hak cipta* copyright. ~ *hari tua* old-age security or pension. ~ *sosial* medical or other financial support from the gvt. **2** security, collateral, bail. *uang* ~ deposit to hold s.t. ~ *hukum* legal guarantee. ~ *tawanan* hostage. **pen-** guarantor. ~ *émisi* underwriter. **pen-an** giving a guarantee.

jamjam see ZAMZAM.

jamnas [*jamboré nasional*] national (Boy or Girl Scout) jamboree.

jampang see CAMBANG.

jampi magic formula or spell, incantation. **ber-1** possess a magic formula. **2** utter the formula. **men-** treat s.o. with an incantation, utter an incantation on behalf of. **men-kan** apply a certain thing as an incantation. **-an** formula chanted. **pen-** o. who utters incantations, sorcerer.

jampuk₁ k.o. owl.

jampuk₂ men- interrupt s.o.

jamput (*Vulg.*) a harsh curse, screw you!

jamrud emerald.

jamu₁ 1 guest. **2** meal, offering (in set phrases). - *laut* offering to the sea. **ber- 1** have or receive visitors. **2** call on. *Bp* ~ *ke rumah guru saya* Father called on my teacher at his home. **men-(i), memper-** entertain s.o. (with a meal). **men-kan** serve. *Ibu* ~ *minuman pd tetamu* Mother served drinks to the guests. **-an** dishes and drinks served to guests. ~ *makan* feast. ~ *minum* cocktail party. **pen-an** holding of a dinner party. **per-an 1** reception, banquet, party. ~ *makan* banquet. **2** a call, visit. ~ *kudus/suci* (*Rel.*) Holy Communion.

jamu₂ tonic made of medicinal herbs. **-²** nostrum, tonic. **-²an** medicinal herbs.

jamung torch.

jamur fungus, mushroom, toadstool. - *karang* moss or polyps growing on coral. - *kulit* skin fungus. - *kuping* k.o. edible fungus, tree ears. - *merang* small round edible mushrooms. - *nasi* edible mushrooms. - *padi* edible mushroom cultivated on the ashes of paddy bran. - *payung* wide mushrooms. **ber-** be covered with mold. *makanan yg* ~ moldy food. **men-** mushroom. *Hotél-hotél baru* ~ New hotels are mushrooming. **-an** moldy. **pen-an** mushrooming. ~ *buku* mushrooming of books.

Jan. [*Januari*] January.

jana see JANA BIJANA.

janabah, janabat (*Isl.*) **1** impure, ceremonially unclean. *Org - tdk boléh msk mesjid* A defiled person may not enter the mosque. **2** impurity after coitus.

jana bijana (*Lit.*) birthplace.

janah, janat see JANNAH.

janangau k.o. rice bug.

jancuk see ANCUK.

janda 1 widow, (less commonly) widower. - *berhias* childless widow. - *laki-laki* widower. **2** divorcee. - *blm berlaki* girl deserted by her lover after being seduced (lit., divorcee that has never been married). - *cerai* divorcee. - *kembang* **1** girl who was divorced prior to consummation of marriage. **2** girlish divorcee. **men-** be a widow or widower, be widowed. **ke-an** widowhood.

jandal-jendul bumpy, with bumps on skin.

jang (*Sd*) form of address to small boys or waiters.

jangak dissolute, licentious. **men-** lead a dissolute life, act dissolute. **pen-** libertine, rake.

jangan₁ 1 do not. **2** should not, ought not to. *Kita - patah hati* We should not be broken hearted. - *mau* be sure not to. - *mau bayar lebih dr seratus* Be sure not to pay more than 100. - *sampai* lest, otherwise. *Hati-hati - sampai jatuh* Be careful you do not fall. *Cepat, nak, - sampai terlambat* Hurry up or you will be late. - *tdk* must, have to. *Engkau - tdk datang nanti malam* You must come this evening. **-² 1** let us hope not. ~ *dia sibuk* Let us hope he is not busy. **2** perhaps, maybe (s.t. bad is the case). *Dia mulai merasa* ~ *itu hukuman Tuhan* She is beginning to feel that perhaps it is a punishment sent from the Lord. **-kan, -pun** let alone, much less. ~ *duduk, berdiripun tdk dpt* He cannot even stand, let alone sit. ~ *rumah, kamar pun blm punya* He does not even have a room yet, much less a house. **men-kan** forbid, prohibit, ban.

jangan₂ (*Jv*) vegetables cooked with soup or gravy. **-an** green vegetables.

jangar vertigo.

jangat 1 skin, hide. - *kepala* scalp. **2** rind. **3** bark (of tree). **4** rawhide rope. **men- 1** skin, flay, fleece. **2** strip bark. **pen-** skinner, flayer.

janggal 1 awkward, clumsy. **2** inelegant, displeasing (of sound or sight), discordant. **3** unbecoming, improper, indecent (of behavior). **men-kan 1** render s.t. awkward, unbecoming, or discordant. **2** consider s.t. awkward, unbecoming, or discordant. **ke-an** awkwardness, discordancy, impropriety.

janggel (*Jv*) corncob, young corn on the cob.

janggelan tentative, provisional.

janggér see JANGIR.

janggi 1 black or exotic person. **2** s.t. bizarre or different from the usual.

janggo cowboy, cowboylike.

janggut 1 beard. **2** chin. **ber-** bearded.

jangir 1 Balinese dancing girl. **2** k.o. Balinese dance and music.

jangka 1 (*Tech.*) compass for describing circles, etc. - *bagi* dividers, calipers. - *kaliber/lengkung* calipers. - *tusuk/ukur* compasses, dividers. **2** period of time. *dlm - satu tahun* within (a period of) o. year. *tdk ada -nya* unlimited. - *jauh* long range. - *kesalahan* range of error. - *panjang* long-range, long-term. *Itu rencana - panjang* That is a long-range plan. - *péndék* short-range, short-term. - *waktu* time span. - *waktu hidup* life expectancy, life span. **3** phase. *Perjuangan kita mencapai - baru* Our struggle is reaching a new phase. **ber- 1** (be a certain) measure. *Jalan ini lébarnya* ~ *lima méter*

This road measures five meters wide. **2** be spaced. **men-(kan) 1** measure (with calipers). **2** plan, work out. *Pemerintah ~ tindakan yg akan dilakukan* The gvt. is planning the action to be taken. **pen-an** planning out. *~ waktu* timing, planning out, the use of time.

jangkah step, stride. **men-** step over, clear s.t.

jangkang men- 1 straddle, stand with legs wide apart. **2** be wide apart (of legs). **ter-** be wide apart (of legs).

jangkap even. *- dua puluh tahun* an even 20 years.

jangkar 1 anchor. *- ayam* k.o. flower, cockscomb. *- darurat (Naut.)* sheet anchor. **2** roots that begin above ground (like mangrove roots). **ber-, men-** anchor. *Kapal ~ di pelabuhan* The ship anchored in the harbor. **men-kan** anchor s.t.

jangkat shallows, ford.

jangkau men- 1 reach. *Période yg mana yg di- dlm buku ini?* What is the historical scope of this book? **2** reach to. *~ propinsi-propinsi di Sulawesi* reach to the provinces of Celebes. **3** reach for. **4** reach out. *Bp ~ memetik bunga* Father reached out to pick flowers. **5** reach out, extend to. *Program itu tdk ~ anggota masyarakat* That program does not extend to members of society. **men-i** reach out to (a shelf, etc.). **men-kan** reach s.t. out. *~ tangannya ke méja itu* reach o.'s hands out to the table. **ter- 1** achieved, reached. *Édisi itu tdk ~ oléh kebanyakan org* That edition is out of the reach of most people. **2** achievable. *Berbagai masalah yg muncul blm dpt ~* The solutions to various problems that have arisen cannot yet be achieved. **-an 1** reach. *~ 2,03 méter* a 2.03-meter reach. **2** extent, scope, range. *~ kaidah* extent to which a rule holds. *~ makna* semantic range. **3** what o. hopes to attain. *~nya terlalu tinggi* She is too ambitious. **se-an, sepen-(an)** as far as s.t. reaches. *~ mata memandang* as far as the eye can see.

jangkerik see JANGKRIK₁.

jangki, jankih cords of a shoulder basket.

jangkih-mangkih scattered around in a disorderly manner.

jangking see JONGKANG₂.

jangkit ber-, men- 1 be contagious. *Koléra adalah penyakit ~* Cholera is a contagious disease. **2** spread (of disease, fire). **3** contagious, infectious (of music, etc.). **ber-an** spread contagion in all directions. **men-i** infect s.o. *Ini penyakit kulit dan kita bisa di-i* That is a skin disease and we might be infected. **men-kan** spread, transmit (a disease). **ter-** spread, infected. **keter-an** state of having gotten infected. **ter-i, ke-an 1** contaminated, infected, smitten by (virus, germ, disease). **2** smitten by. *Mahasiswa itu ~ Beatlemania* The student was bitten by Beatlemania. **pen-an** transmission (of disease). **per-an** outbreak (of disease).

jangkrik₁ cricket.

jangkrik₂ (*Jv*) exclamation used as a euphemism for *diancuk*.

jangkung 1 heron. **2** tall, long-legged (of a person). **-an** stilts.

janik sea urchin.

janin (*Biol.*) fetus, embryo.

janjang₁ (*Jv*) long and slender (of the neck).

janjang₂ (*M*) see JENJANG₁.

janji 1 promise, agreement, agree. *Meréka - utk bertemu lagi* They agreed to meet again. *- kawin* marriage vow. *- keling* false promise. **2** condition. *dgn -* on condition that. **3** engagement, appointment. *Saya punya - jam lima* I have an appointment at five o'clock. **4** delay, deferral. *Ia minta - seminggu* She requested a week's delay. **5** dying hour. *Sdh sampai -mu* Your final hour has arrived. **ber-** promise, pledge to do s.t. *Saya ~ membayar* I promise to pay. *~ setia* pledge allegiance. **(ber)-an** make an appointment with e.o. **men-kan** promise s.t. *Apa yg kau-kan pdnya?* What did you promise to give her? **per-an 1** agreement. **2** pact, covenant. *~ perdamaian* peace treaty. **3** contract. *~ sosial* social contract. *~ Baru (Bib.)* New Testament. *~ Lama (Bib.)* Old Testament. **4** appointment, engagement. **5** last will and testament.

janma see JALMA.

jannah, jannat (*Rel.*) paradise, heaven.

jantan 1 male, masculine (of animals). *ayam -* rooster. **2** bold, brave. *ucapan yg - bold* statement. **3** dashing, valiant. *- teruna* cream of young manhood. **4** virile, manly, macho. *sifat - guts, bravery. **ber-** have sexual intercourse with a man. **men-i** mount, serve a female animal. **ke-an** virility, manhood, machismo. **pe-** stud. *pemeliharaan ~* raising of bulls. **per-an** pederasty.

jantang₁ ber-, men- be clear, stand out (of blood vessels).

jantang₂ ter- blink from bright lights.

jantera see JENTERA.

jantik see JENTIK.

jantung 1 heart. *- cangkokan* transplanted heart. *- mengipas (Med.)* fibrillation. *- pisang* banana blossom. **2** the heart as the seat of the emotions. *Makan hati berulam - suffer greatly (lit., eat liver with the heart as o.'s side dish). *- hati* favorite child, darling, apple of o.'s eyes. **3** thick portion of hands, arms, legs, or feet. *- betis* calf (of leg). *- paha* fleshy part of thigh. *- tangan* heel of the hand. **4** heart-shaped ornament of necklace, watch. **-an 1** suffer a heart attack. **2** heart disease.

jantur 1 magic trick, sleight-of-hand. **2** magic spell. **men-** perform magic tricks. **ter-** enchanted, under a spell. **-an** puppeteer's narration in a shadow play. **pen- 1** sorcerer. **2** (snake) charmer.

Januari January.

janubi see KUTUB.

janur young coconut leaf.

jap 1 completed. **2** in agreement or accord.

Japen [*Jawatan Penerangan*] gvt. information office.

japit tongs, clamp.

japu, japuk k.o. small fish.

jara small drill, auger. **men-** drill, bore.

jarab scabies.

jarah₁ men- plunder. ~ *rajah* plunder and pillage. **-an** plunder, booty, spoils. **pen-** plunder, pillager. **pen-an** pillage, plundering.

jarah₂ see ZARAH, ZIARAH.

jarak₁ distance between, gap. *Rumah sebuah dgn yg lain sembilan méter -nya* The distance between o. house and the other is nine meters. *- antara* clearance, opening (for trucks on highway). *- baris berganda* double margin. *- dekat* short distance. *- jauh* long distance. *- jelajah* cruising range (of ship). *- penglihatan* range of visibility. *- perjalanan* range of movement. *- roda* wheelbase. *- tampak* visibility. *- témbak* firing range. *- tembang* cruising range (of plane). *- tempuh* radius (of missile). **ber-** 1 be at a distance of, have the distance of. *Pohon itu ~ tiga méter dr rumah* The tree is three meters from the house. 2 put distance between. *Anak-anak di baris depan ~ sedikit* The children in the front row moved a bit away from e.o. **men-** go to or keep at a distance from s.t. *Ia suka ~ org yg tdk dikenalinya* He tends to keep a distance from people he does not know. **men-i** put space between things. *Perbédaan pendidikan yg ~ kaum tua dgn anak-anak muda* It is the difference in education that creates a gap between the older generation and the youth. **men-kan** separate. *Wasitnya ~ kedua petinju itu* The referee separated the two boxers. **ter-** 1 separated from. 2 at a distance. **pen-an** spacing (of pregnancy, plants, etc.).

jarak₂ castor oil plant. *minyak -* castor oil.

jaram cold compress. **ber-** cool with cold compress. **men-** apply compress to or dab with s.t. cool. **pen-** cold compress.

jarambab see JEREMBAB.

jaran (*Jv*) horse.

jarang 1 rare, scarce. *Mutiara semacam itu -* That type of pearl is rare. 2 infrequently, rarely, seldom. *Ia - datang kemari* She rarely comes here. 3 spaced, wide apart (of teeth, plants, etc.). 4 coarse in texture (cloth). 5 sparse (of inhabitants), scanty (of hair). **-²** rarely, seldom. **men-** become scarce, widely spaced. *Giginya nampak sdh ~ O.* could see he had lost some of his teeth. **men-kan, memper-** 1 thin out. *Petani itu ~ tanaman di kebunnya* The farmer thins out the plants in his garden. 2 dilute. 3 space. *~ kehamilan* space pregnancies. **ke-an** infrequency, sparseness, rarity. **pen-an** spacing, thinning out.

jaras₁ bunch. *bawang perai se-* a bunch of leeks. **men-** arrange or tie in a bunch.

jaras₂ wicker basket.

jarem bruised, black and blue.

jargon jargon.

jari 1 digit (finger or toe). *- hantu* middle finger. *- jemari* fingers. *- kaki* toe. *- kelingking* little finger. *- lima* starfish. *- malang* middle finger. *- manis* ring finger. *- mati/panjang* middle finger. *- rimpang* widely spaced fingers or toes. *- renik* little finger. *- syahad/telunjuk* index finger. *- tengah* middle finger. 2 digitlike projection (eg. wheelspokes, squid tentacles, etc.). *- ampai* horsewhip.

- buaya k.o. plant. **-²** 1 radius. 2 spokes of a wheel. **men-** stand or stick out (like fingers).

jariah, jariat see AMAL.

jaring dragnet or seine (not a casting net), net used in sports. *memasang -* put out a net, set up a net. *- tadongan* a 40-meter long net. *- sésir* a net 1.5 meters wide. **-²** 1 web. *~ laba-laba* spider web. 2 sports net, mesh net. **men-** 1 catch or pick up in a net. *~ angin* useless act. 2 encompass, embrace (a large area, etc.). **ter-** caught, snared. **-an** 1 net. 2 network (TV, road, radio). *~ jalan* highway network. *~ listrik* electrical circuitry. *~ pembuluh* network of blood vessels. *~ spionase* spy ring. 3 (*Anat.*) tissue. *~ lemak* fatty tissue. **pen-** s.t. to use as a net. *~ burung* bird snare. **pen-an** action of snaring.

jaro bamboo lath or slat.

jarong k.o. of tree.

jarot fiber in fruit or vegetables. **-an** fibrous.

jarum 1 sewing or hypodermic needle. *- cocok* awl. *- goni* coarse needle for sewing sacks. *- jahit* sewing needle. *- kait* crocheting needle. *- kadut/karung* coarse needle for sewing sacks. *- layar* sailmaker's needle. *- penggérék* awl. *- rajut* knitting needle. *- suntik* hypodermic needle. *- tisik* darning needle. 2 pin. *- biku/bundel* pin, straight pin. *- cantél* safety pin. *- pentul* straight pin. *- penyemat* pin. 3 hand of clock, pointer. *- arloji* hand of watch. *- jam* hand of clock. *- panjang* minute hand. *- pedoman* compass needle. *- péndék* hour hand. *- sekon* second hand. 4 trick, ruse. *- halus* sly trick. *melakukan -* play a trick. **-²** 1 needle on pair of scales. 2 nettles. **ber-** 1 have an injection or inoculation. 2 use a needle. 3 thorny, with nettles. **men-** 1 pin. 2 inject, inoculate. 3 prick (the finger, etc.). **men-i** stick into s.t. **-an** 1 needlework. 2 stitch. 3 mild trickery.

jarwa explanation of the meaning, exegesis. *- dosok* (*Ling.*) associative etymology. **men-kan** give a wider explanation.

jas coat. *- buka* open jacket with lapels. *- dingin* overcoat. *- hujan* raincoat. *- kamar* housecoat. *- kerja* working suit. *- luar* overcoat, topcoat. *- mandi* bathrobe. *- minyak* raincoat, slicker. *- tutup* jacket with stiff high collar and no lapels. *-wadi* condom.

jasa 1 merit. 2 service. 3 commendable or meritorious service. *dlm bidang -* in the area of services. *Ia banyak - thd tanah air* She has rendered her country many services. *- baik* good offices. *- raharja* compulsory accident insurance when traveling administered by the state. **ber-** 1 render a service, do a good turn. 2 deserving, meritorious (person).

jasad (*Biol.*) 1 body. 2 organism. *- renik* microorganism.

jasadi bodily, physical.

jasirah see JAZIRAH.

jasmani body. *dlm - yg séhat terdapat rohani yg séhat* a sound mind in a sound body. **ke-an** materialism. **pen-an** 1 materialization. 2 embodiment.

jasmaniah bodily. *kebutuhan -* physical needs.

Jasuka [*Jawa, Sumatera, Kalimantan*] Java, Sumatra, Borneo.
jaswadi see JAS.
jatah 1 allotment, allocation. **2** quota. **3** bribe. **men-kan** allot, allocate. **pen-an 1** alloting, allocating. **2** distributing.
Jateng [*Jawa Tengah*] Central Java.
jati₁ k.o. hardwood tree, teak.
jati₂ see SEJATI.
Jatim [*Jawa Timur*] E. Java.
jatmika 1 polite. **2** modest. **ke-an** politeness, modesty.
jatuh 1 fall. *Ia dr atap* He fell from the roof. - *ke tangan* . . . fall into the clutches of . . . - *tertimpa tangga* have very bad luck (lit., fall and then have the ladder fall on o.). - *cinta pd* fall in love with. **men-cintakan** cause s.o. to fall in love with. - *coloknya* degraded, debased. - *di atas tilam* 1 get off easy. 2 have a lucky break. - *duduk* up and down. - *hati kpd* 1 fall in love with. 2 feel sorry for. - *hujan* rainfall. - *pd* fall for. *Kita* - *pd tipumuslihatnya* We fell for his trick. - *pingsan* keel over, faint. - *sakit* fall ill. - *témpo* be due (of debt payment). **2** fall (of prices, gvt.). - *tekanan* drop in pressure. **3** fall from a high position. - *bangun* 1 fall and rise again, persevere. 2 trial and error. **men-bangunkan** cause s.t. to fall and rise. *Kopra bisa men-bangunkan seorg kepala daérah* Copra can make or break a district head. - *ke atas* be lucky. - *ke bawah* retrogress. - *ke kasur* fall back nicely. - *mérek/nama* lose o.'s good name. - *miskin* become impoverished. **4** fail, flunk. *Ia* - *dlm ujian ilmu pasti* She failed the science exam. **5** lead, reach, arrive. *Jalan ini* - *ke Candi Mendut* This road leads to Candi Mendut. *Kapal itu* - *di Tanjungpriok* That ship arrived at Tanjungpriok. **6** related. *Kau apa -nya dgn Tomo?* How are you related to Tomo? **ber-an** fall (plural). *Buah-buah kastanye ~ ke dlm truk* The chestnuts poured down into the truck. **men-i** fell. *~ hukuman* (*Leg.*) impose a sentence on. *Ia di-i hukuman tujuh tahun* He got seven years. **men-kan** let fall, drop. *Dia ~ diri dlm kursi* He threw himself into the chair. *~ bom atom* drop an atomic bomb. **2** drop, supply a lower level with money. *~ satu juta rupiah utk biaya rutin* drop o. million rupiah for routine expenses. **3** topple, overthrow, bring down (the gvt., regime). **4** ruin, topple, ruin a good name. *Korupsi ~ perusahaan itu* Corruption ruined that firm. *~ nama* ruin o.'s reputation. **5** (*Leg.*) pass (a sentence, judgment), hand down (a verdict, decision). *~ denda* impose a fine. *~ pukulan* deliver a blow. *~ véto* cast a veto. **ter-** fall suddenly or unexpectedly. **ke-an 1** fall, downfall (of a gvt., cabinet). **2** be hit by a falling object. *Kepalanya ~ kelapa* He was hit on the head by a falling coconut. *~ bulan* have a windfall. *Ia ~ bulan* Good fortune befell her. *~ ilham* get an inspiration. *~ penyakit* come down with an illness. **-an** dropping, fall-out. *~ batu* falling or fallen rock. *~ udara* a drop from the air. **pen-an 1** pronouncement of sentence. **2** dropping of s.t.

jauh 1 far, distant, remote. *Indonésia* - *dr Amérika* Indonesia is far from America. *tiga mil -nya* The distance is three miles. - *di mata dekat di hati* gone but not forgotten. **2** far, by far. *Lukisan ini* - *lebih bagus drp yg lain* This painting is far better than the other o. is. - *dicari* exaggerated. - *pemandangan* 1 far-sighted. 2 foreseeing, perceptive. - *umur* advanced in age, along in years. *Ia mati ssdh* - *umur* She died at an advanced age. - *malam* late at night, far into the night. **-²** when o. is far. *~ asal selamat* It does not matter how far (he is away), as long as he is safe. *~ hari* long beforehand. **se-** as far as. *~ manakah?* in how far? to what extent? *~ yg saya ketahui* as far as I know. **se-²** as far as possible. *~ mata memandang* as far as the eye can see. **se-²nya** as far as possible. **ber-** be distant. **ber-an** be far from e.o. *Meskipun kita ~ kita tak akan saling melupakan* Although we're far apart, we will not forget e.o. - **men-i** keep at a distance from e.o. **men-** be or grow distant. *Kapal itu makin ~ dr pantai* The ship drew farther and farther away from shore. **men-i 1** avoid, keep away from. *Ia selalu ~ saya* She always avoids me. **2** be far from. *Senidramanya amat ~ kenyataan* His play is very far from reality. **men-kan, memper-** keep s.t. away. *-kan anak-anak itu dr bahaya* Keep the children away from danger. *~ diri dr* refrain from, avoid. **ke-an 1** distance, distant place. *kelihatan di ~* visible in the distance. **2** too far. *Méja itu ~ dr saya* That table is too far away from me. **-an** distant place. **pen-an 1** avoidance. **2** separation.
jauhar 1 jewel. **2** embryo.
jauhari 1 jeweler. **2** expert, specialist.
Jauza (*Zod.*) Gemini.
Jaw. [*Jawatan*] office, division, bureau.
Jawa 1 Java, Javanese. **2** (*Jv*) s.t. of local origin rather than the imported or foreign kind. *gula* - palm sugar (the local kind, rather than cane sugar). **3** (*Jv*) well-bred. *Anak itu blm* - That child has not learned to behave. **men-kan** Javanize. *~ nama menjadi* Javanize o.'s name to. **ke-an 1** being Javanese. **2** Javanism. **pen-an** Javanization.
jawab reply, answer, response. *"Ndak mungkin," -nya* "Impossible," she answered. - *kedua* rejoinder. **ber- 1** answer, reply, respond. *"Tdk," ia ~* "No," she replied. **2** have, receive an answer. *Pertanyaan yg itu tdk ~* The question received no answer. **ber-an** reply to e.o. **men-** answer, reply. *~ pertanyaan* field questions. *~ perjamuan* return a call. **men-i** answer, respond to (several questions). *Sulit juga ~ pertanyaan sdr* It is quite difficult to answer your questions. **men-kan** give a certain answer. *Tdk tahu saya apa yg hrs di-kan* I do not know what answer to give. **ter-** be answered. **-an** answer, response. **pen-** answerer, replier. *~ dakwaan* (*Leg.*) respondent. **pen-an** answering.
jawahir intrinsic.
Jawanisasi Javanization.
jawat se- colleague. **ber-** *tangan* shake hands. *Petang sdh ~ tangan dng senja* Afternoon was re-

placed by dusk. **men-** 1 hold s.o.'s hand. 2 receive, welcome (gift, etc.). 3 hold an office or position. **men-ankan** convert into an official office. **-an** office, division, bureau. ~ *béa dan cukai* customs and excise service. ~ *distribusi* rationing office. ~ *géologi* geological survey. ~ *imigrasi* immigration service. ~ *keréta api* Indonesian Railways. ~ *luar negeri* foreign service. ~ *pajak* bureau of internal revenue. ~ *pelayaran* navigation service. ~ *penerangan* information service. ~ *penerbangan* aeronautics board. ~ *purbakala* archaeological service. ~ *rahasia* secret service. ~ *tera* bureau of standards. **pen-** *pribadi* privy chamberlain.

jawawut (*Jv*) millet.

jawi₁ ox, cow.

jawi₂ 1 Malaya or Indonesia (as the homeland of Indonesians or Malays who are in Mecca). *Orgnya masih berada di Mekkah. Blm turun ke - lagi* The person was still in Mecca and had not returned to Indonesia yet. 2 the script for writing Malay or Indonesian with Arabic letters. **men-kan** 1 translate into Malay. 2 put into the Malay script.

jawi-jawi k.o. large ficus tree.

jawil men- touch s.o. in order to get attention.

jaya₁ 1 victory. 2 victorious, glorious. *Indonésia -* glorious Indonesia. 3 prosperous. *Dia hidup -* He is prospering. **ber-** 1 victorious, triumphant, glorious. 2 successful, doing very well. **men-kan** glorify, extol. ~ *negara* glorify a country. **ke-an** 1 glory, fame. 2 prosperity, wealth. ~ *udara* air supremacy.

Jaya₂ [*Jkt Raya*] Greater Jkt.

jazirah peninsula.

jazz /jés/ jazz.

jeans /jin, jins/ 1 denim. 2 jeans.

jebah₁ full, broad (of face).

jebah₂ ber- 1 profuse, copious, abundant. 2 assorted, various.

jebai ber- scattered, spread about.

jebak trap. **men-** 1 trap (animals, birds). 2 trap, frame s.o. *Kalian ~ku, ya?* You framed me, didn't you? **ter-** trapped, framed, snared. **-an** trap, snare. **pen-** 1 trapper. 2 trap, snare. **pen-an** 1 trapping, snaring. 2 trapping spot.

jebang long shield made of wood and covered with hide.

jebar-jebur 1 splashing of water while bathing. 2 pouring of water over o.s.

jebat musk. **men-i** anoint. **-²an** fragrant aromas, perfumes.

jebik thick or hanging (of lower lip). **men-** be thick, hang down (of lower lip). **men-kan** curl the lower lip down (to tease).

jeblok₁ muddy. **ke-** 1 be stuck, mired in mud. 2 be tricked, cheated.

jeblok₂ sag, drop (of prices, inflation, etc.).

jeblos give way. *Rém -* The brake gave away. **mem-kan** 1 throw s.t. into. 2 throw (into jail). **ke-, ter-** 1 step or drive into a hole or ditch. 2 cheated, fooled, tricked. *Ia ~ oléh pihak musuh*

He fell into a trap his enemy had set for him. 3 thrown into prison.

jebobok stand on end (of hair), ruffle (of feathers).

jebol 1 broken down. 2 perforated. **men-** 1 break down (a door, etc.). 2 penetrate (enemy lines, etc.). 3 break through (a wall, etc.). **men-kan** 1 make s.t. break down or through. 2 (*Sport*) score. **-an** 1 dropout or graduate. ~ *falkultas hukum* law school dropout. 2 ex, former. ~ *pemain ban* ex-bandplayer. **pen-an** breaking down or through of, inroads, incursion.

jebrét₁ scratched, scrawled. **men-** scratch, scrawl (o's signature).

jebrét₂ sound of a stapler. **men-** staple s.t. **-an** staples.

jebrol men- erupt. *Lahar ~ dr mulut gunung berapi* Lava erupted from the mouth of the volcano. **men-kan** 1 produce, bring forth, give birth to. *Sapi tlh ~ anaknya* The cow had her calf. *Tukang sunglap ~ telur dr mulutnya* The magician produced an egg from his mouth. 2 eject, expel s.t. **pen-an** ejection.

jebuh k.o. fish.

jebul see JEBOL.

jebung k.o. fish, the leatherjacket.

jebur see CEBUR, JEBAR-JEBUR.

jeda 1 rest, respite, take a rest. *- kopi* coffee break. 2 (*Poetry*) caesura. 3 (*Ling.*) juncture. **ber-** take a rest. *tak ~* unceasing, incessant.

jedar-jedor sound of a firearm.

jeding₁ (*Jv*) k.o. tub to store water.

jeding₂ curl upward (of lips).

jedul (*Jv*) sudden appearance.

jégal (*Jv*) **men-** 1 stop, intercept s.o. 2 (*Sport*) keep an opponent from winning. *Inggeris di- Amérika* America stopped England from becoming the winner. **men-i** interfere with, interrupt. ~ *jalannya révolusi* interfere with the course of the revolution. **pen-** o. who interferes with. **pen-an** interfering, stopping.

jegang 1 stiff, inflexible. 2 tense, tight.

jegil men- 1 bulge (of eyes). 2 stab.

jeglég (*Jkt*) sound of clicking. **nge-** make a clicking sound. **men-kan** punch a hole in. **-an** staple for a stapler.

jeglong have a hole in it. **ber-** bumpy, have bumps (of road). **-an** (*Jv*) pothole.

jegog (*Jv*) **men-** to bark.

jegrag (*Jv*) **men-** stand on end (of hair).

jegung (*Naut.*) sea chest, place for storing rigging, sails, etc.

jejadian an invisible animal with supernatural powers, obedient to its human master.

jejak₁ 1 trail, track (of animal). 2 footstep, footprint. *- jari* fingerprint. *- kaki* footprint. *- bara* almost touching the ground. 3 (*Naut.*) wake. **ber-** 1 step, tread on, set foot on. 2 leave tracks. **men-** step, set foot on. *Saya blm ~ Amérika* I have not yet set foot on America. *Rambutnya ~ bahu* She has shoulder-length hair. **men-i** 1 tread, step on. 2 trail, track down (criminal, etc.). 3 investigate.

Polisi ~ kerja biro itu Police investigated that office. **men-kan** set down (o.'s foot). **ter-** trailed, tracked.

jejak₂ 1 straight, erect. **2** stable.

jejaka 1 youth, young man. **2** bachelor, unmarried young man.

jejal ber- 1 crowd, jam. *Tetamu ~ di serambi muka* Guests crowded into the front room. **2** be jampacked (with spectators, etc.). **ber-(an)** thronged, crowded. *Para pembeli karcis ~* The ticket buyers thronged together. **men-** stuff full. *Kondektur ~ bisnya* The conductor crammed the bus full. **men-i 1** fill, crowd, throng (room, auditorium, etc.). *Kota-kota besar makin banyak di-i tunawisma* More and more the homeless are thronging the large cities. **2** fill, stuff (a hole, etc.). **men-kan** stuff, cram s.t. into. **ter-** crowded, jammed. **-an** a throng. **pen-an** filling up, stuffing.

jejala network.

jejamu herbs of various sorts.

jejas lacerated, laceration, lesion. *Ia jatuh tetapi ia tdk - sedikit juapun* She fell but did not receive a single scratch.

jejawi k.o. large ficus tree, the banyan.

jejek stable, sound, firm (of a society, etc.).

jejel see JEJAL.

jejenang frame of door or window.

jejer (*Jv*) a row of leather puppets arrayed in preparation for use in performance.

jéjér series, row, line. **ber-** in a row. *berdiri ~* stand in line. **men-(kan)** arrange in a row. **men-i** get into line with, go up to s.t. to be in a row or line with it. **-an** series, row, line.

jejungkrak, jejungkrakan totally razed.

jék /jék/ (*Crd.*) jack.

jéket jacket.

jéksi see INJÉKSI.

jél (*Coll.*) jail.

jela ber-(²) dangle, swing to and fro (of rope, etc.). **ter-** dangling. *Dasinya ~ di léhérnya* His tie was dangling from his neck.

jeladan k.o. bird that feeds on rice.

jelaga carbon black, soot, lampblack. *- arang* carbon deposit.

jelai₁ 1 k.o. plant, Job's tears. **2** barley.

jelai₂ jam, jelly.

jelajah men-(i) 1 cruise over seas, cross land areas. *Kami tlh ~ belukar hutan bakau* We had already traversed the mangrove swamp scrub. **2** explore (an area, etc.). *Mataku ~ ke segala penjuru* My eyes explored every corner. **3** examine. *Kita ingin ~ pandangannya* We wish to examine his views. **meng-kan** analyze, examine, investigate. **pen- 1** explorer. **2** examiner. **pen-an 1** exploration. **2** examination.

jelak 1 bored, satiated. **2** be tired. **ter-** full, stuffed (with food).

jelalat glance. **-an** glance about, ogle.

jelang men- 1 call on, pay o.'s respects to. *Pd Hari Tahun Baru setiap org berkesempatan ~ Présidén* On New Year's Day everyone has an oppor-

tunity to pay his respects to the president. **2** visit. *béda dgn kota-kota lain yg sdh ku-* different from the other cities I had visited. **3** to (used to address mail). *~ Bp Harsono* to Mr. Harsono. **4** around, toward. *~ Hari Raya harga semua naik* As the fasting month holidays approach everything goes up in price. **5** approach, come close to. *Kurasa waktu itu aku sdh ~ saat ajalku* I felt at that time that I was approaching my final moment. *~ sungai kecil* upon approaching a small river.

jelangak men- look upward.

jelangkung see JAILANGKUNG.

jelantah oil that has been used for frying and will be reused.

jelapak ber-, ter- flop down from weariness.

jelas 1 clear, distinct. *tampak dgn -* clearly visible. **2** unequivocal, explicit (instructions, etc.). *Perkara itu sdh menjadi -* The case has become clear. *- jemelas* very clear. *- terang* **men-terangkan** explain and clarify. **men-** become clear(er). *Bayangan itu ~* The figure became clearer. **men-i** look into a matter, question s.t., seek clarification about. **men-kan 1** clarify, explain s.t. *Ia ~ kedudukan perkara yg sebenarnya* He explained what the real situation of the case was. **2** resolve, settle, clean up (a debt, conflict, etc.). **memper-** clarify. **ke-an** clarity. **pen-** clarifier. *keterangan ~* explanatory material. **pen-an** explanation, clarification.

jelata see RAKYAT.

jelatang 1 stinging nettle. **2** agitator. *- di hulu air* a nuisance from the outset.

jelatik see GELATIK.

jeléh (*Jv*) **nj-i** disgusting, sickening.

jeléjéh ber-an, men- dribble, slobber.

jelék 1 ugly. **2** bad, evil (thoughts, etc.). *- sekali berbuat begitu* It is very bad to do that. **3** bad, poor in quality, not good. *kertas yg -* poor-quality paper. *nasib yg -* bad luck. **-nya** the trouble is, the bad thing is . . . *-²* ugly though o. may be. *~ begini, dia anak duta* He may be ugly, but he is the ambassador's son. **men-i, men-kan** besmirch, sully s.o.'s name, vilify. **memper-** make s.t. worse. **ke-an 1** ugliness. **2** badness, evil. **3** poorness of quality. *~ pendidikan* the poor quality of education. **-²an** of poor quality.

jelempah men- lie scattered about.

jelengar men-, ter- surprised, stunned into silence.

jelentik men- tap or touch s.t. lightly.

jelépak, jelépok men-, ter- fall backward with a plop, lie. *Aku ~ di sisinya* I fell back beside her. *tubuh yg ~ depan pintu* the body lying in front of the door.

jeli 1 charming, ravishing, beautiful (of eyes). **2** sharp (in observation). *Mataku - betul, Tuan. Dua belas semuanya* I have really sharp eyes, Sir. There were 12 of them in all. **ke-an** carefulness of observation or work. *~ sangat perlu dlm pembetulan komputer* Computer repairs require careful work.

jéli cosmetic cream.
jelik see JELÉK.
jelimet hair-splitting, meticulous. **(me)n-** be meticulous. **ke(n)-an** meticulousness.
jeling men- cast a sideways glance, ogle.
jelir men- project, protrude, stick out. **men-kan** stick out (o's tongue).
jelita 1 lovely, sweet. **2** graceful, charming, beautiful. **ke-an** loveliness.
jelititan look around in a confused way. *Ia ~ ketika tlh sadar dan dikelilingi org banyak* He looked around in a daze when he came to and found himself surrounded by a crowd.
jelma men- assume a form. *Nah akan ~ jadi macan gadungan* Nah is going to take the form of a changeling tiger. *Tukang sihir itu ~ menjadi seékor burung* The wizard transformed himself into a bird. *Ssdh mati roh kita akan ~ lagi* After death our souls will be reincarnated. **men-kan 1** create. *Tuhan ~ langit, bulan, dan bintang-bintang* God created the sky, the moon, and the stars. **2** realize, bring about. *~ cita-citanya* realize o.'s ideals. **3** transform s.o. or s.t. **ter-** come into being. **-an 1** incarnation, creation. **2** thing into which s.t. has been transformed. **pen-an 1** incarnation. **2** creation (of). **3** realization, materialization.
jelu (*Jv*) **1** irked, piqued, annoyed. **2** dejected.
jeluak men- vomit.
jeluang bark cloth.
jeluat men- protrude. *Matanya ~* His eyes popped out of his head. *Tulangnya yg patah ~* The broken bone stuck out (of his arm).
jelujur men- 1 baste (a hem). **2** tie or stitch together. *Benang mérah ~ pidato-pidato saya* A red thread held my speeches together. **men-i 1** stitch s.t. on. **2** hold s.t. together with a thread. *Karya Sontani di-i oléh suatu jalur téma yg jelas* A clear thematic line runs through S's writings. **3** go over the length of s.t. **4** investigate. **pen-an 1** going over s.t. **2** investigation.
jeluk cup, container. **men-kan** form a cup, cup. *Ia ~ tangannya menadah air* She cupped her hands to catch the water.
jelum ber- bathe by wetting the body, but not showering. **men-** give s.o. a sponge bath.
jelumat men- mend with fine stitching. **-an** a darn (in socks, etc.).
jelungkap men- 1 spring loose. **2** recoil.
jeluntung, jeluntur see CACAR.
jelunut viscous. **men-** adhere, cohere, stick.
jelus (*Coll.*) jealous, spiteful. **men-kan** cause jealousy, make s.o. jealous.
jelut men- 1 feel upset in the stomach. **2** be upset, annoyed, or irked.
jelutung k.o. tree that produces milky sap from which a rubber substitute can be made.
jém jam, jelly.
jemaah, jemaat 1 community, assembly. **2** (*Rel.*) congregation. - *geréja* parish. - *haji* collective pilgrimage to Mecca.
jemah later on, in the future. *tdk* - never.
jemala 1 head. **2** skull.

jemang se- a moment.
jemantung heart.
jemari finger.
jemawa conceited, arrogant. **ke-an** conceitedness, arrogance.
jemba measure of length, two fathoms or about 2.4 meters. **men-** reach out for, grab at. **-an** two fathoms.
jembak men-, ter-(^{2}) flutter in the wind.
jembalang k.o. supernatural creature, gnome.
jembatan 1 bridge. - *air* aqueduct. - *angkat* vertical lift bridge, drawbridge. - *apung* floating bridge. - *emas* golden bridge, best road or opportunity. - *gantung* suspension bridge. - *jungkatan/jungkit* drawbridge. - *layang* overpass, traffic flyover. - *lengkung* arched bridge, cantilever bridge. - *pelampung* pontoon bridge. - *saluran* aqueduct. - *semanggi* cloverleaf bridge. - *tarik* drawbridge. - *timbangan* truck weighing station. **2** bridge, bond between. **men-i** bridge (river, gap, generation), act as bridge for. *Pemerintah Indonésia ~ pertikaian antara Filipina dan Malaysia* The Indonesian gvt. is acting as a bridge between the Philippines and Malaysia in their dispute.
jémbél 1 poor, shabby, squalid. **2** wanderer, hobo, tramp. *turis/wisatawan* - tourists that look like hippies. **ke-an** squalor.
jémbér (*Jkt*) dirty, muddy.
jembiah k.o. dagger.
jémblem k.o. confection of fried cassava.
jembrot, jembrut see JAMRUD.
jembut (*Jv, Jkt*) pubic hair.
jemeki spangle, sequin.
jempalik, jempalit 1 turn a somersault, tumble over. **2** be upside down. **ber-an** turn somersaults several times.
jemparing (*Jv*) arrow.
jempol 1 thumb. **2** thumbs up, tops, first rate. *paling* - tops, number o. **men-** fingerprint s.o. **ke-an** being tops. **-an** first-rate in quality.
jemput *minta* - ask to be picked up. **se- 1** a pinch. *~ garam* a pinch of salt. **2** a little bit of s.t. *~ saran* a small suggestion. **men- 1** pick up (with fingertips). *Ia ~ kuéh dr piring* He picked up a cake from the plate. **2** pick up (figuratively). *Kata ini di- dr bahasa Jawa* This word has been borrowed from Jv. *Ia ~ sandiwara dr sebuah roman* He took his play from a novel. **3** call for, fetch. *Saya pergi ~ dokter karena Ibu sakit* I went to fetch the doctor because Mother was sick. *Saya di- di pelabuhan* They picked me up at the harbor. *di- yg empunya* meet o.'s maker, die. **men-i 1** pluck repeatedly. **2** pick at, pluck o.'s beard. **-an 1** pick up service, limousine. *Mila menunggu ~* Mila waited to be picked up. *Apakah ada ~ di terminal udara?* Will s.o. pick us up at the airlines terminal? *mobil ~* pick-up car. **2** laundry on the line or in the sun. **3** invitation. **4** (*M*) marriage proposal to a man. *laki-laki ~* man to whom a proposal has been made. *uang ~* dowry. **5** marriage partner. **pen- 1** drying rack for laundry. **2** o. who comes to meet or pick up s.o. *kendaraan*

~ vehicle used to pick up employees, passengers, etc. **pen-an, per-an 1** pick-up service (at airport, etc.). **2** picking up (of).

jemu 1 tired. **2** sick of, fed up with. *Kami - dgn kelakuannya* We are fed up with his behavior. *- hidup* weary of life, tired of living. *- jelak* disgusted, thoroughly fed up. **tdk -²(nya)** tirelessly. *bekerja tdk ~ work tirelessly.* **men-kan 1** bore s.o., boring. **2** tiresome, irksome. **ke-an 1** boredom. **2** be very bored.

jemuas filthy, covered with dirt, mud, or food.

jemuju₁ caraway seed.

jemuju₂ (*Sd*) k.o. timber tree.

jemur 1 sunbathe. **2** dry in the sun. **3** dried rice plant. **ber-** expose o.s. to the sun. **men-** spread out in the sun to dry. *Hém saya yg mérah jangan di-* Do not put my red shirt in the sun to dry. *Krupuk ini hrs di- dulu baru digoréng* You have to dry these chips out first before you fry them. **men-kan** spread out to dry on behalf of s.o. **ter-** dried in the sun. **-an 1** items being dried. **2** the wash, laundry. **pen-an 1** clothesline, rack for drying clothes. **2** action of drying in the sun. *~ makanan dan pakaian* drying of food and clothing.

jen. [*jénderal*] (*Mil.*) general.

jenabah, jenabat see JANABAH, JANABAT.

jenaha, jenahar k.o. fish, red snapper.

jenak₁ a moment. *beberapa - a few instants.* **se-** an instant.

jenak₂ 1 comfortable, at o.'s ease. **2** sound asleep.

jenaka funny, humorous. **ber-** joke, be witty or humorous. **ke-an** humor.

jenakawan humorist, comic.

jenang₁ 1 doorframe or window frame. **2** doorpost.

jenang₂ 1 (*Sport*) referee at cockfight. **2** (*Navy*) steward. **men-(i)** supervise. *Dukun ~ jalannya upacara* The shaman supervised the course of the ceremony. **pen- 1** supervisor, foreman. **2** referee. **3** adjustment.

jenang₃ 1 porridge, pudding, or any food which is thick and viscous. *- gula* k.o. taffy made of sticky rice, palm sugar, and coconut. **2** molten metal or wet cement. **-an** molten material or wet cement.

jenangau k.o. rice bug.

jenasah, jenazah corpse, mortal remains, cadaver. **men-kan** bury, inter. **pen-an** interment.

jendal-jendul bumpy, with a bump on the skin.

jendéla window. *- gésér* sliding window. *- jalusi* Venetian blind. *- (kaca) kubah* bay window. *- kontal-kantil* flap. *- nako* jalousie windows. *- sorong* sliding window. **ber-** have a window.

jénderal 1 general (rank). *gubernur -* governor general. *mayor -* major general. **2** general, comprehensive. *- répétisi* general rehearsal.

jéndol swollen (from a bump). **ber-, men-** stick out (of s.t. round).

jendul see JENDAL-JENDUL.

jeneng (*Jv*) **1** name. **2** status. *- keorangan* personal status.

jénéng slanting, sloping, at an angle. **men-kan** slant, slope, or tilt s.t.

jenéwer Dutch gin.

jeng (*Jv*) polite form of address for a woman the same age or younger than speaker.

jengah 1 embarrassed. **2** reluctant. **ke-an** embarrassment.

jengat see JANGAT.

jengék, jéngék₁ meng-², meng-i mock, ridicule. *Jangan ~ org cacat* Do not make fun of handicapped people. **-an** mockery, ridicule.

jéngék₂ (*M*) woman trader of smuggled or illegal consumer goods.

jenggar-jenggur (*Jkt*) overgrown, overlarge, exceptionally big for o.'s age.

jénggér cock's comb. **ber-** have a comb.

jénggot beard. **ber-** have a beard. **-an** having a beard.

jengguk see JENGUK.

jenggul see JÉNDOL.

jenggur see JENGGAR-JENGGUR.

jengit ber- look startled. *~ getir* look glum.

jengit-jengit men- bob up and down (of dog's tail, head, etc.).

jengkal span (of the hand, about nine inches). *Dr se- mau sedepa* Give him an inch and he will take a mile. **men-** measure s.t. in spans. *~ dada* underestimate s.o.'s courage. *~ muka* do s.t. useless.

jengkang ke-, men-, ter- 1 fall or topple backward. **2** lie on o.'s back. **3** (*Vulg.*) die, kick the bucket.

jéngkang *- jengkot* limp. *Ia - jengkot jalannya* He walks with a limp. **men-** limp.

jengkau see JANGKAU.

jéngkék ber- 1 jump with joy. *Ia ~ mendengar berita itu* She leaped with joy on hearing the news. **2** walk on high heels.

jéngkél annoyed, irritated, irked. *- saya mendengarkan keluh kesahnya* I get annoyed listening to his complaints. **men-i, men-kan** annoy, irritate, annoying, irritating. **ke-an** annoyance, irritation.

jengkelit men- do a handspring, tumble. **-an** handspring, somersault.

jéngkéng₁ ber-an sticking out in every direction.

jéngkéng₂ see JINGKAT.

jengker stiff, rigid (of corpse).

jengkerik see JANGKRIK₁.

jengkét see JINGKAT.

jéngki kind used by cowboys. *celana -* jeans. *sepatu -* high-heeled shoes. *sepéda -* bicycle with a v-shaped frame and double bars running downward from the handlebars.

jengking₁ men- lie with bottom up. **men-(kan)** turn s.t. upside down, tilt s.t.

jengking₂ see KALA₂.

jengkit see JENGKING₁.

jéngkol k.o. tree the beans of which are eaten raw, the *Pithecolobium*. **-an** suffer excessive urination from eating too many of these beans.

jengkolét ber-, men- capsize, turn turtle, tumble over.

jéngkot ber-, men- 1 limp. **2** be lame.

jengkrik see JANGKRIK₁.

jenguk ber-an look or peer out (of many people).

men- 1 look or observe with head thrust forward. *Ia ~ dr jendéla* She looked out of the window. *~ dr belakang pintu* peer from behind a door. 2 pay a call, look in on. *~ si sakit* look in on a patient. **men-kan** stick (the head) out. *~ hidung* stick o.'s nose out.

jengul men- protrude. *Matanya ~* His eyes protrude. **men-kan** stick s.t. out. *Ikan itu ~ kepalanya dr air* The fish stuck its head out of the water.

jeni₁ genius.

jéni₂ see ZENI₁.

jénial brilliant, gifted, talented.

jénialitas genius, talent.

jenis 1 kind, sort, gcnre. *menjual berbagai - dagangan* sell various k.o. merchandise. *- darah* blood type. *- ubah* variety. 2 (*Biol.*) species, race. *- bangsa* race. 3 gender. *- kelamin* sex, gender. **se-** of o. kind, race, type. *Kembang itu adalah ~* Those flowers are of the same species. **ber-(²)** various. *~ org terdapat di sekolah ini* There are all k.o. people in this school. **men-kan** sort, separate. *Ia ~ néker itu menurut besar-kecilnya* He sorted the marbles out according to size. **ke-an** 1 sort, classification s.t. falls in. 2 sex. **pen-an** grouping, classification. *~ kata-kata* grouping of words. *~ ilmu pengetahuan* classification of the sciences.

jenjam tranquil, untroubled, secure.

jenjang₁ 1 ladder, scaffold, trellis. 2 stairs, staircase, flight of stairs. 3 stage, level. *- karier* level of o.'s career. *- usia* age level. *- waktu* time span. **ber-** 1 step by step, gradual. *prosés yg ~* step-by-step process. 2 in tiers, terraced. 3 by ladder. **men-** 1 support. *Balok ini ~ atap* This beam supports the roof. 2 be approaching a certain age, height. *Ia ~ usia empat puluh* He is approaching 40. **-an** span. *~ pengendalian* extent to which s.t. can be kept in control. **-²an** imitation steps. **pen-** supporter. *kursus ~* supporting course. **pen-an** 1 arranging in stages, spacing. *~ hidup manusia* analysis of the stages of a human life. 2 grading. *~ bahan kuliah* arranging lecture materials according to grade of difficulty. **per-an** gradation.

jenjang₂ see JANJANG₁.

jenjang₃ see BURUNG.

jénjéng see JINJING₁.

jentai ter- be caught s.w., situated. *Ia ~ antara basa-basi dan motto dagang* He found himself caught between traditions of saying meaningless pleasantries and a commercial code.

jentaka (*Lit.*) misery.

jentat men- leap, jump (of fleas, etc.).

jentat-jentit (*Jv*) way of walking sexily.

jéntelmén sportsmanlike. *Secara - ia mengaku kesalahannya* In a sportsmanlike manner he admitted his mistake.

jentera 1 wheel in a machine or device. 2 mill, turbine. 3 spinning wheel. **ber-** having wheels.

jentik -² mosquito larva. **men-** 1 pinch, tweak, nip. 2 flick, rap with the fingers. 3 rap, scold, criticize s.o. **men-kan** flick s.t. off.

jéntrét (*Jkt, Jv*) row, line. **-kan** put s.t. in a line

with, add on. *Dia -kan gelar Doktor tanpa sungkan pd diri sendiri* He added the title of PhD to his name without feeling the least bit ashamed of it.

jenuh 1 surfeited, having had too much of s.t., sick and tired. *Aku sdh - mendengarkan pidato-pidato semacam itu* I have had about as much as I can take of listening to speeches like that. *Aku sdh - dgn sistém ini* I am sick of this system. 2 saturated. *Larutan gula itu sdh -* The solution is so full of sugar it is ready to crystallize. **men-kan** 1 satiate. 2 saturate. **ke-an** 1 surfeit, saturation. 2 oversaturated, overfull. **-an** waterlogged. **pen-an** 1 satiation. 2 saturation.

Jepang Japan, Japanese. **men-kan** Japanize.

jepét, jepit 1 tweezers. 2 clip, clamp. *- rambut* hairpin. **men-** hold s.t. by clamping or pinching. *Ia ~ surat itu antara telunjuk dan jari tengahnya* He held the letter between his index and middle finger. **men-kan** 1 squeeze, pinch s.t. *Pelan-pelan saya -kan kancing plastik itu* Slowly I squeezed the plastic button. 2 clip s.t., affix s.t. with clips. *Pak guru ~ peta pulau Jawa di papan tulis* The teacher clipped a map of Java to the blackboard. **ter-, ke-** 1 be squeezed. *Ia ~ di antara org banyak itu* She was hemmed in by the crowd. 2 be in a fix, bind, hemmed in. **keter-an** being in a tight spot. **-an** s.t. which holds by squeezing or clamping: tweezers, clips, tongs, clamps, etc. *~ kertas* paperclip. *~ rambut* hair curler.

jeprat men- sprinkle, splash, splatter (of water). *~ jeprét* snap pictures.

jeprét sound of clicking or snapping. *kancing -* snap (button). **men-** 1 hit with a slingshot. 2 take a snapshot of. **men-kan** snap (a photograph). **-an** stapler. *~kawat* stapler.

Jepun see JEPANG.

jeput₁ se- *hari* all day long.

jeput₂ see JEMPUT.

jera 1 be cured of a habit, learn o.'s lesson. 2 wary, chary, leery. *tak -* undaunted. *tak -²* undaunted, unflinching. **men-kan** 1 teach s.o. a lesson. 2 frighten, intimidate. 3 be wary of, learn to avoid. **ter-** dismayed, intimidated.

jerabai ber-(²) with tattered edges, in tassels.

jeragan see JURAGAN.

jeragih k.o. weed.

jerah₁ 1 abundant, plentiful. *Buah mangga tahun ini sangat -* The mangoes are really plentiful this year. 2 prevalent (of disease, etc.). **ke-an** prevalence, abundance. *~ tenaga térmis* prevalence of thermal energy.

jerah₂ learn a lesson, have had enough. *- jerih* exhausted, tired, worn out. *tak -²nya* never having enough, never tiring.

jerahak ter- neglected, abandoned (of work, a problem, etc.).

jerahap men- lie on o.'s stomach. **ter-** fall into a prone position.

jerait ber-(an) intertwined, interwoven, intergrown (of plants, etc.). *Cocok sanggul ~ pd jala rambut* The hairpin got caught in the hairnet.

jerajak see JERJAK.

jeram₁ rapids, cataract.

jeram₂ see JARAM.

jeramah ber- tug or pull at. **men-** attack viciously, fall upon prey.

jerambab see JEREMBAB.

jerambah platform terrace annexed to a house used for washing things. **men-(kan) 1** use a place as a *jerambah*. **2** treat s.o. without proper respect. **3** make s.o. do drudgery, make o. work like a slave.

jerambai see JERABAI.

jerambang glow that sometimes appears at night over marshy areas.

jerami 1 dried rice stalks. **2** straw.

jeran see JERA.

jerang men- 1 heat s.t. **2** place s.t. on the fire or stove. ~ *air* boil water. ~ *nasi* cook rice. **ter-** heated. **-an** s.t. heated. ~ *sayur* cooked vegetables. **pen-an** place to heat s.t. up.

jerangau the sweet flag, a wild rush with pungent root stock and sweet-smelling flowers, widely used for medicinal purposes.

jerangkak men- crawl on hands and knees.

jerangkang ber- stick up, project upward. *Tiang bendéra ~ sepanjang jalan* Flagpoles were sticking up all along the road. **ber-an** project upward (of several things). *Meréka berbaring di pantai dgn kaki ~* They were lying on the beach with their feet in the air. **men-kan** implant s.t. projecting upward. **ter-** standing, in position projecting upward.

jerangkong (*Jv*) skeleton.

jerap men- absorb. **ter-** absorbed. **keter-an** absorbability.

jerapah giraffe.

jerat 1 snare, lasso. **2** ruse, trick. **se-** a bunch (of flowers, etc.). **men- 1** snare. **2** trick, deceive, round up (criminals). **3** entice, inveigle (customers). **4** snarl, tangle. **ter- 1** snared. **2** tangled. **-an** noose, trap. ~ *pasir* sandtrap (in golf). **pen-** o. who entraps. **pen-an** garroting, strangulation.

jerau florid, deep red.

jeraus nimble, sprightly. **men-kan** make nimble. *Gerak badan ~ serta menyéhatkannya* Physical exercise made him active and healthy.

jerawat pimple, blackhead, acne. **ber-** be pimply. **-an** pimply. *muka yg ~* a face with acne.

Jerbar [*Jerman Barat*] W. Germany.

jerejak adhere, stick.

jerembab, jerembap men- throw o.s. down headlong. ~ *ke ranjang* fall headlong on to the bed. **men-kan 1** cause to fall headlong. **2** hurt, damage s.o. **ter-** fall headlong.

jerémbét see JERÉPÉT.

jerembun ter- suddenly become visible (of huge object).

jerempak ber-, men-, ter- suddenly meet, suddenly come face to face with.

jéréng₁ 1 squinting. **2** cross-eyed.

jéréng₂ men- spread s.t. out.

jerépét ber- 1 linked together (of links in chain).

2 grown together (of fingers, etc.). **-an** coalescence.

jeri 1 frightened, afraid. - *saya msk ke kamar itu* I am afraid to enter that room. **2** waver, be hesitant. *Musuh -, lalu mundur* The enemy wavered, then retreated. **men-kan** fearsome.

jeriau joists used to support floor or roof. **men-** install such joists.

jérigén see JÉRIKÉN.

jerih tired, weary. - *lelah/payah* exertion, effort. **ber-** *lelah/payah* make a great effort, exert to the utmost. - *penat* exhausted, worn out. **ber-(²) 1** exhaust, wear o.s. out. **2** exert, make an effort, put o.s. out. **men-kan** tire s.o., tiring, fatiguing **memper-kan** make s.o. give his utmost efforts, endeavor to help, make exertions for s.t. **ke-an 1** weariness, fatigue. **2** overly fatigued.

jeriji₁ finger. - *kaki* toe.

jeriji₂ see JERUJI.

jérikén jerrycan.

jering₁ *Pithecolobium* tree, with edible seeds considered beneficial to kidneys.

jering₂ k.o. cricket with strong chirping sound. **men-** chirp, cheep (of birds, etc.).

jerit 1 a scream, shriek. - *kegemparan* scream of alarm. **2** clamor. - *rakyat* clamor of the people. **3** strong complaint. **men-** scream, shriek. **men-²** yell at the top of o.'s voice, yell bloody murder. **men-kan** scream s.t. out. **ter-²** come out with a shriek. **-an** screams, shrieks. **pen- 1** screamer. **2** siren.

jerjak bars at window, grid, latticework. - *besi* iron bars, grill. **ber-** having bars.

jerkah snarl, growl. **men-** snarl or snap at s.o.

jermal fish trap consisting of closely spaced stakes behind which the fish get caught when the tide goes out.

Jerman German, Germany.

jermang props for boat on beach.

jernang dragon's blood, red dye obtained from fruit of k.o. rattan.

jernih 1 clear (of water, air, eyes, etc.). *Suasana politik menjadi -* The political atmosphere cleared up. **2** pure (of liquids, etc.). **men-** clear itself up. **men-kan 1** make s.t. clear, clear up (a misunderstanding). ~ *suasana* clear the atmosphere. **2** purify, cleanse. **memper-** clear s.t. up. **ke-an** clarity, purity. **pen-** purifier. ~ *air* water purifier. **pen-an** purification. **per-an** clarification, becoming clear.

jeroan (*Jv*) innards, entrails as food.

jerohok ter- fall or sink into a hole.

jerojol men-, ter- stick out. *Dompétnya ~ dr kantongnya* His wallet protruded from his pocket.

jerongkang - *korang* head over heels. **ter-** fall backward.

jerongkok men- sit with the chin on o.'s knees.

jerongkong men- lean forward and press chest against the knees. **ter-** fall prostrate.

jerubung awning, canopy, tarpaulin.

jeruji 1 trellis, grating, lattice. **2** grating, iron bars. **ber-** supplied with a grating or iron bars.

jeruju k.o. small shrub.

jeruk citrus fruit. - *bali* pomelo. - *bodong* sour lime. - *garut/kepruk* tangerine or orange that peels easily. - *keriput* grapefruit. - *manis* orange. - *nipis* calamondin. - *purut* small fragrant k.o. lime used as medicine. - *siam* orange. **men-** pickle, preserve in salts.

jerukun men- cover or spread over.

jerukup men- overarch.

jerumat men- darn, mend. **-an** a darning, mend. **pen-** darning needle.

jerumbai tassle, fringe. **ber-** tassled, fringed.

jerumun 1 lair of wild boar. **2** shelter, hide-out.

jerumus men-kan 1 drop s.t. on its face. **2** make s.t. fall down or into a hole. ~ *dunia ke dlm perang* plunge the world into war. **ter- 1** fall on o.'s face. **2** plunged into misery, sin, etc. **3** fall into a trap, hole.

jerung k.o. large shark.

jerungkau men- hang down like hair over the face or branches of a willow tree.

jerungkis bent upward. **men-** damage, harm.

jerungkup see JERUKUP.

jét (*Av.*) jet. - *pancar gas* turbojet.

jetis men- make banging noise of firecracker.

jétisasi replacing old fashioned aircraft with jets.

jétsét 1 sophisticated, well trained. **2** (*Sl.*) ugly but fashionable.

jéwang men- snatch s.t. up. *Ia ~ kopernya yg lalu dipikul ke tempat taksi* He snatched his suitcase, which he then carried on his shoulder to the taxi stand.

jewawut see JAWAWUT.

jéwér men- 1 pull or tweak s.o.'s ear. **2** reprimand, scold s.o. **-an 1** tweak (of the ear). **2** reprimand, scolding.

jiarah see ZIARAH.

jiawang k.o. monitor lizard.

jib (*Naut.*) jib sail.

jibaku (*Japanese*) **1** suicide attack. **2** make a suicide attack, participate in a suicide squad. **ber-** engage in a suicide attack.

jibakutai (*Japanese*) suicide squadron.

jiblah aptitude, talent.

jibun ber- 1 pile (of work). **2** teem, swarm (of ants).

jicing opium dust.

jidar 1 border around a letter or printed page. **2** wooden ruler. - *hitung* slide rule. **men-i 1** provide a line. **2** make a line with a ruler.

jidat forehead.

jidor, jidur see TANJIDOR.

jidwal see JADWAL.

jigo (*Ch*) 25.

jigong 1 tartar, plaque, dirt on teeth. **2** dirty person, tramp. **ber-** have dirt on it (of teeth).

jih (*Lit.*) target.

jihad (*Isl.*) holy war. **ber-** engage in a holy war.

jihat side.

jihin see JIN₁.

jiitméh (*Ch*) twenty-first day of the first Ch month (end of the *Cap Go Méh* celebration).

jijak see JEJAK₁.

jijat see JIDAT.

jijik 1 repugnant, abhorrent, nauseating. **2** disgusted, nauseated. *Saya - melihat kotoran itu* I was disgusted at seeing that filth. **men-i** nauseate, loathsome to s.o. **men-kan 1** loathe, abhor, abominate. **2** nauseating, loathsome. *Luka itu ~* That wound is nauseating. **ke-an 1** filthiness. **2** disgust, repugnance. **3** feel disgust.

jijit see JINJIT₂.

jika, jikalau 1 if. - *kauperkenankan, saya mau pulang* If you will permit me, I want to go home. - *... sekalipun* even if. - *benar sekalipun, saya tdk percaya pdmu lagi* Even if it were true, I would never trust you again. **2** when (future, general). - *engkau menjadi déwasa, engkau hrs bekerja* When you grow up, you will have to work. - *kiranya* supposing, in the event that. - *kiranya itu benar, saya girang sekali* If it were true, I would be very happy. **men-** say "if".

jilat men- 1 lick. *Anjing itu ~ kaki saya* The dog licked my foot. ~ *bibir* lick o.'s chops over. *Bual-bual lidah api ~ sampai atap rumah* The flames from the fire licked all the way up to the roof of the house. ~ *air liur* **1** praise s.t. previously despised. **2** flatter excessively. **2** flatter, curry (favor), apple polish. ~ *pantat* (*Vulg.*) kiss s.o.'s ass. **men-i 1** lick s.t. *Ujung kakinya di-i riak ombak* Her toes were licked by the ripples of the waves. ~ *periuk nasi* lick the bottom of the pan. **2** fawning, flattering. **-an 1** a lick. *luput dr ~ bencana* freed from the touch of disaster. ~ *mata* glance. **2** fawning, praise. **pen-** bootlicker. **kepen-an** state of being a bootlicker. **pen-an** apple polishing.

jilatisme mental attitude characterized by seeking benefits by bootlicking.

jilat-jilat men- purr (of cat).

jilbab (*Isl.*) female headgear that exposes face but not ears, neck, or hair.

jilid volume. *dua -* two volumes. - *kedua* volume two. **ber-** bound (of book, etc.). **ber-²** in volumes, by the volume. **men-** bind (book, periodicals). **men-kan** have s.t. bound. **-an** binding. **pen-** bookbinder. **pen-an** bookbinding.

jimak coitus. **ber-, men-** have sexual intercourse.

jimat charm, talisman, amulet.

jimbit se- a pinch, a small amount. **men-** take a pinch.

jin₁ 1 genie. **2** evil spirit.

jin₂ gin.

jina, jinah see ZINA.

jinak 1 tame, domesticated (animal). **2** gentle, docile, moderate. **3** (*Med.*) benign (tumor). **-²** *merpati* pretending to be shy but in reality liking a man. **ber-²** *merpati* act coy. **ber-²an** be on intimate terms with. **men-i** be close to, chum up with s.o. *Ia ~ saya karena ia membutuhkan pertolongan saya* He chummed up with me because he needed my help. **men-kan, memper-** tame. ~ *kaum inteléktuil* tame the intellegentsia. **pen-** (animal) tamer. ~ *bom* bomb-defusing specialist. **pen-an** taming, domestication.

jinawi see GEMAH RIPAH.

jinerap absorbant.

jingau men- peer at.

jingga colors ranging from orange to bright red. **men-** become orange. *Langit ~ di angkasa* The sky turned red in the highest reaches.

jinggering 1 high-heeled (shoes). **2** long-stemmed (glass).

jingkat ber-(²), bersi-, men- stand or walk on tiptoes. **men-kan** make (feet) be on tiptoe. **ter-** be startled.

jingkék 1 tiptoe. **2** high-heeled shoes. **ber-** 1 tiptoe, go on tiptoe. **2** wear high heels.

jingkik ber-² hop on o. leg.

jingklak, jingkrak₁ ber-(²) jump up and down (for joy). *~ kegirangan* jump up and down for joy. **ber-an** jump up and down (of several people).

jingkrak₂ ber-, men- straddle (horse, fence, etc.). **men-i** squat, occupy a place doing as o. likes without having the right to do so. *Kurang ajar. Anak-anak itu ~ taman yg sdh saya atur baik* Those naughty children, playing in the garden that I just finished tidying up.

jinjang₁ slender and tapering (neck).

jinjang₂ 1 leader. **2** necromancer.

jinjang₃ see JENJANG₁.

jinjing₁ men- carry s.t. light in o.'s hand. **men-i** carry several things. **men-kan** carry (s.t. light) for s.o. **ter-** carried. *Dgn tas ~ di tangan kiri dia masih sempat menjéwér telinga adiknya* He still was able to tweak his brother's ear even though he was holding a bag in his left hand. **-an** object carried in the hand.

jinjing₂ k.o. fast-growing tree that yields cheap lumber.

jinjing₃ ber- stand on tiptoes.

jinjit₁ stand on tiptoes. **ber-(²)** go on tiptoe. **men-kan** make s.t. be on tiptoe. *~ sepatu* stand on tiptoe in o.'s shoes.

jinjit₂ men- carry in the hand.

jinjit₃ men- 1 pull s.t. that is not stiff. **2** tweak (an ear).

jinsom ginseng.

jintan, jinten caraway seed. *- hitam* cumin. *- manis* anise seed. *- putih* white cumin.

jip jeep. **ber-** go by jeep.

jipang₁ branch, twig.

jipang₂ melon, gourd.

jipang₃ see BIPANG.

jiplak men- 1 copy. **2** cheat on an exam, crib. **3** plagiarize, fake s.t. by copying it. **-an 1** a copy. **2** plagiarism, imitation that pretends to be the real thing. **pen- 1** plagiarist. **2** duplicator, duplicating machine. **pen-an** plagiarism.

jiprat men- splash, splatter. *Air di jalanan ~ ketika ada mobil liwat* Water splashed when a car passed in the street. *Air ludahnya ~ di wajahku* His spittle spattered on my face. **ter-** splattered, splashed. **ke-an** be splattered with s.t. *Ia ~ rezeki* She received a share of the windfall. **-an** a splash (of water, blood, etc.). *~ api* spark of fire.

jirak k.o. tree with edible fruit.

jiran 1 neighbor. **2** kin, relative. **ber-** be neighbors. **-an** neighbor.

jirangkong see JERANGKONG.

jirat₁ tomb, mausoleum.

jirat₂, jiret see JERAT.

jirian (*Med.*) leucorrhea.

jirigén see JÉRIKÉN.

jirus₁ men- sprinkle water on, pour a small amount of water over.

jirus₂ see TIRUS.

jisim (*Anat.*) body.

jit (*Ch*) seven, in commercial transactions.

jitah see AKAR.

jitak men- slap s.o.

jitpék (*Ch*) 700 (used in commercial transactions).

jitu accurate, precise, exact. *témbakan - ke arah musuh* an accurate shot in the direction of the enemy. *jawaban yg -* a precise answer. **men-kan** make s.t. accurate or precise. **ke-an** accuracy, precision.

jiwa 1 soul, spirit. *-nya melayang* He died (lit., his spirit wafted upward). *rumah sakit -* hospital for mentally sick people. *- raga* body and soul. **ke-ragaan** psychosomatic. *-ku* my beloved. **2** spirit, the principle behind s.t. *- budak* slavish spirit. *- ksatria* warrior spirit. *- Undang-undang Dasar '45* the spirit of the Constitution of 1945. *- perjanjian* spirit of the agreement. **3** inhabitant. *Lebih dr seribu - yg tinggal di kawasannya* More than 1,000 people live in the area. *se- o.* with, of a spirit with. *MPR ~ dgn segala keputusannya* The decisions of the MPR are made in the spirit of the MPR itself. **ber- 1** be alive. *Selama masih ~, janganlah putus asa* Never give up as long as you live. **2** animated, spirited. *Lukisannya mémang bagus tapi tdk ~* The picture shows action, but no spirit. **3** have the spirit of s.t. *~ pahlawan* have the spirit of a hero. **men-i** inspire, be the soul of. *Wayang purwa di-i oléh Mahabharata* The classical shadow play is inspired by the Mahabharata. *Ia ~ pemberontakan itu* He was the inspiration of the uprising. **ke-an** spiritual, psychic, psychological. *pukulan ~* a psychological blow. *AS dgn segala kemampuan ~nya* America with all her spiritual power. **pen-** inspirer. **pen-an 1** animism. **2** inspiration.

jiwani psychic, psychological. *struktur -* psychological makeup.

jiwasraya name of gvt.-owned life insurance company.

JKA [*Jawatan Keréta Api*] see PJKA.

Jkt. [*Jakarta*] Jakarta.

Jkta. [*Jawatan Keréta Api*] Indonesian Railways.

Jl., Jln. [*Jalan*] street, road.

jlimet see JELIMET.

jml. [*jumlah*] amount.

Jng. [*Jatinegara*] a district in Jkt.

jo. [*juncto*] (*Leg.*) connected with.

joang see JUANG.

joanglo, joanlo (*Ch*) chafing dish, food warmer.

joblos see JEBLOS.

jobong (*Jkt*) prostitute.

jodo, jodoh 1 marriage partner, mate. **2** match, be a match, be a mate (to). *Celana ini tak - dgn jas* *itu* These pants do not match that jacket. *Mana - kaos itu?* Where is the mate to that sock? **3** be in agreement over. *Harganya tak -* They cannot come to an agreement about the price. **se-1** twosome, couple. ~ *yg indah* a handsome couple. ~ *bagai cicin* a well-matched couple. **2** a pair. ~ *kuda* a pair of horses. **ber- 1** be paired. **2** be married. **men-i** pair off. *Di kelasku aku di-i sama Ari* In my class I was paired with Ari. **men-kan, memper-kan 1** marry off, give in marriage. **2** pair. *-kan tiap satu anggota himpunan kita dgn satu anggota himpunan meréka* Pair each member of our association with a member of their association. **memper-kan** marry two people to e.o. **per-an 1** marriage, wedlock. **2** mating, pairing.

jogar game of checkers.

jogét 1 k.o. classical Jv dance accompanied by the gamelan. **2** k.o. dance to lively music, us. for couples. **3** o. who performs a dance of this type. **ber-** dance a *jogét.* **pen-** o. who performs a dance of this type.

joglo (*Jv*) steep upper section of roof of traditional Jv mansion.

jogo see KACANG.

jogo tirto (*Jv*) officer in village in charge of distribution of water for irrigation.

jogrog (*Jkt*) **nge-, n-** be in a place without moving. *Sdh sejak tadi dia* ~ *di belakang pintu mendengar semua pembicaraan meréka* He had been behind the door for some time listening to everything they were saying. **-kan** thrust s.t. in front of o. *Mau berlian segedé kacang, gua -in kagak nunggu bésok* If you want a diamond the size of a peanut, OK, I will shove it right under your nose without waiting another minute.

johan 1 world, universe. **2** champion. *- arifin* brilliant person, man or woman of the world. *- pahlawan* universal hero, person of courage.

johar₁ k.o. fast-growing shade tree the crown of which yields firewood.

johar₂ see BINTANG, ZOHRAH.

johar₃ see JAUHAR.

johari see JAUHARI.

joja, jojo k.o. simian.

jojol piling, palisades. **men- 1** protrude (of eyes). **2** protrude upward (of palisades, etc.).

jok /jok/ **1** seat (of car, pedicab, etc.). *- muka* front seat. **2** car upholstery. *- kursi* upholstery.

joki (*Sport*) jockey. **men-kan** make into a jockey.

jolak ber-, men- blaze. *Api itu* ~ The fire blazed. **-an** a blaze. ~ *api* sea of fire.

jolék men- wrap s.t. in leaves.

joli 1 palanquin. **2** team of horses. **se-** a couple, twosome.

joli-joli yawl, k.o. small boat.

jolok men- 1 prod at s.t. with a pole, etc., to knock it down. ~ *buah dgn tongkat* poke at fruit with a stick. ~ *sarang tabuhan* undertake a dangerous venture deliberately (lit., try to knock down a hornet's nest). **2** probe, ferret out. **3** poke finger down throat, into nose, etc. ~ *anak* induce abortion. **pen-** prod for knocking fruit down.

jolong₁ men- project, protrude.

jolong₂ (*M*) see JULUNG₂.

jolong-jolong see IKAN.

jolor men- 1 creep, crawl (of snakes, etc.). **2** inch forward on o.'s belly.

jombang (*M*) handsome, pretty, beautiful. **ke-an** handsomeness, beauty.

jompak ber- rear, prance (of horse, etc.). **ber-an 1** prance about. **2** (*Naut.*) leave a wake. **men-** rear. *Kuda itu* ~ *ketika dipukul keras* The horse leaped when it was hit hard.

jomplang see JUMPLANG.

jompo (*Jv*) old, decrepit, infirm. *rumah org -* old folks' home.

jompong pc-an rallying place.

jong see JUNG.

jongang see JONGKANG₂.

jongét curved upward at the tip or side. **men-** curve upward.

jonggol representative, responsible person. *- pihak législatif* representative for the legislative branch. **men-i** represent s.o. or s.t. **-an** responsibility.

jonghé k.o. weed.

jongkang₁ k.o. boat.

jongkang₂ protruding (of teeth, upper lip, etc.). *--jangking* sticking out right and left. **men-** protrude (of teeth, upper lip, etc.).

jongkang₃ ber-an fall (of several erect things).

jongkar-jangkir sticking out all over (esp. of teeth).

jongkat see JUNGKAT.

jongko stall (in market).

jongkok ber-, men- squat. **ber-²** be obsequious. *Ia selalu* ~ *thd atasannya* He always displays an obsequious attitude toward his superiors. **ter-** in a squatting position. **ter-²** walk in a squatting position.

jongkong k.o. dugout canoe.

jongos (*now considered Derog.*) houseboy, waiter.

jonjot 1 tuft (of hair). **2** flake. **ber-** in flakes. **men-** extract, pluck.

jon towél (*Jkt*) young fellow that puts on airs.

jontrot men- poke, thrust s.t. by poking it. **men-kan** poke with s.t.

joran fishing rod. *- ampai* divining rod.

joréng small piece (of cloth), small clod (of earth). **men-** slice thin.

jori team of horses.

jor-jor (*Jv*) push, elbow aside. **-an** vie with o. another, compete. ~ *drumband* marching band competition.

jornalis see JURNALIS.

jorok₁ 1 slovenly, slipshod. *Pekerjaannya -* His work is slipshod. **2** dirty, untidy. **ke-an** slovenliness, dirtiness, squalor. **pen-** scoundrel, swine.

jorok₂ men- stick out, project, protrude. *Tanah itu* ~ *ke laut merupakan semenanjung* The land sticks out into the sea to form a peninsula. *pohon yg* ~ *ke sungai* a tree that extends out over the river. **men-kan 1** make s.t. protrude. *Kepalanya di-kan keluar jendéla* He stuck his head out of the window. **2** push or shunt aside. *Mendengar perkataannya itu aku merasa di-kan oléh isteriku* Hearing her words I felt that I had been pushed aside by my wife. **ter-** be made to project or protrude. **-an** a protrusion. ~ *atap* eaves.

jorong₁ ellipse, elliptical, oval-shaped.

jorong₂ metal V-shaped holder for betel leaf.

jorong₃ a corner.

jotakan (*Jv*) be on unfriendly terms.

jotos fist. **ber-** fight with the fists. **ber-²** engage in fisticuffs. **men-** strike s.o. with the fist. **men-kan** strike out with (of fists). **-an** boxing, fisticuffs. **-²an** fisticuffs. **per-an** matters pertaining to boxing.

jrang-jreng sound of plucking a guitar, banjo, etc.

jrangkung see JERANGKONG.

jrawut rumpled, disheveled, messed up.

jreng-jreng sound of coins clinking, tinkling sound (of guitar, etc.).

jring-jring sound of tinkling (of guitar, mandolin).

jrs. [*jurusan*] 1 direction. 2 academic field.

jua 1 nothing or nobody but, only. *Meskipun dia bekerja keras sekali, umpatan - yg diterimanya* Although he worked very hard, he got nothing but scoldings. *Hanya dgn kepercayaan itu - ia dpt menyadarkan diri sendiri* Only by means of this belief can he know himself. 2 even if it is, no matter. *Sedikit - jadi* Even a little bit will do. *Apa - yg diperbuatnya, org tuanya tdk puas* No matter what he did, his parents were not satisfied. *Bagaimana - dicobanya, ia tdk berhasil* However much she tried, she failed. *Menghadapi apapun -* Face anything, whatever it may be. *Tak seorg - datang ke rumah saya* Not a single person came to my house. 3 nevertheless. *Dimakan -* She ate it nevertheless. *Lupa - kau pd sumpahmu* You did forget your vow anyway. *Takkan mendatangkan bahagia - pdku* It is not likely to bring me happiness of any sort anyway. *Blm - ia sempat* He still did not get a chance. *Bagaimana pun juga si Amat manusia -* No matter what, Amat is still a human being. 4 also.

juadah 1 delicacy made of rice. 2 cake or cookies. 3 provisions, foodstuffs.

juak₁ ber- compete. **men-** incite, instigate (a fight). **pen-** instigator.

juak₂ men- be projecting upward. **men-kan** hoist a sail, project s.t. upward.

jual sell, sale. **-** *beli* trade. **ber-** *beli* engage in trade, buy and sell. *Indonésia ~ beli dgn India* Indonesia trades with India. **memper-belikan** trade in s.t. **ber-** sell for a living. **ber-an** 1 sell (several things). 2 sell for a living. *Penghidupannya dr ~ sepéda* He earns his living selling bicycles. **men-** sell s.t. *Rumah ini di-* This house is for sale. *~ akad* 1 pawn, hock. 2 sell under certain conditions. *~ aksi* show off. *~ bagus* do nothing (merely sell o.'s looks). *~ bangsa* betray o.'s country. *~ bicara* mere talk (without evidence). *~ kécap* give s.o. a line. *~ kepala* become a mercenary, act as an agent for mercenaries. *~ lagak* show off. *~ lélang* auction off, sell at auction. *~ lepas* sell outright. *~ mahal* be reluctant to grant a favor or part with s.t. *~ nama* trade on s.o.'s

name. *~ omong* mere talk (without evidence). *~ rugi* sell at a loss. *~ rupa/tampang* show off. **men-i** 1 sell repeatedly or many things. 2 sell to. **men-kan** sell on behalf of. **ter-** out of stock, sold out. *Buku itu habis ~* That book is sold out. **-an** merchandise, goods. **pen-** seller, vendor. *~ bangsa* traitor. *~ besar* wholesaler. *~ éceran* retailer. *~ idé* purveyor of ideas. **pen-an** 1 selling. 2 sale, turnover.

juang struggle. *médan -* battlefield. *semangat -* the spirit to keep up the struggle. **ber-** fight, struggle. *~ utk kemerdékaan* fight for freedom. **memper-kan** struggle for s.t. *Irian Barat sedang diperkan* They are fighting (to regain) W. New Guinea. **pe-** fighter, warrior, freedom fighter. **per-an** struggle, fight. *~ hidup* struggle for life. **seper-an** sharing in the same struggle. *temanku ~* my comrade in the revolution.

juang-juang k.o. shrub.

juar see JOHAR₁.

juara 1 champion. *- bertahan* defending champion. *- dunia* world champion. *- gembut* champion eater. *- kedua* runner-up. 2 referee in a cockfight. **men-i** win out, come up as champion. **ke-an** championship.

jubah long flowing robe (including religious habits, Arabic garments, etc.). **ber-** wear such a robe.

jubal, jubel ber-(²), ber-an, -an crowd around. *Di depan tiap gang ~ bécak-bécak* Pedicabs were crowded at the entrance to every alleyway. **men-kan** cram, jam. *Sebuah pisang goréng di-kan ke dlm mulutnya* He crammed a banana fritter into his mouth.

jubin floor tile.

jubir [*jurubicara*] spokesperson.

jubit see CUBIT.

jublek /jublek/ amazed, astonished. **men-** be silent, speechless (us. in bewilderment).

jubur (*Anat.*) anus.

judas, judes 1 cruel, vicious (esp. in speech). 2 harsh and rude, unmannered.

judi gambling. **ber-, men-** gamble. **men-kan** gamble s.t. away. *Di-kannya seluruh hartanya di kasino* He gambled away his entire worldly possessions in the casino. **memper-kan** make a bet on. **pe(n)-** gambler. **pe(r)-an, pen-an** 1 gambling. 2 gambling den.

judo (*Sport*) judo. **pe-** expert in judo.

judoka (*Sport*) expert in judo.

judokang (*Sport*) judo hall.

judul 1 title (of book, etc.). *- tambahan* subtitle. 2 caption (under cartoon, etc.). 3 credits (in movie or on TV). 4 heading. **ber-** be entitled, have the title. **men-i** give a title to, label. **men-kan** enter as an entry.

juga 1 also, too. *Ia - menjadi menteri* He has also become a minister. *Bukan ini saja, tapi - itu* Not only this, but also that. 2 even if. *Terlambat - nggak apa-apa. Pokoknya datang* Even if you are late, it does not matter. So long as you come. 3 no matter what, how, who, etc. *Bagaimana pun - dicobanya tdk berhasil* No matter how she tried doing it, she did not have success. *siapa pun* - no matter who it is. **4** rather. *Berat - kerusakannya* The damage was rather severe. **5** anyway. *Walaupun ia bersalah, saya menolongnya* - Although she was wrong, I helped her anyway. *Sdh malam ia blm - pulang* It is already late, but he has not come home. *Biar mahal, saya masih - mau membelinya* Never mind if it is expensive, I still want to buy it nevertheless. *Marahnya termakan* - Her anger was finally assuaged. *sekarang* - right this minute.

juhi (*Ch*) dried squid.

juih curled (of lips).

juita sweet, lovely, beautiful.

Juja (*Zod.*) Gemini.

jujai (*Lit.*) **ber-** ceaseless, incessant.

jujat (*Lit.*) slander, insult, (verbal) abuse.

juju₁ men- feed (a baby) pre-chewed food. **men-kan** make s.t. soft by chewing it.

juju₂ see TUJU.

jujuh ber-, men- be incessant, unceasing.

jujur₁ honest, on the level. - *belaka* fair and square. **ke-an** honesty, integrity.

jujur₂ men-i present a bride-price to. *Ia ~ bakal mertuanya lima ékor sapi* He gave his future father-in-law five head of cattle as the bride-price. **-an** bride-price.

jujut men- pull, tug at (rope, etc.).

julai slender end of stem of a creeping plant, runner of a creeping plant. **men-kan** dangle s.t. **ber-(²), men-, ter-** dangle.

julak see JOLAK.

julang men- 1 soar, tower. *Gunung itu ~ sampai ke langit* The mountain soared up to the skies. *Api ~ tinggi* The fire soared high. *Harga minyak ~ tinggi* The price of oil soared. **2** carry on the shoulder. *Bp ~ anaknya itu* Father carried his child on his shoulder. **3** hold in high esteem, esteem highly. *Rakyat ~ sang Présidén* The people hold the president in very high esteem.

julat (*Lit.*) range, reach. **se- mata** as far as the eye can see.

Juli July.

julig (*Jv*) cunning, sly (in negative sense).

juling cross-eyed. - *air/bahasa* slanting. *Atapnya - air* The roof was slanting a bit. **men-i** steal a glance at, glance at a bit.

julir harpoon.

julita see JELITA.

julo lottery played by neighborhood wives at monthly get-together. **ber-** play *julo*.

julu - *jalar* in and out, to and fro, back and forth. **ber-an** stretch out (in all directions). **men-** extend, stick out (of tongue, etc.). *Tiba-tiba pintu terbuka dan sebuah kepala ~ ke luar* Suddenly the door opened and a head thrust out. **men-kan** thrust, stick out (o's head, arm, tongue). **-an 1** stick, stave, bar. **2** line, row. **pen-** protruding stick.

juluk named, called. **men-i** dub, give s.o. a nickname. *~nya "ratu dunia"* dub her "queen of the world." **men-kan** give the name of. *Istilah "pop"*

yg di-kan kpd anggota polisi The term "pop" is a nickname which has been given to members of the police force. **-an** sobriquet, nickname.

julung₁ (*Jv*) fated to be unlucky. - *caplok* born at sunset and fated to be attacked by a tiger. - *kembang* born at sunrise and fated to encounter a wild animal.

julung₂ for the first time. *Pohon ini - berbuah* This tree bore fruit for the first time. **-² for the first time.

julung-julung see IKAN.

julur - *jalar* in and out, to and fro, back and forth. **ber-an** stick out (of several things). **men- 1** stick outward. *Kakinya ~ lurus ke depan* His feet stuck out straight in front of him. *Ada sepotong tali dr sana ~ di lantai* A piece of rope was sticking out on the floor. **2** panhandle, beg in street. **men-kan** stick s.t. out. *Ia ~ tangannya mengambil . . .* He stuck out his hands to get . . . *Aku ~ kepala ke luar* I stuck out my head. **ter-** jut out. **-an** s.t. that juts out. *~ wilayah* panhandle. **pen-** panhandler.

jumaah, jumaat₁, juma'ah, juma'at see JEMAAH.

jumaat₂ see JUMAT.

Jumadilakhir the 6th month of the Arabic calendar.

Jumadilawal the 5th month of the Arabic calendar.

jumantara firmament, outer or upper atmosphere.

jumanten emerald.

jumat see JEMAAH.

Jumat 1 Friday. - *Agung/Besar* (*Rel.*) Good Friday. **2** week. *Dia tinggal se- di Mekkah* He stayed a week in Mecca. **ber-** (*Isl.*) engage in the Friday prayers at the mosque.

jumbai tassle, fringe. **se-** a bunch of s.t. that hangs down. *kunci ~* a bunch of keys. **ber-(²) 1** tassled, fringed. **2** frayed. **3** flutter. *Daun-daun kering itu ~ ditiup angin* The dry leaves fluttered in the wind. **men-** be a tassel. *ékornya yg - indah* its tail which was a beautiful tuft. **men-kan** let s.t. hang down loose (of tassles, fringes, etc.). **ter-** hanging down (in a bunch, tassle, etc.). *Rambutnya ~ menutupi kuping* His hair hung down over his ears.

jumblah see JUMLAH.

jumblang cesspool, septic tank.

jumbuh similar, identical. *Jumlahnya* - The amount tallied. **men-kan** make s.t. compatible. *Kedua konsép itu tak dpt ~ cita-cita partai politik yg berselisih* The two concepts could not bring the ideals of the conflicting political parties together. **ke-an** identity.

jumlah 1 sum, amount, total. - *bulat* lump sum. **2** number, quantity. - *dan mutu* quantity and quality. - *terbanyak* majority (of votes, etc.). **3** (*Ling.*) number. - *dualis* (*Math.*) dual number. **-nya** (in) the amount of. **se-** as much as, to the amount of. *hutangnya ~ lima puluh dolar* His debts amount to 50 dollars. *~ besar (kecil)* a large (small) amount. *~ besar penduduk mati kelaparan*

A large number of the population died of starvation. **ber-** number. *Bunga dlm kebun ini ~ ratusan* The flowers in this garden number in the hundreds. **men-** (*Math.*) add. *Ali belajar ~ di sekolah* Ali is learning addition at school. **men-kan** add or count up. *Ia ~ hutangnya* He added up his debts. **ter-** 1 totaled, added up. 2 considered to be among. *Ia ~ anak yg pandai dlm kelasnya* She is considered o. of the bright children in her class. **pen-** adder. **pen-an** adding, totaling. **(per)-an** (*Math.*) addition.

jumpa meet. *sampai - lagi* till we meet again. *- pérs* press conference. **ber-** meet, run into or across. *Saya ~ Ali di jalan* I ran into Ali on the street. **men-i** 1 find. *Di méja ku-i sepucuk surat* On the table I found a letter. 2 go to meet. *Yani hanya ~ aku bila malam datang* Yani only went to meet me after dark. 3 meet with, encounter. *~ kecelakaan* meet with an accident. *~ suasana yg penuh ketegangan* encounter an atmosphere full of tension. **memper-kan** 1 bring together. *Siapa ~ kedua org itu?* Who brought those people together? 2 reconcile (differences, etc.). **ter-** found, exist. *Singa tak ~ di negeri kita* Lions are not to be found in our country. **per-an** meeting, encounter.

jumpalit ber- turn a somersault. **(ber)-an** turn somersaults (of a large number). *Harga ~ ke bawah* Prices fell headlong. **-an** somersault.

jumplang unbalanced, unequal. *Distribusi penghasilan semakin -* The distribution of income is becoming more and more imbalanced. **men-** become unbalanced. **nge-** be unbalanced.

jumpluk se- a pile of. *~ rambut putih* a mop of white hair.

jumpul k.o. mullet.

jumput se- a pinch of s.t. *~ garam* a pinch of salt. *umurnya yg ~* tender age. *tak ~* not a whit. *Ia tak ~ pernah berpikir ttg kesenian* She never gave art a moment's thought. **men-** pick up with thumb and forefinger, get a pinch of.

jumud 1 stiff, rigid, unbending. 2 old-fashioned, resistant to change. **ke-an** 1 obstinacy, unbendingness. 2 being old-fashioned, resistant to change.

junam men- 1 dive (of plane, bird). 2 attack in flight.

juncto /yungkto/ (*Leg.*) in connection with.

jung k.o. boat, Ch junk.

jungat men- tilt upward (of boat, cart, etc.).

jungkal men-kan 1 overturn s.t. 2 overthrow, bring down (a regime, etc.). **ter-** tumble forward. *Ia hampir ~ ke dlm jurang* He almost tumbled into the ravine.

jungkang *--jungkit* bob up and down. **men-** bob up and down.

jungkar men- project, protrude.

jungkat *-jangkit* bob up and down. **men-** slant, tilt. *Lantai itu - The floor slants. hidung yg ~* upturned nose. **ter-** tilt upward. **-an** seesaw.

jungkel, jungkil see JUNGKAL.

jungkir *- balik* 1 upside-down, topsy-turvy. 2 turn a somersault. 3 be in a dither. **men-balikkan**

turn s.t. upside down. **pen-balikan** 1 upset, reversal. 2 somersault. *- jungkal* flip-flop. **ber-(an)** be upside down. *Kenangannya ~* She remembered things exactly the opposite of what they were. **men-** flip over. **men-kan** 1 turn s.t. upside down. 2 reverse s.t. **ter-** be upside down, reversed.

jungkit see JUNGKANG.

jungkrak men- raze (a building). **men-kan** push s.t. aside.

jungkung see JONGKONG.

jungur 1 snout, sword (of swordfish). 2 (*Navy*) bow.

jungut mountain spur.

Juni June.

junjung ber-an have a husband. **men-** 1 carry s.t. on the head, shoulders, or high on the back. *Ibu ~ kendi* Mother carried a water jug on her head. 2 respect, hold in high esteem. *~ nama bangsa dan negara* hold high the name of the race and nation. *~ tinggi* idolize, revere. **men-tinggikan** glorify, revere. *Bp-bp, ibu-ibu yg saya -* Respected ladies and gentlemen. **men-kan** 1 carry on the head for s.o. 2 place s.t. on o.'s head for carrying. **-an** 1 o. who is esteemed. 2 adoration. 3 pole for climbing plants. 4 (*Formal*) o.'s husband. **ter-** be placed on head or high on back. **pen-** respecter, worshiper. **pen-an** respecting, worshiping of.

junta junta.

juntai ber-, men-, ter- dangle. **ber-an** dangle (of many things). **men-kan** dangle s.t. down. *duduk di bangku dan ~ kaki* sit on the bench and let the feet dangle.

juntrung organized, orderly. *dgn -* in an orderly fashion. **men-kan** organize, put in order, arrange. *Ia ~ kursi-kursi yg tadinya berantakan* She arranged the chairs which had been scattered about. **-an** 1 organization, unit. 2 purpose, aim. *Dia bosen mendengar tujuan yg tak jelas ~nya itu* He was sick of hearing about those goals whose purpose was not at all clear.

junub (*Isl.*) ritually impure or soiled (after coitus, giving birth, menstruation, etc.).

junun possessed by a devil.

jup (*Sl.*) yep!

jura men- bow out of respect.

juragan 1 skipper (of small craft). 2 owner of an enterprise. 3 (*in some regions only*) respectful address by villager to man of nobility or higher class. *Mau ke mana, -?* Where are you going, sir?

jurai 1 bunch. *se- bunga* a bunch of flowers. 2 row, sequence. **ber-, ter-, men-** dangle, hang down (of hair, tassels, etc.). *dgn kegondrongan rambut yg ~ ke bahu* with long hair that hung down to the shoulders. **ber-an** hang down (in large numbers).

juran see JORAN.

jurang ravine, gorge, chasm. *- kenistaan* the depths of misery. *- pemisah* gap. *- juriat* generation gap.

juri (*Leg.*) jury. **men-** be a member of the jury in a

competition. **pen-an** judging a case by a jury. *sistim* ~ jury system.
juriat see ZURIAT.
juridiksi see YURIDIKSI.
juridis see YURIDIS.
jurik k.o. supernatural being.
juring, juringan section, segment (of fruit).
juris see YURIS.
jurisprudénsi see YURISPRUDÉNSI.
jurnalis journalist, reporter.
jurnalistik journalism.
juru skilled worker. *- acara* master of ceremonies. *- api (RR.)* locomotive fireman. *- arsip* file clerk. *- azan (Isl.)* muezzin. *- bahasa* interpreter. *- batu* 1 marine pilot. 2 boatswain. *- bayar* cashier. *- berita* reporter. *- bicara* spokesman, spokeswoman. **men-bicarai** serve as a spokesperson for. *Beliau ~ bicarai rakyat itu* He serves as spokesperson for the people. *- buku* bookkeeper. *- bunuh* 1 killer. 2 executioner. *- dakwah (Isl.)* proselytizer. *- damai* peacekeeper, peacemaker. *- dapur* master cook, chef. *- film* cameraman. *- foto* photographer. *- gambar* 1 draftsman. 2 illustrator. *- gendang* drummer. *- gudang* warehouse manager. *- hikmat* practitioner of black arts. *- imbau* announcer. *- injil* evangelist. *- isyarat (RR.)* signal man. *- jalan* road (repair) inspector or foreman. *- jenang* purser, supervisor. *- kabar* journalist, reporter. *- kamera* cameraman. *- kasir* cashier. *- kerah* village messenger. *- ketik* typist. *- kira* 1 accountant. 2 estimator for life expectancy in an insurance firm. *- kirim* forwarding agent. *- kisah* storyteller. *- kuasa* proxy. *- kunci* 1 caretaker in a graveyard. 2 gatekeeper. 3 (*Sport*) the last place. *- laboran* laboratory technician. *- lélang* auctioneer. *- masak* chef, master cook. *- mesin (RR.)* locomotive engineer. *- minyak* oiler. *- mudi (Naut.)* helmsman. *- obat (Mil.)* corpsman. *- penerang* information specialist. *- pijat* masseur, masseuse. *- pisah* 1 arbiter. 2 umpire, referee. *- potrét* photographer. *- pustaka* librarian. *- ramal* fortune-teller. *- rancang* planner, planning expert. *- rawat* nurse. **ke-rawatan** nursing. *- rias* makeup person. *- Selamat (Rel.)* the Savior. *- silat* expert at martial arts. *- situ (Leg.)* bailiff, process-server. *- suara* soundman (in film). *- tafsir* commentator. *- taksir* appraiser, evaluator. *- télpon* telephone operator. *- teluh* utterer of magic formulas. *- tenun* weaver. *- te-*

nung fortune-teller. *- tik* typist. *- tulis* office clerk. *- tunjuk* informer, stool pigeon. *- uang* 1 cashier. 2 bookkeeper. *- ukur* surveyor. *- warta* correspondent, reporter. **ke-an** 1 vocational. 2 vocation, trade.
jurus₁ steps, movements in martial arts. *- pilihan* o.'s favorite steps. **men-** 1 point, lead (in certain direction, etc.). *latihan-latihan bacaan yg ~ pd suatu ilmu tertentu* reading exercises aimed at a specific field of knowledge. 2 go in a certain direction. *Ia ~ ke barat* He went westward. *Matanya ~ tajam ke arah sersan itu* His eyes moved sharply in the direction of that sergeant. **men-i** 1 head toward. 2 investigate, look into. *Pengarang ~ faktor lain* The writer investigated other factors. **men-kan** direct, aim s.t. at, guide. *Pemandu itu ~ tetamu ke pintu gerbang* The guide led the guests toward the portal. **-an** 1 direction. 2 (*Acad.*) department, field, track. *Ia se~ dgn saya* She is in the same field of studies as I am. **pen-** directive, guideline. **pen-an** 1 dividing into departments of a field. *~ menurut ilmunya dan bukan menurut bahasanya* the breaking up into fields according to subject matter and not according to language studied. 2 aiming at, heading toward. *~ ke arah Moskwa* heading in the direction of Moscow.
jurus₂ moment. *beberapa - kemudian* several moments later. *Tunggulah se-* Please wait a moment. **ber-²** repeatedly. *~ anak sakit itu minta air* Again and again the sick child asked for water.
jus₁ sound of steam locomotive.
jus₂ (*Tennis*) deuce.
jus₃ juice. **men-** make a drink out of. *Apokatnya di-* Make the avocado into avocado drink.
jus₄ see JUZ.
justa see DUSTA.
justru exactly, precisely. *- pd saat itu ia tdk beruang sama sekali* Just at that moment he had no money at all. *Itu - kebalikan dr kenyataan* That is precisely the opposite of the facts. *- karena itulah* It is just exactly on account of that.
juta million. **ber-(²)** by the millions. **-an** millions of, by the millions.
jutawan millionaire.
juwang see JUANG.
juz (*Isl.*) section of the Koran. *Qur'an itu terbagi dlm tiga puluh -* The Koran is divided into 30 sections.

K

k /ka/ k, the 11th letter of the alphabet.
k. [*kaca*] page.
K.₁ [*kali*] river.
K.₂ [*kota*] city.
ka see KAH.
Ka. [*kepala*] head, chief.
kaabah see KABAH.
kab. [*kabupatén*] regency (administrative unit).
kaba (*M*) tale, story.
kabag [*kepala bagian*] administrative section head.
kabah /ka'bah/ **1** (*Isl.*) the small cubicle shrine in the Great Mosque of Mecca which contains the famous black Stone of Mecca. It represents the direction (*kiblah*) to which Muslims turn in praying. **2** symbol of the Isl. political party.
kabal see KEBAL.
kabar news, report. - *hari ini* today's news. *Aku cuma mendengar* - I only heard a report. *Apa* -? How do you do? How are you? - *baik* I am fine. *tdk - akan dirinya* be unconscious. - *angin/burung/ selentingan* rumor. **-nya** people say, it is reported. ~ *anda pergi ke luar negeri* They say you went abroad. **ber-** **1** tell, relate. *Ia dpt banyak* ~ She has lots to tell. **2** send news about o.s. *Ia tak pernah* ~ He never sent word of himself. **meng-i** inform, let s.o know. *-i saya nanti* Let me know. **meng-kan** report s.t. *Kau di-kan gugur* You were reported killed in action. *Ia* ~ *kedatangan Bp* He reported your arrival. **ter-** spread, reported. *Berita pemberontakan itu* ~ *ke mana-mana* News of the revolt has spread everywhere. **pe(ng)-** *injil* evangelist. **pe(ng)-an** **1** spreading the news. **2** evangelism. **pe(r)-an** news, news report.
kabarét₁ (*Coll.*) beret.
kabarét₂ see MALAM₁.
kabat see KEBAT.
kabé see KB.
kabel cable. - *penerangan* power cable. - *télpon* telephone cable.
Kabil (*Isl.*) Cain, Abel's brother.
kabilah nomadic tribe.
kabin₁ (*Naut.*) cabin. - *pengemudi* (*Av.*) cockpit.
kabin₂ cream crackers.
kabinét 1 governmental cabinet. - *inti* inner cabinet. - *karya/kerja* cabinet with members chosen for professional expertise rather than political consideration. **2** cabinet (for medicine, etc.).
kabir₁ mighty (of God). *Tuhan al* - Almighty God.
kabir₂ **meng-** reverse the direction of a boat by paddling perpendicular to the hull.
Kabir [*Kapitalis Birokrat*] capitalist bureaucrat. **mengk-kan** consider s.o. a capitalist bureaucrat.

kabisah, kabisat see TAHUN.
kabit thief, pickpocket.
kabriolét (*Auto.*) convertible.
kabu-kabu **1** kapok. **2** fluffy material like kapok. **ber-** fluffy, downy, cottony.
kabul answered, granted (of a prayer, request). **meng-i, meng-kan 1** grant (a wish). **2** answer a prayer, fulfill a request. **ter-** granted, answered. **peng-an** fulfilling (of a request), answering (of a prayer).
kabuli see NASI₁.
kabung₁ white mourning headband. **ber-** mourn, be in mourning for a death in o.'s own family. *misa* ~ funeral mass. **per-an** mourning, grieving.
kabung₂ sugar palm.
kabung₃ measure of four cubits' length.
kabung₄ slice, fragment. **meng-(²)** slice s.t.
kabupatén 1 regency, area headed by a *bupati*. **2** residence or office of the *bupati*.
kabur₁ 1 hazy (view), vague, blurred, clouded (vision). *Penglihatannya menjadi* - Her eyesight became hazy. - *kacau* hazy and confused. **2** fading (of hopes), unclear (of handwriting, speech, etc.). *Harapan utk lepas pingitan* - *lagi* My hopes of leaving the house again faded away. *perasaan yg semula* - feelings that were hazy at first. **3** haze. **meng-** become hazy or blurred, fade away. *Bintangnya* ~ His star began to fade. **meng-kan, memper- 1** blur, make s.t. foggy or hazy. *Asap* ~ *kuda dan pengenendaranya* The smoke made the horse and its rider blurred. **2** obfuscate, obscure s.t. *Sengaja di-kan oléh pengarangnya* It was purposely obscured by the writer. **ke-an** haziness, vagueness, fuzziness. **ke-²an** rather hazy or clouded. **-an** vagueness. **peng-an** blurring of.
kabur₂ 1 bolt (of a horse). **2** run off, flee. *Suaminya - dr rumah* The husband fled the house.
kabus nebulous.
kabut₁ mist, haze, fog. - *asap* smog. **ber-** misty, hazy, foggy. **meng-** become a haze. *Abu tanah liat yg kering berterbangan* ~ *tebal* The dust from the dry clay soil lifted into a thick haze. **meng-i 1** make s.t. foggy, confuse. **2** darken. *Hilanglah sinar temaram yg* ~ *hidupmu pd masa yg silam* The darkness that shadowed your past life has disappeared. **peng- 1** sprayer. **2** atomizer. **3** carburetor. **peng-an** spraying (from the air).
kabut₂ see KEBUT₂.
kaca₁ 1 glass. - *arloji* watch crystal. - *asah* cut glass. - *baur/bening* frosted glass. - *berlekak* stained glass. - *depan* windshield. - *és* ground glass. -

masir frosted glass. - *mata* glasses, spectacles. - *mata debu* goggles. - *mata hitam* sunglasses. - *mati* framed glass. - *mobil* windshield. - *pembakar/pembesar* magnifying glass. - *sahap* cover glass. - *taméng* safety glass. - *teropong* periscope. - *toko* display window (of a store). **2** mirror. - *benggala* large, thick mirror. - *méka* mica. - *muka* pocket mirror. - *spion* rearview mirror. **3** example. *Keasyikannya hendaknya menjadi - bagimu* Her diligence should be an example to you. **ber- 1** look in the mirror. **2** contain glass. *Pintunya yg satu ~ O.* of the doors had glass panes. **ber-² 1** shine, glisten, be glassy. **2** be glistening with tears. *Matanya ~* Her eyes glistened with tears. **ber-kan** *diri* be reflected. *Beringin tua ~ diri di air* An old banyan tree was reflected in the water. **meng-1** become glassy. *Matanya ~* She became glassy-eyed. **2** look in the mirror. **meng-i** glaze. **memper-(i)** scrutinize, place under a magnifying glass. **ter-** be reflected.

kaca₂ page (of book, etc.).

kacak₁ 1 dashing, robust, vigorous. **2** conceited. **ber-** *pinggang* with hands on hips (in a cocky stance). **ke-an 1** dash, drive. **2** conceit, cockiness.

kacak₂ meng- determine the weight or size of s.t. by holding it in the hand. *~ lengan* roll up o.'s sleeves (preparatory to fighting).

kacang pea, bean, peanut. - *arab* small, hard bean, white with black skin, eaten as a snack. - *asin* salted peanuts. - *atom* peanuts fried in batter. - *bandung/cina* k.o. small peanut. - *belimbing* pea. - *Bogor* a large white bean eaten as a snack. - *buas* k.o. very small nut. - *buncis* green beans. - *ganéfo* peanuts fried in batter. - *goréng* peanuts fried crisp. - *hijau/ijo* mung bean. - *(jambu) monyét* cashew. - *jawa* lima bean. - *kara* k.o. oval, flat nut. - *kapri* peas. - *kedelai* soybean. - *lupa kulit* forget o.'s (humble) origin. - *médé/méndé* cashew. - *mérah* kidney bean. - *miang* troublemaker. - *panjang/polong* k.o. legume, the Hindu cowpea. - *rebus* boiled peanuts. - *shanghai* peanuts fried in batter. - *tanah* peanut. **-²** shot, pellet. **ber-** scramble after. *Waktu toko mengobral barang org ~ membelinya* When the shop had a sale people scrambled to buy. **meng-** divide up (profits, booty, catch, etc.). **memper-** make free use of another's property without permission, act irresponsibly. *Meréka ~ simpanan pamannya* They spent their uncle's savings without his permission. **-²an** legumes, pulses.

kacapiring gardenia.

kacapuri main building of a palace.

kacar line used to fish for squid and cuttlefish.

kacau 1 in disorder, in an uproar. *Seluruh negara -* The whole country was in confusion. **2** confused (mind, situation). **3** in disarray. - *balau/bilau* chaotic, disorganized, in total confusion. **ke-balauan** chaos, total confusion. **meng-balaukan** cause chaos and confusion. **ber- 1** be all mixed up. **2** mixed, blended (of food, drink). **bersi-** be in confusion (plural). **meng- 1** stir (a

drink, paint, etc.). **2** stir up trouble. *Rampokkah ini atau mau ~ saja* Is he a thief or does he just want to stir up trouble? **3** bother, disturb. **mengkan, memper-kan 1** mix, stir s.t. up thoroughly. **2** make s.t. confusing. *Otaknya di-kan berbagai macam kesengsaraan* His mind was confused by troubles of all sorts. **3** stir up trouble. *~ perayaan itu* Disturb the celebration. **ke-an** confusion, disorder. **-an** mixture, s.t. mixed and disorganized. *bahasa ~* mixed language. **peng-** agitator, disturber of the peace. **peng-an** commotion, disturbance, stir.

kacék different, dissimilar.

kaci k.o. white cotton cloth from India.

kacip 1 scissors used primarily for cutting areca nut. **2** gardening scissors. **meng- 1** cut with these scissors. **2** hold s.t. between o.'s legs (as in a leghold in wrestling).

kacir see KUCAR-KACIR.

kaco see NGACO.

kacoa, kacoak cockroach.

kacokan see KACUKAN.

kacu₁ handkerchief.

kacu₂ coagulated areca nut juice used in leather tanning.

kacuk meng- mix, put in disorder, muddle. **-an** mixture, s.t. mixed and disorganized. **-²an** all mixed up.

kacung 1 lad, boy. **2** errand boy, houseboy. *Saya jangan dianggap -nya dong, disuruh-suruh kesana kemari* I'm not an errand boy for you to boss around. - *koran* boy that sells or delivers papers.

kada (*Isl.*) **1** divine decree. **2** make up for unobserved days of fasting month or for missing o. of obligatory prayers. - *hajat* defecate.

kadal k.o. lizard.

kadaluarsa, kadaluwarsa see KEDALUWARSA.

kadam see KHADAM.

kadang₁ sometimes. - *kala* occasionally, once in a while. **-²** sometimes. **ter-** occasionally. **keter-an** rarity. *Adalah suatu ~ kalau isterinya menjemputnya di stasiun* It is rare for his wife to pick him up at the station.

kadang₂ meng- *nasi* skim water off the surface of rice to hasten cooking.

kadang₃ blood relationship.

kadar₁ 1 degree, content. - *garam* amount or level of salinity. - *hamud* level of acidity. **2** standard, level, amount. - *ékspansi* degree of expansion. - *jaminan* degree of security. - *keikhlasan* degree of sincerity. **3** value, quality. **4** fate. *Mémang cuma seliran - saya* It is my fate to be no more than a concubine. **se- 1** just enough to. *~ perlu* only as much as is necessary. *Ia berbicara hanya ~ perlu saja* He talked only when it was necessary. *~ tenaga* according to o.'s ability. *Tolonglah ia ~ tenagamu* Help him as much as you can. **2** just for the sake of, just a little. *Bukan dgn maksud sungguh-sungguh. ~ basa basi saja* Not with an earnest intent. Just for the sake of being polite. *Saya ~ bersenda gurau saja* I am just joking around a bit. *Ia datang ~ melihat anaknya* He came to see his son for a moment. **se-nya 1** to the degree necessary (i.e. simply). *Makan dan minumlah* ~ Please help yourself to the simple refreshments. *Pengantin perempuan itu berpakaian* ~ The bride was simply attired. *Pésta itu* ~ The party was as much as o. could expect. *Gajinya cukup utk hidup* ~ His earnings were sufficient for him to lead a simple life. **2** to the best of o.'s ability. *Itu akan saya kerjakan* ~ I will do it to the best of my ability. **meng-kan** destine. *Demikianlah Tuhan* ~ Thus has God destined.

kadar₂ meng- sleep outdoors.

kadas k.o. skin fungus causing white blotches.

kadaster real estate registry.

kadaver 1 cadaver. **2** dead and uninspired. *disiplin* - dead uninspired discipline.

kade quay.

kader 1 cadre. **2** framework. **meng(k)-kan** form cadres. **peng(k)-an** forming of cadres.

kadéra (*E. Indonesia*) chair.

kaderisasi forming of cadres.

Kadés [*kepala desa*] village head.

kadét₁ 1 cadet. **2** midshipman.

kadét₂ pickpocket.

kadét₃ k.o. white bread or roll.

kadi 1 (*Isl.*) judge in religious court. **2** arbiter, referee. **per-an** arbitration.

kadim₁ eternal.

kadim₂ close, intimate. **se-** of close family relationship with.

kadim₃ meng-kan predict, foretell, prophesy.

Kadin [*Kamar Dagang dan Industri*] the Chamber of Commerce and Industry.

Kadinda [*Kamar Dagang dan Industri Daérah*] the Provincial Chamber of Commerce and Industry.

kadipatén (*in the colonial period*) area ruled over by an *adipati* .

kadir almighty.

kado gift, present. **meng(k)-kan** give as a gift. ~ *sebuah rumah* give a house as a gift.

kadok₁ long pepper leaf used as a substitute for the betel leaf.

kadok₂ see KADA.

kadung (*Jv*) **1** go too far, overdo. **2** take an irrevocable step o. should not. *Ia - menjual tanahnya sblm harganya naik* He was too hasty and sold his land before the price went up.

kadut 1 sack, bag. **2** sacking.

kaédah see KAIDAH.

kaf the letters K and Q in the Arabic alphabet. - *besar* q. - *kecil* k.

kafan see KAPAN₂.

kafarat see KEPARAT₁.

kafé café.

kaféin caffeine.

kafétaria small restaurant with a limited menu us. in a school or workplace.

kafilah 1 desert caravan. **2** (*Mil.*) convoy, column, contingent.

kafir infidel, unbeliever. **mengk-kan** consider s.o. an infidel. **ke-an** infidel state, paganism.

kaftan k.o. cloak.

kagak (*Jkt*) no, not. - *aci* no good.

kagét startled, shocked. *Semuanya - mendengar kabar itu* Everybody was startled to hear the news. **meng-** do suddenly, brusquely. **meng-i, meng-kan** shocking, startling. **ke-an** shock, state of being startled.

kagok 1 clumsy, awkward (esp. in feeling o. is doing s.t. improper). *Jangan duduk terlalu dekat supir, nanti dia jadi* - Do not sit too close to the driver. He is going to feel uneasy and embarrassed. **2** speaking a language with a foreign or dialectal accent.

kagol frustrated. **meng-kan** frustrate.

kagum amazed, struck with amazement and admiration. **meng-i** admire, be amazed by. *Saya* ~ *caranya menghormati wanita* I admire his way of showing deference to women. **meng-kan** astonishing, amazing, admirable. *suatu kepahlawanan yg* ~ an act of astonishing heroism. ~ *diri* glorify o.s. **ter-(²)** surprised. **ke-an 1** astonishment, admiration. *rasa* ~ a feeling of amazement. **2** object of o.'s admiration. *org* ~ *saya* the man I admire. **peng-** admirer. **peng-an** act of admiring.

kah birdlime, glue.

-kah 1 particle marking what is being questioned in an interrogative sentence. *Berdosa- aku* Was I sinning? *Pantas- aku menjadi guru?* Is it right that I become a teacher? *Itu- yg dimaksudkan?* Was that what you meant? *Bukan- ia sdh berjanji?* Is it not so that he has already promised? *Siapa- org itu?* Who is that person? **2** whether . . . or. *Semua wajib, kaya- dia, miskin- dia* All are obliged, whether they be rich or poor.

kahaf (*Lit.*) cave.

kahan proboscis monkey.

kahar₁ k.o. vehicle pulled by a draft animal.

kahar₂ all-powerful. *keadaan* - force majeure, inevitable happening.

kahat scarcity, famine.

kahin soothsayer, diviner.

kahiyangan see KAYANGAN.

kahot old-fashioned, ancient.

kahrab amber.

kahwa (*Lit.*) the beverage coffee.

kahwin see KAWIN.

kahyangan see KAYANGAN.

kaidah 1 norm, rule. - *hukum* legal norm. - *kencana* the golden rule. **2** principle. - *bahasa Indonésia* principles of Indonesian. **3** theorem.

kaifiat quality.

kail meng- fish with hook and line. **peng-** angler.

kail-kail tonsilitis.

kaimat quantity.

kain 1 cloth, fabric, material. - *antelas* satin. - *basahan* **1** cloth worn when bathing. **2** everyday clothes. **3** breechcloth, loincloth. - *batik sohan* dyed batik cloth. - *bayang* transparent cloth. - *belacu* unbleached cotton cloth. - *bentangan* banner. - *berkampuh* two pieces of cloth sewn together. - *cap* printed cloth. - *caul* **1** fine cloth from the western coast of India. **2** (silk) scarf. -

cemar menstruation (cloth). - *cindé* dyed Jv fabric. - *cita* chintz. - *déwangga* colored fabric. - *dondang* cloth for rocking the baby. - *dukung* cloth slung over o. shoulder for carrying a child. - *gebar* cover (such as a blanket, sheet, etc.). - *gerim* k.o. coarse flannel. - *gerus(an)* cloth with a bright sheen. - *guni* burlap. - *hapus* 1 cleaning rag. 2 cotton scraps. - *jendéla* window curtain. - *kaci* white cloth. - *kadut* gunny cloth. - *kapur* starched white cloth. - *kasa* muslin. - *kéci* thin white calico. - *képar/képer* denim. - *kerikam* coarse linen cloth. - *kotor* 1 menstruation (cloth). 2 be menstruating. - *linan* linen cloth. - *lurik* handwoven cloth with a striped design. - *merikan* American imported fabric. - *minyak* oilcloth. - *mota* canvas, sailcloth. - *panas* flannel. - *panjang* batik used for a wraparound. - *pelangi* brightly colored tie-dyed cloth used as a scarf. - *penetap* towel. - *piké* piqué cloth. - *pual* voile. - *rahap* pall. - *randi* ribbed silk fabric. - *salut* upholstery. - *sampaian* laundry. - *serkai* filtering cloth. - *songkét/sungkit* embroidered cloth. - *taf* taffeta. - *teriko* tricot. - *terpal* tarpaulin, canvas. - *tik* pillowcase. - *tiras* lint. 2 sarong. - *barut* cloth used to wrap a baby. **ber-** wear a sarong. **-²an** various k.o. fabric.

kaing yelp with pain (of dogs). **ber-, meng-** yelp. **ter-** yelp suddenly.

kais - *pagi* - *petang* eking out a living. **meng-** scratch, scrape for food (of chickens, etc.). *Stlh makanannya habis piringnya di- karena ia masih lapar* He scraped the plate after he finished eating because he was still hungry. **meng-kan** 1 scratch for (mother hen for its chicks). 2 scratch for a living, eke out a living. 3 use s.t. to scratch with. **-an** s.t. scraped up. **peng-an** scraping or scratching of s.t.

kaisar 1 emperor. 2 Caesar. **ke-an** empire.

kaisaryah 1 imperial. 2 (*Med.*) Caesarean.

kait 1 hook, barb. 2 catch. *Hati-hatilah, barangkali ada -nya dlm perjanjian itu* Be careful; there may be a catch in that contract. **- ber-an** interrelated, interconnected. *Prosés ékonomi adalah prosés yg saling ~* The economic process is an interrelated o. **ber-** 1 use a hook or crook. 2 caught, hooked on s.t. **ber-an** 1 link to e.o. 2 be related to. *Huru-hara ini ~ dgn démonstrasi kemarin* The uproar today is connected to the demonstrations yesterday. **ber-²an** related, linked together. *Semua kejadian itu ~ satu sama lain* All those incidents are related to e.o. **meng-** 1 hook. ~ *buah dr pohon* hook fruit from a tree. 2 get caught, hooked on s.t. 3 embezzle. **meng(k)-kan** 1 hook s.t. on to, attach s.t. 2 dock (a ship). 3 connect, relate. ~ *puisinya pd mistik* relates his poetry to mysticism. 4 tie, peg to. *Mata uang rupiah tak lagi di-kan dgn dolar* The Indonesian rupiah is no longer pegged to the dollar. *ékspor yg di-kan* counter-purchase. **ter-** be connected, hooked, interrelated. **keter-an** connection or interrelatedness. **-an** 1 hook, crook, link. 2 connection. ~ *antara peningkatan konsumsi dan pertumbuhan ékonomi* the

connection between a rise in consumption and economic growth. **peng-** hook, crook, linking. *memasang ~ pd bambu utk mengambil layang* attach a hook on a bamboo pole to get a kite down. **peng-an** connecting, obligating s.o. by making a certain action connected to s.o. else. **per-an** state of being docked.

Kaiwan (*Astr.*) Saturn.

kajanah see KHAZANAH.

kajang movable sunshade of bamboo laths, wickerwork or palm thatch. **meng-i** screen in, cover (an area). **pe-an** area covered with simple sunshade, esp. the stern of a boat.

kajat see HAJAT.

kaji₁ knowledge, teaching (esp. religious). *Tersohor -nya ttg Islam* He is famed for his knowledge of Isl. - *pendéta bijaksana itu* the teachings of the wise preacher. **meng(k)-** recite Koranic verses. **meng-kan** read s.t. aloud from the Koran. **peng(k)-an** recitation of the Koran.

kaji₂ mengk- inspect, examine, investigate. ~ *hasil pemilihan* look into the election results. ~ *baik buruknya* weigh the advantages and disadvantages, weigh the pros and cons. ~ *soal lama* go over an old matter. **mengk-²** examine perfunctorily. **tdk ter-** unfathomable, inscrutable. **-an** study, studies. ~ *saya atas Jepang menunjukkan bhw . . .* My study of Japan indicated that . . . **pengk-** examiner, investigator. **pengk-an** investigation, research. *Diadakan ~ ilmiah mengenai penyakit itu* They carried out a scholarly investigation of the disease. *Apakah hasil ~ sebab-sebab kebakaran itu* What is the result of the investigation into the causes of that fire?

kak₁ k.o. glue used in bookbinding.

kak₂ see KAKAK₁.

kakah ber-an burst out laughing. **ter-²** roar with laughter. *Ia tertawa ~* He roared with laughter.

kakak₁ 1 older sibling or cousin. 2 term of address or reference (esp. as *kak*) for a person somewhat older than the speaker. 3 term of address to o.'s husband (in some areas). **ber-** 1 have older brothers or sisters. 2 call s.o. *kakak*.

kakak₂ boisterous laughter. **meng-, ter-²** laugh boisterously. *Tiba-tiba ia ~* Suddenly she burst into gales of laughter.

kakaktua see KAKATUA.

kakanda (*Lit.*) elder brother or sister (esp. in letters).

kakang (*Jv*) elder brother.

kakao cocoa.

Kakao /ka ka o/ see KKO.

kakap₁ 1 name given to many k.o. large fish. 2 big-time criminal, gangster. 3 large-scale (firm, operation).

kakap₂ meng- patrol, scout.

kakap₃ meng- 1 hold, grasp. 2 work a wet ricefield.

kakas meng- scratch, scrape.

kakatua 1 cockatoo. 2 pincers, pliers with pincer shape (like the beak of a cockatoo). 3 k.o. fish.

kakawin k.o. old Jv poetry.

kakéas doubletime, quicktime in marching, jogging.

kakék 1 grandfather or grand-uncle. **2** term of address for an old man. - *moyang* ancestor. *-²* very old, of an age to be a grandfather.

kakén-kakén - *ninén-ninén* grow as old as grandparents. *Semoga hidup panjang umur sampai - ninén-ninén* May you have a long life together (to a newlywed couple).

kakerlak /kakerlak/ (*Coll.*) **1** cockroach. **2** s.o. as vile as a cockroach.

kaki₁ 1 foot, leg. - *ayam* **1** chicken leg. **2** barefooted. **3** wrinkles from o.'s eyes to temples. - *bébék* splay footed. - *beton* concrete base. - *buatan* artificial leg. - *celana* pants leg. - *gigi* root of tooth. - *gips* plaster cast for leg. - *jalan* pincers (of lobster, etc.). - *lilin* candlestick. - *papan lukisan* easel. *ringan* - *tangan* helpful, ready to help. - *rumah* house foundation. - *seribu* flee in fright. - *tangan* accomplice, henchman, stooge. - *tangga* lowest step or rung. - *tiga* tripod. **2** foot (measurement). *Panjang méja itu lima* - The table is five feet long. - *lima* sidewalk. **3** classifier for flowers or umbrellas. *se- payung* an umbrella. **4** edge of an area. - *angkasa* horizon. - *gunung* foot of a mountain. - *hutan* edge of the forest. - *langit* horizon. **ber- 1** have feet or legs. ~ *empat* four-footed. **2** lean, depend on. *Ia masih* ~ *kpd org tuanya* He still leans on his parents. **meng-1** work (as an apprentice, without pay). **2** serve, be submissive. ~ *langit* horizontal. ~ *méja* (*Acad.*) fail to be promoted.

kaki₂ see KAKÉK.

kaki₃ see KHAKI.

kakok (*M*) hold. **meng- 1** hold. **2** work, do.

kaktus cactus.

kaku 1 stiff, rigid. *Lengannya yg patah itu* - Her broken arm was stiff. - *mayat* rigor mortis. - *otot* cramp in leg or arm. - *tangan* callus on hand. **2** clumsy, awkward, ungainly. *Meskipun ia kelihatannya* - , *sebetulnya ia sangat ramah* Although he seems to be socially awkward, he is really very friendly. - *lidah* unable to speak easily. **meng-kan** stiffen s.t. **ke-an 1** stiffness of body, rigidity. **2** clumsiness. **3** awkwardness in company.

kakung (*honorific, Jv*) male.

kakus (*Coll.*) privy, latrine.

kala₁ 1 time, era, period, age. *Pd suatu - ada seorg raja* Once upon a time there was a king. *pd - itu* at that time. - *depan* future. - *és* ice age. - *glasial* glacial age. - *kini* present. - *lampau* past. *ada -nya* sometimes. **2** (*Ling.*) tense. - *lampau* past tense. **ber-** periodic, periodically. **ber-²** from time to time, occasionally.

kala₂ 1 scorpion. - *jengking* scorpion. - *lipan* centipede. **2** (*Zod.*) Scorpio.

kala₃ mare.

kalah 1 defeated. *Negara itu - berperang* That country was defeated in war. **2** lose. *Ia - Rp50.000 dlm penjudian* He lost 50,000 rupiah at gambling. **3** inferior to. *Anak saya tak - dgn anak-anak lain* My child is not inferior to other children. - *angin* on the losing side. - *angka* lose on basis of points, be decisioned (in boxing). - *gertak* be outsnarled, possess too little bluff (to be a leader). - *stém* be outvoted. **meng-stémkan** outvote, defeat at the ballot box. *meng-stémkan suku Cina* outvote the Chinese. - *suara* be defeated in an election. - *takluk* **meng-taklukkan** subjugate. - *tinggi derajatnya* be of lesser rank. **meng- 1** give in, yield. *Ia selalu* ~ *pd adiknya* She always gives in to her younger sister. *Kepentingan idiil terkadang mesti* ~ *kpd kepentingan komersiil* Sometimes ideals have to give way to commercial interests. **2** concede defeat. **meng-kan 1** defeat, best s.o. **2** overcome. *Cinta dpt* ~ *segala-segalanya* Love can overcome everything. **ter-kan** can be defeated. **ke-an** defeat. **-an** underdog. **peng-an** subjugation.

kalai₁ meng- 1 lie down. **2** lean. **men-kan** lay s.t. on, cause s.t. to rest against.

kalai₂ meng- rub, polish s.t. tarnished.

kalak (*Math.*) **1** reciprocal. **2** inverse.

kala-kala (*Naut.*) sea anchor.

kalakat bamboo basket for moist cookies.

kalam₁ 1 pen made from a leaf rib. **2** (*Lit.*) writing instrument.

kalam₂ word, saying. - *Allah/ullah* (*Lit.*) The words of God.

kalam₃ see KALEM.

kalang transverse support, prop. - *hulu* pillow, headrest. **ber-** be supported. *Atap itu hanya* ~ *dua tiang bambu saja* The roof is supported by only two bamboo poles. ~ *tanah* have the earth as o.'s pillow (i.e., be dead). **meng-** support s.t. **meng-kan** prop up, support. ~ *léhér/merih* stick o.'s neck out for s.o. **memper-** use as a prop or support. **ter-** supported, wedged. *lidah* ~ afraid to speak. **-an** shipyard, drydock.

kalangan 1 circle, arena. - *bulan* ring around the moon. - *bola* soccer field. - *ténis* tennis court. - *menari* the dance floor. **2** realm. *di - pengangkutan* in the realm of transportation. **3** circle. - *atas* upper circles of society, business, etc.

kalang-kabut confused, chaotic. *Pikirannya jadi* - His thoughts became confused. *Meréka lari* - They ran helter-skelter. **meng-kan** confuse. **ke-an** confusion, chaos.

kalap 1 possessed by an evil spirit. **2** be beside o.s. with anger. *Tiba-tiba jadi - spt org gila dan bingung* Suddenly he became confused like a crazy person at a loss for what to do. **ke-an** confusion, bewilderment.

kalas 1 thole-strap for an oar. **2** band around the hilt of a machete.

kalau 1 if. - *ia datang panggillah saya* If he comes, call me. - *saja* if only. - *saja saya diberitahu lebih awal* If only I had been told sooner . . . - *tdk* otherwise. - . . ., *bagaimana?* how would it be if . . . ? **2** when (future). - *pekerjaanmu sdh selesai engkau boléh pergi* When you have finished your work you may go. - *musim hujan di sini* . . . When it is the rainy season here . . . **3** as for . . ., in the case of . . . *Kakak saya gemar; - saya, ndak* My older brother likes to; as for me, I do not. - *seribu, bagaimana* If we make it a thousand, how about it? **4** (*Coll.*) whether (introducing an indirect question). *Saya nggak tahu - bisa* I do not know whether it is possible. **5** (*Coll.*) that (introducing an indirect statement). *Dia bilang - hari Senén tdk ada kuliah* He said that there are no classes on Monday. **-pun** even though. ~ *ia sakit, ia pergi juga* Even though she was ill, she went anyway. **-²** **1** in case, lest. *Jangan memanjat pohon itu* ~ *jatuh* Do not climb that tree lest you fall. *Berpakaianlah yg pantas* ~ *ia datang* Get properly dressed in case he comes. **2** maybe, perhaps. *Tanyalah dia,* ~ *dia tahu* Ask him, maybe he knows.

kalawarta 1 magazine, periodical. **2** bulletin.

Kalbar [*Kalimantan Barat*] W. Kalimantan.

kalbu 1 heart. **2** mind. *Keluarkanlah apa yg ada dlm -mu* Please state what is on your mind. - *hati* mind.

kaldéra caldera (of a volcano).

kaldron cauldron.

kaldu broth, stock (for soup).

kalelep (*Jv*) **1** be submerged, lowered. **2** drowned.

kalem calm, cool, patient, relaxed. - *dulu! Jangan gugup* Be calm! Do not get upset.

kalénder calendar.

kaléng 1 tin can. - *penyiram* watering can. - *sampah* dustpan. **2** tin. *atap* - tin roof. **3** tin plate. **mengk-kan** can, preserve food. **-an** canned, in cans. *daging* ~ canned meat. **-²an** canned goods. **peng(k)-an, per-an** canning, preserving.

kalérék see KELERAK.

kalesa source of animal protein.

kali₁ river.

kali₂ 1 time, times. - *ini engkau masih kumaafkan* This time I will forgive you. *beberapa* - several times. *utk pertama -nya* for the first time. **2** (*Math.*) times. *Dua - tiga menjadi enam* Two times three is six. **3** fold (suffix). *sepuluh* - tenfold. **-²** multiplication table. **se-** **1** once, one time. *Ia baru* ~ *pergi ke Jkt* She has only gone to Jkt once. *produksi* ~ *banyak* mass production. ~ *dan selamanya* once and for all. -~ *dua hari* every other day. ~ *jalan* one-way trip. ~ *saja* just once. ~ *teguk* in one swallow. ~ *témpo/waktu* at some time or another. *Kalau* ~ *témpo anda ke Jogja* . . . If some time you should go to Jogja . . . ~ . . . *tetap* . . . once . . . always . . . ~ *merdéka tetap merdéka* once free always free. ~ *tiga uang* six of one, half a dozen of the other. **2** at the same time. **3** when (so-and-so happens), as soon as. *Kita bisa membayar* ~ *uang masuk* We can pay as soon as some money comes in. **se-se-, sese-** occasionally, now and then, once in a while. ~ *ia nonton* She goes to the movies once in a while. **se-²** (*tdk*) never, not at all, under no circumstances. *Pintu itu* ~ *tdk boléh dibuka* That door may not be opened under any circumstances. *Jangan* ~ *berani pergi dgn tdk seizin saya* Don't you dare go without my permission. **se-pun** although. ~ *ia sakit, ia pergi ke sekolah juga* Although he was sick,

he went to school anyway. **ber-²** repeatedly, again and again. *Sdh* ~ *engkau terlambat* You have been late repeatedly. **meng-kan, memperkan** (*Math.*) multiply. ~ *angka-angka* multiply figures. *daftar* ~ multiplication table. **-²an** multiplication. **se-an 1** all. *Meréka* ~ *pergi ke sekolah* All of them went to school. **2** at the same time. *Kita habiskan keduanya* ~ We will finish off both of them at the same time. *Kalau kau ke perpustakaan bawalah buku ini* ~ When you go to the library, would you mind taking this book, too? **peng-** multiplier. **per-an** (*Math.*) **1** multiplication. **2** product.

kali₃ (*Jkt*) probably.

kali₄ (*Jkt*) very.

kalian (*Pl.*) you (form of address to equals, younger persons or persons of lower status).

kaliber 1 caliber (of gun). **2** importance, class. *pemimpin - besar yg dikenalnya* leader of some importance he happened to know. - *kakap* big shot. - *teri* small fry. **ber- 1** have a certain caliber. *meriam* ~ *dua puluh delapan sénti* a 28 cm cannon. **2** be of a certain rank, importance. ~ *besar* be of great importance.

kalibut chaos.

kalifah 1 caliph. **2** caliphate.

kaligrafi calligraphy.

kalimah see SYAHADAT.

Kalimantan Borneo. - *Utara* Sarawak and Sabah.

kalimantang 1 pennant. **2** white beam of light.

kalimat sentence, independent clause. - *ingkar* negative sentence. - *majemuk setara* compound sentence. - *majemuk bertingkat* complex sentence. - *penjelas* declarative sentence. - *tanggap* passive sentence. - *tindak* active sentence. **meng-kan 1** make into a sentence. **2** say or use s.t. in a sentence.

kalingan (*Jv*) partially hidden, with obstructed view.

kalio see KLIO.

kalis 1 dull, lacking luster (of a surface). **2** immune to disease, not allowing air, water, or some other extraneous substance to penetrate. - *air* waterproof. - *udara* airtight. **3** pure. - *dosa* free from sin. **meng-kan** clear or clean out, purify. **ke-an** immunity, resistance to disease.

kalium potassium. - *nitrat* potassium nitrate.

kalkarim, kalkarium wallpaint.

kalkir meng- trace s.t. over s.t.

kalkulasi calculation.

kalkulator calculator.

kalkulir mengk- calculate.

kalkun turkey.

kalo₁ strainer.

kalo₂, kalok see KALAU.

kalong see KELUANG.

kalor (*Phys.*) heat. - *bakar* heat released by combustion.

kalori calorie.

kalpataruh 1 (*Lit.*) k.o. mythological tree that never dies. **2** annual prize awarded to o. who has made an outstanding contribution to preserving the environment.

Kalsel [*Kalimantan Selatan*] S. Kalimantan.
Kalselteng [*Kalimantan Selatan dan Tengah*] S. and Central Borneo.
kalsium calcium.
Kalteng [*Kalimantan Tengah*] Central Borneo.
Kaltim [*Kalimanan Timur*] E. Borneo.
kalu see KALAU.
kalui k.o. fish, gurami.
kalung necklace. **ber-** wear a necklace. *Gadis Hawaii ~ rangkaian bunga* Hawaiian girls wear leis. **ber-kan** use s.t. as necklace. **meng-** be like a necklace. *Di léhernya ~ pita* A ribbon hung around his neck like a necklace. **meng-i** put a necklace on s.o. **meng-kan** drape s.t. around the neck. *-kan baju pelampung* Place o.'s head through the life jacket. *Gubernur ~ medali* The governor placed the medal around his neck. **ter-** be strapped around o.'s neck. **peng-an** putting s.t. around o.'s neck, .
kalurahan see LURAH₁.
kalut confused, chaotic. *Pikiran saya -* My mind is confused. *Rencana perjalanannya - karena banyak tangan ikut mengerjakannya* The itinerary was a mess because too many people were planning it. *- bin kacau* extremely confused. *- malut* chaotic, in great disorder. **meng-kan** upset, confuse s.o., confusing, upsetting. **ke-an** confusion. *~ sosial* social disorganization.
Kalut [*Kalimantan Utara*] N. Borneo.
Kalwan (*Astr.*) Uranus.
kam internment or prison camp.
kama (*Lit.*) love, passion.
kamadéan parasite.
kamar₁ room, chamber. *- (pem)bakar(an)* combustion chamber. *- balut* emergency room, first aid station. *- bedah* operating room. *- belajar* study room, classroom. *- bersalin* delivery room. *- besi* (bank) vault. *- bicara* consulting room. *- bola* pool hall. *- dagang* chamber of commerce. *- depan* front room, anteroom. *- duplo* room with twin beds. *- ganda* double room. *- ganti* dressing room. *- gelap* 1 darkroom. 2 prison cell. *- induk* master bedroom. *- jenazah* morgue. *- haca* greenhouse. *- kecil* W.C., lavatory, toilet, restroom. *- kolong* basement, cellar. *- makan* dining room. *- mandi* bathroom. *- mayat* morgue. *- muka* anteroom. *- pengeram* brooder room. *- petak* partitioned room. *- prakték* doctor's office. *- rias* dressing room. *- tahanan* room of detention. *- tidur* bedroom. *- tunggal* single room. *- tunggu* waiting room. **ber- 1** have a room, room. *Ia ~ di hotél* He roomed in a hotel. **2** have rooms. *hotél yg ~ tujuh* hotel with seven rooms. **ber-²** compartmentalized, be in compartments. **meng- 1** live in (of servants). **2** rent a room (us. for sexual purposes). **ng-** (*Jv*) **1** stay overnight, stay with a family. **2** be admitted to a hospital. **3** rent a room for sexual purposes.
kamar₂ (*Lit.*) moon.
kamar₃ ornamental sash around the waist, cummerbund.
kamariah pertaining to the moon.
kamat₁ (*Isl.*) the call to begin prayer.

kamat₂ k.o. tree.
kambang see AMBANG₂.
kambar k.o. large sea turtle.
kambéh gourd.
kambék 1 make a comeback. *harapan utk bisa -* hopes to make a comeback. **2** (*Coll.*) be reconciled (of lovers).
kambeli k.o. woolen fabric.
kambi 1 rib, frame. **2** paneling, wainscoting.
kambing goat. *- congék* stooge, o. who is present but does not count as taking part. *- domba* sheep. *- gibas/kibas* fat-tailed sheep. *- hitam* 1 black sheep (of the family). 2 scapegoat. **meng-hitamkan** place the blame on, make the scapegoat. *Pemerintah sering meng-hitamkan mahasiswa dlm kesusahan politik* The gvt. often makes the students the scapecoat when there are political problems. *- kacang* k.o. small goat. **meng-²kan** debase, degrade. *Ia ~ karyawannya* He degraded his employees.
kamboja k.o. tree, frangipani.
kambrat 1 comrade. **2** accomplice, party to a crime. **3** small party, get together. *- menyanyi* a singing party. **ber-** have an accomplice, have a companion in an activity. *Dlm kejahatan itu ia ~ dgn temannya itu* He committed that crime together with his friend.
kambuh have or suffer a relapse. *Demamnya - lagi* Her fever flared up again.
kambus blocked, stopped up (of drain).
kambut k.o. woven basket.
kamera camera.
kamerad comrade.
kameraman camera man.
kamerjas, kameryas man's dressing gown.
kamfer see KAMPER.
kamhar camel hair wool.
kami 1 we, us, our (excluding the person addressed). *- akan meninggalkan anda sekalian* We're going to be leaving all of you. *rumah -* our house. **2** I (deferential). *- menghadap Bapak utk minta pertolongan* I have come to see you, sir, to ask for your help. *- sekeluarga* my family and I. *Hormat -*, Yours respectfully.
kamil perfect. *insan -* the perfect man.
Kamis Thursday. *- Putih* Maundy Thursday.
kamis, kamisa shirt.
kamisolen, kamisosolen unable to speak properly from overexcitement.
kamit see KOMAT-KAMIT.
kamitua deputy village chief in Central Java.
kamli see KAMBELI.
kamling [*keamanan lingkungan*] law and order of the neighborhood.
kamp /kém/ see KAM.
kampagne see KAMPANYE.
kampai₁ **ber-(an)** lie supine, stretched out. **meng-kan** stretch s.t. out, put s.o. in a lying position. **ter-** stretched out.
kampai₂ (*Japanese*) Cheers! (on raising a toast).
kampak adze. **meng-** cut with an adze.
kampanye campaign. *- bisik* whisper campaign. **meng-kan** campaign for s.o. or s.t.

kampas see KANVAS.
kampemén military encampment.
kamper camphor, mothballs. - *spiritus* solution of camphor in methylated spirits.
kampil, kampit small sack. - *purun* money pouch of woven grass. **meng-** put in a sack.
kampiun champion, very clever or skilled.
kampleng meng- slap (s.o. in the face). *Mahasiswa itu perlu di-* That student needs to be slapped. **meng-i** slap repeatedly.
kampong see KAMPUNG.
kamprét₁ k.o. small bat.
kamprét₂ shucks!
kampuh 1 shawl, wrap. **2** two thin strips of paper or cloth sewn together, seam. **ber-** see KAIN.
kampung 1 village. **2** quarter. - *Cina* Chinatown. **3** residential area for lower classes in town or city. - *halaman* home, native village, birthplace. **se- 1** the whole village. **2** of the same village. *teman ~ saya* person from my home village. **ber-** gathered, collected. **meng-kan** gather, collect, assemble s.t. **-an** countrified, boorish. *Gadis itu ~ betul* That girl is really a hick. **per-an 1** settlement. **2** gathering place. **3** group of villages. *~ bersama* commune. *~ Olympiade* Olympic village.
kampus campus.
kamrat camshaft.
kamsia (*Ch*) thank you.
kamso (*Jv*) rustic, provincial.
kamtibmas [*keamanan dan ketertiban masyarakat*] peace and order in society.
kamu you, your (*familiar, singular and plural*). - *sekalian* all of you.
kamuflase camouflage. **ber-** camouflage o.s. **meng-** camouflage s.t.
kamufláséring camouflaging.
kamuflir mengk- camouflage.
kamuplase see KAMUFLASE.
kamus dictionary, lexicon. *Pemotongan dana bantuan utk Israél tak ada dlm - Kongrés AS* The word "cut-back" does not exist in the dictionary of the US Congress when it comes to aid for Israel. - *ilmu bumi* gazetteer. **pe-** lexicographer. **per-an** lexicography.
kan₁ 1 It is the case, isn't it? *Ini masih pagi, -?* It is still early, isn't it? **2** because as you well know . . . *Jangan keluar. - gelap* Do not go out. It is dark, you know. *Pantas dia begitu. - baru saja dilantik* No wonder he is like that. He was just appointed, you know.
kan₂ short form for *akan₁. tak - not likely to. Ia tak - datang* She is not likely to come.
kan₃ container for boiling tea.
kan₄ see KANS.
kana preserved olives.
kanak child. *masa -nya* his childhood. **-²** (*Lit.*) small child. *~ anyir* new born baby. **ke-²an** puerile, childish.
kanal 1 canal. **2** channel. *penyeberang -* a swimmer of the channel.
kanan 1 right. *tangan -* right hand. **2** (*Pol.*) rightist. - *luar* (*Sport*) outside right. **meng- 1** turn to the right. **2** keep to the right. *Kendaraan selalu hrs ~ di jalan* Vehicles must keep to the right at all times. **meng-kan** move s.t. to the right, turn (a ship) to starboard. **ke-²an** too much to the right.
kanapé canapé.
kanari₁ the canari tree or its nuts.
kanari₂ see KENARI₂.
kancah 1 large pot for cooking rice. **2** s.t. figuratively comparable to a deep pot: depths (of despair), abyss (of misery). - *informasi* mine of information. - *kesengsaraan* depths of despair. - *peperangan* cauldron of war. - *perjuangan* arena of struggle. - *politik* political arena. **ter-** thrown into the embrace of misery.
kancana see KENCANA.
kancap filled to the brim.
kancil 1 mouse deer. **2** a clever individual.
kancing button. - *baju* shirt button. - *jeprét* 1 snap. **2** push button. - *mansét* cufflinks. - *ritsléting/sorok* zipper. - *gigi/mulut* lockjaw. **meng-(kan) 1** button s.t. **2** lock, latch s.t. **ter-** locked, buttoned. *Mulutnya ~* His jaw was locked from tetanus. **peng-** fastener, catch, lock.
kancut loin cloth, jockstrap.
kanda see KAKANDA.
kandang 1 stable, stall, pen. - *ayam* chicken coop. - *babi* pigpen. - *bermain* playpen. **2** place to keep vehicles, boats, etc. - *bulan* halo around the moon. - *kapal* boathouse. - *mobil* garage. - *monyét* guardhouse. *pulang ke -* return to o.'s original home. *msk -* (*Sport*) be knocked out of a competition. **meng-** go into the stall. *kerbau-kerbau itu ~ kalau hari mulai gelap* The buffalo go into their stalls when it begins to get dark. **meng-i** fence in a yard, pasture, etc. **meng-kan** put into a stable, pen, or the like. *Mobilnya di-kan biar aman* Put the car in the garage so it is safe. *Org hukuman itu di-kan di kantor polisi* The criminal was jailed in the police station. **peng-an** penning up of s.t.
kandar meng-(kan) operate a vehicle. **peng-** driver, operator. *~ sepéda* cyclist. **peng-an** operating a vehicle.
kandas 1 run aground, founder (of a ship etc.). *Kapal itu di pantai* The ship ran aground on the coast. **2** fail. *Segala usahanya -* All her efforts failed. **meng-kan 1** beach (a boat etc.). **2** cause s.t. to fail, frustrate. **ter-** beached, stranded. **ke-an** failure.
kandel 1 thick, heavy. **2** rich, well-to-do.
kandi₁ pouch, small bag.
kandi₂ see ASAM.
kandidat candidate. *ujian -* (doctoral) candidacy exam. **meng-kan** propose as a candidate. **ke-an** candidacy.
kandil 1 lamp. **2** chandelier, candelabra. **3** candlestick.
kandis tree with small sour fruit.
kandung 1 womb, uterus. *anak - o.'s* own child. *sdr - a* brother or sister of the same mother. **2** pouchlike part of the body. - *empedu* gall bladder. - *jantung* pericardium. - *kemih/kencing/(per)ken-*

cingan bladder. **se-** from the same womb. *sdr* ~ a brother or sister of the same mother. **ber-** 1 have contents. 2 be pregnant. **meng-** 1 be pregnant with. *anak yg di-* a child she is carrying. 2 have within it, contain. *Buah-buahan ~ banyak pitamin* Fruit contains many vitamins. *Peristiwa ini ~ ajaran* This event teaches us s.t. *~ hati* bear a grudge, be annoyed. **meng-i** bear in o.'s womb. *Wanita itu ~ benih dr laki-laki yg bukan suaminya* That woman bore in her womb the seeds of a man not her husband. **meng-kan** render pregnant. **ter-** be contained. *merasakan apa yg ~ dlm kata-kata ibarat itu* feel what is contained in words like that. **-an** 1 uterus, womb. 2 contents. *lahar dr ~ gunung api* lava from inside a volcano. *~ hati* contents of the heart. *~ protéin* protein content. 3 unborn child, fetus. *~ terpaksa digugurkan* The fetus must be aborted. 4 pouch. **peng-** s.t. which contains s.t. *~ kuman* carrier of germs.

kang₁ large earthenware container.

kang₂ see KAKANG.

kang₃ see KEKANG.

kangen (*Jv*) long for, miss s.t. *Saya - tanah air* I long for the homeland. *Saya - gudeg* I miss jackfruit stew. **meng-i** 1 long for s.t. 2 make s.o. miss s.t. **ke-an** what o. misses or longs for.

kangka (*Ch*) gambier plantation.

kangkang₁ meng- 1 wide apart (of legs). *duduk ~* sit with legs apart. 2 straddle, sit astride. **meng-i** straddle s.t. **meng-kan** open the legs wide.

kangkang₂ meng- strangle. **meng-i** take by force or illegally. *Wartawan ~ hak démokrasi rakyat dgn tdk mengumumkan sidang pengadilan itu* A journalist deprives the people of their democratic rights if he fails to report the court session.

kangker see KANKER.

kangkung₁ k.o. leafy vegetable, us. growing in water.

kangkung₂ large frog or toad.

kangmas (*Jv*) 1 older brother. 2 term of address for o.'s husband.

kangsa see GANGSA₁.

kangsar k.o. tall tree.

kangsén appointment, have an appointment. *Saya tdk bisa menetapi - kita* I could not keep our appointment. *Saya - dgn dia jam lima* I have an appointment with him at five.

kangtau (*Ch*) chance, opportunity (in business).

kanguru kangaroo.

kanibal cannibal.

kanigara sunflower.

kanin canine.

kanisah see KENISAH.

kanjang ber- persevering, persistent.

kanjar k.o. large dagger.

kanjeng (*Jv*) form of address or reference for a high-ranking noble.

kanji₁ starch. **meng-** starch s.t.

kanji₂ Ch characters used in Japanese.

kanker cancer. *- ganas* malignant tumor.

kano canoe.

kanon₁ cannon.

kanon₂ rent for a plot of ground.

kanonisasi canonization. **mengk-(kan)** canonize.

kanopi canopy.

kanpas see KANVAS.

kans chance, opportunity. *-nya kecil utk diterima* She has little chance of getting accepted.

kanselir chancellor.

kanta lens.

kantang mud flats.

kantih thread, yard.

kantil₁ (*Jv*) the champac, k.o. magnolia.

kantil₂ see KONTAL-KANTIL.

kantin canteen, us. attached to a workplace.

kantong see KANTUNG.

kantor 1 office. *jam -* office hours. 2 office, agency. *- angin* weather station. *- bank* bank office. *- béa* customs office. *- pos* post office. *- pusat* main office. *- télpon* telephone office. **ber-** 1 have o.'s office. 2 open an office. **meng-** work in an office. **ng-** 1 go to the office. 2 have an office. **-an** pertaining to an office. *pegawai ~* office employee. *jam ~* working hours. **per-an** 1 office affairs. 2 office complex.

kantuk sleepiness, drowsiness. **meng-** feel sleepy. **ter-** doze off. **ke-an** drowsiness. **peng-** sleepyhead.

kantung 1 pocket. *- belakang* back pocket. *- dada* breast pocket. 2 bag, pouch. *- kempis/tipis* broke, penniless. *- air panas* hot water bottle. *- kolékte* (*Rel.*) collection plate or bag. 3 pouchlike part of body. *- buah zakar/kemaluan* scrotum. *- empedu* gall bladder. *- kemih/kencing* bladder. **ber-** have a pocket. **meng-i** 1 pocket s.t. *Ia menyusun uang kemenangannya dan ~nya* He gathered the money he won and put it in his pocket. 2 carry in the pocket. *Berhari-hari surat itu di-i* For days he carried the letter in his pocket. **meng-kan** pocket s.t.

kanun (*Rel.*) canon law.

kanvas 1 canvas. *sepatu -* canvas shoes. 2 floor of boxing ring. 3 piece of tire or tube used in patching. 4 brake lining. **mengk-** patch a tire with a piece of rubber. *Ia ~ bannya yg bolong* He put a patch on the hole in his tire. **meng-kan** (*Sport*) floor, knock down to the canvas (in boxing).

Kanwil [*Kantor Wilayah*] regional office.

Kanya (*Zod.*) Virgo.

kaok ber-² 1 cackle (of chickens). 2 yell, shout (of children). **meng-i** yell or scream after. **meng-kan** cackle or yell about. *Pérs ~ kecurangannya* The press screamed about his dishonesty. **-an** s.t. yelled about. **-²an** 1 cackling. 2 yelling, screaming.

kaoliang sorghum.

kaolin kaolin.

kaos 1 sock, stocking. *- kabel* thimble. *- kaki* sock, stocking. *- lampu* mantle of a pressure lantern. *- tangan* glove. 2 singlet, undershirt. *- dlm* undershirt. *- kutang (pria)/oblong* singlet. **ber-** wear an undershirt.

kap 1 (*Auto.*) roof of a car. 2 shade (of lamp, etc.). -

kepala bathing cap. - *lampu* lampshade. 3 cowl. - *cahaya* (*Naut.*) porthole.

kapabel capable, able.

kapabilitas capability.

kapah ter-² 1 startled, trembling from fright. 2 gasping (for breath).

kapai move as if wanting to clutch at s.t. **ter-²** flutter, flail around.

kapak₁ ax.

kapak₂ see KEPAK₁.

kapa-kapa a sunshade on a boat, us. of palm thatch or a temporary sunshade, esp. in the yard for a wedding (or other) feast.

kapal₁ ship, boat, vessel. - *angkasa* space ship. - *angkutan* freighter. - *api* steamship. - *bajak* pirate boat. - *barang* freighter. - *bersayap* hydrofoil. - *capung* spotter plane. - *curah* bulk carrier ship. - *dagang* freighter. - *dayung* rowboat. - *és* icebreaker. - *induk* 1 mother ship. 2 aircraft carrier. - *katung* hovercraft. - *keruk* dredger. - *kincir* paddle boat. - *komando* flagship. - *korék* dredger. - *latih* training vessel. - *laut* ocean vessel. - *layar* sailboat, sailing vessel. - *liar* tramp steamer. - *menyusur* coastal vessel, coaster. - *meriam* gunboat. - *mil* mailboat. - *minyak* fueling ship. - *motor* motorship. - *mualim* pilot boat. - *muatan* freighter. - *pandu* pilot boat. - *panji* flagship. - *pantai* coastal vessel, coaster. - *pemair/pemayar* cruiser. - *pemburu* destroyer. - *penambang* ferryboat. - *pendarat* landing craft. - *penempur* battleship. - *pengangkut* 1 freighter, transport, cargo vessel. 2 troopship. - *pengemas* salvage vessel. - *penggempur* battle cruiser. - *pengiring* escort vessel. - *penjelajah* light cruiser. - *penumpang* passenger ship. - *penyapu ranjau* minesweeper. - *perang* warship, man-of-war. - *peronda* patrol boat. - *perusak* destroyer. - *peti kemas* container ship. - *rambu* tourist ship. - *roda lampung* steamwheeler, paddleboat. - *selam* submarine. - *suar* (*pandu*) lightship. - *tangki* tanker. - *tarik* tugboat. - *terbang* plane. - *torpédo* torpedo boat. - *tunda* tug, tugboat. - *udara* 1 plane. 2 dirigible. - *wisata* cruise ship. **ber-** 1 go by ship. *Ia ~ pergi ke Éropah* She went to Europe by ship. 2 have a boat. **ber-²** several boats. **meng-kan** send s.t. by ship. **peng-an** shipping of s.t. **per-an** 1 shipping, shipping matters. 2 fleet, tonnage. 3 shipyard, dockyard.

kapal₂ 1 callous. 2 stubborn, insensitive. **-an** calloused.

kapan₁ when? - *anda akan pergi?* When will you leave? *Saya blm tahu - bisa* I do not know yet when it will be possible. - *kenalnya? Ketemu aja blm* When could I have gotten to know him? I have not even met him. - *saja* 1 any time whatsoever. *Saya - saja bisa datang* I can come at any time. 2 exactly when. - *saja diadakan?* What times exactly do they put it on? -² at some time or another. *Ya, ~ kita bicarakan* Yes, we will talk about it some time.

kapan₂ shroud of unbleached cotton. **ber-** shrouded. *Mayat itu ~* The corpse was wrapped in a shroud. **meng(k)-i** shroud (a body). **meng(k)-kan** cover with shroud for s.o.

kapan₃ (*Jkt*) because, as you well know . . . *Jangan tanya-tanya lagi, - sekarang sdh jelas* Do not keep asking. Surely it is clear now.

kapanéwon subdistrict of a *kabupatén* (county).

kapang 1 ship worm or worm that gets into rice. 2 mold, mildew. **ber-** have mildew.

kapar flotsam, driftwood. **ber-an** scattered, littered about. *Kotoran ~ di mana-mana* Rubbish was scattered everywhere. **meng(k)-kan** 1 disperse, scatter s.t. 2 deploy (troops). **ter-** scattered, spread out or about. *Ia sdh lama ~ di kursi* He had been spread out in the chair for a long time. *Ia jatuh ~ di tanah* He fell smack on the ground. **-an** 1 flotsam, driftwood. 2 rubbish.

kaparat see KEPARAT₁.

kapas 1 cotton. - *ledak* gun cotton. 2 cotton plant. 3 fleece. 4 (*Med.*) cotton, gauze. - *pembalut* sterilized gauze. **-²an** various k.o. cotton, plants of cotton family.

kapasitas, kapasitét capacity. **ber-** have a certain capacity.

kapatihan see PATIH₁.

kapbir see KABIR.

kapé 1 spatula. 2 putty knife.

kapél chapel.

kapélan chaplain.

kaper (*Jv*) moth.

kapi₁ (*Naut.*) pulley block.

kapi₂ see KAPÉ.

kapilah see KAFILAH.

kapin (*Geol.*) limestone.

kapir see KAFIR.

kapiran (*Jv*) 1 be neglected. 2 let down. 3 beyond help.

kapita see PER.

kapital (*Fin.*) capital.

kapitalis capitalist.

kapitalisme capitalism.

kapitan₁ leader for the Ch, Arabs or certain other local ethnic leaders under the Dutch. - *Cina* the leader of the Ch of a certain area.

kapitan₂, kapitén see KAPTÉN.

kapitulasi capitulation. **ber-** capitulate.

kapling see KAVELING.

kaplok - *dada* beat o.'s breast.

kapoces, kapocis condom.

kapok₁ learn o.'s lesson, be cured. *Ia tak berani lagi ia sdh -* He did not do it again; he has learned his lesson. *Sdh - aku menolong org yg tdk berterima kasih itu* I have had it, trying to help that ungrateful wretch. *Ia membikin - para tamu* (She was so inhospitable) she made her guests feel that they would not want to come back again. *pembohong yg tak ada -nya* an incurable liar. **meng-kan** teach s.o. a lesson.

kapok₂ see KAPUK₁.

kapol see KAPUL.

Kapol [*kepala polisi*] head of the police.

kapolda [*kepala polisi daérah*] head of the provincial police.

kapolrés [*kepala polisi résort*] head of the county police.

kapolri [*kepala polisi Republik Indonésia*] head of the Indonesian police.

kapolsék [*kepala séktor*] head of the district police.

kapolwil [*kepala polisi wilayah*] head of the regional police.

kaporal see KOPRAL.

kaporit chlorine. **meng-** use chlorine, chlorinate. *Apakah kolam ini di-* Has this pool been chlorinated?

kaprah usual, ordinary. *tdk -* unusual.

kapri snow peas.

kapsalon beauty parlor.

kapstok clothes hook, hatrack.

kapsul₁ capsule.

kapsul₂ hair piece.

kapt. [*kaptén*] captain.

kaptén 1 (*Mil.*) captain, lieutenant (in Navy). **2** see KAPITAN₁. **meng-i** be captain of s.t.

kapuk₁ 1 kapok. **2** kapok tree. **per-an** having to do with kapok.

kapuk₂ rice granary or barn.

kapu-kapu k.o. plant, the leaves of which resemble lettuce, formerly found in abundance floating on slow-moving or stagnant water.

kapul, kapulaga, kapulogo cardamom.

kapung see APUNG.

kapur 1 lime. *- barus* 1 camphor. 2 mothballs. *- hidup/kuripan* quicklime. *- mati* slaked lime. *- mentah* quicklime. *- sirih* lime for chewing with betel leaves. *- tohor* quicklime. **2** calcium. *- batu* 1 plaster. 2 gypsum, plaster of paris. 3 chalk. *- belanda* chalk (for writing). *- berwarna* crayon. *- témbok* mortar. **se-** *sirih* 1 a chew of betel leaves. 2 little bit. 3 a few words, a short speech. *Boléhkah kami mengucapkan ~ sirih* I would like to say a few words if I might. **ber-** have calcium deposits. *Paru-parunya ~ kata dokter* The doctor said he had deposits in his lungs. **meng- 1** calcify. 2 prepare the betelnut. 3 whitewash. **meng-i** whitewash (several things). **meng-kan** prepare a chew of betel. **peng-** o. who whitewashes or plasters, instrument for whitewashing or plastering. **pe-an** limekiln, lime pit. **peng-an 1** plastering. 2 whitewashing. 3 calcification. *~ pembuluh darah* hardening of the arteries. **per-an** calcification (in the lungs, etc.).

kapurancang (*Jv*) **ng-** stand with the hands cupped covering the genitals as a sign of deference (of men).

kar map, chart.

kar.₁ [*karangan*] article.

kar.₂ [*karésidénan*] residency.

kara₁ see KACANG.

kara₂ see BATANG.

karaba k.o. fish trap.

karabén, karabin carbine.

karaéng title of nobility in S. Sulawesi.

karaf decanter.

karah 1 stain. **2** tartar (on teeth). **ber- 1** stained. 2 have tartar (on o.'s teeth).

karak see KERAK.

karakter character.

karakterdés [*kader penggerak téritorial désa*] cadre of the Golkar Party assigned to rural areas.

karakterisasi characterization.

karakterisir meng- characterize.

karakteristik characteristic.

karam 1 be shipwrecked, founder, go under. *Kapal itu -* The ship foundered. **2** fail, founder. *Segala usahanya -* All her efforts failed. *perkawinan yg - a marriage* that is on the rocks. **meng-** sink, go under (of a floor, etc.). **meng-kan 1** sink s.t. **2** cause to fail. *Ia hendak ~ usaha musuhnya* He wanted to make his enemy's efforts fail.

karamba basket put in a stream for raising fish.

karambol, karambola billiards game.

karang₁ coral, coral reef, atoll. *- endapan* encrustation. *- gigi* tartar (on teeth). **ber- 1** provided with coral reefs. **2** deeply rooted, chronic (of illness etc.). **ter-** run aground on a coral reef. **-an** coral. **-²an** various types of coral.

karang₂ *- keputrian* neighborhood girls' association. *- taruna* neighborhood youth association. **ber- 1** inset (of diamond, etc.). **2** in bunches (of flowers). *- meng-* composing, writing. *Ia hidup dr ~* She lives from her writing. **meng- 1** string (beads, jewels), arrange (flowers). *~ bunga* arrange flowers. *~ merjan* string beads. **2** compose (music, poetry, fiction). **meng-kan 1** arrange, string s.t. **-an 1** write or compose for s.o. **-an 1** arrangement, floral wreath. *~ bunga* bouquet. **2** composition, s.t. composed or written. *Hamlet ~ Shakespeare* Hamlet by Shakespeare. *~ ilmiah* scholarly or scientific article, research paper. *- acuan* reference article. **peng- 1** author, writer, composer. *~ gigi* gums. *~ jantung* beloved, darling, dearest o. **2** arranger. *~ bunga* flower arranger.

karang₃ stay, sojourn. **pe-an** yard.

karangkitri fruit-producing trees in a yard.

karantina quarantine. **meng(k)-kan** quarantine, isolate.

karap shuttlecomb on a weaving loom.

karapan sapi bull race.

karar 1 calm, peaceful. **2** stable, steadfast, unchanging.

karas aloes wood, camphor tree.

karas-karas k.o. fried cookie made of wheat flour.

karat₁ stain, rust. *- besi* iron rust. **ber- 1** rusty, corroded, corrode, rust. *Keringkanlah pisau itu, nanti ~* Dry off that knife, otherwise it will rust. **2** stained (of teeth, etc.). **3** disgraced, blemished (of reputation). **-an 1** rusty. **2** rusty and old. **3** bad, blemished. **per-an, peng(k)-an** corrosion, corroding.

karat₂ 1 carat. **2** quality, value.

karaté karate.

karatéka o. who engages in karate.
karau ber- be mixed. **meng-** mix, stir s.t.
karavan (*Auto.*) camper.
karawitan (*Jv, Sd*) gamelan music and singing accompanied by a gamelan.
karbit carbide.
karbohidrat carbohydrate.
karbol₁ carbolic acid. **meng(k)-** 1 clean with carbolic acid. 2 bawl out.
karbol₂ Indonesian airforce cadet.
karbon carbon. *kertas -* carbon paper.
karbonaci, karbonacis baking powder.
karburator carburetor.
karcis 1 ticket. *- msk* admission ticket. *- pasar* a daily fee paid for permission to sell in the market. *- pulang pergi/retur* round-trip ticket. *- terusan* through ticket. *- undangan* complimentary ticket. 2 calling card. *- nama* calling card. **ber-** requiring tickets (for an event).
kardamunggu cardamom.
kardan (*Auto.*) differential (of gearing, transmission).
kardinal cardinal.
kardiograf cardiographs.
kardiografi cardiography.
kardiogram cardiogram.
kardiolog cardiologist.
kardiologi cardiology.
kardus 1 cardboard. 2 cardboard box.
karé see KARI.
karédok /karédok/ (*Sd*) cooked vegetable salad.
karena 1 because, because of. *Ia tak mau makan - perutnya sakit* He did not want to eat because he had a stomachache. *Ia lemah - kelaparan* He is weak from hunger. *- itu* therefore. *Ia sakit, - itu ia tdk dpt pergi ke sekolah* He is sick, therefore he could not go to school. 2 reason, cause. *Ia marah dgn tdk ada -nya* She was angry without cause. *- apa* why. *- apa ia menangis?* Why did she cry? **di-kan** caused by. *Ia mati ~ serangan jantung* She died of a heart attack.
karéséh-péséh babble in Dutch.
karésidénan residency (administrative unit of the colonial period).
karét 1 rubber. *- alam* natural rubber. *- ban* rubber band. *- bongkah(an)* crumb rubber. *- buatan* synthetic rubber. *- busa* foam rubber. *- cair* latex. *- kasar* crude (rubber). *- lembaran* sheet rubber. *- penghapus* (pencil) eraser. *- rakyat* rubber produced by smallholder. *- remah* crumb rubber. *- spon* sponge rubber. *- tinta* ink eraser. *- tiruan* synthetic rubber. 2 elastic. 3 condom. **per-an** having to do with rubber.
kargo freight. *- udara* air freight.
kari a dish of meat cooked in a spicy sauce. *- ayam* chicken curry.
karib close, intimate friend. *Persahabatan kita sangat -* Our friendship is very close. *percakapan yg - an* intimate conversation. *- (dan) bait* friends and family. **ber-** be intimate with. *Saya ~ dgn dia* I am close to him. **ber-an** be friends with e.o., be intimate. **meng-i** become intimate with. **meng-**

kan bring people close, make intimate. *Minat meréka yg sama itu ~ meréka* Their mutual interests brought them closer. **ke-an** closeness, intimacy.
kariér career.
kariéris o. who is ambitious for a career.
kariérisme out to promote o.'s career.
karih mix, stir s.t. **meng-** mix, stir s.t.
karikatur caricature.
karikatural caricatural.
karikaturis caricaturist.
karil₁ [*karya ilmiah*] scholarly paper.
karil₂ rabbit.
karim generous, magnanimous (of God).
karir see KARIÉR.
karisma charisma.
karismatik, karismatis charismatic.
karitatif charitable (institution).
karkas carcass (of a slaughtered animal).
karma s.t. (us. bad) that happens to o. because of deeds in a previous life.
karna see KARENA.
karnaval carnival.
karnivor carnivore.
karo [*kepala biro*] head of a department or division.
karosél carousel.
karoséri 1 body of a car. 2 body shop. **ng-** rebuild the body of a vehicle. **meng-kan** send vehicle to the shop to be rebuilt.
karper carp.
karpét carpet.
karpus see KERPUS₂.
karsa (*Lit.*) wish, intention. *- dan karya* will and work.
karsinom, karsinoma carcinoma. *- lambung* stomach cancer.
kartél cartel.
kartika (*Lit.*) star. *- Yudha/Yudo* (*Mil.*) Star Wars.
Kartini Raden Ajeng Kartini, a 19th-century Jv woman, who distinguished herself in fields where women were traditionally excluded.
kartografi cartography.
karton 1 carton. 2 cardboard, hardboard. *- gelombang* corrugated carton. *- jerami* strawboard.
kartoték, kartotik card file.
kartu 1 card. *- anggota* membership card. *- beras* rice ration card. *- berlubang* punchcard. *- indéks* index card. *- indéks kuning* registration card for seekers of employment. *- induk* master card. *- kuning* 1 (*Sport*) warning for rough behavior. 2 citizenship card. *- mérah* 1 (*Sport*) disqualification for roughness. 2 warning for unpaid taxes. *- nama* calling or visiting card. *- natal* Christmas card. *- pemilihan* 1 ballot. 2 voter registration card. *- penduduk* residency card. *- pengenal* identity card. *- peralatan* equipment issue card. *- pindah(an)* change-of-address card. *- pos* postcard. *- suara* ballot. *- tamu* calling card. *- tanda bébas* pass. *- tanda penduduk* residency card. *- tandatangan* signature card. 2 playing card. *- mati* card that cannot be played. **meng-kan** file,

register, or put s.t. on card. **peng-an** placing in a card system.
kartun₁ cartoon.
kartun₂ see KARTON.
kartunis cartoonist.
karu₁ meng- 1 interrupt s.o. 2 stir s.t. **meng-kan** stir s.t. in. ~ *susu ke dlmnya* stir milk into it.
karu₂ -an see KERUAN. *tdk -²an* in complete chaos.
karuhun ancestor.
karun see HARTA.
karung bag, sack. *membeli kucing dlm -* buy a pig in a poke. *- anak* membrane. *- goni* gunny sack. *- rami jute sack. - tidur* sleeping bag. **ber-²** by the sack.
karunia gift, grant from above. **meng-i** favor, reward s.o. **meng-kan** grant s.t. *Raja ~ uang pd saya* The king presented me with money. *Tuhan tlh ~ kpd kami suatu kemerdékaan* God has granted us independence.
karusél see KAROSÉL..
karut 1 confused, muddled. *Ingatannya -* Her mind was confused. 2 chaotic. *- bicaranya* He spoke incoherently. *- marut* totally chaotic. **meng-** 1 confuse s.o. 2 lie, tell a falsehood. **meng- (kan)** make s.t. chaotic, make a shambles of s.t. *Ia ~ susunan acara yg tlh diatur begitu rapi* He made a shambles of a neatly arranged program. **ke-an** confusion.
karya 1 work, opus. *- Shakespeare* the works of Shakespeare. *- agung/besar* magnum opus. *- cerita* film script. *- guna* useful work. **meng-gunakan** make o.s. useful. *Ia ~ diri dlm pembangunan negara* He made himself useful in national development. *- hias* decorative work. *- ilmiah* scholarly paper. *- sastra* literary work. *- tak berkala* occasional papers. 2 work, labor, activity. *- jasa* honorarium, fee. *- nyata/praktikum* laboratory field work. *- wisata* field trip, study tour, working expedition, inspection tour. **ber-** *wisata* go on a field trip. 3 creation (of a designer, etc.). *- jam* timepiece. *- seni* work of art. *- unggul* masterpiece. **ber-** 1 work, do work. 2 produce a masterwork. **mengk-kan** 1 assign s.o to. *Pénsiunan ABRI akan di-kan kpd lembaga pemerintah ataupun swasta* Retirees from the Armed Forces will be assigned to gvt. as well as private institutions. 2 use a possession as a means of earning money. *Mobil dinas meréka di-kan. Malam-malam dipakai sbg taksi* They are earning money with their official cars. They use them as taxis in the evenings. **ke-an** temporary duty in a field outside of o.'s normal duties esp. military officer's assignment to civilian post. **pe-an, pengk-an** assignment to work s.w.
karyawan white collar worker, official employee, functionary. *- bank* bank employee. *- kantor* office worker. *- pérs* journalist. **meng-kan** assign s.o. **ke-an** employment, tenure of service. *bagian ~* personnel division.
karyawati female white collar worker, official employee, functionary.
kas₁ 1 cash, money supply. 2 cashier's window.

Hendaklah membayar pd - Please pay the cashier. 3 treasury. *- negara* gvt. treasury. **ber-** have cash.
kas₂ 1 (wooden) case, (watch) case. 2 wardrobe, armoire.
kasa₁ gauze.
kasa₂ see KASSA.
Kasab [*Kepala Staf Angkatan Bersenjata*] Chief of Staff of the Armed Forces.
kasad intention, purpose.
Kasad [*Kepala Staf Angkatan Darat*] Army Chief of Staff.
kasah-kosoh sound of s.t. cracking against s.t. and breaking.
kasal 1 fragrant shampoo. 2 ointment for the skin. 3 lotion. **ber-** rub with skin ointment.
kasak₁ meng- rub s.t.
kasak₂ meng- persuade s.o.
kasak-kisik, kasak-kusuk 1 whispering, whispers. 2 intrigue. **ber-** 1 plot, conspire. 2 lobby. *Meréka sedang ~ dgn anggota DPR* They are lobbying the members of Parliament.
Kasal [*Kepala Staf Angkatan Laut*] Navy Chief of Staff.
kasam grudge, spite.
kasanah see KHAZANAH.
kasap coarse, rough to the touch.
kasar 1 coarse, rough, rugged (of facial features). 2 crude. *minyak -* crude oil. 3 coarse, uncouth. **meng-i** treat roughly or harshly. **meng-kan** roughen, coarsen s.t. **memper-** make s.t. coarser or rougher. **ke-an** 1 coarseness, roughness. 2 rudeness.
kasasi 1 (*Leg.*) the jurisdiction of the highest court beyond which there is no appeal. 2 appeal to the supreme court. **mengk-** pronounce highest court's decision on a case.
kasatmata in plain view.
kasau rafter. *- betina* common rafters. *- jantan* principal rafters.
kasava cassava.
kasbi see KASPÉ.
kasbon cash receipt.
kasbuk ledger.
kasemak see KASEMEK.
kasemat see KESUMAT.
kasemek k.o. smooth-skinned sweet fruit the size of an apple and eaten fresh.
kasép see KASIP.
kasét cassette. *- vidéo* video cassette. **mengk-kan** record s.t. on a cassette.
kasi₁ (*Coll.*) 1 give. *-lah itu pd saya* Give that to me. *- saya sepiring nasi* Give me a plate of rice. *- tangan* shake hands. *- salam* greet. 2 cause (allow) s.o. to. *- lihat bukunya* Let me see the book. *Mau periksa dulu, nanti saya - tahu* I will look into it and let you know. *- turun semua barang dr dokar* Take all the things off the cart. *- jalan* yield (right of way). 3 put. **di-** 1 give. 2 (*Coll.*) cause to be done. *Ini semua ~ habis* Finish off all of this. *Bukunya ~ lihat* I was shown the book. *Barang ini ~ msk* Bring this inside. *Anjingnya sdh ~ makan* The dog has been fed. 3 (*Coll.*) be put. *Barang-*

barang ini ~ ke mana nanti? Where should these things be put?
kasi₂ [*kepala séksi*] administrative section head.
kasian see KASIH₁.
kasiat see KHASIAT.
kasidah religious chant in Arabic sung to the rhythm of a *gambus.*
kasih₁ love, affection. *Ia - pd anaknya* She loved her child. *- hati* let o. have his way. *- mesra* devoted, great affection. *- sayang* love and affection. *- tak sampai* unrequited love. **ber-(an)** love e.o. *- meng-i* love e.o. **meng-(i)** love. *org yg dinya* the person she loved. *~ mesra* love s.o. dearly, be devoted to s.o. **meng-ani** pity s.o. **ke-an** 1 love. 2 mercy. **-an** 1 mercy. *Apa bédanya antara cinta dan ~?* What is the difference between love and pity? 2 pity s.o. *Saya ~ akan pengemis buta itu* I pitied the blind beggar. 3 poor thing, what a pity! *~ anak itu* That poor child! **pe-** love charm or philter. **peng-** 1 love philter or charm. 2 merciful, compassionate. *yg maha ~* The All Merciful (God).
kasih₂ see KASI₁.
kasim castrated. **meng-** castrate.
kasima ter- upset, disconcerted.
kasino casino.
kasip too late. *Ia datangnya -* Her arrival was too late. **meng-kan** delay, postpone. **ke-an** lateness, tardiness.
kasir cashier.
kasmaran (*Jv*) smitten with love. **meng-i** be madly in love with.
kasno [*bekas cino*] (*Derog.*) Ch who adopts an Indonesian name.
kaso, kasok see KASAU.
kaspé cassava.
kassa 1 cashier, cashier's desk. 2 ticket or box office.
kasta caste in society.
kasténgel cheese stick.
kasti k.o. children's game similar to baseball.
kastil castle.
kastroli castor oil.
kasturi see KESTURI.
kasuari cassowary.
kasumat see KESUMAT.
kasur mattress. *jatuh di -* come out well.
kasus case (legal, medical, grammatical), example. *Ambil - jilbab* Take the Muslim head-covering for example . . .
kasut sandal, slipper. *- belulang* rawhide slipper. *- kayu* clogs. *- kuda* horseshoe. *- roda* rim of a wooden wheel. *- rumput* straw slipper.
kat (*Coll.*) playing card.
kata 1 word. *- adat* traditional proverb. *- asal* root of a word. *- asli* native word. *- bah* unnecessary fullness of language. *- batin* conscience. *- benda* noun. *- bentukan* neologism. *- berlebihan* unnecessary fullness of language. *- bersambungan* derivative. *- bilangan* numeral. *- bilangan pengganda* multiplier. *- dasar* (*Ling.*) base or root of a

word. *- depan* preposition. *- ganti diri* personal pronoun. *- ganti penentuan* determinative pronoun. *- ganti penghubung* relative pronoun. *- ganti penunjuk* demonstrative pronoun. *- ganti org* personal pronoun. *- hati* 1 conscience. 2 (inner) conviction. 3 sincere advice. *- ikatan* definition. *- ingkar* negative. *- istilah* technical term. *- jadian* derivative. *- kerja* verb. *- kerja bantu* auxiliary verb. *- kepala* entry, headword. *- keterangan* adverb. *- kiti* twaddle, rubbish. *- lawan* antonym. *- lontoran* expletive. *- majemuk* compound word. *- masukan* entry, headword. *- mendatang* derivative. *- menyusul* postscript. *- murajif* synonym. *- mufakat* agreement. *- olokan* derision, mockery. *- panggilan* form of address. *- pembimbing* preface. *- pendahuluan* introduction, foreward. *- pengantar* preface. **meng-pengantari** provide s.t. with a preface or introduction. **meng-pengantarkan** say s.t. as a preface. *- pengecil* diminutive. *- pengganti nama benda* pronoun. *- penggolong* collective. *- penghubung* conjunction. *- pengumpul* collective numeral. *- penunjuk* demonstrative pronoun. *- penyambung/penyerta* word that links (e.g. the Jv particle *ing*). *- perangkai* proposition. *- perkenalan* introductory words. *- perpisahan* parting words. *- persembahan* dedication. *- pinjaman* loanword. *- pokok* (*Ling.*) base or root of a word. *- putus* 1 decision to release parties from an agreement. 2 verdict. *- sambung* connective. *- sambutan* 1 foreword, introductory remarks. 2 speech of welcome. 3 words in response to speech of welcome. *- sandang* article. *- sandi* 1 password. 2 code word. *- sapaan* term of address. *- searti* synonym. *- seasal* cognate. *- sebunyi* homophone. *- sebut* noun, name of s.t. *- sepaham/sepakat* agreement. *- seru* interjection. *- sifat* adjective. *- tambahan* adverb. *- tugas* (*Ling.*) function word. *- turunan* derivative. *- utama* entry or headword. 2 says, said. *Makanannya énak di situ org* They say the food is good there. *-ku* I say or said. *-nya* he, she says, they say. *org yg -nya sakti* a person said to have supernatural powers. **se-** alike, of the same tenor. **ber-** talk, speak. *Ia tdk dpt ~* She cannot talk. *~ dgn suara lemah* speak in a soft voice. 2 say. *Ia - bhw ia pergi* He says that he is going. *~ dua* be deceitful, two faced, false hearted. **ber-²** converse, talk to e.o. **di-** be said. *Apa hendak di-?* What is there to say? *jangan di-lagi* not to mention, let alone. *Bangun saja tak mau dia, jangan di- lagi pergi ke sekolah* He does not even want to wake up, let alone go to school. **meng-(²)i** 1 scold s.o., heap abuse upon, jeer at. 2 cast aspersions on. **meng-kan** say s.t., say that . . . *Ia ~ semuanya pd saya* She told me everything. *-kan saja dr Ali* Just tell him it is from Ali. *Boléh di-kan bhw ia tak akan datang* At this point o. could say that he will not come. *~ amin* say yes, agree. **mengk-kan** slur a word in pronunciation. **memper-kan** 1 talk about s.t. 2 explain s.t. verbally. *~ soal yg sulit* give a verbal explanation of a difficult problem. 3 deliberate over s.t., confer

about. **ter-kan** can be expressed. *tdk* ~ indescribable. **per-an** word, words. ~*nya melukai hatinya* Her words hurt him.
katabélece see KATEBÉLECE.
katah ter-² be thrown. *Ia* ~ *di lantai* He was thrown to the floor.
katai 1 midget, dwarf, pygmy. **2** bantam chicken.
katak 1 frog, toad. - *betung* toad. - *di bawah tempurung* shallow-minded. **2** short, stocky, thickset.
katakombe catacomb.
katalis catalyst, catalystic (factor).
katalisasi catalysis. **mengk-kan** catalyze.
katalisator catalyst.
katalog catalog. - *induk* main catalog.
katalogisasi cataloging of books.
katalogus see KATALOG.
katam see KHATAM.
katan see KHITAN.
katang-katang₁ a climbing plant.
katang-katang₂ plaited basket carried on the back.
katapél, katapil see KETAPÉL.
katarak, katarakta (*Med.*) cataract.
katé see KATAI.
katebélece informal note from o. powerful figure to another asking for action (to bypass bureaucracy or the like).
katédral cathedral.
katégis see KATÉKIS.
katégori category. **pengk-an** categorizing. **meng(k)-kan** categorize.
katégoris categorical.
katék₁ armpit. **meng-i** tickle.
katék₂ see KATAI.
katekése catechism.
katekétik catechetical.
katékis catechist.
katékisasi (*Rel.*) confirmation class.
katékismus catechism.
katekumén catechumen.
kutél (*Jv*) k.o. large black spider.
katepél see KETAPÉL.
katéring catering.
katés (*Jv*) papaya.
katétérisasi catheterization.
kati catty (⅓ pounds or 617 grams). **meng-** measure by the catty. **-an** catty scales. **2** by the catty.
katib see KHATIB.
katifah chenille.
katig k.o. knapsack of plaited materials.
katik see KATAI.
katil 1 sleeping platform of solid materials. **2** bier.
katimaha k.o. beautifully grained wood used for making kris sheaths and walking sticks.
katimumul corn on o.'s foot.
katir outrigger.
katistiwa see KHATULISTIWA.
katoda, katode cathode.
katok (*Jv*) shorts, undershorts.

Katolik Catholic. - *Rum/Roma* Roman Catholic. **mengk-kan** Catholicize. **ke-an** catholicism. ~ *geréja* orthodoxy of catholic church.
katrol pulley. **meng(k)- 1** hoist by pulley. **2** raise. *negara-negara yg* ~ *produksi minyak di atas kuota* countries which are raising their oil production above the quota. **-an** s.t. hoisted by a pulley. *Ia naik kelas karena* ~ He only got promoted because s.o. gave him a boost. **peng(k)-an** lifting, hoisting.
katu k.o. bush yielding edible leaves and berries.
katul see BEKATUL.
katulistiwa see KHATULISTIWA.
katun cotton, cloth.
katung (*M*) sea turtle. **ter-² 1** float. *Banyak sampah* ~ *di sungai* A lot of refuse floated in the river. **2** drift, be uncertain, hover. *Pengangkatannya masih* ~ Her appointment is still pending. *Ia* ~ *di antara harapan dan ketakutan* He hovered between hope and fear.
katup 1 valve. - *jantung* heart valve. - *pelepas* release or outlet valve. - *pemasuk* inlet valve. - (*peng)aman* safety valve. - *tenggorok* epiglottis. **2** shut tight. **meng-** shut or close tightly. *Rahangnya* ~ He clenched his jaw. **meng-kan, memperkan 1** close or shut s.t. tightly. **2** clasp. *Ia* ~ *kedua tangannya di dada* He clasped his hands on his chest. **ter-** closed, shut, locked tightly.
kau₁ (*Ch*) nine. - *ban* ninety thousand. - *ban go* ninety-five thousand. - *cap* ninety. - *cap go* ninety-five. - *céng* nine thousand. - *céng go* nine thousand five hundred. - *pék* nine hundred. - *pék go* nine hundred fifty. - *tiau* nine million. - *tiau pua* nine and a half million.
kau₂ see ENGKAU.
kaul 1 a vow. **2** to vow. **ber-** to vow. *Ia* ~ *akan berziarah ke kuburan ayahnya* He vowed to visit his father's grave. **meng-kan** make a vow to do s.t.
kaula, kawula servant, subject. - *negara* national of a country. **ke-negaraan** citizenship. - *swapraja* dependency (of o. nation to another). **ke-swaprajaan** (*Lit.*) having the status of dependency.
kaum₁ social, political, or economic community. *Ia termasuk - bermodal* He belongs to the capitalistic class. - *atasan* **1** the upper class. **2** upper echelon (of executives, etc.). - *awam* the laity. - *bakulan* retailers. - *bangsawan* the nobility. - *bawahan* the lower classes. - *cerdik pandai/cendekia* the intellectuals. - *dahriah* unbelievers, free thinkers, atheists. - *gula* the sugar bloc. - *hawa* women, womenfolk. - *ibu* mothers or housewives. - *kecil* the little people. - *kemajuan* the progressives. - *kerabat* extended family. - *ko* collaborators (those on the Dutch side against the independence movement). - *kolot* the conservatives. - *kromo* proletariat. - *laki-laki/lelaki* the men(folk). - *lunak* the moderates. - *majikan* the employers. - *Marhaén* proletariat. - *mérah* leftists, Reds. - *militér* the militarists. - *murba* the masses, the common people. - *non* noncollaborators, those backing independence from the

Dutch. - *pertengahan* the middle class. - *pertuanan* landed gentry. - *pindahan* emigrants. - *réaksi* reactionaries. - *tani* the peasants or farmers, peasantry. **2** family, clan. **3** ethnic group. - *Batak* the Bataks. **ber-** 1 be related. **2** in groups. **3** pray together with a priest. **ber-²** in groups. **per-an** 1 family, relatives. **2** group. **3** system of dividing a society into small religious or ethnic groups.

kaum₂ religious official who is in charge of the mosque. **-an** the area around the main mosque often settled by the strongly religious.

kaus see KAOS.

Kaus (*Zod.*) Sagittarius.

kausa cause, movement.

kaut meng- scoop up with the hand. **peng-an** drainage by dredging out.

kav. [*kaveling*] lot, parcel of land.

kavaleri cavalry.

kaveling lot, parcel of land. **meng(k)-(kan)** divide land into lots. **peng(k)-an** parceling of land.

kawah 1 cauldron, kettle. **2** crater.

kawak old. **-an** experienced, veteran. *wartawan* ~ veteran reporter.

kawa-kawa spider.

kawal 1 guard, sentry, watchman. **2** watch. - *batas* border guard. **ber-** stand guard, be on guard. **meng-(i)** 1 guard. **2** escort. **3** oversee, patrol an area. **-an** escort, guard. ~ *pasukan kehormatan* honor guard. *melarikan diri dr* ~ *tentara* escape from the army's guards. **peng-** 1 guard, sentry. **2** escort. ~ *kehormatan* guard of honor. ~ *pribadi* personal bodyguard. **peng-an** 1 guarding. **2** escorting. ~ *udara* air escort.

kawalat see KUALAT.

kawan 1 friend, comrade. **2** companion. - *berbuat* accomplice, partner (in crime). - *berlomba* competitor. - *hidup* partner for life. - *roti* spread (jelly, jam, etc. for bread). - *seanggota* fellow member. - *sebaya* peer of the same age. - *sekantor* office colleague. - *seperjuangan* comrade-in-arms. - *sepersekutuan* close ally. - *seregu* teammate. - *sirih* betel set. **3** comrade (of communists). **se-** 1 a herd, flock, school (of fish). ~ *gajah* a herd of elephants. ~ *burung* a flock of birds. **2** a gang (of bandits), group of people. **ber-** 1 have friends, companions. *Ia* ~ *banyak* She has many friends. **2** be friends. *Saya sdh lama* ~ *dgn dia* I have been friends with him for a long time. **ber-²** 1 do in groups. **2** be friends. **meng-i** accompany s.o., keep s.o. company. **memper-** 1 treat s.o. as a friend. **2** (*M*) marry off o.'s daughter. **-an** flock, herd, swarm. **se-an** a flock, herd. **per-an** friendship, comradeship. **perse-an** alliance.

kawang see TENGKAWANG.

kawanisme cronyism.

kawanua fellow countryman (of Menadonese).

kawas ber- border on. *Daérah ini* ~ *dgn Malaysia* This area borders on Malaysia. **meng-i** border on (a river, etc.). *Sebagian dr sawah désa X di-i oléh aréal tanaman Y* Y's plantation borders on a portion of the ricefields which belong to village X. **-an** region, area, sphere. **se-an** of the same region.

kawat 1 wire, filament. *pagar* - wire fence. - *arang* carbon filament. - *(ber)duri* barbed wire. - *has* screen, wire netting. - *jala* wire mesh. - *jeprét* staples. - *kasa* 1 chickenwire. **2** wire netting. - *listrik* electric cable. - *listrik penyambung* extension cord. - *pemanas* heating coil. - *pijar* filament. - *rambut* very fine wire. - *sambungan* extension cord. - *tali* cord. - *télpon* telephone line. **2** cable, telegram. **- meng-** 1 wiring. **2** telegraphing. **meng-** be like a wire. *Garis mukanya* ~ The lines in his face tightened. **meng-kan** wire, cable s.t. *Kabar itu di-kan pd saya* The news was cabled to me. **per-an** having to do with telegraphy.

kawatir see KUATIR.

kawedanan 1 subdistrict within a *kabupatén*. **2** residence of the subdistrict officer.

kawi see BAHASA₁, BATU.

kawin 1 be married. *Apa tuan sdh -?* Are you married? *Ia - dgn kakak saya* He married my older sister. - *batin* married but not officially. - *campuran* mixed marriage. - *dgn keris* marriage by proxy. - *gantung* married in a simple ceremony while consummation awaits an official and more elaborate wedding. - *lari* elopement. - *masal* mass wedding. **meng-masalkan** marry in a mass ceremony. *Tujuh puluh pasang yg saya -masalkan di sini* I performed a mass marriage for 70 couples here. - *mawin* various weddings. *Kalau anak-anak meréka pd besar, meréka akan - mawin antara meréka sendiri* When their children are grown, they will marry among themselves. - *paksa* arranged marriage with an unwilling bride or groom. - *rangkap* being married to more than o. person at a time. - *tamasya* marriage with no ceremony so that the couple may use the funds for a honeymoon. - *tunggal* monogamy. - *tunggu tunang* marriage by proxy. - *wakil* marriage by proxy. **2** copulate. - *suntik* artificial insemination. **di-** *suntik* be artificially inseminated. **meng-i** 1 marry s.o. **2** sleep with s.o. **3** copulate with (of animals). **meng-kan** 1 marry off a son or daughter. **2** mate, breed an animal. **-²an** sleep together out of wedlock. **per-an** 1 marriage. ~ *campuran* mixed marriage. **2** wedding. **3** mating, breeding of animals.

kawiryan (*Jv*) military, having to do with military officers.

kawista k.o. cultivated tree and its fruit, the wood apple (Bengal quince).

kawruh (*Jv*) knowledge.

kawul tinder.

kawung (*Jv*) 1 sugar palm leaf used as wrapper for cigarettes. **2** k.o. motif in batik.

kaya₁ 1 wealthy, rich, well-to-do, well-off. - *baru* newly rich, nouveau riche. - *hati* generous. - *mendadak* get rich quick. - *raya* very rich. **2** rich, having in abundance. *Indonésia - akan hasil bumi* Indonesia is rich in agricultural produce. *Makanan itu - dgn protéin* That food is rich in protein.

3 (*Lit.*) able, having power. *org* - 1 person of rank. **2** (*M*) lady of the house. *Tuhan yg* - Almighty God. **meng-kan** make s.o. rich. **memper-** enrich. ~ *pengalaman politiknya* enrich o.'s political experience. **ter-** wealthiest, richest. **ke-an** 1 wealth, riches. ~ *alam* natural wealth or resources. ~ *hayati* living resources. **2** power, might. ~ *Tuhan* the might of the Lord. ~ *katakata* vocabulary. **pemer-** enrichei. **peng(k)-an** enrichment. **per-an** *berkala tanah* periodic enrichment of soil.

kaya₂, kayak (*Coll.*) like, as. *Tingkah lakunya - org gila saja* IIc behaved like a mad man.

kayal see KHAYAL.

kayangan 1 abode of the Hindu Gods. **2** heaven (as a wonderful place). *tempat ini merupakan suatu - bagiku* This place is heaven for me.

kayap itchy abscess or carbuncle. - *api* small abscess on hands or feet. - *barah* boil, esp. on the abdomen. - *tunggal* small, single abscess on hand or foot.

kayau₁ meng- headhunt. **peng-** headhunter. **peng-an** headhunting.

kayau₂ meng- flood, inundate.

kayu₁ 1 wood, timber. - *anduh* 1 prop, support. 2 splint. - *api* firewood. - *apung* driftwood. - *bakar* firewood. - *bangunan* lumber (for construction). - *basung* a lightweight porous wood. - *besi* ironwood. - *bulat/bundar* log. - *cagak* wooden pole forked at o. end, forked piece of wood. - *cendana* sandalwood. - *daun daérah sedang* deciduous tree. - *gaharu* aloe wood. - *gelondongan* log. - *gergajian* timber used for lumber. - *jawa/jingjing* k.o. soft forest wood. - *karét* hevea pulp. - *kasar* rough lumber. - *kendéka* tree used for making poles. - *kuda-kuda* supporting beam for roof. - *kuning* fustic. - *lat* lath. - *landasan* chopping block. - *lapis* plywood. - *meranti* morantee wood. - *panél* wainscoting. - *pelampung* driftwood. - *pemukul* (*Sport*) ball bat. - *penggaris* wooden ruler. - *penunjuk* pointer. - *pukul* ball bat. - *puter(an)* wood that can be turned. - *ramin* white wood used for furniture. - *rosét* piece of softwood used for attaching electric socket or plug. - *salib* The Cross. - *salib/silang* cross, crossbeam. - *sula* stake (for executions). - *tanduk* k.o. hardwood. - *tas* (*Lit.*) wood of a certain tree thought to frighten tigers. - *topang* 1 prop, support. 2 crutch(es). - *ulin* ironwood. 2 tree. - *angin* tree from which a potion is made. - *ara* cedar. - *arang* ebony. - *geluga* annatto tree. - *hitam* ebony. - *jabon* k.o. of tree. - *jarum* conifer. - *kemuning* Ch myrtle. - *kesturi* Ch juniper. - *kuda* a tree of coastal areas. - *mangir* k.o. tree of forest. - *manis* cinnamon. - *manis cina* licorice. - *penaga* k.o. of tree growing near the beach. - *putih* maleleuca. - *rengas* rosewood. - *sepang* Brazil wood. - *tusam* pine. **ber-1** wooden. *Kapal layar ini tdk* ~ This sailboat is not made of wood. **2** look for wood in the forest. **meng-** 1 become wood. 2 hard as wood. **-²an** various trees or timbers. **pe(r)-an 1** lumber or timber business. **2** house frame.

kayu₂, kayuh₁ bolt (of cloth - us. 40 yards in length).

kayuh₂ 1 paddle. **2** bicycle pedal. **ber-, meng-1** paddle. **2** pedal. ~ *sepéda* pedal a bike. **mengkan** use s.t. as an oar or pedal. **-an** stroke (of oar). **peng-1** oar, paddle. **2** rower, oarsman.

kayun 1 popular, sell well. **2** sold out.

kazanah see KHAZANAH.

KB [*Keluarga Rerencana*] Family Planning. **ber-** practice family planning.

KBRI [*Kedutaan Besar Républick Indonésia*] Embassy of the Republic of Indonesia.

KCK [*Krédit Candak Kulak*] credit extended to small middlemen.

ke to, going to. *Ia pergi - toko* He went to the store. - *atas* upward. - *bawah* downward. - *belakang* 1 to the rear. 2 to the toilet. - *dlm* 1 into. 2 inward. - *muka* to the front. - *pd* to. see PADA. - *samping* to the side. - *sana* in that direction. - *sini* hither.

ké see TAUKÉ.

kéa-kéa king parrot.

kebabal young jackfruit.

kebacut (*Jv*) gone too far, taken an irrevocable step. *Sdh - saya beli* I have gone and bought it already. *Yg satu nangis lantaran - hamil* O. of them was crying because she found she had become pregnant (lit., had taken the irrevocable step and become pregnant).

kebah break out in sweat after a high fever has broken.

kebaji k.o. spell (that makes a married couple love or hate e.o.).

kebal 1 invulnerable (to bullets, etc.). **2** immune (from prosecution, taxes, etc.). - *thd penyakit itu* immune to that disease. **3** insensitive. *Dia tdk mengerti lagi akan sindiran. Sdh* - He does not catch the hints. He has become immune to them. **meng-** become immune to. **meng-kan** immunize, make invulnerable. **ke-an** invulnerability, immunity, resistance (to disease). ~ *parleméntér* parliamentary immunity. **peng-an** immunization.

kebam lead-gray.

kebambam k.o. mango.

kebas₁ 1 paralyzed, paralysis. **2** stiff from fatigue. **3** numb. **meng-kan** cause a feeling of paralysis, stiffness or numbness.

kebas₂ meng-(kan) 1 shake out (a cloth, bedsheet, etc.). **2** flap (wings), wag the tail. *Anjing itu* ~ *ékornya* That dog wagged its tail. **-an** flapping (wings).

kebat bunch, bundle. *bunga se-* a bunch of flowers. - *pinggang* waistband. **meng-** tie s.t. *Di-erat-erat* Tie it tight. **meng-kan** wrap into (a bandage, etc.), use s.t. to tie. **ter- 1** involved. ~ *dlm perkara* involved in a case. **2** wrapped. **-an** 1 bond. 2 tightener, wrapper.

kebat-kebit nervous, agitated.

kebaya k.o. woman's blouse the front of which is pinned together, us. worn with a sarong.

kebayan₁ village official in charge of security.

kebayan₂ see NÉNÉK.

kebel see KEBAL.
kebél k.o. coastal tree.
kebelet (*Coll.*) have an urgent need to do s.t. (esp. defecate or urinate).
kebembem see KEBAMBAM.
kebes wet, soaked.
kebét (*Jv, Jkt*) pages of a book. **meng-** open a book to a certain page.
kébin 1 (*Naut.*) cabin. **2** movie projection booth.
kebiri 1 castrated, neutered. **2** emasculated. **meng- 1** castrate, neuter. **2** emasculate, make powerless. **3** (*Jkt*) short-change. **peng-an 1** castration. **2** emasculation. ~ *hak-hak buruh* emasculation of workers' rights.
keblinger (*Coll.*) **1** confused, dizzy. - *puter-puter* get dizzy and confused from going round and round. *Saya - puter-puter mencari rumahmu* I went around trying to find your house until I became totally confused. **2** come to think the wrong way about s.t., lose perspective on s.t. *Ia sdh - ke dlm aliran politik lain* He has mixed himself up in an opposition political movement.
kebluk (*Sd*) **ng-** be fond of sleeping, sleep soundly.
kebo see KERBAU.
kebon 1 (*Coll.*) gardener. **2** (*Coll.*) janitor. **3** garden.
kebuk cylindrical tool for making rice-flour vermicelli.
kebuli see NASI₁.
kebun 1 garden. - *binatang* zoo. - *bunga* flower garden. - *raya* the botanical garden at Bogor. **2** estate, plantation. - *budidaya* plantation. - *karét* rubber estate. - *tebu* sugar plantation. **3** (*Coll.*) gardener. **ber- 1** farm, plant for a living. **2** have a plantation or garden. **memper-i** use an area for a plantation. **peng-** gardener. **per-an** plantation, commercial agricultural enterprise.
kebur meng- churn, whip up the ocean. **peng-** churner. **peng-an** churning up of s.t. (e.g. the sea).
keburu see BURU.
kebut₁ (me)ng- **1** drive at excessive speed. *Kalau ~ bisa sampai dlm satu jam* If you speed, you can get there in o. hour. **2** race, have a drag race. *Mobilnya di- ke Bogor* He raced his car to Bogor. **3** speed up an activity. *Uang borongan jangan terlalu di-* Do not spend the money for the contract too quickly. **4** compete fiercely, push ahead. **meng-(²), ber-², ter-²** smack o.'s lips. *Kalau makan jangan ~* Do not smack your lips while eating. **-²an 1** wild, reckless speeding. *masalah ~* the problem of speeding. **2** racing, drag racing. **peng- 1** o. who speeds recklessly. **2** drag racer.
kebut₂ meng-(i) dust off (furniture, etc.). ~ *bendéra* wave the flag. *Bendéra di- dan meluncurlah para pembalap sepéda* The flag was waved and the racing cyclists sped off. **meng-kan** shake, beat (dust, crumbs, dirt) off s.t.
kec. [*kecamatan*] subdistrict.
kecah see KECUH-KECAH.
kecai ber-(²), ter- smashed, broken to bits (of glass, pottery, etc.), torn to shreds (of paper, cloth).
kecak₁ make a smacking sound while eating to express astonishment or call an animal. **ber-** smack with the tongue. *Ia ~ kehéranan* She clicked her tongue in astonishment.
kecak₂ ber- pinggang with hands on the waist and arms akimbo.
kécak k.o. Balinese group dance featuring a seated chorus, the monkey dance.
kecam meng-(kan) 1 criticize. **2** investigate, consider carefully. **3** review, write a criticism of (a book, play, etc.). **-an 1** criticism, censure. **2** criticism, critique. **peng- 1** critic, fault finder. **2** critic, commentator.
kecambah shoot, sprout. - *Brusel* Brussel sprouts. **ber-** sprout, germinate. **men-kan** let s.t. sprout or germinate. **per-an** germination.
kecamik sound of murmuring. **ber-** murmur.
kecamuk raging, uproar. **ber-** rage, be in an uproar. *Peperangan ~ dgn hébatnya* The battle raged violently.
kecandan joke, jest. **ber-** a joke, jest.
kecantol see CANTOL.
kecap 1 sound of smacking the tongue. **2** word. *tdk se- pun* not a single word. **meng-** taste (food). ~ *kenikmatan hidup* taste the pleasures of life. **meng-(²), ber-², ter-²** smack o.'s lips. *Kalau makan jangan ~* Do not smack your lips while eating. **-an** taste of s.t. **peng- 1** sense of taste. **2** taster, user.
kécap₁ 1 soy sauce. **2** dish prepared with soy sauce. *ayam -* chicken prepared with soy sauce.
kécap₂ (me)ng- engage in idle talk. **meng-kan** regard as idle talk. *Ia ~ pidato itu* He regarded that speech as nonsense. **peng-an** telling nonsense.
kecapéan see CAPAI₂.
kecapi₁ k.o. plucked stringed instrument. - *mulut* Jew's harp.
kecapi₂ k.o. sour fruit grown commercially in some areas.
kecaprak (*Jv*) **ng-** open o.'s big mouth (when o. should be quiet). *Kalau masih ~ terus, nanti aku karaté buru tahu* If you don't shut up, I'll give you a karate chop to make you learn.
kecar k.o. salad of unripe fruits with a pungent sauce.
kécé 1 (*Jv*) cross-eyed. **2** (*Jkt, Sl.*) great, good-looking.
kecébong₁ tadpole.
kecébong₂ chitchat, small talk. **ber-²** chat. **meng-1** chat. **2** lure with sweet talk. **meng-kan 1** chat about. **2** boast of s.t. **peng-** blabbermouth, chatterbox.
kecelé 1 disappointed, fail to meet s.o. or find s.o. at home and feel bad about it. **2** feel cheated or fooled, feel o. has been made a fool of. - *bulé* completely fooled.
kecelek see KESELEG.
kecelik see KECELÉ.
kécéng with o. eye closed. **se- mata** in the wink of

an eye. ~ *mata pun saya tdk tidur* I did not sleep a wink. **meng-(kan)** *mata* **1** blink the eye. **2** close an eye (to aim).

kécér k.o. cymbal (in the gamelan orchestra).

kecéwa 1 disappointed. **2** fail to meet the success o. had been expecting. *Meréka pulang karena - di daérah transmigrasi* They returned because they were unsuccessful in the resettlement areas. **meng-kan 1** disappoint, disappointing. **2** foil, thwart. **ter-** feel disappointed. **ke-an 1** disappointment. **2** lack of success.

kéci (*Naut.*) ketch.

kooiak ber- cheep, peep (of chickens).

kecibak sound of water splashing. **ber-** splash.

kecicak ber- stamp with the feet.

kecik (*Coll.*) see KECIL.

kecil 1 small. *Rumahnya -* Her house was small. **2** little, young. *anak - itu* that little boy. *Sejak -nya ia suka membaca* He has been fond of reading since early childhood. **3** minor, insignificant, trivial. *perkara yg - a* minor matter. *- hati* **1** annoyed, irritated, offended. **2** hurt, grieved. **3** fainthearted, craven. **4** discouraged. **ber-** *hati* lose heart, be discouraged. **-² 1** though o. may be small. ~ *dia berani juga* He may be small, but he is brave. ~ *cabé rawit* small but brave. ~ *mecil* small but powerful. **2** various small things. **ber-²** in a small way, on a small scale. **ber-²an** do on a small scale. **- meng- 1** disparage e.o., make e.o. look small. **2** various small and large things. **meng-** become small. *Matanya ~* His eyes became small. **meng-kan 1** make s.t. small. ~ *ikat pinggang* tighten o.'s belt. **2** dwarf s.t. **3** turn s.t. down (radio, TV, lights, etc.). ~ *suara* lower the voice. ~ *hati* **1** disparage, belittle s.o. **2** humble (o.'s opponent). **3** dishearten. **memper-** make s.t. smaller, reduce. **ter- 1** smallest. **2** least. **3** minimum. *pasangan ~* (*Ling.*) minimal pair. **ke-an 1** smallness. **2** insignificance. **3** too small. ~ *hati* **1** annoyance. **2** dejection. **3** cowardice. **-an** smaller. **-²an** in a small way, on a small scale. **per-an** becoming small, decrease. **peng-an** making small, reduction, diminution.

kecimpung ber-(an) 1 splash around. ~ *di kolam mandi* splash around in a swimming pool. **2** plunge into an activity. *Ia ~ dlm politik* He is active in politics.

kecimus scorn. **meng-** show scorn with the lips.

kecindan see KECANDAN.

kecipak sound of splashing water. **ber-** splash. *Air ~* The water splattered.

kecipir k.o. four-sided bean eaten as a vegetable.

keciput k.o. small cake sprinkled with sesame seeds.

kecit see KECIL.

keciut whistling, whizzing (of bullets).

kecoak see KACOA.

kecoh meng-kan spit s.t. out. *Air ludahnya dikannya di sepatu saya* He spit on my shoes. **-an** cuspidor.

kécoh₁ fraud, dishonesty, deceit. *- kincang* various k.o. deception. **meng-(kan)** deceive, de-

fraud. *Gerilya itu bisa ~ Belanda* The guerillas succeeded in deceiving the Dutch. **ter-** defrauded, deceived. **peng-** swindler, cheat. **peng-an, per-an** fraud, swindle.

kécoh₂ stir, commotion.

kecomak-kecemik 1 for the mouth to move without uttering anything. *Mulutnya ~ mengucapkan doa* He moved his lips in reciting the prayer without making any sound. **2** chew slowly with lots of food in the mouth.

kecrék (*Jv*) pieces of metal on strings which are made to rattle for sound effects in the *wayang* . **-an 1** (*Jv*) instrument used by an itinerant welder to attract the attention of would-be customers. **2** (*Coll.*) handcuffs.

kecrés (*Jv*) **meng- 1** strike (a match). **2** slash.

kécu (*Jv*) robber, bandit. **meng-** rob, attack in a raid.

kecuak see KACOA.

kecuali 1 except. *Semuanya pergi - saya* All went except me. *Semua org msk tentara - jika meréka tdk layak badannya* Everyone entered the army unless they were physically unfit. **2** aside from, besides. *- merampok ia membunuh pula* Besides robbing he has also committed murder. **-nya** exception. *Semua pemuda msk tentara; tak ada ~* All youths entered the army; there were no exceptions. **ber-** have or be an exception. *tdk ~* without exception. **meng-kan 1** make an exception, exempt. *Saya tdk dpt ~ anda* I cannot make an exception for you. *Peraturan ini ~ saya dr bayar pajak* This regulation exempts me from paying taxes. **2** exclude. *Dr publikasi ini di-kan statistik daérah* Regional statistics have been excluded from this publication. **ter-** with the exception of. *Semua org pergi ~ meréka yg sakit* All went with the exception of those who were ill. **ter-kan** can be excepted. *Tdk seorg pun ~* No o. is excepted. **ke-an** exception. **-an** s.t. excepted or exempted. **per-an** exception. **peng-an** making an exception, exempting from.

kecubung₁ 1 k.o. poisonous plant with large trumpet-shaped flowers, the jimson. **2** cone-shaped.

kecubung₂ see BATU.

kecuh-kecah make a fuss.

kecumbung see BATU.

kecumik ber- mumble, mutter.

kecundang see CUNDANG₁.

kecup sound of a kiss. **ber-an** kiss e.o. **meng-(i)** kiss s.o. **-an** kiss.

kecut₁ 1 wrinkled, shriveled, shrunken. **2** seared (from flames). **3** afraid. *- hati* afraid, frightened, scared. **meng-** shrink, shrivel. *Kulitnya ~* His skin became wrinkled. **meng-kan 1** shrivel, shrink s.t. **2** frighten. ~ *hati* frighten, scare s.o. **peng-** coward. *tindakan ~* cowardly act. **sepeng-** as cowardly as. *Adiknya ~ dia* His little brother is as great a coward as he is.

kecut₂ sour (of taste, face).

kecut₃ ber-² screak, squeak, screech (of a wheel that needs lubricating).

keda see KEDAH.
kedabu k.o. tree producing firewood.
kedadak choleric diarrhea.
kedah open wide (of mouth), spread wide (of legs).
kedai shop, small place that sells s.t. or serves food. - *kopi* cafe. **ber-** 1 shop, market, go shopping. 2 have a shop. **memper-kan, meng-kan** display s.t. for sale. **ter-** displayed. **-an** cabinet or case in shop. **pe-** shopkeeper. **per-an** 1 shop or display window. 2 shop area.
kedal fungoid disease of the hands and feet.
kedaluwarsa 1 superannuated. *Céknya sdh -. Tdk bisa ditunaikan lagi* The check has expired. You cannot cash it anymore. 2 barred by statute of limitations. *waktu -* 1 due or expiration date. 2 statute of limitations. 3 expiration date (on food packages).
kedang₁ 1 outstretched (of hand, arm, etc.). 2 extension (opposite of flection of limbs). **meng-(kan)** stretch s.t. out, straighten s.t. out that is bent or crooked. *~ tinju* raise the fist.
kedang₂ meng- drain, pour water off rice.
kedangkai k.o. plant, the leaves of which are used as medicine.
kedap 1 hermetical, impermeable, watertight. - *abu* dustproof. - *air* waterproof, watertight. - *suara* soundproof. - *udara* airtight. 2 close-meshed, tightly woven (of cloth, wickerwork, etc.). **ke-an** impermeability.
kedar see KADAR₁.
kedasih (*Jv*) k.o. cuckoo.
kedaton see KERATON.
kedau meng- scream (for help).
kedaung, kedawung k.o. large forest tree, the bark, leaves and seeds of which are used medicinally.
kédék ter-² 1 stagger. 2 waddle, toddle.
kedekai a myrobalan, a tree and its fruit, used medicinally.
kedekak-kedekuk not moving freely, stopped up here and there.
kedekar miserly.
kedékeran (*Jkt*) be agitated, kick the feet in agitation.
kedekut stingy.
kedelai, kedelé soybean.
kedempung₁ sound of s.t. falling into water.
kedempung₂ wormy, worm eaten (of fruit, etc.).
kedengkang sound of a gong being struck.
kedengkik very thin, thin as a rail, skin and bones.
kedengkung sound of a deep gong being struck.
kéder (*Jkt*) confused, lose o.'s way.
keder, kedér 1 frightened, scared. 2 trembling, shaking, quivering.
kedera k.o. small mullet.
kederang spiny bush, the roots of which are made into dye.
kedi 1 transvestite. 2 a preadolescent girl. 3 lacking sexual power. **ke-an** transvestitism.
kedian see KEMUDIAN.

kedidi k.o. plover or sandpiper. **bersi-, berse-** hop or skip about.
kedik bent slightly backward (of body). **meng-** be flexible, bend backward. **meng-kan** straighten o.s. up. **ter-** (*Ling.*) retroflex. **peng-an** retroflexion (of tongue).
kedip 1 wink (of an eye). 2 flicker. **ber-(²), ter-(²)** 1 wink, blink. *Edo terus memandanginya tanpa ~* Edo continued to look at him without batting an eye. 2 flicker (of a light), flash. *Bintang-bintang ~* stars flickered. *lampu-lampu ~* flashing lights. **meng-kan** wink, blink (the eye). **-an** 1 wink. 2 flicker.
kedok 1 mask. 2 guise, cover. *dgn - kepentingan pendidikan . . .* under the guise of an interest in education . . . **ber-** wear a mask, masked. *Dgn ~ muka manis ia hendak memikat hati saya* Behind her sweet smiles she wishes to win my heart. *~ sbg pedagang* in the guise of a merchant. **memper-** use s.t. as a mask.
kedombak 1 k.o. forest tree. 2 k.o. fish.
kedompréngan sound of metal objects clattering.
kedondong, kedongdong k.o. tree with edible, but fibrous, sour, plumlike fruit sometimes eaten cooked.
Kedubes [*Kedutaan Besar*] Embassy.
keduduk₁ see SENDUDUK.
keduduk₂ see DUDUK.
keduk (*Jv*) a scoop. *beberapa - beras* several scoops of rice. **meng-** 1 scoop. *Sekop itu gunanya utk ~ tanah* A spade is used to scoop up earth. *~ hasil laut* scoop up the sea's yield. 2 rake in (a profit). *~ keuntungan dr posisi politis yg didudukinya* obtain a (financial) advantage from the political position he occupies.
kedumel ng- grumble, complain under o.'s breath.
kedung 1 pool. 2 center of information.
kedut₁ 1 fold, crease. 2 wrinkled, crumpled (of paper). **ber-** wrinkled, creased (of skin, clothes, etc.). **meng-kan** wrinkle, crease s.t. *~ dahi* knit o.'s brow, frown, scowl.
kedut₂ meng- seize or take by force, snatch.
kedut₃ a twitch. **ber-** twitch.
keeper /kiper/ (*Sport*) goalie.
kegat meng- bite hard.
kéhél ter- 1 crooked, twisted, deformed. 2 off course (of ship, plane, etc.). 3 sprained, twisted (ankle, etc.).
kehendak see HENDAK.
kejai k.o. tree producing rubber. **ber-** stretch (after sleeping). **meng-** stretch (the limbs).
kejam₁ closed (of eyes). **meng-kan** *mata* close the eyes.
kejam₂ 1 cruel, brutal. 2 (*Coll.*) stingy, miserly. **meng-i** treat cruelly or harshly. **ke-an** cruelty, harshness.
kejamas a lotion for rinsing the hair made from water in which the ashes of rice stalks have been immersed.
kejang 1 stiff. *Badannya -* His body was stiff. 2 in convulsions, seized with a cramp or spasm. -

gagau convulsion. - *jantung* angina pectoris. - *mulut* lockjaw. - *otot* muscle cramp. **ber-** be convulsive, seized with a cramp. **meng-** be in convulsions. *Badannya* ~ Her body convulsed. **mengkan** stretch out (a limb, etc. so that it is rigid). **ke-an** being seized by a cramp. **peng-an** contraction, spasm.

kejap a wink of the eye, blink. **se-** (*mata*) a second. *Tunggu* ~ Wait a second. *Ia hilang dlm* ~ *mata* She was gone in a wink. **ber-²** 1 blink. *Matanya* ~ He blinked his eyes. 2 flicker. **ber-an** flicker, twinkle (of stars). **meng-** wink the eyes. **meng-kan** make the eyes blink. **-an** a wink of the eye.

kejar₁ ber-(²) 1 chase e.o. 2 race e.o. 3 compete (in achievement). **(ber)-²an** 1 game of tag. 2 chasing e.o. **bersi-an** come at close intervals o. after another. **- meng-, ber-an** chase e.o. **meng-** 1 run, chase after. ~ *maling* chase a thief. *di-alat-alat negara* be pursued by the authorities. *Nazi -- kaum Yahudi* The Nazis pursued the Jews. 2 pursue, be after. ~ *kesenangan* pursue happiness. 3 catch up with. ~ *waktu* lose no time. ~ *ketinggalan* catch up. *Negara-negara yg sedang membangun diberi kesempatan utk* ~ *ketinggalannya* The developing nations are given a chance to catch up. **meng-i** 1 run or chase after s.o. 2 pursue o.'s ideals. **meng-kan** send s.t. or s.o. in pursuit. **ter-** get caught up with. *Jeep itu masih* ~ It was still possible to catch up with the jeep. **-an** 1 pursuit, chase. 2 object pursued. **peng-** pursuer. **peng-an** pursuing of.

kejar₂ [*kelompok belajar*] study group.

kejat 1 stiff, rigid. 2 firm, sturdy, tight. *Papan itu - terpaku pd tiang* The board was tightly nailed to the beam.

kejawén 1 mysticism associated with the Jv view of the world. 2 general Jv knowledge.

kejeblos see JEBLOS.

kején plowshare.

kejengkang see JENGKANG.

keji despicable, shameful, contemptible (deed). **ber-** *diri* stoop low, demean o.s. **meng-(kan)** 1 despise, consider vile. 2 vilify, call s.o. shameful. **ke-an** meanness, baseness.

kejip see KEDIP, KEJAP.

kejora morning star.

kejot see KEJUT.

kéju cheese. - *kacang* peanut butter.

kejuju meng- flowing, streaming ceaselessly.

kejur stiff, unbending, inflexible (of bristles in a brush, hair, fibers, etc.). **meng-** become stiff. **ke-an** stiffness.

kejut 1 frightened, scared. 2 startled. *si -* the *Mimosa pudica*, a weed with pinnate leaves that contract upon being touched. **ber-** *telinga* prick up or cock o.'s ears. **ber-an** run helter-skelter, scatter, fly apart. **meng-** suddenly, with a start, without warning. **meng-i, meng-kan** startle s.o., startling. ~ *hati* startling, shocking. **ter-** startled, surprised, shocked. **menter-kan** startle. **keter-an** being startled. **ke-an** 1 startled, surprised. 2 surprise. **-an** jolt, shock. ~ *listrik* electric

shock. ~ *otot* sudden stiffening of the muscles. **peng-** shy, skittish.

kék₁ you could have ... or you could have s.t. else, it does not matter if it is ... or if it is ... *Lelaki -, perempuan - pokoknya* ... It could be a man or it could be a woman, the main thing is ... *Makanlah sesuatu, pisang - atau apa -* Eat s.t., I don't care what, even bananas or anything. *Apapun namanya, perploncoan -, perkenalan -, kebaktian -* Whatever name they give it, whether it is hazing, introduction or service, it all amounts to the same thing.

kék₂ see KAKÉK.

kéka, kékah see AKÉKAH.

kekah long-tailed leaf monkey.

kekal 1 eternal, everlasting. *hidup yg -* everlasting life. *persahabatan yg -* eternal friendship. 2 durable, lasting. 3 colorfast. **ber-an** enduring, everlasting. **meng-i, meng-kan** perpetuate, eternalize, make s.t. everlasting. **ke-an** 1 constancy. 2 durability. ~ *énergi* (*Phys.*) conservation of energy.

kekam scum, plankton or algae floating on surface of water.

kekang 1 bridle, reins. - *kuda* reins of a horse. 2 restraint, curb. - *diri* self-restraint. **meng-** 1 pull in the reins, bridle (a horse). 2 curb (o.'s impatience, etc.). ~ *lidahnya* curb his tongue. ~ *kebébasannya* inhibit her freedom. **-an** 1 bridle, reins. 2 restraint, curb. 3 inhibition, hang-up. **peng-an** restraint, curbing. ~ *perdagangan* restraint of trade. ~ *sukaréla* voluntary restraint.

kekap see KEKEP.

kekapas k.o. bird, leafbird.

kekar₁ 1 open, unfolded. 2 spread out. *padi dijemur -* paddy spread out to dry (in the sun). **meng-** open, unfold (of a flower). **meng-kan** spread out (rice to dry).

kekar₂ 1 solid, firm (body, etc.). 2 squat, hefty. 3 tight, close (of weaving, etc.). **ke-an** heftiness, solidity. ~ *tubuhnya* the heftiness of his body.

kekaras see KARAS-KARAS.

kekas see KAKAS.

kekasih beloved, sweetheart.

kekat scum or algae floating on the surface of water.

kekau wake up suddenly from a deep sleep. **ter-** be suddenly awakened.

kekawin see KAKAWIN.

kéké see BURUNG.

kékéh ter-² laugh loudly. **meng-, mengk-** laugh loudly with a high pitch.

kékék₁ ter-² giggle, snicker.

kékék₂ see BURUNG.

kekep (*Jkt*) **ng-in** hold in tight embrace, get hold of. *Karena hanya dua tahun, yg namanya diploma nggak sempat dia -in* Because he had only two years, he did not manage to get hold of what they call a diploma.

kéker 1 binoculars. 2 telescope. **meng-** look through binoculars or a telescope.

kékhi, kéki (*Jkt, Ch*) 1 annoyed, irritated, resentful. *Saya - kalau ia menyombong* I resent it when she brags. **2** ill at ease, uncomfortable. *Murid baru masih merasa - di antara anak-anak lain* The new pupil still feels ill at ease among the other children.

kekisi lattice.

kékok clumsy, awkward, blundering.

kekudung scarf used as head covering.

kel. [*keluarga*] family.

kel- see also entries with **kl-**.

kelab see KLAB MALAM.

kelabakan 1 flounder about, run around like a chicken without a head. **2** be at a loss (what to do). *Ia - karena tiba-tiba kedatangan begitu banyak tamu* She was in a dither because so many guests came at once.

kelabang₁ k.o. centipede.

kelabang₂ braid (of hair). **meng-** braid the hair. **-an** a braid of hair.

kelabat fenugreek, k.o. aromatic seed used as a spice or medicine.

kelabu gray, ash colored. **meng-i** deceive s.o. ~ *mata* misrepresent. **penge-an** deception. ~ *thd konsumén* a deception practiced on the consumer.

keladak dregs, sediment, residue. *- perut* **1** feces excreted upon dying. **2** last child in a family. **meng-** excrete.

keladan the camphor tree.

keladau meng- keep an eye on.

keladi 1 taro. **2** calladium, general name for aroids. *tua-tua - the* older o. gets the worse (or better) he is.

kelagepan chore.

kelah 1 complaint. **2** a charge. *memajukan - thd* press charges against. **3** tell on s.o., complain. **meng-** bring suit against.

kelahi quarrel, argument, fight. *sehabis - teringat silat* too late to be of use (lit., only think of martial arts after having fought). **ber-** fight with the fists, clash, fight over. **memper-kan 1** fight over. **2** pit, cause s.t. to fight. *Ia ~ ayam jantannya* He pitted his cock (against others). **per-an 1** fight, fisticuffs. ~ *bersosoh* hand-to-hand fighting, fracas. **2** quarrel, argument.

kelai see KALAI₁,.

kelajengking scorpion.

kelak₁ later. *- kalau sdh besar* when you are grown up later on. *di - kemudian hari* afterwards, later on. *Mudah-mudahan di - hari tak akan ada perang lagi* Let us hope that in the future there will be no more war.

kelak₂ k.o. bird, cuckoo-dove.

kelak₃ see KELAH.

kelakar a joke, jest, wisecrack. **ber-** crack jokes, wisecrack. **meng-i** make fun of, ridicule.

kelakat see KALAKAT.

kelakatu flying ant.

kelak-kelik flickering (of light, etc.).

kelak keling see KERAKELING.

kelak-keluk 1 curve, curves. **2** details, ins and outs of s.t.

kelakson see KLAKSON.

kelalang slender-necked earthenware bottle, decanter.

kelalap see KELELAP.

kelam₁ 1 dull, overcast. **2** dark, obscure. *- kabut* foggy, murky. *- lebam/membelam/pekat* pitch-dark. **3** dim (of eyesight). *- penglihatannya* His eyesight is dim. **meng-kan** darken. *Awan ~ langit* Clouds darkened the sky. **ke-an** darkness, obscurity. **peng-an 1** darkening. **2** blackout (during air raid).

kelam₂ clamp. **meng-** to clamp.

kelamai see GELAMAI.

kelambai see KELEMBAI.

kelambir₁ see KERAMBIL.

kelambir₂ see GELAMBIR.

kelambit flying fox.

kelambu mosquito net.

kelamin 1 pair, couple (male and female). **2** sex, gender. *Ada dua -* There are two sexes. *alat - sexual* organs. **se- 1** man and wife or a male-female pair. ~ *burung* a pair of birds. **2** of the same sex. *Meréka ~, sama-sama lelaki* They are of the same sex. Both are males. **ber-** in pairs. ~ *burung membuat sarangnya* Birds build their nest in pairs. **meng-** marry s.o. **per-an** sexual affair.

kelamun meng- daydream, muse. **peng-** daydreamer, dreamer. **peng-an** daydreaming, musing.

kélan k.o. vegetable, Ch broccoli.

kelana wanderer, rover. **ber-, meng-** roam, wander. **peng-** o. who roves. **peng-an** roving, roaming, wandering.

kélang see KILANG.

kelang-kabut see KALANG-KABUT.

kelangkan see LANGKAN.

kelangkang crotch, groin.

kelanjar see KELENJAR.

kelantang meng- bleach, whiten, dry in the sun. **ke-an 1** bleached. **2** item put out in the sun to be bleached.

kelantang-kelanting sound of knocking, rattling, chattering, etc.

kelap *- kelip* blinking, flickering. **ber-** *kelip* **1** flicker. **2** sparkle (of a gem), twinkle (of stars). *- kumilap* sparkling, glittering. **se-** *mata* in a wink. **meng-kan** *mata* blink o.'s eye.

kelapa coconut. *- gading* coconut with yellow-colored hull. *- kering* **1** copra. **2** desicated coconut. *- kopyor/puan* a coconut which has developed so that the meat has blended with the juice and is softer and tastier than the others in the bunch. *- sawit* oil palm. **meng-i** put coconut milk or grated coconut on s.t. **per-an** coconut industry.

kelar₁ (*Coll.*) **1** ready, done, finished. *Makan sdh -* Dinner is ready. *Blm - semua. Masih ada yg tinggal* Not everything is finished. There remain some things to do. **2** settled, in order, arranged.

kelar₂ notch, indentation. **ber-(²)** notched, have indentations. **meng-** make a notch or indentation.

kelara the young of the *sembilang*, a catfish with poisonous spine.

kelarah k.o. fruit worm.

kelarai diamond-shaped pattern (of cloth, plaited mat, etc.). **meng-** plait or weave this pattern.

kelarap k.o. small lizard.

kelari k.o. freshwater fish.

kelas₁ 1 class. *Ia berasal dr - ningrat* She comes from the aristocratic class. *- atas(an)* upper class. *- bantam* (*Sport*) bantamweight class. *- bawah(an)* lower class. *- berat* (*Sport*) heavyweight class. *- bulu* (*Sport*) featherweight class. *- kakap* big shot. *- kambing* 1 cheapest class in train, theater, etc. 2 lowest stratum of society. *- layang* lightweight class. *- lose* (*Thea.*) box. *- menengah* 1 (*Sport*) middleweight class. 2 middle class in society. *- ringan* (*Sport*) lightweight class. *- ringan utama* (*Sport*) middleweight class. *- satu* first-class, first-rate. *Ia pemain ténis - satu* She is a first-rate tennis player. *- terbang* (*Sport*) flyweight class. *- teri* unimportant person, small fry. 2 classroom. 3 grade. *Ia duduh di - dua* He is in the 2d grade. 4 (*Biol.*) class.

kelas₂ neap tide.

kelasa₁ camel's hump.

kelasa₂ (*Jv*) mat.

kelasah see KELUSUH-KELASAH.

kelasak (*Lit.*) long body shield.

kelasi₁ sailor, ordinary seaman. *- I* seaman. *- II* apprentice seaman.

kelasi₂ proboscis monkey.

kelat₁ (*Naut.*) brace, sheet (of sailing vessel).

kelat₂ astringent (of fruits).

kelat₃ name given to various myrtaceous trees.

kelat₄ mengk- stuck (of eyes as after waking up).

kelawar₁ (*Crd.*) club.

kelawar₂ see KELELAWAR.

kelayab see KELAYAP.

kelayah ter- be stretched out. ~ *kelelahan* be stretched out because of exhaustion.

kelayang k.o. bird, swallow.

kelayap (*Coll.*) **ber-(an), nge-** roam the streets.

kelayu k.o. tree.

kélder cellar.

kelébat see KELIBAT₂.

kelébék, kelébét folded at the corner or edge (dog-eared pages of a book, tucked-in edge of a bedspread, etc.). **meng-kan** turn back (a page, coverlet).

kelebu 1 taking in water (of foundering ship). 2 sink (of a ship, boat). **meng-kan** sink (a ship).

kelebut 1 shoe last, shoe tree. 2 mold for hats.

kelécé meng-i tease.

keledai donkey, ass.

kelédang 1 k.o. large timber tree, *Artocarpus sp.* 2 k.o. *Artocarpus* tree that produces small, delicious fruit.

keledar ber- approach carefully.

kelédék see UBI.

kéléh see KELIH.

kelejat, kelejet ber-an tremble or shiver strongly, have convulsions.

kélék 1 banister. 2 armrest. 3 armpit. **meng-** carry s.t. under the arm. **meng-i** put s.t. under the arm. **-²an** bannister.

kelelap sink into the water, disappear from sight. *Ia - dlm sungai* He drowned in the river. **meng-kan** immerse s.t.

kelelawar cave bat.

kelelesa chameleon.

kelélot ber- stick out the tongue. **meng-kan** stick s.t. out (o.'s tongue).

kelem (*Coll.*) sunk, foundered, submerged.

kelemapih gangrene.

kelemarin see KEMARIN.

kelemayar k.o. luminous millipede.

kelemayuh gangrene. **ber-** gangrenous.

kelembahang k.o. aroid.

kelembai supernatural being depicted as a giant female with red hair.

kelembak₁ aloes wood.

kelembak₂ Ch rhubarb.

kelémban ber- go roundabout, go around.

kelembuai large dark-shelled snail.

kelembubu whirlwind.

kelembung inflated.

kelempai ter- stretched out weakly.

kelemping (*Jkt*) flabby and sagging (of breasts or belly). **-an** characterized by having flabby or sagging breasts or belly.

kelemumur dandruff.

keléncér (me)ng-, -an take a walk, go on a tour.

kelendara (*Naut.*) ring attaching yard to mast.

kelenéng, kelénéng 1 sound of a bell. 2 small bell (of a bike, etc.). **ber-** clang, tinkle (of bell). **meng-kan** ring (a bell). **-an** 1 high-pitched tinkling sound. 2 an instrument that produces tinkling sound.

kelengar see LENGAR.

kelenggara see SELENGGARA.

keléngkéng₁ longan, k.o. fruit similar to rambutan or lychee, but smaller with smooth brown skin.

keléngkéng₂ small hornbill.

keléngkong intrigue, conspiracy.

kelening see KELENÉNG.

kelenjar, kelénjar gland. *- air mata* tear duct. *- anah ginjal* adrenal gland. *- beguk* thyroid gland. *- buntu* endocrine gland. *- dada* mammary gland. *- di bawah otak* pituitary gland. *- getah bening* lymph gland. *- gondok* thyroid gland. *- kacangan* thymus gland. *- keringat* sweat gland. *- léhér* tonsils. *- liur/ludah* salivary gland. *- ludah perut* pancreas. *- minyak* sebaceous gland. *- peluh* sweat gland. *- prostat* prostate (gland). *- susu* mammary gland.

kelentang₁ sound of a tin can being struck.

kelentang₂ see KELANTANG.

keléntang bean of the *merunggai*.

kelénténg sound of the tinkling of a bell.

kelénténg, kelenting 1 Ch temple. 2 pagoda.

kelentit₁ (*Vulg.*) clitoris.

kelentit₂ ornamental climbing plant with blue flowers.

keléntom, keléntong 1 speech intonation. 2 tone of voice.

kelentung 1 sound of a cowbell. 2 wooden bell.

kelenung 1 sound of a small gong. 2 small gong.

kelép see KLÉP.

kelepai ber-, meng-, ter- hang down limply (of a flag, ears of a hound, broken branch, etc.).

kelepak sound of a hand slapping s.t.

kelépak hang limply. - *baju* lapel.

kelepat meng- (*Naut.*) caulk.

kelepek, kelépék meng-, ter- flutter.

kelépét see KELÉBÉK.

kelepik see KELEPEK.

kelepir testicles.

kelepon k.o. round cake of sticky rice filled with coconut and palm sugar.

kelepuk sound of an object falling to the ground.

kelepur see GELEPUR.

kéler (*Coll.*) a Westerner who converts to Isl. and follows indigenous customs.

kélér box for bottles of liquor, portable bar.

kelerak, kelérak k.o. fruit producing soapy foam used for washing clothes, esp. batik.

kelérek see KLÉRK.

keléréng₁ marbles. **ber-** play or shoot marbles.

keléréng₂ see KELERAK.

kelesa k.o. river fish.

kelésa 1 easygoing. **2** indifferent, apathetic. **ke-an** apathy, indifference, unconcern.

keléséh-péséh see KARÉSÉH-PÉSÉH.

kelésék dried skin of banana trunk (cut up in strips and used as twine for wrapping packages).

kelét be stuck on.

kelétah 1 coquettish. **2** affected (in manner).

keletak sound of a pebble striking wood. **ber-** make a clacking sound with wooden or leather heels.

keletang sound of jingling or tinkling (of silver coins).

keletar see GELETAR.

keletik sound of ticking. **-an** make repeated ticking sound.

keleting sound of tinkling (of coins, etc.).

keletuk₁ 1 sound of rapping on a hollow wooden surface, table, etc. **2** sound of creaking (of wooden furniture, floor, etc.).

keletuk₂ see JAMBU.

keletung sound of a tin can being struck.

keletus (me)ng- bite, chew on hard things.

keléwang see KLÉWANG.

keléwar (*Naut.*) foresail.

keléwat see LÉWAT.

keli edible river catfish.

kelian₁ tin mine.

kelian₂ (*Bali*) village official.

kelian₃ see KALIAN.

keliar ber-an 1 roam or wander about, drift from o. place to another. *taksi yg* ~ a taxi which cruises around. **2** swarm about (of ants, birds, etc.).

kelibang ber- swarm about, fly around (of insects).

kelibat₁ double-bladed paddle. **meng-** use a double-bladed paddle.

kelibat₂ appearing for a flash. **ber-(an)** be visible for only a second, flash by. *drive yg* ~ *melalui garis panjang* a golf drive that flashed by in a long

straight line. **se-(an)** in a moment. *Dlm* ~ *ia menghilang* She disappeared in a flash.

kelibat₃ see LIBAT.

kelici a hard nut (for playing with), marbles.

kelicih, kelicik ter- 1 skid. **2** slip.

kelih meng- look, turn the head to look.

kelik₁ slight curve, turn. **ber-** bend, have curves (of a road, etc.). **meng-** dodge, move abruptly to avoid. **meng-kan 1** bend (o.'s body). **2** dodge s.t. ~ *pukulan musuh* evade an enemy's blow.

kelik₂ ber-² make a loud sound. *Ia menangis* ~ She cried loudly. **ter-** make a gurgling sound (of the stomach).

kelik₃ see KLIK₂.

kelikik meng- giggle, titter.

keliki kanji (*M*) k.o. weed the seeds of which adhere to cloth.

kelikir₁ rattan nose ring (for cattle).

kelikir₂ see KERIKIL.

kelik-kelok k.o. small stinging red ant. - *dlm baju* harbor the enemy in o.'s midst.

keliling 1 circumference, area around. *Di - rumah itu ada kebun yg luas* Around the house was a large garden. **2** periphery. **3** surroundings. *Jkt dan -nya termasuk satu kotapraja* Jkt and its surroundings belong to o. municipality. **se-** the surrounding area. *Rumah dan ~nya habis terbakar* His house and the surrounding buildings were completely burned. **ber-** go around. **meng-i 1** surround. *Musuh* ~ *kota itu* The enemy surrounded the city. **2** travel around (the world, Europe, etc.). **3** circle, go around s.t. **meng-kan 1** distribute, disseminate. **2** move s.t. in a circle. *Dia* ~ *susur besar di dlm mulutnya* She brushed her teeth with the large wad of tobacco (lit., she moved the large wad of tobacco in her mouth in a circle).

kelilip (*Jv, Jkt*) speck in the eye. **-an** get s.t. in the eye.

kelim hem. **ber-** have a hem. **meng-** hem s.t. **-an** hem.

kelimis see KLIMIS.

kelimpungan (*Jv, Jkt*) confused, distraught.

kelimun group, crowd.

kelinci rabbit, hare. - *hutan* black-naped hare. - *percobaan* guinea pig.

kelincir see GELINCIR.

kelindan 1 newly spun thread. **2** conveyor rope of the spinning wheel. **3** thread on a needle. **4** bobbin, spool.

kelindas see LINDAS.

keling₁ (*Derog.*) a person from S. India.

keling₂ rivet. **meng-** rivet s.t.

kelingking little finger, pinkie. - *kaki* little toe.

kelingsir enlargement of the testicles due to hernia and descent of the intestines or accumulation of water.

kelinik see KLINIK.

kelining see KELINTING₁.

kelinjat ter-² move o.'s body nervously.

kelintar (ber)-an 1 walk or roam about, walk up and down or back and forth. **2** hang around,

lurk. *Saya curiga pd org itu, ia ~ saja sekitar kampung kami* I'm suspicious of that man; he just hangs around our neighborhood.
kelinting small bell. **-an** tinkle (of bells).
kelintung rattle (of a snake).
kelip₁ -² **1** firefly. **2** spangles, sequins. **3** flicker. **se-** *mata* in a flash, in the twinkling of an eye. **(ber)-(²)** flicker, glitter. **ber- 1** blink. **2** twinkle, glitter (of spangled things). **ber-an** twinkle (of stars, etc.). *Jika malam, lampu-lampunya ~* In the evening, the lamps twinkled. **meng-²** flicker (of a lamp light). **ter-(²)** flickering (of eyes, stars). **an 1** flickering (of lights), blinking, twinkling (of stars). **2** signal with lights.
kelip₂ a coin valued at five cents (in the colonial period).
kelipat ber- folded, pleated. *tak ~* unable to keep a secret. **ter-** folded.
kelipik speck.
kelir₁ color. **meng-** color (a picture, etc.).
kelir₂ 1 curtain, screen. **2** screen for a movie, shadow play, etc. *- belakang (Thea.)* curtain depicting background. **3** disguise, cover, mask. **ber-, be-** have a curtain over it. *Biji matamu ~ kali* Apparently your eyes have a curtain in front of them (you cannot see).
keliru 1 wrong, erroneous. *- tulis* typographical error. **2** be mistaken, make a mistake. *Org yg terpandai pun dpt -* Even the smartest person can make a mistake. **meng-kan 1** mislead s.o. **2** confuse s.t. with s.t. else. **ke-an** error, mistake.
kelis meng- dodge.
kelis, kelit ber- zigzag, dart back and forth. **ber-²** dart in and out. **meng-** dodge. **meng-kan** quickly get s.t. out of the way.
kelitak sound of seeds rattling inside dried fruit.
keliti *(Naut.)* oarlock, rowlock.
kelitik₁ see GELITIK.
kelitik₂ see WAYANG.
keliwat see LÉWAT.
keliwer see SELIWER.
kelobot see KLOBOT.
kelocak ber- shake.
kelocéh see CELOTÉH.
keloget ber-² wriggle, writhe.
kelojot -an convulse.
kélok curve, bend, turn. **ber-** curve (of a road, etc.). **meng-** turn. *Mobilnya ~* The car turned. **meng-kan** turn s.t. on a curve, make s.t. veer. *Ia ~ mobilnya* She turned the car. **-an** bend, curve, turn. *di ~ jalan* at the bend of the road. **ber-²**, **ber-an** winding, twisting, sinuous (road).
kelola meng-(kan) 1 manage (a business, etc.). **2** carry out, execute (a job, etc.). **-an** management. **peng- 1** manager, organizer. **2** executive (power). **3** organizer. **peng-an** management.
kelom wooden clogs. *- geulis (Sd)* woman's wooden dress slipper.
kelombén see KOLEMBÉN₂, KOLEMBÉNG₂.
kelompang 1 empty. **2** empty eggshell, fruit peel, etc.
kelompok 1 group. *beberapa - org* several groups of people. *- gerilya* a guerrilla band. **2** cluster. *semangga* a cluster of mangoes. *- hutan* forest complex. *- kata (Ling.)* phrase. *- kepentingan* interest group. *- kerja* working group. *- penekan (Pol.)* pressure group. *- penyelidik* investigating team. *- sebaya* peer group. **3** category. *Ia termasuk - petinju di atas seratus kilo* He was in the category of boxers above 100 kg. **ber-** cluster, group, gather. *Meréka ~ di depan rumahnya* They gathered in front of his house. **ber-²** in groups. **meng-** be in groups. **meng-kan** group, arrange. *Guru ~ murid-murid menurut umurnya* The teacher grouped the pupils according to their age. **ke-an 1** cluster. **2** clustering. **-an** a group, agglomeration. **peng-an** grouping.
kelon *(Jv)* accompaniment of s.o. lying down (esp. of a small child by an older person). *minta -* let me get into bed with you. **meng-i 1** hold s.o. close while lying down next to him. **2** harbor (feelings). **3** *(Sl.)* sleep with s.o. for sexual purposes. **-an** embrace while lying down. *dlm ~ ibunya* at his mother's side.
kelonéng sound of a ringing bell. **meng-, ber-** ring (of a bell).
kélong large sea fish trap with two or three compartments.
kelongkong young coconut.
kelongsong 1 husk. *- jagung* cornhusk. *- ular* sloughed snake skin. **2** wrapper (of paper, leaf, etc.). **3** cartridge case. **-an** cartridge case.
kelontang rattling sound of tin cans, clappers, etc. **ber-** rattle (of empty tin cans).
kelontong 1 bamboo clapper (used by peddlers or hawkers). **2** peddler. *Cina - yg menjaja dagangannya di kampung* a Ch peddler selling his wares in the rural areas. **3** sundries, five-and-dime goods.
kelonyo, kelonyor eau de cologne.
kelop 1 jibe, tally, square. *Angka-angka itu - dgn perhitungan saya* Those figures tally with my calculations. **2** balanced. *anggaran belanja yg -* balanced budget. **3** fit together. *Tutupnya tdk - dgn botolnya* The cap does not fit the bottle. *Kedua warna itu - satu sama lain* The two colors go together. **4** be in agreement. *Saya - dgn dia* I am in agreement with him. **mengk-kan** balance, square. *~ pengeluarannya dgn penerimaannya* balance expenditures and receipts.
kelopak 1 *(Biol.)* sheath, spathe, calyx, bract. *- buluh* young bamboo sheath. *- bunga* sepal. **2** calyxlike covering for s.t. other than a plant. *- hati* outer part of the heart. *- kerang* shell of clam, oyster, mussel. *- mata* eyelid. **meng-, ter-** peel or come off.
kélor the *merunggai* tree, a small quick-growing tree cultivated for its edible pinnate leaves. *Dunia tdk sedaun -* The world is bigger than a merunggai leaf (There is plenty of opportunity to find a lover).
kelos reel, spool, bobbin. **meng-** roll, reel s.t. **peng-an** rolling, reeling of s.t.
kelosét see KLOSÉT.

kelosok meng- rub hard, scour.

kelotak - *keloték* bustling about (in the kitchen, etc.). **ber-** rustle, jangle (of silverware, etc.). ~ *keloték* keep busy with small matters.

kelotok meng- fall off, be shed (of skin, feathers, peels). **peng-an** shedding of s.t.

keloyak ber- slough (the skin). **ter-** be peeled (of skin).

keloyang 1 k.o. small bird. **2** a stupid person.

keloyor see KELUYUR.

kelu dumb, mute, speechless (from fright). *Gertakan itu dijawab dgn suara* - He snarled at her and she answered with silence. **meng-kan** keep silent about s.t., be mum about s.t. **ter-** struck speechless.

keluak the fruits of the *kepayang* tree used as a spice.

keluan nose rope (for cattle).

keluang k.o. fruit-eating bat.

keluar 1 go or come out. *Saya - dr kamar* I went out of the room. - *msk* go in and out. **meng-masukkan** take out and put back. *Penjahat itu selalu ~ pistolnya tanda ancaman* The bandit kept taking out his pistol as a threat. - *dr kalam* issue from the pen. - *gigi* cut teeth. *Bayi itu baru - gigi* The baby is cutting his teeth. - *keringat keringnya* with much sweat, with great difficulty. - *tanduknya* get angry. **2** exit, leave, go off (the track). *Keréta api - dr rél* The train left the rails. **3** turn out to be. - *sbg pemenang* come out victorious. **meng-i** go out to face s.o. ~ *lawannya di arena olahraga* go out to face o.'s opponent in the sports arena. **meng-kan 1** take or put outside. *Ia ~ anjing itu* She took the dog outside. ~ *parangnya* take out o.'s machete. **2** expel, eject, remove, discharge (an employee). ~ *usus buntu* remove an appendix. **3** issue (an order, a ticket), publish (a book), say what o. has on o.'s mind. -*kanlah apa yg ada dlm kalbu hatimu* Do say what is on your mind. ~ *suara* vote, cast a vote. **4** export s.t. **5** produce, manufacture. *Paberik itu ~ mesin tulis* That factory produces typewriters. **6** spend, expend money. **7** secrete (a fluid), discharge (blood), exhale s.t. *Cubitan itu ~ darah* That pinch drew blood. **-an 1** s.t. produced, output. *Jam ini ~ Jerman* This watch was made in Germany. *Buku ini ~ penerbitan itu* This book is published by that publishing house. ~ *énérgi* energy production. **2** graduate. *Ia ~ Universitas Indonésia* She is a graduate of the University of Indonesia. ~ *Sukamiskin* a former inmate of Sukamiskin prison. **3** (*Bib.*) Exodus. **peng-an 1** dismissal, expulsion. **2** release (of a new movie), edition. **3** expending of. **4** export. **5** excretion.

keluarga 1 family. - *berencana* family planning. - *inti* nuclear family. **2** relative. *Dia masih - kami* He is a relative of ours. - *sedarah* blood relatives. - *semenda* in-laws. **3** (*Biol.*) genus. **4** group of people like a family. - *besar UI* the community of people connected with the University of Indonesia. **se-** and family, the whole family. *kpd yth Bp*

Oetomo ~ to Mr. Oetomo and his family. *Kami ~ séhat walafiat* The whole family is well. **ber-1** have a family, be married. **2** be related to. *Saya ~ dgn dia* I'm related to him. **ke-an** having to do with family. *pésta yg diadakan dlm suasana ~ a* party held in a family atmosphere. **per-an 1** family affairs. **2** familial relationship.

kelub see KLUB.

kelubak see KUBAK.

kelubi k.o. salacca palm with bitter edible fruit.

kelubung cover, veil. **ber-** covered, veiled. **meng-i 1** cover s.t. **2** conceal s.t.

keluburan pit for trapping animals.

kelucak see KELOCAK.

keluh 1 sigh, moan. **2** complaint. *Ada saja -nya* He always finds s.t. to complain about. - *kesah* complaints and sighs. **ber-** *kesah* moan and complain. **meng-kesahkan** complain about. - *sayu* lamentation, bemoaning. **meng-i** bewail, bemoan s.t. or s.o. *Ia ~ kawannya yg baru meninggal* He bemoaned his friend who had just passed away. **meng-kan 1** complain about s.t. **2** say s.t. in a complaining way. *Dia ~ nama saya* She pronounced my name with a sigh. **-an** complaint. **peng-** complainer, griper.

kelui ramie, k.o. fiber.

keluih see KLUWIH.

keluk curved. **ber- 1** bend. **2** have curves. **meng-** buckle, bend in surface. **-an** buckling.

kelukup k.o. timber-yielding tree.

kelukur ber-(an) abraded, scraped, grazed (of skin).

keluli steel rods for reinforcing cement.

kelulu proper, fitting. *tak* - improper, unseemly, unbecoming.

kelumit bit, part. **se-** a bit. ~ *pikiran* a few thoughts. ~ *prajurit* a handful of soldiers.

kelumpang k.o. tall tree with malodorous flowers that yields soft, cheap wood.

kelumun cover(let), wrapping. **ber-** have a cover, be covered with. **meng-i** cover, envelop. *Kabut ~ puncak bukit* Fog covered the hilltop.

kelun₁ ber- billow (of smoke).

kelun₂ see KELON.

keluna k.o. woody vine.

kelunak k.o. tuber.

kelung 1 bent. **2** hollow, concave.

kelupas ber- get peeled off. **meng- 1** get peeled off. **2** peel s.t. off. ~ *jangat* peel off the skin. **meng-kan 1** peel, skin s.t. **2** peel on behalf of s.o. **ter-** peeled off. *Kakinya sebelah belakang ~* Its hind foot was skinned.

kelupur meng- flutter.

keluron (*Jv*) miscarriage, premature stillbirth. **-an** have a miscarriage, bear a premature baby that dies.

keluruk (*Jv*) crow, go cock-a-doodle-do. **ber-** crow.

kelurut whitlow.

kelus₁ abraded, scraped (of skin).

kelus₂ see KELOS.

kelusuh-kelasah very nervous.

kelut-melut crisis, critical stage (of an illness, political situation, etc.).

kelutum k.o. artocarpus tree the wood of which withstands water.

kelutut k.o. wasplike insect the nests of which exude a sweet sticky substance.

keluwak see KELUAK.

keluyuk (*Ch*) meat dish with sweet sauce. **meng-** make this dish.

keluyur (ber)-an, meng- 1 loaf around, stroll about without purpose. 2 hang around.

Kem. [*Kementerian*] ministry, department.

kémah 1 tent. 2 camp. - *induk* base camp. 3 awning aboard ship. **ber-** 1 camp. 2 put up a tent. **per-an** 1 camping. 2 a camp out. 3 (*Mil.*) camp, encampment, bivouac.

kemah-kemih, kemak-kemik₁ ber- chew.

kemak-kemik₂ mumble. **meng-kan** mumble s.t.

kemal 1 moist, damp, clammy. 2 dingy, grubby.

kemala see GEMALA.

kemam ber- mumble. **meng-** 1 retain in the mouth. 2 mumble.

kemamang (*Jv*) evil spirit in the shape of a flaming head.

kemana see MANA₁.

kemanakan see KEMENAKAN.

kemanan (*Jv*) a percussion instrument used to mark the rhythm.

kemandang see KUMANDANG.

kemang₁ a supernatural being that attacks babies.

kemang₂ k.o. wild mango.

kemangi k.o. basil.

kemantén, kemantin (*Coll.*) newlywed, bride or bridegroom.

kemarau 1 dry (of a season or the hold of a boat after bailing). 2 dry season. - *keras* a long dry spell. 3 having no money. *Kami sedang* - We're broke these days.

kemarén see KEMARIN.

kemari come here. - *sebentar* Come here a minute. **meng-kan** hand, pass this way.

kemarin 1 yesterday. - *dulu* day before yesterday. - *malam* last night. 2 (*Jv*) in the past. *tahun* - last year. --*marin* in the days gone by. **-nya** the day before, the other day.

kemaron k.o. earthenware waterjug.

kemaruk 1 ravenous (esp. after a long illness). 2 greedy, covetous.

kemas 1 orderly, well kept (of a house, etc.), cleared away. 2 crated, boxed. *peti* - shipping container. **ber-(²)** 1 pack. *Meréka ~ utk perjalanan meréka* They packed for their trip. 2 clear things away, put things in order. *~ stl menjamu* clear away after entertaining. **meng-(i)** 1 clear or put s.t. in order. *~ diri* dress o.s. up. *~ rambut* fix o.'s hair. *~ koper* pack the suitcases. 2 care for (the children). **meng-kan** 1 tidy up (a room, etc.). 2 pack s.t. up. **-an** package, packing. **peng-an, per-an** packaging.

kemat see HIKMAH.

kemat-kamit see KOMAT-KAMIT.

kematu hard as stone.

kemawan see AWAN.

kemayu (*Jv*) coquettish.

kembal small wickerwork container (of rattan, bamboo or palm leaves).

kembala-kembali go back and forth.

kembali 1 return, revert to. *Ia - ke negerinya* He returned to his country. *- ke pangkuan Ibu Pertiwi* return to homeland. 2 once again. *Ia hrs mulai* - She has to start over again. *membayar* - pay again. 3 you are welcome. *Terima kasih* - You are welcome. 4 change (of money). *-nya dua ribu* You get 2,000 change. **se-(nya)** upon o.'s return. *~ dia terus mulai bekerja* After his return, he started to work immediately. **meng-kan** 1 return s.t., turn s.t. back. 2 restore s.t. 3 have s.o. return. *Penjagaan di Istana -- kami ke kantor Présidén* The palace guard made us return to the President's office. **-an** pocket change (of money). *Tdk ada uang ~, semua uang besar* We have no change. All our money is in large denominations. **peng-an** 1 return (of s.t.). 2 restitution. 3 reversion.

kemban breast cloth (wrapped around the upper part of a woman's body). **ber-** wear a breast cloth. *~ sarong* wrap a sarong around the top of the body.

kembang 1 flower. *- api* sparkler, fire cracker. *- bangkai* k.o. plant with edible root and malodorous flower. *- biak* **ber-** *biak* 1 multiply, proliferate, grow. 2 breed (of germs, etc.). **meng-biakkan** breed, propagate, proliferate s.t. *~ tunas-tunas baru* grow new shoots. **peng-biakan** breeding of s.t. **per-biakan** proliferation. *- gula* hard candy. *- kol* cauliflower. *- latar/malam* prostitute. *- mayang* palm leaves shaped into ornaments for weddings and other feasts. *- pala* mace (spice). *- wijaya kusuma* k.o. flower. 2 bloom, open like a flower. *- kempis* 1 panting. 2 swell and subside repeatedly. *Kantong kas negara sdh - kempis* The state treasury has gone up and down repeatedly. **meng-kempiskan** cause s.o. to pant. *- ku(n)cup* open and shut. 3 tread (of tire). **ber-** 1 bloom, blossom, unfold. *Bunga-bunga ~* The flowers bloomed. *Dlm masa damai kesenian akan ~* In peacetime art will flourish. *Hatinya ~ karena kegirangan* His heart swelled with joy. *~ mekar* flourish. 2 rise, expand (of dough). 3 develop, expand, burgeon. *Pengetahuannya ~* Her knowledge expanded. 4 having a floral design. **ber-an** 1 in bloom, flowering. 2 expanding. *layar ~* billowing sail. **meng-** 1 expand. *Karena panas hawa akan ~* Air will expand because of heat. 2 unfurl (sail, wings, etc.). *~ bakung* beautiful hair that has been let down. 3 open (an umbrella, book, etc.). 4 swell. *Air mata Ani ~* Ani had tears in her eyes. **meng-i** 1 put flowers on s.t. 2 recap, retread (a tire). **meng-kan** 1 expand. *Panas akan ~ hawa* Heat will expand air. *~ hati* cheer s.o. up. 2 develop s.t. 3 open, unfold (an umbrella, wing, etc.). ~ *layar* unfurl the sails, get under way. **memper-kan** cause s.t. to develop. **peng-** promoter. ~ *Pergerakan* promoter of the (nationalist) Movement. **peng-an** developing of. *mementingkan* ~ *désa* give priority to rural development. **per-an 1** development. *menantikan* ~ *selanjutnya* await subsequent developments. **2** blooming, flowering. **3** expansion.

kembar 1 twin. *Kedua anak itu* - Those two children are twins. - *dampit/démpét* Siamese twins. - *empat* quadruplets. - *Siam* Siamese twins. - *tiga* triplets. **2** in duplicate. **3** identical. *Meréka - dan pakaian meréka pun - juga* They are twins and they dress alike too. **4** match, twin. *Di mana -nya anting-anting saya?* Where is the other earring (of this pair)? **ber- 1** be twins, be a pair. **2** be identical, match e.o. **meng-i 1** match, duplicate. *Saya tak dpt* ~ *kepandaiannya* I cannot match her brilliance. **2** stand up to. *Siapa yg berani* ~ *penggertak itu?* Who dares to stand up to that bully? **meng-kan 1** pair s.t. **2** do s.t. in duplicate. **(ke)-an** twinning. **peng-an** twinning.

kembara see EMBARA.

kemben see KEMBAN.

kembeng meng- flood, overflow.

kembili k.o. large us. purplish edible tuber.

kembira scatter in all directions (of a fleeing army, etc.).

kembiri see KEBIRI.

kemboja see KAMBOJA.

kembok₁ see KOBOK₂.

kembok₂ see GEMBOK.

kémbol meng- bulge (of pockets, etc.).

kembu k.o. small basket for fish.

kembung₁ filled with air, puffed up, puffing, fill. - *kempis* heave up and down, puff up and go down. *Dadanya - kempis* Her chest was heaving. **meng-** puff up. **meng-kan** puff up (o.'s cheeks), inflate, blow up (a balloon, etc.). **peng-an** inflation (of tire, balloon, etc.).

kembung₂ k.o. round rice basket.

kembur ber-, meng- chat, engage in small talk. **ber-²** joke, chat. **meng-kan** talk about s.t.

kemburuan jealous.

kembut k.o. woven basket.

keméja western-style shirt. - *buka* sport shirt. - *kaos/oblong* T-shirt. - *puntung* short-sleeved shirt. - *silir/tamasya* sport shirt. - *tutup* dress shirt.

kemejan see HIU.

kemekmek (*Jkt*) be fascinated.

kemelut crisis, critical stage (of illness, fever, political situation, etc.). - *naik* turn for the worse. - *turun* turn for the better.

kememadaian see PADA₂.

kemenakan nephew, niece.

kemendang mirage or shimmer caused by hot air. **ber-, meng-** see a mirage in the heat.

kemendur 1 (*Naut.*) commander. **2** harbor master. **3** civil official (during the colonial period). **4** overseer, foreman.

kemenis see KOMUNIS.

kementam booming, thundering.

kemenyan incense derived from gum benzoin.

kemeresak sound of rustling.

kemerlap see GEMERLAP.

kemerup flicker.

kemerut see KERUT₁.

kemet o. with the magical power to have intercourse with a woman from afar.

kemi₁ sucking fish, the remora.

kemi₂ see KEMIH.

kemidi see KOMIDI.

kemih (*Formal*) urine. **ber-** urinate. **per-an 1** urination. **2** urinal.

kemik dented. **ber- 1** be all dented. **2** be chapped (of lips). *Bibirnya* ~ His lips are all chapped.

kemil (me)ng- eat snacks. **-an** snacks.

kemilap see GEMILAP.

kemilau sheen, shiny, shining (of metal, jewel, velvet, moon, etc.).

keminting, kemiri candlenut tree and its fruit.

kemis₁ meng- beg. ~ *minta makanan* beg for food. **peng-** beggar. **peng-an** begging.

kemis₂ see PENATU.

Kemis see KAMIS.

kemlandingan the ipil-ipil, a fast-growing tree with edible beans planted to shade coffee and used as cattle feed or for green manure.

kemoceng see KEMUCING.

kemong₁ sunken (of cheeks).

kemong₂ a small gong of the Jv gamelan.

kemot see KEMUT₁,₂.

kempa a press. - *air* hydraulic press. **meng-** press. ~ *kacang tanah utk membuat minyak* press peanuts to make oil. ~ *tangan* keep clenching o.'s fist. **meng-kan** compress s.t. **-an 1** a press. **2** s.t. pressed. **peng-an** pressing. ~ *minyak* pressing for oil.

kempal see KIMPAL.

kempang k.o. canoe.

kempang-kempis pant. *Ia - stl berlari itu* He was panting after his run.

kempas k.o. tree.

kempas-kempis panting for breath.

kémpéitai Japanese military police (or a member of it) during the occupation.

kcmpék bag for betel.

kempelang see KEMPLANG₁.

kempés see KEMPIH.

kempih, kempis 1 deflated, flat (tire, etc.). **2** sunken (of cheeks, chest, etc.). **3** penniless. *kantong -* flat broke. **meng-** collapse (of lung, vein). **meng-i, meng-kan** deflate, let the air out of (a tire, balloon). **peng-an** deflation, collapse (of a lung, etc.).

kempit₁ k.o. earthenware jug.

kempit₂ see KEPIT.

kemplang₁ meng- strike (esp. with the fist). ~ *mulut temannya* hit o.'s friend in the mouth. *Nah, gong terakhir sdh di-* The final bell has rung (The gong was struck for the last time). **-an** blow, hit.

kemplang₂ meng- sell fruit wholesale to middleman before harvesting.

kemplang₃ meng- 1 not pay. *Ia* ~ *hutangnya* He

did not pay his debt. **2** embezzle. *Pegawai tinggi itu ~ uang kas* The high official embezzled the money from the office funds. **-an** embezzled items. *Dua juta rupiah itu adalah uang ~* The two million rupiah were embezzled money.

kempléng twanging sound.

kemplong (*Jv*) mallet for softening batik cloth. **meng-** beat cloth.

kémpo k.o. martial art.

kempos flat, deflated.

kempot₁ sunken, hollow (of cheeks).

kempot₂ broke, penniless.

kempu k.o. round box with lid for clothing.

kempuh 1 soft, mushy (of food which is fully cooked). **2** very ripe (of fruit). **3** rotten, spoiled (of food).

kempul₁ k.o. gamelan instrument containing several small horizontal gongs.

kempul₂ ber-² pant, be out of breath. **ter-²** panting.

kempunan 1 be in a quandary, nervous, desperate. **2** long or yearn for.

kempung sunken (of cheeks from loss of teeth). **-an 1** abdomen. **2** bladder.

kemreket gnash (of teeth).

kemringet (*Jv*) sweaty. **ber-** break into a sweat.

kemrungsung (*Jv*) uncomfortable, ill at ease.

kemu₁ ber-, meng- rinse out the mouth.

kemu₂ meng- mutter, mumble.

kemucak see KEMUNCAK.

kemucing feather duster.

kemudi 1 helm, rudder. **2** steering wheel. *- arah* direction wheel. **3** reins (of gvt., management, etc.). **ber- 1** use a rudder. **2** have a rudder. **3** hold the rudder. **meng-kan** steer, pilot. *- kapal terbang* fly a plane. **2** govern, lead, be at the helm of. **peng- 1** helmsman, driver, pilot. **2** director. **peng-an** piloting, steering. *~ berjarak* remote control.

kemudian afterwards, later, then. *Ia makan, - minum* He ate; afterwards he drank. *- dr itu* afterwards. *(di) - hari* in the future, in coming days. *- ini* recently. **meng-kan 1** postpone, put s.t. off. **2** turn (the clock) back. **3** be subordinate to, place s.t. second to. *Kini ia bekerja keras dan ~ kesenangan* He works hard now, and puts pleasure in 2d place. **ter- 1** last, later than the others. *Ia selalu datang ~* She always comes last. **2** be neglected, made the last thing.

kemudu-kudu see SELAK₂.

kemuka see MUKA.

kemukus k.o. pepper, the cubeb.

kemul₁ (*Jv*) blanket, coverlet. **ber-** cover o.s. (with a blanket), be blanketed. *gunung ~ awan* a mountain blanketed with clouds. **meng-i** blanket, cover with a blanket. *Awan ~ puncak gunung* clouds blanketed the mountain top. **-an** covered with a blanket. *Ia ~ sarung ketika keluar rumah* She covered herself with a sarong when she went outside the house.

kemul₂ munch, gnaw at or on.

kemumu₁ k.o. seaweed.

kemumu₂ k.o. aroid, the leaves and roots of which are eaten.

kemumu₃ dandruff.

kemuncak peak, top, summit, apex.

kemuncup k.o. grass, the seeds of which adhere to o.'s clothing.

kemung see KEMONG₂.

kemungkus addled (of an egg).

kemuning 1 yellow (color). **2** k.o. tree producing beautiful yellow wood.

kemunting the rose-myrtle, a shrub producing dark red edible berries. *- bukit* k.o. creeper.

kemut₁ ter-, meng- 1 throb, beat (of pulse). **2** stagger.

kemut₂ meng- 1 suck on (a piece of candy or as sexual act). **2** move up and down (of mouth when eating). **-an** hard candy that is sucked.

kemutul k.o. hardwood tree.

kén (*Japanese*) regency.

kena 1 be touched adversely, struck, hit, or affected by s.t. unpleasant, come into contact with. *Pabrik itu - bom* The factory was hit by a bomb. *Tangannya - cat basah* He got wet paint on his hands. *- flu* get the flu. *Mau datang soré - ujan* I wanted to come in the afternoon but it rained. *Kakinya - lemari* His leg bumped against the cabinet. *Hatiku masih - pdnya* I am still carrying a torch for him. *- apa?* Why? (What hit or affected you adversely?) *- berapa?* How much did it cost you? *- berapa semua ini?* How much did all of this run? *- cakup* be picked up by police. *- cap* get the label of . . . *Ia - cap kolot* He got labeled as a conservative. *- dakwa* be accused. *- getahnya* have s.t. unpleasant happen to o. because of what s.o. else did. *- jelatang* lascivious. *- jemur* get bleached in the sun. *- kuliah* get a lecture. *- marah* be reprimanded, get a dressing down. *- muka* fall in disgrace. *- rasuk* be possessed by a spirit. *- sakal* be tortured. *- skors* get expelled or fired from a job. *- sogok/suap* be bribed. *- tutup* get closed down. *- undi* get o.'s turn. *Kau - undi utk nyapu* It is your turn to sweep. **2** hit s.t. *begitu kepalanya - bantal* the moment his head hit the pillow. **3** be subject to. *- pajak keméwahan* subject to a luxury tax. *Kampungnya - hukum berkurung* The village was subjected to a curfew. **4** fit, be the right thing, be on the mark. *Baju itu - benar pdmu* That shirt is just right for you. *Tafsiranmu -* Your interpretation is right on the mark. *Prosédur biasa tdk -* The usual procedure does not work. **5** (*Coll., Jv*) be allowed. *Ndak - msk dr belakang* You are not supposed to enter from the back. **-²** to the point. *Kalimatnya péndék dan ~* His sentences are short and to the point. **se-nya** at random, whatever happens to hit. *Ia memukul ~* He hit anywhere he could. *memakai bahasa asing ~* use a foreign language without heeding the rules of grammar and usage. *dr penduduk kota yg disaring ~* of the city residents who were picked at random. **ber-an 1** in connection, in the matter of. *~ dgn Hari Kemerdékaan* in connection with Independence Day. **2** agree (on). **ber-(²)an**

have a connection with. **- meng-** be connected with. *Hal ini tak ~ dgn yg kemarin* This case has no connection with yesterday's. *Apa ~ kelakuan aku dgn semua itu?* What does my behavior have to do with all that? *tdk ~ akan* heedless, regardless. *Tdk ~ akan pengorbanan jiwa, musuh terus menyerang* Heedless of the loss of life, the enemy continued to attack. **meng-** hit the mark, have its effect. *~ jebak kita* Our trap is having its effect. *Terkaanku ~* My guess was on the mark. **meng-i 1** hit, strike, touch. *Jangan -i bajuku* Do not touch my jacket. **2** affect adversely, subject s.o. to. *Ia akan di-i tindakan administratif* They will take administrative measures against him. **3** concern, impinge on. *Surat itu ~ saya* That letter concerns me. **4** about, with respect to. *kuliah ~ sejarah révolusi* a lecture about the history of the revolution. **meng-kan 1** put on clothing. **2** fasten, secure a device to o.s. *Penumpang diwajibkan ~ sabuk* Passengers are required to fasten seat belts. **3** impose (punishment), levy (taxes). *béa cukai yg di-kan pd barang itu* the custom duties which were imposed on that item. **4** aim s.t. **5** subject o. to. *Ia di-kan denda Rp10.000* He was subjected to a fine of 10,000 rupiah. *Kota Madiun juga di-kan momén* They also set up speed traps in Madiun. **meng-²kan** deceive, fool, trick s.o. **ter- 1** hit, struck, accidentally come into contact with. *Ia ~ serangan jantung* He was stricken by a heart attack. *Ia ~ aliran listrik* He came into contact with a power line. **2** exposed. *~ panas* exposed to the heat. **3** affected. *Yg tak bersalah pun ~* People who were not to blame were also affected. **4** be attached. *~ pd dadanya nampak sebaris bintang kehormatan* Attached to his chest was a row of decorations. **5** be subject to. *Baru dua ratus yg ~ peraturan baru* Only 200 people have been affected by the new regulations so far. **peng-** dresser, o. who dresses s.o. **peng-an** imposition. *~ pajak penjualan* imposition of a sales tax.

kenal 1 know, be familiar. *Saya - mobil ini, sdh pernah saya kemudikan* I know this car; I have driven it before. **2** be acquainted with. *Saya - dia* I'm acquainted with him. *tdk - jerih dan payah* tireless, indefatigable. *tdk - malu* thick-skinned, insensitive. **ber-an** be acquainted. **ber-²an, - meng-** know e.o., be friends with e.o. **meng-1** know, be acquainted with. **2** recognize. **3** distinguish, make out. **4** diagnose (an illness). **meng-i** know, recognize, identify. *-ilah bank anda!* Know your bank! **meng-kan** introduce s.o. *Ikan itu di-kan di Jawa oléh Haji Mudjair* That fish was introduced in Java by Haji Mudjair. **member-kan 1** introduce s.o. or s.t. *Boléh saya ~ sdr kpd ibuku?* May I introduce you to my mother? **2** inform s.o. of s.t. **ter-** well known, famed. **keter-an** fame, being famed. **ke-an 1** known, famed. **2** discussed, found out. **-an** an acquaintance. **pemer-** introducer. **peng- 1** identification. *tanda ~* sign of recognition. **2** connoisseur, o. who knows. **peng-an 1** introduction. **2** identi-

fication. **per-an 1** introduction of s.o. to s.o. else. **2** acquaintanceship.

kenalpot see KNALPOT.

kenan₁ birthmark.

kenan₂ ber- 1 have the pleasure of, be so kind as to. *Présidén ~ menghadiri pertemuan kami* The President is pleased to attend our meeting. *Beliau ~ memberi amanat* He is kind enough to present the address. **2** agree, approve of, endorse. *Akhirnya ia ~ pergi bersama-sama dgn saya* She finally deigned to go out with me. *Ayah ~ akan maksud saya utk menjadi perwira* Father approves of my plan to become an officer. **member-kan** permit, allow. *Agamanya tak ~ perceraian* His religion does not permit divorce. *Per-kanlah saya utk . . .* Please permit me to . . . **per-(an)** permission, approval.

kenang be reminded of, think of. **meng-** recall, reminisce about. *~ masa kanak-kanaknya* reminisce about o.'s childhood. **meng-i** remember fondly, commemorate. **meng-kan 1** remember, recall. *~ kembali* recall, recollect. **2** commemorate. **3** remind (o. of s.o.). *Ia ~ saya pd bapak saya* He reminds me of my father. **ter-** be reminded. *Saya ~ pd tanah air* I was reminded of my country. **(²)-an 1** souvenir, keepsake, memento. **2** remembrances, fond memories. **3** ideals of the past. **peng-** reminder, memoir.

kenanga the ylang-ylang or cananga, a shrub the flowers of which produce oils for perfume.

kenap small table.

kenapa 1 why. *- cepat-cepat?* Why the rush? **2** what happened to. *- tanganmu?* What is wrong with your hand? **di-in** (*Coll.*) what happened to . . ., what did they do to . . . *Dia ~ kok sampai menangis?* What did they do to make him cry?

kenari₁ the canari tree and its nuts. *- belanda* almond.

kenari₂ canary.

kencan 1 date, appointment. **2** date. *Ia - saya* She is my date. **ber- 1** have an appointment. **2** have a date, dating.

kencana (*Lit.*) gold. *gelang -* gold bracelet.

kencang 1 fast, quick, speedy. *Mobil itu berjalan dgn -* The car went fast. **2** taut, tight. *Tali itu -* The rope is taut. *pegangan -* a tight grip. *Napasnya -* His breath is constricted. **3** selling well. *pasaran tékstil -* a good market for textiles. **meng-1** increase its speed. *Mobil itu makin ~ larinya* The car went faster and faster. **2** become taut. *Tali ténda itu ~ karena hujan* The tent ropes became taut from the rain. **meng-i** tighten (a belt, rope, etc.). **meng-kan 1** speed up, accelerate. *~ mobilnya* accelerate o.'s car. **2** tighten s.t. *~ ikat pinggang* tighten the belt, economize. **member-(kan)** accelerate, speed up. **ke-an 1** speed, acceleration. **2** tension, tautness. *Ia mengurangi ~ kawat itu* He reduced the tension of the cable.

kencang-kencung clanking sound.

kencar ter-² 1 nervous, agitated. **2** in haste, hastily.

kéncéng₁ bow drill.

kéncéng₂ frying pan.
kencerang-kencering sound of jingling coins or metal ornaments.
kencing 1 urine. **2** urinate. *- batu* kidney stone. *- darah* blood in the urine. *- gula/manis* diabetes. *- nanah* gonorrhea. **ber-** urinate. **meng-i 1** urinate on s.t. **2** (*Coll.*) engage a woman in intercourse. **ter-** urinate involuntarily. **ter-i** get urinated upon. **peng-an, pe-an 1** bladder. **2** urethra.
kénco (*Japanese*) regent.
kéncong₁ crooked, askew, awry. **meng-kan 1** twist, bend (s.o.'s words). **2** curl (o.'s lips).
kéncong₂ pitcher plant.
kencung see KENCANG-KENCUNG.
kencur greater galingale, a root crop resembling ginger, used as spice and medicine. *masih -* still a virgin. *masih bau -* still young and inexperienced.
kendaga 1 cowries, shell money. **2** a chest or oblong box adorned with shell, glass, etc.
kendak lover, mistress. **ber-** have an affair with. **memper-** make s.o. a lover or mistress. **-an** paramour.
kendala constraint, obstacle. *Tdk adanya mas kawin tdk merupakan - utk perkawinan itu* The lack of a dowry was no obstacle to the marriage. **ber-** constrained. *kehidupan yg ~ di masyarakat pedésaan* a life that is restricted in village society. **meng-kan** restrict, constrain.
kendali reins. **ber-** controlled, directed. *peluru/proyéktil -* guided missile. **meng-kan 1** hold the reins (on a horse, etc.). **2** restrain (o.'s desire, etc.). **3** manage, lead (firm, etc.). **ter-** restrained. *ékonomi ~* economy with a lid put on. **ter-kan** can be restrained. **peng- 1** leader, o. who holds the reins. **2** manager. **peng-an 1** restraint, curb. **2** control. *~ harga* price control. *~ kelahiran* birth control. *~ mutu* quality control. *~ nafsu* restraint of the passions. *~ sungai* river control.
kendang₁ k.o. small drum covered with leather at each end. **ber-(an)** play a *kendang*. **-an** membrane in ear.
kendang₂ ream of paper (480 sheets). *kertas se-* a ream of paper.
kendara ber- ride (in or on s.t.). **ber-an 1** have a vehicle. **2** ride in a vehicle. **meng-i 1** drive (a car). **2** ride (a horse). **meng-kan** drive s.t. for s.o. **-an 1** vehicle. *~ berhias* float (in a parade). *~ berlapis baja* armored vehicle. **2** mount. **peng-1** driver, rider. **2** horseman.
kendat, kendatan interruption. *tanpa -* without interruption.
kendati, kendati pun 1 although. *- ia sakit, ia bekerja juga* Although he was sick, he went to work anyway. **2** not to mention, much less. *- serupiah, sésén pun saya tak punya* I do not even have a penny, much less a rupiah.
kendéka see KAYU₁.
kendi k.o. earthenware flask with a neck and spout (us. for drinking water).
kendil (*Jv*) pot for cooking rice.

kendiri (*Coll.*) see SENDIRI.
kendit 1 cloth belt, sash. **2** girdle.
kendo (*Jv*) soft, slow (tone).
kéndo martial arts with Japanese staffs.
kéndong meng- carry s.t. in a cloth.
kendor see KENDUR.
kenduduk₁ see UBI.
kenduduk₂ see SENDUDUK.
kendur 1 slack (of rope, business). **2** loose. *Sepatuku -* My shoe is loose. *roda -* a wobbly wheel. **3** flabby, not trim (of body). *- dagingnya* His flesh was flabby. **4** lifeless, weak, without pep. **5** (*Ling.*) lax. **6** slacken. *Kemauannya belajar -* He has lost his desire to study. *- menyusut* difficult to handle (of situation). **ber-²** slack, loose. *memasang tali ~ pd tiang* attach a rope loosely to a pole. **meng- 1** become loose or slack. **2** relax. *Kekejangan mulutnya ~* The cramp in her face relaxed. **3** become weak (of spirit, voice, etc.). **meng-kan 1** slacken, loosen (a rope). **2** relax (a muscle, regulations). **3** turn down (volume). **4** slow down, lacken (production). **ke-an 1** weakness, laxness (of muscle). **2** relaxation (regulations). **3** slowdown (of work). **peng-** s.t. that loosens or slackens, relaxant. **peng-an 1** slackening, loosening, relaxing of. **2** slowing down, slackening (of production, effort).
kenduri (*Isl.*) ritual meal. *- arwah* ritual feast to mark s.o.'s death. *- maulud* ritual feast on the occasion of Muh.'s birthday. *- meniga* ritual feast on the 3d day after s.o.'s death. **ber- 1** hold a ritual gathering involving a common meal. **2** participate in a ritual gathering. **meng-kan** prepare a ritual feast for.
kenék assistant to a driver.
kenéker marbles. **ber-** play marbles.
kenés 1 coquettish. **2** affected (of female). **ng-** be flirtatious, put on. **ke-an 1** coquettishness, coquetry. **2** being affected, putting on.
kéng bark, yelp (of dogs).
kéngkang see KANGKANG₂.
kéngkéng meng-² 1 yelp, howl (of a dog). **2** whimper, whine.
kenidai name given to several k.o. bushes or trees.
kenikir the cosmos, an ornamental flower with edible leaves.
kening 1 brow, forehead. **2** eyebrow.
kenini see KININE.
kenisah (*Bib.*) the temple in Jerusalem.
kenohong leprosy.
kenong (*Jv*) k.o. small gong of the gamelan.
kenop₁ 1 knob, button. *- lampu* switch of a lamp or light. **2** button (of shirt, etc.).
kenop₂ see KNOP.
kénpéitai see KEMPEITAI.
kénsel *kena -* experience a cancellation (us. of a trip). **meng(k)-** cancel, annul. *Penumpang sering di-* Passengers often do not have their reservations honored.
kental 1 thick (of syrup). **2** strong (of coffee). **3** close (of friendships). **meng-** coagulate, clot

(of blood), curdle (of milk). ~ *pekat* congeal.
meng-kan thicken (gravy, etc.), make blood congeal, curdle (milk). **ke-an** viscosity, thick consistency. **-an** extract. **peng-an** coagulation, congealment, curdling.
kentang potato. - *goréng* fried potatoes. - *puré* mashed potatoes.
kentar unit of weight for gold.
kentara 1 visible. *Pesawat terbang itu hampir tak -* The plane was scarcely visible. 2 discernible, apparent, evident. *Maksud yg sebetulnya -* Her real purpose was apparent. *pengangguran yg tdk -* disguised unemployment. **meng-** become visible. **meng-kan** make visible or discernible.
kentel see KENTAL.
kenténg see GENTÉNG.
kentit (*Jv, Jkt*) **meng-** 1 steal s.t. 2 hide s.t.
kentong, kentung 1 sound of a gong. 2 gong. **-an** 1 drum made from bamboo or wood which is struck to sound an alarm. 2 alarm sounded by this drum.
kentrang-kentring, kentrang-kentrung sound of strumming, strings being plucked.
kentut 1 flatus, stomach gas. 2 break wind, fart. **ber-** break wind. **meng-i** 1 fart on. 2 laugh off, disregard. *Peraturan antikorupsi spt di-i saja oléh para petugas sendiri* The officials themselves just laugh off the anti-corruption regulations. **meng-kan** fart s.t. out. **ter-** break wind suddenly and involuntarily.
kenung 1 sound of gong. 2 a horizontal gong in the gamelan.
kenup₁ truncheon, bludgeon, billy club.
kenup₂ see KENOP₁.
kenyal 1 tough, rubbery (of meat, etc.). 2 elastic (of fibers, etc.). **meng-** 1 be rubbery (of meat). 2 be elastic, spongy. **ke-an** 1 rubberiness. 2 elasticity.
kenyam meng- 1 taste, sample (food). 2 savor s.t. 3 experience, sample. *Masyarakat setempat akan ~ faédahnya kelak* The local community will experience the benefits later. *~ pendidikan formal* undergo a formal education. **meng-i, meng-kan** undergo, experience s.t.
kenyang 1 satisfied, sated. *Ia makan hingga -* He ate until he was satisfied. *Ia - makan garam* He is an old hand. He is very experienced. *Saya sdh - akan nasihatnya* I have had enough of his advice. *makan terlalu -* be overweight. 2 saturated. *Basahilah pasir hingga -* Wet the sand until it is saturated. *tdk -²nya* insatiable. **meng-i** eat o.'s fill of. **meng-kan** satiate, fill s.o. up, filling, surfeiting. **ke-an** 1 satiation. 2 too full, overly full. *Saya sdh ~* I'm too full. **peng-** s.t. that satiates.
kenyat-kenyit, kenyat-kenyut pulsate, throb.
kenyi, kenyih 1 sickly. 2 susceptible to disease.
kenyir crave (food).
kenyit meng- wink. **meng-kan** wrinkle (the brows).
kenyot, kenyut meng- suck (a nipple, etc.). **-an** 1 nipple for baby's bottle. 2 candy to suck on.
kéok₁ defeated, beaten (in sports). **meng-kan** defeat, beat s.o.

kéok₂ cackle, cluck. **ber-(²), ber-an** cackle, cluck (of chickens).
kéong 1 snail. - *daratan* land snail. 2 shape of a snail's shell, coil, or spiral.
kep.₁ [*keputusan*] decision, decree.
kep.₂ [*Kepulauan*] archipelago.
kép₁ cap, detonator, blasting cap.
kép₂ (*Coll.*) form of address to a *kaptén*.
kép₃ cowlick, tuft or similar configuration of hair on animals.
kepada see PADA₁.
kepah k.o. mollusk.
kepai see KAPAI.
kepak₁ wing (of bird, fowl). **ber-** winged. *pintu ~* French door, double door. *tdk ~* powerless. **meng-²kan** flap s.t. **ber-(²), meng-, ter-(²)** with flapping wings.
kepak₂ see PAK₁.
képak₁ meng- carry on the hip.
képak₂ meng-² flutter.
kepaksa (*Coll.*) see PAKSA₁.
kepal 1 lump, clod. 2 fist. - *remas* **meng-remaskan** clench o.'s fist. **se-** a handful or fistful. *tanah ~ a* handful of earth. *~ tanah* a clod of earth. **ber-²** in lumps or clods. **meng-** 1 hold in o.'s fist. *Ia ~ mata uang itu kuat-kuat* He held the coin tightly in his hand. 2 clench. *~ tangannya* clench o.'s fist. 3 knead (dough, clay). **meng-kan** double o.'s fists, clench. **-an** *tangan* fist.
kepala 1 head. - *batok* 1 crew cut. 2 egghead, intellectual. 3 stupid. - *busung* (*Med.*) hydrocephalus. - *dua* 1 two-headed. 2 vacillating, shilly-shallying, fickle. 3 hypocritical. - *pusing* 1 be dizzy. 2 be at wits' end. 2 head, brain. - *angin* 1 empty-headed. 2 windbag, chatterbox. - *batu* obstinate, stubborn. - *berat* numbskull, dumbbell. - *besar* 1 conceited. 2 stubborn, obstinate. - *dingin* calm, cool-headed. - *udang* very stupid, dull-witted. 3 leader, head, chief executive. - *bagian* division head. - *daérah* district head. - *daérah tingkat I* governor. - *daérah tingkat II* 1 regent. 2 mayor. - *désa* village headman. - *dinas* department head. - *gudang* warehouse keeper. - *jaga* commander of the guard. - *jorong* head of section of village. - *kamar* (*Naut.*) cabin steward. - *kampung* village headman. - *keluarga* head of household. - *negara* head of state. - *pasukan* troop commander. - *regu* team leader. - *sekolah* principal, headmaster. - *stasion* station master. 4 the uppermost or foremost, principal part. - *air* edge of flooding water. - *bahu* shoulder blade. - *berita* news headline. - *kain* decorative contrasting band at o. edge of sarong cloth. - *karangan* heading, headline. - *keréta api* locomotive. - *lakon* leading role, leading character (in play or story). - *paha* groin. - *peluru nuklir* nuclear warhead. - *pulau* highest point on an island. - *santan* coconut cream produced at the first straining. - *sarong* contrasting band at o. edge of sarong cloth. - *surat* 1 letter heading. 2 letterhead. - *susu* cream. - *tahun* beginning of the year. - *tangan* 0.32 meters. - *tongkat* handle of cane. 5 person, (per) head. **se- se-** individually.

ber- 1 have a head. *bangkai yg tdk* ~ a headless body. 2 titled (of a book, etc.). **ber-(kan)** have as head. **meng-** act as the head. **meng-i** head, be in charge of. **meng-kan** 1 appoint s.o. as head, make s.t. the head. 2 (*Sport*) hit (a ball) with head. **-an** headline, masthead.

kepalang insufficient, inadequate. *- tanggung* inadequate, halfway done.

kepam 1 musty, stale. 2 faded.

kepang k.o. tree, the rotten xylem of which yields fragrant material.

képang₁ braid, plait. *- képot* 1 crisscross, topsy-turvy. 2 rumpled. **ber-** braided, plaited. **meng-braid, plait** s.t. *Rambutnya di-* Her hair was braided. **-an** s.t. plaited or braided.

képang₂ see KIPANG₁.

kepanggung see PANGGUNG.

kepar k.o. perchlike fish.

képar twilled cloth.

keparat₁ (*Vulg.*) 1 dammit!, damned, accursed. 2 rogue. 3 infidel, heathen.

keparat₂ atonement through good deeds, sacrifice, etc.

kepatang (*M*) yesterday.

kepaya see PAPAYA.

kepayang k.o. large tree which produces the spice *keluwak*.

kepécong fall asleep (of leg or arm).

kepék₁ (*Jv*) notes for cheating on a test. **-an** notes for cheating.

kepék₂ see KEMPÉK.

kempék see KEPIK₁.

kepénak see ÉNAK.

kepéncong fruit of the *kepayang* tree used as spice.

kependudukan see DUDUK.

képéng coin with square hole in center formerly worth ⅛ of a cent (in the colonial era).

kepéngin see KEPINGIN.

kepépét see PÉPÉT.

képer₁ see KÉPAR.

képer₂ see KIPER.

kepergok see PERGOK.

kepet meng-(²)kan shake, manipulate s.t.

képét₁ (*Jkt*) fin (of a fish).

képét₂ fail to clean o.s. after defecating or fail to bathe. **ng-** (*Vulg.*) be a shit ass.

képét₃ ng- magically turn into an animal. *babi* ~ a supernatural being that turns into a pig and steals for his master.

kepetang see KEPATANG.

kepialu migraine headache.

kepiat dried coconut husk.

kepik₁ dented (of fender, etc.).

kepik₂ k.o. insect harmful to agriculture.

kepil near, close or next to, alongside (of a ship). **meng-** go alongside. *Perahu berlayar* ~ *pantai* The boat hugged the coastline. **meng-kan** bring s.t. close. *Ia - mobil nya pd témbok* He parked his car close to the wall. ~ *kapal* berth a ship. **ter-** 1 placed close. 2 (*Naut.*) moored, tied up.

kepincut (*Jv*) attracted, drawn to.

kepinding bedbug.

keping 1 chip, fragment. *- kayu* chip of wood. 2 splinter, sliver, shard. *se- gelas* sliver from a glass. 3 counter for flat thin objects. *dua - papan* two boards. *- rém* brake disc. **ber-²** 1 in pieces or slivers. *Piring itu pecah* ~ The plate broke into pieces. 2 in tatters (of flag, etc.). 3 in tresses, locks. **meng-** 1 split (a plank). 2 slice, cut into thin pieces. **-an** fragment.

kepingin desire, want strongly. *- tahu* curious, eager to know.

kepinis ironwood.

kepinjal flea.

kepiran see KAPIRAN.

kepis k.o. basket for holding freshly caught fish.

kepit pressed between arm and side or between two fingers. **ber-** *tangan* arm in arm. **meng-** 1 carry s.t. under the arm. 2 clasp. *Ia* ~ *anaknya ke dadanya* She clasped her child to her bosom. ~ *dgn pinsét* hold with pincers. 3 pinch. *Sepatu baru ini* ~ These new shoes pinch. **-an** 1 clamp, pincers. 2 o.'s hold.

kepiting crab. *sbg - batu* miserly, stingy, tight-fisted.

keplak meng- slap (us. the head). **meng-i** slap repeatedly. **meng-kan** slap s.t. against. *Ia* ~ *majalah ke kepala adikku* He slapped my little brother's head with a magazine.

keplését slip. *Ia - lalu jatuh* She slipped and fell.

keplok applause. **ber-** clap, applaud. ~ *riuh* applaud loudly. **meng-(kan)** *tangan* applaud, clap o.'s hands. **-an** applause.

kepodang see KEPUDANG.

kepoh, kepok meng-kan deflect, ward off (a blow).

kepompong cocoon, chrysalis, pupa.

keponakan nephew, niece.

kepos see POS.

képot₁ meng- swerve, zigzag. **meng-kan** make s.t. swerve.

képot₂ 1 crumpled, creased. 2 tousled, disheveled.

Kepprés [*Keputusan Présidén*] presidential decree, executive order. **mengk-kan** issue s.t. as a presidential decree.

keprak (*Jv*) small wooden box tapped for a casting-netlike beat. **meng-** hit, tap on s.t.

kepras meng- prune, trim, cut back.

képrét spill, spray. **meng-i** spill or spray on. **meng-kan** make wet, spill s.t., spray s.t. out.

keprétan (*Jkt*) slap with the back of the hand.

keprok₁ see KEPLOK.

keprok₂, kepruk₁ see JERUK.

kepruk₂ meng- smash, break open. *Ia* ~ *kelapa itu pd sebuah batu* He smashed the coconut against a stone. *Polisi* ~ *sarang perampok itu* The police destroyed the bandit's hideout.

kepudang oriole.

kepuh₁ 1 bulging (of briefcase, packet, etc.). 2 billowing (of sails). **meng-** 1 bulge (of a pocket, etc.). 2 billow (of sails). **peng-** s.t. that billows.

kepuh₂ k.o. tree producing soft, cheap wood and striking flowers.

kepuk₁ 1 basket made of bark to hold rice, etc. 2 name given to other baskets.

kepuk₂ dented. **meng-kan** dent s.t. **-an** indentation.

kepul billowing smoke. **ber-(²), meng-(²)** billow forth (of smoke). *reruntuh yg* ~ smoking ruins. **meng-kan** blow s.t. out, emit. **-an** billow of smoke.

kepulaga see KAPUL.

kepulesan see PULAS₁.

kepundan 1 lava. **2** crater. *lubang -* crater.

kepundung a tree with sour fruit similar to the *Lansium.*

kepung ber- encircling, sit or stand around. **meng- 1** surround, encircle. **2** besiege. **ter-1** surrounded, encircled. **2** beleaguered. **-an** encirclement, area surrounded. **peng-** besieger. **peng-an** encirclement, siege. ~ *polisi* police cordon.

kepuyuh see PUYUH₁.

kepuyuk cockroach.

kepyur (*Jv*) **meng-** sprinkle down. *Air hujan* ~ *di kepala kami* We got our heads wet in the rain. **meng-i** sprinkle on. **meng-kan** sprinkle s.t. on. ~ *air suci pd umatnya* sprinkle holy water on the congregation. **-an** s.t. sprinkled.

ker- see also entries with **kr-**.

kera k.o. ape. *- belanda* proboscis monkey.

kerab see AKRAB.

kerabang eggshell.

kerabat relative, family. *mengunjungi - yg tinggal di kota-kota jauh* visit relatives who live in distant cities. **ber- 1** be related to. *Saya* ~ *dgn dia* I am related to him. **2** be allied. **ke-an 1** kinship. **2** (*Ling.*) genetic relationship.

kerabik see KERABIT.

kerabit torn, ripped, rent. **meng-(kan)** rip, tear to shreds.

kerabu₁ salad of raw vegetables or unripe fruits. **meng-** prepare *kerabu.*

kerabu₂ ear studs (jewelry).

keracak₁ elated, jump with joy.

keracak₂ (*Naut.*) make good speed (of sailing vessels).

keracak₃ see KRÉCÉK.

keracap k.o. wooden or bamboo musical instrument.

keraéng see KARAÉNG.

kerah₁ corvée. **ber-** mobilized. **meng-kan 1** mobilize, conscript (workers, militia, etc.). **2** mobilize to do s.t., assemble (to carry out s.t.). *Guru - murid-muridnya membersihkan jalanan* The teacher got the students together to clean the street. ~ *tenaga* **1** recruit, call upon the services of. **2** do o.'s utmost. **peng-** o. who mobilizes, recruits, or drafts. ~ *negeri* state draft boards. **peng-an** conscription. ~ *tenaga* recruitment.

kerah₂ collar. *- lembik* soft collar.

kerahi k.o. small melon.

kerai 1 blinds made of thin bamboo slats. **2** awning.

kerait ber-² creaky (chair, bicycle, etc.).

kerajang gold leaf.

kerak 1 rice crust adhering to the pot. **2** encrustation. *- bumi* the earth's crust. *- besi* iron slag. *- roti* bread crust. **ber-** have a crust, encrust. *Pakaiannya* ~ His clothes are encrusted with dirt. **meng-** become encrusted, become a crust. *Busanya* ~ *di panci* The foam formed a crust in the pan. *Besi tua itu* ~ The old iron rusted. **ter-** completely encrusted.

kerakal gravel (e.g. for roadbed). **meng-i** apply a layer of gravel (to a roadbed).

kerakap betel leaf that has grown thick and tough.

kerakeling brass knuckles.

keram₁ have cramps. *Ia - kaki waktu berenang* He got cramps in his foot when he swam.

keram₂ meng- imprison, incarcerate, lock up.

kerama curse, spell.

keraman see KRAMAN.

keramas shampoo. *- kutu* hair wash for getting rid of lice. **ber-** shampoo o.s. **meng-** shampoo o.'s hair.

keramat 1 sacred, holy. **2** possessing supernatural qualities. **3** shrine, sacred spot. **meng-kan 1** consider sacred. **2** respect highly. *Ijazah sarjana amat di-kan* A master's diploma is highly respected.

kerambil (*Jv*) coconut.

kerambit 1 short clawlike dagger. **2** short sickle.

keramik /keramik/ ceramics.

kerampang perineum, crotch.

keramunting see KEMUNTING.

keran₁ tap, faucet, spigot. *- kebakaran* fire hydrant. *- léding* water faucet.

keran₂ crane, derrick.

keran₃ brazier, portable stove.

keran₄ ng- work as an assistant.

kerana see KARENA.

keranda (*Isl.*) a bier, consisting of a framework of bamboo or wooden laths which support the cloth covering a corpse.

kerang 1 cockle shells. **2** mollusks and their shells. *- hijau* green mussel. **-² 1** loose stones (bricks, etc.) arranged as a path (through muddy ground, shallow water, etc.). **2** shellfish. **ber-** seek or cultivate shellfish. **-²(an)** various k.o. mollusks. **pe(r)-an** heap of shells.

kérang (*Amb*) tortoise shell.

kerangga see KERENGGA.

keranggang see SEMUT.

kerangka 1 skeleton. **2** framework. *- rumah* framework of a house. *- pembakaran* grate for roasting. **3** ship's hull. *- pesawat* fuselage. **4** design, plan. *- acuan* frame of reference. **meng-i** provide with a framework. **ter- 1** still in the framework stage (of houses, ships, etc.). **2** have a plan set. *Repelita sdh* ~ The Five-Year Plan is shaping up.

kerangkai k.o. hard wood used for making wheel rims, hoe handles, etc.

kerangkang₁ see KELANGKANG.

kerangkang₂ see SEMUT.

kerangkéng 1 jail, lock up. **2** cage. **3** playpen.

kerang-keroh 1 crisscross, askew, awry (of lines).

2 irregular (in shape). 3 rambling (of a house, city layout). 4 conniving, scheming.
kerang-kerung clattering (of dishes).
kerani office clerk.
keranjang k.o. basket. - *pakaian* clothes hamper. - *sampah* wastebasket. **ber-²** by the basketful. **meng-kan, meng-i** place in a basket.
keranji k.o. timber tree.
keranjing meng-i be fond of. *gula pasir yg di-i masyarakat* granulated sugar which the public prefers. **meng-kan** incite, whip up (interest, etc.). **ke-an** 1 have a mania for. 2 mania for doing s.t. *Ia terpaksa bayar mahal utk ~nya dlm balapan mobil* He had to pay dearly for his mania for car racing. **-an** have a mania for. *~ menonton bioskop* be crazy about movies.
keranta louse found on a dead or dying body.
kerantong, kerantung bamboo or wooden drum used as an alarm.
kerap₁ 1 close. *Kain itu - tenunannya* That cloth is tightly woven. 2 often, frequently. *Ia - datang ke sini* She often came here. *- kali often, frequently*. **meng-** become frequent. **meng-i** repeat over and over. **meng-kan** tighten, weave closely. **ke-an** frequency.
kerap₂ meng- race bulls. **-an** bull race.
kerapai see GERAPAI.
kerapis see KEROPAS-KERAPIS.
kerap-kerap sound of munching.
kerapu k.o. seafish, the grouper.
keras 1 hard (not soft). 2 (*Phys.*) solid state. - *kematu* hard as a rock. - *makas/mangkas* hard (of fruit). 3 tight, not flexible, taut. *terikat -* tightly bond. *- lidah* have difficulty in pronouncing (lit., stiff tongued). 4 strong. *desakan yg -* a strong urge. *minuman -* strong drink. *keinginan yg -* strong desire. *- batang léhér/insang* stubborn. - *genjur* stern of character. - *hati* firm, persevering, stubborn. - *hidung* narrow-minded, bigoted. - *kepala* stubborn. **ke-kepalaan** obstinacy. 5 hard (with effort). *Ia bekerja -* She works hard. *Hujan -* It rained hard, downpour. 6 gruff (speech, attitude). - *mulut* argumentative, quarrelsome. 7 loud (voice, etc.). 8 stern, stringent (measures). *Ia dijaga -* He was closely watched. *peringatan -* stern warning. - *tegas* rigorous. 9 seriously. *pikiran yg terganggu -* seriously disturbed mind. *panas -* high fever. **bersi-** persist in, absolutely insist on. **ber-** 1 persist. *Ia ~ pd pendiriannya* He persisted in his stand. 2 be hard. *Opsir itu ~ thd anak buahnya* That officer was hard on his men. 3 use force. 4 insist. *Ia ~ spy isterinya meninggalkannya* He insisted that his wife leave him. *~ hati* 1 persevere. 2 be firm. *Meski pun hampir habis tenaganya ia ~ hati* Although he was near the end of his rope, he kept on. *~ kepala* stubborn. **ber-²an** be persistent in opposing e.o. *Kedua org itu ~ mempertahankan pendirian meréka masing-masing* The two persons were persistent in defending their respective viewpoints. *~ mulut* have words, have an argument. **meng-** 1 become hard, harden. *Semén itu ~* The cement

became hard. 2 become louder. *Suaranya ~* Her voice became louder. **meng-i** 1 use force on. *Jangan -i meréka; cobalah cara-cara damai dulu* Do not use force on them; try peaceful means first. 2 treat harshly, roughly. *Anak itu jangan di-i* Don't be harsh with that child. **memper-, meng-kan** 1 harden, stiffen s.t. *Matahari ~ tanah liat itu* The sun hardened the clay. 2 strengthen s.t. 3 force s.o. 4 tighten a screw. 5 amplify the voice. **ke-an** 1 hardness. 2 harshness. 3 loudness. 4 force, violence. *Jika perlu, pergunakanlah ~* Use force if necessary. 5 severity, sternness. 6 stringency, rigor. **peng-** hardener. *Latihan jasmani ~ otot* Physical exercise hardens the muscles. *~ suara* amplifier, loudspeaker. **peng-an** 1 hardening (of s.t.). *~ nadi* arteriosclerosis. 2 amplification (of sound). 3 coercion, force, forceful measure.
kerasan see KRASAN.
keras-keras k.o. crispy cookie.
keras-tulang k.o. plant, the leaves of which are used for medicinal purposes.
kerat₁ 1 slice, piece, part. *daging se-* a slice of meat. 2 part (of a house, road, town). *se- malam* (*Lit.*) a part of the night. **ber-** be cut into pieces. *~ rotan* sever relations, break a friendship. **meng-(i)** 1 cut off pieces, amputate. *~ lidah* interrupt. 2 pare down, reduce. *~ jumlah itu menjadi hanya lima puluh* pare the total down to only 50. **-an** a piece cut off. *daging hasil ~ tadi pagi* meat sliced this morning. **peng-an** the action of cutting s.t. off.
kerat₂ sound of munching. **meng-** nibble, gnaw. **peng-** *binatang ~* rodent.
kerat₃ see KARAT₁.
kerat₄ see KRAT.
keraton palace, esp. of a Jv ruler. **ke-an** having to do with the court. *suasana ~* atmosphere like that of the royal palace.
kerawai₁ k.o. wasp that lives underground or has a nest made of earth.
kerawai₂ k.o. plant.
kerawang 1 filigree. 2 openwork (on cloth, embroidery, lacework). **meng-** do openwork. *~ langit* fantasize (embroider the skies). *Angan-angan ~ kepalanya* Thoughts were embroidering fancies in her mind.
kerawat band of iron or plaited rattan (on the handle of knife or chisel).
kerawit see CACING.
kerbang₁ k.o. wild breadfruit tree.
kerbang₂ see GERBANG₂.
kerbat meng- *mulut* gag s.o.
kerbau 1 carabao, water buffalo. - *péndék* (*Humorous*) pig. *waktu - turun berendam* around five p.m. (when the carabaos wallow to rest). *membeli - di padang* buy a pig in a poke. 2 stupid person.
kercap see KECAP.
kercék crunching sound. **ber-** make a crunching sound.
kercing meng-kan *mata* shut o.'s eyes.
kercit meng-kan *mata* wink.

kercut k.o. rush used for weaving mats, etc.

kerdak 1 dregs, sediment (of coffee, wine, etc.). **2** objects of no value, junk. **3** modest way to refer to o.'s own possessions. *Hanya rumah inilah - saya* The only junk I own is this house.

kerdam boom, loud, resonating sound. **ber-** *loncéng* toll a bell.

kerdil 1 dwarf, stunted. **2** small-minded. **meng-kan** dwarf, stunt (growth, etc.). **ke-an** dwarfishness, smallness. ~ *pendapat bisa disebabkan karena kurangnya pergaulan* Not having social intercourse can make o. petty minded. **-an** petty bickering.

kerdip see KEDIP.

kerdom be(r)-(²) cuss, engage in abusive language. **meng-kan** cuss at s.o.

kerdum booming, resounding sound.

kerdus see KARDUS.

kerdut 1 wrinkled. **2** corrugated.

keré see KERAI.

kéré₁ (*Jv*) puppy.

kéré₂ beggar, vagrant, tramp.

keréat-keréot rickety, squeaking.

kerébok meng- tear s.t.

kerecék see KERCÉK.

kerécéng see KÉCÉNG.

keredak 1 caked, dried-up dirt (on people, animals, etc.). **2** dried mucus in the nose.

kerédép see KEDIP.

kerédok see KARÉDOK.

keredong cover, blanket. **ber-** wrapped, covered (in a blanket, sarong).

keréi see KERAI.

kerék see KERIK.

kérék₁ hoist, pulley (block). - *jalan* motorized crane. - *rantai* chain tackle. **meng- 1** hoist, raise (a flag). **2** lift with a hoist (as of a cargo). **-an** hoist for bucket at well.

kérék₂ a measure for palm sugar. *se- gula enau* 10 lumps of palm sugar.

kerekah see KERKAH.

kerékét sound of squeaking or cracking (of wood, teeth grating, etc.). **ber-** make such a sound. *Papan-papan dipan itu* ~ *sehingga kami tdk dpt tidur* The boards of the couch squeaked so that we could not sleep.

kerékot, kerékut 1 grown deformed (of hands, limbs, fingers, etc.). **2** rough, uneven (of a floor). **3** stingy, avaricious.

keremi pinworms, intestinal worms. **-an, ke-an 1** suffer from pinworms. **2** itch in the anus from pinworms.

keremot wrinkled, furrowed (of the face).

kerempagi 1 straight razor. **2** pocketknife.

kerempang, kerémpéng emaciated, thin. **ke-an** thinness.

kerempung lower abdomen.

keremunting see KEMUNTING.

kerén 1 impressive, handsome (of a man). **2** dashing, well-dressed. *Wah, - betul pakai baju baru nyetir mobil Mercédés!* Hey! Hot stuff! Wearing a new suit and driving a Mercedes! **3** spirited, fast (of a horse).

kéren see KÉRN.

kerena see KARENA.

kerencang, kerencing, kerencung sound of clanging chains, etc.

kerendang k.o. spreading weed with edible leaves used as fodder.

kereneng (*Jv*) a net of bamboo strips for carrying small loose items.

kereng gruff, surly, grumpy.

keréng see KERING₁.

kerengga k.o. large biting red ant.

kerengkam a seaweed.

kerengket shiver with fear.

kereningan tinkling sound.

kerenyam geranium.

kerenyau see KERNYAU₁.

kerenyit see KERNYIT.

kerényot meng- 1 grin. **2** twist or distort o.'s mouth.

kerenyut see KERNYUT₁,₂.

kerepas blind in o. eye. **meng-** *mata* shut o. eye.

kerépés meng- grope for s.t.

kerépot wrinkled. *Sdh - masih ingin kawin lagi* He is old and wrinkled but he wants to marry again.

kererangga see KERENGGA.

keresak, keresek sound of rustling or snapping (of dry leaves). **ber-, ter-** rustle, crunch. *Bunyi langkahnya* ~ *di atas kerikil halamannya* His steps made a rustling sound on the gravel in the yard.

kerések see KERISIK.

keréséng cracked open, slightly open. **meng-, ter-** crack open.

kerésé-pésé see KARÉSÉH-PÉSÉH.

kerésmis see KISMIS.

kerésot wrinkled, furrowed (of forehead).

keret₁ meng- cut s.t.

keret₂ see MENGKERET.

keréta 1 carriage, cart. - *anak* baby carriage. - *angin* (*Lit.*) bicycle. - *api* train. **per-apian** railway affairs. - *api bumel* local train. - *baja* armored car. - *bogi* horse-drawn buggy. - *dorong* pushcart, wheelbarrow. - *gandéngan* trailer. - *gantung* cable car. - *jenazah* hearse. - *kencana* golden chariot. - *léréng* bicycle. - *pasién* hospital cart. - *pengiring* trailer. - *ruang* space ship. - *sétan* ghost train. - *sorong* pushcart, wheelbarrow. - *tambangan* carriage for rent. - *tangan* pushcart, handcart. - *témpél* trailer. - *tolak* hand car. - *waja* armored car. **2** car. **ber- 1** have a carriage. **2** ride in a carriage.

keretak sound of snapping or cracking. - *keretik* creaking. **ber-** *keretik* creak (of stairs). - *kertuk* creak and rattle. **ber-** make a snapping or rattling noise. **meng-kan** cause s.t. to snap or rattle. ~ *gigi* gnash the teeth.

kérétan a pull.

keretek bridge.

keréték₁ (*Jv*) horse-drawn two-wheeled cart.

keréték₂ see KRÉTÉK₁.

keréték₃ see KRITIK.

keretik see KERTIK.

kerétot deformed (of limbs, fingers, etc.), uneven (of a surface).

keréwéng fragment of broken tile.

keri k.o. small sickle for cutting grass. meng- cut grass with this instrument.

keria k.o. cake made of sugar, flour, and potatoes.

keriang-keriut sound of squeezing and creaking (e.g. stairs). ber- make a creaky sound.

keriap ber-an, meng- swarm. *Semut ~ pd makanan* Ants swarmed over the food.

keriat-keriut see KERIANG-KERIUT.

kericau 1 chirp, twitter. 2 chatter.

kericik sound of splashing water. ber-(an) make a splashing sound.

keridas see KADAS.

keridik mole cricket. - *pesan-pesan* k.o. stinging insect.

kerih sound of a screaming monkey. meng- scream like a monkey (from pain, etc.).

kerik meng- scrape or shave off or s.t., scrape s.t. meng-i treat illness by scraping a coin over o.'s back, inducing hyperemia of the skin, chafe s.o. -an 1 scratch. 2 scrapings. 3 have o.'s back rubbed with a coin.

kerikam k.o. linen.

kerikil pebble, gravel. meng-(i) cover with gravel.

kerikit meng- gnaw, nibble. meng-i gnaw or nibble at.

kerimut meng- 1 undo, rumple. 2 hurt (feelings, etc.).

kerincing 1 sound of tinkling, jingling. 2 k.o. musical instrument, the triangle. ber-(an), meng- jingle, tingle. meng-kan make s.t. jingle.

kering₁ 1 dry, dried off or up. *ikan* - dried fish. - *darah(nya)* be shocked (lit., for the blood to dry up). - *embun* between seven and eight a.m. (lit., when the dew dries). - *kerontang* dry as a bone, completely dried up (of a well, creek). - *ringkai* bone-dry (of laundry in the sun). *blm - lidah utk memberi kritik* has not ceased criticizing (lit., the tongue is not to dry to criticize). 2 arid. *Tanah itu - * That soil is arid. - *kersang* barren. 3 not lucrative, poorly paid. *Saya lagi - kantong* I am broke. *jabatan yg - * a gvt. post with little or no chance for kickbacks. 4 crispy. 5 dish made of ingredients chopped up, spiced, and fried until crisp. -² ~ *air* moist, humid. meng- 1 dry out (of s.t. wet). 2 become dry (of a well, etc.). 3 dry up. *Sumber modalnya* ~ The source of capital dried up. meng-i drain s.t. meng-kan 1 dry s.t. out. 2 drain s.t. 3 dry s.t. up. ke-an 1 dryness, aridity. 2 drought. 3 too dry. 4 having a scarcity of wealth, food, etc., dry up on. ~ *binatang sembelihan, meréka makan burung* When they ran out of animals to slaughter, they ate birds. peng- drier, dehumidifier. ~ *rambut* hair dryer. ~ *tinta* blotter. peng-an 1 drainage, draining. 2 drying up, dehydration. 3 desiccation.

kering₂ sound of ringing. ber-² make a ringing sound.

keringat, keringet sweat, perspiration. - *buntat/ buntel* rash, prickly heat. - *dingin* a cold sweat. ber- 1 sweat, perspire. 2 be sweaty. meng-kan 1 expend sweat. 2 sweat over s.t. *yg sdh di-kan* what o. has sweated over. -an sweaty, perspiring.

kerining sound of bicycle bells, carts, etc. ber- sound a bell. -an bicycle bell.

kerinjal kidney.

kerinjing k.o. hardwood tree used for construction.

kerintil hang in clusters or bunches (fruit, etc.).

kerinting₁ salted shellfish.

kerinting₂ see KERITING.

kerinyit ber- see KERNYIT.

kerinyut see KERNYUT₁,₂.

kerip meng- 1 crackle (of gravel, etc.). 2 nibble, gnaw (of rat, squirrel).

keripik crispy chips (of banana, potato, témpéh, etc.). - *éléktronik* microchip. meng- flake, scale s.t.

keriput₁ wrinkled, furrowed, wizened (of face, etc.). ber- wrinkled. meng- become wrinkled. ke-an state of being wrinkled.

keriput₂ see JERUK.

keris kris, k.o. wavy double-bladed dagger. - *pendarah* kris that has drawn blood. - *sakti* magic kris. ber- wear or carry a kris. meng- use a kris, stab with a kris.

kerisik 1 rustling sound. 2 dried banana leaf. ber-, ter- rustle (of leaves, etc.). ~ *dlm semak* make a rustling sound in the bushes. meng- peel because of drying. *Kulit saya* ~ My skin is peeling. -an 1 rustling. 2 peeling off.

kerising meng- grin.

Keristen see KRISTEN.

kerisut see KISUT.

kerit sound of scraping on metal. - *dayung* cricket. ber- make a scraping sound. meng-kan cause s.t. to make a scraping sound. ~ *gigi* gnash the teeth.

keritik₁ sound of crackling. ber-² crackle, sputter (of a lighted candle).

keritik₂ see KRITIK.

keriting curly, kinky (of hair). meng-(i) curl (the hair).

keriuk crowing. ber- crow (of a rooster). ber-², ter-² rumble (of the stomach).

keriut sound of creaking, squeaking, or scraping. ber-an make such a sound. -an the squeaking sound produced by s.t. *Tapi sewaktu* ~ *bunyi rém jip . . .* But at the time that the jeep's brakes made a screeching sound . . .

keriwil see PRIWIL.

kerja 1 work. - *antara* cooperation between. - *bakti* 1 voluntary labor service, work assignment. 2 detail, team. - *borong* contract work. - *halus* 1 white-collar work. 2 fine work (e.g. jewelry-making). - *kasar* manual labor, blue-collar work. - *lembur* overtime (work). - *paksa* forced labor, servitude. - *raja* forced/statute labor. - *tetap* permanent work. - *trampil* skilled labor. 2 occupation, job. -*nya mengetik surat* Her job was typing letters. 3 activity. *Apa -mu datang di kantor pos?* What were you doing at the post office? 4 celebration (of an important rite in life). - *kawinan* a wedding celebration. - *khitanan* celebration of circumcision. **se-** colleague. **be-** 1 work. ~ *keras* work hard. ~ *rodi* do forced labor. ~ *penuh* have a fulltime job. *dpt* ~ *sendiri* able to work without supervision. 2 active (of a volcano, etc.). 3 have a celebration or ceremony. **meng-i** 1 work on s.t. to prepare it. ~ *mayat* prepare a body for burial. 2 (*Coll.*) have sex with. **meng-kan** 1 do, carry out. *Ia* ~ *tugasnya dgn rajin* She did her work diligently. *-kan!* Carry on! 2 work (a field, land, etc.). 3 finish off, eliminate, kill. 4 perform (a task). **-in** (*Jkt*) 1 give a beating. ~ *saja anak bandel itu* Give that naughty child a beating. 2 have sex with. **mempe-kan** employ, put to work, assign. *Ia* ~ *anaknya pd perusahaannya* He put his son to work at his firm. ~ *jantung* exercise the heart. **te-kan** 1 done, performed, carried out. 2 workable, can be carried out. **-an** work. *Saya banyak* ~ I have lots of things to do. **pe-** worker, laborer, employee. ~ *dinas* gvt. employee, civil servant. ~ *halus* white-collar worker. ~ *tangan* manual laborer. **pe-an** 1 work, task, activity. ~ *rumah tangga* household chores. ~ *umum* public works. 2 job, occupation, business, enterprise, line. 3 operation, working, action (of medicine, a chemical, liquor). ~ *kapilér/ pembuluh rambur* capillary action. ~ *mesin mobil* the way in which a car engine operates. 4 celebration, feast (a wedding, anniversary, etc.). 5 endeavor. *lapangan* ~ field of endeavor. 6 employment. ~ *penuh* full employment. **sepe-an** colleague. **peng-an** 1 execution, working on s.t. 2 processing, working. ~ *bahan mentah itu* the processing of raw material.

kerjang see EMAS.

kerjantara employment agency.

kerjap see KEJAP.

kerjasama cooperation. *Program ini dlm rangka - antara AS dan Indonesia* This program is a cooperative o. between the US and Indonesia.

kerkah meng- rip apart with the teeth and eat. **meng-i** crunch on s.t.

kerkak sound of a bone being crushed.

kerkap see KERKAH, KERKAK, KERAKAP.

kerkau meng- seize with a claw.

kérkop (*Coll.*) Christian cemetery.

kerkup sound of cracking. **ber-(²)** crack, crackle. **meng-kan** cause s.t. to make a crackling sound.

kerlap₁ glare, glistening. - *sinar matahari/lampu* the glare of the sunrays or lamp. - *air* glistening of the water. - *kerlip* flickering (of lamplight, candle). **ke-an, meng-** twinkle (of stars), sparkle, glisten.

kerlap₂ meng-, te- doze off for a moment.

kerling₁ glance out of the corner of the eyes. **meng-** 1 glance sidewise. *Ia* ~ *pd saya dan tersenyum* She gave me a side glance and smiled. 2 eye s.t. with a view to obtaining it. **meng-i** steal a glance at. **meng-kan** *mata* throw a side glance. **-an** 1 side glance. 2 eyed, aimed at. *Sinabang makin menjadi* ~ *org-org pemerintah karena hasil cengkéhnya* Sinabang is being more and more eyed by gvt. people because of its clove produc-

tion. **-²an** ogling, side glances, making eyes at s.o.

kerling₂ shining, gleaming, sparkling. **-an** light given off. ~ *mata hari* weak sun rays.

kerlip₁ flickering (of light). **se-** *mata* in a wink. **be-, meng-** 1 flicker (of candle, star). 2 blink (of stars, eyes). **be-an** flicker, twinkle dimly. *Bintang-bintang* ~ *suram* The stars blinked dimly.

kerlip₂ fall in love. *Ia - pd gadis di sebelah rumahnya* He fell in love with the girl next door. **meng-kan** cause s.o. to fall in love.

kerma see KERAMA.

kermak k.o. herb.

kermi see KEREMI.

kérn /kéren/ (*Coll.*) nucleus, nuclear.

kernai meng- cut into small pieces (of meat, vegetables).

kernék see KENÉK.

kernéli vanilla.

kernét see KENÉK.

kernyat-kernyut sound of creaking (of door, shoes, floor, etc.). *Sepatunya masih -* His shoes are so new they squeak.

kernyau₁ sound of crunching, sound of s.o. munching.

kernyau₂ hoarse (of voice).

kernyih grinning, making faces (to show ridicule). **meng-** grin, make faces.

kernying meng- bare the teeth or fangs.

kernyit furrow. **ber-, meng-** frown. **meng-kan** *alis/kening* frown.

kernyut₁ wrinkle. - *muka* crow's feet, wrinkles in the face. **be-, -an** wrinkled. *Keningnya* ~ Her forehead was wrinkled. **meng-** wrinkle, frown. **meng-kan** *dahi* knit o.'s brows.

kernyut₂ gnashing of teeth.

kernyut₃ be- pulsate (of arteries).

kéro₁ bed with springs.

kéro₂ squinting, cross-eyed.

kerobak 1 with holes. *Dinding - kena peluru mortir* The wall had a big hole which was caused by a mortar shell. 2 with a large rip (of a sail, flag, etc.). 3 scarred, pockmarked. - *kerabik/kerabit/ kerobék* 1 in tatters (of flag, sail). 2 badly scarred.

kerobék see ROBÉK.

kerocok rattling noise, sound of liquid being shaken in a bottle, or of light objects falling rapidly.

kerodong see KERUDUNG.

kéroh 1 false, deceptive, crooked. 2 confusing, hazy, unclear.

kerok₁ currycomb. **meng-** 1 curry, rub down, groom (a horse). 2 chafe s.o. with a coin as a medical treatment. **-an** have o.'s back rubbed with a coin.

kerok₂ see KERUK.

kerolok sound of gurgling. **ber-** gurgle.

keromok see KERUMUK₁.

keromong (*Sd*) set of kettle gongs suspended horizontally in a row.

keron (*Coll.*) crown (symbol of Dutch rule).

keroncong₁ 1 sound of clanking, jingling (of cow

bells, etc.). *gelang* - a set of braclets worn together. **2** popular Indonesian music originating from Portuguese songs. **3** k.o. small guitar or ukulele. **ber-** **1** perform *keroncong*. **2** grumble, growl. *Perutnya* ~ His stomach growled. **meng-** make s.t. produce a bubbling sound (e.g. cook rice). **-an** **1** growl, rumble. **2** music produced with bells or jingling.

keroncong₂ deepest recess of a fish trap. *ikan di -* beyond help. **meng-kan** *(bibir)* round the lips (in the shape of a fish trap).

keroncong₃ k.o. plant which furnishes green fertilizer.

keroncor male horseshoe crab.

kerong, kerong-kerang sound of a heavy object being shaken in a tin can.

kérong-kérong k.o. small sea perch.

kerongkongan **1** throat. **2** gullet, esophagus, pharynx.

kerongsang brooch, esp. a set of three brooches used to fasten together women's traditional blouses.

kerongsong see KELONGSONG.

kerontang₁ sound of rattling (of a bucket).

kerontang₂ see KERING₁.

keropak palm leaf manuscript used to write on.

keropas-kerapis small articles or objects of no value. **ber-** do work or activity of no importance.

keropéng scab (of a wound, skin eruption, rash). **meng-** pick a scab.

keropes dried nasal mucus.

keropok₁ **se-** small group.

keropok₂ **1** hollow, empty. **2** eaten at by ants.

keropok₃ see KERUPUK.

keropong hollow, eaten away (of interiors).

keropos **1** porous, spongy. **2** hollow, rotten. **3** rarefied (gas).

kerosak sound of treading on dry leaves or twigs.

kerosang see KERONGSANG.

kerosék sound of swishing (e.g. rinsing uncooked rice).

kerosi see KURSI₁.

kerosin kerosene.

kerosok₁ sound of treading on dry leaves. **ber-, meng-** **1** rustle (of leaves), make this sound. **2** be dry.

kerosok₂ see TEMBAKAU.

kerosong sloughed skin (of reptiles). **meng-** molt, slough the skin.

kerotak sound of things grinding or clashing against e.o.

kerotot **1** grooved (of a file). **2** pockmarked, furrowed, wrinkled (like the skin of a tangerine).

keroyok meng- gang up on, swarm over, overwhelm. **-an** attack by overwhelming numbers. **peng-** attackers. **peng-an** attacking, overwhelming of.

kerpai cartridge pouch.

kerpak sound of cracking (e.g. a branch being snapped).

kerpas sound of rustling, (e.g. treading on bushes, etc.).

kerpik see KERPAK.

kerpis see KERPAS.

kerpu *(Geol.)* blende.

kerpus₁ k.o. headgear, k.o. cap.

kerpus₂ a plastered ridge along the top of a tile roof. **meng-** make a plastered roof ridge. **-an** roof ridge made of plaster.

kerpus₃ guardhouse, cell. **meng-** *(Mil.)* place in a cell.

kerrén see KERÉN.

kersai crumbly, loose (of cooked rice, sand).

kersak sound of treading on dry grass.

kersang see GERSANG.

kérsen cherry.

kersik₁ grit, gravel, coarse sand. **meng-i** cover with a layer of coarse sand.

kersik₂ see KERISIK.

kersip see KEDIP.

kérsmis *(Coll.)* Christmas.

kersuk sound of loud rustling.

kertah k.o land crab.

kertang₁ caked (with mud, dried blood, pus).

kertang₂ sound of striking a tin can. **meng-** bang on a tin can. **meng-kan** *perisai* bang on a shield to make a noise (in battle, etc.).

kertang₃ k.o. sea fish, a large and vicious grouper.

kertap sound of a door being slammed.

kertas₁ paper. *- ampelas* sandpaper. *- atap* roofing paper. *- bertinta* carbon paper. *- bungkus* wrapping paper. *- buram* scratch paper. *- buyar* **1** blotting paper. **2** tissue paper. *- cd* k.o. coarse grade of paper. *- cétak* printing paper. *- corét* scratch paper. *- dinding* wallpaper. *- éfék* stocks, securities. *- embun* blotting paper. *- folio* foolscap. *- isap* blotting paper. *- jernih/jiplak* tracing paper. *- kaca* cellophane. *- kado* gift-wrapping paper. *- karbon* carbon paper. *- karton* cardboard. *- kembang* **1** blotting paper. **2** tissue paper. *- kerja* working paper. *- klosét* toilet paper. *- koordinir* graph paper. *- koran* newsprint. *- kraft* bond paper. *- krép* crepe paper. *- kulit* parchment. *- lap* blotting paper. *- merang* rice paper. *- materai* stamped paper, document with seal. *- minyak* waxpaper. *- pelui/penyerap* blotting paper. *- pérak* tinfoil. *- samak* paper to cover books. *- saring* filter paper. *- ségél* document with an official seal. *- suara* ballot. *- surat* stationery, writing paper. *- tapis* filter paper. *- tebal* cardboard. *- telur* waxpaper. *- tulis* stationery, writing paper. *-* **meng-** **1** wastepaper. **2** various types of paper.

kertas₂ sound of paper being crumpled.

kertau mulberry tree.

kertik ticking sound.

kertika see KARTIKA.

kerting sound of tinging.

kertu see KARTU.

kertuk sound of knocking.

kertus₁ cartridge (of a gun).

kertus₂ sound of paper being crumpled.

keruan known. *Kedatangannya blm -* It is not known for sure if she will arrive. *- saja* of course, by all means. *tdk* - make no sense, erratic, chaotic. *Karangannya itu tdk* - His article did not make any sense. *rencana pekerjaan yg tdk* - a confused working schedule. *Dlm kabut rumah-rumah tdk* - *nampakya* In the fog the houses were very vague. *kegelisahan yg tdk* - extreme nervousness. *berbicara tak* - talk incoherently.

kerubung ber-, meng- encircling in numbers. **meng-i** crowd around. *tahi yg di-i lalat* the feces that the flies swarmed around. **-an** mob that has crowded round.

kerubut₁ meng- gang up on, mob s.o. **meng-i** 1 crowd around. *Murid-murid ~ guru meréka* Pupils crowded around their teacher. 2 swarm over. *Semut-semut ~ kakinya* Ants swarmed over his foot. **-an** crowd.

kerubut₂ k.o. parasite bearing showy flowers.

kerucil see WAYANG.

kerucut 1 cone. 2 conical paper wrapper (for peanuts, etc.). **meng-** conical.

kerudung veil. - *lampu* lampshade. **ber-** veiled. **meng-i** veil s.t.

keruh₁ 1 turbid, muddy. 2 disturbed, clouded (of face). *Mukanya* - His face was disturbed. 3 restless. *Seluruh negara* - The whole country was restless. **meng-** 1 become turbid or muddy. 2 cloud up or over. *Lénsa ~* The lens clouded up. **meng-i** render turbid. *Air di-i oléh warna mérah* The red color made the water turbid. **meng-kan** 1 muddy, make s.t. muddy. *Hujan ~ air kali* The rain made the river muddy. 2 disturb. *Kaum pemberontak ~ keamanan dlm negara* Rebels disturbed the peace of the nation. **ke-an** 1 muddiness, turbidity, cloudiness. 2 unrest, disturbance. 3 irregularity, corruption. *~ dlm pembukuan keuangan* irregularities in the bookkeeping.

keruh₂ snoring. **ber-, meng-** 1 snore. 2 purr (of a cat).

keruing k.o. tree.

keruit ber-² wiggle, wriggle at its end, wag (a tail).

keruk 1 scratching, scraping sound. 2 dredging. *kapal* - a dredge. **meng-** 1 scrape. 2 dredge (a river, etc.). 3 stick o.'s hand into (o.'s pocket, etc. searching for s.t.). *-- untung yg besar* manage to get a huge profit out of s.t. **meng-kan** *tangan* put o.'s hands into s.t. searching for s.t. **peng-** 1 scraper, dredge. 2 exploiter. *~ periuk* glutton. **peng-an** 1 dredging. 2 exploitation. *~ kekayaan negara* exploitation of the nation's resources.

kerukut 1 curled up or over, warped (of wood, etc.), curled (of leaves). 2 deformed (of hands, feet). **meng-** curl up, become warped or deformed. **meng-kan** cause s.t. to curl up.

kerul curl (in the hair, etc.). **meng-** curl the hair.

keruma k.o. itching mite.

kerumit meng- gnaw, nibble (of rabbits, mice). **meng-i** nibble on. *Ia ~ kerak nasi* It nibbled on the rice crust.

kerumuk₁ ber-, meng- be crumpled, wrinkled. **meng-kan** 1 crumple (paper). 2 wrinkle s.t. **ter-** get crumpled, wrinkled.

kerumuk₂ ber- slump (in a chair), sink down.

kerumun ber- 1 swarm over, cluster around, throng, mill about. *Org-org ~ di lapangan* People were swarming over the field. 2 assemble, come together. **meng-i** crowd around s.t. *Meréka ~ tempat penjualan karcis* They crowded around the ticket office. **meng-kan, memper-kan** cause s.t. to swarm around. **-an** throng, crowd, mob. *Ia hilang dlm ~ tubuh-tubuh yg mabok* He disappeared in the mob of drunken bodies. **peng-an** clustering, grouping.

kerumus meng- 1 embrace and kiss. 2 fondle, caress.

kerun see KERON.

kerung concave, hollow, hollowed out (of a spoon, bowl).

kerunia see KARUNIA.

keruntang-pungkang head-over-heels.

keruntung 1 piggy bank (made of a bamboo cylinder). 2 fish basket. **meng-kan** place s.t. in a *keruntung*.

kerunyit see KERNYIT.

kerunyut wrinkle, furrow (in face). **ber-** wrinkled, shriveled (of face).

kerup sound of munching.

kerupuk chips made of flour flavored with fish or shrimp. *- belinjo* chips made from the fruit of the *belinjo*. *- kerak* chips made of hard-boiled rice and fruit. *- kulit* crackled water-buffalo rinds.

kerupung see KEROPÉNG.

kerus k.o. carbonated drink (e.g. orange crush).

kerusi see KURSI₁.

kerusut ber-, meng- 1 shrink (of material). 2 crease, wrinkle.

kerut₁ 1 furrow, wrinkle. *- merut* wrinkled, creased. *memancarkan - merut* show a wrinkled face. **ber-** *merut* frown. 2 curl (in hair). **ber-, ter-** furrowed, wrinkled, creased. *Dahinya ~* His brow was furrowed. **meng(k)-** 1 shrivel, contract (of muscles). 2 wrinkle, crease, furrow. 3 frown. **meng(k)-kan** shrink, contract (o.'s muscles). *~ dahi* frown. *~ gigi* gnash the teeth. *~ kening* knit o.'s brow. *~ kulit* wrinkle the skin. **-an** 1 contraction. *~ otot-otot jantung* contraction of the heart muscles. 2 wrinkling, creasing. *terjadinya ~ mékanis* creasing that took place mechanically.

kerut₂ sound of scraping.

kerutak meng- crunch (on a bone).

kerutu see GERUTU₁.

kerutup sound of crackling (e.g. dry leaves burning).

keruwing see KERUING.

keruyuk₁ see KERIUK.

keruyuk₂ see KEROYOK.

kes.₁ [*kesebelasan*] soccer team.

kes.₂ [*keséhatan*] health.

kés (*Coll.*) cash. *Pembelian itu dibayar* - The purchase was paid for in cash.

kesa first (us. only of planting season).

kesad see KASAD.

kesah moan, sigh. **ber-, meng-** moan, sigh.

késah see KISAH.

kesak meng- 1 shift, move slowly (from o. place to another). **2** move or shift s.t.

kesal 1 fed up. *Saya - melakukan pekerjaan ini* I am fed up with this job. **2** dejected. **3** piqued, peevish, cross. *Ia - karena kalah berdébat* He is cross because he lost the debate. *- gamas* **1** very disappointed. **2** fed up and cross. *- hati* fed up, piqued, annoyed. **ber-** *hati* be fed up, vexed. **meng-kan 1** annoy, peeve, annoying. **2** make s.o., fed up. *Segala kesukaran itu ~ hatinya* All those difficulties made him fed up. **ke-an 1** annoyance. **2** being fed up.

kesambet (*Jv*) be seized with a sudden illness, attributed to possession by an evil spirit.

kesambi k.o. tree yielding wood for charcoal.

kesamping see SAMPING₁.

kesan 1 impression. *- tetap* lasting impression. **2** trace. *- pukulan* traces of a beating. **ber- 1** have the impression. **2** make an impression. *Segala ajaran gurunya tak ~ pdnya* All that her teacher taught her made no impression. **meng- 1** leave traces. **2** leave an impression. *Ceritera itu sangat ~ di hatinya* That story left an impression on him. **meng-kan, memper-kan 1** give an impression. *tanpa ~ perobahan dlm dirinya* without giving any impressions of a change within him. *Ia tdk mau duduk dan itu ~ bhw ia betul-betul marah* He did not want to take a seat and that gave the impression that he was really angry. **2** impress, impressive. *pésta yg ~* an impressive party. **ter-1** impressed. **2** imprinted. *Sikap itu ~ dlm kebijaksanaan pemerintah* That attitude was imprinted on gvt. policy.

kesana see SANA.

kesandung see SANDUNG.

kesang meng- blow o.'s nose by pressing o. nostril with the finger.

kesangsang (*Jv*) be caught (of a kite in a tree, etc.). *Layangan - di pohon* A kite was caught in the tree.

kesap-kesip blink (of the eyes).

kesasar see SASAR.

kesat 1 stiff, rough. **2** rough and dry (of skin). **3** shaggy, hairy. **meng-** wipe dry. *~ dahinya* wipe o.'s brow. **meng-kan** dry off s.t. **peng-** *kaki* doormat.

kesatria 1 noble (caste), knight. **2** acting with noble qualities. **ke-an** gallantry, knighthood, nobleness. **-an** military base, headquarters.

keséd see KÉSÉT₂.

kesejatian see SEJATI.

késék 1 rubbing. **2** door mat. **meng- 1** rub with a coarse object. **2** persuade s.o.

kesel₁ (*Jv*) tired, exhausted.

kesel₂ see KESAL.

keseleg, keselek /keselek/ choke on s.t., swallow s.t. the wrong way.

keseléo be sprained. *Kaki saya - I* sprained my ankle. *- lidah* slip of the tongue. **meng-kan** twist (a regulation).

kesemak see KASEMEK.

kesemat see KESUMAT.

kesemuanya see SEMUA.

kesengsem see SENGSEM.

késéran dolly, cart for moving heavy things.

kését₁ meng- skin, flay (an animal).

kését₂ doormat.

kését₃ see KASÉT.

kesi₁ white, pale, white as a sheet.

kesi₂ see KESU-KESI.

kesian see KASIH₁.

kesiap ter- be startled.

kesik, kesik-kesik sound of whispering.

kesima ter- upset, shaken up, unnerved.

kesimbukan 1 k.o. climbing herbaceous vine, the crushed leaves of which emit an odor. **2** k.o. tree with malodorous leaves.

kesini see SINI.

kesip₁ seedless (of fruit). **meng-** suck (on a juicy fruit, etc.).

kesip₂ ber-² blink o.'s eyes.

kesiur sound of whistling or whizzing. **ber-** whizz (as arrows, etc.). **meng-kan** cause to whizz.

keskul a beggar's bowl.

keslio see KESELÉO.

kesmak see KASEMEK.

kesodo festival of sacrifice held in Tengger during the 10th Jv calendar month.

kesohor see SOHOR.

kesomplok 1 (*Jkt*) hit, bump into. *Dia baru mau lari - polisi* He ran into a policeman just as he was running away. **2** be broke, penniless.

késot ber-, meng- 1 drag o.s. along on the ground (e.g. of a small tot, a disabled person). **2** shuffle, not lift o.'s feet.

kesra [*kesejahteraan rakyat*] the welfare of the people.

kesrakat (*Jv*) suffering from poverty. *Ibu nampak benar-benar -* Mother appeared to be living in misery.

kesturi musk, civet.

kesuari see KASUARI.

kesuh-kesih panting.

kesu-kesi sound of whispering.

kesuk-kesik sound of rustling or treading on leaves.

kesuma (*Lit.*) **1** flower. *- bangsa* flower of the nation (youth killed in battle). **2** beautiful (of a woman), noble.

kesumat 1 conflict, altercation. **2** enmity. **3** hatred.

kesumba 1 various plants that yield a bright red color. **2** bright red in color. *- kuning* yellow food color. **meng-** dye s.t. red.

kesup sound of sucking. **meng-** suck o.'s fingers.

kesusu (*Jv*) in a hurry. *Dia - mau pulang* She was in a hurry to return home.

kesut ter-² in difficulty and frightened.

ketahuan see TAHU₁.

ketai₁ ber-² 1 crumble, fall apart. **2** decompose (of a body, wood, etc.). **meng-** *daging* cut or chop meat into small pieces.

ketai₂ loser (in a card game).

ketak₁ sound of a clack (tapping on a table, etc.). *-*

ketik clickety-clack. **ber-** *ketik* make a ticking sound (of watch, heart, etc.). **ber-(²)** cackle (of hens).

ketak₂ skin fold (of a double chin). **ber-** have folds (of the neck, double chin).

ketakong pitcher plant.

ketam₁ 1 tightly closed. **2** with teeth set. - *mulut* lockjaw. **3** (*in some regions only*) crab. **meng-** close or press tightly. ~ *bibir* press o.'s lips tightly together. ~ *mulut* shut the mouth tightly. **peng-1** pair of pincers. **2** clamp.

ketam₂ meng- harvest rice with a knife held within o.'s palm. **-an** item harvested. **peng-** knife for harvesting rice. **peng-an** harvesting of rice.

ketam₃ a carpenter's tool, the plane. - *kasar* jack plane. **meng-** plane (wood). **-an** item planed. **peng-** instrument for planing. ~ *betina* grooving plane. ~ *panjang* smoothing plane. **peng-an** wood shavings.

ketambak k.o. fish, the pomfret.

ketan sticky or glutinous rice. - *hitam* black sticky rice. - *urap* sticky rice with grated coconut.

ketang tight (of a fit or binding).

ketap₁ meng- *bibir* **1** press o.'s lips together. **2** bite o.'s lips (out of anger).

ketap₂ small knife held in the palm of the hand.

ketap₃ see KETAM₃.

ketapang k.o. almond tree growing near the seashore which bears edible nuts.

ketapél, ketapil 1 catapult, slingshot. **2** a sling to catch landing planes.

ketap-ketip blink o.'s eyes repeatedly. **ber-** blink the eyes repeatedly. **meng-kan** (*mata*) blink (the eyes).

ketar₁ tart, sour (to the taste).

ketar₂ see GETAR.

ketara see KENTARA.

ketarap k.o. fish, a wrasse.

ketat 1 tight (of top on bottle, clothes, ring, embrace, etc.). **2** firm, binding (contract, etc.). **3** strict. *dijaga* - closely guarded. **meng-** become tight, firm, strict. *mengingat -nya waktu* mindful of the strict time limit. **meng-kan, memper-** tighten. **ke-an** tightness. **peng(k)-an 1** tightening. **2** firming up (of a contract, etc.).

ketaton (*Jv*) get injured. *semangat banténg* - the spirit of a wounded buffalo.

ketawa laugh. - *cekikikan* giggle. **meng-i, meng-kan 1** laugh at. *Apa yg kau -kan?* What are you laughing at? **2** make s.o. laugh. **-an** laughter.

ketaya₁ torch made of bamboo filled with resin.

ketaya₂ (*Coll.*) collar made of plaited rattan used as a harness for buffaloes or horses.

ketayalan (*Jv*) do s.t. with a lot of difficulty.

ketayap white rimless cap worn by those who have made the hajj.

ketegar stubborn, obstinate, obdurate.

keték₁ (*Jv*) monkey.

keték₂ see KETIK.

kéték₁ (*Jkt*) armpit. **meng-i** tickle under the arm.

kéték₂ (*M*) small, little.

ketel 1 thick, close together (of leaves, etc.). **2** crowded, dense (of population).

ketél drop (liquid). *se- air* a drop of water. **ber-(²)** in drops, by the drop.

kétél 1 kettle. **2** (*Tech.*) boiler. - *kukus* boiler.

ketéla 1 yams. - *manis* sweet potato. **2** other starchy root crops. - *pohung/kayu* cassava.

kételpak coveralls, jumpsuit.

ketemu see TEMU₂.

kéténg ½ cent coin (of the colonial era). *membeli* - buy on a small scale. **se-** a half cent. **meng- 1** buy o. or a little at a time, buy retail. **2** sell retail o. or a little at a time. **meng-i** distribute merchandise for retailing. **meng-kan** sell s.t. retail. **-an** piecemeal, by the piece. *Saya tak mau membeli satu bungkus, saya mau membeli* ~ *saja* I do not want to buy a pack. I just want to buy a single piece. **peng-** retailer.

ke tengah see TENGAH.

ketepak-ketepak sound of clicking, clickety-clack (of horses on hard surface).

ketepél see KETAPÉL.

ketépéng k.o ornamental shrub.

ketepil see KETAPÉL.

ketepok, ketepuk sound of clicking, clickety-clack (of wooden slippers, horse hooves on a hard surface, etc.). **ber-** go clickety-clack. *Dokar* ~ *di atas aspal* The horse-drawn cab went clickety-clack on the asphalt.

ketés drop (of water, etc.). **meng-** dripping. **meng-i** drip, drip onto.

ketétér, ketétéran 1 fall or lag behind, unable to keep up, left behind. **2** be on the verge of defeat.

keti₁ (*Jv*) 100,000. **se-** 100,000. **ber-(²)** by the hundreds of thousands. **-an** by the 100,000.

keti₂ (*Sport*) wooden ball.

ketiak armpit. **meng-i** put or carry s.t. under the arms.

ketial 1 ponderous, have difficulty in moving about because of obesity or gout. **2** very tight-fitting (of clothes, cork in a bottle, etc.).

ketiap small flat-bottomed boat for river journeys.

ketiau k.o. large tree.

ketib see KHATIB.

ketiban (*Jv*) **1** have s.t. fall on o. *Ia - durian runtuh* He had a ripe durian fall on him (e.g. He had unexpected good luck). - *pulung* **1** have a windfall (in the form of a prize, promotion, substantial gift). **2** have s.t. good or bad befall o. - *rezeki* have good luck or fortune. **2** be struck by.

ketibung see KETIMBUNG.

ketiding k.o. large rattan basket for storing rice.

ketik sound of ticking or clicking (e.g. a watch or typewriter). **meng- 1** tick (of watch). **2** flick (with the fingers). ~ *keléréng* shoot marbles. **3** type (a letter). ~ *sistém buta* touch-type. **meng-kan** type s.t. for s.o. **-an** typing, s.t. typed. **peng-** typist. **peng-an** typing. *ruang* ~ typing room.

ketika₁ 1 point in time, moment. *pd - itu* at that moment. **2** when (at a certain point in time). - *ia pergi, isterinya datang* When he left, his wife came. **se-** an instant, for a moment. ~ *itu juga* that very instant. *Tujuh belas org meninggal* ~ *itu juga* 17 people died that very instant (on the spot). **ber- 1** Godsent, come just at the right time. *Datangnya* ~ His arrival was Godsent. **2** be punctual. **3** be at a set time.

ketika₂ see KARTIKA.

keti-keti k.o. small wasp.

ketil bit. **se-** a tiny piece. **ber-²** in small bits. **meng-** slice or cut into small pieces.

ketilang k.o. bird, a bulbul.

ketimang buckle, clasp.

ketimbang (*Coll.*) **1** compared with, than. *Yg ini lebih baik* ~ *yg kemarin* This is better than yesterday's. **2** better (so-and-so) than . . . ~ *tdk ada* Better than not getting any.

ketimbul k.o. breadfruit with seeds.

ketimbung, ketimpung sound of splashing in water. **ber-(an)** splash around in the water in a playful way.

ketimun see MENTIMUN.

ketimus (*Jv*) cake made of corn or cassava with coconut and palm sugar.

keting tendon of the heel. **meng-** hamstring.

ketip 1 bite or nip (of a small insect). **2** dime. **se-** a dime. **meng- 1** nip, bite. **2** pinch slightly. **-an** worth a dime.

ketipak-ketipuk sound of pitter-patter.

ketiplak sound of clogs. **ber-** make a clackety-clack sound (of clogs). **ber-an** make such a sound (of many objects).

ketipung k.o. small drum in the gamelan ensemble.

ketirah k.o. red-leaved shrub.

ketir-ketir fearful, apprehensive.

ketis meng- flick, flip s.t. with a finger.

ketitir, ketitiran (*Jv*) k.o. spotted dove.

ketiwul (*Jv*) steamed porridge or cake of powdered cassava with palm sugar and grated coconut.

ketok see KETUK₁.

ketok kadal children's game played with bamboo sticks.

ketol see KETUL₂.

ketola k.o. squash, luffa.

ketombé dandruff.

keton k.o. tree.

ketonggéng scorpion.

ketopong helmet. - *besi* steel helmet.

ketoprak₁ a Jv drama depicting historical or pseudo-historical events.

ketoprak₂ (*Jkt*) k.o. salad consisting of bean sprouts, tofu, rice noodles and a peanut sauce.

kétot (*Auto.*) cut-out valve in the engine.

ketrik meng- scrape out prior to spackling. *Lobang di témbok ini hrs di- sblm ditambal* The holes in this wall have to be scraped out before they are spackled. **meng-kan** use s.t. to scrape out. **-an** what has been scraped out.

ketrok meng- strike, hit s.o., beat. **meng-kan** strike s.t. against s.t. (e.g. to loosen it).

kéts see SEPATU.

ketu skull cap. - *mérah* red stocking cap.

ketua 1 chairman. - *harian* executive director. - *induk* national chairman. - *muda* vice or deputy chairman. - *pelaksana* chief executive. **2** elder,

chief. **3** moderator. **meng-i** chair, preside over. **meng-kan** appoint s.o. to be chairman. **peng-** leader, elder.

ketuat wart.

ketuban fetal membrane.

ketuir k.o. bush the seeds of which are used medically to neutralize toxins of ingested seafood.

ketuk₁ knock, tap. - *dan las* bodywork (pounding and welding). - *tilu* (*Sd*) popular melody for *ronggéng* dances. **meng- 1** knock on (a door). ~ *kawat* send a telegram, tap out a message. **2** pound out (a dent, etc.). **meng-i** make a knocking noise on. *klak-klak suara sepatu* ~ *lantai* the clickety-clack of shoes on the floor. **2** knock on. *Lagunya* ~ *pintu hatinya* She was moved by the song. **meng-kan** knock with s.t. ~ *palu* pound the gavel. **-an 1** knock, tapping sound. ~ *motor* engine knock. **2** rap, blow. ~ *palu* rap of the gavel. **3** beat. **peng-** s.t. used to beat.

ketuk₂ (*Jv*) k.o. gamelan instrument, a horizontally suspended bronze kettle.

ketuk₃ sound of a hen clucking. **ber-** cluck.

ketul₁ lump, clod. *se- nasi* a lump of rice. *se- roti* a bun. *se- tanah* a clod of earth. **ber-² 1** in lumps or clods. **2** in clots (of blood). **meng-kan** flex (the muscles). ~ *kaki* draw up the knees.

ketul₂ meng- touch, hit against. **-an** a touch, hit. ~ *arus sungai begitu kuat sehingga menyebabkan longsor* The force of the current was strong enough to cause a landslide.

ketul₃ (*Jv*) dull (of knives, scissors, etc.).

ketulah affliction sent as punishment for disrespect to elderly people, sacred places, etc. *Saya takut - kalau berani dgn bapak sendiri* I am afraid of being punished (by God) when I show disrespect toward my father.

ketumbar coriander.

ketumbé, ketumbi₁ see KETOMBÉ.

ketumbi₂ final dregs. - *tahi ayam* social outcast, lowest of the low.

ketumbit k.o. large weed.

ketumbu k.o. covered basket or hamper.

ketumbuhan see TUMBUH.

ketumpang k.o. weed with malodorous leaves.

ketung a resonant sound. **ber-(²)** make a resonant sound.

ketungging k.o. large black scorpion.

ketup₁ see KATUP.

ketup₂ sound of stamping of feet on planks.

ketupa₁ k.o. owl.

ketupa₂ k.o. flower.

ketupat rice cake boiled in a rhombus-shaped packet of plaited young coconut leaves. - *Ambon/ Bangkahulu* fist (as used in punching s.o.).

ketupuk k.o. owl.

ketur₁ cuspidor, spittoon.

ketur₂ ber- croak (of frogs).

ketus sharp (in reply), speaking in an angry tone. **meng-** speak sharply.

keuring /kéring/ inspection, examination.

kewalahan at a loss what to do (because of a deluge of work, in the face of a superior enemy, etc.), be snowed under.

kéwan see HÉWAN.

kewartal see KUARTAL.

kewatir see KUATIR.

kg. [*kilogram*] kilogram.

Kg. [*kampung*] village, neighborhood.

kh- see also entries with **k-**.

khabar see KABAR.

khadam, khadim (*Lit.*) 1 servant, slave. 2 wage earner.

khaid see HAID.

khaimah see KÉMAH.

khair (*Lit.*) handsome, beautiful.

khaki /kaki/ khaki.

khalaik see KHALAYAK.

khalak (*Lit.*) creation, handiwork, product.

khalayak 1 creature. 2 the public. - *muda* the young crowd. - *pembeli* the buying public. - *ramai* the public, populace. **meng-kan** make public, announce publicly, popularize. *Baju renang ciptaan semacam itu blm berani kita -kan* We do not yet dare distribute this new model of bathing suit to the public.

khali 1 free, unoccupied, unengaged. 2 carefree, easygoing. 3 void, deserted. *tdk - drp* not fail to. *tdk - drp sembahyang magrib* not fail to perform the evening prayers.

khalifah caliph.

khalik (*Isl.*) the Creator.

khalikah 1 creation. 2 character, behavior.

khalil friend, companion.

khalis (*Rel.*) pure, undefiled.

khalkum see HALKUM.

khalwat (*Rel.*) solitude, retirement from the world, retreat. **ber-** retire from the world, go into retreat.

khamar (*Lit.*) wine, liquor.

khamir leavened.

Khamis see KAMIS.

khanduri see KENDURI.

khanjar k.o. large dagger.

khaos chaos.

khaotis chaotic.

kharab (*Lit.*) destroyed, ruined.

kharisma charisma.

kharismatis charismatic.

khas 1 special, exclusive, for private use. 2 special, specific to s.t. *Kerupuk ini - Salatiga* These chips are a specialty of Salatiga. *ciri -* special characteristics. **memper-, meng-kan** reserve for special use. ~ *diri* specialize. **ke-an** special characteristics.

khasah see KASA₁.

khasanah see KHAZANAH.

khasiat 1 special quality or virtue, merit. - *manjur* restorative power. 2 peculiar property. **meng-** scrutinize closely, investigate minutely.

khasis chassis.

khasumat see KESUMAT.

khat 1 line. 2 handwriting. 3 Arabic calligraphy, esp. as an art form.

khatam 1 seal, signet ring. 2 (*Isl.*) final, last. *Ia nabi yg -* He is the last prophet. 3 (*Isl.*) read through to the end (esp. the Koran). - *kaji* recite the verses (of the Koran) to the end. **mengkhkan** finish, conclude (the reading of the Koran). ~ *Koran* complete the reading of the Koran. **-an** ceremony upon completion of reading of the Koran for the first time.

khatan see KHITAN.

khatib 1 preacher at the mosque. 2 a mosque official.

khatifah (*Lit.*) carpet, rug.

khatulistiwa equator.

khaul see KAUL.

khawatir see KUATIR.

khayal 1 fancy, vision, imagination. 2 imaginary. **ber-** 1 see visions. 2 indulge in fancies. **meng-(kan)** imagine s.t., fantasize. *Ia sdh ~ alangkah bahagianya jadi isteri muda seorg Bupati* She fantasized how happy she would be to become the 2d wife of a *Bupati*. ~ *diri* fancy s.o. (in some high position, etc.). **-an** fantasy. **peng-** dreamer, visionary. **peng-an** imagining, fantasizing.

khayali 1 imaginary. *Di mana musuh yg -?* Where is the imaginary enemy? 2 (*Isl.*) in a state of mystic revery.

khayat see HAYAT.

khazanah 1 treasure. 2 treasury. 3 storage area for valuable objects. 4 vocabulary of a language.

khéwan see HÉWAN.

khianat 1 treason, betrayal. 2 treacherous. **ber-** commit treason. ~ *kpd tanah air* betray o.'s country. **meng-** be disloyal or traitorous. **meng-i** betray, be traitorous to s.o. or s.t. **ke-an** treason, betrayal. **peng-** traitor. **peng-an** commiting of treason.

khidmat 1 respect. *diperingati dgn -* be celebrated with respect. 2 humility, submission. **ber-** 1 dutiful, respectful. *Ia ~ kpd perintah* He carried out orders loyally. 2 serve. ~ *kpd negerinya* serve o.'s country. 3 be faithful (to). **meng-i** respect s.o. *suami yg di-i* a respected husband. **ke-an** solemnity, respectfulness, obedience. ~ *ujian* solemnity of the examination.

khilaf 1 wrong, erroneous. 2 commit an error. - *dan alpa* mistakes and oversights. **meng-kan** be uncertain about s.t. **ke-an** mistake, error, slip.

khilafiah 1 wrong. 2 uncertain.

khitan circumcision. **ber-** be circumcised. **meng-i** circumcise several people. **meng-(kan)** circumcise. **-an** feast celebrating a circumcision. **peng-an** circumcising.

khlor chlorine.

khlorida chloride.

khlorinasi chlorination.

khloroform chloroform.

khodrat see KODRAT.

khoja (*Lit.*) 1 Muslim merchant (us. from abroad). 2 title for such a person.

khotbah sermon. **ber-** 1 preach, deliver a sermon. 2 deliver pompous opinions, pontificate. **meng-i** preach at, lecture s.o. *Ia ~ temannya spy tdk mencuri lagi* He lectured his friend not to steal again. **meng-kan** preach s.t. via a sermon. **peng-** 1 preacher. ~ *Injil* evangelist. 2 s.t. to preach with. *kitab ~* book from which to preach.

khotib see KHATIB.
khrom chrome.
khronis chronic.
khrysant see CHRYSANT.
khuatir see KUATIR.
khudu humility.
khulak (*Isl.*) action of returning the bride-price so that o.'s husband will divorce her.
khuldi see BUAH.
khulki genuine.
khuluk nature, character.
khurafat (*Lit.*) myth, superstition.
khurma see KURMA.
khusu, khusuk see KHUSYU, KHUSYUK.
khusus 1 special, different from others. *upacara yg* - a special ceremony. *diberi tugas yg* - be given a special assignment. *hubungan yg* - *antara meréka* a special connection between them. 2 specifically for. *kamar yg* - *utk tamu* a special room for guests. *Ia datang* - *utk menjemputnya* He came expressly to pick her up. -nya in particular, esp. meng-kan 1 set aside, make s.t. be special. *nama kesayangan yg di-kan baginya* the pet name that was esp. reserved for her. ~ *diri* specialize. *Ia* ~ *diri dlm bidang sosiologi pedésaan* He is specializing in rural sociology. 2 give s.t. special treatment. *Produksi tékstil dlm negeri perlu di-kan spy dpt bersaing* Local textile production should be given special preference so that it can be competitive. ter-esp., particularly, specifically. ke-an specific characteristics of. peng-an specialization.
khusyu, khusyuk 1 devout, devoted, humble before God. 2 engrossed in, deeply absorbed in. *Ia* - *menulis tésisnya* He is engrossed in writing his thesis. ber- be devoted to religion. *Ia* ~ *dlm pelajaran agama* She is devoted to the study of religion. meng-kan *diri* devote o.s. to s.t. ke-an humility, devoutness.
khutbah see KHOTBAH.
ki 1 title of respect for men learned in religious matters. 2 title used with certain objects of veneration. - *Jagur* name given to an ancient cannon in Jkt.
kia chain stitch.
kiah meng-(kan) stretch (socks, gloves, etc.). peng- shoehorn.
kiai 1 title or reference for a venerated scholar, teacher of Isl. 2 district head (in S. Kalimantan). 3 title used with certain objects of veneration. - *Jagur* the ancient cannon in Jkt.
kia-kia₁ k.o. shark.
kia-kia₂ (*Ch*) have fun, enjoy o.s., be relaxed.
kiak-kiak k.o. large black ant.
kial gesture. ber- gesture, gesticulate. (ber)-² move vigorously, struggle (of a person trying to free himself). meng-kan act out, dramatize s.t. ter-² be caused to move vigorously, shake with laughter. per-an dramatization, acting out of s.t.
kiam (*Isl.*) erect standing posture during prayer ritual.
kiamat 1 Judgement day, doomsday. *Kau bisa berteriak sampai* - You can shout till doomsday. 2 end of world, disaster. mengk- be like doomsday.

Témbak-menémbak ~ Shooting all over the place as if it were doomsday. mengk-kan *dunia* bring about the end of the world.
kiambang k.o. plant formerly found in abundance in stagnant or slow-moving waters, the leaves of which resemble lettuce.
kiambwee /kyambwé/ (*Ch*) dried salted plums.
kian 1 all the more. *Hatiku - berdebar keras* My heart pounded all the harder. 2 the . . . so much more . . . - *lama - besar juga* the longer the time, the bigger it got. 3 (*Lit.*) (following a number) as many as. *Sepuluh - sekalipun kulawan juga* Even if they are as many as 10 men, I will take them on. - *kemari* up and down, to and fro. *Ia berjalan - kemari* He paced up and down. meng-kemari-kan send back and forth. *Kita sbg pembaca di-kemarikan* As readers we are made to flip back and forth (in the book). se- 1 so-and-so much (an unnamed amount). *Bulan Maret tgl* ~ March on such and such a date. *Kita jual dgn harga pokok. Ini* -, *itu* - We will sell at cost. This o. is so-and-so much. That o. is so-and-so much. *Yg* - *kalinya* the nth time. 2 as much as this. *Rumahnya* ~ *besar* His house was this big. *Baru ini bertemu sejak* ~ *lama* meet for the first time now, after such a long time. ~ *dulu* that is all for this time (often used to conclude an informal letter or speech). kese- 1 the nth, the so-and-so manieth. *isteri* ~ wife number so-and-so. 2 the umpteenth (time). *utk* ~ *kalinya* for the umpteenth time. seperse- such-and-such a percent. ~ *dr penduduk* Such-and-such a percent of the inhabitants. ber-² repeated, again and again. *Rumahnya* ~ He owns countless houses, *kata yg* ~ *itu* . . . the words which came up again and again . . . memper- accelerate, multiply. ~ *merosotnya* accelerate its decline.
kianat see KHIANAT.
kiang - *kiut* sound of creaking. -² creak, screech, squeak, grate.
kiap pieces of wood used to prop s.t. up.
kiara k.o. shade tree.
kias 1 simile, comparison, analogy. 2 analogical reasoning. 3 allusion, hint. ber-²an, meng-² make allusions against e.o. meng- 1 allude to, hint at. 2 criticize (by allusions). meng-kan make an analogy of, analogize, compare. *Ia* ~ *kejadian itu kpd apa yg terjadi di zaman Nabi saw.* He made an analogy of what has happened to happenings from the time of the Prophet. *Ia* ~ *hal itu dgn* . . . She compared that matter with . . . *Saya sekarang akan* ~ *kejadian semacam itu kpd kau sendiri* I will now demonstrate how an event like that applies to your own life. -an 1 figure of speech, allegory, metaphor, analogy. 2 criticism by indirect reference or analogy. 3 lesson, moral. *Ambil* ~ *dr ceritera ini* Take a lesson from this story.
kiasi analogous.
klat₁ stiff, cramped (of neck, limbs, etc.). ber- be stiff, cramped. meng-kan sprain s.t.
kiat₂ trick, secret. *Ada -nya. Begini* There is a trick to it. It is like this.
kiat₃ meng- shuffle cards.

kiaupau (*Ch*) overseas Chinese.

kibar ber-, ber-an 1 wave, flutter, fly (of flags, etc.). **2** be displayed. *Uangnya masih ~ di tangannya* The money was still displayed in his hand. **meng-kan** display, put out (the flag). **-an** fluttering (of flag). **peng-** standard-bearer, waver (of a flag). **peng-an** display (of flags).

kibas₁ meng- wag (tail), sway to and fro, flap (ears, wings). **meng(²)-kan** make s.t. wag, sway, flap. *Pucuk pohon di-²kan angin* The wind made the treetops sway back and forth. *Sapi ~ ékornya utk mengusir lalat* The cow swished its tail to scatter the flies. **-an** wag (of tail), swaying.

kibas₂ see KAMBING.

kibik see KUBIK₂.

kibir arrogant, haughty. **ke-an** arrogance, haughtiness.

kiblah, kiblat 1 direction of Mecca. *Org bersembahyang hrs menghadap - O.* has to face in the direction of Mecca when praying. **2** direction (of the wind). **3** orientation. **ber-, mengk-** oriented toward. *Org-org désa cenderung utk ~ ke kota* The country people have a tendency to follow city models. **meng-kan** orient s.t. to. *Tdk mudah bagi pendidikan tinggi utk ~ diri kpd kebutuhan masyarakat* It is no easy task for higher education to orient itself to society's needs.

kiblik (*Coll.*) republic.

kibul (*Jkt*) bottom, buttocks, rear. **ng-** tell a lie. **meng-i** lie to s.o., cheat, deceive.

kicak see KICAU₁.

kicang-kécoh swindle, deceit of various kinds.

kicap₁ see KICAU₁.

kicap₂ see KÉCAP₁.

kicap-kicup repeated blinking of the eyes. **ber-** blink repeatedly (of eyes). *dgn mata ~* with blinking eyes.

kicau₁ ber- 1 chirp, twitter, warble. **2** chatter. **ber-²an** twitter and chirp (of several birds). **meng-kan 1** talk idly of, chatter about. **2** boast about. **-an** warble, chirp.

kicau₂ ter- swindled.

kicerat (*Jkt*) **meng-** spurt out.

kici (*Naut.*) ketch, brig.

kicu₁ 1 deceit. **2** deceiver. **ber-, meng-** deceive. **peng-** deceiver, swindler. **peng-an** deceiving, swindling.

kicu₂ see KICAU₁.

kicuh see KICU₁.

kicut ber- squeak (of a floor, etc.).

kidal left-handed. *si -* southpaw. **ke-an** left-handedness.

kidam time immemorial, infinite preexistence.

kidang see KIJANG.

kidar, kider see KITAR₁.

kidmat see KHIDMAT.

kidul (*Jv*) south.

kidung ballad. *- geréja* hymn. *- rohani* a spiritual hymn. **meng-** sing a ballad. **meng-kan** sing s.o. a ballad.

kihanat astrology, augury.

kijai k.o. large timber tree.

kijang 1 k.o. small antelope. **2** brand name for k.o. jeep.

kijing₁ k.o. edible mussel.

kijing₂ (*Jv*) gravestone. **meng-i, meng-kan** provide with a gravestone.

kiju see KÉJU.

KIK /ka i ka/ [*Krédit Invéstasi Kecil*] small business loans.

kik₁ loom.

kik₂ /kik/ (*Coll.*) **1** kick. **2** tease, hit s.o. where it hurts. *Sialan, dia - saya di dlm rapat* Damn, he got at me at the meeting where I could not defend myself. *- balik/kembali* getting back at s.o. who has teased o. *Dia - saya, saya - kembali* He got at me and I got back at him. **-²an** tease e.o.

kikih, kikik ber-, meng-, ter-² giggle. **ber-an** giggling at e.o. **-an** a giggle.

kikil 1 foot of an animal (for eating). **2** foot of a person (joking or contemptuous).

kikir₁ file, rasp. *- kuku* nail file. **ber- 1** filed. **2** coarse, wrinkled (of skin). **meng-** file (a metal object). **-an** filings.

kikir₂ stingy, tightfisted. **ke-an** stinginess.

kikis scraped. **meng- 1** erode. *Laut ~ pantai* The sea eroded the coast. **2** make s.t. disappear bit by bit. *~ habis* eliminate s.t. **meng-kan** scrape off. *~ jamur dr kayu* scrape mold from wood. **-an** (*Geol.*) alluvium, what has piled up from erosion. *Pasir tertimbun di muara karena ~ sungai* Sand piled up in the mouth of the river due to the erosion caused by the river. **peng-** scraper. **peng-an 1** erosion. **2** erasure. **3** loss, disappearance.

kikuk clumsy, awkward. **ke-an** clumsiness, awkwardness.

kilaf see KHILAF.

kilah₁ trick, deception, ruse, pretext. **ber-(²) 1** farfetched, forced (argument). **2** spurious (argument). **3** deceitful, fraudulent. **4** argue to defend o. self. **meng-²kan** twist words, distort facts or an argument.

kilah₂ k.o. snaillike mollusk.

kilai spool or reel of thread (for spinning).

kilan₁ span (of the hand). **se-** a span. **meng-(i)** measure s.t. in spans.

kilan₂ ter- be offended.

kilang 1 press, mill, factory for processing or refining natural products. *- getah* rubber factory. *- keruk* dredge. *- minyak* oil refinery. *- tanah liat* clay mill. *- tembakau* tobacco factory. **2** drink made from pressed sugar or palm sugar. **meng-** mill (esp. rice), press (sugar cane), process (natural gas, petroleum). **-an** millstone or other instrument for refining or processing. **per-an** refinery. **peng-an 1** refining. **2** refinery.

kilang-kélok winding, tortuous (road, path).

kilap₁ shine, gloss, sheen, luster. *- baba* afterglow. **se-** *mata* in a flash. **ber-, mengk-** shine. *Sepatunya ~* His shoes were shining. **meng-i** flash s.t. to s.o. **meng(k)-kan** shine, polish (shoes, silver, etc.). **-an** gloss, sheen (e.g. in o.'s hair, etc.).

kilap₂ see KHILAF.

kilar k.o. edible snail.

kilas₁ 1 noose made of rattan. 2 rattan rings used for climbing trees or poles. **meng-** 1 trap (animals, birds). 2 tighten (up). ~ *tali kurung* tighten the string of a bag.

kilas₂ - *balik* flashback. **se-** a glance. ~ *lintas/mata/ pandang* in a flash or wink, in the twinkling of an eye. **meng-** glance at. **meng-kan** release, let s.t. go quickly. ~ *matanya ke pagar* let o.'s glance go quickly along the fence. **-an** glance. ~ *lénsa* flash of the lens.

kilat 1 flash of lightning. 2 shine, gleam, sheen. 3 done in a flash (in set expressions). *kiriman (pos)* - special delivery. - *khusus* express delivery. *informasi* - quick or instant information. *surat* - special delivery letter. **se-** in a flash. **ber-** shine, glisten. ~ *kilau* shining. **mengk-, meng-** 1 shine. *mobil yg* ~ a shiny car. 2 flash. ~*lah pertanyaan itu dlm hatiku* The question flashed into my mind. **meng-i** flash s.t. to s.o. **mengk-kan** 1 make s.t. glitter or shine. *Cahaya matahari* ~ *pedang terhunus* The sunlight made the drawn swords glisten. ~ *kembali* reflect (light). ~ *mobil* polish a car. 2 make a brief reference to. ~ *dlm pidatonya tindakan yg akan diambil* allude in his speech to the measures he would take. **ter-** flash (through the mind). ~ *dlm hati* (it) flashed through her mind. **-an** 1 lightning. 2 a flash. ~ *bom atom* the flash from an atomic bomb. 3 shine, sheen, gloss.

kilau luster, reflected shine, glare. - *kemilau* shine brightly, sparkle (of stars, diamonds). - **mengk-** shine brightly. **(ber)-an** sparkle (plural). **ber-, meng(k)-** sparkle, glitter. *Jendéla kaca itu* ~ *terkena sinar mata hari* The window glass glared in the sun rays. **-an** luster, shine. **-²an** shining brightly but inconstantly.

kiler (*Sl.*) university lecturer who gives killer exams.

kili seam. **meng-** hem s.t.

kilik meng-² 1 tickle. 2 amuse. 3 incite s.o.

kili-kili nose ring of rope or rattan for an ox or water buffalo. - *buaya* sea-nettle. - *dayung* thole.

kilir₁ meng- whet (o.'s knife, etc.). **-an** 1 whetstone, grindstone. 2 whetting, sharpening. ~ *budi* sharpening of the intellect. 3 s.t. made sharp. ~ *taji* sharpened tip of a cockspur.

kilir₂ ter- be sprained. *Lengan saya* ~ I sprained my arm.

kilo 1 kilogram. 2 kilometer. **ber-²** by the kilogram or kilometer. **meng-** measure s.t. in kilograms. **meng-i** weigh s.t. out. **meng-kan** 1 sell s.t. by the kilogram. 2 reckon the weight in kilograms. **-an** by the kilogram. *Beras itu dijual* ~ That rice is sold by the kilogram.

kilogram kilogram.

kilométer 1 kilometer. 2 speedometer.

kilowat kilowatt.

kim k.o. gambling game similar to bingo where the numbers are given out in rhymed verses.

KIM [*Kartu Izin Menetap*] Residence Permit.

kima the giant clam.

kimah, kimat price, value, worth.

kimbang meng-² 1 circle, hover (of a plane, bird, etc.). 2 move back and forth, go to and fro, be very restless. **ter-** hesitating, wavering.

kimblo see KIMLO.

kimia chemistry. - *analitis* analytical chemistry. - *anorganik* inorganic chemistry. - *fisika* physical chemistry. - *hayat* biochemistry.

kimiawi chemical. *campuran* - chemical compound (mixture).

kimis chemical, synthetic.

kimka, kimkha damask.

kimlo k.o. soup with vegetables and meat.

kimono kimono, dressing gown. **ber-** wear a kimono or dressing gown.

kimpal solid, welded. **meng-** forge metal.

kimpul₁ k.o. taro.

kimpul₂ purse, wallet.

kimpus ter- hollow, concave, sunken (of eyes, cheeks).

kina quinine.

kinang a chew of betel. **meng-** chew betel. **-an** betel to chew. **peng-an** set of implements and materials for chewing betel.

kinantan 1 be all white (of cock, horse, etc.). 2 very special.

kinca syrup of palm sugar.

kincah meng- 1 rinse, wash (laundry, etc.). 2 dress, game or fowl. 3 cleanse the genitals.

kincan meng- mix, stir s.t.

kincang fraud, deceit. **ng-** deceive s.o.

kinces (*Jkt*) 1 deflated, burst (of boils). 2 blind.

kincir spool, reel. - *air* waterwheel. - *angin* 1 windmill. 2 propeller. - *menjahit* sewing machine. - *padi* rice mill (operated by water power). - *ria* ferris wheel. **-an** waterwheel.

kincit minor cause of diarrhea.

kincup small, narrow, restricted (of an opening).

kinéskop TV screen.

kinétis kinetic.

king (*Crd.*) king.

kingkit k.o. tiny sour citrus fruit.

kini now, nowadays. *dr* - *dan seterusnya* from now on. *ke-an* the present.

kinine quinine.

kinja ber-² jump with joy.

kinjeng dragonfly.

kintaka archive. **per-an** archival matters.

kintakawan archivist.

kintal₁ see KUINTAL.

kintal₁₁, kintel (*Jv*) bullfrog.

kintil meng- trail s.o.

kintut (*Jkt*) youngest child.

kinurang (*Math.*) subtrahend.

kinyam see KENYAM.

kinyang quartz, rock crystal.

kinyis-kinyis still fresh.

kio (*Ch*) palanquin.

kiong see KÉONG.

kios kiosk. - *buku* bookstall.

kip percussion cap.

KIP [*Kampung Improvement Project*] gvt. sponsored project on the urban ward level.

kipa one-legged.
kipai meng-kan wag s.t.
kipang₁ cake made of fried rice or peanuts or sesame seeds with palm sugar.
kipang₂ see KÉPANG₁.
kipar see KÉPAR.
kipas 1 fan. **2** propeller (of plane, etc.). - *air* windshield wiper. - *angin* 1 electric fan. 2 ventilator. - *hujan/kaca* windshield wiper. - *radiator* (*Auto.*) radiator fan. **ber- 1** use or have a fan. **2** wag, fan, wave. **ber-²** swish (of tail of horse, cow, etc.). **meng-** flutter (of the heart). **meng-i** fan s.o. or s.t. **meng-kan 1** wag (tail, ear). **2** ward off (with wing, hand, etc.).
kipat meng-kan shake, shake off. ~ *tangan karena tersiram air panas* shake o.'s hands because they got splashed with hot water.
kiper goalie, goalkeeper.
kiprah₁ (*Jv*) gait, pace, progress. - *pembangunan* progress in development. **ter-** take action or steps. *Kaum agama ~ melaksananakan perintah Tuhan* The religious group took steps to carry out God's orders.
kiprah₂ part of Jv dance which displays making up and dressing.
kiprat meng- 1 spurt out, jump. **2** hit. **meng-i** splash s.o. or s.t.
kipsiau (*Ch*) teakettle.
kipu craftsman.
kir 1 examination, test. - *badan* physical examination. - *dokter* medical examination. **2** motor vehicle inspection. - *mobil* car inspection. **3** get o.s. examined, get s.t. inspected. *Saya mau - ke Dr. Ong* I want to go to Dr. Ong for an examination. *Sdh waktunya - mobil* It is time to have the car inspected. **mengk-, menge- 1** examine. *Dokter ~ org-org yg hendak msk tentara* The doctor examines those who are about to enter the army. **2** test a car. **mengk-kan, menge-kan** have s.t. examined. *Berlian ini sebaiknya kita -kan dulu, sblm kita beli* We should have this jewel assayed before we buy it.
kira guess, reckon, suppose. *Saya - sdr benar* I guess you are right. *Saya - semua org kenal pdnya* I suppose everyone knows him. -² **1** approximately, about, around. ~ *lima méter* about five meters. **2** estimate. *menurut ~nya* according to her estimate. **3** perhaps, do you think. *Di mana ~ letak rumah itu?* Where do you think the house is located? *Apa ~ meréka sdh kembali?* Do you think they have returned? **4** probably. *mencari barang yg ~ dibutuhkan org* look for things people might need. **5** reasonable, within reason. ~ *ajé dong!* Do not be silly. You should know better! *Kalau memberi harga, yg ~ dong!* If you set a price make it within reason! **-nya 1** I wonder who/when/how/where etc., who/what/how might. *Siapa ~ yg pantas?* I wonder who the right person might be? *Meréka membakar segala apa yg ~ bisa dimakan api* They burned whatever could catch on fire. **2** apparently, it seems. *Tapi ~ perkelahian tdk terhenti di situ* But apparently the quarrel did not

stop there. **3** however. *Apa yg diharapkannya ~ tdk terkabul* What he had been hoping for, however, did not come to being. *Pemburu sangka témbakannya luput, ~ rusa terkena* The hunter thought shot had missed, but the deer had been hit. **4** please, kindly. *Sudilah tuan ~ mengembalikan buku saya?* Would you kindly return my book? **-²nya** possibly, might. **se-** approximately. ~ *jam lima* at around five. *kalau ~* if by some chance. *kalau ~ terjadi* . . . if it should happen . . . **se-nya** if perhaps, in case. **se-²** approximately, about, in the neighborhood of. ~ *seratus rupiah* in the neighborhood of 100 rupiah. **se-²nya** just exactly the right amount. *Diambil ~ saja* Take as much as necessary and no more. **ber-² 1** do some figuring. **2** think over, give some thought. **3** plan, intend. **meng- 1** think, suppose, assume. *Ia ~ saya sdh pergi* She thought I had already gone. **2** guess. *Sebetulnya ia tdk tahu; ia ~ saya* He really does not know; he is just guessing. **3** estimate, calculate s.t. **meng-²** estimate approximately. *Di-²nya lima puluh sén* He reckoned it was around 50 cents. **meng-²(kan) 1** estimate, calculate. **2** guess, figure that. *kecelakaan yg tdk dpt di-²kan* An accident o. could not foresee. **memper-kan** estimate, guess, conjecture. *Sdh diper-kan hasil penjualan itu* They have already calculated how much they will make on the sale. **ter-** estimated. *tak ~ banyaknya* innumerable, countless. *tdk ~* unexpected. **ter-kan** can be calculated. **-an** estimated amount. *tdk msk ~* 1 more than the estimated amount. 2 cannot be calculated. **-²an 1** estimate, calculation. **2** guess, assumption. **per-an 1** estimate, calculation. ~ *belanja* budget. **2** approximation. **peng-an** estimating, calculating.
kirab₁ carnival.
kirab₂ (*Jv*) a ritual procession moving in a circle (e.g. bridal couples, heirlooms, etc.). **ng-** parade s.t. around a room.
kirai₁ meng-(kan) 1 shake out (wet laundry, tablecloth, rug). **2** winnow (rice, etc.). **3** spread (rice) out to dry. **4** flap (its wings, etc.), push open (a door). **ter-² 1** be shaken out (and gotten rid of). **2** hung and spread out (of clothes). **-an** open space. ~ *pintu* door opening.
kirai₂ long strip.
kirai₃ k.o. palm tree.
kirana (*Jv*) **1** ray. **2** beautiful.
kirap₁ meng- 1 hit (with its wings, of an angry goose, hen). **2** flap. **3** flutter (of wings, flag). **meng-kan** flap, spread (wings, a sheet), unfold (cloth), wag (a tail).
kirap₂ meng- disappear, vanish (of ideals, etc.).
kiras k.o. timber tree.
kirau not quite ripe (of fruit).
kirbat bag to hold water, wine etc. - *és* icepack.
kiri 1 left. - *kanan* 1 left and right. 2 from every direction. *tangan -* left hand. **2** (*Naut.*) port. - *kapal* portside. **3** command to driver to pull over to let passenger out. **4** leftist. **5** awkward (behavior). **6** left-handed. **7** unfortunate, unfavor-

able. **meng-** go or keep to the left. *Di Indonésia kendaraan hrs ~* In Indonesia vehicles must keep to the left. *~ menganan* waver. **meng-kan 1** put s.t. to the left. **2** turn down, reject. **3** discard s.t. **ke-²an** somewhat to the left.

kirik₁ mengk- shudder (from fear).

kirik₂ pup.

kirim - *salam/tabik* send greetings or regards. **ber-** send through mail. *~ pesan* send a letter requesting s.t. *~ salam* send o.'s regards. *Kami berjanji akan saling ~ surat* We promised to correspond with e.o. **ber-(²)an** correspond with e.o. - **meng-** send to e.o. **meng 1** send, dispatch s.t. *Kami ~ beras ke seluruh dunia* We ship rice all over the world. **2** leave s.t. for safekeeping, entrust s.t. *~ anak pd tetangga* leave the child with the neighbors. **meng-i** send to. **meng-kan** send or get s.t. off. *Sayang sdh di-kan. Alamatnya salah* It is a pity it has been sent off. The address was wrong. **-an 1** shipment, consignment, s.t. sent. *~ remburs* C.O.D. shipment. **2** missive, missile. **3** item left for safekeeping. **4** rain or some other natural phenomena which comes out of season. *air ~* rain out of season. **peng- 1** sender. *si ~* the sender (of a letter, package). **2** transmitter. **peng-an** shipping, dispatch.

kirmizi (*Lit.*) scarlet, crimson.

kirtya (*Lit.*) society, organization.

kiruh see KERUH₁.

kirut-mirut wrinkles.

kis box, chest.

kisa 1 small purse. **2** small purse net for coastal fishing. **meng-** fish with such a net.

kisah 1 story. **2** narrative. - *bersambung* serialized story. - *perjalanan* travelogue. **ber-** tell a story. **meng-kan** narrate s.t. **peng-** narrator. **peng-an** narration. *~ kembali* retelling.

kisai meng- sift (rice). **-an** sifter, sieve.

kisar rotation (of the earth on its axis). - *kopi* coffee grinder. **ber- 1** revolve, turn. *Roda-roda itu ~* The wheels revolve. **2** change, shift. *Jaman sdh ~* Times have changed. *~ pd* be concerned with, be about or on. *Ceritera ini ~ pd kejadian di Bandung* This story revolves around an event in Bandung. **3** range from a certain amount to another. *~ dr X sampai Y* ranges from X to Y. **meng-(kan) 1** turn s.t., make s.t. revolve. *Mak ~ suntil di antara bibirnya* Mother moved the quid of tobacco around in her mouth. **2** mill (wheat, etc.). **3** turn (the hands of a timepiece). **4** move, shift s.o. or s.t. **5** turn s.t. over to s.o. else. **6** sell s.t. **-an 1** revolution, turn. **2** milling (of wheat, etc.). **3** vortex. *~ air* whirlpool. *~ angin* whirlwind, cyclone. **peng-** miller. **peng-an 1** revolving. **2** milling, grinding. **3** moving, shifting. **per-an 1** revolution. **2** change, shift, turn. *~ jaman* change of the times. *~ abad ini* turn of the century.

kisas retribution.

kisat see KESAT.

kisi 1 grill, lattice, trellis. - *pembakaran* grate (in fireplace). **2** grid, grating. **3** crack of s.t. not closed tight. **-² 1** spokes of a wheel. **2** latticework. **ber- 1** provided with a grating or bars (of a window, etc.). **2** center. *Semua perhatian ~ kpd pidato présidén* All attention centered on the president's speech.

kisik whisper. **-an** gossip.

kismat, kismet 1 fate, destiny. **2** an interjection expressing resignation, What can o. do?

kismis raisin.

kisruh 1 chaotic, anarchic. **2** confused, disorganized. **meng-kan** upset, disrupt. **ke-an** confusion, chaos, muddle.

kissah see KISAH.

kista cyst.

kisut 1 wrinkled, dried up (of skin, etc.). **2** creased (of clothes, etc.). - *mirut* wizened, shrivelled. **meng-(kan) 1** crease, put a crease in s.t. **2** shove or slide the foot. *Ia ~ setelapak dr sisinya* He moved o. footlength from her side.

kiswah (*Isl.*) veil that covers the *Kabah*.

kit (*Coll.*) square, paid up. *Hutangnya sdh - dgn pembayaran ini* With this payment the debt is paid up.

kita 1 we (including person addressed), our, us. **2** (*Coll.*) I (somewhat more humble than *aku/gua*). - *org* we. **-²** we, us (the in-group). *Tdk ada org lain. Hanya ~ saja* There is no o. else (coming). It is just going to be us. **ke-an** state of being the in-group. *rasa ~* feeling of being among the in-group.

kitab₁ (*Lit.*) **1** book. - *kemitab* various books. - *logat* dictionary. - *nujum* **1** book of astrology. **2** astrological tables. **3** book of prophecy. - *undang-undang hukum pidana* penal code. - *usul* book containing a treatise on the true nature of God. **2** holy book. - *Baru* New Testament. - *Injil* the Scripture. - *Lama* Old Testament. - *suci* holy book. - *Ulangan Bibel* Deuteronomy. - *Wasiat Baru/Lama* New/Old Testament. - *Zabur* Book of Psalms. **ber-** be of the Book, having Holy Scriptures. *tdk ~* infidel, not believing in the Book. **peng-** *hukum* compilation of laws, law code.

kitab₂ partition in a cow's stomach.

kitabi possessing the scriptures (of the Christians and Jews).

kitang, kitang-kitang k.o. small sea fish with venomous dorsal spines.

kitar₁ se- 1 around. *Di ~ désa itu banyak sawah* There were many wet rice fields around the village. **2** approximately, about, circa. **se-nya** surroundings, environs. *Jkt dan ~* Jkt and its environs. **ber-** turn, revolve. *Roda itu mulai ~* The wheel began to turn. **meng-²** revolve, turn, rotate. **meng-i** revolve around, orbit. *Bulan ~ bumi* The moon revolves around the earth. **meng-kan, memper-kan** cause s.t. to rotate or revolve. **ter-²** revolved, rolled (of eyes). **-an** orbit. **peng-an** revolving, rotating of s.t. **per-an** rotation, revolution.

kitar₂ memper-kan, meng-kan shove or push s.o. aside.

kitik meng-² tickle s.o.
kiting se- a bit, a little.
kitiran 1 propeller. **2** windmill.
kiu billiard cue.
kiuk dominoes.
kiut see KICUT.
kiwir-kiwir float in the wind. **ter- 1** hang and flap loosely. **2** be made to fall hopelessly in love.
kizib (*Lit.*) lie, falsehood.
KJRI [*Konsulat Jénderal Republik Indonésia*] Indonesian Consulate General.
KK [*Kepala Keluarga*] head of family, households.
KKN [*Kuliah Kerja Nyata*] obligatory (rural) social action internship for advanced university students.
KKO [*Korps Komando*] Marine Corps.
kl- see also entries with **kel-**.
kl.₁ [*kelas*] class.
kl.₂ [*kurang lebih*] more or less, approximately.
klabet see KELABAT.
klab malam nightclub.
klaim claim. *uang* - compensation against a claim. **mengk-** file a claim. **pengk-** claimant. **pengk-an** act of claiming.
klakep see CEP₁.
klak-klak sound of clicking, clickety-clack (e.g. of shoes).
klakson (*Auto.*) horn. **meng(k)-** blow the horn.
klan clan.
klar see KELAR₁.
klaras (*Jv*) dry banana leaf.
klarifikasi clarification.
klarinét clarinet.
klas see KELAS₁.
klasemén classification.
klash /klés/ military clash.
klasi see KELASI₁.
klasifikasi classification. **mengk-kan** classify. **pengk-an** classifying, classification.
klasik, klasika classic.
klasikal classical.
klat rough draft. **mengk-** draft s.t.
klausa (*Ling.*) clause. - *bébas* independent clause. - *terikat* dependent clause.
klausul, klausula (*Leg.*) clause, article (Law).
klaver (*Crd.*) clubs.
klavier, klavir piano.
klawar see KLAVER.
klécam-klécem (*Jv*) smile. *Jeng Sum - tambah ayu* Sum is all the prettier when she smiles.
kledi k.o. mouth organ from Kalimantan.
klelep see KELELAP.
klém₁ clamp. - *besi* iron strap. **meng- 1** clamp together, rivet. **2** stencil s.t.
klém₂ see KLAIM.
klemak-klemék slow and sluggish.
klembak₁ k.o. cigarette in which tobacco is mixed with gum benzene incense.
klembak₂ see KELEMBAK₁,₂.
klén see KLAN.
klénéng k.o. small bell. **-an** concert of gamelan music.
klenger see LENGAR.

klenik secret mystical or magical practices of a questionable nature. **-²an** charlatanism.
klentang sound of a bell.
klenténg 1 Ch temple. **2** pagoda.
klép valve. - *ban* tire valve. - *jantung* heart valve. - *lekum* epiglottis. - *matahari* sun visor. - *pengaman* safety valve.
klepek (*Lit.*) student of the *STOVIA*.
klepon k.o. steamed rice cake filled with palm sugar.
kléptomani kleptomania.
klerek see KELERAK.
kléren hanger (*Coll.*) clothes hanger.
klérikal clerical.
klérk clerk. **mengk-kan** make s.o. a clerk.
klérus clergy.
klés see KLASH.
klésot (*Jv*) **meng-** move squatting close to the ground in a submissive attitude. **-an** sitting on the floor.
klétek (*Jv*) **meng-(i)** peel s.t. **-an** s.t. peeled.
kléwang single-edged sabre, sword with broad, curved blade.
kliar-klior aimless, without direction or goal.
klién client, customer.
klik₁ click (of camera, etc.).
klik₂ clique. **-²an** cliquish.
klimaks climax.
klimatologi climatology.
klimis smooth, shiny, oily (of hair). *Kepala anak itu - gundul* That child's head was smooth and bald.
klimpungan be disoriented, confused.
kling sound of small bells.
klinik clinic. - *berjalan* mobile clinic. - *bersalin* maternity clinic. - *mata* eye clinic.
kliningan see KELENÉNG.
klinis clinical.
klintir 1 clot. - *darah* blood clot. **2** small group. **ber- 1** clot (of blood). **2** in a group, in groups. **ber-an** form a small group. **-an 1** clots. **2** small group.
klio spicy dish of meat stewed with coconut milk.
klip clip.
kliping clipping (as from a newspaper).
klips clips.
klir meng- be clear, become clear. **meng-kan 1** finish s.t. ~ *pekerjaan* get a job out of the way. **2** clear s.t. up. *Kita hrs ~ kesalahpahaman ini* We have to clear up this misunderstanding.
klirak-klirik ogle.
kliring bank clearance, be cleared. **meng-(kan)** clear (checks).
klisé 1 negative of photo. **2** print, picture slide of type shown in movie houses. **3** photographic illustration. **4** cut, engraving. - *kayu* woodcut, woodblock. **5** cliché. **mengk-kan** make a negative or print of s.t.
klisma 1 catch cold. **2** irritation. - *makanan* stomach upset caused by food.
kliwer, kliwir -² hanger (for clothes). **ber-an** hang loosely.
Kliwon (*Jv*) the 5th day of the five-day week.

KLM [*Kapal Layar Motor*] motorized sailing boat.

klobot (*Jv*) dried corn husk used as cigarette wrapper. **mengk-i** husk s.t.

klobotisme tendency toward extensive verbiage without content.

klojotan (*Jv*) shake, tremble (from injury or illness).

klok bell-shaped (of skirts).

klolodan, kloloten choke from getting s.t. stuck in throat.

klompen₁ [*kelompok pendengar*] fans of a certain radio program.

klompen₂ wooden shoes.

klon (*Biol.*) clone. **mengk-** to clone. **pengk-an** cloning.

klontang-klantung hang or go about idly or without purpose.

klonyo see KELONYO.

klop see KELOP.

klorin chlorine. **mengk-** chlorinate.

klos see KELOS.

klosét water closet, toilet bowl.

klosot see KLÉSOT.

klotok small motorized boat ranging in size from a dugout to a small commercial boat.

klub 1 club. **2** clubhouse.

kluing (*Jv*) millipede.

kluntang-kluntung hang around, roam about aimlessly.

klutuk see JAMBU.

kluwek see KELUAK.

kluwih (*Jv*) k.o. breadfruit with many seeds.

kluyar-kluyur hang around, roam about with no purpose.

kluyur see KELUYUR.

KM [*Kapal Motor*] MS (Motorship).

km.₁ [*kilométer*] kilometer.

km.₂ [*kamar*] room.

KMB [*Konperénsi Méja Bundar*] Round Table Conference.

kmd. [*komandan*] commandant.

KMD [*Koran Masuk Désa*] a gvt. policy by which newspapers are given wider distribution in rural areas.

knalpot (*Auto.*) muffler.

KNIL [*Koninklijk Nederlandsch-Indisch Leger*] Dutch colonial army and its members.

KNIP [*Komité Nasional Indonésia Pusat*] the Central Indonesian National Committee.

knop see KENOP₁.

Knop [*Kebijaksanaan Nopémber*] the currency devaluation of November 1978.

ko - *dan non* the o.'s who collaborated (with the Dutch) and the o.'s who did not. *kaum* - collaborators (with the Dutch).

KO /ka o/ [*knock out*] **1** knocked out. **2** (*Humorous*) unconscious, asleep. *Jam delapan saya sdh* - I was out like a light by eight o'clock.

koa (*Ch*) k.o. card game.

koaci see KWACI.

koak sound of a crow, water buffalo, etc. - *hitam* k.o. bird. **ber-(²)** make this noise.

koalisi coalition.

koar ber- 1 scream, shout, yell. **2** talk big, be arrogant.

kobah large drum.

kobak₁ a three-cornered tear (in a shirt, etc.).

kobak₂ -an 1 small hole in the ground into which coins are tossed in a game. **2** puddle, wallow.

kobak₃ see KUBAK.

kobal, kobalt cobalt.

kobar flaming, in flames (forest, etc.). - *nyala* **meng-nyalakan** fire, excite (the spirit). **ber-** flare up, rage (of flames, battle, etc.). **ber-²(an) 1** rage (of fire), be ablaze. **2** vehement. **3** inflammatory (speech). **4** spirited. *Semangatnya* ~ His ardor was exuberant. **meng-kan 1** inspire, fire s.o. up. **2** fan flames, inflame a situation. **3** arouse passions, stir up feelings. **meng-²kan** stir up, arouse (to a heat of passion, etc.). **-an** the raging. ~ *api* raging of a fire. ~ *semangat* exuberance of spirit.

kober (*Jv*) have the opportunity or chance. *Saya belon - bikin betul sepatu tuan* I have not yet had a chance to repair your shoes.

kobér Christian graveyard of colonial times.

kobis see KUBIS.

koboi 1 cowboy. *filem* - a Western film. **2** acting big. - *cacing/céngéng* o. who acts tough (but is not). **(ke)-²an 1** reckless. **2** run wild, commit crimes. **mengk-, ng-** act big and tough.

kobok₁ 1 group (of people). **2** (*Pol.*) party. **ber-²** in groups.

kobok₂ finger bowl. **-an** finger bowl.

kocah-kacih busy doing this and that, niggling, fussing around.

kocai k.o. leek.

kocak₁ 1 hilarious, amusing. **2** smart, classy, dashing. **3** proud, arrogant. **ber-², meng-** joke, jest, be amusing. **ke-an 1** hilarity. **2** smartness. **3** being arrogant.

kocak₂ shaking (of a liquid). **ber- 1** shake. *bunyi air* ~ *di kaléng* the sound of water slushing around in the can. **2** strike (of waves on the shore). **3** become troubled, shook up (of feelings). **meng-(kan)** shake (a bottle, etc.). **ter-1** shaken. **2** troubled. ~ *hati* have o.'s confidence shaken.

kocar-kacir see KUCAR-KACIR.

kocéh ng- talk nonsense. *Ia suka* ~ *pd waktu pelajaran* She likes to talk in class. *Burung itu sdh pandai* ~ That bird knows how to talk.

kocék pocket in clothes. **-an** pocket in clothes.

koci see PURU.

kocik see KOCÉK.

koclok see KOCOK.

kocoh haste. **ter-²** hurriedly, in a hurry.

kocok meng- 1 shake, mix s.t. - *dulu baik-baik sblm dipakai* Shake well before using. *Lawakannya* ~ *perut* His jokes made people shake (with laughter). **2** mix, stir (eggs, dough), shuffle (cards). **3** rub hard. **4** incite s.o. to do s.t. **ng-** (*Coll.*) **1** shake, mix, rub. **2** masturbate. **-an** *kartu* result of shuffling. **peng-** shaker. ~ *perut* joke that makes people laugh. **peng-an 1** shaking. **2** rubbing. **3** mixing, shuffling.

kocolan fry of the *gabus* fish used for bait.

kocong 1 hood (placed over a corpse or s.o. about to be hanged). **2** wrap-around cover with the loose ends bundled up and tied together (e.g. a white cloth wrapped around a corpse in Isl. rites). **meng- 1** enclose in a *kocong*. **2** bind the opening of a bag or the loose ends of a bundle of cloth together.

kocor see KUCUR₁.

Kodaéral [*Komando Daérah Angkatan Laut*] Regional Naval Command.

kodak camera. **meng-** take a picture.

Kodak [*Komando Daérah Kepolisian*] Regional Police Command.

Kodam₁ [*Komando Daérah Militér*] Regional Military Command.

Kodam₂ [*Komando Daérah Angkatan Udara*] Air Force Regional Command.

kodar see KADAR₁.

Kodau [*Komando Daérah Udara*] Regional Airforce Command.

kode code. *- étik* code of ethics. *- pos* zip code. *- télpon* area code. **ber-** using code. *surat ~* a letter in code. **meng-kan** encode. **pengk-an** coding.

kodén 1 in lots of 20. **2** of low quality, of the kind sold in lots of 20. **3** common, ordinary by the score.

koderat see KODRAT.

kodi a score (the normal quantity of wholesale purchase of clothes or clothing). *beli dua - baju* buy 40 shirts. **ber-²** by the score. **-an 1** purchased by the score. **2** mass-produced clothing.

kodifikasi codification. **mengk-kan** codify. **pengk-an** codifying of.

Kodim [*Komando Distrik Militér*] District Military Command.

kodok frog. *- hijau/ijo* frog of the ricefield. *- puru* toad. *-²* piston.

kodrat 1 (*Isl.*) God's will, God's omnipotence. **2** power (of nature). **3** nature or character. **ber-** having the nature or power of.

kodrati see ADI.

kodya [*kota madya*] municipality.

koé see KOWÉ.

koéfisién coefficient.

koék quacking sound. **ber-, meng-** quack like a duck.

koéksisténsi coexistence.

kogel laher ballbearing.

kognossemén see KONOSEMÉN.

koh see ENGKOH.

kohabitasi cohabitation.

Kohanudas [*Komando Pertahanan Udara Nasional*] National Air Defense Command.

kohérén coherent.

kohérénsi coherence.

kohési cohesion.

kohir tax assessment list.

kohol k.o. eye salve.

kohong fetid, stinking (of rotten eggs, etc.).

koin (*Coll.*) coin.

koinsidénsi coincidence.

koit (*Vulg.*) die, dead.

koitus coitus.

koja₁ water jar with a neck.

koja₂ see KHOJA.

kojoh flooded (of ricefields).

kojol ter-² laugh convulsively.

kojor (*Vulg.*) drop dead.

kok₁ 1 why?, how come? *- mau?* How come you were willing? *- banyak lalat di sini?* How come there are so many flies here? **2** a particle at the end of a phrase denying a presumption or statement of the interlocutor. *Bukan -* Not really. *"Jauh, ndak?" "Ndak jauh - "* "Is it far or not?" "No, it is not." *Nggak apa-apa -* Really, it is nothing.

kok₂ /kok/ shuttlecock.

koka k.o. monkey.

kokain cocaine.

kokam [*kontal kambing*] k.o. fried cake.

kokang meng- cock a rifle for firing.

kokas coke.

kokbrut 1 (*Sl.*) have sexual intercourse. **2** (*Sl., Jkt*) damn you!

koki (*Coll.*) cook, chef.

kokila see KUKILA.

koko term of address or reference for o.'s elder brother.

kokoh see KUKUH.

kokok crowing. *- beluk* owl. **ber- 1** crow. **2** boast, brag.

kokol₁ k.o. fern, bracken.

kokol₂ hunched over, doubled up (sitting or lying down). **ber-(²)** shivering (with fever). **meng-** double or hunch up.

kokon cocoon. **peng-an** *ulat sutera* raising of silk worm.

kokop see KUKUP.

kokosan k.o. very sour lansium fruit.

kokot₁ clamp, bent hook. *- betina* eye of clasp. *- buldog* serrated piece of metal for joining two pieces of wood. *- jantan* hook, clasp. **meng-** claw, scratch.

kokot₂ gnarled (of hands, feet through arthritis, scar tissue, etc.). **ter-** badly gnarled.

kokpit (*Av.*) cockpit.

koktil cocktail.

kol₁ cabbage. *- kembang* cauliflower. *- putih* white cabbage.

kol₂ k.o. minibus, name given to passenger vans in general.

kol₃ colt pistol.

kol₄ di- 1 calculated, estimated. **2** collated.

kol₅ brush (of a generator). *- dinamo* generator brush.

kol₆ mengk- (*Bri.*) call.

Kol. [*kolonél*] **1** colonel. **2** (*Navy*) captain.

kolaborasi collaboration, esp. with the enemy. **ber-** collaborate.

kolaborator collaborator.

kolah see KULAH₁.

kolak₁ sweet compote made of starchy fruits (cassava, bananas, etc.) stewed in coconut milk and sugar. **meng-** prepare this dish.

kolak₂ see KULAK₂.
kolam 1 pond, pool. - *air* water reservoir. - *(be)renang* swimming pool. - *ikan* fishpond. - *kaca* aquarium. - *peluncuran* swimming pool provided with a slide. **2** tank.
kolang-kaling₁ the fruit of the sugar palm.
kolang-kaling₂ to and fro, back and forth, up and down.
kolar see KORAL.
koléga colleague.
kolégial colleaguelike.
kolégialitas collegiality.
koléh-koléh 1 tapioca starch. **2** k.o. pastry made from wheat dough rolled into balls.
kolék, kolék-kolék small dinghy. **ber-²** **1** float, bob up and down. **2** go hither and yon. **3** go by dinghy.
kolé-kolé (*Amb*) dug-out canoe.
koléksi 1 collection. **2** church collection.
kolékte church collection.
koléktif collective. *kehidupan* - collective life.
koléktivisme collectivism.
koléktor, koléktur collector of the land tax.
kolembén, kolembéng₁ columbine.
kolembéng₂ k.o. pastry like lady fingers.
koléng ber- 1 float, bob up and down. **2** go hither and yon.
koléra cholera.
kolése 1 lecture. **2** college.
kolésom ginseng.
kolésterol cholesterol.
koli piece, bag, bale. *Barangnya tiga* - Three pieces of luggage.
kolibri hummingbird.
kolik 1 bacterial infection. **2** colic.
kolintang k.o. Minahassan musical instrument similar to the marimba.
koloid, koloida colloid.
kolok see KULUK.
kolokan /kolo'an/ mollycoddled, spoiled so that o. easily cries.
kolokasi collocation.
kolokial colloquial.
kolokium colloquium.
kololit k.o. liquid shoe polish.
kolom printed column. **-an** *harian* daily column.
kolomnis columnist.
kolone (*Mil.*) column.
kolonél 1 colonel. **2** (*Navy*) Captain.
kolong₁ 1 space underneath s.t. (a house, table, sky, etc.). - *jembatan* space beneath a bridge. - *langit* sublunary world. - *layar* banner (for advertisement, etc.). - *rumah* cellar, basement. **2** pit (as in mine). - *timah* tin mine.
kolong₂ -², -an rattan ring or bracelet.
koloni colony.
kolonial colonial.
kolonis colonist.
kolonisasi colonization.
kolonisir meng- colonize.
kolonjono k.o. tall grass used as fodder.
kolonyét perfumed tissue.

kolor 1 drawstring. **2** shorts or undershorts. **ng-bootlick.**
kolosal colossal.
kolot 1 old-fashioned, traditional. *pengertian yg* - old-fashioned idea. **2** conservative. *pendirian yg* - conservative stand. **ke-an** conservatism.
kolporteur, kolportir 1 peddler, hawker. **2** canvasser (of subscriptions).
kolt see KOL₂.
kolumnis see KOLOMNIS.
kom (*Coll.*) cereal bowl.
koma₁ coma.
koma₂ comma. - *atas* apostrophe. - *bernoktah/titik* semicolon.
komak-komik see KOMAT-KAMIT.
koma-koma saffron.
komala see GEMALA.
komaliwan (*Navy*) eating utensils supplied on a boat.
komandan 1 commander. **2** commandant. - *upacara* parade commander. **mengk-i** (*Mil.*) command, have command over.
komandemén commandment.
komandité limited partner (in a business, o. who provides part of the capital without participating in the management).
komanditér limited partnership.
komando 1 command, area of military jurisdiction. **2** military command (to do s.t.). **meng-(kan)** command s.o. to do s.t.
komat-kamit with moving lips but not speaking aloud (as in offering a silent prayer). **ber-** move lips in this way.
kombali see KEMBALI.
kombang see KUMBANG.
kombék /kombék/ (*Coll.*) reconciliation of lovers.
kombi a Volkswagen minibus.
kombinasi combination. - *fitting* combination plug or socket. **meng(k)-kan** combine.
kombong (*Jv*) stable, coop. **-an** feeding trough for horses.
kombor₁ meng- feed a horse.
kombor₂ (*Jv, Jkt*) too big in size, loose fitting.
kombor₃ see ÉS.
Komdak [*Komando Daérah Kepolisian*] Regional Police Command.
komédi see KOMIDI.
komendur 1 troop commander. **2** harbormaster. **3** district head.
koméng dwarfish, stunted in growth, diminutive.
komentar commentary. **meng(k)-i** comment on.
komentator commentator.
komérsial commercial. **mengk-kan** make commercial, commercialize.
komérsialisasi commercialization. **mengk-kan** commercialize.
komérsiil, komérsil see KOMERSIAL.
komés see KUMIS₂.
komét comet.
komfor see KOMPOR.
komfort comfort.
komidi 1 comedy. **2** theater. - *kuda* circus. - *putar*

merry-go-round. - *setambul* touring stage show. **meng-kan** make fun of s.o.

komik 1 clown, humorist, comic. **2** comics.

kominikasi see KOMUNIKASI.

kominiké communiqué.

kominis see KOMUNIS.

komis administrative position immediately senior to that of a clerk.

komisariat 1 office of the commissioner. **2** police headquarters.

komisaris commissioner, superintendent. - *agung* high commissioner. - *polisi* police commissioner.

komisi₁ 1 commission. *pergi* - investigate, inspect s.t. **2** committee (in parliament, etc.). **meng-** inspect, investigate.

komisi₂ 1 commission on a sale. - *borongan* commission on an entire lot or on a wholesale deal. **2** tip, bribe. **mengk-kan** sell s.t. on commission.

komisionér commission agent. - *éfék* stockbroker.

komit see KOMÉT.

komité committee.

komitmen commitment.

komkoma see KOMA-KOMA.

komoditi commodity, raw materials as an item of trade.

komodo 1 an island of the Lesser Sundas. **2** the komodo dragon found on this island.

komodor commodore. - *udara* air commodore (equivalent to brigadier general).

kompa see POMPA.

kompak /kompak/ **1** compact, dense. **2** cohesive (of a group). *salam* - warm greetings. **3** unified. **memper-, mengk-kan 1** firm s.t. up. **2** make a group cohesive. **ke-an 1** compactness. **2** harmony, solidarity. **3** togetherness, cohesiveness.

kompanyi see KOMPENI.

kompanyon associate, colleague (esp. in business). **ber-** have associates, colleagues.

komparatif comparative.

kompartimén two or three departments combined. *menko* - minister in charge of coordination of such combined departments.

kompartiméntasi coordinating of several departments.

kompas₁ compass.

kompas₂ blackmail. **ng-** blackmail.

kompeni 1 popular term for the Dutch E. India Company. **2** Dutch E. Indies soldier or army. **3** Dutch rule (during the early colonial period).

kompénsasi compensation. **meng-(kan)** compensate.

kompénsir mengk- compensate.

komperénsi see KONFERÉNSI.

komperés see KOMPRÉS.

kompés meng- 1 give s.o. the 3rd degree. **2** coerce, torture. **-an 1** the 3d degree. **2** coercion, torture.

kompetén competent. **ber-** be competent, have authority.

kompeténsi competence.

kompétisi competition. **ber-** compete.

kompi (*Mil.*) company.

kompilasi compilation. **mengk-kan** compile, make a compilation of s.t.

komplék, kompléks 1 complex. **2** (psychological) complex. - *perasaan kurang harga diri* inferiority complex. **3** site, complex (of buildings). - *militér* military complex. - *perkantoran* office complex. - *perumahan* housing complex.

kompléksitas complexity.

komplemén complement, supplement. **mengk-i** complement s.t.

kompleméntaritas complementarity.

kompleméntér complementary.

komplét complete. *bistik* - beefsteak with all the trimmings. *Rumahnya - dgn kulkas* His house is complete with an icebox. *kacau* - completely disorganized. **ke-an** completeness, wholeness, totality.

komplikasi complication.

komplimén compliment.

komplit see KOMPLÉT.

komplong₁ (*Jkt*) stupid. **meng-** be agape.

komplong₂ - *Jepang* rubber sole of Japanese slippers (without the bands).

komplot 1 accomplice, henchman. **2** plot. **ber-** plot, conspire. **-an** gang, ring. ~ *Empat* Gang of Four. **peng-** plotter.

kompoi see KONVOI.

kompol see OMPOL.

komponén component.

kompong 1 mutilated, mangled. **2** amputated, only a stump left (of limbs).

komponis composer.

kompor hot plate, stove, brazier.

kompos compost. **meng(k)-kan** turn s.t. into compost. **peng-an** composting. **per-an** becoming compost.

komposisi composition. **ber-** be composed of.

komprador comprador.

komprang (*Jv*) **1** k.o. bell-bottom trousers. **2** loose-fitting (of pants).

kompréhénsi comprehension.

kompréhénsif comprehensive. *sekolah* - comprehensive school. **meng-kan** make s.t. comprehensive.

kompréi comfrey.

komprés compress. - *dingin* cold compress. **meng-** apply a compress to. *Kepalanya di-nya* He applied a compress to his head. **-an** s.t. applied as a compress.

komprési compression. **ber-** have, produce compression.

komprésor compressor.

kompromi, kompromis compromise. **ber-** make a compromise. **mengk-kan** compromise about s.t. **-²an** a sort of a compromise, compromises of various sorts.

kompromistis compromising (situation).

komputasi computation. **mengk-kan** compute.

komputer computer. - *cacahan* digital computer.

komputerisasi computerization. **mengk-kan** computerize.

kompyuter see KOMPUTER.

Komrés [*Komando Résort*] Police District Command.

Komsat [*Kommunikasi Léwat Satelit*] satellite communication.

Komsék [*Komando Séktor*] Police Subdistrict Command.

Komtabes [*Komando Kota Besar*] Metropolitan Police Command.

komunal communal. *tanah* - communal land. **mengk-kan** communalize, collectivize

komunalisme communalism.

komune commune.

komuni (*Rel.*) communion.

komunikasi communication. - *harafiah* literal communication. - *massa* mass communication. **mengk-kan** communicate.

komunikatif communicative.

komuniké communique.

komunis communist. **mengk-kan** communize, make s.t. communistic. **ke-an** state of being a communist. **pengk-an** communizing.

komunisme communism.

komunistofobi irrational fear of communism.

komutasi commutation.

komutator o. who commutes (a juridic sentence).

Komwil [*Komando Wilayah*] Subregional Police Command.

konan meng-i assault, beat up s.o.

konang meng-i discover, find out about. **-an** discovered, found out. *Ia* ~ *waktu melompat pagar* He was discovered when he jumped over the fence.

Konbes [*Konperénsi Besar*] Major Conference.

koncah wavelet. **meng-** fluctuate. **-an** fluctuation.

konci₁ (*Coll.*) female friend.

konci₂ see KUNCI₁.

konco (*Jv*) buddy, crony. **ber- 1** be cronies. **2** have cronies as. **-²an 1** cronies with e.o. **2** crony system.

kondai chignon, hair bun. **ber-** wear a chignon. ~ *dua* having a chignon filled in with an extra switch of hair. **meng-** put (the hair) up in a bun.

kondang₁ 1 famous. *novelis* - famous novelist. **2** high official. - *bagian keuangan* a high official of the finance department. - *kuncara* very famous.

kondang₂ meng- invite. **-an 1** invitation. **2** be invited, go to an affair. *Ia pergi* ~ She went to a party.

kondang₃ ditch, canal, small river.

kondé see KONDAI.

kondektur, kondéktur conductor on public transportation.

kondénsasi condensation. **mengk-kan** condense.

kondénsator condenser.

kondisi condition. **mengk-kan** condition s.t.

kondite see KONDUITE.

kondom condom.

kondomisasi spreading the use of condoms.

kondor, kondoran inguinal hernia.

konduite /konduwite/ efficiency report. *Seorg pegawai negeri hrs mempunyai - yg baik* A civil servant has to have a good efficiency report.

kondum see KONDOM.

konéksi connection with s.o. in power.

konéksitas (*Leg.*) interconnection of jurisdictions.

konéng see KUNING, KUNYIT.

konéométri geometry involving problems.

konfédérasi confederation.

konféksi ready-made clothes.

konferénsi conference. **mengk-kan** make s.t. the subject of a conference. *Apa yg di-kan?* What is the subject of the conference?

konfidénsi confidence.

konfidénsial, konfidénsiil confidential.

konfigurasi configuration.

konfirmasi confirmation. **mengk-kan** confirm s.t.

konfiskasi confiscation. **mengk-** confiscate.

konflik conflict. **ber-** be in conflict with e.o.

konform be in conformity.

konfrontasi 1 the policy of political and armed confrontation with Malaysia of the early 1960s. **2** confrontational (attitude, behavior). **ber-** be in confrontation with e.o. **mengk-kan** engage in a policy of confrontation against s.o.

konfrontir mengk- confront.

kong, kong cu (*Ch*) master, teacher, champion. *Dia tinggal bersama -²nya* He lives with his teachers.

kongésti congestion.

konggrés see KONGRÉS.

Konghucu Confucius.

kongkalikong intrigue, connivance with s.o. in power to get a favor. **ber-** conspire, connive. *Ia* ~ *dgn org dlm* He conspired with the insiders.

kongkang see KUNGKANG₂.

kongkau see KONGKO.

kongking (*Ch*) k.o. card game.

kongko (*Ch*) talk, chat. **ber-, meng-** chat with. **-an 1** a chat. **2** council of Ch Officers (colonial period).

kongkol talking over s.t. **se- 1** be an accessory. *Ia* ~ *dgn penipu itu* He was an accomplice of the thief. **2** scheme, plot with. **berse-/bersi-** plot, conspire. **se-an** collusion, plot. **perse-an 1** intrigue. **2** conspiracy.

kongkong₁ loud bark of a dog. **meng-** bark loudly. **-an** barking of a dog.

kongkong₂ see KUNGKUNG.

kongkow see KONGKO.

kongkrét, kongkrit see KONKRÉT.

kongkur see KONKURS.

kongkurén, kongkurénsi see KONKURÉNSI.

kongkurs see KONKURS.

konglomerat /kon-glomerat/ conglomerate.

kongrégasi congregation.

kongrés congress, convention.

kongruén congruent.
kongsép see KONSÉP$_{1,2}$.
kongsi (*Ch*) 1 commercial association, partnership. 2 group, association. - *perniagaan* trading house. **ber-** enter into a commercial partnership. **per-an** 1 consortium. 2 merchant's association.
kongsol see KONSUL$_1$.
KONI [*Komité Nasional Olah Raga Indonésia*] the Indonesian National Sports Committee.
konifer conifer.
Konjén [*Konsulat Jénderal*] Consulate General.
konjungsi conjunction.
konjungtur 1 business outlook. 2 business cycle. 3 upswing, favorable market.
konklusi conclusion. **ber-** conclude.
konkordansi 1 (*Rel.*) concordance. 2 agreement.
konkrét concrete, tangible, solid. *contoh yg* - a concrete example. **mengk-kan** concretize, objectify. **ke-an** concreteness. **pengk-an** concretization.
konkrétisasi concretization. **mengk-kan** concretize, objectify.
konkrétisir mengk- concretize.
konkurén 1 rivalry. *Toko yg satu tutup dan dgn sendiri* - *habis* O. of the stores closed and so there was no more competition. 2 compete. **ber-** compete.
konkurénsi competition, rivalry.
konkurs match, contest. - *musik* music contest.
konon 1 they say, purportedly. - *ia dipilih menjadi présidén* They say he was elected president. 2 I wonder. *Siapa - memanggil saya tadi?* I wonder who called me just now? 3 perhaps, it seems. *Permintaan itu - diajukan secara mendadak* It seems that the request was made all of a sudden. - *lagi* let alone, much less. *Saya tak berani memotong ayam, - lagi manusia* I do not dare kill a chicken, let alone a human being. **-nya** purportedly. **memper-** mislead with rumors. **meng-kan** report as hearsay.
konosemén bill of lading.
konotasi connotation. **mengk-kan** connote.
konpéksi see KONFÉKSI.
konpénsi see KONVÉNSI.
konperénsi see KONFERÉNSI.
konpergénsi see KONVERGÉNSI.
konpoi see KONVOI.
konsekrasi consecration. **mengk-kan** consecrate s.t.
konsekrir mengk- consecrate. **pengk-an** consecration. ~ *uskup* consecration of a bishop.
konsekuén consistent. **mengk-kan** make consistent. **ke-an** 1 consistency. 2 consequence, result. *Apakah ~ dr tindakan itu?* What are the consequences of that action?
konsekuénsi 1 consistency. 2 consequences.
konsekwén see KONSEKUÉN.
konsekwénsi see KONSEKUÉNSI.
konselét see KORTSLÉTING.
konseling counseling. *Lembaga - Mahasiswa* student counseling agency.

konselor counselor.
konsénsus consensus. **mengk-kan** agree on s.t. by common consent.
konséntrasi concentration. **ber-** concentrate. **mengk-kan** concentrate s.t. on. **ter-** be concentrated on.
konséntrat concentrate.
konséntrik concentric.
konséntrir mengk- concentrate. **ter-** be concentrated on.
konsép$_1$ draft, rough copy. **meng-kan** prepare a draft.
konsép$_2$, **konsépsi** concept, notion, idea. **mengk-kan** conceive of s.t.
konsépsional, **konsépsionil** conceptual. *secara* - conceptually.
konséptor 1 conceiver. 2 drafter (of a plan).
konséptual conceptual.
konséptualisasi conceptualization. **mengk-(kan)** conceptualize.
konsér, **konsért** concert, concerto. - *biola* violin concerto.
konservasi conservation. **mengk-kan** conserve.
konservatif conservative. **ke-an** conservatism.
konservatisme conservatism.
konsérvator curator (of a museum).
konsérvatori conservatory (of music).
konsérven preserves.
konsési 1 concession, special privilege. - *utk menebang hutan* a timber concession. - *tarif* a special tariff agreement. 2 concessions, partial surrender of o.'s own interest. *kedua belah pihak bersedia memberi* - Both sides are prepared to make concessions. **mengk-kan** concede s.t.
konsideran, **konsiderans** preamble.
konsignasi see KONSINYASI$_2$.
konsili (*Rel.*) church council. *di - Trénte* The Council of Trent.
konsinyasi$_1$ confinement to military base. **meng-(kan)** confine to base.
konsinyasi$_2$ consignment. **meng-(kan)** consign.
konsinyator consignor.
konsinyéring confinement to base. **mengk-** confine to base.
konsinyi$_1$ consignee.
konsinyi$_2$ see KONSINYIR$_1$.
konsinyir$_1$ (*Mil.*) on alert. **meng-** put on alert. *Semua tentara di Jkt di- karena ada bahaya* The whole army in Jkt was put on alert because there was a danger.
konsinyir$_2$ meng- consign.
konsistén consistent. **ke-an** consistency.
konsisténsi consistency. **mengk-kan** make s.t. consistent.
konsol see KONSUL$_{1,2}$.
konsolidasi consolidation. **ber-** consolidate o.s. **mengk-kan** consolidate s.t. **pengk-an** consolidating.
konsolidir mengk- consolidate s.t.
konsonan consonant.
konsorsium consortium.
konspirasi conspiracy. **ber-** conspire.

konspiratif conspiratorial.
konstan 1 a constant. **2** constant, fixed. **ke-an** constancy.
konstatasi mengk- draw a conclusion, establish a fact.
konstatéring ascertaining, establishing.
konstatir mengk- 1 mention, state. **2** establish a fact, ascertain.
konstélasi constellation.
konstipasi constipation.
konstituante constituent assembly.
konstitusi constitution. **mengk-kan** establish, constitute s.t.
konstitusional, konstitusionil constitutional.
konstruir mengk- construct.
konstruksi construction. **mengk-(kan)** construct s.t.
konstruktif constructive.
konsul₁ consul. - *jénderal* consul general. - *muda* vice-consul.
konsul₂ consultation. **meng-** consult.
konsulat consulate. - *jénderal* consulate general.
konsulén consultant. - *pajak* tax consultant.
konsulér consular (affairs).
konsult see KONSUL₂.
konsultan consultant.
konsultasi 1 consultation. **2** consult. **ber-** consult, have a consultation. **mengk-** consult s.o. **mengk-kan** consult about s.t.
konsultatif consultative.
konsumén consumer.
konsumerisme consumerism.
konsumir mengk- consume.
konsumsi 1 consumption. - *méwah* conspicuous consumption. **2** refreshments. **mengk-(kan)** consume.
konsumtif consumptive.
kontak₁ contact. *Tdk ada - lagi dgn teman-teman lama* I have not kept in contact with my old friends. - *senjata* armed contact. **meng-** contact s.t. *Dia mencoba ~ temannya* he tried to contact his friend. **meng-kan** bring s.t. into contact. **peng-** connector.
kontak₂ 1 light switch, ignition. *kunci -* ignition key. **2** short circuit. *Listriknya - dan semua lampu mati* There was a short circuit and the lamps went out. **3** electric shock. **meng-kan 1** switch, turn on (a light, engine), plug s.t. in. **2** cause a short circuit. **-an** *listerik* **1** electric switch. **2** short circuit.
kontal-kantil 1 dangle, swing to and fro. **2** flap. **ber-, ter- 1** dangle, swing to and fro. **2** flap.
kontaminasi contamination. **mengk-** contaminate. **ter-** get contaminated.
kontan 1 cash. *membayar dgn -* pay in cash. **2** at that very moment. *Dia minum obat dan - mati* She drank medicine and died on the spot. *menjawab -* reply then and there. - *keras* that very moment. **3** flatly denying s.t. **meng-, meng(k)-i** pay cash for. **-²an** at that very moment.
kontang-kanting dangle. *Jam itu - pd sebuah rantai* The watch dangled on a chain. **ber-, ter-** dangle.

kontéks context.
kontelér, kontelir district officer of the colonial era (controller). **-an** residence of the controller.
kontémplasi contemplation. **ber-** engage in contemplation. **mengk-kan** contemplate s.t.
kontémplatif contemplative.
kontémporér contemporary.
konténsius contentious.
kontés contest. **mengk-kan** hold a contest over. **-²an** contests of various kinds. *Buat apa diadakan ~?* Why do we have to have all these contests?
kontéstan 1 contestant. **2** candidate (in election).
kontéstasi dispute, conflict.
kontét stunted in growth.
kontinén continent.
kontinéntal continental.
kontingén contingent, part.
kontinu, kontinue continuous.
kontinuitas continuity.
kontinyue see KONTINU.
kontol (*Vulg.*) penis. - *bébék* k.o. spiral-shaped machine part. - *kambing* k.o. spherical cake made of red glutinous rice.
kontra contra. *Bukan sekedar non saja, tapi kaum -, kaum anti-Belanda* They were not just uncooperative, but they were the contra's, the o.'s who were really anti-Dutch. - *révolusionér* counterrevolutionary. - *dgn* run into, collide with. *Mobil itu - dgn bis* That car collided with a bus. **meng-(i)** oppose s.t.
kontradiksi contradiction. **mengk-** contradict.
kontradiktif contradictory.
kontradiktoris contradictory.
kontradisi see KONTRADIKSI.
kontrak contract. - *karya/kerja* work contract. **mengk-karyakan, mengk-kerjakan** have s.t. done on contract. - *séwa* **mengk-séwakan** lease s.t. out. **meng-** contract s.t., lease s.t. with a contract. *Ia ~ rumah utk dua tahun* She leased a house by contract for two years. **mengk-kan** contract out. *Penggalian tanah di-kan* The excavation was contracted out. *Saya punya rumah yg mau saya -kan* I have a house I would like to lease out. **-an** s.t. leased (out). *rumah ~* a house leased out, house that was leased. **peng-** o. who works by contract.
kontraksi (*Fin.*) contraction (of money supply). **ber-** contract.
kontraktan contracting party.
kontraktor contractor.
kontraktual, kontraktuil contractual.
kontras contrast. **mengk-kan** contrast s.t. **ke-an** contrast.
kontrasépsi contraception.
kontraséptif contraceptive.
kontrelir see KONTELÉR.
kontribusi contribution, donation.
kontrol, kontrole 1 control, supervision. *bagian -* audit department. **2** trip supervisor. **3** control. *Dia kehilangan - dirinya* He lost control of himself. **ber-** be under control or supervision. **meng- 1** supervise, check on. *Dokter datang ~ jam*

delapan malam The doctor came at eight p.m. to check in. **2** go on o.'s rounds to check up. **3** control. *Ia tak bisa lagi ~ perilakunya* He can no longer control his actions. **ter-** can be controlled, supervised. **peng-** checker, supervisor. *~ banjir* flood control supervisor. **peng-an** act of controlling or supervising.

kontrolir₁ controller, ticket taker.

kontrolir₂ see KONTELÉR.

kontrovérsi controversy.

kontrovérsial, kontrovérsiil controversial.

kontur contour. **meng-** appear in outline.

konvéks convex.

konvéksi convection.

konvénsi 1 convention, congress. **2** agreement. - *Jenéva* the Geneva Convention. **3** convention, custom.

konvensional, konvénsionil conventional.

konvérgén convergent.

konvérgénsi convergence.

konvérsasi conversation.

konvérsi conversion. **mengk-kan** convert. **pengk-an** converting.

konvértibel convertible (car).

konvoi convoy.

konvulsi convulsions.

konyak cognac.

konyan (*Ch*) New Year's celebration.

konyol 1 foolish, inviting problems onto o.s. - *kamu menyimpan péstol tanpa izin* You are crazy to keep a handgun without a permit. *mati -* die for nothing. **2** constant bad luck. - *kita kehabisan bénsin* This is bad luck! We're out of gas. **3** incompetent, not up to snuff. **meng(k)-kan** make o. look foolish. *Dia ~ diri dgn perbuatan itu* He made himself look foolish with what he did. **kean** foolishness, tendency to have bad luck.

konyong se-² sudden, suddenly. *serangan ~* sudden attack. *~ ia memukul saya* Suddenly he hit me.

konyungsi see KONJUNGSI.

konyungtur see KONJUNGTUR.

kooperasi see KOPERASI.

kooperatif see KOPERATIF.

Koops [*Komando Opérasional*] Operational Command.

koordinasi /ko'ordinasi/ coordination. **mengk-kan** coordinate. **pengk-an** coordinating.

koordinat /ko'ordinat/ coordinate.

koordinator /ko'ordinator/ coordinator.

koordinatorat office of coordinating staff. - *Perguruan Tinggi Wilayah Jawa Barat* Coordinating Staff of the Universities of W. Java.

koordinir /ko'ordinir/ **mengk-** coordinate. **pengk-kan** coordinating.

kop₁ 1 head. - *berita* headline. - *télepon* ear and mouthpiece of a phone. **2** letterhead. - *surat* letterhead. **3** head of a recorder. **mengk-, menge-** hit (a ball) with o.'s head. **-²an** strike of a ball with o.'s head.

kop₂ nge- give cupping suction treatment by applying a heated glass to the skin.

kopah quantity of blood. **ber-²** to gush out in quantity (of blood).

kopak₁ meng- peel (potatoes, etc.).

kopak₂ see KUPAK.

Kopasgat [*Komando Pasukan Gerak Cepat*] Rapid Action Force Command.

kopék₁ 1 flaccid (of breasts). **2** (*in some regions only*) teat. **meng-** suckle on an empty breast.

kopék₂ meng- peel with the nails.

kopel₁ (*Auto.*) universal joint.

kopel₂ see RUMAH.

kopeléng, kopeling 1 clutch. **2** connection.

kopelrim a broad army belt (for carrying grenades, etc.).

koper see KOPOR.

koperak see KOPRAK.

koperal see KOPRAL.

koperasi 1 a cooperative (economic enterprise). **2** cooperation. **ber-** cooperate, work in cooperation. **mengk-kan** organize into cooperatives. **kean** cooperativeness. **peng-an, per-an 1** system of cooperatives. **2** system of cooperation.

koperatif cooperative.

koperator cooperator.

kopét narrow (of opening, street, passage).

kopi₁ coffee. - *bubuk* powdered coffee. - *hitam* black coffee (no cream). - *luak* coffee beans collected from the civet cat's feces. - *pahit* **1** black coffee. **2** a scolding, a bawling out. - *susu* coffee with milk. - *tubruk* coffee prepared by pouring boiling water over powdered coffee. **(me)ng-** have a cup of coffee. **peng-** a lover of coffee. **per-an** coffee production.

kopi₂ copy, draft. **mengk-** copy s.t.

kopiah k.o. rimless cap, headdress worn by Muslim men and also by Indonesian men in general as a symbol of national identity. - *setambul* fez.

Kopkamtib [*Komando Pemulihan Keamanan dan Ketertiban*] Command for the Restoration of Security and Public Order.

koplak, koplakan /kopla'an/ place where carts, minibuses, and other vehicles gather to await passengers.

koplam, koplamp headlight.

koplét see KUPLÉT.

kopling see KOPELÉNG.

kopok, kopokan have a runny ear.

kopong (*Jv, Jkt*) empty, hollow.

kopor 1 trunk, footlocker. **2** suitcase.

kopra copra. **meng-kan** turn into copra. **per-an** copra production.

koprak bamboo clapper to frighten birds. **meng-** scare away birds with a clapper. **-an** clapper to frighten birds.

kopral 1 (*Mil.*) corporal. **2** (*Navy*) petty officer 3d class.

koprol somersault, tumble.

kopula (*Ling.*) copula.

kopur (*Fin.*) denomination.

kopure denomination, note of money.

kopyok meng- 1 shake s.t., esp. to blend or mix it up. *Sayur di- dgn air* Rinse the vegetables in water. **2** shake up pieces of paper for lottery. **-an** **1** the thing in which s.t. is shaken up. **2** a lottery, drawing. **3** (*Coll.*) dancing. **peng-** beater, blender.

kopyor a coconut that has developed differently from the others in the bunch and has soft flesh blended with the juice and is esp. tasty and highly prized for snacks.

kor choir.

korah 1 sphere. **2** spherical.

korak [*kommando pérak*] **1** name of a crime organization that specializes in pilfering from delivery trucks. **2** petty extortionist. **meng-** engaging in pilfering from delivery trucks.

koral coral.

Koramil [*Komando Rayon Militér*] Military Headquarters at the ward (*kecematan*) level.

Koran (*Isl.*) the Qur'an.

koran₁ newspaper. *- kuning* yellow journal, scandal sheet. *- pagi* morning paper. *- warawiri* impartial newspaper. **meng-kan** spread information (us. unfavorable). **per-an** newspaper affairs.

koran₂ see RÉKENING.

korat-karit dislocated, scattered, in disorder.

korban 1 sacrifice. **2** (*Isl.*) religious offering, the offering made at rites celebrating *idul adha*. *- misa* (*Rel.*) the sacrifice of the Mass. **3** victims. *- jiwa/manusia* casualty (in war, accident). *- kebakaran* victim of a fire. *- perang* war victim. **ber-** make a sacrifice. *~ pd déwa-déwa* make a sacrifice to the gods. *Dia sdh banyak ~ utkku* He has already made many sacrifices for me. *~ demi kepentingan org lain* make a sacrifice for s.o. else's interests. **meng-kan** sacrifice s.t. *~ jiwanya* sacrifice o.'s life. **peng-an** making a sacrifice. *Tdk ada kasih tanpa ~* There is no love without sacrifice.

kordén see GORDÉN.

kordinasi see KOORDINASI.

kordinat see KOORDINAT.

kordinir see KOORDINIR.

kordon cordon worn with an academic gown.

koréd k.o. small hoe with short handle.

korék₁ matches, cigarette lighter. *- api* matches, cigarette lighter. *- batu* (cigarette) lighter. *- kayu* matches. *- kuping* earpick. **meng-(²) 1** scrape, get s.t. by scraping. *~ nasi* scrape rice out of a container. *Induknya ~ tanah* The mother hen scratched on the ground. *~ kuku* scrape the dirt from under o.'s nails. **2** dig up secrets. *~ rahasia* pry out secrets. *~ peristiwa sepuluh tahun yg lalu* Dig up events of 10 years ago. **meng-i** scrape s.t. out. *~ kaléng itu* scrape out the can. **-an** (cigarette) lighter. **peng-** *telinga* earpick.

korék₂ /korék/ correct.

koréksi correction. **mengk-** correct s.t. *~ cétakan percobaan* proofread. **-an 1** corrected material. **2** papers to be corrected. **peng-an** correcting, proofreading.

koréktif corrective.

koréktor 1 proofreader. **2** correction fluid (for stencils).

korelasi correlation. **mengk-kan** correlate s.t.

Korém [*Komando Résort Militér*] Military Command (at a level below the residency).

koréng 1 sore, ulceration. **2** scab (over a sore). *--moréng* be all scabs. **ber-** have a sore or scab. **meng-** develop a scab. **-an** suffer from skin infections. *sakit ~* scabies.

koréografer choreographer.

koréografi choreography.

Korés [*Komando Résort*] District Police Command.

korés see GORÉS.

koréspondén (newspaper) correspondent.

koréspondénsi correspondence.

Korésta [*Komando Résort Kota*] Metropolitan Police Command.

korét₁ leftovers. **meng-** use the leftovers. **meng-i** scrape the leftovers. **-an** leftovers.

korét₂ see KORÉK₁.

korét₃ see KURÉT.

kori₁ (*Jv*) door.

kori₂ see QARI.

koriah see QARIAH.

koridor corridor.

korma see KURMA.

kornéd see KORNÉT₂.

kornél₁ (*Sport*) corner kick.

kornél₂ see KOLONÉL.

kornét₁ canned corned beef.

kornét₂ see KENÉK.

korok₁ excavation, excavated tunnel. **meng-** dig, excavate s.t.

korok₂ **meng-** snore. **-an** snoring.

koronér a coronary (attack).

korong surroundings. *- kampung* village and surroundings. **ber-** *kampung* have the atmosphere of a village and its surroundings.

korosi corrosion.

korosif corrosive.

Korporasi Corporation.

Korpri [*Korps Pegawai Républik Indonésia*] the Indonesian Civil Service Corps.

korps /korep, koreps/ corps. *- Marinir* Marine Corps.

korsase corsage.

korsél merry-go-round, carousel.

Korsél [*Koréa Selatan*] S. Korea.

korsét corset.

korsi see KURSI₁.

korsléting see KORTSLÉTING.

korting discount. **meng-** give a discount.

kortison cortisone.

kortsléting 1 short circuit. **2** (*Coll.*) misunderstand e.o.

korum see KUORUM.

korup corrupt. **mengk-** misappropriate funds. **mengk-kan** make s.o. corrupt.

korupsi corruption, graft. *- kakap* big-time corruption. *- teri* small-time corruption. **ber-** engage in graft. **mengk-** steal s.t. through graft.

koruptor o. who is corrupt.

Korut [*Koréa Utara*] N. Korea.

korvé corvée.

korvét k.o. warship, a corvette.
kos 1 room and board or just board. *anak* - boarder. *bapak* - landlord. *ibu* - landlady. *rumah* - boarding house. **2** board with s.o. **menge-i** board at. **menge-kan** rent out to roomers or boarders.
kosa kata vocabulary, glossary.
kosak-kasik 1 rustling. **2** fidgeting, restless.
kosambi see KESAMBI.
kosar k.o. autocarpus tree yielding edible fruits and timber.
kosbas landlord, landlady.
kosék door mat. **meng- 1** clean a floor with a brush. **2** rinse or wash food. **3** run water on whetstone while sharpening.
Kosék [*Komando Séktor*] Police Subdistrict Command.
kosél ter-² **1** hem and haw. **2** work in fits and starts. **3** have difficulty with tough meat.
kosén₁ window or door frame.
kosén₂ brave, courageous, daring. **ke-an** daring, bravery, courage.
kosét see KÉSÉT₂.
kosinus (*Math.*) cosine.
kosmétik, kosmétika cosmetics.
kosmografi cosmography.
kosmologi cosmology.
kosmonaut, kosmonot cosmonaut.
kosmopolit, kosmopolitan cosmopolite, a sophisticate.
kosmos cosmos.
kosok - *balik* antonym, opposite, reverse.
kosong 1 empty, blank, zero. *lima-belas* - 15-love. *Nomornya tiga - sembilan* The number is three-zero-nine. *Hasilnya* - There were absolutely no results of any kind. *Kertas* - blank piece of paper. - *losong* completely empty. - *lompong/melompong* **1** empty. **2** idle, empty (words, promises). **2** (*Crd.*) void suit. **3** unoccupied. *Apa tempat ini* -? Is this place free? *Rumah ini sdh lama* - This house has been unoccupied for a long time. **4** hole, empty space. *Ukuran - jendéla ini delapan puluh sénti* The size of the window glass (the hole to be covered by the window) is 80 cm. **meng-kan 1** empty s.t., vacate premises. **2** use s.t. up. **ke-an 1** emptiness. **2** vacancy. **3** hiatus. **peng-an 1** evacuation, vacating (of premises). **2** clearing (of an area). **3** depletion.
kosponsor cosponsor. **mengk-i** to cosponsor.
kost see KOS.
koster manager of a rectory.
kosthuis /koshoys/ boarding house.
kostik caustic (soda).
kostim, kostum 1 costume. **2** woman's Western-style clothing. **3** dress uniform, formal dress. **ber-** wear a costume.
Kostranas [*Komando Strategi Nasional*] National Strategic Command.
kota 1 city, town. - *Bandeng* Semarang. - *Buaya* Surabaya. - *berlibur* resort town. - *Gudeg* Yogyakarta. - *Kembang* Bandung. - *madya/praja* municipality. - *Pahlawan* Surabaya. - *raya* metropolis. -

Révolusi Surabaya. - *satelit* suburbs. **2** fort. **ber-** fortified. **meng-i** wall in a town. **meng-kan** erect a fortress. **-an** urbane, from the city. *org* ~ urbanite. **pe-an** having to do with the city. *daérah* ~ urban areas. **pengk-an 1** urbanization. **2** urban area. **per-an** urban affairs. *pembangunan* ~ urban development.
kotah total. **se-** total, all.
kotai 1 hang down (as of old fruit). **2** left to dry up, desicated. **ter-** hang down.
kotak 1 box. - *ajaib* magic box. - *bergelombang* corrugated box. - *korék api* matchbox. - *makanan otomatis* food dispenser. - *perkakas* accessory kit. - *pos* **1** mailbox. **2** post-office box. - *suara* ballot box. **2** compartment, cubicle. **3** drawer. **4** box-shaped section of a garden divided into beds, of paddy fields, etc.). - *semai* seed box or bed. **-²** checkered (pattern). **ber-² 1** divided into compartments. **2** checkered (pattern). **mengk-kan** put s.t. in a box. **mengk-²kan** compartmentalize (problem, fields of study). **ter-** categorized, put into a certain category. **keter-an** categorization. **pengk-²an** compartmentalizing.
kotak katik motion by which s.o. indicates his presence. *Barangkali ia pergi karena tdk terdengar lagi -nya* Perhaps he has left because we do not hear him moving around any more. **meng-ngatikkan** move, set into motion (an engine, etc.).
kotamara parapet.
kotangén, kotangéns (*Math.*) cotangent.
kotbah see KHOTBAH.
koték₁ 1 tail feather. **2** tail plumed with a tuftlike end (e.g. of a comet). **ber-** have a tail.
koték₂ a cackle (of a hen). **ber-** cackle. *tdk* ~ *lagi* give up.
kotéka penis sheath of Irian.
koténg ter-² alone, friendless.
koterék see KOTRÉK.
kotés bits of thread or lint. **se-** a little bit. **meng-** remove small bits of thread, lint, etc.
Kotipa [*Koléra, Tipes, Paratipes*] immunization against cholera, typhoid, and paratyphoid.
kotok₁ - *ayam* having defective vision, i.e. nearsighted or suffering from night blindness. **-an** night blindness.
kotok₂ short (of pants legs).
kotong cut off, amputated. **meng-kan** amputate.
kotor 1 dirty, soiled, filthy. **2** dirty, vile, filthy (words, etc.). - *mulut* like to talk dirty. **3** gross (of income, profits). **meng-i** contaminate s.t., pollute, foul (a river, the environment). **meng-kan 1** dirty, soil s.t. **2** soil, defile (s.o.'s name). **ke-an** filthiness, dirtiness. **-an 1** feces, dung, manure. ~ *burung* bird droppings. ~ *kuda* horse manure. ~ *manusia* human waste. ~ *mata* sand from the eyes. **2** muck, waste. ~ *dapur* garbage, kitchen refuse. ~ *padat* solid waste. **3** impurity. *datang* ~ menstruate. **peng-** polluter. **peng-an** polluting, littering, dirtying.
kotrék corkscrew.
kotum quota.

kover /kafer, kofer/ **mengk- 1** cover, include. **2** cover (a story). *Ia datang utk ~ pemilihan umum* He came to cover the general elections.

Kowad [*Korps Wanita Angkatan Darat*] Army Women's Corps.

kowak ber-² 1 jabber, chatter. **2** shout (of drunkards, people wild with joy or excitement).

Kowal [*Korps Wanita Angkatan Laut*] Navy Women's Corps.

kowé (*Coll., Derog., Jv, Jkt*) you. **meng-(kan)** address o. with *kowé*.

kowék see KUWÉK.

kowér see KOAR.

Kowil [*Komando Wilayah*] Police Subregion Command.

Kowilhan [*Komando Wilayah Pertahanan*] Defence Territorial Command.

Kowiltabes [*Komando Wilayah Kota Besar*] Metropolitan Police Command.

koyak 1 torn, ripped. **2** lacerated (of the hand, etc.). **-²** in rags or tatters. **meng-(²)kan** rip, tear into tatters. **ter-** get torn, ripped. *kantung yg ~ a* torn bag. **-an** tear, rip, rent. **peng-** o. who tears, violates. **peng-an** lacerating.

koyan measurement of weight or capacity (27-40 piculs).

koyé see KOHIR.

koyer (*Sport*) pitcher in games where a ball is thrown to be batted back.

koyo₁, koyok₁ nonsense. *menjual* - talk nonsense.

koyo₂, koyok₂ (*Ch*) salve put in a medical plaster.

koyok₃ stray dog.

kozyn see KOSÉN₁.

kpd. [*kepada*] to.

KPM [*Koninkliske Paketvaart Maatschappij*] The Royal Mail Packet Lines (of the colonial era).

kr- see also entries with **ker-**.

krah see KERAH₂.

kram see KERAM₁.

krama see KROMO.

kraman rebellion.

kramat see KERAMAT.

kran see KERAN₁.

kranggang k.o. red ant.

krans funerary wreathe.

krasan (*Coll.*) feel at home, like a place o. is new at. *Saya pulang karena tdk - di sana* I went back home because I did not like the other place.

krat crate, case of 24 bottles.

kraton see KERATON.

kré see KERAI.

kréasi creation. *Tarian itu - baru* That dance is a new creation. **ber-** create. **mengk-kan** create, fashion s.t.

kréatif creative.

kréativitas creativity.

kréator creator.

krécék buffalo skin processed for eating.

kréda see KRIDA.

kredap ber-an glitter, shine, flicker.

krédép scintillate.

krédibilitas (*Fin.*) credibility.

krédit credit. *membeli dgn* - buy s.t. on credit. **mengk-kan** sell s.t. on credit. **pengk-an** crediting. **per-an** credit matters.

kréditir, kréditor creditor. **mengk-** credit s.t.

krédo (*Rel.*) credo, creed.

kréi see KERAI.

krém 1 cream of milk. **2** skin-care salve. **3** cream-colored, light-yellow.

krémasi cremation. **mengk-(kan)** cremate.

krématorium crematorium.

kremes k.o. cake made of cassava and palm sugar.

kremi see KEREMI.

krempéng see KEREMPANG.

kremus meng- chew s.t. crispy into small pieces.

kréolin creolin, a preparation of creosol and resin soap used as a deodorant and disinfectant.

kréosot creosote.

krép crépe paper.

krépyak blinds.

kréséh-péséh see KARÉSÉH-PÉSÉH.

kresek₁ see KERESAK.

kresek₂, krésék thin plastic bag with handle.

Kresna central figure of the Mahabharata.

Krésten see KRISTEN.

kréték₁ k.o. cigarette containing chopped cloves.

kréték₂ (*Jv*) horse-drawn cart.

KRI [*Kapal Républic Indonésia*] an Indonesian Flagship.

kriat-kriut see KERIANG-KERIUT.

kribo frizzy (of hair, like Africans, Melanesians, etc.). **ber-** wear o.'s hair in an afro.

Kricika (*Zod.*) Scorpio.

krida activity, physical activity (as opposed to office, school work). *Hari Sabtu hari* - Saturday is a day for extracurricular activities (everybody comes to the office or school but engages in physical activities).

kridit see KRÉDIT.

kriditor pupil who must repeat many school subjects.

kriir mengk- create.

krim see KRÉM.

kriminal, kriminil criminal (law, act, etc.).

kriminalitas, kriminalitét criminality.

kriminologi criminology.

kring₁ cell, small group of believers who work together (e.g. Catholics, etc.).

kring₂ see KERING₂.

kripik see KERIPIK.

krisis crisis. **mengk-kan** cause a crisis.

kristal crystal. **ber-, mengk-** crystallize. **pengk-an** crystallization.

kristalisasi crystallization. **mengk-kan** crystallize. **peng(k)-an** crystallizing.

kristalisir mengk- crystallize.

Kristen 1 Christian. **2** Protestant. *kaum - dan Katolik* Protestants and Catholics. **mengk-kan** Christianize. **ke-an** Christianity. **pengk-an** Christianization, Christianizing.

kristénisasi, kristianisasi Christianization.

Kristus Christ.

kritéria criteria.

kritérium criterion.

kritik 1 criticism. *- sastra* literary criticism. **2** critical. **meng- 1** criticize, give a critical opinion. **2** criticize, say s.t. bad about s.t. **-an** criticism. **peng- 1** critic. **2** fault finder. **peng(k)-an, per-an** criticizing.

kritikal critical.

kritikawan literary critic.

kritikus critic. *- sastra* literary critic.

kritis critical, serious (of patient, situation). **ke-an** in critical condition. *tingkat* ~ critical level.

kritisi see KRITIKUS.

kriuk-kriuk see KERIUK.

kriwil see PRIWIL.

kriya skill. *seni -* artistic skill.

kriyawan male salesclerk.

kriyawati female salesclerk.

kroco 1 k.o. small snail. **2** of little value, of no great importance. *Ia Komandan, dan aku hanya -* He is a commander, and I am a small fry. **3** lowest economic class.

krokét croquettes.

krokot purslane.

krol see KERUL.

kromo 1 the polite form of Jv used to and among upper-class people. *- Inggil* honorific forms. **2** the common people. **ke-an** proletarianism.

kromosom chromosome.

krompyang 1 sound of s.t. crashing to the floor. **2** sound of tin cans.

kron see KERON.

kroncong see KERONCONG₁.

krong see KERONG.

kronik chronicle.

kronis chronic.

kronologi chronology.

kronologis chronological.

kropok 1 empty, without content. **2** soft, weak. **3** moldy.

krosak see KEROSAK.

krosboi (*Coll.*) delinquent youth. *- ingusan* young punk. **ng-** act like a punk.

krosgirl (*Coll.*) female delinquent.

krosmama (*Coll.*) a woman who goes after young men.

krosok see KEROSOK₁.

krospapa a man who goes after young women.

kroto red ant eggs (fed to birds). *- melinjo* blossoms of the *gnenom gnetum* eaten as a vegetable.

kruis crotch.

kruk crutches.

krukas crankcase.

krul see KERUL.

kruntel (*Jv*) rolled up, curled.

krupuk see KERUPUK.

krupukan confused, doing s.t. hastily.

krus see KERUS, KURS.

krutuk bombard.

k.s. [*krédit seméster*] (*Acad.*) semester credit.

KS [*Kepala Staf*] Chief of Staff.

ksatria see KESATRIA.

KTP [*Kartu Tanda Penduduk/Pengenal*] residence identification card.

KTT [*Konperénsi Tingkat Tinggi*] Summit Conference.

ku see KUÉ.

-ku genitive of *aku. rumah-* my house.

ku- first person agent marker of passive verb. *Yg -beli* The o. I bought.

kuaci see KWACI.

kuadé seat at which couples sit in wedding ceremony.

kuadran quadrant.

kuadrat quadrate.

kuah gravy, broth, thin sauce, (thin) dressing. **ber-** with broth. *serabi* ~ waffles with syrup. **meng-i** put broth on s.t. **meng-kan** make a dish with broth.

kuak₁ low (of buffalo), croak (of frogs). **meng-** low, croak, bay (at the moon).

kuak₂ part (in the hair). **ber- 1** open, give way to make an opening. *Waktu angin mulai meniup, awan* ~ When the wind blew, the clouds dispersed. **2** widen, become enlarged (of a hole, rip, etc.). **meng-** become open, get rent. *Blus itu tergaét di tangannya dan* ~ *lebar* The blouse got caught in his hand and tore open. **meng-kan 1** make a rent, opening in. *Peluru itu* ~ *pahanya* The bullet tore through his thigh. **2** break open a window, door, safe, barricade, etc. *Pintu dapur di-kan org dgn paksa* S.o. forced the kitchen door open. **3** push apart (as of people, in order to get through a crowd). *Berjalan* ~ *hutan, menyiang di depan kami* He pushed the brush aside as he walked, making an opening ahead of us.

kuala estuary, river mouth, confluence. **ber-** have an estuary.

kualahan see KEWALAHAN.

kualat 1 accursed, damned. **2** struck down by a calamity.

kuali 1 wide-mouthed clay pot for cooking. **2** (*in some regions only*) iron wok.

kualifikasi 1 qualification, limitation. *tanpa -* without qualification. **2** qualification, fitness, eligibility. **mengk-kan** qualify.

kualitas quality. **ber-** have a certain quality.

kualitatif qualitative.

kualitét quality.

kualon step- (relation). *ibu -* stepmother.

kuangwung k.o. beetle in coconut trees.

kuantitas quantity.

kuantitatif quantitative.

kuantum quantum.

kuap a yawn. **ber-, meng-, ter-** yawn.

kuar meng- loosen or undo with a stick. **meng-kan** use s.t. to pry loose.

kuarsa quartz.

kuarsit quartzite.

kuartal a period of three months. *libur -* the three-month vacation. **-an 1** quarterly examination. **2** s.t. to mark the beginning of a three-month period. *Tiap* ~ *dibelikan sepatu* Each trimester he was bought a pair of shoes.

kuartir quarters.

kuas₁ 1 small brush for painting, writing. - *cat* paintbrush. 2 shaving brush. 3 applicator. - *lém* glue applicator. **meng-** brush.

kuas₂ k.o. lemonade.

kuasa 1 power, might. - *Majapahit* the might of Majapahit. 2 authority given to s.o. - *menteri* proxy for the minister. - *penuh* full powers, power of attorney. - *pos* power of attorney for postal matters. - *Présidén* authority granted by president to act on his behalf. - *usaha* 1 chargé d'affaires. 2 proxy. 3 trustee. 3 capable, able, powerful *tak - powerless, tak - menggunakan kaki* I did not have the strength to make my feet move. **ber-** 1 hold the power. *Ia ~ di negara itu* He holds the power in that country. 2 have the authority. *Polisi ~ menangkap org* The police have the authority to arrest people. *Siapa yg ~?* Who is in charge? *Duta besar ~ penuh* Ambassador plenipotentiary. **meng-i** 1 dominate. *Partai itu ~ seluruh negara* That party dominates the entire country. 2 take charge, be in command. *Bukan kuu yg ~ hidup matimu* You are not in control over whether you live or die. 3 master (a language, a raging fire, etc.). 4 have control over (o.'s feelings). *Kemarahannya tdk dpt di-inya lagi* He could no longer control his anger. **meng-kan** authorize, empower s.o. *UUD ~ Présidén utk mendirikan suatu kabinét* The Constitution empowers the President to set up a cabinet. **ter-i** controllable. *tdk ~* uncontrollable. **ter-kan** can be delegated. *tdk ~* cannot be delegated. **ke-an** 1 power. *dgn ~ uangku* with the power of my money. 2 authority, sway, hegemony, domination. *~ hrs kembali ke tangan Indonésia* Power must be returned to the hands of the Indonesian people. 3 control. *~ org tua atas anaknya* parental control over their children. *~ tertinggi* supreme authority. **peng-** 1 o. in authority. 2 manager, administrator. *~ langit dan bumi* ruler of heaven and earth. *~ pelabuhan* harbormaster. *~ perang* wartime administrator. **peng-an** 1 authority. 2 command, control, mastery. *~ bahasa Indonésia* mastery of the Indonesian language. 3 authorizing of.

kuas-kais scratch the ground (of a chicken, etc.).

kuat 1 strong, powerful. 2 sturdy. 3 forceful (personality), fervent (believer, etc.). *bau -* pungent oder. 4 be able to. *Ia tak - membayar* She cannot afford to pay. *Ia - makan banyak* He can eat a lot. 5 loud (of voice, noise). **se-** as strong or loud as. *~ suara* at the top of o.'s voice. *~ tenaga* to the utmost of o.'s strength. *Saya berdoa ~ tenaga semoga . . .* I prayed with all my heart that . . . **se-²(nya)** as strong or loud as possible. *Aku menjerit ~* I screamed at the top of my lungs. **ber-** persist, stick in there, stick with it. *Ia ~ dlm pendiriannya* She stuck to her point of view. **ber-²an** test e.o.'s strength. **meng-i** 1 take by force. 2 violate (a female). 3 coerce, use coercion against. 4 support (a proposal, etc.). **meng-kan** confirm, corroborate, affirm (a statement, asser-

tion, etc.). **memper-** 1 strengthen, reinforce s.t., brace. 2 support (a proposal, etc.). 3 confirm s.t. 4 sanction, approve. **ke-an** 1 strength, force. *~ batin* spiritual force. *~ bukti* (*Leg.*) weight of evidence. *~ semén* the hardness of the cement. 2 energy. 3 power (e.g., of a magnifying glass). 4 intensity (of light rays, etc.). *~ cahaya* candlepower. *~ dan modal* funds and forces. *~ lilin cahaya* candlepower. *~ mendidik* educational value. *~ pelenting* resilience, elasticity. *~ sembur* thrust. *~ tempur* fighting force. **peng-** 1 strengthener, tonic. *~ suara* loudspeaker. 2 (*Ling.*) intensifier. 3 reinforcement, s.t. that reinforces. **peng-an** 1 strengthening, reinforcing. 2 (*Rel.*) confirmation. *sakramén ~* the sacrament of confirmation. **per-an** 1 reinforcement given. 2 cultivation.

kuatir afraid, apprehensive about. *Ia - suratnya tdk sampai* She was afraid her letter would not arrive. *Jangan -* Do not worry. **meng-kan** 1 cause apprehension, alarm. 2 be worried about. *Itu tdk perlu di-kan* You do not have to worry about that. **ke-an** worry, anxiety.

kuau k.o. pheasant.

kuaya gall, bile.

kuayah k.o. climbing plant.

Kuba Cuba. **mengk-** (*Coll.*) hijack a plane.

kubah 1 dome, vault, cupola. - *geréja* church dome. 2 (*Mil.*) turret. - *jungur* nose turret. **ber-** use or have a dome. *mesjid ~* a domed mosque.

kubak meng- 1 peel (potatoes, etc.). 2 strip (bark from a tree).

kubang mudhole, mudpuddle. **ber-** 1 wallow in a mudhole. 2 be covered with mud. **-an** 1 mudhole. 2 trash dump.

kubat arch.

kubek /kubek/ (*Jkt, Jv*) **meng-** 1 turn s.t. around. 2 stir.

kubik₁ meng- peel (with the fingernails).

kubik₂ cubic.

kubil (*Jkt*) swollen (of eyes).

kubin k.o. flying lizard.

kubis cabbage.

kubit se- a tiny bit. **meng-** 1 pinch s.o. 2 tap s.o on the arm or shoulder to attract his attention. **meng-kan** attract attention with.

kubra 1 unsuccessful, a failure. 2 left undone. **meng-kan** 1 cause s.t. to fail. 2 leave s.t. unresolved or undone.

kubti Coptic.

kubu 1 fortification, fortress, stockade. 2 bunker, entrenchment. - *meriam* turret. - *pertahanan* (*Mil.*) bunker. **ber-** 1 make use of a fortification. 2 fortify o.s. *Stlh meréka mendarat meréka ~ di pantai* After they landed they set up fortifications on the beach. **meng-i** fortify s.t. **per-an** fortification.

kubung₁ flying lemur.

kubung₂ box for raising mushrooms.

kubur grave, tomb. **ber-** 1 buried, entombed. 2 lie (of a hero). **meng-(kan)** bury, inter, lay to rest. *Ia ~ temannya di dekat pantai* He buried his companion near the shore. **peng-an** burial, interment. **(pe)-an, per-an** cemetery, graveyard.

kubus cube.

kucai₁ k.o. leek or green onion.

kucai₂ meng- be isolated from o.'s friends.

kucak see KOCAK₂.

kucam pale, wan, drained (of energy or vitality).

kucar-kacir 1 in disorder, in a mess. **2** disorganized, inadequately supervised. *Musuh lari -* The enemy fled in disorder. **meng-kan** scatter s.t. in confusion. *Serangnya yg sekonyong-konyong itu ~ musuh* The sudden attack scattered the enemy in confusion.

kucek meng- 1 rub. *~ matanya* rub o.'s eyes. **2** do the laundry. **3** crush, grind, mash.

kucel crumpled, creased.

kucerpén [*kumpulan cerita péndék*] collection of short stories.

kucica k.o. small bird.

kucil meng-(kan) 1 expel (from family, clan, relationship, political party, etc.), ostracize, excommunicate. *Perlukah penderita lépra di-kan?* Need a leper be ostracized? **2** squeeze out (toothpaste, glue, etc.). **peng-an** banishment, expulsion, ostracism, excommunication.

kucindan see KECANDAN.

kucing cat, a feline. *- belanda* rabbit. *- garang/hutan/jalang* alley cat. *- kuwuk* cat that eats baby chicks. *- negeri* house cat. *- pekak* mousetrap. *- tupai* rabbit. *menantikan - bertanduk* wait till the cows come home, wait a month of Sundays. **-²an 1** calf (of leg). **2** biceps, muscle of leg or arm. **3** toy kitten. **4** play tag.

kucir 1 cowlick. **2** tuft of hair (left on top of a child's shaved head). **3** tassel. **4** pigtail.

kuco village chief (in Japanese times).

kucung see KOCONG.

kucup₁ be closed (of s.t. that folds up). **meng-kan** close s.t. *~ payung* close an umbrella.

kucup₂ see KECUP.

kucur₁ gushing, pouring forth. **ber-, meng-** gush or pour forth. *Darah ~ dr luka-lukanya* Blood gushed from his wounds. **meng-(i)** pour liquid on s.t. *Ia ~ badannya dgn air* He poured water over his body. **meng-kan 1** pour s.t. out, make s.t. gush forth. *~ darahnya bagi tanah air* shed blood for o.'s country. **2** pour in, contribute. *Ia menyanggupi ~ seratus juta rupiah* He promised to pour 100 million rupiah into the coffers. **-an** stream of s.t. gushed out. *Dgn banyak ~ keringat, sdhlah pekerjaannya* After pouring out much sweat, her task was over.

kucur₂ k.o. fried cake of rice flour. *- kamu* You are stupid.

kucut see KECUT₁.

kuda 1 horse. *- air* Malay tapir. *- andalan* constant winner at the racetrack. *- balap(an)* racehorse. *- beban* packhorse. *- belang* zebra. *- bibit* **1** stud (horse). **2** broad mare. *- hitam* dark horse, unexpected winner. *(main) - kayu* foul play. *- képang* horse made of plaitwork with which men dance themslves into a trance. *- laut* sea horse. *- lump-*

ing horse made of plaitwork with which men dance themslves into a trance. *- loréng* zebra. *- pacu(an)* racehorse. *- pejantan* stallion. *- sandel* horse from the sandlewood island (Sumba). *- semberani/sembrani* winged horse. *- (sungai) Nil* hippopotamus. *- téji* large fast horse. **2** (*Che.*) knight. **-² 1** sawhorse. **2** easel tripod (for blackboard, etc.). **3** a vaulting horse for gymnastics. **4** timbering for a roof. **ber- 1** have a horse. **2** ride a horse. **meng-** become a horse, be like a horse. *Anak-anak ~ pulang dr sekolah* The children trotted like horses as they returned from school. **memper-i** ride a horse. **memper-(²)kan 1** exploit, work s.o. like a horse. **2** use as a horse. **ke-²an** horselike, equine. **-²an 1** ride pickaback, play horsey. **2** hobby horse, toy horse. **3** saw horse. **pe(r)-an 1** stud farm. **2** stable.

kudai 1 small, rattan basket. **2** round silver betel leaf holder.

kudang (*Jv*) **ng-** coo, talk babytalk.

kudangan wish or request by fiancée that her future husband must fulfill.

kudap -² snack, tidbit. **meng- 1** taste s.t. **2** snack, eat between meals. **-an** snack. **peng-** snacker, s.o. who snacks between meals.

kudéta coup d'état. **meng-** carry out a coup d'état.

kudi₁ k.o. machete.

kudi₂ see KODI.

kudian see KEMUDIAN.

kudil, kudis scabies. **ber-, -an** suffer from scabies.

kudrat see KODRAT.

kudrati see ADI.

kudu₁ flower.

kudu₂ (*Jv*) must, have to.

kudu₃ k.o. red dye.

kuduk₁ nape of the neck.

kuduk₂ see NASI.

kudung₁ crippled, maimed. **meng-(kan) 1** chop off (a hand, etc.). **2** maim, mutilate. **peng-an** mutilation.

kudung₂ veil. **ber-** be veiled, wear a veil.

kudus holy, sacred, sacrosanct. *Hari Natal adalah hari -* Christmas is a holy day. **meng-kan** sanctify, makc s.t. hallowed or sacred. **ke-an** sanctity (of home, marriage, etc.). **peng-an** sanctification.

kué, kuéh cooky, cake. *- acuan* cupcake. *- andapita* pastry tidbits. *- apem* k.o. cake of rice flour with leavening. *- basah* deep-fried, boiled, or steamed cake. *- bendéra* a multi-colored layer cake of rice flour. *- bugis* cooky made from sticky rice flour. *- cang* snack consisting of rice wrapped in a bamboo leaf. *- cina* Ch New Year's cake. *- dadar* macaroon. *- dadar gulung* pancake. *- dokok-dokok* cake made of rice flour, coconut, sugar and bananas wrapped in a banana leaf and boiled or steamed. *- donat* doughnut. *- kering* cookies. *- ku* (*Ch*) k.o. rice cake filled with crushed mung beans. *- ladu* a rice dumpling in syrup. *- lapis* layer cake. *- lopis* cake of sticky rice. *- mangkuk* cupcakes. *- pahit* macaroon. *- pancong* k.o. cake of grated coconut and flour. *- putu* steamed cake made of flour and palm sugar eaten with grated coconut. - *ranjang* a cake prepared esp. for the Ch New Year. - *sapit* waffle. - *se(m)prit* S-shaped cookie. - *simping* flat round cracker. - *spékulas* hard brown cooky. - *sus* cream puff. - *tiao* noodle made of rice.

kuék noise, ado, commotion.

kuſu see KUPU, KUPUAN.

kufur infidel, atheist, unbeliever. **mengk-kan** 1 (*Rel.*) excommunicate. 2 consider s.o. an infidel. **ke-an** atheism, heathenism.

KUHAP [*Kitab Undang-Undang Hukum Acara Pidana*] Criminal Code.

KUHD [*Kitab Undang-Undang Hukum Dagang*] code of business law.

KUHP₁ [*Kitab Undang-Undang Hukum Pidana*] Criminal Code.

KUHP₂ [*Kasih Uang Habis Perkara*] (*Coll.*) Give me money and that is that.

kui₁ goldsmith's crucible.

kui₂ genuflect. **ber-** genuflect.

kuih see KUÉ.

kuil temple or shrine currently used by practicing Indian Hindus.

kuin (*Crd.*) queen.

kuing yelping of a dog.

kuini k.o. mango.

kuintal measure of 100 kilograms.

kuintét quintet.

kuir weeding sickle.

kuis₁ **meng-(kan)** 1 kick s.t. aside. 2 scratch the earth (of a chicken, etc.). 3 stir up (a fire).

kuis₂ quiz.

kuit - *gamit* beckon (s.o to approach). - *kapai* scratch through the garbage, rummage through s.t. **meng-** 1 beckon, motion (with fingers, hand, for s.o. to come nearer). *Ia ~ teman-temannya utk berkumpul* He beckoned to his friends to assemble. 2 tap, prod (with a finger or pencil to attract attention). **meng-kan** row (by moving a paddle repeatedly left and right sideways from the stern). ~ *rakit* paddle a raft.

kuitansi see KWITANSI.

kuiz see KUIS₂.

kujang cleaver, chopping knife.

kujur₁ spear for catching fish.

kujur₂ stiff, rigid. **se-** the entire (body). ~ *tubuh/ badan* the whole body.

kujut ber- hang strangle or choke o.s. **ber-²** be involved or implicated. *Baik dia maupun bawahannya ~ dlm pembunuhan itu* Both he and his subordinate are implicated in the murder. **meng-** strangle, garotte.

kuk 1 yoke. 2 collar, harness.

kukai k.o. fish.

kukang₁ see KUNGKANG₂.

kukang₂ see KOKANG.

kukila 1 mynah bird. 2 (*Jv*) bird in general.

kuku 1 fingernail, toenail. - *cengkam* ingrown nail. - *kaki* toenail. - *tangan* fingernail. *bagai - dgn daging* virtually inseparable. *seujung* - very little, a teeny bit. 2 claw, s.t. like a claw. - *macan* staple

remover. - *sauh* fluke of an anchor. - *tikus* young cloves a few months before picking. 3 hoof. - *kuda* horse's hoof. **se-** (*hitam*) very little, a teeny bit. -² the clutches. ~ *demam* the clutches of a fever. **ber-** have nails, claws. *tdk* ~ powerless.

kukuh 1 sturdy, strong (house, etc.), hefty. *perawakan yg* - a strong body. 2 firm, tenacious. *pendirian yg* - a firm stand. **ber-** be firm in, be tenacious. ~ *pd pendapatnya* stick to o.'s opinion. ~ *kata* keep o.'s word. **bersi-** stick to o.'s policy, be stubborn. *Pemerintah ~ menolak meréka mendarat* That gvt. stubbornly refused to let them land. **meng-i** 1 make s.t. firm or strong. 2 hold to (a theory, policy), stand by (a decision). **memper-, meng-kan** 1 strengthen, solidify. 2 brace, fortify s.t. 3 install, inaugurate. *Ia di-kan sbg guru besar* She was installed as a professor. **ke-an** 1 soundness, sturdiness. 2 firmness, tenacity. **peng-an** 1 strengthening, affirmation. 2 inauguration.

kukuk see KOKOK.

kukukbeluk k.o. owl.

kukukeruyuk cock-a-doodle-doo.

kukul₁ acne, pimple.

kukul₂ see KOKOL₂.

kukup alluvium, silt. **meng-** silt up. **peng-an** silting up.

kukur₁ cooing (of a dove).

kukur₂ grater. **meng-** 1 grate s.t. 2 scratch s.t. because it itches. **-an** 1 grater. 2 rasp. **peng-** grater, o. who grates s.t. **peng-an** grating.

kukuruyak see KUKUKERUYUK.

kukus₁ marten.

kukus₂ steam, vapor. - *bekas* exhaust. **ber-** 1 steam. *Kétél itu ~* The kettle steamed. 2 distill. **meng-** steam s.t. **-an** rice steamer.

kukut adopted. *anak* - adopted child.

kul see KOL₂.

kulah₁ a small basin us. built into the bathroom for bathing and other purposes.

kulah₂ k.o. mango.

kulai drooping, hanging down. *senjata yg terpegang - di tangan Anwar* a weapon that Anwar held hanging down from his hands. **ber-** droop, hang limply. **ber-an** (*Pl.*) hang limply. **meng-kan** *kepala* let o.'s head droop. **ter-** drooping. *Bunga-bunga ~ karena kepanasan* The flowers were drooping in the heat.

kulak₁ a cubic measure for rice, etc.

kulak₂ **meng-** buy goods for resale. **-an** wholesale.

kulan k.o. tree of forest that furnishes gutta-percha.

kulansing see BATU.

kulasi see OKULASI.

kulat toadstool, mushroom, fungus. **ber-** with fungus growing on it, covered with mould.

kuldi see BUAH.

kuli coolie, laborer, porter. - *arit* rubber tapper. - *minterad* 1 city employee. 2 street sweeper. - *pelabuhan* dock worker. - *pelat* official porter. - *tinta* journalist. **ber-, meng-** work as a coolie. **per-an** labor affairs.

kuliah university lecture. *memberi - di UI* give lectures at the University of Indonesia. *- kerja nyata* obligatory (rural) social action internships for advanced university students. *- subuh (Isl.)* lecture given at the dawn prayer. **se-** attending the same lecture. *kawan ~mu/kawanmu ~* s.o. you attend classes with. **ber-** follow a lecture. **meng-i** lecture s.o. *Sdr tdk usah ~ Ali agar berhati-hati* You need not lecture Ali to be careful. **meng-kan** lecture on. *Soal itu di-kan di universitas itu* Lectures are given on this problem at the university. **peng-** lecturer.

kulik scream of a bird. **ber-** cry out, scream (of birds of prey).

kulikat disposition, character.

kulim k.o. hardwood.

kulino *(Jv)* **1** be accustomed to. **2** be good at doing s.t.

kulintang see KOLINTANG.

kulipat 1 successor. **2** deputy.

kulir trowel.

kulit 1 skin. *- adam* new skin under the nail. *- ari* epidermis. *- badak* thick-skinned. *- berkikir* goose flesh. *- berwarna* nonwhite people. *- gajah* thick-skinned. *- hitam* **1** black people. **2** dark-skinned, swarthy. **3** soccer ball. *- kelamin* foreskin. *- kepala* scalp. *- lendir* mucous membrane. *- mati* numb, insensitive. *- putih* white people. *- sawo matang* brown-skinned people. *- tanduk* **1** epidermis. **2** cornea. **2** hide, leather. *- buatan* imitation leather. *- bulu* fur pelt. *- bundar* soccer ball. *- gendang* drumhead. *- pegangan* leather strap (on bus, streetcar). *- (peng)gosok* chamois. *- samak* tanned hide. **3** (tree) bark. *- batang/kayu* tree bark. *- lawang/manis* cinnamon bark. **4** peel, husk, shell, crust. *- bumi* the earth's outer crust. *- kara* turtle shell. *- kerang* clamshell. *- kué* pie crust. *- roti* bread crust. *- sekam* rice husk. **5** cover (of a magazine). *- buku* book cover. *- muka* **1** front cover. **2** skin on face. *- sampul* dust jacket. **se-** *sedaging* from the same stock, related. **ber-** have skin. *~ badak* thick-skinned, insensitive. **meng- 1** flay, scalp. **2** slough the skin (of a snake). **meng-i 1** skin s.t., remove the skin, peel s.t. **2** put a cover on. **peng-an** flaying, peeling. **pe(r)-an** tannery. **per-an** cover, jacket.

kulkas refrigerator, icebox. **mengk-kan** refrigerate s.t.

kulliah see KULIAH.

kulminasi culmination. **meng-** be at the pinnacle.

kulon *(Jv)* west. **meng-** westward. *berlayar ~* sail westward.

kulo nuwun 1 *(Jv)* what is called out to announce o.'s arrival at s.o.'s house, ask to come in. **2** *(Coll.)* ask for an OK to proceed. *Harus - dulu* I have to ask permission before I go ahead.

kultivir mengk- cultivate. **pengk-** cultivator.

kultur culture. **ke-an** cultural.

kultural, kulturil cultural.

kultus cult. *- individu* the cult of the individual.

mengk-kan make a cult of. **pengk-an** making a cult. *~ pahlawan* making a cult out of a hero.

kulub₁ heart (as seat of emotions).

kulub₂ boil or steam (vegetables). **-an** steamed vegetables.

kuluk *(Jv)* a man's court headdress shaped like a fez.

kulum meng- 1 suck. *~ gula-gula* suck on candy. **2** mumble (o.'s words). *~ senyum* just be able to smile and not say anything about s.t. o. dislikes. *Kami mengikutinya saja dgn senyum terus di-* We followed him with a smile pasted on our faces. **ter-** be sucked on, be forced (of a smile).

kulum-kulum millipede.

kulup 1 foreskin. **2** appellation for boys. **ber-** not circumcised.

kulur k.o. breadfruit with many seeds.

kulut k.o. hardwood similar to the lansium.

kuluyuk *(Ch)* sweet and sour cooking. *ayam -* sweet and sour chicken.

Kulzum see LAUT.

kumai notch. **ber-** notched. **meng-(kan)** notch, place a notch in s.t. **-an** a notch.

kuma-kuma see KOMA-KOMA.

kumal 1 rumpled, disheveled of clothes. **2** dingy of a room. **3** dog-eared (of magazines). **meng-kan** rumple s.t.

kumala see GEMALA.

kuman germ, microbe. *- bibit* seed strain.

kumandang echo, reverberation. **ber-, meng-** echo, reverberate. *sorak yg ~* resounding cheer. **meng-kan 1** make s.t. reverberate. **2** carry a sound or voice. *Radio ~ suara présidén ke seluruh pelosok negara* The radio carried the president's voice to all corners of the country.

kumanga, kumango see BARANG₁.

kumat have a relapse. *- lagi* recur (of an illness). **ber-²** relapse.

kumat-kamit see KOMAT-KAMIT.

kumba 1 basin, bowl. *- mayang* basin holding water for the washing ceremony of a bride. **2** the protuberance on the forehead of an elephant.

Kumba *(Zod.)* Aquarius.

kumbah meng- 1 wash, do the laundry. **2** rinse. **-an** laundry. **peng-an** laundering, rinsing.

kumbang 1 bumblebee. **2** beetle. *- moncong* weevil. *spt - dgn bunga* attracted to e.o. (of young men and women). **3** black (color of animal). *anjing -* a black dog. **meng-** buzz.

kumbar k.o. thorny, stemless palm resembling the Salacca.

kumbara see EMBARA.

kumbik the candlenut tree and its fruit.

kumbu narrow-mouthed basket for holding freshly caught fish.

kumico head of a quarter (during the Japanese occupation).

kumidi see KOMIDI.

kumilap see KELAP.

kumin granule, mole.

kuminter *(Jv)* think o. is smart when o. is not.

kumis₁ mustache. - *kucing* a herb the leaves of which have diuretic properties. **ber-, -an** have a mustache.

kumis₂ see KOMIS.

kumisi see KOMISI₁,₂.

kumit mote.

kumkuma see KOMA-KOMA.

kumlah see MATI.

kumpal₁ ter-² be tossed about (esp. in a difficult situation).

kumpal₂ see GUMPAL.

kumpar meng- wind (thread, twine, etc.) on a spool. **-an 1** spool, reel. **2** coil, bobbin.

kumpi great grandparent.

kumplit see KOMPLÉT.

kumpul (*Mil.*) fall in! - *kebo* live together out of matrimony. - *satu* **meng-satukan** unite, bring together. **ber- 1** assemble, come together in a place. ~ *di muka sekolah* assemble in front of the school. **2** line up, fall in line. **ber-²** crowd around. **meng- 1** gather, come together in a place. **2** gather, assemble s.t. **meng-kan 1** gather, assemble, concentrate (forces). *Guru ~ murid-murid di muka sekolah* The teacher assembled the pupils in front of the school. **2** collect (stamps, coins, etc.). **3** amass, accumulate (a fortune, an art collection, etc.). **ter-** be gathered, gotten together. *Kalau semua biayanya ~* When all the funds have been collected. **-an 1** collection. ~ *lukisan-lukisan yg ternama* collection of famous paintings. **2** horde, drove. **3** herd (of cattle). **4** (*Coll.*) association. **peng-** collector, gatherer. ~ *catatan* recording secretary. ~ *sampah* garbage collector. **peng-an** collecting. ~ *dana* fund raising. **per-an 1** club, association. ~ *gelap* illegal organization. ~ *rahasia* secret society. **2** meeting.

kumuh dirty, vile, base, low. **meng-kan** debase, defile. **ke-an** dirtiness.

kumulasi cumulation.

kumur ber- rinse the mouth. **ber-²** gargle.

kumus k.o. forest tree yielding good timber and resin.

kun₁ apron, skirt.

kun₂ (*Isl.*) come into being. - *fayakun!* Become! And it came into being!

kuna see KUNO.

kunang -² firefly, glowworm. **ber-(²) 1** sparkle like fireflies. *Bintang ~ di langit* Stars glittered in the sky. **2** see stars. *Matanya ~ ketika ia kena pukulan di kepalanya* He saw stars when he was hit on the head.

kuncah 1 bale of straw. **2** measure for a bale.

kuncara (*Lit.*) famous, renowned. *zaman -* golden age.

kuncén caretaker of a sacred place.

kunci₁ 1 key. - *dobel* duplicate key. - *kontak* ignition key. - *maling* skeleton key. - *pengaman* safety lock (of a grenade, etc.). **2** key, solution. *Inilah - rahasia itu* This is the key to that secret. *tokoh - a* key figure. - *mati* **1** closely guarded secret. **2** im-

passe, deadlock. - *wasiat* secret, mystery. **3** lock, fastening. - *gantung/gembok/kuru-kuru* padlock. - *pengaman* safety catch. **4** wrench. - *Inggeris* monkey wrench. - *pas* open end wrench. - *ring* box wrench. - *roda* lug wrench. - *sok* socket wrench. - *tabung* pipe wrench. **5** joints. - *paha* groin. **6** locked, fastened. -² (*Anat.*) joints. ~ *lutut* patella. **ber-** 1 have a key. **2** be locked. **meng- 1** become locked. *Terdengar detak pintu ~* You could hear the click of a door locking. **2** lock s.t. *Jangan lupa ~ pintu* Do not forget to lock the door. **3** bring s.t. to a close. **meng-kan** lock s.t. in. *Anak itu di-kan di kamarnya* The child was locked up in the room. **ter-** be locked. **peng-** 1 lock, clasp. **2** s.t. said or written in conclusion.

kunci₂ see TEMU₁.

kuncir, kuncit see KUCIR.

kuncung 1 tuft, crest (of feathers). **2** tuft of hair from the crown to the forehead.

kuncup 1 bud (of flower). **2** closed (of flowers). - *jantung* contraction of the heart. - *hatinya* frightened, filled with fear. **3** not circumcised. **meng- 1** close. *Stlh matahari terbenam, bunga-bunga ~* After the sun sets, the flowers close their petals. **2** contract, shrink. **3** cringe, be afraid. **meng-kan** fold up s.t. that closes. ~ *tangan* fold the hands (in greeting). ~ *payung* fold an umbrella.

kundai see KONDAI.

kundang see KONDANG₂.

kundéktur see KONDEKTUR.

kundur₁ wax gourd, a large green melon-shaped fruit growing on vines and eaten as a vegetable.

kundur₂ go home (honorific, *Jv*).

kung (*Jv*) having a properly developed voice (of a dove). *Burung yg kubeli ternyata blm -* The bird I bought turns out to be unable to sing nicely.

kungkang₁ sloth. **meng-** act like a sloth, sluggish.

kungkang₂ k.o. large frog.

kungkang₃ meng- gnaw at s.t.

kungki k.o. large forest tree yielding a hard but undurable timber.

kungkum (*Jv*) **meng-** *diri* bathe submerging o.s. in the water.

kungkung shackles, locks (for a prisoner). **meng- 1** shackle, restrain. **2** impede movement. **3** dominate. **meng-i** put shackles on, enslave. **ter-** be enslaved. **-an 1** shackles. **2** s.t. that imprisons. *Aku ingin lepas dr ~ rumah yg sempit itu* I wanted to be free from the narrow confines of that house.

kuning yellow. - *gading* ivory colored, cream colored. - *kepodang* canary yellow. - *langsat/langsep* creamy yellow (considered a beautiful color of skin). - *mas* golden. - *telur* egg yolk. **meng-** turn yellow. *padi yg sedang ~* the rice that is turning yellow as it ripens. **meng-kan** make s.t. yellow. ~ *nasi dgn kunir* make rice yellow with turmeric. **ke-²an** yellowish. **-an** brass.

kunir (*Jv*) see KUNYIT.

kunjung₁ ber- pay a visit, call on s.o. **ber-an** visit e.o. **meng-i 1** visit, see, call on. **2** attend (a conference, etc.). **-an** visit, call. ~ *balasan* a return visit. **peng-** visitor. **per-an 1** visit. **2** visitation. ~ *kehormatan* courtesy visit.

kunjung₂ *tak* - never (was it, will it be). *Semangat kenasionalan meréka tak - padam* Their national spirit will never be extinguished. *tak - hilang* abiding, will never disappear. *tak - tdk* of course, most certainly. *blm* - never up to now. *alat-alat yg dipesan blm - tiba* the instruments ordered have not arrived yet.

kuno 1 ancient. *kerajaan -* an ancient kingdom. *bahasa Jawa -* Old Javanese. **2** old-fashioned, dated. **ke-an 1** conservatism. **2** antiquity.

kuntal-kantil see KONTAL-KANTIL.

kuntau Ch boxing (kung-fu).

kuntet, kuntét see KONTÉT.

kuntianak, kuntilanak (*Jv*) a malicious supernatural being that is the spirit of a woman who died in childbirth and that appears as a beautiful young woman with a hole in her back.

kuntit meng-(i) tail, shadow, follow s.o. **peng-** tail, shadow. **peng-an** tailing or trailing (of s.o.).

kuntuan Ch silk.

kuntul₁ heron, egret.

kuntul₂ tailless (of fowl).

kuntul₃ see KONTOL.

kuntum 1 flower bud ready to open. **2** (*Lit.*) a budding girl. **3** classifier or counter for flowers. *se- bunga* a flower. **ber-, meng-** bud (of a flower). **ter-** having just reached the stage where it is about to open (of flower).

kuntung pigtail as formerly worn by Ch men.

kunun see KONON.

kunut see DOA.

kunyah meng- 1 chew, masticate. **2** digest (advice, a problem, etc.). **meng-²** chew (a child's) food for him. **meng-kan** chew, masticate for s.o. **ter-** chewed, masticated. ~ *di batu* unfortunate. ~ *di nasi* fortunate, lucky. **-an** cud. **peng-an** chewing, mastication.

kunyam shrunken, sunken (of cheeks from loss of teeth).

kunyit turmeric.

kunyuk 1 monkey. **2** a stupid person, an idiot. - *lu! Mengapa tdk awas?* You stupid fool! Why don't you look! where you are going?

kunyung see KONYONG.

kuorum quorum.

kuota quota. - *ékspor* export quota.

Kuoyu /kwo-i/ (*Ch*) Mandarin Chinese.

kup₁ howdah (on elephant).

kup₂ coup, political power move.

kupak broken, damaged. **ber-** damaged from opening. **meng-** break open, damage.

kupang₁ k.o. shellfish.

kupang₂ a coin of former times.

kupas meng- 1 remove peel or shells. **2** strip s.o. (of clothes). **3** analyze (a problem). **meng-kan 1** peel on behalf of s.o. **2** strip s.o. (of clothes). **ter-** peeled, shelled. **-an 1** peels. **2** analysis. **peng-** o. who analyzes a problem. ~ *kulit* sheller. **peng-an 1** peeling. **2** analyzing.

kupat-kapit 1 wagging (of a tail). **2** dangling limply.

kupel cupola.

kuper [*kurang pergaulan*] (*Sl.*) socially awkward. - *amat sih kamu* You sure are antisocial.

kupét 1 bulb of a thermometer. **2** developing tray (in photography).

kupiah see KOPIAH.

kuping ear. - *gajah* 1 anthurium, caladium. **2** k.o. cookie in the shape of an elephant ear. - *menjangan* perennial herb with bananalike leaves and flowers in spikes. - *tikus* **1** k.o. black fungus used in Ch dishes, earlobe. **2** k.o. fried cassava chip sprinkled with sugar. **meng-** eavesdrop. ~ *sana sini* keep an ear to the ground. **peng-** o. who eavesdrops, instruments to eavesdrop. ~ *télpon* o. who taps a telephone or instrument for tapping.

kupir₁ cutter in a tailor or dress shop.

kupir₂ meng- (*Crd.*) cut (the cards).

kuplét couplet.

kuplok see KULUK.

kupnat dart (in tailoring).

kupon coupon. - *bagasi* baggage check. - *berhadiah* coupon which entitles bearer to receive a prize.

kupu, kupuan rank (by birth, nobility). **se-** equal in rank.

kupui large forest tree with reddish wood and edible fruit.

kupu-kupu butterfly. - *malam* prostitute.

kupur₁ k.o. wild raspberry.

kupur₂ see KUFUR.

kur₁ 1 coo (of a pigeon). **2** sound made in calling chickens to come and eat. - *semangat* **1** expression to call s.o. who has fainted back to consciousness. **2** welcome a newborn baby. **3** phrase expressing mild surprise.

kur₂ see KOR.

kura (*Anat.*) spleen.

kurai 1 grain in wood. **2** vein in marble, damascened veins in a kris blade. **ber-** grained, veined.

kura-kura turtle. - *dlm perahu* pretend not to want to (dance, kiss, etc.) or know (a reference to the phrase it rhymes with: *pura-pura tdk tahu/mau*, pretend not to know or want). - *jendéla* window sill or ledge. - *kaki* instep. - *tangan* back of the hand.

Kuran see KORAN.

kurang₁ 1 less, decrease. *Uangnya - dr lima ratus rupiah* He had less than 500 rupiah. *Kegiatannya makin -* His zeal is decreasing. **2** minus, less, until (of time). *Sepuluh - empat tinggal enam* Ten minus four is six. *Pukul dua belas - sepuluh (menit)* It is 10 (minutes) of 12. **3** lack s.t. *Karena - modal Repelita tak dilaksanakan* For lack of capital the five-year plan was not implemented. *tak - suatu apa* not lacking a thing. **4** not . . . enough, not quite, do not quite. *suaramu - keras* Your voice is not loud enough. *Ia - pandai dr sdrnya* She is not as smart as her sister. *Saya - mengerti* I do not quite understand. - *ajar* **1** (*Derog.*) ill-bred, failing to follow rules of proper conduct. **2** exclamation of annoyance. **ke-ajaran 1** lack of respect, rudeness. **2** wicked conduct. *- asem* euphemism for *kurang ajar.* *- bahasa* impolite. *- bumbu* uninteresting. *- garam* inexperienced, green. *- hati-hati* **1** impudent. **2** careless. *- ingat* **1** careless. **2** forgetful. *Ia - ingat akan janjinya* She forgot her promise. *- jadi* not turn out well. *Bunga mawar - jadi di sini* Roses do not do well here. *Potrét - jadi* The photograph did not turn out well. *- jantan* weak, sissified. *- karat* of inferior quality. *- lebih* more or less, approximately. *- periksa* not known. *Saya - periksa akan hal itu* I have not looked into the matter. **5** about, almost. *Ia bekerja di sini sepuluh tahun -* He has worked here for almost 10 years. **-nya** fault, shortcoming. *Pekerjaannya banyak ~* There is a great deal lacking in his work. *Apa ~ mobil ini?* What is wrong with this car? **-² 1** if there is a lack. *- makan bisa sakit* If you do not eat enough you can get sick. **2** the less (s.t. happens) . . . (the more s.t. else will happen)). *~ diladéninya lebih-lebih ia akan merasa kesalahannya* The less we pay attention to him, the more he will realize his mistake. **se-²nya** at least. *Saya membutuhkan ~ seratus ribu rupiah* I need at least o. hundred thousand rupiah. **ber-** decrease, dwindle, lessen. *Uangnya ~* His money decreased. *Sakitnya ~* Her sickness subsided. **ber-²an** continue to decrease. **meng-** abate (of illness, rain, etc.). **meng-i 1** decrease, lessen s.t. **2** cut back, cut down on, curtail (production, etc.). *~ kebébasannya* abridge freedoms. *~ berat* reduce weight. **3** subtract from, deduct from. *enam di-i dua* six take away two. *Jumlah itu masih di-i dgn pajak* That amount is farther reduced by a tax. **4** dim, turn down (the lights), dampen (o.'s spirits), attenuate, weaken s.t. **meng-kan 1** subtract, take. *~ sepuluh kpd seratus* subtract 10 from o. hundred. **2** lessen, reduce s.t., dim (lights). *~ api* lower the flame. **memper-kan** take s.t. away, subtract s.t. **ke-an 1** lack s.t. *Kami ~ ruangan* We lack space. **2** lack, shortage (of food, etc.). *mengi-si ~* fill out what is lacking. **3** shortcoming, flaw, deficiency. *~ dlm lukisanku* the flaws in my painting. **4** (*Econ.*) deficit. **berke-an** lack, be short of. *Meréka tdk ~ apa-apa* They lacked nothing. **peng-** (*Math.*) subtracter. **peng-an 1** decrease, reduction, cutback. **2** deducting of.

kurang₂ (*Med.*) milt.

kurap ringworm. *- anjing* mange. **ber-, -an 1** covered with scabs (of animals). **2** fraudulent.

kurapat see KHURAFAT.

kuras₁ printed paper folded over several times for binding into a book.

kuras₂ *- otak* brain drain. **meng- 1** drain s.t., clean by draining. *~ sumur* clean a well by draining it. **2** drain, deplete, exhaust. *~ tenaganya* drain o.'s energy. *~ kekayaan negara* drain or use up the country's wealth. *~ minyak* pump out oil. **peng-** drainer (of the country's resources). **peng-an 1** draining, cleaning by draining. **2** giving an enema. **3** exhausting (the resources).

kuratif curative, healing, therapeutic.

kurator 1 curator, keeper. **2** (*Leg.*) receiver (in bankruptcy).

kurau k.o. edible saltwater fish.

kurawal braces (of graphics).

kurban see KORBAN.

kurcaci 1 Brownie Scout. **2** gnome, a small supernatural being.

kurét curette. **mengk-** scrape s.t. (esp. the womb).

kurfa curve.

kuria (*Rel.*) parish (in the Batak area). *- Rumani* The Roman Curia.

kurik speckled. *ayam -* speckled chicken. **ber-²** spotted, speckled.

kurikulér curricular.

kurikulum curriculum.

kuring scabby, with sores.

kuriositas curiosity.

kurir courier.

kuririk cricket.

kurkuma 1 turmeric. **2** saffron.

kurma date palm, dates.

kurnia see KARUNIA.

kurs (*Fin.*) a rate of exchange. *- bébas* free market rate. *- gelap* black-market rate. *- resmi* official rate of exchange. *- tetap* fixed rate.

kursemangat see KUR₁.

kursi₁ 1 chair. *- ayunan* **1** rocking chair. **2** porch swing. *- (be)roda/dorong* wheelchair. *- duduk* chair for sitting. *- gonyét/goyang* rocking chair. *- kantor* desk chair. *- lipat* folding chair. *- malas* easy chair. *- panjang* davenport, sofa. *- putar* swivel chair. *- stalbuis* chair made of steel pipes. *- stélan* set of chairs for receiving visitors. *- ungkang-ungkit* rocking chair. **2** (official) position. **3** seat (in parliament). **- meng-** chair making.

kursi₂ see AYAT.

kursif italics.

kursis course taker, o. who attends courses.

kursus 1 course (of study). **2** nondegree course offered outside of the college or university system. *- kilat* cram course. *- penyegar* refresher course. **meng-** train s.o., give o. a course. **meng-kan** offer s.t. as a course.

kurun 1 century, era. **2** time frame. *- masa/waktu/zaman* period of time, time span.

kurung 1 cage. *- ayam* chicken coop. *- batang* bier. **2** prison. **3** (*Naut.*) cabin. **4** parenthesis, brackets. *- besar* brackets. *- buka* opening parenthesis. *- kecil* parentheses. *- kurawal* braces. *- siku* brackets. *- tutup* closing parenthesis. **ber- 1** be enclosed in. *Rumah itu ~ pagar besi* The house was surrounded by an iron fence. **2** be shut up. *Sejak isterinya meninggal ia ~ di rumahnya* Since his wife died he has shut himself up in his house. **3** enclosed in brackets (of a word). **meng- 1** put in a cage. *Ia ~ burung itu* She put the bird in a cage. **2** imprison, jail, incarcerate s.o. *~ diri dlm biara* shut o.s. up in a monastery. **3** surround s.t. **4** put s.t. between brackets. **meng-i** enclose s.t. in. *Ia ~ ayamnya dgn pagar bambu* He put his chickens in a bamboo stockade. **meng-kan** imprison, encage. **ter-** 1 be enclosed in, imprisoned. *Dgn begitu musuh akan ~ tanpa daya* In that way the enemy will be surrounded and helpless. 2 narrow, restricted. *Pahamnya ~* He has a narrow understanding of things. 3 isolated, out of reach. *Masih delapan kota yg ~ akibat tdk adanya jalan* There are still eight cities out of reach as a result of the lack of roads. **-an** 1 cage. 2 confinement, jail. 3 (*Mil.*) stockade. **peng-an** 1 imprisonment, incarceration, confinement. *~ terpisah* solitary confinement. 2 encirclement.

kurus 1 thin, emaciated, lean. *- kerempeng/kering/ lanjai* thin as a rail, emaciated, scrawny. *- panjang* slim, slender. *- tertulang* very thin. 2 meager. 3 barren, sterile (land). **meng-** become thin. **meng-kan** emaciate, make thin. **ke-an** 1 thinness, slenderness, slimness. 2 too thin.

kurut ber- be wrinkled. *Mukanya ~ menahan sakit* He wrinkled his face in pain.

kuruyuk crow (of a cock).

kus see DEKUS.

kusa elephant goad. **meng-** use an elephant goad.

kusal meng- roll s.t. between the hands (like a cigarette). *~ segumpal adonan* roll a lump of dough between the palms of o.'s hands.

kusam 1 dull, lusterless. *rambut yg -* hair without luster. 2 dim, dull (of light). 3 pallid (of face). **meng-** become dull, dim, pallid. *Mukanya tiba-tiba ~* Her face suddenly become ashen. **ke-an** dullness, dimness, pallor.

kusau ber-(²) 1 confused, mixed up. 2 tousled (of hair).

kusén see KOSÉN₁.

kusir coachman. **meng-** work as a coachman. **meng-i** drive s.t. *Wisatawan ikut ~ andong* The tourists helped drive the horsecart.

kuskus cuscus.

kusta leprosy.

kusuk₁ ber- rub the body with leaves. **meng-** rub s.t.

kusuk₂ see KHUSYU.

kusuma (*Jv, Lit.*) flower. *- bangsa* a nation's heroes.

kusus see KHUSUS.

kusut₁ 1 tousled (of hair). *- mangasai/masai* all in a tangle, disheveled. 2 tangled (of thread, etc.). 3 rumpled (of clothes). 4 complicated, involved, intricate. *- kusau* confused, mixed. *- murut/musut* thoroughly confused, all mixed up. **ber-²** be disheveled. **meng-** become tangled. **meng-kan** tangle, tousle hair. *Angin ~ daun-daun kelapa* The wind piled the coconut leaves into a tangled bunch. **ke-an** 1 confusion. 2 state of being entangled, tousled, rumpled. **-an** kink, twist. **peng-an** 1 entanglement. 2 tangling of s.t.

kusut₂ see USUT.

kutak meng-kan shake s.t. hard.

kutak-katik 1 tinkering with, working on various things. 2 mixing into other people's things. **(me)ng-** 1 work on, mess around with. *Hobinya ~ mobilnya* His hobby is working on his car.

2 tamper with things that do not belong to or concern o. *Jangan ~ barang-barang ini* Keep your hands off these things. **meng-kan** 1 boss, bully s.o. 2 lead s.o. by the nose.

kutang 1 camisole, a woman's underblouse used instead of a brassiere. 2 brassiere. 3 armored vest. *- kebal peluru* bulletproof vest.

kutat-kutet be busily engaged in s.t. **ber-an** 1 be locked tightly together. 2 be deeply involved in a discussion. 3 refuse to give in, maintain a never-say-die attitude. 4 struggle to the utmost for s.t., want s.t. at all costs.

kutet see KUTAT-KUTET.

kuti meng- tear into very small strips.

kutik ber- move slightly. *Saya mendengar tikus ~ di belakang lemari* I heard a mouse make a slight movement behind the cupboard. *Tdk seorg pun berani ~* Not a soul dared move. *Prajurit yg luka parah itu tak ~ lagi* The seriously wounded soldier no longer showed any sign of movement. **meng-** 1 tinker with. *~ mesin mobil* tinker with the car's engine. 2 pick (o.'s nose). 3 cavil, look for faults in another person. **-an** slight nudge or touch.

kutikula cuticle.

kutil wart. **se-** a nibble, tiny piece. **ber-** have warts. **meng-** nibble s.t.

kutilang see KETILANG.

kuting ber-² constantly follow.

kutip meng- 1 pick up small bits (money, rice grains, etc.). 2 copy a portion, cite, excerpt s.t. *Ia ~ dr bukunya* She copied from her book. *Dilarang ~* No quotations permitted. **meng-kan** excerpt s.t. for s.o. **-an** 1 s.t. picked up. 2 citation, quotation, excerpt. **peng-** excerpter. **peng-an** quoting, citing, excerpting.

kutu 1 louse. 2 name for fleas, ticks, and other insects which infest people or animals. *- baru* see KUTU BARU. *- buku* bookworm. *- busuk* bedbug. *- daun* aphids. *- pasar* petty hoodlum. **se-** see SE-KUTU. **ber-** have lice. **ber-(²)** delouse o.s., have o.s. deloused. **ber-²an** delouse e.o. **meng-i** delouse.

kutub pole. *- bergunda* bipolar. *- Janubi/Selatan* S. Pole. *- positif* anode. *- Syamali/Utara* N. Pole. **meng-kan** polarize. **peng-an** polarization.

kutu baru a piece of cloth sewn between the lapels of a *kebaya* to cover the bosom.

kutuk₁ 1 curse, malediction. *Ia kena - ahli sihir jahat itu* He was under the curse of the evil magician. 2 bane, curse (of o.'s existence), blight. **se-beras basah** worthless, useless. **meng-(i)** 1 put a curse on. 2 denounce, condemn, curse. **mem-per-i** curse, denounce. *~ racun agama* denounce the poison of religion. **ter-** accursed, god forsaken. **-an** a curse.

kutuk₂ measure for rice equal to four handfuls.

kutung (*Jv*) amputated, cut off (of limbs).

KUUD /Ku'ut/ [*Koperasi Unit Usaha Désa*] Village Cooperative.

kuwaci see KWACI.

kuwah see KUAH.

kuwalat see KUALAT.

kuwé, kuwéh see KUÉ.
kuwék (*Jv, Humorous*) coming from the regions that have a distinct accent. *Jawa* - a Jv identified as coming from the W. areas.
kuwih see KUÉ.
kuwu village administrative official in charge of water.
kuwuk see KUCING.
kuwung rainbow.
kuya k.o. small turtle.
kuyu dull, lusterless (eye, etc.).
kuyuh urine. **meng-i** urinate on.
kuyung k.o. large timber tree.
kuyup see BASAH. **-²** soaking, sopping wet, soaked through and through.

KV [*kasét vidéo*] video cassette.
kw- see also entries with ku-.
kw.₁ [*kwintal*] 100 kilograms.
kw.₂ [*kawan*] comrade.
kwa qua.
kwaci salted dried watermelon seeds eaten as a snack.
kwalitas see KUALITAS.
kwartal see KUARTAL.
kwas see KUAS₁.
kwitansi receipt.
kwt. [*kawat*] wire, cable.
kyahi, kyai see KIAI.
kyakya see KIA-KIA₂.

L

l /él/ l, twelfth letter of the alphabet.
L [*Laut*] sea, ocean.
la see LHA.
laba 1 profit. **2** benefit, gain. *-nya berapa persén* What is the percentage of profit? - *perang* war profits. - *rugi* profit and loss. **ber-** gainful, profitable. **me-i, me-kan** profit, benefit s.o.
labah k.o. tree yielding wood used to make furniture.
labah-labah spider.
labak k.o. sea fish.
labang me- hammer out iron sheets.
labas exhausted, consumed, used up.
label label.
laberak see LABRAK.
laberang (*Naut.*) rigging.
labial (*Phon.*) labial.
labil labile, changing, unstable.
labi-labi freshwater turtle.
labirin₁ labyrinth.
labirin₂ inner ear.
laboran laboratory assistant.
laboratorium laboratory. - *bahasa* language laboratory.
labrak beating. **me- 1** berate, lay into, lash out at. **2** tackle (a problem). *Bagaimana kita bisa ~ kemiskinan?* How can we tackle poverty? **-an** attack, thrashing.
labu₁ gourd, squash. - *air* 1 vegetable marrow. 2 gourd for carrying water. - *manis* gourd. - *mérah* pumpkin. - *siam* k.o. squash.
labu₂ flask. - *distilasi* retort. - *kencing* urinal. **-²** pipkin.
labuh 1 hanging down, trailing (of shirt sleeve, curtain, etc.). **2** classifier for curtains. **ber- 1** anchor, dock. *Kapal akan ~ pukul enam* The ship will dock at six. **2** be at anchor. **3** be pulled down (of shades, blinds). *Malam ~* Night came upon

(us). **me-** *sauh* drop anchor. **me-kan 1** drop, lower (anchor, blinds). **2** give birth to, drop (a foal, calf, etc.). *~ perhatiannya* focus o.'s attention. **pe-an 1** anchorage. **2** harbor, port, dock. *~ alam* natural harbor. *~ bébas* free port. *~ pertambangan* bunker harbor. *~ udara* airport. **kepe-an** harbor affairs.
labur₁ me- whitewash s.t. **pe-an** resurfacing (of road, street).
labur₂ me- pay laborers in kind or in money. **pe-ration**, portion.
labur₃ ke-an windfall.
lacak₁ me- drag slightly (of anchor).
lacak₂ me- trace, track. *~ rute gerilya waktu perang* trace the guerilla route during war. *~ kembali* retrace (o.'s steps). **me-i** trail, track, trace s.o. **pe-tracker**. *anjing ~* sleuth hound. **pe-an** tracing, reconstruction (of a route).
lacak₃ be-, me- abundant, in great quantity.
laci drawer (in desk, dresser, etc.).
lacur₁ immoral, indecent. *org* - prostitute. **me-carry** on or perform prostitution. **me-kan** prostitute s.t. *~ diri* prostitute o.s. **mempe-kan** prostitute s.t. (figuratively). *~ politiknya* prostitute o.'s politics (to o.'s own interests). **pe-** whore, prostitute. **pe-an, kepe-an** prostitution.
lacur₂ unlucky, working out poorly. *Apa -!* What can be done about it?
lacut me- whip.
lada black or white pepper. - *sulah* black pepper. - *tumbuk* ground pepper. **me-i** put pepper on s.t.
ladah soiled, dirty, polluted.
ladam horseshoe. **me-** shoe (a horse).
ladan see MINYAK.
ladang unirrigated agricultural field. - *minyak* oil field. - *padi* unirrigated rice field. - *tinggal* once used but now abandoned field. **ber-** own or cultivate an unirrigated field. **memper-kan** culti-

vate such a field. **pe-** o. who works or owns such a field. **pe-an, per-an 1** unirrigated agricultural field. **2** cultivation (of such fields). ~ *berpindah-pindah* shifting cultivation, swidden agriculture.

laden (*Jv*) o. who serves. **me-i 1** serve, wait on (a customer, etc.). **2** pay attention, listen to. *Jangan kau-i hinaannya* Do not listen to his insults. **-an** service. **pe-** waiter, servant. **pe-an** act of serving.

lading₁ cleaner.

lading₂ cargo.

ladok haughty, arrogant, overbearing.

ladu lava.

ladung stagnant (water). **me-kan** sprinkle, moisten.

lafadz, lafal, lafaz 1 pronunciation of a word or phoneme. **2** wording, text. **3** the correct version. **me-kan** pronounce. **pe-an** pronunciation, the way a person pronounces.

laga₁ fight. *médan* - (*Lit.*) battlefield. **ber- 1** fight. ~ *nyawa* risk o.'s life in a struggle. **2** wash (of waves against the side of a boat). **me-** (*ayam*) fight cocks. **me(mper)-kan, me-²kan** pit against e.o. *Jangan -²kan temanmu* Do not get your friends fighting. **pe-** fighter (cock, etc.). **per-an 1** fight. **2** collision.

laga₂ be-, **ber-** brag, boast, put on airs. **-²an 1** proud. **2** boastful.

lagak 1 attitude, manner, behavior. - *bahasa* accent. - *lagu* behavior. - *laku* bearing, behavior. **2** mannerism. **3** bluff. **ber- 1** pretend. ~ *spt suami isteri* pretend to be husband and wife. ~ *pilon* pretend to be innocent. **2** put on airs. **me-** impress, show s.o. *Org itu mau ~ pdku rupanya* That person apparently wants to impress me. **me-kan** flaunt (o.'s wealth, etc.). *Binaragawan itu gemar ~ ototnya* That bodybuilder enjoyed showing off his muscles. **pe-** braggart.

lagam₁ horse's bit.

lagam₂ see RAGAM.

lagi₁ 1 again. *Mengapa dia pulang -?* Why is she coming home again? **2** still, further. *Buku ini dibagi - . . .* This book is further divided . . . - *pula/pun* moreover. - *pula, Dahlan adalah kawannya yg karib* Moreover, Dahlan was his close friend. **3** still (when it should not be so). *Saya sdh kerja baik-baik, henapa dimurahi -* I did my work well, and still I get a scolding. *Aduh! Oléh-oléh -* Goodness! You even brought gifts! **4** (with negatives) any more, any longer. *Ia tdk tinggal di sini -* He does not live here any more. **5** more, else, other. *Apa -, kalau ndak itu?* What else if not that? *Siapa -?* Who else? (Anyone else?) *tiga org -* three more men. *Dua hari - baru akan selesai* Two more days and it will be settled. *yg satu(dua) -* the other (o., two, etc.). *Yg satu énak; yg satu - tdk* One is delicious, the other is not. *Mana yg dua -?* Where are the other two? **6** as well (as). *Org itu tampan - pandai* That person is handsome as well as clever. **-² 1** again and again, over and over. ~ *kau memandangku begitu* Again and again you look at me like that. **2** more and more. *Tentu ~ barang-barang listerik* Of course, it is more and more electrical gadgets. **-an** (*Jkt*) moreover.

lagi₂ be in the process of. *Ibu - masak nasi* Mother's cooking rice. **se- 1** during, while. ~ *kecil dia tinggal di sini* During his childhood he lived here. *Pencuri itu datang ~ kami tidur* The thief came while we were sleeping. **2** as long as. ~ *saya hidup, saya tdk akan berkawan kembali dgn dia* I will never be friends with him as long as I live.

lagu 1 melody, tune, song. - *hiburan* light music. - *lagah* booming, roaring. - *langgam* pop song in western-style scale but with Indonesian lyrics. - *Melayu* k.o. popular song influenced by western, Arabic, and Hindi music. - *penghibur* light music. - *rakyat* folksong. - *seriosa* classical, serious music. **2** way, manner. *-nya blm berubah dr dulu* His manner has not changed. - *lagak* behavior. **3** intonation. - *pengucapan* intonation. - *tanya* question intonation. - *tutur* intonation. **ber- 1** melodious. **2** sing. *Kasman ~ bagi janda kecintaannya* Kasman sang for the divorcee he loved. **me-** sing. **me-i** compose a melody for s.t. *Siapa yg ~ sajak itu?* Who composed the melody for the lyrics? **me-kan 1** carry the melody of s.t. *Musik yg riuh ~ mars perjuangan* The noisy music carried the tune of a battle song. **2** sing s.t. ~ *cerita sejarah* singing historical romances.

lah₁ 1 particle urging action. *Minum-. Masih panas!* Please drink it while it is warm! *Mari- kita berangkat!* Let us leave! *Maklum-* Try to understand. **2** That is it! Believe me! (particle requesting belief). *Untung- ada perahu nelayan* Believe me it was good luck that there was a fishing boat. **3** particle of assent. *Baik-, saya kerjakan* OK, I will do it. *Ialah, tapi . . .* Well yes, but . . . **4** particle marking predicate of the sentence (pointing out the main idea of the sentence). *Hancur- générasi kita!* Ruined is our generation! *Itu- pasarnya* That is the market. *Stlh itu iapun berangkat-* After that, he departed. *Jelas tdk- menghérankan jika . . .* Clearly it is not surprising if . . . **5** trivializing particle (with question words). *Lima puluh! Berapa- itu?* Fifty! How much is that anyway?

lah₂ see LHA.

lah₃ see TELAH₁.

lahad (*Isl.*) niche in the wall of a grave for the corpse.

lahak rotten, spoiled (of food).

lahan₁ 1 land, terrain. **2** area. **3** soil. **ber-** have soil. ~ *kering* possess a dry soil. **me-** turn into soil. *Abu gunung ~ di daérah itu* Volcanic ash has turned into soil in that region. **me-kan** let run off. ~ *air ke bagian ladang yg kering* let water run into the dry section of the field.

lahan₂ see PERLAHAN.

lahap ravenous, gluttonous. *Ia - makan dan sebentar-sebentar minum bir* He ate ravenously and every few minutes drank beer. **se-²nya** as gluttonously as possible. ~ *kami berdua makan* The two of us gobbled down our food. **me- 1** be gluttonous. **2** devour, lap up. ~ *isi buku* devour (the contents of) a book. **3** illegally annex. *seakan-akan Afrika Selatan sdh ~ Namibia* as if S.

Africa had annexed Namibia. **me-²** gasp for breath. **ke-an** gluttony. **pe-** glutton.

lahar 1 lava. **2** (*Geol.*) volcanic mudflow. **ber-** expel lava.

lahat see LAHAD.

laher ball-bearing.

lahir₁ 1 external, extrinsic, outward. - *dan batin* matters of the inner self and the outer world. *Maaf - batin* Forgive my sins, both with regard to the world as well as those within me (a greeting for Isl. New Year). **2** worldly, material. *Dia suka yg - saja* He just likes worldly things. **-nya** external aspects. *dlm ~ externally. pd ~* apparently, seemingly. **me-kan 1** express, utter s.t. *~ perasaannya* express o.'s feelings. **2** think out (an idea).

lahir₂ come into being, be born. *Aku - di kampung yg jauh dr sini* I was born in a village far from here. *Dr badan yg séhat -lah kemauan belajar* The urge to study springs from good health. *- mati* still-born. *- pradini* premature birth. **-nya** genesis. **me-kan** give birth to, bear (a child). *Isterinya ~ sejam yg lalu* His wife gave birth an hour ago. *Aku ~ Sari dan Ida* I bore Sari and Ida. **ke-an 1** birth. *kota ~* hometown. *~ mati* stillbirth. *~ sungsang* breech delivery. **2** be born of, spring from. *~ rakyat jelata* of humble origin. *~ Minangkabau* of Minangkabau lineage.

lahiriah 1 external, extrinsic. **2** physical, material.

laici see LÉCI.

laif me-kan attenuate, weaken, enfeeble. **pe-an** attenuation.

laik see LAYAK.

laila, lailah My word! (an exclamation of surprise and us. disapproval). *-! Pakai celana jéngki!* For goodness' sake! Wearing blue jeans!

la ilaha illa'llah, la ilaha illa'llahu 1 (*Isl.*) There is no god but Allah (the beginning of the profession of faith). **2** Good God! (an exclamation uttered when under extreme emotional stress).

lailat - *al hadar* (*Isl.*) The night of the 26th to 27th of the fasting month (the night in which the Koran was revealed).

lain 1 other, another. *Ada org - di sini* There are other people here. *- hari* another day. *- kali* another time, in the future. *tdk -* none other than. *Org itu tdk - adalah paman saya* That man is none other than my uncle. **2** different. *Oto itu - drp oto kami* That car is different from our car. *- drp* unlike. *- drp itu* moreover, besides, apart from that. *- dulu - sekarang* other times other ways. *- halnya dgn org itu* It is another matter with that person. *tak - dan tak bukan* only, nothing else but. *Yg dipikirkannya tak - dan tak bukan uang saja* He thinks about nothing but money. *- rencana, - usaha* Planning is o. thing, implementation another. *- tdk* that is all, nothing more. *Saya hanya mau bilang itu, - tdk* I just want to say that, nothing more. **3** besides, not including. *Séwa rumah ini Rp10.000, - ongkos listriknya* This house rents for 10,000 rupiah, not including electricity. **-²**

various other things. *dan ~* etcetera. **se- 1** besides, in addition to. *~ mendapat pangkat, juga menerima gaji besar* In addition to getting a prestigious position, you are getting a big salary. *~ itu* apart from that. *~ itu, ia masih mempunyai rumah lagi di Bogor* Besides that, she still has a house in Bogor. **2** except. *Tiada pengunjung ~ aku sendiri* There were no visitors except me. **ber-an 1** different. *Meréka masing-masing memandang ke arah yg ~* They each looked in a different direction. *Semuanya ~ dgn hidupnya dulu* Everything was different from his earlier life. **2** be divergent, differ. *Saya tlh bergaul dgn org yg ~ agama dgn saya* I have associated with persons whose religion differs from mine. **me-i** be different from s.t. *~ éjaan resmi* differ from the official spelling. **me-kan 1** but (rather). *Ny. Iskandar tdk menjawab ~ seolah memutuskan pembicaraan dokternya* Mrs. Iskandar did not answer, rather it was as if she interrupted her doctor's conversation. **2** only, except for. *Ia tdk banyak berkata -- makan dan membaringkan diri* He did not say much. He only ate and lay down. **ke-an 1** difference, deviation. **2** aberration, anomaly, disorder. *~ bawaan* congenital defect. *~ wicara* speech impediment. *~ jantung* heart disorder. **keber-an** the amount s.t. deviates. **per-an** (*Lit.*) difference.

lais₁ me- backwater, i.e. to push a paddle or oar toward the bow (to reverse the boat, etc.).

lais₂ k.o. pandanus.

lajang remain unmarried (past usual marrying age). - *tanggung* strapping young man. **me-** remain unmarried.

lajat 1 serious (illness). **2** extreme, very much.

lajim see LAZIM.

lajnah (*Isl.*) committee. - *tanfidziyah* executive committee.

lajo nge- (*Jv*) commute to and from a place of employment or study. **-an** s.t. used to commute on. *keréta api ~* commuter train.

laju 1 fast, quick, rapid. *-nya* speed. **2** rate. - *konsumsi* rate of consumption. - *inflasi* rate of inflation. - *pertumbuhan* rate of growth. **ber-²**, **bersi-/berse-** speed, move fast (of a ship, car, etc.). **me-** move quickly. *Bus terus ~* The bus sped on. *Sampan itu ~ dgn bisu* The dugout glided on silently. **me-kan** accelerate, speed s.t. up. **per-an** acceleration.

lajur 1 row. *se- rumah* a row of houses. **2** strip (of cloth). **3** column (in a paper). - *air* wake (of a boat, etc.). **4** lane. *Ambil - kiri* Stay in the left lane. **5** line (of defense). **-an** neck (of land).

lak₁ 1 sealing wax. - *kuning* shellac. **2** lacquer. - *sténsil* correction fluid. **me- 1** seal s.t. **2** seal with wax.

lak₂ (*Ch*) six. - *ban* 60,000. - *ban go* 65,000. - *cap* 60. - *cap go* 65. - *céng* 6000. - *pék* 600. - *pék céng* 600,000. - *pék go* 650. - *pék go céng* 650,000. - *tiau* six million. - *tiau pua* six and a half million.

laka large liana with red heartwood (used for joss sticks).

lakab title, epithet (for dead or deposed rulers). **me-kan** give a title to a ruler who is dead or has been deposed.

lakak me- strike with a heavy object.

lakan, laken 1 sheet. **2** felt. **3** woolen cloth. **4** velvet.

laki (*Coll.*) husband. - *bini* man and wife. -² **1** man, male (of humans). ~ *jemputan* very eligible bachelor, a good catch. ~ *pengantin* bridegroom. **2** (*Ch, Amb*) male (of animals). *sapi* ~ bull. **ber-** be married (of a woman). **memper-take** as a husband. **memper-kan** marry off (daughter). **ke-(²)an 1** manliness, virility. **2** mannish. **3** manhood.

laklakan throat, gullet.

lakmus litmus.

laknat 1 curse, malediction. **2** anathema. **me-i, me-kan** curse, damn. **pe-an** damnation.

lakon 1 play, drama. **2** act. - *pertama* the first act (of a play). **3** story. - *sedih* tragedy. **ber-** perform in a play. **me-kan 1** present (a play). **2** act out (a story, play, etc.). *Sandiwara itu pernah kami -kan berdua* The two of us once performed that play. **pe-₁ 1** actor, actress. **2** performer. **3** doer.

laksa₁ 10,000.

laksa₂ 1 fine noodles similar to vermicelli. **2** k.o. dish prepared with such noodles.

laksamana admiral. - *madya* vice admiral. - *madya udara* lieutenant general in the Air Force. - *muda* rear admiral. - *muda udara* major general in the Air Force. - *pertama* commodore. - *tertinggi* fleet admiral. - *udara* Air Force general.

laksana 1 quality, characteristic. **2** like, resembling. *Air keran itu putih bening - mata ikan bawal* The tap water was clear and sparkling like a pomfret's eye. **me-kan 1** bring about, cause to materialize. *Mudah-mudahan ia dpt ~ cita-citanya* I hope she will be able to realize her ideals. **2** implement s.t., execute (an order). *Aku tak sanggup ~ instruksinya* I am incapable of implementing his directive. **3** perform (a religious obligation). ~ *sembahyang subuh* perform the dawn prayer. **ter-** carried out. **keter-an** feasibility. **pe-₁ 1** implementer, executor, organizer. **2** producer. **3** manager, director. ~ *pembangunan* building contractor. **pe-an 1** carrying out of s.t., realization. ~ *hukuman mati* execution of the death sentence. **2** implementation.

laksanawan manager, executor.

laktasi /laktasi/ lactation.

laktosa /laktosa/ lactose.

laku 1 behavior, conduct, attitude. - *hidup* behavior. *Bagaimana -nya org bertamu di sini?* How is o. to behave when paying visits here? **2** valid, in effect. *Paspor saya - sampai bulan Agustus saja* My passport is valid only until August. **3** in demand, sell well. *Pd hari panas és - sekali* On hot days ice is very much in demand. *Sejak kau ada, saya tdk - lagi* Ever since you got here, I am not in demand any more. *-nya tdk terkira-kira* The demand was unimaginable. *sdh* - sold out. - *keras* sell well (of a product). - *spt pisang goréng* sell like

hot cakes. **se- 1** as if, like. *Ia menangis ~ anak kecil* He wept like a child. **2** as, in the capacity of. ~ *anggota panitia tésis* as a member of a thesis committee. ~ *ketua* in the capacity of chairman. **se-nya** whatever sells. *Kami jual ~ saja* We just sell whatever sells (i.e., if we do well, it's because of good luck, not because of our abilities). **ber-1** be valid, be in effect. *Undangan ini ~ utk dua org* This invitation is good for two persons. *tetap* ~ hold good. ~ *surut* be retroactive. ~ *mulai bésok* be effective (beginning) tomorrow. **2** occur, happen. *Apa perlunya menyesali yg tlh ~?* What need is there to be sorry for what has already happened? **3** prevail, obtain. *hukum yg ~ di sini* the law which prevails here. *harga yg ~* the prevailing price. **4** behave. *Kau tlh ~ cerdik dgn tdk memanggil polisi* You behaved wisely in not calling the police. *Ibu Nurdin ~ sabar* Nurdin's mother bore herself with forbearance. **5** act as. *Ishak ~ sbg dinas rahasia* Ishak was acting as the secret service. **member-kan** put into effect, cause to be effective. ~ *UUD '45* put the Constitution of 1945 into effect. ~ *surut* make retroactive. ~ *surut surat keputusan sejak 1980* make a decree retroactive from 1980. **keber-an** validity (of a ticket, etc.). **me-kan 1** carry out, execute. ~ *rancangan* carry out a plan. ~ *tugas* fulfill o.'s duty. ~ *abortus* perform an abortion. **2** make, do. ~ *sesuatu* do s.t. *-kanlah perjalanan dgn GIA!* Make a trip with Garuda Indonesian Airways! **3** bring about. ~ *penertiban atas kesemrawutan* bring order out of chaos. **4** commit, perpetrate (a crime). ~ *pembunuhan* commit a murder. **memper-kan** treat, handle. *Org tua jangan kauper-kan demikian* You should not treat an old person like that. **ke-an 1** deed, act. *Jangan prak-tékkan ~ fasis* Do not commit fascist acts. **2** behavior, demeanor. ~ *tak bercela* faultless behavior. **berke-an** have the character of, behaving like. ~ *baik* be of good character. **pe-1** doer, agent. ~ *modernisasi* agent of modernization. **2** (*Ling.*) subject. **3** (*Thea.*) performer, cast. ~ *pentas* stage performer, actor, actress. **per-an** treatment, way of treating s.t. or s.o. ~ *tawanan* treatment of prisoners. ~ *adil* a square deal.

lakum k.o. vine.

lakur (*Lit.*) fuse (of metals). - *baur* mixed, fused. **me-** alloy. **me-kan** mix iron with other metals.

lalab see LALAP.

lalah₁ gluttonous. **pe-** glutton.

lalah₂ me- destroy undergrowth in order to plant.

lalai₁ 1 careless, negligent. - *dlm tugasnya* derelict in o.'s duty. **2** absent-minded, indifferent. **me-kan** neglect, be indifferent to. ~ *tugas* shirk o.'s responsibility. *Asyik menyerang hingga ia ~ per-tahanannya* He was busy attacking to the point that he neglected his self-defense. ~ *hati* comfort, soothe (by trying to forget). ~ *waktu* take it easy, relax and enjoy o.s. **memper-kan 1** neglect. **2** delay, postpone s.t. **3** (*Lit.*) comfort, entertain s.o. **ter-kan** neglected. **ke-an 1** neglect, carelessness. ~ *dlm tugas* dereliction of duty. **2** indifference. **pe-** 1 sluggard, lazybones. **2** an absent-minded person. **pe-an** neglecting of, negligence.

lalai₂ see TALI.

lalang₁ k.o. coarse grass.

lalang₂ see LALU.

lalap dish of raw vegetables and a spicy sauce. **me-** 1 eat such a dish, eat voraciously. **2** utterly destroy, defeat. *di- api* consumed by fire. *Kau sendiri di- musuh* You yourself will be destroyed by the enemy. **3** rape. **-an** dish of raw vegetables and a spicy sauce.

lalar (*Amb*) see LALAT.

lalat a fly. *- hijau* bluebottle. *- kerbau/kuda/langau* horsefly. *Tak ada - langau* There is no o. in sight.

lalau (*Lit.*) **me-, me-i** keep s.o. from trespassing.

laler (*Jv, Jkt*) see LALAT.

lali 1 numb, insensitive (to pain). **2** anesthetized. **3** (*Jv*) forget. **me-** 1 anesthetize. **2** become numb or insensitive. **pe-** o. who is forgetful.

lalim tyrannical, despotic, cruel. **me-i, me-kan** 1 oppress, treat s.o. cruelly. **2** domineer. **ke-an** 1 despotism, tyranny. **2** cruelty. **3** oppression.

lalu 1 pass. *Dilarang - di sini* No passage. *- béa* passage through customs. **me-béakan** pass s.t. through customs. *- lalang/landang* back and forth, to and fro. *Dia - lalang di kamarnya sepanjang hari* She paced back and forth in her room all day long. *Berbagai kendaraan - lalang di jalan* Various vehicles went back and forth over the road. *- lintas* traffic. **per-lintasan** matters pertaining to traffic. *hukum ~* traffic law. *tdk - hujan* rainproof. **2** past, last. *minggu yg -* last week. *Ujian tlh -* The exams are over. *Terlambat, semua sdh -* It is too late, it is all over. **3** then. *Dia datang - pergi lagi* He came and then went away again. **se-** always. *Dia ~ bekerja* She always works. **ber-** 1 pass by. *~ angan* pass through o.'s mind. *~ begitu saja* go by the board. **2** past, overdue. **3** passed away (of s.o.), expired (of a contract). **me-i** 1 pass through (town, diplomatic channels, etc.). *pergi ke Bandung ~ Bogor* go to Bandung via Bogor. **2** by means of. *~ cara légal atau tdk* by legal or illegal means. **me-kan** 1 take through, cause to pass through. *Lemari sebesar itu tdk bisa di-kan di pintu* Such a big cupboard cannot be taken through the door. **2** pass up (profit). **3** put through s.t. *~ tali ke dlm lubang* Put a string in a hole. **ter-** too, exceedingly, very. *~ besar* too large. **keter-an** excessive, far too much. *Saya tlh berbuat ~* I have gone too far.

lama 1 long (of duration). *- sekali dia menunggu* She waited a long time. *Berapa jam -nya?* How many hours will it last? *penyakit - an* illness o. has had a long time. *tak - kemudian* not long afterward. *tdk - lagi* before long, shortly. **2** old, long-standing. *Rumah ini rupanya -* This house seems old. *org - 1* s.o. from the past. **2** s.o. very experienced. *sahabat -* an old friend, a long-time friend. **-² 1** finally, after a long time. **2** take a long time. *Jangan ~ di sana, nak* Do not tarry

while you are there, son. **se-** during, while, as long as. *~ perang* during the war. *~ hayat dikandung badan* as long as I live. *~ ini* up till now, all this time. *~ sembilan tahun* for nine years. **se-²nya** 1 forever, for good. **2** at the longest. *hukuman penjara ~ tiga tahun* maximum imprisonment of three years. **ber-²(an)** 1 for a prolonged period, for a long time. **2** gradually, in the long run. **memper-, me(mper)-kan** drag out, lengthen s.t.'s duration. *Sengaja diper-nya pekerjaan ini* He purposely dragged out this job. **-ke-an** 1 eventually, in the long run. **2** finally, in the end.

laman (*Coll.*) see HALAMAN.

lamang k.o. long straight single-edged sword.

lamar me- 1 ask for the hand of. *Kau berani ~ anakku!* You have the nerve to ask for my daughter in marriage! **2** propose marriage to s.o. **3** apply for (a job). *Dédé ~ kerja di Malang* Dede applied for a position in Malang. **me-kan** apply for a job or another's hand in marriage on s.o. else's behalf. **-an** 1 (marriage) proposal. **2** application. *~ msk* application for admission. **pe-** 1 suitor. **2** applicant. **pe-an** process of applying.

lamat-lamat, lamat-lamatan vague, indistinct, scarcely visible.

lambai ber- wave (of leaves, etc.). **me-** wave o.'s hands. *Ia ~ kpdku* He waved at me. He beckoned me to come. **me-²** 1 wave repeatedly with s.t. (a handkerchief, etc.). **2** summon by waving the hand, wave at. *~ api* fan flames. **me-kan** wave s.t. *Meréka ~ tangan kpdnya* They waved at him. *~ kain* shake out a cloth. **me-²kan** repeatedly wave s.t. *~ karcis* flourish the tickets. **-an** a wave (of the hand, etc.). *~ bendéra* the flapping of a flag.

lambak pile, heap. **ber-(²)** be in a disorderly heap. **me-** rebuild bunds in a rice field. **-an** earth used to build up bunds in a rice field.

lamban 1 languid, indolent. *Laju perkembangan yg masih -* a rate of development which is still sluggish. **2** clumsy, awkward, ungainly. *murid yg - slow learner*. **me-** 1 be indolent, lazy. **2** be clumsy. **memper-** slow (s.o. or s.t.) up or down. **ke-an** 1 indolence. **2** torpor, inertia. **3** laziness. **4** awkwardness, clumsiness.

lambang sign, symbol. *Mérah - apa?* What is red the symbol of? *- keluarga* coat-of-arms. *- kota* city seal, city coat-of-arms. *- martabat* status symbol. **me-kan** 1 symbolize. *Bunga anggrék ~ keabadian* The orchid symbolizes eternity. **2** demonstrate in a graphic way, epitomize. *Setiap rumah ~ kemiskinan rakyat* Each house demonstrates the poverty of the people. **per-** omen. **per-an** symbolism, symbolization.

lambangsari (*Euphemism, Jv*) sexual intercourse. **ber-** have sex.

lambar underlayer. **me-i** provide with an underlayer. **-an** pad, base.

lambat 1 slow-moving, leisurely. *- laun* 1 gradually, in the long run. **2** finally. **3** sooner or later. **2** late. **-² 1** very slowly. **2** be slow. **se-²nya** at the latest. ~ *bésok sampai* At the latest it will be there tomorrow. **me-** slow down, become slow. *Langkahnya* ~ His strides slowed down. **me-kan, memper-** 1 retard, slow s.t. down or up. *Aku* ~ *jalan oto* I slowed the car down. 2 delay. *Hujan* ~ *rencana kami* The rain delayed our plans. **ter-** late. **ke-an** 1 too late. 2 slowness, inertia. 3 delay. **pe-an** decelerating, slowing down. **per-an** 1 retardation. 2 deceleration.

lambau (*Coll.*) farming.

lambo /lambo'/ (*Sulawesi*) k.o. single-masted cargo boat.

lambung₁ 1 side (of ship, person), flank. - *kanan* (*Naut.*) starboard. - *kiri* (*Naut.*) port. 2 an interior cavity. - *perahu* ship's hold. **me-** attack on the flank. **me-i** 1 repair, fix the side of (a ship, house, etc.). 2 (*Naut.*) tack. **-an** side, flank. **pe-an** (*Mil.*) flanking movement.

lambung₂ the bounce (of a ball, etc.). **me-** bounce up, jump up. ~ *kegirangan* leap with joy. ~ *tinggi* soar, zoom. *Harga karét* ~ *tinggi* The price of rubber soared. **me-kan** throw, toss s.t. upward. ~ *dada* boast. **ter-** thrown upward. *Serasa aku* ~ *ke udara* I felt as though I had been tossed skyward. **pe-** pitcher, thrower.

lambur k.o. large jellyfish.

lamin me- decorate the bed of the newlyweds. **pe-an** dais on which the bridal couple sits.

lamp. [*lampiran*] 1 supplement. 2 enclosure.

lampai slim, slender. **me-** graceful (of trees, women, etc.).

lampam k.o. fish.

lampar ber-an be scattered or spread about. *Kabar itu tlh* ~ *ke mana-mana* The news has spread everywhere. **me-** 1 be spread about. 2 spread s.t. out. ~ *babut* spread out the rug.

lampas (*Lit.*) **me-** 1 polish, rub (furniture, etc.). 2 hone, sharpen (a knife).

lampau past. *pd waktu yg* - in the past. *Waktu makan sdh* - Mealtime is over. **me-** 1 pass (of time). *Waktu* ~ *dgn sangat lambat* The time passed very slowly. 2 excessive, go too far. **me-i** 1 pass by s.t., go by way of s.t. *Pengawal itu* ~ *alur kecil* The guard walked by way of a small gully. 2 pass over. *Maut tdk akan* ~ *anakmu* Death will not pass your child over. 3 exceed, overstep. *Ini sdh* ~ *anggaran* This has exceeded the budget. ~ *batas* overstep the bounds (of propriety, etc.). **ter-** too, very much so. ~ *jauh* too far. **ter-i** 1 passed over, overlooked. 2 be overcome. **ke-an** the past. **pe-an** excess. ~ *kekuasaan* excess or abuse of power.

lampias flowing readily. **me-kan** 1 cause s.t. to flow rapidly. 2 release, give full rein to. *Org Sikh* ~ *dendam pd polisi di New Delhi* The Sikhs gave vent to their vengeful feelings toward the New Delhi police. ~ *hawa nafsu* satisfy lust. ~ *kritiknya* give full rein to o.'s criticism. **pe-an** release. ~ *rasa frustrasi* release of a feeling of frustration.

lampin 1 diaper. 2 pot holder. **me-i** 1 put a diaper on (a baby). 2 hold s.t. with a pot holder.

lamping a slope.

lampion Ch paper lantern.

lampir attachments. *memeriksai - dokumén* look carefully at the attachments to the documents. **me-i** 1 attach, append to s.t. 2 enclose. *Surat ini di-i kwitansi sebanyak seribu rupiah* Enclosed is a receipt for 1,000 rupiah. **me-kan** attach, append s.t. *Kwitansinya di-kan pd suratnya* The receipt was enclosed in the letter. **ter-** enclosed. **-an** 1 enclosure. 2 attachment. 3 appendix, annex. 4 supplement.

lampok (*M*) pile of harvested rice.

lampor (*Jv*) howling sound of evil spirits heard on rivers.

lampoyang see LEMPUYANG.

lampu 1 lamp. 2 light. - *baterai* flashlight. - *belakang* tail-light. - *besar* headlight. - *besar dekat* normal headlight. - *besar jauh* bright lights. - *blits* flashbulb. - *busur* arc light. - *corong* headlight, spotlight. - *duduk* table lamp. - *flourénsi* fluorescent lamp. - *isyarat* directional signal. - *kecil* dimmers. - *kerona* chandelier. - *kilat* flashbulb. - *menara* beacon. - *panggung* footlights. - *panjang* bright headlights. - *parkir* parking lights. - *péndék* normal headlights. - *pijar* electric light bulb. - *pilot* pilot light (on gas stove). - *potrét* flashbulb. - *réting/richting* (*Auto.*) directional signals. - *sentolop* flashlight. - *sekat* panel light (on car or plane). - *semboyan* blinker light. - *sein/sén* directional signal. - *sorot* searchlight. - *tangan* directional signal. - *télévisi* TV tube. - *témpél* wall lamp. - *téng/ting* oil lamp. - *TL* fluorescent lamp. - *wasiat* magic lamp. **per-an** lighting.

lampung me- float (of wood, etc.). **pe-** 1 float (on fishing line). 2 float, buoy. ~ *api* flashing buoy. ~ *bénsin* gasoline gauge. ~ *berenang* life belt, life buoy. ~ *pengapil* mooring buoy. ~ *penolong* lifebelt. ~ *suar* light buoy. ~ *tambatan* mooring buoy.

lampus see MAMPUS.

lampuyang see LEMPUYANG.

lamtoro the *Leucaena glauca*, a fast-growing tree used for firewood the leaves of which furnish fodder.

lamtorogung a fast-growing tree similar in use to the *lamtoro* but considerably taller.

lamun₁ (*Lit.*) 1 although. - *sdh dikatakan beberapa kali, masih juga dikerjakannya* Although he was told several times, he did it anyway. 2 provided that, if. *Saya mau pergi, - anda ikut serta* I want to go, provided you go with me.

lamun₂ me- pile up (in a disorderly fashion). **me-i** 1 cover. *Ombak* ~ *pantai* Waves cover the beach. 2 overwhelm.

lamun₃ me-, nge- muse, daydream. **me-kan** daydream about. *Apa yg kau -kan?* What are you dreaming about? **-an** 1 fantasy, daydream. ~ *cabul* obscene thoughts. ~ *kosong* figment of the imagination. 2 speculation. **pe-** daydreamer, woolgatherer.

lamur almost blind.

lanang (*Jv*) male.

lanar mudbank.

lanau silt.
lanca k.o. three-masted ship.
lancana see LENCANA.
lancang₁ 1 dare to do s.t. without proper permission. *Mengapa kamu - meminjamkan bukuku sama temanmu?* Why did you take the liberty of lending my book to your friend? *- tangan* very free with o.'s hands (inclined to steal, aggressive, etc.). *- mulut* prone to say improper things. **2** impudent. *anak -* sassy kid. **me-i** do s.t. which o. does not have the right to do in place of s.o. who does have the right. *Menteri ~ Présidén* The minister went over the president's head. **ke-an 1** presumption, effrontery. **2** impudence, insolence.
lancang₂ k.o. fast sailboat. **-²** toy boat. *bermain ~* skip stones on the surface of the water.
lancang₃ box or container for betel-chewing ingredients.
lancap smooth, slick (of surface). **ter-** slipped out (of a word or statement).
lancar₁ 1 fast, swift (of vessels, cars, etc.). **2** fluent. *Dia - bahasa Inggerisnya* Her English is fluent. **3** smooth (of discussions, etc.). *Ning makin - dgn pelajarannya* Ning was becoming more accomplished in her studies. *Programnya berjalan dgn -* The program is going along smoothly. *- kaji* clever at o.'s studies. *- mulut* talkative, garrulous. **se-, si- ~** *angin* wind-surf. **berse-, bersi-** surf (with a board). **pese-, pesi-** surfer. **me-** speed by (of car, motorcycle). **me-kan, memper- 1** accelerate, speed up (a car, work, etc.). *Ia ~ jalan ceritanya* He sped up the pace of his story. **2** launch (attack, shooting, etc.). *Aku ~ cubitan ke pahanya* I struck back with a pinch on his thigh. *~ tuduh* level a charge (against s.o.). **3** expedite. *~ saluran* open a drain (so it operates freely). **ke-an 1** smoothness. *~ lalu lintas* smooth traffic flow. *~ jalannya pemerintah* smooth running of the gvt. **2** fluency. **pe-** s.t. or s.o. which smooths the way. *uang ~* bribe. **pe-an 1** (*Av.*) runway. **2** expediting of. *~ ékspor* expediting of exports.
lancar₂ pe- girder.
lancaran k.o. swift sailboat.
lancing, lancingan Jv-style trousers.
lancip 1 sharp and pointed. *muka -* face with sharp features. **2** (*Math.*) acute. *sudut -* acute angle. **me-kan** sharpen (a pencil, stick, etc.).
lancong me- go sightseeing, take a pleasure trip. **pe-** tourist, sight-seer. **pe-an** sightseeing, pleasure travel, excursion. **perpe-an** tourism.
lancung₁ 1 false, fake, imitation. *emas -* imitation gold. **2** faithless, untrue (friend). **me-(kan) 1** counterfeit s.t. **2** falsify (a statement, gem), forge (a signature). **ke-an 1** forgery, fake. **2** emptiness (of ideas, etc.). **-an 1** imitation, fake. **2** empty (of peanuts). **3** worthless.
lancung₂ see LANCONG.
landa₁ me- attack violently, knock down s.o. **me-kan 1** crash or ram s.t. into s.t. *bagai benang di-ayam* chaotic, in a mess. **2** pound, overwhelm (of storms, fires, etc.). *Berdebur ombak ~ pantai* Puls-

ing waves pounded on the shore. **ter- 1** knocked down, run into. **2** hit, pounded. *Désa itu di- banjir* The village was hit by a flood. **3** overwhelmed.
landa₂ me- pan (tin, gold). **pe-** s.t. used to pan gold, etc. or o. who does this.
landa₃ lye, alkali.
landai slope slightly (of hillocks, etc.). **-an** hilt of a kris.
landak porcupine. *- laut* sea urchin.
landas 1 base. **2** substratum. *- céncong* meat block. *- kontinén* continental shelf. **ber-kan** rest on s.t., be based on s.t. *lapangan yg ~ tebing batu* field located on a stone slope. *téori ~ fakta* theory resting on facts. **me-i** base s.t. on. *Kepentingan nasional di-i pelaksanaan Pancasila* The national interest is based on the implementation of the Pancasila. **me-kan 1** rest s.t. on s.t. *Léhérnya kukan atas pahaku* I rested his neck on my thigh. **2** base. *Cintanya di-kan pd pematuhan* Faithfulness forms the basis of her love. **-an 1** base. *~ kata* proof. *~ peluncuran* launching pad. *~ terbang/udara* air or landing strip. **2** anvil.
landau me- pan or wash (gold, tin).
landrad (*Coll.*) court of law.
landreform /lénriforem/ land reform.
landskap (*Coll.*) scenery.
landung 1 trailing, hanging down. **2** slack. *- napas* with stamina (lit., breathing easily).
lang₁ table or stand for selling.
lang₂ set of stacked containers for carrying food.
lang₃ see ELANG.
langah me-kan open s.t. widely. **ter(be)- 1** agape (of mouth). **2** ajar (of door).
langau 1 horsefly. **2** bluebottle fly.
langca, langcia (*Ch*) rickshaw.
langgai fishnet.
langgam 1 way, custom, style. *- bahasa* idiom. *- lénggok* customs and movements. **2** melody, tune.
langgan ber- be a customer. **ber-an 1** be(come) a customer of (a store). **2** subscribe to. *~ surat kabar* subscribe to a newspaper. **me-i** be a frequent customer at (a restaurant, etc.). **me-kan, me-ankan** subscribe to s.t. on s.o. else's behalf. **-an 1** customer, client. *Ia sdh ~ dgn RS* She is often hospitalized. *~ adalah raja* The customer is always right. **2** (regular) subscriber.
langgang see TUNGGANG₁.
langgar₁ (*Isl*) prayer house (not used for Friday prayer).
langgar₂ ber- collide (with e.o.). *Kedua mobil itu ~* The two cars collided. **ber-an 1** collide with (of ships, cars, etc.). **2** be in conflict. *Perbuatanmu ~ dgn hukum* Your action conflicts with the law. **me- 1** collide with s.t., run into s.t. *~ anjing* run over a dog. *~ pertahanan musuh* attack enemy defences. **2** break (the law, etc.), contravene. *Pekerjaannya ~ undang-undang* His work is against the law. *~ janji* break a promise. *~ hukum* violate the law. **3** encroach upon (territory). **me-i 1** collide with repeatedly. **2** keep violating (the law).

mem(per)-kan crash s.t. (into s.t.), ram s.t. ~ *perahu* ram a boat. **ter-, ke-** accidentally struck (by a car, pedicab etc.). **pe-** 1 transgressor, offender. ~ *hukum* law breaker. 2 violator. ~ *janji* o. who breaks promises. **pe-an** 1 infraction, violation (of a rule, law). ~ *berat* serious offense. ~ *janji* break of promise. ~ *pidana* 1 criminal offense. 2 punishable offense. ~ *ringan* minor infraction. 2 trespass. 3 infringement (on a patent). 4 (*Sport*) penalty, foul.

langgeng eternal, imperishable. **me-kan** perpetuate, preserve. ~ *kebudayaan tradisional* preserve traditional culture. **ke-an** perpetuity, eternity.

langguk proud, arrogant, haughty.

langi k.o. large mackerel.

langir 1 a shrub, the leaves of which are used for preparing a shampoo. 2 herbal shampoo. **ber-, me-** shampoo (o.'s self). **me-i** shampoo s.o.

langit 1 sky. 2 the heavens. **se-** 1 like the sky. *Harganya* ~ The prices are sky high. 2 extraordinary. *Kemampuannya* ~ His abilities are sensational. **-²** 1 ceiling. 2 s.t. like a ceiling. ~ *tempat tidur* canopy. 3 (*Anat.*) palate. **me-** 1 soar skyward. 2 sky high. ~ *biru* into the wild blue yonder. **-an** (*Anat.*) palate.

langka scarce, rare. *buku* - rare book. - *tapi nyata* rare but true.

langkah 1 step, stride. - *baik* propitious step. - *balik* a step backward. - *kanan* good luck. - *kiri* false step. - *seribu* take to o.'s heels. 2 step, action, measure. *mengambil* - *yg layak* take proper measures. - *laku* behavior, conduct. - *sumbang* false step. **ber-** take a step. **me-** 1 step forward. ~ *msk* step in. 2 stride. **me-i** 1 step over, stride by. ~ *ambang pintu* step over the threshold. ~ *pengemis* walk past a beggar. 2 skip, skip over. *Berhubung dgn kesulitan kertas, beberapa nomor majalah ini terpaksa di-i* Paper difficulties have forced us to skip (the publication of) several issues of this magazine. ~ *kakak* get married before o.'s elder sibling. 3 disregard (instructions, etc.). 4 overstep (propriety, etc.). ~ *moral* overstep the bounds of morality. ~ *mukah* commit adultery. **me-kan** cause (o.'s feet) to stride. ~ *kakinya ke luar* stride out. **ter-** unintentionally stepped into. **ter-kan** have taken strides. **ke-an** 1 overstepped, transgressed. 2 marriage of younger sibling prior to that of his or her older sibling. **pe(r)-an** 1 undertaking. 2 transgression.

langkai slim, slender.

langkan 1 balcony. 2 balustrade, railing.

langkap k.o. palm tree.

langkas₁ dexterous.

langkas₂ (*Lit.*) lose all its fruits (of a tree).

langkat three days from now, the day after the day after tomorrow.

langkau me-i 1 overlook, skip. 2 leave out, omit. **ter-, ter-i** skipped, passed over. ~ *oléh para kritikus* overlooked by the critics.

langkitang k.o. edible mollusc.

langlang nightwatchman. **me-** 1 make the rounds. 2 wander. ~ *buana* roam the world, go abroad.

langsai paid, settled (of bill, accounts).

langsam (*Coll.*) slow. **me-kan** slow s.t. down. *Dikan mobilnya* He slowed down his car.

langsar₁ tall and slender.

langsar₂ 1 fortunate, lucky. 2 happy.

langsat the Lansium tree and its clusters of small, yellow fruit.

langseng me- reheat by steaming.

langsep see LANGSAT.

langsi a shrill sound. **ber-, me-** make a shrill sound, scream. *Peluru* ~ Bullets screamed.

langsing₁ slim, slender, svelte. **me-** become slender, slim down. **me-kan** make s.t. slim, streamline (the body). **ke-an** slimness, slenderness. **pe-an** slimming, slenderizing (of the body).

langsing₂ (*Coll.*) **me-** go back and forth, go up and down.

langsing₃ loud (of sound).

langsir₁ me- 1 (*R.R.*) shunt trains from o. track to another. 2 (*Coll.*) move back and forth. **-an** (*R.R.*) shunt-yard. *pengawas* ~ yardmaster.

langsir₂ thin, slender.

langsir₃ lancer.

langsuir k.o. wailing female vampire, preying on newly delivered mothers in childbirth and their infants.

langsung 1 direct, straight. *Pergi dr sini* - *pulang* Go straight home from here. 2 immediately, straightaway. *Kau* - *menarik kesimpulan yg salah* Straightaway you draw the wrong conclusion. **ber-** go on, take place. *Pertunjukan wayang* ~ *sampai pagi* The puppet show went on till morning. *Négosiasi sedang* ~ Negotiations were under way. *Kejadian ini* ~ *lama . . .* This situation persisted for a long time. **keber-an** persistence, resoluteness. **ber-², me-(²)** continuous, incessant. **me-kan** 1 perform, carry out, hold (an event). 2 perpetuate (the species). **ter-** 1 carried out, implemented. 2 perpetuated. 3 rash, precipitous. **ke-an** 1 performance, execution (of a marriage ceremony, etc.). 2 perpetuity. **per-an** 1 progress, stride. 2 perpetuation. 3 implementation.

langu 1 rotten (of odor). 2 unpleasant (of taste).

langut me- sad, melancholy.

lanja me- go on a visit. **-²an** go anywhere.

lanjai slim, slender.

lanjam plowshare.

lanjang₁ slender.

lanjang₂ see TELANJANG.

lanjar long and tapering. **me-** stretch. **-an** bean pole, trellis.

lanjirat court of law.

lanjung 1 small and slender (of sugarcane, etc.). 2 tall, high.

lanjur protracted, stretched, dragged out. **me-kan** 1 stretch s.t. out, protract s.t. 2 continue s.t. **te-, ter-** too late (of s.t. already past and irreversible). *Leila ~ jatuh cinta pd Rusman* Nothing more can be done, Leila has fallen in love with Rusman. **ter-²** 1 too far, beyond the bounds. 2 continuous. **kete-an** excess, excessively.

lanjut 1 advanced. *pendidikan* - advanced education. - *umur/usia* advanced age. *Sdh* - *malam* It is far into the night. 2 long, detailed. *Ceritanya - sekali* It is a long story. - *ke balik* continued on back (of page). 3 continue, continued. *"Kau lihat bulan?" -nya* "Do you see the moon?" she continued. **se-nya** furthermore. *~ dibicarakannya ttg hal itu* She went on to speak of that matter. *dan ~ etcetera, and so forth. *uth ~* henceforth. **ber-** continue. **ber-²** protracted, extended, prolonged. **keber-an** continuity. **me-** continue (of prices, etc.). *kekacauan yg ~* continuing disorders. **me-kan** 1 continue. *~ perjuangan* continue the struggle. *~ sekolah/studi* continue his studies. 2 lengthen, extend. 3 continue speaking. **ter-** 1 rash, too far. 2 extended, lengthened. **ke-an** 1 repercussion, carry-over, follow-up. *~nya tak akan baik* There will be bad repercussions. 2 continuation, continuity. *~ kisah* continuation of the story. *~ hidup* life's continuation. **-an** 1 continuation. *sekolah ~* secondary school. 2 sequel. **pe-** continuator. *~ kesusastraan Melayu* continuator of Malay literature. **pe-an** continuing of. **per-an** continuation. *~ jenis* perpetuation of the species.

lansét (*Med.*) lancet.

lansir₁ me- 1 launch s.t. 2 spread, distribute (news, etc.).

lansir₂ see LANGSIR₁.

lanskap see LANDSKAP.

lantai 1 floor. - *perahu* ship's bottom. - *rumah* floor of a house. 2 story (of a building). - *dasar* ground floor. - *ketiga* 3d floor. - *puncak* top floor. **me-** 1 floor, install a floor. 2 take the floor (to give a speech), go on to the floor (esp. to dance). 3 hit rock bottom. *Harga ~* Prices hit rock bottom. **pe-** o. who dances before the public.

lantak piston, pile. **me-** 1 hammer s.t. 2 ram, drive (a pile). **me-kan** drum s.t. in. **-an** bar. *~ mas* gold bar. *baja ~* steel bars. **pe-** 1 piston rod. 2 ramrod. 3 ram, jackhammer.

lantam 1 proud. 2 haughty, arrogant. **me-kan** brag, boast of s.t. **ke-an** arrogance, haughtiness.

Lantamal [*Pangkalan Utama Angkatan Laut*] first-class naval base.

lantan me- 1 spoil s.o. 2 care for (o.'s body). 3 economize on (clothing by wearing poorer quality).

lantang 1 shrill, piercing (voice). 2 clear, distinct (of voice, view). - *pandangan* field of vision. **me-** become loud. **ke-an** volume, loudness.

lantar₁ me-kan 1 cause s.t. *Rendahnya daya beli itu di-kan oléh rendahnya penghasilan* Their low rate of production has caused them to have low purchasing power. 2 pass on (a suggestion, etc.). **-an** 1 reason. *Anak itu menangis ~ apa?* Why is that child crying? 2 (*Coll.*) because. *Saya tdk bisa*

datang, ~ tak énak badan I could not come because I was not feeling well. **pe-** 1 mediator, intermediary. 2 (*Ling.*) copula. **pe-an** act of mediation.

lantar₂ ter-, te- neglected. **ter-kan** abandoned (land). **menter-kan** neglect, abandon (s.o. or s.t.). *Bahasa kita tdk akan terus diter-kan* Our language will not continue to be neglected. **keter-an** state of neglect. **peter-an** neglect, abandonment.

lantar₃ see PELANTAR.

lantas 1 straightaway, directly, forthwith, then. *Ia pergi dr sini - ke rumahnya* She went from here directly to her house. 2 and so? *-, kamu mau bikin apa?* And so what are you going to do about it? **me-** go straight to, penetrate. *Naséhat gurunya ~ telinganya* The advice of his teacher went straight to his ears (i.e., he took it to heart). **me-i** penetrate s.t. **me-kan** carry out, execute s.t. *~ angan* do as o. pleases. **ter-** penetrated.

lantéra see LENTÉRA.

lantik me- install, inaugurate s.o. *Ia di- sbg sékretaris* He was installed as the secretary. **pe-an** inauguration, installation,.

lanting₁ me- throw, toss s.t. **me-kan** hurl, throw s.t. *~ nota protés* launch a protest note. **ter-** 1 thrown, tossed. 2 no longer useful, useless. **pe-** slingshot.

lanting₂ hold out at arm's length.

lanting-lanting platform at river bank (for bathing and laundering).

lantun me- 1 rebound (of a ball, spring). 2 reflect. 3 ricochet. **me-kan** make s.t. reflect or ricochet. **-an** 1 rebound. 2 reflection.

lantung₁ putrid, stinking (odor). **me-** emit a bad odor.

lantung₂ 1 a loud bang. 2 verbose. **-²** clang, clash, boom. **ber-** bump against. **me-** 1 make a sound like an explosive. 2 bump against. **ter-** knock or hit against.

lantung₃ nge- laze about, do things without purpose.

lantur me-, nge- 1 stray (from a path). 2 digress. *Jangan bicara ~* Do not get off the subject. **me-²** repeatedly digress. **me-kan** divert, distract s.o. **-an** 1 diversion, digression. 2 aberration.

lanud [*pangkalan udara*] air base.

lanuma [*pangkalan utama*] main base.

lanun pirate.

lanyah muddy.

lanyak me- 1 trample down (earth). 2 step on, run down, disparage (s.o. or s.t.). 3 hit hard.

lanyau soft mud (with a hard crust).

laos galingale, a plant of the ginger family.

laoténg see LOTÉNG.

lap 1 towel. - *piring* dish towel. 2 rag. **me-(kan)**, **menge-** wipe s.t. with a cloth.

lapad see LAFADZ.

lapah me- 1 skin, flay, dress (an animal). 2 devour.

lapal see LAFADZ.

lapan (*Coll.*) see DELAPAN.

lapang 1 open, wide, spacious. *tanah* - open field. - *dada/hati* **1** relieved. **2** patient. **3** relaxed, free from care. - *kira-kira* relieved, eased. **2** free, unoccupied. *Minggu ini saya* - I am not busy this week. **3** roomy. *Tempat duduk ini* - This seat is roomy. - *perut* always hungry, never satiated. **ber-(²)** be unfettered. ~ *hati* be patient. **me-** become spacious. **me-i** make room for, clear away. **me-kan 1** clear space for s.o. **2** relieve s.o. ~ *dr siksaan* free from torture. *Tuhan* ~ *arwahnya di akhirat* May the Lord give her soul peace in the hereafter. **3** broaden widen (a road, etc.). **ke-an 1** emptiness, vacuity. **2** leisure, ease. **3** feel relieved. **-an 1** field, square. *penelitian* ~ field research. ~ *bermain* playing field. ~ *bola* soccer field. ~ *bola baskét* basketball court. ~ *golf* golf course. ~ *hijau* playing field. ~ *perang* battlefield. ~ *rumput* lawn. ~ *sépak bola* soccer field. ~ *témbak* firing range. ~ *ténis* tennis court. ~ *terbang* airfield. **2** sphere, range (of activity). ~ *kerja* opportunities for employment. *Apa* ~ *pekerjaannya?* What is his field of work? **pe-** (*dada*) o. who tends to be relaxed about things.

lapar 1 hungry. **2** hunger. - *gizi* malnutrition. **ber-** go hungry. **me-kan** cause s.o. to be hungry. *Harimau itu sengaja di-kan spy ganas* They purposely starved the tiger to make it fierce. **ke-an 1** hunger. ~ *sangat terasa pd siang hari* O. really feels hunger at midday. **2** famine, starvation. **3** be famished.

lapat-lapat (*Jv, Jkt*) **1** vague, barely visible. **2** barely audible.

lapaz see LAFADZ.

lapih see LAPIS.

lapik 1 base, underlayer. - *cawan* saucer. - *kaki* sandal. **2** lining. **3** mat. - *duduk* mat for sitting. *se- seketiduran* bosom buddies. **ber- 1** have a base. **2** use a mat. **3** serve as a mat. **me-i** line, place a lining in s.t. **me-kan** use (paper, etc.) as a lining.

lapis 1 layer, lining. - *aus* surface layer of a road. - *baja* steel plating. - *cengkam* middle supporting layer in a road between the bed and the surface. - *legit* k.o. layered cake. - *lendir* (*Bot.*) cambium. **2** row. **3** (*Geol.*) stratum. **4** in layers. *kué* - k.o. layered cake. *kayu* - plywood. **ber- 1** have a layer. **2** stratified. **ber-²** in layers. **ber-kan** have s.t. as a layer or lining. ~ *mas* plated with gold. **me-1** line, coat. ~ *jalan dgn aspal* coat the street with asphalt. **2** in layers. **me-i 1** coat s.t. with. **2** plate (a ship). **3** cover s.t. ~ *padi dgn tikar* cover the rice with a mat. **-an 1** layer. ~ *rém* brake lining. **2** stratum, class. ~ *masyarakat* social stratum. **3** coating. ~ *cabé-cabéan* mustard plaster. ~ *dasar* first coat, primer (of paint). ~ *pelindung* protective coating. **4** (*Geol.*) lode, vein, bed. ~ *arang* vein of coal. ~ *batu dasar* bedrock. ~ *bijih* ore deposit. **pe-an 1** coating s.t. or plating. **2** making s.t. be in layers.

lap-lapan (*Sl.*) be in love.

lapor report. - *mata* **me-matakan** give an eyewitness account of s.t. **me-** report. **me-kan** report, notify, inform. *Kecelakaan hrs di-kan* An accident must be reported. *Harap -kan barang-barang yg baru* Please mention the new items. ~ *diri* report, check in. **-an 1** report, account. **2** statement. **pe- 1** reporter, commentator. **2** rapporteur. **pe-an 1** reporting. **2** commentary.

lapuk 1 moldy, putrefied, mildewed. **2** rotten, decayed (of wood, etc.), weakened. - *tumbuh-tumbuhan* peat. **3** obsolete, out-of-date (regulation, etc.). **me- 1** become moldy. **2** become weak, crumble, decay. **ke-an 1** moldiness. **2** mustiness. **pe-an 1** weathering. **2** corrosion.

lapun trap. **me-** trap s.t.

lapur₁ ber- twitch, flutter (of a bird, etc.).

lapur₂ see LAPOR.

lara 1 ill, sick. **2** painful. *hidup yg* - painful existence. *duka* - pain and sorrow. **ter-²** wail, cry bitterly.

larai see LERAI.

larang me- 1 forbid, prohibit, ban. *Di- merokok* No smoking. *Di- msk* No Entrance. **2** interdict. **ter-1** prohibited, forbidden, banned (book, etc.). **2** off limits. *kamar* ~ off-limits room. *bagian-bagian* ~ genitals. **-an 1** prohibition, ban, interdiction. **2** embargo. ~ *perdagangan* trade embargo. **3** (*Ling.*) prohibitive. **pe-an** act of banning, prohibiting.

larang in demand, selling. **me-kan** slacken, pay out (a rope).

laras₁ 1 pitch, key, scale. **2** harmony, harmonious. **se- 1** in accordance with. *Perbuatannya itu tak* ~ *dgn apa yg dijanjikannya* His actions were not in accordance with what he had promised. **2** in harmony, harmonious. *Suara kedua penyanyi itu tak* ~ The voices of the two singers were not in harmony. **3** melodious, tuneful. **menye-kan** adapt, adjust, synchronize. **kese-an 1** harmony. **2** conformity. **penye-an** adjustment, adaption. **me-kan** adjust, adapt, coordinate s.t. **ke-an** harmony. **pe-an** adjustment, adaptation, coordination.

laras₂ 1 barrel (of rifle, cannon, etc.). **2** classifier for rifles. **3** straight and cylindrical.

laras₃ (*M*) district.

larat₁ 1 be protracted, be drawn out (of an illness). **2** drag (of anchor). **3** wander. - *pikiran* **1** very sad, melancholy. **2** let o.'s mind wander. **ber-(²) 1** spread. **2** drag on, be protracted (of a conversation, etc.). **me-** protracted (illness, etc.). **me-kan, memper-** protract, drag out (negotiations, etc.).

larat₂ k.o. Moluccan orchid.

larat₃ see MELARAT.

lari 1 run. - *berantai/beranting/berganti/beregu* relay race. - *cepat* sprint. - *estafét* relay race. - *gawang* hurdles, hurdle race. - *jarak péndék* sprint. - *kencang!* on the double. - *lintas alam* cross-country race. - *lintas gawang* hurdles. - *rintangan* obstacle race. - *santai* jogging. **2** escape, leave. *Berapa org - dr penjara?* How many escaped from prison? *Dia - dr pekerjaannya* She left her job. **-²** run about. **ber-** run. ~ *anjing* trot, jog. **ber-(²)an** run helter-skelter, run in all directions, run every whichway. **me-kan 1** cause s.t. to go, run off with s.t. ~ *uang* abscond with the money. *Ia ~ mobil curian ke Bogor* He fled in the stolen car to Bogor. ~ *diri* flee, escape from. ~ *nyawa* run, flee for o.'s life. **2** kidnap, abduct s.o. **3** drive (a car, etc.) at a high speed. **mempcr-kan 1** drive (a car, etc.). **2** run (a certain distance). **ke-an** escape. **pe-** runner, jogger. ~ *cepat* sprinter. ~ *gawang* hurdler. **pe-an 1** fugitive, escapee. **2** refugee. **3** running, escape, flight.

larih (*Lit.*) **ber-²an** drink together. **me-** pour (a drink). **me-i** pour (a drink) and serve s.o.

larik₁ row, line. **me-** arrange in rows. **-an** row, line.

larik₂ me- 1 turn on a lathe. **2** bore, drill (a hole) in. **pe-, pe-an 1** lathe. **2** potter's wheel.

laring (*Anat.*) larynx.

laringéktomi laryngectomy.

laris popular, in demand, selling well. **me-kan** stimulate the sale of, sell, popularize. **pe-, peng-1** the first item sold in a work day, thought to stimulate later sales. **2** s.t. that sells well, best seller.

laron flying white ant.

lars boot, esp. military boots.

laru (*Jv*) fermenting agent added to make vinegar.

larung (*Jv*) float (esp. of offerings, corpses). **me-kan** dispose of s.t. (a body, an offering, etc.) by floating it away on a raft.

larut₁ 1 soluble. - *hati* broken-hearted. **2** fused, dissolved. **me-** (*Chem.*) become dissolved. **me-kan** dissolve s.t. **ter-kan** soluble. **ke-an** solubility. **-an** (*Chem.*) solution. **pe-** solvent. **pe-an** dissolving.

larut₂ 1 protracted. *kemarau yg* - a protracted dry season. **2** late, far-advanced (of night). **ber-²**, **me- 1** protracted, drawn out. **2** drag on. **me-kan** drag s.t. on, prolong. **ke-an** lateness (of the night). **-an** lateness.

las weld, joint. *tukang* - welder. **me-, nge-** weld s.t. **-an, -²an** (*Coll.*) welded. **penge-an** welding.

lasa 1 numb (of o.'s limbs). **2** paralyzed. **3** callus on the sole.

lasah₁ me- spread flat (mat, fish for drying, etc.). **me-kan, memper- 1** spread s.t. flat for s.o. else. **2** thoroughly exploit s.o. ~ *badan* work to the limits of o.'s endurance.

lasah₂ everyday clothes, work clothes.

lasak₁ 1 restless, restive, fidgety. **2** energetic, hyperkinetic (of a child). **3** peevish, petulant.

lasak₂ see LASAH₂.

lasat (*M*) serious (of illness).

laskar 1 (*Lit.*) pre-modern soldiers. **2** paramilitary troops, guerilla-fighters. - *rakyat* **1** irregulars. **2** paramilitary unit. - *darat* paramilitary ground forces. **ke-an** affairs dealing with paramilitary irregulars.

laso lasso.

lastik see ÉLASTIK.

lasykar see LASKAR.

lat₁ 1 interval. - *dua hari* two-day interval. **2** the space between planks. **-²**, **ber-** at intervals.

lat₂ late.

lat₃ lath.

lata₁ 1 humble, degrading. **2** dirty, ugly. **me-** creep, crawl, slither.

lata₂ see LATAH₁.

lataboga (*Lit.*) herbivore.

latah₁ 1 a nervous condition characterized by erratic involuntary imitative behavior, often pornographic or socially disapproved. **2** (*Coll.*) other irrational imitative behavior (e.g. imitation of speech, etc.). - *mulut* utter absurd statements. *Jangan -, ya?* Do not keep repeating what I say, will you? **3** madly in love.

latah₂ piles of leaves, etc. found under trees in the forest.

latah₃ see LATA₁.

latak residue (in oil or paint).

latam solid, compact. **me-** tamp down (dirt, etc.). **me-kan** cram, stuff.

latang see JELATANG.

latar (*Jv*) **1** yard. **2** surface, plane. **3** background, backdrop. - *belakang* background. **ber-** *belakang* have a background. *Dia ~ belakang pendidikan kejuruan* He has a background in technical training. **ber-belakangkan** have s.t. as a background. *Romannya ber-belakangkan révolusi* His novel has revolution as its background. **me-belakangi** form the background of. *Itulah yg ~ studi ini* That is what forms the background of this study. - *depan* foreground. **ber-kan** be set in. *Cerpén-cerpén ini ~ New York* These short stories are set in New York. **pe-an 1** yard. ~ *utk rapat-rapat militér* an open area for military gatherings. ~ *langsir* (*R.R.*) marshaling or switching yard. ~ *parkir* carpark. **2** background.

latat see MELATAT-MELOTOT.

latéks latex.

latén latent.

latif 1 fine, handsome. **2** gentle, delicate.

latih accustomed, wont. - *tertib* calisthenics. **ber-1** practice, train. **2** rehearse. **me- 1** train s.o. ~ *murid berpikir* train students to think. **2** practice s.t. **ter- 1** trained, skilled. *pemuda yg ~* trained youth. **2** exercised. *Tangan kiri yg lemah tapi sdh ~* The left hand is the weak o. but it has been exercised. **-an** exercise, training, practice. ~ *bahaya udara* air raid drill. ~ *jabatan* on-the-job training. ~ *kemilitéran pertama* (*Mil.*) basic training. ~ *otak* brain stretcher, brain-teaser. ~ *peperangan/perang-perangan* battle, troop maneuvers. ~ *simak* memorization exercises at school. **pe- 1** trainer, instructor. **2** (training) coach. **pe-an** training, giving of exercise. ~ *alih kerja* training for a new skill.

Latin 1 Latin. **2** Roman (type, letters). *huruf* - Roman alphabet letters. **me-kan** romanize (script, etc.). **pe-an** romanization.

lattah see LATAH₁.
latuh edible seaweed.
latung 1 petroleum. 2 kerosene.
latur 1 blistered. 2 blister.
laturahmi (*Isl.*) having close personal relationships.
lauh see LOH₁.
lauk side dish, esp. meat or fish served with rice. - *pauk* a variety of side dishes (including vegetable dishes). **ber-** be served with such side dishes. *Tiada* ~ We have nothing suitable to serve you.
laun -² *hari* 1 several days ago. 2 after several days. **ber-** dawdle, procrastinate, dally. **me-²** postpone, delay s.t.
laung loud voice or sound. **me-** 1 shout, scream, call out loudly. 2 summon, appeal to s.o. **me-kan** call to s.o. **sepe-(an)** the distance a shout can be heard.
laur bent, curved.
laut sea, ocean. - *api* 1 hell. 2 conflagration, sea of fire. - *Karang* Coral Sea. - *Kidul* Indian Ocean (S. of central Java). - *Kulzum* Red Sea. - *lepas* open sea, high seas. - *Mati* Dead Sea. - *pengundak* frontal, head sea. **me-** 1 go to sea. 2 head seaward. 3 resemble a sea (of crowds, etc.). **me-i** ply the seas. **memper-** 1 sail (a vessel). 2 ship by sea. **-an** ocean, sea. ~ *Hindia* Indian Ocean. ~ *Indonésia* Indonesian Ocean. ~ *selebu* the high seas, the open sea. ~ *Teduh* Pacific Ocean. ~ *Tengah* Mediterranean Sea. **pe-** seaman, o. whose livelihood is the sea.
lawa₁ crossbeam. **me-** block the way of the bridegroom and entourage en route to the bride's house.
lawa₂ small bat.
lawa₃, lawah vast, extensive (of view).
lawai thread for weaving.
lawak₁ joke, jest, gag. -² 1 amusing act, a joke. 2 butt (of a joke). **ber-(²), me-(²)** joke, jest, banter. **-an** joke, jest. **pe-** comedian, jokester.
lawak₂ feeding trough. -² *tinggi* fancy o.s. above others, live above o.'s station, live beyond o.'s means, keeping up with the Joneses.
lawak₃ see TEMU₁.
lawalata (*Coll., Amb*) **ber-** trek on foot, walk a considerable distance.
lawa-lawa, lawah-lawah see LABAH-LABAH.
lawamah see NAFSU.
lawan 1 opponent, adversary, rival. - *bicara* interlocutor. 2 enemy, foe. 3 (*Leg.*) respondent. 4 the contrary, the opposite. - *asas* paradox. - *kata* antonym. 5 against, versus. *Sekolahmu bertanding - siapa?* Your school is competing against whom? *enam - dua* six to two (of a score). - *hukum* illegal, against the law. **ber-** 1 contest, compete. *Kepandaiannya tdk* ~ Her cleverness is incontestable. 2 be the opposite of. 3 have an opponent. 4 be pitted against. **ber-an** 1 disagree with, contest s.t. 2 be contrary to. ~ *dgn kenyataan* contrary to the facts. 3 compete. 4 clashing, contradictory (views). **me-** 1 oppose (the enemy, a candidate, etc.), fight. ~ *godaan* resist temptation. 2 versus,

against, compete with. *perang* ~ *narkotika* war against narcotics. 3 be against, be contrary to. *Perbuatan itu* ~ *adat* That act is against customary law. *harga* ~ competitive price. **memper-kan** 1 oppose. 2 pit against. *Di mana org* ~ *ayam di sini?* Where do people fight cocks here? **pe-** 1 opponent, adversary. 2 competitor. 3 opposition. *partai* ~ opposition party. 4 disobedient. **per-an** 1 opposition, resistance. 2 contrast.
lawang₁ door, gate. - *sekéténg* inner gate. **pe-** gatekeeper.
lawang₂ 1 mace. 2 clove flowers.
lawar slice of meat or fish. **me-** slice thinly, cut into thin slices.
lawas₁ 1 long (time). 2 old. **me-** no longer bearing (of fruit tree).
lawas₂ see LUAS.
lawat me- 1 pay a visit. ~ *ke luar negeri* go abroad. 2 make a trip. 3 (*Coll.*) make a visit of condolence. *Ia* ~ *ke tempat kematian* He paid a visit to the place of the deceased. **me-i** visit. *Sdh dua puluh negara di-inya* He has already visited 20 countries. **pe-** visitor, tourist. **per-an** 1 visit, trip. 2 expedition.
lawé 1 yarn, thread. 2 cotton waste. **-an** place where thread is being woven.
lawéan k.o. headless ghost.
lawi, lawi-lawi long tailfeather.
lawon (*Jv*) white cotton. - *tenun* woven material.
layah₁ veil. **me-kan** cover (the face) with a veil.
layah₂ me- bend over backward, bow. **me-kan** cause s.t. to bend down.
layah₃ flat-edged metal plate.
layah₄ see LAYAP₁.
layak 1 proper, suitable. *wanita yg sdh - kawin* a girl of proper marriageable age. *org yg - ditegur o.* who should be told how to behave. - *krédit* creditable. - *laut* seaworthy. - *pakai* usable. - *udara* air worthy. 2 reasonable, fair (price). *hidup yg - a* reasonably comfortable life. 3 like. *menémbak - koboi* shoot like a cowboy. **-nya** as if. *Ia disengat lebah -nya* She acted as if she were stung by a bee. **se-** like. *berkelip* ~ *intan sejuta* sparkle like a million diamonds. **se-nya** 1 proper. *melakukan* ~ do the right, proper or decent thing. *Sdh* ~ *ayahmu membalas demikian* It is only fitting that your father should answer that way. 2 as much as is proper. *uang sumbangan* ~ contribution in the proper amount. **me-kan** 1 make proper. ~ *ruang resépsi* tidy up the reception hall. 2 bring s.t. up to standard. ~ *armada kita* bring our fleet up to standard. **ke-an** 1 worthiness. ~ *udara* air worthiness. 2 fairness (of price). 3 properness. 4 advisability. *studi* ~ feasibility study.
layan me-i 1 serve, wait on (guests), take care of (customers). ~ *suami* adjust o.s. to o.'s husband's wishes. 2 supply. *Kami* ~ *keterangan yg dikehendaki oléh umum* We supply the information requested by the public. 3 man. ~ *meriam pantai tak dpt dilakukan oléh satu dua org saja* Manning the shore battery cannot be done by only o. or

two men. **4** service. *Kita dpt ~ segala jenis mobil* We can service all types of cars. *~ aki* service batteries. **me-kan** serve (a meal). **-an** service. **pe-** 1 waiter, waitress. **2** sales clerk. **3** attendant. *~ lif* elevator operator. *~ pompa* gas station attendant. *~ rém (R.R.)* brakeman. *~ sinyal* railroad-crossing guard. *~ wésél (R.R.)* switchman. **pe-an 1** servicing. *~ di darat (Av.)* ground handling (of baggage). **2** treatment, care. **3** service, waiting (on table).

layang₁ -² 1 kite. **2** k.o. bird, swift. **se-** a little breeze, a passing breeze. *~ lalu/mata/pandang* at a flying glance, in passing. **me- 1** fly. *Tangannya ~ di muka pedagang* His hands flew out at the vendor's face. *Pesawat itu ~ rendah* The plane glided low. *Jiwanya ~* Her soul took flight. **2** drift, waft about. *Pikirannya ~* His mind wandered. **me-²** *(Av.)* fly and swing. **me-kan 1** fly (a kite, plane). *~ pandang* **1** peer, glance at. **2** send dispatch. **2** cause s.t. to fly out. *~ tinju* let fly his fist. **ter-(²) 1** float, drift. *Ingatannya ~ ke mana-mana* Her thoughts wandered everywhere. **2** doze, nod. **-(²)an** kite. **pe-an** flying, soaring.

layang₂ me- cut s.t. in half (e.g. mango, etc.). **pe-an** ferry boat.

layap₁ low (close to the surface). **ber-(²)an 1** fly close to the ground. **2** shake and flutter from the wind (of trees). **me-** fly just above the water's surface seeking fish (of birds). **nge-** *(Jkt)* wander around. **me-i** hover near s.t. or s.o. *Awan ~ pegunungan* Clouds hovered near that range of mountains. **me-(²)kan** cause to float or hover.

layap₂ me- doze, nod.

layar₁ 1 sail. *- agung* mainsail. *- baksi* mizzen sail. *- besar* main sail. *- bubutan (Naut.)* staysail. *- cucur* jib. *- dastur* spanker. *- gusi* spanker. *- padan* storm sail. *- pengapuh* banner on a mast. *- puncak* topsail. *- sabang* spritsail. *- sabur* top gallant sail. *- topana* foresail. **2** screen (TV or movie). *- pérak/putih* movie or silver screen. **me-putihkan** put on the screen. **3** blind, shade (of window, door). **ber-, be- 1** sail, go by boat. *~ ke pulau kapuk* sleep (lit., sail to the island of kapok). **2** have a sail. **me-i** sail, ply (the ocean). **me-kan, memper-kan** sail (a ship). **pe-** sailor, seaman. **pe-an 1** voyage, trip by ship. **2** navigation, shipping. *~ duga (Naut.)* dead reckoning. *~ niaga* merchant shipping. *~ pantai* coastal shipping. *~ wisata* ship's cruise. **3** seamanship.

layar₂ see IKAN.

layat me-, nge- make a visit of condolence. **pe-** o. who pays his respects to the family of the deceased. **pe-an** condolence visit.

layu 1 withered, faded, wilted (of flowers). **2** weak, pale. **me-** wither, wilt. **me-kan** wither, wilt s.t. **ke-an 1** faded, wilted. **2** drooping. **3** pining away (to o.'s death). **4** death, demise. **-²an** withered or wilted material.

layuh 1 paralyzed. **2** weak, feeble, debilitated. *- jantung* cardiac arrest.

layuk me- sway (to the left or right).

layur me- 1 singe, scorch s.t. **2** sear s.t.

lazat see LEZAT.

lazim 1 usual, customary, common. **2** compulsory, obligatory. *sangat tdk -* very or most unusual. **-nya** us. **me-kan 1** make s.t. usual, bring s.t. into vogue. **2** make s.t. compulsory. **ke-an** custom, usage, the fashion, fad.

lazuardi 1 lapis lazuli. **2** azure.

LBH *[Lembaga Bantuan Hukum]* legal aid services.

lbr. *[lébar]* wide, width.

L/C *[letter of credit]*

lé see TOLÉ.

léak see LÉYAK.

lebah bee. *- laut* k.o. jelly fish.

lebai 1 mosque official. *- penghulu* district religious official. **2** mosque servant.

lebak₁ 1 valley. **2** lowlands.

lebak₂ sound of a slap.

lebam sound made by a falling object.

lébam k.o. small edible fish.

leban₁ 1 lead-colored. **2** *(Med.)* hematoma.

leban₂ k.o. tree whose bark and leaves are used for medicinal purposes.

lebap sound of fruit falling to the ground.

lébar 1 broad, wide, extensive. **2** width, breadth. *- sawahnya berapa?* What is the width of the rice field? *- ayunan* amplitude. *- hadapan* frontage. *- kapal* ship's beam. *- laluan* width of passage. *- mulut* big mouth. *- sayap* wingspan, wingspread. *- sepur (R.R.)* gauge. **me-** become wide(r). **me-kan** widen s.t. *Jepang tlh ~ lapangan terbang Mandai* The Japanese widened Mandai airport. **pe-an, per-an** widening, broadening (of road), expansion. *~ sayapnya* spreading of its wings.

Lebaran day of celebration at end of fasting month. *- haji* festival celebrated on the 10th day of the 12th Isl. month. **ber-** celebrate *Lebaran*.

lebas me- whip s.o.

lebat 1 luxuriant, dense (of fruit on trees, hair, etc.). *Pohon jeruk itu - buahnya* That citrus tree is laden with fruit. **2** heavy (of rain). **me- 1** be packed, be luxuriant. *Pohon-pohon mangga ~* Mango trees grow luxuriantly. **2** become thick, luxuriant (of hair). **3** become heavy (of rain). **ke-an 1** luxuriance (hair, fruit, etc.). **2** heaviness (of rain).

lebé see LEBAI.

lébér me- spill or run over.

lebih 1 more, -er. *Dia - besar* He is bigger. *Uangnya - banyak* He has more money. *jam dua - lima* 2:05. *enam puluh lima tahun dan -* 65 and up. *- dulu* prior (in time sequence). *- dulu drp perbuatan itu* prior to the deed. *Saya pergi - dulu* I will leave ahead of you. *- kurang* more or less, approximately. *- lagi* **1** much more. **2** still more. **2** more than. *Setahun - tlh lampau* More than a year has passed. **-² 1** all the more (so). *Saya tdk bisa ~ karena tdk punya uang* I cannot, all the more so because I have no money. **2** *(Coll.)* leftovers, remains. **(se)-nya** rest, remainder. **se-²nya** at most. **ber- 1** remain, be left (over). **2** excessive. *urbanisasi ~* overurbanization. **ber-(²)an 1** copious, profuse. *hidup ~* live in luxury. **2** redundant. *Tdk ~ bila dikatakan* . . . It is no exaggeration to say . . . **me-** increase, become more numerous. **me-i 1** exceed (expectations, etc.). *Tingginya ~ teman lain* His height was greater than his friends'. **2** eclipse, overshadow s.t. **3** add more (to s.t.). **me-²i** exaggerate s.t. **me-kan 1** increase s.t. **2** cause s.t. to be excessive. *Dia ~ berat badannya* He put on an excessive amount of weight. **3** favor, benefit. *Anak laki-laki dlm kebanyakan hal di-kan drp anak perempuan* A boy is, in most cases, favored over a girl. **me-²kan** exaggerate s.t. *Mémang susah tapi jangan di-²kan!* Yes of course it is difficult, but do not exaggerate it! **ter- 1** exceedingly. **2** most. *Siapa yg ~ dulu?* Who is the very first? *~ dulu saya mau* . . . First of all I want to . . . **3** especially. **ter-² 1** above all, esp. **2** all the more so. **ke-an 1** excess, surplus. **2** have s.t. in excess. *Ia ~ duit* He has got too much money. **3** superiority. **berke-an 1** overly abundant, surplus. **2** exaggerated. **3** be superior (to). **-an 1** excess, surplus. *~ lagi* all the more so, even so. **2** remainder.

lebu dust. **ber-** dusty.

lebuh broad road.

lebuk₁ sound of a stone hitting the ground.

lebuk₂ loose (of soil). **me-** *(tanah)* loosen (soil).

lebum sound of a thud.

lebun deceit, fraud. **me-** deceive, defraud.

lebur 1 smelted. **2** dissolved, melted. *panas titik -* melting point. *- binasa* destroyed. *- kiamat* doomsday. **me- 1** melt, fuse. **2** destroy, wipe out. **3** merge. *Semua laskar di- ke dlm TNI* All the paramilitary soldiers were merged with the national army. **me-, me-kan 1** fuse s.t., smelt. **2** join, affiliate s.t. with. *- diri* merge. **3** melt (fat) off. **4** destroy, wipe out. **ke-an** dissolution. **-an** smelting. **pe-an 1** melting, dissolving away. **2** iron works. **3** fusing together, amalgamation. **4** *(Ling.)* coalescence. **5** *(Fin.)* merger.

lecah 1 muddy. **2** glutinous. **ter- 1** get stuck in the mud. **2** get a bad name.

lecak₁ muddy, slushy, miry.

lecak₂ plain, ordinary (of faces).

lecap see BASAH.

lecat₁ raw (of throat).

lecat₂ see LICIN.

lécéh₁ sloppy, unkempt (of dress).

lécéh₂ talkative. **me-** chat along. **me-kan** chat about s.t. **pe-** talkative person.

lécéh₃ vile. **me-** insulting, despising. **me-kan** despise, consider s.t. vile. **pe-an** act of despising, insulting.

lecek 1 disheveled, unkempt. **2** crumpled (of paper, etc.).

lécék worn (of locks, latches, etc.).

lécét 1 chafed. *Kakinya - kena sepatu baru* Her feet are chafed from the new shoes. **2** blister (on foot, etc.). **3** scratched. **be-, me- 1** chafed, become blistered. **2** scratched (a paint job, etc.). **me-kan 1** chafe, rub (the skin, etc.). **2** scuff (o.'s shoes, the floor).

léci the lychee fruit and tree.

lecit me- 1 slip away. **2** ooze through. *Pisang yg diremasnya ~ di sela-sela jarinya* The banana he was squeezing oozed through his fingers.

lecit-lecit snap fastener.

léco dwarf, midget.

lécok very slick.

lecot see LECUT.

lecuh shriveled up (of cooked vegetables).

lecup sound of a kiss.

lecur₁ sound of a whip's lash. *- cambuk* lash of whip.

lecur₂ me- blister. **me-kan** cause a blister.

lecut sound of a whip's lash. *- cambuk* lash of whip. **me- 1** whiplash s.o. or s.t. **2** prod (s.o. into doing s.t.). **3** sound of the lash of a whip. **me-i** give a sound lashing to. **me-kan** whip with s.t. **-an** prod, lash, blow (of a whip). *~ cemeti* lash of a whip.

ledak me- 1 explode (of a bomb, etc.). **2** erupt (of a volcano). **3** break out, burst out. *Tangisnya ~* He burst into tears. *Perang ~* War broke out. **4** *(Sl.)* become a sensation. *Tak duga kasét saya ~* Much to my surprise, my cassette did become a hit. **me-kan 1** explode s.t., cause to explode, blow s.t. up. **2** release (emotions). *~ isi kebencian hatinya* release his pent-up hatred. **-an 1** explosion. **2** eruption. **3** detonation. **pe- 1** explosive. *senjata ~* explosive weapon. **2** explosives expert. **pe-an** explosion.

lédék₁ *(Jv)* **1** k.o. dance performed at feasts by hired dancers joined by honored spectators. **2** such a hired dancer.

lédék₂ *(Jkt)* **me-, nge-** tease. **nge-in** tease s.o.

lédéng see LÉDING.

lédés inflamed, red (of eyes).

leding me- warp, sag (of floors, etc.).

léding plumbing, running water. *air -* running water. *- umum* public water faucet. *tukang -* plumber.

lédor see TELÉDOR.

ledos me- 1 explode, burst. **2** collapse.

leduk me- explode.

ledung me- bend, give (of a bridge). **me-kan** bend s.t.

lega 1 roomy, open. **2** free, not busy. **3** relieved, free of worry. *- dada* unconcerned. *- hati/pikiran* relieved. **me-kan** *(hati)* make o. feel relieved. **ke-an 1** relief. **2** space.

legah see LEGA.

légak-légok see LÉNGGAK-LÉNGGOK.

légal /légal, lékhal/ legal.

légalisasi legalization. **me-kan** legalize.

légalisir me- legalize.

légalistis legalistic.

légalitas legality.

legam *(Lit.)* black.

légar ber- 1 take turn. **2** revolve, circle about. **me-i** rotate, revolve around s.t. **me-kan** circulate s.t. **-an 1** turn. **2** revolution.

légasi legation.
legat straight, fixed.
legén (*Jv*) unfermented toddy.
legénda 1 legend, myth. 2 legend (on maps, etc.).
me-kan make into a legend.
légendaris legendary.
léger /léger, lékher/ ledger.
légér 1 floor joist. 2 wine vat.
Legi (*Jv*) the first day of the five-day week.
légion 1 legion. 2 association. - *Véteran* Veteran's
Association.
législatif legislative.
legit (*Sd*) 1 sweet. 2 sticky.
légitimasi legitimation. me-(kan) legitimatize.
légitimir me- legitimatize.
légiun see LÉGION.
légo release. - *jangkar* drop anchor. me- 1 hand
over, transfer s.t. 2 sell s.t., release for sale.
3 (*Sl.*) sell cheaply, dump. *Mesin tik saya - nanti* I
will dump this typewriter. ter- accidentally cast
away. -an s.t. that has been released. *barang* ~
goods that have been released.
legojo see ALGOJO.
legok 1 concave. *tanah* - uneven land. 2 dented.
3 pothole.
légong k.o. Balinese dance by young girls.
legu me- plait (rug, mat).
legundi k.o. shrub.
legung k.o. tree.
léha, léhah careless, inattentive. (ber)-² (*Coll.*)
take it easy. *ngadem ke Puncak atau* ~ *di Pulau
Putri* go to Puncak to cool off or relax on Putri
Island.
léhér neck. - *baju* collar. - *botol* neck of bottle. -
rahim cervix.
leja me- 1 reprimand. 2 abuse, revile.
lejang 1 fast, swift. 2 flash. 3 (*Sport*) lap. se- *terbang* 1 in a flash, fast as lightning. 2 top speed. ~
kuda berlari the distance a horse can run. me-
kick. me-kan *kaki* stretch out o.'s legs.
lejat₁ me- flip (of a fish). me-² flip-flop, writhe.
-an a flip (of a coin, fish tails, etc.).
lejat₂ see LEZAT.
lejit me- 1 run off, make a dash. ~ *ke depan* thrust
forward. 2 increase suddenly, skyrocket. *Angka
kematian kecelakaan itu* ~ *menjadi seribu org* The
number of casualties jumped to o. thousand.
léka 1 negligent, careless, inattentive. 2 absorbed
in, engrossed, lost in thought.
lekah crack, aperture. me- become chapped,
cracked (of lips, etc.).
lekak-lekuk bumpy (of road, ground).
lekak-liku, lekak-likuk 1 with many bends. 2 intricacies (of a plan, etc.).
lekam me- hold between thumb and index finger.
lekam-lekum a loud noise.
lekang 1 cracked (of hard ground). 2 fission. - *inti*
nuclear fission. 3 easily separated (fruit from its
pit, friends from e.o., etc.). *Pakaiannya tak - dr
badan* He is always wearing the same clothes (lit.,
his clothes never part from his body). *keakraban*

tdk - an inseparable intimacy. me- split, cracked,
cleaved. ter-kan fissionable.
lekap ber- embrace, cuddle up (to s.o.). me-
1 stick, adhere. 2 draw together. me-kan 1 affix
s.t. 2 press. ~ *saputangan ke hidungnya* press a
handkerchief to o.'s nose.
lekap-lekap sound of crunching or rattling.
lekar plaited rattan stand to hold round-bot-
tomed vessels.
lékar 1 reading stand for the Koran. 2 lectern.
lekas 1 fast, swift, quick. 2 soon. *Dia - selesai* He
finished soon. *Keréta api - berangkat* The train
leaves soon. -² very quickly. ~ Hurry up!
se-²nya 1 as quickly as possible. 2 as soon as
possible. ber-² hurry, rush. me-kan, memper-
speed s.t. up, accelerate s.t. -an (*Coll.*) hurry.
lekat sticky, stick. -² 1 adhering, sticking. 2 addicted. 3 close (of friendship). ber-, me- 1 adhere. *dgn kehormatan yg* ~ *pd jabatan ini* with the
respect that adheres to this office. *Hatinya sdh* ~
di Solo He left his heart behind in Solo. 2 close
(of friendship). ~ *dlm hati* remember, recall. me-
kan 1 attach, stick, glue s.t. *Siapa yg* ~ *perangko
ini di sini?* Who stuck this stamp here? 2 put on
(a hat, coat, etc.). 3 invest (money). 4 strike (with
the hand or foot). 5 direct o.'s view or attention
to s.t. or s.o. ke-an 1 adhesiveness, viscosity.
2 have s.t. stuck to. -an 1 adhesion. 2 appendage. pe-an adhering, sticking.
lekéh smudge.
lekir streaky, mottled.
lekit sticky, viscous.
lék-lékan (*Jv*) all-night get-together.
lekok curving, winding (of road, etc.). me-kan
bend s.t., cause s.t. to curve.
Lékra [*Lembaga Kebudayaan Rakyat*] the People's
Cultural Association, a left-wing literary and
cultural organization until the mid-1960s.
léksikograf lexicographer.
léksikografi lexicography.
léksikostatistik (*Ling.*) lexicostatistics.
léktor a rank of university teachers, similar to
associate professor. - *hepala* senior associate professor. - *madya* intermediate associate professor.
- *muda* junior associate professor.
léktris see ÉLÉKTRIS.
léktur reading matter.
leku ber-, me-, te-, berte- lean on o.'s elbow.
lekuh-lekih sound of a cough or of difficult
breathing.
lekuk 1 hollow (in the cheeks), concavity. - *liku*
1 many dents. 2 various tricks. - *lutut* hollow of
the knee. - *mata* 1 eye socket. 2 (*Anat.*) orbit. -
perut pit of the stomach. 2 dent (in a fender,
etc.). 3 depression (in the ground). ber-
1 dented. *mata keris* ~ *tiga* a kris blade with three
curves. 2 have holes. me- 1 become hollow. 2 become dented. me-kan 1 indent s.t. 2 make a
hollow, depression, dent. -an 1 dent. 2 indentation.
lekum₁ see HALKUM.

lekum₂ see LEKAM.

lekung 1 hollow. **2** curved, bent. **me-** curve, bend.

lekup-lekap sound of cracking o.'s knuckles, snapping sticks in two, etc.

léla₁ smart, jaunty. **ber-** act smart. **me- 1** flaunt. **2** swagger, boast. **3** brandish (a sword). **4** challenge with a sword. **5** rampage, storm, tear around. **me-kan** brandish s.t.

léla₂ whim, caprice. **se-²nya** to o.'s heart's content, at o.'s leisure. **ber-** be whimsical. **me-(²)** wander at will. *terbang* ~ fly every whichway.

lelabah spider.

lelabi k.o. fresh-water turtle.

lelah tired, weary, worn-out, exhausted. - *jerih/ letih/payah* very tired. **ber-(²)** tire, wear o.s. out. **me-kan, memper- 1** tire, weary s.o. ~ *diri* tire o.s. **2** tiring, fatiguing, wearying. **ke-an 1** weariness, fatigue, exhaustion. ~ *mata* eyestrain. **2** exhausted, tired.

lelai me- droop (of tree branch, etc.). **me-kan** bend s.t. down.

lelaki man, male. **ke-an** masculinity.

lelakon 1 story (in a shadow play). **2** life story.

lélan k.o. fish.

lelancur 1 half-grown chicken. **2** youngster, young whippersnapper.

lélang auction. *juru* - auctioneer. **me-** auction off, sell at auction. **me(mper)-kan 1** sell at auction. **2** turn s.t. over to an auction. **3** put out to contract, tender. **ter-** auctioned off accidentally. **pe-** auctioneer. **per-an** auction, public sale.

lelangit 1 palate. **2** house ceiling.

lelap sound asleep. - *nyenyak* very sound asleep. **me-kan** put s.o. to sleep. ~ *mata* close o.'s eyes (and sleep). **ter-** be sound asleep. **ter-kan** can be put into a sound sleep. **ke-an 1** deep sleep. **2** too sound (of sleep).

lelar memper-(kan) (*M*) use continually.

lelas 1 smooth (after polishing). **2** blister, blistered (of skin). **me- 1** smooth (by polishing). **2** trim (a cock's comb).

lelatu spark.

lelawa cave bat.

lélé k.o. freshwater catfish.

léléh 1 melt (of wax, etc.). **2** calm down. **ber-an** drip, trickle with (perspiration). **me- 1** trickle, drip (of tears, etc.). *Nanah* ~ *dr telinganya* Pus dripped from his ear. **2** melt. *Lilin* ~ A candle melted (and dripped). **me-kan 1** cause s.t. to trickle, drip. ~ *air mata* weep. **2** cause s.t. to melt (butter, etc.). **-an** a trickle.

lelembut k.o. trouble-making invisible spirit.

lelep₁ (*Jv*) **me-kan 1** submerge, immerse, dip s.t. **2** drown s.o. or s.t. **ke-** submerged. ~ *ke air* drowned.

lelep₂ see LELAP.

lélér ber-an drip with (perspiration). **me- 1** drip, trickle, slobber. **2** stray, wander (of thoughts). **ke-an** scattered around, strewn about. **pe-an** (*Geol.*) effusion.

lelet (*Jv*) **nge-** very slow.

lélét me-kan spread, smear (s.t.).

leléwa ber- 1 show off, put on airs. **2** gaudy, flashy, showy.

léli lily.

lelono broto (*Jv*) lead an ascetic itinerant way of life.

leluasa 1 free, unhampered, unimpeded. **2** lavish, generous, liberal (in giving). **ber-** do as o. pleases. **ke-an** freedom (of action). **berke-an** have freedom of action.

lelucon 1 joke, jest. **2** spoof, farce.

leluhur ancestors, forefathers.

leluing k.o. banyan tree.

lelung see LÉLANG.

leluri 1 ancestor. **2** predecessor.

lém glue. - *tikus* k.o. adhesive mousetrap. **me-** glue s.t.

lemah 1 weak (of body, argument, etc.), low (of battery), fading (of radio). **2** (*Ling.*) unstressed (of syllable). **3** limp, supple. - *gemulai* graceful. - *hati* soft-hearted, meek. - *lembut 1* graceful. **2** gracious, kind-hearted. **ke-** *lembutan 1* gentleness, graciousness. **2** suppleness, gracefulness. - *lantur* flexible, pliant, supple. - *lunglai 1* flexible, pliant. **2** yielding, responsive. **ber-** *diri* weaken o.s. **me-** become weak. **memper-, me-kan 1** weaken, enervate, enfeeble. **2** attenuate. **ke-an 1** weakness, frailty. ~ *perasaan* faintheartedness. ~ *syahwat* impotence. **2** laxity. **3** weakness for s.t., susceptibility. **pe-an** weakening.

lemak 1 fat, grease. - *babi 1* pork fat. **2** lard. - *hewani/jenuh* animal fat. - *ketam* gray. - *nabati* vegetable oil. - *tulang* marrow. **2** greasy. *nasi* - boiled rice with assorted side dishes. **3** sweet (in speech), suave. **ber-** greasy. *makanan* ~ fatty, greasy food. **per-an** fattening (of cattle, etc.).

lemang 1 glutinous rice roasted in bamboo tubes. **2** k.o. cake of grated cassava and coconut with palm sugar steamed in bamboo tubes. **me-** prepare o. of these dishes.

lemari cupboard, wardrobe, case. - *arsip* filing cabinet. - *besi* safe. - *buku* bookcase. - *(pen)dingin/és* icebox, refrigerator. **me-éskan** shelve (a problem), put (a problem) on ice. - *kaca* dresser or chiffonier with mirror. - *kedaian/kodok* display case, showcase. - *laci 1* chest of drawers. **2** filing cabinet. - *makan* kitchen cabinet, cupboard. - *obat* medicine cabinet. - *pajangan/pamér* showcase. - *rias* dresser, dressing table. - *sékering* fuse box.

lemas 1 limp, faint, languid. *mati* - suffocated to death (esp. drowned). **2** supple, pliant, flexible. **me-kan 1** weaken, soften s.t. ~ *kaki* stretch out o.'s legs. **2** smother, stifle, suffocate s.o. **3** refine. **4** accommodate.

lemau 1 soft (of s.t. that should be hard or crisp). **2** weak.

lembab 1 damp, moist, humid. - *lembut* soft and wet (as of sand). **2** dull (of a drum sound). **3** clumsy, awkward. **4** indolent. **me-kan** moisten, dampen, wet s.t. **ke-an** humidity, dampness, mugginess. **pe-** moisturizer, moistener. **pe-an** moisturizing, moistening.

lembaga₁ institute, league, organization, institution. - *Arab* Arab League. - *astronotika* space agency. - *Bantuan Hukum* Legal Aid Society. - *hukuman* penal institution. - *negara* state institution. - *pemasyarakatan* correctional facility, penitentiary. **me-** become institutionalized, become customary. *Korupsi sdh* ~ Corruption has become a way of life. **me-kan 1** institutionalize, commit s o. to an institution. **2** make an institution of s.t. **ter-kan** institutionalize. **ke-an** institutional. **pe-an** institutionalization.

lembaga₂ embryo, sprout. - *daun* sprout of a plant.

lembah valley, dale. - *kehidupan* difficulties of life.

lembai see LAMBAI.

lembak me- 1 boil over. **2** spill over.

lembam₁ 1 weak, tired, languid. **2** swollen from fatigue, weeping, etc. (of facial features). **ke-an** languidness.

lembam₂ see LEBAM.

lembang 1 dent, hollow. **2** dented. **3** valley. **me-** hollow s.t. out.

lembar₁ 1 sheet (of paper). - *percobaan* proofsheet. - *lepas* looseleaf. **2** classifier for paper, etc. **se-** *kertas* a sheet of paper. **se-** *cék* a check. **-an 1** page. ~ *kuning* yellow pages (of telephone directory). **2** sheet (of s.t. thin like paper). ~ *Rp500* 500 rupiah note. ~ *kayu* veneer. ~ *ketikan* typed copy. **3** paper, pamphlet. ~ *buruh* labor organ. ~ *kegiatan* project paper. ~ *negara* gvt. official gazette. ~ *pagi* morning paper. ~ *pembina* data sheet.

lembar₂ 1 thread, string. **2** classifier for hair, thread, etc. **me-kan** twist (of rope, string, etc.).

lembayung 1 the water hyacinth. **2** reddish purple, crimson.

lémbéga k.o. shrub with medicinal qualities.

lembék 1 soft (of a pillow, etc.), flabby (flesh). **2** soft, mushy (of porridge, etc.). **3** loose, slack (of rope, springs). **4** weak. - *ingatan* mentally retarded. **me-** become soft or slack. **me-kan 1** soften s.t. **2** weaken, impair (o.'s health). **ke-an 1** softness. **2** slackness, looseness. **3** weakness.

lémbéng (*Jv*) coquettish.

lembidang edge, rim (of plate, hat, etc.).

lembik see LEMBÉK.

lembing 1 spear, lance. **2** (*Sport*) javelin. **me-** throw the spear or javelin.

lembu ox, cow, bull. - *belang* spotted cow. - *dogol/ dongkol* o. whose bark is worse than his bite. - *hutan* wild bull. - *kasi* ox. - *laut* walrus. - *perahan* dairy cow. - *tampung* piebald cow.

lembung₁ me- swell (of a bruise, balloon, etc.). **me-kan** inflate, blow up (a balloon). ~ *perahu karét* inflate a rubber raft. ~ *dadu* puff up o.'s chest, be haughty, proud. **pe-an** (*Jv*) **1** balloon. **2** blown up gizzard.

lembung₂ see LAMBUNG₂.

lembur₁ work done outside of normal working hours. - *kerja* overtime (work). *upah* - overtime pay. **me-, ng-** work overtime.

lembur₂ see LAMBUR.

lembusir withers, shoulder (of beef, etc.).

lembut 1 soft. **2** meek, tender, gentle. - *hati* gentle, easygoing. **me-** become soft. *Suara paman* ~ *sedikit* Uncle's voice softened a bit. **me-kan** soften, refine s.t. ~ *hati* console, comfort s.o. **ke-an 1** softness. **2** gentleness, tenderness. **pe-an** softening, toning down. ~ *bahasa* euphemism.

lémék protective underlayer. - *kursi* seat cover, pad.

lemes₁ (*Sd*) the most polite speech level.

lemes₂ see LEMAS.

lemét k.o. cake of grated coconut steamed in banana leaves or corn husks.

Lémhanas [*Lembaga Pertahanan Nasional*] National Defense Institute.

Lemigas [*Lembaga Minyak dan Gas Bumi*] Institute for Petroleum and Natural Gas.

lémon see LIMUN₁.

lémot ber-an smeared all over with s.t. *Mulutnya* ~ *és loli* Her mouth was smeared with juice from a popsicle.

lempai see LAMPAI.

lempang straight. - *hati* honest, straight. - *pukang* crisscross. **me-** go straight (of a road, street). **me-kan** straighten s.t. ~ *dgn* adjust to, coordinate with, bring into line with.

lémpar 1 throw. **2** (*Sport*) throwing event. - *cakram* discus throw. - *lembing* javelin toss, throw. - *martil* hammer throw. - *peluru* shotput. **me-1** throw s.t. ~ *peluru* (*Sport*) put the shot. **2** (*Coll.*) dispose of s.t. ~ *tanggung jawab* shift the responsibility, pass the buck. **3** throw at (esp. with stones). ~ *étalase* throw stones at a display window. **me-i** pelt s.o. or s.t. **me-kan** throw, hurl, toss. ~ *kritik kpd* level criticism at. ~ *pandangan* look at s.o. or s.t. briefly. **ter-** tossed aside, flung. ~ *dr truk* flung from the truck. **-an** a pitch, toss, throw. ~ *pisau* a throw of a knife. ~ *hukuman* (*Sport*) foul shot or throw (in basketball). ~ *mata/ pandang* tossing of a glance. **pe- 1** pitcher, hurler, thrower. **2** launcher. ~ *rokét* bazooka. **sepe-** a stone's throw away. **pe-an 1** throwing, hurling. **2** ejection.

lempem see MELEMPEM.

lempeng (*Jv*) see LEMPANG.

lémpéng 1 slab, s.t. broad and flat. - *jam* watch dial. - *kering* peat. - *kulit bumi* (*Geol.*) lithosphere. **2** a classifier for flat broad objects. *se-* *kaca* plate of glass. *se-* *tembakau* plug of tobacco. *se-* *besi* sheet of iron. **3** k.o. pancake with sliced bananas. **me-** be thin and flat. **-an** plaque.

lemper k.o. snack made of steamed glutinous rice with meat or other stuffing and wrapped in a banana leaf.

lemping see LÉMPÉNG.

lempit a fold. **me-** fold s.t. **-an** a fold.

lempok k.o. candied fruit (often durian).

lempuh see LEPUH.
lempuk see LEMPOK.
lempung$_1$ clay.
lempung$_2$ soft and light (of wood).
lempuyang a medicinal plant of the ginger family.
lemukut see MELUKUT.
lemuru k.o. fish, the oil sardine.
lemusir see LEMBUSIR.
lén$_1$ (*Coll.*) lens.
lén$_2$ see LIN$_2$.
léna soundly asleep. - *ayam* 1 doze. 2 late afternoon or early evening. 3 be off guard. **ber-**^{2} dawdle, be unhurried. *Dia ~ berjalan ke pasar* She leisurely walks to the market. **me-kan** put s.o. to sleep. **ter-** fall asleep. **ke-an** somnolent, soporific.
lénan linen.
lencam k.o. small sea fish.
lencana 1 emblem, badge. 2 insignia, ribbon. - *jabatan* official insignia. - *perang* l battle pennant. 2 war decoration.
lencang in a straight line. - *kanan* (*Mil.*) form a straight line by looking to the right. **me-kan** straighten, make s.t. straight.
léncéng me- veer, swerve, turn.
léncér see KELÉNCÉR.
lencing me- flee.
lencir (*Jv*) tall and slim.
lencit me- slip away or out (as of a seed between o.'s fingers).
léncong$_1$ (*Jkt*) **me-** 1 veer, swerve. 2 go astray, depart (from the right path).
léncong$_2$ see BASAH.
lendér, lendir mucus, phlegm.
léndot nge- hang on to (arm, sarong edge, etc., e.g. a child hanging on to his mother).
lendung 1 bent inward, curved. 2 bowed down (from old age). **me-** 1 sag. 2 flex. **-an** deflection. **ke-an** slack.
lenga sesame.
léngah 1 careless, inattentive. 2 carefree, nonchalant. **ber-**^{2} dawdle, dally, relax. **me-** 1 relax, let o.'s guard down. *~ waktu* pass the time. *~ hati* entertain. 2 be inattentive, careless. **me-kan** 1 neglect, ignore. 2 divert. **ter-** 1 neglected, forgotten. 2 absent-minded. **ke-an** 1 neglectfulness, inattentiveness. 2 idleness. **pe-** inattentive person. **pe-**^{2} s.t. diverting. *~ hati* s.t. to soothe the heart. **pe-an** neglect, indifference.
lengai 1 unskilled, maladroit. 2 inactive, dawdling. 3 neglectful.
lengak me- 1 look up. 2 (*Jkt*) look up in surprise.
lengan 1 arm. - *bawah* forearm. - *peraba* tentacle. 2 sleeve. 3 arm (of scales).
lengang 1 lonely, deserted. - *hitam* dark and deserted. 2 quiet, slack (of business). 3 vacant, unoccupied. **me-kan** 1 empty, vacate s.t., clear s.t. out. 2 give s.t. a deserted appearance. **ke-an** 1 quietness, loneliness. 2 deserted.
lengar 1 dazed, drowsy. 2 dizzy. **ter-** unconscious, in a faint (from a blow). **ke-** in a stupor.
lengas 1 moist, damp, humid. 2 moisture. **me-**

become moist. **me-kan** moisten, dampen s.t. **ke-an** humidity.
lengat me- steam (rice, etc.).
lengau see LANGAU.
lenger see LENGAR.
lenggak me- look up. **me-kan** *kepala* raise the head to look up.
lénggak-lénggok a swaying movement. **me-** twist and turn, swing and sway.
lengganan see LANGGAN.
lenggang 1 pause or rest for a moment. 2 be free, have a free moment.
lénggang 1 swinging, swaying. 2 (*Naut.*) roll, wallow (of a boat). - *kangkung* l be casual about s.t. 2 aimless. --*lénggok* swaying (of the hip while o. strides). **ber-, me-** 1 swing (of the arms while walking). 2 roll, pitch (of boats). 3 swish (of tail). **me-kan** (*tangan*) 1 swing (the arms) while walking. 2 bring or carry nothing, be empty-handed. **ter-**^{2} 1 swinging (of arm). 2 rolling or pitching (of ship).
lenggara see SELENGGARA. **me-kan** arrange, take care of.
lénggék$_1$ (*M*) floor, story. **ber-** storied. **memper-kan** pile up, arrange in layers.
lénggék$_2$ **ber-**^{2} scream, shriek.
lénggok swinging, swaying. --*lénggang* swaying (of the hips while walking). **ber-(**^{2}**), me-(**^{2}**)** 1 sway o.'s body. *Tersenyum ia ~ pergi* She left with a smile on her face swaying her hips gracefully. 2 shake o.'s head gracefully. **me-**^{2}**kan** sway, swing (the body) to and fro. **-an** *kepala* toss of the head.
lenggundi see LEGUNDI.
lenggut$_1$ **me-** nod, doze.
lenggut$_2$ (*Phys.*) precession.
lengit 1 crafty, wily, tricky. 2 dishonest.
lengkang see LEKANG.
lengkap 1 complete. *buku* - a full-length book. *Tuliskanlah nama sdr yg -* Please write down your full name. 2 fully equipped. - *persenjataannya* fully armed. 3 comprehensive. *kamus* - a comprehensive dictionary. **se-** a set or suit (of s.t.). **se-nya** in its entirety, properly complete. **se-**^{2}**nya** as complete as possible. **ber-kan** (*Lit.*) equipped with s.t. **me-i, memper-i** 1 equip, fit out s.t. 2 complete, supplement s.t. *Tambahan Dul ~ ongkosnya* Dul's contribution gave him enough for his fare. **me-kan** complete s.t. *~ ilmu dan pengalaman* make o.'s knowledge and experience complete. **memper-** 1 equip, furnish, outfit. *~ kapal* fit out a ship. 2 bring to completion. *~ pelajaran pianonya* complete his piano studies. **ke-an** 1 completeness. *~ persediaan* dowry. 2 comprehensiveness. **-an** installation. **pe-** 1 complement. 2 supplement. *modal ~* supplementary capital. *Kamus itu ~ buku-buku lain* The dictionary is a supplement to other books. 3 (*Ling.*) object. *~ penderita* direct object. *~ penyerta* indirect object. *~ pelaku* doer, subject. **per-an** 1 equipment, outfit. *~ perang* war materiel. 2 equipping. *~ modal* capitalization. 3 supply. *~ jauh dr cukup* The supply is far from sufficient.

léngkéng see KELÉNGKÉNG₁.

léngkét be sticky, adhering. *tanah liat* - sticky clay. **ber-, me-** stick, adhere. **ber-²an** sticking to e.o. *duduk* ~ sit very close to e.o. **me-i** adhere to. *Kaca itu di-i butir air hujan* Raindrops were sticking to the glass. **me-kan** make s.t. adhere. **ke-an** adhesiveness. **per-an** adhesion.

lengkiang see RENGKIANG.

lengkibang millipede.

lengking 1 shrill, strident. 2 say stridently, shriek. *"Hasan! Hasan!" - gadis itu* "Hassan! Hassan!" the girl shrieked. **me-, ter- 1** scream, shriek. **2** be shrill. **3** wail (of siren). *Peluit KA* ~ A railroad whistle wailed. **me-, me-²** strident and shrill. **me-kan** cause s.t. to sound strident. *Pekerja itu ~ besi dgn besi* The worker made a loud clanging sound by striking an iron bar against another. **-an** a wail, a shriek.

lengkitang see LANGKITANG.

léngkok curve, bend. **be(r)-, me-** curve, bend.

lengkuas k.o. ginger plant, the galangale.

lengkung₁ 1 curve, bend. *- kenaikan gaji* the curve of wage increase. **2** arc. **3** hollow. *- kaki gigi* (*Anat.*) alveolus. **me- 1** curve, arch. **2** buckle (of metal). **3** curl (of stamps, etc.). **me-i** surround, encircle s.t. *Jalan yg baru itu ~ daérah Sawahan* The new road encircles the Sawahan district. **me-kan** bend, warp s.t. **-an 1** curve. ~ *bumi* 1 horizon. 2 curvature of the earth. ~ *tulang punggung* curvature of the spine. 2 arc. ~ *suara* modulation, intonation. **pe-** s.t. which causes curving. **pe-an** deflection.

lengkung₂ sound of hammer on iron.

lengkur see DENGKUR.

léngong me- look back at.

léngos me- 1 turn o.'s head to the side. *Aku ~ ke kiri kanan* I turned my head left and right. **2** avoid looking at s.o.

léngsér₁ me- 1 slide down (of the sun, skirt). **2** grease s.t.

léngsér₂ baking pan, cookie sheet.

léngsér₃ (*Sd*) prime minister.

léngsét be- folded outward (of edge of eyelid).

lenguh a bellow (of a bull). **me- 1** gasp for breath. **2** bellow.

lenguk me- hum, buzz.

lengung muse, ponder, brood (over bad news).

lening sounding of a bell.

lenja₁ me- be brazen, become bold. **ke-an** brazenness.

lenja₂ ring, hoop.

lenjuang k.o. small bush.

lénong (*Jkt*) k.o. folk theater.

lénsa lens. *- balur* (*Anat.*) crystalline lens. *- kontak* contact lens. *- mata* 1 (*Optometry*) lens. 2 (*Anat.*) crystalline lens. *- putih* normal eyeglass lens. *- sebar* dispersing, diverging lens.

lénso (*E. Indonesia*) handkerchief. *tarian -* k.o. dance with scarves.

lentang₁ clapper (of bell). **ke-an** clang (of a clapper).

lentang₂ me-kan stretch s.t. out. **mene-** lie on o.'s back. *Ia ~ di tempat tidurnya* He lay stretched out on his bed. **mene-kan** lay s.o. on his or her back. *Dokter ~ si sakit di atas méja bedah* The doctor stretched his patient out face upward on the operating table. **te(r)-** stretched out on o.'s back. *Korban itu tinggal ~, mati di tengah jalan* The victim lay face up, dead in the middle of the road.

léntang-léntok leaning to o. side (of the head).

lentéra lantern. *- laut* lighthouse beacon.

lentik curved, curving. **me-** curve upward or back (esp. of eyelashes). **me-kan** cause s.t. to curve upward. **ke-an** suppleness, pliability.

lenting₁ springy, resilient, bouncy. **me- 1** be bouncy. **2** curl (of leaves, burning paper).

lenting₂ sound of small metal objects hitting a stone. **se-** a tiny (audible) bit. *tak ~ kabarpun* not a bit of news. **ber-** make such a sound.

léntok bent to o. side (of the head).

lentuk me- be flexible. **me-kan** blend s.t. **ke-an** flexibleness.

lentum see DENTUM.

lentun see LANTUN.

lentung₁ sound of clapper or drum. **me-** make such sounds.

lentung₂ me- touch s.o. or s.t. **ter-** nod, doze off.

lentur 1 bent, curved. 2 (*Phys.*) refraction. 3 flexible. 4 warped. **me- 1** bent, curved. **2** be flexible. **me-kan 1** bend s.t. **2** deflect. **3** flex (a muscle). **ke-an** pliancy. **-an 1** (*Phys.*) diffraction. **2** curvature. **pe-** s.t. flexible.

lenyah see LANYAH.

lenyai 1 slack, loose (clothing, etc.). 2 weak, powerless.

lenyak sound asleep.

lenyap disappeared, lost (from sight). *Ia - dr pandangan* She has vanished from sight. *- daratan* lose o.'s head. *- tanpa bekas* vanished without a trace. **me-** disappear. *Wajah itu memucat lantas ~* The face turned pale and disappeared. **me-kan 1** cause s.t. to vanish. ~ *diri* disappear. **2** abolish, repeal, abrogate. **3** destroy, get rid of s.t. ~ *jerawat* get rid of pimples. **ke-an** disappearing. **pe-** remover, eliminator. *Konidin ~ batuk* Konidin gets rid of coughs.

lenyau see LANYAU.

lényéh me- 1 knead (dough). 2 mash (potatoes).

léo (*Coll.*) 1 male lion. 2 astrological sign.

léot me- bend (of wire, etc.).

lépa₁ plaster, mortar, caulking. **ber- 1** be plastered. **2** be engaged in applying plaster or mortar. **me-(kan)** plaster s.t. ~ *obat* stick on a medicinal plaster.

lépa₂ ter- 1 lie sprawled out. 2 be long enough to trail on the ground (of a dress, etc.).

lepai partially paralyzed, withered (of foot, hand).

lepa-lepa the lower part of a palm trunk.

lépa-lépa (*E. Indonesia*) dugout canoe.

lepang cucumber.

lepas 1 free, liberated (of bird, etc.), be rid of. *Keadaan itu sdh - dr bahaya* The situation has become free of danger. - *dr itu* apart from that. *wartawan* - freelance reporter. - *ayam* free as a bird, unencumbered. - *angin* futile, useless (lit., left with no wind). - *béa* duty-free. - *bébas* truly free, independent. - *dr bahaya* off the danger list (of a hospital patient). *Matanya tdk dpt - dr putri yg cantik itu* He could not take his eyes off the pretty girl. - *dr saya* disregarding me. - *landas* take off (of a plane). - *lelas* wholly free. - *pantai* 1 offshore (drilling). 2 off the shore (of). - *renggang* very loose. **me-renggangkan** loosen s.t. - *tangan* 1 stay clear of, avoid. 2 take no responsibility for. *menyetir - tangan* driving no hands. *seorg - seorg* o. by o., o. after the other. 2 undone, detached. *Ikatan itu -* The knot came undone. 3 (*Ling.*) released. *p -* released p. 4 after. - *sekolah menengah* after high school. *Ia akan kembali - seminggu* He will return after a week. - *sekolah* school graduate. 5 past, last. *Nopémber -* last November. *sepuluh tahun yg -* 10 years ago. -² 1 get loose repeatedly. *tak ~* never come free, never stop. *Matanya tak ~ memandang gelang itu* He could not stop looking at the bracelet. 2 freely. **se-** (*Coll.*) after. **se-²** as free as, as far as. *~ mata memandang* as far as the eye can see. *~ hati* as o. wishes. **ber-** be unencumbered. *~ diri* keep free (of controversy, etc.). *~ hati* be satisfied. *~ lelah* relax. **ber-an** become detached from o. another. *Benang itu tlh ~* The thread has become raveled. **me-** 1 remove. *~ topi* take off o.'s hat. *~ hajat/tinja* defecate. *~ kangen* reunion (lit., free o.s. of longing to be with s.o.). 2 escort s.o., see s.o. off. *~ jenazah/mayat* pay o.'s final respects to s.o. 3 fire, dismiss s.o. 4 release s.t. *~ layang-layang* fly a kite. *~ lembu* take cattle (to pasture). *~ kaul* fulfill a vow. *~ pandang* cast a distant glance. *~ uang* lend money at interest. 5 become released or free. *~ bébas* truly free and independent. *hidup yg ~ bébas* a free and independent life. **me-i** 1 discharge (o.'s debt or obligation). 2 fulfill (o.'s promise). **me-kan** 1 free, release. *~ diri* 1 flee. 2 extricate o.s. *~ hati* give rein to, release o.'s passions. *~ jiwa* die. *~ kritik* criticize. *~ mata* look about (for fun). *~ napas yg terakhir* expire, take o.'s last breath. *~ nazar* carry out a promise or vow. *~ niat* carry out an intention. *~ nyawa* die. 2 fire s.o. 3 discharge (a rifle, etc.). *~ pukulan* strike, a blow. *~ témbakan* open fire. *~ tuduhan* charge with or utter an accusation. 4 remove s.t. *~ dahaga* quench o.'s thirst. *~ dendam* take revenge. *~ hajat* defecate. *~ harapan* abandon hope. *~ haus* quench o.'s thirst. *~ keréta* uncouple a railroad car. *~ lapar* assuage o.'s hunger. *~ lelah* take a rest. *~ marah* give vent to o.'s anger. *~ nafsu* vent o.'s passion. *~ perhatian thd* lose sight of. *~ kesan* get rid of an impression. 5 give up, relinquish. *~ kesetiaan* forswear o.'s allegiance. **memper-(kan)** 1 liberate, release. 2 exempt. **ter-** 1 released. *~ dr* 1 apart from. 2 irrespective of. 2 detatched, undone (of a knot). **ter-kan** can be let loose. **ke-an** 1 escape,

the way out. 2 freedom, release. 3 (*Med.*) separation (of the shoulder, etc.). **-an** 1 graduate, alumnus, alumna. *~ sekolah* graduate. 2 former, ex-. *~ tentara* ex-soldier. **pe-** s.t. or s.o. that releases or liberates. *~ kaul* s.t. with which o. fulfills a vow (lit., s.t. which releases o. from a vow). *~ lelah* 1 relaxant. 2 lethargy. **pe-an, peng-an** 1 discharge, dismissal, firing of s.o. *~ hak* give up a right. 2 act of releasing s.t. *~ ketegangan* release of tension. *~ cadangan karét* release of rubber reserves. 3 graduation. *upacara ~* graduation ceremony. 4 (*Anat.*) anus. **per-an** discharge, release.

lepat k.o. snack made of sticky rice wrapped in banana leaves. *spt - dgn daun* inseparable.

lepau food stall.

lepéh me-(kan) chew and spit s.t. out.

lépék₁ soaking wet, drenched.

lépék₂ saucer.

lépék₃ me- slap s.o.

léper see LÉVER₁,₂.

lépér 1 flat, level. 2 shallow (of bowl).

léperansir see LÉVERANSIR.

léperi see RIFRI.

lepih 1 edge of a plaited mat (folded back into the plaitwork). 2 folded back (of a page). **me-kan** fold s.t. back, esp. in plaiting a mat.

lepit folded over. **ber-²** be in folds. **me-** fold s.t. **-an** a fold. *~ sebuah buku* page folded over in a book.

lépoh₁ ter- sprained, twisted (of ankle, etc.).

lépoh₂ me- plaster, daub s.t.

lépot be(r)-an 1 smeared, smudged, soiled (with blood, mud, etc.). 2 be besmirched (of reputation). **me-i** soil, besmirch, smear s.t. with. **ter-**stained.

lépra leprosy.

léprosari leprosarium.

lepu fish with toxic spines, i.e. stone fish, scorpion fish, etc.

lepuh a blister. **me-** get blistered. **me-kan** blister s.t., cause a blister.

lepuk see LAPUK.

lerai me- break up a fight, separate (fighters). *Org datang ~* People came to break it up. **me-kan** separate (fighters, lovers, etc.). **ter-** separated. *tak ~* inseparable. **pe-** 1 o. who moderates. 2 o. who breaks up fights. **pe-an** 1 separation. 2 (*Mil.*) disengagement.

lerak₁ broken open (of house, lock). **me-(kan)** break s.t. open.

lerak₂ see KELERAK.

leram see DERAM.

lérang strip (of cloth).

lérang-lérang stretcher, litter.

lerap see DERAP.

lerek see KELERAK.

léréng₁ 1 slope (of mountain). 2 rim of a wheel, edge (of a coin or of s.t. round). -² caster (of bed, sofa, etc.). **ber-** cycle, ride a bicycle. **me-** slope, incline. *jalan ~* sloping road. **me-i** go along a slope of s.t. *Kita hanya ~ bukit-bukit itu* We only went along the slopes of those hills. **-an** sloping land, slope.

léréng₂ having diagonal stripes (of fabric).

lérét 1 row, line. **2** series. **se-** a row. *~ perasaan* consecutive emotions. **ber-** in a row. *berdiri ~* stand in a row. **me-** stretch out straight. *pedang yg ~ di tanah* a sword lying on the earth as if stretched out. **me-kan** arrange s.t. in a row. **-an** row, series.

lérok me- squint in anger.

lerum see DERUM₁.

lés₁ 1 extracurricular tutorial lesson. **2** non-scholastic course. *- kuda* horse riding lessons. *- ketik* typing course. **3** take lessons. **me-kan** give s.t. as extracurricular lessons. **-²an** various k.o. tutorial lessons.

lés₂ list, roster.

lés₃ 1 picture frame. **2** trim. *- kaca* window trim. *- pinggir* decorative trim on a car. **-²an** framing.

lés₄ reins (for horse).

lesah see LASAH₁.

lesak₁ sound of rustling (of leaves, rain).

lesak₂ see LASAH₂.

lesam softened.

lesan target, goal.

lesap disappeared, vanished. **me- 1** disappear. **2** (*Phys.*) dissipate. **-an** (*Phys.*) dissipation. **pe-an** deletion.

lesat me- fly away, take off. *Pembangunan ~ dgn kecepatan yg menakutkan* Development has taken off at a fearsome speed.

lesau see DESAU.

lésbi, lésbian, lésbis lesbian. **ber-** engage in lesbian activities.

lésbril (*Coll.*) reading glasses.

Lésbumi [*Lembaga Seni Budayawan Muslimin Indonésia*] Muslim Cultural Association of Indonesia, a branch of the Isl. party in the 1960s.

lését me- 1 fall short of (target, estimate). *Témbakannya ~* His shot missed the target. **2** decline (in quality). **keme-an** decline, shortfall. **kepe-, terpe-** slip and lose o.'s balance. *Aku ~ di és I* slipped and fell on the ice.

lesi, lesih see PUTIH. *- pucat* truly pale.

lesing see DESING.

lésing lecture.

lesit₁ me- hum, buzz (of wasps).

lesit₂ me- 1 spray, spout, gush. **2** blow o.'s nose. **me-kan** blow out (o.'s mucous). *-kan ingusmu, Titi* Blow your nose, Titi!

lésnar (*Coll.*) reading desk, lectern.

lésot (*Jv*) **nge-** sit on the ground or floor.

lestari 1 eternal, everlasting. **2** long-lasting. **me-kan 1** continue, perpetuate s.t. **2** conserve, preserve (environment). *Pemerintah berusaha ~ hutan ini* The gvt. is trying to preserve this forest. **ke-an 1** preservation, conservation. *~ lingkungan* environmental conservation. **2** perpetuity, continuance. *menjaga ~ suplai* insure a continuing supply. **pe-an 1** perpetuation.

2 preservation, conservation. *~ satwa* wildlife conservation.

lésték slingshot.

lesu 1 listless, weak (from lack of food or sleep). *- kusam* very tired. **2** sluggish, slack (of business). **3** depressed, blue. **me-** become slow, be sluggish. *Ékonomi dunia sedang ~* The world's economy is slowing down. **ke-an 1** listlessness. **2** sluggishness. **3** lassitude, languor. *~ jiwa* a spiritual languor.

lesung mortar (for pounding rice). *- pipi* dimple (in cheek).

lesus see DESUS.

lésus 1 whirlwind. **2** cyclone.

lesut sound of swishing made by a sword or whip.

let see LAT₁.

lét₁ (*Sport*) let ball.

lét₂ see LÉTNAN.

leta base, shameful, contemptible. **me-kan** despise, hold s.o. in contempt.

letai 1 weak. **2** tired, listless.

letak 1 location, site. *- tempat itu tdk jauh dr sini* The location of the place is not far from here. *-nya di mana?* Where is it located? *- lintang* diagonal position. *- sungsang* breach position. **2** disposition, set up. *Bagaimana -nya hal itu?* What is the situation regarding the matter? **me-kan** put, place s.t. *~ obat pd luka itu* Put medicine on the wound. *~ batu pertama* lay a cornerstone. *~ jabatan* resign from office, give up o.'s post. *~ lunas* lay the keel. *~ pesawat télepon* hang up the phone. *~ senjata* lay down o.'s arms. **ter-** be, be located. *Kabul ~ di Afganistan* Kabul is located in Afghanistan. *Kesalahannya ~ di mana?* Where does the fault lie? *Hak mengambil keputusan tdk ~ pd saya* The right to make a decision does not lie with me. **pe-** o. who places s.t. *~ dasar* founder. **pe-an, per-an** laying down of. *~ batu pertama* laying of a cornerstone. *upacara ~ bunga* wreath-laying ceremony. *~ jabatan* resignation (of o.'s office). *~ lunas* laying of a keel. *~ pekerjaan* work stoppage. *~ senjata* **1** armistice, truce. **2** cease-fire.

létak exhausted, weary, fatigued. *- latai* extremely weary, worn out.

létal lethal.

letang sound of a hammer on iron.

létda [*létnan muda*] 2d lieutenant.

leték me- crack (of earth).

létenan see LÉTNAN.

léter, létér₁ 1 letter. **2** type, font. **me-i** put letters on s.t. (to mark s.t.).

létér₂ be-, me- 1 quack repeatedly (of a duck flock). **2** babble, prattle, talk incessantly.

léterlek (*Coll.*) lit., word for word.

léterséter typesetter.

letih tired, weary, worn out. *- lelah/lesu* completely exhausted. **me-kan 1** tire, weary, exhaust s.o. **2** exhausting, grueling. **ke-an 1** fatigue, exhaustion, weariness. *~ otot* muscle fatigue. **2** overly tired, exhausted.

letik sound of glass cracking from contact with excessive heat. **me-** crack (of glass).

leting₁ me- flap about (of fish in basket).

leting₂ sound of tinkling metallic objects.

létjén [*létnan-jénderal*] lieutenant general.

létkol [*létnan-kolonél*] lieutenant colonel.

létnan 1 lieutenant, often *lét* as a term of familiar address. **2** (*Navy*) lieutenant (junior grade). *- dua* 2d lieutenant. *- jénderal* lieutenant general. *- kolonél* lieutenant colonel. *- muda* ensign. *- satu* first lieutenant.

letoi thin and weak, emaciated.

letok see LETUK.

letos me- stare.

létrasét k.o. lettering sheet rubbed with a pencil.

léttu /létu/ [*létnan satu*] first lieutenant.

letuk sound of knocking. **me-** make a crackling sound.

letum see DENTUM.

letung sound of drumbeats.

letup sound of an explosion. **-²** child's balloon. **me- 1** explode. **2** go off (gun, cannon). **me-kan 1** explode s.t. **2** ignite s.t. **-an** explosion. **pe-an** exploding of.

letus sound of a large explosion. **me- 1** explode, erupt (volcano, boil, etc.). **2** break out, erupt (of a war, quarrel, epidemic). **me-kan 1** explode, detonate (a bomb). **2** blow up (a bridge, etc.). **pe-** (*Ling.*) explosive, stop. **(pe)-an 1** explosion. **2** detonation. **3** eruption. **4** outburst.

leukémi, leukémia /lékémi, lékémia/ leukemia.

léver₁ (*Anat.*) the liver. *Ia sakit -* She suffers from liver trouble.

léver₂ me- supply, provide (goods).

léveransir supplier, purveyor.

lévis (*Coll.*) blue denim jeans.

léwat 1 via, through, by way of. *Saya ke sekolah - Jln Musi* I go to school by way of Musi St. *- darat* overland. *- télepon* by telephone. **2** beyond, past. *Sekarang pukul lima - seperempat* It is now a quarter past five. *- témpo* expired (of time, check, etc.). *- zaman* outmoded, outdated. **3** past, over. *Waktu beristirahat sdh -* The intermission is over. *- jenuh* surfeited, gorged. **me-i 1** pass by s.t., step over. **2** exceed, be excessive. *Ini sdh ~ batas* This is going too far. **3** surpass, exceed. *Kepandaian- nya ~ kawannya* Her intelligence surpasses her friend's. **4** transgress, overstep (the law). **me-kan 1** pass by with (fruits, pastries, etc.). **2** skip, pass up (an opportunity). *~ waktu salat* skip prayer time. **3** spend, pass (time). *Kami ~ akhir minggu di gunung* We spent the weekend in the mountains. **ter- 1** very, exceedingly, too. *~ bagus* very nice. **2** past, overcome. *Kesukaran-kesukaran itu sdh ~* The difficulties have been overcome. **ke-** (*Coll.*) **1** too, excessive. **2** very, exceedingly. *~ besar* very big.

léyak (*Bali*) k.o. evil spirit.

léyéh ber- lie around. **ber-an** lie back.

lezat delicious, luscious. **meng-kan** flavor s.t. **ke-an 1** taste. **2** delicacy. **3** infatuated, enamored. **4** enjoyment, pleasure.

lha (*Jv*) **1** Well, yes, of course! (particle conceding the obvious). *- sepuluh! Tapi di sana dptnya dua puluh* Well yes, you got 10. But if you had gone there you would have gotten 20. *Sudirman nomer satu di kelas. - kalau dia, ndak héran* So, Sudirman is first in class. Well, if he is the o., what else would you expect? **2** well now (particle bringing previous discussion to its conclusion). *Latar bela- kang agamanya tdk sesuai. - kalau itu sdh berbéda, dan dianggap kurang baik oléh keluarga, sdh tdk . . .* She comes from a different religious back- ground. Well now, if that is the case and the family considers it bad, then . . . *Meréka sdh ter- bukti buruk, - kenapa kerja sama?* They have been proven to be bad. Well then, why should you cooperate! **3** That is it! (particle of recognition).

lho (*Jv*) **1** My! (exclamation of surprise at learn- ing s.t. unexpected). *-, sdh di sini!* Goodness, you are here already! **2** Remember? (reminder or warning particle). *Saya tdk bawa uang, -!* Re- member, I did not bring any money with me (so you had better be prepared)! *Terima kasih -!* Oh hey, thanks! **3** Right! (emphatic particle to draw interlocutor's attention). *Ini - uangnya!* Here's the money!

liang 1 hole, pit. *- kubur* grave. *- lahad/lahat* **1** niche in Muslim grave. **2** grave. *- opening*, aperture. *- dubur* anal passage. *- hidung* **1** nostril. **2** nasal passage. *- kemaluan* vagina. *- kumbang* scupperhole. *- mata* eye socket. *- peranakan* va- gina. *- renik/roma* pore (of skin). **ber-** *renik* having to do with pores, exudative. *- telinga* **1** acoustic duct. **2** auditory canal.

liang liong (*Ch*) **1** Ch New Year's dragon dance. **2** paper dragon used in such parades.

liang-liuk ber- sway like a drunken person.

liar 1 wild, primitive (animal, tribe, etc.). **2** wild, illegal, unauthorized (school, organization, etc.). *barisan -* irregulars. *pemogokan -* wildcat strike. **me-** become wild. **me-kan 1** cause s.o. to go wild. *Sikap suaminya ~ Tuti* Her husband's attitude drove Tuti wild. **2** cause s.t. (once do- mesticated) to become wild. *Mawas di-kan oléh petugas pelestarian satwa di hutan* Wildlife conser- vation officers are setting orangutans free in the jungle. **ke-an** wildness.

liat₁ 1 tough, rubbery (of meat). **2** tough, hard- ened (of champion, criminal). **3** clayey (soil). *--liut* meandering (of a river). **me- 1** be tough. **2** be clayey. **ke-an** plasticity. **ke-²an** clayish.

liat₂ see LIHAT.

liau me- suppurate, fester (of a sore).

Libanon Lebanon.

libat ber-² be involved. **me- 1** become wrapped around. *Ular itu ~ di pohon* The snake wrapped itself around a tree. **2** bandage, wrap (a wound). **3** involve. *Perang akan ~ semua negeri* War will involve all countries. **me-kan** involve s.o. or s.t. *Kita dipaksakan ~ diri dlm suatu débat* We were compelled to engage in a debate. **memper-kan** implicate s.o. **ter- 1** bound, wrapped (of a wound). **2** involved, implicated. **ke-** involved.

menter-kan implicate s.o. **keter-an 1** involvement. **2** entanglement. **3** complicity. **-an** tangle, maze. *melepaskan diri dr ~ tali-temali parasyut* free o.s. from the tangle of the parachute cords. **pe-an, per-an** involving s.o.

liberal unconventional. *- mendidik anak* bring up children in an unconventional way.

liberalisasi process of loosening up procedures, etc.

liberalisme (*Pol.*) liberalism.

libur leave, vacation. *- resmi* official leave. **ber-** go on vacation. *Tuan ~ ke mana?* Where did you spend your vacation? **ber-an** take a vacation. **me-kan** send s.o. on vacation. *Kelas itu di-kan dua minggu* The class was given a two-week vacation. **-an 1** leave, liberty. **2** vacation. **3** time off. **pe-**vacationer.

licak crushed flat.

licau shiny, glossy, lustrous.

lichtdruk /likhdruk, lihtdruk/ phototypography.

lici see LÉCI.

licik 1 sly, crafty, tricky. **2** cagey, wily. **ke-an 1** cunning, wiliness, ability to twist words. **2** artifice, scheme.

licin 1 slippery, slick. *Di waktu hujan jalan -* Slippery when wet. *- lecat/licau* very slippery. **2** glossy, smooth. **3** bare, grassless (of land). *- tandas* completely gone, finished. **4** smooth, suave, smooth-tongued. **5** cunning, crafty. *- lidah* fast-talker. **memper-, me-kan 1** make s.t. smooth. *~ jalan* pave the way. **2** make s.t. slippery. **ke-an 1** smoothness. **2** slipperiness. **3** cunning, slyness.

lid (*Lit.*) member of committee, party, etc. *- perkumpulan kematian* member of a funerary association.

lidah tongue. *-nya manis* Her words were sweet. *- air* crest of floodwater. *- api* tongue of flame. *- ayam* herb (used as medicine). *- badak* k.o. plant. *- bayang* tongue and groove (of lumber). *- bercabang/biawak* two-faced, deceitful. *- buaya* aloe, a plant the leaves of which are used as shampoo. *- dacing* tongue of scales, index of a balance. *- gajah* a plant. *- keling* untrustworthy, shifty. *- kucing* 1 a plant. 2 k.o. cookie. *- lembu* k.o. plant. *- ombak* roller, wave. *- pundak* shoulder strap. *- serunai* reed (in a flute, pipe organ). *- tergalang* 1 long-winded. 2 can not say no. *- tdk bertulang* untrustworthy, unreliable. **-²** tonguelike. **ber-1** have a tongue. **2** use the tongue. *~ dua* two-faced. *~ di org* always go along with what others say. **me-²** become tonguelike. *Daun tebu ~* The sugar cane leaves stick out like so many tongues.

lidas itching, sore (esp. around mouth and tongue).

lidi palm leaf rib. *sapu -* a broom made of such splintered ribs.

lift elevator.

liga league. *- Arab* Arab League.

ligas center. **me-** canter.

ligat adept, quick to adjust. **me-** gyrate, spin. **-an** gyration. **pe-** gyroscope.

ligyat (*Ch*) hardworking.

lih. [*lihat*] see.

lihai 1 shrewd, astute. **2** wily, cunning. **3** terrific, tremendous. **ke-an 1** shrewdness, astuteness. **2** caginess. **3** ability.

lihat 1 see. **2** refer to. **ber-²an, - me-** see e.o. **me-1** see s.o. or s.t. *~ film* see a movie. *~ étalase* window shop. *~ hari* look to see what time it is. *~ ke depan* predict. *~ kosong* stare vacantly. **2** observe. *~ kembali* reconsider, take another look. *~ nujum* consult the stars. *~ (dgn) sebelah mata* not take a careful look. **3** discern. **me-²** look around, browse. **me-i 1** look at, scrutinize. *-i baik-baik sblm bercakap* Inspect carefully before you say anything. **2** see, visit, look in on s.o. **me-kan 1** show s.t. **2** observe, look at carefully. **me-²kan** keep an eye on. **memper-, memper-kan** show, display, exhibit. *Karcis hrs diper-kan sblm msk* Tickets must be shown before entering. *~ diri* show o.'s face. **ter- 1** seen. **2** visible. **ke-an 1** visible, in sight. *Rumahnya ~ dr sini* His house is visible from here. **2** discernible. *Dia sdh belajar Bahasa Indonésia dua tahun tapi tdk ada kemajuan yg ~* He has been studying Indonesian for two years but there is no apparent progress. *tak ~ 1* imperceptible. **2** nowhere in sight. *~nya* apparently. **pe(ng)-** seer, prophet. **peng-an 1** sight, vision, eyesight. **2** sight, scene.

lihay see LIHAI.

lijn see LIN₁.

lika-liku 1 details, inner workings. **2** vagaries. *- pemasaran* vagaries of marketing.

likas me- reel in, wind (on a reel). **-an** reel on which newly woven thread is wound.

likat₁ 1 thick and sticky. **2** turbid. **pe-** adhesive.

likat₂ shy.

likeur, likir₁ /likur, likir/ liqueur.

likir₂ k.o. plant with edible tubers.

liku 1 curve, bend (in the road). *--lekuk* intricacies, vagaries. *--lekuk jalan ceritera* plot (twistings and turnings) of a story. **2** coil. **3** bay, inlet. **-² 1** intricacies. **2** vagaries. **ber-** intricate, complicated. **ber-²** 1 winding, curving, tortuous (of road, etc.). **2** sinuous. **ke-an** curvature.

likuida (*Ling.*) liquid.

likuidasi liquidation. **me-** liquidate. **pe-** liquidator.

likuidatur liquidator.

likuide liquid (assets).

likuidir me- liquidate.

likuiditas (*Fin.*) liquidity (of capital).

likur (*Jv*) **se-** 21. **tiga-** 23. **-an** 21 to 29. **se-an** blackjack, 21 (card game).

likw- see also entries with **liku-**.

lila purple.

lilin 1 candle. *enam puluh -* 60 candlepower. **2** wax. *- lebah/tawon* beeswax.

liliput s.t. small. *rumah -* a very small house.

lilit turn, twist. **-nya** circumference. **se- 1** one twist. **2** around. *pergi ~ Bali* go around Bali. **ber-1** twist, wind. **2** be wound around with. **me-** coil around. *Ular ~ dahan kayu* A snake is wound around a tree branch. **me-i** wind, twist around s.t. *selendang yg ~ léhérnya* shawl that wound around her neck. **me-kan** wind (thread, etc.). **-an 1** coil. **2** winding. **3** twist.

lilo-lilo phrase derived from the Arabic for "there is no God but Allah."

lim see LÉM.

lima five. *- belas* fifteen. *- pérakan (Coll.)* five rupiah. *- puluh* fifty. *spt - belas dgn tengah dua puluh* six of o. and half a dozen of the other. **ber-** do s.t. in a group of five, comprise a group of five. *Kami ~ ke Solo* Five of us went to Solo. **ke- 1** 5th. *terbilang yg ~* 5th edition. **2** the five. *~ anak itu* the five children. **-an** *(Coll.)* in fives. *uang ~* five-rupiah note. **seper-** a fifth.

limar *(Jv)* k.o. silk fabric.

limas 1 pyramid. **2** dipper or cup made of young palm leaves.

limau citrus fruit. *- besar* pomelo. *- kedangsa* green-skinned citrus fruit. *- kiai* plant from whose fruit glue is produced. *- kingking* hedge shrub whose fruit is made into syrup. *- manis* orange. *- nipis* sour lime, calamondin. *- purut* rough-skinned lime used as shampoo. *- sundai* lime. **ber-** wash with lime juice. **me-i 1** wash s.o. with lime juice. **2** denigrate, vilify, defame s.o.

limbah 1 waste. *- nuklir* nuclear waste. *- pertanian* compost heap. **2** cesspool. **pe-an** garbage dump, junkyard. *~ industri* industrial cesspool.

limbai me-(kan) wave (the arms).

limban footbridge.

limbang₁ me- wash (gold, rice, etc.). **pe-** implement for washing or o. who washes (gold, rice).

limbang₂ me- loiter, lounge about.

limbat see IKAN.

limbubu see HALIMBUBU.

limbuk emerald dove.

limbung₁ 1 inner harbor. **2** dry dock. **3** fenced-in bathing place.

limbung₂ 1 unsteady because top heavy. **2** bewildered, confused.

limbur₁ me- flood, inundate.

limbur₂ see SABUR.

limitasi limitation.

limosin 1 limousine. **2** minibus serving passengers between hotels and airports.

limpa *(Anat.)* spleen.

limpah 1 abundant. **2** affluent. **3** overflow, plentiful, profuse. *- méwah* a very great amount. *- ruah* crammed full, chockfull. **ber-², ber-an** abound, be plentiful, be in abundance. *pujian ~* compliments or praise galore. **me- 1** overflow. *~ ruah* greatly overflow. **2** be abundant. **3** be redundant. **me-i 1** flood, deluge, inundate. **2** overwhelm with s.t. good or desirable. *Moga-moga aku di-i kesabaran* May I be blessed with quantities of patience. **me-kan 1** shower, give s.t. generously, give in abundance. *~ karunia kpdnya* shower her with blessings. **2** cause s.t. to spill over. **3** delegate (authority). **ke-an** abundance, affluence. **-an 1** overflow. *~ darah di dlm otak*

cerebral hemorrhage. **2** gift. **pe-** spillway. **pe-an 1** act of spilling over. **2** act of extending s.t. to s.o. *~ kewenangan* delegation of authority.

limpas me-kan let run off, let overflow. **-an 1** run-off. *permukaan ~* surface run off. **2** runoff, out-flow (of silt). **pe-an** running off (of water).

limpit layer, lamina, sheet. **ber-** laminated, in layers. **memper-kan 1** laminate. **2** fold.

limpung be in a dither. **ke-an** be in a complete dither.

limun₁ soda pop, carbonated beverage. *- skuas* lemon squash.

limun₂ invisible, dark. **-an** invisibility.

lin₁ line, route. *- 6* no. 6 route. *- cabang* branch line. *- keréta api* railway line.

lin₂ line, edge, boundary line (of sports field, etc.).

lina, linan see LINEN.

linang trickle, drop (of tears, sweat, etc.). **se-²** drop by drop. *~ air mata menjalari pipinya* A teardrop or two trickled down her cheek. **ber-(²)**, **me-** trickle, flow (of tears). *Air mata ~ mengalir pelan* Tears flowed slowly. **ber-an** trickling with (tears, etc.). **me-i** trickle down s.t. *~ pipinya* trickle down his cheeks. **-an** a trickle.

lincah 1 energetic, lively, active. **2** agile. **me-²**, **ter-² 1** flit from o. thing to another. **2** be always on the move. **ke-an 1** liveliness, friskiness. **2** agility.

lincak *(Jv)* low bamboo bench for sitting or sleeping.

lincam me- 1 flash by quickly (lightning, emotions). *rasa malu yg ~* the feeling of shame that swept over him. **2** sudden stab.

lincip pointed (of a pencil).

lincir slick, smooth, slippery. *ban -* bald tire. *- lidahnya* fluent. *- mulut* **1** glib, smooth-spoken. **2** hypocritical, misleading. **me-kan** make s.t. smooth. *Uang ~ segala-segalanya* Money smooths the way to everything. **pe-** lubricant. *uang ~* bribe. **ke-an 1** oiliness. **2** slickness. **3** smoothness.

lindak ber-² boil over.

lindang finished, over. *- tandas* completely gone. **me-kan** run through, squander, dissipate (o.'s wealth).

lindap *(M)* **1** shade. **2** poor (of visibility), overcast. **3** obscure (of a question). **me- 1** become overcast. **2** fade (of light).

lindas, lindes me- 1 knock down, run over. **2** crush (pepper, etc.). **ke-, ter-** be crushed, run over (by a car, etc.). **pe-** mortar.

lindi 1 lye. **2** *(Chem.)* alkali. **me-** leach s.t. **pe-an** leaching.

lindih, lindis me- 1 crush s.t. **2** level, smooth s.t. **3** crush, put down (a rebellion, etc). **pe-** roller.

lindu *(Jv)* earthquake.

lindung₁ ber- 1 take shelter (under a tree, etc.). **2** be under the protection of. *Brunéi ~ pd Britania Raya* Brunei is under the protection of Great Britain. **me-i, memper-i 1** protect s.o. or

s.t., provide shelter for s.o. *Pohon itu ~ kamar ini dr panas matahari* That tree protects the room from the sun's heat. *Hak pengarang di-i oléh undang-undang* The author's rights are protected by the law. **2** cover, conceal (a mistake, etc.). **3** protect, make safe (from danger). **me-kan 1** protect, safeguard. **2** save (o.'s life). **3** use s.t. for shelter or protection. **ter-** protected, sheltered. **ke-an 1** protected. **2** shaded. **-an 1** protection. **2** shelter, refuge. **pe- 1** protector. *~ utk mulut dan hidung* face protector. *~ panas (Tech.)* heat shield. *~ terik matahari* sun visor. **2** patron. **per-an 1** protection. **2** patronage, sponsorship. *di bawah ~* under the aegis of.
lindung₂ eel.
lindur (*Jv, Jkt*) **nge-** talk in o.'s sleep.
linen linen.
lingar me- look about bewildered.
lingga 1 phallus in Hindu temples. **2** commemorative post. *- alam* nature preserve.
linggam see SEDELINGGAM.
linggi (*Lit.*) covered decking at bow and stern of a boat.
linggis k.o. crowbar. **me- 1** use a crowbar, dig with a crowbar. **2** gouge s.t. with a sharp instrument.
lingir (*Jv*) sharp edge.
lingkar 1 circle. *- inti* inner circle. **2** bend, coil. *- ular* coils of a snake. **3** rim (of wheel). **4** hoop (of barrel). **5** circumference. *- dada* chest measurement. **se-** all around. **ber-** coiled, curled up. *duduk ~* sit in a circle. *pér ~* coiled spring, spring coil. **me-(²) 1** form a circle, coil up. **2** go around and round. **3** coil (a rope, cable, etc.). **me-i** be or go around s.t., surround. *~ méja* go all around the table. **me-kan** put s.t. around, embrace with. *Ia ~ lengannya pd bahu anak itu* She put her arm around the child's shoulder. **ter-** encircled, surrounded. **-an 1** circle. *~ arus* circuit. *~ buta/gila* vicious circle. *~ inti/keliling* inner circle. *~ Kutub Selatan* Antarctic Circle. *~ Kutub Utara* Arctic Circle. *~ roda* wheel rim. *~ sétan/tak berujung (ber)pangkal* vicious circle. **2** coil. **3** area, surroundings.
lingkung 1 circle. **2** circumference. **3** perimeter. **se-** around, surrounding. *berjalan ~ kota* walk around town. **me-i 1** surround, encircle s.t. **2** embrace, include. **ter- 1** encircled. **2** included, embraced. **-an 1** circles. *~ yg mengetahui* informed circles. **2** area, surroundings. *~ keluarga* in the circle of the family. *~ sewajarnya* natural surroundings. *~ waktu* time zone. **3** sphere, domain, range. *~ hayat* biological environment. *~ hidup* **1** milieu. **2** living space. *~ kedokteran* medical setting. *~ umur* age bracket.
lingkup scope, range. *ruang - range. - pikirannya luas sekali* The range of his ideas is very wide. *NTR di bawah - Départemén Agama* Marriage, divorce, and reconciliation fall under the scope of the Department of Religious Affairs. **- me-i** overlap. **me-i 1** cover (the head). **2** encompass,

cover, include. *Pembicaraan itu ~ apa saja?* Just what do the discussions cover? **ter- 1** covered, veiled (of head). **2** included, embraced. **-an** scope.
linglung 1 absent-minded, preoccupied. **2** confused, dazed. **3** weak, not aware of things. **me-kan** cause s.o. to become confused or absent-minded. **ke-an** absent-mindedness.
lingsang otter.
lingsir *minyak -* lubrication oil. **me-** set (of the sun). **me-kan** unroll or let down o.'s sleeves.
lini line, edge. *- pertahanan* line of defense.
lino see PAHAT.
linotip linotype.
lintabung k.o. grass.
lintah leech. *- darat* usurer, profiteer. **me-** *darat* work as a profiteer.
lintang₁ 1 across. *Kamar ini -nya empat meter* This room is four meters wide. *- bujur* diagonal. *kedak* zigzag. *- pukang* crisscross. **2** (*Geog.*) latitude. *- utara* north latitude. **me- 1** lie athwart, be in the way, block. *Kursi ~ di muka pintu* A chair is blocking the doorway. **2** crosswise, transverse. **3** hinder. *Saya akan datang kalau tdk ada halangan ~* I will come if nothing stands in my way. **me-i 1** obstruct, block s.t. **2** lie across s.t. *Jembatan bambu ~ sungai itu* A bridge crosses the river. **me-kan** place s.t. athwart. **ter- 1** placed athwart. **2** hampered, hindered. **-an 1** deterrent. **2** hindrance, obstacle, barrier.
lintang₂ (*Jv*) star. *- kemukur* comet.
lintas move (quickly) across. *- alam* cross-country. *- batas* border crossing. *- bébas* free passage. *- cabang* feeder line. *- édar* orbit. *- laut* seaborne. *- léwat* overpass. *- médan* cross-country. *- raya* overpass. *- tapal batas* border crossing. *- sébra* zebra crossing. *- udara* airborne. *- utama* trunk line. **se-** at the same instant. *~ lalu* at a glance. **me- 1** rush by, pass quickly. *Sebuah pedati ~ di depan béngkel* A carriage passed by the workshop. *sekali ~* at first glance, at first thought. **2** take a shortcut. **me-² 1** repeatedly occur. **2** repeatedly occur to o. **me-i 1** rush past, pass in a hurry. **2** flash by s.t. **3** cross (over), traverse. *~ Atlantik* cross the Atlantic. *Ada garis-garis yg tak boléh di-i* There are lines which may not be crossed. **4** overcome (difficulties). *~ mistar* clear the bar. **ter- 1** crossed, passed. **2** cross o.'s mind, occurred to. *Tak ~ dlm hatinya* It did not cross her mind. **ke-an** past. **-an 1** flash (of light, etc.). **2** line. *~ jalan keréta api* grade crossing. *~ naik* incline. *~ sejarah* the course of history. **3** (*Sport*) track, course. **4** orbit, trajectory. **pe-** passerby. **pe-an, per-an** crossover, crossing. *~ keréta api* railroad crossing. *~ perbatasan* crossing of the border.
lintibang (*M*) centipede.
linting me- roll (a cigarette). **-an** hand-rolled cigarette. **pe-** cigarette roller.
lintir me- roll. *Bola yg ditendang ~ dan tiba di kaki temannya* He kicked the ball, and it rolled to the feet of his teammate.

lintuh (*M*) weak, soft.
lintup see LINGKUP.
linu₁ 1 shooting pain (of teeth, nerves, etc). 2 rheumatic pain.
linu₂ earthquake.
linyak (*M*) pressed flat. **me-** flatten (s.t. by pressing, rolling).
linyap see LENYAP.
linyar (*Coll.*) ruler.
lio (*Ch*) brick kiln.
liong (*Ch*) dragon.
liontin medallion, locket, pendant.
lipan centipede. - *bara* poisonous centipede.
lipas cockroach. - *air* water beetle. *spt - kudung* hyperactive, unable to keep o.'s hands still.
lipat fold, crease. - *dua* be doubled, folded double. **me-duakan** double s.t. - *empat* four-fold. **me-empatkan** quadruple. - *ganda* multiple, manifold. **me-gandakan** multiply. **pe-** *ganda* multiplier. **pe-gandaan** multiplication. - *kajang* folded double. - *paha* groin. **ber-** folded, pleated. ~ *ganda* multiple. **ber-²** many times over. *Ia mendapat rezeki* ~ He had good luck many times over. **me-** fold. *Jangan di-* Do not fold. ~ *lutut* 1 bend the knee. 2 (*Coll.*) defeat (the enemy). **me-kan** fold (the hands, etc.), put s.t. in a folded position. **memper-kan** increase (production). **ke-an** (*Math.*) multiple. ~ *persekutuan terkecil* least common denominator. **-an** 1 fold, crease. 2 pack (of playing cards). **pe-** s.t. which folds. ~ *lutut* hollow of the knee. **pe-an** folding (of a newspaper, magazine, etc.). **per-an** 1 multiplication, increase. 2 method of folding.
lipen, lipenstip lipstick.
liperi see RIFRI.
LIPI [*Lembaga Ilmu Pengetahuan Indonésia*] The Indonesian Academy of Sciences.
lipir see LÉPÉR.
lipit me- hem s.t. **pe-** a hem.
liplap 1 in thin layers of various colors. 2 (*Derog.*) Eurasians.
lipstik lipstick.
lipur comfort, consolation, solace. **me-(kan)** 1 comfort, console s.o. 2 entertain. **-an** mitigation. **pe(ng)-** comforter, soother, consoler. - *hati* relief. *memberi* ~ *hati* bring relief. ~ *lara* 1 consoler, s.t. which soothes distress. 2 storyteller. 3 tale told for amusement.
liput me- cover (an event). **me-i** 1 cover, envelop s.t. *di-i ombak* enveloped by waves. *di-i rahasia* surrounded by secrecy. 2 comprise, include. *Kabupatén ini* ~ *dua puluh tiga kecamatan* This regency comprises 23 districts. 3 pervade. *masyarakat yg di-i korupsi* a society pervaded by corruption. **ter-** 1 covered, enveloped, surrounded. 2 overwhelmed. **-an** cover. ~ *berita* news coverage. **pe-** *berita* news reporter.
lir winch.
lirih low, sweet-sounding, gentle, soft (of voice). **-²** softly. **me-kan** 1 lower (o.'s voice). 2 turn down (the radio).

lirik₁ 1 sharp glance. 2 a glance to left or right. **se-** at a glance. **me-** steal a glance at. **-an** sidelong glance, look. ~ *yg berbisa* poisonous look. **pe-an** glancing, looking.
lirik₂ me- pierce, perforate, bore through.
lirik₃ lyrics.
liris k.o. batik pattern consisting of decorated parallel lines.
lis see LÉS₂, LÉS₃, LÉS₄.
lisa louse egg, nit.
lisah see GELISAH.
lisan oral, spoken. *ujian* - oral exam. *dgn* - orally, by word of mouth, verbally. **me-kan** express, utter, put into words.
lisénsi 1 license, permit. 2 franchise.
lisol disinfectant of creosot in soap, Lysol.
lisong cigar.
listrik electricity, electric. - *msk désa* rural electrification. **me-kan** 1 electrify, install electricity. 2 electrocute. **ke-an** electrical matters. **pe-an** 1 electrification. 2 electrical department.
listris electrical, by means of electricity.
lisut 1 withered, wizened, atrophied. 2 wilted, faded. **me-kan** make s.t. withered, wilted, or wrinkled.
litak see LETAK.
litani litany.
Litbang [*Penelitian dan Pengembangan*] Research and Development.
litenan see LÉTNAN.
liter liter. **-an** by the liter.
literator man of letters.
literatur literature.
literér literary.
litnan see LÉTNAN.
litografi lithography.
litup see LINGKUP.
liturgi, liturgia liturgy.
liturgis liturgical.
liuk wriggle. **--***lampai* wind, undulate (as of a snake, dancer, etc.). **me-** 1 bend (of a tree, etc.). 2 flicker. **me-i** bend over to pick up s.t. **me-kan** 1 bend (the body). 2 lean to o. side to dodge s.t. **ter-(²)** bent over. **sepe-** as far as o. can bend.
liuk-liuk whistle made of a rice stalk.
liung-liung k.o. sea fish.
liur saliva. **be(r)-, me-** drool.
liut leathery, tough.
liwaath, liwat₁ /liwa:t/ (*Lit.*) sodomy.
liwat₂ see LÉWAT.
liwet (*Jv*) *nasi* - boiled rice. **me-** boil rice.
liyer-liyer (*Jv*) doze.
lk. [*lebih kurang*] approximately, ca.
LKMD [*Lembaga Ketahanan Masyarakat Désa*] village social activities group.
LN₁ [*Luar Negeri*] abroad, foreign.
LN₂ [*Lembaran Negara*] national statues.
lo see LHO.
loak *barang* - secondhand things. *pasar* - flea market. *tukang* - vendor of used articles. **me-kan** put s.t. used up for sale, resell. ~ *pakaian* sell used

clothing. **-an 1** used. *barang* ~ used item, junk item. *berdagang* ~ deal in junk. **2** flea market.

loba greedy, avaricious, selfish. - *tamak* greedy. **ke-tamakan** greed, greediness. **me-kan** covet, crave. **ke-an** greed, covetousness.

lobak radish. - *mérah* beet.

loban see LUBAN.

lobang see LUBANG.

loberci spangles.

lobi₁ lobby, foyer.

lobi₂ (*Pol.*) s.o. who intervenes at political meetings to argue (informally) for a certain cause. **me-** argue for a cause.

lobiing go around to various people to persuade them to do s.t. *Keputusan rapat itu adalah hasil - berkali-kali* The decision reached in the meeting was the result of repeated lobbying.

lobi-lobi tree with edible fruit (used in fruit salads).

loco (*Coll.*) **me-, nge-** masturbate. **-²an** mutual masturbation.

locok (*Lit.*) **me-** move up and down (of a pump handle, etc.). **pe-** piston rod.

locot₁ chafed, blistered (of hand, foot).

locot₂ see LUCUT₁.

loda [*lotto daérah*] legalized lottery restricted to a certain region.

lodan whale.

lodéh k.o. vegetable dish cooked with coconut milk.

lodoh₁ (*Jv, Jkt*) stripped (threads of screw, etc.).

lodoh₂ **nge-, me-** soften s.t. by sticking it in water.

lodong covered glass jar.

logam metal. - *adi* precious metal. - *campur* alloy. - *hitam* ferrous metal. - *mulia* precious metal. - *tua* scrap metal.

logaritma logarithm.

logat 1 (*Lit.*) word, wordlist. **2** dialect. - *kasar* slang. **3** way of speaking, accent. - *asing* foreign accent. **ber-** speak with a certain dialect or with a certain accent. ~ *Jawa* have a Jv accent.

loge see LOSE.

logika logic.

logis logical, reasonable. **me-kan** make s.t. logical or reasonable. ~ *tindakan* do a logical act. **ke-an** reasonableness, logic.

logistik logistics.

logo logogram.

loh₁ writing tablet.

loh₂ see LHO.

loha see DOHA.

loh jinawi (*Jv*) **1** lush, luxuriant, fertile. **2** well-populated.

lohor 1 (*Isl.*) midday prayer, o. of the five obligatory prayer rituals. **2** midday, noontime.

loji 1 (*Lit.*) warehouse of a colonial trading company. **2** (*Coll.*) large, colonial style house.

lojot ke-an writhing in pain.

lok /lok/ see LOKO.

loka (*Lit.*) place, shop.

lokah see LUKAH.

lokakarya workshop, seminar. **ber-** hold a workshop. **me-kan** hold a workshop about s.t.

lokal 1 local. *dlm wewenang pejabat* - under the jurisdiction of the local official. **2** place. - *kelas* place where the class is held.

lokalisasi 1 prostitution complex organized in order to confine prostitution to only o. area. **2** confinement of prostitution to o. area. **3** complex for confining poor, sick, etc. **me-** confine to o. area (of prostitution, sick, etc.).

lokalisir me- localize.

lokalitas locality.

lokan k.o. edible bivalve. - *laut* conch. **ber-** *dua* bivalve.

lokasi site. **ber-** be located.

lokcan, lokchuan /lokcan, lokcuan/ (*Ch*) silk crepe.

lokék stingy, miserly.

lokét counter (of post offices, immigration offices, etc.), ticket window.

lokio (*Ch*) chives.

lokir (*Che.*) exchange position of s.t. with the rook.

loklok pearl.

loko, lokomotif locomotive. *tempat* - *langsir* yard engine.

lokro loose, slack. **ng-** despondent.

loksun (*Ch*) consumptive with blood in spittle.

loktong prostitute.

lola [*lonté lanang*] (*Sl.*) male prostitute.

lola me- manage, run s.t.

lolak-lolok (*Coll.*) look around uncertain about what to do.

loléng (*Ch*) paper lantern.

loli, lolipop lollipop.

loloh₁ **me-** overfeed s.o.

loloh₂ loose, slack (of clothes).

lolong howling. **me- 1** howl, yelp (of a dog). **2** scream, wail. *meratap dan* ~ weep and wail. **ter-²** howl continuously. **-an** a howl, yelp.

lolos 1 slip off (of a ring, etc.). **2** slip away, bolt (from jail, etc.). *Anjing itu - dr ikatan* The dog slipped out of its leash. **3** be allowed to get through or out. *Pemegang paspor diplomatik - dr pemeriksaan imigrasi* Holders of diplomatic passports do not have to go through immigration formalities. **me-kan 1** slip off s.t. **2** release (s.o., a secret, etc.). ~ *diri* escape, free o.s. **3** allow s.t. to get through or out. ~ *barang selundupan* allow smuggled goods to get through. **ter-** unexpectedly release from s.t. ~ *dr kematian* escaped from (certain) death. **ke-an** breakout (from jail). **pe-** escapee. **pe-an** escape.

lomba a race, contest. - *hias* decoration competition. - *karya-tulis* writing competition. - *lintas médan* cross-country race. - *pacu rintangan* steeplechase. - *perahu layar* yacht race, sailboat competition. - *percobaan* trial run. - *pidato* oratorical contest. **ber-(²), ber-(²)an** compete, race e.o. **me-** race s.t. **memper-kan** race (horse, car, etc.). **pe-1** contestant, competitor. **2** athlete. **per-an**

1 race, contest. 2 racetrack. ~ *beranting* relay race. ~ *senjata* arms race.

lombar me- 1 pay out rope. 2 follow an urge to.

lombok chili. - *rawit* k.o. of small, very hot chili pepper.

lombong 1 mine, quarry. - *batu bara* coal mine. 2 crater. - *gunung berapi* volcanic crater. me-mine s.t.

lomi (*Ch*) k.o. viscous noodle dish.

lomot (*Jkt*) nge- suck in. *Rokoknya di-nya dlm-dlm* He took a deep puff on the cigarette.

lompat a leap, jump. - *galah* pole vault. - *jauh* long jump. - *katak* leapfrog. - *kinja* leap with joy. - *langkah berjingkat* hop, skip and jump. - *sehari* every other day. - *tiga* hop, skip and jump. - *tinggi* high jump. *sekali - sampai ke situ* reach there in o. bound. ber-² jump, leap, hop. ber-(²)an jump about. me- leap, jump. ~ *bangun* jump up. ~ *keluar* (*Av.*) bail out. me-² jump up and down. me-i 1 jump over s.t. 2 spring at. me-kan cause s.o. or s.t. to jump, let s.o. jump. ter-jump accidentally or without thinking. -an 1 (*Sport*) jump, hurdle. 2 leap, jump, bound. pe-jumper. pe-an jumping, leaping (of a fence, etc.). ~ *dr adegan I ke adegan II* jumping from act I to act II.

lompong me- empty, bare.

lompong sagu k.o. sweet made of boiled sago filled with coconut and palm sugar.

lomprot nge- be sloppy. *Dia kian ~ dlm hal ber-pakaian* He is getting more and more sloppy in dress.

loncat₁ leap, jump (esp. high or from a height). - *galah* pole vault. - *indah* fancy diving. - *katak* leapfrog. - *lari* leap out (of a car). - *menara* high diving. - *papan* springboard diving. - *tiga* hop, skip and jump. - *tinggi* high jump. ber-an leap about. ~ *turun ke halaman* jump down to the yard. me- 1 jump, leap, hop. ~ *keluar* (*Av.*) bail out. ~ *pagar* leap over the fence. ~ *tinggi* perform the high jump. ~ *undur* jump back. 2 move, shift. me-² jump about. ~ *kegirangan* leap for joy. me-i 1 leap over s.t., skip over s.t. *Parit itu di-inya* He leapt over the ditch. *Kita ~ saja bab ini* We will just skip this chapter. 2 leap at. *Harimau ~ mangsanya* A tiger leaped at its prey. me-kan cause s.t. to jump. -an 1 jump, leap, bound, hop. 2 antics. pe- jumper. pe(r)-an jumping.

loncat₂ frog.

loncéng 1 bell, chime. - *kematian* death knell. - *penyelamat* warning bell. 2 wall clock. - *angka* digital clock. me- 1 strike (of bells, chimes). 2 ring, call. 3 toll (the death of). -an ring, call.

loncér loose (of a screw). me- be loose.

loncong see LUNCUNG.

loncos tapering.

londang buffalo wallow.

londar locus.

londo (*Jv*) white person.

londong me-(kan) 1 wash away. 2 destroy, wipe out.

londot stripped (of the threads of a screw, etc.).

lonéng (*Jv*) 1 balustrade, railing. 2 low wall before house. me-, nge- 1 sit idle, loaf. 2 get a bit of fresh air.

long₁ k.o. large firecracker.

long₂ (*Lit.*) k.o. bottomless coffin.

long₃ see SULUNG.

longak-longok (*Coll.*) look around unsure of what to do. me- look around unsure.

longgar 1 loose (of rope, clothes, screw, etc.). 2 lax (in discipline). 3 not binding (of contract, friendship). me-i 1 loosen (o.'s clothing). 2 slacken (a rope). 3 make room for. me-kan, memper-1 mitigate, alleviate (a situation). 2 slacken, loosen s.t. 3 relax (discipline, etc.). ke-an 1 laxness, laxity. 2 leeway, room, latitude. 3 dispensation, concession. 4 too loose (of collar, rope, etc.). pe-an relaxing. ~ *politik monetér* relaxing of monetary policy.

longgok heap, pile, stack. - *pasir* sand pile. - *sampah* trash heap. ber-(²) piled (up). me-kan pile, heap, stack s.t. ter- heaped up. -an 1 pile, stack, heap. 2 accumulation. ~ *cebakan* ore deposit.

longgor grow tall. *Anak ini - benar* This child is really growing up.

longkop me- peel (of paint). -an flake (of peeling paint).

longo me- 1 gawk. 2 be open-mouthed (from surprise), bewildered. me-kan surprise, cause o. to be open-mouthed.

longok me- take a peek. *Laki-laki di dlm mobil itu ~ keluar* The man in the car peeked outside. me-kan *kepala* crane o.'s neck in order to see.

longong me- agape, open-mouthed.

longsong me- peel (fruit, etc.). ter- 1 peeled. 2 gone so far as not to be undone. *Saya ~ berjanji jadi terpaksa hrs memenuhinya* I have already promised, so I have to fulfill it. -an shell of spent bullet.

longsor slide (of embankments, hills, etc.). *tanah* landslide. me- slide down, collapse. me-kan erode. *Air ~ tanah* Water eroded the soil. -an 1 landslide. 2 soil erosion. ~ *salju* avalanche. pe-an eroding of.

longtorso strapless bra combined with corset to cover the torso.

lonjak - *anjlok* ups and downs, fluctuation. ber-²(an) bounce about, bounce up and down. me- jump up. *Harga ~ naik* Prices soared. ~ *ria* jump for joy. me-² 1 bounce around. *Rasa mual ~ di perut* A nauseous feeling rumbled in my stomach. 2 be elastic or springy. 3 boast, brag, be haughty. me-kan give a bounce or stimulus to. *Itu akan ~ kegiatan ékonomi* That will give impetus to economic activity. ter- 1 jump up suddenly. ~ *dr korsinya* jump up suddenly from o.'s chair. 2 jump (with joy). -an 1 leap, jump. ~ *harga* a jump in price. 2 bump (in plane flight). pe-an rise, jump (in production, price, etc.).

lonjong 1 tapering, pointed. 2 oval, egg-shaped (esp. of faces).

lonjor 1 stalk, stick. 2 classifier for soap. *se- sabun* a cake of soap. berse- *kaki* stretch o.'s legs. me-kan stick s.t. out. ~ *kepala* stick out o.'s head. -an s.t. straight and long, a stretch of s.t. ~ *rél besi* rail line stretching straight. ~ *kayu* timber.

lonsong see LONGSONG.

lontang-lantung 1 go about with no purpose or destination. **2** neglected, ignored.

lontar₁ 1 palmyra palm the leaves of which may be written on. **2** manuscript of such palm leaves.

lontar₂ - *martil* (*Sport*) hammer throw. **se- 1** a single throw. **2** a little bit of s.t. ~ *kata* a few words. **ber-an** throw at e.o. *Anak ~ batu* Children were throwing rocks at e.o. **me-** throw s.t. **me-i 1** hurl s.t. at repeatedly. **2** throw stones at. ~ *kera* throw stones at a monkey. **me-kan 1** throw s.t. ~ *pandangan* cast a look. ~ *ke orbit* place in orbit. **2** bring up, broach (a subject, idea). ~ *pertanyaan* pose a question. ~ *tuduhan* level an accusation. **ter-** accidently tossed. *mataku ~ ke . . .* my eyes fell on . . . **-an** toss, throw, cast. ~ *tuduhan* leveling of accusations. **pe-** s.t. or s.o. which hurls, thrower. *-* *rocket* rocket launcher. **pe-an 1** hurling. **2** bringing up. ~ *gagasan* introducing an idea. **sepe-an** a stone's throw away.

lonté (*Jv*) prostitute. - *lanang* male prostitute.

lontok squat (of a bottle).

lontong food consisting of rice steamed in a banana leaf.

lontos smooth and cylindrical (of a pillar). **pe-** bald and shiny (head).

loop, lop /lop/ (gun) barrel.

lopakan (*Jkt*) puddle.

lopak-lopak (*Jkt*) woven pouch for tobacco.

lopék k.o. small boat.

loper 1 messenger, errand boy. **2** delivery man. - *susu* milkman. - *koran* newspaper deliverer.

lopis k.o. cake of glutinous rice steamed in banana leaves.

lopong see LOMPONG.

lor (*Jv*) north.

lorék striped.

loréng stripe. - *macan* tiger's stripes. **ber-** striped.

lori (*R.R.*) flatcar us. to transport sugarcane.

lornyét lorgnette.

lorong 1 path, lane, trail. **2** alley(way). **3** hallway, corridor. - *kebakaran* unobstructed fire passage (us. from building to a river). **me-kan** open the way for s.o. or s.t.

lorot₁ me- decline, drop (of prices, etc.). **me-kan** lower, decrease s.t.

lorot₂ me- remove wax fom batik between dyeings.

los₁ (*Naut.*) pilot.

los₂ shed without interior walls, hangar. - *loko* (*R.R.*) roundhouse. - *pasar* market stall.

los₃ (*Coll.*) **1** free, loose. **2** slack, not taut. *Talinya -* The rope is slack. **3** not restrictive, unrestricted. *Orangtuanya -* His parents are permissive. *listrik -* unlimited electricity. **me-kan** release, free, leave alone.

lose, lose₁ box seats, first-class seats in a movie house.

lose₂ house guest.

losin see LUSIN.

losmén inn, cheap hotel.

losong-kosong completely empty.

lot see LOTERÉ.

loték /loték/ k.o. raw vegetable salad served with spicy sauce.

loténg 1 upper story, upstairs. **2** top floor, attic. **3** ceiling. **ber-** storied. *rumah ~* house with more than o. floor.

loteré 1 lottery, raffle, pool. - *buntut* illegal lottery tied to the last (three) numbers of the gvt. sponsored lottery. **2** lottery ticket. **me-** gamble, participate in a lottery. **me-kan** raffle s.t. off.

lotok nge- chip off.

lotong black or gray long-tailed monkey. - *Mentawai* k.o. monkey.

lotot staring (of eyes). **me-** open wide (of eyes), bulge out (of eyes, when angry, etc.). *Ia ~ kehéranan* His eyes bulged in amazement. **me-kan** cause o.'s (eyes) to bulge out.

lotré see LOTERÉ.

lotto k.o. lottery (1960s).

loudspeaker /lotspiker/ (*Coll.*) loudspeaker.

lowak see LOAK.

lowong empty, vacant, unfilled. *Tdk ada pekerjaan - di sini* There is no vacancy here. *Ini mengisi yg -* This fills a gap. **me-i** vacate (a room, building). **-an 1** vacancy, (job) opening. **2** gap, vacuum, void. **ke-an** gap.

loyal loyal.

loyalitas loyalty.

loyang 1 brass. **2** large tray. **3** casserole dish, baking pan.

loyar extravagant, wasteful.

loyo 1 weak, faint. **2** exhausted.

loyong me- stagger, totter.

loyor nge- 1 (*Jkt*) slither. **2** (*Coll.*) leave without saying goodbye.

LP₁ [*Lembaga Pemasyarakatan*] correctional institution, jail.

LP₂ [*long-play*] long-play album.

LSD [*Lembaga Sosial Désa*] village social activity group.

lt.₁ [*lantai*] story, floor.

lt.₂ [*létnan*] lieutenant.

ltd. [*létnan dua*] 2d lieutenant.

lts. [*létnan satu*] first lieutenant.

lu (*Jkt, Ch, Coll.*) you.

luah sickening, nauseating. **me-** be sickened, wish to vomit. **me-kan** vomit (up).

luak₁ (*Jv*) k.o. civet cat.

luak₂ a dug well.

luak₃ me-(i) decrease, reduce s.t.

luak₄ see LOAK.

luak₅ see LUHAK.

luak₆ see LUAH.

luang empty, vacant, free. *hari yg -* a free day. *waktu -* free time. **me-kan 1** vacate. **2** make room for. **3** make time for. ~ *waktu* find time for. **ter-1** free, spare. *Saya akan datang kalau ada waktu ~* I will come if I have spare time. **2** vacant (post, position). **3** uncovered (of body, bridge, etc.). **pe-** opportunity, chance.

luap me- 1 overflow (of a river). **2** boil over (of

water). **3** flare up. *Semangatnya* ~ His fervor flared up. **me-²** be enthusiastic, wild about s.t. **me-i** overflow s.t. **me-kan** cause s.t. to boil over or flare up. **-an 1** overflow. **2** bubbling over. ~ *semangat* enthusiasm that is bubbling over.

luar 1 outside, outer part. - *dlm* inwardly and outwardly. - *dunia* other worldly. - *kampus* off campus. - *kawin* extra marital. - *kelas* 1 out of class. **2** extracurricular. - *kepala* by heart, from memory. - *negeri* abroad. *Départemen - Negeri* Ministry of Foreign Affairs. - *rencana* unplanned, unscheduled. *di* - outside. *Ia berdiri di -* She is standing outside. *ke -* to the outside. see KELUAR. **2** beyond. - *batas* 1 off limits, out of bounds. **2** extraordinary, out of the ordinary. - *biasa* extraordinarily uncommon. **ke-biasaan** peculiarity, extraordinariness. - *dugaan* beyond expectations. - *kanan* (*Sport*) player in the right field. - *kiri* (*Sport*) player in the left field. **-an** outside. *kerja* ~ outside work.

luas 1 wide, broad. *masyarakat* - society at large. **2** extensive, vast (forests, etc.). **3** capacious, commodious (trunk, room). **4** far-ranging (discussion). **-nya 1** width. *Pekarangan itu* ~ *tiga ratus méter persegi* The yard is 300 square meters. **2** area, extent, scope. ~ *ayunan* (*Elec.*) amplitude. ~ *lantai* floorspace. ~ *lingkungan* scope. ~ *sayap* wing spread. ~ *tanaman* planted area. **se-²nya** as widespread as possible. **me-** spread, extend. *Penyakit itu* ~ *ke mana-mana* The disease spread everywhere. ~ *melébar* extend considerably. **mem(per)-(kan) 1** expand, widen. **2** broaden (o.'s experience). **ke-an 1** extent, breadth, width. **2** vastness. **pe(ng)-an, per-an** expansion, broadening.

luat see LUAH.

luban incense.

lubang 1 hole, orifice. - *dubur* anus. - *erong* (*Naut.*) scupperhole. - *hawa* ventilator. - *hidung* nostril. - *kulit* (skin) pore. - *lénsa* aperture of camera. - *pantat* anus. - *pelihat/periksa* peephole. - *silinder* cylinder bore. - *tali* eyelet. - *tubrukan* breach, rupture. **2** cavity, hollow. - *béha* cup of a bra. - *gigi* dental cavity. **3** burrow, pit. - *batu bara* coal mine. - *kepundan* crater. - *perlindungan* 1 foxhole. **2** airraid shelter. **ber- 1** perforated. *gigi* ~ tooth with cavity. **2** hollow. **ber-²** full of holes. **me-** make a hole (in golf). **me-i 1** dig a hole, burrow. **2** pierce (the ears, etc.). **3** punch, perforate. **4** hollow out. **me-²i** riddle s.t., punch full of holes. **me-kan** perforate, punch s.t. **pe-** drill, brace, bit. ~ *kertas* punch, perforator. **pe-an** animal pit-trap.

lubér me- overflow, run over. **pe-an** overflowing (of water, etc.).

lubuk deep pool in a stream. - *hati* the depths of o.'s heart. - *akal lautan ilmu* extremely knowledgeable.

lucah 1 smutty, filthy, obscene. **2** shameless, brazen. **ke-an 1** filthiness, smuttiness. **2** shamelessness.

lucu 1 funny, amusing. --*menggigit* bitingly funny. **2** cute. **ber-, me-** joke, be amusing. **ke-an**

1 humor, joking. **2** cuteness. **-²an** not seriously. **pe-** wag, wit, jokester.

lucup see LUCUT₂.

lucut₁ me- slip off (of a ring, hold, etc.). **me-i** strip s.o., remove from s.o. ~ *pemuda yg bersenjata* strip the youth of their weapons. **me-kan 1** take off (clothes, ring, etc.). **2** loosen, untie (a knot). **ter-** slipped off (of a ring, etc.). *Uang itu* ~ *dr genggamannya* The money slipped from her grasp. **pe-an, per-an** removal. ~ *senjata* disarmament.

lucut₂ me- chafe, rub, cause a blister.

ludah saliva, spittle. **ber-, me-** spit. *Dilarang* ~ No spitting. **me-i** spit on. **me-kan** spit s.t. out. **pe-an** cuspidor, spittoon.

ludang k.o. dugout canoe.

ludas, ludes 1 finished, all gone (of money, etc.). **2** completely destroyed. **3** extinguished (of a flame).

luding Spanish mackerel.

ludruk E. Jv folk theater in which all parts are played by men.

lugas 1 simple, unadorned. **2** businesslike, direct, to the point. *Sikapnya - dan tepat* His attitude was businesslike and correct. **me-kan** simplify. **ke-an 1** matter-of-factness, efficiency. **2** simplicity, uneffectedness.

lugat see LOGAT.

lugu simple, plain, unadorned.

luh see LHO.

luhak district.

luhung 1 noble, supreme. **2** superb, exquisite. **ke-an 1** nobleness, **2** stateliness, magnificence.

luhur 1 glorious, supreme. **2** lofty (ideals). **3** upright, noble. **me-kan** exalt, glorify, ennoble. **ke-an 1** grandeur, majesty. **2** nobleness (of character).

lui (*Ch*) money.

luik me- 1 retch. **2** drip, trickle.

luing k.o. banyan tree.

luk curve (on a kris). **menge-** bend, make s.t. supple.

luka 1 injury, wound. - *baréng* bedsore. - *berat* 1 seriously injured. **2** serious injury. - *hati* insulted, wounded, offended. - *lécét* abrasion, scrape. - *parah* seriously injured. **me-parahkan** injure s.o. seriously. - *sipi* flesh wound. - *telak* slash wound. - *tempur* 1 wounded in action. **2** war wound. **2** (*Coll.*) injured. *Aku menolong kau karena kau -* I will help you because you are wounded. **me-i 1** injure, wound, hurt s.o. ~ *hati* hurt s.o.'s feelings. **2** maul s.o. **me-kan** hurt, injure s.o. **ter- 1** having sustained a wound, hurt. **2** offended. **ke-an** sense of having been hurt.

lukah k.o. fishtrap used in shallow water. **me-** use such a trap.

lukat me- come loose (of adhesive tape).

lukis ber-kan have s.t. painted on. *kain* ~ *tengkorak* cloth painted with a skull. **me- 1** paint, draw. **2** depict, describe. **me-i** paint, draw s.t. **me-kan 1** portray, render. **2** describe. **ter- 1** painted. **2** reflected (of experience, emotions). *penderitaan yg* ~ *pd setiap org* suffering reflected in each

person. **-an 1** painting, drawing, portrayal. **2** design. ~ *dinding* mural. ~ *kejadian* depiction of an event. **pe-** painter, artist. **pe-an** painting, drawing of s.t.
luks luxurious.
luku (*Jv*) plowshare. - *bajak* cultivator. **me-** plow s.t. **pe-an** plowing.
lukup see TELUNGKUP.
lukut various k.o. riverine weeds.
luli₁ spindle for making cotton thread. **me-** wind cotton on spindle.
luli₂ k.o. fish similar to smelt.
lulu see MELULU.
luluh 1 crushed (to powder). - *lantak* smashed to smithereens, completely crushed. **me-lantak-kan** crush s.t. completely. **2** (*Ling.*) assimilated. **me-kan** crush to powder.
luluk mud. **ber-** muddy. **ter-** loose and ready for planting (of soil).
lulum me- suck (o.'s finger).
lulur₁ tenderloin (of beef). - *dlm* fillet of beef.
lulur₂ me- swallow whole, gobble up.
lulur₃ (*Jv*) herbal cosmetic used to lighten o.'s complexion. **me-** apply this cosmetic.
lulus₁ 1 pass (a test). **2** be granted (permission). - *dr* graduate from. **me-i** remove, take away. ~ *pakaian* disrobe. **me-kan 1** permit, allow, grant. **2** yield to (pleas). **3** pass (an exam). **-an 1** graduate. **2** alumnus, alumna. *ikatan* ~ alumni or alumnae association. **ke-an** passing (an examination).
lulus₂ see LOLOS.
lulut₁ obey without questioning.
lulut₂ a scented powder for cleaning babies. **ber-** rub the scented powder on o.'s body. **me-** engage in rubbing on the powder.
lumang ber- smeared. **me-kan 1** smear s.t. **2** defile.
lumas grease. **me-** lubricate. **me-i** smear s.t. with. **me-kan** lubricate (with s.t.). **pe-** lubricant.
lumat fine, pulverized. **me-kan 1** pulverize. **2** smash, destroy. **-an** s.t. crushed to bits. **pe-** pulverizer.
lumayan 1 reasonable, moderate. **2** pretty fair, not bad. *jumlah yg* - a tidy sum.
lumba-lumba cetaceous mammal (i.e. dolphin, etc.).
lumbung rice barn.
lumer, lumér melted. **me-** melt. *Gunung és itu - terus* The iceberg continued to melt. **me-kan** melt. ~ *hatinya* melt o.'s heart.
lumintu without interruption, continuous, uninterrupted. **ke-an** continuousness, uninterruption.
lumpang 1 mortar (used in pestle). **2** rice jar. -² *getah* cups for catching exuding sap.
lumpat see LOMPAT.
lumpia (*Ch*) eggroll. - *basah* an eggroll not fried. - *goréng* a fried eggroll.
lumping see KUDA.
lumpuh paralyzed (of a person, organ or business). - *nier/nir* kidney failure. **me-kan 1** paralyze. **2** incapacitate, disable. **3** deactivate. **ke-an**

paralysis. ~ *saraf* palsy. **pe-an, per-an** paralyzing.
lumpur mud. - *bandang* mud deposited by a flash flood. - *ketam* mud on bank. - *laut* ooze. - *salju* slush. *takut akan - lari ke duri* from the frying pan into the fire. **ber-** muddy. **me-** silt up (of a creek or riverbed). **me-i** cause s.t. to be muddy. *Hujan masih* ~ *kampung-kampung Jkt* Rain is still muddying Jakarta's neighborhoods. **pe-an** mudhole, muddy place.
lumrah 1 normal, customary, usual. **2** commonplace, ordinary. **-nya** us., ordinarily.
lumur a smear. **ber-(an)** smeared. **me-i 1** smear s.t. with. *Aku* ~ *bibirku dgn lipenstip* I smeared lipstick all over my lips. **2** soil, stain. **me-kan 1** smear s.t. **2** soil, stain s.t. **-an** s.t. smeared. ~ *darah* 1 bloodstain. **2** *gorc.* **pe-** lubricant **pe-an 1** staining, smearing. **2** pollution.
lumus soiled (of face).
lumut 1 moss, lichen, bryophyte. - *bahan pembakar* peat moss. - *daun* moss. - *karang* sponge. - *kerah* lichen. **2** algae. **ber-** mossy. **(ber)-an** moss-covered.
lunak 1 soft (food, etc.). - *lidah* pronounce foreign words with ease. **2** easy-going, tractable in disposition. - *hati* gentle, mild. **3** benign (of tumor). **me-** become soft. **2** softening (attitude). **me-i** treat gently. **me-kan 1** soften s.t. ~ *hatinya* soften his heart. **2** weaken s.t. **ke-an 1** softness. **2** gentleness, mildness. ~ *hati* gentleness of heart. **3** moderation. **pe-** softener. **pe-an, per-an** softening. ~ *air* water softening.
lunas₁ paid, settled. **me-i, me-kan** pay, settle (a debt), expiate (a sin), discharge (o.'s duty). **ter-i** paid off. **pe-an** paying off of a debt.
lunas₂ 1 base. **2** (*Naut.*) keel.
lunau mud.
luncas miss or fall short of (the mark).
luncip see LANCIP.
luncung protruding (of chin, snout). **me-kan** cause to protrude. ~ *bibir/mulut* purse o.'s lips.
luncur berse-, bersi- move with gliding action. **me- 1** slide. **2** skim. ~ *di danau* skim along the lake. **me-i** glide over. **me-kan 1** cause s.t. to slip or slide. *Tina* ~ *roknya ke bawah* Tina let her skirt drop. **2** launch, shoot s.t. off. *Angkasawan-angkasawan di-kan ke angkasa* The astronauts were launched into space. **ter-** slipped down. **-an** (*Ling.*) glide. **pe- 1** launcher. **2** o. who slides. ~ *és* skater. **pe-an 1** (*Av.*) blast off, shooting (of artillery). **2** launching. **3** slide, chute.
luncus see LONCOS.
lundi grub, larva (of beetle).
lundu river catfish.
lunduk chameleon.
lung₁ 1 curve, bend. **2** bow and arrow.
lung₂ see LONG₁,₂,₃.
lungguh (*Jv*) **me-** sit at ease. **ke-an** job, position. **-an** land given to officials in lieu of salary.
lungguk see LONGGOK.
lungkrah weak, tired.
lungkum see MUNGKUM.

lungkup see TELUNGKUP.
lunglai weak, exhausted.
lunglit [*balung kulit*] (*Jv*) emaciated.
lungsin warp in a loom.
lungsur₁ me-kan, nge- hand s.t. down (a toy, coat, etc.). **-an** used clothing, hand-me-downs.
lungsur₂ see LUNCUR.
lunjak see LONJAK.
lunjur ber- stretch out (of arms and legs). **me-** protrude, stick out. *Beberapa batang rokok ~ dr bungkusan* Several cigarettes were sticking out of the package.
lunta ter-(²) be in constant difficulty, suffer constantly.
luntang-lanting 1 loaf about, hack around. **2** be out.
luntang-lantung (*Coll.*) go alone.
luntas see BELUNTAS.
luntur 1 faded, become discolored. **2** changeable (of opinion). **3** out-dated (of theory, policy, etc.). **me-kan** cause s.t. to fade.
lup₁ magnifying glass.
lup₂ see LOOP.
lupa forget. *- aku menyediakan asbak* Oh, I forgot to set out an ashtray. *Jangan - linggis* Do not forget the crowbar. *- akan dirinja* not care about o.s. *- daratan* with o.'s head in the clouds. *-² ingat* vaguely remember. **me(nge)-i** (*Lit.*) forget s.t. **me-kan** forget, forget about. *Tdk mungkin aku ~ kau* I could never forget you. **ter-(kan)** forgotten accidentally. **ke-an 1** forget s.t. **2** forgetfulness. **pe-** forgetful person, s.o. absent-minded. **pe-an** tendency to be forgetful.
lupak see LOPAK-LOPAK.
lupa-lupa roll of fatty tissue in a fish's stomach above the roe.
lupat k.o. mollusc.
lupi see PAPAN₁.
lupis see LOPIS.
lupuh me- hammer flat (bamboo for flooring). **pe-** bamboo flooring.
luput 1 slipped away, escaped. *Ia - dr bahaya* He escaped from danger. *tdk - dr fitnah* not spared the slander. **2** not on target. *- tafsiran* wrong interpretation. *Témbakannya -* His shot missed. **me-kan 1** free, release. **2** cause to be off target.
lurah₁ village chief. **ke-an** political district administered by the *lurah*.
lurah₂ 1 ravine, gorge, gully. **2** groove.
lurik (*Jv*) striped woven material. **-an** wear such cloth.
luru (*Lit.*) **me-** chase, run after.

lurub (*Jv*) cloth for covering a bier.
luruban (*Jkt*) see LURUB.
luruh 1 drop (of fruit, leaves, feathers). *Rambutnya -* His hair is falling out. *Air mata -* Tears fell. **2** be touching to the heart. **ber-an** drop in great quantities (of fruit, etc.). **me- 1** shed (of hair, fur). *ayam ~* molting chicken. **2** drop (of leaves, flowers). **3** (*Phys.*) disintegrate. **4** become emotionally affected. *Melihat anak itu hatiku ~* When I saw that child, I was deeply touched. **me-kan 1** cause s.t. to fall. **2** cause s.o. to feel touched. **pe-** s.t. which causes s.t. to drop. **pe-an 1** process of shedding. **2** (*Phys.*) disintegration.
luruk me- assault on a large scale.
lurus straight, undeviating. *Jalan ke Bogor tdk begitu -* The road to Bogor is not so straight. *- hati* honest. *- lempeng* straight, direct. *- tegak* bolt upright. **me- 1** stretch out straight. *Jalanmu ~ panjang* Your path stretches out straight and long. **2** become straight. **me-i** walk straight along s.t. **me-kan** straighten out s.t. *~ roda* align the wheels. **memper-kan** correct s.t. **ke-an 1** honesty, sincerity. **2** justice. **pe-** s.t. which straightens s.t. *sudut ~* supplementary angle. **pe-an** straighting of s.t.
lurut₁ me- 1 draw o.'s hand over s.t. firmly. **2** massage (by pressing in long strokes). **3** strip off (leaves, etc.) by squeezing between the fingers and pulling lengthwise.
lurut₂ see LURUH.
lus see ELUS.
lusa the day after tomorrow.
lusin dozen. **-an** by the dozen.
lustrum 5th anniversary (of an institution).
lusuh old and faded, worn-out (esp. of cloth, paper, etc.). *wajah yg -* a face unkempt and reflecting weariness and disappointment.
lusur see LUNCUR.
lut penetration by a sharp weapon. *tdk -* invulnerable. **te-** penetrated by a sharp weapon.
luti crumpled, wrinkled.
lutung see LOTONG.
lutut knee. **ber- 1** kneel. **2** bow to, give in to. **3** (*Lit.*) surrender.
luwak see LUAK₁.
luwes 1 smooth, well-mannered, sociable. **2** attractive. **3** flexible. **me-kan** smooth out. *Ia ~ rambutnya* He smoothed out his hair. **ke-an 1** smoothness. **2** attractiveness. **3** flexibility.
luyu sleepy. *mata -* droopy eyes.
luyur see KELUYUR.

M

m₁ /ém/ m, 13th letter of the alphabet.
m₂ /ém/ [*méns*] (*Euphemism*) have o.'s period. *Bu, saya tdk ikut olah raga, sedang* - I cannot go to physical education, Teacher. I am having my period.
m.₁ [*méter*] meter. *m²* /méter persegi/ square meter.
m.₂ [*menit*] minute.
M. [*Maséhi*] A.D. - *1939* 1939 A.D.
ma' see MAK.
maab (*Isl.*) place of return.
maaf 1 forgive, pardon. -, *tuan* Pardon me, sir. **2** forgiveness, pardon. *minta* - 1 apologize. 2 ask permission to leave. *Pd hari Lebaran dia minta - kpd org tuanya* On Lebaran day he asked his parents for forgiveness. **ber-²an** forgive e.o. **me-i** forgive s.o. *Tentu saya ~ engkau* Of course I forgive you. **me-kan** forgive s.t. *Kesalahan itu susah di-kan* It is hard to forgive that mistake. *-kanlah kalau ada kesalahan saya* Forgive me if I have done wrong. **ke-an** forgiveness. **pe-** o. who forgives. **kepe-an** quality of being forgiving. **per-an** act of forgiving.
maag /makh/ **1** stomach (as source of sickness). *-nya swak* He has a weak stomach. **2** (*Coll.*) suffer a stomach disorder. *Dia* - He has a gastric problem.
maalim (*Isl.*) religious teacher.
maap see MAAF.
Mabes [*Markas besar*] headquarters.
mabok see MABUK.
mabrur (*Isl.*) accepted by Allah (of o.'s pilgrimage).
mabuk 1 drunk, intoxicated. *Serdadu itu* - the soldier was drunk. *Dia - cinta* He was intoxicated with love. *- bayang* desire the impossible. *- bunga raya* flushed from drinking. *- (bunga) selasih* drunk and unable to stand upright. *- kepayang* 1 madly in love. 2 somewhat tipsy. *- khayal* light headed, intoxicated. *- pukulan* punch drunk. *- uang* dazed from too much money. **2** nauseated, on the verge of vomiting. *- darat* carsick. *- laut/ ombak* seasick. *- udara* airsick. **ber-²(an)** be drunk for a long period, run around drunk. **me-kan** intoxicate. *Minuman itu ~* That drink is intoxicating. **pe-** drunkard, a drunk.
mabur (*Jv*) flee, run away.
macak (*Jv*) dress up.
macam 1 kind, sort, quality, type. *Ini - yg terbaik* This is the best quality. *Org - kau mana mungkin tak lulus?* How can a person like you not pass? - *apa?* What kind? - *mana?* how? - *ragam* diverse.

me-ragamkan diversify s.t. **2** way, method. *Bukan itu -nya* That is not the way. **-² 1** various. **2** do all sorts of things. **se-** a certain kind. *Meréka sdh ada ~ saling mengerti* They had achieved a k.o. mutual understanding. *Ludruk ~ sandiwara* The *ludruk* is a k.o. of stage play. **ber-²** various. ~ *alasan* all k.o. excuses. **memper-²kan** treat differently. *Jangan engkau ~ teman-temanmu* Do not treat your friends differently.
macan (*Jv*) tiger. *- loréng* 1 striped royal tiger. **2** camouflage. *- ompong* a toothless tiger, a high placed person without power to pose a threat. *- tutul* panther. **-²an 1** toy tiger. **2** children's game.
macapat k.o. six-line Jv verse form.
macat, macet, macét 1 stuck, not running smoothly, out of order. *Saluran itu* - The pipe is clogged up. *Payungnya* - His parachute failed. **2** interference, disturbance. **me-kan** clog or jam up. **ke-an 1** jamming, sticking, stagnation. ~ *lalu lintas* traffic jam. ~ *kebudayaan* cultural stagnation. **2** stoppage, shutdown.
macik see MAK.
maci kwé (*Ch*) k.o. pastry filled with fried sesame seeds.
maciok, macok (*Ch*) mahjong.
mada stupid, feebleminded, dull.
ma'da see MAK.
madah 1 eulogy, praise. *- Agung* Song of Songs. **2** stanza. **ber- 1** praise. *Ia duduk di serambi sambil ~* He sits on the veranda praising (God). **2** recite. *Ia - Qur'an* He is reciting the Koran. **me-kan 1** express, pronounce. *Murid itu ~ terima kasih* The pupil expresses his thanks. **2** relate. **-an** songs. **pe-** religious person.
madaliun, madalyun see MÉDALYON.
madan mine. *- mas* gold mine.
madang (*Jv, Jkt*) eat rice.
madap (*Jv*) face.
madarsah see MADRASAH.
madat₁ opium. **ber-** smoke opium. **pe-** opium smoker, addict. **pe-an 1** the use of opium. **2** opium den.
madat₂ watchtower.
maddi (*Isl.*) material rather than spiritual.
madep see MADAP.
madhab see MAZHAB.
madikipé (*Vulg., Jkt*) swear word, mother-fucker.
Madinah Medina.
madipantat (*Vulg., Jkt*) swear word, mother-fucker.
madon (*Jv*) chase after women.
madona madonna.

madrasah 1 Isl. school. **2** (*Isl.*) institution of learning. - *jamiah* university.
madu₁ 1 honey. **2** very sweet (of a smile).
madu₂ co-wife. **ber-** have a co-wife, share o.'s husband with a 2d wife. **me-(i), me-kan, memperkan** give o.'s wife a co-wife. *Pah takut di-(i) kalau tdk melahirkan anak laki-laki* Pah was afraid her husband would take a 2d wife if she did not give birth to a boy. **per-an** polygamy.
madya 1 (*in set formal phrases*) medium, average. *marsekal* - lieutenant general of the air force. *téknologi* - middle-level technology. **2** level of Jv language between *kromo* and *ngoko*.
madzab, madzhab see MAZHAB.
madznun see MAJENUN.
maem (*child language, Jv*) eat.
maén see MAIN.
maésan see MÉSAN.
mafela shawl.
mafhum know, understand, comprehend. *Ia sdh - akan isi buku itu* He now understands the contents of the book. **me-i** know about.
magang₁ 1 candidate, apprentice. **2** clerk. **3** volunteer. **ber-** be an apprentice. **per-an** apprenticeship.
magang₂ overripe.
magel 1 half-ripe. **2** incomplete in knowledge.
magersari 1 tenant. **2** fringe area.
maggi /magi/ bouillon cubes.
maghrib see MAGRIB.
magik /méjik/ magic.
magis magical.
magister master's degree. - *Pendidikan* Master of Education.
magnét, magnit see MAKNIT.
magrib 1 west. **2** at sunset. **3** (*Isl.*) sunset prayer.
magribi western, esp. of western Africa.
magun fixed, permanent. - *angin* porthole.
mah. [*maha*] great.
mah₁ (*Jkt, Sd*) particle to mark the topic. *Kalau dia - tdk berani!* As for him, he wouldn't dare!
mah₂ see MAAG.
maha great, very. - *baik* very good. - *besar* very large, great. **ke-besaran** being very big.
Mahaasih All-loving (God).
Mahabharata the Mahabharata, important story in the literatures of Indonesia.
mahadahsyat tremendous, fantastic.
Mahadéwa 1 the Hindu god Siva. **2** supreme deity.
Mahadéwi the Hindu goddess Batara Durga.
Mahadper [*Mahkamah Angkatan Darat dlm Perang*] Wartime Military Court.
mahaduta ambassador.
Mahaesa The Great Unity, God.
mahaguru professor. **ke-an** professorship.
mahakeramat most sacred or holy.
Mahakuasa the Almighty. **ke-an** almightiness. *kpd ~ Allah* to the almighty power of God.
mahal 1 expensive. *Barang-barang makin -* Things are becoming more and more expensive. **2** scarce, difficult to find. - *mencari org sebaik itu* It is difficult to find s.o. as good as he is. **me-kan**

raise the price. *Penjual-penjual ~ barang-barang meréka* The salesmen raised the price of their merchandise. **ke-an 1** expensiveness. **2** scarcity. *Pd waktu - segala harga naik* During periods of scarcity prices rise. **3** too expensive. *Oléh karena ~ saya tdk beli barang itu* Because it was so expensive I did not buy it.
mahamenteri (*Lit.*) high official at old courts.
Mahaméru the holy mountain, seat of the gods.
mahamulia exalted, lofty, sublime, illustrious. *yg* - His Highness.
mahap see MAAF.
Mahapencipta the Almighty Creator.
mahar (*Isl.*) brideprice.
maharaja sovereign, emperor. **ke-an** empire.
maharajaléla bersi- 1 rage. *Penyakit cacar ~* Smallpox was rampant. **2** rampage, operate unchecked. *Org-org jahat ~ di Sukabumi* Bandits were rampaging in Sukabumi.
maharani, maharatu empress.
maharupa extremely beautiful.
Mahasayang the All-Merciful (of God).
mahasiswa university student. - *pendengar* auditor. **ke-an** university student affairs.
mahasiswi female university student.
Mahasuci the Most Holy (of God).
mahatahu 1 omniscient. **2** (*Coll.*) arrogant.
mahbub (*Lit.*) lover, sweetheart (male).
mahbubah (*Lit.*) beloved (woman).
mahdi (*Isl.*) messianic guide who will come just before the end of the world to lead the faithful.
mahérat see MAIRAT.
mahful stored in the mind. **me-kan** memorize.
mahir skilled, well-versed, clever. *Dia - sekali berbahasa Indonésia* He is very good in Indonesian. **me-kan, memper-kan** practice, learn, acquire. ~ *diri* make o.s. skillful. **ke-an** skill, proficiency.
mahkamah court of law. - *Agung* Supreme Court. - *militér* military court. - *tinggi* high court.
mahkota 1 crown. - *alhajat* life after death. **2** (*Biol.*) corona (in efflorescence). **3** crown of the tooth. **4** sweetheart. **me-i 1** crown (a king). **2** award, crown. *Buku ini di-i hadiah* This book was awarded a prize. **pe-an** coronation.
mahligai palace (us. figuratively). - *harapan* o.'s highest hopes (o.'s castles in the air).
mahluk creature. - *halus* supernatural creatures.
Mahmilub [*Mahkamah Militér Luar Biasa*] special court-martial for members of the armed forces involved in the *G30S* incident or for members of the Communist Party.
mahmud (*Lit.*) praised.
mahoni mahogany.
mahsul see HASIL.
mahsyar see PADANG.
mahyong mahjong.
maido doubt s.t.
maik microphone.
main 1 play. - *piano* play the piano. *Dia - keléréng* He is playing marbles. - *api* play with fire. - *baciluk/bakikuk/bakiluk* play hide-and-seek. - *bola sodok* shoot pool. - *gajah* play chess. - *gayung* fence. - *kenéb* child's game with rubber bands. -

tédéng aling-aling play hide-and-seek. **2** engage in some (us. not quite respectable) activity. - *angin* unpredictable (lit., playing with the wind). - *burit* commit sodomy. - *culik* kidnap. - *curang* unfair play. - *galan-galanan* act chivalrously. - *ganthol* unfair play. - *gila* 1 to joke, fool. 2 be forward, bold, arrogant. - *hakim sendiri* take the law into o.'s own hands. - *judi* gambling. - *jujur* fair play. - *kartu terbuka* lay o.'s cards on the table, be frank. - *kayu* play unfairly. - *kelinci* frequent a prostitute. - *keroyok* gang up on s.o. - *komidi* 1 act in a play. 2 pretend. - *kucing-kucingan* 1 play cat and mouse game. 2 try to avoid s.o. o feels guilty toward. - *mata* wink, flirt. - *mata sérong-sérongan* play unfair, play dirty pool. - *mudah* flirt, court. - *onani* masturbate. - *peran(an)* play a role. - *perempuan* have an illicit affair, chase after women. - *pintu belakang* do things in an underhanded way. - *pompa* have intercourse. - *sabun* 1 bribe, connive to do s.t. illegal. 2 masturbate. - *sapu rata* make a clean sweep, do across the board. - *serobot* do s.t. illegal. - *sikut* elbow o.'s way. - *silap/sulap* 1 juggle. 2 conjure. - *suap* bribe. - *tangan* gesticulate. - *tangan panjang* 1 be impertinent by touching a woman. 2 prone to stealing things. 3 k.o. children's game. - *top* gamble. **3** play (a show). *Bioskop sdh -* The movie has started. *tgl -nya* date of showing. **4** do s.t. unthinkingly, needlessly. - *ambil rokok* take s.o.'s cigarette (without asking permission). *Dokter itu - suntik saja* That doctor just gives injections needlessly. - *témbak* shoot at random, without provocation. *Jangan - tetapi-tetapian* Do not give me any and's, if's, or but's. **5** have sex. -² 1 playful, in fun, not serious. *Dia ~ saja, tdk betul-betul* She is just playing, she is not serious. *Perbédaan kurs resmi utk dolar AS dan kurs gelap ternyata tdk ~* The difference between the official and black market rate of exchange for the US dollar is no joke. **2** drop by for a visit. *~ di rumah nanti* Come see me some time. **ber-** play. *Dia ~ bola* He plays soccer. *~ muda* be unfaithful. **ber-²** playful, all in fun. *Tdk apa, hanya ~ saja* It is nothing serious, it is all in fun. *~ tangan* parry with the hands. **me-kan** 1 play s.t. *~ Indonésia Raya* to play *Indonésia Raya*. *~ peranan penting* play an important role. **2** show, present (a film, show, etc.). *Apa yg di-kan di Ria?* What is playing at the Ria? **memper-kan** make a fool of s.o. **-an, -²an** 1 toy. **2** knickknack. **pe-** player, actor. *Ia ~ tengah* He is a halfback. *~ bayangan* o. who is on the list but does not really ever play. **per-an** 1 game. *~ untung-untungan* game of chance. **2** performance, show. **3** acting. **4** tricks played on o. *Saya jadi korban ~ penipu itu* I was the victim of that swindler's tricks.

mair see MAHIR.

mairat 1 (*Isl.*) ascension. - *Nabi Muh.* the ascension of the Prophet Muh. **2** (*Coll.*) disappear, die.

maiséna cornmeal.

mait (*Jv*) see MAYAT.

mai tua (*in some regions only*) old woman.

maizéna see MAISÉNA.

majadaya in o. piece (of poles, sticks).

majal blunt, dull. *Pisau itu -* That knife is dull.

majalah magazine, periodical, journal. - *bulanan* monthly magazine. - *kejuruan* trade or professional journal.

majas, majasi (just a) figure of speech.

majelis 1 council, committee. - *luhur* high council. - *pengadilan* court of justice. - *Permusyawaratan Rakyat* the People's Advisory Assembly. - *Tinggi dan - Rendah* House of Lords and House of Commons. **2** meeting, session. **3** meeting chamber. - *geréja* vestry.

majemuk (*Ling.*) compound, complex. *Itu kata -* That is a compound word. **me-kan** compound s.t. **ke-an** 1 complexity. **2** plurality, pluralism. **pe-an** compounding.

majenun possessed, insane. **ke-an** state of being possessed.

majikan employer, boss.

majikanisme authoritarian mental attitude.

majir barren, sterile.

ma'jizat see MUKJIZAT.

majong dust cloth.

maju 1 go forward, advance, progress. *Jangan mundur, - terus* Do not back down, keep going forward. - *jalan* Forward march! - *mundur* vacillating. - *penuh* full speed ahead. - *ujian* stand for an examination. **2** thrive, progress. *Toko itu - sekali rupanya* The shop seems to be doing a thriving business. **3** progressive, forward looking. **me-kan** 1 move s.t. forward. *Ayah ~ mobilnya sedikit* Dad moved his car forward a bit. **2** advance, improve. *Ia ingin ~ bahasa Inggerisnya* He wants to improve his English. *~ turisme* promote tourism. **3** propose, suggest. **ke-an** progress, advance, development. **pe-an** furtherance.

majuh 1 gluttonous. **2** overeager.

majun₁ see MAKJUN.

majun₂ see MAJONG.

majung putty.

majusi Persian or Zoroastrian religion.

mak 1 mother. **2** term of address or reference for a woman who is older than the speaker and who might fittingly be called "mother." - *angkat* foster mother. - *bapa* parents. - *bungsu* mother's or father's youngest sister. - *buyung* 1 procuress. 2 used teasingly to indicate a pregnant woman. - *cik* youngest aunt, aunt. - *comblang/jomblang* female go-between for arranging marriages. - *da* aunt (younger sister or younger cousin of parent). - *éték* aunt. - *kecil* aunt (younger sister or younger cousin of parent). - *lung* oldest aunt. - *mentua/mertua* mother-in-law. - *muda* 1 aunt (younger sister or younger cousin of parent). 2 2nd wife. - *sdr* aunt. - *su* father's or mother's youngest sister. - *sulung* oldest aunt. - *téték* foster mother. - *tiri* stepmother. - *cik* aunt (youngest sister of father or mother). - *tua* 1 first wife. 2 mother's or father's older sister.

maka 1 then, so. *Karena itu, - saya tdk mau* Because of that, I am therefore unwilling. **2** particle introducing the main clause which follows a conditional or temporal clause. *Bila dia membacakan doa, - terdengarlah suaranya melaung-laung* When he chanted the prayers his voice could be heard booming. *Kalau kita membacanya, - kita akan mengerti* If we read it, we will understand. *- dr itu* thus, therefore. **-nya** consequently, because of that, no wonder! *O nggak makan sama sekali! ~ sdh lapar* Oh you did not eat anything! No wonder you are already hungry.

makalah working paper (for a conference, etc.), short paper.

makam grave, resting place, burial plot. **ber-** lie buried. **me-kan** bury, inter. **pe-an** funeral, burial, interment. *~ negara* state funeral.

makan 1 eat, eat a meal. *Ia selalu - pisang* He is always eating bananas. *Sdh -? Blm. Baru njajan bakwan* Have you eaten? No. I just had a bit of noodle soup as a snack. *- berpantang* diet, restrictions on what o. may eat religious or medical reasons. *- daging* carnivore. *- darah* fret. *- daun muda* rob the cradle, marry or date a much younger person. *- dawai* very poor, impoverished. **2** take, swallow, ingest. *Saya blm pernah - sirih* I have never chewed betel nut. *- angin* get some fresh air. *- asam* experienced. *- bawang* furious, very angry. *- diri* weaken o.s. by worry, hate, anxiety. *- garam* experienced. *Ia tlh banyak - garam dlm kehidupan* He has savored much of life. *- hak* infringe upon o.'s rights. *- hati* 1 sadden. **2** suffer from s.o.'s act. **3** eat o.'s heart out. **4** be annoying. *- kerawat* very poor, impoverished. *- obat* take medicine. *- pancing* take the bait. *- rumput* graze. *- sabun* fix (a game). *- siku-siku* talk in an indirect way, refer by allusion. *- sumpah* perjure. *- tanah* starve. *- tulang* drive o.s. hard. *- ulam* keep a mistress as well as a wife. **3** meal, food. *- benar* party, large meal. *- besar* have a big party. *- lembu* cattle fodder. *- malam* dinner, supper. *- pagi* breakfast. *- siang* lunch. **4** destroy, consume. *Rumah itu di- api* The house was consumed by fire. *- korban* claimed casualties. **5** take, require, consume. *- waktu tiga jam* It takes three hours. *- ongkos* require an outlay. *- risiko* involve a risk. *- tempat* take up space. **6** make a living by (in set phrases). *- duit/emas* take a bribe. *- gaji* work for wages. *- kuli* work as a day laborer. *- péna* live by the pen. *- riba* lend money at usurious rates. *- sogok/suap* take a bribe. *- upah* 1 work for wages. **2** be open to bribery. **7** hit, strike. *Adik saya di- peluru* My brother was hit by a bullet. *- tangan* 1 struck by a fist. **2** have sudden good fortune. **8** in working condition. *Rém otonya tdk -* The brakes of his car do not hold. **9** range of a weapon, draw of a ship. *- peluru bedil zaman dahulu terbatas* The old-time guns had a limited range. *Kapal itu -nya dua puluh métér* The ship draws 20 meters. **-²** snack. **me-** consume, use up. **me-i 1** feed. *Ibu lagi ~ bayi* The mother is feeding the baby. **2** feed on, nibble at. *buku-buku yg di-i tikus* books that rats nibbled at. **me-kan** feed s.t. to s.o. *Kué itu di-kan pd anaknya* She fed the cake to her child. **ter-**

1 eaten or swallowed accidentally. *Racun itu ~* The poison was accidentally swallowed. **2** edible. **3** influenced by. *Abu betul-betul ~ semua saran Bakri* Abu was totally taken in by Bakri's suggestions. *~ isyu* believe in a rumor. *~ akal* make sense. *Kejadian itu tdk ~ akalnya* He could not understand that event. **-an** food, provisions. *~ baku* staple foods. *~ berpantang* food o. is not allowed to eat. *~ empuk* easy to take advantage of or beat. *~ kecil* hors d'oeuvres. *~ lembu/ternak* fodder. *~ pokok* staple foods. *~ tandon* available food. **-²an** various foods. **pe-** **1** eater. *~ darah* bloodsucker, o. who makes too much profit. *~ bawang* quick to anger. **2** consumer.

makanya see MAKA.

makar₁ 1 trick, tactics. **2** attack, assault. **3** attack against the gvt.

makar₂ 1 hard and tough (of fruits and vegetables). **2** unripe (of fruit).

makara 1 mythological creature said to cause eclipses. *udang -* k.o. crawfish. **2** an astrological sign (Cancer). **3** curvilinear motif like the tail of a shrimp, e.g. as found on ancient temple gargoyles.

makaroni macaroni. *- kruntel* curlicue macaroni. *- skotel* macaroni casserole.

makarya practical.

Makasar Macassar, Macassarese.

makasi see TERIMA KASIH.

Makassar see MAKASAR.

makbul 1 fulfilled, answered. **2** accepted, realized. **3** effective. *Obat itu - sekali* That medicine is very effective. **me-kan 1** accept. *Majikan itu ~ permintaan pegawai-pegawainya* The employer accepted his employees' request. **2** fulfill, realize. *Ia bekerja keras utk ~ cita-citanya* He worked hard to realize his dreams.

makcik see MAK.

makelar broker, intermediary in a sale. *- éfék* share broker. *- rumah* real estate broker. **-an** system of using brokers.

makenah see MUKENAH.

makeruh see MAKRUH.

makét scale model, mockup.

makhdum Sir (honorific, generally used of o. well versed in religion).

makhluk see MAHLUK.

makhudum see MAKHDUM.

maki -² abuse, esp. with vulgar language. **me-** abuse s.o., use abusive language. **-an** abuse, abusive words. **pe-²** s.t. used to abuse. *kata ~* words of abuse.

makin increasingly, the more. *Kota itu - bertambah* The city is growing more and more. *- . . . - the more . . . the more. *- lama - banyak* the longer the time the greater the amount. **se-** more and more. *Suaranya ~ keras* His voice became louder and louder. *~ . . . ~ . . . the more . . . the more . . . ~ banyak gajinya ~ malas ia bekerja* The more he earned the lazier he became.

makjizat see MUKJIZAT.

makjun tonic to increase a man's sexual ability.

maklaf see MALAF.

maklum 1 know, be knowledgeable. *Ttg hal itu sdr tentu sdh -* Of course, you already know about that matter. **2** be understanding of a situation. *-lah, seorg pegawai* You know how it is with an official. **me-i** be understanding of. *Ayah dan ibu saja yg ~ hal itu* Only my parents are understanding about that matter. **me-kan, memper-kan 1** announce, notify. *Diper-kan dgn hormat bhw . . .* It is respectfully announced that . . . **2** declare, proclaim. *Kapan Jepang ~ perang kpd negeri Tiongkok?* When did Japan declare war on China? **per-an, pe-an 1** announcement, declaration, proclamation. **2** statement.

maklumat announcement, declaration. **me-kan** announce, proclaim, declare. *Kementerian itu ~ peraturan baru* The ministry announced a new regulation.

makmal *(in some regions only)* laboratory.

makmum *(Isl.)* congregation, follower of a religious leader in prayer. **ber-** be a follower of a certain leader in prayer. *Saya ~ pd Haji Ali* I will join Haji Ali in praying.

makmur 1 prosperous, rich, wealthy. *Negeri itu - sekali* That country is very prosperous. **2** luxurious. *Org kaya itu - hidupnya* That rich man lives luxuriously. **me-kan** make s.t. prosper. *Penduduk bekerja keras utk ~ daérah itu* The inhabitants work hard to make the area prosper. **ke-an** prosperity. *~ bersama* area which shares in prosperity. *Kementerian ~* Ministry of Welfare. **perse-an** commonwealth.

makna 1 meaning. *- réferénsial* referential meaning. **2** purpose, sense. *Apa -nya bekerja sekeras itu?* What is the purpose of working so hard? **ber-** have meaning, be meaningful, significant. *Tiap kata itu ~* Each word is significant. **me-kan** explain, elucidate. *Org itu ~ Qur'an* That person is explaining the meaning of the Koran. **per-an** matters pertaining to meaning.

maknawi 1 spiritual. **2** meaningful.

maknawiah according to intent rather than literal (of an interpretation).

maknit magnet. **me-kan** magnetize. **ke-an** magnetism. **pe-an** magnetization.

makota see MAHKOTA.

makrifat 1 knowledge. **2** the highest knowledge (in mysticism). **ber- 1** philosophize. *Ia ~ ttg ketuhanan* He philosophizes about divinity. **2** concentrate. *Dia ~ dlm pemujaan Tuhan* He concentrates on worshiping God.

makro- macro.

makruf 1 known. *Itu sdh - ke mana-mana* That has become well known everywhere. **2** good (of deeds). *tindakan yg - good deeds.*

makruh *(Isl.)* s.t. the avoidance of which yields merit but the performance of which is not sinful.

maksi /maksi/ large-scale, major. *Ia merombak secara - perkembangan musik* He has brought about major changes in the development of music.

maksiat in violation of God's law, immoral (esp. sexually immoral). **ber-** engage in immoral acts. **ke-an** sin, wickedness.

maksimal, maksimum /maksimal, maksimum/ maximal, maximum. **me-kan** maximize.

maksud 1 purpose, aim. *Apa -nya datang sepagi ini?* What is his purpose in coming this early? *- perkumpulan itu baik* The aims of that organization are admirable. *- tujuan* objective. **2** intention, plan. *- saya hendak pergi ke bioskop* My intention was to go to the movies. *Apa -nya?* What is he driving at? **3** meaning, sense. *- surat ini* the meaning of this letter. **di-** intend, plan. *Saya ~ ke pasar siang ini* I plan to go to the market this afternoon. **di-** meant, intended. *yg di- dgn istilah itu . . .* what is meant by that term is . . . **me-kan** have in mind, intend. *Entahlah apa yg di-kannya dgn surat itu* I do not know what he meant by that letter. **ter-** the o. in mind. *surat ~* the letter which was meant.

maktab Koranic elementary school.

maktub recorded. **me-kan** write down. **ter-** written down. *Hal itu ~ dlm bukunya* That matter has been written about in his book.

makul /ma'kul/ rational, logical, reasonable.

makulat /ma'kulat/ *(Isl.)* metaphysics.

makzul deposed, dethroned. **me-kan** depose. *~ dirinya* abdicate. **pe-an** deposing.

mal 1 by (in measurements). *tiga - empat* three by four. **2** times (multiplication).

mala 1 disaster, misfortune, accident. **2** spot, stain, flaw, blot on o.'s reputation.

malaékat see MALAIKAT.

malaf, ma'laf manager.

malagizi malnutrition.

malah in fact, instead, on the contrary. *Stlh minum obat - menjadi-jadi sakitnya* He took the medicine but instead became sicker. *- begitu* actually that is the way it was (rather than s.t. not as severe or good). **-an 1** but rather, in fact, instead. *Jangan diputar-putar begitu. Nanti ~ jadi rusak* Do not keep turning it like that. It is going to break instead (of working). **2** in fact, even. *Jangankan rumah, ~ pakaian tdk punya* He does not even have clothing, much less a house.

malaikat angel. *- maut* angel of death. *- pelindung* guardian angel. *- penolong* guiding angel. **me-i** be an angel to.

malaikatulmaut angel of death.

malaise /malése/ see MALÉSE.

malak see MALAIKAT.

Malaka Malacca.

malakalmaut see MALAIKATULMAUT.

malakama, malakamo *buah si -* proverbial fruit which brings bad luck to s.o. who is dear to the possessor if he eats it and equally bad luck to another dear person if he does not eat it. *Bagai makan buah si -* Damned if you do, and damned if you don't.

malakut *(Lit.)* kingdom.

malam₁ 1 evening, night. *- buta* pitchblack night. *- gembira* **1** merry evening. **2** open house. *- hari* night time. - *kemarin* two nights ago. - *menanjak* nightfall. **2** the night an event takes place. - *kabarét* night when a variety show is put on. - *kesenian* evening of cultural entertainment. **3** (preceding the name of a day) eve, the night before an event. - *Kemis* Wednesday night. - *Kudus* Holy Night, Christmas Eve (Dec 24). **4** (following the name of a day) the night of the day. *Kemis* - Thursday night. *kemarin* - last night. - *panjang* **1** Saturday night. **2** any holiday eve when o. can stay up till late. - *takdis* (*Isl.*) night celebrating God's holiness. -² **1** at night. **2** late at night. *Mengapa ~ datang ke sini?* Why did you come here so late at night? **-nya** the night before. **se-** **1** last night. *Énak tidur ~?* Did you sleep well last night? **2** o. night. *Kami tinggal di hotél itu hanya ~ saja* We stayed at the hotel only o. night. *~ suntuk* o. night through. **ber-** **1** spend the night. *Saya ~ di Hotél Garuda* I spent the night at the Hotel Garuda. **2** keep overnight. *Daging itu busuk baunya karena tlh ~* The meat smells spoiled because it was kept overnight (without cooking or refrigerating it). **me-i** spend the night at the bedside of s.o. *Sdh dua malam ibu ~ dia* Mother has spent two nights at her bedside. **me(mper)-kan** keep overnight, leave overnight. *Supnya énak rasanya kalau diper-kan dulu* The soup will taste delicious if you leave it overnight. **ke-an** overtaken by night. *Waktu ke Bogor kami ~ di jalan* We were overtaken by night on our way to Bogor. **se-an** for a night. **se-²an** the whole evening or night. *~ sepicingpun dia tdk tidur* He did not sleep a wink the whole night through. **pe(r)-an** overnight stop, hotel, motel.

malam₂ wax, paraffin.

malan have an uneasy feeling, anxious, concerned.

malang **1** transverse, across. - *melintang* **1** lie across. *Papan - melintang di jalan itu* A plank is lying across the road. **2** unlucky, unfortunate. *Sekali ini mémang - buat dia* It is just bad luck for him this time. - *munjur* at random, haphazardly. **ke-an** **1** bad luck, calamity, distress. **2** struck by disaster or bad luck. *Keluarga itu ~* That family was struck by disaster.

malap **1** dim (of light). *Lampu itu terlalu -* That lamp is too dim. **2** smoldering. - *sbg pelita kekurangan minyak* smoldering like a lamp that is short of oil.

malapetaka misfortune, great disaster.

malar **1** continuous, more and more. *Dia - menangisi anaknya* She cries continuously over her child. **2** but in fact, but instead even . . . *Bukan berhenti, - berlari lebih cepat* He did not stop, but ran even faster. **-²** but instead even . . . **-an** (*Ling.*) continuant.

malari [*Malapetaka 15 Januari*] anti-Japanese riots of January 15, 1974.

malas **1** lazy, indolent. *Murid itu - sekali* That student is very lazy. **2** not feel like, not be up to. *Saya - pergi menonton malam ini* I do not feel up to going to the movies tonight. **ber-** *diri* laze

around. **ber-²**, **(ber)-²an** loaf, take it easy, be idle. *~ di tempat tidur* loafing around in bed. **me-kan** make o. lazy. *Hawa panas ~ saya bekerja* The hot weather makes me feel too lazy to work. **ke-an** laziness. **pe-** sluggard, lazy person.

malaun (*Isl.*) accursed.

Maleman (*Isl.*) last 10 days of the fasting month during which the descent of the divine inspiration is celebrated.

males see MALAS.

malése economic depression.

maligai see MAHLIGAI.

malih (*Jv*) changed, altered. *Ulat sdh - menjadi kupu-kupu* The caterpillar has changed into a butterfly.

malik **1** owner, proprietor. **2** (*Lit.*) king.

malikul maut the angel of death.

malim₁ **1** leader, guide. **2** pilot (of ship). **3** magician.

malim₂ see MAALIM.

ma lima see MO LIMO.

malin (*Rel.*) master. **me-kan** call o. "master." **ke-an** state of being a master in religion.

maling **1** thief. **2** steal. **me-i** steal from, rob. *Ia ~ kawannya* He steals from his friend. **ke-an** **1** robbed. *Saya ~ tadi malam* I was robbed last night. **2** theft, robbery. *Saya tdk tahu bhw ada ~ di rumah sdr* I did not know there was a theft at your house. **pe-** thief, robber.

malinjo see MELINJO₁.

malis **1** faded, pale (of colors). *Warna bajuku sdh -* The color of my dress has faded. **2** vague. *Bau itu masih - tercium dr sini* The odor can be vaguely smelled from here.

malu **1** shy, bashful, embarrassed. *Masuklah, jangan -* Please come in, do not be bashful. *siputri malu* the bashful plant, mimosa pudica. **2** respectful and humble. - *sekali org kampung itu kpd kiyai* The villagers are very humble toward the religious teacher. **3** ashamed. - *diri* ashamed. **4** shame. *tdk tahu -* shameless. **-²** be shy, bashful. *Tdk usah ~* Do not be shy, make yourself at home! *~ bahasa* very bashful. *~ kucing* pretending to be shy, coy. *si ~ Mimosa pudica*, a plant the leaves of which fold upon contact. **ber-** have a feeling of shame. **me-i** **1** embarrass, shame. *Si Amat ~ ayahnya di muka org banyak* Amat embarrassed his father in front of many people. **2** respect. *Walikota kami di-i oléh banyak org* Our mayor is respected by many people. **me-kan** **1** disgraceful, cause shame. *Pakaiannya ~* She is dressed in a disgraceful way. *Anak itu ~ ayahnya* That child disgraced his father. **2** be ashamed of. *Jangan kau-kan rumahmu yg kecil ini* Do not be ashamed of your little house. **memper-kan** be ashamed of. **ke-an** **1** privates, genitals. **2** (*Lit.*) ashamed, shame. **ke-²an** very ashamed. *Tini menundukkan kepalanya ~* Tini bowed her head in shame. **pe-** tending to be shy, timid. *Si Tien ~ sekali. Karena itu tidak punya banyak teman* Tien is very shy. That is why she does not have many friends.

Maluku Moluccas.

ma'lum see MAKLUM.

ma'lumat see MAKLUMAT.

malung k.o. sea fish.

mam₁ (*Coll.*) mother.

mam₂ see MAEM.

mama 1 mother. **2** (*Amb*) aunt. **3** (*Amb*) term of address for women the age of o.'s mother.

mamah chew. **me-** chew, masticate. ~ *biak* chew a cud for the 2d time (of ruminants). **me-kan** chew for. *Ia ~ anaknya kué yg keras* She chewed the hard cake for her child. **-an** cud, s.t. chewed. ~ *hué itu dimakankan pd anaknya* She fed the pre-chewed cake to her child. **pe-** *biak* ruminant.

mamai 1 walk in o.'s sleep. **2** drowsy.

mamak (*M*) mother's brother.

mamalia mammals.

mamanda term of respect for o.'s *mamak*, esp. in letters.

mamang₁ 1 dizzy. *Ssdh jatuh dia merasa* - After he fell, he felt dizzy. **2** frightened, confused. *Anak kecil itu* - The child was frightened.

mamang₂ (*Sd*) **1** term of address for parents' younger brother. **2** term of address for men older than the speaker, esp. as *mang*.

mambang k.o. supernatural being associated with crimson sunsets. - *kuning/soré* ominous reddish dusk.

mambeg (*Jv*) stagnant (of water in a swamp or stream that is stopped up).

mambruk k.o. bird from E. Indonesia with unusual plumage.

mambu (*Jv*) **1** smelling bad. **2** tainted.

mami 1 (*child language*) mother, mommy. **2** madame in a brothel.

mamik tasting bad. *Karena tlh lama disimpan, kué itu sdh - rasanya* Because it was kept so long, the cake does not taste good any more.

mampan see MEMPAN.

mampat, mampet 1 solid, compact, compressed. *Ban - tdk énak dipakai* Solid tires are not comfortable to ride on. **2** clogged up. *Saluran air itu* - The water pipe is clogged up. **3** excellent, fine. *Rencananya - sekali* It is an excellent plan. **me-kan 1** compress. **2** stanch bleeding. **ke-an** congestion. **pem-** compressor. ~ *udara* air compressor. **pem-an** compression.

mampir drop in, come by, call at. *-lah di rumah nanti* Stop by at the house later. **me-i** drop in, at, or on. **me-kan** drop s.t. off on the way. **ke-an** brief visit. **pe-an** stop, place to stay. *Tokio adalah tempat ~nya bilamana ia ke luar negeri* Tokyo is where he stops when he goes abroad. ~ *bis* bus stop.

mampu 1 capable, able. *Saya tdk - menyelesaikan pekerjaan itu hari ini juga* I cannot complete the work this very day. **2** well-to-do, wealthy. *Haji itu org - di désanya* The Haji is a wealthy man in his village. **3** afford, be able. *Banyak ibu yg - utk membeli cat bibir yg mahal* Many ladies can afford to buy expensive lipstick. **se-** as much as (one) is able. ~*ku* to the best of my ability. **ke-an 1** ability, capability, capacity. **2** prosperity. **berke-an** have a certain capacity. **ketidak-an** lack of ability.

mampuh see MAMPU.

mampung porous (of coal, sponge).

mampus (*Vulg.*) **1** die. *-lah kamu!* To hell with you! **2** exclamation about s.t. unfortunate. - *ini, uang habis semua* Darn! The money's all gone. **me-kan** exterminate, finish off.

ma'mur see MAKMUR.

mamut mammoth.

ma'na see MAKNA.

mana₁ 1 where. *Di - dia tinggal?* Where does he live? *Sdr mau ke -?* Where do you want to go? *dr* - from where, whence. *Tuan datang dr -?* Where did you come from? **2** which, which person. *Yg - punya saya?* Which is mine? *Tuan lebih suka kota yg -?* Which town do you prefer? - *kala* whenever. - *kala saya pergi* whenever I go. - *pun* anything, anywhere at all. - *pula* moreover. - *saja* whichever, any. *yg* - *saja kausuka* whichever you like. **3** how (can it be). - *bisa/boléh!* How could it be? (Impossible!) - *boléh! Saya lihat dia tadi pagi* How is it possible! I saw him this morning. - *aku sampai hati!* How could I bring myself to do it! - *suka* as you like it. - *tahan* **1** cannot stand s.t. **2** so good-looking o. cannot restrain o.s. *Asuy! - tahan!* Wow! I cannot restrain myself! - *tahan! Orgnya cakep sih* How could I help myself! She was so good looking! - *tahu* who could know. ~ *tahu dia seorg mata-mata* Who knows, maybe he is a spy. **4** what kind, which kind. *Org -?* What nationality? **-²** wherever, everywhere, anywhere. ~ *itu diucapkan* wherever it is uttered. *terdapat di* ~ available everywhere. *tdk di/ke* ~ nowhere. *Saya tdk ke* ~. *Jalan-jalan saja* I am not going anywhere in particular. Just taking a walk. **-nya** what part of it. ~ *yg énak?* What part of it is good to eat? **dike-kan** where can it be brought? ~ *pembunuh itu?* Where did they bring the murderer? **dike-²kan** brought to some place or other.

mana₂ particle preceding a list of problems o. is facing. - *panas, berdesak-desak* . . . It is hot, crowded . . . - *sendirian lagi* Not only that, I was all alone. - *lagi/pula* moreover. *Dia pintar, - lagi dia punya uang* He is clever and, besides, he has money.

manai pale, colorless (of complexion).

manajemén management.

manalagi name given to esp. good varieties of fruits (esp. mangos). *si* - certain fruit variety which is particularly delicious.

manao k.o. large rattan. **me- 1** collect rattan. **2** prepare rattan for being worked. **3** beat with rattan.

manasik manual, guide. - *haji* guide for those going on the haji.

manasuka as you like, voluntarily.

manat firm and permanent agreement.

manau see MANAO.

ma'nawi see MAKNAWI.

mancanegara foreign countries.

mancawarna varicolored, multicolored.

mancis matches, lighter.

mancung 1 sharp, pointed. *hidung* - a sharp well-formed nose. **2** dry sheath of a coconut. **me-kan** make s.t. sharp or well shaped.

manda₁, mandah₁ bear to do, put up with. *Siapa yg - tinggal lama di tempat itu?* Who could bear to stay in that place long?

manda₂, mandah₂ storage place for rice.

mandah₃ see MALAH.

mandala 1 arena, area in a circle. **2** area or field of operations.

mandam 1 drunk, intoxicated. *Awas! Serdadu -!* Watch out! A drunken soldier! **2** madly in love. *Dia - akan gadis itu* He is madly in love with that girl.

mandar k.o. waterfowl.

Mandar ethnic group in Sulawesi.

mandarsah see MADRASAH.

mandat 1 gvt. orders to make payment. **2** mandate. *Meréka sdh dpt - menémbak siapa saja* They received a mandate to shoot anyone at all. - *blangko* carte blanche.

mandataris o. entrusted with a mandate.

mandau k.o. sword made in Borneo.

mandeg, mandek (*Jv*) **1** stop, get stuck, stall. *Lalu lintas - seluruhnya* Traffic came to a total standstill. **2** stagnate. - *pikiranku kalau aku tinggal di sini lebih lama* I will stagnate if I stay here any longer. **ke-an 1** a halt, standstill. **2** stagnation, inertia.

mandeng (*Jv*) knowing o.'s proper position.

mandering see MINDERING.

mandi 1 bathe, take a bath. *Dia - pagi-pagi benar* He takes a bath very early in the morning. - *darah* shedding of blood. - *junub/wajib* (*Isl.*) bathe after doing s.t. ritually impure (required before performing religious duties). - *keringat* soaked in sweat. - *kucing* bathe perfunctorily. - *Safar* (*Isl.*) the purification ritual held in the month of *Safar*. **2** go swimming. - *laut* bathe in the sea. - *uap* take a steambath. **ber-** bathe. *Dia suka ~ di bawah pancuran* He likes to bathe under a shower. **ber-kan** be bathed in. *~ cahaya matahari* bathed in sunlight. **me-kan 1** bathe s.o. *~ kucing tdk baik* It is not good to wash a cat. **2** stick into water. *-kan panci kotor itu di dlm air agak lama* Soak the dirty pan in water for some time. **member-kan 1** baptize s.o. *Di geréja mana anak itu diper-kan?* In which church was the child baptized? **2** bathe s.o. according to ritual. *Mayatnya diper-kan* His corpse was bathed and prepared for burial. **pe-** bather. **pe-an** bathing place. **per-an 1** bathing place. **2** baptism.

mandiang see MENDIANG.

mandiri stand alone, be autonomous. **ke-an** autonomy.

mandor see MANDUR.

mandraguna invulnerable.

mandu opinion, point of view, thesis.

mandul barren, sterile. *tanah* - barren land. *Isterinya* - His wife is barren. **me-kan** spay. **ke-an** sterility, barrenness. **pe-an** sterilization.

mandung rooster, cock.

mandur foreman, overseer. *Si Amat - air di Jawi* Amat is the foreman of the gang that supervises irrigation at Jawi. **me-i** supervise. *Dia ~ pekerja di ladang* He supervises the workers in the field.

manekén, manekin mannequin.

manfaat 1 use, benefit. *Belajar ada -nya* Studying has its benefits. **2** profit. - *dan mudarat* **1** profit and loss. **2** advantages and disadvantages. **ber-** useful, profitable. **me-i** be beneficial to. *hrs ~ semua pihak* has to benefit all sides. **me-kan 1** make use of, exploit. *pandai - setiap kelemahan dlm pertahanan musuh* know how to exploit every weakness in the enemy's defense. **2** exploit, abuse. *~ kejujurannya* took advantage of her honesty. **memper-kan** make use of.

mang see MAMANG₂.

mangap (*Jv*) **1** gape. *Dia - melihat gedung yg besar itu* He gaped at the large building. **2** yawn. **ter-** agape.

mangau ter- agape.

mangga₁ mango. - *golék* k.o. fibrous, elongated mango.

mangga₂ /manggaq/ (*Sd*) please.

manggan manganese.

manggis, manggistan mangosteen.

manggung 1 coo (of doves). **2** perform (of a band, theater troupe, etc.).

manggut nod (in agreement). **-²** nod the head. *Dokter itu ~ saja mengiakan* The doctor nodded his head in agreement. **me-(²)kan** nod (the head). *~ kepala tanda setuju* nod the head in agreement. **ter-²** inadvertently nod o.'s head.

mangir (*Jv*) k.o. powder to lighten the skin.

mangka see MAKA.

mangkak faded and dull. *Keméja itu sdh -* That shirt is already faded and dull.

mangkal₁ see PANGKAL.

mangkal₂ see MANGKEL.

mangkar 1 green, unripe. **2** not done, raw.

Mangkasar see MAKASAR.

mangkat (*Honorific*) pass away, die, depart this world. *Beliau - tahun yg lalu* He passed away last year. **ke-an** death, demise.

mangkel annoyed, irritated.

mangkin see MAKIN.

mangkir 1 be absent. *Dia - di sekolah seminggu* He was absent from school for a week. **2** be missing, lack. *Satu sekerup - O.* screw is missing. **3** fail. *Dia - ujian* He failed the examination.

mangkok see MANGKUK.

mangku see PANGKU.

mangkubumi o. of the high administrators in the Malay and Jv courts.

mangkuk cup, bowl. - *(pem)bekam* cupping glass. **me-kan** *tangan* cup o.'s hands.

mangkus efficacious, effective.

mangoni see MAHONI.

mangpang-mungpung taking advantage of a favorable situation (us. in an unsavory way).

mangro in a dual capacity. *dlm kedudukan yg - sbg murid dan ibu rumah tangga* in a dual role as student and housewife. **ke-an** duality.

mangsa 1 prey, bait. **2** victim. - *empuk* easy mark, pushover. **me-** prey on, make into a victim. *Seékor macan hendak ~ anaknya* A tiger was about to attack her child.

mangsai see MASAI.

mangsét see MANSÉT.

mangsi 1 (*Lit.*) ink. **2** powdered charcoal for blackening the teeth.

mangu ter-(^{2}) 1 confused, dazed. *Waktu ditanya dia ~* When questioned he was just confused. **2** taken aback, speechless. **3** thoughtful.

mangut 1 confused, dazed. **2** doze. **ber-** be in a daze.

mangut ikan dish of fish in spicy coconut milk.

mani sperm. *pancuran -* ejaculation of sperm. **per-an** insemination. *~ buatan* artificial insemination.

maniak maniac. *- berita* a maniac for news.

manifés bill of lading, manifest.

maniféstasi manifestation. **me-kan** manifest s.t.

manifésto manifesto, political statement.

manik - *mata* pupil. **-^{2} 1** beads. **2** beads of perspiration, small droplets. **ber-^{2}** wear a string of beads.

manikam gem, precious stone. *ratna mutu -* all k.o. precious stones.

Manikebu [*Manifésto Kebudayaan*] anticommunist intellectual manifesto of 1964.

manikur manicure.

manikuris manicurist.

Manipol [*Manifésto Politik*] Sukarno's 1959 manifesto of political orientation. *- Usdék* manifesto of political reorganization. **me-usdékkan** reorganize or retool in accordance with the Political Manifesto and *Usdék*. **ber-** profess this manifesto. **ke-an 1** affected by this manifesto. **2** too much an adherent of this manifesto. **3** quality of being an adherent of this manifesto.

manipolis o. who follows Sukarno's 1959 manifesto.

manipolisasi bringing society into conformity with Sukarno's 1959 manifesto.

manipulasi manipulation. **ber-** engage in manipulation. **me-kan** manipulate s.t.

manipulir me- manipulate.

manis 1 sweet. *Kué itu terlalu -* That cake is too sweet. **2** talking sweetly. *- di mulut jahat di hati* talking sweetly but full of ill-will. **3** attractive, cute. *- benar gadis itu* That girl is very sweet. *-ku* my sweet. *- budi* friendly. *- hati* likable, kindly. *- muka* sweet expression. **4** nicely done. *Dua lagu dibawakan dgn - apik* Two songs were nicely performed. **ber-** act sweet toward. **ber-^{2}** use flattery. **me- 1** decorate, make s.t. look nice. *Ibu lagi ~ méja dgn bunga-bunga utk tamu* Mother is decorating the table with flowers for the guests. **2** smooth s.t. over. **me-kan** sweeten, make s.t. seem nice. *Perempuan itu ~ suaranya spy disukai org* That women modulates her voice so that people will like her. **memper- 1** make sweeter. **2** make cuter or more attractive. *Rénda itu ~ bajunya* The lace makes her blouse cuter. **ke-an 1** sweetness. **2** beauty. *Kesederhanaannya menam-*

bah -nya Her simplicity enhances her beauty. **3** oversweet. *Kopi itu ~* The coffee is oversweet. **-an** candy, sweets. *~ buah* candied fruits. *~ cokelat* chocolate bar, candy. *~ lebah* honey. **pe(r)- 1** sweetener. **2** cosmetics. **3** decoration.

manja 1 spoiled. *Anak itu - sekali* The child is very spoiled. **2** attached, friendly. *Anak itu - sekali kpd ibunya* That child is very much attached to his mother. **3** intimate, close in feeling. *Tak ada -nya thd ayahnya* He and his father are not close. **ber-** ask for affection, ask to be spoiled. *~ spt seorg anak meréngék dlm pelukan ibunya* asking for affection like a child whimpering in his mother's embrace. **ber-^{2}** court, be sweet with o.'s boyfriend or girlfriend. **me- 1** become spoiled (in behavior). **2** ask for affection. **3** spoil s.o. **me(mper)-kan** spoil, baby s.o. **ke-an** comforting familiarity. **ke-^{2}an** pampered. **pe-an** action of pampering.

manjung₁ k.o. large torch used during fishing.

manjung₂ k.o. small boat.

manjur 1 efficacious. *Obat itu -* That medicine is efficacious. **2** strong, effective. *Awas, itu - sekali* Be careful, it is very strong. **3** powerful. *Doanya - rupanya* His prayers seem powerful. **ke-an** efficacy, effectiveness.

manover maneuver.

manpaat see MANFAAT.

mans (*Crd.*) game (in bridge).

mansét 1 cuff. **2** cuff links.

mansuh, mansukh 1 abrogated. **2** expired, null, invalid. **me-kan 1** abrogate. *Peraturan-peraturan lama di-kan* The old regulations were abolished. **2** cancel, annul. *Peraturan baru itu ~ paspor saya* The new regulation makes my passport invalid.

mantab see MANTAP.

mantakan that is why, therefore. *- saya ndak mau* That is why I do not want to!

mantan former. *Dékan -, - Dékan* former Dean.

mantap steady, stable, unwavering. **me-kan** place on a solid footing. *dlm ~ ketahanan nasional* placing national defense on a firm basis. **ke-an** steadiness, stability. *~ politik* political stability. **pe-** means of consolidating. *sarana ~* means for consolidation. **pe-an** stabilization, consolidation.

mantel 1 coat, cardigan, cape. *- hujan* raincoat. **2** casing. **3** condom.

mantep see MANTAP.

mantera magic formula. **me-i** charm, cast a spell on, read a magic formula to affect s.t. *Anak itu di-i* The child was treated with charms. *Penyakit yg di-i* a sickness treated by magic spells.

manteri see MANTRI₁.

mantik logic, thinking based on reason rather than emotion. *ilmu -* logic as a discipline.

mantiki logical. *penalaran -* logical reasoning.

mantol see MANTEL.

mantram see MANTERA.

mantri₁ low-ranking gvt. employee us. a technician. *- hutan* forester. *- héwan* veterinarian's assistant. *- keséhatan* medical aide. *- pajak* tax official. *- pasar* market supervisor who collects fees for rental of space.

mantri₂ see MENTERI.
mantu₁ (*Jv*) hold wedding for o.'s daughter.
mantu₂ see MENANTU.
mantuk₁ the real meaning.
mantuk₂ me-(²) nodding the head.
manuk 1 (*Jv*) bird (in set phrases). - *déwata* bird of paradise. **2** (*child language*) penis.
manunggal be united. **ke-an** total integration.
manusia 1 human being, man. - *angkasa* spaceman, cosmonaut. - *katak* frogman. - *loka* the earth, the abode of humans. **2** human. **ber-manned. me-kan 1** treat like a human. **2** make s.o. into a human being. *Kita pemimpin perlu ~ bawahan kita* We leaders must teach our subordinates to be humane (lit., make human beings out of our subordinates). **memper-** humanize. **ke-an 1** humanity, being a human. **2** human nature. **3** humanism. **perike-an** humaneness, humanitarianism.
manusiawi human, humane.
manut (*Jv*) obedient, tending to follow orders from above. - *pd perintah Tuhan* obedient to the orders of the Lord. **-an** of an obedient type.
manuver see MANOVER.
manyala, manyala bob (*Sl.*) excellent, terrific. *Pukulannya -!* You hit a terrific ball, friend!
manyar see BURUNG.
manyun pout in distaste. *Mulutnya - karena mual* Her mouth puckered in disgust. **ber- (diri) brood.**
manyung k.o. fish.
manzil rest house, a place to spend the night on a trip.
maoni see MAHONI.
map portfolio, file folder. - *ordner* /ortner/ thick folder with clips. - *snelhékhter* binder with clips.
mapak meet s.o., welcome. **me-** meet, welcome. *~ tamu di lapangan terbang* meet the visitors at the airport.
mapalus mutual assistance.
mapan (*Jv*) established, in proper place, order. *Hidupnya sdh -* He is established in life. **me-kan** render s.t. established. **ke-an** state of being established. **pe-an** establishment of s.t.
mapang me-kan show, display. *~ portrét* show a portrait.
Mapram [*Masa Prabakti Mahasiswa*] time of initiating freshmen as full-fledged members of the student body. **di-** be hazed. **pe-an** hazing.
mar (*Che.*) queen.
mara₁ danger, disaster. - *bahaya* **1** disasters, calamities of all sorts. **2** perils.
mara₂ advance, progress, approach. - *sedikit* Step forward a little. **me-kan** advance, move s.t. *Dia ~ piringnya ke arah saya* He moved the plate toward me. **ke-an** progress.
marabunta k.o. voracious African ant.
marah 1 angry. **2** anger, fury. **3** become angry. **-² 1** on the warpath, be angry and disagreeable. **2** in an angry way. **(ber)-an** not on speaking terms. *Aman dan Abu lagi ~* Amat and Abu are not on speaking terms. **me-i** reprimand, scold. *Guru ~ si Ali* The teacher reprimanded Ali. **me-**

kan 1 make angry, infuriate. *Kata-katanya ~ saya* His words infuriated me. **2** be angry at. *Apa yg kau-kan?* What are you angry about? **ke-an 1** fury, anger, wrath. **2** very angry. **ke-²an** very angry, furious. **pe-** hothead, bad-tempered.
Marah title of Minang nobility below *Sutan*.
marajaléle see MAHARAJALÉLA.
marak glow, luster. **se-** bright, lively, lustrous. **me-** glow, flare up. **me-kan** light, brighten up. *Warna ini baik sekali utk ~ bajuku* This color is very good for brightening up my dress.
marakas k.o. percussion instrument, maraca.
maras very anxious, frightened. *Dia - mendengar anaknya blm pulang* He was frightened at hearing his child had not returned.
maraton marathon.
marbut caretaker of the mosque.
marcapada the earth, this world as opposed to heaven (in *wayang* stories).
marem (*Jv*) satisfied, content, complacent.
Maret March.
marga₁ 1 (*Batak*) clan. **2** (*Biol.*) genus. **3** (*S. Sumatra*) district. **4** family name.
marga₂ (*Lit.*) street, way. *bina -* highway construction, road maintenance.
margarin, margarine margarine.
margasatwa wild animals, fauna.
marge /marse/ margin.
marhaban (*Isl.*) Welcome! (esp. used in Isl. school circles). *lagu -* melody for praising the Prophet on *Mikraj.* **me-kan** greet a newborn baby by singing religious melodies to it.
marhaén working classes: peasantry, petty vendors, small-time artisans. *kaum -* the have-nots, little people. **ke-an** proletarianism.
marhaéni female *marhaén.*
marhaénis o. who fights for the interest of the have-nots.
marhaénisme movement to fight for the interests of the have-nots.
marhum see ALMARHUM.
marhumah the late (female). - *ibunda* my late mother.
mari 1 come here. *ke -* here, hither. *Kapan ke - lagi?* When are you coming here again? *ke sana ke -* here and there. **menge-kan** put, bring s.t. here. **2** please (do). - *diminum téhnya!* Please have some tea! **3** goodbye. *-! Sampai bésok!* Bye! See you tomorrow! **4** let us (do). - *kita berangkat* Let us get going.
ma'rifat see MAKRIFAT.
marihuana see MARIJUANA.
marijuana /mariyuana/ marijuana.
Marikan (*Coll.*) American.
Marikh Mars.
marin (*Coll.*) see KEMARIN.
marinir marine, marines.
maritim maritime. **ke-an** maritime affairs.
marjin margin (of profit).
markas 1 station, office. **2** army or police post, barracks. - *besar* headquarters. **pe-an** quartering of soldiers.
markis₁ awning against sun.

markis₂ k.o. setting for gems.
markisa, markisah 1 passion fruit. **2** syrup made from passion fruit.
markonis ship's radio operator.
Marksis Marxist.
Marksisme Marxism.
marmar, marmer marble.
marmot, marmut guinea pig.
maro, maron (*Jv*) system of renting rice fields sharing the crop 50-50.
mars marching tune.
marsda [*marsekal muda*] major general in the air force.
marsdya [*marsekal madya*] lieutenant general in the air force.
marsekal air marshal. - *madya* lieutenant general in the air force. - *muda* major general in the air force. - *pertama* brigadier general in the air force.
marsma [*marsekal pertama*] brigadier general in the air force.
marsosé military police, constabulary of colonial period.
martabak k.o. thick folded crepe filled with spices and pieces of meat.
martabat 1 rank, grade, status. *Org itu tinggi -nya* That person is high ranking. **2** prestige. **3** value. - *kemanusiaan* human values. **4** (*Chem.*) valence. **ke-an** dignity. - *insani* human dignity.
martél see MARTIL.
martelar see MARTIR.
martil hammer. **me-** hammer s.t.
martir (*Rel.*) martyr. **ke-an** martyrdom.
ma'ruf see MAKRUF.
ma'ruh see MAKRUH.
marus clotted blood (as in food).
marwah 1 pride, dignity. **2** manliness.
Marxis see MARKSIS.
Maryam 1 Mariam. **2** (*Rel.*) Mary, the mother of Jesus.
mas₁ 1 sir, brother (used to address or refer to contemporary males, including wife to husband, us. only for Jv). **2** Jv title below *radén*.
mas₂ see EMAS.
masa₁ 1 time, period. *Pd - itu saya di Bandung* At that time I was in Bandung. *di - datang* in the future. - *laku* The duration of validity. - *tenggang* grace period before which interest must be paid on a loan. - *depan* future. - *kini* nowadays. - *laku* time for which s.t. is valid. - *lalu/lampau* the past. - *mula* at the beginning, formerly. - *nifas* postnatal period. - *pancaroba* 1 change of agricultural seasons. **2** puberty. - *perubahan* period of transition. - *percobaan* probation. - *purba* antiquity. - *sekarang* nowadays. - *selam* the past. - *tunas* incubation period. - *waktu* chronology, periodization. **2** during. - *kecil saya bekerja di kantor pos* During my youth I worked in the post office. **3** phase. - *azali* prehistoric times. - *bodoh* indifferent, not care. *Kamu pergi atau tdk - bodoh* Whether you go or not is immaterial to me. **me-bodohkan** let o. do as he pleases. **ke-bodohan** indifference. - *genting* critical phase. - *kesempitan*

depression, slump. - *remaja* puberty, adolescence. - *tapa brata* time o. goes into seclusion to meditate and live as an ascetic. **se- 1** during the time, at the time when. ~ *kecil di kampung* When I was young in the village. **2** contemporary.
masa₂ see MASAK₁.
masaalah see MASALAH.
masa bodoh see MASA₁.
masai tangled. *Rambutnya* - His hair is tangled.
masak₁ impossible, it is inconceivable. - *aku bohong!* How can you think I would lie!
masak₂ 1 ripe. - *mangsai* overripe. **2** cooked, done, *Nasi sdh* - The rice is done. **3** mature. **4** experienced, ready to handle. *Dia sdh - akan segala macam keadaan* He is ready for all k.o. situations. **5** cook. -² carefully, deeply, through and through. *Pikirkan ~, baru kaujawab* Think it over carefully and then answer. **ber-an** be ripe (plural). - **me-** cooking, matters connected with cooking. **me-** cook, bake. ~ *kué* bake a cake. ~ *air* boil water. ~ *telur* cook eggs. **me-²** cooking. **me-kan 1** cook for s.o. *Saya hrs ~ anak-anak* I have to fix dinner for the children. **2** ripen s.t. **ke-an** maturity. ~ *kepribadian* emotional maturity. **-an 1** food, cooking. ~*nya tdk énak* His cooking does not taste good. ~ *héspot* stew. **2** cuisine, cooking method. ~ *Perancis* French cuisine. **pe-1** a cook. **2** cooking utensils. **pe-an** action of cooking. *perusahaan* ~ *roti* bakery.
masakah, masakan see MASAK₁.
masakat difficulty.
masakini the present time.
masal massive. *kuburan* - mass grave. *kawin* - mass marriage. **mengawin-kan** perform a mass marriage. *suntik* - mass injections. **me-kan** spread a practice, method, etc. to the masses. **pe-an** making s.t. massive. ~ *sport* mass participation in sport. *peningkatan* ~ *pembibitan* increasing mass participation in the cultivation of special seedlings.
masalah 1 problem, complication. **2** question. **me-kan, memper-kan** make a problem out of s.t. **per-an** set of problems.
masalla see MASYA ALLAH, MUSHOLLA.
masam sour, acid. *Mangga muda ini* - *sekali* This young mango is very sour. *muka* - sullen, glum. *Jangan* - *saja mukamu* Do not always look so sullen. **me-** become sour. *Susu itu tlh* ~ The milk has become sour. **me-kan 1** make sour, pickle. *Ibu* ~ *timun utk acar* Mother makes pickles out of cucumbers. **2** acidify. ~ *lahan pinus* acidify the terrain in which pines grow. **ke-an 1** unfriendliness. **2** acidity. ~ *tanah* acidity of the soil. **ke-²an** rather sour.
masap me- evaporate.
masarakat see MASYARAKAT.
masdar infinitive.
Maséh Jesus, the Messiah.
maséhi Christian, us. Protestant. **per-an** Christianization.
masgul see MASYGUL.
mashab see MAZHAB.
mashaf handwritten text of the Koran.

mashur see MASYHUR.
ma'siat see MAKSIAT.
Masih see MASÉH.
masih₁ still, yet. *Dia - hidup* He is still alive. *- saja* still despite everything. *Kau - saja senakal dulu* You remain as naughty as ever, despite everything. **se-** when. *teman-teman lama ~ di SMA* my old friends from when I was in high school.
masih₂ (*Jv*) be related in a certain way. *Ia - bibi saya* She is an aunt of mine.
masin (*Jv*) 1 salty, briny. *- lidah/mulut* talkative, verbose. *Blm pernah di - garam* He has not had much experience yet (lit., he hasn't learned about brine and salt). *Garam kami tdk - pdnya* He did not listen to what we said (lit., our salt wasn't salty for him). 2 brackish. **-an** pickles.
masinasi machinations.
masing-masing 1 each. *- mengemukakan pikirannya* Each presented his own idea. 2 respective, respectively.
masinis engineer of a ship or locomotive.
masir granular.
Masir see MESIR.
masjid see MESJID.
masjul see MASYGUL.
maskapai company, enterprise. *- asing banyak sekali di sana* There were many foreign enterprises there. *- anak* subsidiary. *- kapal* shipping concern. *- pengangkutan* transport firm.
maskara mascara.
maskat k.o. shirt or outer jacket.
masker 1 makeup mask (for a facial). 2 gas mask, fencing mask.
maski see MESKI.
maskot mascot.
maskulin masculine.
maslahat use, benefit. *analisa -* cost-benefit analysis. **ke-an** use, benefit, profit.
masmur see MAZMUR.
massa mass. *- aksi* mass action. *- produksi* mass production. *média -* mass media. **me-** mingle, be popular with the masses.
massal see MASAL.
massalisasi spread of s.t. to the masses.
mastautin ber- residc at.
mastika see MESTIKA.
masturbasi masturbation.
masuk 1 enter, go into. *Silakan -* Please come in. *- akal* within reason, stands to reason. *- angin* catch a cold. *- tidur* go to sleep. *- ujian* go in for an examination. 2 set (of the sun). *Matahari - pukul delapan sekarang* The sun goes down at eight now. 3 be present at work. *Hari ini dia tdk -* He will not be in today. *- kuliah* attend class. *- sekolah* go to school. 4 be included. *Dua ribu saja. Ongkos gas sdh -* It is only 2,000. The price of the gas is already included. 5 participate, join. *Kapan dia - perkumpulan itu?* When did he join that organization? *Ia sdh - tentara* He has joined the army. *- Belanda* become a naturalized Dutch citizen. *- bilangan* belonging to, part of. *- Islam/Jawi* become a Muslim. *- latihan* enter military service. *- menjadi* belong to. *- serdadu* join the army.

- ulur become a slave. 6 almost, just about. *- lima tahun* going on five (years old). **ber-an** enter in large numbers. **me-i** 1 enter. *Diam-diam sekali dia ~ kamar itu* Very quietly be entered the room. *~ perkawinan* enter into marriage. 2 meddle in. *Jangan ~ perkara org lain* Do not meddle in others' affairs. **me-kan** 1 take, put into. *Ia ~ barang di lemari* She put the things in the cupboard. *~ anaknya ke universitas* He enrolled his child in the university. 2 import. *Perusahaan itu ~ barang ke dlm negeri* The firm imported goods into the country. 3 enter s.t. in. *O, saya lupa ~ rékening ini* Oh, I forgot to enter this bill (in the books). 4 (*Sport*) enter (a goal). *Regu itu ~ 134 gol* That team made 134 goals. **ter-** included, counted, belonging to. **ke-an** 1 possessed. *~ sétan barangkali* Maybe he is possessed by the devil. 2 entered accidentally, have s.t. manage to get into it. *Botol itu ~ lalat* A fly has gotten into the bottle. *Rumah ~ pencuri* The thief got into the house. **-an** input. **pe-an** 1 registration, entering. 2 import. 3 introduction. *~ berbagai tumbuhan yg berfaédah ke daérah kekeringan* the introduction of various useful plants to the arid regions. 4 income.
masup (*Jkt*) see MASUK.
masya Allah (*Isl.*) Good heavens! My God! (an exclamation expressing strong disapproval).
masyakat see MASAKAT.
masyarakat 1 society, community. *- bahasa* (*ling.*) speech community. *- ramai* the public. 2 inhabitants, people. *- ibu kota* The inhabitants of the capital. **ber-** form a group. **me-** conform to society's norms, be socialized, mingle with society. *perusahaan yg ~* a business that went public. *kelompok élite yg tdk mau ~* the elite that does not want to mingle with the public. **me-kan** 1 socialize, rehabilitate (a criminal). 2 make public (a business). *P.T. Centex ~ 15,1 per sén sahamnya* Centex Inc. is offering 15.1 percent of its shares to the public. **ke-an** social. *soal ~* social problems. **pe-an** socialization. *lembaga ~* correctional institution. *sistém ~* penal system.
masyawarat see MUSYAWARAH.
masygul sad, downhearted. *Hatinya - memikirkan keadaan org tuanya* He is very concerned about his parents. **me-kan** arouse concern. *Keadaan si sakit ~, kata dokter* The doctor says the patient's condition is cause for concern. **ke-an** anxiety, concern.
masyhur well-known, famous. **me-kan** 1 make s.o. or s.t. famous. *Perbuatan itulah yg ~ namanya* It was that deed which made him famous. 2 spread (news), make s.t. well known. *Apakah kabar itu di-kan?* Is that news being spread? **ter-** well-known, famous. **ke-an** fame, renown.
masyrik (*Lit.*) the Orient.
masyuk (*Lit.*) beloved, sweetheart.
Masyumi [*Majlis Syuro Muslimin Indonésia*] a modernist Isl. party prior to 1960.
mat₁ tempo.
mat₂, mat-matan (*Jv*) sitting around enjoying o.s.
mata₁ 1 eye. *di bawah empat -* face to face in pri-

vate. - *ayam* near sighted. - *bakup* black eye. - *bedil* bead (of a gun). - *benda* valuables. - *betung* dumb, uneducated, ignorant. - *buatan* glass eye. - *buaya* o. who is constantly on the lookout for women. - *cipit* slant-eyed. - *dekat* myopic, near-sighted. - *duitan* craving for money. - *elang* eagle-eyed. - *gelap* amuck, in a rage. - *jalan* watchman, scout. - *jauh* farsighted. - *kepala* o.'s own eyes. - *keranjang* be greedy. - *kucing* 1 semi-precious stone. 2 magic eye of radio, TV (the light that turns on). 3 (*in some regions only*) k.o. fruit similar to the lychee. - *sapi* fried egg. - *sapi balik* fried egg over. - *sasaran* bull's eye. - *sipit* slant-eyed. 2 the important part of s.t., source, center. - *air* spring, well. - *alamat* objective, target. - *angin* points of the compass. - *bisul* core of a boil. - *buku* knuckle. - *bulan* dimly visible moon. - *cincin* stone in a ring. - *dacing* gauge (on scales). - *hati* feelings, the mind's eye. - *ikan* 1 corn on toe. 2 holes for shoelaces. - *jala* mesh of a net. - *kain* design on sarong. - *kaki* ankle. - *kayu* knot in wood. - *kérék* knots on a pulley. - *pedoman* points of the compass. - *petir* flash of lightening. - *piano* piano key. - *rantai* link. - *surat* writing in a letter. - *susu* nipple. - *tangga* rung of ladder. 3 type. - *anggaran belanja* line item in a budget. - (*per*)*dagangan* commodities. - *huruf* type of letter, writing. - *kuliah* subject in school. - *pelajaran (tambahan/utama)* (minor, major) subject matter. - *pengajaran* subject of instruction. - *penghidupan/pencarian* means of livelihood. - *uang* currency. 4 cutting edge, point of s.t. sharp. - *bajak* plowshare. - *beliung* cutting edge of ax. - *jarum* 1 eye of needle. 2 point of needle. - *gunting* sharp edge of scissors. - *kail* fishhook, barb. - *panah* arrowhead. - *péna* pen point. - *pisau* knife blade. - *sangkur* bayonet. - *tombak* sharp point of spear. -² 1 spy. 2 detective. **ber-**1 have some k.o. eye. ~ *awas* have sharp eyes. ~ *rabun* have eyes that are almost blind. 2 have as a centerpiece (jewelry). *cincin besar* ~ *batu banyak* a large ring with lots of stones. 3 have a cutting edge. *pisau* ~ *dua* a knife with double-edged blade. **me-²i** 1 investigate, look into. 2 spy on. **ter-²** obvious, very clear.

mata₂ se-(²) only, nothing other than. *dusta* ~ nothing but a lie. ~ *keluar dr hati yg cemburu saja* uttered only because of his jealousy.

matahari the sun. - *berayun* approximately 3:30 p.m. - *hidup* the east. - *msk* sunset. - *mati* the west. - *naik* sunrise. - *tenggelam/terbenam* sunset. - *terbit* sunrise. - *terpijak* noontime.

matalamat objective, target.

mata-mata see MATA₁.

matang 1 ripe. *Buah mangga sdh mulai* - The mangoes have started ripening. 2 done, cooked. *Nasi sdh* -? Is the rice done? 3 mature, adult. *kepribadian yg* - a mature personality. *Bisulnya* - The boil has come to a head. - *biru* black and blue. *Ia sempat dilepas sblm* - *biru di tangan polisi* They managed to get him freed before he was beaten black and blue by the police. **me-kan** 1 cook. 2 let ripen. *Mangga ini di-kan sendiri* This mango was

left to ripen by itself. **memper-** allow to become more mature. **ke-an** 1 overripe. *Jangan dibiarkan di pohon. Nanti* ~ Do not leave it on the tree, it will get overripe. 2 ripeness. 3 maturity. **pe-an** maturation.

matari see MATAHARI.

matématik, matématika mathematics.

matématikus mathematician.

matématis mathematical.

mateng see MATANG.

materai see METERAI.

materi see PATRI.

matéri material, subject matter.

matérialis, matérialistis materialistic

matériil material (help, contribution).

materos see MATROS.

mati 1 die, be dead. *Anjingku* - My dog died. - *angin* weak. - *ayam* die, croak (lit., die like a chicken). - *bersebab* die an unnatural death (murder, drowning, etc.). - *bongkong* die in vain. - *haid* menopause. - *kekam* neap tide. - *honyol* die in vain. - *kumluh* die a natural death. *kutu* powerless, impotent. - *langkah* (*Che.*) checkmated, stymied. - *lelus* 1 a natural death. 2 die in vain. - *lepur* suffocate in mud. - *lidahnya* become speechless. - *mampus* 1 die right away. 2 To hell with you! (Go to hell!) - *modar* (*Vulg.*) kick off. - *pucuk* impotent. - *raga* strengthen o.'s soul by sublimating physical needs in deep meditation. - *rasa* 1 apathetic. 2 numb, anesthetized. - *sabil* die for a worthy cause. - *seajal* die of natural causes. - *sesat* commit suicide. - *syahid* die in a holy war. - *suri* suspended animation. - *tersalai* asphyxiated. 2 stop, go out (of lights, gas, etc.), stop existing. *Perkumpulan itu* - The organization broke up. *Jam itu* - The clock stopped. 3 fixed, inflexible. *Harga itu* - The price is fixed. 4 numb. *Ujung jariku* - My finger tips are numb. 5 (*Ling.*) word-final (of consonants not followed by a vowel). **ber-an** die in numbers. **ber-kan** *diri* pretend to be dying. **me-kan** 1 kill, murder. *Siapa yg* ~ *ular itu?* Who killed the snake? 2 extinguish, put out. *Jangan lupa* ~ *api sblm tidur* Do not forget to put the fire out before you go to bed. **ke-an** 1 death. 2 overtaken by death, bereft of. *Keluarga itu* ~ *anak* The family lost a child. 3 have s.t. die down on o. *Meréka* ~ *angin* They were becalmed. **ke-²an** 1 with every effort. 2 appear dead. **-²an** 1 pretend to be dead. *Dia tdk mati, hanya* ~ *saja* He is not dead, he is just pretending. 2 with all effort, as hard as possible. *Ia* ~ *menyelesaikan pekerjaannya* He is killing himself to finish the job. **pe-an** extinction.

matiné matinée.

Matius 1 Matthew. 2 (*Bib.*) the Book of Matthew.

matlamat see MATALAMAT.

maton (*Jv*) rational. *alasan-alasan yg* - reasons which make sense.

matra 1 dimension. 2 musical measure, bar. 3 ideal, measure. **ke-an** dimensionality.

matras (*Sport*) mattress, mat.

matros sailor.

matu units of weight for gold (= 2.4 carats). *Itu*

emas sepuluh - That is 24-carat gold. **me-kan** determine the purity of gold.

mau 1 shall, will. *Dia - datang soré ini* He will come this evening. **2** wish, want. *Dia - sekali ke Amérika* He very much wishes to go to America. *Tuan apa?* What do you want? **3** wish. *Itu -ku* That is my wish. - *tahu* curious. - *sama* - mutual liking. *Kalau - sama - artinya bukan paksaan* When both like it, there is no saying it was forced. - *tak* - willy-nilly, whether o. wants to or not. - *tak* -, *dia hrs pergi* He has to go, whether he wants to or not. **-nya** would like. *Berapa buah buku ~, pak?* How many books would you like? -²**nya** be willing to do. *Sdh tahu di sana bahaya, kok ~ ke sana juga* You know it is dangerous there. How come you are willing to go there anyway? **se-** as o. likes it. *~mulah* As you wish! *~ gué* as o. likes it, without regard to others' needs or desires. **se-(²)nya** at will, as o. likes. *Dia bekerja ~* He works just as he likes. **me-i 1** demand. **2** want s.t. **me-²kan** force. *Si Ali ~ adiknya makan és krim* Ali forced his younger brother to eat ice cream. **ke-an** wish, desire, will. **berke-an** have a will.

maujud concrete, real, tangible.

maujudat all that has existence, the universe.

maulana (*Isl.*) **1** our Lord. **2** the Honorable (title of a Muslim scholar).

maulid, maulud (*Isl.*) **1** Muh.'s birthday. **2** stories of Muh.'s birth.

maung₁ stinking, disgusting. *Jangan simpan lama-lama, - baunya nanti* Do not keep it too long, it will smell.

maung₂ 1 roar of a tiger. **2** tiger.

maupun, mau pun 1 although, in spite of the fact. *Dia pergi juga - dilarang* He went anyway although it was forbidden. **2** as well as. *baik dia - saya* both he and I. *Tak ada kursi - méja* There was neither a table nor a chair. - . . . - neither . . . nor . . . - *dia - saya boléh* Neither he nor I are allowed to do it.

maut 1 death. **2** hour of death for humans. **3** tremendous, terrible. *Pukulan drivenya -* He has a deadly drive (in golf). **pe-an** mortality.

mawar rose.

mawas₁ orangutan.

mawas₂ - *diri* self-correction through introspection. **me-** *diri* correct o.s. by critical self-appraisal. **pe-an** *diri* engaging in this process.

mawut chaotic, disorganized.

maya illusion, hallucination. -² clear and transparent. **ke-an** illusion.

mayang spadix, palm blossom.

mayapada world of the heavens (in *wayang* stories).

mayat human corpse.

mayeur see MAYOR₂.

mayit see MAYAT.

mayong see MAHYONG.

mayor₁ (*Mil.*) **1** major. - *udara* major in the air force. **2** lieutenant commander.

mayor₂ (*Music*) major (key). *nada* - major key.

mayoritas majority.

mayur see MAYOR₁, SAYUR.

mazbah (*Isl.*) place of ritual slaughter.

mazhab 1 (*Isl.*) school of thought concerning Muslim law. *ulama-ulama yg ~ Safi'i* scholars of the Shafiite persuasion. **2** (*Rel.*) sect. **3** school of thought, school of scientific discipline. - *éksiténsialis* existentialist school. - *mérkantilis* mercantile system.

mazmur 1 (*Bib.*) Book of Psalms. **2** psalm.

MB [*Markas Besar*] headquarters.

MBAD [*Markas Besar Angkatan Darat*] army headquarters.

mbah 1 leader, champion. *Dia adalah -nya komunis* He is a Communist leader. **2** see EMBAH.

mbak, mbakyu term of address to a Jv woman contemporary.

MBAL [*Markas Besar Angkatan Laut*] navy headquarters.

MBAU [*Markas Besar Angkatan Udara*] air force headquarters.

mbék (*Jv, Coll.*) **1** bleat. **2** goat.

mbeling 1 naughty (of children). **2** antiestablishment, tongue-in-cheek literature or policy.

mbengok (*Jv*) shout, yell.

mblekék oversatiated, overfull. *makan sampai -* eat till o. is ready to burst.

mbois behave and dress like a young man.

mbok₁ (*Jv*) a coaxing particle. - *sdh! Jangan nangis!* Come on! Do not cry!

mbok₂ (*Jv*) form of address for older Jv woman of humble origin. - *emban* nursemaid.

mbokmas (*Jv*) see MBOK₂.

MCK [*mandi cuci kakus*] public bathing, washing, and toilet facilities.

mébéa bingo k.o. three-wheeled vehicle with motorcycle engine.

mébel furniture. **per-an** the furniture business.

mébelér 1 pertaining to furniture. **2** furniture.

mecicil opened wide (of eyes) out of illness or bad behavior.

medali, médali medal.

médalyon medallion, pendant.

médan 1 field, plain, square. - *gaya* magnetic field. - *jurit* battlefield. - *laga* battlefield. - *maknit* magnetic field. **2** domain, realm. - *makna* semantic field. - *org pandai-pandai* society of learned people. - *ramai* the public.

medang various *Luarinaceae* trees or of trees bearing similar timber.

médé see MÉNTÉ.

média media. - *massa* mass media.

médian median.

médiasi mediation.

médio- mid-. -*Juni.* mid-June.

médis medical.

medit stingy.

méditasi meditation. **-kan** meditate on.

medok₁ speaking with a heavy Jv (esp. West Jv) accent. **me-kan** say s.t. with a heavy accent. **ke-an** heaviness of accent.

medok₂, meduk 1 porous. **2** dirty, filthy. **3** done,

cooked. *Makin - makin énak* The more it's cooked the better it tastes.
MEE [*Masyarakat Ékonomi Éropa*] European Common Market.
méester see MÉSTER.
méga cloud. *- mendung* rain cloud.
mégafon megaphone.
megah 1 glorious. **2** fame, glory. *-nya bertambah* His fame is growing. **3** luxurious, grandiose. **ber-²** glorify o.s. **ber-²an** do s.t. with grandeur. **me-kan 1** brag about. *Dia selalu ~ kekayaannya* He is always bragging about his wealth. **2** exalt s.t. *~ diri* exalt o.s. **ke-an** greatness, glory
mégal-mégol sway the hips provocatively.
mégan k.o. paste made from fruit.
megap-megap gasp for breath.
mégapon see MÉGAFON.
megar see MEKAR.
megat spin (of a top).
megrék /megrék/ **1** continuously sick. **2** emaciated.
Méi May.
méja 1 table. *- abu* (*Ch*) ancestral altar. *- bilyar/bola* billiard table. *- bundar* round table. *- hijau* court. **me-hijaukan** bring a case to court. *- hias* dressing table. *- kedai* shop counter. *- kursi* furniture. *- makan* dining table. *- tarik* table with leaves, extension table. *- tulis* desk, writing table. **2** (*Crd.*) dummy.
mejam turn, spin.
mejan see MEJEN.
méjan see MÉSAN.
mejen dysentery.
mék /mek/ (*Sl.*) term of address to a friend of either sex. *Aduh, - Nggak lulus jadinya!* Man! I did not pass after all.
Mekah Mecca.
mékanik, mékanika (*Phys.*) mechanics.
mékanis mechanical. *Dia bekerja secara -* He works mechanically.
mékanisasi mechanization. **me-kan** mechanize.
mékanisir me- mechanize.
mékanisme mechanism. *- harga* (*Econ.*) price mechanism.
mekankan, mekangkang see KANGKANG₁.
mékap (*Coll.*) makeup.
mekar 1 open up, blossom. *Kembang melati mulai -* The jasmine has started to blossom. **2** rise. *Adonan kué itu -* The cake dough is rising. **ber-an** blossom in quantity. **me-** blossom forth, rise. *Hatinya yg mulai ~ kuncup kembali* He was just beginning to feel good when he went back into a depression. **me-kan 1** make s.t. blossom or rise. *Ragi dipergunakan utk ~ adonan* They use yeast to make the dough rise. **2** spread out. *Saya ~ payung* I opened the umbrella. **ke-an** efflorescence. **pe-an** process of making s.t. blossom out.
mekasi see TERIMA KASIH.
mekis see MENGKIS.
Méksiko Mexico.
mél₁ report, present o.s. *Jangan lupa - kpd majikanmu* Do not forget to report to your boss.

mél₂ illegal highway toll.
melainkan 1 but, but rather. *Bukan hari ini - bésok* Not today, but rather tomorrow. **2** except. *Tdk ada yg tahu - dia* No o. knows but he.
Melaka Malacca.
melak-melak openly, clearly, obviously (when cheating s.o.). *Ia ditipu (dgn) -* They were very obvious about the way they cheated him.
melambang k.o. flat-bottomed boat.
melanding, melandingan k.o. fast-growing tree used for shading other plants, the beans of which are edible and the leaves of which are used as fodder.
melang anxious, restless.
mélankolik, mélankolis melancholic.
melar 1 stretch, expand, rise. *Adonan itu akan -* The dough will rise. *Sang nyonya yg kondénya - macam martabak manis . . .* The lady with her chignon spread out like a thick pancake . . . **2** expansion. **3** elastic.
melarat poor, miserable. **me-kan** impoverish, make poor and miserable. **ke-an** misery, poverty.
melas miserable, inspiring pity. **me-1** live miserably. *Ia ~ di negeri org* He lived a miserable existence in a foreign land. **2** moving o. to pity. *dgn suara ~* with a pitiful voice.
melasa molasses.
melatat-melotot bulge (of the eyes).
melati jasmine.
Melayu 1 Malay, Malayan. *Ia org -* He is a Malay. *lagu -* k.o. pop music. *- Raya* political union of Malaysia, Indonesia, and Brunei proposed by Sukarno in the 1960s. **2** Indonesian and not Caucasian (self-deprecatory). *Dasar -* No wonder! That's all we Indonesians can do! *spion -* bumbling inept spy. **me-kan** translate into Malay.
melék 1 be awake, have o.'s eyes open. *Bayi sdh -* The baby is awake. **2** be aware of the world, educated. *Ia blm -* He is ignorant. *- huruf* be literate. **ke-an** *huruf* literacy. **me-kan** open o.'s eyes to. *Mata luar negeri di-kan* It opened the world's eyes. **-(²)an** stay up till late.
mélek see MÉLK.
melempem 1 soggy, not properly dry and crisp. *Kué itu jangan ditinggalkan di luar, nanti -* Do not leave the cookies out or they will get soggy. **2** lack hardness, grown weak. *Perjuangan kita tdk boléh -* Our struggle must not be allowed to grow weak.
meléng see MELING.
mélér run (of nose).
melését 1 miss the target, be wrong. *Dugaanya tdklah -* He did not guess wrong. **2** depression, slump.
meligi only, purely.
melik greedy. *- pangkat tinggi* mad desire for a high position. **ke-an** greed, craving.
meling 1 careless, sloppy, untidy. **2** look aside, be inattentive. *Jangan - kalau nyopir* Do not look to the side when driving.
melinjo₁ tree (*Gnetum gnemon*) bearing edible leaves and seeds.

melinjo₂ carelessly negligent.
melionér see MILYUNÉR.
melit curious, inquisitive. **ke-an** inquisitiveness. **pe-an** inquiry.
meliwis see BELIBIS.
mélk canned milk.
mélodi melody.
mélodika k.o. wind instrument with keys like a piano.
melongo see LONGO.
melor k.o two-wheeled carriage.
melukut 1 pieces of rice broken off in pounding. **2** s.t. insignificant. *Soal itu bagi saya bagaikan - saja* That problem is no big thing for me.
melulu exclusively, only. *Uang ini - utk uang makanmu* This money is exclusively for your meals.
melur jasmine.
mem- see also entries with **p-** or **m-**.
mémang 1 yes, you are right, it is indeed so. *Énak, kan? -!* It is delicious, isn't it? Yes it is. *Apa - di sini péstanya?* Is this really the place they're having the party? **2** Yes, I concede the point (but . . .). - *tdk jauh, tapi . . .* You are right, it is not far, but . . . **se-nya** should, the proper thing. *~ dia hrs datang dulu ke rumah kita* He should come to see us first. **-nya 1** What is actually going on? What do you actually think? *~ aku ini buta?* Do you think I am blind? *~ kenapa hrs sekarang juga?* Actually, why does it have to be this minute? **2** actually, yes, (but . . .), You are right (I concede) (but . . .). *Blm ada air lédéng ~* Well, you are right, there is no city water yet (but . . .).
memar bruised. **me-kan** bruise.
memb- see also entries with **b-**.
membasir see MUBASIR.
mémblé 1 pout, be sullen. **2** (*Sl.*) ugly, lousy, no good.
mémbran 1 filter in automobile engine. **2** membrane.
memedi (*Jv*) ghost.
mémék ber-(²) **1** whimper, whine. **2** nag.
memf- see also entries with **f-**.
mémoar memoirs.
mémori explanatory statement, memorandum. - *banding* (*Leg.*) brief for an appeal.
mempan 1 be vulnerable. *Pahlawan itu tdk - kena senjata* The hero was invulnerable to weapons. **2** be sensitive to. *Dia - dinasihati* He is sensitive to criticism. **3** be effective. *Dia - benar dlm pekerjaannya* He is very effective in his work.
mempelai bride and/or bridegroom.
mempelajari see AJAR₁.
mempelam mango.
mempelas see AMPLAS₁.
mempeng persevere.
mémper resemble, be similar to. *Kok nggak - ibunya, ya?* She does not resemble her mother, does she? *Embacang - dgn mangga* An *embacang* is similar to a mango.
memplak extremely white.
mempunyai see PUNYA.
men- see also entries with **t-, n-**.

mena, ména (*tdk*) **se-²** arbitrarily, in a high-handed and unfair fashion. *Musuh membom (tdk) ~* The enemy bombed for no reason. *dikuasai roh yg memperlakukannya dgn (tdk) ~* be controlled by a spirit that treats him capriciously.
Ménag [*Menteri Agama*] Minister of Religious Affairs.
Ménagama [*Menteri Agama*] Minister of Religion.
ménak aristocratic, distinguished, prominent.
menang 1 win, come out on top. *Siapa yg - dlm pertandingannya?* Who won the contest? *- révolusi* win the revolution. *- dgn angka* (*Sport*) win on the basis of points. *- mapan* have an advantage over. *- suara* elected. **2** pass an examination. *Dia - ujian* He passed his examination. **me-i** defeat s.o. or s.t. *Perkumpulan A ~ perkumpulan B* Club A defeated Club B. **me-kan 1** pronounce s.o. a winner. **2** win s.t. *PI ~ beberapa kursi di DPR* The Isl. Party won several seats in Parliament. **3** cause to win. **memper-kan 1** help win, cause to win. *Bom atom yg ~ Amérika di perang dunia kedua* It was the atom bomb which helped the US to win the Second World War. **2** win s.t. *Ia ~ médali emas* He won the gold medal. **ke-an** victory. **pe-** winner.
menantu son- or daughter-in-law. **ber-kan** take as son- or daughter-in-law.
menara tower, minaret. - *air* watertower. - *api* lighthouse. - *bor(an)* drilling rig. - *gading* s.t. that is difficult to attain. *Jangan anggap perguruan tinggi sbg - gading* Do not think that a college education is out of your reach. - *peninjau* observation tower. - *radio* radio tower.
ménat see MINAT.
menatu see PENATU.
menc- see also entries with **c-**.
mencak -² 1 be out of sorts. *Mengapa ~?* Why are you out of sorts? **2** move convulsively. *Binatang itu ~ kepanasan* The animal moved convulsively from the heat. **ber-** do the sword dance.
méncang-méncong not in a straight line, contorted. *mulut yg - contorted* mouth.
méncéng slanted, skewed. **ke-an** slant.
méncerét see CERÉT.
mencit mouse.
méncla-ménclé (*Jv*) inconsistent, unreliable.
ménclok (*Jv*) perch (of birds).
méncok see MÉNCLOK.
méncong 1 askew, aslant. **2** without any specific direction or aim. **me-kan** twist askew. *~ bibir* twist the lips. **ke-an 1** declivity. **2** going off in a skewed direction.
méncos (*Jkt*) miss a target, fail, not be in a straight line.
méncrét see CERÉT.
mend- see also entries with **d-**.
mendadak see DADAK.
Méndagri [*Menteri dlm Negeri*] Minister for Internal Affairs.
mendak 1 sink down, bow down. **2** approach bowing.
mendam drunk. **ke-an** drunkenness.

mendap 1 sink, settle. 2 sediment, deposit.

méndé see MÉNTÉ.

mendéra banyan tree.

mendiang the late. - *tuan Ali* the late Mr. Ali.

mendikai small watermelon.

Méndikbud [*Menteri Pendidikan dan Kebudayaan*] Minister of Education and Culture.

mending 1 fairly good, well off, mild (of climate). *Untung jualan - juga* The profit from the sale is fairly good. 2 average, middling. *Keadaan di sini masih -* The situation here is still tolerable. -an 1 fairing well, well off, 2 average, middling. 3 better, preferable.

mendonan immigrant, stranger.

méndréng see MINDERING.

mendung cloudy, overcast. ber- wrapped in clouds. me-i 1 cloud over. 2 cast a cloud over.

mendusin see DUSIN.

mendut k.o. cake made of sticky rice with grated coconut and brown sugar wrapped in banana leaves.

meneer /menér/ term of address to European or westernized men.

ménéjer manager.

meng- see also entries with k-, ng-, or beginning with a vowel.

mengah (ter)-² huff and puff, out of breath.

mengangah 1 have fiery coals. 2 see API.

mengap gape. -² pant, gasp for breath.

mengapa 1 why? - *bung berangkat?* Why are you leaving? 2 doing what? *Sedang -?* What are you doing?

mengecat see CAT₁.

mengenai 1 concerning, about. 2 see KENA.

mengepas see PAS₁.

mengepél see PÉL₂.

mengerti 1 understand. *Saya kurang -* I do not understand. 2 (*Jv*) know. se- as far as o. knows. ~ *saya* as far as I know. di- be understood. ke-an understanding.

mengetahui see TAHU₁.

mengga complete, perfect. se-² the whole, only. se-²nya completely, perfectly.

menggala 1 (*Lit.*) knight. 2 chief indoctrinator.

ménggok make a turn.

mengi, mengih 1 asthma. 2 pant, have difficulty breathing.

mengiang rainbow.

mengkal 1 unripe (of fruit). 2 improperly ripened because of defect. 3 annoyed, irritated. *Hatinya - sekali* He is very much annoyed. ber-hati be irritated, annoyed. me-kan annoy, irritate. ~ *hati* annoying, irritating. ke-an irritation, annoyance.

mengkali (*Jkt*) see BARANGKALI.

mengkara see MAKARA.

Mengkasar see MAKASAR.

mengkelan ter- get s.t. stuck in the throat.

mengkeret 1 shrink. *Ssdh dicuci bajunya -* After washing the dress shrank. 2 angry. *Jangan -, bung* Do not be angry, my friend. 3 afraid, scared. *Pencuri itu - sekali melihat polisi* The thief

became very afraid when he saw the policeman. 4 double up with pain. *Ia - kesakitan* She doubled up in pain. me-kan make s.t. shrink.

mengkerut me-kan shrink s.t. *Di-kan peranannya* Its role was given less importance.

mengkilap see KILAP₁.

mengkilat see KILAT.

mengking shake with fright.

mengkirik make o.'s flesh creep, shiver.

mengkis 1 challenge. 2 scorn, taunt.

méngkol-péngkol crooked, winding.

mengkuang see BANGKUANG.

mengkudu see BENGKUDU.

mengot crooked, curved.

méngsol 1 askew, aslant. 2 crazy.

mengung see MENUNG.

Ménhankam [*Menteri Pertahanan dan Keamanan*] Minister of Defense and Security.

Ménhub [*Menteri Perhubungan*] Minister of Communication.

méni orange paint used as antirust primer.

menir₁ finely ground grains of rice.

menir₂ see MENEER.

meniran (*Jv, Jkt*) tired from speaking (of the lips).

menit minute.

menj- see also entries with j-.

menjak see SEMENJAK.

menjangan (*Jv, Lit.*) deer.

Ménkéh [*Menteri Kehakiman*] Minister of Justice.

Ménkes [*Menteri Keséhatan*] Minister of Public Health.

Ménkesra [*Menteri Kesejahteraan Rakyat*] Minister of Public Welfare.

Ménkeu /Ménke'u/ [*Menteri Keuangan*] Minister of Finance.

Ménko [*Menteri Koordinator*] Coordinating Minister.

Ménkop [*Menteri Koperasi*] Minister of Cooperatives.

Ménlu [*Menteri Luar Negeri*] Minister of Foreign Affairs.

Ménmud [*Menteri Muda*] Undersecretary. - *Pora* [*Menteri Muda Urusan Pemuda dan Olahraga*] Undersecretary for Youth and Sports.

ménor garish, gaudy in dress or makeup.

Ménpan [*Menteri Negara Penertiban Aparatur Negara*] State Minister for Control of Machinery of the State.

Ménpen [*Menteri Penerangan*] Minister of Information.

Ménpera [*Menteri Negara Urusan Perumahan Rakyat*] State Minister of Public Housing.

Ménperdag [*Menteri Perdagangan*] Minister of Trade.

Ménperhub see MÉNHUB.

Ménpora [*Menteri Negara Pemuda dan Olah Raga*] State Minister of Youth and Sports.

Mén PPLH [*Menteri Negara Pembinaaan dan Pelestarian Lingkungan Hidup*] State Minister of Environmental Affairs.

Ménristék [*Menteri Negara Riset dan Téknologi*] State Minister of Research and Technology.

méns (*Coll.*) menstruation, menstruate.

Ménséknég, Ménsésnég [*Menteri Sékretaris Negara*] Secretary of State.

mensiang k.o. rush.

Ménsos [*Menteri Sosial*] Minister for Social Affairs.

ménstruasi menstruation.

ment- see also entries with **t-**.

mentah 1 unripe, raw, uncooked. *Buah - itu asam* The unripe fruit is sour. **2** incomplete, unfinished. *Sekolahnya masih -* He has not finished school yet. *jadi -* go back to the drawing board, consider undone. **3** raw, unrefined. *minyak -* crude oil. **-² 1** raw, uncooked. *Jangan makan sayuran itu ~* Do not eat the vegetables raw. *air ~* unboiled water. **2** without being thought through, unconditionally. *menolak ~* refuse categorically. *Semua nasihat itu ditelannya ~* She accepts all the advice unconditionally. **me-kan** *kembali* go back to the drawing board, do all over again. *Sastera ini hrs di-kan kembali* This writing has to be redone from the start. **ke-an** rawness, unripeness.

mentak (*Jkt*) probable. **ke-an** probability.

mental 1 bounce off, rebound. *Bola itu - jauh sekali* The ball bounced very far away. **2** be launched (of a vessel). **3** uninjured.

méntal way of thinking. *Dgn - lama tdk mungkin* It is impossible to accomplish anything with the old way of thinking. *- nyonték* having the attitude that o. must cheat.

méntalisme mentalism.

méntalitas, méntalitét mentality.

Méntan [*Menteri Pertanian*] Minister of Agriculture.

mentang - *pun* although. **(se)-², -kan** just because. *~ org kaya, dia berbuat semaunya saja* Just because he is rich he thinks he can do as he likes.

mentari see MATAHARI.

ménté cashew. *kacang -* cashew nut.

mentéga 1 butter. **2** margarine. *- buatan/tiruan* margarine. **me-i 1** smear with butter. *Si Mina ~ roti* Mina butters her bread. **2** butter up, flatter. *Spy dia naik pangkat, pegawai itu selalu ~ majikannya* That employee is always buttering up his boss in order to get a promotion.

menték k.o. plant disease.

Ménténg elite section of Jkt. *babu -* maid that has lots of demands and puts on airs. **-²an** in the mode of s.o. or s.t. from this area.

mentera see MANTERA.

mentéréng 1 dressed up. *- begini, mau kemana?* Where are you going, dressed up like this? **2** luxurious, magnificent. *Rumah menteri itu -* The minister's house is magnificent. **ke-an** luxury, magnificence.

menteri 1 cabinet minister. *- Angkatan Laut* Secretary of the Navy. *- Dlm Negeri* Secretary of the Interior. *- guru* headmaster. *- Luar Negeri* Secretary of State, Minister of Foreign Affairs. *- muda* vice-minister, deputy secretary. *- Negara* Minister of State. *- Urusan Agama* Minister of Religious Affairs. **2** (*Che.*) bishop. **ke-an** ministry,

department. *~ Luar Negeri* Department of State, Ministry of Foreign Affairs.

mentimun cucumber.

mentok (*Jv*) breast of chicken.

méntok (*Jv*) duck.

méntol menthol.

mentua see MERTUA.

mentul-mentul springy. *tempat tidur yg -* bed that is nice and bouncy.

menu 1 diet, what o. eats at a certain meal. *-nya kaya vitamin* His meals are rich in vitamins. **2** what is served at a party. *-nya méwah di pésta tadi* She served fancy food at the party.

menung musing, pondering. **ber- 1** muse, ponder, meditate. *Mengapa ~ saja?* Why are you deep in thought all the time? **2** act gloomy. **me-kan** ponder s.t. deeply. *~ apa lagi engkau sekarang?* What are you pondering about now? **ter-(²)** muse, be lost in thought. *Dia ~ memikirkan penyakit ibunya* He is lost in thought, pondering his mother's illness. **ke-an** meditation. **-an** musing. **pe-** dreamer, ponderer. **per-an** contemplation, musing.

Ménwa [*Résimén Mahasiswa*] students with military training.

meny- see also entries with **s-, n-, c-**.

menyan see KEMENYAN.

menyesal see SESAL.

menyolok see COLOK₂. → **menyolok** see COLOK$_2$.

méong 1 sound made by a cat, meow. **2** cat.

mépét see PÉPÉT.

mérah red. *- bata* brick-red. *- bungsu/bungur* purple. *- dadu* pink. *- darah* blood-red. *- hati* wine-colored. *- jambu* pink. *- lembayung* crimson. *- merang* reddish brown. *- muda* **1** pink. **2** blushing. *- padam* bright red. *- pijar* red hot. *- putih biru* the Red, White, and Blue (Dutch flag). *sang - putih* the Red and the White (Indonesian flag). *- saga/tedas* bright red. *- telur* egg yolk. *- tembaga* copper red. *- tua* dark red. **me-** redden, become red. *Bunga itu ~ sekarang* The flowers are turning red now. **me-kan** make red. *Di-kannya bibirnya sblm berangkat* She put red lipstick on before she left. **ke-²an** reddish. **pe-** reddening agent. *~ bibir* lipstick. *~ pipi* rouge.

merak peacock. *- hati* affable.

meram see MEREM.

merana 1 be miserable and poor. **2** be miserable and lonely. *Hidupnya -* He lived a miserable life (He was poor or He was lonely).

merang rice straw (of paddy).

meranti k.o. timber tree.

mérat see MAIRAT.

merata see RATA.

merawal 1 banner. **2** (*Mil.*) the colors.

merawan k.o. tree good for house parts (*Hopea sp*).

merbah k.o. bird.

merbau k.o. timber tree.

merbuk k.o. turtledove.

mercak-mercik sound of water lapping against the shore.

mercapada see MARCAPADA.

mercon see MERCUN.
mercu 1 top point, summit, crow's nest. - *api* lighthouse. - *gunung* mountain peak. - *suar* lighthouse. 2 tree top.
mercun fireworks. - *bumbung* bamboo cannon using carbide.
mércy /mérsi/ Mercedes-Benz (esp. as a symbol of opulence).
merdéka free, independent, liberated. *Indonésia -* free Indonesia. - *ayam bébas* completely free, free as a bird. **me-kan** 1 liberate, release, set free. 2 acquit, exonerate, absolve. *Penjahat-penjahat perang sdh di-kan* The war criminals were set free. **ke-an** freedom, liberty, independence. **pe-** liberator. **pe-an** liberation, emancipation.
merdésa 1 good, beautiful, decent. *Dia mempunyai watak yg -* He possesses a good character. 2 choosy, fussy. *Dia makan tdk -* He is not fussy about food.
merdu melodious, sweet, clear of voice. *Suara gadis itu -* The girl's voice is sweet. **me-** sound sweet. **ke-an** sweetness of voice.
mére /mér/ (*Rel.*) title for sisters of certain Catholic orders. - *diréktris/kepala* Mother Superior.
mérek see MÉRK.
meréka they, them, their. - *suka minum kopi* They like to drink coffee. *Saya melihat -* I see them. *Ia suka oto -* He likes their car.
merem with closed eyes. **me-kan** close. *Ssdh beberapa jam baru dia bisa ~ matanya* Only after several hours could he close his eyes.
méréng see MIRING.
mérés even, level.
merger /merjer/ (*Fin.*) merger.
meriah merry, gay. **me-kan** make s.t. merry. *di-kan oléh minuman keras* was made lively with liquor.
meriam cannon, artillery piece. - *buluh* long, smooth, and cylindrical cannon. - *penangkis* anti-aircraft cannon. - *penémbak cepat* rapid-fire cannon. - *sundut* ancient type of cannon. **me-i** shell a place.
meriang see RIANG.
merica pepper, esp. white pepper. - *bubuk* ground pepper. - *bulat* peppercorns.
merih throat, windpipe.
mérikan (*Sl.*) American.
meringis grin, show o.'s teeth.
merjan red coral beads for making necklaces.
mérjer (*Fin.*) merger.
mérk 1 brand, make. *Otonya - apa?* What is the make of his car? 2 trade-mark, label. *-nya ada di bagian belakang* The stamp is on the back. 3 quality. 4 signboard. **ber-** 1 have a trademark. *Mainan ini ~ Jepang* This toy has a Japanese trademark. 2 have a sign on it.
merkah-merkah *sarat* (*Naut.*) draft marks.
mérkurokrom Mercurochrome.
merongos see MRONGOS.
merosot see ROSOT.
merpati pigeon, dove. - *jambul* the crested dove. - *mahkota* crown pigeon. - *perdamaian* the dove of peace. - *pos* carrier pigeon.

mersik 1 shrill. *Suara burung itu -* The bird's voice is shrill. 2 crisp and dry. *Krupuk itu -* The shrimp chips are crisp. *selembar daun -* a dry leaf. 3 skinny, lean. *Anak itu kurus -* That child is skinny.
merta see SERTA.
mertamu (*Jv*) pay a visit.
mertéga see MENTÉGA.
mertua parent-in-law. **ber-** have s.o. as a father- or mother-in-law.
méru 1 pagoda of Hindu temple. 2 rice heaped into a mountain shape.
meruah see MARWAH.
meruap 1 steam. 2 bubble up.
merunggai k.o. small tree the leaves of which are eaten as a vegetable (*Moringa sp*).
merutu k.o. small mosquito.
més residence belonging to a concern or gvt. for housing its employees.
mesakat greedy.
mésan tombstone, grave marker.
mésem (*Jv, Jkt*) smile.
mesera see MESRA.
méses chocolate sprinkles (on cookies, etc.).
mesigit see MESJID.
mesin machine, engine. - *bakar* combustion engine. - *bantu* auxiliary engine, motor. - *bicara* phonograph. - *bor* drill. - *bubut* lathe. - *cétak* printing press. - *cuci (pakaian)* washing machine. - *dérék* derrick. - *jahit* sewing machine. - *giling* rolling machine. - *hitung* 1 calculating machine. 2 computer. - *ketik* typewriter. - *las* welding apparatus. - *ngomong nyanyi* phonograph. - *pemecah batu* stone crusher. - *penetas/pengeram* incubator. - *perekam* tape recorder. - *tenaga* power machine. - *terbang* airplane. - *tik/tulis* typewriter. - *tunu* combustion engine. **ber-** motorized. **per-an** having to do with machines. *industri ~* machine industry.
Mesir Egypt.
mesiu ammunition.
mesjid mosque. - *Alharam* principal mosque in Mecca. - *Alaqsa* principal mosque in Jerusalem. - *jami(k)* large mosque used for Friday prayers.
meski, meskipun although, in spite of (the fact that). - *susah, dpt juga* Although it was difficult, he succeeded anyhow. - *begitu* nevertheless.
mesra 1 very close so as to become fused. 2 intimate, very close. *Dia sahabat -* He is a very intimate friend. **ber-** entirely mixed. *Gula itu sdh ~ dgn air* The sugar is dissolved in water. **ber-an** be very close, intimate with e.o. **me-kan** assimilate, fuse. *Meréka ~ naséhatnya* They absorbed his advice entirely. **ke-an** 1 absorption. 2 love, feeling of being intimate. **-²an** in an intimate way.
méss see MÉS.
méster 1 lawyer, jurist. 2 title of those holding a Dutch or Indonesian law degree. 3 teacher.
Méstér Jatinegara, a neighborhood of Jkt.
mesti 1 certain, surely. *Kalau belajar keras, dia - lulus* If he studies hard, he will surely pass. *tdk ~* not certain. 2 must, have to. *Saya - berangkat hari ini juga* I must leave this very day. **se-nya** should have been. *~ selesai hari ini* It should have been

finished today . **me-kan 1** compel, require. *Tiap org di-kan belajar membaca* Everyone is required to learn to read. **2** regard as certain. **ke-an** a must, necessity, obligation.

mestika magic jewel, precious stone. *- hati* sweetheart.

méstis mestizo.

mesum 1 dirty, filthy, polluted. *Pakaiannya tlh* - His clothes are dirty. **2** improper, indecent. *Isi bacaan itu* - The content of the reading is indecent. **3** immoral. *perbuatan* - an immoral act. **ke-an** dirt, indecency, obscenity. **per-an** filthy acts.

meta mad, drunk, in a rage.

métabolisme metabolism.

métafisik metaphysical.

métafisika metaphysics.

métafor, métafora metaphor.

metah see PUTIH.

metal (*Auto.*) bushing.

métalik metallic.

métan, métana methane.

metari see MATAHARI.

métatésis metathesis.

mété see MÉNTÉ.

météorologi meteorology.

méter meter. **-an 1** meter. ~ *air* water meter. ~ *gas* gas meter. **2** by the meter. **3** tape measure. **4** having a meter. *taksi* ~ a taxi with a meter.

meterai, méterai stamp, seal to indicate payment, revenue stamps. *- surat* postage stamp. *- témpél* seal on receipts, checks, etc. *- upah* tax seal or stamp. **ber-** have a seal affixed. **me-(kan)** stamp, put a seal on. **ter-** stamped, sealed. ~ *di dlm hati* sealed in his heart.

méti (*Amb*) low tide.

métoda, métode method. *- kasus* case study method.

métodik methodology.

métodis methodical.

métodologi methodology.

métonimia metonymy.

métrik metric. *ukuran* - metrical scale.

métrika metrics.

métrologi metrology.

métro mini medium-sized city bus.

métropolisasi see MÉTROPOLITANISASI.

métropolitan metropolitan.

métropolitanisasi make s.t. into an urban area.

métrum poetic meter.

meubel see MÉBEL.

mevrouw /mefro/ (*Coll.*) term of address or title for Western or westernized women.

méwah luxurious, extravagant. *jamuan* - an extravagant dinner. *pertumbuhan* - luxuriant growth. **ke-an** luxury, extravagance.

méwék 1 start to cry. **2** torn open.

mezbah see MAZBAH.

mh. [*marah*] (*M*) a title for male nobility.

Mhd. [*Muhammad*]

mhs. [*mahasiswa*] university student.

mi₁ noodles. *- bakso* noodles with meatballs.

mi₂ see MAMI.

miak peeping of chickens.

miang 1 small plant hairs. **2** traitor, slanderer. **se-1** a bit. *Ia tdk takut barang* ~ *juga* He was not a bit afraid. **2** a grain, a drop of s.t.

miara see PELIHARA.

MIB [*Maluku Irian Barat*] Moluccas and Western New Guinea.

midar walk.

midik me- scrutinize.

midodaréni (*Jv*) celebration on the eve before a wedding.

mie see MI₁.

migas [*minyak dan gas bumi*] oil and natural gas.

migran migrant.

migrasi migration. **ber-** migrate.

mihrab niche or chamber in a mosque indicating the direction of Mecca.

mihun 1 thin rice noodles. **2** dish containing dried noodles with bits of vegetables. *- kuah* soup with these noodles.

mijn man /mén man/ (*Coll.*) my husband.

mijn vrouw /mén fro/ (*Coll.*) my wife.

mik /mik/ microphone.

mika mica.

mikin see MAKIN.

mikrab /mi'rab/ see MIHRAB.

mikrad, mikraj /mi'rad/ (*Isl.*) celebration commemorating Muh.'s ascent to Heaven.

mikro micro.

mikroba, mikrobe microbe.

mikrobiologi /mikrobiolokhi, mikrobiologi/ microbiology.

mikrobis, mikrobus medium-sized bus.

mikrofis microfiche.

mikrofon see MIKROPON.

mikrolét k.o. minibus or jitney.

mikron micron.

mikropon microphone.

mikroskop microscope.

mikroskopis microscopic.

mil mile. *- laut* nautical mile.

milénium millennium.

mili millimeter.

miligram milligram.

milik 1 property, possession. *Ini - siapa?* Whose property is this? *- pribadi* private property. *- teralihkan* alienable possession. **2** fate. *Mémang sdh - saya* It is just my fate. **me-i** possess. *Tiada seorgpun* ~ *tanah ini* No o. owns this land. **ke-an 1** property. **2** (*Jv*) greedy for material wealth. **pe-** owner, proprietor. **pe-an** ownership, possession. **kepe-an** ownership.

milimèter millimeter.

milionér see MILYUNÉR.

milir 1 go down to the sea. **2** go down to the city from the outskirts.

milisi 1 militia. **2** military man. **3** military service. **me-kan** draft into the service.

militan militant (as in political movement). **ke-an** militant.

militansi militancy.

militér 1 soldier. **2** military. **ke-an** military. **ke-²an**

affecting a soldierlike stance, trying to be militant in character.

militérisasi militarization. **me-kan** militarize.

militérisme militarism.

militéristis militaristic.

miliun see MILYUN.

milo see MULO.

milukut see MELUKUT.

milyar billion. **-an** by the billions.

milyardér billionaire.

milyun million. **-an** millions.

milyunér millionaire.

mimbar pulpit, speaker's platform, rostrum. - *pembaca* letter to the editor column.

mimi male horseshoe crab. *spt - dan mintuna* unseparable (of married couple), like the male and female horseshoe crab, often found together.

mimik₁ (*child language, Jv*) drink.

mimik₂ facial expression.

mimik₃ mimicry.

mimis round pellet for rifles, beebee.

mimisan suffer from nosebleed.

mimpi dream. - *buruk* nightmare. **ber-** dream. *Bagai ~ di siang hari* It was like a bad dream (lit., like dreaming in the day). **me-kan** dream of, dream about. *~ sesuatu ada artinya* Dreaming about s.t. has significance. *Jangan kau-kan yg bukan-bukan* Do not dream about the impossible. **ter-(2)** dream continually about s.t. *Sebab ingin sekali pergi dia ~* Because he wants to go very much, he dreams about it constantly. **-an** dream, ideal, illusion. *~ keinginan* wishful thinking. **pe-1** dreamer. **2** escapist.

min (*Math.*) minus. *a - b* a minus b.

mina Pisces.

minal'aidin walfaizin congratulations expressed at the end of the fasting month.

Minang of the Minangkabau ethnic group.

minat interest, proclivity. *Ia menaruh - pd musik* He is interested in music. *Dia mempunyai - thd ilmu kimia* He is interested in chemistry. **ber-** have an interest. *Dia tdk ~ lagi utk mengarang* He no longer has any interest in writing. **me-i** be devotee of, be interested in. *Dia ~ politik luar negeri* He is interested in foreign policy. **pe-** devotee, interested person.

minder feel inferior.

mindering sell merchandise on the installment plan traveling through villages. **-an** merchandise bought and sold on this basis.

mindo eat breakfast leftovers with rice at noon.

mindring see MINDERING.

minérologi mineralogy.

mineur /minir/ **1** snide remark. **2** minor key. **3** melancholy (of atmosphere).

minggat (*Jv*) **1** flee, run away. **2** Get out of here!

minggir see PINGGIR.

minggu 1 week. **2** Sunday. **3** go out for a Sunday picnic or walk. **ber-2** for weeks at a time. **-an** weekly. *Majalah itu ~ atau bulanan?* Does that magazine appear once a week or once a month? *dua ~* bi-weekly. **se-an** once weekly.

mingkin -an/se- all the more. *Anak-anaknya jadi ~ kurang ajar* Her children were getting to be more and more outrageous in behavior.

mingser shift, change position. *Sebentar - ke kanan, sebentar lagi - ke kiri* o. moment shifting to the right, the next shifting to the left.

miniatur miniature. **me-kan** make s.t. small.

minicar /minikar/ k.o three-wheeled motorized taxi.

minikata k.o. play using few words.

minim minimum.

minimal minimal. **me-kan** minimize.

minimalisir minimize. **me-** minimize.

minimum minimum. **me-kan** minimize.

minit see MENIT.

minoritas, minoritét minority.

minta 1 ask, request, beg. **2** please. - *air, pak* Please get me a glass of water. - *disambung dgn Pak Ali* Please connect me with Mr. Ali. - *ampun* beg forgiveness. - *banding* appeal to a higher court. - *belét* ask for a letter of appointment. - *berhenti* tender o.'s resignation. - *cerai* file for divorce (of women). - *diri* ask to be excused to leave. - *doa* pray. - *hati* ask for attention, favor. - *jalan* request permission to pass. - *lihat* Let me see it. - *maaf* ask for pardon. - *musyawarat* request consultation. - *nyawa* beg for mercy, beg to be spared. - *pisah* file for divorce (of women). - *sambung* ask to be connected with (by telephone). - *tabik* say goodbye, take leave. - *terima kasih* thank. **3** ask for trouble. *Ia - dilawan* He is asking for a fight. **-2 1** (*Jkt*) I hope. *~ aja kita nggak terlambat nanti* I just hope we're not late. **2** beg for alms. **ber-2** beg for alms. **me- 1** require, demand. *Hal itu ~ perhatian sepenuhnya* The matter requires full attention. **2** request, ask. **3** propose to. *Gadis itu sdh beberapa kali di-* The girl was proposed to several times. **4** claim. *Kejadian itu ~ korban* The incident claimed some victims. **me-2** beg for s.t. **me-i** request from s.o. *Ia di-i tolong* He was asked for help. **me-kan** ask for on behalf of s.o. *Ia ~ adiknya baju baru* He asked for a new jacket for his younger brother. **pe-2** begger. **per-an 1** request. **2** demand. *~ akan dolar Amérika* the demand for American dollars.

mintak (*Coll.*) see MINTA.

mintakat zone, area.

mintaku'lburuj zodiac.

mintal see PINTAL.

mintang see SILANG.

minterad municipal council. *kuli -* workers employed by the city.

mintuna 1 female horseshoe crab. **2** (*Zod.*) Gemini.

minum 1 drink, absorb. *Dia suka - kopi* He likes to drink coffee. *sambil menyelam - air* kill two birds with o. stone. **2** take in (air, smoke). - *hawa* take in fresh air. - *madat* smoke opium. - *obat* take medicine. - *rokok* smoke. **me-** drink s.t. **me-i 1** drink from s.t. **2** drink part of s.t. **me-kan 1** give to drink. *Ibu ~ susu pd bayi* Mother gives the baby milk to drink. **2** water, drench (animals). **ter- 1** drunk accidentally. *Awas! Jangan sampai air di gelas kotor itu* ~ Be careful not to drink the water in that dirty glass. **2** potable, drinkable. **-an 1** a drink. **2** beverage. ~ *keras* alcoholic drink. **pe-** drinker. **pe-an** action of drinking.

minus 1 poor, lacking in economic potential. *daérah* - backward, unproductive region. **2** (*Math.*) minus. **ke-an** unproductiveness.

minyak oil, grease, fat. - *angin* medicinal oil sniffed or rubbed on various places of the head and neck to relieve headaches, nausea, etc. - *atar* perfume. - *babi* lard. - *bakar* fuel oil. - *bumi* petroleum. - *cat* linseed oil. - *gas* kerosene. - *gandapura* k.o. herbal rubbing oil. - *goréng* cooking oil. - *ikan* cod-liver oil. - *jarak* castor oil. - *jelantah* oil left in frying pan. - *kacang* peanut oil. - *kelapa* coconut oil. - *ladan* k.o. fuel made from damar resin. - *lincir/lumas* lubricating oil. - *majemuk* mixture of oils, perfumes. - *mentah* crude oil. - *nyaman* **1** perfumed hair oil. **2** k.o. rubbing oil. - *pelumas* lubricating oil. - *penat* ointment. - *rengas* varnish. - *samin* k.o. cooking oil. - *sapi* suet, beef fat. - *sawit* palm oil. - *semir* lubricating oil. - *serai* citronella. - *suci* chrism. - *tanah* **1** petroleum. **2** kerosene. - *wangi* perfume. **ber-** have oil, be greasy. *Dia pandai* ~ *air* She is very good at making ends meet. **me-i** oil, grease. *Dia* ~ *otonya* He greased his car. **per-an** petroleum or refinery affairs.

minyawak see BIAWAK.

mirah ruby.

mi'raj see MIKRAD.

miring 1 at an angle, aslant, sideways. *Gambar itu* - The painting hangs at an angle. **2** oblique. *cétak, huruf* - italics. **3** crazy. *Sdh - otaknya* She has become somewhat crazy. **me-** become slanted. **me-kan** put at an angle, make aslant. *Ia* ~ *kepalanya* He tilted his head. **ke-an** declivity, slope.

mirip resemble. *Ia - bapaknya* He resembles his father. **ber-an** resemble o. another. **ke-an** resemblance. **-²an** fake or vague resemblance. *Topi itu* ~ *topi saya* That hat resembles mine.

mirjan see MERJAN.

miru (*Jv*) pleat a sarong.

mis. [*misalnya*] for example.

misa (*Rel.*) Mass. - *Agung/Besar* High Mass.

misai mustache. **ber-** have a mustache.

misal example, instance. **-nya** for example. **se-** be like. *Perbuatan anak itu* ~ *org déwasa saja* The behavior of that child is just like an adult's. **me-kan 1** represent, be an example of. *Gambar itu* ~ *apa?* What does that picture represent? **2** assume. *Kita -kan dalil ini benar* We assume that this theory is correct. **3** take as an example. *Anak itu* ~ *kawannya* The child takes his friend as an example. **(di)-kan** for example, let us say . . ., supposing that. **pe-an 1** assumption, premise. **2** taking an example.

misan (*Jkt, Jv*) first cousin.

misbah lamp, light, lantern.

misbar [*grimis bubar*] (*Sl.*) open-air cinema that lets out when it starts to drizzle.

misi₁ 1 (Catholic) mission. **2** mission. - *perdagangan* trade mission.

misi₂ see MISSI.

misih see MASIH₁.

misiologi study of missionizing activities.

misionaris missionary.

miskalkulasi miscalculation.

miskam, miskamp miscarriage.

miskin poor, needy, destitute. - *pupa* very poor. -² very poor. **me-kan** impoverish. *Pajak yg tinggi* ~ *penduduk* High taxes impoverish the population. **ke-an** poverty, destitution. *garis* ~ poverty line. **pe-an** pauperization.

miskram, miskran see MISKAM.

misluk, mislukt be botched, failed.

mismis (*Jkt*) **1** avaricious. **2** overly meticulous.

misoa small rice and egg noodles.

misro k.o. cake made of fried cassava filled with brown sugar.

missa see MISA.

missi ideological role. - *negara* the nation's mission (in history, etc.).

mistar 1 ruler, line. - *hitung* slide rule. **2** crossbar at goal.

mistér 1 term of address or reference for a Caucasian male. **2** (*Coll.*) term of address for male and female Caucasians.

mistéri mysterious.

mistérius mysterious. *penémbakan* - mystery shootings.

misti see MESTI.

mistik 1 mystical. *aliran* - mystical movement (in religion). **2** o. of a pair of numbers which go together as determined by a lottery in gambling. *Dua -nya lima* The number which turns out to go with two is five. **me-** figure out which numbers are going to end up going together. **ke-²an** having to do with mysticallike matters.

mistikus mystic.

mistis mystical.

mistisi mystics.

mistisisme mysticism.

misuh see PISUH.

mité myth.

mitologi mythology.

mitologis mythological.

mitoni (*Jv*) ceremony and feast given for a woman seven months pregnant with her first baby.

mitos myth. **me-kan** make into a myth.

mitra₁ (*Lit.*) friend. *lingkar - budaya* circle of culture lovers. - *usaha* business partner.

mitra₂ miter.

mitraliur, mitralyur machine gun.

mitsal see MISAL.

Mizan (*Zod.*) Libra.

ml- see also entries with **mel-, l-.**

Mobbrig see MOBRIG.

mobil car, automobile. - *dérék* towing truck. - *dinas* office car. - *baja* armored car. - *gerobak* truck. - *kerangkéng* truck for transporting prisoners or animals. **ber-** go by car. **ber-²an** go around in a car. **per-an** having to do with automobiles.

mobilér see MÉBELÉR.

mobilét moped or motorbike.

mobilisasi mobilization. **me-(kan)** mobilize.

mobilisir me- mobilize.

mobilitas, mobilitét mobility.

moblong (*Jkt*) loose, baggy.

Mobrlg [*Mobil Drigade*] paramilitary branch of national police in the Sukarno era.

mocok fill in for a person who is absent. *Blm didapatnya pekerjaan yg tetap. Cuma sekali-sekali ia berhasil -* He has not gotten regular work. He is only able to fill in once in a while.

mocopat see MACAPAT.

modal financial capital. - *(be)kerja* working capital. - *dan poténsi/tenaga* funds and forces. - *dengkul* without any capital or anything of value other than o.'s own will and energy. - *penyertaan* equity capital. - *tetap* real estate. **se-** enter into a partnership. *Dia org ~* He is a partner in the firm. **ber-** have capital. **ber-kan** have s.t. as capital. *~ keberanian* have boldness as (o.'s only) capital. **me-i** finance. *Perusahaan itu di-i pemerintah* The enterprise is financed by the gvt. **ke-an** capitalistic. *Perkumpulan itu bersifat ~* That association has a capitalistic character. **pe-** capitalist. **per-an** capitalization, provision of capital for s.t. *lemahnya ~ petani* the weakness of the peasants in getting access to capital.

modalitas modality.

modalwan capitalist, financier.

modar (*Vulg., Jv*) die.

mode fashion (of clothes).

modél 1 model. **2** the fashion. *Kalung ini - sekarang* This necklace is the fashion now. **3** (*Coll.*) dressed up fancy.

moderat moderate.

moderator moderator in a panel, etc. **me-i** act as moderator for s.t.

modéren see MODÉRN.

modérn modern. **me-kan, memper-** modernize. **ke-an** modernity. **pe-an** modernization.

modérnisasi modernization. **me-(kan)** modernize.

modérnisir me- modernize.

moderok (*Jkt*) **1** mushy (of fruit). **2** damaged, spoiled.

modifikasi modification. **me-(kan)** modify.

modin 1 o. who calls to prayers, muezzin. **2** village religious functionary, esp. o. who officiates at circumcisions.

modis stylish.

modiste dress maker, designer.

modol₁ (*Jkt*) kill.

modol₂ (*Jv, Jkt*) disheveled, untidy.

modul module.

modulasi (*Ling., Phys.*) modulation.

module see MODUL.

modulir me- (*Phys.*) modulate.

modus 1 modus. **2** (*Ling.*) mood.

moga initiative. **-²** May so-and-so happen, I hope that. *~ cita-citanya berhasil* May his ideals be fulfilled. **se-** May it happen, I hope that. *~ suksés* I wish you success.

mogok 1 strike. *Pekerja-pekerja pabrik itu -* The workers of that factory are on strike. *Meréka - pabrik itu* They struck against the factory. - *duduk* sit-down strike. - *makan* hunger strike. **2** stall, fail, break down. *Otonya - di jalan* His car stalled on the road. - *ginjal* kidney failure. **ke-an** stoppage. **pe-** striker. **pe-an** strike.

mogol drop out of school.

moh see EMOH.

Moh. [*Muhammad*]

mohon 1 ask, request. *Dia - izin kpd majikan* He asked permission of the boss. - *diri* take leave. **2** implore, beseech. - *maaf* ask forgiveness. **ber-** beg, plead. *~ diri* take leave. **me-** request, plead for. *~ pekerjaan* ask for work. **me-kan 1** plead for s.t. **2** plead on behalf of. **3** beg from. **pe-1** applicant. **2** supplicant, petitioner. **per-an 1** request, appeal, petition. **2** application. *~ visa* application for a visa.

mohor seal, signet.

mojah 1 socks. **2** stockings.

mojang (*Sd*) young girl.

mok (*Coll.*) mug.

moka mocha.

mokal see MUHAL.

mokhal see MUHAL.

moksa redemption (in Hinduism and Buddhism).

moksai₁ (*Ch*) Pekinese dog.

moksai₂ (*Ch*) a kung fu movement.

molék pretty, cute. *Gadis itu - betul* That girl is very beautiful. **memper-** make more beautiful. **ke-an** loveliness, beauty.

molekul molecule.

molekulér molecular.

molen cement mixer.

molér (*Jkt, Sl.*) prostitute.

molig /molekh/ plump and full (of body). **ke-an** plumpness.

mo limo the five sins in Jv religion: *maling, madat, madon, main, minum.* stealing, opium smoking, womanizing, gambling, drinking. - *madat* take dope.

molor 1 become longer and longer in time or space. **2** laze around. **3** (*Jkt*) sleep. *Sang suami tega banget disuruh - di garasi* The husband put up with being made to sleep in the garage.

molos 1 penetrate. **2** go away without paying.

momén₁ monument.

momén₂ 1 temporary police roadblock or speed trap. **2** check motorists in temporary roadblock.

momén₃ torque. - *gerak/kakas* torque.

momok 1 ghost, spook, specter. **2** haunting danger. - *inflasi* the specter of inflation. **me-i** haunt. **me-kan** make s.t. seem like a danger hanging over o.

momong take care of a baby. **me-** take care of a baby. **-an** child taken care of.

momot (*Jv*) carry (a load, passengers).

Monas [*Monumén Nasional*] the obelisklike national monument in the center of *Lapangan Merdeka* in Jkt.

moncong 1 snout, muzzle. **2** spout. **me-** protrude. *Mulutnya ~ ke depan* His jaw stuck out. **me-kan** make s.t. protrude.

moncor 1 flow out. *Minyak - dr kaléng* The oil flows out of the can. **2** diarrhea.

mondar see MUNDAR-MANDIR.

mondial on a worldwide scale.

mondok₁ fat, squat.

mondok₂ see PONDOK.

monetér monetary.

mong sound of a gong. **-², -²an** k.o. small gong.

monggol knotted, gnarled.

mongkok 1 stick out. *Batu besar - di permukaan air* A big stone protruded out of the water. **2** tower above. *Dia - di antara kawan-kawannya* He towers above his friends. **3** proud. **me-kan 1** make s.t. stick out. **2** make o. proud. *~ hati* make o. proud.

monitor me- monitor s.t.

monoftong monophthong.

monoftongisasi monophthongization.

monogami monogamy.

monografi monograph.

monogram monogram.

monoksida monoxide.

monolitik, monolitis monolithic.

monolog monologue.

monoloyalitas loyalty to only o. thing.

monopoli monopoly. **me-** have a monopoly, monopolize. **pe-an** monopolizing.

monopolisir me- monopolize.

monoril monorail.

monosilabis monosyllabic.

monoton monotonous.

monster₁ sample of merchandise.

monster₂ monster.

monstrans (*Rel.*) monstrance.

montang-manting moving about restlessly.

montase 1 assembly. - *mobil* automobile assembly. **2** editing (of movie).

monté see MOTÉ.

montir 1 mechanic, repairman. - *jam* watch repairman. **2** repair, do mechanical work. *Kalau bisa - udah ndak ada soal* If you know how to make repairs, there is no problem.

montok well built, plump and full (of child's body or breasts). **me-** become full and plump. **ke-an** plumpness.

montor 1 motor. **2** auto, car.

monumén monument (in commemoration of s.t.).

monuméntal grandiose, monumental.

monyét 1 monkey. **2** term of abuse.

monyong₁ sticking out, protruding (of the mouth, from buck teeth or pouting).

monyong₂ humorous term of address to an intimate. *Hé -! Kok lama nggak kelihatan* Hey you! Long time no see!

mopéd moped, motorbike.

mopit Ch writing brush.

mopong me- carry a baby in o.'s arms.

morak-marik see MORAT-MARIT.

moral morality. **ber-** have high moral standards.

moralis moralist.

moralistas morality.

morat-marit confused, disorganized. *Méja itu -* The desk is messy.

morfém (*Ling.*) morpheme.

morfin morphine.

morfinis drug addict.

morfologi /morflokhi, morfologi/ (*Bio., Ling.*) morphology.

mori unbleached plain cloth (used for batik, shrouds, etc.).

moril 1 moral, morality. **2** morale.

moris soursop tree.

morong coffeepot, teapot.

morphin, morphinis see MORFIN, MORFINIS.

morse Morse code.

mortalitas, mortalitét mortality.

mortir artillery mortar. **me-** shell. **pe-an** shelling.

mosaik mosaic.

mosi motion, vote. - *tdk percaya* vote of no confidence.

Moskwa Moscow.

moster₁ mustard. - *basah* prepared mustard.

moster₂ see MONSTER₁.

mota see KAIN.

moté beads (for necklaces).

motif₁ motif, design. **ber-** have a motif.

motif₂ motive. **ber-(kan)** have s.t. as o.'s motive. *Pembunuhan itu ~ iri hati* Jealousy was the motive for the murder.

motip see MOTIF₁,₂.

motivasi motivation. **ber-kan** have as a motivation.

moto₁ motto.

moto₂ (*Coll.*) monosodium glutamate.

motor 1 motor, engine. - *gandéngan/témpél* outboard motor. **2** motorcar, auto. - *pompa* fire engine. **3** motorcycle. **4** moving force behind s.t. **5** (*in some regions only*) motorboat. **ber- 1** motorized. *Sepédanya ~ sekarang* His bicycle is motorized now. **2** go by car, motorcycle. *Kami ~ dr Jkt ke Bogor* We went by car from Jkt to Bogor. **me-i 1** motor, go by car. **2** provide s.o. with a car. **3** be the moving force behind s.t. *Langkah barunya di-i oléh spirit menggali budaya lama* His new direction was inspired by an interest in delving into an old culture. *Ia ~ kesebelasan itu* He was the moving force behind the soccer team.

motorbot motorboat.

motoris engineer, motorman.

motorisasi motorization.

motorkap removable roof of car. *- jip* jeep with convertible roof.

motorpit motorcycle.

moyang great-grandfather, great-grandparents. *- asal* common ancestor of a group. **ber-** have as an ancestor.

mp- see also entries with **emp-**.

M.Pd. [*Magister Pendidikan*] Master of Education.

MPO [*menghitung pajak org*] k.o. sales tax.

mpok (*Jkt*) term of address to young woman of low class.

mpot-mpotan physically or emotionally painful.

MPP [*Masa Persiapan Pensiun*] period prior to retirement.

MPR, MPRS [*Majelis Permusyawaratan Rakyat (Sementara)*] (Provisional) People's Consultative Council.

mps. [*menurut pendapat saya*] in my opinion.

Mr. [*Meester (in de Rechten)*] a law degree used as a title by its holder.

mrongos (*Jv*) bucktoothed.

M'Thai. [*Muang Thai*] Thailand.

MTQ [*Musabaqah Tilawatil Qur'an*] contest of Koranic recitation.

M.Ts. [*Madrasah Tsanawiyah*] (*Isl.*) junior high school.

MU [*Majelis Umum*] General Assembly.

mua₁ eel.

mua₂ see SEMUA.

muafakah, muafakat see MUFAKAT.

muai expand, swell. **me-** expand. **pe-an** expansion. *~ panjang* linear expansion.

muak 1 nauseated, revolted. **2** loathe (food or drink). **me-kan** nauseating, repugnant. **ke-an** feeling of loathing.

mual 1 queasy. *Waktu naik kapal saya -* I feel queasy when I go sailing. **2** feel loathing. *Itu membuat kita jadi - membacanya* It makes us feel nauseous to read it. **me-kan** sickening, make o. feel nauseous. *~ perutku* made me sick to my stomach.

mualaf recent convert to Isl.

mualamat science.

mualim, muallim 1 (religious) teacher. **2** navigator. **3** pilot, guide. **4** (*Navy*) deck officer, mate, first mate.

Muang Thai, Muangthai /muangtai/ Thailand.

muara 1 estuary, mouth. **2** orifice. *- lambung* opening from intestines into stomach. **ber-** empty into. *Kali Ciliwung ~ di Lautan Jawa* The Ciliwung River empties into the Java Sea. **me-kan** empty s.t. out into. *Di sana di-kan tenaga banyak* That place is where they poured in a great deal of manpower.

muasal origin. **ber-** originate.

muat 1 contain, hold, accommodate. *Oto itu - enam org* That car holds six people. **2** be contained in a publication. **3** include. **ber-an 1** have a load of, contain. *Kapal itu ~ gula* The ship is carrying sugar. **2** be charged with electricity. *Besi ini ~ listrik* This iron is carrying an electrical charge. *dua buah zarah ~* two electrically charged particles. **me- 1** hold, contain. **2** accomodate, be able to hold. **3** load, take on. *Kapal itu sedang ~ batu bara* The ship is loading coal. **4** place s.t. in a publication. *Berita itu tdk jadi di-* They ended up not carrying that story. *Tuan - adpertensi di mana?* Where did you place an advertisement? **me-i** load on to. *Sdh dua hari org ~ kapal* They have been loading the ship for two days. **me-kan 1** load s.t. *Org sibuk ~ barang-barang ke kapal* People are busy loading the ship. **2** place. *Sdh berapa lama kamu ~ adpertensi itu?* How long have you had the ad in? **ter-** contained in, placed. *kabar yg ~ di surat kabar* the news contained in the newspaper. **-an 1** load, contents. *~ ledak* explosive charge. **2** capacity. **3** cargo. **pe-an** loading, placing. *~ foto* including a photo (in a publication). **per-an** loading, shipment.

muazin, muazzin muezzin, o. who calls to prayers.

mubadir, mubadzir see MUBASIR.

mubah (*Isl.*) neutral, neither forbidden nor required.

mubalih, muballigh (*Isl.*) preacher, o. who expounds a certain idea.

mubarak blessed, fortunate.

mubarat (*Isl.*) divorce at the request of the wife.

mubasir, mubazir superfluous, waste. *kata-kata -* superfluous words, redundancy. **ke-an** superfluousness, waste.

mubut fragile, brittle. **me-kan** grind, crush, pound.

muci prostitute.

mucikari see MUNCIKARI.

muda 1 young (in age). *Waktu perang dia masih -* During the war he was still young. *- belia* very young, youthful. *- mudi* young people. **2** deputy. *Ketua - di mana?* Where is the deputy chairman? **3** unripe, green. *Buah - itu masam* The green fruit is sour. **4** light, pale. *Saya suka warna hijau -* I like pale green. **ber-²** enjoy o.s. like a young person. **me-kan** rejuvenate. *Katanya obat ini ~* They say this medicine is rejuvenating. **ke-an** youth. **ke-²an** youthful behavior. **pe-** youth, young man. *~ Rakyat* Communist Youth Organization. *~ pelancongan* 1 young drifter. 2 young wanderer, traveler. **kepe-an** matters pertaining to youth.

mudah easy, simple. *Pekerjaan itu -* That job is easy. **ber-²an** take casually. *Bukan ~* It is difficult. **me-kan 1** facilitate, ease. **2** take s.t. lightly. *~ pecahan* reduce a fraction. **memper-** facilitate, make s.t. easier. **ke-an** ease. **pe- 1** easygoing. **2** o. who is easygoing.

mudah-mudahan 1 may it be, I hope (that). *~ anda lekas pulang* May you return soon. **2** maybe, perhaps. *Pergilah ke sekolah, ~ ada manfaatnya bagimu* Go to school. Maybe it will be of value to you.

mudarat, mudharat, mudhorat 1 disadvantage. *Peraturan baru itu memberi - kpd pedagang-pedagang* That new regulation is disadvantageous to the merchants. **2** fail. *Dia - dlm usahanya* He failed in his efforts.
mudi see KEMUDI, MUDA.
mudigah larva.
mudik 1 upstream, upcountry, inland (away from the sea). *Berlayar - tdk mudah* Sailing upstream is not easy. **2** home to the village. *Bujang kami -* Our servant went home. **me-i** go inland on s.t. *Perahu itu berlayar ~ sungai* The prau sailed upstream. **me-kan** sail s.t. upstream. *~ kapal sukar* To sail a boat upstream is hard.
mudin see MODIN.
mudlarat see MUDARAT.
mufaham understand. *Dia - akan hal itu* He understands that matter.
mufakat 1 (hold) discussion to reach an agreement. *Baik kau - dulu dgn org tuamu* You had better have a discussion with your parents first. **2** agreement, consensus. **se- 1** be in agreement. *Kami sdh ~ hendak berangkat bésok* We have agreed to leave tomorrow. **2** unanimously. *Kami ~ mengangktnya sbg ketua* We unanimously appointed him chairman. **menye-i** agree with. **ber-** discuss, agree. *~lah dulu, bung!* Talk it over first, friend! **me-i** agree to s.t. *Ssdh dibicarakan baru meréka ~ hal itu* They agreed with it only after it had been discussed. **me-kan** reach an agreement over. **ke-an** agreement. **per-an 1** discussion, deliberation. **2** agreement. **3** plot, conspiracy.
mufasir (*Isl.*) commentator (on the Koran).
mufrad (*Lit.*) single, simplex.
mufti (*Isl.*) adviser on religious law for a region (above the *kadi* in authority).
Muh. [*Muhammad*]
muhajirin (*Isl.*) those who accompanied Muh. on his flight from Mecca.
muhal impossible, out of the question. **ke-an** impossibility.
muhallil (*Isl.*) man who marries a divorced woman only so that he can divorce her to enable her to remarry her original husband legally.
Muhammadiyah a Muslim movement.
Muharram first month of the Muslim year.
muhibah, muhibbah goodwill. **ber-** go on a goodwill mission.
muhrim (*Isl.*) degree of consanguinity between a man and woman that renders marriage impossible but gives them the right of association. *Siapa -nya ketika janda itu naik haji?* Who was the male relative (who accompanied her) when that widow made the pilgrimage? **ke-an** possessing a *muhrim* relationship.
MUI [*Majelis Ulama Indonésia*] (*Isl.*) Indonesian Council of Religious Scholars.
mujahadah (*Isl.*) war against deviation from the true principles of religion.
mujahid (*Isl.*) defender of the faith.
mujahidin (*Isl.*) defenders of the faith.

mujair k.o. freshwater fish widely stocked in inland waters and an important food.
mujarab effective, efficacious. *Obat itu sangat -* The medicine is extremely effective. **ke-an** effectiveness, efficacy.
mujarad abstract, not concrete.
mujarrab see MUJARAB.
mujarrad see MUJARAD.
mu'jizat see MUKJIZAT.
mujtahid (*Isl.*) expert in Muslim law who gives an independent interpretation of the Koran and Hadith.
mujur 1 straight ahead, straight. *Jalan itu -* The road is straight. **2** luck. *- dia blm sampai!* It was a good thing he had not arrived yet! **3** lucky. *Si Ali - benar kemarén malam* Ali was very lucky last night. **ke-an** luck. **pe-** a lucky person.
muka 1 face. *- anak itu serupa ibunya* That child's face resembles its mother's. *- dua* two-faced. *- kayu* straight-faced. *- papan* imprudent. **2** front. *- lemari itu sdh pecah* The front of the cupboard is broken. *ke -* to the front. *Maju ke - sedikit* Step forward a bit. **3** page, side. *Buku itu berapa -nya?* How many pages does the book have? *- A side A* (of a record). *- atas* top side. **4** surface. *- air tanah* surface watertable. *- bumi* earth's surface. *- laut* sea level. **5** upcoming. *Ia akan datang minggu -* He will come next week. *di - 1* in advance. *Dia membayar di -* He paid in advance. **2** in front of. *Dia berdiri di - rumahnya* He is standing in front of his house. **3** ahead. *Waktu berpacu lari saya jauh di -* During the race I was way ahead of the others. **6** face, reputation. *Kehilangan -* loss of face. *- tebal* not feeling shame. *-²* insincere, hypocritical. **se- 1** having the same appearance. **2** having the same front, fronting in the same direction. *Mesjid dan kantor pos ~ menghadap ke tanah lapang* The mosque and the post office were side by side facing the square. **berse- 1** having the same appearance. **2** facing e.o. **ber-** have a certain k.o. face. *Ia ~ mérah* He has a red face. *~ dua* be hypocritical. **ber-² 1** hypocritical, two-faced. **2** in front of e.o., face to face. **3** telling e.o. frankly face-to-face. **menge-kan 1** suggest, propose, put forward. *Siapa yg ~ hal itu?* Who suggested that? **2** put to the front. *Dia ~ kursi itu* He pushed the chair to the front. **3** confront s.o. *Meréka ~ yg mendakwa dgn yg terdakwa* They confronted the accuser with the accused. *~ diri* thrust o.s. forward. *Dia ~ dirinya utk calon présidén* He thrust himself forward as a candidate for president. **terke-** foremost. *org ~ VIP*, prominent people. **pe-** leader, promoter. **penge-an** presentation, putting forward of s.t. **per-an** surface. *~ air* surface of the water.
mukadimah, mukaddimah introduction, preface.
mukah adultery. **ber-** commit adultery. **per-an** adultery.
mukenah (*Isl.*) white cloak covering a woman's head and body worn at prayer.
mukhalaf (*Isl.*) heresy.

mukhrim see MUHRIM.

mukhtasar summary, resumé.

mukibat 1 k.o. huge cassava bred by a man named Mukibat. **2** s.t. unusually large for the thing it is. *loli* - a monster popsicle.

mukim 1 stay at, be a resident of. *Kawan saya - di hotél Garuda* My friend is staying at the Garuda Hotel. **2** residence, district. *Tempat -nya Jkt* His residence is Jkt. **ber-** live, reside. *Ia ~ di Éropah* He lives in Europe. **me-kan** settle s.o. s.w. **pe-** resident. **pe-an, per-an** settlement, place a group resides.

mukimin residents.

mukjijat see MUKJIZAT.

mukjizat miracle.

mukmin, mukminin (*Isl.*) the believers, the faithful.

mukswa see MOKSA.

muktabar, muktabir respected, venerated.

muktamar congress, conference.

mula 1 beginning. *dr kecil* - from childhood. **2** original cause, basis. *Apa -nya dia marah?* What was the reason for her anger? - *jadi* from the time s.t. came into being. **-²** at first, at the beginning. *~ dia tak mengerti* At first he did not understand. **ber-²** first, at the beginning. **se-** 1 from the beginning. *Semua dilakukan dr ~* Everything was carried out starting at the beginning. **2** since. *~ jadi* since birth. **3** formerly, originally. *Apa yg terjadi lain dr yg disangka ~* What happened is different from what was originally expected. **4** at first. *~ ia malu* At first he was bashful. **se-nya** at the beginning. *Ada ikatan yg tdk jelas ~* There are strings attached which were not made clear at the beginning. **menye-kan** start from the beginning again. **ber- 1** have a beginning. *Cerita itu ~ ketika . . .* The story begins when . . . **2** first. *~ dia pergi ke pasar* First she went to the market. *Kemarén saya terima gaji saya ~* Yesterday I received my first salary. **3** before. *Lain dr ~, bukan?* It is different from before, isn't it? **seber-** at first, at the beginning. **me-i** begin s.t. *Pembacaan Koran di-i jam enam* The reading of the Koran begins at six. **-i 1** begin, start. *Konperénsi sdh ~* The conference has started. **2** from, beginning. *~ tgl 15 sampai 25* from the 15th to the 25th. *dr ~ itu* from that time, beginning then. **me-kan** start, cause. *Yg ~ perkelahian itu bukan dia* He did not start the fight. **pe- 1** initiator, originator. **2** beginner. **per-an 1** beginning, the outset. *Saya tdk dengar ~ cerita itu* I did not hear the beginning of the story. *~ kata* preface. **2** basis, origin. *Hal itu adalah ~ pekerjaannya* That is the basis of his work. *~ kalam* foreword, preface.

mulas slight stomach upset, pain in the stomach. - *perut* stomach upset, colic.

mulek circle around in a closed space.

mules see MULAS.

mulhid heretic.

mulia noble, sublime, lofty. *Dia org yg -* He is a noble person. - *raya* supreme, honorable. *yg -*

His Excellency. **me-kan 1** honor deeply. *Kita hrs ~ nusa dan bangsa kita* We should hold our nation and people in high esteem. **2** improve a breed. **memper-kan** honor deeply, esteem greatly. **ter-** exalted, most respected. *Dia org yg ~ di kota ini* He is the most respected person in this city. **ke-an** magnificence, pomp, glory. **pe-an** breeding to improve the stock. *~ padi* rice breeding. **per-an** magnificence, pomp, glory.

muliawan person worthy of deep esteem.

Mulo /milo/ [*Meer Uitgebreid Lager Onderwijs*] Dutch-language secondary school of colonial times.

multi- multi. *-nasional* multinational. *sistém -partai* multiple party system.

multipléks k.o. plywood.

multiplikasi multiplication.

mulud see MAULID.

muluk 1 high-sounding. **2** bombastic, pompous. **-²** in a pompous or high-sounding way. *Jangan janji ~ kalau tdk bisa ditepati* Do not make high-sounding promises if you cannot keep them. **ber-²** build up in o.'s imagination, dreams, etc. **ke-an** pomposity.

mulur 1 elastic. *Permainan karét itu -* The rubber toy is elastic. **2** flexible. *Orgnya -* She is a flexible person. - *mengkeret* flexible, able to expand and shrink.

mulus 1 flawless, pure. *Salju itu putih -* The snow is pure white. *Honda dlm keadaan -* a Honda in perfect condition. **2** sincere. *Pegawai itu -* The employee is honest.

mulut 1 mouth. - *busuk* saying nasty things. - *manis* gentle in speech. - *ringan* talkative. - *sumbing* harelip. **2** opening. *di -jurang* at the edge of the precipice (lit., at the mouth of the chasm). - *gunung* crater. - *kulit* pore of the skin. - *sungai* estuary. **3** nozzle. - *bedil* mouth of a cannon. - *laras* muzzle. - *meriam* muzzle of a rifle. **ber-1** have an opening. *Pipa itu ~ besar* The pipe has a big opening. **2** talk, chat. *~ besar* talk big, be insolent. **-²an** org object of gossip.

mumbang young coconut.

mumbul (*Jv*) rise, bounce.

mumet 1 headache. **2** (*Jv*) dizzy. *Saya - ssdh jatuh* I became dizzy after I fell. **3** confused.

mumi, mumia mummy.

mu'min see MUKMIN.

mummi see MUMI.

mumpung take advantage while o. can, as long as. *Dpt anda pesan - masih tersedia* You can order it as long as it is available.

mumpungisme opportunism.

munafik 1 (*Isl.*) unbeliever who pretends to be a Muslim. **2** hypocrite. **3** (*Sl.*) liar. **ke-an** hypocrisy.

Munas [*Musyawarah Nasional*] National Deliberative Council.

munasabah, munasabat reasonable, logically acceptable (as an argument, o.'s reaction, etc.).

muncikari procuress, pimp.

muncrat spurt. **me-** spurt. **me-kan** spray, squirt s.t. out.

muncul emerge, appear, turn up. *Ssdh dua tahun dia - lagi* After two years he appeared in public again. **ber-an** appear in numbers, spring up. **me-kan 1** bring up out of the water. *Ia ~ kepalanya dr dlm air* She stuck her head above the water. **2** bring out into view, show. *Dia ~ kepandaiannya* He showed his ability. **3** set in a context, cause s.t. to appear in a certain setting. *Ceritera film itu di-kan pd tahun empat-puluhan* The film was set in the forties. **per-an** appearance, emergence.

muncung see MONCONG.

mundam large bowl, tub.

mundar-mandir move back and forth, esp. aimlessly. *Penjaga itu - di muka pintu* The guard walked up and down (patrolled) in front of the door.

munding (*Sd*) water buffalo.

mundu k.o. small tree and its sour fruit.

mundur 1 go back, back up. *Oto semua disuruh -* All the cars have to back up. **2** decline, decrease, deteriorate. *Keséhatannya -* Her health declined. **3** retreat. **me-kan** make s.t. back up. **ke-an 1** decline, decrease. **2** deterioration. **3** cutback (in production). **pe-an** pulling s.t. back. *~ diri* retreat.

mung see MONG.

munggah see PUNGGAH.

munggu small hill.

munggur k.o. tree.

mungil cute, sweet. **ke-an** cuteness.

mungkam silent.

mungkar 1 deny. *Dia - akan janjinya* He denied (he had made) his promise. **2** ignored. *Pekerjaannya yg - tdk diindahkannya* He did not care about the work he ignored. **me-i 1** deny. *Dia ~ kewajibannya* He denies his responsibility. **2** ignore. *Dia ~ org tuanya* He ignores his parents. **ke-an** denial, disavowal.

mungkeret see MENGKERET.

mungkin possible. *Itu tak -* That is impossible. *se . . . -* as . . . as possible. *sejauh -* as far as possible. *Dia berlari selekas -* He ran as fast as possible. **-²** very possible. **me-kan** enable, make possible. *Pembagian waktu itu ~ saya belajar* The schedule enables me to study. **ke-an** possibility.

mungkir 1 deny, disavow. *Sekali ini jangan -* Do not deny it this time. **2** renege. *Dia - janjinya* He did not keep his promise. **me-i, me-kan 1** deny. *Dia ~ tuduhan* He denied the accusation. *Dia ~ anaknya* He disowned his son. **2** ignore. *Saya ~ hal yg buruk* I ignore the bad things. **3** break (a promise). **-an** denial.

mungkum dome shaped, overarching.

mungkur₁ stretcher, palanquin.

mungkur₂ with o.'s back turned. *Ia duduk -* He sat with his back turned. **me-i** turn o.'s back to. *Ia ~ kami* He turned his back on us.

mungpung see MUMPUNG.

mungsi k.o. herb.

mungsing k.o. shark.

munisi munitions.

munjung heaping full. *delapan séndok makan - garam* eight heaping tablespoons of salt.

Munkar (*Isl.*) o. of two angels who interrogate a dead person soon after he has been buried.

muno keep silent and muse.

munsyi (*Lit.*) language teacher.

muntabér [*muntah bérak*] diarrhea and vomiting, esp. as cholera symptoms.

muntah₁ vomit, throw up. *Dia - karena msk angin* He is vomiting because he caught a flu. *- bérak* intestinal disorder with vomiting and diarrhea. **me-i** vomit on. *Anak itu ~ baju ibunya* The child vomited on his mother's dress. **me-kan** vomit up, out. *~ peluru* spew bullets. **-an** the vomit.

muntah₂ fade, run. *Baju itu dicuci sekali sdh -* The dress was washed only once, but it has faded already.

muntup begin to appear.

munyeng (*Jv*) dizzy.

mupakat see MUFAKAT.

muqaddimah see MUKADIMAH.

Mur Moor.

mur₁ myrrh.

mur₂ nut for a bolt. *- baut* nut and bolt.

murad 1 intention. **2** meaning, significance.

muradif see MURAJIF.

murah 1 cheap, inexpensive. *Di pasar barang-barang lebih -* Things are cheaper at the market. **2** easy, not subject to a number of conditions. *Gadis itu tdk -* That girl is going to be difficult (to marry). **3** generous. *- senyum* smiles readily. *- kata* liking to speak. *- hati* magnanimous. **2** forgiving. **ber-** *hati* **1** generous. **2** tolerant. *- mulut* gentle in speech. **me-kan** lower the price. *Saudagar-saudagar ~ harga-harga barang* The merchants reduce their prices. **memper-** make things cheaper. **ke-an 1** cheapness, inexpensiveness. **2** generosity, magnanimity. *~ hati* generosity. **-an** of a cheap sort. **pe-** generous person.

murai k.o. small bird.

murajif (*Ling.*) synonym.

muram gloomy, depressed. *Dia - sepanjang hari* He is sad all day. **ber-** *durja* look gloomy. **me-kan** depressing. *Apa yg ~ dia?* What is making her gloomy? **ke-an** gloom, dejection.

murang fuse for igniting firecrackers or dynamite.

murat-marit see MORAT-MARIT.

murba common, proletarian. *Meréka termasuk dlm golongan rakyat -* They belong to the common people. *Partai -* Troskyite party. **ke-an** ordinariness.

murbai, murbé mulberry.

muri₁ k.o. metal flute.

muri₂ see MORI.

murid 1 pupil, student of lower grades. *- SD s/d SMA* school children from elementary through high school. **2** disciple, follower of. *Dlm politik saya bekas - Bung Karno* I was a disciple of Sukarno's in my political orientation.

muring in a bad mood.

muris₁ k.o. fabric.

muris₂ greedy, closefisted.
murka 1 anger, fury. **2** (*Lit.*) angry (esp. of royalty). **me-i** be angry with s.o. **me-kan** infuriate s.o. **ke-an 1** fury, rage, anger. **2** greed.
murni pure, clean. *Dia bercita-cita tinggi dan -* He has high and pure ideals. *kebenaran yg -* unvarnished truth. *susu -* unadulterated milk. **me-kan** purify, clean. *Dia sembahyang ~ hatinya* He prays to purify his heart. **ke-an 1** purity, genuineness. **2** chastity. **pe-** cleanser. **pe-an** cleansing, purifying.
mursal₁ (*Isl.*) messengers of God: Abraham, Moses, Jesus, et al.
mursal₂ undisciplinable. *Anak -* The Prodigal Son (of the Gospels).
mursid, mursyid spiritual guide, religious teacher.
murtad 1 (*Isl.*) apostate. **2** renegade from social values. **me-kan** consider o. an apostate. **ke-an** apostasy.
murung melancholy, depressed. **ber-²** in a depressed mood. **me-kan** make depressed. **ke-an** melancholy, depression. **pe-** tending to be depressed.
murup (*Jv*) flame, flaming. *Apinya masih -* The fire is still flaming.
murus have loose bowels.
Musa Moses.
musabab see SEBAB.
musabaqah, musabaqoh contest for reciting the Koran.
musafir traveler. **ber-** travel.
musalla see MUSHOLLA.
musang civet. *- berbulu ayam* wolf in sheep's clothing. *- tenggalung* k.o. civet cat.
musawarah see MUSYAWARAH.
muséum museum.
musholla /musola/ (*Isl.*) small building or room set aside in a public place for performance of religious duties.
musibah calamity, disaster.
musik music. *- kaléng* canned music. *- kamar* chamber music. *- pop* pop music. **ber-** play music. **-an 1** a musical. **2** musician. **pe-** musician.
musikolog musicologist.
musikologi musicology.
musikus musician.
musim 1 season, period. *- barat* W. monsoon. *- bah* flood season. *- bunga* spring. *- dingin* winter. *- gelora* stormy, nasty weather. *- gugur* autumn. *- hujan* rainy season. *- kemarau/kering* dry season. *- panas* summer. *- pancaroba* transitional periods between seasons. *- penghujan* rainy season, monsoon with rain. *- paceklik* period of shortage before harvest. *- rendeng* rainy season. *- rontok/ runtuh* autumn. *- semi* spring. *- tandur* planting time. **2** monsoon. **se-** o. season in length. *Cintanya hanya ~* Her love will last but o. season. **ber-** in season. *Buah-buahan banyak yg ~* Many fruits are in season. **-an** seasonal. **-²an** seasonal.
musisi musicians.
musium see MUSÉUM.

muskil see MUSYKIL.
muslihat 1 trick. **2** strategy, tactics. **me-i** deceive by means of a ruse.
muslim a Muslim.
muslimah, muslimat Muslim woman.
muslimin (*Pl*) Muslims.
musna (*Coll.*) see MUSNAH.
musnah annihilated, destroyed. *Segala kertas-kertas yg berharga tlh -* All valuable papers were destroyed. **me-kan** annihilate, destroy. **ke-an** annihilation, destruction, extinction. **pe-** agent for destroying, disinfectant. **pe-an** annihilation.
musolla see MUSHOLLA.
muson monsoon.
Muspida [*Musyawarah Pimpinan Daérah*] council for provincial and lower level gvt. officials.
mustahak important, crucial.
mustahil impossible, out of the question. *- hal itu terjadi* It is incredible that it could happen. **me-kan** render s.t. impossible. *Pertahanan yg kuat ~ musuh msk* The strong defense makes it impossible for the enemy to invade. **ke-an** impossibility.
mustaid ready, completed, at hand. **me-kan** prepare, complete. *Sblm berangkat meréka ~ segala pekerjaan* Before leaving they completed all their work.
mustajab efficacious, effective. *obat yg -* effective medicine. **ke-an** efficacy.
mustakim straightforward, sincere.
musti see MESTI.
mustika see MESTIKA.
musuh 1 enemy, adversary. *- alam* natural enemy, predator. *- bebuyutan* blood enemy. *- dlm selimut* enemy in disguise. *- masah* enemies. **2** competitor, contestant. *Barang ini tak ada -nya* Nothing can compare with this article. **ber-(an)** be enemies, hostile to e.o. **me-i** compete against. **per-an** hostility.
musyafir see MUSAFIR.
musyarakah, musyarakat partnership.
musyawarah, musyawarat 1 meeting, conference. **2** discussion, deliberation. *- besar* convention. **ber-** engage in deliberations. *Kepala-kepala sekolah ~ ttg murid-murid* The school principals held a meeting about the pupils. **me-kan** discuss, deliberate over. *Kami hrs ~ hal itu dulu* We have to discuss that matter first. **per-an** discussion, conference, deliberation.
musykil difficult to know or prove. **ke-an** abstruseness.
musyrik polytheist. **ke-an** polytheism.
Musytari the planet Jupiter.
mut see KEMUT₂.
mutabar, mutabir see MUKTABAR, MUKTABIR.
mutah see MUNTAH₁.
mutakhir the very latest, most up-to-date (fashion, etc.).
mutalaah study carefully, scrutinize. **me-kan** study s.t.
mutalak see MUTLAK.
mu'tamar see MUKTAMAR.
mutasi 1 (*Biol.*) mutation. **2** transfer of gvt. offi-

cial to a new post or of pupil to a new school, shakeup. **me-kan** effect such a transfer. *Ali Murtopo di-kan* Ali Murtopo has been reassigned.
mutawatir handed down from person to person for generations.
mutiara pearl.
mutlak absolute, unconditional. *jaminan -* unconditional guarantee. *Dia diberi hak -* He was given absolute rights. **me-kan** make s.t. absolutely essential. **ke-an** absoluteness.

mutu 1 pearl. **2** quality, grade. **3** carat. **ber-** high quality, excellent.
mutung 1 burnt, lost by fire. **2** brokenhearted, discouraged. **3** give up.
muwakal proxy.
muwarikh (*Lit.*) historian.
muzhab see MAZHAB.
muzik see MUSIK.

N

n /én/ n, the 14th letter of the alphabet.
n.a. /én a/ [*numpang alamat*] (*Coll.*) c/o, in care of.
na see NAH.
naar boven /nar bofen/ (*Coll.*) go to mountain resort areas, esp. for sexual adventures. *Kalau pikiran tegang, kita mesti - utk santai* If we feel tense, we should head for the resorts to loosen up.
naas unlucky, ill-omened. *saat yg -* unlucky moment. **me-kan** declare s.t. to be ill-omened. **ke-an** bad luck.
nabatah (*Biol.*) vegetable kingdom.
nabati concerning plants, phyto-. *minyak -* vegetable oil.
nabi 1 (*Rel.*) prophet. *- palsu* false prophet. **2** (*Isl.*) Muh. and other important religious figures. *- Isa* (*Isl.*) Jesus. *- Musa* (*Isl.*) Moses. **me-kan 1** make s.o. into a prophet. **2** regard s.o. as a prophet. **ke-an** matters pertaining to prophets. *logika ~* prophetic logic. *cerita ~* a story concerning prophets.
nabiah (*Rel.*) prophetess.
nabrak see TABRAK.
nabtun (*Lit.*) a plant.
naco see NAKO.
nada 1 intonation. **2** tone, note. *- mayeur* major key. *- mineur* minor key. *- rendah* low-key. *- bicara* (*Tel.*) busy signal. *- dasar* keynote. *- pakai* (*Tel.*) busy signal. *- pilih* (*Tel.*) dial tone. *- sumbang* off-key or out-of-tune note. *- tambahan* overtone. *- utama* keynote. **3** (*Ling.*) pitch. **se- 1** monotonous. *Tawanya ~* She laughed in a monotonous way. **2** in harmony with. *Ucapannya ~ dgn ucapan majikannya* What she said was in harmony with what her boss said. **ber- 1** have a tone. *~ sumbang* be off key. **2** smack of. *Pertengkaran sengit itu ~ permusuhan* That violent quarrel smacked of true enmity.
Nadapol [*Narapidana Politik*] political prisoner.
nadar see NAZAR₁.
nadi (*Med.*) pulse, artery. *Dokter memeriksa -* The doctor felt his pulse. *- bersikeras/mengeras* arteriosclerosis. *- ketiak* (*Med.*) arteria axillaris.
nadir₁ rare, unusual.

nadir₂ supervisor, inspector.
nadzar see NAZAR₁.
nafakah see NAFKAH.
nafas breath. *-nya berat* She was breathing hard. *- lelah* short-winded. *- penghabisan* last breath. **se-** be close to e.o., be of o. breath. **menye-kan** make congruent. *dise-kan dgn ajaran Islam* made congruent with Isl. doctrine. **ber- 1** breathe. *~ dlm/panjang* take a deep breath. *~ ke luar badan* rely more on other people. **2** sigh. **me-i** resuscitate, revive. *Ia di-i dgn zat asam* He was revived with oxygen. **me-kan** exhale s.t. **per-an** breathing, respiration. *Bau dupa mewangi menyesakkan ~nya* The fragrant incense made it hard for her to breathe. *~ buatan* artificial respiration. *penyakit ~* respiratory disease.
nafi (*Lit.*) **me-kan** deny.
nafiri 1 k.o. valveless ceremonial trumpet us. part of royal paraphernalia. **2** (*Bib.*) k.o. trumpet.
nafkah 1 basic necessities of life. *Ia mencari -* He is making a living. *- batin* conjugal rights. *- hazir* wife's maintenance. **2** money given to o.'s wife (or divorced wife) for household expenses. **me-kan** spend s.t. for maintenance.
nafsi personal, individual. **-² 1** individual, personal. *perasaan ~* personal feelings. **2** selfish. **ber-² 1** individual, private. **2** egotistic, selfish.
nafsu natural appetite or desire. *Ia berhasil menahan -* He succeeded in controlling his passions. *- beli* urge to buy. *- birahi* sexual desire, lust. *- dukana* lust. *- kebendaan* material desires. *- lawamah* (*Isl.*) ungodly passion (in mysticism). *- makan* appetite for food. *- nafsi* individual desires. *- tabiat* instinct. **ber-** passionate, lustful, desirous. *Stlh saya melihat sampah menumpuk itu, saya tdk ~ makan lagi* After I saw those heaps of garbage, I no longer had a desire to eat. **me-kan** arouse s.o.'s appetite (esp. sexual desires).
naftalin naphthalene.
naga dragon.
naga-naganya apparently.
nagari (*M*) see NEGERI.
nagasari k.o. rice-flour cake stuffed with banana bits and steamed in banana leaves.

nah 1 Here! Take it (with accompanying gesture of offering, etc.). -*! Ini uangnya* Here you are! Here is your money. **2** See! (particle implying acceptance of o.'s advice or opinion, fact, common knowledge, etc.). -*! Apa kata ibu? Kau cantik kalau bersih begitu!* See! What did I tell you? You are pretty when you have cleaned yourself up like that. **3** Now then (a particle introducing a new topic of conversation). -, *pedagang baru itu* . . . Now, that new merchant . . . **4** well! (particle introducing a sentence that concludes a conversation). -, *sekianlah saja* Well, let us stop here.

nahas see NAAS.

Nahdatul Ulama, Nahdlatul Ulama Association of Muslim Scholars, a Muslim political party of 1970's.

nahi (*Isl.*) prohibition, forbidden.

nahu (*Lit.*) grammar.

naib (*Isl.*) mosque official, deputy of local religious affairs. - *kadi* deputy registrar of marriages. **ke-an** office of religious affairs at subdistrict level.

naif naive. **me-kan** make s.o. naive, treat s.o. as naive. *Berani benar kau ~ aku!* You dare to patronize me! **ke-an** naivete.

naik 1 climb, ascend, go up (on). *Kawannya - bukit* His friend climbed the hill. *Raja itu - takhta* The king ascended the throne. *Pesawat itu gagal -* The plane failed to get off the ground. - *apél/ banding* (*Leg.*) appeal to a higher court. - *darat* go ashore. - *haji* (*Isl.*) make the pilgrimage to Mecca. - *kelas* be promoted in school. - *mempelai* get married. - *nobat* installed as ruler. - *panggung* appear on stage. - *pasang* rising tide. - *rumah baru* (*M*) (hold a) housewarming party. - *saksi* (*Leg.*) take the witness stand, bear witness to. - *sorga* ascend to heaven. - *turun* ups and downs. **me-turunkan 1** cause to fluctuate, increase and then reduce s.t. repeatedly. *Perubahan harga minyak ~ pencapaian ékonomi* Changes in the price of oil have caused economic achievement to fluctuate. **2** pick up and drop off. *Kernét itu sibuk ~ muatan penumpang* The bus attendant was busy picking up and dropping off the passengers' belongings. **2** rise, be on the increase. *produksinya - sebanyak empat belas per sén* The production increased by 14 percent. *Matahari -* The sun is rising. - *derajat* increase in prestige, be promoted. - *déwasa* become adolescent. - *gaji* (have a) wage hike. - *harga* rise in price. - *kelas* go up (in school). - *pangkat* be promoted. - *tangan* have good luck. **3** suddenly flare up. - *api* catch fire. - *darah* get angry. - *geram* become excited or angry. - *hati* become conceited. - *marah* get angry. - *marak* **1** start to glow. **2** be at her best (said of a girl). **3** rise to fame. - *pitam/stum* have a fit, get into a rage. **4** ride s.t. - *kuda* ride a horse. - *kuda hijau* be drunk. - *mobil* **1** step into a car. **2** go by car. **me-** be on the increase. *Harga-harga terus ~ akhir-akhir ini* Lately prices have been increasing incessantly. **me-i 1** climb on to s.t., go up into s.t. *Anak itu ~ pohon* The child climbed trees. **2** ride s.t. *mobil yg di-inya* the car he rode. ~

kapal perusak stationed aboard a destroyer. **me-kan 1** cause s.t. to go upward. *Serdadu itu ~ bendéra* The soldier raised the flag. *Ayah ~ doa syukur kpd Tuhan* Father raised prayers of thanks to God. *Ia ~ harga* He raised the price. *Ia ~ tempat duduk* He raised the seat. *Ia di-kan ke atas bécak* She was put in the pedicab. **2** promote s.t., advance s.t. *Ia ~ pangkatnya* She promoted him. **ke-an 1** increase, raise. *~ harga* rise in prices. *~ gaji* salary increase. **2** promotion. *~ kelas* promotion of class (at school). *~ pangkat* promotion, advancement in rank. **3** vehicle, vessel. **4** (*Rel.*) ascension. *~ Nabi Isa* Ascension of Jesus. -*²an* time of promotion to next class. **pe-** climber. *~ darah* hothead. **pe-an 1** increasing. *Rencana ~ jam kerja ditolak buruh* The plan to raise the number of working hours was rejected by the workers. **2** raising. *~ bendéra* flag raising.

naim /na'im/ delightful, pleasant. - *Allah* (*Isl.*) the grace of God.

najam see NUJUM.

najis 1 (*Isl.*) defiling filth, s.t. which, if touched, makes o. unfit for prayer. **2** excrement. - *besar* feces, night soil. - *kecil* urine. **3** (*Coll.*) dirty. *Rumahku ini - diinjak org yg tdk tahu menghormati org tuanya* My house was defiled by people who did not know how to respect their parents. **me-kan 1** soil s.t. **2** consider s.t. dirty. **ke-an 1** state of being ritually unclean. **2** prohibited. **pe-an** contamination, desecration.

nak₁ see ANAK.

nak₂ see HENDAK.

nakal 1 naughty, mischievous. *Anak itu -* That child is naughty. **2** wanton. *perempuan - a* wanton woman. **me-i 1** abuse s.o. sexually. *Hanan mati dibunuh karena ~ seorg perempuan* Hanan was killed because he had sexually assaulted a woman. **2** do s.t. naughty to s.o. **ke-an 1** naughtiness, mischief. **2** delinquency. *~ anak/remaja* juvenile delinquency. -*²an* **1** in a naughty way, mischievously. *"Tunanganmu, ya?" kami bertanya dgn ~* "Is that your fiancé?" we asked in a naughty way. **2** (*Coll.*) do bad things.

naka-naka ber- sing by turns.

Naker [*Tenaga Kerja*] work force, manpower.

nakhoda (*Naut.*) ship's captain. - *Agung* Grand Admiral, admiral of the fleet. **me-i** captain s.t., be the captain of.

nakir see NANGKIR.

nako jalousie window.

nalam song, poetical composition.

nalar see TALAR.

Nalo [*Nasional Loteré*] National Lottery.

naluri instinct. - *kewanitaannya* her female instinct.

naluriah instinctive.

nam see ENAM.

nama 1 name. -*nya siapa?* What is his name? What is your name? *Apa -nya?* What is it called? *atas - keluarganya* in his family's name. *dgn -* by name, with the name of. - *batang tubuh* real name. - *dagang* trade name. - *daging* name given at birth or baptism. - *diri* proper name. - *éjékan/*

julukan nickname, alias. - *kecil* given name. - *keluarga* surname. - *panggilan* nickname. - *pédéngan/samaran* pseudonym. - *sandi* code name. - *sindiran* nickname. - *tambalan* subtitle. - *terang* o.'s name clearly written (as contrasted with signature). - *tubuh* name given at birth or baptism. **2** fame, title. *Ia mendapat* - He became famous. - *baik* good reputation. - *besar* famous, well known. **-nya 1** that is just another name for. *Tdk turut main sandiwara? Itu égois ~!* You do not want to act in the play with us? That is what you call egotistic! **2** what else would o. expect (considering what k.o. thing it is). *Mémang dia rakus, ~ pedagang* Of course he is greedy, after all he is a businessman. **ber- 1** called, named. *Ia ~ Ali* His name is Ali. **2** well known, famous. *spésialis ~* famous specialist. **me-i, me-kan** call, give a name to. *Ia ~ adiknya Zainah* He called his sister Zainah. **ter-** well known, famous. **ke-an** well known, famous. **berke-an** famed, famous. **pe-an** naming, nomenclature.

nambi 1 yaws. **2** skin rash.

nambor (*Coll.*) name-plaque.

namnam k.o. fruit-bearing tree.

nampak visible, evident. *Kepandaiannya tdk* - His ability is not evident. *Ia sdh lama tdk* - He has not been seen for a long time. - *oléh* noticed by, evident to. *Di ruang tamu* - *oléhnya ada org* She noticed s.o. in the guestroom. **-nya** apparently. *~ ia tak mau menunjukkan rumahnya* Apparently she did not want to indicate where she lived. **me-kan** make s.o. or s.t. visible. **pe-an** appearance (of spirits), vision.

nampan tray.

namun yet, however. *Mémang benar, - itu kan blm bisa jadi alasan utk menolaknya?* Of course it is true; however it is not a reason to refuse it, is it? - *apa (juga)* no matter what. - *apa juga diberikannya, selalu ia menolak* No matter what he was given he always refused it. - *demikian* nevertheless. *Tak seorg pun bekerja; - demikian, semuanya mengatakan sibuk* No o. was working; nevertheless they all said they were busy.

nan (*Lit.*) which, a particle between a noun and its modifying adjective. *dgn muka - gembira* with a cheerful face.

nanah suppuration, pus. **ber-, me-** suppurate, fester.

nanak-nunuk (*Jv*) slow-moving (person), slowpoke.

nanap 1 with wide-open eyes. **2** amazed.

nanar 1 confused. *Aku - dan kaku tak sedap perasaanku* I was confused and clumsy and did not feel comfortable. **2** angry. *dgn muka gusar dan pandangan yg* - with an angry face and furious glance.

nanas pineapple. - *seberang* k.o. Sumatran pineapple.

nanda see ANAKANDA.

nangka jackfruit. - *belanda* soursop. - *bubur* k.o. soft-fleshed jackfruit. - *salak* k.o. jackfruit with firm flesh.

nangkir (*Isl.*) o. of the two angels that observe and record o.'s deeds.

nangkring see TANGKRING.

nang-ning-nong sound of metallic resonance (e.g. gamelan, bell, etc.).

nanti 1 wait. - *dulu!* Wait a minute! **2** later, presently. *Aku kuatir kau kecéwa* - I am afraid you will be disappointed later. *Itu soal* - That is a problem for later. **3** presently at (such-and-such a time), to(night), this (noon, afternoon, etc.). *jam tiga* - later at three o'clock. - *malam* tonight. - *soré* this afternoon. **4** next, it might happen that (so watch out). *Jangan ngelamun di jalan, dong!* - *terlanggar bécak!* Do not daydream in the middle of the street! The next thing you know you will get hit by a pedicab. **-nya** later on, eventually. *Mobil yg lama ~ diapkir* The old automobiles eventually were put out of service. **-² *saja*** by and by. **ber-²** repeatedly wait, wait for a long time. *~ dgn gembira* look forward to. **me-** wait. *Aku menyuruhnya ~ sebentar* I told him to wait a moment. **me-² 1** wait a long time, wait on and on. **2** look forward to. **me-kan 1** wait for. *Ia diam ~ kata-kata yg keluar dr mulutku* She was silent and waited for the words to come out of my mouth. **2** watch for. *Mata setiap org ~ mobil itu* All eyes watched for the car. **ter-²** long for, anxiously wait for. **pe-** o. who waits. **pe-an 1** (process of) waiting. *dlm ~ hasilnya* while waiting for the results. **2** waiting room.

nantiasa see SENANTIASA.

nanyang /nan-yang/ the overseas Chinese, esp. of S.E. Asia.

napal k.o. clay (eaten for medicinal purposes).

napas₁ roan (of horses).

napas₂ see NAFAS.

napekah see NAFKAH.

napi₁ [*narapidana*] inmate, prisoner.

napi₂ see NAFI.

Napoli Naples.

napsi see NAFSI.

napsu see NAFSU.

naqli (*Isl.*) reference to relevant citation from Koran.

naradakwa accused, defendant.

naraka see NERAKA.

narapidana 1 convict, prisoner, prison inmate. **2** (*Leg.*) convicted criminal.

narapraja gvt. official.

narasumber resource person, informant.

Narayana 1 a boyhood name of Kresna. **2** (*Lit.*) (time) of o.'s youth.

narkose narcotics.

narkotika narcotics.

narsisisme narcissism.

narwastu spikenard oil.

nas (*Isl.*) authoritative quotation (from the Koran).

nasab 1 lineage, descent (in the male line). **2** (family) tie.

nasabah 1 customer, client. - *utama* best customer. **2** relationship. **per-an** client affairs.

nasakh abrogated. **me-kan** abrogate.

Nasakom [*Nasionalisme, Agama, Komunisme*] "Nationalism, Religion, Communism," political concept in Sukarno era. **me-kan** make s.o. a supporter of *Nasakom*. **pe-an** process of achieving the ideals implied by *Nasakom*. ~ *Angkatan Perang* reforming the armed forces in the spirit of *Nasakom*.

nasar₁ vulture.

nasar₂ see PENASARAN.

nasarani see NASRANI.

naséhat see NASIHAT.

nasgitel [*panas legi kentel*] (*Sl.*) hot, sweet, and syrupy.

nasi₁ 1 cooked rice. - *sdh jadi bubur* no use in crying over spilt milk (lit., the rice has turned to porridge). - *adap-adapan* k.o. ceremonial rice dish. - *angkatan* cooked rice at banquets. - *belantah* insufficiently cooked rice. - *beriani* rice cooked with Indian spices. - *besar* cooked rice for ceremonial purposes. - *biji limau* insufficiently cooked rice. - *damai* rice for wedding parties. - *datang* rice boiled in a leaf. - *dedang* steamed rice. - *godak* rice cooked together with side dishes. - *goréng* fried rice. - *gurih* rice cooked in coconut milk. - *hadap-hadapan* rice served at ceremonies. - *jelantah* insufficiently cooked rice. - *jemah* rice boiled in water. - *kabuli/kebuli* rice cooked served with mutton or goat curry. - *kepal* clotted cooked rice. - *ketupat* rice boiled in coconut fronds plaited in rhomboid shape. - *kuduk* rice cooked in coconut milk. - *kukus* steamed rice. - *kuning* yellow rice for ceremonial occasions. - *lemak* boiled rice with assorted side dishes. - *lemang* rice roasted in bamboo tubes. - *lengat* steamed rice. - *lepat* sticky rice boiled in a leaf. - *lécék* porridge. - *liwet* rice boiled in water. - *minyak* rice boiled in water to which oil is added. - *pelabur* ration of rice as food in prison, military barracks, etc. - *pulan* perfectly cooked rice. - *pulau* rice boiled in broth. - *pulut* cooked glutinous rice. - *ramas* rice and side dishes served together. - *ramsum* ration of rice as food in prison, military barracks, etc. - *rawon* rice served in a beef broth prepared with *keluak*. - *tim* steamed rice cakes served in broth. - *tingkas* white cooked rice with a border of colored rice. - *uduk/wuduk* rice cooked in coconut milk and served with condiments. 2 a meal (of rice). **ber-** with rice. ~ *di balik kerak* There is s.t. behind it (lit., there is rice behind the crust).

nasi₂ see NATIE.

nasib fate, destiny. *Ayahku menjalani -nya* My father accepted his fate. *Ia mencoba -nya* He tried his luck. - *baik* lucky. - *bedebah/celaka/ditimpa malang/malang/sial* bad luck. **se-** of o. destiny. *kawan* ~ o. sharing the same fate. ~ *sepenanggungan* share another's trials and tribulations. -ᵉ**an** at random, relying on o.'s good fortune.

nasihat advice, admonition. *Saya suka ceritera yg mengandung - yg baik* I like a story with a good moral. **me-i** 1 advise s.o. *Nanti saya akan* ~ *Hadi-*

jah spy jangan terlalu rapat dgnnya I will advise Hadijah not to get too close to him. 2 give advice in a scolding way. **me-kan** 1 give as advice. *Tentu yg baik-baik saja yg Bp -kan* surely you only offer the best as advice. 2 advise s.o. *Ia* ~ *anaknya agar tdk putus asa* She advised her child so he would not give up. **pe-** adviser, counselor, consultant. ~ *hukum* legal counsel.

nasion nation.

nasional national. **ke-an** 1 nationality. 2 nationalism. **pe-an** nationalization. *prosés* ~ process of nationalization.

nasionalis nationalist, nationalistic.

nasionalisasi nationalization. **me-kan** nationalize s.t. **pe-an** process of nationalization.

nasionalisir me- nationalize.

nasionalisme nationalism.

nasip see NASIB.

naskah 1 manuscript. 2 document, original text. - *asli* minutes (of meeting). - *ceramah* text of a lecture.

nasofaring (*Anat.*) nasopharynx.

nasrani 1 Christian. 2 (*Lit.*) Portuguese, of Portuguese creole descent. **me-kan** convert to Christianity. **ke-an** Christianity.

Natal Christmas. *Selamat (Hari)* - Merry Christmas. **-an** Christmas celebration.

natalitas birth rate. *angka* - birth rate figures.

natang (*Lit.*) small window, opening.

natar basic color, background. *mérah* - *kuning* red on a yellow background. **pe-an** yard, grounds. ~ *angkatan laut* navy yard.

natie /nasi/ (*Lit.*) nation.

natijah (*Lit.*) core issue (of argument, etc.).

natirlek /natirlek/ (*Coll.*) of course, naturally.

nato [*naskah asli ditepatkan oléh*] (*Leg.*) certified to be a true copy by.

natura in kind.

naturalisasi naturalization. **me-(kan)** naturalize (of citizenship).

naturalisme naturalism.

naturél neutral-colored shoe polish.

naudu-billahi, nauzu-billahi, naudzu-billahi (*Isl.*) I find protection in God, God bless us, God forbid that I should ever do it! (uttered when hearing of a despicable act or fact). *Harga minyak tanah sdh demikian,* ~*!* God bless us! What a price for kerosene!

naung 1 shadow, shade. 2 shelter, protection. **ber-** 1 take shelter. *Kami* ~ *di dlm gua itu* We took shelter in the cave. 2 be in the shelter. ~ *di bawahnya* under its auspices. **me-i** 1 shade. 2 protect, shelter. **-an** shelter, protection. *pohon* ~ shade tree. **pe-an** act of providing shelter. **per-an** shelter.

nautik nautical.

nautika nautical science.

nautis nautical.

navigasi navigation. - *udara* aerial navigation.

navigator navigator.

nayaga see NIYAGA.

nayuban see TAYUB.

nazam poem, composition. **me-kan** compose.
nazar₁ (*Rel.*) vow (to do s.t. if prayer is granted).
ber- make a promise of s.t. *Suami saya ~ memotong kambing kalau dia lulus* My husband has promised to slaughter a goat if he passes. **me-kan** vow to present s.t.
nazar₂ eagle.
nazir see NADIR₂.
n.b. [*nota bene*] nota bene.
ndableg, ndablek (*Jv*) **1** stubborn. **2** thick-skinned.
ndak₁ (*Coll.*) no, not.
ndak₂ see HENDAK.
ndang-ndut see DANG DANG DUT.
ndoro (*Jv*) master, term of address for a member of the aristocracy. *- kakung* master. *- minyak* (*Coll.*) oil baron. *- putri* mistress. **men-kan, -²an** call s.o. *ndoro.*
ndoroisme feudal attitude.
nduk (*Jv*) see GENDUK.
ndut-ndutan (*Coll.*) pulsate, throb (with pain, etc.).
né (*Ch*) term of address for o.'s mother.
nébéng (*Jkt*) **1** sponge off s.o. **2** hitchhike.
nécis (*Coll.*) neat, well groomed.
Néderlan, Néderland the Netherlands.
néfo, néfos [*new emerging forces*] newly independent countries (Sukarno-era term).
Neg.₁ [*Negeri*] country.
Neg.₂ [*Negara*] nation, state.
negara state. *tamu - state guest. - bagian* state in a federal system. *AS terdiri dr lima puluh - bagian* The US consists of 50 states. *- berkembang* developing country. *- hukum* constitutional state. *- kesatuan* unitary state. *- kesejahteraan* welfare state. *- Kangguru* Australia. *- Mabuhay* the Philippines. *- Paman Sam* USA. *- pengékor* client-state. *- Sakura* Japan. *- terbelakang* underdeveloped state. **me-kan 1** create a state. **2** regard as state property. **ke-an** matters pertaining to the state. *urusan ~* affairs of state. **-²an** country that does not measure up to what a country should be.
negarawan statesman. **ke-an** statesmanship.
négasi negation.
négatif, négatip negative.
néger /néher/ (*Coll.*) Negro, a black (esp. in colonial period).
negeri 1 country, land. *- antah-berantah* nevernever land, fairyland. *- awak* native country, homeland. *- di atas angin* **1** a faraway country. **2** an imaginary country, utopia. *- yg baka/kekal* the hereafter. *- luaran/orang* foreign country. **2** (*M, E. Indonesia*) village. **3** state-owned, state-run. *perusahaan - a* state-owned industry. **me-kan** make state-owned. *Universitas swasta itu dikan* The private university was made a state o. **pe-an** act of making s.t. state-owned.
négosiasi negotiation. **ber-** be engaged in negotiations. **me-kan** negotiate s.t.
néher see NÉGER.

nek₁ 1 too rich (of foods). **2** indigestion due to greasy foods.
nek₂ see ENEK.
nék see NÉNÉK.
néka see ANÉKA.
Nékad₁ [*Negara kita pertahankan; Ékonomi kita sosialiskan; Keamanan kita selenggarakan; Agama kita muliakan; Démokrasi terpimpin kita jalankan*] Sukarno-era slogan: The state we will defend; the economy we will socialize; security we will carry out; religion we will esteem; guided democracy we will put into operation.
nékad₂ see NÉKAT.
nékar marbles.
nekara (*Lit.*) kettledrum.
nékat determined, to do s.t. no matter what, ready to take serious risks. *Aku - melarikan diri diikuti tembakan para penjaga* The guards were firing at me, but I did not care. I was determined to escape. *Perampok itu -* The bandit was determined to do it no matter what. **me-** become determined to do s.t. no matter the consequences. **ke-an** determination to do s.t. no matter what. **-²an** undertake s.t. on basis of not heeding consequences and risks.
nékel see NIKEL.
Nékolim [*Néokolonialisme, Kolonialisme, Impérialisme*] Neocolonialism, Colonialism, Imperialism (Sukarno-era term).
néko-néko (*Jv*) **1** all k.o. things. **2** do diverse things unnecessarily.
nékrologi necrology.
nelangsa (*Jv*) arousing pity.
nelayan fisherman.
nelongso pathetic.
nem see ENAM.
nempil (*Jv*) buy s.t. from a place of business that does not normally sell that item, e.g. buy (uncooked) rice from a food stall.
nemplok position o.s. *Ia langsung - di belakang pianonya* She put herself behind the piano immediately. *Pengaruh Barat mulai -* Western influence started to sink in.
nemu see TEMU₂.
nén see NAN.
nenas see NANAS.
nénda see NÉNÉKANDA.
nénék 1 grandmother, great-aunt. *- kebayan* (*Sd*) a figure of legend who carries messages between lovers. **2** (*in some regions*) grandfather, great-uncle. *- mamak* elders. *- moyang* forefather, ancestor. **3** respectful term of reference and address (esp. as *nék*) for elderly persons (esp. women) and, in some areas, dangerous wild animals, e.g. tigers, etc. *- loréng* Grandpa Stripe (in reference to tiger). *- sihir* an old sorceress. **-²** very old, of an age to be a grandmother. **ke-²an** act like or be similar to a very elderly woman.
nénékanda, nénénda grandmother (esp. in letters).
nénér young milkfish.

néng (*Jkt, Sd*) polite form of address to younger woman.

néng-nong sound of metallic ringing (e.g. railway crossing bells, gamelan, etc.).

néo neo-. - *kolonialisme* neocolonialism.

néolitis neolithic.

néologisme neologism.

néon fluorescent or neon light. **me-kan** convert (street lights) to such lighting. - *pusat kota* convert the street lights of the city center to fluorescent lighting.

néonisasi provision of flourescent lamps for street lights.

népotisme nepotism.

neraca 1 pair of scales. **2** balance. - *kekuatan* balance of power. - *niaga* trade balance. - *pembayaran* (*Econ.*) balance of payments. - *utang piutang* (*Econ.*) balance sheet.

neraka 1 hell. **2** destruction, misfortune. **me-** be hell, be horrific. *Témbakan terus* ~ The shooting raged on. **me-i** impose hell on s.o. *Engkaulah yg* ~ *adik-adikmu* It is you who made it hell for your younger brothers and sisters. **me-kan** bring ruin upon.

nerawang translucent, lacy.

nerimo (*Jv*) passive, acquiescent to o.'s fate.

nerocos see CROCOS.

nésan see NISAN.

nestapa sorrow, grief. **ke-an** grief, sorrow.

nét₁ clear, precise.

nét₂ (*Sport*) net.

nétral 1 neutral. **2** uncommitted, nonaligned. **me-kan 1** permit to be neutral. **2** neutralize. **ke-an** neutrality. **pe-an** neutralization.

nétralis neutralist.

nétralisasi neutralization. **me-kan** neutralize.

nétralisir me- neutralize.

nétralisme neutralism.

nétralitas, nétralitét neutrality.

nétron see NÉUTRON.

nétto (*Fin.*) net. *Berapa penghasilan -?* How much is the net income?

neurolog (*Med.*) /nérolokh/ neurologist.

neurologi (*Med.*) /nérologi, nérolokhi/ neurology.

néutron /nétron/ neutron.

néven ancillary (of an organization). *PKI dan - ormasnya dilarang* The Communist party and its ancillary mass organizations were proscribed. **ng-** see also entries with **k-**.

ngabéhi, ngabéi (*Jv*) title of nobility.

ngabén (*Bali*) cremation.

ngabuburit (*Sd*) seek amusement and distractions while waiting for day's fast to end.

ngacau see KACAU.

ngaceng (*Coll.*) **1** be erect. **2** have an erection. **me-kan** set s.t. up erect.

ngacir flee, run away.

ngaco (*Coll.*) talk at random, talk without knowing what o. is talking about. - *bélo* talk at random, dom.

ngadak-ngadak make a fuss.

ngadat break down, sulk, go wrong. *Mobilku* - My car broke down.

ngahari see GAHARI.

ngai (*Ch*) I.

ngakak see KAKAK₂.

ngak-ngik-ngok, ngak-ngik-nguk 1 sound of cacophonic music. **2** low grade music (esp. pop music).

ngalor-ngidul (*Jv*) in all directions, without direction. *ngobrol* - chat on all sorts of topics.

ngambek pout, mope. *Dia -, pacarnya tdk datang* He sulked because his girlfriend did not come.

ngambul (*Jv*) sulk.

ngamén see AMÉN.

ngana (*Coll., Menado, N. Maluku*) you (singular).

nganga agape. **se-²nya** as wide as possible. **me-1** be agape, be wide open. *kawah yg* ~ a gaping crater. *Pintu belakang* ~ The backdoor stood wide open. **2** gape, gawk. *Dgn mulut* ~ *ia menontonnya* He watched her with a gaping mouth. **me-kan** keep s.t. wide open. *Dokter suruh dia* ~ *mulutnya* The doctor told him to open his mouth wide. **ter- 1** open, agape. *Mulutnya* ~ His mouth fell wide open. **2** amazed, flabbergasted. *Ia* ~ *di pintu, tak tahu hendak berbuat apa* She stood amazed at the door, not knowing what to do.

ngangeni see KANGEN.

ngangut me- mumble to o.s.

nganték (*Jv*) until.

ngantuk see KANTUK.

ngapa (*Coll.*) see MENGAPA.

ngap-ngap gasp for breath, pant.

ngarai (*M*) chasm, gorge.

ngarep see HARAP.

ngarit see ARIT.

ngarsa dalem /ngarso dalem/ (*Jv*) the sultan (of Yogya).

ngaung sound of s.t. resonating (airplane, etc.). **me-** make a resonating sound (howl, etc.).

ngawur do s.t. haphazardly or without basis. *lalulintas yg* - traffic patterns where people go whichever way they please. *statistik yg* - statistics that are given without basis in fact. *Kalau ndak tahu, - aja* If you do not know, say whatever comes to your head.

ngayau see KAYAU₁,₂.

nge- see also entries with **e-**. or the root alone.

ngéak sound of a baby crying. **me-(²)** cry, scream (of baby). *Waktu kau dilahirkan, kau* ~ When you were born, you cried.

ngebet (*Coll.*) want s.t. intensely, desire s.t. very strongly. *Dia lagi - sama si Minah* He is still pining for Minah.

ngebluk see KEBLUK.

ngebodoin (*Jkt*) see BODO₂.

ngeden (*Jv, Jkt*) strain during bowel movement.

ngék-ngék sickly.

ngel- see also entries with **ngl-, l-**.

ngélmu esoteric knowledge. - *kadigdayan* knowledge of magical power, us. invulnerability.

ngelonéng see LONÉNG.

ngelotok (*Jkt*) burst open (of fruit).
ngeloyor see KELUYUR.
ngelu (*Jv*) have a headache.
ngeluyur see KELUYUR.
ngemong see EMONG.
ngemot see KEMUT₂.
ngenes (*Jv*) deeply saddened. *Org tua itu mati - karena kelakuan anaknya* The parents died of a broken heart because of what the son had done.
ngengap gasp for breath, pant.
ngengat moth.
ngéngér (*Jv*) live with s.o. (esp. relatives) and do chores in return for room and board.
ngéngkél see ÉNGKÉL.
ngentit (*Coll.*) shortchange s.o., cheat s.o.
ngéntot see ÉNTOT.
ngenyék see ENYÉK.
ngéong meow. **me-** mew.
ngepas see PAS₁.
ngepiah see PIAH.
ngépot see KÉPOT₁.
nger- see also entries with **r-**.
ngeram see ERAM.
ngeran see KERAN₄.
ngerém see RÉM.
ngeres 1 (*Jv*) unpleasant or irritating sensation due to sand or dust (of sand in o.'s sheets, dust in o.'s eyes, etc.). 2 (*Coll.*) touching, sad.
ngeri 1 horrified. 2 horrifying. **me-kan** 1 cause o. to be horrified, blood curdling. *Berita pembantaian massal itu ~* The news of the mass execution was horrifying. 2 be disagreeable to, seem appalling to. *Mentuanya ~ semua teman-temannya* His parents-in-law horrified all his friends. **ke-an** 1 horror. 2 horrified. *Ada yg ketawa ada yg ~* Some laughed, others were horrified. **-an** 1 (*Coll.*) more terrifying. 2 terrified.
nges (*Jv*) very agreeable.
ngeslong see SLONG.
ngéténg see KÉTÉNG.
nggak (*Coll.*) no, not.
ngglenggem see GLENGGEM₂.
nggreges see GREGES.
nggrengseng see GRENGSENG.
ngiang sound of whining or steady humming. **-²** repeatedly whine. *si ~* k.o. supernatural being that whines. **me-** continually whine, hum, or buzz. *Suaranya itu ~ kembali dlm telinganya* That voice of his whined again in her ears. **ter-(²)** 1 whine complainingly. 2 buzz, buzzing. **-an** whining.
ngiau meow.
ngibrit (*Coll.*) run out of a place. *Ia - keluar sidang* He scurried out of the legislative session.
ngicip see ICIP.
ngijo see IJO₁.
ngikik see KIKIH.
ngik-ngik 1 sound of squeaking or screeching (e.g. asthmatic wheezing, violin screeching, etc.). 2 suffer from asthma.
ngiler see ILER.
ngilu pain, smart. *Giginya -* His teeth hurt him. **-²**

kuku lukewarm, tepid. **me-kan** set o. on edge. *~ gigi* set the teeth on edge. **ke-an** smarting pain, hurting feeling.
ngincer see INCAR.
ngirab see KIRAB₂.
ngiung-ngiung 1 sound of a siren, etc. 2 motorcade.
ngl- see also entries with **kl-, l-.**
nglunjak insolent, impertinent.
ngluyur see KELUYUR.
ngo (*Ch*) I.
ngobrol see OBROL.
ngocéh see KOCÉH.
ngok (*Jkt, Sl.*) loud smacking kiss.
ngoko (*Jv*) speech level of Jv used among intimates or when speaking to certain people of lower status.
ngolor see KOLOR.
ngomél see OMÉL.
ngomong see OMONG.
ngompol see OMPOL.
ngomyang grumble angrily (continuously).
ngoni (*Coll., Menado, N. Maluku*) you (plural).
ngorok snore.
ngos-ngosan (*Coll.*) gasp and pant.
ngot-ngotan 1 unpredictable. 2 furious.
ngotot see OTOT₂.
ngowos (*Coll.*) 1 leak (of a tire). 2 talk nonsense.
ngoyo (*Jv*) exert o.s. *Saya tdk - tetapi dpt menggunakan otak semaksimal mungkin* I do not exert myself. Rather I make maximal use of my brains.
ngréh (*Jv*) look down on.
ngréwés (*Jv*) *tdk -* indifferent.
ngublag-ngubleg see UBLAK-UBLEK.
ngubleg-ngubleg see UBLEG-UBLEG.
ngudang see KUDANG.
nguing-nguing sound of siren.
nguler wormlike. *- kambang* very slow.
ngunduh see UNDUH.
ngungu sound of repeated sobbing, choking etc. **ter-** make such noises. *Ia menangis ~ spt anak kecil* He wept in choked sobs like a child.
ngurek 1 (*Jv*) gnaw. 2 (*Coll.*) be inquisitive.
ngutngit gnawing.
ngut-ngut (*Lit.*) nervous movement of mouth, twitch.
ni₁ (*Bali*) respectful title for women.
ni₂ (*Ch*) you.
ni₃ see NIH.
niaga commerce, trade. **ber-** engage in trading. **me-kan, memper-kan** trade s.t. **ter-** traded, sold. *Di situ sdh ~ tdk kurang dr lima ratus sepéda* No less than 500 bicycles were already marketed there. **ke-an** marketing, trade. **pe-** trader. **per-an** trade, commerce. *~ écéran/rincih* retail trade.
niagawan trader.
nian very, really. *Sukar - hitungan ini* This calculation is really difficult. *Bagus - gambar ini* This picture is very beautiful.
niat intention, plan, aim. *-nya tdk dpt dilaksanakan* Her plans cannot be carried out. *membayar -*

fulfill o.'s promise. **ber-** intend. *Aku tdk ~ membunuh kau* I do not intend to kill you. **ber-²** wish intensely. **me-i** intend to get s.t., have a wish for s.t. *Aku ~ mobilmu. Akan kaujual tdk?* I have my eye on your car. Will you sell it or not? **me-kan** make s.t. o.'s intention. **me-²kan** wish intensely to do s.t. **ter-** 1 intended, meant. 2 get an idea, conceive a plan. *~ dlm hatiku akan memberikan lukisan itu kpdnya* I got the idea of giving the painting to her. **-an** s.t. that is intended. *makna ~* intended meaning.

nibung k.o. palm, the nibong.

NICA /nika/ [*Netherlands Indies Civil Administration*] postwar administrative system imposed by the Dutch in occupied territories.

nifas 1 childbirth, parturition. 2 (*Isl.*) the 40-day period after childbirth during which sexual intercourse is forbidden.

nigong dental plaque, film adhering to teeth.

nih 1 particle pointing to s.t. nearby. *Hasilnya ini -* This is the result here. 2 see INI.

nihil nothing, nil. *Hasilnya -* The results are nil. **ke-an** nothingness.

nihilis nihilist.

nihilisme nihilism.

nihistis nihilistic.

nik see NONI.

nikah 1 marriage, wedding. *akad -* marriage contract. *- gantung* marriage formally registered and celebrated but without consummation (pending completion of schooling, reaching legal age, etc.). 2 marry. *Kami sdh sepuluh tahun -* We have been married for 10 years. **ber-** married. **me-** get married. *~ tamasya* wedding with no celebratory meal; the couple leaves immediately for honeymoon. **me-i** marry s.o. *Ia tdk mau ~ Alex* She does not want to marry Alex. **me-kan** marry s.o. off. *Ia ~ anaknya* He married off his child. **-²an** marry repeatedly. **per-an** marriage, wedding ceremony.

nikel nickel (metal).

nikmat 1 comfort, luxury. 2 deeply enjoyable, pleasant. *percintaan yg -* delicious love. *pemandangan yg -* a pleasant view. 3 (*Isl.*) grace. *- bagi tiap-tiap makhluk manusia* a divine gift of grace for each human being. **me-i** 1 enjoy. *-ilah rasa segar di mulut!* Enjoy a fresh feeling in your mouth! 2 benefit from. *Kekayaan alam negara ini blm di-i seluruh rakyatnya* Not all of the people of this country have had a chance to benefit from the wealth of its natural resources. **me-kan** relish s.t., enjoy to the fullest. *Ia ~ és krim* He enjoys ice cream. **ke-an** 1 bliss, enjoyment. *~ perkelaminan* sexual pleasure. 2 comfort, amenity. 3 the privilege of benefiting from s.t. *~ perumahan kantor* the privilege of having a company housing. **pe-** lover, devotee.

nikotin nicotine.

Nil Nile.

nila blue dye, indigo.

nilai 1 price, value. *- uang* the value of money. *- beli* purchase price. *- gizi* nutritive value. *- nomi-* nal face value. *- sastra* quality of literature. 2 school grades. *- Bahasa Indonésiaku selalu jelék* My grades for Indonesian are always low. 3 percentage, proportion. *- kalori* calorie percentage. 4 moral value. *- hidup* 1 values of life (philosophical views). 2 the worth of life. **ber-** valuable, precious. *harta yg betul-betul ~ dlm kehidupan* property which is really valuable in life. **me-(kan)** appraise, evaluate. *Kita bisa objéktip ~ mana roman yg baik* We can evaluate objectively which novels are good. *~ kembali* reevaluate. **ter-** be estimated, given a value. *tdk ~* invaluable, priceless. **-an** estimate, valuation. **pe-** appraiser, assessor. 2 grader, judge (in competition). *Dua ~ pertama memilih Muh. Ali* The first two judges chose Muh. Ali. **per-an** 1 judgment. 2 evaluation, appraisal. *~ kecakapan* performance rating.

nilakandi 1 sapphire. 2 sapphire blue, azure.

nilam₁ k.o. shrub yielding fragrant oil, patchouli.

nilam₂ see BATU.

nilam₃ see BURUNG.

nilem see NILAM₁.

nilon nylon.

nimbrung (*Coll.*) join on in conversation where o. is not wanted, butt into discussion. *É, anak kecil kok - pembicaraan org déwasa* Hey, what is a youngster doing butting into a grown-up's discussion! **me-i** interrupt a conversation.

ninabobo, ninabobok lullaby. **me-kan** lull to sleep. *Ia tdk suka lagi di-kan spt anak kecil* She no longer liked to be put to sleep with a lullaby like a little child. **pe-an** abuse of confidence.

ning see NÉNG.

ning-néng, ning-nong sound of jiggling, such as horse-drawn carriage, etc.

ningrat nobility, aristocracy. *kaum -* aristocratic class. **me-kan** 1 treat s.o. as a noble. 2 raise s.o. to the rank of noble, knight s.o. **ke-an** aristocracy. **ke-²an** aristocraticlike, with aristocratic airs. *Tentulah juga sedikit ~* Of course, it is a little highfalutin. **-²an** feudal.

ningratisme feudal way of thinking and behaving.

nini see NÉNÉK.

ninik (*Ch*) term of address for little girl.

ninik-mamak (*M*) village elders.

ninitowok, ninitowong (*Jv*) 1 k.o. spirit possession involving figure made of coconut shell. 2 such a figure of coconut shell.

NIP [*Nomor Induk Pegawai*] 1 official registry number of civil servants. 2 letter of appointment for civil servants.

nipah thatch palm, nipa palm.

nipis₁ see TIPIS₁.

nipis₂ see JERUK.

Nipon (*Coll.*) Japan.

nir₁ (*Coll.*) kidney. *sakit -* kidney ailment.

nir₂ (*Lit.*) not, non-. *program -gelar* a nondegree program.

nira sap obtained by tapping inflorescences of various palms used to make sugar.

nirair anhydrous.
nirakal insensible.
nirarti meaningless.
nirasa apathy.
nirbangun amorphous.
nirbau odorless.
nirbhaya without danger.
nirgelar nondegree.
nirhawa without air.
nirlaras disharmonious.
nirléka prehistoric.
nirmala clean, pure.
nirmana mode.
niru₁ see TIRU.
niru₂ see NYIRU.
nirwana nirvana.
nirwarna colorless.
nisan gravestone.
nisbah 1 family name, name descriptive of origin or relationship. **2** (*Fin.*) ratio. - *utang* the ratio of indebtedness (to the total capitalization). **ber-** be related to. **me-kan** relate s.t. to.
nisbi, nisbiah relative, proportionate. *lembab -nya angin ini* the relative humidity of the air. **me-kan** make s.t. relative. **ke-an** relativity.
niscaya certainly, surely,. *Apa saja yg dimintanya - akan diberikan oléh Aléx* Surely Alex will give her whatever she asks. **ke-an** certainty.
niskala abstract, immaterial. **me-kan** abstract s.t. **ke-an** abstraction. **pe-an** process of making s.t. abstract.
nista 1 insult, abuse. **2** stigma. **3** insulted, humiliated. *Ia merasa terlalu - diikat begitu* She found it humiliating to be tied up like that. **4** base, low. **me-** insult. **me-i, me-kan** insult s.o. **ke-an 1** insult. **2** feeling of indignity. **-an** insult. **pe-an 1** defamation, (act of) insulting. **2** stigmatization.
nitis see TITIS₁.
nitrat (*Chem.*) nitrate.
Niugini see PAPUA NUGINI.
nivo the level of s.t. - *laut* sea level. - *pendidikan saat ini dianggap rendah* The present level of education is considered low.
niyaga, niyogo (*Jv*) performers in gamelan orchestra.
njelirit (*Jv*) form a thin line, like a thin line. *Kumisnya* - He had a thin line for a mustache.
njlimet see JELIMET.
NKK [*Normalisasi Kehidupan Kampus*] a gvt. measure to reduce student militancy in late 1970's.
Nn. [*nona*] Miss.
no (*Ch, Jkt*) two, in commercial transactions. - *ban* 20,000. - *cap* twenty. - *céng* 2,000.
noban see NO.
nobat royal drum used at installation ceremonies. **me-kan** crown, install. **pe-an** coronation, installation.
nocap, nocéng see NO.
noda 1 stain, spot of dirt. - *matahari* sunspot. **2** shame, disgrace. **ber-** stained, besmirched. *Maria perawan tak* ~ the Virgin Mary undefiled.

me-i 1 stain s.t. *Darah menétés* ~ *bajunya* Blood spots stained his shirt. **2** disgrace. ~ *perempuan* 1 deflower a woman. **2** disgrace a woman. **ter-1** stained, soiled. **2** despoiled, disgraced. *Namanya sdh* ~ His name has been sullied. **pe-an 1** staining, soiling. **2** despoiling, disgracing.
nodul, nodule (*Med.*) nodule.
nok see DENOK.
noktah 1 dot, point. **2** period (of punctuation). **me-i** put small dots on s.t.
nol nought, zero. *Hasilnya* - His efforts amounted to nothing. *tiga puluh derajat di atas* - 30 degrees above zero. - *besar* 1 2d level of preschool, kindergarten. **2** total failure. *Hasilnya - besar* All he got out of it was a goose egg. - *kecil* first level of preschool, nursery school.
nomade, nomaden nomad, nomadic.
nombor see NOMER.
nomenklatur nomenclature.
nomer 1 number. - *bewés* vehicle license. - *bukti* number assigned as proof (of services rendered). - *buncit* finally, last of all. - *buntut* 1 the final two or three digits in illegal lottery. 2 final, last of all. - *dua* 1 runner-up. 2 2d place. **me-duakan** give 2d place to, give less priority. - *induk pokok* official register number of gvt. officials. - *korét* the latter, the last o. - *lingkungan wilayah pos* zipcode. - *pelat* license plate. - *registrasi pokok* (*Mil.*) soldier's registration number. - *satu/utama/wahid* 1 excellent. 2 number o. in importance, priority, etc. **me-satukan** give top priority to. *Sandang pangan hrs di-satukan* Give top priority to basic needs. **2** issue (of a periodical). - *kembar* double issue (of magazine). - *lepas* loose issue, single number of a periodical. - *perdana* first issue of a newly published serial. - *perkenalan* introductory number or issue. **3** number in a musical show. **se-** per number, per issue. **me-** give a number to. *Daftar dan gambar di-* The list and pictures were numbered. **me-i** number several things. *sdr hrs* ~ *barang-barang itu* You must number those things. **pe-an** numbering.
nominal nominal (in statistics, research, mathematics).
nomor see NOMER.
nompang see TUMPANG.
nomplok (*Coll.*) be s.w. in large quantities. *Mengapa semua buku perpustakaan - di rumah dosén?* Why do all the library books wind up in the lecturer's house? *Rejekinya sedang* - Good fortune is piling up on her.
non₁ (*Pol.*) noncooperative. *kaum - dan ko* the non-cooperatives and the cooperatives (i.e. those who did and those who did not cooperate with the Dutch in colonial times).
non₂ nun.
non₃ see NONI.
nona 1 miss, unmarried European, Ch, or Westernized well-to-do Indonesian girl in Western dress. **2** term of address for such women. **3** (*Amb*) unmarried woman.
nonaktif inactive, laid-off. **me-kan** deactivate, de-

commission. **pe-an** deactivating, decommissioning.

non-aliansi nonalliance.

noné (*Jkt*) see NONA.

non-éksakta (*Acad.*) pertaining to humanities and social sciences rather than exact sciences.

nonformal, nonformil 1 outside the regular system, irregular. *pendidikan -* education outside the regular school system. **2** (*Coll.*) informal.

nongkrong see TONGKRONG.

nongol (*Jkt*) stick the head out, appear, be conspicuous. *pengusaha yg sering - di koran* a businessman whose name often appears in the papers. **pe-an** act of appearing.

noni, nonik (*Coll.*) **1** young girl, esp. European or in European clothes. **2** affectionate term of address for such a girl, esp. as *nik* or *non*.

nonius (*Tech.*) vernier.

nonok (*Jkt, Vulg.*) vagina.

nonpri, nonpribumi of foreign descent, nonnative (esp. referring to ethnic Chinese).

nonsén nonsense, ridiculous.

nonton see TONTON.

nonya see NYONYA.

noot /not/ see NOT.

Nopémber November.

nopol [*nomor polisi*] vehicle registration number.

nora, norak (*Jkt*) tacky, in bad taste, vulgar, lower than normal. *corak yg -* garish designs. *Caranya berpakaian - benar* She dresses in very bad taste.

norit general term for carbon-based medicine for stomach problems.

norma norm, standard.

normal normal. *Org itu sptnya nggak -* S.t. is not quite normal about that man. **me-kan** normalize. *~ kegiatan politik* normalize the political activities.

normalisasi normalization. **me-kan** normalize.

norostos sound of firecrackers. *dgn suara - spt petasan* with a voice crackling like a string of firecrackers.

Norwégia Norway.

nostalgi, nostalgia nostalgia.

nostalgis nostalgic.

not musical note. *- angka* musical notation system in which notes are assigned numbers (e.g. do = 1, re = 2, etc.). *- balok* musical note.

nota 1 note. *- krédit* (*Fin.*) note of credit. **2** statement of account, bill. **3** memorandum. *- perubahan* amendment in writing. *- penjelasan* aide-memoire.

nota béné nota bene.

notariat office of notary.

notariil notarial. *surat -* notarial act.

notaris notary public. **ke-an** notarial affairs.

notasi notation. **ber-** annotated. *bibliografi ~* annotated bibliography.

notés small notebook, notepad.

notifikasi notification.

notilen minutes, notes (of a meeting).

notok₁ (*Jv*) to the very end.

notok₂ see TUTUK.

notulen see NOTILEN.

notulis recorder of the minutes of a meeting.

novel novel.

novéla novella.

novelis novelist.

novis novice.

novisiat novitiate.

nr. [*nomor*] number.

NRI [*Negara Républik Indonésia*] Republic of Indonesia.

nrimo see NERIMO.

NRP [*Nomer Régistrasi Pokok*] soldier's registration number.

ntar (*Coll.*) see SEBENTAR.

NTB [*Nusa Tenggara Barat*] Western Lesser Sundas.

NTR [*Nikah, Talak, Rujuk*] be married, divorced, and reconciled.

NTT [*Nusa Tenggara Timur*] E. Lesser Sundas.

NU [*Nahdlatul Ulama*] Association of Muslim Scholars, a Muslim political party of the 1970s.

nuansa nuance.

nubuat (*Rel., Isl.*) prophecy, divine revelation. *tahun tiga puluh -* in the year 30 of the prophet (30 years after the *Hijrah*). **ber-** prophesy. **me-kan** prophesy s.t.

nudis nudist.

nudisme nudism.

nuduh see TUDUH.

nugat nougat.

Nugini see PAPUA NUGINI.

Nuh (*Bib.*) Noah.

nujum fortune-telling, esp. with stars. *ahli -* astrologer. **me-** tell o.'s fortune, consult the stars. *~ takdir* tell o.'s fortune. **me-kan** predict. **memper-kan** consult the stars, cast o.'s horoscope. **-an** prediction. **pe-** fortune-teller. **per-an** astrology.

nukhter objective, balanced (of views, etc.).

nukil 1 quotation, quote. **2** excerpt. **me- 1** quote, cite. **2** excerpt. **me-kan 1** quote s.t. **2** excerpt s.t. **-an 1** quotation, citation. **2** excerpt.

nuklir (*Phys.*) nuclear. **per-an** nuclear affairs.

nul see NOL.

numpang see TUMPANG.

numpleg, numplek see TUMPLEK.

nun (*Lit.*) yonder. *- di balik gunung* yonder, on the other side of the mountain.

nunak-nunuk (*Coll.*) **1** slow in doing s.t. **2** snoop around.

nuntius papal nuncio.

nunut (*Jv*) ride along with. *swarga - neraka katut* the wife shares the husband's fate (lit., go along to heaven, get taken along to hell). **me-i 1** get a ride with s.o. **2** go along with s.o.'s opinion, success, etc. **-an** get a ride. *Boléh saya ~ sampai kota?* Can I get a ride with you as far as the city?

nur (*Lit.*) light, ray of light.

nuraga sympathy.

nurani 1 lustrous, illuminated. **2** pure. **3** inner. *hati -* o.'s inner self.

nurbisa (*Lit.*) antidote, esp. charm or incantation against venom.

nuri k.o. parrot.
nurmala see NIRMALA.
nus k.o. flat-headed squid.
nusa island, esp. in island names. *utk - dan bangsa* for the homeland. - *Nipa* Flores. - *Tenggara* the Lesser Sundas (Bali to Timor).
Nusakambangan a penal island off the S. coast of Java. **me-kan** imprison s.o. at this island.
nusantara 1 archipelago. **2** the Indonesian Archipelago.
Nusra [*Nusa Tenggara*] the Lesser Sundas.
Nusrabar [*Nusa Tenggara Barat*] Western Lesser Sundas.
Nusrateng [*Nusa Tenggara Tengah*] Central Lesser Sundas.
Nusratim [*Nusa Tenggara Timur*] E. Lesser Sundas.
Nusteng [*Nusa Tenggara*] the Lesser Sundas.
nusus, nusyuz (*Isl.*) disobedient (of wives, esp. with regard to granting of conjugal rights).
nutfah (*Biol.*) germ, sperm.
nutrisi nutrition.
nutrisionis nutritionist.
Nuzulul Qur'an (*Isl.*) day commemorating descent of the Koran.
NV [*Naamloze Vennootschap*] Inc., Ltd.
Ny. [*Nyonya*] Mrs.
ny- see also entries with **s-, c-**.
-nya 1 his, her, its, their. *toko-* his (her, their) store. **2** your. *Putra- berapa, pak?* How many children do you have, Sir? **3** him, her, it, them (form of *dia* optionally used after prepositions or verbs with prefix *meng-*). *Saya berikan pd-* I gave it to him. *Terambil oléh-* He accidentally took it. *Saya datang dgn-* I came with him. *Saya tdk melihat-* I cannot see him. **4** the, the o. that we have been talking about or we both know about. *Di situlah rumah-* That is where the house is. *Min, keluarkan és-* Min, take out the ice (that there is). **5** noun-forming affix. *Dr mana datang-* Where do you come from (or where is he coming from)? *Di Surabaya- tiga hari* I was three days in Surabaya. (Lit., the Surabaya stay was three days.). *Tergantung ada tdk-* It depends on whether there are any or not. **6** suffix to adverbs when placed in emphatic position. *Bukan- saya tdk mau* It is not the case that I do not want to. *Mau apa kamu mémang-?* Actually, what is it you want? **7** suffix in words with prefix *se-*. *dikerjakan sebaik-baik-* Do it as well as possible. *Seharus- saya diundang* I should have been invited. *Ditutupi permadani seluruh-* It was covered with a rug, all of it. **8** by him, her, it or them (suffix to verbs with *di-*). *Sdh dilihat-* He has seen it.
nya see NYONYA.
nyabun see SABUN₁.
nyadran see SADRAN.
nyah₁ see ENYAH.
nyah₂ see NYONYA.
nyaho /nyaho'/ (*Jkt*) **1** know, understand. **2** find out the hard way. *Nggak mau dibilangin! Biar dié -*

déh! He does not want to listen! Let him find out the hard way then!
nyai 1 term of reference and address for concubine of European or Ch in colonial period. **2** (*Jv*) respectful term of address to older woman.
nyak₁ (*Jkt*) term of address and reference for o.'s mother.
nyak₂ see NYONYA.
nyala flame. - *lampu* the flame of a lamp. - *matanya* the glow in her eyes. **-²** *hidup* keep going on and off, flicker. *listrik yg ~ hidup* electricity that keeps going on and off. **ber- 1** flame, flare up. **2** burn (of light). *Lampunya tlh ~ dgn terang* The lamp was already burning bright. **ber-²** burn, flare up repeatedly. **me-** flame, flare up. *semangat ~* a burning inspiration. *Api unggun ~ besar* The camp fire flared up. **me-²** **1** flare up violently. **2** spirited, raging. *rasa benci yg ~* a burning hatred. **me-i** ignite, light. **me-kan 1** set fire to, ignite s.t. *~ rokok* light a cigarette. **2** switch on. *~ lampu* switch on a lamp. **3** stir up, inflame (hatred, spirit, etc.). *Pidatonya ~ semangat pendengarnya* His speech stirred up his audience's spirit. **me-²kan** provoke, incite. *~ permusuhan antar golongan* incite interethnic enmity. **pe-an** ignition.
nyalang₁ clear (of vision). *Matanya -* He could see clearly. **me-kan** open (eyes).
nyalang₂ see JALANG.
nyalawadi (*Jv*) arousing suspicion, having s.t. secret about it.
nyalé see SALAI.
nyali 1 gall, bile. **2** guts, daring o. shows in a crisis situation. - *besar* courage. *-nya besar, selalu di depan kalau démonstrasi* She has got pluck, she's always in the front line of a demonstration. - *kecil* cowardice.
nyaman pleasant, comfortable. **me-kan 1** make fit, freshen up. **2** make pleasant or comfortable. *Alat pendingin itu ~ ruangan kantor* The air-conditioner made the office more comfortable. **ke-an 1** freshness, fit feeling. **2** pleasure. **pe-** s.t. which makes s.t. comfortable.
nyambi see SAMBI.
nyamikan /nyami'an/ **1** (*Jv*) sweet snacks, candy. **2** (*Coll.*) mistress.
nyampang in case, just in case, by chance. - *ke kantor pos, belikan perangko utk saya* In case you go to the post office, please buy stamps for me. **-²** on the chance, just in case. **se- 1** supposing that, if. **2** (*Lit.*) although.
nyampoh k.o. tree.
nyamuk mosquito. - *pérs* newspaper reporter.
nyana expect, presume, think. *Tak - ia akan mencuri* I did not expect him to steal. **di-** expected, considered possible. *Tdk ~ dia sdh berumah tangga* I did not realize he was married. **me-kan** expect s.t., suspect s.t. **ter-** expected, thought. *tdk ~ sama sekali* completely unexpected.
nyandu see CANDU.

nyang (*Coll.*) see YANG₁.

nyanyah (*Jv*) **me-** chew.

nyanyi ber-, me- sing. ~ *kecil* hum. **me-kan** sing s.t. *Dia suka ~ lagu geréja* She loved to sing church hymns. **-an** song, melody. ~ *geréja* hymn. **pe-** singer.

nyap-nyap (*Jkt*) angry.

nyaring 1 high-pitched, piercing. *suara -* a high-pitched voice. **2** (*Ling.*) sonorant. **me-kan** make o.'s voice sharp and piercing. **ke-an** (*Ling.*) sonority.

nyaris nearly (of s.t. unpleasant). *- mati* come close to dying. *- ketinggalan* almost left behind.

nyaru disguised. *Ia pencuri - polisi* He was a thief disguised as a policeman.

nyasar see SASAR.

nyata 1 obvious, evident. *Pentingnya perkawinan itu sdh -* The importance of that marriage is obvious. **2** real, tangible. *penghasilan -* real income. *perbuatan -* actual deed. **-²** decidedly. **(se)-nya** as it is, as clear as can be. *~ aku sekarang tdk jadi kapir* It is plain as can be, now I am not a nonbeliever. **me-** getting clearer. *Percakapan yg semula tdk berujung-pangkal itu, kemudian ~lah arahnya* The conversation, which was confused at first, clarified itself later on. **me-kan 1** explain, clarify. **2** declare, assert. *Bangsa Jepang ~ perang* The Japanese declared war. *~ diri* manifest itself. **memper-** make s.t. obvious. **ter- 1** it appears, apparently. **2** it turned out. *Ia merasakan pahanya dan ~ ia kena témbakan* She felt her thigh and it turned out that she had been hit. **ke-an 1** fact, data. *Laporannya berlawanan dgn ~* His report is in contradiction with the facts. **2** truth, reality. *Dia tak mau hidup dlm ~* He does not want to live in reality. *dlm/pd ~(nya)* in fact. **per-an 1** declaration, pronouncement. *~ bersama* joint statement. *~ cinta* declaration of love. *~ perang* declaration of war. **2** expression. *~ terima kasih* expression of gratitude.

nyatut see CATUT.

nyawa life-sustaining principle, soul. *Kau tahu bhw -mu ada di tangan kami?* Don't you know that your life is in our hands? *Dia punya - rangkap* He has nine lives (lit., life twice over). *buang -* risk o.'s life. *satu - dua badan* very close friends. **se-1** of o. soul, completely agreed. **2** (*Chem.*) compound. *~ sianid* cyanide. **se-an** union, complete mixture. **berse- 1** agree completely, see eye to eye. **2** (*Chem.*) become a compound (in a reaction). **memperse-kan** (*Chem.*) perform a reaction creating a compound. **perse-an** fusion of chemical compounds. **ber- 1** have a soul, be alive. *tak ~ lagi* dead. **2** animate.

nyawang see SAWANG₄.

nyekar see SEKAR.

nyelang see NYALANG₁, SELANG₁.

nyelonong see SELONONG.

nyemplak go to a prostitute.

nyengir-nyengir see CENGIR.

nyeni see SENI₁.

nyéntrik 1 eccentric, act in such a way that o. stands out as different. **2** (*Coll.*) stick out, be different from every o. else.

nyenyai loosely woven.

nyenyak be sound (of sleep). **me-kan** put s.o. sound asleep. *Dinginnya udara pagi itu lebih ~ tidur* The early morning chill makes o. sleep even more soundly. **ke-an 1** soundness of sleep. *dlm ~ tidurnya* in the soundness of his sleep. **2** too sound.

nyényéh (*Jv*) suppurating, not healing well (of wound).

nyenyep very quiet.

nyepi₁ last day of Balinese calendar, when no work is done.

nyepi₂ see SEPI.

nyepor see SEPUR.

nyéprét see CÉPRÉT.

nyeri painful, sharp (pain). *- hati* sharply painful (emotion). *- syaraf* neural twinge.

nyerimpung see SERIMPUNG.

nyerocos see CROCOS.

nyeték see SETÉK.

nyi (*Jv*) respectful title for women.

nyilu see NGILU.

nyinyir talkative, fond of chatting. **ke-an** talkativeness, loquacity.

nyiplak see CIPLAK₁.

nyiru k.o. flat basket. **me-** use such a tray to winnow.

nyiur (*Lit.*) coconut. *- kelongkong* young coconut with soft edible flesh adhering to shell's interior.

nylentik see SLENTIK.

nylon see NILON.

nyok (*Jkt*) see AYO.

nyolnyolan (*Coll.*) unladylike (of coarse, mannish behavior).

nyolok see COLOK₂.

nyolong see COLONG.

nyong 1 (*Amb*) young man. **2** (*Amb*) polite term of address for males younger than speaker. **3** (*Jkt*) term of address among intimate male friends.

nyonték cheat on exams. *Kalau ujian dia pasti - pekerjaanmu* He is sure to copy your paper during exams. **me-** cheat on exams.

nyonya 1 Mrs. (esp. of non-Indonesian, i.e. Ch, foreigners). *- Abadi* Mrs. Abadi. **2** lady. *- rumah* 1 lady of the house. 2 housewife. *- besar* 1 Mrs., Madam. 2 old lady. **3** respected woman. **3** (*Coll.*) wife. **4** term of address (esp. as *nya* or *nyah*) for Ch and Western women.

nyora (*E. Indonesia*) term of polite address for certain women of high status (e.g. minister's wife, etc.).

nyrémpét see SERÉMPÉT.

nyunyut (*Jv*) be soggy (of s.t. that was crisp).

nyureng see CURENG.

nyut sensation of stabbing pain. **-²(an)** sharp, throbbing pain. *Tangannya terasa -- sehabis latihan bulutangkis* Her hand throbbed with pain after badminton practice.

O

o₁ /o/ o, the 15th letter of the alphabet.

o₂ 1 Oh, interjection expressing surprise. - *Pak Rusli! Silakan duduk!* Oh, it is Rusli! Please have a seat! - *lihatlah bagaimana bagusnya!* Oh! Look how beautiful it is! **2** oh that, interjection expressing perception or remembering. - *ya, baru saya ingat* Oh yes, now I remember. - *begitu. Bp hanya kerja malam saja?* Oh I see. You only work at night? **3** interjection expressing strong emotional feeling. - *Adil, aku selalu takut ini akan terjadi* Oh Adil, I have always been afraid this might happen.

o₃ (*Lit.*) oh, vocative marker. - *angin,* - *danau, kepunyaan nénék moyang kami* O wind, O lake, which belong to our ancestors.

O. [*Otomat*] (*Tel.*) dial telephone.

oase oasis.

obah see UBAH.

oban see UBAN.

obar see KOBAR.

obat 1 medicine, potion. - *ajaib* wonder drug, elixir. - *angin* cold medicine. - *batuk* cough medicine. - *dlm* medicine for internal use. - *gosok* 1 liniment. **2** scouring powder. - *guna* philter, charm. - *jalan* outpatient treatment. **ber-** *jalan* get outpatient treatment. - *jarum* serum. - *kampung* traditional medicine. - *kimia* chemotherapy. - *kuat* tonic. - *lali* anesthetic. - *lelah* 1 refreshment. **2** tip (lit., medicine for tiredness). - *luar* medicine for external use. - *mérah* iodine, Mercurochrome. - *pelancar* lubricant, Vaseline. - *peluntur* laxative, purgative. - *puru* medicine for boils. - *suntik(an)* injection. - *urus* laxative, purgative. **2** toiletry. - *ketiak* deodorant. - *kumur* mouthwash, gargle. - *rambut* depilatory. **3** chemical preparation (e.g. cleaner, repellent, etc.). - *asah(an)* abrasive. - *hawa* insecticide, pesticide. - *kelantang/pemucat* bleaching powder. - *nyamuk* mosquito repellent. - *potrét* chemicals for photography. **4** gunpowder. - *basah* wet gunpowder. - *bedil/sendawa* gunpowder. **ber-** 1 have treatment. *Ia ~ pd dokter Hasyim* He is being treated by Dr. Hasyim. *Ia ~ di rumah sakit* She got treatment at a hospital. **2** take medicine. *Ia ~ karena sakit perut* He is taking medicine for his stomachache. **meng-(i)** treat s.o. or s.t. *~ org sakit* treat sick people. *~ telinga yg luka* treat a wounded ear. **meng-kan 1** treat s.t. medically. *Ia ~ kakinya yg luka* He treated his injured foot. **2** treat with s.t. **ter-(kan) 1** treated, cured. **2** comforted, tempered. *Kekecéwaannya agak ~ karena kabar ini* Her disappointment was somewhat

tempered by this news. **-²an** medicines. *persediaan* ~ supply of medicines. **peng-** healer, therapist. ~ *hati* consolation. **peng-an** medicinal treatment, therapy. ~ *kimia* chemotherapy. ~ *sarafi* neural therapy.

obéng screwdriver. - *belimbing/bintang/kembang* Philips screwdriver.

oberal see OBRAL.

obituari obituary.

oblak 1 (*Jv, Jkt*) spacious. **2** loose, not firm. *Rodanya sdh* - The wheel has gotten loose.

oblék (*Jkt*) tremble.

obligasi (*Fin.*) debenture, bond. - *berhadiah* k.o. bond paid back by annual drawings.

oblok-oblok 1 dish consisting of leftovers or vegetables mixed with spices. **2** (*Coll.*) offspring of an interethnic marriage.

oblong see KAOS₁.

obor 1 torch. **2** (*Lit.*) guide. **meng-** (*Coll.*) look for fish with a torch. **meng-i** light s.t. with a torch.

obrak-abrik meng- 1 destroy, ruin. **2** upset, tip over, turn upside down.

obral 1 clearance sale. **2** do s.t. without prior consideration, be quick to do s.t. - *ketawa* quick to laugh. **meng- 1** sell out, sell cheaply. *Toko itu ~ barang-barang lama* The shop sold out its old stock. *Aku bukan org yg ~ diri* I am not a person who would sell out to anyone. **2** spend or dispose of s.t. freely. *Ia ~ uangnya* He wasted his money. **-an** sale items. **peng-an** clearance sale.

obras machine hemming. **meng-** hem mechanically. **-an** machine hemming.

obrol (me)ng- chat. *Tetangganya énak-énak duduk merokok dan ~* Her neighbors were sitting there smoking and chatting away. **meng-i** repeatedly talk about, gossip about. *Ia sering di-i oléh ibu tiriku* My stepmother often talked about her. **meng-kan** chat about. *Hamid ~ pelbagai hal* Hamid chatted about various things. **-an 1** chat. **2** gossip.

obros (*Coll.*) lieutenant colonel.

observasi, obsérvasi observation.

obsérvatorium (*Astr.*) observatory.

obsési obsession.

obstétri (*Med.*) obstetrics.

obstétrikus (*Med.*) obstetrician.

obyék₁ 1 object, thing. - *pariwisata* object of interest to tourists. **2** (*Ling.*) object. **3** object, aim.

obyék₂ earning on the side, moonlighting. *Dia suka cari* - He likes to find some side-earnings. - **meng-** dealing in lucrative side-jobs (us. not entirely legal). *Masih lancar juga rupanya ~ di anta-*

ra para pegawai It looks like there are still many officials using their positions to make a fast buck. **(me)ng- 1** do outside work during or outside of office hours, moonlight. **2** misuse gvt. or company property for o.'s own gain. **meng-kan** use s.t. for o.'s own gain. *Kepala bagian ~ uang perusahaan* The section head uses the company money for his own profit. **-an** sideline business, a deal. *menjadi ~ calo-calo asing* a sideline business for foreign go-betweens. **peng-** o. who moonlights or misuses employer's supplies and facilities.

obyéktif 1 objective, unbiased. *Siapa pun yg melawan imperialisme adalah soorg révolusionér* Whoever fights imperialism is, objectively speaking, a revolutionary. **2** objective, goal. **meng-kan** make objective. *utk ~ dasar penilaian* render objective the basis of judgment. **ke-an** objectivity.

obyéktivisme objectivism.

obyéktivitas objectivity.

oc.₁ [*opus citatum*] op. cit.

oc.₂ [*organizing committee*]

ocak-ocak (*Jv*) **meng-** choke.

océanografi see OSÉANOGRAFI.

océanologi see OSÉANOLOGI.

océh babble, talk nonsense. **meng- 1** babble, jabber. *Anak itu ~ pd ibunya* The child babbled to her mother. *Dia ~ mau menjadi bintang filem* He rattled on about becoming a movie star. **2** twitter of bird. **meng-kan** blather about s.t. *Itu saja yg di-kan* That is all that he was jabbering about. **-an** twaddle, gossip. **peng-** talkative person, chatterbox.

odalan (*Bali*) temple festival.

odeklonyo see ODOKLONYO.

odiénsi see AUDIÉNSI.

oditir (*Coll.*) see ODITUR.

oditur (*Mil. Leg.*) military prosecuting attorney, judge advocate. *- jenderal* highest ranking military prosecutor. *- tinggi* military prosecutor at the appeals level. **ke-an** matters pertaining to military prosecutors or prosecuting attorneys.

oditurat the office of the military prosecutor.

odoh 1 ugly. **2** very stupid.

odok (*Coll., Jkt*) take s.t. out from inside.

odoklonyo cologne.

odol (*Coll.*) toothpaste.

ofénsi (*Mil.*) offensive attack.

ofénsif, offénsif 1 offensive (of behavior). **2** (*Mil.*) offensive attack.

oférte (*Coll.*) offer.

ofisial (*Sport*) an official.

ofisiil official, formal.

ogah₁ (*Jv, Jkt*) be averse to. *Ia - bertemu dgn temannya* He does not want to see his friend. **ke-an** aversion. **-²an** reluctantly. *Dia menyapu halaman dgn ~* She swept the yard reluctantly.

ogah₂ meng- shake s.t. to loosen it.

ogak-ogak (*Lit.*) jester. **ber-²** joke. **peng-² 1** jokester. **2** clown.

ogal-agil unsteady, shaky.

ogal-ogalan see UGAL-UGALAN.

oh see O₂.

oha [*orang hukuman*] convict, prisoner.

ohm (*Elec.*) ohm.

oi! 1 hey there! (interjection to call o.'s attention). *-, indah sekali gambar itu!* Look, that is a beautiful picture! **2** interjection to express astonishment or recognition. *"- kau Piter," sahutnya* "Oh, it is you Peter," she shouted.

oja, ojah meng- encourage, incite, egg on.

ojég, ojék /ojék/ motorcycle or bicycle used for public transport. **meng-** earn money by taking people on o.'s bicycle or motorcycle. **meng-kan** use bicycle or motorcycle for passenger service. *Ia sepédanya* He uses his motorbike to convey passengers (for money). **peng-** o. who does this.

ojo (*Jv*) do not. *- ngoyo!* Take it easy, do not work hard!

ojok (*Coll.*) **meng-** make s.o. do s.t. bad.

OK /oké/ OK. **-²** tolerable, all right. **meng-kan** OK s.t.

OKB [*Orang Kaya Baru*] nouveau-riche.

OKD [*Organisasi Keamanan Désa*] village security organization (in the 1960s).

oké see OK.

oker ocher.

okéy see OK.

OKM [*Orang Kaya Mendadak*] nouveau-riche.

oknum 1 a person in a certain capacity, esp. with negative connotation. *Beberapa - militér tersangkut* Some military persons are involved. **2** (*Rel., Lit.*) person (of God). **ke-an** (*Rel., Lit.*) personhood (of God).

okol (*Coll.*) arm-wrestling.

oksid, oksida (*Chem.*) oxide. *- belérang* sulphuric oxide. **meng-kan** oxidize. **peng-** oxidizing agent. **peng-an** oxidization.

oksidasi (*Chem.*) oxidation. **meng-** oxidate.

oksigén (*Chem.*) oxygen.

oktaf octave.

oktan octane.

Oktober October.

oktroi (*Leg.*) **1** patent rights. **2** sole agency or manufacturer rights.

okulasi grafting. **meng-kan** graft s.t.

okulér, okulir ocular.

okulis oculist.

okultisme occultism.

okupasi 1 (*Lit.*) job. **2** illegal occupation of land.

olah₁ 1 manner, way of doing things. *- vokal* vocal training. *- gerak* (*Mil.*) **meng-gerakkan** maneuver. *- rasa* **meng-rasakan** sensitize. **peng-rasaan** sensitizing. **2** trick. *Siapa lagi punya -, kalau bukan Wan Saléh* Who else would play the trick, if not Saleh. **-²** ruse, trick. **se-(²)** as if. *~ tanah seberang gudang emas* as if islands other than Java were warehouses of gold. **-an 1** fickle. **2** whim, caprice.

olah₂ *- data* data processing. *siap -* ready for processing. **meng-** process, turn s.t. into s.t. better. *~ secara kimia* treat chemically. *Tanahnya hendak di- menjadi pusat perumahan* The land is going to be turned into a housing complex. *utk ~ kekaya-*

an alam in order to process the natural wealth. **peng-** processor. **peng-an 1** preparation, manufacture. **2** processing. ~ *ulang* recycling. ~ *sejarah* adaption of history. **3** tabulation (of data).

olahraga 1 sport. **2** physical exercise. **ber-** engage in sports or physical exercise. **meng-kan** make s.t. sports-oriented. ~ *masyarakat* promote sports in society. **ke-an 1** sports. **2** sportsmanlike, athletic. **peng-** athlete.

olahragawan sportsman, athlete.

olahragawati female athlete.

olak circulation of surface water. - *air* whirlpool. - *alik* to and fro. **meng-** *alik* move to and fro. **ber-** turn, whirl. **meng-** stir, turn. **-an** whirling, eddying, turning. ~ *air* whirlpool.

olanda (*Lit.*) the Netherlands, Dutch.

old and new /ol én nu/ (*Coll.*) **ber-** celebrate New Year's Eve with a party.

oldcrack /olkrék/ (*Coll.*) experienced (of old-timer).

Oldéfo [*Old Established Forces*] W. capitalist powers (Sukarno-era phrase).

oléh₁ 1 because of. *Aku merasa kesal - sikapnya itu* I felt angry at his attitude. - *karena/sebab* because, since. - *karena sakit, ia tak pergi ke sekolah* Because she was ill she did not go to school. **2** by (means or agency). *Ia dipukul - ayahnya* He was struck by his father. *disebabkan - angin* caused by the wind. *Nampak -nya* He could see.

oleh₂ -² gift brought back from a trip. **ber-** get, obtain, receive. ~ *untung yg lumayan juga* make a good profit. ~ *hidung* be embarrassed or shy (lit., receive a nose). **meng-²i** bring present from a trip to s.o. **memper-** obtain, get. **teper-** acquired, can be obtained. *perilaku* ~ acquired behavior. **pemer-an** process of acquiring. ~ *bahasa* language acquisition. **per-an** result, achievement, gain, acquisition. *Lumayan juga ~nya hari itu* Her earnings were quite good that day. ~ *bahasa* language acquisition.

oléng 1 shaky. **2** having a strong roll (of ship). - *kemoléng* staggering. **meng-²** shake, rock. **meng-²kan** cause s.t. to rock repeatedly. ~ *kepala* shake o.'s head. **-an, ke-an** rocking (of boat).

olés meng- spread s.t. oily on, lubricate. **meng-i** smear oily substance on s.t. ~ *roti dgn mentéga* spread the bread with butter. **meng-kan** smear with s.t. *Ia* ~ *minyak kelapa ke rambutnya* He smeared coconut oil on his hair. **-an** a smear. ~ *mentéga* a smear of butter.

oli oil, esp. lubricating oil.

olibol k.o. filled doughnut.

olie see OLI.

oligarki oligarchy.

oligarkis oligarchic.

oliman (*Coll.*) person in charge of lubricating (on a ship, in a factory, etc.).

Olimpiade (*Sport*) Olympiad.

Olimpik (*Sport*) Olympic.

olok -² 1 joke, funny remark. **2** ridicule. **ber-²** jest, joke. **meng-²(kan), memper-(²)kan 1** joke with, kid s.o. *Engkau* ~ *saya* You are kidding me.

2 mock, deride, make fun of. *Org tdk berani ~nya* People did not dare make fun of her. **-(²)an 1** joke, jest. **2** ridicule, mockery. *bahan* ~ laughingstock.

Olympiade see OLIMPIADE.

om₁ 1 (*Coll.*) term of address and reference for Western and westernized men, older than the speaker. - *senang* sugar-daddy, middle-aged playboy. **2** uncle, term of reference and address in westernized families and in certain regions.

om₂ (*Elec.*) ohm.

oma 1 (*coll.*) term of address and reference for westernized women of same age as speaker's grandmother. **2** (*Coll.*) grandmother, term of reference and address in westernized families and in certain regions. **3** (*in some regions only*) great-aunt.

ombak wave. - *bunga lepang* whitecaps. - *galur* waves dashing against the cliffs. - *gemulung* rolling waves. - *memecah* breakers. - *pengundak* frontal sea wave. - *selabu* rollers. **ber- 1** be wavy. *Laut* ~ The sea is choppy. **2** undulating, rolling (terrain, etc.). *Rambutnya* ~ He has wavy hair. **ber-² 1** be wavy. **2** in waves. *Musuh menyerang* ~ The enemy attacked in waves. **meng-** wave, undulate. *iramanya yg* ~ the melody which crescendos and descends repeatedly. **-²an** wave effect or motif (on cloth, etc.).

ombang-ambing bob up and down, oscillate. **ber-** bob up and down. **meng- 1** oscillate. **2** toss about helplessly (while adrift, etc.). **3** be uncertain. **meng-kan 1** cause s.t. to toss about. **2** make s.t. uncertain. **ter- 1** be tossed about. ~ *di lautan tujuh hari* adrift and buffeted in the sea for seven days. **2** vacillate. ~ *antara harapan dan kegairahan* vacillate between hope and passion. **-an** vacillation, indecision.

ombyok (*Jv*) bunch. **-an** (*Coll.*) **1** those belonging to a clique, party, etc. **2** commonplace.

omél (me)ng- grumble and complain. ~ *panjang* gripe. **meng-i** complain to or grumble at s.o. **ng-an** always grumbling. **-an** gripe, griping.

omong 1 way of talking. - *Jkt* Jakartanese. - *kasar* rude language. - *kosong* **1** claptrap, nonsense. **2** chatter, gossip. - *punya* - **1** by the way. **2** gradually, as the conversation proceeded. *Mulanya Ayah tdk mau, tapi - punya - akhirnya Ayah setuju juga* At first Father did not want to, but in the course of the conversation he finally consented. **2** talk, say. *Ia banyak - ttg anak-anaknya* He talks a lot about his children. **-² 1** talk, chat. *Ia sering* ~ *ttg tetangga baru ini* He often talks about his new neighbor. **2** idle talk. **3** by the way, speaking of that. ~, *mari kita minum* By the way, let us have a drink. **ber-(²), (ng)-²** talk, chat, converse. **(me)ng-** talk, say. ~ *bahasa Italia* speak Italian. **meng-i** tell s.o. *Kembalilah kami* ~ *sahabat itu* Once more we told that friend of ours about it. **meng-kan** discuss, chat about s.t. *Masih banyak yg hrs kita -kan* We still have lots to talk about. **-an 1** talk. *bahan* ~ food for conversation. **2** gossip. **peng-** talkative person.

ompol (*Coll.*) urine expelled in bed or in o.'s

pants. **ng-** wet the bed or o.'s pants. **ng-i** make s.t. wet by urinating in it.

ompong toothless (of mouths, combs, saws, etc.). *Sisir itu sdh banyak -nya* That comb has a lot of its teeth missing. *- dua/tiga* missing two or three teeth. *Giginya - dua* He is missing two teeth.

ompréng₁ k.o. small basket made of bamboo.

ompréng₂ (me)ng- operate office or gvt. vehicles for personal profit. **meng-kan** use an official or company car illegally as a taxi. *Banyak mobil dinas yg di-kan* Many office cars were illegally used as taxis. **-an** unregistered public transportation. *pekerjaan ~* side-job consisting of this form of transportation. **peng-** s.o. who uses an official car for public transportation.

omprong smoke. *tembakau -* tobacco cured with smoke. **-an** (*Coll.*) lamp chimney. **peng-an** smoking of s.t. *~ tembakau* the smoking of tobacco.

ompu honorary title among the Batak.

omsét turnover (in commercial enterprise).

omslag, omslah /omslakh/ cover (of magazine).

omzét see OMSÉT.

on 1 100 grams. **2** ounce. **-an** by the ounce.

onak curved thorn. *- duri* 1 all k.o. thorns. 2 the sufferings (i.e. thorny parts) of life. **-²** thorny bushes.

onani masturbation. **ber-** masturbate. **meng-** masturbate s.o.

onar noisy sensation, stir. **meng-kan 1** excite, create chaos, agitate. *Perbuatan membuka celananya ~ org sepasar* Taking off his pants caused quite a stir among the people at the market. **2** confuse. **ke-an 1** confusion, boisterousness. **2** sensation. **3** disturbance.

oncar (*Jv*) **meng-i** irrigate.

oncék (*Jv*) **(me)ng-(i)** peel, shell.

oncom fermented cake made from soybean sediment.

oncor (*Jv*) torch. **meng-i** light s.t. with a torch. **-²an 1** toy torch. **2** (*Coll.*) try to outshine e.o., keep up with the Joneses.

ondél-ondél (*Jkt*) giant puppets used in parades.

ondé-ondé, ondéh-ondéh k.o. round fried cake made of rice flour filled with sweetened ground mung beans sprinkled with sesame seeds.

onderdil spare parts.

onderdistrik subdistrict (in colonial area).

ondernéming estate (esp. in colonial era).

onderok slip or other k.o. skirtlike undergarment.

ondo (*Jv*) ladder.

ondok ber- hide. *Kami ~ di belakang gundukan-gundukan tanah* We hid behind heaps of dirt. **meng-(kan)** conceal s.t.

onéng-onéng remote descendants.

onggok₁ ber-² in heaps, stacks, piles. **meng-i** pile up on s.t. *~ piringnya dgn daging* pile her plate with meat. **meng-kan** pile or stack s.t. up. **ter-** heaped up. *Bajunya yg kotor ~ di sudut* His dirty shirts were piled up in a corner. **-an** pile, heap. *~ kayu api* a heap of firewood.

ongkang-ongkang 1 (*Jv*) sit with legs dangling. *Hanya dgn - nyonya rumah dpt memperoléh semua*

keperluan Without lifting a finger the lady of the house can get all she needs (lit., just by sitting with her legs dangling). **2** (*Coll.*) do nothing. *jabatan -* a lucrative position with little work.

ongklok pierced. **meng-** pierce s.t.

ongkok (*M*) **meng-²** walk with a stoop. **meng-i** approach s.o. in a crouching position.

ongkos cost, expenses, charges. *Kami pergi ke Surabaya dgn - sendiri* We went to Surabaya at our own expense. *- damai* financial agreement without 3d party (e.g. between people involved in traffic accident, etc.). *- kirim* forwarding, shipping charges. *- makan* food expenses. *- perusahaan* working expenses. *- siluman* invisible costs, extra costs illegally collected by individuals in gvt. service. *- tetap* 1 fixed costs. 2 overhead. **meng-i, memper-i** finance, pay for. *~ sekolah anaknya* finance o.'s children's schooling. **per-an** cost, expenses.

ongol-ongol k.o. cake made of tapioca.

ONH [*Ongkos Naik Haji*] expenses for pilgrimage to Mecca.

onkol, onkolen meng- decarbonize.

ons see ON.

onslah (*Coll.*) dismissal from a job. **meng-** dismiss, fire.

onta see UNTA.

ontang-anting (*Jv*) only child.

ontologi ontology.

ontong (*Jv*) the whole banana flower including petals.

ontslag, ontslah see ONSLAH.

onyah-anyih (*Jv*) dally, dawdle. *Jangan - waktu pergi ke sekolah!* Do not dally on your way to school!

oom see OM₁.

OP [*Otomat Pemerintah*] gvt. telephone dialing system.

opa 1 (*Coll.*) term of address and reference for westernized men same age as o.'s grandfather. **2** (*Coll.*) grandfather, term of reference and address in westernized families and in certain regions. **3** (*in some regions only*) great-uncle.

opah see UPAH.

opak k.o. fried crispy chip made from a roll of steamed rice or cassava.

opal₁ opal.

opal₂ (*Naut.*) tack.

opas see UPAS₂.

opelét k.o. small urban bus or jitney.

opén₁ (*Jv, Jkt*) attentive, careful. **meng-i** pay attention to. *Dia ingin diladéni, di-i persoalannya* She wants to be taken care of, to get attention for her problem.

opén₂ see OVEN.

openkap 1 (*Auto.*) convertible car. **2** (*Auto.*) convertible with the top down. *Ia lalu di depan rumah dgn -* He drove by the house with the top down. **3** (*Coll.*) scantily dressed, esp. having a low neckline.

oper 1 transfer. **2** (*Auto.*) shift gears. **meng-1** take s.t. over. *Ia ~ pekerjaan temannya* He took over his friend's job. **2** hand over, pass s.t. to. *Ia ~*

bukunya kpd temannya He handed over his book to his friend. *Ia ~ bola* She passed the ball over (to her teammate). **3** transfer. *Majikannya ~nya ke bagian perbekalan* His boss transferred him to the supply department. **meng-kan** transfer, pass down. *tak dpt di-kan* not transferable. *Kitalah yg berkewajiban ~ warisan-warisan ilmiah kpd anak-anak kita* It is our duty to transfer this scientific heritage to our children. **-an** (*Sport*) pass. *Meréka mencoba melakukan ~ panjang* They tried to make a long pass. **peng- 1** o. who takes over. **2** (*Sport*) o. who makes a pass. **peng-an 1** taking over. **2** transferal. **3** delegation (of powers).

opera 1 opera. **2** (*Coll.*) musical drama.

operasi 1 operation, campaign, action. *- Kebersihan* Clean up Campaign. *- gabungan* combined action. **2** (*Med.*) surgical operation. *- plastik* plastic surgery. **ber- 1** (*Mil.*) take action. **2** operate (of bandits, etc.). **meng-(kan)** (*Med.*) operate on. *Dokter ~ kanker di kakinya* The doctor operated on the tumor in her leg. **meng-kan** operate s.t. *~ kilang* operate a refinery. **peng-an** operation (of business, etc.).

operasional operational. **meng-kan** make s.t. operational.

operasionalisasi process of making s.t. operational. **meng-kan** operationalize.

operasionil see OPERASIONAL.

operatif, operatip 1 protocol, set of instructions. **2** operative, come into effect.

operator operator.

operbelas, oper belas overloaded.

operét operetta.

opini opinion.

opisil see OFISIIL.

oplag, oplah, oplak /oplakh/ **1** circulation (of periodical). **2** total printing (of book).

oplét see OPELÉT.

OPM [*Organisasi Papua Merdéka*] Free Papua Organization, secessionist movement of W. New Guinea.

opnaisel tuck (in sewing).

opname₁ 1 photographic shot. **2** shooting. *Bésok akan ada - filem di sana* Tomorrow they are going to shoot a film there. **meng-** shoot (with camera).

opname₂ hospitalization, be hospitalized. *Saya enggan - di situ* I refuse to be hospitalized there. **meng-** hospitalize. *Ia di- di Carolus* She is being hospitalized at Carolus.

opname₃ see STOCK.

oponén (*Sport*) opponent.

opor meat or chicken dish cooked with coconut cream and various spices.

oportunis 1 opportunist. **2** opportunistic.

oposan o. who opposes s.t.

oposisi opposition.

OPR [*Organisasi Pertahanan Rakyat*] civil defense.

opsét₁ typesetting. **meng-** typeset.

opsét₂ (*Sport*) off-sides.

opsét₃ meng- stuff (animals).

opséter₁ typesetter.

opséter₂ supervisor.

opsi option.

opsihter see OPSÉTER₂.

opsinder, opsiner supervisor on plantations, schools, etc. in colonial period, as term of address often *siner.*

opsir (*Mil.*) officer. *- penghubung* liaison officer. *- rendah(an)* noncommissioned officer. *- tinggi* commissioned officer.

Opspék [*Oriéntasi Program dan Pengenalan Kampus*] University Student's Orientation.

Opstib [*Operasi Tertib*] anticorruption operation. **meng-kan** bring order by cracking down on graft.

Opsus [*Operasi Khusus*] special intelligence operation of the military.

optik, optika optics.

optimal best, optimum. **meng-kan** make the best of, optimize. *~ poténsi yg ada* maximize the existing potential.

optimis optimist, optimistic. *pandangan yg - an* optimistic viewpoint. **meng-kan** make s.o. optimistic. **ke-an** optimism.

optimisme optimism.

optimistis optimistic.

optimum optimum. **meng-kan** optimize. **peng-an** optimizing.

optimumisasi optimizing.

opyok (*Jkt*) apply s.t. wet to the head.

opzichter see OPSÉTER₂.

OR [*Olah Raga*] sports.

orak₁ meng- uncoil, unfold. *empat cerita yg ~ dramatik hidup* four stories which unfold the drama of life. *~ tali* uncoil a rope.

orak₂ (*Jkt*) **meng- 1** shake s.t. violently. **2** bring s.t. to disorder. *Barang sdh baik-baik diatur, kok di-!* Everything was all neatly arranged and now suddenly it is a mess!

orak-arik (*Jv*) stir-fried cabbage with eggs.

orang₁ 1 person. *Ini - yg membawa surat itu* This is the person who brought the letter. *- asing* foreigner. *- Jkt* a Jakartan. *- am* general public, the masses. *- antun* dandy, fop. *- asli* **1** s.o. born and bred in a particular area. **2** the real or original person. *- awak* **1** fellow countryman. **2** Minangkabau person. *- awam* lay person, not an expert in the field. *- bambungan* tramp, vagrant. *- banyak* **1** crowd. **2** the public. *- baru* newcomer, recent arrival. *- besar* **1** dignitary, VIP. **2** large person. *- bukit* (*Derog.*) bumpkin. *- bumi* earthling. *- dagang* **1** merchant, tradesman. **2** foreigner. **3** stranger (not from o.'s village). *- dlm* insider, member of an organization, clique, etc. *- dapur* wife. *- datang* outsider, foreigner. *- désa* **1** villager. **2** rustic. *- dompléng* freeloader, sponger. *- dusun* (*Derog.*) bumpkin. *- gajian* wage earner. *- gedéan* big shot. *- gedong(an)* resident in an elite Jkt neighborhood. *- halimun* spirit (of a certain place). *- hanyut* vagrant, tramp. *- helat* stranger, newcomer. *- hobat(an)* sorcerer. *- hulu* (*Derog.*) bumpkin. *- hutan* **1** (*Derog.*) forest dweller. **2** aboriginal peoples of E. Sumatra. *- jauh* foreigner, guest. *- kampung* (*often Derog.*) villager, country fellow. *- kaya* **1** rich person. **2** person of rank.

3 (M) the lady of the house. - *kayo* (M) lady of the house. - *kebanyakan* commoner. - *kecil* 1 common, ordinary person. 2 small-sized person. - *kemit* guard, watchman. - *kepercayaan* confidant. - *lasak* unskilled worker. - *laut* sea nomad, aboriginal peoples in Riau and Sumatra. - *luar(an)* outsider, foreigner. - *mampu* person of means, a well-to-do individual. - *nakal(an)* prostitute, wanton person. - *nguler kambang* o. who takes things easy. - *numpang* outsider. - *pasak kampung* ordinary villager. - *patut-patut* respectable person. - *pedalaman* 1 person who resides in the country. 2 settler, homesteader. - *pendatang* foreigner, newcomer. - *pertandang* traveling salesman. - *perutangan* creditor. - *pesakitan* prisoner. - *ramai* 1 the public, crowd. 2 many people. - *rantai(an)* 1 convict. 2 slave. - *rumah* member of the family. - *sabun* albino. - *sebelah* neighbor. - *sedapur* the family. - *semodal* partner in a firm. - *seorg* an individual, personal. - *séwaan* hireling. - *talang* villager, peasant. - *terlantar* displaced person. - *tua* 1 old person. 2 o.'s parents. **ke-tuaan** parenthood. - *turutan* 1 hitchhiker. 2 o. who goes along with a certain philosophy. - *tutupan* prisoner, inmate. - *udik* (Derog.) bumpkin. - *utangan* debtor. - *yg tdk punya* a have-not. 2 follower, assistant. *salah satu - Pak Saimun* o. of Saimun's men. 3 one, s.o., an indefinite other party. *Ia tinggal di rumah -* He is staying in other people's house. *kampung -* an inhabited village. *Ada - di pintu* There is s.o. at the door. 4 people in general. *kata -* they say. *Tlh merupakan hal yg sangat lumrah jika - menghisap rokok impor* It has become common for people to smoke imported cigarettes. 5 numeral classifier for humans. *Teman saya lima -* My friends number five. *anak se-* o. child. 6 (Ling.) person. - *ketiga jamak* 3d person plural. **-nya** the k.o. person o. is. *Si Bén itu lucu ~* Ben is a fun sort of person. *~ sendiri* the person himself. **se- 1** somebody, s.o. *Ada ~ dokter di pintu* There is a doctor at the door. 2 alone. *Dlm pendirian itu dia tinggal ~* In that opinion he remains alone. *~ diri* alone, on o.'s own. *Dia hidup ~ diri* She lives alone. 3 one (of persons). *Yg ~ putri dan yg ~ lagi putra* One is a girl and the other a boy. **sese- 1** anyone, s.o. or other. 2 a certain person. **kese-an** loneliness, solitude. **se-se-** o. by o., individually. *Biasanya gerilya itu ~, lalu lari undur jauh* Guerillas us. operate individually, then withdraw far away. **ber-an** alone. **per-an 1** individual, personal, private. *pemilikan ~* individual ownership. *Ia pergi secara ~ bukan utk dinas* He went for personal, not business, reasons. 2 an individual person. **-²an 1** dummy, mannequin. 2 puppet, doll. 3 effigy, scarecrow.

orang₂ (Coll., Jv) 1 because. *Dia telat - mobilnya mogok* He is late because his car broke down. 2 What are you (they) talking about! (exclamation of disagreement). - *makanan kaya gini kok dibilang énak* What! Food like this you say is delicious!

orang-orangan mata (Anat.) pupil of the eye.

oranye-krus orange soda pop.
orasi oration. - *ilmiah* scientific oration.
oratoris oratorical.
oratorium reflective gathering with poetry reading, prayers, etc. to commemorate or protest s.t.
Orba [Orde Baru] sociopolitical order in Indonesia since 1965.
orbit orbit. **meng-** orbit. *satelit yg ~* orbiting satellite. **meng-kan** put s.t. or s.o. into orbit. **peng-an** orbiting.
orde₁ sociopolitical or economic system. - *ékonomi internasional* the international economical order. - *Baru* sociopolitical order in Indonesia since 1965. **peng-baruan** making s.t. conform to Orde Baru.
orde₂, order 1 order. - *jual* order to sell. 2 forced labor (colonial period).
ordinat (Math) the y Cartesian coordinate.
ordner ring binder.
ordo 1 Catholic order. - *Fransiskan* Franciscan order. 2 (Biol.) order.
ordonan, ordonans (Mil.) orderly.
ordonansi, ordonnansi decree, ordinance.
orék-orék, orét-orét (Jv, Coll.) 1 doodling, graffiti. 2 doodle. **meng-** doodle in. *Dia ~ buku itu* She doodled in that book. **-an** doodlings, graffiti.
org. [orang] person.
organa organ (musical instrument).
organik, organis₁ organic.
organis₂ organist.
organisasi organization. **ber-** be organized. **meng-(kan)** organize s.t. *Meréka ~ cara bekerja* They organized their working methods. **ter-** organized. **keter-an** being organized, organizational matters. **ke-an** matters concerning organization. **peng-an** organizing.
organisator organizer.
organisatoris organizational. *secara -* organizationally.
organisir meng- organize. **peng-** organizer.
organisma, organisme organism.
organsa k.o. fabric, organdy.
orgel organ (musical instrument). - *putar* hand-organ.
Orhiba [Olahraga Hidup Baru] k.o. aerobics.
ori k.o. bamboo.
ORI [Oeang Répoeblik Indonésia] Indonesian currency used during the revolution.
oriéntalis orientalist.
oriéntasi orientation. **ber-** be oriented. **ber-kan** oriented toward s.t. *~ program-program pengembangan* oriented toward development programs. **meng-kan** orient s.o. *Ayahnya ~ dia ke dunia wiraswasta* His father oriented him to the world of private business.
orijinil, orisinal, orisinil 1 original. *idé -* an original idea. 2 the original (copy) of s.t. **ke-an** originality.
orkeb [organisasi kebudayaan] cultural organization.
orkés musical group. - *gésék* band of stringed instruments. - *Melayu* group playing popular mu-

sic influenced by Indian and Arab music. - *tiup* band of brass instruments.

orkéstra orchestra (of classical music).

Orla [*Ordé Lama*] sociopolitical order during Sukarno era.

orloji see ARLOJI.

orlon a synthetic fabric, orlon.

ormas [*organisasi massa*] mass organization. **ke-an** (matters) pertaining to mass organizations. *UU ~ Dlm Negeri* the Domestic Laws on Mass Organizations.

ornamén 1 ornament. - *pohon Natal* Christmas tree ornament. 2 jewelry. - *telinga* earring.

ornitologi ornithology.

orok₁ (*Jkt, Sd, Jv*) newborn baby.

orok₂ (*Jkt*) **(me)ng-** 1 snort, drone. *Mesin mulai ~* The machine started droning. 2 snore.

orok-orok k.o. sweetmeat made of steamed cassava.

orong see URUNG.

orong-orong (*Jv*) k.o. insect, mole cricket.

oro-oro₁ k.o. legume.

oro-oro₂ (*Jv*) large, empty field.

Orpol [*Organisasi Politik*] political organization.

ortodoks orthodox.

ortodonsi orthodontics.

ortodonti orthodontia.

ortografi orthography.

ortopédi (*Med.*) orthopedics.

Oséania Oceania.

oséanografi oceanography.

oséanologi oceanology.

oséng-oséng stir-fried with chili peppers.

osilasi oscillation.

osio see WÉSIO.

osmosa, osmose osmosis.

OT [*Orang Tahanan*] detained person.

otak brain. - *benak* 1 brains. 2 sense. - *besar* (*Anat.*) cerebrum. - *éncér* smart. - *kecil* (*Anat.*) cerebellum. - *miring* crazy. - *udang* abysmally stupid. **meng-i** be the brains of s.t. *Ia ~ pembajakan pesawat itu* He was the brains behind the plane hijacking. **-²an** 1 boasting. 2 braggart. 3 be mentally disturbed.

otak-atik tinker with s.t.

otak-otak snack made of seafood steamed in banana leaves.

otarki see AUTARKI.

oté see OT.

oték₁ (*Jv, Jkt*) loose, esp. of teeth.

oték₂ see IKAN.

oténg-oténg (*Jkt*) k.o. insect.

oténtik authentic. **ke-an** authenticity.

oténtikasi authentication.

oténtisitas authenticity.

oté-oté k.o. fritter filled with meat or seafood.

oto₁ automotive vehicle, car. - *balap* racing car. - *gerobak* truck. - *pengangkut org sakit* ambulance.

oto₂ cloth binder wrapped around infant's stomach and chest fastened by strings.

otobiografi see AUTOBIOGRAFI.

otobis (*Lit.*) bus.

otodidak autodidact, self-taught person.

otokrasi autocracy.

otokratis autocratic.

otokratisme autocratism.

otokritik self-criticism.

otomat (*Tel.*) automatic dialing. **meng-kan** automatize. *Pemerintah ~ semua télpon di kota Surabaya* The gvt. automatized all telephones in Surabaya.

otomatis 1 automatic. *senjata -* an automatic gun. 2 automatically, of its own. *Pokoknya yg nggak bolos - lulus* As long as you do not cut you automatically pass.

otomatisasi automation. **meng-kan** automatize.

otomobil automobile.

otomotif automotive (industry).

otonom autonomous. **ke-an** autonomy.

otonomi autonomy. **ke-an** matters pertaining to autonomy. *~ daérah itu hanya dlm hal ékonomi* That area has only autonomy in economical matters.

otopét toy scooter.

otopsi see AUTOPSI.

otorisasi authorization.

otorita, otoritas authority.

otoritér 1 authoritative. 2 authoritarian.

otot₁ 1 muscle. - *kawat balung wesi* very powerful (of a man). - *kunyah* masticatory muscle. - *lingkar* sphincter. - *perut* abdominal muscle. 2 tendon, sinew. **ber-** strong, very muscled. *Pegulat itu ~ kuat* That wrestler has strong muscles. **-²an** 1 muscle-bound. 2 muscle not up to standards of a real o. 3 (*Coll.*) strong-arm. 4 (*Coll.*) engage in a fight.

otot₂ **(me)ng-** 1 persevere, persist. 2 be obstinate, stubborn. **ng-²an** (*Coll.*) dispute, have an argument. *Kedua-duanya ~ mempertahankan pendapatnya* The two are fighting over their viewpoints. **keng-an** (*Coll.*) obstinacy.

oval oval. **meng-kan** make s.t. oval-shaped. **ke-an** ovalness.

oven (*Coll.*) oven. **meng-** bake in an oven. *Kalau di- énak jadinya* If you cook it in the oven it will turn out delicious.

overlaping, overléping overlapping authority.

overste /obros/ (*Coll.*) lieutenant colonel.

ovulasi (*Biol.*) ovulation.

owé (*Ch*) 1 I, me (used by men only). 2 yes (used by men in affirmative answers).

oyak₁ (*M*) **meng-²** shake s.t. loose.

oyak₂ (*Jv*) **meng-** chase after.

oyék (*Jv*) k.o. dish made from cassava.

oyok see OYAK₂.

oyong k.o. squashlike vegetable.

oyot-oyotan (*Jv*) various k.o. roots.

ozon ozone.

P

p /pé/ p, the 16th letter of the alphabet.
p.₁ [*pulau*] (*Geog.*) island.
p.₂ [*pangéran*] prince.
P [*pelacur*] prostitute.
P3 see PPP.
P4₁ [*Panitia Penyelesaian Perselisihan Perburuhan*] labor dispute arbitration committee.
P4₂ [*Pedoman Penghayatan dan Pengamalan Pancasila*] guidelines for carrying out the principles of *Pancasila.*
PA [*Port Authority*] the port area as a place of work (e.g. Tanjong Priok in Jkt).
paal act, deed.
pabéan customs office.
paberik see PABRIK.
pabian see PABÉAN.
pabila see APABILA.
pabrik factory. - *kertas* paper mill. - *percobaan* pilot plant. **memp-** manufacture. **ke-an** industrialization. **-an** manufacturer.
pacai sandalwood dust.
pacak₁ roasting spit. **mem-(i) 1** fix upon a spit. **2** impale.
pacak₂ ber- mate (of animals). **mem-(i)** mount for copulation. **pem-** stud, male for breeding.
pacak₃ skilled, experienced.
pacal slave.
pacang mem-kan affiance. **-an 1** fiancé, fiancée. **2** partner (boy or girl).
pacar (*Coll.*) fiancé or fiancée, boyfriend or girlfriend. **ber-an** be engaged, be boy- and girlfriends. **ber-²an** go out with o. of opposite sex. **mem-i** court, make s.o. his girlfriend. **-an 1** go out with members of opposite sex. *Kau pernah ~?* Have you ever had a boyfriend? **2** be boy- and girlfriends. **3** engage in sexual play. *Kau pasti ~ dlm air* You must have been playing around together in the water.
pacat leech. - *kenyang* oblong-shaped and thick in the middle (fountain pen, pencil).
pacé (*Jv*) the *mengkudu* tree and its fruit.
pacek see PACAK₂.
paceklik 1 famine. **2** time of scarcity before harvest. **3** lack of s.t. important. *Kekurangan bahan bacaan mencapai proporsi* - The lack of reading material has reached famine proportions.
pacet see PACAT.
pacinko k.o. gambling game in Japan.
pacombéran see COMBÉRAN.
pacu spur. - *jantung* heart pacemaker. **ber-** race. (*Spo.*) *~ kuda* race on horseback. **ber-an** race against e.o. **mem-(kan) 1** spur. *~ kuda* spur a

horse. **2** spur, push ahead. *Pembangunan pertanian hrs di-* Agricultural development must be pushed. **-an 1** race. *~ persenjataan* arms race. **2** racecourse **pem** s.t. to spur o. on. **per-an** race, rivalry.
pacuk see PATUK.
pacul₁ hoe. **mem-(i)** hoe. **mem-kan** hoe with s.t.
pacul₂ mem- squeeze or press out. **ter-** extracted.
pada₁ 1 at or to (person or institution), have a feeling toward. *Diberikan - saya* Give it to me. *Ia melihat - saya* He looked at me. *Ia bekerja - pemerintah* He works for the gvt. *Buku itu ada - saya* The book is with me. *merasa malu - tetangganya* feel ashamed (to face) her neighbors. *setia - tuannya* loyal to his master. *Terjadi sesuatu - diri saya* S.t. happened to me. **2** in the direction of, to or on, from the surface, tip or edge of. *berpegang - dinding* steady o.s. holding on to the wall. *rangkulan - tubuhnya* the embrace (that held) his body. *bergayutan - tiang* hanging from a pole. *berada - puncaknya* be at its high point. *senyum yg melekat - wajahnya* the smile that was pasted on her face. *kasa stéril yg ditutupkan - hidungnya* the sterile gauze with which she covered her nose. **3** at, in (an abstract place). *Kita dihadapkan - keadaan yg ironis* We come face to face with an ironic situation. *Tergantung - ada tdknya* It depends on whether any is available or not. *Semua ini berpangkal - kekurangan tempat* This is all based on the lack of space. *Perobahan ini dpt dilihat - nama surat kabar itu* This change can be seen in the name of the newspaper. *Pembicaraan yg terbatas - masalah keuangan* A discussion confined to the problem of finances. **4** at (a certain time). - *hari Selasa* on Tuesday. - *ucapan selamat malamnya yg kedua* upon saying good evening for the 2d time. - *waktunya* on time. **5** preposition preceding complement of intransitive verb or of noun. *Ia cinta - warna hijau* She loves the color green. *kenangan - masa dulu* remembrances of former times. **6** preposition in set phrases. - *hakékatnya* in reality. - *hémat/pendapat* in the opinion of. - *umumnya* in general. **dari-** see DARIPADA. **ke-** see KEPADA.
pada₂ enough, sufficient. *Hatinya blm -* He was not satisfied. *Sedikit pun -lah* A little will suffice. **mem-i 1** satisfy, suffice. *Gajinya tdk ~* His salary is not sufficient. *Kemampuannya tdk ~* He does not have sufficient ability. **2** equal. *Tak ada yg dpt ~ kecantikannya* Her beauty cannot be equaled. **kemem-ian** satisfactoriness, sufficiency. **mem-kan 1** satisfy. **2** be content with, make s.t. be

enough. **mem-²kan** make s.t. be just enough. *Gajinya di-²kannya* She stretched his salary just enough to meet their needs.

pada₃ plural marker for verbs or stative adjectives. *Meréka - pergi* They left. *Bunga-bunga - layu* The flowers faded.

padah omen, warning. **-an** unfortunate result, just deserts. *Itulah ~nya* It serves him right.

padahal 1 whereas, but actually the case is. *Katanya ia tdk mampu - uangnya melimpah* He said he could not afford it, whereas in fact he had all k.o. money. *Ia dikatakan pelit - dia sangat pemurah* He was said to be a cheapskate whereas in fact he was very generous. **2** besides.

padam 1 extinguished. *Apinya tlh -* The fire is out. *Lampu -* The light was extinguished. **2** calmed, suppressed, quenched. *Marahnya sdh -* His anger has cooled off. *- nyawanya* He was killed. **mem-** become extinguished, go out. **mem-i, mem-kan 1** extinguish, put out. *~ nyawa* kill. **2** suppress, put out. *Sépnya ~ pemberontakan* The boss suppressed the rebellion. **ter-kan** extinguishable. *Kemarahannya sulit ~* It is difficult to calm down his anger. **pem-** s.t. that extinguishes. *~ api* fire extinguisher. *Jawatan/Dinas ~ Api* Fire Department. **pem-an** extinguishing, putting out (of fire). *~ listrik* blackout.

padan₁ equal, match. **se- 1** suit, match. *Warna itu tak ~ dgn dia* That color did not suit her. **2** match, correspond with. *Perbuatannya tak ~ dgn perkataannya* His behavior does not correspond with his words. **berse-an** be in harmony, go together. **kese-an** correspondence, agreement. **ber-an** harmonize, go together (e.g. colors), be commensurate. *Bentuk pagar dan rumah itu sungguh ~* The fence is of the right proportions for the house. **mem-** compare. **mem-i** compare, correspond, correlate s.t. **-an 1** parable. **2** comparison.

padan₂ border, frontier. **se-** having a common border.

padan₃ promise.

padan₄ dishonest (in gambling).

padang plain, field. *- belantara/gurun* desert. *- golf* golf course. *- lumut* (*Geog.*) tundra. *- mahsyar* (*Isl.*) gathering place on the day of resurrection. *- pasir* (*Geog.*) desert. *- pembidikan* rifle range. *- rumput* **1** meadow. **2** savannah. *- tandus/tiah* (*Geog.*) desert.

padas rock or a layer of hardened soil.

padasan cistern, vat.

padat 1 solid, compact. *acara -* a full agenda. **2** dense. *Kota ini - penduduknya* This city is densely populated. **mem-** come closer together. **mem-i** pack, fill s.t. up until it is compact. *Karyakaryanya ~ majalah Témpo* His works fill up *Tempo* magazine. *Dadanya di-i perasaan beranéka* Her bosom was filled with any number of different feelings. **mem-kan 1** make s.t. solid, hard packed. **2** stuff, cram. **memper-** make s.t. more compact. *~ kantungnya* stuff their pockets. *Org bisa diper- tanpa kehilangan irama* The people

could be made to dance closer together without losing the rhythm. **ke-an 1** density. *~ penduduk* population density. **2** conciseness, intensiveness. **-an** solid matter (in physics). **pem-an** act of cramming or making s.t. more intensive. *~ kuliah* making the course more intensive.

padepokan, padépokan see DEPOK.

paderi 1 (*Rel.*) Catholic priest. *- tentara* army chaplain. **2** Isl. purists from W. Sumatra in the early 19th century.

padi 1 rice plant, unhusked rice. *- baruk* rice from paddy. *- berat* slow-growing rice. *- ceré* quick-ripening small-grained rice. *- gadu* wet field rice. *- gaga/gogo* k.o. dry field rice. *- genjah* k.o. early-yielding rice. *- radin* swamp rice. *- ranap* over-ripe rice. *- ringan* fast-ripening rice. *- séntra* rice from experimental farm. **2** tiny, very small. *tak se-* not a bit. **-an** grain. **-²an** various grains.

padma lotus.

padri see PADERI.

padu 1 solid, compact, fused. **2** in harmony. *satu -* totally united. **bersatu -** form a solid unit. **menyatu-kan** unify. **3** resolute. *Tambah - hatinya utk mengusir siapa saja yg berani* She became all the more determined to drive away anyone who is daring. **se-** being one with, being integrated with. **ber-** be united, unite with e.o., fuse. **mem-1** unite, join. **2** forge, weld, merge. *~ modal* (*Fin.*) get capital together. *~ perkataan* form compound words. *~ suara* sing in harmony. **3** agree. *~ bicara* consult. *~ janji* come to an agreement. *~ janji akan bertemu kembali pd malam* come to an agreement to meet again at night. *~ kasih* love e.o. *~ hati* consult together, negotiate. **mem-kan, memper-kan** meld, integrate. *~ patriotisme dgn internasionalisme* combine patriotism and internationalism into o. **ter-** integrated, fused. *manusia ~* an integrated man. *tim ~ polisi dan hansip* a combined squad of police and constables. **keter-an** integrity. **ke-an** unity, cohesiveness. **-an** fusion, combination, blend, synthesis. *~ suara* choir, chorus. **per-an 1** merger, unification. **2** blend, synthesis.

paduk baseline.

paduka (*Lit.*) excellency. *- Yg Mulia* His Excellency.

padusi (*M*) woman, female.

paédah see FAÉDAH.

paés (*Jv*) makeup (cosmetics). **-an** makeup.

paga (*Jv*) basket (hung up to preserve food).

pagan firm, solid.

pagar 1 fence. **2** hedge. *- ayu* virtue, virginity. *- bedil* (*Mil.*) mopping-up operation. *- betis* volunteer guard against attack or escape of criminals etc. by blocking way without weapons. *- bulan* halo. *- duri kawat* barbed wire. *- hidup/jaro* hedge. *- kapal* ship's railing. *- putar* turnstile. **ber-** be fenced in. **mem-** make a hedge or fence. *~ diri* look after o.s. **mem-i** fence in, put a fence around. *~ tepi jalan* put a fence along the edge of the road. **mem-kan** use as a fence.

pagarisasi program to provide fences.

pagelar mem(p)-kan put on a show, present. **-an** show, presentation. ~ *séks* sex show.
pager see PAGAR.
pagi morning. *Hari baru (masih)* - It is still early. - *buta* very early in the morning. - *hari* in the morning. - *harinya* the following morning. - *ini* this morning. - *tadi* this (past) morning. -² early in the morning. **-nya** that same morning. **se-an** the entire morning. **ter-** the earliest in the morning. **ke-an** too early, too soon. *Sdr ~ datangnya* You came too early. *dgn memberikan ampun ~ kpd Nixon* by pardoning Nixon too soon.
pagina page (of a publication).
pagu ceiling. - *krédit (Econ.)* credit ceiling.
pagut mem- 1 peck **2** bite (of snake). **3** embrace. *Org yg akan tenggelam ~ lalang sehelai* A drowning man clutches at a single straw. **mem-kan** drive s.t. so that it bites deeply. ~ *kapaknya* drive the axe deeply (into the wood). **-an** embrace.
paguyuban (*Jv, Sd*) association.
pah see PAK₂.
paha thigh.
pahala merit, reward for moral conduct. **ber-** bringing a reward. *ibadah yg ~* religious duties which bring merit.
paham 1 understanding. *Ia menaruh - akan soal itu* He shows an understanding of the problem. **2** view, concept. - *ékonomi* economic concept. - *cita* ideology. **3** understand, know. *Saya kurang -* I do not quite understand. - *akan* understand, know about. **se-** like-minded. *Saya ~ dgnnya* I share his views. **ber-** sensible. **mem-i 1** understand. **2** realize, appreciate the facts. **mem-kan 1** explain, make s.o. understand. ~ *benar-benar keadaan daérah yg akan diserang* explain the situation in the area they are going to attack. **2** understand. *Pelajaran itu mudah di-kan* The lesson is easy to understand. *tak* **ter-kan** incomprehensible. **pem-an** comprehension.
pahar teacart, tea wagon.
pahat chisel. - *gérék* plain chisel. - *jantan* a sharp-pointed chisel. **ber-** carved, chiseled. **mem-** chisel, carve, sculpt. **mem-kan** engrave. *Di-kan namanya pd . . .* His name is engraved on . . . **ter-** be engraved. *Di hatinya tlh ~ tékad utk . . .* A determination to . . . was engraved in his heart. **-an** carving, relief. ~ *lino* linecut. **pem-** sculptor, carver.
Pahing see PAING.
pahit 1 bitter (in taste). - *hati* bitter (in feeling). - *getir* unpleasantness. - *getir penghidupan* the gloomy side of life. **ke-getiran** unpleasantness. - *maung* **1** very bitter. **2** bitterness. - *pahang* acrimony. **2** sugarless (of drinks). *téh* - plain tea. **se-** as bitter as. ~ *semanis* for better or for worse. **ber-²** expose o.s. to bitter experiences. **mem-i** provide with bitterness. *Humor itu sdh di-i empedu-empedu penghidupan yg lebih getir* His humor has been lent bitterness by the even greater bitterness of his life. **mem-kan** embitter, exasperate. **ke-an** bitterness, exasperation. **ke-²an** k.o. bitter. **-²an** various things that are bitter.

pahlawan hero, patriot. - *bakiak* o. who espouses causes that have long since become dead issues. - *setia* loyal retainer. **mem-kan** make s.o. into a hero. **ke-an** heroism. **ke-²an** pseudoheroism. **pem-an** lionizing, heroizing.
pahlawati heroine.
pai₁ pie.
pai₂ (*M*) go.
paidah see FAÉDAH.
paido (*Jv*) **m-** disparage, belittle.
paidon (*Jv*) cuspidor.
pailit see PALIT₁.
Paing 2d day of Jv week.
pair₁ - *jantung (Med.)* pulse deviation.
pair₂ see PAYAR.
pais mem- cook in banana leaves over coals.
pait see PAHIT.
paitua 1 (*Amb*) husband. **2** (*Coll.*) old man.
Pajajaran name of kingdom in W. Java.
pajak 1 tax. - *kekayaan* real estate tax. - *pendapatan* income tax. - *rumah tangga* property tax. - *tanah* land tax. - *upah* income tax, withholding tax. **2** monopoly or franchise given by colonial gvt. - *gadai* pawnshop. **mem-i** pay taxes for. **ke-an** revenue. **pem-an 1** taxation. **2** tax system. **per-an** taxation.
pajang mem- dress windows, display. **mem-i** decorate. *di-i bunga* be decorated with flowers. **mem-kan** display. **-an** window-dressing, display. *démokrasi ~* showcase democracy. **pem-an 1** nuptial chamber. **2** place for displaying s.t.
pajar see FAJAR.
paju see AJU.
pajuh mem- stuff, gorge.
pak₁ /pa', pak/ **1** package, parcel. **2** pack. *Sehari dua - kan cukup?* Two packs a day is enough, isn't it? **memp-, menge-(i)** package, pack. **-²an** by the pack. ~ *kartu* packs of cards. **penge-an** packaging up.
pak₂ lease, rent a right. **menge-** hold a franchise, lease the rights to provide a service. *Makanan siang Bu Nurdin yg ~* Mrs. Nurdin has the lunch concession. **mem-kan, menge-kan** rent or lease rights out. **penge-** lease holder. **pem-an, penge-an** leasing.
pak₃ /pak/ charter, pact. - *Atlantik* Atlantic Charter.
pak₄ see BAPA.
pakai 1 involve the use of, with, by means of. *tdk - karcis* without tickets. - *susu, tdk?* With milk or without? *siap -* ready to use. **2** take (a certain food). *Tdk - nasi?* Aren't you having rice? **3** wear. *Tdk hrs - dasi* You are not obliged to wear a tie. **ber-** be dressed. **ber-an 1** get dressed. **2** wearing certain clothes. **mem- 1** wear, apply a dressing. *Ia ~ baju biru* She was wearing a blue dress. ~ *komprés* apply a compress. **2** use, make use of. *Meréka ~ méja itu* They used that table. *tdk ~ otaknya* does not use his brains. *Ia datang ~ mobil* He came by car. **3** require, take. *Itu ~ modal besar* It takes a lot of capital. **di-** (*Coll.*) use for (doing). *Sepréi itu saya - tidur* I used that sheet for

sleeping. **mem-kan** put s.t. on s.o. ~ *baju baru pd anaknya* put a new shirt on his son. **ter-** 1 used (up). 2 canceled, void (passport, visa, etc.). 3 applied. *ilmu-ilmu pengetahuan* ~ applied sciences. *tdk* ~ useless. **-an** 1 clothes, suit, uniform, dress. ~ *adat* traditional dress. ~ *angkatan* military service uniform. ~ *dlm* underwear. ~ *dinas* uniform. ~ *dinas lapangan* battle dress. ~ *jadi* ready-made wear. ~ *kebangsaan* national dress. ~ *kebesaran lengkap* full dress (for wedding, military, etc.). ~ *kuda* harness. ~ *pelasak* work clothes. ~ *seragam* uniform. ~ *taruhan* Sunday clothes. ~ *tekanan* pressurized suit. 2 get dressed. **pem-** 1 user, consumer. 2 wearer. **pem-an** 1 use, consumption. ~ *bahasa Indonésia di SMA* the use of Indonesian in high schools. *izin* ~ *tanah* permission to use the land. 2 application, usage. **sepem-an** complete set of clothes.

pakal putty, caulking. **mem-** caulk (a ship). **pem-** putty, o. who caulks.

pakam see PAKEM₁.

pakan woof. **mem-kan** interweave with s.t.

pakansi holiday, vacation. **ber-** go on vacation.

pakar expert in a certain field. **ke-an** expertise.

pakarya, pakaryan (blue-collar) worker, artisan, craftsman.

pakat₁ 1 agreement. 2 discussion, convention. **se-** 1 agreed. 2 unanimously, in harmony. *Meréka* ~ *menolak usul itu* They unanimously rejected the resolution. **berse-** 1 agree with e.o. 2 discuss. **(ber)se-an** agree with e.o. **menye-i** agree on. *yg pernah kita se-i* what we once agreed to. **kese-an** agreement reached. *Meréka mengadakan* ~ *utk pergi bersama* They made an agreement to go together. **ber-** 1 agree. 2 discuss. **mem-i** agree on.

pakat₂ see PEKAT.

pakcik uncle (younger brother or younger cousin of parent).

pakdé (*Jv*) uncle (older brother or older cousin of o.'s parent).

paké(k) see PAKAI.

pakem₁ taking hold well (of brakes). *Rém mobilnya* - His car has good brakes. **mem-** take hold (of brakes).

pakem₂ source book for the Jv shadow play stories.

pakét 1 parcel. 2 package, set of proposals that go together. - *15 April* The package of (reforms proposed) April 15. **mem-kan** send s.t. by parcel post or delivery service.

pakih see FAKIH.

paking 1 gasket. 2 packaging.

pakir see FAKIR.

pakis k.o. edible fern.

pakking see PAKING.

pakné (*Jv*) term of address to o.'s husband.

pakpué, pakpui (*Ch*) divination.

paksa₁ /paksa/ 1 force. 2 necessity, compulsion. **mem-** 1 be persistent, compelling. 2 force, compel. **mem-²** repeatedly compel. **mem-kan**

1 force, compel s.o. 2 force s.t. on. **ter-** be forced to. *Ia* ~ *pergi* He had to go. **ke-** (*Coll.*) be forced to. **keter-an** the fact of being forced. **-an** compulsion, force exercised. *Permintaanmu merupakan* ~ I felt forced by your request. **pem-an** forcing, applying pressure to do s.t.

paksa₂ /paksa/ favorable opportunity. *angin* - a favorable wind. *Terbukalah - utk . . .* The opportunity presented itself to . . .

paksi 1 axis. 2 pivot.

paksina north.

pakta pact.

pakter stall selling palm wine.

paktor see FAKTOR.

paktur see FAKTUR.

paku₁ nail, spike. - *alam* princely title in Yogyakarta. - *buana* princely title in Yogyakarta. - *jamur/payung* thumbtack. - *keling/sumbat* rivet. - *rapat* **mem-rapat(kan)** nail down or up tight. - *rebana* tack. **ber-** 1 have nails. 2 cling, stick to. **mem-(i)** nail. **mem-kan** nail down or up. *Ia* ~ *plakat pd suatu pohon* He nailed a placard on a tree. **ter-** be stock-still in puzzlement or amazement, fixed in enchantment.

paku₂ k.o. edible fern.

pakuk mem- hit or cut with an axe.

pakum a vacuum.

pal 1 length of about o. mile. 2 milestone. 3 pole. **ber-²** 1 (*Naut.*) tack a vessel. 2 for miles and miles, miles and miles at a time. *Rumahnya* ~ *dr laut* His house is miles away from the sea.

PAL [*Penataran Angkatan Laut*] naval base.

pala₁ nutmeg.

pala₂ (se)-² if so and so has already gotten started, been done to a certain extent (o. might as well go ahead and finish it, do it the whole way). ~ *mencuri, ambil semuanya* While you are stealing, you might as well take everything.

palagan (*Jv*) battleground.

palai mem- stew until tender.

palaikat see PELÉKAT.

palak₁ 1 angry. *Saya - kpdnya* I was angry with him. 2 passionate, easily excited. 3 hot, feverish. **-²** somewhat warm. ~ *dingin* feeling feverish alternating with feeling cold. **pem-** hothead.

palak₂ penis.

palak₃ see FALAK.

palam₁ mem- stop a leak. **pem-** 1 stopper. 2 cork.

palam₂ see PALEM.

palang 1 crossbar. - *atap* cross beam on roof. - *Mérah* Red Cross. 2 bolt. *Ia mendapat - pintu* He got it from his wife for coming home at all hours (He found the doors barricaded). 3 barrier. - *KA* gate at railroad crossing. **mem-i** 1 hamper, block, obstruct. 2 shut with a crossbar. **mem-kan** 1 crucify. 2 lay, position s.t. crosswise.

palapa name of fruit Gajah Madah swore not to eat until kingdom of Majapahit was united.

Palapa name of Indonesian communications satellite.

palar mem-(kan) 1 consider sufficient, all right.

Biarpun sedikit, itu saya -kan Although it was not much, I was pleased with it. **2** count on, hope for.

palawija crops planted as 2d crop in dry season.

paléh (*Sd*) **mem-** take care of a fighting or racing animal.

palem palm.

palén sundries, ready-made merchandise. **-an** sundries.

paléolitik (*Geol.*) paleolithic.

paléontologi (*Geol.*) paleontology.

palét palette.

palindrom palindrome.

paling₁ the most. *yg - baik* the best. *- banyak* the most, at most. *Ia mempunyai yg - banyak* He had the most of all. *- banyak ada lima puluh* At the most there were 50. *- banter* at the absolute most. *- sedikit* the least, at the least. *- tdk* (if nothing else) at the very least. *- tdk saya bersedia, kalau tdk ada yg lain* At least I am willing, if there is no o. else. *-²* at the most. *~ ia dpt menamatkan sekolah menengahnya* At the most he was able to complete his high school education.

paling₂ ber- turn. *~ dr agamanya* turn away from o.'s religion. **mem-(kan)** swing round, alter the course of, divert.

palis₁ ber-, mem- avert o.'s eyes, turn o.'s face away.

palis₂ mem- polish.

palit₁ bankrupt. **mem-kan** declare bankrupt. **ter-²** be mixed up in dirty business. **ke-an** bankruptcy.

palit₂ ointment. **se-** a dab of. *~ lém* a dab of glue. **mem-** smear, daub. **mem-kan** spread evenly. **pem-** *bibir* lipstick.

palka (*Naut.*) hold of a ship.

palma palm (tree).

palsu false, counterfeit. **mem-** falsifying, forging. *~ diploma* falsifying diplomas. **mem-kan 1** forge (documents), counterfeit, falsify s.t. **2** adulterate food. **ke-an** falseness. **pem-** forger, counterfeiter, adulterator. **pem-an 1** counterfeiting, forging. **2** adulteration. **3** falsification.

paltu 1 assistant. **2** acting, temporary holder of position.

palu 1 hammer. *- arit* hammer and sickle (Communist emblem). **2** blow. **3** gavel. *- pimpinan* gavel. *- godam* large hammer. **mem-godamkan** forge, create by hammering out. *~ persatuan bangsa* forge a national unity. **ber-²** barter. **ber-²an** hit e.o. **mem- 1** strike with a hammer, beat (into submission). **2** play a percussion instrument. **-an** blow.

paluh deep pool.

palun ber-² embrace, hug e.o.

palung 1 pool. **2** trough. **3** riverbed. *- ikan* aquarium. **-an** manger.

palut ber- wrapped. **mem-(i)** wrap. **pem-** wrapper.

PAM [*Perusahaan Air Minum*] Municipal Water Corporation. *air -* city water.

paman uncle (esp. younger brother or younger cousin of parent).

pamarta (*Rel.*) savior, redeemer.

pambek /pambek/ (*Jv*) pride.

pamegat patron.

pamén (*Mil.*) an officer of the middle ranks.

paméo 1 slogan. **2** saying, proverb.

pamér show off. **ber-** *diri* exhibit o.s. *Ia ~ diri di depan cermin* She admired herself before the mirror. **mem-i** show off to s.o. **mem(per)-kan 1** model (clothes). **2** exhibit. **3** show off. *~ kepinterannya* show off how clever he is. **-an** exhibition. *~ ilmiah* scientific exhibition. *~ keliling* traveling exhibition. *~ senjata* military review. *~ terapung* floating exhibition.

pamflét pamphlet.

pamili 1 family. **2** relatives. **ber-** *dgn* be related to. **ber-kan** have as o.'s relation.

pamit 1 farewell. **2** say goodbye. **ber-** take leave. **ber-an** say goodbye to e.o. **mem-i** say farewell to. *Semua yg ku-i hanya tersenyum* Everyone I took leave from only smiled. **mem-kan** say good-bye on behalf of s.o. **-an** farewell. *sepatah kata ~* a few words of farewell.

pamong 1 guardian, o. who takes care of (us. gvt. official). *- désa* village administrator. *- praja* civil service, governing bureaucracy. **2** tutor.

pamor 1 pattern inherent in blade of good kris. **2** luster, prestige. *Muh. Ali sdh mulai kehilangan -nya* Muh. Ali is beginning to lose his prestige. **ber-** have this pattern in it, have prestige.

pampang 1 wide, broad. **2** obvious. **mem-kan 1** extend, widen, spread out. **2** explain. **ter-** put up, spread out.

pampas reimbursement, indemnity. **mem-** reimburse. **-an** reparations payment. *~ perang* war reparations. **pem-** compensation. **pem-an** reparation.

pampat mem- press, squeeze. **pem-** press.

pamplét see PAMFLÉT.

pamrih 1 profit, reward o. gets for doing s.t. **2** purpose, what o. is after. **ber-** do s.t with an eye to the reward.

pamungkas 1 (*Jv*) final (part). *Bagian Serat Rama yg -* the final portions of the Ramayana. **2** deadly, s.t. that finishes s.t. off. *senjata -* a lethal weapon.

pamur see PAMOR.

pan₁ oven heated with charcoal. **menge-** bake. **-²an** baked in a charcoal oven.

pan₂ (*Jkt*) see KAN₁.

pana ter- 1 stupified, stunned. **2** stunned, impressed. *Saya ~ oléh keramahannya* I was stunned by her hospitality.

panah bow (and arrow). *- api* rocket firecracker, roman candle. *- kelodan* lightning. *- matahari* sun rays. **mem-(i)** shoot at with bow and arrow. **mem-kan** shoot s.t out like an arrow. *kritik yg di-kan padanya* the criticism which was shot at him. **-an** archery. **pem-** archer. **sepem-** the distance of a bowshot.

panakawan see PUNAKAWAN.

panar stunned, surprised.
panas 1 warm, hot, heat. - *bara* glowing heat. - *kuku* lukewarm. - *pijar* white heat. - *sengangar* noonday heat. - *terik* 1 burning or piercing heat of sun. 2 red-hot (of metal). - *tubuh* body heat. 2 fever, feverish. - *dingin* 1 cold and hot alternatingly. 2 feel uneasy. 3 malaria. 3 critical. 4 fierce. - *hati* quick to anger or hurt feelings. - *hendak* virtually unable to restrain o.s. from doing s.t. *Ia - hendak memukul isterinya* He could hardly keep himself from striking his wife. -² 1 quite new, fresh. 2 when it is hot. 3 when things get hot, times of rebellion. **ber-** expose o.s. to sun. **ber-an** sunbathe. **mem-** heat up, become hot. **mem-i** heat. *-ilah air* Heat some water. **mem-kan** 1 heat. 2 enrage. **ke-an** 1 too hot. 2 heat. 3 suffering from the heat. **-an** place in the sun. **pem-** heater. ~ *surya* solar heater. **pem-an** heating.
panasaran see PENASARAN.
panatik see FANATIK.
panatisme see FANATISME.
panau skin fungus causing white blotches. **(ber)-an** having white blotches from this fungus.
panca 1 penta-, quinti-, five. - *Negara Colombo* the five Colombo countries. - *tunggal* the five top officials in a provincial or county gvt. - *usaha* the five steps taken to implement the Green Revolution. 2 hand. **ber-** wrestle by pushing o.'s opponent with the hands.
pancaindera the five senses.
pancaka crematorium.
pancal **mem-** press down on with foot, step on (the gas). *Kakinya sdh* ~ *pedal gas* His foot was already pressing down on the gas pedal. **-an** pedal.
pancalogi (*Spo.*) five principles.
pancalomba pentathlon.
pancamuka multifaceted.
pancang 1 pole, stake, pile. 2 boundary pole. **ber-an** rooted, implanted (in numbers). **mem-** ram, drive piles. **mem-kan** stick in, fasten. ~ *bendéra di atas puncak* implant the flag on the peak. **ter-** 1 rooted, planted in the ground. 2 established (reputation). **-an** 1 a stake, marker. 2 place to dig s.t. in. ~ *kaki* foothold. **pem-an** 1 marking with a stake. 2 pegging s.t. down.
pancar **ber-²** scattered, dispersed. **ber-an** spout, spray in quantity. **mem-** 1 spout, spray, gush. *Di kaki gunung itu* ~ *air dr dlm tanah* The water spouts out at the foot of the mountain. *Peluhnya* ~ *sehingga bajunya basah* He perspired until his clothes were soaked. 2 sprout. **mem-kan** 1 radiate. *Matahari* ~ *sinarnya* The sun's rays radiate. 2 spout, spray s.t. out. 3 broadcast. *RRI* ~ *siarannya pd gelombang 120 méter* The Indonesian Broadcasting System broadcasts on a wavelength of 120 meters. **ter-** radiated, emitted. **-an** 1 emission, flow. ~ *cinta* outpouring of love. ~ *mani* ejaculation. ~ *mata* a look. 2 broadcast. 3 product. **se-an** homologous. **pem-** 1 fountain.

2 radio or TV transmitter. 3 radiator. **pem-an** action of broadcasting, radiating, emitting.
pancaragam various, motley, all k.o. **ber-** be heterogeneous.
pancargas jet.
pancaroba transition period, esp. between monsoons, periods of life, etc.
Pancasila the five basic principles of the Republic of Indonesia: the belief in o. God Almighty, humanity that is just and civilized, the unity of Indonesia, democracy guided by the wisdom of representative deliberation, social justice for all Indonesians. **mem-kan** make s.t. in accordance with the five basic principles. **ke-an** having to do with the five principles.
pancasilais o. who is an enthusiastic follower or supporter of *Pancasila.*
pancasona invulnerability to death.
pancawarna multicolored.
pancawarsa five-year period.
pancawindu a period of 40 years.
pancer **mem-** 1 keep s.o. waiting. 2 leave s.t. going. *Karena takut mogok mesin, mobilnya diwaktu ia mampir di toko itu* Because he was afraid the car would not start, he kept the motor running while he stopped in the store.
panci pan. - *email* enamelware.
pancing 1 fishing rod. 2 fishhook. **mem-** 1 fish, angle. 2 provoke, start s.t. ~ *ketidak akraban* try to do s.t. to develop a feeling of distance. 3 ferret out secrets, elicit a reaction. ~ *tepuk tangan penonton* elicit the audience's applause. **-an** elicitation, provocation, inducement. ~ *pemikiran* inducing s.o. to think. **pem-** s.t. used to elicit a further reaction. *Uang yg diberikannya sbg* ~ *dlm pembangunan mesjid* The money he gave was to elicit further contributions for the construction of the mosque.
pancit **mem-** squirt little by little.
panco arm wrestling.
pancoléng thief.
pancong see KUÉ.
pancung 1 train of dress, shirttail. 2 angular, cut off sharply. *hukuman* - punishment of decapitation. **mem-** cut off, decapitate, amputate. *Karena mencuri tangannya di-* His hand was cut off for stealing. **mem-kan** make sharp or well shaped. *Dokter bisa* ~ *hidung dgn potongan plastik* With plastic surgery the doctor can make a nose well formed. **-an** a cut. ~ *pedang* a cut with a sword.
pancur **mem-** gush, spout, pour out or down. *Air* ~ *dr saluran bambu* Water poured out of the bamboo pipe. **-an** 1 shower. 2 jet, spray. 3 tap. ~ *air* fountain, spout of water. *Ia mandi di bawah* ~ *air* He is taking a bath under the waterspout.
pancut **mem-** gush. **-an** spray, gush, spurt.
pandai₁ 1 bright, smart. *Anak itu - di kelas* The child is good in school. - *beragak* good at guessing. 2 capable. *Anak itu - membuat layang-layang* The child's capable of making a kite. - *jatuh* able

to shift for o.s. **3** know, know how. *Anak itu - menyenangkan hati org tuanya* That child knows how to please his parents. *Anak itu - berbahasa Inggeris* The child knows English. **se-²** as clever as possible. *~ tupai melompat, sekali akan gawal juga* No matter how good a squirrel is at jumping, he still is going to miss some time. **ke-an** cleverness, skill.

pandai₂ craftsman of metals. *- besi* blacksmith. *- emas* goldsmith.

pandak short. **mem-kan, mem(per)-** shorten, abbreviate.

pandan pandanus.

pandang a look. *sekali -* at first glance. *tdk -* irrespective of. *tdk - bahasa dan bangsa* irrespective of language or nationality. *tak - bulu* not discriminating against, regardless of who or what it is. *ambil tindakan tak - bulu* take necessary steps, no matter who it might be. **ber-an 1** view e.o. **2** have a certain view. **bersi-an** view o. another. **- mem-1** look at e.o. **2** respect e.o. **mem- 1** look at, gaze at. **2** consider, take into account. *Ia ~ hal itu sbg biasa saja* He considered the matter as s.t. ordinary. *tak ~ usia* regardless of age. *Saya ~ rendah pdnya* I have a low opinion of him. *~ hina* look down on s.o. *~ ke atas* glance up. **mem-i** gaze at. **mem-kan** *mata* shift o.'s gaze to. **ter- 1** visible. **2** spot, catch sight of. **3** esteemed, highly regarded. **keter-an** being highly regarded. **-an 1** view, opinion. *~ hidup* view of life, philosophy of life. **2** s.t. o. sees. *laporan ~ mata* eyewitness report. **pem-** spectator. **pem-an 1** view, scenery. **2** observation. **3** viewpoint. *~ umum* the common point of view. **sepem-** as much or far as o. can see at a glance.

pandéga 1 employees on a fishing vessel. **2** Boy or Girl Scouts of highest rank (aged 15-17 years).

pandemén see FONDAMÉN.

pandir stupid, naive. **ke-an** stupidity.

pandita 1 *(Bali)* Hindu priest. **2** *(Lit.)* title of a palace rank.

pandom compass.

pandu 1 guide. *kapal* ship's pilot. **2** Boy or Girl Scout (in former times). **mem-** guide. **mem-kan** pilot, bring a ship into port. **ke-an** scouting, scout movement. **-an 1** escort. **2** pilot (project). *proyék ~* a pilot project. **pem-** guide. *~ wisata* tourist guide. **pem-an** scouting.

panekui *(M)* see PANEKUK.

panekuk crepe, pancake.

panél₁ panel (discussion).

panél₂ panel of wood.

panélis panelist.

panembrama *(Jv)* song welcoming a celebrity opening an important event, etc.

panén 1 harvest. *- susulan* follow-up harvest. **2** reap a nice profit. *Ia sedang - karena jualannya laku sekali* He is reaping a nice profit because his goods sell well. **mem-** harvest. **mem-i** harvest (a field). **-an** harvest gathered. **pem-an** harvesting.

pang sound of drum. *- kutipang* sound of drum.

panga ter- be wide open.

Pangab [*Panglima Angkatan Bersenjata*] Commanderin Chief of the Armed Forces.

pangabekti *(Jv)* homage.

Pangad [*Panglima Angkatan Darat*] Commander in Chief of the Ground Forces.

pangah mem- open the mouth in astonishment. **ter-** open-mouthed.

pangalungan *(Sd)* money thrown by spectators to actors or dancers.

pangan food. *masalah -* problems of providing food.

Pangdam [*Panglima Daérah Militér*] Territorial Military Commander.

pangéran 1 prince, lord. **2** *(Crd.)* jack.

pangéstu *(Jv)* **1** blessing. **2** spiritual movement originating in Central Java.

panggak proud of s.t. or s.o.

panggang 1 baked, roasted. **2** toasted. *Saya suka roti -* I like toast. **mem-** toast, roast, bake. **ter-** scared. **-an 1** place for roasting. **2** s.t. roasted. **pem-an 1** toaster. **2** roasting spit. **pem-** *roti* toaster.

panggar raised framework, us. used for drying fish.

panggeng *(Jkt)* constant, regular, unchanging.

panggih *(Jv)* ritual meeting at the wedding of a couple being married.

panggil mem- 1 call, summon, send for s.o. **2** name, call. *Anak-anak ~ ayah dgn "Pap"* The children call Father "Pap." **mem-i 1** call out s.t. **2** call for, summon. **mem-kan 1** call s.o. by a certain name. **2** summon on behalf of. **-an 1** call, summons. **2** calling, vocation. **sepem-** as far as the voice can reach.

panggul *(Anat.)* hip, pelvis. **mem-** carry on o.'s shoulder. *~ senapan!* *(Mil.)* shoulder arms. *~ senjata* be conscripted (bear arms).

panggung 1 stage, raised platform. **2** grandstand. **3** scaffolding. **ber-** have a stage, platform. **m-** appear on stage. **mem-kan, menge-kan** stage, put on the stage. **-an** lookout tower, post. *~ suara* sound stage. **pem-an** staging, put on the stage.

pangkal 1 base, beginning, starting point. *- air* source of water. *- (ber)tolak* starting point. *- cerita* main point of a story. *- kata kerja* *(Ling.)* infinitive. *- matrial* place that sells construction materials. *- nama* first name. *- pokok* gist, essence. **2** cause. **3** base point. *- bedil* rifle butt. *- kaki* *(Anat.)* tarsus. *- lengan* *(Anat.)* upper arm. *- paha* *(Anat.)* hip. *- pedang* hilt of a sword. *- pohon* foot, base of a tree. *- tenggorok* larynx. **4** *(Elec.)* pole. **ber- 1** have as o.'s base. *tempat ~* home base. **2** originate in. *Masalah itu ~ pd ketidaksanggupannya* The problem originates in his lack of competence. **3** have a cause, basis. *berbicara tdk ~* chatter away (without anything to talk about). **m-** have as o.'s base of operations. *Tukang bécak ~ di pojokan* Pedicab drivers have their base of operations (wait for customers) at the corner. **mem-kan 1** unload, discharge, put ashore. **2** post a person s.w. **-an 1** place to start out from, bridgehead. ~ *peluncur* launch site. **2** quay, anchorage. **3** (*Mil.*) base (for armed forces). ~ *induk* home base. ~ *udara* air base.

pangkas ber- get a haircut. **mem- 1** cut, trim hair. **2** prune, trim. ~ *kata* summarize, recapitulate. **mem-i** mow or trim the plants in an area. ~ *pekarangannya* mow the lawn, trim the plants in the garden. **-an** haircut or other trim given. **pem-** barber. **pem-an 1** barbering. **2** barbershop.

pangkat 1 rank, position. *gila* - overambitious to rise in rank. **2** step, grade (in advancement). **3** floor, story. **4** platform. **5** (*Math.*) degree, power. - *tiga* cubed. *empat* - *lima* four to the 5th power. **ber-** hold an important position. **mem-kan 1** promote s.o. **2** (*Math.*) raise to a power. *dikan tujuh* raised to the 7th power. **ke-an** stratification according to rank. **pem-an** promotion. **per-an** having to do with ranks.

pangkéng, pangking raised area in room for sleeping.

pangkon (*Jv*) wooden base of gamelan.

Pangkopkamtib [*Panglima Komando Pemulihan Keamanan dan Ketertiban*] Commander for the Restoration of Peace, Security, and Order.

pangku lap. **ber-** *tangan* do nothing. **(me)m-1** take on o.'s lap. **2** manage, administer, run. *sblm* ~ *jabatan* before taking office. **-an** lap. **pem-1** manager. **2** functionary. ~ *jabatan* **1** functionary. **2** acting. **pem-an** administration. *wilayah* ~ *hutan* area of forest management.

pangkung mem- hit with a club.

pangkur 1 pickax. **2** mattock, hoe. **mem-** till, work the soil.

panglima (*Mil.*) commander. - *besar* general for life. - *mandala* theater army commander. - *tertinggi* commander in chief. **ke-an** position of commander.

pangling (*Jv*) fail to recognize. **ke-an** failure to recognize.

panglong lumber mill.

pangon shepherd. **-an** pasture.

pangréh praja civil service.

pangsa segment, section (of fruit).

pangsan see PINGSAN.

pangsi₁ reel, drum, shaft.

pangsi₂ 1 k.o. collarless shirt. **2** (*Ch*) k.o. black silk.

pangsit (*Ch*) k.o. wonton or ravioli.

pangsiun see PÉNSIUN.

pangti [*panglima tertinggi*] (*Mil.*) commander in chief.

pangur 1 rasp, file. **2** tooth filing. **mem-** file teeth.

pangus dashing, handsome.

panguyuban see PAGUYUBAN.

panik panic. **ke-an 1** panic. **2** be in a panic. *Meréka* ~ *ketika alarem kebakaran berbunyi* They were in a panic when the fire alarm went off.

panil see PANÉL₂.

panili vanilla.

panitera 1 clerk of a court. - *utama* chief secretary. - *pengadilan* clerk of the court. **2** registrar. **ke-an** secretariat. ~ *pengadilan* office of the clerk of court.

paniteratama chief secretary.

panitia, panitya committee. - *penaskah* draft committee. - *penguji* examining board. - *perumus* formulative committee. **ke-an** having a committee structure. *dlm bentuk* ~ in a committee format.

panjak a player in gamelan.

panjang long, length. - *akal* clever, witty. *Org tua itu* - *akalnya* That old man is very clever. - *bibir* talkative. - *bulat* cylindrical. - *gelombang* wave length. - *kili-kili* full of excuses. - *kira-kira* **1** intelligent, wise. **2** cautious. - *lanjut* wordy, verbose. - *langkah* in a roundabout way. - *lébar* elaborate, at great length. - *lidah* backbiting, slandering. - *mata* immoral. - *napas* with stamina. - *sayap* wingspread. - *tangan* prone to thievery. - *umur* have a long life. - *usus* patient. **se- 1** all along. ~ *jalan* all along the road. **2** as far as. ~ *pengetahuan saya* as far as I know. ~ *hari* all day long. ~ *pikiran saya* in my opinion. **ber-** ~ *kalam* relate in elaborate fashion. ~ *madah* talk a great deal. **ber-an 1** in the long run. **2** for a long time. **mem-1** stretch along a length. *Di depan kami pantai* ~ Before us stretched the seashore. **2** go along, be all along. ~ *jalan-jalan besar* stretch along the highway. **mem-kan** make s.t. long, extend s.t. to its length. ~ *léhér* crane o.'s neck. *Ia* ~ *anyamannya yg hampir selesai* His plait-work was almost finished and he stretched it out to its full length. **memper-** extend s.t., lengthen. ~ *visa* extend o.'s visa. *Pertunjukan itu akan diper-* The performance will be extended. **ke-an 1** too long. **2** length. **3** duration. **4** continuation. **berke-an 1** continuous. **2** prolonged, protracted. **-an** extension. **pem-an** lengthening, extending. **per-an** extension, prolongation.

panjar cash advance. - *pesangon* first payment of o.'s severance or retirement pay. **-an** down payment.

panjat mem- climb. ~ *perkara* (*Leg.*) **1** appeal to a higher court. **2** give notice of appeal. **di-** *kaya* suddenly become rich. **mem-i 1** climb s.t. *pohon yg di-i* the tree being climbed. **2** mount for copulation. **mem-kan 1** cause to climb. *Ia* ~ *keranya* He made his monkey climb up. **2** send up (to the heavens). *Kita -kan doa ke hadirat Illahi* We send a prayer up to God. **pem-an** action of climbing.

panji, panji-panji standard, banner, pennant.

pano see PANAU.

panorama panorama.

panser (*Mil.*) armored vehicle. - *amfibi* landing craft.

pansiun see PÉNSIUN.

pantai beach, coast, seashore. - *Emas* Gold Coast. - *Gading* Ivory Coast. **ber-kan** border on. *lautan yg* ~ *sebagian kepulauan Indonésia* a sea that borders on a portion of the Indonesian archipelago. **mem-** go along the coast or beach.

pantak mem- penetrate. **mem-kan** drive a nail in deeply, rivet.

pantalon (*Lit.*) long trousers.

pantang 1 prohibition, forbidden by taboo. - *mundur!* No retreat! - *kerendahan* want to be first rate. - *larang* various k.o. taboos and restrictions. - *patah di tengah* persevering. - *tersinggung* not easily piqued, offended. *Ia - surut* He never gave up. **2** avoidance of s.t. taboo. **ber-** abstain from. **mem-(i)** abstain from. ~ *makanan gemuk* avoid fatty foods. **-an** prohibition.

pantar se-, (se)-an being of the same age as. *Ia ~ku* He is my age.

pantas 1 proper, suitable. *Baju itu tak - baginya* That dress does not suit her. *perumahan -* suitable housing. **2** reasonable, fair, proper. *Itu harga -* That is a reasonable price. **3** alert, smart. - *pangus* dashing, handsome. - *tangan* clever at picking pockets. **4** of course! no wonder! - *dia jadi miskin!* No wonder he became poor! **se-nya** fitting, proper. ~ *kamu hrs pergi kpdnya* It is fitting you should go to him. *Sdh ~ saya dipilih* I deserve to be chosen. **mem-** dress o.s. up. **mem-kan** make s.t. compatible (of clothes). **ke-an** fairness, properness. **-an** of course! no wonder! ~ *dia tdk pulang-pulang. Punya isteri muda* No wonder he never goes home. He has got himself a 2d wife.

pantat₁ 1 behind, bottom, buttock. - *kuning* tightfisted. **2** back part of s.t. - *truk* back part of a truck. **3** base. - *jarum* eye of needle. **ber-** bottomed, have a bottom.

pantat₂ mem-*getah* gather rubber.

pantau mem- monitor s.t., observe. **ter-** observed, monitored. **-an** observation made. **pem-** observer. **pem-an** monitoring.

panték see PANTIK₁.

Pantékosta (*Rel.*) **1** Whitsuntide, Pentecost. **2** Pentecostal sect.

pantes see PANTAS.

panti 1 (*Lit.*) house, residence. **2** institution, home. - *asuhan* orphanage. - *derma* charitable institution. - *pijat* massage parlor.

pantik₁ mem- 1 strike fire. **2** snap o.'s fingers. **pem-** flintstone. - *api* cigarette lighter.

pantik₂ bamboo nails or dowels. **mem- 1** bleed. **2** drill (a well). **-an** place o. has drilled, s.t. drilled. *sumur* ~ a drilled well. **pem-an** *darah* blood letting.

panting₁ ber-an fall away in numbers. **ter- 1** dart away. **2** fall with thud.

panting₂ see PONTANG-PANTING.

pantis mascara. **mem-** blacken eyebrows.

panto (*Biol.*) annual growth ring (on trees).

pantofel, pantopel slippers (with closed toes).

pantok the endmost, bottommost, furthest point. *Sekolahnya blm -* He has not finished his studies yet.

pantomim pantomime.

pantul mem- bounce back, bounce off. **men-kan** reflect s.t. ~ *pribadi yg lemah* reflects a weak personality. **ter-** be bounced back. **-an 1** reflection. **2** rebound. **pem-an** reflection.

pantun₁ pantun, k.o. traditional poetry, each verse of which consists of two couplets: the first suggests the 2d by sound or other similarity. It is often sung in contests where a boy addresses a quatrain to a girl who must answer with a quatrain of her own. **ber-(an)** recite with two or more persons singing pantuns. **mem-kan** express o.s. by means of pantuns. **-an** recitation of pantuns. **pem-** composer or reciter of pantuns.

pantun₂ se- *tak* ~ *pun* not a single o., not a little bit.

panu (*Jv*) see PANAU.

panus holder for candle or lamp.

panutan s.t. to follow, guide, leader. *Pak guru itu menjadi - masyarakat désanya* The teacher is the leader the villagers follow.

paohi see PAUHI.

pap popping sound.

papa₁ poor, destitute. - *sengsara* destitute. **ke-sengsaraan** poverty, destitution. **ke-an** poverty, destitution.

papa₂ father, esp. in Westernized families.

papah ber- supported. **ber-an** support o.s. on. **mem-** support. *Org sakit itu di- sebab ia tak dpt berjalan sendiri* The sick man was supported because he could not walk by himself. **-an** a support to lean on.

papak₁ flat, level, smooth. **mem-kan** smoothen, flatten.

papak₂ ber- meet. *Saya ~ dgn dia di jalan* I met him on the street. **mem- 1** meet. **2** receive, welcome. **mem-i 1** go to meet. **2** get in way to block, stop. ~ *gerakan tangannya* intercepted the movement of his hand. **-an 1** meeting. **2** welcome, reception. **3** run into, meet. *Saya ~ dgn dia di Surabaya* I ran into him in Surabaya.

papan₁ 1 board, plank. - *asbés* asbestos plate. - *catur* chessboard. - *hubungan* (*Tel.*) switchboard. - *jepit* clipboard. - *jungkat-jungkit* see-saw. - *lupi* boards on front and back of small boat for sitting on. - *lompatan, loncatan* springboard. - *silancar* surfboard. - *tangga* gangplank. - *tongkah* a sledge for use on marshy land. **2** shelf. **3** (road) sign. - *arah* sign indicating the route. - *nama* name plate. - *réklame* billboard. - *tulis* blackboard. **mem-** install boards.

papan₂ housing, shelter (as basic human need). *sandang, pangan,* ~ food, clothing, shelter.

papar flat, level. **mem-kan 1** roll out, flatten. **2** explain, relate. **-an 1** shelf. **2** explanation. **pem-an** explanation.

papas₁ mem- 1 remove, take off. **2** take everything away. **3** resist. **4** criticize. *Ia ~ ceramahnya habis-habisan* He criticized the lecture through and through. **ter-** cut off or out.

papas₂ (ber)-an, ber- meet without stopping. *Meréka ~ di jalan* They met e.o. in passing on the street. **mem-** run into. *Truk itu ~ dinding jembatan* The truck ran into the side of the bridge. **mem-i** meet s.o. (but not stop). *Satu dua org saja yg di-inya* He ran into only o. or two people. **ter-, ke-an** be run into, met.

papaya papaya.

papeda (*Amb*) sago porridge.

papi (*Coll.*) father.

papilyun see PAVILYUN.

papirus papyrus.

papras mem- trim, cut to even out.

Papua-Nugini Papua New Guinea.

para₁ rubber.

para₂ collective plural marker referring to people who comprise a group. - *ahli sejarah* historians. - *domba* flock, congregation. - *hadirin* Ladies and Gentlemen. - *pelaku* cast (of play or movie). - *pembaca* the readers. - *pendengar* the audience, Ladies and Gentlemen. - *penumpang* passengers.

para₃ (*Mil.*) **1** paratrooper. **2** specially trained troops.

parabola (*Math.*) parabola.

parabolis (*Math.*) parabolic.

paradam see PERDOM.

parade parade.

paradigma paradigm.

paradoks, paradoksal paradoxical.

paradom see PERDOM.

paraf initials. **mem-** initial, sign with initials. **pem-an** initialing.

parafin paraffin.

parafrase paraphrase.

paragraf paragraph.

parah in serious condition. *luka -* be seriously injured. *Di samping médan yg mémang -* . . . Besides the field which was really in bad condition . . . **mem-kan** aggravate. *Keadaan yg di-kan dgn adanya* . . . A situation which was aggravated by the existence of . . . **ter-** in the most serious condition. *di tempat musibah ~* in the place hardest hit by the disaster. **ke-an** seriousness of condition.

paraji (*Sd*) midwife. **mem-kan** abort a fetus.

parak 1 difference. *Tabiatnya tak berapa -nya dgn ibunya* Her character does not differ much from that of her mother. **2** partition. **3** interspace. **4** entering a time or era. - *déwasa* entering adulthood. - *siang* late morning. **mem-kan** distinguish.

paralél parallel. **memp-kan** make s.t. go parallel to s.t. else.

paralélogram (*Math.*) parallelogram.

param medicinal powder or ointment, or liquid to rub on body. - *kocok* a hot stinging type of liquid for rubbing which must be shaken before using.

parama arta see AMBEG-PARAMA-ARTA.

paramanusia human race.

paramasastera grammar.

paraméter parameter.

paran 1 direction. **2** goal, aim. **mem-i** approach,

go to. *Gubuk yg ku-i itu kelihatan jelas* The hut I approached was clearly visible.

parang₁ short machete, chopping knife. - *latuk/pelatuk* a machete with a hooked point. **mem-1** cut. **2** cancel. **mem-kan** use s.t. as a machete on.

parang₂ k.o. fish, the wolf-herring.

parap₁ mem- hammer, pound.

parap₂ see PARAF.

para-para loft, shelf over the hearth.

paraplégia (*Med.*) paraplegia.

paras 1 face, countenance. **2** looks, appearance. **3** smooth. **ber-** have a certain appearance. **mem-** make smooth, level.

parasit₁ parasite. *Yg tdk bekerja dipandang sbg - saja* Those who don't work are regarded as mere parasites.

parasit₂ see PARASUT.

parasitisme parasitism.

parasitologi (*Biol.*) parasitology.

parasut parachute.

parasutis parachutist.

parau hoarse. **ke-an** hoarseness.

pardon clemency, pardon. *sonder -* without mercy.

paré bitter melon or momordica, a green bitter and warty squashlike vegetable which grows on vines.

parem see PARAM.

paréwa street-corner loafer.

parfum perfume.

pari₁ rayfish, skate. - *tohok* k.o. rayfish.

pari₂ see BINTANG.

paria pariah.

parik in line, in a queue.

parikan /pari'an/ (*Jv*) aphorism.

paripurna 1 perfect, pure. **2** complete. **3** plenary.

Parisadha Hindu Dharma Pusat highest administrative council of the Hindu-Bali religion.

parit 1 moat, ditch, trench. - *buang/hilir* drainage ditch. **2** furrow, slit, groove. **ber-** grooved. **mem-** dredge.

paritas parity.

paritér having to do with a parity.

pariwara advertisement.

pariwisata 1 tourism. **2** a tour. **ber-** make a trip. **ke-an** tourism business. *unsur ~* the elements of the tourist business.

pariwisatawan tourist. **ke-an** tourism.

parji see FARJI.

parkét parquet.

Parkindo [*Partai Kristén Indonésia*] Indonesian Christian party.

parkir 1 be parked. *Apa mérek mobil yg - di sana?* What k.o. car is parked there? **2** be placed s.w. for a period of time. *dana yg - di bank-bank milik negara* money that is placed in state-owned banks. **mem(p)-(kan)** park. **-an** parking place. *~ taksi* taxi stand. **pem-an** parking. *~ kapal-kapal* the anchoring of ships in a harbor.

parkit parakeet.

parlemén parliament.
parleméntér parliamentary.
parleméntérisme parliamentarism.
parlénte₁ (*Amb*) liar.
parlénte₂ see PERLÉNTÉ.
parmasi see FARMASI.
Parmusi [*Partai Muslim Indonésia*] Indonesian Muslim Party.
paro, paroh half. - *masyarakat* (*Anth.*) moiety. **-²** half-breed, half-and-half. **se-** half, a part. ~ *baya/tuu* middle-aged. **ber-an** sharing 50-50. *Ia menjadikan dirinya batara Wisnu jua ~ dgn batara Krésna* He turned himself into s.t. that was half Vishnu and half Krishna. **mem-** rent land for a half share of the yield. **mem-kan 1** rent out o.'s land for a share of half the yield. **2** halve s.t. **-an 1** half and half, 50-50. *Untungnya ~* The profit was shared 50-50. **2** the half of s.t. *selama ~ kedua abad ke-20* during the 2d half of the 20th century. **pem-** o. who farms on a 50-50 basis.
paroki (*Rel.*) parish.
paron anvil.
parpol [*partai politik*] political parties.
Parpostél [*Pariwisata, Pos, dan Télékomunikasi*] Tourism, Postal, and Telecommunications Department.
Parsi Persia(n).
parsial, parsiil partial (not complete).
partai₁ (*Pol.*) party. *Ia msk - Nasional* He joined the Nationalist party. - *gurem* small, underdog party. **ber-** belonging to a party. *Ia tdk ~* He is nonparty. **ke-an** party system, party affairs.
partai₂ 1 (*Sport*) event. - *perorangan* individual event. - *ganda* doubles. **2** a quantity of. *pesanan dlm - besar* an order for a large quantity.
partikel (*Ling.*) particle, function word. - *ingkar* negative particle. - *pementing/penegas/penentu* emphatic particles.
partikelir private. *Anaknya msk sekolah -* His child entered a private school. **memp-kan** make an organization or private.
partisipasi participation. **ber-** be a participant. **memp-kan** have s.o. participate.
partitur musical score.
partner partner. **ber-** be partners.
partus (*Med.*) delivery.
paruh₁ beak. **mem-** peck at.
paruh₂ see PARO.
parun mem- burn bushes or weeds to clear. **pem-an** burning.
paru-paru lungs. - *basah* pleurisy.
parut 1 rasp, file. **2** scrape, grate. **3** scraper or grater. **ber-** scarred, having lines etched on it. *wajah yg ~ di kening* a face etched with lines on the forehead. **mem- 1** rasp. **2** make into small pieces by grating or scraping. **-an 1** board for scraping or grating. **2** s.t. scraped. *Itu ~ kelapa* That is scraped coconut. **pem-an** process of grating. ~ *batang sago* grating of sago trunks (for flour).
parvinu parvenu, nouveau riche.

parwa chapter of the Mahabharata.
pas₁ 1 fit, be the right size. *Baju itu tdk - baginya* The dress did not fit her. *Jalannya hanya - utk mobilnya* The road was only big enough for his car. **2** exact, exactly. *Itu - spt saya punya* It looked exactly like mine. *uang - exact change. Bayar dgn uang -* Pay with exact change. **3** exactly at. *Ia - dr Magelang* He has just gotten in from Magelang. *Berhenti - di depan rumahnya* Stop exactly in front of her house. **menge-** try s.t. on. **nge- 1** try clothes on. **2** fit (of clothes). **3** be just enough. **-²an** just barely enough and no more. *Utk hidup saja Rp20.000 ~ 20,000 rupiah* is just barely enough to live on.
pas₂ pass, document. - *jalan* travel permit. - *naik* boarding pass.
pas₃ (*Bri.*) pass.
pasah₁ (*Isl.*) divorce granted by religious court at wife's request. **mem-** annul a marriage. **mem-kan** divorce a woman.
pasah₂ ter- land, end up being s.w. *Di mana ~ baju saya?* Where did my dress go to?
pasah₃ mem- plane (wood). **-an** shavings, excelsior.
pasak 1 pin, peg, dowel. *besar - dr tiang* live beyond what o.'s station in life entitles o. to. **2** bolt. - *aman* safety catch. **3** pivot, axis. - *kemudi* tiller. **4** turning point. - *bumi* k.o. aphrodisiac. **mem-peg, pin. mem-kan 1** fasten. **2** impress s.t. on s.o.
pasal 1 paragraph, section. - *pelengkap* addendum. **2** (*Leg.*) article. **3** concerning, regarding, about. - *itu jangan khawatir* Do not worry about that. *Apa -nya itu terjadi?* How did it happen?
pasamuan suci the Catholic community.
pasang₁ pair, set. **se-** *merpati* pair of lovers (lit., turtledoves). **se-** *sepatu* pair of shoes. **se-** *suami isteri* married couple. **ber-²** in pairs. **ber-an** form a pair. **mem-kan 1** make a pair. **2** pair with. **-an 1** pair, set. ~ *minimal* (*Ling.*) minimal pair. **2** partner, counterpart.
pasang₂ - aksi 1 show off. **2** pose, be on o.'s best behavior. *Ia - aksi dgn mobilnya yg baru* He showed off his new car. **mem- 1** install in or on. *Ia ~ ban* He put on a tire. *Ia ~ pakaiannya* He put on his clothes. ~ *radio* turn on the radio. **2** install. *Rék itu blm di-* The shelf has not been installed yet. **3** fasten, pin, post. *Ia ~ Bintang Gerilya di dadanya* He pinned the Guerilla Medal on his chest. ~ *pengumuman* post an announcement. ~ *iklan* insert an advertisement. **4** turn on. ~ *saluran empat* Turn on channel four. **5** put in, enter a wager. *Ia selalu di- dlm pertandingan-pertandingan penting* He is always entered in important contests. ~ *tikaman* stake o.'s money. **6** set. ~ *tarip* set the fare. ~ *wéker* set an alarm clock. ~ *bendéra* hang out the flag. ~ *layar* set sail. ~ *mata* watch closely for s.t. ~ *meriam* fire a gun. ~ *pagar* build a fence. ~ *telinga* listen attentively for s.t. **mem-i** install in or on. ~ *ladam* shoe a horse. **mem-kan 1** install, fit. *Ia ~ lampu*

listerik He installed an electric light. **2** apply. **ter-1** discharged, fired. **2** turned on (light, radio). **-an** s.t. that has been installed, fastened, wagered. ~ *batu mérah* brickwork, masonry. **pem-** fitter, installer. ~ *iklan* advertiser. **pem-an 1** installing, assembling. **2** firing, shooting.

pasang₃ rise (of tide). *Muka laut -* The sea level rose. *- bah* tide causing flooding. *- kering* ebb, low tide. *- mati/perbani* neap tide. *- naik* **1** high tide. **2** increase. *- purnama* tide at full moon. *- surut* the rise and fall of the tides. *Kehidupan ada - surutnya* Life has its ups and downs.

pasanggrahan resthouse for travelers.

pasar market. *- amal/derma* fund-raising bazaar. *- bébas* free market. *- gelap* black market. *- kerja* labor market. *- laris* seller's market. *- malam* fair. *- modal* (*Fin.*) money market. *- pembeli* buyer's market. *- sayur* vegetable market. *- sénggol(an)* a small market so narrow that the people bump into e.o. *- surut* (*Econ.*) a shrinking market. *- tunai* (*Fin.*) spot market. *- uang* (*Fin.*) exchange. **se-** a week. **mem-kan** market s.t. **-an 1** market. *Pisang tdk punya ~ di sini* There is no market for bananas here. ~ *dunia* the world market. **2** (*Jv*) five-day week. **3** hold a market, be market day. *Sekarang sedang ~* It is a market day today. **4** of market quality, not of good enough quality to be sold in a specialty store. **pem-an** marketing.

pasara see PUSARA₁.

pasaréan (*Jv*) cemetery, grave.

pasasi fare (on a bus, etc.).

pasasir passenger. *- gelap* stowaway. *bagian -* check-in counter.

pasca /paska, pasca/ *- sarjana* postgraduate work. *- panén* time after rice harvest.

paséban (*Jv.*) audience hall.

paséh see FASIH.

paser (*Tech.*) compass to measure distance or describe a circle.

pasfoto photo of passport size.

pasi very pale.

pasibraka [*pasukan pengibar bendéra pusaka*] group of model high school students recruited to raise national flag on Independence Day.

pasién medical patient.

pasif passive. **ke-an** passivity, inaction.

Pasifik the Pacific.

pasifikasi pacification. **mem(p)-(kan)** pacify.

pasih see FASIH.

pasik 1 criminal, bad. **2** crazy. **ke-an** sin.

pasilan 1 tree epiphyte. **2** (*Coll.*) freeloader, parasite.

pasilitas see FASILITA.

pasip see PASIF.

pasir 1 sand. *- beton* sand used in preparing concrete. *- hanyut/hidup* quicksand. *- meléla* laterite. *- pasang* sand used in laying bricks. **2** beach or place covered with sand. **ber-** have sand. **mem-** granulated. **-an** sandy.

pasirah (*S. Sumatra*) village chief.

pasisir see PESISIR₁, PASASIR.

Paska, Paskah Easter.

paska sarjana see PASCA.

pasmén lace.

paso see PASU.

pasok mem- supply (a certain commodity). *kontrak utk ~ Arab Saudi dgn persenjataan* contract to supply Saudi Arabia with arms. **pem-** supplier. **pem-an** supplying. ~ *téhnya ke pasar bébas* the supplying of its tea to the open market.

Paspal [*Ilmu Pasti dan Pengetahuan Alam*] (*Acad.*) Mathematics and Natural Sciences.

paspor passport.

pasrah submit to o.'s fate. *Mukanya - dan penuh percaya* She had an expression of submission and complete trust. **mem-i** turn over, entrust to. *Aku yg di-i momong si kecil* I was the o. entrusted to take care of the little o. **mem-kan** submit, entrust s.t. ~ *hal ini kpd Bp* entrust this matter to Father. **ke-an** submission, resignation. **pem-an** act of submission.

passi passion.

passiva liabilities.

pasta paste. *- gigi* toothpaste.

pastéi paté.

pastél meat-filled turnover.

pasti definite, certain. *Ia mau jawaban yg -* He wants a definite answer. *- tdknya* whether it is certain or not. **mem-kan 1** determine, ascertain. **2** confirm, decide. *kemenangan yg ~* a decisive victory. **ke-an 1** certainty. **2** assurance. **3** for sure. *Nanti saya kasih tahu ~nya* I will let you know for sure. **pem-an** ascertainment.

pastiles lozenges.

pastir memp- pasteurize.

pastor, pastur Catholic priest. *- paroki* parish priest. *- praja* diocesan priest. **-an** parish house.

pastoral pastoral. *déwan -* pastoral council.

pastori parish house.

pasu bowl, basin. **-²** cheekbone.

pasukan 1 (*Mil.*) troops. *- gerilya* guerilla troops. *- berkuda* cavalry. *- inti* main force. *- jalan* infantry. *- laut* navy. *- pendamai* peace-keeping force. *- pemadam api* fire brigade. *- pembidas penggempur* shock troops. *- pengawal* guard platoon. *- udara* air force. **2** group. **3** formation. *se- kapal terbang* a formation of planes. *- meriam* artillery. *- musik* band.

Pasundan Sundanese area.

pasung prisoner's stocks. **mem- 1** lock legs between two pieces of wood. **2** repress, muzzle (the press). **-an** stocks. **pem-an 1** placing in stocks. **2** repressing in general. ~ *kréativitas* shackling of creativity.

pat (*Golf*) putt.

pat gulipat, patpat gulipat 1 shady deal. **2** (love) affair. **ber- 1** engage in shady deals. **2** have an affair with.

patah broken. *- arang/batu* completely broken. *- celana* crease in trousers. *- hati* **1** discouraged. **2** brokenhearted. *- lesu* **1** desperate. **2** brokenhearted. *- lidah* **1** speech impediment, defect. **2** speaking unclearly. **3** broken speech. *- mayang* wavy (hair). *- seléra* have no appetite. *- tulang* bone fracture. - *tumbuh hilang berganti* If s.t. breaks it grows back. If it disappears it is replaced. I.e., the struggle renews itself. -² in pieces, broken. *berbahasa Inggeris* ~ speak broken English. **se-** *kata* **1** o. word. **2** a few words. **ber-** *hati* be discouraged, dejected. *Rakyat jangan* ~ *hati* The people should not be discouraged. **mem-kan 1** break. *Ia* ~ *tongkat itu* He broke the cane. **2** discouraging. **ke-an 1** breakdown. **2** discouragement. ~ *rohani* mental breakdown. ~ *hati* discouragement. **-an 1** fracture. **2** broken fragment. **3** (*Geol.*) fault. **pe-** proverb, aphorism, expression. **pem-an** fracture. **per-an** (*Geol.*) place where there is a fracture.

pataka standard, banner.

patal [*pabrik pemintalan*] spinning factory.

patas [*cepat terbatas*] fast semi-express bus or train.

patatas (*Amb*) yams.

paték frambesia, yaws.

patén 1 patent. *obat* - patent medicine. **2** (*Sl.*) admirable, tops. *Teman saya ini - déh* This friend of mine is really cool. *Jahitannya* - Her sewing is first class. **mem-kan** patent s.t.

pater (*Rel.*) priest. - *Jénderal* the highest official in a province of the Society of Jesus.

pateri see PATRI.

paternalisme paternalism.

paternalistis paternalistic.

pateroli see PATROLI.

pati₁ 1 starch. **2** core, essence. - *arak* spirits. **-²an** (*Chem.*) starches.

pati₂ [*perwira tinggi*] (*Mil.*) high-ranking officer.

patih₁ 1 governor. **2** vice regent, chief minister to a king. **ke-an** residence or office of vice-regent.

patih₂ meek, submissive, docile. **ke-an** submissiveness, obedience. **pem-** tending to be submissive or docile.

patihah see ALFATIHAH.

patik 1 slave. **2** (*Lit.*) I, me (very humble).

patil 1 pole, shaft. **2** small adze. **3** stinger of a fish. **mem-** use a pole.

patok pole, stake. - **mem-** setting standards, making determinations. **mem-** determine, define. ~ *garis perbatasan kedua negara* determine the border between the two countries. **-an 1** pole. **2** directive, standard, criterion. ~ *harga* fixity of prices. **3** postulate. ~ *duga* hypothesis.

patologi pathology.

patologik, patologis pathologic.

patri solder. **mem-(kan)** solder s.t. **-an** soldering. *Émbér ini rusak ~nya* The soldering on this bucket is damaged. **pem-an** soldering.

patriot patriot. **ke-an** patriotism.

patriotik patriotic.

patriotis patriotic.

patriotisme patriotism.

patroli patrol.

patrum, patrun₁ cartridge.

patrun₂ (dress) pattern.

patuh obedient, submissive. **mem-** obey. **mem-i** obey s.t., be faithful to. *Ia* ~ *hukum negara* He

obeys the state's laws. **ke-an 1** obedience. **2** discipline, adherence (to rules). **3** faithfulness (to an original).

patuk mem- 1 peck, bite. *Kakinya di- ular* He was bitten on the foot by a snake. **2** grab with the beak. **3** manage to achieve s.t. *Édi* ~ *suksés* Eddy achieved success. **mem-kan** peck at with. ~ *paruhnya ke permukaan tanah* pecked with its beak on the surface of the soil. **-an** bill, beak.

patung₁ 1 image, statue. **2** sculpture. - *dada* bust (sculptured). **mem- 1** be like a statue. *Ia berdiri* ~ He stood like a statue. **2** sculpt. **pem-** sculptor. **pem-an** sculpturing.

patung₂ ber-an chip in together to pay for s.t. *Org* ~ *utk berlangganan surat kabar* People go in together to subscribe to a newspaper. **mem-(kan)** go in together in a money venture. **-an** joint venture. *perusahaan* ~ *antara Isuzu dan GM* a joint venture between Isuzu and GM.

patus mem- drain. **pem-an** drainage.

patut 1 proper, fitting, decent, in line. *Ini harga* - This is a fair price. **2** should, ought to. - *dihukum* liable to punishment. **se-nya** proper, rightly, fittingly. ~ *harganya Rp3.000* The price should be 3,000 rupiah. **ber-an** agree with, be in accordance with. **mem-(²) 1** dress s.t. up. *Nyonya* ~ *diri di muka cermin* Madame fixed herself up in front of the mirror. *Ia* ~ *dasinya di muka kaca* He adjusted his tie before the mirror. **2** take a hard look. **mem-kan** correct, put in order, fit. ~ *diri* dress up. **ke-an 1** fairness, appropriateness. **2** consideration, weighing.

pauh (*Lit.*) mango. *bagai - dilayang* smooth and round (of cheeks). - *janggi* the double coconut.

pauhi (*Ch*) abalone.

pauk₁ mem- hook. **pem-** hook.

pauk₂ see LAUK.

paus₁ (*Rel.*) pope. *Sri* - the Pope. **ke-an** papacy.

paus₂ see IKAN.

pause (*Thea.*) intermission, entr'acte. *Sementara - itu, penonton dihiburkan dgn tari perut* During the intermission, the audience was entertained with a belly dance.

paut closely joined. **ber-** cling to. **ber-an** closely connected, merged. **mem- 1** adhere, stick to. **2** bind. **mem-kan, memper-kan** make s.t. closely joined to s.t. else. **ter- 1** involved. **2** connected. **-an 1** base, origin. **2** home. **per-an** relation, connection.

pauze see PAUSE.

pav. [*pavilyun*]

pavilyun annex, portion (us. an extension) of home set aside as unit for rent.

pawai parade.

pawaka (*Lit.*) fire.

pawana (*Lit.*) wind.

pawang 1 o. endowed with magic powers. - *hujan* o. who controls rainfall. **2** o. with a special skill. - *pukat* expert in catching fish with a dragnet. **3** animal tamer. - *gajah* elephant tamer. **mem-i** put an animal through its paces. *duyung pelacak yg di-i oléh pelatihnya* the jumping porpoise that was being put through its paces by its trainer. **ke-an** the field of animal training. *dinas* ~ police dog unit.

pawiyatan school, training center.

paya swamp, marsh. **ber-(²)** marshy.

payah 1 tired. **2** difficult, troublesome. **3** finding s.t. troublesome. *Kami di Yogya - dgn pembantu* We had trouble with servants when we were in Yogya. *- sesak* asphyxiated. **(ber)-² 1** toil, have a hard time. **2** go to a lot of trouble. **mem-kan** tire s.o., tiring. **mem-²kan** work s.o. to death. **ke-an 1** weariness, fatigue. **2** difficulty. **3** exhausted.

payang₁ large net. *perahu -* boat for fishing with purse seine. **pem-** seine. **pem-an** seining.

payang₂ mem- support s.o. in walking.

payar ber-² cruise back and forth. **mem-** scan. **mem-i** patrol an area. **pem-** cruiser, scanner. **pem-an** patroling, scanning. ~ *radar* radar scanning.

payau 1 brackish. **2** salty, briny.

payit see PALIT₁.

payon shed, lean-to.

payu (*Jv*) in demand, sought after. *sdh -* already sold.

payudara (*Lit.*) (female) breast.

payung 1 umbrella. **2** parachute. **ber-kan** have s.t. as an umbrella. **mem-** take the form of an umbrella. **mem-i 1** screen. **2** protect. **3** drape over. **mem-kan** use s.t. to screen or protect.

PB [*Pengurus Besar*] executive board.

PBB [*Perserikatan Bangsa-bangsa*] United Nations.

PBE [*Pasaran Bersama Éropah*] European Common Market.

PBF [*Pedagang Besar Farmasi*] major pharmaceutical supplier.

PBH [*Pemberantasan Buta Huruf*] literacy campaign.

pc. [*pour condoléance*] legend written on cards expressing condolences.

P'cis. [*Perancis*] France.

PD₁ [*perang dunia*] World War.

PD₂ [*pejabat*] acting.

PD₃ [*Pendidikan Jasmani*] physical education.

PD₄ [*Perusahaan Dagang*] trading company.

PD&K [(*Départmén*) *Pendidikan Dasar dan Kebudayaan*] Department of Basic Education and Culture.

PDAM [*Perusahaan Daérah Air Minum*] Municipal Waterworks.

P dan K [*Pendidikan dan Kebudayaan*] Department of Education and Culture.

PDI [*Partai Démokrasi Indonesia*] Indonesian Democratic party.

PDN [*Perusahaan Dagang Negara*] State Commercial Enterprise.

pdt. [*pendéta*] (*Rel.*) minister.

péang 1 flat (of head). **2** (*Jkt*) worn off. **ter-(²)** worn off.

pebéan, pebian see PABÉAN.

pebila see APABILA.

Pébruari February.

pecah 1 broken, smashed. *- belah* **1** broken into

many pieces. **2** be divided (in opinion). **3** crockery. **ber-** *belah* broken to pieces. **mem-** *belah* divisive, sow discord. **ter-** *belah* become divided. **pem-** *belah* troublemaker. **pem-belahan** dissension, discord. *- hati* brokenhearted. **2** chapped, split open. *Bibirnya -* He has chapped lips. **3** curdled. **4** broken out (of war). **5** hatched out. **ber- (an)** break into pieces. **mem-i 1** break (several things). **2** break on s.t. **mem-(kan) 1** analyze, solve. *Ia ~ soal itu* He solved that problem. **2** split. **3** break. ~ *rékor* break a record. ~ *jerawat dgn kukunya* make the pimples burst with his fingernails. ~ *telur* get o.'s first point (break a zero in tennis). **4** destroy. ~ *angkasa/telinga* deafening. **5** disperse, dissect. **ter-² ** in pieces. **tak ter-kan** insoluble. **ke-an** breakup. **-an 1** piece, fragment, splinter. ~ *saham* shares of a certificate. ~ *granat* shrapnel. *uang* ~ small change. **2** fraction. *bilangan ~* (*Math.*) fraction. ~ *persepuluhan* (*Math.*) decimal fraction. **3** utensils made of glass or porcelain. **4** s.t. broken up on s.t. else. ~ *ombak* breakers. **pem- 1** a breaker. ~ *rékor* record breaker. **2** s.t. that breaks things up. ~ *atom* atom smasher. ~ *kulit* sheller. **pem-an 1** solution, answer. **2** divorce, fission. **per-an** dissension.

pécai vegetable similar to mustard greens.

pécak 1 damaged, dented, flat. **2** blind in o. eye. **mem-kan** flatten.

pecal₁ mem- squeeze, massage.

pecal₂ see PECEL.

pecat fired, discharged. *- nonaktip* suspended with pay. **di-nonaktipkan** be put in the status of suspended with pay. **mem-i** fire (several people). **mem-(kan) 1** discharge. *Ia di- dr pekerjaannya* He was fired from his job. **2** suspend. **pem-an 1** discharge, dismissal. **2** suspension.

peceklik see PACEKLIK.

pecel salad made of blanched vegetables served with peanut sauce.

péci see PICI.

pecik ter- arise. ~ *rasa kasihan di hatinya* A feeling of pity arose in her heart.

pecinan (*Coll.*) Chinatown.

pécok₁ dented.

pécok₂ (*Jv*) axe.

pecombéran see COMBÉRAN.

pécun see PEKCUN.

pecundang be beaten (in a contest). **memp-i** beat s.o.

pecut whip. *-nya diarahkan ke kudanya* He raised his whip at his horse. **mem- 1** whip. **2** urge on. *Itu akan ~ harga pokok ke tingkat yg lebih tinggi* That is going to whip the basic price to a higher level.

peda fish preserved in wet salt. *ikan -* preserved fish. **mem-** preserve fish in salt.

pedadah chest (of medicine, cosmetics).

pedagang see DAGANG₂.

pédagog pedagogue.

pédagogi, pédagogik pedagogy.

pédagogis pedagogical.

pédah see FAÉDAH.
pedal pedal. - *rém* brake pedal. - *gas* accelerator. **ber-** having a pedal. **mem-** step on the pedal.
pedalaman see DALAM.
pedanda Balinese priest.
pedang sword. - *jenawi* long sword with straight blade. - *pora* sword worn by naval cadets. **mem-** strike with a sword. **-an** sword-shaped. **-²an** 1 swordplay. 2 toy or imitation sword.
pedar rancid. - *hati* out of sorts. **mem-kan** put o. in a bad mood. *Meréka ~ gagasan ttg kebahagian* They ruined any thoughts of happiness. **ke-an** out of sorts, displeased.
pedas 1 hot, highly seasoned and spiced 2 severe, biting. *Kritiknya -* His criticism was severe. - *hati* be annoyed, vexed. - *hati saya melihat dia* I hate the very sight of him. **mem-kan** 1 prepare hot, spiced food. 2 cause to smart. *kabut asap yg ~ mata itu* the smog that made the eyes sting. **ke-an** suffer from s.t. hotly spiced.
pedat see PADAT.
pedati horse-drawn cart. **ber-** ride a cart.
pedato see PIDATO.
pédé see PD₃.
pedél marshall, leader of an academic procession.
pédél (*Jkt*) flat.
pédéngan 1 screen, cover. 2 pseudonym. 3 hypocrisy.
pedes see PEDAS.
pedét (*Jv*) calf, heifer. - *jantan* steer.
pédiatri, pédiatrik (*Med.*) pediatrics.
pediatris pediatrician.
pedih 1 smarting. *Matanya - kena sabun* His eyes smart from the soap. 2 poignant. - *hati* mortified, grieved. **mem-** be or become stingingly painful. **mem-i, mem-kan** painful, making s.t. smart. *Putusnya hubungan meréka sangat ~* Their breakup was very painful. **ke-an** pain, smarting, poignancy. *~ hati* heartache.
pedis₁ see PEDAS.
pedis₂ see PEDIH.
pedit see MEDIT.
pedoman 1 compass. - *gasing* gyrocompass. 2 orientation. 3 manual, directive. - *kerja* guidelines for work. 4 catalog, bulletin of a university. **ber-** 1 be guided by. 2 orient o.s. **memp-i** provide guidance for. *~ segenap bangsaku* guide my whole nation. **memp-kan** guide, orient.
pedot (*Jv*) broken off, in two.
pedu see EMPEDU.
peduli 1 pay attention, care about. *Saya tdk - akan perkataannya* I paid no attention to what he said. 2 I do not care. - *amat* Who cares? **memp-kan** pay attention to, mind. *tak -an* indifferent.
pedupan see DUPA.
pedusi (*M*) woman, female.
pedut₁ sticky rice.
pedut₂ (*Jv*) mist, fog.
peduta see DUTA.
pé ér see PR₂.
peg.₁ [*pegunungan*] mountains.

peg.₂ [*pegawai*] employee.
pegagan vine with edible leaves, often planted on sides of rice field bunds to prevent erosion.
pegal 1 stiff, painful (of muscles after overuse). 2 weary, weariness. 3 annoyed, vexed, fed up. **-²** *kejang* completely stiff. **mem-kan** causing painful feeling in muscles after overuse. **-an** 1 tend to be stiff. 2 tend to feel weary. 3 tend to be annoyed.
pegang ber- hold on to. *jalan ~ pd dinding* walk holding on to the wall. *~ tangan* hold hands. *~ pd pendirianya* hold on to his opinion. **ber-an** 1 hold on to e.o. 2 hold on to s.t. (of several people). **mem-** 1 hold, take hold of. *Ia ~ topinya* He is holding his hat. 2 handle. *Ia blm dpt ~ pistol* He is not yet able to handle a pistol. 3 control. *Dahulu Inggeris ~ kekuasaan di laut* Formerly England controlled the seas. 4 occupy, hold. *Siapa ~ jabatan itu?* Who occupied that position? *~ peranan penting* occupy an important role. 5 have on o. *Awas! Org itu ~ pisau* Careful! That man carries a knife. *~ buku* keep accounts. *~ kemudi* steer. **mem-i** take hold of, hold on to. *~ kendali* hold on to the reins. *Ia ketawa sambil ~ perutnya* He laughed while holding on to his stomach. **memper-i** stick, hold to. **mem-kan** hold for s.o. **ter-** manage to hold, can be held. **-an** 1 s.t. to hold on with, handle. *~ tangga* banister, railing. 2 grip, (foot)hold. *lepas dr ~* get free from the grip. 3 s.t. o. can rely on. *Saya belajar komputer spy ada ~ kelak* I will study computers so I will have s.t. to rely on. 4 connection. *Susah memperpanjang visa kalau tdk ada ~ di Imigrasi* It is hard to get your visa extended if you have no connections in the Department of Immigration. 5 guide. *~ hidup* s.t. to guide o.'s life by, ideology. 6 specialty, s.t. o. is expert in. *Mobil itu ~nya. Hanya dia yg bisa membetulkannya* That car is his specialty. He is the only o. who can fix it. **pem-** 1 handle, knob. 2 the o. who holds, holder. *~ adat* adherent, supporter of the traditional law. *~ andil* shareholder. *~ buku* bookkeeper. *~ karcis* ticket holder. *~ kas* cashier, teller. *~ rékor* record holder. *~ saham/séro* shareholder. **pem-an** 1 handle, grip. 2 function, office.
pegar pheasant.
pegari visible. **ke-an** visibility.
pegas 1 spring. 2 carpet beater. 3 pedal in car. - *kopling* clutch pedal. 4 brake. **ber-** be supple, elastic. **mem-** 1 be resilient. 2 spring. **ke-an** elasticity. **pem-an** springiness.
pegat mem- 1 stop, block. 2 intercept, interrupt. 3 divorce, break off engagement with. **-an** (*Jv*) get divorced. **pem-an** 1 interdiction. 2 discontinuity.
pegawai 1 official, gvt. employee. - *bom* customs official. - *negeri/pemerintah* civil servant. 2 employee, worker. - *harian* daily wage earner. - *kantor* office employee. **mem-kan** 1 officially appoint as a civil servant. 2 move a position from private to public sector. **ke-an** 1 officialdom, civil

service. **2** employee affairs. *sejarah* ~ the history of employee affairs.
pegel see PEGAL.
pégépé see PGP.
pegi see PERGI.
pegimana (*Coll.*) see BAGAIMANA.
pégon Javanese written in Arabic characters.
peguyuban see GUYUB₁.
péhak see PIHAK.
péhcun see PÉKCUN.
péhong 1 nasty. **2** k.o. venereal disease.
pejabat see JABAT.
pejajap Buginese war prow.
pejajaran (*Jkt*) **1** evil spirit. **2** damn it!
Pejajaran see PAJAJARAN.
pejal 1 solid, firm (esp. of earth). **2** massive. **mem-kan** press down.
pejam closed (of eyes). **mem- 1** close o.'s eyes. *tanpa* ~ *sebelah mata* without being able to take o.'s eyes off of it. **2** be closed. **mem-kan** close the eyes. **ter-** be closed. *Matanya* ~ Her eyes were closed.
pejera sight of a weapon.
péjét see PIJAT.
pejompongan see JOMPONG.
peju semen, sperm.
pék₁ (*Ch*) hundred (mainly used in commercial transactions). - *go* 150. - *go céng* 150,000.
pék₂ /pi'/ see PIK.
pék₃ see EMPÉK.
peka, péka sensitive. **mem- 1** consider. **2** mind, heed. **ke-an** sensitivity.
pekah see NAFKAH.
pekaja (*Lit.*) lotus.
pekak deaf. - *badak/batu* stone deaf. - *labang* slightly deaf. -² *bahasa* slightly deaf. **se-** measurement for a moment of time. **bersi-** turn a deaf ear to. **mem-(kan), mem-(i)** deafen, deafening. *letusan yg* ~ a deafening explosion.
pekakak kingfisher.
pekakas see PERKAKAS.
pekam brake.
pekan 1 (weekly) market. **2** week. **3** period certain events are held or the events themselves. - *olah raga nasional* national games. **se-** o. week. **ber-²** for weeks.
pekarangan see KARANG₃.
pekasam relish made of meat, fish, or fruit preserved in vinegar or salt and kept for some time.
pekat 1 thick, concentrated. *hitam* - pitch black. *malam* - a dark night. **2** tough. **3** strong (of coffee). **mem-i** inspire certain feelings. **mem-kan** make thick. **ke-an 1** thickness, concentration, density. **2** darkness.
pekau scream.
pékban, pékcap, pékcéng see PIK.
pékcun (*Ch*) the dragon-boat festival on 5th day of 5th lunar month.
pekerti 1 character, nature. *Ya, anak perempuan selalu begitu -nya* Well, as for girls, it is their nature. **2** bad character. *Karena -mu saya merasa dirugikan* I felt I was cheated because of your bad character.

pékgo see PÉK₁.
pekik yell, scream. - *pekuk* various screams. **ber-an** yell repeatedly. **mem-** yell, scream. **mem-kan** scream s.t. out. **ter-** let out a scream. **-an** scream.
peking mem- whine, howl.
pekir see APKIR, FAKIR.
pekis mem- utter a shrill cry.
pekiwan (*Jv*) toilet.
pekojan 1 Arab trader. **2** area where merchants live.
pekoléh efficient.
péktai (*Ch*) leukorrhea.
péktiau see PIK.
pekuk deformed (of hand or foot). - *kaki* clubfooted.
pekung 1 foul-smelling ulceration. **2** tumor. - *inas* carbuncle.
Pekuper [*Pelaksana Kuasa Perang*] military authority under wartime conditions.
pekur memp- muse, meditate.
pel- see also entries with **pl-**.
pél₁ field. **-an** field.
pél₂ *kain* - mop. **mem-, (me)nge-** mop. **-an** mopping.
pél₃ see PIL.
pelabaya hangman, executioner.
pelabi 1 excuse, alibi. **2** dishonest trick.
pelabuhan see LABUH.
pelabur see LABUR₂.
pelaga see KAPUL.
pelah speech impediment.
pelajar, pelajaran see AJAR₁.
pélak 1 k.o. evil spirit. *tak* - cursing expression: a pox on. *Tak - org itu* A curse on that man! **2** there is no mistake. *Dugaannya itu tak* - His guess was right. *tak - lagi* it is obvious. **3** not be able to escape from. *Negara itu tak - lagi dr pengaruh negara lain* That country is clearly not free from the influence of other countries.
pelak, pélak see PÉLEK.
pelakat see PLAKAT.
pelaminan see LAMIN.
pelampang pavilion for outdoor entertainment.
pelan 1 slow. **2** soft (of voice). *suaranya jadi - dan dlm* His voice became soft and deep. -² slow(ly). **mem-kan** slow s.t. down. **-an** slower, more slowly. see PERLAHAN.
pélan see PÉL₁.
pelana saddle. **ber-** saddled. **mem-i** saddle (a horse).
pelanduk mouse deer.
pelanél flannel.
pelang see PLANG.
pelangi rainbow.
pelangki, pelangkin palanquin.
pelangkin tar, pitch.
pelantar platform. **-an 1** unroofed platform attached to house. **2** long bench. **3** scaffolding.
pelanting ber-an roll everywhere. **mem-kan** throw out in all directions. *Bis itu* ~ *penumpangnya ketika tergelincir* When the bus slipped, the passengers where thrown out in every direction.

ter- 1 darted off. 2 shot away. *Namanya ~ ke atas* He shot up to fame. 3 fall with thud.

pelapah see PELEPAH.

pelas mem- tie ropes together.

pelastik see PLASTIK.

pelasuh lazy person.

pelat 1 metal sheet. - *arloji* face of a watch. - *éser* sheet of iron. - *jarum* dial. 2 license plate. - *hitam* black plate, privately owned vehicle, - *kuning* passenger vehicle. - *mérah* gvt.-owned vehicle. - *nomor* license plate. 3 (*Coll.*) phonograph record.

pélat 1 speech defect. 2 speak with an accent.

pelata mackerel.

pelatah see LATAH₁.

Pelatnas [*Pemusatan Latihan Nasional*] Centralization of National Training (for sports).

pelatuk 1 woodpecker. 2 trigger.

pelawak see LAWAK₁.

pelbagai various, all sorts of. - *ragam* various kinds. **memp-ragamkan** diversify. **ke-an** diversity. see BAGAI.

pélbak /pélbak/ refuse bin.

pélbéd, pélbét see FÉLBÉT.

pelbegu pagan, animist.

Példa [*Pembantu Létnan Dua*] lower second lieutenant.

pelebaya see PELABAYA.

peléceh flatterer. **mem-** flatter.

pelécok ter- sprained.

pelék see PLÉK.

pélek /pélek/ rim of wheel.

pelekat see PLAKAT.

pelékat sarong with plaid pattern.

pelékok twisted.

pelekuh crooked.

pelempap breadth of the hand. *se-* a hand's breadth.

pelencit ter- 1 being pressed. 2 be projected by being filliped.

pelengak (*Jkt*) **ter-, m-** surprised.

péléngan (*Anat., Jkt*) temples.

peléngsong (*Jkt*) **m-** deviate.

pelepah stem and midrib of palm, banana leaves, stem of the banana bunch.

pelér see PELIR.

pelés see PLÉS.

pelesat ter- dart away.

pelését see LÉSÉT.

pelesir 1 take a trip. 2 go out for pleasure. 3 pleasure, amusement. **ber-** 1 take a trip. 2 go out for amusement. **ke-an** pleasures. **-an** pleasure, amusement.

pelesit 1 locust. 2 a spirit that sucks blood of unborn or newborn children.

pélét k.o. magic whereby a person is made to fall in love. **mem-** 1 lick, stick out tongue. 2 flatter, play up to s.o. 3 make s.o. fall in love with o. by magical means. **ke-** 1 be made to fall in love by magical means. 2 be seduced.

peletak-peletik make high-pitched knocking noise.

peletak-peletok make a knocking noise.

peleton platoon.

pelihara mem- 1 take care of, protect. 2 raise, rear. ~ *ayam* raise chickens. 3 keep, maintain. **mem-kan** *dr* guard, protect against. ~ *lidah* be careful in what o. says, watch o.'s language. **-an** 1 things to be protected, cared for. 2 mistress. 3 pet, inmate (of zoo), domestic animal, or supernatural being kept by s.o. as a pet. *jin* ~ a spirit under s.o.'s control. **pem-** 1 caretaker. 2 nurseryman. **pem-an** 1 care, maintenance. 2 rearing, cultivation. 3 safeguarding.

pelik 1 peculiar, remarkable. 2 complicated. **ke-an** 1 peculiarity. 2 complexity.

pélikan₁ mineral.

pélikan₂ pelican.

pelikat see PELÉKAT.

peliket (*Jv, Jkt*) sticky. *Badannya terasa - karena ndak sempat mandi* He felt all sticky because he did not have a chance to take a bath.

pelinggam colored marble.

pelintat-pelintut see PLIN-PLAN.

pelinteng (*Jv*) catapult.

pelintir mem- twist. *Ku- tangan kanannya* I twisted her right arm. **mem-kan** spin, cause s.t. turn. ~ *bola* spin the ball. **-an** 1 twisted knot. 2 k.o. cookie shaped into a twist.

pelipir edge. - *jalan* sidewalk.

pelipis, pelipisan (*Anat.*) temples.

pelipit hem. **mem-(i)** hem s.t. *Bajunya tlh selesai. Tinggal ~nya* The shirt is done. I just have to hem it.

pelir penis. - *itik* k.o. screw.

pelisir pleat, pleated. **ber-** pleated. **mem-(i)** put a pleat in.

pelit stingy. **-²an** in a stingy way.

pelita 1 oil lamp. 2 light (in metaphorical sense). - *hati* the light of o.'s heart.

Pelita [*Pembangunan Lima Tahun*] five-year plan.

pelitur mem-, memp- varnish, polish furniture. **-an** varnish.

Pélni [*Pelayaran Nasional Indonésia*] National Shipping Lines.

pélo 1 lisp, babble. 2 have a speech defect.

pélog (*Jv*) seven-tone gamelan scale. **mem-kan** render s.t. on this scale.

pelojok see PELOSOK.

peloksok see PLOKSOK.

pelonci freshman girl.

pelonco o. who is about to get a new status (e.g. as member of entering class, fraternity, etc.), freshman, pledge. **mem(p)-** haze. **per-an** hazing, initiation.

pelopor 1 pioneer. 2 vanguard, forerunner. 3 (*Mil.*) shock troops. 4 ranger, scout. **mem(p)-i** 1 crusade, pioneer, fight for. 2 be at the forefront of. **ke-an** pioneering. **pem(p)-an** initiative.

pélor bullet. - *kesasar* stray bullet.

pelosok 1 outlying place, remote spot. 2 corner. *dr segala* - from every nook and cranny.

pelosot ter- 1 fall down. 2 go down in price.

pélota jai-alai ball.

pélotaris jai-alai player.

peloton see PELETON.

pelotot m- be big (of eyes). **mem-i** look at with big

eyes. ~ *anda dgn nada memaksa* stare at you with a menacing look. **mem-kan** *mata* open the eyes wide.

pélpén measurement used by bricklayer to straighten wall.

pélplés canteen, water container.

pélpolisi rural constabulary.

pelu see PELUH₁.

peluang 1 opportunity. **2** quiet (of wind). **ber-** have an opportunity. **memp-i** give s.o. an opportunity.

pelud [*pelabuhun udara*] airport.

peluh₁ impotent.

peluh₂ perspiration, sweat. **ber-** perspire. **ber-²** sweat and toil.

peluit 1 a whistle (device). **2** whistle (sound). - *bahaya* a whistle signaling danger.

peluk 1 embrace. - *cium* a hug and a kiss. **ber-ciuman** hug and kiss e.o. **2** measurement of length of approximately o. fathom. **ber-** embrace. ~ *lutut* embrace the knees. **ber-(²)an** embrace e.o. **mem-** embrace. *Ia ~ anaknya* She embraced her child. *Meréka ~ agama Islam* They embraced Isl. **mem-i** hold in o.'s embrace. *Ami ~ bonékanya* Ami held her doll in her embrace. **-an** embrace. **pem-** o. who embraces. ~ *agama* adherent of a religion. **sepem-** of such circumference that it can just be embraced by a man's arms.

peluntur laxative.

pelupuh pounded bamboo.

pelupuk cover, wrapper. - *mata* eyelid.

peluru 1 bullet. - *gotri* slug. **2** projectile, missile. - *kendali* guided missile. - *suar* signal flare. **3** (*Sport*) shot-put.

peluruh emetic.

pem- see also entries with **p-, m-**.

pemali s.t. sacred, forbidden, or taboo. *pohon* - taboo tree.

pematah see PEPATAH.

pematang bund, dike between rice fields. *Sawahmu itu se- dgn sawahku* Your rice field shares the same bund as mine.

pemb- see also entries with **b-**.

pemberhentian, pembrentian see HENTI.

pemda, pémda [*pemerintah daérah*] local gvt.

peméo see PAMÉO.

pemeragaan see PERAGA.

pemilu [*pemilihan umum*] general elections.

pemp- see also entries with **p-**.

pemrasaran see PRASARAN.

pemuda see MUDA.

pemudi young woman, girl.

pen- see also entries with **t-, n-**.

pén₁ 1 pin for holding s.t. together in surgery. **2** peg or dowel for joining wood or bamboo. **3** grenade pin.

pén₂ - *atom* ballpoint pen.

péna 1 writing pen. **2** quill.

Penad [*Penerangan Angkatan Darat*] Army Information (Office).

penaga see KAYU₁.

pénak see ÉNAK.

penaka as, for instance.

penakawan see PUNAKAWAN.

Penal [*Penerangan Angkatan Laut*] Navy Information (Office).

penala tuning fork.

pénalti (*Sport*) penalty.

penampan a presentation tray.

penampung cross-section.

penasaran 1 angered (but suppressed), embittered. **2** be anxious to do or find out s.t. **ke-(an)** embitterment.

penat tired, weary, exhausted. - *lelah* worn out, exhausted. **ber-²** toil and sweat. **mem-kan** tire, exhaust, wearying, exhausting. **ke-an 1** tired. **2** weariness, fatigue.

penatu laundryman. - *kemis/kimia* dry cleaner's. **mem-kan** send s.t. to the laundry. **-an** laundry (place).

penatua church elder.

penc- see also entries with **c-**.

penca [*penderita cacat*] disabled person.

pencak₁ system of self-defense. - *silat* k.o. system of self-defense. **ber-** use this system.

pencak₂ m-² jump up and down in a tantrum. *Temanku ~ karena mau pergi mobilnya, dipakai adiknya* My friend jumped up and down in anger because when he wanted to use his car, his little brother had taken it. **mem-(²)** spray out, spurt out in small pieces. *Percikan api ~ dgn riangnya di udara* Sparks of fire burst forth gaily in the air.

pencaka see PANCAKA.

pencar ber- disperse. **ber-²** be dispersed all over. **ber-an** disperse (of many), be dispersed. *Org-org ~ dan bersembunyi* The people dispersed and hid. *ladang-ladang tebu yg ~ antara pétak-pétak sawah* sugar fields dispersed among the plots of rice land. **mem-** dispersed, spread out. **mem-kan** disperse s.t. ~ *tenaga ke daérah-daérah* disperse forces to the local regions. **ter-** be dispersed. *Sinar matahari tlh ~ melalui celah-celah daun kelapa* The sun's rays dispersed through the palm fronds. **-an 1** distribution made. **2** dispersion. **pem-an** act of distribution. **per-an** distribution. ~ *menurut umur* distribution by age.

péncéng skew. **m-** be skewed.

pencét crushed, smashed. **mem- 1** crush, smash. **2** push, press. *Coba di- bél* Please press the bell. ~ *lutut* rub the knees. **mem-i** squeeze (many things repeatedly). **mem-kan** use s.t. to push, press. **-an** pressure.

pencil 1 isolated, secluded. **2** desolate, remote. **mem-** be far from everything. *tempatnya yg ~ a* remote place. **mem-kan** isolate, segregate. ~ *diri* isolate o.s., withdraw. **ter-** isolated, remote, secluded. **keter-an** isolation. **ke-an** isolation. **pem-an** secluding s.t. ~ *diri* withdrawal into seclusion.

pencoléng see PANCOLÉNG.

péncong slanted, skewed. - *méncong* crisscross. **mem-kan** make slanting. **ke-an** skewness.

péncut (*Jv*) **ke-** fall in love, be attracted to.

pend- see also entries with **d-**.

penda *mem-* correct s.t. **-an** correction.

pendam *mem-(kan)* bury, hide away. *Ia ~ uangnya di belakang rumahnya* He hid his money behind his house. *Ia ~ diri selama lima tahun* He hid himself for five years. **ter-** 1 hidden, buried. 2 held in the heart. *Katakanlah apa yg ~ dlm hatimu* Please tell me what you have hidden in your heart. **-an** things hidden away. *~ bisa meletus* Things kept to o.s. can explode. **pem-** o. who buries (feelings). *~ perasaan* o. who keeps his feelings to himself. **pem-an** burial.

Pendam [*Penerangan Daérah Militér*] regional military information (office).

pendamén see FONDAMÉN.

pendapa see PENDOPO.

pendar phosphorescent. **ber-(²)** luminescent.

péndar *ber-(an)* turn, go around. **mem-²kan** turn s.t., turn s.t. around.

pendaringan (*Jv, Jkt*) place to store rice.

pendéga see PANDÉGA.

péndék short. *-nya, - kata* in short, in brief. *- persegi* short and stocky. *- umur* have a short life. **mem-** become shorter. **mem-kan** 1 abbreviate, shorten. 2 make (haircut) short. **memper-** make shorter, cut s.t. back. **ke-an** 1 abbreviation. 2 shortness. 3 too short. *Kakinya ~* His legs were too short. **per-an** making s.t. shorter.

pendékar see DÉKAR.

pendét Balinese dance of welcome.

pendéta 1 Protestant clergyman, Hindu or Buddhist priest. *- Yahudi* rabbi. 2 (*Lit.*) pundit, scholar. **ke-an** clergy, ministry.

pending ornate belt buckle.

pendita see PENDÉTA.

pendopo large open structure in front of Jv mansion, or attached open veranda that serves as an audience hall.

péneng see PÉNING.

pénétrasi penetration.

peng- see also entries with **k-, ng-,** or beginning with a vowel.

penganan snacks.

pengantén, pengantin bride (and) bridegroom. *- baru* newlyweds. *- sarimbit* bridal couple. **ber-** 1 get married, undergo a wedding ceremony. 2 go to a wedding.

pengap close, stuffy, stale, musty. **mem-** close tightly. **mem-kan** oppressive. **ke-an** lack of fresh air.

pengapa see MENGAPA.

pengar have a hangover.

pengaron (*Jv*) large earthenware pot for cooking rice, etc.

pengaruh influence. *- sampingan* side-effect. **ber-** influential. *- memp-i* influence e.o. **memp-i** influence.

pengat 1 fish or meat stewed in spicy sauce. 2 a porridge of tuber, squash, or bananas in coconut milk. **mem-** prepare s.t. in a spicy stew.

pengeboman see BOM₁.

pengecatan see CAT₁.

pengecoran see COR.

pengedokan see DOK₁.

pengemukaan see MUKA.

péngén (*Coll., Jkt*) want s.t.

pengeng migraine headache.

pengepakan see PAK₁.

pengéstu see PANGÉSTU.

pengesyahan see SAH₁.

pengetrapan see TERAP₂.

penggal 1 piece, lump. 2 fragment. **ber-²** in pieces. **mem-** cut off, cut to pieces. *~ kepala* behead. **-an** piece, bit. **pem-an** cutting off the top or head. *~ gedung itu sebanyak tujuh méter* removing topmost seven meters of the building. *~ kata* (*Ling.*) syllabification.

penggawa see PUNGGAWA.

penghulu 1 village chief. 2 Muslim leader. **ke-an** territory of a *penghulu*.

péngin see KEPINGIN.

péngkar crooked (of legs). *- ke dlm* bowlegged. *- ke luar* knock-kneed.

pengki open basket for carrying dirt, garbage, etc.

péngkol bent. **mem-** turn, branch off. **-an** curve.

péngkor crippled, having a shriveled leg.

pengser pincers.

pengulu see PENGHULU.

pening 1 dizzy. *- kepala* headache. 2 upset, rattled. *-² lalat* have a slight headache. **mem-** have a headache. **mem-kan** make dizzy, dizzying. **ke-an** 1 dizziness. 2 feeling dizzy.

péning badge, license (for bicycles, dogs, and pedicabs).

peningset (*Jv*) bride price (paid upon engagement or upon marriage).

pénisilin penicillin.

peniti 1 safety pin. *- cantél* safety pin. 2 brooch to pin a *kebaya* together.

penj- see also entries with **j-**.

penjadan misprint.

penjak₁ *ter-* startled.

penjak₂ *ter-, ber-* glow.

penjara jail, prison. *- anjing* dog pound. **mem-hawa nafsu** restrain o.'s passions. **mem-kan** imprison. **ke-an** prison affairs. **pem-an** incarceration.

penjata heraldry.

pénjol swollen.

penjunan o. who makes pots.

penjurit see PRAJURIT.

penjuru 1 corner, angle. 2 direction from which s.t. comes. *- (mata) angin* directions, points of the compass. *delapan - angin* from all corners of the world. **ber-** having corners, angles. *bintang ~ lima* a five-pointed star.

Pénprés [*penetapan présidén*] presidential decision or directive.

pénsét see PINSÉT.

pénsil 1 pencil. *- isi* mechanical pencil. *- kopi* written in pencil. *- tinta* indelible pen. 2 small brush for drawing.

pensip [*pegawai negeri sipil*] civil servants.

pénsiun pension, retired. *guru* - a retired teacher. **ber-** be retired. **mem-(kan)** pension off, retire. **-an** s.o. retired. ~ *guru* a retired teacher. **peman** pensioning off.

pénstrép penicillin tablets.

pental ke-, ter- flung away. *Ia jatuh ~ dr sepéda motornya* He fell and was flung off his motorcycle.

pentan definite.

pentang mem- open, extend, spread out. **mem-kan** shoot s.t. off, loose (an arrow). **ter-** be spread out, opened, extended. *Pintu masih juga ~* The door was still open. *Di depan kami ~ sebuah jalan yg luas* A broad street stretched out before us.

pentas raised platform, stage. **mem-kan** stage, present. *Sebuah drama akan di-kan bésok* A play will be staged tomorrow. **-an** stage performance. **pem-an 1** showing, presentation. **2** staging.

pentil₁ teat. - *susu* nipple.

pentil₂ mem- pinch s.t. **-an** a pinch.

péntil valve. - *ban* tire valve.

penting₁ important, significant. **mem-kan 1** emphasize. **2** bring to notice, advance. **3** consider important. **ter-** of paramount importance. **ke-an 1** importance. **2** (self-)interest. *utk ~ for the sake of. utk ~ negara* in the interest of the state. *Ia tdk ada ~ di sini* He has no business here. **berke-an** having an interest, be concerned. *Kpd yg ~* To whom it may concern. **pem-** s.t. that gives importance. *partikel ~ (Ling.)* emphatic particle.

penting₂ mem- pluck strings or make s.t. give off a sound of "ting".

pentol, pentul knob. **-an 1** prominent. **2** leader of a gang. **3** leader. **4** bulb.

pentung club, cudgel. **mem-** to club. **mem-i** club repeatedly. **-an** club, cudgel.

penuh 1 full (of), loaded. *Ruangnya -* The room is full. *Botolnya -* The bottle is full. *senyum yg - pergertian* a smile full of understanding. *Hidup yg - dgn kebahagiaan* a life full of happiness. **2** complete. *Dibayar -* It was paid in full. - *montok* shapely. **ke-montokan** shapeliness. - *pekak/pekat/pepak/sesak* crammed, chock-full. - *ruah* bulging out, chock-full. - *tumpah* filled to the brim. **se-** fully. *Saya setuju ~nya* I agree fully. *dgn ~ hati* wholeheartedly. **mem-** crowd, fill a place. *Di dinding lukisan-lukisan ~* Various paintings crowd the walls. **mem-i 1** fill. *Baknya di-i dulu* Fill the tank first. **2** fulfill, comply with a request. *Ia tak dpt ~ janjinya* He could not fulfill his promise. **3** meet a demand. *~ kebutuhnnya* meet his needs. **mem-kan** make s.t. full. **ter-i** compiled with, fulfilled. **ke-an 1** over-full. **2** completeness. *~ hati* wholeheartedness. **pem-an** fulfillment.

peny- see also entries with **c-, s-,** or **ny-.**

penyangkulan see CANGKUL.

penyék, penyét, pényét flattened out, squeezed flat. **me-kan** flatten s.t. **ter-(²)** flattened.

penyok, pényok, pényot dented. **mem-kan** dent s.t.

penyu 1 turtle. **2** tortoise shell.

péok 1 lame. **2** flat. *hidung -* a flat nose.

péon messenger boy.

péot₁ 1 dented. *Mobilnya -* His car was dented. **2** old and battered. *dinding gubuk yg -* the battered walls of the hut.

péot₂ see PÉOK.

pepadang see PADANG.

pepak complete, full. **se-** all of them. **mem-kan, mem-i** make s.t. complete.

pepal concentrated, terse, compact. - *padat* terse and compact. **mem-kan** make s.t terse. **ke-an** terseness.

pepantan group of Christians in new community who combine with existing church temporarily until they can form their own church.

peparu lungs.

pepas mem- fish, angle.

pepat flattened, level, smooth. **mem-** flatten, smooth. - *gigi* tooth filing. **ke-an** flatness.

pepatah aphorism. **ber-** ~ *dan berpetitih* speak with aphorisms. **mem-kan** make an aphorism out of s.t.

pepaya see PAPAYA.

pépé (*Jv*) **m-** expose s.t. to sun, dry in sun. **-an** s.t. dried in sun.

péped see PÉPÉT.

pépék (*Vulg.*) vagina.

péper paper, essay.

Peperda [*Penguasa Perang Daérah*] Regional War Administrator.

Peperpu [*Penguasa Perang Pusat*] Central War Administrator.

Peperti [*Penguasa Perang (Ter)tinggi*] Supreme Military Administrator.

pépés meat or fish wrapped in a banana leaf and roasted. **mem-** cook s.t. in this way.

pepet₁ stopped up (of nose).

pepet₂ see BUNYI.

pépét dead end, no way out. **m- 1** tight (of circumstances). *Waktunya ~* Time is short. **2** press o. self into a corner, against s.o. **mem-kan** corner, trap. **ke-, ter-** cornered, trapped.

pepindan metaphor.

pepohonan see POHON₁.

péptida peptide.

péptidase peptidase.

péptidisasi peptization.

pepuju womb.

pepundén, pepundi (*Jv*) object of worship.

pepura mock, sham.

per 1 per, by the. - *kapita* per capita. - *lusin* by the dozen. **2** as of such and such a date.

per- see also entries with **pr-.**

Per. [*Perusahaan*] enterprise, firm, concern.

pér₁ 1 lightbulb. **2** spring. - *kéong* spiral spring. - *rambut* very fine watch spring. **ber-** with springs. **menge-** be springy.

pér₂ (*Jkt*) **nge-** be scared.

pera the taste of rice that is dry.

perabot 1 utensils. **2** tools. **3** furniture. - *rumah* furniture. - *mobil* spare parts, accessories (of car). **memp-i** furnish a house. **-an** household furnishings.

perabu see PRABU.

perada₁ 1 tin coating. **2** gold leaf. - *pérak* silver leaf.

perada₂ review, parade. - *buku* book review.

Peradin [*Persatuan Advokat Indonésia*] Indonesian Lawyer's Association.

peraga visual aid. **ber-** hold an exhibition. **memp-kan, mem-kan** exhibit, display. **-an** show. **pem-an** exhibit. ~ *visual* a visual presentation.

peragawan male model or mannequin.

peragawati female model or mannequin. **ke-an** modeling.

perah mem- 1 squeeze. **2** milk. - *sapi* milk a cow. ~ *keringat* sweat and toil. **-an 1** milch cow. *Ia memperlakukanku sbg sapi* ~ He used me like a cow to milk dry. **2** s.t. squeezed out. ~ *buah* squeezed fruit juice. **pem-** milker. **pem-an** squeezing.

perahu boat. - *dayung* rowboat. - *gubang* sailing canoe. - *lading* longboat. - *layar* sailboat. - *lépa-lépa* a dugout. - *mayang* deep-sea fishing boat. - *mancung* prow shaped like a sheath. - *motor* motorboat. - *pendarat* landing craft. - *pinisi* k.o. Buginese sailing craft. - *rakit/sasak* raft. - *sérét* barge. - *tambang* ferry boat.

perai₁ 1 free. *Ia mendapat* - *sehari* He had a day off. **2** empty (of a seat). **3** unhampered. **4** broke (without money). **mem-kan 1** set a certain time as time off. **2** give s.o. time off.

perai₂ loose, apart. **ber-² 1** scattered, dispersed. **2** (*Naut.*) tack in sailing.

perajurit see PRAJURIT.

pérak 1 silver. **2** (*Jkt*) rupiah. *tiga puluh* - 30 rupiah. **mem-** white as silver. **ke-an, ke-²an** silvery. *cahaya bulan* ~ silvery moon rays. **-an** a rupiah coin or bill. *lima* ~ a five-rupiah note.

peraktik see PRAKTÉK.

peram ber- shut o.s. off from society. **mem-1** brood. **2** keep s.t. to age or ripen it. **mem-kan** keep fixed to o. place. **pem-an 1** ripening. **2** hatching, brooding. **3** hatchery.

peran 1 actor. **2** character (in novel, play, etc.). **ber-** have a role. **mem-i** play a role in. *Filem yg diinya* The film she played in. **mem-kan, memp-kan 1** play the role of, portray. **2** give s.t. a role. *tindakan utk* ~ *kantor kita* steps to make our office play a role. **-an** role, part. ~ *utama* the lead, leading role. *memainkan* ~ *penting* play an important role. **pem-** player in a film or stage show.

peranakan see ANAK.

perancah scaffolding.

Perancis see PRANCIS.

perandi (*Tech.*) ware. - *lunak* software. - *keras* hardware.

perang war, battle. - *asabat* war of nerves. - *asap* mock battle. - *bersosoh* a battle. - *cakil* scene in Jv shadow play where hero fights demon Cakil. - *dunia* world war. - *gerilya* guerilla warfare. - *kilat* blitzkrieg. - *lidah/mulut* verbal battle. - *paderi* struggle between strict Muslims and adherents of customary law in the Minangkabau area in the early 19th century. - *sabil* (*Isl.*) holy war. - *salib* crusade. - (*urat*) *saraf* war of nerves. - *sdr* civil war. - *sinu* war of nerves. - *tanding* duel. **ber-** wage war. **mem-i** fight against, war on. ~ *pengangguran* fight unemployment. **mem-kan** cause to fight. **-²an** maneuvers, mock warfare. **pe-an 1** battle. **2** war.

pérang colors ranging from reddish blond to auburn (hair of plants, animals, or humans).

perangah ter- be agape with surprise.

perangai 1 nature, disposition. **2** behavior, attitude. **ber- 1** have a (certain) disposition. **2** behave.

perangas-perongos (*Jv*) make a wry expression.

peranggi see PERENGGI.

perangkap see RANGKAP₂.

perangkat see ANGKAT.

perangko see PRANGKO.

peranjak ter- fall on o.'s behind.

peranjat memp-kan startle, surprise. **ter-** startled, surprised. **keter-an** surprise felt.

peranti 1 apparatus, instrument. **2** means. **3** in order to. **4** remedy.

peranye fringe.

perapatan see PRAPATAN.

peras mem- 1 press, squeeze. ~ *keringat* toil, exert o. self. ~ *otak* rack o.'s brains. **2** milk. **3** blackmail, put the squeeze on. **mem-i 1** press (many things). ~ *jeruk* squeeze citrus juice. **2** squeeze juice on to. *Lukanya di-i jeruk nipis agar sakit* Squeeze lemon juice on to his wounds so they hurt. **-an** distillation. **pem- 1** press. **2** exploiter. **pem-an 1** pressing, squeezing. **2** extortion. **3** exploitation.

perasat see FIRASAT.

perasman see PRASMAN.

perawan 1 virgin, girl. *hutan yg masih* - virgin forest. - *sunti* a girl entering puberty. - *yg tak bercela* (*Rel.*) the Holy Virgin. **2** brand new to s.t. *Ia masih* - *dlm kegiatan itu* He is still brand new to that activity. **mem-i** make s.o. or s.t. lose virginity. *hutan yg sdh di-i* a jungle that has lost its virginity (people have entered it). **ke-an 1** spinsterhood, maidenhood. **2** virginity.

perawira see PERWIRA.

perawis ingredients.

perbagai see PELBAGAI.

perbahasa see PERIBAHASA.

perbal 1 official report. **2** ticket. **3** police warrant, summons. **memp-** process a criminal charge.

perban bandage. - *kasa* gauze bandage. **mem-(i)** dress a wound.

Perbanas [*Perhimpunan Bank-bank Nasional Swasta*] association of national private banks.

perbani see BULAN, PASANG₃.

perbawa influence, prestige. ~ *diri* self-expression.

perbegu heathenish.

perbekel (*Bali*) village chief.

perc. [*percétakan*] printing establishment.

perca₁ rag. - *kertas* scraps of paper.

perca₂ see GETAH, PULAU.

percak mem- make rushing noise (of water).

per capita /per kapita/ per capita.

percaya 1 belief, faith. **2** trust, believe. - *angin* vain hope. - *habis* trust completely. *tak - akan diri sendiri* lack self-confidence. - **memp-i** belief in e.o. **di-** be trusted. *yg dpt* ~ what can be trusted. **memp-i** believe in, rely on. **memp-kan** entrust s.t. to. *tugas yg di-kan pd saya* the duties entrusted to me. **te-, ter- 1** reliable, trustworthy. **2** believable. **ke-an 1** s.t. or s.o. whom o. can rely on. **2** faith, trust, confidence, belief. ~ *diri* belief in o.s. ~ *akan Tuhan* faith in God.

percik stain, spot. **se-** a splatter of. ~ *darah* a splattering of blood. ~ *sinar* a small ray of sunlight. **be(r)-an** spattering. **mem- 1** spatter, sprinkle. **2** suddenly arise. *Tiba-tiba* ~ *suatu pengertian* Suddenly a certain understanding came into being. **mem-i** spatter. **mem-kan** splash with s.t. **ter-i** bespattered. ~ *darah* bespattered with blood. **-an** sprinkling, fragment.

percis see PERSIS.

percit mem-, te- spurt forth strongly.

percul te- dart away.

percuma see CUMA.

perdana 1 principal. - *menteri* prime minister, premier. **2** inaugural, first introduction to the public. *penerbangan* - inaugural flight.

perdata (*Leg.*) **1** court of justice. **2** civil (cases). **mem-kan** bring a (civil) case to court. *masalah tanah yg di-kan di depan pengadilan* a problem of land that was adjudicated in the civil court. **ke-an** having to do with civil law.

Perdatam [(*Départemén*) *Perindustrian Dasar dan Pertambangan*] (Department) of Basic Industries and Mining.

perdéo see PRODÉO.

perdikan freed from payment of taxes (in villages) as result of assuming some burden or responsibility.

perdiping story, floor.

perdom (*Coll.*) mild swear word. **mem-** cuss at s.o.

perdu 1 clump (of bamboo, etc.). **2** lowest part of tree trunk.

perduli see PEDULI.

peré see PERAI₁.

peredus te- 1 pregnant. **2** potbellied.

péréh ter-² be overly meticulous.

peréi see PERAI₁.

perek /prek/ [*perempuan ekspériméntal*] loose and freewheeling girl.

perék see PRÉK.

perekat glue.

perékik see PRIKIK.

peréman see PRÉMAN.

perempuan 1 woman, female. - *bergelandang/ gelandangan/jahat* prostitute. - *cabul/jalang* prostitute. - *geladak/jahanam* prostitute. - *pengérét*

gold digger. - *piaraan* mistress. - *yg masih gadis* virgin. **2** feminine. **ke-an** femininity.

perenang see RENANG, CENTANG-PERENANG.

perenggi (*Lit.*) European.

perentang see CENTANG-PERENANG.

peres see PERAS.

pérés leveled off. *delapan séndok makan* - eight level tablespoons.

perétél see PRÉTÉL.

peréwa (*M*) o. who lives outside customary law.

peréwangan see PRÉWANGAN.

pérféksionis perfectionist.

pérféksionisme perfectionism.

pérforasi perforation.

pérforator hole puncher.

pergajul see BERGAJUL.

pergat (*Naut.*) frigate.

pergedél see PERKEDÉL.

pergi 1 go. *Ke mana -nya?* Where has he gone? *datang* - 1 walk up and down. 2 come and go. *Banyak org datang* - Many people were coming and going. **2** leave, be out. *Ia sdh* - He is already left. *Ia sedang* - He is out. **3** (*Coll.*) go to. *Dia* - *Singapura* She went to Singapore. - *haji* (*Coll.*) go on the pilgrimage. - *inspéksi turné* make a tour of inspection. **se-nya** upon leaving. **be-an** go on a trip, travel. ~ *dgn keréta api!* Take a train trip! **ke-an 1** departure. **2** trip, journey. **3** going, passing, death. ~ *beliau dgn mendadak* His passing was sudden.

pergok mem- catch s.o. by surprise. **mem-i, memp-i 1** catch by surprise. **2** catch s.o. red-handed. **te-** detected, caught in the act. ~ *basah* caught red-handed. **ke- 1** surprised, unexpected (meeting). *Saya* ~ *Ali di New York yg kusangka masih di Jkt* I unexpectedly ran into Ali in New York when I thought he was still in Jkt. **2** be caught red-handed. *Pencuri* ~ *polisi* The thief was caught red-handed by the police.

pergol, pergul gold-plated.

perhal see PERI₁.

peri₁ 1 having to do with. - *dolar* (*Fin.*) dollar course. **-hal 1** concerning. **2** events, circumstances. **-hal laku** behavior. - *jam* clockwise. **-keadilan** having to do with justice. **-kehidupan** life. **2** attitude. **-kemanusiaan 1** humanity. **2** humanitarianism. **3** humanism. **ber-kemanusiaan** act in a humanitarian way. **ber-** speak. **ber-²** be in earnest. **mem-** describe. **mem-kan** relate, tell, describe. *tak* **ter-kan** indescribable. **keter-an** accountability. **pem-** (*Ling.*) qualifier. **pem-an** description.

peri₂ (*Lit.*) k.o. female celestial being of exceeding beauty.

peria₁ see PRIA.

peria₂ see PARÉ.

periai see PRIYAYI.

perian bamboo for carrying water.

peribahasa proverb.

peribumi see PRIBUMI.

peridi fertile (of animals).

peridolar see PERI₁.

perigi well, spring. - *buta* 1 dry well. 2 uncovered well.

perih see PEDIH.

perijam see PERI₁.

periksa 1 investigation, inspection, examination. *ruang* - examination room. - *mayat* autopsy. 2 get o.s. examined. *Saya - pd Dokter Go* I went to Dr. Go for an examination. *Kurang* - I do not know. **mem-** 1 investigate, look into. *Polisi ~ hal itu* The police investigated the matter. 2 control, inspect. *~ karcis* look at the tickets. 3 cross-examine, interrogate. **mem-i** search through, check. *dgn mata liar ~ rumah* searching the house with wild eyes. *~ muatan oto* search through the contents of the car. *~ lampiran-lampiran dokumén di atas méja* searching through the piles of documents on top of the table. **mem-kan** have s.t. examined. *Saya ~ anak saya ke Dokter Go* I brought my child to Dr. Go for an examination. *Soal apa yg akan di-kan pd saya?* What problem are they going to have me investigate? **-an** hearing, inquest. **pem-** 1 investigator, inspector. *~ mayat* coroner. 2 (*Leg.*) cross-examiner. **pem-an** 1 (*Leg.*) investigation, inspection. 2 (*Leg.*) cross-examination, interrogation. 3 checkup, examination. *~ air kencing* urinalysis.

perilaku behavior. **ber-** have (a certain) behavior.

Perimnas [*Perumahan Nasional*] National Housing Authority.

perinci see RINCI.

perincis mem-kan specify. **-an** specification.

pering₁ bamboo.

pering₂ stink.

peringkat 1 level. *Kehinaan org setempat tlh sampai ke - yg penghabisan sekali* The degradation of the local population has reached its worst level. 2 rank. **mem-** arrange by rank.

perintah order, command. - *halus* gentle hint (from above), indirect order. *Sepuluh - Tuhan* (*Rel.*) The Ten Commandments. **mem-(i)** 1 order, command. 2 rule, govern. **mem-kan** order, command s.t. *Itu yg di-kan pd saya* That is the order given to me. **ter-** subjected. **pem-** gvt. *~ Indonésia* the Indonesian gvt. *~ bonéka* puppet gvt. *~ darurat* emergency gvt. *~ peralihan* interim gvt. **pem-an** gvt. administration. *di bawah ~ Belanda* under Dutch administration. **kepem-an** having to do with gvt. administration.

perintis see RINTIS.

période period (of time).

périodik periodic, rotating. *pertemuan* - periodic meeting.

périodisasi division of history into periods.

perisai shield.

périskop periscope.

peristiwa 1 event, incident, happening, affair. - *Madiun* the Madiun Affair. *sekali pd suatu* - (*Lit.*) once upon a time. 2 phenomenon. **mem-kan** phenomenalize. *Manusia - diri dlm réalitas* Man phenomenalizes himself in reality.

periuk caldron, cooking pot. - *api* 1 shell. 2 bomb. 3 mine. - *belanga* earthenware.

perjaka young, unmarried man.

Perjanka [*Perusahaan Jawatan Keréta Api*] State Railway Corporation.

perji see FARJI.

perjurit see PRAJURIT.

perkakas tools, implements, apparatus. - *bedah* surgical instruments. - *cap/cétak* printing equipment. - *dapur* kitchen utensils. - *makan* dinnerware. - *rumah* furniture. - *tenun* weaving loom. **be-** equipped. **memp-i** provide with furniture. **-an** tools, apparatus.

perkamén parchment.

perkara 1 matter, case. *duduk - yg sebenarnya* the way the matter really stands. *Habis* - That is that (That will be all). 2 the fact that. - *ia tdk hadir, itu bukan urusan saya* The fact that she did not attend is not my business. 3 (*Leg.*) lawsuit, case. - *gugatan* civil process. - *perdata* civil case. - *pidana* criminal case. **be-** litigate. **memp-kan** bring a case, s.o. to court. *hal yg di-kan* the matter they brought to court.

perkasa 1 brave, courageous. 2 physically powerful, strong and robust. **ke-an** 1 courage. 2 power. *dgn* - with force.

perkedél croquette of spicy ground meat and boiled potatoes or other starch.

perkéneng license for a vehicle.

perkosa 1 violent. *secara* - in a violent manner. 2 violence. **memp-** rape, violate. **-an** rape, violation. **pem-** rapist. **pem-an** raping. *~ hukum* a perversion of the law.

perkusi percussion.

perkutut small turtledove.

perla [*perhubungan laut*] sea communications.

perlahan 1 slow. 2 soft of voice. --*lahan* slow. **memp-kan** slow s.t. down.

perlak₁ varnished, lacquered.

perlak₂ (*Lit.*) garden close to house.

perlak₃ rubber sheet used under bed sheets.

perlambang see LAMBANG.

perlaya die in battle. **mem-i, mem-kan** kill in battle.

perléng mem- extend, prolong.

perlénté (*Coll.*) elegant, swell, dandy. **ke-an** elegance.

perlina lost.

perling te- glitter.

perlintih see PERLÉNTÉ.

perlip fall in love. **-²an** flirt.

perlonco see PELONCO.

perlop 1 leave, furlough. 2 be on leave. **mem-kan** furlough, give a leave. *Kau -kan saja dia seminggu* Simply give him a week off.

perlu 1 necessary, be needed. *Saya pergi jika* - I will go if necessary. *Guru sangat - di sini* Teachers are much needed here. 2 need to. *Kamu tdk - pergi* You do not need to go. 3 (*Coll.*) need. *Saya - uang* I need money. *Ada - apa?* What is it you need? *Apa -nya?* What's the use? (Why?) **se-nya** to whatever extent necessary. *Dia dikasi uang belanja ~* She was given only as much shopping money as she needed. **mem-kan** 1 need. *Ia ~*

banyak uang He needs a lot of money. **2** deem necessary. *Ia ~ kedatanganmu* He thought your coming necessary. **3** require, make compulsory. *Bahasa Inggeris di-kan di sekolah menengah* English was made compulsory in the high schools. **ke-an 1** need, necessity. *Ada ~ dgn siapa?* Whom do you wish to see? *utk ~ on behalf of.* **2** requirement, interests. *Utk ~ siapa?* For whose interests?

perlup be engaged to be married.

perlus te- fall into a hole.

permadani carpet.

permai pretty, beautiful. **ke-an** beauty.

permaisuri consort of king.

permak altered, changed. *baju* - a restyled shirt. **memp- 1** alter, change. *Gudang lama di- dijadikan tempat tinggal* The old warehouse was remodeled into a residence. **2** *(Coll.)* beat up. *Pencopét itu di - org banyak* The crowd beat up the pickpocket. **-an** s.t. which has been remodeled.

perman see FIRMAN.

permana₁ quantity. **te-i** countable. *tak ~* incalculable.

permana₂ *(Jv)* careful.

permanén, pérmanén permanent.

permanénsi, pérmanénsi permanence.

permata jewel, precious stone. *- mata* the apple of o.'s eye. *- nila* sapphire.

permati final, with no further change. *Apa percabutan rébewés ini -?* Is this a permanent suspension of my license? **mem-(kan) 1** make s.t. final. **2** seal, knot s.t. permanently.

permén 1 hard candy. *- batuk* cough drop. **2** candy (in general). *- karét* chewing gum.

Permén *[Peraturan Menteri]* Ministerial Regulation.

Permésta *[Perjuangan Semésta]* The Total Struggle, the uprising in Sulawesi in late 1950's.

Permias *[Persatuan Mahasiswa Indonésia di Amérika Serikat]* Indonesian Students' Association in America.

permil per thousand. *tiga* - three parts in 1,000.

permili see PAMILI.

permisi 1 ask permission. *Tanpa - Ida msk* Ida entered without asking permission. **2** ask to be excused (to leave). *Stlh - pd ayah kami berangkat* We left after taking leave from Father. *Aku - msk ke kamarku* I excused myself to go into my room. **memp-kan** give permission.

pernah₁ once, ever. *Saya - pergi ke Bali* I once went to Bali. *blm -* never up to now. *Saya blm - ke sana tapi saya mau* I have never gone there, but I want to. *tak/tdk -* never (will, was, do). *Ia tak - senang* He was never happy. *Saya tdk - makan babi* I never eat pork.

pernah₂ *(Jv)* be related in a certain way. *- apa dia dgn kamu?* How is she related to you?

pernak-pernik needless complications, complexities.

pernama see PURNAMA.

pernél see PELANÉL.

pernik 1 small beads. **2** little things. *Melengkapi*

rumah baru banyak -nya You need lots of little things to furnish a new house. **3** needless complexity. *Tanpa banyak - lagi ia lalu menyérét kakinya keluar* Without any further fuss and bother he picked himself up and went out.

pernis varnish. **mem-** to varnish.

perocot see PROCOT.

perogol see ROGOL.

peroi crumbly.

péroksida peroxide.

péron railroad platform.

peronyok ter- crushed, crumpled.

pcrop see PROP₁.

perosok ter-, ke- sink in, slip into. *takut ~ ke selokan karena gelap* afraid he would slip the ditch because it was dark. *~ ke dunia kejahatan* fallen in with a group of criminals. **mem(p)-kan** thrust s.t. down into.

perosot see ROSOT.

perotés see PROTÉS.

perpati see MERPATI.

perpelancongan see LANCONG.

Perprés *[Peraturan Présidén]* presidential regulation.

Perpu₁ *[Peraturan Pemerintah Pengganti Undang-undang]* gvt. regulation to replace law number . . .

Perpu₂ *[Peraturan Pemilihan Umum]* Regulations for the General Elections.

pérron see PÉRON.

pérs press.

persada homeland, group of nations that have a connection. *- Indonésia* the Indonesian fatherland. *tersapu dr - Asia Tenggara* ousted from the S.E. Asia family of nations.

persasat like, as if.

persegi see SEGI.

persekot cash advance. **-in 1** *(Coll.)* give an advance to. **2** *(Sl.)* make pregnant before marriage. *Nonot udah dia ~* He has already gotten Nonot pregnant. **mem(p)-i 1** give an advance. **2** engage in premarital intercourse with.

perselah see PERSLAH.

persemakmuran see MAKMUR.

persén 1 percent. **2** tip. **3** present to a subordinate. **mem-(i)** reward s.o. with. *Ia di-(i) pukulan* He was rewarded with a beating. **ke-an** percentage. **-an** percentage or tip given. *"Apa sih komisi?" "~," jawabku* "What is a commission?" "It is a percentage you get," I answered.

perséntage, perséntase /perséntase/ percentage, rate. *- melék huruf* literacy rate.

pérsépsi perception. **mem-** perceive.

perséro 1 share. **2** shareholder, partner. **-an** company. *~ terbatas* limited liability company, Ltd., Inc. see SÉRO.

persétan to hell with. *~ dgn meréka!* To hell with them! **mem-(kan)** damn, send to the devil.

persih see BERSIH.

persik peach.

persil lot, plot. **te-** protrude, bulge.

persis exactly, precisely. *- jam dua* exactly at two

o'clock. *Kau - monyét* You are acting just like a monkey. *Saya tdk tahu (dgn)* - I do not know exactly.

Persit [*Persatuan Isteri Tentara*] army wives' organization.

perslah report, account.

persnéling gear, transmission. - *kedua* 2d gear. - *mundur* reverse. - *otomatis* automatic transmission.

persona see PESONA.

personalia personnel.

persona non grata persona non grata. **mem-kan** consider or make s.o. a persona non grata.

personawi personal. *unsur* - personal element.

pérsonifikasi personification. **memp-(kan)** personify.

personil staff, personnel.

perspéktif perspective.

pérsuasi persuasion.

pérsuasif persuasive.

pertal mem- translate. **-an** translation.

pertama first, the first. *bab yg* - the first chapter. - *kali* the first time. *--tama* first of all. *yg* - the former (not the latter). *yg - sekali* the very first. **memp-kan** give preference to.

Pertamina [*Perusahaan Pertambangan Minyak dan Gas Bumi Negara*] state-owned oil company of Indonesia.

pertanda sign.

pertiwi earth.

pertusis, pertussis (*Med.*) whooping cough.

peruan (*Naut.*) yardarm. - *gema* sonic depth finder.

perugul see ROGOL.

peruk mem- put s.t. in a place. **ter-** collapsed, given away.

perum (*Naut.*) sounding lead. **mem-** sound, gauge the depth. **pem-an** bathymetry, sounding.

Perum₁ [*Perusahaan Umum*] public corporation.

Perum₂ [*perumahan*] housing complex.

perumisasi conversion of state into public corporations.

Perumnas [*Perumahan Nasional*] National Housing Authority.

Perumtél [*Perusahaan Umum Télékomunikasi*] National Telephone and Telegraph Corporation.

perun 1 heap of dried plants for burning. 2 trash, garbage heap. **mem-** 1 burn off weeds, etc. or brush and trees that have been cut down to prepare a field. 2 burn trash.

perunggu bronze. *medali* - bronze medal.

perungus fiery, hot-tempered.

Peruri [*Percétakan Uang Républik Indonésia*] The Indonesian National Mint.

perus stern, grim.

perusa mem- 1 violate, rape. 2 force, compel. 3 annoy, disturb.

perusi see PRUSI.

perut (*Anat.*) 1 stomach, belly. - *buta* appendix. - *gendut* pot-bellied. - *masan* ruminant's stomach. - *muda panjang* intestine. 2 womb. *dlm - ibunya* in his mother's womb. - *besar* 1 stomach. 2 pregnant. 3 lower internal portion of s.t. - *betis* calf of leg. - *bumi* bowels of the earth. - *kaki* calf. - *kapal* hold of a ship. **se-** (*M*) being kin by virtue of having the same maternal grandmother. **mem-i** remove the entrails. **pe-an** intestines.

perwara 1 (*Lit.*) ladies-in-waiting of queen. 2 ancillary.

Perwari [*Persatuan Wanita Républik Indonésia*] Organization of Indonesian Women, a social and charitable woman's club.

perwira 1 (*Mil.*) officer. - *jaga* duty officer. - *menengah* middle ranking officer. - *pertama* officer of the lower ranks. - *tinggi* senior officer. - *utama* high ranking officer. 2 brave, courageous. *pahlawan yg* - a courageous hero. **ke-an** heroism.

pes. [*pesawat*] (*Tel.*) telephone extension.

pés bubonic plague.

pesagi (*Coll.*) see PERSEGI.

pesai ber-² fall to pieces. **mem-** tousle (hair). *Rambutku di-nya dgn tenang* She calmly tousled my hair.

pésak gusset, patch sewn between sleeves and main part of garment or pants legs and main part of trousers.

pesaka see PUSAKA.

pesalin see SALIN.

pesam lukewarm (of water).

pesan 1 order. 2 order, instruction, command. 3 message. **ber-** 1 order. 2 instruct, give a message. **mem-** order (goods, etc.), reserve a place. ~ *dua kamar* reserve two rooms. **mem-i** give a message or order to s.o. *Saya di-i utk menyampaikan kabar ini* I was asked to pass on this news. **mem-kan** order on behalf of, reserve a room for. **-an** 1 order, commission. ~ *percobaan* trial order. ~ *ulangan* repeat order. 2 message. **pem-** buyer, customer. **pem-an** ordering (of goods). ~ *tempat* making reservations.

pesanggrahan see PASANGGRAHAN.

pesangon separation pay. - *tiga bulan gaji* three months' separation pay.

pesan-pesan k.o. poisonous centipede.

pesantrén (*Isl.*) school of Koranic studies for children and young people, most of whom are boarders.

pesara see PUSARA.

pesaréan see PASARÉAN.

pesasir see PASASIR.

pesat quick, speedy, rapid. *dgn sangat -nya* at full speed. **mem-kan** speed up. **ke-an** speed, momentum.

pesawat 1 instrument, machine. - *penerima* radio, radio set. - *uap* steam engine. - *vidéo* video machine. - *wésel* railroad switch. 2 telephone instrument. 3 telephone extension. 4 plane. - *baling-baling* piston plane. - *capung* small single-engine plane. - *pancar gas* jet plane. - *pelémpar bom* bomber. - *peluncur* glider. - *pembom* bomber. - *pemburu* fighter plane. - *penempur* military plane. - *udara* airplane.

peséban see PASÉBAN.

pesegi see SEGI.
pések flat-nosed.
péser half cent of colonial period. *tak punya uang se-pun, tak se- buta* completely broke.
peséro see PERSÉRO.
pesiar 1 trip, journey. *kapal* - tourist boat. 2 take a trip, go for a ride, excursion. - *pengantén baru* honeymoon.
pésimis pessimist, pessimistic.
pésimisme pessimism.
pésimistis pessimistic.
pesindén (*Jv*) woman singer with gamelan orchestra.
pesing stench of urine.
pesirah village chief in S. Sumatra.
pesisir₁ beach, coastal area.
pesisir₂ see PASASIR.
pésok dented. **mem-kan** cause a dent.
pesona 1 enchantment, spell. 2 magic formula. **memp-, memp-kan** 1 enchant, enthrall. 2 hypnotize. **te-, ter-** spellbound.
pésong crooked. **ter-** 1 go off course. 2 miss the target.
pésta party, festivity. - *dansa* a dance. - *fénsi/gila/ maskara* masked ball. - *pora* big celebration. **ber-** celebrate, have a party. **mem-kan** celebrate s.t. **-²an** parties of various kinds. *Duniaku bukan dunia ~ spt itu* My world was not the world of parties like that.
pestaka 1 divining manual. 2 magic formula. 3 magic power investing a weapon or s.t. else.
péstipal festival.
péstisida pesticide.
péstol see PISTOL.
pesuk hole. **ber-²** full of holes. **mem-** make a hole in.
pesut₁ porpoise.
pesut₂ cleaning rag. **mem-** clean, dry with a rag.
pét cap with a visor.
peta 1 map. - *angin* weather map. - *bagan* outline map. - *buta* map with the names of places omitted. - *timbul* relief map. 2 chart. - *laut* nautical chart. 3 picture. **mem-kan** map, chart. **ter-** be outlined, pictured. **pem-an** 1 cartography. 2 mapping.
Péta [*Pembéla Tanah Air*] Indonesian auxiliary troops in the Japanese occupation.
pétah - *lidah* 1 eloquent. 2 witty. **ke-an** *lidah* wittiness.
petai k.o. tree that produces beans with pungent odor, widely eaten raw and cooked. - *cina* k.o. tree planted to shade coffee or other plants, the leaves of which serve as fodder and green manure and beans of which are edible.
pétak₁ 1 compartment, partition, cabin. 2 garden bed, portion of a rice paddy. **se-** a piece of land. **ber-²** compartmentalized, partitioned, sectioned. **-an** plot of land. **pem-an** breaking up into parcels.
pétak₂ white mark, blaze (on horse).
pétak₃ - *umpat* (*Jkt*) hide and seek.
petaka accident, disaster, misfortune.

petakilan (*Jv*) moving about too much, fidgety, improper because of fidgeting too much.
petal mem-kan 1 press s.t. downward. ~ *jarinya pd bedak* press her fingers into the powder. 2 loosen, remove by pressing. ~ *sedikit bedak dgn jarinya* remove some powder with her fingers.
petala 1 layer, stratum. 2 floor, story.
petam band tied around forehead.
petan *main* - play hide and seek.
petang 1 afternoon. - *hari* afternoon. 2 dark. *malam - yg hanya disinari oléh kelipan* a dark night lit only by the twinkling of stars. **se-** o. afternoon. **mem-²kan** *hari* kill time. **ke-an** overtaken by nightfall. **se-²an** all during the afternoon.
pétang divination. **-an** prediction. **ke-an** secret agent.
petani see TANI.
petari see PATRI.
petas see BERAS.
petasan firecracker.
petatah-petitih see PETITIH.
petatas see PATATAS.
peté see PETAI.
petenah see FITNAH.
peténtang-peténténg, peténténgan with o.'s arms on the hips in an arrogant way.
peterah see FITRAH.
peterana 1 throne. 2 bridal chair.
péterséli parsley.
peti case, chest. - *besi* a safe. - *és* refrigerator. **mem-éskan** 1 put on ice. 2 put on the back burner. *Masalah itu di-éskan* Let us put that problem on hold. - *jenazah/mayat* coffin. - *kemas* container (in shipping). **mem-kemaskan** make a shipment with containers. - *mesiu* powder keg. - *nyanyi* phonograph. - *pendingin* freezer. - *pengering* dehumidifier. **ber-²** by the boxful, many boxfuls. **mem-kan** crate, put in chest.
petik pick, pluck. *Boléh - angin!* He can go jump in the lake! (lit., he can pick wind). **mem-** 1 pick flowers. 2 fire (gun). 3 strum, pluck (strings of musical instrument). ~ *gitar* play the guitar. 4 snap o.'s fingers. 5 quote from a book. **mem-i** pick many things. **ter-** be picked up. ~ *kabar . . .* the news was picked up that . . . **-an** 1 playing, plucking (of guitar). 2 quotation, excerpt. **pem-** 1 picker. 2 switch, trigger. ~ *potrét* camera shutter. **pem-an** picking, gathering.
petilan episode, fragment of performance, interview, etc.
petilasan see TILAS.
petinggi see TINGGI.
petir thunderclap, thunderbolt. - *tunggal* heavy crash of thunder.
petis condiment of fermented fish or shrimp.
petisi petition.
petitih proverb, saying. *petatah* - various proverbs and sayings. **ber-** speak with a proverb.
petopan gambling den.
pétor district commissioner.
pétrokimia petrochemical.
pétromax /pétromak/ kerosene pressure lantern.

pétruk (*Jv*) 1 o. of the clowns in the *wayang* stories. 2 funny-looking man.

pétrus [*penémbak misterius*] (*Coll.*) mysterious gunman. mem-(kan) execute s.o. in a mysterious killing.

pétsai (*Ch*) see PÉCAI.

petua, petuah 1 religious advice. 2 advice in general. ber- give advice. mem-i give advice to. mem-kan give certain advice, prescribe. *Métode ilmiah tdk di-kan lagi* They do not prescribe the scientific method any longer.

pétungan reckoning, calculation. *menurut - Cina* the way China reckons it.

peuyeum /peyem/ (*Sd*) fermented cassava.

péyék see REMPÉYÉK.

péyok, péyot see PÉOK, PÉOT₁.

pf. [*pour féliciter*] abbreviation written on card of congratulations.

PGC [*Pasukan Gerak Cepat*] (*Mil.*) shock troops.

PGP, PGPN [*Peraturan Gaji Pegawai (Negeri)*] 1 Regulations regarding civil service grade. 2 officially appointed to a certain grade. men-kan give o. his civil service grade.

PGRI [*Persatuan Guru Républik Indonesia*] Indonesian Teacher's Union.

pH. [*per hektar*] per hectare.

PH [*Piringan Hitam*] phonograph record. memp-kan make a record of.

pharmakologik see FARMAKOLOGI.

pharmasi see FARMASI.

Phb.₁ [*Perhubungan*] communications.

Phb.₂ [*Penghubung*] liaison (officer).

philatélis see FILATÉLIS.

phinisi k.o. Bugis cargo boat.

phobi /fobi/ phobia, opposed to s.t. that o. should favor. *Komunisto-phobi* communist-phobia. -²an various phobias.

photo see FOTO.

pi₁ (*Amb*) see PERGI.

pi₂ see PAPI.

PI [*Perhimpoenan Indonésia*] pre-Independence student organization in the Netherlands.

pia (*Ch*) k.o. tea cake.

piagam charter, contract, deed. - *Jkt* the Jkt charter. mem-kan record in a charter.

piah (*Ch*) take a ride.

pial 1 wattle. 2 gill.

piala 1 (*Lit.*) cup, goblet. 2 loving cup. - *ginjal* (*Anat.*) pelvic region.

pialang intermediary, broker. ber- buy through a broker.

piama see PIYAMA.

piancang (*Ch*) warrior.

pianggang k.o. cricket.

pianica k.o. musical instrument.

pianis pianist.

piano piano. mem-kan play s.t. on the piano. *Tdk pernah saya mendengar musik yg di-kan sebaik itu* I never heard music played on the piano as well as that.

piao (*Ch*) a dart.

piar ter- combed (of hair).

piara see PELIHARA.

piarit 1 harpoon. 2 antenna of insects.

pias₁ margin, line. - *alir* flow chart.

pias₂ pale.

piat-piut descendants.

piatu motherless child. ke-an orphaned.

piau (*Ch*) secret weapon in martial arts.

piawai skilled, expert, sophisticated. ke-an skill, expertise.

pica mem-kan neglect. ter- careless, negligent.

picah see PECAH.

picah-beling k.o. flowering ornamental herb.

picak see PÉCAK.

pici rimless cap, us. of black velvet, similar in shape to an overseas cap. - *lapangan* field cap. ber- wear this cap.

picik 1 narrow. 2 narrow-minded. memper-, mem-kan narrow s.t. ~ *pikiran* make o. narrow-minded. ke-an 1 be in a fix, stuck. 2 narrow-mindedness.

picing se- a wink. *Saya tak tidur ~ jua semalam* I did not sleep a wink last night. ber- *mata* squint, close eye against glare. mem- be closed, squint. *Matanya ~ sebelah* He closed o. eye. mem-kan *mata* close o.'s eyes.

picis amounts in multiples of 10 cents. *tiga -* 30 cents. se- a 10-cent piece. -an 1 10-cent pieces. *Uangnya semuanya ~* All his money consisted of 10-cent pieces. 2 small-time, two-bit. *bandit ~* two-bit bandit. 3 worth 10 cents. *roman ~* cheap, popular novel.

picu trigger, cock, hammer (of gun).

pidana (*Leg.*) 1 criminal. 2 punishment. mem- judge s.o. a criminal, condemn. *Dptkah pengadilan ini ~ org yg melakukan hak-haknya?* Can this court condemn a man who was carrying out his rights? mem(p)-kan make into a criminal case. ~ *perkara yg dulunya perdata* make a criminal case out of a civil case. ke-an penal law, penal law procedure. pem-an condemnation.

pidanawan (*Leg.*) prisoner.

pidato speech, address. - *pembélaan* plea for the defense. - *penerimaan/pengukuhan* (president's) inaugural speech. - *sambutan* welcoming speech. ber- make a speech. mem(p)-i make a speech to. mem(p)-kan declaim. -²an engage in foolish speech-making.

pidi mem- aim, direct.

pigi (*Coll.*) see PERGI.

pigimana see BAGAIMANA.

pigmén /pikmén/ pigment.

pigura 1 picture, painting. 2 figure, representation. - *patung* sculpture. 3 picture frame. mem- frame a picture. ter- be represented, depicted. *Di dasar hatiku tetap namamu ~ dgn indahnya* Your name remains engraved in my heart as a thing of beauty.

pihak 1 side. - *ibu* maternal line. 2 party (in a dispute, etc.). - *yg berperang* belligerents. - *ketiga* 1 a 3d party (in contracts, etc.). 2 outsider. *pd -* 1 siding with, belonging with. 2 with regard to. *di satu - . . . di lain (-) . . .* on the o. hand . . . on the other . . . *di - satunya* . . . *di - lainnya* on the o. hand . . . on the other . . . - *sana/sebelah* opponents, the opposition. **se-** unilateral. **kese-an** one-sidedness. **ber-, mem-** take sides, side with. *Negeri itu ~ pd Barat* That country sides with the W. **mem-kan** isolate.

pihutang see PIUTANG.

piil see FIIL.

pijah ber-, mem- spawn. **mem-kan** hatch (fish, etc.). ~ *ikan* hatch fish. **pem-an** spawning.

pijak -² pedals. **ber-** stand on. *tempatku ~* the place I am at. *Ia yg tdk ~ pd réalitas* He is the o. that does not have his feet firmly planted in reality. **mem-** step on. **mem-kan** *kaki* set o. foot on s.t. **ter-** be stepped on. **-an** place to stand on. **pem-** *kaki* 1 pedal. 2 stirrup.

pijar blazing, red-hot, glowing. **ber-²** glowing. **mem-** 1 glow (of light bulbs). 2 temper steel. **mem-kan** temper steel. **-an** glow given off. ~ *matahari* the sun's glare.

pijar-pijar borax.

pijat get a massage. *Saya - pd Pak Ali* I got a massage from Mr. Ali. **mem-** 1 squeeze, press. ~ *bél* press the bell. 2 massage s.o. or s.t. **mem-i** massage repeatedly. **-an** massage given.

pijat-pijat bedbug.

pijet, pijit see PIJAT.

pik (*Ch*) eight (mainly used in commercial transactions). *- ban* 80,000. *- ban go* 85,000. *- cap* 80. *- cap go* 85. *- céng* 8,000. *- pék* 800. *- pék ceng* 800,000. *- pék go* 850. *- pék go céng* 850,000. *- tiau* 8 million. *- tiau pua* 8,500,000.

pik. [*pikul*] 137 lbs.

pikap (*Coll.*) 1 van, pick-up truck. 2 phonograph, hi-fi.

pikat₁ horsefly.

pikat₂ mem- 1 trap birds with sticky substance. 2 attract, be attractive. *Perkataannya sangat ~ hati* Her words were very enticing. **ter-** attracted. ~ *hati* charmed. **-an** s.t. caught by means of a decoy. **pem-** s.t. that entices, decoy.

pikau ber-an utter cries of fear. **ter-²** gesticulate wildly.

piké see KAIN.

pikep see PIKAP.

piket 1 picket in a strike. 2 posted guard. 3 duty officer, o. on duty during off hours. 4 be on duty during off hours. **mem-i** guard s.t.

pikir 1 opinion, idea. 2 thought. *kurang -* rash, thoughtless. *pd - saya* in my opinion. **-²** think (several times). ~ *dulu!* Think twice! **ber-** think. *Tanpa ~ panjang* . . . Without thinking twice . . . **ber-an** have a certain thought. *tdk ~* thoughtless. **mem-(i)** 1 think about, worry over. 2 be aware, mindful of. **mem-kan** think about, meditate over. **ter-** come to o.'s mind. *Tak pernah ~ oléhnya utk sekali waktu* . . . It never occurred to him at o. time to . . . **ter-kan** can happen to be thought about. *Meskipun medali emas blm ~* . . . Even though no o. has even thought about the gold medal . . . **ke-an** 1 happen to think about

s.t., come to o.'s mind. *Saya blm ~ mau apa* I have not thought about what I am going to do. *Saja blm ~ anak saya mau jadi juara kelas* It never entered my mind that my daughter would become the best in the class. 2 worry. *Aku ~ kamu pulang begini lat* I was worried because you came home so late. **-an** 1 thought, idea. 2 opinion. 3 intelligence, mind. **se-an** be of the same opinion. **pem-an** thinking. *masih dlm ~* still under consideration.

piknik go on an excursion, picnic. *pergi -* go on an excursion. **ber-** go on a picnic.

pikul 137 lbs. **mem-** 1 carry on the shoulders. 2 shoulder, bear. *Berat sama di-, ringan sama dijinjing* Stick together through thick and thin (lit., share equally in carrying heavy and light burdens). ~ *risiko* take the risk. **mem-kan** 1 impose upon, charge s.o. with. 2 load on to s.o. or an animal. 3 bear for s.o. **ter-(kan)** bearable. **-an** 1 carrying pole. 2 load. **pem-** bearer. **pem-an** transporting manually.

pikun senile, senility. **ke-an** senility.

pil pill, tablet.

pilah mem-kan sort, classify. **pem-** sorter. **pem-an** process of sorting.

pilar pillar.

pilek have a cold.

pilem see FILM.

pilih ber-² fastidious, squeamish, choosy. **mem-** 1 choose, select. ~ *muka* discriminate. (*dgn*) *tdk ~ bulu* indiscriminately, irrespective of persons. ~ *kasih* partial. *Jangan suka ~ tebu* Do not be too choosy. 2 elect. 3 vote. **ter-** 1 elected. 2 selected. **-an** 1 choice. ~ *jabatan* choice of profession or calling. 2 selection. ~ *alam* natural selection. ~ *tulisan* selected works. **pem-** 1 voter. 2 particular, fastidious. **pem-an** 1 election. ~ *umum* the general elections. 2 poll.

pilin ber- spiral, twist. **ber-²** twisting around. ~ *dlm kegelisahan* writhing in anxiety. **mem-** 1 wind. 2 entwine, twist. ~ *telinga* twist o.'s ear. **-an** a twist, cord.

Pilipina see FILIPIN.

pilis camphor-based compress applied to forehead.

pilon 1 stupid. 2 innocent, naive.

pilot plane pilot. **ber-** piloted. **mem-i** pilot (a plane).

pilsapat see FILSAFAH.

pilu 1 moved, touched, affected. 2 sympathetic. **mem-(kan)** touch o.'s heart, touching, moving. **ke-an** 1 sadness. 2 emotion, being moved.

pilun see PILON.

pilus k.o. snack made of fried grated sweet potatoes.

pimpin mem- lead, guide. **ter-** be lead by. **-an** 1 leadership, guidance. 2 management, administration. ~ *fakultas* faculty administration. **pem-** 1 leader, guide. ~ *acara* master of ceremonies. ~ *rapat* chairman. ~ *sidang* moderator. 2 manager. ~ *pabrik* factory manager. 3 manual of instructions. **pem-an** action of guiding. **kepem-an** leadership qualities. *sifat ~nya yg tegas* the firm leadership which he provides.

pimping k.o. tall grass.

pimpong see PINGPONG.

pinak descendant.

pinalti see PÉNALTI.

pinang areca nut. *spt - dibelah dua* alike as two peas in a pod. *- muda* matchmaker. *- sirih* mixture for chewing betel. **mem-** 1 propose, ask in marriage. 2 apply for job. **mem-kan** ask for hand in marriage on behalf of s.o. *Suami Munah kawin lagi dgn gadis lepasan SMP. Dia di-kan Munah sendiri* Munah's husband got married again, this time to a girl who had finished junior high. Munah herself had handled the proposal. **-an** 1 proposal submitted. 2 o. whose hand is asked. **pem-** 1 suitor. 2 applicant. 3 betel-nut box. **pem-an** 1 making a proposal. 2 application.

pinatua church elder.

pincang 1 lame, crippled. *kaki - * game leg. 2 having a defect so that things are not even or smooth. *Mesin mobil ini - kedengarannya* This engine sounds as if it is not hitting on all cylinders. **se-** 1.5 cents. **mem-** be imbalanced, weightier on o. side than the other, lean toward. *Kehidupan meréka ~ ke pola-pola yg cenderung materialistis* Their way of life leans towards materialistic tendencies. **mem-kan** cripple s.t. **ke-an** 1 lameness. 2 defect. 3 imbalance. *~ antara yg kaya dan yg miskin* imbalance between the rich and the poor. **pem-an** action of crippling s.t.

pincil bunch, strand.

pincuk₁ 1 a folded-over banana leaf used as a container for portions of food. 2 k.o. fruit salad served with a spicy fish sauce. **mem-(kan)** fold a leaf to make it into a container for food.

pincuk₂ mem- make s.o. fall in love. **ter-** fall in love with.

pincut mem-(kan) enthrall, make s.o. fall in love. **ter-, ke-** be taken with, enchanted by.

pinda see PENDA.

pindah 1 move. *Apa dia sdh -?* Has he already moved? 2 change, transfer to s.t. else. *- keréta* change trains. *- alamat* change of address. *- bola* change serves. *- buku* transfer to another account. **pem-bukuan** transfer to current account. *- kapal* transship. *- nama (Leg.)* transfer a title. *- rumah* change of residence. *- tanam* transplant. **mem-tanamkan** transplant. *- tangan* change hands. **mem-tangankan** transfer to s.o. else. **pem-tanganan** transferal. *- tempat* move to another place. **mem-tempatkan** move s.t. to a different place (e.g. automobile tires, etc.). *- tuang darah* blood transfusion. *- tugas* transfer to a new post. **mem-tugaskan** move s.o. to a new post. *ayah saya di-tugaskan* My father was given a new post. **ber-** 1 move. *~ negeri* emigrate. *burung-burung yg ~* birds that migrate. *~ ke rahmatullah* pass away, die. 2 change to s.t. else. **ber-², -**

mem- 1 keep moving from place to place. 2 spread (of disease), be contagious. **mem-(kan)** move, transfer s.t. *~ gunung* move mountains (do the impossible). **ke-an** 1 transfer. 2 infected. **-an** 1 furniture to be moved. 2 o. who has been transferred. 3 *(Fin.)* balance brought forward. **pem-an** 1 removal, transfer. 2 *(Fin.)* transfer from o. account to another. **per-an** 1 transfer, removal. 2 change.

pindai mem- scrutinize, look at carefully. *Ia ~ parasnya yg cantik di depan cermin* She examined her beautiful appearance in front of the mirror.

pindakas /pindakás/ peanut butter.

pindang preserve large fish or meat with salt without drying. *- bandeng* salted milkfish. *daging - * k.o. beef soup with tamarind. **mem-** make preserved fish or meat. **pem-** material for preparing this dish. **pem-an** 1 this process of fish or meat preservation. 2 place for preserving meat or fish in this way.

pinding see KEPINDING.

pinés thumbtack.

pingai light yellow.

pinggan dish, plate. *- kerang* large platter. *- mangkuk* set of china.

pinggang 1 waist. 2 loins. *- gunung* mountain slope. **pem-** amidships.

pinggir 1 edge, seam. 2 border. **ber-** have an edge, border or seam. **ber-an** have edges or borders. **mem-** go to or along edge. **mem-i** delimit, draw perimeters of. **mem-kan** put at edge or side. **menge-kan** 1 put at edge or side. 2 sweep s.t. aside. **dim-kan** be put at edge or side. **-an** edges, coastal areas, outskirts. *~ kota* outskirts of city. *~ jendéla* windowsill. **pem-(an)** boundary.

pinggul 1 hip. 2 behind, rear.

pingin see KEPINGIN.

pingit secluded (of marriageable girl). **ber-** be secluded, esp. kept in house. **mem-** 1 seclude, keep in house. 2 keep animal in cage. **-an** o. who has been kept secluded.

pingkal see PINGKEL.

pingkau see PIKAU.

pingkel ter-² double up with laughter.

pingpong 1 ping-pong. 2 the football treatment, sending from pillar to post. **mem-** give s.o. the football treatment. *Saya di- ke sana ke mari* They sent me from o. office to another and back again.

pingsan 1 unconscious. 2 fainted. 3 have a fit.

Pingster *(Rel.)* Pentecostal sect.

pinguin, pingwin penguin.

pinhong *(Ch)* screen.

pinisepuh *(Jv)* elders (of a village or any organization).

pinisi see PHINISI.

pinjak see PIJAK.

pinjal flea.

pinjam mem- borrow from. **mem-i** lend to, loan to. *- saya seribu* Lend me 1,000. **mem-kan** lend

s.t. *Berapa yg hrs saya -kan padanya?* How much do I have to lend to him? **memper-kan** lend out s.t. o. has borrowed. *Boléh saja pakai buku saya, tapi jangan diper-kan sama org lain* You may borrow my book but not to lend it out to s.o. else. **-an** loan. **pem-** borrower. **pem-an** action of borrowing or lending. ~ *itu dimulai hari ini* We count interest beginning today.
pinsét tweezers, pincers.
pinsil see PÉNSIL.
pinta₁ request. **-an** request, question.
pinta₂, pintak fate, destiny. **ter-** predestined, fated.
pintal ber-² tangled. **mem-** spin, twine. **-an** ball of twine. **pem-** 1 o. employed in making thread or twine. 2 spinning wheel. **pem-an** 1 spinning. 2 spinning wheel.
pintar 1 clever, smart. - *busuk* cunning, crafty. 2 skilled at, able. *Ia - berbahasa Perancis* He speaks French very well. **se-** as smart as. **ke-an** cleverness, skill.
pintas *sekali* - passing by once. **se-** a second (of time). ~ *lalu* on the face of it, at first glance. ~ *lalu persoalan itu kelihatannya gampang* At first glance the problem seemed easy. **mem-** take a short cut. **mem-i** 1 intercept, interrupt, cut s.o. short. ~ *kesukaran* overcome difficulties. ~ *maksud* beat about the bush. 2 cut off, block o.'s way. *Saya -i jalannya* I blocked his way. 3 cut in (in traffic). ~ *ke kanan* turn to the right. **mem-kan** cut off. **ke-an** 1 overcome, surmounted. 2 cut short. 3 intercepted. **-an** short cut.
pinter see PINTAR.
pintil₁ skein of yarn.
pintil₂ see PÉNTIL.
pintoo (*Ch*) 1 Buddhist priest. 2 term of address to Buddhist priest.
pintu door, gate. - *air* sluice, floodgate, locks. - *angin* porthole, vent. - *belakang* back door. - *darurat* emergency exit. - *geladak* hatchway. - *gerbang* 1 main entrance, front gate. 2 ceremonial gate. - *gésér* sliding door. *ke - kubur* die. - *keluar* exit. - *kolong* trap door. - *kupu-kupu* swinging door. - *maling* side entrance. - *monyét* folding doors. - *msk* entrance. - *putar* revolving door. - *rangkap* folding door. - *sorong* sliding door. - *tani* outer gate of a palace. **se-** *rumah* a house.
pinus k.o. tree, pine.
pinusisasi reforestation with pines.
pion (*Che.*) pawn.
pionir pioneer. **mem-kan** be a pioneer in. **ke-an** pioneering.
pipa 1 pipe, for smoking. - *rokok* cigarette holder. 2 pipe, conduit, tube. - *celana* trouser leg. - *induk air léding* water main. - *kuras* drainpipe. - *minyak tanah* pipeline. - *napas* (*Anat.*) trachea. - *pembuang gas* exhaust pipe. - *pindah* siphon. - *rambut* (*Anat.*) capillary. - *waja* steel pipe.
pipét (*Chem.*) pipette.
pipi cheek.
pipih flat, thin. - *asahan* thin section. **mem-kan** flatten.

pipil mem- loosen beans, grains from shell. *jagung utk di-* corn to remove from the cob. ~ *kedelé* shell soybeans. **-an** s.t. shelled.
pipis₁ (*child language*) urinate.
pipis₂ mem- mash, crush up.
pipit₁ sparrow.
pipit₂ (*child language*) penis.
pipit₃ mouthpiece of a wind instrument. **mem-** press.
pirai (*Med.*) gout.
piramid, piramida pyramid.
piramidal pyramidal.
pirang see PÉRANG.
piranti see PERANTI.
pirasa see RASA.
pirasat see FIRASAT.
pirau dark brown.
Piraun see FIRAUN.
pirdaus see FIRDAUS.
pirik mem- rub down, pulverize.
piring plate. - *cépér* dinner plate. - *dlm* soup plate. - *makan* k.o. shallow dish from which rice is eaten. - *mangkuk* crockery. **(-an)** *hitam* phonograph record. **mem-hitamkan** record on a phonograph record. **(-an)** *terbang* flying saucer.
pirométer pyrometer.
pirsa pem- TV audience.
pirsawan TV audience.
pirsidér refrigerator.
pirus turquoise (gem).
pis₁ bolt of cloth.
pis₂ see PIPIS₁.
pisah - *kebo/méja dan tempat tidur* legal separation (of a couple). **ber-** 1 part. 2 separated. *Meréka itu* ~ They parted. *Meréka itu* ~ *jalan* They took separate ways. **ber-an** part from e.o. **mem-** separate. ~ *kaum lelaki dan kaum perempuan* separate the men and women. **mem-kan** 1 separate, set aside, isolate. *tak dpt di-²kan* inseparable. 2 analyze. **ter-** 1 separate (table, room). 2 get separated accidentally. *tdk* ~ inseparable. **keter-an** state of being separated. **pem-** 1 arbiter. 2 referee. 3 s.t. that separates. *jurang* ~ the chasm that separates (us). **pem-an** 1 separation, division. ~ *meja dan tempat tidur* legal separation (of couple). 2 isolation. 3 discrimination. **per-an** 1 discord. 2 leave-taking, parting. *Kematian bukanlah perceraian, hanya* ~ Death is not a parting. It is just saying goodbye for a while.
pisang banana. - *Ambon* large green banana. - *batu* k.o. banana with seeds. - *goréng* fried banana fritters. - *raja* k.o. large, sweet banana. - *salé* dried banana (as snack). - *serai* an inferior k.o. banana. - *susu* k.o. small, starchy banana with light yellow skin.
pisau knife. - *bedah* scalpel. - *belati* dagger. - *cukur* razor. - *kertas* letter opener. - *lipat* pocket knife. - *raut* carving knife. - *silét* safety razor. - *wali* small knife for wood carving. **ber-** have a knife.
pisik see FISIK.
pisin (*Sd*) saucer.
pisit₁ svelte.

pisit₂ mem- press, compress.
pispot chamber pot.
pistol pistol, revolver. *- air* water pistol. *- angin* air pistol. *- las asétilin* acetylene torch. *- mitralyur* submachine gun. **ber-** carry a pistol. **mem-** shoot with a pistol. **-²an** toy pistol.
pisuh m- curse, use bad language in anger. **mem-i** deride s.o. with bad language. **-an** s.t. said in cussing.
pit₁ (*Ch*) brush pen.
pit₂ bike, motorbike.
pita 1 ribbon. *- mesin tulis* typewriter ribbon. **2** tape. *- cukai* cigarette revenue stamps. *- filem* movie film. *- isolasi* scotch tape. *- mesin* (*Auto.*) driving belt, transmission belt. *- méteran* measuring tape. *- (pe)rekat plastik* cellophane tape. *- suara* vocal cords. *- ukur* measuring tape. *- vidéo* video tape.
pitam 1 dizziness. **2** fit. **3** apoplexy. *- babi* epilepsy. **4** paralytic stroke.
pitar mem- aim a weapon. **pem-** (gun)sight.
pitenah see FITNAH.
pites mem- crush between the fingernails. **mem-i** crush many things, crush repeatedly.
piting₁ (ber)-²an clinch e.o. *Petinju ~* The boxers clinched. **mem-** hold with forearms, clinch. **mem-i** clinch repeatedly. **-an** hold, clinch.
piting₂ see FITING.
pitrah see FITRAH₁.
pituas, pituwas 1 compensation, reward. *Apa -nya dia kerja mati-matian?* What is the reward for working o.s. to death? **2** wage.
piuh distorted. *- pilin* word twisting. **mem-** twist. **ter-** twisted, distorted. **-an** distortion.
piun see PION.
piut descendant 5th removed.
piutang 1 credit. **2** claim, accounts receivable. *- macet* a bad debt, accounts receivable are not coming in. **ber-** have a claim to be collected. **mem-i** lend money to s.o else. **mem-kan** deliver on credit. **pem-** creditor.
piwulang (*Jv, Sd*) lesson, teaching.
piyama pajamas.
piyut choke. **mem-kan** choke or strangle s.t.
Pj. [*Pejabat*] official.
PJKA [*Perusahaan Jawatan Keréta Api*] Indonesian Railway Systems.
Pjs. [*Pejabat sementara*] temporary official.
pk. [*pukul*] o'clock.
PK₁ [*Partai Komunis*] Communist party.
PK₂ [*Paardekracht*] horsepower.
PK₃, P3K [*Pertolongan Pertama pd Kecelakaan*] First Aid.
PKI [*Partai Komunis Indonésia*] Indonesian Communist party.
PKK [*Pendidikan Kesejahteraan Keluarga*] program at village level to educate women on various aspects of family welfare.
pkl. [*pukul*] o'clock.
PKUS [*Partai Komunis Uni Sovyét*] Communist party of the Soviet Union.
pl- see also entries with **pel-**.

PL [*Perjanjian Lama*] (*Bib.*) Old Testament.
plafon, plafond ceiling.
plagiat plagiarism.
plagiator plagiarist.
plak₁ /plak/ sound of slap.
plak₂ plaque (on teeth).
plakat poster.
plakségel receipt stamp or seal.
plamir, plamur putty, spackle for painting. **memp-** spackle.
plane /plein/ airplane.
plang 1 signpost. **2** gate. *- keréta api* railroad crossing gate.
planit planet.
plankton plankton.
planologoi city planning.
plan-plan see PELAN.
plas-plosan see CEPLAS-CEPLOS.
plastik plastic.
plastis plastic. **ke-an** plasticity.
plastisitas plasticity.
plat see PELAT.
platina 1 platinum. **2** (*Auto.*) distributor contact, points.
plébisit plebiscite.
plédooy, plédoy, pléidoi (*Leg.*) defense.
plék stain, spot.
plempem (*Jv*) large pipe (for drainage, etc.).
pléno full, plenary. *sidang -* plenary session. **mem-kan** send to a plenary session. *Semua ini akan di-kan Rabu malam* All of this will be taken up in the plenary session Wednesday night.
plentong lightbulb.
plés bottle, flask.
pléster 1 plaster. **2** adhesive plaster. **-an** covered with plaster.
plestér, pléstér cement. **memp-** cement. **-an** cement floor.
plétat plétot not neat, not straight, not round.
pletik onomatopoetic word for s.t. small ejected. **-an** a small thing ejected. *~ api* sparks.
pliket see PELIKET.
plin-plan, plintat-plintut now this way now that, swaying with the wind, following whatever opinion is dominant.
plin-planisme tendency to follow whatever idea is dominant.
plintir see PELINTIR.
plisir see PELISIR.
PLM [*perahu layar motor*] k.o. sailboat equipped with auxiliary engines.
PLN [*Perusahaan Listrik Negara*] State Electricity Enterprise.
ploi pleat.
ploksok connecting pipe socket with two different sizes.
plombir memp- 1 fill (tooth). **2** stop, plug up. **-an** filling.
plonci, plonco see PELONCI, PELONCO.
plong 1 freed of cares, relieved. *Rasa hatiku bukan main -nya* I was totally relieved. **2** hole. *renda dgn -² yg semarak* lace with decorative holes.

PLP [*Pendidikan Latihan Pertempuran*] (*Mil.*) combat training.

pluit see PELUIT.

pluk, plung sound of splashing water.

plus 1 (*Math.*) plus. *jumlah ini - lima ratus* this sum plus 500. **2** having a surplus. *daérah -* an area that produces a superabundance.

plutokrasi plutocracy.

plutokrat plutocrat.

PM₁ [*Perdana Menteri*] prime minister.

PM₂ [*Polisi Militér*] military police.

PMA [*Penanaman Modal Asing*] foreign investment.

PMDK [*Penelusuran Minat dan Kemampuan*] talent scouting for admission to state university system.

PMDN [*Penanaman Modal Dalam Negeri*] domestic investment.

PMI [*Palang Mérah Indonésia*] Indonesian Red Cross.

PMK [*Pasukan Mencegah Kebakaran*] fire department.

PN [*Perusahaan Negara*] state enterprise. **mem-kan** convert to state enterprise.

pneumonia, pnémonia /pnémonia/ pneumonia.

PNG [*Papua-Nugini*] Papua-New Guinea.

PNI [*Partai National Indonésia*] Indonesian Nationalist party.

po (*Ch*) k.o. card game.

PO [*Perusahaan Otobis*] bus company.

poatang (*Jkt, Ch*) get caught, get found out.

poci teapot.

pocok (*Jv*) **mem-i** fill a certain position temporarily. **mem-kan** fill in for s.o. at his job temporarily. **-an** /poco'an/ fill-in. *cerita ~* story used in publication to fill in when expected o. failed to be submitted.

pocong *sumpah -* (*Leg., Rel.*) an oath of innocence by o. wrapped in a shroud. **mem-** (*Jv*) wrap in a shroud. **-an** (*Jv*) shroud.

podak see PUDAK.

podeng, poding pudding. *- roti* bread pudding.

pof puffed (of sleeves).

pohbor see POPOR.

pohon₁ 1 tree. *- kayu* tree. *- tunjung* lotus tree. **2** origin, cause. *- bahasa* basis of language. *- mata* inner corner of the eye. *- segala kejahatan* the root of all evil. *- telinga* base of ear. **-²an 1** trees, timber. **2** vegetable world. **pe-an 1** trees. **2** reforestation.

pohon₂ see MOHON.

pojok 1 corner. **2** k.o. newspaper column containing pithy comments on the news. **mem-** go to the corner. **mem-kan** force into a corner. *Konsép normalisasi kampus jelas akan ~ mahasiswa* The concept of normalization of the campus is clearly going to force the students into corner. **ter-** be forced into a corner. **keter-an** being forced into a corner. **-an** street corner. **pem-an** act of concerning s.o.

pok see MPOK.

pokal ruse.

pokat see ADVOKAT₂.

pokét (*Mil.*) pocket of uniform.

pokok 1 main, principal, basic, fundamental, base. *-nya* the main thing is. *Tdk perlu bawa apa-apa, -nya datang* You do not have to bring anything. The main thing is that you come. *pd -nya* basically. *Pd -nya anda benar* Basically you are right. *- acara* main point. *- bahasan* topic, subject under discussion. *- hidangan* main course, dish. *- pangkal(an)* main point. *- pembicaraan* topic of conversation. *- pikiran* gist of o.'s thoughts. **2** beginning. *- kata* root, base of a word. *- hujan* rain cloud. **3** capital, stake. *- amal* fund. **4** subject. *- kalimat* subject of the sentence. *- lukisan* l theme, dominant feature, motif. **2** draft. **5** reason, central theme. *- perselisihan* cause of conflict. **6** tree. *- kayu* 1 tree trunk. **2** tree. **7** main or lower part of s.t. *- lampu* fixture of a lightbulb. **ber-** 1 be based on, derived from. **2** have capital. *Meréka berdagang tak ~* They buy and sell without capital. **ber-kan** be based on. *Bahasa Indonésia ~ pd bahasa Melayu* Indonesian is based on Malay. **mem-** be basic, of basic importance. **mem-i** give the capital for s.t. *Ayahnya ~nya utk membuka perusahaan itu* His father gave him the capital to start the business. **mem-kan** focus s.t. (on). **ter-1** cost. *~ berapa bajumu itu?* What did your dress cost? **2** principal, main. *alasan ~* the basic excuse.

pokrol attorney, lawyer. *- bambu* 1 unlicensed lawyer. **2** able debater. **3** cheater. **-²an** pettifoggery.

pol₁ 1 complete, fully done. *Saya bekerja - di situ* I work full-time at that place. *Blm dibayar -* It has not been fully paid for. **2** to the fullest extent. *Putar volume radio itu sampai -* Turn the volume on the radio up as loud as possible. **3** filled up. *Bisnya -* The bus is full. **memp-kan** make s.t. be done fully. *-kan program itu* Make it a full-fledged program.

pol₂ see VOLT.

pola 1 pattern. *- baju* pattern for sewing. **2** system, model of how s.t. is done. *- perkembangan* the way development is taking place. **mem-** form a pattern. *Iklim kemasyarakatan mémang ~ ke arah itu* The social climate does indeed form a pattern in that direction. **mem-kan, memp-kan** pattern, fashion. *~ masyarakat adil dan makmur* to fashion a just and prosperous society. **pem-an** patterning.

polah *- tingkah* behavior. **ber-²** put on.

polan *si -* Mr. So-and-so, Mr. What's-his-name.

Polandia Poland.

polang-paling whirl.

polang-poléng checkered or camouflage pattern.

polantas [*polisi lalu lintas*] traffic police.

polarisasi polarization. **mem-kan** polarize.

polas-polés paint, smear s.t.

poldan 1 paid up. **2** finished! all done! (in card games, etc.).

polémik polemic. **ber-** engage in polemics. **memp-kan** carry out a debate over. *adat lama-baru yg didiskusikan atau di-kan* the old vs. the new customs over which they engaged in polemics.

poléng see POLANG-POLÉNG.
polentér volunteer.
polés polish. **mem-** 1 polish. 2 apply makeup. ~ *segaris tipis pembayang mata di pinggiran matanya* apply a thin line of eye shadow to the eyelids. **mem-i** apply grease, smear on to. *panci yg di-i mentéga* a pan greased with butter. **mem-kan** smear s.t. onto s.t. *Kemudian ia ~ warna yg sering dipakainya* Then he smears on a color he often uses. **-an** 1 s.t. polished. *~mu kasar* You did not polish it smoothly. 2 s.t. smeared on.
polgas at full speed. **memp-** drive at full speed. *Truk itu di-* The truck drove off at full speed.
poli [*poliklinik*] polyclinic.
poliandri polyandry.
poligami polygamy.
poligamis polygamist.
poligon polygon.
poliklinik polyclinic.
polio₁ polio.
polio₂ see FOLIO.
polip (*Med.*) polyp.
polis (insurance) policy.
polisi policeman. *- lalu-lintas* traffic police. *- perairan* 1 coast guard. 2 harbor police. *- tidur* traffic bump. **ke-an** police. *akadémi ~* police academy. **-²an** fake policeman.
polisionil having to do with the police. *aksi -* police action.
politéis polytheist.
politéisme polytheism.
politéknik polytechnic.
politik 1 politics, political. *- praktis* action-oriented politics. 2 policy. *- pasaran/pintu terbuka* free-trade policy. **ber-** engage in politics. **mem-i** manipulate s.o. *Ia pandai ~ rekan-rekannya spy terpilih ketua* He was good at manipulating his friends so that he was chosen chairman. **mem-kan, memper-(kan)** politicize. *~ perbédaan agama* politicize religious differences. **-²an** politics as a game. *main ~* play politics.
politikus politician.
politis political. *tujuan -* political goals.
politisasi politicization.
politisi politicians.
politur see PELITUR.
polmah (*Leg.*) power of attorney. *Siapa memberikan - kpdmu?* Who gave you power of attorney?
polo (*Sports*) polo. *- air* water polo.
polok mem- swallow, bolt down.
polong₁ ghost, evil spirit.
polong₂ pod. **-²an** legumes of various sorts.
polongan outlet, drainpipe.
polos 1 smooth. 2 plain (material, paper, etc.). *mencorat-corét kertas -* doodle on blank piece of paper. 3 straightforward, without guile. *Anak itu masih - sekali* That child is still completely innocent. **ke-an** smoothness, plainness, straightforwardness.
polowijo see PALAWIJA.
Polri [*Polisi Républik Indonésia*] Indonesian Police.
polsus [*polisi khusus*] special police.
polsuska [*polisi khusus keréta api*] railway police.

polusi pollution.
polutan pollutant.
polwan [*polisi wanita*] policewoman.
Polwil [*polisi wilayah*] local police.
Pom [*Polisi Militér*] military police.
POM₁ [*Persatuan Org Tua Murid*] Parents' Association.
POM₂ [*Pengawasan Obat dan Makanan*] Drug and Food Control (of central gvt.).
pomade pomade.
pombénsin gas station.
POMG [*Persatuan Org Tua Murid dan Guru*] Parent-Teacher's Association.
pompa pump. *air watel pump. - bensin* gas pump. **mem-** pump. *~ air* pump out water. **mem-kan** 1 pump s.t. s.w. *téori yg di-kan ke dlm otaknya* theories which were pumped into his brain. 2 pump s.t. up. *~ sepéda* pump up the bicycle (wheel). **pem-an** pumping (up).
pompanisasi provision of water pumps in an area.
pompen push-ups.
pompong see KEPOMPONG.
PON [*Pekan Olahraga Nasional*] National Games.
pon₁ pound (weight and British currency).
pon₂ 3d day of Jv week.
ponakan see KEPONAKAN.
ponco poncho.
pondamén see FONDAMÉN.
pondik arrogant, conceited.
pondoh edible pith of coconut palm trunk.
pondok 1 cottage, hut, cabin. 2 (*Isl.*) Muslim boarding school. **m-** to board. **mem-i** room and board at. *rumah yg di-inya* the house he boarded at. **mem-kan** provide lodgings. **-an** lodgings, rooming house. **pem-** boarder, tenant. **pem-an** lodgings.
pondong mem- carry in o.'s arms.
poném see FONÉM.
pongah conceited, stuck up. **ber-(²)** boast, brag. **ke-an** conceit, arrogance.
ponggang see SIPONGGANG.
ponggawa see PUNGGAWA.
pongo (*Jv*) be open-mouthed from surprise or bewilderment.
poni bangs.
ponim see FONÉM.
ponis see VONIS.
ponok camel's hump.
ponokawan see PUNAKAWAN.
pontang-panting run helter skelter, in any direction. *Dia lari -* He ran away at top speed (without caring where he went).
ponten 1 marks, grades. 2 points in a game. **ber-** have a grade of . . . *Di mata lelaki bangor, meréka ~ sepuluh* In the eyes of lewd men they got an A-plus. **mem-** 1 grade papers, give a mark. 2 regard. *Kok rendah banget sih ~ perempuan kampung* How come you give country girls such low marks?
pontén 1 fountain. 2 public bath and toilet.
ponton pontoon.
ponyard dagger used by naval cadets.

pop pop culture. *musik* - pop music. *nama* - stage name.
popi doll.
popok diaper. **mem-i** put diaper on. **mem-kan** place on as medicine, plaster, etc.
popokan ghost. see MOMOK.
popor rifle butt. **mem-** hit with rifle butt.
popularitas popularity.
populasi population (in a study).
populér popular. **memp-kan** popularize. **ke-an** popularity.
populis of popular culture. *sebuah lakon* - a play of a popular nature.
popuré (*Ch*) talisman.
pora see PEDANG, PÉSTA.
porak-parik, porak-peranda, porak-poranda a mess, in disorder. **memp-kan** bring disorder to. ~ *dunia kita* bring our world into chaos.
pordéo see PRODÉO.
porek see POROK.
pori pore. **ber-** porous. **ke-an** porosity.
Porkas [*Pekan Olahraga utk Kesejateraan Sosial*] weekly lottery based on soccer scores.
pormil see FORMAL.
pormulir see FORMULIR.
porno pornographic. **ke-an** pornography.
pornografi pornography.
porok fork.
poros axis, pivot, shaft. - *belakang* rear axle. - *éngkol* crankshaft. - *halang* (*Sport*) center half (soccer). **se-** ally. *kawan* ~ ally. **menye-kan** create an alliance (esp. ideological). **ber-** have as its center, basis. **ber-kan** be centered around.
porot mem-(i) 1 gnaw at, bite into. **2** steal.
porsekot see PERSEKOT.
porselén china, porcelain.
porsi portion. *pesan nasi dua* - order two portions of rice.
porstél proposal, suggestion.
portal gate (blocking entrance, R.R. crossing, etc.).
portepél portfolio. - *kehakiman* justice portfolio.
portir 1 ticket collector at gate. **2** porter.
porto cost of sending s.t. - *udara* air freight costs. *bébas* - sent free of postage.
portrét see POTRÉT.
Portugés Portuguese.
pos 1 mail. - *kilat* special delivery. - *laut* sea mail. - *réstan* general delivery. - *udara* airmail. **2** item, entry. *Berapa anggaran* - *dana sosial* How much was assigned to charitable contributions? - *débitnya* in the debit column. **3** post, situation. - *penjagaan* guard post. - *polisi* police station. **ber-** have a post at. **memp-kan, menge-kan** send off in the mail. **-²an** guard post.
pose pose (in photo). **ber-** pose for picture taking.
posing see PUSING.
posisi position. - *tawar* bargaining position. *kalah* - be in an unfavorable position.
positif, positip positive. *Saya* - *berangkat bésok* I am sure to leave tomorrow. *Hasil pemeriksaannya* - The medical examination came out positive.
mem-kan affirm. ~ *peranan org buta* affirm the

role of the blind, give the blind a more positive role.
poskar postcard.
Posma [*Pekan Orientasi dan Studi Mahasiswa*] Freshman Orientation Week.
pospakét parcel-post package.
pospor see FOSFOR.
postél [*pos dan télékomunikasi*] postal, telegraph, and telephone service.
poster poster.
postulat postulate. **mem-kan** postulate s.t.
poswésel money order. **memp-kan** send money via money order.
pot 1 pot. - *bunga* flowerpot. **2** chamber pot.
potas potassium.
potéhi (*Ch*) hand puppets.
poténsi potential. - *ékonomi* economic potential.
poténsial, poténsiil potential.
potia (*Ch*) overseer.
potlot pencil. - *isi* mechanical pencil.
poto see FOTO.
potokopi see FOTOKOPI.
potol 1 broke, hard up. **2** cut off.
potong 1 piece. *jumlah* - *barang* number of pieces of baggage. **2** lump. **3** slice. *Saya minta se- roti* I want a slice of bread. - *koréa/sikat/tentara* crewcut. - *rambut* get a haircut. **4** be reduced by. *tiga bulan penjara* - *tahanan* three months of jail including detention. **5** take a short cut. - *kompas* take a short cut by using a compass. **ber-an** have the looks of. *Apa saya* ~ *penipu?* Do I look like a cheat? **mem- 1** cut (off), slice. ~ *bicara* interrupt. **2** slaughter. **3** operate on, amputate. **4** reduce, cut, deduct wages, abbreviate a word. *di- lima puluh persén* reduced 50 percent. **5** take a short cut. **mem-i 1** cut s.t. off from. *Semak hrs di-i* The bushes have to be cut back. **2** cut many things. **-an 1** deduction from wages. **2** discount. **3** way s.t. is made or built, model, cut of clothes. ~ *badannya bagus* He was well built. **4** abbreviation. **5** a cut. ~ *plastik* plastic surgery. **-²an** various parts of a whole. **pem-an 1** butchering, slaughtering. **2** process of cutting, truncation. ~ *pajak* withholding of taxes. ~ *uang* (*Fin.*) devaluation of currency.
potrét 1 photograph, picture, snapshot. - *diri* self-portrait. **2** camera. **3** have o.'s picture taken. **ber-** have o.'s picture taken. - **mem-** photography. **mem-** take a picture, photograph. **mem-i** take pictures of repeatedly. **pem-** photographer. **pem-an** photography. ~ *udara* aerial photography. **per-an** matters or business of photography.
power 1 k.o. four-wheel-drive army truck used in mountainous regions. **2** power of radio or stereo set.
poya see FOYA.
poyang grandfather.
PP₁ [*pulang pergi*] round trip.
PP₂ [*Peraturan Pemerintah*] Governmental Regulations.
PP dan K [*Pendidikan, Pengajaran dan Kebudayaan*] Ministry of Education and Culture.
PPLH [*Pembinaan dan Pelestarian Lingkungan Hi-*

dup] Cultivation and Preservation of the Environment.

PPN [*Pajak Pendapatan Nasional*] National Income Tax.

PPN(B) [*Pusat Perkebunan Negara (Baru)*] (New) Center for Gvt. Estates.

PPP [*Partai Persatuan Pembangunan*] United Development party, a Muslim party.

PPPK [*Pertolongan Pertama pd Kecelakaan*] First Aid.

pr- see also entries with **per-**.

PR₁ [*Penyapu Ranjau*] minesweeper.

PR₂ [*pekerjaan rumah*] homework.

PR₃ [*Pemuda Rakyat*] communist youth movement, the People's Youth

pra- see also entries with **pre-**.

praada preexistence.

praanggapan prejudice, presupposition.

prabakti probationary. *masa -* probationary period.

prabawa see PERBAWA.

prabedah preoperative.

prabu the sovereign.

pracerita opening portion of a story.

pracipta s.t. created beforehand.

prada₁ [*prajurit dua*] (*Mil.*) Private (lowest rank).

prada₂ see PERADA₁.

pradéwasa preadult.

pradini premature in birth, ripening, or flowering. *lahir -* premature birth. **memp-kan** make s.t. flower or ripen early.

praduga presumption. *- tak bersalah* presumption of innocence.

prafabrik prefabricated.

pragaan see RAGA₁.

pragmatis pragmatic.

pragmatisme pragmatism.

prah freight, cargo.

Praha Prague.

prahara hurricane, tempest.

prahoto truck.

prailmiah prescientific.

praja territory of jurisdiction.

prajurit 1 soldier. *- udara* airman. **2** a private. *- I* PFC. *- II* private. **3** soldierlike and brave. *Hendaknya kalian bersikap -* You all must act brave like soldiers. **ke-an 1** military. *latihan ~* military exercises. **2** heroism.

praka [*prajurit kepala*] (*Mil.*) highest rank of private below *kopral*.

prakarsa initiative. **memp-i, memp-kan** initiate. *kerja sama yg di-i (di-kan) oléh Menteri Agama* cooperative program initiated by minister of religion. **pem-** initiator.

prakarya vocational subjects in school (homemaking, sewing, automobile repairing, etc.).

prakasa see PERKASA.

prakata foreword.

prakemerdékaan pre-Independence.

prakira forecast. **memp-kan** forecast s.t. **-an** forecast. *~ cuaca* weather forecast.

prakondisi prerequisite.

prakték, praktik 1 practice of a profession. *buka -* open o.'s practice. **2** practices. *- buruk* evil practices. **ber-** practice (medicine, etc.). **mem-i** practice on. **memp-kan 1** practice, put into practice. *nilai-nilai asing yg di-kan* foreign values which are put into practice. **2** apply. *Di-kan pd keperluan-keperluan lain* It is applied to other needs. **-an** apprentice. *mahasiswa - di rumah sakit* a student apprentice in a hospital. **pem-** practitioner.

praktikum practical work, lab work.

praktis 1 practical. *Kurang - membawa komputer ke hutan* It is impractical to bring a computer to the jungle. **2** practically. *Di sana - tak ada pembangunan* There is practically no development in that place. **-nya** in practice. **ke-an** practicality.

prakualifikasi, prakwalifikasi (*Fin.*) qualifications stipulated for all prospective tenders of a bid.

pralambang prediction, prophecy.

pralon k.o. hard pipe. *pipa -* hard plastic pipe.

prama [*pramahasiswa*] o. who is about to enter university.

pramadara newly registered university freshman (female).

pramana (*Jv*) careful.

pramaria newly registered university freshman.

pramaséhi pre-Christian.

prambos see FRAMBOS.

praméswari see PERMAISURI.

prami newly registered university student (female).

pramubakti, pamubhakti (*Euphemism*) maid servant.

pramugara attendant on long distance transport.

pramugari female attendant on long distance transport.

Pramuka [*(Gerakan) Praja Muda Karana*] Boy Scouts. *- pramuki* Boy and Girl Scouts. **ke-an** scouting movement.

pramukawati Girl Scout.

pramuniaga (*Euphemism*) sales clerk.

pramuria (*Euphemism*) nightclub hostess.

pramuwisata tourist guide.

pramuwisma (*Euphemism*) maid servant.

pranata institution, regulation. *- démokrasi* democratic institution.

Prancis France, French. *bahasa -* the French language.

prangko postage stamp. **mem-i** stamp, affix postage. *-ilah surat ini secukupnya* Put enough postage on this letter.

prapatan crossroads.

prapén (*Jv*) furnace, fireplace, or any place for a fire.

prapendaftaran preregistration.

praperadilan pretrial.

prapertunjukan preview.

prarasa partiality, preference.

prarencana plan in rough, preliminary form.

prasaja straightforward, without guile.

prasangka prejudice. **ber-** prejudiced.

prasantap food served before main course.

prasaran working paper, introductory paper. **mem-i** provide an introductory or working pa-

per for. **men-kan** use s.t. as a working paper. **pem-** 1 keynote speaker. 2 reader of working paper.
prasarana 1 infrastructure. 2 labor done in preparation. *Utk rétribusi dan - hrs dibayar Rp5.000* We have to pay 5,000 rupiah for tolls and overhead.
prasarjana degree awarded after three years of tertiary level study.
prasasti 1 ancient inscription, epigraphy. 2 plaque commemorating inauguration of building.
prasejarah prehistory, prehistorical.
prasekolah preschool.
prasetia, prasetya firm intent, pledge of loyalty, religious vow.
praskripsi (*Acad.*) B.A. thesis.
Prasman (*Coll.*) Frenchman. **-an** buffet.
prasyarat prerequisite. **memp-kan** make as a prerequisite.
pratanda 1 sign, indication. 2 forerunner. **ber-** foreboding.
pratekan (*Ling.*) prestressed.
pratijangkit antiseptic.
pratiwi see PERTIWI.
prat-prit sound of whistle blowing repeatedly.
pratu [*perajurit satu*] (*Mil.*) private first class.
prausul working paper.
prawacana foreword, preface.
prawarsa initiative, impetus.
prawira see PERWIRA.
prayoga decent, suitable.
prayojana purpose, intention, motive.
pré see PERAI₁.
préambul preamble.
prédikat 1 citation, designation. *dgn - "sangat memuaskan"* with the notation "very satisfactory." *dgn - magna cum laude* with the citation magna cum laude. 2 (*Ling.*) predicate. **ber-kan** have a certain title, notation.
préfék (*Rel.*) prefect, the supervisor in a church organization.
préféktur prefecture (in Japan, France, etc.).
préferénsi preference. *tarif -* preferential tariff.
préférensiil preferential.
préhistori prehistory.
préhistoris prehistoric.
préi₁ see PERAI₁.
préi₂ leek.
prék /prék/ (*Vulg.*) Nonsense! Shut up! (exclamation to silence s.o.). **mem-i** tell s.o. to shut up.
prékik see PRIKIK.
prélat prelate.
préliminér preliminary.
prém plum.
préman 1 private, civilian. *mobil -* private vehicle (not for public use). *pakaian -* civies. 2 (*Coll.*) street kids, hoodlums. *bahasa -* argot used by street kids and criminals.
prématur premature.
prémi 1 premium. *- asuransi* insurance premium. 2 bonus.
prémiér (*Thea.*) premier. **memp-kan** premiere s.t.

prémis premise.
prenjak k.o. bird.
préparat (*Med.*) blood smear.
prépéntip see PRÉVÉNTIF.
prérogatif prerogative.
prés₁ - *ban* k.o. procedure for tire repair in which a faulty inner tube is sealed by pressing rubber to it with a hot iron tool. **memp-, menge-** press. **nge-** 1 tight (of clothing). 2 urgent.
prés₂ 1 prize. 2 toy given away as prize in package (of crackerjacks, etc.).
présdir [*présidén diréktur*] president and director of a company.
préseden precedent.
préséntasi presentation. **mem-kan** present s.t.
présidén president. **ke-an** president's residence, pertaining to the president. *hélikopter ~* helicopter of the nation's president. **-an** presidency.
présidénsial, présidénsiil presidential.
présidium presidium.
presis see PERSIS.
présisi precision.
préskripsi prescription. **memp-kan** prescribe s.t.
préstasi achievement, performance. **mem-kan** advance s.t., improve performance of s.t.
préstise prestige.
prétél mem-i 1 dismantle, tear apart. 2 remove, take out. *Arloji dan uangnya di-i oléh perampok* The thief cleaned out his watch and money. 3 find out a secret, question thoroughly. 4 wipe out, clear away. *Pemain top meréka di-i satu persatu* Their top players were knocked out o. at a time. **-an** s.t. that has come off. *Ibu menemukan ~ kancing bajunya* Mother found the button that had come off her dress. **pem-an** tearing apart.
préténsi pretension. **ber-** have pretensions.
préténsius pretentious.
prévéntif, prévéntip preventive.
préviu preview. **memp-kan** preview s.t.
préwangan shaman, o. who has mystical powers.
pri see PRIBUMI.
pria man, male.
priai see PRIYAYI.
pribadi 1 individual, personal. *milik -* personal property. 2 person. **mem-** be internalized. **memp-kan** personify. **ke-an** 1 individuality. 2 personality. 3 identity. **pem(p)-an** 1 personalization. 2 embodiment. 3 personalism.
pribahasa see PERIBAHASA.
pribumi indigene, o. of native stock and not of immigrant blood. **mem-kan** turn over (an enterprise) to natives. **ke-an** the quality of being a native.
pribumisasi the process of turning enterprises over to the indigenous people.
Pries /pris/ Frisian.
prigel (*Jv*) skillful. **ke-an** skill.
prihal see PERI₁.
prihatin concerned, apprehensive. **ber-** be apprehensive, concerned. **memp-kan** be apprehensive about. **ke-an** concern.
prikik (*Sport*) free kick after minor foul.
prilaku see PERI₁.

prilém preliminary.
prima first-rate.
primadona (Coll.) woman who is considered excellent.
primata (Bio.) primate.
primbon (Jv) divining manual.
primér primary.
primitif primitive.
prin, pring (Mil.) answer to the call wérda ("Who goes there?"): friend (not foe).
pringas-pringis grin sheepishly.
pringgitan (Jv) open structure in front of mansion, behind the pendopo, for showing shadow plays or receiving visitors.
pringisan grin.
prinsip principle, tenet. pd -nya in principle. ber- have principles.
prinsipiil, prinsipil principal, basic.
prioritas, prioritét priority. memberikan - jalan yield the right of way. memp-kan give priority to.
prisma prism.
prit sound of blown whistle. - jigo be stopped and made to pay 2,500 rupiah by a traffic cop. di- (Coll.) be stopped by the police.
privat private. lés - private lessons.
privé private.
privilése privilege.
priwil a bicycle gear that allows wheels to turn without engaging pedals.
priya see PRIA.
priyayi (Jv) o. belonging to upper classes. ke-an status of being upper class.
pro pro. - rakyat pro-people. - dan kontra pro's and con's.
probabilitas probability.
problém, problim problem.
problématik set of problems.
procot (Vulg.) be born. mem-kan give birth. tiap tahun ~ anak have a baby every year.
prodéo free, without cost. hotél - (Humorous) prison.
produk product.
produksi production. ber- be in production. Pabrik itu blm ~ The factory is not in production yet. mem- be productive, produce. memp-kan produce, put out.
produktif productive. mem-kan make productive. ke-an productivity.
produktivitas, produktivitét productivity.
produsén producer.
produsér, produsir memp- produce.
profési profession. ber- professional. ke-an professionalism.
profésionalisme professionalism.
profésor professor.
proféssi see PROFÉSI.
profil 1 appearance. 2 profile. ber- have a certain appearance. ~ tentara have a military appearance.
profisiat expression uttered when offering congratulations.
prognosa, prognose prognosis.

program, programa program. - kerja sama a cooperative program. memp-, memp-kan make part of o.'s program, plan.
progrésif progressive. ke-an progressiveness.
progrésivitas, progrésivitét progressiveness.
prohibisionis prohibitionist.
prokém (Jkt) 1 jargon of youth in Jkt. 2 street kids.
proklamasi proclamation. memp-kan proclaim, announce.
proklamator o. who proclaims. - kemerdékaan the proclaimers of independence.
proklamir memp-kan proclaim. pem- o. who proclaims.
prokurasi (Leg.) power of attorney.
proletar proletarian. mem-kan make a proletarian out of. ke-an the quality of being proletarian.
proletariat proletariat.
proletarisasi proletarianization.
proliferasi proliferation.
prolog prologue.
promés (Fin.) promissory note.
promosi 1 promotion of a product. 2 (Acad.) dissertation defense. memp-(kan) promote (a product).
promosional promotional.
promotor (Acad.) dissertation supervisor. 2 o. who champions s.t. - kebébasan wanita champion of women's rights.
promovéndus (Acad.) a candidate for a doctorate.
prop₁ cork, stopper, plug. topi - topee, pith helmet.
prop₂ [propadéus] preparation for entering a university course or profession.
Prop. [propinsi] province.
propadéus, propaedéus, propaedéuse /propadéus/ preparation for entering (a course, a profession).
propaganda propaganda. ber- make publicity, propaganda. memp-i subject s.o. to propaganda or publicity. memp-kan give publicity, plug. Ia ~ produksi pabriknya He plugged the output of this factory.
propagandis propagandist.
propéler (Av.) propeller.
properti property (in TV, film making).
propési see PROFÉSI.
propésor see PROFÉSOR.
propil see PROFIL.
propinsi see PROVINSI.
propokatip see PROVOKATIF.
proporsi proportion.
proporsional, proporsionil reasonable, in accordance with what o. would expect. berpakaian secara - be suitably dressed for the situation. harga - reasonable price.
prosa prose. memp-kan put s.t. in prose.
prosais 1 prose writer. 2 prosaic.
prosedur procedure.
proseduril procedural.
prosén see PERSÉN.
proséntase, proséntasi percentage.

proséntuil on a percentage basis.
prosés 1 process. **2** legal action. - *perbal* verbal official report, minutes, deposition. **memp-kan** process s.t. **pem-** instrument for processing. **pem-an** processing.
prosési procession.
prosodi prosody.
prospék prospect, future chances.
prospéktus promotional leaflet.
prostat, prostata (*Anat.*) prostate.
prostitusi prostitution. **memp-kan** prostitute.
protéina protein.
protéksi economic protection. **memp-** protect (an industry).
protéksionis protectionist.
protéktorat protectorate.
protés protest. **mem-, memp-** protest. **-an** protest made. **-²an** various protests. **pem-** protestor.
Protéstan Protestant.
protokol₁ protocol. *jalan-jalan* - main streets of city (over which official visitor would pass). **ke-an** having to do with protocol. **-²an** various (annoying) protocols. ~ *birokrasi* games o. must play in dealing with bureaucracy.
protokol₂ master of ceremonies at formal functions.
protokolér having to do with protocol.
protol (*Jv*) apart, in pieces. **mem-i** take apart into pieces.
proton (*Phys.*) proton.
provinsi province.
provinsial provincial.
provinsialisme provincialism.
provinsialistis provincial.
provisi (*Fin.*) commission.
provokasi provocation. **memp-(kan)** provoke s.t. **ter-** provoked.
provokatif, provokatip provocative.
provokator provocateur.
provost military police in air force or navy.
proyék project. - *pola* pilot project.
proyéksi projection, forecast. **mem-kan 1** project. ~ *rasa* project a feeling. **2** plan or forecast. *Tingkat produksi utk bulan Januari yg di-kan* the level of production projected for the month of January.
proyéktil missile. - *kendali* guided missile.
proyéktir project s.t. or an image.
proyéktor projector.
PRRI/Permésta [*Pemerintah Révolusionér Républik Indonésia/Perjuangan Semésta*] Total Struggle and the Republic of Indonesia's Revolutionary Gvt., a rebellion in Sumatra and N. Sulawesi against the central gvt. in the late 1950s.
pruf, prup printer's proof. - *bersih/halaman* page proof. - *kotor* galley proof.
prusi verdigris.
ps.₁ [*pasal*] article (in legal documents, etc.).
ps.₂ [*pasar*] market.
ps.₃ [*pejabat sementara*] temporary official.
Psi. [*psikologi*] psychology.

PSI [*Partai Sosialis Indonésia*] Indonesian Socialist party.
PSII [*Partai Serikat Islam Indonésia*] Isl. party of Indonesia.
psikiater psychiatrist.
psikiatri psychiatry.
psikiatrik, psikiatris psychiatric.
psikis psychological, mental.
psikoanalis psychoanalyst.
psikoanalisa psychoanalysis.
psikolinguistik psycholinguistics.
psikolog psychologist.
psikologi psychology.
psikopat psychopath.
psk. [*pasukan*] (*Mil.*) troops.
PSPB [*Pendidikan Sejarah Perjuangan Bangsa*] the History of the National Struggle, a subject in school.
Pt. [*Pendéta*] Rev., title for a minister.
PT₁ [*Perséroan Terbatas*] Inc., Ltd.
PT₂ [*Panglima Tertinggi*] officer the rank of governor of a region.
PT₃ [*Perguruan Tinggi*] Institute of Higher Education.
PTIK [*Perguruan Tinggi Ilmu Kepolisian*] Police Academy.
PTIP [(*Départemén*) *Perguruan Tinggi dan Ilmu Pengetahuan*] Department of Higher Education and Sciences.
PTM [*Persekutuan Tanah Melayu*] Federation of Malaya.
PTP [*Pos, Télékomunikasi (dan) Pariwisata*] Post Office, Telecommunications, and Tourism.
PTT [*Pos, Télgrap dan Télpon*] Postal, Telegraph, and Telephone Service.
PU₁ [*Pejabat Utama*] high official.
PU₂ [*Pembantu Utama*] secretary-general of a ministry.
PU₃ [*Pekerjaan Umum*] Public Works.
puadé see KUADÉ.
puah bah! phooey!
puak group, tribe. **ber-²** in groups. **ke-an** having to do with the group.
puaka gnome, spirit (inhabiting a certain place). **ber-** haunted.
pual₁ voile.
pual₂ vortex.
pualam 1 marble. **2** alabaster. **mem-** be white like alabaster.
puan₁ plate for betel.
puan₂ (*Lit.*) title or deferential term of address for a woman.
puan₃ see KELAPA.
puar cardamom.
puas satisfied, contented. - *lelas* satiated. **ber-** *hati* be satisfied. **mem-i** satisfy. **mem-kan** satisfy, satisfactory, satisfying. **ke-an** satisfaction. **pem-an** satiation.
puasa 1 fast. **2** (*Isl.*) fasting month. **ber-** fast, observe the fasting period.
puatang (*Ch*) have no chance.
puber, pubér, pubertas, pubértas puberty.

publik public.
publikasi publication.
publisir memp- publicize.
publisistik mass communications (as a field of study).
publisitas publicity.
pucat pale due to illness or fright. - *kuam/kusam/ lesi/manai/pasi* deathly pale. - *kelabu* ashen with fright. **mem-** become pale. **mem-kan** bleach s.t. **ke-an** being pale. **pem-an** discoloration.
pucuk 1 tip of a leaf, shoot, sprout. - *dicinta ulam tiba* all that o. wishes for is fulfilled (o. wishes for a shoot, but a whole vegetable appears). *Dendamnya sampai ke - rambut* She hates him from the bottom of her feet to the ends of her hair. - *rebung* pattern of cloth or carving similar to herringbone. 2 tip of s.t. - *api* tongue of flame. *di - kekuasaan* at the peak of power. - *pimpinan* 1 general management. 2 governing board, central board. 3 a classifier. *se- bedil* a rifle. *se- surat* a letter (epistle). **ber-** sprout, bud.
pucung₁ heron.
pucung₂ tree that produces *keluak*.
pudak k.o. pandanus.
pudar 1 pale, faded. 2 weak, dim. **mem-** fade, dim. *Cita-cita Orde Baru* ~ The ideals of the New Order faded. **mem-kan, memp-kan** 1 dim s.t. ~ *makna* make the meaning vague. 2 tarnish (silver). **ke-an** fading away.
pudat full to the brim.
pudék [*pembantu dékan*] assistant dean.
pudel poodle.
puder (face) powder.
pudi powder, dust of precious stones. **mem-kan** pound, grind.
puding₁ croton plant.
puding₂ see PODENG.
pudur extinguished.
pugar mem- restore. **mem-i** restore (several things). **pem-an** restoration.
puguh (*Jkt*) for sure, certain. - *aja* of course. **ke-an** *nggak* ~ out of line, not proper.
puhun see POHON₂.
puing₁ ruins, debris. **mem-** become ruins. **memp- kan** lay s.t. in ruins.
puing₂ see PUYENG.
puisi poetry. **per-an** pertaining to poetry.
puitik, puitis poetic.
puja worship, adoration. **mem-** worship, revere. **-an** 1 adoration, worship. 2 idol. **pem-** worshiper. **pem-an** 1 place of sacrifice, temple. 2 worship, veneration.
pujangga 1 man of letters. 2 poet. **ke-an** literary.
puji praise. **mem-** praise, commend. *Ia suka ~ muridnya di kelas* He is fond of praising his student in class. **mem-²** praise, extol. **mem-kan** recommend. *Buku ini sangat di-kan* This book strongly recommended. **ke-an** praiseworthy. **-an** 1 praise, eulogy. 2 recommendation. ~ *istiméwa* with honors. **-²an** prayers of adoration. **pem-** flatterer.
pujuk see BUJUK.

pujur profligate, dissolute.
pujut strangulation. **mem-(kan)** strangle.
pukal lump, block. *se- mas* a lump of gold.
pukang 1 crotch. 2 thigh of animal. **mem-** tear apart.
pukas see PUKES.
pukat seine, dragnet. - *harimau* large trawling net. **mem-** trawl. **pem-** 1 fisherman. 2 trawler.
pukau drug to make o. sleep. **mem-** 1 drug. 2 mesmerize. - *penonton* mesmerize the audience. **ter-** 1 stunned. 2 mesmerized. **-an** charm. **pem-** s.t. that stuns, holds o. entranced.
pukes vulva.
puki (*Vulg.*) vagina. - *mai/mak* motherfucker.
pukis k.o. butter cake.
puk oping, puk ping menthol inhaler for colds.
pukta excellent.
pukul 1 strike. - *besi* hammer. - *rata* all in all, in general. - *rata dpt dikatakan, buku ini seolah-olah merupakan éséi* In general this book seems only to be an essay. **mem-ratakan** beat all of s.t. *Kita - ratakan saja KNIL* Let us wipe out the Dutch mercenaries! *salah* - 1 miss. 2 make a mistake. *sekali* - with o. blow. 2 blow, o. fell swoop. *Sekali - ia bisa dpt untung jutaan rupiah* In o. fell swoop he was able to make a profit of millions of rupiah. 3 o'clock. - *berapa?* What time is it? - *tiga* It is three o'clock. **ber-²an** hit e.o. - **mem-** hit e.o. **mem-** 1 hit, strike. ~ *bola* (*Sport*) serve (in tennis). ~ *kawat* send a cable. 2 defeat. ~ *mundur* (*Mil.*) repulse. **mem-i** hit (several things or again and again). **mem-kan** hit with. **ter-** be struck. ~ *mundur* beaten back. ~ *rubuh* knocked down. **ke-** stunned, struck by accident. **-an** 1 stroke. ~ *dada* breast stroke. 2 blow, hit, strike. 3 good fortune. *Ia mendapat* ~ *karena mobilnya terjual mahal sekali* He had good luck because his car brought a high price. **pem-** 1 hammer, cudgel, beater. ~ *golf* golf club. 2 o. who strikes.
pul₁ (car)pool.
pul₂ pole.
pula 1 likewise, as well. *Itu benar. Ini benar* - That is true. This is also true. *Ia tertawa. Demikian - temannya* He laughed. So did his friend. *tambahan* - and furthermore. 2 again. *Bisnya berhenti di Hayam Wuruk. Tiba di Harmoni bisnya berhenti* - The bus stopped at Hayam Wuruk. At Harmoni it stopped again. 3 (who, where, how, etc.) else? *Siapa - yg datang?* Who else is coming? 4 (who, where, why, how, etc.) do you think, (what, etc.) in the world. *Bagaimana - bisa dikerjakan kalau tdk begini?* How do you think it can be done, if not this way? *Mengapa - begitu kerjanya?* Why in the world are you doing it like that? 5 do unnecessarily. *Sdh tahu, kenapa tanya* -? You know. Why do you have to ask? *blm* - still not. *Sdh jam sepuluh ia blm - datang* It is already 10 and he still has not come.
pulai k.o. tree whose bark is medicinal and with corklike wood.
pulak see PULA.
pulan 1 good-tasting (of cooked rice or tubers

cooked to proper softness). **2** smooth and mellow. *suara* - a mellow voice.

pulang 1 return home. *Saya mau* - I want to go home. *Ssdh lima tahun baru ia* - He came back only after five years. - *balik* 1 vice versa. 2 to and fro. 3 round trip. - *hari* returning the same day. - *ke alam baka/ke hadirat Tuhan* pass away, die. - *kerja* come home from work. - *pergi* round trip. - *pokok* make no profit, come out even. *Usaha dagang itu hanya* - *pokok* The investment only made enough to return the capital. - *pulih* full recovery. **2** be left up to. *Hal itu* - *kpd Tuan* That is up to you. - *maklum* left to the reader or audience. **se-** upon returning. **ber-** die. ~ *ke rahmatullah* die, pass on. **ber-an** go home (of many people). *Karena kecéwa kaum transmigran* ~ *ke Jawa* The transmigrants returned to Java because they failed. **mem-i** return to a place. **mem-kan 1** give back, return, bring back, send s.t. back to where it came from. *Pembantu saya tdk becus. Saya -kan saja* My servant was incapable. I sent him back home. **2** return what has been expended. ~ *tenaga/pokok* allow o. to recoup o.'s efforts or capital. **ter-** be left up to s.o. else, be thrown back in o.'s court. *Saya hanya memberi informasi; mengenai keputusan terakhir* ~ *pd anda* I only am giving information. As far as the final decision goes that is left up to you. **ke-an** action of going back. **pem-an 1** return, restitution. **2** repatriation.

pulas₁ fast asleep. **ke-an** being fast asleep. ~ *tidurnya amat menyegarkan* Her deep sleep was very refreshing.

pulas₂ se- a dab. **mem-** paint, varnish, smear. *Muka yg di- utk menghadap penonton* A face that has been made up to face the audience. **mem-i** smear on. *roti di-i dgn mentéga* bread smeared with butter. **mem-kan** apply s.t. to, put s.t. on to. **-an 1** outward appearance. **2** s.t. smeared on. ~ *cairan* a liquid smear.

pulas₃ mem- 1 turn, wring. - *telinga* tweak the ears. **2** twist, distort. **3** have colic. **-an** k.o. *rambutan* with short nubbles as if the hair had been tweaked off.

pulasari liana with yellow flowers.

pulau island. - *déwata* the island of the Gods, Bali. - *karang* atoll. - *Perca (Sumatra)* rubber-producing island. **se-** the entire island. *Sekarang* ~ *itu tak kurang dr empat ratus org* Now in the entire island there are no less than 400 people. **mem-kan 1** isolate, insulate. **2** boycott. **ter-** isolated. **ke-an** archipelago.

pulauisme insularity.

pulé see PULAI.

pulen see PULAN.

pules see PULAS₁.

puli₁ o. of the parts of the automobile chassis.

puli₂ rice cracker.

pulih 1 recovered from an illness. **2** restored, repaired. **mem-kan** repair, restore. ~ *ékonomi* put the economy back on its feet. **ter-kan** can be restored. *Hati yg hancur tdk* ~ *kembali* A broken

heart cannot be put back together. **pem-an 1** recovery. **2** repair, restoration.

pulisi see POLISI.

pulkanisir see VULKANISIR.

pulpén fountain pen. - *atom* ballpoint pen.

pulsa beat, throb, pulse. *Biayanya interlokal ke Jkt Rp50 setiap* - The long distance rate to Jkt is 50 rupiah per tick on the meter. *denyut* - the pulse beat.

puluh counter for a multiple of 10. *dua* - twenty. **se-** ten. **se-nya** ten of them. *Berapa* ~? How much are 10 of them? **ber-²** in tens. ~ *tahun yg lalu* several decades ago. ~ *abad* tens of centuries. **-an 1** tens, decades. **2** 10-rupiah note. **per(se)-an** decimal.

pulun ber-, ber-² 1 rise (of smoke). **2** rise like smoke (of thoughts).

pulung₁ pellet. **mem-** roll into pellets. **mem-i** roll into pellets (plural). **-an** s.t. rolled into pellets.

pulung₂ (*Jv*) flash of light which gives o. power enabling him to be legitimized as ruler. *kejatuhan/ketiban* - 1 have power bestowed on o. through this flash. 2 have bad luck (i.e., be given an unwanted task).

pulur see EMPULUR.

pulut 1 glutinous rice. *beras* - sticky rice. **2** birdlime. **si-** sticky rice.

pumigasi see FUMIGASI.

pumpun ber- flock together. **mem-** collect, gather. **ter-** concentrated. **-an 1** meeting place. **2** center.

pun 1 (*Lit.*) then, subsequently. *Tdk lama kemudian ia- matilah* Not long thereafter, he passed away. **2** also. *Ia pergi, saya-pergi* He left and I did, too. **3** even. *Seorg- tak hadir/Tak seorg- yg hadir* Not a soul came. *Makan! Melihat- tdk* I did not eat any. I did not even see it! *O tdk apa-apa! Pénsil- jadi* Oh it does not matter. A pencil will do as well. *Jika mati-, matilah* Even if I die, so be it. *Menembus hutan- saya berani, asal . . .* I would dare go through a jungle, as long as . . . **4** who, where, what, etc. ever it might be, everywhere, everyone, everything, etc. *Ditaruh di mana-* Put it anywhere. *Apa- mahal sekarang ini* Everything is expensive these days. *Bagaimana-, saya tdk bisa* No matter how I try, I cannot do it.

punah extinct. **mem-kan** destroy, exterminate. **ke-an** extinction. **pem-an** extermination.

punai pigeon.

punakawan (*Jv*) servants of royalty in *wayang*.

punat (*Med.*) core of a boil.

punca 1 flap, tail, end. **2** beginning, introduction, elementary. - *bahasa Nippon* elementary Japanese. - *beliung* cyclone. - *tali* the end of a rope. **3** initial cause. - *perselisihan* cause of conflict.

puncak 1 top, summit. - *gigi* crown of tooth. - *paru* upper part of lung. **2** peak, mount. - *Tursina* Mt. Sinai. **3** acme, zenith. **mem-** culminate, reach a crest. **mem-i** allow s.t. to reach its peak, make s.t. the high point. *Kubiarkan dia* ~ *perasaannya* I let her alone to allow her emotions to peak. *Période ini di-i dgn lahirnya Manipol* With the birth of the *Manipol* doctrine, this period reached its peak. **pem-** summit, culminating point.

pundak 1 shoulder. **2** neck. - *bukit* ridge of a hill. **mem-** carry on the back.

pundén (*Jv*) holy place (graves of ancestors, sacred trees, etc.).

pundi 1 earthen jar to hold water. **2** crockery piggy-bank. **-²** purse, bag. ~ *kencing* (*Anat.*) bladder. ~ *udara* air pocket.

punding knot.

pungak-pinguk be or look embarrassed.

punggah mem- load, cargo. **-an** place for loading cargo. **pem-an** loading.

punggal mem- break off the point of s.t.

punggawa court official in Jv shadow play.

pungguk k.o. owl.

punggung back. - *buku* spine of book. - *kuda* bareback (on horse). **mem-i** turn o.'s back to.

punggur tree trunk.

pungkah piece, lump.

pungkasan final, end. *istirahat yg* - final rest.

pungki see PENGKI.

pungkir see MUNGKIR.

pungkur 1 rear end, posterior. **2** residue.

pungli [*pungutan liar*] toll or tariff collected without proper legal authority.

pungliwan o. who extracts illegal tolls.

pungsi see FUNGSI.

pungut adopted. *anak* - adopted child. *sdr* - adopted relative. **mem- 1** pick, pick up. *Jangan di-!* Do not pick it up! **2** collect. *Ia* ~ *pajak* He collected the taxes. **3** harvest. *Ia sekarang* ~ *hasil pekerjaannya* He is harvesting the results of his work now. **4** quote. *Ia* ~ *dr kitab yg lain* He was quoting from other books. **5** adopt (child, etc.). ~ *kembali* recover s.t. ~ *suara* put to the vote, collect votes. **mem-i** pick up, collect many things. **-an 1** pickings, harvest. **2** quotation. **3** tax levied. ~ *pelabuhan udara* airport tax. **4** amount collected, collection (in church). ~ *suara* vote taken. **pem-** collector. **pem-an 1** harvest. **2** collection. ~ *suara* taking of a vote. **3** adoption.

punjul (*Jv*) a bit over in amount. - *lima kilo* a bit more than five kilograms. **ke-an** superiority, being a bit better or more than others. *Ia suka menonjol-nonjolkan* ~*nya* He likes to show off his superiority.

punjung trellis, bower.

punjut mem- tie together.

punktuasi /pungtuasi/ punctuation.

punokawan see PUNAKAWAN.

punsu (*Ch*) able, talented.

punt /pent/ **1** that is the end of it, period. *Dibayar saja.* - Just pay for it; period. **2** period, point.

puntal ber-² 1 winding round. **2** in balls. **mem- 1** wind around. **2** shorten. **-an 1** bobbin, spool. **2** ball of wool.

puntang-panting see PONTANG-PANTING.

punten (*Sd*) excuse me.

punti see BUAH.

puntianak k.o. vampire or blood-sucking supernatural being.

puntil susu nipple.

puntir mem- wind, twist firmly. **-an 1** torsion. **2** s.t. twisted. **ke-** be twisted.

puntul dull, blunt.

puntung 1 blunt. **2** butt, stub, stump. - *rokok* cigarette butt. - *berasap* an impossibility. **3** maimed, crippled, mutilated. **mem-** become blunt. **mem-kan 1** blunt. **2** maim, mutilate.

punuk see PONOK.

punya 1 (*Coll.*) have, possess. *Saya* - *mobil* I have a car. - *hajat* intend to hold a ceremonial meal. - *kerja* celebrate a rite (marriage, circumcision, etc.). **2** belonging. *Siapa* - *ini?/* - *siapa ini?* Who does this belong to? *Itu saya* -/*Itu* - *saya* It is mine. *Itu* -*mu, ini* -*nya* That belongs to you. This belongs to him. *yg* - the owner. *Lampu ini diberikan oléh yg* - *rumah* The landlord provided this lamp. **3** (*Coll.*) a possessive marker. *di saya* - *dada* in my breast. *Siapa lagi* - *olah kalau tdk Wan Saléh* Whose trick was this, if not Wan Saleh's. **4** after, with. *tunggu* - *tunggu* after much waiting. *omong* - *omong* by the way. *Runding* - *runding, rembuk* - *rembuk, meréka mupakatkan* . . . After much discussion and talking, they agreed to . . . **ber-1** have property, be well-to-do. **2** have an owner. *Gadis itu sdh* ~ That girl is already spoken for. **memp-i** possess, have, own. *Para penumpang hrs* ~ *surat cacar* All passengers must have a smallpox certificate. **ke-an** possession, property. *Itu* ~ *saya* That is mine.

pupu degree of consanguinity. (*sdr*) *se-* first cousin. (*sdr*) *dua* - 2d cousin.

pupuh₁ ber- fight. **mem-** beat.

pupuh₂ strophe.

pupuk₁ manure, fertilizer. - *bawang* o. who is the worst in a group. - *buatan* artificial fertilizer. - *hijau* green manure. - *kandang* manure. - *subur* **mem-suburkan** make land fertile. **mem- 1** fertilize, manure. **2** foster, cultivate. ~ *rasa cinta* foster a feeling of love. **pem-** enricher, cultivator. **pem-an** fertilizing, cultivating. ~ *modal* building up of capital.

pupuk₂ (*Jv*) **m-, mem-** put traditional medicines on a wound.

pupun mem- collect (e.g. rubber). **mem-i** gather from. **-an** gathering of rubber. **pem-** s.t. used in collecting.

pupur face powder. **ber-** powder o.'s face. **mem-i** powder s.t. **mem-kan** put on as a powder.

pupus₁ budding leaf, leaf that has just come out.

pupus₂ 1 wiped out, obliterated. **2** disappeared. **mem-(kan)** exterminate, obliterate, wipe out.

puput₁ whistle, flute. **ber-** blow. *Angin* ~ The wind is blowing. **mem-i** make s.t. whistle. **-an 1** pair of bellows. **2** blowing of the wind.

puput₂ crowbar. **mem-** break, pry open. ~ *pintu dgn linggis* break a door open with crowbar.

pura₁ 1 bag. **2** fund.

pura₂ Balinese temple, shrine.

pura-pura 1 pretend. *Ia* - *tdk melihat saya* He pretended not to see me. **2** pseudo, mock. *lambang* - pseudosymbol. *perang* - mock battle. **ber-** feign, pretend. **ke-an** dissimilation, pretense.

purata (*Math.*) mean.

purba old, ancient, antique. *Mesir* - ancient Egypt. *kemurnian* - primeval purity.

purbakala olden times. **ke-an** archaeological. *dinas* ~ archaeological service. ~ *Islam* Isl. monuments.

purbakalawan archaeologist.

purbasangka prejudice. **ber-** prejudiced.

purée purée. **mem-** mash, make into a purée. *Kentangnya di-* Mash the potatoes.

purék [*pembantu réktor*] assistant to the rector.

Purel [*Public Relations*] public relations.

puri 1 castle, royal palace. **2** town. **3** Balinese house of worship.

purifikasi purification.

purik go home for sympathy out of anger. *Isterinya - ke rumah* His wife ran home to her mother.

puring see PUDING₁.

Purn. [*purnawirawan, purnakaryawan*] retired, emeritus.

purna- complete, post- (in formal words or titles). *-jual* after sales. *-sarana* superstructure. *-sarjana* postgraduate. **ke-an** fullness, completeness.

purnakaryawan retired civil servant.

purnakata what is said in conclusion.

purnama full moon.

purnaswasta o. retired in private sector.

purnawirawan retired armed services officer.

puru sore, boil, ulcer. - *koci* syphilitic canker. - *sembilik/sembilit* piles, hemorrhoids.

puruk mem-kan hide s.t. inside. *hanya ku-kan di dlm hati* I only buried it in my heart. **ter-** be hidden, buried. *Matahari* ~ *di balik gunung* The sun sank behind the mountain.

purun k.o. rush used for basket weaving.

purus diarrhea. **mem-** suffer from diarrhea.

purut rough-skinned. *jeruk* - k.o. nubbled lime used as condiment.

purwa see WAYANG.

purwaka in the beginning, formerly.

purwakanti (*Ling.*) assonance, alliteration.

purwocéng k.o. aphrodisiac.

pusa 1 momentum. **2** desire to do s.t.

pusaka heirloom. **mem-i** inherit. **mem-kan** leave behind.

pusar navel. - *kepala* crown at top of head. *-²* whorl (of hair). **ber-** revolve, whirl around. **mem-** whirl s.t. around. **-an 1** rotation. **2** handle, crank. **3** vortex. ~ *air* eddy, whirlpool. ~ *angin* cyclone, whirlwind.

pusara₁ 1 cemetery. **2** grave.

pusara₂ reins. - *negara* reins of gvt.

pusat 1 navel. **2** center. - *pemerintahan* seat of gvt. **3** center, central, main. *kantor* - central office. *Jkt* - central part of Jkt. - *tenaga listrik* electrical power installation. - *berat* center of gravity. - *roda* wheel hub. - *telur* embryo in egg. **se-** concentric. **ber-** *kpd* center, concentrate on. **ber-kan** have a center at. **mem-** be centered. *Pengembangan* ~ *di*

pedésaan Development is concentrated in rural areas. **mem-kan, memper-kan** concentrate on, focus on. ~ *perhatiannya pd studinya* concentrate his attention on his studies. **pem-an 1** concentration. **2** centralization. **per-an** being focused on.

puser (*Jv*) navel.

pusing 1 whirling, dizzy. *Saya - kepala* I am dizzy. **2** be puzzled, confused, worried. *Tak usah - karena itu!* Do not worry about that! *-²* go around trying to get s.t. done. **ber-** turn. **mem-** spin s.t. **mem-kan 1** turn s.t. round. **2** make dizzy. **3** puzzle, confuse s.o. **4** worry about s.t. *Hal itu tdk perlu di-kan* No need to rack your brains about that matter. **ter-²** rotate. **ke-an 1** worry, anxiousness. **2** headache. **-an** rotation. **pem-** centrifuge. **per-an 1** revolution, turning. **2** racking o.'s brains.

Puskesmas [*Pusat Keséhatan Masyarakat*] local gvt. clinic.

puso parched, dried up. *sawah* - rice fields that have dried up. **mem-kan 1** dry s.t. up. **2** fail to pay back (a debt). *Semua krédit Bimas cenderung di-kan* There is a tendency to default on credits from *Bimas*.

puspa (*Lit.*) flower. - *ragam/warna* variegated. **ke-ragaman** variegation.

Puspén [*Pusat Penerangan*] information center.

puspita (*Lit.*) flower.

pustaka 1 book. **2** divining manual. **ke-an 1** literature. **2** documents. *Pemakaian bahasa Belanda sbg bahasa* ~ *masih tetap diperlukan pula* It is still necessary to use Dutch as a language of documentation. **3** bibliography. **per-an** library.

pustakawan librarian.

pusu₁ (*M*) troop, band. **ber-²** gather in crowds.

pusu₂ anthill.

pusung dreamer, dullard.

pusut awl.

putao (*Ch*) rice wine.

putar turning. - *balik* **1** turn around. **2** swindle. **3** constantly changing opinion. **mem-balikkan** twist, pervert. ~ *perkataan* twist o.'s words. **pem-balikan** distortion, twisting. ~ *fakta* twisting of facts. - *belit* ambiguous. - *negeri* revolution, coup d'état. - *pengayuh* go around for pleasure. **se-1** around. ~ *27 Désémber* around Dec. 27. *di* ~ *api* all around the fire. **2** in the vicinity. **3** on the subject of. ~ *persoalan itu* concerning that problem. **ber- 1** rotate. ~ *arah* change directions. **2** insincere, dishonest. *Lidahnya sering* ~ *balik* You cannot rely on what he says. ~ *haluan* **1** take another direction. **2** assume another policy. **ber-²** beat around the bush. **mem- 1** turn, revolve. ~ *tongkat* twirl a cane. **2** wind, twist. ~ *angka* dial a number. ~ *jam* wind a watch. ~ *lidah* pervert words, facts. ~ *otak* trouble o.'s head about s.t. ~ *percakapan* change the subject. ~ *uang* turn over money, make productive use of money. **3** show a film. **mem-i** go around s.t. **mem-kan** turn over (o.'s money). **-an 1** circle. ~ *air* whirlpool. ~ *ganas/sétan* vicious circle. **2** crank, windlass. **3** wheel. **4** showing. ~ *filem* film showing. **pem-** (*Anat.*) neckbone. **pem-an** process of turning s.t. over. ~ *filem* showing, running of a film. ~ *uang* turning over o.'s capital, reinvestment. **per-an 1** rotation. *kecepatan* ~ speed of revolution. **2** change. ~ *nama* change the name (of a license registration).

puter₁ k.o. dove.

puter₂ (*Jv.*) see PUTAR.

putera 1 prince. - *mahkota* crown prince. **2** son, child (of o. who is respected). *-nya berapa?* How many children do you have? **3** a son of (o. from) a certain place. *Kami -² Indonésia* . . . We, the sons of Indonesia . . . **4** male. **ber- 1** have a child. **2** be confined with child. **3** have a son.

puteri 1 princess. **2** daughter, girl (of o. who is respected). **3** female. - *duyung* mermaid. - *malu* a shrub, Mimosa pudica. **ke-an 1** women's affairs. **2** womanhood.

putih 1 white. - *bersih* pure white. - *kuning* cream-colored. - *lesi/lesih* very white. - *mangkak* white that has become greyish. - *metah* snow white. - *telur* egg white. **2** pale, fair skinned. **3** pure. *Buku ini tak - dr segala kekurangan* This book is not free from all shortcomings. **ber-** *mata* **1** be annoyed at having to wait. **2** be disgraced. **ber-** *tulang* dead. *Lebih baik* ~ *tulang drp* ~ *mata* Better dead than disgraced. **mem- 1** turn white all over. **2** fade, turn pale. **mem-kan 1** bleach s.t. **2** whitewash. **3** obtain legal papers for s.t. *rumah yg blm di-kan* house for which a building certificate has not been obtained. ~ *modal gelap* launder money. **ke-²an** whitish. **pem-** whitener, bleach. **pem-an 1** bleaching, whitewashing, purifying. **2** process of obtaining the legal papers for s.t. ~ *pendaftaran tivi* registering the tv set legally through a program of forgiveness of delinquent payments.

putik (*Biol.*) **1** bud, pistil. **2** ovary. **ber-** beginning to bear fruit.

puting 1 handle, hilt. **2** stalk. - *susu* nipple.

puting beliung whirlwind, waterspout.

putra see PUTERA.

putri see PUTERI.

putu steamed cake. - *mayang* k.o. cake made of rice noodles fashioned into a wreath.

putus 1 broken off, severed. *Benangnya sdh* - The thread has broken. - *sekolah* drop out of school. - *arang* irreparable. - *asa/harapan* lose hope. *tak -²(nya)* incessantly. **ber-** *asa* desperate, hopeless. **ke-asaan** despair. - *bicara* be at o.'s wit's end. - *harga* fixed price. - *napas* breathless, exhausted. - *nyawa* die. - *rezeki* lose o.'s livelihood. **2** finished, over. **3** definite, decisive. **mem-** interrupt. **mem-(i), mem-kan 1** decide, resolve. **2** break off, interrupt. ~ *cakap* interrupt. ~ *pertempuran* break off the engagement. **3** finish. **4** break a promise. ~ *harapan* dash o.'s hopes. **5** sever s.t. **(ter)-²** broken, interrupted. **-an 1** decision. **2** (*Leg.*) sentence, verdict. **3** fracture, break. **4** resolution (adopted at meeting). **ke-an 1** decision. ~ *Présidén* a presidential decree. **2** conclusion. **3** (*Leg.*) sentence, finding of a court. ~ *sela* intermediate decision. **4** termination, expiration, end. **berke-an** having a resolution. *tdk* ~ unresolved. **pem-an** cutting, severance. ~ *hubungan diplomatik* severance of diplomatic relations.

puyan body dirt. **ber-** dirty.

puyang see LEMPUYANG.

puyeng 1 headache. **2** confused, dizzy. *Dia sdh - karena tdk bisa menjawab pertanyaan itu* He was confused because he could not answer the question. **ber-²** swirl, whirl around. **ke-an** dizziness.

puyuh₁ quail.

puyuh₂ see ANGIN.

puyunghai see FUYONGHAI.

PWI [*Persatuan Wartawan Indonésia*] Journalists' Association of Indonesia.

PYM [*Paduka Yang Mulia*] Your Excellency.

pyuh-pyuh expression of surprise.

Q

q /ki/ q, the 17th letter of the alphabet.

q- almost all words with **q** may also be written with **k**. For entries with **q-** see **k-**.

Qabil (*Isl.*) Cain, Abel's brother.

qari (*Isl.*) reciter of the Koran.

qariah (*Isl.*) female reciter of the Koran.

Qur'an see KORAN.

R

r /ér/ r, the 18th letter of the alphabet.

R. [*Radén*] (*Jv*) masculine noble title.

ra. [*radiallahu an(hu)*] (*Isl.*) an exclamation uttered after mention of o. of Muh.'s companions or the prophets: May God bless him!

RA.₁ [*Radén Ajeng*] (*Jv*) title of unmarried female nobility.

RA.₂ [*Radén Ayu*] (*Jv*) title of married female nobility.

raad see RAD.

RAB [*Rencana Anggaran Belanja*] 1 budget plan. 2 draft budget.

raba - *rubu* in a hurry. **me-** 1 feel s.t. *Ia ~ di kantongnya* He searched in his pocket. *~ hati sendiri* search o.'s own heart. 2 grope (often with sexual implications). 3 guess. *Ia ~ maksud org lain* He guessed the other's intentions. **me-²** 1 grope, feel o.'s way. *Org buta itu ~* The blind man was feeling his way. 2 fondle. *Ia ~ kepala anaknya* She fondled her child's head. **me-i** carefully or repeatedly touch s.t. *Dokter ~ buah dadanya, kalau-kalau ada kanker* The doctor carefully examined her breasts to make sure there was no tumor. **-an** 1 touch. 2 groping with the hand. 3 guess, estimate. **pe-** organ of touch.

rabah shrike.

rabak 1 large tear, rip. 2 in tatters. **me-** tear.

raban me- 1 jabber, babble. 2 rave, be delirious.

rabas (*M*) drizzle.

rabat rebate, quantity discount.

rabbi (*Bib.*) Lord.

rabiés rabies.

rabik, rabit torn, tattered at the edges. **me-** wear at the edges.

Rabi'ul-akhir (*Isl.*) 4th month of Arabic calendar.

Rabi'ul-awal (*Isl.*) 3d month of Arabic calendar.

rabu₁ (*M*) lungs.

rabu₂ me- seize, carry off (loot, etc.).

Rabu Wednesday.

rabuk 1 fertilizer. - *TSP* k.o. chemical fertilizer. - *buatan/garam* artificial fertilizer. - *hijau* compost, green manure. - *kandang* manure. 2 tinderwood. **me-(i)** fertilize, manure. **pe-an** application of fertilizer.

rabun₁ 1 hazy, dim. - *senja* dusk, twilight. 2 nearsighted. - *ayam/dekat* nearsighted, myopic. - *jauh* farsighted. **ke-an** myopia.

rabun₂ me- 1 (*Lit.*) rise. *Air laut ~* The sea rose. 2 have a ridge.

rabung ridge of a house. **pe-(an)** ridge of a house.

rabut see CABUT.

racau delirious. **me-** rave, delirious.

racek /racek/ (*Jkt*) pockmarked.

racik₁ bird snare. **me-** catch birds with such a snare.

racik₂ me- 1 cut into thin slices. 2 blend various proper ingredients into food, etc. *~ obat-obatan* to compound medicines. 3 eat foods already mixed (rice with vegetables, etc.). 4 make the necessary preparations prior to a main endeavor.

racuk me- tease, entice s.o.

racun poison. **be-** poisonous. **me-i** poison s.o. or s.t. *~ sumur* poison the well. **me-kan** 1 use s.t. to poison. 2 poison s.o. on behalf of another. **ke-an** 1 poisoned. 2 displaying symptoms of having been poisoned. **pe-** 1 poisoner. 2 poisoning agent. **pe-an** poisoning.

rad council. - *agama* religious council.

rada (*Jv, Jkt*) rather, somewhat. **-²** rather.

radak 1 a stab with a spear. 2 an attack. **be-** 1 to stab with a spear. 2 break through in an attack. **me-(kan)** 1 stab (and penetrate) with a weapon. *Ia ~ tombaknya ke karung pasir* He stuck his spear through a bag of sand. 2 poke at (a fire, etc.).

radang 1 inflamed, hot. - *amandel* tonsillitis. - *mata* conjunctivitis. - *paru-paru* pneumonia, inflammation of the lungs. - *gusi* gingivitis. 2 fly into a rage. **me-** 1 become inflamed. *Paru-parunya ~* His lung became inflamed. 2 get excited. *Hatinya ~* He got excited. **pe-an** (*Med.*) infection, inflammation.

radén 1 title of Jv nobility. - *ajeng* title of noble unmarried woman. - *ayu* title of noble married woman. - *aria* title of nobility higher than *radén panji*. - *aria adipati* title given to regents. - *bagus* title of nobility for men, slightly higher than *radén*. - *mas/panji* title of nobility higher than *radén*. - *tumenggung* title given to regents. 2 form of address, esp. as *dén*.

rader rolling pin.

radés radish.

radiallahu anhu (*Isl.*) May God bless him, exclamation uttered after the mention of o. of Muh.'s companions or the prophets.

radiasi radiation. **me-** radiate.

radiator radiator.

radikal (*Pol.*) radical. **ke-an** radicalism.

radikalisasi radicalization. **me-** radicalize.

radikalisir me- radicalize.

radikalisme radicalism.

radin see RADÉN.

radio radio. - *salon* console radio. **me-kan** (send via) radio.

radioaktif radioactive. **me-kan** cause s.t. to be radioactive. **ke-an** radioactivity.

radioaktivitas radioactivity.
radiogram radiogram.
radiologi radiology.
radiowan radioman.
radius circle, radius. *dlm - satu kilo* within the radius of a kilometer.
radmolen ferris wheel.
rafia 1 raffia fibre. 2 k.o. twine made of thin strips of plastic similar to raffia fibre.
raflésia k.o. endotropic parasitic plant, the Rafflesia.
raga₁ be- 1 (*Lit.*) boast, show off. 2 hold an exhibition. mempe-kan 1 boast about, show off. *Ia ~ mobilnya yg baru* He boasted about his new car. 2 model, exhibit. pe- 1 boaster. 2 a model. 3 mock-up, visual aid. pe-an 1 ostentation. 2 show, exhibition. *~ busana/mode* fashion show. 3 modeling. 4 visual display.
raga₂ 1 k.o. simple rattan basket. 2 ball plaited from rattan. be- play rattan ball. me- 1 make rattan baskets. 2 play rattan ball.
raga₃ (*Lit.*) body. *jiwa (dan) -* body and soul.
ragam 1 melody, tune. *- lagu Sunda énak didengar* It is pleasant to listen to the melody of a Sundanese song. 2 manner, kind. *Banyak org banyak -* When there are lots of people there are lots of variations. 3 caprice, whim. *Ia banyak -nya* He has many whims. 4 (*Ling.*) register, style. se- uniform, of o. kind. *pakaian ~* a uniform. *~ sebau* of o. mind. berse- in uniform. menye-kan make uniform, make homogeneous. kese-an uniformity. penye-an act of making s.t. uniform. *~ struktur organisasi* standardizing organizational structure. be- 1 (*Lit.*) sing. 2 various. *Warnanya ~* It is in various colors. be-² various colors, sounds, etc. me- 1 vary. 2 (*Lit.*) sing. 3 give a tinge to. 4 be capricious. me-kan render s.t. heterogeneous. ke-an variety, diversity.
ragangan 1 scaffolding, laths. 2 kite frame. 3 handlebars.
ragas me- 1 pull out (hair, grass, etc.). 2 cut, tear.
ragawi physical. *antropologi -* physical anthropology.
ragbol 1 dust mop, esp. for ceilings. 2 moplike tool for cleaning toilet bowl.
ragi₁ yeast, fermentation agent. be- ferment. *tdk ~* yeastless. me-kan 1 rise (of bread, etc.). 2 add yeast. pe-an fermentation.
ragi₂ design, formulation. se- of o. design, of o. color pattern. *baju wanita ~* dresses of o. design. me- color.
ragib absorbed in an activity.
ragil (*Jv*) youngest (child).
ragu hesitant. *- hati* feel uncertain. -² 1 be wary, uncertain. *Saya ~ apa betul* I am doubtful that it is true. 2 hesitate to do s.t. *Meréka tdk ~ utk memakai bom atom* They did not hesitate to use the atomic bomb. me- 1 disturb. *Ia datang utk ~ saja* He came only to disturb. 2 be doubtful. *Hatinya ~ akan pergi atau tdk* He was doubtful about going or not. me-i, me-kan 1 confuse, make s.o. hesitate. *Surat itu ~ saya* That letter made me hesitant. 2 put s.t. in doubt. *Met ~*

kemungkinan itu Met put that possibility in doubt. me-²kan cast doubt on. ke-an 1 hesitancy. 2 doubt. ke-(²)an 1 hesitation, irresolution. 2 be in doubt. -²an doubtful in nature. pe- doubter.
ragum (*Lit.*) vise, clamp. -an joint (membership, etc.).
ragut see RENGGUT.
rahab see RAHAP₁.
rahang jaw. *- atas* upper jaw. *- bawah* lower jaw.
rahap₁ *kain -* shroud. me- cover a corpse with a cloth. pe- outer covering of a corpse.
rahap₂ me- 1 alight. *Burung ~ di ranting* A bird alights on a twig. 2 kneel down next to. *Anak ~ dekat ibunya* The child knelt near its mother. 3 throw o.s. face down.
raharja (*Jv*) well-being, prosperity.
rahasia secret. *Ia tdk dpt menyimpan -* He cannot keep a secret. *kegiatan -* secret activities. *- dinas/ jabatan* official secret. *dgn -* confidentially, in confidence. me-kan keep s.t. secret. ke-an secrecy.
rahat see ISTIRAHAT.
rahayat see RAKYAT.
rahayu 1 well-being. 2 greeting, esp. used by adherents of Jv folk religion. ke-an state of well-being.
rahib 1 monk. 2 nun.
rahim₁ womb, uterus. *di dlm - ibunya* in his mother's womb.
rahim₂ (*Isl.*) merciful (of God). me-i have mercy on. ke-an mercy.
rahimi (*Isl.*) merciful (of God).
rahman, rahmani (*Isl.*) compassionate (of God).
rahmat (*Isl.*) God's mercy. me-i have mercy on.
rahmatullah (*Isl.*) mercy of God.
rahsia see RAHASIA.
Rahu k.o. monster that causes lunar eclipses by swallowing moon.
rahuh sigh of relief. me- sigh with relief.
raib see GAIB.
rai-gedék (*Jv*) shameless.
raih me- 1 reach for. 2 sweep up, take in toward o.s. *~ dayung* row. *~ hati* be attractive. 3 achieve, manage to obtain. *Ia berhasil ~ gelar kesarjanaan* He succeeded in obtaining a college degree. *Ia ~ keuntungan sebanyak seribu juta* She got a profit of o. million rupiah. *~ impian* achieve o.'s dreams. me-² grope for. *Dgn tangan ~ kami mencari pegangan* Groping with our hands we sought a place to hold on to. -an s.t. o. reached for.
rais₁ me- sweep off.
rais₂ president or chairman, formerly used by the Isl. party. *- am* general chairman.
rait screeching sound. me- screech.
raja 1 king. *- muda* crown prince. *- sehari* bridegroom. *- singa* syphilis. 2 tycoon. *- minyak* oil baron. 3 o. who excels at s.t. *- makan* 1 heavy eater. 2 gourmet. *- tidur* s.o. who sleeps excessively. 4 (*Che.*) king. be- 1 act like a king. *Ia ~ di désanya* He acts like a king in his village. 2 have a king. *Meréka ~ kpd uang* They have money for their king. me- act like a king. me-i 1 rule over.

Singa ~ *rimba* The lion rules over the jungle. **2** control, dominate. *Mitsubishi* ~ *pasaran* Mitsubishi controls the market. *Téori itu* ~ *kuliah* That theory dominates the lecture. **me-kan 1** make into a king. **2** treat like a king. *Ia* ~ *tamunya* He treats his guests like kings. **3** consider highly important. *Ia* ~ *uang* He worships money. **ke-an 1** empire, kingdom. ~ *Inggeris* the British Empire. ~ *Serikat* United Kingdom. **2** royal. *tanda* ~ royal insignia.

Rajab (*Isl.*) 7th month of Arabic calendar.

rajabrana (*Jv*) treasure, riches.

rajah₁ 1 (*Lit.*) figure or design with mystical properties. **2** tattoo. **3** lines in the palm. **me-i** tattoo s.o. **-an** tattoo.

rajah₂ see RAJA.

rajakula dynasty.

rajaléla violent and arbitrary. **me- 1** act violently and arbitrarily. *Lurah bertindak* ~ *di désa itu* The headman acted violently and arbitrarily in that village. **2** break out violently (of disease). *Koléra* ~ *di musim kering* Cholera spread like wildfire in the dry season. **ke-an** violence and arbitrariness.

rajalélé prized variety of rice.

rajam me- stone to death. **-an** stoning.

rajang me- cut into small pieces, mince (vegetables, etc.). **-an** cut tobacco.

rajawali k.o. large black hawk.

rajét (*Coll.*) broken into small pieces. *Bagaimana vas yg sdh - beserpih-serpih bisa kembali utuh?* How could that vase be put back together after being broken into a million pieces?

rajin 1 industrious, diligent. *Anak ini - sekali di sekolah* This child really works hard at school. **2** frequently. *Ia - datang ke rumah* He frequently visited my home. **me-** (*Coll.*) make handicrafts. *bermata pencarian* ~ make handicrafts for a living. **me-kan** cause s.o. to be hardworking. ~ *diri* force o.s. to work to the utmost. **ke-an 1** industry, diligence. ~ *gadis/wanita* domestic science. **2** handicraft. ~ *tangan* handicraft. ~ *kayu* woodcraft. **pe-, peng-** craftsman, artisan. ~ *kuningan* brass artisan. **peng-an** craft industry.

rajuk me- pout, sulk. *Baru dua hari dia pergi, kamu sdh* ~ What's this! He's only been gone two days and you are already moping around. **me-i** pout about s.t. *Ani* ~ *bonékanya yg terputus kepalanya* Ani is pouting over her doll because its head broke off. **pe-** o. who pouts.

rajungan k.o. small crab.

rajut net. - *rambut* hairnet. **me- 1** make a net. **2** crochet, knit. **-an** crocheted or knitted material. **pe-an** process of knitting, crocheting or net making.

rak₁ cracking sound.

rak₂ shelf, rack. - *buku* bookshelf. - *pengering(an)* drying rack.

raka 1 (*Lit.*) elder brother. **2** senior male university student.

rakaat (*Isl.*) essential unit of prayer ritual, consisting of bows and prostrations performed a prescribed number of times. *Kalau sembahyang su-*

buh, diperlukan dua -, ya? For the dawn prayer, two units must be performed, right?

rakam 1 stamping, printing. **2** embroidering. **me- 1** to stamp, print. *Ia* ~ *kain putih utk batik* She stamped white cloth for batik. **2** embroider. *Ia* ~ *kain sutera dgn benang mas* She embroidered the silk with gold thread. **3** record (for posterity), mark down. **4** record on a tape or record. **me-kan** print, embroider s.t. **-an 1** notes, recorded materials. **2** recording (of music, etc.). **pe- 1** recording instrument. ~ *pita* tape recorder. **2** recording technician. **pe(ng)-an** recording of s.t.

rakan see REKAN.

rakanita senior female university student.

rakat see REKAT.

rakawati see RAKANITA.

raker [*rapat kerja*] meeting at which work is accomplished.

rakerda [*rapat kerja daérah*] regional working meeting.

rakernas [*rapat kerja nasional*] national working meeting.

rakét₁ (*Sport*) racket.

rakét₂ see ROKÉT.

rakhman, rakhmani see RAHMAN, RAHMANI.

rakhmat see RAHMAT.

rakit raft. - *penyelamat* life raft. **se-** a pair, set, couple. **be- 1** travel by raft. **2** attached alongside. **me- 1** make a raft. **2** connect, join, assemble. *Mesin ini akan di- di Indonésia dgn lisénsi Prancis* This machine will be assembled in Indonesia with a French patent. **pe-** assembler. **pe-an** assembling. *pabrik* ~ *motor Honda* Honda motorcycle assembly plant.

rakna see RATNA.

raksa see AIR.

raksamala see RASAMALA.

raksasa 1 mythical gigantic demon. **2** giant. *proyék* - an enormous project. **me-** become gigantic. **ke-an** gianthood.

raksasi see RASEKSI.

raksi₁ perfume. **me- 1** mix. *Ia* ~ *air dgn minyak* He mixed water with oil. **2** perfume s.t. **3** cheer s.o. up.

raksi₂ see RASI₁.

rakuk nick, notch, indentation. **be-** be notched, indented.

rakus greedy, voracious. - *makan uang* greedy for money. **ke-an** greed.

rakut me- 1 spin a web, lay a snare. **2** deceive.

rakyat populace, citizenry. - *jelata* masses, common people, proletariat. - *jémbél* the poor. - *murba* common people, proletariat. - *pemilih* electorate. **me-** be close to the people. *TNI diharapkan* ~ The Indonesian army is expected to be o. with the people. *tdk* ~ **1** snobbish. **2** uninspiring and unpopular. **ke-an 1** democracy, rule by the people. **2** populist.

ralat error, mistake, esp. typographical. **me-** correct, rectify. ~ *beberapa kesalahan* correct a number of errors.

ralip me- doze off. **pe-** o. who is always sleepy.
raliwan (*Sport*) participant in sports rally.
rally /réli/ (*Sport*) rally. **pe-an** racing.
RAM [*Républik Arab Mesir*] Egyptian Arab Republic.
ram₁ rumbling sound.
ram₂ 1 window. 2 picture frame.
rama see ROMO.
Ramadan, Ramadhan, Ramadlan (*Isl.*) 9th month of the Arabic calendar, fasting month.
ramah friendly, easy to talk with. - *tamah* hospitable and friendly. *pertemuan - tamah* an informal and friendly meeting. **be-** *tamah* 1 hold an informal meeting. 2 on friendly, intimate terms. **ke-tamahan** friendliness, hospitality. **be-²an** informal, familiar. *Ia suka ~ dgn bawahannya* He likes to be on familiar terms with his subordinates. **me-i** speak to s.o. on friendly terms, engage s.o. in friendly conversation. *Sdh saya coba ~ dia, kok masih acuh tak acuh* I tried to be friendly; why did she act as if she did not care? **ke-an** friendliness, informality. **pe-** a very friendly person.
ramai 1 crowded, busy. - *betul di pasar!* It was really crowded at the market! *org* - the public. *di muka org* - in public. 2 bustling, lively, festive. *Jkt kota yg* - Jkt is a bustling town. *Péstanya - sekali!* The party was really lively! 3 noisy, loud. *Ia - kalau bicara* He is boisterous when he talks. *Percakapannya - sekali* His conversation was loud. 4 interesting. *Pertunjukan itu sangat* - The show was very interesting. **(be)-²** in a lively group. *Kami pergi ~ ke rumahnya* We went in a noisy group to his house. **me-kan** enliven, cheer up. *Meréka ~ perayaan dgn musik* They livened up the celebration with music. **ke-an** 1 festivity. 2 noise, bustle.
ramal me- tell fortunes. *Bintang ~* The stars predict. *Tuan mau di-?* Do you want your fortune told, Sir? **me-kan** 1 predict. *Ia ~ bhw perang akan pecah dlm tahun ini* He predicts that war will break out within this year. 2 portend. *Ledakan bom di pasar ~ huru-hara di kota nanti* An explosion in the market portended future civil disturbances in the city. **-an** 1 prognosis, prediction. 2 fortune-telling. *~ bintang* horoscope. *~ cuaca* weather forecast. **pe-** oracle, fortune-teller. *~ cuaca* weather forecaster. **pe-an** forecast, prediction.
ramanda (*Jv, repsectful*) 1 father (respectful). 2 uncle.
rama-rama butterfly, us. large.
ramas₁ me- 1 press, knead. *~ perut* extremely sorry. 2 (*Coll.*) squeeze. *~ léhér* (*Sl.*) wring his neck.
ramas₂ see RAMES.
Ramayana great Hindu epic from which many themes of Indonesian literature and public life are drawn.
rambah me- clear away, cut down. *Meréka ~ hutan* They cleared away the forest. **-an** what is cut down or cleared away. **pe-** *jalan* pioneer, pathfinder.

rambai₁ k.o. tree bearing edible but undomesticated fruit.
rambai₂ 1 fringe. 2 tuft of hair.
rambak₁ edible portion of beef or pork skin, often fried as chips or used in sauces.
rambak₂ me- multiply, spread in all directions.
ramban (*Jkt*) **me-, me-i** collect grass or leaves for food. **-an** leaves so collected.
rambang₁ broad, wide, extensive. - *mata* sensual. **me-** at random. **ke-an** randomness.
rambang₂ see REMBANG.
rambas me- crush s.t.
rambat spreading, creeping. *ubi* - k.o. yam with spreading vines. **me-** 1 creep and spread (of vines, etc.). *Tumbuhan ini ~ di témbok* This plant is creeping up the wall. 2 spread. *Penyakit itu ~ dgn cepatnya* That disease spread rapidly. **me-i** cover over s.t. by creeping. *Atapnya di-i bugenvil mérah* Red bougainvillea enveloped the roof. *Berbagai prasangka yg bukan-bukan ~ otakku* All k.o. unfounded prejudices crept into my mind. **-an** propagation. **pe-an** process of spreading. *~ imam* the propagation of religious belief.
rambaté rata hayo (*Jv*) heave-ho, phrase uttered in unison by group carrying s.t. heavy.
rambia see RUMBIA.
Rambo /rémbo/ the movie character Rambo. **me-** destroy completely, annihilate.
rambu₁ fringe, tassel. **me-** mark out, plot.
rambu₂ (*Naut.*) short pillar on quay for tying up ships, buoy. - *lalulintas* traffic sign. - *sinar* lighted, flashing buoy. **pe-an** the provision of beacons. *~ lalulintas* the organizing of traffic signals. *Dinas ~* Buoy Service.
rambun tangled undergrowth.
rambut 1 hair of the head. - *palsu* wig. - *kribo* Afro-style hairdo. - *kusut* untidy or tousled hair. - *jangkit* bristling hair. - *remang* bristling hair. - *sasak* bouffant hairdo. *si- panjang* a woman. *si-péndék* a man. 2 (*Coll.*) body hair. - *kelamin* pubic hair. 3 mane. 4 (*Coll.*) thread. 5 (*Coll.*) filament. **be-** 1 possessing (k.o.) hair. *~ panjang* long-haired. 2 (*Biol.*) hirsute, be hairy. **me-** become like hair, stringy. **pe-** lower end of fishing rod.
rambutan k.o. *Nephelium* tree bearing fruit similar to lychee, the rambutan. - *rapiah* highly priced k.o. rambutan of Jkt.
ramé see RAMAI.
Ramelan see RAMADAN.
rames 1 mix by kneading. 2 provide with a mixture. *Makanan di- di atas piring* A mixture of food was provided on the plate. *nasi* - a plate of rice accompanied by a mixture of dishes. **ng-i, me-i** 1 (*Coll.*) try to decipher winning numbers (in gambling). 2 fix mixed rice for s.o.
rami hemp, jute. - *halus* flax.
ramin basket making. **me-kan** make baskets.
rampai various. **-²** mixed, jumble. **me-kan** mix, put various things together. **-an** a collection of various things. *~ musik* medley. *~ karangan* collection of essays.
rampak₁ thick, dense (of foliage, crowd).

rampak₂ completely dressed up.

rampak₃ see REMPAK.

rampas me- seize, carry away. *Pegawai duane ~ semua bagasinya* The customs officer confiscated all her baggage. **me-i** repeatedly seize, take away (from many sources). *Penjahat itu ~ penumpang-penumpang* The bandit held up the passengers. **-an** loot. **pe-** robber. **pe-an 1** robbery, holdup. **2** expropriation. *~ kuasa* coup d'état.

rampat me- swing, brandish. *~ papan* generalize, across the board. *Ia mudah ~ papan dan mengira bhw bangsa itu semua bodoh* He easily made the sweeping generalization that the entire race was stupid.

ramping₁ slender, slightly built. **me- 1** slenderize. **2** worn at the edges.

ramping₂ be- side by side, next to.

ramping₃ 1 disfigured, mutilated. **2** pierced (of ears).

rampok me- rob, plunder. **me-i** repeatedly plunder, rob from several sources. *~ toko-toko* loot shops. **-an** loot. **pe-** robber, plunderer. **pe-an** robbery, looting. *~ lingkungan* despoliation of the environment.

rampung (*Jv*) finished, settled, completed. **me-kan** finish, complete. **pe-an** act of completing s.t. *tahap ~* final stage.

rampus indecent (of language).

ramsum see RANGSUM.

ramu me- gather, collect. **-an** ingredients, concoction.

ramus superfluous hair. **be-** hairy.

rana₁ long-suffering. **me- 1** ailing, suffer chronically. *Ia sakit ~* He suffers chronically. **2** languish, waste away. *Badannya ~* His body is wasting away. **3** keep worrying. *Fikirannya ~ sblm anaknya datang* He kept worrying before his child came. **keme-an** condition of long-term suffering, languishment.

rana₂ see RATNA.

ranah 1 meadow, low-lying valley. **2** domain.

ranai me- drizzle, trickle.

ranap still, quiet. **me-** bend over and touch the ground.

rancah pe- scaffolding.

rancak₁ (*M*) handsome, beautiful. *gadis nan -* a beautiful maiden. *- di labuah/lebuh* dressed up in public (but the household is in disorder).

rancak₂ se- a set. *~ gamelan* set of gamelan instruments. **me- 1** clip. **2** cut into small bits. **-an** stand for a set of small gongs.

rancang stake, post. **be-** plan, intend. *Ia ~ utk perbuatan itu* He is making plans for that deed. **me- 1** stake out, place stakes. *Mereka ~ bambu di tanah utk menandai batas* They placed bamboo in the ground to indicate the boundary. **2** plan, make a schedule. *Ia menghitung dan ~ pesawat Fokker* He made calculations and planned the construction schedule of the Fokker aircraft. **me-kan 1** design. **2** design for s.o. **-an** plan, program. *~ induk* master plan. *~ pola* blueprint. *~ undang-undang* bill (in parliament). **pe-** planner, planning body. *Biro ~ Nasional* National

Planning Bureau. **pe-an** act of planning. *~ alat industri* setting up plans for industrial tools.

rancap 1 pointed. **2** masturbation. **me- 1** sharpen to a point. **2** masturbate. **pe-an** masturbation.

rancu confused. **me-kan** confuse. **ke-an 1** confusion. **2** (*Ling.*) contamination. **pe-an** contamination.

rancung pointed, acute. **me-** be pointed.

randa widow, widower (in some areas of Indonesia). *- kembang* young widow. *- tua* elderly bachelor or spinster. **me-** be unmarried (past usual marrying age).

randai₁ traditional Minangkabau theater. **pe-an** matters pertaining to this folk drama.

randai₂ me- traverse on foot.

randang see RENDANG.

randau me- 1 eat food that has been mixed together or seasoned. **2** make food tasty by mixing several things together. **me-kan** put s.t. into food to make it tastier.

randek /randek/ (*Jkt*) **me-** stop.

randu silk-cotton tree.

randung me-(kan) violate, step on, infringe.

rang₁ rank, position. *Apa -nya?* What is his position? **peng-an** ranking.

rang₂ clanging sound.

rang₃ design, plan. **-²an** rough draft, outline.

rang₄ see ORANG₂.

rangah me- boast.

rangak (*M*) noisy. **me-** make noise.

rangam tomato.

rangas (*Jkt*) termite.

rangda see RANDA.

Rangda (*Bali*) mythological wicked widow.

rangga, ranggah₁ sharp point. *--ranggu* with many sharp points.

ranggah₂ cock's comb.

ranggah₃ me- strip s.t. of all its fruit. *Mereka ~ pohon mangga* They stripped all the fruit off the mango tree.

ranggak (*Naut.*) **me-kan** tow (in embarkation).

ranggas 1 withered, arid. **2** leafless. **me- 1** wither, dry up. **2** molt, shed. *Ayam itu sedang ~* The chicken is molting. *Di musim gugur daun-daun mulai ~* In autumn the leaves begin to fall.

ranggeh me- reach for s.t.

ranggi attractive.

ranggul me- tilt up.

ranggung with legs apart. **me-** sit with legs apart.

rangin long sash (for dancing).

rangka 1 framework. *dlm - penelitian* in the framework of research. *- bakar* grate, grill. *- dasar* framework. *- kepala* (*Anat.*) skull. *- layangan* frame of a kite. *- tubuh* (*Anat.*) skeleton. **2** draft, blueprint. **me-kan** design. *Kantor pembangunan ini ~ bangunan-bangunan di lapangan pasar malam* This construction office designs the buildings on the fair site.

rangkah see RANGKAK.

rangkai bunch (of certain fruits). *- hati/jiwa* sweetheart. **se-** connected, tied together. *tiga ~* triumvirate. **menye-kan** combine into o. *~ jaringan telepon Jawa dan Madura* combine into o.

system the telephone systems of Java and Madura. **be-(²)** attached, tied to e.o. *Dua layangan itu terbang* ~ The two kites are flying attached to e.o. **me-(kan)** combine, attach to e.o. *Ia ~ keréta* He attached the cars to e.o. **-an 1** series. **2** combination. ~ *bunga* floral arrangement. **3** connecting structure (i.e. chain, etc.). **pe-** connector. ~ *rém* (*Auto.*) brake coupling.

rangkak me- 1 crawl on hands and knees. **2** make slow progress. **3** fawn. **me-² 1** cringe. *Ia ~ di hadapan majikannya* He cringes in front of his boss. **2** stumble. *Ia ~ pembacaannya* He reads haltingly. **me-i** crawl along s.t. **me-kan** have s.t. or s.o. crawl. *Ibu ~ bayinya* Mother made her baby crawl.

rangkam me- grasp s.t. in the hands.

rangkang (*Isl.*) religious training center for advanced Isl. studies.

rangkap₁ 1 double. - *dua* 1 double, in duplicate. **2** in two layers. - *lima* in quintuplicate. **2** (*Ling.*) phonetic cluster. **se-** a set of s.t. **be-** double. **be-²** doubles, in sets. **me- 1** wear double layers. *Ia ~ bajunya* He is wearing two layers of clothes. **2** serve concurrently, double as. *Perdana Menteri ~ Menteri Luar Negeri* The prime minister also holds the position of minister of foreign affairs. *Saputangannya ~ anduk* Her handkerchief also served as a towel. **me-²** assume additional, concurrent responsibilities. *Ia sibuk dgn pekerjaan yg ~ itu* He is busy with his work in a double capacity. **me-kan 1** put s.t. over s.t. else. *Ia ~ alas méja baru pd yg lama* She put a new tablecloth over the old o. **2** give s.o. a double task. **-an** s.t. double. ~ *(ke)dua* duplicate. **pe-** a person who holds two jobs. **pe-an** act of assuming additional, concurrent responsibilities.

rangkap₂ me- trap s.t. **pe-** trap, pitfall. ~ *tikus* mousetrap.

rangkas see RANGGAS.

rangkaya, rangkayo (*M*) lady of the house.

rangkét (*Sd*) **me-** thrash, beat up.

rangkiang rice granary.

rangking hood, canopy made of basketry.

rangkok k.o. bird, k.o. hornbill.

rangkuh see RENGKUH.

rangkul se- in o. embrace. **be-²an 1** hug e.o. ~ *pinggang* hug e.o.'s waists. **2** be closely associated with. *Adi ~ dgn Bandrio* Adi was in cahoots with Bandrio. **me-** hug, throw o.'s arms around. **me-kan** entwine s.t. around. **-an** embrace.

rangkum se- an armful. **menye-kan** gather together. **me- 1** embrace, enclose. **2** include, encompass. **me-i** cover s.o. or s.t. in an embrace. **me-kan** wrap up (argument, thesis, etc.). **-an 1** embrace. **2** armful. **3** summary.

rangkung me- squat down, crouch.

rangkungan see KERONGKONGAN.

rangkup 1 hollow, cavity. **2** curve. **me- 1** cup two hands together. **2** cover, embrace. **-an** coverage.

rangrang see SEMUT.

rangsang 1 exciting, stimulating. **2** pungent. - **me-** stimulate e.o. **me-(kan)** excite, stimulate. *Bau minyak wangi itu ~ hidung* The odor of the

perfume titillates the nostrils. *adegan yg ~* a sexually stimulating scene. ~ *hati* excite. **ke-an** irritation. **-an** stimulus. ~ *séks* sex drive. **pe- 1** incentive, spur, stimulus. ~ *pembangunan* an incentive for development. **2** (*Mil.*) shock troops, attackers. **pe-an 1** act of exciting, stimulation. **2** anger, irritation. **3** incentive, motivation.

rangsek (*Jkt*) **me-** attack.

rangsel see RANSEL.

rangsuk see RASUK₂.

rangsum rations. **me- 1** put on rations. **2** ration out. *Pemerintah ~ makanan pd para korban* The gvt. rationed food out to the victims.

rangun observation post, tower.

Rangun Rangoon.

rangup 1 fragile. **2** crisp (i.e. cracker, chip, etc.).

rani₁ queen.

rani₂ rich.

ranjah me- loot, pillage.

ranjam (*Jv*) see RAJAM.

ranjang iron bed. - *bayi* baby's crib. - *kéro/pér* bed with steel springs. - *pengantin* nuptial bed.

ranjau (*Mil.*) **1** bamboo spiked booby traps (set around village to wound enemy). **2** antipersonnel weapon, mine. - *darat* land mine. - *laut* sea mine. **pe-an** mining (of s.t.).

ranjing ke-an 1 possessed (by bad spirit, etc.), mania. **2** have a mania for s.t. *Ia ~ nonton wayang* He is addicted to watching shadow plays.

ranju see RANJAU.

ranjul broken up, bumpy.

ranjungan see RAJUNGAN.

ranking /réngking/ grade ranking (in schools). **me-** arrange grades in a rank. **pe-an** act of ranking grades.

rankus me- collect, gather s.t.

ransel 1 knapsack, backpack. **2** duffle bag.

ransum see RANGSUM.

rantai 1 chain. - *besi* iron chain. - *hukuman* convict's chain. - *kangkang* shackles. - *sepéda* bicycle chain. *Ia memutuskan - perkawinan* He broke the marriage ties. **2** necklace. - *mas* gold chain. **3** series, sequence. - *komando* chain of command. - *peristiwa* sequence of events. **4** a measure of distance, esp. in rice fields. **be- 1** have a chain. *arloji ~* watch with a chain. **2** in sequence. **me-(kan) 1** chain, place to chains. **2** put s.t. into a sequence. **-an** series, sequence, chain. **pe-an 1** imprisonment. **2** convict.

rantam be- do s.t. collectively.

rantang set of stacked containers for transporting food. **me- 1** have a standing order for meals delivered in such containers. **2** deliver food in such containers. **-an** system of getting o.'s food delivered on a standing basis.

rantas 1 broken off. **2** frayed. **me-kan 1** break s.t. off. *Daging selaput itu di-kan oléh pisau cukur* A razor blade cut off the membrane. **2** cause s.t. to be frayed.

rantau 1 (*Geog.*) shoreline. **2** (*Geog.*) reaches (of a river). *Ia berlayar sepanjang -* He sailed along the reaches of the river. **3** abroad, foreign country.

Meréka mau belajar di - They want to study abroad. **me-** 1 leave o.'s home area to make o.'s way in life. 2 wander about. 3 sail along the reaches of a river. **pe-** 1 s.o. wandering about the country. 2 settled foreigner. ~ *Tionghoa* overseas Chinese. **pe-an** not o.'s native place, a foreign country or region.

ranté see RANTAI.

ranting₁ 1 small branch, twig. 2 subsection, branch (of offices, parties, etc.). - *tenggorok* (*Anat.*) bronchiole. **be-** 1 have a twig. *Pohon ini tak* ~ This tree has no twigs. 2 in a chain, sequence, series. **me-** 1 have twigs. *Pohonnya tlh mulai* ~ The tree is beginning to have twigs. 2 protrude like a branch. *Tangannya* ~ *ke atas* His arms stretch upward. 3 prune, lop off.

ranting₂ dried up. **me-** dry up.

ranum overripe. **me-** ripen.

ranyah (*M*) **me-** be difficult, agitated (of infants).

ranyang (*M*) 1 lively. 2 capricious.

ranyuk me- grumble.

raon see RAWON.

rap rapping sound, knocking.

RAP [*Républik Arab Persatuan*] United Arab Republic.

rapah me- walk, step on s.t.

rapak lumuh (*Isl.*) right of woman to appeal to judge if husband refuses to divorce her.

rapal me-i 1 utter a prayer or incantation over s.o. 2 (*Sd*) bless and solemnize a wedding.

rapat 1 close, proximate, dense. *Terpaksa meréka duduk - sekali* They were forced to sit very close to e.o. *anyaman yg* - a close-meshed plaiting. - *penduduknya* The population is dense. 2 close, intimate, familiar. *Ia - sekali pd temannya* He is very close to his friend. *--erat* close and intimate. **me-eratkan** *barisan* close ranks. 3 meeting, assembly. - *antar bagian* interdepartmental meeting. - *gelap* secret meeting. - *kerja* working session. - *kilat* emergency meeting. - *lengkap/pléno* plenary session. - *raksasa/samudera* mass meeting. *Pd tiap-tiap tgl 17 Agustus selalu diadakan - samudera* On the 17th of August of every year a mass meeting is held. **-²** tight, very close. **be-** hold a meeting. **me-** 1 move closer. 2 join together s.t. 3 moor, tie up. **me-i** 1 be on familiar terms with s.o. 2 move s.t. to greater proximity. *Kartini menggésérkan tubuhnya* ~ *Ana* Kartini shifted her body moving closer to Ana. 3 (*Naut.*) tie up. *Kapal asing itu* ~ *dermaga* The foreign ship moored at the pier. **me-kan, memper-** draw s.t. close, make s.t. proximate. *Ia* ~ *léhér mantelnya* He drew the collar of his coat snug to his neck. *Telinga saya di-kan pd radio itu dgn hati dag dig dug* With pounding heart I put my ear next to the radio. ~ *barisan* close ranks. ~ *diri* join, chum up with. **ke-an** density. ~ *pohon per ha* the density of trees per hectare.

RAPBD [*Rencana Anggaran Pendapatan dan Belanja Daérah*] regional budget.

RAPBN [*Rencana Anggaran Pendapatan dan Belanja Negara*] national budget.

rapél back pay. **-an** back pay.

rapi orderly, neat. *Giginya* - His teeth were well spaced. *Ia berpakaian* - He dressed neatly. - *jali* smart (of clothes). **me-kan** put in order, tidy up. **ke-an** neatness, tidiness. **pe-** o. who straightens up. ~ *rambut bermutu* a qualified hairdresser.

rapiah see RAMBUTAN.

rapih see RAPI.

Rapim [*Rapat Pimpinan*] meeting of the armed forces commanders.

rapkol k.o. cabbage.

rapor, raport, rapot school report card.

rapsodi rhapsody.

rapuh brittle, likely to snap. *Jambatan ini* - This bridge is likely to snap. *Keséhatannya* - He is likely to die any minute. - *hati* 1 sensitive, tender. 2 tender hearted. - *mulut* unable to keep a secret. **me-kan** cause to be fragile and brittle. **ke-an** 1 fragility. 2 brittleness, crispness. **pe-** s.t. which causes brittleness.

rapun (*M*) broken, destroyed. **me-** destroy, break s.t.

rapung see APUNG.

rarak see RERAK.

ras₁ sound of rustling (of papers, leaves, etc.).

ras₂ reins. *Ia memegang* - He holds the reins.

ras₃ race. *diskriminasi* - race discrimination.

ras₄ thoroughbred. *anjing* - a thoroughbred dog.

rasa 1 taste, sensation. *Makanan itu -nya énak* That food tastes delicious. - *pedih* stinging or biting sensation. 2 feeling, sense. *Umumnya meréka mempunyai - kedaérahan kuat* In general, they have strong feeling of provincial loyalty. - *hati* heart, mind. - *hormat* (feeling of) respect. - *kehormatan* sense of honor. - *kurang* feeling of inferiority. - *malu* feeling of embarrassment. - *minder* inferiority complex. - *pirasa* emotions, feelings. - *rendah* inferiority complex. - *salah* guilt feeling. - *séntimén* feeling of spite. 3 be of a certain opinion. *Saya - . . .* I think . . . *pd - saya* in my opinion. **-²(nya)** it seems to me. ~ *baru kemarén saja* It seems like it was only yesterday. **be-** 1 feel. *Saya* ~ *lelah* I feel tired. ~ *aral* feel ill at ease. 2 have a certain taste. *Itu* ~ *pahit* That has a bitter taste. **me-** 1 feel, sense. *Saya* ~ *senang di sini* I feel content here. ~ *kasihan pd* feel pity for. ~ *dendam* bear a grudge. ~ *sir* have a crush on s.o. 2 think, believe. **me-²** 1 feel, touch. *Ia* ~ *bonékanya dgn tangannya* She felt the doll with her hands. 2 think over and over. *Kalau di-², ya berat* If you think about it over and over, of course it seems difficult. **me-i** 1 taste. *Ia* ~ *makanan yg sedap itu* He tasted the delicious food. 2 experience, endure. *Ia* ~ *kesukaran di negeri asing* He experienced difficulties in a foreign country. 3 feel, touch. *Ia* ~ *pipinya yg halus dgn jarinya* He felt her soft cheeks with his fingers. 4 feel, intuit. *Kami dpt* ~ *apa yg dipikirkannya* We can intuit his thoughts. **me-kan** 1 cause s.t. to be experienced. 2 experience s.t. *Ia* ~ *pengaruh temannya di daérah ini* He feels his friend's influence in this region. *Ia* ~ *dinginnya di sini* He feels the cold here. **mempe-kan** cause s.t. to be experienced. **-in** (*Coll., Jkt*) Serves you right! *~! Siapa suruh kamu pakai tumit tinggi?* Serves you right! Who told you to wear high heels? **te- 1** felt. *Terik panas matahari tdk ~ oléhnya* He did not feel the heat of the sunrays. **2** feel (of a part of the body). *Kaki saya ~ sakit* My foot hurts. **pe- 1** sense of touch. *~ lidah* sense of taste. *~ tubuh* sense of touch. **2** sensitive person. **pe-an 1** opinion, feeling. *menurut ~ saya* in my opinion. **2** sentiment. **3** experience, sensation. *~ ngeri* sensation of horror. *~ masa bodoh* indifference.

rasai me-kan suffer much. **pe-an** suffering, misfortune.

rasaksa see RAKSASA.

rasam see RESAM₂.

rasamala k.o. tree with fragrant wood.

rasan (*Jv*) **ng-i, -an** backbite, gossip about.

rasé civet cat.

raseksa see RAKSASA.

raseksi female giant.

rasi₁ 1 constellation. **2** lucky. *Ia - dlm perjalanan* He was lucky during his trip. **-an 1** astrology. **2** fortune-telling. **pe-an 1** horoscope. **2** fate. **me-(kan)** consult the stars, cast a horoscope.

rasi₂ se- harmonious, matching, compatible. *Dasinya ~ dgn keméjanya* His tie matches his shirt. *~ air ke air* Birds of a feather flock together. **menye-kan** adapt, make compatible. *~ téknologi baru dgn keadaan lingkungan* make new technology compatible with the environment. *~ diri* adapt o.s. **kese-an 1** harmony. **2** matching appearance. **3** be compatible. **penye-an** adaptation, harmonization.

rasia₁ see RAZIA.

rasia₂ see RAHASIA.

rasial racial.

rasialis racialist.

rasialisme racialism.

rasian dream. **be-** dream. **me-kan** dream of.

rasio 1 reason. *secara -* in a rational manner. **2** (*Math.*) ratio.

rasional, rasionil rational.

rasionalisasi 1 rationalization. **2** reduction in the number of workers in a firm. *Ia kena -* She was laid off.

rasisme racism.

rasmi see RESMI.

rasuah bribery, corruption.

rasuk₁ crossbar, cross beam. *- rakit* crosspiece in a raft. *- rangka* frame. **pe-an** cross piece apparatus.

rasuk₂ possession by a spirit. *Ia kena -* He was possessed. **me- 1** possess s.o. *Jin ~ ke dlm tubuhnya* A spirit entered his body. **2** permeate completely. *Rawonnya énak. Bumbunya sdh ~* The soup is delicious. I can really taste the spices. *Senyumnya ~ sukma* His smile went right to my soul. **me-i** penetrate, possess. *Kebenciannya pd Ali ~ jiwanya* His hatred of Ali obsessed him. *~ hati* trouble the heart, cause psychic turmoil. **me-kan** allow s.t. to take possession. *~ musik ke*

dlm jiwa let music take possession of his soul. **ke-an** possessed. *Stl léwat pohon angker itu, Minah ~ sétan* Right after passing by that eerie tree, Minah was possessed by a devil.

rasul 1 messenger sent by God. **2** (*Isl.*) prophet. **3** (*Rel.*) apostle. **me-** proselytize. **ke-an 1** attribute of a messenger of God. **2** apostolate. *karya ~* apostolic work.

rasuli (*Rel. Isl.*) apostolic.

rasulullah (*Isl.*) the Messenger of God. *Muh. -s.a.w* Muh. the Messenger of God, the blessings of the Lord be upon him.

raswah see RASUAH.

rat₁ see ERAT.

rat₂ see RAD.

rata 1 flat, level. *Permukaan tanah itu -* The surface of the land was flat. **2** even. *Gula-gula itu dibagi -* The candy was divided evenly. **3** average. **-² 1** on the average, mean. *Tiap anggota menerima ~ Rp1.000* Every member receives o. thousand rupiah on an average. **2** quite even. *Org tani memacul tanah ~* The farmer hoed the ground level. **se- 1** everywhere. **2** flat, as even as. *~ cermin* as flat as a mirror. **menye-kan** spread out. **me- 1** smooth. *Muka laut ~ ssdh angin ribut itu* The sea was smooth after the storm. **2** be spread evenly. *Pengaruh pemimpin itu tlh ~ di seluruh negeri* The influence of the leader has spread throughout the land. *kemakmuran yg ~* prosperity which is evenly distributed. *tdk ~* inequitable. **meme-kan** cause s.t. to be spread evenly (wealth, etc.). **keme-an** evenness of distribution. **peme-** s.t. that causes even distribution. **peme-an** even distribution. **me-i 1** cover s.t. completely and evenly, traverse all of s.t. *Dlm perjalanannya ia tlh ~ seluruh kepulauan Indonésia* During his trip he covered all Indonesia. *Bercak mérah ~ seluruh badannya* His body was covered all over with red spots. **2** give equal amounts out to, reach all of a population. *Pembagian gula ~ seluruh penduduk kota* The distribution reached all segments of the city's population. **me-kan 1** level s.t. *Ia ~ jalan di muka rumahnya* He is leveling the surface of the road in front of his house. *Amalia mau ~ diri dgn teman-temannya yg lain* Amalia wanted to put herself on the same level as her friends. **2** distribute evenly. *Ia ~ bahan pakaian kpd seluruh penduduk désa* He is distributing textile goods among the villagers.

ratah simple, plain. **me-** eat o. thing only. *Ia ~ nasi putih* He eats only plain rice.

ratap lamentation. *- tangis* mourning, lamenting. **me-** lament, mourn. *Ayahnya melarang Budi ~* His father forbade Budi to wail. **me-i** lament over s.o. *Dgn hati derita ia ~ anak yg meninggal mendadak* With a sorrowful heart he mourned his daughter who had died suddenly. **-an** lament, wail.

ratas see RETAS.

ratib (*Isl., Lit.*) repeated, chanted recitation of prayer. **me-** recite this prayer. **pe- o.** who recites this prayer.

ratib sadati k.o. traditional dance in Aceh.
ratifikasi ratification. **me-** ratify.
ratifisir me- ratify.
ratio see RASIO.
ratna gem, jewel. - *kendi* precious stone. - *mutu manikam* gems of all kinds. - *cempaka* topaz. - *wilis* emerald.
ratu 1 (*Lit.*) king. - *Adil* (*Jv*) The Just King, a legendary figure. **2** queen. - *Elizabéth* Queen Elizabeth. - *kecantikan* beauty queen. - *malam* moon. - *hatiku* my darling. **me-i** be superior (in beauty, etc.) above other women in a group. *Candra ~ teman-teman sekelasnya* Candra stands out above her fellow classmates. **me-kan** regard as superior above other women in a group. **-²an 1** a queen or king that is not real. **2** pageant queen. *Ada yg bilang ~ tdk sesuai dgn martabat wanita* There are those who say that beauty queens are not respectable.
ratus₁ -hundred. *dua* - 200. **se-** 1 100. **2** 100 rupiah. **be-²** hundreds. *Pohon kelapanya ~* He has hundreds of coconut trees. **me-** in hundreds. *Tentara ~ berbaris di depan istana* Hundreds of soldiers marched in front of the palace. **-an 1** hundreds. *Pekerjanya ~* He has hundreds of workers. **2** a currency note or coin with the value of 100.
ratus₂ (*Jv*) k.o. perfumed powder used as incense. **me-** dry and perfume o.'s hair or clothes by passing it over a censer exuding the smoke of such powder.
rau see DERAU.
raum see RAUNG.
raung sound of a siren, a siren. **me-** **1** a roar. *Kedengaran harimau ~ jauh di hutan* We could hear the tiger roaring far off in the forest. **2** a moan. *~ kesakitan* moan in pain. **me-kan** howl s.t. **-an 1** roar. *~ serigala* the cry of a wolf. *~ mesin jét* the roar of jet engines. **2** moan.
raun-raun (*Sl.*) go on a pleasure trip, stroll about, tour. **me-** promenade. **me-i** go round s.t.
raup me- scoop up s.t. with the hands. *Meréka ~ salju menébarkannya ke mana-mana* They scooped up the snow and scattered it all over. **-an** handful.
raut shape, form. - *muka/wajah* profile. **se-** numerical classifier for faces and some surfaces (moon, etc.). *~ wajah* a face. **me-** shape s.t. by bending it. **me-i 1** repeatedly shape s.t. **2** shape s.t. (of many persons). *Anak-anak ~ pénsil sblm sekolah mulai* The children sharpened their pencils before school began. **-an** s.t. shaped by bendng.
rawa, rawa-rawa, rawah₁ swamp, marsh. **be-** swampy. **me-kan** turn into swamps.
rawah₂ (*M*) basin. *telinga* - o. who does not listen to others' advice (lit., o. who has a basin for ears).
rawai fishing line (with several hooks). **me-** fish with such a device.
rawak (*Lit.*) haphazard. **me-** do s.t. haphazardly. *~ rambang* do s.t. haphazardly.
rawan₁ 1 (*Lit.*) emotional, sensitive. *Aku masih bisa*

- *mendengar bedug* I can still be touched by the sound of the mosque drums. **2** troubled, disturbed. *Daérah ini yg paling - di Indonésia dlm penyalahgunaan narkotika* This is the district most seriously affected by drug abuse. *Kalau malam jangan pergi ke situ; daérahnya - sekali* At night do not go there; the area is extremely dangerous. **me-kan 1** cause alarm. *Balapan motor itu sangat ~* Those motorcycle races are alarming. *Bunyi ledakan di gudang tentara ~ penduduk sekitarnya* The sound of explosions in the military warehouse panicked the nearby inhabitants. **2** (*Lit.*) stir up emotions. **ke-an** crime-infested, unsafe. **pe-** s.t. saddening.
rawan₂ (*Lit.*) classifier for articles of twine. *tiga - jala* three nets.
rawang see RAWA.
rawat me- 1 take care of, nurse. *Ia di- di rumah sakit umum* He is being treated at the general hospital. **2** (*Lit.*) resume o.'s original form. *Syiwa ~ kembali* Shiva resumed his original form. **me-i 1** take care of (s.o. ill). **2** sponge or wipe off (baby, patient, etc.). **me-kan** take s.o. for treatment. *Joni ke Surabaya utk ~ ayahnya* Joni went to Surabaya to have his father treated. **te-** be well taken care of. **-an, pe-an 1** treatment. **2** nursing, care. *~ jantung* treatment of heart. *~ rohani* spiritual care. **pe-** nurse.
rawé k.o. liana causing itching.
rawé-rawé rantas malang-malang putung (*Jv*) strive onward, no matter what (revolutionary slogan).
rawi narrator, writer of story. **me-(kan)** narrate, tell a story. **pe-an** exposition.
rawit₁ fine, small. *cabai* - k.o. very small, very hot chili pepper.
rawit₂ (*Jv*) **ka-an** music, song. **-an** overture (esp. gamelan music).
rawon (*Jv*) k.o. beef stew made with *keluak*. *nasi* - rice served with such a stew and other fixings.
rawuh (*Jv*) come (said of respected person).
rawun overripe.
RAy. see RA₂.
raya (*Lit.*) great, large. *Jkt* - greater Jkt. *hari* - holiday. **me-kan** celebrate. **pe-an** celebration.
Rayagung (*Jv*) the 6th month of the Arabic calendar.
rayah me- plunder, raid.
rayan me-(²) be delirious, dream of s.t. preoccupying. **te-(²)** seen in a dream.
rayang dizzy. **me-** feel dizzy. **pe-an** s.t. that makes the head spin.
rayan-rayan delirious. **me-** delirious. **-an** delirium.
rayap termite. **me-** creep, crawl. *Waktu ~* Time drags. *tanaman yg ~* creeping plant. **me-i** creep over s.t. *Kesunyian kemudian ~ kapal kami* Silence then crept over our ship. *Waktu malam harimau ~ hutan belukar mencari mangsanya* At night the tiger prowls the jungle in search of its prey. **-an** creep, creeping. *~ seékor kura* the creeping of a turtle.

ra'yat see RAKYAT.

rayau me- 1 fumble, grope. 2 rustle. 3 wander around. 4 be troubled.

rayon area, district.

rayonisasi process of dividing into administrative districts. **me-** divide into administrative units.

rayu sad, touched, emotional. **me-** 1 attempt to persuade s.o. *Ia ~ ayahnya* He pleaded with his father. 2 seduce, deceive. **-an** 1 persuasion. 2 flattery, wooing. **pe-** flatterer.

razia, razzia /rasia/ 1 raid by police (in red-light district, etc.). 2 unannounced examination of licenses, documents, etc. by police (in speed trap, during house-to-house search, etc.).

RDJ [*Républik Démokrasi Jerman*] Democratic Republic of Germany.

RDRK [*Républik Démokrasi Rakyat Koréa*] Democratic People's Republic of Korea.

RDV [*Républik Démokrasi Viétnam*] Democratic Republic of Vietnam.

réh (*Jv*) **nge-** boss around. *Jangan ~ adikmu terus-terusan* Don't keep bossing your little brother around.

réagéns (*Chem.*) reagent.

réak see RIAK₂.

réaksi reaction. *- berantai* chain reaction (of events). **be-, me-** react. *Partai oposisi ~ keras thd keputusan pemerintah* The opposition reacted strongly to the gvt.'s decision. **me-kan** cause s.t. to react with another. *Saya ~ natrium dgn asam klorida dan mendapatkan garam* I caused a reaction between sodium and chloride which yielded salt. **pe-** reagent.

réaksionér reactionary.

réaktor (*Phys.*) reactor.

réal see RIAL.

réalis realist.

réalisasi realization. **me-(kan)** bring about s.t. **ter-** be realized.

réalisir me- bring s.t. about. **ter-** be realized.

réalisme realism.

réalistis realistic. **me-kan** make s.o. realistic.

réalitas reality.

réalokasi reallocation. **me-kan** reallocate.

réat-réot sound of squeaking.

rebab two-stringed musical instrument. **be-** play this instrument.

rebah fall down, collapse. *- pingsan* fall into a faint. *- rémpah* stumble along. *- tertumus* fall on o.'s face. **be-an** fall down (plural). **me-** 1 fall down. 2 lie down, rest. **me-i** lie on s.t. **me-kan** 1 knock over, crash into. 2 cause to collapse. *~ kekuasaan Belanda* bring about the downfall of Dutch power. *~ diri* lie down. **-an** 1 things that are overturned. 2 a place to lie down. *Masih terasa ~ kepalanya yg harum di dadaku* I can still feel the place where her sweet-smelling head rested on my breast.

rebak me- be full of tears.

rébak₁ deep cut, wound. **me-** deeply cut, have a bad cut. *Pahanya ~* He has a bad cut on his thigh.

rébak₂ me- spread (of news, disease).

reban chicken coop. **me-kan** place in the chicken house. *Waktu malam ia ~ ayamnya* He puts his chickens in the coop at night.

réban see RÉBÉN.

rebana tambourine. **be-** 1 play the tambourine. 2 have tambourine played (at party, etc.).

rebas see RABAS.

rebat me- enclose, fence in.

rébéh me- hang down loosely. *Pakaiannya ~* His clothes hung loosely on him.

rébék 1 (*Jkt*) dirty, not washed. 2 ugly. 3 disorderly.

rébén o.-way glass.

rébewés (*Coll.*) driver's license.

Rebo see RABU.

réboasasi, réboisasi reforestation. **me-kan** reforest.

rebon k.o. small shrimp.

Rebon (*Jv*) every Wednesday.

Rebu see RABU.

rebung bamboo shoot. **me-** sprout (of bamboo).

rebus boiled. *telor -* boiled eggs. **me-** boil. *Ia ~ kacang* She boiled peanuts. **-an** a boiled food or beverage. *~ jagung* boiled corn on the cob. **pe-** s.t. to make things boil.

rebut be- 1 snatch away, take away by force. 2 struggle to obtain a goal. *Tiap partai ~ kursi di parlemén* Every party fought for a seat in parliament. *~ kata* quarrel. *~ nama/pangkat* vie for fame or position. *~ rezeki* struggle to survive. **be-(²)an** struggle with e.o. *Meréka ~ pangkat* They were vying for postion. *~ makanan* fight over the food. **me-(kan), mempe-(kan)** 1 seize, take by force. *Pejuang-pejuang ~ pasar kota Médan* The patriots seized the market of Medan. 2 fight for, compete for and win s.t. *Meréka ~ piala Thomas* They managed to win the Thomas Cup. **-an** 1 struggle, fight. *~ yg hébat terjadi di antara org-org itu* A violent struggle occurred among those people. *korban ~* victims of the struggle. *~ kekuasaan* 1 coup d'état. 2 struggle for power. *~ pangkat* vying for promotions. 2 object of the struggle. *Gadis itu menjadi ~ semua pemuda di Batusangkar* That girl became the object of intense competition among the young men of Batusangkar. **pe-an** struggle, fight. *~ kuasa* power struggle.

reca see ARCA.

recak₁ light pockmarks.

recak₂ (*M*) **me-** ride (a horse).

recall /rikol/ (*Pol.*) **me-** recall and force resignation of member of parliament for failure to agree with party policies. *Ibu Maramis di- oléh partainya karena terlalu berani bicara di DPR* Mrs. Maramis's party recalled her because she was too outspoken in parliament.

récéh see UANG.

récét cry, protest.

recik droplet. **me-(²)** sprinkle in droplets. **me-i** sprinkle on. **me-kan** sprinkle s.t.

récok 1 noise, uproar. 2 excitement. **me-** be excited, noisy. **me-i** fuss over s.t. **me-kan** cause an uproar, excite. *Dia hanya ~ suasana saja* He just stirred up trouble. **ke-an** excitement, fuss, noise. **pe-** a fussy person.

recup me- burgeon.

red.₁ [*redaksi*] editorial staff.

red.₂ [*redaktur*] editor.

reda abate, subside. *Angin tlh* - The wind has subsided. **me-** calm down, subside. *Kegiatan Gungung Agung tlh ~* The activities of the Gunung Agung volcano have slackened. **me-kan** soothe, calm. *utk ~ situasi yg gawat* to calm a critical situation. **ke-an** ensuing calm. **pe-an** quieting down, slowing down (of activity, etc.).

réda see RÉLA.

redah₁ (*M*) **me-** cut down (trees).

redah₂ me- traverse s.t.

redaksi 1 editorial staff. **2** wording (of text). **me-, me-kan** edit s.t. **ke-an 1** matters pertaining to editing. **2** editorship.

redaksionil pertaining to editing.

redaktris female editor.

redaktur editor.

redam 1 vague, dim, faint. **2** muffled, hushed. **-²** faintly visible. *Kapal yg jauh itu kelihatan ~* The ship in the far distance is faintly visible. **me-muffle**, hush s.t. up. *~ kréativitas* stifle creativity. **me-kan** deaden, muffle. **-an** attenuation. **pe-** k.o. device to reduce noise or light. *~ letus/suara* muffler. **pe-an** damping (noises).

redang₁ lukewarm, tepid.

redang₂ bog.

redap₁ tambourine.

redap₂ me- spread. *Penyakitnya ~ di seluruh tubuhnya* The disease spread throughout his entire body.

redap₃ impenetrable. **ke-an** impenetrability.

redas see REDAH₂.

rédenasi reasoning.

rédha, rédho see RÉLA.

rédi ready.

rédistribusi redistribution. **me-kan** redistribute.

rédla, rédlo see RÉLA.

reduksi, réduksi 1 reduction. **2** discount. **me-kan** reduce s.t. **pe-** reducing agent.

réduktor (*Chem.*) reductor.

redum sound of thumping.

rédundansi redundancy.

redup 1 overcast, dull. *Langit yg tadinya terang mulai* - The sky which had been clear began to become overcast. **2** dull, dreary. *Matanya yg pucat kuning* - His washed-out yellowish eyes were lusterless. **3** extinguished (of embers). **me-** be overcast. **me-kan 1** cloud s.t. **2** muffle. **3** dim the lights. **ke-an** overcast condition.

réduplikasi reduplication. **me-(kan)** reduplicate.

réédukasi reeducation. **me-** reeducate.

réékspor reexport. **me-** reexport.

réévaluasi reevaluation. **me-** reevaluate.

réferat k.o. university level course relying on a single reference book.

réferénsi reference (logical, bibliographical, etc.).

réfléks reflex. **be-** show reflex.

réfléksi reflection. **be-** reflect. **me-kan 1** cause a reflection. **2** reflect on s.t.

réfléktor reflector.

réformasi reformation. **me-(kan)** reform s.t.

réformir me- reform.

réformis reformer.

réformisme reformism.

réformulasi reformulation. **me-(kan)** reformulate s.t.

réformulir me- reformulate s.t.

réfraksi refraction.

refréin (*Music*) refrain, chorus.

réfungsionalisasi refunctionalization, i.e. reorganization of a staff such that the same personnel hold new positions. **me-(kan)** refunctionalize s.t.

rega (*Coll.*) see HARGA.

regang tense, tightly stretched. **be-** in a tense relationship. **be-²** 1 stretch out repeatedly. **2** quarrel with e.o. **berse-/bersi-** quarrel with e.o. **me-** 1 stretch. *~ badan* stretch o.'s body. *~ nyawa* at death's door. *~ telinga* teach s.o. a lesson. **2** intensify. **me-²** repeatedly stretch out. **me-kan** stretch s.t. out. *~ urat* pull a muscle. **-an** tension, strain. **pe-** stretcher. *~ celana* trousers stretcher. **pe-an** process of stretching s.t. till it is tense. *~ nyawa* endangering o.'s life.

regat me- take a shortcut (by following a straight line).

régat regatta.

régel 1 ruler. **2** lath (for tracing).

regén regent. **ke-an** regency.

régénérasi regeneration.

régés (*Jkt*) defoliated.

régi₁ administration. *- garam* salt authority.

régi₂ (film) director.

régiem, régim see RÉZIM.

régiméntasi regimentation. **me-kan** regiment s.t.

régional regional.

régionalisasi regionalization (of power, etc.).

régisir see RÉGI₂.

régistrasi registration. **me-** register s.o. or s.t.

réglemén regulation.

régleméntasi, réglementéring imposition of regulation.

régol 1 (*Jv*) archway, entrance. **2** drainage pipes (under bridges, etc.).

regrési regression.

regu 1 team, group. *- dayung* rowing team. *- penémbak* firing squad. *- penolong/penyelamat* rescue team. *- pramuka* Boy Scout troop. **2** shift. *pekerja tiga* - three shifts of workmen. **be-** in groups, in teams. **me-kan** divide into shifts. **ke-an** team activities.

reguk a slug, a drink. **me-** gulp down. *Beberapa bir di-nya* She gulped down several beers.

régular, régulér regular. **me-kan** regularize.

régularisasi, régulérisasi regularization.

régulasi regulation.

réh see NGRÉH.

réhabilitasi rehabilitation. **me-(kan)** rehabilitate.

réhabilitér, réhabilitir me- rehabilitate.

réhal (*Isl.*) k.o. folding book stand for the Koran during recitations.

réindoktrinasi reindoctrination. me- reindoctrinate.

réinkarnasi reincarnation. be- reincarnate.

réja remains, waste, leftover.

rejah me-kan transgress s.t. pe- transgressor.

rejam see RAJAM.

rejan strained, forced (of coughs, etc.). *batuk -* whooping cough. me- become severe (of coughs, diarrhea, etc.).

rejang₁ horoscope, almanac (for finding favorable days).

rejang₂ see RAJANG.

rejang₃ see LEJANG.

rejasa tin.

Rejeb (*Jv*) see RAJAB.

réjéh red and tearful (of eyes).

rejeki see REZEKI.

rejeng (*Jkt*) me- seize, catch (several people).

réjim see RÉZIM.

réjiméntasi see RÉGIMÉNTASI.

rejuk me- jump forward.

rék₁ row, line.

rék₂ sound of rubbing.

rék₃ see ARÉK.

rék₄ see RAK₂.

réka 1 invention, creative action. 2 trick, ruse. -² a made-up tale. me- 1 invent, devise. 2 plan, schedule. 3 imagine things, indulge in fancies. me-² guess, infer. *Nina ~ sdh tujuh hari Adri sakit* Nina guessed that Adri had been sick for seven days. -an 1 invention, plan. 2 fabricated story, fiction. 3 improvisation. pe- inventor.

reka'at see RAKAAT.

rekah cracked, split, broken. me- split up, crack apart. *Fajar ~* Dawn breaks. *Bibirnya ~* His lips are cracked. *Bibirnya spt delima ~* Her lips parted like a ripe pomegranate (i.e. beautifully red and full). te- open up. -an crack.

rékalsitran recalcitrant.

rekam see RAKAM.

rekan comrade, colleague. *- sekerja/sejawat* colleague. *- serumah* housemate. be-, me- be a comrade of. *Ia ~ gurunya* He is a comrade of his teacher. be-an be partners of. -an 1 partner, friend. 2 partnership. 3 steady customer. pe-an partnership.

rékap, rékapitulasi recapitulation. me- recapitulate.

rekat me- glue s.t. together or to s.t. else. me-kan glue s.t. to s.t. else. ke-an adhesiveness. *~ kertas dinding* adhesiveness of wallpaper. pe- glue, adhesive.

rékayasa me-kan engineer (changes, etc.). pe-an engineering (changes). *~ sosial* social engineering.

réken (*Coll.*) count. me-, ng- 1 count. 2 take into account, bother about s.t. *Ah cuma kecil, kok di-!* Ah, he is just a small kid, why make such a fuss! me-² calculate, count over and over. -an calculation, mathematics.

rékening 1 bill. *Minta -nya* Please give me the bill.

2 (*Fin.*) bank account. *- déposito* fixed deposit account. *- giro* clearing account. *- koran* current account. *- tabungan* savings account.

rekés (*Leg.*) petition, formal request for s.t. me- request, file a petition.

rékisitor, rékisitur see RÉKUISITOIR.

réklamasi reclamation. me- reclaim s.t.

réklame advertisement. me-kan advertise.

réklaséring, réklasifikasi reclassification.

rékoméndasi recommendation. me-kan recommend.

rékoméndir me- recommend.

rékonsiliasi reconciliation. me-kan reconcile s.o.

rékonstruksi 1 (*Ling.*) reconstruction. 2 reconstructing the crime, events, etc. me-(kan) reconstruct.

rékonstruktif reconstructive.

rékor record (in sports, politics, etc.).

rékréasi recreation. be- go out for recreation.

rekrut recruit. me- recruit s.o. pe-an recruiting.

rekrutir me- recruit s.o.

reksa (*Jv*) watch over, guard.

rékstok exercise bars (esp. on walls).

réktifikasi rectification.

réktor (*Acad.*) head of university.

réktorat (*Acad.*) office of university head.

réktorium (*Acad.*) 1 presidium governing university. 2 university president's office.

rekuiém, rekuim requiem.

rekuisisi requisition.

rékuisitoir, rékuisitor /rékwisitoar, rékwisitor/ (*Leg.*) sentence demanded by public prosecutor, prosecutor's summation.

rél railway track. *- mati siding* side track. *- keréta* trolley tracks. *keluar -* derailed.

réla willing, acquiesce in. *Ia - pergi dgn saya* He is willing to go with me. *Dia - akan penderitaannya* He has reconciled himself to his sufferings. *- hati* readily, willingly. *dgn -* 1 readily, willingly. 2 kind(ly), generous. me-i bestow blessing on (of God). *Semoga Allah ~ kepergiannya ke tanah suci* May God bless his journey to Mecca. me-kan 1 allow, consent. *Ia ~ anaknya dirawat di rumah sakit* He allowed his child to be treated at the hospital. *~ waktu* to volunteer time. 2 acquiesce in. ke-an 1 willingness. 2 agreement, consent. 3 blessing, favor (of God). *~ Allah* God's favor.

relai me- crumble, fall to pieces (of cakes, etc.).

rélaks see RILÉK, RILÉKS.

relang₁ me- glitter, flash.

relang₂ rattan hoop.

relap me- shine, glisten.

rélasi 1 customer, client. *- dagang* business connection. 2 relations.

rélatif relative. ke-an relevance.

rélativis relativist.

rélativisme relativism.

rélativitas (*Phys.*) relativity.

rélawan volunteer.

rélban railroad tracks.

rélevan relevant. me-kan make s.t. relevant.

rélevansi relevance.

rélevir me- make s.t. relevant.

reliéf relief on temple walls, etc.
réligi religion.
réligiositas religiosity.
réligius religious. **ke-an** religiousness.
rélikui (*Rel.*) relics.
réliwan participant in a sports rally.
relung niche, recess. - *gua* the recesses of a cave. - *hati* the depths of o.'s heart. **me-** dome-shaped, hollow. **-an** niche, recess, hollow.
rém brake. - *angin* air brakes. - *bahaya* emergency brake. - *cakram* disk brakes. - *kaki* foot brake. - *tangan* hand brake. - *tromel/tromol* disk brakes on bicycles and motorbikes. - *torpédo* back-pedaling brake (on bicycles). **me-, menge-** put on the brakes. **penge-an** braking.
remah crumbs, food remnants. **me-²** crumble. **me-²kan** make crumbs of s.t. *Ia ~ rotinya* He made crumbs of his bread.
remai sharply painful.
remaja adolescent. **me-kan 1** rejuvenate. *~ tanaman* replant with new stock. **2** replace older persons by younger o.'s. *nama-nama pegawai yg akan di-kan* names of employees who will be replaced by younger o.'s. **pe-** rejuvenator. **pe-an** rejuvenation, renovation.
remak preferable, more valued.
remang₁ 1 cloudy, overcast. **2** obscure, vague. **-² 1** blurred, barely visible. **2** dim, obscure. **ke-(²)an 1** vagueness, blur. **2** dimness, obscurity.
remang₂ - *tegak* **me-** *tegak* stand on end. **me-tegak-kan** *bulu* make the hair stand on end, horrify. **me-** stand on end (of hair).
remang₃ me- 1 buzz, hum of insects. **2** stream, flow (of perspiration, tears).
remas see RAMAS₁.
rématik rheumatism.
remba a pair. **be-²** in pairs. *Pesawat itu terbang ~* The planes fly in pairs.
rembah - *rembih* drip. **-²** drip. *Air matanya ~* Her tears flowed freely. **me-** drop down, flow freely.
rembang midpoint of a certain period of time. *waktu matahari -* high noon. - *senja* when dusk falls. **me-** aim at s.t.
rembes me- 1 ooze out, leak. **2** permeate, seep in. **me-i 1** ooze out, leak, filter through s.t. *Air kamar mandi ~ témbok kamar tidur* Bathroom water has leaked through the bedroom wall. **2** permeate s.t., seep into s.t. *Buku-buku saya di-i air banjir* Flood water has permeated all of my books. *Sinar itu mampu ~ benda-benda padat* The ray is capable of penetrating materials of high density. **me-kan** cause s.t. to leak into s.t. **ter-** penetrated. **keter-an** permeability. **-an** oozing liquid, seepage. *~ air dr lédéng bocor membuat témbok penuh lumut* Seepage from a leaky pipe has made moss form on the wall. **pe-** permeating agent. **pe-an 1** oozing, leakage. **2** infiltration.
rémbés (*Jv*) k.o. eye disease in which the eyes are watery.
rémbét₁ hampered, obstructed. **me-, me-kan** hamper, obstruct. *Banjir itu ~ perjalanan kami* The flood hampered our journey.

rémbét₂ me- 1 creep, climb up. *Tanaman itu ~ di pagar* The plant is creeping up the hedge. **2** hang down. *Buahnya ~ ke tanah* The fruits are hanging down to the ground. **3** spread. *Penyakit itu tlh ~ di seluruh kota* The disease has spread to the whole city. *Perkara itu ~ ke seluruh keluarganya* That affair came to involve all his family. **me-kan 1** cause s.t. to creep or hang. **2** spread s.t. *Meréka tak sengaja ~ penyakit* They unintentionally spread the disease. **3** involve. *Ia ~ saya dlm perkara itu* He involved me in the affair. **pe-an** involvement.
rembih see REMBAH. **me-** flow (of tears).
rémbong (*Jv*) **be-²an** be frayed.
rembug, rembuk be- discuss, confer. *Meréka ~ ttg soal perdagangan* They conferred on commercial matters. **me-(kan)** discuss, confer about. **pe-an 1** discussion, deliberation. **2** conference, consultation.
rembulan (*Jv*) moon, s.t. similar to the moon.
rembunai average, normal.
remburs 1 (*Coll.*) reimburse. **2** collect postage on delivery, postage due. *Bukunya dikirim - ke Malang* His books were sent postage-due to Malang.
rembut₁ te-² blink, flicker.
rembut₂ see REBUT.
réméh trifling, of no importance. *perkara yg - a* case of no consequence. - *téméh/céméh* trivial, petty. **me-téméhkan** belittle. **me-kan 1** belittle, disparage s.t. *Taktik itu tdk dpt di-kan* He could not disparage that tactic. **2** take lightly, underestimate. *Syarat-syarat UUD kita janganlah di-kan* Let us not underestimate the preconditions of our constitution. **ke-an** triviality. *~ hati* meanness, pettiness. **pe-an** disparagement.
remen be fond of. **-an** favorite person.
remeng see REMANG₁.
rémét me- ramble on.
remi, rémi rummy.
remiak see RIAK₁.
remis₁ k.o. mussel.
remis₂, remise (*Sport*) draw.
rémisi (*Leg.*) remission.
rempah spices (as a commercial, not culinary object). - *pawah/perawis/piah* various spices or ingredients. - *ratus* medicine consisting of many different items. **-² 1** various spices. **2** (*Lit.*) drugs, ingredients. **me-** make s.t. spicy. **me-i 1** add spices to. **2** embalm. **pe- 1** o. who spices. **2** seasoner. **3** embalmer.
rémpah see REBAH.
rempak se- in unison, all together. *Meréka maju ~* They advanced together. **menye-** advance together in unison. **kese-an** unison, synchronization. **be-** in a row.
rémpak chipped.
rempela (*Jv*) chicken gizzard.
rempelas see REMPLAS.
rempelo see REMPELA.
rempéyék k.o. crisp, thin chip made of flour and peanuts, shrimp or small fish.

remplas 1 fig tree. **2** sandpaper, s.t. to scour with. **me-(i)** scour, sand.

rempu see REMUK.

rempuh see TEMPUH.

remujung k.o. Jv tea.

remuk crushed, shattered. - *redam/rempu* crushed to bits. - *hati* emotionally upset, brokenhearted. -² mutilated, absolutely crushed. **me-(kan)** crush to bits. **ke-an** state of being crushed. **-an** smashing, crushing. *Ia kena ~ jari-jarinya* His fingers were smashed.

remunai see REMBUNAI.

renai see RENYAI.

renang be- swim. *~ kodok* breaststroke. *~ melentang* backstroke. **be-an** swim in groups. **me-i** swim across s.t. *Ia ~ sungai* She swam across the river. **me-kan** cause or allow s.o. to swim. **pe-** swimmer.

rencah₁ me-(²) 1 wade through, slough through. *Ia hrs ~ lumpur* He had to wade through mud. *Kerbau ~ sawah* The water buffalo tread through the wet rice field. **2** face s.t. difficult. *Ia ~ bahaya* He faced the danger. **te-** be trodden on.

rencah₂ mixed, various. **me-** mix. *Ia ~ tepung dgn gula* He mixed flour with sugar. **me-²** do several types (of work, etc.). **pe-** culinary seasoning.

rencana 1 program, plan, schedule. - *kerja* work schedule, work program. - *pelajaran* curriculum. - *Pembangunan Lima Tahun* Five-Year Development Plan. - *perjalanan* itinerary. **2** report, account, article. - *kuno* an old story. - *rapat* program of the meeting. - *surat* contents of the letter. **3** draft. - *anggaran belanja* budget proposal. **ber-** with a plan. *keluarga ~* a planned family (family planning). **me- 1** plan. **2** report. **3** narrate, tell. **me-kan 1** plan, project. *Mereka ~ belanja pemerintah* They planned the governmental budget. *Ia ~ serangan* He planned an attack. **2** relate, give an account, narrate. *Ia ~ surat* He composed a letter. **te-** be planned. **pe-** planner, planning authority. **pe-an 1** planning. *~ kota* city planning. **2** design. *~ rumah* house design.

rencang sound of clanging.

renceh see UANG.

rencek (*Jkt*) **me-kan** clean tree trunk of branches. **-an** branch.

renceng 1 slender. - *badannya* He is of slender build. **2** a string of s.t. - *bunga-bungaan* a string of flowers. **ber-(²)** o. after the other in a line. **me-(kan)** string s.t. **-an** a string, line of s.t. *~ mutiara* a string of pearls. *~ mobil* a line of cars (in traffic).

rencet₁ little by little. **be-², me-** by installments, piecemeal. *Ia membayar utangnya ~* He is paying his debt off in installments.

rencet₂ see RENTET.

rencik see RENIK.

rencis see RENJIS.

rencong Achenese dagger with curved handle.

renda lace. **be-** of lace, decorate with lace. **me-** crochet.

rendabel economically sound.

rendah low. - *budi* of low character. - *pangkat* low in rank. - *diri/hati* modest, unpretentious. **ke-hatian** modesty. *Pastor itu memang menampakkan ~* The priest really showed modesty. **me- 1** descend. *Pesawat itu ~* The plane descended. **2** be modest. *Wataknya selalu ~* He is by nature always modest. *"Saya," katanya ~* "Yes," she said modestly. **me-kan 1** lower. *Penjual itu ~ harganya* The seller lowered his price. *~ diri* humble o.s. *Ia ~ kwalitetnya* He lowered its quality. **2** humiliate, disparage. *Ia ~ temannya* He humiliated his friend. **ke-an 1** too short. *Badannya ~ sehingga tak diterima msk tentara* He was too short to be accepted for military service. **2** lowness. *~ galangan itu menyebabkan banjir* The lowness of the dike caused a flood. *~ budi* bad character, meanness, baseness. *~ hati* modesty. **-an** subordinate, of lower rank. **pe-an** lowering.

rendam be- 1 submerged. *Kerbau suka ~* Water buffalo like to stay submerged. **2** remain in o. place. *Ia selalu ~ di rumahnya* He is always staying in his house. **me-** soak, steep. *Ia ~ pakaian* She soaks the clothes. **me-kan** soak s.t. **te- 1** be soaked, be submerged in water. *Bajunya sdh semalam ~ di air* His clothes were soaked overnight. *~ samudera* engulfed by the ocean. *empat ribu rumah ~* 4,000 houses under water. **2** stay in a place without going out. *Ia selalu ~ di rumahnya* He is always hiding in his house. **pe-** soaking agent or device. *larutan ~* soaking agent solution. **pe-an** soaking, submersion of s.t.

rendang meat simmered in spices and coconut milk. **me-** make such a dish. **pe-an** frying pan.

rendefu rendezvous.

rendem see RENDAM.

rendemen sucrose content of sugar cane crop or sample.

rendeng₁ (*Jv*) rainy season. **-an** pertaining to the rainy season. *padi ~* rice field planted in the rainy season.

rendeng₂ (*Jkt*) **me-** grumble.

rendeng be-(²) be in a line, go s.w. in a line. **me-i** put together in line.

rendet 1 slow. **2** stall, get fouled up. **ke-an** foul-up.

renegosiasi renegotiation.

renek me- vibrate.

reng (*Jv, Sd*) laths used to support or press down roof tiles.

rengas₁ me- varnish.

rengas₂ dried up (of plants).

rengat₁ crack, split. - *hati* furious. **me- 1** crack, split, chap. **2** erupt. **3** have shooting pains. **me-kan** cause s.t. to crack. **-an** crockery.

rengat₂ k.o. insect that eats paper.

rengeh a neigh, whinny. **me-** neigh, whinny.

rengek mosquito.

rengek me- whine, whimper. **me-kan** say s.t. whiningly. **-an** whimper, nagging. **pe-** o. who nags.

rengeng-rengeng soft singing voice, hum.

renggang 1 distantly spaced, wide apart. *persahabatan yg -* a distant friendship. **2** loose (of knot). **me-** be apart, spaced. **me-i** avoid, withdraw from. *Mengapa ia ~ temannya?* Why did he avoid his friend? **me-kan, mempe-kan 1** space s.t. at a distance. *Ia ~ korsi* He spaced the chairs. *Oléh tindakan ini ia ~ diri dr pasukan induk* This move put him far from the main body of the troop. **2** loosen (knot, etc.). *~ ikatan* loosen a knot. *~ tali persahabatan* loosen the ties of friendship. **ke-an** aloofness, distance. *~ hubungan* strained relations. **pe-** s.t. causing aloofness.

renggat ring, concentric grain (in horns, wood).

rénggék see RÉNGÉK.

rengginang k.o. crisp cracker made of glutinous rice.

renggut me- 1 tug at, yank out. *~ nyawa* cause s.o.'s death. **2** obtain s.t. with great endeavor. *Ia ~ gelar juara* He managed to obtain the championship title. **me-²** repeatedly tug at. *Ia ~ jénggotnya sambil memikir soal yg sukar itu* He pulled at his beard when he considered difficult questions. **me-kan** pull s.t. off, make s.t. come off. *batu yg ~ hélem dr kepalanya* the rock that knocked the helmet from his head. *~ diri dr masa lalu* tear o.s. away from the past. **-an** a jerk, tug.

rengit (*Sd*) mosquito.

rengkah see REKAH.

rengkam k.o. seaweed that grows on sea bottom.

réngkéh bent (under burden). **te-(²)** bent (under burden).

rengket very tightly spaced, cramped (of writing). **me-** shiver with fear.

rengkiang elevated rice barn.

rengkuh (*Lit.*) **me-** tear, pull at. **-an** pulling.

réngréngan (*Jv*) blueprint.

réngsa beaten, apathetic. *- sengsara* beaten. **me-** be without will.

réngsék see RINGSEK.

rengus me- sullen, unhappy. **pe-** a sullen person.

rengut see RUNGUT.

renik fine (of rain, rice, etc.). **-²** very fine, delicate, very small. **be-² 1** in drizzles. **2** speckled. *kain putih ~ hitam* white cloth with fine black dots. **me-² 1** in drizzles. *Hujan ~* It is drizzling. **2** fine. *Berasnya ditumbuk ~* The rice is finely pounded. **3** speckled, dotted. *Citanya mérah ~* The cloth is red with fine dots. **ke-an** porosity, delicateness.

renjam see RUNJAM.

renjana 1 emotion. **2** in love, longing. **ke-an** emotionally.

renjis spot, stain. **me-** sprinkle, make spots. **me-i** splash on, besprinkle. **me-kan** sprinkle, spatter s.t. out.

renjul 1 bumpy. **2** crazy, incoherent.

rénovasi renovation. **me-** renovate s.t.

renta me-² speak in a loud voice, raise o.'s voice (in anger).

rénta worn-out. *tua -* very old and decrepit.

réntabilitas potential for producing a profit, remunerativeness.

rentak₁ se- 1 all at once, suddenly. **2** together, in a body. **me-(kan)** tug, pull violently. *Kuda itu ~ tali ingin berlari* The horse tugged at the reins in an effort to run. **te-** pulled off.

rentak₂ stamp o.'s foot. **be-(²)an** be engaged in stamping o.'s foot (in anger, etc.). **me-kan** cause s.t. to pound or stamp. *~ kaki* stamp o.'s foot on the ground. **-an** *kaki* stamping of feet.

rentak₃ rhythm, beat.

rentan susceptible (to illness, tantrums, etc.). **be-** get angry easily. **be-²an** become furiously angry. **ke-an** sensitivity, susceptibility.

rentang se- a distance, part of the way. **me- 1** stretch, extend. *Ia ~ tali* He stretched the cord. **2** build s.t. that spans or extends outward. *Meréka ~ jambatan* They built a bridge. *Mandor itu ~ jalan* The foreman extended the road. **me-i** stretch over s.t. *Ia ~ pintu dgn tali* She stretched a cord over the door. **me-kan** lay out, cause s.t. to extend. *Perusahaan itu ~ pipa minyak hingga ke laut* The firm constructed a pipeline to the sea. *~ sayap perusahaan di Jawa* stretch the wings of Jv industry. **te- 1** extended, stretched out. **2** hindered, obstructed. **-an** stretch, span. *~ harga* range of prizes. *jembatan tiga ~* three-span bridge. *~ waktu/pengendalian* span of time or control. **pe-** a stretching device.

rentas see RETAS.

rénte, rénten (*Fin.*) interest. **me-i** pay interest on. *Ia ~ utangnya* He pays interest on his debt. **me-kan** lend at interest. *Ia ~ uangnya* He lends his money out at interest.

rénténg see RÉNCÉNG.

réntenir creditor, usurer. *Si - suka makan riba* The usurer enjoys obtaining excessive interest.

réntét be-² in line, o. after the other. **me-** line up, extend in a line or series. **-an** series, sequence. *~ témbakan* a volley of gunfire.

renung me- 1 muse, be wistful. **2** daydream. *Sehari-hari ia duduk ~* He sits and stares dreamily every day. **me-i, me-kan 1** meditate upon, muse over. *Ia ~ kekasihnya yg jauh* She was musing about her faraway sweetheart. *saat yg paling tepat utk ~ diri* the best time to reflect upon yourself. **2** gaze at thoughtfully. **ter-** lost in reverie. **-an 1** meditation, reflection. **2** musing. **pe-** daydreamer.

renyah₁ 1 concentration, careful attention. **2** requiring attention. *pekerjaan yg -* a job requiring careful attention. **be-** give special attention. **me- 1** give careful attention. **2** pick and choose tidbits.

renyah₂ 1 melodious (of voices, etc.). *Suaranya -* He has a pleasant voice. **2** crispy (of food).

renyah₃ see RANYAH.

renyai sprinkle, drizzle. **-²** in drizzles. *hujan ~ a* slight shower. **be-an** drip. *Badan olahragawan itu ~ keringat* The athlete's body dripped with sweat.

renyak me- crush, torture s.t. or s.o.

renyang (*M*) **1** restless. **2** feel out of sorts.

rényéh me-(²) whimper.

renyek (*Jkt*) crumpled, shrunk.

renyem 1 (*Sd*) itch. *Seluruh badannya* - He itched over his entire body. 2 desperate, not knowing what to do. *Pikirannya - ketika mengingat soal itu* He became desperate whenever he remembered that problem.

renyoh, renyok see RENYUK.

renyuk (*Lit.*) crumpled (up), crinkled. me- crumple up, cause crinkles. *Angin ~ pasir* The wind stirred the sand into ridges.

renyut see DENYUT.

réog, réok 1 cackle. 2 (*Jv*) k.o. masked dance. 3 (*Sd*) k.o. singing comedy group.

réol see RIOL.

réorganisasi reorganization. me-kan reorganize. pe-an process of reorganizing.

réorganisir me- reorganize.

réoriéntasi reorientation. me-kan reorient s.t.

réot see RÉYOT.

Rep. [*Républik*] republic.

repak crisp, fragile.

réparasi repairs. me- repair s.t. me-kan have s.t. repaired.

repas dry and brittle, crumbly.

répatrian repatriate.

répatriasi repatriation. me-(kan) repatriate s.o.

répék see RÉPÉT.

Repelita [*Rencana Pembangunan Lima Tahun*] Five-Year Development Plan.

réperkusi repercussion.

répertoar, répertoir, répertorium repertory (of dance, drama, etc.).

répés me- 1 fidget. 2 waste time.

répét me- 1 chatter, blabber. 2 splatter (of an oar, etc.). -an 1 empty chatter, gossip. 2 splatter. pe-chatterbox, blatherer.

repetén (*Math.*) phase (of a decimal fraction).

répetir 1 repeat (inoculations). 2 repeating (rifle).

répétisi 1 rehearsal. 2 quiz. 3 repetition.

repih crumbly. -² crumbs, extremely crumbled. me- crumble. me-kan crumble s.t., make crumbs of.

repis see REPIH.

répliek, réplik (*Leg.*) counterplea, rejoinder.

repolper revolver.

répolusi see RÉVOLUSI.

répormir see RÉFORMIR.

réportase 1 way of reporting. 2 article. me-kan report on s.t.

repot (*Coll.*) report. me-kan report, announce. -an a report.

répot 1 busy, occupied. *Ia sangat* - He is very busy. *Jangan* - Do not trouble yourself. 2 troublesome, full of meticulous details. *Pekerjaan ini* - This work is difficult. -² very occupied with details. *O, tak usah ~!* Do not go to any trouble! Do not bother! me-i cause inconvenience to s.o. *Tak ada yg akan ~ kau* There is nothing to inconvenience you. me-kan cause a fuss, make difficulties for. *Perkawinan itu tak sedikit ~ ayahnya* The wedding has caused her father a lot of bother. *Pil itu mahal dan ~ juga* That pill is only expensive and troublesome. *Peraturan ini ~ pekerjaan* This reg-

ulation made the job difficult. ke-an 1 stir, bustle. 2 very busy.

reprep (*Jkt*) torn.

répréséntasi delegation.

répréséntatif representative. ke-an representativeness.

réprési repression.

réprésif repressive.

réproduksi reproduction. me-(kan) reproduce.

réptil reptile.

républik republic. - *Dominika* Dominican Republic. - *Rakyat Cina* People's Republic of China.

républikén republican.

repuh see RAPUH.

repuh-repuh padlock.

reput 1 rotten, crumbling into decay. - *relai* rotten. 2 loose, sandy. 3 (*Geol.*) friable. me- putrefy. pe-an putrefaction.

réputasi reputation.

requisitoir see RÉKUISITOIR.

rerak broken into pieces.

reramuan all k.o. ingredients (in culinary or medicinal preparations).

rerangka framework.

rerantingan all manner of branches and twigs.

rerasan (*Jv*) thinking and talking (about s.o.). - *dan bisik-bisik* backbiting and whispering.

rerata on the average. - *terbobot* (*Math.*) weighted average.

rerep subsided, calmed down.

rérét sound of squeaking. be-an squeak.

reribu thousands.

rerintih moans, groans.

rerintik drizzle, drops.

rerompok see ROROMPOK.

rerongkong, rerongkongan 1 skeleton. 2 carcass, cadaver.

rerongsokan wreckage.

rérot see ÉROT₂.

rerumput, rerumputan grassy field.

reruntuh, reruntuk wreckage, debris, ruins. - *pesawat itu tlh bercampur dgn mayat penumpangnya* The wreckage of the plane was mixed with the passengers' bodies. - *dunia/masyarahat* prostitute. - *mobil* automobile wreckage. -an ruins, debris. *Candi itu tinggal sbg ~ saja* That temple shrine survives only as a ruin.

Rés.₁ [*Résidén*] Resident.

Rés.₂ [*Résimén*] Regiment.

resa movements of baby about to be born.

resah fidgety, restless. *suara* - strained voice, a restless sound. me-kan cause nervousness and uneasiness. *berita yg ~* disturbing news. ke-an unrest, restlessness. *~ sosial* social unrest.

resak k.o. commercial timber tree.

resam₁ k.o. fern.

resam₂ 1 organized, customary ways. 2 equal to. se- equal to.

resan anxious, worried.

resap me- 1 penetrate, infiltrate. *Naséhat itu ~ ke dlm hatinya* That advice penetrated their hearts. 2 ooze out, soak through and out. *Itu ~ keluar* That oozed out. 3 become absorbed, dissipate.

Di tengah hutan, jalan itu ~ tertutup daun-daunan In the middle of the woods, the path vanished, absorbed in the foliage. **me-i 1** penetrate into, be absorbed. *Kopi yg tertumpah tdk dapat ~ kain lap itu* The rag could not absorb the spilt coffee. **2** mentally digest, understand thoroughly. *Tdklah anda ~ buku itu?* Didn't you grasp the contents of that book? **me-kan 1** cause s.t. to penetrate or ooze. *Dingin malam mulai ~ pengaruhnya* The evening cold began to make its influence felt. **2** cause s.t. to dissipate. *Sinar mata hari cepat ~ embun pagi* Sunshine quickly dispersed the morning dew. **-an** absorption. *~ dlm* resorption. **pe-an 1** process of absorbing. **2** infiltration.
résbang bench, cot.
resek cluttered.
résék me- 1 look for s.t. by feeling with the hands. **2** investigate.
résén recent.
résénsi book review. **me-(kan)** write a book-review about. **pe-** reviewer.
résénsor reviewer.
resep₁ (*Sd*) enjoyable.
resep₂ see RESAP.
resép 1 recipe. **2** prescription. **3** recommended program. *- stabilitas ékonomi* a recipe for economic stability. **-²an** bother getting a prescription. *Beli obat di situ nggak usah ~* You can buy medicine there without bothering with getting a prescription.
resépsi reception. **me-kan** hold a reception for s.o.
resépsionis receptionist.
resérse, resérsir detective.
résérvat land set aside for an ethnic group, reservation.
resérve₁ reserve supply.
resérve₂ reticence. *setia tanpa -* completely loyal.
réservoir /réservoar/ reservoir, reserves.
resés recess of parliament. **me-kan** put (parliament) in recess.
resési (*Econ.*) recession.
resi₁ 1 receipt (esp. for mailed or shipped items). **2** baggage check.
resi₂ title for ascetics in *wayang* stories.
resia see RAHASIA.
résidén resident, head of a residency (in colonial administration). **ke-an** residency.
résidivis repeated offender, former convict.
résidu residue.
resik (*Jv*) pure, clean.
résiko see RISIKO.
résim see RÉZIM.
résimén (*Mil.*) regiment.
resiprokatif reciprocal.
resiprositas reciprocity.
résisténsi resistance.
résital music recital.
résitasi recitation. **me-(kan)** recite s.t.
Réskrim [*Resérse Kriminil*] Criminal Investigation Bureau (of police).
resmi 1 official, legitimate. **2** formal. **me-kan**

1 make s.t. official, authenticate s.t. *~ gedung* dedicate a building. *Saya sbg ketua ~ dibukanya kongrés ini* I, as chairman, officially declare this congress open. **2** announce officially. **ke-an 1** official confirmation, official announcement. *Masih blm ada ~ apakah ia benar dinaikkan pangkat atau tdk* There is no official confirmation yet as to whether he has really been promoted or not. **2** of an official character. **-²an** act formally (when it is inappropriate to do so). **pe-an, peng-an 1** official announcement or appointment. **2** official appointment. **3** formal ceremony (of dedication, etc.).
résolusi resolution. **me-(kan)** make a resolution.
résonansi resonance. **me-kan** resonate s.t.
Résopim [*Révolusi Sosialisme Pimpinan Nasional*] Revolution, Socialism, National Leadership (Sukarno-era slogan).
résort 1 police administrative unit at county level (the *kabupatén* level). **2** army administrative unit at level just below division.
résosialisasi resocialization.
réspék respect, to respect. *Saya - pd idé orisinal* I respect original ideas.
réspon, réspons response.
respondén respondent (esp. in surveys).
résponsi review session (at college).
résponsibilitas responsibility.
résponsif responsive, lively.
réstan₁ remainder, remnant.
réstan₂ see POS.
réstitusi repayment of expenses incurred for medical care.
réstoran restaurant. *- kaki lima* sidewalk food-vending stalls. **pe-** restaurateur. **pe-an** restaurant management.
réstorasi₁ food service on a train. *gerbong -* dining car.
restorasi₂ restoration (of monuments, etc.). **me-** restore s.t.
réstriksi restriction. **me-(kan)** restrict.
réstrukturisasi restructuring. **me-(kan)** restructure s.t.
restu blessing. **me-i** bless s.t., approve of. *Usaha itu tdk di-i pemerintah* The gvt. did not look favorably on that project. **pe-an 1** giving a blessing. **2** approval. *~ tujuan-tujuan* approval of the purposes and aims.
restung k.o. boil on nose (us. caused by venereal disease).
resu see RESI₁.
résultan, résultante resultant.
résumé summary. **me-kan** make a summary.
rét (*Bri.*) diamonds.
réta me-(²) talk foolishly and endlessly.
retai crack, fissure.
retak 1 crack, fissure. *- batu* irreparably damaged. *- tangan* lines on the palm of hand. **2** cracked. *Tak ada gading yg tak -* No man is without a fault (Literally, there is no ivory without a crack). *-retai* covered with cracks. **-²** thoroughly cracked. *~ bulu ayam* easy to compromise. **me-** crack,

show a crack. **me-kan 1** cause a crack. **2** cleave, cause a rift. ~ *kesatuan bangsa* split up the unity of the nation. **ke-an** crack, fissure, rift. **-an** a crack. ~ *és* crack in the ice.

retas me- rip open, take apart. *Ia ~ dinding* He broke through the wall. ~ *jahitan* take sewing apart by pulling out the thread. ~ *jalan* cut a road through. **pe- 1** o. who breaks through. ~ *jalan* pioneer. **2** instrument for opening s.t.

rétéh see RETIH₁.

reténsi (*Ling.*) retention.

rétét sound of rattling. **be-** give off a rattling noise.

rététét tétét 1 sound of bugle or trumpet. **2** sound of barrage of gunfire.

retih₁ crackling sound. - *api* crackling of a fire. **me-** crackle.

retih₂ me- form beads (of sweat).

retir see RETUR.

retna see RATNA.

rétok see RÉCOK.

retool /ritul/ see RITUL.

rétorik, rétorika rhetoric.

rétoris rhetorical.

rétorsi retorsion.

retrét (*Rel.*) retreat.

rétribusi 1 toll or fee to use a public facility. - *jalan* road tax. **2** dues (for club).

rétrospéksi retrospection.

rétrospéktif retrospective.

retul see RITUL.

retuling see RITULING.

retur (*Coll.*) round trip (of plane tickets). **me-(kan)** return (a letter) to sender.

réuni reunion.

réunifikasi reunification.

révaluasi revaluation.

révans revenge (esp. in sports, cards, etc.).

révisi revision. **me-** revise.

révisionis revisionist.

révisionisme revisionism.

révisir revise.

révitalisasi revitalization.

révolusi revolution. **me-kan** revolutionize.

révolusionér revolutionary. **me-kan** revolutionize. **ke-an** revolutionariness. **peng-an** revolutionizing.

révolusionérisme an outlook based on revolutionary principles.

révolusionisasi revolutionizing. **peng-an** process of revolutionizing.

réwak see RÉBAK₂.

réwang₁ me- 1 swing. *Ia ~ tongkatnya* He was swinging his walking stick. *Kapal itu ~ pd tali jangkarnya* The ship was swinging on the anchor chain. **2** (*Naut.*) yaw.

réwang₂ (*Jv*) servant, assistant. **me-i** help s.o. to achieve s.t.

réwang₃ (*M*) **me-** grope about.

réwél 1 hard to please, fussy. *Guru ini* - This teacher is hard to please. **2** troublesome. *Mobil tangan kedua sering* - A used car is often trouble-

some. *Bayiku* - *semalaman* My baby was fussy all night through. **me-** become choosy. *Sejak pulang dr kota, Hamid* ~ After coming home from the big city, Hamid has been picky. **ke-an** choosiness, fussiness.

réwes see NGRÉWÉS.

réyal see RIAL.

réyog k.o. E. Jv folk dance.

réyot falling to pieces, decrepit (of houses, etc.).

rezeki 1 livelihood. *mencari* - make o.'s way in life. **2** luck, fortune. *Kalau ada -, tentu saya akan mendapat pekerjaan itu* If I have any luck, I will surely get that job. *Itu sdh -nya* That was his good fortune. - *jangan ditolak* Do not reject any opportunity, invitation, etc. - *batin* richness of inner life. - *mata* things that are nice to look at. - *murah* prosperous. - *nomplok* windfall, s.t. that o. gets in large quantities without expecting it. **3** (*Isl.*) blessing (of God). **ke-an** prosperity.

rézim regime.

RFJ [*Républik Féderal/Féderasi Jérman*] Federal Republic of Germany.

rg. [*regu*] team.

rhéumatik see RÉMATIK.

rhum see RUM₁.

RI [*Républik Indonésia*] Republic of Indonesia.

ria₁ cheerful. - *hati* delight, delightful. - *riuh* merry, happy. **be-(²)** have a good time. **ke-an** joy, cheerfulness, fun.

ria₂ 1 proud, jealously proud. **2** haughty.

riadat (*Isl.*) practice of penance and mortification for spiritual enlightenment.

riah₁ see MERIAH.

riah₂ see RIA₂.

riak₁ 1 ripples. - *air* water ripples. - *gelombang* wavelength. - *remiak* rippling. - *udara* air waves (radio). **2** indication, intention. *Sdh kelihatan -nya bhw ia akan lari* His intention to run away was clear. **be-(²), me-** ripple, move in ripples. **-an** ripples.

riak₂ phlegm, mucus. **be-(²)** cough up phlegm.

riak₃ see RIA₂.

rial 1 Saudi Arabian currency. **2** money.

riam river rapids.

rian measure of yarn or thread equivalent to o. skein or ¹⁄₁₆ of a *tukal* .

riang 1 cheerful, joyful. - *gembira* dizzily happy. *Saya - gembira kamu datang* I am delighted that you are coming. - *hati* in high spirits. **2** dizzy. **me-** feel dizzy and feverish, out of sorts. *Badanku merasa ~* My body feels feverish. ~ *kemelut* (*Med.*) be in a fever moving toward its climax. **me-kan 1** cheer up, make happy, exhilarate. **2** excite. **ke-an** cheerfulness, exhilaration. **pe-** a cheerful person.

riang-riang cicada.

riap me- protrude, swell out. *Tubuhnya pernah ~ subur* She was once buxom. **me-(²)** stick out every which way. *Rambutnya ~* His hair stuck out in every direction.

rias makeup. *méja* - dressing table. - *panggung* stage makeup. - *rupa* makeup. **be-** make up, adorn o.s. ~ *mata* beautify o.'s eyes. ~ *rambut* do o.'s hair. **me-(i)** make s.o. up. *Dia sering* ~ *pengantin* He often does the makeup for bridal couples. **-an** ornament, article of adornment. **pe-** makeup person. ~ *rambut* hairdresser.

riba₁ lap. **me-** take on o.'s lap. *Ia* ~ *anaknya* She took her child on her lap. **-an** lap.

riba₂ usury, excessive interest. **pe-** usurer.

ribak see REBAK.

ribatat family relationship.

ribon (*Sport*) rebound. **me-** cause a rebound (in billiards, etc.).

ribu thousand. *tiga* - 3,000. **se-** 1,000. ~ *satu* a huge number, innumerable. **kese-** thousandth. **seperse-** o. o.-thousandth. **menye-** (*hari*) commemorate the thousandth day of a person's death. **be-** thousands. *bisu* ~ *bahasa* not speak, refuse to say a word. ~ *maaf* a thousand pardons. **be-²** by the thousands, thousands of. **-an** 1 a currency note or coin with the value of 1,000. 2 in thousands, by the thousands. ~ *kilo* thousands of kilometers.

ribut 1 storm, gale. *angin* - squall. 2 noisy, loud. *Jangan* - Do not be noisy. **-²** s.t. noisy, uproar. **be-, me-** 1 be stormy, storm. 2 be noisy, rowdy. **me-i** 1 make a fuss over s.t. or s.o. *Nénék sdh* ~ *kakék ttg jodohku* My grandmother had made a fuss with my grandfather about my prospective spouse. 2 make s.t. noisy. **me-kan** 1 cause a noisy disturbance. 2 make a fuss about s.t. **ke-an** stir, commotion, disturbance. **pe-** troublemaker.

ricau me- chatter, twitter. **me-kan** blather s.t. out. *Ia* ~ *bermacam-macam kalimat anéh* He blathered all k.o. weird sentences.

rices drinking straws.

ricih₁ see RINCIH.

ricih₂, ricik me-(²) make a rushing sound (such as water in terraced ditch). *Airnya mengalir* ~ The water flowed with a rushing sound.

ricis (*Jkt*) **me-** slice, chop (ingredients for a dish).

ricu(h) chaotic, quarrelsome. **ke-an** chaos.

rida see RÉLA.

ridah, ridat, riddah, riddat see MURTAD.

ridha, ridla, ridhlo, ridho see RÉLA.

ridi see RÉDI.

riding (*Lit.*) noose trap.

ridip (dorsal) fins.

ridla, ridlo, ridloh, rido see RÉLA.

rifri (*Sport*) referee.

rigai (*M*) skinny.

rigi -² cog, tooth. **be-²** 1 toothed with cogs. 2 serrated. **me-(kan)** notch.

rigu see TERIGU.

rihal see RÉHAL.

rihat see ISTIRAHAT.

rihting, rihting wéser directional signals (on vehicles).

riil /riyil/ real. *pendapatan* - real income. **me-kan** make s.t. a reality. **ke-an** reality.

rijang (*Geol.*) flint, chert.

rik sound of creaking.

rikosét ricochet.

riksa, riksya rickshaw.

rikuh (*Jv*) feel awkward or ashamed in the presence of o.'s betters. **ke-an** feeling of embarrassment.

ril see RÉL.

rila, rilah see RÉLA.

rilék, riléks /rilék/ 1 relax. 2 carefree.

rilis release (of a tune, record).

rim₁ 1 ream, a measurement for paper. 2 a carton (of cigarettes).

rim₂ (*Coll.*) military style belt (for ammunition, etc.).

rima rhyme. **be-** rhyme. **me-kan** cause to rhyme.

rimas 1 anxious, worried. 2 discontented, irritated. **me-kan** irritate.

rimau see HARIMAU.

rimba jungle, forest. - *belantara* vast forest. - *piatu* jungle. - *raya* vast forest. - *sawang* wilderness. *hilang tak tentu -nya* lost without a trace. **me-** become a jungle or wilderness.

rimbas small adz. **me-** cut with an adz.

rimbit see RÉMBÉT₂.

rimbu forest.

rimbun thick, dense (of foliage, forests, etc.). *Daunnya* - The leaves are thick. **me-** become dense (of foliage, etc.). **me-i** cover s.t. over with dense foliage, etc. *Atap kami di-i pohon bugénfil* Bougainvillea covers our roof. **(ke)-an** lushness, denseness.

rimis (*M*) half a cent.

rimpang rhizome (ginger, tumeric, etc.).

rimpel pleat, pleated. *rok* - *lébar* a skirt with wide pleats (ironed in). **be-** be pleated. **me-** pleat s.t.

rimpi dried fruit slices.

rimpuh tired, exhausted. **me-kan** exhaust s.o.

rimpung me- bind the arms and legs.

rinai₁ (*Lit.*) **me-** hum.

rinai₂ see RENYAI.

rinci detail. **me-(kan)** 1 plan, schedule. *Meréka* ~ *keramaian resmi* They planned an official celebration. 2 break s.t. down into sections, details, etc. *di-in dlm beberapa kecamatan* be broken down into several subdistricts. **mempe-** specify the details. ~ *ongkos yg tlh dihabiskan* give a detailed account of the costs incurred. **te-, terpe-** with details specified. *secara* ~ in detail. **ke-an** specification. **-an** details, breakdown. **pe-an** 1 details, the way s.t. is broken down (of calculation, etc.). ~ *anggaran belanjanya dpt diminta dr Bp diréktur* The details of its budget can be requested from the director. 2 subsection. **peme-an** elaboration, specifying of the details.

rincih small parts, thin slices. **me-** cut into thin slices, small pieces.

rincis me- specify.

rincu, rincuh see RICU(H).

rindang 1 leafy, luxuriant. 2 shady. **-an** luxuriance, lushness.

rinding me- feel suddenly frightened, feel eerie. **me-kan** cause o. to feel eerie.

rindu 1 longing, yearning. *Ia melepaskan -nya pd anaknya* She did it out of her deep longing for her child. - *dendam* deep yearning. 2 feel homesick for, yearn for. - *akan kampung halaman* long for o.'s home town. **me-** become full of yearning. **me-i** long for. **me-kan 1** yearn for, miss. *Ia ~ anaknya* She yearned for her child. **2** cause s.o. to yearn (for s.t.). *Nyanyian itu membuat ayahnya ~ masa kecilnya* That melody awoke in his father a nostalgia for his childhood. **ke-an 1** longing, yearning. **2** (*Coll.*) favorite. *makanan ~ saya* my favorite food. **pe-** o. who yearns for s.t.

ring₁ (*Auto.*) ring. *- séher* piston ring.

ring₂ (*Sport*) boxing ring.

ring₃ sound of ringing.

ringan 1 light in weight. *- kepala* quick-witted, smart. *- tangan* quick to help, generous. *- tulang* active, hard-working. **2** minor in importance. *operasi -* minor operation or surgery. *minuman -* soft drink. **me(mpe)-kan 1** lighten, alleviate. *Ia mau ~ muatan* He wants to lighten the burden. *~ kaki/langkah* be willing to go s.w., accept an invitation. **2** make light of. *Ia ~ kewajibannya* He takes his responsibilities lightly. **ke-an 1** lightness. **2** relief, dispensation. *~ hukuman* (*Leg.*) commutation of a sentence. *~ pajak/perpajakan* tax relief. **3** too light. **pe-** s.t. which lightens s.t. **pe-an 1** lightening of s.t. **2** (*Leg.*) commutation of a sentence.

ringgik see RÉNGÉK.

ringgit₁ 1 two-and-a-half rupiah (note). **2** a gold coin (often used for pendants). **3** national currency of Malaysia and Brunei. **-an** in two and a half rupiah notes.

ringgit₂ (*Lit.*) **me-(i)** notch s.t. **be-(²)** toothed, notched.

ringih me- neigh, whinny.

ringik see RÉNGÉK.

ringis me- grimace, grin. *~ kesakitan* grimace in pain. *tertawa ~* laugh with a sneer. **me-kan** *gigi* show o.'s teeth.

ringkai dry (of leaves), arid. *- ringan* dry and light. **me-** be dry, shriveled up. *Daunnya kering ~* The leaves are dry and shriveled up.

ringkas brief, succinct, concise. *dgn -* briefly, in short, succinctly. **-nya** in brief, in a word. **me-kan 1** shorten, make brief. **2** summarize, contract. **ke-an** succinctness. **-an** résumé, précis, summary. *~ ceritera* the story in short. *~ tésis* dissertation abstract. **pe-** o. who summarizes.

ringkih frail. **me-** become frail. **ke-an** frailty.

ringkik me- neigh, whinny. **-an** a neigh.

ringking me- yell.

ringkok deep dish or shallow bowl to eat from.

ringkuk 1 bent over, stooped. **2** shut up, confined. **me- 1** bend over, stoop over. **2** confined, cooped up. *Dua tahun ia ~ dlm tahanan* He was confined to a prison for two years. **me-kan 1** cause to bend. **2** imprison, jail, confine. **-an 1** stooping over. **2** imprisonment.

ringkus me- 1 catch by binding the limbs. *Ia ~ burung* He caught a bird by snaring its legs. **2** take into custody, catch. *Senjata meréka tlh disemuanya* All their weapons have been confiscated. *Polisi sempat ~ penjahat di Gang VI* The police managed to catch a criminal at Lane VI.

ringsek broken in pieces, totally damaged. *Mobil-*

nya - karena tabrakan His car was totaled in the wreck. **-an** in bad shape, cheap. *perempuan ~* cheap whores.

ringsut decline. *Nilai dollar AS terus -* The value of the US dollar continues to decline. **me-kan** cause s.t. to move slightly.

rintang₁ (*Lit.*) **me-(²)** entertain, distract. *Ia ~ anak itu* She entertained the child. *~ hati* enjoy. *~ pikiran* divert o.'s thoughts. *~ waktu* kill time. **pe-²** distraction. *~ waktu* time killer.

rintang₂ me-i 1 block (o.'s path). **2** interfere with, hamper. *Ia tdk mau ~ perjalanannya* He does not want to interfere with her trip. **me-kan** use s.t. to block (o.'s way, etc.). *Org jahat itu ~ balok di jalan* The bandits barred the road with a barrier. **te-** obstructed. **-an 1** hindrance, obstacle, holdup. *Saya mau datang kalau tak ada ~* I want to come if nothing interferes. **2** barrier, restriction. *~ alam* natural barrier. **pe-** obstacle, o. who hinders.

rintas me- take a short-cut.

rintih a moan, groan. **me-** groan, whimper. **me-kan** bemoan, whimper about s.t. *Bosan aku mendengar dia ~ penderitaanya* I am fed up with listening to him whine about his sufferings. **-an** a groan, moan. **pe-** mourner. *~ séwaan* hired mourner.

rintik 1 spot, fine spot. **2** droplet. **-²** small spots, dots. *~ pd kulitnya* small spots on the skin. **be-² 1** with fine dots. **2** fall in small drops. *Hujan ~* It is drizzling. **me-(²)** drip. *Peluh ~ di dahinya* Sweat dripped down her forehead.

rintis me- 1 clear a way, path. *Ia ~ hutan* He cleared a way through the forest. **2** do pioneering work. *Meréka ~ usaha koperasi itu* They were doing pioneering work in cooperative ventures. **me-kan** clear a path for s.o. **-an 1** pioneering effort. **2** path. **pe-** pioneer. *jalan ~* the first road built in an area. **kepe-an** pioneering work. **pe-an** pioneering.

riol sewer, drain.

rioléring sewers, drainage system.

ripot see REPOT.

ripuh 1 miserable, sad. **2** in a mess.

ripuk broken, damaged.

ri ri ri sound made to call ducks.

RIS [*Républik Indonésia Serikat*] Federal Republic of Indonesia (1949-1950).

risa a callus.

risalah, risalat 1 essay, composition, treatise. **2** circular, brochure. **3** minutes (of meeting), proceedings. **4** report (of assets).

risau restless, nervous. **me-** become worried. **me-i, me-kan 1** worry about. *Aku ~ anak itu* I am worried about that child. **2** make restless, cause worry. *Soal itu ~ pikiran saya* That problem worries me. **ke-an** worry, restlessness. **-an** a cause for worry. **pe-** o. who worries a lot.

riset, risét research. **me-** do research on. *~ faktor démografi* research demographic factors. **pe-** researcher.

risih feel uncomfortable about s.t. risqué, taboo, etc. *Mendengar kata-kata semacam itu kupingnya jadi -* When he heard that sort of talk, his ears began to burn. **me-kan** cause s.o. to feel uncomfortable. *Kata-katanya ~ saya* Her words made me uncomfortable.

risik₁ (*Lit.*) confidential, inquiry. **me-** make secret inquiries, sound out. *Ia ~ dulu sblm melamarnya* He first inquired about her before asking for her hand.

risik₂ be- 1 rustling (noise). **2** be noisy. **me-** rustle. *Daun ~ ditiup angin* The leaves rustle in the wind. **me-kan** cause a rustling sound.

risiko risk, peril. *Ia memikul -* He took the risk. **be-** risky.

riskan, riskant risky.

riskir me- risk s.t.

risoles k.o. croquette, rissole.

risuh embarrassed.

Risték [*Riset dan Téknologi*] Research and Technology.

rit₁ trip made by a public vehicle. *Bis ini jalan empat - sehari* This bus makes four trips a day.

rit₂ sound of creaking.

rit₃ see RICES.

riting see RIHTING.

ritme rhythm.

ritmis rhythmic.

rits, ritsléting zipper.

ritual ritual.

ritul me- 1 (*Coll.*) reorganize. *Cara berpikir pemimpin-pemimpin kita hrs di-* Our leaders' way of thinking has to be refashioned. **2** purge (Sukarno era). **pe-an** retooling, reorganization.

rituling 1 (*Coll.*) reorganization. **2** purge (Sukarno era).

ritus rite.

riuh noisy, vociferous. *- miuh* noise, brouhaha. *- rendah* noisy, boisterous. **me-kan** increase volume of noise, make s.t. noisy. *Ia ~ tertawanya* She laughed louder. **ke-an** din, clamor.

riung₁ range of mountains.

riung₂ me- conduct or gather for a ceremonial meal.

riut₁ sound of s.t. creaking. **me-** creak. **me-kan** cause to creak.

riut₂ me- be bent or folded. **me-kan** bend s.t., fold s.t.

rival (*Lit.*) rival.

rivalitas (*Lit.*) rivalry, competition.

riwan (*Sd*) dream of no significance. *Ah, itu kan cuma -* That was just an insignificant dream, you know.

riwayat 1 story, narrative, tale. *- hidup* biography, curriculum vitae. *- singkat* brief account. **2** history. **be- 1** narrate, relate a story. **2** historic. **me-kan** tell, narrate.

riyep (*Jkt*) **me-** dim (lights).

rizeki, rizki see REZEKI.

RK₁ [*Rum Katolik*] Roman Catholic.

RK₂ [*Rukun Kampung*] **1** village association. **2** a unit of political organization just below the village level.

RKZ [*Rooms Katholieke Ziekenhuis*] a hospital run by the Roman Catholic Church.

R.M. [*Radén Mas*] (*Jv*) title of minor male nobility.

RMS [*Républik Maluku Selatan*] S. Moluccan Republic (secession attempt from central gvt. in 1950s and 1960s).

robah see UBAH.

robak-rabik torn in shreds, in rags.

robék torn. **me-** tear. **me-i** rip repeatedly, tear to shreds. **pe-an** act of tearing. **-an** s.t. torn. *~ kertas* scrap of paper.

Robbi (*Isl.*) God. *Ya ~!* Oh, God!

rober (*Bri.*) rubber.

roboh collapse. *Digergajinya pohon kelapa itu hingga -* They sawed at the coconut tree till it came down. *Témbakan mengena Amin dan ia -* The shot hit Amin and he collapsed. **me-kan 1** cause to come down. *Perusahaan itu ~ gedung itu* The firm demolished the building. *Ia memukul dan ~ adiknya* He hit and knocked down his brother. **2** overthrow, bring down. *Meréka berusaha ~ kabinétnya* They tried to bring down his cabinet. **3** (*Sport*) floor s.o. **ke-an 1** collapse. **2** ruins. **-an** debris, rubble.

robot₁ (*Jkt*) sound of explosion. **me-** explode.

robot₂ 1 robot. **2** unimaginative person.

rocét (*Sd*) disorderly, in a mess. **ke-an** disorder, confusion.

rocok me- 1 flow (forcefully). **2** (*Jkt*) leak.

roda wheel. *- air* water wheel. *- angin* bicycle. *- dua* (motor) bike. *- empat* car. *- gigi* cogwheel. *- gila* (*Auto.*) flywheel. *- penghidupan* wheel of fortune, fate. *- pilih* telephone dial. *- stir* steering wheel. *- tiga* **1** pedicab. **2** three-wheeled vehicle (in general). **be-** wheeled. *motor gerobak ~ enam* a six-wheeled truck. **me-i** put wheels on.

rodan (*Lit.*) painful, tender.

rodat Arabian song accompanied by the tambourine.

rodéntisida rat poison.

rodi forced labor, corvée (of colonial period). **be-, me- 1** do forced labor. **2** (*Coll.*) work extra hard.

rodok me- 1 stab with upward thrust. **2** dash, in a hurry. *Ia ~ ke kantor karena sdh terlambat* He dashed to the office because he was late.

rodong₁ (*Lit.*) **me-** run into, meet by chance. **me-kan** cause to be intimate.

rodong₂ me- wander about.

rofel (*Coll.*) **me-** do more than o. thing at once.

rogoh me- 1 grope, search (in pocket, bag, etc.). *Ia ~ kantongnya* He groped around in his pocket. **2** grope after s.t. *~ gerétan* poke around for a lighter. **me-i** repeatedly grope in s.t. *Meréka ~ saku Amir* They groped in Amir's pocket. **pe-** o. who gropes.

rogol me-, mempe- rape s.o.

roh spirit, soul. *Ia meniupkan - ke dlm badan manusia* He breathed a soul into the human body. *-nya melayang* He died. *- héwani* life spirit in animals. *- insani* spirit of man. *- kudus* (*Rel.*) the Holy Spirit. *- rohani* quickening of spiritual life. *- suci* (*Rel.*) the Holy Spirit.

rohani spiritual. *- dan jasmani* spiritual and physi-

cal. *nyanyian* - church hymn. *santapan* - lessons in religion. **ke-an** spirituality. *préstasi* ~ spiritual achievement.
rohaniah spiritual. **me-kan** spiritualize.
rohaniawan, rohaniwan churchman.
rohaniawati, rohaniwati churchwoman.
rohmat see RAHMAT.
Rohu'l Kudus (*Rel.*) the Holy Spirit.
roi, roilén (*Coll.*) building alignment.
rojok see ROCOK.
rojol me- protrude, jut out, emerge. *Kepalanya* ~ *dr jendéla* His head emerged from a window.
rok skirt. *baju* - women's Western-style dress. - *dlm slip.* - *jadi* ready-made dress. - *jéngki* tight-fitting skirt. - *plisir* skirt with factory-made pleats. - *span* k.o. tight-fitting skirt. **be-** wear a skirt.
rokaat see RAKAAT.
roker rock musician.
rokét rocket. - *bertingkat* multistage rocket. - *kendali* guided missle. - *penggerak* booster rocket. **me-(kan)** rocket s.t. **pe-an** rocketing.
rokh see ROH.
rokhani see ROHANI.
rokhaniah see ROHANIAH.
roki clothes, frock.
rokok cigarette. - *daun/klobot* cigarette made with corn husk or palm leaf wrapper. - *klembak* k.o. cigarette made with tobacco and incense. - *krétek* clove-flavored cigarette. - *linting* rolled cigarette. - *putih* cigarette without clove flavoring. - *serutu/cerutu* cigar. **be-an** smoke (of several people). **me-, nge-** smoke s.t. *Dilarang* ~ No smoking. **pe-** smoker, habitual smoker. **pe-an** pipe or any instrument for smoking.
roko-roko k.o. bird.
rokrak piece of wood.
rol₁ (*Thea.*) role.
rol₂ 1 roll, roller. - *mesin tulis* typewriter platen. - *rambut* roll to put the hair up in. **2** a numerical classifier for rolled things. *dua - film* two rolls of film. *empat - tisu* four rolls of toilet paper. **(me)nge-** roll (o.'s hair). **-²an** hair rollers.
rol₃ k.o. small bread.
rolade k.o. meat loaf.
rolét roulette.
roltar(t) k.o. cylinder-shaped cake served in slices.
rom cream. *mentéga* - butter. *slag* - whipped cream.
roma see BULU.
Roma Rome.
Romadhon, Romadlon, Romadon see RAMADAN.
roman₁ figure, looks. - *cantik* a pretty figure. - *cilik* a petite figure. - *muka* countenance.
roman₂ novel. - *picisan* dime novel. **pe-** novelist.
roman₃ (*Coll.*) **ber-(²an)** be in passionate love with e.o.
romansa romance.
romantik romantic. **be-** full of romanticism.
romantika romance. - *kehidupan* the romance of life.

romantikus romantic thinker.
romantis romantic. **me-kan** romanticize.
romantisir me- romanticize.
romantisme romanticism.
Romawi see RUMAWI.
rombak me- 1 tear down s.t. **2** change the appearance of s.t., remodel. *Pengusaha itu* ~ *rumah* The contractor renovated the house. **3** reorganize. ~ *kabinétnya* change the composition of the cabinet. **-an** result of reorganization. **pe- 1** o. who tears s.t. down. **2** reorganizer. **pe-an 1** reorganizing, making radical changes. ~ *sistém agraria* agrarian reform. **2** destroying and rebuilding. **3** renovation.
rombé see RUMBAI.
rombang-rambing, rombang-rombéng tattered and torn.
rombéng tattered, torn. *Dia cuma punya satu sarung* - He only has o. worn out sarong. **me-** buy and sell secondhand articles. **me-kan** sell s.t. secondhand. **-an 1** junk. *mobil* ~ a junk car, almost inoperable. **2** of a cheap kind.
romboida (*Math.*) rhomboid.
rombong₁ 1 k.o. large rice basket with cover. **2** pushcart (often used by venders).
rombong₂ be-² in large groups. **be-an** come in large groups. **me-** form a group. **-an 1** group, party. ~ *gubernur* the governor's party. ~ *pelajar* student group. ~ *sandiwara* theatrical group, troupe. **2** gang.
romboter butter.
romel, romel-romel (*Coll.*) junk.
roméo handsome, romantic youth.
romét me- work at odd jobs.
romhorn k.o. cone-shaped pastry with sweet filling.
romo term of address or reference to Roman Catholic priest.
romok (*Lit.*) **me-** be uneasy, be upset. *Nita duduk* ~ *di depan, membunyikan harmonika* Nita sat brooding in the front, playing a harmonica.
romong (*Jkt*) torn, in tatters.
rompak me- commit piracy. **pe-** pirate. **pe-an** piracy.
rompal (*Jv, Jkt*) knocked loose, fall apart. *Giginya* - *karena jatuh dr spéda motor* He lost some teeth because he fell off his motorcycle.
rompang see RUMPANG.
rompang-ramping tattered and torn, in shreds.
rompéng, rompés damaged on the edge. *Piring ini* - This plate is chipped on the edge.
rompi waistcoat, vest. - *pelampung/penyelamat/renang* lifejacket.
rompok hut.
rompong 1 cut off, mutilated. **2** mutilation. **me-kan** break off, cut off.
rompyok layer (of a gown). **-²** multilayered (of gowns).
romusa, romusha, romusya 1 program of involuntary labor during Japanese occupation. **2** (*Coll.*) brutally exploited labor. **me-kan** send to forced labor.

rona color. **me-(i)** give color.
roncé tassel, appendage. **be-** tasseled. **me-** make a tassel.
roncét small bits. **be-²** do s.t. bit by bit.
ronda 1 rounds, patrol, beat. - *kampung* village patrol. **2** guard, watchman. **me-** make o.'s rounds, be on patrol. **me-i** patrol an area. **-an** patrol, night watch. *jalan* ~ route of o.'s patrol. **pe-** patrol, watchman. ~ *malam* night watchman. **pe-an** patroling, making the rounds.
rondah-randih be in disorder.
ronde (*Sport*) a round.
rondé k.o. ginger drink with peanuts and rice flour balls.
rondes (*Sport*) rounders.
rondo royal (*Jv*) fried fritters of fermented cassava.
rondok be-, me- hide o.s. **me-kan** hide s.t.
ronéo mimeograph. **me-** mimeograph s.t.
rongak discontinuous, with gaps (of teeth, fences, etc.). *Giginya* - His teeth have spaces in between.
rongga hollow space, cavity, hole. - *dada* thoracic cavity. - *hidung* nasal cavity. - *mata* eye socket. - *mulut* oral cavity. **be-** hollow. **me-** form a hollow space. *Perasaan segar* ~ *di dada Mulyadi* It was as if a refreshing feeling formed a hollow space in Mulyadi's breast.
ronggang see RENGGANG.
ronggéng (*Jv*) paid dancing or singing girl sometimes also available for sex. **me-** dance, serve as a dancing girl.
ronggoh see RUNGGUH₂.
rongkoh, rongkok me- walk stooped over.
rongkongan₁ (*Jv, Jkt*) skeleton.
rongkongan₂ see KERONGKONGAN.
rongong sound of buzzing. **me-** buzz.
rongos see MRONGOS.
rongrong me- 1 gnaw at s.t. **2** undermine s.t., damage s.t. **me-i** disturb, upset. *tdk akan* ~ *pekerjaan PBB* will not disturb the work of the UN. **-an 1** gnawing. ~ *ketidakpastian* gnawing feeling of uncertainty. **2** undermining. **pe-** o. who undermines or pesters. **pe-an** action of undermining.
rongséng sullen, upset, grumbling. **me- 1** grumble, gripe. **2** discontented, unhappy. **me-kan** cause s.o. to feel upset and to grumble. **ke-an** discontent.
rongsok damaged, worn-out. **-an** worn-out articles, wreckage. ~ *besi tua* heap of scrap iron.
ronsel crimp.
ronsen x-ray.
ronta me- struggle to get loose. *Kuda itu* ~ *dr talinya* The horse struggled to free himself from the rope. **me-²** keep struggling to get free. **me-kan** cause to struggle to get loose. **-an** struggle.
rontak see BERONTAK.
rontal see LONTAR₁.
rontgen see RONSEN.
rontog, rontok drop off, fall off, shed. *Gigiku sdh* -

My teeth have fallen out. *musim* - fall, autumn. **me-** drop off, shed. *Rambutnya* ~ *cepat sekali* He is losing his hair very quickly. **me-kan** cause to shed, fall off. *Luka dan kurap tlh* ~ *seluruh bulunya* Sores and scabies made it lose all its fur. ~ *jagung* husk corn. **-an** s.t. fallen off. **pe-** s.t. that causes things to fall off. ~ *pesawat musuh* o. who shoots down enemy planes. *alat* ~ huller.
ronyéh me- grumble.
ronyok crumpled up. **me-** crumple up (paper, etc.).
room see ROM.
roos see ROS₁.
ropak-rapik in disorder, chaotic.
ropel see ROFEL.
rorod me-kan remove husk by shaking.
rorompok (*Sd*) house, in polite, self-deprecating reference to o.'s own house.
ros₁ rose.
ros₂ bull's-eye (in a target).
ros₃ see RUAS.
rosario (*Rel.*) rosary.
rosbang see RÉSBANG.
roséla k.o. fiber used to make sacks and ropes.
roséng see RONGSÉNG.
rosét₁ roselike ornament.
rosét₂ see KAYU₁.
roskam k.o. brush (for horses).
rosok see RONGSOK.
rosot me- 1 slip off. *Celananya* ~ His trousers slipped off. *Saya* ~ *dr tangga* I fell from the ladder. **2** decline, sink. *Harganya* ~ The prices declined. *Namanya* ~ His reputation slipped. **meme-kan** bring s.t. into decline, put s.t. down. *Adik* ~ *diri dr géndongan ibu* Little brother slid down from where Mother was carrying him. **keme-an** decline. **peme-an** bringing s.t. into decline. **me-kan** decrease s.t. *Ia* ~ *harganya* He reduced his price drastically. **pe-an** process of decline (of prices, production, etc.).
roster₁ schedule of classes.
roster₂ opening for ventilation.
rosul see RASUL.
rotan rattan. - *manau* k.o. large rattan. - *ulur* k.o. strong rattan. *Bila tdk ada* - *akarpun jadi* Make do with what you have (lit., when there is no rattan, the root will do). **be-** collect rattan. **me- 1** collect rattan. **2** cane s.o. **3** cane (a chair). **pe-** o. who collects rattan for a living.
rotasi (*Tech.*) rotation.
roti 1 bread. **2** bun. - *Amérika* sliced, white bread. - *bakar* toasted bread. - *kabin* salt crackers. - *kadét* roll. - *kaléng* cracker in form of figure eight. - *kalung* brass knuckles. - *kering* zwieback, dry bread. - *kismis* raisin bread. - *kukus* steamed bread us. in cupcake shape. - *mari* round, plain cookie. - *panggang* toast. - *pisang* bun with a banana roasted inside. - *sobék* sectioned bread with sweet filling. - *sisir* k.o. thin sweet bread. - *tawar* white bread. **pe-an 1** matters concerning bread. **2** bakery.

rotok sound of repeated explosion. **me-** 1 explode repeatedly. 2 grumble.

rotor (*Auto.*) rotor.

rotsoi lousy, rotten. *Kelakuannya benar-benar -* He is really rotten.

royak me- 1 spread. *Mula-mula satu yg tahu, kemudian dua, sdh itu ~* At first o. knew, then, two, finally it spread all over. 2 worsen. *Perasaan muak ~ di dirinya* His feeling of disgust deepened.

royal extravagant, profligate. **be-**(²) splurge, waste money. **me-kan** waste s.t. *Ia ~ uangnya di luar negeri* He wasted his money overseas. **ke-an** extravagance. **pe-** a profligate.

royalis royalist.

royalti royalty.

royan cramps. *- beranak* labor pains. **me-** suffer a cramp.

royokan (*Coll.*) fight e.o. to obtain s.t.

royong see GOTONG-ROYONG.

Rp. [*rupiah*] rupiah.

RPA [*Républik Persatuan Arab*] United Arab Republic.

RPH [*rumah potong héwan*] slaughterhouse.

RPKAD [*Résimén Pasukan Komando Angkatan Darat*] crack troops, storm troops.

RRC, RR Cina [*Républik Rakyat Cina*] People's Republic of China.

RRI [*Radio Républik Indonésia*] Indonesian Broadcasting System.

RRT [*Républik Rakyat Tiongkok*] People's Republic of China.

RS [*Rumah Sakit*] hospital.

RSI [*Rumah Sakit Islam*] Islamic-run hospital.

RSU [*Rumah Sakit Umum*] public hospital.

RSUD [*Rumah Sakit Umum Daérah*] regional public hospital.

RSUP [*Rumah Sakit Umum Pusat*] central hospital.

RSV [*Républik Sosialis Vietnam*] Socialist Republic of Vietnam.

RT [*Rukun Tetangga*] neighborhood association, the lowest administrative unit.

ru₁ 14.49 square meters.

ru₂ see ERU.

rua see RUAK.

ruadat ceremony, sign of respect.

Ruah (*Isl., Coll.*) eighth month of the year.

ruah₁ me- pour out, spill out. **me-kan** empty s.t. **ke-an** overflow (of s.t.).

ruah₂ se- within calling distance. **me-** call, shout at. **-an** a call.

ruak extensive. **me-** expand, widen.

ruam skin eruption. *- saraf* shingles. **me-** break out in a rash.

ruang 1 space. *- angkasa* outer space. *- huruf* space between letters. *- kuburan* tomb. *- lingkup* scope. *- udara* 1 air space. 2 air chamber. *- waktu* leisure. 2 (*Naut.*) ship's well or water that gathers there. 3 column (in a paper, magazine). *- pertama* the first column. *- olahraga* sports column. 4 room, hall. *- baca* reading room. *- belakang*

back room. *- juruterbang* (*Av.*) cockpit. *- kaca* greenhouse. *- kelas* classroom. *- msk* lobby, foyer. *- pamér* exhibition gallery, showroom. *- pariwisata* tourist class (on plane). *- pertama* first class (on plane). *- rumah sakit* hospital ward. *- sidang* conference or seminar room. *- siksaan* torture chamber. *- tunggu* waiting room. **-an** 1 space. 2 room, chamber.

ruap scum, foam. *- bir* beer foam. **me-** 1 bubble (up). 2 steam. *~ darah* very angry.

ruas 1 space between joints, internode. *- bambu* joints of bamboo. *- jari* (*Anat.*) knucklebone. *- tulang belakang* (*Anat.*) vertebrae. 2 (*Math.*) parts of an equation.

ruat₁ shaky, undecided.

ruat₂ (*Jv, Sd*) exorcism ritual. **me-** free s.o. from a spell, exorcise. **-an** exorcism. **peng-an** exorcising.

rubah₁ fox.

rubah₂ see UBAH.

rubai, rubayat (*Lit.*) quatrain.

rubel ruble, Russian currency.

rubiah (*Rel.*) nun.

rubrik 1 heading. 2 column.

rubu see RABA. **me-²** grope around nervously.

rubuh see ROBOH.

rubung flow together in large quantities. **me-** flow together in large quantities, gather around. *Org tambah banyak ~* More and more people crowded around. **me-i** crowd in large numbers, flow over s.t. in large quantities. *Lalat terus ~ lukanya* Flies continued to swarm over his wound. **-an** crowd, large quantity.

rucut me- escape, glide loose. *Wah, ikannya ~* Oh no, the fish escaped.

rudal [*peluru kendali*] guided missile. **me-** shoot with a missile.

rudin impoverished. **me-** become impoverished. **me-kan** impoverish s.o.

rudu 1 stooping, bowed with age. 2 drooping, hanging down.

rudus cutlass, machete.

ruet see RUWET.

rugi 1 suffer a financial loss. *Aku - setengah juta!* I lost a half a million. 2 lose out. *- kamu tdk datang pd pésta* It was your loss you did not come to the party. **be-, me-** suffer losses. **me-kan** 1 inflict a financial loss. *Perobahan harga itu ~ petani* The change in price inflicted a loss upon the farmers. 2 damage, harm. *Perbuatan itu ~ kehormatan negara* That action is damaging to the prestige of the state. **ke-an** 1 financial loss. 2 detriment.

rugos lettering sheet (rubbed with pencil).

ruh see ROH.

ruhak embers.

ruhani see ROHANI.

ruhban (*Rel.*) monk, hermit.

ruhbanat (*Rel.*) nun.

ruit₁ bent, hook-shaped barb. **te-** be bent.

ruit₂ /rét, roit/ (*Crd.*) diamond (suit).

rujah me- stab, poke at a fire.

rujak k.o. fruit salad with pungent dressing. - *cingur* vegetable or fruit salad with slices of beef snout. - *gobét* shredded, unripe mango with tangy sauce. - *manis* fruit salad with sweet sauce. **me-** prepare salad of this sort.

ruji₁ trelliswork, grill. - *sél* bars of a jail cell. **be-** be with trelliswork.

ruji₂ radius. - *ligat* (*Phys.*) radius of gyration.

rujuk₁ 1 reconciliation. 2 be reconciled with o.'s separated wife before divorce is final. **me-** reconcile. **-an** reconciliation.

rujuk₂ reference. *sistém* - reference system. - *silang* cross-reference. **me-** refer. **me-i** refer to s.t. **-an** referral, reference. **pe-an** cross-referencing.

rukaat see RAKAAT.

rukah me- turn over. *Traktor ~ tanah* The tractor turned over the earth.

rukhani see ROHANI.

rukhsah (*Isl.*) dispensation (for elderly, ill, etc.) from observing fast: such a person must donate a day's food to poor.

rukiat₁ magic.

rukiat₂ see RUKYAT.

ruku₁ sound of cooing. **me-** coo.

ruku₂ see RUKUK.

rukuh (*Isl.*) prayer robe for women.

rukuk (*Isl.*) deep bow from the waist during prayer ritual. **me-** perform this bow in prayer.

rukun₁ harmonious. *Meréka hidup* - They live in harmony. - *damai* in peace and harmony. - *kampung* 1 mutual assistance association in the village. 2 administrative unit just below village level. - *tani* farmer's cooperative at neighborhood level. - *tetangga* neighborhood association (the administrative unit). - *warga* administrative unit at the next-to-lowest level in city. **me-kan** appease, bring peace about. **ke-an** harmony, concord.

rukun₂ (*Isl.*) pillar, essential principle. *lima* - Islam five pillars of Isl. - *iman* pillars of faith. - *haji* obligatory ceremony during the hajj. - *syarat* customary, minimally obligatory rules.

ruku-ruku k.o. basil.

rukyat (*Isl.*) determining date by sighting of moon (not by system of *hisab*), esp. to fix beginning and end of fasting period.

rulét see ROLÉT.

rum₁ rum.

rum₂ sound of humming (like that of engine).

rum₃ see ROM.

Rum 1 Byzantium, Istanbul. 2 Rome. - *Katolik* Roman Catholic.

rumah 1 house, dwelling. - *batu/gedung* cement or brick house. - *gadang* traditional Minangkabau house. - *instansi* 1 gvt. official's house. 2 office building. - *kedai* small shop with residence in the rear. - *kembar* duplex house. - *kéong* snail's shell. - *kolong* house perched on piles. - *kopel* duplex consisting of two houses with a common wall. - *lamin* longhouse. - *loténg* house with more than o. floor. - *panggung* house on stilts. - *liar* squatter's house. - *pétak* 1 row houses. 2 apartment. -

selérét long, narrow house. - *tangga* household. **ber-** *tangga* have a household, be married. **ke-tanggaan, pe-tanggaan** household affairs. - *toko* shop with a residence (us. upstairs). - *tumpangan* boardinghouse. 2 (*Coll.*) public building. - *api* lighthouse. - *berhala* temple. - *bola* club (house). - *gadai* pawnshop. - *gambar* exhibition hall. - *gila* insane asylum. - *jaga* guardhouse, sentry post. - *jagal* abattoir. - *kuning* brothel. - *lélang* auction house. - *madat* opium den. - *makan* restaurant. - *monyét* sentry box. - *obat* pharmacy. - *panjang* brothel. - *pangkas* barbershop. - *penginapan* rooming house, inn. - *peranginan* traveler's rest-house. - *perdéo* jail, prison. - *potong* slaughter-house. - *sakit* hospital. - *sakit bantu* auxiliary hospital. - *sakit bersalin* maternity hospital. 3 housing (for machinery, etc.). - *pedoman* housing for a compass. **se-** be under o. roof. **menye-kan** cause o.'s two wives to live under o. roof. **be-** dwell, live. *Ia ~ di kota itu* He lives in that city. **be-²** have a family. *Dgn gaji sekecil itu ia blm bisa ~* With his salary as small as it is, he has not been able to have a family. **me-kan** lay s.o. off (from work). *Banyak buruh di-kan* Many laborers were laid off. **mempe-kan** marry off. *Kemarén ia ~ anaknya* Yesterday he married off his child. **-(²)an** toy or doll house. **pe-an** housing. *~ milik bersama* 1 mutual home ownership. 2 communal housing.

Rumawi Roman. *angka* - Roman numerals. *kaisar* - Roman emperor.

rumba the rumba.

rumbah leaves or salad eaten with rice.

rumbai tuft, tassel. **be-(²)** tasseled, fringed. **me-** grow in strands.

rumbang see ROMBANG-RAMBING.

rumbia sago palm.

rumbing somewhat damaged.

rumét, rumit 1 hard, difficult. 2 complex, intricate, knotty. **me-kan** complicate, make difficult. **ke-an** 1 difficulty, complexity. 2 complication.

Rumi see RUMAWI.

rumpang 1 have gaps. 2 discontinuous (of time).

rumpik 1 wicked, having bad intentions. 2 (*Sl.*) Shit! (interjection used in jest or admiration).

rumpun clump (of herbaceous plants). - *bambu* bamboo cluster. - *bahasa* (*Ling.*) language family. **se-** 1 of o. cluster (of plants). 2 (*Biol.*) of o. family, o. group, o. stock. *Betulkah manusia ~ dgn kera?* Is it true that men are of the same family as apes? **kese-an** oneness of origin. **be-²** grow in clumps. *Bambu tumbuh ~ di pinggir sungai* Bamboo grows in clusters along the river's edge.

rumput 1 grass. - *benggala* pasture grass for cattle. - *gajah* k.o. wide-leaved decorative grass. - *gelagah* k.o. grass. - *Jepang* 1 k.o. fine decorative grass. 2 k.o. plastic string. - *kering* hay. - *laut* seaweed. - *manila* k.o. spongy grass for lawns. - *teki* k.o. grass, the fruit of which is used to make *emping*. 2 weeds. - *air* swamp grass. - *babi* wild heliotrope. **me-** 1 gather grass. 2 weed. **me-i** weed (a garden). **-an** weeds. **-²an** all k.o. grass. **pe-an** grassland, pasture.

rumrum see RUNGRUM.
Rumuhun (*Sd*) ancestor. *Sang* ~ The Ancestors.
rumun see KERUMUN.
rumus 1 (*Chem.*, etc.) formula. **2** abbreviation.
me-kan formulate. **-an** formulation. **pe-** formulator. **pe-an** formulation.
runcing pointed (of pencil, arrowhead, etc.). *bambu* - bamboo spikes. **me- 1** become pointed. **2** become critical, become seriously aggravated. *Keadaan itu* ~ The situation has become critical. **me-i** sharpen (a pencil, etc.). **me-kan 1** sharpen (a point). **2** aggravate, exacerbate. *Kegagalan perundingan itu* ~ *perhubungan* The failure of the negotiations aggravated the bad relationship. **ke-an 1** sharpness (of a point). **2** critical situation. **pe-an 1** act of sharpening to a point. **2** act of increasing tension.
runcit see RONCÉT.
runding be- confer, discuss. **me-kan, mempe-kan** discuss s.t., confer about. *Ia* ~ *rencana baru* He discussed a new plan. **-an 1** discussion. **2** conference. **pe-** negotiator. **pe-an 1** negotiation, deliberation. **2** discussion.
runduk me- stoop, bend, bow. *Ia* ~ *rendah* He made a low bow. ~ *rusa* stalk deer.
rundung me- afflict. *Ia di- malang* He is dogged by bad luck.
rundu randa (*Jkt*) come and go (with a burden).
runggas me- pull out.
rungguh₁ me- squat.
rungguh₂ pledge, guarantee, security. **me-kan** pawn, hock. **pe-an** pawning, hocking.
runggut see RENGGUT.
rungkai see UNGKAI.
rungkau me- hang down like hair over the face or like willow branches. **me-i** hang down over s.t. *Rambutnya* ~ *mukanya* Her hair was hanging down over her face.
rungkuh worn-out, decrepit, aged. **me-** be worn out, decayed, old. **ke-an** dilapidated, decayed, worn-out.
rungkup me-(i) 1 cover up. **2** spread over. *Pohon yg rimbun* ~ *rumahnya* A shady tree covered his house.
rungrum me- fondle, pet.
rungsing see RONGSÉNG.
rungus (*M*) **me-** grumble. **pe-** hothead, spitfire.
rungut be-, me- grumble, gripe.
runjak see LONJAK.
runjam, runjang me- thrust, stab.
runjung cone-shaped. *hantu* - k.o. ghost that grows bigger bit by bit.
runtai me- dangle, hang loosely. **se-** bunch, cluster. ~ *anggur* a bunch of grapes.
runtuh 1 collapse. *Rumah tua tlh* - The old house has collapsed. - *kekuasaannya* His power is destroyed. *tanah* - landslide. - *ripuk* completely destroyed. **2** fall out. *Giginya* - His teeth fell out. **me- 1** collapse, come down. *Gedung tua itu* ~ The old building collapsed. **2** infiltrate. **me-i** collapse onto. **me-kan 1** cause to collapse, demolish. *-kanlah bénténg itu!* Tear down that fort!

2 overthrow, bring down. **ke-an** collapse, fall, debacle. ~ *batin* mental breakdown, collapse. ~ *dinasti Ming* the collapse of the Ming Dynasty. **-an** ruins, debris, rubble. **pe-** o. who causes collapse.
runtuk see RONTOG.
runtun₁ be-(²) o. after the other, in a row. **me-kan** link, join together. **-an** series (of inoculations, regulations, etc.).
runtun₂ me- pull out.
runtut₁ in harmony, harmonious. **ke-an** harmony.
runtut₂ see RUNTUN₁.
runut trace, groove, furrow. **me-(i)** trail, track, follow, trace. **-an** trace. **pe-** (*Chem.*) tracer.
runyam (*Coll.*) be in difficulties. **me-kan 1** make difficult. **2** damage, cause to fail.
rupa 1 form, shape, appearance. - *dan bentuk* appearance and form. - *muka* face, facial expression. **2** sort, kind. **-nya** it seems, apparently. ~ *mau hujan* It looks like rain. **-²** various, diverse, all sorts. ~ *barang yg dijual* Various k.o. articles are sold. **-²nya** probably, seemingly. ~ *dia senang pd gadis itu* Apparently he is taken with that girl. **se- 1** similar, of o. kind, likewise. *modélnya* ~ of o. model. *dua barang yg* ~ two things of the same type. *celana dan jas yg* ~ the trousers and jacket of the same type. *sama dan* ~ congruent. **2** be similar to s.t. *Tingkah lakunya* ~ *saudagar* His attitude is like that of a merchant. ~ *dgn* resemble. **berse-** be alike. *Ia* ~ *dgn ayahnya* He looks just like his father. **menye-i** resemble. *Buatannya* ~ *barang pabrik* His products are as good as manufactured goods. **menye-kan** place on a par, equate. *Karena baiknya ia* ~ *temannya dgn malaikat* Because of her kindness he placed his friend on a par with an angel. **kese-an** similarity. **penye-an** standardization, efforts to forge congruence. **be- 1** shaped, have the shape of. **2** in the form of. *sumbangan* ~ *uang dan barang* contributions in the form of money and goods. **3** handsome, pretty. *Janda itu muda dan* ~ The widow is young and beautiful. **be-²** all sorts, all kinds. **me-** appear, come into o.'s vision. **me-i** resemble. *Badannya* ~ *badan pemain bola* His body resembles that of a soccer player. **me-kan** constitute, form, make up. *Itu* ~ *sebagian besar dr pendapatannya* This forms a large part of his income. **te-** imaginable.
rupawan good-looking person. **ke-an** beauty, handsomeness.
rupek closed in, stuffy.
rupiah Indonesian monetary unit. **me-kan** convert to *rupiah*. **pe-an** conversion to *rupiah*.
rurubai hurried. *Ia - menukar uangnya* He was in a hurry when he changed his money.
rurut me- 1 fall down. **2** slip off. *Cincinnya* ~ Her ring slipped off.
Rus, Ruslan, Rusland Russia.
rusa deer.
rusak 1 damaged, broken, out of order. *Mobilnya* - The car has broken down. - *namanya* His name

is tainted. - *binasa* completely ruined. **me-bina-sakan** utterly destroy s.t. - *hati* 1 depressed. 2 bad character. - *ringan* slightly damaged. 2 depraved, broken down. *Moralnya* - His morals are depraved. 3 (*Coll.*) *Anak itu sdh* - That child has turned into a delinquent. **me-** damage, ruin. *Itu ~ nama perusahaannya* That harmed the good name of the firm. *Nikotin ~ paru-paru* Nicotine damages the lungs. *~ pasaran* spoil the market (that is, pay too much for s.t. so that henceforth others will have to pay too much as well). **me-i** repeatedly damage s.t. **me-kan** destroy, devastate, break s.t. entirely. **ke-an** damage, flaw. *Gedung itu kena ~ besar* The building was heavily damaged. *~ gigi* dental decay. **pe-, peng-** 1 disturber. *~ keamanan* disturber of the peace. 2 destroyer, vandal. *~ tanaman* destroyer of plants. **pe-an, peng-an** act of damaging.

rusbang see RÉSBANG.

rusia see RAHASIA.

Rusia Russia, Soviet Union. **me-kan** Russianize.

rusuh restless, disturbed. *Keadaan negeri* - The situation in the country is unsettled. - *hati* worried. - *resah* anxious. **me-** become unsafe. **me-i** render unsafe. *Gerombolan itu ~ daérah ini* That gang makes this area unsafe. **me-kan** cause a commotion, cause s.o. to worry. **ke-an** 1 disturbance, riot. *~ rasial* racial unrest. 2 turbulence, turmoil. *~ hati* 1 worry, restlessness. 2 excitement. **pe-** 1 rioter. 2 terrorist (in the 1950s). **pe-an** riot, disturbance.

rusuk 1 side, flank. *tulang* - (*Anat.*) rib. - *badan* region of the ribs. - *jalan* side of the road. - *rumah* side of a house. 2 margin, side. - *surat* margin of a letter. **me-** sideways, approach from the side.

rutan [*rumah tahanan*] detention center.

rute route (of bus line, parade, etc.).

rutin routine. **me-** become ordinary, routine. **me-kan** make s.t. a routine. **ke-an** routineness.

rutuk **me-** grumble, cuss. **-an** curse, grumbling.

rutup sound of bubbling.

RUU [*Rencana Undang-Undang*] (*Pol.*) draft of a law.

Ruwah see RUAH.

ruwat see RUAT₂.

ruwet complicated, complex, knotty. - *bundet* extremely complicated. **be-** be complicated. **me-i, me-kan** complicate, render difficult, obscure s.t. **ke-an** complication, complexity.

ruyak see ROYAK.

ru'yat see RUKYAT.

ruyung₁ hard exterior of a palm trunk.

ruyung₂ k.o. clublike weapon.

ruyup 1 heavy-eyed, sleepy. *Matanya* - His eyes are becoming heavy. 2 setting. *Matahari* - The sun is setting.

RW₁ [*Rukun Warga*] administrative unit at the next-to-lowest level in city, consisting of several *RT*'s.

RW₂ a euphemism for cooked dog meat (from Tombulu Minahassan *rintek wuuk* "fine hair" because dog meat is a specialty of the area).

S

s /és/ s, the 19th letter of the alphabet.

S.₁ [*sungai*] river.

S.₂ [*Santa, Santo*] St.

S-0 [*stratum nol*] nonuniversity degree or program.

S-1 [*stratum satu*] undergraduate program.

S-2 [*stratum dua*] master's program.

S-3 [*stratum tiga*] doctorate program.

sa (*Ch*) three, used in bidding and commercial transactions. - *ban* 30,000. - *ban go* 35,000. - *cap* 30. - *cap go* 35. - *céng* 3,000. - *céng go* 3,500. - *pék* 300. - *pék céng* 300,000. - *pék go* 350. - *pék go céng* 350,000. - *tiau* 3,000,000. - *tiau go* 3,500,000.

saadah, saadat bliss. *Baginda* - (*Lit.*) His Majesty.

saal /sal/ see SAL₁.

saat /sa'at/ 1 moment. (*pd*) - *itu* at that moment. *pd* -*nya* in time. *Untunglah pd -nya paman keluar* Fortunately Uncle came out in time. *Sdh sampai -nya* The time has come. - *naas* the evil hour. - *genting* crucial moment. - *teduh* (*Rel.*) meditation time (Protestant). 2 instant. *titik* - instant, moment.

3 at the moment that, when. *Dia sungguh sakit - meninggalkan pacarnya* He felt really hurt when he left his girlfriend. **se-** a moment. *~ itu juga* at the same moment. **se- se-** from time to time. *Dgn ~ memberikan témbakan balasan pasukan gerilya mundur* The guerilla troops withdrew while returning fire from time to time.

saba (*Jv*) frequent a place. **meny-** frequent a place.

sabak₁ 1 sulking, pouting. *Mukanya* - He was sulking. 2 dull. *Matanya* - His eyes were dull. **meny-** wail, lament.

sabak₂ (*Jv*) slate for school.

saban₁ each, every. - *hari* every day. -² 1 time and time again, frequently. *Saya ~ télpon sama dia* I frequently call her on the phone. 2 at some time or another. *~ kita bicarakan* Let us talk about it some time. 3 whenever. *~ saya datang saya dpt uang* Each time I come I get money. 4 (*Med.*) k.o. disease involving incontinence or dribbling of urine.

saban₂ see SYA'BAN.

sabana savannah.

Sabang (*Geog.*) the name of the port on the northernmost island off Sumatra. *dr - sampai Mérauké* from Sabang to Merauke (from o. end of Indonesia to the other, a slogan referring to Indonesia's integrity).

sabar patient, calm. *-lah!* Be patient! *Sdh habis -nya* He ran out of patience. **ber-** (*hati*) be patient, calm. **meny-i** calm s.o. down. **meny-kan** 1 have patience with, put up with. *Penghinaan yg tdk akan saya -kan* An insult I will not tolerate. 2 calm s.o. down. *Tdk apa-apa, jawabku ~* It does not matter, I answered soothingly. **ke-an** (*hati*) 1 patience. 2 tolerance. **ketidak-an** impatience. **-an** (*Jkt*) patient, calm. **peny-** o. with a patient nature.

sabat see SABET.

Sabat 1 (*Bib.*) Saturday. 2 Sabbath.

sabda utterance (of God, Muh., Jesus, or exalted personage). *- Baginda* His Majesty's words. **ber-** speak. *Raja itu ~* The king spoke. **mens-kan, meny-kan** say, state s.t. (of deities, kings).

sabdaillahi (*Isl.*) divine words.

sabel sabre.

saben see SABAN₁.

sabet **meny-** 1 whip. *Ibu ~ anaknya dgn sapu lidi* The mother whipped her son with a bundle of palm midribs. 2 snatch, grab. *Dompétnya di- org di bis* S.o. grabbed his wallet on the bus. *Ia ~ medali emas utk nomor lompat jauh* He managed to sieze the gold medal in the broad jump. **meny-kan** whip s.t. against. **-an** 1 a strike (with a whip), a slash with a whipping motion, action of striking. 2 what is gotten by grabbing. *Hasil ~nya dlm satu hari* What he gets from stealing in a day. **-²an** whipping at e.o. **peny-** (purse) snatcher.

sabil (*Isl.*) the Way.

sabilillah, sabilullah (*Isl.*) The way of God.

sabit₁ sickle. *bulan -* crescent moon (symbol of Islam). **meny-** cut (grass, rice, etc.). *~ hati* heartrending. **meny-kan** cut s.t. with a sickle for s.o. **-an** things cut with a sickle. *rumput ~* grass cut with a sickle.

sabit₂ certain, definitive. **meny-kan** affirm s.t.

sableng (*Jkt*) slightly crazy, silly. **ny-** act slightly crazy.

sablon silk-screening. **mens-, meny-** silk-screen. **pens-, peny-** 1 copier. 2 plagiarist. **peny-an** process of silk-screening.

sabot sabotage. **meny-** to sabotage.

sabotase sabotage. **meny-, mens-** sabotage. *~ program pemerintah* sabotage a gvt. program. **peny-** saboteur. **peny-an** sabotaging.

sabotir **meny-, mens-** sabotage.

sabrang see SEBERANG.

Sabtu Saturday. *- malam* Saturday evening. *malam - Friday evening.*

sabuk belt, sash. *- pengaman/penyelamat* seatbelt, safety belt. **ber-** wear a sash.

sabun₁ soap. *- mandi* bath soap. *- cuci* laundry soap. **ber-** soapy. **meny-** lather. **meny-, ny-** (*Coll.*) 1 connive with s.o. to do s.t. illegal, bribe.

2 masturbate. **meny-i** lather s.t. *Ia ~ mukanya* He lathered his face. **meny-kan** make s.t. into soap. **peny-an** act of lathering.

sabun₂ white, pale, albino.

sabung₁ (*Sport*) competitive fight between two animals (us. with gambling). *ayam -* fighting cock. **ber-** 1 fight, compete (of cocks). 2 compete. *- meny-* 1 fight with e.o. 2 business of cockfighting. **meny-** pit (cocks, kites, etc.) against e.o. *~ jiwa/nyawa* risk o.'s life. **meny-kan** hammer away at s.o. **-an** animal for pitting against another. **peny-** cockfighter. **peny-an** the action of making two cocks etc. fight. **per-an** 1 cock (kite, etc.) fight. 2 conflict. 3 pit for cockfighting.

sabung₂ **ber-** flash. *Kilat ~* The lighting flashed.

sabur 1 dim, vague. *biru -* light blue. 2 confused. *- limbur* dim, confused. **meny-** 1 disappear into the crowd. 2 become confused.

sabut husk, fibrous shell. *- kelapa* coconut fiber. **ber-** fibrous.

sadah betel lime. **ke-an** *air* hardness of water.

sadai **ber-** lay on o.'s back with legs extended. **meny-kan** beach a small boat. **ter-** lying on the back with legs extended.

sadak₁ betel lime.

sadak₂ slanting.

sadap₁ **meny-** 1 make incisions in a tree to obtain sap. 2 sample blood. 3 tap, bug (telephone, information, room, etc.). *~ pembicaraan* tap a conversation. **-an** sap tapped. **peny-** tapper. **peny-an** tapping. *~ suara* bugging.

sadap₂ see SEDAP.

sadaqah see SEDEKAH.

sadar 1 aware. *Ia tak - akan soal ini* He is not aware of this problem. 2 conscious. *Dia - akan dirinya* 1 She regained consciousness. 2 She has self-awareness. *Tanpa - dia terkulai di lantai* He lay unconscious on the floor. **meny-i** realize, be aware (of). *Yg hrs kita -i ialah . . .* What we must bear in mind is . . . *secara di-i atau tdk di-i* consciously or unconsciously. **meny-kan** make s.o. realize. *Sulit ~nya akan pentingnya belajar* It is difficult to make him aware of the importance of studying. *~ diri* come to, regain consciousness. **ter-** 1 come to realize. 2 come to, regain consciousness. *Ibu melihat kpdku spt baru ~* Mother looked at me as if she'd just regained consciousness. **ke-an** 1 awareness, consciousness. 2 realization. 3 come to a realization. **peny-** 1 o. who is aware. 2 s.t. which makes o. aware. **peny-an** awareness, process of making aware.

sadarulkalam (*Lit.*) opening words.

sadel bicycle or motorcycle seat.

sadérék (*Jv*) relation, relative. *-² dr Tanah Air* friends and relatives from the Homeland.

sadik honest, straightforward.

sadir ammonium chloride.

sadis 1 sadist, sadistic. 2 (*Coll.*) terrific, great. *Wah, - makanannya!* What a terrific dish! **ke-an** 1 sadism. 2 being terrifically good.

sadisme sadism.

sadistis sadistic.

sadmatra hexameter.

sado 1 two-wheeled horse-drawn carriage. **2** (*Sumatra*) small motorized jitneys or taxis used for urban transportation. **ber-** ride a *sado*.

sadrah submissive, resigned. **ke-an** submissiveness, resignation.

sadran (*Jv*) ceremony to pay homage to ancestoral spirits. **ny- 1** engage in rites of this ceremony. **2** visit or maintain ancestral graves.

sadsudut (*Math.*) hexagon.

Sadtunggal province or *kabupatén*-level council of the six highest gvt. officials (in the 1960s).

sadur coating of metal. **meny- 1** plate (metal). ~ *emas* gild. ~ *pérak* coat with silver. **2** adapt (a story). ~ *ceritera* adapt a story. **-an 1** metal coating. **2** adaptation. **peny- 1** o. who does plating. **2** adaptor. **peny-an 1** act of plating. **2** the adapting of s.t.

saf line, series, row. *Bila bersolat berjermaah -nya hrs lurus* In group prayers the rows of people should be straight. **-²an 1** column. **2** in layers, in rows. **ber-²(an)** in rows, lined up.

safaat see SYAFAAT.

Safar (*Isl.*) the 2d month of the Arabic calendar.

safari 1 safari. *baju/modél* - style of shirt (with matching pants) that imitates a safari costume. **2** traveling group (of entertainers, etc.). **ber-1** wear a safari costume. **2** go on a safari.

safi clean, pure.

safier, safir sapphire.

saga k.o. tall pinnate tree and its red seeds. *mérah* - bright red.

sagang 1 buttress, support. **2** use a pole to ward off. **ter-** be helped up, supported. *Tangga ~ di témbok* The ladder was propped up against the wall.

sago see SAGU₁.

sagon cookie made of rice flour with coconut and sugar.

sagor see SAGUR.

sagu₁ sago palm or its products. - *belanda/betawi* arrowroot. - *moté* sago which has been refined and made into little colored beads for porridge. **meny-** extract sago. **-²an** plants similar to the sago palm.

sagu₂ (*Coll.*) code name for narcotic powder.

saguér, saguir (*N. Sulawesi*) palm toddy.

sagur dugout canoe.

sah₁ 1 valid, legal. *Itu tdk* - That is not legal (That is invalid). *anak tdk* - illegitimate child. **2** legally, officially. *Fian tlh - menjadi menantu ayahku?* Has Fian legally become my father's son-in-law? **3** certain, for sure. *Ijazah saya - ada di lemari besi* My diploma is definitely in the safe. **menge-kan, mens-kan 1** legalize, approve. **2** authorize. **3** ratify, confirm. **ke-an** legality. **penge-an, pens-an 1** ratification, confirmation. **2** legalization, authorization. *cap jabatan* ~ official stamp for legalization.

sah₂ see SYAH₁.

sahabat friend. - *karib/kental* a close intimate friend. - *Nabi* (*Isl.*) disciples of Muh. - *péna* pen pal. **ber- 1** be friends. **2** friendly. ~ *sekali ditariknya tanganku* In a very friendly way she pulled

my hand toward her. **memper-kan** introduce s.o. *Ia ~ Simin dgn Ali* She introduced Simin to Ali. **per-an** friendship.

sahadat see SYAHADAT.

sahaja₁ simple, natural. **ber-** simple, uncomplicated. *Penghidupannya* ~ His way of living was simple. *suku yg* ~ unacculturated tribe. **memper-kan** simplify s.t. ~ *gaya hidupnya* simplify o.'s life-style. **ke-an, keber-an** simplicity, simpleness. **per-an** simplification.

sahaja₂ memper-kan do s.t. on purpose. *Itu diper-kannya utk mendapat keuntungan* He did it on purpose in order to benefit from it.

sahaja₃ see SAJA.

saham 1 share, stock. **2** contribution. **3** part, role (in an affair, etc.).

sahan large plate, platter.

sahang black pepper.

sahap cover, lid. **ber-** covered. **meny-** cover.

sahaya₁ (*Lit.*) slave, servant.

sahaya₂ see SAYA.

sahbandar see SYAHBANDAR.

sahdan see SYAHDAN.

sahdu see SYAHDU.

sahib (*Lit.*) owner, possessor.

sahibul hikayat (*Lit.*) author. - *yg dirawikan* the author of the chronicle which was being recited.

sahid see SYAHID.

sahifah (*Leg.*) document.

sahih valid, genuine. **ke-an** validity.

sahir see SIHIR.

sahkan₁ see USAH.

sahkan₂ see SAH₁.

sahur₁ (*Isl.*) the meal eaten before daybreak during the fasting month. **ber-** have this meal.

sahur₂ see SAUR₂.

sahut answer s.o.'s call. **ber-(²)an, - meny-** answer back and forth. *Cengkerik di sana-sini ~ dgn katak* The crickets and the frogs called back and forth to e.o. **meny-(i)** answer a call, reply to s.o. **-an** reply. **peny-an** replying.

sahwat see SYAHWAT.

sai₁ inattentive, careless.

sai₂ /sa'i/ ceremony of running between the hills of Sofa and Marwa during the hajj.

said see SAYID.

Sailan Ceylon.

saing₁ ber- compete. *harga* ~ competitive price. *mampu* ~ competitive. **ber-an** compete with e.o. - **meny-i** compete with e.o. **meny-i** compete with. *harga yg tdk dpt di-i* a price no o. can compete with. **memper-kan 1** cause to compete with e.o. **2** compete over s.t. *hal yg patut diper-kan* s.t. worth competing for. **ter-i** get competition from, can be competed with. **-an** competitor, rival. **peny-** competitor. **per-an** competition, rivalry. ~ *bébas* free competition.

saing₂ fang, tusk.

sains science.

sair, sa'ir see SYAIR.

sais (*Lit.*) coachman.

saja 1 only, nothing else than. *Ia bertanya* - He only asked a question. *Kamu suruh diam* - Your job is just to keep quiet. *Ia beli dua* - He only bought two. *Biasa* - It is just the usual thing. *Baik-baik* - Everything is fine. *Begitu - kok marah* All I did was that, and still he is mad. **2** just, only (as the best thing under the circumstances). *Kalau tdk bisa hari ini, bésok* - If you cannot today, just do it tomorrow. *Sekarang - kita bicarakan* Let us just talk about it now. *Biar saya - yg nangani* Let me be the o. to take care of it (if no o. else can). *Kemahalan! Dua ribu* - That is too expensive! Make it 2,000. *Mari makan* - Come on. Let us just eat. **3** exactly, name the things, people, etc. (with interrogative words). *Siapa - yg datang?* Exactly who came? *Apa - yg hrs saya kerjakan?* What exactly do I have to do? **4** just, exactly. *Sama - bagi saya* It is all the same to me. *spt monyét* - just exactly like a monkey. **5** just, alone. *O banyak sekali. Di Jkt - ada seribu* Oh there are lots. In Jkt alone there are 1,000. **6** emphasizing particle. *Saya hampir - mati* I just barely escaped death. *Mudah-mudahan - kamu lulus* I just hope you pass. *Baru - ia datang* He just now came. *Bisa* - Of course it is possible. *Boléh - ikut kalau mau* Of course you can come if you want to. *Kalau diberi, ya mau - saya* If s.o. gives me o., of course I want it. **7** (*Jv*) even. *Saya - tdk bisa, apalagi dia* I cannot do it myself, much less he. *Apa - boléh. Téh boléh. Kopi juga boléh* Anything will do. Tea would be all right. Coffee would be all right, too. *Ditaruh di mana* - Put it anywhere at all. **8** nevertheless, anyway. *Tdk makan apa-apa, tapi tetap gemuk* - He does not eat a thing, but he remains fat anyway. *Ini sdh jam sepuluh, ia blm - muncul* Here it is already 10, and he still has not shown up. *Kok masih - di sini! Kan kamu disuruh pulang?* You were told to go home, weren't you? Why are you still here nevertheless? *kalau* - if only. *Kalau - dokter datang, anaknya tdk mati* If only the doctor had come, the child would not have died.

sajadah (*Isl.*) prayer rug.

sajak 1 poem, verse, lyrics. - *percintaan* love poem. - *ratap* 1 elegy. **2** (*Bib.*) Book of Lamentations. **2** rhyme. - *akhir* end-rhyme. **ber- 1** rhyme (of words, phrases, stories). **2** be in rhyming form. *cerita* ~ a story in rhyme. **3** write poetry. **4** recite poetry. **meny-** write poetry. **meny-kan** make a poem of, put into rhyme. **peny-** poet. **per-an 1** poetry. **2** rhyme.

sajarah see SEJARAH.

sajén (*Rel.*) offering of flowers or food (to spirits, etc.).

saji dishes laid out on the table. **meny-kan 1** serve, dish up. *Ia* ~ *makanan yg énak* He served delicious food. **2** provide, supply, present. *Mingguan itu* ~ *cerita-cerita péndék* The weekly provided short stories. *Ia* ~ *soal-soal baru* She put forward new problems. **ter-** laid out on the table. **ter-kan** can be set out, get set out. **-an 1** dish of food offered to guests. **2** see SAJÉN. **peny-** o. who presents entertainment, a paper, etc. **peny-an** presentation.

sak₁ 1 sack, bag. **2** pocket.

sak₂ see SYAK.

saka 1 heritage. **2** heirloom. - *baka* ancestors.

Saka (*Jv*) year in the calendar beginning 78 A.D. *tahun -...* in the Jv year ...(used to refer to pre-15th century events).

sakadang term of address in fables.

sakaguru see SOKOGURU.

sakal see ANGIN, SAMUN₂.

sakalor (*Sd*) epidemic.

sakap meny- sharecrop. **meny-kan** lease land on a sharecrop basis. **peny-** sharecropper.

sakar (*Chem.*) sugar. - *emping* maltose. - *susu* lactose. **-²** sweets. ~ *produksi* manufactured sweets.

sakaratulmaut, sakarat ulmaut see SAKRATULMAUT.

sakarin saccharin.

sakarosa (*Chem.*) sucrose.

sakat₁ meny-kan tease, annoy. *Ia selalu* ~ *dia* He is always teasing her.

sakat₂ meny-kan beach a boat. **ter-** stranded. *Kapal itu* ~ The ship was stranded.

sakduk /sakduk/ kerchief.

saké k.o. alchoholic beverage, sake.

sakedidi see KEDIDI.

sakelar electric switch.

sakelek (*Coll.*) matter-of-fact, businesslike.

sakharin see SAKARIN.

saking (*Coll.*) on account of. *Ia tak dpt melihat apa-apa - gelapnya* He could not see anything on account of the darkness.

sakit 1 ill, sick, sickness. *Dia jatuh* - He fell ill. - *saya agak berat* I had a rather severe illness. **2** sore, painful. *Tangan saya* - My hand hurts. *Apa yg -? Mana yg -?* Where does it hurt? *Dia menjerit karena - yg tdk terperikan* She shrieked because of her indescribable pain. - *abuh* (*Jv*) (suffering from a) swelling. - *akal/angan-angan* insane. - *batuk kering/kambing* (suffering from) congested coughs. - *céléng* epileptic, epilepsy. - *datang bulan* 1 monthly menstrual period. 2 suffering from menstruation pains. - *gajah-gajahan* (suffering from) elephantiasis. - *gula* diabetes. - *hati* offended, harboring resentment. - *ingatan/pikiran* insane, crazy. - *ingus* (suffer from) glanders (of a horse). - *kepala* (have a) headache. - *keputihan* (suffer from) leucorrhea. - *kuku dan mulut* (suffer from) foot-and-mouth disease. - *kuning* (suffer from) jaundice. - *mangga* (have a) swelling in the groin. - *panas* 1 fever. 2 feverish. - *perempuan* venereal disease. - *perut* have a stomachache. - *sabun* gonorrhea. - *senéwén* 1 nervous disorder. 2 shell shock. - *tujuh keliling* have dizzy spells. *si* - the patient. **se-²** however ill, no matter how suffering or hurt. ~ *hatinya, dia masih menghormatinya* As hurt as she was, she still respects him. **ber-²(an) 1** ail, be sickly. **2** make every effort to do s.t. **meny-i, memper-i** hurt, offend. *Ia* ~ *hatinya* She hurt his feelings. **meny-kan** hurt, painful. *Perkataanya itu* ~ (*hati*) His words hurt. **ke-an 1** be ill. **2** in pain. *Ia menjerit-jerit* ~ He screamed in pain. **3** illness, sickness. **4** hardship, misery, trouble. *Ke mana saja aku datang, selalu menyebabkan* ~ Wherever I go, I cause trouble. **-an** (*Coll.*) more painful. **-²an** sickly, to be in poor health. **peny-** 1 disease, illness. ~ *ayam tetélo* Newcastle disease. ~ *baguk/beguk/gondok* thyroid condition. ~ *dlm* internal disease. ~ *gula* diabetes. ~ *Inggeris* rickets. ~ *karang/batu (ginjal)* kidney stones. ~ *kelamin* venereal disease. ~ *(kencing) manis* diabetes. ~ *kotor/lezat* venereal disease. ~ *mati-mati ayam* epilepsy. ~ *paru-paru* 1 tuberculosis. 2 any lung disease. ~ *pektai* leucorrhea. ~ *pendarahan* hemorrhage. ~ *pitam* apoplexy. ~ *pinggang* nephritis. ~ *saraf* nervous disorder. ~ *senu* neural pain. 2 trouble. *É lu, cari* ~? Hey, are you looking for trouble? 3 bad habit. **berpeny-** 1 suffer from a disease. *Ia* ~ *malaria* He was suffering from malaria. 2 sickly, ailing. **pe-an** prisoner, convict. **peny-an** sickly, easily getting sick. *Anak itu* ~ *karena kurang gizi* That child is sickly because it is undernourished. **berpeny-an** tending to have a certain disease. **per-an** 1 things having to do with illness, disease, suffering. *sahabat* ~ friend in hard times, friend in need. 2 morbidity.

saklar see SAKELAR.

sakral sacred. *Agama merupakan sesuatu yg* - Religion is s.t. sacred. **meny-kan** sanctify, make holy. ~ *Pancasila* make s.t. sacred out of the *Pancasila*.

sakramén (*Rel.*) : sacrament. - *perminyakan (suci)* (*Rel.*) extreme unction.

sakrat ulmaut, sakratul maut, sakratulmaut death agony.

sakristi sacristy.

saksama see SEKSAMA.

saksi 1 witness. - *ahli* expert witness. - *a charge/ pemberat* witness for the prosecutor. - *a décharge/ peringan* witness for the defense. - *mata* eyewitness. 2 testimony. **ber-** 1 have best man or bridesmaid in a wedding. *perkawinan tdk* ~ marriage ceremony performed with no o. but the bride and groom. 2 appeal to s.t. as a witness and proof. ~ *kpd sejarah* appeal to history as proof. 3 testify. **memper-kan, meny-kan** 1 witness. *Malam itu org-org sekampung* ~ *penari itu disérét dr rumahnya* That night the whole village witnessed the dancer being dragged away from his house. 2 watch an event. ~ *sendratari* watch a dance drama. 3 testify. **ke-an** 1 testimony, evidence. 2 (*Rel.*) bearing witness, professing faith. **pe-, peny-** witness. ~ *mata* eyewitness. **peny-an** giving of evidence. **per-an** evidence, testimony.

saksofon saxophone.

saksofonis saxophonist.

saksrak meny- search through s.t. by beating it. *Semak-semak semua di-* They beat the bushes in their search.

sakti /sakti/ 1 supernatural, divine power. *Ia tak dpt luka karena -nya* He was invulnerable because of his supernatural power. 2 having magic or divine power. *Kabarnya rumah itu rumah* - They say that house has magical powers. 3 sacred. *Keris itu - bagi meréka* The dagger was sacred to them. **meny-kan** render supernaturally powerful. **ke-an** supernatural powers.

saku 1 bag, sack. - *kerja* workbag, briefcase. 2 pocket.

sakura 1 cherry tree. 2 (*Coll.*) other trees bearing pink blossoms. *negeri* - Japan.

sakwasangka see SYAK.

sal₁ hospital ward. - *bersalin* lying-in ward.

sal₂ see SYAL.

Sala see SOLO.

salada see SELADA.

salah₁ 1 fault. - *siapa?* Whose fault was it? *Tak ada -nya* There is no harm in it. *Apa -nya aku tahu nama kekasihmu?* What is wrong with my knowing your lover's name? 2 (*Coll.*) be at fault, be guilty. 3 mistake. *Itu adalah suatu - besar* It was a big mistake. *tak - lagi* no doubt about it. *tak - lagi dia yg bersalah* There is no doubt he is the guilty o. - *silih* all sorts of mistakes. 4 wrong. *Terjemahan itu* - The translation is wrong. 5 be in the wrong, mistaken. *Kalau saya tak* - If I am not mistaken. 6 do s.t. the wrong way. - *ambilan* draw wrong conclusion. *Ia* - *ambilan dr percakapan saya itu* He drew the wrong conclusion from my discussion. - *angkuh* 1 indecent. 2 improper. - *arti* misinterpret, misinterpretation. - *bantal* crick in the neck, having stiff neck. - *bebal* mistake, stupidity. - *duga/kira* miscalculate, misjudge, miscalculation, misjudgment. **ke-dugaan** error, mistake. - *faham/mengerti/tangkap/terima/tampa* misunderstand, misunderstanding. **ke-fahaman** misunderstanding. - *guna* **meny-gunakan, mens-gunakan** misuse s.t. **peny-gunaan** misuse, abuse. - *hati* peevish, snappish. - *jalan* 1 lose o.'s way. 2 walk on the wrong side of the road. - *kaprah* (*Jv*) folk-etymology, a deviation from real meaning of word or phrase due to widespread misinterpretation. **ke-kaprahan** (*Jv*) commonly committed error in word usage accepted by custom. - *langkah* (take a) wrong step, (make a) mistake. - *mengerti* misunderstand. **meny-mengertikan** misunderstand s.t. - *omong* say the wrong thing. - *pukul* make the wrong bet. - *raba* be mistaken, bark up wrong tree. - *sambung* (*Tel.*) wrong number. - *sangka* misjudge, misjudgment. - *semat* misunderstanding. - *tafsir* misinterpretation. **meny-tafsirkan** misinterpret s.t. - *terka* misunderstand. - *tingkah* feel awkward, have stage fright. - *urus* mismanagement. - *urat* sprained. - *wésel* 1 bark up wrong tree, miss the point. 2 wrong address. -² if s.t. turns out wrong, if things do not go right. *Jangan dekat-dekat org itu,* ~ *nanti kamu dikira termasuk grombolan meréka* Do not hang around those people. People might just think you are are part of that group. **ber-** be guilty. **ber-an** 1 controversial. 2 be at variance, be in conflict. ~ *paham* have a misunderstanding. **keber-an** guilt. **ber-²an** be in conflict with e.o. **meny-i** 1 conflict with. *Itu* ~ *pendirian saya* It was incompatible with my opinion. 2 violate. ~ *hukum* violate the law. ~ *padan* break o.'s word. 3 do wrong to. *Ia* ~ *saya* He wronged me. **meny-kan** 1 accuse, blame. *Jangan -kan saya dlm hal ini* Do not blame me in this matter. **2** deny. *Tuduhan-tuduhan itu di-kan* The accusations were denied. **3** frustrate s.t. *Serangan itu di-kan* The attack was thwarted. **memper-kan** blame, hold responsible for. *Ia diper-kan atas hal itu* He was blamed for that affair. **ter-** accidentally wrong, mistaken. **ke-an 1** mistake, error, blunder. ~ *dlm hitungan* error in counting. **2** fault. *Ia tdk merasa mempunyai* ~ He did not admit to any faults. **3** guilt. *Apa ~ku?* What did I do wrong? **4** accidentally. *Ia ~ minum obat ibunya* By accident he drank his mother's medicine. **peny-an** refutation.

salah₂ o. of the, o. out of several. *Ambillah - sebuah!* Take o. (any o.)! - *seorg o.* of them.

salai 1 smoked. *ikan* - smoked fish. **2** dried. *pisang* - sun-dried banana chips. **meny- 1** smoke. **2** dry (by fire or in sun). **-an** grill, grate.

salak₁ the Zalacca palm and its fruit.

salak₂ high-pitched bark. **meny-** bark. **meny-i** bark at.

salam₁ 1 peace (in greetings). **2** greetings. *Ia mengirim - kpdmu* He sends you his regards. - *hangat* warm regards. - *kompak/mesra* cordial greetings, warm greetings. - *pembuka* salutation. - *penutup* complimentary close in letter. - *taklim/takzim* sincerely yours. - *témpél/témplék* **1** gift at wedding or circumcision. **2** bribe. *berjabat - témpél* shake hands and leave a bit of money in the other's hands. **ber-** greet (shaking hands, bowing, etc.). **ber-(²)an** shake hands in greeting. **meny-i 1** greet officially. *Ia sedang berpidato ~ meréka yg berhasil* She was making a speech to greet those who succeeded. **2** shake the hand of. *sewaktu tangannya di-i Mulyadi* when Mulyadi shook her hand. **-an 1** handshake. **2** (*Coll.*) greet e.o., shake e.o.'s hand.

salam₂ see DAUN.

salam₃ see IKAN.

salam alaikum, salam lékum see ASSALAM ALAIKUM.

salang meny- stab with a knife, dagger. **peny-** s.t. to stab with.

salap see SALEP.

salasilah genealogy.

salat₁ salad.

salat₂ see SOLAT.

salawat see SELAWAT.

saldo (*Fin.*) balance. - *laba* credit balance.

salé see SALAI.

saléh pious, virtuous, godly. **ke-an** piety.

salem see IKAN.

salémpang see SELÉMPANG.

salep ointment, salve.

salesman salesman.

sali steadfast.

salib 1 (*Bib.*) (Christian) cross. **2** see SALIP. **meny-(kan)** crucify. **peny-an** crucifixion.

salih see SALÉH.

salim healthy.

salin ber- 1 change clothes. ~ *nama* change o.'s name. ~ *rupa* change o.'s appearance. **2** bear a child, give birth. **ber-²** changing continuously, erratic. *Kelakuannya ~ saja* His behavior was er-

ratic. **meny- 1** change s.t. *-lah pakaianmu itu* Change your clothes. **2** copy. *Ia ~ surat perjanjian itu* He copied the contract. **3** translate. *Ia ~ buku itu* She translated the book. **memper-kan** give suit of clothes as a present (lit., cause o. to change clothes). **-an 1** copy. **2** translation. **pe-** new suit of clothes. **peny- 1** copyist. **2** translator. **peny-an** translating, copying. **per-(an)** suit of traditional clothing. **per-an 1** change (of clothes). ~ *rupa* change of appearance. **2** childbirth. **3** gift of clothes.

saling o. another, mutual(ly). *Meréka - menolong* They helped e.o. - *mengerti* understand e.o., mutual understanding. - *menghindari/menolak* mutually exclusive. - *pengertian* mutual understanding. - *tergantung/bergantung(an)* interdependent. **ke-tergantungan** mutual dependence.

salinitas (*Chem.*) salinity.

salip (ber)-²an, - meny- overtake e.o. **meny-** pass, overtake (a car). *Dilarang ~* No passing.

salju snow. - *batu* hail. **ber-** snow-covered.

salla'llahu 'alaihi wasallam (*Isl.*) May Allah bless him and give him peace (said after mentioning Muh.'s name).

salmiak ammonium chloride.

salomé [*satu lobang ramé-ramé*] (*Sl.*) **1** prostitute, loose woman. **2** golf.

salon 1 drawing room. - *kecantikan* beauty parlor. **2** console. - *radio* radio console. **-²an** pertaining to the drawing room. *sosialisme ~* parlor socialism.

salp see SALEP.

salto somersault. - *mortal* sumersault in the air. **ber-** somersault.

saluir salute. **ber-, meny-** salute, greet.

saluk man's kerchief. **ber-** wear such a kerchief.

salung flute. **ber-** play the flute.

salur 1 channel, gutter, duct. **2** (*Tel.*) line (switchboard). **3** lines, stripes. - *biru* blue stripes. **ber-²** having lines. *mata yg ~ mérah* bloodshot eyes. **meny-i** make s.t. pass through s.t. *Selokan itu di-i air lembah* Sewage drains via the ditch. **meny-kan 1** channel s.t. *Aku ~ cintaku ke dunia seni* I channeled my love to the world of art. **2** bring goods on a market, distribute. ~ *bahan baku pd perusahaan* provide raw materials to a factory. ~ *buku* distribute books. **ter-(kan)** find an outlet, channeled. **-an 1** channel. ~ *diplomatik* diplomatic channels. ~ *hukum* legal channels. **2** (*Tel.*) line (switchboard). **3** gutter. **4** tract, duct. ~ *air* waterworks, canal, drain. ~ *air seni/kencing* (*Anat.*) urethra. ~ *empedu* duct for the bile. ~ *pembuangan* sewage system. ~ *(per)nafas(an)* (*Anat.*) respiratory tract. ~ *udara* (*Anat.*) windpipe, trachea. **peny- 1** distributor. ~ *tunggal* sole distributor. ~ *utama* main distributor. **2** conductor. (*Elec.*) ~ *petir* lightning conductor. **peny-an 1** distribution. **2** channeling.

salut₁ 1 cover, envelope. - *surat* envelope. **2** wrapping. **3** casing. **ber-(kan)** covered, plated (with). ~ *emas* plated with gold. **meny-** cover, coat, plate. *di- emas* gold-plated. **-an** coating, plating.

salut₂ 1 salute. 2 greetings. 3 respect, admire. *Saya - akan keberaniannya* I admire her courage.
salvo salvo, volley.
salwat see SELAWAT.
sama₁ same, equal. *Dua tambah tiga - dgn lima* two plus three equals five. *Rupanya - dgn sepuluh tahun yg lalu* He looks the same as he did 20 years ago. *Rumahnya - besarnya dgn rumah saya* His house is the same size as my house. *- saja bagi saya* It is all the same to me. *- arti* having the same meaning. *- dan sebangun* (*Math.*) congruent. *- kaki* (*Math.*) isosceles. *- kuat* a tie. *Pertandingan itu berakhir dgn - kuat* The meet ended with a tie. *- kupuan* equal. *- pusat* homocentric. *- rasa - rata* sharing the same feelings and the same fate. *- rata* equal, having the same treatment. **meny-ratakan** 1 treat alike. 2 generalize. 3 raze to the ground. **peny-rataan** treating the same, generalization, leveling. **meny-rendahkan** treat all with equal condescension. *- sekali* absolutely. *Itu - sekali benar* that is absolutely true. *- sekali tdk mengganggu* It is not the least bit troublesome. *- setentang* level or flush with s.t. *- sisi* (*Math.*) equilateral. *- tengah* impartial. *Dlm perkara itu kita berdiri - tengah* We are impartial in the case. *- ucap* (*Ling.*) homonym. *-²* exactly the same. *Kita ~ berbahaya* We are equally in danger. *"Terima kasih" "~"* "Thank you." "You are welcome. (Thank you, too)". **se-** fellow, peer. *Hargailah perjuangan ~ patriot* Value the struggle of your fellow patriot. *~ narapidana* fellow prisoner. *jangan sampai tertinggal ~nya* lest they be outdone by their peers. **ber-an** 1 be equal to e.o. *Tenaga militér A ~ dgn tenaga militér B* A's military forces are equal to B's. 2 be in conformity with. *Hal itu ~ fasal tiga puluh anggaran dasar* That is in conformity with Article 30 of the statutes. 3 resembling, similar. **meny-** behave like. *Ia ~ bintang filem* She behaved like a movie star. **meny-i** equal, match s.t. *~ rékor dunia* match the world's record. **meny-kan, memper-kan** 1 compare s.t. (with). *Toyota tdk dpt di-kan dgn Ford* You cannot compare a Toyota with a Ford. 2 treat the same as. *Org kelas satu dan org kelas dua di-kan saja* They just treat the people in first class exactly the same as those in 2d class. 3 place on a par, make the same. *Gajinya di-kan dgn gaji menteri* His salary was made the same as that of a state minister. *~ skor* tie the score. *Di jaman penjajahan Indo diper-kan dgn Belanda* In the colonial period the mestizos were placed on a par with the Dutch. **meny-²kan** unjustifiably compare, consider the same, place on a par. **memper-²kan** mistakenly consider the same, mistake s.o. for s.o. else. **ke-an** sameness, similarity. *~ dia dan adiknya* the similarity between her and her sister. *~ derajat* equality of rank. **-an** (*Coll.*) of the same type. **per-an** 1 similarity, agreement. *~ antara kedua bahasa itu* the similarity between the two languages. 2 comparison. 3 equality. *~ hak* having equal rights. 4 (*Math.*) equation. *~ dua*

bilangan yg tdk dikenal an equation with two unknowns. *~ persegi* quadratic equation.
sama₂ 1 (*Coll.*) together, with. *Ia pergi - saya* He went with me. 2 and. *Kedua anak itu jauh bumi - langit* The two children are as different as day and night. *Dikasi minum - makan* Give him s.t. to eat and drink. 3 do together, also do. *Mau ikut -* Want to go along? *Dia ikut melihat -* He looked at it, too. *program kerja -* a cooperative program. *Dia tdk mau bekerja -* He does not want to cooperate. 4 (*Coll.*) regarding (an all-purpose preposition). *Saya kasihan - dia* I feel pity for her. *Kasi saya* Give it to me. *Saya tdk dikasi sekolah lagi - ibu* Mother does not send me to school any longer. *Béda satu - lain* O. is different from the other. *mau - mau* mutually agreeable. *tahu - tahu* connive with e.o. 5 plural marker of adjectives and verbs. *Kita - tahu* We all know . . . **ber-** 1 together with. *saya ~ isteri saya* my wife together with me. 2 herewith. *~ ini saya menyatakan bhw . . .* With this I state that . . . 3 joint, collective. *Ini utk kita ~ This* is for all of us. *perusahaan ~* a joint venture. (**ber-)-²** do together. *Mari kita pulang ~* Let us go home together. **ber-an** do simultaneously. *Beberapa pesawat mendarat ~* Several planes landed at the same time. **keber-an** togetherness.
sama ada (*Lit.*) whether. *Masalah itu tlh dikaji - kita mau merdéka sendiri atau . . .* We have examined the question thoroughly whether we wish to be independent or . . .
samadi see SEMADI.
samak₁ tannin. **meny-** tan s.t. **peny-** tanner. **peny-an** tanning.
samak₂ **ber-** covered, plated. *Ia bersepatu berat ~ besi* He wore heavy shoes with steel taps. **meny-cover.** *~ buku* cover a book. **meny-i** cover s.t. *~ hati* be on o.'s mind.
samapta (*Mil.*) ready, prepared. **ke-an** preparedness, readiness.
samar 1 dim, vague, indistinct. *- muka* twilight. 2 obscure, hidden. 3 disguised, masked. **-²** dimly, vaguely, indistinctly. **meny- 1** be in disguise. *Ia ~ sbg prajurit* He was disguised as a soldier. 2 be incognito. *Raja itu pergi ~* The king went incognito. **meny-kan** conceal, hide s.t. *Ia ~ dirinya di antara org ramai* He hid himself in the crowd. **memper- 1** blur, make vague. 2 make obscure, conceal. *Ia ~ maksudnya* She concealed her intentions. **ter-** disguised. *pengangguran ~* (*Econ.*) disguised unemployment. **ke-an 1** dusk. 2 obscureness, vagueness. 3 camouflage. *~ tempat persembunyian* camouflage of a hiding place. **-an** object of disguise, camouflage. *nama ~ pen* name, pseudonym. **peny-an** camouflage, disguise. *~nya sempurna* His disguise was perfect.
sama rata see SAMA₁.
samas (*Rel.*) deacon (Protestant).
sama sekali see SAMA₁.
sambal condiment us. containing chili peppers. *- bajag/bajak* fried spices. *- déndéng* dish with dried

meat in a spicy sauce. - *goréng* k.o. of food fried in a spicy sauce. - *terasi* sauce made with shrimp paste. - *ulek* sauce made by crushing spices in a mortar. **meny-** prepare this sauce. **-²an** various spicy side dishes.

sambaléwa done half-heartedly. **meny-** half-heartedly. **meny-kan** carry s.t. out in a half-hearted way.

sambang₁ watch, guard, patrol. **ber-** 1 keep watch. 2 make o.'s rounds. **meny-i** patrol s.t.

sambang₂ (*Jv*) disease or affliction caused by evil spirits.

sambang₃ empty honeycomb.

sambang₄ (*Jv, Jkt*) visit. **meny-i** visit.

sambar - meny- strike o. after the other (as of flash of lightning). **meny-** 1 swoop down and seize. *Burung elang itu ~ anak ayam* The hawk swooped down and seized the baby chick. *Pisaunya di- lawannya* His opponent seized the knife. *Sialan, jamku di- org* What bad luck! My watch was stolen. 2 strike, attack. *Pohon itu di-hulilintar* The tree was struck by lightning. *Ia di-dgn pisau* He was attacked with a knife. *Api ~ atapnya* The fire attacked the roof. - *glédék* an imprecation (lit., be struck by lightning). 3 steal, rob. **meny-kan** grab with a forceful swoop on behalf of s.o. **ter-** 1 be seized. 2 be struck. **-an** strike, stroke.

sambat₁ (*Jv, Jkt*) **ber-, meny-** ask for help. **-an** 1 (mutual) assistance. 2 assistant. 3 help e.o.

sambat₂ ber- connected, joined. **meny-** join s.t. *Ia ~ kedua potong tali itu* He spliced the two pieces of rope.

sambékala (*Jv*) accident. *mengalami -* have an accident.

sambel see SAMBAL.

sambén 1 sideline, part-time extra job. 2 side issue.

samber see SAMBAR.

sambet ke- 1 struck by a sharp object. 2 struck with disease.

sambi meny-, ny- 1 do at the same time. 2 have a side job.

sambil while, at the same time. *Ia menyanyi - bermain piano* She sang while playing the piano. *Ia tertawa - menangis* He laughed and cried at the same time. - *lalu* in passing. *Jika ada disebut, maka hanyalah - lalu* If it was mentioned, it was only in passing. **meny-lalukan** consider s.t. as of secondary importance. *pendidikan anak tak boléh di-lalukan* The upbringing of a child should not be considered of secondary importance. - *menyelam minum air* kill two birds with o. stone. **meny-** engage in secondary employment, moonlight. *Ia terpaksa ~ karena gajinya tdk mencukupi* He had to moonlight because his wage did not meet his needs. **meny-kan** 1 do s.t. at the same time. 2 do s.t. as a sideline. *Waktu ia bepergian ke luar negeri, ia ~ berdagang* While he was traveling abroad, he did a little business on the side. **ter-** 1 unimportant, incidental, secondary in importance.

Baginya uang adalah soal ~ saja Money is of incidental importance to him. 2 held as a sideline. *pekerjaan ~* side job. **-an** 1 side line. 2 part-time. 3 pretext.

sambit ber-(²)an throw at e.o. *Kedua pengantin itu ~ dgn daun sirih* The bride and groom threw betel leaves at e.o. **meny-** lash. **meny-(i)** throw at. *Lelaki itu ~ kanak-kanak dgn kulit jeruk* The man threw orange peels at the children. **meny-kan** throw s.t. *Pisau itu di-kannya ke pintu belakang* She threw the knife into the back door.

sambuk a whip. **meny-** whip. **-an** whipping. *Kemarahan majikannya merupakan ~ baginya spy bekerja lebih keras* His employer's anger whipped him to work harder.

sambung 1 continue, go on (in conversation). *"Seratus saja," -nya* "It was only a hundred," he continued. 2 be connected. *Maaf, salah -* Sorry, wrong number. **ber-** 1 continued, prolonged. 2 connected. *cerita ~* a story with several episodes, serial. *~ kembali* knit (of bones). *~ tangan* obtain assistance. *~ keluarga dgn* be related to. *~ dr mulut ke mulut* spread by word of mouth. **ber-²** successively, in a row, continuously. **ber-an** connected. *Kamar ini ~ dgn kamar tidurnya* This room connects with his bedroom. - **meny-** in a row, continuously. **meny-** 1 continue, connect on to s.t. *Ceritera itu akan di-* The story will be continued. *Ia ~ tali itu* She connected the pieces of string. 2 reply to. *~ surat bp yg terakhir* in reply to your last letter. *~ hidup/nyawa* work to make both ends meet. *~ silaturrahim* strengthen a friendship. *~ keturunan* continue the family line. **meny-i** connect several things. **meny-kan** connect s.t. on to or with. *Minta di-kan dgn Keterangan* Connect me with Information. **ter-** connected. *tdk ~ lagi* (*Tel.*) disconnected. **-an** 1 continuation, extension. 2 connection. *~ tangan* helper. *~ terakhir* final installment (of a serial). *~ langsung jarak jauh* (*Tel.*) long distance connection. **peny-** 1 connector, link. *~ lidah* conveyor of a message, mouthpiece. *~ nyawa* means of livelihood. 2 o. who connects. *~ télpon* telephone operator. **peny-an** connecting, connection, linking-up. *~ aliran air dan listrik* connection of water and electricity. **per-an** 1 connection. 2 continuation.

sambur see SABUR.

sambut answer. - **ber-** alternate (lit., answering each other). *Hélaan napas terdengar ~ seolah-olah saling berjawaban* O. could hear (them) breathing alternately, as if responding to e. o. **ber-** 1 answered. 2 parried, intercepted. *~ pd* appeal to. *Meréka ~ pd kakék spy dilindungi* They appealed to their grandfather for protection. **ber-an** 1 respond to e.o. 2 be in accordance. *Hal itu ~ dgn apa yg dikatakannya* It was in accordance with what he said. **ber-²an 1** answer e.o. 2 do alternately, continually back and forth. *Meriam kedua belah pihak ~* The artillery of both sides answered e.o. in turn. - **meny-** 1 answer e.o. 2 receive e.o. *Tangan-tangan* ~ Hands reached out to o. another. **meny-** 1 welcome, receive. *Org banyak ~ kedatangan Présidén* The crowd welcomed the president's arrival. 2 accept. *Usulusul perdamaian itu di- dgn gembira* The peace terms were gladly accepted. 3 parry, reply. *Ia ~ tuduhan-tuduhan* He parried the accusations. 4 on the occasion of. *~ ulang tahun kemerdékaan* on the occasion of the anniversary of independence. **-an** 1 welcome, reception. *~ meluap* rousing welcome. *~ hangat* warm reception. 2 answer, response, reaction. 3 agreement, approval. *Sayangnya prinsip si Ujang tdk dpt ~* Unfortunately Ujang's way of thinking did not meet with approval. 4 speech given in formal setting where a representative from every group attending says a few words. **peny-** s.o. that welcomes. *sorak ~* cheer of welcome. **peny-an** reception, welcoming.

samédi see SEMADI.

samenléven live together like husband and wife without benefit of matrimony.

samen wérking cooperation.

sami mawon (*Jv, Humorous*) It is just the same.

samin see MINYAK.

samirana breeze.

Samiri (*Bib.*) Samaritan.

samodera see SAMUDERA.

sampah rubbish, trash. *- hijau* compost. *- masyarakat* scum of society. *- sarap* trash, refuse. **meny-** become trash, rot. **per-an** trash heap, trash can.

sampai₁ 1 to, till, as far as. *Ia dpt menghitung dr satu - sepuluh* He can count from o. to 10. *Ia berjalan - Bogor* She walked as far as Bogor. *- bésok!* See you tomorrow! *- botak/tua* forever, until hell freezes over. *- dgn* up to and including. *- dgn 15 Maret* up to and including March 15. *- jangka waktu* exact, right on time. *- ketemu lagi* So long. *- nanti!* See you later! *- sekarang* up to now. *- umur* come of age. 2 arrive. *Pukul enam pagi kami -* We arrived at six a.m. 3 reach, extend far enough. *Saya tak dpt - pd langit-langit kamar itu* I could not reach the ceiling of the room. *Pendapatannya tak -* His earnings are insufficient. *- (di) akal* reasonable, plausible. *Cerita itu tak - di akal* That story is implausible. 4 arrive, materialize. *Maksudnya - juga* He reached his goal. 5 go as far as to, get to the point of. *Kalau PSSI - kalah, susah juga* If PSSI should lose, that would be pretty bad. *- sakit tenggorokan aku memanggilnya* I called him till I got a sore throat. *jangan - lest. Belajarlah baik-baik jangan - kalah dlm ujian nanti* Study hard or you will fail your exams. *- hati* have the heart to. *Ia tak - hati memukul anaknya* He did not have the heart to strike his child. *-² 1* so that, to such an extent that. *Ia asyik berjudi ~ ia lupa akan anaknya* She was so busy gambling that she forgot about her children. 2 even. *~ baju anaknya disita* Even his child's clothes were confiscated. **se-** upon arriving. *~nya di penginapan dia mandi* Upon arriving at the hotel, she

took a bath. **- meny-** sufficient. *Gajinya tiada ~* He could not make ends meet on his salary. **ny-** 1 reach. *Wah, kabelnya tdk ~* The cable is not long enough. 2 (*Coll.*) understand. *Gua nggak ~ kuliah itu* I did not understand the lecture. **meny-kan** 1 convey, extend (information, etc.). *Akan saya -kan salammu itu* I will give him your regards. *Ada org yg ~ bhw skuternya dicuri org* S.o. informed her that her scooter had been stolen. *~ pidato* give a speech. 2 hand over, give. *Ia ~ sepucuk surat* He handed over a letter. 3 deliver. *Sdh kamu -kan kiriman dr Toko Murah itu?* Did you deliver the goods from Toko Murah? **ke-an** achieved, accomplished. *Maksudnya ~* His goal was achieved. **peny-** o. who conveys. **peny-an** delivery.

sampai₂ meny- hang up to dry. **meny-kan** 1 put on (a dress). 2 carry on a pole. **-an** 1 rack, hatrack. 2 drying frame, clothesline.

sampak metal band around a knife handle.

sampan small boat, dugout. *- lundang* k.o. sampan. *- tunda* towed sampan. **ber-** ride in this k.o. boat. **ber-²** ride in these boats for fun.

sampang₁ brown varnish.

sampang₂ meny- paddle at stern of the boat.

sampang₃ stock to hold water buffalo's neck. **meny-** hold a water buffalo by the neck. *~ léhér kerbau utk dilobangi hidungnya* Hold the buffalo's neck tight so that a hole can be put through its nose. **ter-** (*M*) 1 get stuck, caught. 2 be hanging out.

sampang₄ k.o. tree.

sampanye champagne.

sampar plague, pest.

sampé see SAMPAI₁.

sampéan (*Jv*) you (polite).

sampék see SAMPAI₁.

sampel sample.

samper (*Coll.*) **meny-i** call on s.o., drop by to pick s.o. up. *Tolong -i saya kalau anda pergi ke mesjid* Stop by for me when you go to the mosque. **ke-** get hit by s.t., afflicted by s.t. evil.

sampéyan see SAMPÉAN.

sampi see SAPI.

samping₁ side. *Ia duduk di - saya* She sat beside me. *Aku melihat dr -* 1 looked from the side. *di - (itu)* besides, apart from (that). *Di - sepéda dia juga punya mobil* Besides a bicycle, she also has a car. *ke -* to the side. **- meny-** side by side. *rumah yg ~ rumah itu* houses on either side of that house. **ber-an** side by side. *Meréka berjalan ~* They walked side by side. **meny-, ny-** (be) on the edge, (go) along the side. **meny-i** be beside, next to. *Ajudannya selalu ~nya* His adjutant was always at his side. **meny-kan** 1 put aside. 2 bypass, ignore. 3 place side by side. **menge-kan** 1 put aside. *Ia ~ beberapa rupiah sebulan* He put a few rupiah aside monthly. 2 bypass s.t., ignore. *Ia ~ keinginan rakyat* He ignored the will of the people. **terke-kan** shunted aside. *hal yg ~ dr pembicaraan* a matter shunted out of the conversation. **ter-** pushed aside. *Di mana-mana ia ~ saja*

He was pushed aside whereever he went. **-an** side-, secondary. *hasil* ~ by-product. *kegiatan* ~ side activity. *pekerjaan* ~ side job.
samping₂ ceremonial sarong (us. silk with gold threads).
sampir meny-kan hang. *Ia ~ jasnya pd korsi* He hung his coat over a chair. **-an 1** place to hang clothes, a rack, peg, hook. **2** first two lines of a pantun, couplet.
sampo, sampu₁ shampoo.
sampu₂ (*Med.*) anemia. *- pening* epilepsy.
sampuk meny- run into s.o., fly at. **meny-kan** use s.t. to flail with.
sampul cover, wrapper. *- bantal* pillowcase. *- buku* book cover. *- surat* envelope. *- tertutup* sealed envelope. **ber-** covered, wrapped, placed in an envelope. **meny-(i)** wrap, place in an envelope, put a cover on. **ter-** wrapped.
sampur (*Jv*) sash, k.o. long scarf worn by female dancer. *mendapat -* be given the scarf by a dancer and have the obligation to dance with her.
samroh k.o. Isl. music sung in chorus (us. by women).
samséng 1 gamecock. **2** rowdy, bully.
samsi₁ (*Ch*) lion dance.
samsi₂ sun.
samsir (*Lit.*) k.o. sword.
samsonit attaché case.
samudera, samudra ocean. *- Indonésia* Indian Ocean.
samudrawi oceanic.
samun₁ bushes, shrubs.
samun₂ *- sakal* robbery accompanied by violence. **meny-** rob s.o. **ke-an** robbed. *Ia ~ kemarin malam* He was robbed last night. **meny-i** go to in order to rob. **peny-** robber. **(peny)-an** robbery.
samurai 1 samurai sword. **2** samurai. **meny-** use a samurai sword.
san see SÉRSAN.
sana there, yonder. *Ia sedang duduk di -* He is sitting there. *ke -* there, thither. *Ia pergi ke -* She went there. *di bawah -* down there. *ke - kemari* to and fro, back and forth. *tdk ke - tdk ke sini* impartial, neutral. *sebelah/bagian -* the other side. *seberang -* opposite side (of street, river, etc.). *- sini* here and there, everywhere. *Di - sini kedengaran bunyi rététan senapang* The sound of rattling gunfire was everywhere. **menge-kan** bring there, send there. *Meréka sdh dike-kan* They have been sent there.
sanak relative. **ber-** *sdr/keluarga* o.'s relatives. *tanpa -* *tanpa sdr* all alone. **se-** *sdr* be related. *Saya ~ sdr dgn dia* I am related to him. *~ jangan berkelahi* People who are related should not quarrel. **ber-sdr 1** have relatives. **2** be related to. *Kami ~ sdr dgn dia* We are related to him.
sanat (*Isl.*) Muslim year. *- Maséhi* A.D.
sanatorium sanatorium, health resort.
sanca see ULAR.
sandal sandal, open-toe slipper. *-jepit/Jepang* sandals with a thong. **ber-** wear sandals.
sandang₁ shoulder strap. **meny- 1** carry s.t.

strapped over the shoulder. *Ia ~ senapannya* He carried his gun over the shoulder. **2** bear (a title). *Ia cukup mampu ~ titel doktor* Her qualifications are high enough to deserve the title of PhD. **meny-i** attribute to. *Jénderal itu di-i gelar Doktor Honoris Causa* The general was given an honorary doctorate. **meny-kan** strap on, gird. **memper-kan** carry over o.'s shoulders. **-an** sling. **peny-** shoulder strap.
sandang₂ clothing. *- pangan* food and clothing, basic necessities. **meny-i** clothe. **-an** clothing.
sandar *kursi -* armchair. **ber- 1** lean on. *Ia ~ pd dinding* He leaned against the wall. **2** (*Naut.*) moor, tie up (ship). *Kapal berbélok ke kiri utk ~ di pelabuhan* The ship veered left to dock in the harbor. **3** be dependent on, be based on. *Ia ~ pd pendapatan isterinya* He relied on his wife's earnings. *Hal itu ~ pd téori lama* That is based on old theory. **ber-an** lean on. **ber-kan** be based on. *~ téori saya . . .* Based on my theory . . . **- meny-1** lean on e.o. **2** depend on o. another. *Kedua negeri itu ~* The two countries were dependent on e.o. **meny-** buttress, lean against s.t. or s.o. *Aku bangkit dan duduk ~ ke dinding* I got up and sat leaning against the wall. **meny-i 1** support o.s. on. *Org tua itu ~ anaknya kalau berjalan* The old man was supported by his son when he walked. **2** lean against. *Jangan kau-i pintu yg baru dicat itu* Do not lean against the newly painted door. **3** (*Naut.*) moor to. *sebuah dermaga yg dpt di-i kapal* a pier which ships can moor to. **meny-kan 1** base s.t. on. *Ia ~ nasibnya pd keadilan hakim* He based his fate on the judge's sense of justice. **2** prop, lean s.t. *Ia ~ sepedanya ke dinding* She put her bicycle against the wall. **memper-i** lean against. **-an 1** support, assistance. **2** abutment, prop, back. *~ buku* book end. *~ jembatan* parapet. *~ kursi* back of a chair. **3** basis. *~ hukum* The basis for the law.
sandel₁ *kayu -* sandalwood.
sandel₂ see KUDA.
sandel₃ see SANDAL.
sandera 1 hostage. **2** debt bondsman. **meny-(kan)** take as a hostage. **ter-** be taken hostage. **peny-an** taking of hostages.
sandi code. *kata -* codeword. **ber-** in code. **meny-(kan)** encode. *~ balik* decode. **per-an** encoding.
sanding₁ close, near. *- kata* (*Ling.*) collocation. **ber-** sit in state (of bride and groom at marriage ceremony). *duduk ~* sit next to e.o. in marriage ceremony. **meny-i 1** accompany, be next to. **2** be married to. **meny-kan, memper-kan** place newlyweds next to e.o. (in marriage ceremony). **-an** partner, o. who accompanies.
sanding₂ sharp angle. **ber- 1** angular. **2** sharp, biting. *Perkataannya ~* Her words were sharp.
sandiwara 1 play, drama. **2** theatrical troupe. *- keliling* traveling show. **ber- 1** be on the stage. *Tiap malam ia ~* Every evening she was on the stage. **2** pretend, play-act. *Ia biasanya ~ saja* She us. just pretends. **meny-kan 1** dramatize. **2** adapt for the stage. **peny-an** dramatization (of

novel, etc.). **per-an, ke-an** matters concerning plays.

sandiwarawan dramatist.

sando k.o. chest-exercise device, consisting of springs attached to handles.

sandra see SANDERA.

sandung pedal of weaving loom. **meny- 1** make s.o. stumble, trip up. **2** undermine. ~ *program pemerintah* undermine gvt. programs. **ter-, ke-** stumble. *Kakinya ~ pd batu* He stumbled over a stone. **-an** stumbling block.

sanépa (*Jv*) figure of speech to express a superlative by referring to a quality the opposite of the expected and using it as o. of the standards of comparison; that is, saying that in comparison to the thing described the characteristic thing has the opposite quality. *Pait madu (dibandingkan senyummu)* (Your smile is) sweeter than honey. Honey is bitter (compared to your smile).

sanéring (*Fin.*) currency reform.

sang honorific epithet or article (also used in sarcastic or derogatory way). *- atas* superiors. *- déwi* Goddess. *- Hyang/Yang* title for God. *- Mérah Putih/Dwiwarna* the Indonesian flag. *- Nata* His Majesty. *- pencuri* the thief. *- Penebus* (*Bib.*) the Redeemer. *- Prabu* His Majesty. *- suami* the (honorable) husband. *- Surya* **1** sun. **2** sun god.

sanga₁ dross.

sanga₂ ter-² nervous and in a hurry.

sanga₃ see WALI.

sangai₁ lid, cover, top.

sangai₂ ber- warm o.s. **meny-** warm s.t.

sangan (*Jv*) earthen pot. **meny-** heat in utensil without oil or water. *Kacang kedelai di- sampai kering* The soybeans are roasted dry.

sangar₁ ill-fated, bringing misfortune, spooky.

sangar₂ heated in utensil without oil. *kacang -* roasted peanuts. **meny-** roast in utensil without oil.

sangat 1 very, extremely. *Ia - sakit/Ia sakit -* She is very ill. *- kurang* very much lacking. *Dia - mengerti* She understood very well. **2** intense, violent, vehement. *wangi yg amat -* strong fragrance. *atas permintaan yg -* on urgent request. **-²** critical, important. *soal ~* burning questions. **memper-** intensify. *Itu ~ perselisihan* That intensified the quarrel. **ter-** excessive, extreme. **ke-an** excessive, extreme. *Hampir saya lupa karena ~ gembira* I almost forgot because of my excessive enthusiasm.

sangawali see WALI.

sangga prop, support. *- buku* book rest. *- kejutan* (*Auto.*) shock absorber. *- bunuh* charm against death in battle. *- mara* **1** crossbar. **2** (*Naut.*) gaff (sailing vessel). **meny-** support, prop. **peny-** support, buffer.

sanggah₁ (*Bali*) house-shrine.

sanggah₂ meny- protest, oppose, contradict. *Ia ~ kebenaran berita itu* He contradicted the truth of the report. **-an** protest, rejoinder, rebuttal. **peny- 1** opponent. **2** discussant. **3** o. who protests. **peny-an** act of opposing.

sanggama see SENGGAMA.

sanggar 1 small house temple. **2** studio. *- kerja* workshop, atelier. *- poto* photo studio.

sanggat run aground. **ter-** run aground.

sanggerah₁ bloodletting. **meny-** bleed s.o.

sanggerah₂ pe-an traveler's rest house.

sanggit meny- *gigi* gnash o.'s teeth.

sanggul knot of hair, hair bun. *- duduk* hair bun worn low. **ber-** wear o.'s hair in a knot. **meny-(kan)** put hair up in a knot. *Ibu mau di-kan sekalian?* Would you like to have your hair done up at the same time? **-an** wear a hair bun. **ter-** put up in a bun. *Rambutnya ~ rapi* Her hair was put up in a neat bun.

sanggup 1 able, capable. *Polisi tak - mengamankan pemberontakan itu* The police were unable to pacify the uprising. **2** be prepared to do. *Ia tdk - bertanggung jawab* He was not willing to take responsibility. **meny-i** promise. *Roni ~ saya bantuan* Roni promised me help. **meny-kan 1** enable. *Undang-undang itu ~ Indonésia keluar dr persekutuan itu* The decree enabled Indonesia to withdraw from the alliance. **2** promise. *Ia ~ utk memberi Rp1.000* He promised to contribute 1,000 rupiah. **ke-an 1** power, capability, performance. *Jangan khawatir akan ~ tentara kita* Do not doubt the power of our forces. **2** readiness to do s.t. **-an** promise. *~ Belanda utk merundingkan kedudukan Irian Barat* the promise of the Dutch to discuss the West New Guinea situation.

sanggurdi stirrup.

sangit 1 smelling burnt or scorched, burnt or scorched (smell). **2** see WALANG.

sangka 1 supposition, idea. *pd - saya* in my opinion. **2** suspicion. *- itu hendaklah dihilangkan* That suspicion should be abandoned. **ber-** mean, think. *Ia tiada ~ demikian* She did not expect it to be so. **meny- 1** think, suppose. *Saya tdk ~ kamu akan . . .* I never imagined you would . . . **2** suspect. *Ia di- turut dlm pemberontakan itu* He was suspected of taking part in the rebellion. **3** take s.o. for, consider to be. *Ia di- org Pilipina* He was taken for a Filipino. **tak meny-²** never expect. *Saya tak ~ mendapat uang sebanyak ini* I never expected to obtain this much money. **meny-kan** take s.o. for, consider. **ter- 1** suspected. *Ia ~ mencuri* He's suspected of stealing. *si ~* (*Leg.*) the suspect. **2** expected. *Tak ~ kau ada di sini* I did not expect to see you here. **-an** supposition, idea. **per-an 1** suspicion. **2** presupposition, expectation, estimate.

sangkak₁ forked, fork shaped. *- kayu* tree branch. *- ayam* hen's nest.

sangkak₂ meny- have goose flesh, ruffle feathers. *Ayamnya ~ bulunya* The chicken ruffled its feathers. *Bulu saya ~ karenanya* It made my flesh creep. *Hatinya ~* He was angry. **meny-i** prevent, stop.

sangkakala 1 valveless trumpet used in ceremonies. **2** (*Rel.*) Last Trumpet.

sangkal₁ handle (of hammer, adz, etc.).

sangkal₂ ber- be unwilling. *Ia ~ akan janjinya* He

was unwilling to keep his promise. **meny-1** deny. *Ia ~ berita itu* He denied the report. *tak dpt di-* undeniable. **2** reject. *Ia ~ permohonan itu* He rejected the request. **-an** disavowal, denial. **peny-** denier. *~ Allah* atheist. **peny-an** denial, refusal.

sangkala see SENGKALAN.

sangkar₁ **1** bird cage. **2** chicken coop. **meny-kan** cage s.t. **-an 1** bird cage, chicken coop. **2** encagement.

sangkar₂ diagonal.

sangking see SAKING.

sangkur bayonet. **ber-** have a bayonet. *bedil yg ~* rifle with bayonet attached. **meny-** bayonet s.o.

sangkut hook onto. *- paut* relation, connection, relevance. *Penahanan itu itu ada - pautnya dgn pembunuhannya* His arrest had s.t. to do with the murder. **ber-** *paut* **1** closely joined, connected. **2** relevant. *Hal-hal yg tak ~ paut disebutkannya panjang lébar* She discussed irrelevant topics at great length. **meny-pautkan** involve, relate to. *Soal-soal ini ~ seluruh dunia* These issues involve the whole world. **ter-** *paut* be involved. **ber-(an)** be concerned with, involved with or in, relevant. *Meréka yg ~ dgn pemberontakan itu ditahan* Those involved in the rebellion were arrested. *Kpd yg ~* To whom it may concern. **ny-** (*Jkt*) drop in for a while. *Seorang teman léwat dan ~* A friend came along and dropped in for a while. **meny-** relate to, involve, concern. *Soal ini tdk ~ saya* This problem does not concern me. **meny-kan 1** hang, hook. *Ia ~ bajunya pd sangkutan* He hung his coat on a peg. **2** involve s.o. in s.t., implicate. *Ia ~ saya dlm pembunuhan itu* He involved me in the murder. **ter- 1** involved. *Ia ~ dlm perkara itu* He was involved in the case. *~ hati* like very much, be attracted to, be hooked on. *yg ~* (*Leg.*) The accomplice. **2** get caught. **ter-²** jerky, move with erratic starts and stops. *Saking tuanya mobil itu ~ mesinnya* Because it is old the car has a jerky motor. **keter-an** involvement. **ke-** (*Coll.*) **1** involved in, dragged into s.t. *Ia ~ juga* He too was involved. **2** be caught on, stuck, attached to. *Layang-layangnya ~ di dahan kayu* The kite was caught on a tree branch. **3** stumble over s.t. or s.o. *Kakinya ~ batu* He stumbled over a stone. **-an 1** relation, connection. **2** involvement. **3** peg, hook. **4** obstacle. **per-an 1** connection, relation. **2** involvement.

sangling (*Jv*) **meny-** polish, burnish.

sangoni see SANGU.

sangra (*Sd, Jkt*) **meny-i** fry without oil.

sangsai poor, miserable.

sangsaka [*Sang Saka Merah Putih*] the first Indonesian flag.

sangsang meny- hook onto s.t. *Layang-layangnya ~ di pohon* His kite got caught in a tree. **ter-, ke-** get caught.

sangsara see SENGSARA.

sangsekerta see SANSKERTA.

sangsi₁ doubt. *Saya - apakah ia akan dpt menamatkan sekolahnya itu* I doubt whether he will be able to complete his studies. *- ragu* doubtful. **meny-kan** question, be doubtful about. *Saya ~ kepandaiannya* I doubted his ability. **ke-an** doubt, skepticism. **peny-an** doubting.

sangsi₂ sanction.

sangsing meny- hold in o.'s hands.

sangu 1 provisions. **2** traveling funds. **ny-oni** (*Jv, Jkt*) give s.o. provisions or money for a trip.

sangyang see SANG.

sani sublime.

sanitair see SANITÉR.

sanitasi sanitation.

sanitér sanitary.

sanjai tall and handsome.

sanjak see SAJAK.

sanjakala see SENJA.

sanjung honor, praise. **meny-** laud. **meny-kan 1** praise s.o. or s.t. to s.o. **2** appease, cater to. **-an 1** flattery. **2** s.o. praised. **peny-** o. who gives praise. **peny-an** act of giving praise.

sanksi see SANGSI₂.

sans (*Bri.*) no trump.

sansai nostalgia. *lagu -* nostalgic song.

Sanskerta Sanskrit.

santa (*Rel.*) (female) saint. *- Maria* Saint Mary.

santai relaxed, relax. *Ia - dlm pergaulan* He is relaxed when dealing with people. **ber-** relax. *duduk ~* sit in a relaxed atmosphere. **ber-²** relax, enjoy o.'s leisure. *pusat ~ bagi warganya* a leisure center for the residents. **meny-kan** cause to relax. *~ diri dgn membaca* relax o.s. by reading. **ke-an** state or quality of being relaxed. *suasana ~ an* atmosphere of relaxation.

santak see SENTAK₂.

santan milk squeezed from coconut.

santana (*Sd*) title of lower nobility.

santap ber- 1 dine (of royalty). **2** have a meal (written or formal speech). *~ malam* eat dinner. **meny-** eat, partake of. **-an** food, meal. *~ Perancis* French cuisine. *~ rohani* spiritual nourishment. *~ siang* luncheon.

santek (*Jv*) latch. **-an** latch.

santél see CANTÉL.

santen see SANTAN.

santeng (*Jv*) sash worn around waist of traditional woman's dress. **ber-** wear a sash.

santer 1 strong, heavy (of meteorological phenomena). *Angin yg -* strong wind. **2** lively (conversation). *berita -* hot news. *pembicaraan -* lively discussion. **meny-kan** spread (news, etc.).

santét black magic. **meny-** practice black magic. **peny-** practitioner of black magic. **peny-an** practicing black magic.

santiaji briefing, indoctrination, or coaching given by o.'s superiors. **meny-** give a briefing. **peny-** o. who gives a briefing. **peny-an** briefing, indoctrination (esp. in ideology).

santiran image, thing like s.t. else. *Ia adalah - ayahnya* He is the image of his father. *Tiada -nya* There is nothing like it.

santiu k.o. Ch fabric.

santo (*Rel.*) (male) saint. *- Petrus* Saint Peter.

santri 1 student at traditional Muslim school. **2** strict adherent of Isl.
santrinisasi process of making conduct (esp. of public affairs) strictly in accordance with principles and ceremonies of Isl.
santu see SANTO.
santun 1 well mannered, well behaved. **2** good manners. *Ia tahu -* He is well mannered. **meny-i 1** sympathize with. *Ia ~ kesusahanku* He sympathized with my problems. **2** help, assist. *Ia ~ org-org terlantar* She helps homeless people. **ke-an** good manners, modesty. **-an 1** help, sympathetic care. **2** compensation paid by insurance company. **peny-** o. who is benevolent, inclined to help. *Déwan ~* board of trustees. **peny-an 1** giving help. **2** compensation payment (in insurance).
santung k.o. rough silk cloth, Shantung.
sanubari inner person, o.'s inner self.
saos see SAUS.
sap see SAF.
sapa₁ ber-²an, - meny- greet e.o. **meny-** address, speak to in greeting. *Ia ~ saya* He addressed me. **ter-** bewitched, ill because of being addressed by spirits. **-an** greeting. **peny-an** extending a greeting.
sapa₂ *(Coll.)* see SIAPA.
sapah see SEPAH.
Sapar see SAFAR.
saparila see SARSAPARILA.
sapat₁ k.o. saltwater fish eaten dried and salted.
sapat₂ *(Sd)* chopped, broken off.
sapérsi asparagus.
sapi 1 cow, bull, ox. *- bantai/potong* beef cattle. *- dara* heifer. *- hutan* dwarf buffalo. *- pemacak* stud bull. *- perahan* dairy cow. **2** *(Zod.)* Taurus.
sapih meny- wean a child. **-an** child that has been weaned. **peny-an** weaning.
sapir see SAFIER.
sapit see SEPIT.
saprodi [*sarana produksi padi*] infrastructure for rice production.
saprotan [*sarana produksi pertanian*] infrastructure for agricultural production.
sapta seven (in slogans or other coined expressions). *- Usaha Tama* Seven Basic Efforts.
Saptamarga The Seven Articles, Armed Forces oath.
saptamargais o. who has taken the Armed Forces oath (a follower of the seven articles).
Saptu see SABTU.
sapu broom. *- ijuk* broom of sugar palm fiber. *- kaca* windshield wiper. *- lidi* broom of split coconut midribs. *sistém - lidi* strongly united. *- tangan* handkerchief. **meny- 1** wipe off, brush off. **2** sweep. **3** finish s.t. *~ bersih* sweep clean, wipe out. *~ rata* level off, demolish. **meny-kan 1** sweep, brush s.t. away. *Di-kannya kotornya yg di bajunya* She wiped off the dirt on her dress. **2** smear (medicine) on to. *Minyak itu di-kan pd dadanya* He wiped the oil on his chest. **ter-** be swept away. *~ banjir* swept away in a flood. **-an**

wiper, s.t. to wipe with. **-²an** sweepings, gleanings. *~ jalan* street sweepings. **peny- 1** wiper, broom. *~ ranjau* mine sweeper. *~ kaki* doormat. **2** sweeper. *~ jalan* street sweeper. **peny-an** cleaning up, reform. *Bang Ali melakukan ~ kantor Gubernuran* Bang Ali undertook a reform of the governor's office.
saput cover, shroud, veil. **meny-(i) 1** cover thinly with s.t. *Padang itu di- oléh salju* The field was dusted with snow. **2** paint with s.t. watery, whitewash. **meny-kan** paint with s.t. **ter-** covered with a thin coat of paint.
saputangan see SAPU.
sara pension, support. **ber- 1** share. **2** pensioned.
SARA [*suku, agama, ras, antar-golongan*] matters pertaining to ethnic, religious, and racial relations. *Pamplét itu bernada hasutan dan isyu -* The pamphlet had a provocative tone which spread rumors regarding ethnic, religious, and racial relations.
sara-bara confused, in disorder, in disarray. *Bukunya - terletak di lantai* His books were scattered all around the floor.
saraf₁ *(Anat.)* nerve. *- mata* optical nerve. *- baja* nerves of steel. **per-an** having to do with the nerves. *sistém ~ manusia* the human nervous system.
saraf₂ *(Ling.)* derivation of Arabic words from the same root.
sarafi neural.
sarak *(Leg.)* separated, parted. **ber-** separate, part. **meny-(i)** divorce o.'s wife.
sarakah see SERAKAH.
saran suggestion. *- yg baik* a good idea. **meny-i** suggest to, suggestive. *nada ~* suggestive tone. **meny-kan** propose, suggest s.t. **-an** suggestion, proposition.
sarana medium, tool, means. *- kebijaksanaan* instrument of policy. *- komunikasi* means of communication. *- perhubungan* means of communication and transportation.
sarang₁ 1 nest, lair, web. *- semut* ant hill. *- lebah* beehive. *- burung* bird's nest. *- laba(h)* spider web. *- madu* honeycomb. **2** hide-out, hideaway. **3** hotbed, breeding place. *- penyakit* breeding place of disease. *- perzinaan* den of adultery. **4** *(Mil.)* emplacement (for machine gun, etc.). **ber- 1** nest, make a nest, nestle. **2** lodged. *Sebuah peluru ~ di pahanya* A bullet was lodged in his thigh. *Dendam ~ dlm dirinya* She harbored feelings of revenge. **meny- 1** become (like) a nest. *Barang-barangnya begitu banyak sampai ~ di kamarnya* His room is like a rat's nest with all the junk he has in it. **2** nestle. **meny-i** make a nest in or on s.t. *Bangsat-bangsat kecil ~ rumah dan perabot kami* Bedbugs built their nests in our house and furniture. **meny-kan** put in a nest or in nestlike thing, lodge. *~ bola (Sport)* kick or throw the ball in (goal, basket, etc.). **-an** *~ kenalpot* vehicle muffler.
sarang₂ porous. **ber-²** be full of holes. **ke-an** porosity.

sarangan (*Jv*) chestnut.
sarap₁ k.o. skin rash.
sarap₂ litter. - *sampah* litter, trash. **meny-** 1 litter. *Kertas-kertas ~ di lantai* Papers littered the floor. 2 just be present s.w., be useless.
sarap₃ ber-an have breakfast. **(me)ny-** feed, stuff, gorge (us. of animals). **meny-i** serve breakfast. **-an** 1 breakfast. 2 have breakfast. *Marilah ~ dulu* Let us have breakfast first.
sarap₄ (*Coll.*) crazy.
saraséhan (*Jv*) informal discussion, meeting.
saraswati female singer.
sarat₁ 1 loaded, laden, full. *Prahoto itu sdh - berisi pasir* The truck was loaded with sand. *Hati saya - dgn kesusahan* My heart was filled with sorrow. 2 (*Naut.*) draft (of a ship). **meny-i** load s.t. with. *Truk itu di-i muatan banyak* That truck was heavily loaded. **meny-kan** load s.t. on to. **ke-an** 1 too loaded, too full. 2 density. *~ makna* density of meaning.
sarat₂ see SYARAT.
sarau (*M*) unfortunate. **meny-kan** render unfortunate.
sardén, sardéncis, sardine tinned sardines.
saréan (*Jv*) grave, graveyard.
saréat see SYARIAH.
Sarékat Islam Isl. league, an early nationalistic organization of 1910s and 1920s.
saréngat see SYARIAH.
sargut meny- rip with o.'s teeth.
sari 1 concentrate, essence. - *nanas* essence of pineapple. - *susu* cream. 2 nucleus, main point. - *berita* the main point of the news. - *pati* main point, core, gist. *Apakah - pati pidatonya?* What was the essence of her speech? 3 (*Biol.*) pollen. **meny-** 1 reduce to an essence. 2 quote, abstract from. 3 sum up. **meny-kan** summarize. **ter-kan** be summarized. **per-an** digest, summary.
sariawan see SERIAWAN.
saridelé (*Jv*) soybean milk.
sarikat see SERIKAT.
saring meny- 1 filter, strain, sift. 2 refine, distill. -- *minyak* refine petroleum. 3 sift, separate, sort out (information, meaning, etc.). *Meréka tak mampu ~ berita yg msk akal dan yg tdk* They are not able to tell which reports make sense and which do not. 4 screen (personel for job). **ter-** strained, filtered. **-an** 1 sieve, strainer, filter. *~ minyak* oil filter. *~ udara* air filter. 2 screening. **peny-** filter, strainer. *~ air* water filter. **peny-an** 1 sifting. 2 filtering. 3 screening, selection (of personnel).
sarip see SYARIF.
saripati see SARI.
sari-sari (*Coll.*) daily, everyday. *tak -nya* unusual, extraordinary.
sarit (*M*) difficult. -² rarely.
sarjana 1 scholar, academician degree-holder. 2 title of degree similar to the Bachelor's. - *Hukum* Master of Law. - *lengkap* PhD Candidate (pre-1980s). - *Kimia* BS in chemistry. - *muda* Bachelor (of Arts, Science, etc.) (pre-1980s). - *Pendidikan* Master of Education. - *Sastera* Master

of Arts. **ke-an** scholarship, quality of being a scholar.
sarjananisasi the process of requiring employees to get Bachelor's degrees.
sarkasme sarcasm.
sarkastis sarcastic.
sarkofagus sarcophagus (esp. in archaeology).
sarmud [*sarjana muda*] a Bachelor (of Arts, Law, etc.).
saroja see SEROJA.
saron (*Jv*) o. of the metallophone instruments of gamelan.
sarong see SARUNG.
sarsaparila, sarsaparilla sarsasparilla drink.
Sartan (*Zod.*) Cancer.
saru₁ dim, vague. **meny-** disguise o.s. *Penyelidik itu ~ sbg seorg pedagang* The detective disguised himself as a merchant. **peny-** s.o. in disguise. **peny-an** disguise.
saru₂ k.o. Australian pine.
saru₃ (*Jv*) indecent, obscene.
saruk₁ -² dragging of feet. *Kedengaran ~ langkahnya menjauh* O. can hear her dragging her feet as she walks away. **meny-** make o.'s way through (bushes, jungle etc.). **ter-²** with the noise of dragging feet.
saruk₂ meny- have luck (in game), win.
sarundéng see SERUNDÉNG.
sarung 1 sarong. - *pelékat* sarong with block patterns. 2 case, container. - *jari* thimble. - *pélor* cartridge shell. 3 sheath. - *gigi* crown of tooth. 4 wrapper. - *bantal* pillowcase. - *korsi* slip cover. - *pistol* holster. - *sepatu* overshoes. - *tangan* glove. - *tinju* boxing gloves. 5 condom. **ber-** 1 wear a sarong. 2 sheathed. **meny-i** 1 encase. 2 put s.t. on. 3 sheathe. *Bantalnya blm di-i* No o. has put a pillowcase on the pillow. **meny-kan** use as a sheath, pillowcase, casing, etc. *Sarung bantal kok di-kan ke guling!* How come you wrapped a pillowcase over a bolster! **-an** wearing a sarong. *org ~* (*Coll.*) orthodox Muslim man.
sarut₁ (*M*) k.o. grass. *Sebatang rumput - dipuput oléh angin* o. strong in times of trouble (lit., a tall grass blown by the wind).
sarut₂ meny- bite.
sarwa all, the whole. (*Tuhan*) - *sekalian alam* (*Rel.*) (Lord of) the whole world.
sarwaboga omnivore.
sasa robust, strong. *Tubuhnya tegap* - He was well built.
sasak 1 wattle, coarse plaitwork of split bamboo. 2 bouffant (women's hairdo). **meny-** (*rambut*) tease up o.'s hair in a bouffant, comb back. **-an** bouffant.
sasakala (*Sd*) legend.
sasana 1 (*Jv*) auditorium, public center. - *krida* university auditorium, student center. 2 gymnastics training camp. - *tinju* boxing arena.
sasanti see SESANTI.
sasap₁ meny- pull up weeds.
sasap₂ see SUSUP.
sasar 1 mad, insane. 2 dazed. **(me)ny-** 1 miss o.'s

target. *Serangan kapal terbang itu ~ saja* The plane missed its target when it attacked. **2** go astray. *Ia kena peluru ~* He was hit by a stray bullet. **meny-kan** (*Jv*) cause s.t. to go astray or miss the target. **ter-, ke-** lost, strayed away. *Saya ~ di kota* I lost my way in the town. *Kelihatannya spt seékor anjing yg ~* It looked like a stray dog.

sasaran₁ target, aim, objective. *~ pokok* main objective.

sasaran₂ (*M*) playing field, field for practicing sports, shooting etc.

sasat see PERSASAT.

sasis chassis.

sasmita hint, divine signal, omen.

sas-sus rumor.

sastera see SASTRA.

sasterakanta (*Lit.*) thesis.

sasterawan, sasterawati see SASTRAWAN, SASTRAWATI.

sastra books, literature. *- Jawa* Jv literature. *Fakultas -* School of Letters. **ber-** compose literature. **ke-an** (things pertaining to) literature. *memenuhi syarat-syarat ~* meet the criteria of literature.

sastrawan man of letters. **ke-an** matters pertaining to men of letters.

sastrawati woman of letters.

sat₁ large measure for rice of five or ten *gantang.*

sat₂ see ZAT.

sata (*Lit.*) hundred.

satah (*Math.*) plane.

satai see SATÉ.

Satal [*Sangir dan Talaud*] two island groups N.E. of Sulawesi.

satan see SÉTAN.

satang pole, stick, stake.

satar a line.

saté small pieces of meat roasted on skewer. **(me)ny-** **1** prepare or eat brochettes. **2** make brochettes of. *Bisa tdk daging anjing di-?* Can you make brochettes out of dog meat? **ter-** be skewered. **per-an** dissension (divisions into small pieces like *saté*).

satelit satellite. *kota -* satellite city. *- antariksa* space satellite. **per-an** matters concerning satellites. *di bidang ~* the field of satellite study.

satén see SATIN.

sateria see KESATRIA.

sateru see SETRU.

satgas [*satuan tugas*] task force.

satin satin.

satir satyr.

satiris satirical.

sato (*Jv*) wild animal.

Satpam [*satuan pengamanan*] security guard.

satria see KESATRIA.

satron (*Jv*) **meny-i** be hostile toward.

satru₁ k.o. cookie made with mung beans and palm sugar.

satru₂ (*Jv*) see SETRU.

satu one. *- buyut* (*Jv*) of the same great-grandparent. *- dua* one or two, a few. *Dia pergi utk - dua*

hari She went for o. or two days. *- demi -* o. at a time. *- golongan* o. group. **meny-golongkan** treat as o. category or class. *Aliran ini bisa digolongkan dgn . . .* The school of thought can be put in the same category as *. . . - jalan* 1 one way. **2** having the same orientation. **ber-** *jalan* of the same orientation (mind, etc.). *- nada* monotone. **ke-nadaan** monotony. *- padu* unified. **ber-** *padu* unite (with e.o.) firmly. *Kami hendaklah ber- padu dlm menghadapi kesulitan ini* We should be firmly united in facing this problem. **meny-padukan** unite firmly. **ter-** *padu* be firmly united. *- per - o.* at a time. *- per - penumpang bis turun* O. by o. the passengers got off the bus. *- ragam* uniform. **peny-ragaman** the process of making s.t. uniform. *- sama lain* mutual, o. another. *Meréka tak setuju - sama lain* They did not agree with o. another. *- segi* o. aspect. **ke-segian** one-sidedness. *- sisi* unilateral. **ke-sisian** one-sidedness. *- waktu* o. time. **meny-waktukan** synchronize. *- warna* of the same color. *yg - lagi* the other o. *Berapa harga yg - lagi?* What is the price of the other o.? **-²** 1 o. by o. *Bicaranya ~* She speaks syllable by syllable. **2** some, a few. *Di sana tak banyak rumah. Hanya ~ saja* There were not many houses there. Just a few. **-²nya** only. *Kaulah ~ kawanku yg dpt kupercayai* You are the only friend I can trust. *anak ~* an only child. **ber-** allied, united. *~ hati* be of o. mind, be in agreement. *Meréka ~ dlm peperangan itu* They were allies during the war. **ber-an** form a unit. **meny-** become or be one. *Kedua jalur ~ di sebelah utara* The two lanes join to the N. **memper-kan, meny-kan** 1 unite, join, ally. *Ia berhasil ~ negerinya* He succeeded in uniting his country. *Ia ~ dirinya dgn angkatan darat* He joined the ground forces. **2** concentrate s.t. on. *Ia ~ segala tenaganya utk memecahkan soal itu* He concentrated all his efforts toward resolving the problem. **ke-** (*Coll.*) the first. **ke-an** 1 (*Mil.*) unit. *Beberapa ~ musuh berhasil mendarat* Several enemy units succeeded in landing. **2** totality. **3** unity, oneness. *negara ~* unitary state. **-an 1** unit. *~ berat* unit of weight. *~ hitung* number by which o. counts. *~ hitung sepuluh* count by tens. **2** (*Mil.*) unit, squad. **pemer-** unifier, integrationist. *alat ~* unifying forces. **pemer-an, peny-an** unification. **per-an** 1 association, club, union. **2** unity. *cinta ~ bangsa* love for the unity of the people. *~ dan kesatuan* unity and integrity.

satwa wild animal, fauna. *- lindungan* protected species.

satwaboga carnivore.

satwacarita animal fable.

Satyalancana Indonesian award for merit, Medal of Honor.

sau rustling sound. *- angin* rustling of wind.

saudagar large-scale merchant.

saudara 1 brother, sister, cousin of same generation. *- dua pupu/misan* 2d cousin. *- sebapak (seibu)* half-brother, half-sister with same father (mother). *- sejalan/sejadi/(se)kandung* full sibling.

- sepupu first cousin. **2** relative (us. of same generation). *- anjing* half-brother, half-sister (with same mother). *- belahan* descendant. *- bau embacang/daging* distant relative. *- dekat* close relative. *- jauh* distant relative. *perang -* civil war. **3** formal term of address for s.o. of same age group or younger with whom o. is not acquainted. *- datang bésok. Maksud kami mempekerjakan -* Come tomorrow. Our intention is to employ you. *- saudari* ladies and gentlemen. **4** term of address in official situations. *- pendengar* to all the listeners (address on radio). *-² yg saya hormati* Ladies and Gentlemen. **ber- 1** be siblings. *Saya dan Rusli ~ Rusli and I are* brothers. **2** be related. *Saya ~ dgn dia* I am related to him. **memper-kan** make friends of s.o. **per-an 1** relationship. **2** friendship. **3** fraternity, brotherhood.

saudari formal term of address to female of same age or younger with whom o. is not acquainted.

sauh₁ (*Naut.*) anchor. *membongkar -* weigh anchor. *membuang -* cast anchor. **ber-** be at anchor.

sauh₂ see SAWO.

sauk 1 ladle. **2** scoop. **-²** bucket, scoop. **meny-1** dip up, scoop up. **2** lasso.

saum 1 (*Isl.*) the Fast. **2** (*Rel.*) Lent.

saung cave, grotto.

saur₁ ber- interlocking, entangled. **meny-i** grow over densely. **ter-** get caught on, stumble.

saur₂ meny- repay a debt. **ter-** paid off (of a debt).

saur₃ see SAHUR₁.

saus 1 sauce, gravy. *- tomat* tomato catsup. **2** mixture to give flavor to s.t. else.

saut₁ (*Jv*) snatch.

saut₂ see SAHUT.

saw. (*Isl.*) [*salla'llahu 'alaihi wasallama*] May Allah bless him and give him peace (said after uttering Muh.'s name).

sawa see ULAR.

sawah wet rice field. *- basah/bencah* irrigated rice field. *- bengkok/lungguh* (*Jv*) rice field given in usufruct to village officials. *- (ber)bandar langit* dry rice field. *- bera* fallow rice field. *- kas* village-treasury land. *- lebak* rice field in swampy area. *- tadah(an) hujan* rice field dependent on rain. **ber-1** own rice fields. **2** live by working the rice fields (as an occupation). **meny-** work the rice fields. **peny-, pe-** rice grower, farmer of wet rice fields. **per-an 1** rice cultivation. **2** fields for rice cultivation, cluster of rice fields.

Sawal see SYAWAL.

sawala debate. **ber-** debate.

sawan (*Med.*) **1** epilepsy. *- babi* epilepsy. **2** fit, convulsions. *- bangkai* apoplectic stroke.

sawang₁ cobweb.

sawang₂ atmosphere. **-an** atmosphere.

sawang₃ forest. **ber-** forest-covered. **pe(r)-an** (*M*) wasteland, dangerous wilderness.

sawang₄ (*Jv*) **ny-** look.

sawar barricade, fence. **meny-** bar.

sawat₁ shoulder strap, sling.

sawat₂ pe- see PESAWAT.

sawi mustard greens. *- putih* Ch cabbage, lighter colored mustard greens. *- hijau* darker colored mustard greens.

sawit see KELAPA.

sawo 1 k.o. fruit-bearing tree, sapodilla. *- kecik* k.o. sapodilla with firm flesh. *- Manila* sapodilla. **2** tan, brown like the skin of sapodilla. *- mateng/tua* dark brown.

sawut snack of steamed grated cassava with palm sugar.

saya 1 I, me, my. *- mau pergi* I want to go. *Ia melihat -* He saw me. *Itu buku -* That is my book. **2** yes (deferential). *Apa anda sopirnya? -* Are you the driver? Yes, I am. *- sendiri!* (*Tel.*) Speaking!

sayambara see SAYEMBARA.

sayang 1 pity. *Aku - melihat dia* I felt pity on seeing her. **2** love. *Ia sangat - kpd anaknya* He loves his child very much. *- meréka pdku* their love for me. **3** dear, darling. *Tidurlah dulu, -* Go to sleep, darling. *suamiku -* my dear husband. **-(nya)** it is a pity. *~ saya tdk melihatnya* Unfortunately I did not see him. **ber-²an** love e.o. **di-** be loved. *sbg murid yg ~* as a student who is loved. **meny-i 1** pity. *-ilah saya ini* Pity me. *-ilah binatang* Be kind to animals. **2** love, be attached to. *Abu bertambah ~ Bakri* Abu grew more attached to Bakri. **meny-kan 1** regret, deplore, consider s.t. to be a pity. *Kejadian itu sangat di-kan* That incident is deeply regretted. **2** spare from s.t. bad. *Semua bukunya dibakar. Tak ada yg di-kan* All his books were burned. Nothing was spared. **ke-an 1** pity, sorrow. **2** love, affection. **3** darling, favorite. *nyanyian ~ku* my favorite song. *nama ~* pet name. *tanah ~* beloved land. **peny- 1** charitable, merciful, loving. *Tuhan Yg Maha ~* (*Isl.*) the All-merciful Lord. **2** lover, amateur, devotee. *~ burung* bird lover.

sayap 1 wing. *- belakang* rear wing. *- dua* biplane. *- roda* (*Auto.*) **1** mudguard. **2** fender. **2** (*Pol.*) wing of a political party. *- kiri* the left wing. **ber-** winged. **meny-** outflank.

sayarah, sayarat see BINTANG.

sayat slice. **meny- 1** slice, slash into. **2** touch profoundly. *suara ~* a very touching voice. *~ hati* heartrending. **meny-i** cut in multiple slashes. *~ daging sapi* cut beef in slices. **ter- 1** be sliced into, slashed. **2** deeply wounded. **-an 1** slice. **2** slicing.

sayembara prize contest. **meny-kan** make a contest of an activity. *Pembacaan puisi yg di-kan* They held a contest for poetry reading. **2** hold a contest over. *Mobil yg di-kan* He held a contest in which the winner got a car.

sayét see SIYÉT.

sayid (*Isl.*) lord, sir: title given to Muh.'s direct descendants.

sayidi my lord. *Ya -!* O (my) Lord!

sayonara (*Japanese, Coll.*) goodbye.

sayu 1 melancholy, downcast. *Hatinya -* She was downcast. **2** droopy. *Matanya -* Her eyes were droopy. *- rayu* sad, melancholy. **ber-²** ask for pity. **meny-** become melancholy or droopy. *Matanya ~ karena terlalu banyak minum* His eyes drooped because he drank too much. **meny-kan 1** touch, move s.o. **2** make vague. ~ *pemandangan* be vague about o.'s view. **ke-an** sadness, melancholy, wistfulness.

sayup soft, faint (of sound), blurred. **-² 1** blurred, indistinct, faintly heard. **2** scarcely, hardly. **3** (*Lit.*) faintly seen. ~ *sampai* barely, extremely vague. *Bunyi musik kedengaran* ~ *sampai* A vague sound of music was barely heard. *Tangannya* ~ *sampai pd buku itu* His hand almost reached the book. **se-(²)** *mata (memandang)* as far as the eye can see. **meny-** become faint or blurred (of sound). *Suaranya* ~ *ditelan keramaian* Her voice became faint as it was swallowed up by the noise of the crowd. **ke-an 1** blurredness, indistinctness, faintness. **2** dreaminess. *Aku merenung dgn* ~ *yg biasa terdapat pd si penyair* I was reflecting with the dreaminess that is usual for a poet.

sayur 1 vegetable. - *mayur* all k.o. vegetables. - *asinan* spiced raw vegetable salad. *spt* - *dgn rumput* as different as day and night (lit., like weeds and vegetables). **2** vegetable soup. - *asam/asem* sour vegetable soup. **meny-** prepare as a vegetable dish. *Nangka ini masih dpt di-* You can still make a vegetable dish from this jackfruit. **-an** vegetables (in general). **-²an** various k.o. vegetables.

SB [*serikat buruh*] labor or trade union.

S'baya. [*Surabaya*] Surabaya.

sbb. [*sebagai berikut*] as follows.

sbg. [*sebagai*] as.

schat /sxat/ (*Coll.*) darling (term of endearment).

schors see SKORS.

schorsing see SKORSING.

s/d, s.d. [*sampai dgn*] up to and including.

SD [*Sekolah Dasar*] elementary school.

sda. [*seperti di atas*] as above.

sdg. [*sedang*]

sdr. [*saudara*] Mr., Ms. (as a title).

sdri. [*saudari*] Ms. (as a title).

se- 1 one. *-menit* o. minute. **2** same. *Ia -umur dgn saya* He is the same age as I. **3** all. *-Indonésia* All-Indonesian. **4** when, as soon as. *Saya akan beri kabar -terimanya balasan* I will let you know when the reply is received. **5** as . . . as. *-kecil itu sdh pandai membaca* As small as he is, he already reads well.

SE₁ [*Sarjana Ékonomi*] o. who holds a Bachelor's degree in Economics.

SE₂ [*Surat Édaran*] circular (memorandum).

sé (*Ch*) surname.

seantéro see ANTÉRO.

séba ber- present o.s. before a king.

sebab 1 because. *Ia tdk pergi - ia sakit* He did not go because he was sick. **2** cause, motive, reason. - *mati* cause of death. *Apa -nya kaukatakan itu?* What is the reason for your saying that? *Itulah -nya maka ia tak datang* That is why he did not come. *Oléh - ia sakit ia tak pergi* Because he was ill he did not go. - (*dan*) *akibat* cause and effect. - *apa?* Why? - *apa ia menangis?* Why is she crying? - *kahar* force majeure, act of god, inevitable acci-

dent. - *musabab* various reasons. *Tentu ada - musababnya maka ia mengatakan demikian* Of course there were various reasons for his saying so. **ber-** with reason, justly. **meny-kan** evoke, cause. *Apa yg* ~ *rumah itu terbakar?* What caused that house to burn down? *Pertengkaran itu di- oléh salah pengertian* The quarrel was caused by misunderstanding. **ter-(kan)** caused, occasioned. **peny-1** cause. *faktor* ~ causal factor. **2** (*Chem.*) agent.

sebagai see BAGAI.

sebagaimana see BAGAIMANA.

sebak full of water to the point of overflowing. *Matanya - penuh air mata* Her eyes were brimming with tears.

sébak see SIBAK.

sebal₁ resentful. *Hatinya - ketika permintaannya tak diluluskan* He was resentful when his wish was not granted. **meny-i** make s.o. resentful. **meny-kan 1** resent s.t. **2** cause resentment. **ke-an** resentment.

sebal₂ (*Jv*) **meny-** deviate (from a principle).

sebaliknya see BALIK.

sebam 1 gray. **2** dark. *Matanya - karena kurang tidur* His eyes had black circles because he lacked sleep.

sebanding see BANDING.

sebangun see BANGUN.

sebar₁ asleep, numb (of arms or legs).

sebar₂ - *luas* **meny-luaskan** spread, disseminate, propagate. **peny-luasan** dissemination, spread, promulgation. ~ *ilmu pd masyarakat* dissemination of knowledge in society. **ber-an** lie all over, be spread all over. *Piringan hitam* ~ *di atas bupét* Records were lying all over the sideboard. **meny-** spread. *Rasa kaku itu* ~ *ke lain otot* Stiffness spread to the other muscles. **meny-kan 1** strew, scatter. *Ia* ~ *benih* He scattered seeds. **2** spread, distribute. *Ia* ~ *kabar bohong* He spread false news. *Surat-surat selebaran di-kan* Leaflets were distributed. **ter-** spread, scattered, dispersed. **-an** s.t. spread. ~ *péstisida* an application of pesticide. **peny-** disseminator. ~ *penyakit* spreader of disease. ~ *candu* **1** s.o. who disseminates opium. **2** s.o. who spreads bad things in general. **peny-an** distributing, spreading, disseminating. ~ *agama* proselytization. **per-an** the spread, dissemination. ~ *kebudayaan asing ke Indonésia* the spread of foreign culture to Indonesia.

sebarang see BARANG₂.

sebat₁ **meny- 1** brush s.t. away with flip of hands. **2** shake hands to dry them. **3** whip with long, slender rod. *Anaknya di-nya dgn belebas* He whipped his child with a ruler. **4** steal by snatching. *Ia* ~ *dompét saya* He snatched my wallet.

sebat₂, sébat quick in movement. **ke-an** quickness in movement.

sebatangkara see BATANG.

sebaya see BAYA.

sebel see SEBAL₁.

sebelah see BELAH.

sebelas 11. **ke-an** soccer team.

sebelum see BELUM.

sebentar 1 for a moment. *Saya mau singgah di sini* - I want to stop in here for a moment. *Tunggu* - Wait a moment. *Kami - saja* We just need a moment, we will not be long. *- ini* a moment ago, just now. *Saya berjumpa dgn dia - ini* I met him just a short while ago. *- lagi* **1** a little longer. **2** in a few minutes. *Tunggulah - lagi* Please wait a little longer. *Ia akan berangkat - lagi* He will be going in a few minutes. **2** later in the same day. *- malam kita nonton* We're going to the movies tonight. *- soré* this evening. **-², se-, - -bentar 1** frequently, again and again. **2** every now and then. *Ia datang - utk minta uang pd ayahnya* He came every now and then to ask his father for money. **3** for a few moments. *Ia kalau datang hanya ~ saja* If he came he only stayed for a few moments. *Lampu itu ~ mati ~ hidup* The light went off and on. **-an** for a moment.

seberang 1 across, opposite. *di vila - rumahku* in the cottage opposite my house. *di - jalan* across the street. *- laut* overseas. **2** foreign (from outside the island or across the seas). **ber-an** on both sides, opposite e.o. *- meny-* facing, opposite e.o. *Rumah kami ~* Our houses face e.o. **meny-(i)** cross to the other side. *Ia ~ sungai* He crossed the river. *Dilarang ~ jalan di sini* It is forbidden to cross here. **meny-kan** take across. *Ia ~ saya dgn perahunya* He took me across in his boat. **ter-1** crossed. **2** accessible. **ter-i** manage to be crossed. **ter-kan** can be brought across. *Dia tdk tenggelam karena ~ oléh arus* he did not drown because the current carried him to the other shore. **peny-** s.o. who goes across s.t. *~ kanal* channel swimmer. **peny-an** crossing.

seberhana a suit of clothes.

seberot see SEBROT₁.

sébet fast, quick.

sebih see TASBEH.

sebit see SABIT₁.

sebodo see MASA BODOH.

sébra see ZÉBRA.

sebrang see SEBERANG.

sebrot₁ meny- rob, pick pockets.

sebrot₂ meny- burst out.

sebu full. *Tempat sampah itu -* The trash can was full. **meny-** fill, stuff s.t. **meny-kan** fill up, plug up.

sebuk meny- 1 infiltrate, penetrate. **2** interrupt a conversation. **peny-an** infiltration.

sebul blow. **meny-kan** blow s.t. *~ asap ke udara* blow smoke into the air.

seburit see BURIT.

sebut meny- 1 mention. *Jangan ~ namaku* Do not mention my name. **2** name, call. *Kertas ini dikertas minyak* This paper is called "wax paper." **meny-² 1** bruit about. *Dia di-² sbg calon pengganti Présidén* His name was bruited about as possible successor to the president. **2** keep mentioning. **meny-kan** name, list names of. *-kan nama gunung-gunung pulau Jawa* Name the mountains of Java. **ter- 1** mentioned. *Tlh ~ tadi bhw . . .* It was

mentioned earlier that . . . *Rumah ~ tlh terjual* The above mentioned house has been sold. *yg ~ belakangan* the latter. **2** talked about. *Ia ~ di-mana-mana* He was talked about everywhere. *~lah (Lit.)* it is said, once upon a time. *~lah cerita di jaman Yunani . . .* It is said that in the time of the Greeks . . . **-an 1** term, expression, designation. **2** quotation. *Bukunya itu berisi ~ dr buku-buku lain* His book is filled with quotations from other books. **3** designation, appellation. *Nduk adalah ~ utk anak perempuan* Nduk is a designation for a young girl. **4** (*Ling.*) comment, predicate. *Yg mana ~ kalimat ini?* Which is the predicate of this sentence? **-²an 1** much-talked-of. **2** title. **peny- 1** o. who calls, mentions. **2** (*Math.*) denominator. **peny-an** addressing, mentioning. *~ yg masih menggunakan "saudara"* continuing to address people as "saudara".

Secaba [*Sekolah Calon Bintara*] (*Mil.*) training school for noncomissioned officers.

secang see SEPANG.

secara see CARA.

sedak ter-, ke-, ke-an choke, swallow the wrong way. *Makanlah pelahan-lahan nanti ~ kamu* Eat slowly or you will choke on your food. *~ hidung* stuffy nose.

sédak rattan band around top of drum to keep the head taut.

sedan sob. **ter-²** sobbing.

sédan (*Auto.*) sedan. *- buka atap/atap terbuka* a convertible.

sedang₁ 1 average, moderate, medium. *Kepandaiannya -* He was an average person in ability. *katégori - medium* (category). *Setasiun - jauhnya dr rumah saya* The station was not so far away from my house. **2** sufficient, fit. *Dua ratus dolar sebulan - baginya* 200 dollars a month was sufficient for him. *Baju itu - baginya* The jacket fits him fine. **-²(nya)** average, moderate. **se-nya** just enough. *Diberi garam ~* salt to taste. *- meny-* barely adequate, scarcely sufficient. *Gajinya tdk ~* His salary was insufficient. **meny-** try on. *Ia ~ sepatunya* He tried on his shoes. **meny-(²)kan** try to make ends meet. **-an** medium (sized). *jenis yg ~* medium-sized variety.

sedang₂ 1 while, the time that. *- ia mengucapkan kata-katanya itu, isterinya menjerit* While he was uttering those words, his wife screamed. **2** be in the process of. *Ia - membaca ketika saya datang* He was reading when I came. *- bicara* (*Tel.*) The line is busy. *- dicétak* in press. *- mengapa ia?* What is she doing? **3** while, whereas. *Kucingnya putih - kucing saya hitam* His cat was white whereas mine was black. **-kan 1** while, at the time that. **2** whereas, but. *Di sana répot ~ di sini tdk* They're busy over there, but here we're not.

sedap 1 delicious, tasty. *Makanan itu -* The food was delicious. **2** (*Coll.*) nice, pleasing. *Bau bunga itu -* The flower had a pleasing fragrance. *pemandangan yg - a* nice view. *- malam* **1** k.o. flower, tuberose. **2** prostitute. **3** well, refreshed. *Badan saya tak merasa - ketika itu* I did not feel well then.

- hati pleased, amused. *Tak - hatinya mendengar perkataanmu itu* He was not pleased with what you said. **meny-kan 1** season, make s.t. tasty. *Bumbu ~ makanan* Spices make food tasty. **2** please s.o. *Perkataannya itu ~ hati* His words were pleasing. **-²an** delicacies. **ke-an 1** pleasantness. **2** refreshed feeling. **peny-** s.t. used as flavoring. *bumbu ~* flavoring spice.

sedar see SADAR.

sedari see DARI.

sedarum all together, in unison. *Meréka menjawab -* They answered all together.

sedasi sedation.

sedat 1 slow in thinking, sluggish. *Pikirannya -* He thinks slowly. **2** stopped, stopped up.

sedekah *(Rel.)* **1** alms, give alms. **2** religious meal, offering to spirits, give a religious meal. *- bumi* thanksgiving ceremony performed by farmers or fishermen. *- désa* rural thanksgiving ceremony after harvest. *Kami mau - malam Jumaat nanti* We want to have a religious feast on Thursday night. **ber- 1** give alms. **2** give a religious meal. **meny-i 1** give alms to. *Ia ~ pengemis itu* He gave alms to the beggar. **2** give a religious meal on the behalf of. *Ia bermaksud ~ anaknya* He intends to give a religious meal for his son. **meny-kan** give s.t. as alms. **-an** alms given.

sedekala see SEDIAKALA.

sedelinggam red lead used as antirust paint.

sédeng part in hair.

sédéng *(Jkt)* crazy.

séder cedar tree.

sederhana simple, plain, unpretentious. *pakaian -* simple clothes. *makanan -* plain food. *Hidupnya -* She lives modestly. **meny-kan 1** simplify. **2** economize. **ke-an** simplicity. **peny-an** simplification.

sedia 1 ready. *Ia sdh - utk berangkat* She was ready to leave. *Makanan sdh -* Dinner was ready. **2** willing. *Ia selalu - utk menolong* He was always ready to help. **-nya** actually, as a matter of fact, properly speaking. *~ ia tak suka kawin* As a matter of fact, he did not want to marry. *Acara yg ~ akan mulai bésok diundurkan* The activity which should have begun tomorrow has been postponed to a later time. *~ ... tetapi ...* it is true ... but ... **ber- 1** be ready, prepared. *Ibunya sama sekali tak ~ menghadapi nasib itu* Her mother was not at all prepared to face her fate. **2** disposed (to), willing. *Aku selalu ~ membantumu* I am always willing to help you. **meny-i** provide s.o. with. *Di kamar ini kami di-i téh* In this room we are provided with tea. **memper-kan, meny-kan 1** prepare. *Ibu sedang ~ makanan* Mother was preparing the food. *Kapal-kapal itu sdh di-kan utk mengangkut prajurit* The ships were made ready to transport the troops. **2** set aside (food, funds, etc.) in preparation. *~ beras di rumah* have a supply of rice at home. **3** equip, supply, make available. *~ béasiswa* provide scholarships. *Hotél itu ~ selimut* The hotel furnished the blankets.

ter- on hand, available. *Tak ada uang ~ utk projék itu* There was not any money on hand for that project. *Bir selalu ~ di kulkas* There is always beer available in the refrigerator. **keter-an** availability. **ke-an** readiness, willingness. *Terima kasih atas ~nya utk membantu* Thank you for your willingness to help. **peny-an 1** act of preparing. **2** equipping, supplying. *~ ruangan pembaca* provision of a reading room. **per-an 1** stock, supply. *Saya masih punya ~ enam botol brandi* I still have six bottles of brandy in stock. *~ makanan itu tak cukup* The food supply was insufficient. **2** preparations. *Tlh diadakan ~ utk memulai perundingan itu* Preparations had been made to hold the consultations.

sediakala former, of old. *Kemudian ia kembali ke tempatnya -* Afterward he went back to his former place. *Hidupnya spt - saja* His life is just as it used to be.

sedih 1 sad, distressed. *Hatinya -* He was sad. **2** tragic. *Peristiwa itu sangat -* The event was very tragic. *- pedih* sorrow, sorrowful. **ber-** *(hati)* be sad. **meny-kan** sadden. *cerita yg ~ a* sad story. **ke-an** sorrow, sadness. *Ia berhasil mengatasi ~ hidup* He managed to overcome the sadness of life. **peny-** o. who tends to be sad.

sedikit 1 a little, a bit, some. *Beri saya -* Give me a little. *- banyak* more or less. *- demi -* little by little. *- lagi* **1** a little more. **2** just a moment (please). *- hari lagi* in a few days, before long. *Sekolah itu - hari lagi akan dibuka kembali* The school will be reopened in a few days. **2** little, few. *Ia berkata -* He said little. **3** a bit, slightly. *Kepalanya terasa - pusing* She was a bit dizzy. *Dia tdk -pun mirip ayahnya* She did not resemble her father in the least. *terlalu besar -* somewhat too large. **-² 1** a little bit. *Ia ~ saja makan* He eats very little. **2** little by little. *Anak itu memakan kuénya ~* The child ate the cake little by little. **-nya** at least. *Walaupun tak kaya, ~ ia dpt membeli makanan sehari-hari* Though he was not rich, he could at least buy his daily bread. **meny-i** decrease. **meny-kan, memper-(kan)** lessen s.t. *Jumlah ini diper- utk mempermudah kontrol* We have lessened the quantity to make control easier. *Ia ~ pengeluaran uangnya* He reduced his expenditures.

sédimén sediment.

sédiméntasi sedimentation.

sedot meny- 1 suck. *Anak itu ~ minuman dr gelasnya* The child slurped the drink from the glass. **2** inhale, sip from. **ter-** sucked up. *Anak itu ~ pusaran air* The child was sucked into the whirlpool. **peny-** instrument to absorb. *pompa ~* sump pump, drainage pump. **peny-an** suction. *~ rahim (Med.)* suction curettage. **-an 1** a straw. **2** a puff, inhalation. *~ hidung* inhaler.

sedu₁ 1 a sob. *- sedan* sobbing, sobs. **ter-** *sedan* sob. **2** a hicup. **3** *(Lit.)* sad. **ter-(²)** sob.

sedu₂ see SEDUH₁.

sedua meny-i share part of the farm yield. *Sejak kematian bapak itu, ibu ~ tanah sawah seorg har-*

tawan After Father died, Mother worked in the rice fields of a rich man for a share in the harvest. **meny-kan** lease out on a part-time basis.

seduh₁ (*M*) **meny-** pour boiling water on s.t. *téh yg jika di- menghasilkan cairan pekat* a tea which yields a thick brew when suffused with boiling water. **ter-** steeped. **-an** steepings, produced by pouring hot water on s.t. ~ *jamu itu diminum sementara masih panas* The steeping from the mixture should be drunk hot. **peny-an** scalding.

seduh₂ see SEDU₁.

seduk scoop.

sedut see SEDOT.

seeded /sɪdèd/ *pemain* - (*Sport*) seeded player. **meny-** seed a player. **-an** a seeded player.

séf see SÉP₁.

ség₁ /sékh/ (*Coll.*) you know. *Aku jéngkél* - I was annoyed, you know.

ség₂ see SÉK.

segah full, satiated.

segak meny- blurt out.

ségak 1 recovered from illness. **2** fresh. *Mukanya - ssdh sembuh dr sakitnya* He looked fresh after recovering from his illness. **3** proud. **meny-kan** make s.t. fresh. ~ *diri* perk o.s. up.

segal ter-² breathless, out of breath.

segala 1 all, all of them (of things that are not uniform). - *rumahnya sdh dijualnya* He had sold all his houses. - *sedikit* a little of everything. - *sesuatu* everything, each and every. - *sesuatu yg diceriterakannya itu tak ada yg benar* Everything he said was a lie. **2** entirely, wholly. *Ia berpakaian - mérah* She was dressed entirely in red. **3** (*Coll.*) and all, (do) unnecessarily. *Kok macak benar hari ini pakai dasi* - You are all dressed up today. You are even wearing a tie. *Kok bawa oléh-oléh* - Oh my! You brought s.t. back for us. You should not have. **-²nya, -galanya** everything. *Barangnya habis* ~ He lost everything he had. **ke-an** everything concerned.

segan 1 keep in o.'s place, feel that person o. is dealing with has a higher position. *Murid-murid-nya - kpd guru itu* The pupils give the teacher proper respect. - *hormat* awe, respect. **meny-hormati** respect. **2** be reluctant to do s.t. others might consider above o. or in regard to a person of higher status. *Saya - utk menegur kepala kantor* I do not dare criticize the office head. **3** unwilling to do s.t. not quite proper. *tdk* - willing even to . . . *Dlm keadaan sulit ia tdk - menjadi tukang bécak* In his difficult situation he was willing even to become a pedicab driver. **-² 1** shy, be ashamed to do s.t. o. thinks o. has no right to do. *Jangan* ~ Make yourself at home, do not be shy. **2** be unwilling to do s.t. not proper. *tdk* ~ not hesitate. *Ia tdk akan* ~ *membunuh ibunya sendiri* He would not hesitate to kill his own mother. **meny-i** have mutual respect. *Meréka* ~ They respect e.o. **meny-i** respect, stand in awe of. *Ia di-i dan dicintai anak buahnya* He was respected and loved by his crew. *Suaranya tdk di-i* No o.

heeded his voice. **ke-an 1** reluctance, aversion. **2** respect, awe. **peny-** o. who is shy, retiring.

segar 1 fresh. *Sayur-sayuran itu masih* - The vegetables were still fresh. *Saya merasa - kembali* I feel like a new person again. - *bugar 1* safe and sound. **2** fit, like new. **2** refreshing. *Minuman itu* - The drink was refreshing. **3** delicious. - *makanannya di rumah makan Hong Kong* The Hong Kong has good food. **meny-kan, memper-** refresh. *Minuman itu* ~ *badan* The drink was refreshing. **ke-an 1** freshness. **2** health. ~ *jasmani* physical fitness. ~*nya terbayang di mukanya* Her face reflected her health. **peny-** freshener. ~ *napas* breath freshener. **peny-an** act of refreshing. *kursus* ~ *kembali* refresher course.

segara (*Lit.*) ocean. - *Kidul* the Java Sea.

ségel₁ 1 seal, stamp (notarizing, etc.). - *témpél* receipt stamp. **2** ration coupon. **ber-** be sealed. **meny-** seal, stamp. *Meréka* ~ *surat perjanjian itu* They sealed the contract. *Rumahnya di- karena tak ada izin tinggal* His house was sealed because he had no residence permit. **peny-an** sealing.

ségel₂ (*Naut.*) length of anchor chain of about 12 meters.

segen (*Jkt*) see SEGAN.

segenap see GENAP.

séger see SÉHER.

segera quickly, immediately. - *kemudian iapun datang* Immediately afterwards he came. **se-** as soon as. *Datanglah* ~ *mungkin* Come as soon as possible. ~*nya* as soon as possible. **ber-** hurry. *Tak usah* ~ No need to hurry. **meny-kan, memper-(kan) 1** speed up, accelerate. *Tindakannya itu* ~ *jatuhnya kabinét* His action speeded up the fall of the cabinet. **2** urge s.o. to work fast. **ke-an** being available or done immediately. ~*nya utk menolong org lain* the way she helps people immediately. **per-an** speeding up, acceleration.

segi 1 side. - *empat* (*Math.*) quadrangle. - *tiga* triangle. **2** angle, aspect, facet. *Ditinjau dr - kemanusiaan* . . . Seen from the humane point of view . . . **3** sector. - *ékspor* export sector. **ber-** with sides. ~ *tiga* triangular. *Pertempuran meréka* ~ *banyak* They fought on many fronts. **per-(Math.) 1** sided. ~ *tiga* triangular. *empat* ~ square. *empat* ~ *panjang* rectangular. **2** square. *enam méter* ~ six square meters.

segini see GINI.

segitu see GITU.

ségmén segment.

ségméntasi segmentation.

séh see SÉG₁, SYÉKH.

séhat 1 healthy. *Anaknya* - His child was healthy. *Makanan itu* - The food was healthful. - *badan dan - pikiran* sound of body and sound of mind. - *bugar* hale and hearty. - *rungu* with normal hearing. - *walafiat* hale and healthy, safe and sound. **2** sound. *ékonomi yg* - a healthy economy. **-²** in good health, in good condition. *Semua famili* ~ *saja* The whole family is in good health. **meny-kan** make healthy. *Makanan itu* ~ That food is healthful. **memper-** make healthier. **ke-an** health. ~ *masyarakat* public health. ~ *jiwa* mental health. **peny-an** sanitation. ~ *pantai* clearing up of the shore. *téknik* ~ health technology.

séher piston.

sehingga see HINGGA.

seia see IA₂.

seimbang see IMBANG.

séin see SÉN₂.

séinéndan (*Japanese*) youth army.

séinéndojo (*Japanese*) youth training center.

séismik (*Geol.*) seismic.

séismograf (*Geol.*) seismograph.

sejahtera 1 prosperous. 2 safe. **mens-kan, meny-kan** 1 make prosperous. *Pemerintah* ~ *kehidupan buruh* The gvt. gave the working class a more prosperous life. 2 make safe. **ke-an** 1 prosperity. 2 safety. **pe-an** well-being.

sejajar see JAJAR₁.

sejak₁ since, from the time that. *Ia sakit-sakit saja - minggu yg lalu* He has been ill since last week. - *itu* since then. - *kecil* since childhood. - *tadi* from a little while ago.

sejak₂ see SAJAK.

sejaman see JAMAN.

sejarawan, sejarahwan historian.

sejarah history. - *perang* military history. - *Pertumbuhan* (*Bib.*) Book of Genesis. **ber-** historic(al), full of history. *Hari 17 Agustus adalah hari yg* ~ *bagi org Indonésia* August 17 is a historic day for Indonesians. *Yogya adalah kota* ~ Yogya is a historical city. **meny-kan** tell or write the history of. **ke-an** things having to do with history. *alasan* ~ historical basis.

sejati true, real, genuine. *pahlawan* - a true hero. **ke-an** authenticity, genuineness.

seji see SAJI.

sejoli see JOLI.

sejuk cool, chilly. - *benar dlm kamar ini* It is quite cool in this room. - *hati* comfortable, relaxed. **meny-** become cool. **meny-i, meny-kan** cool s.t. *Ia* ~ *kamarnya* He cooled his room off. ~ *hati* comfort, cheer up s.o. *Perangainya itu* ~ *hati org tuanya* His behavior was a comfort to his parents. **ke-an** 1 cold, coolness. 2 numb with cold. *Anak itu* ~ The child was numb with cold. **peny-** cooler.

sék /sék/ shag. *tembakau* - shag tobacco.

séka ber- rub o.s. clean. **meny-** rub, wipe, polish. *Ia* ~ *mukanya dgn handuk* He wiped his face with a towel. **meny-kan** 1 brush away (tears). 2 use to wipe. **peny-** s.t. to rub or wipe with.

sekadar see KADAR₁.

sékah hearty, dashing.

sekak 1 chess. 2 checkmate.

sekakar stingy.

sekakelar see SAKELAR.

sekaker see SEKAKAR.

sekakmat (*Che.*) checkmate.

sekal scale of a map.

sekala see SKALA.

sekali₁ very. *baik* - very good.

sekali₂ (*Kalimantan*) apparently. **-nya** as it turned out.

sekali₃, sekalian see KALI₂.

sekaligus all at once. *Meréka menangis* - They all cried at once.

sekalipun see KALI₂.

sekalor k.o. herbal medicine.

sekam husk, chaff, hull of rice. **meny-** shut in, repress.

sekang a plug. - *mata* annoying, a nuisance. **meny-** put a plug in s.t. **ter-** stuck, plugged up.

sekap meny- 1 ripen fruit by enclosing it in s.t. 2 lock s.o. up. *Pembunuh itu di- dlm penjara* The murderer was locked up in prison. **ter-** get locked up or trapped in. *Ia* ~ *dlm gua* He was trapped in a cave. **-an** 1 ripe fruit. 2 prisoner. **peny-an** locking up (of s.o.).

sekar (*Jv*) flower. - *mayang* palm blossom (esp. used in wedding ceremonies). - *suhun* k.o. necklace. **meny-** bring flowers to a place for decoration, etc.

sekarang 1 now. *Mari kita pergi* - Let us go now. 2 nowadays. - *ini mudah saja bepergian* Nowadays it is very easy to travel. - (*ini*) *juga* this very moment, right now. *Kerjakan itu - ini juga* Do that this very moment. *dr - dan seterusnya* from now on. **-²** right now, at this very moment.

sekarat agony, be in agony. **ber-** be in death's throes. ~ *maut* risk o.'s life.

sekat₁ 1 screen. 2 (*Anat.*) partition. - *tembuni* section of afterbirth. - *rongga badan* diaphragm, midriff. - *rongga hidung* internasal septum. **ber-** partitioned off. **meny-** get stuck fast. **meny-(i)** 1 partition off. *Kedua buah kamar itu di-* The two rooms were partitioned off. 2 bar. *Dipisi kedua* ~ *gerakan musuh* The 2d division barred the enemy's movements. 3 isolate, insulate. *Ia* ~ *dirinya selama setahun* She went into seclusion for a year. **ter-** be obstructed. *Kerongkonganku* ~ I have a lump in my throat. **-an** 1 partition, screen. ~ *buku* flyleaf (in book). 2 obstruction. **peny-** 1 s.t. that partitions off, partition, screen. 2 insulator. **peny-an** isolation.

sekat₂ ice skates.

sekata see KATA.

sekatén a festival held in Solo and Yogya in honor of Muh.'s birthday.

sekatér tax collector.

sekaut police inspector.

Sekdalopbang [*Sékretaris Pengendalian Operasi Pembangunan*] supra-cabinet-level coordinator of development operations.

sekedar see KADAR₁.

sekédeng see SÉDENG.

sekeduduk see SENDUDUK.

sekehendak see HENDAK.

sekel (*Jv*) robust.

sekelar see SAKELAR.

sekelat woolen cloth.

sekelébatan see KELIBAT₂.

sekeliling see KELILING.

sekéma see SKÉMA.

sékéng (*Jv*) poor.
sekerat see SEKARAT.
sekeri hinge.
sékering see SÉKRING.
sekerja see KERJA.
sékertariat see SÉKRETARIAT.
sékertaris see SÉKRETARIS.
sekerup see SEKRUP.
sekésel screen, partition.
sekét sketch. **peny-** sketcher.
sékher see SÉHER.
sekian see KIAN.
sekilas see KILAS$_2$.
sekilwak (*Mil.*) sentinel, sentry.
sekin knife.
sekip 1 (*Mil.*) target. 2 firing range.
sekir **meny-** sand s.t., grind. ~ *klép* grind the valves.
sekiranya see KIRA.
sekis (*Geol.*) schist.
sekitar see KITAR$_1$.
sékjén [*sékretaris-jénderal*] secretary-general.
séko 1 scout. *Létnan itu mengirim tiga org* - The lieutenant sent three scouts. 2 spy. - *itu ditémbak mati* The spy was shot. 3 espionage.
sekoci$_1$ (*Naut.*) boat, sloop. - *penolong* lifeboat.
sekoci$_2$ bobbin, shuttle.
sekoi k.o. grass yielding grain similar to millet.
sekolah 1 school. - *aliyah* Isl. school, senior high school level. - *bruderan* school operated by Catholic brothers. - *frobel* kindergarten. - *ibtidaiyah* Isl. school, elementary level. - *kejuruan* vocational school. - *kepandaian puteri kesejahteraan keluarga* home economics high school. - *lanjutan* secondary school. - *menengah atas* senior high school. - *menengah pertama* junior high school. - *pertukangan* junior technical school. - *rakyat/rendah* elementary school. - *tinggi* college, university. - *Tinggi Théologia* divinity school, theological seminary. - *tingkat* public school. - *vak* vocational school. 2 attend school. *Ia tdk* - He does not go to school. He never went to school. **ber-** go to school. **meny-kan** send to school. *Ia tak ~ anaknya* He did not send his children to school. **-an 1** schooling. 2 school (building). **peny-an** schooling, sending s.o. to school. **per-an** school system.
sekon second (of time). *Dlm semenit ada enam puluh* - A minute is sixty seconds.
sekonar (*Naut.*) k.o. two-masted boat, schooner.
sekonéng beveling in a piece of wood so that it fits into another.
sekongkel, sekongkol see KONGKOL.
sekonyong see KONYONG.
sekop see SKOP.
sekopong (*Crd., Coll.*) spade suit.
sekores see SKORS.
sekorsing see SKORSING.
sekoteng, sekoténg (*Jv*) ginger-flavored drink served hot.
sekout see SEKAUT.
sékr. [*sékretariat*] secretariat.

sekrési secretion. **mens-kan** secrete.
sékretarésse woman secretary.
sékretariat secretariat. - *Negara* State Secretariat. **ke-an** things pertaining to a secretariat. *tugas ~* secretarial tasks.
sékretaris secretary. - *jénderal* secretary-general, undersecretary. - *Negara* State Secretary.
sékring fuse for electric circuit.
sekrop$_1$ scrub floor with soap and water.
sekrop$_2$ see SKOP.
sekrup screw, bolt. **meny-(kan)** screw s.t.
séks sex, sexual activity. *main* - have sexual intercourse. *film* - pornographic or erotic movie.
seksama accurate, exact, thorough. *Perkara itu diperiksa dgn* - The case was studied thoroughly. **meny-kan 1** arrange in an orderly way. 2 deal with s.t. thoroughly. **ke-an** accuracy, precision.
séksi$_1$ 1 (*Biol.*) dissection. 2 section. - *tiup* wind section (of orchestra). - *perkusi* percussion section. 3 platoon.
séksi$_2$ (*Coll.*) sexy. **ke-an** sexiness.
séksofon, séksopon see SAKSOFON.
sékstan sextant.
séksual sexual.
séksualitas, séksualitét sexuality.
séksuil see SÉKSUAL.
séktaris sectarian.
séktarisme sectarianism.
sékte sect.
séktor sector.
séktoral by sector.
sékuéns sequence (in movie).
sékularis secularistic.
sékularisasi secularization.
sékularisme secularism.
sékulér, sékulir secular. **mens-kan** secularize.
sekunar see SEKONAR.
sekundér secondary.
sekuriti (*Mil.*) security, security forces.
sekuteng see SEKOTENG.
sekuter see SKUTER.
sekutu 1 partner. *Ali dan -nya tlh bercerai* Ali and his partner had separated. 2 ally. *Tentera - meninggalkan pulau itu* The allied forces left the island. **ber-** united, allied. *Kedua negara itu ~ melawan musuhnya bersama* The two countries united to oppose their common enemy. *makhluk ~* a social being. *~ dgn* side with e.o., join forces. *Dlm perang dunia kedua Amérika ~ dgn Rusia* During World War II the US and Russia joined forces. **meny-i** join, ally o.s. with. *Dulu negeri Inggeris ~ Rusia* Formerly England allied herself with Russia. **meny-kan 1** consider as an ally. 2 provide forces as an ally. *Inggeris ~ angkatan daratnya pd Perancis dlm perang itu* Great Britain joined her ground forces with the French in that war. **memper-kan** make s.t. or s.o. an ally, connect. *~ Tuhan dgn keindahan* identify God with beauty. **per-an 1** federation. *~ Tanah Melayu* Federation of Malaya. 2 partnership. 3 league, alliance.
sekyuriti see SEKURITI.

sél 1 cubicle, cell (in prison, etc.). - *macan* death row. **2** (*Tech.*) cell. - *aki* battery cell. - *darah* corpuscle. - *raba* taste bud. **3** (*Pol.*) political cell. *sistém - dlm partai Komunis* the cell system in the Communist party. **men(ge)-, men-kan** put into a prison cell.

sela₁ 1 crack, opening, gap. - *gunung* mountain pass. **2** interval. - *hari* every other day. *Si miskin makan nasi - hari* The poor eat rice every other day. **3** interrupt. *"Benar sekali," - Patiwiri* "That is very true," Patiwiri interrupted. **4** catch crop, auxiliary crop. **ber-** with gaps or intervals. *tdk ~* unbroken, uninterrupted. *Pagar itu tdk ~ There* were no gaps in the fence. **- meny-** alternate, intermittent. **meny-(i) 1** vary, put intervals in s.t. **2** interrupt. *Boléh saya ~?* Excuse me, may I interrupt? **meny-kan, memper-kan** insert. **-an** break, interruption. **peny-an** interruption.

sela₂ mixture.

séla₁ saddle.

séla₂ stone. **meny-kan** throw stones.

séla₃ squinting.

selada lettuce. - *air* watercress.

seladang k.o. wild ox.

seladeri, seladri see SELÉDERI.

selagi see LAGI₂.

selai jelly, jam. - *kacang* peanut butter.

selain see LAIN.

selaju see LAJU.

selak₁ bolt, bar to hold door closed. **meny-** bolt or bar a door.

selak₂ - *kemudu-kudu* (*Jv*) have to do s.t. immediately without delay.

selak₃ meny- insist. **ke-, ter-** choked.

sélak meny-(kan) 1 open (o.'s shirt, etc.). **2** reveal.

selakangan crotch.

sélakarang (*Jv*) k.o. medicinal preparation.

selaku see LAKU.

selalu see LALU.

selam₁ dive. **ber-** *air* test witch, etc. by submerging in water to ascertain guilt. **meny- 1** dive. *Ia ~ ke dlm air* She dove into the water. **2** be under water. *Ia ~ di dlm air* He stayed under water. *Sambil ~ minum air* Kill two birds with o. stone. **meny-i 1** dive into. *Ia ~ laut* She dived into the sea. **2** dive for. *Ia ~ mutiara* He dived for pearls. **3** penetrate, fathom. *Saya tak dpt ~ perasaannya* I could not penetrate her feelings. **meny-kan** immerse s.t. *tak ter-i* unfathomable. *spt laut dlm yg tak ~* like the unfathomable deep sea. **peny-** diver. **peny-an 1** diving. - *indah* fancy diving. **2** immersion, submersion.

selam₂ (*Coll.*) Islam. *org - a* Muslim. **meny-(kan) 1** convert s.o. to Isl. **2** circumcise. **peny-an 1** conversion to Isl. **2** circumcision.

selama see LAMA.

selamat 1 safe. *Ia datang - dr peperangan* He returned safe from the war. - *asrakal* burying the placenta. **2** welfare, happiness, prosperity. **3** happy, pleasant, blessed. *Hidupnya - sekali* Her life was very happy. *Saya - saja* I am just fine. **4** congratulations, wish for good luck, happiness, or prosperity. *Ia mengucapkan - kpd saya* He congratulated me. *Meréka membaca doa -* They prayed for happiness and prosperity. - *(ber)bahagia* congratulations. - *belajar* happy studying. - *datang* Welcome. - *erat* warm regards. - *hari lahir* Happy birthday! - *Hari Lebaran* Congratulations (said at end of fasting month). - *Hari Natal* Merry Christmas. - *jalan* goodbye (to o. leaving), have a nice trip. - *makan* enjoy your meal. - *malam* good evening, good night. - *siang* good day (around noontime). - *tidur* good night, sleep well. - *tinggal* goodbye (to o. staying behind). **-²** *saja* take care of yourself. **(ber)-an** hold a ceremonial meal. **meny-i 1** hold a ceremonial meal for s.o. *Kami ~ arwah nénék kami* We hold a ceremonial meal to commemorate our deceased. **2** congratulate s.o. **meny-kan 1** save, rescue. *Ia ~ semua penumpang* He saved all the passengers. **2** bury. **ter-kan** can be saved. **ke-an 1** happiness, welfare. **2** safety. *~ kerja* job safety. **3** salvation. *Bala ~* The Salvation Army. **-an** ceremonial meal. **peny- 1** rescuer. **2** (*Rel.*) Savior, Redeemer. **peny-an** rescuing, redemption.

selamba (*Lit.*) rude, uncivilized. **ke-an** rudeness.

selampai, selampé 1 scarf, kerchief. **2** handkerchief. **meny-kan** sling s.t. over the arm or shoulder.

selampit braid. **meny-** braid.

Sélan Sri Lanka.

selancar see LANCAR.

Sélandia Baru New Zealand.

selang₁ interval, break. - *beberapa hari kemudian . . .* After several days . . . - *sehari* every other day, with a day intervening. - *seminggu* with a week intervening. - *seling* **1** alternatingly. **2** without cease. **ber-** *seling* **1** alternating, alternately. *Gadis itu memakai benang mérah dan biru ~ seling dlm jahitannya* The girl used red and blue thread alternately in her sewing. **2** intermittent. **meny-nyeling(kan)** alternate, vary s.t. *Ia ~ hari kerjanya di kantor dan di rumah* He alternates between working at home and at the office. **meny-nyelingi** alternate with. *Pembicaraan itu di-selingi tawa yg segar* The conversation was punctuated by cheerful laughter. **ber- 1** at intervals, at an equal distance from e.o., intermittently. *~ tiga hari* at three-day intervals. **2** ago. *tiga hari ~* three days ago. **ber-² 1** alternating. **2** intermittent. **meny- 1** interrupt, intercede. *Ia selalu ~ pembicaraan saya* He is always interrupting my speech. **2** alternate two things. *Ia ~ benang mérah dgn benang biru* She alternated red and blue thread. **meny-i** interrupt. *Ceritanya kadang-kadang di-i tangis ibunya* His story was sometimes interrupted by his mother's sobs. **meny-kan** alternate with s.t., put s.t. in between at intervals. **-an 1** an object between other objects. **2** space between two things.

selang₂ meny- lend. **meny-i, memper-i** lend to s.o. **meny-kan, memper-kan** lend s.t.

selang₃ see SLANG₁.

selangka see TULANG.

selangkang, selangkangan groin.

selap possessed. meny-(i) take possession of (of a spirit). *Ia di- hantu* He was taken over by a spirit. meny-kan arouse o.'s fury.

selapan (*Jv*) 35 days. -an ritual conducted when a baby is 35 days old.

selaput 1 (*Anat.*) membrane, film. - *bening* cornea. - *dara* hymen. - *jala* retina. - *jantung* pericardium. - *kegadisan* hymen. - *mata* cornea. - *otak* cerebral membrane. - *pelangi* iris. - *renang* web (of ducks, etc.). - *tanduk* cornea. 2 coating. ber- covered with a membrane. meny-i form a thin layer around s.t., coat. *Wajahnya di-i asap sampah yg sedang dibahar* His face was covered with a thin layer of smoke from the trash that was being burnt. -an coating, casing. ~ *kartu mahasiswa* laminate for a student's ID card.

selar meny-(kan) 1 brand. 2 singe, sear. 3 fry (without oil).

selaras see LARAS₁.

selar bagat k.o. mackerel.

Selasa Tuesday. - *Kliwon* Tuesday that coincides with *Kliwon*, first day of Jv week, considered a sacred day.

selasar open veranda.

selasih basil.

selat 1 straits, narrows, sound. - *Sunda* Sunda Straits. 2 passage. meny- sail through a strait. meny-kan insert, thrust between. *Di-kan sesuatu pd keruntung pengemis itu* S.t. was thrust into the beggar's basket. peny- s.t. inserted.

selatan south. - *daya* S.-S.W. - *menenggara/tenggara* S.-S.E. meny- southward. meny-kan move s.t. further to the south. ter- southernmost.

selawat (*Isl.*) invocation, short prayer us. consisting of verses from the Koran.

selawé (*Jv*) 25.

selayang see LAYANG₁.

séldri see SELÉDERI.

selé see SELAI.

selebaran leaflet. - *gelap* illegal and unsigned leaflet.

selébor see SLÉBOR.

selebu see LAUT.

seléderi celery.

seleguri k.o. small bush.

selejang see LEJANG.

selek see SELAK₂.

selékéh stain, spot. ber- stained, dirty. meny-(i) smear, stain.

selekit (*Jv*) ny- offensive, tending to hurt o.'s feeling. *Omongan dia selalu ~!* The way she talks is always offensive!

selékoh 1 a bend. 2 bastion, work in fortress that thrusts outward.

seléksi, seléksi selection. men-, meny- select.

seléktif selective. ke-an selectiveness.

selembubu turbulence, tornado.

selempada k.o. large red ant.

selempang₁ afraid, frightened. meny-kan worry about.

selempang₂ ter- fall astraddle.

selémpang shoulder belt, sash worn across the body. - *tanda dokter* (*Acad.*) doctor's hood. ber- wear a belt or sash over o. shoulder or over the shoulders and across the body. ber-kan wear s.t. as a shoulder sash. meny-kan put s.t. over a shoulder. ~ *sarung di tubuhnya* wear a sarong over o.'s shoulders. -an banner.

selempit meny-kan tuck in. -kan *kain sepré pd tempat tidur itu* Tuck in the sheets of that bed. ter- tucked in. *Mesjid ~ di belakang gedung-gedung* The mosque was tucked in behind some buildings.

seléndang shawl or stole worn over o. shoulder or diagonally across body. ber- wear a shawl or stole. meny- wear s.t. as a shawl or stole over the shoulder. meny-i put a shawl or stole on s.o. meny-kan hang, carry on the shoulder. ~ *tas buku* carry a book bag over the shoulder. mem-per-kan use s.t. for a shawl or stole.

selénder see SILINDER.

selénger (*Auto.*) crank.

selenggara meny-kan 1 run s.t., take care of, operate. *Ayahnya ~ kebun* His father ran a plantation. 2 organize. *Meréka ~ sebuah pésta* They organized a party. ~ *sayembara* hold a contest. 3 execute, carry out, implement. ~ *undang-undang* enforce the law. *Ia ~ pekerjaannya dgn baik* He executed his job properly. ter- carried out. peny- 1 caretaker. 2 executor. 3 organizer, operator. peny-an 1 implementation. 2 organization, coordination.

selentang-selenting rumor.

selentik see SLENTIK.

selentingan in passing, incidentally. *"Apa rencanamu sekarang?" tanyanya* - "What are your plans now?" he asked in passing. *kabar* - rumors.

seléo see KESELÉO.

selep irony.

selepa cigarette case, betel box.

selepétan slingshot.

seléra₁ 1 appetite. *Saya ndak ada - pagi begini* I have no appetite this early in the morning. 2 taste. - *pemuda-pemudi* the taste of the younger generation. 3 lust, desire. *Gadis macam itu membuat Mat Coléng tdk tahan* - Girls like that made Mat Coléng experience an uncontrollable lust. ber- 1 have appetite, feel like. 2 attractive, appetizing. 3 have a taste for. *Org yg ~ baik memilih jam Pagol* People with the right taste choose a Pagol watch.

seléra₂ (*Lit.*) body.

selérang skin, hide.

selésa 1 space, room. 2 opportunity, occasion. *Ia tdk* - He had no opportunity. 3 wide.

selesai 1 finished, done. *Pekerjaannya sdh* - His work was finished. *Sekolahnya sdh* - He had finished his education. 2 done and over with, paid off (of debt), finished (of quarrel). *Perkaranya blm* - The case has not been settled. meny-kan 1 finish s.t. *Ia tak pernah ~ pekerjaannya* She never finished her job. 2 solve, settle, discharge (debt, etc.). *Meréka berikhtiar ~ pertengkaran itu*

They tried hard to settle the dispute. **peny-** s.o. who settles a matter, solves a problem. ~ *pertikaian* arbiter. **peny-an 1** arrangement. **2** solution, settlement, completion. ~ *gedung* the completion of a building. ~ *anjuran* the disposition of a proposal. ~ *utang* settling of a debt.

selesma, selésma a cold, sniffles.

seletuk see CELETUK.

seléwéng meny- 1 deviate, digress. *Apa kita sdh ~?* Have we digressed from the subject? **2** engage in improper activity. **3** be unfaithful in an amorous relationship. **meny-kan** divert, deflect, s.t. ~ *uang* divest money into o.'s own pocket. *Ékspor tdk akan di-kan ke daérah lain* Exports will not be diverted to other areas. **ter-kan** diverted, deflected. **peny-** crook. **peny-an 1** deviation (from task or duty). **2** irregularity, corruption.

selewir see SELIWER.

sélf-kritik self-criticism.

sélibat celibate. **ber-** (be) celibate.

selidik 1 accurate, careful. **2** critical, observant. *Ia sangat - akan segala perkataan saya* He paid very close attention to everything I said. **meny-** be investigating, act in an investigative capacity. **meny-i 1** investigate. *Ia ~ pembunuhan itu* He investigated the murder. **2** do research. **3** spy, pry into. **ter-i** investigated. **peny- 1** investigator, research worker. **2** examiner, detective. **3** scout, spy. **peny-an 1** research. ~ *ilmiah* scientific research. **2** inquiry, investigation. **3** survey.

seligi javelin. **meny-** throw a javelin.

seligit swarm, swarm over.

selimpang meny- deviate from the right path.

selimpat - *selimput* sneak around to avoid s.t. **ber-an** sneak away (in numbers). *Setiap org ~ keluar* Everyone snuck out of the place. **meny-** stay clear of, avoid s.t.

selimpet ber-an crowd, press together. *tempat rumah-rumah sederhana ~* where simple houses crowded e.o.

selimut 1 blanket. **2** camouflage, cover. **ber-1** covered over. **2** camouflaged. **ber-kan** covered with. ~ *salju* blanketed with snow. **meny-i 1** cover s.t. with a blanket. **2** cover, hide s.t. *Ia ~ maksudnya yg jahat itu dgn kata-kata yg manis* He concealed his evil intentions behind nice words. *Ia ~ kegugupannya* She concealed her nervousness. **meny-kan 1** hide behind, use as a cover. **2** cover, blanket with s.t. *Basri ~ jasnya kpdku* Basri put his coat over me. **ter-i** be blanketed. *Puncaknya ~ kabut* The peak is blanketed in clouds. **peny-an 1** covering. **2** camouflaging.

selinap - *sana - sini* slither in all directions. **meny-1** slither, move stealthily. *Ular itu ~ ke dlm semak-semak* The snake crawled into the bushes. **2** get, slip away or into s.t. *Pencopét itu dgn segera ~ dr polisi* The thief immediately slipped away from the policemen. **meny-i 1** crawl, move stealthily into s.t. **2** get, slip into s.t. *Rasa sedih ~ hatiku* A feeling of sadness came into my heart. **meny-kan** introduce s.t. stealthily.

selindung ber- be hidden, hide o.s. *Musuhnya ~ dlm kegelapan* The enemy was hidden in the dark.

seling interspace, interval. **ber-** take turns, alternate. *Nyanyian-nyanyian barat ~ dgn nyanyian-nyanyian timur* Western songs alternated with eastern o.'s. **ber-** *ganti* alternating(ly). **meny-(i)** intervening, go in between. *Obrolan meréka di-i tawa riang* Cheerful laughter punctuated their conversation. *Ada rumah ~ bangunan Caltex* There were houses interspersed between the Caltex buildings. **meny-kan** put s.t. in between. **ter-(i)** have s.t. interspersed in it. **-an 1** interlude, s.t. put in between. **2** variation from the routine. *Sbg ~ kafétaria juga menjual hamburger* For a change, the cafeteria also has hamburgers on the menu. **peny-** alternative.

selingkar see LINGKAR.

selingkuh (*Jv*) dishonest, corrupt.

selingkung see LINGKUNG.

selingkup meny-(kan) enclose, cover.

selip₁ meny- slip into a place. *Kami ~ di antara org ramai* We slipped into the crowd. **meny-i** insert between. *Majalah ini di-i brosur perusahaannya* He inserted his business brochure in the journal. **meny-kan** insert s.t. in between. *Ia ~ sehelai kertas di bukunya* He slipped a piece of paper into his book. **ter- 1** enclosed. **2** inserted, slipped in. ~ *rasa kekesalan dlm hatiku* A feeling of spite slipped into my heart. **-an** slip (in magazine, etc.).

selip₂ skid. *Mobilnya -* His car skidded. **ter-** skid. ~ *keluar* **1** protrude. **2** leak out. ~ *keluar dr mulut* say s.t. inadvertently.

selip₃ meny- drag, tow.

seliput meny-i cover, envelope. *Kabut pagi ~ kota Bandung* A morning fog covered Bandung. **ter-i** covered with.

selir₁ mistress, concubine. **ber-kan** have s.o. as a concubine. **memper-kan** take as concubine. **per-an** concubinage.

selir₂ sound of breeze. **ber-an, meny-** murmur (of a breeze).

selira see SELÉRA₂.

selirat ber- confused.

selisih 1 difference. *Umur kami tak banyak -nya* Our ages do not differ much. *dua puluh sénti - a* difference of 20 centimeters. *- basah* moving in traffic back and forth (of ships). **2** quarrel, dispute. *- kata* quarrel. *- faham* difference of understanding. **ber- 1** be at certain interval in time or space. *Saya ~ dua tahun dgn dia* I am two years older (or younger) than he is. ~ *jalan* pass e.o. without meeting, cross (of letters). *Surat sdr ~ jalan dgn surat saya* Our letters crossed. **2** quarrel, disagree, be at odds with. **memper-kan, meny-kan** disagree over s.t. **per-an** disagreement, quarrel, dispute.

selisik meny- 1 go through the hair to pick lice or nits. **2** investigate, get at the bottom of. *Ia ~ perkara itu* He investigated the case.

selisip meny- slip in. **meny-kan** insert s.t.

selisir meny- go along the edge of s.t.

selit meny- be wedged or inserted in between. *Uang sepérak saja ~ dlm kantongku* I had only a rupiah in my pocket. **meny-kan** insert between two objects. *Ia ~ sebatang rokok di bibirnya* She put a cigarette between her lips. **ter-(kan)** inserted between. **-an** space between two objects.

seliwar-seliwar to and fro.

seliwer (ber)-an crowd, mill about. *Org banyak pd ~* The crowd milled about. *Kendaraan ~ di kota* Traffic was heavy in the town.

séllis cellist.

sélo cello.

selobok meng-kan slip s.t. into s.t.

seloka archaic short witty poem ending in an aphorism. **ber-** recite or compose such a poem.

selokan 1 gutter, drain. **2** sewer. **3** ditch. **per-** drainage system.

seloki see SLOKI.

selomot (*Jv*) **meny-** fool, hoodwink. **meny-i** burn, touch fire to s.t.

selomprét₁ mild swear word. *-lu!* Damn you!

selomprét₂ see SLOMPRÉT₁.

Sélon, Sélong Ceylon. **meny-** exile, deport.

selongkar meny- 1 turn over, put in disorder. **2** rummage through.

selongsong 1 cover. **2** a muzzle (dog). **3** shell of bullet.

selonjor in a position with o.'s legs stretched forward. **ber-** with outstretched legs. **meny-kan** stretch (the legs). **ter-** be stretched out (of legs).

selonong meny-, ny- 1 go astray, slide into (by accident). **2** (*Coll.*) go through, in, or out without permission. *É, ini anak ny- ajé kagak paké permisi* Hey, here is a child going through (my property) without permission.

selop₁ slipper, sandal with closed toes. *- jéngkék* high-heeled slippers.

selop₂ see SLOF.

seloro, seloroh 1 funny, amusing. **2** joke, witty remark. **ber-** joke, crack jokes.

selot bolt or lock. *- gantung* padlock. **meny-** lock.

sélotip cellophane tape.

sélsius Celsius.

seluang k.o. freshwater fish.

seluar (*Lit.*) trousers.

selubung 1 cover, veil. **2** wrapper. *- anak* (*Biol.*) placenta. **ber-** cover o.s. up. **meny-i** cover with a veil or wrapper. *~ rahasia* hide a secret. **meny-kan** use s.t. as a covering. *Ku-kan selimut pdnya* I threw a cover over her. **ter-** veiled, covered. *Banyak pertanyaan ~ yg diajukan* They asked many veiled questions. **-an** covering, wrapping. *~nya kurang rapi* It was not well wrapped. **peny-an** act of covering.

seludang sheath or spathe of inflorescence of palm tree.

seluduk meny- crawl under s.t. *Ia ~ ke bawah méja* He crawled under the table.

seludup see SELUNDUP.

selujur see SELONJOR.

seluk₁ curve, bend, coil. *- beluk* **1** details. **2** complications. **ber-** *beluk* **1** complicated. **2** be related to. *Ia masih ~ beluk dgn keluarga présidén* He is related in some way to the president's family. **ber-** twisted, winding.

seluk₂ meny- feel (around) for.

séluler (*Biol.*) cellular.

sélulosa, sélulose (*Chem.*) cellulose.

selulup dive, plunge. **ber-** dive, plunge.

selumbar wood splinters.

selumur snakeskin that has been shed.

selundup meny- 1 duck into, hide. **2** smuggle. **3** infiltrate. **meny-i** infiltrate. **meny-kan** smuggle s.t. in. **-an** things that are smuggled. *barang ~* contraband. **peny-** smuggler. **peny-an** smuggling

selungkang fake (of metal).

selungkap detached, worked loose (of skin, etc.).

selungkup meny- cover, close.

selunjur see SELONJOR.

selup₁ (*Naut.*) sloop.

selup₂ see CELUP.

selupat see SELAPUT.

seluruh entire, whole. *- kampung itu sepi* The entire village was quiet. *- hidupnya diabdikan pd negara* He devoted his entire life to the state. **-nya** all of it. *Lantainya ~ ditutupi permadani* The entire floor was covered with a rug. **meny-1** spread all over. *Kabar ini sdh ~ di tanah air* This news has spread throughout our country. **2** comprehensive. *peraturan ~* a comprehensive or exhaustive regulation. *pendekatan yg ~* a comprehensive approach. **meny-i** enclose completely. **ke-an** totality, whole. *dlm ~nya* as a whole, in its totality. *secara ~* on the whole.

selusuh 1 slide. **2** s.t. to ease childbirth (lit., s.t. to make the child slide out).

selusup meny- penetrate, infiltrate. *Ia ~ ke daérah musuh* He penetrated into the enemy territory. *Ia ~ ke dlm semak* He disappeared into the underbrush. **meny-i** penetrate or infiltrate into s.t. **meny-kan** slip s.t. s.w. on the sly. **ter-i** get infiltrated. **peny- 1** infiltrator. **2** s.t. that infiltrates. *pesawat pembom ~* an infiltrating bomber. **peny-an** penetration.

selusur *- (pegangan) tangga* handrail, banister. **meny-** slide. *Anak itu ~ dr pegangan tangga* The boy slid down the banisters. **meny-i 1** go along, follow. *Meréka ~ jalan dan lorong ibukota* They went through the streets and the alleys of the capital. **2** go through s.t. carefully. *Di-inya koran* He went through the newspaper carefully.

selut mud, ooze.

sélwagon patrol wagon.

selwir see SELIWER.

semacam see MACAM.

semadi 1 meditation. **2** meditate. **ber-** meditate. **meny-kan** meditate over s.t. **peny-an** meditating.

sémah an offering to guard against demons. **meny-** make an offering. **meny-kan** sacrifice s.t. **-an** a religious offering.

semai seedling. **meny-(kan)** raise seedlings, make seeds germinate. **-an** seedling. **peny-an**

process of raising seedlings. **per-an** seedbed, nursery.

semak₁ bushes, underbrush. - *belukar* underbrush, scrub. - *samun* bushes, shrubbery. *dr - ke belukar* six of o. and half a dozen of the other (lit., from the thicket to the underbrush). **meny-** 1 be like underbrush. *Bunga-bungaan ~ di kebunnya* Various flowers have turned into underbrush in his garden. 2 entangled. *Rambutnya ~* Her hair was tangled. 3 confused. 4 worried. **meny-kan** 1 allow to become a wilderness, let (a garden, etc.) run wild. 2 confuse, worry.

semak₂ feeling comfortable, at o.'s ease. *Arjuna mémang kurang -, tak begitu senang bertemu dgn para pejabat* Arjuna felt ill at ease; he was not fond of meeting gvt. officials.

sémak see SIMAK₁.

semakin see MAKIN.

semalu see SIMALU.

semampai slender.

séman 1 failed. 2 aborted. **ke-an** 1 failure. 2 abortion.

semanak jovial, friendly.

semandan bridesmaid.

semandéra pennant at the stern of a boat.

semang see ANAK, INDUK.

semangat 1 zest, spirit, enthusiasm, have enthusiasm. *-nya utk belajar tak ada lagi* He has lost all his zest for study. *Ia kalah -* He lost courage. *- kambing* coward. *- kampung* having a village-oriented mentality. *- kedaérahan* provincialism. *- pelaut* enthusiastic about naval matters. *- perang* warlike, militant. *- perkampungan* group loyalty. 2 soul, spirit. **ber-** 1 conscious. *Ia tdk ~* He is unconscious. 2 enthusiastic, energetic. *Tdk ~* listless. **memper-kan, meny-i** inspire. *Rakyat hrs di-i* The people must be inspired.

semanggi 1 edible herb with trifoliate leaf. 2 (*Jv*) dish of vegetables steamed with spices.

semangka watermelon.

semangkin see MANGKIN.

sémantik semantics.

sémantis semantic.

semaput (*Coll.*) 1 unconscious, fainted. 2 have a fit.

Semar chief of the servants of the Pandawas in *Wayang*.

semarai cracked, broken, damaged.

semarak 1 shine, luster. 2 ornament. 3 shining, glittering. *prosési ~ a* gala procession. **ber-** radiant, splendid. **memper-, meny-kan** 1 embellish, adorn. 2 cheer up, brighten. **ke-an** splendor.

semasa see MASA₁.

sema-sema a cold, sniffles.

semasih see MASIH₁.

semat pin, peg, hook. **meny-(i)** pin on s.t. *Murdani di-i tanda pangkat jénderalnya oléh présidén sendiri* The president himself fastened the insignia of general on Murdani. **meny-kan** fasten, pin, attach. *Ia ~ peniti hiasannya ke bajunya* She fastened her brooch to her dress. **ter-** be fastened on. **-an** appendix to a book. **peny-** pin.

peny-an 1 pinning (of medals, etc.). 2 (*Ling.*) embedding.

semata, semata-mata see MATA₂.

semau, semaunya see MAU.

semayam lie down, lie. **ber-** reside, sit (of royalty). **meny-kan** bury. *Para jenazah di-kan* The dead were buried. **per-an** 1 throne. 2 residence.

sembab swollen (of facial features from physical or emotional fatigue). *Matanya - karena tangis* His eyes were swollen from weeping. **ber-** swollen. *~ mata* have o.'s eyes swollen.

sembabat fitting, matching.

sembada capable, able to carry through.

sembah 1 respectful greeting (made with palms together, fingertips upward and touching the forehead). 2 homage, obeisance. *- sungkem* deepest respect. *Dgn -, ananda* Most respectfully, your son. 3 words, saying (to king, etc.). **ber-** address respectfully. **meny-** 1 pay homage. 2 worship. *~ Tuhan* worship God. **meny-²** beg or entreat in a polite way. *Ia ~ Retno agar mengampuni kesalahannya* She begged Retno to forgive her for her mistakes. **meny-kan** put (the hands or s.o.'s hands) in the position of respectful greeting. **memper-kan** 1 offer or present s.t. to a high personnage. *Sebuah patung kayu diper-kan kpd présidén* A wooden statue was presented to the president. *~ kurban misa* (*Rel.*) celebrate mass. 2 (*Lit.*) inform or report to a royal personnage. *Ia ~ segala kejadian itu kpd rajanya* He reported on all events to his king. 3 dedicate. *Saya per-kan buku ini kpd ibu saya* I dedicate this book to my mother. 4 present a performance. *Malam ini filem itu akan diper-kan* That film will be presented tonight. **-an** object or person worshipped. **peny-** worshipper. *~ berhala* idolater. **peny-an** adoration, worship. **per-an** 1 tribute, gift. 2 dedication.

sembahyang (*Rel.*) prayer service, prayer. *- asar* (*Isl.*) afternoon prayer (3-5 p.m.). *- doha* (*Isl.*) optional Muslim prayer performed before noon. *- hajat* (*Isl.*) prayer service held for the fulfillment of a wish. *- isa/isya* (*Isl.*) evening prayers. *- lima waktu* (*Isl.*) the five obligatory prayers. *- sunat* (*Isl.*) optional prayer. *- tahajut* (*Isl.*) optional midnight prayer. *- wajib* (*Isl.*) the five obligatory prayers. **ber-** pray, worship. **meny-i, meny-kan** pray for, conduct services for. **-an** praying. **peny-an** act of praying for s.o.

sembam₁ swollen in body or face.

sembam₂ **meny-** roast in hot ashes.

sembap see SEMBAB.

sembarang of any kind, no particular o. *Ia percaya pd - org* He trusted anyone at all. *bukan batu -* not just any old rock. *- waktu* any (old) time. *dgn -* haphazardly. **ke-an** arbitrariness, doing things any old way. **-an** 1 at random. *Jangan ~ buang sampah* Do not throw garbage anywhere you feel like it. *Cakapnya ~ saja* He says anything that comes to his head. 2 just anyone, anything. *Ahsan bukan pelukis -* Ahsan is not just any old painter.

sembari while. *Biarkan mesin itu hidup - kita menunggu* Let the engine run while we're waiting.

sembat see SEBAT₁.

sémbat meny- 1 whip up with a jerk. *Rotan itu ~* The rattan whipped up with a jerk. 2 grab while passing.

sembayan (*M*) co-wife, woman married to same man as another. **ber-** be co-wives of same man.

sembelih meny- slaughter. *Ia ~ ayam* He killed a chicken. **-an** an animal to be slaughtered, slaughtered animal. *ternak ~* beef-cattle. **peny-** a butcher. **peny-an** slaughter, butchering.

sembelit 1 constipation. 2 constipated.

sembér raucous, hoarse, cracked (voice)

semberani see SEMBRANI.

semberono see SEMBRONO.

semberut scowl.

sembilan nine. *- belas* 19. *- puluh* 90. **ber-** do s.t. in a group of nine.

sembilang k.o. fish with poisonous spines.

sembilik see PURU.

sembilu blade of split bamboo (traditionally used to cut umbilical chord). **meny-** 1 cut (with such a blade). *Kematian isterinya turut ~ hati* His wife's death further cut his heart. 2 be cutting (of words). **-an** having the cutting quality of a bamboo knife.

sembir edge, margin. *nilai -* marginal value. *catatan -* marginal note. **meny-** deviate. **-an** margin, suburb.

sembirat tinge of color.

sembodo see SEMBADA.

semboja see KAMBOJA.

semboyan 1 slogan, motto, catchword. 2 sign, signal. **ber-(kan)** have as a slogan. **meny-kan** 1 give a prearranged signal. 2 use s.t. as a slogan.

sembrani see KUDA, BESI.

sembrono doing things any way that comes to o.'s head, at random, not in accordance with the rules of society. *Jangan bicara - saja* Do not just say whatever comes to your head. *Jangan berlaku -* Do not do whatever you happen to feel like doing. **ke-an** frivolity, doing things without heeding the rules, recklessness.

sembuang (*Naut.*) mooring buoy.

sembuh recover, heal. *Ia sdh - dr penyakitnya* He has recovered from his illness. *Si sakit itu - oléh Dokter Go* The sick person was cured by Dr. Go. **meny-kan** cure. *Dokter tak dpt ~ penyakit anak itu* The doctor could not cure the child's illness. **ke-an** recovery. **ter-kan** curable. *penyakit yg tdk ~ an* incurable disease. **peny-** s.t. to heal. *~ gangguan pencernaan* s.t. to get rid of indigestion. **peny-an** healing. **per-an** 1 recovery (from illness). 2 cure, healing.

sembul ber-(an) emerge, appear partially. **meny-** 1 appear partially, emerge. *Seékor ular ~ dr lubang itu* A snake appeared from the hole. 2 swell, bulge, protrude. *Matanya ~* His eyes bulged. **meny-kan** 1 hold out or up. *Ia ~ lengannya* He held his arm out. *Ia ~ kepalanya* He held up his

head. 2 make s.t. protrude, appear. *Pintu sél terbuka. Mési ~ kepalanya dan msk* The door of the cell was open. Mesi stuck in her head and entered. **ter-** 1 emerge, appear. 2 be outstanding. *Dlm keluarga itu ~ seorg gadis manis* In the family a beautiful girl stood out.

sembuni, sembunyi 1 hidden, concealed. 2 hide. *Ia pergi - karena menyangka kita tentara* She went into hiding because she thought we were soldiers. **-²** secretly. *Ia menulis surat itu dgn ~* She wrote the letter in secret. *~ puyuh* head-in-the-sand policy. **ber-** hide o.s. *Ia ~ di bawah tempat tidur* She hid under the bed. **meny-kan** 1 hide s.t. *Ia ~ uangnya* He hid his money. 2 conceal, suppress. *Ia ~ kesalahannya* He concealed his faults. **ter-** 1 hidden. *perasaan ~* hidden feelings. 2 stealthily. **ke-an** secret, mystery. **-²an** hide-and-seek. **peny-an** act of hiding s.t. **per-an** shelter, hiding place, hide-away.

sembur spittle, esp. when sprayed as a charm to cure s.o. **ber-(²)an** be spit out in quantity, be sprayed out. **meny-** 1 squirt, spurt. *Keringat dingin ~* He broke out in a cold sweat. 2 spray spit at. *Ia ~ muka polisi* He spat all over the policeman's face. **meny-²** keep spraying out. **meny-kan** spray or spout s.t. out. *Kompor gas ~ api yg lebih panas* A gas stove gives off a better flame. **ter-** 1 sprayed, sprinkled, squirted. 2 be scolded. *~ gelak* burst into laughter. **-an** 1 outpouring, spraying out. *~ lava* outpouring of lava. 2 scolding. **peny-** instrument for spraying. *~ api* flame thrower. **peny-an** act of spraying.

semburat 1 tinge. *berwarna - kelabu* tinged with gray. 2 disperse. **ber-kan** be tinged with. **meny-** sparkle.

semburit sodomy. *main -* engage in sodomy. **ber-** engage in sodomy. **meny-i** sodomize.

semedi, semédi see SEMADI.

semek soggy. **ny-²** become soggy.

seméméh soiled, dirty.

semén cement. *- bata/mérah* pulverized bricks. *- beton* concrete. **meny-** cement.

semena see MENA.

semenanjung (*Geog.*) peninsula.

semenda related by marriage. **ber-, meny-** be related by marriage. *Ia ~ ke raja Minangkabau di Pagaruyung* He was related (by marriage) to the Minangkabau sultan in Pagaruyung.

semendal (*Geog.*) mica.

semenggah proper, seemly. *Kelakuannya tdk -* He did not behave properly.

semenjak (*Lit.*) since.

semenjana mediocre.

sementang see MENTANG.

sementara₁ 1 while. *- menunggu ibunya ia mendengarkan radio* While he was waiting for his mother, he listened to the radio. *- itu* 1 in the meantime. 2 at the same time. 2 provisional, temporary, interim. *tindakan -* temporary measure. *Undang-undang Dasar -* provisional constitution. *laporan -* interim report. *utk - for the time being. *Ia datang utk - saja* He just came for a while. *Itu sdh cukup utk* - It was enough for the time being. *utk - (waktu)* for the moment. **ke-an** transitoriness, temporariness. *status* ~ temporary status.

sementara₂ a certain unnamed party. *Kalau ini tdk disenangi - org . . .* If there are certain parties that do not like this . . .

semér see SEMIR.

semerap absorbent, absorptive.

semerbak 1 fragrant. *Bunga-bungaan itu - baunya* The flowers were fragrant. **2** pervade (fragrance).

semesta, semésta whole, entire, total. *- alam* universe. *atlas - dunia* world atlas. *rencana pembangunan -* overall development plan. **ke-an** totality. **-an** universalism.

semi young shoot. **ber-, meny-** sprout. *Di hatinya ~ harapan lagi* Hope sprouted anew in her heart.

sémi loose, improperly fixed, unbalanced, out of gear. *Stirnya sdh -* Its steering wheel is out of balance.

semiang see MIANG.

sémi-final 1 (*Sport*) semi-finals. **2** semifinal.

sémi-finalis semifinalist.

semilih alternating. **meny-** alternate.

semilir breezy (of wind).

seminar see SINAR.

séminar seminar. **meny-kan** hold a seminar on. *Tatabahasa Indonésia di-kan* They held a seminar on Indonesian grammar.

séminari (*Rel.*) seminary.

séminaris (*Rel.*) seminarian.

semingkin see MINGKIN.

sémiotika semiotics.

semir polish. *- oli* lubricating oil. *- sepatu* shoe polish. **meny- 1** to polish. **2** spread s.t. oily or greasy on, lubricate. *Ayahnya ~ roti utk anak-anaknya* Her father spread butter on the children's bread. **3** bribe, grease the palm. *Pegawai itu hrs di- spy izin kita cepat ke luar* That official has to have his palms greased in order to have our permit issued fast. **meny-kan** polish, smear on to s.t. **ter-** polished. **peny- 1** s.o. who polishes shoes. **2** s.t. to polish with.

semisal see MISAL.

semoga see MOGA.

semokel smuggling. **meny-** smuggle.

semokelar (*Coll.*) smuggler.

sempadan 1 border, demarcation. **2** (*Sport*) finishing line. **ber-** border on. **meny-i** delimit.

sémpak₁ chipped.

sémpak₂ see SWÉMPAK.

sempal₁ meny-, ter- 1 stick. *Sebatang jarum ~ dlm kerongkongannya* A needle stuck in his throat. **2** gag. *Ia ~ mulut saya dgn sehelai kain* He gagged me with a piece of cloth.

sempal₂ (*Jv*) broken, chipped. **-an** fragment. *kelompok ~* (*Pol.*) splinter group.

sempana see SEMPENA.

sémpang meny- trip s.o.

sémpar meny- push, hurl s.t.

sempat 1 have sufficient time, opportunity. *Ia tak - datang* He did not have time to come. *Tdk semua cerpén - diterbitkan* Not all short stories can be published. **2** still be able to do s.t. *Kau masih kecil ketika ayahmu meninggal. - kau ingat muka-nya?* You were small when your father died. Do you still remember what he looked like? **meny-** await an opportunity. **meny-i** find opportunity for s.t. **meny-kan 1** make use of. *Ia ~ waktu mengunjungiku di rumah sakit* She used the time to visit me in the hospital. **2** give o. time. *Ia tiada ~ saya belajar* He did not give me time to study. **ke-an 1** opportunity. *~ utk bertanya diberikan* There was opportunity to ask questions. *~ kerja* work opportunity. **2** occasion. *~ resmi* official occasion. **berke-an** have an opportunity, time. *Ia tiada ~ menyelesaikan pelajarannya* He had no opportunity to complete his studies.

sempé k.o. waffle, wafer.

sémpé (*Amb*) k.o. earthenware bowl.

sempelah 1 rubbish, dregs. **2** useless, of no value.

sempena blessing. **meny-kan** bless s.t.

sempena hati conscience.

sémpér paralyzed.

semperit see SEMPRIT₁.

semperong see SEMPRONG.

semperot see SEMPROT₁.

sempil meny-, ter- stick out so that a small part can be seen. *Dr bawah bantal putih itu kelihatan ~ sebuah buku mérah* You could see a red book sticking out from underneath the white pillow.

sempit 1 narrow, tight. *Jalan itu -* The street was narrow. *pandangan -* a narrow-minded viewpoint. *- ketat* tight-fitting (of dress, etc.). **2** pressed, limited. *Waktu saya - sekali* I was pressed for time. *- hati* a hothead. **ber-²** packed like sardines. **meny-** tighten, narrow, constrict. *Jalan ~* The road narrows. **meny-kan, memper-** narrow, constrict, tighten s.t. *Méja itu ~ kamar saya* The table made my room small. **ke-an 1** narrowness, narrow-mindedness. **2** being hard-pressed, shortage. *~ hidup* poverty, straitened circumstances. **3** too narrow. **-an** narrow passage. **peny-an** constriction, stricture. *~ pembuluh nadi* (*Med.*) arteriosclerosis.

sempoa (*Ch*) abacus.

sempor see CEMPOR.

sempoyongan totter, stagger from drunkenness.

semprit₁ a whistle. **meny-** blow (a whistle). **meny-i** blow a whistle at. *Polisi itu - saya* The policeman blew a whistle at me. **-an** whistle (sound).

semprit₂ S-shaped cookie made of sago or tapioca flour.

semprong 1 lamp chimney. **2** chimney, smokestack, ship's funnel. **3** tube, telescope.

semprot₁ syringe, squirt gun. **meny- 1** spray. **2** scold. *Pak guru ~ muridnya dgn kata-kata kasar* The teacher scolded the children with harsh words. **meny-i** spray. *Pohon itu di-i* The tree was sprayed. **meny-kan 1** squirt s.t. out. *Air mandi di-kan dr atas* Water for bathing was squirted out from above. **2** inject, spray. **ter-** sprayed, squirted. **-an 1** syringe, squirt gun. **2** scolding. **peny-** syringe, sprayer. **peny-an** spraying. ~ *tanah* landfill activities.

semprot₂ S-shaped cookie made of sago or tapioca flour.

semprul (*Jv*) mild swear word: you jerk!

sempurat see SEMBURAT.

sempurna 1 perfect. *Pekerjaannya selalu dikerjakan dgn -* He always did his job perfectly. **2** complete. *Kalimatmu itu blm -* Your sentence is not complete yet. *- umur* grown-up. **se-** as complete or perfect as. **meny-kan 1** perfect. **2** complete s.t. **3** be given a proper ceremony. *Ia minta di-kan, dikubur spt manusia makhluk ilahi* He asked to have a proper funeral ceremony, to be buried like o. of God's creatures. **ke-an 1** perfection. **2** completeness. **peny-1** s.t. to perfect. **2** o. who perfects s.t. **peny-an** action of perfecting, completing, finishing (articles, products).

semrawut chaotic, disorganized. *Lalulintas di Vietnam sangat -* Traffic in Vietnam is totally disorganized. *Koran-koran - di pasaran* Newspapers were lying around all over the market. **ke-an 1** chaos, lack of organization. **2** be chaotic, disorderly.

semsem see SENGSEM.

semu 1 appearance, micn. *Negara itu mempunyai pemerintahan démokrat yg - saja* The gvt. of that country was democratic in appearance only. **2** apparent, pseudo-, quasi-. *kemenangan - a* pseudovictory. **3** deceit, trick. *Ia kena - kemarin* He was deceived yesterday. **-²** more or less, roughly like this. **ber-** having the appearance of being (but not being so). *Dgn wajah ~ sedih dia datang ke upacara pemakaman musuhnya* She came to her enemy's funeral with a face that appeared sad (but was not). *air yg ~ biru* water that appears to be blue. **meny-i, meny-kan** deceive, trick. *Ia suka ~ org lain* He likes to deceive others. **ter-** tricked, deceived. **peny-** impostor.

semua all. *- katanya itu bohong belaka* All his words were just lies. **-nya** all (of them), everything. *Berikan dia ~* Give him all of them. **-muanya** anything and everything. *~ selalu dibandinghan nya dgn Éropah* He always compares everything with Europe. **ke-nya** all of it, everything. *Topi détéktip, kaca mata, sepatu, celana yg ~ berwarna hitam* A detective hat, glasses, shoes, pants, all of them black. **ke-an** totality. *~ penyelenggaraan* totality of implementation.

semudera see SAMUDERA.

semuhun-dawuhisme see SUMUHUN-DAWUHISME.

semuka see MUKA.

semula see MULA.

semur dish of meat and sometimes bean curd, tempeh, etc. stewed with spices. **meny-** stew.

semut ant. *- yg jauh kelihatan tapi gajah di depan mata tak tampak* see the mote in o.'s brother's eye and not the beam in o.'s own (lit., see an ant from afar but not the elephant in front of o.'s eyes). *- gatal* small red ant with a toxic bite. *- keranggal*

keranggang/kerangkang/rangrang k.o. red ant. *- sentada* k.o. ant. **meny-** swarm, teem. *Org ~ di tanah lapang itu* People were swarming over the square. **ke-(²)an, -an** go to sleep, become numb (as of arm or leg). *Kaki saya ~* My foot's gone to sleep.

sén₁ cent. **-an 1** o.-cent piece. **2** in cents.

sén₂ (*Auto.*) mechanical turning signal. *lampu -* turning signal.

sena k.o. timber tree, narra.

senak 1 tight, oppressed. *Napasnya -* He had a tightness in his chest. **2** having a stuffed feeling (from overeating). **meny-** be pressing, be oppressive. **meny-kan** oppress. *Ia tak tahu apa yg ~ dadanya* He did not know what was oppressing his chest. **ter-** tongue-tied, having a lump in the throat such that o. has difficulty speaking. **ke-an 1** having a stuffed feeling (from overeating). **2** having an oppressed feeling. **ke-²an** suffer from s.t. oppressive.

senam₁ (*Sport*) gymnastics, calisthenics. *- jantung* panic, pounding of the heart. **ber- 1** do physical exercises. **2** stretch (after resting). **pe-** gymnast.

senam₂ indigo blue.

senamaki senna, a purgative.

senandung a hum. **ber-** hum. **meny-kan** hum s.t. *Aku ~ lagu itu* I hummed that song.

senang 1 happy, contented. *- hati* contented, satisfied. **ber-** *hati* be pleased. **2** like. *Aku - rumah ini, dan aku - akan ketenangannya* I like this house and I like its peacefulness. **3** comfortable. *tak - ill* at ease. **-²** gladly. *Belanda ~ mengambil hak kita* The Dutch didn't mind depriving us of our rights. **ber-²** enjoy o.s., have a good time. *Kau melarang dia ~ dan bermain-main* You forbid him to relax and have a good time. **meny-i** like s.t. *Saya ~ pekerjaan saya* I like my work. **meny-kan** please, gratify. *jawaban yg ~ a* satisfying answer. *Saya hanya senyum utk ~ hati suamiku* I only smile to please my husband. **memper-(kan)** amuse, do s.o. a favor. **ke-an 1** happiness, contentment, pleasure. *mencari ~ pd laki-laki lain* seek pleasure with other men. **2** favorite. *Rokok kréték ~ Abu* Clove cigarettes were Abu's favorite. **peny- 1** s.o. or s.t. which gives pleasure or comfort. **2** entertainer.

senantiasa always.

senapan, senapang rifle, gun. *- angin* air rifle. *- buluh* bamboo toy gun. *- cis* k.o. small-cartridge rifle. *- kembar* double-barreled shotgun. *- lantak(an)* k.o. rifle loaded at the muzzle. *- mesin* machine gun. *- mimis* air rifle. **ber-** have a rifle.

sénapati (*Jv*) commander in chief.

senar string (of musical instrument, racquet, for fishing, etc.). *- hati* heartstrings.

sénat 1 (*Acad.*) faculty senate. **2** (*Pol.*) senate.

senawi boat passenger who is working his way.

senda *- canda/gurau* joke, banter. **ber-** *canda/gurau* joke, banter back and forth. **per-gurauan** butt of jokes. **ber-** joke. **memper-kan** make fun of s.o.

sendal see SANDAL.

sendang (*Jv*) spring, source.

sendat stagnant, not flowing freely (water or, figuratively, s.t. else). *Suaranya* - Her voice is choked. **meny-²** be choked off. *Napasnya mengengah dan* ~ He huffed and puffed (his breath came in bursts). **meny-kan** cause s.t. to be choked up or stagnante. **ter-** 1 choked up. *Jono* ~ *dlm bercerita ini* Jono was choked up (with emotion) as he told his story. **2** clogged up. **3** stagnating, at a standstill. *Pelaksanaannya masih* ~ Action on it is still at a standstill. **ter-²** choked off again and again. *irama yg* ~ a choppy rhythm. *Kali itu tetap mengalir walaupun* ~ The river continues to flow, although it was sluggish and erratic. **ke-an** 1 clogged up. **2** stagnation.

sendawa₁ saltpeter, gunpowder.

sendawa₂ a burp. **ber-** belch.

séndél lean on.

séndéng 1 slanting, leaning. **2** mentally off. **meny-** lean, slant. **meny-kan** tilt s.t. **ter-²** totter, stagger.

sénder (*Coll.*) transmitting station.

séndér see SANDAR.

sendera see SANDERA.

sendi 1 hinge, joint. - *éngsél* hinge (joint). - *peluru* (*Anat.*) ball-and-socket joint. - *rangka* spinal column. - *tulang* every bone in o.'s body. **2** socket. **3** pivotal strength, principle. - *Pakét April 9* the principles underlying the economic reforms of April 9. - *negara* pivotal strength of the state (that which the state hinges on). **ber-** hinged on, based. *Bukankah adat* ~ *agama?* Does not traditional law hinge on religion? **ber-kan** have as a pivotal point. **ber-²** with joints. **meny-kan, memper-kan** make s.t. pivotal. **per-an** 1 pivot, base. **2** the body joints. *gerakan* ~ movement of the joints.

sendiri 1 self (the intensifier). *Dia - tdk mau* He himself does not want to. *dgn -(nya)* automatically, it is taken for granted. **2** own. *Itu anaknya -* That is her own child. *Saya lihat dgn mata saya -* I saw it with my own two eyes. **3** on o.'s own. *berdiri -* stand on o.'s own. **4** (*Jv*) most. *yg pandai* - the cleverest. *tempat duduk yg di muka -* The seat that is at the very front (of the bus). **-²** individual, apart. *Tiap-tiap benda hrs diterangkan* ~ Every article must be declared individually. *Masing-masing dgn maksudnya* ~ Each with his own individual goal. **ber-, meny-** 1 be alone, apart, separated. **2** be aloof, isolate o.s. *Ia* ~ *tak mau bergaul* He isolated himself, unwilling to mix with others. **meny-kan** isolate s.o. or s.t. **ter-** 1 alone, individual, separate. *Dia duduk agak di pojok* ~ He was sitting away in a corner, all by himself. **2** special, different from others. *Bibiku mempunyai filsafat* ~ My aunt has her own special philosophy. **keter-an** solitude, isolation. **ke-an** aloneness, solitude. **-an** alone. *Ambé berani jalan* ~? Aren't you afraid to walk all by yourself, Ambé? **peny-** solitary, liking to be alone, loner. **peny-an** isolation. ~ *golongan* group isolation.

séndok 1 spoon. - *bubur* a spoon intermediate in size between a tablespoon and a teaspoon. -

makan tablespoon. - *téh* teaspoon. **2** ladle. **3** spoonlike tool (e.g. trowel, etc.). - *ban* (*Auto*) metal bar used in taking tires off the rim. - *sepatu* shoe horn. **ber-²** by the spoonful. **meny-** 1 ladle up, ladle out, spoon. ~ *gula* spoon in sugar. **2** scoop up, scoop out. *Ia* ~ *sirih tumbukan itu ke dlm mulutnya* She scooped the pounded betel leaf into her mouth. **meny-i** 1 skim. **2** spoonfeed. **meny-kan** spoon out on behalf on s.o.

sendorong ter- slide forward.

sendratari [*seni, drama, dan tari*] (*Thea.*) dance-drama, ballet. **meny-kan** perform s.t. as a dance-drama.

sendu sad. **ke-an** sadness.

senduduk k.o. flowering shrub, melastoma.

senduk see SÉNDOK.

senél see SEPUR.

Senén Monday. *berpuasa - (dan) Kemis* fast on Mondays and Thursdays. *--kemis* precarious (that is, in a situation where o. should intensify religious duties, e.g. fast on Mondays and Thursdays). *Napasnya sdh --kemis* He is on his last legs.

senentiasa see SENANTIASA.

senéwen nervous, have a nervous fit.

séng 1 zinc. **2** iron sheeting. - *atap/gelombang/kerdut* corrugated iron sheets (used for roofing). **3** roofing. - *asbés* asbestos-tiled roof.

sengaja intentional, deliberate, expressly. *Orang yg - ditugaskan utk . . .* A person who was expressly given the duties of . . . **meny-** do on purpose. *Meletus di mulutku dgn tdk di- . . .* I blurted out unintentionally . . . **meny-kan** do s.t. on purpose. *Dulu aku -kan memilih ayat yg panjang* Formerly, I deliberately chose verses that were long. **ke-an** deliberateness, doing s.t. on purpose. *unsur* ~ an element of deliberateness.

sengak₁ 1 pungent, piercing in smell (like vinegar, etc.). *--senguk* repeatedly sniff. **2** obnoxious.

sengak₂ ter- 1 have a spasm in o.'s limb. **2** be surprised.

sengal painful joints. **-²** pains. ~ *pinggang* lumbago.

sengal-sengal out of breath, having difficulty breathing. **ter-** being difficult (of breathing). *Napasnya* ~ She breathed with difficulty.

sengam meny- eat up, devour gluttonously.

sengap quiet, silent. **meng-** stop noise, shut s.o. or s.t. up.

sengat the sting (organ) of certain insects. **ber-** have a stinger. **meny-** sting s.o. or s.t. *di- lebah* stung by a bee. *Panas matahari itu* ~ The heat of the sun is stinging. **ter-** stung. **-an** pain or wound resulting from a sting. ~ *lebah* bee sting. ~ (*terik*) *matahari* the sting inflicted by the heat of the sun. **peny-** 1 s.t. that stings. *bangsat-bangsat* ~ stinging bedbugs. **2** wasp.

sengau talk through the nose, nasal. **meny-(kan)** nasalize, make a sound come through the nose. **ter-kan** nasalized. **-an** nasalized sound. **peny-an, per-an** nasalization.

séngét 1 slanted. *matahari - di belakang méga* The sunrays slanted from behind the clouds. 2 placed on o. side. **meny-** slant, be at an angle. **meny-kan** put s.t. on an angle. **ter-** slanting. *Selimutnya ~, karena itu ia kedinginan* His blanket was arranged on an angle so he was cold.

senggak₁ snarl. *"Diam kau!" - Haris galak* "Shut up!" Haris snarled fiercely. **meny-(²)** speak harshly, growl. *Serdadu itu ~ berkata pd Ibu* That mercenary snarled what he had to say to Mother.

senggak₂ (*Jv*) applaud, cheer (in dancing and singing).

senggama coitus. *- terputus* coitus interruptus. **ber-** have coitus. **per-an** coital act.

sengganen k.o. flowering shrub, melastoma.

senggang be free, unoccupied (of time). *waktu -* free time. **ber-²** relax, pass o.'s free time. **meny-kan** free (time), allow (time) for. **ke-an** leisureliness, leisure.

senggara see SELENGGARA.

senggayut **ber-** swing o.s. while hanging from the arms, dangle. *Beruk-beruk ~ dr dahan ke dahan* The monkeys swung from branch to branch.

senggeruk (tobacco) snuff.

sénggol *pasar -* market packed so that people brush against e.o. **ber-(an)** touch e.o. **meny-1** nudge with the elbow, brush against. *Yg satu masih ~ sang gadis* O. of them kept allowing himself to brush against the girl. 2 brush against. *Ia hampir ~ kendaraan lain* He nearly scraped another vehicle. **ter-, ke-** touched, hit. *~ motor* bumped into by a motorbike. **-an** a shove, push, nudge. **-²an** repeated nudging.

senggugut irregular menstrual periods.

sengguk₁ **meny-** repeatedly nod (often from weariness). **ter-** 1 nod (from sleepiness). 2 hit o.'s head (on a door frame, etc.).

sengguk₂ see SESENGGUKAN.

senggulung millipede.

senggut strike sideways (e.g. a gong, etc.).

sengih **meny-** 1 open o.'s mouth a little. 2 smile, grin. **meny-kan** cause to open (the mouth). *~ gigi* grin. *~ senyum* force a smile.

sengir₁ turpentinelike, having the sharp acrid taste of an orange peel. **meny-, ny-** turn up o.'s nose, make a wry face (due to s.t. distasteful). *Ia pernah ~ di hadapan yg empunya warung* She once turned up her nose at the owner of the stall.

sengir₂ see CENGIR.

sengit 1 k.o. stinging insect. 2 sharp (odor, words, etc.). *Kata-katanya -* Her words were stinging. 3 violent. *pertempuran -* a bitter fight. 4 poignant, bitter (emotions). **ber-** feel bitter. **ber-²an** feel angry at e.o. *Sdh lama kedua tetangga itu ~* For a long time the two neighbors had bitter feelings toward e.o. **ke-an** acrimony, fierceness.

séngit see SÉNGÉT.

sengkak **meny-** massage the abdomen with an upward motion.

sengkala see SANGKAKALA.

sengkalan (*Jv*) chronogram. *- memet* pictorial rebus suggesting a date. *- sastra* rebus of letters suggesting a date.

sengkang 1 crossbar. 2 spoke of wheel. 3 (*Math.*) diameter of a circle. 4 dash, hyphen. **meny-1** arrange a crossbar on s.t. *~ mulut buaya* put a vertical bar in a crocodile's mouth (to keep it from closing). 2 have a fish bone, etc. caught in the throat.

séngkang with legs far apart.

sengkar (*Lit.*) removable plank deck on a sail boat.

sengkarut chaos. **ber-** 1 intertwined, interlaced. 2 confused.

séngkéh see SINGKÉH.

sengkelang, sengkeling crossing (of arms or legs). **meny-kan** cross (arms or legs).

sengkelit₁ a loop worn around o.'s legs for shimmying up tree trunks.

sengkelit₂ (*Jv*) the wearing of a kris stuck in a belt at the back of o.'s waist. **meny-** be worn in this way. *Keris ~ di pinggang Ayah* Dad had a kris in the back of his belt. **meny-kan** attach to o.'s waist-belt. *Seruling itu di-kan di pinggangnya* The flute was attached to his belt.

sengkenit k.o. jungle tick.

sengkéta 1 (*Leg.*) lawsuit, legal action. 2 quarrel, dispute. **ber-** have a legal dispute. **meny-kan, memper-kan** dispute, quarrel over s.t. *Keluarga itu mau ~ tanah itu* The family wanted to dispute the (ownership of the) land. **per-an** contention, dispute, conflict. *~ perburuhan* labor dispute.

sengkilit (*Jkt*) **meny-** 1 trip up by tying or grabbing a leg. 2 cheat s.o.

séngkong see SINGKONG.

sengkuang 1 plant with a white edible tuber (*Pachyrrhizus sp.*). 2 k.o. tree.

sengkuap (*Lit.*) shed, awning.

sengsai wretched.

séngsai see SINSÉ.

sengsara 1 misery, suffering. 2 suffer, be miserable. **meny-kan** torment s.o. **ke-an** misery, suffering, torment.

sengsé see SINSÉ.

sengsem (*Jv*) **ke-** 1 highly attracted to s.t. 2 absorbed, engrossed in. *Ia ~ mengurusi hotél ini* She was engrossed in managing the hotel.

senguk (*Jv*) **meny-** sniff.

sengut frown. **ter-²** sob uncontrollably.

seni₁ 1 refined, fine. *suara yg -* high-pitched voice. 2 art. *- pahat/patung* sculpture. *- sungging* enameling. *- taman* landscaping. *- lukis* art of painting. **ke-lukisan** matters pertaining to the art of painting. *dunia ke-lukisan* the world of painting. *- rupa* plastic arts (painting, sculpture, etc.), fine arts. *- suara* 1 art of music. 2 singing (as subject in school). **ber-** artistic. **ny-** (*Coll.*) arty. **ke-an** things having to do with art. *cita-cita ~* artistic aspirations.

seni₂ see AIR.

séni see ZÉNI₁,₂.

seniah artistic. **ke-an** artistry.

seniman artist. *Lagaknya spt - sinting* He puts on airs, thinking he is some k.o. artist or s.t. **ke-an** artistic, matters pertaining to artists. *citra ~* artistic image.

Senin see SENÉN.

sénior 1 senior, o. who has more authority, o. with more experience, etc. 2 Sr. (after a name). 3 (*Coll.*) male university seniors. 4 (*Coll.*) hazing of incoming freshmen.

sénioren (*Coll.*) hazing of incoming freshmen.

séniorita (*Coll.*) female university seniors.

senirupa plastic arts, fine arts.

senirupawan artist.

seniwati female artist.

senja twilight, dusk. *- buta* late twilight. *- kala* twilight.

senjak see SEJAK₁.

senjang₁ 1 asymmetrical, imbalanced. 2 differing, unlike. **ke-an** asymmetry, discrepancy. *mempertajam ~ sosial* exacerbate social imbalance. *~ antara negara industri dan dunia ketiga* the gap between the developed and the 3d world nations. *~ génerasi* generation gap.

senjang₂ see SENJA.

senjata₁ 1 weapon. *- makan tuan* 1 s.t. that backfires, turns against o. 2 Evil done to others comes back to the perpetrator. 2 rifle, gun. *- angin* air rifle. *- api* firearms. *- berat* heavy artillery. *- lantak* a barrel-loaded gun. *- lengkung* mortar. *- ringan* small arms. **ber-** 1 armed. *gerombolan ~* armed band. *~ lengkap* fully armed. 2 armed with s.t. *Hasan ~ panah dan adiknya ~ pedang* Hassan was armed with a bow and his brother with a sword. **ber-kan** armed with .s.t. *serdadu ~ bedil* a mercenary armed with a gun. **memper-i** arm s.t. *Kapal selam yg di-i peluru kendali* submarines armed with guided missiles. **ke-an** weaponry, matters pertaining to weapons. *sistém ~* weapons system. **per-an** armament, arms, weaponry.

senjata₂ (*Lit.*) a vowel sign in Arabic script.

senjolong see IKAN.

senonoh proper, polite. *tdk -* improper, obscene.

sénopati see SÉNAPATI.

sénsasi sensation, sensational news.

sénsasional, sénsasionil sensational.

sénsé see SINSÉ.

sénsitif sensitive.

sénsitivitas sensitivity.

sénsor, sénsur censor. **meny-** censor s.t. **peny-** censor. **peny-an** censoring.

sénsus census. **meny-** take a census.

senta wooden beam attached lengthwise to the ribs of a boat to support the deck.

sentadu see BELALANG₁.

sentak₁ (*Jv*) **meny-** snap at s.o., verbally abuse s.o., tongue-lash.

sentak₂, séntak pull, pull out. **meny-** pull at s.t. **meny-kan** 1 pull at, jerk at. *Meréka ~ pintu jeriji itu* They rattled the grated door. 2 startle s.o. *Itulah suara yg ~ dia dr alam mimpi* That was the voice that startled him out of his dreams. **meny-²**

repeatedly jerk at s.t. *Tali di léhérnya di-²* The rope around her neck was yanked over and over. **ter-** give a start, be startled. *~ bangun* wake up with a start. *Frédi ~ dr lamunannya* Freddy snapped out of his daydreams. **-an** a jerk, jolt. *Oléh suatu ~, senjata itu terpelanting* Because of the backfire, the gun fell to the floor.

sental₁ meny- rub hard, scour, scrub.

sental₂ see SINTAL.

sentana₁ (*Lit.*) possible. *kalau -* suppose, if for instance. **ber-** with the possibility. *dgn tdk ~* without further ado.

sentana₂ (*Jv*) relative by birth or adoption.

sentana₃ (*Jv*) cemetery.

sentana₄ see SANTANA₁.

sentap see SENTAK₁.

sentara see SEMENTARA₁.

sentausa see SENTOSA.

sénténg₁ in short supply, fall short, insufficient. **ke-an** scarcity, shortage.

sénténg₂ see SINTING.

sénter₁ flashlight, spotlight. **meny-** shine, light. *Proyéktor ~ ke arah témbok* The projector shone in the direction of the wall. **meny-i** 1 light with a flashlight. 2 expose (in photography). **-an** s.t. shone, s.t. projected as a focused light. *menghindari cahaya ~ proyéktor* avoid the projector's light beam.

sénter₂ (*Sport*) center. **meny-** 1 center (a ball). 2 play as a center.

sénterhaf (*Sport*) center half-back.

senteri see SANTRI.

sénterpor (*Sport*) center forward.

sénti centimeter.

sentiasa see SENANTIASA.

sentil₁ ter- protrude a little.

sentil₂ meny- 1 (*Jkt*) snap o.'s fingers. 2 flick s.t. with o.'s finger, snap o.'s fingers at s.t. *~ kuping* hit the ear with a fillip. *Mardi ~ dua ékor pacat dr kakinya* Mardi flicked two leeches from his leg. 3 criticize, reprimand. **-an** scolding, criticism.

séntimén 1 grudge, bad feeling, bias. 2 have or hold a grudge, have ill feelings. *Jangan - begitu!* Do not hold a grudge! **ber-** bear grudges, have ill feelings. **meny-i** have bad feelings toward or on account of.

séntiméntal sentimental. **ke-an** sentimentality, bathos.

séntiméntalitas, sentimentalitét sentimentality.

séntiméntil see SÉNTIMÉNTAL.

séntiméter centimeter.

senting₁ k.o. shrub used for fences or fertilizer.

senting₂ (*M*) difficult.

sentiong (*Jkt*) Ch graveyard.

sentolop flashlight.

sentong (*Jv*) small inner room of a house (traditionally used for family ceremonies or as a storage room).

sentosa 1 quiet, tranquil. 2 safe. **ber-** peaceful, safe. **meny-kan** 1 protect. 2 provide rest and safety. **ke-an** 1 peace, tranquillity, rest. 2 safety.

séntral 1 central. *pasar -* the central market.

2 center. - *industri* industrial center. - *listrik* central power station.
séntralisasi centralization. **meny-kan** centralize.
séntralisér mens- centralize.
séntralisme centralism.
séntralistis centralistic.
sentrap-sentrup (*Jv*) nasal, esp. of s.o. speaking while weeping or suffering from a cold.
séntrifugal centrifugal.
séntrifuse centrifuge. **mens-kan** centrifuge s.t. ~ *latéks* put latex through a centrifuge.
séntris centrally (located). *daérah* - centrally located area.
séntrum 1 center. - *pengolahan berita* news processing center. **2** (*Geol.*) centrum.
sentuh ber- touch, be in physical contact. **ber-an** have contact with, touching e.o. **ber-²an** repeatedly come in contact with e.o. *Cangkir-cangkir mulai* ~ The cups began to rattle against e.o. **meny-** touch s.t., nudge. *Aku takkan* ~ *tubuhmu!* I will not even touch your body! *Golok itu* ~ *kakinya* That machete was touching her leg. ~ *jiwa* touch o.'s soul. **meny-(²)kan** cause s.t. to touch, touch with s.t. *Berani dia* ~ *kakinya pd kakiku!* He had the nerve to brush his foot up next to mine. **ter- 1** touched. **2** slightly nudged. **-an** touch, contact. ~ *hati* emotional sensitivity. ~ *terakhir* finishing touch. **peny-** s.t. that touches, s.t. touching. ~ *hati nurani* s.t. that touches o.'s deepest feelings. **per-an** contact, touch.
sentul k.o. tall, tree bearing yellow fruit similar to the mangosteen but sour.
sentung pelalai a charm which prevents a woman from obtaining a husband.
senuh full feeling from overeating.
senut-senut feeling of gnawing pain.
senyak see NYENYAK.
senyampang see NYAMPANG.
senyap₁ 1 very quiet, deserted. **2** silent, quiet. **3** sound asleep. **ke-an** silence. ~ *alam* silence of nature.
senyap₂ see LENYAP.
senyar funny bone, numb sensation from bumping the ulnar nerve in o.'s elbow.
senyawa see NYAWA.
senyum 1 a smile. - *hambar* 1 expressionless smile. **2** forced smile. - *kambing* grin. - *kecut* a grim smile. - *kuda* sheepish smile. - *sumbang* cynical smile. - *simpul* smile out of embarrassment. - *sinis* cynical smile. - *tipis* a slight smile. **2** smile. **-²** repeatedly smile. **ber-(²)an** smile at e.o. *Meréka minum kopi berduaan,* ~ They drank coffee together, smiling at e.o. **meny-i** smile at s.o. *Dia selalu* ~ *saya* She always smiles at me. **meny-kan** make s.o. smile. *Kaulah yg akhirnya* ~ *aku* It is you who finally made me smile. **ter-** smile. *Ia memaksa dirinya* ~ He forced himself to smile. *Amin* ~ *kecut mendengar ujiannya gagal* Amin smiled grimly when he heard he had failed the exam. **-an** a smile.
senyur₁ see SINYO.

senyur₂ see INSINYUR.
séok-séok, séot-séot sound of s.t. dragged. *Terdengarlah - langkah dr luar* O. could hear dragging footfalls outside. **ber-** make a dragging sound. **ter-** drag o.'s feet. *Aku* ~ *menuju ke bundaran Harmoni* I dragged my feet heading for the Harmoni traffic circle.
sep- see also entries with **sp-**.
sép₁ (*Coll.*) o. in charge (of an office, railway station, etc.). **ber-** acknowledge as o.'s superior.
sép₂ see SIP.
sépa (*Jv, Jkt*) flat, uninteresting, with no spices.
sepada (*Coll.*) anybody in? (said when entering shop or home).
sepadan see PADAN₁.
sepah a chew of s.t., remains of s.t. already chewed or sucked on. - *raja* k.o. bird of paradise. - *tebu* indigestible fibers that remain after chewing on a piece of sugarcane. - *tembakau* quid of tobacco spit out after chewing it. **meny-** chew on s.t. to extract its juices.
sépah ter- in disorder, scattered around.
sépak a kick. - *bola* soccer. **per-bolaan** soccer affairs. - *raga* k.o. game, similar to kickball, played with a plaited rattan ball, traditional in Sulawesi and Sumatra. - *takraw/takro* k.o. game similar to *sépak raga* but with a specific number of players in opposing teams which play on opposite sides of a net. - *terjang* 1 kick, ill-treat. 2 behavior, activity. - *terjangnya sopan* Her behavior is modest. **meny-** kick. *Mayat-mayat di-nya barangkali ada yg masih hidup* He kicked the corpses to be sure that no o. was still alive. ~ *sila* kick with the inside of o.'s foot. ~ *singkur* kick with the outside of o.'s foot. **-an 1** kicking. **2** kick. ~ *kakinya mengenai tubuh nona Tionghoa* In his kicking he hit a young Ch woman.
sepakat see PAKAT₁.
sepakbor see SPATBOR.
sepala-pala see PALA₂.
sepalek see SPALEK.
sepan tightly, tight. *rok* - tight-fitting skirt. **meny-** fit tightly.
sepandri private first class (in the colonial army).
sepanduk see SPANDUK.
sepang k.o. tree the wood of which produces a red dye.
sepanjang see PANJANG.
sepantun see PANTUN₂.
Sepanyol Spain, Spanish.
séparasi separation.
séparatis separatist.
séparatisme separatism.
separo, separoh, separuh see PARO.
sepasan see SEPESAN.
sepasar see PASAR.
sepasi see SPASI.
sepat₁ astringent to the taste.
sepat₂ k.o. fresh water fish found in flooded rice fields.
sepatbor see SPATBOR.
sepatu shoe, footwear. - *air* water ski. - *big boss/*

Bruce Lee kung fu slippers, cotton slip-ons. - *(ber)duri* spiked shoes. - *bola* soccer shoes. - *és* skis. - *hak* high-heeled shoes. - *jéngki* short boots. - *jinjit* high-heeled shoes. - *karét* canvas shoes. - *katak* scuba flippers. - *kéts* canvas shoes. - *kuda* horseshoes. - *luar* overshoe, galosh. - *pantofel* slippers. - *rém* brake lining. - *roda* roller skates. **ber-** shod, wear shoes. **per-an** matters pertaining to shoes and shoemaking.

sepéda bicycle. - *balap* racing bicycle. - *érobik* exercise bicycle. - *jéngki* k.o. old-fashioned bicycle with a v-shaped bar connecting the seat and rear wheel with the handle-bars and front wheel. - *kumbang/motor* motorcycle. - *tandem* tandem bicycle. - *torpédo* bicycle with pedal brakes. **ber-** bike.

sepél (*Coll.*) **meny-** spell. **-an** spelling.

sepélé unimportant and trivial. *Anggap ini barang* - Consider this to be of no consequence. **meny-kan** belittle, consider insignificant (of s.t. which is worth consideration). *Dia jéngkél pekerjaannya di-kan* She was annoyed because her work was not considered important. **ke-an** triviality.

sepéling see SPÉLING.

sepemeluk see PELUK.

sepén 1 storage cupboard. **2** series of rooms in back used for storage, servants quarters, etc.

sepenggalah see GALAH₁.

sepeninggal see TINGGAL.

seperah see SUFRAH.

seperai, seperéi see SEPRAI.

seperti like, as. - *biasa* as usual. **-nya 1** as it should be, fittingly. *Kalau mau dpt hasil baik kerjakanlah yg* ~ If you want to get good results you should work properly. **2** it seems that, it is as if. ~ *saya tlh kenal wajah itu* It is as if I have seen that face before.

sepesan centipede.

sepésial see SPÉSIAL.

sepet see SEPAT₁.

sepi 1 quiet, still. **2** desolate, lonely. **3** slack (business market). *Dagang* - Business is dull. **meny-, ny- 1** grow still, become desolate. **2** retire into seclusion. *Ia suka* ~ *ke puncak gunung Lawu* She often goes in seclusion to the peak of Mt. Lawu. **memper-** make quieter or lonlier. **meny-kan 1** cause to be lonely. *Kehidupan ini* ~ *dan memencilkannya* This life made her lonely and isolated. **2** cause to be quiet. *Percakapan yg tak keruan dpt di-kannya* He made all that irresponsible talk die down. **ke-an 1** solitude, loneliness. *Hidupnya penuh* ~ Her life was full of loneliness. **2** deserted, lonely, (too) quiet.

sepidol see SPIDOL.

sepih see SERPIH.

sepintas see PINTAS.

sepion see SPION.

sepir see SIPIR, SPIR.

sepit 1 pincer (of lobster, crab, etc.). **2** tongs, tweezers. - *angkup* **1** pair of tweezers. **2** clothes peg. **meny-(kan)** pinch, squeeze. **ter-** be in a tight place. *Di ujung jarinya* ~ *rokok* She held a

cigarette between her fingertips. **-an** tongs, pincers, etc. **peny- 1** tweezers. **2** pincer (of lobster, crab, etc.).

sepoa see SEMPOA.

sepoi₁ (*Lit.*) sepoy, Indian mercenary soldier of colonial period.

sepoi₂ -² basa be gentle (of wind). **ber-** blow softly (of breeze).

sepon see SPON.

sepor see SEPUR.

seporos see POROS.

seprai, sepré, sepréi 1 bedsheet. **2** coverlet.

seprit see KUÉ.

Sept. [*Séptémber*] September.

Séptémber September.

sepuh₁ plating material. - *pérak* silver plating. - *emas* gilt. **meny-** plate s.t., gild s.t. **ter-** gilded. **-an** gilt. **peny-an 1** gilding s.t. **2** (*Phys.*) plating. *prosés* ~ *éléktrolitis* electrolytic process of plating.

sepuh₂ 1 (*Jv*) old. **2** older person. *para* - *yg mengamati remaja* old people who pay close attention to teenagers. **-an** (*Coll.*) old.

sepuluh see PULUH.

sepur (*R.R.*) **1** rail, railroad. - *simpang* siding. - *mati* siding with no egress. **2** train. - *balas* freight train. - *senél/snél* express train. *stasiun* - railroad station. **3** railway platform. **ny-** (*Coll.*) go by train. **-an** (*Jv*) railway fare.

seput (*Coll.*) fast, quick.

ser- see also entries with **sr-**.

sera ter-² hastily, in a hurry.

serabai, serabi k.o. rice flour pancake.

serabut 1 fiber. **2** fibrous, coarse. **-an 1** fibrous, coarse. *pakaian* ~ coarse clothing. **2** chaotic, mixed. *lari* ~ run in confusion (of many people).

seragam see RAGAM.

serah - *pakai* surrender for use. - *terima* transfer (of a function or command). **meny-terimakan** hand over (o.'s job officially). *meny-terimakan jabatannya* step down o.'s office, change the reins of authority. **ber-** surrender. ~ *diri* yield, surrender. **meny- 1** surrender. *Para gerilya tdk mau* ~ *pd tentara* The guerillas did not want to surrender to the army. ~ *kalah* admit defeat. **2** give in, accede. *Ia* ~ *pd kemauan ibunya* She gave in to her mother. **meny-i** hand over to s.o., deliver to s.o., submit to s.o. *Suharto di-i tugas menyelenggarakan kekuasaan pemerintah* Suharto was entrusted with the task of coordinating the power of the gvt. **meny-kan** hand s.t. over, transfer s.t. *Ia* ~ *arsip kantor kpd diréktur yg baru* She submitted the office archives to the new director. ~ *diri* give o.s. up, surrender. **ter- 1** surrendered, submitted. **2** as you will! up to you! ~ *pdmu* It is up to you. (I leave it to you.). **peny-** s.o. who surrenders or transfers. **peny-an 1** transfer, delivery. ~ *kedaulatan* transfer of sovereignty. ~ *dlm tiga bulan* on delivery in three months. **2** surrender, yielding. **3** resignation to a situation. ~ *diri* acceptance of o.'s fate.

sérah (*M*) bright red.

serahi k.o. long-necked flask.
serai lemongrass, citronella.
sérai ter- scattered, dispersed.
serak hoarse, husky (of voice). **ke-an** rasp (in voice).
sérak ber-(^{2}) scattered. **ber-an** be scattered around. *Puntung rokok* ~ Cigarette butts were scattered around. **meny-i** scatter s.t. on s.t. *Halaman sekitarnya di-i bunga* The surrounding yard was scattered with flowers. **meny-kan** scatter s.t. around. **ter-** scattered. *Banyak majalah yg* ~ *di méja* A lot of magazines were scattered all over the table. **-an** garbage scattered about.
serakah greedy. **meny-i** covet. **ke-an** greed.
serakahisme greedy mentality.
seram hair-raising. - *kulit* goose flesh. **meny-kan** 1 cause o.'s hair to stand on end. 2 terrify. **ke-an** frightfulness.
Séram the S. Moluccan island of Ceram.
serambi 1 front porch, veranda. - *jantung* (*Anat.*) auricle of the heart. 2 platform (in station).
serampang₁ trident. **meny-** harpoon s.t. with a trident.
serampang₂ (*Coll.*) strike at random. **-an** at random, any old way. *contoh* ~ (*Tech.*) random sample. **ke-an** randomness.
serampang dua belas k.o. traditional Indonesian social dance.
serampangisme mentality marked by doing whatever o. likes to do without regard to societal norms.
séran stripe.
Séran see SÉRAM.
seranah (*Lit.*) a curse. **meny-** curse.
serandang trestle, sawhorse. **meny-** support with a trestle.
serandung ter- stumble.
serang₁ - **meny-** attack e.o. **meny-** attack. *Pada hari ketiganya, kembali Sekutu* ~ *kota Makassar* On the 3d day, the Allied Forces once again attacked Macassar. *Ibu di- penyakit paru-paru* Mother fell ill with lung disease. **ter-** 1 attacked. 2 fell ill. ~ *histéri* came down with hysteria. **-an** attack, aggression. ~ *balasan* counterattack. ~ *pancingan* diverting attack. ~ *jantung* heart attack. **peny-** attacker, aggressor. ~ *tengah* (*Sport*) center forward. **peny-an** attack, aggression. ~ *tentara sekutu* the allied attack.
serang₂ (*Naut.*) boatswain's mate.
serang₃ (*M*) **ber-** become more, increase.
serangga insect.
seranggung ber- sit bent forward.
serangkak barbs used to prevent s.o. from climbing a (fruit) tree. - *payung* umbrella ribs.
serani 1 (*Lit., Amb*) Christian. *Ia msk* - He became a Christian. 2 (*Lit.*) Portuguese-speaking Christians of pre-19th century Jkt. **meny-kan** 1 convert s.o. to Christianity. 2 legally marry an Indonesian wife (in the colonial period).
seranta (*Lit.*) **meny-kan** proclaim widely.
serap - *mesra* intimate. **meny-** 1 absorb a fluid. 2 pervade. ~ *jiwa* pervade the soul. **meny-kan**

cause s.o. or s.t. to absorb. *Dia* ~ *moral baik pd anaknya* He implanted good morals into his children (caused his children to absorb good morals). **ter-(kan)** absorbable, absorbed. **ke-an** absorbency. **keter-an** absorbability. **-an** 1 s.t. absorbed. 2 absorption. **peny-** 1 absorbent. 2 absorber. ~ *goncangan* (*Auto*) shock absorber. **peny-an** absorption.
sérap reserve, spare. *ban* - (*Auto.*) spare tire. **meny-kan** hold in reserve, lay aside.
serapah curse. **meny-** be abusive, curse. **meny-i** curse s.o. or s.t.
serasah₁ manure, offal.
serasah₂ k.o. printed cotton fabric from India.
serasah₃ mountain rapids.
serasi see RASI₂.
serat₁ 1 fibrous parts of fruit, etc. 2 fiber. *tali dgn - kukuh* a rope with strong fibers. **ber-** fibrous. *Mangga bangsa ini selalunya* ~ This k.o. mango is always fibrous.
serat₂ tight, jammed. **meny-i** make tight. **ter-** stuck fast.
seratus see RATUS₁.
serawak (*Chem.*) antimony.
Serawak Sarawak in Malaysia.
seraya₁ while.
seraya₂ **meny-** ask for help.
serba completely, very much so. *segalanya* - *luks* Everything was deluxe. - *ada* having everything. *toko* - *ada* general store. - *aku* egotistic. - *anéka* all different varieties. *Barang-barang* - *anéka dipamérkan di situ* All sorts of goods are displayed there. **ke-anékaan** diversity. - *béda* heterogeneous. - *bisa* all-round, versatile. - *déwa* heterogeneous. - *dua* dualism. - *omongan* just idle chatter. - *salah* 1 all wrong. 2 at a loss as to what to do. - *sama* homogeneous. **ke-samaan** homogeneity. - *sedikit* very little. - *serbi* all sorts of (things), miscellaneous. - *tunggal* one of each.
serbak **meny-** be perfumed, be good-smelling. **meny-kan** spread s.t. (fragrance, etc.). **meny-i** perfume s.o. **peny-an** smelling good.
serban turban. *Ia sdh memakai* - He wears a turban now (i.e., he has made the pilgrimage to Mecca). **ber-** wear a turban.
serbanéka all k.o., diverse. **ke-an** extreme diversity.
serbat 1 sherbet. 2 k.o. ginger drink with spices. 3 (*Jv*) k.o. drink of shredded young coconut and syrup.
serbét napkin. **meny-(i)** wipe off with a napkin.
serbu **meny-** attack or invade in a throng. ~ *perkubuan musuh* attack fortifications of the enemy. *Anak-anak sdh mulai* ~ *santapan* The children already started to attack the refreshments. **meny-kan** induce to attack. **-an** 1 attack. 2 stampede, rush. **peny-** attacker. **peny-an** attacking, invasion.
serbuk 1 dust - *besi* iron filings. - *gergaji* sawdust. - *héroin* heroin powder. 2 (*Biol.*) pollen. - *sari* pollen. 3 powder. - *kelantang* bleaching powder. **meny-** become pulverized, become powder.

meny-i pollinate. **meny-kan 1** cause s.t. to become powder, pulverize s.t. **2** pollinate s.t. **peny-** pollinator. *agén* ~ pollinating agent. **peny-an** pollination.

sérda [*sérsan dua*] (*Mil.*) sergeant 2d class.

serdadu 1 soldier. **2** mercenary in foreign pay (during the colonial period). **ke-an** soldiery.

serdak fine dust.

serdawa see SENDAWA₂.

serdih protruding (of chest or belly).

seré see SERAI.

seregang see REGANG.

seréh see SERAI.

sérelak k.o. lacquer.

serem see SERAM.

serembab ter- fall flat on o.'s face.

serempak see REMPAK.

serempeng see SREMPENG.

serémpét (ber)-an brush against e.o. *Kol* ~ *dengan bus* A passenger van and a bus brushed against e.o. **meny-, ny-** graze, brush against s.t. *Sebuah témbakan* ~ *pergelangan tangannya* A shot grazed his wrist. ~ *bahaya* risk danger. ~ *wilayah filsafat* touch on the border of philosophy. **meny-², ny-²** *bahaya* brush close against danger. **meny-kan** cause s.t. to brush against. *Sopir* ~ *truknya ke sédan* The driver caused his truck to graze the sedan. **ke-, ter-** get grazed. *Anak yg bermain sepatu roda* ~ *truk* The child was sideswiped by a truck as he was roller-skating. ~ *bahaya* brushed by danger. **-an 1** abrasion. **2** stumble over e.o.

seréng (*Jv*) rocket (firecracker).

serenjang (*Lit.*) stand up straight.

serenta (*Jv*) as soon as. - *mendengar mobilnya, kami berhamburan keluar* As soon as we heard her car, we all rushed outside. *dgn* - immediately.

serentak 1 jointly, together, at once. *Petugas Hansip dan RK berjalan - ke sana* The civil guard and neighborhood watchmen headed in that direction together. *jawaban* - simultaneous answers. - *dgn itu* at the same time as that. **2** all at once. - *kosong rasa hatiku mendengar pernyataan itu* All at once I was depressed when I heard that statement. **3** as soon as. - *saya selesai bicara, ia pergi* As soon as I had spoken, she left. **ke-an** unison, simultaneity.

sérep see SÉRAP.

seret 1 dry (of throat) so that o. has difficulty swallowing. **2** (*Coll.*) sluggish (of traffic, the movement of goods, business). *Bulan ini penghasilannya* - This month there has been very little production. **meny-kan** make business sluggish, make sales slow. **ke-an** sluggishness. ~ *penyaluran* sluggishness of distribution.

sérét₁ dragging, trailing behind. **meny- 1** drag s.t. or s.o. *Aku* ~ *Iwan berlindung di rumpun pandan* I dragged Iwan to a hiding place in a pandanus clump. **2** cause s.t. to drag. *Di-nya sandalnya* He shuffled along in his sandals. *Burhan* ~ *kakinya* Burhan dragged his feet. **meny-²** drag along, carry away. *Suaranya* ~ *hati* His voice

carries the heart away. **meny-i 1** drag along. *Rumpun-rumpun bambu di-i banjir kali* Stands of bamboo were swept away by the flooded river. **2** grab forcibly. **ter- 1** dragged along. *Dia jatuh dr mobil dan* ~ *hampir sepuluh méter* She fell out of the car and was dragged along for almost 10 meters. **2** involved (in unsavory affair). **-an** dragging. ~ *langkahnya* the dragging of his step.

sérét₂ the unadorned edge of a batik cloth.

sergah say s.t. with a snarl. *"Kau tidur seharian, ya?"* - *Mak Haji* "You sleep all day long, don't you?" the hajji's wife snarled. **meny-** suddenly snarl at s.o., speak harshly unexpectedly. *Ia* ~ *gerombolan anak yg mengikutinya* He suddenly yelled at the gang of children following him. **-an** harsh words.

sergap meny- 1 attack, ambush. *Anak buah saya* ~ *Létnan Taha dr belakang* My followers attacked Lieutenant Taha from the rear. *Ia lebih doyan* ~ *perempuan drp musuh* He'd rather attack a woman than the enemy. **2** catch (in a raid, etc.). *Mulyadi* ~ *senjata itu* Mulyadi lunged at and snatched the weapon. *Polisi* ~ *maling malam tadi* The police caught a thief last night. **3** snarl at. **-an** attack, ambush. **peny-** o. who attacks. **peny-an** attack on s.o. or s.t. ~ *pos-pos tentara* the capture of military posts.

seri₁ 1 honorific royal title. - *Paduka* His Majesty. - *Paus* the Pope. **2** shining splendor, gleam. *Matahari menambah - dan cantiknya* The sun increased her charm and beauty. - *panggung* star of the stage, prima donna. - *wajahnya* the gleam in his face. **ber-** shine, beam. *Mukanya* ~ Her face beamed. *mérah* ~ *tanda cukup vitamin* glowing and rosy, a sign of sufficient vitamins. **ber-²** beam, gleam. *Wajahnya* ~ *karena bangga akan menantunya* Her face gleamed because of her pride in her son-in-law. **meny-kan** brighten s.t. *Kehadiran tamu itu* ~ *pésta kami* The guest's presence livened up our party. **ke-an** brilliance.

seri₂ (*Sport*) be a tie. *Permainan kita* - We played to a draw.

seri₃ see SARI.

seri₄ see HILANG.

séri series. **ber-** in a series. *Cerita ini* ~ This story is a series.

seriawan (*Med.*) sprue, oral ulceration. - *mulut* ulcer in the mouth. - *usus* dysentery.

seribu see RIBU.

serigala jackal, wolf.

serigunting k.o. bird with a forked tail.

serik₁ sore (of throat).

serik₂ learn o.'s lesson, refuse to do s.t. because of a former bad experience.

serikat 1 united. *Amérika* - the USA. **2** union, league, alliance. - *Afrika Selatan* Union of S. Africa. - *buruh/sekerja* labor or trade union. - *Islam* Isl. League. - *Yésus* the Jesuit Order. **ber-** united, allied. **meny-kan, memper-kan** join together, cause persons to unite. *Partai Komunis* ~ *buruh tani* The Communist party brought together the workers and peasants. ~ *Allah* (*Rel.*) be polytheistic. **per-an** organization, association, union. ~ *Bangsa-bangsa* the United Nations.

serikaya₁ annona, the sweetsop fruit.

serikaya₂ k.o. jam made of eggs, sugar, and coconut cream.

serimpat, serimpet see SERÉMPÉT.

serimpung (*Jkt, Jv*) **meny-** 1 tie or entangle another's feet. 2 block s.t., impede s.t. *Golongan oposisi ~ program pemerintah* The opposition impede the gvt.'s programs. 3 make o. stumble (by hurling s.t. to entangle the feet). **ber-(²)an, -²an** trip e.o. up. **ter-** tripped, stumbled. **peny-an** act of tripping up or impeding.

serindit k.o. parakeet.

sering₁ often. *Lagu itu - kami nyanyikan* We often sang that song. *- kali* often. **-²** often, over and over. *Pemuda tampan itu ~ mengajak aku berpiknik* That good-looking youth often invited me to go on a picnic. **-nya** frequency. *Saking ~ dia tdk makan teratur, dia sakit perut* He had stomach problems because he frequently failed to eat properly. **se-** as often as. **ke-an** frequency.

sering₂ (*M*) slender.

sering₃ firm and tight (of plaited or braided materials). **meny-** plait or twine s.t.

seringai 1 a grin, grimace. 2 say with a grin or grimace. *"Kena" -nya puas* "Got it!" he said with a smug grin. *"Patah!" - Mulyadi* "It is broken!" said Mulyadi with a grimace. **meny-** 1 grin, grimace. *Ia ~ ketika memandang ke dadaku* He grinned when he stared at my bosom. 2 curl into a grin or grimace. *Mulutnya ~ dgn keramahan palsu* His mouth curled into a grin of phony friendliness.

sériosa semiclassical and classical (of music).

serit k.o. fine-toothed louse comb. **meny-** remove lice with this comb.

sérius 1 serious, solemn. 2 wholehearted. *Waktu itu aku bermain -* At that time I was playing with all my heart. **meny-kan** take seriously. *Karyanya baru mulai di-kan tahun-tahun terakhir* Her works have begun to be taken seriously only in the last years. **ke-an** seriousness.

serkah torn or broken off. **meny-** break or tear off.

serkai meny- 1 wring out (wet clothes, etc.). 2 squeeze out liquid (from cheesecloth, etc.).

serkap₁ 1 cone-shaped fish trap that is thrust down on fish in shallow water. 2 cone-shaped bird cage. **meny-** 1 catch fish with such a fish trap. 2 cover with s.t. (us. cone-shaped). **meny-i** cover s.t.

serkap₂ see SERGAP.

serkup meny- seize or cover with a concave object (a cone, cupped hand, etc.).

serling pitfall. **ter-** fallen into a pitfall.

séro₁ (*Fin.*) 1 a share (business). 2 have a share interest in a firm or business. **be-** have a share or interest. **pe-** shareholder. *~ diam* sleeping partner. **pe(r)-an** company, partnership. *~ terbatas* incorporated, limited. *~ komanditér* limited partnership.

séro₂ k.o. large stationary fish trap.

serobok see SIROBOK.

serobot (ber)-an (*Coll.*) 1 grab for e.o.'s possessions. 2 try to get ahead of e.o. **meny-** 1 get in front of. *Orang lain antri tapi dia ~ juga* Everyone else was waiting in line but she cut in (and went straight to the head of the line). *Sopir ~ lampu mérah* The driver kept on going right through a red light. *~ antrian* butt into a line. 2 interfere with or take arbitrarily. *Aku akan ~ mobilnya* I'm going to steal his car. **-an** s.t. snatched. *Mobil-mobil yg kaulihat itu adalah ~ dr sana* Those cars you see were stolen from that place. **peny-** 1 o. who snatches. 2 o. who acts highhandedly. **peny-an** illegal occupancy or annexation, snatching away of s.t.

serodok see SERUDUK.

seroja k.o. lotus.

sérok₁ (*Lit.*) bay, inlet. **-an** drain, ditch.

sérok₂ (*Jv*) scoop, round spatula. **meny-** 1 scoop up (food, etc.). 2 round up in a swoop. *Aktivis-aktivis PKI di- lagi* They rounded up Communist activists again.

sérok₃ see SÉRO₂.

serombong 1 hollow cylinder. 2 pipe, tube.

serondol see SONDOL.

serondong see SONDONG.

sérong 1 askew, slanting. *garis* - a slanting line. *Tariklah garis - dr sudut A* Draw a diagonal from angle A. 2 unfaithful. *Permainan - ini terjadi di rumah saya* This act of unfaithfulness occurred in my home. *berbuat/main -* commit adultery. *ngomong -* talk dirty. **- meny-** crisscross. **meny-go** askew. **meny-kan** tilt s.t., slant s.t. **ke-an** 1 insincerity, disloyalty. 2 adultery. **-an** incline. **peny-an** beveling, act making s.t. go at an angle.

seronok (*Lit., Humorous*) pleasant, agreeable.

seropot (*Jkt*) **meny-** sip s.t. noisily.

serpih 1 splinter, flake, shard. *- kayu* chips, wood shavings. 2 (*Geol.*) shale. *- minyak* oil shale. **meny-** 1 splinter. 2 fragment. *Awan-awan ~ menjadi awan kecil* The clouds broke into small clouds. **-an** chip, piece, shard.

sérpis see SÉRVIS₁,₂.

sérsan (*Mil.*) sergeant or naval petty officer, in address, esp. as *san. - dua* lower-ranking sergeant. *- kadét* sergeant in military training. *- kepala* sergeant first class. *- mayor* 1 sergeant major, highest ranking noncommissioned officer. 2 chief petty officer. *- satu* higher-ranking sergeant. *- udara* master sergeant (air force).

sérse, sérsi₁ see RESÉRSE.

sérsi₂ serge.

serta 1 with, along with. *Beliau - rombongan tiba di sini* He and his party arrived here. *- rasa* 1 sympathy. 2 empathy. 2 and, as well as. *Obrolannya selalu anéh - hébat* His conversation was always odd as well as intense. *menggerakkan otot - urat* exercise every muscle in a body (lit., muscles together with sinews). 3 as soon as. *- ia mendengar berita itu, ia pergi* As soon as he heard the report, he went. *--merta* immediately, all of a sudden. **be-** 1 along with, as well as. *Ia mesti* *berangkat* ~ *saya* He has to leave along with me. *Dikeluarkannya cat bibir* ~ *cermin* She took out lipstick and a mirror. **2** attached (of letters), enclosed with. *surat* ~ *surat cerai* a letter to which was attached a divorce document. **meny-i 1** participate in. *Ia* ~ *rapat itu* She participated in the meeting. *Aku tak* ~ *kegirangannya* I did not share her joy. **2** accompany s.o. or s.t. *Jururawat itu selalu* ~ *dokter* That nurse always accompanies the doctor. **mempe(r)-kan, meny-kan** enclose s.t. *Fotonya di-kan* His photograph is enclosed. **ke-an** participation. **pe-** participant. **pe-an** participation. **peny-an 1** participation. ~ *masyarakat dlm pengembangan pendidikan* the participation of society in the development of education. **2** attaching s.t., enclosing s.t. *Tanpa* ~ *surat kelahiran lamaran tak dpt diurus* Applications that do not have a birth certificate enclosed cannot be processed.

sertarasa see SERTA.

sértifikat, sértipikat certificate. **meny-kan** (*Leg.*) formalize (ownership of land, etc.) with a certificate. *Luas tanahnya tlh di-kan* The area of his land was officially registered and he received a deed.

sertu (*Isl.*) ritual ablution after touching s.t. impure (e.g. pig, etc.). **meny-** undergo such ablutions.

sértu [*sérsan satu*] (*Mil.*) first sergeant.

seru 1 utter a shout, yell s.t. *"Masuklah!" -nya* "Come in!" he called. **2** sharp, violent. *pertempuran yg* - violent clash. **ber-** call, shout out. ~ *kpd* appeal to s.o. **meny- 1** call. **2** hail (a cab, etc.). **meny-kan 1** call, shout out s.t. *Meréka* ~ *perkataan-perkataan cabul kpd jogét-jogét* They shouted out obscenities to the dancing girls. **2** proclaim s.t. ~ *azan* (*Isl.*) proclaim the call to prayer. ~ *dagangannya* proclaim o.'s wares. ~ *damai* proclaim peace. **-an 1** call, cry. **2** (*Ling.*) exclamation. **3** appeal. **peny-** announcer. **peny-an 1** calling, crying. **2** appeal.

seruak meny- 1 make o.'s way through a narrow passage or dense foliage or a crowd. *Amin melompat* ~ *mencari jalan dr kepungannya* Amin leapt up, pushing his way through (the underbrush), trying to find a way out of the ambush. **2** waft out through narrow spaces. *Uap* ~ *dr kolong-kolong ranjang yg tergenang air* Steam wafted up from the puddles under the bed. *Radio* ~ *dr jendéla* The sound of a radio wafted out through the window.

serual see SELUAR.

seru alam the universe. *Tuhan* - Lord of the universe.

serudi ber- ground, polished (precious stones). **meny-** polish by grinding.

seruduk meny- 1 go with the head lowered. **2** (*Jv, Jkt*) ram into. *Dua org téwas di- bis kota* Two people died after a city bus had run into them. **3** go into a place unobstrusively. **meny-i** ram into s.o. again and again. **ter-, ke-** rammed into. *mati* ~ *sapi jantan* died after being gored by a bull. **-an** attack, ramming.

serudung k.o. monkey.

seruit₁ harpoon. **meny-** harpoon s.t.

seruit₂ (*Jkt*) **meny-** blow a whistle. **-an** a whistle.

seruling k.o. flute.

sérum serum. **meny-** treat with serum.

serumah see RUMAH.

serunai₁ a wind instrument with a reed.

serunai₂ k.o. flowering plant.

serundéng, serunding relish of grated coconut and spices.

seruni k.o. seashore flower.

serunting k.o. vine.

serupa see RUPA.

serusuk meny- go through (bushes, crowds, etc). *Ia* ~ *kerumunan, mencari anaknya* He went through the crowd, looking for his child.

serut (*Jkt*) k.o. carpentry tool, a plane. *és* - a refreshment of shaved ice. **meny-** plane s.t. **-an** shavings.

serutu see CERUTU.

sérvis₁ 1 service (in a hotel, etc.). **2** provide with repair or maintenance service. *Dia - mobilku baik-baik* He serviced my car well. - *aki* offer a battery changing service. - *besar* give a 1,000-mile checkup to a car. - *kecil* give a perfunctory checkup to a car. **meny-, men-** service (of engines, etc.). **peny-** o. who services.

sérvis₂ set of crockery (for tea, dessert, dinner, etc.).

sesah₁ meny- wash clothes by pounding them. *kain yg di-* faded and worn cloth (from repeated laundering).

sesah₂ ber- bertinju (*M*) have a violent fight.

sesajén, sesaji, sesajian (*Rel.*) ritual offerings.

sesak 1 narrow, close. - *dada/napas* short-winded. **2** crowded, tight. - *kencing* an urge to urinate. **ber-(²)** crowd e.o., pack o.s. in. *Meréka* ~ *di muka lokét* They pressed against e.o. in front of the ticket booth. **ber-²an** be crowded, packed in tightly. *naik keréta api* ~ ride the train packed in like sardines. **meny- 1** become tight, constricted. ~ *napas* sultry, close. **2** urge. **meny-i** fill up s.t. so that it becomes tight. *perasaan yg* ~ *dada* oppressive feeling. *Ia sedang di-i geram* Anger was stifling her. **meny-kan** oppress, tighten, constrict. *Perasaannya* ~ *napasnya* She could hardly breathe because of what she felt. *Perusahaan téxtil Jepang* ~ *perusahaan batik Jabar* Japanese textile factories are having an adverse constrictive effect on W. Java's batik industry. **ter- 1** be hard pressed. **2** constricted. **ke-an 1** oppressiveness, tightness. **2** oppressed.

sesal regret, remorse, repentance. **meny-** be sorry, regret. *Saya* ~ *mengirim surat kpdnya* I'm sorry I wrote her a letter. **meny-i 1** blame s.t. or s.o. ~ *diri* blame, reproach o.s. **2** regret s.t. o. did. *Ia* ~ *perlakuannya terhadapku* She repents what she did to me. **meny-kan** deplore, regret s.t. *Hal itu sangat saya -kan* I very much regret that matter. **peny-an 1** regret, remorse. **2** reproach.

sesama see SAMA₁.

sesanti (*Jv*) slogan, motto.
sesap₁ meny- 1 sip, lap up. 2 suck. *Anak itu ~ susu ibunya* The baby was sucking its mother's breast. **-an** 1 s.t. sucked, lapped up. *~ burung* birdbath. 2 sucking.
sesap₂ (*M*) abandoned field.
sesar₁ meny-kan move or push s.t. aside. *Ia ~ tutup jendéla* She moved the curtain aside.
sesar₂ (*Geol.*) fault. **per-an** faulting, faulting system.
sésar (*Med.*) cesarean. *operasi -* cesarean section.
sesat 1 lose o.'s way. *Ia - di jalan* He lost his way. *- barat* lose o.'s bearings. 2 go astray, deviate. *Ia - dlm agamanya* His religious beliefs began to deviate. *anasir-anasir nasional yg -* deviating nationalist elements. *perempuan -* wayward woman, prostitute. *imam yg -* Muslim leader fallen into heresy. **ber-** 1 be on the wrong track. 2 lost. **meny-kan** lead astray, mislead. *Dia ~ kami spy mudah diserang Belanda* He misled us so it would be easy for the Dutch to attack us. **ter-** 1 be lost. *Kami ~ di hutan itu* We lost our way in the forest. 2 have gone astray, deviate. *Pikirannya ~* Her thoughts have gone astray. **ke-an** 1 losing o.'s way. 2 slip, digression, error. *Geréja itu sedang dilanda ~* That church is overcome with heresy. *~ pengadilan* miscarriage of justice. **peny-** s.o. or s.t. that leads astray. *ajaran ~* teachings which lead o. up the wrong path.
sesawi k.o. green vegetable.
Sesdalopbang see SEKDALOPBANG.
sésé centimeter.
sesekali see KALI₂.
sesembahan (*Jv, Rel.*) s.o. or s.t. worshiped.
sesenap k.o. plant.
sesenggukan in gasps, choking. *menangis -* weep with choking sobs.
seseorang see ORANG₁.
sesepuh (*Jv*) elders.
sésér k.o. fish net. **peny-** o. who catches fish with such a net.
sését₁ (*Jv*) skinned, scraped. **meny-** skin, peel.
sését₂ dragonfly.
Sésko [*Sekolah Staf Komando*] Staff College of the Armed Forces.
Séskogab [*Sésko gabungan*] Joint Staff College of the Armed Forces.
séspan side-car (of motorcycle). **ber-** with a side-car.
sesuai 1 appropriate. *Baju itu tak - baginya* 1 The dress does not fit her. 2 The dress is not suitable for her. *Perbuatannya tak - dgn kedudukannya dlm masyarakat* His behavior did not conform to his social position. *- dgn permintaan* in accordance with o.'s request. 2 agree with. *Meréka tak - dlm perundingan itu* They did not agree in the discussion. **ber-an** be in mutual accord. *Pekerjaannya tak ~ dgn kemauan kapténnya* His work did not match his captain's expectations. **meny-kan** adjust, adapt, bring into line. *Ia tak dpt ~ diri dgn lingkungan itu* She could not adjust to the environment. *Meréka ~ pendapat meréka masing-*

masing They reconciled their opinions. *-kanlah jam anda dgn waktu Indonésia Barat* Set your watch to W. Indonesian time. **ke-an** 1 uniformity, conformity. 2 suitability, concord, congruity, compatibility. **berke-an** be in mutual accord. *Keindahannya mesti ~ dgn abad yg akan datang* Its beauty must be appropriate for the coming century. **peny-an** adaptation, adjustment, accommodation. *~ diri* self-adaptation. **per-an** agreement, concurrence, compatibility. *~ faham/pendapat* meeting of the minds, agreement.
sesuatu see SUATU.
sesudah see SUDAH.
sesumbar see SUMBAR.
sesungguhnya see SUNGGUH.
set- see also entries with **st-**.
sét₁ (*Tech.*) set. *- rambut* hairset. *- ténis* tennis set. **(me)nge-** 1 arrange s.t., set s.t. *~ rambut* set hair. 2 typeset.
sét₂ menge- trick s.o.
seta (*Coll.*) see HASTA.
setabelan (*Mil.*) artillery.
setabil see STABIL.
setadion see STADION.
setaf see STAF.
setagén see STAGÉN.
setahu see TAHU₁.
setakona see ASTAKONA.
setala see TALA.
setalén see TALÉN.
setali see TALI.
setambuk see STAMBUK.
setambul₁ (*Jkt*) k.o. fez.
setambul₂ see STAMBUL.
sétan 1 (*Rel.*) satan, devil. *Kemasukan -* possessed by the devil. *- alas* an evil spirit of the forest. *- liwat* sudden simultaneous spontaneous halt in conversation. 2 s.o. evil. *Kau - yg paling gila!* You are a crazy devil! **meny-** behave like a devil, become evil or reckless. **memper-(kan)** tell s.o. to go to hell. *Ia tak mempunyai keberanian utk ~ gurunya* She did not have the courage to tell her teacher to go to hell. **ke-an** possessed. **per-** Damm it! To hell! *~ sama kritik* To hell with the critics!
setandar see STANDAR₁.
setang see STANG.
setangan kerchief.
setangga see TANGGA.
setanggi incense, incense-stick.
setap see STAF.
setar see STAR.
setara see TARA₁.
setaraf see TARAF.
sétarter see STARTER.
setasi see STASI.
setasion, setasiun 1 railway station, depot. 2 public transportation terminal. *- bis* bus terminal. *- motor* public motorboat harbor for riverine transport. *- pengamatan* tracking or monitoring transport.

setat list, roll, statement. - *gaji* payroll.

setater see STARTER.

setawar k.o. medicinal plant. - *dan sedingin* 1 medicinal leaves against fever. 2 consolation, comforting words.

setégér 1 (*Coll.*) step-ladder. 2 scaffolding.

seték cutting, slip of a plant. **meny-** cut a slip. **peny-an** grafting.

setéker see STÉKER.

setél₁ 1 set, suit (of clothes, cards, etc.). - *kartu* deck of cards. *satu - pakaian* a suit of clothes. 2 match, be compatible. *Celana dan jasnya tdk -* His trousers and coat do not match. 3 (*Sl.*) be stylish. **ber-an** have or wear a suit. **meny-** match. *Ia pandai ~ warna* She was good at matching colors. **-an** set, suit of clothes.

setél₂ meny- 1 tune up, adjust. *Ia pandai ~ mesin* He was good at tuning up the engine. *~ arloji* set a watch. *~ mik* adjust a microphone. 2 turn on. *Ia ~ radio* He turned on the radio. **-an** radio dial, tuning knob, etc. **peny-an** installation, adjustment, tuning. *~ kacamata* fitting of glasses.

setéléng exhibition. **meny-kan** exhibit.

setéling see STÉLING.

setém₁ vote. **meny-** vote for s.o. or s.t. **-an** voting.

setém₂ tune, in tune. *Pianonya tdk -* The piano is not in tune. **meny-** tune up. *Ia ~ piano* He tuned the piano.

setempat see TEMPAT.

setémpel official stamp, seal. **meny-** stamp s.t. officially.

setén (*Jv*) assistant to a district head.

setengah see TENGAH.

seténsil see STÉNSIL.

setér see STÉR.

seterap see SETRAP.

setérek see STÉREK.

seterék éser (*Coll.*) clothes iron.

seteréng see STRÉNG.

setéréotip see STÉRÉOTIP.

seteria see KESATRIA.

seterik see SETRIK₁.

seterika iron, flatiron. - *listrik* electric iron. **ber-** ironed. *keméja yg ~* an ironed shirt. **meny-** 1 iron s.t. *Pakaiannya di- licin oléh binatu* The launderer ironed his clothes so they were crisp and neat. 2 (*Coll.*) flatten, smash. *Kita - negeri itu!* We'll flatten that country! *Bulldozer ~ hutan lébar* Bulldozers leveled a wide stretch of forest. **ter-** ironed. **-an** 1 iron. 2 clothes for ironing.

seterimin see STRIMIN.

seterip see SETRIP₁.

seterom see SETRUM.

seteru see SETRU.

seterum see SETRUM.

seterup see SETROP.

setia loyal, faithful. - *kawan* 1 solidarity. 2 be in solidarity with. **ber-kawanan** be in solidarity with. **ke-kawanan** solidarity. **ber-** be loyal. **meny-i** adhere faithfully to. *hal-hal yg di-i pengarang* things the author remained faithful to. **ke-an** loyalty, allegiance.

setiap see TIAP₁.

setiar (*Coll.*) see IKHTIAR.

setiawan 1 a loyal person. 2 faithful.

setik stitch. - *hiasan* ornamental stitch. - *silang* cross-stitch. - *balik* seam.

setikan game of marbles.

setil see STIL.

setimbang see TIMBANG₁.

setimbal, setimpal see TIMBAL₁.

setinggil (*Jv*) audience hall.

setip₁ k.o. convulsive child disease.

setip₂ eraser. **meny-** erase (with rubber eraser).

setir steering wheel (of a motor-vehicle). - *kiri* left-hand drive. **meny-** 1 drive, steer. 2 (*Coll.*) control, wield control over. *Minah ~ suaminya* Minah has control over her husband. **meny-kan** drive a vehicle on behalf of s.o. **peny-** driver.

setiren (*Coll.*) drive a car.

setiwal, setiwel leggings, puttee.

setolop see SENTOLOP.

setop₁ stop. **meny-** stop s.t. **ke-** have o.'s way obstructed. *~ pawai* held up by a parade. **-an** a stop (bus, streetcar). *~ gantung* 1 hanging traffic light. 2 traffic light (in general). **peny-an** stopping.

setop₂ see SETUP.

setopelés, setoplés see STOPLÉS.

setor deposited. **meny-** 1 make a deposit. *Ia ~ uang di bank* He deposited the money in a bank. 2 pay a rental fee. 3 put in storage. *~ lima ratus ékor sapi* store (the meat of) 500 cattle. 4 (*Sl.*) defecate. **meny-kan** 1 deposit s.t., pay s.t. 2 turn over s.t. o. has produced to the person who has paid to have it made. *~ pakaian jadi* turn in orders of clothing o. was given to sew. **-an** 1 deposit. 2 rental fee (for taxi drivers, etc., who rent their vehicles). 3 stored commodity. *~ sapi potong* stockpile of beef cattle (meat). **peny-** 1 purveyor, supplier. 2 depositor. **peny-an** depositing, payment.

setori 1 (*Jkt, Coll.*) quarrel, bicker. *Ia selalu - dgn majikannya* He was always quarreling with his boss. *cari -* look for a fight. 2 (*Amb*) talk. *Jangan - dgn meréka* Do not talk to them.

setoter (*Coll.*) stutter.

setrap (*Coll.*) punishment. **meny-** punish. *Ia di-oléh gurunya* He was punished by his teacher. **-an** 1 punishment. 2 prisoner.

setrat see STRAT.

setrék see SETERÉK ÉSER.

setrép see SETRIP₁.

setrik₁ hair ribbon.

setrik₂ (*Coll.*) strict.

setrika see SETERIKA.

setrip₁ 1 line. 2 decorative stripe. 3 stripe (insignia of rank). 4 slash (as a mark of punctuation). *tiga - enam ⅜.* 5 (*Sport*) straight (in golf). *Pukulannya -* He hit the ball straight. **ber-(²)** with stripes. *baju putih ~ biru* a white shirt with blue stripes.

setrip₂ (*Coll.*) crazy.

setrop fruit syrup for drinks.

setru enemy, foe. ber- hostile. *Meréka ~ dgn tetangganya* They are at odds with their neighbors. meny-i be hostile toward s.o. *Ia ~ tetangganya* He assumed a hostile attitude toward his neighbor. meny-kan, memper-kan treat as an enemy, be hostile toward. *Ia ~ gurunya* He was hostile toward his teacher. per-an enmity, hostility.

setrum (*Elec.*) electric current. meny- 1 induce. 2 electrify, charge. *Ia ~ aki* He charged the battery. ke- get a shock (from electricity).

setu (*Jv*) see RESTU.

setubuh see TUBUH.

setudén see STUDÉN.

setuju scc TUJU.

setum steam. meny- 1 dry-clean with steam. 2 let steam off.

setung see RESTUNG.

setup k.o. fruit-stew. meny- stew fruit. -an fruit-stew.

seturi see SETORI.

setyakawan see SETIA.

séwa 1 rent, hirc. - *rumah* house rent. 2 rented. *kamar* - rented room. - meny- business of renting things out. meny- 1 rent. *Ia ~ rumah baru* He rented a new house. 2 hire. *~ bécak* hire a pedicab. *~ advokat* engage a lawyer. meny-kan, memper-kan hire out, rent out, let. *Ia ~ mobilnya* He hired out his car. -an rented articles, hired people. *rumah ~* a rented house. *serdadu-serdadu ~* mercenaries. peny- 1 tenant, lessee. 2 rental payment. *uang ~ stan* money for the payment of the rent of the stand. peny-an renting out. per-an rental.

séwah see SÉWAR.

séwaka₁ (*Lit.*) tribute, homage. ber- pay homage, honor.

séwaka₂ see SUAKA₁,.

séwar k.o. curved dagger.

séwot (*Jv, Jkt*) furious.

séyot see SÉOK-SÉOK.

SGA [*Sekolah Guru Atas*] senior normal school.

SGB [*Sekolah Guru Bawah*] junior normal school.

SGKP [*Sekolah Guru Kepandaian Putri*] school for training home economics teachers.

SH [*Sarjana Hukum*] (*Acad.*) Master of Law.

shalat see SOLAT.

shampo see SYAMPO.

shé /sé/ see SÉ.

shio /sio, syo/ (*Ch, Zod.*) any of the 12 astrological signs.

shodanco /syodanco/ (*Japanese*) section commander.

sholat /solat/ see SOLAT.

si₁ 1 definite article used before the names of those with whom the speaker and interlocutor is intimate. *Mana - Mat?* Where is Mat? 2 definite article used before a noun referring to a particular person in a category. *- alamat* addresse. *- anu* such-and-such a person. *- pengirim* sender. 3 definite article used before an adjective referring to a person whose well-known characteristics are referred to by the adjective. *hikayat -*

miskin the story of the poor man. *Ini - gendut lagi* The fat o. is here again. *- gesit - loyo* the dynamic o. and the weak o.

si₂ (*Ch*) four. *- ban* 40,000. *- ban go* 45,000. *- cap* 40. *- cap go* 45. *- céng* 4,000. *- céng go* 4,500. *- pék* 400. *- pék go* 450. *- pék go bang* 450,000. *- pék go céng* 405,000. *- tiau* four million. *- tiau pua* four and a half million.

si₃ see SIH.

siaga₁ ready, alert, prepared. ber- be on the alert. meny-kan alert s.o., prepare s.o. for action. ke-an readiness, preparedness.

siaga₂ Boy or Girl Scout (9-13 years old).

siah - *layah* move from side to side, oscillate. *Pohon itu - layah ditiup angin* The trees were swaying in the wind. *Org mabuk itu berjalan - layah* The drunkard staggered and veered along. meny- part s.t. *Ia ~ kelambu* She parted the mosquito net. meny-kan push aside. *Mobilnya ~ mobil lain ke pinggir* His car forced other cars to the side.

siak₁ (*Isl.*) mosque caretaker.

siak₂ see SIAH.

sial 1 be unlucky, unfortunate. *Hari ini - baginya* This day was unfortunate for him. 2 bad luck. *Gang 13 membawa - saja utk kita semua* 13th Street only brings bad luck to all of us. meny-kan cause bad luck. *Semuanya gagal! Siapa yg mendatangkan ~ pagi-pagi begini?* Everything has gone wrong! Who is bringing bad luck so early in the morning? -an 1 s.o. unfortunate, s.t. ill-fated. *negeri-negeri ~* countries with bad luck. *~ dangkalan* (*Jkt*) term of abuse, damn! 2 s.o. or s.t. bringing bad luck. *Aduh, ~ déh! Saya tunggu bis satu jam* Hey, this is really bad luck! I have been waiting for the bus an hour. 3 Damn it, exclamation of dissatisfaction.

sialang 1 beehive. 2 k.o. tree in which bees commonly build their nest. ber- 1 swarm (of bees). 2 gather honey. (me)ny- gather honey. peny- honey gatherer.

sialat see CIAKLAT.

siamang₁ gibbon.

siamang₂ (*Chem.*) wolfram, tungstcn.

siang₁ 1 day, daylight period. *- hari* daytime. *- malam* day and night. *masih - 1* still broad daylight. 2 still quite early (in the evening). 2 period from about 11 a.m. to three p.m. *makan -* lunch. *sekolah -* afternoon session. *jam dua -* two p.m. *- dinihari* noon. *- (hari) bolong* 1 precisely at noontime. 2 broad daylight. -² early, in time. *Datanglah ~ spy dpt tempat* Come early so you will get a place. se- a whole day. *~ suntuk* all day long. ke-an 1 caught by daylight. *Rupanya pucat spt bulan ~* He looked as pale as the moon in the daytime. 2 overslept. *Ia ~ terlambat pergi ke kelas* He overslept and went to school late. 3 do s.t. late in the morning which should have been done earlier. -an later in day (said before noon), earlier in afternoon (said at noon or later). *Kau sih yg terlambat, tadi kuajak lebih ~* It is you who is late, I asked you to come earlier in the afternoon.

siang₂ 1 weeded (of garden). **2** cleaned (of fish). **ber-** clean. **meny- 1** clear away (weeds, undergrowth, etc.). *Ia ~ rumput gajah di halaman rumahnya* He cleared away the weeds in his yard. **2** clear (a place), weed (a place). *Ia ~ hutan utk meladang* He cleared away the jungle in order to cultivate it. **3** gut, clean (fish, birds, etc.). *Ia ~ ikan sblm menggoréngnya* He cleaned the fish before frying it. **meny-i** clear s.t. of weeds. *Bésok aku mau ~ kebunku* Tomorrow I want to weed my garden.

sianu see SI₁.

siap 1 ready, prepared. *Meréka - utk pergi* They were ready to go. *- cétak* ready to print. **meny-cétak(kan)** make ready for publication. *Makalah ini di-cétakkan oléh penulis* The author prepared this article for publication. *- pakai* ready to wear. *- sedia* completely prepared. **ber-** *sedia* make preparations. **ke-sediaan** preparedness. *- siaga* prepared and completely alert. *prajurit-prajurit yg - siaga* mobilized soldiers. **ber-** *siaga* be prepared, be on the alert. **ke-siagaan** state of being prepared and on the alert. **2** finished, done. *Pekerjaannya sdh -* His job was finished. **3** (*Mil.*) attention. **-²** get ready. *Aku hrs ~ utk berangkat ke luar kota bésok pagi* I have to get ready to leave town tomorrow morning. **ber- 1** get ready, get prepared. *Ayo Muh, lekas ~* Come on Muh, get ready quickly. **2** (*Sport*) on your mark. **ber-²** make preparations. *Para penumpang ~ utk turun ke darat* The passengers were making preparations to go ashore. **meny-kan, memper-kan 1** prepare. *Ia - laporan* He prepared a report. *Guru ~ murid-muridnya utk ujian* The teacher prepared his pupils for the examination. *~ pasukan* place troops in a state of alert. *Rumah itu di-kan utk diséwakan* The house was equipped for renting out. **2** finish s.t. *Saya blm sempat ~ pekerjaan saya* I have not had a chance to finish my work. **ke-an** readiness. **-²an** not fully prepared, only half prepared. *Utk ujian minggu depan dia hanya ~ saja* For next week's exam she is only half prepared. **per-an 1** preparations. *~ perang tlh selesai* Preparations for a war have been made. **2** set-up, arrangement. *~ pengurus kumpulan itu tdk lengkap* The setup of the board of the association is not complete. **3** supply, equipment, etc., prepared for some purpose.

siapa who. *- itu?* Who is that? *- namanya?* What is his name? *- konon* whoever, who. *- lu - gua* (*Coll.*) every person for himself. *- pun* whoever, anyone at all. *Ia tak pernah berkompromi pd - pun* She has never made compromises to anyone. *- saja* **1** who all, name everyone who. **2** anyone at all. **-²** whoever, just anyone. *~ tdk membeli karcis tdk boléh msk* Anyone who fails to buy a ticket cannot be admitted. *O, Met! Kirain ~ tadi* Oh, Met! I was wondering who it was! *bukan ~* **1** no o. else. **2** not just anyone. *Yg datang bukan ~ melainkan teman-temannya yg karib* The people who came were not just anybody. They were his close friends.

siapuh interjection expressing disappointment.

siar₁ ber-an broadcast, be on the air. **meny-kan 1** spread (news), broadcast. *Ia ~ kabar* He spread the news. *Kabar itu di-kan semalam* The news was broadcast last night. **2** broadcast. *Kabar itu di-kan semalam* The news was broadcast last night. **3** announce, promulgate. *Pemerintah ~ peraturan baru* The gvt. announced a new regulation. **ter- 1** broadcasted, announced. **2** spread around, circulated about. *~ berita kematiannya* The news of her death had spread. **-an 1** broadcast. *~ luar negeri* foreign broadcast. **2** announcement. *~ pemerintah* gvt. announcement. *~ pérs* press release. **3** publication, issue. **4** circulation, spread. **peny- 1** announcer. **2** publisher. **3** (*Tech.*) transmitter. **peny-an** broadcasting. *kantor ~ radio* radio broadcasting office. **per-an** matters concerning broadcasting. *~ radio* radio broadcast. *~ kilat* bulletin, leaflet.

siar₂ ber-(²) stroll about.

siarah₁ see ZIARAH.

siarah₂ see BINTANG.

siar-siur rustling sound.

siasat₁ 1 investigation. **2** tactics, strategy. *- perang* war strategy. *- mengajar* teaching methods. **3** policy for achieving s.t. *- pemasaran* marketing policy. **ber- 1** be full of stratagems, investigative plans, etc. **2** have s.t. as a strategy. **meny-i** pry into s.o.'s affairs or get the better of s.o. (by questioning, using certain tactics or approaches, etc.). *Polisi ~ pengédar morfin itu dgn pura-pura menjadi pembelinya* The police investigated the morphine dealer by pretending to be a buyer. **peny- 1** (*Lit.*) investigator. **2** strategist, tactician. **peny-an 1** (*Lit.*) investigation. **2** bringing tactics or stratagems to bear.

siasat₂ (*Lit.*) punishment. **meny-kan** punish.

sia-sia 1 in vain, useless, without result. *Usahanya - saja* His efforts were all in vain. *- ia datang kemari* It was futile for him to come here. **2** meaningless. *Ia kira perjanjian kita - saja* He thought our promise was meaningless. **ber-** (*Lit.*) useless. **meny-kan** make s.t. useless, cause s.t. to have no result, neglect. *Ia ~ uang* She wasted money. *Tentu kau tdk ~ harapanku ini* Of course you will not neglect my expectations. **ter-** wasted, not put to proper use. *Usahanya ~* Her efforts were wasted. *waktu yg ~* wasted time. **ke-an** (*Lit.*) futility, uselessness.

sibak part (in hair), a division. **ber-** parted, separated. *rambut yg ~* parted hair. *Meréka ~ di luar kota* They separated outside the city. *Awan ~* The clouds parted. *~ mata* be teary-eyed due to prolonged weeping. **meny- 1** separate s.t. **2** cleave s.t. apart. *Perahu ~ gelombang* The prow parted the waves. **meny-²** repeatedly part s.t. (i.e. separate leaves of a book, repeatedly part s.o.'s hair to search for lice, etc.). **meny-kan** move s.t. aside. *Ia ~ semua piring yg ada di atas méja* She pushed aside all the plates that were on the table.

siban see SI₂.

sibango /siban-go/ see SI₂.

sibar 1 piece of cloth sewn as border. **2** porch or annex to house.

sibar₂ see SÉBAR₂.

sibernétik, sibernétika cybernetics.

sibir (*M*) a small slice. *se- kuéh* a small slice of cake. **-an** a small slice. ~ *tulang* the apple of o.'s eye (lit., a slice of o.'s bones).

sibuk busy. *Ia - bekerja* She is busy working. **meny-i** keep s.o. busy. *Kita di-i oléh prospék hari depan* Prospects of the future keep us busy. **meny-kan 1** stir up, incite. *Banjir itu ~ penduduk utk pindah* The flood stirred the people to move. **2** occupy, busy o.s. with. *Ia ~ soal temannya* He gave a lot of thought to his friends problems. *pekerjaan yg ~* work that keeps o. fully occupied. **memper-** cause s.o. to be busy. *Rini ~ dirinya dgn mencuci piring* Rini occupied herself with washing dishes. **ke-an** stir, bustle, activity. ~ *kota* city activity.

sibur ladle, scoop. **meny-** ladle, scoop.

sibur-sibur dragonfly.

SIC [*Surat Ijin Cétak*] gvt. printing permit.

sicap see SI₂.

sice complete set of living room furniture consisting of table and four chairs or table, settee, and some chairs.

sicéng see SI₂.

sicérék k.o. small shrub.

sidai meny- hang out to dry.

sidak [*inspéksi mendadak*] surprise inspection (of gvt. offices).

sidang 1 session, meeting. - *paripurna/pléno* plenary session. - *gabungan* joint session. - *geréja* synod. - *jemaat* congregation. **2** council, group. - *hakim* members of the courts. - *pembaca* 1 the reading public. 2 the reader of a certain magazine, etc. - *pengarang* editorial board. - *perang* council of war. **ber-** convene, sit in session. *Parlemén ~* Parliament convened. **meny-** try s.o. in court. **meny-kan 1** convene on a matter. **2** (*Leg.*) bring s.o. or s.t. to trial. **peny-an** (*Leg.*) summoning (of accused). ~ *Héri Akhmadi* the summoning to court of Heri Akhmadi. **per-an 1** meeting, assembly. **2** court session (over several days).

siddik see FAJAR.

sidekap ber- fold o.'s arms over o.'s chest.

sidi 1 confirmation (Protestant). - *besar* confirmation. - *kecil* infant baptism. **2** o. who has been confirmed. **di-** confirmed.

sidik₁ investigation, examination. - *jari* 1 finger print. 2 the study of finger prints, dactyloscopy. - *midik* scrutiny, close examination. - *selidik* investigation, inquiry. **meny-** investigate. **peny-** (*Leg.*) investigating officer. **peny-an** police investigation.

sidik₂ see FAJAR.

sidomukti (*Jv*) k.o. batik design of dark symmetrical patterns.

siduk see CÉDOK.

sifat 1 characteristic. - *khas* special characteristic. - *jantan* male characteristic. - *kelanjutan* con-

tinuity. **2** identifying feature. *Ia menguraikan - anjingnya yg hilang itu* He gave a description of his lost dog. - *perawakan* personal description. **3** nature, disposition. - *kemanusiaan* human nature. - *partai kami* the nature of our party. - *pendiam* quiet disposition. - *tabiat* character. **4** (*Rel.*) attribute (of God). **ber-** have the quality, character(istic) of. *Itu ~ bundar* It has a round shape. *Ia ~ penakut* He is cowardly by nature. ~ *menyerang* aggressive in nature. ~ *tetap* permanent. ~ *sementara* temporary. ~ *gado-gado* heterogeneous. **men-i 1** characterize, be characteristic of. *Ringan dan mudah panas ~ logam aluminium* Light weight and heat conductivity characterize aluminum. **2** characterize s.t. or s.o. **ter-kan** describable. **pens-an** characterization, description.

sifon siphon.

sigai (*Lit.*) **1** pegs inserted in pole for climbing. **2** small ladder, peg ladder. **meny-** climb up on such a ladder.

sigak Shoo! exclamation used to drive away dogs.

sigap efficient, always ready. *Kerjanya cepat, - dan rapi* She works fast, efficiently, and methodically. **ber-** be in readiness. *Ia sdh ~ utk perjalanan itu* He was ready for the trip. **ke-an 1** efficiency. **2** energy.

sigar (*Jv*) a slice (of fruit that is split open). **meny-** part (hair).

sigi₁ torch. **meny-** **1** light with a torch. *Meréka ~ kodok di sungai* They went frog hunting in the river with a torch. **2** investigate. *Ia ~ soal pelarian* He investigated the problem of refugees.

sigi₂ pull out, pry out.

sigung₁ k.o. polecat.

sigung₂ see SINGGUNG.

sih (*Coll.*) **1** particle used to soften questions. *Berapa - ini?* How much is this, by the way? *Ada apa -?* Hmm, what is wrong? **2** particle used to mark a topic. *Capék -, tdk. Tapi mari kita duduk dulu sebentar* I am not tired, but let us sit down for a minute. *Murah - murah. Tapi barangnya bagaimana?* It may be cheap, but of what quality is it? *Saya - nggak nyangka begini jadinya* Well I did not expect it to turn out like this. **3** you know! particle to emphasize a reason given. *Jangan dimakan itu! Pedes -* Do not eat that! It is too spicy.

sihir black magic, witchcraft. **meny-(kan)** practice black magic on s.o. *Katanya ia sakit karena diorg* They said he was ill because s.o. had practiced black magic on him. **ter-** suffer from black magic. *Kami spt ~!* We were as if bewitched! **-an** sorcery.

sihung see SIUNG₂.

siip see SIP.

siji (*Jv*) one.

sijil certificate.

sijingkat ber- stand or walk on tiptoe.

sijundai magic charm that drives o. mad. **ber-** sing as though out of o.'s mind.

Sik, Siq /sik/ Sikh.

sikap 1 attitude, demeanor. *Bagaimana - pemerin-*

tah? What is the gvt.'s attitude? - *méntal* mental outlook. - *budi* kind attitude. - *laku* 1 gesture. 2 way of behaving. **2** posture. *-nya tegap* He has an erect posture. *memperbaiki - duduknya* adjust o.'s sitting position. **ber-** 1 have a certain attitude. *Partai ini ~ kanan* This party has a rightist attitude. **2** (*Mil.*) stand at attention.

sikat 1 brush. - *gigi* toothbrush. **2** (*in some regions*) comb. **3** rake, harrow. **4** bunch (of bananas). **meny-** 1 brush s.t. *Ia ~ giginya* She brushed her teeth. **2** comb s.t. **3** rake out, harrow s.t. *Ia ~ ladang itu* He harrowed the field. **4** (*Coll.*) take away. *Ia berhasil ~ sebuah mesin jahit* She managed to steal a sewing machine. *Ia suka sekali ~ hak org lain* He likes to snatch away other's rights. **5** (*Coll.*) wipe out, clean out. *Meréka ~ kaum pelarian* They massacred the refugees. - *bersih sisa-sisa kolonial!* Wipe out the colonialist remnants! *~ makanan di méja* devour the food on the table. **6** (*Sport*) defeat completely. **-an** stolen goods. **peny-an** 1 brushing, combing, etc. 2 stealing. 3 abrupt removal.

sikatan k.o. bird.

sikeras see KERAS.

sikit (*Coll.*) see SEDIKIT.

siklamat cyclamate.

siklis cyclical.

siklon cyclone.

siklopédia see ÉNSIKLOPÉDI.

siklotron cyclotron.

siklus (*Tech.*) cycle.

sikon, si-kon [*situasi dan kondisi*] situation and conditions, circumstances. *tergantung pd* - depending on the circumstances.

sikongkol see KONGKOL.

siksa torture. **meny-, meny-i** 1 torture s.o. *Dgn seribu satu alat tubuhku di-* They tortured my body with 1001 instruments. **2** (*Coll.*) annoy, irritate. *Itulah hal yg paling ~* That is the most troublesome part of it. *~ otaknya* prey on o.'s mind. **ter-** tortured. **-an** torture, mistreatment. **peny-** tormentor, torturer. **peny-an** torturing, mistreating. *Itu ~ thd diri sendiri, Mas Mul!* That is torturing yourself, Mul!

siku 1 elbow. **2** (*Math.*) right angle. **3** s.t. at right angles (carpenter's or draftman's square; curve in road, etc.). - *bedil* rifle butt. - *biku* zigzag. - *jalan* a bend in the road. - *kain pembalut* sling (for the arm). - *keluang* zigzag design. **-²** 1 (*Math.*) having a 90-degree angle. *~ segi tiga* a right-angled triangle. *Tdk makan ~* not acceptable (i.e. does not fit all the angles). **2** a piece of wood or s.t. else added to an irregular piece to square it off. **ber-** have an angle or curve. **ber-²** have many bends and turns. *Jalannya ~* The road has a lot of curves. - **meny-** 1 nudge e.o. **2** (*Math.*) opposite (of angles). **meny-** 1 nudge, elbow o.'s way. **2** form a rectangle. **3** curve or bend at a right angle. *Jalan ini ~* This road makes a right-angle curve. **meny-kan** make s.t. into a right angle, square s.t. off. **-²an** nudge e.o. **peny-** 1 s.t. to square off. **2** (*Math.*) complementary. *sudut ~* complementary angle.

sikudidi see KEDIDI.

sikut (*Jv*) elbow. - *jalan* intersection, crossroad. **meny-** 1 nudge with elbow. *Ia ~ sahabatnya* She elbowed her friend. **2** (*Coll.*) deceive, cheat.

sila₁ 1 cross-legged. **2** such a sitting posture. *Di muka - masing-masing penjudi itu bertumpukan uang* Each gambler had stacks of money lying before his crossed legs. **ber-** sit with the legs crossed. *~ panggung* sit with crossed legs and the knees pulled up.

sila₂ moral principle, esp. of the Pancasila.

sila₃ meny-kan, memper-kan invite, ask. *Ia ~ tamunya makan* He invited his guest to eat. *Ketua ~ para terdakwa utk membéla diri* The chairman called on the accused to defend themselves. **-kan** please, a word used to urge s.o. to do s.t., esp. to benefit himself. *~ duduk* Please sit down. *~ minum* Please have a drink. *~ maju* Please move forward. *Boléh? ~!* May I? Please do!

silabus syllabus.

silaf, silah₁ see SILAP₁.

silah₂ see SILA₃.

silam₁ 1 set (of the sun). *Hari tlh -* The day is gone. *Matahari tlh -* The sun has gone down. **2** ago, of the past. *sekitar tiga tahun -* about three years ago. *masa yg -* the past. **meny-** disappear. **meny-kan** darken (o.'s vision). **ter-** caught by darkness. *Ia ~ di tengah hutan* He was caught by the darkness in the middle of the jungle. **ke-an** 1 darkness. **2** past. *Ia keluar dr kekinian dan msk ~* She left the present and began to discuss the past.

silam₂ see SELAM₁.

silancar see LANCAR.

silang crosswise, intersecting. *tanda -* sign of crossing. - *datar* (*R.R.*) level, crossing. - *empat* crossroads. - *melintang/mintang* (lie about) in disorder. - *selimpat* 1 complicated. 2 crumpled, rumpled. - *selisih/sengkéta* conflict, dispute. - *siur* crisscrossing. **ber-** *siur* cross back and forth, crisscross. *Berbagai keraguan ~ siur dlm kepalanya* Several doubts crisscrossed in her mind. **ber-** 1 crossed. *Ia ~ kaki* He had his legs crossed. *jalan ~* intersecting roads. *~ mata* look e.o. in the eyes. **2** piled up in a crisscross way. *Kursi ~ di halaman* The chairs were piled up in the yard. **ber-an** cross e.o., pass e.o. *Ketika naik sepéda ia ~ dgn kawannya* While riding his bicycle he passed his friend going in the other direction. - **meny-** crisscross. **meny-i** intersect or cross s.t. *Keméjanya di-i sarung* A sarong hung (like a bandoleer) from o. shoulder across his shirt. **meny-(kan), memper-kan** lay s.t. in the form of a cross. *Garpu dan séndok di-kannya di atas piring* She put the fork and spoon crosswise on the plate. **ter-** crossed. *dgn kakinya ~* with legs crossed. **-an** crossing (of legs or hands). **peny-an** crossing, mutation (in agriculture). *~ buatan* artificial crossbreeding. **per-an** 1 crossing. *~ jalan keréta* railroad crossing. *~ ras* racial mixture. **2** contradiction, conflict. *Timbullah ~ kemauan dlm hatinya* Conflicting desires arose in her heart.

silap₁ wrong, false, mistaken. *Anda - waktu memi-*

lih nomor télepon? Did you dial the wrong number? - *mata* mistaken in what o. saw. **-²** (*Coll.*) be in error. ~ *nanti bisa dipukulin org ramai-ramai* If you slip up, everyone will gang up on you and beat you. **ter-** done by mistake. **ke-an** mistake, slip, error.

silap₂ see SULAP₁.

silat traditional self-defense arts. **ber- 1** engage in such self-defense. ~ *kata/lidah* argue, debate. **2** mime the actions of self-defense. **meny-** parry, fend off. **per-an** matters pertaining to systems of self-defense.

silaturahim, silaturrahim, silaturahmi, silaturrahmi friendship, good relationship. *tali* the bonds of friendship.

silau dazzled, temporarily blinded by the glare. *Ia - karena sinar matahari* He was blinded by the sun. - *mata* dazzled. **ber-** *mata* blinded temporarily. **meny-** become glaring. **meny-kan** cause a glare, blind s.o. *Sinar matahari soré* ~ *sopir mobil* The afternoon sun blinded the driver. **ke-an 1** glare. **2** blinded.

silét razor blade. **meny-** slice with a razor blade. *Org gila itu* ~ *kakinya sendiri* The madman slit his own legs with a razor blade.

silhuét silhouette.

silih - (*ber*)*ganti* alternately, in turns. *Seluruh badanku terasa dingin panas - berganti* My whole body felt cold and hot in turns. **ber-** (*ber*)*ganti* by turns, changing. *Tilpun berdering* ~ *berganti* Phones were ringing alternately. - *rugi* indemnify. - *semilih* by turns. **ber-** turn, change into. *Malam* ~ *dgn siang* Night turns into day. **meny-1** change. *Ia* ~ *baju* She changed her dress. **2** shed skin, molt. **peny-an** alternating s.t., alternation.

silik (*M*) **meny-** observe, note carefully.

silikat silicate.

silikon silicon.

silinder cylinder.

silinderkop (*Auto.*) cylinder head.

silir₁ soft breeze. - *semilir* soft blowing of a breeze. **ber-²** blowing softly (of a breeze). **meny-** become breezy (wind). **-an** the blowing (of a breeze).

silir₂ (*Biol.*) membrane.

siliwer see SELIWER.

silo see SILA₁.

silsilah genealogy, family tree.

silu 1 twinge felt on hearing a grating sound (e.g. chalk drawn across a blackboard). **2** timid, modest. **ber-** be modest. **meny-kan 1** cause such a twinge. **2** move, affect.

siluman 1 a human who has taken the appearance of an animal for nefarious purposes. **2** invisible.

silungkang k.o. woven cloth made in Silungkang, W. Sumatra.

SIM [*Surat Izin Mengemudi*] driver's license.

simaharajaléla see MAHARAJALÉLA.

simak₁ meny- scrutinize, observe attentively. ~ *visum* scrutinize a visa. **-an** s.t. scrutinized. **peny-** good listener. **peny-an** listening attentively, monitoring.

simak₂ ber- gather, group. *Meréka* ~ *di kamar muka* They gathered in the front room. **meny-** gather, collect. *Ia* ~ *barang-barang yg tlh dipakai* She gathered the used things together. **-an** gathering.

simalu k.o. weed, sensitive plant (*Mimosa pudica*).

simbah ber- be drenched, bespattered. *Ia* ~ *darah* He was bespattered with blood. **meny-1** splash, bespatter. *Ombak* ~ *pesisir* Waves splashed on the beach. **2** break out, appear. *Keringatnya* ~ *di mukanya* Sweat broke out on his face. **ter-** drenched, spattered.

simbang k.o. children's game. **ber-** play such a game. **meny-** toss s.t. up.

simbar k.o. plant. - *badak* k.o. tree.

simbok (*Jv*) see MBOK₂.

simbol symbol. **ber-(kan)** have s.t. as a symbol. ~ *arit* have a sickle as a symbol. **meny-kan** symbolize.

simbolik, simbolis symbolic. *tanda* - a symbolic sign.

simbolisasi symbolization.

simbul see SIMBOL.

simbur ber- 1 splash up on. *Laut* ~ *ke pantai* The sea splashed up on the beach. **2** be partially enveloped by s.t. similar to waves. *Pemandangan* ~ *kabut* The view was obscured by a fog which seemed to wash up around it. **ber-an** splash on e.o. *Gadis-gadis itu mandi* ~ Those girls bathed while splashing e.o. **meny-(i)** splash on s.t., sprinkle with water. *Ia* ~ *daun tembakau spy basah* He sprinkled the tobacco leaves to dampen them. **meny-kan** splash s.t. out. *Ia* ~ *air yg dimanterainya pd anak itu* He splashed the child with the water he had cast a spell on. **ter-, ke-an** be splashed accidentally.

simétris symmetrical.

simfoni symphony.

simpai₁ fastening which encircles. - *beduk* hoop on a big drum. - *besi* iron band. - *tong* barrel hoop. **meny-(kan)** put a band around s.t. *Ia* ~ *gendang* He put a band around a drum.

simpai₂ k.o. monkey.

simpan meny- 1 store, lay away. *Ia* ~ *bahan makanannya di gudang* He stored the food supplies in the storehouse. *Ia* ~ *bukunya di peti* He put away his books in a box. ~ *uang* save money. **2** have inside, keep s.t. in storage. *Para peronda menggelédah rumah-rumah kalau-kalau* ~ *kedua org itu* The patrols searched houses to check that the two persons were not being kept in them. *Ia* ~ *rahasia* She kept a secret. ~ *dendam* bear a grudge. ~ *di hati* keep s.t. to o.s. **2** keep s.t. alive in o.'s heart. **meny-kan** lay s.t. away for s.o. *Ia* ~ *uang anaknya* He saved money for his son. **ter-1** stored, laid away, saved. **2** kept within, borne. *Sdh terlalu lama dendamnya* ~ She had borne her grudge for too long. **ter-kan** can be stored. **-an 1** savings, goods laid away. *uang* ~ money savings. **2** storage place. **3** mistress. *isteri* ~ a secret wife. **peny- 1** o. who saves, a depositor. ~ *arsip*

archivist, keeper of records. **2** storage place. **peny-an** storage, laying away. *tempat ~ peluru* a place for storing bullets.
simpang branch (of road, etc.), deviation. *- empat/jalan* road intersection, crossroads. *- sungai* tributary. *- siur* crisscross. *Banyak mobil yg - siur menuju ke Kebayoran* Many cars crossed back and forth in front of e.o. on the way to Kebayoran. **ber-** *siur* crisscross. **ke-siuran** confusion. **per-siuran 1** crisscrossing. **2** confusion, mix-up. **ber-1** branch off. *jalan ~* a branch road. **2** deviate from e.o. *Meréka ~ pendapat* They had different opinions. *~ jalan* go separate ways. *~ kata* hold a different opinion. **ber-an** intersect. *jalan yg ~* intersecting roads. **meny- 1** deviate, diverge. *Ia ~ dr adat* She deviated from the traditional custom. *Ia ~ spy tdk ditabrak* He deviated so he would not get hit by a car. *tak ~* unswerving. **2** take a side route. *Ia ~ dr jalan besar* She avoided the main highway. *Ia agak ~ dr pokok acara* He departed somewhat from the topic under discussion. **meny-i** isolate. *mana yg perlu di-i, mana yg perlu ditambah* those which should be isolated and those which should be added. **meny-kan** divert s.t., distract s.o. **ter-kan** possible to distract or deviate. **-an 1** branching off. **2** byway, side route. **3** crossroads. **4** (*Math.*) deviation. *~ baku* standard deviation. **peny-an** deviation, divergence. *~ dasar* standard deviation (in science). **per-an** intersection, branching off. *~ jalan* road intersection.
simpansé chimpanzee.
simpati sympathy. **ber-** sympathetic. *Ada pihak yg menuduh bhw meréka ~ pd gerombolan* Certain people accuse them of being sympathetic toward the gang.
simpatik congenial, likeable. *Dia mémang gadis yg - * She is really a likeable girl.
simpatisan sympathizer (of a party, cause, etc.).
simpel (*Coll.*) simple, modest, small in amount.
simping k.o. mollusc with a flat shell.
simplifikasi simplification.
simpoa see SEMPOA.
simponi see SIMFONI.
simposion, simposium symposium.
simpuh ber- sit with the knees bent and folded back to o. side. **ter-** fall down on o.'s knees. *Ia sampai di perbatasan, ~ letih di tanah airnya* He reached the border and in exhaustion, he fell down on his knees in his homeland.
simpul₁ knot, node. *- hidup* slipknot. *- mati* a firm knot. *- pulih* slipknot. **meny- 1** button clothing. **2** form a knot. **meny-kan 1** form s.t. into a knot. *Parjo duduk dan ~ kain pd léhérnya* Parjo sat down and tied a sarong around his neck. **2** conclude, summarize. *Ia ~ bhw temannya tak akan membayar utangnya* He concluded that his friend was not going to pay his debt. **ter- 1** knotted. *~ mati* irrevocably knotted. *Tali celananya ~ mati* The drawstring of his shorts was impossible to untie. **2** implied, included. *Penghargaan yg tinggi ~ dlm hadiah itu* Great esteem was implied in that gift.

ke-an conclusion. **berke-an** have as a conclusion. **-an 1** knot, node. **2** act of buttoning. **peny-** s.o. or s.t. which brings s.t. (discussion, etc.) to a conclusion. *artikel ~* concluding article (in magazine, etc,). **peny-an** process of drawing a conclusion.
simpul₂ see SENYUM. **meny-** form an embarrassed smile. *Senyum ~ di bibirnya* An embarrassed smile formed on his lips.
sim-sala-bim, simsalabim magical formula, abracadabra.
simultan simultaneous.
sinaga k.o. acute viral disease affecting the skin, shingles.
sinagoga synagogue.
sinambung continuous. *fase -* connected stage, serial. *tak -* (*Phys., Math.*) discrete. **ber-** continuous, serial. **ke-an** continuity. **berke-an** continuous, without interruption. *Programnya hrs ~ spy éféktif* The program has to be carried out without interruption if it is to be effective.
sinar 1 ray, beam. *- kosmik* cosmic ray. *- laser* laser beam. *- matahari* sunray. **2** gleam. *- api* light from a fire. *- seminar* glittering, radiating (of light). **- meny-** glitter and gleam. **ber-, meny-** shine. *mata ~* shining eyes. *Lampu lalulintas itu ~ mérah* The traffic light gleams red. **meny-i 1** illuminate s.t., gleam on s.t. *Matahari ~ bumi* The sun illuminates the earth. **2** irradiate s.t. *~ film* expose film. **meny-kan 1** radiate, send off. *Bom itu ~ panas* That bomb radiates heat. *Matanya ~ kelaparan cintanya* His eyes radiated his hunger for love. **2** cause s.t. to shine. *Ia ~ lampunya* She let her lamp shine. **ke-an 1** well-lightedness. **2** shone upon. **-an 1** glow, gleam. *~ mata lembutnya* the glow of her soft eyes. **2** ray. **peny-an 1** illumination. **2** radiation.
sinau sparkle, shine. *- seminau* glittering and sparkling. **ber-²** glitter and sparkle.
sincia (*Ch*) lunar New Year.
sincunkionghi (*Ch*) Happy Lunar New Year.
sindap dandruff.
sindén see PESINDÉN.
sinder see OPSINDER.
sindikat syndicate.
sindir s.t. said by allusion in order to tease. *"Kau sdh tahu tapi kau masih saja mau bertanya," -nya* "You know the answer already but you want to ask anyway," he teased. **- meny-** make allusions to e.o. to tease. *Meréka menembang ~* They teased each other by citing poetry full of allusions. **meny-** tease us. by insinuation and allusion. **peny-** teaser. **-an 1** teasing allusion. **2** satire. *~ nasib* irony of fate.
sindroma syndrome.
sinduk see SÉNDOK.
sinéas film-maker.
sinématék film library.
sinématografi cinematography.
sinématografis cinematographic.
siner see OPSINDER.
sinerap (*Tech.*) absorbate.

sing sound of buzzing.
singa 1 lion. - *laut* walrus. 2 (*Zod.*) Leo.
Singapura Singapore.
singelar (*Sport*) single player.
singga see SEHINGGA.
singgah stop by, stop in. *Saya mau - sebentar* I want to stop in for a moment. **meny-i** stop in. *Ia ~ Délhi dlm perjalanannya ke Éropa* She stopped at Delhi on her way to Europe. *Ia ~ temannya di kota itu* He stopped in at his friend's in that town. **meny-kan** 1 cause s.t. to stop. *Ia ~ bis di jalan* He stopped a bus on the street. 2 stop to deliver. *Mobil itu ~ kiriman org tuanya* The car stopped to deliver a parcel from his parents. **per-an** 1 stopover, transit. 2 port of call.
singgang k.o. culinary method for cooking meats in coconut milk. *ayam -* chicken prepared in this way.
singgasana throne. **ber-** be on the throne. **meny-kan** enthrone.
singgat, singget meny- divide, part. **-an** partition.
singgul see SÉNGGOL.
singgung ber- touch, nudge. **ber-an** touch, contact e.o. *~ kulit* be so close that skin touches skin. **meny-** 1 touch, contact. *Di- begitu saja menangis* As soon as he is touched he starts crying. 2 offend, insult, hurt (o.'s feelings). *~ perasaan* hurt o.'s feelings. 3 touch on, treat (a subject, problem). *Ia ~ soal harta warisan* He touched on the problem of inheritance. **ter-** offended. *mudah ~* easily offended, sensitive, touchy. **keter-an** 1 touchiness. 2 state of having been offended. **-an** 1 s.t. touched upon. 2 (*Coll.*) mutually acquainted. **peny-an** act of offending. **per-an** point of contact.
singit₁ (*Jv*) sacred, no trespassing. *Tempat itu - org tdk boléh msk begitu saja* This place is sacred and may not be entered at will.
singit₂ see SÉNGÉT.
singkap meny- 1 unveil, expose, open. *~ kordén* open the curtains. *~ tirai* 1 unveil a monument. 2 open a blind. 2 reveal. *Ia ~ rahasia* She revealed a secret. 3 be turned back and open a bit (sheets, skirts, etc.). *Di atas kasur seprénya ~* On the mattress the sheets lay drawn open. **meny-kan** 1 disclose, reveal. *Buku ini ~ dunia baru* This book discloses a new world. *Pandangannya seolah ~ ketuaan hati* His gaze seemed to reveal a heart which had grown old. 2 turn s.t. back (of cloth, sheets, etc.). **ter-** opened, disclosed. *Hari tlh ~* It has become day. **-an** 1 s.t. folded back or drawn to o. side. *~ roknya membuat banyak lelaki menoléh* The folded-back slit of her skirt caused several men to steal glances at her. 2 exposure. **peny-** s.o. or s.t. that uncovers or discloses. *~ rahasia* discloser of secrets. **peny-an** uncovering, disclosure.
singkat 1 brief, concise. - *akal/paham* dumb, mentally limited. - *pengetahuan* narrow-minded. 2 short in length. *Bajunya -* She has a short blouse on (i.e., she is not wearing the *baju ku-*

rung, the coat-length blouse). 3 short in time. - *sungu* hot-tempered. - *umur* have a short life. **-nya** in short, in brief. **meny-** make brief or short. *~ waktu* shorten the time. **meny-kan** abbreviate, shorten. *Itu di-kan dr kata pengantar* That is a condensed version of the preface preface. **memper-** shorten. **ke-an** shortness. **-an** 1 abbreviation. 2 abstract, résumé.
singkéh, singkék (*Derog.*) a Ch (immigrant) that is still very Ch in his ways.
singkir meny- 1 step aside, yield. *Ia ~ waktu mobil liwat* He stepped aside when the car passed. 2 evacuate, move to. *Banyak pengungsi ~ ke tempat yg aman* Many refugees evacuated to a safe place. **meny-i** avoid s.t., evade s.t. *Meréka ~ tempat yg berbahaya* They avoided the dangerous place. **meny-kan** 1 evacuate s.t. *Ia ~ barang-barangnya ke désa* He evacuated his belongings to the village. 2 remove, put away, lay aside. *Ia ~ buku-buku yg tdk dipakai* He removed all unused books. *Meréka ~ perselisihannya waktu perayaan itu* They laid aside their differences at the celebration. 3 eliminate, purge, get rid of s.o. or s.t. *Ada kekuatan dlm perusahaan yg ~nya dr jabatannya* There are forces in the firm which are eliminating her from her position. *Dia berhasil ~ isyu-isyu buruk ttg dirinya* He managed to lay to rest all the nasty rumors about himself. **ter-** 1 prevented, safeguarded. *Ia ~ dr bahaya* She was kept safe from danger. 2 eliminated, gotten rid of. *Pégawai itu ~ karena tdk becus* The employee was removed because of incompetence. **ter-kan** be shoved aside by s.t. *Masalah pembangunan ~ oléh masalah politik* Problems of development became overshadowed by political problems. **peny-an** 1 evacuation. 2 elimination, purge. 3 exclusion. *~ Amat dr kepemimpinan partai* the exclusion of Amat from the party leadership.
singkong cassava. - *gendruwo* k.o. very big cassava. - *mukibat* k.o. large cassava first bred by a man named Mukibat.
singkron see SINKRON.
singkup shovel. - *keruk* dredging bucket.
singkur meny-i turn o.'s back to s.o. or s.t., ignore.
singlét sleeveless undershirt.
singsat tight. *Bajunya -* His clothing is tight. **meny-** shrink. *Keméjanya ~* His shirt shrank. **meny-kan** 1 tighten. *Ia ~ tali* She tightened the rope. 2 roll up. *Ia ~ lengan bajunya* He rolled up his sleeves. 3 shrink s.t.
singsé see SINSÉ.
singset see SINGSAT.
singshé see SINSÉ.
singsing meny- rise, lift, break clear. *Awan tlh ~* The cloud has lifted. *Fajar ~* The dawn is breaking (It is daybreak). **meny-(kan)** roll, tuck up. *~ lengan* 1 roll up o.'s sleeves. *Ia ~ lengan bajunya* He rolled up his sleeves. 2 get to work. *Angkatan muda mesti ~ lengan menyelesaikan répolusi ini* The young generation must work hard in order to

complete the revolution. **ter-** rolled up. *Dgn ce-lana ~ ia msk WC* He entered the washroom with his pants rolled up.

singsring meny- blow o.'s nose.

sini 1 here. *Bawa -* Bring it here. *dr -* from here. *di -* here. *Ia sdh lama di -* He has been here for a long time. *ke -* 1 to here. **2** (*Coll.*) come here! **dike-kan** be sent here. *Kalau ia tdk mau terima boléhlah barang itu ~* If he will not accept it you may send it here. **2** there, where the recipient is (in letters only). **3** (*Coll.*) I, we. *- tdk keberatan; bagaimana sana?* We have no objections; how about the others?

sinis 1 sarcastic, scornful. *Suaminya menyambut-nya dgn senyum - yg menikam-nikam hatinya* Her husband received her with a sarcastic smile that stabbed right through her heart. **2** cynical. *Dia - dan tak perduli* She is cynical and does not care. **ke-an 1** sarcasm, scorn. **2** cynicism.

sinisme 1 sarcasm, scorn. **2** cynicism.

sinkrétisme syncretism.

sinkron synchronous. **meny-kan** synchronize.

sinkronisasi synchronization. **mens-kan** synchronize some event or project.

sinode (*Rel.*) synod.

sinom young tamarind leaves.

sinonim synonym. **ke-an** synonymy.

sinopsis synopsis.

sinoptik synoptics.

sinsé, sinshé, sinsyé Ch physician, purveyor of Ch herbal medicines. *- guamia/kuamia* (*Ch*) fortune-teller. *- kuritan* (*Ch*) kung fu master.

sintak see SÉNTAK₂.

sintaksis syntax.

sintal well-fed, full, well rounded, having an attractive figure.

sintang 1 short. **2** weird, eccentric.

sinterklas (*Coll.*) Santa Claus.

sintése synthesis. **meny-kan, mens-kan** synthesize.

sintétis synthetic.

sinting rather crazy. *Banyak org mengatakan bhw Abu itu setengah -* Many people say that Abu is half-crazy. **ke-an** craziness, oddness.

sintir 1 dice. **2** dice game.

sintok see SINTUK₁,₂.

sintuh see SENTUH.

sintuk₁ k.o. cinnamon tree the bark of which is used as a medicine.

sintuk₂ (*Lit.*) **ber-** rub o.s. with s.t. *Ia sedang ~ badan* He was rubbing his body.

sintung meny- touch with the elbow.

sinu nerve.

sinuhun (*Jv, Sd*) term of address for a sovereign.

sinus sine.

sinyal 1 signal. *- bahaya* danger signal. **2** railway crossing light. **mens-kan** give a signal.

sinyalemén 1 indication. *Ada - bhw dia anggota PKI* There are indications that she is a member of the Communist Party. **2** assumption, suspicion. *Menurut - polisi barang selundupan itu akan msk di pelabuhan* According to the assumptions

of the police the smuggled goods will enter the harbor.

sinyalir mens- call attention to, point out. *Parlemén ~ bahaya inflasi* Parliament pointed out the dangers of inflation.

sinyo 1 (*Coll.*) term of address and reference for European or Westernized youth. **2** term of address used by servant to master's son.

Sinyoklas, Sinyokolas (*Coll.*) Father Christmas.

sio₁ (*Amb*) Alas!

sio₂ see SHIO.

siocia (*Ch*) term of address and reference for unmarried woman.

siocu k.o distilled alcoholic beverage.

sioh see SHIO.

siomai (*Ch*) k.o. steamed ravioli filled with meat and open on the top.

sip (*Coll.*) **1** OK. *Kalau enam org, -!* If there are six persons, that is fine! **2** great, admirable. *Orgnya -, deh!* That guy's really fantastic!

sipai see SEPOI₁.

sipaku gelang (*M*) k.o. traditional bangle worn by brides.

sipat₁ *- datar* device to ascertain whether s.t. is level. **meny-(kan)** (*Lit.*) measure with a plumb.

sipat₂ mascara. *- mata* mascara.

sipat₃ see SIFAT.

sipat kuping (*Jv*) helter-skelter, frantically fast.

sipedas (*M*) ginger.

sipék see SI₂.

Sipenmaru [*séléksi penerimaan mahasiswa baru*] entrance test to the state university system.

sipi be just off the mark, a little off center, glancing (blow). *- sekali* a hair's breadth. **meny-** graze, be just off center. *Témbakannya ~* His shot just missed the bull's-eye.

sipil 1 civil. *bagian -* civil engineering. **2** civilian.

sipilis syphilis.

sipir jailer.

sipit₁ slanting (of the eyes). **meny-** become squinted or narrowed (of eyes). *Matanya mengedip-ngedip cepat dan ~* She blinked fast and narrowed her eyes. **meny-kan** squint. **ke-an** narrowness (of eyes).

sipit₂ see SEMPIT.

sipolan see POLAN.

sipon see SIFON.

siponggang echo. **ber-** echo, echoing.

sipu₁ ter-(²), ke-(²)an embarrassed, shy, bashful. *Ia mérah mukanya ~* His face was flushed from embarrassment.

sipu₂ ter-² in a hurry.

sipulut see PULUT.

siput snail. *- memuji buntut* praise o.s. (lit., The snail praise its tail.).

SIPVA [*Surat Izin Pembelian Valuta Asing*] permit for purchase of foreign exchange.

sir₁ (*Lit.*) mystical.

sir₂ (*Coll.*) **1** like s.t. or s.o., lust after. *Ia ~ pd perempuan itu* He lusts after that woman. **2** fall in love with s.o. **3** aim, what o. is after. **-²an** fall in love. *Pemuda itu yg pernah ~ dgn gadis-gadis itu*

That is the young man who had fallen in love with those girls.
sir₃ sound of hissing.
sirafa see JERAPAH.
sirah see SÉRAH.
sirak see SERAK.
siram ber- 1 be cascaded (with water, liquid). *Ia mandi ~ air* He took a shower (He bathed, pouring water over himself). **2** (*Lit.*) bathe (of royalty). **meny-** pour (water) over s.t., flush. *~ kakus* flush the toilet. **meny-i** pour (water) on s.t., sprinkle on. *~ halaman* water the garden. **meny-kan** pour out (water, liquid). *Anak itu ~ air ke tanah* The child poured water on the ground. **ter-** get s.t. splashed on it. *Mukanya kecut bagai maling ~ air kencing* He had an expression on his face like that of a thief s.o. had emptied a chamber pot on. **-an 1** a splash of water. **2** (*Jv*) ceremony of bathing a bride prior to the wedding. **peny-** s.t. to pour water (or other liquids) with, o. who waters the plants. *kendi ~* a vessel to pour out water with. **peny-an** pouring of liquids, watering. **per-an** (*Lit.*) bathing place.
sirap₁ slightly raised. **meny-kan 1** raise slightly. *Angin ~ atap* The wind lifted the roof slightly. **2** scare s.o. **ter-** *darah* suddenly startled and terrified, scared to death. *Setiap kali bél tilpun berdering darahnya ~* Each time the phone rang he was scared to death.
sirap₂ shingle. *atap -* shingle roof. **ter-** shingled. *Atapnya ~* The roof is shingled.
sirap₃ see SIREP.
sirat mesh, network. **meny-** make a knot. **meny-kan** imply. *Apa yg di-kan pernyataannya?* What was implied by his statement? **ter- 1** knotted. *tali yg ~* knotted string. **2** implied, implicit. *yg ~ dlm kalimat ini* which is implied in this sentence. **-an 1** s.t. knotted or knitted. *~ benang* net. **2** implication.
siratulmustakim (*Isl.*) path for believers on the Last Day.
siréne siren. *- kebakaran* fire alarm.
sirep 1 (*Jv*) quiet, silent. **2** (*Jv*) fallen (of temperature). **3** magic formula to induce sleep. **meny-(kan) 1** cast a sleeping spell over s.o. **2** (*Jv*) calm s.o.
siri /siri'/ (*Sulawesi*) suffer humiliation. **peny-an** taking revenge because of humiliation.
Siria see SURIAH.
sirih k.o. plant, betel vine. *- kuning* a pretty girl. *- pulang ke gagang* proper, fitting. **2** a quid us. consisting of betel leaf, areca nut, and lime (often with other ingredients, e.g. gambier, tobacco, etc.). *makan -* chew betel. **meny-** chew betel. **meny-i 1** offer betel to s.o. *Meréka ~ tamunya* They offered betel to their guests. **2** offer s.t. to s.o. (esp. guests). **meny-kan** *rokok* offer s.o. a cigarette.
sirik₁ envious. *Ia - pd temannya yg kaya* He was jealous of his wealthy friend.
sirik₂ see SYIRIK.
siring₁ k.o. shrimp net. **meny-** scoop up care-

fully. *Ia ~ minyak dr wajan* He scooped up oil from the frying pan.
siring₂ hem of cloth. **ber-** have a hem.
siring₃ gutter, drain, ditch.
sirip fish fin. *sop - ikan hiu* shark fin soup. *- dada* pectoral fin. *- sayap* flap (on plane).
sirkam k.o. small ornamental comb.
sirkaya see SERIKAYA₁.
sirkel circle.
sirkit, sirkuit circuit.
sirkol sauerkraut.
sirkulasi circulation.
sirkulér circular.
sirkus circus.
sirlak varnish.
sirna disappeared. **meny-kan 1** make disappear. **2** abolish. **3** destroy, kill.
sirobok ber- meet for an instant (of eyes, glance).
sirop see SIRUP.
sirsak k.o. fruit, soursop.
sirup fruit syrup concentrate for drinks.
sis sound of hissing.
sisa 1 residue, remainder. *- uang* the rest of the money. **2** remnant. *- makanan* leftovers from a meal. *- rasa* aftertaste. **ber-** remain, be left over. *Kalau diambil dua, ~ tiga* If you take away two, you will have three left. **meny-kan 1** leave behind. *Pembelian itu ~ dua dolar saja* That purchase left just two dollars. **2** set aside (for later). **ter-** left(over). *tdk ~* without remainder.
sisal sisal hemp.
sisalak (*Coll.*) **ber-** be cantankerous, prone to fits of anger.
sisi side, flank. *- rumah* side of the house. *- kanan dan kiri* right and left side. *Ia duduk di - pamannya* He sat beside his uncle. *- miring* (*Math.*) hypotenuse. *di - itu* besides. *ke -* to the side. **menge-kan** ignore. *Ia merasa dike-kan* He felt ignored. **ber-(an)** side by side. *Meréka duduk ~* They sat side by side. **meny- 1** move to the side. *Ia ~ karena ada mobil léwat* He moved to the side because a car was passing. **2** go along the side of s.t. *Perahu itu ~ sepanjang sungai* The boat went along the river's edge. **meny-kan** move s.t. to the side. *Ia ~, mobilnya utk diparkir* He moved his car to the side to park it. **peny-an** movement to the side.
sisih meny- 1 give way, get out of the way. *Ia ~ ke pinggir jalan waktu ada mobil léwat* He went to the side of the road when a car passed. **2** be separate, aloof from. *Rumahnya ~ dr bagian ramai* Her house is separate from the busy section. **3** set s.t. aside, put s.t. to the side. *Di-nya rambutnya yg terurai di atas telinganya* She pushed away the hair that hung over her ear. **meny-kan 1** set aside, separate out. *Ia ~ buah yg busuk dr yg lainnya* He separated the rotten fruit from the others. *~ uang* set money aside. **2** reject, ignore. *Ia ~ murid yg tdk disukai itu* He cold-shouldered the unpopular student. **3** (*Sport*) eliminate. *Tim RI sdh ~ kebanyakan lawannya* The Indonesian team had already eliminated most of its adver-

saries. **ter-** isolated, set apart, ignored. *Anwar merasa ~ dr masyarakat kampung itu* Anwar felt isolated from village society. **ter-kan** (*Sport*) eliminated. *Ia ~ dlm babak semi-final* She was eliminated in the semifinals. **peny-an 1** isolation. **2** elimination.

sisihan (*Jv*) spouse.

sisik 1 scales of fish, reptile, etc. **2** turtle shell, esp. as article of commerce. **ber-** scaly. **meny-** become (like) scales. *Air danau meriak kecil ~ pérak* The water of the lake rippled and became a silvery sheath of scales. **meny-(i)** remove scales. *Ia ~ ikan* He removed scales from the fish. *Ia minta ~ limbat* She wants the impossible (lit., remove scales from a catfish, which is scaleless).

sisip ber-an have an insert. **ber-kan** have a certain thing inserted in it. *majalah yg ~ kupon berhadiah* a magazine with coupons inserted in it. **meny-** penetrate between two objects or into a narrow space. *Jarum ~ daging* The needle penetrated the flesh. *~ ke daérah musuh* slip into enemy territory. **meny-i 1** insert into s.t. **2** repair s.t. by putting s.t. flat in between, e.g. insert new parts in roof, etc. *Ia ~ atap* He repaired the thatch (by inserting new pieces here and there). **meny-kan, memper-kan** insert s.t. in. *Ia ~ penunjuk halaman di bukunya* He inserted a bookmark in the book. *Ia ~ pistol di bawah sabuknya* He slipped a pistol under his belt. **ter- 1** inserted. **2** implied, interpolated. **ke-an 1** get a splinter under the skin. **2** get s.t. inserted into it by accident. *Dompétnya ~ uang temannya* His wallet has some of his friend's money in it. **-an 1** s.t. inserted. **2** s.t. implied. **3** (*Ling.*) infix. **peny-an 1** insertion. *~ komentar yg humoristis* insertion of humorous comments. **2** (*Ling.*) infixation.

sisir₁ 1 comb. **2** harrow. **3** bunch (of bananas). *-pisang* a bunch of bananas. **ber- 1** use a comb. **2** combed. *Rambutnya jarang ~* His hair is seldom combed. **meny- 1** comb s.t. *~ rambut* comb hair. **2** harrow s.t. *~ tanah* harrow the ground. **meny-kan** comb s.t. for s.o. *Mari aku -kan rambutmu* Let me comb your hair for you. **ter-** combed.

sisir₂ see SUSUR₁.

Siskamling [*Sistém Keamanan Lingkungan*] **1** neighborhood security system. **2** participate in this system.

sispan see SÉSPAN.

sistém system. *- angkum* court-martial system (in which military personnel are not directly subject to civil law). *- famili* nepotism. *- go-go* system of making a passenger pay a bribe to get a seat. *- kartu* card system (in computers, etc.). *- kawan* spoils system. *- kecakapan* merit system. *- témbak* **1** dealing with crime by simply shooting the suspect. **2** outspoken, direct. *- lingkungan* ecosystem.

sistématik 1 systematic. **2** systematics. **men-kan** systematization.

sistématis systematic.

sistématisasi systematization. **mens-kan** systematize.

sister see SUSTER.

sistim see SISTÉM.

sistol (*Med.*) systole.

sisurut see SURUT.

siswa 1 student (at secondary school). **2** student (at academies, training institutes, but not at universities). **3** male student at such institutions. *--siswi* male and female students.

siswi female student at a secondary school or nonuniversity institutions of tertiary education.

sit master sheet for mimeographing. **menge-** type s.t. in a master sheet.

SIT [*Surat Izin Terbit*] written authorization to publish s.t.

sita seizure, confiscation. **meny-, men- 1** seize, confiscate. *Rumahnya dibakar dan ternaknya di-* His house was burnt and his cattle confiscated. **2** consume (o.'s time or attention). *Seluruh perhatiannya di- oléh hari perkawinannya* The day of her wedding took all her attention. *~ waktu* take time, time-consuming. **ter-** confiscated. *Obat bius yg ~* confiscated drugs. **-an** confiscated goods. **peny-an, pen-an** (*Leg.*) seizure, confiscation.

sitar see SITER.

sitegang see TEGANG.

sitekan see TEKAN.

sitén see SETÉN.

siter zither.

siti 1 title for a woman of noble lineage. *- Hawa* Eve. *- Mariam* (*Isl.*) Mary, the mother of Jesus. **2** a woman's name.

sitiau see SI₂.

sitir meny-(kan), mens- cite, quote. **-an** citation, quotation (from book).

sitokar see STOKER.

sitologi (*Med.*) cytology.

sitronella k.o. plant, citronella.

sitrun citron.

sitti see SITI.

situ₁ 1 there (not very far away and near person addressed). *dr -* from there. *ke -* to that place. *anak-anak kampung -* the children of the village there. *di -* **1** there, over there (within sight). *Taruh di -* Put it over there. **2** then, at the moment. *di - baru ia mengerti* Only then did he understand. **3** (*Coll.*) you. *Di - yg bayar* You pay! **3** (Coll.) you. *Kan - tahu siapa yg ngambil!* But you know who it was that took it!

situ₂ (*Sd*) lake.

situasi 1 situation, circumstances. **2** location, the way s.t. is located. **men-kan, meny-kan** situate s.t. (on a site, etc.).

situn (*Lit.*) k.o. earthenware pot.

situs archaeological site.

siuk meny- groan, moan. *Org sakit itu ~* The patient was groaning.

siul sound of whistling. **ber-** whistle (of people, trains, etc.). *Keréta api ~* The train whistles.

men-kan whistle s.t. ~ *lagu romantis* whistle a romantic tune. **-an** whistling. ~ *burung* twitter of a bird. **peny-** whistler.

siuman 1 become sober. 2 recover consciousness. *Ia - dr pingsannya* She came to after her fainting spell.

siung₁ 1 canine tooth. 2 fang, tusk. 3 clove (of garlic). *- bawang putih* clove of garlic.

siung₂ sound of buzzing. **ber-** whiz by. *Peluru ~ di dekat telinganya* Bullets whizzed by his ears.

siur₁ sound of leaves rustling. **ber-** make a rustling sound. **ber-an, berke-an** rustle, whistle (of many things). *Peluru* ~ Bullets were whistling. *Angin sepanjang malam* The wind rustled all night.

siur₂ see SILANG.

siut sound of sizzling, whizzing, etc. **ber-** produce a sizzling or whistling sound. *Api ~ jika disiram air* Fire gives off a hissing sound when water is poured on it. *Ia ~ kepedasan* He is blowing air out of his mouth because of the hot spices. **men-(²)** make sizzling sounds. *Ia suka ~ di dlm pertemuan* He likes to hiss at meetings. **-an** whizzing sound. ~ *peluru* the whizzing sound of a bullet.

SIVA [*Surat Impor Valuta Asing*] foreign exchange import permit.

sivil see SIPIL.

sivilisasi civilization.

siwak₁ (*Lit.*) bundle of young twigs or roots used to clean teeth.

siwak₂, siwakan (*Jv*) not on speaking terms.

siwalan (*Jv*) k.o. fan palm or its edible fruit.

siwar [*psychological war*] psychological warfare.

siwer (*Jv*) squinting. *mata -* cross-eyed.

siyét 1 k.o. knitting. 2 wool for knitting. **meny-** knit.

sk. [*surat kabar*] newspaper.

SK [*Surat Keputusan*] decree. **meng-kan** issue a decree for s.t. **peng-an** issuing of a decree.

skak see SEKAK.

skakelar see SAKELAR.

skala scale (of map, etc.).

skandal scandal.

skap tool to plane wood.

skat 1 ice skates. 2 skating. *- indah* figure-skating.

skéma 1 scheme, sketch. 2 chart, diagram.

skématis schematic.

skéna (*Thea.*) scene.

skénario scenario. *- politik* political scenario.

sképtikus a skeptic.

sképtis skeptical.

sképtisi skeptic.

skét, skéts, skétsa sketch. **men-(kan)** sketch.

skétsel partition.

skizofrén schizophrenic.

skizofrénia schizophrenia.

SKKA [*Sekolah Kesejahteraan Keluarga Atas*] upper secondary school for training home economics teachers.

SKM [*Sarjana Keséhatan Masyarakat*] Master of Public Health.

SKN [*Staf Keamanan Nasional*] National Security Staff.

skop shovel, spade.

skor (*Sport*) score. **peng-an** scoring.

skorbut (*Med.*) scurvy.

skorkar score card.

skors **men-, meny-** 1 suspend s.o. *Ia di- dr pekerjaannya* She was suspended from her job. 2 adjourn. *Rapat di- selama sejam* The meeting was adjourned for an hour. **pen-an** suspension.

skorsing suspension (of student, sportsman, etc.).

SKP [*Sekolah Kepandaian Puteri*] home economics school.

skrining screening (of applicants, us. for security reasons). **men-** screen.

skrip (*Thea.*) script.

skripsi k.o. minithesis to obtain *dokterandus* degree.

skuadron, skwadron squadron.

skup see SKOP.

skuter (*Coll.*) motor-scooter.

sl- see also entries with **sel-**.

sla₁ salad.

sla₂ see SLAH.

slada see SELADA.

slagorde (*Mil.*) battle-array.

slah (*Crd.*) trick.

slahrom, slahrum whipped cream.

slametan (*Coll., Jv*) ceremonial meal, esp. at marriages, promotions, etc.

slang₁ tube, hose. *- kebakaran* fire hose.

slang₂ /sléng/ slang.

slébor₁ (*Jkt*) mudguard, fender. *- baru* 1 (*Sl.*) new haircut. 2 new mudguard.

slébor₂ (*Coll.*) unconventional.

slék women's slacks often tight.

sléndro five-tone tuning system of Jv gamelan.

slénger (*Auto.*) crank, starting-handle. **men-** crank, start a car with a crank.

slentik (*Jv*) **meny-, ny-** 1 snap s.o. or s.t. with o.'s index finger. 2 reprimand s.o.

slintru (*Jv*) screen to partition a room.

slip see SELIP₂.

sliwar-sliwer to and fro.

SLJJ [*Sambungan Langsung Jarak Jauh*] (*Tel.*) direct-dial long distance network.

slof carton of cigarettes (unit of 10 packs). **-²an** by the carton.

slogan slogan. **men-kan** utter s.t. as a slogan, make s.t. into a slogan.

sloganisasi sloganizing.

sloganisme mentality characterized by excessive use of slogans.

sloki 1 shot glass. 2 a shot (of liquor). **ber-²** by the shot.

slomprét₁ trumpet (us. made of paper). *- kabut* foghorn. **men-kan** propagandize, be the mouthpiece of.

slomprét₂ see SOMPRÉT₁.

slong nge- not working (of brakes).

slop see SLOF.

slot see SELOT.

slt. [*selatan*] south.

sM. [*sebelum Maséhi*] B.C., before Christ.

SM₁ [*Sekolah Menengah*] secondary school.

SM₂ [*Sarjana Muda*] academic degree similar to the baccalaureate.

SMA [*Sekolah Menengah Atas*] upper secondary school.

smir see SEMIR.

smokel see SEMOKEL.

SMP [*Sekolah Menengah Pertama*] lower secondary school.

snél (*Coll.*) fast.

snélvarband long gauze bandage.

snur (*Coll.*) cable, wire, cord.

so (*E. Indonesia*) see SUDAH.

soal /so'al/ **1** problem, matter. *Itu - yg sukar* That is a difficult problem. **2** question. *Meréka memajukan banyak - kpd pembicara* They asked the speaker a lot of questions. *- jawab* question-and-answer. **ber-** *jawab* engage in question-and-answer session, discuss. *Ia ~ jawab dgn Hasan ttg sikap hidupnya* He discussed his attitude toward life with Hassan. **-nya** The thing is . . . , The issue is . . . *~ saya tdk punya uang* The problem is I do not have any money. **ber-** engage in a question and answer session. *Yésus ~ dgn para imam di kenisah* Jesus engaged in a discussion with the religious leaders in the synagogue. **ber-²** **1** discuss. **2** argue, debate. **meny-kan** set questions about s.t. (in an exam, etc.). *hal yg di-kan di ujian itu* the topic he asked about in the test. **memper-kan** **1** question s.t. *Kejujurannya diper-kan* His honesty is questioned. **2** discuss, deal with. *Meréka sedang ~ rencana itu* They were discussing the plan. *Makalah ini ~ tradisi banci di Sulawési* This paper deals with the transvestite tradition in Sulawesi. **per-an** **1** problem, matter, issue. **2** discussion, debate.

SOB [*Staat van Oorlog en Beleg*] (*Pol.*) state of war and siege. **meng-kan** bring s.t. under military authority during war. *Perusahaan asing itu di-kan* The foreign enterprise was seized by the military authority.

sobat **1** friend. *- kental* close friends. **2** comrade (among communists). **ber-** be friends. **meny-i** make friends with s.o. *Ia pandai ~ org kaya* He is good at making friends with wealthy people. **per-an** friendship.

sobék torn, ripped. **meny-** tear, rip. **meny-(²)** repeatedly tear. **meny-kan** **1** cause s.t. to be torn. *Waktu mencuci, tak sengaja dia ~ baju anaknya* While she was laundering, she unintentionally tore her child's shirt. **2** tear s.t. on s.o.'s behalf. **ter-** torn. *Karcis yg sdh ~ tdk dpt dipakai lagi* The tickets which have been torn cannot be used again. **-an** a torn piece. *~ kain* a torn piece of cloth. *~ karcis* ticket stub. **peny-** o. who takes (and tears) tickets, ticket-taker.

sobok alloy. **ber-** encounter, fall in with.

SOBSI [*Séntral Organisasi Buruh Seluruh Indonésia*] All-Indonesia Federation of Labor Organizations.

soda soda (of various substances containing sodium). *- api* caustic soda. *- kué* baking soda. *- gembira* k.o. drink of sodawater with red syrop.

sodét₁ spatula.

sodét₂ see SUDÉT.

sodok₁ shovel, spade. **meny-** shovel, scoop up. **peny-** shovel, spade.

sodok₂ **ber-²an**, **- meny-** poke e.o. **meny-** thrust, poke. *Ia ~ perut saya dgn siku* He poked my stomach wth his elbow. **meny-i** poke (several times in several places). **meny-kan** poke with s.t., thrust s.t. *Ia ~ laras bedilnya ke dlm perutku* He thrust his gun barrel into my belly. **-an 1** a poke. **2** (*Sport*) shot in billiards. **3** instrument to poke or thrust.

sodomi sodomy.

sodor **meny-i** hand to s.o. *Para peserta konperénsi itu di-i program yg cukup padat* The participants of the conference were given a busy program. *Tukang catut ~ aku karcis seharga Rp1.000* The scalper handed me a a ticket for 1,000 rupiah. **meny-kan** **1** thrust s.t. forward, stretch s.t. out. *Ia ~ kakinya* He stretched out his legs. *Ia ~ surat kpd temannya* He handed a letter to his friend. *~ kucing dlm karung* hand s.o. a pig (lit., cat) in a poke, make s.o. accept s.t. without getting a look at it beforehand. **2** put forth. *Ia ~ usulnya kpd hadirin* He put forward his proposal to those present. **peny-** o. who hands in s.t. **peny-an** offer.

soé (*Ch*) bringing misfortune, unlucky.

soék see SOBÉK.

soen /sun/ see SUN.

sofa sofa.

sofball, sofbol (*Sport*) softball. **per-an** matters pertaining to softball.

sofis sophist.

sofisme sophism.

soga k.o. tree from which red dye used for batik is made.

sogang fence, palisade.

sogok₁ (*Coll.*) bribery. *- suap* bribe, bribery. **meny-** bribe s.o. *Paman tdk mau di- pedagang-pedagang itu* My uncle did not want to accept bribes from those merchants. **-an** bribe. **-²an** bribe e.o. *sistém ~ system* based on bribery. **peny-an** bribery.

sogok₂ stab, pierce through.

sohon see SOHUN.

sohor famous. **meny-kan** make s.o. or s.t. famous. *Partai itu ~ diri sbg satu-satunya partai* That political party made itself famous as the only party. **ke-, ter-** famous. **keter-an** fame.

sohun (*Ch*) transparent bean flour vermicelli.

sok₁ **1** as if, pretending. *Ia - jagoan* He pretends to be a tough guy. *Ia - tahu* She pretends to know. *- aksi* act pompous. **2** put on airs. *Org itu - aja* That guy's just showing off. **-²an** putting on airs, showing off. ~ *filosofis* putting on philosophical airs.

sok₂ /sok/ stocking, sock.

sok₃ /sok/ socket, waterpipe connection.

sok₄ see SYOK₂.

soka k.o. flowering tree.

sokbréker (*Auto.*) shock absorber.

soklat (*Coll.*) see COKLAT.

sokoguru 1 (*Jv*) central pillar (of house). **2** principal factor.

sokong prop, support. **meny- 1** prop up, support. *Tiang itu ~ rumahnya* That post is propping up her house. **2** aid. *~ pemberontakan* support a rebellion. **-an** support, aid, contribution. **peny-** supporter, contributor.

sok-sok (*Jv*) often. *Kalau - msk organisasi, lekas sekali terjebak* You're going to wind up in trouble if you constantly join organizations.

sol₁ sole (of a shoe). **men-** sole s.t.

sol₂ the musical note sol.

solar diesel fuel.

solat (*Isl.*) **1** ritual prayers and actions performed five times daily. *- Id* prayer ritual celebrating end of fasting month. **2** perform such prayers. **ber-** perform such ritual prayers.

soldadu see SERDADU.

soldér men- solder. **-an** soldering tool. **pen-an** soldering.

soléh see SALÉH.

solék well-dressed, stylish. **ber- 1** apply o.'s makeup. **2** dress up (of women). **meny-i** apply makeup to s.o. **pe- 1** o. who uses makeup. **2** a woman who likes to dress up.

solidaritas, solidaritét solidarity.

solidér in solidarity with. **meny-i** be in solidarity with, join in solidarity. **ke-an** solidarity.

solis soloist.

solo single, solo.

Solo city in central Java, Surakarta.

solok gift, contribution in kind. **peny-** gift, contribution in kind.

solokan see SELOKAN.

solot (*Jkt, Jv*) heatedly angry. **ny-** be blazing with anger. *Saking ~nya dia ambil sebuah cermin dan dibantingnya* In her wild fury she grabbed a mirror and slammed it down.

solvabilitas solvency.

som a hem. **mens-** hem s.t.

somah household. *- seperut* maternally related family (but with different fathers).

somatis somatic.

sombar (*Amb*) shade, shadow.

sombol meny- cram food into the mouth.

sombong arrogant, conceited. **ber-** act in an arrogant or conceited way. **meny-** be arrogant, be self-assertive, boast. **meny-i** be arrogant to s.o. *Dia ~ tetangganya* He is snobbish with his neighbor. **meny-kan** boast, brag about. *Ia selalu ~ kehayaannya* He is always boasting about his wealth. *~ diri* boast about o.s. **ke-an 1** arrogance, boasting. **2** vanity, conceit. **3** arrogant, conceited. *"Nggak," katanya agak ~* "No," she

said in a rather arrogant way. **ke-²an** act arrogantly, boast. **peny-** an arrogant conceited person, a braggart.

sompék chipped, broken off. *Piringnya -* The plate is chipped.

somplok, sompok ber- run into, meet unexpectedly. **ber-an** pass e.o. on the way. **ter-** be trapped. *Ia tak dpt lari ketika ~ polisi* He could not get away when he was trapped by the police.

somprét₁ (*Jkt*) dammit!, term of verbal abuse.

somprét₂ see SLOMPRÉT₁.

somsom (*Jkt*) conceited, arrogant.

sondak see SUNDAK.

sondang meny- lift, raise on o.'s head or shoulders.

sonder (*Coll.*) without.

sondol meny- 1 charge by lowering the head, butt s.t. **2** (*Sport*) hit the ball with the head. **-an** a forceful push (with the head).

sondong k.o. net for catching shrimp. **meny-** catch shrimp. **peny-** net for catching shrimp.

sondor see SODOR.

sonebril (*Coll.*) sunglasses.

sonéta sonnet.

songar proud, arrogant. **ke-an** pride, arrogance.

songél meny- protrude, jut out.

songgéng₁ protrude.

songgéng₂ see SUNGGING.

songkét see SUNGKIT₁.

songkok rimless fezlike cap us. made of velvet.

songpia (*Ch*) k.o. small fried spring-roll us. filled with finely shredded meat.

songsang see SUNGSANG.

songsong₁ (*Jv*) k.o. ceremonial umbrella of royalty. **ber-** carry or use the royal umbrella. **meny- 1** welcome. *Rakyat ~ kedatangan présidén* The people welcomed the arrival of the president. **2** commemorate. *pidato ~ Hari Kemerdékaan* speech commemorating Independence Day. **3** carry out (s.o.'s wishes, etc.). *Ia pergi ke makam ayahnya ~ permintaan ibunya* He went to his father's grave to carry out his mother's wish. **-an** welcome. **peny- 1** greeter. **2** greetings. *sepatah kata ~* some words of welcome. **peny-an** greeting, welcoming.

songsong₂ against. **ber-** go out against s.t. **meny-** go against. *Ia berlayar ~ angin yg keras* He sailed against a strong wind. *Ia ~ tindakan pemerintah* He opposed the gvt.'s action. *Ia berjalan ~ musuh* He went out to meet the enemy.

sono₁ (*Jkt*) place of origin.

sono₂ (*Jkt*) see SANA.

sontak₁ torn, damaged, broken off. **meny-kan** mutilate, disfigure.

sontak₂ meny-kan tug at, give a (sudden) jerk at. *Ia tiba-tiba ~ kudanya* He gave his horse a sudden jerk. **ter- 1** all of a sudden. *~lah tangisku* Suddenly I cried. **2** shocked.

sonték₁ meny- push away.

sonték₂ meny- copy, cheat in class, crib.

sontok akal see SUNTUK.

sontoloyo (*Coll.*) exclamation of disapproval or dislike, damn you!

soon see SOHUN.

sop soup. - *ayam* chicken soup. - *buntut* oxtail soup. - *tito* pork-tripe soup. **(me)nge-** make soup for dinner. **meny-kan** make soup of. -*kanlah tulang ini!* Make soup of this bone!

sopak₁ k.o. discoloration of the skin.

sopak₂ (*Jv*) hairpiece.

sopan 1 respectful. *Ia - pd org tuanya* He was respectful to his parents. 2 well mannered, decorous. *Ia - sekali dlm tingkah-lakunya* He has a courteous approach. *Org yg - tak akan berbuat spt itu* A decent person would not do anything like that. -*santun* 1 be correct in behavior, courteous, polite. 2 etiquette. **meny-i** be courteous to s.o. *Buat apa ~ org itu?* Why bother being polite to that person? **meny-kan** 1 make or render s.t. polite. 2 civilize. *~ bangsa lain* civilize other peoples. **meny-²kan** make (o.'s actions) falsely polite. *Ah, mau mengambil hati ibu pacarnya, maka di-²kannya tingkah lakunya* Heck, she is trying to get in good with her boyfriend's mother, so she is behaving with exaggerated politeness. **ke-an** good manners, polite behavior.

sopék k.o. small traditional fishing boat.

sopi 1 distilled palm wine. 2 (*Lit.*) liquor.

sopia see SONGPIA.

sopir chauffeur, driver. - *maut* reckless driver. **meny-, ny-** drive a motor vehicle (us. as chauffeur). **meny-i** drive s.t. *Bis yg di-i Amir meledak* The bus driven by Amir exploded.

sopran soprano.

sorak applause, cheering. - *semarai/sorai* loud cheering. **ber-*sorai*** cheer, yell (loudly). *Meréka ~ sorai, berteriak, "Bapak datang!"* They cheered and screamed "Father is coming!" **ber-(²)** cheer, shout. *Meréka ~ hingga suaranya habis* They cheered until their voices disappeared. **meny-i** cheer s.o., acclaim s.o. *Meréka ~ juara itu* They cheered the champion. **meny-kan** yell out s.t. *Meréka ~ nama org yg hrs datang* They yelled out the names of those who had to come forward. **-an** cheers, yells. **peny-** o. who yells, vocal supporter.

sorang (*Coll.*) alone. *Nyonya itu datang -* The lady came alone. **-an** (*Sd*) alone, on o.'s own. *~ waé* all alone, single.

sorban see SERBAN.

soré afternoon, early evening (between three and six p.m.). - *hari* in the afternoon. *nanti -* this afternoon or evening. -² toward evening. **-nya** the following afternoon. *Waktu pagi ia bekerja ~ bersekolah* He worked in the mornings and went to school in the afternoons. **ke-an** too late (in the afternoon). *Datangnya ~* She arrived too late in the afternoon.

soréh see SURIH.

sorék bamboo.

sorga see SURGA.

sorgaloka (*Lit.*) heaven, paradise.

sori (*Coll.*) Excuse me!

sorjan see SURJAN.

sorok₁ see SOGOK₁.

sorok₂ see SURUK.

sorong 1 sliding, pushing. *pintu -* sliding door. *keréta -* pushcart. 2 bribe. *Ia makan -* He accepted a bribe. **meny-** 1 push, slide. *Ia ~ pintu* He slid the door back. *Ia ~ keréta* He pushed the cart. 2 urge. *Ia ~ temannya spy pergi ke sana* He insisted that his friend go there. 3 propose, suggest. *~ damai* offer to make peace. 4 bribe s.o. **meny-kan** 1 slide s.t. forward. *Ia ~ pisau belatinya ke arah perutku* He slid his dagger toward my belly. 2 shove, push forward, hand. *Ia ~ usul* He pushed a proposal. *Ia ~ karcis kpdnya* She handed the tickets to him. **ter-** 1 put or slid forward. 2 forced, pushed into doing. *Dia berbuat jahat ~ oléh keadaan* She was pushed by the circumstances into doing evil. **-an** 1 s.t. pushed or shoved (e.g. a bolt). 2 a bribe. 3 a push, shove.

sorot ray, beam of light (of lamp, sun, etc.). - *mata* look, gaze. *nonton -* see a movie. **meny-** 1 shine, gleam, irradiate. *Lampunya ~ keluar* The lamp shone outside. 2 project (pictures). 3 gaze, look (of eyes). *Matanya tajam ~ ke dlm mataku* Her sharp eyes gazed into mine. 4 draw attention to, highlight. *~ masalah tapol* draw attention to the problem of political prisoners. **meny-i** 1 illuminate s.t., light up. *Ia ~ gang dgn lampu mobilnya* He illuminated the alley with his car lights. 2 spotlight s.t. or s.o., give prime importance to. *Mengapa kamu beranggapan bhw org lain selalu ~ dirimu?* Why do you think that other people are always focusing their attention on you? **meny-kan** 1 radiate s.t. *Matanya ~ sinar keramahan* His eyes radiated cheerfulness. 2 illuminate with s.t. *Dia ~ sénter ke rumah itu* She shone a flashlight on the house. **ter-** gaze, look at, be directed to (eyes). *Matanya ~ ke arahku* Her eyes were directed toward me. **-an** 1 ray, beam. 2 radiation, spotlight. 3 attention (in press, public, etc.). **peny-** 1 reflector, projector. 2 commentator, reviewer. *~ soal kebudayaan* a commentator on cultural affairs. **peny-an** 1 illumination, spotlighting. 2 elucidation.

sortasi sorting, grading.

sortir mens-, **meny-** sort. **(peny)-an, pen-an** sorting (of mail, etc.).

sos. [*sosial*] social studies division.

sosbud [*sosial budaya*] sociocultural.

sosi (*Ch*) key (to lock, etc.).

sosial 1 social. *fungsi -* societal function. 2 charitable. **men-kan** socialize s.o. **ke-an** 1 friendliness. 2 social. **pen-an** socialization.

sosialis socialist, socialistic. **meny-kan** make socialistic (the economy, etc.).

sosialisasi socialization.

sosialisme socialism.

sosialitas charitableness, charity.

sosiatri measurement of social behavior, esp. as a field of study.

sosiawan a social-minded or altruistic man.

sosiawati a social-minded or altruistic woman.

sosio-budaya sociocultural.
sosiografi social ethnography.
sosiolinguistik sociolinguistics.
sosiolog sociologist.
sosiologi sociology.
sosiologis sociological.
sosio-nasionalisme socialist nationalism.
sosio-psikologi social psychology.
sosis sausage.
sositét social club (colonial period).
soska [*sosialis kanan*] right-wing socialist.
soski [*socialis kiri*] left-wing socialist.
sosoh₁ meny- whiten or clean rice. **peny-** s.t. for hulling rice. *mesin* ~ huller. **peny-an** process of hulling rice.
sosoh₂ meny- **1** fight, engage in combat. **2** do s.t. with vigor.
sosok₁ **1** buttonhole, eye. **2** noose, loop. **pe-** eye, loop.
sosok₂ **1** form, shape, frame. - *tubuh* shape of the body, figure. **2** numeral classifier for body. *Tiga - badan bergelimpangan di jalan* Three bodies were sprawled on the street. **ber-** have the shape of. *Badannya ~ tinggi besar* He is tall and large. **meny-** set up the framework (of house), lay the keel (of ship).
sosong see SONGSONG₂.
sosor bill (of duck, etc.). **meny-** use the bill to scoop up or to peck at.
Sospol [*Sosial dan Politik*] **1** social and political science. **2** university division of social and political sciences.
soto k.o. clear soup. - *ayam* chicken soup. - *babat* tripe soup. - *daging* beef soup. - *mi/mie* noodle soup. - *madura* Madurese-style soup (with potato croquettes). **meny-** make *soto* of s.t. *Ia ~ ayamnya* He made his chicken into *soto*.
sotoh flat roof, roof-terrace.
sotong cuttlefish, squid.
so'un see SOHUN.
Sovyét-Uni Soviet Union.
sowan (*Jv*) visit (s.o. of higher status). *Ny. Suwarni - pd Ny. Kartini* Mrs. Suwarni called on Mrs. Kartini.
sp- see also entries with sep-.
SP [*Sri Paduka*] His Excellency, title for kings and at o. time the president of Indonesia.
spada a call to announce o.'s arrival at a house, anybody home?
spak wheel spoke.
spalek, spalk splints. **men-** put splints in, splint s.t.
span see SEPAN.
spanduk street banner affixed on both ends.
spaneng, spaning voltage.
spanrok k.o. tight skirt.
Spanyol see SEPANYOL.
sparepart /spérpar/ spare parts.
spasi space (in typing, etc.). - *rangkap/renggang* double-spaced.
spatbor, spatbord (*Auto.*) fender, mudguard.
speedometer /spidométer/ speedometer.

spékkuk see SPÉKUK.
spéktakulér spectacular.
spéktograf spectograph.
spéktogram spectogram.
spéktrum spectrum.
spékuk k.o. multilayered butter cake.
spékulan (*Fin.*) speculator.
spékulasi **1** speculation, conjecture. **2** risky commercial venture. **3** undertake a risky venture. **ber-** **1** speculate, conjecture. **2** undertake a risky venture.
spékulatif speculative.
spékulator speculator.
spéling **1** synchronization of mechanical parts. *Mobil ini hrs direparasi; -nya kurang baik* This car needs to be repaired; the timing is off. **2** erratic (of o.'s behavior).
spérma (*Biol.*) sperm.
spési (*Biol.*) species.
spésial special.
spésialis specialist.
spésialisasi specialization.
spésialitas specialty.
spésiés (*Biol.*) species.
spésifik **1** specific. **2** characteristic (of certain place or ethnic group). *makanan - Sunda* characteristically Sundanese cuisine.
spésifikasi specification. **mengs-** specify.
spidol felt-tip marker.
spiku see SPÉKUK.
spion **1** spy. - *Melayu* **1** very obvious or unprofessional undercover agent. **2** obviously prying busybody. **2** rearview mirror.
spionase espionage.
spir unus. well-developed muscle. - *lengan* biceps.
spiral **1** spiral. **2** (*Med.*) intrauterine birth control device.
spiralisasi program for getting the population to accept intrauterine birth control devices.
spiran (*Ling.*) spirant.
spirit (*Coll.*) enthusiasm, vigor.
spiritual, spirituil spiritual.
spiritus, spirtus methylated spirit, rubbing alcohol.
spon, spons foam rubber sponge.
sponse see BESI.
sponsor sponsor (of contest, etc.). **men-i** sponsor s.t.
spontan spontaneous. **ke-an** spontaneity.
spontanitas spontaneity.
spor, sport (*Coll.*) **1** sports. **2** exercise.
spora (*Biol.*) spore.
sporadis sporadic.
sportif **1** sportsmanlike, fair. **2** casual (of clothing). **ke-an** sportsmanship.
sportifitas, sportivitas sportsmanship.
sportip see SPORTIF.
spréi see SEPRAI.
spréken (*Coll.*) speak Dutch.
S.Psi. [*Sarjana Psikologi*] bachelor's degree in psychology.

spt. [*seperti*] as, like.
spuit /spoit/ syringe.
spura see SPORA.
S'pura [*Singapura*] Singapore.
sput see SEPUT.
spy. [*supaya*] so that.
sr- see also entries with **ser-**.
Sr. [*Suster*] title of Catholic nun.
SR [*Sekolah Rakyat/Rendah*] elementary school.
sreg (*Jv*) **1** well fitting, comfortable. - *melekat pd badan* fitting the body comfortably. **2** comfortable, at ease. *Dia merasa sdh - kalau memanggil saya Tom* She has become comfortable with calling me Tom. **3** appropriate (of o.'s behavior).
srempeng (*Jv*) enthusiastic. -² very enthusiastic. *Kami masih ~ mengikuti kuliah* We're still quite enthusiastic about going to classes. **meny-** do s.t. with enthusiasm, concentrate on s.t. *Pekerjaan ini mesti di-; bésok diambil* You will have to concentrate on this job; it was promised for tomorrow.
srémpét see SERÉMPÉT.
sri see SERI₁.
sribombok (*Jv*) k.o. long-necked waterbird.
srikandi 1 a heroine, Arjuna's wife, in some old romances and *wayang* . **2** heroine.
srikaya see SERIKAYA₁.
srimpét see SERÉMPÉT.
srimpi (*Jv*) k.o. court dance.
srimpung see SERIMPUNG.
sripah₁ (*Jv*) the deceased. **ke-an** suffer the death of a loved o.
sripah₂ see SYARIFAH.
sripanggung see SERI₁.
srrrt written representation of sound of zipping or squirting.
srt. [*surat*] letter (correspondence).
srudug meny- ram or butt with o.'s head. **ke-** suffer a head on blow or head on collision. *Ia meninggal seketika akibat ~ bis* She died immediately after being hit head-on by a bus.
sruput sound of a slurp. **ny-** sip noisily, slurp.
SS [*Sarjana Sastra*] bachelor's degree in literature.
ssk. [*surat-surat kabar*] newspapers.
SSKAD [*Sekolah Staf dan Komando Angkatan Darat*] (*Mil.*) Army Command and Staff School.
SSS [*suka sama suka, senang sama senang*] by mutual consent (esp. with regard to sex and marriage).
sssst, st Hush! (sound made to silence s.o.).
st- see also entries with **set-**.
St. [*Sutan*] (*M*) title of nobility.
staar see STAR.
stabil stable. **meny-** become stable, stabilize. *Ékonominya sedang ~* The economy is now stabilizing. **meny-kan** stabilize s.t. *~ ékonomi* stabilize the economy. **ke-an** stability. **pen-** stabilizer.
stabilisasi stabilization. **mens-kan** stabilize.
stabilisator stabilizer, stabilizing factor.
stabilitas stability.
stabilo 1 light color marking pen to highlight text. **2** neon-colored. **men-** mark a text with a highlighting pen. **-an** traces of marking with such a pen.

stadia (*Med.*) stages of a disease.
stadion stadium.
stadium (*Med.*) stage of a disease. *Penyakitnya sdh dlm - lanjut* Her illness was in an advanced stage.
staf staff.
stagén (*Jv*) women's waist sash or cummerbund.
stagnasi stagnation.
staking (*Coll.*) a strike (work stoppage).
stalles (*Coll.*) center seats in a theater.
stambom 1 lineage. - *raja-raja Perancis* the lineage of French royalty. **2** pedigree (of animals).
stambuk ledger.
stambul k.o. stage show often featuring indigenous versions of western drama.
Stambul Istanbul.
stamina stamina.
stan₁, stand₁ (*Sport*) score. *dgn - 2-0* with a 2-0 score. *-nya berapa?* What is the score?
stan₂, stand₂ stand, small shop (in recreation or shopping centers).
standar₁ standard. **men-kan** standardize. **pen-an** standardization.
standar₂ bicycle or motorcycle kickstand.
standar₃ (*Mil.*) standards, emblems of an army, etc.
standardisasi standardization.
stang 1 bar (of vehicle, engine, etc.). **2** handlebar of a bicycle. - *stir* bicycle handlebar. **3** (*Coll.*) control s.o. or s.t.
stanplas, stanplat bus stop.
stansa stanza.
star (*Med.*) cataract.
start 1 (*Coll.*) begin a journey. **2** (*Sport*) start.
starter 1 (*Auto.*) starter. **2** (*Elec.*) flourescent light starter. **men-, meny-** (*Coll.*) start an engine.
stasi (*Rel.*) station of the Way of the Cross.
stasionér stationary.
stasiun see SETASION.
stater see STARTER.
statif stative.
statis static, stationary. **ke-an** the state of being static.
statistik 1 statistics. **2** statistical, according to statistics. *Islam -* Muslim by statistics but not really practicing. **per-an, ke-an** matters pertaining to statistics. *kegiatan ~* statistics activities.
statistikus statistician.
statistisi statisticians.
status status.
statuta, statuten statutes. - *universitas* statutes of a university.
sték see SETÉK.
stéker 1 electrical plug, light switch. **2** cigarette lighter.
stél see STIL.
stéling (*Mil.*) **1** installation, camps. **2** position. **3** take a position. **mens- 1** set up barricades around s.t. **2** (*Mil.*) take up a position.
stélsel system.
stémbat see STIMBAT.
stémpel see SETÉMPEL.
stémpét lubricating grease.
stén, stén gun k.o. machine gun.

sténo, sténografi shorthand.
sténotipis, sténotypist stenographer.
sténsil men- mimeograph. **-an 1** a stencil. *ruang* ~ mimeograph room. **2** mimeographed materials. ~ *kuliah* mimeographed lecture notes. **pen-an** mimeography.
stépa (*Geog.*) steppe.
stér (*Che.*) queen.
stérek (*Coll.*) **1** strong, full-flavored (of beverages). **2** strong and healthy.
stéreométri geometry.
stéréoskopis stereoscopic.
stéréotip stereotype. *arguméntasi yg* - a stereotypical argument. **men-kan** categorize, stereotype. **pen-an** categorization, stereotyping.
stéril sterile. **men-kan** sterilize. **ke-an** sterility.
stérilisasi sterilization.
stétoskop stethoscope.
steup see STUIP.
stéwal see SETIWAL.
S.Th. [*Sarjana Théologi*] Master of Theology.
stiker sticker, decal.
stil 1 (*Sl.*) stylishly dressed. **2** have a certain attitude. *Dia - tenang saja menghadapi boss* He had a calm attitude in facing the boss. **nye-** be fashionable.
stilistika stylistics.
stimbat (*Coll.*) steam bath.
stimulans stimulant, stimulus.
stimulasi stimulation. **men-kan** stimulate.
stimulir men- stimulate.
stip see STUIP.
stir see SETIR.
STKI [*Surat Tanda Kewarganegaraan Indonésia*] Indonesian citizenship card.
stl. [*setelah*] after.
STM [*Sekolah Téhnik Menengah*] technical high school.
STNK [*Surat Tanda Nomor Kendaraan*] motor vehicle license.
stock, stok stock, supply. - *jagung* supply of corn. - *opname* inventory check.
stoker (*R.R.*) engineer's helper.
stoking women's stockings.
stop see SETOP₁.
stopkontak electric socket, plug.
stoplés stoppered glass jar for storing food.
stopmap folio-sized folder.
stor see SETOR.
storemking see STROMKING.
storing radio static, disturbance.
strap see SETRAP.
strat (*Coll.*) street.
strata levels (in society, education). - *satu* BA degree. - *dua* MA degree. - *tiga* PhD degree.
stratégi strategy.
stratégis strategic.
stratifikasi stratification.
stratigrafi stratigraphy.
stratosfér see STRATOSFIR.
stratosfir stratosphere.
stratum stratum (of soil, society, etc.).
stréng (*Coll.*) strict, severe.

stréples strapless (bra, gown, etc.).
strimin k.o. coarsely woven fabric used for lining.
strip see SETRIP₁.
striptis (*Sl.*) strip-tease.
stromking, strongking high-pressure kerosene lantern.
stroom, strom /strom/ see SETRUM.
struktur structure. - *batin* (*Ling.*) deep structure. - *lahir* (*Ling.*) surface structure. *organisasi* organizational chart. **men-kan** structure s.t. **ke-an** structure. **pen-an** structuring.
struktural structural.
strukturalisme structuralism.
strukturil see STRUKTURAL.
struma (*Med.*) goiter.
STTB [*Surat Tanda Tamat Belajar*] diploma for primary or secondary school.
studén (*Coll.*) student.
studi 1 study. *bahan* - study material. *melanjutkan -nya* continue o.'s study. **2** research.
studio studio. - *pelukis* artist's studio.
studium géneralé k.o. introductory general studies course.
stuip /stép/ convulsions, fits (esp. accompanying children's fevers).
stupa stupa, dome enclosing an effigy of Buddha.
su₁ see SUDAH.
su₂ see BUNGSU.
SU₁ [*Sékretaris Umum*] general secretary.
SU₂ [*Sidang Umum*] General Session.
SU₃ [*Staf Umum*] General Staff.
sua ber- 1 meet, run into. *Ia* ~ *adiknya* He met his younger brother. ~ *muka* meet face to face. **2** meet up with, find. *Ia tak dpt* ~ *dgn apa yg dicarinya* He could not find what he was looking for. *Mudah-mudahan keuntungan itu* ~ *pdmu* Let us hope that good fortune will befall you. **memper-kan, meny-kan 1** cause to meet. **2** bring into contact with, confront. **ter-** accidentally met up with. **per-an** meeting.
suai see SESUAI. **ber-** fitting, appropriate.
suak₁ (*Lit.*) inlet, small bay.
suak₂ (*M*) cancel.
suak₃ see SWAK.
suaka₁ 1 asylum. *minta - politik* request political asylum. **2** sanctuary. - *alam/margasatwa* wildlife reserve.
suaka₂ see SÉWAKA₁.
sual see SOAL.
suam warm. *Badannya* - He has a fever. **-²** rather warm. ~ *kuku* lukewarm. **ke-an 1** warmth. **2** feverishness.
suami husband. - *isteri* married couple, husband and wife. **ber-** *isteri* live as a married couple. **ber-** be married, i.e. have a husband. **ber-kan** be married to s.o., have s.o. as a husband. *Bahagialah perempuan yg* ~ *Aléx* Happy is the woman who has Alex as a husband. **memper-** take a husband. *Ia tak suka* ~ *org itu* She did not want to take that man as her husband. **memper-kan** marry o.'s daughter off. *Ia* ~ *anaknya* He married off his daughter. **per-an** matters pertaining

to husbands (us. with humorous implications). *Kalau bicara mengenai* ~, *dialah ahlinya* Talking about husband-business, she is the expert!

suangi (*Lit., Amb*) k.o. prowling, nocturnal evil sorcerer.

suang-suang (*Lit.*) *tak* - not easy. *Pintu itu tak - dibukanya* That door was not easy to open.

suap 1 a mouthful. **2** bribe. **se-** a mouthful. ~ *nasi* a mouthful of rice. *Ia mencari ~ nasi* He was looking for a living (a mouthful of rice). ~ *pagi (dan)* ~ *petang* a meager or modest living. **ber-** eat with o.'s hands. **ber-²an** feed e.o. (a custom in some marriage rituals). **meny- 1** eat with the hand. **2** bribe s.o. *Kalau kepala kantor tdk di- suratnya tdk akan keluar* The office manager will not release the letter if you do not bribe him. **3** give s.t. as a bribe. *ia ~ seratus ribu kpd ketua jurusan* She paid a bribe of l00 thousand to the head of the department. **meny-i** feed s.o., esp. by placing food into the mouth. **meny-kan** feed s.t. to s.o. *Ia ~ nasi kpd yg sakit* She fed the patient rice. **-an 1** act of eating with the hand. **2** bribe. **peny-an 1** feeding or eating with the hand. **2** bribery.

suar signal light, flare. **ber- 1** light a signal flare. **2** signal. **meny-** light, illuminate.

suara 1 voice. - *gadis itu lembut halus* That girl's voice is smooth and refined. - *basah* a low earthy voice. - *hati* conscience. *membuka -* 1 make a speech. **2** offer an opinion. - *rangkap* a duet. **2** sound. *nyanyian yg merdu -nya* a sweet-sounding melody. - *témbakan* the sound of shooting. - *mengalun* a voice that is intermittently audible, a wafting sound. - *pokok* fundamental tone. **3** vote. - *blanko* abstaining vote. - *bulat* unanimously. - *terbanyak* majority vote. - *timbang rasa* vote of confidence. **se-** unanimously. **ber- 1** have a voice. *Pendapat rakyat blm ~ di parlamén* The people's opinion has not been voiced in parliament. **2** produce a sound. *Akhirnya Boyik ~ "Sandiwara macam apa ini?"* At last Boyik said, "What k.o. play is this?" *Abu hanya tertawa tdk ~* Abu only laughed without saying anything. **3** (*Ling.*) voiced. *tak ~* (*Ling.*) voiceless. **meny-kan 1** give voice to s.t., express s.t. ~ *kehendak rakyat* voice the will of the people. ~ *keluh* raise a complaint. **2** utter. **ter-** sound, be audible. *Tanyanya ~ dr relung hati yg paling dlm* Her question resonated from the innermost depths of her heart. **peny-an 1** declamation. **2** dubbing. **3** (*Ling.*) voicing.

suarang (*M*) joint property of husband and wife acquired during marriage.

suargaloka see SORGALOKA.

suari see KASUARI.

suasa gold with large alloy mixture, pinchbeck.

suasana 1 milieu. - *kanak-kanak* children's world. **2** ambience, atmosphere. - *politik* the political atmosphere. - *jiwa* mood. **ber-** have a certain atmosphere. **meny-i 1** give an atmosphere to s.t. *Ancaman perang ~ dunia* The threat of war encompasses the world. **2** convey the atmosphere of s.t. *Utk ~ kesenangan hatinya Lumbat terpaksa juga tertawa* Lumbat forced himself to laugh to

allow the joy which he felt to color the mood of the gathering.

suatu a certain (unspecified). - *désa* a certain village. *pd - hari, di - tempat* on a certain day, in a certain place. **se- 1** a certain, an unspecified. ~ *surat kabar* a certain (unspecified) newspaper. **2** a certain s.t. *Barangkali ada ~ yg kaubutuhkan* Maybe there is s.t. you need. *tak ~ pun* nothing at all, not a thing. *Meréka tak pernah mengatakan ~ pun* They never said anything.

subahat see SYUBHAT.

subak (*Bali*) water-control system. **per-an** matter pertaining to this water-control system.

subal meny- substitute with fake material. *Dia ~ kursi sofa itu dgn potongan kain* She stuffed the sofa with pieces of cloth (instead of proper material). **peny-** s.t. used to mix with, or substitute s.t. else.

suban splinter, sliver of wood.

subang ear-plug. **ber-** wear ear-plugs.

subhanahu wa taala 1 (*Isl.*) Praise be unto Thee the Almighty, a laudation uttered upon completion of o.'s ritual prayers or upon mentioning one of God's names. **2** (*Isl., Coll.*) Lord! exclamation of surprise.

subjék see SUBYÉK.

subjéktif subjective.

subjéktivisme subjectivism.

subjéktivitas, subjéktivitét subjectivity.

subkomisi subcommission.

subkutis subcutaneous.

sublim sublime.

sublimasi sublimation.

sublimir men- sublimate.

subordinasi subordination. **men-kan** subordinate. ~ *dirinya* subordinate o.s.

subordinat (*Ling.*) subordinate.

subsidér 1 (*Leg.*) with the option of. *Ia dihukum denda Rp300.000 - empat bulan kurungan* She was sentenced to a fine of 300,000 rupiah or four months imprisonment. **2** subsidiary, secondary.

subsidi subsidy, subsidized. *sekolah -* subsidized school. **meny-** subsidize s.t. **meny-kan** subsidize with s.t. ~ *buku pd sekolah itu* subsidize the school with books.

substantif substantive. **men-kan** make into a substantive.

substitusi substitution. **men-kan** substitute.

substratum (*Ling.*) substratum.

subtil subtle.

subtropis subtropical.

subuh 1 dawn, daybreak. **2** (*Isl.*) the early morning prayer. **-²** very early in the morning.

subur 1 fertile. *tanah yg -* fertile soil. **2** thriving, prosperous. *Kelihatannya - dan makmur* He looked as if he was thriving and prosperous. *Pohon ini - tumbuhnya* This tree was growing rapidly. **3** healthy. *Badannya tinggi dan -* He was tall and healthy. **meny-** become fertile, be fertile. **meny-kan 1** make s.t. fertile, make s.t. grow. *Mana mungkin tanah begitu kering bisa dikan!* How can such dry land possibly be made fertile! **2** make s.t. prosper. **memper-** increase the prosperity or productivity of s.t. ~ *usahanya* invigorate o.'s efforts. **ke-an 1** fertility. **2** prosperity. **peny-** s.t. that makes fertile. *pupuk ~ tanah* fertilizer to enrich soil.

suburban /suburbén/ k.o. automobile formerly used for interurban passenger transportation.

subvérsi subversion.

subvérsif subversive.

subyék 1 subject, topic of discussion. **2** (*Ling.*) subject. - *gabungan* compound subject.

subyéktif, subyéktip see SUBJÉKTIF.

subyéktivisme see SUBJÉKTIVISME.

suci 1 pure, purified. - *hama* sterile, aseptic. **men-hamakan** sterilize, make germ-free. **2** holy. **ber- 1** live a pure life. **2** cleanse o.s. of impurities. **3** (*Isl.*) cleanse o.s. after defilement (defecation, giving birth, sexual congress, etc.). **meny-kan, men-kan 1** purify, disinfect, clean. *Ia ~ tulang belulang itu dgn air* He cleaned the bones with water. **2** sanctify. **memper-kan** bless. **ter-** most pure or holy. *Yg ~* His Holiness. **ke-an 1** purity, chastity. *~ jiwa* purity of the soul. **2** holiness. **peny-** a purifying agent. **peny-an, per-an** purification, cleansing.

suda bamboo spikes sticking upward to form a mantrap.

sudah 1 already, as of a certain point in time. *Ia - pergi* He has already gone. *Uangnya - habis* His money is gone. *Baru datang, - mau pergi lagi* He has just arrived and he is leaving already. *Pd tgl 1 Agustus ia - akan berdinas tiga puluh tahun* On August 1 he will have put in 30 years' service. - (*barang*) *tentu* of course, indeed. - *léwat* expire, run out. - *pd tempatnya* fitting, proper. - *semestinya* it goes without saying. - . . . *lagi* not only is (so-and-so) the case (which is enough) but even . . . - *dpt duit minta jajan lagi* You already got money. Isn't that enough? Now you want sweets! **2** past, last. *tahun yg -* the past year, last year. *Yg -,* - What is past is past. **3** done, finished. - *itu timbul répolusi* After that the revolution broke out. *Percakapannya tak akan - jika kami blm pergi* The discussions would never have been over if we had not left. *barang-barang -* finished goods. -*!* That is enough! **4** Good-bye. **5** All right, I agree. -*lah. Ambillah.* All right. Take it. **6** never mind, don't. -*lah. Jangan dihiraukan lagi.* Never mind. Don't pay any attention to it. .-² bygone. *Hal yg ~ jangan dipercakapkan lagi* Do not talk about bygone things. *tak ~* without end, endless. -**nya** finally. *~ bagaimana?* How was it finally? **se-** after. *~ makan pagi ia bekerja* After breakfast she works. *~ itu dia pulang* After that, he went home. **se-nya** afterwards, thereafter. *sehari ~* the day afterwards. **se-²nya** to o.'s heart's content. *Ia makan ~* He ate to his heart's content. **ber- 1** come to an end. *~lah muktamar itu dgn pidato* The conference was closed with a speech. **2** have an end. *Ceritanya tiada ~* The story has no end. **meny-i 1** conclude s.t. *Ia ~ pidatonya dgn doa* He ended his speech with a prayer. **2** fulfill, bring to its (proper) ending. *Ia ~ perintah majikannya* He fulfilled the orders of

his boss. **meny-kan** end, conclude, finish s.t. *Lega dia dpt ~ studinya* He was relieved that he was able to conclude his studies. **memper-kan** bring s.t. to a close, conclude s.t. **ke-an 1** conclusion, result, consequence. *Akhirnya kami cuma menunduk sambil menantikan ~nya* In the end we gave in and waited for the conclusion. **2** in the end, finally. *Ia memandangku. ~nya katanya, "Bagus kalungmu."* She looked at me. Finally she said, "Your necklace is beautiful." **berke-an** having an end. **peny- 1** final act, s.t. to conclude with. **2** conclusion. **peny-an** conclusion, act of concluding or completing.

sudara, sudaré see SAUDARA.

sudét (*Jv*) **meny- 1** make an incision (e.g. on a boil, ulcer). **2** make a connecting passage between canals. -**an 1** incision. **2** waterway diversion. **peny-an** cutting between canals, diverting (water).

sudi₁ 1 acquiesce, be agreeable. -*kah sdr pindah ke Jkt?* Are you willing to move to Jkt? *Ia tak - berjumpa dgn ayahnya lagi* He was not willing to see his father anymore. - *tak - willy-nilly.* - *tak - ia hrs datang* He has to come whether he likes it or not. **2** please (formal). -*lah tuan duduk!* Please take a seat, sir! **ber-kan** be willing to. **meny-kan 1** invite, request. *Ia ~ tamu-tamu msk* He invited his guests to come in. **2** make s.o. willing. *Kejadian itulah yg ~ ayahnya menemui dokter* That incident made his father willing to see the doctor. **memper-kan** cause s.o. to stoop or deign to do s.t. **ke-an** willingness.

sudi₂ (*M*) - *siasat* interrogation. **meny-** interrogate, examine.

sudip k.o. spoon used for mixing culinary ingredients. **meny-** stir s.t.

sudit see SODÉT.

sudra (*Lit.*) lowest Hindu caste.

sudu 1 goosebeak, duckbill. **2** k.o. large spoon. **3** convex blade, (of machine, etc.). - *turbin* blade of a turbine. **meny- 1** scoop up, ladle up. *Meréka ~ sari sagu dgn tangan meréka* They scooped up the sago meal with their hands. **2** scoop up (with bill). *Itik itu ~ ikan di air* The duck scooped up fish in the water. **ter-** nipped by a duck or goose.

suduk see SODOK₂.

sudung 1 hut, esp. in agricultural fields. **2** polite self-deprecating term for o.'s own house.

sudut 1 corner. - *rumah* corner of a house. - *mata* the corner of o.'s eye, angle of vision. **2** (*Math.*) angle. - *30 derajat* a 30-degree angle. - *lancip* acute angle. - *siku* right angle. - *penyiku* complementary angle. - *tumpul* obtuse angle. **3** direction. *Org datang dr segala -* People came from all directions. **4** point of view. *Dilihat dr - itu . . .* Seen from that point of view . . . **ber-** have angles, corners. - **meny- 1** on diagonally opposite corners, kitty-corner. **2** aspects, angles. *~ industri ringan* aspects of light industry. **meny- 1** form an angle. **2** retire to a corner. *Silahkan ke mari. Jangan ~* Please come here. Do not sit in a corner. **meny-kan** put s.t. into a corner. *Pertanyaan-pertanyaan itu ~ dosén muda itu* Those questions boxed the young lecturer into a corner. **ter-** pushed in a corner, cornered. *Ia merasa* ~ He felt cornered.

suf wool cloth.

sufi 1 mystical, esp. related to Sufism. **2** a Sufic mystic.

sufiks (*Ling.*) suffix.

Sufisme Sufism.

sufrah floorcloth or carpet on which ceremonial meals are spread out.

sugésti power (hypnotic, etc.) to direct another's actions. **men-kan** persuade s.o. to be of the same opinion.

sugéstif 1 having the power to direct another's actions. **2** suggestive (of lewd dances, etc.).

sugi$_1$ toothpick. **ber-** use a toothpick. **meny-** pick o.'s teeth with a toothpick. **pe-** toothpick.

sugi$_2$ (*M*) tobacco quid, esp. chewed with betel. **ber-** have a tobacco quid in the mouth. **meny-** wipe betel juice from o.'s mouth.

sugih (*Jv*) wealthy.

suguh - *sumbangsih* contribution in honor of s.o. **meny-** place before s.o., esp. a guest. *Tamunya di- téh dan pisang goréng* Tea and fried bananas were placed before the guests. **meny-i** present to s.o. (esp. guests). *Turis di-i tari-tarian tradisionil* They presented traditional dances to the tourists. **meny-kan** serve (a guest, etc.) with s.t. *Ibunya* ~ *nasi* His mother set out rice. **-an** s.t. presented (e.g. food served to guests, a drama performance, etc.). **peny-an** presentation. ~ *sendratari itu sangat baik* The dance drama presentation was excellent.

sugul (*Coll.*) see MASYGUL.

sugun (*Lit.*) tangled, tousled (of hair).

suh$_1$ Shoo! (exclamation to drive away animals, esp. chickens).

suh$_2$ 1 (*Jv*) broom binding (of plaited rattan, etc.). **2** a binding factor which keeps diverse elements together. *Bung Karno menjadi - satu-satunya bagi persatuan dan kesatuan rakyat* Sukarno became the sole binding force to unite and unify the people. *spt lidi kehilangan -nya* without a leader or guide (like a broom without its binding).

suhanura [*suara hati nurani*] the voice of o.'s inner heart.

suhu$_1$ temperature.

suhu$_2$ 1 teacher of the art of self-defence. **2** (*Ch*) healer.

suhuf (*Isl.*) scriptures inspired by God.

suhun (*Jv*) **meny-** show great respect for s.o.

suikher see SÉHER.

suit sound of whistling. **ber-** whistle, esp. with o.'s fingers in the mouth. **ber-^{2}** whistle repeatedly. *Pemuda itu* ~ *mengganggu gadis-gadis yg léwat* That young man always whistles to bother the girls passing by. **meny-i** whistle at. **-an** a whistle, whistling. ~ *keréta api* whistling of a locomotive.

sujadah see SAJADAH.

sujén (*Jv*) skewer (for meat).

suji ber- have embroidery on it. **meny-** embroi-

der s.t. **ter-** be embroidered in or on. **-an** embroidery.

sujud (*Isl.*) **1** bow from kneeling position so that forehead touches floor, a part of prayer ritual. - *tawakal* bow in resignation (to God's will). **meny-tawakalkan** resign s.t. (to God). *Diri-pribadi baru ada artinya apabila di-tawakalkan ke hadirat Allah* O.'s personhood only acquires value when it is resigned to the presence of God. **2** (*Isl., Coll., Jv*) perform ritual prayers. **ber- 1** perform this bow. **2** admit o.'s humble station. *Hidup tenteram selalu* ~ *pd Tuhan* A calm, even life always acknowledges God's authority. *Dia kira saya mau* ~ *di kakinya* He thinks I want to grovel at his feet.

suka 1 happiness, joy, pleasure. - (*dan*) *duka* happiness and sorrow, the ups and downs of life. - *hati* pleasure, delight. **se-hati** as o. pleases. - *sama suka* by mutual agreement, esp. with regard to sex and marriage. **2** like, be fond of. *Ia - (pd) ibunya* She likes her mother. *Ia - (akan) coklat* He is fond of chocolate. - *tak* - indifferent, averse to. **3** be willing, would like. *Kalau tuan - datang, silakan datang* If you'd like to come, please do. *-lah kiranya* if you will be so kind as to. **4** be apt to. *Ia - lupa pd pekerjaannya* He was apt to forget about his work. - *ribut* tend to be noisy. **se-nya, se-^{2}** as o. wishes, whatever o. likes. *Ia belajar* ~ He studies as he wishes. **ber-^{2}** enjoy o.s. *Meréka* ~ *di pantai* They enjoyed themselves at the beach. **ber-^{2}an 1** enjoy o.s. **2** be in love with e.o., be enthralled with e.o., be courting. *Ketika itu, aku* ~ *dgn ibumu* At that time, I courted your mother. **meny-i** like, love. *Ia tak di-i temannya* He is not liked by his friends. **meny-kan 1** cheer s.o. up. *Ia selalu mencoba* ~ *temannya* He is always trying to cheer up his friend. **2** cause s.o. to like s.t. *Ia* ~ *anaknya pd anjing* She taught her child to like dogs. **ke-an 1** joy, pleasure. **2** s.t. o. is fond of, hobby. *lagu ~nya* her favorite song. **-an 1** sweetheart, darling. **2** favorite.

sukabumi meny-kan kill.

sukacita 1 happy, glad, merry. **2** joy, happiness. **ber-** rejoice. **ke-an** joy, state of being glad.

sukamandi (*Jv*) k.o. dark cotton cloth.

sukar hard, difficult. **meny-kan, memper-kan** cause s.o. or s.t. difficulty. *Tingkah-lakunya* ~ *ayahnya* His behavior caused his father difficulties. **ke-an 1** difficulty, hardship. ~ *hidup* the hardships of life. **2** have difficulties, suffer hardship. *Dia* ~ *mengerjakan tugas ini* He had difficulties in doing this task.

sukaréla voluntary. *Dgn - org mau bekerja utk itu* People want to work for it voluntarily. **ke-an** volunteering.

sukarélawan a volunteer.

sukarélawati woman volunteer.

sukaria 1 happy. **2** delight, pleasure. **ber-** be happy, celebrate.

sukat 1 unit of measure of four *gantang* or 12.6 liters. **2** measure. **ber-** measured by this measure. **meny-** measure s.t. by this measure. **-an** measure.

suklih (*Coll.*) searchlight.
sukma life spirit, soul.
suksés 1 success. *Mudah-mudahan kamu mencapai* - May you achieve success! **2** be successful. *Dia - dlm ujian* She was successful in her exams. **mens-kan, meny-kan** make s.t. successful. **ke-an** success. **pens-an, peny-an** the act of making s.t. successful.
suku₁ 1 a quarter, one-fourth. **2** a part. - *cadang* spare parts. (*bilangan*) - *dua* number consisting of two digits, group of two digits. **3** extended family, ethnic group. - *Sunda* the Sundanese ethnic group. - *bangsa* ethnic group. - *terasing* unacculturated tribal groups in Sumatra, Sulawesi, etc. **4** (*Biol.*) family. **5** (*Lit.*) 50 cents. **se- 1** half a rupiah. **2** of the same ethnic group. **ber-²** be grouped in tribes or ethnic groups. **ke-an** clique mentality. *prasangka* ~ ethnic prejudices. **sepe-an** of the same ethnic group. **per-an** things concerning the division into ethnic groups.
suku₂ (*Jv*) leg.
suku₃ (*Ling.*) syllable. *buka/hidup* open syllable. - *kata* syllable. - *mati/tertutup* closed syllable. **pen-an** syllabification.
sukuisme communalism, ethnocentricity.
sukun₁ breadfruit.
sukun₂ (*Jv*) toothless gum.
sukun₃ diacritical mark in Arabic script to indicate presence of a vowel.
sukur see SYUKUR.
sukwan [*sukarélawan*] volunteer.
sukwati [*sukarelawati*] female volunteer.
sula sharp vertical stake (for impalement or for husking coconuts). **meny- 1** shear off coconut husks by exerting downward pressure on such a stake. **2** (*Lit.*) impale s.o. **-an** sharp stake.
sulah (*Lit.*) bald, hairless.
Sulaiman (*Bib., Isl.*) Solomon.
sulak a (feather) duster. **meny-i** clean s.t. with such a duster.
sulalat 1 descent, lineage. **2** family tree.
sulam₁ embroidery. **ber-** embroidered. *kain ~* embroidered cloth. **ber-kan 1** embroidered with s.t. **2** be added to with s.t., sprinkled with s.t., laden with (additions). *Suratku ~ dorongan semangat kpdnya utk belajar lebih tekun* My letter was sprinkled with encouragements to her to study harder. **meny-** embroider. **meny-kan** embroider s.t. on to. *Saya mau ~ tulisan ini dgn benang emas* I want to embroider this writing with gold thread. **ter-** embroidered. **-an** embroidery, embroidered goods.
sulam₂ **meny-** replace dead rice seedlings with new ones.
sulang₁ lampblack, soot. - *lampu* lampblack. **ber-** be dirty with soot.
sulang₂ **ber-²an** (*Lit.*) give e.o. food or drink. - **meny-** feed e.o. (custom for bride and groom in some areas). *Meréka cinta-mencintai, ~* They were deeply in love, sharing their food (like newlyweds). **meny-kan** (*Lit.*) feed s.t. to. *Ia ~ jagung kpd anaknya* She fed corn to her child.

sulap₁ conjuring, sleight of hand. **ber-** engage in conjury. **meny- 1** conjure up s.t. *Ia ~ kué yg lazat* She conjured up a delicious cake. **2** (*Coll.*) cause s.t. to disappear (esp. in embezzlements, etc.). **-an** conjuring. **peny-** conjurer. **pe-an** matters pertaining to conjuring or juggling. **peny-an** conjuring, methods of sleight of hand.
sulap₂ (*Jv*) dazzled (as if by magic).
sulap₃ (*Jv*) **ber-** find a defect in the weaving.
sulat-salit (*Lit.*) irregular (of teeth).
Sulawési Celebes, Sulawesi.
sulbi (*Anat.*) the vertebrae. *tulang -* coccyx.
sulfa medicinal powder containing a sulfanilamide drug
sulfur sulphur.
sulih (*Jv*) a substitute.
suling₁ flute. - *keréta api* train whistle. **ber-, meny-** play the flute.
suling₂ **meny-** distill. ~ *minyak wangi* distill perfume. **-an 1** distillate. *air ~* distilled water. **2** refinery. **peny-** instrument to refine. **peny-an** distilling, refining. ~ *minyak* **1** oil distillation. **2** oil refinery.
suling₃ (*M*) **ber-** tumbled upside down. **meny-kan** turn s.t. upside down.
sulit 1 difficult, hard, complicated. *soal yg - a* difficult problem. *keadaan - a* critical situation. **2** (*Lit.*) secret, hidden, secluded. **meny-kan, memper- 1** complicate s.t., render s.t. difficult. **2** cause difficulties for s.o. *Kenapa kauper- dirimu sendiri?* Why do you make it difficult for yourself? *Ia menyesal karena sangat ~mu* He regrets to have made things difficult for you. **ke-an** difficulty, trouble. ~ *air* water shortage (i.e. difficulties in obtaining water). ~ *hidup* life's hardships. ~ *perumahan* housing difficulties. **peny-1** complicating factor. **2** (*Med.*) complication.
Sulselra [*Sulawési Selatan dan Tenggara*] S. and S.E. Sulawesi.
sultan sultan. **ke-an** sultanate.
sultanat sultanate.
suluh 1 torch. **2** (*Lit.*) scout, spy. **ber-** light with a torch. **meny-(i) 1** light s.t. with a torch, cast a light upon s.t. ~ *ikan* fish by torch. **2** inform, instruct. ~ *rakyat* inform the people. **3** investigate. *Ia ~ soal tanah* He investigated the land problem. **peny- 1** o. who provides elucidation. **2** (*Lit.*) investigator, spy. **peny-an 1** illumination. **2** information, elucidation. ~ *pertanian* agricultural extension.
suluk 1 mysticism. **2** (*Jv*) recitation of a *wayang* narrator. **ber-** retreat from the world.
sulung oldest, first-born. *anak yg -* first-born child. *buah -* first fruit of the season. *gigi -* milk teeth. - *tahun* first of the year.
sulur 1 spiraling upward (of plants). - *batang* spiral-shaped. **2** shoots. **ber-** spiral, climb upward. **meny-** climb, creep. **-an** climbing plant. **-²an** various vines and creepers.
sulur-bulur confused, incoherent (of speech).
sulut **meny- 1** (*Jv*) kindle, ignite. ~ *api* set afire. ~ *rokok* light a cigarette. **2** become heatedly an-

gry. **meny-kan** ignite or light s.t. on s.o.'s behalf. **ter-** lit, set afire. *Api permusuhan sdh* ~ The flames of hatred have been lit. **peny-** instrument or person that ignites a fire.

Sulut [*Sulawési Utara*] N. Sulawesi.

Sulutteng [*Sulawesi Utara dan Tengah*] N. and Central Sulawesi.

Sum. [*Sumatera*] Sumatra.

sumang feverish, esp. of children.

sumangat see SEMANGAT.

sumarak see SEMARAK.

sumba see KESUMBA.

sumbang₁ 1 incestuous. *anak* - child of incest. - *dgn sdrnya* commit incest with o.'s sibling. **2** illicit (esp. in sexual matters). - *langkah* illicit act. **3** out of tune, discordant. *lagu yg* - a discordant song. **meny-kan** *langkah* **1** do s.t. illicit or indecent. **2** make irregular moves (in martial arts). **meny-²kan** make slightly out of time, distort slightly. *dgn suara yg di-²kan* with a slightly distorted voice. **ke-an 1** impropriety, indecency. **2** falseness, discordance. **3** cynicism.

sumbang₂ - *saran* brainstorming. **meny- 1** contribute. *Kalau aku kawin nanti, Hamid akan* ~ *tiga ékor ayam* When I get married, Hamid will contribute three chickens. **2** help, assist. **meny-kan 1** offer s.t. as a contribution. *Hidup saya akan saya -kan utk membangun tanah air saya* I will contribute my life to build my nation. **2** give s.t. as help. **-an** contribution. **peny-** contributor, supporter.

sumbangsih contribution.

sumbar (*Jv*) boast, brag. **se-** boast, show off. *Ia* ~ *pasti lulus* She boasts that she will certainly pass her exam. **ber-, berse-, meny-, ny-** boast, brag, challenge. *Ia* ~ *bisa mengalahkan lawannya* She boasted that she could defeat her adversaries. **meny-kan** boast, brag about.

Sumbar [*Sumatera Barat*] W. Sumatra.

sumbat stopper, plug. - *botol* bottle stopper. **meny-** stop, close up, plug up. ~ *mulut botol* cork a bottle. ~ *telinga* plug o.'s ears. **meny-kan** obstruct with s.t., close up with s.t. *Dia* ~ *gabus pd botol itu* She put a cork on the bottle. **ter-** stopped up, gagged, clogged up. *Lédingnya* ~ The pipe is clogged up. *Kerongkongnya rasa* ~ It feels as if she has a lump in her throat. **-an** s.t. to plug or close up with. **peny-an** clogging, obstruction, blockage.

sumber 1 well. **2** source. - *penghasilan* source of income. - *yg boléh dipercaya* a reliable source. **3** resources. - *alam* natural resource. - *daya* resources. - *daya perikanan* fishery resources. **ber-** have (as) a source, be based (on). *Apa yg saya tulis, adalah juga* ~ *pd masyarakat, pd kehidupan sebenarnya* What I write is also rooted in society, in real life. **ber-kan** have s.t. as its source.

sumbi rod used in weaving to hold edge taut. **meny-** repair the edge of s.t. damaged (e.g. crown a tooth, etc.).

sumbing jagged, dented, chipped. *pisau* - a knife with a jagged edge. *bibir* - harelip.

sumbu₁ 1 wick. - *kumpai/lampu* lamp wick. **2** fuse. - *meriam* fuse of a cannon. **pe-an, peny-an 1** place of wick or fuse. **2** touchhole of a cannon.

sumbu₂ 1 wagon axle. **2** pivot, axis. - *bumi* the earth's axis. - *datar* (*Math.*) abscissa. - *tegak* (*Math.*) coordinates.

sumbu₃ horn of a rhinoceros.

sumbul (*Jv*) k.o. basket with a lid.

sumbur meny- 1 protrude. **2** emerge. **meny-kan 1** extend s.t. (hand, leg, tongue, etc.). **2** hang out or raise the flag. **ter-** bulge.

sumbut (*Jv*) in balance with the efforts or costs, worthwhile. *Hasilnya tdk* - The results were not worthwhile.

sumilir see SEMILIR.

sumir short, brief, succinct. *perkara* - (*Leg.*) clear-cut cases (e.g. stealing, etc.). **meny-kan** shorten a matter.

sumirat (*Sd*) beam, glowing.

sumpah 1 oath. - *dokter* Hippocratic oath. - *setia* oath of allegiance. *mengatakan dgn* - state under oath. - *jabatan* oath of office. - *besar* very serious (about s.t.). - *besar dia ttg perjalanannya* She was dead serious about her trip. - *palsu* perjury. - *pocong* oath taken while dressed in a shroud (the strongest form of oath). **2** curse. *sakit karena - org tuanya* become ill from the curse of his parents. - *serapah* curses of all sorts. **ber-** swear, take the oath. *Ia* ~ *utk tak berjumpa dgn temannya* He swore that he did not meet his friend. **meny-1** curse. *Ia* ~, "*Anak gila ini lagi!*" She cursed, "That crazy kid again!" **2** swear in. *Penghulu itu* ~ *pegawai baru* The official swore in the new employees. **meny-²** curse in anger. *Saya* ~ *karena barangnya tdk ketemu* I cussed and cussed because I could not find the thing. **meny-i** curse s.o. *Ia* ~ *anaknya* He cursed his son. **memper-kan 1** declare under oath. **2** swear in, administer the oath to s.o. **peny-an** swearing in, administration of an oath. **per-an** act of taking an oath.

sumpah-sumpah k.o. flying lizard.

sumpal (*Jv*) stopper. **meny- 1** plug s.t., fill a gap. **2** (*Vulg.*) feed. ~ *empat mulut* feed four mouths. **meny-kan** plug up, with s.t. *Ia* ~ *batu pd lobangnya* He plugged the hole with a stone. **ter-** clogged, stopped up. **-an** s.t. obstructing a passage.

sumpek /sumpek/ (*Jv*) **1** crowded. **2** feel stifled, have o.'s head in a whirl because of problems. **ke-an** confusion of thought, feeling of being troubled.

sumpel see SUMPAL.

sumping (*Jv*) k.o. ear ornament worn in classical dance.

sumpit₁ chopsticks.

sumpit₂ meny- shoot with a blowpipe. **meny-kan** use as a blowpipe. **-an** blowpipe.

sumpit₃, sumpit-sumpit k.o. coarse, plaited storage bag, esp. for rice or salt.

Sumsel [*Sumatera Selatan*] S. Sumatra.

sumsum (*Anat.*) marrow. - (*tulang*) *belakang* spinal cord.

Sumteng [*Sumatera Tengah*] Central Sumatra.
sumuhun-dawuhisme mentality characterized by sycophancy.
sumur well. - *digali air terbit* exceed o.'s expectations. - *bor* artesian well. - *di (tepi) jalan* prostitute. - *mati* dry well. - *panték* well drilled in ground.
sumurung outstanding.
Sumut [*Sumatera Utara*] N. Sumatra.
sun kiss on the cheek. *Jangan lupa -nya nanti!* Do not forget that kiss later! **meng-, nge-** kiss lightly, peck s.o.'s cheek. **-²an 1** kisses (on cheek). **2** give kisses (on cheek).
sunah see SUNAT₂.
Sunah (*Isl.*) orthodox law based on teachings and practices of Muh. as reported by tradition, supplement to Koran. *ahli* - Sunnite Muslims.
sunam meny- slip in. **meny-kan** smuggle s.t. in. *Ia berhasil ~ obat-obatan dr luar negeri* He succeeded in smuggling medicine in from abroad.
sunan₁ title for the holy men who first brought Isl. to Java.
sunan₂ (*Jv*) ruler of Surakarta. **ke-an** dominion of the *Sunan*, i.e. Surakarta.
sunat₁ circumcision. **ber-** circumcised. **meny-1** circumcise s.o. **2** skim money off the top of a budget so that the grantee gets only a portion. *Anggaran yg lima belas juta itu di- lima* Five million were taken away from the budgeted 15 (so that the department received only 10 million of the amount allotted). **meny-i** circumcise (several people). **meny-kan** have s.o. circumcised. **-an** circumcision. *pésta ~* celebration of a circumcision.
sunat₂, sunatrasul (*Isl.*) optional, but meritorious if performed (of pious deeds, prayers, etc.). **meny-kan 1** consider a deed meritorious. **2** prescribe for s.o. as a meritorious deed. *Kaum Islam di-kan utk berkhitan* Muslims prescribe circumcision, but it is not obligatory.
sunbulat (*Zod.*) Virgo.
Sunda Sundanese, the Sunda area (W. Java).
sundai see LIMAU₂.
sundak meny- 1 (*M*) bump o.'s head. **2** rise. *Pasang ~* The tide has come in. **ter-** bump accidentally. *~ pd lampu* bumped against a lamp.
sundal, sundel 1 prostitute. - *bolong* k.o. evil female spirit (with a hole in her back). - *malam* tuberose that gives off a pleasant scent in the evening. **2** lewd, immoral. **3** (*Vulg.*) Whore!, a strong exclamation of disapproval. *Anak -!* Bastard!, strong exclamation of disapproval. **ber-, meny-** carry on prostitution. **per-an 1** prostitution. **2** fornication.
sundul see SONDOL.
sundut₁ (*M*) generation, descent. **ber-** hereditary.
sundut₂ (*M*) **meny-** carry.
sundut₃ (*Lit.*) **meny-** light, kindle.
sungai river, stream. - *mati* **1** dry river. **2** road full of holes and stones. *(pergi) ke* - defecate. **per-an** river system.
sungga (*Lit.*) spike or sharp stake implanted at angle to impede enemy's progress. **meny-** stick with a spike.
sunggi meny- carry on the head.
sungging painting, decoration. *se- senyum* faint or forced smile. **meny-** produce s.t. decorative with delicate details. *~ wayang* make a *wayang* figure with its intricate decorations. **meny-kan** *senyum* give a faint smile. *Dia kembali ~ senyumnya yg memikat itu* Again she gave this charming faint smile of hers. **ter- 1** painted. **2** faint, forced (of a smile).
sunggit see SUNGKIT₂.
sungguh 1 true. *Perkataanmu mémang -* What you say is true. - *hati* earnest. **2** really, truly. *Ia - sakit rupanya* He really seems to be sick. *Kehidupan di sini - mahal* Life here is indeed expensive. - *pun* although. - *pun panas, saya pergi juga* Even though it was hot, I went anyway. - *pun begitu* nevertheless. - *pun mati* I swear to it by my life. - *pun mati saya tdk tahu* I swear to God, I do not know. **3** actually, in fact. - *ia mengatakan itu pd saya, tetapi saya lupa* As a matter of fact he told me so, but I forgot it. **-² seriously, wholeheartedly.** *Mémang ~ ia sama sekali tdk sakit* He is actually not ill at all. *Ia belajar ~* He studies seriously. **se-hati** with earnestness, with all o.'s heart. **se-nya** actually, in truth. **ber-² make every effort, try seriously.** *Dlm permainan bilyar ia jarang ~* He rarely makes a serious effort when he plays billiards. **meny-i, memper-i** take s.t. seriously, do s.t. in a serious way. *Ia ~ pekerjaannya* He takes his work seriously (He does his utmost in his work). **meny-kan 1** take s.t. seriously. **2** establish the seriousness of s.t., justify. **ke-an 1** truth, sincerity. **2** seriousness. **3** in all seriousness, earnestly. *Maman mengangguk ~* Maman nodded very seriously. **ke-²an** seriousness. *dgn wajah ~* with a serious face. **-an** (*Coll.*) serious, in earnest. *Kali ini aku ~* This time I am serious. **peny-an** affirmation, verification.
sungguhpun see SUNGGUH.
sungkah meny-(kan) devour s.t. greedily.
sungkal (*Lit.*) - *bajak* plowshare. **meny-** plow, dig up.
sungkan (*Jv*) reluctant to approach or take action toward s.o. of higher status. *Ia - menegor anak gurunya* He did not quite dare scold his teacher's child. **-² embarrassed before o.'s betters.** *Mari makan dong! Jangan ~!* Come on! Help yourself! Do not be shy. **meny-i** feel reluctant toward s.o.
sungkawa see BÉLASUNGKAWA.
sungkem₁ (*Jv*) show respect by kneeling and pressing o.'s face to another's knees. **meny-** pay respect in such a way.
sungkem₂ (*Lit.*) prop up.
sungkit₁ embroidered with bits of gold or silver thread. *kain* - cloth produced in such a way. **meny-** embroider in such a way.
sungkit₂ pry out. **peny-** tool for prying.
sungkup concave cover or shelter. **ber-** be covered. *botol yg ~ mangkok* a bottle covered with an overturned bowl. **meny-(i)** cover with s.t. *Ia ~*

botol dgn telapak tangan He covered the bottle with his cupped hand. **meny-kan** apply s.t. as a cover. *Ia ~ tangan pd mukanya* He covered his face with his cupped hands. **-an** k.o. basket. **peny-** 1 concave cover. 2 bell jar.

sungkur₁ spade, shovel.

sungkur₂ meny- 1 root up, grub up (earth). *Babi hutan ~ tanah* A wild boar rooted up the soil. 2 lower the head (as if to root up). *Kerbau ~ menyerang lawannya* The water buffalo lowered its head to attack its opponent. **meny-kan** put down, lower. *Kepalanya di-kan ke pangkuan Onik* He laid his head on Onik's lap. **ter-** fall headfirst. *Aku ~; hidung dan mulutku berdarah* I fell headlong; my nose and mouth were bleeding. **ter-²** headlong. *lari ~* run pell-mell.

sunglap see SULAP₁.

sungpia see SONGPIA.

sungsang 1 upside down. *- kalak* upside down. 2 against the grain. **meny-** 1 be upside down. 2 go against the grain. **meny-kan** place s.t. upside down.

sungsep ny- fall or slip down in mud headfirst. *Mobilnya kecebur sungai, ~ ke lumpur* He drove his car into the river and it went down headfirst into the mud.

sungsum see SUMSUM.

sungu (*Jv*) horn of animal.

sungut₁ 1 (*Biol.*) a specialized organ of touch in an animal or insect (e.g. tentacle, antenna, feeler, etc.). *- jangkerik* a cricket's antennae. *- ikan* fish barbels. 2 moustache. *- kucing* cat's whiskers.

sungut₂ *- létér* nagging, grumbling. **ber-(²)** grumble, complain. *Biasanya org terus juga membayarkannya, meskipun dgn ~* Usually people pay it right away, albeit with grumbling. **-an** grumbling complaint.

suni (*Isl.*) pertaining to the Sunnite movement.

sunjam (*Lit.*) head downward. **ter-** with head downward, headfirst. *Ia jatuh -* He fell headfirst.

sunnah see SUNAT₂.

sunni see SUNI.

sunti knob on ginger root. *- halia* ginger.

suntih (*M*) **meny-** cut into small pieces.

suntik meny- 1 inject. *Ia di- sblm dibedah* He got an injection before the operation. 2 inoculate, vaccinate. *Ia di- sblm perjalanananya keluar negeri* He was inoculated before his trip abroad. *~ cacar* vaccinate against smallpox. 3 incite. *Ia ~ pemuda-pemuda spy melawan* He incited the youths to fight back. **-an** injection, vaccination. **peny-** 1 s.o. who gives injections. 2 syringe. **peny-an** injecting, vaccinating injection.

suntil chewing tobacco.

sunting₁ ornament or flower worn behind the ear. **ber-** wear s.t. behind the ear. **meny-kan** place behind the ear or in the hair. *Ia ~ bunga* She stuck a flower in her hair. **memper-** 1 place s.t. in o.'s hair as an ornament. 2 adorn s.o. or s.t. 3 place s.t. in o.'s possession, obtain s.t. abstract. *~ ilmu dan pengalaman* obtain knowledge and experience.

sunting₂ meny- 1 proofread and correct. *Kamus ini perlu di- lagi* This dictionary needs to be proofread again. 2 insert s.t., edit s.t. into. *Kini tinggal ~ kata pendahuluan pd bukunya* Now only the preface to his book remained. **-an** editing. *~ naskah* editing of a text. **peny-** editor.

sunting₃ meny- marry s.o. (of men). *Ia berhasil ~ Ingrid* He succeeded in marrying Ingrid. **meny-kan** have s.o. as a wife. *Untung benar ia ~ isteri cantik* He is very lucky to have such a pretty wife.

suntuk 1 too late. *waktu yg - too late. - akal* narrow-minded, short-sighted. 2 be overtaken by events or time. *Ia lekas pulang karena takut - malam* He hurried home because he was afraid he'd be overtaken by darkness. 3 entire length of time. *sehari -* the whole day. *semalam -* the whole night. **ter-** 1 be late. *Trém ~ datangnya* The streetcar was late. 2 be overtaken by events or time. *Ia ~ malam di jalan* He was overtaken by darkness along the way.

sunyata (*Lit.*) true. **ke-an** the truth in a religious sense.

sunyi 1 lonely. *Ia merasa - di negeri asing itu* He felt lonely in the strange country. 2 quiet. *malam yg -* a quiet night. 3 deserted, desolate. *jalan yg -* a deserted road. *- senyap/sepi* deathly still, desolate. **ber-(²)** withdraw, retire. *Muhammad, sblm beliau menjadi nabi, sering ~ diri di gua Hira* Before he became a prophet, Muh. often withdrew to the cave of Hira. **meny-** become quiet. **ke-an** 1 loneliness. 2 quiet, solitude. *memecah -* break silence. 3 feel lonely. *Kalau engkau pergi, ibu sendirian, Maman, ibu ~* If you go, I will be all by myself, Maman, I will feel all alone.

sup see SOP.

supaya 1 so that. *Katakan pd temanmu - ia tahu* Tell your friend so that he will know. *Mari kita cepat - jangan terlambat* Let us hurry so we are not late. 2 please, particle introducing a polite command. *Penonton - mundur* If the onlookers would be so kind as to step back!

supel 1 flexible. *hukum yg -* a flexible law. 2 sociable. **ke-an** 1 flexibility. 2 sociability.

super 1 high-octane (of gasoline). 2 (*Coll.*) superior.

superioritas superiority.

supermi instant noodles.

supersemar [*Surat Perintah Sebelas Maret*] document handing over the gvt. power from Sukarno to Suharto.

supervisi supervision.

supir see SOPIR.

supit see SUMPIT₁.

suplai supply. **men-, meny-** supply s.t. **peny-** supplier.

suplemén supplement.

suporter (*Sport*) enthusiast, fan.

supra-alami supernatural.

suprémasi supremacy. *Pasar itu sdh lengang karena - perniagaan pindah ke tempat lain* That shopping center is dying because the center of commerce has moved elsewhere.

sur see SYUR₁.

sura see ASYURA.
surabi see SERABAI.
surah (*Isl.*) division of the Koran, a sura.
surai (*Lit.*) dressed or parted (of hair, animal fur, etc.). **ber-** break up, disperse. *Rapat* ~ The meeting broke up. **meny-(kan)** break s.t. up, disperse s.t. *Polisi* ~ *rapat* Police broke up the meeting.
Surakarta Solo, city in central Java.
suralaya (*Lit.*) dwelling of the gods.
suram 1 vague, hazy. *Ingatannya tlh* - His memory has become hazy. *cahaya yg* - a dim light. **2** gloomy, dark, dull *cuaca yg* - gloomy weather. **-²** rather dark or gloomy. ~ *gelap* 1 quite dark. **2** dusk. **meny-** become dim, become blurred. **meny-kan 1** darken s.t. **2** make s.t. gloomy. *Berita duka itu* ~ *suasana pertemuan itu* The sad news spread a pall over the meeting. **ke-an 1** vagueness, indistinctness. **2** dullness.
surat 1 letter, epistle. *dgn* - in writing. - *budek/buta* unsigned letter. *cepat* special-delivery letter. - *édaran* 1 circular (letter). **2** (*Rel.*) encyclical. - *gelap/kaléng* anonymous letter. - *kilat* express letter. - *kilat khusus* overnight delivery letter. - *pengantar* 1 letter of introduction. **2** a cover letter. **3** invoice. **4** bill of lading. - *penghargaan* testimonial letter (upon retirement, etc.). - *Puasa* (*Rel.*) episcopal letter before fasting begins. - *puji(an)* 1 letter of recommendation, testimonial. **2** attestation. - *selebaran* pamphlet. **2** certificate, receipt, document. - *anggota* membership card. - *angkutan* bill of lading. - *bébas* letter of authorization, permit. - *bébas Gestapu* certificate of noninvolvement in 30th of September 1965 coup. - *fiskal* document proving payment of taxes. - *gadai/gadén* pawnshop receipt. - *ijin* permit. - *kabar* newspaper. **per-kabaran** press. - *kawin* marriage certificate. - *keberatan* petition. - *kepercayaan* credentials. - *keterangan* identity card, identification papers. - *kir* inspection certificate. - *kiriman* notice of delivery. - *kuasa* (*Leg.*) power of attorney, authorization, warrant. - *lepas* 1 (*Mil.*) discharge papers. **2** (*Leg.*) divorce certificate. - *mentéga* letter of dismissal, walking papers. - *pajak* document stating that taxes were paid. - *paksa* warrant, write. - *panggilan* 1 summons. **2** post office notification of parcel or registered letter. - *pas* a pass (to enter military base, etc.). - *pemilihan* voter registration card. - *perintah* 1 mandate, instruction. **2** commission, mission. - *suara* ballot for voting. - *tugas* 1 instruction, mandate. **2** mission, commission. - *ukur* 1 property title. **2** map of premises. - *undian* lottery ticket. - *wali* letter of authorization. - *wésél* bill of exchange, postal money order. **ber-1** written, inscribed. *batu* ~ inscribed stone. **2** (*Lit.*) compose a letter. *Saya akan* ~ *pd Léti* I will write to Leti. **ber-an** correspond with e.o. - **meny- 1** correspond, write to e.o. **2** correspondence. **meny-** write letters. **meny-i 1** inscribe. **2** write a letter to s.o. *Sdh lama ia tdk* ~*mu* He has not written to you for a long time. **meny-kan** make s.t. a letter or document. *Ia* ~ *perjanjian-*

nya pd tembaga He formalized the agreement in a copper plaque. **ter- 1** written. **2** destined, fated, written in the palms of o.'s hand. *Sdh* ~ *rupanya bhw engkau akan mengawini dia* It seems to have been destined for you to marry her. **-an 1** writing. **2** fate, destiny. *Ah, malam yg amat duka! Mengapakah* ~ *hrs begini?* Oh sorrowful night! Why does fate have to be like this? **3** lines of the palm of the hand. **-²an** (*Coll.*) correspond, write to e.o. *Meréka saling* ~ They write to e.o. **pe(r)-an 1** matters pertaining to correspondence. **2** (*Lit.*) literature.
surau (*Isl.*) prayer-house, communal building suitable for any devotion except Friday prayer.
suren see JALAK.
surén (*Jv*) see SURIAN.
surga heaven. - *dunia* an earthly paradise.
surgawi heavenly, pertaining to heaven.
suri₁ shuttle comb on a weaving loom.
suri₂ see IBU.
Suriah Syria.
surian k.o. tree.
surih (*M*) a scratch or line. **ber-** ruled, lined. **meny-** draw lines, trace. **meny-kan** make a line or scratch. ~ *jalan* give directions. ~ *percakapan* change the subject.
suri teladan good example, model.
surjan (*Jv*) long-sleeved man's jacket us. of woven, striped material.
sursak see SIRSAK.
suruh 1 (*Coll.*) be ordered to. *Kamu - diam aja* You were told just to keep quiet. **2** order s.o. to do s.t. - *buat* have s.t. made. *Pak Guru - buat sepuluh kopi dr péperku* Teacher had 10 copies of my paper made. **meny-** order s.o. to do s.t. *Ia* ~ *adiknya menulis surat* He had his brother write a letter. *Org itu sulit di-* It is difficult to tell that person to do anything. **-an 1** message, order. *Tak lama kemudian iapun pulang membawa* ~ *ibu* Soon afterward she brought home mother's orders. **2** messenger, delegate. ~ *itu mengerjakan perintahnya* The messenger carried out his order. **-²an** errand boy, messenger. **pe-** messenger. **peny-** o. who gives orders.
suruk ber-²an play hide-and-seek. **meny- 1** duck the head. *spt anak ayam* ~ *di bawah sayap induknya* like a chick that ducks its head under its mother's wings. **2** hide. *Dia* ~ *di antara rumput* She hid among the weeds. **meny-i** creep under. *Ia* ~ *pagar* He crept under the fence. **meny-kan 1** bend s.t. down, keep s.t. down. *Ia* ~ *kepalanya* He bent his head down. **2** hide s.t. *Ia* ~ *buku di bawah tempat tidur* He hid the book under the bed. **ter-** hidden (away). *Rumahnya kecil dan* ~ *di sebuah kampung yg sunyi* His house was small and hidden in a quiet village. **ter-²** bent down, esp. because of tiredness, etc. **-an 1** hiding place, shelter. **2** (*Coll.*) drawer.
surung see SORONG.
surup₁ (*Jv*) fitting, proper, appropriate.
surup₂ (*Jv*) **meny-** set, sink (of heavenly bodies). **ke-an** possessed (by a spirit). *mati* ~ dead because of being entered by a spirit.

surut 1 withdraw. *Sekali maju tak dpt - lagi* Once it advances it cannot withdraw again. *Ia - ke rumahnya* He withdrew to his house. **2** lessened, subsided. *Anginnya tlh -* The wind has died down. *Penyakitnya tlh -* His illness has subsided. *air -* ebb tide. **ber-** withdraw, take leave of s.o. of higher rank. **bersi-** withdraw little by little. **meny-** lessen, subside. *Peminat ke dinas ketentaraan ~ akhir-akhir ini* The number of people who are interested in military careers has decreased in recent times. **meny-kan 1** withdraw s.t. *~ pasukannya* withdraw o.'s troops. **2** decrease, lessen. *~ jam bekerja* decrease the working hours. *Ia ~ kemarahan gurunya* He calmed down his teacher's anger. *~ api* diminish a blaze. **ter- 1** retired. **2** diminished.

survai, survé 1 research. *disain -* research design. **2** to survey.

surya (*Lit.*) sun.

Suryahi (*Lit.*) Syrian.

suryakanta magnifying glass.

sus₁ see KUÉ.

sus₂ see ZUS.

susah 1 troubled. *Ia - karena uangnya hilang* He was unhappy because he lost his money. *Jangan -* Do not worry. *- hati* worried. **2** hard to get. *Uang agak - sekarang ini* Money is hard to get these days. **3** difficult, bothersome. *pekerjaan yg - a* difficult job. *- payah* **1** great difficulty. **2** much effort, pains. **ber-** *payah* make every effort. *Ia ber- payah menekan perasaan harunya* With great difficulty, he suppressed his deep emotions. **-²** go to a lot of trouble. *Buat apa ~ ke Jkt kalau cuma itu yg dicari* Why make such a fuss to go to Jkt if that is all you want. **ber-²** make every effort. *Ia tlh ~ belajar* He has put all his efforts into his studies. **meny-i 1** make s.o. sad, become a burden to. **2** become sad about s.o. **meny-kan 1** make s.t. difficult. *Suaminya terlalu ~ pekerjaan org itu* Her husband made the work of those people too difficult. *Perumahan masih ~* Housing is still causing problems. *pekerjaan yg ~ a* troublesome job. **2** worry about. *"Jadi apa yg kaukan?" ibu mendesak* "So what is it you are worrying about?" mother demanded. **memper-(kan)** render s.t. difficult. *~ hati* cause o. to worry. **ke-an 1** difficulty. **2** worry, grief. **3** be in trouble, have difficulties. *Kami tak pernah ~ air* We have never had any water problems.

susastera literature. **ke-an** literature. **per-an** matters pertaining to literature.

susi sister, term of address to Catholic nun.

susila 1 decent, well behaved. *nilai-nilai -* moral values. **2** decency, morality. *polisi séksi -* morals squad. **ber-** have good morals. **ke-an 1** ethics. **2** decency, morality.

susis see SOSIS.

suspénsi₁ (*Leg.*) suspension, adjournment.

suspénsi₂ (*Phys.*) suspension. **men-kan** turn s.t. into suspension. *Serat-serat asbés di-kan dlm air* Asbestos fibers were turned into a suspension in (the) water.

suster 1 Catholic nun. **2** term of reference and address for a female nurse. *- Hayati* Nurse Hayati. **-an** convent. *sekolah ~* convent school.

susu 1 breast. **2** milk. *- bubuk* powdered milk. *- kaléngan* canned milk. **meny-** suckle on the breast. **meny-i** give suck. *Induk babi ~ anaknya* The sow suckled her piglets. *Ia ~ anaknya dgn botol* She bottle-fed her baby. **peny-** wet nurse. **sepe-an** of those who have suckled at the same breast.

susuan (*Jv*) nest.

susuh 1 large projecting thorn or hook. **2** spur.

susuhunan (*Jv*) title of the ruler of Surakarta.

susuk₁ 1 small piece of gold or diamond inserted in the face as a magical charm to improve o.'s beauty. **2** pin, nail. **3** (*Med.*) implant. **ber- 1** insert a small piece of gold (for medicinal or magical purposes). **2** wear a hairpin. **meny- 1** magically insert s.t. subcutaneously to improve o.'s attractions. **2** (*Jv*) stab with a pin. **meny-kan** stick s.t. in. *~ hidung dlm saputangan* stick o.'s nose in a handkerchief.

susuk₂ (*Jv*) surplus change after payment.

susuk₃ see SOSOK₂.

susukan (*Jv*) channel between two rivers.

susul ber-²an, - meny- following e.o. successively. **meny- 1** follow, come afterward. *Yg satu ~ yg lain* O. followed the other. *Surat -* Letter follows (in telegrams). **2** follow and catch up with. *Ia ~ temannya* He caught up with his friend. *Ia hrs ~ pelajaran-pelajaran waktu ia sakit* He had to catch up on his lessons when he was sick. *Ia ~ ayahnya ke Mekah* He followed his father to Mecca. *~ asal* trace origins. *Tdk mudah ~ asal-mulanya ceritera itu* It was not easy to trace the origin of that story. **meny-i 1** follow on. *~ surat saya bulan yg lalu* following up on my letter of last month. **2** add s.t. *Ia ~ keterangan lain pd pidatonya* He added some other information to his speech. **3** add to s.t. *Ia ~ pidatonya dgn keterangan lain* He followed his speech up with other information. **meny-kan 1** add s.t. written. *Ia ~ pasal baru* He added a new paragraph. **2** cause s.o. or s.t. to follow. *Anaknya akan di-kan ke negeri Belanda* His child will be sent to Holland later. **ter-** be caught up with. *Mobil penjahat ~ oléh polisi* The police managed to catch up with the criminal's car. **-an 1** appendix, supplement. **2** continuation. *panén ~* 2d harvest. **peny-** o. who follows.

susun 1 stack, orderly pile. *dua - buku* two stacks of books. **2** row, series. *- tangga* arranged in a gradient order from small to large, etc. **3** arranged in a stack. *rumah -* a house with several stories. **ber- 1** stacked (o. on the other). *piring ~* plates stacked o. on the other. **2** in layers, stories or rows. *kué ~* layer cake. *hotél ~ sepuluh* a 10-story hotel. *berdiri ~ lima* be standing in five rows. **3** arranged in orderly fashion. *kata-kata yg tdk ~* words that are not in orderly arrangement. **meny-** arrange s.t. in orderly fashion. *~ acara* prepare the agenda. *~ batu* pile up stones. *~ kalimat* compose a sentence. *~ kamus* compile a dictionary. ~ *piring* stack plates o. on the other. **meny-kan** arrange s.t. in an orderly fashion on s.o.'s behalf. **ter-** 1 arranged in orderly fashion. *bajunya yg ~ di lemari* shirts stacked up neatly in a wardrobe. *wawancara* ~ a structured interview. 2 composed, formed, compiled. ~ *atas tiga unsur* composed of three elements. **-an** 1 composition, compilation. 2 formation, structure. ~ *masyarakat kita* the fabric of our society. ~ *kartu* the order of cards. ~ *kata* wording. ~ *tindih* overlapping order. **peny-** composer, compiler. ~ *bibliografi* bibliographer. ~ *huruf* compositor, typesetter. **peny an** 1 arranging, compiling. 2 composing.

susup - *sasap* infiltrate, creep under things. **meny-** 1 move (below s.t.), pass in a low posture. *Anak-anak* ~ *di bawah méja itu* The children crawled under the table. 2 penetrate, infiltrate. *Meréka* ~ *ke dlm rimba* They penetrated into the forest. *Sétan* ~ *ke tubuhnya* The devil entered his body. **meny-i** enter into s.t. stealthily. **meny-kan** 1 place s.t. below s.t. else. *Ia* ~ *peti ke bawah lemari* He pushed the box under the cupboard. *Ia* ~ *wajahnya ke dada suaminya* She buried her face in her husband's chest. 2 smuggle, have infiltrate. *Ia* ~ *pasukan ke belakang garis musuh* He smuggled troops behind the enemy lines. **peny-** infiltrator. **peny-an** penetration, infiltration.

susur₁ edge, fringe, margin. - *bantal* edge of a pillow. - *galur* pedigree, genealogy. - *kota* city's edge. - *pantai* shore's edge. - *tangga* banister of a staircase. **meny-, meny-i** 1 go along the edge. *berjalan* ~ *pantai* walk along the shore. 2 trace, follow. ~ *jejak* follow trail, trace a path. ~ *riwayat Banjarmasin yg sebenarnya* trace the real history of Banjarmasin. **ter-, ter-i** followed, traced. **-an** edge, margin, fringe. ~ *atas* edge of a roof. **peny-** o. who follows up. **peny-an** act of tracing.

susur₂ (*Jv*) quid of tobacco, often mixed with betel ingredients. **meny-** chew tobacco.

susut shrink, decrease. **meny-** 1 decrease in size, shrink (of cloth, etc.). *Tubuhnya yg semula berisi sekarang* ~ Her body which had been well-rounded was now shrunken. 2 subside (of a wind, storm, swelling, etc.). 3 wipe off. ~ *hidung* wipe o.'s nose. **meny-i** 1 reduce, decrease. ~ *perbelanjaan negara* reduce the national budget. ~ *badan* lose weight. 2 wipe off (repeatedly). **meny-kan** decrease s.t.'s size. *Obat ini* ~ *badannya* This medicine reduced his weight. **ke-an** shrinkage, decrease. **-an** reduction. ~ *nilai* (*Fin.*) reduction in (capital) value. **peny-an** 1 shrinkage, contraction. 2 reduction, decrease.

sut₁ flapping sound, sound of s.t. thin jerked rapidly.

sut₂ ber- draw lots, play paper-rock-scissors.

sutan 1 title of Minangkabau nobility above the rank of *marah*. 2 term of address to o. of this rank, us. as *tan*. **ber-(²)** act in a high-handed fashion.

suten see SUT₂.

sutera silk. - *déwangga* k.o. very fine silk. **per-an**

matters pertaining to silk. *industri* ~ silk industry.

sutil (*Jkt, Jv*) frying spatula.

sutra see SUTERA.

sutradara film or play director. **meny-i** direct a film or play. **peny-an** 1 play or film direction. 2 directing.

sutuh see SOTOH.

suun see SOHUN.

suvenir souvenir.

suwar-suwir (*Jv*) k.o. sweetmeat.

suwir meny- shred. **-an** shred. ~ *daging* a shred of meat.

suwuk (*Jv*) **meny-** heal magically by blowing on s.t. **-an** healing by blowing. **peny-an** action of blowing to heal magically.

sw. [*subhanahu wa taala*] (*Isl.*) the Almighty and most worthy of praise, written after God's name.

swa- self-, a prefix in formal neologisms.

swadaya innate strength or effort, self-supporting. **ber-** do s.t. on a self-supporting basis (i.e. without outside funds). *Masyarakat setempat* ~ *membangun jembatan* The local population built a bridge on their own, without outside funds.

swadési Gandhian movement of *swadeshi*, the confining of consumption to goods of village production.

swak (*Coll.*) 1 sickly and weak, exhausted. 2 weak (of batteries).

swakarsa o.'s own will. *atas -nya* of her own accord. *transmigrasi* - spontaneous transmigration, transmigration not sponsered or funded by the gvt.

swakarya self-developing (of projects without gvt. funding).

swakelola self-management (i.e. community construction of public buildings).

swalayan self-service. *pasar* - supermarket.

swapraja autonomous area or region.

swara see SUARA.

swarga see SURGA.

Swarnadipa (*Lit.*) the Golden Isle, Sumatra.

swartepit k.o. card game of Dutch origin.

swasembada self-supporting, self-sufficient.

swasiswa an autodidact.

swasta private. *pengusaha* - private entrepreneur. **mengs-kan** make s.t. private. ~ *perusahaan negara* convert a state enterprise into a private o. **pengs-an** conversion to private ownership. ~ *perkebunan* conversion of estates to private ownership.

swat. [*swatantra*] autonomy.

swatantra autonomy, autonomous. **ke-an** autonomy.

Swédia Sweden, Swedish.

swémbak (*Coll.*) swimming pool.

swémpak swimming suit.

SWI [*Sumbangan Wajib Istiméwa*] k.o. motor-vehicle tax levied in the 1960s.

swt.₁ [*subhanahu wa taala*] (*Isl.*) the Almighty and most worthy of praise, written after God's name.

swt.₂ [*swatantra*] autonomy, autonomous.

swt.₃ [*swasta*] private (not public, of businesses, etc.).

sy- see also entries with **s-**.

Syaban /sya'ban/ (*Isl.*) the eighth month of the Arabic calendar.

syabas (*in some regions only*) good! well done!

syafaat 1 (*Rel.*) mediation, intercession (in communication with God). **2** blessing.

syafakat₁ kindness, sympathy.

syafakat₂ see SEPAKAT.

syah₁ (*Lit.*) ruler.

syah₂ see SAH₁.

syahadah see SYAHADAT.

syahadan see SYAHDAN.

syahadat 1 confession, testimony. **2** (*Isl.*) the profession of faith: There is no God other than Allah, and the Prophet Muh. is His messenger. *kalimah* - The Isl. profession of faith.

syahbandar harbormaster, port officer. **ke-an 1** matters pertaining to port authorities and harbormasters. **2** office of harbormaster.

syahdan (*Lit.*) so it happened, the next thing in the story. - *sampailah raja itu di tempat yg dituju* So it happened that the king arrived at his destination.

syahdu 1 eminent, excellent. **2** serene, calm. **ke-an** serenity.

syahid (*Isl.*) martyr or warrior killed while fighting for Isl. principles. *mati* - die a martyr's death (and so be guaranteed immediate admission to heaven). **ke-an** martyrdom.

syahmat see SEKAKMAT.

syahwat 1 lust, voluptuous feeling. **2** orgasm. *mencapai* - achieve an orgasm.

syair 1 story related in verse form using o.-end-rhyme quatrains. **2** poem. **3** rhyme containing clues to the lottery. **ber- 1** write poetry, poetize. **2** recite poetry. **meny-, meny-kan** compose a poem about s.t., make a historical poem of s.t. ~ *cerita si Kantan* make a poem of the story of Kantan. **peny-** poet. **kepeny-an** poetizing.

syaitan see SÉTAN.

syak suspicion, doubt, distrust. *tiada - lagi* no doubt whatsoever. - *wasangka* 1 suspicion. 2 doubt, distrust. *menaruh - wasangka* doubt, suspect. **mensy-i** suspect s.o.

syakti see SAKTI.

syal shawl, muffler.

syalat see SOLAT.

syaléh, syalih see SALÉH.

syalwat see SELAWAT.

Syam (*Lit.*) Syria.

syaman shaman.

syamanisme shamanism.

syampo shampoo.

syaraf see SARAF₁.

syarahan (*Lit.*) edition.

syarak (*Isl.*) canon law.

syarat condition, prerequirement, requisite. - *hidup* necessary requirement for living. *Ia tak dpt memenuhi - persetujuan itu* He was not able to fulfill the terms of the agreement. *Apa -nya utk*

ikut ujian itu? What are the requirements for taking this exam? **-²** qualifications. ~ *kawin* prerequisites for marriage. ~ *mutlak* an absolute condition. **ber-** conditional. *penyerahan yg tak* ~ unconditional surrender. **ber-kan** have s.t. as a condition. **mensy-kan, memper-kan** set s.t. as a condition, require s.t. *Pak Guru* ~ *murid-murid berseragam* The teacher requires the pupils to wear uniforms. **per-an** rules and regulations.

syariah, syariat /syari'ah, syari'at/ Isl. law. **mensy-kan** declare a certain deed to be Isl. law. *Msk ke gréja bagi org Islam di-kan sbg tindakan murtad* It has been declared apostasy according to Isl. law to enter a church.

syarif (*Isl.*) title of a male descendant of Muh.

syarifah 1 title of a female descendant of Muh. **2** (*Coll.*) Arab women.

syarikat see SERIKAT.

syasis see SASIS.

syatriya see KESATRIA.

Syawal, Syawwal (*Isl.*) the 10th month of the Arabic calendar.

syékh (*Isl.*) **1** sheikh. **2** title of a Isl. scholar.

syelawat see SELAWAT.

syéti (*in some regions only*) moneylender of Indian descent.

syiar /syi'ar/ (*Isl.*) magnificence, greatness (of God and religion). - *Allah* God's greatness.

syiir see SYAIR.

syinkék see SINGKÉH.

syirik, syirk (*Isl.*) **1** belief in more than o. God, polytheism. **2** s.t. to be avoided on religious grounds. **men-kan** make s.t. taboo. *Sejak dia bertengkar dgn saya, dia* ~ *datang ke rumah saya* He has avoided coming to my house like the plague ever since he quarreled with me.

syit see SIT.

symposion, symposium /simposion, simposium/ see SIMPOSION.

syok₁ 1 very attractive. **2** very absorbed in s.t., interested and excited.

syok₂ /syok/ (*Med.*) shock.

syok₃ see SOK₁.

syolat see SOLAT.

syor see SYUR₁.

syorga see SURGA.

syubhat s.t. dubious.

syuco (*Japanese*) administrator of a residency.

syuhada 1 (*Isl.*) persons who died for Isl. (martyrs, warriors in religious war, etc.). *Para - banyak dimakamkan di Mekah* Many of the people who died for Isl. are buried in Mecca. **2** heroic martyrs of a just cause.

syuk see SYOK₁.

syukur 1 thank God, thanks be to God. - *alhamdulillah* (*Isl.*) thank God. **2** happily, fortunately. *-lah ia hanya luka-luka ringan* Fortunately she was only slightly injured. **ber- 1** thank God. *Ia* ~ *karena luput dr bahaya maut* He thanked God to have escaped from mortal danger. **2** (*Coll.*) be grateful. *Saya* ~ *kpdnya* I am grateful to her. **keber-an** gratitude to God. **men-i 1** be grateful to God about s.t. *perbuatan yg di-i org* a deed for which people have thanked God. ~ *nikmat* be grateful for God's blessings. **2** (*Coll.*) thank s.o. **ke-an** gratitude to God. **-an** expression of gratitude to God. *malam* ~ a night event to express thanks to God.

syur₁ 1 exciting, absorbing. *perasaan -* exciting rush (sensation). **2** sexually arousing. *Badannya -!* His body is sexy! **men-i** be attracted to, delight in. *Bukunya di-i oléh pembacanya* This book was thoroughly enjoyed by its readers. **men-kan 1** attract, absorb o.'s interest. **2** arouse sexual desire. *Di klab malam banyak penari yg ~ penonton-penontonnya* In nightclubs there are many dancers who excite the audience.

syur₂ (*Lit.*) advice, suggestion. **men-kan** advise, recommend.

syurga see SURGA.

syuriah advisory.

syuur see SYUR₁.

T

t /té/ t, the 20th letter of the alphabet.

t. [*tanpa*] without.

ta₁ see TO₁.

ta₂ see TAK₁.

taajal see TAKJAL.

taajub see TAKJUB.

taala see ALLAH.

taalim see TAKZIM.

taart see TART.

taassub fanatical, dogmatic, bigoted.

taat 1 obedient. *Meréka - pd perintah opsir meréka* They obeyed their officer's commands. **2** loyal. *Ia - kpd negaranya* He was loyal to his country. **ber-** be obedient, be loyal. **men(t)-i 1** adhere to, obey s.t. *Ia tak ~ seruan pemerintah utk menyerah* He did not follow the gvt.'s call to surrender. **2** be faithful to. **ke-an** loyalty, fidelity. **pen-** o. who is obedient. **pen-an** adherence, obedience. ~ *peraturan-peraturan* adherence to the rules.

taawuz (*Isl.*) prayer recited before reading the Koran.

tabah₁ 1 determined, resolute. **2** able to endure (hardship, etc.). *Ia - sekali menghadapi kemalangan itu* He is very resolute in facing the misfortune. **men-kan** make firm, make determined. *Nasihat-nasihat itu ~ hati teman-temannya* The advice strengthened his friends' determination. *Tuhan, -kan aku!* God, give me strength! **memper-** make firmer. **ke-an** firmness, determination. ~ *hati* firmness, determination. **pen-** o. who is resolute or able to endure difficulties.

tabah₂ see TEBAH.

tabak k.o. tray used to present s.t.

tabal 1 k.o. drum used at royal installations. **2** formal installation ceremony. **men-** crown or declare s.o. king. **men-kan** install s.o. as king. **pen-an, per-an** installation or investiture (of a king).

taban the gutta-percha tree.

Tabanas [*Tabungan Pembangunan Nasional*] savings for national development, a gvt.-insured savings account program. **men-kan** deposit s.t. into such an account.

tabas see TEBAS₁.

tabé see TABIK.

tabéat see TABIAT.

tabék see TABIK.

tabél table, list. *- tegakan* (*Fin.*) yield table.

tabernakel (*Rel.*) tabernacle.

tabiat /tabi'at, tabiyat/ **1** character, nature. **2** behavior. **ber-** be of a certain character or behavior. *anak yg ~ buruk* a child with bad behavior.

tabib 1 traditional healer. **2** (*Lit.*) physician. **ke-an** matters pertaining to such healing.

tabik 1 greeting, salute given in greeting. **2** hello, good morning (afternoon, etc.). **ber-** extend a greeting. **ber-an** greet e.o. **men-, men-i** greet s.o. *Ia ~ kawannya* He greeted his friend.

tabir screen, partition. *- asap* smoke screen. *- besi* the iron curtain. *- mabir* all sorts of partitions. **ber- 1** be separated by a screen. **2** be in disguise. **men-i** screen off s.t. *Asap ~ léréng gunung itu* Smoke screened the slope of the mountain.

tablét tablet, pill. *- hisap/isap* lozenge.

tablig, tabligh (*Isl.*) **1** sermon at a religious meeting. **2** such a religious meeting. **ber-** preach at such meetings. **ment-kan** preach s.t.

tablo (*Thea.*) pantomime.

tabok men- slap, esp. the head. **men-i** repeatedly slap s.o. **-an** a slap.

tabrak - *lari* hit and run. **ber-, ber-an** collide. *Kedua mobil itu ~* The two cars collided. *Mobil ~ dgn gerobak* The car collided with a truck. **men-** hit against. *Mobil itu ~ témbok* The car struck the wall. *Pemain bola itu ~ penjaga gawang* The soccer player slammed into the goalie. **men-i, n-(²)** repeatedly run into obstacles or hit things. **men-kan** make collide, let strike. *Kapal sengaja di-kan ke pantai* They purposely ran the ship aground. **ter-** accidentally crashed into. *Pohon ~ mobil* A car crashed into a tree. **-an** collision. ~ *berantai/beruntun* chain collision. **pen-** s.o. who collides, esp. a driver.

tabu 1 taboo. **2** consider taboo, avoid doing. *Ibu tabu masak dgn moto* Mother avoids cooking with monosodium glutamate. **men(t)-kan** consider s.t. taboo. *Ibu ~ perbuatan semacam itu* Mother considers s.t. like that taboo.

tabuan see TABUHAN.

tabuh₁ s.t. used to strike percussion instruments, esp. a gong. **men-** strike a gong, etc. *Ia ~ gamelan* He plays the gamelan. **-an** k.o. percussion instrument. **-²an** 1 music to accompany a dance. 2 various k.o. percussion instruments.

tabuh₂ k.o. large mosque drum used to summon people to prayer. **men-** 1 strike such a drum. 2 drum on s.t. with o.'s fingers. **pen-** o. who strikes such a drum.

tabuhan (*Lit.*) k.o. wasp. *~ meminang anak lebah* out of proportion (lit., the hornet courts the baby bee).

tabulasi tabulation. **men-kan** tabulate. **pen-an** process of tabulation.

tabun men- collect and burn s.t. *Ia ~ sampah* He burned trash. **-an** the heaping and burning of rubbish.

tabung 1 k.o. bamboo tube used for storage. - *gambar* TV picture tube. - *kimia* (*Chem.*) test tube, retort. - *madat* opium pipe. - *pemilihan* ballot box. - *surat* mailbox. 2 money box. - *pérak* savings box. **men-(kan)** save. *Ia ~ uang di bank* She saves money in the bank. **ter-** put into savings. **-an** 1 money box. 2 savings. *~ Asuransi Berjangka* k.o. life insurance. *~ Pembangunan Nasional* savings for national development, a gvt.-insured savings account program. *~ pos* postal savings account. **pen-** a depositor. **pen-an** 1 savings. 2 process of saving money, setting aside s.t.

tabur - *bunga* ceremony of placing flowers on a grave. **ber-(an)** scattered, spread. *Bintang-bintang ~ di langit* Stars were scattered across the sky. **ber-kan** be spread over with s.t. *Perhiasannya ~ intan permata* Her jewelry was inlaid with all sorts of precious stones. *~ sari* strewn with flowers. **men-** 1 sow, broadcast (seed). 2 scatter s.t. about. *~ bunga* strew flowers. **men-i** 1 sow s.t. (a field, etc.). *Ia ~ tanahya dgn biji* He sowed his land with seed. 2 spread over s.t., scatter all over s.t. **men-kan** 1 sow with s.t. 2 scatter, spread. **-an** sowing. **pen-** sower, spreader. **pen-an** diffusion, strewing.

tabut 1 (*Bib.*) ark. 2 (*Isl., M*) effigy representing Muh.'s steed, carried in procession on the 3d day of Muharam. 3 (*Isl., M*) procession on the 3d day of Muharam.

taci, tacik 1 (*Ch*) term of address or reference for o.'s elder sister. 2 (*Coll.*) term of address or reference for Ch woman.

tada see TIADA.

tadah 1 storage receptacle. - *keringat* 1 undershirt. 2 sweat shirt. - *cangkir* saucer. 2 cistern, reservoir. - *hujan* 1 cistern. 2 dependent on rain water for irrigation. **ber-** use a receptacle or reservoir. *~ amin* say amen (us. with hands extended, palms upward). **men-** 1 store liquids, collect liquids in receptacles. *Ia ~ air dgn tangan-*

nya He held out his hands to get some water. 2 (*Coll.*) receive stolen goods. **men-kan** obtain s.t. (esp. liquids) or with s.t. *~ piring* hold a plate up to receive s.t. *~ tangannya* 1 receive in the hands. 2 hold out o.'s hands with palms upward. **-an** stolen goods bought by a fence. **pen-** 1 container, receptacle. 2 buyer of stolen goods. 3 (*Sport*) catcher. 4 (*Sport*) a bat. **pen-an** 1 process of storing liquids, etc. *Di daérah kering itu, ~ air hujan dianjurkan* In that dry region, storing rain water is recommended. 2 passing on or buying of stolen goods.

tadarus see TEDARUS.

tadbir management. **men(t)-kan** manage, administer. **pen(t)-** manager. **pen(t)-an** administering, managing. **per-an** administration, management.

tadi 1 a while ago, some time ago. - *ia di sini, sekarang tdk* He was here a while ago; now he is not. *dr/sejak* - since some time ago. 2 this (morning, evening, etc.) just past, last (night), this past (two, three, etc. o'clock). *Saya ke sana jam satu* - I went there at o. o'clock (just now). - *malam* last night. - *siang* this (past) noon. 3 the o. from a while ago, the aforementioned. *Apa ini setrop saya -?* Was this my drink? *Saya ke sana dgn Pak Pomo* - I went there with Mr. Pomo, whom I told you about a while ago. **-nya** formerly, just before. *Pantai yg ~ agak besar, kini bertambah kecil* The shore which a while ago loomed large, was now growing smaller and smaller.

tadrus see TEDARUS.

taduh see TEDUH.

taék 1 (*Jv, vulg.*) Bullshit! exclamation of surprise or disagreement. 2 see TAHI.

tafahus 1 a search. 2 examination. **ment-** 1 search s.t. 2 examine s.t.

tafakur, tafakkur, tafkur 1 contemplation. 2 reflective, contemplative. *Meréka duduk* - They sat in contemplation. **ber-** 1 be reflective. 2 observe silence out of respect for s.o. **men(t)-kan** reflect on s.t. **-an** 1 meditation. 2 engage in meditation.

taferil scene, picture.

tafsir 1 (*Isl*) explanation of passages of Koran by supplying additional information. - *Bukhari* Bukhari's exegesis. 2 exegesis (of Christian scriptures). **men(t)-kan** interpret s.t. (esp. scriptures). **ter-kan** interpreted, explained. **-an** 1 interpretation, explanation. 2 commentary, exegesis. **pent-** 1 commentator, exegete. 2 evaluator. **pen(t)-an** 1 explanation, interpretation. 2 commentary, exegesis.

taftan taffeta.

tagal pebble.

tagan stake in gambling.

tagar sound of thunder. **ber-** thunder and rumble.

tagih₁ 1 addicted to s.t. - *rokok* addicted to smoking. 2 habitually accustomed to s.t. *Ia - bekerja* He has an addiction to work. - *membaca koran* obsessed with reading the newspaper. **ke-** (*Coll.*) 1 addicted to. 2 habitually accustomed to. **ke-an**

1 addiction. ~ *minuman keras* alcoholism. 2 addicted to. *Ia* ~ *madat* He is addicted to opium. 3 (*Coll.*) crave for.

tagih₂ men- 1 dun, collect o.'s debts. *Ia* ~ *hutangnya* He pressed for payment of the debt. 2 demand fulfillment of (a promise, etc.). ~ *janji* demand the fulfillment of an agreement. **menkan** collect a debt for s.o. **ter-** collected. **-an** a claim. **pen-** creditor, dunner. **pen-an** pressing a claim.

-tah (*Lit.*) I wonder, particle in interrogative sentences, expressing reflectiveness. *Siapa- yg man bergaul dgn org itu?* Who would want to go around with that person? *Apa- nasibku kiranya?* I wonder what in the world my fate is going to be?

tah see ENTAH.

tah. [*tahun*] year.

tahadi see TADI.

tahajud, tahajut see SEMBAHYANG.

tahak a belch. **ber-** belch.

tahakik see TAHKIK.

tahalil see TAHLIL₂.

tahan 1 endure, put up with. *Ia - menderita* He can stand suffering. *Badannya tak - lagi* His body could not take any more. *- air* waterproof, watertight. *- banting* be able to take it. *- besi* invulnerable. *- cuci* washable. *- harga* 1 with self-respect. 2 stable in price. *- hati* persistent, firm. *- kias* able to take teasing. *- lama* keeping for a long time, imperishable. *- lembab* moisture-resistant. *- nafsu* with self-control. *- palu/pukulan* able to take a beating. *putih - sesah, hitam - serpa* unchanging, resistant to change. *- tangan* invulnerable. *- turut* (*Naut.*) backstay (sailing). *- uji* tested, tried. 2 last, hold out. *Itu bisa - lima minggu* That can last five weeks. *- lama* durable, lasting. *- warna* fast (of color). **ber-** hold out. *Musuh masih ~ di daérah itu* The enemy is still holding out in that area. *~ hidup* survive. *~ diri* defend o.s. *~ larat* hold out, last. **men-** 1 hold back, restrain , withhold. *Penjaga ~ org banyak* The guard held back the crowd. *Ia ~ hawa nafsu* He restrained his desire. *Meréka ~ meningkatnya harga* They checked the rise in prices. *~ diri/hati* restrain o.s. *Meréka ~ sepuluh per sén dr gaji saya* They withheld 10 percent of my wage. 2 detain, arrest. *Polisi ~ pencuri itu* The police detained the thief. 3 provide support for, hold up. *Ia ~ tiang yg hampir roboh itu* He stopped the pole from falling by holding it up. **men-i** arrest or detain (many people). **men-kan** be strong enough to endure s.t. *Bisakah engkau ~ nasib spt ini?* Are you strong enough to endure a fate such as this? **memperkan** defend, maintain. *Ia ~ pendiriannya* He defended his stand. *~ kehidupan* sustain life. *~ tésisnya* defend o.'s thesis. **ter-** 1 endured. *kemarahan yg ~* restrained anger. 2 detained, impeded. *Kita akan ~ dan mati di sini* We will be detained, and we will die here. *tak ~* irresistible.

ter-² 1 repeatedly restrained. 2 repeatedly break down (of car). *Baru ganti busi kok ~ lagi!* We just put in a new spark plug but there it is stalling

again! 3 faltering (of speech, o.'s breath, etc.),. *Karena émosi yg meluap-luap itu, pidatonya ~* Because of his strong emotions, his speech faltered. **ter-kan** 1 checked, restrained. 2 endured. *tak* ~ irresistible, unbearable. **ke-an** tenacity, endurance. *~ ékonomi* stamina of the economy. **-an** 1 resistance, opposition, obstruction. 2 arrest, detention. *dlm ~* in custody. 3 detainee. **pen-** s.o. or s.t. that restrains or resists. *pér ~ bantingan* (*Auto.*) shock-absorber. *~ kerusuhan* police that stops rioting. **pen-an** 1 restraint. *~ nafsu* forbearance. *dinding ~* restraining wall. 2 detention, arrest. **per-an** 1 defense. *Départemén ~* Ministry of Defense. 2 stronghold, fortress.

tahang₁ (*Lit.*) ravine.

tahang₂ 1 barrel, cask, drum. 2 tank, reservoir.

tahap stage, phase. *pd - awal* at a preliminary stage. **ber-(²)** in stages, phases. *Réncana ini hrs dilaksanakan ~* This plan must be implemented gradually. **men-kan** do s.t. in phases. *PU ~ pembangunan dlm tiga fase* The Public Works Department phased construction in three stages. **-an** stage, phase. **pen-an** arranging in phases. *~ kembali* temporarily stopping work on a project by saying what was completed was the "first stage."

tahayul see TAKHYUL.

tahbis (*Rel.*) **men(t)-kan** consecrate, ordain. *Bp uskup ~ sebelas pastor baru* The bishop ordained 11 new priests. **-an** ordination, consecration. **pent-an** consecration or ordination ceremony. *~ uskup* consecration of a bishop.

tahdiriyah (*Isl.*) kindergarten.

tahfidz know by heart.

tahi 1 excrement, feces. *- kucing!* Bullshit! 2 filth, dregs. *- air* scum on water. *- angin* 1 light drifting clouds. 2 a plant used for diarrhea. *- besi* iron rust. *- bintang* meteorite. *- gergaji* sawdust. *- gigi* tartar on teeth. *- kikir* iron filings. *- kontol* smegma. *- kotok* chicken droppings. *- kuku* dirt under the nails. *- kuping* ear wax. *- lalat* small moles, freckles. *- mata* mucus in the eye. *- minyak* dregs that remain after making (coconut) oil. *- telinga* ear wax.

tahil 1 a measure of weight equal to 16 *kati*. 2 a measure of gold, silver , or opium.

tahir (*Lit.*) pure. **ke-an** purity. **pen-an** purification.

tahiti k.o. rattan.

tahiyat (*Isl.*) 1 prayer greeting God. 2 greetings.

tahkik verification. **ment-kan** (*Lit.*) verify.

tahlil₁ 1 (*Isl.*) repeated recitation of the confession of faith: there is no god but God: (*la ilaha illallah*). 2 (*Rel.*) songs of praise (Protestant).

tahlil₂ (*Isl.*) legalize remarriage of husband and wife (who already have divorced 3 times) by arranging for the wife to marry and divorce another man (*muhallil*) before remarriage to her original husband.

tahmid (*Isl*) devotional repetition of the ejaculation, "Praise God," *alhamdulillah*, often as part of a mystic exercise.

tahsil acquisition, esp. collection of rents, taxes, etc.

tahta see TAKHTA.

tahu₁ /tahu, tau/ **1** know, be cognizant of. *Aku - (bhw) dia mau datang* I know that she wants to come. *- ada(nya)* sure of o.s. *- adat* well mannered. *- akal* have an idea. *- balas* grateful. *- bérés* not care whether s.t. gets done or not, too lazy to join in a worthwhile effort. *- madu* know where the profit lies. *- sama -* **1** silent agreement between two persons participating in a mutually advantageous (illegal) deal. **2** we know among ourselves. *Kita - sama - bhw itu tak benar, bukan?* We know it is not true, don't we? *tdk - diri* **1** unconscious. **2** insolent. **2** (*Coll.*) I do not know (often accompanied by a shrug etc.). *-, ya* Dunno. **3** you understand? *Aku bukan budakmu, -?* I am not your slave, you get it? **-nya** (*Coll.*) **1** o.'s knowledge. *~ cuma minta uang saja* All he knows how to do is ask for money. **2** it turned out, to my surprise. *~ istrinya pemain sépak bola!* It turned out his wife is a soccer player! *tak ~* unexpectedly. **se-** as far as o. knows. *~ saya ia tak ada di sini lagi* As far as I know he is no longer here. *dgn ~* with the knowledge. *Meréka pergi dgn ~ saya* They left with my knowledge. **ber-** **1** well informed. **2** conceited. **- men-** *tdk ~* **1** know absolutely nothing about s.t. **2** not be mutually acquainted. **menge-i** **1** know, understand s.t. *Ia blm ~ apa salahnya* He does not know yet what his mistake was. *Ke-ilah! Aku pasti pulang* You'd better understand this! I will surely return home. *kalangan yg sangat ~* well-informed sources. **2** detect, find out. *Ibu marah waktu ~ aku mendengarkan pembicaraan meréka* Mother was angry when she found out that I was listening to their conversation. **memper-kan** (*Lit.*) announce s.t. **ke-an** be found out, detected. *Ia mau pergi diam-diam, tapi ~ juga* He wanted to go quietly, but he was found out anyway. *tdk ~* be erratic, be uncertain. *tdk ~ ayahnya* of an unknown father. **penge-an** **1** knowledge. *ilmu ~* science. *~ dagang* business education. **2** skill, ability. **berpenge-an** knowledgeable.

tahu₂ /tau/ (*Coll.*) ever, once. *Aku - pergi ke Jkt* I have been to Jkt. *Dia nggak - marah* He never gets angry.

tahu₃ /tahu/ tofu, soybean curd. *- goréng* fried tofu. *- isi* tofu filled with meat. *- kuning* firm yellow tofu. *- pong* deep-fried puffy tofu. *- témpé* bean curd and tempeh.

tahua /tahua, tawa/ (*Ch*) k.o. by-product of tofu, similar to yoghurt in consistency.

tahun /tahun, taun/ year. *- ajaran* academic year. *- anggaran* budgetary fiscal year. *- baru* new year. *- berikutnya* the following year. *- buku* fiscal year according to book-keeping operations. *- datang/ depan/hadapan* next year. *- fiskal* fiscal year. *- hijriah* (*Isl.*) **1** a date in the Muslim calendar. **2** the Muslim calendar. *- jagung* approximately three months (from corn crop to corn crop). *umur se-jagung* just a youngster. *- kabisah/kabisat* leap year. *- kamariah* lunar year. *- Maséhi* **1** a date in the Gregorian calendar. **2** the Gregorian calendar. *- pajak* fiscal year according to taxes. *- pelajaran/pengajaran* academic year. *- pembukuan* fiscal year according to the books. *- takwim* calendar year. **se-(²)nya** every year. *~ produksinya lima ratus ton* The yearly production is 500 tons. **ber-²** for many years. *Ia ~ tinggal di negeri asing* He lived abroad for many years. **men-** chronic, lasting for years. *Penyakit itu sdh ~* The disease is chronic. **-an** **1** approximate years of age (after a number). *dua puluh ~ (in)* o.'s twenties. *Umurnya kira-kira sdh lima puluh ~* She must be in her fifties. **2** annual. *rapat ~* annual meeting. **3** perennial. **4** anniversary. **se-²an** the entire year.

tahu-tahu /tau-tau/ suddenly and unexpectedly. *~ ia datang* He came unexpectedly.

tahyul see TAKHYUL.

tai see TAHI.

taifun see TOPAN.

taik₁ see TAHI.

taik₂ see NAIK.

taiko (*Ch*) leprosy.

taipak **1** (*Ch*) gambling. **2** financier in gambling.

taipun see TOPAN.

tais dirty.

taisén (*Ch*) **1** the other number in a fixed pair of numbers in a numbers game or lottery. **2** the beloved.

taiso (*Japanese*) group calisthenics.

tajak k.o. hoe used to remove weeds, esp. in paddy field. **men-, men-i** work soil or chop down weeds with such a tool.

tajali, tajalli (*Isl.*) k.o. vision of truth.

tajam **1** sharp. *pisau -* a sharp knife. *berujung -* sharp-pointed. *sudut -* a sharp corner. **2** incisive, acute. *- akalnya* sharp-witted. *- mulutnya* sharp-tongued. *- otaknya* keen, intelligent. *- perasaan* sensitive. **men-** intensify, reach a critical point. *Segala kontradiksi makin ~* The contradictions are becoming more and more critical. **men-kan** sharpen s.t., whet s.t. **memper-** exacerbate. *Pertentangan itu ~ hubungan antara kedua negeri itu* The disagreement aggravated the relationship between the two countries. **ke-an** **1** too sharp. **2** sharpness. **3** acuteness. *~ mata* visual acuity. **pen-an** **1** sharpening. **2** exacerbation.

taji cock's spur. **2** metal spur attached to fighting cock's leg. *- bentuk* spur with slightly curved blade. *- golok* cock's spur with blade like a dagger. **ber-** with the spur on.

tajin **1** thick water from cooked rice often fed to infants as milk substitute. **2** water with starch for ironing. **men-** **1** feed rice water (to an infant). **2** starch o.'s clothes. **men-i** starch s.t. **men-kan** make rice water or starch out of s.t.

tajong men- strike (with the arm).

tajub see TAKJUB.

tajuk **1** crown. *- gigi* crown of tooth. *- mahkota* **1** a part of a royal crown. **2** beloved, darling. *- rencana* editorial. **2** (*Lit.*) ornamental aigrette. **3** (*Naut.*) outward projection on small craft. **ber-**

have (a topic) as an editorial. *Hari ini Jawa Pos ~ masalah pemboman Borobudur* Today the *Java Post* featured the bombing of Borobudur in an editorial. **men-** 1 protrude. 2 prominent, well known. **men-kan** make s.t. into an editorial. *~ kunjungan délégasi RRT* make the visit of the Ch delegation the editorial (topic).

tajwid (*Isl.*) proper pronunciation for correct recitation of the Koran.

tak₁ no, not. *- acuh* indifferent. **ke-acuhan** indifference, apathy. *- akan, -kan* not likely to. *Kau jangan kuatir! Aku - akan/kan menyentuh tubuhmu!* Do not be afraid! I am not about to touch your body! *- boléh/dpt tdk* absolutely must. *Ia - dpt tdk pergi* He cannot help but go. *- dpt tdk hrs* must. *- lain - bukan* nothing other than. *- tau* never. *Turis barat mémang - tau mandi* Western tourists never bathe. *- organik* (*Chem.*) inorganic. *- sengaja* unintentional.

tak₂ (*Jv*) I, by me. *Berani bohong - pukul kamu* Try lying and I will beat you up!

tak₃ see TAKT.

takabur arrogant, haughty. **ke-an** arrogance.

takah₁ (*M*) 1 appearance, attitude. 2 of suitable bearing.

takah₂ see TAKUH.

takak **men-** sew two ends of sarong together (to yield tube shape). **ber-** formed by sewing ends together.

takal block and tackle.

takan, ta'kan see TAK₁.

takar 1 k.o. pottery container. 2 variable unit of liquid or solid measure between o. quart to o. gallon. *- coba* test batch. **se-** of the same capacity. *Kepandaiannya tak ~ dgn keberaniannya* His ability does not match his courage. **men-(i)** measure out. **ke-an** standard of living. **-an** 1 measuring container. 2 measurement, dosage. **pen-an** act of measuring out.

takat (*Lit.*) limit, end point. **se-** up to (a point). *~ léhér* up to o.'s neck.

takbir (*Isl.*) recitation of laudation, "God is great" (*Allahu akbar*) us. at opening of prayers. *- di pangkal lidah* be on verge of death. **ber-(an)** engage in such recitation. **-an** 1 laudations in the form of such recitations. 2 night of last day of fasting month.

takbirul-ihram (*Isl.*) opening laudation of prayer ritual.

takbur see TAKABUR.

takdim (*Isl.*) opening (of prayer).

takdir divine decree, fate. **men-kan** predestine, preordain. *Kita di-kan Tuhan hidup bersama* God has predestined us to live together.

takdis holiness.

takel see TAKAL.

taker see TAKAR.

takéyari (*Japanese*) bamboo spear.

takhayul see TAKHYUL.

takhlik (*Lit.*) **ment-kan** create (of God).

takhta throne. *- Suci* (*Rel.*) Holy See. **ber-** reign. *Ia ~ selama sepuluh tahun* He reigned for 10

years. **men(t)-kan** crown, enthrone. *Raja tua itu ~ putera mahkota* The old king enthroned the crown prince. **ke-an** things concerning the throne. *tongkat ~* royal scepter.

takhyul superstitious, superstition. *Segala hantu itu - belaka* All that belief in ghosts is just superstition. **ke-an** belief in superstitions.

takik notch. **ber-(²)** notched, incised. **men-** 1 make incisions to extract sap. *~ darah di batu* get blood from a turnip. *~ getah* tap rubber. 2 notch s.t. *~ batang kelapa* cut footholds in a coconut trunk. **-an** extraction of sap. *Tiap ~ menghasilkan setengah liter* Each incision produces a half a liter. **pen-** o. who makes such incisions. *~ getah* rubber-tree tapper.

takil see PETAKILAN.

takir (*Jv, Jkt*) water container made of banana leaves, palm fronds, etc. *se- nasi* a portion of rice wrapped in a banana leaf.

takjal hastily, hurriedly.

takjil (*Isl.*) sweet food eaten upon breaking the fast.

takjim see TAKZIM.

takjub astonishment, astonished. **men(t)-i** be astonished at. *Ia ~ kepandaian temannya* He was pleasantly surprised at his friend's ability. **men(t)-kan** astonish, amaze. *Keindahan kota itu ~ para wisatawan* The city's beauty astonished the tourists. **ke-an** astonishment, amazement.

takkan see TAK₁.

taklid 1 (*Rel.*) unquestioning acceptance of traditional religious interpretations. 2 (*Coll.*) gullible. *- buta* follow s.o. blindly.

taklif imposition of responsibility or duty.

taklik 1 (*Lit.*) addendum, attachment. 2 (*Isl.*) conditions attached to an agreement, esp. marriage contracts so that, e.g., divorce is effected if husband fails to return after a certain time, etc. *nikah - a* marriage with such conditions. 3 (*Leg.*) probationary (sentence). **men-** read diligently, peruse carefully. **pen-an** collation.

taklikat (*Lit.*) addendum, marginal notes.

taklim see TAKZIM.

takluk subject, subjection. *- kpd hukum negara* subject to the laws of the country. *- kpd permintaan ayahnya* yielding to his father's request. **men(t)-kan** subjugate, subdue. *Penjajah baru ~ Pulau Bali pd abad kedua puluh* The colonial power subjugated Bali only in the 20th century. *~ nafsu séksuil* subdue the sexual appetite. **-an** s.t. subjected. *daérah ~nya* conquered territories. **pen-** conqueror, subjugator. **pen(t)-an** subjection, submission.

takoa, takoah see TAKUA.

takrau, takraw (*Sport*) rattan plaited into a rough ball (used in traditional games).

takrif (*Lit.*) definition. **men(t)-kan** define. **ke-an** (*Ling.*) definition.

takrim see TAKZIM.

takrir (*Leg.*) evidence, proof.

takro see TAKRAU.

taksa equivocal. **ke-an** being equivocal.

taksi taxi. **ber-** ride a taxi. **men-** drive a cab. **men-kan** use s.t. as a cab. *Ia ~ mobilnya utk mencari pendapatan tambahan* He used his car as a cab to obtain extra income. **per-an** taxi matters.

taksir men- estimate, value, appraise. *Dr raut wajahnya ku- ia berumur dua puluh tahun* From her features I took her to be 20. **n-** (*Sl.*) have an eye for, be attracted to. *~ anak org gedé ngapain, sih?* What is the use of setting your sights on a rich man's kid, anyway? **-an** appraisal. *menurut ~nya* according to her estimation. *~ kasar* rough appraisal. **pen-** appraiser. **pen-an** appraising, evaluation. *panitia ~* evaluation committee.

taksiun (*Coll.*) station.

taksonomi taxonomy.

takt (*Auto.*) stroke. *motor dua -* two-stroke engine.

tak-tak /tak tak/ sound of cracking, bullet shots, toy machine gun, etc.

taktik (*Mil.*) tactics.

taktis tactical. *dana -* operating funds.

tak tok /tak tok/ sound of clicking.

takua (*Ch*) k.o. firm spiced tofu.

takuh notch. *--takah* all k.o. notches.

takuk notch. **ber-** notched. **men-** cut a notch, incision. **men-(kan)** fix, determine. *Ia ~ hari berangkat* He fixed the departure date.

tak-umpet see PÉTAK₃.

takung men- 1 let s.t. settle. *Ia ~ air sungai spy bersih* He let the river water settle so it would be clean. **2** cause liquid to accumulate. **ter-** accumulated (of liquids). **-an** accumulated water, puddle, etc.

takup men- close itself together firmly. **men-kan** close s.t. (two symmetrical things) together firmly. *~ bibir* purse the lips firmly. **ter-** be closed firmly (of two symmetrical things).

takur see TEKUR.

takut be afraid. *Jangan -!* Do not be afraid! *Ia - kalau-kalau perasaanku akan tersinggung* She was afraid that my feelings would be hurt. *Saya - ular* I am afraid of snakes. *Ia sama sekali tdk - gelap* She was absolutely not afraid of the dark. **-²** somewhat afraid, cautious. *~ berani* hesitating. **men-i 1** frighten s.o. *Ia ~ dan membentak org bawahannya* She intimidated her subordinates and spoke harshly to them. **2** fear s.t. *Yg paling ku-i ialah . . .* What I most fear is . . . *Hanya Tuhan yg sewajarnya kita -i* We need fear only God. **men-²i** scare off, try to intimidate. *Dia ~ anakku!* He is blustering at my child. **men-kan 1** cause s.o. to fear, frighten s.o. *Bermimpi jahat tentu ~nya* He surely was frightened by a nightmare. *Perlombaan senjata nuklir sangat ~* The nuclear arms race is terrifying. **2** fear s.t. *Itu dikannya* That is what he is afraid of. **ke-an 1** fear, anxiety. **2** frightened, anxious. *Meréka sedih hati dan ~* They are sad and anxious. *Ia ~ melihat gurunya* He was terrified upon seeing his teacher. **-²an** tend to be afraid. **pen-** coward, s.o. fainthearted. *Bp sdh tua dan ~* Father had grown old and timorous.

takwa₁ piety. **ber-** pious. *Stlh kematian ibunya*

Hasan tambah ~ kpd Tuhan Upon his mother's death Hassan became increasingly devout.

takwa₂ see TAKUA.

takwim (*Lit.*) almanac, calendar. *tahun -* calendar year.

takziah 1 visit the home of people suffering death or injury in the family. **2** sympathy, condolence.

takzim respect, esteem. *Terimalah salam - saya* Please accept my respectful greetings. **ment-kan** respect or esteem s.o. **ke-an** matters pertaining to honor and respect.

takzir (*Isl.*) punishment imposed by a religious court.

tal (*Jv*) k.o. fan palm, the leaves of which were formerly used for writing on.

tala in tune, harmonious. *garpu -* tuning fork. *- suara* voice modulation. **se-** in tune. **menye-kan** put in the same scale. **men-** tune an instrument. **pen- 1** s.o. or s.t. which tunes. *~ piano* piano tuner. **2** tuning fork. **pen-an** tuning.

talaah see TELAAH.

talah (*M*) **ter-²** hastily, hurriedly.

talak₁ 1 (*Isl.*) divorce (o.'s wife). **2** divorce formula used by Muslim husband. *- tiga* divorce pronounced for 3rd time (after two reconciliations); remarriage is prohibited, except through *tahlil.* **men(t)-** divorce s.o. *Si Ali tdk berani ~ bininya* Ali is not brave enough to divorce his wife.

talak₂ see TALK.

talam tray. *- dua muka* two-faced.

talang₁ (*Jkt, Jv*) middleman. *- kuda* horse trader. **men-** lend money as a profession. **men-i** advance s.o. money. **pen-** *~ (uang)* moneylender.

talang₂ eaves trough, gutter.

talar ber- 1 think logically, reason. **2** deliberate a problem. **n- 1** logical reasoning. *~ sangat penting dlm pendidikan* Reasoning is important in education. **2** reasonable. **men-kan** reason or think s.t. out. **pen-an** reasoning, intellectual activity.

talas taro.

talek see TALK.

talén 25 cents, a quarter (of a *rupiah*). *uang se-* 25 cents. **-an** a quarter, 25 cents.

talenan chopping block, cutting board.

tales see TALAS.

tali 1 string, cord, rope. *- alit* string for spinning a top. *- anak* small auxiliary rope. *- ari-ari* umbilical cord. *- batong* sash. *- belati* rope of European hemp. *- busur* 1 bowstring. 2 (*Math.*) chord in geometry. *- dahi layar* ropes serving as bridle. *- jentera* thread in process of being spun. *- duga* (*Naut.*) sounding line. *- dugang* supporting rope. *- kail* fishing line. *- kang/kangkang/kekang* 1 reins. 2 guideline. *- kelat* (*Naut.*) boat's sheet. *- lalai/pangkal* mast rope. *- pancing* fishing line. *- peduga* (*Naut.*) sounding line. *- pendarat* (*Naut.*) hawser. *- pengangguk* (*Naut.*) forestay. *- penyidai kain* clothesline. *- (pen)cemat* towrope. *- perut* 1 bellyband. 2 intestines. *- pusar/pusat* umbilical cord. *- putri* k.o. long thin parasitical weed. *- ruai* a thin, weak rope. *- sabut* fiber rope. *- sepatu* shoelace, shoestring. *- sipat* carpenter's plumb. *-*

suai a stay rope. - *tandur* cords for blinds. - *temali* all sorts of ropes, cordage, rigging. - *tunda* tow-rope. - *umban* a sling rope. **2** line, connection. - *air* 1 small stream, creek. 2 current. 3 perineum. - *api* fuse. - *jiwa* source of life, heart. - *nyawa* heart, source of life. - *suci* holy bonds (of matrimony). **3** belt, strap. - *ambin* a strap around a load. - *bahu* shoulder straps of knapsack. - *bawat* brace. - *dahi* browband of a horse. - *kepala* straps attaching a burden carried on the back to head. - *lés* reins. - *tom* reins. - *tudung* chin strap for hat. -² s.t. like a rope. **se-** 1 connected to e.o. **2** 25 cents, a quarter of a rupiah. ~ *tiga uang* six of o. and half dozen of the other. - **ber-** continuously. ~ *org yg datang ke lapangan itu* People keep coming to the field. **ber-** equipped with a rope, with a rope attached. **ber-²** 1 with all k.o. ropes. 2 interconnected, involved. *Banyak hal ~ dgn soal ini* Many things are involved in this matter. **3** continuous. *Ia menyebutkan namanya ~* He mentioned his name continuously. **ber-an** 1 tied to e.o. *Tubuh-tubuh itu ~* The bodies were tied to e.o. **2** related. **3** relevant, germane. **men-** tie with a rope. *Payah aku ~ pakétmu* I had trouble tying your package. **men-kan** tie s.t. or s.o. to. *Ia ~ kudanya ke pohon* He bound his horse to a tree. **memper-kan** 1 tie to. **2** link, connect. *Rumah-rumah baru itu ~ désa dgn kota* The new houses link the village with the town. *Meréka ~ kematiannya dgn peminuman obat itu* They linked his death to his drinking the medicine. **3** join s.o. (in marriage). *Ingin aku ~ engkau dgn adikku* I want to join you in marriage to my brother. -²*an* vines. **pen-** 1 binder. ~ *kuda* rope for a horse. **2** (*Lit.*) conclusion. ~ *permusyawaratan* conclusion of the conference. **per-an** 1 relation, relationship. ~ *bahasa* relationship of languages. ~ *darah* blood relationship. ~ *jiwa* congeniality. **2** connection.

talibun k.o. old poetry with a distinctive rhyme pattern.

taligram see TÉLÉGRAM.

taligrap see TÉLÉGRAP.

ta'lim see TAKZIM.

talipun see TÉLEPON.

talk talcum powder.

talkin (*Isl.*) instructions to the dead us. at close of funeral to offer advice on what to say when questioned by the angels of death. **men(t)-(kan)** whisper instructions in the ear of the dead or dying.

talu₁ 1 opening melody at a *wayang* show. **2** k.o. gong. **ber-** play this opening melody or gong.

talu₂ ber-² continuously, incessantly. *Beduk Jumat dipukul ~* The Friday prayer drum was beaten incessantly.

taluk, ta'luk see TAKLUK.

talun - *temalun* various resounding noises. **ber-** resound. *Suara kentongan ~* The sound of the wooden drum resounded. -**an** resonance.

tam plinking sound of small stones hitting s.t. metallic.

tama see PERTAMA.

tamadun, tamaddun (*Lit.*) civilization. **ber-** 1 civilized. ~ *Islam* with a Muslim civilization. **2** cultured, refined.

tamah see RAMAH.

tamak 1 greed. - *menghilangkan malu* Greed has no shame. **2** greedy, covetous. - *akan upah* eager for pay. - *kedekut* greed and avarice. **ke-an** greed.

taman garden, park. - *bacaan* reading room. - *bunga* flower garden. - *sari* pleasure park, garden. - *indria/kanak-kanak* kindergarten. - *margasatwa* 1 game preserve. 2 zoo. - *makam pahlawan* military cemetery. - *pustaka* library. **per-an** 1 gardens. 2 horticulture. 3 garden affairs.

tamasya 1 view, scenery. **2** spectacle, performance. **3** go on an excursion. **ber-** go on an excursion, go sight-seeing. *Meréka pergi ~ ke gunung* They went on a trip to the mountains.

tamasyawan (*Lit.*) tourist.

tamat 1 finished, completed. *Ceritanya - begitu saja* The story ended just like that. *sdh - sekolah* graduated. - *riwayatnya* demise, decease. **2** end, conclusion. **se-** upon ending, as soon as it ended. *Dia kawin dgn aku ~ kami dr SMA* She married me as soon as we finished high school. **men-kan** conclude s.t. ~ *sekolah rakyat* graduate from grammar school. *AS ~ segala bantuan militér pd Israél* America cut off all military assistance to Israel. *Sebentar saja dia sdh ~ vidéo silat tiga puluh jilid itu* In no time at all he finished (viewing) the 30 installment kung fu video. -**an** 1 graduation. **2** a graduate. *Suaminya ~ UI* Her husband is a graduate of the University of Indonesia.

tamatalkalam, tamatu'lkalam (*Lit.*) end of the story.

tambah 1 add. *"Tapi itu suamiku!"* - *Ira gemetar* "But that is my husband!" added Ira quivering with emotion. *Lima - satu ada enam* five plus o. is six. **2** additional amount. *Lima rupiah tdk cukup; minta* - Five rupiah is not enough; I want more. **3** more, increasingly. *wajahnya yg - pucat* his face which became increasingly pale. - *besar* larger. - *rusak* more damaged. - . . . - . . . the more . . . the more . . . *lama - kuat* The longer it was, the stronger he became. - *pula* moreover, in addition. - *pula ia sakit* Moreover, he fell ill. **ber-** 1 increase. *Séwa ~ jadi tiga juta rupiah* The rent increased to three million rupiah. **2** increasingly, more and more. ~ *banyak* increasing in number. ~ . . . ~ . . . the more . . . the more . . . ~ *besar ~ congkak* The older he became the more arrogant he got. **ber-²** 1 increase steadily. *Kekayaanya ~* His wealth increased steadily. **2** all the more so. *Ia sedang bingung ~ anaknya sakit* He was even more upset because his child was sick. **men-** add to, increase. *satu di- dua* o. plus two. *Sebuah tahi lalat kecil ~ kemanisannya* A small freckle added to her beauty. *Segala cerita itu ~ bimbang hati Dullah* All these stories increased Dullah's anxiety. **men-i** increase s.t. *Ia ~ sup dgn air* She increased the amount of soup by adding water. **men-kan** 1 add s.t. *Ia ~ gula ke dlm téh* She added sugar to the tea. **2** cause s.t. to increase. *Obat itu ~ sakitnya* The medicine increased the pain. *Lembah yg curam ~ keseraman perjalanan* The steep valley compounded the fearsomeness of the trip. **memper-** cause s.t. to increase. *~ hasil bumi* increase the agricultural yield. **ter- 1** inadvertently added. *Tadi rambutannya ~* Just now a few extra rambutan got included. **2** augmented. **ke-an** have s.t. added to it. *bakat bangsa Indonésia yg ~ daya penyatu* the talent of the Indonesian people augmented by the power to become united. **-an 1** addition. *~ buku-buku baru* acquisition of new books. **2** supplement, extra amount. *~ kuota* an additional quota. *mencari uang ~* find additional funds. **3** furthermore. *Engkau tdk setia ~ dengki!* You are not loyal, what is more you are spiteful! *~ lagi/pula* furthermore. **pen- 1** (*Math*) enumerator, counter. **2** addition, extra. *~ belanja* addition to the budget. *sbg ~ utk mencukupi hidup* as s.t. extra to make ends meet. **pen-an** increment, increasing. *~ gaji* increasing salaries. **per-an** increase, growth, accretion. *~ nilai* (*Fin.*) added value. *~ pengangguran* increase in unemployment.

tambak 1 earthen dam, embankment. **2** fishpond (made by damming). *- pesisir* coastal pond. **3** banking, leveling off. **men- 1** bank up earth to control water flow or irrigate fields, etc. *Meréka ~ sungai* They dammed up the river. **2** apply a poultice. *Ia ~ luka* He put a plaster on the wound. **3** obstruct movement. *Pemerintah berusaha ~ arus msknya morfin ke California* The gvt. is trying to reduce the flow of drugs into California.

tambal a patch or mend. *- ban* tire repair. *- sulam* **1** repair by patching (clothing, etc.). **2** do s.t. in an ad hoc manner. **ber-** patched. *Keméja itu ~ di bahu* The shirt is patched on the shoulder. **ber-²** be patched all over. **ber-kan** have as a patch. **men-** patch, mend. *Ia ~ lobang di témbok* He patched the hole in the wall. *~ pakaian* mend clothes. *Gigi saya akan di-* I am going to have my tooth filled. **men-i** apply a patch to s.t. *Belakangnya di-i dgn obat yg baru* They patched up his back with a new medication. **men-kan 1** patch with s.t. **2** patch on behalf of s.o. **-an** patch, repairs. *Celananya penuh ~* His pants were full of patches. *~ gigi* tooth filling. **pen- 1** o. who patches. **2** s.t. to patch with. **pen-an** act of patching.

tambang₁ mine. *- besi* iron mine. **men-** mine, dig. *Di Sumatera Tengah org ~ batu bara* In central Sumatra people mine coal. **ter-** mined. **pen-** miner. **pen-an** the activity of mining. *~ timah* tin mining. **per-an** mining, mine workings.

tambang₂ 1 cross (river) by small boat, dugout, etc. *sampan* - dugout used for ferrying passengers across a river. **2** (*Lit.*) fare. **men-** cross a body of water by a small passenger boat. *setiap hari saya hrs ~ ke sekolah* Every day I have to go to school by riding a small boat. **men-kan 1** transport across (a body of water). **2** operate a passenger vehicle. *Ia ~ taksinya* He operated his taxi. **-an** ferrying, conveyance for ferrying. **pen- 1** ferryman. **2** ferry. **3** s.o. engaging in transporting a small number of passengers (taxi drivers, pedicab drivers, etc.). **pen-an** ferrying, transport.

tambang₃ (*Jkt*) thick rope. *perlombaan tarik* - tug-of-war. **men-** fasten with a thick rope. *Ia ~ perahunya pd tiang* He fastened his boat to a pole.

tambang₄ men- separate from but refuse to support or divorce o.'s wife.

tambat tether. **ber-** tethered, tied up. **ber-an** connected with. **men-(kan)** tether, tie up. *~ hati* enthrall s.o., cause s.o. to fall in love. *tempat ~ kerbau* the thing to tie the buffalo to. **ter-** tethered, tied up. *~ hati* enthralled, in love. *~ hatinya melihat gadis itu* She fell in love when she saw that fisherman. **keter-an** attachment. *~ budaya* state of being culture-bound. **-an 1** mooring buoy or post. **2** tether. *~ hati* lover, sweetheart. **pen-** s.t. to tie with. *tali ~ ayamnya* a rope to tie his chicken with. **pen-an** act of tethering or mooring. **per-an 1** ship moorings. **2** connection, relationship.

tambeng (*Jv*) disobedient.

tambera₁ 1 (*Lit.*) bronze. **2** bronze inscription.

tambera₂ see IKAN.

tambi 1 Indian. **2** (*in some regions only*) term of address for young males from India.

tambo (*M*) legend, historical traditions.

tamborin see TAMBURIN.

tambuh (*M*) *- ciék* have another plate of rice. **ber-** have another serving of rice. **-an** additional serving of rice.

tambul₁ 1 dessert. **2** snacks that accompany beverages. **3** beverage refreshment. *Ia mengeluarkan - berupa téh dan kopi* She offered refreshments of tea and coffee. **ber- 1** served with a light snack. **2** enjoy refreshments. *Sblm rapat dilanjutkan, marilah ~ dahulu* Before we go on with the meeting, let us have some refreshments.

tambul₂ (*Thea.*) **ber-, men-** do theatrical stunts (magic shows, farces, etc.). **pen-** theatrical performer, artiste.

tambun₁ chubby, well fed. *Mukanya - sekarang* His face has fleshed out (It is not skinny and drawn). **men-kan** cause to put on some needed weight.

tambun₂ (*M*) see TIMBUN.

tambung rude, impertinent.

tambur 1 drum, esp. of European origin. **2** (*Isl.*) mosque drum. **ber-, men-** beat a drum. **men-i** beat on s.t. *Anak-anak itu ~ kaléng dan tong* Those children were beating out a rhythm on cans and casks.

tamburin tambourine.

tambus see TIMBUS.

taméng (*Jv*) a shield for combat. **ber- 1** shelter or protect o.s. behind a shield. **2** use s.t. as a pretext.

tammat see TAMAT.

tammatu'lkalam see TAMATALKALAM.

tampa₁ men- 1 understand. 2 think, suppose.
tampa₂ see TANPA.
tampah (*Jv*) winnowing tray.
tampak₁ appear, be visible. *Gedungnya - dr sini* The building is visible from here. *Engkau sdh lama tdk -* We have not seen you for a long time. **-²** 1 show up. *tak ~* just never show up. *Kenapa ia tdk ~?* Why doesn't he show up? 2 vaguely visible. *~ apung* not readily visible. **-nya** apparently. *~ ia melawan* Apparently, he is resisting. **men-** (*Coll.*) see. *Ia ~ gunung di kejauhan* He saw the mountain in the distance. **men-kan** make s.t. visible, show. *Ia ~ giginya yg ompong* He showed that he had lots of teeth missing. *~ kesopanan berlalulintas di Jkt* show courtesy in traffic in Jkt. *~ diri* show up, appear. *Sdh lama engkau tak ~ dirimu* You have not shown up for a long time. **ter-** visible. *Beberapa tentara Indonesia ~ dlm sinar* A number of Indonesian soldiers were visible in the moonlight. **pen-an** appearance.
tampak₂ (*Med.*) measles.
tampal 1 patch. 2 a mend. **men-** 1 patch or mend (clothes, inner tube, etc.). 2 patch, plaster. *Ia ~ témbok* He plastered the wall. **men-kan** 1 affix a patch, etc. so that it adheres. *~ pléster pd dahinya* affix an adhesive poultice to o.'s forehead. 2 cause s.t. to adhere. *Ia ~ gambar ke témbok* He pasted pictures on the wall. **-an** 1 s.t. affixed or stuck on (i.e. a patch, etc.). 2 appendix of a book.
tampan 1 of suitable bearing (esp. of males). *Tahu-tahu - juga ia memakai sorjan* Quite unexpectedly he looked great in a Jv jacket. *- muka* 1 features. 2 appearance. *- rupa* appearance, looks. 2 appropriate, fitting. *Ia - sekali menjadi ketua* It is very appropriate that he become chairman. **-nya** at first sight. **-²nya** apparently, seemingly. **men-** 1 assume a proper bearing. 2 spruce up, groom o.s. **ke-an** handsomeness.
tampang₁ (*M*) 1 planting seed, cutting for planting. 2 source. *Inilah - segala kejahatan* This is the source of all evil. **men-** cut in slices. **pen-** 1 diameter or longitudinal plane through the center. 2 longitudinal section.
tampang₂ (*Jkt*) wad, roll. *se- tembakau* a wad of tobacco.
tampang₃ 1 appearance of a person. *nggak -* looking like a tramp. 2 put on, show off. **men-** 1 look at o.s. in the mirror. 2 show off, put on. *Ia memakai baju potongan Dior utk ~* She was wearing a Dior dress just to show off. **pen-(an)** profile. *~ tanah* soil profile.
tampar a slap with the flat of the hand. **ber-** slap. *~ tangan* applaud. *- men-* slap e.o. **men-** beat, slap. *Ya, aku ~ muka halusnya* So what! I slapped her smooth face. **men-i** slap repeatedly. **men-kan** use s.t. to slap. *Ia ~ popor senapannya ke punggung pencuri itu* He jammed the rifle butt into the thief's back. **ter-** slapped accidently. **-an** a slap. *~ nyamuk* (*Lit.*) shoulder blade. **pen-** s.t. or s.o. that slaps. **pen-an** action of slapping.
tampas (*Lit.*) **men-** lop off.

tampek see TAMPAK₂.
tampél slight hit, bump. *Rokoknya jatuh kena - tangan org* He dropped his cigarette because s.o. bumped into it. **men-** (*Sport*) hit a ball or shuttlecock.
tampi winnowing. **men-** winnow s.t. *Jangan tumpah padinya kalau ~* Do not overdo it (lit., don't spill the rice while winnowing). *Darahnya ~* He got angry, excited (lit., his blood winnowed). **-an** 1 s.t. winnowed. *beras ~* winnowed rice. 2 winnowing basket. **pen-** winnowing basket.
tampik₁ men- reject, refuse. *Ia ~ tawaran saya* He rejected my offer. *Ajakan kami selalu di-nya dgn macam-macam alasan* She always declines our invitations on all k.o. pretexts. **-an** rejection. **pen-an** act of refusing or rejecting.
tampik₂ see TEMPIK₁.
tampil 1 step forward. *Ia - ke muka utk berceramah* He stepped forward to give the lecture. *Ketika aku - di hadapan meréka, pertengkaran reda* When I appeared before them, the quarrel calmed down. 2 appear before. 3 appear, come into being. **men-kan** 1 put s.o. or s.t. forward. *Angkatan muda ~ W.S. Rendra sbg pujangga meréka* The younger generation puts forward W.S. Rendra as its literary figure. 2 bring forward to show to the public, show. *celana yg pantas di-kan di disko* pants that are suitable to wear to a disco. **ke-an** appearance, presence. **pen-an** 1 presentation. 2 making o.'s appearance. *~ tokoh-tokoh itu* the appearance of those figures.
tampin k.o. rough container made of plaited palm leaves, esp. for sago.
tampuk 1 (*Biol.*) calyx, s.t. like a calyx. *- lampu listerik* light socket. *- pemerintahan* state leadership, supreme power. *- pimpinan* (*Pol.*) 1 supreme authority. 2 central leadership. **ber-** *pimpinan* have its central authority. *Indonésia ~ pimpinan di Jkt* The central authority of Indonesia is in Jkt. *- pistol* handgun barrel. 2 any calyxlike design (rosettes, etc.) or calyx-like lid. *- susu* aureole surrounding the nipple.
tampung₁ men- 1 intercept and retain falling water (rain, waterfall, spigot, etc.). *Ia ~ air hujan* He caught the falling rain. 2 receive, accommodate, take in. *Ruang ini bisa ~ dua ribu penonton* This hall can hold 2,000 spectators. *Tong ini bisa ~ segala sarap sampah sekitarnya* This drum can hold all the rubbish in the area. *Pertanian ~ sepuluh persén tenaga kerja* Agriculture absorbs 10 percent of manpower. **men-kan** intercept and retain (water) with s.t. *Ia ~ tangan di bawah pancuran* He caught the water under the pipe with his hand. **ter-** accommodated. *Tdk semua lulusan SMA ~ di perguruan tinggi negeri* Not all high school graduates can be accommodated in public universities. **pen-** s.t. or s.o. who intercepts. **pen-an** 1 collecting and saving water, etc. *wadah ~ rainwater* reservoir. 2 place that receives. *kota ~ pengungsi* a city which takes in refugees. 3 act of receiving or accommodating.
tampung₂ a patch.

tampur see TEMPUR.
tampus (*M*) sorrel color.
tamsil 1 parable. 2 example. **men(t)-kan** 1 compare. *Siti ~ kejadian yg menimpa dirinya dgn pengalaman ibunya* Siti compared the misfortune that befell her to her mother's experience. 2 relate in a parable or analogous manner. *Cerita itu ~ keburukan fanatisisme* That story presented a parable on the evils of fanaticism. **-an** comparison.
tamsir (*Lit.*) armor.
tamtam indigo.
tam-tam small bongo drum.
tamtama (*Mil.*) 1 lower-ranking noncomissioned officer, corporal. 2 lower-ranking comissioned officer (below Colonel).
tamu guest, visitor, s.o. who comes to another person's place. *Ada -, Bu. Penjual keliling* There is s.o. at the door, Mom. A door-to-door salesman. *- agung* VIP, high-ranking visitor. *- negara* a guest of the nation, state visitor. *- tak diundang* an unwanted guest (lit., uninvited guest). **ber-** 1 visit. *Ia sering ~ ke rumah Mimi* He often visits Mimi's house. 2 be a guest. **men-** be a guest of s.o. **men-i** visit a place or person. *Masak, Bibi tdk pernah kamu -i!* Are you serious! You mean you have never visited Auntie! **ke-an** be visited by. *Ia ~ tiga org penjahat* He was visited by three bandits.
tamyiz (*Lit.*) discernment of good and bad. **ment-kan** discern.
tamzil see TAMSIL.
tan see SUTAN.
tan- (*Jv*) a privative prefix, a-. *-suara* soundless.
tanah 1 land. *- datar* flat country. *- goyang* earthquake. *- hidup* cultivated land. *- kampung* communal land. *- kosong* unused, uncultivated land. *- kuripan* privately owned land. *- lapang* 1 field, plain. 2 a square. *- mati* wasteland. *- milik* privately owned land. *- rata* level ground. *- raya* continent. *- rembang* open, exposed ground. *- usaha* 1 hereditary landed property. 2 cultivated land. 3 land for an enterprise. *- wakaf* land given for public purpose. 2 country, land. *- air* fatherland. *- Arab* Arabia. *- Jawa* Java. *- Melayu* 1 Malaya. 2 (*Coll.*) Malaysia. *- Réncong* Acch. *- seberang* 1 areas beyond Java (e.g. Sumatra). 2 Malacca (from Sumatra). *- Suci* (*Isl.*) the Holy Land (Mecca and religious shrines of Mideast). *- tumpah darah* birthplace. 3 soil, ground. *- kering* a dry, unirrigated field. *- longsor* landslide. *- pekat* clay, loam. *- tesirah* fresh grave. **ber-** 1 take root. 2 put down roots, own land. *Saya sdh ~ di sini* I have already put down roots here. **menge-kan** 1 cause s.t. to come to the ground. *~ bendéra* haul down a flag. *~ toko* raze a store to the ground. 2 bury. **per-an** land affairs, land matters.
tanahair see TANAH.
tanahulayat (*M*) community land.
tanak cooked (of rice). *Jangan pergi dulu, nasi sdh -* Do not go yet; the rice is cooked. **ber-** boil rice.

Tunggu dulu Ibu sedang ~ Wait awhile; mother is cooking rice. **men-** 1 cook rice (by boiling). 2 boil. *~ minyak* render coconut flesh into oil. **-an** cooked rice. **-²an** play at cooking rice. **pen-** s.t. to boil rice in. **sepe(r)-, sepen-** the time needed to boil rice, about 20 minutes.
tanam ber- engage in planting or cultivating. *musim ~* planting season. **ber-²an** be engaged in planting. *~ kasih* love e.o. *- men-* planting, gardening. **men-** 1 plant s.t. *Ia ~ padi* She planted rice. *~ mumbang* undertake s.t. hopeless (lit., plant young coconuts). 2 cover with earth. *Ia ~ senjata gelap* He buried smuggled weapons. *~ mayat* bury a corpse. 3 (*Fin.*) invest. *Ia ~ uangnya* He invested his money. **men-i** plant on s.t. *Ia ~ tanahnya dgn kacang* He planted his field with peanuts. **men-kan** 1 implant s.t. *Pengertian politik yg di-kan Bakri menjadi bertambah teguh* The political ideas Bakri had implanted became stronger and stronger. 2 (*Fin.*) invest. **ter-**planted, buried. *Akibat tanah longsor, rumahnya ~* Due to the landslide his house was buried. *Pakaiannya mémang kasar dan kotor tetapi bukankah di balik itu ~ kelembutan?* Sure, his clothes are shabby and dirty but isn't there a gentleness beneath all that? **-an** 1 plants. *~ merambat* vine. 2 crop. **-²an** all k.o. plants. **pen-** planter. **pe-an** planting area. **pen-an** 1 planting. 2 (*Fin.*) investment.
tanang men- carry s.t. with the hands underneath it.
tanbiat (*Rel.*) prophecy.
tanbih (*Lit.*) note the following (of s.t. to be clarified in the following paragraph).
tancap 1 embed s.t. sharp. 2 (*Coll.*) step on the gas, floor it. **men-** 1 embed s.t., implant s.t. 2 implanted, stick (of s.t. sharp). *Pisau ~ beberapa miliméter di luar lingkaran* The knife stuck a few millimeters outside the target. *Punggungku terasa luka oléh pandangan-pandangan yg ~ dr belakang* It felt like my back was being wounded by the many glances from behind. **men-kan** 1 implant s.t., embed s.t. *Aku mampu ~ pisau pd léhérnya* I was able to plunge a knife into his neck. *Ia ~ tombaknya di tanah* He stuck his spear in the ground. 2 transfix with o.'s eyes. **ter-** embedded, stuck.
tanda 1 sign, token, mark. *- cintaku* a token of my love. *- hormat* 1 sign of respect. 2 salute. *- penerimaan/terima* receipt. *- bakti* testimonial. *- jasa* 1 decoration. 2 reward. *- esrar* (*Rel.*) the sacraments. *- hajat/hidup* memento. *- kutip (pembuka)* (opening) quotes. *- msk* admission stub. *- mata* memento, souvenir. *- pangkat* (*Mil.*) insignia, chevrons. *- pengenal* identification tag. *- sah (diri)* validation, verification. **men-sahkan** validate. *- selar* 1 brand. 2 stigma. *- serah* legal expenses. 2 signal. *- berangkat keréta api* the train's signal of departure. *- bahaya* danger signal. 3 omen. *- bahaya* an omen of danger. 4 typographic symbol. *- akar* (*Math.*) root sign. *- alangan* dash. *- bagi* division sign. *- baca(an)* punctuation mark. *-*

bunyi (Ling.) phonetic sign. - *cerai* hyphen. - *garis* dash. - *hubung* hyphen. - *kali (Math.)* multiplication sign. - *kurang (Math.)* minus sign. - *kurawal (Ling.)* brace. - *kurung* parentheses. - *kurung besar/siku* brackets. - *kutip* quotation mark. - *penghubung/penyambung* hyphen. - *penyeru* exclamation point. - *petik* double quotation marks. - *petik tunggal* single quotation marks. - *pisah* dash. - *sengkang* dash, hyphen. - *seru* exclamation point. - *tambah (Math.)* plus sign. - *tanya* question mark. - *ujar* quotation mark. - *ulang (Ling.)* superscript "2" to indicate repetition. **ber-** 1 marked, labeled. *Koperku ~ gambar garuda* My bag had the picture of a *garuda* as a lable. 2 signify. **men-i** 1 sign s.t., make a mark on s.t. *Ia ~ kopernya dgn potlot* He marked his bags with a pencil. *Kehadirannya di-i dgn perkelahian* His presence was marked by a fight. 2 remark, perceive. *Ia ~ suara Ripin dlm sorak-sorai yg riuh* She noted Ripin's voice in the loud cheering. **men-kan** signify, indicate. *Huru-hara itu ~ kemerosotan ékonomi akhir-akhir ini* That riot indicates the recent economic decline. *Ia hrs ~ bhw ia kepala jawatan* He must show that he is the department head. *~ irama* beat, keep time. **ter-** marked, signed. **keter-an** *(Ling.)* markedness. **pen-** 1 s.t. used as a sign. 2 *(Ling.)* marker. *~ satuan sintaksis* phrase marker. *~ suara* voice or tonal quality. **pe(r)-** 1 indication, sign, augury. *Bendéra mérah ~ bahaya* A red flag signifies danger. *Fajar menyingsing, ~ hari tlh pagi* It is dawn; that means it is already morning. 2 landmark. *Gunung ini menjadi ~ bagi pelaut-pelaut* This mountain is a landmark for seamen. **pen-an** 1 signaling, giving a sign, designating. 2 *(Ling.)* markedness. **per-an** indication. *~ zaman* sign of the times.

tandak *(Jv)* k.o. dance. **ber-** perform such a dance. **pen-** female dancer in this dance.

tandan the stem of the banana (coconut, etc.) plant from which bunches grow. - *ékor* solid part of tail.

tandang ber- visit, make a social call. *Ia ~ ke rumah néneknya* He visited his grandmother. **men-i** visit. *Ia ~ ibunya* She visited her mother. **pe(r)-** *(M)* visitor.

tandas₁ absolutely wiped out, demolished. - *hartanya karena hutang* Debts have wiped him out. *licin/lindang* - finished without a trace. -² completely finished off. *Hidangannya disikat ~* He gobbled up the serving to the last morsel. **men-kan** spend everything, completely finish s.t.

tandas₂ latrine over a stream.

tandas₃ firm. *sikap yg* - a firm attitude. **men-kan** state s.t. firmly, stress s.t. *Pejabat itu ~ sikap pemerintah* The official explicitly stated the gvt. policy. *Ku-kan perlunya bersatu Nasionalisme, Agama, dan Komunisme* I explicitly stated the necessity of uniting nationalism, religion, and communism. **pen-an** emphasizing.

tandatangan signature. **ber-** signed. *surat yg tdk ~ an* unsigned letter. *yg ~ di bawah ini* the undersigned. **men-i** sign s.t. *Titiek mau juga ~ fotonya* It turned out Titiek was willing to autograph her photo. **pen-** the signer, signatory. *~ persetujuan* the signatory to the treaty. **pen-an** the signing.

tandem see SEPÉDA.

tandes see TANDAS₃.

tandil *(Lit.)* foreman, overseer.

tanding₁ match, equal, counterpart. **se-** be equal to, be comparable to. *Ya, tentu kota Palopo tdk ~ kota Parépare* Well, of course the city of Palopo is not on the same level as Parepare. **ber-** 1 be the equal of, match. *Negeri sebesar itu tak ~ kekuatannya dgn negeri kami* A country of that size does not compare in power with ours. 2 compete. *Pasti kalau ~ dgn kesatuan Surabaya, Denpasar kalah* Without a doubt, if they compete with the Surabaya team, Denpasar will lose. *semangat ~* competitive spirit. 3 fight a duel. **men-i** 1 be equal to, be comparable with. *Tak ada yg ~ kepandaiannya* No o. equals his cleverness. 2 stand up to. *Meréka bersekutu utk ~ musuhnya* They united in order to stand up to 3 compete with. **men-kan** compare. *~ kebaikan ibu dan ketegasan ayahnya* compare o.'s mother's kindness with o.'s father's sternness. **memper-kan** 1 compare s.t. with. 2 put into combat. *Akhirnya ia ~ pasukannya* Finally he placed his troops in combat. **ter-i** can be matched. **-an** match, equal. *lelaki ~ a* suitable husband. *Mana ~nya Rudy Hartono?* Where is there anyone who is Rudy Hartono's equal? **per-an** 1 contest, competition. 2 comparison.

tanding₂ pile, heap. *se- kacang* a pile of peanuts. **men-** pile, heap up.

tandon 1 *(Fin.)* security for a loan, collateral. 2 *(Jv)* stock, provision, goods provided. 3 *(Jv)* reservoir.

tandu a litter or sedan chair. **ber-** ride in a sedan chair. **men-** carry in a litter.

tanduk₁ animal horns. - *tegak* horns vertical with points near e.o. - *tilpon* telephone receiver. - *kuda* expect the impossible (lit., horns on a horse). *spt telur di ujung* - precarious. **ber-** horned. **men-** 1 butt. 2 *(Sport)* shoot (at billiards). **-an** *kepala (Sport)* headshot.

tanduk₂ see TINDAK.

tandur *(Jv)* - *alih* transplanting. **men-** plant s.t. *~ padi* plant rice. **men-i** plant on or in. *~ sawah* plant the rice field.

tandus 1 empty and infertile (of land), nonarable. 2 wiped out. **ke-an** barrenness.

tanfidziah, tanfiziah *(Isl.)* executive (of religious organization).

tang₁ 1 pliers. 2 tongs, pincers.

tang₂ *(Mil.)* tank.

tang₃ clanging sound of falling metal.

tangan 1 hand, arm. *Meréka berjabat -* They shook hands. *dr - ke tangan* passed from o. hand to another. - *besi* strict, ruthless. *Ia memerintah dgn - besi* He ruled with an iron fist. - *dingin* successful in planting, healing, etc. - *hampa* empty-handed. - *kanan* right-hand man. - *lébar* open-handed, generous. - *panas* unlucky, a failure. - *pertama*

1 (*Leg.*) first owner. 2 instigator. - *terbuka* generous. *-nya berulas* He has a good assistant. 2 s.t. resembling a hand or arm in shape or function. - *baju* sleeves. - *kemudi* (*Naut.*) helm, rudder. - *korsi* arms of a chair. - *manis* the right hand. - *panjang* long-sleeved (of shirts). - *tangga* stair rail, handrail. -² s.t. resembling an arm or hand, i.e. handlebars of a bicycle, arm of a pair of scales, etc. **ber-** have hands. *Dia pulang ~ kosong* He returned empty-handed. **- men-** pass through many hands. *Arloji ini kelihatan baru; sebenarnya ia tlh ~* This watch looks new; actually it has passed through many hands. **men-i 1** handle, take in hand (job, problem, etc.). *tdk dpt ~ masalah lalulintas* unable to handle the traffic problem. 2 strike with the hand. *Pencopét itu di-i dan diténdang beramai-ramai* Everyone joined in beating and kicking that pickpocket. **ter-i** handled, taken care of. **-an 1** handmade product. 2 s.t. resembling a hand or arm. **pen-an** handling.

tangas vaporization. - *kukus* steambath. **ber-** take a steam bath. **men-** steam s.t. **pen-** steam bath. **pen-an** steaming.

tangéh (*Jv*) far off, away. *Masih - dr waktunya* It is still far ahead of the time.

tangén (*Math.*) tangent line or plane.

tangénsial (*Math.*) tangential.

tangga 1 ladder. *Jatuh tertimpa -* o. misfortune after the other (lit., fall and have the ladder fall on top of o.). - *pengait* flexible portable ladder for climbing trees. - *sigai* portable ladder. 2 staircase, stairs. - *pilin* winding staircase, stairs. - *sokong* a notched climbing pole. 3 s.t. arranged in levels, s.t. scaled. - *pelajaran bahasa Jepang* lessons in Japanese arranged according to difficulty. - *bunyi/nada* (*Music*) scale. - *gaji* pay scale. **se-** neighbor. **ber-** with steps. **ber-² 1** gradually, by degrees, step by step. 2 terraced, graduated. *sawah ~* terraced rice field.

tanggah (*Lit.*) kitchen.

tanggal₁ fall out, come loose. *Giginya -* His teeth fell out. *Celananya - terus* His trousers kept slipping down. *Daun pohon - pd musim rontok* The leaves fall off in the fall. **men-i 1** strip s.o. or s.t. *Ia ~ terdakwa* He stripped the suspect. *~ pabrik* dismantle a factory. 2 strip s.t. off. *Ia ~ pakaiannya* He stripped off his clothes. **men-kan 1** strip off, take off. *Ia ~ pakaiannya* He took off his clothes. 2 pull out. *Ia ~ paku* She pulled out a nail. **pen-an 1** stripping, removal (of a cover, etc.). *~ kewarganegaraan* stripping of o.'s citizenship. 2 (*Lit.*) k.o. ghost whose head separates and flies independently.

tanggal₂ date. - *berapa?* What is the date? - *6 Agustus* (It is) August 6. - *pengembalian buku* return due date. **ber-** dated. *surat yg tdk ~ an* undated letter. **men-kan** date. *Ia tak sempat ~ suratnya* He had no opportunity to date his letter. **ter-** dated. *suratmu ~ 9 Maret 1989* your letter dated March 9, 1989. **-an** calendar. **pen-an 1** calendar, almanac. *~ dinding* wall calendar. 2 dating.

tanggam dovetail (in carpentry). **ber-** dovetailed. **men-** dovetail s.t.

tanggang (*M*) **ber-** refrain from a normal activity. *~ malam* keep watch through the night. *~ suami* refuse conjugal pleasures to o.'s husband. **men-** restrain o.'s appetites. *~ perut* fast.

tanggap₁ perceptive. **men- 1** listen carefully. 2 note attentively. **men-i** receive, perceive. *kelemahannya utk ~ cinta itu dlm bentuknya yg wajar* her inability to receive that love in its natural form. *Hamidah ~ kontras antara dirinya dgn gadis itu* Hamidah perceived the contrast between her and that girl. **-an 1** idea, conception. *~ dunia* conception of the world. 2 reaction. *~ méntal* mental response.

tanggap₂ (*Jv*) 1 summon a *dalang*. 2 perform a *wayang* . **men-** hire a performer. **-an** performance of a *wayang* .

tanggon (*Jv*) reliable.

tangguh₁ 1 strong, hard to defeat. *lawan yg -* a strong opponent. 2 firm, sturdy, of integrity. *pemimpin yg -* a leader of integrity. **ke-an 1** strength, tenacity. 2 integrity, honesty.

tangguh₂ postponement, delay. **ber- 1** postpone, put off. *Ia tdk ~ lagi minta perlop* He did not put off asking for leave. 2 hesitant, reluctant. *~ memanggil pacarnya* hesitant about calling o.'s sweetheart. **men-kan, memper-kan** postpone, delay s.t., put off. *Ia ~ pembayarannya* He postponed his payment. **ter-²** hesitatingly. **pen-an, per-an** postponement, deferment.

tangguk small fish scoop or scoop-net. **men-** fish with such a net or scoop. **pen- 1** fisherman who uses such a device. 2 o. who takes unfair advantage. *~ keuntungan berkeliaran mencari kurban* The crooks swarmed about in search of victims.

tanggul dike, embankment. **men-** build a dike, embankment.

tanggulang (*Jv*) sluice-gate. **men-i** ward off, cope with. *Walikota tdk dpt ~ gerakan-gerakan pengrusak itu* The mayor was not able to cope with those vandalistic activities. **pen-** o. who tackles a problem, etc. **pen-an** tackling. *~ kejahatan* crime prevention. *~ kemerosotan ékonomi* dealing with economic decline.

tanggung₁ 1 guaranteed. *Perkerjaannya - baik* His work is guaranteed to be good. 2 bear s.t. - *derita* **men-deritakan** suffer, endure, put up with. 3 responsible. *Ia tdk - akan selesainya pekerjaan itu* He will not be responsible for the completion of the job. - *bérés* take care of s.t. *Dia - bérés* He will take care of it. - *jawab* 1 responsible for. *Kpd siapa ia - jawab?* To whom is he responsible? 2 responsibility. **ber-***jawab* be responsible, be liable. *Menteri negara ~ jawab pd parlemén* A state minister is responsible to parliament. *tak ~ jawab* irresponsible. **men-***jawab* accept responsibility. **memper-jawabkan** account for, justify. *Ia tak dpt memperjawabkan segala pengeluarannya* He could not account for all his expenditures. **per-jawaban 1** responsibility. 2 justification, accounting. - **men-**

be mutually responsible. **men- 1** carry on o.'s shoulders. ~ *muatan yg berat* carry a heavy burden. **2** bear s.t. (emotion, duty, etc.). ~ *rugi* bear the loss. ~ *sakit* endure an illness. ~ *sabar* bear up with patience. ~ *malu* endure the shame. ~ *ragam* endure tribulations. ~ *rindu* bear the yearnings. **3** guarantee, assume liability for. *Siapa yg ~ pengeluaran ini?* Who guarantees these expenses? *Ia ~ ongkos kirim* He is responsible for shipping costs. ~ *risiko* take the risk. *Pemerintah ~ keamanan negeri* The gvt. assumes responsibility for the country's security. *Kebersihannya di Its cleanliness* is guaranteed. ~ *rahasia* keep a secret. **men-kan 1** bear. *Itulah beban yg harus ku han seorg diri* That is the burden I alone must bear. **2** be responsible for s.t. *Prétensi itu tak berani saya -kan* Such a claim I do not dare take upon myself. **memper-kan** make s.o. responsible for s.t. *Rupanya rumah Naim yg terbakar itu diper-kan kpd kantor assuransi* Apparently an insurance company will be responsible for covering Naim's house that burned down. **ter-** endured, borne. *Keremukan hatiku tak ~* My depression was unbearable. **ter-kan** endured, bearable. *Akibat terakhir tak ~* The final result was unbearable. **-an 1** burden, load. *Menyekolahkan anak ~ berat bagi org tua* To send a child to school is a heavy burden for the parents. **2** s.t. or s.o. o. is responsible for. *~nya banyak* He has many dependents (or responsibilities). *atas ~ sendiri* at o.'s own risk. **3** guarantee, bail, security. *Ia memberi cincinnya sbg ~* He gave his ring as security. *memberi ~ enam bulan* give a six-months' guarantee. **4** insurance. ~ *jiwa* life insurance. **pen- 1** guarantor, backer. ~ *jawab* responsible (legally liable) person or agency. ~ *kebakaran* marine underwriter. ~ *varia* accident underwriter. **2** sufferer. **3** o. who is insured. **pen-an 1** trials and tribulations. **2** assumption of responsibility. **per-an 1** responsibility. ~ *jawab* responsibility. **2** guarantee, security. ~ *bunga tahunan* annuity. **3** insurance. ~ *jiwa* life insurance. ~ *jiwa kelompok* group life insurance.

tanggung₂ 1 large but not large enough. *Kamar ini - besarnya* This room is inadequate in size. *hujan* - a rain heavy enough to get things wet but not give a thorough soaking. *pemuda* - young man near full adulthood. **2** ill-timed, soon but not soon enough. *- sekali kedatanganmu ini* Your arrival was ill-timed (You came a bit too late). *- bulan* be broke around the end of the month. **-²** halfway, halfhearted. *Kalau bekerja jangan ~* If you are going to do s.t., do it right.

tangis 1 weeping. *Tapi ia sendiri tahu bhw - itu dibuat-buat* But she knew herself that her weeping was fake. *Begitu keras - dan jerit ibu Sybil* The weeping and screaming of Sybil's mother was so extreme. **2** wail. *"Tapi kau sdh mati, Adil," - nénék* "But you are dead now, Adil," grandmother wailed. **ber-(²)an 1** weep for e.o. **2** cry on and on. **men-** weep. *Ia menjerit dan ~ ketakutan* He

screamed and wept from fear. **men-i** weep over, bemoan. *Ia ~ anaknya yg meninggal* He wept over his dead child. **men-kan 1** weep over, bemoan. *Apa lagi yg kau-kan?* What in the world are you crying about? **2** make o. weep. *Ia ~ adiknya* He made his little brother cry. **-an** weeping, crying. **pen-** a crybaby.

tangkai 1 stalk, stem. - *bunga* flower stalk. - *hati* sweetheart, beloved. - *kering* a miser. **2** stock, shaft, handle. - *bedil* rifle butt. - *péna* penholder. **3** numeral classifier used with slender objects. *tiga - dayung* three paddles.

tangkal talisman, amulet. **men-** avoid, ward off a (catastrophe). *utk ~ gangguan hantu* to ward off disturbances from spirits. **pen- 1** amulet, charm **2** preventive. ~ *petir* lightning rod. ~ *mata hari* sun visor. **pen-an** preventive measure, esp. refusal of entry to a country to a potentially dangerous foreigner.

tangkap men- 1 catch. ~ *bola* catch a ball. *Roda gigi itu saling ~ dgn baik* The gears meshed well. ~ *angin* undertake s.t. impossible to achieve (lit., sieze the wind). **2** seize, arrest. *Polisi ~ penjahat* The police caught the criminal. ~ *basah* catch red-handed. **3** comprehend, grasp. *Ia ~ maksud pembicaraan itu* He understood the meaning of the conversation. **men-i 1** arrest repeatedly. **2** seize or arrest a large number of people. *Banyak perahu di-i Jepang* Many boats were caught by the Japanese. **men-kan** capture on behalf of. **ter-** get caught. *Ayah ~ dan dibawa ke tangsi besar* Father got caught and was brought to the main barracks. ~ *basah* caught in the act. *Pengédar morfin itu ~ basah* The drug dealer got caught red-handed. ~ *muka* meet face to face unexpectedly. **-an 1** capture, arrest. *Hati-hati! Banyak ~ sepéda tak berlampu sekarang!* Be careful! They have been confiscating lots of bicycles lately because they lacked headlights! **2** haul, catch. **3** prisoner. *~nya tetap ada di tangan tentara* The prisoners were still in the hands of the army. **ke-** (*Coll.*) seized, arrested. *Pembikin uang palsu ~* The counterfeiter was seized. **pen-** captor, capturer, s.t. that catches. ~ *ikan* 1 fisherman. **2** fish net, trap. ~ *suara* recorder. **pen-an 1** catching. **2** arrest, seizure. **3** haul, catch (fish). *alat-alat ~ ikan* tools for catching fish.

tangkar see TENGKAR.

tangkas deft, adroit, agile. **ke-an** adroitness, skill, dexterity. ~ *lidah* quick wittedness, quickness at repartee. ~ *jasmani* physical agility.

tangki tank for liquids.

tangkis men- 1 ward off, parry. ~ *pukulan* ward off the blows. **2** repulse, repel. ~ *serangan* repulse an attack. ~ *tuduhan* reply (by denying) an accusation. **men-i** parry or repulse several things. **ter-** repulsed, parried. **-an** defense, resistance. **pen-** s.t. which wards off. ~ *serangan udara* antiaircraft defense. ~ *petir* lightning rod. **pen-an 1** repelling. ~ *serangan musuh* repulsing an enemy attack. **2** fending off (blows, etc.).

tangkring (me)n- 1 (*Coll.*) sit, sit high where easily visible. *Bola golfnya ~ di rumput, énak utk dipukul* The golf ball sat high in the grass making it easy to hit. *Ia ~ di pagar* He sat (high) on the fence.

tangkué (*Ch*) chunks of sweetened squash used in baking.

tangkul k.o. large net. men- fish with a net.

tangkup (*Lit.*) hollow space. - *telentang* 1 back and forth. 2 thorough. men-telentangkan consider thoroughly. *Meréka ~ soal itu* They considered the problem thoroughly. se- 1 a cupped handful. 2 symmetrical. ber-, men- 1 close (of two sides uniting). *~ lalat* catch a fly by cupping both hands together. 2 fall face downward. *Ia ~ ke tanah* He fell face down to the ground. men-kan lay s.t. face down. *Ia ~ diri ke balé-balé* She threw herself face down on the bench. ter- 1 closed. 2 laid face down.

tangkur (*Jv*) seahorse.

tanglung (*Ch*) paper lantern.

tangpu (*Jv*) pawnshop.

tangsel (*Jv*) a wedge. men- (*Coll.*) 1 wedge s.t. 2 insert s.t. di- (*Jkt*) stuffed to the gills. pen- s.t. used to fill s.t. up. *~ perut* (*Coll.*) s.t. to fill the stomach.

tangsi (*Coll., Mil.*) barracks. meng-kan confine to quarters. *Tentaranya di-kan* The troops were confined to quarters.

tangsin (*Ch*) spiritualism, medium.

tani farmer. *pak* - farmer. ber- engage in farming. *~ sayuran* grow vegetables. pe- farmer. per-an agriculture. *~ rakyat* small-scale farming. *tanah ~* farmland.

tanjak slanting upward. ber- rise in a sloping manner. *~ kaki* rise up on o.'s tiptoes. (me)n- 1 slope upward. *Jalannya ~* The road goes steadily upward. *Layarnya dipasang ~* He set the sail pointing upward. *berjalan ~* walk on o.'s tiptoes. 2 ascend, climb. *~ gunung* climb a mountain. *~ déwasa* enter adulthood, undergo puberty. men-kan 1 cause s.t. to slope upward. *Ia ~ layar* He hoisted the sail. *Ia ~ kakinya* He stood on his toes. 2 bring s.t. upward. *~ bahan ke atas gunung* bring supplies up the mountain. -an 1 steep grade. 2 ascent, climb. pen-an ascending, climbing.

tanji see TUKANG.

tanjidor, tanjidur k.o. brass music popular in Jkt.

tanjul k.o. noose attached to a pole to snare animals, esp. snakes. men- snare s.t. with such a noose.

tanjung₁ (*Geog.*) cape, promontory. - *Harapan* Cape of Good Hope. - *Hijau* Cape Verde. - *Pérak* the port of Surabaya. - *Priok* the port of Jkt. men- 1 look like a cape. *Apa nama daérah yg ~ ke laut itu?* What is the name of the area that extends into the sea like a cape? 2 sail along the cape. *berlayar ~* sail along the cape.

tanjung₂ see BUNGA.

tanjur (*M*) ladle made of coconut shell.

tank /téng/ (*Mil.*) army tank.

tanker /téngker/ tanker (ship).

tanki see TANGKI.

tanpa without. - *prasangka* without prejudice. ke-prasangkaan nondiscriminatory. - (*ber*)*syarat* unconditionally. - *bobot* weightlessness. - *perkelahian* without fighting.

tanpanama anonymous.

tanpanegara stateless.

tanpasta toothpaste.

tanta see TANTE.

tantama see TAMTAMA.

tantang men- challenge. *Ia ~ anak-anak asrama lain utk bertinju* He challenged the other children in the dormitory to a fist fight. *pernyataan yg ~ a* defiant statement. -an challenge, defiance. pen-challenger. pen-an act of challenging.

tante 1 Ma'am, form of reference and address for European, Ch, or Westernized women 30 or older. - *girang* middle aged, Westernized woman partial to gigolos. 2 aunt. -² of an age to be an aunt. ke-²an acting like an aunt.

tanting men- carry in the palms of the hands.

tantra (*Rel.*) the tantric sect of Buddhism.

tanur oven, furnace. - *tinggi* blast furnace.

tanya 1 question. *Numpang -, bung!* May I ask a question, friend? *dgn wajah yg penuh -* with a look of questioning on the face. - *jawab* 1 interview, question and answer. 2 discussion. 2 inquire. *Ia - ttg suamiku* She asked about my husband. ber- ask a question. *Boléh saya ~?* May I ask a question? *Ia ~: "Kenapa kau masih menatapku sedemikian?"* He asked: "Why do you keep looking at me that way?" ber-² 1 repeatedly ask. 2 wonder, be quizzical. *Ia ~ dlm hatinya mengapa ayahnya tak datang* He wondered to himself why his father did not come. men- 1 (*Coll.*) ask. *Ia ~ temannya* He asked his friend. 2 ask for a woman's hand in marriage. men-i repeatedly question, interrogate. *Ia ~ temannya ttg keadaan itu* He asked his friend in detail about the situation. *Aku di-i lama oléh polisi setempat* The local police interrogated me for a long time. men-kan ask about s.t. *Ia ~ soal keuangan kpd gurunya* He asked his teacher about financial matters. *Aku takkan ~ hal itu lagi pdmu* I will not ask you about that issue again. memper-kan call s.t. into question. *Saya ~ pendapatnya* I question her opinion. ter-² 1 repeatedly ask. *Karena tadi tdk diberitahu, pasti beliau ~ saja* Because no o. gave any explanations, of course he kept asking questions. 2 wonder, be curious. pen- interrogator, questioner. *~ jawab* interviewer. pen-an (*Lit.*) interrogation. per-an question, query. *~ keliling* questions from the floor.

tanzil (*Isl.*) o. who has received a revelation.

taoci, taoco see TAUCI.

taogé see TAUGÉ.

taokéh see TAUKÉ.

taola see TUALA.

taosi see TAUCI.

tap (*Coll.*) k.o. distilled alcoholic beverage.

tapa asceticism, esp. in order to acquire magical powers. - *brata* highest form of asceticism. - *sungsang* a form of mortification characterized by hanging upside down. **ber-** 1 live as an ascetic. 2 isolate o.s. (to meditate, to acquire magical power, etc.). 3 (*Coll.*) imprisoned. *Terpaksa ia ~ lima tahun di LP* He was imprisoned for five years. **memper-kan** achieve through asceticism. *Ia ~ maksudnya* Through asceticism he achieved his aim. **per-** hermit, ascetic. **per-an** 1 hermit's abode, retreat. 2 asceticism. 3 penance.

tapai 1 k.o. sweet cake made of slightly fermented rice or tubers. - *keladi* such a cake made of taro. 2 k.o. alcoholic beverage made by fermenting rice or tubers. *air* - this alcoholic beverage. **men-** 1 become fermented. *Ketéla itu ~* The cassava became fermented. 2 ferment s.t. *Ia ~ ketéla* He let some cassava ferment. **pen-an** fermentation. **per-an** matters pertaining to fermentation.

tapak 1 palm of hand, sole of foot. *lari putih -nya* run very fast (lit., run with the white of the soles). - *besi* horseshoe. - *lépér rata* flatfooted. - *sepatu* sole of shoe. - *tangan* palm of hand. 2 a rough lineal measure. *Lébarnya dua* - It was two hands wide. 3 tracks, footprints. - *kaki* footprints. 4 site. - *bangunan* building site. - *catur* the squares of a chessboard. - *rumah* house sites. **se-** 1 a footstep. *~ demi ~* step by step. 2 o. palm's or sole's breadth. *jalan ~* narrow trail (where o. must walk single file). **ber-** 1 step, tread on. *Kakinya ~ ke permadani* His feet tread on the carpet. 2 have an underlayer. 3 have a foot hold. *Terayun-ayun di léréng yg curam itu ia berusaha ~ di tonjolan batu* As she swung from the steep cliff face she tried to get a foothold on a protruding rock. *Kekuasaannya ~ di mana-mana* His power has a firm hold everywhere. **ber-(kan)** be based on, supported. *Pemerintah mesti ~ kehendak rakyat* A gvt. must be based on the will of the people. **men-** 1 measure with the palm of the hand or sole of the foot. *~ lébarnya méja* measure the width of the table with the palm of the hand. 2 step, tread on. 3 follow in the footsteps of, do same thing s.o. else did. *Ia ~ ayahnya* He is following in his father's footsteps. **men-i** follow in the footsteps of. **men-kan** set (foot) down. *~ kakinya ke tanah* set o.'s feet on the ground. **-an** layer, foundation.

tapak-tapak (*Sumatra*) k.o. wooden patten or clog.

tapal paste, poultice, plaster. - *gigi* toothpaste. **men-** apply a poultice or plaster. *Giginya di- utk cétakan membuat gigi baru* They put gypsum on his teeth to make a cast for his false teeth.

tapal batas frontier, border.

tapal kuda horseshoe. **men-** make horseshoes.

tapé see TAPAI.

tapékong see TEPÉKONG.

tapelak see TAPLAK.

tapi see TETAPI.

tapian (*M*) see TEPI.

tapih (*Jv*) k.o. woman's ankle-length batik wraparound.

tapioka tapioca.

tapir tapir, esp. Asian species.

tapis men- 1 filter s.t. *Ia ~ air itu* She filtered the water. 2 sort through s.t. 3 censor s.t. *~ berita sensitif* censor sensitive news. **-an** 1 filtered material, filtrate. 2 a filter, sieve. **pen-** a filter, sieve. **pen-an** filtering.

taplak tablecloth. **ber-** covered with a tablecloth. *méja yg ~* a table with a tablecloth. **men-i** cover s.t. with a tablecloth.

tapol [*tahanan politik*] political prisoners.

tapsir see TAFSIR.

tap-tap 1 sound of water trickling on water. 2 sound of s.t. small closing (a cigarette case, etc.).

taptu (*Mil.*) taps, retreat.

tapuk₁ (*Jv*) **men-** slap.

tapuk₂ scar, pockmark. **ber-²** 1 heavily pockmarked. 2 have a bad reputation. *Namanya sdh ~* He has a bad reputation.

tapuk₃ see TAMPUK.

tar₁ snapping sound of whip, firecracker, or pistol shot. *-! -! Kudanya lari di atas aspal* With a crack of the whip, the horse ran on the pavement.

tar₂ see TÉR₁.

tar₃ see TART.

tara₁ 1 matching, equal. *tiada - bagusnya* unequaled in beauty. *laki-bini yg -* a husband and wife on a par. 2 counterpart. **se-** 1 be equal, equivalent. *Usahanya tdk ~ dgn hasilnya* His results do not equal his efforts. 2 made for e.o., suited. *dua teman yg ~* two friends made for e.o. **ber-** matching. *tiada ~* unequaled, unmatched. **ter-** equal, matched. *tiada ~* unrivaled, unequaled.

tara₂ 1 the weight of the wrapping, etc., containing goods. 2 tare, a deduction from the total weight to allow for this weight.

taraf 1 standard. - *hidup* standard of living. 2 degree, level. - *peradaban* level of civilization. *menurut - dan umur* according to status and age. - *perang penghabisan* final phase of the war. - *dua* two stages, two levels. **ber- dua** two-stage. - *warna* shade of color. **se-** equal, equivalent, on a par. *Pangkatnya ~ dgn gubernur* His rank is equal to that of a governor. **menye-kan** 1 make equal, make equivalent. 2 consider on a par with. *Ia ~ negerinya dgn negeri-negeri yg tlh maju* He considers his country on a par with advanced countries. 3 balance. *Ia ~ keperluan dgn keuangannya* He balances his needs against his finances. **men-kan** 1 evaluate, grade s.t. 2 give the rank of. **pen-an** ranking, grading in ranks.

tarah planed smooth. **ber-** planed. **men-** plane s.t. smooth. **-an** s.t. that has been planed smooth. **pen-** a plane.

tarak 1 abstinence. 2 abstain from, avoid (eating, etc.). *Nénék - garam karena bludréknya tinggi*

Grandmother abstains from salt because of severe hypertension. **ber-** abstain. **per-an** abstinence.

taram (*Lit.*) dim. *cahaya* - dim light. - *temaram* dark.

tarap see TARAF.

taraté see TERATAI.

tarawéh, tarawih (*Isl.*) nonobligatory evening prayers during fasting month.

tarbiah (*Isl.*) education.

tarbus Turkish-style fez.

tarékat 1 (*Isl.*) path for mystics to follow, esp. Sufism. **2** (*Lit.*) an order of mystics.

targét target. **ment-kan** aim for s.t., target s.t. *Kita ~ pembangunan pedésaan* We are aiming at village development. **-²an** (*Coll.*) do s.t. only to fulfill a quota.

tari a dance. - *gambus* k.o. dance to Arabian music. - *gebyar* k.o. Balinese dance. - *kejang* break dance. - *lénso* handkerchief dance, a folk dance of E. Indonesia popular nationally. **ber-, men-** dance, esp. non-Western dances. **men-²** jump (with joy), dance up and down. *Jari-jemarinya ~ di atas papan tuts* Her fingers danced over the keyboard. **men-kan** dance s.t., dance a certain k.o. dance. **-an** a dance. **-²an** dances, a variety of dances. *~ daérah* regional or folk dances. **pen-** dancer. **pen-an** dancing.

tarif see TARIP.

ta'rif see TAKRIF.

tarih see TARIKH.

tarik₁ pull. - *muka* grin. - *muka dua belas* be disappointed. - *tambang* tug-of-war. **ber-²an** mutually tug. *~ tali* play tug-of-war. **men-** 1 draw, pull. *Ia ~ keréta* He pulled a wagon. *~ diri* withdraw. *~ kembali* 1 withdraw s.t. 2 reverse a decision. *~ ke pengadilan* (*Leg.*) bring s.o. to court. *~ kesimpulan* draw a conclusion. *~ mundur* withdraw. *~ napas* breathe, inhale. *~ napas yg terakhir* breathe o.'s last. *~ napas panjang* heave a sigh. *~ nyawa* die. *~ otot* stubborn, obstinate. *~ panjang* stretch, prolong. *~ senyum kecil* smile a bit. *~ surut* withdraw s.t. *~ urat léhér* stubborn, obstinate. **2** draw out, extract. *~ pedang* pull out o.'s sword. *~ akar* (*Math.*) extract the root. *~ garis* (*Math.*) draw a line. *~ lagu/nyanyi/suara* sing (in public). *O, dia bisa juga ~ suara, ya?* Oh! he is able to sing (in public)? *~ layar* unfurl a sail. *~ loteré* win a prize at the lottery. *~ undian* win a prize. **3** drive. *~ mobil* drive a car. **4** collect. *~ bayaran* collect payment. *Bank itu ~ bunga sebesar lima belas persén* That bank draws an interest at the rate of 15 percent. *~ ongkos* charge a fee. *~ untung* earn a profit. *~ cék kosong* write a bad check. **5** attractive, interesting. *Uang tdk ~ bagiku* Money does not appeal to me. *Orgnya ndak ~ sih!* The guy's just not interesting! *~ hati* interesting, appealing. *~ minat* attract o.'s attention. *~ perhatian* draw attention. **n-** (*Coll.*) make o.'s living as a driver. **men-²** 1 repeatedly drag, pull. *Anak kecil itu ~ tas bukunya* The child dragged along his book bag. **2** implicate s.o. *Ia ~ teman-nya ke dlm soal itu* He involved his friend in that matter. **men-i** pull repeatedly on. **men-kan** draw or pull for s.o. **memper-kan 1** drag s.t. away. **2** stretch s.t. **ter-** 1 extracted. *Giginya ~ juga* His tooth was finally extracted. **2** attracted, interested. *Ia ~ pd gambar itu* She was attracted by the picture. **ter-²** be dragged along in an erratic way. **ke-** (*Coll.*) drawn, attracted. *Meréka mulai ~ pd sastera* They're beginning to be attracted to literature. **-an 1** pulling, drawing. *~ kuda* pulling by a horse. *~ cerobong* draft (of a chimney). **2** attraction. **-²an 1** tug-of-war. **2** pull on e.o. **pen- 1** s.o. or s.t. that pulls, extracts, drags, etc. *~ beca* pedicab driver. **2** s.t. interesting. **pen-an 1** drawing, pulling. *~ picu* pulling of a trigger. **2** collection, drawing in. *~ pajak* taxation. *~ diri* withdrawal from an activity.

tarik₂ see TARIKH.

tarikah, tarikat see TARÉKAT.

tarikh 1 era. - *hijrah/hijriah* (*Isl.*) A.H., the era beginning with Muh.'s flight to Medina. - *Maséhi* (*Rel.*) A.D., the era beginning with Jesus. **2** in the year. - *1526* in the year 1526. **3** (*Lit.*) date. **4** (*Lit.*) chronicle, annals. - *perang Acéh* chronicles of the Achehnese war. **men(t)-kan 1** date s.t. **2** record as a historical event.

taring 1 tusk, fang. - *babi* boar's tusk. **2** canine tooth.

tarip fare, rate. - *angkutan* rate for transporting. - *béa pos* postal rates. - *bis* bus fare. - *harga* price list. - *makan(an)* menu. - *sepur* 1 railroad timetable. **2** railroad fare.

tarjamah, tarjemah see TERJEMAH.

taro₁ small tarts, cakes.

taro₂ see TARUH.

tarok₁ see TARO₁.

tarok₂ see TARUH.

tarompét see TROMPÉT.

tarpentin see TÉRPENTÉN.

tart European-style cake. - *kelapa* coconut cake, us. frosted.

tar-tar sound of repeated pistol fire.

tar-tor sound of repeated gunfire.

tarub see TARUP.

taruh (*Coll.*) place s.t., put s.t. - *beras dlm padi* keep a secret. **-lah** supposing that **-lah dia tdk mau ikut** supposing he does not want to go along - *mata* watch, see. - *muka* meet people. **ber- 1** bet, wager. *Saya berani ~ ia tak akan datang* I bet he will not come. **2** bet s.t. *~ lima ratus rupiah* bet 500 rupiah. *~ jiwa* pledge o.'s life. **ber-kan** bet s.t. **men- 1** put, place. *Ia ~ buku di méja* He put the book on the table. *~ harapan atas sesuatu* place o.'s hope in s.t. *Ia ~ uang di bank* He deposited the money in the bank. *Ia ~ belas kasihan kpd anaknya* She took pity on her child. *~ cinta* love. *~ hati* be interested. *Ia ~ hati kpd sejarah* She is interested in history. *~ hormat* give respect. *~ kasih* love, pity. *~ kepercayaan* place o.'s trust. *~ perhatian akan* be interested in. *~ syakwasangka* suspect s.o. **2** maintain. *Ia ~ mobil* He has a car. *Ia ~ rahasia* She kept a secret. *~ ayam* raise chickens. **men-i 1** put s.t. on s.t. *Méja itu di-i dgn buku* The table was covered with books. **2** bet on s.t. *Ia ~ ayam putih* He bet on the white cock. **men-kan 1** place, put. *~ uang ke dlm tabungan* put money in a money box. *Besar sekali harapan yg di-kan kpd sdr* The expectations we have of you are very great. **2** bet. **memper-kan 1** pawn. *Ia ~ arlojinya* He pawned his watch. **2** entrust. *Ia ~ barang-barangnya kpd org lain* He entrusted his goods to other people. **3** risk. *Ia ~ jiwanya* He risked his life. *Ia ~ perkawinannya* She is putting her marriage on the line. *Kehormatan kitalah yg diper-kan* It is our honor that is at stake. **-an 1** bet, wager. *Saya berani ~* I am willing to bet. **2** stake. *~nya cuman lima rupiah* The stake was just five rupiah. **3** s.t. saved. *uang -* savings. **4** security, deposit. **pe- 1** final instructions, last will and testament. **2** security. **pen-** s.o. who places s.t. *~ perhatian* o. who is interested. **pen-an** money box, strongbox. **per-an 1** s.t. placed s.w. *~ senjata* (*Mil.*) cease-fire. **2** bet. **3** savings. **4** articles entrusted to s.o.

taruk₁ sprout, bud. **ber-** sprout.

taruk₂ see TARUH.

tarum indigo plant.

taruna see TERUNA.

tarung₁ sound of metallic clashing (swords, etc.). **ber- 1** dispute, fight. *~ di pengadilan* dispute before the court. **2** fight. *Ia ~ dgn lawannya* He fought with his opponent. **men-kan, memper-kan 1** cause persons or animals to fight. *Ia ~ ayamnya* He entered his rooster in a cockfight. **2** risk. *Ia ~ jiwanya* He risked his life. **pen-** obstacle. **per-an** fight, struggle.

tarung₂ stumble. **ter-** stumbled on s.t. *Kakinya ~ batu* His foot bumped against a stone.

taruni (*Mil.*) female cadet.

tarup (*Jv*) temporary structure (for weddings, etc.). *- agung* grandstand.

tarwih see TARAWÉH.

tas₁ bag, handbag, briefcase. *- kresek* k.o. plastic bag.

tas₂ sound of whizzing (bullets or stones hitting a wall, a small explosion, etc.). *-! Peluru kena dinding séng* Zing! A bullet ricocheted from the tin siding. *--tus* sound of repeated whizzing or a small explosion.

tas₃ see KAYU₁.

tasak styptic. **men-** stanch bleeding. **pen-** styptic pencil.

tasalsul genealogy.

tasauf, tasawuf (*Isl.*) mysticism, esp. of Sufist school. *ahli -* mystic. **ke-an** (things) having to do with mysticism.

tasbéh, tasbih 1 (*Isl.*) a formula extolling God's perfection (*subhanahu wa taala*). **2** (*Isl.*) a string of 100 beads to recite this laudation. **3** (*Rel.*) rosary. **ber-** tell o.'s beads. **men-kan** extol God. **pen-an** praising God.

tasdid see TASYDID.

tasdik affirmation, verification. **men-kan** verify.

tasik lake.

tasiun (*Coll.*) see SETASION.

tasmak see TESMAK.

tasrif (*Ling.*) **1** conjugation of Arabic verbs. **2** inflection. **ment-kan** conjugate.

tasydid (*Isl.*) diacritical mark used to indicate gemination in Arabic script.

tasyhid (*Isl.*) pronouncement of the *syahadat.*

tata order, arrangement, system. *- acara* agenda. *- adab* good manners, politeness. *- bahasa* grammar. *- bentuk* (*Biol., Ling.*) morphology. *- boga* food science. *- buku* bookkeeping, accounting. *- bumi* land use or utilization. *- bunyi* phonetics. *- busana* dressmaking. *- cara* customs and manners. *- geréja* church ritual. *- graha* homemaking. *- guna* the method of making use of s.t. **pen-gunaan** use. *- hukum* legal structure. *- istilah* terminology. *- kaca* stained glass. *- kalimat* (*Ling.*) syntax. *- karya* organization. *- kata* (*Ling.*) morphology. *- krama* etiquette. *- laksana* managing. **ke-laksanaan** management. *- masyarakat* social structure. *- nama* nomenclature. *- negara* **1** form of gvt. **2** state structure. **3** public institutions. **ke-negaraan** matters pertaining to form of gvt. or constitution. *- niaga* business administration. *- perdésaan* structure of rural regions. *pembangunan - perdésaan yg démokratis* democratic rural development. *- personalia* personnel management. *- pimpinan* management. *- praja* public administration. *- puspa* flower arrangement. *- rias* art of cosmetics. *- ruang* (*Art, Printing*) layout. *- rupa* makeup, format. *- surya* (*Astr.*) solar system. *- susila* **1** good manners, good conduct. **2** ethics. *- susunan* organization, structure, hierarchy. *- syarat* requirements. *- tentrem karta raharja* orderly, peaceful with complete wellbeing. *- tenteram/tertib* discipline, order, regulations (for conduct). *- tingkat* hierarchy. *- usaha* administration, management. *- warna* technicolor. **men-** put in order, organize. *Pemerintah sedang ~ kembali kurikulum SMA* The gvt. is currently reorganizing the curriculum of senior high schools. **-an** arrangement, planning. **pen-** s.t. or s.o. that puts s.t. in order. *~ buku* bookkeeper. *~ praja* administrator. *~ rambut* hairdresser. *~ tertib* moderator (of discussion), leader (of meeting). **pen-an** ordering, structuring. *~ kembali orde ékonomi internasional* the restructuring of the international economic order.

tatabahasa see TATA.

tatah₁ inlaid work. **ber-(kan)** inlaid, studded. *takhta ~ ratna* a crown set with jewels. **men-** inlay s.t. **-an** inlaid work. **pen-an** carving, inlaying s.t.

tatah₂ see TATIH.

tatakan /tataan/ (*Jv*) **1** base of a tray, etc. **2** s.t. underneath, underlayer. *- gelas* coaster for glasses.

tatal wood shavings.

tatanama see TATA.

tatanan (*Jv*) arrangement, order. *- sosial masyarakat* the social order of society.

tatang men- carry in outstretched palm of hands. *Ia ~ sebuah baki* He carried a tray.

tatap - *muka* face to face. *pertemuan* - *muka* a face-to-face encounter. **bersi-** look at e.o. *Mata meréka* ~ *sesaat* Their eyes met for o. second. **beran** be face to face. *Dihindarinya benar matanya* ~ *dgn Ny. Budiono* He made it a point to avoid looking into Mrs. Budiono's eyes. ~ *pandang* exchanging glances. **men-** observe intently. *Ia* ~ *gambar di témbok* He examined the picture on the wall. *Matanya* ~ *saya* He observed me intently. **men-i** examine s.t. closely. ~ *buku* examine the books closely. **men-kan** let o.'s eyes, gaze, etc. rest on s.t. *Ia* ~ *pandangannya thd témbok* She focused her gaze on the wall. **ter-** stared at, eyed. *Saya* ~ *oléh seorg gila* I was stared at by a madman. **-an** close observation, gaze, stare. ~ *matanya sendu* His gaze was sad. ~ *radar* radar observation. **pen-an** gazing, staring.

tatar men- upgrade s.t. *Séminar ini direncanakan utk* ~ *tata buku di kantor wilayah* The seminar was planned to upgrade bookkeeping in regional offices. **-an** rank, level. **pe-** trainee. **pen-** trainer, upgrader. **pen-an 1** upgrading. **2** refresher course.

tatawarna see TATA.

tatih unsteady steps (of toddler, etc.). **ber-** toddle along. **men- 1** teach s.o. to walk by holding his hands. **2** give support with the hand to s.o. walking. *Jalanan tambah naik dan org yg ku- jatuh* The road became steeper and steeper and the person whom I was helping to walk fell. **ter-²** wobbly.

tating see TATANG.

tatkala (*Lit.*) when, at the time. - *sampai di kamar, ia cuma menjumpai kekosongan* When he reached the room he only found emptiness. *Dulu - ia masih suka membikin syair, . . .* Before when she was still fond of composing poetry, . . . - *itu* at that time.

taton see KETATON.

tatu (*Jv*) wound(ed). **men-i** injure. **ter-** wounded.

tau (*Coll.*) see TAHU₁,₂.

taubat see TOBAT.

taucang (*Ch*) pigtail.

tauci, tauco, taucyo (*Ch*) fermented bean paste used as condiment.

taufan see TOPAN.

taufik (*Isl.*) God's guidance. - *dan hidayah* divine direction and guidance.

taugé (*Ch*) bean sprouts.

tauhid (*Rel.*) unity of God. **ber-** acknowledge the o.ness of God. **ment-kan 1** acknowledge God's o.ness. **2** concentrate on s.t. **ke-an** o.ness (of God).

tauk see TAHU₁.

tauké 1 Ch shop proprietor. **2** employer, boss.

tauladan see TELADAN.

taulan see TOLAN.

taun₁ /ta'un/ (*Lit.*) epidemic, esp. cholera.

taun₂ see TAHUN.

taup see TAUT.

taurat 1 (*Isl.*) the scripture revealed to prophet Moses. **2** (*Rel.*) Old Testament, esp. Pentateuch.

tausi see TAUCI.

taut ber- 1 fit together. *Lukanya* ~ The wound closed. ~ *jaminan* hostage. *Rantai kakinya* ~ *dgn borgol tangannya* The chain on his feet was linked to his handcuffs. *Dua macam tumbuh-tumbuhan* ~ The two plants grew together. ~ *tangan* shake hands. **2** fuse, become one. *Semua aliran politik* ~ *menjadi satu perkumpulan* All political factions fused into o. group. **ber-an** be linked with, related to. *ilmu yg* ~ related sciences. *Sajak yg disajikan itu cukup* ~ The poems which were presented were quite interrelated. **memper-kan, men-kan 1** combine s.t. **2** sew up a wound. **3** attach s.t. ~ *biduk ke dermaga* moor the boat to the pier. ~ *gerbong keréta makan ke induk lain* hook the dining car to the other cars. **-an** link. **pen-an** act of linking up. **per-an 1** contact, bond. **2** joining, uniting. **3** (*Chem.*) linkage.

Tavip [*Tahun Viveré Pericoloso*] the Year of Living Dangerously (Sukarno's speech of August 17, 1964).

tawa laughter, laugh. - *gemuruh* roaring laughter. - *kecil* smile. - *sumbang* laughing on the outside but crying on the inside. - *terkékéh* giggle. **men(t)er-i, men(t)-kan** laugh at. *Saya jéngkél pd gadis itu karena dia* ~ *saya* I am mad at that girl because she laughed at me. **ter-** laugh. ~ *dekah-dekah* laugh uproariously. ~ *terpingkal-pingkal* shake with laughter. **ter-an** object of ridicule. *bahan/buah* ~ laughingstock. **ke-** laugh. ~ *cekikikan* giggle. **menge-i, menge-kan 1** laugh at. *Apa yg kau -kan?* What are you laughing at? **2** make s.o. laugh. **-an 1** laughingstock, object of ridicule. **2** mockery. *Nada pertanyaan itu mengandung* ~ The tone of that question contained mockery.

tawadu (*Isl.*) prescribed ablutions before performing prayer ritual.

tawaf ceremony of circumambulation of the Ka'abah in Mecca seven times.

tawak (*Lit.*) **men-i** throw stones at.

tawakal, tawakkal (*Isl.*) resignation, trust in God who orders everything. **ber-** place o.'s trust in God. **ke-an** attitude of resignation. *ketabahan dan* ~ *yg luhur* deep patience and resignation.

tawak-tawak k.o. gong used to summon people.

tawan men- 1 capture in war. *Ia* ~ *musuhnya* He captured the enemy. **2** subdue. ~ *hati* captivating. *senyum yg* ~ a captivating smile. **3** intern, imprison. **ter- 1** interned. **2** captivated. **-an 1** military internee. *barang* ~ captured goods. **2** prisoner. ~ *jaminan* hostage. **3** captivation, detention. *Ia tdk mau mengusut perkara* ~*ku* He does not want to investigate the case of my detention. ~ *kota* city arrest. ~ *rumah* house arrest. **pen-** o. who arrests or subdues. ~ *hati* o. who captivates the heart. **pen-an** captivation.

tawar₁ 1 tasteless, insipid. *Tanpa ilham filemnya jadi* - Without inspiration the film became dull. *air* - freshwater. *roti* - unsweetened bread. *kopi* - unsweetened coffee. - *hambar* utterly insipid. **2** ineffective (of poison, magic spells, incantations, etc.). *Dgn ajimat pusaka ini segala mantranya*

- *saja* With this magic charm, all of his incantations can do us no harm. **3** undisturbed, at an even temper. *Mukanya - saja melihat suaminya kembali* She appeared indifferent to her husband's return. - *hati* **1** discouraged. **2** calmed down. **3** uninterested. -² **1** unmoved, emotionless. *Mukanya ~ saja menerima tamu* He appeared unmoved while receiving his guests. **2** moderate, average. *Perdagangan ~ saja hari ini* Business is just average today. **men-** weaken (strength or effectiveness of s.t.). **men-i 1** make magic or venom ineffective by using spells, charms, potions, etc. **2** seduce, tempt. ~ *hati janda* win the widow's heart. **3** pacify, calm down. ~ *amarah temannya* pacify his friend's anger. **men-kan** make (magic, etc.) ineffective. ~ *guna-guna* neutralize the effects of black magic. **pen-1** magic or charm to remove effects of black magic. **2** antidote, disinfectant. ~ *bisa ular* antidote for snake poison. **3** neutralizer. *seteguk ~ haus* a sip to assuage o.'s thirst. **pen-an 1** cure. **2** treatment of magic by incantations, etc. **3** neutralization.

tawar₂ bargain. *Boléh saya -?* May I bargain? **ber-²an** be engaged in bargaining with s.o. - **men-** bid(ding) back and forth, bargain(ing). **men- 1** bargain. **2** offer a price for s.t. *Blm ada yg ~ mobil ini* No o. has made an offer on this car yet. **men-i 1** offer to s.o. *Saya di-i rumah* I was offered a house. **2** repeatedly bargain. **men-kan** offer s.o. or s.t. (for sale, use, in marriage, etc.). *Ia ~ rokok Koa kpdku* He offered me a Koa cigarette. **-an** offer, bid. ~ *rumah* an offer to buy the house. ~ *pekerjaan* an offer of a job. **pen-** bidder, bargainer. **pen-an 1** offer, bid, deal. **2** bargaining.

tawarikh (*Lit.*) history. *ahli -* historian.

tawar-tawar k.o. plant.

tawas alum.

tawes k.o. freshwater fish.

tawon bee.

tawur₁ engage in a gang fight. **men-i** attack in a group. **-an** engage in a gang fight.

tawur₂ see TABUR.

tayammun, tayamum (*Isl.*) ritually purify o.s. with sand in absence of water.

tayang men- 1 carry s.t. resting on o.'s palms. **2** (*Lit.*) carry, waft. *Suara indahnya di- angin* Her beautiful voice was carried by the wind. **men-kan** (*Lit.*) present. *Program itu di-kan kpd umum* The program was presented to the public. **-an 1** s.t. held in the palms. **2** (*Lit.*) presentation.

taypak see TAIPAK.

tayub (*Jv*) *tarian* - k.o. dance with a professional entertainer. **men-** dance with a professional dancer in k.o. traditional dance. **-an** k.o. dance in which male members of audience are invited to join female professional dancers. **pen-** the dancer.

ta'zim see TAKZIM.

tbc /tébésé/ [*tuberculosis*] tuberculosis.

TC /tésé/ [*Training Center*] (*Sport*) Training Center. *Ia msk -* He entered a training center. **men(t)-(kan)** put or train in a training center. *Pembalap asuhannya sedang di-kan* The racer under his care has been enrolled in a training center. **pen(t)-an** causing o. to enter a sports training center.

té see SATÉ.

team /tim/ **1** (*Sport*) team. **2** team, group for carrying out a project.

téater drama theater.

téaterawan dramatist.

tebah men- strike a flat surface. *Ia ~ babut* He beat the rug. ~ *dada* beat o.'s breast (in anger or disappointment). **-an** beating. ~ *org yg tak berdosa* the beating of an innocent person. **pen-** (rug) beater. *kayu ~* **1** beating stick. **2** (*Sport*) bat.

tebak -² repeatedly guess. ~ *manggis* **1** gamble by guessing the number of segments a particular mangosteen fruit contains. **2** keep guessing. **men-** guess. ~ *warna kucing dlm karung* guess the color of a cat in a bag, i.e. be very difficult. **ter-1** guessable. **2** be guessed. **-an 1** guess, conjecture. **2** riddle. **pen-** guesser.

tébak men- chop off, cut off. ~ *tarah* turn over the soil with a hoe.

tebal 1 thick. *buku - a* thick book. *mantel - a* heavy overcoat. *cétak/huruf -* boldface type. **2** dense. *kabut yg - a* dense fog. **3** strong. *iman yg - a* strong faith. **4** insensitive. - *hati/kulit* cruel, pitiless. - *muka* **1** insensitive. **2** shameless. **ber-** *muka* be insensitive or shameless. - *telinga* stubborn. **men-** become thick. *Kabut ~* The fog thickened. **men-kan 1** thicken s.t. **2** reinforce. ~ *keyakinan kita* reinforce our belief. **memper-** strengthen, reinforce. *Arsiték itu ~ fondasi gedungnya* The architect strengthened the foundation of the building. *Musibah itu ~ imannya kpd Tuhan* That accident strengthened her faith in God. **ke-an** thickness. ~ *air* density of water. **pen-an** process of thickening. **per-an** thickening.

tebang men- fell. **men-i** repeatedly chop down. **-an** felled tree. *Tanah itu bekas ~ pohon di hutan* That land was once a site for extracting forest timber. **pen-** o. who fells trees. **pen-an** felling of trees. ~ *liar* illicit timber industry.

tébar ber-(an) spread around, scattered about. *Majalah ini ~ di seluruh Jawa* This magazine is distributed over all of Java. *beberapa daérah yg ~ puluhan kilométer dr ibu kota* several regions that are scattered tens of kilometers away from the capital. **keber-an** (*Phys.*) dispersity. **men-i** scatter in or on s.t. *Petani itu ~ ladangnya dgn benih bayam* The farmer scattered spinach seeds in his garden. **men- 1** spread around, disperse. ~ *bau busuk* exude a bad odor. **2** spread and throw s.t. out. *Ia ~ jalanya* He cast his net. **memper-kan** spread around. ~ *kabar* spread the news. **ke-an** (*Phys.*) dispersity. **-an 1** circular, bulletin. **2** seed. **pen-** (*Phys.*) s.t. that disperses. **pen-an 1** spread, spreading. *prosés ~ pengetahuan* the process of spreading knowledge. **2** (*Phys.*) dispersion. **per-an** (*Phys.*) dispersion.

tebas₁ men- cut down (shrubs, vegetation, etc. but not large trees). *Meréka ~ rerumput di jalan* They cleared the road by cutting away the undergrowth. *~ menebang* cut down shrubs and fell trees. **men-kan** cut with s.t., use s.t. to cut down. *Ia ~ parangnya ke tali-talian yg menghalangi jalannya* He used his machete to cut away the vines obstructing his way.

tebas₂ - *mentah* ask for money of the same value as the gift offered in place of the gift. *Tdk usah dipéstakan - mentah aja, Pak* Do not hold a celebration for us, Dad. Let us have the money instead. **men-** 1 buy up a harvest's yield before it has been harvested. *Tengkulak sdh ~ padinya yg masih hijau itu* The middleman contracted for the whole rice harvest while it was still unripe. 2 (*Jv*) buy up all of s.t. produced. **men-kan** contract to sell o.'s harvest while it is still in the fields. **-an** produce bought before harvesting. **pen-** 1 middleman who buys crops still standing in the field and who employs his own labor. 2 wholesale buyer of a product.

tebat 1 dam. 2 fishpond created by such a dam. **men-** create a pond with dam. **pen-an** damming up of s.t.

tébécé /tébésé/ tuberculosis.

tébéng₁ protective temporary screen (e.g. a mat to provide shade, etc.). - *jendéla* window hangings. - *topi* wide brim of sun hat. **men-** 1 put up temporary screen (mat, sail, etc.). 2 spread out cloth, mats, etc. for display. *~ babut* spread out carpets. **men-i** protect or screen s.t.

tébéng₂ (*Coll.*) **men-** sponge s.t., freeload, ride or live with (for free). *~ rokok* mooch cigarettes. *Selama menganggur dia ~ temannya* For the time he was unemployed he lived off his friend. **men-kan** allow or arrange for s.o. to live for free, mooch, etc. *Ia ~ anaknya ke mobil tetangganya* He had his daughter get a ride with his neighbor (to school).

teberau k.o. reedlike plant.

tébésé see TÉBÉCÉ.

tebi see RUMPUT.

tebing steeply sloping riverbank or mountainside.

tebir see TABIR.

tébok men- firmly strike with fist.

tebu 1 sugar cane. *dpt - rebah* be in luck (lit., get sugar cane already cut down). - *keprasan* sucker rising from the roots of a sugar cane plant which has already been cut down. 2 name for various k.o. reeds. - *kera* k.o. plant. -² encircling design on hilt, bangle, etc., similar to sugar cane joints.

tebuan see TABUHAN.

tebuk perforation (e.g. eyelet for shoelace, etc.). **men-** 1 perforate s.t. 2 bore through s.t. *Tupai ~ kelapa itu* A squirrel gnawed into that coconut.

tebus men- 1 redeem s.t. by paying cash or exchanging some other object. *~ cincin* redeem o.'s ring (from a pawnshop). *~ wésel* redeem (postal) money order. 2 compensate for some wrong. *~ dosa* (*Rel.*) expiate a sin. *~ malu* wipe out a disgrace. *~ kepengecutan itu dgn suatu laku kepahlawanan* compensate for that act of cowardice by an act of heroism. *~ talak* (*Lit.*) obtain a divorce from o.'s husband by returning the bride price. 3 fulfill. *~ janji* fulfill a promise. *~ kata* keep o.'s word. **-an** 1 ransom. 2 compensation. **pen-** 1 ransom. 2 o. who pays a ransom or makes compensation. *Sang ~* (*Rel.*) the Redeemer. **pen-an** 1 redemption. 2 compensation.

tedarus (*Isl.*) group recitation of Koran us. by taking turns, often performed during fasting month.

tedas (*Coll.*) clear, distinct. *berkata -* speak clearly, distinctly.

tédéng (*Jv*) protective screen (i.e. to shield from heat). - *aling-aling* s.t. used to cover up a criminal or secret act. **ber-(an)** covered up.

teduh 1 calm (following s.t. noisy or violent). *Angin -* The wind has died down. *Hujan tlh -* The rain has stopped. 2 shaded, shade. *istirahat di tempat yg -* rest in a shaded place. *matahari -* cloudy day. **ber-** take shelter. *~ di bawah pohon* take shelter under a tree. **ber-kan** make a shelter of s.t. *hanya ~ secarik plastik* with only a torn piece of plastic for shelter. **men-** 1 be shady. 2 become calm. **men-i** provide shade or shelter for. *Matanya di-i alis yg amat tebal* His bushy eyebrows shaded his eyes. **men-kan** 1 calm s.o. down. *Ia berhasil ~ amarahku* She succeeded in calming my anger. 2 make s.t. sheltered or shaded. *Pohon nangkanya ~ gubuk itu* That jackfruit tree shaded the hut. **ke-an** 1 calm, quietness. 2 shelter, shade. *~ pohon* the shelter of a tree. 3 sheltered, shaded. **-an** shade, shelter. **pen-** s.t. that shades or shelters. *pohon ~* shade tree. **pen-an** providing shade or shelter.

tedun (*Jv*) hernia.

téécu (*Ch, Lit., humble*) I.

tefakur, tefekur see TAFAKUR.

téga 1 bring o. self to, have the heart to. *Ia tak - melihat luka parah itu* He could not bring himself to look at that terrible wound. 2 do s.t. without worrying about the consequences. *Ia - meninggalkan anaknya* She left her child behind without giving it a 2d thought.

tegah men-(kan) forbid, prevent s.t. *"Jangan ke sini," Mamat ~* "Do not come this way," Mamat forbade. **pen-an** prohibition.

tegak 1 upright, erect. *Ia berdiri -* He stood upright. - *sbg alif* straight as a ramrod. - *cancang* pointed upward. - *damar* torch stand. - *lurus* upright. 2 standing. - *sama tinggi duduk sama rendah* equal in all respects. -² quite upright. **se-** height of standing man. **ber-nya** existence. *~ hukum* the existence of laws to uphold. **bersi-** uphold o.'s opinion with tenacity. **men-** become upright. *~ tiang* stand straight as a ramrod. **men-kan** 1 erect, build. *~ rumah* erect a house. 2 cause s.t. to be upright. *~ léhér baju* turn up the coat collar. *sesuatu yg ~ bulu kudukku* s.t. that set my hair on end. *~ tiang* erect a pole. 3 maintain. *~ semangat berjuang* maintain a fighting spirit. ~ *hukum* uphold the law. **ter-** in an erect position. **ke-an** uprightness. **-an** an upright cluster, a stand. ~ *jati* a stand of teak. **pen-** upholder. ~ *pendapat* holder of an opinion. ~ *hukum* (*Leg.*) o. who upholds the law. **pen-an** maintenance. ~ *haknya* maintenance of o.'s rights. ~ *hukum lalulintas* traffic law enforcement.

tegal₁ (*Lit.*) because. *Ada empat puluh bayi mati - sebab yg sama* 40 babies died for the same reason.

tegal₂, **tegalan** dry (not irrigated) field near the rice fields but used for vegetables and other secondary crops. **pen-an** cultivation without irrigation. *persawahan dan* ~ wet and dry land cultivation.

tegang 1 taut, tight. *Talinya -* The rope is taut. 2 tense, strained. *perhubungan yg - a* tense situation. *wajah -* a strained face. **ber(si)-** 1 persevere. 2 be stubborn, insist uncompromisingly. ~ *urat lehér* be stubborn. **men-** tighten, become tight, be tight, tense. *Sarafku ~ melihat kejadian ngeri itu* My nerves tautened when I saw that horrifying event. **men-i** tighten s.t. **men-kan** 1 tighten, make taut. ~ *otot-ototnya* contract o.'s muscles. 2 strain, make tense. *Peristiwa itu ~ hubungan kedua negeri itu* The incident strained the relations between the two countries. ~ *seluruh badan* tense o.'s whole body. **memper-** make tenser. **ke-an** 1 strained situation, tension. ~ *antara dua kekasih itu* the tension between the two lovers. 2 strain, stress. ~ *mata* eye strain. ~ *jiwa* mental stress. 3 suspense. **-an** tension, stress. ~ *tinggi* high tension.

tegap 1 well built, sturdy. *Badannya -* He is well built. 2 steady and unshakable. *pimpinan yg -* firm guidance. **men-kan** 1 make sturdy. ~ *badan* assume an erect, tense posture, to come to attention. 2 strengthen s.t. **ke-an** sturdiness.

tegar₁ stiff, rigid. *semangat -* a rigid spirit. *- hati/ tengkuk* stubborn. **men-kan** stiffen s.t. **ke-an** obstinacy, rigidity.

tegar₂ see TAGAR.

tegas 1 clear, distinct, explicit. *Sekarang pilihlah dgn -, dia atau aku* Now make a clear choice, him or me. *- bergas* straight to the point. *- ringkas* brief but clear. 2 firm, resolute. *sikap yg -* firm attitude. *tindakan yg -* a resolute step. **-nya** explicitly, in other words. ~ *ia mau kerja sedikit, tapi mendapat untung banyak* In other words, she wants to get a great profit with little work. **bersi-** maintain, state firmly. *"Tdk usah!" laki-laki itu ~* "That is not necessary!" the man maintained. **men-** ask. *"Benar?" Héri ~* "True?" Heri asked. **men-kan** 1 explain, clarify. *Ia ~ bhw "hantu" itu manusia juga spt ia sendiri* She explained that the "ghost" was just a human being like herself. 2 assert, insist. *Ia ~ bhw Sri hrs jadi isterinya* He asserted that Sri had to become his wife. **memper-** 1 clarify, explain. *Hal tersebut diper- oléh pasal 44(1)* That question is clarified by article 44(1). 2 affirm. *Perdagangan bébas kembali diper-* Free trade was reaffirmed. **ke-an** 1 firmness, reso-

luteness. 2 clearness, explicitness. 3 explanation. **-an** 1 affirmation. 2 emphasis. **pen-an** confirmation. *Perlu minta penentuan dan ~* (We) should ask for determination and confirmation.

tegel (*Jv*) capable of doing s.t. despicable. *Tentara hrs - makan ular* Soldiers must be able to stomach eating snakes.

tégel /tégel, tékhel/ floor tile. **men-** cover with floor tiles.

tégelté a briquet of tea leaves.

teges (*Jkt*) see TEGAS.

tegor see TEGUR.

teguh 1 firm, solidly made or done. *Diikat -* It was tied up firmly. *- bedegap* robust, strong. *janji yg - a* firm promise. 2 tenacious. *Meréka masih memegang - adatnya* They are still holding on firmly to their customs. 3 dependable. *- dlm perjoangan* reliable in struggle. **se-²nya** 1 as firm as possible, tenaciously. 2 with all o.'s might. *Bung juga memegang ~ sesuatu yg dicekokkan sejak kecil* You too just cling with all your might to what was taught to you when you were a kid. **ber-** 1 hold to, be firm in. 2 strengthen o.s. **ber-²an** mutually strengthen. ~ *persahabatan* mutually shore up a friendship. **men-kan, memper-kan** 1 confirm s.t. ~ *niatnya* affirm o.'s intentions. 2 strengthen s.t. ~ *lekat warna itu* strengthen the fixing power of that dye. **ke-an** 1 firmness, strength. ~ *iman* unassailability of his faith. 2 dependability. *~nya memegang rahasia* her dependability in keeping a secret. **pen-an** 1 confirmation. 2 the act of strengthening.

teguk a swallow or gulp. *se- air* a swallow of water. **men-** swallow s.t., gulp down. **men-i** repeatedly swallow or gulp s.t. **-an** swallow, gulp.

tegun startled. **se-** for a moment, suddenly. ~ *langkahnya terhenti* For a moment he stopped. **ter-** 1 startled to the point standing still a moment, stupefied. *Ia ~ mendengar langkah org yg sedang naik ke atas* She was startled and stopped moving when she heard the steps of s.o. coming up. 2 stop suddenly. *Pembicara itu ~* The speaker stopped abruptly. *Tiba-tiba jalan meréka ~* All of a sudden they stopped short. **ter-²** keep stopping. *Mobilnya itu ~, malahan mogok* That car of his kept faltering, in fact it broke down completely. **keter-an** startled amazement. *Blm hilang ~nya* Her amazement was not over yet. **-an** astonishment.

tegur expressions used to engage o. in a conversation. *- sapa* words used to open a conversation (greetings, etc.). *org yg baik - sapanya* a polite and well-mannered person. **ber-** *sapa* be on speaking terms. *Blm pernah aku ~ sapa dgn dia* I have never spoken with him. **ber-², ber-an** address e.o. **men-** 1 address s.o. (in order to open a conversation). *Ia melangkah mendekati gadis itu tapi tdk berani ~nya* He walked up to the girl but did not dare to address her. 2 admonish, reprimand. *Ia ~ temannya spy bekerja* He admonished his friend to do his work. **ke-an** suffer illness because of coming in contact with a ghost. **-an**

1 warning, reprimand. *mendapat ~ dr atasan* get a warning from o.'s superiors. **2** greeting. *Ia tdk menyahut ~ku* She did not respond to my greeting. **pen-** o. who addresses a meeting.

téh tea (both beverage and leaves). *- botol* bottled or packaged tea. *- és* iced tea. *- kotak* tea to drink in cartons. *- pahit* unsweetened tea. *- susu* tea with milk. *- tawar* unsweetened tea. *- tok* **1** unsweetened tea. **2** tea served without snacks.

téhnik, téhnis see TÉKNIK.

téhnikus see TÉKNIKUS.

téhnisi see TÉKNISI.

téhnologi see TÉKNOLOGI.

téja yellowish sunset glow. *- keluang* brightness after a rain.

téji see KUDA.

ték see TIK₁.

Tékab [*Team Khusus Anti Banditisme*] special antibanditry team of police.

tékad **1** determined to do s.t. despite the consequences. **2** strong will, resolve. *- (yg) bulat* very determined will. **ber- (hati)** be determined, be bent on. *Ia ~ akan pulang* She was resolved on going back. **men-kan** make (a decision, o.s.) resolute. *Ia ~ diri utk terus memperjuangkan haknya* He resolved to continue struggling for his rights. **ke-an** determination.

tekak (*Anat.*) **1** soft palate. **2** throat. *- haus/kering* dry throat. **3** taste. *- languk* nasty taste in the mouth. **men-** stick to the palate. *Manisnya ~* Its sweetness sticks to o.'s throat.

tekan pressure. **ber-** lean on. *~ pd tongkatnya* He leaned on his cane. *~ pinggang* with arms akimbo. **ber-an** exerting pressure. *~ tinggi* having high pressure or voltage. **men- 1** press, push down. *~ kenop* pressed a button. **2** suppress, repress, oppress. *~ harga* keep prices down. *Ia tak ~ perasaan tdk puas itu* He did not repress his feelings of dissatisfaction. *Kesepian terasa tambah ~* The loneliness felt increasingly oppressive. **3** compress. *Saya mencoba ~ pekerjaan seminggu menjadi sehari* I try to compress the work of a week in a day. **men-kan 1** stress, emphasize s.t. *Ia ~ kebenaran kataku* She emphasized the truth of what I said. *"Bukan," jawab Simun ~* "No," Simun answered emphatically. **2** press with s.t. *Ia ~ jarinya ke témbok* He pressed his finger onto the wall. **ter-** suppressed, oppressed. *Émosinya ~* His emotions were pent up. **-an 1** pressure. *~ udara* atmospheric pressure. *~ darah tinggi* hypertension *~ tinggi* (*Med.*) high pressure. **2** emphasis, stress. **3** tension, stress. *~ émosi* emotional stress. **4** (*Ling.*) stress. **pen-** s.t. or s.o. that stresses or emphasizes. *partikel ~* (*Ling.*) emphatic particle. **pen-an 1** pressing, pressuring. **2** stressing, emphasizing.

tékan see TÉKEN₁,₂.

tekap cover. **ber-** be covered. **men-(i)** cover. *Ia ~ mulut mangsanya yg berteriak itu* He covered the mouth of his screaming victim. **-an 1** cover. **2** dome, cupola.

tekat embroidery. **men-** embroider s.t.

tékat see TÉKAD.

teka-teki 1 riddle. *- jenaka* conundrum. **2** puzzle. *- silang* crossword puzzle. **ber- 1** play riddles. **2** ask a riddle.

tékdung 1 k.o. homemade rifle used in the revolution. **2** (*Jkt*) pregnant out of wedlock.

tekebur see TAKABUR.

tekék see TOKÉ₂.

tékel men- manage, handle. *Hal-hal berurusan dgn polisi di- oléh Rob* Rob will handle matters having to do with the police.

tékelék see TÉKLÉK.

teken (*Jkt*) see TEKAN.

téken₁ (*Coll.*) **1** signature. **2** sign. *Abang perlu - laporan itu* You must sign that report. **men-** sign s.t. *~ serdadu* sign up for military service (colonial period). *~ mati* risk o.'s life for s.t. **-an** registration for military service. *~ serdadu* enlist (in a foreign army).

téken₂ drawing, sketch. **-an** picture, drawing.

téker *batu -* flint. **men-** light a fire with a flint. **-an** flint.

tékhnik, tékhnis see TÉKNIK.

tékhnokrat see TÉKNOKRAT.

tékhnologi see TÉKNOLOGI.

teki k.o. grass the root of which is used in the preparation of *emping*.

tékidanto (*Japanese*) grenade hurler.

tekis (*Lit.*) nearly happen.

teklak-tekluk (*Jv*) bobbing up and down. *- nganatuk* keep nodding drowsily.

téklék (*Jv*) wooden clog with leather straps.

téknik 1 technique. **2** technology, engineering. *- éléktro* electrical engineering. *- kelautan* marine engineering. *- listrik* electrical engineering. *- perkapalan* marine engineering. **3** technical.

téknikus technician.

téknis technical.

téknisi technician.

téknokrasi technocracy.

téknokrat technocrat.

téknokratis technocratic.

téknologi technology, engineering.

téknologis technological.

téko, tékoh teapot.

tékong see TIKUNG.

tekor (*Coll.*) show a deficit. *Uangnya - lima puluh dolar* He is short fifty dollars. **ke-an 1** deficit. **2** be short of. *Saya ~ uang* I am short of money.

tekoran container made of banana or palm leaves.

tékosi (*Coll.*) tea cozy.

téks text. *buku -* textbook. *- pidato* the text of the speech.

tékstil textile. **per-an** matters pertaining to textiles or textile industry.

tékstur texture.

ték-ték sound of tapping. *bakmi -* Ch noodle dish sold by street vendors who tap on their woks to attract customers.

téktonis (*Geol.*) tectonic.

tekuk (*Jkt*) crumpled, bent up. *- lutut* bending of

the knee. **ber-** *lutut* bend the knees, surrender. *Belanda ~ lutut pd Jepang* The Dutch surrendered to the Japanese. **men-lutut(kan)** bring to the knees, subdue. *~ pemerintah* bring a gvt. to its knees. **ber-** folded roughly, crumpled. *~ tangan* fold o.'s arms across the chest. **men-** fold s.t. stiff. *Ia ~ surat itu* He folded the letter. **men-kan** fold s.t., bend s.t. over. *Setiap pagi saya ~ pinggang dua puluh lima kali* Every morning I do 25 deep bends from the waist. **ter-** folded. **-an** 1 fold. 2 tool for folding.

tekukur large turtledove.

tekun 1 diligent, zealous. *Ia belajar dgn -* He studied diligently. *Meréka - bekerja* They work diligently. 2 diligence. **ber-** 1 be diligent. 2 hold fast, adhere to. *~ pd adat kuno* hold on to old-fashioned customs. **men-i** occupy o.s. diligently with s.t. *Bahasa Sunda hanya di-i oléh org Sunda* Only the Sundanese people really work at the Sundanese language. *Berhari-hari dia ~ buku-bukunya* She occupied herself with her books for days on end. **ke-an** 1 diligence, application. 2 perseverance. **pen-** s.o. who is diligent about s.t. *~ buku-buku agama* a devotee of religious books. **pen-an** acting diligent about s.t.

tekur bend over (of head). **ber-** with head bowed. *duduk ~* sit with bowed head. **men-** 1 bend, bow. *Ia ~ pd méja di depannya* She bowed her head down on the table in front of her. 2 meditate. **men-i** 1 stare at. *~ panorama* gaze steadily at a view. 2 bend, bow o.'s head over s.t. *Kembali di-inya diktatnya* She bent her head over her lecture notes again. **men-kan** bow s.t. *~ kepala* bow the head. **ter-** be bowed (of the head).

tékwan k.o. soup with fishballs.

Tel. [*Teluk*] (*Geog.*) bay, gulf.

tél. [*télfon*] telephone.

tela (*Lit.*) pavilion for women in a palace complex.

téla₁ **per-an** proceedings, report.

téla₂ see KETÉLA.

telaah study, research. **men(t)-** analyze, study carefully. *~ buku pelajaran* carefully go over o.'s school books. **-an** research paper. **pen-** researcher. **pen-an** research.

telabang (*Lit.*) k.o. shield.

teladan model, example. *mahasiswa -* a model student. **men-** follow the example of. *Ia ~ kakaknya yg pandai itu* He followed the example of his brilliant sister. **men-i** set an example for. *Guru mesti ~ muridnya* The teacher must set an example for his pupils. **men-kan** make s.t. an example, provide a model. *Bung Hatta ~ sikap yg baik sbg mahasiswa* Bung Hatta provided a model for the best attitude for a student.

telaga 1 lake, pond. 2 stagnant pit, well. *- tahi* cesspool.

telah₁ already (marker indicating a completed action). *Ia - besar* He is already grown. **se-** after. *~ makan ia tidur* After eating he went to sleep.

telah₂ **men-(kan)** predict. *Kita blm dpt ~ hasil-hasil pemilihan* We cannot predict the results of the elections yet. **pen-** prophesier, forecaster. **pen-an** prophecy, prediction.

telak right on target, unequivocally. *Team sépak bola kita kalah - empat nol* Our soccer team was trounced four to nothing. *Sepatunya - menghantam perutnya* The shoe hit him right smack in the stomach.

telan swallow. *- mentah-mentah* utterly defeat. *- spt kasuari* (*Amb*) swallow s.t. without chewing. **men-** 1 swallow. *~ makanan* swallow food. *~ ludah* be anxious. 2 swallow up. *hilang di- malam* disappear in the night. *Empat org meloncat ke laut dan hilang di- ombak* Four people jumped into the sea and were swallowed by the waves. 3 endure patiently (insults, etc.). *Ia hrs ~ tuduhan yg berat* She had to take the grave accusations. 4 require, consume. *Perjalanan itu ~ banyak ongkos* The trip cost a lot of money. *Perjoangan ini banyak ~ korban* This struggle is causing heavy losses. *~ waktu* take up time. *~ waktu lima hari* take five days. **ter-** 1 swallowed accidentally. 2 swallowed up, consumed. *Tenaga dan waktu yg tlh ~ di dlmnya* It has consumed energy and time. 3 be caught up, taken along by the rush of events. *Kau hanya ~ sbg korban kekejaman manusia pd jamannya* You were simply caught up, a victim of the human cruelty that existed at the time. **pen-an** swallowing.

telangkai matchmaker.

telangkup see TELUNGKUP.

telanjang bare, naked. *- kaki* barefoot. *- bugil/ bulat* stark naked. **ber-** *bulat* be stark naked. *~ bulat ia berjalan sepanjang jalan raya* He walked stark naked along the main street. *- dada* bare breasted. **ber-** *dada* be bare breasted. **ber-** be naked. **men-i** 1 strip s.o. or s.t. *~ rahasia* uncover a secret. 2 strip s.o of. *~ penumpang dr barangnya* strip the passenger of his goods. **ter-i** found out (of an evil practice), be laid bare. **ke-an** nakedness, nudity. **pen-an** stripping, denudation.

telanjur see LANJUR.

telantar see LANTAR₂.

telap 1 cause injury (by knives, etc.). 2 vulnerable. *Ia tdk -* He is invulnerable. 3 (*Phys.*) permeable. **men-** 1 cause injury (by sharp weapons). 2 (*Phys.*) permeate. **ke-an** (*Phys.*) permeability. **-an** (*Phys.*) permeance.

telapak, telapakan 1 palm of hand, sole of foot. *- kuda* hoof. 2 bottom part of s.t. *- ban* tread of a tire. *- kembar* 1 dual tread. 2 two-ply.

telasih see SELASIH.

telat (*Coll.*) overdue, too late. *Keréta api datang -* The train was overdue. **ke-an** tardiness.

telatah o.'s characteristic ways, gestures, movements, etc. *- Sutarji sungguh menjijikkan!* Sutarji's mannerisms are disgusting!

telatén 1 patient, persevering. *Ia tak - menunggu* He waited impatiently. 2 painstaking. **men-i** persevere in s.t. *Kita hrs siap ~ pekerjaan rumit ini* We must be prepared to perservere in this complicated work. **ke-an** patience.

telau a spot, stain of color. **ber-(²) 1** with spots (of a lighter color). *tangan yg* ~ a hand covered with spots. *kebiruan* ~ spotty blue color. *cahaya lentéra jalan* ~ with streetlight illumination here and there.

télé ber-² long-winded, excessively long and trivial. *kalimat-kalimat yg panjang* ~ needlessly long sentences.

telédék (*Jv*) dancing girl.

telédor negligent, careless. *Ia - dlm pekerjaannya* He is negligent in his work. **men(t)-kan** neglect, be careless about. ~ *soal-soal kebudayaan* neglect cultural matters. **men-kan** neglect s.t. **ke-an 1** negligence, carelessness. **2** default (payment, etc.).

teledu k.o. a small badgerlike mammal of Sumatra.

téléfon see TÉLEPON.

téléfonis by telephone. *Ia bisa dihubungi secara -* He can be contacted by telephone.

téléfoniste female telephone operator.

télégraf see TÉLÉGRAP.

télégrafis 1 telegraphy operator. **2** telegraphic.

télégram, télegram telegram. **men-** send a telegram.

télégrap, télegrap telegraph.

télégrapis see TÉLÉGRAFIS.

telek (*Jkt*) see TELAK.

telék (*Jv*) bird droppings.

telekan ber- lean o.'s hand, elbow, etc. s.w. **bersi-** rest both hands. *Tangan gadis itu masih* ~ *pd piano* The girl's hands still rested on the piano. **men-kan** rest a part of the body s.w. *Ia* ~ *kepala di tangannya memandangi aku* She rested her head on her hands while looking at me.

télékomunikasi telecommunications.

téléks telex.

telekung (*Isl.*) outermost robe worn by women when praying.

telempap breadth of hand (a measure). **se-** as large as o.'s hand. **men-** measure with o.'s hand.

telémpong (*M*) k.o. percussion instrument.

telenan see TALENAN.

teleng (*Anat.*) pupil (of eye).

téléng at an angle. *mata -* (*Sd*) cross-eyed. **men-i** cause s.t. to slope at an angle. *Kepalanya tertoléh sedikit* ~ *bahunya* Her head was slightly turned causing her shoulder to slope. **men-kan** cause s.t. to be at an angle. ~ *kepalanya* cock o.'s head at an angle. ~ *topi* tip o.'s hat.

telengkup lie on o.'s stomach.

telentang see LENTANG₂.

telep (*Sl.*) take s.t. without permission.

télépati telepathy.

télépisi see TÉLÉVISI.

télepon, télépon telephone. **ber-** talk by phone, use the phone. **(ber)-²an** telephone e.o. **men-** phone s.o. **men-kan** phone on s.o.'s behalf. *Ia minta tolong di-kan kantornya* He asked s.o. to call his office. **pen-** caller. **per-an** pertaining to telecommunication.

telepuk design printed onto cloth with gold or silver foil.

télépun see TÉLEPON.

télér₁ (*Med.*) foul discharge from an infected ear.

télér₂ 1 overexhausted. *Wah, saya naik gunung sampai - déh!* Hey, I was mountain climbing till I was really exhausted! **2** intoxicated. **-²an** get plastered, get completely drunk.

télér₃ see ÉS.

téléskop telescope.

telétong (*Jv*) manure, dung.

télévisi television. **men-kan** show s.t. on TV. **per-an** matters pertaining to television.

télgram see TÉLÉGRAM.

telik see TILIK.

telikung men- bind hand and foot, wrap s.t. up entirely. *Dua-duanya di-* oléh pikirannya sendiri Both of them were wrapped up in their own thoughts.

telimpuh ber- (*Lit.*) sit with legs bent back beside body.

telinga 1 ear. *- gajah* large ears. *msk - kiri, keluar - kanan* in o. ear and out the other. *- tipis* easily offended. **ber-** *tipis* be easily offended. **2** ear-shaped handle. *- panci* handle of a pan. *- tempayan* ears that do not hear (lit., ears of a jug).

telingkah (*Lit.*) behavior. **ber-** quarrel.

telingkup see TELUNGKUP.

teliti careful, thorough. *memeriksa dgn -* examine carefully. **se-²nya** as careful as possible. *Meskipun telah dirawat dgn* ~ *keadaannya tak tampak sembuh* Although she was treated with all possible care, there was no improvement in her condition. **men- 1** examine carefully. *Meréka* ~ *jejak-jejak harimau* They carefully examined the footprints of the tiger. **2** research s.t. **memper-** scrutinize. ~ *setiap angka* scrutinize each figure. **ter-** be examined. **ke-an** carefulness. ~ *bekerja* meticulousness. **pen-** researcher. ~ *ilmiah* scientific researcher. **pen-an 1** thorough, detailed examination. **2** research. ~ *guna* applied research. ~ *permulaan* pilot study. ~ *lapangan* fieldwork.

Télkom [*Télekomunikasi*] Telecommunications (a public corporation).

télop still photographs shown on television.

telor see TELUR.

télor having a speech defect.

télp. [*télpon*] telephone.

télpon see TÉLEPON.

telu (*Lit., Jv*) three.

teluh magical formula.

teluk (*Geog.*) bay, cove, gulf. *- Benggala* Bay of Bengal. *- Iran* Persian Gulf. *- rantau* **1** district, region. **2** river bend. **men-** curve around, be curved.

teluk belanga (*M*) k.o. traditional tunic for men.

teluki see BUNGA.

telukup see TELUNGKUP.

telumpang men- overlap.

telungkup face downward. **men-** lie face downward. *Minah* ~ *di tempat tidur menangis* Minah lay face downward on the bed weeping. **men-i** lie face downward on s.t. *Ia ~ persada Ibu Pertiwi* She lay face downward on the regal soil of the motherland. **men-kan** place s.t. face downward. *Ia ~ mukanya ke atas tuts piano itu* He laid his face down on the keyboard of the piano. **ter-** flat on o.'s face.

telunjuk index finger. - *lurus kelingking berkait* two-faced, hypocritical (lit., the index finger is straight but the little finger is hooked around s.t.).

telur 1 egg, roe, etc. - *asin* salted egg. - *ceplok* fried egg. - *dadar* omelette. - *kocokan* scrambled eggs. - *kol* cauliflower. - *lo* hard-boiled egg with soy sauce. - *masak setengah* soft-boiled egg. - *mata sapi* egg fried sunny-side up. - *pindang* egg boiled in water spiced with chili, tamarind, and other spices. - *di ujung tanduk* critical, precarious. **2** (*Biol.*) ovum. **3** a grade or score of zero. - *besar* 2d level of kindergarten. - *kecil* first level of kindergarten. **ber-** lay eggs. **men-kan** produce s.t. as if laying an egg (s.t. new, s.t. dropped, etc.). *Kapal terbang ~ bom* The plane dropped a bomb. *Ia ~ penemuan baru* He brought forth a new invention. *~ hasil* produce results. **pe-** egg-layer. *ayam ~* layer hen. **pen-an** egg laying, egg production.

telusur men- 1 unravel s.t. **2** investigate, explore. *~ kemungkinan* explore a possibility. **men-i 1** go along, follow. *Ia ~ sungai sejauh lima kilométer* She went five km along the river. **2** trace, follow. *~ sejarah* follow the course of history. *Gejala itu dpt di-i sejak tahun 1905* This symptom can be traced back to the year 1905. **3** research, investigate. *~ sistém pendidikan* do research on the education system. *~ perkara pembunuhan* investigate a murder case. **pen-** o. who traces paths. **pen-an** investigation.

telut₁ ber- 1 kneel down. **2** surrender.

telut₂ see LUT.

telutut (*Lit.*) **men-** kneel.

tém (*Jkt*) **nge-** wait for sufficient numbers (of passengers). *Sopir ~ penumpang* The driver waited for enough passengers to fill the vehicle.

téma theme, topic. **ber-(kan)** have as a theme.

temaah (*M*) greedy.

temabur scattered.

temadun see TAMADUN.

temaha, temahak see TEMAAH.

temali see TALI.

temambah (*Math.*) additive.

teman friend, companion. - *hidup* life's companion, helpmate. - *sekerja* colleague. - *sekelas* classmate. - *setanahair/senegara* fellow countryman. --*temin* (*Sl.*) male and female friends. **ber- 1** with friends. *Ia datang ~* He came with his friends. **2** be friends to e.o. *Meréka udah ~* They have become friends. *Ia ~ dgn anak saya* He has become a friend of my son. **3** be married. *Ia sdh ~, bukan bujang lagi* He is married and not a bachelor anymore. **ber-kan** have as a friend. *~ seorg*

isteri have o.'s wife as a friend. **men-i** accompany s.o. *Siapa yg ~ ibumu ke Bandung?* Who is accompanying your mother to Bandung? **pen-an** companionship.

temantén (*Jv*) bride, bridegroom. - *baru* newlyweds.

temara (*Lit.*) k.o. spear.

temaram dark (obscure). *Ia mencari wajahku di - malam* She looked for my face in the dark of the night.

temarang see TERANG.

temasa, temasya see TAMASYA.

tembaga copper. - *kuning* brass. - *mérah* copper. - *perunggu* bronze. - *putih* pewter. **men-** become copper-colored.

témbak shoot at. *Aku maklum ke mana - kata-katanya* I knew what his words were aiming at. - *di tempat* shoot on sight. *hukum -* death by a firing squad. - *jitu* (*Mil.*) direct hit. - *mati* sentence to death by firing squad. **ber-²an** shoot at e.o. - **men-** shoot at e.o. **men- 1** fire a gun. *~ jatuh* shoot s.t. down. **2** aim at, intend. **3** (*Sport*) shoot (a basket), make a goal, etc. **men-i** repeatedly fire on s.t. *Kapal itu di-i pesawat udara* The ship was fired on by a plane. **men-kan 1** shoot with s.t. *Ia ~ bedilnya* He fired his rifle. **2** shoot s.t. out. *Ia ~ peluru penghabisan* He shot his last bullet. **ter- 1** shot. *Ia ~ mati* He was shot to death. **2** struck (as if by a projectile). *Rumahnya ~ petir* His house was struck by lightning. **-an 1** shooting. *~ meréka tdk ada hentinya* There was no end to their shooting. **2** shot. *~ kehormatan* salvo. *~ pengampunan* coup de grace. **-²an 1** shooting, rifle drill. **2** shooting at e.o. **pen-** rifleman, marksman. *~ jitu/mahir* sharpshooter. **pen-an 1** bombardment, shooting. *peristiwa ~ anjing itu* the incident of the shooting of that dog. **2** firing (of a missile).

tembakau, tembako tobacco. - *belati* imported tobacco. - *kerosok* dried tobacco leaf. - *jawa* native-grown tobacco. - *rajangan* cut tobacco. - *sék* shag tobacco. **per-an** tobacco affairs.

tembam puffed-up (of face).

tembang sung or recited Jv poetry. **men-** recite or sing Jv poetry us. accompanied by gamelan music. *Utk mengisi waktu meréka ~* To pass the time they recited *tembang*. **men-kan** sing or recite (a *tembang*). *~ lagu-lagu sedih* sing sad songs. **pen-** singer with gamelan orchestra.

tembékar see TEMBIKAR.

témbél₁ sty (in eye).

témbél₂ see TAMBAL.

tembelék see TELÉK.

tembem see TEMBAM.

témbérang garrulous, bombastic, given to boasting.

témbéréng 1 potsherd. **2** earthenware. **3** (*Math.*) segment. - *lingkaran* segment of a circle. **4** outer edge, borderline.

tembesi k.o. tree yielding timber.

tembikai watermelon.

tembikar 1 glazed porcelain, ceramics, china. 2 earthenware. 3 sherds.

tembilang spade (for digging).

tembilu see SEMBILU.

témbok₁ masonry wall. - *beton* concrete wall. - *penahan* retaining wall. - *kering* miser (lit., a dry wall). men-, men-i wall s.t. up. *Perkarangan sebelah rumah kami di-* The yard beside our house was walled in. -an stone dam.

témbok₂ (*Jv*) men- cover batik with wax to resist dye.

tembola k.o. game of chance, tombola.

tembolok 1 craw, crop. 2 (*Coll.*) paunch.

témbong (*Jv*) spot, esp. facial birthmark.

tembuk see TEBUK.

tembung (*Lit.*) cudgel. men- hit with a cudgel.

tembuni (*Biol.*) afterbirth, placenta.

tembus 1 perforate. 2 emerge. *Jalan ini - ke pasar* This street comes out at the market. 3 penetrated. *Pertahanan musuh tlh -* The enemy's defense was penetrated. ber-an filled with holes. men- 1 pierce, stab. *Ia ~ dada musuhnya dgn bayonét* He pierced his opponent's chest with a bayonet. 2 penetrate, break through. *Meréka tlh ~ pertahanan musuh* They have penetrated the enemy's defense. *~ rékor lama* (*Sport*) beat a record. 3 emerge, come out. *Sungai ini ~ di tengah kota* This river emerges in the center of town. *Air hujan ~ témbok* Rain water is seeping through the wall. men-i penetrate s.t. *Matanya ~ badan Nah* His eyes seemed to pierce Nah's body. *Kata-katanya ~ hatiku* Her words cut into my heart (and irritated me). men-kan pierce with s.t. *~ jarum ke kulit* prick the skin with a needle. ter- perforated, pierced. -an 1 perforation, penetration. 2 thoroughfare, passage, tunnel. 3 carbon copy, esp. for forwarding to s.o. *~ bermeterai* stamped, certified copy. pen-an penetration.

temebar 1 (*Jv*) spread out, dispersed. *Baunya ~ di seluruh ruangan* The odor dispersed throughout the room. 2 dispersive.

temen see TEMAN.

temenan (*Jv*) really, truly. *ibu yg ayu ~ a* really beautiful mother.

temenggung 1 (*Lit.*) title of high-ranking royal official. 2 title of regent (in colonial period).

temerang see TERANG.

temin₁ metal band (for reinforcing a handle, etc.).

temin₂ (*Sl.*) female friend.

tempa metal handiwork. - *Malaka* k.o. short kris. men- make metal objects, manufacture knives, etc. *~ barang dapur* make kitchen utensils. *~ diri* undergo severe discipline and training. *Ia ~ diri mempersiapkan utk ujian* He underwent severe training in preparation for his examinations. ter- forged. ter-kan malleable. -an s.t. made. *barang ~ Bali* articles made in Bali. pen- smith. pen-an forging. *~ méntal* forging of the intellect.

tempah in advance. *uang -* prepayment. men-

(kan) 1 book ahead of time. 2 make to order. -an an order (of some item).

témpang see TIMPANG.

tembilu see TELEMPAP.

tempat place, spot, location. - *persembunyian* hideaway. - *kediaman/kedudukan* place of residence. *Ia tiba di pintu penjara - isterinya ditahan* He arrived at the gate of the prison, the place his wife was detained. *Ialah - kami bertanya* It was to him we directed our questions (He was the locus of questioning). - *abu* ashtray. - *bertaut* point of contact. - *hiburan* amusement park. - *kelahiran* place of birth. - *lapang* a square, plaza. - *menyeberang* pedestrian crossing. - *pemberian* place of issue. - *pemberian suara* poll, voting booth. - *pengasingan* 1 internment camp. 2 isolation ward. - *pengumpulan* depot. - *tidur* bed. - *tinggal* residence. ber- tinggal live, stay. *Ia ~ tinggal di pinggir laut* She lived by the seashore. - *tujuan* destination. - *tumpah darah* birthplace. *Sdh pd -nya It* is fitting. *Tidak pd -nya It* is not proper. *di - istirahat* at ease, at rest. se- 1 local. *jam 15.00 waktu ~* three p.m. local time. *polisi ~* local police. 2 of the same place. *Ia ~ dgn saya* He comes from the same place I come from. se-² some places. *Tanamannya hanya ~ yg rusak* His plants are damaged in some spots only. menye-kan localize. *~ penyakit menjalar* localize a contagious disease. ber- 1 be (placed), located. *Tetangga ini sdh lama ~ tinggal di sebelah rumahku* She has been my next-door neighbor for a long time. 2 take place. *Pertemuan ini ~ di gedung bioskop* This meeting took place at the movie theater. men-i occupy. *Rumah ini siap utk di-i* This house is ready to be occupied. *Ia ~ jabatan yg baru* He occupies a new post. *~ lowongan* fill a vacancy. men-kan put s.t. in a certain place. *~ topi di méja* place a hat on the table. *Penolakan saya ~ meréka ke dlm keadaan sulit* My refusal places them in a difficult position. ter-i be occupied. pen-an 1 appointment, placement. *~ tenaga* staffing, placement. *Jawatan ~ Tenaga* employment placement office. 2 stand, place to set s.t. *~ sepéda* bicycle stand. 3 occupying, settling. *izin ~* occupancy permit. 4 placing. *~ iklan* placing of an ad.

tempaus k.o. fragrance used in cigarettes.

tempawan forged, beaten.

tempayak maggots.

tempayan k.o. large water jar.

témpé 1 k.o. fermented soybean cake, tempeh. 2 s.t. trivial and unimportant or low grade in quality. men-kan 1 make s.t. into this foodstuff. 2 consider s.t. trivial or low grade. *Dlm jaman penjajahan org Indo ~ pribumi* During the colonial times the Eurasians considered the natives to be no better than tempeh.

témpél 1 adhere. 2 patch. - *ban* inner tube patching service. ber- stick, be next to. men- 1 adhere, cling. *Perangkonya tdk ~* The stamp does not stick. *Anak itu ~ kpd ibunya* That child clings to his mother. *cecak yg ~ di dinding* a gecko clinking to the wall. **2** (*Coll.*) patch. ~ *ban* patch a tire. **3** (*Coll.*) be right up next to. *Halamannya ~ sungai* His yard is right next to the river. **men-i 1** stick to, make s.t. stick to. *Amplop itu blm di-i perangko secukupnya* That envelope does not have sufficient stamps stuck on it. ~ *ibunya* cling to o.'s mother. **2** sponge, freeload on s.t. **3** cover s.t. by sticking materials. ~ *témbok dgn gambar* cover the wall with pictures. **4** (*Sl.*) bribe. **men-kan** stick s.t. on. ~ *gambar ke témbok* stick pictures on the wall. **ter-** stuck, attached. *Pd halaman itu ~ kertas guntingan* A clipping was attached to that page. **-an 1** sticker, poster. **2** attached to s.o. or s.t. **3** revenue stamp. **pen-** instrument or person that sticks s.t. up. **pen-an** attachment, sticking. ~ *plakat* attachment of a poster.

tempelak blame, reproach. **men-** reproach s.o.

tempéléng slapping on the face or ears. **men-(i)** slap s.o. on the face or side of the head. *Prajurit itu mengangkat tangannya utk ~ lawannya* The soldier lifted his hand to slap his adversary. **-an** a slap administered.

témperamén temperament.

temperas (*Lit.*) in complete disarray. **ber-an** spread about in disorder.

témperatur temperature.

tempiar ber-an splashed in all directions.

tempias a splash, a spray. *Ia menepi-nepi trotoar, menghindarkan - air* She kept to the far edge of the sidewalk to avoid splashes (from passing cars). **men- 1** splash up. **2** splash on s.t. *Hujan ~ daun-daunan* Rain splashed the leaves. **men-kan** splash s.t. onto. *Selesai mandi, ia ~ air ke mukanya* After bathing, he splashed some water on his face.

tempik₁ a shout. *- sorak* all k.o. yells and cheers. **ber-** yell, shout. **-an** a cry, a shout.

tempik₂ (*Jv*) vagina.

tempil see TAMPIL.

témplék men- attached to, hanging on or against. *Lampu yg ~ di témbok* a lamp attached to the wall. **-²an 1** (*Jv*) be close to o. **2** assembling.

templok men-, n- 1 lean on. ~ *di dinding* lean against the wall. **2** depend. ~ *pd perempuan* depend on a woman (for o.'s living, etc.).

témpo, témpoh 1 time. *Kalau ada -, silakan datang* If you have time, do come over. *Ada -nya ia menangis* At times he cries. *Sdh -nya utk pulang* It is time to go home. *minta -* ask for a delay. *- doeloe/dulu* in olden days, formerly. *- hari* 1 the other day. **2** formerly. *Kenapa kau - hari mengeluarkan kata-kata yg kasar* Why did you say those nasty things the other day? *bekas teman sekolahku - hari* a former schoolmate of mine. **2** period of time. *Ia diberi - tiga bulan* He was given a period of three months. *- berlaku* period of validity. **3** (*Coll.*) when. *- saya datang, ia pergi* When I came, he was gone. **4** tempo. **5** break, interruption. *waktu - tahun baru* at New Year's vacation. *Ia dpt - sehari* He gets a day off. **-²** sometimes, now

and then. *Ia datang ~* He came sometimes. ~ *dia muak mendengar kuliah* At times she was fed up with hearing lectures.

témpohari see TÉMPO.

tempolong cuspidor, spittoon.

témporér temporary.

tempoyak k.o. salty condiment made of fermented durian.

tempua weaverbird.

tempuh ber-² (*Lit.*) attack e.o. **men- 1** attack, assail. ~ *musuh* attack the enemy. **2** go through, endure by passing through. ~ *hutan yg lebat* penetrate a thick jungle. ~ *segala kesukaran* endure all difficulties. ~ *ujian* take an examination. ~ *berbagai-bagai pelajaran* take various courses of study. ~ *jalan* go o.'s way. ~ *jarak* cover a distance. ~ *bahaya* face danger. *berjalan ~ angin* walk into the wind, brave the wind. **3** take on, take up. *Negara itu ~ politik koéksisténsi* That state follows a policy of peaceful coexistence. **men-kan** make s.o. responsible for s.t. *Ia ~ tetangganya karena kerusakan itu* He said his neighbor was responsible for the damage. **ke-an 1** be responsible for. *Ia ~ Rp100.000 karena kerusakan itu* He was held responsible for damages of 100,000 rupiah. **2** be blamed. *Saya yg ~ kesalahan itu* I was the o. blamed for the mistake. **-an** an attack. **pen-** o. who attacks, assumes some difficult task, or goes a certain distance. ~ *lari seratus méter* the o. who undertook to run the 100-meter dash. **pen-an** the traveling of a certain distance, the undertaking of a difficult task.

tempuling harpoon, trident.

tempur combat. *semangat -* fighting spirit. *médan -* battlefield. *pesawat -* jet-fighter. **ber-** be engaged in combat. ~ *dgn pasukan musuh* fight enemy troops. *Ombak ~ dgn karang* Waves raged against the reefs. **bersi-an** (*Lit.*) fight e.o. **men-** attack, assail. **memper-kan 1** fight for s.t. *Meréka ~ kenaikan gaji* They fought for a salary increase. **2** cause s.o. to fight (on behalf of another). ~ *pasukan persediaan* have the reserve troops fight. **pen-** assailant. *kapal ~* battleship. **per-an** battle, combat. *daérah ~* combat area. ~ *darah* bloodshed.

tempurung piece of coconut shell. *- biola* body of a violin. *- kepala* (*Anat.*) cranium, skull. *- lutut* (*Anat.*) kneecap. *spt katak di bawah -* narrowminded.

tempuyung k.o. medicinal plant.

temu₁ wild ginger, generic term for many *Curcuma* species and similar plants. *- giring* k.o. medicinal root. *- kunci* k.o. root used for spice and medicine. *- kuning/kunyit* tumeric. *- lawak* k.o. wild ginger.

temu₂ come together. **ber- 1** meet. *Saya ~ dia* I met him. *Pandangan kami ~* Our glances met. *Saya ingin ~ guru saya* I want to see my teacher. *Mungkin itu hilang, tiada ~ lagi* Possibly it is lost, it cannot be found. *Sampai - lagi* So long, until we meet again. ~ *mata/muka* meet face to face. *Ia* *menoléh dan ~ mata dgn musuhnya* He turned and came face to face with his enemy. **2** match, agree. *Perkataannya tak ~ dgn perbuatannya* His words do not match his deeds. **men-i 1** go to meet s.o. *Ia ~ temannya* He went to see his friend. **2** come upon, run into. *~ soal baru* come upon a new problem. **3** experience s.t. (us. unpleasant). *Ia ~ kegagalan* He met with failure. *~ ajalnya* die, meet o.'s end. **men-kan 1** find, meet with. *~ kekecéwaan* meet with disappointment. **2** find, discover. *Columbus ~ Amérika* Columbus discovered America. *~ métode pemberantasan butahuruf* discover a method to fight illiteracy. *~ akal* devise a trick. **memper-kan 1** (*Lit.*) unite s.o. or s.t. *Mamaknya ~ meréka dlm jodoh* Her uncle united them in marriage. **2** confront. *Hakim ~ saksi itu dgn bukti* The judge confronted the witness with evidence. **ke- 1** accidentally meet. *Saya ~ dia di jalan* I happened to meet her on the way. *Sampai ~ lagi* Till we meet again. **2** be found. *Dicari setengah jam, ndak ~ juga!* I looked for it for a half an hour but it still did not turn up. **menge-i 1** meet, join s.o. **2** find s.t. **menge-kan 1** meet s.o. **2** find s.t. **3** unite, bring two people together. **ter-i** can be found. **-an** finding, s.t. found. *~ batu bertulis* the finding of an inscription. **pen-** discoverer. *~ métode baru* the discoverer of a new method. **pen-an 1** invention, innovation. **2** discovery. **per-an 1** meeting. *~ dgn gurunya* a meeting with his teacher. *~ ramah-tamah* social gathering. **2** companionship.

temurun see TURUN.

tenaga 1 power, energy. *- atom* atomic energy. *- batin* spiritual power. *- dlm* inner, invisible power in martial arts. *- gerak* kinetic energy. *- hidup* vitality. *- kuda* horsepower. *- listerik* electric power. *- luar* exterior, visible power in martial arts. *- panas bumi* geothermic energy. *- pembeli* purchasing power. *- tempat* (*Phys.*) potential energy. **2** personnel, staff, force. *- ahli* expert. *- kerja* manpower, labor force. *- kerja trampil* skilled manpower. **ke-kerjaan** matters pertaining to manpower. *dlm bidang ~* in the field of manpower. *- pekerja* workers, labor force. *- pengajar* teaching staff. *- terdidik* trained staff. **ber-1** powerful, have strength. *Untunglah aku masih ~ memegang kau* Fortunately I still had the strength to hold you. **2** equipped with a power source. *~ listrik* electrified. **di-i** (*Lit.*) powered. *Pesawat itu ~ oléh motor jét* That plane is powered by jet engines.

tenang 1 calm, composed. **2** quiet, still. *Saya minta -* Silence, please. (**ber-**)**-²** face s.t. calmly. **men-kan** calm s.o. down. *Coba -kan anak itu* Please calm that child down. **ke-an 1** calm and quiet. **2** composure. **pen-** s.o. or s.t. that soothes and calms. *~ saraf* sedative.

tenar, ténar 1 noise. **2** well known. *penyanyi - a* popular singer. **ment-kan** make s.o. well-known. **ke-an 1** noise. **2** popularity, fame.

ténda 1 tent. **2** awning. **3** top of a pedicab.

tendang a kick with the heel or side of the foot. *-*

terajang kicking and stamping. *- tumit* stamping the foot. **men- 1** kick. *~ pantat* kick s.o.'s behind. **2** (*Coll.*) expel s.o. *Karena ketagihannya, Rauf didr sekolah* Because of his addiction, Rauf was expelled from school. **ter-** kicked. **-an** (*Sport*) kick. *~ pertama* kick-off. *~ sudut* corner kick. **pen-** s.t. to kick with.

tendas (*Lit.*) decapitation. **men-** decapitate.

téndéns, téndensi tendency. **ber-** tendentious.

téndénsius tendentious.

ténder bid, offer.

téner paint thinner.

téng₁ tank (container). *- bénsin* gasoline tank.

téng₂ (*Ch*) lantern.

téng₃ sound of a bell.

tengadah gaze upward. **men-** look up. *Ia ~ melihat pesawat itu* He looked up to see the plane. **men-i** look up at s.t. *Plafon itu yg ku-i dlm tidur telentang* That was the ceiling I looked at while lying on my back. **men-kan** cause s.t. to face upward. *Ia ~ mukanya* He tilted his face upward. *Ia ~ tangannya sambil beramin* He lifted the palms of his hands and said amen.

tengah 1 middle, center. *di - kamar* in the middle of the room. *berdiri di - 1* stand in the middle. **2** take a neutral stance. *- bulanan* semimonthly. *- dua ratus* 150. *- empat puluh* 35. *- hari* noon. *- hari rembang* high noon. *- jalan* on the way, halfway through. *Di - jalan hujan!* Halfway there and it rained! *- malam* midnight. *- naik* about nine a.m. *- rumah* inner room. *- tiga* half past two. *- turun* about three p.m. **2** among, midst. *Di - kami ada org Amérika* There was an American among us. *ke -* to the fore, into the midst of things. *Anaknya dibawa ke -* His child was brought forward. *memperlihatkan ke - masyarakat* bring into the midst of society for their observation. **3** in the process of. *Ia memperhatikan para pegawai yg - bekerja* He was observing his employees who were going about their work. *- ia menari kecil, datang majikannya* Just as he was in the process of doing a little dance, his boss came in. **-²** middle. *Pohon itu berdiri di ~ alun-alun itu* The tree stands in the middle of the square. *di ~ kami* in our midst. *di ~ terang* in the middle of broad daylight. **se-1** half. *~ jalan* halfway. *-- jam* half an hour. *~ masak* half-done. *jam ~ empat* half past three, 3:30. *kerjaan ~ hari* half-day work. *~ hati* half-hearted. *Kalau ~ hatimu, janganlah kamu pergi* If you feel halfhearted about it, do not go. *~ matang* 1 half-ripe. 2 half-cocked. 3 soft-boiled, not cooked through. *~ miring otak/tiang* somewhat crazy. *~ umur* middle-aged. **2** some. *~ penduduk tak percaya kpdnya* Some of the inhabitants do not believe him. *~ org* some people. **se- se- 1** some. **2** vaguely, not entirely. *Kalau bekerja jangan ~* If you do s.t. do not do it halfway. **men- 1** move to the center. *Dr pinggir ia ~* From the edge he moved to the center. **2** middle, intermediate. *kelas ~* middle class. *sekolah ~* secondary school. *Anak yg ~ lelaki* The middle child is a boy. **3** average. **4** be neutral. *politik ~* a neutral policy. **5** intercede, mediate. *Ia akan ~ dlm soal ini* He will mediate this problem. **men-i, menge-i 1** intercede, mediate. *PBB ~ pertengkaran itu* The UN interceded in the conflict. **2** intervene. *~ pendébatan* intervene in a debate. *"Diam!" bentak Nurdin* ~ "Silence!" snapped Nurdin, intervening. **men-kan** come between. *Datanglah keluarga ~ dan menyabarkan kami* The family came between us and got us to calm down. **menge-kan 1** set forth. *~ bukti yg kuat* present strong evidence. *Dlm rapat itu dike-kannya apa-apa yg terasa oléhnya* In the meeting he set forth everything he felt. **2** (*Leg.*) subpoena, summon. **-an 1** middle level. *pegawai ~* middle level employee. **2** 50 cent piece. **pen- 1** mediator, arbiter. **2** o. with neutral attitude. **3** s.t. used to separate two sections. *Lemari itu dipakai sbg ~ antara kamar makan dan kamar duduk* They used the cupboard as a divider between the dining and living rooms. **per-an 1** the middle. *Abad ~* Middle Ages. *pd ~ bulan* in the middle of the month. *~ jalan* halfway. *kelas ~* middle class. **2** the average. *diambil ~nya, . . .* on the average, . . .

téngak-téngok look about repeatedly.

tengal (*Jkt*) badly cooked, tough.

tengara signal, sign.

tengari noon.

tenggak men- swallow, gulp down.

tenggala a plow. **men-** plow. **pen-** plowman.

tenggalung k.o. civet cat.

ténggang *- hati/rasa* considerate, thoughtful. **ber-** endeavor to carry on. **ber-²(an)** show respectful restraint toward e.o. *- men-* be mutually considerate. **men-** restrain. *~ rasa* restrain o.'s feelings. **memper-kan 1** get along on, be economical. **2** consider. **ke-an** consideration.

tenggara S.E. *Asia - S.E.* Asia. **men- 1** in a S.E. direction. *angin selatan ~* S.-S.E. wind. **2** go S.E. *Stl meninggalkan pelabuhan, kapalnya ~* After leaving the harbor, the boat sailed in a S.E. direction.

ténggék ber-, men- to squat.

tenggelam 1 sink, be under water. *Kapal -* The ship sank. *Ssdh hujan lebat kampung-kampung di pinggir sungai -* After the heavy rain the villages along the river were underwater. **2** sink below a surface, disappear. *Matahari -* The sun set. *Masing-masing - dlm pikiran sendiri-sendiri* Each was lost in his own thoughts. **men-kan 1** cause s.t. to sink. *Kapal selam ~ kapal penjelajah* The submarine sank the cruiser. **2** make s.t. disappear. *Waktu sekian lama itu hampir ~ kenangannya* Such a long time almost made the memory of it disappear. **pen-an** sinking, torpedoing.

ténggér ber- 1 be perched on a branch, roost. **2** settle down, stay. *Tapi mobil itu tdk mau pergi, tetap ~ di situ* But the car would not leave; it was as if it had settled there. **-an** perch, roost.

tenggérét cicada.

tenggiling scaly anteater.

tenggiri Spanish mackerel. *- luding* k.o. mackerel.

ténggok (*Jv, Jkt*) basket.

tenggorok, tenggorokan (*Anat.*) throat, larynx.

tengguli molasses.

tengik 1 rancid, pungent. **2** (*Coll.*) spiteful. **ke-an 1** rancidity. **2** (*Coll.*) spitefulness.

tengil₁ (*Jv*) swell, bulge. **men-** swell.

tengil₂ tending to be sarcastic in a hurtful way.

tengkalang k.o. rice storage shed on stilts.

tengkar dispute. *- mulut* **ber-** *mulut* **1** quarrel, dispute, squabble. **2** conceited. **ber-(an)** quarrel (with e.o.). *Kalau ~ dgn adik, saya selalu yg disalahkan* When my little sister and I have a quarrel, I am always blamed for it. **men-i** fight over s.t. *Nasib kita di tangan Tuhan, tdk ada siapapun yg dpt ~nya* Our fate is in God's hands, no o. can dispute that. **memper-kan** make s.t. the subject of a dispute. *Meréka ~ soal Irian* They argued over the problem of New Guinea. **-²an** quarrel often. *Sering-sering aku lihat dia ~ dgn diréktur* I often saw her quarrel with the director. **pen-** a conceited person. **per-an** dispute, fracas.

tengkawang name of several k.o. *Dipterocarpaceae* trees, including those which yield illipe nuts.

téngkék k.o. bird.

téngki 1 (*R.R.*) tank car. **2** (gas) tank. *~ air* water tank.

téngkoh (*Ch*) prepared opium.

tengkok see TENGKUK.

tengkorak (*Anat.*) skull, cranium.

tengku term of address and reference for certain Malay nobility.

tengkuk 1 nape of neck. **2** bunch (of bananas). **3** stalk of rice.

tengkulak broker, middleman.

tengkuluk headcloth, turban.

tengkurap lying flat on o.'s stomach. **ber-, men-** lie flat, face down on the ground. *Ia menyuruh kawan-kawannya ~ di celah-celah rumpun padi* He commanded his friends to lie prostrate between rice plant clusters.

tengkuyung k.o. mollusk.

tenglang (*Ch*) a Chinese person.

téngloléng (*Ch*) paper lantern.

téng-néng sound of railway crossing warning bell.

téngok *- kanan* (*Mil.*) Eyes right! **men- 1** view s.t. *~ tanaman di ladang* view the plants in the field. *~ pakaiannya, ia org asing* Based on what his clothes look like (lit., when o. looks at his clothing) he is a foreigner. **2** visit. *~ teman yg sakit* visit a sick friend. **3** look. *~ ke kanan* look to the right. **4** make predictions. *~ peruntungan* tell fortunes. **men-i** repeatedly look at or visit. **men-kan** turn o.'s head to look. *Ia ~ kepalanya memandang ambinnya* She turned her head to look at her sling. **pen- 1** visitor. **2** observer.

téngténg₁ k.o. chewy sweet confection. *- gepuk* k.o. sweet made with peanuts and sugar. *- jahé* confection with ginger. *- kacang* k.o. peanut brittle.

téngténg₂ see TÉNTÉNG₁.

tengu k.o. tiny mite or bug.

ténis, ténnis tennis. - *méja* ping-pong, table tennis. **pe-** tennis player. **per-an** matters pertaining to tennis. *dunia* ~ world of tennis.

ténong large, covered container to carry food in.

ténor tenor.

ténsi (*Med.*) **1** tension. **2** blood pressure.

ténsiméter device to measure blood pressure.

téntamen (*Acad.*) preliminary examination.

téntamina (*Acad.*) preliminary examinations.

tentang 1 place directly opposite, facing, or above. *Kantornya di - setasiun* His office is across the street from the station. *Matahari di - kepala* The sun was directly overhead. **2** exactly at or on. - *dadanya di sebelah kiri* on the left side of the chest. **3** about, regarding. *Ia tak tahu suatu juapun - itu* He did not know a thing about it. **se-1** exactly opposite. *Ia duduk ~ saya* He sat just opposite me. **2** just exactly at. *sama ~* flush up against. **ber-** be opposite. *Rumahnya ~ dgn mesjid* His house is opposite the mosque. *~ mata* face to face. **ber-an 1** be in contradiction, be incompatible. *Uraiannya ~ dgn kenyataan* His explanation contradicted the facts. *Tarian itu ~ dgn agama kita* That dance is incompatible with our religion. **2** be in conflict. *Ia selalu ~ dgn majikannya* He is always in conflict with his boss. *~ paham* have conflicting opinions. **3** be face to face. *~ musuh* be face to face with the enemy. **men- 1** gaze directly at. *~ muka ibunya* look into his mother's face. *~ matahari* look at the sun. **2** facing toward. *duduk di muka pintu ~ laut* sit in front of the door facing the sea. *~ angin* against the wind. **3** oppose. *~ politik pemerintah* oppose gvt. policy. *Dua suara ~* Two votes were against. **4** defy. *tindakan yg ~ hukum* a action which defied the law. *~ bahaya maut* defy death. **men-i** repeatedly oppose. *~ musuh* face the enemy. *Ia ~ usul semacam itu* He opposes proposals of that kind. **men-kan 1** bring o.s. face to face with. *Ia ~ pintu* He faced the door. **2** cause s.o. to face. *Ia ~ adiknya ke pintu* He had his brother face the door. **memper-kan 1** oppose. **2** contrast. *Istilah ini diper-kan dgn istilah itu* This term was contrasted with that term. **ter-** contradicted. *Kebenarannya tak ~ pula* The truth could not be contradicted any longer. **-an 1** rcsistance, opposition. **2** at stake. *Jiwa anakmu menghadapi ~nya* Your child's life is at stake. **3** challenge. **pen-** the opposition, opponent. **pen-an 1** resistance. **2** opposition, conflicting. *~ kemauan* a conflict of desires. **per-an 1** conflict, controversy. *~ kesukuan* ethnic conflict. **2** contradiction, contrast. *Segala tindakan selalu merupakan ~* Everything he did was the opposite of what was wanted. **3** opposition, resistance.

tentara (*Mil.*) army. - *pendudukan* occupation army. - *tetap* regular army. - *payung* paratroop unit. - *pilihan* elite troops. **ke-an 1** military. *lagu-lagu ~* military songs. **2** military forces. **pe(r)-an 1** military barracks. **2** army base.

ténténg₁ men- carry in o.'s hand, while walking.

-an things carried in the hand, carry-on luggage. *barang ~* hand-carried goods.

ténténg₂ see PETÉNTANG-PETÉNTÉNG.

tentera see TENTARA.

tenteram quiet, peaceful. *hidup ~* a peaceful life. **men-kan 1** pacify. **2** reassure, calm. *Ia ~ hati anak-anak itu dgn kata-kata manis* He appeased the children with sweet words. **ke-an** calm, tranquillity. *~ di gang dan kampung ini* peace and quiet in this alley and neighborhood. **pen-** s.t. that soothes. **pen-an** reassurance.

téntir 1 tutorial. **2** preliminary exam. **men- 1** give s.o. a tutorial or preliminary exam. *Mbak Sri ini perlu di- dulu* Sri has to pass her mid-terms first. **2** (*Sl.*) educate.

tentram, tentrem see TENTERAM.

tentu 1 fixed, definite. *menurut masa yg -* according to a specified time. *Jawabnya blm -* His answer is not definite yet. *tak - arahnya* **1** no fixed direction. **2** every which way. **2** sure, certain. *Sdh -* That is for sure. *Ia - menang* He is certain to win. - *saja* certainly. **-nya** certainly, of course. *~ tdk semua laki-laki begitu* Of course not all men are like that. **ber-²** certainly, positively. **men-** certain, stabilized. *tdk ~* variable, indeterminate, vague. *angin tdk ~* variable winds. *perasaan yg tak ~* a vague feeling. *Ia blm bekerja; jadi hidupnya blm ~* He does not have a job yet; so his life has not stabilized yet. **men-kan 1** determine, establish. *~ hari berangkatnya* determine the day of departure. *~ syarat* set a condition. **2** make certain about s.t. *~ suatu penyakit* diagnose a disease. *~ idéntitas* determine an identity. *~ sebab-sebab* establish the causes. **ter- 1** certain, sure. *suatu hal yg ~* a sure thing. *Setiap celaan, ~ buat kami* Each criticism was surely meant for us. **2** certain, s.t. or s.o. specific but unnamed. *Kami dlm hal-hal ~ selalu berpendapat sama* On certain matters we always have the same opinion. *~ jumlahnya* a fixed amount. *kecuali pd saat-saat ~* except on fixed times. **ke-an 1** certainty. *Ia ditémbak sblm ada ~ ia bersalah atau tdk* She was shot before it was certain that she was guilty. **2** stipulation. *Ia bertindak di luar ~ tugasnya* He acted against the stipulations of his job. **3** determinate, clear, certain. *lilin yg tdk ~ sinarnya* candle with a wavering light. **berke-an** be sure, certain. *tdk ~* unsure, uncertain. **pen- 1** o. who determines s.t. *~ alokasi bantuan* s.o. who allocates aid. **2** s.t. determining. *faktor ~* decisive factor. **pen-an** act of determining s.t. *Bésok ~nya. Siapa yg beruntung* The decision will be made tomorrow. Who will be the lucky o.? *~ kebijaksaan* policy formulation.

tenuk k.o. tapir.

tenun weaving affairs. *tukang -* weaver. *kain -* woven cloth. **ber-, men-** weave. **-an** fabric, woven product. *kain ~* woven cloth. **pen-** weaver. **pen-an** weaving. **per-an 1** textile mill. **2** textiles.

tenung 1 fortune-telling. **2** horoscope. **3** enchantment, wizardry or witchcraft. **ber-** tell fortunes. **men-(kan) 1** tell fortunes. **2** bewitch s.o. **-an** fortune-telling. **pen-** fortune-teller. **pen-an, per-an** fortune-telling, soothsaying.

téodolit (*Tech.*) theodolite.

téokrasi theocracy.

téolog theologian.

téologi, téologia theology.

téologis theological.

téorém (*Math.*) theorem.

téorétikus theoretician.

téorétis theoretical.

téorétisi theoretician.

téori theory. - *himpunan* (*Math.*) set theory. **ber-** theorize. **ber-²an** theorizing, **ment-kan** theorize about s.t.

téoris theorist.

téorisasi theorizing.

téoritikus see TÉORÉTIKUS.

téoritisi see TÉORÉTISI.

téosof theosopher.

téosofi theosophy.

tép₁ see TIP₁.

tép₂ see TIK₁.

tepak a light slap. **men-** slap slightly. ~ *air di dulang, terpecik muka sendiri* Slapping a tray full of water will only get your own face splashed. **-an** slap.

tépak betel box. - *rokok* cigarette case. - *tembakau* tobacco pouch.

tepas₁ bamboo wickerwork (used as railing, wall, etc.). *empat - dunia* the four points of the compass. **ber-** protected by bamboo wickerwork. **men-(i)** screen s.t. with such a screen.

tepas₂ (*Jv, Sd*) veranda, porch.

tepa slira (*Jv*) principle of putting o.s. in another's place, i.e. not doing s.t. o. would not want done to o.s.

tepat 1 exact, precise. *perhitungan yg - an* exact calculation. - *jam empat* exactly four o'clock. *utara -* due north. *Ia duduk - di muka saya* He sat right in front of me. - *guna* efficient, effective. **ber- guna** be efficient. **ke-gunaan** efficiency. **2** appropriate. *pilihan -* most appropriate choice. **-²** directly, precisely. *Bibi itu memandang ~ muka suaminya* The woman looked her husband straight in the eye. **-nya** to be exact. *Ia ke Jkt hari ini. ~ jam sembilan* He is going to Jarkarta today; at nine to be exact. **ber-an** coincide. *Datangnya ~ dgn hadirnya Pak Ayub di kantor itu* His arrival coincided with the presence of Mr. Ayub in the office. *Pendapatnya ~ dgn pikiran saya* His opinion coincides with my views. *Hari berangkatnya ~ dgn tgl satu Muharram* His departure date happened to fall on the first of *Muharram*. **men-** go straight. *Ia ~ ke rumahnya* He went straight to his house. *Jalan ini ~ ke pasar* This road leads straight to the market. **men-i 1** head straight for s.t. **2** fulfill. ~ *janji* fulfill a promise. **men-kan 1** aim, direct. *Ia ~ pasangannya ke rumah itu* He directed his aim at that house. **2** set, adjust. ~ *jam* set a clock. **ke-an 1** happen to be,

coincidentally. *Ia ~ ada di rumah* He happened to be at home. **2** accuracy, exactness, precision. ~ *waktu* punctuality. **berke-an** coincidentally, accidentally. *Perkawinannya ~ pd bulan puasa* His marriage coincided with the fasting month. **-an 1** destination. **2** aim, purpose. **pen-an** adjustment, correction. **per-an** coincidence.

tepaut difference between two quantities, time between two events. *Bédanya - lima rupiah* The difference amounts to five rupiah.

tépdék tape deck.

tépék numeral classifier for thin, sticky objects. *dua - tembakau* two quids of tobacco. *empat - mentéga* four pats of butter. **ber-²** soiled with sticky smears (of mud, sap, etc.). **men-** sticky, stick on.

tepékong (*Ch*) idol.

tepekur see TAFAKUR.

tepi side, edge, periphery. *ke -* (placed) to o. side. - *baju* hem of jacket. - *jalan* side of the road. - *langit* horizon. - *laut* seashore. - *sungai* riverbank. **ber-** be bordered by s.t. *péci ~ emas* rimless cap with gold trim. **ber-kan** have s.t. along the edge. *kain ~ mérah* cloth with a red border. *jalan ~ pepohonan* a road lined with plantings. **men-1** move to o. side. *Meréka menanti rakit ~* They waited for the raft to move aside. **2** go along the side of (road, etc.). **men-kan** move s.t. to o. side, pull s.t. over. ~ *sepéda ke trotoar* pull o.'s bike over to the sidewalk. **menge-kan 1** place s.t. at the side. ~ *mobil* park a car at the side of the road. **2** ignore, neglect. ~ *kewajiban* ignore o.'s responsibility. **-an 1** edge, border, hem. ~ *ilmu* learned person, scholar. ~ *mata* sweetheart. **2** bathing place by the riverbank.

tepis₁ men-1 skim, glide low. *Burung ~ di laut* The birds skimmed over the sea. **2** skim s.t. ~ *susu* skim the milk. **-an** s.t. skimmed. ~ *susu* skim milk.

tepis₂ men- ward off s.t. *Témbakannya di- oléh penjaga gawang* His shot was blocked by the goalie. **men-(²)kan 1** ward off with the back of o.'s hand. **2** push s.t. aside. *Terpaksa ia ~ dedaunan yg menghalangi jalanan* He was forced to push aside the shrubbery obstructing the path again and again. **ter-** warded off. **pen-an** (act of) warding off.

tepok₁ worn-out, run-down.

tepok₂ see TEPUK.

tépok lame.

tépos flat-bottomed.

tepo sliro see TEPA SLIRA.

tepuk light blow. - *persahabatan* a friendly tap. - *berbalas* tit for tat. - *dada* beating o.'s breast. - *sebelah tangan* do s.t. which cannot be successful, to love without hope of having o.'s love requited (lit., clapping with o. hand). - *sorak/tangan* applause. - *tari* dance accompanied by hand clapping. - *tepak* all k.o. clapping. **ber-** engage in clapping. *Para hadirin ~ tangan riuh* The audience applauded loudly. ~ *sebelah tangan* effort made in vain, receive no love in return (lit., clap with o. hand). **ber-²** repeatedly make clapping noises. *Sepanjang malam ombak* ~ All night long the waves splashed. **men-** clap, slap. ~ *dada* thump o.'s chest. *Ia* ~ *bahuku* He slapped my shoulder. **men-²** slap repeatedly. *Ia* ~ *pistolnya* He patted his pistol. **men-kan** slap with s.t. ~ *tangannya* clap o.'s hands. **-an 1** clapping, applause. **2** beater. ~ *kasur* mattress beater.

tepung 1 flour, esp. rice flour. - *larut* k.o. cassava flour. - *tawar* rice flour mixed with water and the leaves of the *setawar* plant, used in ritual purifications. **men-tawari** ritually purify s.o. with such a flour mixture. **2** powder. - *kanji* cornstarch. - *ragi* baking powder. - *tulang* bonemeal. **men- 1** pound into flour. ~ *beras* pulverize rice. **2** powdery. **men-kan** make s.t. into flour. *Kedelénya di-kan* The soybeans are made into flour.

ter- see also entries with **tr-**.

tér₁ tar. **men-** tar (a street, etc.).

tér₂ see TIR₁.

tera official seal. **men- 1** seal s.t. **2** calibrate. ~ *pipét* calibrate a pipette. **3** print s.t. **men-kan 1** calibrate. **2** stamp, seal, imprint s.t. **ter- 1** officially stamped. **2** printed. *tdk* ~ indescribable. *Kegembiraannya tak* ~ His joy was indescribable. **-an 1** seal. **2** imprint. **pen-** inspector of weights and measures. **pen-an** calibration. **per-an** print office.

terabas men- 1 take a shortcut, bypass. **2** (*Coll.*) bypass red tape or other obstacles by bribing. **-an** shortcut.

terada see TIADA.

terajang see TERJANG.

teraju (*Lit.*) a balance, pair of scales.

terak slag, cinder. - *api* cinders. - *dapur* kitchen rubbish. - *nasi* hard crust adhering to the rice pot.

terali latticework, bars (of window), trellis. - *kapal* ship's railing.

teraling k.o. bird.

terampil see TRAMPIL.

teram-temeram (*Lit.*) overcast.

terang 1 clear, bright. - *benderang* very bright, clear. - *bulan* 1 moonlight. **2** k.o. pancake with peanuts and other ingredients. - *cuaca* a clear sky, nice weather. - *gemblang* bright and clear. - *hari* bright day. - *hati* bright, smart. - *lampu* lamplight. - *lengkap* full particulars. - *mata* clairvoyant. - *matahari* sunlight, sunshine. - *tanah* twilight. - *temarang/temerang* radiant, brilliantly clear. - *terus* transparent. **2** evident. *Sdh -lah* It goes without saying. - *jelas* absolutely clear. **men-jelaskan** clarify. ~*jelaskan cita-cita luhur* clarify noble aspirations. **-² 1** very clear, bright. **2** frank, aboveboard. *Abang* ~ *menolak bujukanku* My older brother openly rejected my attempts to persuade him. ~ *gelap* dusk, twilight. ~ *kain* not too clear. ~ *laras* vague, unclear light, e.g. twilight. **-nya** i.e., in other words. *utk* ~ for clarity's sake. **ber-²** bluntly, frankly. *Ia* ~ *mengatakan segala keluhannya* He frankly stated all his complaints. **men-** dawn, become light. *Hari mulai* ~

The day has begun to dawn. **men-i 1** light s.t. *Lampu* ~ *jalan* The lamp illuminated the street. *-ilah jalan!* Light the way! **2** remove undergrowth. ~ *kebun* weed a garden. **men-kan 1** explain, clarify. *Ia* ~ *keadaannya* He explained his situation. ~ *sikapnya dlm suatu perselisihan* explain his attitude in a dispute. **2** declare, state. *Ia* ~ *dirinya tak mampu* He declared himself financially insolvent. **3** illuminate s.t. **4** indicate. *Tanda-tanda ini* ~ *akan datangnya hujan* These signs indicate rain. **ke-an 1** information. ~ *dasar* baseline data. *utk* ~ *lbh lanjut* for further information. **2** explanation. ~ *tanda-tanda* legend of the symbols on a map. ~ *ahli* an expert's explanation. ~ *kerja* (*Ling.*) grammatical object. **3** official statement. ~ *pemerintah* the gvt.'s statement. ~ *kelakuan baik* statement of good conduct. ~ *pabéan* customs declaration. **-²an** frank, open, blunt. *Saya akan* ~ *pdmu* I will be very frank with you. *Meréka* ~ *memihak Jepang* They openly sided with the Japanese. **pen-** o. who explains. **pen-an 1** providing information. *Kementerian* ~ Ministry of Information. **2** explanation, clarification. **3** illumination, lighting. ~ *jalan* street illumination.

terap₁ k.o. tree, the bark of which is used in making bark cloth.

terap₂ arranging, applying. **men-** adjust, apply, arrange. **men-kan** apply. ~ *prinsip Pancasila pd hidup sehari-hari* apply the principles of *Pancasila* to daily life. **-an** applied. *ilmu bahasa* ~ applied linguistics. **pen-** o. who applies s.t. **pen-an/penge-an 1** assembling. **2** application.

terap₃ groove along blade of kris. **ber-** inlaid. **men-** do inlaid work. **-an** inlayed design.

terap₄ see TIARAP.

térapéutik, térapéutis therapeutic.

térapi therapy.

térapis therapist.

teras 1 (*Biol.*) hard core of certain trees, xylem. **2** essence, nucleus. - *penampang réaktor atom* the nucleus of the cross-section of a nuclear pile. **3** principal element, elite. *pejabat-pejabat* - key officials. **men-** take the essence only.

téras porch, terrace. **ber-** have a porch or terrace.

terasi condiment made from pounded and fermented shrimp or small fish.

teratai k.o. lotus.

teratak shed, temporary hut.

terawang₁ ber- full of holes. **men-** make holes (in s.t.). **-an** s.t. full of holes. *bahan tipis* ~ thin fleecy material.

terawang₂ men- muse, be lost in thought. *Matanya* ~ *memandangi lembah* Lost in thought, he gazed at the valley. ~ *langit/udara* daydream, build castles in the air. **men-i** cause s.o. to be lost in thought, trouble o.

terawéh, terawih see TARAWÉH.

terban collapse (dam, riverbank). *Hampir semua pematang - di hujan keras* Almost all the bunds in the paddy gave way in the heavy rain.

terbang₁ 1 fly. *Burung elang itu - tinggi* That hawk

is flying high. - *layang* glider flying. *pagi blm - lalat* early dawn. **2** disappear. - *pikiran* losing o.'s mind. *minyak harum yg* - perfume that evaporates. **3** rapidly ascending. *inflasi yg - ini* this rapidly escalating inflation. **be(r)-an** fly (of many things), fly every which way. *Peluru-peluru ~ di sekitarnya* Bullets were flying all around him. **men-i** fly over. *~ laut* fly over the sea. *~ lin Jkt-Singapura* fly the Jkt-Singapore route. **men-kan 1** cause s.t. to fly, blow s.t. away. *Ia ~ burung* He let the bird fly. *Atapnya di-kan angin* The wind blew their roof away. *~ astronaut ke angkasa luar* put an astronaut into outer space. *~ layang-layang* fly a kite. **2** flee with s.t. *Ia ~ uang bank* He fled with the bank's money. **pen-** flyer, aviator. *~ uji* test pilot. **pen-an** (*Av.*) flight. *~ yg lima jam lamanya* a five-hour flight. *~ lanjutan* connecting flight. *~ perintis* flight to remote areas.
terbang₂ (*Jv*) k.o. tambourine.
terbis (*Lit.*) landslide.
terbit 1 rise, emerge. *Matahari -* The sun is rising. **2** arise, well up. - *keinginan utk berjalan* A desire to travel arises. - *dr hati yg suci* from the bottom of o.'s heart. **3** appear, come out. *Surat kabar tdk - hari ini* The paper did not come out today. *Majalah itu - tiap minggu* The magazine is published every week. **men-kan 1** cause, produce. *Soal itu ~ kekacauan* That matter has caused unrest. *Éjékannya ~ tawa org ramai* Her mockery caused general laughter. **2** publish. *~ majalah Détéktif dan Romantika* publish the magazine *Detektif dan Romantika*. **3** put in print. *Ia ~ pendapatnya di ruang "Kontak Pembaca"* He published his opinions in the *Kontak Pembaca* column. **-an 1** publication. *Buku ini ~ Bandung* This book is published in Bandung. **2** edition, issue. *~ berséri* serial. **pen-** publisher. **pen-an 1** publication. *dlm ~* in press. **2** publishing house. **3** edition, issue.
terbus a fez.
terbut large bolt, stud.
teréak see TERIAK.
terém see TRÉM.
térem see TIRAM.
teri 1 k.o. tiny sea fish. **2** of small importance. *koruptor kelas -* small-fry hoodlums.
teriak 1 a scream. - *org kesakitan* the scream of s.o. in pain. **2** yell s.t., shout s.t. *"Ceritakan Bu!" - anak-anak serempak* "Tell us, Ma'am!" the children shouted simultaneously. **ber-** scream, shout. *Meréka semakin riuh, bersorak dan ~* They were increasingly noisy, cheering and shouting. **ber-²** keep shouting. *Ia ~ minta tolong* He kept shouting for help. **men-i** shout at s.o. *Ia ~ adik-nya* He shouted at his brother. **men-kan 1** yell out s.t. *Ia ~ tiap-tiap kata* He yelled out each word. **2** show off. *Ia ~ kepandaiannya kpd teman-temannya* He was showing off his skill to his friends. **-an** scream, shout. *~ di luar masih saja terdengar riuh* The loud shouting outside kept up.
terigu wheat.
terik₁ 1 extreme, intense. *Tangannya diikat -* Her

hands were tied tightly. *panas -* suffocating heat. **2** intenseness. - *panas matahari* the intensity of the heat of the sun. **men-kan** intensify s.t. *~ ikatan* tighten the knot. *~ bantal* make the pillow firmer. **ke-an** extreme heat (of sun).
terik₂ fried spiced beef.
terima acceptance. - *jadi* ready for occupancy, use, etc. (of house, manufactured product, etc.). - *kasih* thank you. **ber-** *kasih* be grateful, express o.'s thanks. *~ kasih atas kemurahan Tuhan* be grateful for God's generosity. *Jangan kalian ~ kasih kpdku* You do not have to say thank-you to me. - *salah* admit guilt. **men- 1** accept, approve. *Ia ~ segala tuduhan* He accepted all charges. *~ nasib* accept o.'s fate. **2** receive. *~ surat* receive a letter. *Kabinét ~ baik laporan Menlu* The cabinet agreed with the foreign minister's report. *~ télpon* take a call. **3** (*Coll.*) be passive. *Rakyat kecil masih ~* The ordinary folks still take it all passively. **men-kan** hand s.t. over. *Ia ~ suratnya kpd ayahnya* He handed his letter to his father. *Gubernur ~ penghargaan kpd para bupati* The governor handed out commendations to the district heads. **pen- 1** receiver. *~ tamu* o. who receives guests. *alat ~* (*Tech.*) receiver (radio, telephone, etc.). **2** (*Coll.*) resigned, acquiescent. **pen-an 1** acceptance. *~ anggota baru* the acceptance of new members. **2** revenue. *~ dr minyak bumi* oil revenues. **3** reception. *~ tamu* reception of guests. **4** receipt. *~ surat* receipt of a letter.
teripang sea cucumber, sea slug.
teritip k.o. barnacle.
teritis, teritisan covered passageway (under eaves of house, within covered bridge, etc.).
téritor territory.
téritorial territorial.
téritorium territory.
terjal steep, sheer. *Léréng gunung itu -* The mountain slope was steep. **ke-an** steepness.
terjang thrust with part of body, kick the feet, attack, lunge. - *tumit* driving the heel into the ground for firmer support. **men-** lunge, attack. *Serdadu itu ~nya sampai jatuh* The soldier knocked him down. **men-i** trample on. *~ belukar* trample on the underbrush. **men-kan** lunge at with. *Ia ~ kakinya* He kicked with his foot. **pen-an** act of lunging.
terjemah (*Isl.*) translation of the Koran. **men(t)-kan** translate. *Roman-roman Pramudya di-kan ke dlm bahasa-bahasa asing* Pramudya's novels are translated into foreign languages. **-an** translation. *~ ke dlm Bahasa Indonésia* a translation into Indonesian. **pen(t)-** translator. *~ lisan* interpreter. **pen(t)-an** translating.
terjun 1 jump down. *Ia - ke dlm air* She dived into the water. - *bébas/indah* free fall. - *payung* parachute jumping. **2** enter a field of study or activity. *Ia - ke dunia politik* He entered into the world of politics. **ber-an** jump in large numbers. *Meréka ~ dr langit* They jumped down in large numbers from the sky. **men-i 1** jump in(to). *~ danau* dive into a lake. **2** occupy o.s. with s.t. *Ia*

~ *soal yg sulit itu* She threw herself into that difficult problem. **men-kan** cause s.t. to dive downward. *Ia ~ anjingnya ke dlm air* He dropped his dog into the water. *Ia di-kan di Irbar* He was dropped by parachute in W. Irian. ~ *diri* throw o.s. *Léna ~ diri ke dunia pendidikan* Lena threw herself into education. **pen-** jumper. ~ *(payung)* parachutist. **pen-an** jumping. ~ *payung* parachute jumping.

terka a guess, conjecture. **men-** guess, surmise. *Anda bisa ~ ada berapa kacang di botol ini?* Can you guess how many beans there are in this bottle? **-an** guess, conjecture, supposition. **-²an** game of guessing. **pen-** o. who guesses. **pen-an** guess, conjecture, supposition.

terkadang see KADANG₁.

terkam springing leap of a predator. **men-** pounce on. *Tiba-tiba kucing itu ~ tikus* Suddenly the cat pounced on a mouse. *Ia ~ léhér bajuku sambil menggertak giginya* He grabbed the collar of my shirt while grinding his teeth. **-an 1** a pounce. **2** grip of a predator. ~ *bius* the grip of drugs.

terkun [*dokter dukun*] doctor practicing traditional folk medicine.

terkup (*Lit.*) **men-** fall on s.t.

termala suffering, languishing.

térmik thermal.

términal terminal. - *bis* bus terminal.

términologi terminology.

termis thermal.

térmit termite.

térmodinamika (*Phys.*) thermodynamics.

térmométér thermometer.

térmonuklir (*Phys.*) thermonuclear.

térmos thermos bottle.

ternak livestock. - *potong* beef cattle. **be(r)-** breed. ~ *ayam* raise chickens. **men(t)-kan** breed animals. **pe-** breeder. ~ *unggas* poultry breeder. **pe-an** animal husbandry.

ternang (*Lit.*) jug.

terobos men-, men-i 1 break through. *Pencuri ~ pagar* A thief broke through the fence. *Angin dingin ~ dr celah dinding* A cold wind penetrated the cracks in the wall. **2** cut in a line or queue (at a bank, etc.). **pen- 1** piercer. **2** burglar. **3** o. who cuts into a line or breaks a regulation. ~ *peraturan* o. who does not adhere to regulations. **pen-an 1** a break-in, burglary. **2** breakthrough, act of penetration. **-an** penetration.

teromel see TROMEL.

teromok pleasingly plump.

teromol see TROMEL.

terompah k.o. rough wooden or leather clog. - *kuda* horseshoe.

terompét trumpet, bugle. **men-kan** proclaim loudly.

térong see TERUNG.

teropong 1 telescope, binoculars. **2** tube. **men- 1** look through a telescope. *Nakhoda ~ pulau* The captain looked at the island with his spyglass. **2** observe carefully, study, scrutinize. *Pani-*

tia itu ~ keadaan negeri The committee studied the country's situation. **men-i** examine carefully, focus carefully on s.t. **pen-an 1** telescopic research. **2** study, close observation.

téror terror. **men(t)-** terrorize. **pen-** terrorist. **pen(t)-an** terrorizing.

téroris terrorist.

térorisme terrorism.

terowongan tunnel.

terpa men- 1 (*Lit.*) jump at (often in anger or passion). **2** attack (of meteorological phenomenon). *Angin dingin ~nya* A cold wind caught up with her. **-an** attack. ~ *matahari* The blows of the sun.

terpal tarpaulin, canvas.

terpaut see TEPAUT.

terpédo see TORPÉDO.

terpekur see TAFAKUR.

terpelajar see AJAR₁.

térpentén turpentine.

térsiér tertiary.

tertawa see TAWA.

tertib 1 order. - *hukum* legal order. **2** ceremony. - *acara* 1 standing orders. 2 program. - *nikah* marriage ceremony. **3** orderly, correct. - *sopan* well mannered, decent. **- men-** regarding orderliness. *masalah ~* the problem of law and order. **men-kan 1** straighten up, put in order. *Ia ~ kamar tidur* She straightened up the bedroom. **2** control, curb. ~ *diri* keep o.s. under control. **ke-an 1** orderliness, law and order. ~ *umum* public order. **2** correct conduct. **pen-** s.o. who keeps order. **pen-an** control, curb.

terubuk k.o. fish with highly prized roe.

teruf see TERUP.

teruk (*Lit.*) extreme, excessive. *penyakit -* a violent disease.

terum see DERUM₂.

terumbu ridge of rock exposed at low tide.

teruna 1 youth, youthful. **2** (*Mil.*) cadet.

terung, térung eggplant.

terungku (*Lit.*) prison. **men-kan** imprison. **ke-an** imprisonment.

terup (*Crd.*) **1** trump. **2** k.o. game similar to whist or bridge.

terus 1 straight, direct. *Ia pergi dr rumah - ke rumah sakit* He went from home straight to the hospital. - *saja!* Straight ahead! - *mata* clear-sighted. - *terang* candid, straightforward. *Ia mengatakan - terang bhw ialah yg mencuri uang* He frankly admitted that he stole the money. - *terang saja, Etsa!* Out with it, Etsa! **ber-** *terang* mince no words, be frank. **ke-terangan** candor, straightforwardness. **2** straight away, immediately. *Sampai di rumah ia - makan* As soon as he arrived home he ate. **3** continue, keep on. *Ia bekerja -* He kept on working. *Anginnya - menghébat* There continued to be a strong wind. **4** (*Coll.*) then, next. - *dia bilang saya nggak mau* Then she said I did not want to. **se-nya** from now on, henceforth. *Dan ~ meréka hidup senang* And they lived happily ever after. *Mudah-mudahan ia séhat ~* Let us hope he will be healthy from now on. *dan begitulah/lain-lain* ~ and so forth, etc. **ber-²** continually. *Ia ~ meminta uang pd ayahnya* He continually asked his father for money. **ber-an** continually, uninterruptedly. **- men-, -²an** continuous, on and on, constant. *hujan yg* ~ continuous rain. *Ia ~ mengikuti meréka* She constantly follows them. **men-i** break through s.t., penetrate. **men-kan 1** continue. *ia ~ perjalanan* He continued the trip. **2** forward, pass (on). *Ia ~ surat kpd majikannya* He forwarded a letter to his boss. **ke-an 1** inadvertently go straight ahead. *É! Mau bélok kanan, kok* ~ Hey, you were supposed to turn right, but somehow you went straight ahead. **2** (*Tech.*) transmissivity. **-an 1** continuation, sequel. *Cerita ini tak ada ~nya* This story has no sequel. ~ *Jl. Kawi/Jl.* ~ *Kawi* the extension of Kawi St. **2** canal, channel. ~ *Panama* Panama Canal. ~ *Inggeris* English Channel. **pen-** s.o. or s.t. that continues s.t. ~ *cita-cita révolusi* those who carry on the aspirations of the revolution. *génerasi* ~ the next generation (which will continue s.t.). **pen-an 1** continuation, sequel, resumption. ~ *suara* projection of the voice. **2** continuity.

terusi verdigris, copper sulfate.

terwélu (*Jv*) hare.

tés (*Coll.*) a test. **men(ge)-, nge-** test. **pen(ge)-** o. who administers tests. **pen(ge)-an** testing. ~ *mengenai beberapa hipotésa* testing of several hypotheses.

tésaurus thesaurus.

tési (*Ch*) teaspoon.

tésis thesis. - *sarjana* master's thesis.

tesmak (*Coll.*) glasses, spectacles.

téstamén, téstamént will, testament. - *politik* political testament.

tetabuhan music with percussion to accompany dancing.

tetak 1 chop, hack. *luka* - wound caused by a chop (of machete, etc.). **2** circumcized. *Adikku baru saja* - My little brother has just been circumcised. **men-(i)** hack. **men-kan 1** hack at s.t. **2** hack with s.t. ~ *parangnya ke pohon* hack into a tree with a machete. **-an 1** a chopping blow. **2** a notch from hacking. **3** (*Jv*) circumcise. **pen-** o. who chops or hacks. **pen-an** hacking.

tetal men- be compact, compressed. *Isinya* ~ The contents are compact. **men-kan** compact s.t. ~ *karung dgn jagung* fill up a sack with corn. **pen-an** making s.t. compact.

tetampah sieve, winnowing basket.

tetamu (*Lit.*) guest.

tetanaman crops.

tetangga neighbor. **ber-** be neighbors. *Saya senang sekali* ~ *dgn Ibu* I am delighted to be your neighbor. **ber-kan** have s.o. or s.t. as a neighbor. ~ *dokter anak* have a pediatrician for a neighbor.

tétanus tetanus.

tetap₁ 1 permanent, constant. *penduduk* - permanent resident. *Keséhatannya - baik* His health remained good. *Keadaannya - spt dulu* The situation is the same as before. *pd kepanasan* - at a stable temperature. *karyawan* - permanent employee. *- hati* steadfast, firm, resolute. **2** settled, decided. *Soal itu masih blm* - That matter has not been settled yet. *Pajaknya blm* - The tax has not been decided yet. *pendirian* - consistent opinion. **3** persistent, unchanged. *Meréka - tdk mau bayar* They persisted in not wanting to pay. *Kami - pd keputusan itu* We will abide by the decision. - *hidup* still manage to stay alive. **men- 1** settle at, maintain a permanent residence at. *Ia ~ di kota ini* He is a permanent resident of this city. **2** stabilize. *Pukul enam suhu menurun dan* ~ At six o'clock the temperature decreased and became constant. **men-i 1** fulfill. ~ *janji* keep a promise. **2** carry out. ~ *peraturan pemerintah* carry out a gvt. regulation. **men-kan 1** decide, determine. *Rapat ~ ia menjadi utusan luar negeri* At the meeting he was appointed to be overseas representative. ~ *peraturan* draw up a regulation. ~ *undang-undang* pass a law. **2** maintain, establish, secure. *Ia ingin ~ kedudukannya di parlemén* He wanted to maintain his position in parliament. *Ia ~ janji utk datang hari ini* He kept his promise to come today. ~ *hati/tékad* encourage. **3** determine. *Ia bertugas ~ harga-harga* He was in charge of fixing the prices. *spt yg di-kan dlm pasal satu* as stipulated in article o. **ke-an 1** decision. ~ *pajak* tax assessment. **2** firmness, determination. **3** constancy, steadiness. **berke-an** be determined. **-an** (*Math., Tech.*) a constant. **pen-** permanent resident. **pen-an 1** determining, decision, decree. ~ *waktu kunjungan* establishment of visiting hours. ~ *harga* price regulation. ~ *ketua panitia* appointment of a committee chairman. **2** fulfillment. ~ *janji* fulfillment of a promise or agreement.

tetap₂ (*Lit.*) **men-** blot up a liquid (ink, water, etc.). **pen-** absorber (blotter, dishrag).

tetapi but, yet. *Ia miskin - suka menolong org* He is poor but he likes to help people. *murah - bagus* cheap but nice. **-²an** (*Coll.*) ands, ifs, or buts. *Datang segera, tanpa ~!* Come immediately, without ands, ifs, or buts!

tetarub (*Jv*) stage with decorations (of leaves, papers, and fruits).

tetas men- 1 crack or slit s.t. open by force from the interior. *Ia ~ témbok* He cracked open the wall from the inside. **2** hatch. *Telor ayamku blm* ~ My hen has not hatched her egg yet. **men-kan 1** cause s.t. to break out. *kejadian yg ~ huru-hara* an event that caused a riot to break out. **2** hatch s.t. **-an** s.t. hatched. *sejumlah ~ ayam* a number of newly hatched chicks. **pen-an** hatching. *tempat ~* hatchery.

téték teat. **men-** suckle. *Bayi itu ~ pd bibinya* The infant suckled at his aunt's breast. **men-i** give suck to, breast-feed. ~ *anaknya* breast-feed o.'s child. **men-kan** have s.o. else breast-feed a baby. *Terpaksa saya ~ bayi saya pd bahu susu* I was forced to have my baby breast-fed by a wet nurse.

téték-bengék trivial matters and details of various

kinds. *Saya tak mau memperhatikan segala ~ itu* I did not want to pay any attention to all those trifling matters.

tetel (*Jv*) glutinous rice steamed in coconut milk.

tetélan (*Jv*) bones with a bit of adhering meat.

tetélo a poultry disease, Newcastle disease.

tetér (*Jv*) **men-** hit repeatedly. **ke-an** in chaos, dispersed, disordered.

tetés 1 drop. *se- darah* a drop of blood. **2** (*Jv*) molasses. **ber-an** full of drips, dripped with. *Mahkotanya ~ embun* Its corona dripped with dew. **men-** drip. *Air ~ dr méja* Water dripped from the table. **men-i** sprinkle on s.t. *~ luka dgn spiritus* sprinkle alcohol on a wound. **men-kan** expel a liquid drop by drop. *~ obat* dispense medicine with a dropper. *~ air mata* shed tears. **-an** drop. *~ air* drops of water. *~ darah* 1 drop of blood. **2** descendant. *~ darah Diponegoro* a descendant of Diponegoro. *~ péna* writings. **pen-** dropper. **pen-an** sprinkling, dispensing drop by drop.

tetirah (*Jv*) go s.w. for a cure. **ber-** vacation in a health resort area. **pe-an** vacation resort for health. *Panti ~ Anak* Institution for Children's Health Resorts.

tétoron k.o. synthetic material.

tetua₁ (*Jkt*) moles, age spots.

tetua₂ elder, head.

tetuang (*Lit.*) bamboo wind instrument.

tetumbuhan all k.o. plants.

Teuku, Teungku /teku, tengku/ title of leader in Aceh.

tévé₁ (*Coll.*) television.

tévé₂ [*tweede vrouw*] (*Coll.*) 2d wife, mistress.

téwas 1 killed in action, slain. *- dlm pertempuran* killed in battle. *Seratus delapan penumpang pesawat DC-8 -* 108 passengers of a DC-8 perished. **2** lose. *- perangnya* lose the war. **3** (*Lit.*) defect, flaw. **men-kan 1** defeat, overcome. *Ia ~ musuhnya* He defeated the enemy. **2** kill, slay. *Harimau ini tlh ~ sepuluh org* This tiger has killed 10 people. **ke-an 1** defeat. **2** disaster, mishap.

téwél (*Jv*) unripe jackfruit.

téyol (*Jv*) exhausted.

Tg. [*Tanjung*] (*Geog.*) cape.

Tgk. [*Tengku*] a title of certain nobility.

tgl. [*tanggal*] calender date.

th. [*tahun*] year.

thd., thdp. [*terhadap*] toward, with regard to.

théma see TÉMA.

théologi, théologia, théologis see TÉOLOGI, TÉOLOGIS.

thérapi see TÉRAPI.

thérapis see TÉRAPIS.

Thian /tian/ (*Ch*) heaven, God.

THT [*Telinga, Hidung, Tenggorokan*] ear, nose, and throat specialist.

thn. [*tahun*] year.

T'hoa. [*Tionghoa*] Chinese.

thok /tok/ (*Jv*) only, so much and not a bit more. *Tiga hari -* Three days and no more.

thp. [*terhadap*] toward, to.

THR₁ [*Tunjangan Hari Raya*] bonus received near holidays.

THR₂ [*Taman Hiburan Rakyat*] public recreation and entertainment park.

THT [*Telinga, Hidung, Tenggorokan*] ear, nose and throat specialist.

tiada not, not existing. *- besar* not large. *- org di sini* There is no o. here. *- mampu* unable to afford or do s.t. **ke-mampuan** condition of inability to achieve or do s.t. *- mupakat* lack of consensus. **ke-mupakatan** lacking consensus. **-nya** the nonexistence of. *~ sarana yg baik* the lack of good facilities. **men-kan, memper-kan 1** abolish, destroy, nullify. *~ perhubungan ke tempat itu* break off communications to that place. *~ kerja malam* abolish the night shift. **2** consider nonexistent. *Ia ~ Tuhan* He denies the existence of God. **ke-an 1** lack, non-existence. *~ kerja* unemployment. **2** nothingness. *hilang dlm ~* all gone. **pen-an 1** negation. **2** abolition, discontinuance.

tian (*Anat.*) womb. *dlm -* pregnant. **ber-** pregnant. **men-i** make s.o. pregnant.

tiang 1 pole, post, mast. *- bendéra* flagpole. *- pagar* fence post. *- kapal* ship's mast. *- agung* (*Naut.*) main mast. *- gantungan* gallows. *- ibu rumah* the main pillars of a house. *- salib* a cross. *- seri* chief pillar of a house (to which honor is given). *- tanam* house pillars implanted in the ground. *- topang* (*Naut.*) foremast. **2** s.t. essential in an endeavor. *- keluarga* backbone of the family. *- negara* pillars of state. *- penghidupan* main source of income. **ber-** propped up, supported. **men-i** provide with poles, posts, masts, etc.

tiap₁ 1 every, each. *- hari* every day. *- org* each person. *- meréka yg membacanya* each of them who read it. **2** each time. *- saya muncul, pasti dia minta uang* As soon as I appear, he is sure to ask for money. **se-, -²** each and every.

tiap₂ 1 (*Ch*) dosage. **2** key money (to enable o. to rent quarters). **men-** give key money.

tiarap face downward. **ber-** lie prone. **men-** (lie) face downward. *Prajurit-prajurit itu ~ di tanah yg basah* The soldiers lay face downward on the wet ground. *Pendéta ~ di hadapan Syiwa* The priest lay prostrate before Shiva. **men-kan** place s.o. or s.t. face downward. *Ia ~ adiknya; dan kemudian memeriksa lukanya* He made his brother lie face downward and then examined the wound. **ter-** fallen face downward. *Korban bom mati ~* The bombing victims fell dead face downward.

tiba arrive. *Ia - di Bandung dgn selamat* He arrived safely in Bandung. *Saatnya tlh -* The moment has come. *-²* suddenly, unexpectedly. *~ saja dia jatuh* All of a sudden she fell. **se-** upon arrival. *~nya di hotél ia menélpon rumahnya* Upon his arrival at the hotel he telephoned home. **ke-²an** suddenness.

tiban see DUKUN.

Tibum [*Ketertiban Umum*] Public Order.

tidak no, not. *-, ia - dpt pergi* No, he cannot go. *- besar* not big. *dgn - adanya perencanaan khusus* without special planning. - *adil* unjust, unfair. **ke-adilan** injustice. - *boléh/dpt* - 1 no doubt. 2 it is inevitable. - *boléh* - *org Jepang sangat penting di Asia* There is no doubt that the Japanese are very important in Asia. *Saya hrs ikut,* - *boléh* - I must go, I cannot do otherwise. - *cocok* not fitting, incompatible. **ke-cocokan** incompatibility. - *jelas* unclear. **ke-jelasan** obscurity. - *jujur* dishonest. **ke-jujuran** dishonesty. - *kunjung* never. - *lain* - *bukan* nothing else than. *Penyakit ini* - *lain bukan disebabkan kurang tidur* This illness has been caused by nothing other than lack of sleep. - *. . . lagi* no longer. *Saya* - *tinggal di sini lagi* I do not live here anymore. - *pun* if not. *Kalau boléh, saya minta ujian hari Senén,* - *pun tak apa* If possible, I request the test on Monday, if not, that is all right. -² nonsense. *Ia mengatakan hal yg* ~ *di rapat* He talked nonsense at the meeting. **se-(²)nya 1** at the least. ~ *ia akan mengirim kartu pos kpd saya* At least she will send me a postcard. **2** in any case. *Namun* ~ *keamanan dan nyawa meréka lebih berharga lagi* But in any case their safety and lives are even more valuable. **men-kan, memper-kan** deny, reject (as a reality, possibility). *Ia* ~ *semua perkataanku* She denied every word of mine. **3** ignore. **4** abolish, cancel.

tidur 1 sleep. *Baru jam berapa kok sdh -!* What time is it anyway? How come you are already sleeping! - *ayam* 1 doze, nap. 2 sleep lightly. - *léna/ lenap/nyenyak* sound asleep. - *miring* sleep on o.'s side. **2** slumber, sleep. *bangun dr* - *yg sangat nyenyak* wake up from a very deep sleep. - *siang* afternoon nap. -² lie about, nap. *Ia* ~ *saja di gubuk* He is just lying around in a shed. **(ber)-an** lie down. **men-i 1** (of a man) to have intercourse with s.o. *Mansur* ~ *anak tetangganya* Mansur slept with (had sex with) his neighbor's daughter. **2** lie or sleep on s.t. *Dataran rumput itu biasanya di-i gadis remaja itu* The young girl us. slept on that grassy field. **men-kan 1** put to bed. ~ *anaknya* put o.'s child to bed. *tembang* ~ lullaby. **2** lay s.t. down. ~ *tongkat* lay a cane down. **ter-** fall asleep. *Lama-lama capai juga dan* ~ Finally she became exhausted and fell asleep. **ke-an 1** slumber. **2** bed. **3** oversleep, doze off. *Guru tak datang di kelas karena* ~ The teacher did not come to class because she overslept. *Para pendengar* ~ The audience fell asleep. **seke-an** sleeping together, sharing the same bed. *selapik* ~ be bosom friends, always be together. **ber-seke-an** (*Lit.*) have intercourse. -(²)an lying down. *Burhan membaca koran sambil* ~ Burhan read a newspaper while he was lying down. **pen-** o. who sleeps a great deal. **pe(n)-an** place to sleep.

tifa k.o. drum in E. Indonesia.

tiga three. - *belas* thirteen. - *hari* 1 three days. 2 3d day of s.o.'s death. **men-** *hari* commemorate the 3rd day of a person's death. - *persegi* (*Math.*) triangle, triangular. - *puluh* 30. - *ratus* 300. - *sekawan* be in a clique of three friends together. - *sekawan itu menonjol di sekolah* It is striking the way those three hang around together in school. - *serangkai* triad. - *warna* the tricolor, i.e. the Dutch flag. **ber-** do s.t. in a group of three. *Kami* ~ *tinggal di rumah ini* The three of us are staying at this house. **ber-²** do s.t. three at a time. **men-** do s.t. for the 3d time. **memper-(kan)** divide into three. **ke- 1** third. *buku* ~ the 3d book. ~ *dr kiri* 3d from the left. **2** all three. ~ *buku itu* the three books. *Meréka* ~ *pergi ke rumahnya* The three of them went to his house. **(ke)-²nya** all three. ~ *jatuh di sungai* All three of them fell in the river. **per-** third. *dua* ~ *hasil sawah* ⅔ of the yield of the rice-field. **per-an** T-intersection, three-way intersection. **seper-** a third. *mendapat hasil* ~ get a third of the share. **ke-an** (*Rel.*) trinity.

tijak (*M*) step on, tread on.

tik see KETIK.

tikai difference. **ber-** differ in opinion, quarrel. *Wah! Ramai juga org* ~ *ttg perkara korupsi itu* Say! There was quite a fuss with everyone arguing about that graft case. **men-** (*Lit.*) contradict. **memper-kan 1** differentiate. **2** make s.t. a subject for a quarrel. *Déwan Juri itu senantiasa dpt diper-kan* That panel of judges could always be argued about. **per-an** conflict, controversy, disagreement.

tikam 1 wound s.o. by stabbing (us. overhanded). **2** sword or knife thrust. **ber-²an** stab e.o. - **men-** stab e.o. **men- 1** stab s.o. ~ *musuhnya dgn pisau* stab o.'s opponent with a knife. **2** be cutting, be biting (words, wind, etc.). *Kata-katanya* ~ *hati anaknya* His words hurt his child's feelings. *Angin* ~ *sampai ke tulang* The wind cut right through to the bone. **3** put up a stake in a card game, etc. **men-kan** stab with s.t. -*kan pedang hingga ke hulu!* Thrust a sword to its hilt! **ter-** stabbed. *Ia mati* ~ *dadanya* He died from a stab in the chest. **-an 1** a stab, thrust, jab. **2** stake in gambling. **3** cutting (of wind). ~ *angin gunung* the cutting mountain wind. **pen- 1** o. who stabs. **2** s.t. o. stabs with. **pen-an** a stab, stabbing. **per-an** a fight with daggers or similar weapons.

tikar a plaited mat. - *bantal* bedding. - *ladang* a rough woven mat. - *sembahyang* prayer mat. - *tidur* sleeping mat. **ber-kan** use s.t. as a mat. *hanya* ~ *koran* using only a newspaper for a mat.

tikas (*Geol.*) impression, imprint.

tika-tika skein of yarn.

tikét ticket (us. for transportation but not entertainment).

tikpi (*Ch*) trident.

tiktak sound of a clock, ticktock. **ber-** tick. *jam* ~ the clock's ticking away.

tikung men- 1 curve or bend. **2** make a turn. *Ban G800 Radial* ~ *lebih cermat* G800 Radial tires take curves better. **-an** a bend in the road.

tikus mouse, rat. - *percobaan* experimental mouse. - *belanda* guinea pig. - *kesturi* musk shrew. - *mondok* mole. - *tanah* field mouse. -²an toy mouse.

tilam s.t. to sleep on (mat, blanket, but esp. mattress). **ber-** have s.t. to sleep on. ~ *pasir* homeless.

tilang [*bukti pelanggaran*] traffic ticket. **men-** issue a traffic ticket. *7.988 pengemudi di- dan 1.165 kendaraan ditahan selama razzia itu* 7,988 drivers got traffic tickets and 1,165 cars were detained during that roundup.

tilas (*Jv*) trace. **pe-an** remains of the past. ~ *Diponegoro sedang dipugar* They are restoring the ruins of Diponegoro's (fort).

tilawat (*Isl.*) recitation of the Koran.

tilawatil, tilawatul (*Isl.*) recitation of the Koran. **ment-kan** recite (Koran) in a competition. *Al-Quran di-kan di Médan* The Koranic recitation competition will be in Medan.

tilem-timbul up and down.

tilep n- take s.t. on the sly. *Dia kayak babu yg kepergok* ~ *roti oléh majikannya* She was like a maid who was caught snitching bread by her employer.

tilgram see TÉLÉGRAM.

tilgrap see TÉLÉGRAP.

tilia lime tree.

tilik 1 glance at s.t. (often with supernatural connotation). *baik -nya* keen-eyed. *tukang -* fortuneteller. *kurang -nya* not very observant. *- jahat* evil eye. *pd -nya* in his opinion. **2** visit s.o. **men- 1** tell the future. ~ *nujum* tell o.'s fortune based on astrology. **2** observe carefully, watch. *Ia* ~ *muka-nya di cermin* She observed her face carefully in the mirror. **3** consider, examine carefully. *Ia* ~ *perbuatan itu sbg perbuatan yg salah* He regarded that act as an evil deed. **4** supervise. ~ *org bekerja/pengeluaran* supervise workers, expenditures. **-an 1** prediction. **2** examination, observation. **3** control, supervision. **pen- 1** fortuneteller. **2** supervisor, inspector. ~ *sekolah* school inspector. **pen-an 1** supervision, control. *di bawah* ~ *pemerintah* under gvt. control. **2** observation. *pd* ~ *saya* in my opinion.

tilp. [*tilpon*] telephone.

tilpon see TÉLÉPON.

TIM [*Taman Ismail Marzuki*] Ismail Marzuki Cultural Center in Jkt.

tim₁ men(ge)- 1 boil meat until very tender. **2** steam rice in a certain way. **pc-an** k.o. utensil for cooking rice in this way.

tim₂ team.

timah tin, lead. *- daun* tin foil. *- hitam* lead. *- putih* tin. *- wurung* bismuth.

timang₁ men- rock (a child) in o.'s arms or a cradle. *Ia* ~ *anaknya spy tidur* She lulled her child to sleep. **-an** o.'s favorite child. *dgn* ~ *ibu* coddled. *nama* ~ nickname, nursery name. **-²an** repeated rocking motion. *Perahu kami terkatung-katung dlm* ~ *ombak* Our boat was helplessly floating about in rocking waves.

timang₂ men-(²) 1 (*Lit.*) test the balance of s.t. by shifting it in o.'s hand. **2** observe by holding in the hand. *Ia* ~ *barang itu sblm membelinya* He looked at it carefully in his hand before he bought it. **3** consider an issue carefully.

timba pail, bucket, dipper. *- ruang* **1** container used to bail a boat. **2** the center (and deepest) part of a boat's hull. **ber-** use a dipper, etc. ~ *karang* start a row (lit., scoop up coral). ~ *uang* live in luxury. **men- 1** bail out (a boat). **2** draw (water) from a well, etc. **pen- 1** a container for scooping liquids. **2** o. who scoops out water, etc. **pen-an** scooping, dipping.

timbal₁ balancing. *- balik* on both sides. *Kertas itu tertulis - balik* This paper is written on on both sides. *Meréka bersurat-suratan - balik* They are carrying on a mutual correspondence. *hubungan - balik* reciprocal relationship. **ber-** *balik* be on both sides. **se- 1** in balance, proportionate. *Besarnya tak* ~ They are not of the same weight. **2** equitable, just. *Hukumannya* ~ He deserves his punishment. **ber-(an) 1** be in balance, be mutually equal. *Beratnya* ~ The weights are in balance. *Ia dipelihara* ~ *dgn anaknya sendiri* He was brought up like his own son. **2** be on both sides. *Pohon-pohon itu berdiri* ~ *jalan* Trees stand on both sides of the road. **3** ambivalent. *kata* ~ ambivalent words. **ber-²an** balance e.o. *Meréka menyanyi* ~ They sang alternating with e.o. **men-(i)** counterbalance, counter s.t. **-an** (counter)balance.

timbal₂ see TIMBEL.

timbang₁ weighing. *- rasa* sympathy, consideration of other's feelings. **ber-** *rasa* be sympathetic. *- terima* transfer. *- terima pimpinan* the transfer of command. **men-terimakan** hand over, transfer. ~*terimakan jabatan* hand over an office or post. *- tunai* C.O.D. **se- 1** in balance. *Beratnya* ~ The weight's balanced. **2** in proportion. *Ongkosnya* ~ *dgn beratnya pekerjaan* The cost is in proportion to the hard labor. **menye-kan** harmonize, balance. **memperse-kan** compensate, counterbalance. **kese-an** harmony, balance, equilibrium. **ber-(an)** be of equal weight or importance. *upah yg* ~ *dgn jasanya* a wage commensurate with his services. ~ *kata* exchange words. ~ *pandang* exchange glances. ~ *tanda* exchange engagement rings. *- men- 1* repeatedly weigh (shipment, problem, etc.). **2** weigh e.o.'s feelings. **men- 1** weigh. *Ia sedang* ~ *beras* He is weighing the rice. **2** consider, take into account. *Ia* ~ *perlunya mengadakan rapat* He considered the necessity of calling a meeting. **men-²** play with the idea of. **men-i 1** repay, counterbalance. *Utk* ~ *kebaikannya saya memberi uang Rp500 kpdnya* To repay his kindness I gave him 500 rupiah. **2** be in proportion to. *Upahnya* ~ *usahanya* His wage was in proportion to his efforts. **men-kan** weigh out on behalf of s.o. **memper-kan** consider s.t., mull s.t. over. ~ *kembali* reconsider. *Ia* ~ *permintaan adiknya* He mulled over his sister's request. **-an 1** pair of scales, weights. ~ *daging* meat scales. **2** opinion, criticism, judgment. ~ *buku* book review. **3** equal. *Ia bukan* ~ *isterinya yg terpelajar itu* He is not the equal of his educated wife. **4** rather than. *kerja* ~ *nganggur* work rather than do nothing. **pen-** 1 pair of scales. *roda* ~ balance wheel. 2 counselor. **pen-an** 1 (act of) weighing, balancing. ~ *air* weighing water. 2 considering. **per-an** 1 judgment, opinion. ~ *nilai* value judgment. *menurut* ~ *saya* in my opinion. 2 consideration. ~ *psikologis* psychological consideration. 3 review (of books, etc.).

timbang₂ see KETIMBANG.

timbel 1 (*Jv*) lead (metal). 2 weight on a scale.

timbil sty in eye. **-an** (*Coll.*) suffer from a sty.

timbrung (*Jv*) **men-** 1 interfere in s.o.'s affairs. 2 butt in on a conversation. **-an** interference.

timbul 1 float to the surface, emerge. *Stl dilepaskan pelampung itu - juga* After it was untied, the float rose to the surface after all. *- perasaan yg tdk énak* An unpleasant feeling emerged. *Kursus-kursus politik - di mana-mana* Political courses sprang up everywhere. *- marah* become angry. *- tenggelam* 1 rise and sink, bob up and down. 2 be heavily in debt. 3 unsure. *- tenggelam kerajaan-kerajaan* rise and fall of kingdoms. 2 appear. *penulis yg baru -* an up-and-coming writer. **men-kan** 1 make s.t. to come to the surface. ~ *barang yg sdh lama ditanam* to bring to the surface things that have long been in the ground. ~ *perahu* raise a (sunken) boat. 2 cause s.t. to occur or appear. ~ *kekacauan* bring about chaos. *Kejadian-kejadian itu dpt* ~ *perang* Those events can lead to war. ~ *kesan* give an impression. ~ *kecurigaan* arouse suspicion.

timbun heap, pile. **se-** a pile. ~ *pasir* a pile of sand. ~ *kayu* pile of wood. **ber-** in piles. *Kekayaannya* ~ *di mana-mana* He has wealth piled up all over. **ber-²** piled up, in heaps. *Bukunya* ~ His books were piled high. **men-** 1 be heaped up, become piles. *Di médan pertempuran mayat pemuda* ~ On the battlefield the corpses of young men were piled high. *Hartanya* ~ Her wealth accumulated. 2 be piled up on. *Tanahpun diturunkan* ~ *kubur itu* They tossed earth down, heaping it on the grave. 3 heap s.t. up. ~ *pohon-pohon* heap up trees. **men-i** heap piles on s.t. *Mayatnya di-i dgn tanah* Dirt was heaped over the corpse. *- jurang* fill up a ravine. **men-kan** 1 pile s.t. up. ~ *tanah* pile up dirt. 2 accumulate s.t. *Ia* ~ *bahan makanan* He accumulated food supplies. **ter-** 1 heaped up. *Barangnya* ~ *di muka rumahnya* His goods were piled up in front of his house. 2 buried under, covered with. *Badannya* ~ *pasir* His body was buried under the sand. **-an** a pile, heap. ~ *kerja* piles of work. **pen-** a hoarder. **pen-an** 1 accumulation, piling up. ~ *tuduhan-tuduhan* an accumulation of accusations. 2 hoarding. 3 process of reclaiming land from the sea by piling up earth.

timbus men-(i) fill up s.t. ~ *lobang* fill up a hole.

Timor the island of Timor. *- Timur* E. Timor.

timpa (*Jkt*) punch s.o. **- ber-** fall on top of e.o. *Di hatiku penyedihan dan penyesalan* ~ Sorrow and regret came o. after another in my heart. **ber-²** press in, come in large quantities. ~ *suratnya yg datang* The letters came pouring in. **men-(i)**

1 fall on. *Batu besar* ~ *kakinya* A big stone fell on his foot. 2 descend upon, strike down. *Kecelakaan* ~ *keluarganya* An accident befell his family. *Ia* ~ *musuhnya dgn batu* He struck down his opponent with a sword. **men-kan** 1 cause s.t. to fall upon. ~ *batu ke kakinya* drop a stone on his foot. *Ia merenung-renungkan hukuman apa yg bakal dikan pdnya* Over and over he thought about the punishment that was about to befall him. 2 blame. *Ia* ~ *segala kekeliruan kpd temannya* He blamed all his mistakes on his friend. **ter-, ke-** struck down. ~ *kemalangan* stricken by misfortune. *Seorang penjaga mati* ~ *atap yg runtuh* A guard died when the roof collapsed on him. **-an** befalling of, s.t. which pins down. *- atap itu menyebabkan kematiannya* The collapse of the roof caused his death.

timpal see TIMBAL₁.

timpang unstable, unbalanced. *Méja itu -, kakinya hanya tiga* That table is unstable; it has only three legs. *Ia - jalannya* He is limping. *keadaan yg - an* unstable situation. *pendapat yg - an* a biased or one-sided opinion. *- neraca* unbalanced budget. **men-** 1 be unbalanced. 2 limp. *Mengapa ia* ~? Why is he limping? **men-²** pretend to limp. **ke-an** 1 imbalance. ~ *dlm keseluruhan komposisi* imbalance in the overall composition. 2 lameness. 3 partiality, one-sidedness.

timpas dried up. *sumur -* a dry well.

timpé (*Jkt*) **men-** swipe, pilfer. *Dompét saya di-* S.o. swiped my wallet.

timpuh see SIMPUH.

timpuk (*Jkt*) **men-(i), n-in** throw at. **men-kan** throw s.t. **-an** a throw. ~*nya tepat mengenai mata* Her throw hit him directly in the eyes.

timpus tapering.

Timteng [*Timur Tengah*] Middle E.

Timtim [*Timor Timur*] E. Timor.

timun see MENTIMUN.

timung traditional herbal bath of Kalimantan.

timur east - *Dekat* Near E. - *Jauh* Far E. - *laut* N.E. - *menenggara* E.-S.E. - *Tengah* Middle E. - *tenggara* E.-S.E. **-²** *laut* E.-N.E. **men-** 1 go to the east. 2 eastward. **ke-an** eastern, Asian. *cara* ~ the way of doing things in Asia.

tinambah (*Math.*) addend.

tindak act, action. *- balas* reaction. *- pelaksanaan* executive action. *- pidana* criminal act. *- tanduk* behavior, conduct. **se-** o. step. ~ *demi* ~ step by step. **ber-** 1 take steps, measures. *Polisi* ~ *keras thd perampok itu* The police took harsh measures against the robbers. 2 act. *Ia tak berani* ~ *kalau tak ada perintah* He would not have dared act if he had not been ordered to. **men-** take action against. *Kalau bersalah Présiden Sukarno pun hrs di-* They would even have taken action against President Sukarno if he had been guilty. **men-kan** carry out s.t. ~ *kekerasan* take strong measures. **-an** 1 measure, step. ~ *darurat* emergency measure. ~ *balasan* reprisal. 2 action. ~ *yg nyata* a clear action. ~ *kelanjutan* follow-up. ~ *keras* stern measures. **pen-an** taking measures. *Thd* *pelanggaran ini tlh dilakukan* ~ Against these transgressions action has already been taken. ~ *huru-hara* riot control.

tindas men- 1 crush with snapping action (esp. insects). ~ *kutu* crack a louse. ~ *kala dgn kayu* crush a scorpion with a piece of wood. 2 oppress. ~ *rakyatnya* oppress the people. 3 suppress violently. ~ *pemberontakan* crush a revolt. **ter-** suppressed, downtrodden. **-an** 1 oppression. 2 carbon copy. **pen-** oppressor, tyrant. **pen-an** 1 oppression. 2 suppression.

tindih overlapping. **ber-(an)** 1 be superimposed. *Huruf "O"* ~ *pd titik itu* The letter "O" had been (typed) superimposed on the period. 2 lie on e.o. 3 overlap e.o. *Maknanya* ~ The meanings overlap. **ber-²** 1 all over e.o., strewn on top of e.o. *Korban pengeboman mati* ~ The bombing victims lay dead, entwined and heaped on e.o. 2 dense, crowded. *Org* ~ *di pasar* It was very crowded in the market. **- men-** be placed on top of e.o. **men-, men-i** 1 press with s.t. heavy, place a weight on s.t. ~ *kertas yg kerenyut* press a crumpled piece of paper. 2 suppress. ~ *perasaan hati* suppress o.'s feelings. 3 oppress. *pajak yg* ~ *rakyat* an oppressive tax. **men-kan** press with s.t. ~ *besi pd kertas* press paper with an iron weight. **ter-** be pinned under. *Kakinya* ~ *batu besar* His foot was pinned under a large rock. **ke-an** 1 pressed down, crushed under. *Badannya* ~ *pohon yg rebah* His body was pinned under a fallen tree. 2 have a cramp. *Kakinya* ~ He had a cramp in his leg. **-an** 1 pressure. ~ *yg berat* a heavy pressure. 2 oppression. **pen-** oppressor. ~ *kertas* paperweight. **pen-an** 1 applying pressure or weight on s.t. 2 suppressing. **per-an** overlapping. *Akan dihindari* ~ *masalah yg dibahas* We will avoid overlapping in the issues under discussion.

tindik ber-, men- pierce. *upacara* ~ *telinga* ear-piercing ceremony.

tindis see TINDIH.

tinébar (*Phys.*) dispersoid.

ting₁ sound of a light metallic ring.

ting₂ (*Jv*) lantern.

tinggal 1 live, stay. *Ia - di Garut* He lives in Garut. 2 remain, keep, stay. *Jangan diam, ambillah tindakan!* Do not keep sitting still, do s.t.! *Teman - teman* A friend remains a friend. *- hidup* survive, subsist. 3 be left, remaining. *Sepuluh yg - akan saya kirim bésok* The remaining 10 I will send tomorrow. *Uangnya - berapa?* How much money do you have left? *Lima diambil tiga - dua* five minus three leaves two. *- kelas* be held back a class. 4 all that is left, all that remains. *Karcisnya sdh dibeli, kamu - berangkat saja* The tickets have been purchased, all that is left is for you to go. *- ke popak salak* broke, penniless. *- kulit pembalut tulang* be skin and bones. *- nadi* critically ill. *- pakai* ready to wear. *- tulang* very thin. 5 except. *Semua sdh di sini, - Tono* Everyone's here, except Tono. 6 leave (in set phrases). *- landas/landasan* 1 take off (of planes, projects, etc.). *Dlm Pelita VI*

Indonésia - landas utk menjadi negara industri In the 6th Five-Year Plan Indonesia will take off to become an industrialized nation. 2 lose o.'s perspective. **men-** die, pass away. *Ia tlh lama* ~ She died a long time ago. ~ *dunia* die, pass away. **men-i** 1 live in, stay at. *Ia sdh lama* ~ *rumah itu* He has lived in that house for a long time. 2 leave behind to, bequeath. *Ia* ~ *anaknya sebidang tanah* He left his son a piece of land. **men-kan** 1 leave s.t. behind. *Ia* ~ *dua anak* He left two children (when he died). *Ia tdk* ~ *adat waktu menemui mentuanya* He did not leave behind his good manners when he went to meet his in-laws. 2 leave. *Ia* ~ *negerinya* He left his country. *Ia* ~ *pekerjaannya* He left his job. *Kapan ia* ~ *rumahnya?* When did he leave his house? **ter-** left behind. *Buku saya* ~ *di rumah* I left my book at home. *daérah* ~ backward district (left behind by progress). **keter-an** fact of having fallen behind. ~ *ékspor jati* having been surpassed in the export of teakwood. **ke-an** 1 remainder. ~*nya akan saya berikan lain kali* I will give you the remainder another time. 2 be left out, inadvertently omitted. *Dua kalimat* ~*; tdk ditik* Two sentences were omitted; they were not typed. 3 be left behind. *Ia* ~ *bis* She missed the bus. *Semuanya datang. Basri pun tdk* ~ Everyone came. Even Basri was not left behind. *Bukunya* ~ *di rumah* She accidentally left her book at the house. *Negeri itu sangat* ~ *dlm hal téknik* That country is very much behind in technical matters. ~ *zaman* out of date. **-an** 1 inheritance, bequest. 2 remainder. **pen-** 1 death, passing away. 2 separation. **sepen-** 1 upon or after the departure of. ~ *sdr ke Makassar kami sdh pindah* After your departure to Makassar we moved. 2 after o.'s death. ~ *ayahnya* after her father's passing. **pen-an** 1 estate, inheritance. 2 relic, archaeological remains. 3 remainder, rest.

tinggam (*M*) k.o. conjuration which causes death by piercing o.'s likeness with a stinger from a ray fish.

tinggi 1 high, tall. *menara - a* high tower. *berbadan - be* tall. *perguruan - institute* of higher education. *harga - high* prices. *-nya delapan méter* The height is eight meters. *- awan* sky-high. *- cakap* brag. *- hati* 1 proud, boastful. 2 conceited. *- rasi* have a lucky star. 2 advanced. *umur yg tlh - an* advanced age. *peradaban yg - advanced* civilization. *pegawai - high-ranking* official. *- hari* late in the morning. **se-²** no matter how high. ~ *burung bangau terbang, tentu kembali ke kubangan* O. always comes back to o.'s place of origin. **se-²nya** the highest possible. *jasa* ~ the highest service. **men-** 1 go high, rise, advance. *Matahari makin* ~ The sun rose higher and higher. 2 boast, be boastful. *Percakapannya makin* ~ His conversation became more and more boastful. *Ia selalu* ~ *thd teman-temannya* He was always boasting to his friends. **men-kan** 1 raise, heighten. *Bantal Tono di-kan* They elevated Tono's pillow. *Kenaikan harga minyak tanah turut* ~ *tingkat inflasi negara*

The rise in the cost of oil had a part in raising the national inflation rate. ~ *diri* boast. **2** increase, enhance. ~ *martabat negara* enhance national prestige. **memper-(kan) 1** make s.t. higher. **2** enhance. ~ *produksi* boost production. **ter-** highest, supreme, top-level. **ke-an 1** (*Coll.*) too high, very high. **2** elevated place (podium, plateau, etc.). *Rumahnya terletak di ~ bukit itu* His house was situated on the top of the hill. **3** altitude, height. **4** boastful. ~ *cakapnya* boastful language. ~ *hati* boastfulness. **pe-** s.o. with formal authority or acknowledged influence within a certain region. **pen-an** heightening, raising, enhancement. ~ *taraf hidup* raising of living standards.

tinggir see TÉNGGÉR.

tinggung ber- to squat.

tingkah₁ 1 behavior, action. *-nya baik* His behavior is good. - *laku/langkah/perangai/polah* behavior. **2** caprice, whim. *gadis yg banyak ~nya* a girl of many whims. **ber- 1** act, behave. ~ *anéh* act strange. **2** be capricious, fickle. **3** act up, put on airs. *Motor itu sdh ~ pula* The engine has begun acting up again. *Hati-hati di kota besar, jangan ~* Be careful in a big city; do not act like you know everything. *Blm puas Hanafi ~ dgn pakaiannya* Hanafi never tires putting on airs with his clothes. **men-i** put on airs toward s.o., contradict.

tingkah₂ k.o. drum. **ber-²** alternate in a musical presentation. *Meréka ~ memperdengarkan piano dan gitar* They played the piano and guitar by turns. **men-** answer. *"Ia ya, Bu Sulami," Bu Abdullah ~ dgn terpaksa* "Well, Mrs. Sulami," Mrs. Abdullah replied grudgingly. **men-(i)** strike a musical instrument to accompany other instruments. **-an** musical accompaniment.

tingkal borax.

tingkalak (*M*) k.o. fish trap.

tingkap 1 (*Lit.*) window. **2** blinds. **men-** (*Lit.*) peer from a window. **-an** small window.

tingkar (*Sd*) **men-** surround. **ter-** surrounded.

tingkat 1 floor, story. *rumah tiga* - a three-story house. - *kapal* ship's deck. **2** rung, step. *tangga sepuluh* - a 10-rung ladder. **3** level, degree. *kebudayaan yg tinggi -nya* high level of civilization. *pegawai negeri - tiga* gvt. official at the 3d level. - *pertumbuhan* growth rate. - *kecerdasan* IQ level. - *tiga* Third Estate (of the French Revolution). - *tinggi* high level. **men-tinggikan** step up. *mentinggikan produksi* step up production. **4** phase, stage. **se- 1** o. level. *Ia naik ~* She advanced o. level. **2** of the same level. *Kamarnya ~ dgn kamar saya* Our rooms are on the same floor. **ber-(²) 1** multistoried. *Rumahnya ~* He has a multistoried house. **2** with many consecutive levels. *masyarakat yg ~* a stratified society. *sawah yg ~* terrace wet rice fields. *Pekerjaan ini hrs dikerjakan ~* This job must be done in stages. **men- 1** rise, mount. *Panasnya ~* The temperature rose. *Harga beras ~* The price of rice went up. *Jumlah kematian ~* The number of dead is mounting.

Umurnya ~ He became older. **2** be promoted, advance. *Ia ~ kelasnya* He went up on the social scale. **3** terrace. *Petani di Bali biasa ~ sawahnya* Farmers in Bali us. terrace their wet rice fields. **men-² keep increasing. men-kan 1** increase s.t., raise. ~ *produksi* increase production. ~ *tawaran* raise the bid. ~ *taraf penghidupan* raise the standard of living. **2** upgrade. *Semua fasilitas akan dikan* All facilities will be upgraded. **-an 1** floor, story. **2** class, level, standard. **3** stage, phase. ~ *permulaan* initial stage. ~ *terakhir* final phase. **pen-an 1** raising (a level), upgrading. ~ *keséhatan* improvement of health conditions. **2** rise, increase, escalation. ~ *produksi pangan* increase of food production.

tingkepan (*Jv*) traditional ceremony held for a woman seven months pregnant.

tingting see TÉNGTÉNG₁.

ting-tong sound of repeated, varied metallic ringing. **ber-²** make such sounds. *Loncéng stasiun berbunyi ~* The station bells kept on going "dingdong."

tingwé [*nglinting déwé*] **1** roll o.'s own cigarette. **2** cigarettes rolled by o.s.

tinja 1 feces, excrement. **2** sewage. *bak -* cesspool.

tinjak stride, step. **bersi-** (*Lit.*) step by step.

tinjau ber-² observe, be on o.'s guard. - **men-** observe at a distance. **men- 1** watch, observe at a distance. ~ *kapal liwat* watch a passing ship. **2** view, consider. *di- dr sudut ékonomi soal ini boléh disebut kurang penting* Looking at it from an economic point of view, this problem can be called unimportant. ~ *kembali* reconsider, review. **3** observe s.t., reconnoiter s.t., survey s.t. *Wakil pemerintah pusat ~ keadaan di tempat* A central gvt. representative studied the local situation. **4** guess from afar. *Ia dpt ~ perasaan ayahnya* He could guess his father's feelings. **-an 1** observation. **2** contemplation, consideration. ~ *buku* book review. ~ *atas buku Umar Kayam semua sangat sarat dgn pujian* All the reviews of Umar Kayam's book are full of praise. **pen-** observer. **pen-an 1** observation, survey. **2** consideration, contemplation. ~ *kembali* (*Leg.*) judicial review. **3** reconnoitering.

tinju 1 fist. **2** (*Sport*) boxing. *Nanti malam ada -* There is a boxing match tonight. **ber-, men-** be engaged in a fist fight. **ber-²an** strike e.o. with the fists. - **men- 1** punch e.o. **2** (*Coll.*) engage in a fist fight. **men-i** punch at. *Kepalan komandan jaga itu terus saja ~* The commander's fist continued to strike out. **ter-** be accidentally struck with the fist. **pe-** boxer. **per-an 1** matters pertaining to fist fighting. *sejarah ~* the history of boxing. **2** fist fight.

tinta ink. **men-i** apply ink to s.t.

Tionggoan (*Ch*) (ancient) China.

Tionghoa Chinese. - *peranakan* Chinese of mixed Indonesian descent. - *totok* Chinese with no Indonesian ancestral background. **ke-an 1** (*Lit.*) Chineseness. **2** act characteristically Chinese. **per-an** Chinese affairs.

Tiongkok China.

tip₁ monetary remuneration.
tip₂ tape recorder.
tip₃ a bit of information. **di-kan** receive some information.
tip₄ adhesive tape.
tip₅ see KETIK.
tipak (*M*) portion, quota, allotment.
tipar (*Jkt*) dry rice field.
tipe type, kind.
tipes (*Med.*) typhus.
tipi see TÉVÉ₁.
tipifikasi typification.
tipikal typical.
tipis₁ 1 thin. *kertas yg* - thin paper. *kain yg* - sheer material. - *telinga* 1 touchy, irritable. 2 sensitive. 2 slight, very small. *harapan yg* - a slight hope. *keuntungan yg* - a slight profit. 3 fine (of thread). **men-** 1 become thin. 2 diminish, become less and less. *Persediaan makanan sdh* ~ The food supply is running low. *Kenangan itu* ~ *hilang dr ingatan saya* That memory has faded away from my memory. **men-kan** 1 make s.t. thin. *Ia* ~ *kayu* He thinned out the woods. 2 dilute s.t. 3 reduce, decrease. ~ *keinginan utk menyerang* reduce the desire to attack. ~ *harapan* reduce hope.
tipis₂ see TYPIS.
tipografi typography.
tipografis typographical.
tipologi typology.
tipologis typological.
tipp-éx /tip ék/ white-out, white correction fluid. **ment-** apply white-out to s.t. **-an** s.t. which has been corrected with white-out.
tipu trick, deceit, fraud. - *daya/muslihat* deceit, trickery. - *tépok* ruse, trick. **men-** deceive s.o. **ter-** cheated, tricked. **-an** 1 deceit, swindle. 2 sham. *dgn* ~ *penyakit* simulating illness. **pen-** deceiver, impostor. **pen-an** deception.
tir₁ (*Che.*) rook, castle.
tir₂ see TÉR₁.
tirah ber- stay in a health resort. **pe-an** health resort.
tirai 1 curtain, blinds. - *bantal* pillow fringe. - *kelambu* mosquito net. - *mirai* blinds of all sorts. 2 partition, screen. - *Besi* Iron Curtain. 3 backdrop. **ber-** with curtains or partitions.
tirakat (*Jv*) do s.t. ascetic (fast, etc.) in order to fulfill a wish or commemorate an event. **ber-** perform asceticism to reach o.'s goal. **-an** jointly perform some ascetic act to achieve or commemorate s.t.
tiram oyster. **pe-an** oyster field or bed.
tiran tyrant.
tirani tyranny.
tiras (*Lit.*) unraveled thread.
tirau (*M*) gnome.
tiri step-, related by the remarriage of a parent and not by blood. *ibu* - stepmother. *anak* - stepchild.
tiris leak through. *Atapnya* - The roof is leaking. **men-kan** 1 cause to leak through. 2 drain. *Beras*

dicuci bersih, direndam, di-kan dan dimasukkan dlm panci The rice is washed clean, soaked, drained, and put in a pan. **ke-an** 1 get wet from a leak. *Kamarnya basah* ~ *hujan* The room got wet from a leak. 2 leak. **-an** a leak. **pen-an** place for draining.
tirta (*Lit.*) water. - *amerta* elixir of life. - *kencana* golden water.
tiru men- imitate, do as s.o. does. ~ *kebudayaan asing* imitate foreign cultures. **men-kan** imitate s.t. ~ *tiap kata* imitate every word. **-an** 1 imitation, simulation. 2 counterfeit, forgery. **pen-** imitator, simulator. **pen-an** imitation.
tirus 1 pointed. *Ékornya panjang dan* - Its tail is long and pointed. 2 haggard. *seorg pria berwajah* - *a man with a haggard face.* **men-** taper, come to a point.
tisik men-(i) darn, mend. ~ *kaus* mend stockings. **men-kan** give to s.o. to mend. *Ini di-kan sama bibi* Give this to the maid to mend. **-an** a mend.
tit sound of a car horn.
titah royal word or command. **ber-** speak, utter (of kings, etc.). **men-kan** command, decree s.o. *Raja itu* ~ *bhw . . .* The king decreed that . . .
titan titanium.
titar (*Lit.*) **ber-²** move quickly back and forth.
tité ham hock.
titel 1 title. 2 column heading. **ber-** have a degree, titled. *Ia* ~ *dokter* He has a medical degree.
titi wooden or bamboo foot bridge. **men-** walk on s.t. elevated, narrow, and long. ~ *jembatan yg sempit* walk along a small narrow bridge. ~ *batang kayu/buih/kawat* perform a very difficult task. **-an** 1 footbridge. 2 narrow path or passageway. ~ *batu* stepping stones.
titih see PETITIH.
titik 1 drop. - *air mata* teardrop. - *api* focus (of a lens). 2 period, point. *menaruh* - *di akhir kalimat* place a period at the end of a sentence. - *beku* freezing point. - *berat* 1 center of gravity. 2 heart, center. - *berat dr pembélaan negeri itu dipusatkan kpd kekuatan angkatan udara* The heart of the country's defense was centered in the air force. **mem-beratkan** 1 stress, emphasize. 2 count heavily on. *Negeri itu mem-beratkan pembélaanya pd dua kapal perang* That country relied heavily on two battleships for its defense. **pen-beratan** stressing, accentuation. *pen-beratan yg terlalu besar di séktor industri modérn* too big an emphasis on the modern industrial sector. - *biaya kembali* break-even point. - *buhul* meeting point of beams in roof. - *cair* melting point. - *didih* boiling point. - *dua* colon (punctuation). - *impas* break-even point. - *jenuh* saturation point. - *kata* decision. - *koma* semicolon. *tdk karuan* - *komanya* unfathomable, difficult to figure out. - *lebur/ léléh/luluh* melting point. - *lidah* a saying. - *mata* point of view. - *nol* zero level. - *pangkal* basic stand from which to initiate a discussion. - *perubahan pokok* turning point. - *potong* point of intersection. - *pusat* center. - *seléra* have o.'s mouth water. - *sentuh* (*Av.*) point of touch down. - *tolak*

point of departure. **ber-** *tolak* have as a starting point. **ber-** 1 drip. *Darahnya masih* ~ His blood is still dripping. 2 have a period. *Kalimat ini tdk* ~ This sentence has no period. **ber-²** dotted. **men-** 1 drip. *Darahnya terus-menerus* ~ The blood drips continuously. 2 place a period. **men-i** sprinkle on s.t. ~ *luka dgn obat* sprinkle the wound with medicine. **men-kan** cause s.t. to drip. ~ *airmata* shed tears. **-an** drops, s.t. which was dripped. ~ *air dr genténg* the stream of water dripping from the roof.

titilaras scale of notes.

titimangsa (*Jv*) chronicle, date.

titinada musical note. *pola* - pitch.

titip men-, men-kan entrust s.t. to s.o. for a short period. *Kalau ke Indonésia nanti, saya* ~ *oléh-oléh buat adik saya?* When you go to Indonesia, can I entrust a present for my sister to you? *Boléhkan saya - beli karcis nanti?* Could you pick up a ticket for me later? *Aku - tasku di sini, ya?* I will leave my bag here in your custody, okay? **men-i** entrust to s.o. *Kalau ada teman baik yg bisa di-i pulangnya, ayah tdk usah menjemput lagi* But if there is a good friend with whom we can entrust her for her trip home, Father does not have to go and pick her up. **ke-an** have s.t. left with o. *Saya* ~ *barang yg berharga* I was entrusted to watch some valuable things. **-an** 1 entrusted goods. 2 deposit. **pen-** (*uang*) depositor. **pen-an** 1 depositing. 2 storage place. ~ *pakaian* cloakroom.

titir alarm signal beaten out on drum, gong, etc. **men-** sound an alarm in such a way.

titiran (*Jv*) 1 propeller. 2 k.o. mill.

titis₁ (me)n- 1 (*Jv*) become incarnate. 2 (*Coll.*) descend into o.'s offspring (of traits, etc.). *Sifat kebaikannya* ~ *ke anak bungsunya* His good characteristics were inherited by his youngest child. **-an** (*Jv*) reincarnation. ~ *péna* essay, composition. **pen-an** (*Jv*) reincarnation.

titis₂ see TÉTÉS.

titit₁ sound made by car or motorcycle horn.

titit₂ (*child language*) penis.

titulatur system of titles.

titulér titular. *kaptén* - titular captain.

tiung k.o. bird, mynah and other similar birds.

tiup 1 related to wind instruments. *kwintét* - wind quintet. 2 blow (of wind). - *besar* **men-besarkan** blow up (an affair, event) out of proportion. *Peristiwa itu di-besarkan oléh pemerintah* That event was inflated all out of proportion by the gvt. **ber-** blow. *Angin* ~ *sepanjang malam* The wind blew the whole night. **men-** 1 blow. *Angin soré* ~ *agak keras* The evening wind blew very hard. 2 blow air into or through. ~ *pluit* blow a whistle. ~ *trompét* play a trumpet. ~ *balon-balonan* blow up a balloon. **men-²** blow a problem out of proportion. *Masalah itu jangan di-² agar tdk berkepanjangan* Do not blow that problem up so it will get out of proportion. **men-i** 1 blow on s.t. ~ *api* blow on a fire. 2 blow on s.o. as part of a healing ritual. *Dukun itu* ~ *org yg sakit* The shaman blew on the sick man. **men-kan** 1 cause

to spread, cause to fan out. *Jangan suka* ~ *kabar angin* Do not spread rumors. 2 blow on or up on behalf of s.o. **ter-** blown. ~ *angin* blown by the wind. **-an** 1 blast of wind, blowing. 2 s.t. blown on. **pen-** o. who blows. ~ *gelas* glass blower. ~ *suling* flute player.

tivi see TÉVÉ.

tiwas see TÉWAS.

tiwikrama (*Jv, Wayang*) the process whereby Kresna turns himself into Wisnu in a crisis. **ber-** 1 transform o.s. in a moment of crisis. 2 do o.'s utmost.

tiwul k.o. snack made from dried cassava.

tk. [*tingkat*] 1 level. 2 floor, story.

TK [*Taman Kanak-Kanak*] kindergarten.

TKI [*Tenaga Kerja Indonesia*] Indonesian blue-collar workers and craftsmen employed overseas.

TKS [*Tenaga Kerja Sukaréla*] volunteer worker.

tkt. [*tingkat*] 1 level. 2 floor, story.

tkw. [*tdk kawin*] unmarried.

TKW₁ k.o. cheap liquor.

TKW₂ [*Tenaga Kerja Wanita*] female worker.

TL [*Timur Laut*] N.E.

tlédék see LÉDÉK₁.

tlésék ber-an scattered here and there.

tlh. [*telah*] already.

tlola-tlolo (*Jv*) move (o.'s head) around in fear or worry. *Kepalanya - kuatir kalau-kalau ada org lain yg melihatnya* He moved his head about in fear that s.o. could see him.

tlundak, tlundakan steps, stairs.

Tn. [*tuan*] Mr., esp. for non-Indonesians.

TNI [*Tentara Nasional Indonésia*] Indonesian National Armed Forces.

to₁ (*Jv*) Right? (particle eliciting agreement). *Kan maunya ke sana, -?* You wanted to go there, didn't you?

to₂ (*Ch*) close or fail (of businesses).

to₃ see DATUK.

toalét see TOILÉT₁,₂.

toapékong see TEPÉKONG.

tobat 1 (*Rel.*) repent and forswear. - *dr dosanya* repent o.'s sins. - *pd Tuhan* swear to God to change o.'s sinful ways. 2 learn o.'s lesson and swear off. *Sakit perut sekali itu, aku - minum és apokat* After getting diarrhea once, I learned my lesson and stopped drinking iced avocado. 3 I have had it! That does it! (exclamation of surprise and regret). *O, -! Berapa harga lémon sebotol?* Well, that is it, I give up. How much does a bottle of soda pop cost? **ber-** 1 repent and forswear. *Suami-isteri* ~ *mohon ampun kpd Tuhan* Husband and wife repented and asked God for forgiveness. 2 learn o.'s lesson. **men(t)-kan** cause s.o. to repent and change behavior.

tobel see TOBIL.

toberos see TEROBOS.

tobil My God! (a mild exclamation of surprise and concern). -, *tanamanku mati semua!* Heavens! All my plants are dead.

toblos see TEROBOS.

toboh group.

tobong limekiln.

tobros see TEROBOS.

todak k.o. fish, the gar. *hiu - * sawfish.

todong *tukang - * armed robber. **men- 1** threaten s.o. by pointing a weapon. *Kerjanya cuma ~ pedagang* His only job is strong-arming merchants. *Tangan kanannya ~ ke muka* He thrust his right hand out in a threatening way. **2** commit armed robbery. **men-kan** threaten by pointing with s.t. *Ia ~ pistolnya kpd temannya* He pointed his gun at his friend. **-an 1** threat consisting of s.t. pointed (weapon, etc.). *Ia tdk melawan karena ~ pistol di dadanya* He could not resist because of the pistol pointed at his chest. **2** hold-up, stick-up. **-²an** all k.o. armed robberies. **pen-** hold-up man. **pen-an** hold-up.

toets see TUTS.

tofan see TOPAN.

toga 1 academic gown. **2** judge's robe. **ber-** wear an academic gown or judge's robe.

togé see TAUGÉ.

togél tail-less.

Togog 1 (*Wayang*) a servile character who changes allegiance. **2** opportunist.

togok₁ 1 a log trimmed of all its branches, a rough post or stake. **2** torso, statue of a torso. **3** (*Jkt*) stupid. **ber-, n-** (*Coll.*) sit dully like a bump on a log.

togok₂ k.o. taper lamp.

toh₁ (*Coll.*) nevertheless, after all. *Ia - juga manusia dan makan nasi spt kita* He is, after all, a human being and has to eat just like the rest of us. *Sejahat-jahat anak kita, - dia pancaran darah kita* No matter how bad our child is, he is after all our own flesh and blood.

toh₂ see TO₁.

tohok₁ 1 harpoon or javelin with rope attached. **2** a downward stab. **men-** stab downward. *~ kawan seiring* betray o.'s associates. **men-kan** use s.t. in a downward piercing motion. *Ia ~ tombaknya ke arah musuhnya* He cast his spear down at his enemy.

tohok₂ see BINTANG, PARI₁.

tohor 1 dried up (e.g. after tide has gone out). **2** superficial. *Pengetahuannya - * His knowledge is superficial. **ber-** dry up. *~ air liur* talk a great deal. *tdk ~ kaki* work hard with no time to rest. **men-kan** dry s.t. up. *~ sungai* dry up a river.

toilét₁ /twalét/ process of grooming.

toilét₂ /twalét/ toilet, W.C. *kertas - * toilet paper.

tojin (*Ch*) Taoist priest.

tojok men- thrust (s.t. long) into s.t. **men-kan** thrust s.t. (of long things). **-an** a thrust.

tojor men- hit with a fist.

tojos n- (*Jkt*) perforate, pierce. **pen-an** perforation. *~ tanda gambar* indication of o.'s election choice by perforating the appropriate party symbol on the ballot.

tok₁ just, only. *Berjuang - dgn tdk memakai siasat, adalah ketololan besar* Just fighting without using strategy is very foolish. *Dia hanya bisa makan -!* All he can do is just eat! *Anak saya satu - I* have only got o. child.

tok₂ sound of knocking. *-, -, -, kedengaran suara org mengetuk pintu* Knock, knock, knock, o. could hear the sound of s.o. knocking on the door.

tokcer, tokcér 1 working well, easy to start (of engine), lighting easily (of matches), getting pregnant easily, etc. *Mobil itu kalau distart, - * As far as starting that car goes, it is a snap. **2** the right thing, most efficacious. *Yg paling - adalah mufakat sama Tuhan* The thing which is the most efficacious is to consult with the Lord.

toké₁, tokéh see TAUKÉ.

toké₂, tokék 1 k.o. house lizard with distinctive call. **2** call of such a lizard. **3** term of abuse. *- lu!* You jerk!

tokh see TOH₁.

Tokio Tokyo.

toko shop, store. *- buku* bookstore, bookshop. *- emas* jewelry store. *- kelontong* store selling notions. *- keriting rambut* beauty parlor. *- loak* secondhand shop. *- sandang-pangan* shop selling food and clothing. *- serba ada* department store. *- swalayan* self-service supermarket. **ber-** have or manage a store. **per-an 1** shop matters. **2** shopping complex.

tokoh₁ 1 (*Lit.*) shape, form. *- badan* bodily shape. *- bulat* round shape. **2** personage, prominent figure. *- sastra* literary figure. *Ia - yg penting di konperénsi* He is an important figure at the conference. *- baja* steel magnate. **3** character in a story. **ber-** have the shape of. *rumah yg ~ kapal* a house in the shape of a boat. **men-i** run, lead (a group). *Sudirman ~ pembentukan tentara nasional Indonésia* Sudirman organized the formation of Indonesia's national army. **men-kan** feature s.t. *Amir di-kan sbg calon bupati* Amir was put up as a candidate for resident. **pen-an** characterization.

tokoh₂ men- cheat, deceive. **pen-** cheater, deceiver.

tokok₁ s.t. extra, s.t. added. **ber-** (*Lit.*) with an addition. *~ pula* furthermore. **men-** give or say s.t. extra.

tokok₂ (*M*) hammer. **- men- 1** strike e.o. **2** blame e.o. **men-** tap, pound at. *~ batu* crush stones into gravel. *Berkali-kali Uju ~ pintu* Over and over Uju tapped on the door. *~ kawat* send a telegram.

tokolan (*Jv*) bean sprouts.

tokong₁ 1 (*Lit.*) shaving a woman's hair as punishment. **2** (*Coll.*) short hair (of women). **men-** shave.

tokong₂ rocky islet.

tokong₃ (*Lit.*) Ch temple.

tokowan shopkeeper, store owner.

toksik toxic.

toksikologi toxicology.

toksikosis toxicosis.

toksin toxin.

tol toll, esp. on highways. *jalan - * tollroad.

tolak push away. *- angsur* give and take (esp. in bargaining). *- bala* warding off misfortune. *ratib - bala* recitation of prayers to ward off misfortune. *- bahara/bara* ballast. *- belakang* taking leave of e.o. *- peluru* (*Sport*) shotput (event). *- pinggang* with arms akimbo. - *raih* bargaining. **ber-** 1 (*Lit.*) leave, depart. *Ia ~ ke Singapura* He left for Singapore. *~ belakang* be exactly the opposite of e.o. *Meréka itu kembar tapi sifatnya ~ belakang* They are twins but the exact opposite of e.o. 2 start from s.t., take s.t. as a starting point. *~ dr dalil-dalil* taking the theses as a point of departure. **ber-²** 1 accuse e.o. 2 impose tasks on e.o. **ber-²an** jostle e.o. **- men-** push or parry e.o. **men-** 1 push. *~ keréta* push a handcart. *Pintu di- di muka hidungnya* The door was shut right in her face. 2 push aside, prevent. *Sial tdk bisa di-* Bad luck cannot be avoided. *~ bahaya kebakaran* prevent danger of fire. 3 repel. *~ pukulan musuh* repel the enemy's blows. 4 reject, refuse. *Permintaan saya di-* My request was refused. 5 (*Math.*) subtract. *~ lima dr sepuluh* subtract five from 10. **men-kan** 1 push away. *Kutepiskan tangannya dan ku-kan dadanya kuat-kuat* I warded off his hand and pushed against his chest with all my might. 2 push off on to. *Ia ~ kesalahan itu pd temannya* He threw the blame on his friend. **-an** 1 a push, shove, or parry. 2 a reject. *barang ~* rejected articles. 3 (*Coll.*) rejection. *~ Siti tdk membuat Tono terlalu kecéwa* Siti's rejection did not cause Tono too much disappointment. **pen-** 1 rejecter. 2 repellent. *~ serangga* insect repellent. *~ bisa* antidote, antitoxin. **pen-an** 1 refusal, rejection. 2 warding off.

tolan acquaintance, friend.

tolé (*Jv*) 1 boy. 2 term of address for boys, esp. as *lé*.

toléh men- 1 turn o.'s head. *~ ke kanan* look to the right. 2 look toward by turning the head. *Ia ~ pd seorg pemuda yg berpantalon wol* She glanced toward a young man in woolen pants behind her. **men-kan** cause o.'s head or attention to turn somewhat. *~ wajah* turn o.'s face. *Saya ~ perhatian meréka ke soal lain* I turned their attention to other problems. **-an** a turn of the head.

toleran, toléran tolerant.

toleransi, toléransi 1 tolerance. 2 (*Coll.*) consideration, understanding. *Saya minta -, Pak; saya ndak bisa lebih dr seribu* I am asking for your understanding, sir; I cannot come up with more than 1,000. **men(t)-kan** tolerate.

tolerér, tolérér, tolerir, tolérir men- tolerate.

tolk /tolek/ (*Coll.*) interpreter.

tolok 1 equal, match. 2 standard. *- ukur* measuring rod. **se-** on the same footing. **ber-** with an equal, matched. *tdk ~* peerless. **men-** compare. **pen-** 1 an equal. 2 standard.

tolol stupid, simple-minded. *- benar kamu* You are really stupid. **men(t)-kan, memper-kan** consider s.o. a fool, make a fool of. *~ diri* make a fool of o.s. *Kok mau kamu diper-kan sama si Musa* What is this! You want that Musa to think you are a fool? **ke-an** stupidity, foolishness.

tolong 1 help. *Minta -* Ask for help. 2 please. *- sampaikan pesan saya pd Tities* Please deliver my message to Tities. *- panggilkan Romo* Please call the priest. **ber-²an** give mutual assistance. **- men-** give mutual aid. **men-** help, aid, assist s.o. *Meréka ~ Mulyadi merawat Sérsan Lumbato* They

helped Mulyadi to take care of Sergeant Lumbato. **men-i** repeatedly help with s.t. *Minah ~ mengambil sayuran* Minah helped in collecting vegetables. **ter-, ke-an** 1 helped. *Yg luka itu masih blm ~* The wounded were still not given help. 2 can be helped. *Dia sakit keras; tdk ~ lagi* He is very sick. He is beyond help. **pen-** 1 helper, auxiliary. *bahan baku dan bahan ~* basic and auxiliary goods. 2 rescuer. *regu ~* rescue team. **per-an** help, aid. *~ pertama dlm kecelakaan* first aid.

tom (*Jkt*) bridle.

toma move directly against current or wind (of boats).

tomat tomato. *saus -* ketchup.

tombak 1 spear, lance. *- bertungguh* forked lance. 2 a linear measure of around 3.6 meters. **ber-** armed with a lance. **men-** stab with a spear. **ter-** speared.

tombok additional sum of money. **men-** 1 (*Jkt*) pay extra, pay an additional fee. 2 stake out money in gambling. **men-i** 1 add a sum of money to. *Karena uang yg dibawanya kurang, terpaksa saya -i* Because he did not bring enough money, I had to add some. 2 pay extra (of many persons). *Sdh disepakati org kampung ~ hanya delapan ratus ribu* All the villagers agreed to pay only 800,000 extra. 3 bet on. *Nomer berapa yg kamu -i?* Which number did you bet on?

tombol 1 knob. *- pintu* door knob. 2 button for mechanical devices, push button switch. *- penyetél* dial (of TV, etc.). *- tekan* push button. *Tekanlah - utk membunyikan bél* Push the button to ring the bell.

tombong₁ mortar, artillery.

tombong₂ see TUMBUNG₁.

tomong see TOMBONG₁.

tompang see TUMPANG.

tompél (*Jkt*) birthmark.

tomplok see NOMPLOK.

ton₁ ton. **ber-²** by the ton.

ton₂ [*peleton*] (*Mil.*) platoon.

tonase tonnage. **ber-** have a certain tonnage.

tonér millionaire (in colonial era).

tong₁ barrel, vat, cask. *se- bir* a barrel of beer. *- paku* a keg of nails. *- kosong nyaring bunyinya* An empty barrel resounds loudly. *- sampah* trash bin, garbage can. **-an** by the barrel.

tong₂ sound of a gong, clang.

tongak see DONGAK.

tongcai, tongcoi (*Ch*) k.o. salted greens.

tonggak₁ 1 tree stump. 2 post, pole. *- gantungan* gallows. *- rumah* house pillar. 3 milestone. *- sejarah* historical milestone. *Peristiwa itu merupakan - sejarah sekolah kita* That event was a milestone in the history of our school. **men-** make s.t. erect. *Pancang-pancang utk lampu sdh di- teguh* The stake for the lantern had been firmly implaced.

tonggak₂ men- drink from a container by pouring its contents down o.'s throat.

tonggerét k.o. cicada.

tonggok₁ (*Lit.*) heap, pile. **se-** a heap of. *~ tahi kerbau* a heap of buffalo dung.

tonggok₂ (M) **ber-** perch (of birds).
tonggos (Jkt) bucktoothed.
tongkang barge.
tongkat cane, stick. - *jalan* walking stick. - *militér* swagger stick. - *ampai* divining rod. - *ketiak* crutches. - *komando* baton. **ber-** use (as) a cane. *Org tua itu ~ besi* The old man had an iron walking stick. *~ senduk* be far along in years. **ber-kan** rest on. *rumah yg ~ batu* a house resting on stones. **men-** 1 raise high. 2 cane s.o. **men-kan** 1 hold up with s.t. *~ jas pd bantalnya* use a jacket to prop up o.'s pillow. 2 raise. **pen-** assistant.
tongkéng (Anat.) small of the back. *tulang* - coccyx.
tongkol₁ tuna fish.
tongkol₂ 1 knob (of wood). *se- mas* a gold nugget. 2 stem of an ear of corn.
tongkrong n- 1 (Coll.) squat. 2 (Coll.) sit around doing nothing, hang out. 3 idle, not in use. *kol yg ~ di lapangan menunggu penumpang* a minibus sitting on the square waiting for passengers. **men-i** 1 squat on s.t., hang out around at. *~ warung sambil membaca komik* hang around a stand, reading comic books. 2 squat on land. *Tanah org kok di-i!* That land belongs to s.o. How come they are settled there? **men-kan** let s.t. remain idle. *~ mobil yg kempés bannya* Let a car with a flat tire sit idle. **-an** place where s.o. sits around idly. *Lapangan parkir itu adalah ~ si jagoan itu* The parking lot was where the tough character hung out.
tongol see NONGOL.
tongong (Coll.) nincompoop, blockhead.
tongpés [kantong kempés] (Sl.) broke, penniless.
Tongsan (Ch) China.
tongséng k.o. dish prepared with cabbage and meat us. lamb.
tongtong signal drum made from a bamboo or hollowed-out log.
tonikum tonic (tonic).
tonil 1 theater, the stage. 2 show. **men(t)-kan** 1 act, perform. 2 dramatize, put into a play. *Meréka ~ bukunya* They dramatized his book.
tonjok (Jkt) fist. **(me)n-** hit with the fist, fight. *Oké! Kalau tdk mau bayar, aku -* OK! If you are not going to pay, I will use my fists.
tonjol (Lit.) protrusion, bump (on the skin). **ber-²** bumpy. *jalan yg ~* a bumpy road. **ber-an** stick or bulge out (plural). **men-** 1 protrude, stick out. *Badannya ~ dr jendéla* His body stuck out the window. *Urat-urat léhérnya ~* His neck muscles stood out. 2 conspicuous, prominent. *Sifat pendiamnya makin ~ kalau ada org lain di dekatnya* Her taciturnity is even more conspicuous if there are other people around. *Ia ~ di antara kawan-kawannya karena kepintaran* She stood out among her friends because of her intelligence. **kemen-an** 1 state of protruding or bulging. 2 conspicuousness. **men-kan** 1 stick s.t. out, cause s.t. to protrude. *Ia ~ kepalanya dr jendéla* He stuck his head out the window. *~ diri* thrust o.s. forward. *Saya rasa barang keras di-kan ke tulang rusuk saya* I felt s.t. sharp being thrust into my ribs. 2 show,

present. *~ angka-angkanya* show off o.'s grades. *Ia ~ begitu banyak teka-teki dlm sikapnya!* She poses so many riddles about her behavior! 3 feature, accentuate s.t. **men-²kan** show s.t. off which is not worth showing off. **ter-** 1 pushed or thrust forward. 2 conspicuous. *Warna yg mérah itu ~ jelas* The red color was conspicuous. **-an** protrusion, protuberance. *~ keluar dr tulang yg patah* a protrusion from a broken bone. 2 s.o. or s.t. outstanding. *tokoh ~ minggu ini* this week's outstanding figure. **pen-an** 1 making s.t. stand out, accentuation. *lawakan yg dialasi ~ keganjilan bentuk tubuh* humor based on accentuation of physical aberrations. 2 conspicuousness. *~ fakta* obviousness of the facts.
tonton (me)n- 1 watch for entertainment, observe. *Ia ~ kesibukan di pasar* He watched the hustle and bustle in the marketplace. *~ bola* watch soccer matches. 2 go to the movies. *Mari kita ~* Let us go to the movies. *~ di mana?* To which show are you going? **men-i** 1 visit the family of o.'s future in-laws (to obtain information). 2 meet e.o. for mutual inspection (of future bridal pairs in arranged marriages). **men-kan, memper-kan** 1 show (off), exhibit. *~ kepandaiannya* show off his cleverness. 2 play, perform. *Meréka ~ tari Jawa* They performed Jv dances. **-an** 1 show, performance. 2 spectacle. **pen-** 1 spectator. *~ filem* movie goer. *~ ténis* spectator of a tennis match. 2 onlooker. *~ di pinggir jalan* sidewalk superintendent.
tonus tone (of muscles).
top₁ (Coll.) superlative. *lagu yg -* the most popular song. **nge-** be on top. *Ia mendadak jadi ~* All of a sudden he was at the top.
top₂ k.o. game of chance. **pe-an** gambling place.
topan typhoon, hurricane.
topang₁ prop, support, abutment. **ber-** lean on, be supported on. *Rumah itu ~ pd batu besar* The house was supported by a large stone. *~ dagu* sit with o.'s chin leaning on o.'s hand. **men-** prop up, shore up. *~ kepala dgn tangannya* support the head with the hands. **men-kan** lean s.t. on. *~ harapannya pd sdr* pin all his hopes on a relative. **-an, pen-** support, prop, abutment.
topang₂ tdk **ber-** be in conflict. *Ia tdk ~ dgn temannya dlm soal itu* He was in conflict with his friend in that matter. *Perkataannya tdk ~ pd yg dikatakannya semula* His words contradicted what he had said previously. *tdk* **men-** contradict. **per-an** 1 contradiction. 2 conflict, dispute.
topas topaz.
topdal ship's log.
topékong see TEPÉKONG.
topéng mask. - *gas* gas mask. **ber-** 1 have or wear a mask. 2 put on a front, cover up. *dgn ~ sbg pedagang* pretending to be a merchant. **ber-kan** use s.t. as a cover-up. **memper-** 1 mask, hide, disguise. *~ kesusahannya* disguise o.'s sorrow. 2 use as a mask. *Org kota melakukan kemesuman dgn ~ nama cinta* City folks do filthy things masquerading under the name of love.

topi hat. - *baja* steel helmet. - *gabus* pith helmet. - *jaksi* Panama hat. - *keselamatan* safety helmet. - *pandan/rumput/tikar* straw hat. **ber-** wear a hat.

topik topic. **men(t)-kan** use as a topic. *Gadis-gadis Timor Timur yg akan kami -kan* . . . The girls of E. Timor which will be our topic . . .

toples topless, bare-breasted.

toplés see STOPLÉS.

topo (*Jkt*) rag (for wiping, dusting).

topobroto (*Jv*) lead a sedentary, ascetic way of life.

topografi topography.

topong₁ a small basket. **2** conical.

topong₂ (*Jv*) k.o. rimless hat.

torah (*Bib.*) **1** Pentateuch. **2** tablet (of the law).

torak 1 bobbin holder. **2** piston. **-²** (*Auto.*) cylinder.

torat see TAURAT.

torbus see TARBUS.

toréh - *kayu* woodcut. **men-** 1 make a shallow cut. *Di- dgn pisau tak berdarah mukanya* Though it was scored with a knife, his face did not bleed. ~ *getah* tap rubber. **2** slit open. ~ *sampul* slit open an envelope. **-an 1** a notch, incision. **2** slit. **pen-** 1 scoring or slitting tool. **2** o. who taps rubber. **pen-an** process of rubber tapping.

torék (*Jkt*) hard of hearing.

torés see TORÉH.

torné see TURNÉ.

toros see TURUS.

torpedir ment- torpedo s.t.

torpédo torpedo. **men(t)-** torpedo s.t. **pen(t)-an** torpedoing.

torsi torsion.

tortor k.o. Batak dance.

tosera, toserba [*toko serba ada*] department store.

total 1 total. - *jéndral* grand total. **2** completely. *gila* - completely crazy. *hancur* - totally destroyed. **men(t)-kan** add s.t. up, total s.t. **ke-an** totality.

totalisator 1 sweepstakes. **2** soccer pool.

totalitas totality.

totalitér 1 total. *peperangan* - total war. **2** totalitarian.

totalitérisme totalitarianism.

totalitét totality.

toto k.o. lottery.

totok₁ 1 full-blooded. *Belanda* - a full-blooded Dutchman. **2** (*Coll.*) a full-blooded Chinese. **3** (*Coll.*) newcomer. *Saya masih - di sini* I am still a newcomer here.

totok₂ see TUTUK.

totokromo proper conduct, etiquette.

totol (*Jkt*) freckles. **men-kan** cause s.t. to splatter on s.t. *spt pupur yg di-kan* like face powder speckled all over.

tour see TUR.

tournooi /turnoi/ see TURNOI.

tour of duty /tur op duti/ **ment-kan** transfer s.o. to another post.

towél (*Jkt*) touch slightly with finger.

toya (*Ch*) k.o. staff for fighting.

toyor (*Jkt*) **men-** strike, punch.

t.p. [*tanpa penerbit*] no indication of publisher (in bibliographies, etc.).

TPS [*Tempat Pemungutan Suara*] poll, voting place.

tracee see TRASÉ.

trachom see TRAKHOM.

trada (*Moluccas*) see TIADA.

tradisi tradition.

tradisionil, tradisional traditional.

trafo 1 neon-light transformer. **2** voltage regulator.

tragédi tragedy.

tragédis tragic.

tragik tragedy.

tragis tragic.

trah (*Coll.*) having a lineage. *ayam* - pure-breed chicken. - *Hamengku Buwono* of the Yogyanese royal family.

trak sound of click (of key in lock, etc.). *-! Kunci diputar* Click! S.o. turned a key. *--trok* sound of footsteps, shuffling shoes, etc.

trakhom, trakhoma, trakhum (*Med.*) trachoma.

traksi traction.

traktat treaty.

traktir men- treat s.o. *Ia* ~ *aku makan bakmi dua porsi* He treated me to two servings of noodles. **-an** treating. *Nanti sewaktu* ~, *ajak kita, ya!* When you decide to pick up the bill, be sure to ask me along!

traktor tractor. - *tangan* hand-operated tractor, rototiller. **ment-i** do work with a tractor. **pent-an** bulldozing.

traktorisasi program to popularize the use of tractors in agricultural production.

trali, tralis see TERALI.

trampil skilled, competent. **men-kan** train s.o. *Ramlan di-kan dlm hal peternakan* Ramlan was trained in cattle raising. **ke-an** skill, know-how. ~ *otak* mental skill.

transaksi transaction, deal.

transdisiplin, transdisiplinér (*Lit.*) cross-disciplinary.

transéndén transcendent.

transéndéntal transcendental.

transfer transfer. - *télégrafis* telegraphic transfer. **ment-(kan)** transfer s.t.

transfigurasi transfiguration.

transformasi transformation. **ment-kan** transform.

transformator (*Tech.*) transformer.

transfusi transfusion.

transisi transition.

transistor transistor.

transito transit. *pelabuhan* - transit harbor.

Transkopemada [(*Départemén*) *Transmigrasi, Koperasi dan Pembangunan Masyarakat Désa*] Ministry of Resettlement, Co-operatives, and Village Development.

transkrip transcript.

transkripsi transcription. **ment-kan** transcribe. **pent-an** the process of transcribing s.t.

transliterasi transliteration. **ment-(kan)** transliterate.

transmigran o. who has been resettled in another region.

transmigrasi system of resettling inhabitants of overpopulated islands to less populated regions. - *musim* seasonal relocation. - *swakarsa* spontaneous relocation. **ment-kan** resettle s.o. **ke-an** matters pertaining to organized resettlement. **pent-an** process of relocating s.o.

transmisi transmission.

transmutasi (*Biol.*) transmutation. **ment-kan** transmute.

transparan 1 transparent. 2 transparency.

transparansi transparency.

transplantasi transplantation.

transpor transport.

transportasi transportation.

trap₁ (*Coll.*) stairs.

trap₂ see TERAP₂.

trapésium (*Math.*) trapezoid.

trapo see TRAFO.

tras trass, k.o. rock used for cement.

trasé 1 (ground) plan. 2 path. **ment-** trace. **pent-an** tracing.

trasi see TERASI.

trasir ment- trace.

tratak see TERATAK.

trayék 1 designated route for public transportation. 2 license to operate a vehicle on that route. 3 (*R.R.*) section. **ber-** operate on a certain route.

tréak see TERIAK.

trék designated route for public vehicles. **nge-** 1 operate a public vehicle along such a route. 2 drive a vehicle very fast. **-²an** 1 operation of such a vehicle. 2 drive a vehicle very fast.

trékbom land mine.

tréker trigger (coll.).

trékpén technical design pen.

trék sando (*Sport*) arm-stretcher.

trém streetcar, tram.

tréma (*Ling.*) diacritical mark indicating diaeresis.

trembesi (*Jv*) k.o. tree.

trémos see TÉRMOS.

trenggiling see TENGGILING.

trengginas (*Jv*) swift, quick-moving.

tréningspak athlete's sweatsuit, tracksuit.

trenyuh (*Jv*) moved to pity. **men-kan** move to pity. *pengalaman yg* ~ a moving experience.

tresno (*Jv*) feel love. *Sekian dr adik yg selalu -, Tuti* That is all from your ever-loving sweetheart, Tuti (at close of letter). **ke-an** love.

trét sound of metallic objects colliding. - *tét tét* sound of rapid gunfire. *Témbakan brén pemuda menyusul - tét tét* There followed the rattling noise of the youth brigade's machine gun.

tri- tri-, used in some compounds.

TRI₁ [*Tebu Rakyat Inténsifikasi*] smallholder's sugarcane intensification, an agricultural program.

TRI₂ [*Tentara Rakyat Indonésia*] Indonesian People's Army (1945-50).

triangulasi (*Tech.*) triangulation.

trias politika Montesquieu's threefold division of political authority: the legislative, judicial, and executive powers.

tribulan quarterly.

tribun, tribune 1 stand (part of stadium). - *terbuka* bleachers, open stands. 2 reviewing stand (for officials).

tribut plonco see ATRIBUT.

trica(k) three-wheeled pedicab.

tridasawarsa 30th anniversary.

Tridharma 1 religious sect incorporating the three streams of Ch religio-ethical principals: Taoism, Confucianism, Buddhism. 2 the three responsibilities of institute of higher education: research, teaching, and social service.

triftong (*Ling.*) triphthong.

trigu see TERIGU.

trik (*Crd.*) trick.

trikembar (*Lit.*) triplet.

triko k.o. fabric, tricot.

Trikora [*Tri Komando Rakyat*] strategy for mobilization of country in order to wrest W. New Guinea from Dutch (pre-1963).

trik-trak sound of s.t. creaking.

trilala 1 hum a cheerful tune. 2 act cheerful. - *trilili* be light-hearted. 3 careless, haphazard. *Pakaiannya - déh!* Really! Her clothes are ill-matched and carelessly worn.

trilingga (*Ling.*) k.o. reduplication with triple repetition of o. element, e.g. *cas-cis-cus*.

trilipat threefold.

trilogi trilogy.

trilyun quintillion.

trima see TERIMA.

trimatra three-dimensional.

trimo see NERIMO.

trimurti (*Rel.*) the oneness of the three Hindu gods, Brahma, Vishnu, and Siva.

trindil (*Jkt*) robbed, fleeced. **men(t)-i** rob s.o. *Ia di-i cincin emasnya* He was robbed of his golden ring.

trinitas (*Rel.*) trinity.

trio trio.

trip (*Coll.*) trip, journey.

TRIP [*Tentara Républik Indonésia Pelajar*] Student Army of the Republic of Indonesia (1945-1950).

Tripida [*Tri Pimpinan Daérah*] Regional Leadership Triumvirate, consisting of the leaders of police, army, and village.

triplék, tripléks plywood.

triprogram (*Lit.*) a program consisting of three points.

trirangkap (*Lit.*) triple.

trisila (*Lit.*) threefold. *sumpah* - threefold oath.

trisilabis trisyllabic.

trisula trident, a three-pronged spear.

tritugas (*Lit.*) three functions.

tritunggal 1 (*Rel.*) trinity. - *yg mahakudus* Holy Trinity. 2 tripartite, triumvirate.

Tritura [*Tri Tuntutan Rakyat*] political slogan of 1960s, the People's Three Demands: Banning the Indonesian Communist party, Purging

Communist elements from the *Dwikora* cabinet, and Lowering prices of basic commodities.

triunsur (*Lit.*) triadic.

triwarsa (*Lit.*) three years.

triwindu (*Lit.*) 24 years.

triwulan see TRIBULAN.

trm. [*transmigrasi*] resettlement.

trol trawl. *kapal* - trawler.

trombon trombone.

trombosa (*Med.*) thrombosis.

tromel metal lunch-box.

tromol pos postal box.

trompét 1 trumpet, esp. of European origin. 2 automobile horn. -*2 truk di jalanan mengaung tinggi* Truck horns on the street blasted shrilly. **men(t)-kan** trumpet out s.t. (a song, etc.).

trompétis trumpet player.

trondol (*Jv*) 1 featherless, esp. of live avians. 2 leafless. **men-i** defeat s.o.

trop see TERUP.

tropika tropics.

tropikalisasi making s.t. suitable for the tropics.

tropis tropical.

tropua (*Ling.*) trope.

trotoar, trotoir /trotoar/ sidewalk.

trubuk see TERUBUK.

truf see TERUP.

truk truck. **ber-2** by the truckload.

trusi see PRUSI.

T.s. [*teman sejawat*] colleague (used in professional correspondence by doctors). - *dr. Poli Mata* (to my) colleague in the Eye Clinic.

Tsanawiyah (*Isl.*) junior high school.

tsb. [*tersebut*] above-mentioned.

TSP₁ [*toko sandang pangan*] shops selling clothing and food.

TSP₂ k.o. chemical fertilizer.

tst [*tahu sama tahu*] unspoken agreement between two persons participating in a mutually advantageous, often illegal, deal.

tt.₁ [*tertanda*] signed.

tt.₂ [*tertanggal*] dated.

tt.₃ [*tanpa tahun*] no year of publication (in bibliographies, etc.).

TT₁ [*Timur Tengah*] Middle E.

TT₂ [*Teritorium Tentara*] military administrative unit at provincial level, used until early 1950s.

ttd. [*tertanda*] signed.

ttg.₁ [*tentang*] about, concerning.

ttg.₂, ttgl. [*tertanggal*] dated.

tth. [*tanpa tahun*] no year of publication (in bibliographies, etc.).

TTS [*Teka Teki Silang*] crossword puzzle.

ttt. [*tanpa tahun terbitan*] no date of publication (in bibliographies, etc.).

TU [*Tata Usaha*] administration.

tu₁ see SATU.

tu₂, 'tu see ITU.

tua 1 old. *Ia sdh* - He is old. *Ia - lima bulan dr saya* He is five months older than I. - *bangka* very old, senile. - *bangkot* old in years but young in spirit. - *catuk* feeble-minded from old age. - *datuk* old and dignified. - *ganyut* trying to look younger

than o.'s years. - *kutuk* old scoundrel. - *lara* a wretched person. - *lélér* 1 run-down, dilapidated. 2 past o.'s prime. - *lontok* senile. - *renta* 1 decrepit, in o.'s dotage. 2 dilapidated. - *suntuk* old, aged. - *uzur* very old. 2 ripe. *Buahnya masih masam karena blm* - The fruit is still sour because it is not ripe yet. 3 head, chief. - *kampung* village elder. - *rumah* head of the family. 4 pure. *mas* - pure gold. 5 dark (of color). *mérah* - dark red. -*2* 1 older. ~ *kelapa/keladi* the older the better (smarter, sexier, etc.) o. becomes. 2 (*Jv*) although old. ~ *keluyuran tak keruan* Old as he is, he just hangs around aimlessly. ~ *terung asam* old man who tries to act young. 3 age spots. **se-** of the same age, as old as. *Org ~ itu hrs hidup berhati-hati* A man of that age has to live carefully. **ber-²(an)** 1 (*M*) according to seniority. *Meréka berjéjér* ~ They lined up according to seniority. 2 grow old together (of husband and wife). **men-** 1 become old. 2 ripen, come to head. *Jerawatnya tumbuh dan* ~ His pimples grew and ripened. **ment-, mer-** see MERTUA. **men-kan** 1 let s.t. grow older, riper, etc. ~ *buah di pohonnya let die fruit ripen on the tree.* ~ *emas* make the gold purer. ~ *warnanya* let the color get deeper. *mendéwasakan dan* ~ *pemikiran org* make people's way of thinking more mature. 2 make s.o. a full adult by marrying that person off. *Ia salah seorg yg di-kan di kampung itu* She was o. of the persons who was married off in that village. 3 make or consider s.o. head. *Rapat* ~ *Pak Karto* The meeting put Pak Karto in charge. *Dlm keluarganya ia lebih di-kan drp saya* In his family he was considered older than me. **ter-** oldest. **ke-, menge-i, penge-** see KETUA. **ke-an** 1 too old. *Ia merasa* ~ *utk mendaki* She feels too old to go mountain climbing. 2 age. *Itu hanya menandakan* ~*nya* That only shows his age. *prosés* ~ the process of aging. **ke-²an** elderly, oldish. *suara* ~ an old-sounding voice. **-an** (*Coll.*) older, too old. **pen-an** aging.

tuah 1 good luck, good fortune. 2 magic power. 3 respect, honor, prestige. - *seorg pahlawan naik ssdh matinya* A hero's prestige increases after his death. **ber-** 1 lucky, fortunate. *Ia* ~ *menarik loteré* He was lucky to hit the jackpot. 2 bring good luck. *Mengapa aku yg* ~ Why is it me who is supposed to bring good luck? 3 have magic power. *makam yg* ~ a grave which has magic power. *kata* ~ *"pembangunan"* the magic word "development." **ke-an** 1 supernatural power. 2 lucky, fortunate. *Meréka* ~ *dgn datangnya di negeri itu* They were very lucky to come to that country.

tuai k.o. crescent-shaped reaping knife that fits in the palm of the hand. **men-** 1 harvest rice by cutting each stalk individually close to the ear with such a reaping knife. 2 reap. *Yg membeli itu kelak yg* ~ The buyer is the o. who reaps later on. **pen-** 1 rice harvest knife. 2 o. who reaps or gathers in a harvest. *perempuan* ~ *lada* a woman who harvests pepper. **pen-an** harvesting of rice.

tuak fermented palm wine, esp. of sugar or coconut palm. - *keras* strongly alcoholic palm wine. - *manis* slightly alcoholic palm wine.

tual a block of wood. **ber-²** cut up into blocks.

tuala (*Lit.*) towel.

tualang 1 fly about (of bees, etc.). **2** without permanent residence. **ber- 1** swarm (of bees). **2** wander, roam, tramp around. *Ia sdh ~; hari sdh menjelang soré* He had been wandering about; dusk was about to fall. **3** engage in an adventure (often recklessly). *Penjajah Portugis ~ mencari jaringan niaga* The Portuguese colonials undertook an adventurous search for trade routes. **pe- 1** wanderer, tramp. **2** adventurer who is trying to make a better life for himself. ~ *yg kecéwa hidup* adventurers disappointed in life. **pe-an 1** wandering about. **2** adventure, escapade. ~ *gila Don Kisot* the crazy escapades of Don Quixote.

tuam hot compress. **ber-, men-** be treated with a hot compress. *Karena tangannya bengkak, Abu hrs ~* Because of his swollen arm, Abu had to use hot compresses. **men-i** apply a hot compress on s.t.

tuan₁ 1 Mr., term of reference and address for Western and (occasionally) Westernized adult males. - *Ali* Mr. Ali. *Apa - suka ini?* Do you like this, sir? *Sdh, -* Yes, sir. **2** (*Coll.*) Ma'am, for Western women (in some areas). **3** (*Lit.*) master. *budak dan -nya* a slave and his master. - *besar* 1 boss, head. 2 important individual. - *pabrik* factory owner. - *puteri* princess. - *rumah* 1 family head. 2 host. - *tamu* host. - *tanah* landlord. **ber- 1** act as boss. *Semeninggal ayahnya ia ~ di rumahnya* After the death of his father he acted as boss at home. **2** have a master. *Kpd siapa meréka ~?* Whom do they serve as master? *daérah tdk ~* no man's land. **3** use the term of address *tuan. Meréka selalu ~* They always call e.o. *tuan.* **ber-kan** have s.t. as a master. *Anjing itu ~ org buta* That dog has a blind man as a master. **men-i, memper-i** dominate, exercise control over. *Dialah yg ~ gerombolan itu* He was the o. in charge of the gang. **memper-(kan) 1** respect. *Ia diper- oléh anak buahnya* He was respected by his crew. **2** address s.o. as *tuan. Yg Diper- Agung* the ruling king of Malaysia. **ke-²an** like a master, make a pretense at being a *tuan. Ah, pelayan saja berlagak ~!* All you are is a waiter. Why do you give yourself airs like that? **per-an 1** sovereignty, suzerainty. ~ *tanah* landlordism, landownership. **2** ruling class, upper class. **3** rule, gvt.

tuan₂ see TUHAN.

tuang pour. **men-** pour s.t. liquid. ~ *kopi ke cangkir* pour coffee into a cup. ~ *besi* cast iron. **men-i** pour into s.t. ~ *cangkir dgn air panas* pour hot water into a cup. **men-kan 1** pour s.t. out. ~ *kopi ke cangkir* pour coffee into a cup. **2** cause to pour forth. *Oplét ~ penumpangnya dan menadah yg lain* The minibus poured out its passengers and piled in new o.'s. *Pacat di-kan keluar dr sepatunya* He poured leeches out from his shoe. **3** mold, cast. *Utk dpt ~ pendidikan di Indonésia, perlu di-*

adakan risét It requires research to give shape to education in Indonesia. **ter-** poured forth. *kopi ~ ke dlm pocinya* coffee poured into its pot. *dukacita ~ meléwati péna* sorrows poured out through a pen. **-an 1** s.t. poured or cast. **2** a mold used in casting. **pen-an** pouring, molding, casting. ~ *pertama fundamén* the first pouring of the foundations.

tuangku see TUANKU.

tuang-tuang k.o. bamboo horn.

tuan hamba (*Lit.*) you, very respectful and servile.

tuanku (*Lit.*) title of royalty.

tuarang (*Lit.*) dry season.

tuas lever. **men-** lever s.t. up.

tub tube (of paint, toothpaste, etc.).

tuba 1 name of plants from which a stupefying drug is obtained. **2** stupefying drug used in fishing. - *tikus* arsenic. - *dibalas dgn susu* returning good for evil. **men-** spread this poison s.w. to catch fish. ~ *kolam* spread fish poison in a pond. **men-i** poison fish, etc. with such a poison.

tubagus title of a nobility in Banten, W. Java.

tuban-tuban (*Anat.*) amnion, fetal membrane.

tube see TUB.

tuberculosa (*Med.*) tuberculosis.

tubi ber-(²) repeatedly. *Témbakan-témbakan ~ terus-menerus* The shots came o. after the other without stopping. ~ *saja pukulanku jatuh* Again and again my punches landed on their mark. *Abu ditanyai ~* They asked Abu over and over again. **men- 1** keep at s.t. **2** repeat. *Ia ~ pertanyaannya* He repeated his question. **memper-²** intensify by repetition. *Ia ~ pukulannya* He increased the rate of delivering his blows.

tubin (*Lit.*) four days from now.

tubir 1 ravine, gully. **2** sea chasm. **3** precipice, edge of s.t. deep. - *bibir* outline of the lips. **men-** deep, steep. **men-i** trace the edge of s.t. precipitous. *Minah di-i wasangkanya sendiri* Minah was edged in by her own suspicions.

tubruk₁ 1 a lunge. **2** a slamming action, collision. **ber-an** have a collision. *Mobil ~ dgn truk* The car collided with a truck. **men- 1** lunge at s.o. *Ia berusaha lari tapi perampok itu lebih cepat ~nya* He tried to run away but the bandit was faster and managed to lunge at him. **2** collide with, run into. *Hati-hati, nanti kita ~ pohon* Be careful, or we will crash into a tree. **3** run over, hit s.o. *spt ayam di- mobil* like a chicken run over by a car. **men-kan** make s.t. crash into. **ke-, ter-1** slammed into. *Kepalanya ~ témbok* His head knocked against the wall. **2** struck, run over. *Ada org ~ mobil* S.o. was hit by a car. **-an 1** collision, crash. **2** impact. ~ *begitu kecil hingga tdk ada kerugian* The impact was so slight there was no loss. **pen-an** colliding, crashing, striking.

tubruk₂ see KOPI₁.

tubuh 1 body. - *halus* diminutive build. *Sekujur -ku mandi keringat* My whole body dripped with sweat. - *badan* the whole body. **2** (*Lit.*) person. *menghadap -* appear in person. *jas bekas -* a worn-out jacket. **se- 1** (*Lit.*) in harmony. **2** copulation.

berse- have sexual intercourse. **menye-i** copulate with s.o. **perse-an** copulation. **ber-** with a body of certain characteristics. *Wartawan itu ~ kukuh* The reporter was well built. *~ langsing* of slender build. **men-kan 1** realize, bring to realization. *~ cita-citanya* realize o.'s ideals. **2** bring into existence. **per-an** organization.

tuding₁ sloping, at an angle. **men-kan** make s.t. slant.

tuding₂ (*Jv*) index finger. **men- 1** point at s.t. *Héru ~ bénjolan biru di wajahnya* Heru pointed at the bruise on his face. **2** accuse. **men-i** point at repeatedly. *Yg ingin kita -i di sini adalah . . .* What we'd like to point out here is . . . **men-kan** point with s.t. *~ telunjuknya ke bulan* point o.'s finger to the moon. *~ senapang ke arah musuh* point a gun toward the enemy. **-an 1** s.t. which is pointed at. *mengikut arah ~* follow the indicated direction. **2** accusation.

tuduh accuse. **- men-** mutual recrimination, mutually recriminate. **men-** accuse s.o. *Aku yg dikaum kapitalis oléh org politik* It is me the politicians accuse of being a capitalist. *Apa! Kau ~ aku punya tunangan!* What! You are accusing me of having a fiancée! *Meréka ~ perbuatan saya sbg pengkhianatan* They charged that my actions were treason. **men-kan** accuse of, charge with s.t. *Ia ~ kegagalan itu kpd temannya* He accused his friend of the failure. *dlm perkara yg di-kan kpd Parman* in the matter with which Parman is charged. *Bibi Tarmi ~ wasangka-wasangka jahat* Tarmi's aunt made accusations based on her worst suspicions. **ter-** accused. *si ~* (*Leg.*) the accused. **-an** accusation, complaint, charge. *atas ~* on a charge of. **pen- 1** (*Leg.*) prosecutor. **2** accuser, plaintiff. **pen-an** accusation.

tudung 1 veil, cover. *- lampu* lampshade. *- lingkup* veil used by some Isl. women. *- muka* veil. *- saji* movable cone-shaped cover for food. **2** sun hat. **ber- 1** be covered. **2** use a veil. **ber-kan** covered with. *~ daun pisang* covered with a banana leaf. **men-i** cover s.t. up carefully, repeatedly shade s.t. *Keranda mayat itu di-i dgn payung* The coffin was shaded by an umbrella. **men-kan** use s.t. for a cover or shade. *~ kain putih pd méja* put a white cloth over the table. *Ia ~ tapak tangannya menahan silau matahari* He used his palms to deflect the sun's rays. **ter-** covered. **pen-** cover. **pen-an** covering.

tufah (*Lit.*) apple.

tugal a dibble. **men-** dibble with a pointed stick in order to sow seeds. **men-kan** sow seeds in this way. *Benih-benih yg besar dpt di-kan* Good-sized seedlings can be planted by preparing a place with a dibble. **-an** s.t. dibbled. *padi ~* rice planted by dibbling.

tugas 1 duty. *-nya kpd Tuhan* her duty to God. *- kewajiban* **1** duty. **2** task. **3** function. **2** order, assignment. *Dia dpt - berangkat ke daérah garis depan* He received orders to leave for the front line. **3** task. **ber-** have s.t. as a duty. *Ia pergi tiada ~* He left without an assignment. *Saya ~ men-*

jaga kubu ini I have the duty of guarding this fortification. **men-i** give an assignment to. **men-kan 1** assign s.t. as a task. *Présidén ~ pembérésan keamanan di daérah itu kpdnya* The president gave him the task of restoring security in that area. **2** assign, place s.o. in an assignment. *Saya di-kan di bagian radio* I was assigned in the radio section. **pe- 1** functionary, official. *~ keamanan* security guard or agent. *~ pabéan* customs official. **2** employee. *~ parkir* parking attendant. **pen-an** giving an assignment.

tugu 1 post, column, pillar. **2** monument. *- peringatan* memorial, monument.

tuguran stand guard during a commemoration.

tuh *see* ITU.

Tuhan God. *- Allah* God. *- yg Esa* the o. God. **ber-1** believe in God. *tdk ~* atheistic. **2** have a certain god. *Meréka ~ pd lembu* They worship the cow as a god. **ber-kan** have s.t. as a god. *Di kota banyak yg ~ uang saja* In cities there are many who have made money their god. **men-kan, memper-kan** consider as a god, deify. *Ia ~ dirinya sendiri* He made himself into a god. *~ téknik* deify technology. **ke-an** divinity, deity. **berke-an** devout. **-²an** false deity.

tuhfah (*Lit.*) gift.

tuil a lever. **men-** lever s.t. up.

tuit tweed.

tujah (*Lit.*) **men-** stab downward.

tuju (*Lit.*) k.o. bewitchment by pointing at the victim. **se- 1** agree. *Meréka ~ dgn usul* They agreed with the proposal. *tanda tdk ~nya* a sign of disagreement. *231 ~ dan 164 menentang* 231 in favor and 164 opposed. *warna témbok yg ~ dgn warna perkakas rumah* a color of the wall which harmonized with the furniture. **2** (*Coll.*) like. *Ambillah kalau ~ dgn barang itu* Take it if you like it. **berse- 1** have o. and the same aim or purpose. **2** agree. *Saya ~ dgn permintaan tuan* I agree with your request. **menye-i** agree to s.t., approve s.t. *~ usul* agree with a proposal. *~ belanja tahunan* approve the annual budget. *Parlemén ~ tindakan pemerintah* Parliament ratified the gvt.'s action. **memperse-kan** bring into line, coordinate. **ber-an 1** have s.t. as a purpose. *Kehidupannya tiada ~* His life has no purpose. *Ia ~ menyelesaikan pekerjaannya* He intends to finish his work. *katakerja ~* (*Ling.*) transitive verb. **2** head for, go in a certain direction. *Sdr ~ ke mana?* Where are you headed? **men- 1** go in the direction of. *Ia berangkat ~ Paris* He headed for Paris. **2** aim, strive. *Meréka giat berusaha ~ ke keamanan dunia* They were striving hard for world peace. **3** concern, aim (accusations, etc.) at. *Engkau yg di-nya dgn sindirannya* You are the o. he was aiming at with his jibes. **4** (*Lit.*) practice a k.o. sorcery on s.o. *Ia sakit di- org* He was made ill by sorcery. **men-kan 1** point with s.t. *Ia ~ pistolnya kpd saya* He pointed his gun at me. **2** cause s.t. to point in a direction. *Ia ~ perahunya ke pelabuhan* He directed his boat toward the harbor. *Ia ~ sindirannya kpd saya* He directed his jibes at me. **-kan**

perhatian direct o.'s attention. *Ia ~ langkahnya ke selatan* He headed (lit., aimed his steps) south. **ter-** directed. *Semua mata ~ pdnya* All eyes were directed to him. **-an 1** aim, purpose, objective. *~ apa sdr datang ke mari?* What is your purpose in coming here? *satu ~ dlm hidup ini* a single purpose in this life. **2** direction, destination. *dgn ~ Bandung* with the destination of bandung. **3** (*Ling.*) object. *~ penderita* direct object. **se-an 1** of o. purpose. *Banyak jalan yg ~ maksudnya* There are many means to the same end. **2** having the same direction. *Kapal-kapal itu berlayar ~* The ships sailed in the same direction. **perse-an 1** treaty, agreement. *~ Versailles* Treaty of Versailles. **2** approval, agreement. *~ parlémén* approval of parliament. *Dgn ~ org tuanya . . .* With the permission of his parents . . . **pen-** *hati* to o.'s liking. *makanan ~ hati* o.'s favorite dish.

tujuh seven. *- belas* 17. *- puluh* 70. *- bulan* solemnization of the 7th month of pregnancy. **men-bulani** solemnize the 7th month of pregnancy. *- hari* commemoration of the 7th day after o.'s death. **men-** *hari* commemorate the 7th day of death. *Keluarganya ~ hari kematian ayahnya* His family commemorated the 7th day of his father's death. *- keliling* severe dizzy spells (lit., dizzy seven times over). **ber-** be in a group of seven. *Meréka ~ pergi ke kota* The seven of them went to town. **ber-²** seven at a time. **ke-** **1** seventh. *anak ~ itu* the 7th child. **2** all seven. *~ anak itu* the seven children.

tuk₁ sound of knocking on wood. *--tak* sound of repeated tapping. **-²** sound of repeated tapping.

tuk₂ see DATUK.

tukai (*Vulg.*) female sex organs.

tukak sore, ulcer. **men-** fester.

tukal a variable measure of length for thread equivalent to 16 *rian*.

tukang 1 skilled laborer or craftsman. *- azan* o. who summons to. *- besi* blacksmith. *- bubut* a fitter. *- catut* ticket scalper. *- gigi* o. who makes false teeth. *- jahit* tailor. *- jambrét* purse snatcher. *- khatan/khitan* circumciser. *- kulak* o. who buys goods for resale. *- loak* secondhand dealer. *- potong* butcher. *- rém* brakeman. *- silap mata* conjurer, magician. *- sunat* circumciser. *- sulap/sunglap* **1** juggler. **2** magician. *- tadah* a fence, s.o. who receives stolen goods. *- tanji* musician. **2** o. who has the bad habit of doing s.t. *- amin* a yes man. *- bohong* liar. *- boncéng* sponger, parasite. *- cuplik* plagiarizer. *- mabuk* drunkard. *- ngacau* agitator, troublemaker. *- nrimo* o. who accepts whatever comes. *- pidato* speechifier. *- riba* usurer. *- serobot* **1** o. who cuts in line or breaks into a conversation. **2** o. who grabs others possessions. *- tidur* o. who likes to sleep. **ber-, men-** be an artisan, skilled laborer. **- men-** matters pertaining to craftsmanship. **men-i 1** craft s.t. *~ korsi* make a chair. **2** repair s.t. *~ korsi rusak* repair a broken chair. **ke-an** skill, craftsmanship. **per-an 1** trade. *sekolah ~* trade school. *~ kayu* carpentry.

2 handicraft, craftsmanship. *perkakas ~* tools of o.'s trade. **3** craft, guild, association.

tukar exchange. *- cincin* exchange rings. *- ganti* substitution. *- jaga* changing of the guard. *- menjadi* change into. *- tambah* exchange and add an amount. **ber-** change. *~ akal* change o.'s mind. *~ bulu* molt. *~ dr yg sdh-sdh* be different from before. *~ haluan* (*Naut.*) tack, turn (a ship). *~ kapal* transship. *~ keréta* change trains. *Malam ~ dgn siang* Night has changed into day. *~ pakaian* change clothes. *~ pikiran* **1** change o.'s mind. **2** exchange ideas, discuss. **3** lose o.'s head, get crazy. *~ tangan* change hands. *~ warna* change color. **ber-² 1** alternating. **2** keep changing. *Pikirannya selalu ~* She is always changing her mind. **ber-(²)an** mutually exchange s.t. *Banyak negeri ~ pelajar* Many countries have student exchange programs. **- men-** exchange with e.o. *program ~ mahasiswa* student exchange program. **men-1** change. *~ ban* change a tire. *~ uang* change money. *Ini di- dgn yg bersih* Exchange this for a clean o. **2** exchange, barter. **men-kan** give s.t. in exchange. *~ cék* cash a check. *Mobil yg lama di-kan dgn yg baru* The old car was traded in for a new o. **memper-kan 1** barter. *Org Kubu dan pedagang ~ hasil bumi dgn barang dagangan* The Kubu people and merchants barter natural products for commercial goods. **2** vary, alternate. **ter-** get accidently exchanged. *Bajunya ~ dgn milik adiknya* He accidently got his brother's shirt instead of his own. **pen-** *uang* money-changer. **pen-an 1** alteration, process of making a change. *~ agama* religious conversion. *~ uang* monetary conversion. *~ hawa* ventilation. *~ zat* metabolism. **2** exchange. *~ barang* exchange of goods. **per-an 1** exchange. *~ pikiran* exchange of thoughts. **2** change. *~ hawa* a change in the weather.

tukas₁ (*M*) **1** false accusation, aspersion. **2** say accusingly. *"Kau membéla si Minah," - bibi Tarmi* "You are defending that Minah," shouted Tarmi's aunt accusingly. **men-** calumniate. **-an** false accusation, slander.

tukas₂ **ber-²** repeatedly. (*M*) **men-** say in repetition. *"Aku lalu tertangkap Belanda." "Tertangkap!" kata Mulyadi ~* "I was then caught by the Dutch." "Caught!" Mulyadi repeated.

tukas₃ 1 say in rejection (of earlier discourse). *"Aku belikan kau baju." "Aku tdk mau," - Minah* "I will buy you a dress." "I do not want o.," countered Minah. **2** respond. *"Ya, Mak Haji," - Dullah dgn hormat* "Yes, Ma'am," responded Dullah respectfully.

tukas₄ k.o. rattan.

tukik₁ men- dive. *Pesawat itu ~, terus menyerang* The plane dived, then attacked. **men-i** dive at. **men-kan 1** let dive, point s.t. downward. *~ telunjuknya ke sebuah lembah* point his index finger toward a valley. **2** point s.t. at, direct s.t. to. *Kita -kan perhatian kita pd ceramah itu* We directed our attention to the lecture.

tukik₂ notch, nick, indentation. **men-** make a notch. *Meréka ~ tebing mencari logam* They chipped away at the riverbank looking for ore.

tukik₃ woodpecker.

tukil see NUKIL.

tukuk see TOKOK₁.

tukul hammer. - *kayu* mallet. **men-** hammer. **pen-** hammerer.

tul see BETUL.

tulah₁ calamity brought on by a curse or breaking a taboo. **men-i** curse s.o. or s.t. **ke-an** struck by a curse.

tulah₂ see TUSLAH.

tulang bone. - *air mata* lachrymal. - *baji sphenoid bone.* - *belakung* spine, backbone. - *belulang/berbalut kulit* skin and bones. - *bercagak* cheekbone. - *cenak* clavicle, collarbone. - *daun* veins of a leaf. - *empat kerat* the extremities. - *halus* cartilage. - *hasta* ulna. - *kelangkang* sacrum. - *kering* shinbone. - *ketok jari* knuckles. - *ketul* cartilage. - *lembusir* shoulder blade. - *muda* cartilage. - *papan* breastbone. - *punggung* spinal column. - *selangka* collarbone. - *sendi* joint. - *sumsum* bone with marrow. - *tongkéng* coccyx. - *tunjang* 1 leg bone of fowls. 2 bony part of haunches. - *tungging* coccyx. **ber-** bony. *daging tiada ~* boneless meat. *tiada ~* weak, lacking spunk. **men-(²)** become bone. *kurus dan ~* thin and wasted away. **men-i** debone s.t. *~ ikan* remove the bones from a fish. **ter-** 1 feel to the marrow. *sakitnya ~* pained to the bone. 2 down to skin and bones. **ke-an** have a fishbone stuck in the throat. **-²an** 1 all k.o. bones. 2 skeleton. 3 carcass, frame. **pen-an** erecting a framework. *~ konstruksi beton* providing the steel frame underlying cement construction.

tular men- 1 infect, contaminate. *Penyakit itu ~ ke mana-mana* That disease spread everywhere. 2 spread. *Pemogokannya ~ di seluruh negeri* The strike spread over the entire nation. **men-i** spread to s.o. or s.t., contaminate. *Penyakit akimu ~ku* Your grandfather's disease has spread to me. **men-kan** cause s.t. to spread. *Hawa yg panas ~ penyakit* Hot weather spreads the disease. **ke-an** infected, contaminated. **-an** 1 contagion. *bersih dr ~* untouched by contagion. 2 s.o. or s.t. that is infected. *setengah juta ~* half a million contaminated people. *daérah ~ cacar* an area struck by smallpox. **pen-** infector, infecting agent. **pen-an** spreading. *cara ~ penyakit* the transmission of a disease.

tulat (*Lit.*) three days from now (the day after tomorrow).

tule k.o. fabric, tulle.

tulén pure, genuine. *mas -* pure gold. *org Surabaya - a* real Surabayan. **ke-an** authenticity, genuineness.

tuli deaf. - *bisu* deaf mute. **men-kan** make deaf. *~ telinga* close o.'s ears, refuse to listen. *Bunyi itu ~ telinga saya* That sound deafened my ears. **ke-an** suffer from deafness. *Org itu pendengarannya*

jadi rusak dan agak ~ That person's hearing was damaged and she is rather deaf.

tulis write. *"Banyak terima kasih," begitu - kakakku* "Thanks very much," my sister writes. **ber-** written on. *Kertas ini tdk ~* This sheet is not written on. *batu ~* ancient stone inscription. **ber-an** written on with some notice. *Papan itu ~: "Awas anjing galak"* The board said: "Beware of the vicious dog." **ber-kan** inscribed with s.t. *baki ~ kata-kata* a tray inscribed with words. - **men-** writing (of articles, stories, etc.). **men-** 1 write. *~ surat* write a letter. 2 draw. *~ gambar* draw a picture. **men-i** 1 write on s.t. *~ kertas putih* write on white paper. 2 doodle on s.t., jot graffiti on s.t. *Semua pemuda sedang asyik ~ témbok gedung itu* All the youths were busy scribbling graffiti on the walls of the building. **men-kan** 1 write s.t. down. *~ pikirannya di kertas* write down o.'s thoughts on paper. 2 write with s.t. *~ kapur pd papan* write with chalk on the board. **ter-** written. *hukum ~* written law. *Di dlm notés ini ~ rahasia* A secret was written in this notebook. **-an** 1 s.t. written. *~ tangan* handwriting. *dgn ~* in writing. 2 article, writing. *~nya dlm majalah yg baru terbit* his article in a recent issue of a magazine. **pen-** 1 writer (of letter, etc.). 2 secretary (of association). *~ cepat* stenographer. **pen-an** process of writing. *~ kembali* rewriting. *~ sejarah* historiography. **per-an** inscription.

tuli-tuli (*Lit.*) k.o. silver cord decoration on some kris sheaths.

tul-tul polka-dot.

tulung see TOLONG.

tulup men- blow with a pipe.

tulus honest, sincere. - *ikhlas* honest and straightforward. **se-²nya** as sincerely as possible. **ke-an** honesty, sincerity, integrity.

tuma louse, esp. human head lice.

tuman (*Jkt*) be accustomed to. *Ia - pergi ke sana* He was accustomed to going there.

tumang₁ 1 k.o. peg or stake. 2 rock or stick to support pan on a brazier.

tumang₂ (*Amb*) leaf container for sago meal.

tumbak see TOMBAK.

tumbal 1 (*Jv, Jkt*) s.t. used to prevent disease or misfortune. *sesaji kepala kerbau sbg - bagi roh-roh di sekitarnya* an offering of a water buffalo head as a pacifying gift for the surrounding spirits. 2 protective agent. *Rakyat dijadikan - pembangunan* The people become the protective guarantee of development. *Simin gugur sbg - révolusi* Simin died as a protector of the revolution.

tumbang fall down with a crash (of s.t. large and erect). *Kekuasaannya - ssdh perang itu* Its power collapsed after the war. *Pohon-pohon besar - kena angin ribut* Big trees were toppled by the storm. *rékor-rékor dunia yg -* world records that were smashed. **ber-an** fall (in numbers). **men-kan** 1 cause to come crashing down. *Sengaja kami ~ pohon asem itu* We purposely felled that tamarind tree. *~ rékor dunia* break a world's record.

2 slaughter (cattle, etc.). **pen-** *rékor* record breaker. **pen-an** causing s.t. to crash down. **per-an** collapse.

tumbén (*Jkt*) **1** for the first time. *Cip - minum bir Cip* drank beer for the first time. **2** How odd! (exclamation of surprise). - *jam dua, sdh mau pulang* How strange! You already want to go home at two o'clock.

tumbu (*Jv*) k.o. small basket.

tumbuh 1 grow, sprout up. *Pohon ini dpt - di mana-mana* This tree can grow anywhere. *Perusahaan-nya - dgn suburnya* His business has developed rapidly. - *luas* grow extensively. **men-luaskan** make flourish. *Ia mencoba men-luaskan kemer-dékaan kritik* He tried to extend and stimulate freedom of criticism. '**2** appear from below, arise. *Gigi bayinya* - The baby's teeth emerged. *Di sini - perselisihan* Conflict arose here. **ber-** grow. *Kelapa ~ di hawa yg panas* Coconuts grow in a warm climate. **ber-an** grow (several things). **men-i** sprout up over s.t. *Lapangan itu di-i rumput* The field was overgrown with grass. **men-kan 1** make s.t. grow. *obat utk ~ rambut* medicine to make the hair grow. *Ia ~ bunga-bungaan di halamannya* She grows various k.o. flowers in the yard. **2** cause to emerge or sprout up. *Kesederha-naan Susy ~ perasaan cinta di hatinya* Susy's down-to-earth ways caused a feeling of love to rise in him. **ke-an 1** growth. **2** smallpox, skin eruption, etc. **3** grown over. *Halamannya ~ cendawan* His yard was grown over with mushrooms. **-an 1** a plant. *~ obat* medicinal plant. **2** a growth. *~ daging mungkin kembang-kembang kanker* a fleshy growth, maybe an early cancer tumor. **-²an** all k.o. plants. **pen-** s.t. that stimulates growth. *~ dan pencegah rambut rontok* s.t. to stimulate growth and prevent the loss of hair. **pen-an 1** the act of growing. **2** emergence. **per-an** growth, development.

tumbuk pound. **ber- 1** fight, come to blows. *Ia ~ dgn musuhnya* He fought with his opponent. **2** slam against e.o. *Mobil ~ cikar* A car collided with a bullock cart. **3** coincide. *Perayaannya diun-durkan karena ~ dgn rapat umum* The celebration was postponed because it coincided with the general meeting. **ber-an** collide, slam against e.o. *Kotak-kotak ~* The boxes collided. **men-1** pound, crush. *Ia ~ kopi* She pounded coffee. **2** strike, deliver a blow to. *Ia ~ lawannya di muka-nya* He struck his opponent on the face. **3** crash into. *Mobil ~ témbok* A car crashed against a wall. **4** let the eyes alight on s.t. *Dia ~ méja dgn mata yg bersinar* He looked down at the table with glistening eyes. *Di mana-mana dia di- dgn pandangan benci* Everywhere he was met with looks of hatred. **men-kan 1** pound with s.t., beat s.t. against. *Ia ~ kepalanya ke témbok* He smashed his head against the wall. **2** crush for s.o. *Ia ~ ayahnya kopi* She pounded coffee for her father. **ter- 1** accidentally made to collide. *Badannya ~ pohon* Her body struck a tree. **2** pounded, crushed. *~ akal* at the end of o.'s wits. **3** light on

s.t. (of eyes, gaze, etc.). *Mataku ~ pd jari-jarinya* Involuntarily my eyes lighted on her fingers. **-an 1** blow, pounding. **2** s.t. pounded or crushed. *sirih ~* crushed betel leaf. **3** crash, collision. *~ kepentingan* clash of interest. **4** impact. **pen-** crusher, pounder. **pen-an 1** pounding, crushing. *~ beras di lesung* the pounding of rice in a mortar. **2** blow, stroke. **3** act of colliding.

tumbung₁ lump, bulge. - *dubur* prolapse. - *kelapa* coconut seed-bud.

tumbung₂ see TOMBONG₂.

tumenggung see TEMENGGUNG.

tumis a culinary procedure similar to sautéing but at a higher temperature. **men-** sauté at high temperatures. *di- dgn minyak kelapa* Stir fry with coconut oil.

tumit heel. - *sepatu* shoe heel.

tumor (*Med.*) tumor.

tumpah spilled. *Airnya -* The water spilled out. *tanah - darah* o.'s place of birth, motherland. *- ruah* 1 spilled, poured out everywhere. **2** filled to the brim. **men-i** spill on s.t. *Air ~ bajunya* Water spilled on his clothes. *Gaun barunya di-i dgn anggur* She spilled wine on her new dress. **men-kan 1** cause s.t. to spill. *~ darah* shed blood. *~ tinta* spill ink. **2** spill s.t. out, concentrate s.t. *Ia ~ segala perhatiannya kpd pekerjaan* He poured all his concentration into his work. *Ia ~ kemengkalannya kpd suaminya* She poured out her irritation on her husband. **ter- 1** spilled, shed. *Airnya ~* The water's spilled. **2** be concentrated on. *Segala tenaganya ~ kpd tujuannya itu* All his strength was concentrated on his goal. **ke-an** have s.t. spilled on it. *Tangannya ~ minyak* He spilled oil on his hands. **-an 1** s.t. spilled. *~ darah* blood that has been spilled. **2** concentration (of efforts). *~ pikiran* burst of thought. **pen-an 1** acts of spilling or shedding. *~ darah* bloodshed. **2** concentration. **per-an** spillage. *~ darah* bloodshed.

tumpak batch, collection. - *peragaan* demonstration batch. *se- sawah* rice field (consisting of many divisions). **ber-(²)** in groups.

tumpang join with others. - *sari* intercropping. **men-sarikan** intercrop. *Hasil kacang-kacangan berkurang jika di-sarikan dgn jagung* The yield of legumes decreases if they are planted in rows alternating with corn. - *suh/tindih* overlapping, piling up on o. another. **ber-** *suh/tindih* overlap, be piled up on o. another. **(me)n- 1** ride in, go by. *Dgn ~ bis Sulastri pulang ke kampungnya* Sulastri went back to her village by bus. **2** join in, go along with, use s.t. belonging to s.o. else. *Ia pergi ~ dgn temannya* He got a ride with his friend. *~ alamat* use another's address. *~ makan* join s.o. in his or her meal. *~ surat* place a letter inside s.o. else's for mailing. **3** stay with. *Ia ~ di rumah pamannya* He lived with his uncle. **4** please, may I, (particle preceding polite queries). *~ ber-tanya?* May I ask a question? *~ jalan?* Excuse me, may I pass here? (said when passing in front of or going around s.o.). **men-i** ride in, be a passenger in. *Bécak yg ku-i rasanya tak mau jalan cepat* The pedicab I rode in seemed unwilling to go fast. **men-kan 1** cause s.o. or s.t. to go with, cause s.o. to be a passenger. *Ia ~ anaknya di mobil itu* He arranged for his child to ride in the car. *Ia ~ surat dgn temannya* He sent a letter via his friend. **2** cause s.o. to stay with. *Ia ~ tamu-tamunya di hotél* He put his guests up at a hotel. *Ia ~ anaknya pd temannya* He arranged to have his child stay with his friend. *~ diri kpd* entrust o.s. to. **ter-** included. *~ salam Trisno* Trisno adds his greetings. **-an 1** lodging. *rumah ~ Hamidah* the place where Hamidah stays. **2** fare, passenger, load, *Ia mencari ~ buat mobilnya* He is seeking passengers (or a load) for his car. **3** inclusion, addition. *dgn ~ salam Trisno* with the added greetings of Trisno. **pen- 1** passenger. *~ gelap* a stowaway. *~ geladak* steerage passenger. **2** boarder, hotel guest. **berpen-** have passengers or boarders. **pen-an 1** act of being over s.t. *~ lapisan X di atas logam Y* the placing of an X layer on the surface of the Y metal. **2** place to stay.

tumpas destroyed, annihilated, exterminated. **men- 1** destroy, eradicate. *Ia ditugaskan ~ gerombolan Mat Coléng* He was assigned the task of eradicating Mat Coleng's gang. **2** extinguish. *~ api* extinguish a fire. **men-kan 1** destroy s.t. on s.o.'s behalf. **2** destroy, exterminate. **pen-** destroyer. **pen-an** annihilation, extermination.

tumpat 1 stopped up, clogged up. **2** crammed, solid. *- padat* dense, compact. **3** be at the end of o.'s rope. *penderitaan batin yg - itu* a pressing inner grief. **men-kan** cram s.t., stuff s.t. **ter-** crammed, stuffed.

tumpeng (*Jv*) ceremonial dish of yellow rice served in a cone shape. **-an** ritual in which this dish is served.

tumpes see TUMPAS.

tumpil (*Jkt*) supporting pole, prop. **men-** prop up.

tumplek /tumplek/ (*Jv*) spilled all over. *Semuanya - di klosét* Everything spilled out in the toilet. *- bleg* spilled all over. **n- 1** pour out, empty all at o. time. *kertas-kertas yg di- di depan pintu* papers that had been emptied out all in a pile in front of the door. **2** be spilled out, be in a huge crowd in a place. *para pegawai yg - di situ* the employees who crowded around in that place.

tumpu 1 footing. **2** foothold, support. **3** springboard. **ber- 1** rest on. *Patung itu ~ pd batu besar* The statue rests on a large stone. *Badannya ~ di kedua sikunya* She rested, leaning on her elbows. **2** have support. *Kekuasaannya ~ pd kepopulérannya* His power is supported by his popularity. *Ia ~ pd batu sblm melompat* He pushed off from a stone before leaping. **3** touch upon, come in contact with. **4** concentrate, focus. *Angan-anganku ttg wanita ~ pdnya* All my daydreams about women focus on her. **men- 1** become concentrated. *Ia dikuasai rasa kasih sayang yg ~* He was controlled by a concentrated feeling of love. **2** support, sustain. *Pras ~ kepalanya dgn kedua*

tangannya Pras supported his head with his hands. **men-kan 1** lean with s.t., lean s.t. on to. *Ia ~ tangannya pd méja* He leaned on the table with his hands. **2** provide support for s.t. or s.o. *Batu besar ~ tangga ke rumah* A large stone supported the steps to the house. *Dialah yg ~ ibunya* It was he who supported his mother. **3** cause s.t. to rest. *Témbok itu di-kan pd alasan yg kokoh* The wall rested on a strong foundation. **4** concentrate. *~ segala perhatian pd* concentrate all o.'s attention on. *~ segala usahanya* concentrate all o.'s efforts. **ter-** concentrated on. *Pikirannya ~ pd gadis itu* His thoughts were concentrated on the girl. **-an 1** support, pillar, prop. *~ pantai* beachhead. *~ gelombang* breakwater (on ship). **2** stepping-stone. **3** focus, center. *~ perhatian* center of interest. **pen-** support. *~ kaki* **1** footstool. **2** kneeler (in a church pew).

tumpuk heap, pile, stack. *se- pekerjaan* a stack of work. **ber-(²) 1** be in piles or stacks. *Bukunya ~ di kamarnya* His room was piled high with books. *Uangnya ~* He has a lot of money. **2** in groups, clusters. *Meréka datang ~* They came in groups. *pulau kecil-kecil yg ~* tiny islands in clusters. **men- 1** pile up, accumulate. *Di sudut kamar satu-satu puntung rokok mulai ~* Cigarette butts were accumulating o. by o. in a corner of the room. **2** pile s.t. up. **men-i** pile up on top of s.t. *nasi yg di-i dua ékor ayam goréng* rice on top of which two fried chickens were added. **men-kan 1** pile s.t. up. *Buruh Tionghoa ~ beras di bangsal dapur* Ch laborers piled rice up in the makeshift kitchen. *~ kesalahan pd* heap the blame on. **2** hoard, accumulate. *Org dilarang ~ bahan makanan* People are forbidden to hoard foodstuffs. **ter- 1** piled up. **2** hoarded. **ke-an** accidentally piled on. *Wah, tanamannya ~ batu* Oh no! His plants got covered with rocks. **-an 1** stack, heap, mound. *~ salju* a mound of snow. *~ selimut* a pile of blankets. **2** group. **pen-an** accumulation, hoarding. *~ lemak pd permukaan kulit* the accumulation of oils on the surface of the skin. *~ kayu jati* the piling up of teakwood.

tumpul 1 dull, blunt. *pisau -* a blunt knife. **2** dull, stupid. *Pikirannya -* He is dull. **3** obtuse (of angles). **men- 1** become blunt. **2** become stupid. *Pikirannya ~* His thoughts became dull. **men-kan** blunt s.t. **ke-an** bluntness, dullness. *~ otak* dullness, stupidity. **-an** stub, s.t. blunt.

tumpur 1 ruined, destroyed. **2** (*Coll.*) broke, penniless. **men-kan** destroy.

tun (*Lit.*) title for noblemen.

tuna (*Lit.*) a wound. **ter-** hurt. *Kakinya ~* His foot was hurt. *Hatinya ~* His feelings were hurt.

tuna- privative affix forming literary and fancy compounds.

tunaaksara (*Lit.*) illiterate.

tunabusana (*Lit.*) naked, without clothing.

tunadiri (*Lit.*) without personality.

tunai cash. *membayar -* pay cash. **men-kan 1** fulfill, carry out. *~ perjanjian* fulfill a promise. *~ perintah* carry out orders. *~ kewajiban/tugas* accomplish o.'s task. **2** cash. ~ *cék* cash a check. **pen-an 1** (cash) payment. **2** settlement. **3** fulfillment. ~ *tugas* discharge of a duty. **per-an** matters pertaining to cash.

tunakarya (*Lit.*) unemployed. **ke-an** unemployment.

tunakawaca (*Lit.*) barely dressed.

tunalaras (*Lit.*) unsociable.

tunanétra (*Lit.*) blind. **ke-an** blindness.

tunang ber-(an) engaged, betrothed. *Sdh lama meréka* ~ They have been engaged for a long time. **men-i** take s.o. as o.'s betrothed. *Anak saya* ~ *Tuti* My son got engaged to Tuti. **memperkan, men-kan** affiancé. *Ia* ~ *anaknya* He arranged for his daughter's engagement. **-an** fiancé, fiancée. **pen-an** act of becoming engaged, betrothal. **per-an** engagement.

tunarungu (*Lit.*) deaf. - *wicara* deaf and mute.

tunas shoot, bud. - *melati* a jasimine bud. - *harapan* ray of hope, the new generation. - *muda/ mudi* children. **ber-** sprout, bud. *masa* ~ time of budding. **men-(i)** prune.

tunasusila (*Lit.*) immoral. *wanita* - prostitute.

tunawicara (*Lit.*) mute.

tunawisma (*Lit.*) homeless, without housing.

tunda₁ tow. *kail* - tow line (for fishing). **men-** tow. *Sepanjang hari kami* ~ *K.M. Tirtalana ke pelabuhan Ambon* All day we towed the Tirtalana to Ambon harbor. ~ *mobil mogok* tow a stalled car. **pen-** s.t. used for towing. *kapal* ~ tugboat or boat assisting another vessel (by towing it).

tunda₂ men-(kan) 1 postpone, delay. *Rapat di-* The meeting was postponed. **2** adjourn. **ter-** delayed. *Pesawatnya* ~ Her plane was delayed. **ter-²** repeatedly delayed. **pen-an** postponement, deferment, adjournment.

tunda₃ (*M*) push s.t.

tundangan (*Jkt*) see TUNANG.

tunduk 1 be bent down. *Hérman - malu* Herman was bent over in shame. - *tengadah* 1 ponder s.t. **2** nod o.'s head. **2** be bent in submission, submit to a higher authority. *Musuhnya tlh* - The enemy surrendered. *Ia memilih merdéka drp - pd Belanda* She chose freedom over surrendering to the Dutch. - *pd suatu pemerintahan Islam* obey a certain Islamic rule. **men-** bow. *Kepala Ibu* ~ *ke lantai mencari jarum yg jatuh* Mother's head bent over the floor as she looked for the needle that fell. **men-²** bow repeatedly, humble o.s. **men-i** bow over s.t. *Aku terus* ~ *halaman majalah itu* I kept my head bent over the pages of that magazine. **men-kan 1** cause s.o. or s.t. to bow. *Ia* ~ *kepalanya* He bowed his head. **2** cause s.o. to submit. *Ia* ~ *musuhnya dgn mudah* He conquered his opponent with ease. *Jerman Barat* ~ *US duasatu* W. Germany defeated the Soviet Union 2-1. **ter-** bowed, bent. *dgn kepala* ~ with a bent head. *Munah* ~ *mendengar nasihatku* Munah hung her head while listening to my advice. **ke-an 1** submission. **2** loyalty, obedience. **pen-an 1** submission, subjection. **2** subjugation.

tundun (*Jv*) bunch of fruit. *se- pisang* a bunch of bananas.

tundung men- expel, exile. *Ia di- oléh ayahnya* He was chased away by his father. **-an** exile, exiled.

tungau k.o. mite that infests fowls, mite.

tunggak₁ men- be in arrears. *Ia* ~ *bulan ini* He was in arrears this month. *Hutangnya di-* The debt is not paid. **-an 1** arrears. ~ *hutang* back debts, arrears. *Banyak* ~ *bulan ini* There were many delinquent payments this month. ~ *pajak* delinquent tax. **2** remainder. **pen-** o. who is arrears in payments. ~ *krédit* s.o. behind in his credit payments.

tunggak₂ see TONGGAK₁.

tunggal₁ 1 one and only, just one. *berdiri berkaki* - stand on o. foot. *Batara* - the supreme deity of Hinduism. *anak* - an only child. *penyanyi* - a solo singer. *paméran* - one-man show. - *berbéléng* quite alone. - *ika* unity, single. **ke-ikaan** unity, singleness. - *nada* monotonous. **ke-nadaan, pen-nadaan** monotony. **2** (*Ling.*) singular. *diri ketiga* - 3d person singular. *kalimat* - a simple sentence. **4** whole, complete, unconditional. *dgn hati* - wholeheartedly. **se-** of o. k.o. quality. *bapak dan anaknya* ~ like father like son. ~ *banjar dgn* (*Bali*) be a neighbor of. ~ *darah dgn* be related to. **men- 1** be alone. **2** be a single entity. *usaha ABRI yg mau* ~ *dgn Rakyat* the efforts of the Armed Forces to be o. with the people. **men-kan** concentrate into o. **ke-an 1** left alone. **2** singleness, oneness. **pen-an** concentration.

tunggal₂ banner.

tunggang₁ 1 upside down. **2** steep. *jalan yg amat* - a very steep road. - *balik* head over heels. **men-balikkan** turn s.t. upside down. - *hati* 1 keen about. **2** steadfast. - *langgang* head over heels. **men-langgangkan 1** let s.t. dive or tumble. **2** cause to run helter-skelter. *Bunyi pistol men-langgangkan musuhnya* The sound of a pistol caused the enemy to run helter-skelter. - *tunggik/tunggit* bob up and down, pitch. - **men-** head over heels. **men-kan** turn s.t. over. *Ia* ~ *pancinya spy isinya keluar* She turned the pan over to pour out its contents. **memper-kan** hold upside down.

tunggang₂ - *gunung* around sunset. **men-** ride, mount. *Ia* ~ *kuda* He rode horseback. **men-i 1** ride s.t. **2** use an existing activity or situation for o.'s own purpose or profit, get a free ride out of. *Présidén mendapatkan informasi bhw protés-protés itu di-i oléh kekuatan yg menentanginya* The president got the information that those protests were being exploited by forces that were opposed to him. **-an 1** mount, riding animal. **2** carriage, vehicle. **pen-** rider, passenger. ~ *kuda* horseman.

tunggik see TUNGGANG₁.

tungging₁ with tail end up. **men- 1** move with the rear end higher than the front. **2** sink bow first. **3** be upside down. *Botol* ~ *di méja* The bottles stood upside down on the table. **4** dive. *Pesawat itu* ~ *utk menjatuhkan bom* The plane dived to drop a bomb. **5** bulge toward the bottom. *Sakunya* ~ *penuh berisi* His pocket bulged. **men-kan 1** place s.t. upside down. *Botol di-kan di atas méja*

The bottle was placed upside down on the table. **2** lift or raise rear portion. *Kuda itu ~ kaki belakangnya* The horse lifted its hind legs. *Ia ~ pesawatnya* He put his plane into a dive. **3** overthrow (a high authority). *~ pemerintah* overthrow the gvt. **ter-** be in a position with rear end up.
tungging₂ four days from now.
tunggit with the posterior facing outward.
tunggu wait. *- dulu dong!* Hey, wait a minute! **ber-** guard, keep watch. **men- 1** wait for. *Ia ~ ayahnya* He waited for his father. **2** look forward to. **3** (*Jv*) stay at a place to take care of what has to be done there. *Dia lagi ~ réstorannya* She is taking care of the restaurant. **men-²** look forward to eagerly for some time. *Ia sdh lama ~ kedatangan surat itu* He'd been eagerly looking forward to that letter for a long time. **men-i 1** watch over, look after, guard. *~ rumah kosong* watch over an empty house. *Meréha ~ barang-barangnya di setasiun* They were guarding their luggage at the station. *Ada jin yg ~ sumur itu* There is a spirit watching over that well. **2** take care of, tend, nurse. *~ org sakit* nurse a sick person. *~ org makan* tend people eating. **men-kan** watch over on behalf of s.o. *Saya ~ kopernya* I watched his suitcase for him. **pen- 1** watchman, guard. *wanita ~ rumah* a woman who looks after the house. **2** attendant. *~ org sakit* hospital orderly. **3** tutelary spirit. **pen-an** act of waiting.
tunggul tree stump, stubble. **ke-an** *silsilah* **1** lineage. **2** dynasty.
tungkai leg. **men-** kick.
tungku hearth, fireplace. *- arang* charcoal stove. *- listrik* electric stove.
tungkul₁ (*Lit.*) **men- 1** bow o.'s head. **2** submit. **men-kan** bow s.t. *Ia ~ kepalanya* He lowered his head.
tungkul₂ (*Jv*) **men- 1** push from behind. **2** do s.t. to s.o. from behind. **-an** a push from behind.
tungkul₃ see TONGKOL₂.
tungkup (*M*) face downward. *- telentang* every which way (downward and upward facing). **men-telentangkan** consider s.t. from every angle. **men-** be in a face-downward position. *Ia ~ di tanah* She lay prostrate on the ground. **men-kan** place s.t. or s.o. face downward. *Perempuan itu ~ mukanya di dada suaminya* The woman put her face on her husband's chest. **ter-** in a face-downward position.
tungkus₁ parcel, package. **men-** wrap s.t.
tungkus₂ immersed. **ber-** *lumus* (*Lit.*) struggle against great odds.
tunjal ber-an receive support or subsidy. **men-** (*Lit.*) find footing for a leap.
tunjang₁ ber-an receive support or subsidy. **men-1** support. *Besi panjang ~ témbok itu* An iron bar supported that wall. **2** support financially. *Ia ~ ayahnya tiap bulan* He gave his father financial support every month. **-an 1** support, aid. **2** subsidy. *~ anak* dependent's allowance. *~ apkir/kecelakaan* disability allowance. *~ belajar* subsidy for study, scholarship. *~ jabatan* extra allowance o. gets for holding a high-ranking office. *~ ke-*

mahalan cost-of-living allowance. **3** alimony. **pen-** s.t. supporting. *fakta-fakta ~* supporting facts. **pen-an** the act of supporting. *~ krédit* credit support. *~ tercapainya sasaran* support toward achieving the goals.
tunjang₂ (*M*) leg. **men-** kick s.o. or s.t. **-an** a kick. *Ia didorong dgn ~ lutut seorg serdadu* He was shoved ahead with a knee kick from a soldier.
tunjuk 1 index finger. **2** show s.t. *- muka* appear before. *- silang* cross-reference. **men-silangkan** cross-reference s.t. **pen-silangan** cross-referencing. **men- 1** point toward, indicate. *Ia ~ ke selatan* He pointed toward the south. **2** show, indicate. *Papan ini ~ jalan ke utara* This sign indicates the road to the north. *Ia ~ halaman* He showed the page. *Ia ~ kpd kesalahan saya* She pointed to my mistake. **3** appoint, designate. *Pemerintah tlh ~nya selaku sékretaris* The gvt. appointed him as a secretary. **4** raise o.'s hand. *Yg blm dpt bagian harap ~* Those who have not received their share, please raise their hands. **5** with reference to (your letter). **men-i** advise s.o., train s.o. *Niscaya aku ~mu ke jalan yg lurus* I will surely provide you with advice to keep to the straight and narrow. **men-kan 1** point out s.t. *Ia ~ cara yg benar* He showed the right way. **2** indicate. *Sikapnya itu ~ asalnya* His attitude indicated where he came from. *Air mukanya ~ kegembiraan* Her face showed happiness. *Jam tlh ~ pukul setengah dua malam* The clock indicated 1:30 a.m. *~ bulunya* show o.'s real colors. **3** refer. *Indéks itu ~ nomor lima belas* The index refers to no. 15. **memper-kan 1** show, exhibit. *Filem itu diper-kan di kota ini* That film has been shown in this town. **2** demonstrate. *Ulfah ~ keboléhannya berkarat* Ulfah demonstrated her karate skills. **-an** indication. **pe- 1** instruction, guideline. *Obat ini hrs diminum menurut ~ dokter* This medicine must be taken according to the doctor's directions. **2** advice, guidance. *~ ayahnya* his father's advice. **3** indication, clue, hint. *~ kecelakaan* an omen of disaster. *tanpa bukti-bukti atau ~ yg kuat* without evidence or strong indications. *~ Tuhan* inspiration, divine guidance. **4** direction. *~ navigasi* navigation aids. **pen- 1** s.t. which indicates. *~ angin* weather vane. *~ arah* directional signal. *~ halaman* bookmark. *~ jalan* signpost, road sign. *~ télepon* telephone directory. **2** o. who indicates. *seorg ~ jalan* o. to show the way, a guide. **pe-an** appointment (to job, etc.). **pen-an 1** indication. **2** reference, pointing to s.t. *sumber ~* reference source. **3** appointment, assignment. *~ tugas* assignment of duties. **per-an 1** show, exhibition. **2** performance. *~ amal* charity performance. *~ bioskop* movie show. *~ perdana* premiére, opening performance.
tunjung lotus tree.
tuntas complete, total, thorough. *berantas korupsi secara -* eradicate corruption completely. *suatu penelitian yg -* a thorough investigation. **se-²nya** as thoroughly as possible. *menikmati dunia ini ~* enjoy this world to the full. **men-kan** treat exhaustively. *~ kasus korupsi* investigate the brib-

ery case to the very bottom. **ke-an 1** completeness, thoroughness. **2** (*Ling.*) exhaustiveness.

tuntun₁ ber- guided by means of s.t. *Ia berjalan ~ pd tongkatnya* He walked along, guiding himself by his cane. *Ia ~ pd petunjuk-petunjuk temannya* He was guided by his friend's instructions. **men- 1** guide s.o. or s.t. by a line, the hand, etc. *~ sepéda* push a bicycle by hand. *Ia ~ org buta* He guided a blind person by the hand. *Sérsan Lumbato ~ seékor kambing* Sergeant Lumbato led a goat by a rope. **2** give guidance to. *Paman selalu ~ kami spy tetap jujur* Uncle always taught us to remain honest. **-an** guidance. *~ agama* **1** religious guidance. **2** the guidance provided by religion. **pen- 1** guide. **2** manual, guide. **pen-an 1** leading with a line, etc. **2** providing guidance.

tuntun₂ (*M*) close o.'s eyes.

tuntung 1 point (of needle, etc.). **2** small box or case. **men- 1** cut into tiny pieces. **2** empty.

tuntut men- 1 demand. *Ia ~ kpdnya spy utangnya dibayar* He demanded from her that the debt be paid. *~ haknya* claim o.'s rights. *Jaksa ~ saya sembilan tahun* The public attorney demanded a sentence of nine years for me. *~ balas/béla/malu* demand revenge, avenge s.t. **2** (*Leg.*) prosecute, sue. *Ia di- di muka pengadilan* He was prosecuted in court. *~ dakwa* bring a charge (against s.o.). **3** strive for. *~ ilmu* pursue knowledge. **-an 1** demand. *~ kenaikan gaji* demands for a salary increase. *~ darah* vendetta. **2** striving, pursuit. **3** (*Leg.*) indictment, claim. *~ hukum* criminal procedure. **pen- 1** o. who demands s.t., petitioner. **2** (*Leg.*) claimant, prosecutor. *~ Umum* general prosecutor. **3** o. who strives after. *~ ilmu* scholar, student. **pen-an 1** demanding. *~ imbalan jasa* demanding repayment of services. **2** pursuit, study. **3** (*Leg.*) prosecution.

tunu men- roast in a fire. **men-kan** roast for s.o. **ter-** get burnt or roasted. **pen-** o. who roasts. **pen-an** roasting.

tupai squirrel. *- belang* striped squirrel. *- cerlih* k.o. small squirrel. *- kerawak* k.o. large squirrel with reddish fur.

tupai-tupai clamps on a boat.

tupang see TOPANG₁.

tur 1 tour (of inspection, etc.). **2** organized travel. *Ia ikut - ke AS* He joined a tour to the US.

tura-tura (*M*) **ber- 1** get very angry, go into a rage. *Ia akan ~ dan membusuk-busukkan nama pengurus itu* She will be furious and slander the manager's good name. **2** talk in o.'s sleep.

turba [*turun ke bawah*] **1** visit by officials to villages (in the 1960s). **2** trend (among political leaders) to maintain channels of communication with the people. *Dr. Idham Khalid sibuk - memimpin umat Islam* Dr. Idham Khalid is busy visiting villages and giving guidance to the Isl. leaders. **ber- 1** be in close contact with the people. **2** engage in joint projects with the ordinary citizens (of students helping peasants to harvest, etc.). **men-kan** cause close contacts with the people. *Mahasiswa-mahasiswa yg di-kan* The students who

have been sent to associate with the people in joint projects. **pen-an** going down to the people.

turbin turbine.

turi sesbania, ornamental shrub or small tree with white or red pealike flowers.

turih see TORÉH.

turis₁ tourist.

turis₂ notch, scratch. **men-** make a notch or scratch.

turisme tourism.

Turki Turk, Turkish, Turkey.

turnamén tournament.

turné 1 tour, esp. on official business. **2** go on tour (for business, work, etc.). *Ia sdh lama - mengelilingi dunia* He has been touring around the world for a long time. **ber-** make a tour.

turnoi tournament.

tursa [*turun ke desa*] trend (among political leaders) to maintain channels of communication with the rural people.

Tursina Sinai.

turun 1 go down, descend. *- gunung* go down a mountain. *Ia - dr sepédanya* He got off his bicycle. *- ke sampan* get down into a dugout. *Hujan -* The rain fell. *- bérok* hernia. *- derajat* demoted. *- ke air* bathe in the river. *- ke darat* go ashore. *- ke bumi* ceremonial occasion of child's touching the earth for the first time. *- ke sawah* go to work in the rice fields. *- mandi* **1** take a bath (in the river). **2** a child's first bath in the river. *- mesin* overhaul a machine. *- mobil* get out of a car. *- pangkat* get demoted. *- tangan* **1** meddle, interfere. **2** lend a hand. *Kalau ada kesukaran lain baru lurah akan - tangan* Only if there were other difficulties would the village head step in. *- tangga* **1** descend steps or a ladder. **2** staircase fashion. *Meréka berjéjér - tangga* They lined up in staircase fashion. *- takhta* abdicate. **2** decrease, decline. *Panasnya -* His temperature went down. *Penghasilannya -* Her income decreased. *Préstasi atlit kita -* The performance of our athletes slumped. *- naik* **1** go up and down. **2** fluctuate. **men-naik-kan** cause to go up and down, cause fluctuation. *- temurun* **1** hereditary. **2** for generations. **di-temurunkan** passed on from o. generation to the other. *Naskah itu di-temurunkan sejak jaman Diponegoro* That manuscript was handed down from o. generation to the next ever since the time of Diponegoro. **3** befall, descend upon. *Kemalangan itu - kpd org yg tak berdosa* That tragedy befell innocent people. **4** set (of sun). *Matahari sdh -* The sun has set. *matahari tengah -* mid-afternoon. **5** (*Coll.*) dance. *Di pésta tadi malam, Totok - dgn Mimi* At last night's party, Totok danced with Mimi. **6** move from o. place to another (of respected persons). *Para haji blm - dr Mekah* The Muslim pilgrims have not arrived from Mecca yet. **7** take a break. *- main* school recess. *- minum* rest period, time out. **ber-an 1** (*Coll.*) have offspring. **2** get off a vehicle (of several). **men- 1** go down, descend, down (in crossword puzzles). *Jalan ini ~* This road slopes downward. **2** decline, sink, decrease. *Kualitétnya ~* The quality declined. **3** be herditary. *Penyakitnya ~ pd cucunya* His illness was passed down to the grandchildren. **4** (*Ling.*) falling (of tones). **men-i 1** go down along s.t. *~ sungai* go down along the river. *~ tangga* go down the stairs. **2** go down to, descend to. *Aku ~ dusun itu* I went down to the hamlet. *~ sumur* go down into a well. **mcn-kan 1** cause s.t. to go down. *~ tentara payung* drop paratroopers. *~ sauh* drop anchor. *~ bendéra* haul down the flag. *~ peti jenazah* lower a casket. *Caprina ~ pemain-pemain baru ke lapangan* Caprina put their new players on the field. *~ laporan* file a report. **2** discharge passenger or cargo. *~ muatan* unload a cargo. *Ia ~ temannya di muka setasiun* He dropped his friend off in front of the station. **3** reduce, lower. *~ harga* reduce the price. *~ kewaspadaannya* lower o.'s guard. *~ pangkat* demote. **4** send down s.t. to o.'s inferiors. *~ peringatan* hand down a warning. *~ Kitab Injil* reveal the New Testament. **5** generate (descendants), produce a hereditary line of. *~ raja-raja Perancis* beget a line of French kings. **ke-an 1** decline. *~ harga-harga* decline in prices. **2** descent, offspring, scion. *~ bahasa* linguistic affiliation. *~ raja* royal descent. *penyakit ~* hereditary disease. **3** generation. **4** inherit. *Ia ~ penyakit org tuanya* He has inherited his parent's disease. **5** possessed, seized. *~ org halus* possessed by a spirit. **berke-an 1** for generations. **2** of a certain ethnic heritage. *~ Arab* of Arab blood. **-an 1** descendant. *~ raja-raja* s.o. of royal descent. *penyakit ~* hereditary disease. **2** generation. *menetap di sana tiga ~* reside there for three generations. **3** copy. **4** (*Ling.*) derivative. **5** slope, descent. *~ yg curam* a steep slope. **pen-an 1** slope, descent. **2** discharge, unloading. *~ dr kapal* disembarkation. **3** lowering, taking down. *~ bendéra* lowering of the flag. *~ gambar-gambar Sukarno* taking down pictures of Sukarno. **4** derivation, deriving. *Prosés ~ dalil ini kita namakan déduksi* The process of deriving this argument is what we call deduction. **5** reduction, decline (of cost, prices, etc.).

turus 1 pillar, post, stake. **2** numerical classifier for long narrow objects. *se- sabun cuci* o. long bar of laundry soap. **men-** straight and erect. **men-kan** (*Lit.*) tie s.o. to a post as a punishment.

turut join in. *- campur* interfere. *- makan* join in eating. *- pergi* go along with. *Ia hrs - bertanggung jawab* He must share the responsibility. *Aku dipaksanya - ke rumah* He forced me to follow him to his house. *- menentukan* have a share in deciding. *- serta* go along with, participate. **men-sertakan** draw s.o. or s.t. into. *Dia di-sertakan dlm rapat* They involved him in the meeting. **pe-sertaan** drawing s.o. or s.t. into, involving. **-²** join in. **ber-² 1** in succession, in a row. *Meréka berjalan ~* They walked o. after the other. *pendekatan-pendekatan ~* successive approaches. *tiga jam ~* three hours at a stretch. *Ia ~ diminta*

pulang Over and over again he was asked to come home. **2** continued. *cerita ~* a continued story. **men- 1** follow. *~ jejak pamannya* follow in his uncle's footsteps. **2** according to. *~ kata org* according to what people say. *~ waktu* chronological. *~ akal* reasonable, rational. **3** imitate, follow along. *Ia ketawa-tawa ~ kakaknya* He was laughing in imitation of his older brother. *~ contoh di papan* copy an example on the board. **4** obey, follow. *Ia ~ kata ayahnya* He obeyed his father's words. *~ keadaan* adapt to the situation. *Anjing ini perlu diikat karena masih blm ~* This dog has to be tied up because it does not obey yet. **men-i 1** follow. *~ pencuri yg lari* follow the fleeing thief. *~ perkabaran dgn teliti* follow the news closely. **2** grant. *~ permintaan* grant a request. **3** comply with, observe (regulations, etc.). *~ kemauan org tua* comply with o.'s parents' wishes. **men-kan 1** obey, follow. *Ia ~ perintah* He obeyed the order. *~ nafsu berahinya* follow o.'s sensual impulse. **2** copy, imitate. *Ia ~ tingkah laku temunnya* He copied his friend's behavior. **3** cause s.o. to follow or join in. **memper-kan** follow, obey. *~ hati* give way to o.'s emotions. **memper-²kan** have s.o. get involved. *Ia diper-²kan dlm soal itu* He was forced to become involved in that matter. **-an 1** example. **2** sequence, succession. **3** s.t. joining in. **-²an** accommodating, merely following others. *Ia tak pernah ada pendapat sendiri; selalu ~ saja* He never has an opinion of his own; he just follows others. **pen- 1** s.o. obedient and docile. *seorg yg pendiam dan ~* a taciturn and docile person. **2** a follower. **per-an 1** continuation. **2** repetitiveness.

tus sound of whizzing (bullets, etc.).

tusam see KAYU₁.

tuslah 1 extra allowance, wage supplement. **2** excess fare, extra charge on tickets.

tusor, tussor k.o. fabric.

tustél camera.

tusuk 1 a pin. **2** stick, skewer. *dua - saté* two skewers of barbecued meat. *- gigi* toothpick. *- jarum* acupuncture. *- kondé* hairpin. **men- 1** stab s.o. *Isteriku tlh ~nya dgn pisau dapur* My wife stabbed him with a kitchen knife. **2** prick, stick. *~ dgn jarum* prick with a needle. *~ jarum* apply acupuncture. *ucapan yg ~* biting words. *~ hati* hurt o.'s feelings. **3** skewer s.t. **4** vote by perforating the symbol of o.'s choice on the ballot, punch a ballot. *~ PDI* vote PDI. **5** penetrate. *Pisauku ~ badannya* My knife penetrated his body. *bau keringat yg ~* a penetrating smell of sweat. **men-i 1** perforate s.t. in many places. **2** penetrate s.t. *Bau kemenyan ~ hidungku* A smell of incense was pungent (penetrated my nostrils). **men-kan** stab or prick with s.t. *Ia ~ pisau ke musuhnya* He jabbed a knife into his opponent. *~ jarum ke bantal* stick a needle into a pillow. **ter-** get stabbed. **-an 1** a stab, a prick. **2** puncture. **3** a bite, a twinge. **pen-** s.t. to perforate or stab with. **pen-an 1** stabbing, jabbing. **2** perforation.

tuter auto horn. **men-, ment-** blow a horn.

tutor tutor.
tuts 1 mechanical buttons. - *trompét* trumpet valves. - *mesin tik* typewriter keys. **2** piano key.
tutuh men- lop off, trim.
tutuk men- 1 tap, knock on. **2** strike with o.'s fingers (in martial arts). **ter-** struck, knocked. **-an** a knock, a tap.
tutul 1 pockmarked. *Mukanya -* His face was pockmarked. **2** spotted, stained. *harimau -* k.o. spotted leopard. **men-²kan** dab on. *di-²kan hanya di tempat yg ada jerawatnya* to be dabbed on only where there are pimples.
tutup 1 closed, shut. *Kantor sdh -* The office is closed. - *buku* balanced (of books). - *tahun* annual balancing of books. **2** cover, lid. - *panci* pan lid. - *kepala* head gear. - *jendéla* curtain. - *malu* a means of concealing an embarrassment. **3** complete, full. *setahun -* a full year. **ber-** have a cover. *cangkir ~* cup with cover. *Jip kami tdk ~* Our jeep did not have a roof. **men-** 1 close, shut. *~ buku* close a book. *~ kantor* close the office. *~ pintu* close or shut the door. *Rapat di- pd jam dua belas malam* The meeting was concluded at midnight. *~ mata* die. *~ jalan* block a road. **2** cover. *~ muka* cover the face. *~ ongkos* cover expenses. *~ méja* set the table. **3** hide, conceal. *~ maksud yg buruk* hide o.'s bad intentions. **4** fill in, cover over. *~ selokan* fill in a ditch. *~ lowong(an)* fill a gap, vacuum, vacancy. **5** lock, shut up in jail. *Ia di- dlm penjara* He was locked up in jail. **men-i** 1 provide a cover for. *Lantainya di-i permadani* A carpet covered the floor. **2** cover up. *~ dosa-dosanya* cover up o.'s sins. **3** cover or shut repeatedly. *Ia coba ~ jendéla dan pintu* He kept trying to shut the windows and doors. **men-²i** cover s.t. up. **men-kan** 1 cover with s.t. *Ia ~ topinya ke muka anaknya* He covered his child's face with his hat. **2** close or cover on s.o.'s behalf. *Ia ~ surat itu utk ibunya* He sealed the letter for his mother. **ter-** 1 shut, closed. *sampul ~* a closed (sealed) envelope. **2** locked, secured. **3** reclusive, closed (of o.'s personality or feelings). **4** closed off, not available. *Ia ~ pd idé baru* He is closed to new

ideas. *Kesempatan meneruskan di perguruan tinggi sdh ~ bagi meréka yg kurang mampu* The opportunity to study at the university level has become closed off for those who do not have the means.
keter-an reticence, closedness. *Kita tahu bhw ~ adalah lawan démokrasi* We know that concealment is the enemy of democracy. **-an** 1 cover, lid. **2** place where people are locked up (prison, etc.). *Kedua tawanan ditempatkan pd sebuah ~ darurat* The two prisoners were placed in a temporary lock-up. **pen-** 1 cover, lid, casing. *~ botol* bottle cap. *~ badan* body covering. **2** closing. *sbg ~* in closing (of letters or speeches). *ucapan ~* closing address. **pen-an** 1 covering. *~ tanaman* covering a plant. **2** closing, shutting, occlusion, shut down. *pésta-pésta ~* closing festivities. *~ sidang* the closing of the session.
tutur₁ speech, talk. - *bayi* infant talk. - *kata* words, phrases, sayings. *menjadi buah -* the talk of the town. - *sapa* form of address. **ber-** talk, speak. *Ia ~ dlm bahasa asing* He spoke in a foreign language. **ber-²** talk, converse. **men-kan** 1 relate, narrate, tell about. *Ia ~ pengalamannya* He related his experiences. **2** pronounce, express. **3** inform, announce. **-an** 1 story, narrative, discourse. **2** information, announcement. **pen-** speaker, narrator, pronouncer. *~ bahasa Indonésia* a speaker of Indonesian. *~ ceritera* a storyteller. **pen-an** 1 talk, speech. *~nya langsung* Her speech is direct. **2** discussion, narrative. **3** announcement, information. **per-an** 1 conversation. **2** word, phrase. **3** pronunciation. **4** (*Ling.*) speech act.
tutur₂ -an lowest part of thatched roof. **pe-an, pen-an** (*Lit.*) descendant.
tuyul k.o. spirit that obtains wealth for its human master.
TV [*télévisi*] television. **ber-** have a TV. **per-an** television business.
TVRI [*Télévisi Républik Indonésia*] Television Service of the Republic of Indonesia.
twédehan, twédehans (*Coll.*) secondhand, used.
typis /tipis/ typical.

U

u /u/ u, the 21st letter of the alphabet.
ua, uak₁ 1 (*Coll.*) term of address for (Jv or Sd) men and women of o.'s parent's age. **2** (*Sd*) uncle or aunt, term of address for o.'s parents' elder siblings. **3** (*Ch*) term of address and reference for o.'s elder aunt.
uak₂ see KUAK₂.
uang 1 money. - *administrasi* administrative costs. - *angus* 1 bridegroom's share in wedding ex-

penses. **2** unspent portion of budgeted expenses which must be returned to budgeting agency. - *bandar* stake (in gambling). - *bangku* school contribution. - *bedol* financial support for people resettled by the gvt. - *buta* 1 unemployment compensation. **2** official half pay. - *capé* tip. - *cegatan* bribe paid to be admitted. - *céndol* spending money. - *duduk* money o. gets for attending a meeting. - *duka* donation to relatives of deceased person. - *ikhlas* money given in compensation to s.o. who has suffered an injury. - *jajan* pocket money. - *jalan* travel expenses. - *jasa* honorarium. - *jerih* tip. - *jujur(an)* 1 token sum of money. 2 money given to bride and groom. - *kancing* deposit. - *kas* funds of an organization. - *kecil* small change. - *kembali(an)* change. - *kematian* donation to family of dead person. - *keras* strong currency. - *kontan* cash. - *kopi* 1 tip. 2 bribe. - *kuliah* university tuition. - *kunci* 1 key money, bribe to tenants to persuade them to vacate premises. 2 deposit. - *kupatan/Lebaran* extra charges levied just prior to the *Lebaran* festival. - *lauk-pauk* military subsistence. - *lelah* compensation. - *makan* (*Mil.*) money for food while on duty. - *mati* uninvested capital, capital not earning interest. - *muka* advance payment. - *panas* 1 a loan at high interest rate. 2 hot money, money earned through gambling or corruption. - *pangkal* entrance fee in schools. - *panjar* down payment. - *pecah* small change. - *pelicin* bribe. - *pitingan* road tariff collected illegally. - *plécét* bribe. - *rapat* honorarium for attending a meeting. - *récéh/réncéh* small change. - *saku* pocket money. - *sembah* money given to girl's parents after breaking an engagement. - *semir/senin* bribe. - *sidang* honorarium for court officials or members of parliament when in session. - *siluman* money from unclear source, bribe. - *sirih* 1 tip. 2 bribe. - *sogok(an)/sorok/suap* bribe. - *susuk* small change. - *téh* 1 tip. 2 bribe. - *thiap/tiap* key money (presented to previous tenants to persuade them to vacate a house). - *tikaman* stake (in gambling). - *tinta* 1 tip for a clerk. 2 bribe. - *tunai* cash. - *pecah* small change. 2 coin. - *bolong* coin with a hole in the center. - *mas ukon* gold coin used as an ornament. *setali tiga* - six of o. and half dozen of the other. - *tali* 25-cent piece. **ber-** 1 have money. 2 be well off. **meng-i** finance s.t. *Ia ~ perusahaan anaknya* He financed his son's business. **meng-kan** 1 cash in s.t. *~ poswésel* cash a postal money order. 2 sell s.t. (jewelry, etc.) for cash. **ke-an** finances, things having to do with money. *Saya tdk keberatan asal ~ mengizinkannya* I have no objections if the finances allow it. **-²an** 1 counterfeit money. 2 play money. **peng-an** cashing of checks, money orders, etc. **per-an** monetary affairs.

uap₁ 1 steam, vapor. 2 fume. **ber-** 1 steam. 2 carbonated (drinks). **meng-** 1 evaporate, vaporize. 2 become steam. **meng-i** steam s.t. *Utk menjaga kesegaran kulit, ibu-ibu spy ~ muka* Ladies, apply steam to your faces to ensure freshness of the skin. **meng-kan** 1 steam. 2 let evaporate. *~ air laut* let sea water evaporate. **-an** s.t. steamed. **peng-an** 1 evaporation. *Buah-buahan itu dikeringkan dgn cara ~* They dried the fruits by means of dehydration. 2 distillation process.

uap₂ see KUAP.

uar announcement, proclamation. **ber-, meng-(²)** cry out, proclaim. **meng-kan** proclaim s.t.

ub. [*untuk beliau*] on behalf of him (used when signing on behalf of a higher authority). *Gubernur Jawa Timur, - Sékwilda* On behalf of the governor of E. Java, the regional secretary.

uba vessel for sago meal.

ubah difference. *tak - dgn/spt* the same as, no different from. **ber-** change, become different. *Bunga itu ~ warna* The flower changed color. *Ia ~ hatinya* She changed her mind. *Angin ~* The wind shifted. *~ akal/ingatan* be crazy, go insane. *~ pikiran* change o.'s mind. **ber-²** be fickle, changeable, fluctuate. *Pendapatnya ~* His opinion often changes. **meng-** 1 change, become different. 2 alter, modify. *~ sikapnya* change o.'s attitude. *Hukum mati di- menjadi seumur hidup* The death sentence was commuted to life imprisonment. **meng-i** change or modify several things. *Utk apa pula ia selalu ~ rencana yg sdh matang?* Why in the world does he always change plans that are already set? **meng-kan** alter on behalf of s.o. **ter-** changed. **-an** 1 variation. 2 change, alteration. **pe-** variable. **peng-** 1 o. who changes. 2 corrector. *~ arus listrik* instrument to change alternating current into direct current. **peng-an** process of altering, modification. **per-an** change, alteration. *~ haluan* change of opinion or policy. *zaman ~* transitional era.

ubal see UBEL.

uban gray hair. **ber-** have gray hair. **meng-** be graying. **meng-i** 1 pull out gray hairs. *Ia ~ ayahnya* She pulled out her father's gray hairs. 2 cause gray hair (through worry, etc.). **-an** gray-headed. *Kalau sdh ~ jangan melirik gadis lagi* What are you doing looking at young girls when you are already all gray!

ubar₁ 1 k.o. tree the bark of which is used for dye or paint. 2 dye or paint derived from such a tree. **meng-** paint or dye s.t. with such material.

ubar₂ **meng-** unroll s.t. and spread it out.

ubat see OBAT.

ubek /ubek, ube'/ **meng-** stir vigorously by hand. **-an** s.t. stirred or mixed up with the hands.

ubel, ubel-ubel 1 anything wrapped around part of the body. 2 head-wrap, turban.

uber **meng-(²)** go after, pursue. **-²an** chase e.o. **peng-an** pursuit.

ubi 1 edible tuber. - *jalar/jawa* sweet potato. - *kayu/kasbi/kaspé* cassava. - *kelédék* sweet potato. - *kenduduk* k.o. tuber. - *kentang* potato. - *perancis* cassava. - *rambat* sweet potato. 2 sweet potato. *Ada - ada talas* tit for tat (lit., if there are sweet potatoes there is taro). **-²an** various k.o. tubers.

ubin floortile. **meng-i** tile s.t.

ublak-ublek (*Jv*) **ng-** turn upside down to find s.t.

ubleg-ubleg (*Jv*) **ng-** pester s.o.

ubrak-abrik see OBRAK-ABRIK.

ubub, ububan a pair of bellows.

ubudiah (*Isl*) matters pertaining to prayer ritual.

ubun **ber-** loom. *Gedung besar ~ di muka kami* A large building loomed before our eyes.

ubun-ubun₁ 1 fontanel. 2 crown of head. *matahari di -* midday.

ubun-ubun₂ (*Lit.*) nun.
ubur-ubur jellyfish.
ucap saying, word. - *siapa?* Who said that? **ber-1** (*Lit.*) say, utter. ~ *doa* utter a prayer. ~ *pidato* make a speech. ~ *selamat* congratulate. **2** pronounce. *Ia* ~ *kata dgn jelas* He pronounced the word clearly. **meng-** (*Isl.*) worship God by pronouncing His names and attributes. **meng-i 1** say s.t. to s.o. *Ia* ~ *selamat murid-murid kelas tiga* She congratulated the 3d grade pupils. **2** recite spells over s.o., treat s.o. who is ill by reciting prayers and invocations. *Dukun itu* ~ *anak Bu Wati yg sedang sakit* The shaman recited spells over Mrs. Wati's sick child. **meng-(kan)** express. *Saya* ~ *terima kasih banyak-banyak* I express my deepest thanks. **ter-** have been pronounced. **terkan 1** mentionable. **2** happen to be uttered. **-an 1** utterance, expression. ~ *selamat* congratulations. **2** statement, communication. **3** pronunciation. **peng-an** pronouncing.
ucek (*Jkt, Jv*) **meng-(²)** rub with o.'s hands. *Dr tadi saya* ~ *baju ini tapi fléknya tdk hilang-hilang* I have been rubbing this shirt for a while now but the stain will not come out. ~ *mata* rub o.'s eyes.
ucus see USUS.
uda₁ (*M*) older brother or male cousin.
uda₂, udah (*Jkt*) see SUDAH.
udak meng- chase after, pursue. *Payah wartawan* ~ *berita dr menteri itu* With difficulty the reporters chased after the minister for news.
udak-udak meng- stir. *Di-nya tumpukan nasi* He stirred the heap of rice.
udal-adul meng- rumple hair, string, or other hairlike material. *Rambut gondrongnya di- dgn jari-jarinya* He ran his fingers through his shoulder-length hair.
udan k.o. batik pattern.
udang shrimp. *Ada - di balik batu* There is s.t. behind it (lit., there is a shrimp behind the rock). - *batu* rock shrimp. - *galah* 1 k.o. large prawn. **2** (*Coll.*) lobster. - *geragau/gerangau* k.o. small shrimp used for shrimp paste. - *goréng tepung* batter-fried shrimp. - *tak tahu dibungkuknya* not to know o.'s own defects (lit., the shrimp doesn't know it is crooked). - *dlm tangguk* worried, uneasy (lit., a shrimp in a scoop). **-²an 1** various k.o. shrimps. **2** imitation shrimp.
udap-udapan salad made of various k.o. vegetables, often bought as a snack on the street.
udar (*Jv*) reel. **meng- 1** reel, wind. **2** disentangle.
udara 1 air. - *melingkungi bumi* Air surrounds the earth. **2** atmosphere. - *politik* political atmosphere. **3** sky, air space. **4** weather. **ber-** have a certain k.o. weather. *kota yg* ~ *dingin* a city with cold weather. **meng- 1** go on the air (radio, etc.). **2** go up in the air (balloons, etc.). **meng-kan 1** air (programs). *Acara ini di-kan tiap Sabtu malam* This program is broadcast every Saturday night. **2** put s.t. in the air, let s.t. fly. **ke-an** matters pertaining to air. **peng-an 1** airing. ~ *radio pendidikan* putting educational radio on the air,

school radio. **2** releasing s.t. into the air. ~ *pesawat layang* releasing of a balloon ship into the air.
udé, udéh (*Jkt*) see SUDAH.
udek (*Jv, Jkt*) **meng-** stir.
udel (*Jv*) navel. *seénak -nya sendiri* do as o. likes without regard for propriety (lit., do as o.'s own navel pleases).
udeng (*Jv, Jkt*) headcloth (for men).
udet (*Jv*) belt.
udi (*M*) unfortunate.
udik 1 upper course of a river. *di - sungai* on the upper course of a river. **2** interior, inland country. **3** (*Jkt*) backward, countrified. *Dia - sekali déh! Masak malam-malam pakai kaca hitam* He is really a bumpkin! Imagine wearing sunglasses in the middle of the night. **meng- 1** go upstream. **2** return to o.'s ancestral village. **-an** s.o. raised in a rural area.
udu see WUDHU.
uduh see ODOH.
uduk see NASI.
udur see UZUR.
udut (*Jv*) **meng-** smoke s.t. **-an** pipe to smoke. **peng-** o. who smokes.
udzur see UZUR.
uék see UIK.
ufuk horizon.
ugahari (*Lit.*) moderate, frugal, temperate.
ugal-ugal ke-an 1 naughtiness, mischief. **2** recklessness, inconsiderateness. **-an 1** mischievous, naughty. **2** reckless, inconsiderate.
ugama see AGAMA.
ugem (*Jv*) property. **meng-** claim as o.'s own. *Ia* ~ *kekuasaan pemerintah* He claims governmental authority.
ugeran (*Jv*) rule, norm.
UGM [*Universitas Gadjah Mada*] Gadjah Mada University in Yogyakarta.
ugut intimidation, threat. **meng-** threaten, intimidate.
uhu 1 sound of an owl. **2** owl.
uhuk sound of s.o. crying and sobbing. **meng-²** sob.
UI [*Universitas Indonésia*] University of Indonesia in Jkt.
uih see WIH.
uik meng- squeal (of pigs).
uir-uir k.o. locust.
uja see OJA.
ujan see HUJAN.
ujang (*in some regions only*) term of familiar address for boys.
ujar 1 statement. *-nya ia akan datang nanti* He said he would come later. **2** (*Ling.*) utterance. **berspeak. meng-kan** say s.t. **-an** statement, pronouncement.
ujat see HUJAT.
uji test, experiment. - *coba* a try-out. **meng-** *coba* try s.o. or s.t. out. **meng- 1** examine. *Ia* ~ *mas itu* He tested the gold. *Ia* ~ *murid baru itu* He tested the new student. **2** put to the test, try. *Pengala-*

man itu ~ *kesabaran saya* That experience tried my patience. **ter-** put to a test. **ke-an** (*M*) found out, discovered. **-an 1** examination. ~ *lisan* oral examination. ~ *pendadaran* comprehensive exam. ~ *persiapan* 1 examination at end of first university year (in older, now-defunct system). 2 preliminary examination, entrance examination. **2** test, trial, experiment. *Kejujurannya sedang dlm* ~ His honesty is being tested. **3** assay. **4** (*Coll.*) take an exam. **peng-** examiner. **peng-an** trial, testing. ~ *keséhatan* medical examination.

ujud see WUJUD.

ujung 1 tip, point, top. *di - mulut* be much talked of. *- jari* finger tip. *- kuku* a little bit. *- lidah* 1 tip of the tongue. **2** spokesman. *- mata* outer corner of the eye. *- tanah* (*Geog.*) cape. **2** end. *- bulan Januari* end of January. *di pulau yg paling - sebelah barat* on the westernmost island. *- kota* suburbs, outskirts. *- pangkal* lower and upper ends, beginning and end. *Jawabnya itu tak tentu - pangkalnya* His answer was incoherent (undecipherable as to the beginning and end). *tak* **ber-** *pangkal* incoherent. **ber-** 1 pointed. *besi yg* ~ *tajam* iron bar with sharp point. **2** culminate in. **meng-1** reach an end or a top. **2** become sharp or pointed. **3** intensify. *Perselisihan tlh* ~ *dan mungkin perang akan meletus* The conflict has intensified and war will probably break out. **ter-** the furthest end or tip. *di bahagian* ~ *dr perkampungan* in the furthest reaches of the settlement. **peng-** extreme end. ~ *minggu* end of the week.

ujur see UZUR.

ujut see WUJUD.

ukhrowi (*Isl.*) eschatological matters.

ukhuwah (*Isl.*) 1 fraternity (of believers). 2 association, organization.

ukir ber-² 1 embellished with all manner of carving. **2** pockmarked. *wajah yg* ~ a pockmarked face. **ber-an** having a carving in it. *-* **meng-** carve repeatedly. **meng-** carve s.t., engrave. *Dia* ~ *kayu itu* He carved the piece of wood. **meng-kan** carve into or on s.t. *Ia* ~ *namanya pd cincin* He engraved her name on the ring. ~ *dlm hati* imprint in the heart. *Ia* ~ *pelajaran itu dlm hatinya* He implanted that lesson in his mind. **ter-** carved **-an** a carved object. ~ *kayu* a wood carving. ~ *timbul* bas-relief. **peng-** engraver, carver. **peng-an** act of carving.

ukon coin worth ½ rupiah.

ukup 1 incense, perfume. **2** scent. **ber-** be perfumed or incensed. **meng-, meng-i** perfume s.t., incense s.t. *Pengantin wanita di-i dgn dupa* The bride was made fragrant with incense. **-an 1** perfume, scent. **2** censer. **per-an** censer.

ukur 1 measure. *- alit* rules and regulations. *- baju di badan sendiri* judge others by o.s. **2** measuring tape. **se-** in agreement. *Adi* ~ *dgn rencana kita* Adi is in agreement with our plan. **ber-an** have a measurement of. *Peluru itu* ~ *tiga puluh méter* The missile measures 30 meters. **meng-1** measure, survey. ~ *jalan* go strolling or riding

(in car, on motorbike). *kalau di- dgn* in comparison with. **2** read a meter. ~ *suhu* take o.'s temperature. **meng-kan** measure against s.t. *Garis P di-kan pd garis Q* Take line P and measure it against line Q. **ter-** measured, measurable. **-an 1** measurement, measure. ~ *induk* standard measure. ~ *isi* cubic measure. ~ *luas* square measure. ~ *panjang* linear measure. **2** size, dimension. *satu kamar* ~ *sedang* a medium sized room. **3** format. **4** norm, criterion, standard. *Kecantikan bukanlah* ~ *yg mutlak* Beauty is not an absolute criterion *menurut* ~ *ku* according to my standards. **5** measuring stick. ~ *jangka* geometric compass. **peng- 1** meter, gauge. ~ *jarak* odometer. ~ *lengas* hygrometer. **2** o. who measures. ~ *tanah* surveyor. **peng-an** measuring, gauging.

ulah manner, way, act. **meng-** prepare.

ulai see KULAI.

ulak see ULEG.

ulak-ulak (*Anat.*) *- pinggang* pelvis, hollow above the hips. **ber-** whirl, bubble (water, etc.).

ulam raw vegetable side dish with rice. *- mencari sambal* women looking for a husband (lit., raw vegetable looking for dressing). **-²** concubine. **ber-** have a raw vegetable side dish.

ulama, ulamak (*Isl.*) 1 scholar of Isl. 2 Muslim religious teacher or leader.

ulang frequent, repeatedly. *- alik* go back and forth. **ber-** *-alik* shuttle (aircrafts). *- aling* to and fro. *- tahun* birthday, anniversary. **ber-** *tahun* have a birthday, commemorate an anniversary. **ber-** happen again, recur. *Ia takut bhw sejarah akan* ~ She was afraid that history would repeat itself. ~ *kali* repeatedly. **ber-²(an)** be repeated. *Anak-anak itu* ~ *menyajikan pantun jenaka* The children repeatedly exchanged humorous pantuns. **meng- 1** repeat s.t. *Ia* ~ *pertanyaannya* He repeated his question. *Aku terpaksa* ~ *Tahun I* I had to repeat the first year at the university. **2** study over again. *Meréka* ~ *pelajaran utk besok* They studied their lessons for tomorrow. **meng-i 1** repeat, do s.t. again **2** visit frequently. **meng-kan** repeat for s.o. **ter-** repeated, repeatable. **-an 1** s.t. that is done again, repetition. *cétakan* ~ reprint. *Kitab* ~ (*Bib.*) Deuteronomy. **2** test. *Bésok kan ada* ~ *aljabar?* Isn't there an algebra test tomorrow? ~ *umum* test administered at end of quarter (pre-university). **3** refrain. **peng- 1** s.o. who repeats. **2** coach, tutor. **peng-an** repeating s.t. **per-an** repetition, recurrence. ~ *kata* (*Ling.*) word reduplication.

ulap-ulap (*Jv*) k.o. hand gesture in traditional dances. **meng-kan** perform such a gesture with (the hand).

ular snake. *- ari* k.o. venomous snake. *- beludak* viper. *- danau* k.o. water snake. *- kepak* viper. *- mengiang* rainbow. *- patola* (*Amb*) python. *- puspo kajang* k.o. big, long python. *- sanca/sawa* python. *- séndok/tedung* cobra. *- welang* k.o. poisonous snake. *- bukan, ikan pun bukan* neither

fish nor fowl (lit., neither snake nor fish). - *kepala dua* uncertain attitude (lit., two-headed snake). **-²** **1** snakes. **2** rubber hose or tube. **-an** rubber hose or tube. **-²an 1** toy snake. **2** all k.o. snakes.
ular-ularan (*M*) cramp.
ulas₁ 1 wrapper, covering. - *surat* envelope. - *méja* tablecloth. - *kasur* bed sheet. **2** (*Coll.*) pillowcase. **ber- 1** wrapped, covered. *Bantalnya tiada* ~ The pillow has no pillowcase. **2** be painted with. *Bibirnya* ~ *mérah* Her lips were painted red. **meng-1** cover, wrap. **2** daub (in painting). **meng-i 1** put a cover on s.t. *Ia* ~ *bukunya* She put a cover on her book. **2** daub over and over. **meng-kan** use s.t. to cover. ~ *kuas* move the brush (in painting). **-an 1** envelope, cover. **2** daubing (in painting).
ulas₂ 1 section of citrus fruit. **2** clove (of garlic, shallot, etc.). **se-** o. section (of fruit). ~ *senyum* a smile. **meng- 1** review, comment on. **2** explain, analyze. **meng-kan** divide into sections. ~ *senyum* smile. **-an 1** review, commentary. **2** remark. **peng-** reviewer.
ulat 1 caterpillar. - *sutera* silkworm. **2** maggot, larva. **ber-** worm-eaten. ~ *mata melihat* repulsed at the sight of.
ulayah see WILAYAH.
uleg, ulek /ulek/ **-²** pestle. **meng-** pulverize, grind. *Ia* ~ *sambal itu* She pulverized the condiments. **-an 1** pestle. **2** s.t. crushed with a pestle.
ulem (*Jv*) **-²** invitation. **meng-, meng-i** invite. **-an** invitation.
uler (*Jv*) worm. - *kambang* **1** leech. **2** s.t. very slow. **ng-** wormlike. ~ *kambang* go or work slowly.
ulet₁ tough, persevering. **meng-** stretch (after sleeping). **memper-** make tough, cause to persevere. **ke-an** tenacity, perseverance.
ulet₂ see ULAT.
uli₁ meng- knead (dough).
uli₂ 1 glutinous rice. **2** k.o. sweetmeat made with cooked glutinous rice, sugar and coconut.
ulia see AULIA.
ulik₁ meng- investigate. **peng-an** investigation.
ulik₂ see ULIT.
ulin k.o. very hard wood.
ulir thread of a screw. **meng-** put in a screw. **-an** s.t. with a thread (screw, lightbulb, etc.).
ulit ber- put a child to sleep with lullabies. **meng-i, meng-kan** put s.o. to sleep by singing lullabies. *Ia sedang* ~ *anaknya* She is singing her child to sleep. **peng-** lullaby singer.
ulos traditional Batak cloth worn covering shoulder.
ultah. [*ulang tahun*] anniversary, birthday.
ultimatum ultimatum.
ultra ultra-, extremely. - *modéren* ultramodern.
ulu see HULU₂.
ulubalang see HULUBALANG.
ulu hati pit of the stomach, solar plexus.
uluk (*Jv*) - *salam* extend greetings. **ber-, meng-salam** extend greetings. **meng-** *layang-layang* fly a kite.

ulung 1 capable, skilled, experienced. **2** excellent, superior. *cap yg* - a superior product, labeled superior. **ke-an 1** experience, skill. **2** superiority, excellence.
ulup (*Naut.*) hawser.
ulur₁ meng- 1 pay out. *Ia* ~ *tali itu* He paid out the rope. **2** extend. **3** make concessions. **meng-²** repeatedly extend s.t. ~ *perjanjian* stall a promise, not keep a promise. **meng-i** hand over to s.o. *Ia* ~ *saya buku* She handed over a book to me. **meng-kan 1** pay out (a rope, etc.). **2** pass s.t. out, stick s.t. out. *Ia* ~ *kertas itu pd saya* She handed me a sheet of paper. *Ia* ~ *lidah* He put out his tongue. ~ *tangan* extend o.'s hand. **3** extend, stretch. *Maskapai itu* ~ *perjanjian* The company extended its contract. ~ *bendéra* put out the flag. **ter- 1** stretched out. **2** protruding, projecting. **-an 1** part of rope which has been payed out. **2** slackening, concession. **3** assistance, contribution. ~ *tangan* a helping hand.
ulur₂ (*Lit.*) bondsman.
ulu-ulu (*Jv*) official responsible for irrigation.
um see UMMI₂.
uma see HUMA.
umak-umik (*Jv*) **meng-** silently mouth words.
umang-umang 1 hermit crab. **2** o. who likes to dress in fine, but borrowed, clothes.
umaro (*Isl.*) gvt. *ulama dan* - Isl. leaders and the gvt.
umat the members of a religious community. - *Katolik* Catholics. - *manusia* mankind, humanity.
umbai tassle, fringe. - *cacing* (*Anat.*) appendix. **ber- 1** fringed. **2** swing, dangle. *Ranting* ~ *di kawat télepon* A branch was dangling from the telephone wire. **meng-²kan** swing, dangle s.t. **ter-²** dangling, swinging. *Ia* ~ *di antara langit dan bumi* He was dangling between heaven and earth.
umban sling. **meng- 1** sling. **2** throw away. **peng-** missile, sling.
umbang meng- float. *Kayu* ~ *di air* Wood floats on water.
umbang-ambing see OMBANG-AMBING.
umbar meng- free s.t., let loose. *Kambingnya di- di halaman* The goat was let loose in the yard. ~ *hawa nafsu* give o.'s passion free rein. ~ *tubuhnya* let o.'s body grow fat. ~ *nafas* waste breath.
umbi tuber, root. - (*dan*) *akar* **1** the very roots. **2** complete, drastically. - *bunga* bulb. - *iles-iles* k.o. tuber. **se-** of one plant. **ber-** rooted. **-²an 1** all k.o. tubers. **2** belonging to the tuber group.
umbuk - *umbai/umbi* swindle. **meng- 1** swindle. **2** persuade. **3** appease, talk in a friendly way to s.o. **peng-** swindler.
umbul₁ meng- bubble up, rise rapidly.
umbul₂ (*Jv*) children's game played with picture cards which are tossed in the air.
umbul-umbul 1 (*Jv, Bali*) banner. **2** (*Jv, Bali*) pennants or palm fronds decorating doorways on feast days. **3** tassle (of hat etc.).
umbun see UBUN.

umbut edible topmost and innermost frond of a palm, palm-cabbage. **meng-** extract s.t. difficult to remove. ~ *nyawa* take s.o.'s life.

ummat see UMAT.

ummi₁ illiterate.

ummi₂ term of address for mother in families of Arab descent.

umpak 1 foot, step. **2** pedestal, fundament, base. **meng-(²)** extol a person to the skies. **-²an** praise, flattery.

umpama 1 example. *sbg* - as an example. - *kata* for example. **2** like, as. **se- 1** like, equal. *Ia mati* ~ *tikus* He died like a rat. **2** supposing. **(se)-nya** for example, supposing. **ber-** talk hypothetically. *Meréka* ~ *menang undian* They talked about what would happen if they were to win the lottery. **meng-kan 1** compare. **2** take as an example. *Ia* ~ *ayahnya dlm menjalankan tugas itu* He followed his father's example in carrying out the task. *Ia cukup di-kan di kota itu* He was sufficiently respected in that city. **3** assume, suppose. *Kami* ~ *kapal itu bergerak* We assumed the ship was moving. **per-an** parable.

umpan bait, food. - *pancing* fish bait. - *balik* feedback. - *keris/pisau* doomed to death (at the end of weapon). - *peluru* cannon fodder. - *tekuk* appetizer. **ber-** have bait in it. **meng-** tempt, lure. ~ *bola* (*Sport*) pass the ball to s.o. who will score. **meng-i 1** bait s.t. ~ *pancing* put bait on a fishing hook. **2** entice. *Ia* ~ *temannya dgn ucapan-ucapan yg manis* He entices his friend with sweet words. **meng-kan** use s.t. as bait. ~ *kera* put a monkey out as bait. **peng-** o. who uses a bait. ~ *bola* (*Sport*) o. who passes the ball to s.o. who will score.

umpat curse, swearword. **meng-** swear, curse (in reproach). **meng-i** swear at s.o. **-an** curse, verbal abuse. **peng-** s.o. who curses.

umpel-umpelan (*Jv*) crowded.

umpet (*Coll.*) **meng-** go hide, lie low. ~ *rahasia* keep a secret. **meng-kan** hide s.t. ~ *muka* avoid public shame (hide o.'s face). **-²an 1** in secret, on the sly. **2** hide-and-seek.

umpil meng- 1 lift, raise. **2** row, scull. **peng-** lever, crowbar.

umpuk heap, pile, stack. **se-** *batu* a pile of stones. **ber-** in a pile.

umrah, umroh (*Isl.*) perform a pilgrimage to Mecca (us. not during the hajj season) omitting some of the ritual (e.g. the visit to the fields of Arafah). **ber-** make such a pilgrimage.

umuk (*Jv*) brag, boast.

umum 1 general, common. *rapat* - general (public) meeting. *Keméja ini sdh* - *dipakai* This shirt is now commonly worn. **2** the public. *tdk terbuka pd* - not open to the public. *télpon* - public telephone. *penuntut* - public prosecutor. **-nya** us., by and large. ~ *ia bekerja pd pagi hari* Usually he works in the morning. *pd* ~ generally. **se-nya** generally. **meng-kan 1** announce, notify. ~ *perang* declare war. **2** publish. **ke-an** generality.

peng-an announcement, notification. ~ *perang* declaration of war. **per-an 1** generalizing. **2** generalization.

umur 1 age. *Berapa* -*nya?* How old is he? (*di*) *bawah* - under age. *cukup* - come of age. *sdh sampai* - adult. *setengah* - middle-aged. **2** lifespan. *Sebagian besar dr* -*ku kuhabiskan di sana* I spent a large part of my life there. **3** at the age of. *Ayahnya dulu kawin* - *lapan belas* Her father got married when he was 18. **se-** of the same age. *Ia* ~ *dgn anak saya* He is the same age as my child. ~ *hidup* lifelong, for life. *dihukum* ~ *hidup* sentenced for life. ~ *jagung* **1** three-and-a-half months. **2** three-and-a-half years (in reference to the Japanese occupation). **3** very young. *Kamu baru* ~ *jagung!* You are still wet behind the ears! ~ *jaman* a very long time. **ber- 1** attain the age of. *Ia* ~ *tiga tahun* She is three years old. **2** be old, be grown up. *Orangnya tlh* ~ He was an old man. **se-an** the same age. *Saya* ~ *dgn suami saya* I am the same age as my husband.

unam k.o. sea mollusc.

uncang bag (for traveling, etc.). - *uang* money bag.

uncang-uncit restless, unsettled.

unclik (*Jv, Jkt*) **meng-** walk without looking left or right.

uncué, uncui see HUNCUÉ.

undak (*Jv*) **1** step. **2** terrace. **ber-(²) 1** have stairs. *Rumahnya tdk* ~ The house has no stairs. **2** have stories. *Rumah itu* ~ *tiga* That house has three stories. **-²an** stairs, steps.

undan₁ level. **ber- 1** protracted, drawn out in stages. **2** in different levels (as the roof of certain houses). **ber-²** curly (hair).

undan₂ pelican.

undang₁ meng- invite, summon. *Ia* ~ *temannya utk makan malam* He invited his friend for dinner. ~ *tawa* provoke laughter. **-an 1** invitation. **2** invited guest.

undang₂ -² law, ordinance, act. ~ *darurat* emergency regulations. ~ *dasar* constitution. **meng-kan** legislate, establish by law. *Pemerintah* ~ *peraturan baru* The gvt. legislated new regulations. **peng-²** legislator. **peng-an** enactment (of a law). **per-(²)an** legislation.

undat (*Jv*) **meng-²** dig up old grievances.

unda-unda ber- being in tow o. behind the other. **meng-** tow o. behind the other.

undi a lot (in a drawing). **meng-** draw (lots, straws, etc.). ~ *suara* vote. **memper-kan** raffle off s.t. **ter-** drawn (of lots, etc.). **-an 1** lottery. ~ *uang* money lottery. ~ *suara* voting. **2** lottery prize. **peng-** o. who draws (a lot, ticket, etc.). **peng-an** lottery, raffle.

unduh (*Jv*) **meng-** pick (fruit from tree).

unduk-unduk sea horse.

undung-undung veil over the head. **ber-** wear a veil over the head. **meng-kan** use as a head covering. *Ia* ~ *kain itu pd kepalanya* She used the cloth as a veil over her head.

undur 1 go back, withdraw. **2** be out of circulation or publicity, out of trend. *Sayang, film itu sdh - dr perédaran* What a pity, that movie is out of circulation. **meng-kan 1** cause s.t. to go back. *Ia ~ mobilnya* He backed his car up. *Ia ~ tentaranya* He withdrew his troops. *Ia ~ jam* He set the clock back. *~ diri* **1** withdraw, retire. **2** resign, retire. *Ia ~ diri dr pekerjaannya* He retired from work. *~ suara* withdraw o.'s vote. **2** postpone. *Ia ~ hari berangkatnya* He postponed the day of departure. **meng-²(kan)** keep postponing. **peng-an** retreat, withdrawal, putting or setting back, postponement.

undur-undur (*Jv*) ant-lion.

uneg-uneg, unek-unek (*Jv*) grudges.

ungap meng- gasp for breath.

unggah-ungguh (*Jv*) etiquette.

unggang-unggit go up and down (seesaw, rocking chair, etc.).

unggas bird, fowl, esp. as scientific term. **per-an** poultry husbandry.

unggat-unggit see UNGGANG-UNGGIT.

unggis meng- nibble, gnaw at.

ungguk see ONGGOK.

unggul superior, excellent. *kepandaian yg - superior* ability. *bibit -* prime seed. *Isterinya lebih - mencari duit dr dirinya sendiri* His wife was better than he was at earning money. **meng-i** surpass. *Team Nasional ~ lawannya* The national team surpassed its rivals. **meng-kan** use o.'s superior qualities for o.'s own advantage. *Amir ~ suaranya yg merdu* Amir cashed in on his sweet voice. **di-kan 1** be considered or proposed as superior. **2** (*Sport*) seeded. *pemain ~* a seeded player. **meng-²kan** show off. *Apa-apaan, baju kayak gitu aja di-²kan!* What is going on, showing off a shirt like that! **ter-** most superior. **ke-an** superiority, special quality. **-an** s.o. or s.t. considered superior. *sastrawan ~ Shakespeare* the supreme literary figure, Shakespeare.

unggun 1 woodpile. **2** campfire. **ber-(²) 1** in heaps. **2** make a campfire or bonfire. *Meréka ~ di dekat sungai* They made a campfire near the river. **meng-kan** pile (wood, etc.). **-an 1** campfire. **2** heap, pile.

unggut ber-²an tug a rope, play tug of war. **meng-** pull at, tug.

ungka k.o. gibbon.

ungkai come undone, come off (of clothing). **meng- 1** untie, undo, loosen. *Ia ~ tali* He untied the rope. **2** break open. **3** undo, take off. *Ia ~ bajunya* He took off his jacket. **4** disclose. *Ia ~ soal lama* He disclosed an old matter.

ungkak (*Naut.*) post for fastening the hawser.

ungkang-ungkang see ONGKANG-ONGKANG.

ungkang-ungkit see UNGGANG-UNGGIT.

ungkap meng- 1 express (with words, face or gestures). *Kehidupan yg di- pengarang itu berlawanan dgn kenyataan* The life depicted by that author conflicts with reality. **2** reveal, uncover. *Meréka tdk berhasil ~ korupsinya* They did not succeed in uncovering the corruption. **meng-i** dig up. *Saya tdk mau ~ kembali jalan hidupku* I do not want to dig my past up again. **meng-kan 1** give expression to. *Kemarahan tdk perlu di-kan dlm bentuk kekerasan* Anger need not be expressed in the form of violence. **2** utter, pronounce. *Kalimat-kalimatnya di-kan dgn lambat dan jelas* She pronounced her sentences slowly and clearly. **3** uncover, reveal. *Ia takut ~ simpanannya* She was afraid to reveal her savings. **ter- 1** expressed, pronounced. **2** revealed (of a secret). **-an 1** expression. **2** idiom. *~ pelembut* euphemism. *~ pengeras* emphasizing or intensifying expression. **peng-an** act of expressing.

ungkat --ungkit repeated oscillating motions. **meng-(²)** bring up old sore points.

ungkil meng- pry up. **peng-** lever. **peng-an** leverage.

ungkir see MUNGKIR.

ungkit -² bob up and down. **meng- 1** pry up. **2** pry (into other people's business). *Buat apa ~ urusan orang!* Why stick your nose in other people's affairs! **meng-² 1** bob up and down. **2** open up old sore points. **ter-** get pried up, opened up (of secrets, problems, etc.). **peng-** lever. **peng-an** leverage.

ungku see ENGKU.

ungkur ber-²(an) 1 (*Jv*) back to back. *Rumah Pak Marto ~ dgn rumah Pak Mustafa* Marto and Mustafa's houses are back to back. **2** be somewhat poorly timed so that people fail to meet. *Edhi ~ dgn Han* Edhi no sooner left then Han arrived.

ungsi meng- flee. **meng-kan** evacuate s.o. **peng-** refugee, evacuee. **peng-an 1** evacuation. **2** asylum, refuge.

ungu purple. *- muda* violet. **meng-** become purple. **ke-²an** purplish.

uni₁ (*M*) older sister.

uni₂ union, esp. in names of political entities. *- Afrika Selatan* Union of S. Africa. *- Soviét* The Soviet Union.

uni₃ see HUNI.

unifikasi unification.

uniform 1 standardized. **2** a uniform. **ber-** wear a uniform. **meng-kan** make uniform. **peng-an** process of standardization.

uniformisasi uniformization.

uniformitas uniformity.

unik unique. **ke-an 1** uniqueness. **2** unique thing or phenomenon.

unit /yunit, unit/ *unit. Penjualan sdh mencapai seribu -* The sales have reached 1,000 units. *Kantornya di - II* His office is in Unit II.

univérsal, univérsil universal. **meng-kan** make s.t. universal. **ke-an** universality.

universitas, univérsitas university. **ke-an** matters pertaining to the university. *di kalangan ~* in university circles.

universitér, univérsitér concerning universities. *urusan ~* university affairs.

universitét, univérsitét see UNIVERSITAS.

unjam see HUNJAM.

unjuan see UNJUKAN.

unjuk show s.t. - *beritahu* inform. - *gigi* show o.'s teeth. - *periksa* (*Jv*) inform s.o. of high status. - *rasa/perasaan* demonstration. **meng- 1** extend the hand. *Yg blm dpt bagian disuruh* ~ Anyone who failed to get his share was asked to raise his hand. **2** indicate, point out. **meng-kan 1** raise or extend o.'s hand. **2** present, hand over, pass. *Ia* ~ *surat kpd ayahnya* He handed the letter to his father. **3** indicate, point out, show (us. to s.o. of high status). *Ia* ~ *kpd bulan* He pointed at the moon. *Ia* ~ *gambar-gambar perjalanannya* He showed pictures of his trip. **peng-** o. who presents or points out. **peng-an 1** offer, presentation. **2** indication.

unjukan /unju'an/ (*Jv*) drinks offered to a respected person.

unjung see KUNJUNG₁.

unjur extended, stretched out (of legs). **bel-, bersit** with o.'s legs stretched out. *Ia duduk* ~ *di tanah* He sat on the ground with his legs stretched out. **meng-** stretch o.s. **meng-kan** stretch s.o. or s.t. out. *Ia* ~ *yg sakit itu di tempat tidur* She stretched the patient out on the bed. *Ia* ~ *kakinya* He stretched out his legs. **-an** foot of the bed.

unjut small bag or bundle tied at the end with knots. **meng-** wrap up in a bundle, make into a bundle.

unsur element, substance. - *kimia* chemical element. - *pembangun* constituent element. **ber-** has as an element. **meng-i** be an element of. *Pegawai negeri* ~ *Golkar* Civil servants form a part of the Functionaries' party.

unsuri, unsuriah 1 elementary, elemental. **2** elemental.

unta camel. *burung* - ostrich.

untai 1 string, lace. **2** numerical classifier for stringlike objects (garlands, rosaries, etc.). *lima - kalung mutiara* five pearl necklaces. **ber-(²), ber-an 1** hang loosely. **2** on a string. *biji* ~ beads on a string. **meng- 1** dangle, hang down. **2** string s.t. *Ia* ~ *biji* She strung beads. **-an 1** series. **2** string, chain, garland. **3** strophe. **4** (*Ling.*) string.

untal₁ 1 pellet. **2** pill, tablet. **meng-** roll s.t. into pellet shape. **meng-²** wad up.

untal₂ meng- 1 swallow a large quantity. **2** (*Vulg.*) eat. **meng-i** swallow s.t. repeatedly.

untang-anting swinging to and fro.

until₁ meng- dangle, hang down.

until₂ see UNTAL₁.

unting 1 strand, skein. - *rambut* strand of hair. - *benang* skein of thread. **2** numeral classifier for hanging objects, tied together (such as corn, etc.). **-²** plumb. **meng-** sound, plumb. **-an** bunch of things tied together at o. end.

untir meng- twist. **ter-** sprained. *Lututnya* ~ Her knee was sprained.

untuk 1 for, on behalf of. *Buku ini - siapa?* Who is this book for? **2** to, in order to. *Ia pergi - menemui ayahnya* He went to meet his father. - *gampangnya (lekasnya)* to make it simple (quick). *Uang itu - membeli nasi* That money is for buying rice. **ber-** have o.'s share. **meng-kan, memper-kan** allo-

cate, assign. *Buku ini di-kan bagi pelajar* This book is intended for students. *Ia* ~ *bahan makanan kpd pengungsi* She allocated the foodstuff to the evacuees. **ter-** intended for, destined for. **per-an** allotment, allocation. ~ *penggunaan tanah* the allotment of the land use.

untung 1 luck, fortune. *bukan - tapi buntung* not good luck but bad luck. - *malang* whether it is good or bad luck. **2** good luck, have good luck. *-lah pd saatnya paman keluar* Fortunately uncle came out in time. *Kau lebih - dr Khadijah* You are more fortunate than Khadijah. - *akan celaka* to o.'s great misfortune. **3** advantage, profit. - *lima ribu dolar* a 5,000-dollar profit. - *bersih* net profit. - *kotor* gross profit. - *rugi* profit and loss. - *séro* dividend. **4** gain profit. *Aminah - Rp3.000* Aminah made a profit of 3,000 rupiah. **-²** it is lucky. ~ *kalau tdk habis dicaci-makinya* We will be lucky if he does not really chew us out. ~ *kita tdk mati* It was just luck that we did not die. **se-²nya** as profitable as possible. ~ *jadi pedagang, lebih untung jadi bankir* No matter how profitable it is to be a trader, it is more profitable to be a banker. **ber- 1** lucky. *Ia* ~ *mendapat rumah* He was lucky to get a house. **2** successful. *Ia* ~ *dlm usahanya* She was successful in her efforts. **3** make a profit. *Ia* ~ *dua juta rupiah* He made a profit of two million rupiah. **keber-an** luck. ~*nya baik; dagangannya laris* He had good luck; all his goods found a buyer. **meng-kan** cause s.o. to enjoy a profit or benefit. *Peraturan itu sangat* ~ *penduduk* That regulation was exceptionally beneficial to the people. **ke-an 1** profit. **2** luck. **-²an** undertake s.t. hoping for the best. ~, *kalau karcis masih dpt* Let us take our chances. Maybe there are still some tickets available. **per-an** fortune, luck.

untut elephantiasis.

unyai (*M*) softly, gently. **ber-(²) 1** softly, gently. **2** little by little. **meng-** do s.t. slowly.

up. [*untuk perhatian*] for the attention of (used in letter addresses).

upacara 1 ceremony, ritual. - *ngruwet* (*Jv*) ritual to ward off evil. - *pelantikan* inaugural ceremony. **2** regalia. **meng-i, meng-kan** hold a ceremony for.

upah 1 pay, wages. - *bulanan* monthly wage. - *jahit* wages for sewing s.t. *Itulah -nya!* That is what you get! (for ignoring good advice, etc.). - *pokok* base pay. - *pokok terendah* minimum subsistance wage. **2** fee, commission. **ber-** be paid a fee. *menolong org dgn tiada* ~ help people without pay. **meng-(i)** pay s.o. wages or some remuneration. *Ia* ~ *temannya mengambil surat* She paid her friend for getting her letter for her. **meng-kan** have s.t. done upon payment. *Ia* ~ *bajunya* He paid s.o. to make a suit. **-an 1** wages. **2** hired worker. **per-an** wage matters.

upam meng- polish, burnish. *Ia* ~ *mas dan pérak* She polished the gold and silver. **-an** s.t. polished, burnished.

upama see UMPAMA.

upas₁ k.o. toxin derived from the sap of certain plants.
upas₂ 1 messenger, attendant. - *pos* postman. 2 policeman.
upat see UMPAT.
upaya 1 efforts (to attain a certain aim). 2 means. - *hukum* legal remedy. ber- make serious efforts (to do s.t.). meng-kan strive for, seek. *Ia ~ terca-painya keamanan* He strove for the attainment of peace.
upet (*Jv*) wick, fuse.
upeti 1 tribute paid by subjects. 2 (*Coll.*) bribe to higher-ranking official.
upgrade /apgréd/ meng- upgrade s.t.
upgrading /apgréding/ upgrading.
upih (*Biol.*) leaf-sheath.
upik (*M*) term of address for a little girl. *si- jantan* tomboy. *si- sibuyung* whether it is a male child or a female child. *Blm tentu si- sibuyungnya* The final decision was not yet certain.
upil 1 dried snot. 2 scab on a wound. (me)ng-1 pick o.'s nose. 2 form scab on a wound.
upleg (*Jv, Jkt*) be extremely busy. -²an rush about very busy.
urah₁ (*M*) meng- demolish, tear down. *Ia ~ rumah lama* He demolished an old house.
urah₂ meng- relate. *Ia ~ pengalamannya di masa Jepang* He related his experiences during the Japanese period.
urai apart, asunder. - *sendi* dislocation. ber- 1 fall apart, fall or hang down in strands. *Karena ia lari gelungnya ~* Because she was running, her hair came undone. 2 scatter, disperse. *Penonton pasar malam ~ ketika hujan turun* The audience at the night market dispersed when the rain fell. *~ air mata* shed tears. meng- become disentangled. *Kerumitan itu pun ~* Even that knotted problem became disentangled. meng-kan 1 loosen, disentangle (o.'s hair, a fastening, etc.). *Ia ~ kantong* She untied her bag. 2 scatter. *Ia ~ air matanya* She let her tears flow. 3 explain, analyze. *Coba -kan soal ini* Please analyze this problem. ter- hang loosely. *Rambutnya ~* Her hair hung loosely. -an 1 analysis. *~ kalimat* (*Ling.*) sentence parsing. 2 explanation. *~ peker-jaan* job description. -²an strands, pieces. peng-1 o. who analyzes or disentangles. 2 chemicals used for decomposing. peng-an the action of disentangling or analyzing. per-an disentanglement.
urakan rowdy, unconventional. *Kaum -* name of a literary group of the 1970s.
urang-aring k.o. herb used for the hair.
uranium uranium.
urap₁ ointment, salve. ber-²an rub ointment on o.s. meng-(i) rub with ointment. *Ia ~ badannya sblm tidur* She rubbed her body with ointment before going to sleep. meng-kan apply s.t. to the body. *Ia ~ bedak wangi di badannya* She applied scented powder to her body. -an 1 ointment. 2 (*Rel.*) ordination, consecration. *~ Imamat Suci* ordination to the priesthood.
urap₂ grated coconut with spices. -² salad of

mixed vegetables (cabbage, beansprouts, string-beans) with coconut. -an vegetables to make this salad.
urat 1 tendon. - *keting* (*Anat.*) Achilles' tendon. 2 nerve. - *daging* sinews in meat. - *saraf* nerve. 3 vein. - *darah* blood vessel. - *darah halus* vein. - *merih* jugular vein. - *nadi* artery. ber- muscular, sinewy. *~ keras* 1 sinewy (of people). 2 tough (of wood). *~ berakar* deeply rooted. *Agama Islam ~ berakar pd org Bantam* Isl. is deeply rooted in the people of Bantam. meng- 1 be rooted. *Mencuri ~ kpdnya* Stealing is rooted in him. 2 become tough.
urban o. who has moved to the city from the country.
urbanisasi migration to the city. ber- migrate to the city.
uréa urea-based fertilizer.
urét (*Jv*) larva, white grub.
urgén urgent.
urgénsi urgency.
URI see ORI.
uri₁ (*Anat.*) placenta, afterbirth.
uri₂ meng- revolve rapidly.
urik (*Jv*) meng- pick, pluck.
urine (*Med.*) urine.
uring (*M*) groove between nose and upper lip.
uring-uringan (*Jv*) grumble angrily, be angry.
uris dash. - *datar* dash. - *miring* slant, virgule.
urolog urologist.
urologi urology.
uro-uro chant Jv poetry.
URSS [*Uni Républik Sovyét Sosialis*] USSR.
uruk meng- 1 bury. 2 fill (with soil, sand, etc.). *~ bagian ladang yg rendah* fill in the lower part of the field. meng-i put sand or soil on. *~ tai anak-nya dgn tanah* put earth on her child's feces. -an mound.
urun - *rembug* participate in decision making. *Ibunya - rembug dlm persoalan itu* Her mother gave an opinion regarding the issue. -an (*Jv*) 1 contribution. 2 contribute.
urung 1 failed, unsuccessful. *Ia - jadi duta besar di negeri itu* He was unsuccessful in becoming ambassador to that country. *tak -* for sure. *Ia tak - dinaikkan pangkat* He is sure to be promoted. 2 not take place, be canceled. *Pertemuannya - karena perselisihan meréka itu* The meeting did not take place because of that disagreement of theirs. meng-kan 1 cause to fail. 2 abandon, cancel. *Ujiannya di-kan karena gurunya sakit* His examination was canceled because the teacher was sick.
urup meng- 1 barter, exchange. *Ia ~ barang itu* He exchanged the goods. 2 change money. -an 1 the thing exchanged. 2 change (money). peng- money-changer.
urus ber-an 1 get in touch with, contact. 2 be concerned with, have business with. *Ia tdk ~ dgn perdagangan lagi* He has nothing to do with business anymore. *Ia ~ dgn polisi* He has to deal with the police. meng- 1 arrange matters (with a higher-up). *~ visa* arrange for o.'s visa. 2 take

care of, manage. ~ *perusahaan* manage a business. *Ia ~ ladang peninggalan bapak* He runs the field he inherited from his father. *Ia ~ bayinya* He looks after his baby. *Polisi ~ pencurian* The police dealt with the theft. **meng-i** take care of. *~ anak-isterinya* take care of o.'s family. *~ hubungan kemasyarakatan* be in charge of public relations. **meng-kan 1** manage, run. **2** take care of on s.o.'s behalf, handle for s.o. **ter-** organized, taken care of, looked after. *sebidang sawah yg tak ~ a* neglected rice field. **-an 1** affair, matter. *Itu bukan ~ saya* That is not my affair. *~ kemasyarakatan* social affairs, problems. *~ pegawai* personnel affairs. *~ belakang* a matter to be taken care of later. *~ agama* religious affairs. **2** arrangement. *~nya kurang baik* The arrangements were poor. **3** division of administration. *~ keuangan* finance division. **peng- 1** board, management. *~ besar* board of directors, executive board. **2** manager. *~ tata usaha* manager. **peng-an 1** management handling, treatment. **2** arrangement. **kepeng-an** management, leadership (of an organization).

urus-urus purgative, laxative.

urut₁ ber- get massaged. **meng- 1** massage, rub. *Ia ~ lengan adiknya* He massaged his little brother's arm. *~ dada* feel sad, disappointed. **2** caress, stroke. *Ia ~ kepala adiknya spy berhenti menangis* He rubbed his little brother's head so that he would stop crying.

urut₂ (*Coll.*) in a series, well organized. *dlm - kacang* in a line, in a queue. *- tgl* chronology. **ber-(an) 1** in a series. *Dia sdh berlangganan Témpo ~ dr nomor pertama* She has subscribed to *Tempo* from the first issue on. **2** chronological. *Kami belajar peristiwa-peristiwa sejarah itu secara ~* We studied those historical events in chronological order. **meng- 1** put in the right order. **2** trace s.t. *~ garis keturunan* trace a line of descent. **meng-kan** put s.t. in the right order. *Mengembalikannya salah, sekarang aku mesti ~ semuanya!* They put it back incorrectly. Now I have to straighten it all up. **-an** order, sequence. *~ kata* (*Ling.*) word order. **-²an 1** consecutively, in sequence. **2** (*Sport*) seeded. *pemain ~* a seeded player.

US [*Uni Sovyét*] Soviet Union.

usah it is not necessary, no need to. *tdk -* it is not necessary. *Tdk - anda datang* You do not have to come. **-kan 1** let alone, not to mention. *~ makan, minum pun tak dihidangkannya* He did not even serve drinks, let alone food. **2** instead of.

usaha 1 effort, exertion. *- pemerintah* gvt. initiative. *- patungan* joint venture. *atas -* at the instigation of. **2** labor, work, trade. *- tani* farm operations, farm enterprises. *- tamasya* excursion service. **ber- 1** try, endeavor. *~lah, spy adikmu jangan mengalami kesengsaraan* Try to see that your sister does not run into trouble. *Meréka ~ sebaik-baiknya* They are making every effort. **2** be running a business. *Ia ~ dlm bidang pertanian* She is in the agricultural business. **meng-kan 1** carry on, expend o.'s energy at s.t. *Ia ~ pertanian* He is carrying on farming. *Ia ~ tanah* She

works the land. *~ diri* exert o.s. *Ia ~ dirinya spy lulus ujian* He exerted himself in order to pass the examination. *~ kekuasaan* employ force. **2** organize, manage. *Ia ~ rapat* He organized a meeting. *Meréka yg ~ minuman dan makanan itu adalah wanita-wanita muda* Those who take care of the food and drinks are young women. **3** make an effort. *Pemerintah ~ penurunan harga* The gvt. made an effort to lower prices. **mem-per-kan 1** carry on, do business in. *Ia ~ perdagangan* She is carrying on trade. **2** cultivate, raise. **peng-** industrialist, entrepreneur. **peng-an** effort, exertion. **per-an** business, enterprise, undertaking, concern. *~ air* waterworks. *~ negara* state enterprise. *~ pelayaran* shipping firm. *~ pertanian negara* state farm. *~ tanah* plantation, estate.

usahawan 1 entrepreneur. **2** industrialist.

usai 1 finished, ready. **2** dispersed. *Rapat - pd tengah malam* The meeting broke up at midnight. **se-** after. *~ sekolah dia menjajakan koran* After school he peddles newspapers.

usak decrease, lessen.

usali, usalli 1 (*Isl.*) firm intention to pray. **2** (*Isl.*) word uttered upon beginning a prayer. **3** intention.

usam₁ 1 dregs. **2** waste remaining after the oil has been pressed from coconut meat.

usam₂ vague, dull (of color).

usang 1 worn out, decrepit. *kaus kaki -* worn-out stockings. **2** obsolete. *pendirian -* an obsolete view. **3** dry, barren, withered. **meng-** dry up, wither. **ke-an 1** decrepitude, obsolescence. **2** dryness.

usap meng- 1 wipe s.t. off. *Ia ~ keringatnya dgn saputangan* He wiped off his sweat with a handkerchief. **2** caress, stroke. *Ia ~ rambut anaknya* He caressed his child's hair. *~ dada* stroke o.'s chest (to express disappointment or sorrow). **meng-i 1** wipe s.t. *Ia ~ dahinya dgn lap* He mopped his brow with a rag. **2** caress, stroke. *Pak Modin ~ pipi yg kena jotos* Pak Modin stroked his cheek which had been punched. **3** rub in. *Tubuh meréka di-i minyak* Their bodies received an oil rubbing. **meng-kan** wipe with s.t. *Di-kannya saputangan ke dahinya* She wiped her forehead with a handkerchief. **-an** stroke, caress.

usar k.o. grass used to make fragrant oil.

USDÉK [*Undang-undang dasar 1945; Sosialisme a la Indonésia; Démokrasi terpimpin; Ékonomi terpimpin; Kepribadian Indonésia*] the five guiding principles of Sukarno's gvt. after 1960: the 1945 Constitution; Socialism a la Indonesia; Guided democracy; Guided economy; National identity.

usdékisme politics on the basis of *USDÉK*.

ushuludin see USULUDIN.

usia age. *- sekolah* school age. *-mu berapa tahun?* How old are you? **se-** of the age of. **ber-** attain the age of. *Ia ~ lima belas tahun* He is 15 years old.

usik meng- 1 tease. **2** touch on. *Ia ~ soal lama* He touched on an old problem. **3** (*Phys.*) perturb. **ter-** be disturbed. *Itik itu ~ oléh hardikannya* His shouts disturbed the ducks. **-an 1** annoyance, disturbance. **2** meddling, criticism. **3** (*Phys.*) perturbance. **peng- 1** disturber. **2** meddler.

usil annoying, bothering others doing s.t. not desired. *Kamu ini - bukan main! Siapa suruh kamu corét-corét buku Bp!* You sure are a brat! Who told you to scribble in Daddy's book? *mulut -* bigmouthed. **ke-an** annoyance, naughtiness. **-an** annoyance, bothering.

usir ber-²an chase e.o. **- meng-** chase e.o. **meng-** chase away, drive out, expel. *Ia di- dr kantornya karena sering terdapat mabuk di sana* He was thrown out of the office because he often turned up drunk there. *Ia di- oléh pemerintah itu* She was expelled by the gvt. **ter-** evicted, driven out. **-an** fugitive. **peng-** s.o. or s.t. that chases away. *~ burung* scarecrow. **peng-an** eviction, expulsion.

uskup (*Rel.*) bishop. *- agung* archbishop. **ke-an 1** diocese, bishopric. *~ agung* archdiocese. **2** office or residence of a bishop.

usolli see USALI.

ustad, ustadz, ustaz (*Isl.*) **1** term of address for Isl. teacher. **2** (*Lit.*) lord, master.

ustadah, ustadzah, ustazah (*Isl.*) term of address for a female Isl. teacher.

Ustrali (*Coll.*) Australia.

Ustria (*Coll.*) Austria.

usuk (*Jv*) rafter.

usul₁ 1 proposal, suggestion. *Ia memajukan - yg berikut* He suggested the following proposal. *- balasan* counterproposal. **2** motion. *- perubahan* amendment. **-²** proposals. *~ perdamaian* peace terms. **meng-kan** propose, suggest. *Aris ~ spy kita pindah saja* Aris suggested that we just move. **-an** proposal, suggestion. *daftar ~ proyék* project proposal form. **peng-** proposer.

usul₂ nature, characteristic. *- periksa* investigation. *Dia ditangkap dgn tiada - periksa lagi* He was arrested without due investigation. *- menunjukkan asal* O.'s characteristics reflect o.'s ancestry. **meng-(i)** examine s.o. **peng-an** inquiry, examination.

usuludin (*Isl.*) o. of the branches of theology pertaining to law and philosophy.

usung meng- carry (together with others) on the shoulders. *Meréka ~ mayat* They carried a corpse. **-an** stretcher, litter. *~ mayat* bier. **peng-** o. who carries s.t. on his shoulders. *~ peti jenazah* pall-bearer. **peng-an** act of carrying s.t. on the shoulders.

usur see UZUR.

usus intestines. *- besar* large intestine. *- buntu* appendix. *- dua belas jari* duodenum. *- halus* small intestine.

usut meng- 1 feel all over, handle. **2** examine. *Perkara ini di- oléh seorg jaksa* The case was examined by a public prosecutor. **meng-(²)** feel all over, handle. **ter-** investigate. **peng-** investigator. **peng-an** examination, investigation.

utak-atik, utak-utik tinker with s.t. **meng-** tinker with s.t. **peng-** o. who tinkers.

utama 1 prominent, eminent. *pemain -* top player. **2** principal, prime. *saksi -* chief witness. *setasiun -* main station. *hasil -* main product. **meng-kan** consider as most important, give priority to. *Meréka ~ pembuatan alat perang* They gave top priority to the production of war materials. **ter-1** superior, best. *Ia pelajar yg ~ di kelasnya* He was the best student in his class. **2** especially, particularly. *Kesukaran ini ~ disebabkan oléh perang* This hardship was caused esp. by the war. **3** most important. *Sebab yg ~ ialah kemiskinan* The most important cause was poverty. **ter-nya** especially. **menter-kan** consider as most important, give the highest priority to. **ke-an 1** superiority, excellence. *~ kekuasaan udara mendatangkan kemenangan* Superiority of air power brought victory. **2** virtue, decency, moral excellence. **peng-an** act of giving priority to s.t.

utan see HUTAN.

utang see HUTANG.

utara₁ north. *- barat laut* N.-N.W.

utara₂ meng-kan present, state in public. *~ ceramah* deliver a talk or lecture. **peng-an 1** explanation. **2** communication.

Utarid (*Astr.*) Mercury.

utar-utar small round shield.

utas₁ skilled, capable.

utas₂ 1 cord, string, strand. **2** numeral classifier for long, thin, and supple things (such as ropes, straw, etc.). *se- tali* a length of rope or string. **ber-** in a strand or string. *~ permata* with gems strung together.

utik-utik meng- touch with a finger, poke into s.t. to examine it. *~ mesin* tinker with an engine. *~ persoalan* look for the solution of a problem.

utilitas utility, usefulness.

utk. [*untuk*] for, in order to.

utopi, utopia utopia.

utopis utopian.

utuh whole, intact. *Tradisi itu masih hidup dgn -nya* The tradition lives on unimpaired. **meng-kan** make sound, make a whole. *~ wilayah RI dr Sabang ke Mérauké* make Indonesian territory intact from Sabang to Merauke. **ke-an** totality, wholeness. **-an** (*Math.*) integer. **peng-an** process of unifying.

utus meng-(kan) delegate s.o. **-an 1** messenger. *~ Allah* (*Isl.*) God's messenger. *~ injil* evangelistic missionary. *~ Yésus* (*Bib.*) disciples. **2** envoy. **3** delegate. **peng-an** mission. **per-an** delegation, deputation.

UU [*Undang-undang*] law, decree.

UUD [*Undang-undang Dasar*] the Constitution.

UUDS [*Undang-undang Dasar Sementara*] provisional constitution.

uwar see UAR.

uyel-uyel (ber)-an (*Jv*) jostle e.o. **meng-kan** cause to jostle.

uzur enfeebled (from old age or illness). **ke-an 1** suffer from weakness and illness. *Ia ~ tak dpt datang* He was too weak to come. **2** agedness.

V

v /fé/ v, the 22d letter of the alphabet.
vadémécum comprehensive handbook (for medical students, etc.).
vagina /tagina, fakhina/ (*Med.*) vagina.
vak /fak/ **1** subject of study. *Ambil berapa -?* How many courses are you taking? **2** discipline, field of study. *sekolah -* vocational school.
vakansi vacation.
vakature /fakatur/ vacancy.
vaksin (*Med.*) vaccine.
vaksinasi vaccination. **mem-(kan)** vaccinate.
vaksinator o. who vaccinates.
vakum₁ vacuum. **mem-kan** put in a vacuum. *Présidén lebih suka ~ jabatan kementerian itu* The president prefers to keep that ministerial position vacant. **ke-an** a situation in which a vacuum exists.
vakum₂ (*Med.*) suction device to abort the fetus.
valénsi valence.
validasi validation.
validitas validity.
valuta currency. *- asing* foreign currency.
vandalisme vandalism.
vandel souvenir pennant.
varan monitor lizard. *- Komodo* Komodo dragon.
varia variety, varied.
variabel 1 subject to change. **2** statistical variable.
variabilitas variability.
varian variant.
variasi variation. *- mobil* car accessories. **ber-** have variation.
variétas variety, kind (of plants, etc.). *- unggul* high-yielding variety.
varisés (*Med.*) varicose veins.
varitas see VARIÉTAS.
Varuna see BARUNA.
vas vase.
vaselin vaseline.
VB [*Vestiging Besluit*] permission to occupy a company house (in the colonial period).
véém wharfage and transport business. **per-an** wharfage business.
végétaris vegetarian.
végétarisme vegetarianism.
véktor (*Math.*) vector.
vélar (*Ling.*) velar.
vélbak see PÉLBAK.
véldbéd /félbét/ see FÉLBÉT.
véldflés /pélplés, félflés/ water-bottle, canteen.
vélg see PÉLEK.
véntilasi ventilation.
véntilator ventilator.

ver- see also entries with **per-**.
vérba (*Ling.*) verb. *- teratur* regular verb.
vérbal 1 verbal, oral. *ujian -* oral examination. **2** (*Ling.*) verbal. **mem-kan** verbalize, put into words.
verdah suspected of having a disease. *- tifus* suspected of having typhus. **mem-** suspect.
verdieping see PERDIPING.
vergunning /verkhéning/ see PERKÉNING.
vérifikasi verification. **mem-kan** verify.
verkénéng, verkéning reconnaissance, reconnoitering.
vermaak /permak/ see PERMAK.
vernis see PERNIS.
verpleegster see VERPLÉHSTER.
verpléger, verpléher male hospital attendant.
verpléhster nurse.
verpolitisir mem-(kan) politicize.
vérsi version.
versnéleng, versnéling see PERSNÉLING.
vérsus versus.
vértikal vertical.
vét (*Coll.*) grease, esp. engine lubricators. **menge-(i)** grease (an engine).
véter shoelaces.
véteran veteran, esp. of the Revolution of 1945. **mem-kan** retire s.o. from the army.
véto veto. **mem-** veto.
vétsin monosodium glutamate.
via via.
viaduk, viadukt 1 viaduct. **2** fly-over, overpass.
vibrasi vibration.
vidé refer to, see.
vidéo 1 video cassette. **2** video performance.
Viétsel [*Viétnam Selatan*] S. Vietnam.
Viétut [*Viétnam Utara*] N. Vietnam.
vihara see WIHARA.
vikariat (*Rel.*) vicariate.
vikaris jénderal (*Rel.*) vicar general.
vila, villa house in the country, us. for weekend use.
vilt felt.
vinyét vignette.
violét violet in color.
violis violinist.
VIP /fip/ s.t. reserved for VIPs. **mem-kan 1** reserve s.t. for VIPs. **2** give s.o. VIP status.
VIPwan VIP. *Para - diberi prioritas utama* The VIPs are given top priority.
Virgo (*Zod.*) Virgo.
virulén virulent.
virulénsi virulence.

virus virus.
visa visa.
visi point of view, perspective.
visual visual.
visualisasi visualization. mem-kan visualize.
visuil see VISUAL.
visum 1 visa. 2 any written document from relevant authorities stating that a certain matter has been considered and approved of. - *dokter* medical report. - *et repertum* official report of an autopsy.
vital vital. ke-an vitality.
vitalitas vitality.
vitrage /fitrasye/ lace curtain.
vivéré périculoso live dangerously (Sukarno-era slogan). ber- flirt with danger.
vla k.o. rich custard us. used as a topping for cakes and puddings.
vlék see PLÉK.
VOC /fé o sé/ [*Verenigde Oostindische Compagnie*] Dutch E. India Company (a trading company that held a monopoly in Indonesia 1602-1799).
voile /foal/ k.o. cloth, voile.
vokabulér 1 vocabulary, wordlist. 2 o.'s verbal knowledge.
vokal (*Ling.*) vowel. - *hampar* unrounded vowel. - *kendur* lax vowel. - *tengah* central vowel.
vokalis vocalist.
vol see POL₁.

vol. [*volume*] volume.
voli volleyball.
volt volt.
Volta Hulu Upper Volta.
voltase voltage.
volume 1 volume, amount of liquid content. 2 volume, loudness.
voluntér a volunteer.
vonis verdict. mem- sentence, condemn s.o. *Hakim ~ mati Subandrio* The judge sentenced Subandrio to death.
votum vote. - *kepercayaan* vote of confidence.
vrij /fré, pré/ see PERAI₁.
vs /fé és/ [*vérsus*] versus.
vulgair /fulkhér/ vulgar.
vulgarisasi vulgarization. mem- vulgarize.
vulkan volcano.
vulkanik, vulkanis volcanic.
vulkanisasi vulcanization.
vulkanisir mem- 1 retread. 2 vulcanize. -an s.t. retreaded (tire).
vulkanisme (*Geol.*) volcanic activity.
vulkanolog expert in vulcanology.
vulkanologi study of volcanic activity.
vulpén see PULPÉN.
vuring lining of clothing.
VUTW [*Varitas Unggul Tahan Wereng*] a high-yielding pest-proof variety of rice (much used in the 1970s).

W

w /wé/ w, the 23d letter of the alphabet.
w. [*waktu*] time (zone). - *Indonésia Barat* W. Indonesian time.
waad, waadat (*Lit.*) treaty, contract.
wabah epidemic. me- become an epidemic. me-i plague s.o. or s.t. *Ketidakadilan ~ berjuta-juta manusia* Injustice plagues millions of people. me-kan 1 spread an epidemic disease. 2 cause s.t. to spread like an epidemic. *~ idé yg berbahaya ke rakyat yg lugu* spread dangerous ideas to an innocent population.
wabakdahu, wabakdu (*Lit.*) furthermore, then.
wacana 1 (*Lit.*) word, expression. 2 (*Ling.*) discourse.
wadag body, bodily. - *kasar* corporeal reality, body (as opposed to soul).
wadah 1 container. - *gula* sugar bowl. 2 coordinating institution, umbrella organization. ber-kan have a certain organization as the umbrella. me-i contain, provide a place for. *Organisasi ini bermaksud ~ semua organisasi pemuda* This organization aims to provide an umbrella for all

youth organizations. pe-an provision of a place or container.
wadal sacrifice (upon completion of a new building, to obtain magical powers, etc.).
wadam [*wanita adam*] transvestite homosexual, transsexual.
wadas stony ground.
wadat 1 celibacy. 2 live a celibate life. ber- live as a celibate.
wadduh (*Jv*) see ADUH.
wader k.o. small freshwater fish.
wadi wadi, a stream in desert.
wadon (*Jv*) female.
waduh (*Jv*) see ADUH.
waduk 1 rumen. 2 (*Coll.*) paunch. 3 basin, reservoir.
wadul (*Jv*) tell on s.o., be a tattletale.
wadung ax.
waé 1 (*Sd*) also, even. 2 (*Jv*) only.
wafat pass away. me-kan cause s.o.'s death. ke-an death, demise.
Wagé fourth day of the Jv five-day week.
wagen /wakhen/ carriage (of typewriter).

wagon (*R.R.*) coach, car. - *réstorasi* dining car.
wagub [*wakil gubenur*] vice-governor.
wah Well! Hey! (exclamation of surprise or exasperation). -! *Énak betul!* Say! This is delicious! -, *susah ini!* Hey! This is really difficult!
waha, wahah oasis.
wahadah, wahadat (*Rel.*) oneness (of God).
wahai (*Lit.*) 1 alas! (particle to emphasize distress). - *nasibku yg malang!* Alas, I am unfortunate. 2 Oh! (particle to draw attention). - *kaum muslimin yg beriman!* O, ye Muslim believers!
waham suspicious, suspicion. **me-kan** suspect.
wahana 1 (*Lit.*) mode, vehicle (for conveying thoughts, ideas, or for realizing ideals). *Koperasi adalah - utk menuju masyarakat yg makmur* A cooperative is a vehicle to attain a prosperous society. 2 vehicle (in automotive workshop names).
wahid 1 one, unique (of God). 2 alone, without peer. *nomor -* (*Sl.*) first-class, excellent.
wahon see WAGON.
wahyu (*Rel.*) divine revelation, vision from God to man. **me-i** inspire s.o. *Tuhan ~ Musa* God made a revelation to Moses. **me-kan** reveal s.t. (in a vision). *Tuhan ~ sepuluh perintahnya kpd Musa* God revealed His 10 commandments to Moses.
wai₁ river (in place names in Lampong, Ambon, and elsewhere).
wai₂ see WAHAI.
Waisak, Waisyak see WÉSAK.
waja see BAJA₁.
wajah countenance, face. - *baru* newcomer. **ber-** have a face of a certain kind.
wajan wok.
wajar₁ 1 natural, proper. 2 genuine, without deceit. **se-nya** fittingly, properly. *Mémang ~ dia naik pangkat* It is natural that he should be promoted. *Sdh ~ org berjasa diganjar* It is only proper that meritorious people be rewarded. *melakukan ~* do the proper thing. **me-kan** make natural, make proper. *~ harga* bring prices to what they should be. **ke-an** fittingness. **kesc-an** 1 genuineness. 2 naturalness.
wajar₂ [*wajib belajar*] compulsory education.
wajib 1 (*Isl.*) obligatory (of certain pious acts, e.g. praying at the appointed times, etc.). 2 must. *Tiap org - membayar pajak* Everyone must pay taxes. 3 duty, obligation. - *belajar* compulsory education. - *daftar* registration requirement. - *dinas* service requirement. - *latih* military training requirement (for civilians in the 1970s). - *latih mahasiswa* military training requirement (for students in the 1970s). - *militér* draft. - *muat* obligation of transport companies to do services for the gvt. - *pajak* tax obligation. **ber-** have the obligation of. *yg ~* the authorities. **me-kan** make s.t. compulsory. *Pemerintah ~ tiap anak bersekolah* The gvt. requires every child to go to school. **ke-an** obligation, duty. *Jangan lupa ~ Do not forget your duties. ~ belajar/bersekolah* compulsory education. **berke-an** have the duty of. **pe-** s.o. who is liable.

wajik 1 rhomboid shape. 2 (*Crd.*) diamond. 3 k.o. cake made of sticky rice and palm sugar, cut in rhomboid shapes.
wak see UA.
waka [*wakil kepala*] deputy head.
wakaf₁ (*Isl.*) 1 property donated for religious or community use. 2 religious foundation. **ber-** donate for religious community use. **me-kan** donate s.t. to be used for religious or community use. *Org kaya itu ~ tanahnya utk mesjid* The rich man donated his land as a site for a mosque.
wakaf₂ (*Isl.*) pause in reading the Koran.
wakap see WAKAF₁.
wakhen see WAGEN.
wakif (*Isl.*) o. who donates property to the Isl. community.
wakil 1 representative. 2 vice-, deputy-. - *présidén* vice-president. - *gubernur* deputy governor. 3 agent (on behalf of a firm). - *tunggal* sole agent. **ber-(an)** 1 be represented. *Rakyat ~ di parlemén* The people are represented in parliament. 2 have as a deputy. *Bp Présidén ~ Umar Zain* The president has Umar Zain as a deputy. **me-i** represent, look after the interests of s.o. or s.t. *Indonésia di-i oléh menteri dlm negeri* Indonesia was represented by the minister of home affairs. **me-kan** 1 appoint s.o. as a representative. *Présidén ~ Adam Malik utk menghadiri pemakaman Sadat* The president used Adam Malik as a representative to Sadat's funeral. 2 do s.t. by proxy. *Pengambilan ijazah tdk boléh di-kan* The diploma cannot be collected by proxy. **ter-** be represented. *Koréa blm ~ di PBB* Korea has no representation in the UN. **per-an** 1 delegation. *~ Tiongkok di Washington* the Ch delegation in Washington. 2 agency. *~ mutlak/tunggal* sole agent. 3 representation. *Déwan ~ Rakyat* house of representatives. *~ berimbang* proportional representation. 4 (*Mil.*) liaison unit.
waktu 1 time. *pd - itu* at that time. *beberapa - yg lalu* some time ago. *dlm - dekat yg singkat* soon. *(kaum) - telu/tiga* group of Muslims in Lombok who perform only three of the five prescribed prayers. *sdh -(nya)* it is time, time's up. *Sdh -nya berangkat* It is time to leave. - *(ter)luang* spare time. - *tolok* standard time. 2 when. - *saya pergi, temanku tiba* When I left, my friend came. 3 while. *Jangan bicara dgn sopir - bis berjalan* Do not talk to the driver while the bus is in motion. 4 time zone. - *Indonésia Tengah* Central Indonesian Time (zone). **se-** when, at the time that. **sese-, se-²** 1 from time to time. *Susy ~ melirik ke arah Irwan* From time to time Susy glanced stealthily at Irwan. 2 at any time. *Bom dinamit itu ~ bisa meletus* That dynamite bomb can explode at any time.
wakuncar [*wajib kunjung pacar*] (*Coll.*) have a date with o.'s lover.
Wala [*wajib latih*] military training requirement for civilians (1970s).
walaah /wala:h/ (*Coll.*) 1 Come on get serious! (exclamation of belittlement). -, *gitu aja kok*

ribut! C'mon now, how can you make such a fuss over s.t. like that! **2** Oh no! (exclamation expressing disapproval of a situation). *-, kecil-kecil kok sdh tdk beribu!* What a pity, still so young and already motherless! *- saya lupa! Seharusnya saya ke rumahnya!* Oh no! I forgot; I was supposed to go to her house!

walafiat see SÉHAT.

walah ke-an overwhelmed (by a task, a person), unable to handle. *Amir nakal sekali; ibunya ~ Amir* is very unruly; his mother cannot do a thing about it.

walaikum salam (*Isl.*) And peace be to you (in reply to the greeting *assalam alaikum*).

walakhir (*Lit.*) (and) in the end, finally.

walakin (*Lit.*) although.

walama [*Wajib Latih Mahasiswa*] military training requirement for students (in the 1970s).

walang (*Jv*) grasshopper, locust. *- hati* anxious, concerned. *- sangit* k.o. insect that releases a pungent smell.

walau although. *- diberi uang, dia tak mau melakukannya* Although he will get money for it, he does not want to do it.

walaupun although. *- dia sakit, dia mau nonton juga* Even though he is ill, he still intends to go to the movies. *- demikian* **1** nevertheless, yet. **2** in spite of that.

walawa [*wajib latih mahasiswa*] military training requirement for students (in the early 1970s).

waled (*Jv*) ooze, alluvium. **-an** arrears (in payment, salary).

walét (*Jv*) k.o. swallow.

walhasil (*Lit.*) with the result that . . .

wali 1 (*Isl.*) male relative legally responsible for a bride, us. her father. *- hakim* person who acts on behalf of the father of a bride. **2** guardian, proxy. *- kelas* homeroom teacher. *- murid* person responsible for a pupil (not a parent). **3** high civil servant. *- kota* mayor. *- nagari* (*M*) head of a country. *- negara* head of state during the period of the United States of Indonesia. *- negeri* **1** provincial head. **2** governor. **3** former governor-general. **4** religious leader. *- geréja* Catholic bishop. *- sanga/sanga -* the nine pious leaders who spread Isl. in Java. **me-kan, memper-kan 1** act as guardian for. **2** appoint s.o. to be guardian. **ke-an** status as guardian. **per-an 1** guardianship. **2** custody (of child), trusteeship. **3** protectorate.

walikota mayor. **me-kan** make s.o. a mayor. **ke-an** having to do with the mayor. **per-an** matters pertaining to the mayor's job.

walimah wedding party.

waliullah (*Isl.*) holy person.

wallah see WALAAH.

wallahi I swear by God! *-! Saya tdk mengambil* I swear I did not take it.

wallahu alam 1 God knows best. *- bissawab* God knows the truth. **2** Heaven knows! (I do not). *Apa dia sdh kawin atau blm, -!* Whether he is married or not, only God knows!

wals, walsa waltz.

waluh (*Jv*) squash, gourd, pumpkin.

waluku (*Jv*) plow.

wamil [*wajib militér*] conscription. **me-kan** conscript, draft.

wamilda [*Wajib Militér Darurat*] emergency military obligation. **me-kan** engage in an emergency military obligation.

Wampa [*Wakil Menteri Pertama*] deputy chief minister.

wan 1 term of reference or address for males of Arab descent. **2** title for nobility in some areas.

wana (*Ch*) an indigenous Indonesian.

wang see UANG.

wangi fragrant. **me- 1** fragrant. **2** scent, perfume. **me-kan** perfume s.t. **ke-an** fragrance. **-an 1** fragrance, scent. **2** perfume. **-²an** perfumery, all k.o. scents. **pe-** s.t. to impart fragrance. *~ ruangan* air freshener.

wangkang ocean-going sailboat.

wangsa dynasty. **ke-an** kinship.

wangsat expression of reproach: you animal!

wangsit (*Jv*) divine inspiration.

wanita woman. *- adam* transvestite. *- P/tuna susila/T/TS* prostitute. **ke-an 1** femininity. **2** womanhood. **ke-²an** effeminate.

Wanra [*Perlawanan Rakyat*] people's militia.

wanti-wanti (*Jv*) repeatedly, time after time. **me-** tell s.o. repeatedly, warn.

wantunas see WATUNAS.

wap see UAP₁.

wapat see WAFAT.

waperdam [*wakil perdana menteri*] vice-premier.

waprés [*wakil présidén*] vice-president.

WARA [*Wanita Angkatan Udara*] women's section of the Air Force and its members.

warak (*Isl.*) observant of religious obligations, esp. regarding abstinence.

warakat see WARKAH.

warakawuri (*Lit.*) army widow.

warangan see BERANGAN₁.

waranggana (*Jv*) singer in gamelan orchestra.

waras 1 having full possession of o.'s senses. *Engkau tak -, Mas Noto?* Are you out of your mind, Noto? *kurang -* (a bit) crazy. **2** healthy. **ke-an** health (physical and mental).

warawiri₁ (*Lit.*) hibiscus.

warawiri₂ 1 back and forth. **2** fickle, unstable.

warek /warek/ (*Jv, Jkt*) satiated, full.

warembol k.o. sweet roll.

warga 1 accredited member of an association. *- AURI* a member of the Indonesian Air Forces. *- masyarakat* a member of society. *- désa* villager. **2** citizen. *- dunia* world citizen. **ke-duniaan** cosmopolitanness. *- kota* city resident. *- negara* citizen of a country. *- negara bunglon* (*Sl.*) citizen who is not committed to the country. *- negara Indonésia* **1** naturalized Indonesian citizen. **2** Indonesian citizen of Ch descent. **3** (*Leg.*) Indonesian citizen. *- negara asing* citizen of foreign country (us. referring to Chinese). **ber-** *negara* have certain k.o. citizens. **me-negarakan** naturalize. **ke-negaraan 1** citizenship. **2** civics (as subject in school). **berke-negaraan** holding citizenship. *tak berke-negaraan* stateless. **pe-negera-an** naturalization. **ke-an 1** membership. **2** citizenry.

waria [*wanita pria*] transsexual, transvestite homosexual.

waringin (*Jv*) see BERINGIN.

waris heir. - *asli* lineal heir. - *sah* legal heir. **me-i** inherit s.t. *Dia ~ semua kehayaan pamannya* He inherited all his uncle's wealth. **me-kan** bequeath s.t. *Dia ~ semuanya kpd anaknya* He bequeathed everything to his child. **-an** legacy, inheritance. **pe-** heir. **pe-an 1** inheriting. **2** inheritance. **per-an, ke-an** matters pertaining to inheritance.

warkah, warkat (*Lit.*) letter. - *pos* **1** aerogram. **2** postal form for domestic mail similar to an aerogram.

warmbol see WAREMBOL.

warna 1 color. - *bahasa* (*Ling.*) speech level. - *keramat* Indonesian national colors, red and white. - *nada* timbre. - *riang* bright colors. - *sari* anthology. - *suara* timbre. - *warni* all k.o. colors. - *warta* miscellany, all k.o. news. **2** (*Crd.*) suit. **ber-** colored. *bangsa ~* non-Caucasian race. **ber-²** **1** multicolored. *pakaian ~* multicolored clothes. **2** various. **me-** acquire color. *Wajahnya mulai ~* His face began to get some color. **me-i 1** apply a color to s.t., color. *Adik suka sekali ~* Little Brother really likes to color. *Pintu dan jendéla diinya hijau* He painted the doors and windows green. **2** slant (a story), color s.t. **me-kan** color, paint. **pe-** dye. *~ alami* natural dye.

warni see WARNA.

warok (*Jv*) k.o. ascetic expert of martial arts, often homosexual.

warong see WARUNG.

warsa (*Lit.*) year.

warta 1 report, communication. - *harian* daily newspaper. **2** news. - *berita* news broadcast. - *sepekan* weekly news. **me-kan** report, inform. **pe-1** correspondent, reporter. **2** news bulletin. **pe-an** reporting.

wartawan journalist, correspondent. **ke-an** journalism.

wartawati woman reporter or journalist.

warteg [*warung Tegal*] food stall with cheap food (us. with little or no meat).

waru₁ (*Crd.*) spades.

waru₂ see BARU₂.

Waruna see BARUNA.

warung small shop, stall. - *keliling* itinerant food stall. - *kopi* coffee shop. - *nasi* food stall. - *remeng-remeng* **1** dimly lit food stall. **2** food stall for assignations in a prostitution complex. - *Tegal* food stall with cheap food. **ber-** run a small shop.

wasalam see WASSALAM.

wasana (*Lit.*) final. *laporan -* final report. - *kata* finally (in ending discourse).

wasangka suspicion. **ber-** suspicious.

waserai dry-cleaners and laundry. **me-kan** dry-clean. **-an** dry-cleaned clothes.

wasiat 1 dying exhortation, last will and testament (spoken or written). - *Baru* New Testament. - *Lama* Old Testament. **2** magic power (of an ancient heirloom). *lampu -* magic lamp. **ber-make o.'s will. me-kan** will, bequeath.

wasilah, wasilat relation, connection, bond.

wasir see BAWASIR.

wasit 1 referee, umpire. **2** arbiter. **me-i** be the referee in. *Siapa yg ~ pertandingan itu?* Who refereed that match? **per-an** matters pertaining to referees. *déwan ~* (*Sport*) board of referees.

wasitah medium, spirit.

waskita clairvoyant, psychic.

waskom see BASKOM.

waslap washcloth, scrubbing towel.

waspada wary, on guard. **me-i** keep on guard against. **me-kan** alert s.o. *ABRI ~ rakyat akan bahaya ékstrémisme* The armed forces alerted the people about the dangers of extremism. **ke-an 1** vigilance, alertness. **2** caution.

wassalam Peace be with you! (used to conclude letters), sincerely yours.

wassalamualaikum (*Isl.*) And peace be with you (used to close letters and speeches). - *warakhmatullahi wabarakatuh* And peace be with you and God's blessings (used to close letters and speeches).

wasserij /waserai/ see WASERAI.

wastafel bathroom sink, wash basin.

waswas, waswisu anxious, uneasy to the point of being suspicious. **ke-an** anxiety, uneasiness.

wat Thai Buddhist temple.

watak 1 nature, disposition. **2** character (of novel, etc.). **me-i** form the character of. *Sifat-sifat ayahnya ~ kepribadian anak itu* His father's attitudes have thoroughly permeated the child's personality. **per-an** characterization.

watas₁ limit. **pe-** (*Ling.*) modifier, qualifier. **per-an** (*Ling.*) modification.

watas₂ see BATAS.

watermantel water-cooled machine gun.

waterpas carpenter's level.

waterpoken (*Coll.*) chicken pox.

waterpruf, waterprup waterproof.

watt watts.

wattase wattage.

watunas [*wanita tuna susila*] prostitute.

wau the 25th letter of the Arabic alphabet.

wauw (*Coll.*) wow!

wauwau k.o. gibbon.

wawancara interview. **ber-** hold an interview. **me-i** interview s.o. **me-kan** make the topic of an interview, interview about. *Meréka ~ soal pangan* They held an interview about the food problem. **pe-** interviewer. **pe-an** interviewing.

wawansantap (*Lit.*) friendly, informal meal or banquet.

wawasan 1 insight, perception. **2** concept. - *Nusantara* the Archipelago concept (i.e. the maritime territory of Indonesia includes all the water between the islands). **ber-** have a conception. *Pemuda yg ~ luas diperlukan negara* The state needs young people with a wide perspective.

way see WAI₁.

wayang 1 shadow play with leather puppets often

dramatizing themes from Hindu epics, the *wayang*. **2** leather puppet. **3** traditional drama performance of Java and Bali. - *bébér* performance using a picture scroll. - *golék* wooden puppet show. - *kelitik/kercil/kerucil* show with flat wooden puppets. - *kulit* shadow play with leather puppets. - *org* Jv stage show us. with *wayang* themes. - *potéhi* Ch hand-puppet (show). - *purwa* classical shadow play. - *suluh* puppet show in Indonesian language. - *titi* Ch hand-puppet (show). - *topéng* stage show with masked players. - *wahyu* shadow play with leather puppets performing biblical stories. - *wong* Jv stage show us. with *wayang* themes. **me-kan 1** put into a *wayang* format for presentation. *Pada waktu itu slogan politik di-kan di désa kami* At that time they made *wayang* stories out of political slogans and performed them in our village. **2** act, perform. **-an 1** a *wayang* performance. **2** attend a *wayang* performance. **pe-an** things pertaining to the *wayang* .
wayer electric fan.
wayuh (*Jv*) **ber-** have more than o. wife.
wazir 1 (*Lit.*) vizier. **2** (*Che.*) queen.
wb. see WR. (WB.).
WC /wésé/ [*water closet*] toilet, restroom.
wé₁ (*Jv*) Gosh!
wé₂ see OWÉ.
wedana (*Jv*) district chief. **ke-an 1** district. **2** residence of district chief.
wedar (*Jv*) disclose. **ter- 1** disclosed. *Rahasia itu ~* The secret was disclosed. **2** be let down. *Rambutnya ~* Her hair was let down.
wedel (*Jv.*) **me-** dye. **-an** s.t. dyed.
wedung (*Jv*) cleaver.
wegah see OGAH₁.
wejang me-(i) advise, instruct. **me-kan** use s.t. to advise or instruct. *Para gubernur ~ nilai-nilai Pancasila kpd anak buahnya* The governors use the values of *Pancasila* to instruct their staff. **-an 1** advice. **2** speech containing advice.
wéker, wékker see BÉKER₁.
welang (*Jv*) see BELANG.
welasan (*Jv*) custom of giving or buying 10 units (of same item) with an extra o. as a gift.
welas asih (*Jv*) mercy.
weling last will and testament.
welirang see BELÉRANG.
weluku see WALUKU.
Wenang Syiwa's father (in the *wayang*).
wenang, wénang entitled to, qualified. **se-²(nya)** arbitrarily, without compunction. *Tindakannya yg ~ itu menyakiti hati penduduk* His cruel deeds made the people resentful. **berse-² 1** act arbitrarily, at o.'s own discretion. **2** act cruelly, despotically. **menye-²i** treat s.o. arbitrarily. *Rakyat tdk boléh di-²i di negara ini* In this country the people cannot be treated arbitrarily. **kese-²an 1** arbitrariness. **2** despotism. **ber-** have the power to, be competent to. **ke-an** competence, authority. **ke-²an 1** arbitrariness. **2** despotism, tyranny. *~ merajaléla* Despotism prevails. **pe-**s.o. who gives authority.

wérak recruiter of laborers.
wérda (*Mil.*) a guard's call: "Who is there?"
werdha see WISMA.
wérék see WÉRAK.
wérek kontrak (*Coll.*) contract labor.
wereng k.o. rice pest.
Wésak holiday marking Buddha's birth, enlightenment, and death.
wésel₁ money order, draft. **me-kan** send money by means of a money order.
wésel₂ (*R.R.*) railway switch.
wéselbor (*Tel.,R.R.*) switchboard.
wésélpos see POSWÉSEL.
wesi (*Jv*) see BESI.
wésio (*Ch*) Buddhist monk.
wésternisasi Westernization.
wét (*Coll.*) law.
wétan (*Jv*) east.
wewangian perfumery.
wéwé, wéwé gombél (*Jv.*) k.o. ugly female ghost with sagging breasts.
wewenang authority, competence. **ber-** have authority.
wiara see WIHARA.
WIB [*Waktu Indonésia Bagian Barat*] W. Indonesian Time (zone).
wibawa authority, power. **ber- 1** with authority. **2** having an authoritative bearing. **ke-an** authority. *~ pemerintah pusat tdk diakui* The authority of the central gvt. was not acknowledged.
wicara (*Ling.*) speech. *cacat -* speech defect. - *buatan* artificial speech.
widara see BIDARA.
widuri (*Jv*) k.o. shrub.
widyakarya (*Lit.*) university-level work-study.
widyawisata (*Lit.*) study tour.
Wiéna see WINA.
wih (*Coll.*) exclamation to show surprise or call attention to s.t. -*! Takut déh gué* Boy! I was really afraid.
wihara Buddhist monastery or nunnery.
wijaya (*Lit.*) victory. **ke-an** victory.
wijayakusuma see BUNGA.
wijén (*Jv*) see BIJAN.
wiku see BIKSU.
wiladah confinement, childbirth.
wilayah 1 region, district (below the province but larger than a county in size). **2** zone. - *industri* industrial estate. - *pinggiran* peripheral area, frontier zone. - *waktu* time zone. **ber-** have a certain area. *Daérah ~ dua ratus héktar* This area comprises 200 hectares. **pe(ng)-an** division into territories. **per-an** matters relating to districts.
wildop hubcap.
wilis see BURUNG.
Wina Vienna.
windu cycle of eight years in Jv calendrical reckoning. *Indonésia merayakan panca - kemerdékaannya* Indonesia celebrated the 40th anniversary of its independence. **ber-²** decade after decade.
wing 1 (*Mil.*) decoration (for those who have flown or parachuted a certain number of times).

2 wing in air formation.
wiper /waiper/ windshield wiper.
wira (*Lit.*) man, hero. - *tamtama* a low military rank. **ke-an** manliness.
wiracarita, wiracerita (*Lit.*) epic.
wirama see IRAMA.
wiraniaga salesperson.
wiraswasta 1 entrepreneur. 2 run a private enterprise. **ber-** run a private enterprise. **ke-an** entrepreneurship.
wiraswastawan entrepreneur.
wirausaha businessman.
wirawan hero, heroic.
wirid (*Isl.*) passage of Koran. **ber-, -an** recite Koranic passages.
wiron (*Jv*) pleats in a batik wraparound. **ber-** pleated.
wiru ber-² pleated. **me-** pleat s.t.
wiryaan see HAL₁.
wisata a tour. **ber-** make a tour.
wisatawan tourist.
wisel see WÉSEL₁.
wisik (*Jv*) inspiration.
wiski whisky.
wisma public building. - *budaya* art gallery. - *tamu* guesthouse. - *werdha/wreda* (*Lit.*) old people's home.
wisuda graduation ceremony. - *gelar* conferral of degrees at graduation ceremony. **me-(kan)** award a degree at graduation ceremony.
wisudawan male graduate at commencement.
wisudawati female graduate at commencement.
WIT [*Waktu Indonésia Bagian Timur*] E. Indonesian Time (zone).
WITA [*Waktu Indonésia Bagian Tengah*] Central Indonesian Time (zone).
wiyaga (*Jv*) gamelan player.
wiyata (*Lit.*) education. - *bhakti* practice teaching.
wk(l). [*wakil*] vice-, deputy, assistant.
wkt. [*waktu*] time.
WMP see WAMPA.
WN [*warga negara*] citizen.
WNA [*Warga Negara Asing*] foreign citizen, us. referring to Chinese.
WNI [*Warga Negara Indonésia*] 1 (*Leg.*) citizen of Indonesia. 2 naturalized Indonesian citizen, esp. of Ch descent. **me-kan** cause s.o. to become an Indonesian citizen (us. of Ch). **ke-an** matters pertaining to Indonesian citizenship (us. in relation to Ch minority).
woki-toki walkie-talkie.
wol wool.
Wolanda see BELANDA.
wong₁ (*Jv*) person.
wong₂ (*Jv*) because. *Saya nggak ngerti - baru datang* I do not understand; after all, I just got here.
wong₃ (*Jv*) what are you talking about! (expression of disagreement). - *makanannya kayak gini kok dibilang énak* What do you mean calling food like this delicious!
wortel carrot.
wr. (**wb.**) [*warakhmatullahi (wabarakatuh)*] may God be merciful (and bless you) (for formal conclusions to letter and speeches).
wreda see WISMA.
wredatama (*Lit.*) retired person.
WTS [*wanita tuna susila*] prostitute.
wudhu, wudlu, wudu (*Isl.*) ritual ablution before prayers. **ber-** perform such ablutions.
wuduk see NASI₁.
wujud shape into which s.t. has been formed. - *kréasi tarinya* shape of the choreography. **ber-** 1 have the shape of. *Méja itu ~ bundar* The table is round. *Kursus itu akan ~ pelajaran tertulis* The lessons will be in the form of a correspondence course. 2 concrete, tangible. **me-** materialize. **me-kan** 1 give shape to, create. 2 bring into reality. *Susah dia ~ cita-citanya* It is difficult for him to realize his ideals. **ter-** materialized. **keter-an** materialization. **per-an** 1 shape, form. 2 realization, materialization. 3 phenomenon.
wuku (*Jv*) o. of the 30 seven-day periods which make up the 210-day calendar cycle.
wukuf (*Isl.*) ceremony of gathering on the field of Arafah during the hajj. **ber-** perform this ceremony.
wuluh₁ (*Zod.*) Pleiades.
wuluh₂ see BELIMBING.
wuluh₃ (*Jv*) see BULUH.
wungkul (*Jv*) whole, unbroken.
wungu (*Jv*) see UNGU.
wutuh see UTUH.
wuwu (*Jv*) see BUBU.
wuwung (*Jv*) see BUBUNG.

Y

y /yé, ai, i grék/ y, the 25th letter of the alphabet.
ya₁ 1 yes. *Bp guru? -, betul* Are you a teacher? Yes,
I am. *-, boléh saja* Yes, of course you may.
2 What? (a response to s.o.'s call). *-! Apa?* Yes!
What is it? **3** OK?, will you? (particle indicating a
softened command). *Saya boléh datang, -?* It is
OK for me to come, isn't it? *Jangan marah, -?* Do
not be angry, OK? *Boléh. Tapi, -, jangan lama-
lama* OK. But do not be long now. *Bu, ini berapa,
-* How much is it? (May I ask). *Tahu, -* I do not
know. (Is it OK if we leave it at that?) *Terima
kasih, -* Thanks. **4** right? isn't it? (question tag
word). *Itu mahal sekali, -?* That is really expensive, isn't it? *Masa, -* It is impossible, isn't it? **5** Let
us see now . . . what? how? who? etc. *Bagaimana,
-?* Hum, how shall we do it? *Berapa, -, tadi?* How
much was it now? **6** hmm (hesitation particle).
*Sdh berapa lama sebenarnya? -, sdh sejak saya tamat,
saya kira* How long has it been? Um, since I
graduated, I think. **7** as for (topic marker). *Saya
-, saya sdh tiga bulan di sini* As for me, I have been
here for three months. **8** well then that is the
way it is. *Kalau tdk mau, - sdh* If you do not want
to, then do not. *- itu! Mémang itu!* Yes, that is the
o. That is really the o.! *Di jalan raya, di muka
rumah makan, - di mana-mana!* On the highways,
in front of restaurants, in fact everywhere . . .
9 (*Jv*) also, too. *Di Surabaya gitu. Di Yogya - gitu* In
Surabaya that is the way it is. In Yogya it is that
way, too.
ya₂ Oh (vocative marker). *- Robbi!* O my Lord! *-
Allah* 1 O God! **2** My God! (exclamation of displeasure, painful surprise, etc.).
yad. [*yg akan datang*] the future, coming.
yah₁ well . . . (particle of resignation, exasperation, etc.). *-, beginilah nasib janda* Well, that is the
fate of a widow.
yah₂ see AYAH.
yahud (*Sl.*) OK, excellent, great. **ber-²** agree with
e.o. *tempat ~* place where lovers meet.
Yahudah Judaic.
Yahudi Jew, Jewish. **memper-kan** treat in inferior
fashion. **ke-an** Judaism.
yahudiah Jewish.
yahut see YAHUD.
Yahya 1 male name. **2** (*Bib.*) the Gospel of John.
yaini see YAKNI.
yais menopause.
yaitu that is, i.e., viz.
yak 1 (*Coll.*) yes. **2** (*Sport*) catch! (i.e. a ball).
yakin sure, certain, convinced. *Saya - hal ini tdk
mudah diurus* I am certain it will not be easy to

arrange this matter. **se-²nya** absolutely convinced, as convinced as can be. **me-i** be convinced about s.t. *Saya ~ Kitab Suci itu* I believe in
the scriptures. **me-kan 1** convince s.o. *Ia ~ temannya bhw mobilnya baik* He convinced his
friend that the car was all right. *Tampangnya
cukup ~* He has an appearance that inspires
trust. **2** make convincing. *utk ~ katanya* in order
to make his words convincing. **ke-an** conviction,
firm belief. **berke-an** be convinced. **pe-an** act of
convincing. *cara ~ diri sendiri* way of convincing
o.s.
yakis baboon.
yakni that is, namely, viz.
yakut hyacinth.
yalah see IALAH.
Yaman Yemen.
yang₁ 1 nominalizing particle: the o. who, the
thing which, etc. *- datang siapa?* Who was it that
came? *- saya beli besar* The o. I bought was big. *-
lebih murah sih banyak* There are plenty that are
cheaper. *Saya ambil - biru saja* I will just take the
blue o. **2** particle forming a specific adjective
clause: "which is, who are," etc. *Saya di rumah -
kecil itu, bukan di rumah - besar ini* I stay in the
house that is little there, not in the o. that is big
over here. *Itu org - datang tadi* That is the man
who came a little while ago. *- lalu* ago. *Dua bulan
- lalu* two months ago. **3** with numerals or de-
monstratives: the o. or the two, etc. (as opposed
to others), this or that o. (as opposed to others).
Bukan - itu! - ini koper saya Not that o. This o. is
my suitcase. *- mana* Which o.? *- satu (dua, tiga,
etc.) lagi* the other o. (two, three, etc.). *- satu
mahal - satu lagi tdk* O. was expensive. The other
o. was not. **4** (*Coll.*) (do) in such-and-such a manner. *- baik, ya, kalau kerja* Do a good job when you
work, will you?
yang₂ see SAYANG.
yapon 1 bathrobe (for women). **2** Western-style
woman's dress.
yareh, yarig /yareh/ (*Coll.*) have o.'s birthday.
yasan k.o. rice field that is cultivated individually.
Yasin (*Isl.*) chapter 37 of the Koran often read
while s.o. is dying.
yasmin jasmine.
Yassin see YASIN.
yatim fatherless child. *- piatu* orphan.
yaumuddin (*Isl.*) doomsday.
yaumulkiamah (*Isl.*) Day of Judgment.
yayasan foundation, institute. *- Ford* Ford Foundation.

yayi (*Jv*) younger brother or sister.
yb. [*yg berikut*] next, following.
ybl. [*yg baru lalu*] last.
ybs. [*yg bersangkautan*] the person concerned.
yéksi see INJÉKSI.
yél yell (in demonstrations, etc.).
yellow paper /yélo péper/ sensation-oriented newspaper.
Yeremiah (*Bib.*) Jeremiah.
Yésuit (*Rel.*) Jesuit.
yét see JÉT.
yg. [*yang*] which, who.
yi. [*yaitu*] that is, namely, viz, i e
yl.₁ [*yg lain*] the other.
yl.₂ [*yg lalu*] past, last.
YME [*Yang Maha Esa*] the One God.
ymj. [*yg menjalankan jabatan*] acting, holding office temporarily.
yo see AYO.
yodium iodine.
yodiumisasi program for providing iodized salt.
yoga meditation.
yogia, yogya proper, fitting. **se-nya** properly, obviously. ~ *kamu pergi ke rumahnya* You should have gone to his home. **mense-kan** make s.t. proper.
Yohanes, Yohannes 1 male name. 2 (*Bib.*) the gospel of John.
yojana distance, field of vision. **se-** as far as. ~ *mata* as far as the eye can see.
yok see AYO.
yoker (*Crd.*) joker.
yon. [*Batalyon*] battalion.
yongenskop short haircut (for women).
yongker see YOKER.
yong tahu (*Ch*) tofu filled with meat.
you /yu/ you (distant but informal).
yth. [*yg terhormat*] the honorable (on letter addresses and salutations).

yts. [*yg tersebut*] mentioned.
yu₁ see MBAK.
yu₂ see HIU.
yu₃ see YOU.
yu₄ see AYO.
yubilaris o. who celebrates his or her jubilee (wedding, ordination, etc.).
yubiléum jubilee.
yuda, yudha (*Lit.*) war.
yudisium 1 Latinate citation on a diploma (*cum laude*, etc.). 2 graduation exercise (at divisional level).
yudo judo.
Yugo Yugoslav, Yugoslavia.
yuh, yuk see AYO.
Yuli see JULI.
Yunani Greek, Greece.
yuncto /yungkto/ (*Leg.*) in connection with.
yunior 1 (*Sport*) junior, pertaining to or concerning youth. *sépak bola* - youth football competition. 2 son of. *Joni* - son of Joni, little Joni. **ke-an** being a junior.
yuniorat k.o. college preparatory school emphasizing classics (esp. in colonial period and formerly in Jesuit training).
yuran 1 contribution. 2 dues.
yuridiksi jurisdiction, competency of a certain court.
yuridis juridical. *secara - formil* (*Leg.*) in a formal sense.
yuris 1 jurist, lawyer. 2 law student.
yurisprudénsi legal administration, jurisdiction.
yurk /yurek/ dress, frock, shirt.
Yusak (*Bib.*) Joshua.
yuta see JUTA.
yuwelir jeweler.
yuyu k.o. small soft-shelled crab.

Z

z /zét, sét, jét/ z, the 26th letter of the alphabet.
zaal /sal/ see SAL₁.
zabarjad topaz.
zabib (*Lit.*) raisins.
zabur psalm. *Kitab* - (*Bib.*) Book of Psalms.
zadah see JADAH.
zadat (*Phys.*) solid.
zadir (*Chem.*) sal ammoniac.
zahid ascetic.
zahir see LAHIR₁.
zair (*Phys.*) liquid.
zait, zaitun olive tree and its fruit.
zak /sak/ see SAK₁.

zakar penis. *batang* - shaft of the penis, penis. *buah* - testicles.
zakat (*Isl.*) tithe. *-fitrah* (*Isl.*) tithe in rice or money paid on last day of fasting month. - *maal* tithe paid by rich people. **men-kan** donate s.t.
zakelijk /sakelek/ (*Coll.*) businesslike.
zakiah sincere, pure.
zalf /salep/ see SALEP.
zalim see LALIM.
zalir fluid.
zaman see JAMAN.
zamrud emerald.
zamzam 1 a sacred well in Mecca's mosque, Ha-

gar's well. **2** water from Mecca's sacred well. - *durja* facial expression.

zanggi see JANGGI.

zantara (*Phys.*) medium.

zarafah see JERAPAH.

zarah, zarrah 1 particle, crumb, matter. **2** atom. **se-** a bit. **men-** *pecah* pulverized.

zat (*Chem.*) essence, substance. - *air* hydrogen. - *air belérang* hydrogen sulphide. - *alir* fluid. - *asam* oxygen. - *cair* liquid. - *hijau* chlorophyl. - *lemas* nitrogen. - *makanan* vitamin. - *padat* (*Phys.*) solid matter. - *pelemas* nitrogen. - *pembakar* oxygen. - *putih telur* albumen. - *sendawa* nitrogen. - *telur* protein, albumen. - *yg mahatinggi* the supreme substance (God).

zébra zebra. *jalur* - zebra (pedestrian) crossing.

zénding (*Rel.*) /sénding/ Protestant missionary or mission.

zéni₁ (*Mil.*) detachment of army engineers. - *tempur* combat engineers.

zéni₂ (*Coll.*) genius.

zénit zenith.

zéro (*Ling.*) zero allomorph.

zét /sét/ **menge-** set type.

ziadah addition, excess.

ziarah make a devotional visit to a sacred place. **ber-** visit a sacred place. *Ia ~ ke makam Pangéran Diponegoro* He made a devotional visit to the grave of Prince Diponegoro. **men-i** visit (a sacred place). **pe(n)-** visitor to a sacred place or grave. **pen-an, per-an** act of going s.w. sacred.

zib₁ (*Lit.*) k.o. wolf.

zib₂ see JIB.

zig-zag zig-zag. **ber-** to zig-zag.

zikir see DIKIR.

zina, zinah any sexual act outside of marriage. - *mata* sin with lustful looks. **ber-** engage in illicit sex. **pe-** adulterer, fornicator. **per-an** sexual acts outside of marriage.

zindik heretic.

zinkwit /singkwit/ zinc-white.

zirafah see JERAPAH.

zirah (*Lit.*) coat of chain-mail.

zirnikh /sirnikh/ arsenic.

zitje /sice/ see SICE.

Zohal (*Astr.*) Saturn.

Zohrah (*Astr.*) Venus.

zolim see LALIM.

zonder /sonder/ see SONDER.

zoologi /sologi/ zoology.

zuadah see JUADAH.

Zuhal see ZOHAL.

Zuhrah, Zuhrat see ZOHRAH.

zuhur see LOHOR.

Zulhijah 12th month of Arabic calendar.

Zulkaédah 11th month of Arabic calendar.

zunub see JUNUB.

zurafah see JERAPAH.

zuriat 1 (*Biol.*) seed. **2** descendant, posterity.

zus /sus, ses/ **1** term of address for Christian or Westernized adult women. **2** term of address for female nurses and midwives.

zuster /suster, sester/ see SUSTER.